Pocket Oxford American Dictionary

Pocket Oxford American Dictionary

SECOND EDITION

OXFORD

UNIVERSITY PRESS

OXFORD
UNIVERSITY PRESS

Oxford University Press, Inc., publishes works that further
Oxford University's objective of excellence
in research, scholarship, and education.

Oxford New York

Auckland Cape Town Dar es Salaam Hong Kong Karachi
Kuala Lumpur Madrid Melbourne Mexico City Nairobi
New Delhi Shanghai Taipei Toronto

With offices in

Argentina Austria Brazil Chile Czech Republic France Greece
Guatemala Hungary Italy Japan Poland Portugal Singapore
South Korea Switzerland Thailand Turkey Ukraine Vietnam

Copyright © 2008 by Oxford University Press

First edition 2002
Second edition 2008

Published by Oxford University Press, Inc.
198 Madison Avenue, New York, NY 10016
www.oup.com

Oxford is a registered trademark of Oxford University Press

The Library of Congress Cataloging-in-Publication Data

Data available

ISBN 978-0-19-530163-2

1 3 5 7 9 8 6 4 2

Printed in the United States of America
on acid-free paper

Contents

Contributors

Project Manager
Maurice Waite

Senior Editor
Christine A. Lindberg

Editor
Benjamin G. Zimmer

Lexicographers
Orin Hargraves
Sue Ellen Thompson

Preface

This new edition of the *Pocket Oxford American Dictionary* is the result of a collaboration harnessing both the expertise of experienced lexicographers who are native speakers of American English and the worldwide resources of Oxford University Press. This has ensured that the dictionary is fully informed by analysis of both the Oxford English Corpus, a two-billion-word database of many different types of real English, and the database of the Oxford Reading Program.

The dictionary covers a broad range of vocabulary: while the focus is on the core language of contemporary English, there is also a wide selection of technical terms from specialist areas such as medicine, computing, and the environment—for example, *endorphin*, *mirror site*, and *carbon sink*.

The definitions are written in a clear, natural style, with few abbreviations. Grammatical information is presented straightforwardly, and pronunciations are shown using easily understandable respellings.

Specially written usage notes answer questions about English to help you write well and effectively. For instance, should you say *they didn't ought to*? Is it *different from*, *different than*, or *different to*?

The central supplement contains a selection of frequently needed information, such as weights and measures and countries of the world.

Trademarks

This dictionary includes some words that have, or are asserted to have, proprietary status as trademarks or otherwise. Their inclusion does not imply that they have acquired for legal purposes a nonproprietary or general significance, nor any other judgment concerning their legal status. In cases where the editorial staff have some evidence that a word has proprietary status, this is indicated in the entry for that word by the label trademark, but no judgment concerning the legal status of such words is made or implied thereby.

Guide to the Dictionary

1. Structure of entries

Here are examples of the major types of information in entries:

part of speech (word class)

headword ···⊱ **ac·quit** /əˈkwit/ ▸ v. **(acquits, acquitting, acquitted):1** formally declare that someone is not guilty of a criminal charge. **2 (acquit oneself)** behave or perform in a particular way: *he acquitted himself very well on his debut.*

verb forms (inflections)

pronunciation (see section 4 for key)

ad·ver·sar·y /ˈadvərˌserē/ ▸ n. (pl. **adversaries**) an opponent in a contest, dispute, or conflict.

plural form

syllable breaks (see section 5)

aer·o·plane /ˈe(ə)rəˌplān/ ▸ n. Brit. an airplane.

geographical label showing where the headword is used (see section 3)

grammatical information

aes·thet·ics /esˈTHetiks/ (also **esthetics**) ▸ pl.n. (usu. treated as sing.) **1** a set of principles concerned with the nature of beauty, especially in art. **2** the branch of philosophy that deals with questions of beauty and artistic taste.

variant (alternative) spelling

a use or form of the headword that has its own definition

different words with the same spelling, numbered

···⊱ **a·light¹** /əˈlīt/ ▸ v. **1 (alight on)** (of a bird) land or settle on something. **2** formal get off a train or bus. **3 (alight on)** happen to notice something.

···⊱ **a·light²** ▸ adv. & adj. **1** on fire. **2** shining brightly.

register label indicating the style of English in which the headword is used (see section 3 for explanations)

subject label

an·i·on /ˈanˌīən/ ▸ n. Chemistry an ion with a negative charge. The opposite of **CATION**. ◂··· ■ **an·i·on·ic** /ˌanīˈänik/ adj.

cross reference to another entry (in bold capital letters)

ap·ple /ˈapəl/ ▸ n. the round fruit of a tree of the rose family, with green or red skin and crisp flesh. ■ **ap·pley** adj.

phrases and expressions

– PHRASES **the apple of one's eye** a person of whom one is extremely fond and proud. **a rotten** (or **bad**) **apple** informal a corrupt person in a group, likely to have a bad influence on the others. **upset the apple cart** spoil a plan.

example of use, to help distinguish different senses

numbered sense of the headword

···⊱ **ap·praise** /əˈprāz/ ▸ v. **1** assess the quality or nature of: *she appraised the damage and groaned.* **2** give an employee an appraisal. **3** (of an official valuer) set a price on something. ■ **ap·prais·ee** /əˌprāzˈē/ n. **ap·prais·er** n.

derivatives (words derived from the headword)

note giving help with using the headword

USAGE
Appraise is often confused with **apprise**.
Appraise means 'assess someone or something', whereas **apprise** means 'inform someone' (*psychiatrists were apprised of his condition*).

2. Spelling and forms of nouns and verbs

Alternative spellings

The main form of each word given in the dictionary is the accepted American spelling. Although there is only one way that most words can be spelled, sometimes other spellings (called *variants*) are also acceptable. Such spellings are given after the headword, e.g., **adaptor** (also **adapter**), or before a particular sense if the spelling variant is only used in that sense. In all such cases the spelling given as the headword is the one that most people use. The label Brit. shows spellings that are used in British English, e.g. **color** (Brit. **colour**).

Hyphenation

Although standard spelling in English is fixed, the use of hyphens is not. There are a few general rules that should be followed, and these are outlined below.

Noun compounds: there are no set rules as to whether a compound (a word such as **airstream**) should be written as one word, two words, or with a hyphen (unless the hyphen is used to show the word's grammatical function; see the next section): **airstream**, **air stream**, and **air-stream** are all acceptable. However, in modern English people are tending to use hyphens less than before and are writing compounds either as one word (**airstream**) or two words (**air raid**) rather than with a hyphen. There is also a tendency to write compounds as one word in American English and as two words in British English.

To save space and avoid confusion, the dictionary gives only the standard American form. This does not, however, mean that other forms are incorrect or not used.

Grammatical information: hyphens are also used to show a word's grammatical function. When a noun compound made up of two separate words (e.g. **credit card**) is placed before another noun, the rule is that the compound has a hyphen, so you should write, for example, *I used my credit card* but *credit-card debt*. You will see this in some example phrases and sentences, but it is not otherwise mentioned in the dictionary entries.

There is a similar rule with compound adjectives such as **well known**. When they are placed after the verb (in the *predicative* position) such adjectives are not written with a hyphen, but when they are placed before the noun (in the *attributive* position) they should have a hyphen: *he is well known* but *he is a well-known painter*.

A verb compound formed from a noun compound that is two words (e.g. **hero worship**) should normally be written with a hyphen (to **hero-worship**). Compound verbs of this type are always shown in the dictionary entries.

Forms of nouns and verbs (inflections)

Plurals of nouns

The plurals of most nouns are formed by adding -*s*, or -*es* when they end in -*s*, -*x*, -*z*, -*sh*, or -*ch* (as in *church*). These kinds of plurals are not shown in the dictionary.

All irregular and difficult plural forms are shown, for example: **fly** (pl. **flies**), **foot** (pl. **feet**).

Verbs

Most verbs change their form (inflect) by adding -*s*, -*ing*, and -*ed* to the infinitive (the basic unchanged part of the verb), e.g. **jump** → **jumps, jumping, jumped**. Most verbs ending in -*e* add -*s*, -*ing* (dropping the -*e*), and -*d*, e.g. **bake** → **bakes, baking, baked**.

Neither of the above patterns of verb forms is shown in the dictionary.

Irregular and difficult verb forms are shown, e.g., **sing** (past **sang**; past part. **sung**), **bat** (**bats, batting, batted**).

Adjectives

Most adjectives form their comparatives and superlatives in the following ways, and these are not shown in the dictionary:

- words of one syllable adding -*er* and -*est*, e.g., **great** → **greater, greatest**
- words of one syllable ending in silent (unspoken) -*e*, which drop the -*e* and add -*er* and -*est*, e.g., **brave** → **braver, bravest**
- words that form the comparative and superlative by adding "more" and "most," e.g., *more beautiful, most beautiful.*

In all other cases the forms are shown in the dictionary, e.g., **hot** (**hotter, hottest**), **happy** (**happier, happiest**).

3. Labels

The majority of the words and senses in this dictionary are part of standard English, which means that they are the kinds of words we use in every type of situation, whether at home, with friends, or in a formal work situation. Some words, however, are suitable only for certain situations or are found only in certain types of writing, and where this is the case a label (or a combination of labels) is used.

Register labels

Register labels refer to the particular level of use in the language—indicating whether a term is informal, formal, historical, and so on.

- **formal:** normally used only in writing, such as in official documents (e.g., **missive**)
- **informal:** normally used only in speaking or writing to friends (e.g., **cornball**)
- **dated:** no longer used by most English speakers, but still used by older people or to give a humorous or other effect (e.g., **domestic science**)
- **old use:** old-fashioned language, not in ordinary use today, though sometimes used to give an old-fashioned or humorous effect and also found in the literature of the past (e.g., **damsel**)
- **historical:** only used today to refer to something that is no longer part of modern life (e.g., **blunderbuss**)
- **literary:** found only or mainly in literature (e.g., **foe**)
- **technical:** normally used only in technical language, though not restricted to a particular subject field (e.g., **dorsal**)
- **humorous:** used to sound funny or playful (e.g., **beauty sleep**)
- **euphemistic:** used instead of a more direct or rude term (e.g., **powder room** instead of "women's toilet")
- **dialect:** only used in certain local regions of the English-speaking world (e.g., **bide**)
- **derogatory:** deliberately intended to express a low opinion or insult someone else (e.g., **bimbo**)
- **offensive:** likely to cause offence, especially racial offence, whether the person using it means to or not
- **vulgar slang:** very informal language, usually relating to sexual activity or bodily functions, which most people regard as taboo and which may cause offence.

Geographical labels

English is spoken throughout the world, and while most of the words used in American English will be the same as those used in, say, Canadian or British English, there are some words which are only found in one type of English. For example, the normal word in British English for a sidewalk is **pavement**. This dictionary includes a selection of words of this kind with geographical labels. The label Brit. means that the word is found typically in British English but is not found in American English, though it may be found in other varieties such as Australian English.

Subject labels

Subject labels are used to show that a word or sense is associated with a particular subject field or specialist activity, such as Music, Chemistry, or Baseball.

4. Pronunciations

This dictionary uses a simple respelling system to show how entries are pronounced, using the symbols listed below. If two or more identical headwords are pronounced identically, only the first has a pronunciation given. Where a derivative simply adds a common suffix such as **-less**, **-ness**, or **-ly** to the headword, the derivative may not have a pronunciation shown unless some other element of the pronunciation also changes.

Symbol	Example	Symbol	Example	Symbol	Example
a	**hat** /hat/	i	**fit** /fit/	ou	**mouse** /mous/
ā	**day** /dā/	ī	**time** /tīm/	p	**put** /pŏŏt/,
ä	**lot** /lät/	i(ə)r	**beer** /bi(ə)r/		**cap** /kap/
b	**big** /big/	j	**judge** /jəj/	r	**run** /rən/, **fur** /fər/
CH	**church** /CHərCH/	k	**cut** /kət/	s	**sit** /sit/
d	**dog** /dôg/	l	**lap** /lap/	SH	**shut** /SHət/
e	**men** /men/	m	**main** /mān/	t	**top** /täp/
ē	**feet** /fēt/	n	**need** /nēd/	TH	**thin** /THin/
e(ə)r	**care** /ke(ə)r/	NG	**sing** /siNG/,	TH	**then** /THen/
ə	**about** /ə'bout/,		**anger** /'aNGgr/	v	**very** /'verē/
	curt /kərt/	ō	**go** /gō/	w	**wait** /wāt/
f	**free** /frē/	ô	**law** /lô/	y	**yet** /yet/,
g	**get** /get/	oi	**boy** /boi/		**accuse** /ə'kyŏŏz/
h	**her** /hər/	ŏŏ	**wood** /wŏŏd/,	z	**zipper** /'zipər/
(h)w	**when** /(h)wen/		**sure** /SHŏŏr/	ZH	**measure** /'mezHər/
		ōō	**food** /fōōd/		

Foreign Sounds

KH **Bach** /bäKH/ A "guttural" consonant pronounced with the tongue in the same position as for /k/, as in German *Buch*, or Scottish *loch*.

N **en route** /än 'rōōt/, **Sauvignon** /'sōvin'yôN/ The /N/ does not represent a separate sound: it indicates that the preceding vowel is nasalized, as in French *bon*.

œ **hors d'oeuvre** /ôr 'dœvrə/, **adieu** /ä'dyœ/ A vowel made by rounding the lips as with /ô/ while saying /e/, as in French *feu* or German *Höhle*.

Y **mot juste** /,mō 'zHYst/, **Übermensch** /'Ybər,menCH/ A vowel made by rounding the lips as with /ōō/ while saying /i/, as in French *rue* or German *fühlen*.

Stress Marks

Stress (or accent) is indicated by the mark ' before the syllable with the heaviest stress, and by ˌ before a syllable with weaker stress, e.g., **oversee** /ˌōvər'sē/.

Variant Pronunciations

There are several ways in which variant pronunciations are indicated in the respellings.

Some respellings show a pronunciation symbol within parentheses to indicate a possible variation in pronunciation; for example, in **sandwich** /'san(d)wicH/ sometimes the /d/ is pronounced, while sometimes it is not.

Variant pronunciations may be respelled in full, separated by semicolons. The more common pronunciation is listed first, if this can be determined, but it many cases it cannot.

Variant pronunciations may be indicated by respelling only the part of the word that changes; then a hyphen replaces the part of the pronunciation that remains the same, as in **quasiparticle** /ˌkwäzī'pärtikəl; ˌkwäzē-/

A partial respelling for a derivative refers back to the headword respelling, not the preceding derivative, as in **annotate** /'anəˌtāt/... ■ **annotation** /ˌanə'tāsHən/ **annotator** /-ˌtātər/.

A hyphen is sometimes used to separate syllables because the respelling might otherwise look confusing, as in **allowedly** /ə'lou-idlē/.

5. Syllable breaks

Syllable breaks are shown for headwords and derivatives, e.g. **de·flect**, **de·flec·tion**. They can be used as a guide for dividing words at the end of lines, but it is best **not** to divide:

- a word of five or fewer letters, e.g., **mor·al**
- a proper name, e.g., **Al·ex·an·der**
- a contraction, e.g., **could·n't**
- after the first letter of a word, e.g., **a·float**
- before the last letter of a word, e.g., **catch·y**
- anywhere other than at the hyphen in a word that is already hyphenated, e.g., **arm-twist·ing**
- if the result would be misleading or distracting, e.g., **leg·end**

6. Abbreviations used in the dictionary

abbr.	abbreviation	contr.	contraction	pron.	pronoun
adj.	adjective	exclam.	exclamation	pronunc.	pronunciation
adv.	adverb	fem.	feminine	sing.	singular
Austral.	Australian	n.	noun	usu.	usually
Brit.	British	part.	participle	v.	verb
comb.	combining	pl.	plural		
conj.	conjunction	prep.	preposition		

Abbreviations in general use (such as e.g., cm, and UK) are explained in their own entries.

A¹ (also **a**) ► n. (pl. **As** or **A's**) **1** the first letter of the alphabet. **2** indicating the first, best, or most important in a set. **3** Music the sixth note of the scale of C major.
– PHRASES **from A to B** from one place to another. **from A to Z** covering or including the entire range or scope of something.

A² ► abbr. **1** ampere(s). **2** (**Å**) angstrom(s). **3** answer.

a¹ /ā, ə/ (**an** before a vowel sound) ► determiner **1** used when mentioning someone or something for the first time; the indefinite article. **2** one single: *a hundred.* **3** per: *typing 60 words a minute.* **4** someone that (the name specified): *you're no better than a Hitler.*

a² ► abbr. **1** (in travel timetables) arrives. **2** (used before a date) before.

a- (often **an-** before a vowel) ► prefix not; without: *atheistic.*

@ /at/ ► symbol 'at,' used: **1** to indicate cost or rate per unit. **2** in Internet addresses between the user's name and the domain name: *john.smith@oup.com.*

A1 ► adj. informal excellent.

A4 ► n. a standard European size of paper, 297 × 210 mm.

AA ► abbr. **1** Alcoholics Anonymous. **2** antiaircraft. **3** administrative assistant. **4** Associate of Arts. **5** /ˌdubəl ˈā/ a dry cell battery of a size commonly used in digital cameras.

AAA /ˌtripəl ˈā/ ► abbr. **1** American Automobile Association. **2** a dry cell battery of a size commonly used in TV remote controls.

aard·vark /ˈärdˌvärk/ ► n. an African mammal with a tubular snout and a long tongue, feeding on ants and termites.

AB ► abbr. **1** able seaman. **2** Alberta.

a·back /əˈbak/ ► adv. (in phrase **take someone aback**) shock or surprise someone: *I was taken aback by the question.*

ab·a·cus /ˈabəkəs/ ► n. (pl. **abacuses**) a frame with rows of wires or dowels along which beads are slid, used for counting.

a·baft /əˈbaft/ ► adv. & prep. Nautical in or behind the stern of a ship.

ab·a·lo·ne /ˌabəˈlōnē, ˈabəˌlōnē/ ► n. an edible sea creature that has a shell lined with mother-of-pearl.

a·ban·don /əˈbandən/ ► v. **1** desert or leave permanently: *he abandoned his family and moved to London.* **2** give up a course of action completely. **3** (**abandon oneself to**) make no attempt to resist something: *she abandoned herself to his kiss.* ► n. complete lack of self-control or self-consciousness: *dancers swung their bodies with wild abandon.* ■ **a·ban·don·ment** n.

a·ban·doned /əˈbandənd/ ► adj. wild and uninhibited.

a·base /əˈbās/ ► v. (**abase oneself**) behave in a way that is demeaning or degrading. ■ **a·base·ment** n.

a·bashed /əˈbasHt/ ► adj. embarrassed or ashamed.

a·bate /əˈbāt/ ► v. (of something bad) become less severe or widespread: *the epidemic showed no sign of abating.* ■ **a·bate·ment** n.

ab·at·toir /ˈabəˌtwär/ ► n. Brit. a slaughterhouse.

ab·bé /aˈbā/ ► n. (in France) an abbot or other clergyman.

ab·bess /ˈabis/ ► n. a woman who is the head of an abbey of nuns.

ab·bey /ˈabē/ ► n. (pl. **abbeys**) a building occupied by a community of monks or nuns.

ab·bot /ˈabət/ ► n. a man who is the head of an abbey of monks.

ab·bre·vi·ate /əˈbrēvēˌāt/ ► v. shorten a word, phrase, or text.

ab·bre·vi·a·tion /əˌbrēvēˈāsHən/ ► n. a shortened form of a word or phrase.

ABC ► n. **1** the alphabet. **2** an alphabetical guide to something. **3** the basic facts of a subject.

ab·di·cate /ˈabdiˌkāt/ ► v. **1** (of a king or queen) give up the throne. **2** fail to fulfill or carry out a duty or responsibility. ■ **ab·di·ca·tion** /ˌabdiˈkāsHən/ n.

ab·do·men /ˈabdəmən, abˈdōmən/ ► n. **1** the part of the body that contains the stomach, intestines, and reproductive organs. **2** the rear part of the body of an insect, spider, or crustacean. ■ **ab·dom·i·nal** /abˈdämənl/ adj. **ab·dom·i·nal·ly** adv.

ab·duct /abˈdəkt/ ► v. take someone away, typically using force to do so. ■ **ab·duct·ee** n. **ab·duc·tion** n. **ab·duc·tor** n.

a·beam /əˈbēm/ ► adv. at right angles to a ship's or an aircraft's length.

a·bed /əˈbed/ ► adv. old use in bed.

ab·er·rant /ˈabərənt, əˈber-/ ► adj. not normal or acceptable: *his aberrant behavior.*

ab·er·ra·tion /ˌabəˈrāsHən/ ► n. **1** an action, event, or way of behaving that is not normal or acceptable. **2** a temporary failure of judgment or concentration: *a mental aberration.*

a·bet /əˈbet/ ► v. (**abets, abetting, abetted**) (usu. in phrase **aid and abet**) encourage or assist someone to do something wrong, in particular to commit a crime. ■ **a·bet·ment** n. **a·bet·tor** (also **abetter**) n.

a·bey·ance /əˈbāəns/ ► n. (in phrase **in/into abeyance**) temporarily suspended or not in use.

ab·hor /abˈhôr/ ► v. (**abhors, abhorring, abhorred**) hate or detest: *he abhorred sexism.*

ab·hor·rent /ab'hôrənt, -'här-/ ▶adj. disgusting or hateful. ■ **ab·hor·rence** n.

a·bide /ə'bīd/ ▶v. 1 (**abide by**) accept or obey a rule or decision. 2 (**cannot abide**) dislike very much: *I can't abide lies.* 3 (of a feeling or memory) last for a long time. 4 old use live in a place.

a·bid·ing /ə'bīdiNG/ ▶adj. lasting a long time; enduring: *an abiding love of the countryside.* ■ **a·bid·ing·ly** adv.

a·bil·i·ty /ə'bilitē/ ▶n. (pl. **abilities**) 1 the power or capacity to do something. 2 skill or talent.

ab·ject /'abjekt, ab'jekt/ ▶adj. 1 very unpleasant and degrading: *families living in abject poverty.* 2 completely without pride or dignity: *an abject apology.* ■ **ab·ject·ly** adv.

ab·jure /ab'jŏŏr/ ▶v. formal swear to give up a belief or claim.

ab·la·tion /ab'blāsHən/ ▶n. 1 the surgical removal of body tissue. 2 the loss of solid material such as ice or rock by melting, evaporation, or erosion.

ab·la·tive /'ablətiv/ ▶adj. Grammar (of a case) indicating an agent, instrument, or source, expressed by 'by,' 'with,' or 'from' in English.

a·blaze /ə'blāz/ ▶adj. burning fiercely.

a·ble /'ābəl/ ▶adj. (**abler, ablest**) 1 having the power, skill, or means to do something. 2 skillful and competent: *a very able public speaker.* ■ **a·bly** adv.

a·ble-bod·ied /'ābəl,bädēd, ,ābəl'bädēd/ ▶adj. physically fit and healthy.

ab·lu·tions /ə'bloōsHənz/ ▶pl.n. formal or humorous the process of washing oneself.

ABM ▶abbr. antiballistic missile.

ab·ne·ga·tion /,abni'gāsHən/ ▶n. formal the giving up of something that is valuable or desired. ■ **ab·ne·gate** /'abni,gāt/ v.

ab·nor·mal /ab'nôrməl/ ▶adj. differing from what is normal or typical. ■ **ab·nor·mal·ly** adv.

ab·nor·mal·i·ty /,abnôr'malitē/ ▶n. (pl. **abnormalities**) 1 a feature or event that is not normal: *babies with congenital abnormalities.* 2 the state of being abnormal.

A·bo /'abō/ ▶n. (pl. **Abos**) Austral. informal, offensive an Aboriginal.

a·board /ə'bôrd/ ▶adv. & prep. on or into a ship, train, or other vehicle.

a·bode /ə'bōd/ ▶n. formal or literary a person's house or home.

a·bol·ish /ə'bälisH/ ▶v. officially put an end to a system, law, or practice.

ab·o·li·tion /,abə'lisHən/ ▶n. the official ending of a system, law, or practice: *the abolition of the death penalty.*

ab·o·li·tion·ist /,abə'lisHənist/ ▶n. a person who supports the abolition of something, especially capital punishment or (in the past) slavery. ■ **ab·o·li·tion·ism** n.

A-bomb ▶n. an atom bomb.

a·bom·i·na·ble /ə'bäm(ə)nəbəl/ ▶adj. 1 very unpleasant and causing disgust: *an abominable crime.* 2 informal very bad; terrible. ■ **a·bom·i·na·bly** adv.

A·bom·i·na·ble Snow·man ▶n. the yeti.

a·bom·i·nate /ə'bämə,nāt/ ▶v. formal detest something or someone.

a·bom·i·na·tion /ə,bämə'nāsHən/ ▶n. 1 a thing that causes disgust or hatred. 2 a feeling of hatred.

ab·o·rig·i·nal /,abə'rijənl/ ▶adj. 1 inhabiting or existing in a land from the earliest times or from before the arrival of colonists. 2 (**Aboriginal**) relating to the Australian Aboriginals. ▶n. 1 a person who has inhabited a land from the earliest times. 2 (**Aboriginal**) a member of one of the original peoples of Australia.

ab·o·rig·i·ne /,abə'rijənē/ ▶n. an original inhabitant of a land, especially (**Aborigine**) an Australian Aboriginal.

a·bort /ə'bôrt/ ▶v. 1 carry out the abortion of a fetus. 2 (of a pregnant woman or female animal) have a miscarriage. 3 bring to a premature end because of a problem or fault: *the helicopter was forced to abort its mission owing to a blizzard.*

a·bor·ti·fa·cient /ə,bôrtə'fāsHənt/ Medicine ▶adj. (of a drug) causing an abortion. ▶n. a drug that causes an abortion.

a·bor·tion /ə'bôrsHən/ ▶n. 1 a surgical operation in which a human pregnancy is deliberately brought to an end. 2 the natural ending of a pregnancy before the fetus is able to survive on its own.

a·bor·tion·ist /ə'bôrsHənist/ ▶n. derogatory a person who carries out abortions.

a·bor·tive /ə'bôrtiv/ ▶adj. (of an action) failing to achieve the intended result; unsuccessful: *an abortive military coup.*

a·bound /ə'bound/ ▶v. 1 exist in large numbers or amounts. 2 (**abound in/with**) have in large numbers or amounts: *woodlands abounding with spring flowers.*

a·bout /ə'bout/ ▶prep. & adv. 1 on the subject of; concerning. 2 used to indicate movement within an area or location in a place; around: *she looked about the room.* 3 approximately.
– PHRASES **be about to** be on the point of.

a·bout-face (also Brit. **about-turn**) ▶n. 1 a complete change of opinion or policy. 2 Military a turn made so as to face the opposite direction.

a·bove /ə'bəv/ ▶prep. & adv. 1 at a higher level than. 2 rather or more than: *he valued safety above comfort.* 3 (in printed text) mentioned earlier.
– PHRASES **above oneself** having too high an opinion of oneself. **not be above** be capable of doing something dishonest or dishonorable.

a·bove-board /ə'bəv,bôrd/ ▶adj. legitimate, honest, and open. ▶adv. legitimately, honestly, and openly: *the accountants acted completely aboveboard.*

ab·ra·ca·dab·ra /,abrəkə'dabrə/ ▶exclam. a word said by magicians when performing a trick.

a·brade /ə'brād/ ▶v. scrape or wear away the surface of something.

a·bra·sion /ə'brāzHən/ ▶n. 1 a patch of skin that has been damaged by being scraped. 2 the scraping or wearing away of the surface of something.

a·bra·sive /ə'brāsiv, -ziv/ ▶adj. 1 able to polish or clean a hard surface by rubbing or grinding. 2 showing little concern for the feelings of other people; harsh or unkind: *a politician renowned for his abrasive manner.* ▶n. a substance used for cleaning or polishing hard surfaces. ■ **a·bra·sive·ly** adv. **a·bra·sive·ness** n.

a·breast /ə'brest/ ▶adv. 1 side by side and facing the same way. 2 (**abreast of**) up to date with: *I shall keep you abreast of any developments.*

a·bridge /ə'brij/ ▶v. shorten a text or filmed production. ■ **a·bridg·ment** (also **abridgement**) n.

a·broad /ə'brôd/ ▸ adv. **1** in or to a foreign country or countries. **2** felt or talked about by many people: *there was a new mood abroad.* **3** over a wide area: *millions of seeds are scattered abroad.* **4** old use out of doors.

ab·ro·gate /'abrə,gāt/ ▸ v. formal cancel or end a law or agreement. ■ **ab·ro·ga·tion** /,abrə'gāSHən/ n.

ab·rupt /ə'brəpt/ ▸ adj. **1** sudden and unexpected: *the car came to an abrupt halt.* **2** brief to the point of rudeness: *an unnecessarily abrupt response.* ■ **ab·rupt·ly** adv. **ab·rupt·ness** n.

ABS ▸ abbr. antilock braking system.

abs /abz/ ▸ pl.n. informal the abdominal muscles.

ab·scess /'ab,ses/ ▸ n. a swelling on the skin or in the body, containing pus.

ab·scis·sa /ab'sisə/ ▸ n. (pl. **abscissae** /-'sisē/ or **abscissas**) Mathematics the distance from a point on a graph to the vertical or y -axis; the x -coordinate.

ab·scond /ab'skänd/ ▸ v. leave a place hurriedly and secretly to escape from custody or avoid arrest. ■ **ab·scond·er** n.

ab·sence /'absəns/ ▸ n. **1** the state of being away from a place or person. **2** (**absence of**) the nonexistence or lack of: *the absence of reliable information.*

ab·sent ▸ adj. /'absənt/ **1** not present: *the number of students absent from school.* **2** showing that someone is not paying attention: *an absent expression.* ▸ v. /ab'sent/ (**absent oneself**) leave or stay away from somewhere. ■ **ab·sent·ly** /'absəntlē/ adv.

ab·sen·tee /,absən'tē/ ▸ n. a person who is absent.

ab·sen·tee·ism /,absən'tē,izəm/ ▸ n. frequent absences from work or school without good reason.

ab·sent·mind·ed /'absənt,mīndid/ ▸ adj. forgetful or tending not to pay attention. ■ **ab·sent·mind·ed·ly** adv. **ab·sent·mind·ed·ness** n.

ab·sinthe /'ab,sinTH/ ▸ n. a green anise-flavored liqueur, formerly made with wormwood.

ab·so·lute /'absə,lōōt, ,absə'lōōt/ ▸ adj. **1** not qualified or reduced in any way; total: *absolute silence.* **2** having unlimited power: *an absolute ruler.* **3** not related or compared to anything else: *absolute moral principles.* **4** Law (of a decree) final. ▸ n. Philosophy a value or principle that is universally valid or that can be viewed without relation to other things.

ab·so·lute·ly /,absə'lōōtlē/ ▸ adv. **1** completely; entirely: *she trusted him absolutely.* **2** used for emphasis or to express agreement.

ab·so·lute ma·jor·i·ty ▸ n. a majority over all rivals or opposition considered as a group; more than half.

ab·so·lute pitch ▸ n. Music **1** perfect pitch. **2** pitch according to a fixed standard defined by the frequency of the sound vibration.

ab·so·lute tem·per·a·ture ▸ n. a temperature measured from absolute zero in kelvins.

ab·so·lute ze·ro ▸ n. the lowest temperature theoretically possible (zero kelvins, −273.15°C, −459.67.15°F).

ab·so·lu·tion /,absə'lōōSHən/ ▸ n. formal forgiveness of a person's sins.

ab·so·lut·ism /'absəlōō,tizəm/ ▸ n. the political principle that a ruler or government should have unlimited power. ■ **ab·so·lut·ist** n. & adj.

ab·solve /ab'zälv, -'sälv/ ▸ v. declare someone to be free from guilt, responsibility, or sin.

ab·sorb /ab'zôrb, -'sôrb/ ▸ v. **1** take in or soak up liquid or another substance. **2** understand information fully. **3** incorporate something smaller or less powerful: *the family firm was absorbed into a larger group.* **4** use up time or resources. **5** reduce the effect or strength of sound or an impact. **6** interest someone and hold their attention completely: *she was absorbed in her work.* ■ **ab·sorb·a·ble** adj. **ab·sorb·er** n.

ab·sorb·ent /ab'zôrbənt, -'sôr-/ ▸ adj. able to soak up liquid easily. ■ **ab·sorb·en·cy** n.

ab·sorb·ing /ab'zôrbiNG, -'sôr-/ ▸ adj. holding someone's interest completely; very interesting.

ab·sorp·tion /ab'zôrpSHən, -'sôrp-/ ▸ n. **1** the process by which one thing absorbs or is absorbed by another. **2** the state of being engrossed in something. ■ **ab·sorp·tive** adj.

ab·stain /ab'stān/ ▸ v. **1** restrain oneself from doing or enjoying the pleasure of something: *they abstained from alcohol for two months.* **2** formally choose not to vote. ■ **ab·stain·er** n.

ab·ste·mi·ous /ab'stēmēəs/ ▸ adj. deliberately limiting one's consumption of food or alcohol. ■ **ab·ste·mi·ous·ly** adv. **ab·ste·mi·ous·ness** n.

ab·sten·tion /ab'stenSHən/ ▸ n. **1** a deliberate decision not to vote. **2** abstinence.

ab·sti·nence /'abstinəns/ ▸ n. the avoidance of something enjoyable, such as food or alcohol. ■ **ab·sti·nent** adj.

ab·stract ▸ adj. /'ab'strakt, 'ab,strakt/ **1** relating to ideas or qualities rather than physical things. **2** (of art) using color and shapes to create an effect rather than attempting to represent reality accurately. ▸ v. /ab'strakt/ take out or remove something. ▸ n. /'ab,strakt/ **1** a summary of a book or article. **2** an abstract work of art. ■ **ab·stract·ly** adv.

ab·stract·ed /ab'straktid/ ▸ adj. not concentrating on what is happening; preoccupied. ■ **ab·stract·ed·ly** adv.

ab·strac·tion /ab'strakSHən/ ▸ n. **1** the quality of being abstract. **2** something that exists only as an idea. **3** a preoccupied state of mind. **4** the action of removing something.

ab·struse /ab'strōōs/ ▸ adj. difficult to understand: *an abstruse philosophical controversy.*

ab·surd /ab'sərd, -'zərd/ ▸ adj. completely unreasonable or illogical; ridiculous. ■ **ab·surd·i·ty** n. **ab·surd·ly** adv.

a·bun·dance /ə'bəndəns/ ▸ n. **1** a very large quantity of something. **2** the state of having a very large quantity of something: *vines grew in abundance.*

a·bun·dant /ə'bəndənt/ ▸ adj. **1** existing or available in large quantities; plentiful. **2** (**abundant in**) having plenty of: *riverbanks abundant in beautiful wild plants.*

a·bun·dant·ly /ə'bəndəntlē/ ▸ adv. **1** in large quantities; plentifully. **2** extremely: *he made it abundantly clear that he would not tolerate racism.*

a·buse ▸ v. /ə'byōōz/ **1** use badly or wrongly: *he had abused his position as a doctor.* **2** treat a person or animal with cruelty or violence. **3** speak to someone in an insulting and offensive way. ▸ n. /ə'byōōs/ **1** the wrong use of something: *an abuse of public funds.* **2** cruel and violent treatment of a person or animal. **3** insulting and offensive language. ■ **a·bus·er** n.

a·bu·sive /ə'byōōsiv, -ziv/ ▸ adj. **1** very offensive

and insulting. **2** involving cruelty and violence: *an abusive relationship.* ■ **a·bu·sive·ly** adv.

a·but /əˈbət/ ▸ v. (**abuts, abutting, abutted**) be next to or touching: *the states that abut the Great Lakes.*

a·bu·ti·lon /əˈbyōōtlˌän/ ▸ n. an herbaceous plant or shrub with showy yellow, red, or mauve flowers.

a·but·ment /əˈbətmənt/ ▸ n. a structure supporting the side of an arch, especially at the end of a bridge.

a·buzz /əˈbəz/ ▸ adj. filled with talk or activity: *the city was abuzz with rumors.*

a·bys·mal /əˈbizməl/ ▸ adj. **1** extremely bad. **2** literary very deep. ■ **a·bys·mal·ly** adv.

a·byss /əˈbis/ ▸ n. a very deep chasm or hole.

a·byss·al /əˈbisəl/ ▸ adj. relating to the depths of the ocean.

Ab·ys·sin·i·an /ˌabəˈsinēən/ historical ▸ adj. relating to Abyssinia (the former name of Ethiopia). ▸ n. a person from Abyssinia.

AC ▸ abbr. **1** alternating current. **2** air conditioning. **3** athletic club.

Ac ▸ symbol the chemical element actinium.

a/c ▸ abbr. **1** account. **2** (also **A/C**) air conditioning.

a·ca·cia /əˈkāshə/ ▸ n. a tree or shrub with yellow or white flowers, found in warm climates.

ac·a·deme /ˌakəˈdēm, ˈakəˌdēm/ ▸ n. (often in phrase **the groves of academe**) literary academia.

ac·a·de·mi·a /ˌakəˈdēmēə/ ▸ n. the world of teaching and research conducted at universities and colleges or the people involved in it.

ac·a·dem·ic /ˌakəˈdemik/ ▸ adj. **1** relating to education and scholarship. **2** not connected to a real situation; of theoretical interest only. ▸ n. a teacher or scholar in a college or university. ■ **ac·a·dem·i·cal·ly** adv.

ac·a·de·mi·cian /ˌakədəˈmishən, əˌkadə-/ ▸ n. **1** an academic. **2** a member of an academy.

ac·a·dem·i·cism /ˌakəˈdeməˌsizəm/ ▸ n. the practice of keeping to formal or conventional rules and traditions in art or literature.

a·cad·e·my /əˈkadəmē/ ▸ n. (pl. **academies**) **1** a place of study or training in a special field. **2** a society or institution of distinguished scholars, artists, or scientists. **3** a secondary school.

A·cad·e·my A·ward ▸ n. an award given by the Academy of Motion Picture Arts and Sciences for achievement in the motion-picture industry; an Oscar.

A·ca·di·an /əˈkādēən/ ▸ adj. relating to the former French colony of Acadia (now Nova Scotia) or its people. ▸ n. **1** a person from Acadia. **2** a descendant of the Acadians deported to Louisiana in the 18th century; a Cajun.

a·can·thus /əˈkan(t)həs/ ▸ n. a plant or shrub with spiny decorative leaves.

a cap·pel·la /ˌä kəˈpelə/ ▸ adj. & adv. (of music) sung without instrumental accompaniment.

ac·cede /akˈsēd/ ▸ v. (usu. **accede to**) formal **1** agree to a demand or request. **2** take up an office or position: *he acceded to the throne in 1972.*

ac·cel·er·an·do /äkˌseləˈrändō, ak-, äˌCHelə-/ ▸ adv. & adj. Music with a gradual increase of speed.

ac·cel·er·ant /akˈselərənt/ ▸ n. a substance used to help fire spread.

ac·cel·er·ate /akˈseləˌrāt/ ▸ v. **1** begin to move more quickly. **2** increase in rate, amount, or extent: *inflation started to accelerate.*

ac·cel·er·a·tion /akˌseləˈrāshən/ ▸ n. **1** the rate at which a vehicle increases speed. **2** an increase in the rate, amount, or extent of something: *the acceleration of economic reform.*

ac·cel·er·a·tor /akˈseləˌrātər/ ▸ n. **1** a foot pedal that controls the speed of a vehicle. **2** Physics a piece of equipment that causes charged particles to move at high speeds.

ac·cel·er·om·e·ter /akˌseləˈrämitər/ ▸ n. an instrument for measuring the acceleration of a moving vehicle.

ac·cent ▸ n. /ˈakˌsent/ **1** a distinctive way of pronouncing a language, associated with a country, area, or social background. **2** an emphasis given to a syllable, word, or note. **3** a mark on a letter or word showing how a sound is pronounced or stressed. **4** a special importance, value, or prominence: *the accent is on participation.* ▸ v. /ˈakˌsent, akˈsent/ **1** (as adj. **accented**) spoken with a foreign accent: *he spoke heavily accented English.* **2** stress or emphasize something.

ac·cen·tu·ate /akˈsenchōōˌāt/ ▸ v. make more noticeable or prominent: *a deep tan that accentuated his blue eyes.* ■ **ac·cen·tu·a·tion** n.

ac·cept /akˈsept/ ▸ v. **1** agree to receive or do something offered. **2** believe to be valid or correct: *the committee accepted his explanation.* **3** admit responsibility or blame for something. **4** make someone welcome. **5** come to terms with an unwelcome situation: *she had to accept the fact that he might not return.* ■ **ac·cept·ance** n. **ac·cep·tor** n.

USAGE

Do not confuse **accept** with **except**. Accept means 'agree to receive or do something' (*she accepted the job*), whereas **except** means 'not including; apart from' (*I work every day except Sunday*).

ac·cept·a·ble /akˈseptəbəl/ ▸ adj. **1** able to be accepted. **2** good enough; adequate: *the food was just about acceptable.* ■ **ac·cept·a·bil·i·ty** /akˌseptəˈbilitē/ n. **ac·cept·a·bly** adv.

ac·cess /ˈakˌses/ ▸ n. **1** the means or opportunity to approach or enter a place. **2** the right or opportunity to use something or see someone: *do you have access to a computer?* **3** the process of obtaining information stored in a computer's memory. **4** literary an attack or outburst of an emotion: *an access of rage.* ▸ v. **1** enter a place. **2** obtain data stored in a computer.

ac·ces·si·ble /akˈsesəbəl/ ▸ adj. **1** able to be reached or used. **2** friendly and easy to talk to. **3** easily understood or enjoyed: *her writing is straightforward and very accessible.* ■ **ac·ces·si·bil·i·ty** /-ˌsesəˈbilitē/ n. **ac·ces·si·bly** adv.

ac·ces·sion /akˈseshən/ ▸ n. **1** the gaining of an important position or rank: *her accession to the throne.* **2** the process of formally joining a group or organization. **3** a new item added to a library or museum collection.

ac·ces·so·rize /akˈsesəˌrīz/ ▸ v. add a fashion accessory to a garment.

ac·ces·so·ry /akˈses(ə)rē/ ▸ n. (pl. **accessories**) **1** a thing that can be added to something else to make it more useful or attractive. **2** a small article carried or worn to improve the look of a garment. **3** Law a person who helps someone commit a crime without taking part in it.

ac·ci·dent /'aksidənt/ ▶ n. **1** an unexpected and unpleasant event. **2** an event that is unforeseen or has no apparent cause.
– PHRASES **by accident** in a way that is not planned or organized.

ac·ci·den·tal /ˌaksi'dentl/ ▶ adj. happening by accident: *a verdict of accidental death.* ▶ n. a sign attached to a musical note indicating a momentary departure from the key signature. ■ **ac·ci·den·tal·ly** adv.

ac·ci·dent-prone ▶ adj. tending to be involved in a greater than average number of accidents.

ac·claim /ə'klām/ ▶ v. praise enthusiastically and publicly: *the car was acclaimed as the best in its class.* ▶ n. enthusiastic public praise.

ac·cla·ma·tion /ˌaklə'māsHən/ ▶ n. loud and enthusiastic approval or praise.

ac·cli·ma·tize /ə'klīməˌtīz/ ▶ v. adapt to a new climate or new conditions. ■ **ac·cli·ma·ti·za·tion** /əˌklīmətə'zāsHən/ n.

ac·co·lade /'akəˌlād, -ˌläd/ ▶ n. something given as a special honor or as a reward for excellence.

ac·com·mo·date /ə'käməˌdāt/ ▶ v. **1** provide lodging or space for: *the boat accommodates 40 passengers.* **2** adapt to or fit in with: *they tried hard to accommodate the children's needs.*

ac·com·mo·dat·ing /ə'käməˌdātiNG/ ▶ adj. willing to help or fit in with someone's wishes.

ac·com·mo·da·tion /əˌkämə'dāsHən/ ▶ n. **1** (**accommodations**) a place where someone may live or stay. **2** (**accommodations**) lodging; room and board. **3** an action of accommodating or the process of being accommodated. **4** a settlement or compromise.

ac·com·pa·ni·ment /ə'kəmp(ə)nimənt/ ▶ n. **1** a musical part played to support a voice, group, or other instrument. **2** something that adds to or improves something else: *the sauce is a perfect accompaniment to all fish dishes.*

ac·com·pa·nist /ə'kəmpənist/ ▶ n. a person who plays a musical accompaniment.

ac·com·pa·ny /ə'kəmp(ə)nē/ ▶ v. (**accompanies, accompanying, accompanied**) **1** go somewhere with someone. **2** be present or occur at the same time as: *violent winds accompanied by rain, hail, or snow.* **3** play musical support or backing for a voice, group, or other instrument.

ac·com·plice /ə'kämplis/ ▶ n. a person who helps another commit a crime.

ac·com·plish /ə'kämplisH/ ▶ v. achieve or complete something successfully.

ac·com·plished /ə'kämplisHt/ ▶ adj. highly skilled: *an accomplished musician.*

ac·com·plish·ment /ə'kämplisHmənt/ ▶ n. **1** something that has been achieved successfully: *his military accomplishments.* **2** a skill or special ability. **3** the successful achievement of a task.

ac·cord /ə'kôrd/ ▶ v. **1** give power or status to someone. **2** (**accord with**) be in agreement or consistent with: *his views accorded with those of Harris.* ▶ n. **1** an official agreement or treaty. **2** agreement in opinion or feeling: *we are in accord on all points.*
– PHRASES **of one's own accord** willingly. **with one accord** in a united way.

ac·cord·ance /ə'kôrdns/ ▶ n. (in phrase **in accordance with**) in a way conforming with: *a ballot held in accordance with union rules.*

ac·cord·ing /ə'kôrdiNG/ ▶ adv. (**according to**) **1** as stated by someone. **2** following or agreeing with: *the event did not go according to plan.*

ac·cord·ing·ly /ə'kôrdiNGlē/ ▶ adv. **1** in a way that is appropriate. **2** therefore.

ac·cor·di·on /ə'kôrdēən/ ▶ n. a musical instrument played by stretching and squeezing with the hands to work a bellows, the notes being sounded by buttons or keys. ■ **ac·cor·di·on·ist** n.

ac·cost /ə'kôst, ə'käst/ ▶ v. approach someone and speak to them, especially in a rude or aggressive way.

ac·count /ə'kount/ ▶ n. **1** a description of an event or experience. **2** a record of money spent and received. **3** a service through a bank or firm by which funds are held on behalf of a customer, or goods or services are supplied on credit. **4** importance: *money was of no account to her.* ▶ v. regard in a particular way: *her visit could not be accounted a complete success.*
– PHRASES **account for 1** supply or form a particular amount or part of: *the industry accounts for 11 percent of the US economy.* **2** give a satisfactory explanation of. **call someone to account** ask someone to explain a mistake or bad performance. **on someone's account** for someone's benefit: *don't trouble yourself on my account.* **on account of** because of. **on no account** under no circumstances. **take account of** take something into consideration. **turn something to (good) account** turn something to one's advantage.

ac·count·a·ble /ə'kountəbəl/ ▶ adj. responsible for one's actions and expected to explain them. ■ **ac·count·a·bil·i·ty** /əˌkountə'bilitē/ n.

ac·count·ant /ə'kount(ə)nt/ ▶ n. a person who keeps or checks financial accounts. ■ **ac·count·an·cy** n.

ac·count·ing /ə'kountiNG/ ▶ n. the keeping of financial accounts.

ac·cou·tered /ə'kŌŌtərd/ (Brit. **accoutred**) ▶ adj. clothed or equipped.

ac·cou·ter·ment /ə'kŌŌtərmənt, -trə-/ (Brit. **accoutrement**) ▶ n. an item of clothing or equipment required for a particular activity.

ac·cred·it /ə'kredit/ ▶ v. (**accredits, accrediting, accredited**) **1** (**accredit something to**) attribute something to someone. **2** give official authorization to someone or something. **3** send a diplomat or journalist to a particular place or post. ■ **ac·cred·i·ta·tion** /əˌkredi'tāsHən/ n.

ac·crete /ə'krēt/ ▶ v. grow or be formed by a gradual buildup of new layers.

ac·cre·tion /ə'krēsHən/ ▶ n. **1** the process of growing or increasing in size as the result of a gradual buildup of new layers of something. **2** a thing formed or added in this way.

ac·crue /ə'krŌŌ/ ▶ v. (**accrues, accruing, accrued**) **1** (of money) be received in regular or increasing amounts. **2** collect or receive payments or benefits. ■ **ac·cru·al** n.

ac·cul·tur·ate /ə'kəlCHəˌrāt/ ▶ v. successfully absorb someone or something into a different culture or social group. ■ **ac·cul·tur·a·tion** /əˌkəlCHə'rāsHən/ n.

ac·cu·mu·late /ə'kyŌŌmyəˌlāt/ ▶ v. **1** gather together a number or quantity of something. **2** increase in number or quantity: *very large debts accumulated.* ■ **ac·cu·mu·la·tion** /əˌkyŌŌmyə'lāsHən/ n. **ac·cu·mu·la·tive**

/ə'kyŏŏmyələtiv, -ˌlātiv/ adj.

ac·cu·mu·la·tor /ə'kyŏŏmyəˌlātər/ ▶ n. 1 a person or thing that accumulates things. 2 Computing a register used to contain the results of an arithmetical or logical operation. 3 Brit. a large rechargeable electric cell.

ac·cu·rate /'akyərit/ ▶ adj. 1 correct in all details: *an accurate description.* 2 reaching an intended target: *an accurate shot.* ▪ **ac·cu·ra·cy** /'akyərəsē/ n. **ac·cu·rate·ly** adv.

> USAGE
> On the distinction between **accurate** and **precise**, see the note at **PRECISE**.

ac·curs·ed /ə'kərst, ə'kərsid/ ▶ adj. 1 literary under a curse. 2 informal horrible.

ac·cu·sa·tion /ˌakyə'zāsHən, ˌakyŏŏ-/ ▶ n. a claim that someone has done something illegal or wrong.

ac·cu·sa·tive /ə'kyŏŏzətiv/ ▶ n. a grammatical case used for the object of a verb.

ac·cu·sa·to·ry /ə'kyŏŏzəˌtôrē/ ▶ adj. suggesting that one believes a person has done something wrong: *an accusatory stare.*

ac·cuse /ə'kyŏŏz/ ▶ v. claim that someone has committed a crime or done something wrong: *he was accused of attempted murder.* ▪ **ac·cus·er** n.

ac·cus·tom /ə'kəstəm/ ▶ v. 1 (**accustom someone/thing to**) make someone or something used to. 2 (**be accustomed to**) be used to.

ac·cus·tomed /ə'kəstəmd/ ▶ adj. customary; usual: *his accustomed route.*

AC/DC ▶ adj. 1 alternating current/direct current. 2 informal bisexual.

ace /ās/ ▶ n. 1 a playing card with a single spot on it, the highest card in its suit in most games. 2 informal a person who is very good at a particular activity: *a snowboarding ace.* 3 a war pilot who has shot down many enemy aircraft. 4 Tennis a service that an opponent is unable to return. 5 Golf, informal a hole in one. ▶ adj. informal very good. – PHRASES **ace up one's sleeve** a plan or piece of information kept secret until needed.

a·cel·lu·lar /ā'selyələr/ ▶ adj. Biology 1 not divided into or containing cells. 2 consisting of one cell only.

a·cer /ā'sər/ ▶ n. a maple or related tree, having leaves with five lobes.

a·cer·bic /ə'sərbik/ ▶ adj. (of a person or their remarks) sharply critical and forthright. ▪ **a·cer·bi·cal·ly** adv. **a·cer·bi·ty** /-bitē/ n.

a·ce·ta·min·o·phen /əˌsētə'minəfən/ ▶ n. a drug used to relieve pain and reduce fever.

ac·e·tate /'asiˌtāt/ ▶ n. 1 Chemistry a salt or ester of acetic acid. 2 fiber or plastic made of a substance produced from cellulose.

a·ce·tic ac·id /ə'sētik/ ▶ n. the acid that gives vinegar its characteristic taste.

ac·e·tone /'asiˌtōn/ ▶ n. a colorless liquid used as a solvent.

a·ce·tyl·cho·line /əˌsētl'kō,lēn, ˌasitl-/ ▶ n. Biochemistry a compound that occurs throughout the nervous system, in which it functions as a neurotransmitter.

a·cet·y·lene /ə'setlən, -ˌēn/ ▶ n. a gas that burns with a bright flame, used in welding.

ACH ▶ abbr. Automated Clearinghouse, the system in the US that handles check transactions between banks.

ache /āk/ ▶ n. a continuous or long-lasting dull

pain. ▶ v. 1 suffer from an ache. 2 (**ache for/to do**) feel great desire for or to do: *he ached to see her again.* ▪ **ach·ing** adj.

a·chieve /ə'CHēv/ ▶ v. succeed in doing something by effort, skill, or courage. ▪ **a·chiev·a·ble** adj. **a·chiev·er** n.

a·chieve·ment /ə'CHēvmənt/ ▶ n. 1 a thing that is done successfully: *the government's greatest economic achievement.* 2 the process of achieving something.

Achil·les heel /ə'kilēz/ ▶ n. a weak or vulnerable point.

Achil·les ten·don /ə'kilēz/ ▶ n. the tendon that connects the calf muscles to the heel.

a·chon·dro·pla·sia /āˌkändrə'plāzH(ē)ə/ ▶ n. a hereditary condition in which the bones of the arms and legs fail to grow to the normal size.

ach·ro·mat·ic /ˌakrə'matik, ˌākrə-/ ▶ adj. 1 transmitting light without separating it into its constituent colors. 2 without color.

ach·y /'ākē/ (also **achey**) ▶ adj. (**achier, achiest**) suffering from an ache or aches.

ac·id /'asid/ ▶ n. 1 a substance with chemical properties that include turning litmus red, neutralizing alkalis, and dissolving some metals. 2 informal the drug LSD. ▶ adj. 1 having the properties of an acid; having a pH of less than 7. 2 sharp-tasting or sour. 3 (of a remark) bitter or cutting. ▪ **ac·id·ly** adv. **ac·id·y** adj.

ac·id house ▶ n. a kind of fast, repetitive synthesized dance music.

a·cid·ic /ə'sidik/ ▶ adj. 1 containing acid. 2 having a sour taste.

a·cid·i·fy /ə'sidəˌfī/ ▶ v. (**acidifies, acidifying, acidified**) make or become acid. ▪ **a·cid·i·fi·ca·tion** /əˌsidəfi'kāsHən/ n.

a·cid·i·ty /ə'siditē/ ▶ n. 1 the level of acid in something. 2 bitterness or sharpness in a person's remarks or tone.

ac·id jazz ▶ n. a kind of dance music incorporating elements of jazz, funk, soul, and hip-hop.

ac·i·doph·i·lus /ˌasi'däfələs/ ▶ n. a bacterium used to make yogurt.

ac·id rain ▶ n. rainfall made acidic by atmospheric pollution resulting from the burning of coal or oil in factories.

ac·id re·flux ▶ n. a condition in which gastric acid is regurgitated.

ac·id test ▶ n. a conclusive test of the success, truth, or value of something.

a·cid·u·late /ə'sijəˌlāt/ ▶ v. make something slightly acidic.

a·cid·u·lous /ə'sijələs/ ▶ adj. (of a remark) cutting; bitter.

ack-ack /'ak ˌak/ ▶ n. Military, informal antiaircraft gunfire or guns.

ac·kee ▶ n. variant spelling of AKEE.

ac·knowl·edge /ak'nälij/ ▶ v. 1 accept or admit that something exists or is true: *he acknowledged that he had made mistakes.* 2 confirm that one has received or is grateful for: *please acknowledge receipt of this letter.* 3 show that one has noticed someone by making a gesture of greeting.

ac·knowl·edg·ment /ak'nälijmənt/ (also chiefly Brit. **acknowledgement**) ▶ n. 1 the action of acknowledging something or someone. 2 something done or given to express gratitude.

ACLU ▶ abbr. American Civil Liberties Union, a nonprofit advocacy organization.

ac·me /'akmē/ ▶ n. the point at which something is at its best or most highly developed.

ac·ne /'aknē/ ▶ n. a skin condition causing many red pimples on the face.

ac·o·lyte /'akə,līt/ ▶ n. **1** an assistant or follower. **2** a person helping a priest in a religious service.

ac·o·nite /'akə,nīt/ ▶ n. **1** a poisonous plant with pink or purple flowers. **2** (also **winter aconite**) a small spring-flowering plant with yellow flowers.

a·corn /'ā,kôrn/ ▶ n. the fruit of the oak tree, a smooth oval nut in a cuplike base.

a·cous·tic /ə'kōōstik/ ▶ adj. **1** relating to sound or hearing. **2** not having electrical amplification: *an acoustic guitar.* ▶ n. (**acoustics**) **1** the features of a room or building that affect how it transmits sound. **2** the branch of physics concerned with the properties of sound. ■ **a·cous·ti·cal** adj. **a·cous·ti·cal·ly** adv.

ac·quaint /ə'kwānt/ ▶ v. **1** (**acquaint someone with**) make someone aware of or familiar with: *take time to acquaint yourself with your new surroundings.* **2** (**be acquainted**) know someone personally.

ac·quaint·ance /ə'kwāntns/ ▶ n. **1** a person one knows slightly. **2** familiarity with or knowledge of someone or something.

ac·qui·esce /,akwē'es/ ▶ v. accept something without protest.

ac·qui·es·cent /,akwē'esənt/ ▶ adj. ready to accept or do something without protest. ■ **ac·qui·es·cence** n.

ac·quire /ə'kwī(ə)r/ ▶ v. **1** come to have; obtain: *I managed to acquire a copy of the tape.* **2** learn or develop a quality or skill: *he acquired a taste for whiskey.* ■ **ac·quire·ment** n. **ac·quir·er** n.

ac·quired taste ▶ n. a thing that one at first dislikes but comes to like over time.

ac·qui·si·tion /,akwə'zisHən/ ▶ n. **1** an object that has recently been obtained. **2** the action of acquiring or obtaining something.

ac·quis·i·tive /ə'kwizitiv/ ▶ adj. too interested in obtaining money or possessions. ■ **ac·quis·i·tive·ly** adv. **ac·quis·i·tive·ness** n.

ac·quit /ə'kwit/ ▶ v. (**acquits, acquitting, acquitted**) **1** formally declare that someone is not guilty of a criminal charge. **2** (**acquit oneself**) behave or perform in a particular way: *he acquitted himself very well on his debut.*

ac·quit·tal /ə'kwitl/ ▶ n. an official judgment that a person is not guilty of the crime with which they have been charged.

a·cre /'ākrə, 'äkər, 'ākər/ ▶ n. a unit of land area equal to 4,840 square yards (0.405 hectare).

a·cre·age /'āk(ə)rij/ ▶ n. an area of land, typically when used for agricultural purposes, but not necessarily measured in acres.

ac·rid /'akrid/ ▶ adj. having an unpleasantly strong and bitter smell or taste.

ac·ri·mo·ni·ous /,akrə'mōnēəs/ ▶ adj. angry and bitter: *a long and acrimonious debate.*

ac·ri·mo·ny /'akrə,mōnē/ ▶ n. feelings of anger and bitterness.

ac·ro·bat /'akrə,bat/ ▶ n. an entertainer who performs spectacular gymnastic feats.

ac·ro·bat·ic /,akrə'batik/ ▶ adj. involving or performing spectacular gymnastic feats. ▶ n. (**acrobatics**) spectacular gymnastic feats. ■ **ac·ro·bat·i·cal·ly** adv.

ac·ro·nym /'akrə,nim/ ▶ n. a word formed from the initial letters of other words (e.g., *laser*).

ac·ro·pho·bi·a /,akrə'fōbēə/ ▶ n. extreme fear of heights. ■ **ac·ro·pho·bic** /-'fōbik/ adj.

a·crop·o·lis /ə'kräpəlis/ ▶ n. the citadel of an ancient Greek city, built on high ground.

a·cross /ə'krôs, ə'kräs/ ▶ prep. & adv. from one side to the other of something. – PHRASES **across the board** affecting or applying to everyone or everything.

a·cros·tic /ə'krôstik, ə'kräs-/ ▶ n. a poem or puzzle in which certain letters in each line form a word or words.

a·cryl·ic /ə'krilik/ ▶ adj. (of a synthetic fabric, plastic, or paint) made from acrylic acid.

a·cryl·ic ac·id ▶ n. Chemistry a strong-smelling liquid organic acid.

ACT ▶ abbr. American College Test.

act /akt/ ▶ v. **1** take action; do something. **2** take effect or have a particular effect: *a substance that acts on nerves in the digestive system.* **3** behave in a particular way: *he acts as if he owns the place.* **4** (**act as**) fulfill the function of: *she often acted as an interpreter.* **5** (**act for/on behalf of**) represent the interests of someone. **6** (as adj. **acting**) temporarily doing the duties of another person: *the acting president.* **7** perform a role in a play, movie, or television production. ▶ n. **1** a thing done. **2** a law passed formally by a parliament. **3** a way of behaving that is not genuine or sincere: *she's putting on an act.* **4** a main division of a play, ballet, or opera. **5** a short piece of entertainment in a show: *a comedy act.* **6** a performer or performing group. – PHRASES **act of God** an event caused by natural forces beyond human control. **act up** informal behave badly. **get in on the act** informal become involved in an activity to share its benefits.

ac·ti·nide /'aktə,nīd/ ▶ n. any of the series of fifteen radioactive metallic elements from actinium to lawrencium in the periodic table.

ac·tin·i·um /ak'tinēəm/ ▶ n. a rare radioactive metallic chemical element found in uranium ores.

ac·tion /'aksHən/ ▶ n. **1** the process of doing something to achieve an aim. **2** a thing done. **3** the effect or influence of something such as a chemical. **4** a lawsuit. **5** armed conflict: *servicemen missing in action.* **6** the way in which something works or moves. **7** informal exciting activity: *a preview of the weekend's sporting action.* ▶ v. deal with something: *your request will be actioned.* – PHRASES **in action** performing an activity; in operation. **out of action** not working.

ac·tion·a·ble /'aksHənəbəl/ ▶ adj. Law giving someone grounds to take legal action.

ac·ti·vate /'aktə,vāt/ ▶ v. make something act or start working: *the security alarms had been activated.* ■ **ac·ti·va·tion** /,aktə'vāsHən/ n. **ac·ti·va·tor** n.

ac·ti·vat·ed car·bon (also **activated charcoal**) ▶ n. charcoal that has been treated to increase its ability to absorb gases and dissolved substances.

ac·tive /'aktiv/ ▶ adj. **1** moving or tending to move about often or energetically. **2** (of a person's mind) alert and lively. **3** doing something regularly: *sexually active adults.* **4** functioning: *the watermill was active until 1960.* **5** (of a volcano) erupting or having erupted in the recent past. **6** having a chemical or biological effect: *salicylic acid is the active ingredient in aspirin.* **7** Grammar referring to verbs in which the subject is the person or thing performing the action and which can take a direct object (e.g., *she loved him* as opposed to the passive form *he was loved*). ■ **ac·tive·ly** adv.

ac·tive serv·ice ▶ n. direct involvement in military operations as a member of the armed forces.

ac·tiv·ist /'aktə,vist/ ▶ n. a person who campaigns for political or social change. ■ **ac·tiv·ism** /'aktə,vizəm/ n.

ac·tiv·i·ty /ak'tivitē/ ▶ n. (pl. **activities**) **1** a situation in which things are happening or being done. **2** busy or energetic action or movement. **3** a thing that a person or group does or has done: *sporting and social activities.*

ac·tor /'aktər/ ▶ n. a person whose profession is acting. ■ **ac·tor·ish** adj.

ac·tress /'aktris/ ▶ n. a female actor. ■ **ac·tress·y** adj.

ac·tu·al /'akchōōəl/ ▶ adj. **1** existing in fact: *those were his actual words.* **2** existing now; current: *actual income.*

ac·tu·al·i·ty /,akchōō'alitē/ ▶ n. (pl. **actualities**) **1** the state of existing in fact; reality: *the $100 mentioned was in actuality $100,000.* **2** (**actualities**) existing conditions or facts.

ac·tu·al·ize /'akchōōə,līz/ ▶ v. make something real. ■ **ac·tu·al·i·za·tion** /,akchōōələ'zāshən/ n.

ac·tu·al·ly /'akchōōəlē/ ▶ adv. **1** in reality. **2** used to emphasize or contradict something: *he actually expected me to be pleased!*

ac·tu·ar·y /'akchōō,erē/ ▶ n. (pl. **actuaries**) a person who compiles and analyzes statistics in order to calculate insurance risks and premiums. ■ **ac·tu·ar·i·al** /,akchōō'e(ə)rēəl/ adj.

ac·tu·ate /'akchōō,āt/ ▶ v. **1** cause a machine to operate. **2** motivate someone to act: *they were actuated by malice.* ■ **ac·tu·a·tion** /,akchōō'āshən/ n. **ac·tu·a·tor** n.

a·cu·i·ty /ə'kyōoitē/ ▶ n. keenness of thought, vision, or hearing.

a·cu·men /ə'kyōomən, 'akyə-/ ▶ n. the ability to make good judgments and quick decisions.

ac·u·pres·sure /'akyə,preshər/ ▶ n. a form of alternative therapy related to acupuncture in which specific points of the body are pressed to stimulate the flow of energy.

ac·u·punc·ture /'akyə,pəNGkchər/ ▶ n. a system of complementary medicine in which fine needles are inserted in the skin at specific points along supposed lines of energy. ■ **ac·u·punc·tur·ist** n.

a·cute /ə'kyōot/ ▶ adj. **1** (of something bad) serious or severe: *an acute housing shortage.* **2** (of an illness) coming sharply to a crisis. Often contrasted with CHRONIC. **3** showing or having insight; perceptive. **4** (of a sense) highly developed: *an acute sense of smell.* **5** (of an angle) less than 90°. ■ **a·cute·ly** adv. **a·cute·ness** n.

a·cute ac·cent ▶ n. a mark (´) placed over certain letters in some languages to indicate pronunciation (e.g., in *fiancée*).

AD ▶ abbr. Anno Domini (used to show that a date comes the specified number of years after the traditional date of Jesus's birth).

USAGE
AD is normally written in small capitals and should be placed **before** the numerals, as in AD *375.* However, when the date is spelled out, you should write *the third century* AD.

ad /ad/ ▶ n. informal an advertisement.

ad·age /'adij/ ▶ n. a popular saying expressing a widely accepted truth.

a·da·gio /ə'däjō, ə'däzhē,ō/ Music ▶ adv. & adj. in slow time. ▶ n. (pl. **adagios**) a passage in slow time.

ad·a·mant /'adəmənt/ ▶ adj. refusing to be persuaded or to change one's mind: *he is adamant that he is not going to resign.* ■ **ad·a·mant·ly** adv.

ad·a·man·tine /,adə'man,tīn, -tin-, -,tēn/ ▶ adj. literary unable to be broken.

Ad·am's ap·ple /'adəmz/ ▶ n. a projection at the front of the neck formed by the thyroid cartilage.

a·dapt /ə'dapt/ ▶ v. **1** make something suitable for a new use or purpose. **2** become adjusted to new conditions: *older workers are struggling to adapt to change.* ■ **a·dap·tive** adj.

a·dapt·a·ble /ə'daptəbəl/ ▶ adj. able to adjust to or be altered for new conditions or uses. ■ **a·dapt·a·bil·i·ty** /ə,daptə'bilitē/ n.

ad·ap·ta·tion /,adap'tāshən, ,adəp-/ (also **adaption**) ▶ n. **1** the action of adapting. **2** a movie or play adapted from a written work.

a·dapt·o·gen /ə'daptəjən/ ▶ n. (in herbal medicine) a natural substance believed to help the body adapt to stress. ■ **a·dapt·o·gen·ic** /ə,daptə'jenik/ adj.

a·dap·tor /ə'daptər/ (also **adapter**) ▶ n. **1** a device for connecting pieces of equipment. **2** a device for connecting several electric plugs to one socket.

ad·bot /'ad,bät/ ▶ n. a computer program that caches advertising on personal computers and then displays the advertising when certain linked programs are being used.

ADC ▶ abbr. **1** aide-de-camp. **2** analog-to-digital converter.

ADD ▶ abbr. **1** attention deficit disorder. **2** analog digital digital, indicating that a music recording was made in analog format before being mastered and stored digitally.

add /ad/ ▶ v. **1** join to or put with something else: *a new wing was added to the building.* **2** put together two or more numbers or amounts to calculate their total value. **3** (**add up**) increase in amount, number, or degree: *watch those air miles add up!* **4** say something as a further remark. **5** (**add up**) informal make sense.

ad·den·dum /ə'dendəm/ ▶ n. (pl. **addenda** /-də/) an extra item added at the end of a book or other publication.

ad·der /'adər/ ▶ n. a poisonous snake with a dark zigzag pattern on its back.

ad·dict /'adikt/ ▶ n. a person who is addicted to something.

ad·dict·ed /ə'diktid/ ▶ adj. **1** physically dependent on a particular substance. **2** devoted to a particular interest or activity: *I'm addicted to crime novels.*

ad·dic·tion /ə'dikshən/ ▶ n. the fact or condition of being addicted to something.

ad·dic·tive /ə'diktiv/ ▶ adj. **1** (of a substance or activity) causing someone to become addicted to it. **2** relating or prone to addiction. ■ **ad·dic·tive·ly** adv.

ad·di·tion /ə'dishən/ ▶ n. **1** the action of adding. **2** a person or thing that is added: *the mirror would make a handsome addition to a bathroom.*

ad·di·tion·al /ə'disHənl/ ▸ adj. extra to what is already present or available: *we need additional information.* ■ **ad·di·tion·al·ly** adv.

ad·di·tive /'aditiv/ ▸ n. a substance added to something to improve or preserve it.

ad·dle /'adl/ ▸ v. **1** confuse someone. **2** (as adj. **addled**) (of an egg) rotten. ▸ adj. (in combination) not clear; muddled: *an addle-brained adolescent.*

ad·dress /ə'dres, 'a,dres/ ▸ n. **1** the details of the place where someone lives or an organization is situated. **2** a formal speech. **3** a number identifying a location in a data storage system or computer memory. **4** a string of characters that identifies a destination for email messages. ▸ v. **1** write a name and address on an envelope or parcel. **2** formal speak to someone. **3** think about and begin to deal with: *the computer industry has started to address the problem.* ■ **ad·dress·a·ble** adj. **ad·dress·er** n.

ad·dress·ee /,adre'sē, ə,dre'sē/ ▸ n. the person to whom something is addressed.

ad·duce /ə'd(y)ōōs/ ▸ v. refer to something as evidence.

ad·dy /'adē/ ▸ n. (pl. **addies**) informal an address, especially an email address.

ad·e·nine /'adn,ēn, -,īn/ ▸ n. Biochemistry a compound that is one of the four constituent bases of nucleic acids.

ad·e·noids /'adn,oidz/ ▸ pl.n. a mass of tissue between the back of the nose and the throat, sometimes hindering speaking or breathing in children. ■ **ad·e·noi·dal** /,adn'oidl/ adj.

a·dept ▸ adj. /ə'dept/ very good at doing something; skilled: *I became adept at inventing excuses.* ▸ n. /'adept, ə'dept/ a person who is skilled at doing something. ■ **a·dept·ly** adv. **a·dept·ness** n.

ad·e·quate /'adikwit/ ▸ adj. satisfactory or acceptable in quality or quantity: *an adequate supply of fuel.* ■ **ad·e·qua·cy** /-kwəsē/ n. **ad·e·quate·ly** adv.

à deux /ä 'dœ/ ▸ adv. for or involving two people: *dinner à deux.*

ADHD ▸ abbr. attention deficit hyperactivity disorder.

ad·here /ad'hi(ə)r/ ▸ v. (**adhere to**) **1** stick firmly to something. **2** follow, observe, or support: *members must adhere to a code of practice.* **3** represent something truthfully. ■ **ad·her·ence** n.

ad·her·ent /ad'hi(ə)rənt, -'her-/ ▸ n. a person who supports a particular party, person, or set of ideas. ▸ adj. sticking firmly to something.

ad·he·sion /ad'hēzHən/ ▸ n. **1** the action of adhering to something. **2** Medicine an abnormal joining of surfaces in the body as a result of inflammation or injury.

ad·he·sive /ad'hēsiv, -ziv/ ▸ n. a substance used for sticking things together. ▸ adj. able to stick to something; sticky. ■ **ad·he·sive·ly** adv. **ad·he·sive·ness** n.

ad hoc /'ad 'häk, 'hōk/ ▸ adj. & adv. formed or done for a particular purpose only: *an ad hoc committee.*

ad ho·mi·nem /'ad 'hämənəm/ ▸ adv. & adj. (of an argument) personal rather than objective.

a·dieu /ə'd(y)ōō, ä'dyœ/ ▸ exclam. chiefly literary goodbye.

ad in·fi·ni·tum /,ad infə'nītəm/ ▸ adv. forever in the same way: *I could quote Dylan lyrics ad infinitum.*

ad·i·os /,ädē'ōs, ,adē-/ ▸ exclam. (in Spanish-speaking countries) goodbye.

ad·i·pose /'adə,pōs/ ▸ adj. technical (of body tissue) used for storing fat.

ad·it /'adit/ ▸ n. a horizontal access or drainage passage in a mine.

ad·ja·cent /ə'jāsənt/ ▸ adj. next to or adjoining something else. ■ **ad·ja·cen·cy** n.

ad·jec·tive /'ajiktiv/ ▸ n. a word used to describe a noun, such as *sweet, red,* or *technical.* ■ **ad·jec·ti·val** /,ajik'tīvəl/ adj.

ad·join /ə'join/ ▸ v. be next to and joined with: *the dining room adjoins a conservatory.*

ad·journ /ə'jərn/ ▸ v. **1** break off a meeting or legal case with the intention of resuming it later. **2** postpone a judicial sentence. **3** (of a group) go to another room or place, especially to relax: *they adjourned to the local bar.* ■ **ad·journ·ment** n.

ad·judge /ə'jəj/ ▸ v. (especially of an authority) make a decision about someone or something: *she was adjudged guilty.*

ad·ju·di·cate /ə'jōōdi,kāt/ ▸ v. **1** make a formal judgment on a disputed matter. **2** judge a competition. ■ **ad·ju·di·ca·tion** /ə,jōōdi'kāsHən/ n. **ad·ju·di·ca·tor** /,ajik'kātər/ n.

ad·junct /'ajəNGkt/ ▸ n. an additional and supplementary part: *computer technology is an adjunct to learning.* ■ **ad·junc·tive** /ə'jəNG(k)tiv/ adj.

ad·jure /ə'jŏŏr/ ▸ v. formal solemnly urge someone to do something.

ad·just /ə'jəst/ ▸ v. **1** alter something slightly so as to achieve a desired result: *he adjusted his tie.* **2** become used to a new situation. **3** assess loss or damages when settling an insurance claim. ■ **ad·just·a·bil·i·ty** /ə,jəstə'bilitē/ n. **ad·just·a·ble** adj. **ad·just·er** n.

ad·just·ment /ə'jəstmənt/ ▸ n. **1** a minor change made so as to correct or improve something: *the company will make adjustments to its packaging.* **2** the action of adjusting.

ad·ju·tant /'ajətənt/ ▸ n. a military officer acting as an administrative assistant to a senior officer.

ad·ju·vant /'ajəvənt/ ▸ adj. (of medical treatment) applied after initial treatment for cancer to prevent secondary tumors. ▸ n. a substance that improves the body's immune response to an infection or foreign body.

ad-lib /'ad'lib/ ▸ v. (**ad-libs, ad-libbing, ad-libbed**) speak or perform in public without preparing beforehand. ▸ adv. & adj. **1** spoken without previous preparation. **2** as much and as often as required: *the price includes meals and drinks ad lib.* ▸ n. an unprepared remark or speech.

ad li·tem /ad 'lītəm/ ▸ adj. Law acting in a lawsuit on behalf of people who cannot represent themselves.

ad·man /'ad,man/ ▸ n. (pl. **admen**) informal a person who works in advertising.

ad·min /'ad,min/ ▸ n. informal administration.

ad·min·is·ter /əd'minəstər/ ▸ v. **1** manage or put into effect: *the abatement program is administered by the EPA.* **2** give out a drug or remedy.

ad·min·is·trate /əd'minə,strāt/ ▸ v. manage an organization. ■ **ad·min·is·tra·tor** /əd'minə,strātər/ n.

ad·min·is·tra·tion /əd,minə'strāsHən/ ▸ n. **1** the organization and running of a business or system. **2** the action of giving out or applying something. **3** the government in power.

ad·min·is·tra·tive /əd'miniˌstrātiv, -strātiv/ ▶adj. relating to the running of a business, organization, etc. ■ **ad·min·is·tra·tive·ly** adv.

ad·mi·ra·ble /'admərəbəl/ ▶adj. deserving respect and approval. ■ **ad·mi·ra·bly** adv.

ad·mi·ral /'admərəl/ ▶n. **1** the most senior commander of a fleet or navy. **2** a naval or coast guard officer of the second most senior rank, ranking above a vice admiral.

Ad·mi·ral·ty /'admərəltē/ ▶n. (pl. **Admiralties**) (in the UK) the government department formerly in charge of the Royal Navy.

ad·mire /əd'mī(ə)r/ ▶v. **1** regard with respect or approval: *I admire your courage.* **2** look at something with pleasure. ■ **ad·mi·ra·tion** /ˌadmə'rāsHən/ n. **ad·mir·er** /əd'mī(ə)rər/ n. **ad·mir·ing** /əd'mī(ə)riNG/ adj.

ad·mis·si·ble /əd'misəbəl/ ▶adj. **1** acceptable or valid. **2** having the right to be admitted to a place. ■ **ad·mis·si·bil·i·ty** /əd,misə'bilitē/ n.

ad·mis·sion /əd'misHən/ ▶n. **1** entry to or permission to enter a place or organization: *many victims are refused admission to the shelter.* **2** a confession. **3** a person admitted to a hospital for treatment.

ad·mit /əd'mit/ ▶v. (**admits, admitting, admitted**) **1** confess to be true or to be the case: *I admit that I was relieved when he went.* **2** allow someone to enter a place or organization. **3** accept someone into a hospital for treatment. **4** accept something as valid. **5** (**admit of**) allow the possibility of: *the narrative can admit of no deviation.*

ad·mit·tance /əd'mitns/ ▶n. the process of entering or the fact of being allowed to enter: *we were unable to gain admittance to the hall.*

ad·mix·ture /ad'miksCHər/ ▶n. technical a mixture. ■ **ad·mix** /ad'miks/ v.

ad·mon·ish /əd'mänisH/ ▶v. **1** reprimand someone firmly. **2** earnestly urge or warn someone. ■ **ad·mon·ish·ment** n. **ad·mo·ni·tion** /ˌadmə'nisHən/ n.

ad·mon·i·to·ry /əd'mänəˌtôrē/ ▶adj. giving or expressing a warning or reprimand: *she lifted an admonitory finger.*

ad nau·se·am /ad 'nôzēəm/ ▶adv. to an annoyingly excessive extent: *they recycle one idea ad nauseam.*

a·do /ə'do͞o/ ▶n. trouble; fuss: *I left without further ado.*

a·do·be /ə'dōbē/ ▶n. a kind of clay used to make sun-dried bricks.

ad·o·les·cent /ˌadl'esənt/ ▶adj. in the process of developing from a child into an adult. ▶n. an adolescent boy or girl. ■ **ad·o·les·cence** n.

A·don·is /ə'dänis/ ▶n. a very handsome young man.

a·dopt /ə'däpt/ ▶v. **1** legally take another person's child and bring it up as one's own. **2** choose an option or course of action. **3** take on an attitude or position: *he adopted a patronizing tone.* **4** formally approve or accept someone or something. ■ **a·dopt·a·ble** adj. **a·dopt·ee** /əˌdäpt'tē/ n. **a·dopt·er** n. **a·dop·tion** n.

a·dop·tive /ə'däptiv/ ▶adj. **1** (of a child or parent) in that relationship by adoption. **2** (of a place) chosen by a person as their permanent place of residence.

a·dor·a·ble /ə'dôrəbəl/ ▶adj. very lovable or charming. ■ **a·dor·a·bly** adv.

a·dore /ə'dôr/ ▶v. **1** love and respect someone greatly. **2** informal like very much: *she adores Mexican cuisine.* ■ **ad·o·ra·tion** /ˌadə'rāsHən/ n. **a·dor·er** n. **a·dor·ing** adj.

a·dorn /ə'dôrn/ ▶v. make something more attractive or beautiful. ■ **a·dorn·ment** n.

ADP ▶abbr. **1** Biochemistry adenosine diphosphate, a compound involved in metabolic energy transfer. **2** automatic data processing.

ad·re·nal /ə'drēnl/ ▶adj. relating to a pair of glands above the kidneys that produce adrenaline and other hormones.

a·dren·al·ine /ə'drenl-in/ (also **adrenalin**) ▶n. a hormone produced by the adrenal glands that increases rates of blood circulation, breathing, and carbohydrate metabolism.

a·dre·nal·ized /ə'drēnlˌīzd/ ▶adj. excited, tense, or highly charged.

A·dri·at·ic /ˌādrē'atik/ ▶adj. relating to the region of the Adriatic Sea, between Italy and the Balkans.

a·drift /ə'drift/ ▶adj. & adv. **1** (of a boat) drifting without control. **2** no longer fixed in position. **3** lost and confused; without purpose or guidance: *the band has been adrift ever since her departure.*

a·droit /ə'droit/ ▶adj. clever or skillful: *an adroit administrator.*

ad·sorb /ad'zôrb, -'sôrb/ ▶v. (of a solid) hold molecules of a gas, liquid, or dissolved substance in a layer on its surface. ■ **ad·sorb·ent** adj. & n. **ad·sorp·tion** n.

ad·u·la·tion /ˌajə'lāsHən/ ▶n. excessive admiration. ■ **ad·u·late** /'ajəˌlāt/ v. **ad·u·la·to·ry** /'ajələˌtôrē/ adj.

a·dult /ə'dəlt, 'adˌəlt/ ▶n. **1** a person who is fully grown and developed. **2** Law a person who has reached the age of majority. ▶adj. **1** fully grown and developed. **2** for or typical of adults: *adult education.* ■ **a·dult·hood** n.

a·dul·ter·ate /ə'dəltəˌrāt/ ▶v. make something poorer in quality by adding another substance. ■ **a·dul·ter·ant** /ə'dəltərənt/ adj. **a·dul·ter·a·tion** /ə,dəltə'rāsHən/ n.

a·dul·ter·er /ə'dəltərər/ ▶n. (fem. **adulteress**) a person who has committed adultery.

a·dul·ter·y /ə'dəlt(ə)rē/ ▶n. sexual intercourse between a married person and a person who is not their spouse. ■ **a·dul·ter·ous** adj.

ad·um·brate /'adəmˌbrāt, ə'dəm-/ ▶v. formal **1** give a general idea of; outline: *his essay developed the arguments adumbrated in his earlier message.* **2** be a warning of a future event. ■ **ad·um·bra·tion** /ˌadəm'brāsHən/ n.

ad·vance /əd'vans/ ▶v. **1** move forward. **2** make progress. **3** put forward a theory or suggestion. **4** hand over payment to someone as a loan or before it is due: *he advanced me a month's salary.* ▶n. **1** a forward movement. **2** a development or improvement. **3** an amount of money advanced to someone. **4** (**advances**) approaches made to someone with the aim of starting a sexual or romantic relationship. ▶adj. done, sent, or supplied beforehand.

ad·vanced /əd'vanst/ ▶adj. **1** far on in development or progress: *an advanced computer network.* **2** complex; not basic.

ad·vance·ment /əd'vansmənt/ ▶n. **1** the promotion of a cause or plan: *the advancement of science.* **2** the promotion of a person in rank or status. **3** a development or improvement.

ad·van·tage /əd'vantij/ ▶ n. **1** a condition or factor that puts one in a more favorable position: *our technology will help you build a competitive advantage.* **2** Tennis a score marking a point between deuce and winning the game.
– PHRASES **take advantage of 1** make unfair use of something for one's own benefit. **2** make good use of the opportunities offered by something.

ad·van·ta·geous /ˌadvən'tājəs, -van-/ ▶ adj. good or useful in a particular situation. ■ **ad·van·ta·geous·ly** adv.

ad·vent /'adˌvent/ ▶ n. **1** the arrival of an important person or thing: *the days before the advent of air conditioning.* **2** (**Advent**) (in Christian belief) the coming or second coming of Jesus. **3** (**Advent**) the first season of the Church year, leading up to Christmas.

Ad·vent·ist /'adˌventist/ ▶ n. a member of a Christian sect who believes that the second coming of Jesus is about to happen. ■ **Ad·vent·ism** n.

ad·ven·ti·tious /ˌadven'tiSHəs/ ▶ adj. **1** happening by chance. **2** (of roots) growing directly from the stem or other upper part of a plant.

ad·ven·ture /ad'venCHər, əd-/ ▶ n. **1** an unusual, exciting, and daring experience. **2** excitement arising from danger or risk: *she traveled the world in search of adventure.* ■ **ad·ven·ture·some** adj.

ad·ven·tur·er /ad'venCHərər, əd-/ ▶ n. (fem. **adventuress**) **1** a person willing to take risks or use dishonest methods to gain wealth or power: *a political adventurer.* **2** a person who enjoys or looks for adventure.

ad·ven·tur·ism /ad'venCHəˌrizəm, əd-/ ▶ n. willingness to take risks in business or politics. ■ **ad·ven·tur·ist** n. & adj.

ad·ven·tur·ous /ad'venCHərəs, əd-/ ▶ adj. open to or involving new or daring methods or experiences: *an adventurous cook.* ■ **ad·ven·tur·ous·ly** adv. **ad·ven·tur·ous·ness** n.

ad·verb /'adˌvərb/ ▶ n. a word or phrase that gives more information about an adjective, verb, other adverb, or a sentence (e.g., *gently, very, fortunately*). ■ **ad·ver·bi·al** /ad'vərbēəl/ adj. & n.

ad·ver·sar·i·al /ˌadvər'se(ə)rēəl/ ▶ adj. involving conflict or opposition: *the media's adversarial attitude toward the military.*

ad·ver·sar·y /'advərˌserē/ ▶ n. (pl. **adversaries**) an opponent in a contest, dispute, or conflict.

ad·verse /ad'vərs, 'advərs/ ▶ adj. preventing success or progress; harmful or unfavorable. ■ **ad·verse·ly** adv.

USAGE
Do not confuse **adverse** with **averse**. **Adverse** means 'harmful' or 'unfavorable' (*adverse publicity*), whereas **averse** means 'strongly disliking' or 'opposed' (*I am not averse to helping out*).

ad·ver·si·ty /ad'vərsitē/ ▶ n. (pl. **adversities**) a difficult or unpleasant situation.

ad·vert /ad'vərt, əd'vərt/ ▶ v. (**advert to**) formal refer to something.

ad·ver·tise /'advərˌtīz/ ▶ v. **1** present or describe a product, service, or event in the media so as to promote sales. **2** publicize information about a job vacancy. **3** make a quality or fact known: *she coughed to advertise her presence.* ■ **ad·ver·tis·er** n. **ad·ver·tis·ing** n.

ad·ver·tise·ment /'advərˌtīzmənt, əd'vərtiz-/

▶ n. a notice or display advertising something.

ad·ver·to·ri·al /ˌadvər'tôrēəl/ ▶ n. an advertisement in the style of an editorial or objective journalistic article.

ad·vice /əd'vīs/ ▶ n. **1** guidance or recommendations about what someone should do. **2** a formal notice of a financial transaction.

USAGE
Do not confuse **advice** with **advise**. **Advice** means 'recommendations about what someone should do' (*your doctor can give you advice on diet*), whereas **advise** means 'recommend that someone should do something' (*I advised him to leave*).

ad·vis·a·ble /əd'vīzəbəl/ ▶ adj. to be recommended; sensible: *it's advisable to book in advance.* ■ **ad·vis·a·bil·i·ty** /-ˌvīzə'bilitē/ n.

ad·vise /əd'vīz/ ▶ v. **1** recommend that someone should do something; offer advice: *I advised him to go home.* **2** inform someone formally about a fact or situation. ■ **ad·vis·er** (also **advisor**) n.

USAGE
On the confusion of **advise** and **advice**, see the note at ADVICE.

ad·vised /əd'vīzd/ ▶ adj. behaving as someone would recommend; sensible. ■ **ad·vis·ed·ly** adv.

ad·vi·so·ry /əd'vīzərē/ ▶ adj. having the power to make recommendations but not to ensure that they are carried out.

ad·vo·caat /'advəˌkärt, 'advəˌkär/ ▶ n. a liqueur made with eggs, sugar, and brandy.

ad·vo·cate ▶ n. /'advəkit/ **1** a person who publicly supports or recommends a particular cause or policy: *he was an untiring advocate of reform.* **2** a person who pleads a case on someone else's behalf. **3** Scottish term for BARRISTER. ▶ v. /'advəˌkāt/ publicly recommend or support something. ■ **ad·vo·ca·cy** /'advəkəsē/ n.

adz /adz/ (also **adze**) ▶ n. a tool similar to an ax, with an arched blade at right angles to the handle.

Ae·ge·an /i'jēən/ ▶ adj. relating to the region of the Aegean Sea, between Greece and Turkey.

ae·gis /'ējis/ ▶ n. the protection, backing, or support of someone: *the negotiations were conducted under the aegis of the UN.*

ae·on /'ēən, 'ē,än/ ▶ n. chiefly British spelling of EON.

aer·ate /'e(ə)rāt/ ▶ v. introduce air into something. ■ **aer·a·tion** /e(ə)r'āSHən/ n. **aer·a·tor** n.

aer·at·ed /'e(ə)rātid/ ▶ adj. (of a liquid) made fizzy by being charged with carbon dioxide.

aer·i·al /'e(ə)rēəl/ ▶ n. a structure that sends or receives radio or television signals. ▶ adj. **1** existing or taking place in the air. **2** involving the use of aircraft.

aer·i·al·ist /'e(ə)rēəlist/ ▶ n. a person who performs acrobatics on a tightrope or trapezes.

aer·ie /'e(ə)rē, 'i(ə)rē/ (also **eyrie**) ▶ n. a large nest of an eagle or other bird of prey, typically built high in a tree or on a cliff.

aero- ▶ comb. form **1** relating to air: *aerobic.* **2** relating to aviation: *aeronautics.*

aer·o·bat·ics /ˌe(ə)rə'batiks/ ▶ pl.n. (treated as sing. or pl.) skillful and exciting movements performed in an aircraft for entertainment. ■ **aer·o·bat·ic** adj.

aer·o·bic /ə'rōbik, e(ə)'rō-/ ▶ adj. **1** relating to physical exercise intended to improve the intake of oxygen and its movement around the body. **2** Biology using oxygen from the air: *aerobic bacteria.* ■ **aer·o·bi·cal·ly** adv.

aer·o·bics /əˈrōbiks, e(ə)ˈrō-/ ▶ pl.n. (treated as sing. or pl.) aerobic exercises.

aer·o·drome /ˈe(ə)rəˌdrōm/ ▶ n. Brit. a small airport or airfield.

aer·o·dy·nam·ic /ˌe(ə)rōdīˈnamik/ ▶ adj. **1** relating to aerodynamics. **2** (of an object) having a shape that reduces the drag from air moving past. ■ **aer·o·dy·nam·i·cal·ly** adv.

aer·o·dy·nam·ics /ˌe(ə)rōdīˈnamiks/ ▶ pl.n. **1** (treated as sing.) the branch of science concerned with the movement of solid bodies through the air. **2** (treated as pl.) the aspects of an object that make it aerodynamic. ■ **aer·o·dy·nam·i·cist** /-ˈnaməsist/ n.

aer·o·nau·tics /ˌe(ə)rəˈnôtiks/ ▶ pl.n. (usu. treated as sing.) the study or practice of travel through the air. ■ **aer·o·nau·tic** adj. **aer·o·nau·ti·cal** adj.

aer·o·plane /ˈe(ə)rəˌplān/ ▶ n. Brit. an airplane.

ae·ro·pon·ics /ˌe(ə)rəˈpäniks/ ▶ n. a plant-growing technique in which the roots of a plant hang suspended in air and nutrient solution is delivered to them in the form of a fine mist.

aer·o·sol /ˈerəˌsôl, -ˌsäl/ ▶ n. a substance sealed in a container under pressure and released as a fine spray.

aer·o·space /ˈe(ə)rōˌspās/ ▶ n. the branch of technology and industry concerned with aviation and space flight.

aes·thete /ˈesˌтнēt/ (also **esthete**) ▶ n. a person who is appreciative of art and beauty.

aes·thet·ic /esˈтнetik/ (also **esthetic**) ▶ adj. **1** concerned with beauty or the appreciation of beauty. **2** having a pleasant appearance. ▶ n. a set of principles underlying the work of a particular artist or artistic movement. ■ **aes·thet·i·cal·ly** adv. **aes·thet·i·cism** n.

aes·thet·ics /esˈтнetiks/ (also **esthetics**) ▶ pl.n. (usu. treated as sing.) **1** a set of principles concerned with the nature of beauty, especially in art. **2** the branch of philosophy that deals with questions of beauty and artistic taste.

a·far /əˈfär/ ▶ adv. literary at or to a distance.

AFB ▶ abbr. Air Force Base.

AFC ▶ abbr. **1** American Football Conference. **2** automatic frequency control, a system in radios and television that keeps them tuned to an incoming signal.

af·fa·ble /ˈafəbəl/ ▶ adj. good-natured and sociable. ■ **af·fa·bil·i·ty** /ˌafəˈbilitē/ n. **af·fa·bly** adv.

af·fair /əˈfe(ə)r/ ▶ n. **1** an event of a specified kind or that has previously been referred to: *I want the wedding to be a family affair.* **2** a matter that a person is responsible for. **3** a love affair. **4** (**affairs**) matters of public interest. **5** (**affairs**) business and financial dealings.

af·fect[1] /əˈfekt/ ▶ v. **1** make a difference to: *the mold has affected my health.* **2** move someone emotionally. ■ **af·fect·ing** adj.

> **USAGE**
> **Affect** and **effect** are often confused. **Affect** is a verb meaning 'make a difference to' (*the mold has affected my health*). **Effect** is used both as a noun meaning 'a result' (*the substance has a painkilling effect*) and as a verb meaning 'bring about a result' (*I effected a cost-cutting exercise*).

af·fect[2] ▶ v. **1** pretend to have or feel something. **2** use or wear in an artificial way or so as to impress: *he'd affected a British accent.*

af·fec·ta·tion /ˌafekˈtāsнən/ ▶ n. behavior, speech, or writing that is artificial and designed to impress.

af·fect·ed /əˈfektid/ ▶ adj. artificial and designed to impress. ■ **af·fect·ed·ly** adv.

af·fec·tion /əˈfeksнən/ ▶ n. a feeling of fondness or liking.

af·fec·tion·ate /əˈfeksнənit/ ▶ adj. readily showing affection. ■ **af·fec·tion·ate·ly** adv.

af·fec·tive /əˈfektiv/ ▶ adj. Psychology relating to moods, feelings, and attitudes.

af·fi·ance /əˈfīəns/ ▶ v. (**be affianced**) literary be engaged to marry.

af·fi·da·vit /ˌafiˈdāvit/ ▶ n. Law a written statement for use as evidence in court, sworn on oath to be true.

af·fil·i·ate ▶ v. /əˈfilēˌāt/ officially link a person or group to an organization. ▶ n. /-it/ a person or group linked to a larger organization. ■ **af·fil·i·a·tion** /əˌfilēˈāsнən/ n.

af·fin·i·ty /əˈfinitē/ ▶ n. (pl. **affinities**) **1** a natural liking or sympathy for someone or something. **2** close similarity in structure, qualities, or origin: *there is a stylistic affinity between the mosaics.* **3** the tendency of a substance to combine with another.

af·firm /əˈfərm/ ▶ v. state something firmly or publicly.

af·fir·ma·tion /ˌafərˈmāsнən/ ▶ n. **1** the action or process of affirming or being affirmed. **2** Law a formal declaration by a person who declines to take an oath for reasons of conscience.

af·firm·a·tive /əˈfərmətiv/ ▶ adj. agreeing with a statement or a request: *an affirmative answer.* ▶ n. a statement or word indicating agreement. ▶ exclam. yes. ■ **af·firm·a·tive·ly** adv.

af·firm·a·tive ac·tion ▶ n. action favoring people who are often discriminated against.

af·fix ▶ v. /əˈfiks/ attach or fasten something to something else. ▶ n. /ˈaˌfiks/ Grammar a letter or letters added to a word in order to alter its meaning or create a new word. ■ **af·fix·a·tion** /ˌafikˈsāsнən/ n.

af·flict /əˈflikt/ ▶ v. cause pain or trouble to: *the problems that afflict inner-city communities.*

af·flic·tion /əˈfliksнən/ ▶ n. **1** something that causes pain or suffering: *a crippling affliction of the nervous system.* **2** pain or suffering.

af·flu·ent /ˈaflo͞oənt, əˈflo͞o-/ ▶ adj. having a great deal of money; wealthy. ■ **af·flu·ence** n.

af·ford /əˈfôrd/ ▶ v. **1** (**can/could afford**) have enough money, time, or other resources for something. **2** provide or supply: *the rooftop terrace affords beautiful views.*

af·ford·a·ble /əˈfôrdəbəl/ ▶ adj. reasonably priced; not expensive. ■ **af·ford·a·bil·i·ty** /əˌfôrdəˈbilitē/ n. **af·ford·a·bly** adv.

af·for·est·a·tion /əˌfôrəˈstāsнən, əˌfär-/ ▶ n. the process of planting trees on an area of land in order to form a forest.

af·fray /əˈfrā/ ▶ n. Law, dated a breach of the peace by fighting in a public place.

af·front /əˈfrənt/ ▶ n. an action or remark that causes offense. ▶ v. offend or insult: *she was affronted by his familiarity.*

Af·ghan /ˈafˌgan/ ▶ n. a person from Afghanistan. ▶ adj. relating to Afghanistan.

Af·ghan hound ▸ n. a silky-haired breed of dog used for hunting.

af·ghan·i /afˈgänē, -ˈgä-/ ▸ n. (pl. **afghanis**) the basic monetary unit of Afghanistan.

a·fi·ci·o·na·do /əˌfiSH(ē)əˈnädō, əˌfisyə-/ ▸ n. (pl. **aficionados**) a person who is very knowledgeable and enthusiastic about an activity or subject.

a·field /əˈfēld/ ▸ adv. to or at a distance.

a·fire /əˈfī(ə)r/ ▸ adj. & adv. chiefly poetic/literary on fire; burning.

a·flame /əˈflām/ ▸ adj. in flames.

a·float /əˈflōt/ ▸ adj. & adv. **1** floating in water. **2** on board a ship or boat. **3** out of debt or difficulty: *he takes odd jobs to keep afloat.*

a·flut·ter /əˈflətər/ ▸ adj. in a state of agitated excitement.

a·foot /əˈfoŏt/ ▸ adv. & adj. **1** happening or in preparation: *plans are afoot for a festival.* **2** on foot.

a·fore /əˈfôr/ ▸ prep. old use or dialect before.

afore- ▸ prefix before; previously: *aforementioned.*

a·fore·men·tioned /əˈfôrˌmensHənd/ (also **aforesaid** /əˈfôrˌsed/) ▸ adj. referring to a thing or person previously mentioned.

a·fore·thought /əˈfôrˌTHôt/ ▸ adj. see MALICE AFORETHOUGHT.

a for·ti·o·ri /ˌä ˌfôrtēˈôrē, ˈä ˌfôrtēˈôrī/ ▸ adv. for an even stronger reason.

a·foul /əˈfoul/ ▸ adv. (in phrase **run/fall afoul of**) come into conflict or difficulty with: *he ran afoul of the boss and resigned.*

a·fraid /əˈfrād/ ▸ adj. feeling fear or anxiety.
– PHRASES **I'm afraid** expressing polite regret.

a·fresh /əˈfresH/ ▸ adv. in a new or different way.

Af·ri·can /ˈafrikən/ ▸ n. **1** a person from Africa, especially a black person. **2** a person descended from black African people. ▸ adj. relating to Africa or Africans. ∎ **Af·ri·can·ize** /ˈafrikəˌnīz/ v.

Af·ri·can A·mer·i·can ▸ n. an American of African origin, especially one descended from slaves. ∎ **Af·ri·can-A·mer·i·can** adj.

Af·ri·can vi·o·let ▸ n. a small East African plant with velvety leaves and violet, pink, or white flowers.

Af·ri·kaans /ˌafriˈkänz/ ▸ n. a language derived from Dutch, one of the official languages of South Africa.

Af·ri·ka·ner /ˌafriˈkänər/ ▸ n. an Afrikaans-speaking white person in South Africa. ∎ **Af·ri·ka·ner·dom** n.

Af·ro /ˈafrō/ ▸ n. (pl. **Afros**) a hairstyle consisting of a mass of very tight curls all around the head.

Afro- ▸ comb.form African: *Afro-American.*

Af·ro-A·mer·i·can ▸ adj. & n. another term for AFRICAN AMERICAN.

Af·ro·beat /ˈafrōˌbēt/ ▸ n. a style of popular music incorporating elements of African music and jazz, soul, and funk.

Af·ro-Car·ib·be·an ▸ n. a person descended from African people who lives in or comes from the Caribbean. ▸ adj. relating to Afro-Caribbeans.

aft /aft/ ▸ adv. & adj. at, near, or toward the stern of a ship or tail of an aircraft.

af·ter /ˈaftər/ ▸ prep. **1** in the time following an event or another period of time. **2** next to and following something in order or importance. **3** behind someone. **4** so as to have, get, or find: *most of them are after money.* **5** in reference to:
he was named after his grandfather. ▸ conj. & adv. in the time following an event. ▸ adj. nearer the stern of a ship.
– PHRASES **after all** in spite of any suggestion otherwise. **after hours** after normal working or opening hours.

af·ter·birth /ˈaftərˌbərTH/ ▸ n. the placenta and other material that is discharged from the uterus after a birth.

af·ter·burn·er /ˈaftərˌbərnər/ ▸ n. an auxiliary burner in the exhaust of a jet engine.

af·ter·care /ˈaftərˌke(ə)r/ ▸ n. care of a person after a stay in a hospital or on release from prison.

af·ter·ef·fect /ˈaftəriˌfekt/ ▸ n. an effect that follows some time after its cause.

af·ter·glow /ˈaftərˌglō/ ▸ n. **1** light remaining in the sky after the sun has set. **2** good feelings remaining after a pleasant experience: *basking in the afterglow of victory.*

af·ter·im·age /ˈaftərˌimij/ ▸ n. an impression of a vivid sensation (especially a visual image) retained after the stimulus has ceased.

af·ter·life /ˈaftərˌlīf/ ▸ n. (in some religions) life after death.

af·ter·mar·ket /ˈaftərˌmärkit/ ▸ n. **1** the market for spare parts, accessories, and components, especially for motor vehicles. **2** Stock Market the market for shares and bonds after their original issue.

af·ter·math /ˈaftərˌmaTH/ ▸ n. the results of an unpleasant or important event: *prices soared in the aftermath of the drought.*

af·ter·noon /ˌaftərˈno͞on/ ▸ n. the time from noon or lunchtime to evening.

af·ter·shave /ˈaftərˌSHāv/ ▸ n. a scented lotion for putting on a man's face after shaving.

af·ter·shock /ˈaftərˌSHäk/ ▸ n. a smaller earthquake following the main shock of a large earthquake.

af·ter·taste /ˈaftərˌtāst/ ▸ n. a strong or unpleasant taste lingering in the mouth after eating or drinking.

af·ter·tax ▸ adj. relating to income that remains after the deduction of taxes due.

af·ter·thought /ˈaftərˌTHôt/ ▸ n. something thought of or added later.

af·ter·ward /ˈaftərwərd/ (also **afterwards** /ˈaftərwərdz/) ▸ adv. at a later or future time.

af·ter·word /ˈaftərˌwərd/ ▸ n. a section at the end of a book.

af·ter·world /ˈaftərˌwərld/ ▸ n. a world that a person enters after death.

AG ▸ abbr. **1** adjutant general. **2** attorney general.

Ag ▸ symbol the chemical element silver.

a·gain /əˈgen, əˈgān/ ▸ adv. **1** once more. **2** returning to a previous position or condition: *he closed the locker and sat down again.* **3** in addition to what has already been mentioned.

a·gainst /əˈgenst, əˈgänst/ ▸ prep. **1** opposing or disagreeing with. **2** close to or touching. **3** so as to anticipate and prepare for a difficulty. **4** as protection from: *I turned up my collar against the wind.* **5** in contrast to: *the benefits must be weighed against the costs.* **6** so as to reduce, cancel, or secure money owed, due, or lent. **7** (in betting) in anticipation of the failure of: *the odds were 5–1 against England.*
– PHRASES **have something against someone** dislike or bear a grudge against someone.

a·gape /ə'gāp/ ▶ adj. (of a person's mouth) wide open.

a·gar /'ä,gär, 'ä,gär/ (also **agar-agar**) ▶ n. a jellylike substance obtained from seaweed, used as a thickener in foods and in biological cultures.

ag·a·ric /'agərik, ə'gar-/ ▶ n. a fungus with gills on the underside of the cap, e.g., a mushroom.

ag·ate /'agit/ ▶ n. a semiprecious variety of quartz with a striped appearance.

a·ga·ve /ə'gävē/ ▶ n. an American plant with narrow spiny leaves and tall flower stems.

age /āj/ ▶ n. **1** the length of time that a person or thing has existed. **2** a particular stage in someone's life: *children of elementary school age.* **3** old age. **4** a distinct period of history: *the Elizabethan age.* ▶ v. (**ages, aging** or **ageing, aged**) **1** grow or cause to appear old or older: *some foods may protect your eyes as you age.* **2** (of an alcoholic drink, cheese, etc.) mature.
– PHRASES **come of age** be legally recognized as an adult (in US law at 18).

aged ▶ adj. **1** /ājd/of a specified age: *the driver, aged 42, was taken into custody.* **2** /'ājid/having lived or existed for a long time; old.

age·ism /'āj,izəm/ ▶ n. prejudice or discrimination on the grounds of a person's age. ■ **age·ist** adj. & n.

age·less /'ājlis/ ▶ adj. not aging or appearing to age.

a·gen·cy /'ājənsē/ ▶ n. **1** an organization or government department providing a particular service: *an advertising agency.* **2** action or intervention producing a result: *channels carved by the agency of running water.*

a·gen·da /ə'jendə/ ▶ n. **1** a list of items to be discussed at a meeting. **2** a list of matters to be dealt with. **3** the underlying intentions or motives of a particular person or group. **4** a diary for listing appointments.

a·gent /'ājənt/ ▶ n. **1** a person who provides a service, typically by organizing dealings between two other parties: *a travel agent.* **2** a spy. **3** a person or thing that takes an active role or produces a particular effect: *bleaching agents.*

a·gent pro·vo·ca·teur /ä,zнän(t) prə,väkə'tər/ ▶ n. (pl. **agents provocateurs** pronunc. same) a person employed to tempt others to break the law and therefore be convicted.

age of con·sent ▶ n. the age at which a person's consent to sexual intercourse is legally valid.

age-old /'āj,ōld/ ▶ adj. very old.

ag·glom·er·ate ▶ v. /ə'glämə,rāt/ collect or form into a mass. ▶ n. /-rit/ a mass or collection of things. ■ **ag·glom·er·a·tion** /ə,glämə'rāshən/ n.

ag·glu·ti·nate /ə'glōōtn,āt/ ▶ v. firmly stick together to form a mass. ■ **ag·glu·ti·na·tion** /ə,glōōtn'āshən/ n.

ag·gran·dize /ə'gran,dīz/ ▶ v. increase the power or importance of: *the description "subediting" aggrandizes the nature of my task.* ■ **ag·gran·dize·ment** /-,dīzmənt, -diz-/ n.

ag·gra·vate /'agrə,vāt/ ▶ v. **1** make worse: *military action would only aggravate the situation.* **2** informal annoy someone. ■ **ag·gra·va·ting** adj. **ag·gra·va·tion** /,agrə'vāshən/ n.

USAGE
Some people think that it is incorrect to use **aggravate** to mean 'annoy someone'. However, this sense dates back to the 17th century and is widely used in modern English.

ag·gra·vat·ed /'agrə,vātid/ ▶ adj. Law (of an offense) made more serious by related circumstances.

ag·gre·gate ▶ n. /'agrigit/ a whole formed by combining several different elements: *the council is an aggregate of three regional assemblies.* ▶ v. /-,gāt/ combine into a whole. ▶ adj. /'agrigit/ formed or calculated by combining many separate items. ■ **ag·gre·ga·tion** /,agri'gāshən/ n.

ag·gre·ga·tor /'agri,gātər/ ▶ n. Computing an Internet company that collects information about competing products and services and distributes it through a single website.

ag·gres·sion /ə'greshən/ ▶ n. hostile or violent behavior or attitudes: *a link between extensive TV viewing and aggression in children.*

ag·gres·sive /ə'gresiv/ ▶ adj. **1** very hostile or angry. **2** determined and forceful: *an aggressive campaign to reduce energy use.* ■ **ag·gres·sive·ly** adv. **ag·gres·sive·ness** n.

ag·gres·sor /ə'gresər/ ▶ n. a person or country that attacks without being provoked.

ag·grieved /ə'grēvd/ ▶ adj. resentful because of unfair treatment.

a·ghast /ə'gast/ ▶ adj. filled with horror or shock: *he looked aghast at the blood on his blazer.*

ag·ile /'ajəl/ ▶ adj. **1** able to move quickly and easily. **2** quick-witted or shrewd. ■ **ag·ile·ly** adv. **a·gil·i·ty** /ə'jilitē/ n.

ag·ing /'ājiNG/ (also **ageing**) ▶ n. **1** growing old. **2** change in a material over a period, either spontaneous or caused deliberately. ▶ adj. **1** (of a person) growing old; elderly. **2** (of a thing) reaching the end of its useful life: *the world's aging fleet of oil tankers.*

ag·i·tate /'aji,tāt/ ▶ v. **1** make someone troubled or nervous. **2** campaign to arouse public concern about something: *they have begun to agitate for better living conditions.* **3** stir or disturb a liquid briskly.

ag·i·ta·tion /,aji'tāshən/ ▶ n. **1** a state of anxiety or nervous excitement. **2** the action of agitating to arouse concern about something.

ag·i·ta·tor /'aji,tātər/ ▶ n. a person who urges others to protest or rebel.

ag·it·prop /'ajit,präp/ ▶ n. political propaganda, especially in the arts.

ag·let /'aglit/ ▶ n. a metal or plastic tube fixed around each end of a shoelace.

a·glow /ə'glō/ ▶ adj. glowing.

AGM ▶ abbr. air-to-ground missile.

ag·nos·tic /ag'nästik/ ▶ n. a person who believes that one cannot know whether or not God exists. ■ **ag·nos·ti·cism** /-tə,sizəm/ n.

a·go /ə'gō/ ▶ adv. before the present (used with a measurement of time).

USAGE
When **ago** is followed by a clause, you should use **that** rather than **since**, e.g., *it was ten years ago that I left home* (not *it was ten years ago since I left home*).

a·gog /ə'gäg/ ▶ adj. very eager to hear or see something: *I was agog with curiosity.*

ag·o·nist /'agənist/ ▶ n. **1** Biochemistry a substance that initiates a physiological response when combined with a receptor. **2** Anatomy a muscle whose contraction moves a part of the body directly.

ag·o·nize /'agə,nīz/ ▸ v. **1** worry greatly: *I didn't agonize over the problem.* **2** (often as adj. **agonizing**) cause great pain to: *an agonizing death.*

ag·o·ny /'agənē/ ▸ n. (pl. **agonies**) great pain or distress.

ag·o·ra /ə'gôrə, ,ägô'rä/ ▸ n. (pl. **agorot** /ə'gôrōt, ,ägô'rōt/ or **agoroth** /ə'gôrōt, ,ägô'rōt/) a unit of money of Israel, equal to one hundredth of a shekel.

ag·o·ra·pho·bi·a /,agərə'fōbēə/ ▸ n. irrational fear of open or public places. ■ **ag·o·ra·pho·bic** adj. & n.

a·grar·i·an /ə'gre(ə)rēən/ ▸ adj. relating to agriculture.

a·gree /ə'grē/ ▸ v. (**agrees, agreeing, agreed**) **1** have the same opinion as another person or people. **2** (**agree to/to do**) be willing to do something suggested by another person. **3** (of two or more people) decide on something. **4** (**agree with**) be consistent with: *your body language doesn't agree with what you're saying.* **5** (**agree with**) be good for: *he ate something that didn't agree with him.*

a·gree·a·ble /ə'grēəbəl/ ▸ adj. **1** enjoyable or pleasant. **2** willing to agree to something. **3** able to be agreed on; acceptable: *a compromise that is agreeable to both employers and unions.* ■ **a·gree·a·ble·ness** n. **a·gree·a·bly** adv.

a·gree·ment /ə'grēmənt/ ▸ n. **1** the act of agreeing or the state of being agreed: *we failed to reach agreement.* **2** an arrangement or contract agreed between people, typically one that is legally binding.

ag·ri·busi·ness /'agrə,biznis/ ▸ n. **1** agriculture run on strictly commercial principles. **2** the group of industries concerned with agricultural produce and services.

ag·ri·cul·ture /'agri,kəlchər/ ▸ n. the science or practice of farming, including the rearing of crops and animals. ■ **ag·ri·cul·tur·al** /,agri'kəlchərəl/ adj. **ag·ri·cul·tur·al·ist** /,agri'kəlchərəlist/ n. **ag·ri·cul·tur·al·ly** /,agri'kəlchərəlē/ adv. **ag·ri·cul·tur·ist** /'agri,kəlchərist/ n.

ag·ri·mo·ny /'agrə,mōnē/ ▸ n. a plant with slender stalks of yellow flowers.

ag·ri·tour·ism /,agri'tŏŏrizəm/ ▸ n. tourism in which farms are open to the public for agricultural activities and as lodgings for vacationers.

ag·ro·chem·i·cal /,agrō'kemikəl/ ▸ n. a chemical used in agriculture.

a·gron·o·my /ə'gränəmē/ ▸ n. the science of soil management and crop production. ■ **ag·ro·nom·ic** /,agrə'nämik/ adj. **a·gron·o·mist** n.

a·ground /ə'ground/ ▸ adj. & adv. (with reference to a ship) on or onto the bottom in shallow water.

a·gue /'ā,gyōō/ ▸ n. old use malaria or another illness involving fever and shivering.

ah /ä/ ▸ exclam. used to express a range of emotions including surprise, pleasure, sympathy, and realization.

a·ha /ä'hä/ ▸ exclam. used to express satisfaction, triumph, or surprise.

a·head /ə'hed/ ▸ adv. **1** farther forward in space or time: *we should plan ahead.* **2** in the lead. – PHRASES **ahead of 1** in front of; before. **2** earlier than.

a·hem /ə'hem, ə'hm/ ▸ exclam. used to represent the noise made when clearing the throat,

typically to attract attention or express disapproval or embarrassment.

a·him·sa /ə'him,sä/ ▸ n. (in the Hindu, Buddhist, and Jain tradition) the principle of nonviolence toward all living things.

a·his·tor·i·cal /,āhi'stôrikəl, -'stär-/ ▸ adj. lacking historical perspective; not historical.

a·hoy /ə'hoi/ ▸ exclam. Nautical a call to attract attention.

AI ▸ abbr. artificial intelligence.

AID ▸ abbr. **1** Agency for International Development. **2** artificial insemination by donor.

aid /ād/ ▸ n. **1** help or support. **2** money or resources given to help a country in need. ▸ v. help or support: *women, aided by their children, cleaned the fish.* – PHRASES **in aid of** in support of.

aide /ād/ ▸ n. an assistant to a political leader.

aide-de-camp /'ād də 'kamp/ ▸ n. (pl. **aides-de-camp** pronunc. same) a military officer acting as a personal assistant to a senior officer.

aide-me·moire /'ād mem'wär/ ▸ n. (pl. **aides-memoires** or **aides-memoire** pronunc. same) **1** a note or book used to help one remember something. **2** an informal diplomatic message.

AIDS /ādz/ ▸ n. a disease, caused by the HIV virus and transmitted in body fluids, in which the sufferer's natural defenses against infection are destroyed.

ai·ki·do /,īkē'dō, ī'kēdō/ ▸ n. a Japanese martial art that uses locks, holds, throws, and the opponent's own movements.

ail /āl/ ▸ v. old use cause suffering or trouble to someone.

ai·ler·on /'ālə,rän/ ▸ n. a hinged part on the back of an aircraft's wing, used to control the balance of the aircraft.

ail·ing /'āliNG/ ▸ adj. in poor health or condition: *the country's ailing economy.*

ail·ment /'ālmənt/ ▸ n. a minor illness.

aim /ām/ ▸ v. **1** point a weapon or camera at a target. **2** direct something at someone or something: *the program is aimed at a wide audience.* **3** try to achieve something. ▸ n. **1** a purpose or intention. **2** the aiming of a weapon or missile. – PHRASES **take aim** point a weapon at a target.

aim·less /'āmlis/ ▸ adj. without purpose or direction: *aimless wandering.* ■ **aim·less·ly** adv. **aim·less·ness** n.

ain't /ānt/ ▸ contr. informal **1** am not; are not; is not. **2** has not; have not.

USAGE
The use of **ain't** was widespread in the 18th century and is still perfectly normal in many dialects and informal contexts in both North America and Britain. Today, however, it does not form part of standard English and should not be used in formal contexts.

air /e(ə)r/ ▸ n. **1** the invisible mixture of gases surrounding the earth, mainly oxygen and nitrogen. **2** the open space above the earth's surface: *I threw the ball up in the air.* **3** the earth's atmosphere as a medium for transmitting radio waves. **4** (**an air of**) an impression of: *there was an air of sadness about her.* **5** (**airs**) an affected and condescending manner. **6** a tune or short song. ▸ adj. using aircraft: *air travel.* ▸ v. **1** express an opinion or complaint publicly. **2** broadcast a program on radio or television.

3 expose a room or washed laundry to fresh or warm air. ■ **air·less** adj.

– PHRASES **on** (or **off**) **the air** being (or not being) broadcast on radio or television. **up in the air** (of an issue) still to be settled. **walk on air** feel very happy or pleased.

air·bag /'e(ə)r‚bag/ ▶ n. a safety device that inflates rapidly when there is a sudden impact, so protecting a vehicle's occupants in a collision.

air·base /'e(ə)r‚bās/ ▶ n. a base for military aircraft.

air·borne /'e(ə)r‚bôrn/ ▶ adj. **1** carried through the air. **2** (of an aircraft) flying.

air brake /'e(ə)r‚brāk/ ▶ n. a vehicle brake worked by air pressure.

air·brush /'e(ə)r‚brəsн/ ▶ n. an artist's device for spraying paint by means of compressed air. ▶ v. **1** paint a picture or alter a photograph with an airbrush. **2** alter or remove undesirable elements or people to present an improved version of reality: *the failures are airbrushed from history.*

air con·di·tion·ing ▶ n. a system for controlling the humidity, ventilation, and temperature in a building or vehicle. ■ **air-con·di·tion·ed** adj. **air con·di·tion·er** n.

air cor·ri·dor ▶ n. a route over a foreign country that aircraft must take.

air·craft /'e(ə)r‚kraft/ ▶ n. (pl. same) an airplane, helicopter, or other machine capable of flight.

air·craft car·ri·er /'e(ə)r‚kraft'karẽər/ ▶ n. a large warship from which aircraft can take off and land.

air·crew /'e(ə)r‚krōō/ ▶ n. (pl. **aircrews**) (treated as sing. or pl.) the crew of an aircraft.

air cush·ion ▶ n. the layer of air supporting a hovercraft or similar vehicle.

air·drop /'e(ə)r‚dräp/ ▶ n. an act of dropping supplies, troops, or equipment by parachute.

Aire·dale /'e(ə)r‚dāl/ ▶ n. a large rough-coated black-and-tan breed of terrier.

air·fare /'e(ə)r‚fe(ə)r/ ▶ n. the price to be paid by an airline passenger for a journey.

air·field /'e(ə)r‚fēld/ ▶ n. an area of land set aside for the takeoff, landing, and maintenance of aircraft.

air·flow /'e(ə)r‚flō/ ▶ n. the flow of air, especially that encountered by a moving aircraft or vehicle.

air·foil /'e(ə)r‚foil/ ▶ n. a curved structure, such as a wing, designed to give an aircraft lift in flight.

air force /'e(ə)r‚fôrs/ ▶ n. a branch of the armed forces concerned with fighting or defense in the air.

air·frame /'e(ə)r‚frām/ ▶ n. the body of an aircraft as distinct from its engine.

air·freight /'e(ə)r‚frāt/ ▶ n. the carriage of goods by aircraft.

air fresh·en·er ▶ n. a scented substance or device for disguising unpleasant smells in a room, automobile, etc.

air gun /'e(ə)r‚gən/ ▶ n. **1** a gun that uses compressed air to fire pellets. **2** a tool using very hot air to strip paint.

air·head /'e(ə)r‚hed/ ▶ n. informal a stupid person.

air·ing /'e(ə)riNG/ ▶ n. **1** an act of exposing laundry or a place to warm or fresh air. **2** a public expression of an opinion or discussion of a subject.

air kiss /'e(ə)rkis/ ▶ n. a kiss close to a person's face, but without making contact.

air·lift /'e(ə)r‚lift/ ▶ n. an act of transporting supplies by aircraft, typically in an emergency.

air·line /'e(ə)r‚līn/ ▶ n. **1** an organization providing a regular passenger air service. **2** (**air line**) a pipe supplying air.

air·lin·er /'e(ə)r‚līnər/ ▶ n. a large passenger aircraft.

air·lock /'e(ə)r‚läk/ ▶ n. **1** a stoppage of the flow in a pump or pipe, caused by an air bubble. **2** a compartment with controlled pressure and airtight doors at each end, to allow people to move between areas at different pressures.

air·mail /'e(ə)r‚māl/ ▶ n. a system of transporting mail by air.

air·man /'e(ə)rmən/ (or **airwoman**) ▶ n. (pl. **airmen** or **airwomen**) **1** a pilot or member of the crew of an aircraft in an air force. **2** a member of the US Air Force of the lowest rank, below sergeant.

air mat·tress ▶ n. an inflatable mattress.

air mile ▶ n. **1** a nautical mile used as a measure of distance flown by aircraft. **2** (**Air Miles**) trademark points (equivalent to miles of free air travel) collected by buyers of airline tickets and other products.

air pis·tol ▶ n. a pistol that uses compressed air to fire pellets.

air·plane /'e(ə)r‚plān/ ▶ n. a fixed-wing powered flying vehicle that is heavier than the air.

air plant /'e(ə)r‚plant/ ▶ n. a tropical American plant that grows on trees, with long narrow leaves that absorb water and nutrients from the atmosphere.

air·play /'e(ə)r‚plā/ ▶ n. broadcasting time devoted to a particular recording, performer, or type of music.

air pock·et /'e(ə)r‚päkət/ ▶ n. **1** a hollow space containing air. **2** a region of low pressure causing an aircraft to lose height suddenly.

air·port /'e(ə)r‚pôrt/ ▶ n. a complex of runways and buildings for the takeoff, landing, and maintenance of civil aircraft, with facilities for passengers.

air pow·er ▶ n. airborne military forces.

air pump /'e(ə)r‚pəmp/ ▶ n. a device for pumping air into or out of an enclosed space.

air qual·i·ty ▶ n. the degree to which the air in a place is pollution-free.

air raid /'e(ə)r‚rād/ ▶ n. an attack in which bombs are dropped from aircraft onto a ground target.

air ri·fle ▶ n. a rifle that uses compressed air to fire pellets.

air-sea res·cue ▶ n. a rescue from the sea using aircraft.

air·ship /'e(ə)r‚sнip/ ▶ n. a power-driven aircraft kept aloft by a body of gas (usually helium) that is lighter than air.

air·sick /'e(ə)r‚sik/ ▶ adj. feeling sick due to air travel.

air·side /'e(ə)r‚sīd/ ▶ n. the area beyond passport and customs control in an airport terminal.

air·space /'e(ə)r‚spās/ ▶ n. the part of the air above and subject to the laws of a particular country.

air·speed /'e(ə)r‚spēd/ ▶ n. the speed of an aircraft relative to the air through which it is moving.

air·stream /'e(ə)r‚strēm/ ▶ n. a current of air.

air·strip /'e(ə)r‚strip/ ▶ n. a strip of ground for

the takeoff and landing of aircraft.

air·tight /'e(ə)r͵tīt/ ▶ adj. 1 not allowing air to escape or pass through. 2 having no weaknesses: *an airtight alibi.*

air·time /'e(ə)r͵tīm/ ▶ n. 1 the time during which a broadcast is being transmitted. 2 the time during which a cell phone is in use.

air traf·fic con·trol ▶ n. the ground-based staff and equipment concerned with controlling air traffic within a particular area. ■ **air traf·fic con·troll·er** n.

air·waves /'e(ə)r͵wāvz/ ▶ pl.n. the radio frequencies used for broadcasting.

air·way /'eər͵wā/ ▶ n. 1 the passage by which air reaches the lungs. 2 a tube for supplying air to the lungs in an emergency. 3 a recognized route followed by aircraft.

air·wor·thy /'e(ə)r͵wərTHē/ ▶ adj. (of an aircraft) safe to fly. ■ **air·wor·thi·ness** n.

air·y /'e(ə)rē/ ▶ adj. (**airier, airiest**) 1 (of a room or building) spacious and well ventilated. 2 not treating something as important; casual: *her airy unconcern for economy.* ■ **air·i·ly** adv. **air·i·ness** n.

air·y-fair·y /͵e(ə)rē'fe(ə)rē/ ▶ adj. informal, chiefly Brit. vague and unrealistic.

aisle /īl/ ▶ n. 1 a passage between rows of seats in a public building, aircraft, or train. 2 a passage between sets of shelves in a store. ■ **aisled** adj.

aitch /āCH/ ▶ n. the letter H.
– PHRASES **drop one's aitches** fail to pronounce the letter *h* at the beginning of words.

aitch·bone /'āCH͵bōn/ ▶ n. 1 the buttock or rump bone of cattle. 2 a cut of beef lying over the rump bone.

a·jar /ə'jär/ ▶ adv. & adj. (of a door or window) slightly open.

AK ▶ abbr. Alaska.

aka ▶ abbr. also known as.

AKC ▶ abbr. American Kennel Club.

a·kee /a'kē, 'akē/ (also **ackee**) ▶ n. the fruit of a West African tree, eaten as a vegetable.

a·kim·bo /ə'kimbō/ ▶ adv. with hands on the hips and elbows turned outward.

a·kin /ə'kin/ ▶ adj. similar in nature or type: *a road more akin to an army assault course.*

AL ▶ abbr. Alabama.

Al ▶ symbol the chemical element aluminum.

à la /'ä ͵lä, 'ä lə/ ▶ prep. in the style or manner of: *a publicity stunt à la Joan Crawford.*

al·a·bas·ter /'alə͵bastər/ ▶ n. a white, semitransparent form of the mineral gypsum, often carved into ornaments. ▶ adj. literary smooth and white: *pale, alabaster skin.*

à la carte /͵ä lä 'kärt, lə/ ▶ adj. (of a menu) listing dishes that can be ordered as separate items, rather than part of a set meal.

a·lac·ri·ty /ə'lakritē/ ▶ n. brisk eagerness or enthusiasm: *she accepted the invitation with alacrity.*

A·lad·din's lamp /ə'ladnz/ ▶ n. an object that brings its holder the promise of having a wish fulfilled.

à la mode /͵ä lä 'mōd/ ▶ adv. & adj. up to date; fashionable.

a·larm /ə'lärm/ ▶ n. 1 anxious or frightened awareness of danger. 2 a warning of danger: *I hammered on the door to raise the alarm.* 3 a warning sound or device. ▶ v. 1 frighten or disturb someone or something. 2 (**be alarmed**)

be fitted or protected with an alarm.

a·larm clock ▶ n. a clock that can be set to sound an alarm at a particular time, used to wake someone up.

a·larm·ist /ə'lärmist/ ▶ n. a person who exaggerates a danger, so causing needless alarm. ▶ adj. creating needless alarm. ■ **a·larm·ism** /-͵mizəm/ n.

a·las /ə'las/ ▶ exclam. literary or humorous an expression of grief, pity, or regret: *I, alas, am dieting.*

alb /alb/ ▶ n. a long white robe worn by clergy and servers in some Christian Churches.

al·ba·core /'albə͵kôr/ ▶ n. a tuna of warm seas that is an important food fish.

Al·ba·ni·an /al'bānēən, ôl-/ ▶ n. 1 a person from Albania. 2 the language of Albania. ▶ adj. relating to Albania.

al·ba·tross /'albə͵trôs, -͵träs/ ▶ n. (pl. **albatrosses**) 1 a very large seabird with long narrow wings, found chiefly in the southern oceans. 2 a burden: *the radioactive albatross around the nuclear power industry's neck.*

al·be·do /al'bēdō/ ▶ n. (pl. **albedos**) the proportion of the incident light or radiation that is reflected by a surface, typically that of the earth, the moon, or some other celestial object.

al·be·it /ôl'bē-it, al-/ ▶ conj. although: *I got up, albeit rather groggily.*

al·bi·no /al'bīnō/ ▶ n. (pl. **albinos**) a person or animal born without pigment in the skin and hair (which are white) and the eyes (which are usually pink). ■ **al·bi·nism** /'albə͵nizəm/ n.

Al·bi·on /'albēən/ ▶ n. literary Britain or England.

al·bum /'albəm/ ▶ n. 1 a blank book in which photographs, stamps, or other items can be kept. 2 a collection of musical recordings issued as a single item.

al·bu·men /al'byōōmən/ ▶ n. egg white, or the protein contained in it.

al·bu·min /al'byōōmən/ ▶ n. a form of protein that is soluble in water and is found especially in blood serum and egg white.

al·che·my /'alkəmē/ ▶ n. 1 the medieval forerunner of chemistry, concerned particularly with attempts to convert common metals into gold. 2 a seemingly magical or mysterious process: *watching the great chef create culinary alchemy.* ■ **al·chem·i·cal** /al'kemikəl/ adj. **al·che·mist** n.

al·co·hol /'alkə͵hôl, -͵häl/ ▶ n. 1 a colorless volatile liquid that is the intoxicating ingredient in drinks such as wine, beer, and liquor. 2 drink containing alcohol. 3 Chemistry any organic compound containing a hydroxyl group –OH: *propyl alcohol.*

al·co·hol·ic /͵alkə'hôlik, -'häl-/ ▶ adj. 1 relating to alcohol. 2 affected by alcoholism. ▶ n. a person affected by alcoholism.

al·co·hol·ism /'alkəhô͵lizəm, -hä-/ ▶ n. addiction to alcoholic drink.

al·cove /'al͵kōv/ ▶ n. a recess in the wall of a room.

al·de·hyde /'aldə͵hīd/ ▶ n. Chemistry an organic compound formed by the oxidation of an alcohol.

al den·te /äl 'dentä, al/ ▶ adj. & adv. (of food) cooked so as to be still firm when bitten.

al·der /'ôldər/ ▶ n. a tree of the birch family that bears catkins and has toothed leaves.

al·der·man /'ôldərmən/ ▶ n. (pl. **aldermen**) 1 (or

alderwoman) an elected member of a city council. **2** historical a member of an English county or borough council, next in status to the mayor.

ale /āl/ ▶n. **1** a type of beer with a bitter flavor and a higher alcoholic content. **2** chiefly Brit. beer, other than lager, stout, or porter.

a·le·a·to·ry /'ālēə,tôrē, 'al-/ (also **aleatoric** /,ālēə'tôrik, ,al-/) ▶adj. depending on the throw of a dice or on chance.

ale·house /'āl,hous/ ▶n. dated an inn or tavern.

a·lem·bic /ə'lembik/ ▶n. a container with a long, downward-sloping spout leading from the top, formerly used in distilling.

a·lert /ə'lərt/ ▶adj. **1** quick to notice and respond to danger or possible problems: *be alert to early signs of stress.* **2** quick-thinking; intelligent. ▶n. **1** the state of being watchful for danger or possible problems: *we should be on the alert for terrorists.* **2** a warning of danger. ▶v. warn someone about a danger or problem. ■ **a·lert·ly** adv. **a·lert·ness** n.

Al·ex·an·der tech·nique /,alig'zandər/ ▶n. a system designed to promote well-being through retraining one's habits of posture.

al·ex·an·drine /,alig'zandrin, -,drēn/ ▶adj. (of a line of verse) having six iambic feet. ▶n. an alexandrine line.

al·fal·fa /al'falfə/ ▶n. a plant with cloverlike leaves and bluish flowers, grown in warm climates for fodder.

al·fres·co /al'freskō, äl-/ ▶adv. & adj. in the open air: *an alfresco meal.*

al·ga /'algə/ ▶n. (pl. **algae** /-jē/) a simple plant of a large group that contain chlorophyll but lack true stems, roots, and leaves, e.g., seaweed. ■ **al·gal** /-gəl/ adj.

al·ge·bra /'aljəbrə/ ▶n. the branch of mathematics in which letters and other symbols are used to represent numbers and quantities. ■ **al·ge·bra·ic** /,aljə'brā-ik/ adj. **al·ge·bra·ist** /-,brā-ist/ n.

Al·ge·ri·an /al'ji(ə)rēən/ ▶n. a person from Algeria. ▶adj. relating to Algeria.

-algia ▶comb.form used to form nouns referring to pain in a specified part of the body: *neuralgia.* ■ **-algic** comb.form.

Al·gon·qui·an /al'gäɴɢk(w)ēən/ (also **Algonkian** /-kēən/) ▶n. **1** a large family of North American Indian languages, including Cree, Blackfoot, and Cheyenne. **2** a speaker of Algonquian. ▶adj. relating to Algonquian.

Al·gon·quin /al'gäɴɢk(w)in/ (also **Algonkin** /-kin/) ▶n. **1** a member of an American Indian people living in Canada along and westward of the Ottawa River. **2** the language of the Algonquins. ▶adj. relating to the Algonquins.

al·go·rithm /'algə,riᴛᴍəm/ ▶n. a process or set of rules used in calculations or other problem-solving operations. ■ **al·go·rith·mic** /,algə'riᴛᴍik/ adj.

a·li·as /'ālēəs/ ▶adv. also known as: *Eric Blair, alias George Orwell.* ▶n. **1** a false identity. **2** an identifying label used to access a computer file, command, or address.

a·li·as·ing /'ālēəsiɴɢ/ ▶n. **1** Physics & Telecommunications the misidentification of a signal frequency, introducing distortion or error. **2** the use of aliases to identify computer files, commands, etc.

al·i·bi /'alə,bī/ ▶n. (pl. **alibis**) **1** a claim or piece of evidence that one was elsewhere when an alleged act took place. **2** informal an excuse: *there can be no more alibis for failure.* ▶v. (**alibis, alibiing, alibied**) informal provide an alibi for someone.

USAGE
Alibi means 'a claim by a person that they were elsewhere'. The informal meaning 'an excuse' is regarded as incorrect by some people and should be avoided in careful writing.

a·li·en /'ālyən, 'ālēən/ ▶adj. **1** belonging to a foreign country. **2** unfamiliar or unacceptable: *extravagance is alien to his measured approach to life.* **3** relating to beings from other worlds. ▶n. **1** a foreigner. **2** a being from another world. ■ **al·ien·ness** n.

al·ien·a·ble /'ālēənəbəl, 'ālyənə-/ ▶adj. Law able to be transferred to new ownership.

al·ien·ate /'ālēə,nāt, 'ālyə-/ ▶v. **1** make someone feel isolated or estranged. **2** lose the support or sympathy of: *I wanted to keep the friends I had and not alienate any of them.* ■ **al·ien·a·tion** /,ālēə'nāsHən, ,ālyə-/ n.

a·light¹ /ə'līt/ ▶v. **1** (**alight on**) (of a bird) land or settle on something. **2** formal get off a train or bus. **3** (**alight on**) happen to notice something.

a·light² ▶adv. & adj. **1** on fire. **2** shining brightly.

a·lign /ə'līn/ ▶v. **1** put things in a straight line or in the correct position in relation to something else. **2** (**align oneself with**) give support to: *newspapers align themselves with certain political parties.* ■ **a·lign·ment** n.

a·like /ə'līk/ ▶adj. similar to each other: *the brothers were very much alike.* ▶adv. in a similar way.

al·i·men·ta·ry /,alə'ment(ə)rē/ ▶adj. relating to food or nutrition.

al·i·men·ta·ry ca·nal ▶n. the whole passage along which food passes through the body during digestion.

al·i·mo·ny /'alə,mōnē/ ▶n. court-ordered financial support for a spouse after separation or divorce.

A-line /'ā ,līn/ ▶adj. (of a garment) slightly flared from a narrow waist or shoulders.

al·i·quot /'alikwət/ ▶n. **1** technical a portion or sample taken for analysis or treatment. **2** (also **aliquot part** or **portion**) Mathematics a quantity that divides into another a whole number of times.

A-list /'ā ,list/ (or **B-list**) ▶n. a list of the most (or second most) famous or sought-after people, especially in show business.

a·live /ə'līv/ ▶adj. **1** living; not dead. **2** continuing in existence or use: *keeping hope alive.* **3** alert and active. **4** (**alive to**) aware of and willing to respond to: *I am very alive to the challenges we face.* **5** (**alive with**) teeming with something.

al·ka·li /'alkə,lī/ ▶n. (pl. **alkalis**) a compound, such as lime, with particular chemical properties including turning litmus blue and neutralizing or effervescing with acids.

al·ka·line /'alkəlin, -,līn/ ▶adj. containing an alkali or having the properties of an alkali; having a pH greater than 7. ■ **al·ka·lin·i·ty** /,alkə'linitē/ n.

al·ka·loid /'alkə,loid/ ▶n. Chemistry any of a class of organic compounds containing nitrogen that have significant physiological effects on humans.

al·kane /'al,kān/ ▶n. Chemistry any of the series of saturated hydrocarbons whose simplest members are methane and ethane.

al·kene /ˈalˌkēn/ ▸ n. Chemistry any of the series of unsaturated hydrocarbons containing a double bond, of which the simplest member is ethylene.

al·kyl /ˈalkəl/ ▸ n. Chemistry a hydrocarbon radical derived from an alkane by removal of a hydrogen atom.

all /ôl/ ▸ predeterminer & determiner 1 the whole quantity or extent of. 2 any whatever: *he denied all knowledge.* 3 the greatest possible. ▸ pron. everything or everyone. ▸ adv. 1 completely. 2 used to show an equal score: *one-all.*
– PHRASES **all along** from the beginning. **all and sundry** everyone or everything. **all around** (also chiefly Brit. **all round**) 1 in all respects: *all around, I think it's a good idea.* 2 for or by each person: *drinks all around.* **all but** very nearly. **all for** informal strongly in favor of. **all in** informal exhausted. **all in all** on the whole. **all out** using every effort. **all over the place** informal 1 everywhere. 2 in a disordered state. **all told** in total. **at all** in any way. **in all** in total. **on all fours** on hands and knees. **one's all** one's greatest effort.

Al·lah /ˈälə, ˈalə/ ▸ n. the name of God among Muslims (and Arab Christians).

all-A·mer·i·can ▸ adj. 1 possessing qualities characteristic of American ideals, such as honesty, industriousness, and health: *his all-American wholesomeness.* 2 having members or contents drawn only from the Americas or the US: *an all-American anthology.* 3 (of an athlete) honored as one of the best amateur competitors in the US: *an all-American wrestler.* ▸ n. an athlete honored as one of the best amateurs in the US.

all-a·round /ˈôləˌround/ (also chiefly Brit. **all-round** /ˈôlˌround/) ▸ adj. 1 having a wide range of abilities or uses. 2 in many or all respects: *his all-around excellence.*

al·lay /əˈlā/ ▸ v. reduce or end fear, concern, or difficulty.

all-clear ▸ n. a signal that danger or difficulty is over.

al·le·ga·tion /ˌaliˈgāSHən/ ▸ n. an unproven claim that someone has done something illegal or wrong.

al·lege /əˈlej/ ▸ v. claim that someone has done something illegal or wrong: *he alleged that he'd been assaulted.* ■ **al·leged** /əˈlejd/ adj. **al·leg·ed·ly** /-idlē/ adv.

al·le·giance /əˈlējəns/ ▸ n. loyalty or commitment to a superior person or to a group or cause: *I have no allegiance to any political party.*

al·le·go·rize /ˈaligəˌrīz/ ▸ v. interpret or represent something symbolically.

al·le·go·ry /ˈaləˌgôrē/ ▸ n. (pl. **allegories**) a story, poem, or picture that contains a hidden symbolic meaning. ■ **al·le·gor·i·cal** /ˌaliˈgôrikəl, -ˈgär-/ adj. **al·le·gor·i·cal·ly** /ˌaliˈgôrikəlē, -ˈgär-/ adv. **al·le·go·rist** n.

al·le·gret·to /ˌaliˈgretō/ ▸ adv. & adj. Music at a fairly brisk speed.

al·le·gro /əˈlegrō/ Music ▸ adv. & adj. at a brisk speed. ▸ n. (pl. **allegros**) a piece of music to be performed at a brisk speed.

al·lele /əˈlēl/ ▸ n. each of two or more alternative forms of a gene that arise by mutation and are found at the same place on a chromosome. ■ **al·lel·ic** /əˈlēlik, əˈlel-/ adj.

al·le·lu·ia /ˌaləˈlo͞oyə/ ▸ exclam. variant spelling of HALLELUJAH.

Al·len wrench /ˈalən/ ▸ n. a wrench designed to fit into and turn an **Allen screw** (one with a hexagonal socket in the head).

al·ler·gen /ˈalərjən/ ▸ n. a substance that causes an allergic reaction. ■ **al·ler·gen·ic** /ˌalərˈjenik/ ▸ adj. likely to cause an allergic reaction.

al·ler·gic /əˈlərjik/ ▸ adj. 1 caused by or relating to an allergy. 2 having an allergy.

al·ler·gy /ˈalərjē/ ▸ n. (pl. **allergies**) a medical condition in which the body reacts badly when it comes into contact with a particular substance. ■ **al·ler·gist** n.

al·le·vi·ate /əˈlēvēˌāt/ ▸ v. make pain or a problem less severe: *yoga can help alleviate insomnia.* ■ **al·le·vi·a·tion** /əˌlēvēˈāSHən/ n.

al·ley /ˈalē/ ▸ n. (pl. **alleys**) 1 a narrow passageway between or behind buildings. 2 a long, narrow area in which games such as bowling are played. 3 a path in a park or garden.
– PHRASES **up** (or **right up**) **one's alley** informal well suited to one's interests or abilities.

al·ley·way /ˈalēˌwā/ ▸ n. an alley between or behind buildings.

al·li·ance /əˈlīəns/ ▸ n. 1 a relationship established between countries or organizations for a joint purpose: *Saudi Arabia's alliance with the United States.* 2 the state of being joined or associated.

al·lied /əˈlīd, ˈalˌīd/ ▸ adj. 1 relating to or part of an alliance. 2 (**Allied**) relating to the US and its allies in World Wars I and II, and in global military actions since. 3 (**allied to/with**) combined or together with: *skilled craftsmanship allied to technology.*

al·li·ga·tor /ˈaliˌgātər/ ▸ n. a large reptile similar to a crocodile but with a broader and shorter head.

al·li·ga·tor pear ▸ n. an avocado.

all-in·clu·sive ▸ adj. 1 including everything or everyone. 2 relating to a vacation or resort in which all or most meals, drinks, and activities are included in the overall price.

all-in-one ▸ adj. combining two or more items or uses in a single unit.

al·lit·er·a·tion /əˌlitəˈrāSHən/ ▸ n. the occurrence of the same letter or sound at the beginning of words that are close together, as in *sing a song of sixpence.* ■ **al·lit·er·a·tive** /əˈlitərətiv, -ˌrātiv/ adj.

al·li·um /ˈalēəm/ ▸ n. (pl. **alliums**) a plant of a genus that includes onions, leeks, and garlic.

al·lo·cate /ˈaləˌkāt/ ▸ v. give or distribute something: *all the tickets have been allocated to tour operators.* ■ **al·lo·ca·ble** /-kəbəl/ adj. **al·lo·ca·tor** /-ˌkātər/ n.

al·lo·ca·tion /ˌaləˈkāSHən/ ▸ n. 1 the action of allocating something. 2 an amount of a resource given to someone.

al·lop·a·thy /əˈläpəTHē/ ▸ n. the conventional treatment of disease, using drugs that have effects opposite to the symptoms. ■ **al·lo·path** /ˈaləˌpaTH/ n. **al·lo·path·ic** /ˌaləˈpaTHik/ adj.

al·lot /əˈlät/ ▸ v. (**allots**, **allotting**, **allotted**) give or share out something: *equal time was allotted to each task.*

al·lot·ment /əˈlätmənt/ ▸ n. 1 an amount allotted to someone. 2 the action of allotting something. 3 historical a plot of land deeded by the government to an American Indian. 4 Brit. a plot of land rented by a person from a local authority, for growing vegetables or flowers.

al·lo·trope /'alə,trōp/ ▸ n. Chemistry each of two or more different physical forms in which an element can exist (e.g., graphite, charcoal, and diamond as forms of carbon). ■ **al·lo·trop·ic** /,alə'träpik, -'trō-/ adj.

al·low /ə'lou/ ▸ v. **1** let someone have or do something. **2** decide that something is legal or acceptable. **3** provide or set aside: *allow an hour or so for driving.* **4** (**allow for**) take into consideration: *income rose by 11 percent allowing for inflation.* **5** accept that something is true. ■ **al·low·a·ble** adj. **al·low·ed·ly** /ə'lou-idlē/ adv.

> **USAGE**
> On the confusion of **allowed** and **aloud**, see the note at **ALOUD**.

al·low·ance /ə'lou-əns/ ▸ n. **1** the amount of something allowed: *the recommended daily allowance of 1,300 mg calcium.* **2** a sum of money paid regularly to a person.
– PHRASES **make allowances for 1** take something into consideration. **2** treat someone less harshly because of their difficult circumstances.

al·loy ▸ n. /'a,loi/ **1** a mixture of two or more metals. **2** an inferior metal mixed with a precious one. ▸ v. /'a,loi, ə'loi/ mix metals to make an alloy.

all-pur·pose ▸ adj. having many uses, especially all that might be expected from something of its type: *an all-purpose kitchen knife.*

all right ▸ adj. **1** satisfactory; acceptable. **2** able to be done or to happen; allowable. ▸ adv. fairly well. ▸ exclam. expressing or asking for agreement or acceptance.

All Saints' Day ▸ n. a Christian festival in honor of all the saints, held on November 1.

All Souls' Day ▸ n. a Catholic festival with prayers for the souls of the dead in purgatory, held on November 2.

all·spice /'ôl,spīs/ ▸ n. the dried fruit of a Caribbean tree, used as a spice in cooking.

all-star ▸ adj. composed wholly of outstanding performers or players: *an all-star cast.* ▸ n. a member of such a group or team.

all-ter·rain ve·hi·cle ▸ n. a motorcycle with four wheels and large tires, for off-road use.

all-time /'ôl,tīm/ ▸ adj. not bettered or surpassed: *the all-time record.*

al·lude /ə'lōōd/ ▸ v. (**allude to**) **1** mention briefly: *offering no evidence, he alluded airily to 'scientific findings'.* **2** refer to someone or something in an indirect way.

al·lure /ə'lōōr/ ▸ n. powerful attractiveness or charm. ▸ v. (often as adj. **alluring**) strongly attract or charm: *the alluring scent of lemon.* ■ **al·lure·ment** n. **al·lur·ing·ly** adv.

al·lu·sion /ə'lōōzHən/ ▸ n. an indirect reference to something.

al·lu·sive /ə'lōōsiv/ ▸ adj. using or containing indirect references to something: *elaborate, allusive prose.* ■ **al·lu·sive·ly** adv. **al·lu·sive·ness** n.

al·lu·vi·um /ə'lōōvēəm/ ▸ n. a fertile deposit of clay, silt, and sand left by floodwater. ■ **al·lu·vi·al** adj.

al·ly ▸ n. /'alī/ (pl. **allies**) **1** a person, organization, or country that cooperates with another. **2** (**the Allies**) the countries that fought with the US in World Wars I and II. ▸ v. /ə'lī/ (**allies, allying, allied**) **1** (**ally something to/with**) combine a

resource or quality with another in a way that benefits both: *he allied his racing experience with his father's business skill.* **2** (**ally oneself with**) side with or support something.

-ally ▸ suffix forming adverbs from adjectives ending in *-al* (such as *radically* from *radical*).

al·ma ma·ter /'älmə 'mätər, 'almə/ ▸ n. the school, college, or university that one once attended.

al·ma·nac /'ôlmə,nak, 'al-/ (also **almanack**) ▸ n. **1** a calendar giving important dates and information, such as the phases of the moon. **2** an annual handbook containing information of general or special interest.

al·might·y /ôl'mītē/ ▸ adj. **1** having complete or very great power: *an almighty army.* **2** informal very big; enormous. ▸ n. (**the Almighty**) a name or title for God.

al·mond /'ä(l)mənd, 'a(l)-/ ▸ n. the oval edible nutlike seed (kernel) of the almond tree.

al·mond paste ▸ n. marzipan.

al·most /'ôl'mōst, 'ôl,mōst/ ▸ adv. very nearly.

alms /ä(l)mz/ ▸ pl.n. old use money or food given to poor people.

alms·house /'ä(l)mz,hous/ ▸ n. historical a house founded by charity, offering accommodations for poor people.

al·oe /'alō/ ▸ n. **1** a succulent tropical plant with thick tapering leaves. **2** (**aloes** or **bitter aloes**) a strong laxative obtained from the bitter juice of some kinds of aloe.

al·oe ver·a /'alō 'verə, 'vi(ə)rə/ ▸ n. a jellylike substance obtained from a kind of aloe, used to soothe the skin.

a·loft /ə'lôft/ ▸ adj. & adv. up in or into the air.

a·lo·ha /ə'lō,hä/ ▸ exclam. & n. a Hawaiian word used when greeting or parting from someone.

a·lone /ə'lōn/ ▸ adj. & adv. **1** on one's own; by oneself. **2** isolated and lonely. **3** only; exclusively: *it was a smile for him alone.* ■ **a·lone·ness** /ə'lōn(n)əs/ n.
– PHRASES **leave** (or **let**) **someone/thing alone 1** abandon someone or something. **2** stop interfering with someone or something.

a·long /ə'lôNG, ə'läNG/ ▸ prep. & adv. **1** moving forward on. **2** extending in a horizontal line on. **3** in or into company with other people: *she'd brought along a friend.*
– PHRASES **along with** together with or at the same time as. **be** (or **come**) **along** arrive.

a·long·side /ə'lôNG,sīd, ə'läNG-/ (often **alongside of**) ▸ prep. **1** close to the side of; next to. **2** at the same time as.

a·loof /ə'lōōf/ ▸ adj. cool and distant: *they were polite but faintly aloof.* ■ **a·loof·ly** adv. **a·loof·ness** n.

al·o·pe·ci·a /,alə'pēsH(ē)ə/ ▸ n. Medicine abnormal loss of hair; baldness.

a·loud /ə'loud/ ▸ adv. out loud; so as to be heard.

> **USAGE**
> Do not confuse **aloud** with **allowed**. **Aloud** means 'out loud' (*I read the letter aloud*), whereas **allowed** means 'permitted' (*smoking is not allowed in the office*).

alp /alp/ ▸ n. **1** a high mountain. **2** (**the Alps**) a high range of mountains in Switzerland and adjoining countries.

al·pac·a /al'pakə/ ▸ n. (pl. same or **alpacas**) **1** a long-haired domesticated South American mammal related to the llama. **2** the wool of the alpaca.

al·pen·stock /'alpən,stäk/ ▸ n. a long iron-tipped stick used by walkers in hilly country.

al·pha /'alfə/ ▸ n. the first letter of the Greek alphabet (A, α), represented as 'a'. ▸ adj. referring to the dominant animal or person in a group: *an alpha male.*
– PHRASES **alpha and omega** the beginning and the end.

al·pha·bet /'alfə,bet, -bit/ ▸ n. an ordered set of letters or symbols used to represent the basic speech sounds of a language.

al·pha·bet·i·cal /,alfə'betikəl/ ▸ adj. in the order of the letters of the alphabet. ■ **al·pha·bet·ic** adj. **al·pha·bet·i·cal·ly** adv.

al·pha·bet·ize /'alfəbi,tīz/ ▸ v. arrange words in alphabetical order.

al·pha·nu·mer·ic /,alfən(y)oo'merik/ ▸ adj. made up of or using both letters and numerals.

al·pha par·ti·cle ▸ n. Physics a helium nucleus, especially as given out by some radioactive substances.

al·pine /'al,pīn/ ▸ adj. **1** relating to or found on high mountains. **2** (**Alpine**) relating to the Alps. ▸ n. a plant that grows on high mountains.

al·read·y /ôl'redē/ ▸ adv. **1** before the time in question. **2** as surprisingly soon or early as this: *you aren't leaving already?*

al·right /ôl'rīt/ ▸ adj., adv., & exclam. variant spelling of ALL RIGHT.

> USAGE
> Many people consider the spelling **alright** (rather than **all right**) to be unacceptable in formal writing, even though other single-word forms such as **altogether** have long been accepted as standard.

Al·sa·tian /al'sāSHən/ ▸ n. Brit. a German shepherd dog.

al·so /'ôlsō/ ▸ adv. in addition.

al·so-ran ▸ n. a person who is unsuccessful in a race or contest.

alt. /alt/ ▸ prefix referring to a version of something that is intended as a challenge to the traditional version: *an alt.country band.*

al·tar /'ôltər/ ▸ n. **1** the table in a Christian church at which the bread and wine are consecrated in communion services. **2** a table or other structure on which religious offerings are made.

al·tar boy ▸ n. a boy who assists a priest during a service.

al·tar·piece /'ôltər,pēs/ ▸ n. a painting or other work of art set above and behind an altar.

al·ter /'ôltər/ ▸ v. make or become different: *she had to alter her vacation plans.*

al·ter·a·tion /,ôltə'rāSHən/ ▸ n. a change or modification.

al·ter·ca·tion /,ôltər'kāSHən/ ▸ n. a noisy disagreement.

al·ter e·go /,altər 'ēgō, ,ôltər 'ēgō/ ▸ n. **1** another side to someone's normal personality. **2** a close friend who is very like oneself.

al·ter·nate ▸ v. /'ôltər,nāt/ **1** occur or do in turn repeatedly: *the narrative alternates personal observation with historical fact.* **2** change repeatedly between two contrasting states: *his mood alternated between aggression and morose despair.* ▸ adj. /'ôltərnit/ **1** every other: *the service runs on alternate days.* **2** (of two things) each following and succeeded by the other in a regular pattern: *put alternate layers of potatoes and fish in the casserole.* **3** another term for ALTERNATIVE. ■ **al·ter·nate·ly** /-nitlē/ adv. **al·ter·na·tion** /,ôltər'nāSHən/ n.

> USAGE
> The use of **alternate** to mean **alternative** (as in *we will need to find alternate sources of fuel*) is common in American English, although it is still regarded as incorrect by many people in Britain.

al·ter·nate an·gles ▸ pl.n. two equal angles on opposite sides of a line crossing two parallel lines.

al·ter·nat·ing cur·rent ▸ n. an electric current that reverses its direction many times a second. Compare with DIRECT CURRENT.

al·ter·na·tive /ôl'tərnətiv/ ▸ adj. **1** (of one or more things) available as another possibility. **2** differing from the usual or traditional form of something: *people attracted to alternative lifestyles.* ▸ n. one of two or more available possibilities. ■ **al·ter·na·tive·ly** adv.

> USAGE
> Some people say that you can have a maximum of only two alternatives (because the word **alternative** comes from Latin *alter* 'other of two'). References to more than two alternatives are, however, normal in modern standard English.

al·ter·na·tive en·er·gy ▸ n. energy produced in ways that do not use up natural resources or harm the environment.

al·ter·na·tive med·i·cine ▸ n. medical treatment that does not follow the usual practices of Western medicine, e.g., herbalism.

al·ter·na·tor /'ôltər,nātər/ ▸ n. a dynamo that generates an alternating current.

al·though /ôl'THō/ ▸ conj. **1** in spite of the fact that. **2** however; but.

al·tim·e·ter /al'timitər/ ▸ n. an instrument that indicates the altitude reached by something, especially an aircraft.

al·ti·pla·no /alti'plänō/ ▸ n. (pl. **altiplanos**) a broad, high, level region in central South America.

al·ti·tude /'alti,t(y)ood/ ▸ n. the height of an object or point above sea level or ground level.

al·ti·tude sick·ness ▸ n. illness resulting from a shortage of oxygen in places that are high above sea or ground level.

al·to /'altō/ ▸ n. (pl. **altos**) the highest adult male or lowest female singing voice. ▸ adj. referring to the second or third highest of a family of instruments: *an alto sax.*

al·to·geth·er /,ôltə'geTHər/ ▸ adv. **1** completely. **2** in total. **3** on the whole.
– PHRASES **in the altogether** informal naked.

> USAGE
> Note that **altogether** and **all together** do not mean the same thing. **Altogether** means 'in total' (*there are six bedrooms altogether*), whereas **all together** means 'all in one place' (*it was good to have a group of friends all together*) or 'all at once' (*they came in all together.*).

al·tru·ism /'altroo,izəm/ ▸ n. unselfish concern for the needs and well-being of other people. ■ **al·tru·ist** n. **al·tru·is·tic** /,altroo'istik/ adj. **al·tru·is·ti·cal·ly** /,altroo'istikəlē/ adv.

a·lum /'aləm/ ▸ n. a crystalline compound of aluminum and potassium, used in dyeing and tanning animal skin.

a·lu·mi·na /ə'lōōmənə/ ▶ n. aluminum oxide, a chemical compound found in many types of rock.

a·lu·mi·nize /ə'lōōmə,nīz/ ▶ v. coat something with aluminum.

al·u·mi·num /ə'lōōmənəm/ (Brit **aluminium** /,alyə'minēəm/) ▶ n. a lightweight silvery-gray metallic element that is resistant to rust and corrosion.

a·lum·nus /ə'ləmnəs/ ▶ n. (pl. **alumni** /-nī, -nē/; fem. **alumna** /ə'ləmnə/, pl. **alumnae** /-nī, -nē/) a former student of a particular school, college, or university.

al·ve·o·lus /al'vēələs/ ▶ n. (pl. **alveoli** /-,lī/) 1 any of the many tiny air sacs in the lungs. 2 the bony socket for the root of a tooth. ■ **al·ve·o·lar** /al'vēələr/ adj.

al·ways /'ôl,wāz, -wēz/ ▶ adv. 1 on all occasions; at all times. 2 forever. 3 repeatedly. 4 failing all else.

a·lys·sum /ə'lisəm/ ▶ n. (pl. **alyssums**) a plant with small flowers, most commonly white.

Alz·hei·mer's dis·ease /'älts,hīmərz, 'ôlts-, 'älz-, 'ôlz-/ ▶ n. a disorder that causes progressive mental deterioration, typically affecting older people.

AM ▶ abbr. amplitude modulation.

Am ▶ symbol the chemical element americium.

am /am/ ▶ first person singular present of BE.

a.m. ▶ abbr. before noon.

AMA ▶ abbr. American Medical Association.

a·mal·gam /ə'malgəm/ ▶ n. 1 a mixture or blend. 2 an alloy of mercury with another metal, especially one used for dental fillings.

a·mal·ga·mate /ə'malgə,māt/ ▶ v. 1 combine or unite to form one organization or structure: *the paper later amalgamated with other publications.* 2 mix a metal with mercury to make an alloy. ■ **a·mal·ga·ma·tion** /ə,malgə'māsHən/ n.

a·man·u·en·sis /ə,manyōō'ensis/ ▶ n. (pl. **amanuenses** /-,sēz/) a writer's assistant.

am·a·ranth /'amə,ranTH/ ▶ n. a plant of a family that includes love-lies-bleeding.

am·a·ret·to /,amə'retō, ,äm-/ ▶ n. a brown almond-flavored Italian liqueur.

am·a·ryl·lis /,amə'rilis/ ▶ n. a plant with large trumpet-shaped flowers.

a·mass /ə'mas/ ▶ v. build up over time: *he amassed a fortune of more than $13 million.*

am·a·teur /'amətər, -,tər, -,cHŏŏr, -cHər/ ▶ n. 1 a person who takes part in a sport or other activity for pleasure, rather than as a profession or job. 2 a person who is not skilled at a particular activity. ▶ adj. 1 nonprofessional: *an amateur photographer.* 2 done in an unskillful way. ■ **am·a·teur·ism** n.

am·a·teur·ish /,amə'tərisH, -'t(y)ŏŏr-, -'cHŏŏr-/ ▶ adj. not done or made skillfully.

am·a·to·ry /'amə,tôrē/ ▶ adj. relating to sexual love or desire.

a·maze /ə'māz/ ▶ v. surprise someone very much. ■ **a·maze·ment** n.

a·maz·ing /ə'māziNG/ ▶ adj. 1 very surprising: *it's amazing how quickly she adapted.* 2 informal very good or impressive. ■ **a·maz·ing·ly** adv.

Am·a·zon /'amə,zän, -zən/ ▶ n. 1 (in Greek mythology) a member of a race of female warriors. 2 a very tall, strong woman.

Am·a·zo·ni·an /,amə'zōnēən/ ▶ adj. 1 relating to the Amazon River. 2 (of a woman) very tall and strong.

am·bas·sa·dor /am'basədər, -,dôr/ ▶ n. 1 a diplomat sent by a government as its permanent representative in a foreign country. 2 a person who represents or promotes something: *he is a great ambassador for football.* ■ **am·bas·sa·do·ri·al** /am,basə'dôrēəl/ adj.

am·ber /'ambər/ ▶ n. 1 a hard translucent yellowish substance formed from the fossilized resin of certain ancient trees, used in jewelry. 2 a honey-yellow color.

am·ber·gris /'ambər,gris, -,grē(s)/ ▶ n. a waxy substance produced by sperm whales, used in perfume manufacture.

am·bi·dex·trous /,ambi'dekst(ə)rəs/ ▶ adj. able to use the right and left hands equally well.

am·bi·ence /'ambēəns/ (also **ambiance**) ▶ n. the character and atmosphere of a place: *the gentle color scheme creates a relaxing ambience.*

am·bi·ent /'ambēənt/ ▶ adj. 1 relating to the surrounding area: *the ambient temperature.* 2 referring to a style of electronic instrumental music with no persistent beat, used to create a relaxed atmosphere.

am·bi·gu·i·ty /,ambi'gyōō-itē/ ▶ n. (pl. **ambiguities**) the quality of having more than one possible meaning or interpretation.

am·big·u·ous /am'bigyōōəs/ ▶ adj. 1 (of language) having more than one possible meaning. 2 not clear or decided: *a European nation whose position had long been ambiguous.* ■ **am·big·u·ous·ly** adv.

am·bit /'ambit/ ▶ n. the scope or extent of something: *the need to bring the activity within the ambit of federal law.*

am·bi·tion /am'bisHən/ ▶ n. 1 a strong desire to do or achieve something: *her burning ambition was to be world champion.* 2 the desire or determination to become successful or rich.

am·bi·tious /am'bisHəs/ ▶ adj. 1 having or showing a determination to succeed. 2 requiring a great deal of effort, time, or money to succeed: *an ambitious six-year development plan.* ■ **am·bi·tious·ly** adv.

am·biv·a·lent /am'bivələnt/ ▶ adj. having mixed feelings about something or someone. ■ **am·biv·a·lence** n. **am·biv·a·lent·ly** adv.

am·ble /'ambəl/ ▶ v. walk at a leisurely pace. ▶ n. a leisurely walk.

am·bro·sia /am'brōzH(ē)ə/ ▶ n. 1 Greek & Roman Mythology the food of the gods. 2 something that tastes or smells very pleasant. ■ **am·bro·sial** adj.

am·bu·lance /'ambyələns/ ▶ n. a vehicle equipped for taking sick or injured people to and from a hospital.

am·bu·lance chas·er ▶ n. derogatory a lawyer who encourages accident victims to make claims for damages in a court of law.

am·bu·lant /'ambyələnt/ ▶ adj. Medicine able to walk around; not confined to bed.

am·bu·la·to·ry /'ambyələ,tôrē/ ▶ adj. 1 relating to walking or able to walk: *ambulatory patients.* 2 movable; mobile: *an ambulatory data recorder.* ▶ n. (pl. **ambulatories**) an aisle or cloister in a church or monastery.

am·bush /'am,bŏŏsH/ ▶ n. a surprise attack made by people lying in wait in a concealed position. ▶ v. attack a person or group of people from a concealed position.

a·me·ba /ə'mēbə/ (also chiefly Brit. **amoeba**) ▶ n. (pl. **amebas** or **amebae**) a single-celled animal that catches food and moves by extending fingerlike projections of protoplasm. ■ **a·me·bic** /-bik/ adj. **a·me·boid** /-boid/ adj.

a·me·lio·rate /əˈmēlyəˌrāt, əˈmēlēə-/ ▶ v. formal make something that is bad or unsatisfactory better. ■ **a·me·lio·ra·tion** /əˌmēlyəˈrāsHən/ n.

a·men /äˈmen, āˈmen/ ▶ exclam. said at the end of a prayer or hymn, meaning 'so be it'.

a·me·na·ble /əˈmēnəbəl, əˈmen-/ ▶ adj. **1** willing to cooperate or be persuaded to do something. **2** (**amenable to**) able to be affected by: *conditions that are amenable to medical intervention.* ■ **a·me·na·bil·i·ty** /əˌmēnəˈbilitē, əˌmen-/ n.

a·mend /əˈmend/ ▶ v. make small changes or improvements to a document, proposal, etc.

a·mend·ment /əˈmen(d)mənt/ ▶ n. **1** a small change or improvement made to a document, proposal, etc. **2** (**Amendment**) an article added to the US Constitution.

a·mends /əˈmendz/ ▶ pl.n. (in phrase **make amends**) do something to show that one regrets a wrong or unfair action: *I want to make amends for the way I treated her.*

a·men·i·ty /əˈmenitē, əˈmē-/ ▶ n. (pl. **amenities**) a useful or desirable feature of a place: *a convenient location, close to all local amenities.*

a·men·or·rhe·a /āˌmenəˈrēə/ ▶ n. the abnormal absence of menstrual periods.

Am·er·a·sian /ˌamərˈāzHən/ ▶ adj. having one American and one Asian parent. ▶ n. an Amerasian person.

A·mer·i·can /əˈmerikən/ ▶ adj. relating to the US or to the continents of America. ▶ n. a person from the US or any of the countries of North, South, or Central America. ■ **A·mer·i·can·ize** /əˈmerikəˌnīz/ v.

A·mer·i·ca·na /əˌmeriˈkänə, -ˈkanə/ ▶ pl.n. things associated with the US.

A·mer·i·can dream ▶ n. the ideal of equality of opportunity associated with the US.

A·mer·i·can In·di·an ▶ n. a member of the native peoples of America.

> **USAGE**
> **American Indian** has been steadily replaced by the term **Native American**, especially in official contexts. However, **American Indian** is still widespread in general use and is generally acceptable to American Indians themselves.

A·mer·i·can·ism /əˈmerikəˌnizəm/ ▶ n. a word or phrase used or originating in the US.

am·er·i·ci·um /aməˈrisHēəm/ ▶ n. a radioactive metallic chemical element made by high-energy atomic collisions.

Am·er·in·di·an /ˌaməˈrindēən/ (also **Amerind** /ˈamərind/) ▶ n. & adj. another term for AMERICAN INDIAN.

am·e·thyst /ˈaməTHəst/ ▶ n. a precious stone consisting of a violet or purple variety of quartz.

Am·har·ic /amˈharik/ ▶ n. the Semitic official language of Ethiopia.

a·mi·a·ble /ˈāmēəbəl/ ▶ adj. friendly and pleasant. ■ **a·mi·a·bil·i·ty** /ˌāmēəˈbilitē/ n. **a·mi·a·bly** adv.

am·i·ca·ble /ˈamikəbəl/ ▶ adj. friendly and without disagreement or dispute: *an amicable working relationship.* ■ **am·i·ca·bly** adv.

am·ice /ˈamis/ ▶ n. a white cloth worn on the neck and shoulders by a priest celebrating Holy Communion.

a·mi·cus (in full **amicus curiae** /ˈkyōōrēˌī, -ēˌē/)

▶ n. (pl. **amici** /əˈmēkē, əˈmīkī/, **amici curiae**) an impartial adviser, often voluntary, to a court of law in a particular case.

a·mid /əˈmid/ (or **amidst**) ▶ prep. surrounded by; in the middle of.

am·ide /ˈamīd, -id/ ▶ n. Chemistry **1** an organic compound containing the group −C(O)NH₂. **2** a saltlike compound containing the anion NH₂⁻.

a·mid·ships /əˈmidˌsHips/ ▶ adv. & adj. in the middle of a ship.

a·mi·go /əˈmēgō/ ▶ n. (pl. **amigos**) informal a friend.

a·mine /əˈmēn, ˈamēn/ ▶ n. Chemistry an organic compound obtained from ammonia.

a·mi·no ac·id /əˈmēnō/ ▶ n. any of about twenty organic compounds that form the basic constituents of proteins.

a·mir /əˈmi(ə)r/ ▶ n. variant spelling of EMIR.

A·mish /ˈämisH/ ▶ pl.n. a strict Protestant sect living mainly in the US states of Pennsylvania and Ohio.

a·miss /əˈmis/ ▶ adj. not quite right: *he didn't notice that anything was amiss.* ▶ adv. wrongly or badly: *everything had gone amiss.*
− PHRASES **take something amiss** be offended by something that is said.

am·i·ty /ˈamitē/ ▶ n. formal friendly relations between people or countries.

am·me·ter /ˈa(m)ˌmētər/ ▶ n. an instrument for measuring electric current in amperes.

am·mo /ˈamō/ ▶ n. informal ammunition.

am·mo·nia /əˈmōnyə, -nēə/ ▶ n. a colorless, strong-smelling gas that forms an alkaline solution in water, and that is used as a cleaning fluid.

am·mo·nite /ˈaməˌnīt/ ▶ n. an extinct sea creature with a spiral shell, found as a fossil.

am·mo·ni·um /əˈmōnēəm/ ▶ n. Chemistry the ion NH₄⁺, present in solutions of ammonia and in salts obtained from ammonia.

am·mo·noid /ˈaməˌnoid/ ▶ n. an extinct cephalopod mollusk with a flat-coiled spiral shell, found commonly as a fossil in marine deposits.

am·mu·ni·tion /ˌamyəˈnisHən/ ▶ n. **1** a supply of bullets and shells. **2** points used to support one's case in an argument or debate: *the analysis provided vital ammunition to anti-nuclear campaigners.*

am·ne·sia /amˈnēzHə/ ▶ n. loss of memory. ■ **am·ne·si·ac** /amˈnēzēˌak, -zHēˌak/ n. & adj.

am·nes·ty /ˈamnistē/ ▶ n. (pl. **amnesties**) **1** an official pardon given to people convicted of political offenses. **2** a period during which people admitting to particular offenses are not punished: *there will be no amnesty for people who have not paid the tax.*

am·ni·o·cen·te·sis /ˌamnē-ōsenˈtēsis/ ▶ n. (pl. **amniocenteses** /-sēz/) a medical procedure in which a sample of amniotic fluid is taken from a pregnant woman's uterus in order to check for abnormalities in the fetus.

am·ni·on /ˈamnēˌän, -ən/ ▶ n. (pl. **amnions** or **amnia**) the innermost membrane surrounding an embryo. ■ **am·ni·ot·ic** /ˌamnēˈätik/ adj.

am·ni·ot·ic flu·id /ˌamnēˈätik/ ▶ n. the fluid surrounding a fetus before birth.

a·moe·ba, etc. /əˈmēbə/ ▶ n. (pl. **amoebas** or **amoebae** /-bē/) chiefly British spelling of AMEBA, etc.

a·mok /əˈmək, əˈmäk/ (also **amuck**) ▶ adv. (in

phrase **run amok**) behave in an uncontrolled and disorderly way.

a·mong /əˈməNG/ (chiefly Brit. also **amongst**) ▶ prep. **1** surrounded by; in the middle of. **2** included or occurring in. **3** shared by; between.

a·mon·til·la·do /əˌmäntlˈädō, -təˈyädō/ ▶ n. (pl. **amontillados**) a medium dry sherry.

a·mor·al /āˈmôrəl/ ▶ adj. without morals; not concerned about right or wrong. ■ **a·mo·ral·i·ty** /ˌāməˈralitē/ n.

USAGE

Amoral does not mean the same as **immoral**: while **immoral** means 'not following accepted standards of morality,' **amoral** means 'without morals.'

am·o·rous /ˈamərəs/ ▶ adj. showing or feeling sexual desire. ■ **am·o·rous·ly** adv.

a·mor·phous /əˈmôrfəs/ ▶ adj. without a definite shape or form.

am·or·tize /ˈamərˌtīz/ ▶ v. Finance gradually pay off a debt. ■ **am·or·ti·za·tion** /ˌamərtiˈzāsHən, əˌmôrti-/ n.

a·mount /əˈmount/ ▶ n. **1** the total number, size, or value of something. **2** a quantity: *add a small amount of water.* ▶ v. (**amount to**) **1** add up to a total. **2** be the equivalent of: *a degree of carelessness that amounted to gross negligence.*

a·mour /əˈmoŏr, äˈmoŏr/ ▶ n. a secret love affair.

amp[1] /amp/ ▶ n. short for AMPERE.

amp[2] ▶ n. informal short for AMPLIFIER. ▶ v. (**amp up**) informal **1** make a quality, feeling, etc., more intense. **2** make a person very excited or energetic through, or as if through, the consumption of amphetamines or another stimulant.

am·per·age /ˈamp(ə)rij/ ▶ n. the strength of an electric current, measured in amperes.

am·pere /ˈamˌpi(ə)r/ ▶ n. the base unit of electric current in the SI system.

am·per·sand /ˈampərˌsand/ ▶ n. the sign &, standing for *and*.

am·phet·a·mine /amˈfetəˌmēn, -min/ ▶ n. a drug used illegally as a stimulant.

am·phib·i·an /amˈfibēən/ ▶ n. a cold-blooded animal such as a frog or toad that lives in water when young and on land as an adult.

am·phib·i·ous /amˈfibēəs/ ▶ adj. **1** living in or suited for both land and water. **2** (of a military operation) involving forces landing at a place from the sea.

am·phi·the·a·ter /ˈamfəˌTHēətər/ (also **amphitheatre**) ▶ n. a round building consisting of tiers of seats surrounding a central space for dramatic or sporting events.

am·pho·ra /ˈamfərə/ ▶ n. (pl. **amphorae** /-ˌrē/ or **amphoras**) an ancient Greek or Roman jar with two handles and a narrow neck.

am·pi·cil·lin /ˌampiˈsilin/ ▶ n. Medicine a semisynthetic form of penicillin used chiefly to treat infections of the urinary and respiratory tracts.

am·ple /ˈampəl/ ▶ adj. **1** enough or more than enough; plentiful: *there was ample room for storage.* **2** large: *her ample bosom.* ■ **am·ply** /-p(ə)lē/ adv.

am·pli·fi·er /ˈampləˌfīər/ ▶ n. an electronic device for increasing the strength of electrical signals.

am·pli·fy /ˈampləˌfī/ ▶ v. (**amplifies, amplifying, amplified**) **1** increase the strength of sound

or electrical signals. **2** add details to a story or statement. ■ **am·pli·fi·ca·tion** /ˌampləfiˈkāsHən/ n.

am·pli·tude /ˈampliˌt(y)oŏd/ ▶ n. **1** Physics the maximum amount by which an alternating current or electromagnetic wave can vary from its average level. **2** great size or extent.

am·pli·tude mod·u·la·tion ▶ n. the modification of a radio wave by varying its amplitude, used as a method of broadcasting an audio signal.

am·poule /ˈamˌp(y)oŏl/ (also **ampule** or **ampul**) ▶ n. a small sealed glass capsule that contains a measured quantity of liquid ready for an injection.

am·pul·la /amˈpoŏlə, -ˈpələ/ ▶ n. (pl. **ampullae** /-ˌlē/) **1** a roughly spherical ancient Roman flask with two handles. **2** a flask holding the consecrated oil in a church.

am·pu·tate /ˈampyəˌtāt/ ▶ v. cut off a limb in a surgical operation. ■ **am·pu·ta·tion** /ˌampyəˈtāsHən/ n.

am·pu·tee /ˌampyəˈtē/ ▶ n. a person who has had a limb amputated.

Am·trak /ˈamˌtrak/ ▶ n. trademark the national passenger railroad service in the US, a government-subsidized corporation.

a·muck /əˈmək/ ▶ adv. variant spelling of AMOK.

am·u·let /ˈamyəlit/ ▶ n. an ornament or small piece of jewelry worn as protection against evil, illness, or danger.

a·muse /əˈmyoŏz/ ▶ v. **1** make someone laugh or smile. **2** provide someone with an enjoyable or interesting activity: *he amused himself by writing poetry.* ■ **a·mused** adj. **a·mus·ing** adj.

a·muse·ment /əˈmyoŏzmənt/ ▶ n. **1** the state or experience of finding something funny. **2** something that causes laughter or provides entertainment.

a·muse·ment park ▶ n. a large outdoor area with fairground rides and other entertainments.

am·yl·ase /ˈaməˌlās, -ˌlāz/ ▶ n. Biochemistry an enzyme found in saliva that converts starch into sugars.

am·yl ni·trite /ˈaməl ˈnītrīt/ ▶ n. a liquid used in medicine to expand blood vessels and sometimes inhaled for its stimulant effect on the body.

an /an/ ▶ determiner the form of the indefinite article 'a' used before words beginning with a vowel sound.

USAGE

It is better to use **a** rather than **an** before words beginning with an initial **h** that is sounded, such as *historical* and *hotel*. **An** was common in the 18th and 19th centuries because the initial **h** in such words was then often not pronounced.

an- ▶ prefix variant spelling of A- before a vowel (as in *anemia*).

An·a·bap·tist /ˌanəˈbapˌtist/ ▶ n. a member of a Protestant religious group believing that only adults should be baptized.

an·a·bol·ic ste·roid /ˌanəˈbälik/ ▶ n. a synthetic hormone taken illegally to improve a competitor's performance in a sport.

a·nab·o·lism /əˈnabəˌlizəm/ ▶ n. a metabolic process in which complex molecules are formed from simpler ones and energy is stored. The opposite of CATABOLISM. ■ **an·a·bol·ic** /ˌanəˈbälik/ adj.

a·nach·ro·nism /əˈnakrəˌnizəm/ ▶ n. a thing that belongs or is appropriate to a period of time other than the one in which it exists or is placed: *such lavish houses seemed anachronisms, relics of a long-gone era.* ■ **a·nach·ro·nis·tic** /ə,nakrə'nistik/ adj. **a·nach·ro·nis·ti·cal·ly** /-'nistik(ə)lē/ adv.

an·a·con·da /,anə'kändə/ ▶ n. a very large snake of the boa family, found in tropical South America.

a·nae·mi·a, etc. /ə'nēmēə/ ▶ n. British spelling of ANEMIA, etc.

an·aer·o·bic /,ane(ə)'rōbik, ,anə-/ ▶ adj. Biology not using oxygen from the air. ■ **an·aer·o·bi·cal·ly** adv.

an·aes·the·sia, etc. /,anəs'THēzHə/ ▶ n. British spelling of ANESTHESIA, etc.

an·a·gram /'anə,gram/ ▶ n. a word or phrase formed by rearranging the letters of another.

a·nal /'ānl/ ▶ adj. **1** relating to the anus. **2** fussily concerned about minor details and orderliness. ■ **a·nal·ly** adv.

an·al·ge·si·a /,anl'jēzēə, -zHə/ ▶ n. Medicine the loss of sensitivity to pain.

an·al·ge·sic /,anl'jēzik, -sik/ ▶ n. a pain-relieving drug. ▶ adj. having a pain-relieving effect.

an·a·log /'anl,ôg, -,äg/ (also **analogue**) ▶ adj. relating to electronic information or signals represented by a varying physical effect (e.g., voltage or the position of a pointer) rather than by a digital display. ▶ n. a person or thing that is like or comparable to another.

a·nal·o·gous /ə'naləgəs/ ▶ adj. alike or comparable in certain ways: *an analogous situation.*

a·nal·o·gy /ə'naləjē/ ▶ n. (pl. **analogies**) **1** a way of explaining or clarifying something by comparing it to something else: *an analogy between the workings of nature and those of human societies.* **2** a partial similarity. ■ **an·a·log·i·cal** /,anə'läjikəl/ adj.

a·nal-re·ten·tive ▶ adj. Psychoanalysis excessively fussy and concerned with orderliness (supposedly because of problems with toilet-training in infancy).

a·nal·y·sand /ə'nalə,sand, -,zand/ ▶ n. a person who is undergoing psychoanalysis.

a·nal·y·sis /ə'naləsis/ ▶ n. (pl. **analyses** /-,sēz/) **1** a detailed examination of the features or structure of something: *an analysis of the causes of unemployment.* **2** the separation of something into its component parts. **3** psychoanalysis.

an·a·lyst /'anl-ist/ ▶ n. **1** a person who carries out an analysis. **2** a psychoanalyst.

an·a·lyt·i·cal /,anl'itikəl/ (also **analytic** /,anl'itik/) ▶ adj. relating to or using analysis. ■ **an·a·lyt·i·cal·ly** adv.

an·a·lyze /'anl,īz/ (Brit. **analyse**) ▶ v. **1** examine something in detail in order to explain it or discover its structure or composition. **2** psychoanalyze someone.

a·naph·o·ra /ə'nafərə/ ▶ n. the repetition of a word or phrase at the beginning of successive statements, used for rhetorical effect.

an·a·phy·lac·tic shock /,anəfə'laktik/ ▶ n. Medicine a severe allergic reaction to something that the body has become extremely sensitive to.

an·ar·chic /a'närkik/ ▶ adj. having no controlling rules or principles.

an·ar·chist /'anərkist/ ▶ n. a person who believes that all forms of government should

be abolished. ■ **an·ar·chism** /'anər,kizəm/ n. **an·ar·chis·tic** /,anər'kistik/ adj.

an·ar·chy /'anərkē/ ▶ n. a state of disorder due to the lack of any form of government or control.

A·na·sa·zi /,anə'säzē/ ▶ n. (pl. same or **Anasazis**) a member of an ancient American Indian people of the Southwest who flourished between c. 200 BC and AD 1500. The present day Pueblo culture developed from their later stage.

a·nath·e·ma /ə'naTHəmə/ ▶ n. something that one detests: *racism was anathema to her.*

a·nath·e·ma·tize /ə'naTHəmə,tīz/ ▶ v. curse or condemn: *a church council anathematized those who refused to conform.*

a·nat·o·mize /ə'natə,mīz/ ▶ v. examine and analyze in detail: *successful comedy is notoriously difficult to anatomize.*

a·nat·o·my /ə'natəmē/ ▶ n. (pl. **anatomies**) **1** the scientific study of bodily structure. **2** the bodily structure of a person, animal, or plant. **3** a detailed examination or analysis: *an anatomy of the disaster.* ■ **an·a·tom·i·cal** /ə'natəmē/ adj. **an·a·tom·i·cal·ly** adv. **a·nat·o·mist** n.

ANC ▶ abbr. African National Congress.

an·ces·tor /'an,sestər/ ▶ n. **1** a person from whom one is descended. **2** something from which a later species or version has developed: *an ancestor of the horse.*

an·ces·tral /an'sestrəl/ ▶ adj. relating to or inherited from a person's ancestor or ancestors: *his ancestral home.*

an·ces·try /'an,sestrē/ ▶ n. (pl. **ancestries**) a person's ancestors or the people from which they are descended: *her Irish ancestry.*

an·chor /'aNGkər/ ▶ n. a heavy metal object used to moor a ship to the sea bottom. ▶ v. **1** moor a ship with an anchor. **2** fix firmly in position: *the rope was anchored to the rocks.*

an·chor·age /'aNGk(ə)rij/ ▶ n. a place where ships may be anchored safely.

an·cho·rite /'aNGkə,rīt/ ▶ n. historical a person who lives in isolation from others for religious reasons.

an·chor·man /'aNGkər,man/ (or **anchorwoman** /'aNGkər,wŏŏmən/) ▶ n. (pl. **anchormen** or **anchorwomen**) a person who presents a live television or radio program and coordinates the contributions of participants.

an·cho·vy /'an,cHōvē, an'cHōvē/ ▶ n. (pl. **anchovies**) a small fish of the herring family, with a strong flavor.

an·cien ré·gime /än'syän rā'zHēm/ ▶ n. (pl. **anciens régimes** pronunc. same) a political or social system that has been replaced by a more modern one.

an·cient /'āncHənt/ ▶ adj. **1** belonging to or dating from the very distant past: *an ancient civilization.* **2** very old: *an ancient pair of jeans.* ▶ n. (**the ancients**) the people of ancient times. ■ **an·cient·ly** adv.

an·cil·lar·y /'ansə,lerē/ ▶ adj. **1** providing support to the main activities of an organization: *ancillary staff.* **2** additional; extra: *ancillary accommodations.*

and /and/ ▶ conj. **1** used to connect words, clauses, or sentences. **2** used to connect two identical words to show gradual change, continuing action, or great extent: *getting better and better.* **3** (connecting two numbers) plus. **4** informal (after a verb) to: *try and do it.*

> **USAGE**
> Some verbs, especially **try**, **come**, and **go**, can be followed by **and** rather than **to** in sentences like *we should try and help them.* The use with **and** is very common but in formal writing or speech it is best to say **to**: *we should try to help them.*
> Many people think that **and**, together with other conjunctions such as **but** and **because**, should not be used to start a sentence, the argument being that such a sentence expresses an incomplete thought. However, **and** has long been used in this way in both written and spoken English, and it is quite acceptable to do so.

an·dan·te /än'dän,tā/ Music ▶ adv. & adj. in a moderately slow tempo. ▶ n. a passage to be performed at a moderately slow tempo.

An·de·an /'andēən, an'dē-/ ▶ adj. relating to the Andes mountains of South America.

and·i·ron /'an,dīərn/ ▶ n. either of a pair of metal stands used to support wood burning in a fireplace.

An·dor·ran /an'dôrən/ ▶ n. a person from Andorra, a small self-governing principality in the southern Pyrenees. ▶ adj. relating to Andorra.

an·dro·gen /'andrəjən/ ▶ n. a male sex hormone, such as testosterone.

an·drog·y·nous /an'dräjənəs/ ▶ adj. partly male and partly female. ■ **an·drog·y·ny** /-nē/ n.

an·droid /'an,droid/ ▶ n. (in science fiction) a robot with a human appearance.

an·ec·do·tal /,anik'dōtl/ ▶ adj. (of a story) not necessarily true because based on someone's personal account of an event rather than on facts. ■ **an·ec·do·tal·ly** adv.

an·ec·dote /'anik,dōt/ ▶ n. a short entertaining story about a real incident or person.

a·ne·mi·a /ə'nēmēə/ (Brit. **anaemia**) ▶ n. deficiency of red blood cells or of hemoglobin in the blood, resulting in weariness.

a·ne·mic /ə'nēmik/ ▶ adj. **1** suffering from anemia. **2** not lively or exciting: *an anemic performance.*

an·e·mom·e·ter /,anə'mämitər/ ▶ n. an instrument for measuring the speed of the wind.

a·nem·o·ne /ə'nemənē/ ▶ n. a plant having brightly colored flowers with dark centers.

an·er·oid ba·rom·e·ter /'anə,roid/ ▶ n. a barometer that measures air pressure by the action of air on the flexible lid of a box containing a vacuum.

an·es·the·sia /,anəs'THēzhə/ (Brit. **anaesthesia**) ▶ n. insensitivity to pain, especially as artificially induced by the administration of gases or the injection of drugs before surgical operations.

an·es·the·si·ol·o·gy /,anəs,THēzē'äləjē/ ▶ n. the branch of medicine concerned with anesthesia and anesthetics. ■ **an·es·the·si·ol·o·gist** /-jist/ n.

an·es·thet·ic /,anəs'THetik/ (Brit. **anaesthetic**) ▶ n. a drug or gas that makes one unable to feel pain.

an·es·the·tize /ə'nesTHi,tīz/ (Brit. **anaesthetize**) ▶ v. give an anesthetic to a patient.
■ **an·es·the·ti·za·tion** /-THitə'zāSHən/ n.

an·eu·rysm /'anyə,rizəm/ (also **aneurism**) ▶ n. Medicine an excessive swelling of the wall of an artery.

a·new /ə'n(y)oō/ ▶ adv. **1** in a new or different way. **2** once more; again.

an·gel /'ānjəl/ ▶ n. **1** a spiritual being acting as an attendant or messenger of God, represented as being of human form with wings. **2** a very beautiful, kind, or good person. **3** informal a person who gives financial backing to a theatrical production.

an·gel dust ▶ n. informal the hallucinogenic drug phencyclidine hydrochloride.

an·gel·fish /'ānjəl,fiSH/ ▶ n. (pl. same or **angelfishes**) a tropical fish with large fins, often vividly colored or patterned.

an·gel food cake ▶ n. a very light, pale sponge cake made with no egg yolks.

an·gel hair ▶ n. a type of pasta consisting of very fine long strands.

an·gel·ic /an'jelik/ ▶ adj. **1** relating to angels. **2** very beautiful, innocent, or kind: *his small, angelic face.* ■ **an·gel·i·cal·ly** adv.

an·gel·i·ca /an'jelikə/ ▶ n. the stalks of a sweet-smelling plant, preserved in sugar and used in cake decoration.

an·ge·lus /'anjələs/ ▶ n. **1** a Roman Catholic prayer commemorating the Incarnation of Jesus, said at morning, noon, and sunset. **2** a ringing of bells to signal the times of the angelus.

an·ger /'aNGgər/ ▶ n. a strong feeling of extreme displeasure. ▶ v. make someone angry.

an·gi·na /an'jīnə/ (also **angina pectoris** /'pektəris/) ▶ n. a condition marked by severe pain in the chest, caused by an inadequate supply of blood to the heart.

an·gi·o·gram /'anj(ē)ə,gram/ ▶ n. an X-ray photograph of blood or lymph vessels, made after injection of a marking substance.

an·gi·o·plas·ty /'anjēə,plastē/ ▶ n. (pl. **angioplasties**) a surgical operation to repair or unblock a blood vessel, especially an artery in the heart.

an·gi·o·sperm /'anjēə,spərm/ ▶ n. a plant of a large group that have flowers and produce seeds enclosed in a carpel, including herbaceous plants, shrubs, grasses, and most trees.

An·gle /'aNGgəl/ ▶ n. a member of an ancient Germanic people who founded kingdoms in the north and east of England in the 5th century AD.

an·gle¹ /'aNGgəl/ ▶ n. **1** the space between two intersecting lines or surfaces at or close to the point where they meet. **2** a position from which someone or something is viewed: *the camera angle shifted from side view to a full-face closeup.* **3** a particular way of considering something: *let's look at the issue from a different angle.*
▶ v. **1** move or place something in a slanting position. **2** present information from a particular point of view: *angle your answer so that it is relevant to the job for which you are applying.*
■ **an·gled** adj.

an·gle² ▶ v. **1** fish with a rod and line. **2** try to get something by indirectly prompting someone to offer it: *she was angling for sympathy.* ■ **an·gler** n. **an·gling** n.

an·gle brack·et ▶ n. either of a pair of marks in the form<>, used to enclose words or figures so as to separate them from their context.

an·gle grind·er ▶ n. a device with a rotating abrasive disk, used to grind, polish, or cut metal and other materials.

an·gle i·ron ▶ n. a building material consisting of pieces of iron or steel with an L-shaped cross section, able to be bolted together.

an·gler·fish /'aNGglər,fiSH/ ▶ n. (pl. same or **anglerfishes**) a marine fish that lures prey within reach of its mouth with a fleshy filament projecting from its snout.

An·gli·can /'aɴɢglikən/ ▶ adj. relating to the Church of England or any Church associated with it. ▶ n. a member of the Anglican Church. ■ **An·gli·can·ism** n.

An·gli·cism /'aɴɢglə,sizəm/ ▶ n. a word or phrase that is peculiar to British English.

an·gli·cize /'aɴɢglə,sīz/ ▶ v. make English in form or character: *he anglicized his name from Gutman to Goodman.* ■ **an·gli·ci·za·tion** /,aɴɢgləsə'zāsHən/ n.

An·glo /'aɴɢglō/ ▶ n. (pl. **Anglos**) a white, English-speaking American as distinct from a Hispanic American.

Anglo- /,aɴɢglō-/ ▶ comb.form **1** English: *anglophone.* **2** English or British and ...: *Anglo-Latin.*

An·glo-Cath·o·lic ▶ adj. a member of a section of the Church of England that is close to Catholicism in its beliefs and worship. ■ **An·glo-Ca·thol·i·cism** n.

An·glo·cen·tric /,aɴɢglō'sentrik/ ▶ adj. considered in terms of England or Britain; seeing English or British culture as most important.

An·glo-In·di·an ▶ adj. **1** relating to or involving both Britain and India. **2** of mixed British and Indian parentage. **3** chiefly historical of British descent or birth but having lived for a long time in India. ▶ n. an Anglo-Indian person.

An·glo-I·rish ▶ adj. **1** relating to both Britain and Ireland (or specifically the Republic of Ireland). **2** of mixed English and Irish parentage. **3** of English descent but born or living in Ireland.

An·glo·phile /'aɴɢglə,fīl/ ▶ n. a person who likes or greatly admires England or Britain. ■ **An·glo·phil·i·a** n.

an·glo·phone /'aɴɢglə,fōn/ ▶ adj. English-speaking.

An·glo-Sax·on ▶ n. **1** a Germanic inhabitant of England between the 5th century and the Norman Conquest. **2** an English person. **3** a white, English-speaking person. **4** the Old English language.

An·glo·sphere /'aɴɢglō,sfi(ə)r/ ▶ n. the group of countries where English is the main native language.

An·go·lan /aɴɢ'gōlən, an'gōlən/ ▶ n. a person from Angola, a country in SW Africa. ▶ adj. relating to Angola.

an·go·ra /aɴɢ'gôrə/ ▶ n. **1** a cat, goat, or rabbit of a long-haired breed. **2** a fabric made from the hair of the angora goat or rabbit.

an·gos·tu·ra /,aɴɢgə'st(y)ŏŏrə/ ▶ n. **1** a bitter bark from a South American tree, used as a flavoring. **2** (also **Angostura bitters** trademark) a kind of tonic.

an·gry /'aɴɢgrē/ ▶ adj. (**angrier, angriest**) **1** feeling or showing anger. **2** (of a wound or sore) red and inflamed. ■ **an·gri·ly** adv.

angst /aɴɢ(k)st, äɴɢ(k)st/ ▶ n. a strong feeling of anxiety about life in general. ■ **angst·y** adj.

ang·strom /'aɴɢstrəm/ ▶ n. Physics a unit of length equal to one hundred-millionth of a centimeter, 10^{-10} meter.

an·guish /'aɴɢgwisH/ ▶ n. severe pain or distress. ▶ v. be very distressed: *I was anguishing about whether I'd made the right decision.*

an·guished /'aɴɢgwisHt/ ▶ adj. feeling or expressing severe pain or distress.

an·gu·lar /'aɴɢgyələr/ ▶ adj. **1** having angles or sharp corners. **2** (of a person) lean and bony. **3** Physics measured by means of an angle. ■ **an·gu·lar·i·ty** n. **an·gu·lar·ly** adv.

an·hy·drous /an'hīdrəs/ ▶ adj. Chemistry containing no water.

an·i·line /'anl-in/ ▶ n. an oily liquid used in making dyes, drugs, and plastics.

an·i·mad·vert /,anəmad'vərt/ ▶ v. (**animadvert on/against**) formal speak out against or criticize someone or something. ■ **an·i·mad·ver·sion** /,anəmad'vərzHən/ n.

an·i·mal /'anəməl/ ▶ n. **1** a living organism that can move about of its own accord and has specialized sense organs and nervous system. **2** a mammal, as opposed to a bird, reptile, fish, or insect. **3** a brutal or uncivilized person. **4** a particular type of person or thing: *she's a political animal.* ▶ adj. physical rather than spiritual or intellectual: *animal lust.*

an·i·mal·cule /,anə'mal,kyōōl/ ▶ n. chiefly literary a microscopic animal.

an·i·mal·ism /'anəmə,lizəm/ ▶ n. physical and instinctive behavior; animality. ■ **an·i·mal·is·tic** /,anəmə'listik/ adj.

an·i·mal mag·net·ism ▶ n. a quality of powerful sexual attractiveness.

an·i·mate ▶ v. /'anə,māt/ **1** bring life or new vigor to: *Christianity animated a society and reshaped it.* **2** give a movie or television show, or a character, the appearance of movement using animation. ▶ adj. /-mit/ alive; having life. ■ **an·i·ma·tor** /'anə,mātər/ n.

an·i·mat·ed /'anə,mātid/ ▶ adj. **1** full of interest or energy; lively: *an animated conversation.* **2** (of a movie or television show) made using animation. ■ **an·i·mat·ed·ly** adv.

an·i·ma·tion /,anə'māsHən/ ▶ n. **1** the state of being full of life or energy; liveliness. **2** the technique of filming a sequence of drawings or positions of models to create the appearance of movement. **3** (also **computer animation**) the creation of moving images by means of a computer.

an·i·ma·tron·ics /,anəmə'träniks/ ▶ pl.n. (treated as sing.) the creation and operation of lifelike robots, especially for use in movies. ■ **an·i·ma·tron·ic** adj.

an·i·me /'anə,mā/ ▶ n. Japanese animated films, typically having a science fiction theme.

an·i·mism /'anə,mizəm/ ▶ n. the belief that all things in nature, such as plants and hills, have a soul. ■ **an·i·mist** /'anəmist/ n. **an·i·mis·tic** /,anə'mistik/ adj.

an·i·mos·i·ty /,anə'mäsitē/ ▶ n. (pl. **animosities**) strong hostility; hatred.

an·i·mus /'anəməs/ ▶ n. hatred or hostility.

an·i·on /'an,īən/ ▶ n. Chemistry an ion with a negative charge. The opposite of CATION. ■ **an·i·on·ic** /,anī'änik/ adj.

an·ise /'anis/ ▶ n. **1** a plant grown for its aromatic seeds (aniseed). **2** the flavoring extracted from aniseed: *a light glaze with a hint of anise.*

an·i·seed /'anə(s),sēd/ ▶ n. the seed, or seeds, of the plant anise, used as a flavoring.

ankh /äɴɢk/ ▶ n. an ancient Egyptian symbol of life in the shape of a cross with a loop instead of the top arm.

an·kle /'aɴɢkəl/ ▶ n. **1** the joint connecting the

foot with the leg. **2** the narrow part of the leg between the ankle joint and the calf.

an·klet /'aNGklit/ ▸ n. a chain or band worn around the ankle.

an·na /'ana/ ▸ n. a former unit of money of India and Pakistan, equal to one sixteenth of a rupee.

an·nal /'anl/ ▸ n. **1** (**annals**) a historical record of events year by year. **2** a record of the events of one year. ∎ **an·nal·ist** n.

an·nat·to /a'nätō/ ▸ n. an orange-red dye obtained from a tropical fruit, used for coloring foods.

an·neal /a'nēl/ ▸ v. heat metal or glass and allow it to cool slowly, to remove internal stresses.

an·ne·lid /'anl,id/ ▸ n. a worm with a body made up of segments, such as an earthworm.

an·nex ▸ v. /a'neks, 'aneks/ **1** seize territory and add it to one's own. **2** (usu. as adj. **annexed**) add or attach something: *the annexed document.* ▸ n. /'aneks, -iks/ (chiefly Brit. also **annexe**) (pl. **annexes**) **1** a building attached or near to a main building, used for additional space. **2** an addition to a document. ∎ **an·nex·a·tion** /,anek'sāsHən, ,anik-/ n.

an·ni·hi·late /a'nī-ə,lāt/ ▸ v. **1** destroy completely: *this bomb could annihilate them all.* **2** defeat someone completely. ∎ **an·ni·hi·la·tion** /ə,nīə'lāsHən/ n. **an·ni·hi·la·tor** /-,lātər/ n.

an·ni·ver·sa·ry /,anə'vərsərē/ ▸ n. (pl. **anniversaries**) the date on which an event took place in a previous year.

An·no Dom·i·ni /'anō 'dämənē, -nī, 'änō/ ▸ adv. full form of **AD.**

an·no·tate /'ana,tāt/ ▸ v. add explanatory notes to a piece of writing. ∎ **an·no·ta·tion** /,ana'tāsHən/ n. **an·no·ta·tor** /-,tātər/ n.

an·nounce /a'nouns/ ▸ v. **1** make a public statement about something. **2** be a sign of: *lilies announce the arrival of summer.*

an·nounce·ment /a'nounsmənt/ ▸ n. **1** a public statement. **2** the action of announcing something.

an·nounc·er /a'nounsər/ ▸ n. a person who announces something, especially someone who introduces or gives information about programs on radio or television.

an·noy /a'noi/ ▸ v. make someone slightly angry. ∎ **an·noyed** adj. **an·noy·ing** adj. **an·noy·ing·ly** adv.

an·noy·ance /a'noi-əns/ ▸ n. **1** the feeling or state of being annoyed. **2** a thing that annoys someone.

an·nu·al /'anyōōəl/ ▸ adj. **1** happening once a year. **2** calculated over or covering a year: *annual income.* **3** (of a plant) living for a year or less. ▸ n. **1** a book published once a year under the same title but with different contents. **2** an annual plant. ∎ **an·nu·al·ly** adv.

an·nu·al·ized /'anyōōə,līzd/ ▸ adj. (of a rate of interest, inflation, or return on investment) recalculated as an annual rate.

an·nu·i·ty /a'n(y)ōōitē/ ▸ n. (pl. **annuities**) a fixed sum of money paid to someone each year.

an·nul /a'nəl/ ▸ v. (**annuls, annulling, annulled**) declare a law, marriage, or other legal contract to be invalid. ∎ **an·nul·ment** n.

an·nu·lar /'anyələr/ ▸ adj. technical ring-shaped.

an·nun·ci·a·tion /ə,nənsē'āsHən/ ▸ n. **1** (**the Annunciation**) the announcement by the angel Gabriel to the Virgin Mary that she was

to be the mother of Jesus. **2** a Church festival commemorating the Annunciation, held on March 25.

an·nus hor·ri·bi·lis /'anəs hə'ribəlis/ ▸ n. a disastrous or unlucky year for someone or something.

an·ode /'anōd/ ▸ n. an electrode with a positive charge. The opposite of **CATHODE.**

an·o·dized /'anə,dīzd/ ▸ adj. (of metal, especially aluminum) coated with a protective oxide layer by electrolysis.

an·o·dyne /'anə,dīn/ ▸ adj. unlikely to cause offense or disagreement; bland: *anodyne tales of small-town life.* ▸ n. a painkilling drug or medicine.

a·noint /a'noint/ ▸ v. **1** smear or rub someone with oil, especially as part of a religious ceremony. **2** choose someone to replace another in a job or role: *he's been anointed country rock's poster boy.*

a·nom·a·lous /a'nämələs/ ▸ adj. differing from what is standard or normal: *anomalous results.* ∎ **a·nom·a·lous·ly** adv.

a·nom·a·ly /a'näməlē/ ▸ n. (pl. **anomalies**) something that differs from what is standard or normal.

an·o·mie /'anə,mē/ ▸ n. lack of the usual standards of expected or good behavior.

a·non /a'nän/ ▸ adv. old use or informal soon; shortly.

anon. ▸ abbr. anonymous.

a·non·y·mous /a'nänəməs/ ▸ adj. **1** with a name that is not known or made known: *an anonymous letter.* **2** having no outstanding or individual features: *an anonymous building on an anonymous street.* ∎ **an·o·nym·i·ty** /,anə'nimitē/ n. **a·non·y·mous·ly** adv.

a·noph·e·les /a'näfə,lēz/ ▸ n. a mosquito of a genus that is particularly common in warmer countries and includes the mosquitoes that transmit the malarial parasite to humans.

an·o·rak /'anə,rak/ ▸ n. a waterproof cold-weather jacket with a hood.

an·o·rex·i·a /,anə'reksēə/ (also **anorexia nervosa** /nər'vōsə/) ▸ n. a psychological disorder in which a person refuses to eat because they are afraid of becoming fat.

an·o·rex·ic /,anə'reksik/ (also **anorectic** /,anə'rektik/) ▸ adj. **1** relating to anorexia. **2** informal very thin. ▸ n. a person with anorexia.

an·oth·er /a'nəTHər/ ▸ determiner & pron. **1** one more. **2** different from the one already mentioned.

an·ox·i·a /a'näksēə/ ▸ n. **1** an absence of oxygen. **2** Medicine an absence or deficiency of oxygen reaching the tissues; severe hypoxia. ∎ **an·ox·ic** /-sik/ adj.

an·swer /'ansər/ ▸ n. **1** something said or written in reaction to a question or statement. **2** a solution to a problem: *the hormone has been touted as the answer to aging.* ▸ v. **1** give an answer. **2** (**answer back**) give an insolent reply. **3** satisfy a need. **4** (**answer to**) be responsible to someone. **5** defend oneself against an accusation. **6** (**answer for**) be responsible or to blame for: *Larry has got a lot to answer for.* ∎ **an·swer·er** n.

an·swer·a·ble /'ansərəbəl/ ▸ adj. **1** (**answerable to**) responsible to someone. **2** (**answerable for**) responsible for something.

an·swer·ing ma·chine ▸ n. a machine that gives a recorded answer to a telephone call and can record a message from the caller.

an·swer phone ▶ n. Brit. an answering machine; voicemail.

ant /ant/ ▶ n. a small insect, usually wingless, living with many others in a highly organized group.

ant·ac·id /ant'asid/ ▶ adj. (of a medicine) preventing excess stomach acid.

an·tag·o·nism /an'tagə,nizəm/ ▶ n. open hostility or opposition.

an·tag·o·nist /an'tagənist/ ▶ n. an open opponent or enemy of someone or something. ■ **an·tag·o·nis·tic** /an,tagə'nistik/ adj.

an·tag·o·nize /an'tagə,nīz/ ▶ v. make hostile: *Louis had no wish to antagonize his parents.*

Ant·arc·tic /ant'är(k)tik/ ▶ adj. relating to the region surrounding the South Pole.

an·te /'antē/ ▶ n. a stake put up by a player in poker and similar games before receiving cards. ▶ v. (**antes, anteing, anted**) (**ante up**) put up an amount as an ante in poker and similar games. – PHRASES **up** (or **raise**) **the ante** increase what is at stake or under discussion.

ante- ▶ prefix before; preceding: *antecedent.*

ant·eat·er /'ant,ētər/ ▶ n. a mammal with a long snout, feeding on ants and termites.

an·te·bel·lum /,antē'beləm/ ▶ adj. occurring or existing before a war, especially the US Civil War.

an·te·ced·ent /,antə'sēdnt/ ▶ n. **1** a thing that occurs or exists before another: *the antecedents to aggressive actions.* **2** (**antecedents**) a person's ancestors and social background. **3** Grammar an earlier word, phrase, or clause to which a following pronoun refers back. ▶ adj. coming before in time or order.

an·te·cham·ber /'antē,chāmbər/ ▶ n. a small room leading to a main one.

an·te·date /'anti,dāt/ ▶ v. **1** come before something in time. **2** indicate that a document or event belongs to an earlier date.

an·te·di·lu·vi·an /,antēdə'lōōvēən/ ▶ adj. **1** belonging to the time before the biblical Flood. **2** ridiculously old-fashioned: *antediluvian video games.*

an·te·lope /'antl,ōp/ ▶ n. **1** a swift deerlike animal with upward-pointing horns, native to Africa and Asia. **2** (also **pronghorn antelope**) inaccurate term for PRONGHORN.

an·te·na·tal /,antē'nātl/ ▶ adj. Brit. during pregnancy; before birth.

an·ten·na /an'tenə/ ▶ n. (pl. **antennae** /-'tenē/) **1** each of a pair of long, thin parts on the heads of some insects, shellfish, etc., used for feeling. **2** (pl. also **antennas**) an aerial.

an·te·pe·nul·ti·mate /,antēpə'nəltəmit/ ▶ adj. last but two in a series.

an·te·ri·or /an'ti(ə)rēər/ ▶ adj. technical at or nearer the front. The opposite of POSTERIOR.

an·te·room /'antē,rōōm, -,rŏŏm/ ▶ n. a small room leading to a larger one.

an·them /'anthəm/ ▶ n. **1** an uplifting song associated with a group or cause, especially one chosen by a country to express patriotic feelings. **2** a musical setting of a religious text to be sung by a choir during a church service. ■ **an·the·mic** /an'THēmik, -'THemik/ adj.

an·ther /'anthər/ ▶ n. the part of a flower's stamen that contains the pollen.

ant·hill /'ant,hil/ ▶ n. a mound-shaped nest built

by ants or termites.

an·thol·o·gy /an'THäləjē/ ▶ n. (pl. **anthologies**) a collection of poems or other pieces of writing or music. ■ **an·thol·o·gist** n. **an·thol·o·gize** v.

an·thra·cite /'anthrə,sīt/ ▶ n. hard coal that burns with little flame and smoke.

an·thrax /'an,thraks/ ▶ n. a serious disease of sheep and cattle, caused by a bacterium and able to be transmitted to humans.

an·thro·po·cen·tric /,anthrəpō'sentrik/ ▶ adj. regarding humankind as the most important element of existence. ■ **an·thro·po·cen·trism** /-,trizəm/ n.

an·thro·poid /'anthrə,poid/ ▶ adj. referring to the higher primate mammals, including monkeys, apes, and humans.

an·thro·pol·o·gy /,anthrə'päləjē/ ▶ n. the study of societies, cultures, and human origins. ■ **an·thro·po·log·i·cal** /-pə'läjikəl/ adj. **an·thro·pol·o·gist** n.

an·thro·po·mor·phic /,anthrəpə'môrfik/ ▶ adj. treating a god, animal, or object as if they were human. ■ **an·thro·po·mor·phism** /,anthrəpə'môr,fizəm/ n.

an·thro·poph·a·gy /,anthrə'päfəjē/ ▶ n. the eating of human flesh by other humans; cannibalism.

an·ti /'an,tī, 'antē/ ▶ prep. opposed to; against.

anti- ▶ prefix **1** opposed to; against: *antiaircraft.* **2** preventing or relieving: *antibacterial.* **3** the opposite of: *anticlimax.*

an·ti·air·craft /,antē'er,kraft, ,antī-/ ▶ adj. (especially of a gun or missile) used to attack enemy aircraft.

an·ti·bac·te·ri·al /,antēbak'ti(ə)rēəl, ,antī-/ ▶ adj. active against bacteria.

an·ti·bi·ot·ic /,antēbī'ätik, ,antī-/ ▶ n. a medicine that destroys bacteria or slows their growth.

an·ti·bod·y /'anti,bädē/ ▶ n. (pl. **antibodies**) a protein produced in the blood to destroy an antigen (harmful substance).

An·ti·christ /'antē,krīst, 'antī-/ ▶ n. an enemy of Jesus believed by the early Church to appear before the end of the world.

an·tic·i·pate /an'tisə,pāt/ ▶ v. **1** be aware of a future event and prepare for it. **2** regard as probable: *she anticipated scorn on her return to acting.* **3** look forward to something. **4** happen or do something before: *he anticipated Bates's theories on mimicry.* ■ **an·tic·i·pa·tor** /-,pātər/ n. **an·tic·i·pa·to·ry** /an'tisəpə,tôrē/ adj.

an·tic·i·pa·tion /an,tisə'pāsHən/ ▶ n. the action of anticipating something.

an·ti·cli·max /,antē'klī,maks, ,antī-/ ▶ n. a disappointing end to an exciting series of events. ■ **an·ti·cli·mac·tic** /,antēklī'maktik/ adj.

an·ti·cline /'antē,klīn, 'antī-/ ▶ n. a ridge or fold of rock in which the strata slope downward from the crest. Compare with SYNCLINE.

an·ti·clock·wise /,antē'kläk,wīz, ,antī-/ ▶ adv. & adj. British term for COUNTERCLOCKWISE.

an·ti·co·ag·u·lant /,antēkō'agyələnt, ,antī-/ ▶ n. a substance that prevents the blood from clotting.

an·ti·con·vul·sant /,antēkən'vəlsənt, ,antī-/ ▶ n. a drug that prevents or reduces the severity of epileptic fits or other convulsions.

an·tics /'antiks/ ▶ pl.n. foolish, outrageous, or amusing behavior.

an·ti·cy·clone /,antē'sīklōn, ,antī-/ ▶ n. an area of high atmospheric pressure around which air slowly circulates, usually resulting in calm, fine weather. ■ **an·ti·cy·clon·ic** /-sī'klänik/ adj.

an·ti·de·pres·sant /,antēdə'presnt, ,antī-/ ▶ n. a drug used to relieve depression.

an·ti·dote /'anti,dōt/ ▶ n. 1 a medicine taken to counteract a poison. 2 something that counteracts an unpleasant feeling or situation: *laughter is a good antidote to stress.*

an·ti·freeze /'anti,frēz/ ▶ n. a liquid added to water to prevent it from freezing, used in the radiator of a motor vehicle.

an·ti·gen /'antijən/ ▶ n. a harmful substance that causes the body to produce antibodies. ■ **an·ti·gen·ic** /,anti'jenik/ adj.

an·ti·glob·al·i·za·tion /,antē,glōbələ'zāshən, ,antī-/ ▶ n. opposition to the agendas and actions of groups perceived to favor globalization.

An·ti·guan /an'tēgwən/ ▶ n. a person from Antigua, or the country of Antigua and Barbuda, in the West Indies. ▶ adj. relating to Antigua or Antigua and Barbuda.

an·ti·he·ro /'antē,hi(ə)rō, 'antī-/ (or **antiheroine** /'antē,herōin, 'antī-/) ▶ n. a central character in a story who lacks typical heroic qualities.

an·ti·his·ta·mine /,antē'histəmin, -mēn/ ▶ n. a drug that counteracts the effects of histamine, used in treating allergies.

an·ti·in·flam·ma·to·ry /,antēin'flamə,tôrē, ,antī-/ ▶ adj. (of a drug) used to reduce inflammation.

an·ti·lock /,antē'läk, ,antī-/ ▶ adj. (of brakes) designed so as to prevent the wheels from locking and the vehicle from skidding if applied suddenly.

an·ti·log·a·rithm /,antē'lôgə,riTHəm, -'läg-, ,antī-/ ▶ n. Mathematics the number of which a given number is the logarithm.

an·ti·ma·cas·sar /,antēmə'kasər/ ▶ n. a cloth put over the back of a chair to protect it from grease and dirt.

an·ti·ma·lar·i·al /,antēmə'le(ə)rēəl, ,antī-/ ▶ adj. used to prevent malaria. ▶ n. an antimalarial drug.

an·ti·mat·ter /'antē,matər, 'antī-/ ▶ n. Physics matter consisting of the antiparticles of the particles that make up normal matter.

an·ti·mi·cro·bi·al /,antēmī'krōbēəl, ,antī-/ ▶ adj. active against microbes. ▶ n. a substance that acts against microbes.

an·ti·mo·ny /'antə,mōnē/ ▶ n. a brittle silvery-white metallic element.

an·ti·no·mi·an /,anti'nōmēən/ ▶ adj. believing that Christians are released by grace from obeying moral laws. ▶ n. a person with such a belief. ■ **an·ti·no·mi·an·ism** /-,nizəm/ n.

an·tin·o·my /an'tinəmē/ ▶ n. (pl. **antinomies**) formal a contradiction between two beliefs or conclusions that are reasonable in themselves; a paradox.

an·ti·ox·i·dant /,antē'äksidənt, ,antī-/ ▶ n. a substance that counteracts oxidation.

an·ti·par·ti·cle /'antē,pärtikəl, 'antī-/ ▶ n. Physics a subatomic particle with the same mass as a given particle but an opposite electric charge or magnetic effect.

an·ti·pas·to /,antē'pästō, ,än-/ ▶ n. (pl. **antipasti** /-'pästē/) an Italian appetizer, usually including an assortment of olives, cheeses, and meats.

an·tip·a·thy /an'tipəTHē/ ▶ n. (pl. **antipathies**) a strong feeling of dislike. ■ **an·ti·pa·thet·ic** /,antipə'THetik/ adj.

an·ti·per·son·nel /,antē,pərsə'nel, ,antī-/ ▶ adj. (of weapons) designed to kill or injure people rather than to damage buildings or equipment.

an·ti·per·spi·rant /,anti'pərspərənt/ ▶ n. a substance applied to the skin to prevent or reduce sweating.

an·ti·phon /'antə,fän/ ▶ n. (in the Christian Church) a short chant sung before or after a psalm or canticle.

an·tiph·o·nal /an'tifənl/ ▶ adj. sung or recited alternately between two groups.

An·tip·o·des /an'tipədēz/ ▶ pl.n. (**the Antipodes**) Australia and New Zealand (in relation to the northern hemisphere). ■ **An·tip·o·de·an** /an,tipə'dēən/ adj. & n.

an·ti·psy·chot·ic /,antēsī'kätik, ,antī-/ ▶ n. a drug used to treat psychotic disorders.

an·ti·py·ret·ic /,antē,pī'retik, ,antī-/ ▶ adj. (of a drug) used to prevent or reduce fever.

an·ti·quar·i·an /,anti'kwe(ə)rēən/ ▶ adj. relating to the collection or study of antiques, rare books, or antiquities. ▶ n. (also **antiquary** /'anti,kwerē/) a person who studies or collects antiquarian items. ■ **an·ti·quar·i·an·ism** /-,nizəm/ n.

an·ti·quat·ed /'anti,kwātid/ ▶ adj. old-fashioned or outdated.

an·tique /an'tēk/ ▶ n. a decorative object or piece of furniture that is valuable because of its age. ▶ adj. 1 (of an object) valuable because of its age. 2 old-fashioned or outdated.

an·tiq·ui·ty /an'tikwitē/ ▶ n. (pl. **antiquities**) 1 the distant past, especially before the Middle Ages. 2 an object from the distant past. 3 great age: *a church of great antiquity.*

an·ti·re·tro·vi·ral /,antē,retrō'vīrəl, ,antī-/ ▶ adj. working against or targeted against retroviruses, especially HIV: *antiretroviral therapy.* ▶ n. an antiretroviral drug.

an·tir·rhi·num /,anti'rīnəm/ ▶ n. (pl. **antirrhinums**) a snapdragon.

an·ti·Sem·i·tism ▶ n. hostility to or prejudice against Jews. ■ **an·ti·Sem·ite** n. **an·ti·Se·mit·ic** adj.

an·ti·sep·tic /,anti'septik/ ▶ adj. 1 preventing the growth of microorganisms that cause disease or infection. 2 so clean or pure as to lack character: *the antiseptic modernity of a conference center.* ▶ n. an antiseptic substance.

an·ti·se·rum /'anti,si(ə)rəm/ ▶ n. (pl. **antisera** /-,si(ə)rə/) a blood serum containing antibodies against specific antigens (harmful substances).

an·ti·so·cial /,antē'sōshəl, ,antī-/ ▶ adj. 1 (especially of behavior) conflicting with accepted standards and causing annoyance. 2 not wanting to mix with other people. ■ **an·ti·so·cial·ly** adv.

an·ti·ter·ror·ism /,antē'terə,rizəm, ,antī-/ ▶ n. activities or measures designed to prevent or thwart terrorism. ■ **an·ti·ter·ror·ist** adj.

an·tith·e·sis /an'tiTHəsis/ ▶ n. (pl. **antitheses** /-,sēz/) 1 a person or thing that is the direct opposite of another. 2 the putting together of contrasting ideas or words to produce an effect in speaking or writing.

an·ti·thet·i·cal /,antə'THetikəl/ ▶ adj. opposed to or incompatible with each other: *those whose religious beliefs are antithetical to mine.*

an·ti·tox·in /,antē'täksin/ ▶ n. an antibody that counteracts a toxin.

an·ti·trust /ˌantēˈtrəst, ˌantī-/ ▸ adj. (of laws) preventing or controlling monopolies, so assisting fair competition.

an·ti·tus·sive /ˌantēˈtəsiv/ ▸ n. a drug or other preparation that cures or relieves a cough.

an·ti·ven·in /ˌantēˈvenin, ˌantī-/ ▸ n. an antiserum containing antibodies against poisons in the venom of snakes.

an·ti·vi·ral /ˌantēˈvīrəl, ˌantī-/ ▸ adj. (of a drug or treatment) effective against viruses.

an·ti·viv·i·sec·tion·ist /ˌantēˌvivīˈseksHənist, ˌantī-/ ▸ n. a person who is opposed to the use of live animals for scientific research.

ant·ler /ˈantlər/ ▸ n. each of a pair of branched horns on the head of an adult male deer.

an·to·nym /ˈantəˌnim/ ▸ n. a word opposite in meaning to another (e.g., *bad* and *good*).

ant·sy /ˈantsē/ ▸ adj. agitated, impatient, or restless: *he was too antsy to stay in one place for long.*

a·nus /ˈānəs/ ▸ n. the opening at the end of the digestive system through which solid waste leaves the body.

an·vil /ˈanvil/ ▸ n. a heavy iron block on which metal can be hammered and shaped.

anx·i·e·ty /aNGˈzī-itē/ ▸ n. (pl. **anxieties**) 1 a feeling of unease or worry. 2 strong concern or eagerness: *the housekeeper's anxiety to please.*

anx·ious /ˈaNG(k)sHəs/ ▸ adj. 1 feeling or causing worry or unease: *she became anxious about his debts.* 2 very eager and concerned to do something. ■ **anx·ious·ly** adv. **anx·ious·ness** n.

an·y /ˈenē/ ▸ determiner & pron. 1 one or some of a thing or things, no matter how much or how many. 2 whichever or whatever one chooses. ▸ adv. at all.

USAGE

When used as a pronoun **any** can be used with either a singular or a plural verb, depending on the rest of the sentence: *we needed more sugar but there wasn't any left* (singular verb, to match 'sugar') or *are any of the new videos available?* (plural verb, to match 'videos').

---

an·y·bod·y /ˈenēˌbädē, -ˌbədē/ ▸ pron. anyone.

an·y·how /ˈenēˌhou/ ▸ adv. 1 anyway. 2 in a careless or haphazard way.

an·y·more /ˌenēˈmôr/ ▸ adv. to any further extent; any longer: *she refused to listen anymore.*

an·y·one /ˈenēˌwən/ ▸ pron. any person or people.

an·y·place /ˈenēˌplās/ ▸ adv. informal term for **ANYWHERE.**

an·y·thing /ˈenēˌTHiNG/ ▸ pron. a thing of any kind, no matter what.
– PHRASES **anything but** not at all.

an·y·time (also **anytime**) ▸ adv. 1 at whatever time: *she can come any time.* 2 without exception or doubt: *I can handle a shrimp like him anytime.*

an·y·way /ˈenēˌwā/ ▸ adv. 1 used to emphasize something just said or to change the subject. 2 nevertheless.

an·y·where /ˈenē(h)we(ə)r/ ▸ adv. in or to any place. ▸ pron. any place.

An·zac /ˈanˌzak/ ▸ n. a soldier in the Australian and New Zealand Army Corps (1914–18).

A-OK informal ▸ n. in good order or condition; all right. ▸ adv. in a good manner or way; all right: *we hit it off A-OK.*

a·or·ta /āˈôrtə/ ▸ n. the main artery supplying blood from the heart to the rest of the body.

■ **a·or·tic** adj.

a·pace /əˈpās/ ▸ adv. literary quickly: *sales are growing apace.*

A·pach·e /əˈpaCHē/ ▸ n. (pl. same or **Apaches**) a member of an American Indian people living chiefly in New Mexico and Arizona.

a·part /əˈpärt/ ▸ adv. 1 separated by a distance in time or space. 2 having distinctive qualities: *wrestlers were a breed apart.* 3 into pieces.
– PHRASES **apart from** 1 except for. 2 as well as.

a·part·heid /əˈpärt,(h)āt, -,(h)īt/ ▸ n. the official system of segregation or discrimination on racial grounds formerly in force in South Africa.

a·part·ment /əˈpärtmənt/ ▸ n. 1 a set of rooms forming an individual home within a larger building. 2 (**apartments**) a private suite of rooms in a very large house.

ap·a·thet·ic /ˌapəˈTHetik/ ▸ adj. not interested or enthusiastic. ■ **ap·a·thet·i·cal·ly** adv.

ap·a·thy /ˈapəTHē/ ▸ n. lack of interest or enthusiasm: *the task of overcoming voter apathy.*

ap·a·to·sau·rus /ˌapətōˈsôrəs/ ▸ n. a huge plant-eating dinosaur with a long neck and tail; a brontosaurus.

APC ▸ abbr. armored personnel carrier.

ape /āp/ ▸ n. 1 an animal similar to a monkey but without a tail, such as a gorilla or chimpanzee. 2 informal a stupid or clumsy person. ▸ v. imitate in an absurd or unthinking way: *his sons aped those who were more westernized.*

a·per·çu /ˌāperˈso͞o/ ▸ n. (pl. **aperçus** pronunc. same) a comment that makes a clever or entertaining point.

a·pe·ri·tif /ˌäˌperiˈtēf, -ə,per-/ ▸ n. a drink of alcohol taken before a meal.

ap·er·ture /ˈapərˌCHər/ ▸ n. 1 an opening, hole, or gap. 2 the variable opening by which light enters a camera.

A·pex /ˈāpeks/ (also **APEX**) ▸ n. a system of reduced fares for air or rail journeys booked in advance.

a·pex /ˈāpeks/ ▸ n. (pl. **apexes** or **apices** /ˈāpəˌsēz, ˈapə-/) the top or highest point: *the paper was regarded as the apex of journalism.*

a·pha·sia /əˈfāZHə/ ▸ n. the inability to understand or produce speech, as a result of brain damage. ■ **a·pha·sic** /-zik/ adj. & n.

a·phe·li·on /əˈfēlyən, aˈfēlēən/ ▸ n. (pl. **aphelia** /əˈfēlyə, aˈfēlēə/) the point in the orbit of a planet, asteroid, or comet at which it is farthest from the sun. The opposite of **PERIHELION.**

a·phid /ˈāfid, ˈaf-/ ▸ n. a greenfly or similar small insect feeding on the sap of plants.

aph·o·rism /ˈafəˌrizəm/ ▸ n. a short clever phrase that states something true. ■ **aph·o·ris·tic** /ˌafəˈristik/ adj.

aph·ro·dis·i·ac /ˌafrəˈdizēˌak, -ˈdēzē-, -ˈdēzHē-/ ▸ n. a food, drink, or other thing that arouses sexual desire. ▸ adj. acting as an aphrodisiac: *the root of the plant is said to have aphrodisiac properties.*

a·pi·ar·y /ˈāpēˌerē/ ▸ n. (pl. **apiaries**) a place where bees are kept. ■ **a·pi·a·rist** n.

a·pi·cal /ˈāpikəl, ˈap-/ ▸ adj. technical relating to or forming an apex.

a·pi·ces /ˈāpəˌsēz, ˈapə-/ ▸ plural of **APEX.**

a·pi·cul·ture /ˈāpiˌkəlCHər/ ▸ n. technical beekeeping.

a·piece /əˈpēs/ ▸ adv. to, for, or by each one; each.

a·plen·ty /ə'plentē/ ▶ adj. in abundance: *he has work aplenty.*

a·plomb /ə'pläm, ə'pləm/ ▶ n. calm self-confidence: *he took the penalty with aplomb.*

ap·ne·a /'apnēə, ap'nēə/ ▶ n. a medical condition in which a person temporarily stops breathing, especially during sleep.

APO ▶ abbr. Army Post Office.

a·poc·a·lypse /ə'päkə,lips/ ▶ n. **1** an event involving great and widespread destruction. **2** (**the Apocalypse**) the final destruction of the world, as described in the biblical book of Revelation.

a·poc·a·lyp·tic /ə,päkə'liptik/ ▶ adj. relating to or resembling the destruction of the world: *an apocalyptic war.* ■ **a·poc·a·lyp·ti·cal·ly** adv.

A·poc·ry·pha /ə'päkrəfə/ ▶ pl.n. (treated as sing. or pl.) those books of the Old Testament not accepted as part of Hebrew scripture and excluded from the Protestant Bible at the Reformation.

a·poc·ry·phal /ə'päkrəfəl/ ▶ adj. **1** widely known but unlikely to be true: *an apocryphal story.* **2** relating to the Apocrypha.

ap·o·gee /'apəjē/ ▶ n. **1** the highest point in the development of something: *they regarded Alexandria as the apogee of civilization.* **2** the point in the orbit of the moon or a satellite at which it is farthest from the earth. The opposite of **PERIGEE**.

a·po·lit·i·cal /,āpə'litikəl/ ▶ adj. not interested or involved in politics.

a·pol·o·get·ic /ə,pälə'jetik/ ▶ adj. admitting and showing regret for wrongdoing. ■ **a·pol·o·get·i·cal·ly** adv.

a·pol·o·get·ics /ə,pälə'jetiks/ ▶ pl.n. (treated as sing. or pl.) reasoned arguments defending a theory or doctrine.

ap·o·lo·gi·a /,apə'lōj(ē)ə/ ▶ n. a formal written statement defending one's opinions or behavior.

a·pol·o·gist /ə'päləjist/ ▶ n. a person who offers an argument in defense of something controversial: *an apologist for fascism.*

a·pol·o·gize /ə'pälə,jīz/ ▶ v. say sorry for something that one has done wrong: *we apologize for any inaccuracy.*

a·pol·o·gy /ə'päləjē/ ▶ n. (pl. **apologies**) **1** an expression of regret for a wrongdoing. **2** (**an apology for**) a very poor example of: *it's an apology for a bridge, built of leftover stones.*

ap·o·phthegm ▶ n. British spelling of **APOTHEGM**.

ap·o·plec·tic /,apə'plektik/ ▶ adj. **1** overcome with anger. **2** dated relating to apoplexy (stroke).

ap·o·plex·y /'apə,pleksē/ ▶ n. (pl. **apoplexies**) **1** extreme anger. **2** dated unconsciousness or inability to move or feel, caused by a stroke.

ap·op·to·sis /,apə(p)'tōsis/ ▶ n. Physiology the death of cells that occurs as a normal and controlled part of an organism's growth or development.

a·pos·ta·sy /ə'pästəsē/ ▶ n. the abandonment of a belief or principle.

a·pos·tate /ə'päs,tāt, -tit/ ▶ n. a person who abandons a belief or principle.

a pos·te·ri·o·ri /'ä pä,sti(ə)rē'ôr,ē, -'ôr,ī/ ▶ adj. & adv. involving reasoning based on known facts to deduce causes.

a·pos·tle /ə'päsəl/ ▶ n. **1** (**Apostle**) each of the twelve chief disciples of Jesus. **2** a pioneering advocate or enthusiastic supporter of an idea or cause: *he's an apostle of positive thinking.*

a·pos·to·late /ə'pästə,lāt, -lit/ ▶ n. **1** the position or authority of a religious leader. **2** evangelistic activity.

ap·os·tol·ic /,apə'stälik/ ▶ adj. **1** relating to the Apostles. **2** relating to the Pope, regarded as the successor to St. Peter.

a·pos·tro·phe /ə'pästrəfē/ ▶ n. **1** a punctuation mark (') used to show either possession or the omission of letters or numbers. **2** a passage in a speech or poem that turns away from the subject to address an absent person or thing.

> **USAGE**
> The apostrophe should be used to show that a person or thing relates or belongs to someone or something (*Sue's cat, yesterday's weather*) or that letters or numbers have been omitted (*he's gone; the winter of '99*). Do not use an apostrophe to form the plural of ordinary words, as in *apple's*, or in the possessive pronouns **its, hers, yours,** or **theirs**.

a·pos·tro·phize /ə'pästrə,fīz/ ▶ v. **1** punctuate a word with an apostrophe. **2** address a separate passage in a speech or poem to an absent person or thing.

a·poth·e·car·y /ə'päTHi,kerē/ ▶ n. (pl. **apothecaries**) old use a person who prepared and sold medicines.

ap·o·thegm /'apə,THem/ (Brit. **apophthegm**) ▶ n. a short phrase stating a general truth.

a·poth·e·o·sis /ə,päTHē'ōsis, ,apə'THēəsis/ ▶ n. (pl. **apotheoses** /-,sēz/) **1** the highest point: *science is the apotheosis of the intellect.* **2** the raising of someone to the rank of a god. ■ **a·poth·e·o·size** /ə'päTHēə,sīz, ,apə'THēə-/ v.

ap·pall /ə'pôl/ (Brit. **appal**) ▶ v. **1** cause great shock or dismay to: *I am appalled at his lack of understanding.* **2** (as adj. **appalling**) informal shockingly bad. ■ **ap·pall·ing·ly** /ə'pôlinGlē/ adv.

Ap·pa·loo·sa /,apə'lōōsə/ ▶ n. a horse of a North American breed having dark spots on a light background.

ap·pa·rat·chik /,äpə'rächik/ ▶ n. **1** chiefly derogatory an official in a large political organization. **2** chiefly historical a member of the administrative system of a communist party.

ap·pa·rat·us /,apə'ratəs, -'rätəs/ ▶ n. (pl. **apparatuses**) **1** the equipment needed for a particular activity or purpose. **2** the complex structure of an organization: *the apparatus of government.*

ap·par·el /ə'parəl/ ▶ n. formal clothing. ▶ v. (**apparels, appareling, appareled**) old use clothe someone.

ap·par·ent /ə'parənt, ə'pe(ə)r-/ ▶ adj. **1** clearly seen or understood; obvious. **2** seeming real, but not necessarily so: *his apparent lack of concern.* ■ **ap·par·ent·ly** adv.

ap·pa·ri·tion /,apə'rishən/ ▶ n. a remarkable thing that makes a sudden appearance, especially a ghost.

ap·peal /ə'pēl/ ▶ v. **1** make a serious or earnest request. **2** be attractive or interesting: *activities that appeal to all.* **3** ask a higher court of law to reverse the decision of a lower court. **4** (in sports) call on an umpire or referee to rule on a completed play or move. ▶ n. **1** an act of appealing. **2** the quality of being attractive or interesting: *the popular appeal of football.*

ap·peal·ing /ə'pēlinG/ ▶ adj. attractive or interesting. ■ **ap·peal·ing·ly** adv.

ap·pear /əˈpi(ə)r/ ▶ v. **1** come into sight or existence: *Pat appeared at the door.* **2** give a particular impression; seem: *she appeared antisocial.* **3** perform in a movie, play, etc. **4** present oneself formally in a court of law. **5** be published.

ap·pear·ance /əˈpi(ə)rəns/ ▶ n. **1** the way that someone or something looks or seems: *you can improve your appearance with makeup.* **2** an act of appearing.
– PHRASES **keep up appearances** keep up an impression of wealth or well-being.

ap·pease /əˈpēz/ ▶ v. make someone calmer or less hostile by agreeing to their demands.
■ **ap·pease·ment** n. **ap·peas·er** n.

ap·pel·lant /əˈpelənt/ ▶ n. Law a person who appeals to a higher court to reverse the decision of a lower court.

ap·pel·late /əˈpelit/ ▶ adj. Law (of a court) dealing with appeals.

ap·pel·la·tion /ˌapəˈlāSHən/ ▶ n. formal a name or title.

ap·pend /əˈpend/ ▶ v. add something to the end of a document or piece of writing.

ap·pend·age /əˈpendij/ ▶ n. a thing attached to or projecting from something larger or more important.

ap·pen·dec·to·my /ˌapənˈdektəmē/ (Brit. also **appendicectomy** /əˌpendəˈsektəmē/) ▶ n. (pl. **appendectomies**) a surgical operation to remove the appendix.

ap·pen·di·ci·tis /əˌpendəˈsītis/ ▶ n. inflammation of the appendix.

ap·pen·dix /əˈpendiks/ ▶ n. (pl. **appendices** /-diˌsēz/ or **appendixes**) **1** a small tube of tissue attached to the lower end of the large intestine. **2** a section of additional information at the end of a book.

ap·per·tain /ˌapərˈtān/ ▶ v. (**appertain to**) formal relate to: *the law appertaining to businesses is rather different.*

ap·pe·tite /ˈapiˌtīt/ ▶ n. **1** a natural desire to satisfy a bodily need, especially for food. **2** a liking or inclination: *the nation's growing appetite for the Internet.* ■ **ap·pe·ti·tive** /ˈapiˌtītiv/ adj.

ap·pe·tiz·er /ˈapiˌtīzər/ ▶ n. a small dish of food or a drink taken before a meal to stimulate the appetite.

ap·pe·tiz·ing /ˈapiˌtīziNG/ ▶ adj. causing a pleasant feeling of hunger.

ap·plaud /əˈplôd/ ▶ v. **1** show approval by clapping. **2** express approval of: *the world applauded his courage.*

ap·plause /əˈplôz/ ▶ n. approval shown by clapping.

ap·ple /ˈapəl/ ▶ n. the round fruit of a tree of the rose family, with green or red skin and crisp flesh. ■ **ap·pley** adj.
– PHRASES **the apple of one's eye** a person of whom one is extremely fond and proud. **a rotten** (or **bad**) **apple** informal a corrupt person in a group, likely to have a bad influence on the others. **upset the apple cart** spoil a plan.

ap·ple-pie or·der ▶ n. perfect neatness or order.

ap·plet /ˈaplit/ ▶ n. Computing a small application running within a larger program.

ap·pli·ance /əˈplīəns/ ▶ n. a device designed to perform a specific task: *a gas appliance.*

ap·pli·ca·ble /ˈaplikəbəl, əˈplik-/ ▶ adj. relevant or appropriate: *most of the book is applicable to any country.* ■ **ap·pli·ca·bil·i·ty** /ˌaplikəˈbilitē/ n.

ap·pli·cant /ˈaplikənt/ ▶ n. a person who applies for something.

ap·pli·ca·tion /ˌapliˈkāSHən/ ▶ n. **1** a formal request to an authority. **2** the action of applying something. **3** practical use or relevance: *this principle has no application to the present case.* **4** sustained effort; hard work. **5** a computer program designed to fulfill a particular purpose.

ap·pli·ca·tor /ˈapliˌkātər/ ▶ n. a device for inserting or applying something.

ap·plied /əˈplīd/ ▶ adj. practical rather than theoretical: *applied chemistry.*

ap·pli·qué /ˌapliˈkā/ ▶ n. decorative needlework in which fabric shapes are sewn or fixed onto a fabric background. ■ **ap·pli·quéd** adj.

ap·ply /əˈplī/ ▶ v. (**applies, applying, applied**) **1** make a formal request: *he applied for a job as a plumber.* **2** bring something into operation or use. **3** be relevant: *the regulations apply to all member nations.* **4** put a substance on to a surface. **5** (**apply oneself**) put all one's efforts into a task.

ap·point /əˈpoint/ ▶ v. **1** give a job or role to someone. **2** decide on a time or place.
■ **ap·point·ee** /əˌpoinˈtē/ n.

ap·point·ed /əˈpointid/ ▶ adj. **1** (of a time or place) prearranged. **2** equipped or furnished: *a luxuriously appointed lounge.*

ap·point·ment /əˈpointmənt/ ▶ n. **1** an arrangement to meet someone. **2** a job or position. **3** the action of appointing someone to a job. **4** (**appointments**) the furniture or fittings in a room.

ap·por·tion /əˈpôrSHən/ ▶ v. share something out.
■ **ap·por·tion·ment** n.

ap·po·site /ˈapəzit/ ▶ adj. very appropriate; apt.

ap·po·si·tion /ˌapəˈziSHən/ ▶ n. **1** chiefly technical the positioning of things next to each other. **2** Grammar a relationship in which a word or phrase is placed next to another in order to qualify or explain it (e.g., *my friend Sue*).

ap·prais·al /əˈprāzəl/ ▶ n. **1** an act of assessing someone or something. **2** a formal assessment of an employee's performance.

ap·praise /əˈprāz/ ▶ v. **1** assess the quality or nature of: *she appraised the damage and groaned.* **2** give an employee an appraisal. **3** (of an official valuer) set a price on something. ■ **ap·prais·ee** /əˌprāˈzē/ n. **ap·prais·er** n.

USAGE
Appraise is often confused with **apprise**. **Appraise** means 'assess someone or something,' whereas **apprise** means 'inform someone' (*psychiatrists were apprised of his condition*).

ap·pre·ci·a·ble /əˈprēSH(ē)əbəl/ ▶ adj. large or important enough to be noticed. ■ **ap·pre·ci·a·bly** adv.

ap·pre·ci·ate /əˈprēSHēˌāt/ ▶ v. **1** recognize the worth of: *that's a son who appreciates his mother.* **2** understand a situation fully. **3** be grateful for something. **4** rise in value or price. ■ **ap·pre·ci·a·tor** n.

ap·pre·ci·a·tion /əˌprēSHēˈāSHən/ ▶ n. **1** recognition of the worth of something. **2** gratitude. **3** a favorable written assessment of a person or their work. **4** increase in value.

ap·pre·cia·tive /əˈprēSH(ē)ətiv/ ▶ adj. feeling or showing gratitude or pleasure.

■ **ap·pre·cia·tive·ly** adv. **ap·pre·cia·tive·ness** /ə'prēsʜ(ē)ətiv,nəs/ **n.**

ap·pre·hend /,apri'hend/ ▸ v. **1** seize or arrest someone for a crime. **2** understand something.

ap·pre·hen·sion /,apri'hensʜən/ ▸ n. **1** worry or fear about what might happen. **2** understanding. **3** the action of arresting someone.

ap·pre·hen·sive /,apri'hensiv/ ▸ adj. worried or afraid about what might happen: *she was apprehensive about attending classes.* ■ **ap·pre·hen·sive·ly** adv.

ap·pren·tice /ə'prentis/ ▸ n. a person learning a skilled practical profession from an employer. ▸ v. employ someone as an apprentice. ■ **ap·pren·tice·ship** /-,sʜip/ n.

ap·prise /ə'prīz/ ▸ v. inform or tell: *I had better apprise you of the situation.*

USAGE

On the confusion of **apprise** and **appraise**, see the note at **APPRAISE**.

---

ap·proach /ə'prōcʜ/ ▸ v. **1** come near to someone or something in distance, time, or standard. **2** go to someone with a proposal or request. **3** start to deal with in a particular way: *one must approach the matter with caution.* ▸ n. **1** a way of dealing with something. **2** an initial proposal or request. **3** the action of approaching. **4** a way leading to a place.

ap·proach·a·ble /ə'prōcʜəbəl/ ▸ adj. **1** friendly and easy to talk to. **2** able to be reached from a particular direction or by a particular means: *the peak is approachable via a six-mile hike.* ■ **ap·proach·a·bil·i·ty** /ə,prōcʜə'bilitē/ n.

ap·pro·ba·tion /,aprə'bāsʜən/ ▸ n. approval; praise.

ap·pro·pri·ate ▸ adj. /ə'prōprē-it/ suitable or proper in the circumstances: *there is an appropriate time for training.* ▸ v. /-,āt/ **1** take something for one's own use without permission. **2** allocate money for a special purpose. ■ **ap·pro·pri·ate·ly** /-itlē/ adv. **ap·pro·pri·ate·ness** /-itnis/ n. **ap·pro·pri·a·tion** /-'āsʜən/ n. **ap·pro·pri·a·tor** /-,ātər/ n.

ap·prov·al /ə'prōōvəl/ ▸ n. **1** the belief that someone or something is good. **2** official acceptance that something is satisfactory. – PHRASES **on approval** (of goods) able to be returned to a supplier if unsatisfactory.

ap·prove /ə'prōōv/ ▸ v. **1** believe that someone or something is good or acceptable: *I don't approve of romance.* **2** officially accept something as satisfactory.

ap·prox·i·mate ▸ adj. /ə'präksəmit/ almost but not completely accurate. ▸ v. /-,māt/ **1** come close in nature or quantity to: *shoppers can create a computer image that approximates their body shape.* **2** estimate something fairly accurately. ■ **ap·prox·i·mate·ly** adv.

ap·prox·i·ma·tion /ə,praksə'māsʜən/ ▸ n. **1** an approximate figure or result. **2** the action of estimating something fairly accurately.

ap·pur·te·nan·ces /ə'pərtn-ənsiz/ ▸ pl.n. formal accessories associated with a particular activity.

APR ▸ abbr. annual (or annualized) percentage rate.

a·près-ski /,äprā 'skē/ ▸ n. social activities following a day's skiing.

ap·ri·cot /'apri,kät, 'āpri-/ ▸ n. an orange-yellow fruit resembling a small peach.

A·pril /'āprəl/ ▸ n. the fourth month of the year.

A·pril Fool's Day ▸ n. April 1, traditionally an occasion for playing practical jokes.

a pri·o·ri /'ä prē'ôrē, prī'ôrī, 'ā/ ▸ adj. & adv. based on theoretical reasoning rather than actual observation.

a·pron /'āprən/ ▸ n. **1** a protective garment covering the front of one's clothes and tied at the back. **2** an area on an airfield used for maneuvering or parking aircraft. **3** (also **apron stage**) a strip of stage projecting in front of the curtain. – PHRASES **tied to someone's apron strings** dominated or excessively influenced by someone, especially one's mother.

ap·ro·pos /,aprə'pō/ ▸ prep. with reference to: *she kept smiling down at her plate, apropos of nothing.* ▸ adj. very appropriate.

apse /aps/ ▸ n. a large recess with a domed or arched roof at the eastern end of a church. ■ **ap·si·dal** /'apsidl/ adj.

apt /apt/ ▸ adj. **1** appropriate; suitable. **2** having a tendency to: *junior recruits are most apt to have low morale.* **3** quick to learn. ■ **apt·ly** adv. **apt·ness** n.

ap·ti·tude /'apti,t(y)ōōd/ ▸ n. a natural ability or tendency: *a youth with a remarkable aptitude for math.*

aq·ua /'äkwə, 'ak-/ ▸ n. a light bluish-green color; aquamarine.

aqua- ▸ comb.form relating to water: *aqualung.*

aq·ua·cul·ture /'äkwə,kəlcʜər, 'ak-/ ▸ n. the rearing of aquatic animals or the cultivation of aquatic plants for food.

aq·ua·lung /'äkwə,ləNG, 'ak-/ ▸ n. another term for SCUBA.

aq·ua·ma·rine /,äkwəmə'rēn, ,ak-/ ▸ n. **1** a precious stone consisting of a light bluish-green variety of beryl. **2** a light bluish-green color.

aq·ua·naut /'äkwə,nôt, 'ak-/ ▸ n. a diver.

aq·ua·plane /'äkwə,plān, 'ak-/ ▸ v. **1** (of a vehicle) slide uncontrollably on a wet surface. **2** ride on an aquaplane. ▸ n. a board for riding on water, pulled by a speedboat.

aq·ua re·gi·a /'äkwə 'rejēə, 'ak-/ ▸ n. a highly corrosive mixture of concentrated nitric and hydrochloric acids.

aq·ua·relle /,äkwə'rel, ,ak-/ ▸ n. the technique of painting with thin, transparent watercolors.

a·quar·ist /ə'kwe(ə)rist/ ▸ n. a person who keeps an aquarium.

a·quar·i·um /ə'kwe(ə)rēəm/ ▸ n. (pl. **aquariums** or **aquaria** /-ēə/) a water-filled glass tank for keeping fish and other water creatures and plants.

A·quar·i·us /ə'kwe(ə)rēəs/ ▸ n. **1** a constellation and the eleventh sign of the zodiac (the Water Carrier), which the sun enters about January 21. **2** (**an Aquarius**) a person born when the sun is in this sign. ■ **A·quar·i·an** /ə'kwe(ə)rēən/ n. & adj.

a·quat·ic /ə'kwätik, ə'kwat-/ ▸ adj. **1** relating to water. **2** living in or near water. ▸ n. an aquatic plant or animal.

aq·ua·tint /'äkwə,tint, 'ak-/ ▸ n. a print resembling a watercolor, made using a copper plate etched with acid.

aq·ua·vit /'äkwə,vēt, 'ak-/ ▸ n. an alcoholic spirit made from potatoes.

aq·ue·duct /'äkwə,dəkt, 'ak-/ ▸ n. a long channel or raised bridgelike structure, used for carrying water across country.

a·que·ous /'ākwēəs, 'ak-/ ▸ adj. relating to or containing water.

a·que·ous hu·mor ▸ n. the clear fluid in the eyeball in front of the lens.

aq·ui·fer /'äkwəfər, 'ak-/ ▸ n. a body of rock that holds water or through which water flows.

aq·ui·le·gi·a /ˌakwə'lēj(ē)ə/ ▸ n. a garden plant bearing showy flowers with backward-pointing spurs; columbine.

aq·ui·line /'akwəˌlīn, -lin/ ▸ adj. 1 (of a nose) curved like an eagle's beak. 2 like an eagle.

AR ▸ abbr. Arkansas.

Ar ▸ symbol the chemical element argon.

Ar·ab /'arəb/ ▸ n. 1 a member of a Semitic people inhabiting much of the Middle East and North Africa. 2 a breed of horse originating in Arabia. ■ **Ar·ab·ize** /'arəˌbīz/ v.

ar·a·besque /ˌarə'besk/ ▸ n. 1 a ballet posture in which one leg is extended horizontally backward and the arms are outstretched. 2 an ornamental design consisting of intertwined flowing lines. 3 a musical passage with a highly ornamented melody.

A·ra·bi·an /ə'rābēən/ ▸ adj. relating to Arabia or its people. ▸ n. historical an Arab.

Ar·a·bic /'arəbik/ ▸ n. the Semitic language of the Arabs, written from right to left. ▸ adj. relating to the Arabs or Arabic.

a·rab·i·ca /ə'rabikə/ ▸ n. a type of coffee bean widely grown in tropical Asia and Africa.

Ar·a·bic nu·mer·al ▸ n. any of the numerals 0, 1, 2, 3, 4, 5, 6, 7, 8, and 9.

Ar·ab·ism /'arəˌbizəm/ ▸ n. 1 Arab culture or identity. 2 an Arabic word or phrase. ■ **Ar·ab·ist** n. & adj.

ar·a·ble /'arəbəl/ ▸ adj. 1 (of land) used or suitable for growing crops. 2 (of crops) able to be grown on arable land.

a·rach·nid /ə'raknid/ ▸ n. an invertebrate animal of a class including spiders, scorpions, mites, and ticks.

a·rach·no·pho·bi·a /əˌraknə'fōbēə/ ▸ n. extreme fear of spiders. ■ **a·rach·no·phobe** /ə'raknəˌfōb/ n.

ar·ak ▸ n. variant spelling of ARRACK.

Ar·a·ma·ic /ˌarə'māik/ ▸ n. an ancient Semitic language still spoken in parts of the Middle East. ▸ adj. relating to Aramaic.

Ar·an /'arən/ ▸ adj. (of knitwear) featuring patterns of cable stitch and diamond designs, as made traditionally in the Aran Islands off the west coast of Ireland.

A·rap·a·ho /ə'rapəˌhō/ ▸ n. (pl. same or **Arapahos**) 1 a member of a North American Indian people living on the Great Plains. 2 the language of the Arapaho.

Ar·a·wak /'arəˌwäk/ ▸ n. (pl. same or **Arawaks**) 1 a member of a group of native peoples of the Greater Antilles and northern and western South America. 2 any of the languages of the Arawak.

ar·bi·ter /'ärbitər/ ▸ n. 1 a person who settles a dispute. 2 a person who has influence in a particular area: *an arbiter of taste.*

ar·bi·trage /'ärbiˌträzh/ ▸ n. the buying and selling of assets at the same time in different markets or in derivative forms, taking advantage of the differing prices. ■ **ar·bi·tra·geur** /ˌärbiträ'zhər, 'ärbiˌträzhər/ n.

ar·bi·trar·y /'ärbiˌtrerē/ ▸ adj. 1 not appearing to be based on any reason or system: *an arbitrary*

decision. 2 (of power or authority) used without restraint. ■ **ar·bi·trar·i·ly** /ˌärbi'tre(ə)rəlē/ adv. **ar·bi·trar·i·ness** n.

ar·bi·trate /'ärbiˌträt/ ▸ v. (of an independent person or body) officially settle a dispute. ■ **ar·bi·tra·tion** /ˌärbi'träSHən/ n.

ar·bi·tra·tor /'ärbiˌträtər/ ▸ n. an independent person or body officially appointed to settle a dispute.

ar·bor[1] /'ärbər/ (Brit. **arbour**) ▸ n. a garden shelter formed by trees or climbing plants trained over a framework.

ar·bor[2] ▸ n. 1 an axle on which something revolves. 2 a device holding a tool in a lathe.

Ar·bor Day ▸ n. a day dedicated annually to public tree-planting in the US, Australia, and other countries. It is usually observed in late April or early May.

ar·bo·re·al /är'bôrēəl/ ▸ adj. 1 living in trees. 2 relating to trees.

ar·bo·re·tum /ˌärbə'rētəm/ ▸ n. (pl. **arboretums** or **arboreta**) a botanical garden devoted to trees.

ar·bor·i·cul·ture /'ärbəriˌkəlCHər, är'bôri-/ ▸ n. the cultivation of trees and shrubs.

ar·bour, etc. ▸ n. British spelling of ARBOR[1], etc.

ARC ▸ abbr. 1 AIDS-related complex. 2 American Red Cross.

arc /ärk/ ▸ n. 1 a curve forming part of the circumference of a circle. 2 a curving passage of something in the air: *he swung his torch in a wide arc.* 3 a luminous electrical discharge between two points. ▸ v. (**arcs, arcing, arced**) 1 move in an arc: *the ball arced over the goal.* 2 (as n. **arcing**) the forming of an electrical arc.

ar·cade /är'kād/ ▸ n. 1 a covered passage with arches along one or both sides. 2 a covered walk with stores along one or both sides. 3 Architecture a series of arches supporting a wall. ■ **ar·cad·ing** n.

Ar·ca·di·an /är'kādēən/ ▸ adj. literary rural in an unrealistically pleasant way.

ar·ca·na /är'känə/ ▸ pl.n. (sing. **arcanum** /-nəm/) mysteries or secrets.

ar·cane /är'kān/ ▸ adj. understood by few people; mysterious: *arcane arguments about economics.* ■ **ar·cane·ly** adv.

arch[1] /ärCH/ ▸ n. 1 a curved structure spanning an opening or supporting the weight of a bridge, roof, or wall. 2 the inner side of the foot. ▸ v. form or make a curved shape. ■ **arched** adj.

arch[2] ▸ adj. self-consciously playful or teasing. ■ **arch·ly** adv. **arch·ness** n.

arch- ▸ comb.form 1 chief; main: *archbishop.* 2 foremost: *archenemy.*

Ar·chae·an /är'kēən/ ▸ adj. British spelling of ARCHEAN.

ar·chae·ol·o·gy /ˌärkē'äləjē/ (also **archeology**) ▸ n. the study of human history and prehistory through the excavation of sites and the analysis of objects found in them. ■ **ar·chae·o·log·ic** /-ə'läjik/ adj. **ar·chae·o·log·i·cal** /-ə'läjikəl/ adj. **ar·chae·ol·o·gist** /-'äləjist/ n.

ar·chae·op·ter·yx /ˌärkē'äptəriks/ ▸ n. the oldest known fossil bird, of the late Jurassic period, which had feathers and wings like a bird, but teeth and a bony tail like a dinosaur.

ar·cha·ic /är'kāik/ ▸ adj. 1 very old or old-fashioned. 2 belonging to former or ancient times. ■ **ar·cha·i·cal·ly** adv.

ar·cha·ism /'ärkēˌizəm, 'ärkā-/ ▸ n. 1 an old or old-fashioned word or style of art or language.

2 the use of old or old-fashioned features or styles in language or art.

arch·an·gel /'ärk,ānjəl/ ▸ n. an angel of a high rank.

arch·bish·op /'ärcH'bishəp/ ▸ n. the chief bishop responsible for a large district.

arch·dea·con /'ärcH'dēkən/ ▸ n. a senior Christian priest ranking immediately below an archbishop.

arch·di·o·cese /,ärcH'dīəsis, -,sēz/ ▸ n. the district for which an archbishop is responsible. ■ **arch·di·oc·e·san** /,ärcHdī'äsəsən/ adj.

arch·duke /'ärcH'd(y)ook/ ▸ n. **1** a chief duke. **2** historical a son of the emperor of Austria.

Ar·che·an /är'kēən/ (Brit. **Archaean**) ▸ adj. relating to the earlier part of the Precambrian eon (before about 2,500 million years ago).

arch·en·e·my /'ärcH'enəmē/ ▸ n. a chief enemy.

ar·che·ol·o·gy ▸ n. variant spelling of ARCHAEOLOGY.

arch·er /'ärcHər/ ▸ n. a person who shoots with a bow and arrows.

ar·cher·y /'ärcHərē/ ▸ n. the activity or sport of shooting with a bow and arrows.

ar·che·type /'ärk(i),tīp/ ▸ n. **1** a very typical example: *she's the archetype of the single American female.* **2** an original model from which other forms are developed. **3** a recurrent symbol in literature or art. ■ **ar·che·typ·al** /,ärk(i)'tīpəl/ adj. **ar·che·typ·i·cal** /,ärk(i)'tipikəl/ adj. **ar·che·typ·i·cal·ly** /,ärk(i)'tipikəlē/ adv.

ar·chi·e·pis·co·pal /,ärkēə'piskəpəl/ ▸ adj. relating to an archbishop.

Ar·chi·me·des' prin·ci·ple /,ärkə'mēdēz/ ▸ n. Physics a law discovered by the Greek mathematician Archimedes (*c.* 287–212 BC), stating that a body immersed in a fluid is subject to an upward force equal to the weight of fluid the body displaces.

ar·chi·pel·a·go /,ärkə'pelə,gō/ ▸ n. (pl. **archipelagos** or **archipelagoes**) a group of many islands.

ar·chi·tect /'ärki,tekt/ ▸ n. **1** a person who designs buildings and supervises their construction. **2** a person who originates or realizes an idea or project: *the architects of the green revolution.*

ar·chi·tec·ton·ic /,ärkitek'tänik/ ▸ adj. **1** relating to architecture or architects. **2** having a clearly defined and artistically pleasing structure: *architectonic cheekbones.* ▸ n. (**architectonics**) (treated as sing.) the scientific study of architecture.

ar·chi·tec·ture /'ärki,tekcHər/ ▸ n. **1** the art or practice of designing and constructing buildings. **2** the style in which a building is designed and constructed: *Gothic architecture.* **3** the complex structure of something. ■ **ar·chi·tec·tur·al** /,ärki'tekcHərəl/ adj.

ar·chi·trave /'ärki,trāv/ ▸ n. **1** (in classical architecture) a main beam resting across the tops of columns. **2** the frame around a doorway or window.

ar·chive /'är,kīv/ ▸ n. **1** a collection of historical documents or records. **2** a complete record of the data in a computer system, stored on a less frequently used medium. ▸ v. place or store something in an archive. ■ **ar·chi·val** /är'kīvəl/ adj.

ar·chi·vist /'ärkəvist, -,kī-/ ▸ n. a person who is in charge of archives.

arch·ri·val ▸ n. the chief rival of a person, team, or organization.

arch·way /'ärcH,wā/ ▸ n. a curved structure forming a passage or entrance.

arc lamp (also **arc light**) ▸ n. a light source using an electric arc.

Arc·tic /'ärktik, 'ärtik/ ▸ adj. **1** relating to the regions around the North Pole. **2** living or growing in the regions around the North Pole. **3** (**arctic**) informal (of weather) very cold. ▸ n. (**the Arctic**) the regions around the North Pole.

ar·cu·ate /'ärkyōoit, -,āt/ ▸ adj. technical curved.

ar·dent /'ärdnt/ ▸ adj. **1** very enthusiastic; passionate: *an ardent supporter of organic agriculture.* **2** old use burning or glowing. ■ **ar·dent·ly** adv.

ar·dor /'ärdər/ (Brit. **ardour**) ▸ n. great enthusiasm; passion.

ar·du·ous /'ärjōoəs/ ▸ adj. difficult and tiring. ■ **ar·du·ous·ly** adv. **ar·du·ous·ness** n.

are /är/ ▸ second person singular present and first, second, third person plural present of BE.

ar·e·a /'e(ə)rēə/ ▸ n. **1** a part of a place, object, or surface. **2** the extent or measurement of a surface. **3** a space allocated for a specific use: *a picnic area.* **4** a subject or range of activity. ■ **ar·e·al** adj.

ar·e·a code ▸ n. a telephone dialing code.

a·re·na /ə'rēnə/ ▸ n. **1** a level area surrounded by seating, in which sports and other public events are held. **2** an area of activity: *conflicts within the political arena.*

aren't /är(ə)nt/ ▸ contr. **1** are not. **2** am not (only used in questions): *I'm right, aren't I?*

a·re·o·la /ə'rēələ/ ▸ n. (pl. **areolae** /-,lē/) Anatomy a small circular area, especially the darker skin surrounding a human nipple.

a·rête /ə'rāt/ ▸ n. a sharp mountain ridge.

ar·gent /'ärjənt/ ▸ adj. & n. literary & Heraldry silver.

Ar·gen·tin·i·an /,ärjən'tinēən/ (also **Argentine** /'ärjən,tīn, -,tēn/) ▸ n. a person from Argentina. ▸ adj. relating to Argentina.

ar·gon /'är,gän/ ▸ n. an inert gaseous chemical element, present in small amounts in the air.

ar·go·sy /'ärgəsē/ ▸ n. (pl. **argosies**) literary a large merchant ship, originally one from Ragusa (now Dubrovnik) or Venice.

ar·got /'ärgō, -gət/ ▸ n. the jargon or slang of a particular group or area of activity: *the argot of city planning.*

ar·gu·a·ble /'ärgyooəbəl/ ▸ adj. **1** able to be argued or asserted: *it is arguable that the company was already experiencing problems.* **2** open to disagreement. ■ **ar·gu·a·bly** adv.

ar·gue /'ärgyoo/ ▸ v. (**argues, arguing, argued**) **1** exchange conflicting views heatedly. **2** give reasons or evidence in support of something. ■ **ar·gu·er** n.

ar·gu·ment /'ärgyəmənt/ ▸ n. **1** a heated exchange of conflicting views. **2** a set of reasons given in support of something.

ar·gu·men·ta·tion /,ärgyəmən'tāsHən/ ▸ n. systematic reasoning in support of something.

ar·gu·men·ta·tive /,ärgyə'mentətiv/ ▸ adj. apt to argue.

ar·gyle /'är,gīl/ ▸ n. a pattern used in knitwear, consisting of colored diamonds on a plain background.

a·ri·a /'ärēə/ ► n. a long accompanied song for a solo voice in an opera or oratorio.

ar·id /'arid/ ► adj. **1** very dry because having little or no rain. **2** uninteresting; unsatisfying. ■ **a·rid·i·ty** /ə'riditē/ n.

Ar·ies /'e(ə)rēz, 'e(ə)rē-ēz/ ► n. **1** a constellation and the first sign of the zodiac (the Ram), which the sun enters about March 20. **2** (**an Aries**) a person born when the sun is in this sign. ■ **Ar·i·an** /'e(ə)rēən/ n. & adj.

a·right /ə'rīt/ ► adv. dialect correctly; properly.

a·rise /ə'rīz/ ► v. (past **arose** /ə'rōz/; past part. **arisen** /ə'rizən/) **1** come into being or come to notice: *new difficulties had arisen.* **2** (**arise from/out of**) occur as a result of: *back pain can arise from a multitude of problems.* **3** formal get or stand up.

a·ris·toc·ra·cy /,ari'stäkrəsē/ ► n. (pl. **aristocracies**) the highest social class, consisting of people of noble birth with hereditary titles.

a·ris·to·crat /ə'ristə,krat/ ► n. a member of the aristocracy.

a·ris·to·crat·ic /ə,ristə'kratik/ ► adj. relating to or typical of the aristocracy. ■ **a·ris·to·crat·i·cal·ly** adv.

Ar·is·to·te·lian /ə,ristə'tēlyən, ,aristə-, -lēən/ ► adj. relating to the theories of the Greek philosopher Aristotle (384–322 BC). ► n. a student or follower of Aristotle or his philosophy.

a·rith·me·tic ► n. /ə'riтHmə,tik/ **1** the branch of mathematics concerned with the properties and manipulation of numbers. **2** the use of numbers in counting and calculation. ► adj. /,ariтH'metik/ relating to arithmetic. ■ **ar·ith·met·i·cal** /,ariтH'metikəl/ adj. **ar·ith·met·i·cal·ly** /,ariтH'metikəlē/ adv. **a·rith·me·ti·cian** /ə,riтHmə'tishən/ n.

ar·ith·met·ic pro·gres·sion /,ariтH'metik/ (also **arithmetic series**) ► n. a sequence of numbers in which each differs from the preceding one by a constant quantity (e.g., 9, 7, 5, 3, etc.).

ark /ärk/ ► n. **1** (in the Bible) the ship built by Noah to save his family and two of every kind of animal from the Flood. **2** (also **Holy Ark**) a chest or cupboard housing the Torah scrolls in a synagogue. **3** (**Ark of the Covenant**) the chest that contained the laws of the ancient Israelites.

ARM ► abbr. adjustable rate mortgage.

arm¹ /ärm/ ► n. **1** each of the two upper limbs of the human body from the shoulder to the hand. **2** a side part of a chair supporting a sitter's arm. **3** a narrow strip of water or land projecting from a larger area. **4** a branch or division of an organization. ■ **arm·ful** n. **arm·less** adj. **arm·load** /'ärm,lōd/ n.
– PHRASES **arm in arm** with arms linked. **cost an arm and a leg** informal be very expensive. **keep someone/thing at arm's length** avoid close contact with someone or something. **with open arms** with great affection or enthusiasm.

arm² ► v. **1** supply someone with weapons. **2** provide with essential equipment or information: *we were armed with all sorts of statistics.* **3** activate the fuse of a bomb or missile so that it is ready to explode.

ar·ma·da /är'mädə/ ► n. a fleet of warships.

ar·ma·dil·lo /,ärmə'dilō/ ► n. (pl. **armadillos**) an insect-eating mammal of Central and South America, with a body covered in bony plates.

Ar·ma·ged·don /,ärmə'gedn/ ► n. **1** (in the New Testament) the last battle between good and evil before the Day of Judgment. **2** a catastrophic conflict or event: *the threat of nuclear Armageddon.*

Ar·mag·nac /,ärmən'yak, -'yäk/ ► n. a type of brandy made in Aquitaine in SW France.

ar·ma·ment /'ärməmənt/ ► n. **1** (also **armaments**) military weapons and equipment. **2** the equipping of military forces for war.

ar·ma·ture /'ärməсHər, -,сHŏŏr/ ► n. **1** the rotating coil of a dynamo or electric motor. **2** any moving part of an electrical machine in which a voltage is induced by a magnetic field. **3** a piece of iron placed across the poles of a magnet to preserve its power. **4** the protective covering of an animal or plant.

arm·band /'ärm,band/ ► n. **1** a band worn around the upper arm to indicate something, such as a person's role or identity. **2** an inflatable plastic band worn around the upper arm as a swimming aid.

arm·chair /'ärm,сHe(ə)r/ ► n. an upholstered chair with side supports for the sitter's arms. ► adj. experiencing something through reading, television, etc., rather than doing it: *an armchair traveler.*

armed /ärmd/ ► adj. equipped with or involving a firearm.

armed forc·es ► pl.n. a country's army, navy, and air force.

Ar·me·ni·an /är'mēnēən, -yən/ ► n. **1** a person from Armenia. **2** the language of Armenia. ► adj. relating to Armenia.

arm·hole /'ärm,hōl/ ► n. each of two openings in a garment through which the wearer puts their arms.

ar·mi·stice /'ärməstis/ ► n. a truce.

arm·let /'ärmlit/ ► n. a bracelet worn around the upper arm.

arm·lock /'ärm,läk/ ► n. a method of restraining someone by holding their arm bent tightly behind their back.

ar·moire /ärm'wär, 'ärm,wär/ ► n. a large cabinet used especially for storing clothes; a wardrobe.

ar·mor /'ärmər/ (Brit. **armour**) ► n. **1** the metal coverings formerly worn to protect the body in battle. **2** (also **armor plate**) the tough metal layer covering a military vehicle or ship. **3** military vehicles as a whole. **4** the protective layer or shell of some animals and plants. ■ **ar·mored** adj.

ar·mor·er /'ärmərər/ ► n. **1** a maker or supplier of weapons or armor. **2** an official in charge of the arms of a warship or regiment.

ar·mo·ri·al /är'môrēəl/ ► adj. relating to heraldry or coats of arms.

ar·mor·plat·ed ► adj. covered with armor plate.

ar·mor·y /'ärmərē/ ► n. (pl. **armories**) **1** a store or supply of arms. **2** a set of resources available for a purpose: *their armory of tax-gathering methods.*

ar·mour, etc. /'ärmər/ ► n. British spelling of ARMOR, etc.

arm·pit /'ärm,pit/ ► n. a hollow under the arm at the shoulder.

arm·rest /'ärm,rest/ ► n. an arm of a chair.

arms /ärmz/ ► pl.n. **1** guns and other weapons. **2** the heraldic emblems on a coat of arms.
– PHRASES **a call to arms** a call to prepare for conflict. **up in arms** strongly opposed to and protesting about something.

arms con·trol ► n. international agreement to limit the production and accumulation of arms.

arms race ▶ n. a situation in which nations compete for superiority in developing and stockpiling weapons.

arm-twist-ing ▶ n. informal persuasion by the use of physical force or moral pressure: *eight years of arguing and diplomatic arm-twisting.* ■ **arm-twist v.**

arm-wres-tling ▶ n. a contest in which two seated people clasp hands and try to force each other's arm down onto a surface.

ar-my /'ärmē/ ▶ n. (pl. **armies**) **1** an organized military force equipped for fighting on land. **2** a large number of similar people or things: *an army of cleaners.*

ar-ni-ca /'ärnikə/ ▶ n. a plant with yellow daisylike flowers, used for the treatment of bruises.

a-ro-ma /ə'rōmə/ ▶ n. **1** a pleasant and distinctive smell. **2** a particular quality or atmosphere: *the aroma of officialdom.*

a-ro-ma-ther-a-py /ə,rōmə'тнerəpē/ ▶ n. the use of aromatic oils obtained from plants for healing or to promote well-being. ■ **a-ro-ma-ther-a-peu-tic** /-,тнerə'pyōōtik/ adj. **a-ro-ma-ther-a-pist** n.

ar-o-mat-ic /,arə'matik/ ▶ adj. **1** having a pleasant and distinctive smell. **2** (of an organic compound such as benzene) containing a flat ring of atoms in its molecule. ▶ n. an aromatic plant, substance, or compound. ■ **ar-o-mat-i-cal-ly** adv.

a-rose /ə'rōz/ ▶ past of ARISE.

a-round /ə'round/ ▶ adv. **1** with circular movement; so as to rotate. **2** so as to cover the whole area surrounding a particular center: *she glanced around admiringly at the decor.* **3** so as to turn and face in the opposite direction. **4** used in describing the relative position of something: *the pieces are the wrong way around.* **5** on every side; so as to surround or give support. **6** in or to many places throughout. **7** so as to reach a new place or position. **8** available or present. **9** approximately. ▶ prep. **1** on every side of. **2** in or to many places throughout. **3** so as to encircle or surround. **4** following a circular route. **5** from or on the other side of. **6** so as to cover the whole area of.

a-rouse /ə'rouz/ ▶ v. **1** bring about a feeling or response: *the invitation had aroused my curiosity.* **2** excite someone sexually. **3** awaken someone from sleep. ■ **a-rous-al** n.

ar-peg-gi-o /är'pejē,ō/ ▶ n. (pl. **arpeggios**) the notes of a musical chord played in rapid succession.

arr. ▶ abbr. **1** (of a piece of music) arranged by. **2** (with reference to the arrival time of a bus, train, or airplane) arrives.

ar-rab-bi-a-ta /ə,räbē'ätə/ ▶ n. a spicy pasta sauce made with tomatoes and chili peppers.

ar-rack /'arək, ə'rak/ (also **arak**) ▶ n. an alcoholic spirit made in Eastern countries from the sap of the coconut palm or from rice.

ar-raign /ə'rān/ ▶ v. call someone before a court to answer a criminal charge. ■ **ar-raign-ment** n.

ar-range /ə'rānj/ ▶ v. **1** put tidily or in a particular order: *the columns are arranged in rows.* **2** organize or plan for something. **3** adapt a musical composition for performance with instruments or voices other than those originally specified. ■ **ar-range-a-ble** adj. **ar-rang-er** n.

ar-range-ment /ə'rānjmənt/ ▶ n. **1** a plan for a future event: *I made arrangements to meet him.*

2 an agreement to do something. **3** something made up of items placed in an attractive or ordered way: *a flower arrangement.* **4** an arranged musical composition.

ar-rant /'arənt/ ▶ adj. utter; complete: *what arrant nonsense!*

ar-ras /ä'räs, 'arəs/ ▶ n. a tapestry wall hanging.

ar-ray /ə'rā/ ▶ n. **1** an impressive display or range: *a bewildering array of choices.* **2** an ordered arrangement of troops. **3** literary elaborate or beautiful clothing. ▶ v. **1** display or arrange in a neat or impressive way: *bottled waters are arrayed on crushed ice.* **2** (**be arrayed in**) be elaborately clothed in something.

ar-rears /ə'ri(ə)rz/ ▶ pl.n. money owed that should already have been paid.
– PHRASES **in arrears 1** behind with paying money that is owed. **2** (of wages or rent) paid at the end of each period of work or occupation.

ar-rest /ə'rest/ ▶ v. **1** seize someone by legal authority and take them into custody. **2** stop or delay progress or a process: *the spread of the disease can be arrested.* **3** (as adj. **arresting**) attracting attention. ▶ n. **1** an act of arresting someone. **2** a sudden stop. ■ **ar-rest-ing-ly** adv.

ar-rhyth-mi-a /ā'riтнmēə, ə'riтн-/ ▶ n. a medical condition in which the heart beats with an irregular or abnormal rhythm. ■ **ar-rhyth-mic** /ə'riтнmik/ adj.

ar-ri-val /ə'rīvəl/ ▶ n. **1** the action of arriving. **2** a person or thing that has just arrived or appeared.

ar-rive /ə'rīv/ ▶ v. **1** reach a destination. **2** be brought or delivered. **3** (of a moment or event) happen: *spring has finally arrived.* **4** (**arrive at**) reach a conclusion or decision. **5** informal become successful and well known.

ar-ri-vi-der-ci /,ärivə'dercнē/ ▶ exclam. goodbye until we meet again.

ar-ri-viste /,ärē'vēst/ ▶ n. often derogatory a person who has recently become wealthy or risen in social status or is ambitious to do so.

ar-ro-gant /'arəgənt/ ▶ adj. having an exaggerated sense of one's own importance or abilities. ■ **ar-ro-gance** n. **ar-ro-gant-ly** adv.

ar-ro-gate /'arə,gāt/ ▶ v. take or claim something for oneself without justification. ■ **ar-ro-ga-tion** /,arə'gāsHən/ n.

ar-ron-disse-ment /ə'rändismənt, ä'rändēs,mäN/ ▶ n. **1** (in France) a subdivision of a local government department. **2** an administrative district of Paris.

ar-row /'arō/ ▶ n. **1** a stick with a sharp pointed head, designed to be shot from a bow. **2** a symbol resembling an arrow, used to show direction or position. ■ **ar-rowed** adj.

ar-row-head /'arō,hed/ ▶ n. **1** the pointed end of an arrow, typically wedge-shaped. **2** a decorative device resembling an arrowhead. **3** an aquatic or semiaquatic plant with arrow-shaped leaves and three-petaled white flowers.

ar-row-root /'arō,rōōt, -,rŏŏt/ ▶ n. a plant that yields a fine-grained starch used in cooking and medicine.

ar-roy-o /ə'roi,ō/ ▶ n. (pl. **arroyos**) a deep gully cut by the action of fast-flowing water in an arid area.

arse /ärs/ ▶ n. British form of ASS[2].

ar-se-nal /'ärs(ə)-nl/ ▶ n. a store of weapons and ammunition.

ar-se-nic /'ärs(ə)nik/ ▶ n. a brittle steel-gray chemical element with poisonous compounds.

■ **ar·sen·i·cal** /är'senikəl/ adj. **ar·se·nide** /'ärs(ə)ˌnīd/ n.

ar·son /'ärsən/ ▸ n. the criminal act of deliberately setting fire to property. ■ **ar·son·ist** n.

art[1] /ärt/ ▸ n. **1** the expression of creative skill in a visual form such as painting or sculpture. **2** paintings, drawings, and sculpture as a whole. **3** (**the arts**) the branches of creative activity, such as painting, music, and drama. **4** (**arts**) subjects of study mainly concerned with human culture (as contrasted with scientific or technical subjects). **5** a skill: *the art of conversation.*

art[2] ▸ old-fashioned or dialect second person singular present of **BE.**

art dec·o /'dekō/ ▸ n. a decorative art style of the 1920s and 1930s, characterized by geometric shapes.

ar·te·fact /'ärtəˌfakt/ ▸ n. British spelling of ARTIFACT.

ar·te·ri·al /är'ti(ə)rēəl/ ▸ adj. **1** relating to an artery or arteries. **2** relating to an important transport route.

ar·te·ri·o·scle·ro·sis /ärˌti(ə)rēōsklə'rōsis/ ▸ n. thickening and hardening of the walls of the arteries.

ar·ter·y /'ärtərē/ ▸ n. (pl. **arteries**) **1** any of the tubes through which blood flows from the heart around the body. **2** an important transport route.

ar·te·sian well /är'tēzHən/ ▸ n. a well bored vertically into a layer of water-bearing rock that is lying at an angle, the water coming to the surface by natural pressure.

art·ful /'ärtfəl/ ▸ adj. clever, especially in a cunning way. ■ **art·ful·ly** adv. **art·ful·ness** n.

art house ▸ n. a movie theater that shows independently made artistic or experimental films.

ar·thri·tis /är'THrītis/ ▸ n. painful inflammation and stiffness of the joints. ■ **ar·thrit·ic** /-'THritik/ adj. & n.

ar·thro·pod /'ärTHrəˌpäd/ ▸ n. an invertebrate animal with a body divided into segments and an external skeleton, such as an insect, spider, or crab.

ar·thro·scope /'ärTHrəˌskōp/ ▸ n. Medicine an instrument through which the interior of a joint may be inspected or operated on. ■ **ar·thro·scop·ic** /ˌärTHrə'skäpik/ adj. **ar·thros·co·py** /är'THräskəpē/ n.

Ar·thu·ri·an /är'THŏŏrēən/ ▸ adj. relating to the reign of the legendary King Arthur of Britain.

ar·ti·choke /'ärtiˌCHōk/ ▸ n. (also **globe artichoke**) a vegetable consisting of the unopened flowerhead of a thistlelike plant.

ar·ti·cle /'ärtikəl/ ▸ n. **1** a particular object. **2** a piece of writing in a newspaper or magazine. **3** a separate clause or paragraph of a legal document. **4** Brit. (**articles**) a period of professional training as a solicitor, architect, surveyor, or accountant. ▸ v. Brit. (**be articled**) (of a solicitor, architect, etc.) be employed under contract as a trainee.
– PHRASES **article of faith** a firmly held belief.

ar·tic·u·lar /är'tikyələr/ ▸ adj. Anatomy relating to a joint.

ar·tic·u·late ▸ adj. /är'tikyəlit/ **1** able to speak fluently and clearly. **2** having joints or jointed segments. ▸ v. /-ˌlāt/ **1** pronounce words distinctly. **2** clearly express in words: *the president articulated the feelings of the vast majority.* **3** form a joint. **4** (as adj. **articulated**)

having sections connected by a flexible joint. ■ **ar·tic·u·la·cy** /-ləsē/ n. **ar·tic·u·late·ly** adv. **ar·tic·u·late·ness** n. **ar·tic·u·la·tor** /-ˌlātər/ n.

ar·tic·u·la·tion /ärˌtikyə'lāsHən/ ▸ n. **1** the expression of an idea or feeling in words. **2** the formation of distinct sounds in speech. **3** the state of being jointed.

ar·ti·fact /'ärtəˌfakt/ (Brit. **artefact**) ▸ n. a useful or decorative man-made object.

ar·ti·fice /'ärtəfis/ ▸ n. the use of skill or cunning in order to trick or deceive: *the writing is deliberately free of artifice.*

ar·ti·fi·cial /ˌärtə'fisHəl/ ▸ adj. **1** made as a copy of something natural: *artificial flowers.* **2** not sincere; affected. ■ **ar·ti·fi·cial·i·ty** /-ˌfisHē'alitē/ n. **ar·ti·fi·cial·ly** adv.

ar·ti·fi·cial in·sem·i·na·tion ▸ n. the injection of semen into the vagina or uterus of a woman or female animal, as a medical method of fertilizing an egg.

ar·ti·fi·cial in·tel·li·gence ▸ n. the performance by computers of tasks normally requiring human intelligence.

ar·ti·fi·cial res·pi·ra·tion ▸ n. the forcing of air into and out of a person's lungs to make them begin breathing again.

ar·til·ler·y /är'tilərē/ ▸ n. **1** large-caliber guns used in warfare on land. **2** a branch of the armed forces trained to use artillery.

ar·ti·san /'ärtizən/ ▸ n. a skilled worker who makes things by hand. ■ **ar·ti·san·al** adj.

art·ist /'ärtist/ ▸ n. **1** a person who paints or draws as a profession or hobby. **2** a person who practices or performs any of the creative arts. **3** informal a person who practices a particular activity: *a con artist.*

ar·tiste /är'tēst/ ▸ n. a professional singer or dancer.

ar·tis·tic /är'tistik/ ▸ adj. **1** having creative skill. **2** relating to or characteristic of art or artists: *an artistic temperament.* **3** pleasing to look at: *artistic designs.* ■ **ar·tis·ti·cal·ly** adv.

art·ist·ry /'ärtistrē/ ▸ n. creative skill or ability: *the artistry of the pianist.*

art·less /'ärtlis/ ▸ adj. **1** sincere, straightforward, or unpretentious: *an artless, naive girl.* **2** without skill; clumsy. ■ **art·less·ly** adv.

art nou·veau /är(t) nōō'vō/ ▸ n. a style of art and architecture of the late 19th and early 20th centuries, having intricate linear designs and flowing curves.

art·sy /'ärtsē/ (also **arty** /'ärtē/) ▸ adj. (**artsier, artsiest**) informal interested or involved in the arts in an affected way. ■ **art·si·ness** n.

art·work /'ärtˌwərk/ ▸ n. illustrations for inclusion in a publication.

a·ru·gu·la /ə'rōōgələ/ ▸ n. an edible Mediterranean plant eaten in salads.

ar·um /'ärəm/ ▸ n. jack-in-the-pulpit or a related plant.

ar·um lil·y ▸ n. a tall lilylike African plant of the arum family.

Ar·y·an /'e(ə)rēən, 'ar-, -yən/ ▸ n. **1** a member of a people speaking an Indo-European language who spread into northern India in the 2nd millennium BC. **2** the language of the ancient Aryans. **3** (in Nazi ideology) a non-Jewish person of Caucasian race. ▸ adj. relating to the Aryan people.

As ▸ symbol the chemical element arsenic.

as /az/ ▸ adv. used in comparisons to refer to the extent or amount of something. ▸ conj. **1** while. **2** in the way that. **3** because. **4** even though. ▸ prep. **1** in the role of; being: *a job as a cook.* **2** while; when.
– PHRASES **as for** with regard to. **as yet** until now or that time.

USAGE
Some people think that you should say *he's not as shy as I* (rather than *he's not as shy as me*), but this sounds stilted and is now rarely used in normal speech. For more information, see the note at PERSONAL PRONOUN.

a·sa·fet·i·da /ˌasəˈfetidə/ (Brit. **asafoetida**) ▸ n. an unpleasant-smelling gum obtained from the roots of a plant, used in herbal medicine and Indian cooking.

a·sa·na /ˈäsənə/ ▸ n. a posture adopted in hatha yoga.

ASAP ▸ abbr. as soon as possible.

as·bes·tos /asˈbestəs, az-/ ▸ n. a fibrous silicate mineral used in fire-resistant and insulating materials.

as·bes·to·sis /ˌasbesˈtōsis, ˌaz-/ ▸ n. a serious lung disease, often accompanied by cancer, resulting from breathing asbestos dust.

as·cend /əˈsend/ ▸ v. **1** go up; rise or climb: *I ascended the stairs.* **2** move up in rank or status. ■ **as·cend·er** n.

as·cend·ant /əˈsendənt/ ▸ adj. **1** rising in power or influence. **2** Astrology (of a planet or sign of the zodiac) just above the eastern horizon. ■ **as·cend·an·cy** n.
– PHRASES **in the ascendant** rising in power or influence.

as·cen·sion /əˈsensHən/ ▸ n. **1** the action of rising in status. **2** (**Ascension**) the ascent of Jesus into heaven after the Resurrection.

as·cent /əˈsent/ ▸ n. **1** an act of ascending something: *the first ascent of the Matterhorn.* **2** an upward slope.

as·cer·tain /ˌasərˈtān/ ▸ v. find out for certain: *an investigation to ascertain the cause of the accident.* ■ **as·cer·tain·a·ble** adj. **as·cer·tain·ment** n.

as·cet·ic /əˈsetik/ ▸ adj. strictly self-disciplined and avoiding any pleasures or luxuries. ▸ n. an ascetic person. ■ **as·cet·i·cism** /-ˌsizəm/ n.

ASCII /ˈaskē/ ▸ abbr. Computing American Standard Code for Information Interchange.

a·scor·bic ac·id /əˈskôrbik/ ▸ n. vitamin C.

as·cot /ˈasˌkät, -kət/ ▸ n. a man's broad silk necktie.

as·cribe /əˈskrīb/ ▸ v. (**ascribe something to**) **1** consider something to be caused by: *he ascribed his fits of depression to the divorce.* **2** consider that a particular quality belongs to someone or something: *those who ascribe great importance to his theories.* ■ **as·crip·tion** n.

ASEAN /ˈäsēˌän, -as-/ ▸ abbr. Association of Southeast Asian Nations.

a·sep·tic /āˈseptik/ ▸ adj. free from harmful bacteria, viruses, and other microorganisms.

a·sex·u·al /āˈsekshŌŌəl/ ▸ adj. **1** not having sexual feelings or associations. **2** (of reproduction) not involving sexual activity. **3** not having sexual organs. ■ **a·sex·u·al·ly** adv.

ash¹ /asH/ ▸ n. **1** the powder remaining after something has been burned. **2** (**ashes**) the remains of a human body after cremation.

■ **ash·y** adj.

ash² ▸ n. a tree with winged fruits and hard pale wood.

a·shamed /əˈsHāmd/ ▸ adj. feeling embarrassed or guilty.

A·shan·ti /əˈsHäntē, əˈsHantē/ (also **Asante** /əˈsäntē, əˈsantē/) ▸ n. (pl. same) a member of a people of south central Ghana.

ash blonde (also **ash blond**) ▸ adj. very pale blond.

ash·en /ˈasHən/ ▸ adj. very pale as a result of shock, fear, or illness.

Ash·ke·naz·i /ˌasHkəˈnazē, ˌäsHkəˈnäzē/ ▸ n. (pl. **Ashkenazim** /-ˈnazim, -ˈnäzim/) a Jew of central or eastern European descent. Compare with SEPHARDI.

ash·lar /ˈasHlər/ ▸ n. large square-cut stones used as the surface layer of a wall.

a·shore /əˈsHôr/ ▸ adv. to or on the shore or land.

ash·ram /ˈäsHrəm/ ▸ n. a Hindu religious retreat or community.

ash·tan·ga /əsHˈtäNGə/ ▸ n. a type of yoga based on eight principles and consisting of a series of poses performed in rapid succession, combined with deep, controlled breathing.

ash·tray /ˈasHˌtrā/ ▸ n. a small receptacle for tobacco ash and cigarette butts.

Ash Wednes·day ▸ n. the first day of Lent in the Christian Church.

A·sian /ˈāzHən/ ▸ n. a person from Asia or a person of Asian descent. ▸ adj. relating to Asia.

A·si·at·ic /ˌāzHēˈatik, ˌāzē-/ ▸ adj. relating to Asia.

USAGE
Although it is standard in scientific and technical use, **Asiatic** can be offensive when used of individual people: use **Asian** instead.

a·side /əˈsīd/ ▸ adv. **1** to one side; out of the way. **2** in reserve. ▸ n. **1** an actor's remark spoken to the audience rather than the other characters. **2** a remark that is not directly related to the main subject of discussion.
– PHRASES **aside from** apart from.

A-side ▸ n. the side of a pop single regarded as the main one.

as·i·nine /ˈasəˌnīn/ ▸ adj. extremely stupid or foolish.

-asis (also **-iasis**) ▸ suffix forming the names of diseases: *psoriasis.*

ask /ask/ ▸ v. **1** say something in order to get an answer or some information. **2** say that one wants someone to do, give, or allow something: *she asked me to help her.* **3** (**ask for**) request to speak to someone. **4** expect or demand something from someone: *you are asking too much of her.* **5** invite someone to a social occasion. **6** (**ask someone out**) invite someone out on a date. **7** (**ask after**) chiefly Brit. make polite inquiries about someone's health and well-being.
– PHRASES **for the asking** for little or no effort or cost: *the job was his for the asking.*

a·skance /əˈskans/ ▸ adv. with a suspicious or disapproving look.

a·skew /əˈskyŌŌ/ ▸ adv. & adj. not straight or level.

ask·ing price ▸ n. the price at which something is offered for sale.

a·slant /əˈslant/ ▸ adv. & prep. at or across at a slant.

a·sleep /əˈslēp/ ▸ adj. & adv. in or into a state of sleep.

a·so·cial /āˈsōsHəl/ ▸ adj. avoiding social

interaction; inconsiderate of or hostile to others.

asp /asp/ ▶ n. **1** a small viper with an upturned snout. **2** the Egyptian cobra.

as·par·a·gus /əˈsparəgəs/ ▶ n. a vegetable consisting of the tender young shoots of a tall plant.

as·par·tame /ˈaspärˌtām/ ▶ n. a low-calorie artificial sweetener.

ASPCA ▶ abbr. American Society for the Prevention of Cruelty to Animals.

as·pect /ˈaspekt/ ▶ n. **1** a particular part or feature of something: *a training course covering all aspects of the business.* **2** a particular appearance or quality: *the black eyepatch gave his face a sinister aspect.* **3** the side of a building facing a particular direction.

as·pect ra·tio ▶ n. the ratio of the width to the height of an image on a television screen.

as·pen /ˈaspən/ ▶ n. a poplar tree with small rounded leaves.

As·per·ger's syn·drome /ˈaspərgərz/ ▶ n. a mild form of autism.

as·per·i·ty /əˈsperitē/ ▶ n. harshness of tone or manner.

as·per·sions /əˈspərzнən/ ▶ pl.n. (in phrase **cast aspersions on**) make critical or unpleasant remarks about: *no one is casting aspersions on you or your officers.*

as·phalt /ˈasfôlt/ ▶ n. a dark tarlike substance used in surfacing roads or waterproofing buildings.

as·pho·del /ˈasfəˌdel/ ▶ n. a plant of the lily family with clusters of yellow or white flowers on a long stem.

as·phyx·i·a /asˈfiksēə/ ▶ n. a condition arising when the body is deprived of oxygen, causing unconsciousness or death.

as·phyx·i·ate /asˈfiksēˌāt/ ▶ v. **1** kill someone by depriving them of oxygen. **2** die as a result of a lack of oxygen. ■ **as·phyx·i·a·tion** /asˌfiksēˈāsнən/ n.

as·pic /ˈaspik/ ▶ n. a savory jelly made with meat stock.

as·pi·dis·tra /ˌaspiˈdistrə/ ▶ n. a plant of the lily family with broad tapering leaves.

as·pir·ant /ˈaspərənt, əˈspī-/ ▶ n. a person with strong ambitions to do or be something.

as·pi·rate ▶ v. /ˈaspəˌrāt/ **1** pronounce a word with the sound of the letter *h* at the start. **2** remove fluid from a part of the body using suction. **3** technical inhale. ▶ n. /ˈasp(ə)rit/ the sound of the letter *h*.

as·pi·ra·tion /ˌaspəˈrāsнən/ ▶ n. a strong desire to do or have something; an ambition: *he never showed any aspirations for political office.*

as·pi·ra·tion·al /ˌaspəˈrāsнənl/ ▶ adj. **1** having a strong desire to do or have something: *young, aspirational women.* **2** referring or relating to something that people strongly desire to do or have: *an aspirational lifestyle.*

as·pi·ra·tor /ˈaspəˌrātər/ ▶ n. an instrument or device for removing fluid from a part of the body by suction.

as·pire /əˈspī(ə)r/ ▶ v. have strong ambitions to be or do something: *she aspired to study at Cambridge.* ■ **as·pir·ing** adj.

as·pi·rin /ˈasp(ə)rin/ ▶ n. (pl. same or **aspirins**) a medicine used in tablet form to relieve pain and reduce fever and inflammation.

ass¹ /as/ ▶ n. a donkey or related small wild

horse. **2** informal a stupid person.

ass² ▶ n. vulgar slang **1** a person's buttocks or anus. **2** a stupid, irritating, or contemptible person. **3** women regarded as a source of sexual gratification.

as·sail /əˈsāl/ ▶ v. **1** attack someone or something violently. **2** (of an unpleasant feeling) come upon someone suddenly and strongly: *she was assailed by doubts and regrets.*

as·sail·ant /əˈsālənt/ ▶ n. an attacker.

as·sas·sin /əˈsasin/ ▶ n. a person who assassinates someone.

as·sas·si·nate /əˈsasəˌnāt/ ▶ v. murder an important person for political or religious reasons. ■ **as·sas·si·na·tion** /ə,sasəˈnāsнən/ n.

as·sault /əˈsôlt/ ▶ n. **1** a violent attack. **2** Law an act that threatens physical harm to a person. **3** a determined attempt to do something difficult: *a winter assault on Mt. Everest.* ▶ v. attack someone violently.

as·sault and bat·ter·y ▶ n. Law the action of threatening a person together with making physical contact with them.

as·sault ri·fle ▶ n. a lightweight rifle that may be set to fire automatically or semiautomatically.

as·say /ˈaˌsā, aˈsā/ ▶ n. the process of testing a metal or ore to establish its composition or purity. ▶ v. **1** test a metal or ore to establish its composition or purity. **2** old use attempt.

as·sem·blage /əˈsemblij/ ▶ n. **1** a collection or gathering of things or people: *a rich assemblage of 16th-century paintings.* **2** something made of pieces fitted together.

as·sem·ble /əˈsembəl/ ▶ v. **1** come or bring together: *a crowd assembled outside the gates.* **2** fit together the component parts of: *supplied in flat-pack form, the shed is easily assembled.*

as·sem·bler /əˈsemblər/ ▶ n. **1** a person who assembles a machine or its parts. **2** Computing a program for converting instructions written in low-level symbolic code into machine code.

as·sem·bly /əˈsemblē/ ▶ n. (pl. **assemblies**) **1** a group of people gathered together. **2** a body of people with powers to make decisions and laws. **3** a regular gathering of teachers and students in a school. **4** the action of assembling the component parts of something.

as·sem·bly line ▶ n. a series of workers and machines in a factory that assemble the component parts of identical products in successive stages.

as·sent /əˈsent/ ▶ n. approval or agreement. ▶ v. agree to a request or suggestion: *both parties assented to the terms of the agreement.*

as·sert /əˈsərt/ ▶ v. **1** state a fact or belief confidently and firmly: *he asserted that he had no intention of stepping down.* **2** make other people recognize something by behaving confidently and forcefully: *a young woman seeking to assert her independence.* **3** (**assert oneself**) behave in a confident and forceful way.

as·ser·tion /əˈsərsнən/ ▶ n. **1** a confident and forceful statement. **2** the action of asserting something.

as·ser·tive /əˈsərtiv/ ▶ adj. having or showing a confident and forceful personality. ■ **as·ser·tive·ly** adv. **as·ser·tive·ness** n.

as·ses /ˈasiz/ ▶ plural of ASS¹, ASS².

as·sess /əˈses/ ▶ v. **1** calculate or estimate the value, importance, or quality of: *a survey to*

assess the damage caused by the oil spill. **2** set the value of a tax for a person or property.
■ **as·sess·ment** n. **as·ses·sor** n.

as·set /'aset/ ▶ n. **1** a useful or valuable thing or person. **2** (**assets**) the property owned by a person or company.

as·set-strip·ping ▶ n. the practice of taking over a company that is in financial difficulty and then selling its assets separately at a profit.

as·sev·er·a·tion /əˌsevəˈrāSHən/ ▶ n. formal a solemn or emphatic declaration or statement.
■ **as·sev·er·ate** /əˈsevəˌrāt/ v.

ass·hole /'asˌhōl/ ▶ n. vulgar slang **1** the anus. **2** an irritating or contemptible person.

as·sid·u·ous /əˈsijəwəs/ ▶ adj. showing or done with great care and thoroughness: *he was assiduous in his duties.* ■ **as·si·du·i·ty** /ˌasiˈd(y)o͞oitē/ n. **as·sid·u·ous·ly** adv.

as·sign /əˈsīn/ ▶ v. **1** give a task or duty to someone: *work duties were assigned at the beginning of the shift.* **2** give someone a job or task: *she had been assigned to a new post.* **3** regard something as belonging to or being caused by: *a mosaic assigned to the late third century* BC.

as·sig·na·tion /ˌasigˈnāSHən/ ▶ n. a secret meeting, especially one between lovers.

as·sign·ee /əˌsīˈnē/ ▶ n. chiefly Law **1** a person to whom a right or liability is legally transferred. **2** a person appointed to act for another.

as·sign·ment /əˈsīnmənt/ ▶ n. **1** a task allocated to someone as part of a job or course of study. **2** the assigning of a job or task to someone.

as·sim·i·late /əˈsiməˌlāt/ ▶ v. **1** take in and understand information or ideas. **2** absorb and integrate people or ideas into a wider society or culture: *they were assimilated into mainstream American society.* **3** absorb and digest food or nutrients. ■ **as·sim·i·la·ble** /-ləbəl/ adj. **as·sim·i·la·tion** /əˌsiməˈlāSHən/ n.

as·sist /əˈsist/ ▶ v. give help or support to someone.

as·sis·tance /əˈsistəns/ ▶ n. help or support.

as·sis·tant /əˈsistənt/ ▶ n. **1** a person who ranks below a senior person. **2** a person who provides help in a particular role or type of work: *an administrative assistant.*

as·size /əˈsīz/ (also **assizes**) ▶ n. historical a court that sat at intervals in each county of England and Wales.

ass·kick·ing informal ▶ n. forceful or aggressive behavior; an instance of this; a beating.
▶ adj. dominant or powerful, especially exceptionally so: *she makes an ass-kicking hot sauce.*

as·so·ci·ate ▶ v. /əˈsōsēˌāt, -SHē-/ **1** connect in one's mind: *I associated wealth with freedom.* **2** frequently meet or have dealings with: *she began associating with Marxists.* **3** (**be associated with** or **associate oneself with**) be involved with. ▶ n. /-it/ a work partner or colleague. ▶ adj. /-it/ **1** connected with an organization or business. **2** belonging to an organization but not having full membership.

as·so·ci·a·tion /əˌsōsēˈāSHən, -SHē-/ ▶ n. **1** a group of people organized for a joint purpose. **2** a connection or relationship: *his close association with the university.* **3** an idea, memory, or feeling that is connected to someone or something: *the name had unpleasant associations for him.*

as·so·ci·a·tive /əˈsōsēˌātiv, -SHē-, -sēətiv, -SHətiv/ ▶ adj. **1** relating to or involving association.

2 Mathematics producing the same result however quantities are grouped, as long as their order remains the same, as in the equation $(a \times b) \times c = a \times (b \times c)$.

as·so·nance /'asənəns/ ▶ n. the rhyming of vowels only (e.g., *hide, line*) or of consonants but not vowels (e.g., *cold, killed*).

as·sort·ed /əˈsôrtid/ ▶ adj. of various different sorts put together: *a plate of assorted vegetables.*

as·sort·ment /əˈsôrtmənt/ ▶ n. a collection of different things: *an assortment of boots and shoes.*

as·suage /əˈswāj/ ▶ v. **1** make an unpleasant feeling less intense: *his letter assuaged the fears of most members.* **2** satisfy an appetite or desire.

as·sume /əˈso͞om/ ▶ v. **1** accept as true or being the case without having proof: *he assumed she was married.* **2** take responsibility or control. **3** begin to have: *foreign trade has assumed greater importance in recent years.* **4** pretend to have: *he assumed an air of indifference.*

as·sum·ing /əˈso͞omiNG/ ▶ conj. based on the assumption that.

as·sump·tion /əˈsəm(p)SHən/ ▶ n. **1** a thing that is assumed to be true. **2** the assuming of responsibility or control. **3** (**Assumption**) the taking up of the Virgin Mary into heaven, according to Roman Catholic doctrine.

as·sur·ance /əˈSHo͞orəns/ ▶ n. **1** a statement or promise intended to give someone confidence. **2** confidence in one's own abilities. **3** chiefly Brit. life insurance.

as·sure /əˈSHo͞or/ ▶ v. **1** tell someone that something is definitely true or will be the case: *she assured him that everything was under control.* **2** make something certain to happen: *victory would assure their promotion.* **3** Brit. insure a person's life.

as·sured /əˈSHo͞ord/ ▶ adj. **1** having or showing confidence: *her calm, assured voice.* **2** protected against change or danger: *an assured tenancy.*
■ **as·sur·ed·ly** /əˈSHo͞oridlē/ adv.

As·syr·i·an /əˈsi(ə)rēən/ ▶ n. an inhabitant of Assyria, an ancient country in what is now Iraq.

as·ta·tine /'astəˌtēn, -tin/ ▶ n. a very unstable radioactive chemical element belonging to the halogen group.

as·ter /'astər/ ▶ n. a garden plant of the daisy family, typically having purple or pink flowers.

as·ter·isk /'astəˌrisk/ ▶ n. a symbol (*) used in text as a pointer to a note elsewhere.

a·stern /əˈstərn/ ▶ adv. behind or toward the rear of a ship or aircraft.

as·ter·oid /'astəˌroid/ ▶ n. a small rocky planet orbiting the sun.

asth·ma /'azmə/ ▶ n. a medical condition causing difficulty in breathing. ■ **asth·mat·ic** /azˈmatik/ adj. & n.

a·stig·ma·tism /əˈstigməˌtizəm/ ▶ n. a defect in an eye or lens that prevents it from focusing properly. ■ **as·tig·mat·ic** /ˌastigˈmatik/ adj.

a·stil·be /əˈstilbē/ ▶ n. a plant with plumes of tiny white, pink, or red flowers.

a·stir /əˈstər/ ▶ adj. **1** in a state of excited movement. **2** awake and out of bed.

as·ton·ish /əˈstäniSH/ ▶ v. surprise or impress someone greatly. ■ **as·ton·ished** adj. **as·ton·ish·ing** adj. **as·ton·ish·ment** n.

as·tound /əˈstound/ ▶ v. shock or greatly surprise someone. ■ **as·tound·ed** adj. **as·tound·ing** adj.

as·tral /ˈastrəl/ ▸ adj. relating to the stars.

a·stray /əˈstrā/ ▸ adv. away from the right path or direction.

a·stride /əˈstrīd/ ▸ prep. & adv. 1 with a leg on each side of something. 2 (as adv.) (of a person's legs) wide apart.

as·trin·gent /əˈstrinjənt/ ▸ adj. 1 (of a substance) making body tissue contract. 2 harsh or severe in manner or style: *her astringent comments.* ▸ n. an astringent lotion used medically or as a cosmetic. ■ **as·trin·gen·cy** n. **as·trin·gent·ly** adv.

astro- ▸ comb.form relating to the stars or to outer space: *astronaut.*

as·tro·bi·o·lo·gy /ˌastrōbīˈäləjē/ ▸ n. the branch of biology concerned with the discovery or study of life on other planets or in space. ■ **as·tro·bi·o·lo·gist** n.

as·tro·labe /ˈastrəˌlāb/ ▸ n. an instrument formerly used for measuring the altitudes of stars and calculating latitude in navigation.

as·trol·o·gy /əˈsträləjē/ ▸ n. the study of the supposed influence of stars and planets on human affairs. ■ **as·trol·o·ger** n. **as·tro·log·i·cal** /ˌastrəˈläjikəl/ adj. **as·tro·log·i·cal·ly** /ˌastrəˈläjik(ə)lē/ adv.

as·tro·naut /ˈastrəˌnôt/ ▸ n. a person trained to travel in a spacecraft.

as·tro·nau·tics /ˌastrəˈnôtiks/ ▸ pl.n. (treated as sing.) the science and technology of space travel and exploration.

as·tro·nom·i·cal /ˌastrəˈnämikəl/ ▸ adj. 1 relating to astronomy. 2 informal extremely large: *astronomical fees.* ■ **as·tro·nom·ic** adj. **as·tro·nom·i·cal·ly** /-ik(ə)lē/ adv.

as·tro·nom·i·cal u·nit ▸ n. a unit of measurement equal to the mean distance from the earth to the sun, 149.6 million kilometers.

as·tron·o·my /əˈstränəmē/ ▸ n. the science of stars, planets, and the universe. ■ **as·tron·o·mer** n.

as·tro·phys·ics /ˌastrōˈfiziks/ ▸ pl.n. (treated as sing.) the branch of astronomy concerned with the physical nature of stars and planets. ■ **as·tro·phys·i·cal** adj. **as·tro·phys·i·cist** /-ˈisist/ n.

As·tro·Turf /ˈastrōˌtərf/ ▸ n. trademark an artificial grass surface, used for sports fields.

as·tute /əˈst(y)o͞ot/ ▸ adj. good at making accurate judgments; shrewd. ■ **as·tute·ly** adv. **as·tute·ness** n.

a·sun·der /əˈsəndər/ ▸ adv. literary apart.

a·sy·lum /əˈsīləm/ ▸ n. 1 protection from danger, especially for people who leave their own country as a result of suffering persecution for their political beliefs. 2 dated an institution for the care of people who are mentally ill.

a·sym·met·ri·cal /ˌāsəˈmetrikəl/ ▸ adj. having sides or parts that do not correspond in size, shape, or arrangement; lacking symmetry. ■ **a·sym·met·ric** adj. **a·sym·met·ri·cal·ly** adv.

a·sym·me·try /āˈsimitrē/ ▸ n. (pl. **asymmetries**) lack of symmetry between the sides or parts of something.

a·symp·to·mat·ic /ˌāsim(p)tə'matik/ ▸ adj. producing or showing no symptoms of a disease or condition.

a·syn·chro·nous /āˈsiNGkrənəs/ ▸ adj. not existing or occurring at the same time. ■ **a·syn·chro·nous·ly** adv. **a·syn·chro·ny** n.

At ▸ symbol the chemical element astatine.

at /at/ ▸ prep. (used to express:) 1 location, arrival, or time. 2 a value, rate, or point on a scale. 3 a

state or condition. 4 the object or target of a look, shot, action, or plan. – PHRASES **at that** in addition; furthermore.

at·a·vis·tic /ˌatəˈvistik/ ▸ adj. related or reverting to the feelings or behavior of the earliest humans: *an atavistic fear of the dark.* ■ **at·a·vism** /ˈatəˌvizəm/ n. **at·a·vis·ti·cal·ly** /-ˈtik(ə)lē/ adv.

a·tax·i·a /əˈtaksēə/ ▸ n. Medicine the loss of the ability to control or coordinate one's movements.

ATC ▸ abbr. 1 air traffic control or controller. 2 Air Training Corps.

ate /āt/ ▸ past of EAT.

at·el·ier /ˌatlˈyā/ ▸ n. a workshop or studio used by an artist or designer.

a·the·ism /ˈāTHēˌizəm/ ▸ n. disbelief in the existence of a god or gods. ■ **a·the·ist** n. **a·the·is·tic** /ˌāTHēˈistik/ adj.

A·the·ni·an /əˈTHēnēən/ ▸ n. a person from Athens in Greece. ▸ adj. relating to Athens.

ath·er·o·scle·ro·sis /ˌaTHərōskləˈrōsis/ ▸ n. a disease of the arteries in which fatty material is deposited on their inner walls. ■ **ath·er·o·scle·rot·ic** /-ˈrätik/ adj.

ath·lete /ˈaTHˌlēt/ ▸ n. 1 a person who is good at sports. 2 a person who competes in track and field events.

ath·lete's foot ▸ n. a contagious fungal infection affecting the skin between the toes.

ath·let·ic /aTHˈletik/ ▸ adj. 1 fit and active; good at sports. 2 relating to athletes or athletics. ■ **ath·let·i·cal·ly** /-ik(ə)lē/ adv. **ath·let·i·cism** /-ˌsizəm/ n.

ath·let·ics /aTHˈletiks/ ▸ pl.n. (usu. treated as sing.) 1 physical sports and games of any kind. 2 chiefly Brit. the sport of competing in track and field events.

a·thwart /əˈTHwôrt/ ▸ prep. & adv. from side to side of something; across.

At·kins di·et /ˈatkinz/ ▸ n. trademark a high-protein, high-fat diet in which carbohydrates are severely restricted.

At·lan·tic /ətˈlantik/ ▸ adj. relating to the Atlantic Ocean.

at·las /ˈatləs/ ▸ n. a book of maps or charts.

ATM ▸ abbr. automated teller machine.

at·mos·phere /ˈatməsˌfi(ə)r/ ▸ n. 1 the gases surrounding the earth or another planet. 2 the quality of the air in a place: *the smoky atmosphere of an industrial town.* 3 an overall tone or mood: *a hotel with a friendly, relaxed atmosphere.* 4 a unit of pressure equal to the pressure of the atmosphere at sea level, 101,325 pascals (roughly 14.7 pounds per square inch).

at·mos·pher·ic /ˌatməsˈfi(ə)rik, -ˈferik/ ▸ adj. 1 relating to the atmosphere of the earth or another planet. 2 creating a distinctive mood, especially one of romance, nostalgia, or excitement: *a very atmospheric location.* ■ **at·mos·pher·i·cal·ly** adv.

at·mos·pher·ics /ˌatməsˈfi(ə)riks, -ˈferiks/ ▸ pl.n. electrical disturbances in the atmosphere that interfere with telecommunications.

at·oll /ˈaˌtôl, ˈaˌtäl, ˈāˌtôl, ˈāˌtäl/ ▸ n. a ring-shaped coral reef or chain of islands.

at·om /ˈatəm/ ▸ n. 1 the smallest particle of a chemical element that can exist. 2 an extremely small amount: *she did not have an atom of strength left.*

at·om bomb ▸ n. (also **atomic bomb**) a bomb whose explosive power comes from the fission (splitting) of the nuclei of atoms.

a·tom·ic /əˈtämik/ ▸ adj. 1 relating to an atom or

atoms. **2** relating to nuclear energy or weapons.

a·tom·ic mass u·nit ► n. a unit of mass used to express atomic and molecular weights, equal to one twelfth of the mass of an atom of carbon-12.

a·tom·ic num·ber ► n. the number of protons in the nucleus of a chemical element's atom, which determines its place in the periodic table.

a·tom·ic the·o·ry ► n. the theory that all matter is made up of tiny indivisible particles (atoms).

a·tom·ic weight ► n. another term for RELATIVE ATOMIC MASS.

at·om·ize /'atə,mīz/ ► v. convert a substance into very fine particles or droplets. ■ **at·om·i·za·tion** /,atəmə'zāSHən/ n.

at·om·iz·er /'atə,mīzər/ ► n. a device for sending out water, perfume, or other liquids as a fine spray.

a·ton·al /ā'tōnl/ ► adj. not written in any musical key. ■ **a·to·nal·i·ty** /,ātō'nalitē/ n.

a·tone /ə'tōn/ ► v. (**atone for**) make amends for a sin, crime, or other wrongdoing.

a·tone·ment /ə'tōnmənt/ ► n. **1** the action of making amends for a sin, crime, or other wrongdoing. **2** (**the Atonement**) the reconciliation of God and humankind brought about through the death of Jesus.

a·top /ə'täp/ ► prep. on the top of.

ATP ► abbr. Biochemistry adenosine triphosphate.

at-risk ► adj. vulnerable, especially to abuse or delinquency: *a church-run school for the most at-risk children.*

a·tri·um /'ātrēəm/ ► n. (pl. atria /'ātrēə/ or atriums) **1** a central hall rising through several stories and having a glazed roof. **2** an open area in the center of an ancient Roman house. **3** each of the two upper cavities of the heart. ■ **a·tri·al** /'ātrēəl/ adj.

a·tro·cious /ə'trōSHəs/ ► adj. **1** horrifyingly cruel or wicked. **2** extremely bad or unpleasant. ■ **a·tro·cious·ly** adv.

a·troc·i·ty /ə'träsitē/ ► n. (pl. atrocities) an extremely cruel or wicked act.

at·ro·phy /'atrəfē/ ► v. (atrophies, atrophying, atrophied) **1** (of body tissue or an organ) waste away. **2** gradually become weaker: *the local shipbuilding industry had atrophied.* ► n. the condition or process of atrophying.

at·ro·pine /'atrə,pēn/ ► n. a poisonous compound found in deadly nightshade.

at·tach /ə'taCH/ ► v. **1** fasten or join one thing to another. **2** include a condition as part of an agreement. **3** attribute importance or value to: *they attached great importance to this research.* **4** appoint someone for special or temporary duties: *I was attached to another working group.* ■ **at·tach·a·ble** adj.

at·ta·ché /,atə'SHā, ,ata-/ ► n. a person on an ambassador's staff who has a specific responsibility or works in a particular area of activity: *a military attaché.*

at·ta·ché case ► n. a small, flat briefcase for carrying documents.

at·tached /ə'taCHt/ ► adj. very fond of someone: *Mark became increasingly attached to Tara.*

at·tach·ment /ə'taCHmənt/ ► n. **1** an extra part attached to something in order to perform a particular function: *a detachable roof rack with attachments for carrying bikes.* **2** a computer file sent with an email. **3** the action of attaching one thing to another. **4** affection or fondness.

at·tack /ə'tak/ ► v. **1** take violent action against someone or something. **2** (of a disease, chemical, etc.) act harmfully on: *meningitis attacks the brain.* **3** criticize fiercely and publicly: *he attacked the government's defense policy.* **4** begin to deal with a problem or task in a determined way. **5** (in sports) attempt to score goals or points. ► n. **1** an act of attacking someone or something. **2** a sudden short period of an illness: *a bad attack of the flu.* **3** the players in a team whose role is to attack. ■ **at·tack·er** n.

at·tain /ə'tān/ ► v. **1** succeed in achieving something one has worked for: *he attained the rank of brigadier.* **2** reach a particular age, size, or level: *the cheetah can attain speeds of 68 mph.* ■ **at·tain·a·ble** adj.

at·tain·der /ə'tāndər/ ► n. historical the forfeiting of land and civil rights as a result of being sentenced to death.
– PHRASES **bill of attainder** a piece of legislation inflicting attainder without judicial process.

at·tain·ment /ə'tānmənt/ ► n. **1** the achieving of something. **2** something that one has achieved: *his educational attainments.*

at·tar /'atər/ ► n. a sweet-smelling oil made from rose petals.

at·tempt /ə'tem(p)t/ ► v. make an effort to do something. ► n. an effort to do something.

at·tend /ə'tend/ ► v. **1** be present at an event. **2** go regularly to a school, church, etc. **3** (**attend to**) deal with or pay attention to: *he had important business to attend to.* **4** occur at the same time as or as a result of: *the unfortunate events that attended their arrival.* **5** escort and assist an important person. ■ **at·tend·ee** /ə,ten'dē, ,aten-/ n. **at·tend·er** n.

at·tend·ance /ə'tendəns/ ► n. **1** the action of attending a place or event: *her infrequent attendance at church.* **2** the number of people present at a particular occasion.

at·tend·ant /ə'tendənt/ ► n. **1** a person employed to provide a service to the public: *a museum attendant.* **2** an assistant to an important person. ► adj. occurring at the same time or as a result of: *obesity and its attendant health problems.*

at·ten·tion /ə'tenSHən/ ► n. **1** the mental faculty of considering or taking notice of someone or something: *he turned his attention to the educational system.* **2** special care or consideration: *a child in need of medical attention.* **3** (**attentions**) things done to express an interest in or please someone: *she was flattered by his attentions.* **4** an erect position taken by a soldier, with the feet together and the arms straight down the sides of the body.

at·ten·tion def·i·cit dis·or·der ► n. a condition found in children, marked by hyperactivity, poor concentration, and learning difficulties.

at·ten·tive /ə'tentiv/ ► adj. **1** paying close attention to something: *an attentive audience.* **2** considerate and helpful: *the staff were friendly and attentive.* ■ **at·ten·tive·ly** adv. **at·ten·tive·ness** n.

at·ten·u·ate /ə'tenyōō,āt/ ► v. **1** make something weaker or less effective. **2** make someone or something thin or thinner. ■ **at·ten·u·a·tion** /ə,tenyōō'āSHən/ n.

at·test /ə'test/ ► v. **1** provide or act as clear evidence of: *the collection attests to his interest in mythology.* **2** declare that something is true or is the case. ■ **at·tes·ta·tion** /,ate'stāSHən/ n.

At·tic /'atik/ ▶ adj. relating to Attica in Greece, or to ancient Athens.

at·tic /'atik/ ▶ n. a space or room inside the roof of a building.

at·tire /ə'tī(ə)r/ formal or literary ▶ n. clothes of a particular kind: *formal evening attire.* ▶ v. (**be attired**) be dressed in clothes of a particular kind: *he was attired in a dark suit.*

at·ti·tude /'ati̱t(y) o͞od/ ▶ n. **1** a way of thinking or feeling: *his attitude to the job had changed.* **2** a position of the body. **3** informal self-confident or uncooperative behavior. ■ **at·ti·tu·di·nal** /ˌati't(y)o͞odn-əl/ adj.

at·ti·tu·di·nize /ˌati't(y)o͞odnˌīz/ ▶ v. adopt or express an attitude for effect.

at·tor·ney /ə'tərnē/ ▶ n. (pl. **attorneys**) **1** a person appointed to act for another in legal matters. **2** a lawyer.

at·tor·ney gen·er·al ▶ n. (pl. **attorneys general**) the most senior legal officer in some countries or states.

at·tract /ə'trakt/ ▶ v. **1** cause someone to come to a place or event or participate in an undertaking. **2** cause a particular reaction: *the decision attracted widespread criticism.* **3** cause someone to have a liking for or interest in: *many men were attracted to her.* **4** draw something closer by exerting a force on it. ■ **at·trac·tor** n.

at·tract·ant /ə'traktənt/ ▶ n. a substance that attracts something.

at·trac·tion /ə'traksʜən/ ▶ n. **1** the action or power of attracting someone or something. **2** an interesting or appealing feature or quality: *the apartment's main attraction is the large pool.* **3** Physics a force under the influence of which objects tend to move toward each other.

at·trac·tive /ə'traktiv/ ▶ adj. **1** pleasing in appearance: *a very attractive man.* **2** having features or qualities that arouse interest: *an attractive investment proposition.* **3** relating to attraction between physical objects. ■ **at·trac·tive·ly** adv. **at·trac·tive·ness** n.

at·trib·ute ▶ v. /ə'triˌbyo͞ot/ (**attribute something to**) regard something as belonging to, made, or being caused by: *he attributed his success to his parents' unwavering support.* ▶ n. /'atrəˌbyo͞ot/ **1** a characteristic quality or feature: *she has the key attributes of any journalist.* **2** an object that is traditionally associated with a person or thing: *the hourglass is an attribute of Father Time.* ■ **at·trib·ut·a·ble** /ə'tribyətəbəl/ adj. **at·tri·bu·tion** /ˌatrə'byo͞osʜən/ n.

at·trib·u·tive /ə'tribyətiv/ ▶ adj. Grammar (of an adjective) coming before the word that it describes, as *old* in *the old dog.* Contrasted with PREDICATIVE. ■ **at·trib·u·tive·ly** adv.

at·tri·tion /ə'trisʜən/ ▶ n. **1** the gradual reduction of something's strength or effectiveness through prolonged attack or pressure. **2** the wearing away of something by friction. ■ **at·tri·tion·al** adj.

at·tune /ə't(y)o͞on/ ▶ v. (**be attuned**) be receptive to and able to understand someone or something: *a royal family more attuned to the feelings of the public.*

Atty. ▶ abbr. attorney.

ATV ▶ abbr. all-terrain vehicle.

a·typ·i·cal /ā'tipikəl/ ▶ adj. not representative of a type, group, or class. ■ **a·typ·i·cal·ly** adv.

Au ▶ symbol the chemical element gold.

au·ber·gine /'ōbərˌzʜEn/ ▶ n. chiefly Brit. term for EGGPLANT.

au·bre·ti·a /ō'brēsʜ(ē)ə/ (also **aubrietia**) ▶ n. a trailing plant with purple, pink, or white flowers, commonly grown in rock gardens.

au·burn /'ōbərn/ ▶ n. a reddish-brown color.

auc·tion /'ōksʜən/ ▶ n. a public sale in which goods or property are sold to the highest bidder. ▶ v. sell an item or items at an auction.

auc·tion·eer /ˌōksʜə'ni(ə)r/ ▶ n. a person who conducts auctions.

au·da·cious /ō'dāsʜəs/ ▶ adj. **1** willing to take daring risks. **2** showing a lack of respect; rude or impudent. ■ **au·da·cious·ly** adv. **au·da·cious·ness** n. **au·dac·i·ty** /ō'dasitē/ n.

au·di·ble /'ōdəbəl/ ▶ adj. able to be heard. ■ **au·di·bil·i·ty** /ˌōdə'bilitē/ n. **au·di·bly** adv.

au·di·ence /'ōdēəns/ ▶ n. **1** the people gathered to see or listen to a play, concert, movie, etc. **2** a formal interview with a person in authority.

au·di·o /'ōdēˌō/ ▶ adj. relating to sound, especially when recorded, transmitted, or reproduced: *audio equipment.*

audio- ▶ comb.form relating to hearing or sound: *audiovisual.*

au·di·o fre·quen·cy /'ōdēˌō/ ▶ n. a frequency capable of being perceived by the human ear, generally between 20 and 20,000 hertz.

au·di·ol·o·gy /ˌōdē'äləjē/ ▶ n. the branch of science and medicine concerned with the sense of hearing. ■ **au·di·o·log·i·cal** /-ə'läjikəl/ adj. **au·di·ol·o·gist** /-jist/ n.

au·di·o·phile /'ōdē-ōˌfīl/ ▶ n. an enthusiast of recorded music.

au·di·o·tape /'ōdē-ōˌtāp/ ▶ n. magnetic tape on which sound can be recorded.

au·di·o·vis·u·al /ˌōdē-ō'vizʜo͞oəl/ ▶ adj. using both sight and sound.

au·dit /'ōdit/ ▶ n. an official examination of an organization's accounts. ▶ v. (**audits, auditing, audited**) make an official examination of an organization's accounts.

au·di·tion /ō'disʜən/ ▶ n. an interview for an actor, singer, etc., in which they give a practical demonstration of their skill. ▶ v. assess or be assessed by means of an audition.

au·di·tor /'ōditər/ ▶ n. **1** a person who carries an audit of an organization's accounts. **2** a listener.

au·di·to·ri·um /ˌōdi'tôrēəm/ ▶ n. (pl. **auditoriums** or **auditoria** /-'tôrēə/) **1** the part of a theater or hall in which the audience sits. **2** a large hall or room used for public gatherings, especially at a school.

au·di·to·ry /'ōdiˌtôrē/ ▶ adj. relating to the sense of hearing.

au fait /ˌō 'fe/ ▶ adj. (**au fait with**) having a good or detailed knowledge of something: *she was au fait with all the latest technology.*

au·ger /'ōgər/ ▶ n. a tool resembling a large corkscrew, for boring holes.

> **USAGE**
> On the confusion of **auger** and **augur**, see the note at AUGUR.

aught[1] /awt/ (also **ought**) ▶ pron. old use anything at all.

aught[2] ▶ n. **1** the digit 0; zero. **2** (**the aughts**) informal the years from 2000 to 2009, or corresponding years in another century.

aug·ment /'ōg'ment/ ▶ v. increase the amount, size, or value of: *many people work overtime* *to augment their income.* ■ **aug·men·ta·tion** /ˌôgmen'tāsHən/ **n.**

au grat·in /ˌō 'grätn, 'grätn, gra'taN/ ▶ **adj.** sprinkled with breadcrumbs and/or grated cheese and browned: *ratatouille au gratin.*

au·gur /'ôgər/ ▶ **v.** (augur **well/badly**) be a sign of a good or bad outcome: *the announcement does not augur well for the economy.*

> **USAGE**
> Do not confuse the verb **augur**, meaning 'be a sign of a good or bad outcome', with the noun **auger**, which is a tool for boring holes.

au·gu·ry /'ôgyərē/ ▶ **n.** (pl. **auguries**) a sign of what will happen in the future; an omen.

Au·gust /'ôgəst/ ▶ **n.** the eighth month of the year.

au·gust /ô'gəst/ ▶ **adj.** inspiring respect and admiration.

Au·gus·tan /ô'gəstən/ ▶ **adj.** 1 relating to or written during the reign of the Roman emperor Augustus. 2 relating to a classical style of 17th- and 18th-century English literature.

auk /ôk/ ▶ **n.** a black and white seabird with short wings.

auld lang syne /ôld laNG 'zīn/ ▶ **n.** times long past.

au na·tu·rel /ˌō ˌnacHə'rel/ ▶ **adj. & adv.** 1 in the most simple or natural way. 2 humorous naked.

aunt /ant, änt/ ▶ **n.** the sister of one's father or mother or the wife of one's uncle.

aunt·ie /'antē, 'än-/ (also **aunty**) ▶ **n.** (pl. **aunties**) informal a person's aunt.

au pair /ˌō 'pe(ə)r/ ▶ **n.** a foreign girl employed to look after children and help with housework in exchange for room and board.

au·ra /'ôrə/ ▶ **n.** (pl. **auras**) 1 the distinctive atmosphere or quality associated with someone or something: *the hotel had an aura of glamour and excitement.* 2 a supposed invisible force surrounding a living creature.

au·ral /'ôrəl/ ▶ **adj.** relating to the ears or the sense of hearing. ■ **au·ral·ly** **adv.**

> **USAGE**
> Do not confuse **aural** with **oral**. **Aural** means 'relating to the ears or sense of hearing' (*her new album provides pure aural pleasure*), whereas **oral** means 'spoken' or 'relating to the mouth' (*oral communication*).

au·re·ate /'ôrē-it, -ˌāt/ ▶ **adj.** made of or having the color of gold.

au·re·ole /'ôrēˌōl/ ▶ **n.** 1 (in paintings) a bright circle surrounding a person to indicate that they are holy. 2 a circle of light around the sun or moon.

au re·voir /ˌō rəv'wär/ ▶ **exclam.** goodbye.

au·ri·cle /'ôrikəl/ ▶ **n.** 1 the external part of the ear. 2 an upper cavity of the heart.

au·rochs /'ouräks, 'ô̩räks/ ▶ **n.** (pl. same) a large extinct European wild ox.

au·ro·ra /ə'rôrə, ô'rôrə/ ▶ **n.** a phenomenon characterized by streamers of colored light in the sky near the earth's magnetic poles, known as the Northern Lights (**aurora borealis**) near the North Pole and the Southern Lights (**aurora australis**) near the South Pole.

aus·cul·ta·tion /ˌôskəl'tāsHən/ ▶ **n.** listening to sounds from the heart, lungs, or other organs with a stethoscope.

aus·pice /'ôspis/ ▶ **n.** (in phrase **under the**

auspices of) with the support or protection of: *elections held under the auspices of the United Nations.*

aus·pi·cious /ô'spisHəs/ ▶ **adj.** suggesting that there is a good chance of success: *his new assignment has not had an auspicious start.* ■ **aus·pi·cious·ly** **adv.**

Aus·sie /'ôsē/ (also **Ozzie**) ▶ **n.** (pl. **Aussies**) **& adj.** informal Australia or Australian.

aus·tere /ô'sti(ə)r/ ▶ **adj.** 1 severe or strict in appearance or manner. 2 without comforts or luxuries: *their austere living conditions.* ■ **aus·tere·ly** **adv.**

aus·ter·i·ty /ô'steritē/ ▶ **n.** (pl. **austerities**) 1 strictness or severity of appearance or manner. 2 difficult economic conditions resulting from a cut in public spending.

aus·tral /'ôstrəl/ ▶ **adj.** technical of the southern hemisphere.

Aus·tral·a·sian /ˌôstrə'lāzHən/ ▶ **adj.** relating to Australasia, a region made up of Australia, New Zealand, and islands of the SW Pacific.

Aus·tral·ian /ô'strālyən/ ▶ **n.** a person from Australia. ▶ **adj.** relating to Australia.

Aus·tral·ian Rules ▶ **pl.n.** (treated as sing.) a form of football played on an oval field with teams of eighteen players.

Aus·tri·an /'ôstrēən/ ▶ **n.** a person from Austria. ▶ **adj.** relating to Austria.

au·tar·chy /'ôˌtärkē/ ▶ **n.** (pl. **autarchies**) 1 another term for **AUTOCRACY**. 2 variant spelling of **AUTARKY**.

au·tar·ky /'ôˌtärkē/ (also **autarchy**) ▶ **n.** (pl. **autarkies**) 1 economic independence or self-sufficiency. 2 an economically independent country, state, or society. ■ **au·tar·kic** /ô'tärkik/ **adj.**

au·teur /ô'tər/ ▶ **n.** a movie director regarded as the author of their movies.

au·then·tic /ô'THentik/ ▶ **adj.** 1 of undisputed origin; genuine: *the letter is now accepted as an authentic document.* 2 based on facts; accurate. ■ **au·then·ti·cal·ly** /-ik(ə)lē/ **adv.** **au·then·tic·i·ty** /ˌôTHen'tisitē/ **n.**

au·then·ti·cate /ô'THentiˌkāt/ ▶ **v.** prove or show something to be genuine. ■ **au·then·ti·ca·tion** /ôˌTHenti'kāsHən/ **n.** **au·then·ti·ca·tor** /-ˌkātər/ **n.**

au·thor /'ôTHər/ ▶ **n.** 1 a writer of a book or article. 2 a person who thinks of a plan or idea. ■ **au·thor·ess** /'ôTHəris/ **n.** **au·tho·ri·al** /ô'THôrēəl/ **adj.** **au·thor·ship** /'ôTHərˌsHip/ **n.**

au·thor·i·tar·i·an /əˌTHôri'te(ə)rēən, ôˌTHär-/ ▶ **adj.** in favor of or demanding strict obedience to authority. ▶ **n.** an authoritarian person. ■ **au·thor·i·tar·i·an·ism** **n.**

au·thor·i·ta·tive /ə'THôriˌtātiv, ə'THär-/ ▶ **adj.** 1 true or accurate and so able to be trusted: *authoritative information.* 2 commanding and self-confident; likely to be respected and obeyed: *his quiet but authoritative voice.* 3 coming from an official source. ■ **au·thor·i·ta·tive·ly** **adv.** **au·thor·i·ta·tive·ness** **n.**

au·thor·i·ty /ə'THôritē, ô'THär-/ ▶ **n.** (pl. **authorities**) 1 the power to give orders to other people and enforce their obedience. 2 a person or organization with official power. 3 official permission to do something: *the money was spent without congressional authority.* 4 recognized knowledge about or expertise in something. 5 a person with expert knowledge of a particular subject: *he was an authority on the stock market.*

au·thor·ize /'ôTHə,rīz/ ▸ v. give official permission for: *the UN Security Council authorized the use of force.* ■ **au·thor·i·za·tion** /,ôTHərə'zāSHən/ n.

Au·thor·ized Ver·sion ▸ n. an English translation of the Bible made in 1611.

au·tism /'ô,tizəm/ ▸ n. a mental condition in which a person has great difficulty in communicating with others. ■ **au·tis·tic** /ô'tistik/ adj.

au·to /'ôtō/ ▸ adj. & n. **1** short for AUTOMOBILE. **2** short for AUTOMATIC.

Au·to·bahn /'ôtə,bän/ ▸ n. a German expressway.

au·to·bi·og·ra·phy /,ôtəbī'ägrəfē/ ▸ n. (pl. **autobiographies**) an account of a person's life written by that person. ■ **au·to·bi·og·ra·pher** n. **au·to·bi·o·graph·i·cal** /,ôtəbīə'grafikəl/ adj.

au·toch·tho·nous /ô'täkTHənəs/ ▸ adj. inhabiting a place from the earliest times; indigenous.

au·to·clave /'ôtə,klāv/ ▸ n. a strong heated container used for processes using high pressures and temperatures, e.g., steam sterilization.

au·toc·ra·cy /ô'täkrəsē/ ▸ n. (pl. **autocracies**) **1** a system of government in which one person has total power. **2** a country, state, or society governed by a person with total power.

au·to·crat /'ôtə,krat/ ▸ n. **1** a ruler who has total power. **2** a person who insists on complete obedience from others.

au·to·crat·ic /,ôtə'kratik/ ▸ adj. **1** relating to a ruler who has total power. **2** taking no account of other people's wishes and insisting on complete obedience: *his autocratic management style.* ■ **au·to·crat·i·cal·ly** adv.

au·to·da·fé /'ôtō də 'fā/ ▸ n. (pl. **autos-da-fé** pronunc. same) the burning of a heretic by the Spanish Inquisition.

au·to·di·al /'ôtō,dī(ə)l/ ▸ v. (**autodials**, **autodialing**, **autodialed**) Computing (of a modem) automatically dial a telephone number or establish a connection with a computer.

au·to·di·dact /,ôtō'dī,dakt/ ▸ n. a self-taught person.

au·to·fo·cus /'ôtō,fōkəs/ ▸ n. a device focusing a camera or other device automatically.

au·to·gi·ro /,ôtō'jīrō/ (also **autogyro**) ▸ n. (pl. **autogiros**) a form of aircraft with unpowered freely rotating horizontal blades and a propeller.

au·to·graph /'ôtə,graf/ ▸ n. **1** a celebrity's signature written for a fan or admirer. **2** a manuscript or musical score in an author's or composer's own handwriting. ▸ v. write one's signature on something.

au·to·im·mune /,ôtōə'myōōn/ ▸ adj. (of disease) caused by antibodies or lymphocytes produced by the body to counteract substances naturally present in it.

au·to·mate /'ôtə,māt/ ▸ v. convert a process or facility so that it can be operated by automatic equipment.

au·to·mat·ed tell·er ma·chine ▸ n. a machine that provides cash and other banking services when a special card is inserted.

au·to·mat·ic /,ôtə'matik/ ▸ adj. **1** operating by itself without human control. **2** (of a firearm) able to load bullets automatically and fire continuously. **3** done or occurring without conscious thought or as a matter of course: *an automatic decision.* **4** enforced without question because of a fixed rule: *murder carries an automatic life sentence.* ▸ n. an automatic machine. ■ **au·to·mat·i·cal·ly** /-ik(ə)lē/ adv. **au·to·mat·ic·i·ty** /-mə'tisitē/ n.

au·to·mat·ic pi·lot ▸ n. a device for keeping an aircraft on a set course.
– PHRASES **on automatic pilot** doing something out of habit and without thinking.

au·to·ma·tion /,ôtə'māSHən/ ▸ n. the use of automatic equipment in manufacturing or similar processes.

au·tom·a·tism /ô'tämə,tizəm/ ▸ n. action that does not involve conscious thought or intention.

au·tom·a·ton /ô'tämətən, -,tän/ ▸ n. (pl. **automata** /-tə/ or **automatons**) **1** a moving mechanical device resembling a human being. **2** a machine that operates according to coded instructions.

au·to·mo·bile /,ôtəmō'bēl/ ▸ n. a powered road vehicle designed to carry a small number of people.

au·to·mo·tive /,ôtə'mōtiv/ ▸ adj. relating to motor vehicles.

au·to·nom·ic /,ôtə'nämik/ ▸ adj. relating to the part of the nervous system that controls involuntary bodily functions such as digestion.

au·ton·o·mous /ô'tänəməs/ ▸ adj. self-governing or independent. ■ **au·ton·o·mous·ly** adv.

au·ton·o·my /ô'tänəmē/ ▸ n. **1** the possession or right of self-government. **2** freedom of action: *a structure that gives greater autonomy to employees.*

au·to·pi·lot /'ôtō,pīlət/ ▸ n. short for AUTOMATIC PILOT.

au·top·sy /'ô,täpsē/ ▸ n. (pl. **autopsies**) an examination of a dead body to discover the cause of death.

au·to·sug·ges·tion /,ôtōsə(g)'jesCHən/ ▸ n. the hypnotic or subconscious adoption of an idea that one has originated oneself.

au·tumn /'ôtəm/ ▸ n. the season after summer and before winter; fall. ■ **au·tum·nal** /ô'təmnəl/ adj.

aux·il·ia·ry /ôg'zilyərē, -'zil(ə)rē/ ▸ adj. providing extra help and support. ▸ n. (pl. **auxiliaries**) a person or thing that provides extra help or support.

aux·il·ia·ry verb ▸ n. a verb used in forming the tenses, moods, and voices of other verbs (e.g., *be, do,* and *have*).

AV ▸ abbr. **1** audiovisual. **2** Authorized Version.

a·vail /ə'vāl/ ▸ v. **1** (**avail oneself of**) formal use or take advantage of: *she did not avail herself of my advice.* **2** help or benefit someone. ▸ n. use or benefit: *his protests were to little avail.*

a·vail·a·ble /ə'vāləbəl/ ▸ adj. **1** able to be used or obtained. **2** free to do something: *the nurse is only available in the mornings.* ■ **a·vail·a·bil·i·ty** /ə,vālə'bilitē/ n.

av·a·lanche /'avə,lanCH/ ▸ n. **1** a mass of snow and ice falling rapidly down a mountainside. **2** an overwhelming amount: *an avalanche of gifts.*

a·vant-garde /'avänt 'gärd, ,avän/ ▸ adj. (in the arts) new and experimental. ▸ n. (**the avant-garde**) new and experimental ideas or artists. ■ **a·vant-gard·ism** /-,dizəm/ n. **a·vant-gard·ist** /-dist/ n.

av·a·rice /'avəris/ ▸ n. extreme greed for wealth or material things.

av·a·ri·cious /,avə'riSHəs/ ▸ adj. very greedy for wealth or material things.

a·vast /ə'vast/ ▸ exclam. Nautical stop; cease.

av·a·tar /'avə,tär/ ▶ n. Hinduism **1** a god or goddess appearing in bodily form on earth. **2** Computing a two- or three-dimensional on-screen graphic that represents an Internet user.

A·ve Ma·ri·a /'ävä mə'rēə/ ▶ n. a prayer to the Virgin Mary used in Catholic worship.

a·venge /ə'venj/ ▶ v. punish or harm someone in return for a wrong. ■ **a·veng·er** n.

av·e·nue /'avə,n(y)ōō/ ▶ n. **1** a broad road or path. **2** a way of approaching or achieving something: *the discovery has opened up new avenues of research.*

a·ver /ə'vər/ ▶ v. (**avers, averring, averred**) formal declare something to be the case.

av·er·age /'av(ə)rij/ ▶ n. **1** the result obtained by adding several amounts together and then dividing the total by the number of amounts. **2** a usual amount or level. ▶ adj. **1** being an average. **2** usual or ordinary. **3** not very good; mediocre. ▶ v. **1** amount to or achieve as an average: *her website averaged 30,000 hits a day.* **2** calculate the average of something. ■ **av·er·age·ly** adv. **av·er·age·ness** n.

a·verse /ə'vərs/ ▶ adj. (**averse to**) strongly disliking or opposed to: *he's not averse to change.*

> **USAGE**
> On the confusion of **averse** and **adverse**, see the note at **ADVERSE**.

a·ver·sion /ə'vərzHən/ ▶ n. strong opposition or dislike. ■ **a·ver·sive** /-siv, -ziv/ adj.

a·vert /ə'vərt/ ▶ v. **1** turn away one's eyes. **2** prevent an undesirable event.

a·vi·an /'āvēən/ ▶ adj. relating to birds.

a·vi·an flu ▶ n. formal term for **BIRD FLU**.

a·vi·ar·y /'āvē,erē/ ▶ n. (pl. **aviaries**) a large enclosure for keeping birds in.

a·vi·a·tion /,āvē'āsHən/ ▶ n. the activity of operating and flying aircraft.

a·vi·a·tor /'āvē,ātər/ ▶ n. a pilot.

a·vi·cul·ture /'āvi,kəlcHər, 'avi-/ ▶ n. the breeding of birds. ■ **a·vi·cul·tur·al** /,āvi'kəlcHərəl, ,avi-/ adj. **a·vi·cul·tur·ist** /-rist/ n.

av·id /'avid/ ▶ adj. keenly interested or enthusiastic: *avid baseball fans.* ■ **a·vid·i·ty** /ə'viditē/ n. **av·id·ly** adv.

a·vi·on·ics /,āvē'äniks/ ▶ pl.n. (usu. treated as sing.) electronics used in aviation.

av·o·ca·do /,avə'kädō, ,ävə-/ ▶ n. (pl. **avocados**) a pear-shaped fruit with a rough dark green skin, pale green flesh, and a large stone.

av·o·ca·tion /,avə'kāsHən/ ▶ n. formal a hobby or minor occupation.

av·o·cet /'avə,set/ ▶ n. a long-legged wading bird with an upturned bill.

a·void /ə'void/ ▶ v. **1** keep away from or stop oneself from doing something. **2** prevent from happening: *book early to avoid disappointment.* ■ **a·void·a·ble** /ə'voidəbəl/ adj. **a·void·a·bly** /ə'voidəblē/ adv. **a·void·ance** /ə'voidns/ n.

av·oir·du·pois /,ävərdə'poiz/ ▶ n. a system of weights based on a pound of 16 ounces or 7,000 grains. Compare with **TROY**.

a·vow /ə'vou/ ▶ v. declare or confess something openly. ■ **a·vow·al** /ə'vouəl/ n. **a·vowed** adj.

a·vun·cu·lar /ə'vəNGkyələr/ ▶ adj. (of a man) friendly and kind toward a younger person.

AWACS /'ā,waks/ ▶ abbr. airborne warning and control system.

a·wait /ə'wāt/ ▶ v. **1** wait for an event. **2** be in

store for: *many dangers await them.*

a·wake /ə'wāk/ ▶ v. (past **awoke** /ə'wōk/; past part. **awoken** /ə'wōkən/) **1** stop sleeping. **2** make or become active again. ▶ adj. not asleep.

a·wak·en /ə'wākən/ ▶ v. **1** stop sleeping; awake. **2** stir up a feeling. ■ **a·wak·en·ing** n. & adj.

a·ward /ə'wôrd/ ▶ v. give something officially as a prize, payment, or reward. ▶ n. **1** a payment, prize, or honor given to someone. **2** the giving of an award.

a·ware /ə'we(ə)r/ ▶ adj. having knowledge of a situation or fact: *everyone is aware of aging.* ■ **a·ware·ness** n.

a·wash /ə'wôsH, ə'wäsH/ ▶ adj. covered or flooded with water.

a·way /ə'wā/ ▶ adv. **1** to or at a distance. **2** into a place for storage. **3** until disappearing: *the sound died away.* **4** continuously or persistently. ▶ adj. (of a sports contest) played at the opponents' park: *this is the Twins' last away game of the season.*

awe /ô/ ▶ n. a feeling of great respect mixed with fear. ▶ v. fill someone with awe.

a·weigh /ə'wā/ ▶ adj. (of a ship's anchor) raised just clear of the seabed.

awe·some /'ôsəm/ ▶ adj. **1** very impressive or daunting: *the awesome power of the sea.* **2** informal excellent.

awe·struck /'ô,strək/ ▶ adj. filled with awe.

aw·ful /'ôfəl/ ▶ adj. **1** very bad or unpleasant. **2** used for emphasis: *an awful lot.* **3** old use causing awe. ■ **aw·ful·ness** n.

aw·ful·ly /'ôf(ə)lē/ ▶ adv. **1** informal very or very much. **2** very badly or unpleasantly.

a·while /ə'(h)wīl/ ▶ adv. for a short time.

awk·ward /'ôkwərd/ ▶ adj. **1** hard to do or deal with: *awkward questions.* **2** causing embarrassment or inconvenience. **3** feeling embarrassed. **4** not graceful; clumsy. ■ **awk·ward·ly** adv. **awk·ward·ness** n.

awl /ôl/ ▶ n. a small pointed tool used for piercing holes.

awn /ôn/ ▶ n. a stiff bristle growing from the ear or flower of barley, rye, and grasses.

awn·ing /'ôniNG/ ▶ n. a sheet of canvas stretched on a frame, used for shelter.

a·woke /ə'wōk/ ▶ past of **AWAKE**.

a·wo·ken /ə'wōkən/ ▶ past participle of **AWAKE**.

AWOL /'ā,wôl/ ▶ adj. Military absent but without intent to desert.

a·wry /ə'rī/ ▶ adv. & adj. away from the expected course or position.

ax /aks/ (also **axe**) ▶ n. **1** a tool with a heavy blade, used for chopping wood. **2** (**the ax**) severe cost-cutting action: *thirty workers are facing the ax.* ▶ v. **1** cancel or reduce something by a large amount. **2** dismiss someone ruthlessly.

– PHRASES **have an ax to grind** have a private reason for doing something.

ax·el /'aksəl/ ▶ n. Figure Skating a jump with a forward takeoff from the forward outside edge of one skate to the backward outside edge of the other, with one and a half turns in the air.

ax·es /'ak,sēz/ ▶ plural of **AXIS**.

ax·i·al /'aksēəl/ ▶ adj. relating to or forming an axis. ■ **ax·i·al·ly** adv.

ax·il /'aksəl/ ▶ n. the upper angle where a leaf joins a stem.

ax·i·om /'aksēəm/ ▶ n. a statement regarded

as accepted or obviously true. ■ **ax·i·o·mat·ic** /ˌaksēəˈmatik/ **adj.**

ax·is /ˈaksis/ ▶**n.** (pl. **axes** /ˈaksēz/) **1** an imaginary line through a body, about which it rotates. **2** an imaginary line about which a regular figure is symmetrically arranged. **3** Mathematics a fixed reference line for the measurement of coordinates.

ax·le /ˈaksəl/ ▶**n.** a rod passing through the center of a wheel or group of wheels.

ax·on /ˈakˌsän/ ▶**n.** the long threadlike part of a nerve cell.

a·yah /ˈäyə/ ▶**n.** a nanny employed by Europeans in India or another former British territory.

a·ya·tol·lah /ˌäyəˈtōlə/ ▶**n.** a Shiite religious leader in Iran.

aye /ī/ (also **ay**) ▶**exclam.** old use or dialect yes. ▶**n.** a vote in favor of a proposal.

A·yur·ve·da /ˌäyərˈvädə, -ˈvēdə/ ▶**n.** the traditional Hindu system of medicine, using diet, herbal treatment, and yogic breathing. ■ **A·yur·ve·dic** /-ˈvedik/ **adj.**

AZ ▶**abbr.** Arizona.

a·zal·ea /əˈzālyə/ ▶**n.** a shrub with brightly colored flowers.

A·zer·bai·ja·ni /ˌazərbīˈjänē, ˌäzər-/ ▶**n.** (pl. **Azerbaijanis**) a person from Azerbaijan. ▶**adj.** relating to Azerbaijan or Azerbaijanis.

az·i·muth /ˈazəməth/ ▶**n.** Astronomy the horizontal direction of a celestial object, measured from the north or south point of the horizon. ■ **az·i·muth·al** /ˌazəˈməthəl/ **adj.**

Az·tec /ˈazˌtek/ ▶**n.** a member of the American Indian people dominant in Mexico before the Spanish conquest.

az·ure /ˈazнər/ ▶**n.** a bright blue color.

Bb

B[1] (also **b**) ▶ n. (pl. **Bs** or **B's**) **1** the second letter of the alphabet. **2** Music the seventh note of the scale of C major.

B[2] ▶ abbr. **1** (in chess) bishop. **2** black (used in describing grades of pencil lead). ▶ symbol the chemical element boron.

b ▶ abbr. **1** (**b.**) born. **2** billion.

B2B ▶ abbr. business-to-business, referring to trade carried out via the Internet between businesses.

BA ▶ abbr. **1** Bachelor of Arts. **2** Baseball batting average.

Ba ▶ symbol the chemical element barium.

baa /bä/ ▶ v. (**baas, baaing, baaed**) (of a sheep or lamb) bleat. ▶ n. the cry of a sheep or lamb.

bab·ble /'babəl/ ▶ v. **1** talk rapidly in a foolish or confused way. **2** (of a stream) flow with a continuous murmur. ▶ n. **1** foolish or confused talk. **2** a babbling sound. ■ **bab·bler** n.

babe /bāb/ ▶ n. **1** literary a baby. **2** informal an attractive young woman. **3** informal an affectionate form of address for a lover.

ba·bel /'babəl, 'bā-/ ▶ n. a confused noise made by a number of voices.

ba·boon /ba'bo͞on/ ▶ n. a large monkey with a long snout, large teeth, and a pink rump.

ba·bush·ka /bə'bo͞osHkə/ ▶ n. (in Russia) an old woman or grandmother.

ba·by /'bābē/ ▶ n. (pl. **babies**) **1** a child or animal that is newly or recently born. **2** a timid or childish person. **3** informal a person's lover. **4** (**one's baby**) one's particular responsibility or concern. ▶ adj. small or immature in comparison with others of the same kind: *baby carrots*. ▶ v. (**babies, babying, babied**) treat someone too protectively. ■ **ba·by·hood** n. **ba·by·ish** adj. – PHRASES **throw the baby out with the bathwater** discard something valuable while getting rid of the inessential or unwanted.

ba·by boom ▶ n. informal a temporary marked increase in the birth rate, especially the one following World War II. ■ **ba·by boom·er** n.

ba·by bug·gy ▶ n. a baby carriage.

ba·by car·riage ▶ n. a four-wheeled carriage for a baby, typically with a retractable hood and pushed by a person on foot.

ba·by-doll ▶ adj. referring to a style of women's clothing resembling that traditionally worn by a young child.

bab·y fat ▶ n. fat on a child's body which disappears around adolescence.

ba·by grand ▶ n. the smallest size of grand piano, about 4.5 feet (1.5 m) long.

Bab·y·lo·ni·an /ˌbabə'lōnēən/ ▶ n. a person from Babylon or Babylonia, an ancient city and kingdom in Mesopotamia (part of what is now Iraq). ▶ adj. relating to Babylon or Babylonia.

ba·by·sit /'bābē,sit/ ▶ v. (**babysits, babysitting,** babysat) look after a child or children while the parents are out. ■ **ba·by·sit·ter** n.

bac·ca·lau·re·ate /ˌbakə'lôrēit/ ▶ n. **1** an exam that qualifies candidates for higher education. **2** a bachelor's degree.

bac·ca·rat /'bäkəˌrä, ˌbakə'rä/ ▶ n. a gambling card game in which players bet against a banker.

bac·cha·nal /ˌbäkə'näl, ˌbak-, 'bakənl/ ▶ n. chiefly literary a wild and drunken party or celebration.

Bac·cha·na·li·a /ˌbakə'nālyə, ˌbäk-/ ▶ pl.n. (also treated as sing.) **1** the ancient Roman festival of the god Bacchus. **2** (**bacchanalia**) drunken celebrations. ■ **bac·cha·na·li·an** adj.

ba·cha·ta /bä'cHätä/ ▶ n. a style of romantic music originating in the Dominican Republic.

bach·e·lor /'bacH(ə)lər/ ▶ n. **1** a man who has never been married. **2** a person who holds an undergraduate degree from a college or university. ■ **bach·e·lor·hood** n.

bach·e·lor·ette /ˌbacH(ə)lə'ret/ ▶ n. a young unmarried woman.

Bach flow·er rem·e·dies /bäkH, bäk/ ▶ pl.n. preparations of the flowers of various plants used in a system of complementary medicine.

ba·cil·lus /bə'siləs/ ▶ n. (pl. **bacilli** /-'silī/) a rod-shaped bacterium. ■ **bac·il·lar·y** /'basəˌlerē/ adj.

back /bak/ ▶ n. **1** the rear surface of a person's body from the shoulders to the hips. **2** the upper surface of an animal's body, equivalent to a person's back. **3** the side or part of something that is farthest from the front or that is not normally seen or used. **4** a player in a team game who plays in a defensive position behind the front line. ▶ adv. **1** in the opposite direction from that in which one is facing or traveling. **2** so as to return to an earlier or normal position or state. **3** into the past. **4** in return. ▶ v. **1** give support to: *the scheme is backed by the education secretary.* **2** walk or drive backward. **3** bet money on a person or animal winning a race or contest. **4** (**back on/onto**) (of a building or other structure) have its back facing or adjacent to something. **5** cover the back of an object. **6** provide musical accompaniment to a singer or musician. **7** (of the wind) change direction counterclockwise around the points of the compass. ▶ adj. **1** of or at the back. **2** in a remote or less important position. **3** relating to the past. ■ **back·er** n. **back·less** adj. – PHRASES **back and forth** to and fro. **the back of beyond** a very remote place. **back down** admit defeat. **back off** draw back from confrontation. **back out** withdraw from a commitment. **back to front** Brit. with the back at the front and the front at the back. **back something up** Computing make a spare copy of data or a disk. **behind someone's back** without a person's knowledge. **get** (or **put**) **someone's back up** annoy someone. **put one's**

back into tackle a task in a determined and energetic way. **turn one's back on** ignore; reject. **with one's back to** (or **up against**) **the wall** in a desperate situation.

back·ache /'bak.āk/ ▶ n. prolonged pain in one's back.

back·beat /'bak.bēt/ ▶ n. Music a strong accent on one of the normally unaccented beats of the bar.

back·bench·er /'bak'benchər/ ▶ n. (in the UK) a member of parliament who does not hold a government or opposition post and who sits behind the front benches in the House of Commons. ■ **back·bench** adj.

back·bit·ing /'bak.bītiNG/ ▶ n. spiteful talk about a person who is not present.

back·board /'bak.bôrd/ ▶ n. 1 a board placed at or forming the back of something, such as a collage or piece of electronic equipment. 2 Basketball an upright board behind the basket, off which the ball may rebound.

back·bone /'bak.bōn/ ▶ n. 1 the spine. 2 the chief support of a system or organization: *small customers are the backbone of a profitable business.* 3 strength of character.

back·break·ing ▶ adj. (of manual labor) physically demanding.

back burn·er ▶ n. (in phrase **on the back burner**) set aside because low priority.

back cat·a·log ▶ n. all the works previously produced by a recording artist, record company, or movie director.

back·coun·try /'bak.kəntrē/ ▶ n. sparsely inhabited rural areas; wilderness.

back·cross /'bak.krôs/ Genetics ▶ v. cross a hybrid with one of its parents or an organism with the same genetic characteristics as one of the parents. ▶ n. 1 an instance of backcrossing. 2 the product of such a cross.

back·date /'bak.dāt/ ▶ v. 1 make something valid from an earlier date. 2 put an earlier date on a document than the actual one.

back·door /'bak.dôr/ ▶ adj. underhanded or secret.

back·drop /'bak.dräp/ ▶ n. 1 a painted cloth hung at the back of a theater stage as part of the scenery. 2 the setting or background for an event.

back·field /'bak.fēld/ ▶ n. Football the area of play behind either the offensive or defensive line.

back·fill /'bak.fil/ ▶ v. refill an excavated hole with the material dug out of it.

back·fire /'bak.fī(ə)r/ ▶ v. 1 (of a vehicle or its engine) undergo a mistimed explosion in the cylinder or exhaust. 2 produce the opposite effect to what was intended: *his trick backfired on him.*

back·gam·mon /'bak.gamən/ ▶ n. a board game in which two players move their pieces around triangular points according to the throw of dice.

back·ground /'bak.ground/ ▶ n. 1 part of a picture, scene, or description that forms a setting for the main figures or events. 2 information or circumstances that influence or explain something: *the historical background to the rebellion.* 3 a person's education, experience, and social circumstances. 4 a persistent low level of radioactivity, noise, etc., present in a particular environment. ▶ v. form a background to something.

back·hand /'bak.hand/ ▶ n. (in racket sports) a stroke played with the back of the hand facing in the direction of the stroke. ▶ v. strike someone or something with a backhanded blow or stroke.

back·hand·ed /'bak.handid/ ▶ adj. 1 made with the back of the hand facing in the direction of movement. 2 expressed in an indirect or ambiguous way: *a backhanded compliment.*

back·hand·er /'bak.handər/ ▶ n. 1 a backhand stroke or blow. 2 Brit. informal a bribe.

back·hoe /'bak.hō/ (Brit. also **backhoe loader**) ▶ n. a mechanical digger with a bucket attached to a hinged boom.

back·ing /'bakiNG/ ▶ n. 1 help or support. 2 a layer of material that forms or strengthens the back of something. 3 (especially in popular music) music or vocals accompanying the main singer.

back·ing track ▶ n. a recorded musical accompaniment.

back·lash /'bak.lasH/ ▶ n. 1 a strong and adverse reaction by a large number of people: *the backlash against conservatism.* 2 recoil between parts of a mechanism.

back·list /'bak.list/ ▶ n. a publisher's list of books published before the current season and still in print.

back·lit /'bak.lit/ ▶ adj. illuminated from behind.

back·log /'bak.lôg, -.läg/ ▶ n. a buildup of matters needing to be dealt with.

back·lot /'bak.lät/ ▶ n. an outdoor area in a movie studio where large sets are made and some outside scenes are filmed.

back·pack /'bak.pak/ ▶ n. a bag with shoulder straps that allow it to be carried on someone's back. ▶ v. travel carrying one's belongings in a backpack. ■ **back·pack·er** n.

back·ped·al /'bak.pedl/ ▶ v. 1 reverse a previous action or opinion. 2 move the pedals of a bicycle backward (formerly so as to brake).

back·room /'bak.rōōm/ ▶ adj. relating to secret work or planning.

back·seat driv·er /'bak'sēt/ ▶ n. informal a passenger in a car who gives the driver unwanted advice.

back·side /'bak.sīd/ ▶ n. informal a person's buttocks.

back·slap·ping /'bak.slapiNG/ ▶ n. the offering of hearty congratulations or praise.

back·slash /'bak.slasH/ ▶ n. a backward-sloping diagonal line (\).

back·slide /'bak.slīd/ ▶ v. (past and past part. **backslid**) return to bad ways. ■ **back·slid·er** n. **back·slid·ing** n.

back·space /'bak.spās/ ▶ n. a key on a typewriter or computer keyboard used to move the carriage or cursor backward. ▶ v. move a typewriter carriage or computer cursor backward.

back·spin /'bak.spin/ ▶ n. a backward spin given to a moving ball, causing it to stop more quickly or rebound at a steeper angle.

back·splash /'bak.splasH/ ▶ n. a panel behind a sink or stove that protects the wall from splashes.

back·stab·bing /'bak.stabiNG/ ▶ n. the action of criticizing someone while pretending to be friendly.

back·stage /'bak'stāj/ ▶ adv. & adj. behind the stage in a theater.

back·stairs /'bak'ste(ə)rz/ ▶ adj. secret or underhanded: *backstairs deals.*

back·stitch /'bak.stich/ ▶ n. a method of sewing with overlapping stitches.

back·stop /'bak,stäp/ ▶ n. **1** a person or thing placed at the rear of or behind something as a barrier, support, or reinforcement. **2** Baseball a high fence or similar structure behind the home plate area. **3** informal Baseball a catcher.

back·sto·ry /'bak,stôrē/ ▶ n. (pl. **backstories**) a history or background created for a fictional character in a movie or television program.

back·street /'bak,strēt/ ▶ n. a minor street. ▶ adj. acting or done secretly and typically illegally: *backstreet abortions.*

back·stroke /'bak,strōk/ ▶ n. a swimming stroke in which the swimmer lies on their back and lifts their arms alternately out of the water in a backward circular movement.

back·swing /'bak,swiNG/ ▶ n. a backward swing, especially of an arm or of a golf club when about to hit a ball.

back·talk /'bak ,tôk/ ▶ n. informal rude or impertinent remarks made in reply to someone in authority.

back-to-back ▶ adj. following one after the other. ▶ adv. (**back to back**) **1** (of two people) facing in opposite directions with backs touching. **2** in succession.

back·track /'bak,trak/ ▶ v. **1** retrace one's steps. **2** reverse one's previous opinion or position: *he denied that he was backtracking on his promise.*

back·up /'bak,əp/ ▶ n. **1** help or support. **2** a person or thing kept ready to be used if necessary.

back·ward /'bakwərd/ ▶ adj. **1** directed toward the back. **2** having made less progress than is normal or expected. ▶ adv. (also **backwards**) **1** toward one's back. **2** back toward the starting point. **3** opposite to the usual direction or order. – PHRASES **bend over backward** informal try one's hardest to be fair or helpful. **know something backward and forward** be completely familiar with something. ■ **back·ward·ly** adv. **back·ward·ness** n.

back·wash /'bak,wôsh, -,wäsh/ ▶ n. waves flowing outward behind a ship.

back·wa·ter /'bak,wôtər, -,wätər/ ▶ n. **1** a stretch of stagnant water on a river. **2** a place or state in which no development is happening: *the country remains an economic backwater.*

back·woods /'bak,woodz/ ▶ pl.n. **1** remote uncleared forest land. **2** a region that is remote or has few inhabitants. ■ **back·woods·man** n. (pl. **backwoodsmen**).

back·yard /'bak,yärd/ ▶ n. a yard at the back of a house or building. – PHRASES **in one's** (**own**) **backyard** informal the area close to where one lives.

ba·con /'bākən/ ▶ n. salted or smoked meat from the back or sides of a pig. – PHRASES **bring home the bacon** informal make money or achieve success.

bac·te·ri·a /bak'ti(ə)rēə/ ▶ plural of BACTERIUM.

bac·te·ri·o·log·i·cal /bak,ti(ə)rēə'läjikəl/ ▶ adj. **1** relating to bacteriology or bacteria. **2** relating to germ warfare.

bac·te·ri·ol·o·gy /bak,ti(ə)rē'äləjē/ ▶ n. the study of bacteria. ■ **bac·te·ri·ol·o·gist** n.

bac·te·ri·um /bak'ti(ə)rēəm/ ▶ n. (pl. **bacteria**) a member of a large group of microscopic single-celled organisms, many of which can cause disease. ■ **bac·te·ri·al** /-'ti(ə)rēəl/ adj. **bac·te·ri·al·ly** /-'ti(ə)rēəlē/ adv.

USAGE
Bacteria is the plural form of **bacterium** and should always be used with the plural form of the verb: *the bacteria are killed by thorough cooking.*

Bac·tri·an cam·el /'baktrēən/ ▶ n. a camel with two humps, native to central Asia.

bad /bad/ ▶ adj. (**worse, worst**) **1** of poor quality or a low standard. **2** unwelcome or unpleasant: *bad news.* **3** severe or serious. **4** wicked or evil. **5** (**bad for**) harmful to: *fatty food is bad for you.* **6** injured, ill, or diseased. **7** (of food) decayed. **8** (**badder, baddest**) informal excellent. ■ **bad·ness** n. – PHRASES **too bad** informal regrettable but unable to be changed.

bad blood ▶ n. hostility or hatred between people.

bad debt ▶ n. a debt that will not be repaid.

bad·dy /'badē/ (also **baddie**) ▶ n. (pl. **baddies**) informal a wicked or evil person in a book, movie, or play.

bade /bad, bād/ ▶ past of BID².

bad faith ▶ n. intention to deceive: *they were accused of negotiating in bad faith.*

bad form ▶ n. an offense against accepted behavior.

badge /baj/ ▶ n. a small flat object worn by a person to show who they are or what they do.

badg·er /'bajər/ ▶ n. a heavily built mammal with a gray and black coat and a white-striped head that lives underground. ▶ v. pester someone to do something.

bad hair day ▶ n. informal a day on which everything goes wrong.

bad·i·nage /,badn'äzh/ ▶ n. witty conversation.

bad·lands /'bad,landz/ ▶ pl.n. poor land with very little soil.

bad·ly /'badlē/ ▶ adv. (**worse, worst**) **1** in a way that is not acceptable or satisfactory. **2** severely; seriously. **3** very much. – PHRASES **badly off** not wealthy; poor.

bad·min·ton /'badmintn/ ▶ n. a game with rackets in which a shuttlecock is hit back and forth across a net.

bad-mouth ▶ v. informal criticize someone.

bad-tem·pered ▶ adj. easily angered or annoyed.

baf·fle /'bafəl/ ▶ v. make someone feel bewildered or puzzled. ▶ n. a device for controlling or stopping the flow of sound, light, gas, or a fluid. ■ **baf·fle·ment** n. **baf·fling** adj.

bag /bag/ ▶ n. **1** a flexible container with an opening at the top. **2** (**bags**) loose folds of skin under a person's eyes. **3** (**bags of**) informal, chiefly Brit. plenty of. **4** informal, derogatory an unpleasant or unattractive woman. ▶ v. (**bags, bagging, bagged**) **1** put something in a bag. **2** succeed in getting: *get there early to bag a seat.* **3** succeed in killing or catching an animal. **4** (of clothes) form loose bulges. ■ **bag·ful** n. **bag·ger** n. – PHRASES **in the bag** informal sure to be gained.

bag·a·telle /,bagə'tel/ ▶ n. **1** a game in which small balls are hit into numbered holes on a board. **2** something unimportant.

ba·gel /'bāgəl/ ▶ n. a ring-shaped bread roll with a heavy texture.

bag·gage /'bagij/ ▶ n. **1** luggage packed with belongings for traveling. **2** past experiences or long-held attitudes regarded as having an undesirable influence: *emotional baggage.* **3** dated a disagreeable girl or woman.

bag·gy /'bagē/ ▶ adj. (**baggier**, **baggiest**) loose and hanging in bulges or folds. ■ **bag·gi·ness** n.

bag la·dy ▶ n. informal a homeless woman who carries her possessions in shopping bags.

bag·man /'bag,man, -mən/ ▶ n. (pl. **bagmen**) informal an agent who collects or distributes the proceeds of illicit activities.

bag·pipe /'bag,pīp/ (also **bagpipes**) ▶ n. a musical instrument with pipes that are sounded by wind squeezed from a bag. ■ **bag·pip·er** n.

ba·guette /ba'get/ ▶ n. a long, narrow loaf of French bread.

bah /bä/ ▶ exclam. an expression of contempt.

Ba·ha·'i /bə'hī/ (also **Bahai**) ▶ n. (pl. **Baha'is**) **1** a religion founded in Persia, emphasizing that there is one god and that humankind and all religions are essentially one. **2** a follower of the Baha'i faith.

Ba·ha·mi·an /bə'hāmēən, -'häm-/ ▶ n. a person from the Bahamas. ▶ adj. relating to the Bahamas.

Bah·rain·i /bä'rānē/ ▶ n. (pl. **Bahrainis**) a person from Bahrain. ▶ adj. relating to Bahrain.

baht /bät/ ▶ n. (pl. same) the basic unit of money of Thailand.

Ba·hu·tu /bä'hoo,too/ ▶ plural of **HUTU**.

bail[1] /bāl/ ▶ n. **1** the temporary release of an accused person before they are tried, often on condition that a sum of money is promised to the court to ensure they attend the trial. **2** money paid to a court for this reason. ▶ v. release an accused person on payment of bail.
– PHRASES **jump bail** informal fail to appear for trial after being released on bail. **post bail** provide bail money for an accused person.

bail[2] ▶ n. **1** a bar on a typewriter or computer printer that holds the paper steady. **2** a bar separating horses in an open stable. **3** an arched handle.

bail[3] (Brit. also **bale**) ▶ v. **1** scoop water out of a ship or boat. **2** (**bail out**) make an emergency parachute descent from an aircraft. **3** (**bail someone/thing out**) rescue from a difficulty: *the state will not bail out loss-making enterprises.*

bai·ley /'bālē/ ▶ n. (pl. **baileys**) the outer wall of a castle.

bail·iff /'bālif/ ▶ n. an official in a court of law who keeps order, looks after prisoners, etc.

bail·i·wick /'bālə,wik/ ▶ n. **1** (**one's bailiwick**) one's area of activity or interest: *after the war, the Middle East remained his bailiwick.* **2** Law a district over which a bailiff has authority.

bail·out /'bāl,out/ ▶ n. informal an act of giving financial assistance to a failing business or economy to save it from collapse.

bain-ma·rie /,ban mə'rē/ ▶ n. (pl. **bains-marie** or **bain-maries** pronunc. same) a pan of hot water in which a cooking container is placed for slow cooking.

bait /bāt/ ▶ n. food put on a hook or in a trap to attract fish or other animals. ▶ v. **1** taunt or tease someone. **2** set dogs on an animal that is trapped or tied up. **3** put bait on a hook or in a trap or net.
– PHRASES **rise to the bait** react to taunting or temptation exactly as someone intended.

baize /bāz/ ▶ n. a green feltlike material, used for covering billiard and card tables.

bake /bāk/ ▶ v. **1** cook food by dry heat in an oven. **2** heat something so as to dry or harden it. **3** informal be or become very hot in hot weather.

▶ n. a social gathering at which baked food is eaten: *a lobster bake.*

baked beans ▶ pl. n. haricot beans cooked in a sauce.

Ba·ke·lite /'bāk(ə),līt/ ▶ n. trademark an early brittle form of plastic.

bak·er /'bākər/ ▶ n. a person who makes bread and cakes. ■ **bak·er·y** n. (pl. **bakeries**)
– PHRASES **baker's dozen** a group of thirteen.

bak·ing pow·der ▶ n. a mixture of sodium bicarbonate and cream of tartar, used in baking to make cakes rise.

bak·ing so·da ▶ n. sodium bicarbonate.

ba·kla·va /,bäklə'vä/ ▶ n. a Middle Eastern dessert made of filo pastry filled with chopped nuts and soaked in honey.

bak·sheesh /'bakshēsh, bak'shēsh/ ▶ n. (in India and some eastern countries) a small sum of money given as charity, a tip, or a bribe.

bal·a·cla·va /,balə'klävə/ ▶ n. a close-fitting woolen hat covering the whole head and neck except for the face.

bal·a·fon /'balə,fon/ ▶ n. a large xylophone with hollow gourds as resonators, used in West African music.

bal·a·lai·ka /,balə'līkə/ ▶ n. a Russian musical instrument like a guitar with a triangular body and three strings.

bal·ance /'baləns/ ▶ n. **1** a state in which weight is distributed evenly, enabling a person or thing to remain steady and upright. **2** a situation in which different elements are equal or in the correct proportions: *elections left the political balance almost unchanged.* **3** mental or emotional stability. **4** a device for weighing. **5** a predominating amount: *the balance of opinion was that work was important.* **6** an amount that is the difference between money received and money spent in an account: *a healthy bank balance.* **7** an amount still owed when part of a debt has been paid. ▶ v. **1** be or put in a steady position. **2** compare the value of one thing with another. **3** establish a balance of proportions or elements in: *she manages to balance work and family life.* **4** compare sums of money owed and paid to an account to ensure that they are equal. ■ **bal·anc·er** n.
– PHRASES **balance of payments** the difference in total value between payments into and out of a country over a period. **balance of power** **1** a situation in which nations of the world have roughly equal power. **2** the power held by a small group when larger groups are of equal strength. **balance of trade** the difference in value between a country's imports and exports. **be** (or **hang**) **in the balance** be in an uncertain state. **on balance** when everything is considered.

bal·ance sheet ▶ n. a written statement detailing what a business owns and what it owes at a particular point in time.

bal·bo·a /bal'bōə/ ▶ n. the basic unit of money of Panama.

bal·co·ny /'balkənē/ ▶ n. (pl. **balconies**) **1** an enclosed platform projecting from the outside of a building. **2** the highest tier of seats in a theater or movie theater. ■ **bal·co·nied** adj.

bald /bôld/ ▶ adj. **1** having very little or no hair on the head. **2** (of an animal) not covered by the usual fur, hair, or feathers. **3** (of a tire) having the tread worn away. **4** without any extra detail or explanation: *the bald facts.* ■ **bald·ing** adj. **bald·ish** adj. **bald·ly** adv. **bald·ness** n.

bal·da·chin /'bôldəkin/ (also **baldaquin** pronunc. same) ▶ n. a ceremonial canopy over an altar, throne, or doorway.

bald ea·gle ▶ n. a white-headed North American eagle; it is the national emblem of the US.

bal·der·dash /'bôldər,dasн/ ▶ n. senseless talk or writing; nonsense.

bale¹ /bāl/ ▶ n. a large wrapped or bound bundle of paper, hay, or cotton. ▶ v. make up paper, hay, or cotton into bales. ∎ **bal·er** n.

bale² ▶ v. Brit. variant spelling of BAIL³.

ba·leen /bə'lēn/ ▶ n. whalebone.

ba·leen whale ▶ n. any of the kinds of whale that have plates of whalebone in the mouth for straining plankton from the water.

bale·ful /'bālfəl/ ▶ adj. causing or threatening to cause harm: *she watched him with baleful eyes.* ∎ **bale·ful·ly** adv.

Ba·li·nese /,bälə'nēz, ,bal-, -'nēs/ ▶ n. (pl. same) a person from Bali. ▶ adj. relating to Bali.

balk /bôk/ (Brit. also **baulk**) ▶ v. 1 (**balk at**) hesitate to accept an idea. 2 thwart or hinder a plan or person. ▶ n. a roughly squared timber beam.

Bal·kan /'bôlkən/ ▶ adj. relating to the countries on the peninsula in SE Europe surrounded by the Adriatic, Ionian, Aegean, and Black Seas. ▶ n. (**the Balkans** /'bôlkənz/) the Balkan countries.

Bal·kan·ize /'bôlkə,nīz/ ▶ v. divide a region or organization into smaller states or groups who oppose each other. ∎ **Bal·kan·i·za·tion** /,bôlkənə'zāsнən/ n.

ball¹ /bôl/ ▶ n. 1 a rounded object that is kicked, thrown, or hit in a game. 2 a single throw or kick of the ball in a game. 3 a rounded part or thing: *the ball of the foot.* ▶ v. 1 squeeze or form something into a ball. 2 (**ball something up**) bungle something.
– PHRASES **the ball is in your court** it is up to you to make the next move. **keep one's eye on** (or **take one's eye off**) **the ball** keep (or fail to keep) one's attention focused on the matter in hand. **on the ball** alert to new ideas or methods. **play ball** informal cooperate. **start** (or **get** or **set**) **the ball rolling** make a start.

ball² ▶ n. a formal social gathering for dancing.
– PHRASES **have a ball** informal enjoy oneself very much.

bal·lad /'baləd/ ▶ n. 1 a poem or song telling a popular story. 2 a slow sentimental or romantic song. ∎ **bal·lad·eer** /,balə'di(ə)r/ n. **bal·lad·ry** /'balədrē/ n.

bal·lade /bə'läd/ ▶ n. 1 a poem with three eight-line stanzas, each ending with the same line, and a short stanza (envoy) in conclusion. 2 a short, lyrical piece of music, especially one for piano.

ball-and-sock·et joint ▶ n. a joint in which a rounded end lies in a socket, allowing movement in all directions.

bal·last /'baləst/ ▶ n. 1 a heavy substance carried by a ship or hot-air balloon to keep it stable. 2 gravel or coarse stone used to form the base of a railroad track or road.

ball bear·ing ▶ n. 1 a bearing in which the parts are separated by a ring of small metal balls that reduce friction. 2 a ball used in such a bearing.

ball·boy /'bôl,boi/ (or **ballgirl** /'bôl,gərl/) ▶ n. a boy (or girl) who retrieves balls that go out of play during a tennis match or baseball game.

ball·cock /'bôl,käk/ ▶ n. a valve that automatically fills up a tank when liquid is drawn from it.

bal·le·ri·na /,balə'rēnə/ ▶ n. a female ballet dancer.

bal·let /ba'lā/ ▶ n. 1 an artistic form of dancing performed to music, using set steps and gestures. 2 a creative work of this form. ∎ **bal·let·ic** /ba'letik, bə-/ adj.

bal·let·o·mane /bə'letə,mān, ba-/ ▶ n. a ballet enthusiast.

ball game ▶ n. a game played with a ball.
– PHRASES **a different** (or **whole new**) **ball game** informal a situation that is completely different from a previous one.

bal·lis·tic /bə'listik/ ▶ adj. 1 relating to projectiles or their flight through the air. 2 moving under the force of gravity only.
– PHRASES **go ballistic** informal fly into a rage.

bal·lis·tic mis·sile ▶ n. a missile that is initially powered and guided but falls under gravity onto its target.

bal·lis·tics /bə'listiks/ ▶ pl.n. (treated as sing.) the science of projectiles and firearms.

bal·loon /bə'lōōn/ ▶ n. 1 a small rubber bag that is inflated and used as a toy or a decoration. 2 (also **hot-air balloon**) a large bag filled with hot air or gas to make it rise in the air, with a basket for passengers hanging from it. 3 a rounded outline containing the words or thoughts of characters in a comic strip. ▶ v. 1 swell outward. 2 increase rapidly: *the company's debt ballooned in the last five years.* 3 (usu. as n. **ballooning**) travel by hot-air balloon. ∎ **bal·loon·ist** n.

bal·lot /'balət/ ▶ n. 1 a way of voting secretly on something, usually by placing paper slips in a box. 2 (**the ballot**) the total number of votes cast in such a way. ▶ v. (**ballots, balloting, balloted**) 1 obtain a secret vote from members. 2 cast one's vote on an issue.

ball·park /'bôl,pärk/ ▶ n. 1 a baseball field or stadium. 2 informal an area or range within which an estimate is likely to be correct. ▶ adj. informal approximate: *a ballpark figure.*

ball·point pen /'bôl,point/ ▶ n. a pen with a tiny ball as its writing point.

ball·room /'bôl,rōōm, -,rōŏm/ ▶ n. a large room for formal dancing.

ball·room danc·ing ▶ n. formal social dancing in couples.

balls /'bôlz/ vulgar slang ▶ pl.n. 1 testicles. 2 courage; nerve.

balls-out ▶ adj. informal without moderation or restraint.

balls·y /'bôlzē/ ▶ adj. (**ballsier, ballsiest**) informal bold and confident.

ball valve ▶ n. a one-way valve opened and closed by pressure on a ball that fits into a cup-shaped opening.

bal·ly·hoo /'balē,hōō/ ▶ n. informal excessive publicity or fuss.

balm /bä(l)m/ ▶ n. 1 a fragrant ointment used to heal or soothe the skin. 2 something that soothes or heals: *the story was balm to American hearts.*

balm·y /'bä(l)mē/ ▶ adj. (**balmier, balmiest**) 1 (of the weather or a period of time) pleasantly warm. 2 informal mad or foolish.

ba·lo·ney /bə'lōnē/ ▶ n. informal nonsense.

bal·sa /'bôlsə/ (also **balsa wood**) ▶ n. very lightweight wood from a tropical American tree, used for making models.

bal·sam /'bôlsəm/ ▶ n. **1** a scented resin obtained from certain trees and shrubs, used in perfumes and medicines. **2** a plant grown for its pink or purple flowers. ■ **bal·sam·ic** /bôl'samik/ adj.

bal·sam·ic vin·e·gar ▶ n. dark, sweet Italian vinegar that has been matured in wooden barrels.

Bal·tic /'bôltik/ ▶ adj. relating to the Baltic Sea or the countries on its eastern shores.

bal·us·ter /'baləstər/ ▶ n. a short pillar forming part of a series supporting a rail.

bal·us·trade /'balə,strād/ ▶ n. a railing supported by balusters. ■ **bal·us·trad·ed** adj.

bam·bi·no /bam'bēnō/ ▶ n. (pl. **bambini** /-nē/ or **bambinos**) a baby or young child.

bam·boo /,bam'bōō/ ▶ n. a giant tropical grass with hollow woody stems.

bam·boo shoot ▶ n. a young shoot of bamboo, eaten as a vegetable.

bam·boo·zle /bam'bōōzəl/ ▶ v. informal cheat or deceive someone.

ban¹ /ban/ ▶ v. (**bans, banning, banned**) officially forbid something or prevent someone from doing something. ▶ n. an official order forbidding something.

ban² /bän/ ▶ n. (pl. **bani** /'bänē/) a unit of money of Romania, equal to one hundredth of a leu.

ba·nal /'bānl, bə'nal, -'näl/ ▶ adj. very ordinary and unoriginal: *songs with banal, repeated words.* ■ **ba·nal·i·ty** /bə'nalitē/ n. (pl. **banalities**) **ba·nal·ly** adv.

ba·nan·a /bə'nanə/ ▶ n. a long curved fruit of a tropical or subtropical treelike grass, with yellow skin and soft flesh.

– PHRASES **go bananas** informal become (or be) insane or angry.

ba·nan·a re·pub·lic ▶ n. derogatory a small country that is politically unstable because its economy is dominated by a single export controlled by foreign businesses.

ba·nan·a split ▶ n. a dessert made with bananas cut down the middle and filled with ice cream, sauce, whipped cream, and nuts.

band¹ /band/ ▶ n. **1** a flat, thin strip or loop of material used as a fastener, for reinforcement, or as decoration. **2** a stripe or strip of a different color or nature from its surroundings: *a band of cloud.* **3** a range of frequencies or wavelengths in a spectrum: *the UHF band.* ▶ v. **1** fit a band on or around something. **2** mark something with a stripe or stripes. ■ **band·ing** n.

band² ▶ n. **1** a small group of musicians and singers who play pop, jazz, or rock music. **2** a group of musicians who play brass, wind, or percussion instruments. **3** a group of people with a shared interest or purpose. ▶ v. form a group to achieve the same aim: *people banded together to help each other.*

band·age /'bandij/ ▶ n. a strip of material used to bind up a wound or to protect an injury. ▶ v. bind a wound or part of the body with a bandage.

Band-Aid /'band ,ād/ ▶ n. trademark **1** an adhesive bandage with a gauze pad in the center, used to cover minor wounds. **2** a makeshift or temporary solution.

ban·dan·na /ban'danə/ (also **bandana**) ▶ n. a square of brightly colored fabric worn on the head or around the neck.

B. & B. ▶ abbr. bed and breakfast.

band·box /'band,bäks/ ▶ n. a circular cardboard box for carrying hats.

ban·deau /ban'dō/ ▶ n. (pl. **bandeaux** /-'dōz/) **1** a narrow band worn around the head to hold the hair in position. **2** a woman's strapless top consisting of a band of fabric fitting around the bust.

ban·di·coot /'bandi,kōōt/ ▶ n. an insect-eating marsupial of Australia and New Guinea.

ban·dit /'bandit/ ▶ n. a member of a gang of armed robbers. ■ **ban·dit·ry** n.

band·lead·er /'band,lēdər/ ▶ n. a player at the head of a musical band.

ban·do·lier /,bandə'li(ə)r/ (also **bandoleer**) ▶ n. a shoulder belt with loops or pockets for cartridges.

band·saw /'band,sô/ ▶ n. a power saw consisting of an endless moving steel belt with a serrated edge.

band·stand /'band,stand/ ▶ n. a platform for a band to play on, covered if out of doors.

band·wag·on /'band,wagən/ ▶ n. an activity or cause that has suddenly become fashionable or popular: *the company is jumping on the Green bandwagon.*

band·width /'band,widTH/ ▶ n. **1** a range of frequencies used in telecommunications. **2** the ability of a computer network or other telecommunication system to transmit signals.

ban·dy¹ /'bandē/ ▶ adj. (**bandier, bandiest**) (of a person's legs) curved outward so that the knees are wide apart.

ban·dy² ▶ v. (**bandies, bandying, bandied**) pass on or discuss an idea, rumor, or name in a casual or uninformed way: *$40,000 is the figure that has been bandied about.*

– PHRASES **bandy words** exchange angry remarks.

bane /bān/ ▶ n. a cause of great distress or annoyance: *the phone was the bane of my existence.*

bang /baNG/ ▶ n. **1** a sudden loud sharp noise. **2** a sudden painful blow. **3** (**bangs**) a fringe of hair cut straight across the forehead. ▶ v. **1** hit or put down something forcefully and noisily. **2** make or cause to make a bang. **3** vulgar slang (of a man) have sex with someone. ▶ adv. informal, chiefly Brit. exactly: *bang in the middle of town.*

– PHRASES **bang for one's** (or **the**) **buck** value or performance for cost: *get more bang for your buck by ordering the three-course lunch menu for $21.* **with a bang** suddenly or impressively.

bang·er /'baNGər/ ▶ n. Brit. informal **1** a sausage. **2** an old car. **3** a loud explosive firework.

Bang·la·desh·i /,bäNGglə'deSHē, ,baNGglə-/ ▶ n. (pl. **Bangladeshis**) a person from Bangladesh. ▶ adj. relating to Bangladesh.

ban·gle /'baNGgəl/ ▶ n. a rigid bracelet worn around the arm.

bang-up ▶ adj. informal excellent: *for a novice, he has done a bang-up job.*

ba·ni /'bänē/ ▶ plural of **BAN²**.

ban·ish /'baniSH/ ▶ v. **1** make someone leave a place as an official punishment. **2** get rid of: *I banished the thought from my mind.* ■ **ban·ish·ment** n.

ban·is·ter /'banəstər/ (also **bannister**) ▶ n. **1** (also **banisters**) the uprights and handrail at the side of a staircase. **2** a single upright at the side of a staircase.

ban·jo /'banjō/ ▶ n. (pl. **banjos** or **banjoes**) a musical instrument like a guitar, with a circular body and a long neck. ■ **ban·jo·ist** /-ist/ n.

bank¹ /baNGk/ ►n. **1** the land alongside a river or lake. **2** a long, high slope, mound, or mass: *mud banks.* **3** a set of similar things grouped together in rows. ►v. **1** heap or form a substance into a mass or mound. **2** (of an aircraft or vehicle) tilt sideways in making a turn. **3** build a road, railroad, or sports track higher at the outer edge of a bend.

bank² ►n. **1** an organization offering financial services, especially loans and the safekeeping of customers' money. **2** a stock or supply available for use: *a blood bank.* **3** a place where something may be safely kept: *the computer's memory bank.* **4** (**the bank**) the store of money or tokens held by the banker in some gambling or board games. ►v. **1** deposit money or valuables in a bank. **2** have an account at a bank. **3** (**bank on**) rely on confidently: *he can't bank on their support.* – PHRASES **break the bank** informal cost more than one can afford.

bank·a·ble /'baNGkəbəl/ ►adj. certain to bring profit and success. ■ **bank·a·bil·i·ty** /,baNGkə'bilitē/ n.

bank card ►n. a credit card, debit card, or ATM card issued by a bank.

bank·er /'baNGkər/ ►n. **1** a person who manages or owns a bank. **2** the person who keeps the bank in some gambling or board games.

bank hol·i·day ►n. Brit. a public holiday, when banks are officially closed.

bank·ing /'baNGkiNG/ ►n. the business activity of a bank.

bank·note /'baNGk,nōt/ ►n. a piece of paper money issued by a central bank.

bank rate ►n. the rate of discount set by a central bank.

bank·roll /'baNGk,rōl/ ►n. **1** a roll of banknotes. **2** available funds. ►v. informal support someone or something financially.

bank·rupt /'baNGk,rəpt, -rəpt/ ►adj. **1** declared in law as unable to pay one's debts. **2** completely lacking in a particular good quality or value: *their cause is morally bankrupt.* ►n. a person judged by a court to be bankrupt. ►v. make a person or organization bankrupt. ■ **bank·rupt·cy** /'baNGk,rəp(t)sē, -rəp(t)sē/ n. (pl. **bankruptcies**)

bank swal·low ►n. another term for SAND MARTIN.

ban·ner /'banər/ ►n. **1** a long strip of cloth bearing a slogan or design, hung up or carried on poles. **2** an advertisement on a website in the form of a bar, column, or box. ►adj. excellent; outstanding: *a banner year.*

ban·nis·ter /'banəstər/ ►n. variant spelling of BANISTER.

banns /banz/ ►pl.n. a public announcement of an intended marriage read out in a parish church.

ban·quet /'baNGkwit/ ►n. an elaborate and formal meal for many people. ►v. (**banquets, banqueting, banqueted**) give or take part in a banquet.

ban·quette /baNG'ket/ ►n. an upholstered bench along a wall.

ban·shee /'banshē/ ►n. (in Irish legend) a female spirit whose wailing warns of an impending death in a house.

ban·tam /'bantəm/ ►n. a chicken of a small breed.

ban·tam·weight /'bantəm,wāt/ ►n. a weight in boxing and other sports between flyweight and featherweight.

ban·ter /'bantər/ ►n. the good-humored exchange of teasing remarks. ►v. exchange remarks in a good-humored teasing way.

Ban·tu /'bantōō/ ►n. (pl. same or **Bantus**) **1** a member of a large group of peoples of central and southern Africa. **2** the group of languages spoken by the Bantu.

USAGE
Bantu is a strongly offensive word in South African English, especially when used to refer to individual black people.

ban·yan /'banyən/ (also **banian** pronunc. same) ►n. an Indian fig tree with spreading branches from which roots grow downward to the ground and form new trunks.

ban·zai /'ban'zī/ ►exclam. a cry used by the Japanese when going into battle or in greeting their emperor.

ba·o·bab /'bāō,bab, 'bä-ō-/ ►n. a short African tree with a very thick trunk and large edible fruit.

bap·tism /'bap,tizəm/ ►n. the Christian rite of sprinkling a person with water or dipping them in it, as a sign that they have been cleansed of sin and have entered the Church. ■ **bap·tis·mal** /bap'tizməl/ adj. – PHRASES **baptism of fire** a difficult new experience.

Bap·tist /'baptist/ ►n. a member of a Protestant group believing that only adults should be baptized and that this should be by total immersion in water.

bap·tis·tery /'baptəstrē/ (also **baptistry**) ►n. (pl. **baptisteries**) a building or part of a church used for baptism.

bap·tize /'bap,tīz, bap'tīz/ ►v. **1** admit someone to the Christian Church by the rite of baptism. **2** give a name or nickname to: *the media baptized the murderer 'The Babysitter.'*

bar¹ /bär/ ►n. **1** a long rigid piece of wood, metal, etc. **2** a counter, room, or place where alcoholic drinks or refreshments are served. **3** a small shop or counter serving refreshments or providing a service: *a snack bar.* **4** a barrier or obstacle: *her humble beginnings were no bar to becoming head of state.* **5** any of the short units into which a piece of music is divided, shown on a score by vertical lines. **6** (**the bar**) the place in a courtroom where an accused person stands during a trial. **7** (**the Bar**) the legal profession. **8** (**the Bar**) lawyers as a group. ►v. (**bars, barring, barred**) **1** fasten something with a bar or bars. **2** forbid from doing something or prevent from going somewhere: *they were barred from entering the room.* ►prep. chiefly Brit. except for. ■ **barred** adj. – PHRASES **bar none** with no exceptions. **behind bars** in prison.

bar² ►n. a unit of pressure equivalent to a hundred thousand newtons per square meter.

bar·a·the·a /,barə'тнēə/ ►n. a fine woolen cloth.

barb /bärb/ ►n. **1** a sharp backward-pointing part of the head of an arrow, a fishhook, etc., that makes it difficult to remove from something it has pierced. **2** a spiteful remark. **3** a barbel at the mouth of some fish. ■ **barb·less** adj.

Bar·ba·di·an /bär'bādēən/ ►n. a person from Barbados. ►adj. relating to Barbados.

bar·bar·i·an /bär'be(ə)rēən/ ►n. **1** (in ancient times) a member of a people not belonging to the Greek, Roman, or Christian civilizations. **2** an uncivilized or cruel person. ▸ adj. uncivilized or cruel.

bar·bar·ic /bär'barik/ ▸ adj. **1** savagely cruel. **2** lacking sophistication; primitive. ■ **bar·bar·i·cal·ly** adv.

bar·ba·rism /'bärbə,rizəm/ ▸ n. **1** extreme cruelty. **2** an uncivilized or primitive state. **3** a word or expression that is badly formed according to traditional rules, e.g., the word *television*, which is formed from two different languages.

bar·bar·i·ty /bär'baritē/ ▸ n. (pl. **barbarities**) **1** extreme cruelty. **2** lack of culture and civilization.

bar·ba·rous /'bärbərəs/ ▸ adj. **1** extremely cruel. **2** primitive; uncivilized. ■ **bar·ba·rous·ly** adv.

bar·be·cue /'bärbi,kyōō/ ▸ n. **1** an outdoor meal or party at which food is grilled over an open fire. **2** a structure or device for grilling food outdoors. ▸ v. (**barbecues, barbecuing, barbecued**) cook on a barbecue.

bar·be·cue sauce ▸ n. a spicy sauce made from tomatoes, chilies, etc.

barbed /bärbd/ ▸ adj. **1** having a barb or barbs. **2** (of a remark) spiteful.

barbed wire ▸ n. wire with clusters of short, sharp spikes along it.

bar·bel /'bärbəl/ ▸ n. **1** a long, thin growth hanging from the mouth or snout of certain fish. **2** a large freshwater fish with barbels hanging from the mouth.

bar·bell /'bär,bel/ ▸ n. a long metal bar to which discs of varying weights are attached at each end, used for weightlifting.

bar·ber /'bärbər/ ▸ n. a person who cuts men's hair and shaves or trims beards as an occupation. ▸ v. cut or trim a man's hair.

bar·ber·ry /'bär,berē, -bərē/ ▸ n. (pl. **barberries**) another term for BERBERIS.

bar·ber·shop /'bärbər,sHäp/ ▸ n. a style of singing in which four men sing in close harmony without musical accompaniment.

bar·bi·can /'bärbikən/ ▸ n. a double tower above a gate or drawbridge of a castle or fortified city.

bar·bi·tu·rate /bär'bicHərit, -ə,rāt/ ▸ n. a kind of sedative drug derived from a synthetic compound (**barbituric acid** /,bärbi'cHŏŏrik/).

barb·wire /'bärb'wīr/ ▸ n. barbed wire.

bar code ▸ n. a set of stripes printed on a product, able to be read by a computer to provide information on prices and quantities in stock.

bard /bärd/ ▸ n. **1** old use or literary a poet. **2** (**the Bard**) Shakespeare. **3** (**Bard**) the winner of a prize for Welsh verse at an eisteddfod. ■ **bard·ic** adj.

bare /be(ə)r/ ▸ adj. **1** not clothed or covered. **2** without the appropriate or usual covering or contents: *a big, bare room.* **3** without detail; basic. **4** only just enough: *a bare majority.* ▸ v. uncover or reveal: *the dog bared its teeth.* ■ **bare·ness** n.
– PHRASES **with one's bare hands** without using tools or weapons.

> USAGE
> On the confusion of **bare** and **bear**, see the note at BEAR¹.

bare·back /'be(ə)r,bak/ ▸ adv. & adj. on a horse without a saddle.

bare·boat /'be(ə)r,bōt/ ▸ adj. (of a ship) hired without a crew.

bare·faced /'be(ə)r,fāst/ ▸ adj. shameless and undisguised: *a barefaced lie.*

bare·foot /'be(ə)r,fŏŏt/ (also **barefooted** /-,fŏŏtid/) ▸ adj. & adv. wearing nothing on one's feet.

bare·head·ed /'be(ə)r,hedid/ ▸ adj. & adv. without a covering for one's head.

bare·ly /'be(ə)rlē/ ▸ adv. **1** only just; almost not: *she nodded, barely able to speak.* **2** only a short time before: *they had barely sat down when forty policemen swarmed in.* **3** in a simple and sparse way: *their barely furnished house.*

barf /bärf/ ▸ v. informal vomit.

bar·fly /'bär,flī/ ▸ n. (pl. **barflies**) informal a person who spends much time drinking in bars.

bar·gain /'bärgən/ ▸ n. **1** a thing offered for sale or bought for a low price. **2** an agreement made between people as to what each will do for the other. ▸ v. **1** negotiate the terms of an agreement. **2** (**bargain for/on**) expect: *I got more information than I'd bargained for.* ■ **bar·gain·er** n.
– PHRASES **drive a hard bargain** press hard for a deal in one's favor. **into the bargain** in addition.

bar·gain base·ment ▸ n. a part of a store where goods are sold cheaply, typically because they are old or imperfect: *investors snapped up shares at bargain-basement prices.*

barge /bärj/ ▸ n. **1** a long flat-bottomed boat for carrying freight on canals and rivers. **2** a large ornamental boat used for pleasure or on ceremonial occasions. ▸ v. **1** move forcefully or roughly: *she barged into the room and accosted him.* **2** (**barge in**) intrude or interrupt rudely or awkwardly.

bar graph (also **bar chart**) ▸ n. a diagram in which different quantities are represented by rectangles of varying height.

ba·ris·ta /bə'rēstə/ ▸ n. a person who serves in a coffee bar.

bar·i·tone /'bari,tōn/ ▸ n. an adult male singing voice between tenor and bass. ▸ adj. referring to an instrument that is second lowest in pitch in its family: *a baritone sax.*

bar·i·um /'be(ə)rēəm, 'bar-/ ▸ n. a soft, reactive metallic chemical element.

bark¹ /bärk/ ▸ n. the sharp sudden cry of a dog, fox, or seal. ▸ v. **1** give a bark. **2** shout something in a fierce or abrupt way.
– PHRASES **one's bark is worse than one's bite** one is not as fierce as one seems. **be barking up the wrong tree** informal be pursuing a mistaken idea or course of action.

bark² ▸ n. the tough protective outer covering of the trunk and branches of a tree. ▸ v. scrape the skin off one's shin by accidentally hitting it.

bark³ ▸ n. (also **barque**) old use or literary a ship or boat.

bar·keep·er /'bär,kēpər/ ▸ n. a person who owns or serves drinks in a bar.

bark·er /'bärkər/ ▸ n. informal a person at a fair who calls out to passersby to persuade them to visit a sideshow.

bar·ley /'bärlē/ ▸ n. a cereal plant with bristly heads, the grains of which are used in brewing and animal feed.

bar·maid /'bär,mād/ ▸ n. a woman who serves drinks in a bar.

bar·man /'bärmən/ ▸ n. (pl. **barmen**) chiefly Brit. a man who serves drinks in a bar.

bar mitz·vah /,bär 'mitsvə/ ▸ n. a religious

ceremony in which a Jewish boy aged 13 takes on adult responsibilities under Jewish law.

barn /bärn/ ▶ n. a large farm building used for storage or for housing livestock.

bar·na·cle /'bärnəkəl/ ▶ n. a small shellfish that attaches itself permanently to underwater surfaces. ■ **bar·na·cled** adj.

barn dance ▶ n. a party with country dancing.

barn owl ▶ n. a pale-colored owl with a heart-shaped face.

barn·storm /'bärn,stôrm/ ▶ v. **1** tour rural districts putting on shows or giving flying displays. **2** make a rapid tour as part of a political campaign.

barn·yard /'bärn,yärd/ ▶ n. a farmyard.

bar·o·graph /'barə,graf/ ▶ n. a barometer that records its readings on a moving chart.

ba·rom·e·ter /bə'rämitər/ ▶ n. **1** an instrument that measures atmospheric pressure, used in forecasting the weather. **2** an indicator of change: *furniture is a barometer of changing tastes.* ■ **bar·o·met·ric** adj.

bar·on /'barən/ ▶ n. **1** a man belonging to the lowest rank of the British nobility. **2** historical a man who held lands or property from the sovereign or an overlord. **3** a powerful person in business or industry: *a press baron.* ■ **ba·ro·ni·al** /bə'rōnēəl/ adj.

bar·on·ess /'barənis/ ▶ n. **1** the wife or widow of a baron. **2** a woman holding the rank of baron.

bar·on·et /'barənit, ,barə'net/ ▶ n. a man who holds a title below that of baron, with the status of a commoner. ■ **bar·on·et·cy** n.

bar·o·ny /'barənē/ ▶ n. (pl. **baronies**) the rank and estates of a baron.

ba·roque /bə'rōk/ ▶ adj. **1** relating to a highly decorated style of European architecture, art, and music of the 17th and 18th centuries. **2** very elaborate or showy. ▶ n. the baroque style or period.

ba·rouche /bə'rōōsн/ ▶ n. historical a four-wheeled horse-drawn carriage with a collapsible hood over the rear half.

barque /bärk/ ▶ n. **1** a sailing ship with three masts, one of which is rigged fore-and-aft while the others are square-rigged. **2** literary a boat.

bar·rack /'barək/ ▶ v. provide soldiers with accommodations.

bar·racks /'barəks/ ▶ pl.n. (often treated as sing.) a large building or group of buildings for housing soldiers.

bar·ra·cu·da /,barə'kōōdə/ ▶ n. (pl. same or **barracudas**) a large, slender predatory fish of tropical seas.

bar·rage /bə'räzн/ ▶ n. **1** a continuous artillery bombardment over a wide area. **2** an overwhelming number of things coming in rapid succession: *a barrage of questions.* **3** a barrier built across a river to control the water level. ▶ v. bombard someone with questions or complaints.

barre /bär/ ▶ n. a horizontal bar at waist level used by ballet dancers as a support during exercises.

bar·rel /'barəl/ ▶ n. **1** a large cylindrical container bulging out in the middle and with flat ends. **2** a measure of capacity for oil and beer (36 imperial gallons for beer and 35 for oil). **3** a tube forming part of an object such as a gun or a pen. ▶ v. (**barrels**, **barreling**, **barreled**) **1** put something into a barrel or barrels. **2** informal drive

or move very fast.
– PHRASES **over a barrel** informal at a great disadvantage.

bar·rel or·gan ▶ n. a small pipe organ that plays a preset tune when a handle is turned.

bar·rel vault ▶ n. a vault in a roof forming a half cylinder.

bar·ren /'barən/ ▶ adj. **1** (of land) too poor to produce vegetation. **2** (of a female animal) unable to bear young. **3** bleak and lifeless: *huge barren rooms.* **4** lacking meaning or value: *heads stuffed with barren facts.* ■ **bar·ren·ness** n.

bar·rette /bə'ret/ ▶ n. a hair clip.

bar·ri·cade /'bari,kād/ ▶ n. a makeshift barrier erected to block a road or entrance. ▶ v. block or defend something with a barricade.

bar·ri·er /'barēər/ ▶ n. **1** an obstacle that prevents movement or access. **2** something that prevents or hinders communication or progress: *a language barrier.*

bar·ri·er meth·od ▶ n. contraception using a device or preparation that prevents sperm from reaching an ovum.

bar·ri·er reef ▶ n. a coral reef close to the shore but separated from it by a channel of deep water.

bar·ring /'bäriNG/ ▶ prep. except for; if not for.

bar·ri·o /'bärē,ō/ ▶ n. (pl. **barrios**) **1** (in a Spanish-speaking country) a district of a town. **2** (in the US) the Spanish-speaking quarter of a town or city.

bar·ris·ter /'barəstər/ ▶ n. chiefly Brit. a lawyer qualified to argue a case in court, especially in the higher courts. Compare with SOLICITOR.

bar·room /'bär,rōōm, -,rŏŏm/ ▶ n. a room where alcoholic drinks are served over a counter.

bar·row[1] /'barō/ ▶ n. **1** a metal frame with two wheels used to carry objects such as luggage. **2** a wheelbarrow.

bar·row[2] ▶ n. an ancient burial mound.

bar·tend·er /'bär,tendər/ ▶ n. a person serving drinks at a bar. ■ **bar·tend·ing** n.

bar·ter /'bärtər/ ▶ v. exchange goods or services for other goods or services. ▶ n. trading by bartering.

bar·y·on /'barē,än/ ▶ n. Physics a subatomic particle with a mass equal to or greater than that of a proton.

ba·sal /'bāsəl, -zəl/ ▶ adj. chiefly technical forming or belonging to a bottom layer or base.

ba·sal met·a·bol·ic rate ▶ n. the rate at which the body uses energy while at rest to maintain vital functions such as breathing.

ba·salt /bə'sôlt/ ▶ n. a dark fine-grained volcanic rock. ■ **ba·sal·tic** /-tik/ adj.

bas·cule bridge /'baskyōōl/ ▶ n. a type of bridge with a section that can be raised and lowered using counterweights.

base[1] /bās/ ▶ n. **1** the lowest or supporting part of something. **2** a foundation, support, or starting point: *the town's economic base collapsed.* **3** the main place where a person works or stays. **4** a center of operations: *a military base.* **5** a main element or ingredient to which others are added. **6** Chemistry a substance capable of reacting with an acid to form a salt and water. **7** Mathematics the number on which a system of counting is based, e.g., 10 in conventional notation. **8** Baseball each of the four stations that must be reached in turn to score a run. ▶ v. **1** use something as the foundation for: *the film is based on a novel.*

2 situate something at a center of operations. ∎ **based** adj.
– PHRASES **touch base** informal briefly make or renew contact.

base² ▸adj. **1** without moral principles: *the baser instincts of greed and selfishness.* **2** old use of low social class. ∎ **base·ness** n.

base·ball /ˈbāsˌbôl/ ▸n. a team game played with a bat and ball on a diamond-shaped circuit of four bases, to all of which in turn a batter must run to score.

base·ball cap ▸n. a cotton cap with a large bill.

base·board /ˈbāsˌbôrd/ ▸n. a narrow wooden board running along the base of an interior wall.

base hit ▸n. Baseball a fair ball hit such that the batter can advance safely to first base without aid of an error committed by the fielding team or a fielder's choice.

base jump ▸n. a parachute jump from a fixed point, e.g., a high building.

base·less /ˈbāslis/ ▸adj. not based on fact; untrue.

base·line /ˈbāsˌlīn/ ▸n. **1** a minimum or starting point used for comparisons. **2** (in tennis, volleyball, etc.) the line marking each end of a court. **3** Baseball the line between bases, which a server must stay close to.

base·man /ˈbāsmən/ ▸n. (pl. **basemen**) Baseball a fielder designated to cover first, second, or third base.

base·ment /ˈbāsmənt/ ▸n. a room or floor below ground level.

base met·al ▸n. a common nonprecious metal such as copper, tin, or zinc.

base on balls ▸n. Baseball another term for **WALK** (sense 5 of the noun).

ba·ses /ˈbāsēz/ ▸ plural of **BASE¹** and **BASIS**.

bash /bash/ informal ▸v. **1** hit someone or something hard. **2** (**bash something out**) produce something rapidly and carelessly. ▸n. **1** a heavy blow. **2** a party. ∎ **ba·sher** n.

bash·ful /ˈbashfəl/ ▸adj. shy and easily embarrassed. ∎ **bash·ful·ly** adv. **bash·ful·ness** n.

BASIC /ˈbāsik/ ▸n. a simple high-level computer programming language.

ba·sic /ˈbāsik/ ▸adj. **1** forming an essential foundation; fundamental: *certain basic rules must be obeyed.* **2** consisting of the minimum required or offered: *a basic wage.* **3** Chemistry containing or having the properties of a base; alkaline. ▸n. (**basics**) essential facts or principles of a subject.

ba·si·cal·ly /ˈbāsik(ə)lē/ ▸adv. **1** in the most fundamental respects. **2** used to sum up a more complex situation: *I basically did the same thing.*

bas·il /ˈbāzəl, ˈbazəl/ ▸n. an herb of the mint family, used in cooking.

ba·sil·i·ca /bəˈsilikə/ ▸n. **1** (in ancient Rome) a large oblong public building with two rows of columns and a domed recess at one end. **2** a Christian church of a similar design.

bas·i·lisk /ˈbasəˌlisk, ˈbaz-/ ▸n. **1** a mythical reptile whose gaze or breath could kill. **2** a long, slender Central American lizard.

ba·sin /ˈbāsən/ ▸n. **1** a large bowl or open container for preparing food or holding liquid. **2** a circular valley or natural depression. **3** an area drained by a river and its tributaries. **4** an enclosed area of water for mooring boats.

ba·sis /ˈbāsis/ ▸n. (pl. **bases** /-sēz/) **1** the underlying support for an idea or process. **2** the

principles according to which an activity is carried on: *she needed coaching on a regular basis.*

bask /bask/ ▸v. **1** lie in warmth and sunlight for pleasure. **2** (**bask in**) take great pleasure in: *he was basking in the glory of his first book.*

bas·ket /ˈbaskit/ ▸n. **1** a container for holding or carrying things, made from interwoven strips of cane or wire. **2** Basketball a net fixed on a hoop, used as the goal. **3** Basketball a goal scored. **4** a group or range of currencies or investments.

bas·ket·ball /ˈbaskitˌbôl/ ▸n. a team game in which goals are scored by throwing a ball through a net fixed on a hoop.

bas·ket case ▸n. informal a useless person or thing.

bas·ket·ry /ˈbaskitrē/ ▸n. **1** the craft of basketmaking. **2** baskets as a whole.

bas·ket·work /ˈbaskitˌwərk/ ▸n. material woven in the style of a basket.

bask·ing shark ▸n. a large shark that feeds on plankton and swims slowly close to the surface.

bas·ma·ti rice /bäsˈmätē/ ▸n. a kind of long-grain Indian rice with a delicate aroma.

Basque /bask/ ▸n. **1** a member of a people living in the western Pyrenees in France and Spain. **2** the language of the Basques.

bas-re·lief /ˌbä rəˈlēf/ ▸n. Art low relief.

bass¹ /bās/ ▸n. **1** the lowest adult male singing voice. **2** informal a bass guitar or double bass. **3** the low-frequency output of transmitted or reproduced sound. ▸adj. referring to an instrument that is lowest in pitch in its family: *a bass clarinet.* ∎ **bass·ist** n.

bass² /bas/ ▸n. (pl. same or **basses**) **1** the common European freshwater perch (fish). **2** an American fish of the freshwater sunfish family. **3** a sea bass.

bass clef /bās klef/ ▸n. Music a clef placing F below middle C on the second-highest line of the staff.

bas·set /ˈbasit/ (also **basset hound**) ▸n. a breed of hunting dog with a long body, short legs, and long ears.

bas·si·net /ˌbasəˈnet/ ▸n. a child's wicker cradle.

bas·so /ˈbasō, bä-/ ▸n. (pl. **bassos** or **bassi** /ˈbasē/) a bass voice or vocal part.

bas·soon /bəˈsoōn, ba-/ ▸n. a large bass woodwind instrument of the oboe family. ∎ **bas·soon·ist** n.

bas·so pro·fun·do /ˈbasō prōˈfəndō, ˈbäsō/ ▸n. (pl. **bassos profundos** or **bassi profundi** /ˈbäsē prōˈfəndē/) a bass singer with an exceptionally low range.

bass·wood /ˈbasˌwoŏd/ ▸n. any of the linden trees native to North America.

bas·tard /ˈbastərd/ ▸n. **1** old use or derogatory a person born to parents who are not married to each other. **2** informal an unpleasant person. **3** informal a person of a specified kind: *the poor bastard.* ▸adj. no longer in a pure or original form: *a bastard language.*

bas·tard·ize /ˈbastərˌdīz/ ▸v. (often as adj. **bastardized**) make something impure by adding new elements: *a bastardized form of French.* ∎ **bas·tard·i·za·tion** /ˌbastərdiˈzāshən/ n.

bas·tar·dy /ˈbastərdē/ ▸n. old use illegitimacy.

baste¹ /bāst/ ▸v. pour fat or juices over meat during cooking. ∎ **ba·ster** n.

baste² ▸v. sew something with long, loose stitches in preparation for permanent sewing.

bas·ti·na·do /ˌbastəˈnādō, -ˈnädō/ ▸n. chiefly historical a form of punishment or torture that involves caning the soles of someone's feet.

bas·tion /'bascHən/ ► n. **1** a projecting part of a fortification allowing an increased angle of fire. **2** something that preserves particular principles or activities: *the town was a bastion of conservatism.*

bat¹ /bat/ ► n. an implement with a handle and a solid surface, used in sports for hitting the ball. ► v. (**bats, batting, batted**) **1** (in sports) take the role of hitting rather than fielding the ball. **2** hit someone or something with the flat of one's hand. **3** (**bat something around/about**) informal casually discuss an idea.
– PHRASES **bat a thousand** informal produce consistently favorable outcomes; be consistently correct about something or a series of things. **go to bat for** informal support.

bat² ► n. **1** a flying mammal with wings that extend between the fingers and limbs, active at night. **2** (**old bat**) informal an unattractive and unpleasant woman.
– PHRASES **have bats in the belfry** informal be eccentric or crazy.

bat³ ► v. (**bats, batting, batted**) flutter one's eyelashes.
– PHRASES **not bat an eyelid** informal show no surprise or concern.

batch /bacH/ ► n. **1** a quantity of goods produced or dispatched at one time. **2** a group of people or things. **3** Computing a group of records processed as a single unit. ► v. arrange things in batches.

bat·ed /'bātid/ ► adj. (in phrase **with bated breath**) in great suspense.

> **USAGE**
> The correct spelling is **with bated breath** (not *baited*).

bath /baTH, bäTH/ ► n. **1** a large tub that is filled with water for washing one's body. **2** an act of washing in a bath. **3** (also **baths**) Brit. a building containing a public swimming pool or washing facilities. **4** a container holding a liquid in which an object is immersed in chemical processing.

bathe /bāTH/ ► v. **1** wash by immersing one's body in water. **2** chiefly Brit. take a swim. **3** soak or wipe something gently with liquid to clean or soothe it. **4** fill with or envelop in something: *my desk is bathed in sunlight.* ■ **bath·er** n.

bath·house /'baTH,hous/ ► n. **1** a building with baths for communal use. **2** a building where swimmers change clothes.

bath·ing suit (Brit. also **bathing costume**) ► n. a swimsuit.

ba·thos /'bāTHäs/ ► n. (in literature) an unintentional change in mood from the important and serious to the trivial or ridiculous. ■ **ba·thet·ic** /bə'THetik/ adj.

bath·robe /'baTH,rōb/ ► n. a robe, typically made of terrycloth.

bath·room /'baTH,rōōm, -,rŏŏm/ ► n. **1** a room containing a bathtub or shower and usually also a washbasin and toilet. **2** a room containing a toilet.

bath salts ► pl.n. crystals that are dissolved in bathwater to soften or perfume it.

bath·tub /'baTH,təb/ ► n. a tub in which to bathe.

bath·y·sphere /'baTHə,sfir/ ► n. a manned spherical vessel for deep-sea observation.

ba·tik /bə'tēk/ ► n. a method of producing colored designs on cloth by waxing the parts not to be dyed.

ba·tiste /bə'tēst/ ► n. a fine linen or cotton fabric.

bat mitz·vah /bät 'mitsvə/ ► n. a religious ceremony in which a Jewish girl aged twelve years and a day takes on adult responsibilities under Jewish law.

ba·ton /bə'tän/ ► n. **1** a thin stick used to conduct an orchestra or choir. **2** a short stick passed from runner to runner in a relay race. **3** a stick carried and twirled by a drum major. **4** a police officer's club.

bats·man /'batsmən/ ► n. (pl. **batsmen**) a player who bats in cricket.

bat·tal·ion /bə'talyən/ ► n. a large body of troops, forming part of a brigade.

bat·ten¹ /'batn/ ► n. a long wooden or metal strip for strengthening or securing something. ► v. strengthen or fasten something with battens.
– PHRASES **batten down the hatches 1** secure a ship's tarpaulins. **2** prepare for a difficult situation.

bat·ten² ► v. (**batten on**) thrive or prosper at the expense of: *multinational monopolies batten on the working classes.*

bat·ter¹ /'batər/ ► v. **1** hit someone or something hard and repeatedly. **2** damage or harm: *the space program has been battered by bureaucratic wrangling.* ■ **bat·ter·er** n.

bat·ter² ► n. a mixture of flour, egg, and milk or water, used for making pancakes or coating food before frying. ■ **bat·tered** adj.

bat·ter³ ► n. a player who bats in baseball.

bat·ter·ing ram ► n. a heavy object swung or rammed against a door to break it down.

bat·ter·y /'batərē/ ► n. (pl. **batteries**) **1** a device containing one or more electrical cells, for use as a source of power. **2** an extensive series: *a battery of tests.* **3** Law unlawful physical contact with another person. **4** a group of heavy guns.

bat·ting or·der ► n. Baseball the fixed order in which batters take their turn at bat.

bat·tle /'batl/ ► n. **1** a prolonged fight between organized armed forces. **2** a long and difficult struggle or conflict: *a battle of wits.* ► v. fight or struggle with determination: *the city's two tabloids are battling for survival.* ■ **bat·tler** n.
– PHRASES **battle royal** a fierce fight or dispute.

battle·ax /'batl,aks/ (also **battleaxe**) ► n. **1** a large ax used in ancient warfare. **2** informal an aggressive older woman.

bat·tle·dress /'batl,dres/ ► n. combat uniform worn by soldiers.

bat·tle·field /'batl,fēld/ (also **battleground**) ► n. the piece of ground on which a battle is fought.

bat·tle·ment /'batlmənt/ ► n. a parapet at the top of a wall with gaps for firing from, forming part of a fortification. ■ **bat·tle·ment·ed** adj.

bat·tle·ship /'batl,sHip/ ► n. a heavily armored warship with large-caliber guns.

bat·ty /'batē/ ► adj. (**battier, battiest**) informal crazy. ■ **bat·ti·ness** n.

bat·wing /'bat,wiNG/ ► adj. (of a sleeve) having a deep armhole and a tight cuff.

bau·ble /'bôbəl/ ► n. a small, showy trinket or decoration.

baud /bôd/ ► n. (pl. same or **bauds**) Computing a unit of transmission speed for electronic signals, corresponding to one information unit or event per second.

baulk ► v. & n. chiefly British spelling of BALK.

baux·ite /ˈbôksīt/ ▸ n. a claylike rock from which aluminum is obtained.

bawd·y /ˈbôdē/ ▸ adj. (**bawdier, bawdiest**) dealing with sex in a comical way. ▪ **bawd·i·ness** n.

bawd·y house ▸ n. old use a brothel.

bawl /bôl/ ▸ v. 1 shout out noisily. 2 (**bawl someone out**) reprimand someone angrily. 3 weep noisily. ▸ n. a loud shout.

bay¹ /bā/ ▸ n. a broad curved inlet of the sea.

bay² (also **bay laurel** or **sweet bay**) ▸ n. an evergreen Mediterranean shrub with aromatic leaves that are used in cooking.

bay³ ▸ n. 1 a window area that projects outward from a wall. 2 an area allocated for a purpose: *a loading bay*. 3 a compartment with a particular function in an aircraft, motor vehicle, or ship: *a bomb bay*.

bay⁴ ▸ adj. (of a horse) reddish-brown with black points. ▸ n. a bay horse.

bay⁵ ▸ v. (of a dog) howl loudly. ▸ n. the sound of baying.
– PHRASES **at bay** trapped or cornered. **hold** (or **keep**) **someone/thing at bay** prevent someone or something from approaching or having an effect.

bay·ber·ry /ˈbā‚berē/ ▸ n. (pl. **bayberries**) a North American shrub with aromatic leathery leaves and waxy berries.

bay leaf ▸ n. the aromatic, usually dried, leaf of a bay, used in cooking.

bay·o·net /ˈbāənit, ‚bāə'net/ ▸ n. a long blade fixed to the muzzle of a rifle for hand-to-hand fighting. ▸ v. (**bayonets, bayoneting, bayoneted**) stab someone with a bayonet. ▸ adj. referring to a type of fitting for a light bulb that is pushed into a socket and then twisted into place.

bay·ou /ˈbīoo, ˈbīō/ ▸ n. (pl. **bayous**) (in the southern US) a marshy outlet of a lake or river.

bay rum ▸ n. a perfume for the hair, distilled originally from rum and bayberry leaves.

bay win·dow ▸ n. a window built to project outward from a wall.

ba·zaar /bəˈzär/ ▸ n. 1 a market in a Middle Eastern country. 2 a sale of goods to raise funds for charity.

ba·zoo·ka /bəˈz‍ookə/ ▸ n. a short-range rocket launcher used against tanks.

BB ▸ n. a lead pellet of a standard size, used in air rifles.

BBC ▸ abbr. British Broadcasting Corporation.

BBQ ▸ abbr. barbecue.

BC ▸ abbr. 1 before Christ (used to show that a date comes the specified number of years before the traditional date of Jesus's birth). 2 British Columbia.

USAGE
BC is normally written in small capitals and placed **after** the numerals, as in *72 BC*.

bcc ▸ abbr. blind carbon copy.

BCE ▸ abbr. before the Common Era (indicating dates before the Christian era).

BCG ▸ abbr. Bacillus Calmette-Guérin, an anti-tuberculosis vaccine.

BD ▸ abbr. Bachelor of Divinity.

BDSM ▸ abbr. bondage, domination, sadism, masochism.

BE ▸ abbr. 1 Bachelor of Education. 2 Bachelor of Engineering.

Be ▸ symbol the chemical element beryllium.

be /bē/ ▸ v. (sing. present **am; are; is**; pl. present **are**; 1st and 3rd sing. past **was**; 2nd sing. past and pl. past **were**; present subjunctive **be**; past subjunctive **were**; present part. **being**; past part. **been**) 1 (usu. **there is/are**) exist; be present. 2 take place. 3 have the specified state, nature, or role: *the floor was uneven.* 4 come; go; visit. ▸ auxiliary v. 1 used with a present participle to form continuous tenses: *they are coming.* 2 used with a past participle to form the passive voice. 3 used to indicate something that is due to, may, or should happen.
– PHRASES **the be-all and end-all** informal the most important aspect. **-to-be** of the future: *his bride-to-be.*

be- ▸ prefix forming verbs. 1 all over; all around: *bespatter.* 2 thoroughly; excessively: *bewilder.* 3 expressing transitive action: *bemoan.* 4 affect with or cause to be: *becalm.* 5 (forming adjectives ending in *-ed*) having; covered with: *bejeweled.*

beach /bēcH/ ▸ n. a pebbly or sandy shore at the edge of the sea or a lake. ▸ v. bring or come onto a beach from the water.

beach ball ▸ n. a large, light inflatable ball used for playing games on the beach.

beach·comb·er /ˈbēcH‚kōmər/ ▸ n. a person who searches beaches for articles of interest or value.

beach·head /ˈbēcH‚hed/ ▸ n. a defended position on a beach taken from the enemy by landing forces.

beach·wear /ˈbēcH‚we(ə)r/ ▸ n. clothing suitable for wearing on the beach.

bea·con /ˈbēkən/ ▸ n. 1 a fire lit on the top of a hill as a signal. 2 a signal light for ships or aircraft. 3 a radio transmitter signaling the position of a ship or aircraft.

bead /bēd/ ▸ n. 1 a small piece of glass, stone, etc., threaded in a string with others to make a necklace or rosary. 2 a drop of a liquid on a surface. 3 a small knob forming the front sight of a gun. 4 the reinforced inner edge of a tire. ▸ v. (often as adj. **beaded**) decorate or cover with beads: *a beaded bag.*

bead·y /ˈbēdē/ ▸ adj. (of a person's eyes) small, round, and observing things clearly. ▪ **bead·i·ly** adv.

bea·gle /ˈbēgəl/ ▸ n. a small, short-legged breed of hound.

beak /bēk/ ▸ n. a bird's horny projecting jaws; a bill. ▪ **beaked** adj. **beak·y** adj.

beak·er /ˈbēkər/ ▸ n. a cylindrical glass container used in laboratories.

beam /bēm/ ▸ n. 1 a long piece of timber or metal used as a support in building. 2 a narrow horizontal length of timber for balancing on in gymnastics. 3 a ray or shaft of light or particles. 4 a radiant smile. 5 a ship's breadth at its widest point. ▸ v. 1 transmit a radio signal or broadcast. 2 shine brightly. 3 smile radiantly.
– PHRASES **off beam** informal on the wrong track; mistaken.

bean /bēn/ ▸ n. 1 an edible seed growing in long pods on certain plants. 2 the hard seed of a coffee or cocoa plant. 3 informal a very small amount or nothing at all: *there is not a bean of truth in the report.*
– PHRASES **full of beans** informal lively; in high spirits. **old bean** Brit. informal, dated a friendly form of address to a man.

bean·bag /ˈbēn‚bag/ ▸ n. 1 a small bag filled with

dried beans and used in children's games. **2** a large cushion filled with polystyrene beads, used as a seat.

bean count·er ▶ n. informal an accountant or bureaucrat who is excessively concerned with controlling expenditure.

bean curd ▶ n. another term for TOFU.

bean·ie /'bēnē/ ▶ n. (pl. **beanies**) a small close-fitting hat worn on the back of the head.

bean·pole /'bēn,pōl/ ▶ n. informal a tall, thin person.

bean sprouts ▶ pl.n. the edible sprouting seeds of certain beans.

bear¹ /be(ə)r/ ▶ v. (past **bore**; past part. **borne**) **1** carry someone or something. **2** have something as a quality or visible mark. **3** support a weight. **4** (**bear oneself**) behave in a specified way: *she bore herself with dignity.* **5** manage to tolerate: *the grief was more than he could bear.* **6** (**cannot bear**) strongly dislike someone or something. **7** give birth to a child. **8** (of a tree or plant) produce fruit or flowers. **9** turn and go in a specified direction: *bear left.*
– PHRASES **bear down on** approach in a purposeful or threatening way. **bear fruit** have good results. **bear someone a grudge** feel resentment against someone. **bear something in mind** remember something and take it into account. **bear on** be relevant to. **bear something out** support or confirm something. **bear up** stay cheerful in difficult circumstances. **bear with** be patient or tolerant with. **bear witness** (or **testimony**) **to** provide evidence of.

> USAGE
> Do not confuse **bear** with **bare**. **Bear** means 'carry' (*he was bearing a tray of food*) or 'tolerate,' whereas **bare** is an adjective that means 'naked' or a verb meaning 'uncover or reveal' (*he bared his chest*).

bear² ▶ n. **1** a large, heavy mammal with thick fur and a very short tail. **2** Stock Exchange a person who sells shares hoping to buy them back later at a lower price. Often contrasted with BULL¹.
– PHRASES **loaded for bear** informal fully prepared for a confrontation or challenge.

bear·a·ble /'be(ə)rəbəl/ ▶ adj. able to be endured. ■ **bear·a·bly** adv.

bear-bait·ing ▶ n. historical a form of entertainment that involved setting dogs to attack a captive bear.

bear claw ▶ n. a semicircular sweet pastry, usually flavored with almond and often containing raisins.

beard /bi(ə)rd/ ▶ n. **1** a growth of hair on the chin and lower cheeks of a man's face. **2** a tuft of hairs or bristles on certain animals or plants. ▶ v. boldly confront or challenge someone daunting. ■ **beard·ed** adj. **beard·less** adj.

bear·er /'be(ə)rər/ ▶ n. **1** a person or thing that carries something. **2** a person who presents a check or other order to pay money.

bear hug ▶ n. a rough, tight embrace.

bear·ing /'be(ə)riNG/ ▶ n. **1** a person's way of standing, moving, or behaving: *a man of dignified bearing.* **2** the way in which something is related to or influences something else: *past accidents can have a bearing on back problems.* **3** (usu. **bearings**) a part of a machine that allows one part to rotate or move in contact with another. **4** direction or position relative to a fixed point. **5** (**one's bearings**) awareness of one's position in relation to one's surroundings: *I checked my map to get my bearings.* **6** a heraldic emblem.

bear·ish /'be(ə)risH/ ▶ adj. resembling a bear, especially in being surly or clumsy.

bear mar·ket ▶ n. Stock Exchange a market in which share prices are falling.

Bé·ar·naise sauce /,ber'nāz/ ▶ n. a rich sauce thickened with egg yolks and flavored with tarragon.

bear·skin /'be(ə)r,skin/ ▶ n. a tall cap of black fur worn ceremonially by certain troops.

beast /bēst/ ▶ n. **1** an animal, especially a large or dangerous mammal. **2** a very cruel or wicked person.

beast·ie /'bēstē/ ▶ n. (pl. **beasties**) Scottish or humorous a small animal or insect.

beast·ly /'bēstlē/ ▶ adj. informal very unpleasant. ■ **beast·li·ness** n.

beast of bur·den ▶ n. an animal used for carrying loads.

beat /bēt/ ▶ v. (past **beat**; past part. **beaten**) **1** hit someone repeatedly and violently. **2** hit something repeatedly to flatten it or make a noise. **3** defeat someone or overcome something. **4** do or be better than: *he beat his own world record.* **5** informal baffle someone. **6** (of the heart) throb. **7** (of a bird) move the wings up and down. **8** stir cooking ingredients vigorously. **9** move across land striking at the vegetation to raise game birds for shooting. ▶ n. **1** a main accent in music or poetry. **2** a throb of the heart. **3** a movement of a bird's wings. **4** a brief pause. **5** an area patrolled by a police officer. ▶ adj. informal completely exhausted. ■ **beat·a·ble** adj. **beat·er** n.
– PHRASES **beat around** (or **about**) **the bush** discuss a matter without coming to the point. **beat a dead horse** waste energy on something that can never be successful. **beat down** shine very brightly. **beat someone down** force someone to reduce the price of something. **beat it** informal leave. **beat someone up** attack someone and hit them repeatedly. **beat a retreat** withdraw quickly to avoid something. **off the beaten track** isolated.

beat·box /'bēt,bäks/ ▶ n. informal **1** a drum machine. **2** a radio or radio cassette player for playing loud music, especially rap.

beat gen·er·a·tion ▶ n. a movement of young people in the 1950s and early 1960s who rejected conventional society.

be·a·tif·ic /,bēə'tifik/ ▶ adj. **1** feeling or expressing intense happiness. **2** (in the Christian Church) bestowing spiritual blessedness. ■ **be·a·tif·i·cal·ly** adv.

be·at·i·fy /bē'atə,fī/ ▶ v. (**beatifies, beatifying, beatified**) (in the Roman Catholic Church) announce that a dead person is in a state of spiritual bliss, the first step toward making them a saint. ■ **be·at·i·fi·ca·tion** /bē,atəfi'kāsHən/ n.

be·at·i·tude /bē'ati,t(y)ōōd/ ▶ n. very great happiness or blessedness.

beat·nik /'bētnik/ ▶ n. a young person associated with the beat generation.

beat-up ▶ adj. informal worn out by overuse.

beau /bō/ ▶ n. (pl. **beaux** /bōz/ or **beaus** /bōz/) dated **1** a boyfriend or male admirer. **2** a dandy.

Beau·fort scale /'bōfərt/ ▶ n. a scale of wind speed ranging from force 0 to force 12.

Beau·jo·lais /,bōzHə'lā/ ▶ n. a light red wine produced in the Beaujolais district of SE France.

beau monde /ˌbō 'mônd/ ► n. fashionable society.

beau·te·ous /'byōōtēəs/ ► adj. literary beautiful.

beau·ti·cian /byōō'tishən/ ► n. a person whose job is to give beauty treatments.

beau·ti·ful /'byōōtəfəl/ ► adj. 1 very pleasing to the senses or to the mind. 2 of a very high standard; excellent. ■ **beau·ti·ful·ly** adv.

beau·ti·fy /'byōōtə,fī/ ► v. (beautifies, beautifying, beautified) make someone or something beautiful. ■ **beau·ti·fi·ca·tion** /ˌbyōōtəfi'kāshən/ n.

beau·ty /'byōōtē/ ► n. (pl. beauties) 1 a combination of qualities that is very pleasing to the senses or to the mind. 2 a beautiful woman. 3 an excellent example of something. 4 an attractive feature or advantage. ► adj. intended to make someone more attractive: *beauty treatment.*

beau·ty con·test ► n. a contest in which the winner is the woman judged the most beautiful.

beau·ty mark (also **beauty spot**) ► n. a dark facial mole, especially one near a woman's upper lip, or an artificial mole applied to the face.

beau·ty queen ► n. the winner of a beauty contest.

beau·ty sa·lon (also **beauty parlor**) ► n. an establishment in which hairdressing and beauty treatments are carried out.

beau·ty sleep ► n. humorous sleep that helps one remain young and attractive.

beaux /bōz/ ► plural of BEAU.

bea·ver /'bēvər/ ► n. (pl. same or **beavers**) 1 a large rodent with a broad tail and strong teeth that lives partly in water. 2 a hat made of beaver fur. 3 a very hard-working person. ► v. informal work hard: *she beavered away to keep things running smoothly.*

be·bop /'bē,bäp/ ► n. a type of jazz characterized by complex harmony and rhythms.

be·calm /bi'kä(l)m/ ► v. (be becalmed) (of a sailing ship) be unable to move through lack of wind.

be·came /bi'kām/ ► past of BECOME.

be·cause /bi'kôz, -'kəz/ ► conj. for the reason that; since.
– PHRASES **because of** by reason of.

> **USAGE**
> Confusion can arise when **because** follows a negative such as *not.* For example, the sentence *he didn't go because he was ill* could mean either 'the reason he didn't go was that he was ill' or 'being ill wasn't the reason for him going; there was another reason.' Use a comma when the first meaning is intended (*he didn't go, because he was ill*), or avoid using **because** after a negative altogether.
> On starting a sentence with **because**, see the note at AND.

bé·cha·mel /ˌbāshə'mel/ ► n. a rich white sauce flavored with herbs and other seasonings.

beck /bek/ ► n. (in phrase **at someone's beck and call**) always having to be ready to obey someone's orders.

beck·on /'bekən/ ► v. 1 make a gesture to encourage or instruct someone to approach or follow. 2 seem appealing or inviting: *the wide-open spaces of Australia beckoned.*

be·come /bi'kəm/ ► v. (past **became** /bi'kām/; past part. **become**) 1 begin to be. 2 develop into: *the child will become an adult.* 3 (**become of**)

happen to: *what would become of her now?* 4 suit or be appropriate to: *celebrity status did not become him.*

be·com·ing /bi'kəmiNG/ ► adj. 1 (of clothing) looking good on someone. 2 appropriate or suitable. ■ **be·com·ing·ly** adv.

bec·que·rel /ˌbek(ə)'rel/ ► n. Physics a unit of radioactivity in the SI system.

BEd /ˌbē 'ed/ ► abbr. Bachelor of Education.

bed /bed/ ► n. 1 a piece of furniture for sleeping on. 2 an area of ground where flowers and plants are grown. 3 a part or layer on which something rests or is supported: *roast chicken on a bed of herbs.* 4 a layer of rock. 5 the bottom of the sea or a lake or river. 6 informal a bed as a place for sexual activity. ► v. (**beds, bedding, bedded**) 1 provide someone with or settle in sleeping accommodations. 2 fix something firmly. 3 informal have sex with someone. 4 (**bed something out**) transfer a plant from a pot to the ground. ■ **bed·ded** adj.
– PHRASES **a bed of roses** (usu. with negative) a comfortable or easy situation or activity.

bed and board ► n. lodging and food.

bed and break·fast ► n. 1 sleeping accommodations and breakfast in a guest house or hotel. 2 a guest house.

be·daz·zle /bi'dazəl/ ► v. greatly impress someone with brilliance or skill.

bed·bug /'bed,bəg/ ► n. a wingless bug that sucks the blood of sleeping humans.

bed·cham·ber /'bed,CHāmbər/ ► n. old use a bedroom.

bed·clothes /'bed,klō(TH)z/ ► pl.n. coverings for a bed, such as sheets and blankets.

bed·ding /'bediNG/ ► n. 1 bedclothes. 2 straw or similar material for animals to sleep on.

bed·ding plant ► n. an annual plant produced for planting in a garden in the spring.

be·deck /bi'dek/ ► v. decorate lavishly: *the town was bedecked with flags.*

be·dev·il /bi'devəl/ ► v. (bedevils, bedeviling, bedeviled) cause continual trouble to: *the devices were bedeviled by mechanical failures.*

bed·fel·low /'bed,felō/ ► n. 1 a person or thing closely associated with another: *laughter and tragedy are not such strange bedfellows.* 2 a person sharing a bed with another.

bed head ► n. informal a casual hairstyle resulting from failure to comb or arrange the hair after sleep.

be·di·zen /bi'dīzən/ ► v. literary decorate someone or something gaudily.

bed·lam /'bedləm/ ► n. a scene of uproar and confusion.

bed linen ► n. sheets and pillowcases.

Bed·ou·in /'bed(ə)win/ (also **Beduin**) ► n. (pl. same) an Arab living as a nomad in the desert.

bed·pan /'bed,pan/ ► n. a container used as a toilet by a bedridden patient.

bed·post /'bed,pōst/ ► n. any of the four upright supports of a bedstead.

be·drag·gled /bi'dragəld/ ► adj. untidy or disheveled.

bed·rid·den /'bed,ridn/ ► adj. having to stay in bed because of sickness or old age.

bed·rock /'bed,räk/ ► n. 1 solid rock underlying loose deposits such as soil. 2 underlying or basic principles: *self-sufficiency was the bedrock of the regime.*

bed·roll /'bed,rōl/ ▶ n. a sleeping bag or other bedding rolled into a bundle.

bed·room /'bed,rōōm, -,rŏŏm/ ▶ n. a room for sleeping in.

bed·side man·ner /'bed,sīd/ ▶ n. a doctor's approach to a patient.

bed·sore /'bed,sôr/ ▶ n. a sore caused by lying in bed in one position for a long time.

bed·spread /'bed,spred/ ▶ n. a decorative cloth used to cover a bed.

bed·stead /'bed,sted/ ▶ n. the framework of a bed.

bed·straw /'bed,strô/ ▶ n. a plant with small flowers and slender leaves, formerly used for stuffing mattresses.

bed·time /'bed,tīm/ ▶ n. the usual time when someone goes to bed.

bed-wet·ting ▶ n. urinating unintentionally while asleep.

bee /bē/ ▶ n. 1 a stinging winged insect that collects nectar and pollen and produces wax and honey. 2 a meeting for communal work or amusement: *a sewing bee.*
– PHRASES **the bee's knees** informal an outstandingly good person or thing. **have a bee in one's bonnet** informal be obsessed with something.

beech /bēCH/ ▶ n. a large tree with gray bark and hard, pale wood.

bee-eat·er ▶ n. a brightly colored insect-eating Old World bird with a curved bill and a long tail.

beef /bēf/ ▶ n. 1 the flesh of a cow, bull, or ox, used as food. 2 informal strength or power: *he was brought in to give the team more beef.* 3 informal flesh with well-developed muscle. 4 (pl. **beefs**) informal a complaint or grievance. ▶ v. informal 1 (**beef something up**) make stronger or more substantial: *rifles were supplied to the police to beef up security.* 2 complain about someone or something.

beef·cake /'bēf,kāk/ ▶ n. informal men with well-developed muscles.

beef·eat·er /'bēf,ētər/ ▶ n. a Yeoman Warder or Yeoman of the Guard in the Tower of London.

beef·steak /'bēf,stāk/ ▶ n. a thick slice of steak, especially rump steak.

beef·steak to·ma·to ▶ n. a large, firm variety of tomato.

beef·y /'bēfē/ ▶ adj. (**beefier, beefiest**) 1 informal muscular or powerful. 2 tasting like beef.

bee·hive /'bē,hīv/ ▶ n. 1 a structure in which bees are kept. 2 a woman's domed and lacquered hairstyle popular in the 1960s.

bee·keep·ing /'bē,kēpiNG/ ▶ n. the occupation of owning and breeding bees for their honey.
■ **bee·keep·er** n.

bee·line /'bē,līn/ ▶ n. (in phrase **make a beeline for**) hurry directly to.

Be·el·ze·bub /bē'elzə,bəb/ ▶ n. the Devil.

been /bin/ ▶ past participle of BE.

beep /bēp/ ▶ n. a short, high-pitched sound made by electronic equipment or a vehicle horn. ▶ v. produce a beep.

beep·er /'bēpər/ ▶ n. another term for PAGER.

beer /bi(ə)r/ ▶ n. an alcoholic drink made from fermented malt flavored with hops.

beer bel·ly (also **beer gut**) ▶ n. informal a man's fat belly caused by excessive beer-drinking.

beer gar·den ▶ n. a yard next to a bar or tavern, where drinks are served.

beer·y /'bi(ə)rē/ ▶ adj. informal 1 smelling or tasting of beer. 2 influenced by the drinking of beer: *a burst of beery laughter.*

bee-stung ▶ adj. informal (of a woman's lips) full and red.

bees·wax /'bēz,waks/ ▶ n. 1 wax produced by bees to make honeycombs, used for wood polishes and candles. 2 informal a person's concern or business.

beet /bēt/ ▶ n. a plant with a fleshy root, grown for food and for processing into sugar.

bee·tle[1] /'bētl/ ▶ n. an insect with the forewings modified into a hard case that covers the hind wings and abdomen. ▶ v. informal make one's way hurriedly.

bee·tle[2] ▶ n. a very heavy mallet.

bee·tle[3] ▶ v. (usu. as adj. **beetling**) project or overhang: *his beetling brows.*

beet·root /'bēt,rōōt/ ▶ n. chiefly Brit. the edible dark-red root of a variety of beet.

BEF ▶ abbr. British Expeditionary Force.

be·fall /bi'fôl/ ▶ v. (past **befell**; past part. **befallen**) literary (especially of something bad) happen to: *a terrible tragedy befell him.*

be·fit /bi'fit/ ▶ v. (**befits, befitting, befitted**) be appropriate for: *as befits a Quaker, he was a humane man.* ■ **be·fit·ting** adj.

be·fore /bi'fôr/ ▶ prep., conj., & adv. 1 during the time preceding. 2 in front of. 3 rather than.

be·fore·hand /bi'fôr,hand/ ▶ adv. in advance.

be·friend /bi'frend/ ▶ v. become a friend to someone.

be·fud·dle /bi'fədl/ ▶ v. (often as adj. **befuddled**) muddle or confuse someone.
■ **be·fud·dle·ment** n.

beg /beg/ ▶ v. (**begs, begging, begged**) 1 ask someone earnestly or humbly for something. 2 ask for food or money as charity. 3 (**beg off**) withdraw from something planned or promised: *they went to see the fireworks—I begged off.*
– PHRASES **beg the question 1** invite an obvious question. 2 assume the truth of something without arguing it. **go begging** be available because unwanted by others.

be·gan /bi'gan/ ▶ past of BEGIN.

be·gat /bi'gat/ ▶ old-fashioned past of BEGET.

be·get /bi'get/ ▶ v. (**begets, begetting, begot** /bi'gät/; past part. **begotten** /bi'gätn/) literary 1 cause: *vengeance begets vengeance.* 2 produce a child.
■ **be·get·ter** n.

beg·gar /'begər/ ▶ n. 1 a person who lives by begging for food or money. 2 informal a person of a particular type: *lucky beggar!* ▶ v. make someone very poor.
– PHRASES **beggar belief** (or **description**) be too extraordinary to be believed or described.

beg·gar·ly /'begərlē/ ▶ adj. 1 very small in amount. 2 very poor.

beg·gar·y /'begərē/ ▶ n. a state of extreme poverty.

be·gin /bi'gin/ ▶ v. (**begins, beginning, began** /-'gan/; past part. **begun** /-'gən/) 1 perform or undergo the first part of an action or activity. 2 come into being. 3 have as its starting point: *the track begins at the village.* 4 (**begin on**) set to work on something. 5 informal have any chance of doing: *I can't begin to describe my confusion.* ■ **be·gin·ner** n. **be·gin·ning** n.

be·gone /bi'gôn, -'gän/ ▶ **exclam.** old use go away at once.

be·go·nia /bi'gōnyə, -nēə/ ▶ n. a garden or house plant with brightly colored flowers.

be·got /bi'gät/ ▶ past of BEGET.

be·got·ten /bi'gätn/ ▶ past participle of BEGET.

be·grudge /bi'grəj/ ▶ v. 1 feel envious that someone possesses or enjoys something: *I've never begrudged my father his achievements.* 2 give something reluctantly or resentfully.

be·guile /bi'gīl/ ▶ v. 1 charm or trick someone. 2 literary help time pass pleasantly. ■ **be·guil·ing** adj.

be·guine /'begēn, 'bā,gēn, bə'gēn/ ▶ n. a popular dance of Caribbean origin, similar to the foxtrot.

be·gum /'bāgəm, 'bē-/ ▶ n. Indian 1 a Muslim woman of high rank. 2 (**Begum**) the title of a married Muslim woman.

be·gun /bi'gən/ ▶ past participle of BEGIN.

be·half /bi'haf/ ▶ n. (in phrase **on behalf of** or **on someone's behalf**) 1 in the interests of a person, group, or principle. 2 as a representative of someone.

be·have /bi'hāv/ ▶ v. 1 act or operate in a specified way: *he always behaved like a gentleman.* 2 (also **behave oneself**) act in a polite or proper way.

be·haved /bi'hāvd/ ▶ adj. acting in a specified way: *a well-behaved child.*

be·hav·ior /bi'hāvyər/ (Brit. **behaviour**) ▶ n. the way in which someone or something behaves: *he was shocked by the behavior of the fans.* ■ **be·hav·ior·al** adj.

be·hav·ior·ism /bi'hāvyə,rizəm/ ▶ n. the theory that behavior can be explained in terms of conditioning, and that psychological disorders are best treated by altering behavior patterns. ■ **be·hav·ior·ist** n. & adj.

be·head /bi'hed/ ▶ v. execute someone by cutting off their head.

be·held /bi'held/ ▶ past and past participle of BEHOLD.

be·he·moth /bi'hēməth, 'bēəməth/ ▶ n. 1 a huge creature. 2 something very large, especially an organization.

be·hest /bi'hest/ ▶ n. (in phrase **at the behest of**) literary at the request or command of.

be·hind /bi'hīnd/ ▶ prep. & adv. 1 at or to the back or far side of. 2 farther back than other members of a group. 3 in support of. 4 responsible for an event or plan. 5 less advanced than. 6 late in achieving or paying something. 7 remaining after the departure or death of. ▶ n. informal a person's buttocks.

be·hold /bi'hōld/ ▶ v. (past and past part. **beheld**) old use or literary see or observe someone or something. ■ **be·hold·er** n.

be·hold·en /bi'hōldən/ ▶ adj. owing a debt of thanks to someone in return for a favor: *they don't want to be beholden to anyone.*

be·hoove /bi'hoōv/ ▶ v. (**it behooves someone to do**) formal it is necessary or appropriate for someone to do something: *if my brother is ill, then it behooves me to see him.*

beige /bāzH/ ▶ n. a pale whitish-brown color.

be·ing /'bēiNG/ ▶ n. 1 the state of existing; existence: *the town came into being because there was gold nearby.* 2 the nature of a person. 3 a living creature: *alien beings.*

be·jew·eled /bi'jōōəld/ ▶ adj. decorated with jewels.

be·la·bor /bi'lābər/ ▶ v. 1 attack someone physically or verbally. 2 argue or discuss in excessive detail: *there's no need to belabor the point.*

Be·la·rus·ian /,belə'rōōsiən, ,bä-/ (also **Belarussian** /,belə'rəsHən/) ▶ n. 1 a person from Belarus in eastern Europe. 2 the Slavic language of Belarus. ▶ adj. relating to Belarus.

be·lat·ed /bi'lātid/ ▶ adj. coming or happening late or too late: *a belated birthday present.* ■ **be·lat·ed·ly** adv. **be·lat·ed·ness** n.

be·lay /bi'lā/ ▶ v. 1 fix a rope around a rock, pin, or other object to secure it. 2 nautical slang stop! ▶ n. an act of belaying.

bel can·to /bel 'käntō, 'kan-/ ▶ n. a style of operatic singing using a full, rich, broad tone.

belch /belCH/ ▶ v. 1 noisily expel wind from the stomach through the mouth. 2 give out smoke or flames with great force. ▶ n. an act of belching.

be·lea·guered /bi'lēgərd/ ▶ adj. 1 in difficulties: *the beleaguered telecom industry.* 2 (of a place) under siege.

bel·em·nite /'beləm,nīt/ ▶ n. a type of extinct marine mollusk with a bullet-shaped internal shell, found as a fossil.

bel·fry /'belfrē/ ▶ n. (pl. **belfries**) the place in a bell tower or steeple in which bells are housed.

Bel·gian /'beljən/ ▶ n. a person from Belgium. ▶ adj. relating to Belgium.

Be·li·al /'bēlēəl/ ▶ n. the Devil.

be·lie /bi'lī/ ▶ v. (**belies, belying, belied**) 1 fail to give a true idea of: *her fast reflexes belied her age.* 2 show something to be untrue or unjustified.

be·lief /bi'lēf/ ▶ n. 1 a feeling that something exists or is true, especially one without proof. 2 a firmly held opinion. 3 (**belief in**) trust or confidence in: *we must have belief in our own capabilities.* 4 religious faith. – PHRASES **beyond belief** astonishing; incredible.

be·lieve /bi'lēv/ ▶ v. 1 accept that something is true or someone is telling the truth. 2 (**believe in**) feel certain that someone or something exists. 3 think that something is the case: *I believe we've already met.* 4 have religious faith. ■ **be·liev·a·bil·i·ty** /bi,lēvə'bilitē/ n. **be·liev·a·ble** /bi'lēvəbəl/. **be·liev·a·bly** adv. **be·liev·er** n.

be·lit·tle /bi'litl/ ▶ v. dismiss someone or something as unimportant.

Be·li·ze·an /bə'lēzēən/ (also **Belizian**) ▶ n. a person from Belize, a country in Central America. ▶ adj. relating to Belize.

bell /bel/ ▶ n. 1 a metal cup-shaped object that sounds a clear musical note when struck. 2 a device that buzzes or rings to give a signal. 3 a bell-shaped thing. 4 (**bells**) a musical instrument consisting of a set of metal tubes, played by being struck. 5 Nautical the time as indicated every half-hour of a watch by the striking of the ship's bell one to eight times. ▶ v. spread or flare outward like the lip of a bell. – PHRASES **bells and whistles** attractive additional features or trimmings. **ring a bell** informal sound vaguely familiar.

bel·la·don·na /,belə'dänə/ ▶ n. 1 deadly nightshade. 2 a drug made from deadly nightshade.

bell-bot·toms ▶ pl.n. pants with a marked flare below the knee.

bell·boy /'bel,boi/ (also **bellhop**) ▶ n. a porter in a hotel.

belle /bel/ ▶ n. a beautiful girl or woman.

belle é·poque /,bel ā'pôk/ ▶ n. the period of settled and comfortable life before World War I.

belles-let·tres /,bel 'letrə/ ▶ pl.n. literary essays written and read for their elegant style.

bell·flow·er /'bel,flou(-ə)r/ ▶ n. a plant with blue, purple, or white bell-shaped flowers.

bell·hop /'bel,häp/ ▶ n. an attendant in a hotel who performs services such as carrying guests' luggage; a bellboy.

bel·li·cose /'beli,kōs/ ▶ adj. aggressive and ready to fight. ■ **bel·li·cos·i·ty** /,belə'käsitē/ n.

bel·lig·er·ence /bə'lijərəns/ (also **belligerency**) ▶ n. aggressive or warlike behavior.

bel·lig·er·ent /bə'lijərənt/ ▶ adj. **1** hostile and aggressive. **2** engaged in a war or conflict. ▶ n. a nation or person engaged in war or conflict. ■ **bel·lig·er·ent·ly** adv.

Bel·li·ni /bə'lēnē/ ▶ n. (pl. **Bellinis**) a cocktail consisting of peach juice mixed with champagne.

bell jar ▶ n. a bell-shaped glass cover used in a laboratory.

bel·low /'belō/ ▶ v. **1** give a loud, deep roar of pain or anger. **2** shout or sing something very loudly. ▶ n. a loud, deep shout or sound.

bel·lows /'belōz/ ▶ pl.n. **1** a device consisting of a bag with two handles, used for blowing air into a fire. **2** an object or device with folded sides that allow it to expand and contract.

bell-ring·ing ▶ n. the activity or pastime of ringing church bells or handbells. ■ **bell-ring·er** n.

Bell's pal·sy /belz/ ▶ n. paralysis of the facial nerve, causing muscular weakness in one side of the face.

bell-weth·er /'bel,weᴛʜər/ ▶ n. **1** the leading sheep of a flock, with a bell on its neck. **2** a leader or indicator: *university campuses are often the bellwether of change.*

bel·ly /'belē/ ▶ n. (pl. **bellies**) **1** the front part of the human body below the ribs, containing the stomach and bowels. **2** a person's stomach. **3** the rounded underside of a ship or aircraft. **4** the top surface of a violin or similar instrument, over which the strings are placed. ▶ v. (**bellies, bellying, bellied**) swell or bulge: *the sails bellied out in the breeze.* ■ **bel·lied** adj.
– PHRASES **go belly up** informal go bankrupt.

bel·ly·ache /'belē,āk/ informal ▶ n. a stomach pain. ▶ v. complain noisily or persistently.

bel·ly·but·ton ▶ n. informal a person's navel.

bel·ly dance ▶ n. a dance originating in the Middle East, typically performed by a woman and involving undulating movements of the belly and rapid gyration of the hips. ■ **bel·ly danc·er** n. **bel·ly danc·ing** n.

bel·ly·flop /'belē,fläp/ ▶ n. informal a dive into water, landing flat on one's front.

bel·ly·ful /'belē,fŏŏl/ ▶ n. a sufficient amount to eat.
– PHRASES **have a bellyful of** informal have more than enough of something.

bel·ly laugh ▶ n. a loud unrestrained laugh.

be·long /bi'lông/ ▶ v. **1** (**belong to**) be the property of someone. **2** (**belong to**) be a member of a group or organization. **3** be rightly put into a particular position or category: *I put the chair back where it belonged.* **4** feel at ease in a particular place or with a particular group.

be·long·ings /bi'lôngiNGZ/ ▶ pl.n. a person's movable possessions.

Be·lo·rus·sian /,belō'rəsHən/ ▶ adj. of or relating to Belarus, its people, or its language. ▶ n. **1** a person from Belarus. **2** the East Slavic language of Belarus.

be·lov·ed /bi'ləv(i)d/ ▶ adj. dearly loved. ▶ n. a much loved person.

be·low /bi'lō/ ▶ prep. & adv. **1** at a lower level than. **2** mentioned further on in a piece of writing.

belt /belt/ ▶ n. **1** a strip of leather or other material worn around the waist to support or hold in clothes or to carry weapons. **2** a continuous band in machinery that transfers motion from one wheel to another. **3** a strip or encircling area: *the asteroid belt.* **4** informal a heavy blow. **5** informal a gulp or shot of liquor. ▶ v. **1** fasten or secure something with a belt. **2** hit someone or something very hard. **3** (**belt something out**) informal sing or play something loudly and forcefully. **4** informal rush or dash. **5** gulp a drink quickly. ■ **belt·ed** adj.
– PHRASES **below the belt** disregarding the rules; unfair. **tighten one's belt** cut one's spending. **under one's belt** safely or satisfactorily achieved or acquired.

belt·way /'belt,wā/ ▶ n. a highway encircling an urban area.

be·lu·ga /bə'lōōgə/ ▶ n. (pl. same or **belugas**) **1** a small white toothed whale of Arctic waters. **2** a very large sturgeon from which caviar is obtained.

bel·ve·dere /'belvi,di(ə)r/ ▶ n. a summer house or open-sided gallery positioned to command a fine view.

be·ly·ing /bi'lī-iNG/ ▶ present participle of BELIE.

be·moan /bi'mōn/ ▶ v. express discontent or sorrow about something.

be·muse /bi'myōoz/ ▶ v. confuse or bewilder someone. ■ **be·mused** adj. **be·muse·ment** n.

bench /bencH/ ▶ n. **1** a long seat for more than one person. **2** a long worktable in a workshop or laboratory. **3** (**the bench**) the office of judge or magistrate. **4** (**the bench**) a seat at the side of a sports field for coaches and players not taking part in a game.

bench·mark /'bencH,märk/ ▶ n. **1** a standard against which things may be compared: *champagne will remain the quality benchmark for all sparkling wines.* **2** a surveyor's mark cut in a wall and used as a reference point in measuring altitudes.

bench press ▶ n. an exercise in which one lies on a bench with feet on the floor and raises a weight with both arms.

bench test ▶ n. a test carried out on a product before it is released.

bend[1] /bend/ ▶ v. (past and past part. **bent** /bent/) **1** give or have a curved or angled shape, form, or course: *the road bends right and then left.* **2** lean or curve the body downward. **3** force or be forced to give in: *a refusal to bend to mob rule.* **4** interpret or modify a rule to suit someone. **5** direct one's attention or energies to a task. ▶ n. **1** a curved or angled part or course. **2** a kind of knot used to join two ropes together, or one rope to another object. **3** (**the bends**) (treated as sing.) decompression sickness. ■ **bend·a·ble** adj.
– PHRASES **bend someone's ear** informal talk to

someone at length or to ask a favor. **around the bend** informal crazy.

bend[2] ▸ n. Heraldry a broad diagonal stripe from top left to bottom right of a shield.

bend·er /'bendər/ ▸ n. informal a drinking session.

bend sin·is·ter ▸ n. Heraldry a broad diagonal stripe from top right to bottom left of a shield (a supposed sign of illegitimacy).

bend·y /'bendē/ ▸ adj. (**bendier, bendiest**) 1 capable of bending; flexible. 2 having many bends: *bendy country roads.*

be·neath /bi'nēTH/ ▸ prep. & adv. extending or directly underneath. ▸ prep. of lower status or worth than.

Ben·e·dic·tine /ˌbeni'dik,tēn, -tin/ ▸ n. 1 a monk or nun of a Christian religious order following the rule of St. Benedict. 2 trademark a liqueur based on brandy, originally made by Benedictine monks in France. ▸ adj. relating to St. Benedict or the Benedictines.

ben·e·dic·tion /ˌbeni'dikSHən/ ▸ n. 1 the speaking of a blessing. 2 the state of being blessed.

ben·e·fac·tion /ˌbenə'fakSHən/ ▸ n. formal a donation or gift.

ben·e·fac·tor /'benə,faktər, ˌbenə'faktər/ ▸ n. a person who gives money or other help. ■ **ben·e·fac·tress** /'benə,faktris, ˌbenə'faktris/ n.

ben·e·fice /'benəfis/ ▸ n. (in the Christian Church) an office whereby a member of the clergy receives accommodations and income in return for their duties.

be·nef·i·cent /bə'nefəsənt/ ▸ adj. doing or resulting in good: *a beneficent democracy.* ■ **be·nef·i·cence** n.

ben·e·fi·cial /ˌbenə'fiSHəl/ ▸ adj. having a good effect; favorable. ■ **ben·e·fi·cial·ly** adv.

ben·e·fi·ci·ar·y /ˌbenə'fiSHē,erē/ ▸ n. (pl. **beneficiaries**) a person who benefits from something, especially a trust or will.

ben·e·fit /'benəfit/ ▸ n. 1 advantage or profit gained from something: *the benefits of a private education.* 2 a payment made by the government or an insurance company to someone entitled to receive it. 3 a public performance to raise money for a charity. ▸ v. (**benefits, benefiting** or **benefitting, benefited** or **benefitted**) 1 receive an advantage: *areas that would benefit from regeneration.* 2 bring advantage to someone or something.
– PHRASES **the benefit of the doubt** an acceptance that a person is truthful or innocent if the opposite cannot be proved.

be·nev·o·lent /bə'nevələnt/ ▸ adj. 1 well meaning and kindly. 2 (of an organization) charitable rather than profit-making. ■ **be·nev·o·lence** n. **be·nev·o·lent·ly** adv.

Ben·ga·li /beNG'gälē/ ▸ n. (pl. **Bengalis**) 1 a person from Bengal in the northeast of the Indian subcontinent. 2 the language of Bangladesh and West Bengal. ▸ adj. relating to Bengal.

be·night·ed /bi'nītid/ ▸ adj. 1 lacking understanding of cultural, intellectual, or moral matters: *you're a provincial, benighted fool.* 2 old use unable to travel further because night has fallen.

be·nign /bi'nīn/ ▸ adj. 1 kind and gentle. 2 not harmful or harsh; favorable: *Spain's benign climate.* 3 (of a tumor) not malignant. ■ **be·nig·ni·ty** /bi'nignitē/ n. **be·nign·ly** adv.

be·nig·nant /bi'nignənt/ ▸ adj. less common term for BENIGN.

Be·ni·nese /ˌbenə'nēz, -'nēs/ ▸ n. a person from Benin, a country in West Africa. ▸ adj. relating to Benin.

ben·i·son /'benəsən, -zən/ ▸ n. literary a blessing.

bent /bent/ past and past participle of BEND[1] ▸ adj. 1 having an angle or sharp curve. 2 (**bent on**) determined to do or have something. ▸ n. a natural talent or inclination: *a man of a religious bent.*

bent·wood /'bent,wŏŏd/ ▸ n. wood that is artificially shaped for making furniture.

be·numb /bi'nəm/ ▸ v. deprive someone of feeling.

ben·zene /'ben,zēn, ben'zēn/ ▸ n. a volatile liquid hydrocarbon present in coal tar and petroleum.

ben·zine /'ben,zēn, ben'zēn/ (also **benzin** /'benzin/) ▸ n. a mixture of liquid hydrocarbons obtained from petroleum.

ben·zo·di·az·e·pine /ˌbenzō,dī'azə,pēn/ ▸ n. any of a class of organic compounds used as tranquilizers, such as Valium.

be·queath /bi'kwēTH, -'kwēTH/ ▸ v. 1 leave property to someone by a will. 2 pass on: *he ditched the unpopular policies bequeathed to him.*

be·quest /bi'kwest/ ▸ n. 1 a legacy bequeathed to someone. 2 the action of bequeathing something.

be·rate /bi'rāt/ ▸ v. scold or criticize someone angrily.

Ber·ber /'bərbər/ ▸ n. a member of a people native to North Africa.

ber·be·ris /'bərbəris/ ▸ n. a spiny shrub with yellow flowers and red berries.

be·reave /bi'rēv/ ▸ v. (**be bereaved**) be deprived of a close relation or friend through their death. ■ **be·reave·ment** n.

be·reft /bi'reft/ ▸ adj. 1 (**bereft of**) deprived of or lacking: *her room was bereft of color.* 2 sad and lonely because someone has died or gone away.

be·ret /bə'rā/ ▸ n. a flat round cap of felt or cloth.

ber·ga·mot /'bərgə,mät/ ▸ n. 1 an oily substance extracted from Seville oranges, used as flavoring in Earl Grey tea. 2 an herb of the mint family.

ber·i·ber·i /'berē'berē/ ▸ n. a disease causing inflammation of the nerves and heart failure, due to a deficiency of vitamin B_1.

ber·ke·li·um /bər'kēlēəm/ ▸ n. a radioactive metallic chemical element.

berm /bərm/ ▸ n. a raised bank or flat strip of land on the edge of a river, canal, or road.

Ber·mu·dan /bər'myŏŏdn/ (also **Bermudian** /bər'myŏŏdēən/) ▸ n. a person from Bermuda. ▸ adj. relating to Bermuda.

Ber·mu·da shorts /bər'myŏŏdə/ ▸ pl.n. casual knee-length shorts.

ber·ry /'berē/ ▸ n. (pl. **berries**) 1 a small round juicy fruit without a stone. 2 Botany a fruit that has its seeds enclosed in a fleshy pulp, e.g., a banana or tomato.

ber·serk /bər'zərk, -'sərk/ ▸ adj. out of control with anger or excitement: *the crowd went berserk.*

berth /bərTH/ ▸ n. 1 a place for a ship to moor at a wharf or harbor. 2 a bunk on a ship or train. ▸ v. moor a ship in a berth.
– PHRASES **give someone/thing a wide berth** stay well away from someone or something.

ber·yl /'berəl/ ▶ n. a transparent pale green, blue, or yellow mineral used as a gemstone.

be·ryl·li·um /bə'rilēəm/ ▶ n. a hard, gray, lightweight metallic chemical element.

be·seech /bi'sēCH/ ▶ v. (past and past part. **besought** /bi'sôt/ or **beseeched**) literary ask someone urgently or pleadingly to do or give something: *they beseeched him to stay.*

be·set /bi'set/ ▶ v. (**besetting**; past and past part. **beset**) (of an unwelcome or unpleasant situation) affect or trouble someone or something: *the consortium has been beset by financial difficulties.*

be·side /bi'sīd/ ▶ prep. **1** at the side of; next to. **2** compared with. **3** in addition to; apart from.
– PHRASES **beside oneself** frantic with worry. **beside the point** irrelevant.

be·sides /bi'sīdz/ ▶ prep. in addition to; apart from. ▶ adv. in addition; as well.

be·siege /bi'sēj/ ▶ v. **1** surround a place with armed forces in order to force it to surrender. **2** crowd around someone oppressively: *she was besieged by newsmen.* **3** overwhelm with requests or complaints: *the radio station was besieged with calls.* ■ **be·sieg·er** n.

be·smirch /bi'smərCH/ ▶ v. damage someone's reputation.

be·som /'bēzəm/ ▶ n. a broom made of twigs tied around a stick.

be·sot·ted /bi'sätid/ ▶ adj. completely infatuated with someone.

be·sought /bi'sôt/ ▶ past and past participle of BESEECH.

be·spat·ter /bi'spatər/ ▶ v. splash something with liquid: *his shoes were bespattered with mud.*

be·speak /bi'spēk/ ▶ v. (past **bespoke** /bi'spōk/; past part. **bespoken** /bi'spōkən/) formal **1** be evidence of: *the attractive tree-lined road bespoke money.* **2** order something in advance.

be·spec·ta·cled /bi'spektəkəld/ ▶ adj. wearing eyeglasses.

best /best/ ▶ adj. **1** of the highest quality. **2** most suitable or sensible. ▶ adv. **1** to the highest degree or standard; most. **2** most suitably or sensibly. ▶ n. **1** (**the best**) that which is of the highest quality. **2** (**one's best**) the highest standard one can reach. ▶ v. informal outwit or defeat someone.
– PHRASES **at best** taking the most optimistic view of a situation. **the best of three** (or **five**, etc.) victory achieved by winning the majority of a specified odd number of games. **the best part of** most of. **get the best of** overcome: *the disease almost got the best of her.* **had best** find it most sensible to do something: *I'd best be going.* **make the best of** get what limited advantage one can from a situation.

best boy ▶ n. the assistant to the chief electrician of a movie crew.

bes·tial /'bēsCHəl, 'bes-/ ▶ adj. **1** relating to or like an animal or beast. **2** savagely cruel: *bestial and barbaric acts.* ■ **bes·tial·ly** adv.

bes·ti·al·i·ty /ˌbēsCHē'alitē, ˌbes-/ ▶ n. **1** savagely cruel behavior. **2** sexual intercourse between a person and an animal.

bes·ti·ar·y /'bēsCHē͵erē, 'bes-/ ▶ n. (pl. **bestiaries**) a medieval collection of descriptions of various kinds of animals.

be·stir /bi'stər/ ▶ v. (**bestirs**, **bestirring**, **bestirred**) (**bestir oneself**) make a physical or mental effort; rouse oneself to activity.

best man ▶ n. a man chosen by a bridegroom to assist him at his wedding.

be·stow /bi'stō/ ▶ v. award an honor, right, or gift to someone: *he wore the medals bestowed upon him by the president.* ■ **be·stow·al** n.

be·stride /bi'strīd/ ▶ v. (past **bestrode** /bi'strōd/; past part. **bestridden** /bi'stridən/) have a leg on either side of something.

best·sell·er /ˌbest'selər/ ▶ n. a book or other product that sells in very large numbers.
■ **best·sell·ing** adj.

be·suit·ed /bi'sōōtid/ ▶ adj. (of a man) wearing a suit.

bet /bet/ ▶ v. (**bets, betting**; past and past part. **bet** or **betted**) **1** risk money or property against someone else's on the outcome of an unpredictable event such as a race. **2** informal feel sure: *I bet she made it all up.* ▶ n. **1** an act of betting money on something. **2** an amount of money bet: *a $10 bet.* **3** informal an option: *Austria is your best bet for summer skiing.* **4** (**one's bet**) informal one's opinion: *my bet is that she'll stay.* ■ **bet·tor** (also **better**) n.
– PHRASES **you bet** informal of course; certainly.

be·ta /'bātə/ ▶ n. **1** the second letter of the Greek alphabet (Β, β), represented as 'b.' **2** short for BETA TEST.

be·ta block·er ▶ n. a drug used to treat angina and reduce high blood pressure.

be·take /bi'tāk/ ▶ v. (past **betook** /bi'tōōk/; past part. **betaken**) (**betake oneself to**) literary go to a place.

be·ta par·ti·cle (also **beta ray**) ▶ n. Physics a fast-moving electron given off by some radioactive substances.

be·ta test ▶ n. a trial of machinery, software, etc., in the final stages of its development, carried out by people not connected with its development. ▶ v. (**beta-test**) subject a product to such a test.

be·tel /'bētl/ ▶ n. the leaf of an Asian plant, chewed as a mild stimulant.

be·tel nut ▶ n. the seed of a tropical areca palm tree, often chewed with betel leaves.

bête noire /ˌbāt 'nwär, ˌbet/ ▶ n. (pl. **bêtes noires** pronunc. same) (**one's bête noire**) a person or thing that one particularly dislikes.

be·think /bi'THiNGk/ ▶ v. (past and past part. **bethought** /bi'THôt/) (**bethink oneself**) formal come to think about something.

be·tide /bi'tīd/ ▶ v. literary happen, or happen to someone.

be·times /bi'tīmz/ ▶ adv. literary in good time; early.

be·to·ken /bi'tōkən/ ▶ v. literary be a warning or sign of: *the blue sky betokened a day of good weather.*

bet·o·ny /'betn-ē/ ▶ n. (pl. **betonies**) a plant of the mint family with purple flowers.

be·took /bi'tōōk/ ▶ past of BETAKE.

be·tray /bi'trā/ ▶ v. **1** endanger one's country, a person, or group of people by treacherously helping an enemy. **2** be disloyal to: *many of the unemployed felt betrayed by the government.* **3** unintentionally reveal something: *Lou's heightened color betrayed her embarrassment.* ■ **be·tray·al** n.

be·trothed /bə'trōTHd, -'trôTHd/ formal ▶ adj. engaged to be married. ▶ n. (**one's betrothed**) the person to whom one is engaged to be married. ■ **be·troth·al** /bə'trōTHəl, -'trôTHəl/ n.

bet·ter /'betər/ ▶ adj. **1** more satisfactory or

effective. **2** partly or fully recovered from an illness or injury. ▸ **adv. 1** in a more satisfactory or effective way. **2** to a greater degree; more. ▸ **n. 1** something that is better. **2** (**one's betters**) dated or humorous people who are superior to oneself in social status. ▸ **v. 1** improve on: *a record bettered by only one other nonleague team.* **2** (**better oneself**) improve one's social status. – PHRASES **better off** in a more favorable position, especially financially. **the better part of** most of. **get the better of** defeat or overcome: *no one had ever gotten the better of her.* **had better** ought to do something: *I'd better get on with my work.*

> USAGE
> In the phrase **had better do something** the word **had** is often dropped in informal speech, as in *you better not come tonight.* In writing, the **had** may be shortened to **'d** but it should not be dropped altogether (*you'd better not come tonight*).

bet·ter half ▸ **n.** informal a person's husband, wife, or partner.

bet·ter·ment /'betərmənt/ ▸ **n.** the improvement of someone or something: *the betterment of society.*

be·tween /bi'twēn/ ▸ **prep. & adv. 1** at, into, or across the space separating two things. **2** in the period separating two points in time. ▸ **prep. 1** indicating a connection or relationship. **2** by combining the resources or actions of two or more parties. – PHRASES **between you and me** (or **between ourselves**) in confidence.

> USAGE
> A preposition such as **between** takes the object case and is correctly followed by object pronouns such as **me** rather than subject pronouns such as **I**. It is therefore correct to say **between you and me** rather than **between you and I**.

be·twixt /bi'twikst/ ▸ **prep. & adv.** old use between. – PHRASES **betwixt and between** informal neither one thing nor the other.

bev·el /'bevəl/ ▸ **n. 1** (in carpentry) a sloping surface or edge. **2** (also **bevel square**) a tool for making angles in carpentry and stonework. ▸ **v.** (**bevels, beveling, beveled**) cut a sloping edge on an object.

bev·er·age /'bev(ə)rij/ ▸ **n.** a drink other than water.

bev·y /'bevē/ ▸ **n.** (pl. **bevies**) a large group of people or things: *a bevy of children.*

be·wail /bi'wāl/ ▸ **v.** express great regret or sorrow over: *she wept copiously and bewailed her bad luck.*

be·ware /bi'we(ə)r/ ▸ **v.** be cautious and alert to risks or dangers: *beware of pickpockets at the train and bus stations.*

be·wil·der /bi'wildər/ ▸ **v.** puzzle or confuse someone. ■ **be·wil·der·ing** adj. **be·wil·der·ment** n.

be·witch /bi'wiCH/ ▸ **v. 1** cast a spell over someone. **2** enchant and delight someone. ■ **be·witch·ing** adj. **be·witch·ment** n.

bey /bā/ ▸ **n.** (pl. **beys**) historical the governor of a province in the Ottoman Empire.

be·yond /bē'änd, bi'yänd/ ▸ **prep. & adv. 1** at or to the farther side of. **2** outside the range or limits of. **3** to or in a state where something is impossible: *the engine was beyond repair.* **4** happening or continuing after. **5** apart from.

bez·el /'bezəl/ ▸ **n.** a groove holding a gemstone or the glass cover of a watch in position.

be·zique /bə'zēk/ ▸ **n.** a card game for two players, played with a double deck of 64 cards.

Bh ▸ symbol the chemical element bohrium.

bha·ji /'bäjē/ (also **bhajia** /'bäjēə/) ▸ **n.** (pl. **bhajis, bhajia**) (in Indian cooking) a small flat cake or ball of vegetables, fried in batter.

bhan·gra /'bäNGgrə/ ▸ **n.** a type of popular music combining Punjabi folk traditions with Western pop music.

b.h.p. ▸ abbr. brake horsepower.

Bhu·tan·ese /ˌbo͞otn'ēz, -'ēs/ ▸ **n.** a person from Bhutan, a small kingdom in the Himalayas. ▸ **adj.** relating to Bhutan.

Bi ▸ symbol the chemical element bismuth.

bi /bī/ ▸ **adj.** informal bisexual.

bi- ▸ comb. form **1** two; having two: *biathlon.* **2** occurring twice in every one or once in every two: *bicentennial.* **3** lasting for two: *biennial.*

bi·an·nu·al /bī'anyo͞oəl/ ▸ **adj.** occurring twice a year. ■ **bi·an·nu·al·ly** adv.

bi·as /'bīəs/ ▸ **n. 1** an inclination or prejudice in favor of or against a particular person or thing: *some people alleged there was a bias toward the Democrats.* **2** a slanting direction across the grain of a fabric. **3** the tendency of a ball in the game of lawn bowling to swerve because of the way it is weighted. **4** Electronics a steady voltage, applied to an electronic device, that can be adjusted to change the way the device operates. ▸ **v.** (**biases, biasing, biased** or **biassing, biassed**) cause someone to have an opinion or prejudice in favor of or against: *he claimed the judge was biased against him.*

bi·ath·lon /bī'aTHlän/ ▸ **n.** a sporting event combining cross-country skiing and rifle shooting.

bib /bib/ ▸ **n. 1** a piece of cloth or plastic fastened under a child's chin to keep its clothes clean while it is eating. **2** the part of an apron or pair of dungarees that covers the chest. – PHRASES **one's best bib and tucker** informal one's smartest clothes.

bi·be·lot /'bib(ə)ˌlō/ ▸ **n.** a small ornament or trinket.

Bi·ble /'bībəl/ ▸ **n. 1** the Christian scriptures, consisting of the Old and New Testaments. **2** the Jewish scriptures. **3** (**bible**) informal a book regarded as giving comprehensive and reliable information about something: *the professional electrician's bible.*

Bi·ble Belt ▸ **n.** the areas of the southern and midwestern US and western Canada where many Protestants believe in a literal interpretation of the Bible.

bib·li·cal /'biblikəl/ ▸ **adj.** relating to or found in the Bible. ■ **bib·li·cal·ly** adv.

bib·li·og·ra·phy /ˌbiblē'ägrəfē/ ▸ **n.** (pl. **bibliographies**) **1** a list of the books or articles referred to in a scholarly work. **2** a list of books on a particular subject or by a particular author. **3** the study of books and their production. ■ **bib·li·og·ra·pher** n. **bib·li·o·graph·ic** /ˌbiblēə'grafik/ adj.

bib·li·o·phile /'biblēəˌfīl/ ▸ **n.** a person who collects or loves books.

bib·u·lous /'bibyələs/ ▸ **adj.** formal very fond of drinking alcohol.

bi·cam·er·al /bī'kamərəl/ ▸ **adj.** (of a parliament or other legislative body) having two chambers.

bi·car·bo·nate /bī'kärbə,nāt, -nit/ ▶ n. **1** Chemistry a compound containing HCO₃ negative ions together with a metallic element. **2** (also **bicarbonate of soda**) sodium bicarbonate.

bi·cen·ten·ar·y /,bīsen'tenərē/ ▶ n. another name for BICENTENNIAL.

bi·cen·ten·ni·al /,bīsen'tenēəl/ ▶ n. the two-hundredth anniversary of an event.

bi·ceps /'bī,seps/ ▶ n. (pl. same) a large muscle in the upper arm that flexes the arm and forearm.

bi·chon frise /'bēsнän 'frēz/ ▶ n. a breed of toy dog with a curly white coat.

bick·er /'bikər/ ▶ v. argue about unimportant things.

bi·cus·pid /bī'kəspid/ ▶ n. a tooth with two cusps or points. ▶ adj. having two cusps or points.

bi·cy·cle /'bīsikəl/ ▶ n. a vehicle with two wheels held in a frame one behind the other, propelled by pedals. ▶ v. ride a bicycle. ■ **bi·cy·clist** n.

bid¹ /bid/ ▶ v. (**bids, bidding**; past and past part. **bid**) **1** offer a price for something, especially at an auction. **2** (**bid for**) offer to do work or supply goods for a stated price. **3** try to get or achieve: *the two boys are bidding for places on the swim team.* ▶ n. **1** an offer to buy something. **2** an offer to do work or supply goods at a stated price. **3** an effort to get or achieve something: *a bid for power.* ■ **bid·der** n. **bid·ding** n.

bid² /bid/ ▶ v. (**bids, bidding**; past **bid** or **bade** /bad, bād/; past part. **bid**) **1** utter a greeting or farewell to someone. **2** old use order someone to do something.

bid·da·ble /'bidəbəl/ ▶ adj. meekly ready to obey instructions.

bid·den /'bidn/ ▶ old-fashioned past participle of BID².

bid·dy /'bidē/ ▶ n. (pl. **biddies**) informal an old woman.

bide /bīd/ ▶ v. old use or dialect remain or stay in a place.
– PHRASES **bide one's time** wait patiently for a good opportunity to do something.

bi·det /bi'dā/ ▶ n. a low basin used for washing one's genital and anal area.

bi·en·ni·al /bī'enēəl/ ▶ adj. **1** taking place every other year. Compare with BIANNUAL. **2** (of a plant) living for two years. ▶ n. **1** a biennial plant. **2** an event celebrated or taking place every two years. ■ **bi·en·ni·al·ly** adv.

bi·en·ni·um /bī'enēəm/ ▶ n. (pl. **bienniums** or **biennia** /-'enēə/) a specified period of two years.

bier /bi(ə)r/ ▶ n. a movable platform on which a coffin or dead body is placed before burial.

biff /bif/ informal ▶ v. hit someone or something hard with the fist. ▶ n. a sharp blow with the fist.

bi·fid /'bīfid/ ▶ adj. technical (of a part of a plant or animal) divided into two parts by a deep cleft or notch.

bi·fo·cal /'bī,fōkəl/ ▶ adj. (of a lens) made in two sections, one with a focus for seeing distant things and one for seeing things that are close. ▶ n. (**bifocals**) a pair of glasses with bifocal lenses.

bi·fur·cate /'bīfər,kāt/ ▶ v. (of a road, river, etc.) divide into two branches or forks. ■ **bi·fur·ca·tion** /,bīfər'kāsнən/ n.

big /big/ ▶ adj. (**bigger, biggest**) **1** of great size, power, or extent. **2** very important or serious: *a big decision.* **3** older or grown-up: *my big sister.* **4** informal very popular: *fast food isn't big in Iceland.* ■ **big·gish** adj. **big·ness** n.

– PHRASES **be big with child** old use be in a late stage of pregnancy. **the Big Apple** informal New York City. **the big screen** informal the cinema. **think big** informal be ambitious. **too big for one's britches** informal conceited.

big·a·my /'bigəmē/ ▶ n. the crime of marrying someone while already married to another person. ■ **big·a·mist** n. **big·a·mous** adj.

big band ▶ n. a large group of musicians playing jazz or swing music.

Big Bang ▶ n. the rapid expansion of extremely dense matter that, according to current cosmological theories, marked the origin of the universe.

big box ▶ n. (also **big-box store**) a superstore. ▶ adj. relating to or functioning as a superstore: *big-box retailers will dominate the landscape.*

Big Broth·er ▶ n. a person or organization exercising total control over people's lives.

Big·foot /'big,foot/ ▶ n. (pl. same) a large, hairy apelike creature, supposedly found in NW America.

big game ▶ n. large animals hunted for sport.

big·head /'big,hed/ ▶ n. informal a conceited person. ■ **big·head·ed** adj.

big hit·ter ▶ n. another term for HEAVY HITTER.

big·horn /'big,hôrn/ ▶ n. a stocky brown North American wild sheep, found in the Rocky Mountains and other western ranges.

bight /bīt/ ▶ n. **1** a long inward curve in a coastline. **2** a loop of rope.

big mouth ▶ n. informal a person who boasts, or one who cannot keep secrets.

big·ot /'bigət/ ▶ n. a person with strong and prejudiced views who will not listen to the opinions of others. ■ **big·ot·ed** adj. **big·ot·ry** n.

big shot (also **big noise**) ▶ n. informal an important person.

big top ▶ n. the main tent in a circus.

big wheel ▶ n. another term for BIGWIG.

big·wig /'big,wig/ ▶ n. informal an important person.

bi·jou /'bēzhoo/ ▶ adj. small and elegant: *a bijou apartment.*

bike /bīk/ informal ▶ n. a bicycle or motorcycle. ▶ v. ride a bicycle or motorcycle. ■ **bik·er** n.

bi·ki·ni /bi'kēnē/ ▶ n. (pl. **bikinis**) a women's two-piece swimsuit.

bi·ki·ni line ▶ n. the area of skin around the pubic mound as revealed by the high-cut legs of a bikini.

bi·lat·er·al /bī'latərəl/ ▶ adj. **1** having two sides. **2** involving two parties: *bilateral discussions.* ■ **bi·lat·er·al·ly** adv.

bil·ber·ry /'bil,berē/ ▶ n. (pl. **bilberries**) the small blue edible berry of a shrub closely related to the blueberry.

Bil·dungs·ro·man /'bildoongzrō,män, 'beldoongks-/ ▶ n. a novel about one person's formative years or spiritual education.

bile /bīl/ ▶ n. **1** a bitter fluid that helps digestion, produced by the liver and stored in the gall bladder. **2** anger or irritability.

bile duct ▶ n. the tube that conveys bile from the liver and the gall bladder to the duodenum.

bilge /bilj/ ▶ n. **1** the bottom of a ship's hull. **2** (also **bilge water**) dirty water that collects in the bilge. **3** informal nonsense.

bil·har·zi·a /bil'härzēə/ ▶ n. a disease caused by infestation of the body with a type of parasitic flatworm.

bi·lin·gual /bī'liNGgwəl/ ▶ adj. **1** speaking two languages fluently. **2** expressed in or using two languages: *a bilingual dictionary.* ■ **bi·lin·gual·ism** n. **bi·lin·gual·ly** adv.

bil·ious /'bilyəs/ ▶ adj. **1** affected by nausea or vomiting. **2** relating to bile. **3** spiteful or bad-tempered. ■ **bil·ious·ly** adv. **bil·ious·ness** n.

bil·i·ru·bin /'bili,roōbin/ ▶ n. Biochemistry an orange-yellow pigment formed in the liver by the breakdown of hemoglobin and excreted in bile.

bilk /bilk/ ▶ v. informal cheat or defraud someone.

bill[1] /bil/ ▶ n. **1** a printed or written statement of the money owed for goods or services. **2** a draft of a proposed law presented to a legislature for discussion. **3** a program of entertainment at a theater or movie theater. **4** a banknote. **5** an advertising poster. ▶ v. **1** list a person or event in a program of entertainment. **2** (**bill someone/thing as**) describe someone or something as: *the vehicle has been billed as the car of the future.* **3** send a statement of charges to a person or organization. ■ **bill·ing** n.
– PHRASES **a clean bill of health** a statement confirming that someone is in good health or that something is in good condition. **fit the bill** be suitable for a particular purpose.

bill[2] ▶ n. **1** the beak of a bird. **2** a stiff brim at the front of a cap.
– PHRASES **bill and coo** informal behave or talk in a loving and sentimental way.

bill·a·ble /'biləbəl/ ▶ adj. (of activities or time devoted to them) chargeable to an account or customer: *billable hours.*

bil·la·bong /'bilə,bôNG/ ▶ n. Austral. a branch of a river forming a backwater or stagnant pool.

bill·board /'bil,bôrd/ ▶ n. a large outdoor board used to display advertisements.

bil·let[1] /'bilit/ ▶ n. a civilian house where soldiers live temporarily. ▶ v. (**billets, billeting, billeted**) provide soldiers with temporary accommodations in a civilian house.

bil·let[2] ▶ n. **1** a thick piece of wood. **2** a small bar of metal.

bil·let-doux /'bilā 'doō, 'bēyā-/ ▶ n. (pl. **billets-doux** /-'doōz/) chiefly humorous a love letter.

bill·fold /'bil,fōld/ ▶ n. a man's wallet.

bill·hook /'bil,hoōk/ ▶ n. a tool with a curved blade, used for pruning.

bil·liards /'bilyərdz/ ▶ pl.n. (treated as sing.) a game for two people, played on a rectangular cloth-covered table with three balls.

bil·lion /'bilyən/ ▶ cardinal number (pl. **billions** or (with numeral or quantifying word) same) **1** a thousand million; 1,000,000,000 or 10^9. **2** (**billions**) informal a very large number or amount: *billions of tiny sea creatures.* ■ **bil·lionth** ordinal number.

bil·lion·aire /'bilyə,ne(ə)r/ ▶ n. a person owning money and property worth at least a billion dollars (or pounds, etc.).

bill of at·tain·der ▶ n. Law an item of legislation (prohibited by the US Constitution) that inflicts attainder without judicial process.

bill of ex·change ▶ n. a document instructing a person to pay a stated sum of money to someone on a particular date.

bill of fare ▶ n. dated a menu.

bill of goods ▶ n. a consignment of merchandise.
– PHRASES **sell someone a bill of goods** deceive someone, usually by persuading them to accept something untrue or undesirable: *she was sold a*

bill of goods about that dog's pedigree.

bill of lad·ing ▶ n. a document giving full details of a ship's cargo.

bill of rights ▶ n. a written statement of the basic rights of a country's citizens.

bil·low /'bilō/ ▶ v. **1** (of smoke, cloud, or steam) roll outward: *smoke was billowing from the chimney.* **2** (of fabric or a garment) fill with air and swell out: *her dress billowed out around her.* ▶ n. **1** a large rolling mass of cloud, smoke, or steam. **2** old use a large wave. ■ **bil·low·y** adj.

bil·ly /'bilē/ ▶ n. (pl. **billies**) **1** short for BILLY GOAT. **2** (also **billy club**) a truncheon; a cudgel.

bil·ly goat ▶ n. a male goat.

bim·bo /'bimbō/ ▶ n. (pl. **bimbos**) informal, derogatory an attractive but unintelligent young woman. ■ **bim·bette** /bim'bet/ n.

bi·me·tal·lic /,bīmə'talik/ ▶ adj. made or consisting of two metals.

bi·month·ly /bī'mənTHlē/ ▶ adj. & adv. appearing or taking place twice a month or every two months.

bin /bin/ ▶ n. **1** a large storage container: *a bread bin.* **2** a partitioned stand or case for storing bottles of wine. ▶ v. (**bins, binning, binned**) place something in a bin.

bi·na·ry /'bī,nerē, -nərē/ ▶ adj. **1** composed of or involving two things. **2** using or relating to a system of numbers with two as its base, using the digits 0 and 1. ▶ n. (pl. **binaries**) **1** the binary system of notation. **2** Astronomy a system of two stars revolving around their common center.

bind /bīnd/ ▶ v. (past and past part. **bound**) **1** tie or fasten something tightly together. **2** restrain someone by tying their hands and feet: *he was bound and gagged.* **3** wrap or encircle tightly: *her blond hair was bound with a scarf.* **4** stick together in a single mass: *mix the flour with the coconut and enough egg white to bind them.* **5** hold together as a united group: *the religious and social rituals that bind people together.* **6** require someone to do something by law or because of a contract. **7** (**bind someone over**) (of a court of law) require someone to do something: *he was bound over to keep the peace.* **8** fix together and enclose the pages of a book in a cover. **9** trim the edge of a piece of material with a fabric strip. ▶ n. informal an annoying or difficult situation.

bind·er /'bīndər/ ▶ n. **1** a cover for holding magazines or loose papers together. **2** a reaping machine that binds grain into sheaves. **3** a bookbinder.

bind·er·y /'bīndərē/ ▶ n. (pl. **binderies**) a workshop or factory in which books are bound.

bin·di /'bindē/ ▶ n. (pl. **bindis**) a decorative mark worn in the middle of the forehead by Indian women.

bind·ing /'bīndiNG/ ▶ n. **1** a strong covering holding the pages of a book together. **2** fabric cut or woven in a strip, used for binding the edges of a piece of material. ▶ adj. (of an agreement) putting someone under a legal obligation.

bind·weed /'bīnd,wēd/ ▶ n. a plant with trumpet-shaped flowers that twines itself around things.

binge /binj/ informal ▶ n. a short period of uncontrolled indulgence in an activity, especially eating or drinking. ▶ v. (**binges, bingeing** or **binging, binged**) do something, especially eat, without being able to control oneself. ■ **bing·er** n.

bin·go /'biNGgō/ ▶ n. a game in which players mark off randomly called numbers on printed cards, the winner being the first to mark off all their numbers. ▶ exclam. 1 a call by someone who wins a game of bingo. 2 said to express satisfaction at a sudden good event.

bin·na·cle /'binəkəl/ ▶ n. a casing for holding a ship's compass.

bin·oc·u·lar /bi'näkyələr/ ▶ adj. adapted for or using both eyes.

bin·oc·u·lars /bi'näkyələrz/ ▶ pl.n. an instrument with a separate lens for each eye, used for viewing distant objects.

bi·no·mi·al /bī'nōmēəl/ ▶ n. Mathematics an algebraic expression consisting of two terms linked by a plus or minus sign. ▶ adj. consisting of two terms.

bi·o /'bīō/ ▶ n. (pl. **bios**) informal 1 biology. 2 biography.

bio- ▶ comb.form 1 relating to life or living beings: *biosynthesis.* 2 biological; relating to biology: *biohazard.*

bi·o·ac·tive /ˌbīō'aktiv/ ▶ adj. (of a substance) having a biological effect. ■ **bi·o·ac·tiv·i·ty** /-ak'tivitē/ n.

bi·o·chem·is·try /ˌbīō'keməstrē/ ▶ n. the branch of science concerned with the chemical processes that occur within living organisms. ■ **bi·o·chem·i·cal** /ˌbīō'kemikəl/ adj. **bi·o·chem·ist** n.

bi·o·cide /'bīə,sīd/ ▶ n. a substance that is poisonous to living organisms, such as a pesticide.

bi·o·de·grad·a·ble /ˌbīōdi'grādəbəl/ ▶ adj. (of a substance or object) capable of being decomposed by bacteria or other living organisms. ■ **bi·o·de·grad·a·bil·i·ty** /-,grādə'bilitē/ n. **bi·o·deg·ra·da·tion** /ˌbīōdegrə'dāsHən/ n. **bi·o·de·grade** /ˌbīōdi'grād/ v.

bi·o·die·sel /'bīō,dēzəl, -səl/ ▶ n. a biofuel intended as a substitute for diesel.

bi·o·di·ver·si·ty /ˌbīōdi'vərsitē/ ▶ n. the variety of plant and animal life in the world or in a particular habitat.

bi·o·en·gi·neer·ing /ˌbīō,enjə'ni(ə)riNG/ ▶ n. 1 genetic engineering. 2 the use of artificial tissues or organs in the body. 3 the use of organisms or biological processes in industry. ■ **bi·o·en·gi·neer** n. & v.

bi·o·eth·ics /ˌbīō'eTHiks/ ▶ pl.n. (treated as sing.) the ethics of medical and biological research. ■ **bi·o·eth·i·cal** /-'eTHikəl/ adj. **bi·o·eth·i·cist** /-'eTHəsist/ n.

bi·o·feed·back /ˌbīō'fēd,bak/ ▶ n. the electronic monitoring of a normally automatic bodily function in order to train someone to control that function of their own accord.

bi·o·fla·vo·noid /ˌbīō'flāvə,noid/ ▶ n. any of a group of compounds occurring mainly in citrus fruits and black currants, sometimes regarded as vitamins.

bi·o·fu·el /'bīō,fyōōəl/ ▶ n. fuel obtained directly from living matter.

bi·o·gas /'bīō,gas/ ▶ n. gaseous fuel, especially methane, produced by the fermentation of organic matter.

bi·o·gen·e·sis /ˌbīō'jenəsis/ ▶ n. the synthesis of substances by living organisms. ■ **bi·o·ge·net·ic** /-jə'netik/ adj.

bi·o·graph·i·cal /ˌbīə'grafikəl/ ▶ adj. relating to

or dealing with a particular person's life: *detailed biographical information.*

bi·og·ra·phy /bī'ägrəfē/ ▶ n. (pl. **biographies**) an account of a person's life written by someone else. ■ **bi·og·ra·pher** n.

bi·o·haz·ard /'bīō,hazərd/ ▶ n. a risk to human health or the environment resulting from biological research.

bi·o·in·for·mat·ics /ˌbīō,infər'matiks/ ▶ pl.n. (treated as sing.) the science of collecting and analyzing complex biological data such as genetic codes.

bi·o·log·i·cal /ˌbīə'läjikəl/ ▶ adj. 1 relating to biology or living organisms. 2 (of a parent or child) related by blood. 3 relating to the use of harmful microorganisms as weapons of war. 4 (of a detergent) containing enzymes to help in the removal of stains. ■ **bi·o·log·i·cal·ly** adv.

bi·o·log·i·cal clock ▶ n. a natural mechanism that controls certain regularly recurring physical processes in an animal or plant, such as sleeping.

bi·o·log·i·cal con·trol ▶ n. the control of a pest by nonchemical means, by bringing a natural enemy or predator of the pest into the environment.

bi·ol·o·gy /bī'äləjē/ ▶ n. 1 the scientific study of living organisms. 2 the features of a particular organism or class of organisms: *the biology of marine plants.* ■ **bi·ol·o·gist** n.

bi·o·lu·mi·nes·cence /ˌbīō,lōōmə'nesəns/ ▶ n. the production of light by living creatures such as fireflies and deep-sea fishes. ■ **bi·o·lu·mi·nes·cent** adj.

bi·o·mark·er /'bīō,märkər/ ▶ n. a measurable substance in an organism whose presence indicates disease, infection, or environmental exposure.

bi·o·mass /'bīō,mas/ ▶ n. 1 the total quantity of organisms in a given area. 2 organic matter used as a fuel, especially in the production of electricity.

bi·o·ma·te·ri·al /ˌbīōmə'ti(ə)rēəl/ ▶ n. synthetic or natural material that can be used in constructing artificial organs and prostheses or to replace bone or tissue.

bi·ome /'bī,ōm/ ▶ n. a large community of plants and animals occupying a major habitat, such as forest or tundra.

bi·o·me·chan·ics /ˌbīōmə'kaniks/ ▶ n. (treated as sing.) the study of the mechanical laws relating to the movement or structure of living organisms.

bi·o·met·rics /ˌbīō'metriks/ ▶ n. the application of statistical analysis to biological data. ■ **bi·o·met·ric** /ˌbīō'metrik/ adj. **bi·o·met·ri·cal** /ˌbīō'metrikəl/ adj. **bi·o·me·tri·cian** /ˌbīōmə'trisHən/ n.

bi·o·mi·met·ics /ˌbīōmə'metiks/ (also **biomimicry**) ▶ n. the design and production of materials, structures, and systems that are modeled on biological entities and processes. ■ **bi·o·mi·met·ic** adj.

bi·o·morph /'bīō,môrf/ ▶ n. a design or decorative form resembling or representing a living organism. ■ **bi·o·mor·phic** /ˌbīō'môrfik/ adj.

bi·on·ic /bī'änik/ ▶ adj. 1 relating to the use of electrically powered artificial body parts. 2 informal having ordinary physical powers increased by the use of such artificial body parts.

bi·o·pharm·a·ceut·i·cal /ˌbīō,färmə'sōōtikəl/ ▶ n. a pharmaceutical substance, especially a protein or peptide, produced by biotechnology.

bi·o·pic /ˈbīōˌpik/ ▶ n. informal a movie about the the life of a particular person.

bi·op·sy /ˈbīˌäpsē/ ▶ n. (pl. **biopsies**) an examination of tissue taken from the body, to discover the presence, cause, or extent of a disease.

bi·o·rhythm /ˈbīōˌriᴛʜəm/ ▶ n. a recurring cycle in the physiology or functioning of the body, such as the daily cycle of sleeping and waking.

bi·o·se·cur·i·ty /ˌbīōsiˈkyo͝orətē/ ▶ n. procedures intended to protect humans or animals against disease or harmful substances.

bi·o·sphere /ˈbīəˌsfi(ə)r/ ▶ n. the parts of the earth's surface and atmosphere that are inhabited by living things.

bi·o·syn·the·sis /ˌbīōˈsinᴛʜəsis/ ▶ n. the production of complex molecules within living organisms or cells. ▪ **bi·o·syn·thet·ic** /-ˌsinˈᴛʜetik/ adj.

bi·o·ta /bīˈōtə/ ▶ n. the animal and plant life of a particular region, habitat, or geological period.

bi·o·tech /ˌbīōˈtek, ˈbīōˌtek/ ▶ n. informal biotechnology.

bi·o·tech·nol·o·gy /ˌbīōtekˈnäləjē/ ▶ n. the use of microorganisms in industry and medicine for the production of antibiotics, hormones, etc. ▪ **bi·o·tech·no·lo·gi·cal** /ˌbīōˌteknəˈläjikəl/ adj. **bi·o·tech·nol·o·gist** n.

bi·o·ter·ror·ism /ˌbīōˈterəˌrizəm/ ▶ n. the use of harmful biological or biochemical substances as weapons of terrorism. ▪ **bi·o·ter·ror·ist** /ˌbīōˈterəˌrist/ n.

bi·o·ther·a·py /ˌbīōˈᴛʜerəpē/ ▶ n. (pl. **biotherapies**) the treatment of disease using substances obtained or derived from living organisms.

bi·ot·ic /bīˈätik/ ▶ adj. relating to living things and the effect they have on each other.

bi·o·tin /ˈbīətin/ ▶ n. a vitamin of the B complex, found in egg yolk, liver, and yeast.

bi·o·war·fare /ˌbīōˈwôrˌfe(ə)r/ ▶ n. biological warfare.

bi·o·weap·on /ˈbīōˌwepən/ ▶ n. a harmful organism or biological substance used as a weapon of war.

bi·par·ti·san /bīˈpärtəzən/ ▶ adj. involving the agreement or cooperation of two political parties. ▪ **bi·par·ti·san·ship** /-ˌsʜip/ n.

bi·par·tite /bīˈpärˌtīt/ ▶ adj. 1 involving two separate parties: *a bipartite agreement*. 2 technical consisting of two parts.

bi·ped /ˈbīped/ ▶ n. an animal that walks on two feet. ▪ **bi·ped·al** /bīˈpedl/ adj.

bi·plane /ˈbīˌplān/ ▶ n. an early type of aircraft with two pairs of wings, one above the other.

bi·po·lar /bīˈpōlər/ ▶ adj. 1 (especially of an electronic device) having two poles. 2 having two opposite extremes: *a bipolar view of the world*. ▪ **bi·po·lar·i·ty** /ˌbīpōˈlaritē, -pə-/ n.

bi·po·lar dis·or·der ▶ n. a mental disorder marked by alternating periods of elation and depression.

birch /bərcʜ/ ▶ n. 1 a slender tree with thin peeling bark and hard fine-grained wood. 2 (**the birch**) historical a punishment in which a person was beaten with a bundle of birch twigs.

bird /bərd/ ▶ n. 1 a warm-blooded egg-laying animal that has feathers, wings, and a beak, and typically is able to fly. 2 informal a person of a particular kind: *she's a sharp old bird*.

– PHRASES **the birds and the bees** informal basic facts about sex, as told to a child.

bird·brain /ˈbərdˌbrān/ ▶ n. informal a stupid person.

bird·cage /ˈbərdˌkāj/ ▶ n. a cage for pet birds.

bird·er /ˈbərdər/ ▶ n. informal a birdwatcher. ▪ **bird·ing** n.

bird flu ▶ n. an often fatal flu virus of birds that is transmissible from them to humans, in whom it may also prove fatal.

bird·ie /ˈbərdē/ ▶ n. (pl. **birdies**) 1 informal a little bird. 2 Golf a score of one stroke under par at a hole. ▶ v. (**birdies, birdying, birdied**) Golf play a hole with a score of one stroke under par.

bird of par·a·dise ▶ n. (pl. **birds of paradise**) a tropical bird, the male of which has brightly colored plumage.

bird of prey ▶ n. (pl. **birds of prey**) a bird that feeds on animal flesh, such as an eagle, hawk, or owl.

bird·seed /ˈbərdˌsēd/ ▶ n. a blend of seeds for feeding birds.

bird's-eye view ▶ n. a general view of something from a high position above it.

bird's nest soup ▶ n. (in Chinese cooking) a soup made from the dried gelatinous coating of the nests of swifts and other birds.

bird·song /ˈbərdˌsônG/ ▶ n. the musical sounds made by birds.

bird·watch·ing /ˈbərdˌwäcʜinG/ ▶ n. the hobby of observing birds in their natural environment. ▪ **bird·watch·er** n.

bi·ret·ta /bəˈretə/ ▶ n. a square cap with three flat projections on top, worn by Roman Catholic clergymen.

birth /bərᴛʜ/ ▶ n. 1 the emergence of a baby or other young from the body of its mother. 2 the beginning of something: *the birth of modern jazz*. 3 a person's origin or ancestry: *he is of noble birth*. ▪ **birth·ing** n.

– PHRASES **give birth** produce a child or young animal.

birth cer·tif·i·cate ▶ n. an official document recording a person's name, their place and date of birth, and the names of their parents.

birth con·trol ▶ n. the prevention of unwanted pregnancies, especially through the use of contraception.

birth·date /ˈbərᴛʜˌdāt/ ▶ n. the date on which a person is born.

birth·day /ˈbərᴛʜˌdā/ ▶ n. the annual anniversary of the day on which a person was born.

birth de·fect ▶ n. a physical or biochemical abnormality that is present at birth and that may be inherited or the result of environmental influence.

birth·mark /ˈbərᴛʜˌmärk/ ▶ n. an unusual, typically permanent, mark on the body that is there from birth.

birth moth·er ▶ n. a woman who has given birth to a child, as opposed to an adoptive mother.

birth·place /ˈbərᴛʜˌplās/ ▶ n. 1 the place where a person was born. 2 the place where something began or originated: *the birthplace of feminism*.

birth rate ▶ n. the number of live births per thousand of population per year.

birth·right /ˈbərᴛʜˌrīt/ ▶ n. 1 a right or privilege that a person has as a result of being born into a particular family, social class, or place. 2 a natural or basic right possessed by all people: *a* *college education should be regarded as everyone's birthright.*

birth·stone /'bərth,stōn/ ▶ n. a gemstone popularly associated with the month or astrological sign of a person's birth.

bi·ry·a·ni /,birē'änē/ (also **biriani**) ▶ n. an Indian dish made with highly seasoned rice and meat, fish, or vegetables.

bis·cuit /'biskit/ ▶ n. **1** a small, round cake of bread leavened with baking powder or soda. **2** a light brown color. **3** porcelain or other pottery that has been fired but not glazed. ■ **bis·cuit·y** adj.

bi·sect /bī'sekt, 'bī,sekt/ ▶ v. divide something into two parts. ■ **bi·sec·tion** n. **bi·sec·tor** n.

bi·sex·u·al /bī'seksнōōəl/ ▶ adj. **1** sexually attracted to both men and women. **2** Biology having characteristics of both sexes. ▶ n. a person who is sexually attracted to both men and women. ■ **bi·sex·u·al·i·ty** /,bīseksнōō'alitē/ n.

bish·op /'bisнəp/ ▶ n. **1** a senior member of the Christian clergy, usually in charge of a diocese. **2** a chess piece with a top shaped like a miter, that can move diagonally in any direction.

bish·op·ric /'bisнəprik/ ▶ n. the position or diocese of a bishop.

bis·muth /'bizməth/ ▶ n. a brittle reddish-gray metallic element resembling lead.

bi·son /'bīsən, -zən/ ▶ n. (pl. same) a shaggy-haired wild ox with a humped back.

bisque¹ /bisk/ ▶ n. a rich soup made from lobster or other shellfish.

bisque² ▶ n. another term for **BISCUIT** (sense 3).

bis·tro /'bistrō, 'bē-/ ▶ n. (pl. **bistros**) a small, inexpensive restaurant.

bit¹ /bit/ ▶ n. **1** a small piece or quantity of something. **2** (**a bit**) a short time or distance. – PHRASES **a bit** rather; slightly: *you're a bit late.* **bit by bit** gradually. **do one's bit** informal make a useful contribution to a task or enterprise. **to bits 1** into pieces. **2** informal very much: *he was thrilled to bits.*

bit² ▶ past of **BITE**.

bit³ ▶ n. **1** a metal mouthpiece attached to a bridle, used to control a horse. **2** a tool or part of a tool for boring or drilling. **3** the part of a key that engages with the lock lever. – PHRASES **get the bit between one's teeth** begin to tackle a task with determination.

bit⁴ ▶ n. Computing a unit of information expressed as either a 0 or 1 in binary notation.

bitch /bicн/ ▶ n. **1** a female dog, wolf, fox, or otter. **2** informal a spiteful or unpleasant woman. **3** (**a bitch**) informal a difficult or unpleasant thing or situation: *working the night shift is a bitch.* ▶ v. informal make spiteful comments.

bitch·y /'bicнē/ ▶ adj. (**bitchier, bitchiest**) informal spiteful. ■ **bitch·i·ly** adv. **bitch·i·ness** n.

bite /bīt/ ▶ v. (past **bit**; past part. **bitten**) **1** cut into something with the teeth. **2** (of a snake, insect, or spider) wound someone or something with a sting, pincers, or fangs. **3** (of a fish) take the bait or lure on the end of a fishing line into the mouth. **4** (of a tool, tire, etc.) grip a surface. **5** (of a policy or situation) take effect, with unpleasant consequences: *in hospitals, the strike action was beginning to bite.* **6** (**bite something back**) stop oneself saying something. ▶ n. **1** an act of biting. **2** a piece of food bitten off. **3** Dentistry the bringing together of the teeth when the jaws are closed. **4** informal a quick snack. **5** a sharpness

or strength of flavor: *chicory leaves add color and bite to a salad.* **6** a feeling of cold in the air. ■ **bit·er** n. – PHRASES **bite the bullet** make oneself do something difficult or unpleasant that can no longer be avoided. **bite the dust** informal die or be killed. **bite the hand that feeds one** deliberately hurt or offend a person who is trying to help. **bite off more than one can chew** take on a commitment one cannot fulfill. **bite one's tongue** make a desperate effort to avoid saying something.

bit·ing /'bītiNG/ ▶ adj. **1** (of a wind) very cold and unpleasant. **2** harshly critical: *a biting commentary on contemporary society.* ■ **bit·ing·ly** adv.

bit·map /'bit,map/ ▶ n. the information used to control an image or display on a computer screen, in which each item corresponds to one or more bits of information.

bit part ▶ n. a small acting role in a play or movie.

bit·ten /'bitn/ ▶ past participle of **BITE**.

bit·ter /'bitər/ ▶ adj. **1** having a sharp taste or smell; not sweet. **2** causing pain or unhappiness: *the decision came as a bitter blow.* **3** feeling anger, hurt, and resentment. **4** (of a conflict) intense and full of hatred: *a long and bitter dispute.* **5** (of wind or weather) intensely cold. ▶ n. **1** Brit. bitter-tasting beer that is strongly flavored with hops. **2** (**bitters**) (treated as sing.) alcohol flavored with bitter plant extracts, used as an ingredient in cocktails. ■ **bit·ter·ly** adv. **bit·ter·ness** n. – PHRASES **to the bitter end** to the very end, in spite of severe difficulties.

bit·tern /'bitərn/ ▶ n. a marshland bird of the heron family, noted for the male's deep booming call.

bit·ter or·ange ▶ n. another term for **SEVILLE ORANGE**.

bit·ter·sweet /'bitər,swēt/ ▶ adj. **1** sweet with a bitter aftertaste. **2** bringing pleasure mixed with a touch of sadness.

bit·ty /'bitē/ ▶ adj. (**bittier, bittiest**) tiny.

bi·tu·men /bi't(y)ōōmən, bī-/ ▶ n. a black sticky substance obtained naturally or from petroleum, used for road surfacing. ■ **bi·tu·mi·nous** /bi't(y)ōōmənəs, bī-/ adj.

bi·tu·mi·nous coal ▶ n. a type of black coal that burns with a characteristically bright smoky flame.

bi·valve /'bī,valv/ ▶ n. a mollusk that lives in water and has a hinged double shell, such as an oyster, mussel, or scallop. ▶ adj. (also **bivalved**) having a hinged double shell.

biv·ou·ac /'bivōō,ak, 'bivwak/ ▶ n. a temporary camp without tents, used especially by soldiers or mountaineers. ▶ v. (**bivouacks, bivouacking, bivouacked**) stay in a bivouac.

bi·week·ly /bī'wēklē/ ▶ adj. & adv. appearing or taking place every two weeks or twice a week.

biz /biz/ ▶ n. informal business.

bi·zarre /bi'zär/ ▶ adj. very strange or unusual. ■ **bi·zarre·ly** adv. **bi·zarre·ness** n.

Bk ▶ symbol the chemical element berkelium.

blab /blab/ ▶ v. (**blabs, blabbing, blabbed**) informal reveal information that should have been kept secret.

blab·ber /'blabər/ ▶ v. informal talk at length about foolish or unimportant things.

blab·ber·mouth /'blabər,mouTH/ ► n. informal a person who reveals secrets or talks too much.

black /blak/ ► adj. **1** of the very darkest color. **2** (of coffee or tea) served without milk. **3** relating to the human group having dark-colored skin. **4** marked by tragedy, disaster, or despair: *the blackest day of the war.* **5** (of humor) presenting tragic or distressing situations in comic terms. **6** full of anger or hatred: *he threw me a black look.* ► n. **1** black color. **2** a member of a dark-skinned people. ► v. make something black, especially by applying black polish or makeup. ■ **black·ish** adj. **black·ly** adv. **black·ness** n.

– PHRASES **black out** lose consciousness; faint. **black something out** make a room or building dark by switching off all the lights and covering the windows. **in the black** not owing any money.

> **USAGE**
> **Black**, designating Americans of African heritage, became the most widely used and accepted term in the 1960s and 1970s, replacing **Negro**. It is not usually capitalized: *black Americans.* Through the 1980s, the more formal **African American** replaced **black** in much usage, but both are now generally acceptable.

black and white ► adj. (of a situation or debate) involving clear-cut opposing opinions or issues.

black art (also **black arts**) ► n. black magic.

black·ball /'blak,bôl/ ► v. reject a candidate applying to become a member of a private club.

black bean ► n. a cultivated variety of soybean.

black belt ► n. a black belt worn by an expert in judo, karate, and other martial arts.

Black·Ber·ry /'blak,berē/ ► n. trademark a hand-held wireless electronic device that provides Internet access along with email, telephone, and text messaging services.

black·ber·ry /'blak,berē/ ► n. (pl. **blackberries**) the purple-black edible fruit of a prickly climbing shrub.

black·ber·ry·ing /'blak,berēiNG, 'blak,brēiNG/ ► n. the activity of picking blackberries.

black bile ► n. (in medieval science and medicine) one of the four bodily humors, believed to be associated with a melancholy temperament.

black·bird /'blak,bərd/ ► n. an American songbird, the male of which has black plumage that is iridescent or has patches of red or yellow.

black·board /'blak,bôrd/ ► n. a large board with a dark surface for writing on with chalk.

black box ► n. a flight recorder in an aircraft.

black cur·rant ► n. the small round edible black berry of a shrub.

black e·con·o·my ► n. the part of a country's economic activity that is not recorded or taxed by its government.

black·en /'blakən/ ► v. **1** become or make black or dark. **2** damage or destroy someone's reputation.

black eye ► n. **1** an area of bruised skin around the eye caused by a blow. **2** a mark or source of dishonor or shame.

black-eyed pea ► n. a plant of the pea family native to the Old World tropics. It is an important forage and human food crop.

black·fly /'blak,flī/ ► n. (pl. **blackflies**) a small black fly that sucks blood and can transmit diseases.

Black·foot /'blak,foŏt/ ► n. (pl. same or **Blackfeet**) a member of an allied group of North American Indian peoples of the northwestern plains.

black·guard /'blagərd, 'blak,gärd/ ► n. dated a man who behaves in a dishonorable or dishonest way.

black·head /'blak,hed/ ► n. a lump of oily matter blocking a hair follicle.

black hole ► n. a region of space that has a gravitational field so intense that no matter or radiation can escape from it.

black ice ► n. a transparent layer of ice on a road surface.

black·ing /'blakiNG/ ► n. black paste or polish.

black·jack /'blak,jak/ ► n. **1** a gambling card game in which players try to acquire cards with a face value as close as possible to 21 without going over. **2** a flexible lead-filled club.

black light ► n. ultraviolet or infrared radiation, invisible to the eye.

black·list /'blak,list/ ► n. a list of people or groups seen as unacceptable or untrustworthy. ► v. put the name of a person or group on a blacklist: *the author was blacklisted for his political beliefs.*

black mag·ic ► n. a type of magic that involves the summoning of evil spirits.

black·mail /'blak,māl/ ► n. **1** the crime of demanding money from someone in return for not revealing information that could disgrace them. **2** the use of threats or other pressure in an attempt to persuade someone to do something they do not want to do: *she resorted to emotional blackmail.* ► v. **1** demand money from someone in return for not revealing information that could disgrace them. **2** force someone to do something by using threats or other pressure: *he blackmailed her into marrying him.* ■ **black·mail·er** n.

Black Ma·ri·a /mə'rīə/ ► n. informal a police vehicle for transporting prisoners.

black mark ► n. informal a record of the fact that someone has done something that is disapproved of by others.

black mar·ket ► n. the illegal buying and selling of goods that are officially controlled or hard to obtain. ■ **black mar·ke·teer** n.

black mass ► n. an imitation of the Roman Catholic Mass, performed in worship of the Devil.

Black Mus·lim ► n. a member of the Nation of Islam.

black·out /'blak,out/ ► n. **1** a period when all lights must be turned off during an enemy air raid. **2** a sudden failure of an electrical power supply. **3** a temporary loss of consciousness. **4** an official suppression of information: *a total news blackout.*

Black Pan·ther ► n. a member of a militant political organization set up in the US in 1966 to fight for black rights.

black sheep ► n. informal a member of a family or group who is regarded by the other members as a source of shame or embarrassment.

black·shirt /'blak,SHərt/ ► n. a member of a Fascist organization.

black·smith /'blak,smiTH/ ► n. **1** a person who makes and repairs things in iron by hand. **2** a person who shoes horses; a farrier.

black·thorn /'blak,THôrn/ ► n. a thorny shrub with white flowers and blue-black fruits (sloes).

black tie ► n. men's formal evening clothes, specifically a black bow tie worn with a dinner jacket.

black·top /'blak,täp/ ▶ n. **1** asphalt or other black material used for surfacing roads. **2** a road or area surfaced with such material.

black wid·ow ▶ n. a highly poisonous American spider having a black body with red markings.

blad·der /'bladər/ ▶ n. **1** a sac in the abdomen that receives urine from the kidneys and stores it for excretion. **2** an inflated or hollow flexible bag.

blad·der·wort /'bladər,wərt, -,wôrt/ ▶ n. a water plant with small air-filled sacs that keep it afloat.

blad·der·wrack /'bladər,rak/ ▶ n. a type of seaweed with long, flat brown fronds that contain sacs filled with air.

blade /blād/ ▶ n. **1** the flat part of a knife or other tool or weapon that has a sharp edge for cutting. **2** the broad flat part of an oar, leaf, or other object. **3** a long narrow leaf of grass. **4** informal, dated a dashing young man.

blame /blām/ ▶ v. feel or state that someone or something is responsible for a bad or unfortunate act, situation, or occurrence: *he blamed Francis for his mother's death.* ▶ n. responsibility for a bad or unfortunate act, situation, or occurrence: *she's trying to put the blame on me.* ■ **blame·wor·thy** /'blām,wərTHē/ **adj.** – PHRASES **be to blame** be responsible for a bad or unfortunate act, situation, or occurrence.

blame game ▶ n. the act of individuals or groups assigning blame to one another rather than taking a constructive position: *we should all stop this blame game and start the negotiations process.*

blame·less /'blāmlis/ ▶ adj. free from responsibility for any bad or unfortunate act, situation, or occurrence.

blanch /blanCH/ ▶ v. **1** make or become white or pale. **2** prepare vegetables by plunging them briefly in boiling water. **3** peel almonds by scalding them.

blanc·mange /blə'mänj, -'mänZH/ ▶ n. Brit. a sweet jellylike dessert made with cornstarch and milk.

bland /bland/ ▶ adj. **1** lacking strong qualities and therefore uninteresting: *bland, mass-produced pop music.* **2** showing little emotion: *his bland expression.* ■ **bland·ly** adv. **bland·ness** n.

bland·ish·ments /'blandiSHmənts/ ▶ pl.n. flattering remarks intended to persuade someone to do something.

blank /blaNGk/ ▶ adj. **1** not marked or decorated; bare or plain: *a blank piece of paper.* **2** not understanding or reacting: *he gave me a blank look.* **3** complete; absolute: *a blank refusal.* ▶ n. **1** a space left to be filled in a document. **2** a cartridge containing gunpowder but no bullet. **3** an empty space or period of time. ▶ v. **1** hide or cover: *the sun had gone, blanked out by the smoke.* **2** defeat (a sports opponent) without allowing the opposition to score: *Baltimore blanked Toronto in a 7-0 victory.* ■ **blank·ly** adv. **blank·ness** n. – PHRASES **draw a blank** get no response or result.

blank check ▶ n. **1** a signed check with the amount left for the person cashing it to fill in. **2** complete freedom of action.

blan·ket /'blaNGkit/ ▶ n. **1** a large piece of woolen or similar material used as a warm covering. **2** a thick mass or layer of something: *a blanket of cloud.* ▶ adj. covering all cases; total: *a blanket ban on tobacco advertising.* ▶ v. (**blankets, blanketing, blanketed**) cover completely with a thick layer: *the countryside was blanketed with snow.* ■ **blan·ket·ing** n.

blank verse ▶ n. poetry written in iambic pentameter that does not rhyme.

blare /ble(ə)r/ ▶ v. sound loudly and harshly: *a police car with its siren blaring.* ▶ n. a loud, harsh sound.

blar·ney /'blärnē/ ▶ n. talk intended to be charming, flattering, or persuasive.

bla·sé /blä'zā/ ▶ adj. unimpressed with or indifferent to something because one has seen or experienced it many times before.

blas·pheme /blas'fēm, 'blas,fēm/ ▶ v. speak disrespectfully about God or sacred things. ■ **blas·phem·er** n.

blas·phe·mous /'blasfəməs/ ▶ adj. disrespectful toward God or sacred things. ■ **blas·phe·mous·ly** adv.

blas·phe·my /'blasfəmē/ ▶ n. (pl. **blasphemies**) disrespectful talk about God or sacred things.

blast /blast/ ▶ n. **1** an explosion, or the destructive wave of air spreading outward from it. **2** a strong gust of wind or air. **3** a single loud note of a horn or whistle. **4** informal an enjoyable experience. ▶ v. **1** blow something up with explosives. **2** (**blast off**) (of a rocket or spacecraft) take off. **3** produce loud music or noise. **4** strike a ball hard. **5** informal criticize someone or something fiercely. ■ **blast·er** n. – PHRASES (**at**) **full blast** at maximum power or volume.

blast·ed /'blastid/ ▶ adj. **1** informal used to express annoyance: *make your own blasted coffee!* **2** informal drunk.

blast fur·nace ▶ n. a smelting furnace using blasts of hot compressed air.

blast-off /'blast,ôf, -,äf/ ▶ n. the launch of a rocket or spacecraft.

bla·tant /'blātnt/ ▶ adj. (of an act considered to be bad) done in an open, obvious, and unashamed way: *a blatant abuse of human rights.* ■ **bla·tan·cy** /'blātnsē/ n. **bla·tant·ly** adv.

blath·er /'blaTHər/ (also **blither**) ▶ v. talk at length without making much sense. ▶ n. rambling talk.

blaze /blāz/ ▶ n. **1** a very large or fiercely burning fire. **2** a very bright light or display of color. **3** a conspicuous display or outburst of something: *a blaze of publicity.* **4** a white stripe down the face of a horse or other animal. **5** (**blazes**) informal a euphemism for 'hell': *go to blazes!* ▶ v. **1** burn or shine fiercely or brightly. **2** (of guns) be fired repeatedly or wildly. **3** informal achieve something in an impressive manner. ■ **blaz·ing** adj. – PHRASES **blaze a trail 1** mark out a path or route. **2** be the first to do something.

blaz·er /'blāzər/ ▶ n. **1** a jacket worn by schoolchildren or team members as part of a uniform. **2** a man's sports jacket that does not form part of a suit.

bla·zon /'blāzən/ ▶ v. **1** display or describe prominently or vividly: *his name was blazoned all over the newspapers.* **2** Heraldry depict a coat of arms. ▶ n. old use a coat of arms.

bleach /blēCH/ ▶ v. **1** make something white or lighter by the use of chemicals or by exposing it to sunlight. **2** clean or sterilize a drain, sink, etc., with bleach. ▶ n. a chemical used to lighten things and also to sterilize drains, sinks, etc.

bleach·er /'blēCHər/ ▶ n. (usu. **bleachers**) a cheap bench seat in an uncovered part of a sports arena.

bleak /blēk/ ▶ adj. **1** bare and exposed to the weather: *the bleak snow-covered hillside.* **2** empty or unwelcoming; without pleasant features: *a bleak room in a grimy hotel.* **3** (of a situation) not hopeful or encouraging: *HIV patients in the town face a bleak future.* ■ **bleak·ly** adv. **bleak·ness** n.

blear·y /'bli(ə)rē/ ▶ adj. (**blearier, bleariest**) (of a person's eyes) dull and not focusing properly, especially as a result of tiredness. ■ **blear·i·ly** adv.

bleat /blēt/ ▶ v. **1** (of a sheep or goat) make a weak, wavering cry. **2** speak or complain in a weak or petulant way. ▶ n. a bleating sound.

bleed /blēd/ ▶ v. (past and past part. **bled** /bled/) **1** lose blood from the body. **2** take blood from someone as a former method of medical treatment. **3** informal deprive of money or resources: *bogus refugees bled the country of $100 million.* **4** (of dye or color) seep into an adjoining color or area. **5** allow fluid or gas to escape from a closed system through a valve. ▶ n. an instance of losing blood from a part of the body.

bleed·ing /'blēdiNG/ ▶ adj. Brit. informal used for emphasis or to express annoyance.

bleed·ing heart ▶ n. informal, derogatory a person considered to be too softhearted or liberal.

bleep /blēp/ ▶ n. a short high-pitched sound made by an electronic device. ▶ v. **1** make a bleep. **2** substitute a bleep or bleeps for (a censored word or phrase).

blem·ish /'blemiSH/ ▶ n. **1** a small mark or flaw that spoils the appearance of something. **2** a fault or failing. ▶ v. spoil the appearance of something.

blench /blenCH/ ▶ v. flinch suddenly through fear or pain.

blend /blend/ ▶ v. **1** mix a substance with another substance so that they combine together. **2** combine with something in an attractive or harmonious way: *costumes, music, and lighting all blend together.* **3** be an unobtrusive or attractive part of something by being similar in appearance or behavior: *a tourist resort designed to blend in with the natural surroundings.* ▶ n. a mixture of different things or people.

blend·er /'blendər/ ▶ n. an electric device used for liquidizing or chopping food.

blen·ny /'blenē/ ▶ n. (pl. **blennies**) a small sea fish with spiny fins and a scaleless skin.

bless /bles/ ▶ v. **1** ask God to protect someone or something: *may God bless you and keep you.* **2** make holy by performing a religious rite: *the priest had broken the bread and blessed the wine.* **3** praise God. **4** (**be blessed with**) have or be given something that is greatly wished for: *we have been blessed with a baby boy.* – PHRASES **bless you!** said to a person who has just sneezed.

bless·ed /blest, 'blesid/ ▶ adj. **1** made holy. **2** protected by God. **3** bringing welcome pleasure or relief: *blessed sleep.* **4** informal used in mild expressions of exasperation. ■ **bless·ed·ly** /'blesidlē/ adv. **bless·ed·ness** /'blesidnis/ n.

bless·ing /'blesiNG/ ▶ n. **1** God's favor and protection. **2** a prayer asking for this. **3** something for which one is very grateful: *it's a blessing we're alive.* **4** a person's approval or support: *he gave the plan his blessing.*

– PHRASES **a blessing in disguise** something that at first seems unfortunate but eventually has good results.

blew /blōō/ ▶ past of BLOW¹.

blight /blīt/ ▶ n. **1** a plant disease, especially one caused by fungi. **2** a thing that spoils or damages something: *an ugly building that is a blight on the landscape.* **3** ugly or neglected urban landscape. ▶ v. **1** infect plants with blight. **2** spoil or destroy: *lives blighted by economic hardship.*

bli·mey /'blīmē/ ▶ exclam. Brit. informal expressing surprise or alarm.

blimp /blimp/ ▶ n. **1** a small nonrigid airship. **2** informal an obese person. ■ **blimp·ish** adj.

blind /blīnd/ ▶ adj. **1** not able to see. **2** done without being able to see or without having certain information: *a blind tasting of eight wines.* **3** not noticing or realizing something: *I am not blind to her shortcomings.* **4** not controlled by reason: *they left in blind panic.* **5** (of a corner or bend in a road) impossible to see around. ▶ v. **1** make someone or something blind. **2** make someone no longer able to think clearly or sensibly: *they were blinded by hatred.* **3** (**blind someone with**) confuse or overawe someone with something they do not understand: *a manual that does not blind you with computer science.* ▶ n. **1** a screen for a window. **2** something designed to conceal one's real intentions. ▶ adv. without being able to see clearly. ■ **blind·ly** adv. **blind·ness** n.

– PHRASES **blind drunk** informal extremely drunk. **turn a blind eye** pretend not to notice.

blind al·ley ▶ n. **1** a cul-de-sac. **2** a course of action that does not produce useful results.

blind date ▶ n. a meeting with a person one has not met before, with the aim of developing a romantic relationship.

blind·ers /'blīndərz/ ▶ pl.n. **1** a pair of small pieces of leather attached to a horse's bridle to prevent the horse seeing sideways. **2** something that prevents someone from fully understanding a situation.

blind·fold /'blīnd,fōld/ ▶ n. a piece of cloth tied around the head to cover someone's eyes. ▶ v. put a blindfold on someone so that they cannot see. ▶ adv. with a blindfold covering the eyes: *I could find my way around the place blindfold.*

blind·ing /'blīndiNG/ ▶ adj. **1** (of light) very bright. **2** (of pain) very intense: *a blinding headache.* **3** informal very skillful and exciting: *a blinding performance.* ■ **blind·ing·ly** adv.

blind man's buff (also **blind man's bluff**) ▶ n. a children's game in which a blindfolded player tries to catch others while being pushed around by them.

blind side ▶ n. a direction in which a person has a poor view of approaching traffic or danger.

blind spot ▶ n. **1** a small area of the retina in the eye that is insensitive to light. **2** an area where a person's view is obstructed. **3** an area or subject about which a person lacks understanding or impartiality: *he has a blind spot where his daughter is concerned.*

blind·worm /'blīnd,wərm/ ▶ n. another term for SLOW-WORM.

bling-bling /'bliNG ,bliNG/ (also **bling**) ▶ n. & adj. informal used to refer to expensive, showy clothing and jewelry, or the style or attitudes associated with them.

blin·i /'blinē, 'blē-/ (also **blinis**) ▸ pl.n. pancakes made from buckwheat flour.

blink /bliɴɢk/ ▸ v. **1** shut and open the eyes quickly. **2** (of a light) flash on and off. ▸ n. an act of blinking the eyes.
– PHRASES **on the blink** informal out of order.

blink·er /'bliɴɢkər/ ▸ n. **1** a device that blinks, especially a vehicle's turn signal. **2** (**blinkers**) another term for **BLINDERS**. ▸ v. put blinders on a horse.

blink·ered /'bliɴɢkərd/ ▸ adj. **1** (of a horse) wearing blinders. **2** having or showing a narrow or limited outlook or point of view: *a small-minded, blinkered approach.*

blip /blip/ ▸ n. **1** a very short high-pitched sound made by an electronic device. **2** a small flashing point of light on a radar screen. **3** an unexpected and usually temporary change in the pattern of a situation or process: *a blip in what has otherwise been a successful career.* ▸ v. (**blips**, **blipping**, **blipped**) (of an electronic device) make a blip.

bliss /blis/ ▸ n. **1** a state or feeling of perfect happiness. **2** a state of spiritual blessedness.

bliss·ful /'blisfəl/ ▸ adj. extremely happy.
■ **bliss·ful·ly** adv.

B-list ▸ n. see **A-LIST**.

blis·ter /'blistər/ ▸ n. **1** a small bubble on the skin filled with watery liquid, typically caused when the skin is rubbed against another surface or by burning. **2** a similar swelling, filled with air or fluid, on the surface of painted wood, heated metal, etc. ▸ v. form or cause to form blisters: *his skin was beginning to blister with the heat.*

blis·ter·ing /'blistəriɴɢ/ ▸ adj. **1** (of heat) intense. **2** (of criticism) very forceful: *a blistering attack on the government.* **3** extremely fast, energetic, or impressive: *he set a blistering pace.* ■ **blis·ter·ing·ly** adv.

blithe /blīᴛʜ, blīᴛʜ/ ▸ adj. **1** showing a casual lack of concern about something: *a blithe disregard for the rules of the road.* **2** literary happy.
■ **blithe·ly** adv. **blithe·ness** n.

blith·er·ing /'bliᴛʜəriɴɢ/ ▸ adj. informal complete: *you blithering idiot.*

blitz /blits/ ▸ n. **1** an intensive or sudden military attack. **2** (**the Blitz**) the German air raids on Britain in 1940–41. **3** informal a sudden and concentrated effort to deal with something: *the Department launched a blitz on drunk drivers.* ▸ v. attack or seriously damage a place in a blitz.

blitz·krieg /'blits,krēg/ ▸ n. an intense military campaign intended to bring about a rapid victory.

bliz·zard /'blizərd/ ▸ n. a severe snowstorm with high winds.

bloat /blōt/ ▸ v. swell or cause to swell with fluid or gas. ■ **bloat·ed** adj.

blob /bläb/ ▸ n. **1** a drop of a thick liquid or sticky substance. **2** a roundish mass or shape.
■ **blob·by** adj.

bloc /bläk/ ▸ n. a group of countries or political parties who have formed an alliance.

block /bläk/ ▸ n. **1** a large piece of a solid material with flat surfaces on each side. **2** a building, usually part of a complex, used for a particular purpose: *a cell block.* **3** a group of buildings with streets on all four sides. **4** a large quantity of things regarded as a unit: *a block of shares.* **5** a thing that makes movement or progress difficult: *a block to career advancement.* **6** a solid area of color on a surface. **7** (also **cylinder block** or

engine block) a large metal molding containing the cylinders of an internal-combustion engine. **8** a pulley or system of pulleys mounted in a case. ▸ v. **1** prevent movement or flow in a road, passage, pipe, etc.: *all three lanes were blocked with traffic.* **2** hinder or prevent: *unions threatened to block the deal.* ■ **block·er** n.
– PHRASES **block something out** exclude something unpleasant from one's thoughts or memory. **knock someone's block off** informal hit someone on the head. **put one's head** (or **neck**) **on the block** informal put one's position or reputation at risk by doing or saying something.

block·ade /blä'kād/ ▸ n. an act of sealing off a place to prevent goods or people from entering or leaving. ▸ v. seal off a place to prevent goods or people from entering or leaving.

block·age /'bläkij/ ▸ n. an obstruction that makes movement or flow difficult or impossible.

block and tack·le ▸ n. a lifting mechanism consisting of ropes, a pulley block, and a hook.

block·bust·er /'bläk,bəstər/ ▸ n. informal a movie or book that is a great commercial success.
■ **block·bust·ing** adj.

block cap·i·tals ▸ pl.n. plain capital letters.

block·head /'bläk,hed/ ▸ n. informal a very stupid person.

block·house /'bläk,hous/ ▸ n. a reinforced concrete shelter used as an observation point.

block let·ters ▸ pl.n. block capitals.

blog /bläg/ ▸ n. a personal website on which someone regularly records their opinions or experiences and creates links to other sites.
▸ v. (**blogs**, **blogging**, **blogged**) (usu. as n. **blogging**) regularly update a blog. ■ **blog·ger** n.

blog·o·sphere /'blägə,sfi(ə)r/ ▸ n. the world of weblogs.

blog·roll /'bläg,rōl/ ▸ n. (on a weblog) a list of hyperlinks to other weblogs.

bloke /blōk/ ▸ n. Brit. informal a man.

blonde /bländ/ ▸ adj. (also **blond**) **1** (of hair) fair or pale yellow. **2** having fair hair and a light complexion. ▸ n. a woman with blond hair.

blood /bləd/ ▸ n. **1** the red liquid that circulates in the arteries and veins, carrying oxygen and carbon dioxide. **2** a person's family background: *she must have Irish blood.* **3** dated a fashionable and dashing young man. ▸ v. initiate someone in an activity: *clubs are too slow in blooding young players.*
– PHRASES **be** (or **run**) **in one's blood** be a natural or fundamental part of one's character and, typically, of the character of other family members: *writing is in her blood.* **blood, sweat, and tears** extremely hard work. **first blood 1** the first shedding of blood in a fight. **2** the first point or advantage gained in a contest. **have blood on one's hands** be responsible for someone's death. **make someone's blood boil** informal make someone extremely angry. **make someone's blood run cold** horrify someone. **new** (or **fresh** or **young**) **blood** new (or younger) members of a group or organization, especially those seen as having new and invigorating ideas or skills. **someone's blood is up** someone is angry and in a fighting mood.

blood bank ▸ n. a place where supplies of blood or plasma for transfusion are stored.

blood·bath /'bləd,baᴛʜ/ ▸ n. an event in which many people are killed violently.

blood broth·er ▸ n. a man who has sworn to treat another man as a brother.

blood count ▸ n. a calculation of the number of corpuscles (red and white blood cells) in a particular quantity of blood.

blood·cur·dling /'bləd,kərd(ə)liNG/ ▸ adj. horrifying; extremely frightening.

blood feud ▸ n. a lengthy conflict between families involving a cycle of revenge killings.

blood group ▸ n. any of the various types into which human blood is classified for medical purposes.

blood·hound /'bləd,hound/ ▸ n. a large hound with a very keen sense of smell, used in tracking.

blood·less /'blədlis/ ▸ adj. **1** without violence or killing: *a bloodless coup.* **2** (of the skin) looking very pale; drained of color. **3** lacking emotion or vitality: *a pedantic, bloodless character.* ▪ **blood·less·ly** adv.

blood·let·ting /'bləd,letiNG/ ▸ n. **1** historical the surgical removal of some of a patient's blood for medical purposes. **2** violence during a war or conflict.

blood·line /'bləd,līn/ ▸ n. a pedigree, set of ancestors, or line of descent.

blood mon·ey ▸ n. **1** money paid to compensate the family of a murdered person. **2** money paid to a hired killer.

blood or·ange ▸ n. an orange of a variety with red flesh.

blood poi·son·ing ▸ n. a serious illness that occurs when harmful microorganisms have infected the blood.

blood pres·sure ▸ n. the pressure of the blood in the circulatory system, which is closely related to the force and rate of the heartbeat.

blood re·la·tion (also **blood relative**) ▸ n. a person who is related to another by birth.

blood sau·sage (also **blood pudding**) ▸ n. sausage made from pork and dried pig's blood.

blood·shed /'bləd,sHed/ ▸ n. the killing or wounding of people.

blood·shot /'bləd,sHät/ ▸ adj. (of the eyes) having the whites tinged with blood.

blood sport ▸ n. a sport involving the hunting, wounding, or killing of animals.

blood·stain /'bləd,stān/ ▸ n. a stain or a spot caused by blood. ▪ **blood·stained** adj.

blood·stock /'bləd,stäk/ ▸ n. thoroughbred horses.

blood·stream /'bləd,strēm/ ▸ n. the blood circulating through the body.

blood·suck·er /'bləd,səkər/ ▸ n. **1** an animal or insect that sucks blood. **2** informal a person who extorts money from other people. ▪ **blood·suck·ing** adj.

blood sug·ar ▸ n. the concentration of glucose in the blood.

blood·thirst·y /'bləd,THərstē/ ▸ adj. taking great pleasure in violence and killing.

blood ves·sel ▸ n. a vein, artery, or capillary carrying blood through the body.

blood·y /'blədē/ ▸ adj. (**bloodier, bloodiest**) **1** covered with or containing blood. **2** involving much violence or cruelty: *a bloody military coup.* **3** informal, chiefly Brit. used to express anger or shock, or for emphasis. ▸ v. (**bloodies, bloodying, bloodied**) cover or stain something with blood. ▪ **blood·i·ly** /'blədəlē/ adv. **blood·i·ness** n.

Bloody Mar·y ▸ n. (pl. **Bloody Marys**) a drink consisting of vodka and tomato juice.

bloom /bloom/ ▸ v. **1** produce flowers; be in flower. **2** be or become very healthy: *she had bloomed during her pregnancy.* ▸ n. **1** a flower. **2** the state or period of blooming: *the apple trees were in bloom.* **3** a youthful or healthy glow in a person's complexion: *the rosy bloom in her cheeks.* **4** a delicate powdery deposit on the surface of fruits or leaves.

bloom·er /'bloomər/ ▸ n. **1** a plant that flowers at a specified time. **2** a person who matures or flourishes at a specified time: *he was a late bloomer.*

bloo·mers /'bloomərz/ ▸ pl.n. **1** women's loose-fitting knee-length underpants. **2** historical women's loose-fitting trousers, gathered at the knee or ankle.

bloom·ing /'bloomiNG/ ▸ adj. Brit. informal used to express annoyance or for emphasis: *of all the blooming nerve!*

bloop·er /'bloopər/ ▸ n. informal an embarrassing mistake.

blos·som /'bläsəm/ ▸ n. **1** a flower or a mass of flowers on a tree or bush. **2** the state or period of flowering: *the cherry trees are in blossom.* ▸ v. **1** (of a tree or bush) produce flowers. **2** develop in a promising or healthy way: *their friendship blossomed into romance.*

blot /blät/ ▸ n. **1** a mark or stain, especially one made by ink. **2** a thing that spoils something that is otherwise good or attractive: *the only blot on his dazzling career.* ▸ v. (**blots, blotting, blotted**) **1** dry a wet surface or substance with an absorbent material. **2** mark, stain, or spoil: *the eyesores that have blotted our cityscapes.* **3** (**blot something out**) cover or hide something from view. **4** (**blot something out**) try to keep an unpleasant memory or thought from one's mind: *he tried to blot out the image of Helen's sad face.*

blotch /bläcH/ ▸ n. a large irregular mark. ▪ **blotched** adj. **blotch·y** adj.

blot·ter /'blätər/ ▸ n. a sheet or pad of blotting paper kept on a desk.

blot·ting pa·per ▸ n. absorbent paper used for soaking up excess ink when writing.

blot·to /'blätō/ ▸ adj. informal extremely drunk.

blouse /blous, blouz/ ▸ n. **1** a garment like a shirt, worn by women. **2** a type of jacket worn as part of a military uniform. ▸ v. make a garment hang in full, loose folds.

blous·on /'blou,sän, -,zän/ ▸ n. a short loose-fitting jacket.

blo·vi·ate /'blōvēāt/ ▸ v. talk at length, especially using inflated or empty rhetoric.

blow[1] /blō/ ▸ v. (past **blew**; past part. **blown**) **1** (of wind) move, creating a current or air. **2** carry or be carried by the wind: *my tent had blown away.* **3** send out air through pursed lips. **4** force air through the mouth into a musical instrument. **5** sound the horn of a vehicle. **6** (of an explosion) force something out of place: *the blast blew out the windows.* **7** burst or burn out through pressure or overheating: *the fuse in the plug had blown.* **8** shape molten glass by forcing air into it through a tube. **9** informal spend money recklessly. **10** informal waste an opportunity: *they blew their championship chances.* **11** informal reveal or expose something: *one mistake could blow his cover.* ▸ n. **1** an act of blowing something. **2** a strong wind.

– PHRASES **blow a fuse** (or **gasket**) informal lose one's temper. **blow hot and cold** keep changing one's mind. **blow someone's mind** informal impress or affect someone very strongly. **blow one's nose** clear one's nose of mucus by blowing through it. **blow over** (of trouble) fade away without having any serious effects. **blow one's top** informal lose one's temper. **blow up 1** explode. **2** lose one's temper. **3** develop suddenly and violently: *a crisis blew up between the two countries in 1967.* **blow something up 1** make something explode. **2** inflate something.

blow² ▶ n. **1** a powerful stroke with a hand or weapon. **2** a sudden shock or disappointment: *the news came as a crushing blow.*
– PHRASES **come to blows** start fighting after a disagreement.

blow-by-blow ▶ adj. (of a description of an event) giving all the details in the order in which they happened.

blow-dry ▶ v. dry the hair with a hand-held dryer, arranging it into a particular style.

blow·er /ˈblōər/ ▶ n. a device that creates a current of air to dry or heat something.

blow·fish /ˈblō.fish/ ▶ n. (pl. same or **blowfishes**) a fish that is able to inflate its body when it is alarmed.

blow·fly /ˈblō.flī/ ▶ n. (pl. **blowflies**) a bluebottle or similar large fly that lays its eggs on meat and carcasses.

blow·hard /ˈblō.härd/ ▶ n. informal a boastful or pompous person.

blow·hole /ˈblō.hōl/ ▶ n. **1** the nostril of a whale or dolphin, on the top of its head. **2** a hole in ice for breathing or fishing through. **3** a vent for air or smoke in a tunnel.

blow job ▶ n. vulgar slang an act of fellatio.

blown /blōn/ ▶ past participle of BLOW¹.

blow·out /ˈblō.out/ ▶ n. **1** an occasion when a vehicle tire bursts or an electric fuse melts. **2** informal a large meal or social gathering.

blow·pipe /ˈblō.pīp/ ▶ n. **1** a weapon consisting of a long tube through which an arrow or dart is blown. **2** a long tube used for blowing glass.

blows·y /ˈblouzē/ (also **blowzy**) ▶ adj. (of a woman) red-faced and untidy in appearance.

blow·torch /ˈblō.tôrch/ ▶ n. a portable device producing a very hot flame, used to burn paint off a surface.

blow·up /ˈblō.əp/ ▶ n. **1** an enlargement of a photograph. **2** informal an outburst of anger.
▶ adj. inflatable: *a blowup neck pillow.*

BLT ▶ n. a sandwich filled with bacon, lettuce, and tomato.

blub·ber¹ /ˈbləbər/ ▶ n. the fat of sea mammals, especially whales and seals. ■ **blub·ber·y** adj.

blub·ber² ▶ v. informal sob noisily.

bludg·eon /ˈbləjən/ ▶ n. a thick stick with a heavy end, used as a weapon. ▶ v. **1** hit someone repeatedly with a bludgeon or other heavy object. **2** bully into doing something: *he bludgeoned Congress into approving the measures.*

blue /blōō/ ▶ adj. (**bluer, bluest**) **1** of the color of the sky on a sunny day. **2** informal sad or depressed. **3** informal having sexual or pornographic content: *a blue movie.* ▶ n. **1** blue color or material. **2** (**the blue**) literary the sky or sea; the unknown. ■ **blue·ness** n.
– PHRASES **blue on blue** Military referring to an attack made by one's own side that accidentally harms one's own forces. **once in a blue moon** informal very rarely. **out of the blue** informal unexpectedly.

blue ba·by ▶ n. a baby born with bluish skin as the result of a lack of oxygen in the blood.

blue·bell /ˈblōō.bel/ ▶ n. a woodland plant with clusters of blue bell-shaped flowers.

blue·ber·ry /ˈblōō.berē/ ▶ n. (pl. **blueberries**) the dark blue edible berry of a North American shrub.

blue·bird /ˈblōō.bərd/ ▶ n. an American songbird, the male of which has a blue head, back, and wings.

blue blood ▶ n. **1** noble birth: *blue blood is no guarantee of any particular merit, competence, or expertise.* **2** a person of noble birth. ■ **blue-blood·ed** adj.

blue book ▶ n. **1** a listing of socially prominent people. **2** a reference book listing the prices of used cars. **3** a blank book used for written examinations in high school and college.

blue·bot·tle /ˈblōō.bätl/ ▶ n. a large fly with a metallic-blue body.

blue cheese ▶ n. cheese containing veins of blue mold, such as Stilton.

blue-chip ▶ adj. (of a company or shares) considered to be a reliable investment.

blue-col·lar ▶ adj. relating to manual work or workers.

blue crab ▶ n. a large edible swimming crab of the Atlantic coast of North America.

blue-eyed boy ▶ n. informal, chiefly derogatory a person who is held in high regard by someone else and treated with special favor.

blue·grass /ˈblōō.gras/ ▶ n. **1** (also **Kentucky bluegrass**) a meadow grass grown for fodder in North America. **2** a kind of traditional American country music played on banjos and guitars.

blue-green al·gae ▶ pl.n. cyanobacteria.

blue·ish /ˈblōō.ish/ ▶ adj. variant spelling of BLUISH.

blue jay ▶ n. a common North American jay with a blue crest, back, wings, and tail.

blue·print /ˈblōō.print/ ▶ n. **1** a design plan or other technical drawing. **2** something that acts as a plan or model: *a blueprint for an integrated transport system.*

blue rib·bon ▶ n. a blue silk ribbon given to the winner of a competition or as a mark of great distinction. ▶ adj. (**blue-ribbon**) of the highest quality; first-class.

blues /blōōz/ ▶ pl.n. **1** (treated as sing. or pl.) a type of mainly slow, sad music that originated among black Americans in the southern US. **2** (**the blues**) informal feelings of sadness or depression. ■ **blues·y** adj.

blue-sky ▶ adj. informal creative or visionary and not yet having a practical use or application: *blue-sky research.*

blues·man /ˈblōōzmən/ ▶ n. (pl. **bluesmen**) a male performer of blues music.

blue state ▶ n. a US state that has or is thought to have more Democratic than Republican voters.

blue·stock·ing /ˈblōō.stäkiNG/ ▶ n. often derogatory an intellectual or literary woman.

blue whale ▶ n. a bluish-gray whale that is the largest living animal.

blu·ey /ˈblōōē/ ▶ adj. almost or partly blue.

bluff¹ /bləf/ ▶ n. an attempt to deceive someone into believing that one knows or will do something. ▶ v. try to deceive someone about what one knows, or about what one can or is going to do: *she knew him well enough to suspect* *that he was bluffing.* ■ **bluff·er** n.

– PHRASES **call someone's bluff** challenge someone to do what they are threatening to do, in the belief that they will not in fact be able to.

bluff² ▶ adj. (of a person or their manner) frank and direct but in a good-natured way. ■ **bluff·ness** n.

bluff³ ▶ n. a steep bank or slope.

blu·ish /'bloōĭsh/ (also **blueish**) ▶ adj. having a blue tinge.

blun·der /'bləndər/ ▶ n. a stupid or careless mistake. ▶ v. **1** make a blunder. **2** move clumsily or as if unable to see.

blun·der·buss /'bləndər,bəs/ ▶ n. historical a gun with a short, wide barrel, firing balls or lead bullets.

blunt /blənt/ ▶ adj. **1** lacking a sharp edge or point. **2** very frank and direct: *a blunt statement of fact.* ▶ v. **1** make or become blunt. **2** make weaker or less effective: *this coming and going between home and school blunted his alertness.* ■ **blunt·ly** adv. **blunt·ness** n.

blur /blər/ ▶ v. (**blurs, blurring, blurred**) make or become unclear or less distinct: *tears blurred her vision.* ▶ n. something that cannot be seen, heard, or recalled clearly. ■ **blur·ry** adj. (**blurrier, blurriest**).

blurb /blərb/ ▶ n. informal a short description written to promote a book, movie, or other product.

blurt /blərt/ ▶ v. say something suddenly and without careful thought.

blush /bləsh/ ▶ v. become red in the face through shyness or embarrassment. ▶ n. **1** an instance of blushing. **2** literary a pink tinge. **3** blusher. ■ **blush·ing** adj.

blush·er /'bləsHər/ ▶ n. a cosmetic used to give a warm color to the cheeks.

blus·ter /'bləstər/ ▶ v. **1** talk in a loud or aggressive way with little effect. **2** (of wind or rain) blow or beat fiercely and noisily. ▶ n. loud and empty talk. ■ **blus·ter·er** n. **blus·ter·y** adj.

blvd. ▶ abbr. boulevard.

BMI ▶ abbr. body mass index, a measure of whether someone is over- or underweight calculated by dividing their weight in kilograms by the square of their height in meters.

B-mov·ie ▶ n. a low-budget movie, especially one supporting the main attraction in a double feature.

BMX ▶ abbr. bicycle motocross (referring to bicycles designed for cross-country racing).

bo·a /'bōə/ ▶ n. **1** a large snake that winds itself around its prey and crushes it to death. **2** a long, thin stole of feathers or fur worn around a woman's neck.

boar /bôr/ ▶ n. (pl. same or **boars**) **1** (also **wild boar**) a wild pig with tusks. **2** an uncastrated domestic male pig.

board /bôrd/ ▶ n. **1** a long, thin, flat piece of wood used in building. **2** a thin, flat, rectangular piece of stiff material used for various purposes. **3** a group of people who control an organization. **4** the provision of regular meals in return for payment: *room and board.* ▶ v. **1** get on or into a ship, aircraft, or other vehicle. **2** receive meals and accommodations in return for payment. **3** (of a student) live at school during the semester. **4** (**board something up/over**) cover or seal something with pieces of wood.

– PHRASES **go by the board** (of a plan or principle) be abandoned or rejected. **on board**

on or in a ship, aircraft, or other vehicle. **take something on board** informal fully consider or accept a new idea or situation. **tread the boards** informal appear on stage as an actor.

board·er /'bôrdər/ ▶ n. **1** a student who lives at school during the semester. **2** a person who receives regular meals and lodging in return for payment.

board game ▶ n. a game that involves the movement of pieces around a board.

board·ing house ▶ n. a private house providing food and lodging for paying guests.

board·ing school ▶ n. a school at which the students live during the semester.

board·room /'bôrd,roōm/ ▶ n. a room in which a board of directors meets regularly.

board·sail·ing /'bôrd,sāliNG/ ▶ n. another term for WINDSURFING. ■ **board·sail·or** /-,sālər/ n.

board·walk /'bôrd,wôk/ ▶ n. **1** a wooden walkway across sand or marshy ground. **2** a promenade along a beach or waterfront.

boast /bōst/ ▶ v. **1** talk about oneself with excessive pride. **2** possess an impressive or admirable feature: *the resort complex boasts ten pools.* ▶ n. an act of boasting. ■ **boast·er** n.

boast·ful /'bōstfəl/ ▶ adj. showing excessive pride in oneself. ■ **boast·ful·ly** adv. **boast·ful·ness** n.

boat /bōt/ ▶ n. a vessel for traveling on water. ▶ v. travel in a boat for pleasure. ■ **boat·ing** n. **boat·load** n.

– PHRASES **be in the same boat** informal be in the same difficult situation as others. **rock the boat** informal disturb an existing situation.

boat·er /'bōtər/ ▶ n. **1** a flat-topped straw hat with a brim. **2** a person who travels in a boat.

boat·house /'bōt,hous/ ▶ n. a shed at the edge of a river or lake used for housing boats.

boat·man /'bōtmən/ ▶ n. (pl. **boatmen**) a person who provides transport by boat.

boat peo·ple ▶ pl.n. refugees who have left a country by sea.

boat·swain /'bōsən/ (also **bo'sun** or **bosun** pronunc. same) ▶ n. a ship's officer in charge of equipment and the crew.

boat train ▶ n. a train scheduled to connect with the arrival or departure of a boat.

boat·yard /'bōt,yärd/ ▶ n. a place where boats are built, maintained, or stored.

bob¹ /bäb/ ▶ v. (**bobs, bobbing, bobbed**) **1** make or cause to make a quick, short movement up and down. **2** curtsy briefly. ▶ n. a quick, short movement up and down.

bob² ▶ n. **1** a short hairstyle hanging evenly all around. **2** a weight on a pendulum, plumb line, or kite-tail. **3** a bobsled. ▶ v. (**bobs, bobbing, bobbed**) cut hair in a bob.

bob³ ▶ n. (pl. same) Brit. informal a shilling.

bob·bin /'bäbin/ ▶ n. a cylinder, cone, or reel holding thread.

bob·ble¹ /'bäbəl/ ▶ v. **1** informal move with an irregular bouncing motion. **2** mishandle (a ball).

bob·ble² ▶ n. chiefly Brit. a small ball made of strands of wool; a pom-pom. ■ **bob·bly** adj.

bob·by /'bäbē/ ▶ n. (pl. **bobbies**) Brit. informal a police officer.

bob·by pin ▶ n. a sprung hairpin or small clip.

bob·cat /'bäb,kat/ ▶ n. a small North American lynx with a striped and spotted coat and a short tail.

bob·sled /'bäb,sled/ ▶ n. a sled with brakes and

a steering mechanism, used for racing down an ice-covered run. ■ **bob·sled·ding** n.

bob·tail /'bäb,tāl/ ▶ n. a docked tail of a horse or dog.

bod /bäd/ ▶ n. informal a body.

bo·da·cious /bō'dāsHəs/ ▶ adj. informal excellent, admirable, or attractive.

bode /bōd/ ▶ v. (**bode well/ill**) be a sign of a good or bad outcome: *recent sales trends bode well for the coming year.*

bo·de·ga /bō'dāgə/ ▶ n. (in Spanish-speaking countries) a grocery store.

bo·dhi tree /'bōdē/ ▶ n. a fig tree native to India and SE Asia, regarded as sacred by Buddhists because it was under such a tree that Buddha's enlightenment took place.

bod·ice /'bädis/ ▶ n. 1 the part of a woman's dress that is above the waist. 2 a woman's sleeveless undergarment, often laced at the front.

bod·ice-rip·per ▶ n. informal, humorous a sexually explicit historical novel or movie.

bod·i·ly /'bädl-ē/ ▶ adj. relating to the body. ▶ adv. by taking hold of a person's body with force: *the blast lifted me bodily off the floor.*

bod·kin /'bädkin/ ▶ n. a thick, blunt needle with a large eye, used for drawing tape or cord through a hem.

bod·y /'bädē/ ▶ n. (pl. **bodies**) 1 the whole physical structure of a person or an animal. 2 the trunk of the body. 3 a corpse. 4 the main or central part: *the body of the plane filled with smoke.* 5 a mass or collection. 6 an organized group of people with a common function: *a regulatory body.* 7 technical an object: *the path taken by the falling body.* 8 a full flavor in wine. 9 fullness of a person's hair. ▶ v. (**bodies, bodying, bodied**) (**body something forth**) formal give physical form to something abstract. ■ **bod·ied** adj.
– PHRASES **keep body and soul together** stay alive in difficult circumstances.

bod·y bag ▶ n. a bag used for carrying a corpse from a battlefield, accident, or the scene of a crime.

bod·y blow ▶ n. 1 a heavy punch to the body. 2 a severe setback.

bod·y·board /'bädē,bôrd/ ▶ n. a short, light surfboard ridden in a prone position. ■ **bod·y·board·er** n. **bod·y·board·ing** n.

bod·y·build·er /'bädē,bildər/ ▶ n. a person who strengthens and enlarges their muscles through exercise such as weightlifting.

bod·y clock ▶ n. a person's biological clock.

bod·y dou·ble ▶ n. a stand-in for a movie actor during stunt or nude scenes.

bod·y·guard /'bädē,gärd/ ▶ n. a person employed to protect an important or famous person.

bod·y lan·guage ▶ n. the communication of one's feelings by the movement or position of one's body.

bod·y pol·i·tic ▶ n. the people of a nation or society considered as an organized group of citizens.

bod·y shop ▶ n. a garage where repairs to the bodies of vehicles are carried out.

bod·y·snatch·er /'bädē,snacHər/ ▶ n. historical a person who illegally dug up corpses for dissection.

bod·y stock·ing ▶ n. a woman's one-piece undergarment covering the torso and legs.

bod·y·suit /'bädē,sōōt/ ▶ n. a close-fitting one-piece stretch garment for women, typically worn for sports or exercise.

bod·y·surf /'bädē,sərf/ ▶ v. surf without using a board.

bod·y·work /'bädē,wərk/ ▶ n. 1 repairs done to the bodies of motor vehicles. 2 the metal outer shell of a vehicle.

Boer /bôr, bōōr/ ▶ n. an early Dutch or Huguenot settler of southern Africa. ▶ adj. relating to the Boers.

boff /bäf/ informal ▶ v. have sex with someone. ▶ n. an act of sexual intercourse.

bog /bäg, bôg/ ▶ n. an area of soft, wet, muddy ground. ▶ v. (**be/get bogged down**) 1 be or become stuck in mud. 2 be prevented from progressing: *we are hopelessly bogged down in bureaucracy.* ■ **bog·gi·ness** n. **bog·gy** adj.

bo·gey¹ /'bōgē/ Golf ▶ n. (pl. **bogeys**) a score of one stroke over par at a hole. ▶ v. (**bogeys, bogeying, bogeyed**) play a hole in one stroke over par.

bo·gey² (also **bogy**) ▶ n. (pl. **bogeys**) 1 an evil or mischievous spirit. 2 a cause of fear or alarm: *the bogey of recession.*

bo·gey·man /'bōōgē,man, 'bō-/ (also **bogyman**) ▶ n. (pl. **bogeymen**) an evil spirit.

bog·gle /'bägəl/ ▶ v. informal 1 be astonished or baffled: *the mind boggles at the spectacle.* 2 (**boggle at**) hesitate to do something.

bo·gus /'bōgəs/ ▶ adj. not genuine or true: *a bogus police officer.*

bo·gy /'bōgē, bōōgē/ ▶ n. (pl. **bogies**) variant spelling of BOGEY².

Bo·he·mi·an /bō'hēmēən/ ▶ n. 1 a person, especially an artist or writer, who does not follow accepted standards of behavior. 2 a person from Bohemia, a region of the Czech Republic. ▶ adj. 1 unconventional: *the Bohemian life of Montparnasse.* 2 relating to Bohemia. ■ **Bo·he·mi·an·ism** n.

bo·ho /'bō,hō/ ▶ n. (pl. **bohos**) & adj. informal term for BOHEMIAN (sense 1 of the noun).

bohr·i·um /'bôrēəm/ ▶ n. a very unstable chemical element made by high-energy atomic collisions.

boil¹ /boil/ ▶ v. 1 (with reference to a liquid) reach or cause to reach the temperature at which it bubbles and turns to vapor. 2 cook or be cooked in boiling water: *boil the potatoes for 20 minutes.* 3 seethe or bubble; be turbulent. 4 (of a person or emotion) be stirred up. 5 (**boil down to**) amount to: *everything boils down to money in the end.* ▶ n. 1 the action of boiling; boiling point. 2 a state of great activity or excitement: *the housing market has gone off the boil.*

boil² ▶ n. an inflamed pus-filled swelling on the skin.

boil·er /'boilər/ ▶ n. a fuel-burning device for heating water.

boil·er·plate /'boilər,plāt/ ▶ n. 1 rolled steel plates for making boilers. 2 standardized pieces of writing for use as clauses in contracts. 3 stereotyped or clichéd writing.

boil·ing /'boiliNG/ ▶ adj. 1 at or near boiling point. 2 informal extremely hot. 3 (of an emotion) intense.

boil·ing point ▶ n. the temperature at which a liquid boils.

bois·ter·ous /'boist(ə)rəs/ ▶ adj. 1 noisy, lively, and high-spirited: *boisterous gangs of youths.*

2 literary (of weather or water) wild or stormy.
■ **bois·ter·ous·ly** adv. **bois·ter·ous·ness** n.

bok choy /ˌbäk 'CHoi/ ▶ n. a variety of Chinese cabbage with smooth-edged tapering leaves.

bo·la /'bōlə/ ▶ n. (also **bolas**) (especially in South America) a missile consisting of a number of balls connected by cord, thrown to entangle the limbs of animals.

bold /bōld/ ▶ adj. 1 confident and brave: *the company's bold new approach.* 2 (of a color or design) strong or vivid. 3 dated lacking respect; impudent. 4 (of type) having thick strokes. ▶ n. a bold typeface. ■ **bold·ly** adv. **bold·ness** n.
– PHRASES **as bold as brass** so confident as to be disrespectful.

bole /bōl/ ▶ n. a tree trunk.

bo·le·ro /bə'le(ə)rō/ ▶ n. (pl. **boleros**) 1 a Spanish dance in simple triple time. 2 a woman's short open jacket.

bo·le·tus /bō'lētəs/ (also **bolete** /bō'lēt/) ▶ n. (pl. **boletuses** /bō'lētəsəz/) a toadstool with pores rather than gills on the underside of the cap.

bol·i·var /bə'lē,vär, 'bäləvər/ ▶ n. the basic unit of money of Venezuela.

Bo·liv·i·an /bə'livēən/ ▶ n. a person from Bolivia. ▶ adj. relating to Bolivia.

boll /bōl/ ▶ n. the rounded seed capsule of plants such as cotton.

bol·lard /'bälərd/ ▶ n. 1 a short post on a ship or wharf for securing a rope. 2 Brit. a short post used to prevent traffic from entering an area.

bol·locks /'bäləks/ (also **ballocks**) ▶ pl.n. Brit. vulgar slang 1 the testicles. 2 (treated as sing.) nonsense; rubbish.

Bol·ly·wood /'bälē,wŏŏd/ ▶ n. the Indian movie industry, based in Bombay (now Mumbai).

bo·lo·gna /bə'lōnē/ ▶ n. a large smoked, seasoned sausage made of various meats, especially beef and pork.

bo·lo tie /'bōlō/ ▶ n. a tie consisting of a cord around the neck with a large ornamental fastening at the throat.

Bol·she·vik /'bōlSHə,vik/ ▶ n. historical 1 a member of the majority group within the Russian Social Democratic Party, which seized power in the Revolution of 1917. 2 a person with revolutionary or politically radical views.
■ **Bol·she·vism** /-,vizəm/ n. **Bol·she·vist** /-vist/ n.

bol·ster /'bōlstər/ ▶ n. 1 a long, firm pillow. 2 a part in a tool, vehicle, or structure providing support or reducing friction. ▶ v. support or strengthen: *the conservation zones should help to bolster tourism.* ■ **bol·ster·er** n.

bolt[1] /bōlt/ ▶ n. 1 a long metal pin with a head that screws into a nut, used to fasten things together. 2 a bar that slides into a socket to fasten a door or window. 3 a flash of lightning. 4 a short, heavy arrow shot from a crossbow. 5 the sliding piece of the breech mechanism of a rifle. ▶ v. 1 fasten something with a bolt. 2 run away suddenly: *they bolted down the stairs.* 3 eat food quickly. 4 (of a plant) grow quickly upward and stop flowering as seeds develop. ■ **bolt·er** n.
– PHRASES **a bolt from** (or **out of**) **the blue** a sudden and unexpected event. **bolt upright** with the back very straight. **have shot one's bolt** informal have done everything possible but still not succeeded. **make a bolt for** try to escape by running suddenly toward something.

bolt[2] ▶ n. a roll of fabric, originally as a measure.

bo·lus /'bōləs/ ▶ n. (pl. **boluses**) 1 a small rounded mass of something, especially of food being swallowed. 2 a large pill used in veterinary medicine. 3 a single dose of a medicinal drug given all at once.

bomb /bäm/ ▶ n. 1 a container of material capable of exploding or causing a fire. 2 (**the bomb**) nuclear weapons as a whole. 3 (**da** (or **the**) **bomb**) informal an outstandingly good person or thing. ▶ v. 1 attack someone or something with a bomb or bombs. 2 informal fail badly: *the film bombed, losing ten million dollars.*
– PHRASES **it looks like a bomb hit it** (or **went off**) informal used to describe a place that is extremely messy or untidy in appearance.

bom·bard ▶ v. /bäm'bärd/ 1 attack someone or something continuously with bombs or other missiles. 2 direct a continuous flow of questions or information at: *they were bombarded with complaints.* 3 Physics direct a stream of high-speed particles at a substance. ▶ n. /'bäm,bärd/ an early form of cannon, which fired a stone ball.
■ **bom·bard·ment** /bäm'bärdmənt/ n.

bom·bar·dier /ˌbämbə(r)'di(ə)r/ ▶ n. 1 a rank of noncommissioned officer in certain Canadian and British artillery regiments, equivalent to corporal. 2 a member of a bomber crew in the US Air Force responsible for aiming and releasing bombs.

bom·bast /'bämbast/ ▶ n. language that sounds impressive but has little meaning.
■ **bom·bas·tic** /bäm'bastik/ adj. **bom·bas·ti·cal·ly** /bäm'bastik(ə)lē/ adv.

bombe /bäm(b)/ ▶ n. a frozen dome-shaped dessert.

bombed /bämd/ ▶ adj. informal intoxicated by drink or drugs.

bomb·er /'bämər/ ▶ n. 1 an aircraft that drops bombs. 2 a person who plants bombs, especially as a terrorist.

bomb·er jack·et ▶ n. a short jacket, usually leather, gathered at the waist and cuffs by elasticized bands and having a zipper front.

bomb·shell /'bäm,SHel/ ▶ n. 1 something that comes as a great surprise or shock. 2 informal a very attractive woman.

bo·na fide /'bōnə ,fīd, 'bänə/ ▶ adj. genuine; real: *she was a bona fide expert.* ▶ adv. chiefly Law without intention to deceive.

bo·na fi·des /'bōnə ,fīdz, 'fīdēz, 'bänə/ ▶ n. (treated as pl.) evidence proving that a person is what they claim to be; credentials.

bo·nan·za /bə'nanzə/ ▶ n. 1 a situation creating an increase in wealth, profit, or good luck: *a natural gas bonanza.* 2 a large amount of something desirable.

bon ap·pé·tit /'bōn ,apə'tē/ ▶ exclam. used to wish someone an enjoyable meal.

bon·bon /'bän,bän/ ▶ n. a piece of candy.

bond /bänd/ ▶ n. 1 a thing used to tie or fasten things together. 2 (**bonds**) ropes or chains used to hold someone prisoner. 3 a force or feeling that unites people: *the bonds between mother and daughter.* 4 an agreement with legal force. 5 a certificate issued by a government or a public company promising to repay borrowed money at a fixed rate of interest and at a specified time. 6 a sum of money paid as bail. 7 (also **chemical bond**) a strong force of attraction holding atoms together in a molecule. ▶ v. 1 join or be joined securely to something else. 2 form a relationship based on shared feelings or experiences: *you*

naturally bond with people in that sort of situation.
— PHRASES **in bond** (of goods) stored by customs until the importer pays the duty owing.

bond·age /'bändij/ ▶ n. **1** the state of being a slave. **2** sexual practice that involves the tying up of one partner.

bond·ed /'bändid/ ▶ adj. **1** joined securely together. **2** bound by a legal agreement.

bond pa·per ▶ n. high-quality writing paper.

bonds·man /'bändzmən/ ▶ n. (pl. **bondsmen**) **1** a person who takes responsibility for the payment of a bond. **2** old use a slave.

bone /bōn/ ▶ n. **1** any of the pieces of hard, whitish tissue making up the skeleton in vertebrates. **2** the hard material of which bones consist. **3** a thing made or formerly made of bone, such as a strip of stiffening for an undergarment. ▶ v. **1** remove the bones from meat or fish before cooking. **2** (**bone up on**) informal study a subject intensively. ■ **bone·less** adj.
— PHRASES **bone of contention** a subject over which there is continuing disagreement. **close to the bone 1** (of a remark) accurate to the point of causing discomfort. **2** (of a joke or story) near the limit of decency. **have a bone to pick with someone** informal have reason to quarrel or be annoyed with someone. **in one's bones** felt or believed deeply or instinctively. **make no bones about** be straightforward in stating or dealing with something. **work one's fingers to the bone** work very hard.

bone chi·na ▶ n. white porcelain containing the mineral residue of burned bones.

bone dry ▶ adj. very or completely dry.

bone·head /'bōn,hed/ ▶ n. informal a stupid person.

bone·meal /'bōn,mēl/ ▶ n. ground bones used as a fertilizer.

bon·er /'bōnər/ ▶ n. **1** informal a stupid mistake. **2** vulgar slang an erection of the penis.

bon·fire /'bän,fīr/ ▶ n. an open-air fire lit to burn trash or as a celebration.

Bon·fire Night ▶ n. (in the UK) November 5, on which fireworks are set off, bonfires lit, and figures representing Guy Fawkes burned, in memory of the Gunpowder Plot of 1605.

bong /bäNG/ ▶ n. a water pipe used for smoking marijuana or other drugs.

bon·go /'bäNGgō, 'bôNG-/ ▶ n. (pl. **bongos**) each of a pair of small drums, held between the knees and played with the fingers.

bon·ho·mie /'bänə,mē, ,bänə'mē/ ▶ n. good-natured friendliness. ■ **bon·ho·mous** adj.

bo·ni·to /bə'nētō/ ▶ n. (pl. **bonitos**) a small tuna with dark stripes.

bonk /bäNGk/ informal ▶ v. **1** hit someone or something. **2** have sex. ▶ n. **1** an act or sound of hitting someone or something. **2** an act of sexual intercourse.

bon·kers /'bäNGkərz/ ▶ adj. informal mad; crazy.

bon mot /'bän 'mō, ,bôn 'mō/ ▶ n. (pl. **bons mots** pronunc. same or /'mōz/) a clever or witty remark.

bon·net /'bänit/ ▶ n. **1** a woman's or child's hat tied under the chin and with a brim framing the face. **2** (also **war bonnet**) the ceremonial feathered headdress of an American Indian. ■ **bon·net·ed** adj.

bon·sai /'bän'sī, 'bänsī/ ▶ n. the art of growing ornamental trees or shrubs kept very small by pruning.

bo·nus /'bōnəs/ ▶ n. **1** a sum of money added to a person's wages for good performance. **2** an unexpected and extra benefit: *as an added bonus, prizewinners will have their adventures videotaped.*

bon vi·vant /'bän vē'vänt, ,bôn vē'väN/ ▶ n. (pl. **bon vivants** or **bons vivants** pronunc. same) a person who enjoys a sociable and luxurious lifestyle.

bon vi·veur /'bän vē'vər, ,bôn vē'vœr/ ▶ n. (pl. **bon viveurs** or **bons viveurs** pronunc. same) another term for **BON VIVANT**.

bon vo·yage /'bän voi'äzн, 'bôn, bôn/ ▶ exclam. have a good journey.

bon·y /'bōnē/ ▶ adj. (**bonier, boniest**) **1** relating to or containing bones. **2** so thin that the bones can be seen. ■ **bon·i·ness** n.

bon·y fish ▶ n. a fish with a skeleton of bone rather than cartilage.

boo /boō/ ▶ exclam. **1** said suddenly to surprise someone. **2** said to show disapproval or contempt. ▶ v. (**boos, booing, booed**) say 'boo' to show disapproval.

boob[1] /boōb/ informal ▶ n. a foolish or stupid person.

boob[2] ▶ n. informal a woman's breast.

boo-boo ▶ n. **1** informal a mistake. **2** informal a minor injury.

boob tube ▶ n. informal television; a television set.

boo·by[1] /'boōbē/ ▶ n. (pl. **boobies**) **1** informal a stupid person. **2** a large tropical seabird of the gannet family.

booby[2] ▶ n. (pl. **boobies**) informal a woman's breast.

boo·by prize ▶ n. a prize given to the person who comes last in a contest.

boo·by trap ▶ n. an object containing a hidden device that is designed to explode when someone touches it. ▶ v. (**booby-trap**) place a booby trap in or on an object or area.

boog·ie /'boōgē/ ▶ n. (also **boogie-woogie** /-'woōgē/) (pl. **boogies**) **1** a style of blues played on the piano with a strong, fast beat. **2** informal a dance to pop or rock music. ▶ v. (**boogies, boogieing, boogied**) informal dance to pop or rock music.

boog·ie board ▶ n. a short, light surfboard ridden in a prone position.

book /boōk/ ▶ n. **1** a written or printed work consisting of pages fastened together along one side and bound in covers. **2** a main division of a literary work or of the Bible. **3** a bound set of blank pages for writing in: *an exercise book.* **4** (**books**) a set of records or accounts. **5** a set of tickets, stamps, matches, etc., bound together. **6** a bookmaker's record of bets accepted and money paid out. ▶ v. **1** reserve accommodations, a ticket, etc. **2** engage a performer or guest for an event. **3** (**be booked up**) have all places or dates reserved. **4** make an official note of the details of someone who has broken a law or rule. ■ **book·a·ble** adj. **book·er** n. **book·ing** n.
— PHRASES **bring someone to book** officially ask someone to explain their behavior. **by the book** strictly according to the rules. **on the books** contained in a book of laws or records. **take a leaf out of someone's book** imitate someone in a particular way. **throw the book at someone** informal charge or punish someone as severely as possible.

book·bind·er /'boōk,bīndər/ ▶ n. a person skilled in the craft of binding books. ■ **book·bind·ing** n.

book·case /'bŏŏk,kās/ ▸ n. an open cabinet containing shelves on which to keep books.

book club ▸ n. an organization that sells its members selected books at reduced prices.

book·end /'bŏŏk,end/ ▸ n. a support placed at the end of a row of books to keep them upright.

book·ie /'bŏŏkē/ ▸ n. (pl. **bookies**) informal a bookmaker.

book·ish /'bŏŏkĬsH/ ▸ adj. 1 devoted to reading and studying: *a bookish, intellectual young man.* 2 (of language) literary in style.

book·keep·ing /'bŏŏk,kēpĬNG/ ▸ n. the activity of keeping records of financial dealings.
■ **book·keep·er** /-,kēpər/ n.

book learn·ing ▸ n. knowledge gained from books or study; mere theory.

book·let /'bŏŏklĬt/ ▸ n. a small, thin book with paper covers.

book·mak·er /'bŏŏk,mākər/ ▸ n. a person whose job is to take bets, calculate odds, and pay out winnings.

book·mark /'bŏŏk,märk/ ▸ n. 1 a strip of leather or cardboard used to mark a place in a book. 2 a record of the address of a computer file, Internet page, etc., enabling quick access by a user. ▸ v. record the address of a computer file, Internet page, etc., for quick access.

book·sell·er /'bŏŏk,selər/ ▸ n. a person who sells books, especially as the owner or manager of a bookstore.

book·shelf /'bŏŏk,sHelf/ ▸ n. (pl. **bookshelves** /-,sHelvz/) a shelf on which books can be stored.

book·store /'bŏŏk,stôr/ ▸ n. a store that sells new or used books.

book val·ue ▸ n. the value of a security or asset as entered in a company's books. Often contrasted with MARKET VALUE.

book·worm /'bŏŏk,wərm/ ▸ n. informal a person who greatly enjoys reading.

Bool·e·an /'bŏŏlēən/ ▸ adj. (of a system of notation) used to represent logical operations by means of the binary digits 0 (false) and 1 (true), especially in computing and electronics.

boom[1] /bŏŏm/ ▸ n. 1 a loud, deep, resonant sound. 2 a period of great prosperity or rapid economic growth. ▸ v. 1 make a loud, deep, resonant sound. 2 experience a period of rapid economic growth: *business is booming.*
■ **boom·y** adj.

boom[2] ▸ n. 1 a pivoted spar to which the foot of a vessel's sail is attached. 2 a movable arm carrying a microphone or movie camera. 3 a floating beam used to contain oil spills or to form a barrier across the mouth of a harbor.

boo·mer·ang /'bŏŏmə,raNG/ ▸ n. a curved flat piece of wood that can be thrown so as to return to the thrower, used by Australian Aboriginals as a hunting weapon.

boom·town /'bŏŏm,toun/ ▸ n. a town undergoing rapid growth due to sudden prosperity: *a former mining boomtown.*

boon /bŏŏn/ ▸ n. 1 something that is helpful or beneficial: *the detailed information is a boon to researchers.* 2 old use a favor or request.

boon·docks /'bŏŏn,däks/ ▸ pl.n. (the boondocks) informal rough or isolated country.

boon·dog·gle /'bŏŏn,dägəl, -,dôgəl/ ▸ n. informal an unnecessary, wasteful, or fraudulent project.

boon·ies /'bŏŏnēz/ ▸ pl.n. short for BOONDOCKS.

boor /bŏŏr/ ▸ n. a rude, ill-mannered person.
■ **boor·ish** adj. **boor·ish·ly** adv. **boor·ish·ness** n.

boost /bŏŏst/ ▸ v. 1 help or encourage to increase or improve: *praise certainly boosts confidence.* 2 push someone from below. ▸ n. 1 a source of help or encouragement. 2 an increase. 3 a push from below.

boost·er /'bŏŏstər/ ▸ n. 1 a source of help or encouragement: *the rodeo is a morale booster for employees.* 2 a dose of a vaccine that increases or renews the effect of an earlier one. 3 the part of a rocket or spacecraft used to give acceleration after liftoff. 4 a device for increasing electrical voltage or signal strength.

boot[1] /bŏŏt/ ▸ n. 1 an item of footwear covering the foot and ankle, and sometimes the lower leg. 2 short for DENVER BOOT. 3 informal a hard kick. 4 Brit. an automobile's trunk. ▸ v. 1 kick something hard. 2 (**boot someone out**) informal force someone to leave. 3 start a computer and put it into a state of readiness for operation.
■ **boot·a·ble** adj. **boot·ed** adj.
– PHRASES **give someone** (or **get**) **the boot** informal dismiss someone (or be dismissed) from a job.

boot[2] ▸ n. (in phrase **to boot**) as well.

boot·black /'bŏŏt,blak/ ▸ n. a person who makes a living by polishing boots and shoes.

boot camp ▸ n. 1 a military training camp with very harsh discipline. 2 a military-style prison for young offenders.

boot-cut ▸ adj. (of jeans or other pants) flared very slightly below the knee, so as to be worn over boots.

booth /bŏŏTH/ ▸ n. 1 an enclosed compartment allowing privacy when telephoning, voting, etc. 2 a small temporary structure used for selling goods or staging shows at a market or fair.

boot·ie /'bŏŏtē, bŏŏ'tē/ (also **bootee**) ▸ n. 1 a baby's soft shoe. 2 a woman's short boot.

boot·lace /'bŏŏt,lās/ ▸ n. a cord or leather strip for lacing boots.

boot·leg /'bŏŏt,leg/ ▸ adj. (of liquor, computer software, or a recording) made or distributed illegally. ▸ v. (**bootlegs, bootlegging, bootlegged**) make or distribute illicit goods. ▸ n. an illegal musical recording.
■ **boot·leg·ger** n.

boot·less /'bŏŏtlĬs/ ▸ adj. old use (of an action) not successful or useful.

boot·lick·er /'bŏŏt,likər/ ▸ n. informal a person who tries to gain favor by servile behavior.

boot·strap /'bŏŏt,strap/ ▸ n. a loop at the back of a boot, used to pull it on.
– PHRASES **pull oneself up by one's bootstraps** improve one's position by one's own efforts.

boo·ty[1] /'bŏŏtē/ ▸ n. valuable stolen goods.

boo·ty[2] ▸ n. informal a person's buttocks.

boo·ty·li·cious /,bŏŏtĬ'lisHəs/ ▸ adj. informal sexually attractive.

booze /bŏŏz/ informal ▸ n. alcohol, especially hard liquor. ▸ v. drink large quantities of alcohol.
■ **booz·y** (**boozier, booziest**) adj.

booz·er /'bŏŏzər/ ▸ n. informal a person who drinks large quantities of alcohol.

bop[1] /bäp/ informal ▸ n. 1 a dance to pop music. 2 a social occasion with dancing. ▸ v. (**bops, bopping, bopped**) dance to pop music.
■ **bop·per** n.

bop[2] informal ▸ v. (**bops, bopping, bopped**) hit or punch someone quickly. ▸ n. a quick blow or punch.

bo·rac·ic /bə'rasik/ ▶ adj. consisting of or containing boric acid.

bor·age /'bôrij, 'bär-/ ▶ n. a plant with bright blue flowers and hairy leaves.

bo·rax /'bôraks/ ▶ n. a white mineral that is a compound of boron, used in making glass and as a flux in soldering or smelting.

Bor·deaux /bôr'dō/ ▶ n. (pl. same /bôr'dōz/) a wine from the Bordeaux region of SW France.

bor·del·lo /bôr'delō/ ▶ n. (pl. **bordellos**) literary a brothel.

bor·der /'bôrdər/ ▶ n. 1 a boundary between two countries or other areas. 2 a decorative band around the edge of something. 3 a strip of ground along the edge of a lawn for planting flowers or shrubs. ▶ v. 1 form a border around or along: *a pool bordered by palm trees.* 2 (of a country or area) be next to another. 3 (**border on**) come close to being: *he fought the war with a ruthlessness that bordered on the maniacal.*

bord·er·line /'bôrdər,līn/ ▶ n. a boundary. ▶ adj. on the boundary between two states or categories: *references may be requested in borderline cases.*

bore¹ /bôr/ ▶ v. 1 make a hole in something with a drill or other tool. 2 hollow out a gun barrel or other tube. ▶ n. 1 the hollow part inside a gun barrel or other tube. 2 the diameter of a bore: *a small-bore rifle.*

bore² ▶ n. a dull and uninteresting person or activity. ▶ v. make someone feel tired and uninterested by dull talk or behavior.
■ **bor·ing** adj.

bore³ (also **tidal bore**) ▶ n. a steep-fronted wave caused by the meeting of two tides or by a tide rushing up a narrow estuary.

bore⁴ ▶ past of BEAR¹.

bo·re·al /'bôrēəl/ ▶ adj. chiefly technical of the North or northern regions.

bored /bôrd/ ▶ adj. feeling tired and impatient because one is doing something dull or one has nothing to do.

bore·dom /'bôrdəm/ ▶ n. the state of being bored.

bore·hole /'bôr,hōl/ ▶ n. a deep, narrow hole in the ground made to find water or rock.

bor·er /'bôrər/ ▶ n. 1 a worm, mollusk, insect, or insect larva that bores into wood, other plant material, or rock: *a squash vine borer.* 2 a tool for boring.

bo·ric /'bôrik/ ▶ adj. Chemistry of boron.

bo·ric ac·id ▶ n. a compound derived from borax, used as a mild antiseptic.

Bo·ri·cua /bô'rēkwə/ ▶ n. informal a Puerto Rican, especially one living in the US.

born /bôrn/ ▶ adj. 1 existing as a result of birth. 2 (**-born**) having a particular nationality: *a German-born philosopher.* 3 having a natural ability to do a particular job: *a born engineer.* 4 (**born of**) existing as a result of: *a confidence born of success.*
– PHRASES **born and bred** by birth and upbringing. **in all one's born days** throughout one's life (used for emphasis). **I** (or **she**, etc.) **wasn't born yesterday** I am (or she, etc., is) not foolish or easily deceived.

born-a·gain ▶ adj. 1 (of a person) newly converted to a personal faith in Jesus. 2 newly converted to and very enthusiastic about a cause: *born-again environmentalists.*

borne /bôrn/ past participle of BEAR¹.
▶ adj. (**-borne**) carried by the thing specified: *soil-borne bacteria.*

Bor·ne·an /'bôrnēən/ ▶ n. a person from Borneo. ▶ adj. relating to Borneo.

bo·ron /'bôrän/ ▶ n. a crystalline chemical element used in making alloy steel and in nuclear reactors.

bor·ough /'bərō/ ▶ n. 1 an administrative division of London or of New York City. 2 a municipal corporation in certain US states.

bor·row /'bärō, 'bôrō/ ▶ v. 1 take and use something belonging to someone else with the intention of returning it. 2 have money on loan from a person or bank. 3 take and use a word or idea from another language or person.
■ **bor·row·er** n.
– PHRASES **be (living) on borrowed time** be surviving beyond the time that one was expected to do so.

borscht /bôrsHt/ (also **borsch** /bôrsH/) ▶ n. a Russian or Polish soup made with beets and served with sour cream.

bor·zoi /'bôrzoi/ ▶ n. (pl. **borzois**) a breed of large Russian wolfhound with a narrow head and silky coat.

Bos·ni·an /'bäznēən/ ▶ n. a person from Bosnia. ▶ adj. relating to Bosnia.

bos·om /'boozəm/ ▶ n. 1 a woman's breasts or chest. 2 loving care or protection: *he went home to the bosom of his family.* ▶ adj. (of a friend) very close. ■ **bos·om·y** adj.

boss¹ /bôs, bäs/ informal ▶ n. a person who is in charge of a worker or organization. ▶ v. give orders in a domineering way: *now you're an adult I can't boss you around.* ▶ adj. excellent.

boss² ▶ n. 1 a projecting knob or stud, especially on the center of a shield. 2 an ornamental carving at the point where the ribs in a ceiling cross.

bos·sa no·va /'bäsə 'nōvə, 'bô-/ ▶ n. 1 a Brazilian dance like the samba. 2 music composed for this dance.

boss·y /'bôsē, 'bäs-/ ▶ adj. (**bossier, bossiest**) informal fond of giving orders; domineering.
■ **boss·i·ly** adv. **boss·i·ness** n.

Bos·ton baked beans /'bôstən/ ▶ pl.n. a dish of baked beans with salt pork and molasses.

bo·sun (also **bo'sun**) ▶ n. variant spelling of BOATSWAIN.

bot /bät/ ▶ n. an autonomous program on a computer network that can interact with systems or users.

bo·tan·i·cal /bə'tanikəl/ ▶ adj. relating to botany. ▶ n. a substance obtained from a plant and used in cosmetic and medicinal products.
■ **bo·tan·i·cal·ly** adv.

bo·tan·i·cal gar·den (also **botanic garden**)

▶ n. a place where plants are grown for scientific study and display to the public.

bot·a·ny /'bätn-ē/ ▶ n. the scientific study of plants. ■ **bo·tan·ic** /bə'tanik/ adj. **bot·a·nist** n.

botch /bäCH/ informal ▶ v. perform an action or task badly or carelessly. ▶ n. (also **botch-up**) a badly performed action or task. ■ **botch·er** n.

both /bōTH/ ▶ predeterminer, determiner, & pron. two people or things, regarded together. ▶ adv. applying equally to each of two alternatives.
– PHRASES **have it both ways** benefit from two conflicting ways of thinking or behaving.

USAGE
When **both** is used with **and**, the structures following the two words should be symmetrical: *both at home and at work* is better than *both at home and work*.

both·er /'bäTHər/ ▶ v. **1** take the trouble to do something. **2** worry, disturb, or upset someone. **3** (**bother with/about**) feel concern about or interest in: *she has never bothered about boys before.* ▶ n. **1** trouble or effort. **2** (**a bother**) a cause of trouble or annoyance.

both·er·some /'bäTHərsəm/ ▶ adj. troublesome; annoying.

Bo·tox /'bō,täks/ ▶ n. trademark a drug prepared from botulin (the toxin involved in botulism), used cosmetically to remove wrinkles by temporarily paralyzing the muscles of the face. ■ **Bo·toxed** adj.

Bot·swa·nan /bät'swänən/ ▶ n. a person from Botswana, a country of southern Africa. ▶ adj. relating to Botswana.

bot·tle /'bätl/ ▶ n. **1** a container with a narrow neck, used for storing liquids. **2** the contents of such a container: *he managed to put away a bottle of wine.* ▶ v. **1** put liquid in bottles. **2** (**bottle something up**) repress or hide one's feelings.
– PHRASES **hit the bottle** informal start to drink alcohol heavily.

bot·tle-feed ▶ v. (**bottle-feeds, bottle-feeding, bottle-fed**) feed a baby with milk from a bottle.

bot·tle green ▶ adj. dark green.

bot·tle·neck /'bätl,nek/ ▶ n. **1** a narrow section of road where traffic flow is restricted. **2** a cause of delay in a process or system.

bot·tom /'bätəm/ ▶ n. **1** the lowest point or part. **2** the farthest point or part. **3** the lowest position in a competition or ranking: *life at the bottom of society.* **4** a person's buttocks. **5** (also **bottoms**) the lower half of a two-piece garment. ▶ adj. in the lowest or farthest position. ▶ v. **1** (**bottom out**) reach the lowest point before stabilizing or improving: *the real estate market has probably bottomed out.* **2** (of a ship) touch the bottom or bed of the sea. ■ **bot·tom·less** adj. **bot·tom·most** /-,mōst/ adj.
– PHRASES **at bottom** basically. **be at the bottom of** be the basic cause of something. **the bottom falls** (or **drops**) **out** something suddenly fails or collapses. **bottoms up!** informal said as a toast before drinking. **get to the bottom of** find an explanation for a mystery.

bot·tom feed·er ▶ n. **1** any marine creature that lives on the seabed and feeds by scavenging. **2** informal a member of a group of very low social status who survives by any means possible.

bot·tom line ▶ n. informal **1** the final total of an account or balance sheet. **2** the basic and most important factor: *the bottom line is that the economy is recovering.*

bot·u·lism /'bäCHə,lizəm/ ▶ n. food poisoning caused by a bacterium growing on preserved foods that have not been properly sterilized.

bou·clé /,bōō'klä/ ▶ n. yarn with a looped or curled strand.

bou·doir /'bōō,dwär/ ▶ n. a woman's bedroom or small private room.

bouf·fant /bōō'fänt/ ▶ adj. (of hair) styled so as to stand out from the head in a rounded shape. ▶ n. a bouffant hairstyle.

bou·gain·vil·le·a /,bōōgən'vilyə, -'vēə, ,bō-/ (also **bougainvillaea**) ▶ n. a tropical climbing plant with brightly colored modified leaves (bracts) surrounding the flowers.

bough /bou/ ▶ n. a main branch of a tree.

bought /bôt/ ▶ past and past participle of **BUY**.

USAGE
On the confusion of **bought** and **brought**, see the note at **BROUGHT**.

bouil·la·baisse /,bōō(l)yə'bäs, 'bōō(l)yə,bäs/ ▶ n. a rich fish stew or soup, as made originally in Provence.

bouil·lon /'bōŏlyən, -yän/ ▶ n. thin soup or stock made by stewing meat, fish, or vegetables.

boul·der /'bōldər/ ▶ n. a large rock. ■ **boul·der·y** adj.

bou·le /bōōl/ (also **boules** pronunc. same) ▶ n. a French game similar to lawn bowling, played with metal balls.

boul·e·vard /'bōŏlə,värd/ ▶ n. a wide street, typically one lined with trees.

bou·le·var·dier /,bōŏləvär'di(ə)r/ ▶ n. a wealthy, fashionable person who is fond of social activities.

bounce /bouns/ ▶ v. **1** move quickly up or away from a surface after hitting it. **2** move or jump up and down repeatedly. **3** (**bounce back**) recover well after a setback. **4** informal (of a check) be returned by a bank when there is not enough money in an account for it to be paid. **5** eject (from a nightclub or similar establishment) a troublemaker. ▶ n. **1** an act of bouncing. **2** energy or self-confidence: *the bounce was back in Jane's step.* **3** health and body in a person's hair.

bounc·er /'bounsər/ ▶ n. a person employed by a nightclub, etc., to prevent troublemakers entering or to remove them from the building.

bounc·ing /'bounsiNG/ ▶ adj. (of a baby) lively and healthy.

bounc·y /'bounsē/ ▶ adj. (**bouncier, bounciest**) **1** able to bounce or making something bounce: *a bouncy ball.* **2** confident and lively. ■ **bounc·i·ly** adv. **bounc·i·ness** n.

bound¹ /bound/ ▶ v. walk or run with leaping strides. ▶ n. a leaping movement toward or over something.

bound² ▶ n. a boundary or limit: *her grief knew no bounds.* ▶ v. **1** form the boundary of something. **2** place something within limits.
– PHRASES **out of bounds 1** (in sports) beyond the field of play. **2** beyond permitted limits.

bound³ ▶ adj. going toward somewhere: *a train bound for New York City.*

bound⁴ past and past participle of **BIND** ▶ adj. **1** (**-bound**) restricted to a place or by a situation: *his job kept him city-bound.* **2** certain to be, do, or have: *there's bound to be a bar open somewhere.* **3** obliged to do something.

bound·a·ry /'bound(ə)rē/ ▶ n. (pl. **boundaries**)

1 a line marking the limits of an area. **2** a limit, especially of a subject or area of activity.

bound·en /'boundən/ ▸ adj. (in phrase **one's bounden duty**) a responsibility that cannot be ignored; something one feels morally obliged to do.

bound·less /'boundlis/ ▸ adj. unlimited or immense: *a man of boundless enthusiasm.*

boun·te·ous /'bountēəs/ ▸ adj. old use bountiful.

boun·ti·ful /'bountəfəl/ ▸ adj. **1** large in quantity; abundant: *bountiful crops.* **2** giving generously.
■ **boun·ti·ful·ly** adv.

boun·ty /'bountē/ ▸ n. (pl. **bounties**) **1** literary something given or occurring in generous amounts. **2** literary generosity: *people along the Nile depend on its bounty.* **3** a reward paid for killing or capturing a person or animal. **4** historical a sum paid by the government to encourage trade.

boun·ty hunt·er ▸ n. a person who pursues a criminal for a reward.

bou·quet /bō'kā, bōō-/ ▸ n. **1** a bunch of flowers. **2** the characteristic scent of a wine or perfume.

bou·quet gar·ni /bō'kā gär'nē, bōō-/ ▸ n. (pl. **bouquets garnis**) a bunch of herbs used for flavoring a stew or soup.

bour·bon /'bərbən/ ▸ n. an American whiskey distilled from corn and rye.

bour·geois /bōōr'ʒwä, 'bōōrʒwä/ (also **bourgeoise** /bōōr'ʒwäz, 'bōōrʒwäz/) ▸ adj. **1** belonging to or characteristic of the middle class, especially in being materialistic or conventional: *they are the epitome of bourgeois complacency.* **2** (in Marxism) capitalist. ▸ n. (pl. same) a bourgeois person.

bour·geoi·sie /ˌbōōrʒwä'zē/ ▸ n. (treated as sing. or pl.) **1** the middle class. **2** (in Marxism) the capitalist class.

bourn /bôrn, bŏŏrn/ (also **bourne**) ▸ n. literary a boundary or limit.

bourse /bōŏrs/ ▸ n. a stock market in a non-English-speaking country, especially France.

bout /bout/ ▸ n. **1** a short period of illness or intense activity. **2** a wrestling or boxing match.

bou·tique /bōō'tēk/ ▸ n. a small store selling fashionable clothes.

bou·tique ho·tel ▸ n. a small stylish hotel situated in a fashionable location in a town or city.

bou·zou·ki /bōō'zōōkē/ ▸ n. (pl. **bouzoukis**) a long-necked Greek form of mandolin.

bo·vine /'bōvīn, -vēn/ ▸ adj. **1** relating to cattle. **2** sluggish or stupid: *a look of bovine contentment.* ▸ n. an animal of the cattle group, which also includes buffaloes and bison.
■ **bo·vine·ly** adv.

bo·vine spon·gi·form en·ceph·a·lop·a·thy ▸ n. see BSE.

bow[1] /bō/ ▸ n. **1** a knot tied with two loops and two loose ends. **2** a weapon for shooting arrows, made of curved wood joined at both ends by a taut string. **3** a rod with horsehair stretched along its length, used for playing some stringed instruments. ▸ v. play a stringed instrument using a bow.

bow[2] /bou/ ▸ v. **1** bend the head or upper body as a sign of respect, greeting, or shame. **2** bend with age or under a heavy weight. **3** give in to pressure: *the company bowed to public pressure and withdrew its product.* **4** (**bow out**) withdraw or retire from an activity. ▸ n. an act of bowing.
– PHRASES **bow and scrape** behave in a servile

way. **take a bow** acknowledge applause by bowing.

bow[3] /bou/ (also **bows**) ▸ n. the front end of a ship.

bowd·ler·ize /'bōdlə,rīz, 'boud-/ ▸ v. remove indecent or offensive material from a written work.

bow·el /'bou(ə)l/ ▸ n. **1** the intestine. **2** (**bowels**) the deepest inner parts of something.

bow·el move·ment ▸ n. an act of defecation.

bow·er /'bou(-ə)r/ ▸ n. **1** a pleasant shady place under climbing plants or trees. **2** literary a woman's private room.

bow·er·bird /'bou(-ə),bərd/ ▸ n. an Australasian bird noted for the male's habit of building an elaborate structure to attract the female.

bow·head /'bō,hed/ ▸ n. a black Arctic right whale that feeds by skimming the surface for plankton.

bow·ie knife /'bōōē, 'bōē/ ▸ n. a long knife with a blade double-edged at the point.

bowl[1] /bōl/ ▸ n. **1** a round, deep dish or basin. **2** a rounded, hollow part of an object. **3** a hollow or depression in the landscape. **4** a stadium for sporting or musical events.

bowl[2] ▸ v. **1** roll a round object along the ground. **2** move rapidly and smoothly: *we bowled along the country roads.* **3** (**bowl someone over**) knock someone down. **4** (**bowl someone over**) informal greatly impress or overwhelm someone. **5** play a game of tenpin bowling. ▸ n. a large heavy ball used in tenpin bowling, lawn bowling, or skittles.

bow·leg·ged ▸ adj. having legs that curve outward at the knee.

bowl·er[1] /'bōlər/ ▸ n. a player at tenpin bowling, lawn bowling, or skittles.

bowl·er[2] ▸ n. a man's hard felt hat with a round dome-shaped crown.

bow·line /'bōlin, 'bō,līn/ ▸ n. **1** a simple knot for forming a nonslipping loop at the end of a rope. **2** a rope attaching the windward side of a square sail to a ship's bow.

bowl·ing /'bōliNG/ ▸ n. the game of tenpin bowling, lawn bowling, or skittles.

bowl·ing al·ley ▸ n. a building containing lanes for bowling.

bowl·ing green ▸ n. an area of closely mown grass on which the game of lawn bowling is played.

bowls /bōlz/ ▸ pl.n. (treated as sing.) British name for LAWN BOWLING.

bow·man /'bōmən/ ▸ n. (pl. **bowmen**) an archer.

bow·sprit /'bou,sprit, 'bō-/ ▸ n. a pole projecting from a ship's bow, to which the ropes supporting the front mast are fastened.

bow·string /'bō,striNG/ ▸ n. the string of an archer's bow. ▸ v. (past and past participle **bowstrung**) historical strangle with a bowstring (a former Turkish method of execution).

bow tie /bō/ ▸ n. a necktie in the form of a bow.

bow win·dow /bō/ ▸ n. a curved bay window.

box[1] /bäks/ ▸ n. **1** a container with a flat base and sides and a lid. **2** an area enclosed within straight lines on a page or computer screen. **3** an enclosed area reserved for a group of people in a theater or sports ground, or for witnesses or the jury in a court of law. **4** a mailbox at a post office, newspaper office, or other facility for

box 89 **braid**

keeping letters until collected. **5** (**the box**) Soccer the penalty area. **6** (**the batter's box**) Baseball the rectangular area occupied by the batter. ▶ v. **1** put something in a box. **2** (**box someone in**) restrict or confine someone. – PHRASES **think outside the box** informal have original or creative ideas.

box[2] ▶ v. fight an opponent with the fists in padded gloves as a sport. ▶ n. a slap on the side of a person's head. ■ **box·ing** n. – PHRASES **box someone's ears** slap someone on the side of the head.

box[3] ▶ n. an evergreen shrub with small glossy leaves and hard wood.

box·car /'bäks,kär/ ▶ n. an enclosed railroad freight car.

box·er /'bäksər/ ▶ n. **1** a person who boxes as a sport. **2** a medium-sized breed of dog with a smooth brown coat and puglike face. **3** (**boxers**) another term for BOXER SHORTS.

box·er shorts ▶ pl. n. men's loose-fitting underpants resembling shorts.

Box·ing Day ▶ n. (in Canada and the UK) a public holiday on the first day after Christmas Day.

box of·fice ▶ n. **1** a place at a theater or other arts establishment where tickets are sold. **2** (often as adj. **box-office**) used to refer to the commercial success of a play, movie, or actor: *the movie was a huge box-office hit.*

box score ▶ n. the tabulated results of a baseball game or other sporting event, with statistics given for each player's performance.

box seat ▶ n. a seat in a box in a theater or sports stadium.

box spring ▶ n. each of a set of vertical springs housed in a frame in a mattress or upholstered chair base.

box·y /'bäksē/ ▶ adj. (**boxier, boxiest**) **1** squarish in shape. **2** (of a room or space) cramped.

boy /boi/ ▶ n. **1** a male child or youth. **2** a man, especially one who comes from a particular place or who does a particular job: *the inspector was a local boy.* **3** (**boys**) informal men who mix socially or belong to a particular group. ▶ exclam. used to express admiration, surprise, etc. ■ **boy·hood** n. **boy·ish** adj.

bo·yar /bō'yär/ ▶ n. a member of the old aristocracy in Russia, next in rank to a prince.

boy·cott /'boi,kät/ ▶ v. refuse to deal with a person, organization, or country as a punishment or protest. ▶ n. an act of boycotting.

boy·friend /'boi,frend/ ▶ n. a person's regular male companion in a romantic or sexual relationship.

Boyle's law /boilz/ ▶ n. Chemistry a law stating that the pressure of a given mass of an ideal gas is inversely proportional to its volume at a constant temperature.

Boy Scout ▶ n. **1** a member of the Boy Scouts of America. **2** an honest, friendly, and typically naive man.

boy·sen·ber·ry /'boizən,berē/ ▶ n. (pl. **boysenberries**) a large red edible blackberrylike fruit.

bo·zo /'bōzō/ ▶ n. (pl. **bozos**) informal a stupid or insignificant man.

BP ▶ abbr. **1** before the present (era). **2** blood pressure.

bp ▶ abbr. **1** Biochemistry base pair(s), as a unit of length in nucleic acid chains. **2** Finance basis point(s).

bps ▶ abbr. Computing bits per second.

Bq ▶ abbr. becquerel.

Br ▶ symbol the chemical element bromine.

Br. ▶ abbr. **1** British. **2** (in religious orders) Brother.

bra /brä/ ▶ n. a woman's undergarment worn to support the breasts. ■ **bra·less** adj.

brace /brās/ ▶ n. **1** a strengthening or supporting device or part. **2** (**braces**) a wire device fitted in the mouth to straighten the teeth. **3** (pl. same) a pair of things: *a brace of grouse.* **4** either of two connecting marks, { and }, used in printing and music. **5** (also **brace and bit**) a drilling tool with a crank handle and a socket to hold a bit. ▶ v. **1** make something stronger or firmer with a brace. **2** press one's body firmly against something to stay balanced. **3** prepare for something demanding or unpleasant: *he braced himself for the interview.*

brace·let /'brāslit/ ▶ n. an ornamental band or chain worn on the wrist or arm.

bra·chi·al /'brākēəl, 'brak-/ ▶ adj. Anatomy of or relating to the arm, specifically the upper arm, or an armlike structure: *the brachial artery.*

bra·chi·o·pod /'brākēə,päd, 'brak-/ ▶ n. an invertebrate sea creature with two hinged shells and tentacles used for filter-feeding.

bra·chi·o·sau·rus /,brākēə'sôrəs, ,brak-/ ▶ n. a huge plant-eating dinosaur with forelegs much longer than the hind legs.

brac·ing /'brāsiNG/ ▶ adj. refreshing; invigorating: *bracing winds.* ■ **brac·ing·ly** adv.

brack·en /'brakən/ ▶ n. a tall fern with coarse fronds.

brack·et /'brakit/ ▶ n. **1** each of a pair of marks, [and], used to enclose words or figures. **2** a category of similar people or things: *a high income bracket.* **3** a right-angled support projecting from a wall. ▶ v. (**brackets, bracketing, bracketed**) **1** enclose words or figures in brackets. **2** place in the same category: *being bracketed with the world's greatest movie director was thrill enough.* **3** hold or attach something by means of a bracket.

brack·ish /'brakiSH/ ▶ adj. (of water) slightly salty.

bract /brakt/ ▶ n. a modified leaf with a flower in the angle where it meets the stem.

brad /brad/ ▶ n. a nail with a rectangular cross section and a small head.

brad·y·car·di·a /,bradi'kärdēə/ ▶ n. Medicine abnormally slow heart action.

brag /brag/ ▶ v. (**brags, bragging, bragged**) say something boastfully. ▶ n. **1** a boastful statement. **2** a simplified form of poker.

brag book ▶ n. informal an album of photographs intended to show the subjects, especially one's family, to others in an admiring way.

brag·ga·do·ci·o /,bragə'dōsHē,ō/ ▶ n. boastful or arrogant behavior.

brag·gart /'bragərt/ ▶ n. a person who boasts about their achievements or possessions.

Brah·man /'brämən/ ▶ n. (pl. **Brahmans**) **1** (also **Brahmin** /-min/) a member of the highest Hindu caste, that of the priesthood. **2** (also **Brahma**) (in Hinduism) the ultimate reality underlying all phenomena.

Brah·min /'brämin/ ▶ n. **1** variant spelling of BRAHMAN (sense 1). **2** a socially or culturally superior person. ■ **Brah·min·i·cal** /brä'minikəl/ adj.

braid /brād/ ▶ n. **1** threads woven into a

decorative band for trimming garments. **2** a length of hair made up of three or more interlaced strands. ▸ v. **1** interlace three or more strands of (hair or other flexible material) to form a length. **2** edge or trim a garment with braid.

Braille /brāl/ ▸ n. a written language for the blind, in which characters are represented by patterns of raised dots.

brain /brān/ ▸ n. **1** an organ of soft nervous tissue inside the skull, functioning as the coordinating center of the nervous system. **2** the ability to use one's intelligence: *she's got brains, that child.* **3** (**the brains**) informal a clever person who is the main organizer in a group. ▸ v. informal hit someone hard on the head with an object.
– PHRASES **have something on the brain** informal be obsessed with something.

brain·child /'brān,CHīld/ ▸ n. (pl. **brainchildren**) informal an idea or invention originated by a particular person.

brain-dead ▸ adj. **1** having suffered brain death. **2** informal very stupid.

brain death ▸ n. irreversible brain damage causing the end of independent breathing.

brain drain ▸ n. informal the emigration of highly skilled or qualified people from a country.

brain·less /'brānlis/ ▸ adj. stupid; very foolish.

brain·pow·er /'brān,pouər/ ▸ n. mental ability; intelligence.

brain·stem /'brān,stem/ ▸ n. the central trunk of the brain, consisting of the medulla oblongata, pons, and midbrain.

brain·storm /'brān,stôrm/ ▸ n. **1** informal a moment in which one is suddenly unable to think clearly. **2** a group discussion to produce ideas. ▸ v. have a group discussion to produce ideas.

brain-teas·er ▸ n. informal a problem or puzzle.

brain·wash /'brān,wôsh, -,wäsh/ ▸ v. force someone to accept an idea or belief by using mental pressure, constant repetition, etc.

brain·wave /'brān,wāv/ ▸ n. **1** an electrical impulse in the brain. **2** informal a sudden clever idea.

brain·y /'brānē/ ▸ adj. (**brainier, brainiest**) informal intelligent; clever. ■ **brain·i·ness** n.

braise /brāz/ ▸ v. fry food lightly and then stew it slowly in a closed container.

brake[1] /brāk/ ▸ n. a device for slowing or stopping a moving vehicle. ▸ v. slow or stop a vehicle with a brake.

USAGE
Do not confuse **brake** with **break. Brake** means 'a device for slowing or stopping a vehicle' or 'slow or stop a vehicle' (*I had to brake hard*), whereas **break** mainly means 'separate into pieces' or 'a pause or interruption' (*a coffee break*).

brake[2] ▸ n. historical an open horse-drawn carriage with four wheels.

brake[3] ▸ n. a thicket.

brake drum ▸ n. a broad, short cylinder attached to a wheel, against which the brake shoes press to cause braking.

brake horse·pow·er ▸ n. an imperial unit equal to one horsepower, used in expressing the power available at the shaft of an engine.

brake shoe ▸ n. a long curved block that presses on a brake drum.

bram·ble /'brambəl/ ▸ n. **1** a prickly shrub of the rose family, especially a blackberry. **2** any rough,

prickly vine or shrub.

bran /bran/ ▸ n. pieces of grain husk separated from flour after milling.

branch /branCH/ ▸ n. **1** a part of a tree that grows out from the trunk or a bough. **2** a river, road, or railroad extending out from a main one. **3** a division of a large organization, subject, etc. ▸ v. **1** divide into one or more branches. **2** (**branch out**) extend one's activities in a new direction: *the company is branching out into Europe.*

brand /brand/ ▸ n. **1** a type of product manufactured by a company under a particular name. **2** a brand name. **3** an identifying mark burned on livestock with a heated iron. **4** a piece of burning wood. ▸ v. **1** mark livestock with a branding iron. **2** mark out as having a particular shameful quality: *she was branded a liar.* **3** give a brand name to a product.

bran·dish /'brandish/ ▸ v. wave or flourish something as a threat or in anger or excitement.

brand name ▸ n. a name given by the maker to a product or range of products.

brand new ▸ adj. completely new.

bran·dy /'brandē/ ▸ n. (pl. **brandies**) a strong alcoholic spirit distilled from wine or fermented fruit juice.

brash /brash/ ▸ adj. **1** self-assertive in a rude, noisy, or overbearing way. **2** showy or tasteless in appearance: *the cafe was a brash new building.* ■ **brash·ly** adv. **brash·ness** n.

brass /bras/ ▸ n. **1** a yellow alloy of copper and zinc. **2** a brass memorial plaque in the wall or floor of a church. **3** brass wind instruments forming a band or section of an orchestra. **4** (also **top brass**) informal people in authority.
– PHRASES **get down to brass tacks** informal start to consider the basic facts.

brass band ▸ n. a group of musicians playing brass instruments.

bras·se·rie /,brasə'rē/ ▸ n. (pl. **brasseries**) an inexpensive French or French-style restaurant.

bras·si·ca /'brasikə/ ▸ n. a plant of a family that includes cabbage, turnip, and Brussels sprouts.

bras·siere /brə'zi(ə)r/ ▸ n. full form of BRA.

brass knuck·les ▸ n. a metal guard worn over the knuckles in fighting, especially to increase the effect of the blows.

brass rub·bing ▸ n. the copying of the design on an engraved brass by rubbing crayon or chalk over paper laid on it.

brass·y /'brasē/ ▸ adj. (**brassier, brassiest**) **1** bright or harsh yellow. **2** tastelessly showy or loud: *a tawdry, brassy woman.* **3** harsh or blaring like a brass instrument.

brat /brat/ ▸ n. derogatory or humorous a badly behaved child. ■ **brat·tish** adj.

brat·wurst /'brät,wərst/ ▸ n. a type of fine German pork sausage.

bra·va·do /brə'vädō/ ▸ n. confidence or a show of confidence that is intended to impress.

brave /brāv/ ▸ adj. ready to face and endure danger, pain, or difficulty. ▸ n. dated an American Indian warrior. ▸ v. endure or face unpleasant conditions with courage: *more than 1,000 visitors braved a downpour to get in.* ■ **brave·ly** adv. **brav·er·y** n.

bra·vo[1] /brä'vō/ ▸ exclam. shouted to express approval for a performer.

bra·vo² /'brävō/ ▶ n. (pl. **bravos** or **bravoes**) dated a thug or hired assassin.

bra·vu·ra /brə'v(y)o͞orə/ ▶ n. **1** great skill and brilliance, typically shown in a performance. **2** the display of great daring.

brawl /brôl/ ▶ n. a rough or noisy fight or quarrel. ▶ v. fight or quarrel in a rough or noisy way. ■ **brawl·er** n.

brawn /brôn/ ▶ n. physical strength as opposed to intelligence. ■ **brawn·y** adj.

bray /brā/ ▶ v. **1** (of a donkey) make a loud, harsh cry. **2** (of a person) speak or laugh loudly and harshly. ▶ n. a loud, harsh cry of a donkey.

braze /brāz/ ▶ v. solder something with an alloy of copper and zinc.

bra·zen /'brāzən/ ▶ adj. **1** bold and shameless. **2** old use made of brass. ▶ v. (**brazen it out**) endure a difficult situation with apparent confidence and lack of shame. ■ **bra·zen·ly** adv.

bra·zier¹ /'brāzhər/ ▶ n. a portable heater holding lighted coals.

bra·zier² ▶ n. a person who works in brass.

Bra·zil·ian /brə'zilēən/ ▶ n. a person from Brazil. ▶ adj. relating to Brazil.

Bra·zil nut ▶ n. the large three-sided nut of a South American tree.

breach /brēCH/ ▶ v. **1** make a gap or hole in something. **2** break a law, rule, or agreement. ▶ n. **1** a gap made in a wall or barrier. **2** an act of breaking a rule or agreement. **3** a break in relations: *a sudden breach between father and son.*
– PHRASES **breach of the peace** public disturbance, or an act considered likely to cause one. **step into the breach** replace someone who is suddenly unable to do a job.

bread /bred/ ▶ n. **1** food made of flour, water, and yeast mixed together and baked. **2** informal money.
– PHRASES **bread and butter** a person's main source of income. **break bread** celebrate Holy Communion. **know which side one's bread is buttered (on)** informal know where one's advantage lies.

bread·bas·ket /'bred,baskit/ ▶ n. **1** a part of a region that produces cereals for the rest of it. **2** informal a person's stomach, considered as the target for a blow.

bread·crumb /'bred,krəm/ ▶ n. a small fragment of bread.

bread·ed /'bredid/ ▶ adj. (of food) coated with breadcrumbs and fried.

bread·fruit /'bred,fro͞ot/ ▶ n. a large round starchy fruit of a tropical tree, used as a vegetable.

bread·line /'bred,līn/ ▶ n. a line of people waiting to receive free food.

bread·stick /'bred,stik/ ▶ n. a crisp stick of baked dough.

breadth /bredTH/ ▶ n. **1** the distance or measurement from side to side of something. **2** wide range: *they have talent but no breadth of vision.*

bread·win·ner /'bred,winər/ ▶ n. a person who supports their family with the money they earn.

break /brāk/ ▶ v. (past **broke**; past part. **broken**) **1** separate into pieces as a result of a blow, shock, or strain. **2** make or become unable to function: *you've broken the stereo.* **3** interrupt a sequence or course. **4** fail to observe a law, regulation, or agreement. **5** crush the spirit of someone. **6** beat a record. **7** decipher a code. **8** make a rush or dash. **9** lessen the impact of a fall. **10** suddenly make or become public: *once the news broke, emails circulated worldwide.* **11** (of a person's voice) falter and change tone. **12** (of a boy's voice) change in tone and register at puberty. **13** (of the weather) change suddenly, especially after a fine spell. **14** (of a storm, dawn, or day) begin. **15** use a bill to pay for something and receive change. ▶ n. **1** an interruption, pause, or gap. **2** a short rest or vacation. **3** an instance of breaking, or the point where something is broken. **4** a sudden rush or dash: *she made a break for the door.* **5** informal an opportunity or chance. **6** (also **break of serve** or **service break**) Tennis the winning of a game against an opponent's serve. **7** make the first stroke at the beginning of a game of pool, snooker, or billiards. ■ **break·a·ble** adj. & n.
– PHRASES **break away** escape from someone's control or influence. **break the back of** accomplish the main or hardest part of something. **break cover** (of people or animals being hunted) suddenly leave shelter. **break down 1** suddenly fail or stop functioning. **2** lose control of one's emotions when upset. **break even** reach a point in a business when the profits are equal to the costs. **break in 1** force entry to a building. **2** interrupt with a remark. **break something in 1** make a horse used to being ridden. **2** make new shoes comfortable by wearing them. **break into** burst into laughter, song, or faster movement. **break of day** dawn. **break something off** suddenly stop or end something. **break out 1** (of something unwelcome) start suddenly. **2** escape from confinement. **break something out** informal open and start using something. **break out in** be suddenly affected by: *I broke out in a rash.* **break someone's serve** win a game in a tennis match against an opponent's service. **break up** (of a gathering or relationship) end or part. **break wind** release gas from the anus. **break with someone/thing 1** quarrel with someone. **2** go against a custom or tradition. **give someone a break** informal stop putting pressure on someone.

> **USAGE**
> On the confusion of **break** and **brake**, see the note at **BRAKE**.

break·age /'brākij/ ▶ n. the action of breaking something or the fact of being broken.

break·a·way /'brākə,wā/ ▶ n. **1** a departure from something established or long-standing. **2** (in sports) a sudden attack or forward movement. ▶ adj. having separated from a larger group or country: *a breakaway republic.*

break·beat /'brāk,bēt/ ▶ n. a sampled electronic drumbeat repeated to form a rhythm used as a basis for dance music or hip-hop.

break·danc·ing ▶ n. an energetic and acrobatic style of street dancing.

break·down /'brāk,doun/ ▶ n. **1** a failure or collapse. **2** an explanatory analysis of figures or costs.

break·er /'brākər/ ▶ n. **1** a heavy sea wave that breaks on the shore. **2** a person who breaks or breaks up something.

break·fast /'brekfəst/ ▶ n. a meal eaten in the morning, the first of the day. ▶ v. eat breakfast.

break-in ▶ n. an illegal forced entry in order to steal something.

break·ing point ▶ n. the moment of greatest strain at which someone or something gives way.

break·neck /'brāk,nek/ ▶ adj. dangerously fast.

break·out /'brāk,out/ ▶ n. 1 a forcible escape, especially from prison. 2 an outbreak.

break point ▶ n. 1 a place or time at which an interruption or change is made. 2 Tennis the state of a game when the side receiving service needs only one more point to win the game. 3 Tennis a point of this nature. 4 Computing a place in a computer program where the sequence of instructions is interrupted.

break·through /'brāk,THroō/ ▶ n. a sudden important development or success.

break-up ▶ n. 1 the breaking up of something into several parts. 2 an end to a relationship.

break·wa·ter /'brāk,wôtər, -,wätər/ ▶ n. a barrier built out into the sea to protect a coast or harbor from the force of waves.

bream /brim, brēm/ ▶ n. (pl. same) a deep-bodied greenish-bronze freshwater fish.

breast /brest/ ▶ n. 1 either of the two protruding organs on a woman's chest that produce milk after childbirth. 2 a person's or animal's chest region. ▶ v. 1 face and move forward against or through: *I watched him breast the wave.* 2 reach the top of a hill. ■ **breast·ed** adj.

breast·bone /'brest,bōn/ ▶ n. a thin, flat bone running down the center of the chest, to which the ribs are attached; the sternum.

breast·feed /'brest,fēd/ ▶ v. (**breastfeeds, breastfeeding, breastfed** /'brest,fed/) feed a baby with milk from the breast.

breast·plate /'brest,plāt/ ▶ n. a piece of armor covering the chest.

breast·stroke /'brest,strōk/ ▶ n. a style of swimming in which the arms are pushed forward and then swept back while the legs are tucked in and then kicked out.

breast·work /'brest,wərk/ ▶ n. a low temporary defense or parapet.

breath /breTH/ ▶ n. 1 air taken into or sent out of the lungs. 2 an instance of breathing in or out. 3 a slight movement of air. 4 a hint or suggestion: *he avoided the slightest breath of scandal.*
– PHRASES **breath of fresh air** a refreshing change. **hold one's breath** stop breathing temporarily. **out of breath** gasping for air. **take someone's breath away** astonish or inspire someone. **under one's breath** in a very quiet voice.

breath·a·ble /'brēTHəbəl/ ▶ adj. 1 (of air) fit to breathe. 2 (of clothing or material) allowing air to the skin so that sweat may evaporate. ■ **breath·a·bil·i·ty** n.

breath·a·lyz·er /'breTHə,līzər/ ▶ n. trademark a device used by police for measuring the amount of alcohol in a driver's breath. ■ **breath·a·lyze** v.

breathe /brēTH/ ▶ v. 1 take air into the lungs and send it out again as a regular process. 2 say something quietly. 3 let air or moisture in or out. 4 give an impression of: *the room breathed an air of efficiency.*
– PHRASES **breathe down someone's neck** 1 follow closely behind someone. 2 constantly check up on someone.

breath·er /'brēTHər/ ▶ n. informal a brief pause for rest.

breath·ing space ▶ n. an opportunity to pause, relax, or decide what to do next.

breath·less /'breTHlis/ ▶ adj. 1 gasping for breath. 2 feeling or causing great excitement, fear, etc.:

breathless enthusiasm. ■ **breath·less·ly** adv. **breath·less·ness** n.

breath·tak·ing /'breTH,tāking/ ▶ adj. astonishing or awe-inspiring. ■ **breath·tak·ing·ly** adv.

breath test ▶ n. a test in which a driver is made to blow into a breathalyzer.

breath·y /'breTHē/ ▶ adj. (of a voice) having an audible sound of breathing. ■ **breath·i·ly** adv.

brec·ci·a /'brechēə, 'bresh-/ ▶ n. rock consisting of angular fragments cemented by finer chalky material.

bred /bred/ ▶ past and past participle of BREED.

breech /brēCH/ ▶ n. the back part of a rifle or gun barrel.

breech birth ▶ n. a birth in which the baby's buttocks or feet are delivered first.

breech·es /'brichiz, 'brē-/ ▶ pl.n. short trousers fastened just below the knee, now worn for riding or as part of ceremonial dress.

breed /brēd/ ▶ v. (past and past part. **bred**) 1 (of animals) mate and then produce offspring. 2 keep animals to produce offspring. 3 bring up in a particular way: *Penny had been beautifully bred.* 4 develop a variety of plant. 5 produce or lead to. ▶ n. 1 a distinctive type within a species of animals or plants, especially one deliberately developed. 2 a sort or kind: *a new breed of executive.* ■ **breed·er** n.

breed·ing /'brēding/ ▶ n. upper-class good manners regarded as being passed on from one generation to another.

breeze /brēz/ ▶ n. 1 a gentle wind. 2 informal a thing that is easy to do. ▶ v. informal 1 come or go in a casual way. 2 (**breeze through**) deal with or accomplish something with ease.

breez·y /'brēzē/ ▶ adj. (**breezier, breeziest**) 1 pleasantly windy. 2 relaxed and cheerily brisk. ■ **breez·i·ly** adv. **breez·i·ness** n.

bre·sao·la /bre'sōlə, bri'zō-/ ▶ n. an Italian dish of sliced raw beef that has been cured by salting and air-drying.

breth·ren /'breTH(ə)rin/ old-fashioned plural of BROTHER ▶ pl.n. fellow Christians or members of a group: *their baseball brethren.*

Bret·on /'bretn/ ▶ n. 1 a person from Brittany. 2 the Celtic language of Brittany.

breve /brēv, brev/ ▶ n. 1 Music a note twice as long as a whole note. 2 a written or printed mark (˘) indicating a short or unstressed vowel.

bre·vi·ar·y /'brēvē,erē, 'brev-/ ▶ n. (pl. **breviaries**) a book containing the service for each day, used in the Roman Catholic Church.

brev·i·ty /'brevitē/ ▶ n. 1 concise and exact use of words. 2 shortness of time.

brew /broō/ ▶ v. 1 make beer by soaking, boiling, and fermentation. 2 make tea or coffee by mixing it with hot water. 3 begin to develop: *a real crisis is brewing.* ▶ n. 1 a drink that has been brewed. 2 a mixture of different things: *her smell was a powerful brew of cheap perfume and mothballs.* ■ **brew·er** n.

brew·er·y /'broōərē/ ▶ n. (pl. **breweries**) a place where beer is made.

bri·ar¹ /'brī(ə)r/ (also **brier**) ▶ n. a prickly shrub, especially a wild rose.

bri·ar² (also **briar pipe, brier**) ▶ n. a tobacco pipe made from the woody nodules of a shrub of the heather family.

bribe /brīb/ ▶ v. dishonestly persuade someone to act in one's favor, especially by giving them money. ▶n. something offered or given to bribe someone. ■ **brib·er·y** n.

bric-a-brac /'brik ə ˌbrak/ ▶n. various objects and ornaments of little value.

brick /brik/ ▶n. **1** a small rectangular block of fired or sun-dried clay, used in building. **2** informal, dated a helpful and reliable person. ▶v. block or enclose something with a wall of bricks.
– PHRASES **bricks and mor·tar** buildings, especially housing.

brick·bat /'brik ˌbat/ ▶n. **1** a critical remark. **2** a piece of brick used as a missile.

brick·lay·er /'brik ˌlāər/ ▶n. a person whose job is to build structures with bricks. ■ **brick·lay·ing** n.

brick red ▶n. a deep brownish red.

brick·work /'brik ˌwərk/ ▶n. the bricks in a wall or building.

brick·yard /'brik ˌyärd/ ▶n. a place where bricks are made.

bri·co·lage /ˌbrēkō'läzн, ˌbrikə-/ ▶n. (in art or literature) the creation of something from a diverse range of available things.

brid·al /'brīdl/ ▶adj. relating to a bride or a newly married couple.

bride /brīd/ ▶n. a woman on her wedding day or just before and after the event.

bride·groom /'brīd ˌgro͞om/ ▶n. a man on his wedding day or just before and after the event.

brides·maid /'brīdz ˌmād/ ▶n. a girl or woman who accompanies a bride on her wedding day.

bridge[1] /brij/ ▶n. **1** a structure carrying a route or railroad across a river, road, or other obstacle. **2** the platform on a ship from which the captain and officers direct its course. **3** the upper bony part of a person's nose. **4** a false tooth or teeth supported by natural teeth on either side. **5** the part on a stringed instrument over which the strings are stretched. ▶v. **1** be or make a bridge over or between something. **2** make a difference or gap between two groups or things less significant: *how do we bridge the gap between politicians and people?*

bridge[2] ▶n. a card game related to whist, played by two partnerships of two players.

bridge·head /'brij ˌhed/ ▶n. a strong position secured by an army inside enemy territory.

bridge loan ▶n. a sum of money lent by a bank to cover the period of time between the buying of one thing and the selling of another.

bri·dle /'brīdl/ ▶n. the headgear used to control a horse, consisting of buckled straps to which a bit and reins are attached. ▶v. **1** put a bridle on a horse. **2** bring something under control. **3** show resentment or anger: *she bridled at being given an order.*

bri·dle path ▶n. a path or track along which horses are ridden.

Brie /brē/ ▶n. a kind of soft, mild, creamy cheese.

brief /brēf/ ▶adj. **1** lasting a short time. **2** using few words; concise. **3** (of clothing) not covering much of the body. ▶n. **1** a set of instructions about a task. **2** a summary of the facts in a case, filed by an attorney before arguing the case in court. **3** a letter from the Pope on a matter of discipline. ▶v. give someone information so as to prepare them to deal with something. ■ **brief·ly** adv.

brief·case /'brēf ˌkās/ ▶n. a flat rectangular case for carrying books and documents.

brief·ing /'brēfɪɴɢ/ ▶n. a meeting for giving information or instructions.

briefs /brēfs/ ▶pl.n. short, close-fitting underpants.

bri·er[1] ▶n. variant spelling of BRIAR[1].

bri·er[2] ▶n. variant spelling of BRIAR[2].

brig /brig/ ▶n. **1** a two-masted square-rigged ship. **2** informal a prison on a warship.

Brig. ▶abbr. **1** brigade. **2** brigadier.

bri·gade /bri'gād/ ▶n. **1** a subdivision of an army, typically consisting of a small number of battalions and forming part of a division. **2** informal, often derogatory a particular group of people: *the anti-smoking brigade.*

brig·a·dier /ˌbrigə'di(ə)r, 'brigəˌdi(ə)r/ ▶n. a rank of officer in the British army, above colonel and below major general.

brig·a·dier gen·er·al ▶n. a rank of officer in the US Army, Air Force, and Marine Corps, above colonel and below major general.

brig·and /'brigənd/ ▶n. a member of a gang of bandits. ■ **brig·and·age** n.

brig·an·tine /'brigənˌtēn/ ▶n. a two-masted sailing ship, with the foremast square-rigged and the mainmast fore-and-aft rigged.

bright /brīt/ ▶adj. **1** giving out or filled with light. **2** (of color) vivid and bold. **3** intelligent and quick-witted. **4** cheerful and lively. **5** (of future prospects) good. ■ **bright·ly** adv. **bright·ness** n.

bright·en /'brītn/ ▶v. **1** make or become brighter. **2** make or become happier and more cheerful.

brill /bril/ ▶n. a European flatfish similar to the turbot.

bril·liant /'brilyənt/ ▶adj. **1** (of light or color) very bright or vivid. **2** exceptionally clever or talented. **3** Brit. informal excellent; marvelous. ■ **bril·liance** /'brilyəns/ (also **brilliancy** /-sē/) n. **bril·liant·ly** adv.

brim /brim/ ▶n. **1** the projecting edge around the bottom of a hat. **2** the lip of a cup, bowl, or other container. ▶v. (**brims, brimming, brimmed**) fill or be full to the point of overflowing: *he's brimming with ideas.* ■ **brim·ful** adj.

brim·stone /'brim ˌstōn/ ▶n. **1** a large bright yellow or greenish-white butterfly. **2** old use sulfur.

brin·dle /'brindl/ (also **brindled**) ▶adj. (of a domestic animal) brownish or tawny with streaks of other color.

brine /brīn/ ▶n. water containing dissolved salt.

bring /briɴɢ/ ▶v. (past and past part. **brought**) **1** take or go with someone or something to a place. **2** cause to be in a particular position or state: *the agreement brought an end to hostilities.* **3** cause someone to receive money as income or profit. **4** (**bring oneself to do**) force oneself to do something unpleasant. **5** begin legal action. ■ **bring·er** n.
– PHRASES **bring something about** cause something to happen. **bring someone along** encourage or help someone to develop or improve. **bring someone around 1** cause an unconscious person to become conscious. **2** persuade someone to agree to something. **bring something forward 1** move something planned to an earlier time. **2** propose an idea for consideration. **bring something on** cause something unpleasant to happen. **bring something out 1** produce and launch a new product or publication. **2** emphasize something. **bring the house down** make an audience

laugh or applaud very enthusiastically. **bring someone to** cause an unconscious person to become conscious. **bring something to bear** use influence or pressure to achieve a result. **bring something to pass** chiefly literary cause something to happen. **bring to the table** (or **party**) contribute something of value to a discussion, project, etc. **bring someone/thing up 1** look after a child until it is an adult. **2** raise a matter for discussion.

brink /briNGk/ ▶ n. **1** the extreme edge of land before a steep slope or a body of water. **2** the point at which a new or unwelcome situation is about to begin: *companies on the brink of bankruptcy.*

brink·man·ship /'briNGkmən,sHip/ (also **brinksmanship**) ▶ n. the pursuit of a dangerous policy to the limits of safety before stopping.

brin·y /'brīnē/ ▶ adj. relating to brine; salty. ▶ n. (**the briny**) Brit. informal the sea.

bri·o /'brēō/ ▶ n. energy or liveliness.

bri·oche /brē'ōsH, -'ôsH/ ▶ n. a small, round, sweet French roll.

bri·quette /bri'ket/ (also **briquet**) ▶ n. a block of compressed coal dust or peat used as fuel.

brisk /brisk/ ▶ adj. **1** quick, active, or lively. **2** practical and efficient: *a brisk, businesslike tone.* **3** (of wind or the weather) cold but refreshing. ■ **brisk·ly** adv. **brisk·ness** n.

bris·ket /'briskit/ ▶ n. meat from the breast of a cow.

bris·ling /'brizliNG, 'bris-/ ▶ n. (pl. same or **brislings**) a sprat, typically one smoked and canned.

bris·tle /'brisəl/ ▶ n. **1** a short, stiff hair on an animal's skin or a man's face. **2** a stiff animal or artificial hair, used to make a brush. ▶ v. **1** (of hair or fur) stand upright away from the skin. **2** react angrily or defensively. **3** (**bristle with**) be covered with or full of: *the island bristles with forts.* ■ **bris·tly** adj.

Brit /brit/ ▶ n. informal a British person.

Bri·tan·ni·a /bri'tanyə, -'tanēə/ ▶ n. a woman wearing a helmet and carrying a shield and trident, used to represent Britain.

Bri·tan·nic /bri'tanik/ ▶ adj. dated relating to Britain or the British Empire.

Brit·ish /'britisH/ ▶ adj. relating to Great Britain or the United Kingdom. ■ **Brit·ish·ness** n.

Brit·ish·er /'britisHər/ ▶ n. informal (especially in North America) a British person.

Brit·ish ther·mal u·nit ▶ n. a unit of heat equal to the amount of heat needed to raise 1 lb of water at maximum density through one degree Fahrenheit.

Brit·on /'britn/ ▶ n. **1** a British person. **2** a Celtic inhabitant of southern Britain before and during Roman times.

brit·tle /'britl/ ▶ adj. **1** hard but likely to break or shatter easily. **2** sharp or artificial and showing signs of nervousness: *a brittle laugh.* ■ **brit·tle·ness** n.

brit·tle bone dis·ease ▶ n. a disease in which the bones become brittle, especially osteoporosis.

bro /brō/ ▶ n. informal short for BROTHER.

broach /brōCH/ ▶ v. **1** raise a subject for discussion. **2** pierce or open a cask or container to draw out liquid.

broad /brôd/ ▶ adj. **1** having a distance larger than usual from side to side; wide. **2** of a particular distance wide. **3** large in area or range: *a broad expanse of water.* **4** without detail; general: *a broad outline.* **5** (of a hint) clear and unmistakable. **6** (of a regional accent) very strong. ▶ n. informal a woman. ■ **broad·ly** adv. **broad·ness** n.
– PHRASES **broad daylight** full daylight; day.

broad·band /'brôd,band/ ▶ n. a high-capacity telecommunications technique that uses a wide range of frequencies, enabling messages to be sent simultaneously.

broad bean ▶ n. a large flat green bean.

broad-brush ▶ adj. dealing with something in a general way; lacking in detail: *a broad-brush approach to the problem.*

broad·cast /'brôd,kast/ ▶ v. (past **broadcast;** past part. **broadcast** or **broadcasted**) **1** transmit a program or information by radio or television. **2** tell something to many people. **3** scatter seeds rather than placing them in rows. ▶ n. a radio or television transmission. ■ **broad·cast·er** n.

broad·cloth /'brôd,klôtH/ ▶ n. a fine wool or cotton cloth.

broad·en /'brôdn/ ▶ v. make or become broader.

broad gauge ▶ n. a railroad gauge that is wider than the standard gauge of 4 ft. 8½ in. (1.435 m.).

broad-leaved /'brôd,lēvd/ (also **broadleaf** /'brôd,lēf/) ▶ adj. (of trees or herbaceous plants) having relatively wide flat leaves, as opposed to conifers or grasses.

broad·loom /'brôd,lōōm/ ▶ n. carpet woven in wide widths.

broad-mind·ed ▶ adj. tolerant of views or behavior different from one's own; not easily offended.

broad·sheet /'brôd,sHēt/ ▶ n. **1** a newspaper with a large format. **2** another term for BROADSIDE.

broad·side /'brôd,sīd/ ▶ n. **1** a strongly worded critical attack. **2** historical a firing of all the guns from one side of a warship. **3** the side of a ship above the water between the bow and quarter. **4** a large sheet of paper printed on one side only.
– PHRASES **broadside on** sideways on.

broad-spec·trum ▶ adj. referring to antibiotics, pesticides, etc., effective against a large variety of organisms.

broad·sword /'brôd,sôrd/ ▶ n. a sword with a wide blade, used for cutting rather than thrusting.

Brob·ding·nag·i·an /,brabdiNG'nagēən/ ▶ adj. gigantic.

bro·cade /brō'kād/ ▶ n. a rich fabric woven with a raised pattern, usually with gold or silver thread. ■ **bro·cad·ed** adj.

broc·co·li /'bräk(ə)lē/ ▶ n. a vegetable with heads of small green or purplish flower buds.

bro·chette /brō'sHet/ ▶ n. a dish of meat or fish chunks barbecued, grilled, or roasted on a skewer.

bro·chure /brō'sHŏŏr/ ▶ n. a small book or pamphlet containing pictures and information about a product or service.

bro·de·rie an·glaise /,brōdə'rē äNG'glez, -'gläz/ ▶ n. open embroidery on fine white cotton or linen.

brogue /brōg/ ▶ n. **1** a strong outdoor shoe with perforated patterns in the leather. **2** a noticeable accent, especially Irish or Scottish, when speaking English.

broil /broil/ ▶ v. cook meat or fish using direct heat, especially heat that radiates downward.

broil·er /'broilər/ ▶ n. **1** a young chicken suitable for roasting, broiling, or barbecuing. **2** a frame or device used for cooking meat or fish with direct radiant heat, especially the broiling unit in an oven.

broke /brōk/ past (and old-fashioned past participle) of BREAK ▶ adj. informal having no money.
– PHRASES **go for broke** informal risk everything in one determined effort.

bro·ken /'brōkən/ past participle of BREAK ▶ adj. (of a language) spoken hesitantly and with many mistakes, as by a foreigner. ■ **bro·ken·ly** adv. **bro·ken·ness** n.

bro·ken-down ▶ adj. **1** worn out and in a bad condition. **2** not working.

bro·ken-heart·ed ▶ adj. overwhelmed by grief or disappointment.

bro·ken home ▶ n. a family in which the parents are divorced or separated.

bro·ker /'brōkər/ ▶ n. a person who buys and sells goods or assets for other people. ▶ v. arrange or negotiate a deal or plan. ■ **bro·ker·age** n.

bro·me·li·ad /brō'mēlē,ad/ ▶ n. a member of a family of tropical American plants.

bro·mide /'brōmīd/ ▶ n. **1** a compound of bromine with another chemical element or group. **2** dated a preparation containing potassium bromide, used as a sedative. **3** an unoriginal idea or remark.

bro·mine /'brōmēn/ ▶ n. a dark red liquid chemical element of the halogen group, with a strong, irritating smell.

bron·chi /'brängkī, -kē/ ▶ plural of BRONCHUS.

bron·chi·al /'brängkēəl/ ▶ adj. relating to the bronchi or bronchioles.

bron·chi·ole /'brängkē,ōl/ ▶ n. any of the minute branches into which the bronchi in the lungs divide.

bron·chi·tis /bräng'kītis/ ▶ n. inflammation of the mucous membrane in the bronchial tubes. ■ **bron·chit·ic** /bräng'kitik/ adj. & n.

bron·chus /'brängkəs/ ▶ n. (pl. **bronchi** /-kī, -kē/) any of the major air passages of the lungs that spread out from the windpipe.

bron·co /'brängkō/ ▶ n. (pl. **broncos**) a wild or half-tamed horse of the western US.

bron·to·sau·rus /,bräntə'sôrəs/ ▶ n. former term for APATOSAURUS.

bronze /bränz/ ▶ n. **1** a yellowish-brown alloy of copper and tin. **2** a yellowish-brown color. **3** an object made of bronze. ▶ v. make a person or part of the body suntanned. ■ **bronz·y** adj.

Bronze Age ▶ n. a historical period that followed the Stone Age and preceded the Iron Age, when tools were made of bronze.

bronze med·al ▶ n. a medal made of or colored bronze, awarded for third place in a race or competition.

brooch /brōch, brōōch/ ▶ n. an ornament fastened to clothing with a hinged pin and catch.

brood /brōōd/ ▶ n. **1** a family of young animals produced at one hatching or birth. **2** informal all the children in a family. ▶ v. **1** think deeply about an unpleasant subject. **2** (as adj. **brooding**) mysterious or menacing: *the dark, brooding atmosphere.* **3** (of a bird) sit on eggs to hatch them. ▶ adj. (of an animal) kept for breeding: *a brood mare.*

brood·y /'brōōdē/ ▶ adj. (**broodier, broodiest**) **1** (of a hen) wanting to lay or sit on eggs. **2** informal (of a woman) wanting very much to have a baby. **3** thoughtful and unhappy. ■ **brood·i·ly** adv. **brood·i·ness** n.

brook¹ /brōōk/ ▶ n. a small stream.

brook² ▶ v. formal tolerate or allow: *she would brook no criticism.*

brook trout ▶ n. a freshwater fish of the salmon family, common throughout much of N America and popular with anglers.

broom /brōōm, brŏŏm/ ▶ n. **1** a long-handled brush used for sweeping. **2** a shrub with many yellow flowers and small or few leaves.

broom·stick /'brōōm,stik, 'brŏŏm-/ ▶ n. a brush with twigs at one end and a long handle, on which witches are said to fly.

Bros. ▶ pl. n. brothers (in names of companies).

broth /bräth, brôth/ ▶ n. soup made from meat or vegetables cooked in stock.

broth·el /'bräthəl, 'brôthəl/ ▶ n. a house where men visit prostitutes.

broth·er /'brəthər/ ▶ n. **1** a man or boy in relation to other children of his parents. **2** a male associate or fellow member of an organization. **3** (pl. also **brethren**) a (male) fellow Christian. **4** a member of a religious order of men: *a Benedictine brother.* ■ **broth·er·ly** adj.

broth·er·hood /'brəthər,hŏŏd/ ▶ n. **1** the relationship between brothers. **2** a feeling of fellowship and understanding. **3** a group of people linked by a shared interest or belief: *a religious brotherhood.*

broth·er-in-law ▶ n. (pl. **brothers-in-law**) **1** the brother of one's wife or husband. **2** the husband of one's sister or sister-in-law.

brought /brôt/ ▶ past and past participle of BRING.

USAGE
Do not confuse **bought** and **brought**. **Bought** is the past tense and past participle of **buy** (*she bought a bar of chocolate*), whereas **brought** is the past tense and past participle of **bring** (*the article brought a massive response*).

brou·ha·ha /'brōōhä,hä, brōō'hähä/ ▶ n. a noisy and overexcited reaction.

brow /brou/ ▶ n. **1** a person's forehead. **2** an eyebrow. **3** the summit of a hill or pass.

brow·beat /'brou,bēt/ ▶ v. (past **browbeat**; past part. **browbeaten**) bully or intimidate someone by using stern or abusive words.

brown /broun/ ▶ adj. **1** of a color produced by mixing red, yellow, and blue, as of dark wood or rich soil. **2** dark-skinned or suntanned. ▶ n. brown color or material. ▶ v. make or become brown by cooking. ■ **brown·ish** adj. **brown·y** adj.

brown bear ▶ n. a large bear with a coat color ranging from cream to black.

brown belt ▶ n. a brown belt marking a level of skill below that of a black belt in judo, karate, or other martial arts.

brown coal ▶ n. lignite.

brown dwarf ▶ n. Astronomy a celestial object midway in size between a large planet and a small star.

brown·field /'broun,fēld/ ▶ adj. (of an urban site) having been previously built on. Compare with GREENFIELD.

brown goods ▶ pl. n. television sets, audio equipment, and similar household appliances.

Compare with **WHITE GOODS**.

Brown·i·an mo·tion /'brounēən/ ▶n. Physics the erratic movement of microscopic particles in a fluid, as a result of collisions with the surrounding molecules.

Brown·ie /'brounē/ ▶n. (pl. **Brownies**) 1 a member of the junior branch of the Girl Scouts. 2 (**brownie**) a small square of rich chocolate cake. 3 (**brownie**) a kind elf that supposedly does housework secretly.
– PHRASES **brownie point** informal an imaginary good mark given for an attempt to please someone.

brown-nose ▶n. (also **brown-noser**) informal a person who behaves in a very servile or ingratiating way toward someone in an attempt to gain their approval.

brown·out /'broun,out/ ▶n. a partial blackout.

brown rice ▶n. unpolished rice with only the husk of the grain removed.

Brown·shirt /'broun,SHərt/ ▶n. a member of a Nazi military force founded by Hitler in 1921 and suppressed in 1934, with brown uniforms.

brown·stone /'broun,stōn/ ▶n. 1 a kind of reddish-brown sandstone used for building. 2 a building faced with this kind of sandstone.

brown sug·ar ▶n. unrefined or partially refined sugar.

brown trout ▶n. (pl. same) the common trout of European lakes and rivers, typically with dark spotted skin.

browse /brouz/ ▶v. 1 look at goods or text in a leisurely way. 2 read or look at computer files via a network. 3 (of an animal) feed on leaves, twigs, etc. ▶n. an act of browsing. ■ **brows·a·ble** adj.

brows·er /'brouzər/ ▶n. 1 a person or animal that browses. 2 a computer program used to navigate the World Wide Web.

bru·cel·lo·sis /,brōōsə'lōsis/ ▶n. a disease caused by a bacterium, which chiefly affects cattle.

bruise /brōōz/ ▶n. 1 an area of discolored skin on the body, caused by a blow or impact that bursts underlying blood vessels. 2 a similar area of damage on a fruit, vegetable, or plant. ▶v. 1 inflict a bruise on someone or something. 2 develop a bruise.

bruis·er /'brōōzər/ ▶n. informal, derogatory a tough, aggressive person.

bruis·ing /'brōōziNG/ ▶adj. conducted in an aggressive way and likely to be stressful: *a bruising cabinet battle over public spending.* ▶n. bruises on the skin.

bruit /brōōt/ ▶v. spread a story or rumor widely.

brume /brōōm/ ▶n. literary mist or fog.

brunch /brənCH/ ▶n. a late morning meal eaten instead of breakfast and lunch.

Bru·nei·an /brōō'nīən/ ▶n. a person from the sultanate of Brunei. ▶adj. relating to Brunei.

bru·nette /brōō'net/ (also **brunet**) ▶n. a woman or girl with dark brown hair.

brunt /brənt/ ▶n. the chief impact of something bad or unwelcome: *the island bore the brunt of the storm.*

bru·schet·ta /brōō'sketə/ ▶n. toasted Italian bread drizzled with olive oil and often topped with tomatoes or other ingredients.

brush[1] /brəSH/ ▶n. 1 an implement with a handle and a block of bristles, hair, or wire, used especially for cleaning, smoothing, or painting. 2 an act of brushing. 3 a brief encounter with something bad or unwelcome: *a brush with death.* 4 the bushy tail of a fox. 5 a piece of carbon or metal serving as an electrical contact with a moving part in a motor or alternator. ▶v. 1 clean, smooth, or apply with a brush. 2 touch something lightly. 3 (**brush someone/thing off** (or **aside**)) dismiss someone or something in an abrupt way: *he brushed aside their questions.* 4 (**brush up on something**) work to improve a skill that has not been used for some time.

brush[2] ▶n. undergrowth, small trees, and shrubs.

brushed /brəSHt/ ▶adj. 1 (of fabric) having a soft raised nap. 2 (of metal) finished with a nonreflective surface.

brush-off ▶n. informal a rejection or dismissal.

brush-stroke /'brəSH,strōk/ ▶n. a mark made by a paintbrush drawn across a surface.

brush·wood /'brəSH,wŏŏd/ ▶n. undergrowth, twigs, and small branches.

brush·work /'brəSH,wərk/ ▶n. the way in which a painter uses a brush.

brusque /brəsk/ ▶adj. abrupt or offhand in manner or speech. ■ **brusque·ly** adv. **brusque·ness** n.

Brus·sels sprout /'brəsəlz/ (also **Brussel sprout** /'brəsəl/) ▶n. the bud of a variety of cabbage, eaten as a vegetable.

brut /brōōt/ ▶adj. (of sparkling wine) very dry.

bru·tal /'brōōtl/ ▶adj. 1 savagely violent. 2 not attempting to disguise something unpleasant: *he replied with brutal honesty.* ■ **bru·tal·i·ty** /brōō'talitē/ n. **bru·tal·ly** adv.

bru·tal·ism /'brōōtl,izəm/ ▶n. 1 cruelty and savagery. 2 a stark style of architecture that makes use of massive blocks of steel and concrete.

bru·tal·ize /'brōōtl,īz/ ▶v. 1 make someone cruel, violent, or callous by repeatedly exposing them to violence. 2 treat someone in a violent way. ■ **bru·tal·i·za·tion** /'brōōtli'zāSHən/ n.

brute /brōōt/ ▶n. 1 a violent or savage person or animal. 2 informal a cruel or insensitive person. ▶adj. 1 involving physical strength alone, rather than thought or intelligence: *brute force.* 2 unpleasant and inescapable: *the brute facts of the human condition.* ■ **brut·ish** adj.

bry·o·ny /'brīənē/ ▶n. (pl. **bryonies**) a climbing plant with red berries.

bry·o·phyte /'brīə,fīt/ ▶n. any of a division of small, simple plants that comprises the mosses and liverworts.

bry·o·zo·an /,brīə'zōən/ ▶n. any of a group of sedentary aquatic invertebrates.

BS ▶abbr. 1 Bachelor of Science. 2 vulgar slang bullshit.

BSE ▶abbr. bovine spongiform encephalopathy, a fatal disease of cattle that affects the central nervous system and is believed to be related to Creutzfeldt–Jakob disease in humans.

B-side ▶n. the side of a pop single regarded as the less important one.

Btu (also **BTU**) ▶abbr. British thermal unit(s).

btw ▶abbr. by the way.

bub·ble /'bəbəl/ ▶n. 1 a thin sphere of liquid enclosing air or another gas. 2 an air- or gas-filled spherical cavity in a liquid or a solidified liquid such as glass. 3 a transparent cover or enclosure in the shape of a dome. ▶v. 1 (of a liquid) contain rising bubbles of air or gas.

2 (**bubble with**) be filled with an irrepressible feeling: *she was bubbling with excitement.*

bub·ble bath ▸ n. sweet-smelling liquid added to bathwater to make it foam.

bub·ble·gum /'bəbəl,gəm/ ▸ n. chewing gum that can be blown into bubbles.

bub·ble wrap ▸ n. trademark protective plastic packaging in the form of sheets containing numerous small air pockets.

bub·bly /'bəb(ə)lē/ ▸ adj. (**bubblier, bubbliest**) **1** containing bubbles. **2** cheerful and high-spirited. ▸ n. informal champagne.

bu·bo /'b(y)o͞obō/ ▸ n. (pl. **buboes**) a swollen inflamed lymph node in the armpit or groin. ■ **bu·bon·ic** /b(y)o͞o'bänik/ adj.

bu·bon·ic plague ▸ n. a form of plague transmitted by rat fleas, causing swellings (buboes) in the groin or armpits.

buc·cal /'bəkəl/ ▸ adj. technical relating to the cheek or mouth.

buc·ca·neer /,bəkə'ni(ə)r/ ▸ n. **1** historical a pirate, originally one operating in the Caribbean. **2** a recklessly adventurous and unscrupulous person. ■ **buc·ca·neer·ing** adj.

buck¹ /bək/ ▸ n. **1** the male of some animals, e.g., deer and rabbits. **2** a vertical jump performed by a horse, with the back arched and the back legs thrown out behind. **3** old use a fashionable young man. ▸ v. **1** (of a horse) perform a buck. **2** resist or go against: *utility shares bucked the trend and rallied.* **3** (**buck someone up** or **buck up**) informal make or become more cheerful.

buck² ▸ n. informal a dollar.

buck³ ▸ n. an object placed in front of a poker player whose turn it is to deal.
– PHRASES **the buck stops here** informal the responsibility for something cannot be avoided. **pass the buck** informal shift responsibility to someone else.

buck·a·roo /,bəkə'ro͞o/ ▸ n. dated or humorous a cowboy.

buck·board /'bək,bôrd/ ▸ n. an open horse-drawn carriage with four wheels and seating that is attached to a plank between the front and rear axles.

buck·et /'bəkit/ ▸ n. **1** a cylindrical open container with a handle, used to carry liquids. **2** (**buckets**) informal large quantities of liquid. **3** a scoop on a dredger, or one attached to the front of a digger or tractor. ■ **buck·et·ful** n.

buck·et·load /'bəkit,lōd/ ▸ n. informal a large amount or number.

buck·et seat ▸ n. a vehicle seat with a rounded back to fit one person.

buck·eye /'bək,ī/ ▸ n. **1** a North American tree or shrub related to the horse chestnut, with showy yellow, red, or white flowers. **2** (**Buckeye**) a native of Ohio.

buck·le /'bəkəl/ ▸ n. a flat frame with a hinged pin, used for fastening a belt or strap. ▸ v. **1** fasten a belt or strap with a buckle. **2** bend and give way under pressure. **3** (**buckle down**) tackle a task with determination.

buck na·ked ▸ adj. informal completely naked.

buck·ram /'bəkrəm/ ▸ n. coarse linen or other cloth stiffened with paste, used in bookbinding.

buck·shot /'bək,SHät/ ▸ n. coarse lead shot used in shotgun shells.

buck·skin /'bək,skin/ ▸ n. **1** soft leather made from the skin of deer or sheep. **2** (**buckskins**)

clothes or shoes made from buckskin. **3** thick smooth cotton or woolen fabric.

buck teeth ▸ pl.n. upper teeth that project over the lower lip. ■ **buck-toothed** adj.

buck·thorn /'bək,тнôrn/ ▸ n. a thorny shrub or small tree that bears black berries.

buck·wheat /'bək,(h)wēt/ ▸ n. a plant producing starchy seeds used for animal fodder or milled into flour.

bu·col·ic /byo͞o'kälik/ ▸ adj. relating to country life.

bud¹ /bəd/ ▸ n. **1** a growth on a plant that develops into a leaf, flower, or shoot. **2** Biology an outgrowth from an organism that separates to form a new individual without sexual reproduction taking place. ▸ v. (**buds, budding, budded**) form a bud or buds.

bud² ▸ n. informal a companion or friend: *Johnson and Rooney are buds.*

Bud·dhism /'bo͞odizəm, 'bo͝od-/ ▸ n. a religion or philosophy, founded by Siddartha Gautama (Buddha; *c.* 563–*c.* 483 BC), that teaches that enlightenment may be reached by the elimination of earthly desires. ■ **Bud·dhist** n. & adj.

bud·ding /'bədiNG/ ▸ adj. beginning to develop and showing signs of promise or success: *their budding relationship.*

bud·dle·ia /'bədlēə, bəd'lēə/ ▸ n. a shrub with clusters of lilac, white, or yellow flowers.

bud·dy /'bədē/ ▸ n. (pl. **buddies**) informal a close friend.

budge /bəj/ ▸ v. **1** make or cause to make the slightest movement. **2** change or cause to change an opinion.

budg·et /'bəjit/ ▸ n. **1** an estimate of income and expenditure for a set period of time. **2** the amount of money needed or available for a particular purpose: *a $1 million advertising budget.* **3** a regular estimate of national or state income and expenditure put forward by a government. ▸ v. (**budgets, budgeting, budgeted**) allow for in a budget: *they budgeted for a new roof.* ▸ adj. inexpensive. ■ **budg·et·ar·y** adj.

budo /'bo͞odō, 'bo͝odō/ ▸ n. Japanese martial arts, or the code on which they are based.

buff¹ /bəf/ ▸ n. **1** a yellowish-beige color. **2** a dull yellow leather with a velvety surface. ▸ v. **1** polish something. **2** give a velvety finish to leather.
– PHRASES **in the buff** informal naked.

buff² ▸ n. informal a person who is interested in and very knowledgeable about a particular subject: *a movie buff.*

buf·fa·lo /'bəfə,lō/ ▸ n. (pl. same or **buffaloes**) **1** a heavily built wild ox with backward-curving horns. **2** the North American bison.

buff·er¹ /'bəfər/ ▸ n. **1** a person or thing that lessens the impact of something harmful or forms a barrier between adversaries: *she often had to act as a buffer between father and son.* **2** (also **buffer solution**) Chemistry a solution that resists changes in pH when acid or alkali is added to it. **3** Computing a temporary memory area or queue used when creating or editing text, or when transferring data.

buff·er² ▸ n. Brit. informal a foolish or incompetent elderly man.

buff·er zone ▸ n. a neutral area serving to separate hostile forces or nations.

buf·fet[1] /bəˈfā/ ▶ n. **1** a meal consisting of several dishes from which guests serve themselves. **2** a room or counter selling light meals or snacks.

buf·fet[2] /ˈbəfit/ ▶ v. (**buffets, buffeting, buffeted**) (especially of wind or waves) strike or push someone or something repeatedly and violently. ▶ n. dated a blow.

buf·foon /bəˈfo͞on/ ▶ n. a ridiculous but amusing person. ■ **buf·foon·er·y** n. **buf·foon·ish** adj.

bug /bəg/ ▶ n. **1** a small insect. **2** informal a harmful microorganism or an illness caused by a microorganism. **3** informal an enthusiasm for something: *they caught the sailing bug.* **4** a microphone used for secret recording. **5** an error in a computer program or system. ▶ v. (**bugs, bugging, bugged**) **1** conceal a microphone in a room or telephone. **2** informal annoy or bother someone.

bug·a·boo /ˈbəgəˌbo͞o/ ▶ n. a cause of fear.

bug·bear /ˈbəgˌbe(ə)r/ ▶ n. a cause of anxiety or irritation.

bug-eyed ▶ adj. with bulging eyes.

bug·ger /ˈbəgər, ˈbo͞og-/ vulgar slang, chiefly Brit. ▶ n. **1** a person regarded with contempt or pity. **2** an annoying or awkward thing. **3** derogatory a person who commits buggery. ▶ v. **1** (**bugger off**) go away. **2** cause serious harm or trouble to someone or something. **3** have anal intercourse with someone.

bug·ger·y /ˈbəgərē, ˈbo͞og-/ ▶ n. anal intercourse.

bug·gy[1] /ˈbəgē/ ▶ n. (pl. **buggies**) **1** historical a light horse-drawn vehicle for one or two people. **2** short for BABY BUGGY. **3** a small motor vehicle with an open top; a motorized cart.

bug·gy[2] ▶ adj. **1** infested with bugs. **2** (of a computer program or system) faulty in operation.

bu·gle[1] /ˈbyo͞ogəl/ ▶ n. a brass instrument like a small trumpet with no valves, traditionally used for military signals. ■ **bu·gler** n.

bu·gle[2] ▶ n. a creeping plant with blue flowers on upright stems.

bu·gloss /ˈbyo͞oglôs, -läs/ ▶ n. a bristly plant with bright blue flowers.

build /bild/ ▶ v. (past and past part. **built**) **1** construct something by putting parts or materials together. **2** (often **build up**) increase in size or intensity over time. **3** (**build on**) use something as a basis for further progress or development. **4** (**build something in/into**) incorporate something as a permanent part of a larger structure. ▶ n. the size and shape of a person's or animal's body: *a man of stocky build.* ■ **build·er** n.

build·ing /ˈbilding/ ▶ n. **1** a structure with a roof and walls. **2** the process or profession of building houses and other structures.

build·out /ˈbildˌout/ ▶ n. **1** the growth, development, or expansion of something: *the rapid buildout of digital technology.* **2** the state of maximum development as permitted by a plan or regulations: *concerns about water as the community approaches its buildout.* **3** the execution of a building or community development plan.

build·up /ˈbildˌəp/ ▶ n. **1** a gradual increase in something over a period of time. **2** a period of excitement and preparation before an event.

built /bilt/ past and past participle of BUILD ▶ adj. of a particular physical build: *a slightly built woman.*

built-in ▶ adj. included as part of a larger structure.

built-up ▶ adj. (of an area) covered by many buildings.

bulb /bəlb/ ▶ n. **1** the rounded underground base of the stem of some plants, from which the roots grow. **2** a light bulb. **3** an expanded or rounded part at the end of something such as a thermometer.

bul·bous /ˈbəlbəs/ ▶ adj. **1** round or bulging in shape. **2** (of a plant) growing from a bulb.

Bul·gar·i·an /ˌbəlˈge(ə)rēən, ˌbo͞ol-/ ▶ n. **1** a person from Bulgaria. **2** the Slavic language spoken in Bulgaria. ▶ adj. relating to Bulgaria.

bulge /bəlj/ ▶ n. **1** a rounded swelling on a flat surface. **2** informal a temporary increase: *a bulge in the birth rate.* ▶ v. **1** swell or stick out. **2** be full of: *a bag bulging with papers and letters.* ■ **bulg·y** adj.

bul·gur /ˈbəlgər/ ▶ n. (also **bulgar**) a cereal food made from whole wheat partially boiled and then dried.

bu·lim·i·a /bo͞oˈlimēə, ˈlē-/ ▶ (also **bulimia nervosa** /nərˈvōsə/) ▶ n. an emotional disorder that causes bouts of overeating, followed by fasting or self-induced vomiting. ■ **bu·lim·ic** /-ˈlimik, ˈlē-/ adj. & n.

bulk /bəlk/ ▶ n. **1** the mass or size of something large. **2** the greater part of something: *the bulk of the club's supporters are well behaved.* **3** a large mass or shape. **4** roughage in food. ▶ adj. large in quantity: *bulk orders.* ▶ v. (**bulk something up/out**) treat a product so that its quantity appears greater than it really is.
– PHRASES **in bulk** (of goods) in large quantities.

bulk·head /ˈbəlkˌhed/ ▶ n. a barrier between separate compartments inside a ship or aircraft.

bulk·y /ˈbəlkē/ ▶ adj. (**bulkier, bulkiest**) large and awkward to handle.

bull[1] /bo͞ol/ ▶ n. **1** an uncastrated male animal of the cattle family. **2** a large male animal, e.g., a whale or elephant. **3** Stock Exchange a person who buys shares hoping to sell them at a higher price later. Often contrasted with BEAR[2].
– PHRASES **like a bull in a china shop** behaving clumsily in a delicate situation. **take the bull by the horns** deal decisively with a difficult situation.

bull[2] ▶ n. an order or announcement issued by the Pope.

bull[3] ▶ n. informal nonsense.

bull·dog /ˈbo͞olˌdôg/ ▶ n. a breed of dog with a protruding lower jaw, a flat wrinkled face, and a broad chest.

bulldog clip ▶ n. trademark a metal device with two flat plates held together by a spring, used to hold papers together.

bull·doze /ˈbo͞olˌdōz/ ▶ v. **1** clear ground or destroy buildings with a bulldozer. **2** informal use force to do something or deal with someone: *he bulldozed his way to his first Formula One victory.*

bull·doz·er /ˈbo͞olˌdōzər/ ▶ n. a tractor with a broad curved blade at the front for clearing ground.

bul·let /ˈbo͞olit/ ▶ n. **1** a projectile fired from a small firearm. **2** a solid circle printed before each item in a list.

bul·le·tin /ˈbo͞olitn, -ˌtin/ ▶ n. **1** a short official statement or summary of news. **2** a regular newsletter or report.

bul·le·tin board ▶ n. **1** a site on a computer system where users can read or download files supplied by others and add their own files. **2** a board, typically made of cork, for displaying notices, posters, etc.

bul·let·proof /ˈbo͝olitˌpro͞of/ ▶ adj. able to resist the penetration of bullets.

bull·fight·ing /ˈbo͝olˌfītiNG/ ▶ n. the sport of baiting and killing a bull for public entertainment. ■ **bull·fight** n. **bull·fight·er** n.

bull·finch /ˈbo͝olˌfinCH/ ▶ n. a Eurosian finch with mainly gray and black plumage, the male having a pink breast.

bull·frog /ˈbo͝olˌfrôg, -ˌfräg/ ▶ n. a very large frog with a deep croak.

bull·head·ed /ˈbo͝olˌhedid/ ▶ adj. determined and obstinate.

bull·horn /ˈbo͝olˌhôrn/ ▶ n. a megaphone.

bul·lion /ˈbo͝olyən/ ▶ n. gold or silver in bulk before being made into coins.

bull·ish /ˈbo͝oliSH/ ▶ adj. **1** aggressively confident and self-assertive. **2** Stock Exchange characterized or influenced by rising share prices. ■ **bull·ish·ly** adv. **bull·ish·ness** n.

bull mar·ket ▶ n. Stock Exchange a market in which share prices are rising.

bull-necked ▶ adj. (of a man) having a thick neck.

bul·lock /ˈbo͝olək/ ▶ n. a castrated male animal of the cattle family, raised for beef.

bull·pen /ˈbo͝olˌpen/ ▶ n. **1** an enclosure for bulls. **2** a warmup area for baseball pitchers. **3** the relief pitchers on a baseball team.

bull·ring /ˈbo͝olˌriNG/ ▶ n. an arena where bullfights are held.

bulls·eye /ˈbo͝olsˌī/ (also **bull's-eye**) ▶ n. the center of the target in sports such as archery and darts.

bull·shit /ˈbo͝olˌSHit/ vulgar slang ▶ n. nonsense. ▶ v. (**bullshits, bullshitting, bullshitted**) talk nonsense in an attempt to deceive someone. ■ **bull·shit·ter** n.

bull ter·ri·er ▶ n. a dog that is a crossbreed of bulldog and terrier.

bul·ly¹ /ˈbo͝olē/ ▶ n. (pl. **bullies**) a person who intimidates or persecutes weaker people. ▶ v. (**bullies, bullying, bullied**) intimidate or persecute someone.

bul·ly² ▶ n. (pl. **bullies**) (also **bully off**) the start of play in field hockey, in which two opponents strike each other's sticks three times and then go for the ball.

bul·ly³ ▶ adj. informal very good; first-rate. ▶ exclam. (**bully for**) an expression of admiration or approval: *he got away—bully for him.*

bul·ly boy ▶ n. a tough or aggressive man.

bul·ly pul·pit ▶ n. a public office or position of authority that provides its occupant with an opportunity to speak out on any issue.

bul·rush /ˈbo͝olˌrəSH/ (also **bullrush**) ▶ n. a tall waterside plant with a long brown head.

bul·wark /ˈbo͝olˌwərk/ ▶ n. **1** a defensive wall. **2** a person or thing that acts as a defense: *a bulwark against fascism.* **3** an extension of a ship's sides above deck level.

bum¹ /bəm/ informal ▶ n. **1** a homeless person or beggar. **2** a lazy or worthless person. ▶ v. (**bums, bumming, bummed**) **1** get something by asking or begging for it: *I bummed a cigarette off him.* **2** (**bum around**) travel or spend one's time with no particular aim or plan. ▶ adj. bad; wrong: *the first bum note she'd played all evening.*

bum² ▶ n. Brit. informal a person's buttocks.

bum·ble /ˈbəmbəl/ ▶ v. move or speak in an awkward or confused way.

bum·ble·bee /ˈbəmbəlˌbē/ ▶ n. a large hairy bee with a loud hum.

bum·mer /ˈbəmər/ ▶ n. informal an annoying or disappointing thing.

bump /bəmp/ ▶ n. **1** a light blow or collision. **2** a hump or swelling on a level surface. ▶ v. **1** knock or run into someone or something with a jolt. **2** travel with a jolting movement: *the car bumped along the rutted track.* **3** (**bump into**) meet someone by chance. **4** (**bump someone off**) informal murder someone. **5** (**bump something up**) informal increase or raise something: *the company bumped up the prices.* ■ **bump·y** adj. (**bumpier, bumpiest**).

bump·er /ˈbəmpər/ ▶ n. a horizontal bar fixed across the front or back of a motor vehicle to reduce damage in a collision. ▶ adj. exceptionally large or successful: *a bumper crop.*

bump·er car ▶ n. a small electrically powered car with rubber bumpers, driven within an enclosure at an amusement park with the aim of bumping other such cars.

bump·er stick·er ▶ n. an adhesive label carrying a slogan or advertisement, made to go on a vehicle's bumper.

bump·kin /ˈbəmpkin/ ▶ n. an unsophisticated person from the countryside.

bump·tious /ˈbəmpSHəs/ ▶ adj. irritatingly confident or self-important. ■ **bump·tious·ly** adv. **bump·tious·ness** n.

bum rap ▶ n. informal a false charge or unfair criticism.

bun /bən/ ▶ n. **1** a bread roll of various shapes and flavorings. **2** a hairstyle in which the hair is drawn into a tight coil at the back of the head. **3** (**buns**) informal a person's buttocks. – PHRASES **have a bun in the oven** informal be pregnant.

bunch /bənCH/ ▶ n. **1** a number of things growing or fastened together. **2** informal a group of people. **3** informal a lot. ▶ v. collect or form into a bunch.

bun·dle /ˈbəndl/ ▶ n. **1** a collection of things or quantity of material tied or wrapped up together. **2** a set of nerve, muscle, or other fibers that run parallel to each other. **3** informal a large amount of money. ▶ v. **1** tie or roll something up in a bundle. **2** (**be bundled up**) be dressed in many warm clothes. **3** informal push or carry forcibly: *they bundled him into a van.*

Bundt cake /ˈbənt/ ▶ n. trademark a ring-shaped cake made in a fluted tube pan, called a **Bundt pan**.

bung /bəNG/ ▶ n. a stopper for a hole in a container. ▶ v. **1** close a container with a bung. **2** (**bung something up**) block something up.

bun·ga·low /ˈbəNGgəˌlō/ ▶ n. a house with only one story.

bun·gee /ˈbənjē/ (also **bungee cord** or **rope**) ▶ n. a long rubber band encased in nylon, used for securing luggage and in bungee jumping.

bun·gee jump·ing ▶ n. the sport of leaping from a high place, held by a bungee around the ankles. ■ **bun·gee jump** n. **bun·gee jump·er** n.

bun·gle /ˈbəNGgəl/ ▶ v. **1** perform a task clumsily or incompetently. **2** (as adj. **bungling**) tending to make many mistakes. ▶ n. a mistake or failure. ■ **bun·gler** n.

bun·ion /ˈbənyən/ ▶ n. a painful swelling on the big toe.

bunk¹ /bəNGk/ ▸ n. a narrow shelflike bed.

bunk² ▸ n. informal, dated nonsense.

bunk bed ▸ n. a piece of furniture consisting of two beds, one above the other.

bun·ker /'bəNGkər/ ▸ n. **1** a large container for storing fuel. **2** an underground shelter for use in wartime. **3** a hollow filled with sand, forming an obstacle on a golf course.

bunk·house /'bəNGk,hous/ ▸ n. a building with sleeping accommodations for workers.

bun·kum /'bəNGkəm/ ▸ n. informal nonsense.

bun·ny /'bənē/ ▸ n. (pl. **bunnies**) (also **bunny rabbit**) informal a child's term for a rabbit.

Bun·sen burn·er /'bənsən/ ▸ n. a small adjustable gas burner used in laboratories.

bunt¹ /bənt/ ▸ v. **1** Baseball (of a batter) gently tap a pitched ball without swinging in an attempt to make it more difficult to field. **2** (of a batter) help a base runner to progress to a further base by tapping a ball in such a way: *he bunted Davis to third.* **3** (of a person or animal) butt with the head or horns. ▸ n. **1** Baseball an act or result of tapping a pitched ball in such a way. **2** an act of flying an aircraft in part of an outside loop.

bunt² ▸ n. a disease of wheat caused by a smut fungus, the spores of which give off a smell of rotten fish.

bunt·ing¹ /'bəntiNG/ ▸ n. a songbird with brown streaked plumage and a boldly marked head.

bunt·ing² ▸ n. flags and streamers used as decorations.

bu·oy /'bōō-ē, boi/ ▸ n. a floating object anchored to the seabed that marks safe navigation channels for boats. ▸ v. **1** keep someone or something afloat. **2** make or remain cheerful and confident: *he was buoyed up by his success.*

buoy·ant /'boi-ənt, 'bōōyənt/ ▸ adj. **1** able to keep afloat. **2** cheerful and optimistic. **3** (of an economy or market) involved in much successful trade or activity. ■ **buoy·an·cy** /'boi-ənsē, 'bōōyənsē/ n. **buoy·ant·ly** adv.

bur /bər/ ▸ n. see BURR.

bur·ble /'bərbəl/ ▸ v. **1** make a continuous murmuring noise. **2** speak at length in a way that is difficult to understand. ▸ n. a continuous murmuring noise.

bur·bot /'bərbət/ ▸ n. a fish that is the only freshwater member of the cod family.

bur·den /'bərdn/ ▸ n. **1** a heavy load. **2** a cause of hardship, worry, or grief: *the tax burden on low-income families.* **3** the main responsibility for a task. **4** the main theme of a speech, book, or argument. ▸ v. **1** load someone or something heavily. **2** cause someone worry, hardship, or grief: *I don't want to burden you with my problems.*

– PHRASES **burden of proof** the obligation to prove that something is true.

bur·den·some /'bərdn'səm/ ▸ adj. causing worry or difficulty.

bur·dock /'bərdäk/ ▸ n. a plant of the daisy family, with large leaves and prickly flowers.

bu·reau /'byōōrō/ ▸ n. (pl. **bureaux** or **bureaus** /'byōōrōz/) **1** a chest of drawers. **2** an office that carries out a particular type of business: *a news bureau.* **3** a government department. **4** Brit. a slant top desk.

bu·reauc·ra·cy /byōō'räkrəsē/ ▸ n. (pl. **bureaucracies**) **1** a system of government in which most decisions are made by bureaus and officials rather than by elected representatives.

2 administrative procedures that are too complicated.

bu·reau·crat /'byōōrə,krat/ ▸ n. an official in an organization or government department who is seen as being too concerned with following administrative guidelines. ■ **bu·reau·crat·ic** /,byōōrə'kratik/ adj.

bu·reauc·ra·tize /byōō'räkrə,tīz/ ▸ v. run a government or organization by implementing or following administrative procedures that are too complicated. ■ **bu·reauc·ra·ti·za·tion** /-,räkrəti'zäsHən/ n.

bu·reau de change /'byōōrō də 'sHänzH/ ▸ n. (pl. **bureaux de change** pronunc. same) a place where foreign money can be exchanged.

bu·rette /byōō'ret/ (also **buret**) ▸ n. a glass tube with measurements on it and a tap at one end, for delivering known amounts of a liquid.

burg /bərg/ ▸ n. **1** informal a town or city: *a bucolic burg framed by snowcapped mountains.* **2** an ancient or medieval fortress or walled town.

bur·geon /'bərjən/ ▸ v. grow or increase rapidly.

burg·er /'bərgər/ ▸ n. a hamburger.

bur·gess /'bərjis/ ▸ n. chiefly historical a person with municipal authority or privileges, such as a member of the assembly of colonial Maryland or Virginia.

burgh·er /'bərgər/ ▸ n. old use a citizen of a town or city.

bur·glar /'bərglər/ ▸ n. a person who commits burglary.

bur·glar·ize /'bərglə,rīz/ ▸ v. enter a building illegally with the intention of committing a crime.

bur·gla·ry /'bərglərē/ ▸ n. (pl. **burglaries**) the crime of entering a building illegally with the intent of stealing something inside.

bur·gle /'bərgəl/ ▸ v. chiefly Brit. burglarize.

bur·gun·dy /'bərgəndē/ ▸ n. (pl. **burgundies**) **1** a red wine from Burgundy, a region of east central France. **2** a deep red color.

bur·i·al /'berēəl/ ▸ n. the burying of a dead body.

bu·rin /'byōōrin/ ▸ n. **1** a steel tool used for engraving. **2** Archaeology a flint tool with a chisel point.

bur·ka /'bōōrkə/ (also **burkha** or **burqa**) ▸ n. a long, loose garment covering the whole body, worn in public by some Muslim women.

Bur·ki·nan /bər'kēnən/ ▸ n. a person from Burkina, a country in western Africa. ▸ adj. relating to Burkina or its people.

burl /bərl/ ▸ n. a rounded knotty growth on a tree, often polished and used for handcrafted objects and veneers.

bur·lap /'bərlap/ ▸ n. coarse canvas woven from jute or hemp, used to make sacks.

bur·lesque /bər'lesk/ ▸ n. **1** a performance or piece of writing that makes fun of something by representing it in a comically exaggerated way. **2** a variety show, typically including bawdy humor and striptease. ▸ v. (**burlesques, burlesquing, burlesqued**) make fun of someone or something by representing them in a comically exaggerated way.

bur·ly /'bərlē/ ▸ adj. (**burlier, burliest**) (of a person) large and strong. ■ **bur·li·ness** n.

Bur·man /'bərmən/ ▸ n. (pl. **Burmans**) & adj. another term for BURMESE.

Bur·mese /bər'mēz, -'mēs/ ▸ n. (pl. same) **1** a member of the largest ethnic group of

Burma (now Myanmar) in SE Asia. **2** a person from Burma. **3** (also **Burmese cat**) a cat of a short-coated breed that originated in Asia. ▶ **adj.** relating to Burma or the Burmese.

burn[1] /bərn/ ▶ **v.** (past and past part. **burned** or chiefly Brit. **burnt**) **1** (of a fire) flame or glow while using up a fuel. **2** be or cause to be harmed or destroyed by fire. **3** use a fuel as a source of heat or energy. **4** (of the skin) become red and painful as a result of exposure to the sun. **5** (**be burning with**) experience a very strong desire or emotion: *she was burning with curiosity.* **6** (**burn out**) become exhausted through overwork. **7** produce a CD by copying from an original or master copy. ▶ **n.** an injury caused by burning. – PHRASES **burn one's bridges** do something that makes it impossible to return to the previous situation. **burn the candle at both ends** go to bed late and get up early. **burn the midnight oil** work late into the night.

burn[2] ▶ **n.** Scottish & N. English a small stream.

burn·er /'bərnər/ ▶ **n. 1** a part of a stove, lamp, etc., that gives out a flame. **2** a heating element on a stovetop. **3** a device for burning something. **4** short for CD BURNER.

burn·ing /'bərniNG/ ▶ **adj. 1** very strong or deeply felt: *her burning ambition to win.* **2** of great interest and importance; requiring immediate action or attention: *the burning issues of the day.* ■ **burn·ing·ly** adv.

bur·nish /'bərnisH/ ▶ **v.** polish something by rubbing it. ▶ **n.** the shine on a polished surface.

bur·noose /bər'noos/ ▶ **n.** a long hooded cloak worn by Arabs.

burn·out /'bərn,out/ ▶ **n. 1** physical or mental collapse. **2** overheating of an electrical device or component.

burn rate ▶ **n.** the rate at which an enterprise spends money, especially venture capital, in excess of income.

burnt /bərnt/ chiefly Brit. past and past participle of BURN[1].

burp /bərp/ informal ▶ **v. 1** belch. **2** make a baby belch after feeding. ▶ **n.** a belch.

bur·qa /'boorkə/ ▶ **n.** variant spelling of BURKA.

burr /bər/ ▶ **n. 1** a whirring sound. **2** a rough pronunciation of the letter *r*, as in some regional accents. **3** (also **bur**) a prickly seed case or flowerhead that clings to clothing and animal fur. **4** (also **bur**) a rough edge left on a metal object by the action of a tool. ▶ **v.** make a whirring sound.

bur·ri·to /bə'rētō/ ▶ **n.** (pl. **burritos**) a Mexican dish consisting of a tortilla rolled around a filling of beans or chopped or shredded beef.

bur·ro /'bərō, 'boorō/ ▶ **n.** (pl. **burros**) a small donkey used as a pack animal.

bur·row /'bərō/ ▶ **n.** a hole or tunnel dug by a small animal as a home. ▶ **v. 1** dig a hole or tunnel. **2** hide underneath or nestle into something. **3** search for something: *he was burrowing among his files.* ■ **bur·row·er** n.

bur·sar /'bərsər/ ▶ **n.** a person who manages the financial affairs of a college or university.

bur·si·tis /bər'sītis/ ▶ **n.** inflammation of a bursa (fluid-filled sac), typically in a shoulder joint.

burst /bərst/ ▶ **v.** (past and past part. **burst**) **1** break suddenly and violently apart. **2** be very full: *her closet was bursting with clothes.* **3** move or be opened suddenly and forcibly. **4** (**be bursting with**) feel a very strong emotion or

impulse. **5** suddenly begin doing or producing something: *she burst into tears.* ▶ **n. 1** an instance of bursting. **2** a sudden brief outbreak: *a burst of activity.* **3** a period of continuous effort.

Bu·run·di·an /bə'roondēən/ ▶ **n.** a person from Burundi, a country in central Africa. ▶ **adj.** relating to Burundi.

bur·y /'berē/ ▶ **v.** (**buries, burying, buried**) **1** put or hide something underground. **2** place a dead body in the earth or a tomb. **3** cover someone or something completely. **4** hide or try to ignore something: *I buried the memories for years.* **5** (**bury oneself**) involve oneself deeply in something. – PHRASES **bury one's head in the sand** ignore unpleasant realities.

bus /bəs/ ▶ **n.** (pl. **buses** or **busses**) **1** a large motor vehicle carrying customers along a fixed route. **2** a distinct set of conductors within a computer system, to which pieces of equipment may be connected in parallel. ▶ **v.** (**buses, busing, bused** or **busses, bussing, bussed**) **1** transport or travel in a bus. **2** clear dirty dishes in a restaurant or cafeteria. ■ **bus·load** n.

bus·boy /'bəs,boi/ ▶ **n.** a young man who clears tables in a restaurant or cafeteria.

bus·by /'bəzbē/ ▶ **n.** (pl. **busbies**) a tall fur hat worn by certain military regiments.

bush /boosH/ ▶ **n. 1** a shrub or clump of shrubs with stems of moderate length. **2** (**the bush**) (in Australia and Africa) wild or uncultivated country. **3** a thick growth of hair.

bush·ba·by /'boosH,bābē/ ▶ **n.** (pl. **bushbabies**) a small African mammal with very large eyes.

bushed /boosHt/ ▶ **adj.** informal very tired; exhausted.

bush·el /'boosHəl/ ▶ **n. 1** a measure of capacity equal to 64 US pints (35.2 liters). **2** Brit. a measure of capacity equal to 8 gallons (36.4 liters).

bu·shi·do /'boosHēdō/ ▶ **n.** the code of honor and morals of the Japanese samurai.

bush·ing /'boosHiNG/ ▶ **n. 1** a metal lining for a hole into which something fits or revolves. **2** a sleeve that protects an electric cable.

Bush·man /'boosHmən/ ▶ **n.** (pl. **Bushmen**) **1** a member of any of several aboriginal peoples of southern Africa. **2** (**bushman**) a person who lives or travels in the Australian bush.

bush·whack /'boosH,(h)wak/ ▶ **v. 1** live or travel in wild or uncultivated country. **2** work clearing scrub and felling trees. **3** ambush someone. ■ **bush·whack·er** n.

bush·y /'boosHē/ ▶ **adj.** (**bushier, bushiest**) **1** growing thickly. **2** covered with bush or bushes. ■ **bush·i·ly** adv. **bush·i·ness** n.

busi·ness /'biznis/ ▶ **n. 1** a person's regular occupation or profession. **2** commercial activity. **3** a commercial organization. **4** work to be done or matters to be attended to. **5** a person's concern: *that's none of your business.* **6** informal a difficult matter. **7** (**the business**) informal harsh verbal criticism. – PHRASES **in business** (of a commercial organization) operating. **mind one's own business** avoid interfering in other people's affairs.

busi·ness end ▶ **n.** informal the functional part of a tool or device.

busi·ness·like /'biznis,līk/ ▶ **adj.** efficient and practical.

busi·ness·man /'biznis,man, -mən/ (or

businesswoman) ▶ n. (pl. **businessmen** or **businesswomen**) a person who works in commerce, especially at an executive level.

busi·ness mod·el ▶ n. a design for the successful operation of a business, identifying revenue sources, customer base, products, and details of financing.

busk /bəsk/ ▶ v. play music in the street in order to be given money by passersby. ■ **busk·er** n.

bus·man's hol·i·day /'bəsmən/ ▶ n. leisure time spent doing the same thing that one does at work.

bust[1] /bəst/ ▶ n. 1 a woman's breasts. 2 a sculpture of a person's head, shoulders, and chest.

bust[2] informal ▶ v. (past and past part. **busted** or **bust**) 1 break, split, or burst. 2 hit someone hard. 3 (of the police) raid or search a building. 4 arrest someone. ▶ n. 1 a period of economic difficulty. 2 a police raid. ▶ adj. bankrupt.

bus·tard /'bəstərd/ ▶ n. a large swift-running bird found in open country.

bust·er /'bəstər/ ▶ n. informal 1 a form of address to a man or boy. 2 a person or thing that stops a specified thing: *a crime-buster.*

bus·tier /boos'tyā/ ▶ n. a woman's close-fitting strapless top.

bus·tle[1] /'bəsəl/ ▶ v. 1 move in an energetic and busy way. 2 (often as adj. **bustling**) (of a place) be full of activity. ▶ n. excited activity and movement.

bus·tle[2] ▶ n. historical a pad or frame worn under a skirt to puff it out behind.

bust-up ▶ n. informal a serious quarrel or fight.

bust·y /'bəstē/ ▶ adj. (**bustier, bustiest**) informal having large breasts.

bus·y /'bizē/ ▶ adj. (**busier, busiest**) 1 having a great deal to do. 2 currently occupied with an activity. 3 full of activity: *busy streets.* 4 excessively detailed or decorated. ▶ v. (**busies, busying, busied**) (**busy oneself**) keep oneself occupied. ■ **bus·i·ly** adv. **bus·y·ness** n.

bus·y·bod·y /'bizē,bädē/ ▶ n. (pl. **busybodies**) an interfering or nosy person.

bus·y sig·nal ▶ n. a sound indicating that a telephone line is in use, typically a repeated single bleep.

but /bət/ ▶ conj. 1 in spite of that; nevertheless. 2 on the contrary. 3 (with negative or in questions) other than; otherwise than. 4 (with negative) old use without it being the case that. ▶ prep. except; apart from. ▶ adv. no more than; only. ▶ n. an objection.
– PHRASES **but for 1** except for. **2** if it were not for. **but then** on the other hand.

USAGE
On starting a sentence with **but**, see the note at AND.

bu·tane /'byoo,tān/ ▶ n. a flammable hydrocarbon gas present in petroleum and natural gas and used as a fuel.

butch /booch/ ▶ adj. informal masculine in a conspicuous or aggressive way.

butch·er /'boochər/ ▶ n. 1 a person who cuts up and sells meat as a profession. 2 a person who slaughters animals for food. 3 a person who kills brutally. ▶ v. 1 slaughter or cut up an animal for food. 2 kill someone brutally. 3 spoil something by doing it badly. ■ **butch·er·y** n. (pl. **butcheries**).

but·ler /'bətlər/ ▶ n. the chief manservant of a house.

butt[1] /bət/ ▶ v. 1 hit someone or something with the head or horns. 2 (**butt in**) interrupt a conversation or activity. ▶ n. a rough push with the head.

butt[2] ▶ n. 1 a person or thing that is the target of criticism or ridicule. 2 a target or range in archery or shooting.

butt[3] ▶ n. 1 the thicker end of a tool or a weapon. 2 the stub of a cigar or a cigarette. 3 informal a person's buttocks. ▶ v. 1 adjoin or meet end to end. 2 join pieces of wood or other building materials with the ends or sides flat against each other.
– PHRASES **butt naked** informal completely naked.

butt[4] ▶ n. a cask used for wine, ale, or water.

butte /byoot/ ▶ n. technical an isolated hill with steep sides and a flat top.

but·ter /'bətər/ ▶ n. a pale yellow fatty substance made by churning cream. ▶ v. 1 spread something with butter. 2 (**butter someone up**) informal flatter someone.
– PHRASES **look as if butter wouldn't melt in one's mouth** informal appear innocent while being the opposite.

but·ter bean ▶ n. a large flat white edible bean.

but·ter·cream /'bətər,krēm/ ▶ n. a mixture of butter and powdered sugar used as a filling or topping for a cake.

but·ter·cup /'bətər,kəp/ ▶ n. a plant with bright yellow cup-shaped flowers.

but·ter·fat /'bətər,fat/ ▶ n. the natural fat contained in milk and dairy products.

but·ter·fin·gers /'bətər,fiNGgərz/ ▶ n. informal a person who often drops things.

but·ter·fly /'bətər,flī/ ▶ n. (pl. **butterflies**) 1 an insect with two pairs of large wings that feeds on nectar and is active by day. 2 a showy or frivolous person: *a social butterfly.* 3 (**butterflies**) informal a fluttering sensation felt in the stomach when one is nervous. 4 a stroke in swimming in which both arms are raised out of the water and lifted forward together.

but·ter·milk /'bətər,milk/ ▶ n. the slightly sour liquid left after butter has been churned.

but·ter·nut /'bətər,nət/ ▶ n. 1 a North American walnut tree valued for its nuts and its light-colored wood. 2 the edible, oblong, sticky fruit of this tree.

but·ter·nut squash ▶ n. a pear-shaped variety of winter squash with light yellowish-brown rind and orange flesh.

but·ter·scotch /'bətər,skäch/ ▶ n. a candy or syrup made with melted butter and brown sugar.

but·ter·y[1] /'bətərē/ ▶ adj. containing, tasting like, or covered with butter.

but·ter·y[2] ▶ n. (pl. **butteries**) a room for storing wine and liquor.

but·tock /'bətək/ ▶ n. either of the two round fleshy parts that form the lower rear area of a human trunk.

but·ton /'bətn/ ▶ n. 1 a small disk or knob sewn onto a garment to fasten it by being pushed through a buttonhole. 2 a knob on an electrical or electronic device that is pressed to operate it. 3 a decorative badge pinned to clothing. 4 an object placed in front of a poker player whose turn it is to deal. ▶ v. 1 fasten or be fastened with buttons. 2 (**button something**

up) informal complete something satisfactorily. ■ **but·toned** adj.
– PHRASES **button one's lip** informal stop or refrain from talking. **buttoned-up** informal conservative or inhibited. **on the button** informal precisely.

but·ton·hole /'bətn,hōl/ ▶ n. a slit made in a garment to receive a button for fastening. ▶ v. informal stop someone so as to begin a conversation.

but·ton mush·room ▶ n. a young unopened mushroom.

but·tress /'bətris/ ▶ n. **1** a projecting support built against a wall. **2** a projecting portion of a hill or mountain. ▶ v. **1** support something with buttresses. **2** support or reinforce: *I was hoping that facts would buttress my point of view.*

bu·tyl /'byōōtl/ ▶ n. Chemistry the radical $-C_4H_9$, derived from butane.

bux·om /'bəksəm/ ▶ adj. (of a woman) attractively plump and large-breasted.

buy /bī/ ▶ v. (**buys, buying, bought**) **1** obtain something in exchange for payment. **2** get by sacrifice or great effort: *greatness is dearly bought.* **3** informal accept the truth of: *I don't buy the claim that the ends justify the means.* ▶ n. informal something bought; a purchase.
– PHRASES **buy someone out** pay someone to give up an interest or share in something. **buy time** delay an event so as to have longer to improve one's own position. **have bought it** informal be killed.

> **USAGE**
> For an explanation of the difference between **brought** and **bought**, see the note at BROUGHT.

buy·er /'bīər/ ▶ n. **1** a person who buys something. **2** a person employed to buy stock for a retail or manufacturing business.

buy·er's mar·ket ▶ n. an economic situation in which goods or shares are plentiful and buyers can keep prices down.

buy·out /'bī,out/ ▶ n. the purchase of a controlling share in a company.

buzz /bəz/ ▶ n. **1** a low, continuous humming or murmuring sound. **2** the sound of a buzzer or telephone. **3** an atmosphere of excitement and activity. **4** informal a thrill. ▶ v. **1** make a humming sound. **2** call someone with a buzzer. **3** move quickly. **4** (**buzz off**) informal go away. **5** be full of excitement or activity: *the department was buzzing with the news.* **6** informal (of an aircraft) fly very close to something at high speed.

buz·zard /'bəzərd/ ▶ n. **1** a large bird of prey that soars in wide circles. **2** a vulture.

buzz cut ▶ n. a very short haircut in which the hair is clipped close to the head.

buzz·er /'bəzər/ ▶ n. an electrical device that makes a buzzing noise to attract attention.

buzz·word /'bəz,wərd/ ▶ n. informal a technical word or phrase that has become fashionable.

buzz·y /'bəzē/ ▶ adj. informal (of a place or atmosphere) lively and exciting.

bwa·na /'bwänə/ ▶ n. (in East Africa) a form of address for a boss or master.

by /bī/ ▶ prep. **1** indicating the person or thing performing an action or the means of achieving something. **2** indicating a quantity or amount, or the size of a margin. **3** expressing multiplication, especially in dimensions. **4** indicating the end of a time period. **5** near to; beside. **6** past and beyond. **7** during. **8** according to. ▶ adv. so as to go past. ▶ n. (pl. **byes**) variant spelling of BYE[1].
– PHRASES **by and by** before long. **by the by** (or **bye**) incidentally. **by and large** on the whole.

by- (also **bye-**) ▶ prefix less important; secondary: *by-election.*

bye[1] /bī/ (also **by**) ▶ n. the transfer of a competitor directly to the next round of a competition because they have no opponent assigned to them.
– PHRASES **by the bye** variant spelling of BY THE BY (see BY).

bye[2] (also **bye-bye**) ▶ exclam. informal goodbye.

by·gone /'bī,gôn/ ▶ adj. belonging to an earlier time.
– PHRASES **let bygones be bygones** forget past disagreements and be reconciled.

by·law /'bī,lô/ ▶ n. **1** a rule made by a company or society to regulate the actions of its members. **2** a regulation made by a local authority; an ordinance.

by·line /'bī,līn/ ▶ n. a line in a newspaper naming the writer of an article.

by·pass /'bī,pas/ ▶ n. **1** a road passing around a town for through traffic. **2** a secondary channel or connection to allow a flow when the main one is closed or blocked. **3** a surgical operation to make an alternative passage to aid the circulation of blood. ▶ v. **1** go past or around something. **2** avoid a problem or obstacle.

by·play /'bī,plā/ ▶ n. secondary action in a play or movie.

by·prod·uct /'bī,prädəkt/ ▶ n. **1** an incidental or secondary product made in the manufacture of something else. **2** an unintended but unavoidable secondary result.

by·road /'bī,rōd/ ▶ n. a minor road.

By·ron·ic /bī'ränik/ ▶ adj. **1** characteristic of Lord Byron (1788–1824) or his poetry. **2** (of a man) attractively mysterious and moody.

by·stand·er /'bī,standər/ ▶ n. a person who is present at an event but does not take part.

byte /bīt/ ▶ n. a unit of information stored in a computer, equal to eight bits.

by·way /'bī,wā/ ▶ n. a minor road or path.

by·word /'bī,wərd/ ▶ n. **1** a notable example: *his name became a byword for luxury.* **2** a proverb or saying.

Byz·an·tine /'bizən,tēn, bə'zan-, -,tīn/ ▶ adj. **1** relating to Byzantium (now Istanbul), the Byzantine Empire, or the Eastern Orthodox Church. **2** excessively complicated. **3** very crafty or underhanded. ▶ n. a citizen of Byzantium or the Byzantine Empire.

C¹ (also **c**) ▶ n. (pl. **Cs** or **C's**) **1** the third letter of the alphabet. **2** indicating the third item in a set. **3** Music the first note of the scale of C major. **4** the Roman numeral for 100.

C² ▶ abbr. **1** (**C.**) (on maps) Cape. **2** Celsius or centigrade. **3** (©) copyright. **4** a dry cell battery of a size commonly used in flashlights and toys. **5** Physics coulomb(s). ▶ symbol the chemical element carbon.

c ▶ abbr. **1** cent(s). **2** (preceding a date or amount) circa. **3** (**c.**) century or centuries. ▶ symbol Physics the speed of light in a vacuum.

CA ▶ abbr. California.

Ca ▶ symbol the chemical element calcium.

ca. ▶ abbr. (preceding a date or amount) circa.

cab /kab/ ▶ n. **1** (also **taxi cab**) a taxi. **2** the driver's compartment in a truck, bus, or train. **3** historical a horse-drawn vehicle for public hire.

ca·bal /kəˈbäl, -ˈbal/ ▶ n. a small group of people who plot secretly to gain political power.

Cab·a·la /kəˈbälə, ˈkabələ/ ▶ n. variant spelling of KABBALAH.

ca·ban·a /kəˈban(y)ə/ ▶ n. a cabin, hut, or shelter, especially one at a beach or swimming pool.

cab·a·ret /ˌkabəˈrā, ˈkabəˌrā/ ▶ n. **1** entertainment held in a nightclub or restaurant while the audience sits at tables. **2** a nightclub or restaurant where cabaret is performed.

cab·bage /ˈkabij/ ▶ n. a vegetable with thick green or purple leaves surrounding a heart or head of young leaves.

cab·bage white ▶ n. a white butterfly whose caterpillars are pests of cabbages and related plants.

Cab·ba·la /kəˈbälə, ˈkabələ/ ▶ n. variant spelling of KABBALAH.

cabb·a·lis·tic /ˌkabəˈlistik/ ▶ adj. relating to or associated with the Kabbalah.

cab·by /ˈkabē/ (also **cabbie**) ▶ n. (pl. **cabbies**) informal a taxi driver.

Ca·ber·net Sau·vi·gnon /ˌkabərˈnā ˌsōvinˈyôn, -vēˈnyôn/ ▶ n. a variety of black wine grape originally from the Bordeaux area of France.

cab·in /ˈkabən/ ▶ n. **1** a private room on a ship. **2** the passenger compartment in an aircraft. **3** a small wooden shelter or house.

cab·in boy ▶ n. chiefly historical a boy employed to wait on a ship's officers or passengers.

cab·in cruis·er ▶ n. a motorboat with living accommodations.

cab·i·net /ˈkabənit/ ▶ n. **1** a cupboard with drawers or shelves for storing or displaying articles. **2** a wooden box or piece of furniture housing a radio, television, or speaker. **3** a body of advisers to the president. ■ **cab·i·net·ry** /ˈkabənitrē/ n.

cab·i·net·mak·er /ˈkabənitˌmākər/ ▶ n. a skilled joiner who makes furniture or similar high-quality woodwork.

cab·in fe·ver ▶ n. informal depression and irritability resulting from long confinement indoors during the winter.

ca·ble /ˈkābəl/ ▶ n. **1** a thick rope of wire or hemp. **2** an insulated wire or wires for transmitting electricity or telecommunication signals. **3** a cablegram. **4** Nautical a length of 200 yards (182.9 m) or (in the US) 240 yards (219.4 m). ▶ v. dated send a cablegram to someone.

ca·ble car ▶ n. a small car suspended on a moving cable and typically traveling up and down a mountainside.

ca·ble·gram /ˈkābəlˌgram/ ▶ n. historical a telegraph message sent by cable.

ca·ble-knit ▶ adj. (of an item of clothing) knitted using cable stitch.

ca·ble mo·dem ▶ n. a modem that uses a cable television connection to provide high-speed Internet service.

ca·ble stitch ▶ n. a combination of knitted stitches resembling twisted rope.

ca·ble tel·e·vi·sion ▶ n. a system in which television programs are transmitted to subscribers by cable.

cab·o·chon /ˈkabəˌsHän/ ▶ n. a gem that is polished but not cut in facets.

ca·boo·dle /kəˈbōōdl/ ▶ n. (in phrase **the whole caboodle** or **the whole kit and caboodle**) informal the whole number or quantity of people or things in question.

ca·boose /kəˈbōōs/ ▶ n. **1** a railroad car with accommodations for the crew, typically at the end of a train. **2** informal a person's buttocks.

cab·ri·o·let /ˌkabrēəˈlā/ ▶ n. **1** a car with a roof that folds down. **2** historical a light two-wheeled carriage with a hood, drawn by one horse.

ca·ca·o /kəˈkou, kəˈkāō/ ▶ n. the beanlike seeds of a tropical American tree, from which cocoa and chocolate are made.

ca·cha·ca /kəˈsHäsə/ ▶ n. a Brazilian white rum made from sugarcane.

cache /kasH/ ▶ n. **1** a hidden store of things. **2** Computing an auxiliary memory from which high-speed retrieval is possible. ▶ v. store something in a cache.

ca·chet /kaˈsHā/ ▶ n. **1** the state of being respected or admired; prestige: *he would miss the cachet of working at one of the world's best companies.* **2** a distinguishing mark or seal.

ca·chex·i·a /kəˈkeksēə/ ▶ n. Medicine weakness and wasting of the body.

ca·cique /kəˈsēk/ ▶ n. **1** (in Latin America or the Spanish-speaking Caribbean) a native chief. **2** (in Spain or Latin America) a local political boss.

cack·le /'kakəl/ ▶v. **1** laugh in a noisy, harsh way. **2** (of a hen or goose) make a noisy clucking cry. ▶n. a noisy clucking cry or laugh.

ca·coph·o·ny /kə'käfənē/ ▶n. (pl. **cacophonies**) a mixture of loud and unpleasant sounds. ■ **ca·coph·o·nous** /-nəs/ adj.

cac·tus /'kaktəs/ ▶n. (pl. **cacti** /-tī, -tē/ or **cactuses**) a succulent plant with a thick fleshy stem bearing spines but no leaves.

CAD /kad/ ▶abbr. computer-aided design.

cad /kad/ ▶n. dated or humorous a man who behaves dishonorably, especially toward a woman. ■ **cad·dish** adj.

ca·dav·er /kə'davər/ ▶n. Medicine or literary a corpse.

ca·dav·er·ous /kə'davərəs/ ▶adj. very pale, thin, or bony.

cad·die /'kadē/ (also **caddy**) ▶n. (pl. **caddies**) a person who carries a golfer's clubs and provides other assistance during a match. ▶v. (**caddies**, **caddying**, **caddied**) work as a caddie.

cad·dis·fly /'kadis,flī/ ▶n. (pl. **caddisflies**) a small winged insect having larvae that live in water and build cases of sticks, stones, etc.

cad·dy /'kadē/ ▶n. (pl. **caddies**) a small storage container, especially for tea.

ca·dence /'kādns/ ▶n. **1** the rise and fall in pitch of a person's voice. **2** a sequence of notes or chords making up the end of a musical phrase. ■ **ca·denced** adj.

ca·den·za /kə'denzə/ ▶n. a difficult solo passage in a concerto or other musical work, typically near the end.

ca·det /kə'det/ ▶n. **1** a young trainee in the armed services or police. **2** formal or old use a younger son or daughter. ■ **ca·det·ship** /-,SHip/ n.

cadge /kaj/ ▶v. informal ask for or get something without giving anything in return. ■ **cadg·er** n.

cad·mi·um /'kadmēəm/ ▶n. a silvery-white metallic chemical element resembling zinc.

ca·dre /'kadrē, 'käd-, -,rä/ ▶n. **1** a small group of people trained for a particular purpose or profession. **2** a group of activists in a revolutionary organization.

ca·du·ce·us /kə'd(y)ōōsēəs, -sHəs/ ▶n. (pl. **caducei** /-sē,ī, -sHē,ī/) an ancient Greek or Roman herald's wand, typically one with two serpents twined around it, carried by the messenger god Hermes or Mercury.

cae·cum ▶n. (pl. **caeca**) British spelling of CECUM.

Caer·phil·ly /kär'filē/ ▶n. a kind of mild white cheese, originally made in Caerphilly in Wales.

Cae·sar /'sēzər/ ▶n. a title of Roman emperors, especially those from Augustus to Hadrian.

cae·sar·e·an ▶n. variant spelling of CESAREAN.

Cae·sar sal·ad ▶n. a salad consisting of romaine lettuce and croutons served with a dressing of olive oil, lemon juice, raw egg, and Worcestershire sauce.

cae·su·ra /si'zHŏŏrə, -'zŏŏrə/ ▶n. a pause near the middle of a line of verse.

ca·fe /ka'fā, kə-/ (also **café**) ▶n. a small restaurant selling light meals and drinks.

ca·fe so·ci·e·ty ▶n. people who spend a lot of time in fashionable restaurants and nightclubs.

caf·e·te·ri·a /,kafi'ti(ə)rēə/ ▶n. a self-service restaurant.

caf·feine /ka'fēn, 'kaf,ēn/ ▶n. a substance found in tea, coffee, and other plants that stimulates the central nervous system. ■ **caf·fein·at·ed** /'kafə,nātid/ adj.

caf·tan ▶n. variant spelling of KAFTAN.

cage /kāj/ ▶n. **1** a structure of bars or wires in which birds or other animals are confined. **2** any similar structure, especially the compartment in an elevator. ▶v. confine someone or something in a cage.

cag·ey /'kājē/ ▶adj. (**cagier, cagiest**) informal cautiously reluctant to give information: *airlines are cagey about their policy on free upgrades to business class.* ■ **cag·i·ly** /'kājilē/ adv. **cag·i·ness** (also **cageyness**) n.

ca·hoots /kə'hōōts/ ▶pl.n. (in phrase **in cahoots**) informal secretly working to achieve something dishonest or underhanded with others.

cai·man /'kāmən/ (also **cayman**) ▶n. a tropical American reptile similar to an alligator.

Cain /kān/ ▶n. (in phrase **raise Cain**) informal create trouble or a commotion.

ca·ique /kä'ēk, kīk/ ▶n. **1** a light rowboat used on the Bosporus. **2** a small eastern Mediterranean sailing ship.

cairn /ke(ə)rn/ ▶n. **1** a mound of rough stones built as a memorial or landmark. **2** (also **cairn terrier**) a small breed of terrier with a shaggy coat.

cais·son /'kā,sän, 'kāsən/ ▶n. **1** a large watertight chamber in which underwater construction work may be carried out. **2** a vessel or structure used as a gate across the entrance of a dry dock or basin.

ca·jole /kə'jōl/ ▶v. persuade someone to do something by coaxing or flattery. ■ **ca·jol·er·y** n.

Ca·jun /'kājən/ ▶n. a member of a French-speaking community in areas of southern Louisiana, descended from French Canadians. ▶adj. relating to the Cajuns.

cake /kāk/ ▶n. **1** an item of soft sweet food made from baking a mixture of flour, shortening, eggs, and sugar. **2** a flat round item of savory food that is baked or fried. ▶v. (of a thick or sticky substance) cover and form a hard layer on something: *my clothes were caked with mud.* ■ **ca·key** adj. (informal).

– PHRASES **a piece of cake** informal something easily achieved. **sell like hot cakes** informal be sold quickly and in large quantities. **take the cake** surpass or exceed all others.

cake·hole ▶n. chiefly Brit. informal a person's mouth: *shut your cakehole.*

cake·walk /'kāk,wôk/ ▶n. informal a very easy task.

Cal ▶abbr. large calorie(s).

cal ▶abbr. small calorie(s).

cal·a·bash /'kalə,basH/ ▶n. a water container, tobacco pipe, or other object made from the dried shell of a gourd.

cal·a·brese /'kalə,brēz/ ▶n. a bright green variety of broccoli.

cal·a·mine /'kalə,mīn/ ▶n. a pink powder consisting of zinc carbonate and ferric oxide, used to make a soothing lotion.

ca·lam·i·ty /kə'lamitē/ ▶n. (pl. **calamities**) a sudden event causing great damage or distress. ■ **ca·lam·i·tous** /-itəs/ adj. **ca·lam·i·tous·ly** adv.

cal·car·e·ous /kal'ke(ə)rēəs/ ▶adj. containing calcium carbonate; chalky.

cal·cif·er·ol /kal'sifə,rôl, -,rōl/ ▶n. vitamin D_2, essential for the deposition of calcium in bones.

cal·cif·er·ous /kal'sifərəs/ ▶adj. containing or producing calcium salts, especially calcium carbonate.

cal·ci·fy /'kalsə,fī/ ▶ v. (**calcifies, calcifying, calcified**) harden something by a deposit of calcium salts. ■ **cal·ci·fi·ca·tion** /,kalsəfi'kāsHən/ n.

cal·cine /'kal,sīn/ ▶ v. reduce, oxidize, or dry a substance by exposure to strong heat. ■ **cal·ci·na·tion** /kalsə'nāsHən/ n.

cal·cite /'kal,sīt/ ▶ n. a white or colorless mineral consisting of calcium carbonate.

cal·ci·um /'kalsēəm/ ▶ n. a soft gray reactive metallic chemical element.

cal·ci·um car·bon·ate ▶ n. a white insoluble compound occurring naturally as chalk, limestone, marble, and calcite.

cal·cu·late /'kalkyə,lāt/ ▶ v. **1** determine the amount or number of something mathematically. **2** intend an action to have a particular effect: *his words were calculated to hurt her.* **3** (**calculate on**) include something as an essential element in one's plans. ■ **cal·cu·la·ble** /'kalkyələbəl/ adj.

cal·cu·lat·ed /'kalkyə,lātid/ ▶ adj. done with awareness of the likely consequences: *a calculated act of terrorism.* ■ **cal·cu·lat·ed·ly** adv.

cal·cu·lat·ing /'kalkyə,lātiNG/ ▶ adj. shrewdly planning things so as to benefit oneself.

cal·cu·la·tion /,kalkyə'lāsHən/ ▶ n. **1** an act of calculating the amount or number of something mathematically. **2** an assessment of the effects of a course of action.

cal·cu·la·tor /'kalkyə,lātər/ ▶ n. something used for making mathematical calculations, in particular a small electronic device.

cal·cu·lus /'kalkyələs/ ▶ n. **1** (pl. **calculuses**) the branch of mathematics concerned with problems involving rates of variation. **2** (pl. **calculi** /-,lī, -,lē/) a hard mass formed by minerals in the kidney, gall bladder, or other organ of the body.

cal·de·ra /kal'derə, kôl-, -'di(ə)rə/ ▶ n. a large volcanic crater, especially one formed by the collapse of the volcano's mouth.

cal·dron ▶ n. variant spelling of CAULDRON.

Cal·e·do·ni·an /,kalə'dōnēən/ ▶ adj. relating to Scotland or the Scottish Highlands.

cal·en·dar /'kaləndər/ ▶ n. **1** a chart or series of pages showing the days, weeks, and months of a particular year. **2** a system by which the beginning, length, and subdivisions of the year are fixed. **3** a list of special days, events, or activities. ■ **ca·len·dri·cal** /kə'lendrikəl/ adj.

cal·en·der /'kaləndər/ ▶ n. a machine in which cloth or paper is pressed by rollers to glaze or smooth it.

cal·ends /'kaləndz, 'kā-/ (also **kalends**) ▶ pl.n. the first day of the month in the ancient Roman calendar.

ca·len·du·la /kə'lenjələ/ ▶ n. a plant of a family that includes the common marigold.

calf[1] /kaf/ ▶ n. (pl. **calves**) **1** a domestic cow or bull in its first year. **2** the young of some other large mammals, such as elephants.

calf[2] ▶ n. (pl. **calves**) the fleshy part at the back of a person's leg below the knee.

calf·skin /'kaf,skin/ ▶ n. leather made from the hide or skin of a calf.

cal·i·ber /'kaləbər/ (Brit. **calibre**) ▶ n. **1** the quality of something, especially a person's ability: *scholars of the highest caliber.* **2** the diameter of the inside of a gun barrel, or of a bullet or shell.

cal·i·brate /'kalə,brāt/ ▶ v. **1** mark a gauge or instrument with a standard scale of readings.

2 compare the readings of an instrument with those of a standard. ■ **cal·i·bra·tion** /kalə'brāsHən/ n. **cal·i·bra·tor** /-brātər/ n.

cal·i·co /'kali,kō/ ▶ n. (pl. **calicoes** or **calicos**) printed cotton fabric. ▶ adj. (of a cat) multicolored.

cal·i·for·ni·um /,kalə'fôrnēəm/ ▶ n. an unstable, artificially made radioactive metallic chemical element.

cal·i·per /'kaləpər/ (also **calliper**) ▶ n. **1** (also **calipers**) a measuring instrument with two hinged legs and in-turned or out-turned points. **2** a motor-vehicle or bicycle brake consisting of two or more hinged components. **3** a metal support for a person's leg.

ca·liph /'kālif, 'kal-/ ▶ n. historical the chief Muslim civil and religious ruler, regarded as the successor of Muhammad. ■ **cal·iph·ate** /'kālə,fāt, 'kal-, -fit/ n.

cal·is·then·ics /,kaləs'THeniks/ (Brit. **callisthenics**) ▶ pl.n. gymnastic exercises to achieve bodily fitness and grace of movement.

calk ▶ n. & v. variant spelling of CAULK.

call /kôl/ ▶ v. **1** cry out to someone so as to summon them or attract their attention. **2** telephone someone. **3** order or ask someone to go or come somewhere. **4** pay a brief visit. **5** give a specified name or description to: *they called their son David.* **6** fix a date or time for a meeting, election, or strike. **7** predict the outcome of a future event. **8** (of a bird or animal) make its typical cry. **9** inspire or urge someone to do something. ▶ n. **1** an act or instance of calling. **2** the typical cry of a bird or animal. **3** a brief visit. **4** (**call for**) demand or need for: *there is little call for antique furniture.* **5** a vocation: *his call to be a disciple.* ■ **call·er** n. – PHRASES **call for** require; demand. **call something in** require payment of a loan. **call something off** cancel an event or agreement. **call on/upon** turn to someone as a source of help. **call of nature** euphemistic a need to go to the bathroom. **call the shots** (or **tune**) take the initiative in deciding how something should be done. **call someone/thing up 1** summon someone to serve in the army or to play in a team. **2** bring something stored into use. **on call** available to provide a professional service if necessary.

cal·la /'kalə/ ▶ n. a plant of the arum family with a showy white spathe.

call cen·ter ▶ n. an office in which telephone calls are handled for an organization.

call girl ▶ n. a female prostitute who accepts appointments by telephone.

cal·lig·ra·phy /kə'ligrəfē/ ▶ n. decorative handwriting or handwritten lettering. ■ **cal·lig·ra·pher** n. **cal·li·graph·ic** /,kali'grafik/ adj.

call-in ▶ n. a radio or television program during which listeners or viewers can make comments or ask questions by telephoning the studio.

call·ing /'kôliNG/ ▶ n. **1** a profession or occupation. **2** a vocation.

call·ing card ▶ n. **1** a visiting card or business card. **2** a prepaid card allowing the user to make calls from a public telephone.

cal·li·o·pe /kə'līəpē/ ▶ n. chiefly historical an American keyboard instrument resembling an organ but with the notes produced by steam whistles.

call·i·per ▶ n. variant spelling of CALIPER.

call op·tion ▶ n. Stock Market an option to buy assets at an agreed price on or before a particular date.

cal·los·i·ty /kə'läsitē/ ▶ n. (pl. **callosities**) technical a thickened and hardened part of the skin; a callus.

cal·lous /'kaləs/ ▶ adj. insensitive and cruel.
■ **cal·lous·ly** adv. **cal·lous·ness** n.

cal·loused /'kaləst/ (also **callused**) ▶ adj. having hardened skin.

cal·low /'kalō/ ▶ adj. (of a young person) inexperienced and immature.

call sign (also **call signal**) ▶ n. a message or tune that is broadcast by radio to identify the broadcaster or transmitter.

call-up ▶ n. **1** an act of summoning someone or of being summoned to serve in the armed forces or on a sports team. **2** a person so summoned: *De La Rosa was a surprise call-up after the injury to Cabrera.*

cal·lus /'kaləs/ ▶ n. a thickened and hardened part of the skin or soft tissue.

calm /kä(l)m/ ▶ adj. **1** not showing or feeling nervousness, anger, or other emotions. **2** peaceful, quiet, or undisturbed: *the comfortable, calm atmosphere of my home.* **3** (of the weather) without wind. ▶ n. a calm state or period. ▶ v. make or become tranquil and quiet: *I tried to calm her down.* ■ **calm·ly** adv. **calm·ness** n.

calm·a·tive /'kä(l)mətiv/ ▶ adj. (of a drug) having a sedative effect.

ca·lor·ic /kə'lôrik, -'lär-/ ▶ adj. technical relating to heat or calories; calorific.

cal·o·rie /'kal(ə)rē/ ▶ n. (pl. **calories**) **1** (also **large calorie**) a unit of energy equal to the energy needed to raise the temperature of 1 kilogram of water through 1°C (4.1868 kilojoules). **2** (also **small calorie**) a unit of energy equal to one-thousandth of a large calorie.

cal·o·rif·ic /ˌkalə'rifik/ ▶ adj. **1** relating to the amount of energy contained in food or fuel. **2** (of food or drink) high in calories.

cal·o·rim·e·ter /ˌkalə'rimitər/ ▶ n. a device for measuring the amount of heat involved in a chemical reaction or other process.
■ **cal·o·ri·met·ric** /ˌkalərə'metrik/ adj. **cal·o·rim·e·try** /-'rimitrē/ n.

ca·lum·ni·ate /kə'ləmnē,āt/ ▶ v. formal make false and defamatory statements about someone.
■ **ca·lum·ni·a·tor** /-,ātər/ n.

cal·um·ny /'kaləmnē/ ▶ n. (pl. **calumnies**) the making of false statements about someone in order to damage their reputation.
■ **ca·lum·ni·ous** /kə'ləmnēəs/ adj.

Cal·va·dos /ˌkalvə'dōs/ ▶ n. apple brandy, traditionally made in the Calvados region of Normandy.

calve /kav/ ▶ v. **1** give birth to a calf. **2** (of a mass of ice) split off from an iceberg or glacier.

calves /kavz/ ▶ plural of CALF¹, CALF².

Cal·vin·ism /'kalvə,nizəm/ ▶ n. the form of Protestantism of John Calvin (1509–64), centering on the belief that God has decided everything that happens in advance. ■ **Cal·vin·ist** n. **Cal·vin·is·tic** /ˌkalvə'nistik/ adj.

ca·lyp·so /kə'lipsō/ ▶ n. (pl. **calypsos**) a kind of West Indian music or song, typically with improvised words on a topical theme.

ca·lyx /'kāliks, 'kal-/ ▶ n. (pl. **calyces** /'kālə,sēz/ 'kal-/ or **calyxes**) the sepals of a flower, forming a protective layer around a flower in bud.

cal·zo·ne /kal'zōn(ē)/, ▶ n. (pl. **calzoni** /-'zōnē/ or **calzones**) a type of pizza that is folded in half before cooking to contain a filling.

CAM /kam/ ▶ abbr. computer-aided manufacturing.

cam /kam/ ▶ n. **1** a projecting part on a wheel or shaft, designed to come into contact with another part while rotating and cause it to move. **2** a camshaft.

ca·ma·ra·de·rie /ˌkäm(ə)'rädərē, ˌkam-, -'rad-/ ▶ n. trust and friendship between people.

cam·ber /'kambər/ ▶ n. **1** a slightly convex or arched shape of a road or other horizontal surface. **2** the slight sideways inclination of the front wheels of a motor vehicle. ■ **cam·bered** adj.

cam·bi·um /'kambēəm/ ▶ n. (pl. **cambia** /-bēə/ or **cambiums**) a layer of cells in a plant stem, from which new tissue grows by the division of cells.

Cam·bo·di·an /kam'bōdēən/ ▶ n. **1** a person from Cambodia. **2** the Khmer language. ▶ adj. relating to Cambodia.

Cam·bri·an /'kambrēən, 'kām-/ ▶ adj. **1** Welsh. **2** Geology relating to the first period in the Paleozoic era, about 570 to 510 million years ago.

cam·bric /'kāmbrik/ ▶ n. a lightweight, closely woven white linen or cotton fabric.

cam·cord·er /'kam,kôrdər/ ▶ n. a portable combined video camera and video recorder.

came /kām/ ▶ past tense of COME.

cam·el /'kaməl/ ▶ n. a large mammal of arid country, with a long neck and either one or two humps on the back.

cam·el hair ▶ n. **1** a fabric made from the hair of a camel. **2** fine, soft hair from a squirrel's tail, used in artists' brushes.

ca·mel·lia /kə'mēlyə/ ▶ n. an evergreen shrub with showy flowers and shiny leaves.

Cam·em·bert /'kaməm,be(ə)r/ ▶ n. a kind of rich, soft, creamy cheese originally made near Camembert in Normandy.

cam·e·o /'kamē,ō/ ▶ n. (pl. **cameos**) **1** a piece of jewelry consisting of a carving of a head shown in profile against a background of a different color. **2** a short descriptive written sketch. **3** a small part in a play or movie for a distinguished actor.

cam·er·a /'kam(ə)rə/ ▶ n. a device for taking photographs or recording moving images.
■ **cam·er·a·man** n. (pl. **cameramen**).
– PHRASES **in cam·er·a** chiefly Law in private, in particular in the private rooms of a judge.

cam·er·a ob·scu·ra /əb'skyo͝orə/ ▶ n. a darkened box or building with a lens or opening for projecting the image of an external object onto a screen inside.

cam·er·a-read·y ▶ adj. (of material to be printed) in the right form to be reproduced photographically onto a printing plate.

Cam·e·roon·i·an /ˌkamə'ro͞onēən/ ▶ n. a person from Cameroon, a country on the west coast of Africa. ▶ adj. relating to Cameroon.

cam·i·sole /'kamə,sōl/ ▶ n. a woman's loose-fitting undergarment for the upper body.

cam·o·mile /'kamə,mēl, -,mīl/ ▶ n. variant spelling of CHAMOMILE.

cam·ou·flage /'kamə,fläzн, -,fläj/ ▶ n. **1** the disguising of military forces and equipment by painting or covering them to make them blend in with their surroundings. **2** clothing or materials used as camouflage. **3** the natural coloring or form of an animal that enables it to blend in with its surroundings. ▶v. hide or disguise someone or something by means of camouflage.

camp[1] /kamp/ ▶n. **1** a place with temporary accommodations of tents, huts, etc., for soldiers, refugees, or travelers. **2** a recreational facility with outdoor activities, sports, crafts, etc., and rustic overnight accommodations. **3** the supporters of a particular party or set of beliefs: *the liberal and conservative camps.* ▶v. stay in a tent or camper while on vacation.
– PHRASES **break camp** take down a tent or the tents of an encampment ready to leave.

camp[2] informal ▶adj. **1** (of a man) effeminate in an exaggerated or flamboyant way. **2** deliberately exaggerated and theatrical in style. ▶n. camp behavior or style. ▶v. (usu. **camp it up**) behave in a camp way. ■ **camp·y** adj.

cam·paign /kamˈpān/ ▶n. **1** a series of military operations intended to achieve an objective in a particular area. **2** an organized course of action to achieve a goal. ▶v. work in an organized way toward a goal: *groups that campaigned for cheaper anti-AIDS drugs.* ■ **cam·paign·er** n.

cam·pa·ni·le /ˌkampəˈnēlē, -ˈnēl/ ▶n. a bell tower, especially one that is separate from a church or other building.

cam·pa·nol·o·gy /ˌkampəˈnäləjē/ ▶n. the art or practice of bell-ringing. ■ **cam·pa·nol·o·gist** n.

cam·pan·u·la /kamˈpanyələ/ ▶n. another term for BELLFLOWER.

camp·er /ˈkampər/ ▶n. **1** a person who spends a vacation in a tent or camp. **2** a large motor vehicle with facilities for sleeping and cooking while camping.
– PHRASES **happy camper** a comfortable, contented person.

cam·pe·si·no /ˌkampəˈsēnō, ˌkäm-/ ▶n. (pl. **campesinos**) (in Spanish-speaking countries) a peasant farmer.

camp·fire /ˈkampˌfī(ə)r/ ▶n. an open-air fire in a camp.

camp fol·low·er ▶n. **1** a civilian working in or attached to a military camp. **2** a person who associates with a group without making a full contribution to its activities.

camp·ground /ˈkampˌground/ ▶n. a place used for camping, especially one with some common facilities for campers.

cam·phor /ˈkamfər/ ▶n. a white substance with an aromatic smell and bitter taste, used in insect repellents.

cam·pi·on /ˈkampēən/ ▶n. a plant of the pink family, typically having pink or white flowers with notched petals.

camp·site /ˈkampˌsīt/ ▶n. a place used for camping, especially one equipped for vacationers.

cam·pus /ˈkampəs/ ▶n. (pl. **campuses**) **1** the grounds and buildings of a college or university. **2** a branch or area of a university away from the main site.

cam·py·lo·bac·ter /ˈkampələˌbaktər, kamˈpilə-/ ▶n. a genus of bacterium that sometimes causes food poisoning in humans and abortion in animals.

cam·shaft /ˈkamˌSHaft/ ▶n. a shaft with one or more cams attached to it, especially one operating the valves in an internal-combustion engine.

can[1] /kan/ ▶modal v. (3rd sing. present **can**; past **could** /kŏŏd/) **1** be able to. **2** used to express doubt or surprise: *he can't have finished.* **3** used to indicate that something is typically the case: *he could be very moody.* **4** be permitted to.

USAGE
The verb **can** is chiefly used to mean 'be able to,' as in *can he move?* (i.e. is he physically able to move?). Although it is not wrong to use **can** when requesting permission, it is more polite to say **may** (i.e. *may we leave now?* rather than *can we leave now?*).

can[2] ▶n. **1** a cylindrical metal container, in particular one in which food or drink is sealed for long-term storage. **2** (**the can**) informal prison. **3** (**the can**) informal the toilet. ▶v. (**cans, canning, canned**) **1** preserve food in a can. **2** informal dismiss (someone) from their job. ■ **can·ner** n.
– PHRASES **a can of worms** a complex matter that is full of possible problems. **in the can** informal on tape or film and ready to be broadcast or released.

Can·a·da goose /ˈkanədə/ ▶n. a common brownish-gray North American goose with a black head and neck and a loud trumpeting call.

Ca·na·di·an /kəˈnādēən/ ▶n. a person from Canada. ▶adj. relating to Canada. ■ **Ca·na·di·an·ism** /kəˈnādēəˌnizəm/ n.

ca·nal /kəˈnal/ ▶n. **1** a waterway cut through land for the passage of boats or for conveying water for irrigation. **2** a tubular passage in a plant or animal conveying food, liquid, or air.

can·al·ize /ˈkanəlˌīz/ ▶v. **1** convert a river into a canal. **2** convey something through a duct or channel. ■ **ca·nal·i·za·tion** /ˌkanl-əˈzāSHən/ n.

can·a·pé /ˈkanəˌpā, -ˌpē/ ▶n. a small piece of bread or pastry with a savory topping, often served with drinks.

ca·nard /kəˈnär(d)/ ▶n. an unfounded rumor or story.

ca·nar·y /kəˈne(ə)rē/ ▶n. (pl. **canaries**) **1** a bright yellow finch with a tuneful song, popular as a cage bird. **2** (also **canary yellow**) a bright yellow color.

ca·nas·ta /kəˈnastə/ ▶n. a card game resembling rummy, using two packs and usually played by two pairs of partners.

can·can /ˈkanˌkan/ ▶n. a lively, high-kicking stage dance originating in 19th-century Parisian music halls.

can·cel /ˈkansəl/ ▶v. (**cancels, canceling, canceled**) **1** decide that a planned event will not take place. **2** withdraw from or end a formal arrangement. **3** (**cancel something out**) have an equal but opposite effect on: *the heat given off by the fan motor probably cancels out any cooling effect.* **4** mark a stamp, ticket, etc., to show that it has been used and is no longer valid. ■ **can·cel·la·tion** /ˌkansəˈlāSHən/ n. **can·cel·er** /ˈkansələr/ n.

Can·cer /ˈkansər/ ▶n. **1** a constellation and the fourth sign of the zodiac (the Crab), which the sun enters about June 21. **2** (**a Cancer**) a person born when the sun is in this sign. ■ **Can·cer·i·an** /kanˈse(ə)rēən, -ˈsi(ə)r-/ n. & adj.

can·cer /ˈkansər/ ▶n. **1** a disease caused by an uncontrolled division of abnormal cells in a part of the body. **2** a malignant growth or tumor resulting from an uncontrolled division of cells. **3** something evil or destructive that is hard to contain or destroy: *the cancer of racism.* ■ **can·cer·ous** adj.

can·de·la /kan'dēlə, -'delə/ ▶ n. Physics the SI unit of luminous intensity.

can·de·la·brum /ˌkandə'läbrəm, -'lab-/ ▶ n. (pl. **candelabra** /-'läbrə, -'labrə/) a large candlestick or other holder for several candles or lights.

> **USAGE**
> **Candelabrum** is a Latin word, and the correct plural is **candelabra**, but people often incorrectly think that the singular form is **candelabra** and therefore its plural is **candelabras**.

can·did /'kandid/ ▶ adj. truthful and straightforward; frank. ■ **can·did·ly** adv.

can·di·da /'kandidə/ ▶ n. a yeastlike parasitic fungus that sometimes causes thrush.

can·di·date /'kandi,dāt, -dit/ ▶ n. 1 a person who applies for a job or is nominated for election. 2 a person or thing regarded as suitable for something or likely to experience a particular fate: *she was the perfect candidate for a biography.* ■ **can·di·da·cy** /'kandidəsē/ n.

can·di·di·a·sis /ˌkandi'dīəsis/ ▶ n. infection with candida, especially as causing oral or vaginal thrush.

can·died /'kandēd/ ▶ adj. (of fruit) preserved in a sugar syrup.

can·dle /'kandl/ ▶ n. a stick or block of wax or tallow with a central wick that is lit to produce light as it burns.
– PHRASES **cannot hold a candle to** informal be not nearly as good as: *the song can't hold a candle to James Taylor's 'Fire and Rain.'*

can·dle·light /'kandl,līt/ ▶ n. dim light provided by a candle or candles. ■ **can·dle·lit** /'kandl,lit/ adj.

Can·dle·mas /'kandlməs/ ▶ n. a Christian festival held on February 2 to commemorate the purification of the Virgin Mary and the presentation of Jesus in the Temple.

can·dle·pow·er /'kandl,pou(ə)r/ ▶ n. the illuminating power of a light source, expressed in candelas (formerly candles).

can·dle·stick /'kandl,stik/ ▶ n. a support or holder for a candle.

can·dle·wick /'kandl,wik/ ▶ n. a thick, soft cotton fabric with a raised, tufted pattern.

can·dor /'kandər, -,dôr/ ▶ n. the quality of being open and honest.

can·dy /'kandē/ ▶ n. (pl. **candies**) a sweet food made with sugar or syrup combined with fruit, chocolate, or nuts.

can·dy ap·ple ▶ n. 1 an apple coated with a thin layer of cooked sugar or caramel and fixed on a stick. 2 (also **candy-apple red**) a bright red color.

can·dy-striped ▶ adj. patterned with alternating stripes of white and another color, typically pink.

can·dy-strip·er /'strīpər/ ▶ n. informal a teenage girl who does volunteer nursing in a hospital.

can·dy·tuft /'kandē,təft/ ▶ n. a plant with small heads of white, pink, or purple flowers.

cane /kān/ ▶ n. 1 the hollow jointed stem of tall reeds, grasses, etc., especially bamboo. 2 the slender, flexible stem of plants such as rattan. 3 a woody stem of a raspberry or related plant. 4 a length of cane or a stick used as a support for plants, a walking stick, or for hitting someone as a punishment. ▶ v. hit someone with a cane as a punishment. ■ **can·er** n.

caned /kānd/ ▶ adj. (of furniture) made or repaired with cane.

can·id /'kanid, 'kā-/ ▶ n. Zoology a mammal of the dog family; a canine.

ca·nine /'kā,nīn/ ▶ adj. relating to or resembling a dog or dogs. ▶ n. 1 a dog or other animal of the dog family. 2 (also **canine tooth**) a pointed tooth between the incisors and premolars.

can·is·ter /'kanəstər/ ▶ n. a round or cylindrical container.

can·ker /'kaNGkər/ ▶ n. 1 a destructive fungal disease of trees that results in damage to the bark. 2 a condition in animals that causes open sores. 3 an evil or corrupting influence: *you're tainted with the canker of rebellion.* ▶ v. become infected with canker.

can·na /'kanə/ ▶ n. a lilylike tropical American plant with bright flowers and ornamental leaves.

can·na·bis /'kanəbəs/ ▶ n. a drug obtained from the hemp plant.

canned /kand/ ▶ adj. 1 preserved in a sealed can. 2 informal, chiefly derogatory (of music, applause, or laughter) prerecorded.

can·nel·li·ni bean /ˌkanl'ēnē/ ▶ n. a kidney-shaped bean of a creamy-white variety.

can·nel·lo·ni /ˌkanl'ōnē/ ▶ pl.n. rolls of pasta stuffed with a meat or vegetable mixture, typically cooked in a cheese sauce.

can·ner·y /'kanərē/ ▶ n. (pl. **canneries**) a factory where food is canned.

can·ni·bal /'kanəbəl/ ▶ n. a person who eats the flesh of other human beings. ■ **can·ni·bal·ism** /-,lizəm/ n. **can·ni·bal·is·tic** /ˌkanəbə'listik/ adj.

can·ni·bal·ize /'kanəbə,līz/ ▶ v. 1 use a machine as a source of spare parts for another machine. 2 (of an animal) eat an animal of its own kind. ■ **can·ni·bal·i·za·tion** /ˌkanəbələ'zāsHən/ n.

can·no·li /kə'nōlē/ ▶ pl.n. Italian pastries in the form of tubular shells filled with sweetened ricotta cheese and often containing nuts, citron, or chocolate bits.

can·non /'kanən/ ▶ n. (pl. usu. same) 1 a large, heavy gun formerly used in warfare. 2 a heavy automatic gun that fires shells from an aircraft or tank.

can·non·ade /ˌkanə'nād/ ▶ n. a period of continuous heavy gunfire.

can·non·ball /'kanən,bôl/ ▶ n. a metal or stone ball fired from a cannon.

can·non fod·der ▶ n. soldiers regarded only as a resource to be used up in war.

can·not /kə'nät, 'kan,ät/ ▶ contr. can not.

can·nu·la /'kanyələ/ ▶ n. (pl. **cannulae** /-lē, -lī/ or **cannulas**) a thin tube put into the body to administer medication, drain off fluid, or insert a surgical instrument.

can·ny /'kanē/ ▶ adj. (**cannier, canniest**) shrewd, especially in financial or business matters. ■ **can·ni·ly** adv. **can·ni·ness** n.

ca·noe /kə'noo/ ▶ n. a narrow shallow boat with pointed ends, propelled by a paddle or paddles. ▶ v. (**canoes, canoeing, canoed**) travel in or paddle a canoe. ■ **ca·no·er** n. **ca·noe·ist** n.

can·o·la /kə'nōlə/ ▶ n. oilseed rape of a variety developed in Canada and grown in North America. It yields a valuable cooking oil.

can·on¹ /'kanən/ ▶ n. 1 a general rule or principle by which something is judged: *his designs break the canons of fashion.* 2 the works of a particular author or artist that are recognized as genuine.

3 a list of literary works considered to be permanently established as being of the highest quality. **4** a Church decree or law. **5** a piece of music in which a theme is taken up by two or more parts that overlap.

can·on² ▶ n. **1** a member of the clergy on the staff of a cathedral. **2** (also **canon regular** or **regular canon**) (fem. **canoness**) a member of certain orders of Roman Catholic clergy that live communally like monks or nuns.

ca·non·ic /kə'nänik/ ▶ adj. **1** in the form of a musical canon. **2** another term for CANONICAL. ■ **can·on·ic·i·ty** /ˌkanə'nisitē/ n.

ca·non·i·cal /kə'nänikəl/ ▶ adj. **1** accepted as being authentic or established as a standard: *the canonical works of science fiction.* **2** according to the laws of the Christian Church. ■ **ca·non·i·cal·ly** adv.

can·on·ize /'kanəˌnīz/ ▶ v. (in the Roman Catholic Church) officially declare a dead person to be a saint. ■ **can·on·i·za·tion** /ˌkanənə'zāsHən/ n.

can·on law ▶ n. the laws of the Christian Church.

ca·noo·dle /kə'no͞odl/ ▶ v. informal kiss and cuddle amorously.

can·o·py /'kanəpē/ ▶ n. (pl. **canopies**) **1** a cloth covering hung or held up over a throne or bed. **2** a rooflike projection or shelter. **3** the part of a parachute that opens. **4** the top branches of the trees in a forest, forming an almost continuous layer of foliage. ■ **can·o·pied** adj.

cant¹ /kant/ ▶ n. **1** insincere talk about moral or religious matters. **2** derogatory the language specific to a particular group: *thieves' cant.*

cant² ▶ v. be or cause to be in a slanting position; tilt. ▶ n. a slope or tilt.

can't /kant/ ▶ contr. cannot.

can·ta·bi·le /kän'täbəˌlā/ ▶ adv. & adj. Music in a smooth singing style.

can·ta·loupe /'kantlˌōp/ ▶ n. a small round variety of melon with orange flesh and ribbed skin.

can·tan·ker·ous /kan'taNGkərəs/ ▶ adj. bad-tempered, argumentative, and uncooperative. ■ **can·tan·ker·ous·ly** adv. **can·tan·ker·ous·ness** n.

can·ta·ta /kən'tätə/ ▶ n. a narrative or descriptive piece of accompanied vocal music, typically for solos, chorus, and orchestra.

can·teen /kan'tēn/ ▶ n. **1** a restaurant in a military camp, workplace, school, or factory. **2** a small water bottle, as used by soldiers or campers.

can·ter /'kantər/ ▶ n. a pace of a horse between a trot and a gallop, with not less than one foot on the ground at any time. ▶ v. move at a canter.

Can·ter·bur·y bell /'kantərˌberē, -bərē/ ▶ n. a tall cultivated bellflower with large pale blue flowers.

can·ti·cle /'kantikəl/ ▶ n. a hymn or chant forming a regular part of a church service.

can·ti·le·ver /'kantlˌēvər, -ˌevər/ ▶ n. **1** a long projecting beam or girder fixed at only one end, used in bridge construction. **2** a bracket or beam projecting from a wall to support a balcony, cornice, etc. ▶ v. support something by a cantilever or cantilevers.

can·to /'kanˌtō/ ▶ n. (pl. **cantos**) one of the sections into which some long poems are divided.

can·ton /'kantn, 'kanˌtän/ ▶ n. a political or administrative subdivision of a country, especially in Switzerland.

Can·ton·ese /ˌkantn'ēz, -'ēs/ ▶ n. (pl. same) **1** a person from Canton (another name for Guangzhou), a city in China. **2** a form of Chinese spoken mainly in SE China and Hong Kong. ▶ adj. relating to Canton or Cantonese.

can·ton·ment /kan'tōnmənt, -'tän-/ ▶ n. (especially in the Indian subcontinent) a military garrison or camp.

can·tor /'kantər/ ▶ n. **1** an official who sings liturgical music and leads prayer in a Jewish synagogue. **2** a person who sings solo verses to which the choir or congregation in a Christian service responds.

Ca·nuck /kə'nək/ ▶ n. informal, often derogatory in the US a Canadian, especially a French Canadian.

can·vas /'kanvəs/ ▶ n. (pl. **canvases** or **canvasses**) **1** a strong, coarse unbleached cloth used to make sails, tents, etc., and as a surface for oil painting. **2** an oil painting on canvas. **3** (**the canvas**) the floor of a boxing or wrestling ring, having a canvas covering. **4** either of the tapering ends of a rowboat used in racing.
– PHRASES **under canvas** in a tent or tents.

can·vas·back /'kanvəsˌbak/ ▶ n. a North American diving duck with a long, sloping black bill and a light gray back.

can·vass /'kanvəs/ ▶ v. **1** visit someone to seek their vote in an election. **2** question someone to find out their opinion. ▶ n. an act of canvassing. ■ **can·vass·er** n.

can·yon /'kanyən/ ▶ n. a deep gorge, especially one with a river flowing through it.

can·yon·eer·ing /'kanyənˌniNG/ ▶ n. (also **canyoning**) the sport of following the stream down a canyon by means of such techniques as climbing, rappelling, jumping, and swimming.

CAP ▶ abbr. Civil Air Patrol.

cap¹ /kap/ ▶ n. **1** a soft, flat hat with a peak. **2** a soft, close-fitting head covering worn for a particular purpose: *a shower cap.* **3** a lid or cover for a bottle, pen, etc. **4** the broad upper part of a mushroom or toadstool. **5** an upper limit imposed on spending or borrowing. **6** (also **percussion cap**) a small amount of explosive powder in a metal or paper case that explodes when struck. ▶ v. (**caps, capping, capped**) **1** put or form a cap, lid, or cover on something. **2** provide a fitting climax to: *she capped a phenomenal year with three Oscar nominations.* **3** place a limit on prices or expenditure. ■ **cap·ful** n. **cap·per** n.
– PHRASES **cap in hand** humbly asking for a favor. **set one's cap at someone** dated (of a woman) try to attract a man.

cap² /kap/ ▶ n. Finance short for CAPITALIZATION: *mid-cap companies.*

ca·pa·bil·i·ty /ˌkāpə'bilitē/ ▶ n. (pl. **capabilities**) the power or ability to do something.

ca·pa·ble /'kāpəbəl/ ▶ adj. **1** (**capable of**) having the ability or quality necessary to do: *I'm quite capable of taking care of myself.* **2** able to achieve whatever one has to do; competent. ■ **ca·pa·bly** /-blē/ adv.

ca·pa·cious /kə'pāsHəs/ ▶ adj. having a lot of space inside; roomy.

ca·pac·i·tance /kə'pasitəns/ ▶ n. the ability of a system to store electric charge, equivalent to the ratio of the change in electric charge to the corresponding change in electric potential.

ca·pac·i·tor /kə'pasitər/ ▸ n. a device used to store electric charge.

ca·pac·i·ty /kə'pasitē/ ▸ n. (pl. **capacities**) **1** the maximum amount that something can contain or produce: *the room was filled to capacity.* **2** the ability or power to do something. **3** a specified role or position: *I was engaged in a voluntary capacity.* ▸ adj. fully occupying the available space: *a capacity crowd.*

ca·par·i·son /kə'parəsən/ ▸ v. (**be caparisoned**) be dressed in rich decorative coverings or clothes.

cape[1] /kāp/ ▸ n. a short cloak. ■ **caped** adj.

cape[2] ▸ n. a piece of land that projects into the sea; a headland.

Cape goose·ber·ry ▸ n. the edible yellow berry of a tropical South American plant, enclosed in a lantern-shaped husk.

cap·e·lin /'kap(ə)lən/ ▸ n. a small food fish of the smelt family, found in North Atlantic coastal waters.

cap·el·li·ni /ˌkapə'lēnē/ ▸ pl.n. pasta in the form of very thin strands.

ca·per[1] /'kāpər/ ▸ v. skip or dance around in a lively or playful way. ▸ n. **1** a playful skipping movement. **2** informal a lighthearted or illicit activity, or a movie or novel portraying one: *a futuristic crime caper.* ■ **ca·per·er** n.

ca·per[2] ▸ n. a pickled flower bud of a southern European shrub, used in sauces and as a garnish.

cap·er·cail·lie /ˌkapər'kāl(y)ē/ ▸ n. (pl. **capercaillies**) a large turkeylike grouse of pine forests in northern Europe.

cap·il·lar·i·ty /ˌkapə'laritē/ ▸ n. the tendency of a liquid in a narrow tube or absorbent material to rise or fall as a result of surface tension.

cap·il·lar·y /'kapəˌlerē/ ▸ n. (pl. **capillaries**) **1** any of the fine branching blood vessels that form a network between the arteries and veins. **2** (also **capillary tube**) a tube with an internal diameter of hairlike thinness.

cap·il·lar·y ac·tion ▸ n. another term for CAPILLARITY.

cap·i·tal[1] /'kapitl/ ▸ n. **1** the main city or town of a country or region, typically where the government is based. **2** wealth owned by a person or organization or invested, lent, or borrowed. **3** the amount by which a company's assets exceeds its liabilities. **4** a capital letter. ▸ adj. **1** (of an offense) punishable by death. **2** (of a letter of the alphabet) large in size and of the form used to begin sentences and names. **3** informal, dated excellent. – PHRASES **make capital out of** use something to one's advantage.

cap·i·tal[2] ▸ n. the top part of a pillar or column.

cap·i·tal gain ▸ n. a profit from the sale of property or an investment.

cap·i·tal goods ▸ pl.n. goods that are used in producing other goods, rather than being bought by consumers.

cap·i·tal·ism /'kapətlˌizəm/ ▸ n. an economic and political system in which a country's trade and industry are controlled by private owners for profit. ■ **cap·i·tal·ist** /'kapətlist/ n. & adj. **cap·i·tal·is·tic** /ˌkapətl'istik/ adj.

cap·i·tal·ize /'kapətlˌīz/ ▸ v. **1** (**capitalize on**) take advantage of: *the software lets you capitalize on new customer opportunities.* **2** provide a company with financial capital. **3** convert income into financial capital. **4** write or print a word or letter in capital letters or with an initial capital. ■ **cap·i·tal·i·za·tion** /ˌkapətl-ə'zāSHən/ n.

cap·i·tal pun·ish·ment ▸ n. the punishment of a crime by death.

cap·i·tal sum ▸ n. a lump sum of money payable to an insured person or paid as an initial fee or investment.

cap·i·ta·tion /ˌkapi'tāSHən/ ▸ n. the payment of a fee or grant to a doctor, school, etc., the amount being determined by the number of people that are served.

cap·i·tol /'kapitl/ ▸ n. **1** a building housing a legislative assembly. **2** (**the Capitol**) the seat of the US Congress in Washington DC.

ca·pit·u·late /kə'piCHəˌlāt/ ▸ v. give in to an opponent or an unwelcome demand. ■ **ca·pit·u·la·tion** n. **ca·pit·u·la·tor** n.

cap'n /'kapn/ ▸ n. informal contraction of captain, used in representing speech.

ca·po[1] /'kāpō, 'käpō/ ▸ n. (pl. **capos**) a clamp fastened across all the strings of a guitar or similar instrument to raise their tuning.

ca·po[2] ▸ n. (pl. **capos**) the head of a branch of the Mafia.

ca·po·ei·ra /ˌkäpōō'ārə/ ▸ n. a martial art and dance form originating among Angolan slaves in Brazil.

ca·pon /'kā,pän, -pən/ ▸ n. a domestic cock that has been castrated and fattened for eating.

cap·puc·ci·no /ˌkäpə'CHēnō, ˌkap-/ ▸ n. (pl. **cappuccinos**) coffee made with milk that has been frothed up with pressurized steam.

ca·pric·ci·o /kə'prēCHē,ō, -CHō/ ▸ n. (pl. **capriccios**) **1** a lively piece of music, typically one that is short and free in form. **2** a painting or other work of art representing a fantasy or a mixture of real and imaginary features.

ca·price /kə'prēs/ ▸ n. a sudden change of mood or behavior.

ca·pri·cious /kə'priSHəs, -'prē-/ ▸ adj. prone to sudden changes of mood or behavior. ■ **ca·pri·cious·ly** adv. **ca·pri·cious·ness** n.

Cap·ri·corn /'kaprē,kôrn/ ▸ n. **1** a constellation and the tenth sign of the zodiac (the Goat), which the sun enters about December 21. **2** (**a Capricorn**) a person born when the sun is in this sign. ■ **Cap·ri·corn·i·an** /ˌkaprē'kôrnēən/n. & adj.

ca·prine /'kap,rīn/ ▸ adj. relating to or resembling a goat or goats.

ca·pri pants /kə'prē/ (also **capris**) ▸ pl.n. close-fitting calf-length tapered pants for women.

caps /kaps/ ▸ abbr. capital letters.

cap·si·cum /'kapsikəm/ ▸ n. (pl. **capsicums**) a sweet pepper or chili pepper.

cap·size /'kap,sīz, kap'sīz/ ▸ v. (of a boat) be overturned in the water.

cap sleeve ▸ n. a sleeve that extends a short distance from the shoulder and tapers to nothing under the arm.

cap·stan /'kapstən/ ▸ n. a broad revolving cylinder with a vertical axis, used for winding a rope or cable.

cap·stone /'kap,stōn/ ▸ n. a stone fixed on top of a wall or prehistoric tomb.

cap·sule /'kapsəl, 'kap,sŏŏl/ ▸ n. **1** a small case or container. **2** a small case of gelatin containing a dose of medicine, which dissolves after it is swallowed. **3** Botany a dry fruit that releases its seeds by bursting open when ripe. ▸ adj. brief, condensed, or compact: *a capsule review of the movie.* ■ **cap·su·lar** adj.

cap·sul·ize /'kapsə,līz/ ▶v. put information in compact form.

Capt. ▶abbr. captain.

cap·tain /'kaptən/ ▶n. 1 the person in command of a ship or civil aircraft. 2 a rank of naval officer above commander and below commodore. 3 a rank of officer in the US Army, Marine Corps, or Air Force above lieutenant and below major. 4 the leader of a team, especially in sports. 5 a police officer in charge of a precinct. ▶v. be the captain of a ship, aircraft, or team. ■ **cap·tain·cy** /-tənsē/ n.

cap·tion /'kapsHən/ ▶n. 1 a title or brief explanation accompanying an illustration or cartoon. 2 a piece of text appearing on screen as part of a movie or television broadcast. ▶v. provide an illustration with a title or explanation.

cap·tious /'kapsHəs/ ▶adj. formal tending to find fault or raise petty objections.

cap·ti·vate /'kaptə,vāt/ ▶v. attract and hold the interest of someone; charm. ■ **cap·ti·va·ting** adj. **cap·ti·va·tion** /,kaptə'vāsHən/ n.

cap·tive /'kaptiv/ ▶n. a person who has been taken prisoner or held in confinement. ▶adj. 1 imprisoned or confined. 2 not free to choose an alternative: *a captive audience.* ■ **cap·tiv·i·ty** /kap'tivitē/ n.

cap·tor /'kaptər, -,tôr/ ▶n. a person who captures or confines another.

cap·ture /'kapcHər/ ▶v. 1 take control of something by force. 2 take someone prisoner. 3 record accurately in words or pictures: *the illustrations capture the dogs' antics.* 4 cause data to be stored in a computer. ▶n. the action of capturing or the state of being captured. ■ **cap·tur·er** n.

Cap·u·chin /'kap(y)əsHən, kə'p(y)ōō-/ ▶n. 1 a friar belonging to a strict branch of the Franciscan order. 2 (**capuchin**) a South American monkey with a hoodlike cap of hair on the head.

cap·y·ba·ra /'kapə,berə, -,bärə/ ▶n. (pl. same or **capybaras**) a large South American rodent resembling a long-legged guinea pig.

car /kär/ ▶n. 1 an automobile. 2 a vehicle that runs on rails, especially one that is part of a train.

car·a·bi·ner /,karə'bēnər/ ▶n. variant spelling of KARABINER.

ca·ra·bi·nie·re /,karəbən'ye(ə)rē/ ▶n. (pl. **carabinieri** pronunc. same) a member of the Italian paramilitary police.

car·a·cal /'karə,kal/ ▶n. a brown lynxlike cat with black tufted ears, native to Africa and western Asia.

car·a·cul ▶n. variant spelling of KARAKUL.

ca·rafe /kə'raf, -'räf/ ▶n. an open-topped glass flask used for serving wine or water in a restaurant.

ca·ram·bo·la /,karəm'bōlə/ ▶n. a golden-yellow fruit with a star-shaped cross section; starfruit.

car·a·mel /'karəməl, -,mel, 'kärməl/ ▶n. 1 a soft toffee made with sugar and butter. 2 sugar or syrup heated until it turns brown, used as a flavoring or coloring for food. ■ **car·a·mel·ize** /'karəmə,līz, 'kärmə-/ v.

car·a·pace /'karə,pās/ ▶n. the hard upper shell of a tortoise, lobster, or other animal.

car·at /'karət/ ▶n. 1 a unit of weight for precious stones and pearls, equivalent to 200 milligrams. 2 chiefly British spelling of KARAT.

car·a·van /'karə,van/ ▶n. 1 a group of people traveling together. 2 Brit. a recreational vehicle or camper; a travel trailer. ■ **car·a·van·ner** n. **car·a·van·ning** n.

car·a·van·sa·ry /,karə'vansərē/ (chiefly Brit. also **caravanserai** /-sə,rī/) ▶n. (pl. **caravansaries** or **caravanserais**) 1 a group of people traveling together; a caravan. 2 historical an inn with a central courtyard in the deserts of Asia or North Africa.

car·a·vel /'karə,vel, -vəl/ (also **carvel** /'kärvel/) ▶n. a small, fast Spanish or Portuguese sailing ship of the 15th–17th centuries.

car·a·way /'karə,wā/ ▶n. the seeds of a plant of the parsley family, used for flavoring.

car·bide /'kär,bīd/ ▶n. a compound of carbon with a metal or other element.

car·bine /'kär,bīn, -,bēn/ ▶n. 1 a light automatic rifle. 2 historical a short rifle or musket used by cavalry.

car·bo·hy·drate /,kärbə'hī,drāt/ ▶n. any of a large group of compounds (including sugars, starch, and cellulose) that contain carbon, hydrogen, and oxygen, found in food and used to give energy.

car·bol·ic ac·id /kär'bälik/ (also **carbolic**) ▶n. phenol, used as a disinfectant.

carbo-load /'kärbō,lōd/ ▶v. eat large amounts of carbohydrates, especially in preparation for athletic endurance.

car·bon /'kärbən/ ▶n. 1 a nonmetallic chemical element that has two main forms (diamond and graphite) and is present in all organic compounds. 2 carbon dioxide or other gaseous substances released into the atmosphere.

car·bo·na·ceous /,kärbə'nāsHəs/ ▶adj. consisting of or containing carbon or its compounds.

car·bo·na·ra /,kärbə'närə, -'narə/ ▶n. a pasta sauce made with bacon or ham, egg, and cream.

car·bo·nate /'kärbənət, -,nāt/ ▶n. a compound containing CO_3 negative ions together with a metallic element. ■ **car·bo·na·tion** /,kärbə'nāsHən/ n.

car·bo·nat·ed /'kärbə,nātid/ ▶adj. (of a drink) containing dissolved carbon dioxide and therefore fizzy.

car·bon black ▶n. a fine carbon powder used as a pigment.

car·bon cop·y ▶n. 1 a copy made with carbon paper. 2 a person or thing identical to another.

car·bon dat·ing (also **radiocarbon dating**) ▶n. a method of determining the age of an organic object by measuring the amount of radioactive carbon-14 that it contains.

car·bon di·ox·ide ▶n. a colorless, odorless gas produced by burning carbon and organic compounds and by breathing, and absorbed by plants in photosynthesis.

car·bon fi·ber ▶n. a material consisting of thin, strong crystalline filaments of carbon.

car·bon foot·print ▶n. the amount of carbon dioxide emitted due to the the consumption of fossil fuels by a particular person or group.

car·bon·ic /kär'bänik/ ▶adj. relating to carbon or carbon dioxide.

car·bon·ic ac·id ▶n. a very weak acid formed when carbon dioxide dissolves in water.

Car·bon·if·er·ous /ˌkärbəˈnifərəs/ ▶ adj. Geology relating to the fifth period of the Paleozoic era (about 363 to 290 million years ago), when extensive coal-bearing strata were formed.

car·bon·ize /ˈkärbəˌnīz/ ▶ v. convert something into carbon, typically by heating or burning. ■ **car·bon·i·za·tion** /ˌkärbənəˈzāsʜən/ n.

car·bon mon·ox·ide ▶ n. an odorless toxic flammable gas formed by incomplete burning of carbon.

car·bon-neu·tral ▶ adj. making no net release of carbon dioxide to the atmosphere, especially through offsetting emissions by planting trees.

car·bon off·set·ting ▶ n. the counteracting of carbon dioxide emissions by doing something that reduces carbon dioxide in the atmosphere by an equivalent amount, e.g., planting trees.

car·bon pa·per ▶ n. thin paper coated with carbon, used for making a copy as a document is being written or typed.

car·bon sink ▶ n. a forest, ocean, or other natural environment viewed in terms of its ability to absorb carbon dioxide from the atmosphere.

car·bon steel ▶ n. steel in which the main alloying element is carbon.

car·bon tax ▶ n. a tax on gasoline and other fossil fuels.

car·bon tra·ding ▶ n. another term for EMISSIONS TRADING.

car·bon·yl /ˈkärbəˌnil/ ▶ n. Chemistry a radical consisting of a carbon atom linked to an oxygen atom, present in aldehydes and many other organic compounds.

car·bo·run·dum /ˌkärbəˈrəndəm/ ▶ n. a very hard black solid consisting of silicon and carbon, used for grinding, smoothing, and polishing.

car·box·yl /kärˈbäksəl/ ▶ n. Chemistry a radical consisting of a carbon atom linked to an oxygen atom and a hydroxyl group, present in organic acids.

car·box·yl·ic ac·id /ˈkärbäkˈsilik/ ▶ n. an acid containing a carboxyl group, such as formic and acetic acids.

car·boy /ˈkärˌboi/ ▶ n. a large globular glass bottle with a narrow neck, used for holding acids.

carbs /kärbz/ ▶ pl.n. informal dietary carbohydrates.

car·bun·cle /ˈkärˌbəNGkəl/ ▶ n. 1 a severe abscess or multiple boil in the skin. 2 a polished garnet (gem). ■ **car·bun·cu·lar** /ˈkärˈbəNGkyələr/ adj.

car·bu·re·tor /ˈkärb(y)əˌrātər/ ▶ n. a device in an internal combustion engine for mixing air with a fine spray of liquid fuel.

car·cass /ˈkärkəs/ (Brit. also **carcase**) ▶ n. 1 the dead body of an animal, especially one prepared for cutting up as meat. 2 the remains of a cooked bird after all the edible parts have been removed. 3 the structural framework of a building, ship, or piece of furniture.

car·cin·o·gen /kärˈsinəjən, ˈkärsənəˌjen/ ▶ n. a substance that can cause cancer. ■ **car·cin·o·gen·ic** /ˌkärsənəˈjenik/ adj.

car·ci·no·ma /ˌkärsəˈnōmə/ ▶ n. (pl. **carcinomas** or **carcinomata** /-ˈnōmətə/) a cancer arising in the tissues of the skin or of the lining of the internal organs.

card¹ /kärd/ ▶ n. 1 thick, stiff paper or thin cardboard. 2 a piece of card for writing on or printed with information. 3 a small rectangular piece of plastic containing personal data in a form that can be read by a computer: *a credit*

card. 4 a playing card. **5** (**cards**) a game played with playing cards. **6** informal, dated an odd or amusing person.
- PHRASES **in the cards** informal possible or likely.
play the —— card exploit a particular issue, especially for political advantage: *he played the race card to win votes.* **play one's cards right** make the best use of one's assets and opportunities. **put** (or **lay**) **one's cards on the table** state one's intentions openly.

card² ▶ v. comb and clean raw wool or similar material with a sharp-toothed instrument to disentangle the fibers before spinning. ▶ n. a toothed implement or machine for combing and cleaning wool. ■ **card·er** n.

car·da·mom /ˈkärdəməm/ ▶ n. the seeds of a SE Asian plant, used as a spice.

card·board /ˈkärdˌbôrd/ ▶ n. thin board made from layers of paper pasted together or from paper pulp. ▶ adj. (of a fictional character) not realistic.

card-car·ry·ing ▶ adj. 1 registered as a member of a political party or labor union. 2 informal confirmed in or dedicated to a specified pursuit or outlook: *a card-carrying pessimist.*

car·di·ac /ˈkärdēˌak/ ▶ adj. relating to the heart.

car·di·gan /ˈkärdigən/ ▶ n. a knitted long-sleeved sweater that fastens down the front.

car·di·nal /ˈkärd-nl, ˈkärdn-əl/ ▶ n. 1 a leading Roman Catholic clergyman, nominated by and having the power to elect the Pope. 2 a deep scarlet color like that of a cardinal's robes. 3 a New World songbird of the bunting family, with a stout bill and typically with a conspicuous crest. The male is mostly red in color. ▶ adj. of the greatest importance; fundamental.

car·di·nal hu·mor ▶ n. see HUMOR (sense 3 of the noun).

car·di·nal num·ber ▶ n. a number expressing quantity (one, two, three, etc.) rather than order (first, second, third, etc.).

car·di·nal point ▶ n. each of the four main points of the compass (north, south, east, and west).

car·di·nal sin ▶ n. 1 (in Christian tradition) any of the seven deadly sins. 2 a serious error of judgment.

car·di·nal vir·tue ▶ n. each of the chief moral virtues in medieval philosophy: justice, prudence, temperance, and fortitude.

card in·dex ▶ n. a catalog in which each item is entered on a separate card.

car·di·o·gram /ˈkärdēəˌgram/ ▶ n. a record of muscle activity within the heart made by a cardiograph.

car·di·o·graph /ˈkärdēəˌgraf/ ▶ n. an instrument for recording heart muscle activity. ■ **car·di·og·ra·pher** /ˌkärdēˈägrəfər/ n. **car·di·og·ra·phy** /-ˈägrəfē/ n.

car·di·ol·o·gy /ˌkärdēˈäləjē/ ▶ n. the branch of medicine concerned with the heart. ■ **car·di·o·log·i·cal** adj. **car·di·ol·o·gist** n.

car·di·o·pul·mo·nar·y /ˌkärdēōˈpoolməˌnerē, -ˈpəl-/ ▶ adj. relating to the heart and the lungs.

car·di·o·vas·cu·lar /ˌkärdēōˈvaskyələr/ ▶ adj. relating to the heart and blood vessels.

car·doon /kärˈdoon/ ▶ n. a tall thistlelike plant related to the globe artichoke, with edible leaves and roots.

card sharp (also **card sharper** or **card shark**) ▶ n. a person who cheats at cards.

CARE /ke(ə)r/ ▸ abbr. Cooperative for American Relief Everywhere, a large private organization that provides emergency and long-term assistance.

care /ke(ə)r/ ▸ n. 1 the provision of welfare and protection. 2 serious attention applied to avoid damage, risk, or error: *handle with care.* 3 a feeling of or cause for anxiety. ▸ v. 1 feel concern or interest. 2 feel affection or liking. 3 (**care for/to do**) like to have or be willing to do: *would you care for some tea?* 4 (**care for**) look after and provide for the needs of someone or something. ■ **car·ing** n. & adj.
– PHRASES **care of** at the address of. **take care 1** be careful. **2** make sure to do something. **take care of someone/thing 1** keep someone or something safe and provided for. **2** deal with something.

ca·reen /kə'rēn/ ▸ v. 1 tilt a ship on its side for cleaning or repair. 2 move quickly and in an uncontrolled way.

ca·reer /kə'ri(ə)r/ ▸ n. an occupation undertaken for a significant period of a person's life, usually with opportunities for progress. ▸ adj. 1 (of a woman) choosing to pursue a profession rather than devoting herself to childcare or housekeeping. 2 working with long-term commitment in a particular profession: *a career diplomat.* ▸ v. move swiftly and in an uncontrolled way: *I careered across the desert at 150 mph.*

ca·reer·ist /kə'ri(ə)rist/ ▸ n. a person whose main concern is to progress in their profession. ■ **ca·reer·ism** /-,izəm/ n.

care·free /'ke(ə)r,frē/ ▸ adj. free from anxiety or responsibility.

care·ful /'ke(ə)rfəl/ ▸ adj. 1 taking care to avoid harm or trouble; cautious. 2 sensible in the use of something: *he'd always been careful with money.* 3 done with or showing thought and attention. ■ **care·ful·ly** adv. **care·ful·ness** n.

care·giv·er /'ke(ə)r,givər/ ▸ n. a family member or paid helper who regularly looks after a child or a sick, elderly, or disabled person. ■ **care·giv·ing** n. & adj.

care·less /'kerlis/ ▸ adj. 1 not giving sufficient attention or thought to avoiding harm or mistakes. 2 (**careless of/about**) not concerned or worried about: *he was careless of the truth.* 3 showing no interest or effort. ■ **care·less·ly** adv. **care·less·ness** n.

CARE pack·age ▸ n. 1 a box of food and relief supplies sent by CARE. 2 (**care package**) a box of small gifts for a relative or friend, typically of something not readily available: *convince Aunt Alice to send me a care package full of homemade goodies.*

ca·ress /kə'res/ ▸ v. touch or stroke someone or something lovingly. ▸ n. a gentle or loving touch. ■ **ca·ress·ing** adj. **ca·ress·ing·ly** adv.

car·et /'karit/ ▸ n. a mark (ʌ, ʌ) placed below or in a line of text to indicate an insertion.

care·tak·er /'ke(ə)r,tākər/ ▸ n. a person employed to look after a public building or a house in the owner's absence. ▸ adj. holding power temporarily: *a caretaker government.*

care·worn /'ke(ə)r,wôrn/ ▸ adj. tired and unhappy because of prolonged worry.

car·go /'kärgō/ ▸ n. (pl. **cargoes** or **cargos**) freight carried on a ship, aircraft, or motor vehicle.

car·go pants ▸ pl. n. loose-fitting casual cotton pants with large patch pockets halfway down each leg.

Car·ib /'karib/ ▸ n. 1 a member of a South American people living mainly in coastal regions of French Guiana, Suriname, Guyana, and Venezuela. 2 the language of the Carib.

Car·ib·be·an /,karə'bēən, kə'ribēən/ ▸ adj. relating to the region consisting of the Caribbean Sea, its islands, and the surrounding coasts.

car·i·bou /'karə,bōō/ ▸ n. (pl. same) a large North American reindeer.

car·i·ca·ture /'karikəchər, -,chŏŏr/ ▸ n. a picture or description in which a person's distinctive features are exaggerated for comic effect. ▸ v. make a caricature of someone. ■ **car·i·ca·tur·al** /,karikə'chŏŏrəl/ adj. **car·i·ca·tur·ist** /-,chŏŏrist/ n.

car·ies /'kerēz/ ▸ n. decay and crumbling of a tooth or bone. ■ **car·i·ous** /'karēəs/ adj.

car·il·lon /'karə,län, -lən/ ▸ n. a set of bells sounded from a keyboard or by an automatic mechanism.

car·jack·ing /'kär,jakiNG/ ▸ n. the action of stealing a car after violently ejecting its driver.

car·load /'kär,lōd/ ▸ n. 1 the number of people that can travel in an automobile. 2 the quantity of goods that can be carried in a railroad freight car.

Car·mel·ite /'kärmə,līt/ ▸ n. a friar or nun of an order founded at Mount Carmel in Israel during the Crusades (c. 1154). ▸ adj. relating to the Carmelites.

car·min·a·tive /kär'minətiv, 'kärmə,nātiv/ ▸ n. a drug that relieves flatulence.

car·mine /'kärmən, -,mīn/ ▸ n. a vivid crimson color.

car·nage /'kärnij/ ▸ n. the killing of a large number of people.

car·nal /'kärnl/ ▸ adj. relating to physical, especially sexual, needs and activities. ■ **car·nal·i·ty** /kär'nalitē/ n. **car·nal·ly** adv.

car·nal know·ledge ▸ n. dated, chiefly Law sexual intercourse.

car·na·tion /kär'nāshən/ ▸ n. a cultivated variety of pink, with double pink, white, or red flowers.

car·nel·ian /kär'nēlyən/ (also **cornelian**) ▸ n. a dull red or pink semiprecious variety of chalcedony (a form of quartz).

car·ni·val /'kärnəvəl/ ▸ n. 1 an annual public festivity involving processions, music, and dancing. 2 a traveling amusement show or circus. ■ **car·ni·val·esque** /,kärnəvə'lesk/ adj.

car·ni·vore /'kärnə,vôr/ ▸ n. an animal that feeds on meat.

car·niv·o·rous /kär'nivərəs/ ▸ adj. (of an animal) feeding on meat.

car·ob /'karəb/ ▸ n. the edible brownish-purple pod of an Arabian tree, from which a substitute for chocolate is made.

car·ol /'karəl/ ▸ n. a religious song or popular hymn sung at Christmas. ▸ v. (**carols, caroling, caroled**) 1 (**go caroling**) sing carols in the streets. 2 sing or say something happily. ■ **car·ol·er** n.

Car·o·lin·gi·an /,karə'linj(ē)ən/ ▸ adj. relating to the dynasty founded by Charlemagne's father, which ruled in western Europe from 750 to 987.

car·om /'karəm/ ▸ n. 1 Billiards a stroke in which the cue ball strikes two balls successively. 2 any of the billiard games played on a table without pockets. ▸ v. make a carom; strike and rebound.

car·o·tene /'karə,tēn/ ▶ n. an orange or red substance found in carrots and many other plants, important in the formation of vitamin A.

ca·rot·e·noid /kə'rätn,oid/ ▶ n. any of a group of mainly yellow, orange, or red pigments, including carotene, that give color to plant parts such as ripe tomatoes and autumn leaves.

ca·rot·id /kə'rätid/ ▶ adj. relating to the two main arteries carrying blood to the head and neck.

ca·rouse /kə'rouz/ ▶ v. drink alcohol and enjoy oneself with others in a noisy, lively way. ■ **ca·rous·al** n. **ca·rous·er** n.

car·ou·sel /,karə'sel, 'karə,sel/ ▶ n. 1 a merry-go-round at a fair. 2 a conveyor system at an airport from which arriving passengers collect their luggage.

carp[1] /kärp/ ▶ n. (pl. same) a freshwater fish, often kept in ponds and sometimes farmed for food.

carp[2] ▶ v. complain about something continually. ■ **carp·er** n.

car·pac·cio /kär'päcH(ē)ō/ ▶ n. an Italian hors d'oeuvre consisting of thin slices of raw beef or fish served with a sauce.

car·pal /'kärpəl/ ▶ adj. relating to the bones in the wrist. ▶ n. a bone in the wrist.

car·pal tun·nel syn·drome ▶ n. a painful condition of the hand and fingers caused by compression of a major nerve where it passes over the bones in the wrist.

car park ▶ n. Brit. a parking lot or parking garage.

car·pe di·em /,kärpā 'dē,em/ ▶ exclam. make the most of the present time.

car·pel /'kärpəl/ ▶ n. the female reproductive organ of a flower, consisting of an ovary, a stigma, and usually a style.

car·pen·ter /'kärpəntər/ ▶ n. a person who makes wooden objects and structures. ■ **car·pen·try** /'kärpəntrē/ n.

car·pet /'kärpit/ ▶ n. 1 a floor covering made from thick woven fabric. 2 a large rug. 3 a thick or soft expanse or layer of something: *a carpet of snow and ice.* ▶ v. (**carpets, carpeting, carpeted**) 1 cover a floor with a carpet. 2 figurative cover with a thick or soft expanse or layer of something. – PHRASES **on the carpet** informal being reprimanded by someone in authority. **sweep something under the carpet** conceal or ignore a problem in the hope that it will be forgotten.

car·pet·bag /'kärpit,bag/ ▶ n. a traveling bag of a kind originally made of thick carpetlike fabric.

car·pet·bag·ger /'kärpit,bagər/ ▶ n. informal, derogatory 1 a politician who tries to get elected in an area where they have no local connections. 2 historical a person from the northern states who went to the South after the Civil War to profit from Reconstruction.

car·pet-bomb ▶ v. bomb an area intensively.

car·pet·ing /'kärpiting/ ▶ n. material for making carpets or carpets in general.

car·pet slip·per ▶ n. a soft slipper with an upper of wool or thick cloth.

car·pool /'kär,pool/ ▶ n. 1 an arrangement among people to make a regular trip in a single vehicle, typically with each person taking turns to drive the others. 2 a group of people with such an arrangement. ▶ v. form or participate in a carpool.

car·port /'kär,pôrt/ ▶ n. an open-sided shelter for a car, projecting from the side of a house.

car·pus /'kärpəs/ ▶ n. (pl. **carpi** /-,pī, -,pē/) the group of small bones in the wrist.

car·ra·geen /'karə,gēn/ ▶ n. an edible red seaweed with flattened branching fronds.

car·rel /kä'rel/ ▶ n. 1 a small cubicle with a desk for a reader in a library. 2 historical a small enclosure or study in a cloister.

car·riage /'karij/ ▶ n. 1 a four-wheeled passenger vehicle pulled by two or more horses. 2 a baby carriage. 3 a person's way of standing or moving. 4 a moving part of a machine that carries other parts into the required position. 5 a wheeled support for moving a heavy object such as a gun.

car·ri·er /'karēər/ ▶ n. 1 a person or thing that carries or holds something. 2 a company that transports goods or people for payment. 3 a person or animal that transmits a disease to others without suffering from it themselves.

car·ri·er pig·eon ▶ n. a homing pigeon trained to carry messages.

car·ri·on /'karēən/ ▶ n. the decaying flesh of dead animals.

car·ri·on crow ▶ n. a common black crow.

car·rot /'karət/ ▶ n. 1 the tapering orange root of a plant of the parsley family, eaten as a vegetable. 2 something tempting offered to someone as a means of persuasion: *training that relies more on the carrot than on the stick.*

car·rot·y /'karətē/ ▶ adj. (of a person's hair) orange-red.

car·ry /'karē/ ▶ v. (**carries, carrying, carried**) 1 move or take someone or something from one place to another. 2 have on one's person: *he is believed to be carrying a gun.* 3 support the weight of someone or something. 4 take or accept responsibility or blame. 5 have as a feature or result: *a crime that carries a maximum penalty of 20 years.* 6 take or develop an idea or activity to a particular point: *he carried the criticism much further.* 7 approve a proposal by a majority of votes: *the motion was carried by one vote.* 8 publish or broadcast something. 9 (of a sound or voice) travel. 10 (**carry oneself**) stand and move in a particular way with: *she was carrying twins.* 11 be pregnant with: *she was carrying twins.* – PHRASES **be/get carried away** lose one's self-control. **carry the day** be victorious or successful. **carry something forward** transfer figures to a new page or account. **carry someone/something off 1** take someone away by force. **2** (of a disease) kill someone. **carry something off** succeed in doing something. **carry on 1** continue. **2** informal be engaged in a love affair. **carry something on** take part in something: *it's difficult to carry on a conversation with him.* **carry something out** perform a task. **carry something over 1** keep something to use or deal with in a new context. **2** postpone an event. **carry something through** bring a project to completion. **carry weight** be influential.

car·ry-on n. ▶ 1 a bag or suitcase suitable for taking onto an aircraft as hand-held luggage. 2 (also **carryings-on**) improper behavior.

car·ry-out ▶ n. another term for TAKEOUT.

car·sick /'kär,sik/ ▶ adj. feeling sick as a result of traveling in a car.

cart /kärt/ ▶ n. 1 an open horse-drawn vehicle with two or four wheels, used for carrying loads or passengers. 2 a shallow open container on wheels, pulled or pushed by hand. ▶ v. 1 carry something in a cart or similar vehicle. 2 informal

carry a large, heavy, or unwieldy object somewhere with difficulty. **3** take someone somewhere roughly: *the demonstrators were carted off by the police.*
– PHRASES **put the cart before the horse** do things in the wrong order.

carte blanche /ˌkärt ˈbläNSH, ˈbläNCH/ ▸ n. complete freedom to do whatever one wants to do.

car·tel /kärˈtel/ ▸ n. an association of manufacturers or suppliers formed to keep prices high and restrict competition.

Car·te·sian /kärˈtēzHən/ ▸ adj. relating to the French philosopher René Descartes (1596–1650) and his ideas. ▪ **Car·te·sian·ism** /-ˌnizəm/ n.

Car·te·sian co·or·di·nates ▸ pl.n. a system for locating a point by reference to its distance from axes intersecting at right angles.

Car·tha·gin·i·an /ˌkärTHəˈjinēən/ ▸ n. a person from the ancient city of Carthage on the coast of North Africa. ▸ adj. relating to Carthage or its people.

Car·thu·sian /kärˈTH(y)o͞ozHən/ ▸ n. a monk or nun of a strict order founded at Chartreuse in France in 1084. ▸ adj. relating to this order.

car·ti·lage /ˈkärtl-ij/ ▸ n. firm, flexible tissue that covers the ends of joints and forms structures such as the larynx and the external ear.
▪ **car·ti·lag·i·nous** /ˌkärtlˈajənəs/ adj.

car·ti·lag·i·nous fish ▸ n. a fish with a skeleton of cartilage rather than bone, e.g., a shark or ray.

car·tog·ra·phy /kärˈtägrəfē/ ▸ n. the science or practice of drawing maps. ▪ **car·tog·ra·pher** n. **car·to·graph·ic** /ˌkärtəˈgrafik/ adj.

car·ton /ˈkärtn/ ▸ n. a light cardboard box or container.

car·toon /kärˈto͞on/ ▸ n. **1** a humorous or satirical drawing in a newspaper or magazine. **2** (also **cartoon strip**) a comic strip. **3** a film made from a sequence of drawings, using animation techniques to give the appearance of movement. **4** a full-size drawing made as a preliminary design for a painting or other work of art.
▪ **car·toon·ist** n.

car·touche /kärˈto͞oSH/ ▸ n. **1** a carved decoration or drawing in the form of a scroll with rolled-up ends. **2** an oval or oblong containing Egyptian hieroglyphs that represent the name and title of a monarch.

car·tridge /ˈkärtrij/ ▸ n. **1** a container holding a spool of film, a quantity of ink, or other item or substance, to be inserted into a mechanism. **2** a casing containing a charge and a bullet or shot for a gun.

cart·wheel /ˈkärt,(h)wēl/ ▸ n. a circular sideways handspring with the arms and legs extended.
▸ v. perform cartwheels.

carve /kärv/ ▸ v. **1** cut into or shape a hard material to produce an object or design: *the tools used to carve marble.* **2** produce a design or object by carving: *I carved my initials on the tree.* **3** cut cooked meat into slices for eating. **4** (**carve something out**) develop a career, reputation, etc., through great effort. **5** (**carve something up**) divide something ruthlessly into separate parts or areas.

car·vel /ˈkärvel/ ▸ n. variant spelling of CARAVEL.

car·ver /ˈkärvər/ ▸ n. a person or tool that carves.

car·ver·y /ˈkärvərē/ ▸ n. (pl. **carveries**) a buffet or restaurant where cooked roasts of meat are carved as required.

carv·ing /ˈkärviNG/ ▸ n. an object or design carved from wood or stone as a work of art.

car wash ▸ n. a structure containing equipment for washing vehicles automatically.

car·y·at·id /ˌkarēˈatid, ˈkarēəˌtid/ ▸ n. Architecture a supporting pillar in the form of a clothed female figure.

Cas·a·no·va /ˌkazəˈnōvə, ˌkasə-/ ▸ n. a man notorious for seducing women.

cas·bah /ˈkas,bä/ ▸ n. variant spelling of KASBAH.

cas·cade /kasˈkād/ ▸ n. **1** a small waterfall, especially one in a series. **2** a mass of something that falls, hangs, or occurs in large quantities: *a cascade of raindrops.* **3** a succession of devices or stages in a process, each of which triggers the next. ▸ v. pour downward rapidly and in large quantities.

cas·car·a /kasˈkarə/ (also **cascara sagrada** /səˈgrädə/) ▸ n. a laxative made from the dried bark of a North American shrub.

case¹ /kās/ ▸ n. **1** an instance of a particular situation: *a case of mistaken identity.* **2** an instance of a disease, injury, or problem: *1,000 new cases of cancer.* **3** an incident being investigated by the police. **4** a legal action that is to be or has been decided in a court of law. **5** a set of facts or arguments supporting one side of a debate or lawsuit. **6** a person or problem requiring or receiving the attention of a doctor, social worker, etc. **7** Grammar a form of a noun, adjective, or pronoun expressing the relationship of the word to other words in the sentence: *the possessive case.*
– PHRASES **be the case** be so. **in case** so as to allow for the possibility of something happening or being true.

case² ▸ n. **1** a container or protective covering. **2** Brit. a suitcase. **3** a box containing twelve bottles of wine or other drink, sold as a unit.
▸ v. **1** enclose something within a case. **2** informal look around a place before carrying out a robbery.

case·book /ˈkās,bo͝ok/ ▸ n. a book containing a selection of source materials on a particular subject.

case-hard·ened ▸ adj. made callous or tough by experience: *a case-hardened politician.*

case his·to·ry ▸ n. a record of a person's background or medical history kept by a doctor or social worker.

ca·sein /ˈkā,sēn, ˈkāsēən/ ▸ n. the main protein present in milk and (in coagulated form) in cheese.

case law ▸ n. the law as established by the outcome of former cases rather than by legislation.

case·load /ˈkās,lōd/ ▸ n. the number of cases being dealt with by a doctor, lawyer, or social worker at one time.

case·ment /ˈkāsmənt/ ▸ n. a window set on a vertical hinge so that it opens like a door.

case-sen·si·tive ▸ n. Computing **1** (of a program or function) differentiating between capital and lowercase letters. **2** (of input) treated differently depending on whether it is in capitals or lowercase text.

case stud·y ▸ n. **1** a detailed study of the development of a particular person, group, or situation over a period of time. **2** a particular instance of something used or analyzed to illustrate a theory or principle.

case·work /'kās‚wərk/ ▶ n. social work involving the study of a particular person's family history and personal circumstances. ■ **case·work·er** n.

cash /kash/ ▶ n. **1** money in the form of coins or bills. **2** money in any form: *he was always short of cash.* ▶ v. **1** give or get bills or coins for a check or money order. **2** (**cash something in**) convert an insurance policy, savings account, etc., into money. **3** (**cash in on**) informal take advantage of a situation. ■ **cash·less** adj.
– PHRASES **cash in hand** payment in cash rather than by check or other means.

cash and car·ry ▶ n. a system of wholesale trading in which goods are paid for in full and taken away by the buyer.

cash·back /'kash‚bak/ ▶ n. **1** a service offered by a store by which a customer may withdraw cash when buying goods with a debit card. **2** a cash refund offered as an incentive to buyers of certain products.

cash book ▶ n. a book in which amounts of money paid and received are recorded.

cash cow ▶ n. informal a business or investment that provides a steady income or profit.

cash crop ▶ n. a crop produced for selling rather than for use by the grower.

cash·ew /'kash‚ōō, kə'shōō/ ▶ n. (also **cashew nut**) the edible kidney-shaped nut of a tropical American tree.

cash flow ▶ n. the total amount of money passing into and out of a business.

cash·ier[1] /ka'shi(ə)r/ ▶ n. a person whose job is to pay out and receive money in a store, bank, or business.

cash·ier[2] ▶ v. dismiss someone from the armed forces because of a serious wrongdoing.

cash·mere /'kazh‚mi(ə)r, 'kash-/ ▶ n. fine soft wool, originally that obtained from a breed of Himalayan goat.

cash reg·is·ter ▶ n. a machine used in stores for adding up and recording the amount of each sale and storing the money received.

cash-strapped ▶ adj. informal very short of money.

cas·ing /'kāsiNG/ ▶ n. **1** a cover or shell that protects or encloses something. **2** the frame around a door or window.

ca·si·no /kə'sēnō/ ▶ n. (pl. **casinos**) a public building or room for gambling.

cask /kask/ ▶ n. a large barrel for storing alcoholic drinks.

cas·ket /'kaskit/ ▶ n. **1** a small ornamental box or chest for holding valuable objects. **2** a coffin.

Cas·san·dra /kə'sandrə/ ▶ n. a person who makes pessimistic predictions.

cas·sa·va /kə'sävə/ ▶ n. the starchy root of a tropical American tree, used as food.

cas·se·role /'kasə‚rōl/ ▶ n. **1** a large dish with a lid, used for cooking food slowly in an oven. **2** a kind of stew cooked slowly in an oven. ▶ v. cook food slowly in a casserole.

cas·sette /kə'set/ ▶ n. a sealed plastic case containing audiotape, videotape, film, etc., to be inserted into a recorder, camera, or other device.

cas·sia /'kasHə/ ▶ n. **1** a tree or plant of warm climates from which senna (a mild laxative) is obtained. **2** the bark of an East Asian tree, from which an inferior kind of cinnamon is obtained.

cas·sis /ka'sēs/ (also **crème de cassis** /‚krem də ka'sēs/) ▶ n. a syrupy black currant liqueur.

cas·sock /'kasək/ ▶ n. a long garment worn by some Christian clergy and members of church choirs.

cas·sou·let /‚kasə'lā/ ▶ n. a stew made with meat and beans.

cas·so·war·y /'kasə‚werē/ ▶ n. (pl. **cassowaries**) a very large flightless bird related to the emu, native mainly to New Guinea.

cast /kast/ ▶ v. (past and past part. **cast**) **1** throw something forcefully. **2** cause light or shadow to appear on a surface. **3** direct one's eyes or thoughts toward something. **4** express: *journalists cast doubt on this account.* **5** register a vote. **6** give a part to an actor or allocate parts in a play, movie, or television show. **7** leave aside: *he jumped in, casting caution to the winds.* **8** throw the hooked and baited end of a fishing line out into the water. **9** shape metal or other material by pouring it into a mold while molten. **10** produce an object by casting metal: *a figure cast in bronze.* **11** describe or present in a particular way: *he cast himself as the embodiment of the American dream.* **12** cause a magic spell to take effect. ▶ n. **1** the actors taking part in a play, movie, or television show. **2** an object made by casting metal or other material. **3** (also **plaster cast**) a bandage stiffened with plaster of Paris, molded to support and protect a broken limb. **4** the appearance or nature of someone or something: *minds of a philosophical cast.* **5** a slight squint.
– PHRASES **be cast away** be stranded after a shipwreck. **be cast down** feel depressed. **cast about** (or **around**) search far and wide. **cast off** Knitting take the stitches off the needle by looping each over the next. **cast something off** release a boat or ship from its moorings. **cast on** Knitting make the first row of loops on the needle.

cas·ta·nets /‚kastə'nets/ ▶ pl.n. a pair of small curved pieces of wood, ivory, or plastic, clicked together by the fingers as an accompaniment to Spanish dancing.

cast·a·way /'kastə‚wā/ ▶ n. a person who has been shipwrecked and stranded in an isolated place.

caste /kast/ ▶ n. each of the hereditary classes of Hindu society.

cas·tel·lat·ed /'kastə‚lātid/ ▶ adj. having battlements. ■ **cas·tel·la·tion** /‚kastə'lāsHən/ n.

cast·er /'kastər/ ▶ n. **1** each of a set of small swiveling wheels fixed to the legs or base of a piece of furniture. **2** a small container with holes in the top, used for sprinkling salt, sugar, etc.

cas·ti·gate /'kastə‚gāt/ ▶ v. reprimand someone severely. ■ **cas·ti·ga·tion** /‚kastə'gāsHən/ n.

Cas·til·ian /kə'stilyən/ ▶ n. **1** a person from the Spanish region of Castile. **2** the language of Castile, the standard form of both spoken and literary Spanish. ▶ adj. relating to Castile or Castilian.

cast·ing /'kastiNG/ ▶ n. an object made by casting molten metal or other material.

cast·ing vote ▶ n. an extra vote used by a chairperson to decide an issue when votes on each side are equal.

cast i·ron ▶ n. a hard alloy of iron and carbon that can be readily cast in a mold. ▶ adj. firm and unchangeable: *a cast-iron guarantee.*

cas·tle /'kasəl/ ▶ n. **1** a large fortified building or group of buildings constructed during medieval times. **2** Chess, informal old-fashioned term for ROOK[2].

– PHRASES **castles in the air** (or **in Spain**) plans or dreams that are never likely to be achieved or fulfilled.

cast-off /'kast,ôf/ ▶ adj. no longer wanted; abandoned or discarded. ▶ n. a garment that is no longer wanted.

cas-tor /'kastər/ ▶ n. variant spelling of CASTER.

cas-tor oil ▶ n. an oil obtained from the seeds of an African shrub, used as a laxative.

cas-trate /'kas,trāt/ ▶ v. 1 remove the testicles of a male animal or person. 2 deprive someone or something of power or vitality. ■ **cas-tra-tion** /ka'strāsʜən/ n. **cas-tra-tor** /-,trātər/ n.

cas-tra-to /kas'trä,tō/ ▶ n. (pl. **castrati** /-tē/) historical a male singer castrated before puberty so that he kept a soprano or alto voice.

ca-su-al /'kazʜōōəl/ ▶ adj. 1 relaxed and unconcerned. 2 done or made without much thought: *a casual remark.* 3 not regular or firmly established; occasional or temporary: *casual jobs.* 4 happening by chance; accidental. 5 (of clothes) suitable for informal everyday wear: *a casual short-sleeved shirt.* ▶ n. 1 a person who does something irregularly, especially a temporary worker. 2 (**casuals**) clothes or shoes suitable for informal everyday wear. ■ **cas-u-al-ly** adv. **cas-u-al-ness** n.

cas-u-al-ty /'kazʜ(ōō)əltē/ ▶ n. (pl. **casualties**) 1 a person killed or injured in a war or accident. 2 a person or thing badly affected by an event or situation: *the firm was one of the casualties of the recession.*

cas-u-ist-ry /'kazʜōōəstrē/ ▶ n. the use of clever but false reasoning. ■ **cas-u-ist** /'kazʜōōist/ n. **cas-u-is-tic** /,kazʜōō'istik/ adj. **cas-u-is-ti-cal** /,kazʜōō'istikəl/ adj.

CAT /'kat/ ▶ abbr. Medicine computerized axial tomography.

cat /'kat/ ▶ n. 1 a small domesticated mammal with soft fur. 2 a wild animal related to or resembling this, e.g., a lion or tiger. ■ **cat-like** adj.

– PHRASES **the cat's meow** (or **pajamas** or **whiskers**) informal an excellent person or thing. **let the cat out of the bag** informal reveal a secret by mistake. **like a cat on a hot tin roof** informal very agitated or anxious.

ca-tab-o-lism /kə'tabə,lizəm/ ▶ n. a metabolic process in which complex molecules are broken down to form simpler ones and energy is released. The opposite of ANABOLISM. ■ **cat-a-bol-ic** /,katə'bälik/ adj.

cat-a-clysm /'katə,klizəm/ ▶ n. a violent upheaval or disaster. ■ **cat-a-clys-mic** /,katə'klizmik/ adj. **cat-a-clys-mi-cal-ly** /-mik(ə)lē/ adv.

cat-a-comb /'katə,kōm/ ▶ n. an underground cemetery consisting of tunnels with recesses for tombs.

cat-a-falque /'katə,fô(l)k, -,falk/ ▶ n. a decorated wooden framework used to support a coffin.

Cat-a-lan /'katl,an, 'katl-ən/ ▶ n. 1 a person from Catalonia in NE Spain. 2 the language of Catalonia. ▶ adj. relating to Catalonia.

cat-a-lep-sy /'katl,epsē/ ▶ n. a medical condition in which a person suffers a loss of consciousness and their body becomes rigid. ■ **cat-a-lep-tic** /,katl'eptik/ adj. & n.

cat-a-log /'katl,ôg, -,äg/ (also **catalogue**) ▶ n. 1 a complete list of items arranged in alphabetical or other systematic order. 2 a publication containing details of items for sale. 3 a series of

bad things: *a catalog of disasters.* ▶ v. (**catalogs, cataloging, cataloged**; also **catalogues, cataloguing, catalogued**) list an item or items in a catalog. ■ **cat-a-log-er, cat-a-log-uer** n.

Cat-a-lo-ni-an /,katl'ōnēən/ ▶ adj. & n. another term for CATALAN.

ca-tal-pa /kə'talpə/ ▶ n. a tree with heart-shaped leaves, native to North America and east Asia.

ca-tal-y-sis /kə'taləsis/ ▶ n. the speeding up of a chemical reaction by a catalyst. ■ **cat-a-lyt-ic** /,katl'itik/ adj.

cat-a-lyst /'katl-ist/ ▶ n. 1 a substance that increases the speed of a chemical reaction without undergoing any permanent chemical change itself. 2 a person or thing that causes something to happen: *his speech had acted as a catalyst for debate.*

cat-a-lyt-ic con-vert-er ▶ n. a device in the exhaust system of a motor vehicle, containing a catalyst for converting pollutant gases into less harmful ones.

cat-a-lyze /'katl,īz/ (Brit. **catalyse**) ▶ v. cause or speed up a reaction by acting as a catalyst. ■ **cat-a-lyz-er** n.

cat-a-ma-ran /,katəmə'ran, 'katəmə,ran/ ▶ n. a sailboat or other boat with twin parallel hulls.

cat-a-mite /'katə,mīt/ ▶ n. old use a boy kept by an older man as a homosexual partner.

cat-a-plex-y /'katə,pleksē/ ▶ n. a medical condition in which strong emotion or laughter causes a person to experience sudden weakness in the muscles.

cat-a-pult /'katə,pəlt, -,pōōlt/ ▶ n. 1 historical a military machine for hurling large stones or other missiles. 2 a mechanical device for launching a glider or aircraft. ▶ v. 1 throw something forcefully. 2 move suddenly or very fast.

cat-a-ract /'katə,rakt/ ▶ n. 1 a large waterfall. 2 a medical condition in which the lens of the eye becomes opaque, resulting in blurred vision.

ca-tarrh /kə'tär/ ▶ n. excessive mucus in the nose or throat. ■ **ca-tarrh-al** adj.

ca-tas-tro-phe /kə'tastrəfē/ ▶ n. an event causing great damage or suffering. ■ **cat-a-stroph-ic** /,katə'sträfik/ adj. **cat-a-stroph-i-cal-ly** /-ik(ə)lē/ adv.

cat-a-to-ni-a /,katə'tōnēə/ ▶ n. a condition resulting from schizophrenia or another mental disorder, in which a person experiences both periods of unconsciousness and overactivity.

cat-a-ton-ic /,katə'tänik/ ▶ adj. 1 suffering from catatonia. 2 informal inert or completely unresponsive.

cat-bird /'kat,bərd/ ▶ n. a long-tailed American songbird of the mockingbird family, with mainly gray plumage and catlike calls.

– PHRASES **in the catbird seat** informal in a superior or advantageous position.

cat bur-glar ▶ n. a thief who enters a building by climbing to an upper story.

cat-call /'kat,kôl/ ▶ n. a shrill whistle or shout of mockery or disapproval. ▶ v. make a catcall.

catch /kacʜ, kecʜ/ ▶ v. (past and past part. **caught**) 1 seize and take hold of a moving object. 2 capture a person or animal. 3 be in time to board a train, bus, etc., or to see a person or event. 4 entangle or become entangled: *she caught her foot in the bedspread.* 5 surprise someone in the act of doing something wrong or embarrassing: *she caught him flirting with another woman.* 6 (**be caught in**) unexpectedly

find oneself in an unwelcome situation.
7 become infected with an illness. **8** see, hear, or understand: *I couldn't catch what he said.* **9** gain a person's interest or attention. **10** hit someone or something: *she fell and caught her head on the hearth.* **11** start burning. ▶ n. **1** an act of catching something. **2** a device for fastening a door, window, etc. **3** a hidden problem. **4** a break in a person's voice caused by emotion. **5** informal a person thought of as being desirable or suitable as a husband or wife. **6** an amount of fish caught.
– PHRASES **catch one's breath 1** breathe in sharply as a result of a strong emotion. **2** recover one's breath after exercise. **catch someone's eye 1** be noticed by someone. **2** attract someone's attention by making eye contact. **catch on** informal **1** become popular. **2** understand what is meant. **catch up 1** do tasks that one should have done earlier. **2** (**be/get caught up in**) become involved in. **catch someone up** succeed in reaching a person ahead.

catch-22 ▶ n. a difficult situation from which there is no escape because it involves situations that conflict with or are dependent on each other.

catch-all ▶ n. a term or category intended to cover all possibilities.

catch·er /'kaCHər, 'keCH-/ ▶ n. Baseball a fielder positioned behind home plate to catch pitches not hit by the batter and to execute other defensive plays.

catch·ing /'kaCHiNG, 'keCH-/ ▶ adj. (of a disease) infectious.

catch·ment /'kaCHmənt, 'keCH-/ ▶ n. **1** the action of collecting water, especially the collection of rainfall over a natural drainage area. **2** the area from which rainfall flows into a river, lake, or reservoir. **3** the activity of collecting something in a place it gathers. **4** (also **catchment area**) the area of a city, town, etc., from which a hospital's patients or school's students are drawn.

catch·pen·ny /'kaCH,penē, 'keCH-/ ▶ adj. having a superficially attractive appearance so as to sell quickly.

catch·phrase /'kaCH,frāz, 'keCH-/ ▶ n. a well-known sentence or phrase.

catch-up ▶ n. informal an instance of catching up to someone in a particular activity.
– PHRASES **play catch-up 1** fall behind continually with work or financial matters: *I'm always playing catch-up with my homework.* **2** try to equal a competitor in a sport or game.

catch·word /'kaCH,wərd, 'keCH-/ ▶ n. a frequently used word or phrase that is associated with or encapsulates a particular thing: *perestroika was the catchword of the Gorbachev era.*

catch·y /'kaCHē, 'keCHē/ ▶ adj. (**catchier, catchiest**) (of a tune or phrase) instantly appealing and easy to remember. ■ **catch·i·ness** n.

cat door ▶ n. a small hinged flap in an outer door through which a cat may pass in and out.

cat·e·che·sis /,katə'kēsis/ ▶ n. religious instruction given to prepare someone for Christian baptism or confirmation.

cat·e·chism /'katə,kizəm/ ▶ n. a summary of the principles of the Christian religion in the form of questions and answers, used for teaching.

cat·e·chist /'katəkist/ ▶ n. a Christian teacher, especially one using a catechism.

cat·e·chize /'katə,kīz/ ▶ v. teach someone about the principles of the Christian religion by means of question and answer, especially by using a catechism.

cat·e·gor·i·cal /,katə'gôrikəl/ (also **categoric**) ▶ adj. completely explicit and direct. ■ **cat·e·gor·i·cal·ly** /-ik(ə)lē/ adv.

cat·e·go·rize /'katəgə,rīz/ ▶ v. place someone or something in a particular category: *the population is categorized according to age, sex, and socioeconomic group.* ■ **cat·e·go·ri·za·tion** /,katəgərə'zāSHən/ n.

cat·e·go·ry /'katə,gôrē/ ▶ n. (pl. **categories**) a class or group of people or things with shared characteristics.

cat·e·nar·y /'katə,nerē, 'katn,erē/ ▶ n. (pl. **catenaries**) a curve formed by a wire, chain, etc., hanging from two points on the same horizontal level. ▶ adj. involving or referring to a curve of this type.

ca·ter /'kātər/ ▶ v. **1** provide food and drink at a social event. **2** (**cater to**) provide with what is needed or required: *the school caters to children with special needs.* **3** (**cater to**) satisfy a need or demand. ■ **ca·ter·er** n.

cat·er·pil·lar /'katə(r),pilər/ ▶ n. **1** the larva of a butterfly or moth. **2** (also **caterpillar track** or **tread**) trademark a segmented steel band passing around the wheels of a vehicle for travel on rough ground.

cat·er·waul /'katər,wôl/ ▶ v. make a shrill howling or wailing noise.

cat·fight /'kat,fīt/ ▶ n. informal a fight between women. ■ **cat·fight·ing** n.

cat·fish /'kat,fiSH/ ▶ n. (pl. same or **catfishes**) a freshwater or sea fish with whiskerlike growths around the mouth.

cat·gut /'kat,gət/ ▶ n. material used for the strings of musical instruments and formerly for surgical sutures, made of the dried intestines of sheep or horses (but not cats).

Cath. ▶ abbr. **1** Cathedral. **2** Catholic.

ca·thar·sis /kə'THärsis/ ▶ n. the process of releasing strong but repressed emotions so as to be relieved of them.

ca·thar·tic /kə'THärtik/ ▶ adj. providing psychological relief through the expression of strong but previously repressed emotions: *writing the book was a very cathartic experience.*

ca·the·dral /kə'THēdrəl/ ▶ n. the principal church of a diocese.

cath·e·ter /'kaTHətər/ ▶ n. a flexible tube inserted into the bladder or another body cavity to remove fluid.

cath·e·ter·ize /'kaTHitə,rīz/ ▶ v. Medicine insert a catheter into (a patient or body cavity). ■ **cath·e·ter·i·za·tion** /,kaTHitərə'zāSHən/ n.

cath·ode /'kaTH,ōd/ ▶ n. an electrode with a negative charge. The opposite of ANODE.

cath·ode ray ▶ n. a beam of electrons sent out from the cathode of a vacuum tube.

cath·ode ray tube ▶ n. a high-vacuum tube in which cathode rays produce a luminous image on a fluorescent screen, used in televisions and visual display units.

cath·o·lic /'kaTH(ə)lik/ ▶ adj. **1** including a wide variety of things: *catholic tastes.* **2** (**Catholic**) Roman Catholic. **3** (**Catholic**) of or including all Christians. ▶ n. (**Catholic**) a Roman Catholic. ■ **Ca·thol·i·cism** /kə'THälə,sizəm/ n. **cath·o·lic·i·ty** /,kaTH(ə)'lisətē/ n.

cat·i·on /'kat,īon, -,īän/ ▶ n. Chemistry an ion with a positive charge. The opposite of ANION. ■ **cat·i·on·ic** /,katī'änik/ adj.

cat·kin /'katkin/ ▸ n. a spike of small soft flowers hanging from trees such as willow and hazel.

cat lit·ter ▸ n. see LITTER (sense 4 of the noun).

cat·nap /'kat,nap/ ▸ n. a short sleep during the day. ▸ v. (**catnaps, catnapping, catnapped**) have a catnap.

cat·nip /'kat,nip/ ▸ n. a plant with a strong smell that is very attractive to cats.

cat-o'-nine-tails ▸ n. historical a whip consisting of a rope made from nine knotted cords, used for flogging people.

cat's cra·dle ▸ n. a child's game in which patterns are formed in a loop of string held between the fingers of each hand.

cats·eye /'kats,ī/ ▸ n. a semiprecious stone, especially chalcedony or chrysoberyl.

cat's paw ▸ n. a person used by someone else to carry out an unpleasant task on their behalf.

cat·suit /'kat,sōōt/ ▸ n. a woman's close-fitting jumpsuit that covers the body from the neck to the feet.

cat·sup /'kechəp, 'kachəp, 'katsəp/ ▸ n. another term for KETCHUP.

cat·tail /'kat,tāl/ ▸ n. a tall, reedlike marsh plant with straplike leaves and a dark brown, velvety cylindrical head of numerous tiny flowers.

cat·tle /'katl/ ▸ pl.n. large domesticated animals with horns and cloven hoofs; cows, bulls, and oxen.

cat·tle guard ▸ n. a metal grid covering a trench across a road, allowing vehicles and pedestrians to cross but not animals.

cat·tle·man /'katlmən, -,man/ ▸ n. (pl. **cattlemen**) a person who tends or rears cattle.

cat·ty /'katē/ ▸ adj. (**cattier, cattiest**) spiteful. ■ **cat·ti·ly** adv.

CATV ▸ abbr. community antenna television (cable television).

cat·walk /'kat,wôk/ ▸ n. 1 a narrow platform along which models walk to display clothes. 2 a raised narrow walkway or open bridge.

Cau·ca·sian /kô'kāzhən/ ▸ adj. 1 relating to a division of humankind covering peoples from Europe, western Asia, and parts of India and North Africa. 2 white-skinned; of European origin. ▸ n. a Caucasian person.

cau·cus /'kôkəs/ ▸ n. (pl. **caucuses**) 1 a meeting of a policy-making committee of a political party. 2 a group of people with shared concerns within a larger organization.

cau·dal /'kôdl/ ▸ adj. of, at, or near the tail or the rear part of an animal's body. ■ **cau·dal·ly** adv.

cau·dil·lo /kô'dēlyō, -'dēō, kou'dē,(y)ō/ ▸ n. (pl. **caudillos**) (in Spanish-speaking regions) a military or political leader.

caught /kôt/ ▸ past and past participle of CATCH.

caul /kôl/ ▸ n. the membrane enclosing a fetus, part of which is sometimes found on a baby's head at birth.

caul·dron /'kôldrən/ (also **caldron**) ▸ n. a large metal pot, used for cooking over an open fire.

cau·li·flow·er /'kôli,flou(-ə)r, 'käli-/ ▸ n. a variety of cabbage with a large flowerhead of small creamy-white flower buds.

cau·li·flow·er ear ▸ n. a person's ear that has become thickened or deformed as a result of repeated blows.

caulk /kôk/ (also **calk**) ▸ n. a waterproof substance used in building work to fill cracks and seal

joints. ▸ v. 1 seal something with caulk. 2 make a boat or its seams watertight.

caus·al /'kôzəl/ ▸ adj. relating to or being a cause of something: *a causal connection between smoking and lung cancer.* ■ **caus·al·ly** adv.

cau·sal·i·ty /kô'zalətē/ ▸ n. the relationship between something that happens and the effect it produces.

cau·sa·tion /kô'zāshən/ ▸ n. 1 the action of causing something. 2 another term for CAUSALITY.

caus·a·tive /'kôzətiv/ ▸ adj. acting as a cause of something.

cause /kôz/ ▸ n. 1 a person or thing that produces an effect. 2 good reason for thinking or doing something: *there is no cause for concern.* 3 a principle, aim, etc., that one is prepared to support or fight for: *the socialist cause.* 4 a lawsuit. ▸ v. make something, especially something bad, happen.
– PHRASES **cause and effect** the relationship between an action or event and the effect it produces.

cause cé·lè·bre /'kôz sə'leb(rə), 'kôz/ ▸ n. (pl. **causes célèbres** pronunc. same) a controversial issue arousing great public interest.

cause·way /'kôz,wā/ ▸ n. a raised road or track across low or wet ground.

caus·tic /'kôstik/ ▸ adj. 1 able to burn or corrode living tissue by chemical action. 2 bitterly critical or sarcastic. ■ **caus·ti·cal·ly** /-ik(ə)lē/ adv.

caus·tic so·da ▸ n. sodium hydroxide.

cau·ter·ize /'kôtə,rīz/ ▸ v. burn the skin or flesh of a wound to stop bleeding or prevent infection. ■ **cau·ter·i·za·tion** /,kôtərə'zāshən/ n.

cau·tion /'kôshən/ ▸ n. 1 care taken to avoid danger or mistakes. 2 warning: *advisers sounded a note of caution.* ▸ v. warn or advise: *economic advisers cautioned against a tax increase.*
– PHRASES **throw caution to the wind** (or **winds**) act in a reckless way.

cau·tion·ar·y /'kôshə,nerē/ ▸ adj. acting as a warning.

cau·tious /'kôshəs/ ▸ adj. careful to avoid possible problems or dangers. ■ **cau·tious·ly** adv. **cau·tious·ness** n.

ca·va /'kävə/ ▸ n. a Spanish sparkling wine made in the same way as champagne.

cav·al·cade /,kavəl'kād/ ▸ n. a procession of vehicles or people on horseback.

cav·a·lier /,kavə'li(ə)r/ ▸ n. (**Cavalier**) historical a supporter of King Charles I in the English Civil War. ▸ adj. showing a lack of proper concern: *the president's cavalier attitude to America's international obligations.* ■ **cav·a·lier·ly** adv.

cav·al·ry /'kavəlrē/ ▸ n. (pl. **cavalries**) (usu. treated as pl.) soldiers who formerly fought on horseback, but who now use armored vehicles. ■ **cav·al·ry·man** /-mən/ n. (pl. **cavalrymen**).

cave /'kāv/ ▸ n. a large natural hollow in the side of a hill or cliff, or underground. ▸ v. (**cave in**) 1 give way or collapse. 2 finally agree to someone's demands: *the bank caved in to pressure from local community groups.*

ca·ve·at /'kavē,ät, 'käv-/ ▸ n. a warning that certain conditions or provisos need to be taken into account.

ca·ve·at emp·tor /'emp,tôr/ ▸ n. the principle that the buyer is responsible for checking the quality and suitability of goods before buying them.

cave-in ▸ n. **1** a collapse of a roof or similar structure, typically underground. **2** an instance of yielding or submitting under pressure: *the government's cave-in to industry pressure.*

cave·man /'kāv,man/ (or **cavewoman**) ▸ n. (pl. **cavemen** or **cavewomen**) a prehistoric person who lived in caves.

cav·ern /'kavərn/ ▸ n. a large cave, or chamber in a cave.

cav·ern·ous /'kavərnəs/ ▸ adj. (of a room or space) like a cavern in being very large and empty or dark.

cav·i·ar /'kavē,är/ (also **caviare**) ▸ n. the pickled roe of the sturgeon (a large fish), eaten as a delicacy.

cav·il /'kavəl/ ▸ v. (**cavils, caviling, caviled**) make trivial complaints or objections. ▸ n. a trivial complaint or objection.

cav·ing /'kāviNG/ ▸ n. another term for SPELUNKING. ■ **cav·er** n.

cav·i·ta·tion /,kavə'tāSHən/ ▸ n. the formation of bubbles in a liquid.

cav·i·ty /'kavitē/ ▸ n. (pl. **cavities**) **1** a hollow space within a solid object. **2** a decayed part of a tooth.

cav·i·ty wall ▸ n. a wall formed from two layers of bricks with a space between them.

cav·ort /kə'vôrt/ ▸ v. jump or dance around excitedly.

ca·vy /'kāvē/ ▸ n. (pl. **cavies**) a guinea pig or related South American rodent.

caw /kô/ ▸ n. the harsh cry of a crow, rook, or similar bird. ▸ v. (of a crow, rook, or similar bird) make a harsh cry.

cay /kē, kā/ ▸ n. a low bank or reef of coral, rock, or sand.

cay·enne /kī'en, kā'en/ (also **cayenne pepper**) ▸ n. a hot-tasting red powder prepared from dried chilies.

cay·man ▸ n. variant spelling of CAIMAN.

CB ▸ abbr. Citizens' Band (radio frequencies).

CC ▸ abbr. **1** closed-captioned. **2** Cape Cod.

cc (also **c.c.**) ▸ abbr. **1** carbon copy (an indication that a duplicate has been or should be sent to another person). **2** cubic centimeter(s).

CCTV ▸ abbr. closed-circuit television.

CCU ▸ abbr. **1** cardiac care unit. **2** coronary care unit. **3** critical care unit.

CD ▸ abbr. **1** compact disc. **2** certificate of deposit.

Cd ▸ symbol the chemical element cadmium.

cd ▸ abbr. candela.

CD burner ▸ n. a device for producing a compact disc by copying from an original or master copy.

CDC ▸ abbr. Centers for Disease Control.

CD-R ▸ abbr. compact disc recordable, a CD that can be recorded on once only.

CD-ROM /,sē ,dē 'räm/ ▸ n. a compact disc used in a computer as a read-only device for displaying data.

CD-RW ▸ abbr. compact disc rewritable, a CD on which recordings can be made and erased a number of times.

CDT ▸ abbr. Central Daylight Time.

CE ▸ abbr. **1** Church of England. **2** Common Era. **3** Corps of Engineers.

Ce ▸ symbol the chemical element cerium.

ce·a·no·thus /,sēə'nōTHəs/ ▸ n. a North American shrub with dense clusters of small blue flowers.

cease /sēs/ ▸ v. come or bring to an end; stop. – PHRASES **without cease** without stopping.

cease·fire /'sēs,fīr/ ▸ n. a temporary period when fighting is stopped.

cease·less /'sēslis/ ▸ adj. constant; never stopping. ■ **cease·less·ly** adv.

ce·cum /'sēkəm/ (Brit. **caecum**) ▸ n. (pl. **ceca** /-kə/) a pouch connected to the junction of the small and large intestines. ■ **ce·cal** /-kəl/ adj.

ce·dar /'sēdər/ ▸ n. a tall coniferous tree with hard, sweet-smelling wood.

cede /sēd/ ▸ v. give up power or territory.

ce·dil·la /sə'dilə/ ▸ n. a mark (¸) written under the letter c, especially in French, to show that it is pronounced like an s (e.g., *soupçon*).

cei·lidh /'kālē/ ▸ n. a social event with Scottish or Irish folk music and singing, traditional dancing, and storytelling.

ceil·ing /'sēliNG/ ▸ n. **1** the upper inside surface of a room. **2** an upper limit set on prices, wages, or spending. **3** the maximum altitude to which an aircraft can climb.

cel·an·dine /'selən,dīn, -,dēn/ ▸ n. a yellow-flowered plant of the buttercup family.

ce·leb /sə'leb/ ▸ n. informal a celebrity.

cel·e·brant /'seləbrənt/ ▸ n. **1** a person who performs a religious ceremony, especially a priest who leads the service of Holy Communion. **2** a person who celebrates something.

cel·e·brate /'selə,brāt/ ▸ v. **1** mark an important occasion with a social gathering or enjoyable activity. **2** (often as adj. **celebrated**) honor or praise publicly: *a celebrated mathematician.* **3** perform a religious ceremony, in particular the Christian service of Holy Communion. ■ **cel·e·bra·tion** /,selə'brāSHən/ n. **cel·e·bra·tor** /-,brātər/ n. **cel·e·bra·to·ry** /sə'lebrə,tôrē, 'seləbrə-/ adj.

ce·leb·ri·ty /sə'lebrətē/ ▸ n. (pl. **celebrities**) **1** a famous person. **2** the state of being famous.

ce·ler·i·ac /sə'lerē,ak/ ▸ n. a variety of celery that forms a large edible root.

ce·ler·i·ty /sə'leritē/ ▸ n. old use or literary speed of movement.

cel·er·y /'sel(ə)rē/ ▸ n. a plant with crisp juicy stalks, eaten in salads or as a vegetable.

ce·les·ta /sə'lestə/ (also **celeste** /sə'lest/) ▸ n. a small keyboard instrument in which felt-covered hammers strike a row of steel plates.

ce·les·tial /sə'lesCHəl/ ▸ adj. **1** belonging or relating to heaven. **2** positioned in or relating to the sky or outer space. ■ **ce·les·tial·ly** adv.

ce·les·tial e·qua·tor ▸ n. the projection into space of the earth's equator.

ce·les·tial pole ▸ n. Astronomy the point on the celestial sphere directly above either of the earth's geographic poles, around which the stars appear to rotate.

ce·les·tial sphere ▸ n. an imaginary sphere of which the observer is the center and on which all celestial objects are considered to lie.

ce·li·ac dis·ease /'sēlē,ak/ ▸ n. a condition in which the small intestine fails to digest and absorb food, caused by excessive sensitivity to gluten.

cel·i·bate /'seləbət/ ▸ adj. **1** not marrying or having sex, especially for religious reasons. **2** not having or involving a sexual relationship. ▸ n. a person who is celibate. ■ **cel·i·ba·cy** /-bəsē/ n.

cell /sel/ ▸ n. **1** a small room for a prisoner, monk, or nun. **2** the smallest unit of a living organism that is able to reproduce and perform other functions. **3** a small compartment in a larger structure such as a honeycomb. **4** a small group of people working as part of a large political organization, usually in secret: *a terrorist cell.* **5** a device or unit in which electricity is produced using chemical energy or light, or in which electrolysis takes place.

cel·lar /'selər/ ▸ n. **1** a storage space or room below ground level in a building. **2** a stock of wine.

cell·mate /'sel‚māt/ ▸ n. a person with whom one shares a cell.

cel·lo /'chelō/ ▸ n. (pl. **cellos**) a large instrument of the violin family, held upright on the floor between the legs of the seated player. ■ **cel·list** n.

cel·lo·phane /'selə‚fān/ ▸ n. trademark a thin transparent wrapping material made from viscose.

cell phone (also **cellular phone**) ▸ n. a portable telephone using a cellular radio system.

cel·lu·lar /'selyələr/ ▸ adj. **1** relating to or made up of living cells. **2** relating to a mobile telephone system that uses a number of short-range radio stations to cover the area it serves. **3** (of fabric) woven so as to form holes or hollows that trap air and provide extra insulation. **4** consisting of small compartments or rooms.

cel·lu·lite /'selyə‚līt/ ▸ n. fat that accumulates under the skin, causing a dimpled effect.

cel·lu·loid /'selyə‚loid/ ▸ n. **1** a transparent plastic formerly used for movie film. **2** motion pictures considered as a type of art.

cel·lu·lose /'selyə‚lōs, -‚lōz/ ▸ n. a substance found in all plant tissues, used in making paint, plastics, and artificial fibers. ■ **cel·lu·lo·sic** /‚selyə'lōsik, -'lōzik/ adj.

Cel·si·us /'selsēəs, 'selshəs/ ▸ adj. relating to a scale of temperature on which water freezes at 0° and boils at 100°.

> **USAGE**
> **Celsius** rather than **centigrade** is the standard accepted term when giving temperatures.

Celt /kelt, selt/ ▸ n. **1** a member of a group of peoples inhabiting much of Europe and the western peninsula of Asia in pre-Roman times. **2** a native of a modern region in which a Celtic language is (or was) spoken.

Celt·ic /'keltik, 'sel-/ ▸ n. a group of languages including Irish, Scottish Gaelic, Welsh, Breton, Manx, and Cornish. ▸ adj. relating to Celtic or to the Celts.

Celt·ic cross ▸ n. a Latin cross with a circle around the center.

ce·ment /si'ment/ ▸ n. **1** a powdery substance made by strongly heating lime and clay, used in making mortar and concrete. **2** a soft glue that hardens on setting. ▸ v. **1** fix something with cement. **2** establish firmly: *the occasion cemented our friendship.* ■ **ce·men·ta·tion** /‚sē‚men'tāshən/ n.

cem·e·ter·y /'semə‚terē/ ▸ n. (pl. **cemeteries**) a large burial ground.

cen·o·taph /'senə‚taf/ ▸ n. a monument to members of the armed forces killed in a war.

Ce·no·zo·ic /‚senə'zōik/ (also **Cainozoic** /‚kīnə-/) ▸ adj. Geology relating to the era following the Mesozoic era (from about 65 million years ago to the present).

cen·ser /'sensər/ ▸ n. a container in which incense is burned during a religious ceremony.

cen·sor /'sensər/ ▸ n. an official who examines material that is to be published and suppresses parts considered offensive or a threat to security. ▸ v. officially suppress unacceptable parts of a book, movie, etc. ■ **cen·sor·ship** n.

cen·so·ri·ous /sen'sôrēəs/ ▸ adj. severely critical.

cen·sure /'senshər/ ▸ v. criticize someone or something severely. ▸ n. strong disapproval or criticism.

> **USAGE**
> **Censure** and **censor** are often confused. **Censure** means 'criticize severely' (*the country was censured for human rights abuses*) or 'strong disapproval,' while **censor** means 'officially suppress unacceptable parts of a book, movie, or similar work' or 'an official who censors books and other material.'

cen·sus /'sensəs/ ▸ n. (pl. **censuses**) an official count or survey of a population.

cent /sent/ ▸ n. a unit or money equal to one hundredth of a dollar, euro, or other decimal currency unit.

cen·taur /'sen‚tôr/ ▸ n. Greek Mythology a creature with the head, arms, and torso of a man and the body and legs of a horse.

cen·ta·vo /sen'tävō/ ▸ n. (pl. **centavos**) a unit of money of Mexico, Brazil, and certain other countries, equal to one hundredth of the basic unit.

cen·te·nar·i·an /‚sentn'e(ə)rēən/ ▸ n. a person who is a hundred or more years old.

cen·ten·ar·y /sen'tenərē, 'sentn‚erē/ ▸ n. (pl. **centenaries**) Brit. the hundredth anniversary of an event.

cen·ten·ni·al /sen'tenēəl/ ▸ adj. relating to a hundredth anniversary. ▸ n. a hundredth anniversary.

cen·ter /'sentər/ (Brit. **centre**) ▸ n. **1** a point or part in the middle of something. **2** a place devoted to a specified activity: *a conference center.* **3** a point from which something spreads or to which something is directed: *the city was a center of discontent.* **4** the middle player in some team games. ▸ v. **1** place something in the center. **2** (**center on/around**) have as a major concern or theme: *several questions center on funding.*
− PHRASES **center of gravity** the central point in an object, around which its mass is evenly balanced.

cen·ter back ▸ n. a player in the middle of the back line of some sports, such as volleyball.

cen·ter·board /'sentər‚bôrd/ ▸ n. a board lowered through the hull of a sailboat to reduce sideways movement.

cen·ter field ▸ n. Baseball **1** the central part of the outfield, behind second base. **2** the position of an outfielder in this area. ■ **cen·ter field·er** n.

cen·ter·fold /'sentər‚fōld/ ▸ n. **1** the two middle pages of a magazine, often containing a single illustration or feature. **2** an illustration on such pages, typically a picture of a naked or scantily clad model.

cen·ter for·ward ▸ n. Soccer & Field Hockey an attacker who plays in the middle of the field.

cen·ter half ▸ n. Soccer a center back.

cen·ter·piece /ˈsentərˌpēs/ ▶ n. **1** an object or item that is intended to be a focus of attention: *the centerpiece of the project is the construction of a new theater*. **2** a decorative piece or display placed in the middle of a dining or serving table.

cen·ter stage ▶ n. the most prominent position. ▶ adv. in or toward the most prominent position.

cen·tes·i·mal /senˈtesəməl/ ▶ adj. relating to division into hundredths.

centi- ▶ comb.form **1** one hundredth: *centiliter*. **2** hundred: *centipede*.

cen·ti·grade /ˈsentəˌgrād/ ▶ adj. relating to the Celsius scale of temperature.

> **USAGE**
> On using **centigrade** or **Celsius**, see the note at **CELSIUS**.

cen·ti·gram /ˈsentəˌgram/ ▶ n. a metric unit of mass equal to one hundredth of a gram.

cen·ti·li·ter /ˈsentəˌlētər/ (Brit. **centilitre**) ▶ n. a metric unit of capacity equal to one hundredth of a liter.

cen·time /ˈsänˌtēm, ˈsent-/ ▶ n. a unit of money equal to one hundredth of a franc or some other decimal currency units (used in France, Belgium, and Luxembourg until the introduction of the euro in 2002).

cen·ti·me·ter /ˈsentəˌmētər, ˈsän-/ (Brit. **centimetre**) ▶ n. a metric unit of length equal to one hundredth of a meter.

cen·ti·mo /ˈsentəmō/ ▶ n. (pl. **centimos**) a unit of money of a number of Latin American countries (and formerly of Spain), equal to one hundredth of the basic unit.

cen·ti·pede /ˈsentəˌpēd/ ▶ n. an insectlike creature with a long body composed of many segments, most of which have a pair of legs.

cen·tral /ˈsentrəl/ ▶ adj. **1** in or near the center. **2** very important; essential. ■ **cen·tral·i·ty** /senˈtralətē/ n. **cen·tral·ly** adv.

cen·tral bank ▶ n. a national bank that provides services for its country's government and commercial banking system and issues currency.

cen·tral heat·ing ▶ n. a system for warming a building by heating water or air in one place and circulating it through pipes and radiators or vents.

cen·tral·ize /ˈsentrəˌlīz/ ▶ v. bring something under the control of a central authority. ■ **cen·tral·ism** /ˈsentrəˌlizəm/ n. **cen·tral·ist** /ˈsentrəˌlist/ n. & adj. **cen·tral·i·za·tion** /ˌsentrələˈzāSHən/ n.

cen·tral nerv·ous sys·tem ▶ n. the complex of nerve tissues that controls the activities of the body.

cen·tral proc·ess·ing u·nit (also **central processor**) ▶ n. the part of a computer in which operations are controlled and executed.

Cen·tral time ▶ n. the standard time in a zone that includes the central states of the US and parts of central Canada.

cen·tre, etc. ▶ n. British spelling of **CENTER**, etc.

-centric ▶ comb.form **1** having a specified center: *geocentric*. **2** originating from a specified viewpoint: *Eurocentric*. ■ **-centricity** comb.form.

cen·trif·u·gal /senˈtrif(y)əgəl/ ▶ adj. Physics moving away from a center. ■ **cen·trif·u·gal·ly** adv.

cen·trif·u·gal force ▶ n. Physics a force that appears to cause a body traveling around a central point to fly outward from its circular path.

cen·tri·fuge /ˈsentrəˌfyōōj/ ▶ n. a machine with a rapidly rotating container, used to separate liquids from solids.

cen·trip·e·tal /senˈtripətl/ ▶ adj. Physics pulling toward a center. ■ **cen·trip·e·tal·ly** adv.

cen·trip·e·tal force ▶ n. Physics a force that causes a body traveling around a central point to maintain its circular path.

cen·trist /ˈsentrəst/ ▶ n. a person having moderate political views or policies. ■ **cen·trism** /-ˌtrizəm/ n.

cen·tu·ri·on /senˈt(y)ŏŏrēən/ ▶ n. the commander of a hundred men in the ancient Roman army.

cen·tu·ry /ˈsenCH(ə)rē/ ▶ n. (pl. **centuries**) **1** a period of one hundred years. **2** a company of a hundred men in the ancient Roman army.

> **USAGE**
> Strictly speaking, centuries run from 01 to 100, meaning that the new century begins on the first day of the year 01 (e.g. January 1, 2001). In practice and in popular belief, however, the new century is regarded as beginning when the significant digits in the date change, e.g. on January 1, 2000, when 1999 became 2000.

CEO ▶ abbr. chief executive officer.

cep /sep/ ▶ n. an edible mushroom with a smooth brown cap.

ce·phal·ic /səˈfalik/ ▶ adj. technical relating to the head.

ceph·a·lo·pod /ˈsefələˌpäd/ ▶ n. a mollusk of a class including octopuses and squids.

ce·ram·ic /səˈramik/ ▶ adj. made of clay that is permanently hardened by heat. ▶ n. (**ceramics**) **1** ceramic articles. **2** (usu. treated as sing.) the art of making ceramic articles. ■ **ce·ram·i·cist** /səˈraməsist/ n.

ce·re·al /ˈsi(ə)rēəl/ ▶ n. **1** a grain used for food, for example wheat, oats, or corn. **2** a grass producing a cereal grain. **3** a breakfast food made from a cereal grain or grains.

cer·e·bel·lum /ˌserəˈbeləm/ ▶ n. (pl. **cerebellums** or **cerebella** /-ˈbelə/) the part of the brain at the back of the skull that coordinates muscular activity. ■ **cer·e·bel·lar** adj.

ce·re·bral /səˈrēbrəl, ˈserəbrəl/ ▶ adj. **1** relating to the cerebrum of the brain. **2** intellectual rather than emotional or physical. ■ **ce·re·bral·ly** adv.

ce·re·bral pal·sy ▶ n. a condition in which a person has difficulty in controlling or moving their muscles, caused by brain damage before or at birth.

cer·e·bra·tion /ˌserəˈbrāSHən/ ▶ n. chiefly formal the working of the brain; thinking.

ce·re·bro·spi·nal /səˌrēbrōˈspīnl, ˌserəbrō-/ ▶ adj. relating to the brain and spine.

ce·re·bro·spi·nal flu·id ▶ n. the clear watery fluid that fills the space between membranes in the brain and the spinal chord.

ce·re·bro·vas·cu·lar /səˌrēbrōˈvaskyələr, ˌserəbrō-/ ▶ adj. relating to the brain and its blood vessels.

ce·re·brum /səˈrēbrəm, ˈserə-/ ▶ n. (pl. **cerebra** /-brə/) the main part of the brain, located in the front of the skull.

cer·e·mo·ni·al /ˌserəˈmōnēəl/ ▶ adj. **1** relating to or used for ceremonies. **2** (of a position or role) in name only; without real authority or power. ▶ n. another term for **CEREMONY**. ■ **cer·e·mo·ni·al·ly** adv.

cer·e·mo·ni·ous /ˌserəˈmōnēəs/ ▶ adj. relating or appropriate to grand and formal occasions. ■ **cer·e·mo·ni·ous·ly** adv.

cer·e·mo·ny /ˈserəˌmōnē/ ▶ n. (pl. **ceremonies**) **1** a formal religious or public occasion, typically celebrating a particular event. **2** the set procedures performed at grand and formal occasions: *the new president was welcomed with due ceremony.*
– PHRASES **stand on ceremony** insist on formal behavior.

ce·rise /səˈrēs, -ˈrēz/ ▶ n. a light, clear red color.

ce·ri·um /ˈsi(ə)rēəm/ ▶ n. a silvery-white metallic chemical element.

cert. ▶ abbr. **1** certificate. **2** certified. **3** Law certiorari.

cer·tain /ˈsərtn/ ▶ adj. **1** able to be relied on to happen or be the case: *it's certain that more changes are in the offing.* **2** completely sure that something is the case. **3** specific but not actually stated: *he raised certain personal problems.* ▶ pron. (**certain of**) some but not all.

cer·tain·ly /ˈsərtnlē/ ▶ adv. **1** without doubt; definitely. **2** yes; by all means.

cer·tain·ty /ˈsərtntē/ ▶ n. (pl. **certainties**) **1** the quality or state of being certain or sure. **2** a fact that is true or an event that is definitely going to take place.

cer·ti·fi·a·ble /ˌsərtəˈfīəbəl/ ▶ adj. **1** able or needing to be officially confirmed or recorded. **2** officially recognized as needing treatment for a mental disorder. ■ **cer·ti·fi·a·bly** adv.

cer·tif·i·cate /sərˈtifikit/ ▶ n. **1** an official document recording a particular fact, event, or achievement. **2** a document attesting ownership of a certain item. ■ **cer·ti·fi·ca·tion** /ˌsərtəfiˈkāshən/ n.

cer·tif·i·cate of de·pos·it (abbr.: **CD**) ▶ n. a certificate issued by a bank to a person depositing money for a specified length of time.

cer·ti·fied pub·lic ac·count·ant /ˈsərtəˌfīd/ (abbr.: **CPA**) ▶ n. a member of an officially accredited professional body of accountants.

cer·ti·fy /ˈsərtəˌfī/ ▶ v. (**certifies**, **certifying**, **certified**) **1** confirm or state something in a formal document. **2** officially recognize that someone or something meets certain standards. **3** officially declare someone insane. ■ **cer·ti·fi·er** n.

cer·ti·o·ra·ri /ˌsərsH(ē)əˈrärē, -ˈre(ə)rī/ ▶ n. Law a writ or order by which a higher court reviews a decision of a lower court.

cer·ti·tude /ˈsərtəˌt(y)o͞od/ ▶ n. a feeling of absolute certainty.

ce·ru·le·an /səˈro͞olēən/ ▶ adj. deep blue in color.

cer·vi·cal /ˈsərvikəl/ ▶ adj. **1** relating to the neck of the uterus. **2** relating to the neck: *the fifth cervical vertebra.*

cer·vix /ˈsərviks/ ▶ n. (pl. **cervices** /-vəˌsēz/) the narrow necklike passage forming the lower end of the uterus.

ce·sar·e·an /siˈze(ə)rēən/ (also **caesarean**) ▶ n. a cesarean section.

ce·sar·e·an sec·tion ▶ n. a surgical operation for delivering a child by cutting through the wall of the mother's abdomen.

ce·si·um /ˈsēzēəm/ (Brit. **caesium**) ▶ n. a soft, silvery, extremely reactive metallic chemical element.

ces·sa·tion /seˈsāsHən/ ▶ n. the ending of something.

ces·sion /ˈsesHən/ ▶ n. the formal giving up of rights, power, or territory by a country or state.

cess·pool /ˈsesˌpo͞ol/ (also **cesspit** /ˈsesˌpit/) ▶ n. an underground tank or covered pit where liquid waste and sewage are stored before disposal.

c'est la vie /ˌsā lä ˈvē/ ▶ exclam. expressing resigned acceptance of an undesirable situation.

ce·ta·cean /siˈtāsHən/ ▶ n. a sea mammal of an order including whales and dolphins.

ce·vi·che /səˈvēCHē, -CHā/ (also **seviche**) ▶ n. a South American dish of marinaded raw fish or seafood.

CF ▶ abbr. **1** cystic fibrosis. **2** center field(er).

Cf ▶ symbol the chemical element californium.

cf. ▶ abbr. compare with.

CFA ▶ abbr. **1** chartered (or certified) financial analyst. **2** Consumer Federation of America.

CFC ▶ abbr. chlorofluorocarbon, a gas that is a compound of carbon, hydrogen, chlorine, and fluorine, used in refrigerators and aerosols and harmful to the ozone layer.

CFS ▶ abbr. chronic fatigue syndrome.

CGI ▶ abbr. **1** computer-generated imagery. **2** Computing common gateway interface.

ch. ▶ abbr. chapter.

Cha·blis /sHaˈblē, sHə-, sHä-/ ▶ n. a dry white burgundy wine from Chablis in France.

cha-cha /ˈCHä ˌCHä/ ▶ n. a ballroom dance with swaying hip movements, performed to a Latin American rhythm.

cha·conne /sHäˈkôn, -ˈkän, -ˈkən/ ▶ n. **1** a musical composition in a series of varying sections in slow triple time. **2** a stately dance performed to a chaconne.

Chad·i·an /ˈCHadēən/ ▶ n. a person from Chad in central Africa. ▶ adj. relating to Chad or Chadians.

chad·or /ˈCHədər, ˈCHädˌôr/ (also **chadar** or **chuddar**) ▶ n. a piece of dark cloth worn by Muslim women around the head and upper body, so that only part of the face can be seen.

chafe /CHāf/ ▶ v. **1** make or become sore or worn by rubbing against something. **2** rub a part of the body to warm it. **3** become impatient because of a restriction or disadvantage: *the women chafed at earning less than the men.*

chaf·er /ˈCHāfər/ ▶ n. a large flying beetle of a group including the Japanese beetle.

chaff[1] /CHaf/ ▶ n. **1** the husks of grain separated from the seed by winnowing or threshing. **2** chopped hay and straw used as cattle fodder.
– PHRASES **separate the wheat from the chaff** distinguish valuable people or things from worthless ones.

chaff[2] ▶ n. light-hearted joking. ▶ v. tease someone.

chaf·finch /ˈCHafˌinCH/ ▶ n. a European finch, the male of which has a bluish head, pink underparts, and dark wings.

chaf·ing dish /ˈCHāfiNG/ ▶ n. **1** a cooking pot with an outer pan of hot water, used for keeping food warm. **2** a metal pan with a heating device below it, used for cooking at the table.

cha·grin /sHəˈgrin/ ▶ n. annoyance or shame at having failed. ▶ v. (**be chagrined**) feel annoyed or ashamed.

chain /CHān/ ▶ n. **1** a connected series of metal links used for fastening or pulling something, or as jewelry. **2** a connected series, set, or sequence: *a chain of restaurants.* **3** a part of a molecule consisting of a number of atoms bonded together in a series. **4** a measure of length equal to 66 ft. ▶ v. **1** fasten or confine someone or something with a chain. **2** restrict or limit to a situation or place: *the chef was chained to his stove six days a week.*

chain gang ▶ n. a group of convicts chained together while working outside the prison.

chain let·ter ▶ n. a letter sent to a number of people, all of whom are asked to make copies and send these to other people, who then do the same.

chain-link ▶ adj. made of wire in a diamond-shaped mesh: *a chain-link fence.*

chain mail ▶ n. historical armor made of small metal rings linked together.

chain re·ac·tion ▶ n. **1** a series of events, each caused by the previous one. **2** a chemical reaction in which the products of the reaction cause other changes.

chain·saw /'CHān,sô/ ▶ n. a power-driven saw with teeth set on a moving chain.

chain-smoke ▶ v. smoke cigarettes one after the other.

chain store ▶ n. one of a group of stores owned by the same company and selling the same goods.

chair /CHe(ə)r/ ▶ n. **1** a separate seat for one person, with a back and four legs. **2** the person in charge of a meeting or an organization. **3** a professorship. **4** (**the chair**) the electric chair. ▶ v. act as chairperson of a meeting or organization.

chair·lift /'CHe(ə)r,lift/ ▶ n. a series of chairs hung from a moving cable, used for carrying passengers up and down a mountain.

chair·man /'CHe(ə)rmən/ (or **chairwoman** /'CHe(ə)r,wŏŏmən/) ▶ n. (pl. **chairmen** or **chairwomen**) a person in charge of a meeting or organization.

chair·per·son /'CHe(ə)r,pərsən/ ▶ n. a chairman or chairwoman.

chaise /SHāz/ ▶ n. **1** chiefly historical a two-wheeled horse-drawn carriage for one or two people. **2** a chaise longue.

chaise longue /'SHāz 'lôNG/ (also **chaise lounge** /'SHāz 'lounj, 'CHās/) ▶ n. (pl. **chaises longues** pronunc. same) a sofa with a backrest at only one end.

chak·ra /'CHäkrə/ ▶ n. (in Indian thought) each of seven centers of spiritual power in the human body.

chal·ced·o·ny /kal'sedn,ē, CHal-, 'kalsə,dōnē, 'CHalsə-/ ▶ n. (pl. **chalcedonies**) a type of quartz with very small crystals, such as onyx.

cha·let /SHa'lā, 'SHa,lā/ ▶ n. **1** a wooden house with overhanging eaves, typically in the Swiss Alps. **2** a similar building used as a ski lodge.

chal·ice /'CHaləs/ ▶ n. **1** historical a goblet. **2** the wine cup used in Holy Communion.

chalk /CHôk/ ▶ n. **1** a white soft limestone formed from the skeletal remains of sea creatures. **2** a similar substance made into sticks and used for drawing or writing. ▶ v. **1** draw or write something with chalk. **2** (**chalk something up**) achieve something noteworthy. **3** (**chalk something up**) ascribe something to a particular cause. ■ **chalk·y** adj.

chalk·board /'CHôk,bôrd/ ▶ n. another term for BLACKBOARD.

chal·lah /'hälə, 'KHälə/ ▶ n. (pl. **challahs**) a braided loaf of white bread, traditionally baked to celebrate the Jewish sabbath.

chal·lenge /'CHalənj/ ▶ n. **1** a demanding task or situation. **2** a call to someone to participate in a contest. **3** an action or statement that calls something into question: *a legal challenge to the ruling failed in the High Court.* **4** an attempt to win a contest or championship in a sport. ▶ v. **1** raise doubt as to whether something is true or genuine. **2** invite someone to do something demanding or take part in a fight. **3** (of a sentry) call on someone to prove their identity. **4** Law object to a jury member. ■ **chal·leng·er** n.

chal·lenged /'CHalənjd/ ▶ adj. **1** euphemistic having a particular disability or impairment: *physically challenged.* **2** humorous lacking in a specified respect: *vertically challenged.*

chal·leng·ing /'CHalənjiNG/ ▶ adj. presenting a test of one's abilities: *a challenging job.*

chal·lis /'SHalē/ ▶ n. a lightweight soft clothing fabric made from silk and worsted.

cham·ber /'CHāmbər/ ▶ n. **1** a large room used for formal or public events. **2** one of the parts of a lawmaking body. **3** (**chambers**) Law rooms used by a judge or judges. **4** old use a private room, especially a bedroom. **5** an enclosed space or cavity. **6** a cavity in the body, an organ, or a plant. **7** the part of a gun bore that contains the charge. ▶ adj. relating to or for a small group of musical instruments: *a chamber orchestra.* ■ **cham·bered** adj.

cham·ber·lain /'CHāmbərlən/ ▶ n. historical an officer who managed the household of a monarch or noble.

cham·ber·maid /'CHāmbər,mād/ ▶ n. a woman who cleans rooms in a hotel.

cham·ber mu·sic ▶ n. instrumental music played by a small ensemble, such as a string quartet.

cham·ber of com·merce ▶ n. a local association to promote the interests of the business community.

cham·ber pot ▶ n. a bowl kept in a bedroom and used as a toilet.

cham·bray /'SHam,brā, -brē/ ▶ n. a cloth with a white weft and a colored warp.

cha·me·le·on /kə'mēlyən, -lēən/ (also **chamaeleon**) ▶ n. a small lizard that can change color according to its surroundings. ■ **cha·me·le·on·ic** /kə,mēlē'änik/ adj.

cham·fer /'CHamfər/ ▶ v. Carpentry cut away a right-angled edge or corner to make a symmetrical sloping edge.

cham·ois /'SHamē/ ▶ n. (pl. same, pronounced /'SHamēz/) **1** an agile goat-antelope found in mountainous areas of southern Europe. **2** (also **chamois leather**) soft pliable leather made from the skin of sheep, goats, or deer.

cham·o·mile /'kamə,mēl, -,mīl/ (also **camomile**) ▶ n. a plant with white and yellow flowers, used in herbal medicine.

champ¹ /CHamp/ ▶ v. **1** munch noisily. **2** fret impatiently.
– PHRASES **champ at the bit** be very impatient to start doing something.

champ² ▶ n. informal a champion.

cham·pagne /SHam'pānyə, SHam'pān/ ▶ n. a white sparkling wine from the Champagne region of France.

cham·pi·on /'CHampēən/ ▶ n. **1** a person who has won a sporting contest or other competition. **2** a person who actively supports or defends another person or cause. ▶ v. actively support: *priests who championed human rights.*

cham·pi·on·ship /ˈCHampēən,SHip/ ▶ n. **1** a contest for the position of champion in a sport. **2** the active support of a person or cause.

chance /CHans/ ▶ n. **1** a possibility of something happening. **2** (**chances**) the probability of something happening: *spelling errors could jeopardize your chances of promotion.* **3** an opportunity. **4** the way in which things happen without any obvious plan or cause: *they met by chance at a youth hostel.* ▶ v. **1** do something by accident. **2** informal do something even though it is risky.
– PHRASES **on the** (**off**) **chance** just in case. **stand a chance** have a likelihood of success. **take a chance** (or **chances**) take a risk.

chan·cel /ˈCHansəl/ ▶ n. the part of a church near the altar, reserved for the clergy and choir.

chan·cel·ler·y /ˈCHans(ə)lərē/ ▶ n. (pl. **chancelleries**) the post or department of a chancellor.

chan·cel·lor /ˈCHans(ə)lər/ ▶ n. **1** a senior government or legal official of various kinds. **2** the president or chief administrative officer of a college or university. **3** (**Chancellor**) the head of the government in some European countries. ■ **chan·cel·lor·ship** /-,SHip/ n.

Chan·cel·lor of the Ex·cheq·uer ▶ n. the chief finance minister of the United Kingdom.

Chan·cer·y /ˈCHans(ə)rē/ (also **Chancery Division**) ▶ n. (pl. **Chanceries**) (in the UK) the Lord Chancellor's court, a division of the High Court of Justice.

chan·cre /ˈkaNGkər, ˈSHaNG-/ ▶ n. a painless ulcer, especially one developing on the genitals in syphilis.

chanc·y /ˈCHansē/ ▶ adj. (**chancier, chanciest**) informal uncertain; risky.

chan·de·lier /,SHandəˈli(ə)r/ ▶ n. a large hanging light with branches for several light bulbs or candles.

chan·dler /ˈCHan(d)lər/ (also **ship chandler**) ▶ n. a dealer in supplies and equipment for ships. ■ **chan·dler·y** n. (pl. **chandleries**).

change /CHānj/ ▶ v. **1** make or become different. **2** exchange something for another: *he scarcely knew how to change a spark plug.* **3** move from one to another: *I had to change trains.* **4** (**change over**) move from one system or situation to another. **5** exchange a sum of money for the same sum in a different currency or denomination. ▶ n. **1** the action of changing. **2** a different experience: *heated pools make a welcome change from a chilly beach.* **3** money returned to someone as the balance of the sum paid. **4** money given in exchange for the same sum in larger units. **5** coins as opposed to paper currency. **6** a clean set of clothes. **7** an order in which a peal of bells can be rung. ■ **change·less** adj. **chang·er** n.
– PHRASES **change hands** pass to a different owner. **change one's tune** express a very different attitude. **ring the changes** vary the ways of doing something.

change·a·ble /ˈCHānjəbəl/ ▶ adj. **1** likely to change in an unpredictable way. **2** able to be changed. ■ **change·a·bil·i·ty** /,CHānjəˈbilətē/ n.

change·ling /ˈCHānjliNG/ ▶ n. a child believed to have been secretly substituted by fairies for the parents' real child.

change·o·ver /ˈCHānj,ōvər/ ▶ n. a change from one system or situation to another.

chan·nel /ˈCHanl/ ▶ n. **1** a band of frequencies used in radio and television transmission, or a station using such a band. **2** a means of communication: *apply through the proper channels.* **3** a passage along which liquid or a watercourse may flow. **4** a wide stretch of water joining two seas. **5** a passage that boats can use in a stretch of water that is otherwise unsafe. **6** an electric circuit that acts as a path for a signal. ▶ v. (**channels, channeling, channeled**) **1** direct toward a particular purpose: *the money has been channeled into the establishment of DNA banks.* **2** pass something along or through a specified route or medium.

chan·nel-surf ▶ v. informal change frequently from one television channel to another.

chant /CHant/ ▶ n. **1** a repeated rhythmic phrase that is shouted or sung together by a group. **2** a tune to which the words of psalms or other works with irregular rhythm are fitted by singing several syllables or words to the same note. ▶ v. say, shout, or sing in a chant.

chant·er /ˈCHantər/ ▶ n. the pipe of a bagpipe with finger holes, on which the melody is played.

chan·te·relle /,SHantəˈrel, ,SHänt-/ ▶ n. an edible woodland mushroom with a yellow funnel-shaped cap.

chan·teuse /,SHänˈtœz, ˈtœz/ ▶ n. a female singer of popular songs.

chant·ey /ˈSHantē/ (also **chanty, shanty,** or **sea chantey**) ▶ n. a song in which a solo part alternates with a chorus, sung by sailors when working together.

chan·try /ˈCHantrē/ ▶ n. (pl. **chantries**) a chapel or other part of a church established by an endowment in order for masses to be said for the donor's soul.

chant·y ▶ n. (pl. **chanties**) variant spelling of **CHANTEY**.

Cha·nuk·kah /ˈKHänəkə, ˈhänəkə/ ▶ n. variant spelling of **HANUKKAH**.

cha·os /ˈkā,äs/ ▶ n. **1** complete disorder and confusion. **2** the formless matter supposed to have existed before the creation of the universe.

cha·os the·o·ry ▶ n. the branch of science concerned with the behavior of complex systems in which tiny changes can have major effects.

cha·ot·ic /kāˈätik/ ▶ adj. in a state of complete confusion and disorder. ■ **cha·ot·i·cal·ly** adv.

chap[1] /CHap/ ▶ v. (**chaps, chapping, chapped**) **1** (of the skin) crack and become sore through exposure to cold weather. **2** (as adj. **chapped**) (of the skin) cracked and sore through exposure to cold weather.

chap[2] ▶ n. Brit. informal a man.

chap·ar·ral /,SHapəˈral/ ▶ n. vegetation consisting of tangled shrubs and thorny bushes.

cha·pat·ti /CHəˈpätē/ ▶ n. (pl. **chapattis**) (in Indian cooking) a flat cake of wholemeal bread cooked on a griddle.

chap·el /ˈCHapəl/ ▶ n. **1** a small building or room for Christian worship in an institution or large private house. **2** a part of a large church with its own altar.

chap·er·one /ˈSHapə,rōn/ ▶ n. **1** a person who accompanies and looks after another person or people. **2** dated an older woman who accompanies and supervises an unmarried girl at social occasions. ▸v. accompany and supervise someone.

chap·lain /ˈCHaplən/ ▸n. a member of the clergy attached to a chapel in a private house or an institution, or to a military unit. ■ **chap·lain·cy** n.

chap·let /ˈCHaplət/ ▸n. a decorative circular band worn on the head.

chaps /CHaps, sHaps/ ▸pl.n. leather pants without a seat, worn by a cowboy over ordinary pants to protect the legs.

chap·ter /ˈCHaptər/ ▸n. **1** a main division of a book. **2** a particular period in history or in a person's life. **3** the governing body of a cathedral or other religious community. **4** a local branch of a society.
– PHRASES **chapter and verse** an exact reference or authority.

char¹ /CHär/ ▸v. (**chars, charring, charred**) partially burn something so as to blacken the surface.

char² ▸n. variant spelling of CHARR.

char³ Brit. informal , dated ▸n. a charwoman.

char·ac·ter /ˈkariktər/ ▸n. **1** the qualities that make a person different from others. **2** the particular nature of something: *the picturesque character of the village.* **3** strength and originality in a person's nature. **4** a person's good reputation. **5** a person in a novel, play, movie, or television show. **6** informal an eccentric or amusing person. **7** a printed or written letter or symbol. ■ **char·ac·ter·ful** /-fəl/ adj. **char·ac·ter·less** adj.

char·ac·ter ac·tor ▸n. an actor who specializes in playing unusual people rather than leading roles.

char·ac·ter·is·tic /ˌkariktəˈristik/ ▸n. a feature or quality typical of a person, place, or thing. ▸adj. typical of a particular person, place, or thing: *the characteristic tilt of her head.* ■ **char·ac·ter·is·ti·cal·ly** adv.

char·ac·ter·ize /ˈkariktəˌrīz/ ▸v. **1** describe the character of someone or something. **2** be typical of: *the rugged hills that characterize New England.* ■ **char·ac·ter·i·za·tion** /ˌkariktərəˈzāsHən/ n.

cha·rade /sHəˈrād/ ▸n. **1** an absurd pretense. **2** (**charades**) a game of guessing a word or phrase from written or acted clues.

char·broil /ˈCHärˌbroil/ ▸v. grill food, especially meat on a rack over charcoal.

char·coal /ˈCHärˌkōl/ ▸n. **1** a black form of carbon obtained when wood is heated in the absence of air. **2** a dark gray color.

char·cu·te·rie /sHärˌko͞otəˈrē, -ˈko͞otərē/ ▸n. (pl. **charcuteries**) **1** cold cooked meats. **2** a store selling cold cooked meats.

chard /CHärd/ (also **Swiss chard**) ▸n. a variety of beet with edible, slightly bitter, broadly ribbed leaves.

Char·don·nay /ˌsHärdnˈā/ ▸n. a white wine made from a variety of grape used for making champagne and other wines.

char·ette /sHəˈret/ ▸n. a meeting or conference devoted to a concerted effort to solve a problem or plan something.

charge /CHärj/ ▸v. **1** ask an amount of money as a price for goods or a service. **2** formally accuse someone of something. **3** rush forward so as to attack someone or something. **4** rush in a particular direction: *he charged up the stairs.* **5** entrust someone with a task. **6** store electrical energy in a battery. **7** load or fill a container, gun, etc. **8** fill with a quality or emotion: *the air was charged with menace.* ▸n. **1** a price asked. **2** a formal accusation made against a prisoner brought to trial. **3** responsibility for care or control: *she felt out of touch with the youngsters in her charge.* **4** a person or thing entrusted to someone's care. **5** a headlong rush forward. **6** the property of matter that is responsible for electrical phenomena, existing in a positive or negative form. **7** energy stored chemically in a battery for conversion into electricity. **8** a quantity of explosive to be detonated in order to fire a gun or similar weapon. ■ **charge·a·ble** adj. **charged** adj.
– PHRASES **press charges** accuse someone formally of a crime so that they can be brought to trial.

charge·back /ˈCHärjˌbak/ ▸n. **1** a demand by a credit-card provider for a retailer to make good the loss on a fraudulent or disputed transaction. **2** an act or policy of allocating the cost of an organization's centrally located resources to the individuals or departments that use them.

charge card ▸n. a credit card issued by a chain store or bank.

char·gé d'af·faires /sHärˌzHä däˈfer/ (also **chargé**) ▸n. (pl. **chargés d'affaires** pronunc. same) **1** an ambassador's deputy. **2** a government's diplomatic representative in a country to which an ambassador has not been sent.

charg·er¹ /ˈCHärjər/ ▸n. **1** a device for charging a battery. **2** historical a horse ridden by a knight or cavalryman.

charg·er² ▸n. old use a large flat dish.

char·i·ot /ˈCHarēət/ ▸n. a two-wheeled vehicle drawn by horses, used in ancient warfare and racing. ■ **char·i·ot·eer** /ˌCHarēəˈti(ə)r/ n.

cha·ris·ma /kəˈrizmə/ ▸n. **1** attractiveness or charm that can inspire admiration or enthusiasm in other people. **2** (pl. **charismata** /-ˌmətə/) (in Christian belief) a special gift given by God.

char·is·mat·ic /ˌkarizˈmatik/ ▸adj. **1** having a charm that can inspire admiration in other people. **2** relating to a Christian movement that emphasizes special gifts from God, such as the healing of the sick. ■ **char·is·mat·i·cal·ly** adv.

char·i·ta·ble /ˈCHaritəbəl/ ▸adj. **1** relating to the assistance of people in need. **2** not judging others too severely; tolerant. ■ **char·i·ta·bly** adv.

char·i·ty /ˈCHaritē/ ▸n. (pl. **charities**) **1** an organization set up to help people in need. **2** the voluntary giving of money or other help to people in need. **3** help or money given to people in need. **4** tolerance in judging others.

char·la·tan /ˈsHärlətən, ˈsHärlətn/ ▸n. a person who falsely claims to have a particular skill. ■ **char·la·tan·ism** /-lətəˌnizəm, -lətnˌizəm/ n. **char·la·tan·ry** n.

Charles's law /CHärlz, CHärlziz/ ▸n. a law stating that the volume of an ideal gas at constant pressure is directly proportional to the absolute temperature.

charles·ton /ˈCHärlstən/ ▸n. a lively dance of the 1920s that involved turning the knees inward and kicking out the lower legs.

char·lotte /ˈsHärlət/ ▸n. a pudding made of stewed fruit with a casing or covering of bread, sponge cake, or cookies.

charm /CHärm/ ▸n. **1** the power or quality of delighting or fascinating others. **2** a small ornament worn on a necklace or bracelet. **3** an object, act, or saying believed to have magic power. ▶v. **1** delight greatly: *she charmed me with her intelligence.* **2** use one's charm in order to influence someone. ■ **charm·er** n. **charm·less** adj.

charmed /CHärmd/ ▶adj. (of a person's life) unusually lucky as though protected by magic. ▶exclam. dated expressing polite pleasure at an introduction.

charm·ing /'CHärmiNG/ ▶adj. **1** delightful; attractive. **2** very polite, friendly, and likable. ▶exclam. used as an ironic expression of displeasure. ■ **charm·ing·ly** adv.

charm of·fen·sive ▶n. a campaign of flattery and friendliness designed to achieve the support of others.

char·nel house /'CHärnl/ ▶n. historical a building or vault in which corpses or bones were piled.

Cha·ro·lais /,SHarə'lā/ ▶n. (pl. same) an animal of a breed of large white beef cattle.

charr /CHär/ (also **char**) ▶n. (pl. same) a troutlike northern freshwater or sea fish.

chart /CHärt/ ▶n. **1** a sheet of information in the form of a table, graph, or diagram. **2** a geographical map, especially one used for navigation by sea or air. **3** (**the charts**) a weekly listing of the current best-selling pop records. ▶v. **1** make a map of an area. **2** plot or record something on a chart.

char·ter /'CHärtər/ ▶n. **1** a document granted by a ruler or government, by which an institution such as a university is created or its rights are defined. **2** a written constitution or description of an organization's functions. **3** the hiring of an aircraft, ship, or motor vehicle. ▶v. **1** hire an aircraft, ship, or motor vehicle. **2** grant a charter to a university or organization. ■ **char·ter·er** n.

char·ter flight ▶n. a flight by an aircraft chartered for a specific journey, not part of an airline's regular schedule.

char·ter mem·ber ▶n. an original or founding member of an organization.

Chart·ism /'CHärt,izəm/ ▶n. a UK movement (1837–48) for social and legislative reform, the principles of which were set out in *The People's Charter*. ■ **Chart·ist** /'CHärtəst/ n. & adj.

char·treuse /SHär'trŌōz, -'trŌōs/ ▶n. a pale green or yellow liqueur made from brandy.

char·wom·an /'CHär,wŏŏmən/ ▶n. (pl. **charwomen**) Brit. dated a woman employed as a cleaner in a house or office.

char·y /'CHe(ə)rē/ ▶adj. cautiously reluctant: *leaders are chary of reform.*

chase¹ /CHās/ ▶v. **1** pursue someone or something so as to catch them. **2** hurry or cause to hurry somewhere: *she chased him out of the house.* **3** try to obtain something owed or required. ▶n. **1** an act of chasing. **2** (**the chase**) hunting as a sport.
– PHRASES **give chase** pursue someone or something so as to catch them.

chase² ▶v. engrave metal or a design on metal.

chas·er /'CHāsər/ ▶n. **1** a person or thing that chases someone or something. **2** informal a weak alcoholic drink taken after a stronger one.

chasm /'kazəm/ ▶n. **1** a deep crack or opening in the earth. **2** a marked difference between people, opinions, or feelings: *the chasm between rich and poor.*

chas·sis /'CHasē, 'SHasē/ ▶n. (pl. same /-sēz/) the base frame of a car or other wheeled vehicle.

chaste /CHāst/ ▶adj. **1** refraining from all sex, or from sex outside marriage. **2** without unnecessary decoration; simple.

chas·ten /'CHāsən/ ▶v. (often as adj. **chastened**) make someone feel ashamed or sorry: *you walk like a chastened but defiant kid.*

chas·tise /CHas'tīz/ ▶v. reprimand someone severely. ■ **chas·tise·ment** /CHas'tīzmənt, 'CHastəz-/ n.

chas·ti·ty /'CHastətē/ ▶n. the practice of refraining from all sex, or from sex outside marriage.

chas·ti·ty belt ▶n. historical a garment or device designed to prevent the woman wearing it from having sex.

chas·u·ble /'CHazəbəl, 'CHazh-, 'CHas-/ ▶n. a sleeveless outer garment worn by a Christian priest when celebrating Mass.

chat /CHat/ ▶v. (**chats, chatting, chatted**) **1** talk in an informal way. **2** (**chat someone up**) informal talk to someone flirtatiously. ▶n. an informal conversation.

cha·teau /SHa'tō/ ▶n. (pl. **chateaux** or **chateaus** pronunc. same or /-'tō(z)/) a large French country house or castle.

chat·e·laine /'SHatl,ān/ ▶n. dated a woman in charge of a large house.

chat room ▶n. an area on the Internet or other computer network where users can communicate.

chat·tel /'CHatl/ ▶n. a personal possession.

chat·ter /'CHatər/ ▶v. **1** talk informally about minor matters. **2** (of a bird or monkey) make a series of quick high-pitched sounds. **3** (of a person's teeth) click repeatedly together from cold or fear. ▶n. **1** informal talk. **2** a series of quick high-pitched sounds. ■ **chat·ter·er** n.
– PHRASES **the chattering classes** derogatory educated people considered as a social group prone to expressing liberal opinions.

chat·ter·box /'CHatər,bäks/ ▶n. informal a person who talks too much, especially about trivial matters.

chat·ty /'CHatē/ ▶adj. (**chattier, chattiest**) **1** fond of chatting. **2** (of a letter) informal and lively. ■ **chat·ti·ly** adv. **chat·ti·ness** n.

chauf·feur /'SHōfər, SHō'fər/ ▶n. a person employed to drive a car. ▶v. drive a car or a passenger in a car, especially as one's job.

chau·vin·ism /'SHōvə,nizəm/ ▶n. **1** extreme or aggressive support for one's own country or group. **2** the belief held by some men that men are superior to women. ■ **chau·vin·ist** /'SHōvənist/ n. & adj. **chau·vin·is·tic** /,SHōvə'nistik/ adj.

Ch.E. ▶abbr. chemical engineer.

cheap /CHēp/ ▶adj. **1** low in price. **2** charging low prices. **3** low in price and of poor quality. **4** having no value because achieved in a regrettable way: *her moment of cheap triumph.* ▶adv. at or for a low price. ■ **cheap·ly** adv. **cheap·ness** n.

cheap·en /'CHēpən/ ▶v. **1** lower the price of something. **2** reduce the worth of someone or something.

cheap·jack /'CHēp,jak/ ▶adj. of inferior quality.

cheap·skate /'CHēp,skāt/ ▶n. informal a stingy person.

cheat /CHēt/ ▶v. **1** act dishonestly or unfairly in order to gain an advantage. **2** deprive someone of something by dishonest or unfair means.

3 manage to avoid something bad or unwelcome: *he cheated death after falling 20 feet to the pavement.* ▶ n. **1** a person who cheats. **2** an act of cheating.

Che·chen /'CHeCHən/ ▶ n. (pl. same or **Chechens**) a person from Chechnya, a self-governing republic in SW Russia.

check[1] /CHek/ ▶ v. **1** examine the accuracy, quality, or condition of something. **2** make sure that something is the case: *I checked that all the doors were secure.* **3** stop or slow the progress of: *measures to check the growth in crime and violence.* **4** Chess move a piece or pawn to a square where it directly attacks the opposing king. ▶ n. **1** an act of checking the accuracy, quality, or condition of something. **2** a means of controlling or restraining something. **3** Chess a position in which a king is directly threatened. **4** the bill in a restaurant.
– PHRASES **check in** register at a hotel or airport. **check out** settle one's hotel bill before leaving. **check something out** investigate or find out about something. **check up on** investigate something. **in check 1** under control. **2** Chess (of a king) directly attacked by an opponent's piece or pawn.

check[2] ▶ n. a pattern of small squares. ▶ adj. (also **checked**) having a pattern of small squares.

check[3] /CHek/ (Brit. **cheque**) ▶ n. a written order to a bank to pay a stated sum from an account to a particular person.

check·book /'CHek,boŏk/ ▶ n. a book of blank checks with a register for recording the checks written.

check·er[1] /'CHekər/ ▶ n. **1** a person or thing that verifies or examines something. **2** a cashier in a store or supermarket.

check·er[2] (Brit. **chequer**) ▶ n. **1** (often **checkers**) a pattern of squares, typically alternately colored: *a geometric shape bordered by checkers.* **2** (**checkers**) (treated as sing.) a game for two players, with twelve pieces each, played on a checkerboard. **3** a round flat piece, usually red or black, used to play checkers.

check·er·board /'CHekər,bôrd/ ▶ n. **1** a board for playing checkers and similar games, having a regular checkered pattern in black and white. **2** a pattern resembling such a board.

check·ered /'CHekərd/ ▶ adj. **1** having a pattern of alternating squares of different colors. **2** marked by periods of varied fortune or discreditable incidents: *his checkered past might hurt his electability.*

check·ered flag ▶ n. a flag with a black-and-white checkered pattern, shown to racing drivers at the end of a race.

check-in ▶ n. the place at an airport where a passenger registers before departure.

check·ing ac·count ▶ n. an account at a bank against which checks can be drawn by the account holder.

check·list /'CHek,list/ ▶ n. a list of items required or things to be done or considered.

check mark ▶ n. a mark (✓) used to indicate that a written item is correct or has been chosen or verified.

check·mate /'CHek,māt/ Chess ▶ n. a position of check from which a king cannot escape. ▶ v. put a king into checkmate.

check·out /'CHek,out/ ▶ n. **1** a place where goods are paid for in a supermarket or similar store.

2 the procedure followed when a guest leaves a hotel at the end of a stay.

check·point /'CHek,point/ ▶ n. a barrier where security checks are carried out on travelers.

check·up /'CHek,əp/ ▶ n. a thorough examination to detect any problems, especially medical or mechanical ones.

ched·dar /'CHedər/ ▶ n. a kind of firm, smooth cheese originally made in Cheddar in SW England.

cheek /CHēk/ ▶ n. **1** either side of the face below the eye. **2** either of the buttocks. **3** remarks or behavior seen as rude or disrespectful.
– PHRASES **cheek by jowl** close together. **turn the other cheek** choose not to retaliate after one has been attacked or insulted.

cheek·bone /'CHēk,bōn/ ▶ n. the bone below the eye.

cheek·y /'CHēkē/ ▶ adj. (**cheekier**, **cheekiest**) showing a lack of respect, often in an amusing way. ■ **cheek·i·ly** adv. **cheek·i·ness** n.

cheep /CHēp/ ▶ n. a shrill, squeaky cry made by a young bird. ▶ v. make a cheep.

cheer /CHi(ə)r/ ▶ v. **1** shout for joy or in praise or encouragement. **2** praise or encourage a person, team, etc., with shouts. **3** (**cheer up** or **cheer someone up**) become or make less miserable. **4** give comfort or support to someone. ▶ n. **1** a shout of joy, encouragement, or praise. **2** (also **good cheer**) a feeling of happiness or optimism.

cheer·ful /'CHi(ə)rfəl/ ▶ adj. **1** noticeably happy and optimistic. **2** bright and pleasant: *cheerful colors.* ■ **cheer·ful·ly** adv. **cheer·ful·ness** n.

cheer·i·o /,CHi(ə)rē'ō/ ▶ exclam. Brit. informal goodbye.

cheer·lead·er /'CHi(ə)r,lēdər/ ▶ n. **1** a person belonging to a group that performs organized chanting and dancing in support of a team at a sports event. **2** an enthusiastic and vocal supporter.

cheer·less /'CHi(ə)rlis/ ▶ adj. gloomy and depressing.

cheers /CHi(ə)rz/ ▶ exclam. informal **1** expressing good wishes before drinking. **2** chiefly Brit. said to express thanks or on parting.

cheer·y /'CHi(ə)rē/ ▶ adj. (**cheerier**, **cheeriest**) happy and optimistic. ■ **cheer·i·ly** adv. **cheer·i·ness** n.

cheese[1] /CHēz/ ▶ n. a food made from the pressed curds of milk, either firm or soft in texture.

cheese[2] (also **big cheese**) ▶ n. informal an important person: *he was a big cheese in the business world.*

cheese[3] ▶ (**be cheesed off**) chiefly Brit. informal be irritated or bored.

cheese·burg·er /'CHēz,bərgər/ ▶ n. a hamburger with a slice of cheese on it.

cheese·cake /'CHēz,kāk/ ▶ n. **1** a rich sweet cake made with cream and soft cheese on a cookie or pastry crust. **2** informal pictures of scantily dressed women posing in a sexually attractive way.

cheese·cloth /'CHēz,klôTH/ ▶ n. thin, loosely woven cotton cloth.

cheese·steak /'CHēz,stāk/ ▶ n. (also **Philly cheesesteak**) a submarine sandwich containing thin-sliced sautéed beef, melted cheese, and sautéed onions.

chees·y /'CHēzē/ ▶ adj. (**cheesier**, **cheesiest**) **1** like cheese in taste, smell, or consistency. **2** informal cheap and low in quality. **3** informal unoriginal or sentimental: *an album of cheesy pop hits.* ■ **chees·i·ly** adv. **chees·i·ness** n.

chee·tah /'cʜētə/ ▶ n. a large fast-running spotted cat found in Africa and parts of Asia.

chef /sʜef/ ▶ n. a professional cook, especially the chief cook in a restaurant or hotel.

chef-d'œu·vre /sʜā 'dœv(rə), 'də(r)v/ ▶ n. (pl. **chefs-d'œuvre** pronunc. same) a masterpiece.

chem. ▶ abbr. **1** chemical. **2** chemistry.

chem·i·cal /'kemikəl/ ▶ adj. relating to chemistry or chemicals. ▶ n. a compound or substance that has been artificially prepared or purified. ■ **chem·i·cal·ly** adv.

chem·i·cal en·gi·neer·ing ▶ n. the branch of engineering concerned with the design and operation of industrial chemical plants.

che·mise /sʜə'mēz, -'mēs/ ▶ n. **1** a dress hanging straight from the shoulders, popular in the 1920s. **2** a woman's loose-fitting petticoat or nightdress.

chem·ist /'kemist/ ▶ n. **1** a person engaged in chemical research. **2** Brit. a person who is authorized to dispense medicinal drugs. **3** Brit. a drugstore.

chem·is·try /'keməstrē/ ▶ n. (pl. **chemistries**) **1** the branch of science concerned with the nature and properties of substances and how they react with each other. **2** the chemical properties of a particular substance: *the patient's blood chemistry was monitored regularly.* **3** the interaction between two people, especially when experienced as a strong mutual attraction: *sexual chemistry.*

che·mo /'kēmō/ ▶ n. informal chemotherapy.

che·mo·ther·a·py /ˌkēmō'ʜʜerəpē, ˌkemō-/ ▶ n. the treatment of disease, especially cancer, by the use of chemical substances.

che·nille /sʜə'nēl/ ▶ n. fabric with a long velvety pile.

Che·nin blanc /'sʜenan 'blängk, 'sʜenan / (also **Chenin**) ▶ n. a white wine made from a variety of grape native to the Loire valley in France.

cheong·sam /'cʜông,säm/ ▶ n. a straight, close-fitting silk dress with a high neck, worn by Chinese and Indonesian women.

cheque ▶ n. British spelling of CHECK³.

cheq·uer ▶ n. British spelling of CHECKER².

cher·ish /'cʜerisʜ/ ▶ v. **1** protect and care for someone or something lovingly. **2** keep in one's mind: *he had long cherished a secret fantasy about his future.*

Cher·o·kee /'cʜerəkē/ ▶ n. (pl. same or **Cherokees**) a member of an American Indian people formerly living in much of the southern US.

che·root /sʜə'rōōt/ ▶ n. a cigar that has both ends open.

cher·ry /'cʜerē/ ▶ n. (pl. **cherries**) **1** a small, round bright or dark red fruit with a stone. **2** a bright, deep red color.
– PHRASES **a bowl of cherries** a pleasant or enjoyable situation or experience.

cher·ry-pick ▶ v. selectively choose the best things or people from those available.

cher·ry to·ma·to ▶ n. a miniature tomato.

cher·ub /'cʜerəb/ ▶ n. **1** (pl. **cherubim** /'cʜer(y)əbim/ or **cherubs**) a type of angel, represented in art as a chubby child with wings. **2** (pl. **cherubs**) a beautiful or innocent-looking child. ■ **che·ru·bic** /cʜə'rōōbik/ adj. **che·ru·bi·cal·ly** /-bik(ə)lē/ adv.

cher·vil /'cʜərvəl/ ▶ n. an herb with an anise flavor, used in cooking.

Chesh·ire /'cʜesʜər, 'cʜesʜ,ir/ ▶ n. a kind of firm, crumbly cheese, originally made in Cheshire, England.

Chesh·ire cat ▶ n. a cat with a broad fixed grin, as described in Lewis Carroll's *Alice's Adventures in Wonderland* (1865).

chess /cʜes/ ▶ n. a board game for two players, the object of which is to put the opponent's king under a direct attack, leading to checkmate.

chess·board /'cʜes,bôrd/ ▶ n. a square board divided into sixty-four checkered squares, used for playing chess or checkers.

chest /cʜest/ ▶ n. **1** the front surface of a person's body between the neck and the stomach. **2** a large strong box in which things may be stored or transported. ■ **chest·ed** adj.
– PHRASES **get something off one's chest** informal say something that one has wanted to say for a long time. **keep** (or **play**) **one's cards close to one's chest** informal be extremely secretive about one's plans.

ches·ter·field /'cʜestər,fēld/ ▶ n. a sofa whose back and outward-curving arms are padded and of the same height.

chest·nut /'cʜes(t),nət/ ▶ n. **1** a shiny brown edible nut that develops within a bristly case. **2** (also **sweet chestnut** or **Spanish chestnut**) the large tree that produces chestnuts. **3** a deep reddish-brown color. **4** a reddish-brown horse. **5** (**old chestnut**) a joke or story that has become uninteresting because it has been repeated too often.

chest of drawers ▶ n. a piece of furniture consisting of an upright frame fitted with a set of drawers.

chest·y /'cʜestē/ ▶ adj. **1** informal (of a woman) having large or prominent breasts. **2** produced deep in the chest. **3** conceited and arrogant. ■ **chest·i·ness** n.

che·val glass /sʜə'val/ (also **cheval mirror**) ▶ n. a tall mirror fitted at its middle to an upright frame so that it can be tilted.

chev·a·lier /sʜə'val,yā, sʜəval'yā/ ▶ n. **1** historical a knight. **2** a member of the French Legion of Honor.

chè·vre /'sʜev(rə)/ ▶ n. French cheese made with goat's milk.

chev·ron /'sʜevrən/ ▶ n. **1** a V-shaped line or stripe, especially one on the sleeve of a soldier's or police officer's uniform to show their rank. **2** Heraldry a broad upside-down V-shape.

chew /cʜōō/ ▶ v. **1** bite and work food in the mouth to make it easier to swallow. **2** (**chew something over**) discuss or consider something at length. ▶ n. **1** an act of chewing something. **2** something other than food that is meant for chewing: *a dog chew.* ■ **chew·a·ble** adj. **chew·er** n.
– PHRASES **chew the fat** informal chat in a leisurely way. **chew the scenery** see SCENERY.

chew·ing gum ▶ n. a flavored gum that is chewed but not swallowed.

chew·y /'cʜōōē/ ▶ adj. (**chewier, chewiest**) (of food) needing much chewing before it can be swallowed. ■ **chew·i·ness** n.

Chey·enne /sʜī'an, sʜī'en/ ▶ n. (pl. same or **Cheyennes**) a member of an American Indian people formerly living between the Missouri and Arkansas Rivers.

chez /shā/ ▸ prep. chiefly humorous at the home of.

chi /chē/ (also **qi** or **ki** pronunc. same) ▸ n. the circulating life force whose existence and properties are the basis of much Chinese philosophy and medicine.

Chi·an·ti /kē'äntē, -'antē/ ▸ n. (pl. **Chiantis**) a dry red Italian wine.

chi·a·ro·scu·ro /kē,ärə'sk(y)ŏŏrō, kē,arə-/ ▸ n. the treatment of light and shade in drawing and painting.

chic /shēk/ ▸ adj. (**chicer, chicest**) elegant and stylish. ▸ n. elegance and stylishness. ▪ **chic·ly** adv.

chi·cane /shi'kān, chi-/ ▸ n. a sharp double bend created to form an obstacle on an auto-racing course.

chi·can·er·y /shi'kānərē, chi-/ ▸ n. trickery or deception.

Chi·ca·no /chi'känō, shi-/ ▸ n. (pl. **Chicanos**; fem. **Chicana** /chi'känə, shi-/, pl. **Chicanas**) (in North America) a person of Mexican origin or descent.

chi-chi /'shēshē, 'chēchē/ ▸ adj. intended to be stylish or elegant but seeming over-elaborate or artificial.

chick /chik/ ▸ n. **1** a young bird, especially one newly hatched. **2** informal a young woman.

chick·a·dee /'chikədē/ ▸ n. a North American titmouse with a black head and white breast, widely distributed in the US and Canada.

chick·en /'chikən/ ▸ n. **1** a domestic fowl kept for its eggs or meat. **2** informal a coward. ▸ adj. informal cowardly. ▸ v. (**chicken out**) informal be too scared to do something.
– PHRASES **chicken-and-egg** referring to a situation in which each of two things appears to be necessary to the other.

chick·en feed ▸ n. informal a very small sum of money.

chick·en·pox /'chikən,poks/ ▸ n. an infectious disease causing a mild fever and a rash of itchy inflamed pimples.

chick·en wire ▸ n. wire netting with a hexagonal mesh.

chick·pea /'chik,pē/ ▸ n. a yellowish seed cooked and eaten as a vegetable.

chick·weed /'chik,wēd/ ▸ n. a small white-flowered plant, often growing as a garden weed.

chic·le /'chikəl, 'chiklē/ ▸ n. the milky latex of the sapodilla tree, used to make chewing gum.

chic·o·ry /'chikərē/ ▸ n. (pl. **chicories**) **1** a blue-flowered plant with edible leaves and a root that can be used as an additive to or substitute for coffee. **2** another term for ENDIVE (sense 1).

chide /chīd/ ▸ v. (past **chided** or **chid**; past part. **chided**) scold or rebuke someone.

chief /chēf/ ▸ n. **1** a leader or ruler of a people. **2** the head of an organization. ▸ adj. **1** having the highest rank or authority. **2** most important: *the chief reason.* ▪ **chief·dom** n.

chief·ly /'chēflē/ ▸ adv. mainly; mostly.

chief of staff ▸ n. the senior staff officer of an armed service or command.

chief·tain /'chēftən/ ▸ n. the leader of a people or clan. ▪ **chief·tain·cy** /-sē/ n. (pl. **chieftaincies**) **chief·tain·ship** /-,ship/ n.

chif·fon /shi'fän, 'shif,än/ ▸ n. a light, transparent silk or nylon fabric.

chif·fo·nier /,shifə'ni(ə)r/ ▸ n. a tall chest of drawers.

chig·ger /'chigər/ (also **jigger** /'jigər/) ▸ n. a tropical flea, the female of which lays eggs

beneath the host's skin, causing painful sores.

chi·gnon /'shēn,yän, shēn'yän/ ▸ n. a knot or coil of hair arranged on the back of a woman's head.

chig·oe /'chigō, 'chē-/ ▸ n. another term for CHIGGER.

chi·hua·hua /chə'wäwə, shə-/ ▸ n. a very small breed of dog with smooth hair and large eyes.

chil·blain /'chil,blān/ ▸ n. a painful, itching swelling on a hand or foot caused by poor circulation in the skin during exposure to cold weather.

child /chīld/ ▸ n. (pl. **children**) **1** a young human being below the age of full physical development. **2** a son or daughter of any age. **3** (**children**) old use the descendants of a family or people. ▪ **child·less** adj.
– PHRASES **child's play** an easy task. **with child** old use pregnant.

child·bed /'chīld,bed/ ▸ n. old use childbirth.

child·birth /'chīld,bərth/ ▸ n. the action of giving birth to a child.

child·care /'chīld,ke(ə)r/ ▸ n. the care of children while the parents are working.

child·hood /'chīld,hŏŏd/ ▸ n. the state or period of being a child.

child·ish /'chīldish/ ▸ adj. **1** like or appropriate to a child. **2** silly and immature. ▪ **child·ish·ly** adv. **child·ish·ness** n.

child·like /'chīld,līk/ ▸ adj. (of an adult) having the good qualities associated with a child, such as innocence.

child·proof /'chīld,prŏŏf/ ▸ adj. designed to prevent children from injuring themselves or doing damage.

chil·dren /'chīldrən/ ▸ plural of CHILD.

Chil·e·an /'chilēən, chə'lāən/ ▸ n. a person from Chile. ▸ adj. relating to Chile.

chil·i /'chilē/ (also **chile**, Brit. **chili**) ▸ n. (pl. **chilies, chiles**, or Brit. **chillies**) **1** a small hot-tasting kind of pepper, used in cooking and as a spice. **2** chili con carne.

chil·i con car·ne /kän 'kärnē, kən/ ▸ n. a stew of ground meat and beans flavored with chili.

chil·i pow·der ▸ n. a mixture of ground dried red chilies and other spices.

chill /chil/ ▸ n. **1** an unpleasant feeling of coldness. **2** a feverish cold. ▸ v. **1** make someone or something cold. **2** horrify or frighten someone. **3** (usu. **chill out**) informal calm down and relax. ▸ adj. chilly.
– PHRASES **take a chill pill** informal calm down; relax.

chill·er /'chilər/ ▸ n. a cold cabinet or refrigerator for keeping stored food a few degrees above freezing.

chilli ▸ n. British spelling of CHILI.

chill·y /'chilē/ ▸ adj. (**chillier, chilliest**) **1** unpleasantly cold. **2** unfriendly. ▪ **chill·i·ness** n.

chi·mae·ra ▸ n. variant spelling of CHIMERA.

chime /chīm/ ▸ n. **1** a tuneful ringing sound. **2** a bell or a metal bar or tube used in a set to produce chimes when struck. ▸ v. **1** (of a bell or clock) make a tuneful ringing sound. **2** (**chime in**) interrupt a conversation with a remark.

chi·me·ne·a /,shimi'nēə/ (also **chiminea**) ▸ n. an earthenware outdoor fireplace shaped like a light bulb, with the bulbous lower part housing the fire and typically supported by a wrought-iron stand.

chi·me·ra /kī'mi(ə)rə, kə-/ (also **chimaera**)
▶ n. **1** an unrealistic hope or idea. **2** Greek Mythology a fire-breathing female monster with a lion's head, a goat's body, and a serpent's tail.

chi·mer·i·cal /kī'mi(ə)rikəl, kə-/ ▶ adj. impossible to achieve; unrealistic.

chim·ney /'CHimnē/ ▶ n. (pl. **chimneys**) **1** a vertical channel or pipe that takes smoke and gases up from a fire or furnace. **2** a steep, narrow cleft by which a rock face may be climbed.

chim·ney pot ▶ n. an earthenware or metal pipe at the top of a chimney.

chim·ney stack ▶ n. the part of a chimney that sticks up above a roof.

chim·ney sweep ▶ n. a person whose job is cleaning out the soot from chimneys.

chimp /CHimp/ ▶ n. informal a chimpanzee.

chim·pan·zee /,CHim,pan'zē, -pən'zē, -'panzē/ ▶ n. an ape native to west and central Africa.

chin /CHin/ ▶ n. the part of the face below the mouth.
– PHRASES **keep one's chin up** informal remain cheerful in difficult circumstances. **take it on the chin** informal accept a difficult or unpleasant situation without complaining.

chi·na /'CHīnə/ ▶ n. **1** a fine white ceramic material. **2** household objects made from china.

chi·na clay ▶ n. another term for KAOLIN.

Chi·na·man /'CHīnəmən/ ▶ n. (pl. **Chinamen**) chiefly old use or derogatory a native of China.

Chi·na syn·drome ▶ n. a hypothetical chain of events following the meltdown of a nuclear reactor, in which the core melts deep into the earth.

Chi·na tea ▶ n. tea made from a type of tea plant grown in China, often smoked or with flower petals added.

Chi·na·town /'CHīnə,toun/ ▶ n. a district of a non-Chinese town in which the majority of the population is of Chinese origin.

chinch bug /CHinCH/ ▶ n. a plant-eating ground bug that forms large swarms on grasses and rushes.

chin·chil·la /CHin'CHilə/ ▶ n. **1** a small South American rodent with soft gray fur and a long bushy tail. **2** a breed of cat or rabbit with silver-gray or gray fur.

chine¹ /CHīn/ ▶ n. the backbone of an animal, or a cut of meat containing part of it.

chine² ▶ n. the angle where the planks or plates at the bottom of a boat or ship meet the side.

Chi·nese /CHī'nēz, -'nēs/ ▶ n. (pl. same) **1** the language of China. **2** a person from China. ▶ adj. relating to China.

Chi·nese check·ers ▶ pl.n. (treated as sing.) a board game in which players attempt to move marbles or counters from one corner to the opposite one on a star-shaped board.

Chi·nese lan·tern ▶ n. **1** a collapsible paper lantern. **2** a plant with white flowers and round orange fruits enclosed in a papery orange-red calyx.

Chi·nese puz·zle ▶ n. an intricate puzzle consisting of many interlocking pieces.

Chi·nese wall ▶ n. something that prevents information passing from one person or group to another.

Chink /CHiNGk/ ▶ n. informal, offensive a Chinese person. ■ **Chink·y** adj.

chink¹ /CHiNGk/ ▶ n. **1** a narrow opening or crack. **2** a beam of light entering through a chink.

chink² ▶ v. make a light, high-pitched ringing sound, like that of glasses or coins striking each other. ▶ n. a high-pitched ringing sound.

chin·less /'CHinlis/ ▶ adj. **1** (of a man) having a very small chin. **2** informal having a weak character.

chi·no /'CHēnō/ ▶ n. **1** a cotton twill fabric. **2** (**chinos**) casual cotton pants, originally made from this fabric.

chi·noi·se·rie /,SHēn,wäz(ə)'rē, ,SHēn'wäzərē/ ▶ n. **1** the use of Chinese images and styles in Western art, furniture, and architecture. **2** objects or decorations made in this style.

Chi·nook /SHə'nŏŏk, CHə-/ ▶ n. (pl. same or **Chinooks**) a member of an American Indian people originally living in Oregon.

chi·nook /SHə'nŏŏk, CHə-/ ▶ n. **1** a warm, dry wind that blows down the east side of the Rocky Mountains at the end of winter. **2** a large North Pacific salmon that is an important food fish.

chintz /CHints/ ▶ n. multicolored cotton fabric with a shiny finish, used for curtains and upholstery.

chintz·y /'CHintsē/ ▶ adj. (**chintzier, chintziest**) **1** decorated with or resembling chintz. **2** decorated in a colorful but gaudy and tasteless way: *a chintzy little hotel.*

chin·wag /'CHin,wag/ ▶ n. chiefly Brit. informal a chat.

chip /CHip/ ▶ n. **1** a small, thin piece cut or broken off from a hard material. **2** a mark left by the removal of such a piece. **3** a thin slice of food made crisp by being fried, baked, or dried and typically eaten as a snack. **4** a microchip. **5** a counter used in certain gambling games to represent money. **6** (in soccer or golf) a short, high kick or shot. ▶ v. (**chips, chipping, chipped**) **1** cut or break a small piece from a hard material. **2** break at the edge or on the surface. **3** (**chip away**) gradually and relentlessly make something smaller or weaker: *rival firms are chipping away at their market share.* **4** (in soccer or golf) strike the ball to produce a short, high shot or pass.
– PHRASES **chip in** contribute money to a joint fund. **a chip off the old block** informal someone who resembles their mother or father in character. **a chip on one's shoulder** informal a long-held grievance. **when the chips are down** informal when a very serious situation occurs.

chip·board /'CHip,bôrd/ ▶ n. material made from compressed wood chips and resin.

chip·mak·er /'CHip,mākər/ ▶ n. a company that manufactures microchips.

chip·munk /'CHip,məNGk/ ▶ n. a burrowing ground squirrel with light and dark stripes running down the body.

chi·pot·le /CHi'pōtlā/ ▶ n. a smoked hot chili pepper used especially in Mexican cooking.

Chip·pen·dale /'CHipən,dāl/ ▶ adj. (of furniture) designed by or in the style of the English furniture-maker Thomas Chippendale (1718–79).

chip·per¹ /'CHipər/ ▶ adj. informal cheerful and lively.

chip·per² ▶ n. **1** a machine for chipping the trunks and limbs of trees. **2** a person or device that produces chips.

chip·py /'CHipē/ (also **chippie**) ▶ n. (pl. **chippies**) informal a promiscuous young woman, especially a prostitute.

chip·set /'CHip,set/ ▶ n. a collection of integrated circuits that form the set needed to make an electronic device.

chi·rop·o·dy /kə'räpədē, SHə-/ ▶ n. the medical treatment of the feet. ■ **chi·rop·o·dist** n.

chi·ro·prac·tic /ˌkīrə'praktik/ ▶ n. a system of complementary medicine based on the manipulation of the joints, especially those of the spinal column. ■ **chi·ro·prac·tor** /'kīrə,praktər/ n.

chirp /CHərp/ ▶ v. **1** (of a small bird) make a short, sharp, high-pitched sound. **2** say something in a lively and cheerful way. ▶ n. a chirping sound.

chirp·y /'CHərpē/ ▶ adj. (**chirpier, chirpiest**) informal cheerful and lively. ■ **chirp·i·ly** adv. **chirp·i·ness** n.

chirr /CHər/ (also **churr**) ▶ v. (of a bird or insect) make a low trilling sound. ▶ n. a low trilling sound.

chir·rup /'CHi(ə)rəp, 'CHərəp/ ▶ v. (**chirrups, chirruping, chirruped**) (of a small bird) make repeated short high-pitched sounds. ▶ n. a chirruping sound.

chis·el /'CHizəl/ ▶ n. a hand tool with a long blade and a beveled cutting edge, used to cut or shape wood, stone, or metal. ▶ v. (**chisels, chiseling, chiseled**) **1** cut or shape wood, stone, or metal with a chisel. **2** informal swindle: *do you think you can chisel me out of a fortune?*

chit[1] /'CHit/ ▶ n. derogatory a rude or impudent young woman.

chit[2] ▶ n. a short official note recording a sum of money owed.

chit-chat informal ▶ n. conversation about unimportant things. ▶ v. talk about unimportant things.

chi·tin /'kītn/ ▶ n. a tough substance that forms the external covering of the bodies of arthropods. ■ **chi·tin·ous** /'kītn-əs/ adj.

chi·ton /'kītn, 'kī,tän/ ▶ n. **1** a long woolen tunic worn in ancient Greece. **2** a marine mollusk that has a shell of overlapping plates.

chit·ter /'CHitər/ ▶ v. make a twittering or chattering sound.

chit·ter·lings /'CHitlənz/ ▶ pl.n. the smaller intestines of a pig, cooked for food.

chiv·al·rous /'SHivəlrəs/ ▶ adj. (of a man) polite and gallant, especially toward women. ■ **chiv·al·rous·ly** adv.

chiv·al·ry /'SHivəlrē/ ▶ n. **1** (in medieval times) the religious, moral, and social code of behavior that a knight was expected to follow. **2** polite behavior, especially that of a man toward women. ■ **chi·val·ric** /SHə'valrik/ adj.

chives /CHīvz/ ▶ pl.n. an herb with long tubular leaves, used in cooking.

chla·myd·i·a /klə'midēə/ ▶ n. (pl. same) a very small parasitic bacterium that can cause various diseases.

chlo·ral /'klôrəl/ ▶ n. a colorless liquid used as a sedative.

chlo·rate /'klôr,āt/ ▶ n. Chemistry a salt containing ClO_3 negative ions together with a metallic element: *sodium chlorate.*

chlo·ride /'klôr,īd/ ▶ n. a compound of chlorine with another element or group.

chlo·ri·nate /'klôrə,nāt/ ▶ v. put chlorine in something. ■ **chlo·ri·na·tion** /ˌklôrə'nāSHən/ n.

chlo·rine /'klôr,ēn/ ▶ n. a poisonous pale green gaseous chemical element that may be added to water as a disinfectant.

chlo·ro·fluor·o·car·bon /ˌklôrō,flŏŏrō'kärbən/ ▶ n. see CFC.

chlo·ro·form /'klôrə,fôrm/ ▶ n. a sweet-smelling liquid used as a solvent and formerly as a general anesthetic.

chlo·ro·phyll /'klôrə,fil/ ▶ n. a green pigment that enables plants to absorb light so as to provide energy for photosynthesis.

chlo·ro·plast /'klôrə,plast/ ▶ n. a structure in green plant cells that contains chlorophyll and in which photosynthesis takes place.

chlo·ro·sis /klô'rōsəs/ ▶ n. Botany abnormal reduction or loss of the normal green coloration of leaves of plants, typically caused by mineral deficiency, disease, or lack of light.

choc·a·hol·ic ▶ n. variant spelling of CHOCOHOLIC.

chock /CHäk/ ▶ n. a wedge or block placed against a wheel to prevent it from moving.

chock-a-block ▶ adj. informal completely full of people or things pressed close together.

chock-full /'CHäk 'fŏŏl, 'CHək-/ ▶ adj. informal filled to overflowing.

choc·o·hol·ic /ˌCHäkə'hôlik, ˌCHô-, -'hälik/ (also **chocaholic**) ▶ n. informal a person who is very fond of chocolate.

choc·o·late /'CHäk(ə)lit, 'CHôk-/ ▶ n. **1** a food made from roasted and ground cacao seeds, eaten as a candy or mixed with milk and water to make a drink. **2** a candy made of or covered with chocolate. **3** a deep brown color. ■ **choc·o·lat·ey** (also **chocolaty**) adj.

cho·co·la·tier /ˌCHôk(ə)lə'ti(ə)r, ˌSHôkəlä'tyä/ ▶ n. (pl. pronounced same) a person who makes or sells chocolate.

choice /CHois/ ▶ n. **1** an act of choosing. **2** the right or ability to choose. **3** a range from which to choose: *a menu offering a wide choice of dishes.* **4** a person or thing that has or can be chosen: *this disk drive is the perfect choice for your computer.* ▶ adj. **1** of very good quality. **2** (of language) rude and abusive.
– PHRASES **of choice** chosen as one's favorite or the best: *champagne was his drink of choice.*

choir /'kwīr/ ▶ n. **1** an organized group of singers, especially one that takes part in church services. **2** the part of a large church between the altar and the nave, used by the choir and clergy.

choir·boy /'kwīr,boi/ (or **choirgirl** /'kwīr,gərl/) ▶ n. a boy (or girl) who sings in a church or cathedral choir.

choke /CHōk/ ▶ v. **1** prevent someone from breathing by squeezing or blocking their throat or depriving them of air. **2** have trouble breathing. **3** fill a space so as to make movement difficult or impossible: *the roads were choked with traffic.* **4** (**choke something back**) suppress a strong emotion: *she choked back tears of rage.* **5** (**choke up** or **be choked up**) feel tearful or very upset. ▶ n. a valve in the carburetor of a gasoline engine used to reduce the amount of air in the fuel mixture.

chok·er /'CHōkər/ ▶ n. a necklace or band of fabric that fits closely around the neck.

chok·y /'CHōkē/ ▶ adj. **1** having or causing difficulty in breathing. **2** having difficulty speaking as a result of strong emotion.

cho·le·cal·cif·er·ol /ˌkōlə,kal'sifə,rôl, -,rōl/ ▶ n. a form of vitamin D (vitamin D_3), produced naturally in the skin by the action of sunlight.

chol·er /'kälər/ ▶ n. **1** (in medieval science and medicine) one of the four bodily humors, believed to be associated with an irritable temperament. **2** old use anger or bad temper.

chol·er·a /'kälərə/ ▶ n. an infectious disease of the small intestine that causes severe vomiting and diarrhea.

chol·er·ic /'kälərik, kə'lerik/ ▶ adj. bad-tempered or irritable.

cho·les·ter·ol /kə'lestə,rôl, -,rōl/ ▶ n. a compound that occurs normally in most body tissues and is believed to lead to disease of the arteries if present in high concentrations in the blood (e.g., as a result of a diet high in animal fat).

cho·line /'kō,lēn/ ▶ n. Biochemistry a strongly basic compound occurring widely in living tissues and important in the synthesis and transport of lipids.

chomp /CHämp, CHômp/ ▶ v. munch or chew food noisily or vigorously.

choose /CHōōz/ ▶ v. (past **chose**; past part. **chosen**) **1** pick someone or something out as being the best of two or more alternatives. **2** decide on a course of action: *the men chose to ignore his orders.*

choos·y /'CHōōzē/ ▶ adj. (**choosier, choosiest**) informal very careful when making a choice and so hard to please. ■ **choos·i·ness n.**

chop /CHäp/ ▶ v. (**chops, chopping, chopped**) **1** cut something into pieces with repeated sharp, heavy blows of an ax or knife. **2** strike something with a short, heavy blow. **3** get rid of something or reduce it by a large amount: *the share price was chopped from $10 to $7.* ▶ n. **1** a thick slice of meat, especially pork or lamb, next to and usually including a rib. **2** a downward cutting blow or movement. **3** the broken motion of water, typically due to the action of the wind against the tide.

chop·per /'CHäpər/ ▶ n. **1** a short ax with a large blade. **2** informal a helicopter. **3** (**choppers**) informal teeth. **4** informal a type of motorcycle with high handlebars.

chop·py /'CHäpē/ (**choppier, choppiest**) ▶ adj. (of the sea) having many small waves. ■ **chop·pi·ness n.**

chops /CHäps/ ▶ pl.n. informal a person's or animal's mouth, jaws, or cheeks.

chop·stick /'CHäp,stik/ ▶ n. each of a pair of thin, tapered sticks held in one hand and used as eating utensils by the Chinese and Japanese.

chop su·ey /,CHäp 'sōōē/ ▶ n. a Chinese-style dish of meat with bean sprouts, bamboo shoots, and onions.

cho·ral /'kôrəl/ ▶ adj. relating to or sung by a choir or chorus. ■ **cho·ral·ly adv.**

cho·rale /kə'ral, -'räl/ ▶ n. a simple, stately hymn tune for a choir or chorus.

chord¹ /kôrd/ ▶ n. a group of three or more musical notes sounded together in harmony. ■ **chord·al adj.**

> USAGE
> Do not confuse **chord** with **cord**. Chord means 'a group of musical notes' (*an E major chord*), whereas **cord** means 'thin string or rope' or 'a part of the body resembling string or rope' (*the spinal cord*).

chord² ▶ n. a straight line joining the ends of an arc.

– PHRASES **strike** (or **touch**) **a chord** say or do something that arouses sympathy, enthusiasm, etc., in others.

chor·date /'kôrdət, -,dāt/ ▶ n. an animal of a large group, including all the vertebrates, with a skeletal rod of cartilage supporting the body.

chore /CHôr/ ▶ n. a routine or boring task, especially a household one.

cho·re·a /kə'rēə/ ▶ n. a disorder of the nervous system characterized by uncontrollable jerky movements.

cho·re·o·graph /'kôrēə,graf/ ▶ v. compose the sequence of steps and moves for a ballet or other dance.

cho·re·og·ra·pher /,kôrē'ägrəfər/ ▶ n. a person who designs the steps and movements for a ballet or other dance.

cho·re·og·ra·phy /,kôrē'ägrəfē/ ▶ n. **1** the sequence of steps and movements in a ballet or other dance. **2** the art of designing such sequences. ■ **cho·re·o·graph·ic** /,kôrēə'grafik/ adj.

cho·rine /'kôr,ēn/ ▶ n. a chorus girl.

chor·is·ter /'kôrəstər, 'kär-/ ▶ n. a member of a church choir.

cho·ri·zo /CHə'rēzō, -sō/ ▶ n. (pl. **chorizos**) a spicy Spanish pork sausage.

chor·tle /'CHôrtl/ ▶ v. laugh loudly with pleasure or amusement. ▶ n. a loud laugh of pleasure or amusement.

cho·rus /'kôrəs/ ▶ n. (pl. **choruses**) **1** a part of a song that is repeated after each verse. **2** a piece of choral music, especially one forming part of an opera or oratorio. **3** a large group of singers performing with an orchestra. **4** a group of singers or dancers in a musical or an opera. **5** (in ancient Greek tragedy) a group of performers who comment on the main action of the play. **6** something said at the same time by many people. ▶ v. (**choruses, chorusing, chorused**) (of a group of people) say the same thing at the same time.

cho·rus girl ▶ n. a young woman who sings or dances in the chorus of a musical.

chose /CHōz/ ▶ past of **CHOOSE**.

cho·sen /'CHōzən/ ▶ past participle of **CHOOSE**.

chough /CHəf/ ▶ n. a black Old World bird of the crow family with a red or yellow bill.

choux pas·try /SHōō/ ▶ n. very light pastry made with egg, used for eclairs and profiteroles.

chow /CHou/ ▶ n. **1** informal food. **2** (also **chow chow**) a Chinese breed of dog with a tail curled over its back, a bluish-black tongue, and a thick coat.

chow·der /'CHoudər/ ▶ n. a rich soup containing fish, clams, or corn with potatoes and onions.

chow mein /'CHou 'mān/ ▶ n. a Chinese-style dish of fried noodles with shredded meat or seafood and vegetables.

chrism /'krizəm/ ▶ n. a consecrated oil used for anointing in rites such as baptism in the Catholic, Orthodox, and Anglican Churches.

Christ /krīst/ ▶ n. the title given to Jesus. ▶ exclam. used to express irritation, dismay, or surprise. ■ **Christ·like adj. Christ·ly adj.**

chris·ten /'krisən/ ▶ v. **1** name a baby at baptism as a sign of admission to a Christian Church. **2** informal use something for the first time. ■ **chris·ten·ing** /'kris(ə)niNG/ n.

Chris·ten·dom /'krisəndəm/ ▶ n. literary the worldwide body of Christians.

Chris·tian /'krisCHən/ ▶ adj. relating to or believing in Christianity or its teachings. ▶ n. a person who has received Christian baptism or is a believer in Christianity. ■ **Chris·tian·ize** /-ˌnīz/ (or **Christianise**) v.

Chris·tian e·ra ▶ n. the era beginning with the traditional date of Jesus's birth.

Chris·ti·an·i·ty /ˌkrischē'anitē/ ▶ n. the religion based on the teachings and works of Jesus.

Chris·tian name ▶ n. a first name, especially one given at baptism.

Chris·tian Sci·ence ▶ n. the beliefs and practices of the Church of Christ Scientist, a Christian sect. ■ **Chris·tian Sci·en·tist** n.

Christ·mas /'krisməs/ ▶ n. (pl. **Christmases**) 1 (also **Christmas Day**) the annual Christian festival celebrating Jesus's birth, held on December 25. 2 the period immediately before and after December 25.

Christ·mas cac·tus ▶ n. a succulent South American plant with red, pink, or white flowers.

Christ·mas rose ▶ n. a small white-flowered winter-blooming hellebore.

Christ·mas tree ▶ n. an evergreen or artificial tree decorated with lights and ornaments at Christmas.

chro·ma /'krōmə/ ▶ n. purity or intensity of color.

chro·mate /'krō,māt/ ▶ n. Chemistry a salt in which the anion contains both chromium and oxygen.

chro·mat·ic /krō'matik/ ▶ adj. 1 relating or referring to a musical scale that rises or falls by half steps. 2 relating to or produced by color.

chro·ma·tin /'krōmətən/ ▶ n. Biology the material of which nonbacterial chromosomes are composed, consisting of DNA and protein (and RNA at certain times).

chro·ma·tog·ra·phy /ˌkrōmə'tägrəfē/ ▶ n. Chemistry a technique for separating and analyzing a mixture by passing it through a medium in which the components move at different rates. ■ **chro·mat·o·gram** /krō'matə,gram/ n. **chro·mat·o·graph** /krō'matə,graf/ n. **chro·mat·o·graph·ic** /krō,matə'grafik/ adj.

chrome /krōm/ ▶ n. a hard shiny metal coating made from chromium. ▶ adj. referring to compounds or alloys of chromium: *chrome steel*. ■ **chromed** adj.

chro·mite /'krō,mīt/ ▶ n. the main ore of chromium, a brownish-black oxide of chromium and iron.

chro·mi·um /'krōmēəm/ ▶ n. a hard white metallic chemical element used in stainless steel and other alloys.

chro·mo·some /'krōmə,sōm/ ▶ n. a threadlike structure in a cell nucleus, carrying the genes. ■ **chro·mo·so·mal** /ˌkrōmə'sōməl/ adj.

chron·ic /'kränik/ ▶ adj. 1 (of an illness or problem) lasting for a long time. 2 having a bad habit: *a chronic liar*. ■ **chron·i·cal·ly** /-ik(ə)lē/ adv.

chron·ic fa·tigue syn·drome ▶ n. a medical condition of unknown cause, with fever, aching, and prolonged tiredness and depression.

chron·i·cle /'kränikəl/ ▶ n. a written account of historical events in the order of their occurrence. ▶ v. record a series of events in a factual way. ■ **chron·i·cler** n.

chron·o·graph /'kränə,graf, 'krō-/ ▶ n. an instrument for recording time with great accuracy.

chron·o·log·i·cal /ˌkränl'äjikəl/ ▶ adj. 1 (of a record of events) following the order in which they occurred: *the video shows all his goals in chronological order*. 2 relating to the establishment of the dates of past events. ■ **chron·o·log·i·cal·ly** /-ik(ə)lē/ adv.

chro·nol·o·gy /krə'näləjē/ ▶ n. (pl. **chronologies**) 1 the arrangement of events in the order of their occurrence. 2 the study of records to establish the dates of past events. 3 a list of events or dates in chronological order. ■ **chro·nol·o·gist** /-jist/ n.

chro·nom·e·ter /krə'nämətər/ ▶ n. an instrument for measuring time accurately in spite of motion or varying conditions.

chrys·a·lis /'krisələs/ ▶ n. (pl. **chrysalises**) 1 a dormant insect pupa, especially of a butterfly or moth. 2 the hard outer case enclosing an insect pupa.

chry·san·the·mum /kri'sanтнəməm/ ▶ n. (pl. **chrysanthemums**) a garden plant of the daisy family with brightly colored flowers.

chthon·ic /'тнänik/ (also **chthonian** /'тнōnēən/) ▶ adj. literary relating to or inhabiting the underworld.

chub /chəb/ ▶ n. (pl. same or **chubs**) a thick-bodied river fish with a gray-green back and white underparts.

chub·by /'chəbē/ ▶ adj. (**chubbier, chubbiest**) plump and rounded. ■ **chub·bi·ness** n.

chuck¹ /chək/ ▶ v. informal 1 throw something carelessly or casually. 2 (**chuck something away/out**) throw something away. 3 (**chuck someone out**) force someone to leave a building. 4 give up suddenly: *he chucked his history course*. ■ **chuck·er** n.

chuck² ▶ v. touch someone playfully under the chin. ▶ n. a playful touch under the chin.

chuck³ ▶ n. 1 a device for holding a workpiece in a lathe or a tool in a drill. 2 (also **chuck steak**) a cut of beef extending from the neck to the ribs.

chuck⁴ ▶ n. food or provisions.

chuck·le /'chəkəl/ ▶ v. laugh quietly or inwardly. ▶ n. a quiet laugh.

chuck·le·head /'chəkəl,hed/ ▶ n. informal a stupid person.

chuck wag·on ▶ n. a wagon or other vehicle with cooking facilities providing food on a ranch, worksite, or campsite.

chuff /chəf/ ▶ v. (of a steam engine) move with a regular puffing sound.

chug¹ /chəg/ ▶ v. (**chugs, chugging, chugged**) move with a series of muffled explosive sounds, as of an engine running slowly.

chug² (also **chugalug** or **chug-a-lug** /'chəgə,ləg/) ▶ v. informal consume a drink in large gulps without pausing.

chuk·ker /'chəkər/ (also **chukka**) ▶ n. each of a number of periods into which a game of polo is divided.

chum¹ /chəm/ informal ▶ n. a close friend. ▶ v. (**chums, chumming, chummed**) form a friendship with someone: *they started chumming around in high school*. ■ **chum·my** adj.

chum² ▶ n. chopped fish and other material thrown overboard as angling bait.

chump /chəmp/ ▶ n. informal a foolish or easily deceived person.

chunk¹ /chənɢk/ ▶ n. 1 a thick, solid piece. 2 a large amount.

chunk² ▶ v. make a muffled, metallic sound.

chunk·y /'chənɢkē/ ▶ adj. (**chunkier, chunkiest**) 1 (of a person) short and sturdy. 2 bulky and thick. **3** containing chunks. ▪ **chunk·i·ly** /-kəlē/ adv. **chunk·i·ness** n.

church /CHərCH/ ▶ n. **1** a building used for public Christian worship. **2** (**Church**) a particular Christian organization: *the Catholic Church.* **3** the Christian religion as an institution with political or social influence: *the separation of church and state.*

church·go·er /'CHərCH,gōər/ ▶ n. a person who attends church services regularly.

church·man /'CHərCHmən/ (or **churchwoman** /'CHərCH,wŏŏmən/) ▶ n. (pl. **churchmen** or **churchwomen**) a member of the Christian clergy or of a Church.

Church of Eng·land ▶ n. the English branch of the Western Christian Church, which has the king or queen as its head.

Church of Scot·land ▶ n. the national (Presbyterian) Christian Church in Scotland.

church·ward·en /'CHərCH,wôrdn/ ▶ n. either of two people who are elected by an Anglican congregation to take care of church property and keep order.

church·y /'CHərCHē/ ▶ adj. **1** excessively pious. **2** resembling a church.

church·yard /'CHərCH,yärd/ ▶ n. an enclosed area surrounding a church, especially as used for burials.

churl /CHərl/ ▶ n. **1** a rude and surly person. **2** old use a peasant.

churl·ish /'CHərliSH/ ▶ adj. rude and surly. ▪ **churl·ish·ly** adv. **churl·ish·ness** n.

churn /CHərn/ ▶ v. **1** (of liquid) move about vigorously: *the water churned and foamed.* **2** (**churn something up**) break up the surface of an area of ground. **3** (**churn something out**) produce something in large quantities and without much thought. **4** (as adj. **churned up**) upset or nervous. **5** shake milk or cream in a churn to produce butter. ▶ n. a machine for making butter by shaking milk or cream.

chur·ro /'CHŏŏrō/ ▶ n. a Spanish sweet snack consisting of a strip of fried dough dusted with sugar or cinnamon.

chute¹ /SHŏŏt/ (also **shoot**) ▶ n. **1** a sloping channel for conveying things to a lower level. **2** a water slide into a swimming pool.

chute² ▶ n. informal a parachute.

chut·ney /'CHətnē/ ▶ n. (pl. **chutneys**) a spicy condiment made of fruits or vegetables with vinegar, spices, and sugar.

chutz·pah /'hŏŏtspə, 'KHŏŏtspə, -spä/ ▶ n. informal extreme self-confidence or audacity.

chyle /kīl/ ▶ n. a milky fluid that drains from the small intestine into the lymphatic system during digestion.

chyme /kīm/ ▶ n. the fluid that passes from the stomach to the small intestine, consisting of gastric juices and partly digested food.

Ci ▶ abbr. curie.

CIA ▶ abbr. Central Intelligence Agency.

cia·bat·ta /CHə'bätə/ ▶ n. a flattish Italian bread made with olive oil.

ciao /CHou/ ▶ exclam. informal hello or goodbye.

ci·ca·da /sə'kädə, sə'kädə/ ▶ n. a large insect with long wings that makes a shrill droning noise after dark.

cic·a·trix /'sikə,triks/ (also **cicatrice** /-,tris/) ▶ n. (pl. **cicatrices** /,sikə'trīsēz, sə'kātrə,sēz/) a scar.

cic·a·trize /'sikə,trīz/ ▶ v. heal a wound by scar formation.

cic·e·ly /'sisilē/ (also **sweet cicely**) ▶ n. (pl. **cicelies**) a white-flowered plant with fernlike leaves.

cic·e·ro·ne /,sisə'rōnē, ,CHēCHə-/ ▶ n. (pl. **ciceroni** pronunc. same) a guide who gives information to sightseers.

cich·lid /'siklid/ ▶ n. a perchlike freshwater fish of a large family.

-cide ▶ comb.form **1** referring to a person or substance that kills: *insecticide.* **2** referring to an act of killing: *suicide.*

ci·der /'sīdər/ ▶ n. **1** (also **sweet cider**) an unfermented drink made from crushed apples. **2** (also **hard cider**) an alcoholic drink made from fermented crushed apples.

cig /sig/ ▶ n. informal a cigarette.

ci·gar /si'gär/ ▶ n. a cylinder of tobacco rolled in tobacco leaves for smoking.

cig·a·rette /,sigə'ret, 'sigə,ret/ ▶ n. a cylinder of finely cut tobacco rolled in paper for smoking.

cig·a·ril·lo /,sigə'rilō, -'rē(y)ō/ ▶ n. (pl. **cigarillos**) a small cigar.

cil·i·um /'silēəm/ ▶ n. (pl. **cilia** /'silēə/) Biology a microscopic hairlike vibrating structure, occurring on the surface of certain cells. ▪ **cil·i·ar·y** /'silē,erē/ adj.

cim·ba·lom /'simbələm/ ▶ n. a large Hungarian dulcimer (musical instrument).

CINC ▶ abbr. Commander in Chief.

C. in C. ▶ abbr. Commander in Chief.

cinch /sinCH/ ▶ n. informal **1** a very easy task. **2** a certainty.

cin·cho·na /siNG'kōnə, sin'CHōnə/ ▶ n. a medicinal drug obtained from the bark of a South American tree, containing quinine.

cin·der /'sindər/ ▶ n. a small piece of partly burned coal or wood. ▪ **cin·der·y** adj.

cin·der block ▶ n. a lightweight building brick made from small cinders mixed with sand and cement.

Cin·der·el·la /,sində'relə/ ▶ n. a person or thing that is undeservedly neglected.

cin·e /'sinē/ ▶ adj. chiefly Brit relating to filmmaking: *a cine camera.*

cin·e·aste /'sinē,ast/ ▶ n. a person who is fond of or knowledgeable about movies or filmmaking.

cin·e·ma /'sinəmə/ ▶ n. **1** the production of movies as an art or industry. **2** Brit. a movie theater. ▪ **cin·e·mat·ic** /,sinə'matik/ adj. **cin·e·mat·i·cal·ly** /-ik(ə)lē/ adv.

cin·e·mat·o·graph /,sinə'matəgraf/ ▶ n. historical, chiefly Brit. an early movie projector.

cin·e·ma·tog·ra·phy /,sinəmə'tägrəfē/ ▶ n. the art of making motion pictures. ▪ **cin·e·ma·tog·ra·pher** /-fər/ n. **cin·e·ma·to·graph·ic** /-,matə'grafik/ adj.

cin·e·phile /'sini,fīl/ ▶ n. a movie enthusiast.

cin·e·plex /'sini,pleks/ ▶ n. trademark a movie theater with several separate screens; a multiplex.

cin·e·rar·i·a /,sinə're(ə)rēə/ ▶ n. a winter-flowering plant of the daisy family.

cin·e·rar·y urn /'sinə,rerē/ ▶ n. an urn for holding a person's ashes after cremation.

cin·na·bar /'sinə,bär/ ▶ n. **1** a bright red mineral consisting of mercury sulfide. **2** (also **cinnabar moth**) a moth with black and red wings.

cin·na·mon /'sinəmən/ ▸ n. **1** a spice made from the dried bark of an Asian tree. **2** a reddish- or yellowish-brown color.

cinque·foil /'siNGk,foil, 'saNGk-/ ▸ n. **1** a plant with leaves made up of five leaflets and five-petaled yellow flowers. **2** a decorative design of five arcs arranged inside a circle.

ci·pher /'sīfər/ (also **cypher**) ▸ n. **1** a code, especially one in which a set of letters or symbols is used to represent others. **2** a key to a code. **3** an unimportant person. **4** dated a zero. ▸ v. put a message into code.

cir·ca /'sərkə/ ▸ prep. approximately.

cir·ca·di·an /sər'kādēən/ ▸ adj. (of biological processes) recurring on a twenty-four-hour cycle.

cir·cle /'sərkəl/ ▸ n. **1** a round plane figure whose boundary consists of points at an equal distance from the center. **2** a thing or group of people or things shaped like a circle. **3** a curved upper tier of seats in a theater. **4** a group of people with a shared profession, interests, or friends. ▸ v. **1** move or be situated all the way around: *the cat circled the room twice.* **2** draw a line around something.
– PHRASES **come** (or **turn**) **full circle** return to a previous position or situation.

cir·clet /'sərklət/ ▸ n. an ornamental circular band worn on the head.

cir·cuit /'sərkət/ ▸ n. **1** a roughly circular line, route, or movement. **2** a system of conductors and components forming a complete path for an electric current. **3** an established series of sporting events or entertainments: *the comedy circuit.* **4** a series of physical exercises performed in one training session. **5** a regular journey by a judge around a district to hear court cases. ▸ v. move all the way around something.

cir·cuit board ▸ n. a thin rigid board containing an electric circuit; a printed circuit.

cir·cuit break·er ▸ n. an automatic safety device for stopping the flow of current in an electric circuit.

cir·cu·i·tous /sər'kyo͞oətəs/ ▸ adj. (of a route) longer than the most direct way.

cir·cuit·ry /'sərkətrē/ ▸ n. (pl. **circuitries**) a system of electric circuits.

cir·cu·lar /'sərkyələr/ ▸ adj. **1** having the form of a circle. **2** (of an argument) false because it uses as evidence the point that is to be proved. **3** (of a letter or advertisement) for distribution to a large number of people. ▸ n. a circular letter or advertisement. ■ **cir·cu·lar·i·ty** /,sərkyə'laritē/ n. **cir·cu·lar·ly** adv.

cir·cu·lar·ize /'sərkyələ,rīz/ ▸ v. distribute circulars to a large number of people.

cir·cu·lar saw ▸ n. a power saw with a rapidly rotating toothed disk.

cir·cu·late /'sərkyə,lāt/ ▸ v. **1** move continuously through a closed system or area: *antibodies circulate in the bloodstream.* **2** pass from place to place or person to person. **3** move around a social function and talk to many people. ■ **cir·cu·la·tor** /-,lātər/ n.

cir·cu·la·tion /,sərkyə'lāsHən/ ▸ n. **1** movement around something. **2** the continuous motion of blood around the body. **3** the public availability of something: *a large number of counterfeit tickets are in circulation.* **4** the number of copies sold of a newspaper or magazine. ■ **cir·cu·la·to·ry** /'sərkyələ,tôrē/ adj.
– PHRASES **in** (or **out of**) **circulation** (of a

person) seen (or not seen) in public.

circum- ▸ prefix about; around: *circumambulate.*

cir·cum·am·bu·late /,sərkəm'ambyə,lāt/ ▸ v. formal walk all the way around something. ■ **cir·cum·am·bu·la·tion** /-,ambyə'lāsHən/ n.

cir·cum·cise /'sərkəm,sīz/ ▸ v. **1** cut off the foreskin of a young boy or man as a Jewish or Islamic rite. **2** cut off the clitoris, and sometimes the labia, of a girl or young woman. ■ **cir·cum·ci·sion** /,sərkəm'sizHən, 'sərkəm,sizHən/ n.

cir·cum·fer·ence /sər'kəmf(ə)rəns/ ▸ n. **1** the boundary that encloses a circle. **2** the distance around something. ■ **cir·cum·fer·en·tial** /sər,kəmfə'renCHəl/ adj.

cir·cum·flex /'sərkəm,fleks/ ▸ n. a mark (^) placed over a vowel in some languages to indicate a change in the way it is pronounced.

cir·cum·lo·cu·tion /,sərkəm,lō'kyo͞osHən/ ▸ n. the use of many words where fewer would do. ■ **cir·cum·loc·u·to·ry** /-'läkyə,tôrē/ adj.

cir·cum·nav·i·gate /,sərkəm'navə,gāt/ ▸ v. go all the way around something, especially by sail. ■ **cir·cum·nav·i·ga·tion** /-,navə'gāsHən/ n.

cir·cum·po·lar /,sərkəm'pōlər/ ▸ adj. situated or occurring around one of the earth's poles.

cir·cum·scribe /'sərkəm,skrīb/ ▸ v. **1** put limits on; restrict: *the joys of country life were circumscribed by foot-and-mouth disease.* **2** Geometry draw a figure around another, touching it at points but not cutting it. ■ **cir·cum·scrip·tion** /,sərkəm'skripsHən/ n.

cir·cum·spect /'sərkəm,spekt/ ▸ adj. wary and unwilling to take risks; cautious. ■ **cir·cum·spec·tion** /,sərkəm'speksHən/ n. **cir·cum·spect·ly** adv.

cir·cum·stance /'sərkəm,stans, -stəns/ ▸ n. **1** a fact or condition connected with an event or action. **2** unforeseen and influential events that are outside one's control: *a victim of circumstance.* **3** (**circumstances**) a person's financial or personal situation. **4** old use ceremony and public display: *pomp and circumstance.*

cir·cum·stan·tial /,sərkəm'stanCHəl/ ▸ adj. **1** (of evidence) strongly suggesting something, but not proving it conclusively. **2** related to the particular circumstances of something: *a circumstantial log of our travels.* ■ **cir·cum·stan·ti·al·i·ty** /-,stansHē'alətē/ n. **cir·cum·stan·tial·ly** adv.

cir·cum·vent /,sərkəm'vent/ ▸ v. find a way of avoiding a problem, regulation, or obstacle. ■ **cir·cum·ven·tion** /-'venCHən/ n.

cir·cus /'sərkəs/ ▸ n. (pl. **circuses**) **1** a traveling company of acrobats, trained animals, and clowns. **2** informal a scene of hectic activity: *a media circus.* **3** (in ancient Rome) a circular sports arena lined with seats.

cirque /sərk/ ▸ n. a steep-sided hollow at the head of a valley or on a mountainside.

cir·rho·sis /sə'rōsəs/ ▸ n. a chronic liver disease typically caused by alcoholism or hepatitis. ■ **cir·rhot·ic** /sə'rätik/ adj.

cir·ro·cu·mu·lus /,sirō'kyo͞omyələs/ ▸ n. cloud forming a broken layer of small fleecy clouds at high altitude.

cir·ro·stra·tus /,sirō'stratəs, -'strātəs/ ▸ n. cloud forming a thin, uniform layer at high altitude.

cir·rus /'sirəs/ ▸ n. (pl. **cirri** /'sir,ī, 'sirē/) **1** cloud forming wispy streaks at high altitude. **2** Zoology & Botany a slender tendril or filament.

CIS ▸ abbr. Commonwealth of Independent States.

cis·co /'siskō/ ▸ n. (pl. **ciscoes**) a northern freshwater whitefish, important as a food fish.

Cis·ter·cian /sis'tərsHən/ ▸ n. a monk or nun of an order that is a stricter branch of the Benedictines. ▸ adj. relating to the Cistercians.

cis·tern /'sistərn/ ▸ n. a water storage tank, especially as part of a flushing toilet.

cistus /'sistəs/ ▸ n. a shrub with large white or red flowers.

cit·a·del /'sitədl, -,del/ ▸ n. a fortress protecting or overlooking a city.

ci·ta·tion /sī'tāsHən/ ▸ n. 1 a quotation from or reference to a book or author. 2 a mention of a praiseworthy act in an official report. 3 a note accompanying an award, giving reasons for it.

cite /sīt/ ▸ v. 1 quote a book or author as evidence for an argument. 2 praise someone for a courageous act in an official report. 3 summon someone to appear in court.

cit·i·fied /'siti,fīd/ ▸ adj. chiefly derogatory characteristic of a city: *the obligations of citified life.*

cit·i·zen /'sitizən, -sən/ ▸ n. 1 a person who is legally recognized as a subject or national of a country. 2 an inhabitant of a town or city. ■ **cit·i·zen·ry** /-rē/ n. **cit·i·zen·ship** /-,sHip/ n.

cit·i·zen's ar·rest ▸ n. an arrest by an ordinary person without a warrant, allowable in certain cases.

Cit·i·zens' Band ▸ n. a range of radio frequencies that are allocated for local communication by private individuals.

cit·rate /'si,trāt/ ▸ n. a salt or ester of citric acid.

cit·ric /'sitrik/ ▸ adj. related to citrus fruit: *a sharp, citric flavor.*

cit·ric ac·id ▸ n. a sharp-tasting acid present in the juice of lemons and other sour fruits.

cit·ron /'sitrən/ ▸ n. the large, lemonlike fruit of an Asian tree.

cit·ron·el·la /,sitrə'nelə/ ▸ n. a fragrant oil obtained from a South Asian grass, used as an insect repellent and in perfume.

cit·rus /'sitrəs/ (also **citrus fruit**) ▸ n. (pl. **citruses**) a fruit of a group that includes lemons, limes, oranges, and grapefruit. ■ **cit·rus·y** adj.

cit·y /'sitē/ ▸ n. (pl. **cities**) 1 a large town. 2 an incorporated municipal center.

cit·y fa·ther ▸ n. a person concerned with the administration of a city.

cit·y hall ▸ n. municipal offices or officers.

cit·y·scape /'sitē,skāp/ ▸ n. a city landscape.

cit·y slick·er /'slikər/ ▸ n. informal, derogatory a person with the sophisticated tastes or values associated with people who live in cities.

cit·y-state ▸ n. chiefly historical a city and surrounding territory that forms an independent state.

cit·y·wide /'sitē,wīd/ ▸ adj. & adv. extending throughout a city.

civ·et /'sivət/ ▸ n. 1 a slender cat native to Africa and Asia. 2 a strong musky perfume obtained from the scent glands of the civet.

civ·ic /'sivik/ ▸ adj. relating to a city or town or to the duties or activities of its citizens. ■ **civ·i·cal·ly** /-ik(ə)lē/ adv.

civ·ic cen·ter ▸ n. a municipal building or building complex consisting of government or other public-use buildings.

civ·ics /'siviks/ ▸ pl.n. (treated as sing.) the study of the rights and duties of citizenship.

civ·il /'sivəl/ ▸ adj. 1 relating to ordinary citizens, as distinct from military or church matters. 2 Law noncriminal: *a civil court.* 3 courteous and polite. ■ **civ·il·ly** adv.

civ·il de·fense ▸ n. the organization and training of civilians for their protection during wartime.

civ·il dis·o·be·di·ence ▸ n. the refusal to obey certain laws as a political protest.

civ·il en·gi·neer ▸ n. an engineer who designs roads, bridges, dams, and similar structures.

ci·vil·ian /sə'vilyən/ ▸ n. a person not in the armed services or the police force. ▸ adj. relating to a civilian.

ci·vil·i·ty /sə'vilətē/ ▸ n. (pl. **civilities**) 1 politeness and courtesy. 2 (**civilities**) polite remarks used in formal conversation.

civ·i·li·za·tion /,sivələ'zāsHən/ ▸ n. 1 an advanced stage or system of human social development: *the Victorians equated the railroads with progress and civilization.* 2 the process of achieving a civilized stage of human development. 3 a civilized nation or region.

civ·i·lize /'sivə,līz/ ▸ v. 1 bring a place or people to an advanced stage of social development. 2 (as adj. **civilized**) polite and well-mannered. ■ **civ·i·liz·er** n.

civ·il law ▸ n. 1 law concerned with ordinary citizens, rather than criminal, military, or religious affairs. 2 the system of law predominant on the European continent, influenced by that of ancient Rome.

civ·il lib·er·ty ▸ n. 1 freedom of action and speech subject to laws established for the good of the community. 2 (**civil liberties**) a person's right to be subject only to laws established for the good of the community. ■ **civ·il lib·er·tar·i·an** n.

civ·il mar·riage ▸ n. a marriage solemnized without a religious ceremony.

civ·il rights ▸ pl.n. the rights of citizens to political and social freedom and equality.

civ·il serv·ant ▸ n. a member of the civil service.

civ·il serv·ice ▸ n. the branches of government administration, excluding military and judicial branches and elected politicians.

civ·il u·ni·on ▸ n. (in some countries and in some US states) a legally recognized union of a couple of the same sex, with rights similar to those of marriage.

civ·il war ▸ n. a war between citizens of the same country.

civ·vy /'sivē/ ▸ n. (pl. **civvies**) informal 1 a civilian. 2 (**civvies**) civilian clothes, as distinct from uniform.

CJD ▸ abbr. Creutzfeldt–Jakob disease.

Cl ▸ symbol the chemical element chlorine.

cl ▸ abbr. centiliter.

clack /klak/ ▸ v. make a sharp sound as of a hard object striking another. ▸ n. a clacking sound.

clad /klad/ old-fashioned or literary past participle of CLOTHE ▸ adj. 1 clothed: *leather-clad boys.* 2 covered with cladding.

clad·ding /'klading/ ▸ n. a covering or coating on a structure or material.

clade /klād/ ▸ n. a group of organisms comprising all the evolutionary descendants of a common ancestor.

cla·dis·tics /klə'distiks/ ▶ pl.n. (treated as sing.) a method of classifying animals and plants based on only those shared characteristics that can be deduced to have originated in the common ancestor of a group of species during evolution. ■ **cla·dis·tic** adj.

claim /klām/ ▶ v. **1** state that something is the case, without being able to give proof. **2** ask for something that one has a right to have: *she went to Germany, where she claimed asylum.* **3** cause the loss of someone's life. **4** request money under the terms of an insurance policy. **5** call for someone's attention. ▶ n. **1** a statement that something is the case. **2** a demand for something to which one has a right. **3** a request for compensation under the terms of an insurance policy. ■ **claim·a·ble** adj. **claim·ant** n.

claims ad·just·er ▶ n. an insurance agent who assesses the amount of compensation that should be paid to a person making a claim.

clair·voy·ance /kle(ə)r'voiəns/ ▶ n. the supposed ability of being able to see future events or to communicate with people who are dead or far away.

clair·voy·ant /kle(ə)r'voiənt/ ▶ n. a person claiming to be able to predict the future or communicate with the dead. ▶ adj. able to predict the future.

clam /klam/ ▶ n. a large shellfish with two shells of equal size. ▶ v. (**clams, clamming, clammed**) (**clam up**) informal stop talking abruptly.

clam·bake /'klam,bāk/ ▶ n. an outdoor social gathering at which clams and other seafood are baked or steamed.

clam·ber /'klambər, 'klamər/ ▶ v. climb or move in an awkward and laborious way: *Saul clambered into the back of the truck.* ▶ n. an act of clambering.

clam·dig·gers /'klam,digərz/ ▶ pl.n. close-fitting calf-length pants for women.

clam·my /'klamē/ ▶ adj. (**clammier, clammiest**) **1** unpleasantly damp and sticky. **2** (of air) cold and damp. ■ **clam·mi·ly** adv. **clam·mi·ness** n.

clam·or /'klamər/ (Brit. **clamour**) ▶ n. **1** a loud and confused noise. **2** a strong protest or demand. ▶ v. (of a group) shout or demand loudly: *the surging crowds clamored for attention.* ■ **clam·or·ous** /-ərəs/ adj.

clamp /klamp/ ▶ n. a brace, band, or clasp for strengthening or holding things together. ▶ v. **1** fasten a thing or things in place or together with a clamp. **2** (**clamp down**) take firm or harsh action to prevent something: *a plan to clamp down on smuggling.* ■ **clamp·er** n.

clamp·down /'klamp,doun/ ▶ n. informal a firm or harsh attempt to prevent something.

clan /klan/ ▶ n. **1** a close-knit group of related families, especially in the Scottish Highlands. **2** a group with a shared interest or characteristic: *a clan of born-again Christians.*

clan·des·tine /klan'destən, -,tīn, -,tēn, 'klandəs-/ ▶ adj. kept secret or done secretively. ■ **clan·des·tine·ly** adv. **clan·des·tin·i·ty** /,klandes'tinitē/ n.

clang /klaNG/ ▶ n. a loud metallic sound. ▶ v. make a clang.

clang·or /'klaNGər/ (Brit. **clangour**) ▶ n. a continuous clanging sound. ■ **clang·or·ous** /'klaNGərəs/ adj.

clank /klaNGk/ ▶ n. a loud, sharp metallic sound. ▶ v. make a clank.

clan·nish /'klaniSH/ ▶ adj. (of a group) tending to exclude others outside the group. ■ **clan·nish·ness** n.

clans·man /'klanzmən/ (or **clanswoman** /'klanz,wŏŏmən/) ▶ n. (pl. **clansmen** or **clanswomen**) a member of a clan.

clap[1] /klap/ ▶ v. (**claps, clapping, clapped**) **1** strike the palms of one's hands together repeatedly, especially to applaud. **2** slap someone encouragingly on the back. **3** put someone or something somewhere quickly or suddenly: *he clapped a hand to his forehead.* ▶ n. **1** an act of clapping. **2** a sudden loud noise, especially of thunder.
– PHRASES **clap someone in jail** (or **irons**) put someone in prison (or in chains).

clap[2] ▶ n. informal a sexually transmitted disease, especially gonorrhea.

clap·board /'klabərd, 'klap,bôrd/ ▶ n. one of a series of planks of wood with edges horizontally overlapping, used to cover the outer walls of buildings.

clap·per /'klapər/ ▶ n. the free-swinging metal piece inside a bell that strikes the bell to produce the sound.

clap·per·board /'klapər,bôrd/ ▶ n. hinged boards that are struck together at the beginning of filming to enable the picture and sound to be synchronized during editing.

clap·trap /'klap,trap/ ▶ n. nonsense: *feminist claptrap.*

claque /klak/ ▶ n. **1** a group of people who follow someone in an obsequious way. **2** a group of people hired to applaud or heckle a performer.

clar·et /'klarit/ ▶ n. **1** a red wine, especially from Bordeaux. **2** a deep purplish red color.

clar·i·fy /'klarə,fī/ ▶ v. (**clarifies, clarifying, clarified**) **1** make easier to understand: *the judges' ruling had clarified the law of rape.* **2** melt butter to separate out the impurities. ■ **clar·i·fi·ca·tion** /,klarəfi'kāSHən/ n. **clar·i·fi·er** n.

clar·i·net /,klarə'net/ ▶ n. a woodwind instrument with holes stopped by keys and a mouthpiece with a single reed. ■ **clar·i·net·ist** /-'netist/ n.

clar·i·on /'klarēən/ ▶ adj. literary loud and clear. ▶ n. historical a shrill war trumpet.
– PHRASES **clarion call** a strongly expressed demand for action.

clar·i·ty /'klaritē/ ▶ n. **1** the state or quality of being easy to understand, see, or hear: *she analyzes the pros and cons with admirable clarity.* **2** transparency or purity.

clash /klaSH/ ▶ n. **1** a conflict or disagreement. **2** an inconvenient occurrence of dates or events at the same time. **3** a loud discordant sound. ▶ v. **1** (of opposing groups) come into conflict. **2** disagree or be at odds: *Shanghai's decadent culture once clashed with Maoist principles.* **3** (of colors) appear discordant when placed together. **4** (of dates or events) occur inconveniently at the same time: *he was invited to a dinner party, but it clashed with one of his seminars.* **5** strike cymbals together, producing a loud discordant sound.

clasp /klasp/ ▶ v. **1** grasp something tightly with one's hand. **2** place one's arms tightly around someone or something. **3** fasten something with a clasp. ▶ n. **1** a device with interlocking parts used for fastening. **2** an act of embracing or grasping.

class /klas/ ▶ n. **1** a set or category of people or things having a common characteristic: *a* *new class of antibiotics.* **2** a system that divides members of a society into sets based on social or economic status. **3** a social division based on social or economic status: *the ruling class.* **4** a group of students who are taught together. **5** a lesson. **6** informal impressive stylishness. **7** Biology a principal category into which animals and plants are divided, ranking below phylum or division. ▶ v. put someone or something in a particular category. ▶ adj. informal showing stylish excellence: *a class player.*

class ac·tion ▶ n. Law a lawsuit filed or defended by an individual acting on behalf of a group.

clas·sic /'klasik/ ▶ adj. **1** judged over time to be of the highest quality. **2** typical: *the classic symptoms of flu.* ▶ n. **1** a work of art that is recognized as being of high quality. **2** a thing that is an excellent example of its kind: *tomorrow's game should be a classic.* **3** (**Classics**) the study of ancient Greek and Latin literature, philosophy, and history. **4** (**the classics**) the works of ancient Greek and Latin writers.

clas·si·cal /'klasikəl/ ▶ adj. **1** relating to ancient Greek or Latin literature, art, or culture. **2** (of a form of art or a language) representing the highest standard within a long-established form. **3** (of music) of long-established form or style or (more specifically) written in the European tradition between approximately 1750 and 1830. **4** relating to the first significant period of an area of study: *classical Marxism.* ■ **clas·si·cal·ly** /-ik(ə)lē/ adv.

clas·sic car ▶ n. an old car, generally one built before 1948 and in good condition.

clas·si·cism /'klasə,sizəm/ ▶ n. the following of ancient Greek or Roman principles and style in art and literature, generally associated with harmony and restraint.

clas·si·cist /'klasəsist/ ▶ n. **1** a person who studies Classics. **2** a follower of classicism.

clas·si·ciz·ing /'klasə,sīziNG/ ▶ adj. imitating a classical style.

clas·si·fi·ca·tion /,klasəfə'kāSHən/ ▶ n. **1** the action of classifying something. **2** a category into which something is put. ■ **clas·si·fi·ca·to·ry** /'klasəfikə,tôrē/ adj.

clas·si·fied /'klasə,fīd/ ▶ adj. **1** (of newspaper or magazine advertisements) organized in categories. **2** (of information or documents) officially classed as secret. ▶ n. (**classifieds**) classified advertisements.

clas·si·fy /'klasə,fī/ ▶ v. (**classifies, classifying, classified**) **1** arrange a group in classes according to shared characteristics. **2** put in a particular class or category: *it's the only French winery classified as a National Monument.* **3** categorize documents or information as officially secret. ■ **clas·si·fi·a·ble** /,klasə'fīəbəl/ adj. **clas·si·fi·er** n.

class·less /'klasləs/ ▶ adj. **1** (of a society) not divided into social classes. **2** not showing characteristics of a particular social class. ■ **class·less·ness** n.

class·mate /'klas,māt/ ▶ n. a fellow member of one's school or college class.

class·room /'klas,rōōm, -,rŏŏm/ ▶ n. a room in which a class of students is taught.

class·y /'klasē/ ▶ adj. (**classier, classiest**) informal stylish and sophisticated. ■ **class·i·ly** adv. **class·i·ness** n.

clat·ter /'klatər/ ▶ n. a loud rattling sound as of hard objects striking each other. ▶ v. make or move with a clatter.

clause /klôz/ ▶ n. **1** a group of words that includes a subject and a verb, forming a sentence or part of a sentence. **2** a particular and separate item of a treaty, bill, or contract. ■ **claus·al** adj.

claus·tro·pho·bi·a /,klôstrə'fōbēə/ ▶ n. extreme or irrational fear of being in an enclosed place. ■ **claus·tro·pho·bic** /,klôstrə'fōbik/ adj.

clav·i·chord /'klavə,kôrd/ ▶ n. a small early keyboard instrument with a soft tone.

clav·i·cle /'klavikəl/ ▶ n. technical term for COLLARBONE.

claw /klô/ ▶ n. **1** a curved pointed nail on each digit of the foot in birds, lizards, and some mammals. **2** the pincer of a crab, scorpion, or similar creature. ▶ v. **1** (usu. **claw at**) scratch or tear something with the claws or fingernails. **2** (**claw something back**) regain or recover money or power with difficulty. ■ **clawed** adj.

claw ham·mer ▶ n. a hammer with one side of the head split and curved, used for extracting nails.

clay /klā/ ▶ n. **1** a heavy sticky earth that can be molded when wet and baked to make bricks and pottery. **2** literary the substance of the human body: *this lifeless clay.* ■ **clay·ey** adj.

clay pig·eon ▶ n. a saucer-shaped piece of baked clay or other material thrown up in the air as a target for shooting.

clean /klēn/ ▶ adj. **1** free from dirt, stains, or harmful substances. **2** maintaining good personal hygiene. **3** not immoral or obscene: *good clean fun.* **4** showing or having no record of offenses or crimes: *a clean driving license.* **5** done according to the rules: *a good clean fight.* **6** free from irregularities; smooth. **7** (of an action) smoothly and skillfully done. ▶ v. **1** make someone or something clean. **2** (**clean someone out**) informal use up or take all someone's money. **3** (**clean up**) informal make a substantial gain or profit. ▶ adv. **1** so as to be free from dirt. **2** informal completely: *I clean forgot her birthday.* ▶ n. an act of cleaning. ■ **clean·a·ble** adj. **clean·ness** n.
– PHRASES **clean and jerk** a weightlifting exercise in which a weight is raised above the head following an initial lift to shoulder level. **a clean slate** an absence of existing restraints or commitments. **come clean** (or **make a clean breast of it**) informal fully confess something. **keep one's hands clean** remain uninvolved in something immoral or illegal. **make a clean sweep 1** remove all unwanted people or things ready to start afresh. **2** win all of a group of related sports contests.

clean-cut ▶ adj. **1** (of a person, especially a man) neat and respectable. **2** sharply outlined.

clean·er /'klēnər/ ▶ n. **1** a person or thing that cleans something. **2** (**the cleaners**) a place of business where clothes and fabrics are dry-cleaned.
– PHRASES **take someone to the cleaners** informal cheat or defraud someone of all their money or possessions.

clean·ly /'klēnlē/ ▶ adv. in a clean way. ■ **clean·li·ness** /'klenlēnis/ n.

cleanse /klenz/ ▶ v. **1** make something thoroughly clean. **2** remove something unpleasant or unwanted from: *he wanted to cleanse the town of immorality.*

cleans·er /'klenzər/ ▶ n. **1** a powder or liquid for scouring sinks, toilets, and bathtubs. **2** a cosmetic product for cleansing the skin.

clean-shav·en ▸ adj. (of a man) without a beard or moustache.

clean-up /ˈklēnˌəp/ ▸ n. 1 an act of cleaning a place. 2 an act of removing or putting an end to disorder, immorality, or crime. 3 Baseball the fourth position in a team's batting order, typically reserved for a power hitter likely to clear the bases by enabling any runners to score.

clear /ˈkli(ə)r/ ▸ adj. 1 easy to see, hear, or understand. 2 leaving or feeling no doubt. 3 transparent: *a stream of clear water.* 4 free of obstructions or unwanted objects. 5 (of a period of time) free of commitments. 6 free from disease or guilt. 7 (**clear of**) not touching; away from. 8 complete: *seven clear days' notice.* 9 (of a sum of money) net: *a clear profit of $1,100.* ▸ adv. 1 so as to be out of the way of or uncluttered by. 2 with clarity. ▸ v. 1 make or become clear. 2 get past or over something safely or without touching it. 3 show or declare someone to be innocent. 4 give official approval to; authorize: *I cleared him to return to his squadron.* 5 cause people to leave a building or place. 6 (of a check) pass through a clearinghouse so that the money enters a person's account. 7 earn an amount of money as a net profit. 8 pay off a debt. ■ **clear·ness** n.
‒ PHRASES **clear the air** 1 make the air less humid. 2 defuse a tense situation by frank discussion. **clear the decks** prepare for something by dealing with possible obstacles to progress. **clear off** (or **out**) informal go away. **clear something out** informal empty something. **clear up** 1 (of an illness or other medical condition) become cured. 2 (of the weather) become fine and dry. **clear something up** 1 tidy something by removing unwanted items. 2 solve or explain something. **in the clear** no longer in danger or under suspicion.

clear·ance /ˈkli(ə)rəns/ ▸ n. 1 the action of clearing. 2 official authorization for something. 3 clear space allowed for a thing to move past or under another.

clear-cut ▸ adj. easy to see or understand.

clear·ing /ˈkli(ə)riNG/ ▸ n. an open space in a forest.

clear·ing·house /ˈkli(ə)riNGˌhous/ ▸ n. 1 a bankers' establishment where checks and bills from member banks are exchanged. 2 an agency that collects and distributes information.

clear·ly /ˈkli(ə)rlē/ ▸ adv. 1 in a clear way. 2 without doubt; obviously.

clear-sight·ed ▸ adj. thinking clearly.

cleat /klēt/ ▸ n. 1 a T-shaped projection to which a rope may be attached. 2 a projecting piece of metal or rubber on the sole of a shoe, to prevent a person from slipping. ■ **cleat·ed** adj.

cleav·age /ˈklēvij/ ▸ n. 1 the space between a woman's breasts. 2 a marked difference or division between people. 3 cell division, especially of a fertilized egg cell.

cleave¹ /klēv/ ▸ v. (**cleaves, cleaving, clove** /klōv/ or **cleft** /kleft/ or **cleaved**; past part. **cloven** /ˈklōvən/ or **cleft** or **cleaved**/klēvd/;) 1 split something along a natural grain or line. 2 move forcefully through: *they watched a coot cleave the smooth water.*

cleave² ▸ v. (**cleave to**) literary 1 stick fast to. 2 become strongly involved with or emotionally attached to: *sport was something he could cleave to.*

cleav·er /ˈklēvər/ ▸ n. a tool with a heavy broad blade, used for chopping meat.

clef /klef/ ▸ n. Music any of several symbols placed on a stave, indicating the pitch of the notes written on the stave.

cleft /kleft/ past and past participle of CLEAVE¹ ▸ adj. split, divided, or partially divided into two. ▸ n. 1 a crack or split in rock or the ground. 2 a narrow vertical indentation in the chin or other part of the body.

cleft lip ▸ n. a split in the upper lip on one or both sides of the center, present from birth.

cleft pal·ate ▸ n. a split in the roof of the mouth that is present from birth.

clem·a·tis /ˈklemətəs, kləˈmatəs/ ▸ n. a climbing plant with white, pink, or purple flowers.

clem·en·cy /ˈklemənsē/ ▸ n. the quality of being clement or merciful.

clem·ent /ˈklemənt/ ▸ adj. 1 (of weather) mild. 2 showing mercy.

clem·en·tine /ˈklemənˌtīn, -ˌtēn/ ▸ n. a deep orange-red variety of tangerine.

clench /klenCH/ ▸ v. 1 close or press one's teeth or fists together tightly, as a reaction to stress or anger. 2 contract a set of muscles sharply. 3 hold something tightly: *he clenched the steering wheel.*

clere·sto·ry /ˈkli(ə)rˌstôrē/ (also **clearstory**) ▸ n. (pl. **clerestories**) the upper part of the nave, choir, and transepts of a large church, with a series of windows that allow light into the central parts of the building.

cler·gy /ˈklərjē/ ▸ n. (pl. **clergies**) (usu. treated as pl.) the people ordained for religious duties considered as a group, especially those in the Christian Church.

cler·gy·man /ˈklərjēmən/ (or **clergywoman** /ˈklərjēˌwŏŏmən/) ▸ n. (pl. **clergymen** or **clergywomen**) a Christian priest or minister.

cler·ic /ˈklerik/ ▸ n. a priest or religious leader.

cler·i·cal /ˈklerikəl/ ▸ adj. 1 relating to the routine work of an office clerk. 2 relating to the clergy. ■ **cler·i·cal·ly** adv.

cler·i·cal col·lar ▸ n. a stiff upright white collar that fastens at the back, worn by the clergy in some Christian churches.

cler·i·cal er·ror ▸ n. a mistake made in copying or writing out a document.

cler·i·hew /ˈklerəˌhyōō/ ▸ n. a short comic verse consisting of two rhyming couplets, usually referring to a famous person.

clerk /klərk/ ▸ n. 1 a person employed in an office or bank to keep records or accounts and to carry out other routine administrative duties. 2 a person in charge of the records of a local council or court. 3 (also **desk clerk**) a receptionist in a hotel. 4 (also **sales clerk**) an assistant in a store. ■ **clerk·ly** adj.

clev·er /ˈklevər/ ▸ adj. (**cleverer, cleverest**) 1 quick to understand and learn things. 2 skilled at doing something: *he's very clever with his hands.* ■ **clev·er·ly** adv. **clev·er·ness** n.

clew /klōō/ ▸ n. the lower corner of a sail or that nearest the stern of the boat.

cli·ché /klēˈSHā, kli-, ˈklēˌSHā/ (also **cliche**) ▸ n. a phrase or idea that has been used so often that it is no longer interesting or effective. ■ **cli·chéd** adj.

click /klik/ ▸ n. 1 a short, sharp sound. 2 Computing an act of pressing one of the buttons on a mouse. ▸ v. 1 make or cause to make a click: *the cameras started clicking.* 2 Computing press a mouse button. 3 informal become suddenly clear or understandable. 4 informal (of two people) become friends, especially at the first meeting. ■ **click·a·ble** adj.

cli·ent /'klīənt/ ▶ n. a person using the services of a professional person or organization.

cli·en·tele /ˌklīən'tel, ˌklē-/ ▶ n. all the clients or customers of a particular store, restaurant, or other business.

cli·ent-serv·er ▶ adj. Computing referring to a computer system in which a central server provides data to a number of networked workstations.

cliff /klif/ ▶ n. a steep rock face, especially at the edge of the sea.

cliff·hang·er /'klif,haNGər/ ▶ n. 1 a dramatic ending to an episode of a serial drama, leaving the audience in suspense. 2 an exciting situation in which the outcome is uncertain.

cli·mac·ter·ic /klī'maktərik, ˌklīmak'terik/ ▶ n. 1 the period of life when fertility is in decline; (in women) menopause. 2 a critical period or event.

cli·mac·tic /klī'maktik, klə-/ ▶ adj. forming an exciting climax. ■ **cli·mac·ti·cal·ly** /-ik(ə)lē/ adv.

USAGE
Do not confuse **climactic** with **climatic**. **Climactic** means 'forming a climax' (*the thrilling climactic scene*), whereas **climatic** means 'relating to climate' (*climatic and environmental change*).

cli·mate /'klīmit/ ▶ n. 1 the general weather conditions in an area over a long period. 2 a general trend, attitude, or situation: *the current economic climate*. ■ **cli·ma·tol·o·gy** /ˌklīmə'täləjē/ n. **cli·ma·to·log·i·cal** /ˌklīmətl'läjikəl/ adj.

cli·mate change ▶ n. long-term, significant change in the climate of an area or of the earth, usually seen as resulting from human activity.

cli·mat·ic /klī'matik/ ▶ adj. relating to climate. ■ **cli·mat·i·cal·ly** /klī'matik(ə)lē/ adv.

cli·max /'klī,maks/ ▶ n. 1 the most intense, exciting, or important point of something. 2 an orgasm. ▶ v. reach a climax.

climb /klīm/ ▶ v. 1 go or come up to a higher position. 2 go up a hill, rock face, etc. 3 (of a plant) grow up a supporting structure by clinging to or twining around it. 4 move somewhere, especially with effort or difficulty: *he climbed out through the kitchen window*. 5 increase in amount, value, or power: *the shares climbed more than $3*. 6 (**climb down**) withdraw from a position taken up in an argument or negotiation; admit that one was wrong. ▶ n. 1 an act of climbing. 2 a route up a mountain or cliff. ■ **climb·a·ble** adj.

climb·er /'klīmər/ ▶ n. a person who climbs rocks or mountains as a sport.

climb·ing wall ▶ n. a wall at a sports center or in a gymnasium fitted with attachments to simulate a rock face for climbing practice.

clime /klīm/ ▶ n. chiefly literary a region with a particular climate: *people leaving the Northwest for sunnier climes*.

clinch /klinCH/ ▶ v. 1 succeed in achieving or winning: *he clinched a $5 million sponsorship deal*. 2 settle an argument or debate. ▶ n. 1 an act of grappling at close quarters in a fight. 2 informal an embrace.

clinch·er /'klinCHər/ ▶ n. informal a fact, argument, or event that settles something decisively.

cline /klīn/ ▶ n. a continuum with an infinite number of gradations from one extreme to the other. ■ **clin·al** /'klīnl/ adj.

cling /kliNG/ ▶ v. (past and past part. **clung** /kləNG/) (**cling to/on to**) 1 hold on tightly to. 2 stick to: *her hair clung to her damp skin*. 3 be unwilling to give up a belief or hope: *she clung to her convictions*. 4 be emotionally dependent on someone.

cling·y /'kliNGē/ ▶ adj. (**clingier, clingiest**) 1 (of a garment) clinging to the body. 2 (of a person) too emotionally dependent on someone else. ■ **cling·i·ness** n.

clin·ic /'klinik/ ▶ n. 1 a place where or time when specialized medical treatment or advice is given. 2 an occasion at which advice and training in a particular subject or activity is given: *a tennis clinic*.

clin·i·cal /'klinikəl/ ▶ adj. 1 relating to the observation and treatment of patients (rather than theoretical studies). 2 without feeling or sympathy: *she looked at him with clinical detachment*. 3 (of a place) very clean and plain. ■ **clin·i·cal·ly** /'klinik(ə)lē/ adv.

clin·i·cal psy·chol·o·gy ▶ n. the branch of psychology concerned with the assessment and treatment of patients of mental illness and behavioral problems.

cli·ni·cian /klə'nisHən/ ▶ n. a doctor having direct contact with and responsibility for treating patients, rather than one involved with theoretical studies.

clink[1] /kliNGk/ ▶ n. a sharp ringing sound, like that made when metal or glass is struck. ▶ v. make or cause to make a clink.

clink[2] ▶ n. informal prison.

clink·er[1] /'kliNGkər/ ▶ n. the stony remains from burned coal or from a furnace.

clink·er[2] ▶ n. informal something that is unsatisfactory, of poor quality, or a failure: *marketing couldn't save such clinkers as these films*.

clip[1] /klip/ ▶ n. 1 a flexible or spring-loaded device for holding an object or objects together or in place. 2 a piece of jewelry that can be fastened onto a garment with a clip. 3 a metal holder containing cartridges for an automatic firearm. ▶ v. (**clips, clipping, clipped**) fasten something with a clip or clips.

clip[2] ▶ v. (**clips, clipping, clipped**) 1 cut or trim something, or cut something out with shears or scissors. 2 trim an animal's hair or wool. 3 strike someone or something with a sharp blow. ▶ n. 1 an act of clipping something. 2 a short sequence taken from a movie or broadcast. 3 informal a sharp blow. 4 informal a rapid speed: *they went by at a fast clip*.

clip art ▶ n. digital pictures and symbols provided with word-processing software.

clip·board /'klip,bôrd/ ▶ n. a small board with a spring clip at the top, used for holding papers and providing support for writing.

clip joint ▶ n. informal a nightclub or bar that charges extremely high prices.

clipped /klipt/ ▶ adj. (of speech) having short, sharp vowel sounds and clear pronunciation.

clip·per /'klipər/ ▶ n. 1 (**clippers**) an instrument for clipping. 2 a fast sailing ship of the 19th century.

clip·ping /'klipiNG/ ▶ n. 1 a small piece trimmed from something: *grass clippings*. 2 an article cut out of a newspaper or magazine.

clique /klēk, klik/ ▶ n. a small group of people who spend time together and are unwilling to allow others to join them. ■ **cli·quey** adj. **cli·quish** adj.

clit·o·ris /ˈklitərəs/ ▶ n. a small sensitive organ at the front end of the female external genitals. ■ **clit·o·ral** /ˈklitərəl/ adj.

clo·a·ca /klōˈākə/ ▶ n. (in some animals) a cavity at the end of the digestive tract into which the urinary and reproductive systems also open, leading to a single opening in the body.

cloak /klōk/ ▶ n. 1 an outer garment that hangs loosely from the shoulders over the arms to the knees or ankles. 2 something that hides or covers: *a cloak of secrecy.* ▶ v. 1 hide or cover: *the summit was cloaked in thick mist.* 2 (as adj. **cloaked**) wearing a cloak.

cloak-and-dag·ger ▶ adj. involving intrigue and secrecy.

cloak·room /ˈklōkˌro͞om, -ˌro͝om/ ▶ n. a room in a public building where outdoor clothes and bags may be left.

clob·ber /ˈkläbər/ ▶ v. 1 hit someone hard. 2 defeat a person or team heavily.

cloche /klōsH/ ▶ n. 1 a small glass or plastic cover for protecting outdoor plants or making them develop faster than usual. 2 (also **cloche hat**) a woman's close-fitting bell-shaped hat.

clock /kläk/ ▶ n. 1 an instrument that measures and indicates the time by means of a dial or a digital display. 2 informal a measuring device resembling a clock, such as a speedometer. ▶ v. 1 reach or achieve a particular time, distance, or speed. 2 (**clock in/out**) record the time of one's arrival at or departure from work, especially by inserting a card in a special clock. 3 informal, chiefly Brit. hit someone on the head. – PHRASES **around the clock** all day and all night. **turn back the clock** return to the past or to a previous way of doing things.

clock-watch·er ▶ n. a person who constantly checks the time to make sure that they do not work longer than they are supposed to.

clock·wise /ˈkläkˌwīz/ ▶ adv. & adj. in the direction of the movement of the hands of a clock.

clock·work /ˈkläkˌwərk/ ▶ n. a mechanism with a spring and toothed gearwheels, used to drive a mechanical clock, toy, or other device. – PHRASES **like clockwork** very smoothly and easily.

clod /kläd/ ▶ n. 1 a lump of earth. 2 informal a stupid person.

clod·dish /ˈklädisH/ ▶ adj. foolish, awkward, or clumsy.

clod·hop·per /ˈklädˌhäpər/ ▶ n. informal 1 a large, heavy shoe. 2 a foolish, awkward, or clumsy person.

clog /kläg, klôg/ ▶ n. a shoe with a thick wooden sole. ▶ v. (**clogs, clogging, clogged**) block or become blocked: *the gutters were clogged with leaves.*

cloi·son·né /ˌkloizəˈnā, ˌkläwäz-/ ▶ n. enamel work in which the different colors in the design are separated by strips of flattened wire placed on a metal backing.

clois·ter /ˈkloistər/ ▶ n. 1 a covered passage around an open courtyard in a convent, monastery, college, or cathedral, usually having a row of columns on the inner side. 2 (**the cloister**) the secluded life of a monk or nun.

clois·tered /ˈkloistərd/ ▶ adj. 1 having or enclosed by a cloister: *a cloistered walkway.* 2 protected from the problems of ordinary life.

clomp /klämp, klômp/ ▶ v. walk heavily.

clone /klōn/ ▶ n. 1 an animal or plant produced from the cells of another, to which it is genetically identical. 2 a person or thing regarded as an exact copy of another. ▶ v. 1 create an animal or plant as a clone. 2 make an identical copy of something.

clonk /kläNGk, klôNGk/ ▶ n. a loud sound made by heavy things hitting each other. ▶ v. 1 move with or make a clonk. 2 informal hit.

clop /kläp/ ▶ n. a sound made by a horse's hooves on a hard surface. ▶ v. (**clops, clopping, clopped**) move with such a sound.

close¹ /klōs/ ▶ adj. 1 only a short distance away or apart in space or time. 2 (**close to**) almost doing or being something: *she was close to tears.* 3 (of a connection or resemblance) strong. 4 (of a person) part of someone's immediate family: *a close relative.* 5 (of a relationship or the people in it) very affectionate or intimate. 6 (of observation or examination) done in a careful and thorough way. 7 uncomfortably humid or airless. ▶ adv. so as to be very near. ■ **close·ly** adv. **close·ness** n. – PHRASES **at close quarters** (or **range**) very near to someone or something. **close-knit** (of a group of people) united by strong relationships and common interests. **close-run** (of a contest) won or lost by a very small amount. **close shave** (also **close call**) informal a narrow escape from danger or disaster.

close² /klōz/ ▶ v. 1 move something so as to cover an opening. 2 bring two parts of something together: *she closed the book.* 3 (**close on/in on**) gradually get nearer to or surround someone or something. 4 (**close in**) (of bad weather or darkness) gradually surround someone. 5 (**close in**) (of days) get successively shorter with the approach of the winter solstice. 6 (**close around/over**) encircle and hold. 7 bring or come to an end. 8 finish speaking or writing. 9 (often **close down/up**) (with reference to a business or other organization) stop or cause to stop trading or operating. 10 bring to a conclusion: *he closed a deal with one of the supermarkets.* ▶ n. the end of an event or of a period of time or activity.

closed /klōzd/ ▶ adj. 1 not open or allowing access. 2 not communicating with or influenced by others: *a closed society.* – PHRASES **behind closed doors** in private. **a closed book** a subject or person about which one knows nothing.

closed cap·tion ▶ n. one of a series of subtitles to a television program, accessible through a decoder. ■ **closed-cap·tion·ing** n.

closed-cir·cuit tel·e·vi·sion ▶ n. a television system in which the signals are transmitted from one or more cameras by cable to a restricted set of monitors.

closed shop ▶ n. a place of work where all employees must belong to a particular labor union.

close har·mo·ny /klōs/ ▶ n. Music harmony in which the notes of the chord are close together, typically in vocal music.

close-mouthed /ˈklōs ˈmou͟THd, ˈmou͟THt/ ▶ n. reticent; not communicating freely: *the candidates have been close-mouthed about their fund-raising goals.*

clos·et /'kläzit/ ▸ n. **1** a tall cupboard or wardrobe. **2** a small room. **3** old use a toilet. ▸ adj. secret: *a closet socialist*. ▸ v. (**closets, closeting, closeted**) **1** shut oneself away in private to talk to someone or to be alone: *he closeted himself in his room*. **2** (as adj. **closeted**) keeping the fact of being homosexual secret.
– PHRASES **in** (or **out of**) **the closet** not admitting (or admitting) that one is homosexual.

close-up /'klōs ,əp/ ▸ n. a photograph, movie, or video taken at close range.

clo·sure /'klōzHər/ ▸ n. **1** an act or process of closing something. **2** a device that closes or seals something. **3** (in a parliament) a procedure for ending a debate and taking a vote. **4** a feeling that an emotional or upsetting experience has been resolved.

clot /klät/ ▸ n. a thick semisolid mass formed from a liquid substance, especially blood.
▸ v. (**clots, clotting, clotted**) form into clots.

cloth /klôTH/ ▸ n. (pl. **cloths**) **1** fabric made by weaving or knitting a soft fiber such as wool or cotton. **2** a piece of cloth used for a particular purpose. **3** (**the cloth**) Christian priests as a group.

clothe /klōTH/ ▸ v. (past and past part. **clothed** or old use or literary **clad** /klad/) **1** provide someone with clothes. **2** (**be clothed in**) be dressed in.

clothes /klō(TH)z/ ▸ pl. n. things worn to cover the body.

clothes horse ▸ n. **1** a frame on which washed clothes are hung to dry. **2** informal a person who models or is over-concerned with wearing fashionable clothes.

clothes·line /'klō(TH)z,līn/ ▸ n. a rope or wire on which washed clothes are hung to dry.

clothes moth ▸ n. a small brown moth whose larvae can damage fabric, especially wool.

clothes·pin /'klō(TH)z,pin/ ▸ n. a wooden or plastic clip for securing clothes to a clothesline.

cloth·ier /'klōTHyər, -THēər/ ▸ n. a person who makes or sells clothes or cloth.

cloth·ing /'klōTHiNG/ ▸ n. clothes.

clot·ted cream ▸ n. chiefly Brit. thick cream made by heating milk slowly and then allowing it to cool while the cream rises to the top in lumps.

clo·ture /'klōcHər/ ▸ n. (in a legislature) a procedure for ending a debate and taking a vote.

cloud /kloud/ ▸ n. **1** a white or gray mass of condensed watery vapor floating in the atmosphere. **2** a mass of smoke, dust, etc. **3** a large number of insects or birds moving together. **4** a state or cause of gloom or anxiety: *injury worries cast a cloud over the team's preparations*. ▸ v. **1** (**cloud over**) (of the sky) become full of clouds. **2** make or become less clear: *all sorts of doubts clouded my mind*. **3** (of someone's face or eyes) show sadness, anxiety, or anger. ■ **cloud·less** adj.
– PHRASES **have one's head in the clouds** be full of idealistic dreams. **on cloud nine** extremely happy. **under a cloud** under suspicion of having done wrong.

cloud·burst /'kloud,bərst/ ▸ n. a sudden violent rainstorm.

cloud·y /'kloudē/ ▸ adj. **1** covered with clouds; having many clouds. **2** (of a liquid) not clear or transparent. ■ **cloud·i·ness** n.

clout /klout/ informal ▸ n. **1** a heavy blow. **2** influence or power. ▸ v. hit someone hard.

clove¹ /klōv/ ▸ n. **1** the dried flower bud of a tropical tree, used as a spice. **2** (**oil of cloves**) a strong-smelling oil extracted from these flower buds and used for the relief of toothache.

clove² ▸ n. any of the small bulbs making up a compound bulb of garlic.

clove³ ▸ past of CLEAVE¹.

clove hitch ▸ n. a knot used to fasten a rope to a spar or another rope.

clo·ven /'klōvən/ ▸ past participle of CLEAVE¹.

clo·ven hoof (also **cloven foot**) ▸ n. the divided hoof or foot of animals such as cattle, sheep, goats, and deer.

clo·ver /'klōvər/ ▸ n. a plant with round white or deep pink flowerheads and leaves with three rounded parts.
– PHRASES **in clover** living a comfortable life with plenty of money.

clo·ver·leaf /'klōvər,lēf/ ▸ n. a junction of roads intersecting at different levels with connecting sections forming the pattern of a four-leaf clover. ▸ adj. having a shape or pattern resembling a leaf of clover, especially a four-leaf clover.

clown /kloun/ ▸ n. **1** a comic entertainer, especially one in a circus, wearing a traditional costume and exaggerated makeup. **2** a playful and amusing person. ▸ v. behave in a silly or playful way. ■ **clown·ish** adj.

cloy·ing /'kloi-iNG/ ▸ adj. so sweet or sentimental as to be unpleasant. ■ **cloy·ing·ly** adv.

club¹ /kləb/ ▸ n. **1** an association of people who meet regularly to take part in a particular activity. **2** an organization where members can meet, eat meals, and stay overnight. **3** a nightclub with dance music. ▸ v. (**clubs, clubbing, clubbed**) informal go out to nightclubs. ■ **club·ber** n.

club² ▸ n. **1** a heavy stick with a thick end, used as a weapon. **2** (also **golf club**) a club used to hit the ball in golf, with a heavy wooden or metal head on a slender shaft. **3** (**clubs**) one of the four suits in a conventional deck of playing cards, represented by a design of three black leaves on a short stem. ▸ v. (**clubs, clubbing, clubbed**) beat someone or something with a club or similar object.

club·by /'kləbē/ ▸ adj. (**clubbier, clubbiest**) informal friendly and sociable with fellow members of a group or organization but not with outsiders.

club foot ▸ n. a deformed foot that is twisted so that the sole cannot be placed flat on the ground.

club·house /'kləb,hous/ ▸ n. a building having a bar and other facilities for the members of a club.

club·moss /'kləb,mos, -,man/ ▸ n. a low-growing flowerless plant.

club·root /'kləb,rōōt, -,rŏŏt/ ▸ n. a disease of cabbages, turnips, etc., in which the root becomes swollen and distorted.

club sand·wich ▸ n. a sandwich consisting typically of ham, turkey, or chicken and bacon, tomato, and lettuce, layered between three slices of bread.

club so·da ▸ n. another term for SODA (sense 2).

cluck /klək/ ▸ v. **1** (of a hen) make a short, low sound. **2** (**cluck over/around**) express fussy concern about someone. ▸ n. the short, low sound made by a hen.

clue /klōō/ ▸ n. a fact or piece of evidence that helps to clear up a mystery or solve a problem.

▶ v. (**clues, clueing, clued**) (**clue someone in**) informal inform someone about something.
– PHRASES **not have a clue** informal not know about something, or about how to do something.

clue·less /'klŌŌləs/ ▶ adj. informal having no knowledge, understanding, or ability. ■ **clue·less·ness** n.

clump /kləmp/ ▶ n. **1** a small group of trees or plants growing closely together. **2** a mass or lump of something. **3** the sound of heavy footsteps. ▶ v. **1** form into a clump or mass. **2** walk or tread heavily.

clump·y /'kləmpē/ ▶ adj. **1** containing or tending to form clumps. **2** (of shoes or boots) heavy and clumsy-looking.

clum·sy /'kləmzē/ ▶ adj. (**clumsier, clumsiest**) **1** not smooth or graceful in movement or action. **2** difficult to handle or use. **3** tactless. ■ **clum·si·ly** /-zəlē/ adv. **clum·si·ness** n.

clung /kləNG/ ▶ past and past participle of CLING.

clunk /kləNGk/ ▶ n. a dull, heavy sound like that made by thick pieces of metal striking together. ▶ v. move with or make a clunk.

clunk·y /'kləNGkē/ ▶ adj. (**clunkier, clunkiest**) informal **1** solid, heavy, and old-fashioned. **2** making a clunking sound.

clus·ter /'kləstər/ ▶ n. a group of similar things positioned or occurring closely together. ▶ v. form a cluster.

clus·ter bomb ▶ n. a bomb that releases a number of smaller bombs when it explodes.

clutch[1] /kləCH/ ▶ v. grasp something tightly. ▶ n. **1** a tight grasp. **2** (**clutches**) power or control: *he had fallen into her clutches.* **3** a mechanism for connecting and disconnecting the engine and the transmission system in a vehicle.

clutch[2] ▶ n. **1** a group of eggs fertilized at the same time and laid in a single session. **2** a brood of chicks. **3** a small group of people or things.

clutch bag ▶ n. a slim, flat handbag without handles or a strap.

clut·ter /'klətər/ ▶ v. cover or fill something with an untidy collection of things. ▶ n. **1** things lying around untidily. **2** an untidy state.

Cm ▶ symbol the chemical element curium.

cm ▶ abbr. centimeter or centimeters.

Cmdr. ▶ abbr. commander.

Cmdre. ▶ abbr. Commodore.

CNN ▶ abbr. Cable News Network.

CO ▶ abbr. **1** Colorado. **2** Commanding Officer.

Co ▶ symbol the chemical element cobalt.

Co. ▶ abbr. **1** company. **2** county.

c/o ▶ abbr. care of.

co- ▶ prefix **1** (forming nouns) joint; mutual; common: *co-driver.* **2** (forming adjectives) jointly; mutually: *coequal.* **3** (forming verbs) together with another or others: *co-produce.*

coach[1] /kōCH/ ▶ n. **1** a closed horse-drawn carriage. **2** a railroad car. **3** Brit. a bus with comfortable seats, used for longer journeys.

coach[2] ▶ n. **1** an athletic instructor or trainer. **2** a tutor who gives private or specialized teaching. ▶ v. train or teach someone as a coach.

coach·man /'kōCHmən/ ▶ n. (pl. **coachmen**) a driver of a horse-drawn carriage.

co·ag·u·lant /kō'agyələnt/ ▶ n. a substance that causes a fluid to coagulate.

co·ag·u·late /kō'agyə,lāt/ ▶ v. (of a fluid, especially blood) change to a solid or semisolid state. ■ **co·ag·u·la·tion** /kō,agyə'lāsHən/ n.

coal /kōl/ ▶ n. **1** a black rock consisting mainly of carbon formed from the remains of ancient trees and other vegetation and used as fuel. **2** a red-hot piece of coal or other material in a fire.

co·a·lesce /,kōə'les/ ▶ v. come or bring together to form one mass or whole. ■ **co·a·les·cence** n.

coal·face /'kōl,fās/ ▶ n. an exposed area of coal in a mine.

coal·field /'kōl,fēld/ ▶ n. a large area rich in underground coal.

co·a·li·tion /,kōə'lisHən/ ▶ n. a temporary alliance, especially of political parties forming a government. ■ **co·a·li·tion·ist** n.

coal tar ▶ n. a thick black liquid distilled from coal, containing various organic chemicals.

coam·ing /'kōmiNG/ (also **coamings**) ▶ n. a raised border around the cockpit or hatch of a boat to keep out water.

coarse /kôrs/ ▶ adj. **1** rough or harsh in texture. **2** consisting of large grains or particles. **3** rude or vulgar in behavior or speech. ■ **coarse·ly** adv. **coarse·ness** n.

coars·en /'kôrsən/ ▶ v. make or become coarse.

coast /kōst/ ▶ n. land next to or near the sea. ▶ v. **1** move easily without using power. **2** achieve something without making much effort: *the team coasted to victory.* ■ **coast·al** adj.
– PHRASES **the coast is clear** there is no danger of being seen or caught.

coast·er /'kōstər/ ▶ n. **1** a small mat for a glass. **2** a ship carrying cargo along the coast from port to port.

coast guard ▶ n. **1** (**Coast Guard**) a branch of the US armed forces responsible for the enforcement of maritime law and for the protection of life and property at sea. **2** a civilian or volunteer organization keeping watch on the sea near a coast in order to assist people or ships in danger and to prevent smuggling.

coast·line /'kōst,līn/ ▶ n. a stretch of coast: *a rugged coastline.*

coat /kōt/ ▶ n. **1** a full-length outer garment with sleeves. **2** an animal's covering of fur or hair. **3** an enclosing or covering layer or structure. **4** a single application of paint or similar substance. ▶ v. provide with or form a layer or covering: *vanilla ice cream coated with chocolate.*

co·a·ti /kō'ätē/ ▶ n. (pl. **coatis**) a raccoonlike animal found in Central and South America, with a long flexible snout and a tail with circular stripes.

co·a·ti·mun·di /kō,ätiˈməndē/ ▶ n. (pl. **coatimundis**) another term for COATI.

coat·ing /'kōtiNG/ ▶ n. a thin layer or covering of something.

coat of arms ▶ n. the distinctive heraldic design or shield of a person, family, corporation, or country.

coat of mail ▶ n. historical a jacket made of metal rings or plates, used as armor.

coat·tail /'kōt,tāl/ ▶ n. each of the flaps formed by the back of a tailcoat.
– PHRASES **on someone's coattails** benefiting from someone else's success.

coax[1] /kōks/ ▶ v. **1** gradually or gently persuade someone to do something. **2** manipulate something carefully into a particular situation or position.

coax² /'kō-aks, kō'aks/ ▶ n. informal coaxial cable.

co·ax·i·al /kō'aksēəl/ ▶ adj. **1** having a common axis. **2** (of a cable or line) transmitting by means of two concentric conductors separated by an insulator.

cob /käb/ ▶ n. **1** a corncob. **2** (also **cobnut**) a hazelnut or filbert. **3** a powerfully built, short-legged horse. **4** a male swan.

co·balt /'kō,bôlt/ ▶ n. a hard silvery-white metallic chemical element, used in alloys.

co·balt blue ▶ n. a deep blue pigment containing cobalt and aluminum oxides.

cob·ble¹ /'käbəl/ ▶ n. (also **cobblestone**) a small round stone used to cover road surfaces. ∎ **cob·bled** adj.

cob·ble² ▶ v. (**cobble something together**) produce something quickly and without great care: *the movie was cobbled together from two separate stories.*

cob·bler /'käblər/ ▶ n. **1** a person whose job is mending shoes. **2** a fruit pie with a rich crust on top.

COBOL /'kō,bôl/ ▶ n. a computer programming language designed for use in commerce.

co·bra /'kōbrə/ ▶ n. a highly poisonous snake that spreads the skin of its neck into a hood when disturbed, native to Africa and Asia.

cob·web /'käb,web/ ▶ n. a spider's web, especially an old or dusty one. ∎ **cob·webbed** adj.

cob·web·by adj.

co·ca /'kōkə/ ▶ n. a tropical American shrub grown for its leaves, which are the source of cocaine.

Co·ca-Co·la ▶ n. trademark a carbonated nonalcoholic drink.

co·caine /kō'kān, 'kō,kān/ ▶ n. an addictive drug obtained from coca or prepared synthetically, used as an illegal stimulant and sometimes in medicine as a local anesthetic.

coc·cus /'käkəs/ ▶ n. (pl. **cocci** /'käk,(s)ī, 'käk,(s)ē/) Biology any rounded bacterium.

coc·cyx /'käksiks/ ▶ n. (pl. **coccyges** /'käksə,jēz/ or **coccyxes** /'käksiksiz/) a small triangular bone at the base of the spinal column in humans and some apes. ∎ **coc·cyg·e·al** /käk'sijēəl/ adj.

coch·i·neal /'käcнə,nēəl, 'kō-/ ▶ n. a scarlet dye used for coloring food, made from the crushed dried bodies of a kind of insect.

coch·le·a /'kōklēə, 'käk-/ ▶ n. (pl. **cochleae** /-lē,ē, -lē,ī/) the spiral cavity of the inner ear, containing an organ that produces nerve impulses in response to sound vibrations. ∎ **coch·le·ar** adj.

cock /käk/ ▶ n. **1** a male bird, especially of a domestic fowl. **2** vulgar slang a man's penis. **3** a firing lever in a gun that can be raised to be released by the trigger. ▶ v. **1** tilt or bend something in a particular direction. **2** raise the cock of a gun to make it ready for firing. – PHRASES **cock one's ear** (of a dog) raise its ears to an erect position.

cock·ade /kä'kād/ ▶ n. a rosette or knot of ribbons worn in a hat as a badge of office or as part of a livery. ∎ **cock·ad·ed** adj.

cock-a-hoop /,käk ə 'hōop, 'hōop/ ▶ adj. extremely pleased.

cock-a-leek·ie /,käk ə 'lēkē/ ▶ n. a soup traditionally made in Scotland with chicken and leeks.

cock and bull sto·ry ▶ n. informal an unbelievable story, especially one used as an excuse.

cock·a·tiel /'käkə,tēl/ ▶ n. a small crested Australian parrot with a mainly gray body and a yellow and orange face.

cock·a·too /'käkə,tōō/ ▶ n. a crested parrot found in Australia and Indonesia.

cock·a·trice /'käkətris, -,trīs/ ▶ n. **1** another term for BASILISK (sense 1). **2** Heraldry a mythical animal represented as a two-legged dragon with a cock's head.

cock·chaf·er /'käk,cнāfər/ ▶ n. a large brown flying beetle.

cock·crow /'käk,krō/ ▶ n. literary dawn.

cock·er·el /'käkərəl/ ▶ n. a young domestic cock.

cock·er span·iel /'käkər/ ▶ n. a small breed of spaniel with a silky coat.

cock·eyed /'käk'īd/ ▶ adj. informal **1** crooked or askew; not level. **2** absurd; impractical. **3** drunk.

cock·fight·ing /'käk,fītiNG/ ▶ n. the sport (illegal in some countries) of setting two cocks to fight each other. ∎ **cock·fight** n.

cock·le /'käkəl/ ▶ n. **1** an edible shellfish with a strong ribbed shell. **2** (also **cockleshell** /'käkəl,sнel/) literary a small, shallow boat. – PHRASES **warm the cockles of one's heart** give one a feeling of contentment.

cock·ney /'käknē/ ▶ n. (pl. **cockneys**) **1** a person from the East End of London, traditionally one born within the sound of Bow Bells. **2** the dialect or accent used in this area.

cock·pit /'käk,pit/ ▶ n. **1** a compartment for the pilot and crew in an aircraft or spacecraft. **2** the driver's compartment in a race car. **3** a place where cockfights are held.

cock·roach /'käk,rōcн/ ▶ n. a beetlelike insect with long antennae and legs, some kinds of which are household pests.

cocks·comb /'käks,kōm/ ▶ n. **1** the crest or comb of a domestic cock. **2** a tropical plant with a showy crest of flowers.

cock·sure /'käk'sнōr/ ▶ adj. arrogantly confident.

cock·tail /'käk,tāl/ ▶ n. **1** an alcoholic drink consisting of a spirit mixed with other ingredients, such as fruit juice. **2** a dish consisting of a mixture of small pieces of food: *shrimp cocktail.* **3** a mixture of different substances or factors, especially when dangerous or unpleasant: *a cocktail of drugs.*

cock·y /'käkē/ ▶ adj. (**cockier, cockiest**) conceited in a bold or impudent way. ∎ **cock·i·ly** adv. **cock·i·ness** n.

co·coa /'kōkō/ ▶ n. **1** a powder made from roasted and ground cacao seeds. **2** a hot drink made from cocoa powder mixed with milk or water.

co·coa bean ▶ n. a cacao seed.

co·coa but·ter ▶ n. a fatty substance obtained from cocoa beans, used in confectionery and cosmetics.

co·co·nut /'kōkə,nət/ ▶ n. **1** the large brown seed of a tropical palm, consisting of a hard woody husk surrounded by fiber, lined with edible white flesh and containing a clear liquid (**coconut milk**). **2** the edible white flesh of a coconut.

co·coon /kə'kōon/ ▶ n. **1** a protective silky case spun by the larvae of many insects, in which the pupa develops. **2** a covering that prevents the corrosion of metal equipment. **3** something that envelops someone in a protective or comforting way: *a cocoon of sheets and blankets.* ▶ v. envelop in a protective or comforting way: *we were cocooned in our sleeping bags.*

co·cotte /kô'kôt, kə'kät/ ▶ n. (usu. in phrase **en cocotte** /äɴ/) a small dish in which individual portions of food can be cooked and served.

COD ▶ abbr. cash on delivery.

cod /käd/ (also **codfish**) ▶ n. (pl. same) a large sea fish that is important as a food fish.

co·da /'kōdə/ ▶ n. **1** Music the concluding passage of a piece or movement. **2** a concluding event, remark, or section.

cod·dle /'kädl/ ▶ v. **1** treat someone in an indulgent or overprotective way. **2** cook an egg in water below the boiling point.

code /kōd/ ▶ n. **1** a system of words, figures, or symbols used to represent others, especially for the purposes of secrecy. **2** a series of numbers or letters used to classify or identify something. **3** (also **area code**) a sequence of numbers dialed to connect a telephone line with another exchange. **4** Computing program instructions. **5** a set of moral principles or rules of behavior: *a strict code of conduct*. **6** a systematic collection of laws or statutes: *the penal code*. ▶ v. **1** convert the words of a message into a code. **2** (usu. as adj. **coded**) express the meaning of something in an indirect way: *his coded criticism of the prime minister*. ■ **cod·er** n.

co·deine /'kō,dēn/ ▶ n. a painkilling drug obtained from morphine.

code name ▶ n. a word used for secrecy or convenience instead of the usual name.

co·de·pend·en·cy /,kōdə'pendənsē/ ▶ n. the state of being too emotionally or psychologically dependent on a partner, especially one who has an illness or addiction and needs care or support. ■ **co·de·pend·ence** /-dəns/ n. **co·de·pend·ent** /-dənt/ adj. & n.

code·share /'kōd,sHe(ə)r/ ▶ n. **1** a marketing arrangement in which two airlines sell seats on a flight that one of them operates. **2** a flight or aircraft in which such an arrangement is in effect. ■ **code·shar·ing** n.

co·dex /'kō,deks/ ▶ n. (pl. **codices** /'kōdə,sēz, 'käd-/ or **codexes**) **1** an ancient manuscript in book form. **2** an official list of medicines, chemicals, etc.

cod·fish /'käd,fisH/ ▶ n. (pl. same or **codfishes**) another term for COD.

codg·er /'käjər/ ▶ n. informal, derogatory an elderly man.

cod·i·cil /'kädəsəl, -,sil/ ▶ n. an addition or supplement that explains, changes, or cancels a will or part of one.

cod·i·fy /'kädə,fī, 'kōd-/ ▶ v. (**codifies, codifying, codified**) organize procedures or rules into a system. ■ **cod·i·fi·ca·tion** /,kädəfə'kāsHən, ,kōd-/ n.

cod·ling /'kädliNG/ ▶ n. a young cod.

cod·ling moth ▶ n. a small grayish moth whose larvae feed on apples.

cod liv·er oil ▶ n. oil obtained from the fresh liver of cod, which is rich in vitamins D and A.

co·don /'kō,dän/ ▶ n. Biochemistry a sequence of three nucleotides that together form a unit of genetic code in a DNA or RNA molecule.

cod·piece /'käd,pēs/ ▶ n. (in the 15th and 16th centuries) a pouch covering the genitals, attached to a pair of man's breeches.

co·ed /'kō,ed/ ▶ n. dated a female student at a co-educational institution. ▶ adj. (of an institution or system) co-educational.

co·ed·u·ca·tion /,kō,ejə'kāsHən/ ▶ n. the education of students of both sexes together. ■ **co·ed·u·ca·tion·al** adj.

co·ef·fi·cient /,kōə'fisHənt/ ▶ n. **1** Mathematics a quantity placed before and multiplying the variable in an algebraic expression (e.g., 4 in $4x^2$). **2** Physics a multiplier or factor that measures a particular property.

coe·la·canth /'sēlə,kanTH/ ▶ n. a large bony sea fish with a tail fin in three rounded parts, known only from fossils until one was found alive in 1938.

coe·len·ter·ate /si'lentə,rāt, -rət/ ▶ n. Zoology a member of a large group of invertebrate sea animals that usually have a tube- or cup-shaped body with a single opening fringed with tentacles, such as jellyfish, corals, and sea anemones.

co·en·zyme /kō'en,zīm/ ▶ n. Biochemistry a compound that is essential for the functioning of an enzyme.

co·e·qual /kō'ēkwəl/ ▶ adj. (of two or more people or things) having the same rank or importance. ▶ n. a person or thing equal with another.

co·erce /kō'ərs/ ▶ v. persuade an unwilling person to do something by using force or threats. ■ **co·er·cion** /kō'ərzHən, -sHən/ n. **co·er·cive** /kō'ərsiv/ adj.

co·e·val /kō'ēvəl/ ▶ adj. having the same age or date of origin; contemporary. ▶ n. a person or roughly the same age as oneself; a contemporary.

co·ex·ist /,kō-ig'zist/ ▶ v. **1** exist at the same time or in the same place. **2** exist together in a peaceful or harmonious way. ■ **co·ex·ist·ence** /-'zistəns/ n. **co·ex·ist·ent** /-'zistənt/ adj.

co·ex·ten·sive /,kō-ik'stensiv/ ▶ adj. formal extending over the same area, extent, or time: *we are not separate from but coextensive with nature*.

cof·fee /'kôfē, 'käfē/ ▶ n. **1** a hot drink made from the roasted and ground beanlike seeds of a tropical shrub. **2** the seeds used to make this drink.

cof·fee break ▶ n. a short rest from work during which refreshments are usually taken.

cof·fee cake ▶ n. a cake, often cinnamon-flavored, with a drizzled white icing or crumb topping and usually eaten with coffee.

cof·fee ta·ble ▶ n. a small, low table.

cof·fee-ta·ble book ▶ n. a large book with many pictures or photographs.

cof·fer /'kôfər, 'käfər/ ▶ n. **1** a small chest for holding valuables. **2** (**coffers**) used to refer to the money that a government or organization has available to spend: *the company's coffers have run dry*. **3** a decorative sunken panel in a ceiling.

cof·fer·dam /'kôfər,dam, 'käfər,dam/ ▶ n. a watertight enclosure pumped dry to allow construction work below the waterline, e.g., when building bridges or repairing a ship.

cof·fin /'kôfən, 'käfən/ ▶ n. a long, narrow box in which a dead body is buried or cremated.

cog /käg/ ▶ n. **1** a wheel or bar with a series of projections on its edge, which transfers motion by engaging with projections on another wheel or bar. **2** any one of these projections.

co·gent /'kōjənt/ ▶ adj. (of an argument or case) clear, logical, and convincing. ■ **co·gen·cy** /'kōjənsē/ n. **co·gent·ly** adv.

cog·i·tate /'käjə,tāt/ ▶ v. formal think deeply. ■ **cog·i·ta·tion** /,käjə'tāsHən/ n.

co·gnac /'kōn,yak, 'kän-, 'kòn-/ ▶ n. a high-quality brandy made in Cognac in western France.

cog·nate /'kägˌnāt/ ▶ adj. **1** (of a word) having the same original form as another in a different language (e.g., English *father*, German *Vater*, and Latin *pater*). **2** formal related; connected. ▶ n. a word that has the same original form as another in a different language.

cog·ni·tion /ˌkägˈnisHən/ ▶ n. the process of obtaining knowledge through thought, experience, and the senses.

cog·ni·tive /'kägnətiv/ ▶ adj. relating to the process of obtaining knowledge through thought, experience, and the senses. ■ **cog·ni·tive·ly** adv.

cog·ni·tive ther·a·py ▶ n. a type of psychotherapy based on the belief that psychological problems are caused by negative ways of thinking, which can be avoided or changed.

cog·ni·zance /'kägnəzəns/ ▶ n. formal knowledge or awareness. ■ **cog·ni·zant** /'kägnəzənt/ adj.

cog·no·men /käg'nōmən, 'kägnəmən/ ▶ n. **1** a name or nickname. **2** (in ancient Rome) an extra name given to a citizen, functioning rather like a nickname and often passed down from father to son.

co·gno·scen·ti /ˌkänyōˈsHentē, ˌkägnə-/ ▶ pl.n. people who are well informed about a particular subject.

cog·wheel /'kägˌ(h)wēl/ ▶ n. another term for COG (sense 1).

co·hab·it /kōˈhabit/ ▶ v. (**cohabits, cohabiting, cohabited**) **1** live together and have a sexual relationship without being married. **2** coexist. ■ **co·hab·i·ta·tion** /kōˌhabəˈtāsHən/ n. **co·hab·it·ant** n. **co·hab·it·er** n.

co·here /kōˈhi(ə)r/ ▶ v. form a unified whole; be logically consistent.

co·her·ent /kōˈhi(ə)rənt/ ▶ adj. **1** (of an argument or theory) logical and consistent. **2** able to speak clearly and logically. ■ **co·her·ence** /kōˈhi(ə)rəns/ n. **co·her·ent·ly** adv.

co·he·sion /kōˈhēzHən/ ▶ n. the action or fact of holding together or forming a unified whole.

co·he·sive /kōˈhēsiv, -ziv/ ▶ adj. **1** forming a unified whole: *a cohesive group.* **2** causing people or things to form a unified whole: *a cohesive force.* ■ **co·he·sive·ness** n.

co·hort /'kōˌhôrt/ ▶ n. **1** an ancient Roman military unit equal to one tenth of a legion. **2** a group of people with a shared characteristic: *a cohort of students.* **3** a supporter or companion.

co·hosh /'kōˌhäsH/ ▶ n. a North American plant with medicinal properties.

co-host ▶ n. a person who hosts an event or broadcast with another or others. ▶ v. be the co-host of an event or broadcast.

coif /koif/ ▶ n. **1** a close-fitting cap worn by nuns under a veil. **2** informal coiffure. ▶ v. /kwäf, koif/ (**coifs, coiffing** or **coifing, coiffed** or **coifed**) style or arrange someone's hair.

coif·feur /kwäˈfər/ ▶ n. (fem. **coiffeuse** /kwäˈf(y)o͞oz, -ˈfə(r)z/) a hairdresser.

coif·fure /kwäˈfyo͝or/ ▶ n. a person's hairstyle. ■ **coif·fured** adj.

coign /koin/ ▶ n. a projecting corner or angle of a wall.

coil /koil/ ▶ n. **1** a length of something wound in a joined sequence of loops. **2** a contraceptive device in the form of a coil, placed inside the uterus. **3** an electrical device consisting of a coiled wire, for converting the level of a voltage, producing a magnetic field, or adding inductance to a circuit. ▶ v. arrange or form into a coil.

coin /koin/ ▶ n. a flat disk or piece of metal with an official stamp, used as money. ▶ v. **1** invent a new word or phrase. **2** make coins by stamping metal.

coin·age /'koinij/ ▶ n. **1** coins as a whole. **2** the process of producing coins. **3** a system or type of coins in use. **4** a newly invented word or phrase.

co·in·cide /ˌkōənˈsīd, ˈkōənˌsīd/ ▶ v. **1** happen at the same time or place. **2** be the same or similar.

co·in·ci·dence /kōˈinsədəns, -ˌdens/ ▶ n. **1** a remarkable concurrence of events or circumstances without apparent connection. **2** the fact of two or more things happening at the same time or being the same.

co·in·ci·dent /kōˈinsədənt, -ˌdent/ ▶ adj. **1** happening at the same time or in the same place. **2** in agreement or harmony.

co·in·ci·den·tal /kōˌinsəˈdentl/ ▶ adj. resulting from a coincidence; not planned or intentional. ■ **co·in·ci·den·tal·ly** adv.

Coin·treau /kwänˈtrō/ ▶ n. trademark a colorless orange-flavored liqueur.

coir /'koi(ə)r/ ▶ n. fiber from the outer husk of the coconut, used in potting compost and for making ropes and matting.

co·i·tus /'kōətəs, kōˈētəs/ ▶ n. technical sexual intercourse. ■ **co·i·tal** /'kōətl, kōˈētl/ adj.

co·i·tus in·ter·rup·tus /intəˈrəptəs/ ▶ n. sexual intercourse in which the man withdraws his penis before ejaculation.

Coke /kōk/ ▶ n. trademark short for COCA-COLA.

coke[1] /kōk/ ▶ n. **1** a solid fuel made by heating coal in the absence of air. **2** carbon residue left after the incomplete combustion of gasoline or other fuels.

coke[2] ▶ n. informal cocaine.

col /käl/ ▶ n. the lowest point between two peaks of a mountain ridge.

Col. ▶ abbr. Colonel.

COLA ▶ abbr. cost-of-living adjustment, an increase made to wages or Social Security benefits to keep them in line with inflation.

co·la /'kōlə/ ▶ n. **1** a brown carbonated drink flavored with an extract of cola nuts, or with a similar flavoring. **2** (also **kola**) a small tropical evergreen tree whose seed (the **cola nut**) contains caffeine.

col·an·der /'kələndər, 'käl-/ ▶ n. a bowl with holes in it, used for draining food.

cold /kōld/ ▶ adj. **1** of or at a low or relatively low temperature. **2** not feeling or showing emotion or affection. **3** not influenced by personal feeling or emotion: objective: *the cold facts.* **4** (of a color) containing pale blue or gray and giving no impression of warmth. **5** (of a scent or trail) no longer fresh and easy to follow. **6** without preparation or rehearsal; unawares: *they went into the test cold.* **7** informal unconscious: *she was out cold.* ▶ n. **1** cold weather or surroundings. **2** an infection in which the mucous membrane of the nose and throat becomes inflamed, causing sneezing and a runny nose. ■ **cold·ly** adv. **cold·ness** n.

– PHRASES **cold comfort** little or no consolation under the circumstances. **get cold feet** lose one's nerve. **the cold shoulder** deliberate unfriendliness or rejection. **in cold blood** without pity; in a deliberately cruel way.

cold-blood·ed ▸ adj. **1** (of animals, e.g., reptiles and fish) having a body whose temperature varies with that of the environment. **2** without emotion or pity. ■ **cold-blood·ed·ly** adv.

cold-call ▸ v. visit or telephone someone without being asked to do so in an attempt to sell them goods or services.

cold chis·el ▸ n. a toughened chisel used for cutting metal.

cold cream ▸ n. a cream for cleansing and softening the skin.

cold cuts /ˈkōld ˌkəts/ ▸ pl.n. slices of cold cooked meats.

cold frame ▸ n. a frame with a glass top in which small plants are grown and protected.

cold fu·sion ▸ n. nuclear fusion supposedly occurring at or close to room temperature.

cold-heart·ed ▸ adj. lacking affection or warmth; unfeeling.

cold snap ▸ n. a brief spell of cold weather.

cold sore ▸ n. an inflamed blister in or near the mouth, caused by a virus.

cold stor·age ▸ n. preservation of something in a refrigerated room.
– PHRASES **in/into cold storage** so as to be postponed temporarily.

cold sweat ▸ n. a state of sweating caused by nervousness or illness.

cold tur·key ▸ n. informal the abrupt withdrawal from a drug to which one is addicted, often accompanied by sweating and nausea.

cold war ▸ n. a state of hostility between the countries allied to the former Soviet Union and the Western powers after World War II.

cole·slaw /ˈkōlˌslô/ ▸ n. a salad dish of shredded raw cabbage and carrots mixed with mayonnaise.

co·le·us /ˈkōlēəs/ ▸ n. a tropical plant with brightly colored variegated leaves.

col·ic /ˈkälik/ ▸ n. severe pain in the abdomen caused by gas or obstruction in the intestines. ■ **col·ick·y** adj.

col·i·se·um /ˌkäləˈsēəm/ (also **colosseum**) ▸ n. (in names) a large theater, movie theater, or stadium.

co·li·tis /kəˈlītis, kō-/ ▸ n. inflammation of the lining of the colon.

col·lab·o·rate /kəˈlabəˌrāt/ ▸ v. **1** work jointly on an activity or project. **2** betray one's country by cooperating with an enemy. ■ **col·lab·o·ra·tion** /kəˌlabəˈrāshən/ n. **col·lab·o·ra·tion·ist** /kəˌlabəˈrāshənist/ n. & adj. **col·lab·o·ra·tive** /kəˈlabərətiv/ adj. **col·lab·o·ra·tor** /kəˈlabəˌrātər/ n.

col·lage /kəˈläzh, kô-, kō-/ ▸ n. **1** a form of art in which various materials are arranged and stuck to a backing. **2** a combination of various things: *the collage of cultures within our nation.*

col·la·gen /ˈkäləjən/ ▸ n. any of a group of proteins that form the main structural component of animal connective tissue.

col·lapse /kəˈlaps/ ▸ v. **1** suddenly fall down or give way. **2** (of a person) fall down as a result of illness or fatigue. **3** fail suddenly and completely: *when he died the family business collapsed.* ▸ n. **1** an instance of a structure collapsing. **2** a sudden failure or breakdown.

col·laps·i·ble /kəˈlapsəbəl/ ▸ adj. able to be folded into a small space.

col·lar /ˈkälər/ ▸ n. **1** the part around the neck of a garment, either upright or turned over. **2** a band put around the neck of a dog or other domestic animal. **3** a connecting band or pipe in a piece of machinery. ▸ v. informal stop or arrest someone. ■ **col·lar·less** adj.

col·lar·bone /ˈkälərˌbōn/ ▸ n. either of the pair of bones joining the breastbone to the shoulder blades; the clavicle.

col·late /kəˈlāt, ˈkōˌlāt, ˈkälˌāt/ ▸ v. **1** collect and combine documents or information. **2** compare and analyze two or more sources of information. ■ **col·la·tor** n.

col·lat·er·al /kəˈlatərəl, kəˈlatrəl/ ▸ n. something that is promised to someone if one is not able to repay a loan. ▸ adj. **1** additional but less important. **2** situated side by side; parallel. ■ **col·lat·er·al·ly** adv.

col·lat·er·al dam·age ▸ n. unintentional casualties and destruction in civilian areas caused by military operations.

col·la·tion /kəˈlāshən, kō-, kä-/ ▸ n. **1** the action of collating something. **2** formal a light informal meal.

col·league /ˈkälˌēg/ ▸ n. a person with whom one works.

col·lect¹ /kəˈlekt/ ▸ v. **1** bring or come together: *a crowd collected at the door.* **2** find or buy items of a particular kind as a hobby. **3** call for and take away someone or something. **4** ask for money or receive a prize or award. **5** (**collect oneself**) regain control of oneself. ▸ adv. & adj. (of a telephone call) to be paid for by the person receiving it.

col·lect² /ˈkälˌekt, -likt/ ▸ n. (in the Christian Church) a short prayer used on a particular day or during a particular period.

col·lect·a·ble /kəˈlektəbəl/ (also **collectible**) ▸ adj. **1** worth collecting; of interest to a collector. **2** able to be collected. ▸ n. (usu. **collectibles**) an item valued by collectors. ■ **col·lect·a·bi·li·ty** /kəˌlektəˈbilitē/ n.

col·lect·ed /kəˈlektid/ ▸ adj. **1** calm and self-controlled. **2** (of works) brought together in one volume or edition.

col·lec·tion /kəˈlekshən/ ▸ n. **1** the action of collecting. **2** a number of things that have been collected. **3** a new range of clothes produced by a designer. **4** a regular removal of mail or garbage.

col·lec·tive /kəˈlektiv/ ▸ adj. **1** done by or involving all the members of a group. **2** taken as a whole: *the collective power of the workforce.* ▸ n. a business or farm owned or run as a cooperative venture. ■ **col·lec·tive·ly** adv. **col·lec·tiv·i·ty** /kəˌlekˈtivitē, ˌkälˌek-/ n.

col·lec·tive bar·gain·ing ▸ n. negotiation of wages and other conditions of employment by an organized body of employees.

col·lec·tive farm ▸ n. a farm or group of farms owned by the government and run by a group of people.

col·lec·tive noun ▸ n. a noun that refers to a group of individuals (e.g., *assembly*, *family*).

> **USAGE**
> In the US, a **collective noun** is usually used with a singular verb (*my family was always hard-working*), while in Britain it is often used with a plural verb (*his family were disappointed in him*). It is important to remember that, if the verb is singular, any following pronouns (words such as 'he,' 'she,' or 'they') must be too: *the government is prepared to act, but not until it knows the outcome of the talks* (not *...until they know the outcome...*).

col·lec·tiv·ism /kə'lektə,vizəm/ ▸ n. the ownership of land, business, and industry by the people or the government. ■ **col·lec·tiv·ist** adj. & n. **col·lec·ti·vize** /kə'lektə,vīz/ v.

col·lec·tor /kə'lektər/ ▸ n. **1** a person who collects things of a specified type. **2** an official who is responsible for collecting money owed.

col·leen /kə'lēn, 'käl,ēn/ ▸ n. Irish a girl or young woman.

col·lege /'kälij/ ▸ n. **1** an educational establishment providing higher education or specialized training. **2** any of the independent institutions into which some universities are separated. **3** an organized group of professional people: *the College of Fellows of the Society.*

col·le·gi·al /kə'lēj(ē)əl/ ▸ adj. **1** relating to a college or its students; collegiate. **2** involving shared responsibility.

col·le·gian /kə'lējən/ ▸ n. a member of a college.

col·le·giate /kə'lējət/ ▸ adj. **1** relating to a college or its students. **2** (of a university) composed of different colleges.

col·lide /kə'līd/ ▸ v. **1** hit by accident when moving. **2** come into conflict: *the culture of the two companies collided.*

col·lie /'kälē/ ▸ n. (pl. **collies**) a breed of sheepdog with a long, pointed nose and long hair.

col·lier /'kälyər/ ▸ n. chiefly Brit. **1** a coal miner. **2** a ship carrying coal.

col·lier·y /'kälyərē/ ▸ n. (pl. **collieries**) a coal mine.

col·lin·e·ar /kə'linēər, kä-/ ▸ adj. Geometry (of points) lying in the same straight line.

col·li·sion /kə'lizнən/ ▸ n. **1** an instance of a person or object colliding with another. **2** a conflict of ideas, qualities, or groups: *a calculated collision of science and humanity.*

col·lo·cate ▸ v. /'kälə,kāt/ (of a word) frequently occur with another: *'maiden' collocates with 'voyage.'* ▸ n. a word that frequently occurs with another.

col·lo·ca·tion /,kälə'kāshən/ ▸ n. **1** the frequent occurrence of a word with another word or words. **2** a pair or group of words that frequently occur together (e.g., *heavy drinker*).

col·loid /'käl,oid/ ▸ n. a homogeneous substance consisting of submicroscopic particles of one substance dispersed in another, as in an emulsion or gel. ■ **col·loi·dal** /kə'loidl/ adj.

col·lo·qui·al /kə'lōkwēəl/ ▸ adj. (of language) used in ordinary conversation; not formal or literary. ■ **col·lo·qui·al·ly** adv.

col·lo·qui·al·ism /kə'lōkwēə,lizəm/ ▸ n. an informal word or phrase.

col·lo·qui·um /kə'lōkwēəm/ ▸ n. (pl. **colloquiums** or **colloquia** /-kwēə/) an academic conference or seminar.

col·lo·quy /'käləkwē/ ▸ n. (pl. **colloquies**) formal a conference or conversation.

col·lude /kə'lood/ ▸ v. cooperate secretly for a dishonest or underhanded purpose: *the president accused his opponents of colluding with foreigners.*

col·lu·sion /kə'loozнən/ ▸ n. secret cooperation in order to deceive others. ■ **col·lu·sive** /-siv, -ziv/ adj.

col·o·bus /'käləbəs/ ▸ n. (pl. same) a slender African monkey with silky fur.

co·logne /kə'lōn/ ▸ n. eau de cologne or other scented toilet water.

Co·lom·bi·an /kə'lәmbēən/ ▸ n. a person from Colombia. ▸ adj. relating to Colombia.

co·lon[1] /'kōlən/ ▸ n. a punctuation mark (:) used before a list, a quotation, or an explanation.

co·lon[2] ▸ n. the main part of the large intestine, which passes from the cecum to the rectum. ■ **co·lon·ic** /kō'länik, kə-/ adj.

colo·nel /'kərnl/ ▸ n. a rank of officer in the US Army, Air Force, and Marine Corps above a lieutenant colonel and below a brigadier or brigadier general. ■ **colo·nel·cy** n. (pl. **colonelcies**).

co·lo·ni·al /kə'lōnyəl, -nēəl/ ▸ adj. **1** relating to a colony or colonialism. **2** in a neoclassical style characteristic of the period of the British colonies in America before independence. ▸ n. a person who lives in a colony. ■ **co·lo·ni·al·ly** adv.

co·lo·ni·al·ism /kə'lōnēə,lizəm, kə'lōnyə,lizəm/ ▸ n. the practice of acquiring control over another country, occupying it with settlers, and exploiting it economically. ■ **co·lo·ni·al·ist** /-list/ n. & adj.

co·lon·ic ir·ri·ga·tion ▸ n. a therapeutic treatment in which water is inserted via the anus to flush out the colon.

col·o·nist /'kälənist/ ▸ n. an inhabitant of a colony.

col·o·nize /'kälə,nīz/ ▸ v. **1** establish a colony in a place. **2** take over for one's own use: *his work has colonized the space outside his studio.* ■ **col·o·ni·za·tion** /,kälənə'zāsнən/ n. **col·o·niz·er** n.

col·on·nade /,kälə'nād/ ▸ n. a row of evenly spaced columns supporting a roof or other structure. ■ **col·on·nad·ed** adj.

co·lon·os·co·py /,kōlə'näskəpē/ ▸ n. (pl. **colonoscopies**) examination of the colon with a fiber-optic instrument inserted through the anus.

col·o·ny /'kälənē/ ▸ n. (pl. **colonies**) **1** a country or area under the control of another country and occupied by settlers from that country. **2** a group of people of one nationality or race living in a foreign place. **3** a place where a group of people with the same interest live together: *a nudist colony.* **4** a community of animals or plants of one kind living close together.

col·o·phon /'käləfən, -,fän/ ▸ n. a publisher's emblem or imprint.

col·or /'kələr/ (Brit. **colour**) ▸ n. **1** the property possessed by an object of producing different sensations on the eye as a result of the way it reflects or emits light. **2** one, or any mixture, of the constituents into which light can be separated: *a rich brown color.* **3** the use of all colors, not only black and white, in photography or television. **4** the shade of the skin as an indication of someone's race. **5** redness of the complexion. **6** interest, excitement, and vitality: *a town full of color and character.* **7** (**colors**) an item or items of a particular color worn for identification in sports. **8** (**colors**) the flag of a regiment or ship. ▸ v. **1** change the color of something. **2** show embarrassment by becoming red; blush. **3** influence, especially in a negative way: *the experience had colored her whole existence.*

– PHRASES **show one's true colors** reveal one's real character or intentions.

Col·o·rad·o po·ta·to bee·tle /,kälə'rädō, -'radō/ ▸ n. a yellow- and black-striped beetle whose larvae are highly destructive to potato plants.

col·or·ant /'kələrənt/ ▶ n. a dye or pigment used to color something.

col·or·a·tion /ˌkələ'rāsHən/ ▶ n. 1 the natural coloring of something. 2 character or tone: *he gives each performance its own emotional coloration.*

col·o·ra·tu·ra /ˌkələrə'tŏŏrə, ˌkäl-/ ▶ n. 1 elaborate ornamentation of a vocal melody, especially in opera. 2 a soprano skilled in coloratura singing.

col·or-blind ▶ adj. unable to distinguish certain colors. ■ **col·or blind·ness** n.

col·ored /'kələrd/ ▶ adj. 1 having a color or colors. 2 offensive wholly or partly of nonwhite descent. 3 (usu. **Coloured**) S. African historical of mixed ethnic origin. ▶ n. 1 offensive a person who is wholly or partly of nonwhite descent. 2 (usu. **Coloured**) S. African a person of mixed descent, usually speaking Afrikaans or English as their mother tongue. 3 (**coloreds**) clothes or household linen that are any color but white.

col·or·fast ▶ adj. dyed in colors that will not fade or be washed out.

col·or·ful /'kələrfəl/ ▶ adj. 1 having many or varied colors. 2 lively and exciting; vivid. ■ **col·or·ful·ly** /-f(ə)lē/ adv.

col·or·ing /'kələriNG/ ▶ n. 1 the process or art of applying color. 2 the appearance of something with regard to its color. 3 the natural colors of a person's skin, hair, and eyes. 4 a substance used to color something, especially food.

col·or·ist /'kələrist/ ▶ n. an artist or designer who uses color in a special or skillful way.

col·or·is·tic /ˌkələ'ristik/ ▶ adj. 1 showing a special use of color. 2 having a variety of musical expression.

col·or·less /'kələrləs/ ▶ adj. 1 without color. 2 lacking character or interest; dull.

col·or scheme ▶ n. an arrangement or combination of colors.

col·or·way /'kələrˌwā/ ▶ n. any of a range of combinations of colors in which something is available.

co·los·sal /kə'läsəl/ ▶ adj. extremely large. ■ **co·los·sal·ly** adv.

col·os·se·um /ˌkälə'sēəm/ ▶ n. variant spelling of COLISEUM.

co·los·sus /kə'läsəs/ ▶ n. (pl. **colossi** /-'läsˌī/) 1 a person or thing of great size or importance. 2 a statue that is much bigger than life size.

co·los·to·my /kə'lästəmē/ ▶ n. (pl. **colostomies**) a surgical operation in which the colon is shortened and the cut end diverted to an opening in the abdominal wall.

co·los·trum /kə'lästrəm/ ▶ n. the first fluid produced by the mammary glands after giving birth.

col·our, etc. ▶ n. & v. British spelling of COLOR, etc.

col·pos·co·py /käl'päskəpē/ ▶ n. surgical examination of the vagina and the neck of the uterus.

colt /kōlt/ ▶ n. a young uncastrated male horse.

col·ter /'kōltər/ ▶ n. a vertical cutting blade attached to the front of a plowshare.

colt·ish /'kōltisH/ ▶ adj. lively but awkward in one's movements or behavior.

colts·foot /'kōltsˌfŏŏt/ ▶ n. a plant with yellow flowers and large heart-shaped leaves.

co·lum·bine /'käləmˌbīn/ ▶ n. an aquilegia with long-spurred flowers.

col·umn /'käləm/ ▶ n. 1 an upright pillar supporting an arch or other structure or standing alone as a monument. 2 a line of people or vehicles moving in the same direction. 3 a vertical division of a page. 4 a regular section of a newspaper or magazine on a particular subject or by a particular person: *a weekly column in a Sunday newspaper.* 5 an upright shaft used for controlling a machine. ■ **col·um·nar** /kə'ləmnər/ adj. **col·umned** adj.

col·um·nist /'käləmnist/ ▶ n. a journalist who writes a column in a newspaper or magazine.

com- (also **co-, col-, con-,** or **cor-**) ▶ prefix with; together; altogether: *combine.*

co·ma /'kōmə/ ▶ n. a state of prolonged deep unconsciousness.

Co·man·che /kə'manCHē/ ▶ n. (pl. same or **Comanches**) a member of an American Indian people of the southwestern US.

com·a·tose /'kōməˌtōs, 'kämə-/ ▶ adj. 1 relating to or in a state of coma. 2 humorous very tired or lethargic.

comb /kōm/ ▶ n. 1 an object with a row of narrow teeth, used for untangling or arranging the hair. 2 a device for separating and dressing textile fibers. 3 the red fleshy crest on the head of a domestic fowl, especially a cock. 4 a honeycomb. ▶ v. 1 untangle or arrange the hair with a comb. 2 search carefully and systematically: *I combed the stores for a leather jacket.* 3 prepare wool, flax, or cotton for manufacture with a comb.

com·bat /'kämˌbat/ ▶ n. fighting, especially between armed forces. ▶ v. (**combats, combating, combated;** also **combats, combatting, combatted**) take action to reduce or prevent: *equipping people to combat crime.*

com·bat·ant /kəm'batnt, 'kämbətənt/ ▶ n. a person or nation taking part in fighting during a war.

com·bat fa·tigue ▶ n. 1 psychological disturbance caused by prolonged exposure to active warfare, especially being under bombardment. 2 (**combat fatigues**) a uniform of a type to be worn into combat.

com·bat·ive /kəm'bativ/ ▶ adj. ready or eager to fight or argue. ■ **com·bat·ive·ly** adv. **com·bat·ive·ness** n.

comb·er /'kōmər/ ▶ n. a long curling sea wave.

com·bi·na·tion /ˌkämbə'nāsHən/ ▶ n. 1 something made up of distinct elements: *a combination of drama, dance, and music.* 2 the combining of two or more different things. 3 a sequence of numbers or letters used to open a combination lock. ■ **com·bi·na·tion·al** adj.

com·bi·na·tion lock ▶ n. a lock that is opened by using a specific sequence of letters or numbers.

com·bine ▶ v. /kəm'bīn/ 1 join or mix to form a whole. 2 join with others for a common purpose. 3 do at the same time: *an ideal place to combine shopping and sightseeing.* 4 Chemistry unite to form a compound. ▶ n. /'kämˌbīn/ a group of people or companies acting together for a commercial purpose. ■ **com·bin·er** /kəm'bīnər/ n.

com·bine har·ves·ter ▶ n. a machine that reaps, threshes, and cleans a cereal crop in one operation.

com·bin·ing form /kəm'bīniNG/ ▶ n. a form of a word used in combination with another element to form a word (e.g., *bio-* 'life' in *biology*).

com·bo /'kämbō/ ▶ n. (pl. **combos**) informal 1 a small jazz, rock, or pop band. 2 a combination.

com·bust /kəm'bəst/ ▶ v. burn or be burned by fire. ■ **com·bus·tor** n.

com·bus·ti·ble /kəm'bəstəbəl/ ▶ adj. able to catch fire and burn easily. ▶ n. a substance that is able to catch fire and burn easily.

com·bus·tion /kəm'bəsCHən/ ▶ n. 1 the process of burning. 2 rapid chemical combination with oxygen, producing heat and light.

come /kəm/ ▶ v. (past **came**; past part. **come**) 1 move or reach toward or into a place. 2 arrive at a place. 3 happen; take place. 4 have or achieve a specified position in order or priority: *she came second.* 5 pass into or reach a specified state, situation, or state of mind: *my shirt came undone.* 6 be sold or available in a specified form: *the tops come in three sizes.* 7 (also **come, come**) said to correct, reassure, or urge someone on. 8 informal have an orgasm. ▶ prep. informal when a specified time is reached or event happens.
– PHRASES **come about** 1 take place. 2 (of a ship) change direction. **come across** 1 give a specified impression. 2 meet or find someone or something by chance. **come back** respond, especially vigorously. **come by** manage to get something. **come down on** criticize or punish someone harshly. **come down to** be dependent on a factor. **come forward** volunteer for a task or to give evidence. **come from** originate in something. **come in** prove to be: *I'm sure the money will come in handy.* **come in for** receive a negative reaction. **come into** inherit money or property. **come of** 1 result from something. 2 be descended from someone. **come off** 1 be accomplished. 2 end up in a specified situation: *he always came off worse in a fight.* **come off it** informal said when expressing strong disbelief. **come on** 1 (of a situation or condition) start to arrive or happen. 2 (also **come upon**) meet or find someone or something by chance. **come on to** informal make sexual advances toward someone. **come out** 1 (of a fact) become known. 2 declare oneself as being for or against something. 3 end up in a specified situation. 4 (of a photograph) be produced satisfactorily or in a specified way. 5 (of the result of a calculation or measurement) emerge at a specified figure. 6 informal openly declare that one is homosexual. 7 dated (of a young upper-class woman) make one's debut in society. **come out with** say something in a sudden or incautious way. **come over** (of a feeling) begin to affect someone. **come around** 1 recover consciousness. 2 be converted to another person's opinion. **come to** 1 recover consciousness. 2 (of an expense) reach an amount in total. 3 (of a ship) come to a stop. **come to pass** literary happen. **come up** 1 (of a situation or problem) occur or arise. 2 (of a time or event) draw near. **come up with** produce something, especially when pressured or challenged. **come upon** 1 attack someone by surprise. 2 see COME (sense 2 of the verb). **come what may** no matter what happens. **have it coming (to one)** informal be due to face the unpleasant results of one's behavior.

> **USAGE**
> On the use of **come** followed by **and**, see the note at AND.

come·back /'kəm,bak/ ▶ n. 1 a return to fame or fashionability. 2 informal a quick reply to a critical remark.

co·me·di·an /kə'mēdēən/ ▶ n. (fem. **comedienne**) 1 an entertainer whose act is intended to make people laugh. 2 a comic actor.

come·down /'kəm,doun/ ▶ n. informal 1 a loss of status or importance. 2 a feeling of disappointment or depression.

com·e·dy /'kämədē/ ▶ n. (pl. **comedies**) 1 entertainment consisting of jokes and sketches intended to make people laugh. 2 an amusing movie, play, or television show. 3 a humorous play in which the characters find happiness after experiencing difficulty. ■ **co·me·dic** /kə'mēdik/ adj.

com·e·dy of man·ners ▶ n. a play, novel, or movie that satirizes behavior in a particular social group.

come-hith·er ▶ adj. informal flirtatious: *a come-hither look.*

come·ly /'kəmlē/ ▶ adj. (**comelier, comeliest**) old use or humorous pleasant to look at; attractive. ■ **come·li·ness** n.

come-on ▶ n. informal a gesture or remark intended to attract someone sexually.

com·er /'kəmər/ ▶ n. 1 a person who arrives somewhere: *feeding every comer is still a sacred duty.* 2 informal a person or thing likely to succeed.

co·mes·ti·ble /kə'mestəbəl/ ▶ n. formal or humorous an item of food.

com·et /'kämit/ ▶ n. an object that moves around the solar system, consisting of a nucleus of ice and dust and, when near the sun, a long tail. ■ **com·et·ar·y** /'kämi,terē/ adj.

come·up·pance /kə'məpəns/ ▶ n. informal a punishment or fate that someone deserves.

com·fit /'kəmfit, 'kämfit/ ▶ n. dated a candy consisting of a nut or other center coated in sugar.

com·fort /'kəmfərt/ ▶ n. 1 a state of being physically relaxed and free from pain. 2 (**comforts**) things that contribute to physical ease and well-being. 3 relief for unhappiness or worry: *a few words of comfort.* ▶ v. make someone feel less unhappy. ■ **com·fort·ing** adj.

com·fort·a·ble /'kəmfərtəbəl, 'kəmftərbəl/ ▶ adj. 1 providing or enjoying physical comfort. 2 free from financial worry. 3 (of a victory) easily achieved. ■ **com·fort·a·bly** /-blē/ adv.

com·fort·er /'kəmfərtər/ ▶ n. 1 a warm quilt. 2 a person or thing that provides relief from grief or worry.

com·frey /'kəmfrē/ ▶ n. (pl. **comfreys**) a plant with clusters of purplish or white bell-shaped flowers.

com·fy /'kəmfē/ ▶ adj. (**comfier, comfiest**) informal comfortable: *a comfy chair.* ■ **com·fi·ly** adv. **com·fi·ness** n.

com·ic /'kämik/ ▶ adj. 1 causing or meant to cause laughter. 2 relating to or in the style of comedy. ▶ n. 1 a comedian. 2 a children's magazine containing comic strips.

com·i·cal /'kämikəl/ ▶ adj. causing laughter, especially through being ridiculous. ■ **com·i·cal·ly** /-ik(ə)lē/ adv.

com·ic op·er·a ▶ n. an opera that portrays humorous situations and characters, with much spoken dialogue.

com·ic re·lief ▶ n. humorous content in a play or novel that offsets more serious parts.

com·ic strip ▶ n. a sequence of drawings in boxes that typically tell an amusing story.

com·i·ty /'kämitē/ ▶ n. (pl. **comities**) 1 formal polite and considerate behavior toward others. 2 (also comity of nations) the mutual recognition by nations of the laws and customs of others.

comm. ▶ abbr. **1** commercial. **2** commission. **3** committee. **4** communication. **5** community.

com·ma /ˈkämə/ ▶ n. a punctuation mark (,) showing a pause between parts of a sentence or separating items in a list.

com·mand /kəˈmand/ ▶ v. **1** give an order. **2** be in charge of a military unit. **3** be in a position that gives a good view or control of something: *I climbed up a rocky outcrop commanding a view of the valley.* **4** be in a position to have or secure: *emeralds command a high price.* ▶ n. **1** an order. **2** authority, especially over armed forces: *the officer in command.* **3** the ability to use or control something: *her poor command of English.* **4** a group of officers having control over a particular group or operation. **5** an instruction causing a computer to perform one of its basic functions.

com·man·dant /ˈkämənˌdant, -ˌdänt/ ▶ n. an officer in charge of a force or institution.

com·mand e·con·o·my ▶ n. an economy in which production, investment, prices, and incomes are determined centrally by the government.

com·man·deer /ˌkämənˈdi(ə)r/ ▶ v. **1** officially take possession of something for military purposes. **2** seize for one's own purposes: *the men in the family have commandeered my other computer.*

com·mand·er /kəˈmandər/ ▶ n. **1** a person in authority, especially in a military situation. **2** a rank of naval officer next below captain. **3** (in certain metropolitan police departments) the person in charge of a district, precinct, or squad. **4** a member of a higher class in some orders of knighthood.

com·mand·er-in-chief ▶ n. (pl. **commanders-in-chief**) an officer in charge of all of the armed forces of a country.

com·mand·ing /kəˈmandiNG/ ▶ adj. **1** having or expressing authority. **2** possessing or giving superior strength: *a commanding lead.* ■ **com·mand·ing·ly** adv.

com·mand·ment /kəˈmandmənt/ ▶ n. a rule given by God, especially one of the Ten Commandments.

com·man·do /kəˈmandō/ ▶ n. (pl. **commandos**) **1** a soldier specially trained for carrying out raids. **2** a unit of commandos.

com·mand per·for·mance ▶ n. a presentation of a play, concert, or other show at the request of royalty.

com·me·dia dell'ar·te /kəˈmädēə del ˈärtē/ ▶ n. an Italian kind of improvised comedy popular in the 16th–18th centuries, based on stock characters.

comme il faut /ˌkôm ēl ˈfō/ ▶ adj. correct in behavior or etiquette.

com·mem·o·rate /kəˈmeməˌrāt/ ▶ v. take action to honor the memory of: *the town held a silent march to commemorate the dead.* ■ **com·mem·o·ra·tion** /kəˌmeməˈrāSHən/ n.

com·mem·o·ra·tive /kəˈmem(ə)rətiv, kəˈmeməˌrātiv/ ▶ adj. acting to honor the memory of an event or person.

com·mence /kəˈmens/ ▶ v. start or be started; begin.

com·mence·ment /kəˈmensmənt/ ▶ n. **1** the beginning of something. **2** a ceremony in which

degrees or diplomas are conferred on graduating students.

com·mend /kəˈmend/ ▶ v. **1** praise someone or something formally. **2** present as suitable or good; recommend: *I commend you to her without reservation.* **3** (**commend someone/thing to**) chiefly old use entrust someone or something to. ■ **com·men·da·tion** /ˌkämənˈdāSHən, -ˌen-/ n.

com·mend·a·ble /kəˈmendəbəl/ ▶ adj. deserving praise and approval. ■ **com·mend·a·bly** adv.

com·men·sal /kəˈmensəl/ ▶ adj. Biology (of two organisms) having an association in which one benefits and the other derives neither benefit nor harm.

com·men·su·ra·ble /kəˈmensərəbəl, kəˈmensHərəbəl/ ▶ adj. **1** formal measurable by the same standard: *not every chapter is commensurable with every other.* **2** Mathematics (of numbers) in a ratio equal to a ratio of integers.

com·men·su·rate /kəˈmensərət, -ˈmensHə-/ ▶ adj. corresponding in size or degree; in proportion: *salary will be commensurate with experience.* ■ **com·men·su·rate·ly** adv.

com·ment /ˈkämˌent/ ▶ n. **1** a remark expressing an opinion or reaction. **2** discussion of an issue or event. ▶ v. express an opinion or reaction.

com·men·tar·y /ˈkämənˌterē/ ▶ n. (pl. **commentaries**) **1** a broadcast spoken account of an event as it happens. **2** the expression of opinions or offering of explanations about an event: *a piece marrying fact and commentary from the paper's Paris correspondent.* **3** a set of explanatory or critical notes on a written work.

com·men·tate /ˈkämənˌtāt/ ▶ v. provide a commentary on a sports contest or other event.

com·men·ta·tor /ˈkämənˌtātər/ ▶ n. **1** a person who comments on events, especially in the media. **2** a person who provides a commentary on a live event.

com·merce /ˈkämərs/ ▶ n. **1** the activity of buying and selling, especially on a large scale. **2** dated social dealings between people.

com·mer·cial /kəˈmərSHəl/ ▶ adj. **1** concerned with or engaged in commerce. **2** making or intended to make a profit. **3** (of television or radio) funded by broadcast advertisements. ▶ n. a television or radio advertisement. ■ **com·mer·ci·al·i·ty** /kəˌmərSHēˈalitē/ n. **com·mer·cial·ly** adv.

com·mer·cial·ism /kəˈmərSHəˌlizəm/ ▶ n. emphasis on making maximum profit.

com·mer·cial·ize /kəˈmərSHəˌlīz/ ▶ v. manage or exploit something in a way designed to make a profit. ■ **com·mer·cial·i·za·tion** /kəˌmərSHələˈzāSHən/ n.

com·mer·cial space ▶ n. an area rented or sold as business premises.

Com·mie /ˈkämē/ ▶ n. (pl. **Commies**) informal, derogatory a communist.

com·min·gle /kəˈmiNGgəl, kä-/ ▶ v. literary mix; blend.

com·mi·nut·ed /ˈkäməˌn(y)oōtəd/ ▶ adj. technical reduced to minute particles or fragments. ■ **com·mi·nu·tion** /ˌkäməˈn(y)oōSHən/ n.

com·mis·er·ate /kəˈmizəˌrāt/ ▶ v. express sympathy or pity; sympathize. ■ **com·mis·er·a·tion** /kəˌmizəˈrāSHən/ n.

com·mis·sar /ˈkäməˌsär, ˌkäməˈsär/ ▶ n. a Communist official responsible for political education.

com·mis·sar·i·at /ˌkämə'se(ə)rēit/ ▶ n. a military department for the supply of food and equipment.

com·mis·sar·y /'käməˌserē/ ▶ n. (pl. **commissaries**) 1 a restaurant or food store in a military base or other institution. 2 a deputy or delegate.

com·mis·sion /kə'mishən/ ▶ n. 1 an instruction, command, or duty. 2 a formal request for something to be designed or made. 3 a group of people given official authority to do something. 4 a sum paid to an agent for selling something: *foreign banks may charge a commission.* 5 a warrant conferring the rank of military officer. 6 the committing of a crime or offense. ▶ v. 1 order or authorize the production of: *the council commissioned a study of the issue.* 2 bring something newly produced into working order. 3 appoint someone to the rank of military officer. – PHRASES **in** (or **out of**) **commission** in (or not in) use or working order.

com·mis·sion·er /kə'mish(ə)nər/ ▶ n. 1 a person appointed by, or as a member of, an official commission. 2 a representative of the highest authority in an area. 3 a person appointed to regulate a particular sport: *the baseball commissioner.*

com·mit /kə'mit/ ▶ v. (**commits, committing, committed**) 1 do something wrong, bad, or illegal. 2 dedicate or allocate to a course or use: *the Government should commit more money to training judges.* 3 (**commit oneself**) promise to do something. 4 (**be committed to**) be in a long-term emotional relationship with someone. 5 (**commit something to**) put something somewhere to preserve it: *she committed each detail to memory.* 6 send someone to prison or a psychiatric hospital, or for trial in a higher court.

com·mit·ment /kə'mitmənt/ ▶ n. 1 dedication to a cause or activity. 2 a promise to do something. 3 an engagement or duty that restricts freedom of action.

com·mit·tal /kə'mitl/ ▶ n. 1 the sending of someone to prison or a psychiatric hospital, or for trial. 2 the burial of a corpse.

com·mit·ted /kə'mitid/ ▶ adj. dedicated to a cause, activity, job, etc.: *a committed democrat.*

com·mit·tee /kə'mitē/ ▶ n. (treated as sing. or pl.) a group of people appointed for a specific function by a larger group.

com·mode /kə'mōd/ ▶ n. 1 a piece of furniture containing a concealed chamber pot. 2 a chest of drawers of a decorative type popular in the 18th century.

com·mod·i·fy /kə'mädəˌfī/ ▶ v. (**commodifies, commodifying, commodified**) turn into or treat as a mere commodity: *a culture in which sexuality is commodified.* ■ **com·mod·i·fi·ca·tion** /kəˌmädəfə'kāshən/ n.

com·mo·di·ous /kə'mōdēəs/ ▶ adj. formal roomy and comfortable.

com·mod·i·ty /kə'mäditē/ ▶ n. (pl. **commodities**) 1 a raw material or agricultural product that can be bought and sold. 2 something useful or valuable.

com·mo·dore /'käməˌdôr/ ▶ n. 1 a naval rank above captain and below rear admiral. 2 the president of a yacht club.

com·mon /'kämən/ ▶ adj. (**commoner, commonest**) 1 occurring, found, or done

often; not rare: *remedies for common ailments.* 2 without special qualities or position; ordinary. 3 shared by two or more people or things: *working toward our common goal.* 4 belonging to or affecting the whole of a community: *common land.* 5 showing a lack of taste and refinement supposedly typical of lower-class people; vulgar. ▶ n. a piece of open land for public use. ■ **com·mon·ness** n. – PHRASES **in common** in joint use or possession; shared. **in common with** in the same way as.

com·mon·al·i·ty /ˌkämən'alitē/ ▶ n. (pl. **commonalities**) the sharing of common features: *the commonality of grief.*

com·mon·al·ty /'kämənl-tē/ ▶ n. (treated as pl.) (**the commonalty**) chiefly historical people without special rank or position.

com·mon de·nom·i·na·tor ▶ n. 1 Mathematics a common multiple of the denominators of several fractions. 2 a feature shared by all members of a group.

com·mon·er /'kämənər/ ▶ n. one of the ordinary or common people, as opposed to the aristocracy or to royalty.

Com·mon E·ra ▶ n. another term for CHRISTIAN ERA.

com·mon frac·tion ▶ n. a fraction expressed by a numerator and a denominator (numbers above and below the line), not decimally.

com·mon ground ▶ n. views shared by each of two or more parties.

com·mon law ▶ n. the part of English law that is based on custom and judicial decisions rather than created by Parliament.

com·mon-law hus·band (or **wife**) ▶ n. a man or woman who has lived with a person long enough to be recognized as a husband or wife, but has not been married in a civil or religious ceremony.

com·mon·ly /'kämənlē/ ▶ adv. very often; frequently.

com·mon mar·ket ▶ n. 1 a group of countries imposing few or no duties on trade with one another. 2 (**the Common Market**) the European Union.

com·mon noun ▶ n. a noun referring to a class of things (e.g., *tree, cat*) as opposed to a particular person or thing. Often contrasted with PROPER NOUN.

com·mon·place /'kämənˌplās/ ▶ adj. not unusual or original; ordinary. ▶ n. 1 a usual or ordinary thing. 2 an unoriginal remark; a cliché.

com·mon room ▶ n. 1 a room in a school or college for use of students or staff outside teaching hours. 2 a room in a residential facility for the recreational use of all residents.

com·mons /'kämənz/ ▶ pl.n. 1 a dining hall in a residential school or college. 2 (treated as sing.) land or resources belonging to or affecting the whole of a community. 3 a public park of a town or city.

com·mon salt ▶ n. see SALT.

com·mon sense ▶ n. good sense and sound judgment in practical matters.

com·mon·sen·si·cal /ˌkämən'sensikəl/ ▶ adj. having or showing common sense.

com·mon stock ▶ n. shares entitling their holder to dividends that vary in amount and may even be missed, depending on the fortunes of the company. Compare with PREFERRED STOCK.

com·mon time ▶ n. a rhythmic musical pattern in which there are two or four beats in a measure.

com·mon·weal /'kämən‚wēl/ ▶ n. (**the commonweal**) old use the welfare of the public.

com·mon·wealth /'kämən‚welтн/ ▶ n. **1** an independent country or community. **2** a grouping of countries or other bodies. **3** (**the Commonwealth** or in full **the Commonwealth of Nations**) an association consisting of the UK together with countries that were previously part of the British Empire, and dependencies. **4** the formal title of the US states of Massachusetts, Pennsylvania, Virginia, and Kentucky.

com·mo·tion /kə'mōsнən/ ▶ n. a state of confused and noisy disturbance.

com·mu·nal /kə'myōōnl/ ▶ adj. **1** shared or done by all members of a community. **2** (of conflict) between different communities, especially those having different religions or ethnic origins. ■ **com·mu·nal·i·ty** /‚kämyə'nalitē/ n. **com·mu·nal·ly** adv.

com·mu·nal·ism /kə'myōōnl‚izəm/ ▶ n. **1** a principle of political organization based on federated communes. **2** the principle or practice of living together and sharing possessions and responsibilities.

com·mu·nard /‚kämyə'när(d)/ ▶ n. **1** a member of a commune. **2** (**Communard**) historical a supporter of the Paris Commune.

com·mune¹ /'käm‚yōōn/ ▶ n. **1** a group of people living together and sharing possessions and responsibilities. **2** (in France) the smallest district for administrative purposes. **3** (**the Paris Commune**) the short-lived government elected in Paris in 1871, advocating communal organization of society.

com·mune² /kə'myōōn/ ▶ v. (**commune with**) share one's intimate thoughts or feelings with: *visitors can stroll the fields and commune with nature.*

com·mu·ni·ca·ble /kə'myōōnikəbəl/ ▶ adj. (especially of a disease) able to be communicated to others.

com·mu·ni·cant /kə'myōōnikənt/ ▶ n. a person who receives Holy Communion.

com·mu·ni·cate /kə'myōōnə‚kāt/ ▶ v. **1** share or exchange information or ideas. **2** pass on, transmit, or convey an emotion, disease, heat, etc. **3** (as adj. **communicating**) (of two rooms) having a common connecting door. **4** receive Holy Communion. ■ **com·mu·ni·ca·tor** n.

com·mu·ni·ca·tion /kə‚myōōnə'kāsнən/ ▶ n. **1** the action of communicating. **2** a letter or other message. **3** (**communications**) the means of sending or receiving information, such as telephone lines or computers. **4** (**communications**) means of traveling or of transporting goods, such as roads or railroads. ■ **com·mu·ni·ca·tion·al** adj.

com·mu·ni·ca·tive /kə'myōōnə‚kātiv, -nikətiv/ ▶ adj. willing or eager to talk or impart information.

com·mun·ion /kə'myōōnyən/ ▶ n. **1** the sharing of intimate thoughts and feelings: *man's mystical communion with the divine.* **2** (also **Holy Communion**) the service of Christian worship at which bread and wine are consecrated and shared; the Eucharist. **3** an allied group of Christian Churches or communities: *the*

Anglican communion.

com·mu·ni·qué /kə‚myōōnə'kā, kə'myōōnə‚kā/ ▶ n. an official announcement or statement, especially one made to the media.

com·mu·nism /'kämyə‚nizəm/ ▶ n. **1** a political and social system whereby all property is owned by the community and each person contributes and receives according to their ability and needs. **2** a system of this kind derived from Marxism, practiced in China and formerly in the Soviet Union. ■ **com·mu·nist** n. & adj. **com·mu·nis·tic** /‚kämyə'nistik/ adj.

com·mu·ni·tar·i·an·ism /kə‚myōōni'te(ə)rēə‚nizəm/ ▶ n. a theory that emphasizes the responsibility of the individual to the community and the importance of the family unit. ■ **com·mu·ni·tar·i·an** adj. & n.

com·mu·ni·ty /kə'myōōnitē/ ▶ n. (pl. **communities**) **1** a group of people living together in one place. **2** (**the community**) the people of an area as a social group; society. **3** a group of people with a common religion, race, or profession: *the scientific community.* **4** the holding of certain attitudes and interests in common: *the sense of community that organized religion can provide.* **5** a group of interdependent plants or animals growing or living in the same place.

com·mu·ni·ty care ▶ n. long-term care for mentally ill, elderly, and disabled people within the community rather than in hospitals or other institutions.

com·mu·ni·ty cen·ter ▶ n. a place providing educational or recreational activities for the residents of a particular community.

com·mu·ni·ty col·lege ▶ n. a nonresidential junior college offering courses to people living in a particular area.

com·mu·ni·ty serv·ice ▶ n. **1** voluntary work intended to help people. **2** socially useful work that an offender is required to do instead of going to prison.

com·mu·tate /'kämyə‚tāt/ ▶ v. regulate or reverse the direction of an alternating electric current, especially to make it a direct current. ■ **com·mu·ta·tion** /‚kämyə'tāsнən/ n.

com·mu·ta·tive /'kämyə‚tātiv, kə'myōōtətiv/ ▶ adj. Mathematics unchanged in result by interchanging the order of quantities, as in the equation $a \times b = b \times a$.

com·mu·ta·tor /'kämyə‚tātər/ ▶ n. an attachment, connected to the armature of a motor or generator, that ensures the current flows as direct current.

com·mute /kə'myōōt/ ▶ v. **1** travel some distance between one's home and place of work on a regular basis. **2** reduce a judicial sentence, especially a death sentence, to a less severe one. **3** change one kind of payment or obligation for another. ■ **com·mut·a·ble** adj. **com·mu·ta·tion** /‚kämyə'tāsнən/ n. (in senses 2 and 3) **com·mut·er** n.

co·mor·bid·i·ty /‚kōmôr'biditē/ ▶ n. the simultaneous presence of two chronic diseases or conditions in a patient: *the comorbidity of anxiety and depression in Parkinson's disease.*

comp /kämp/ informal ▶ n. **1** short for a complimentary ticket or voucher. **2** short for composition. **3** short for a comprehensive examination. **4** short for computation. **5** (in real estate) short for a comparable property. ▶ v. **1** play music as an accompaniment, especially in jazz or blues. **2** give something away free, especially as part of a promotion: *the management graciously comped our wine selection.*

com·pact[1] ▶ adj. /kəm'pakt, käm-, 'käm,pakt/ **1** closely and neatly packed together; dense. **2** having all the necessary parts or features fitted into a small space. ▶ v. /kəm'pakt, käm-/ press firmly together; compress: *the waste is compacted and buried.* ▶ n. /'käm,pakt/ **1** a small flat case containing face powder, a mirror, and a powder puff. **2** a compact car. ■ **com·pac·tion** /kəm'paksHən/ n. **com·pact·ly** adv. **com·pact·ness** n. **com·pac·tor** /kəm'paktər, käm-, 'käm,paktər/ n.

com·pact[2] /'käm,pakt/ ▶ n. a formal agreement or contract.

compact car ▶ n. a medium-sized car.

com·pact disc ▶ n. (also **compact disk**) a small plastic disc on which music or other digital information is stored in a form that can be read by a laser.

com·pa·dre /kəm'pädrā/ ▶ n. (pl. **compadres**) informal a friend or companion.

com·pan·ion /kəm'panyən/ ▶ n. **1** a person with whom one spends time or travels. **2** each of a pair of things intended to complement or match each other. **3** (**Companion**) a member of the lowest grade of certain orders of knighthood. ■ **com·pan·ion·ship** /kəm'panyən,sHip/ n.

com·pan·ion·a·ble /kəm'panyənəbəl/ ▶ adj. friendly and sociable. ■ **com·pan·ion·a·bly** /-blē/ adv.

com·pan·ion·way /kəm'panyən,wā/ ▶ n. a set of steps leading from a ship's deck down to a cabin or lower deck.

com·pa·ny /'kəmpənē/ ▶ n. (pl. **companies**) **1** a commercial business. **2** the fact of being with another person or other people: *she is excellent company.* **3** a guest or guests: *we're expecting company.* **4** a gathering of people. **5** a body of soldiers, especially the smallest subdivision of an infantry battalion. **6** a group of actors, singers, or dancers who perform together. – PHRASES **in company with** together with. **keep someone company** spend time with someone to prevent them feeling lonely or bored.

com·pa·ra·ble /'kämp(ə)rəbəl/ ▶ adj. **1** able to be compared. **2** similar: *prices online and in the shops are broadly comparable.* ■ **com·pa·ra·bil·i·ty** /,kämp(ə)rə'bilitē/ n. **com·pa·ra·bly** /-blē/ adv.

com·par·a·tive /kəm'parətiv/ ▶ adj. **1** measured or judged by comparing one thing with another; relative: *I returned to the comparative comfort of my own home.* **2** involving comparison between two or more subjects or branches of science. **3** (of an adjective or adverb) expressing a higher degree of a quality, but not the highest possible (e.g., *braver*, *more fiercely*). Contrasted with POSITIVE, SUPERLATIVE.

com·par·a·tive·ly /kəm'parətivlē/ ▶ adv. to a moderate degree as compared with something else; relatively.

com·par·a·tor /kəm'parətər/ ▶ n. a device for comparing something measurable with a reference or standard.

com·pare /kəm'pe(ə)r/ ▶ v. **1** estimate, measure, or note the similarity or difference between: *revenues will amount to $138 million this year, compared with $147 million last year.* **2** (**compare something to**) describe the resemblances of something with something else.

3 be similar to or have a specified relationship with another thing or person: *salaries compare favorably with those of other professions.* – PHRASES **beyond** (or **without**) **compare** better than all others of the same kind. **compare notes** exchange ideas or information.

com·par·i·son /kəm'parəsən/ ▶ n. **1** an instance of comparing things or people. **2** the quality of being similar or equivalent: *there is no comparison between the two offenses.*

com·part·ment /kəm'pärtmənt/ ▶ n. **1** a separate section of a structure or container. **2** a division of a railroad car marked by partitions. ■ **com·part·men·tal** /kəm,pärt'mentl/ adj.

com·part·men·tal·ize /kəm,pärt'mentl,īz/ ▶ v. divide something into categories or sections. ■ **com·part·men·tal·i·za·tion** /kəm,pärt,mentl-ə'zāsHən/ n.

com·pass /'kəmpəs/ ▶ n. **1** an instrument containing a magnetized pointer that shows the direction of magnetic north. **2** (also **pair of compasses**) an instrument for drawing circles and arcs and measuring distances between points, consisting of two arms linked by a movable joint. **3** range or scope: *it would be impossible to bring all the subjects within the compass of a single volume.*

com·pas·sion /kəm'pasHən/ ▶ n. sympathetic pity and concern for the sufferings or misfortunes of others.

com·pas·sion·ate /kəm'pasHənət/ ▶ adj. feeling or showing sympathy and concern for others. ■ **com·pas·sion·ate·ly** adv.

com·pas·sion·ate leave ▶ n. leave from work granted to someone as a result of personal circumstances, especially the death of a close relative.

compass saw ▶ n. a handsaw with a narrow blade for cutting curves.

com·pat·i·ble /kəm'patəbəl/ ▶ adj. **1** able to exist or be used together without problems or conflict: *a contemporary design theme that's compatible with any decor.* **2** (of two people) able to have a good relationship; well suited. **3** consistent or in keeping: *the symptoms were compatible with a peptic ulcer.* ■ **com·pat·i·bil·i·ty** /kəm,patə'bilitē/ n. **com·pat·i·bly** adv.

com·pa·tri·ot /kəm'pātrēət/ ▶ n. a fellow citizen or national of a country.

com·pel /kəm'pel/ ▶ v. (**compels, compelling, compelled**) **1** force or oblige someone to do something. **2** cause by force or pressure: *ground troops would be necessary to compel capitulation.*

com·pel·ling /kəm'peliNG/ ▶ adj. **1** strongly arousing attention or admiration. **2** not able to be resisted or doubted: *a compelling argument.* ■ **com·pel·ling·ly** adv.

com·pen·di·ous /kəm'pendēəs/ ▶ adj. formal presenting the essential facts in a detailed but concise way. ■ **com·pen·di·ous·ly** adv.

com·pen·di·um /kəm'pendēəm/ ▶ n. (pl. **compendiums** or **compendia** /-dēə/) **1** a collection of concise but detailed information about a subject. **2** a collection of similar items.

com·pen·sate /'kämpən,sāt/ ▶ v. **1** give someone something in recognition of loss, suffering, or injury. **2** (**compensate for**) reduce or counteract something undesirable by having an opposite force or effect. ■ **com·pen·sa·tor** /-,sātər/ n. **com·pen·sa·to·ry** /kəm'pensə,tôrē/ adj.

com·pen·sa·tion /ˌkämpənˈsāsHən/
▶ n. **1** something given to someone to compensate for loss, suffering, or injury. **2** something that makes up for an undesirable situation: *getting older has its compensations.* **3** the action of compensating.

com·pete /kəmˈpēt/ ▶ v. **1** try to gain or win something by defeating or being better than others. **2** be able to rival another or others: *in this business no one can compete with Schumacher.*

com·pe·tence /ˈkämpətəns/ (also **competency**) ▶ n. **1** the ability to do something well. **2** the authority of a court or other body to deal with a particular matter.

com·pe·tent /ˈkämpətənt/ ▶ adj. **1** having the necessary skill or knowledge to do something successfully. **2** acceptable and satisfactory: *she spoke quite competent French.* **3** having legal authority to deal with a particular matter. ■ **com·pe·tent·ly** adv.

com·pe·ti·tion /ˌkämpəˈtisHən/ ▶ n. **1** the activity of competing against others. **2** an event or contest in which people compete. **3** the person or people with whom one is competing.

com·pet·i·tive /kəmˈpetətiv/ ▶ adj. **1** relating to competition. **2** strongly desiring to be more successful than others. **3** as good as or better than others of a similar nature: *we offer prompt service at competitive rates.* ■ **com·pet·i·tive·ly** adv. **com·pet·i·tive·ness** n.

com·pet·i·tor /kəmˈpetətər/ ▶ n. **1** a person who takes part in an athletic contest. **2** an organization or country that competes with others in business or trade.

com·pi·la·tion /ˌkämpəˈlāsHən/ ▶ n. **1** the action of compiling something. **2** a thing, especially a book or record, compiled from different sources.

com·pile /kəmˈpīl/ ▶ v. **1** produce a book, report, etc., by assembling material from other sources. **2** gather material to produce a book, report, etc.

com·pil·er /kəmˈpīlər/ ▶ n. **1** a person who compiles information. **2** a computer program that translates instructions from a high-level language into a form that can be executed by the computer.

com·pla·cent /kəmˈplāsənt/ ▶ adj. satisfied with oneself in a smug or uncritical way. ■ **com·pla·cen·cy** /kəmˈplāsənsē/ (also **complacence**) n. **com·pla·cent·ly** adv.

USAGE
Do not confuse **complacent** with **complaisant**. **Complacent** means 'smugly self-satisfied' (*don't be complacent about security*), whereas **complaisant** means 'willing to please' (*the local people were complaisant and cordial*).

com·plain /kəmˈplān/ ▶ v. **1** express dissatisfaction or annoyance about something. **2** (**complain of**) state that one is suffering from a symptom of illness. ■ **com·plain·er** n.

com·plain·ant /kəmˈplānənt/ ▶ n. Law a person who brings a case against another in certain lawsuits.

com·plaint /kəmˈplānt/ ▶ n. **1** an act of complaining. **2** a reason for being dissatisfied with something. **3** the expression of dissatisfaction: *a letter of complaint.* **4** an illness or medical condition, especially a minor one.

com·plai·sant /kəmˈplāsənt/ ▶ adj. willing to please others or to accept their behavior without protest. ■ **com·plai·sance** n.

USAGE
On the difference between **complaisant** and **complacent**, see the note at COMPLACENT.

com·ple·ment ▶ n. /ˈkämpləmənt/ **1** a thing that contributes extra features to something else so as to improve it. **2** the number or quantity that makes something complete: *we have a full complement of staff.* **3** a word or words used with a verb to complete the meaning of the subject (e.g., *happy* in the sentence *we are happy*). **4** Geometry the amount by which a given angle is less than 90°. ▶ v. /-ˌment, -mənt/ add extra features to someone or something in a way that improves. ■ **com·ple·men·ta·tion** /ˌkämpləmenˈtāsHən/ n.

USAGE
The words **complement** and **compliment** are often confused. As a verb, **complement** means 'add extra features to someone or something in a way that improves' (*a classic blazer complements a look that's smart or casual*), while **compliment** means 'politely congratulate or praise someone or something' (*he complimented Kate on her appearance*).

com·ple·men·tar·i·ty /ˌkämpləmenˈtaritē/ ▶ n. (pl. **complementarities**) a situation in which two or more different things improve each other or form a balanced whole.

com·ple·men·ta·ry /ˌkämpləˈment(ə)rē/ ▶ adj. **1** combining so as to form a whole or to improve each other: *they have different but complementary skills.* **2** relating to complementary medicine.

USAGE
On the confusion of **complementary** and **complimentary**, see the note at COMPLIMENTARY.

com·ple·men·ta·ry an·gle ▶ n. either of two angles whose sum is 90°.

com·ple·men·ta·ry col·or ▶ n. either of two colors that, when combined, produce white (in the case of light) or black (in the case of pigments).

com·ple·men·ta·ry med·i·cine ▶ n. medical therapy that is not part of scientific medicine but may be used alongside it, e.g., acupuncture.

com·plete /kəmˈplēt/ ▶ adj. **1** having all the necessary or appropriate parts; entire. **2** having run its full course; finished. **3** to the greatest extent or degree; total: *a complete ban on smoking.* **4** (also **compleat**) chiefly humorous skilled at every aspect of an activity: *the compleat mathematician.* **5** (**complete with**) having something as an additional part or feature. ▶ v. **1** finish making or doing something. **2** provide with the items necessary to make entire or complete: *quarry tiles complete the look.* **3** write the required information on a form. ■ **com·plete·ness** n.

com·plete·ly /kəmˈplētlē/ ▶ adv. totally; utterly.

com·ple·tion /kəmˈplēsHən/ ▶ n. **1** the action of completing something or the state of being completed. **2** Football a successful forward pass.

com·ple·tist /kəmˈplētist/ ▶ n. an obsessive, typically indiscriminate, collector or fan.

com·plex ▶ adj. /ˈkämˌpleks, kəmˈpleks, ˈkämˌpleks/ **1** consisting of many different and connected parts. **2** difficult to understand; complicated. ▶ n. /ˈkämˌpleks/ **1** a group of similar buildings or facilities on the same site. **2** an interlinked system; a network. **3** a group of repressed feelings that lead to abnormal mental states or behavior. **4** informal a strong concern or anxiety about something. ■ **com·plex·i·ty** /kəmˈpleksitē/ n. (pl. **complexities**) **com·plex·ly** adv.

com·plex·ion /kəmˈpleksHən/ ▶n. **1** the natural color and texture of the skin of a person's face. **2** the general character of something: *he can single-handedly change the complexion of a game.* ■ **-com·plex·ioned** adj.

com·plex num·ber ▶n. Mathematics a number containing both a real and an imaginary part.

com·pli·ance /kəmˈplīəns/ ▶n. the action of obeying an order, rule, or request.

com·pli·ant /kəmˈplīənt/ ▶adj. **1** tending to be excessively obedient or ready to accept something. **2** in accordance with rules or standards. ■ **com·pli·ant·ly** adv.

com·pli·cate /ˈkämpləˌkāt/ ▶v. make something more intricate or confusing.

com·pli·cat·ed /ˈkämpləˌkātid/ ▶adj. **1** consisting of many interconnecting elements; intricate. **2** involving many confusing aspects.

com·pli·ca·tion /ˌkämpləˈkāsHən/ ▶n. **1** a thing that complicates something; a difficulty. **2** an involved or confused state: *companies offering a variety of solutions with a minimum of complication.* **3** a secondary disease or condition that makes an already existing one worse.

com·plic·it /kəmˈplisit/ ▶adj. involved with others in an unlawful activity: *the militant group may be complicit in ten violent incidents.*

com·plic·i·ty /kəmˈplisitē/ ▶n. involvement with others in an unlawful activity.

com·pli·ment ▶n. /ˈkämpləmənt/ **1** a polite expression of praise or admiration. **2** (**compliments**) formal greetings. ▶v. /ˈkämpləˌment/ politely congratulate or praise: *he complimented Kate on her appearance.* – PHRASES **return the compliment** retaliate or respond in a similar way. **with one's compliments** provided free of charge.

USAGE
On the confusion of **compliment** and **complement**, see the note at COMPLEMENT.

com·pli·men·ta·ry /ˌkämpləˈmentərē, -ˈmentrē/ ▶adj. **1** praising or approving: *a complimentary remark.* **2** given free of charge.

USAGE
Do not confuse the words **complimentary** and **complementary**. **Complimentary** means 'praising' or 'given free of charge' (*a complimentary breakfast*), whereas **complementary** means 'combining to form a whole or to improve each other' (*they have different but complementary skills*).

com·pline /ˈkämplin, -ˌplīn/ ▶n. (in the Roman Catholic and High Anglican Church) an evening service traditionally said before retiring for the night.

com·ply /kəmˈplī/ ▶v. (**complies, complying, complied**) (often **comply with**) **1** act in accordance with a request or order. **2** meet specified standards: *engines designed to comply with state emissions standards.*

com·po·nent /kəmˈpōnənt/ ▶n. a part or element of a larger whole. ▶adj. being part of a larger whole.

com·port /kəmˈpôrt/ ▶v. (**comport oneself**) formal behave in a particular way: *students*

who comported themselves well in television interviews.

com·port·ment /kəmˈpôrtmənt/ ▶n. formal a person's behavior or bearing.

com·pose /kəmˈpōz/ ▶v. **1** make up a whole: *the committee is composed of ten senators.* **2** create a work of art, especially music or poetry. **3** form a whole by arranging parts in an orderly or artistic way. **4** phrase a letter or other piece of writing with care and thought. **5** (often as adj. **composed**) settle one's features or thoughts. **6** prepare a written work for printing by setting up the characters to be printed.

com·pos·er /kəmˈpōzər/ ▶n. a person who writes music.

com·pos·ite /kəmˈpäzət, käm-/ ▶adj. **1** made up of various parts. **2** (**Composite**) relating to a classical style of architecture consisting of elements of the Ionic and Corinthian orders. **3** (of a plant) having flowerheads consisting of numerous florets, such as a daisy. ▶n. **1** a thing made up of several parts. **2** a motion for debate composed of two or more related resolutions.

com·po·si·tion /ˌkämpəˈzisHən/ ▶n. **1** the way in which something is made up from different elements: *the molecular composition of cells.* **2** a work of music, literature, or art. **3** a thing made up of various elements. **4** the composing of something. **5** the artistic arrangement of the parts of a picture. ■ **com·po·si·tion·al** adj.

com·pos·i·tor /kəmˈpäzitər/ ▶n. a person who arranges type for printing or who keys text into a composing machine.

com·pos men·tis /ˌkämpəs ˈmentəs/ ▶adj. having full control of one's mind.

com·post /ˈkämˌpōst/ ▶n. **1** decayed organic material used as a fertilizer for plants. **2** a mixture of compost with soil used for growing plants. ▶v. make organic matter into compost. ■ **com·post·er** n.

com·po·sure /kəmˈpōzHər/ ▶n. the state of being calm and self-controlled.

com·pote /ˈkämˌpōt/ ▶n. fruit preserved or cooked in syrup.

com·pound¹ ▶n. /ˈkämˌpound/ **1** a thing composed of two or more separate elements. **2** a substance formed from two or more elements chemically united in fixed proportions. **3** a word made up of two or more existing words. ▶adj. /ˈkämˌpound, kämˈpound, kəmˈpound/ **1** made up or consisting of several elements. **2** (of interest) payable on both capital and the accumulated interest. Compare with SIMPLE. **3** (of a leaf, flower, or eye) consisting of two or more simple parts or individuals in combination. ▶v. /kəmˈpound, kämˈpound, ˈkämˌpound/ **1** make up a composite whole. **2** mix ingredients to form a whole. **3** make something bad worse. ■ **com·pound·er** n.

com·pound² ▶n. /ˈkämˌpound/ a large open area enclosed by a fence, for example within a prison.

com·pound eye ▶n. an eye consisting of an array of numerous small visual units, as found in insects and crustaceans.

com·pound frac·ture ▶n. an injury in which a broken bone pierces the skin.

com·pre·hend /ˌkämpriˈhend/ ▶v. **1** fully understand something. **2** formal include or encompass: *a divine order comprehending all men.*

com·pre·hen·si·ble /ˌkämpriˈhensəbəl/ ▶adj. able to be understood; intelligible.

■ **com·pre·hen·si·bil·i·ty** /-ˌhensəˈbilitē/ n.

com·pre·hen·sion /ˌkämpriˈhenchən/ ▶ n. the ability to understand something.

com·pre·hen·sive /ˌkämpriˈhensiv/ ▶ adj. 1 including or dealing with all or nearly all aspects of something: *a comprehensive guidebook*. 2 (also **comprehensive examination** or **comp**) an examination testing a student's command of a special field of knowledge. 3 (of motor-vehicle insurance) providing cover for most risks. ■ **com·pre·hen·sive·ly** adv. **com·pre·hen·sive·ness** n.

com·press ▶ v. /kəmˈpres/ 1 squeeze or press so as to occupy less space: *the skirt can be compressed into a small bag.* 2 squeeze or press two things together. ▶ n. /ˈkämˌpres/ a pad of absorbent material pressed onto part of the body to relieve inflammation or stop bleeding. ■ **com·press·i·bil·i·ty** /kəmˌpresəˈbilitē/ n. **com·press·i·ble** adj. **com·pres·sive** /-ˈpresiv/ adj.

com·pressed air ▶ n. air that is at more than atmospheric pressure.

com·pres·sion /kəmˈpreshən/ ▶ n. 1 the action of compressing something. 2 the reduction in volume (causing an increase in pressure) of the fuel mixture in an internal-combustion engine before ignition. ■ **com·pres·sion·al** adj.

com·pres·sor /kəmˈpresər/ ▶ n. 1 an instrument or device for compressing something. 2 a machine used to supply air or other gas at increased pressure.

com·prise /kəmˈprīz/ ▶ v. 1 be made up of; consist of: *the country comprises twenty states.* 2 (also **be comprised of**) make up a whole: *this breed comprises 50 percent of the Swiss cattle population.*

USAGE

Traditionally, **comprise** means 'consist of' and should not be used to mean 'make up a whole.' However, a passive use of **comprise** (as in *the country is comprised of twenty states*) is now becoming part of standard English: this has broadly the same meaning as the traditional active sense (*the country comprises twenty states*).

---

com·pro·mise /ˈkämprəˌmīz/ ▶ n. 1 an agreement reached by each side making concessions. 2 something that is halfway between conflicting elements: *a compromise between greed and caution.* ▶ v. 1 settle a dispute by each side making concessions. 2 accept standards that are lower than is desirable for practical reasons: *we weren't prepared to compromise on safety.* 3 bring someone into disrepute or danger by reckless behavior. ■ **com·pro·mis·er** n.

com·pro·mis·ing /ˈkämprəˌmīziNG/ ▶ adj. revealing an embarrassing or incriminating secret.

comp·trol·ler /kənˈtrōlər, ˌkäm(p)ˈtrōlər, ˈkäm(p)ˌtrōlər/ ▶ n. a controller (used in the title of some financial officers).

com·pul·sion /kəmˈpəlshən/ ▶ n. 1 the compelling of someone to do something. 2 an irresistible urge to do something.

com·pul·sive /kəmˈpəlsiv/ ▶ adj. 1 resulting from or acting on an irresistible urge: *compulsive eating.* 2 powerfully interesting or exciting. ■ **com·pul·sive·ly** adv. **com·pul·sive·ness** n.

com·pul·so·ry /kəmˈpəlsərē/ ▶ adj. required by law or a rule; obligatory. ■ **com·pul·so·ri·ly** /-sərəlē/ adv.

com·punc·tion /kəmˈpəNG(k)shən/ ▶ n. a feeling of guilt that prevents or follows wrongdoing: *he felt no compunction about deceiving them.*

com·pu·ta·tion /ˌkämpyo͞oˈtāshən/ ▶ n. 1 mathematical calculation. 2 the use of computers, especially as a subject of research or study. ■ **com·pu·ta·tion·al** /ˌkämpyo͞oˈtāshənl/ adj.

com·pute /kəmˈpyo͞ot/ ▶ v. calculate a figure or amount.

com·put·er /kəmˈpyo͞otər/ ▶ n. an electronic device capable of storing and processing information according to a predetermined set of instructions.

com·put·er·ize /kəmˈpyo͞otəˌrīz/ ▶ v. convert something to a system or form that is controlled, stored, or processed by computer. ■ **com·put·er·i·za·tion** /kəmˌpyo͞otərəˈzāshən/ n.

com·put·er·lit·er·ate ▶ adj. having enough knowledge and skill to be able to use computers.

com·put·ing /kəmˈpyo͞otiNG/ ▶ n. the use or operation of computers.

com·rade /ˈkämˌrad, ˈkämrəd/ ▶ n. 1 (among men) a colleague or a fellow member of an organization. 2 (also **comrade-in-arms**) a fellow soldier. ■ **com·rade·ly** adj. **com·rade·ship** /-ˌship/ n.

con¹ /kän/ *informal* ▶ v. (**cons, conning, conned**) persuade someone to do or believe something by lying to them. ▶ n. an act of deceiving or tricking someone.

con² ▶ n. (usu. in phrase **pros and cons**) a disadvantage of or argument against something.

con³ ▶ n. *informal* a convict.

con⁴ ▶ v. variant spelling of **CONN**.

con·cat·e·nate /kənˈkatnˌāt/ ▶ v. *formal or technical* link things together in a chain or series.

con·cat·e·na·tion /kənˌkatnˈāshən/ ▶ n. a series of interconnected things: *a concatenation of events that had led to the murder.*

con·cave /känˈkāv, ˈkänˌkāv/ ▶ adj. having an outline or surface that curves inward like the inside of a ball. Compare with **CONVEX**. ■ **con·cav·i·ty** /känˈkavitē/ n.

con·ceal /kənˈsēl/ ▶ v. 1 prevent someone or something from being seen. 2 keep something secret. ■ **con·ceal·er** n. **con·ceal·ment** n.

con·cede /kənˈsēd/ ▶ v. 1 finally admit or agree that something is true. 2 give up a possession, advantage, or right. 3 admit defeat in a match or contest. 4 fail to prevent an opponent scoring a goal or point.

con·ceit /kənˈsēt/ ▶ n. 1 excessive pride in oneself. 2 an artistic effect or device. 3 a complicated metaphor.

con·ceit·ed /kənˈsētid/ ▶ adj. excessively proud of oneself.

con·ceiv·a·ble /kənˈsēvəbəl/ ▶ adj. capable of being imagined or understood. ■ **con·ceiv·a·bly** /-blē/ adv.

con·ceive /kənˈsēv/ ▶ v. 1 become pregnant with a child. 2 form a plan or idea in the mind: *the project was conceived by a Dutch businessman.*

con·cen·trate /ˈkänsənˌtrāt/ ▶ v. 1 focus all one's attention on a particular object or activity: *she couldn't concentrate on the movie.* 2 gather together in large numbers or a mass at one point: *resources should be concentrated in areas where unemployment is highest.* 3 increase the strength of a substance or solution. ▶ n. a concentrated substance or solution. ■ **con·cen·tra·tor** n.

con·cen·tra·tion /ˌkänsənˈtrāsHən/ ▸ n. **1** the action or power of concentrating. **2** a close gathering of people or things. **3** the relative amount of a particular substance within a solution or mixture.

con·cen·tra·tion camp ▸ n. a camp for holding political prisoners, especially in Nazi Germany.

con·cen·tric /kənˈsentrik, kän-/ ▸ adj. (of circles or arcs) sharing the same center.

con·cept /ˈkänˌsept/ ▸ n. an abstract idea: *the concept of justice.*

con·cep·tion /kənˈsepsHən/ ▸ n. **1** the process of conceiving a child. **2** the forming of a plan or idea. **3** the way in which something is viewed or regarded: *our conception of democracy.* **4** ability to imagine or understand something: *the administration had no conception of women's problems.*

con·cep·tu·al /kənˈsepCHōōəl/ ▸ adj. relating to ideas or concepts. ■ **con·cep·tu·al·ly** adv.

con·cep·tu·al·ize /kənˈsepCHōōəˌlīz/ ▸ v. form an idea or concept of something in the mind. ■ **con·cep·tu·al·i·za·tion** /kənˌsepCHōōələˈzāsHən/ n.

con·cern /kənˈsərn/ ▸ v. **1** relate to; be about. **2** affect or involve: *stop interfering in matters that don't concern you.* **3** make someone anxious or worried. ▸ n. **1** worry or anxiety. **2** a matter of interest or importance: *the court's primary concern is her welfare.* **3** a business or company.

con·cerned /kənˈsərnd/ ▸ adj. worried or anxious.

con·cern·ing /kənˈsərniNG/ ▸ prep. about.

con·cert /ˈkänˌsərt, ˈkänsərt/ ▸ n. a musical performance given in public. – PHRASES **in concert 1** acting together. **2** giving a live public performance.

con·cert·ed /kənˈsərtəd/ ▸ adj. **1** jointly arranged or carried out: *a concerted campaign.* **2** done with great effort or determination.

con·cer·ti·na /ˌkänsərˈtēnə/ ▸ n. a small musical instrument played by stretching and squeezing a central bellows, each note being sounded by a button. ▸ v. (**concertinas, concertinaing** /ˌkänsərˈtēnəiNG/, **concertinaed** or **concertina'd**) compress something into folds like those of a concertina.

con·cer·to /kənˈCHertō/ ▸ n. (pl. **concertos** or **concerti** /-tē/) a musical composition for an orchestra and one or more solo instruments.

con·cert pitch ▸ n. **1** an international standard for the tuning of musical instruments. **2** a state of readiness and keenness.

con·ces·sion /kənˈsesHən/ ▸ n. **1** a thing given up or allowed to settle a dispute: *the union was reluctant to make any concessions.* **2** a reduction in price for a certain kind of person. **3** a commercial operation set up within the premises of a larger business. **4** the right to use land or other property for a particular purpose, granted by a government or other controlling body. ■ **con·ces·sion·ar·y** adj.

con·ces·sion·aire /kənˌsesHəˈne(ə)r/ ▸ n. someone who holds a concession.

conch /käNGk, känCH, käNGk/ ▸ n. (pl. **conchs** /käNGks, kôNGks/ or **conches** /ˈkänCHiz/) a mollusk of tropical seas, with a spiral shell.

con·cierge /kônˈsyerzH, ˌkänsēˈerzH/ ▸ n. **1** (especially in France) a resident caretaker of an apartment block or small hotel. **2** a hotel employee who assists guests by booking tours, making theater and restaurant reservations, etc.

con·cil·i·ate /kənˈsilēˌāt/ ▸ v. **1** make someone calmer or less angry. **2** act as a mediator in a dispute. ■ **con·cil·i·a·tion** /kənˌsilēˈāsHən/ n. **con·cil·i·a·tor** /-ˌātər/ n.

con·cil·i·a·to·ry /kənˈsilēəˌtôrē/ ▸ adj. intended to make someone calmer or less angry: *a conciliatory tone of voice.*

con·cise /kənˈsīs/ ▸ adj. giving information clearly and in few words. ■ **con·cise·ly** adv. **con·cise·ness** n. **con·ci·sion** /-ˈsizHən/ n.

con·clave /ˈkänˌklāv/ ▸ n. **1** a private meeting. **2** (in the Roman Catholic Church) a meeting of cardinals in order to elect a pope.

con·clude /kənˈklōōd/ ▸ v. **1** bring or come to an end. **2** arrive at a judgment or opinion by reasoning: *doctors concluded that she had suffered a stroke.* **3** formally settle or arrange a treaty or agreement.

con·clu·sion /kənˈklōōzHən/ ▸ n. **1** an end or finish. **2** the summing-up of an argument or text. **3** a judgment or decision reached by reasoning: *she came to the conclusion that her husband was right.* **4** the settling of a treaty or agreement.

con·clu·sive /kənˈklōōsiv, -ziv/ ▸ adj. decisive or convincing: *conclusive evidence.* ■ **con·clu·sive·ly** adv.

con·coct /kənˈkäkt/ ▸ v. **1** make a dish or meal by combining different ingredients. **2** invent a story or plan. ■ **con·coc·tion** /kənˈkäksHən/ n.

con·com·i·tant /kənˈkämitənt/ formal ▸ adj. occurring or naturally connected with something else: *the Gulf crisis and the concomitant rise in oil prices.* ▸ n. a phenomenon that occurs or is naturally connected with something else. ■ **con·com·i·tant·ly** adv.

con·cord /ˈkäNGˌkôrd, ˈkän-/ ▸ n. **1** literary agreement; harmony. **2** a treaty.

con·cord·ance /kənˈkôrdns/ ▸ n. **1** an alphabetical list of the important words in a text, usually with quotations from or references to the passages concerned. **2** formal agreement.

con·cord·ant /kənˈkôrdnt/ ▸ adj. in agreement; consistent.

con·cor·dat /kənˈkôrˌdat/ ▸ n. an agreement or treaty, especially one between the Vatican and a government.

con·course /ˈkänˌkôrs, ˈkäNG-/ ▸ n. **1** a large open area inside or in front of a public building. **2** formal a crowd of people.

con·crete /känˈkrēt, ˈkänˌkrēt, kənˈkrēt/ ▸ adj. **1** existing in a physical form; not abstract. **2** specific; definite: *concrete proof.* ▸ n. a building material made from gravel, sand, cement, and water, forming a stonelike mass when dry. ▸ v. cover a surface with concrete. ■ **con·crete·ly** adv. **con·crete·ness** n.

con·crete jun·gle ▸ n. an urban area with many large, unattractive, modern buildings.

con·cre·tion /kənˈkrēsHən, kän-/ ▸ n. a hard solid mass.

con·cu·bine /ˈkäNGkyōōˌbīn/ ▸ n. **1** chiefly historical (in societies in which a man may have more than one wife) a woman who lives with a man but has lower status than his wife or wives. **2** old use a man's mistress.

con·cu·pis·cence /känˈkyōōpisəns, kən-/ ▸ n. formal lust. ■ **con·cu·pis·cent** /känˈkyōōpisənt, kən-/ adj.

con·cur /kənˈkər/ ▸ v. (**concurs, concurring, concurred**) **1** agree: *the Council concurred with this decision.* **2** happen at the same time.

con·cur·rent /kənˈkərənt, -ˈkə-rənt/
▶ adj. **1** existing or happening at the same time. **2** Mathematics (of three or more lines) meeting at or approaching one point. ■ **con·cur·rence** n. **con·cur·rent·ly** adv.

con·cuss /kənˈkəs/ ▶ v. hit someone on the head, making them temporarily unconscious or confused.

con·cus·sion /kənˈkəsHən/ ▶ n. **1** temporary unconsciousness or confusion caused by a blow on the head. **2** a violent shock as from a heavy blow.

con·demn /kənˈdem/ ▶ v. **1** express complete disapproval of someone or something. **2** sentence someone to a punishment: *the rebels had been condemned to death.* **3** force someone to endure something unpleasant: *he was condemned to a lifelong struggle with depression.* **4** officially declare something to be unfit for use. ■ **con·dem·na·tion** /ˌkändemˈnāsHən, -dəm-/ n. **con·dem·na·to·ry** /-ˈdemnəˌtôrē/ adj.

con·den·sa·tion /ˌkänˌdenˈsāsHən, -dən-/ ▶ n. **1** water from humid air collecting as droplets on a cold surface. **2** the conversion of a vapor or gas to a liquid.

con·dense /kənˈdens/ ▶ v. **1** change from a gas or vapor to a liquid. **2** make something denser or more concentrated. **3** express a piece of writing or speech in fewer words.

con·densed milk ▶ n. milk that has been thickened by evaporation and sweetened.

con·dens·er /kənˈdensər/ ▶ n. **1** a piece of equipment for condensing vapor. **2** a lens or system of lenses for concentrating and directing light. **3** another term for CAPACITOR.

con·de·scend /ˌkändəˈsend/ ▶ v. **1** behave as if one is better than other people. **2** do something that one believes to be below one's dignity or level of importance: *he condescended to see me at my hotel.* ■ **con·de·scen·sion** /-ˈsenCHən/ n.

con·de·scend·ing /ˌkändəˈsendiNG/ ▶ adj. feeling or showing that one thinks one is better than other people. ■ **con·de·scend·ing·ly** adv.

con·dign /kənˈdīn/ ▶ adj. formal (of punishment) fitting and deserved.

con·di·ment /ˈkändəmənt/ ▶ n. a substance such as salt, mustard, or ketchup, used to flavor food.

con·di·tion /kənˈdisHən/ ▶ n. **1** the state of something or someone, with regard to appearance, fitness, or working order. **2** (**conditions**) the circumstances affecting something: *the health risks associated with poor living conditions.* **3** a state of affairs that must exist before something else is possible: *for a country to borrow money, three conditions must be met.* **4** an illness or medical problem. ▶ v. **1** train or accustom to behave in a certain way: *some students may have been conditioned to respond to authority figures.* **2** have a significant influence on or determine something. **3** bring something into a good or desired state or condition. **4** apply conditioner to the hair. – PHRASES **on condition that** as long as certain requirements are fulfilled.

con·di·tion·al /kənˈdisHənl/ ▶ adj. **1** subject to one or more conditions or requirements being fulfilled; depending on other factors: *a conditional offer.* **2** (of a clause, phrase, conjunction, or verb form) expressing a condition. ▶ n. the conditional form of a verb, for example *should* in *if I should die.* ■ **con·di·tion·al·ly** adv.

con·di·tion·er /kənˈdisH(ə)nər/ ▶ n. a thing used to improve the condition of something, especially a liquid applied to the hair after shampooing.

con·do /ˈkändō/ ▶ n. (pl. **condos**) informal short for CONDOMINIUM (sense 1).

con·dole /kənˈdōl/ ▶ v. (**condole with**) express sympathy for someone.

con·do·lence /kənˈdōləns/ ▶ n. an expression of sympathy for someone, especially when a relative or close friend has died.

con·dom /ˈkändəm, ˈkən-/ ▶ n. a thin rubber sheath worn on the penis during sex as a contraceptive or to protect against infection.

con·do·min·i·um /ˌkändəˈminēəm/ ▶ n. (pl. **condominiums**) **1** a building or complex containing a number of individually owned apartments or houses. **2** an apartment or house in a condominium. **3** the joint control of a country's affairs by other countries.

con·done /kənˈdōn/ ▶ v. overlook or forgive an offense or wrongdoing.

con·dor /ˈkänˌdôr, -dər/ ▶ n. a very large South American vulture with a bare head and mainly black plumage.

con·duce /kənˈd(y)o͞os/ ▶ v. (**conduce to**) formal help to bring something about.

con·du·cive /kənˈd(y)o͞osiv/ ▶ adj. (**conducive to**) contributing to or helping to bring something about: *an environment that is conducive to learning.*

con·duct ▶ n. /ˈkänˌdəkt/ **1** the way in which a person behaves. **2** management or direction: *the conduct of foreign affairs.* ▶ v. /kənˈdəkt/ **1** organize and carry something out. **2** direct the performance of a piece of music or an orchestra or choir. **3** guide someone to or around a place. **4** (**conduct oneself**) behave in a particular way. **5** transmit heat, electricity, etc., by conduction.

con·duct·ance /kənˈdəktəns/ ▶ n. the degree to which a material conducts electricity.

con·duc·tion /kənˈdəksHən/ ▶ n. the transmission of heat or electricity directly through a substance. ■ **con·duc·tive** /kənˈdəktiv/ adj.

con·duc·tiv·i·ty /ˌkänˌdəkˈtivitē, kən-/ ▶ n. the degree to which a particular material conducts electricity or heat.

con·duc·tor /kənˈdəktər/ ▶ n. **1** a person who conducts an orchestra or choir. **2** a material or device that conducts heat or electricity. **3** a person who sells tickets and collects fares on a train, streetcar, or other public conveyance. ■ **con·duc·tress** /kənˈdəktrəs/ n.

con·duit /ˈkänˌd(y)o͞oət, ˈkänd(w)ət/ ▶ n. **1** a channel for carrying water or other fluid from one place to another. **2** a tube or trough protecting electric wiring.

cone /kōn/ ▶ n. **1** an object that tapers from a circular base to a point. **2** (also **traffic cone**) a plastic cone used to separate off sections of a road. **3** the cone-shaped dry fruit of a conifer. **4** a cone-shaped wafer for holding ice cream. **5** one of two types of light-sensitive cell in the retina of the eye, responsible for sharpness of vision and color perception. Compare with ROD.

co·ney /ˈkōnē/ (also **cony**) ▶ n. (pl. **coneys**) a rabbit.

con·fab /ˈkänˌfab, kənˈfab/ ▶ n. informal an informal conversation or discussion.

con·fab·u·late /kənˈfabyəˌlāt/ ▶ v. formal have a conversation. ■ **con·fab·u·la·tion** /-ˌfabyəˈlāsHən/ n.

con·fect /kənˈfekt/ ▸ v. formal make something by putting together various elements.

con·fec·tion /kənˈfeksʜən/ ▸ n. 1 an elaborate sweet dish. 2 an elaborately constructed thing: *an extravagant confection of marble and gilt.*

con·fec·tion·er /kənˈfeksʜənər/ ▸ n. a person who makes or sells candy and other sweets.

con·fec·tion·ers' sug·ar (also **confectioner's sugar**) ▸ n. finely powdered sugar used to make icing.

con·fec·tion·er·y /kənˈfeksʜəˌnerē/ ▸ n. candy and other sweets.

con·fed·er·a·cy /kənˈfedərəsē/ ▸ n. (pl. **confederacies**) 1 a league or alliance, especially of confederate states. 2 (**the Confederacy**) the Confederate States of America.

con·fed·er·ate ▸ adj. /kənˈfedərət/ 1 joined by an agreement or treaty. 2 (**Confederate**) referring to the southern states that separated from the US in 1860–1861. ▸ n. /kənˈfedərət/ an accomplice or fellow worker. ▸ v. /-ˌrāt/ (usu. as adj. **confederated**) bring states or groups of people into an alliance.

con·fed·er·a·tion /kənˌfedəˈrāsʜən/ ▸ n. 1 an alliance of a number of parties or groups. 2 a union of states with some political power belonging to a central authority.

con·fer /kənˈfər/ ▸ v. (**confers, conferring, conferred**) 1 grant a title, award, benefit, or right to someone: *an honorary degree was conferred on her.* 2 have discussions. ■ **con·fer·ment** n. **con·fer·ral** /-ˈfərəl/ n.

con·fer·ee /ˌkänfəˈrē/ ▸ n. a person who attends a conference.

con·fer·ence /ˈkänf(ə)rəns/ ▸ n. a formal meeting for discussion or debate.

con·fess /kənˈfes/ ▸ v. 1 admit to a crime or wrongdoing. 2 acknowledge something reluctantly. 3 declare one's sins formally to a priest.

con·fes·sion /kənˈfesʜən/ ▸ n. 1 an act of confessing, especially a formal statement admitting to a crime. 2 an account of one's sins given privately to a priest. 3 (also **confession of faith**) a statement setting out essential religious beliefs.

con·fes·sion·al /kənˈfesʜənl/ ▸ n. 1 an enclosed stall in a church, in which a priest sits to hear confessions. 2 a confession. ▸ adj. 1 referring to speech or writing in which a person admits to private thoughts or incidents in their past. 2 relating to religious confession.

con·fes·sor /kənˈfesər/ ▸ n. 1 a priest who hears confessions. 2 a person who makes a confession.

con·fet·ti /kənˈfetē/ ▸ n. small pieces of colored paper traditionally thrown over a bride and groom after a marriage ceremony.

con·fi·dant /ˈkänfəˌdant, -ˌdänt/ ▸ n. (fem. **confidante** pronunc. same) a person in whom one confides.

con·fide /kənˈfīd/ ▸ v. 1 tell someone about a secret or private matter in confidence: *he decided to confide in Elizabeth.* 2 (**confide something to**) dated entrust something to the care of someone.

con·fi·dence /ˈkänfədəns, -fəˌdens/ ▸ n. 1 the belief that one can have faith in or rely on someone or something. 2 self-assurance resulting from a belief in one's own ability to achieve things. 3 a feeling of trust that someone will not reveal private information to others:

things I had told her in confidence. 4 a private matter told to someone under the understanding that they will keep it secret.
– PHRASES **in someone's confidence** in a position of trust with someone.

con·fi·dence game ▸ n. an act of cheating someone by gaining their trust.

con·fi·dent /ˈkänfədənt, -fəˌdent/ ▸ adj. 1 feeling confidence in oneself. 2 feeling certainty about something. ■ **con·fi·dent·ly** adv.

con·fi·den·tial /ˌkänfəˈdencʜəl/ ▸ adj. 1 intended to be kept secret: *confidential information.* 2 entrusted with private information: *a confidential secretary.* ■ **con·fi·den·ti·al·i·ty** /-ˌdencʜēˈalitē/ n. **con·fi·den·tial·ly** adv.

con·fig·u·ra·tion /kənˌfig(y)əˈrāsʜən/ ▸ n. an arrangement of the parts of something in a particular way.

con·fig·ure /kənˈfigyər/ ▸ v. 1 arrange something in a particular way. 2 arrange a computer system so that it is able to perform a particular task. ■ **con·fig·ur·a·ble** adj.

con·fine ▸ v. /kənˈfīn/ 1 (**confine someone/thing to**) keep someone or something within certain limits of space, scope, or time. 2 (**be confined to**) be unable to leave one's bed, home, etc., due to illness or disability. 3 (**be confined**) dated (of a woman) remain in bed for a period before, during, and after giving birth. ▸ n. /ˈkänˌfīn/ (**confines** /ˈkänˌfīnz/) limits or boundaries.

con·fined /kənˈfīnd/ ▸ adj. (of a space) small and enclosed.

con·fine·ment /kənˈfīnmənt/ ▸ n. 1 the state of being confined. 2 dated the time at which a woman gives birth.

con·firm /kənˈfərm/ ▸ v. 1 state or show that something is true or correct: *the Stock Exchange confirmed that it was investigating the rumors.* 2 make something definite or formally valid: *hotels usually require a deposit to confirm a booking.* 3 (**confirm someone in**) make someone feel or believe something more strongly: *the experience confirmed her in her decision not to employ a nanny.* 4 administer the religious ceremony of confirmation to someone. ■ **con·firm·a·to·ry** /-məˌtôrē/ adj.

con·fir·ma·tion /ˌkänfərˈmāsʜən/ ▸ n. 1 the action of confirming something. 2 the religious rite at which a baptized person is admitted as a full member of the Christian Church. 3 the Jewish ceremony of bar mitzvah.

con·firmed /kənˈfərmd/ ▸ adj. firmly established in a habit, belief, or way of life: *a confirmed bachelor.*

con·fis·cate /ˈkänfəˌskāt/ ▸ v. take or seize property with authority. ■ **con·fis·ca·tion** /ˌkänfəˈskāsʜən/ n.

con·fit /kônˈfē/ ▸ n. duck or other meat cooked very slowly in its own fat.

con·fla·gra·tion /ˌkänfləˈgrāsʜən/ ▸ n. a large and destructive fire.

con·flate /kənˈflāt/ ▸ v. combine two or more things into one. ■ **con·fla·tion** /ˈflāsʜən/ n.

con·flict ▸ n. /ˈkänˌflikt/ 1 a serious disagreement or argument. 2 a long-lasting armed struggle. 3 a lack of agreement between opinions, principles, etc.: *a conflict of interests.* ▸ v. /kənˈflikt, ˈkänˌflikt/ be different or in opposition: *his theory conflicted with those generally accepted at the time.*

con·flu·ence /'kän,flōōəns, kən'flōōəns/ ▶ n. **1** a place where two rivers join. **2** an act or the process of two or more things merging.

con·form /kən'fôrm/ ▶ v. **1** obey or follow rules, standards, or conventions: *the kitchen does not conform to hygiene regulations.* **2** be similar in form or type: *families that do not conform to the conventional stereotype.*

con·form·ance /kən'fôrməns/ ▶ n. another term for CONFORMITY.

con·for·ma·tion /,känfôr'māshən, -fər-/ ▶ n. the shape or structure of something.

con·form·ist /kən'fôrmist/ ▶ n. a person who behaves or thinks in the same way as most other people, rather than in an original or unconventional way. ▶ adj. conventional. ■ **con·form·ism** /-,mizəm/ n.

con·form·i·ty /kən'fôrmitē/ ▶ n. **1** the fact of following or obeying conventions, rules, or laws. **2** similarity in form or type.

con·found /kən'found/ ▶ v. **1** surprise or confuse someone. **2** prove a theory or expectation wrong. **3** defeat a plan, aim, or hope.

con·found·ed /kən'foundəd, kän-/ ▶ adj. informal, dated used to express annoyance. ■ **con·found·ed·ly** adv.

con·fra·ter·ni·ty /,känfrə'tərnitē/ ▶ n. (pl. **confraternities**) a brotherhood, especially with a religious or charitable purpose.

con·frère /'kän,frer, kän'frer, kôn'frer/ ▶ n. a fellow member of a profession.

con·front /kən'frənt/ ▶ v. **1** come face to face with someone in a hostile or defiant way: *he was confronted by a police officer.* **2** (of a problem) present itself to someone: *the government was confronted with many difficulties.* **3** face up to and deal with a problem. **4** force someone to face or consider something: *she confronted him with her suspicions.*

con·fron·ta·tion /,känfrən'tāshən/ ▶ n. a situation of angry disagreement or opposition. ■ **con·fron·ta·tion·al** adj.

Con·fu·cian /kən'fyōōshən/ ▶ adj. relating to the Chinese philosopher Confucius (551–479 BC) or his philosophy. ▶ n. a follower of Confucius or his philosophy. ■ **Con·fu·cian·ism** /kən'fyōōshə,nizəm/ n. **Con·fu·cian·ist** n. & adj.

con·fuse /kən'fyōōz/ ▶ v. **1** make someone unable to think clearly or understand something. **2** make something less easy to understand. **3** mistake one person or thing for another. ■ **con·fus·a·ble** adj.

con·fused /kən'fyōōzd/ ▶ adj. **1** unable to think clearly or understand something. **2** lacking order and so difficult to understand or make sense of. ■ **con·fus·ed·ly** /-'fyōōzədlē/ adv.

con·fu·sion /kən'fyōōzhən/ ▶ n. **1** the state of being confused; uncertainty or lack of understanding. **2** a situation of panic or disorder. **3** the mistaking of one person or thing for another.

con·fute /kən'fyōōt/ ▶ v. formal prove a person or an accusation or assertion to be wrong. ■ **con·fu·ta·tion** /,känfyōō'tāshən/ n.

con·ga /'känggə/ ▶ n. **1** a Latin American dance performed by people in single file and consisting of three steps forward followed by a kick. **2** (also **conga drum**) a tall, narrow drum beaten with the hands.

con·geal /kən'jēl/ ▶ v. (of a liquid substance) become semisolid, especially by cooling.

con·ge·ner /kən'jēnər/ ▶ n. a chemical constituent, especially one that gives a distinctive character to a wine or liquor or is responsible for some of its effects on the body.

con·gen·ial /kən'jēnyəl/ ▶ adj. **1** (of a person) pleasant to be with because their qualities or interests are similar to one's own: *congenial company.* **2** pleasant because suited to one's taste or character: *congenial working conditions.* ■ **con·ge·ni·al·i·ty** /-,jēnē'alitē/ n. **con·gen·ial·ly** adv.

con·gen·i·tal /kən'jenətl/ ▶ adj. **1** (of a disease or abnormality) present from birth. **2** having a particular trait as an apparently permanent part of one's character: *a congenital liar.* ■ **con·gen·i·tal·ly** adv.

con·ger /'känggər/ (also **conger eel**) ▶ n. a large eel of coastal waters.

con·ge·ries /'känjərēz/ ▶ n. (pl. same) a disorderly collection.

con·gest·ed /kən'jestid/ ▶ adj. **1** so crowded as to make movement difficult or impossible. **2** abnormally full of blood. **3** blocked with mucus.

con·ges·tion /kən'jeschən/ ▶ n. the state of being congested: *the new bridge should ease congestion in the area.*

con·ges·tive /kən'jestiv/ ▶ adj. Medicine involving or occurring as a result of a part of the body becoming abnormally full of blood.

con·glom·er·ate ▶ n. /kən'glämərət/ **1** something consisting of a number of different and distinct things. **2** a large corporation formed by the merging of separate firms. **3** a type of sedimentary rock consisting of rounded fragments cemented together. ▶ v. /-,rāt/ gather into or form a conglomerate. ■ **con·glom·er·a·tion** /kən,glämə'rāshən/ n.

Con·go·lese /,känggə'lēz, -'lēs/ ▶ n. (pl. same) **1** a person from the Congo or the Democratic Republic of Congo (formerly Zaire). **2** any of the languages spoken in the Congo region. ▶ adj. relating to the Congo or the Democratic Republic of Congo.

con·grat·u·late /kən'grachə,lāt, -'grajə-/ ▶ v. **1** express good wishes or praise at the happiness or success of someone. **2** (**congratulate oneself**) think oneself lucky or clever. ■ **con·grat·u·la·to·ry** /-lə,tôrē/ adj.

con·grat·u·la·tion /kən,grachə'lāshən, -,grajə-/ ▶ n. **1** (**congratulations**) praise or good wishes on a special occasion. **2** the action of congratulating someone.

con·gre·gant /'känggrəgənt/ ▶ n. a member of a congregation.

con·gre·gate /'känggrə,gāt/ ▶ v. gather into a crowd or mass.

con·gre·ga·tion /,känggrə'gāshən/ ▶ n. **1** a group of people gathered together for religious worship. **2** a gathering of people or things. ■ **con·gre·ga·tion·al** adj.

Con·gre·ga·tion·al·ism /,känggrə'gāshənl,izəm/ ▶ n. a system of organization among Christian churches in which individual churches are largely self-governing. ■ **Con·gre·ga·tion·al** adj. **Con·gre·ga·tion·al·ist** n. & adj.

con·gress /'känggrəs, ,kän-/ ▶ n. **1** a formal meeting or series of meetings between delegates. **2** (**Congress**) the national lawmaking body of the US. **3** formal the action of coming together. ■ **con·gres·sion·al** /kən'greshənl/ adj.

con·gress·man /'kaNGgrəsmən, 'kän-/ (or **congresswoman** /'käNGgrəs,wŏŏmən, 'kän-/) ▶ n. (pl. **congressmen** or **congresswomen**) a member of the US Congress.

con·gru·ent /kən'grōōənt, 'käNGgrōōənt/ ▶ adj. 1 in agreement or harmony. 2 Geometry (of figures) identical in form. ■ **con·gru·ence** n.

con·gru·ous /'käNGgrōōəs/ ▶ adj. in agreement or harmony. ■ **con·gru·i·ty** /kən'grōōitē/ n.

con·i·cal /'känikəl/ ▶ adj. shaped like a cone.

con·ic sec·tion /'känik/ ▶ n. the figure of a circle, ellipse, parabola, or hyperbola formed by the intersection of a plane and a circular cone.

co·ni·fer /'känəfər, kō-/ ▶ n. a tree bearing cones and evergreen needlelike or scalelike leaves, e.g., a pine or cypress. ■ **co·nif·er·ous** /kə'nifərəs/ adj.

con·jec·ture /kən'jekCHər/ ▶ n. an opinion or conclusion based on incomplete information; a guess. ▶ v. form a conjecture; guess. ■ **con·jec·tur·al** /kən'jekCHərəl/ adj.

con·join /kən'join, kän-/ ▶ v. formal join; combine.

con·joined twins ▶ pl.n. technical term for SIAMESE TWINS.

con·joint /kən'joint, kän-/ ▶ adj. formal combined or united.

con·ju·gal /'känjəgəl/ ▶ adj. relating to marriage or the relationship between husband and wife.

con·ju·gate /'känjə,gāt/ ▶ v. give the different forms of a verb. ■ **con·ju·ga·tion** /,känjə'gāsHən/ n.

con·junct ▶ adj. /kən'jəNGkt, kän-/ joined together, combined, or associated. ▶ n. /'känjəNGkt/ each of two or more things that are joined or associated.

con·junc·tion /kən'jəNGksHən/ ▶ n. 1 a word used to connect words or clauses (e.g., *and*, *if*). 2 an instance of two or more events occurring at the same point in time or space. 3 Astronomy & Astrology an alignment of two planets so that they appear to be in the same place in the sky. – PHRASES **in conjunction** together.

con·junc·ti·va /,känjəNG(k)'tīvə, kən-/ ▶ n. (pl. **conjunctivae**) the mucous membrane that covers the front of the eye and lines the inside of the eyelids.

con·junc·tive /kən'jəNG(k)tiv/ ▶ adj. relating to or forming a conjunction.

con·junc·ti·vi·tis /kən,jəNG(k)tə'vītis/ ▶ n. inflammation of the conjunctiva.

con·junc·ture /kən'jəNGkCHər/ ▶ n. 1 a combination of events. 2 a state of affairs.

con·jure /'känjər, 'kən-/ ▶ v. (usu. **conjure something up**) 1 cause a spirit or ghost to appear by magic. 2 cause something to appear as if by magic. 3 create an image of something in the mind: *the books conjure up nostalgic memories of Christmases past.*

con·jur·ing /'känjəriNG, 'kən-/ ▶ n. a form of entertainment involving apparently magical tricks, typically ones that seem to make objects appear or disappear.

con·ju·ror /'känjərər, 'kən-/ (also **conjurer**) ▶ n. a person who performs conjuring tricks.

conk[1] /käNGk, kôNGk/ ▶ v. (**conk out**) informal 1 (of a machine) break down. 2 faint or go to sleep. 3 die.

conk[2] ▶ v. informal hit someone on the head.

con man ▶ n. informal a man who cheats people by using a confidence game.

conn /kän/ (also **con**) ▶ v. direct the steering of a ship.

con·nect /kə'nekt/ ▶ v. 1 bring together so as to establish a link. 2 join together so as to provide access and communication: *the buildings were connected by underground passages.* 3 (**be connected**) be related in some way: *bonuses are connected to the firm's performance.* 4 (of a train, bus, etc.) arrive at its destination just before another leaves so that passengers can transfer. ■ **con·nect·or** n.

con·nect·ing rod ▶ n. the rod connecting the piston and the crankshaft in an engine.

con·nec·tion /kə'neksHən/ ▶ n. 1 a link or relationship. 2 (**connections**) influential people with whom one has contact or to whom one is related. 3 an opportunity for catching a connecting train, bus, etc. – PHRASES **in connection with** concerning.

con·nec·tive /kə'nektiv/ ▶ adj. connecting one thing to another.

con·nec·tive tis·sue ▶ n. body tissue that connects, supports, binds, or separates other tissues or organs.

con·nec·tiv·i·ty /,kə,nek'tivitē/ ▶ n. 1 the state or extent of being connected. 2 Computing capacity for the interconnection of systems, applications, etc.

conn·ing tow·er ▶ n. a raised structure on a submarine, containing the periscope.

con·nive /kə'nīv/ ▶ v. 1 (**connive at/in**) secretly allow a wrongdoing. 2 (often **connive with**) conspire. ■ **con·niv·ance** /kə'nīvəns/ n.

con·nois·seur /,känə'sər, -'sŏŏr/ ▶ n. an expert in matters involving the judgment of beauty, quality, or skill: *a connoisseur of Renaissance art.*

con·no·ta·tion /,känə'tāsHən/ ▶ n. an idea or feeling suggested by a word in addition to its main or literal meaning.

con·note /kə'nōt/ ▶ v. (of a word or phrase) imply or suggest something in addition to its main or literal meaning (e.g., the word *mother* connotes qualities such as protection and affection).

con·nu·bi·al /kə'n(y)ōōbēəl/ ▶ adj. literary relating to marriage; conjugal.

con·quer /'käNGkər/ ▶ v. 1 overcome and take control of a territory or its people by military force. 2 successfully overcome a problem or climb a mountain. ■ **con·quer·or** n.

con·quest /'kän,kwest, 'käNG-/ ▶ n. 1 the action of conquering a territory or its people. 2 a conquered territory. 3 a person whose affection or favor has been won.

con·quis·ta·dor /kôNG'kēstə,dôr, kän'k(w)istə-, kən-/ ▶ n. (pl. **conquistadores** /-,kēstə'dôrēz, -äs, -,k(w)istə-/ or **conquistadors**) a Spanish conqueror of Mexico or Peru in the 16th century.

con·san·guin·i·ty /,kän,saNG'gwinitē/ ▶ n. formal descent from the same ancestor. ■ **con·san·guin·e·ous** /,kän,saNG'gwinēəs/ adj.

con·science /'känCHəns/ ▶ n. a person's moral sense of right and wrong, chiefly as it affects their own behavior. – PHRASES **in (good) conscience** by all that is fair.

con·sci·en·tious /,känCHē'enCHəs/ ▶ adj. 1 diligent and thorough in carrying out one's work or duty. 2 relating to a person's conscience. ■ **con·sci·en·tious·ly** adv. **con·sci·en·tious·ness** n.

con·sci·en·tious ob·jec·tor ▶ n. a person who refuses to serve in the armed forces for moral reasons.

con·scious /'känCHəs/ ▶ adj. 1 aware of and responding to one's surroundings. 2 (usu.

conscious of) aware of something: *I was very conscious of his disappointment.* **3** deliberate: *a conscious effort.* ■ **con·scious·ly** adv.

con·scious·ness /'känCHəsnəs/ ▶ n. **1** the state of being conscious. **2** one's awareness or perception of something.

con·script ▶ v. /kən'skript/ call someone up for compulsory military service. ▶ n. /'kän,skript/ a conscripted person. ■ **con·scrip·tion** /kən'skripSHən/ n.

con·se·crate /'känsi,krāt/ ▶ v. **1** make or declare something to be holy or sacred. **2** ordain someone to a sacred office, typically that of bishop. **3** (in Christian belief) declare that bread or wine represents or is the body and blood of Jesus. ■ **con·se·cra·tion** /,känsi'krāSHən/ n.

con·sec·u·tive /kən'sekyətiv/ ▶ adj. following in unbroken sequence.

con·sen·su·al /kən'senCHŌŌəl/ ▶ adj. relating to or involving consent or consensus.

con·sen·sus /kən'sensəs/ ▶ n. general agreement about something.

con·sent /kən'sent/ ▶ n. permission or agreement. ▶ v. **1** give permission for something. **2** agree to do something.

con·sent·ing a·dult ▶ n. an adult who willingly agrees to engage in a sexual act.

con·se·quence /'känsikwəns, -,kwens/ ▶ n. **1** a result or effect, especially one that is unpleasant. **2** importance or relevance: *the past is of no consequence.* **3** dated social distinction.

con·se·quent /'känsikwənt, -,kwent/ ▶ adj. following as a result or effect of something. ■ **con·se·quen·tial** /,känsə'kwenCHəl/ adj. **con·se·quent·ly** adv.

con·serv·an·cy /kən'sərvənsē/ ▶ n. (pl. **conservancies**) **1** an organization concerned with the preservation of natural resources. **2** the conservation of wildlife and the environment.

con·ser·va·tion /,känsər'vāSHən/ ▶ n. **1** preservation or restoration of the natural environment and wildlife. **2** preservation and repair of archaeological, historical, and cultural sites and objects. **3** careful use of a resource: *energy conservation.* **4** Physics the principle by which the total value of a quantity (e.g., mass or energy) remains constant in a closed system. ■ **con·ser·va·tion·ist** n.

con·serv·a·tive /kən'sərvətiv/ ▶ adj. **1** opposed to change and holding traditional values. **2** (in politics) favoring free enterprise and private ownership. **3** (**Conservative**) relating to the Conservative Party of Great Britain. **4** (of an estimate) deliberately low or high for the sake of caution. ▶ n. **1** a conservative person. **2** (**Conservative**) a supporter or member of the Conservative Party. ■ **con·serv·a·tism** /kən'sərvə,tizəm/ n. **con·serv·a·tive·ly** adv.

Con·serv·a·tive Par·ty ▶ n. a major British right-wing political party that favors free enterprise and private ownership.

con·ser·va·toire /kən'sərvə,twär/ ▶ n. a college for the study of classical music.

con·ser·va·tor /kən'sərvətər, -,tôr, 'känsər,vātər/ ▶ n. a person involved in conservation.

con·serv·a·to·ry /kən'sərvə,tôrē/ ▶ n. (pl. **conservatories**) **1** a room with a glass roof and walls, attached to a house and used as a sunroom or greenhouse. **2** a conservatoire.

con·serve /kən'sərv/ ▶ v. **1** protect something from harm or waste. **2** Physics maintain a quantity

at a constant overall total. ▶ n. /'kän,sərv/ jam or marmalade.

con·sid·er /kən'sidər/ ▶ v. **1** think carefully about something. **2** believe or think: *people considered to be at risk of contracting the disease.* **3** take something into account when making a judgment: *his record is even more remarkable when you consider his age.* **4** look attentively at someone or something.

con·sid·er·a·ble /kən'sidər(ə)bəl, -'sidrəbəl/ ▶ adj. great in size, amount, or importance. ■ **con·sid·er·a·bly** adv.

con·sid·er·ate /kən'sidərət/ ▶ adj. careful not to harm or inconvenience others. ■ **con·sid·er·ate·ly** adv.

con·sid·er·a·tion /kən,sidə'rāSHən/ ▶ n. **1** careful thought. **2** a fact taken into account when making a decision. **3** thoughtfulness toward others. **4** a payment or reward. – PHRASES **take something into consideration** think about something when making a decision or forming an opinion.

con·sid·er·ing /kən'sidəriNG/ ▶ prep. & conj. taking something into consideration. ▶ adv. informal taking everything into account.

con·sign /kən'sīn/ ▶ v. **1** (**consign someone/ thing to**) put someone or something in a place so as to be rid of them. **2** deliver someone or something to someone's possession or care.

con·sign·ment /kən'sīnmənt/ ▶ n. a batch of goods delivered or sent somewhere.

con·sist /kən'sist/ ▶ v. **1** (**consist of**) be composed of. **2** (**consist in**) have as an essential feature: *poetry consists in the use of emotive language.*

con·sist·en·cy /kən'sistənsē/ (also **consistence**) ▶ n. (pl. **consistencies**) **1** the state of being consistent. **2** the degree of thickness of a substance.

con·sist·ent /kən'sistənt/ ▶ adj. **1** always acting or done in the same way. **2** unchanging over a period of time: *consistent growth in the manufacturing sector of the economy.* **3** in agreement with something: *the results are consistent with other research.* ■ **con·sist·ent·ly** adv.

con·sis·to·ry /kən'sistərē/ ▶ n. (pl. **consistories**) **1** (in the Roman Catholic Church) the council of cardinals, with or without the Pope. **2** (also **consistory court**) (in the Church of England) a court presided over by a bishop, for the administration of ecclesiastical law in a diocese.

con·so·la·tion /,känsə'lāSHən/ ▶ n. **1** comfort received after a loss or disappointment. **2** a person or thing providing such comfort. ■ **con·sol·a·to·ry** /kən'sōlə,tôrē/ adj.

con·so·la·tion prize ▶ n. a prize given to a competitor who narrowly fails to win.

con·sole¹ /kən'sōl/ ▶ v. comfort someone in a time of grief or disappointment.

con·sole² /'kän,sōl/ ▶ n. **1** a panel or unit containing a set of controls. **2** a cabinet for television or radio equipment. **3** (also **games console**) a small machine for playing computerized video games. **4** the cabinet containing the keyboards, stops, etc., of an organ. **5** an ornamental bracket used to support a structure or fixture on a wall.

con·sol·i·date /kən'sälə,dāt/ ▶ v. **1** make something stronger or more stable: *the company consolidated its position in the market.* **2** combine two or more things into a single unit: *arrangements can be made to consolidate your debts.* ■ **con·sol·i·da·tion** /-ˌsälə'dāsHən/ n. **con·sol·i·da·tor** /-ˌdātər/ n.

con·som·mé /ˌkänsə'mā/ ▶n. a clear soup made with concentrated stock.

con·so·nance /'känsənəns/ ▶n. agreement or compatibility.

con·so·nant /'känsənənt/ ▶n. **1** a speech sound in which the breath is at least partly obstructed and which forms a syllable when combined with a vowel. **2** a letter representing such a sound (e.g., *c*, *t*). ▶adj. (**consonant with**) in agreement or harmony with: *the findings are consonant with recent research.* ■ **con·so·nan·tal** /ˌkänsə'nantl/ adj.

con·sort¹ ▶n. /'kän,sôrt/ a wife or husband, especially of a reigning monarch. ▶v. /kən'sôrt, 'kän,sôrt/ (**consort with**) regularly associate with someone.

con·sort² /'kän,sôrt/ ▶n. a small group of musicians performing together, typically playing Renaissance music.

con·sor·ti·um /kən'sôrsH(ē)əm, -'sôrtēəm/ ▶n. (pl. **consortia** /-tēə, -sH(ē)ə/ or **consortiums**) an association of several companies.

con·spec·tus /kən'spektəs/ ▶n. a summary or overview of a subject.

con·spic·u·ous /kən'spikyōōəs/ ▶adj. **1** clearly visible. **2** attracting notice; notable: *his conspicuous bravery.* ■ **con·spic·u·ous·ly** adv.

con·spir·a·cist /kən'spirəsist/ ▶n. a supporter of a conspiracy theory.

con·spir·a·cy /kən'spirəsē/ ▶n. (pl. **conspiracies**) **1** a secret plan by a group to do something unlawful or harmful. **2** the action of conspiring to do something.

con·spir·a·cy the·o·ry ▶n. a belief that some secret but influential organization is responsible for an unexplained event.

con·spire /kən'spīr/ ▶v. **1** jointly make secret plans to commit a wrongful act. **2** (of circumstances) seem to be acting together to bring about an unfortunate result: *the illness and her failing marriage conspired to make her life intolerable.* ■ **con·spir·a·tor** /kən'spirətər/ n. **con·spir·a·to·ri·al** /kən,spirə'tôrēəl/ adj. **con·spir·a·to·ri·al·ly** /kən,spirə'tôrēəlē/ adv.

con·sta·ble /'känstəbəl/ ▶n. **1** a peace officer with limited authority, typically in a small town. **2** Brit. a police officer of the lowest rank.

con·stab·u·lar·y /kən'stabyə,lerē/ ▶n. (pl. **constabularies**) the constables of a district.

con·stant /'känstənt/ ▶adj. **1** occurring continuously: *a constant stream of visitors.* **2** remaining the same: *a constant speed.* **3** faithful and dependable. ▶n. **1** an unchanging situation. **2** Mathematics & Physics a number or quantity that does not change its value. ■ **con·stan·cy** n. **con·stant·ly** adv.

con·stel·la·tion /ˌkänstə'lāsHən/ ▶n. a group of stars forming a recognized pattern and typically named after a mythological or other figure.

con·ster·na·tion /ˌkänstər'nāsHən/ ▶n. a feeling of anxiety or dismay.

con·sti·pat·ed /'känstə,pātid/ ▶adj. suffering from constipation.

con·sti·pa·tion /ˌkänstə'pāsHən/ ▶n. the condition of having difficulty in emptying the bowels.

con·stit·u·en·cy /kən'sticHōōənsē/ ▶n. (pl. **constituencies**) **1** the group of voters in a particular area who elect a representative to a lawmaking body. **2** the area represented in this way.

con·stit·u·ent /kən'sticHōōənt/ ▶adj. **1** being a part of a whole: *the constituent republics of the USSR.* **2** having the power to appoint or elect a representative. **3** able to make or change a political constitution. ▶n. **1** a voter in a constituency. **2** a component part of something: *the essential constituents of the human diet.*

con·sti·tute /'känstə,t(y)ōōt/ ▶v. **1** be a part of a whole: *women constitute more than half the workforce.* **2** be or be equivalent to: *his failure to act constituted a breach of duty.* **3** (**be constituted**) be established by law.

con·sti·tu·tion /ˌkänstə't(y)ōōsHən/ ▶n. **1** a body of principles according to which a country, state, or organization is governed. **2** the composition or formation of something. **3** a person's physical or mental state.

con·sti·tu·tion·al /ˌkänstə't(y)ōōsHənl/ ▶adj. **1** relating to or according to the principles of a constitution. **2** relating to a person's physical or mental state. ▶n. dated a walk taken regularly to maintain good health. ■ **con·sti·tu·tion·al·i·ty** /-,t(y)ōōsHənə'nalitē/ n. **con·sti·tu·tion·al·ly** adv.

con·sti·tu·tive /'känstə,t(y)ōōtiv, kən'sticHətiv/ ▶adj. **1** having the power to establish something. **2** forming a constituent of something.

con·strain /kən'strān/ ▶v. **1** force someone to do something: *he felt constrained to explain.* **2** (as adj. **constrained**) appearing forced or unnatural. **3** severely restrict the scope, extent, or activity of: *most developing countries are constrained by limited resources.*

con·straint /kən'strānt/ ▶n. **1** a limitation or restriction: *tight financial constraints.* **2** strict control of one's behavior or repression of one's feelings.

con·strict /kən'strikt/ ▶v. **1** make or become narrower or tighter: *a drug that constricts the blood vessels.* **2** limit or restrict: *political parties constricted by the need to appeal to public opinion.* ■ **con·stric·tion** n.

con·stric·tor /kən'striktər/ ▶n. **1** a snake that kills by squeezing and choking its prey, such as a boa or python. **2** a muscle whose contraction narrows a vessel or passage in the body.

con·struct ▶v. /kən'strəkt/ **1** build or make something. **2** form something from different elements: *he constructed his own theory of the universe.* ▶n. /'kän,strəkt/ **1** an idea or theory containing various elements. **2** a thing that has been built or made. ■ **con·struc·tor** /kən'strəktər/ n.

con·struc·tion /kən'strəksHən/ ▶n. **1** the action or process of constructing something. **2** a building or other structure. **3** the industry of erecting buildings or other structures. **4** an interpretation or explanation of something. ■ **con·struc·tion·al** adj.

con·struc·tive /kən'strəktiv/ ▶adj. useful and helpful: *constructive suggestions.* ■ **con·struc·tive·ly** adv.

con·strue /kən'strōō/ ▶v. (**construes**, **construing**, **construed**) interpret something in a particular way: *his silence could be construed as an admission of guilt.* ■ **con·stru·al** n.

con·sul /'känsəl/ ▶n. **1** a government official living in a foreign city and protecting the government's citizens and interests there.

2 (in ancient Rome) one of two elected chief magistrates who ruled the republic jointly for a year. ■ **con·su·lar** /'käns(y)ələr/ adj.

con·su·late /'känsələt/ ▶ n. **1** the place where a consul works. **2** (in ancient Rome) the period of office of a consul or the system of government by consuls.

con·sult /kən'səlt/ ▶ v. **1** ask someone for information or advice. **2** discuss something with someone, especially in order to get their approval or permission: *patients are entitled to be consulted about their treatment.* **3** (as adj. **consulting**) acting as a professional adviser to others in the same field. ■ **con·sul·ta·tive** /-'səltətiv/ adj.

con·sult·an·cy /kən'səltnsē/ ▶ n. (pl. **consultancies**) a company giving expert advice in a particular field.

con·sult·ant /kən'səltnt/ ▶ n. a person who provides expert advice professionally.

con·sul·ta·tion /ˌkänsəl'tāsHən/ ▶ n. **1** the process of consulting someone or discussing something. **2** a meeting to discuss something or to get advice or treatment.

con·sume /kən'sōōm/ ▶ v. **1** eat or drink something. **2** use up a resource: *a smaller vehicle that consumes less fuel.* **3** (especially of a fire) completely destroy something. **4** (of a feeling) completely fill the mind of someone: *she was consumed with guilt.* ■ **con·sum·a·ble** /kən'sōōməbəl/ adj. **con·sum·ing** adj.

con·sum·er /kən'sōōmər/ ▶ n. a person who buys a product or service for personal use.

con·sum·er·ism /kən'sōōməˌrizəm/ ▶ n. **1** the preoccupation of society with acquiring goods. **2** the protection of the interests of consumers. ■ **con·sum·er·ist** adj. & n.

con·sum·er price in·dex ▶ n. an index of the variation in prices paid by typical consumers for retail goods and other items.

con·sum·mate ▶ v. /'känsəˌmāt/ **1** make a marriage or relationship complete by having sex. **2** complete a transaction. ▶ adj. /'känsəmət, kən'səmət/ showing great skill and flair. ■ **con·sum·mate·ly** /'känsəmətlē, kən'səmətlē/ adv. **con·sum·ma·tion** /ˌkänsə'māsHən/ n.

con·sump·tion /kən'səm(p)sHən/ ▶ n. **1** the action or process of consuming something. **2** an amount of something that is consumed: *she had managed to reduce her alcohol consumption.* **3** dated a wasting disease, especially tuberculosis. ■ **con·sump·tive** /kən'səm(p)tiv/ adj. & n. (dated).

cont. ▶ abbr. **1** continued. **2** contents.

con·tact ▶ n. /'kän,takt/ **1** the state of touching something. **2** the state of communicating or meeting: *she had lost contact with her son.* **3** a relationship or communication established with someone: *we have good contacts with the local community.* **4** a person who may be asked for information or help. **5** a person who has associated with a patient suffering from a contagious disease. **6** a connection for the passage of an electric current from one thing to another. ▶ v. /'kän,takt, kən'takt/ get in touch or communication with someone. ▶ adj. /'kän,takt/ caused by or operating through physical touch: *contact dermatitis.* ■ **con·tact·a·ble** /'kän,taktəbəl, kən'tak-/ adj.

con·tact lens ▶ n. a thin plastic lens placed directly on the surface of the eye to correct visual defects.

con·tact sport ▶ n. a sport in which bodily contact between the participants is a necessary feature.

con·ta·gion /kən'tājən/ ▶ n. the passing of disease from one person to another by close contact.

con·ta·gious /kən'tājəs/ ▶ adj. **1** (of a disease) spread by direct or indirect contact between people or organisms. **2** having a contagious disease. **3** (of an emotion, attitude, etc.) likely to spread to and affect others: *her enthusiasm is contagious.*

con·tain /kən'tān/ ▶ v. **1** have or hold within: *a wallet containing cash and credit cards.* **2** control or restrain oneself or a feeling. **3** prevent a problem from becoming worse. ■ **con·tain·a·ble** adj.

con·tain·er /kən'tānər/ ▶ n. **1** a box, cylinder, or similar object for holding something. **2** a large metal box for the transport of goods by road, rail, sea, or air.

con·tain·er·ize /kən'tānəˌrīz/ ▶ v. pack cargo into containers or transport it in containers. ■ **con·tain·er·i·za·tion** /-ˌtānərə'zāsHən/ n.

con·tain·ment /kən'tānmənt/ ▶ n. the action of keeping something harmful under control.

con·tam·i·nate /kən'taməˌnāt/ ▶ v. pollute something by exposing it to or adding a substance that is poisonous or carries disease. ■ **con·tam·i·nant** /-'tamənənt/ n. **con·tam·i·na·tion** /-ˌtamə'nāsHən/ n.

con·tem·plate /'käntəmˌplāt/ ▶ v. **1** look at someone or something thoughtfully. **2** think about: *the idea was too awful to contemplate.* **3** think deeply and at length.

con·tem·pla·tion /ˌkäntəm'plāsHən/ ▶ n. **1** the process of contemplating something. **2** religious meditation.

con·tem·pla·tive /kən'templətiv/ ▶ adj. showing or involving contemplation: *a contemplative mood.* ▶ n. a person whose life is devoted to prayer, especially in a monastery or convent.

con·tem·po·ra·ne·ous /kənˌtempə'rānēəs/ ▶ adj. existing at or occurring in the same period of time. ■ **con·tem·po·ra·ne·i·ty** /-rə'nēitē, -rə'nāitē/ n.

con·tem·po·rar·y /kən'tempəˌrerē/ ▶ adj. **1** living, occurring, or originating in the same time: *Greek literature contemporary with the New Testament.* **2** belonging to or occurring in the present. **3** modern in style or design. ▶ n. (pl. **contemporaries**) **1** a person or thing existing at the same time as another. **2** a person of roughly the same age as another.

con·tempt /kən'tem(p)t/ ▶ n. **1** the feeling that a person or a thing is worthless or deserves no respect at all. **2** (also **contempt of court**) the offense of being disobedient to or disrespectful of a court of law.
– PHRASES **beneath contempt** utterly worthless. **hold someone/thing in contempt** despise someone or something.

con·tempt·i·ble /kən'tem(p)təbəl/ ▶ adj. deserving to be hated or despised: *a display of contemptible cowardice.* ■ **con·tempt·i·bly** adv.

con·temp·tu·ous /kən'tem(p)CHōōəs/ ▶ adj. showing or feeling a lack of respect for someone or something. ■ **con·temp·tu·ous·ly** adv.

con·tend /kən'tend/ ▶ v. **1** (**contend with/against**) struggle to deal with a difficulty: *they may have to contend with racism and* *discrimination.* **2** (**contend for**) struggle or campaign to achieve something. **3** put forward a position in an argument: *he contends that the judge was wrong.* ■ **con·tend·er** n.

con·tent¹ /kən'tent/ ▶ adj. happy and satisfied. ▶ v. **1** satisfy or please someone. **2** (**content oneself with**) accept something as adequate despite wanting something more or better. ▶ n. a state of happiness or satisfaction. ■ **con·tent·ment** n.
– PHRASES **to one's heart's content** as much as one wants.

con·tent² /'kän,tent/ ▶ n. **1** (**contents**) the things that are contained in something. **2** the amount of a particular thing occurring in a substance: *soy milk has a low fat content.* **3** (**contents** or **table of contents**) a list of chapters or sections at the front of a book or periodical. **4** the material dealt with in a speech or text as distinct from its form or style.

con·tent·ed /kən'tentəd/ ▶ adj. happy and satisfied. ■ **con·tent·ed·ly** adv.

con·ten·tion /kən'tenCHən/ ▶ n. **1** heated disagreement between people. **2** a point of view expressed or asserted.
– PHRASES **in** (or **out of**) **contention** having (or not having) a good chance of success in a contest.

con·ten·tious /kən'tenCHəs/ ▶ adj. **1** causing or likely to cause disagreement or controversy. **2** tending to provoke arguments.

con·tent pro·vid·er ▶ n. a person or organization who supplies information for use on a website.

con·test ▶ n. /'kän,test/ **1** an event in which people compete to try to win something. **2** a struggle to win power or control: *the Republican leadership contest.* ▶ v. /kən'test, 'kän,test/ **1** take part in a competition, election, or struggle for a position of power: *one of the first women to contest a parliamentary seat.* **2** challenge or dispute: *he intended to contest his father's will.* ■ **con·test·a·ble** /kən'testəbəl/ adj.
– PHRASES **no contest 1** another term for NOLO CONTENDERE: *he pleaded no contest to two misdemeanor counts.* **2** a competition, comparison, or choice whose outcome is a foregone conclusion.

con·test·ant /kən'testənt/ ▶ n. a person who takes part in a contest.

con·text /'kän,tekst/ ▶ n. **1** the circumstances that form the setting for an event, statement, or idea. **2** the parts that immediately precede and follow a word or passage and make its meaning clear. ■ **con·tex·tu·al** /kən'teksCHōōəl/ adj. **con·tex·tu·al·ly** adv.

con·tex·tu·al·ize /kən'teksCHōōə,līz/ ▶ v. consider something together with the surrounding words or circumstances.

con·tig·u·ous /kən'tigyōōəs/ ▶ adj. **1** sharing a border. **2** next or together in sequence. ■ **con·ti·gu·i·ty** /,käntə'gyōōitē/ n.

con·ti·nent¹ /'käntn-ənt, 'käntnənt/ ▶ n. **1** any of the world's main continuous expanses of land (Europe, Asia, Africa, North and South America, Australia, Antarctica). **2** (also **the Continent**) the mainland of Europe as distinct from the British Isles.

con·ti·nent² ▶ adj. **1** able to control the bowels and bladder. **2** self-restrained, especially sexually. ■ **con·ti·nence** n.

con·ti·nen·tal /,käntn'entl/ ▶ adj. **1** forming or belonging to a continent. **2** (also **Continental**) coming from or typical of mainland Europe. ▶ n. (also **Continental**) a person from mainland Europe.

con·ti·nen·tal break·fast ▶ n. a light breakfast of coffee and bread rolls.

con·ti·nen·tal cli·mate ▶ n. a relatively dry climate with very hot summers and very cold winters, characteristic of the central parts of Asia and North America.

con·ti·nen·tal drift ▶ n. the gradual movement of the continents across the earth's surface through geological time.

con·ti·nen·tal shelf ▶ n. an area of seabed around a large landmass where the sea is relatively shallow.

con·tin·gen·cy /kən'tinjənsē/ ▶ n. (pl. **contingencies**) **1** a future event or circumstance that is possible but cannot be predicted with certainty. **2** something done in case of a possible event or circumstance occurring: *supplies were kept as a contingency against a blockade.*

con·tin·gent /kən'tinjənt/ ▶ n. **1** a group of people with a common feature, forming part of a larger group. **2** a body of troops or police sent to join a larger force. ▶ adj. **1** (**contingent on**) dependent on something: *the merger is contingent on government approval.* **2** subject to or happening by chance.

con·tin·u·al /kən'tinyōōəl/ ▶ adj. **1** constantly or frequently occurring. **2** having no interruptions: *a continual process of growth.* ■ **con·tin·u·al·ly** adv.

USAGE
On the distinction between **continual** and **continuous**, see the note at CONTINUOUS.

con·tin·u·ance /kən'tinyōōəns/ ▶ n. formal **1** the state of continuing. **2** the time for which a situation or action lasts.

con·tin·u·a·tion /kən,tinyə'wāSHən/ ▶ n. **1** the action or state of continuing. **2** a part that is attached to and is an extension of something else.

con·tin·ue /kən'tinyōō/ ▶ v. (**continues, continuing, continued**) **1** keep existing or happening without stopping: *the rain continued to pour down.* **2** carry on with: *he returned to America to continue his work.* **3** carry on traveling in the same direction. **4** start again: *the trial continues tomorrow.*

con·ti·nu·i·ty /,käntn'(y)ōōətē/ ▶ n. (pl. **continuities**) **1** the uninterrupted and unchanged existence or operation of something. **2** a logical connection or smooth line of development between things. **3** the maintaining of continuous action and consistent details in the scenes of a movie or broadcast. **4** the linking of broadcast items by a spoken commentary.

con·tin·u·o /kən'tinyə,wō/ ▶ n. (pl. **continuos**) (in baroque music) an accompanying part that includes a bass line and harmonies, typically played on a keyboard instrument.

con·tin·u·ous /kən'tinyōōəs/ ▶ adj. forming an unbroken whole or sequence without interruptions or exceptions. ■ **con·tin·u·ous·ly** adv.

USAGE
Continuous and **continual** can both mean 'without interruption' (*years of continuous/*

continual warfare), but only **continual** can be used to mean 'happening frequently' (*the continual arguments*).

con·tin·u·um /kən'tinyŏŏəm/ ▶ n. (pl. **continua** /-yŏŏə/) a continuous sequence in which the elements next to each other are very similar, but the last and the first are very different.

con·tort /kən'tôrt/ ▶ v. twist or bend something out of its normal shape. ■ **con·tor·tion** /kən'tôrsʜən/ n.

con·tor·tion·ist /kən'tôrsʜənist/ ▶ n. an entertainer who twists and bends their body into strange and unnatural positions.

con·tour /'kän,tŏŏr/ ▶ n. 1 an outline of the shape or form of something. 2 (also **contour line**) a line on a map joining points of equal height. ▶ v. mold something into a particular shape.

con·tour line ▶ n. a line on a map joining points of equal height above or below sea level.

contra- ▶ prefix against; opposite: *contraception*.

con·tra·band /'käntrə,band/ ▶ n. 1 goods that have been imported or exported illegally. 2 trade in smuggled goods.

con·tra·cep·tion /,käntrə'sepsʜən/ ▶ n. the use of contraceptives to prevent pregnancy.

con·tra·cep·tive /,käntrə'septiv/ ▶ n. a device or drug used to prevent a woman becoming pregnant. ▶ adj. 1 preventing pregnancy. 2 relating to contraception.

con·tract ▶ n. /'kän,trakt/ 1 a written or spoken agreement intended to be enforceable by law. 2 informal an arrangement for someone to be killed by a hired assassin. ▶ v. 1 decrease in size, number, or range. 2 (of a muscle) become shorter and tighter in order to move part of the body. 3 catch or develop a disease. 4 enter into a legally binding agreement with someone. 5 (**contract something out**) arrange for work to be done by another organization. 6 become liable to pay a debt. ■ **con·trac·tu·al** /kən'trakcʜŏŏəl/ adj. **con·trac·tu·al·ly** adv.

con·tract bridge /'kän,trakt/ ▶ n. the standard form of the card game bridge, in which only tricks bid and won count toward the game.

con·tract·i·ble /kən'traktəbəl/ ▶ adj. able to be shrunk or capable of contracting.

con·trac·tile /kən'traktəl, -,tīl/ ▶ adj. technical able to contract or produce contraction.

con·trac·tion /kən'traksʜən/ ▶ n. 1 the process of contracting. 2 a shortening of the muscles of the uterus occurring at intervals during childbirth. 3 a shortened form of a word or group of words.

con·trac·tor /'kän,traktər/ ▶ n. a person who undertakes a contract to provide materials or labor for a job.

con·tra·dict /,käntrə'dikt/ ▶ v. deny the truth of a statement made by someone by saying the opposite.

con·tra·dic·tion /,käntrə'diksʜən/ ▶ n. 1 an opposition or lack of agreement between statements, ideas, or features. 2 the action of saying the opposite to something that has already been said.

– PHRASES **contradiction in terms** a statement containing words or ideas that are incompatible in meaning.

con·tra·dic·to·ry /,käntrə'dikt(ə)rē/ ▶ adj. 1 opposed or inconsistent. 2 containing opposing or inconsistent elements.

con·tra·dis·tinc·tion /,käntrədə'stiɴɢksʜən/ ▶ n. distinction made by contrasting the different qualities of two things.

con·tra·in·di·cate /,käntrə'ində,kāt/ ▶ v. Medicine (of a condition or circumstance) suggest or indicate that a particular technique or drug should not be used. ■ **con·tra·in·di·ca·tion** /-,ində'kāsʜən/ n.

con·tral·to /kən'traltō/ ▶ n. (pl. **contraltos**) the lowest female singing voice.

con·trap·tion /kən'trapsʜən/ ▶ n. a machine or device that appears strange or unnecessarily complicated.

con·tra·pun·tal /,käntrə'pəntl/ ▶ adj. Music relating to or in counterpoint. ■ **con·tra·pun·tal·ly** adv.

con·trar·i·an /kən'tre(ə)rēən, kän-/ ▶ n. a person who opposes or rejects popular opinion.

con·tra·ri·e·ty /,käntrə'rīətē/ ▶ n. opposition or inconsistency between two things.

con·trar·i·wise /'kän,trerē,wīz, kən'tre(ə)rē-/ ▶ adv. 1 in the opposite way. 2 on the other hand.

con·trar·y ▶ adj. /'kän,tre(ə)rē/ 1 opposite in nature, direction, or meaning. 2 (of two or more statements, beliefs, etc.) opposed to one another. 3 /kən'tre(ə)rē/ deliberately inclined to do the opposite of what is expected or desired. ▶ n. /'kän,tre(ə)rē/ (**the contrary**) the opposite. ■ **con·trar·i·ly** /-əlē/ adv. **con·trar·i·ness** n.

– PHRASES **to the contrary** with the opposite meaning or implication.

con·trast ▶ n. /'kän,trast/ 1 the state of being noticeably different from something else when put or considered together: *in contrast to karate, tae kwon do is characterized by its high kicks*. 2 a thing or person noticeably different from another. 3 the degree of difference between tones in a television picture, photograph, or other image. ▶ v. /'kän,trast, kən'trast/ 1 differ noticeably. 2 compare people or things so as to emphasize differences. ■ **con·tras·tive** /kən'trastiv, 'kän,tras-/ adj.

con·tra·vene /,käntrə'vēn/ ▶ v. 1 commit an act that is not allowed by a law, rule, treaty, etc. 2 conflict with a right or principle. ■ **con·tra·ven·er** n. **con·tra·ven·tion** /,käntrə'vencʜən/ n.

con·tre·temps /'käntrə,tän, ,kôntrə'tän/ ▶ n. (pl. same or /-,tän(z), -'tän(z)/) a minor disagreement.

con·trib·ute /kən'tribyŏŏt, -byət/ ▶ v. 1 give something in order to help achieve or provide something. 2 (**contribute to**) help to cause: *all of these factors can contribute to depression*. 3 give one's views in a discussion. ■ **con·trib·u·tive** /-yətiv/ adj. **con·trib·u·tor** n.

con·tri·bu·tion /,käntrə'byŏŏsʜən/ ▶ n. 1 a gift or payment to a common fund or collection. 2 the part played by a person or thing in causing or advancing something: *his contribution to 20th century music cannot be overstated*. 3 an item that forms part of a journal, book, broadcast, or discussion.

con·trib·u·to·ry /kən'tribyə,tôrē/ ▶ adj. 1 playing a part in bringing something about. 2 (of a pension or insurance scheme) operated by means of a fund into which people pay.

con·trite /kən'trīt/ ▶ adj. very sorry or regretful for having done wrong. ■ **con·trite·ly** adv. **con·tri·tion** /kən'trisʜən/ n.

con·triv·ance /kən'trīvəns/ ▶ n. **1** a clever or inventive device or scheme. **2** the use of skill to create or achieve something.

con·trive /kən'trīv/ ▶ v. **1** plan or achieve something in a clever or skillful way. **2** manage to do something foolish. ■ **con·triv·er** n.

con·trived /kən'trīvd/ ▶ adj. deliberately created rather than arising naturally, and typically seeming artificial.

con·trol /kən'trōl/ ▶ n. **1** the power to influence people's behavior or the course of events. **2** the restriction of something: *crime control*. **3** a means of limiting or regulating something: *controls on spending*. **4** a device by which a machine is regulated. **5** the place where something is checked or from which an activity is directed: *passport control*. **6** a person or thing used as a standard of comparison for checking the results of a survey or experiment. ▶ v. (**controls, controlling, controlled**) **1** have control of; direct or supervise: *she was appointed to control the firm's marketing strategy.* **2** limit or regulate something. ■ **con·trol·la·bil·i·ty** /kən,trōlə'bilitē/ n. **con·trol·la·ble** adj. **con·trol·la·bly** /-əblē/ adv.
– PHRASES **in control** able to direct a situation, person, or activity. **out of control** no longer manageable. **under control** (of a danger or emergency) being dealt with or contained successfully.

con·trol·ler /kən'trōlər/ ▶ n. a person in charge of an organization's finances.

con·trol·ling in·ter·est ▶ n. the holding by one person or group of a majority of the stock of a business.

con·trol tow·er ▶ n. a tall building from which the movements of air traffic are controlled.

con·tro·ver·sial /,käntrə'vərsHəl, -'vərsēəl/ ▶ adj. causing or likely to cause much debate and conflicting opinions. ■ **con·tro·ver·sial·ist** /-list/ n. **con·tro·ver·sial·ly** adv.

con·tro·ver·sy /'käntrə,vərsē/ ▶ n. (pl. **controversies**) debate about a matter that arouses conflicting opinions.

con·tro·vert /'käntrə,vərt, ,käntrə'vərt/ ▶ v. deny the truth of something.

con·tu·ma·cious /,känt(y)ə'māsHəs/ ▶ adj. old use or Law willfully disobedient to authority. ■ **con·tu·ma·cy** /kən't(y)o͞oməsē, 'känt(y)əməsē/ n.

con·tu·me·ly /kən't(y)o͞omələ, 'känt(y)ə,mēlē, 'kän,t(y)o͞omlē/ ▶ n. (pl. **contumelies**) old use insolent or insulting language or treatment.

con·tu·sion /kən'to͞ozHən/ ▶ n. Medicine a bruise. ■ **con·tuse** /kən'to͞oz/ v.

co·nun·drum /kə'nəndrəm/ ▶ n. (pl. **conundrums**) **1** a confusing and difficult problem or question. **2** a riddle.

con·ur·ba·tion /,känər'bāsHən/ ▶ n. an extended urban area consisting of several towns merging with the suburbs of a central city.

con·va·lesce /,känvə'les/ ▶ v. gradually recover one's health after an illness or medical treatment.

con·va·les·cent /,känvə'lesənt/ ▶ adj. recovering from an illness or medical treatment. ▶ n. a person who is recovering from an illness or medical treatment. ■ **con·va·les·cence** n.

con·vec·tion /kən'veksHən/ ▶ n. transference of mass or heat within a fluid caused by the tendency of warmer and less dense material

to rise. ■ **con·vect** /kən'vekt/ v. **con·vec·tive** /kən'vekshən/ adj.

con·vec·tor /kən'vektər/ ▶ n. a heating appliance that circulates warm air by convection.

con·vene /kən'vēn/ ▶ v. come or bring together for a meeting or activity.

con·ven·er /kən'vēnər/ (also **convenor**) ▶ n. a person who arranges the meetings of a committee.

con·ven·ience /kən'vēnyəns/ ▶ n. **1** freedom from effort or difficulty: *food today is more about convenience than nourishment.* **2** a useful or helpful thing. **3** Brit. a public toilet.
– PHRASES **at one's convenience** when or where it suits one. **at one's earliest convenience** as soon as one can without difficulty.

con·ven·ience food ▶ n. a food that has been preprepared commercially and so requires little preparation by the consumer.

con·ven·ience store ▶ n. a store with extended opening hours and in a convenient location, stocking a limited range of household goods and groceries.

con·ven·ient /kən'vēnyənt/ ▶ adj. **1** fitting in well with a person's needs, activities, and plans. **2** involving little trouble or effort. ■ **con·ven·ient·ly** adv.

con·ve·nor ▶ n. variant spelling of CONVENER.

con·vent /'kän,vent/ ▶ n. **1** a Christian community of nuns living under monastic vows. **2** (also **convent school**) a school attached to and run by a convent.

con·ven·tion /kən'venchən/ ▶ n. **1** a way in which something is usually done: *he is at his best working within the established conventions.* **2** socially acceptable behavior. **3** an agreement between countries. **4** a large meeting or conference. **5** an assembly of the delegates of a political party to select candidates for office. **6** a body set up by agreement to deal with a particular issue.

con·ven·tion·al /kən'venchənl/ ▶ adj. **1** based on or in accordance with what is generally done or believed. **2** following social conventions; not individual or adventurous. **3** (of weapons or power) nonnuclear. ■ **con·ven·tion·al·i·ty** /-,venchə'nalitē/ n. **con·ven·tion·al·ize** /-,īz/ v. **con·ven·tion·al·ly** adv.

con·verge /kən'vərj/ ▶ v. **1** come together from different directions so as eventually to meet. **2** (**converge on**) come from different directions and meet at a place. ■ **con·ver·gent** adj.

con·ver·sant /kən'vərsənt/ ▶ adj. (**conversant with**) familiar with or knowledgeable about something.

con·ver·sa·tion /,känvər'sāsHən/ ▶ n. an informal spoken exchange of news and ideas between people. ■ **con·ver·sa·tion·al** adj.

con·ver·sa·tion·al·ist /,känvər'sāsHənl-ist/ ▶ n. a person who is good at or fond of engaging in conversation.

con·verse[1] /kən'vərs/ ▶ v. hold a conversation.

con·verse[2] /'kän,vərs/ ▶ n. the opposite of a situation, fact, or statement. ▶ adj. /'kän,vərs, kən'vərs/ opposite. ■ **con·verse·ly** /'kän,vərslē, kən'vərslē/ adv.

con·ver·sion /kən'vərzHən/ ▶ n. **1** the action of converting someone or something. **2** Football the act of scoring an extra point or points after having scored a touchdown.

con·vert ▶v. /kən'vərt/ **1** change in form, character, or function: *grazing lands are being converted to farming.* **2** change money, stocks, or units into others of a different kind. **3** adapt a building for a new purpose. **4** change one's religious faith or other beliefs. **5** Football score extra points after a touchdown. ▶n. /'kän,vərt/ a person who has changed their religious faith or other beliefs. ■ **con·vert·er** (also **convertor**) n.

con·vert·i·ble /kən'vərtəbəl/ ▶adj. **1** able to be changed in form, character, or function. **2** (of a car) having a folding or detachable roof. ▶n. a car with a folding or detachable roof. ■ **con·vert·i·bil·i·ty** /-,vərtə'bilitē/ n.

con·vex /kän'veks, 'kän,veks, kən'veks/ ▶adj. having an outline or surface that curves outward. Compare with CONCAVE. ■ **con·vex·i·ty** /kän'veksitē, kən-/ n.

con·vey /kən'vā/ ▶v. **1** transport or carry something to a place. **2** communicate an idea, quality, or feeling. **3** Law transfer the title to property. ■ **con·vey·or** (also **conveyer**) n.

con·vey·ance /kən'vāəns/ ▶n. **1** the action of conveying something. **2** formal a means of transport. **3** the legal process of transferring property from one owner to another. ■ **con·vey·anc·er** n. **con·vey·anc·ing** n.

con·vey·or belt ▶n. a continuous moving belt for transporting objects within a building.

con·vict ▶v. /kən'vikt/ declare someone to be guilty of a criminal offense by the verdict of a jury or the decision of a judge in a court of law. ▶n. /'kän,vikt/ a person found guilty of a criminal offense and serving a sentence of imprisonment.

con·vic·tion /kən'viksHən/ ▶n. **1** an instance of formally being found guilty of a criminal offense in a court of law. **2** a firmly held belief or opinion. **3** the feeling or appearance of being sure in one's belief: *his voice lacked conviction.*

con·vince /kən'vins/ ▶v. **1** cause someone to believe firmly in the truth of something: *he tried to convince her that everything would be all right.* **2** persuade someone to do something. ■ **con·vinc·er** n.

con·vinc·ing /kən'vinsiNG/ ▶adj. **1** able to convince. **2** (of a victory or a winner) leaving no margin of doubt. ■ **con·vinc·ing·ly** adv.

con·viv·i·al /kən'vivēəl, kən'vivyəl/ ▶adj. **1** (of an atmosphere or event) friendly and lively. **2** cheerful and sociable. ■ **con·viv·i·al·i·ty** /kən,vivē'alitē/ n. **con·viv·i·al·ly** adv.

con·vo·ca·tion /,känvə'kāsHən/ ▶n. a large formal assembly of people.

con·voke /kən'vōk/ ▶v. formal call together an assembly or meeting.

con·vo·lut·ed /'känvə,lōōtid/ ▶adj. **1** (of an argument, statement, or story) very complex. **2** twisted or coiled in a complex way.

con·vo·lu·tion /,känvə'lōōsHən/ ▶n. **1** a coil or twist. **2** the state of being coiled or twisted. **3** a complex argument, statement, etc. ■ **con·vo·lu·tion·al** adj.

con·vol·vu·lus /kən'välvyə,ləs, -'vōl-/ ▶n. (pl. **convolvuluses**) a twining plant with trumpet-shaped flowers.

con·voy /'kän,voi/ ▶n. a group of ships or vehicles traveling together under armed protection. ▶v. (of a warship or armed troops) accompany a group of ships or vehicles for protection.

– PHRASES **in convoy** traveling as a group.

con·vulse /kən'vəls/ ▶v. **1** suffer convulsions. **2** (**be convulsed**) make sudden uncontrollable movements because of emotion, laughter, etc. ■ **con·vul·sive** /kən'vəlsiv/ adj. **con·vul·sive·ly** adv.

con·vul·sion /kən'vəlsHən/ ▶n. **1** a sudden irregular movement of the body, caused by the muscles contracting involuntarily. **2** (**convulsions**) uncontrollable laughter. **3** a violent social or natural upheaval.

co·ny ▶n. (pl. **conies**) variant spelling of CONEY.

coo /kōō/ ▶v. (**coos, cooing, cooed**) **1** (of a pigeon or dove) make a soft murmuring sound. **2** speak in a soft gentle voice. ▶n. a cooing sound.

cook /kŏŏk/ ▶v. **1** prepare food or a meal by mixing and heating the ingredients. **2** (of food) be heated so as to reach an edible state. **3** informal alter something dishonestly. **4** (**cook something up**) informal invent a story, excuse, or plan. ▶n. a person who cooks food.

– PHRASES **cook someone's goose** informal spoil someone's plans.

cook·book /'kŏŏk,bŏŏk/ ▶n. a recipe book.

cook·er /'kŏŏkər/ ▶n. Brit. an appliance for cooking food; a kitchen stove.

cook·er·y /'kŏŏkərē/ ▶n. the practice or skill of preparing and cooking food.

cook·house /'kŏŏk,hous/ ▶n. a building used for cooking, especially on a ranch or military camp.

cook·ie /'kŏŏkē/ ▶n. (pl. **cookies**) **1** a small sweet cake, typically round, flat, and crisp. **2** informal a person of a specified kind: *she's a tough cookie.*

– PHRASES **that's the way the cookie crumbles** informal that's the situation, and it must be accepted, however undesirable.

Cook's tour ▶n. informal a rapid tour of many places.

cook·ware /'kŏŏk,we(ə)r/ ▶n. pots, pans, or dishes in which food can be cooked.

cool /kōōl/ ▶adj. **1** fairly cold. **2** keeping one from becoming too hot. **3** not excited, angry, or emotional: *he kept a cool head.* **4** not friendly or enthusiastic. **5** informal fashionably attractive or impressive. **6** informal excellent. **7** informal used to express acceptance or agreement. **8** (**a cool ——**) informal used to emphasize a specified large amount of money: *they pocketed a cool $1 million each.* ▶n. (**the cool**) a fairly low temperature, or a fairly cold place or time: *the cool of the day.* ▶v. **1** make or become cool. **2** make or become less excited or angry. ■ **cool·ish** adj. **cool·ly** adv. **cool·ness** n.

– PHRASES **keep** (or **lose**) **one's cool** informal stay (or fail to stay) calm and controlled.

cool·ant /'kōōlənt/ ▶n. a fluid used to cool an engine or other device.

cool·er /'kōōlər/ ▶n. **1** a device or container for keeping things cool. **2** (**the cooler**) informal prison.

cool·head·ed /'kōōl,hedəd/ ▶n. not easily worried or excited.

coo·lie /'kōōlē/ ▶n. (pl. **coolies**) dated an unskilled native laborer in some Asian countries.

cool·ing-off pe·ri·od ▶n. **1** a period during which the people in a dispute can try to settle their differences before taking further action. **2** a period after a sale contract is agreed upon during which the buyer can decide to cancel without losing any money.

cool·ing tow·er ▶n. an open-topped, cylindrical concrete tower, used for cooling water or condensing steam from an industrial process.

coolth /ko͞olтн/ ▶ n. **1** pleasantly low temperature. **2** informal the quality of being fashionable.

coon /ko͞on/ ▶ n. **1** short for RACCOON. **2** informal, offensive a black person.

coop /ko͞op, ko͝op/ ▶ n. a cage or pen for poultry. ▶ v. confine in a small space: *I'm sick of being cooped up at home.*

co-op /'kō,äp, kō'äp/ ▶ n. informal a cooperative organization.

coop·er /'ko͞opər, 'ko͝opər/ ▶ n. a person who makes or repairs casks and barrels. ■ **coop·er·age** /'ko͞opərij, 'ko͝op-/ n.

co·op·er·ate /kō'äpə,rāt/ (also **co-operate**) ▶ v. **1** work together to achieve something. **2** do what is requested. ■ **co·op·er·a·tion** /kō,äpə'rāsн∂n/ n. **co·op·er·a·tor** n.

co·op·er·a·tive /kō'äp(ə)rətiv/ (also **co-operative**) ▶ adj. **1** involving cooperation. **2** willing to help. **3** (of a farm or business) owned and run jointly by its members, with profits or benefits shared among them. ▶ n. an organization owned and run jointly by its members. ■ **co·op·er·a·tive·ly** adv.

co-opt /kō'äpt, 'kō,äpt/ ▶ v. **1** make someone a member of a committee or other body by invitation of the existing members. **2** divert to a role different from the usual one: *can a government co-opt private industry to promote its policies?* **3** adopt an idea or policy for one's own use. ■ **co-op·ta·tion** n. **co-op·tion** n.

co·or·di·nate (also **co-ordinate**) ▶ v. /kō'ôrdə,nāt/ **1** bring the different elements of a complex activity or organization into an efficient relationship. **2** (**coordinate with**) negotiate with others in order to work together effectively. **3** match or harmonize attractively. ▶ n. /kō'ôrdn-ət/ **1** Mathematics each of a group of numbers used to indicate the position of a point, line, or plane. **2** (**coordinates**) matching items of clothing. ▶ adj. /kō'ôrdənət/ equal in rank or importance. ■ **co·or·di·na·tor** /-'ôrdn,ātər/ n.

co·or·di·na·tion /kō,ôrdn'āsн∂n/ (also **co-ordination**) ▶ n. **1** the organization of things so as to work together effectively. **2** the ability to move different parts of the body smoothly and at the same time.

coot /ko͞ot/ ▶ n. **1** (pl. same) a black waterbird with a white bill. **2** (usu. **old coot**) informal a foolish person, typically an old man.

coot·ie /'ko͞otē/ ▶ n. informal a children's term for an imaginary germ or repellent quality transmitted by undesirable or repugnant people.

cop /käp/ informal ▶ n. a police officer. ▶ v. (**cops, copping, copped**) **1** arrest an offender. **2** experience or receive something unwelcome: *the team's captain copped the blame.* **3** steal. **4** (**cop out**) avoid doing something that one ought to do.
– PHRASES **cop a feel** informal fondle someone sexually. **cop a plea** engage in plea bargaining.

co·pal /'kōpəl/ ▶ n. resin from certain tropical trees, used to make varnish.

co-par·ent ▶ v. (especially of a separated or unmarried couple) share the duties of bringing up a child. ▶ n. a person who co-parents a child.

cope¹ /kōp/ ▶ v. deal effectively with something difficult. ■ **cop·er** n.

cope² ▶ n. a long cloak worn by a priest or bishop on ceremonial occasions. ▶ v. (in building) cover a joint or structure with a coping.

co·peck /'kō,pek/ ▶ n. variant spelling of KOPEK.

Co·per·ni·can sys·tem /kə'pərnikən/ (also **Copernican theory**) ▶ n. the theory proposed by the Polish astronomer Nicolaus Copernicus that the sun is the center of the solar system, with the planets orbiting around it. Compare with PTOLEMAIC SYSTEM.

cop·i·er /'käpēər/ ▶ n. a machine that makes exact copies of something.

co·pi·lot /'kō,pīlət/ ▶ n. a second pilot in an aircraft.

cop·ing /'kōpiNG/ ▶ n. the curved or sloping top course of a brick or stone wall.

co·pi·ous /'kōpēəs/ ▶ adj. abundant in supply or quantity: *drinking copious amounts of beer.* ■ **co·pi·ous·ly** adv. **co·pi·ous·ness** n.

co·pol·y·mer /kō'päləmər/ ▶ n. Chemistry a polymer made by reaction of two different monomers, with units of more than one kind.

cop-out ▶ n. informal an instance of avoiding a commitment or responsibility.

cop·per¹ /'käpər/ ▶ n. **1** a red-brown metallic chemical element that is used for electrical wiring and as a component of brass and bronze. **2** (**coppers**) Brit. coins of low value made of copper or bronze. **3** a reddish-brown color. ▶ v. cover or coat something with copper. ■ **cop·per·y** adj.

cop·per² ▶ n. Brit. informal a police officer.

cop·per beech ▶ n. a variety of beech tree with purplish-brown leaves.

cop·per·head /'käpər,hed/ ▶ n. any of a number of stout-bodied venomous snakes with coppery-pink or reddish-brown coloration, in particular a North American pit viper.

cop·per·plate /,käpər'plāt, 'käpər,plāt/ ▶ n. **1** a polished copper plate with a design engraved or etched into it. **2** a neat, looped style of handwriting.

cop·per sul·phate ▶ n. a blue crystalline solid used in electroplating and as a fungicide.

cop·pice /'käpəs/ ▶ n. an area of woodland in which the trees or shrubs are periodically cut back to ground level to stimulate growth. ▶ v. cut back a tree or shrub to ground level.

cop·ra /'käprə/ ▶ n. dried coconut kernels, from which oil is obtained.

co·proc·es·sor /kō'prä,sesər, ,kō'präsəsər/ ▶ n. Computing a microprocessor designed to supplement the capabilities of the primary processor.

co·pro·duce /,kōprə'd(y)o͞os/ ▶ v. produce a theatrical work or a radio or television program jointly. ■ **co·pro·duc·er** n. **co·pro·duc·tion** /-'dəksн∂n/ n.

copse /käps/ ▶ n. a small group of trees.

Copt /käpt/ ▶ n. **1** a member of the Coptic Church, the native Christian Church in Egypt. **2** a native Egyptian in the periods of Greek and Roman rule.

cop·ter /'käptər/ ▶ n. informal a helicopter.

Cop·tic /'käptik/ ▶ n. the language of the ancient Copts, which survives only in the Coptic Church. ▶ adj. relating to the Copts or their language.

cop·u·la /'käpyələ/ ▶ n. a verb, especially the verb *be*, that links a subject and complement (e.g., *was* in the sentence *I was happy*).

cop·u·late /'käpyə,lāt/ ▶ v. have sexual intercourse. ■ **cop·u·la·tion** /,käpyə'lāsн∂n/ n. **cop·u·la·to·ry** /-lə,tôrē/ adj.

cop·y /'käpē/ ▶ n. (pl. **copies**) **1** a thing made to be similar or identical to another. **2** a single specimen of a particular book, record, etc. **3** material to be printed in a book, newspaper, or magazine. **4** the written part of an advertisement. ▶ v. (**copies, copying, copied**) **1** make a copy of something. **2** imitate the behavior or style of: *this view of leadership is copied from business.*

cop·y·book /'käpē,bŏŏk/ ▶ n. a book containing models of handwriting for learners to imitate. ▶ adj. exactly in accordance with established standards: *a copybook landing.*

cop·y·cat /'käpē,kat/ ▶ n. informal a person who copies another. ▶ adj. (of an action, especially a crime) done in imitation of another: *copycat attacks.*

cop·y·ed·it ▶ v. edit written material by checking its consistency and accuracy. ■ **cop·y ed·i·tor** n.

cop·y·ist /'käpē-ist/ ▶ n. **1** a person who makes copies. **2** a person who imitates the styles of others, especially in art.

cop·y·right /'käpē,rīt/ ▶ n. the exclusive legal right, given to the originator for a fixed number of years, to print, publish, perform, film, or record literary, artistic, or musical material.

cop·y·writ·er /'käpi,rītər/ ▶ n. a person who writes advertisements or publicity material.

coq au vin /,kōk ō 'van, ,käk/ ▶ n. a casserole of chicken pieces cooked in red wine.

co·quette /kō'ket/ ▶ n. a woman who flirts. ■ **co·quet·ry** /'kōkətrē, kō'ketrē/ n. **co·quet·tish** adj. **co·quet·tish·ly** adv.

cor·a·cle /'kôrəkəl, 'kär-/ ▶ n. a small, round boat made of wickerwork covered with a watertight material, propelled with a paddle.

cor·al /'kôrəl, 'kär-/ ▶ n. **1** a hard stony substance produced by certain sea creatures as an external skeleton, typically forming large reefs. **2** precious red coral, used in jewelry. **3** a pinkish-red color.

cor·al snake ▶ n. a brightly colored venomous snake of the cobra family, typically having conspicuous bands of red, yellow, white, and black.

cor an·glais /,kôr 'äNglā/ ▶ n. (pl. **cors anglais** pronunc. same) a woodwind instrument of the oboe family, sounding a fifth lower than the oboe.

cor·bel /'kôrbəl/ ▶ n. a projection jutting out from a wall to support a structure above it. ■ **cor·beled** adj. **cor·bel·ing** n.

cord /kôrd/ ▶ n. **1** thin string or rope made from several twisted strands. **2** a length of cord. **3** a structure in the body resembling a cord (e.g., the spinal cord). **4** a flexible insulated cable used for carrying electric current. **5** corduroy. **6** (**cords**) corduroy pants. **7** a measure of cut wood (usually 128 cu. ft., 3.62 cubic meters). ■ **cord·ing** n.

> **USAGE**
> On the confusion of **cord** and **chord**, see the note at **chord**[1].

cor·date /'kôr,dāt/ ▶ adj. Botany & Zoology heart-shaped.

cord blood ▶ n. blood from the human umbilical cord, a source of stem cells.

cor·dial /'kôrjəl/ ▶ adj. **1** warm and friendly. **2** strongly felt: *I earned his cordial loathing.* ▶ n. **1** another term for LIQUEUR. **2** a pleasant-tasting medicine. ■ **cor·dial·i·ty** /,kôrjē'alitē/ n. **cor·dial·ly** adv.

cor·dil·le·ra /,kôrdl'(y)erə/ ▶ n. a system or group of parallel mountain ranges together with the intervening plateaus and other features, especially in the Andes or the Rockies.

cord·ite /'kôr,dīt/ ▶ n. a smokeless explosive used in ammunition.

cord·less /'kôrdləs/ ▶ adj. (of an electrical appliance) working without connection to a main supply or central unit.

cor·do·ba /'kôrdəbə, -dəvə/ ▶ n. the basic unit of money of Nicaragua.

cor·don /'kôrdn/ ▶ n. **1** a line or circle of police, soldiers, or guards forming a barrier. **2** a fruit tree trained to grow as a single ropelike stem. ▶ v. (**cordon something off**) close somewhere off by surrounding it with police or other guards.

cor·don bleu /,kôrdôN 'blœ/ ▶ adj. **1** (of a cook or cooking) of the highest class. **2** referring to a dish consisting of veal or chicken rolled, filled with cheese and ham, and then fried in breadcrumbs.

cor·don sa·ni·taire /kôrdôN ,sänē'ter/ ▶ n. (pl. **cordons sanitaires** pronunc. same) **1** a line of guards positioned around an area infected by disease, preventing anyone from leaving. **2** a measure designed to prevent communication or the spread of undesirable influences.

cor·du·roy /'kôrdə,roi/ ▶ n. a thick cotton fabric with velvety ribs.

core /kôr/ ▶ n. **1** the tough central part of various fruits, containing the seeds. **2** the central or most important part: *mysticism was the core of his faith.* **3** the dense metallic or rocky central region of a planet. **4** the central part of a nuclear reactor, which contains the fissile material. ▶ v. remove the core from a fruit. ■ **cor·er** n.

co·re·op·sis /,kôrē'äpsəs/ ▶ n. a plant of the daisy family, cultivated for its rayed, typically yellow, flowers.

co·re·spond·ent ▶ n. a person named in a divorce case as having committed adultery with the husband or wife of the person who wants a divorce.

cor·gi /'kôrgē/ (also **Welsh corgi**) ▶ n. (pl. **corgis**) a breed of dog with short legs and a foxlike head.

co·ri·an·der /'kôrē,andər, ,kôrē'andər/ ▶ n. a Mediterranean plant of the parsley family, used as an herb in cooking.

Co·rin·thi·an /kə'rinTHēən/ ▶ adj. **1** relating to Corinth, a city in southern Greece and a city-state in ancient Greece. **2** relating to an ornate classical style of architecture having flared capitals with rows of acanthus leaves. ▶ n. a person from Corinth.

cork /kôrk/ ▶ n. **1** a buoyant, light brown substance obtained from the bark of a kind of Mediterranean oak tree. **2** a bottle stopper made of cork. ▶ v. **1** close or seal a bottle with a cork. **2** (as adj. **corked**) (of wine) spoiled by tannin from the cork.

cork·age /'kôrkij/ ▶ n. a charge made by a restaurant for serving wine that has been brought in by a customer.

cork·er /'kôrkər/ ▶ n. informal an excellent person or thing. ■ **cork·ing** adj.

cork·screw /'kôrk,skrōō/ ▶ n. a device with a spiral metal rod, used for pulling corks from bottles. ▶ v. move or twist in a spiral.

corm /kôrm/ ▶ n. the underground storage organ of plants such as crocuses, consisting of a swollen stem base covered with scale leaves.

cor·mo·rant /'kôrmərənt/ ▶ n. a large diving seabird with a long neck, long hooked bill, and mainly black plumage.

corn¹ /kôrn/ ▶ n. 1 a North American cereal plant that yields large kernels set in rows on a cob. 2 the grains of this plant. 3 informal something unoriginal or sentimental: *the movie is pure corn.* – PHRASES **corn on the cob** corn when cooked and eaten straight from the cob.

corn² ▶ n. a small, painful area of thickened skin on the foot, caused by pressure.

corn·ball /'kôrn,bôl/ ▶ adj. trite and sentimental: *a cornball movie.* ▶ n. a person with trite or sentimental ideas.

corn·bread /'kôrn,bred/ ▶ n. a type of bread made from cornmeal and typically leavened without yeast.

corn·cob /'kôrn,käb/ ▶ n. the central woody part of an ear of corn, to which the grains are attached.

cor·ne·a /'kôrnēə/ ▶ n. the transparent layer forming the front of the eye. ■ **cor·ne·al** adj.

corned beef ▶ n. beef brisket cured in brine and boiled, typically served cold.

cor·ner /'kôrnər/ ▶ n. 1 a place or angle where two or more sides or edges meet. 2 a place where two streets meet. 3 a remote area. 4 a difficult or awkward position: *Mick thought it was a crazy idea, but he was in a corner.* 5 Baseball first or third base on a baseball diamond. 6 Boxing & Wrestling each of the diagonally opposite ends of the ring, where a contestant rests between rounds. ▶ v. 1 force into a place or situation from which it is hard to escape: *my landlord cornered me as I was going upstairs.* 2 go around a bend in a road. 3 control a market by dominating the supply of a particular commodity.

cor·ner·back /'kôrnər,bak/ ▶ n. Football a defensive back positioned to the outside of the linebackers.

cor·ner·stone /'kôrnər,stōn/ ▶ n. 1 a vital part or basis: *sugar was the cornerstone of the economy.* 2 a stone that forms the base of a corner of a building, joining two walls.

cor·net /kôr'net/ ▶ n. 1 a brass instrument resembling a trumpet but shorter and wider. 2 British term for ICE CREAM CONE (sense 1). ■ **cor·net·ist** /-'netəst/ (also **cornettist**) n.

corn·flakes /'kôrn,flāks/ ▶ pl.n. a breakfast cereal consisting of toasted flakes made from corn.

corn·flow·er /'kôrn,flouər/ ▶ n. a plant of the daisy family with deep blue flowers.

cor·nice /'kôrnis/ ▶ n. 1 an ornamental molding around the wall of a room just below the ceiling. 2 a horizontal molded projection crowning a building or structure. ■ **cor·niced** adj. **cor·nic·ing** n.

cor·niche /'kôrnish, kôr'nēsh/ ▶ n. a road cut into the edge of a cliff and running along a coastline.

Cor·nish /'kôrnish/ ▶ adj. relating to Cornwall. ▶ n. the ancient Celtic language of Cornwall.

corn·meal /'kôrn,mēl/ ▶ n. meal made from ground, dried corn.

corn·rows /'kôrn,rōz/ ▶ pl.n. (especially among black people) a style of braiding the hair in narrow strips to form geometric patterns on the scalp.

corn sal·ad ▶ n. a small plant with soft roundish leaves that are eaten in salads.

corn·starch /'kôrn,stärch/ ▶ n. finely ground corn flour, used for thickening sauces.

cor·nu·co·pi·a /,kôrn(y)ə'kōpēə/ ▶ n. 1 an abundant supply of good things. 2 a symbol of plenty consisting of a goat's horn overflowing with flowers, fruit, and cereals. ■ **cor·nu·co·pi·an** adj.

corn·y /'kôrnē/ ▶ adj. (**cornier**, **corniest**) informal unoriginal or very sentimental: *corny jokes.* ■ **corn·i·ness** n.

co·rol·la /kə'rälə, kə'rōlə/ ▶ n. the petals of a flower, typically forming a whorl within the sepals.

cor·ol·lar·y /'kôrə,lerē, 'kärə-/ ▶ n. (pl. **corollaries**) 1 a direct consequence or result. 2 a logical proposition that follows from one already proved. ▶ adj. associated; supplementary.

co·ro·na /kə'rōnə/ ▶ n. (pl. **coronae** /-nē, -nī/) 1 the envelope of gas around the sun or another star. 2 a small circle of light seen around the sun or moon. 3 (also **corona discharge**) Physics the glow around a conductor at high potential. 4 a long, straight-sided cigar. ■ **cor·o·nal** /'kôrənl, 'kär-/ adj.

cor·o·nar·y /'kôrə,nerē, 'kär-/ ▶ adj. relating to the arteries that surround and supply the heart. ▶ n. (pl. **coronaries**) (also **coronary thrombosis**) a blockage of the flow of blood to the heart, caused by a clot in a coronary artery.

cor·o·na·tion /,kôrə'nāshən, ,kär-/ ▶ n. the ceremony of crowning a sovereign or a sovereign's consort.

cor·o·ner /'kôrənər, 'kär-/ ▶ n. an official who holds inquests into violent, sudden, or suspicious deaths.

cor·o·net /,kôrə'net, ,kär-/ ▶ n. 1 a small or simple crown. 2 a circular decorative band worn on the head.

Corp. ▶ abbr. 1 Corporal. 2 Corporation.

cor·po·ra /'kôrpərə/ ▶ plural of CORPUS.

cor·po·ral¹ /'kôrp(ə)rəl/ ▶ n. a rank of noncommissioned officer in the US Army or Marine Corps, above lance corporal or private first class and below sergeant.

cor·po·ral² ▶ adj. relating to the human body.

cor·po·ral pun·ish·ment ▶ n. physical punishment, such as caning.

cor·po·rate /'kôrp(ə)rət/ ▶ adj. 1 relating to a business corporation. 2 relating to or shared by all members of a group: *corporate responsibility.* ■ **cor·po·rate·ly** adv.

cor·po·rate raid·er ▶ n. a financier who makes a practice of making hostile takeover bids for companies, either to control their policies or to resell them for a profit.

cor·po·rate tax ▶ n. tax paid by companies on their profits.

cor·po·ra·tion /,kôrpə'rāshən/ ▶ n. 1 a large company or group of companies recognized by law as a single unit. 2 (also **municipal corporation**) a group of people elected to govern a city, town, or borough.

cor·po·rat·ism /'kôrp(ə)rə,tizəm/ ▶ n. the control of a government or organization by large interest groups. ■ **cor·po·rat·ist** adj. & n.

cor·po·re·al /kôr'pôrēəl/ ▶ adj. relating to a person's body; physical rather than spiritual. ■ **cor·po·re·al·i·ty** /kôr,pôrē'alitē/ n.

corps /kôr/ ▶ n. (pl. **corps** /kôrz/) 1 a main subdivision of an army in the field, consisting of two or more divisions. 2 a branch of an army assigned to a particular kind of work. 3 a group of people engaged in a particular activity: *the press corps.*

corps de bal·let /ˌkôr də baˈlā/ ▸ n. (treated as sing. or pl.) **1** the members of a ballet company who dance together as a group. **2** the lowest rank of dancers in a ballet company.

corpse /kôrps/ ▸ n. a dead body, especially of a person.

cor·pu·lent /ˈkôrpyələnt/ ▸ adj. (of a person) fat. ▪ **cor·pu·lence** n.

cor·pus /ˈkôrpəs/ ▸ n. (pl. **corpora** /-pərə/ or **corpuses**) **1** a collection of written works. **2** a collection of written or spoken material in a form that is readable by a computer.

Cor·pus Chris·ti /ˌkôrpəs ˈkristē/ ▸ n. a Christian feast commemorating the institution of Holy Communion, observed on the Thursday after Trinity Sunday.

cor·pus·cle /ˈkôrˌpəsəl/ ▸ n. a red or white blood cell. ▪ **cor·pus·cu·lar** /ˈkôrˈpəskyələr/ adj.

cor·ral /kəˈral/ ▸ n. a pen for livestock on a farm or ranch. ▸ v. (**corrals, corralling, corralled**) **1** put or keep livestock in a corral. **2** gather a group together.

cor·rect /kəˈrekt/ ▸ adj. **1** free from error; true; right: *they came up with the correct answer.* **2** meeting accepted social standards. ▸ v. **1** put right an error or fault. **2** mark the errors in written work. **3** tell someone that they are mistaken. **4** adjust a result or reading to allow for departure from standard conditions. ▪ **cor·rect·a·ble** adj. **cor·rect·ly** adv. **cor·rect·ness** n. **cor·rec·tor** n.

cor·rec·tion /kəˈreksHən/ ▸ n. **1** the action of correcting something. **2** a change that puts right an error or inaccuracy.

cor·rec·tion·al /kəˈreksHənl/ ▸ adj. relating to punishment intended to rectify criminals' behavior: *a correctional institution.*

cor·rec·tive /kəˈrektiv/ ▸ adj. designed to put right something undesirable.

cor·re·late /ˈkôrəˌlāt, ˈkär-/ ▸ v. have or bring into a relationship in which one thing depends on another and vice versa: *success in the educational system correlates highly with class.* ▸ n. each of two or more related or complementary things.

cor·re·la·tion /ˌkôrəˈlāsHən/ ▸ n. **1** a relationship in which one thing depends on another and vice versa. **2** the process of correlating two or more things.

cor·rel·a·tive /kəˈrelətiv/ ▸ adj. **1** having a relationship in which one thing affects or depends on another. **2** (of words such as *neither* and *nor*) corresponding to each other and regularly used together.

cor·re·spond /ˌkôrəˈspänd, ˌkär-/ ▸ v. **1** match or agree almost exactly. **2** be comparable or equivalent in character or form: *many companies assign employees numbers that correspond to their date of hire.* **3** communicate by exchanging letters.

cor·re·spond·ence /ˌkôrəˈspändəns, ˌkär-/ ▸ n. **1** a close similarity, link, or equivalence. **2** letters sent or received.

cor·re·spond·ence course ▸ n. a course of study in which student and teachers communicate by mail.

cor·re·spond·ent /ˌkôrəˈspändənt, ˌkär-/ ▸ n. **1** a journalist reporting on a particular subject or from a particular country: *a White House*

correspondent. **2** a person who writes letters on a regular basis.

cor·ri·da /kôˈrēdə/ ▸ n. a bullfight.

cor·ri·dor /ˈkôrədər, ˈkär-, -ˌdôr/ ▸ n. **1** a passage in a building, with doors leading into rooms. **2** a strip of land linking two other areas or following a road or river.

– PHRASES **the corridors of power** the senior levels of government or administration.

cor·rob·o·rate /kəˈräbəˌrāt/ ▸ v. confirm or give support to a statement or theory. ▪ **cor·rob·o·ra·tion** /kəˌräbəˈrāsHən/ n. **cor·rob·o·ra·tive** /-ˈräb(ə)rətiv/ adj.

cor·rob·o·ree /kəˈräbərē/ ▸ n. an Australian Aboriginal dance ceremony in the form of a sacred ritual or informal gathering.

cor·rode /kəˈrōd/ ▸ v. **1** (with reference to metal or other hard material) wear or be worn away slowly by chemical action. **2** gradually weaken or destroy: *the criticism corroded his reputation.*

cor·ro·sion /kəˈrōzHən/ ▸ n. **1** the process of wearing away something. **2** damage caused by this process.

cor·ro·sive /kəˈrōsiv, -ziv/ ▸ adj. causing corrosion. ▪ n. a corrosive substance.

cor·ru·gate /ˈkôrəˌgāt, ˈkär-/ ▸ v. **1** contract into wrinkles or folds: *his brow corrugated in a frown.* **2** (as adj. **corrugated**) shaped into alternate ridges and grooves: *corrugated iron.* ▪ **cor·ru·ga·tion** /ˌkôrəˈgāsHən, ˌkär-/ n.

cor·rupt /kəˈrəpt/ ▸ adj. **1** willing to act dishonestly in return for money or personal gain. **2** evil or very immoral. **3** (of a written work or computer data) made unreliable by errors or alterations. ▸ v. **1** make dishonest or depraved: *he was corrupted by power.* **2** introduce errors into a written work or computer data. ▪ **cor·rupt·er** n. **cor·rupt·i·ble** adj. **cor·rup·tive** adj. **cor·rupt·ly** adv.

cor·rup·tion /kəˈrəpsHən/ ▸ n. **1** dishonest or illegal behavior. **2** the action of corrupting someone or something.

cor·sage /kôrˈsäzH, -ˈsäj/ ▸ n. a spray of flowers worn pinned to a woman's clothes.

cor·sair /ˈkôrˌse(ə)r/ ▸ n. **1** old use a pirate. **2** historical a privateer, especially one operating in the Mediterranean in the 17th century.

cor·set /ˈkôrsət/ ▸ n. **1** a woman's tight-fitting undergarment extending from below the chest to the hips, worn to shape the figure. **2** a similar garment worn to support a weak or injured back. ▪ **cor·set·ed** adj. **cor·set·ry** n.

Cor·si·can /ˈkôrsikən/ ▸ n. **1** a person from Corsica. **2** the language of Corsica. ▸ adj. relating to Corsica.

cor·tège /kôrˈtezH, ˈkôrˌtezH/ ▸ n. a solemn funeral procession.

cor·tex /ˈkôrˌteks/ ▸ n. (pl. **cortices** /-təˌsēz/) the outer layer of a bodily organ or structure, especially the outer, folded layer of the brain (**cerebral cortex**). ▪ **cor·ti·cal** /ˈkôrtikəl/ adj.

cor·ti·co·ster·oid /ˌkôrtikōˈsterˌoid, -ˈsti(ə)rˌoid/ ▸ n. any of a group of steroid hormones produced by the cortex of the adrenal glands.

cor·ti·sol /ˈkôrtəˌsôl, -ˌsōl/ ▸ n. another name for **HYDROCORTISONE**.

cor·ti·sone /ˈkôrtəˌsōn/ ▸ n. a steroid hormone used to treat inflammation and allergies.

co·run·dum /kəˈrəndəm/ ▸ n. an extremely hard form of aluminum oxide, used as an abrasive.

cor·us·cate /ˈkôrəˌskāt, ˈkär-/ ▶v. literary (usu. as adj. **coruscating**) **1** flash; sparkle. **2** be brilliant or exciting: *a coruscating attack on the rock tradition.* ■ **cor·us·ca·tion** /ˌkôrəˈskāsHən/ n.

cor·vette /kôrˈvet/ ▶n. a small warship designed for convoy escort duty.

cor·vine /ˈkôrˌvīn/ ▶adj. relating to or like a raven or crow.

cos[1] /käs, kôs/ (also **cos lettuce**) ▶n. chiefly Brit. another term for ROMAINE.

cos[2] ▶abbr. cosine.

co·se·cant /kōˈsēˌkant, -kənt/ ▶n. (in a right triangle) the ratio of the hypotenuse to the side opposite an acute angle.

cosh /käsH/ Brit. ▶n. a thick heavy stick or bar used as a weapon. ▶v. hit someone with a cosh.

co·sig·na·to·ry /kōˈsignəˌtôrē/ ▶n. a person or country signing a treaty or other document jointly with others.

co·sine /ˈkōˌsīn/ ▶n. (in a right triangle) the ratio of the side adjacent to a particular acute angle to the hypotenuse.

cos·met·ic /kazˈmetik/ ▶adj. **1** relating to treatment intended to improve a person's appearance. **2** improving only the appearance of something: *the reforms were merely a cosmetic exercise.* ▶n. (**cosmetics**) substances used to improve the appearance of the face and body. ■ **cos·met·i·cal·ly** /-(ə)lē/ adv.

cos·me·tol·o·gy /ˌkäzməˈtäləjē/ ▶n. the professional skill or practice of beautifying the face, hair, and skin. ■ **cos·me·tol·o·gist** /-jist/ n.

cos·mic /ˈkäzmik/ ▶adj. relating to the universe or cosmos. ■ **cos·mi·cal** adj. **cos·mi·cal·ly** /-(ə)lē/ adv.

cos·mic rays ▶pl.n. highly energetic atomic nuclei or other particles traveling through space at a speed approaching that of light.

cos·mog·o·ny /käzˈmägənē/ ▶n. (pl. **cosmogonies**) the branch of science concerned with the origin of the universe, especially the solar system. ■ **cos·mo·gon·ic** /ˌkäzməˈgänik/ adj. **cos·mog·o·nist** /-nist/ n.

cos·mog·ra·phy /käzˈmägrəfē/ ▶n. (pl. **cosmographies**) **1** the branch of science that deals with the general features of the universe, including the earth. **2** a description or representation of the universe or the earth. ■ **cos·mog·ra·pher** n. **cos·mo·graph·i·cal** /ˌkäzməˈgrafikəl/ adj.

cos·mol·o·gy /käzˈmäləjē/ ▶n. (pl. **cosmologies**) **1** the science of the origin and development of the universe. **2** a theory of the origin of the universe. ■ **cos·mo·log·i·cal** /ˌkäzməˈläjikəl/ adj. **cos·mol·o·gist** n.

cos·mo·naut /ˈkäzməˌnôt, -ˌnät/ ▶n. a Russian astronaut.

cos·mo·pol·i·tan /ˌkäzməˈpälitn/ ▶adj. **1** consisting of people from many different countries and cultures: *Barcelona is a cosmopolitan city.* **2** familiar with and at ease in different countries and cultures. ▶n. **1** a person who is familiar with different countries and cultures. **2** a cocktail made with Cointreau, vodka, cranberry juice, and lime juice. ■ **cos·mo·pol·i·tan·ism** /-ˌizəm/ n.

cos·mos[1] /ˈkäzməs, -ˌmōs, -ˌmäs/ ▶n. the universe seen as a well-ordered whole.

cos·mos[2] ▶n. an ornamental plant of the daisy family with single dahlialike flowers.

Cos·sack /ˈkäsˌak, -ək/ ▶n. a member of a people of southern Russia, Ukraine, and Siberia, noted for their horsemanship and military skill.

cos·set /ˈkäsət/ ▶v. (**cossets, cosseting, cosseted**) care for and protect someone in an overindulgent way.

cost /kôst/ ▶v. (past and past part. **cost**) **1** be able to be bought or done for a specific price: *tickets cost $15.* **2** involve the loss of: *his heroism cost him his life.* **3** (past and past part. **costed**) estimate the cost of something. ▶n. **1** an amount given or required as payment. **2** the effort or loss necessary to achieve something. **3** (**costs**) legal expenses.
–PHRASES **at all costs** (or **at any cost**) regardless of the price or the effort needed. **at cost** without profit to the seller.

cost ac·count·ing ▶n. the recording of all the costs arising in a business in a way that can be used to improve its management. ■ **cost ac·count·ant** n.

co·star /ˈkōˌstär, kōˈstär/ ▶n. a movie or stage star appearing with another or others of equal importance. ▶v. **1** appear in a movie or play as a co-star. **2** (of a movie or play) include someone as a co-star.

Cos·ta Ri·can /ˌkôstə ˈrēkən, ˌkôstə, ˌkästə/ ▶n. a person from Costa Rica, a republic in Central America. ▶adj. relating to Costa Rica.

cost-ef·fec·tive (also **cost-efficient**) ▶adj. effective or productive in relation to its cost.

cost·ly /ˈkôstlē/ ▶adj. (**costlier, costliest**) **1** expensive; not cheap. **2** causing suffering, loss, or disadvantage: *her most costly mistake.* ■ **cost·li·ness** n.

cost of liv·ing ▶n. the level of prices relating to a range of everyday items.

cos·tume /ˈkäsˌt(y)o͞om, -təm/ ▶n. **1** a set of clothes in a style typical of a particular country or historical period: *authentic Elizabethan costumes.* **2** a set of clothes worn by an actor or performer for a role. **3** a set of clothes, particularly a woman's ensemble, for a particular occasion. ▶v. dress someone in a set of clothes.

cos·tume dra·ma ▶n. a television or movie production set in a historical period.

cos·tume jew·el·ry ▶n. jewelry made with inexpensive materials or imitation gems.

cos·tum·er /ˈkäsˌt(y)o͞omər, käsˈt(y)o͞o-/ (also chiefly Brit. **costumier** /käsˈt(y)o͞omēər/) ▶n. a maker or supplier of theatrical or party costumes.

co·sy, etc. ▶adj. British spelling of cozy, etc.

cot[1] /kät/ ▶n. **1** a portable, collapsible bed. **2** Brit. a baby's crib.

cot[2] ▶n. **1** a small shelter for livestock. **2** old use a small, simple cottage.

cot[3] ▶abbr. Mathematics cotangent.

co·tan·gent /kōˈtanjənt/ ▶n. (in a right triangle) the ratio of the side (other than the hypotenuse) adjacent to a particular acute angle to the side opposite the angle.

cote /kōt, kät/ ▶n. a shelter for mammals or birds, especially pigeons.

co·te·rie /ˈkōtərē, ˌkōtəˈrē/ ▶n. (pl. **coteries**) a small exclusive group of people with shared interests or tastes.

co·ter·mi·nous /kōˈtərmənəs/ ▶adj. having the same boundaries or extent: *on the east the area is coterminous with Sweden.*

co·to·ne·as·ter /kə'tōnē,astər, 'kätn,ēstər/ ▶n. a shrub with bright red berries, often grown as a hedge.

cot·tage /'kätij/ ▶n. a small house, typically one in the country. ∎ **cot·tag·ey** adj.

cot·tage cheese ▶n. soft, lumpy white cheese made from the curds of skimmed milk.

cot·tage in·dus·try ▶n. a business or manufacturing activity carried on in people's homes.

cot·tag·er /'kätijər/ ▶n. a person living in a cottage.

cot·ter pin /'kätər/ ▶n. **1** a metal pin used to fasten two parts of a mechanism together. **2** a split pin that is opened out after being passed through a hole.

cot·ton /'kätn/ ▶n. the soft white fibers that surround the seeds of a tropical and subtropical plant, used to make cloth and thread for sewing. ▶v. informal (**cotton on**) begin to understand or realize: *I cottoned on to what Bill was saying.* ∎ **cot·ton·y** adj.

cot·ton ball ▶n. a fluffy soft wad of cotton, used for applying or removing cosmetics or bathing wounds.

cot·ton can·dy ▶n. a mass of artificially colored spun sugar wrapped around a stick.

cot·ton·mouth /'kätn,mouтн/ ▶n. a large, dangerous semiaquatic pit viper that inhabits lowland swamps and waterways of the southeastern US.

cot·ton·tail /'kätn,tāl/ ▶n. a North American rabbit that has a speckled brownish coat and a white underside to the tail.

cot·ton·wood /'kätn,wŏŏd/ ▶n. any of several North American poplars with seeds covered in white cottony hairs.

cot·y·le·don /,kätl'ēdn/ ▶n. the first leaf to grow from a germinating seed.

couch[1] /koucн/ ▶n. **1** a long upholstered piece of furniture for several people to sit on. **2** a long seat with a headrest at one end on which a psychoanalyst's subject or doctor's patient lies during treatment. ▶v. **1** express in language of a specified type: *the announcement was couched in technical language.* **2** literary lie down.

couch[2] (also **couch grass**) ▶n. a coarse grass with long creeping roots.

cou·chette /kŏŏ'sнet/ ▶n. **1** a railroad car with seats convertible into sleeping berths. **2** a berth in a couchette car.

couch po·ta·to ▶n. informal a person who spends a great deal of time watching television.

cou·gar /'kŏŏgər/ ▶n. a large American wild cat with a plain tawny to grayish coat.

cough /kôf/ ▶v. **1** expel air from the lungs with a sudden sharp sound. **2** (of an engine) make a sudden harsh noise. **3** (**cough something up**) informal give something, especially money, reluctantly. ▶n. **1** an act of coughing. **2** a condition of the throat or lungs causing coughing. ∎ **cough·er** n.

cough drop ▶n. a medicated lozenge sucked to relieve a cough or sore throat.

could /kŏŏd/ ▶modal v. past of CAN[1].

USAGE
For advice on **could have** versus **could of**, see the note at HAVE.

could·n't /'kŏŏdnt/ ▶contr. could not.

cou·lomb /'kŏŏ,läm, -,lōm/ ▶n. the SI unit of electric charge, equal to the quantity of electricity conveyed in one second by a current of one ampere.

coun·cil /'kounsəl/ ▶n. **1** an assembly of people that meets regularly to discuss, advise on, or administer something. **2** a group of people elected to manage a city, county, or district.

USAGE
Do not confuse **council** with **counsel**. **Council** means 'a group of people who manage an area or advise on something' (*the city council*), whereas **counsel** means 'advice' or 'advise someone' (*we counseled him on estate planning*).

coun·cil·man /'kounsəlmən/ (or **councilwoman** /'kounsəl,wŏŏmən/) ▶n. (pl. **councilmen** or **councilwomen**) a member of a council, especially a municipal one.

coun·ci·lor /'kouns(ə)lər/ (Brit. **councillor**) ▶n. a member of a council.

coun·sel /'kounsəl/ ▶n. **1** advice given to someone. **2** (pl. same) a lawyer or other legal adviser conducting a case. ▶v. (**counsels, counseling, counseled**) **1** give advice to: *we counseled him on estate planning.* **2** give professional help and advice to someone with personal or psychological problems. **3** recommend a course of action. – PHRASES **keep one's own counsel** not reveal one's plans or opinions.

coun·se·lor /'kouns(ə)lər/ (Brit. **counsellor**) ▶n. **1** a person trained to give advice on personal or psychological problems. **2** a person who supervises children at a camp. **3** a senior officer in the diplomatic service. **4** a trial lawyer.

count[1] /kount/ ▶v. **1** calculate the total number of a collection of people or things. **2** say numbers in ascending order. **3** include someone or something when calculating a total. **4** regard or be regarded as being: *people she had counted as her friends.* **5** be important; matter: *it's the thought that counts.* **6** (**count on**) rely on someone or something. **7** (**count someone in** or **out**) include (or exclude) someone in a planned activity. ▶n. **1** an act of counting. **2** the total found by counting. **3** a point for discussion or consideration: *she is unsuitable on every count.* **4** Law each of the charges against an accused person. ∎ **count·a·ble** adj. – PHRASES **count the days** (or **hours**) be impatient for time to pass. **keep** (or **lose**) **count** take note of (or forget) the number or amount when counting. **down for the count 1** Boxing defeated by being knocked to the ground and unable to rise within ten seconds. **2** unconscious or sound asleep.

count[2] ▶n. a European nobleman whose rank corresponds to that of an English earl.

count·down /'kount,doun/ ▶n. **1** an act of counting in reverse order to zero, especially before the launch of a rocket. **2** the final moments before a significant event.

coun·te·nance /'kountn-əns/ ▶n. a person's face or facial expression. ▶v. tolerate or agree to: *his mother would never countenance such a marriage.*

coun·ter[1] /'kountər/ ▶n. **1** a long flat fixture over which goods are sold or served or across which business is conducted with customers. **2** a small disk used in board games for keeping the score or as a place marker. **3** a person or thing that counts something. **4** a token representing a coin.

– PHRASES **over the counter** by ordinary sale in a store, with no need for a prescription or license. **under the counter** (or **table**) bought or sold secretly and illegally.

coun·ter² ▶ v. **1** speak or act in opposition or response to: *they will bolster the resources needed to counter terrorism.* **2** Boxing give a return blow while parrying. ▶ adv. (**counter to**) in the opposite direction or in opposition to. ▶ adj. responding to something of the same kind, especially in opposition: *argument and counter argument.* ▶ n. an act that opposes or prevents something else.

coun·ter- ▶ prefix **1** opposing or done in return: *counterattack.* **2** in the opposite direction: *counterpoise.* **3** corresponding: *counterpart.*

coun·ter·act /'kountər,akt/ ▶ v. act against something so as to reduce its force or cancel it out. ■ **coun·ter·ac·tion** /,kountər'aksнən/ n. **coun·ter·ac·tive** /kountər'aktiv/ adj.

coun·ter·at·tack /'kountərə,tak/ ▶ n. an attack made in response to one by an opponent. ▶ v. attack someone in response to an attack.

coun·ter·bal·ance ▶ n. /'kountər,baləns/ **1** a weight that balances another. **2** a factor that has the opposite effect to that of another and so balances it out. ▶ v. /,kountər'baləns/ have an opposing and balancing effect on: *his steadiness would counterbalance the kid's nervous manner.*

coun·ter·charge /'kountər,cнärj/ ▶ n. **1** an accusation made in turn by someone against their accuser: *charges and countercharges concerning producers, quotas, and affidavits.* **2** a charge by police or an armed force in response to one made against them.

coun·ter·claim /'kountər,klām/ ▶ n. a claim made in response to and opposing a previous claim.

coun·ter·clock·wise /,kountər'kläk,wīz/ ▶ adv. & adj. in the opposite direction to the way in which the hands of a clock move around.

coun·ter·cul·ture /'kountər,kəlcнər/ ▶ n. a way of life and set of attitudes that are at variance with those accepted by most of society.

coun·ter·es·pi·o·nage /,kountər'espēə,näzн, -,näj/ ▶ n. activities designed to prevent or thwart spying by an enemy.

coun·ter·feit /'kountər,fit/ ▶ adj. made in exact imitation of something valuable with the intention to deceive or defraud others. ▶ n. a forgery. ▶ v. **1** imitate something fraudulently. **2** pretend to feel or possess an emotion or quality. ■ **coun·ter·feit·er** n.

coun·ter·in·tel·li·gence /,kountərin'teləjəns/ ▶ n. activities designed to prevent or thwart spying, intelligence gathering, and sabotage by an enemy or other foreign entity.

coun·ter·in·tu·i·tive /,kountərin't(y)ōōitiv/ ▶ adj. at variance with intuition or common-sense expectation.

coun·ter·mand /,kountər'mand, 'kountər,mand/ ▶ v. cancel an order.

coun·ter·meas·ure /'kountər,mezнər/ ▶ n. an action taken to counteract a danger or threat.

coun·ter·of·fen·sive /'kountərə,fensiv/ ▶ n. an attack made in response to one from an enemy, typically on a large scale or for a prolonged period.

coun·ter·pane /'kountər,pān/ ▶ n. a bedspread.

coun·ter·part /'kountər,pärt/ ▶ n. a person or

thing that corresponds to another: *the minister held talks with his French counterpart.*

coun·ter·point /'kountər,point/ ▶ n. **1** the technique of writing or playing a melody or melodies together with another, according to fixed rules. **2** a melody played together with another. **3** a pleasing or notable contrast to something: *dill crème fraiche was a nice counterpoint to the fish.* ▶ v. **1** add counterpoint to a melody. **2** contrast with something.

coun·ter·poise /'kountər,poiz/ ▶ n. & v. another term for COUNTERBALANCE.

coun·ter·pro·duc·tive /,kountərprə'dəktiv/ ▶ adj. having the opposite of the desired effect.

Coun·ter-Ref·or·ma·tion ▶ n. the reform of the Church of Rome in the 16th and 17th centuries that was stimulated by the Protestant Reformation.

coun·ter·rev·o·lu·tion /'kountər,revə'lōōsнən/ ▶ n. a revolution opposing a former one or reversing its results. ■ **coun·ter·rev·o·lu·tion·ar·y** /-,nerē/ adj. & n.

coun·ter·sign /'kountər,sīn/ ▶ v. sign a document already signed by another person.

coun·ter·sink /'kountər,siNGk/ ▶ v. (past and past part. **countersunk** /-,səNGk/) **1** enlarge the rim of a drilled hole so that a screw or bolt can be inserted level with the surface. **2** drive a screw or bolt into such a hole.

coun·ter·ten·or /'kountər,tenər/ ▶ n. the highest male adult singing voice.

coun·ter·ter·ror·ism /,kountər'terə,rizəm/ ▶ n. political or military activities designed to prevent or thwart terrorism. ■ **coun·ter·ter·ror·ist** /,kountər'terərist/ n.

counter·top /'kountər,täp/ ▶ n. the flat top of a counter, especially when regarded as a work or storage space: *countertop appliances.*

coun·ter·vail /,kountər'vāl/ ▶ v. (usu. as adj. **countervailing**) counteract something with something of equal force: *a profusion of countervailing opinions.*

coun·ter·weight /'kountər,wāt/ ▶ n. a weight that counterbalances another.

count·ess /'kountəs/ ▶ n. **1** the wife or widow of a count or earl. **2** a woman holding the rank of count or earl.

count·ing /'kountiNG/ ▶ prep. taking account of; including.

count·less /'kountləs/ ▶ adj. too many to be counted; very many.

count noun ▶ n. a noun that can form a plural and, in the singular, can be used with *a* (the indefinite article), e.g., *books, a book.* Contrasted with MASS NOUN.

coun·tri·fied /'kəntri,fīd/ (also **countryfied**) ▶ adj. characteristic of the country or country life.

coun·try /'kəntrē/ ▶ n. (pl. **countries**) **1** a nation with its own government, occupying a particular territory. **2** districts outside large urban areas. **3** an area with regard to its physical features: *hill country.* **4** country music.

– PHRASES **across country** not keeping to roads.

coun·try and west·ern ▶ n. country music.

coun·try club ▶ n. a club with sporting and social facilities, set in a suburban area.

coun·try code ▶ n. a sequence of numbers prefixed to a telephone number to connect to an exchange in another country.

coun·try cous·in ▶ n. an unsophisticated and provincial person.

coun·try dance ▶ n. a traditional type of English dance, in particular one performed by couples facing each other in long lines.

coun·try·fied ▶ adj. variant spelling of COUNTRIFIED.

coun·try·man /ˈkəntrēmən/ (or **countrywoman**) ▶ n. (pl. **countrymen** or **countrywomen**) 1 a person from the same country as someone else. 2 Brit a person living or born in a rural area.

coun·try mu·sic ▶ n. a form of popular music originating in the rural southern US, typically featuring ballads and dance tunes accompanied by a guitar.

country rock ▶ n. a type of popular music that is a blend of country and rock.

coun·try·side /ˈkəntrēˌsīd/ ▶ n. the land and scenery of a rural area.

coun·try·wide /ˈkəntrēˈwīd/ ▶ adj. & adv. extending throughout a nation.

coun·ty /ˈkountē/ ▶ n. (pl. **counties**) 1 each of the main areas into which some countries are divided for the purposes of local government. 2 a political and administrative division of a state.

coun·ty seat ▶ n. the town that is the administrative capital of a county.

coup /ko͞o/ ▶ n. (pl. **coups** /ko͞oz/) 1 (also **coup d'état** /ˌko͞o dāˈtä/) a sudden violent seizure of power from a government. 2 a successful move that achieves something difficult: *the ten-year agreement is a major coup for the company.*

coup de grâce /ˌko͞o də ˈgräs/ ▶ n. (pl. **coups de grâce** pronunc. same) a final blow or shot given to kill a wounded person or animal.

coupe /ko͞op/ (also **coupé** /ko͞oˈpā/) ▶ n. a car with a fixed roof, two doors, and a sloping rear.

cou·ple /ˈkəpəl/ ▶ n. 1 two people or things of the same sort considered together. 2 (treated as sing. or pl.) two people who are married or in a romantic or sexual relationship. 3 informal an indefinite small number. ▶ v. 1 link or combine: *anger control coupled with relaxation therapy significantly lowered blood pressure.* 2 have sex. ■ **cou·ple·dom** n. **cou·pler** /ˈkəp(ə)lər/ n.

cou·plet /ˈkəplət/ ▶ n. a pair of successive lines of verse, typically rhyming and of the same length.

cou·pling /ˈkəp(ə)liNG/ ▶ n. a device for connecting railroad vehicles or parts of machinery together.

cou·pon /ˈk(y)o͞oˌpän/ ▶ n. 1 a voucher entitling the holder to a discount or to buy something. 2 a detachable portion of a bond that is given up in return for a payment of interest.

cour·age /ˈkərij, ˈkə-rij/ ▶ n. 1 the ability to do something that frightens one. 2 strength in the face of pain or grief.
– PHRASES **have the courage of one's convictions** act on one's beliefs despite danger or disapproval.

cou·ra·geous /kəˈrājəs/ ▶ adj. not deterred by danger or pain; brave. ■ **cou·ra·geous·ly** adv.

cour·gette /ˌko͞orˈzHet/ ▶ n. Brit. a zucchini.

cou·ri·er /ˈko͞orēər, ˈkərēər/ ▶ n. 1 a person employed to deliver goods or documents quickly. 2 chiefly Brit. a person employed to guide and assist a group of tourists. ▶ v. send goods or documents by courier.

course /kôrs/ ▶ n. 1 a direction taken or intended to be taken. 2 the way in which something

progresses or develops: *the course of history.* 3 (also **course of action**) a way of dealing with a situation: *my decision represented the wisest course open to me at the time.* 4 a dish forming one of the stages of a meal. 5 a series of lectures or lessons in a particular subject. 6 a series of repeated treatments or doses of medication. 7 an area of land or water prepared for racing, golf, or another sport. 8 a continuous horizontal layer of brick or stone in a wall. ▶ v. 1 (of liquid) flow. 2 (often as n. **coursing**) pursue game, especially hares, with greyhounds using sight rather than scent.
– PHRASES **in (the) course of** 1 in the process of. 2 during. **of course** 1 as expected. 2 certainly; yes.

cours·er[1] /ˈkôrsər/ ▶ n. literary a swift horse.

cours·er[2] ▶ n. a person who goes coursing with greyhounds.

course·work /ˈkôrsˌwərk/ ▶ n. work done during a course of study, usually counting toward a final grade.

court /kôrt/ ▶ n. 1 (also **court of law**) the judge, jury, and law officers before whom legal cases are heard. 2 the place where a court of law meets. 3 a quadrangular area marked out for ball games such as tennis. 4 a quadrangle surrounded by a building or group of buildings. 5 the residence, councilors, and household of a sovereign. ▶ v. 1 pay special attention to someone to try to win their support. 2 try hard to win favorable attention. 3 behave in a way that makes one vulnerable to: *he has often courted controversy.* 4 dated be involved with someone romantically, especially with a view to marriage. 5 (of a male bird or other animal) try to attract a mate.
– PHRASES **hold court** be the center of attention. **out of court** before a legal hearing can take place. **pay court to** pay flattering attention to someone.

cour·te·ous /ˈkərtēəs/ ▶ adj. polite, respectful, and considerate. ■ **cour·te·ous·ly** adv. **cour·te·ous·ness** n.

cour·te·san /ˈkôrtəzən, ˈkər-/ ▶ n. a prostitute with wealthy or upper-class clients.

cour·te·sy /ˈkərtəsē/ ▶ n. (pl. **courtesies**) 1 polite and considerate behavior. 2 something said or done for politeness in a formal social situation: *there was a ritual exchange of courtesies with the lawyers.*
– PHRASES **(by) courtesy of** given or allowed by someone.

cour·te·sy ti·tle ▶ n. a title given to someone as a mark of courtesy, such as Mr. or Mrs.

court·house /ˈkôrtˌhous/ ▶ n. 1 a building in which a court of law meets. 2 a building containing the administrative offices of a county.

cour·ti·er /ˈkôrtēər, ˈkôrcHər/ ▶ n. a sovereign's companion or adviser.

court·ly /ˈkôrtlē/ ▶ adj. (**courtlier, courtliest**) very polite and dignified. ■ **court·li·ness** n.

court mar·tial ▶ n. (pl. **courts martial**) a court for trying members of the armed services accused of breaking military law. ▶ v. (**court-martial**) (**court-martials, court-martialing, court-martialed**) try a member of the armed services by court martial.

court or·der ▶ n. a direction issued by a court or a judge requiring a person to do or not do something.

court re·port·er ►n. a stenographer who makes a verbatim record and transcription of the proceedings in a court of law.

court·room /'kôrt,rōōm, -,rŏŏm/ ►n. the room or building in which a court of law meets.

court·ship /'kôrt,SHip/ ►n. **1** a period during which a couple develop a romantic relationship. **2** the courting of a person to win their support. **3** the behavior of male birds and other animals aimed at attracting a mate.

court·yard /'kôrt,yärd/ ►n. an open area enclosed by walls or buildings, especially in a castle or large house.

cous·cous /'kōōs,kōōs/ ►n. a North African dish of steamed or soaked semolina, usually served with spicy meat or vegetables.

cous·in /'kəzən/ ►n. **1** (also **first cousin**) a child of one's uncle or aunt. **2** a person of a similar or related people or nation: *our American cousins*. ■ **cous·in·ly** adj. **cous·in·ship** /-,SHip/ n.
– PHRASES **second cousin** a child of one's parent's first cousin. **third cousin** a child of one's parent's second cousin.

cou·ture /kōō'tŏŏr, -'tʏr/ ►n. **1** the design and manufacture of fashionable clothes to a client's specific requirements. **2** fashionable made-to-measure clothes.

cou·tu·ri·er /kōō'tŏŏrēər, -'tŏŏrē,ā/ ►n. (fem. **couturière** /kōō'tŏŏrēər, -,tŏŏrē'e(ə)r/) a person who designs and sells fashionable made-to-measure clothes.

cou·ver·ture /,kōōvər't(y)ŏŏr/ ►n. chocolate with extra cocoa butter to give a high gloss, used to cover candies and cakes.

co·va·lent /,kō'vālənt/ ►adj. (of a chemical bond) formed by the sharing of electrons between atoms. Often contrasted with IONIC. ■ **co·va·len·cy** n. **co·va·lent·ly** adv.

cove /kōv/ ►n. **1** a small sheltered bay. **2** a concave arch or arched molding at the junction of a wall with a ceiling. ■ **coved** adj. **cov·ing** n.

cov·en /'kəvən/ ►n. a group of witches who meet regularly.

cov·e·nant /'kəvənənt/ ►n. **1** a formal agreement, especially a written contract by which one agrees to make regular payments to a charity. **2** (in Judaism and Christianity) an agreement that brings about a commitment between God and his people. ►v. agree or pay something by a formal written contract. ■ **cov·e·nan·tal** /,kəvə'nantl/ adj.

cov·er /'kəvər/ ►v. **1** put something over or in front of someone or something so as to protect or hide them. **2** spread or extend over: *the grounds covered eight acres*. **3** deal with or report on: *the course will cover a range of subjects*. **4** travel a specified distance. **5** (of money) be enough to pay for something. **6** (of insurance) protect against a liability, loss, or accident. **7** disguise or hide: *I laughed to cover my embarrassment*. **8** (**cover something up**) try to hide or deny something illegal or wrong. **9** (**cover for**) temporarily take over the job of a colleague. **10** aim a gun at someone to prevent them from moving or escaping. **11** protect an exposed person by shooting at the enemy. **12** (in team games) take up a position ready to defend against an opponent. **13** record or perform a cover version of a song. ►n. **1** something that covers or protects. **2** a thick protective outer part or page of a book or magazine. **3** shelter or protection: *they ran for cover*. **4** military support for someone in danger. **5** a means of concealing an illegal or secret activity: *we are not using science as a cover for commercial whaling*. **6** (also **cover version**) a recording or performance of a song previously recorded by a different artist. **7** a place setting at a table in a restaurant. ■ **cov·er·ing** n.
– PHRASES **cover one's back** informal take steps to avoid attack or criticism. **under cover of 1** concealed by something. **2** while pretending to do something.

cov·er·age /'kəv(ə)rij/ ►n. **1** the treatment of a subject by the media. **2** the extent to which something is covered: *eighty transmitters would give nationwide coverage*.

cov·er·all /'kəvər,ôl/ ►n. (also **coveralls**) a full-length protective outer garment.

cover charge ►n. a service charge per person added to the bill in a restaurant.

cov·er girl ►n. a female whose picture appears on a magazine cover.

cov·er·let /'kəvərlət/ ►n. a bedspread.

cover let·ter ►n. a letter sent with, and explaining the contents of, another document or a parcel.

co·vert ►adj. /'kōvərt, kō'vərt, 'kəvərt/ not done openly; secret. ►n. /'kəvər(t), 'kōvərt/ a thicket in which game can hide. ■ **co·vert·ly** /'kōvərtlē, kō'vərtlē, 'kəvərtlē/ adv.

cov·er-up ►n. an attempt to conceal a mistake or crime.

cov·et /'kəvət/ ►v. (**covets, coveting, coveted**) long to possess something belonging to someone else. ■ **cov·et·a·ble** adj.

cov·et·ous /'kəvətəs/ ►adj. longing to possess something. ■ **cov·et·ous·ly** adv. **cov·et·ous·ness** n.

cov·ey /'kəvē/ ►n. (pl. **coveys**) a small flock of game birds, especially partridge.

cow[1] /kou/ ►n. **1** a fully grown female animal of a domesticated breed of ox. **2** the female of certain other large animals, such as the elephant. **3** informal, derogatory a disliked or unpleasant woman.
– PHRASES **till the cows come home** informal for an indefinitely long time.

cow[2] ►v. frighten someone into giving in to one's wishes.

cow·ard /'kou-ərd/ ►n. a person who is afraid to do dangerous or unpleasant things. ■ **cow·ard·li·ness** /'kou-ərdlēnis/ n. **cow·ard·ly** /'kou-ərdlē/ adv.

cow·ard·ice /'kou-ərdəs/ ►n. lack of courage.

cow·bell /'kou,bel/ ►n. a bell hung around a cow's neck.

cow·boy /'kou,boi/ ►n. **1** a man on horseback who herds cattle, especially in the western US. **2** a reckless or careless person.

cow·boy boot ►n. a high-heeled boot of a style originally worn by cowboys, typically with a pointed toe.

cow·catch·er /'kou,kaCHər, -,keCHər/ ►n. a metal frame at the front of a locomotive for pushing aside obstacles.

cow·er /'kou(-ə)r/ ►v. shrink back or crouch down in fear.

cow flop ►n. informal a cowpat.

cow·hand /'kou,hand/ ►n. a person employed to tend or ranch cattle.

cow·herd /'kou,hərd/ ►n. a person who looks after grazing cattle.

cow·hide /'kou̇ˌhīd/ ▸ n. a cow's hide.

cowl /kou̇l/ ▸ n. **1** a large loose hood forming part of a monk's habit. **2** a hood-shaped covering for a chimney or ventilation shaft. **3** another term for COWLING. ■ **cowled** adj.

cow·lick /'kou̇ˌlik/ ▸ n. a lock of hair that grows in a direction different from the rest and that resists being combed flat.

cowl·ing /'kou̇liNG/ ▸ n. a removable cover for a vehicle or aircraft engine.

cow·pat /'kou̇ˌpat/ ▸ n. a flat, round piece of cow dung.

cow·pea /'kou̇ˌpē/ ▸ n. a black-eyed pea, especially when grown as a forage or cover crop.

cow·poke /'kou̇ˌpōk/ ▸ n. informal a cowboy.

cow·pox /'kou̇ˌpäks/ ▸ n. a disease of cows' udders spread by a virus, which can be caught by humans and resembles mild smallpox.

cow·rie /'kou̇rē/ ▸ n. (pl. **cowries**) a sea mollusk having a glossy, domed shell with a long, narrow opening.

cow·slip /'kou̇ˌslip/ ▸ n. a wild primula with clusters of yellow flowers in spring.

cox /käks/ ▸ n. a coxswain. ▸ v. act as a coxswain for a racing boat or crew. ■ **cox·less** adj.

cox·comb /'käksˌkōm/ ▸ n. old use a vain and conceited man; a dandy.

cox·swain /'käksən/ ▸ n. a person who steers a boat.

coy /koi/ ▸ adj. (**coyer**, **coyest**) **1** pretending to be shy or modest. **2** reluctant to give details about something sensitive: *he's coy about his age.* ■ **coy·ly** adv. **coy·ness** n.

coy·o·te /'kīˌōt, kīˈōtē/ ▸ n. (pl. same or **coyotes**) a wolflike wild dog native to North America.

coy·pu /'koiˌpoō/ ▸ n. (pl. **coypus**) a large beaverlike South American rodent, farmed for its fur.

coz /kəz/ ▸ conj. informal short for BECAUSE.

co·zy /'kōzē/ (Brit. **cosy**) ▸ adj. (**cozier**, **coziest**) **1** comfortable, warm, and secure. **2** not seeking or offering challenge or difficulty: *the cozy belief that man is master.* **3** (of a transaction or arrangement) working to the mutual advantage of the people involved (used to convey a suspicion of corruption): *a cozy deal.* ▸ n. (pl. **cozies**) a cover to keep a teapot or a boiled egg hot. ▸ v. (**cozies**, **cozying**, **cozied**) informal (**cozy up to**) try to gain the favor of someone. ■ **co·zi·ly** adv. **co·zi·ness** n.

CPA ▸ abbr. certified public accountant.

CPI ▸ abbr. consumer price index.

Cpl. ▸ abbr. corporal.

CPR ▸ abbr. cardiopulmonary resuscitation.

cps (also **c.p.s.**) ▸ abbr. **1** Computing characters per second. **2** cycles per second.

Cpt. ▸ abbr. captain.

CPU ▸ abbr. Computing central processing unit.

Cr ▸ symbol the chemical element chromium.

crab /krab/ ▸ n. **1** a marine shellfish, some kinds of which are edible, with a broad shell and five pairs of legs, the first of which are modified as pincers. **2** (**crabs**) informal an infestation of crab lice. ▸ v. (**crabs**, **crabbing**, **crabbed**) **1** move sideways or at an angle. **2** fish for crabs. ■ **crab·ber** n. **crab·like** /-ˌlīk/ adj. & adv.

– PHRASES **catch a crab** make a faulty stroke in rowing in which the oar is jammed under the water or misses the water completely.

crab ap·ple ▸ n. a small, sour kind of apple.

crab·bed /'krabəd/ ▸ adj. **1** (of writing) very small and hard to read. **2** bad-tempered; crabby.

crab·by /'krabē/ ▸ adj. (**crabbier**, **crabbiest**) bad-tempered; irritable. ■ **crab·bi·ly** adv. **crab·bi·ness** n.

crab·grass /'krabˌgras/ ▸ n. a creeping grass that can become a serious weed.

crab louse ▸ n. a louse that infests human body hair.

crab·meat /'krabˌmēt/ ▸ n. the flesh of a crab as food.

crack /krak/ ▸ n. **1** a narrow opening between two parts of something that has split or been broken. **2** a sudden sharp noise. **3** a sharp blow. **4** informal a joke, especially a critical one. **5** informal an attempt to do something: *she's made the most of her first crack at stardom.* **6** (also **crack cocaine**) a very strong form of cocaine broken into small pieces. ▸ v. **1** break apart or without complete separation of the parts. **2** give way under pressure or strain. **3** make a sudden sharp sound. **4** hit someone or something hard. **5** (of a person's voice) suddenly change in pitch, especially through strain. **6** informal solve or decipher: *he took less than a day to crack the code.* **7** tell a joke. ▸ adj. very good or skillful: *he is a crack shot.*

– PHRASES **crack down on** informal take strong action against someone or something. **crack of dawn** daybreak. **crack up** informal **1** suffer an emotional breakdown under pressure. **2** burst into laughter. **3** (**be cracked up to be**) informal be claimed to be: *acting isn't as glamorous as it's cracked up to be.* **get cracking** informal begin immediately and work quickly.

crack·brained /'krakˌbrānd/ ▸ adj. informal very foolish.

crack·down /'krakˌdou̇n/ ▸ n. a set of severe measures against undesirable or illegal behavior.

cracked /krakt/ ▸ adj. **1** having cracks. **2** informal insane; crazy.

cracked wheat ▸ n. grains of wheat that have been crushed into small pieces.

crack·er /'krakər/ ▸ n. **1** a thin, crisp wafer. **2** a firework that explodes with a crack. **3** Brit. informal an excellent example of something.

crack·er·jack /'krakərˌjak/ ▸ n. exceptionally good: *the actors do a crackerjack job.*

crack·ers /'krakərz/ ▸ adj. informal insane; crazy.

crack·le /'krakəl/ ▸ v. make a series of slight cracking noises. ▸ n. a series of slight cracking noises. ■ **crack·ly** adj.

crack·ling /'kraklən, -liNG/ ▸ n. the crisp fatty skin of roast pork.

crack·pot /'krakˌpät/ informal ▸ n. an eccentric or foolish person. ▸ adj. eccentric; impractical.

-cracy ▸ comb.form referring to a particular form of government or rule: *democracy.*

cra·dle /'krādl/ ▸ n. **1** a baby's bed, especially one on rockers. **2** a place in which something originates or flourishes: *the Middle East is believed to be the cradle of agriculture.* **3** a supporting framework, in particular for a boat under repair. **4** the part of a telephone on which the receiver rests when not in use. ▸ v. hold something gently and protectively.

cra·dle-rob·ber ▸ n. informal, derogatory a person who has a sexual relationship with a much younger person.

craft /kraft/ ▸ n. **1** an activity involving skill in making things by hand. **2** the skill needed for one's work: *he learned his craft in Holland.*

3 (**crafts**) things made by hand. **4** skill in deceiving others; cunning. **5** (pl. same) a boat, ship, or aircraft. ▶v. make something skillfully. ∎ **craft·er** n.

crafts·man /'kraf(t)smən/ (or **craftswoman** /'kraf(t)s,wŏŏmən/) ▶n. (pl. **craftsmen** or **craftswomen**) a worker skilled in a particular craft. ∎ **crafts·man·ship** /-,SHip/ n.

craft·work /'kraft,wərk/ ▶n. **1** the making of things by hand. **2** items produced by hand. ∎ **craft·work·er** n.

craft·y /'kraftē/ ▶adj. (**craftier**, **craftiest**) clever at deceiving people; cunning. ∎ **craft·i·ly** adv. **craft·i·ness** n.

crag /krag/ ▶n. a steep or rugged cliff or rock face.

crag·gy /'kragē/ ▶adj. (**craggier**, **craggiest**) **1** having many crags. **2** (of a man's face) attractively rugged.

crake /krāk/ ▶n. a bird of the rail family with a short bill, such as the corn crake.

cram /kram/ ▶v. (**crams**, **cramming**, **crammed**) **1** force too many people or things into a place or container. **2** fill to overflowing: *the hut was crammed with sacks of wheat or corn.* **3** study intensively just before an exam.

cramp /kramp/ ▶n. **1** painful involuntary contraction of a muscle or muscles. **2** a tool for clamping two objects together. ▶v. **1** restrict the development of: *tighter rules will cramp economic growth.* **2** fasten something with a cramp or cramps.

cramped /kram(p)t/ ▶adj. **1** uncomfortably small or crowded. **2** (of handwriting) small and difficult to read.

cram·pon /'kram,pän/ ▶n. a metal plate with spikes, fixed to a boot for climbing on ice or rock.

cran·ber·ry /'kran,berē, -bərē/ ▶n. (pl. **cranberries**) a small sour red berry used in cooking.

crane /krān/ ▶n. **1** a tall machine used for moving heavy objects by suspending them from a projecting arm. **2** a gray or white wading bird with long legs and a long neck. ▶v. stretch out one's neck to see something.

crane fly ▶n. a slender fly with very long legs; a daddy longlegs.

cra·ni·al /'krānēəl/ ▶adj. relating to the skull or cranium.

cra·ni·o·sa·cral ther·a·py /,krānēō'sakrəl, -'sākrəl/ ▶n. a system of alternative medicine intended to relieve pain and tension by gentle manipulations of the skull.

cra·ni·um /'krānēəm/ ▶n. (pl. **craniums** or **crania** /'krānēə/) the skull, especially the part enclosing the brain.

crank¹ /kraNGk/ ▶v. **1** turn a crankshaft or handle to start an internal combustion engine. **2** (**crank something up**) informal increase the intensity of something. **3** (**crank something out**) informal, derogatory produce something regularly and routinely. ▶n. a right-angled part of an axle or shaft, for converting linear to circular motion or vice versa.

crank² ▶n. an eccentric or obsessive person.

crank·case /'kraNGk,kās/ ▶n. a case or covering enclosing a crankshaft.

crank·shaft /'kraNGk,SHaft/ ▶n. a shaft driven by a crank.

crank·y /'kraNGkē/ ▶adj. (**crankier**, **crankiest**) informal **1** bad-tempered; irritable. **2** Brit. eccentric or odd. ∎ **crank·i·ly** adv. **crank·i·ness** n.

cran·ny /'kranē/ ▶n. (pl. **crannies**) a small, narrow space or opening.

crap¹ /krap/ vulgar slang ▶n. **1** something that is of extremely poor quality. **2** excrement. **3** nonsense. **4** clutter; junk. ▶v. (**craps**, **crapping**, **crapped**) defecate. ∎ **crap·py** adj.

crap² ▶n. a losing throw of 2, 3, or 12 in craps. ▶v. (**crap out**) informal **1** make a losing throw at craps. **2** fail in what one is attempting to do: *the Rams almost crapped out late in the game.* **3** (of a machine) break down: *the laptop crapped out.*

crape /krāp/ ▶n. black silk, formerly used for mourning clothes.

craps /kraps/ ▶pl.n. (treated as sing.) a gambling game played with two dice.

crap·shoot /'krap,SHŏŏt/ ▶n. **1** a game of craps. **2** a risky or uncertain matter.

crash /kraSH/ ▶v. **1** (of a vehicle) collide violently with an obstacle or another vehicle. **2** (of an aircraft) fall from the sky and hit the land or sea. **3** move with force, speed, and sudden loud noise: *the cup crashed to the floor.* **4** make a sudden loud noise. **5** (of shares) fall suddenly in value. **6** (of a computer, system, or software) fail suddenly. **7** informal fall deeply asleep. **8** informal gate-crash a party. ▶n. an instance or sound of crashing. ▶adj. rapid and concentrated: *a crash course in Italian.*

crash-dive ▶v. (of an aircraft or submarine) dive rapidly or uncontrollably.

crash hel·met ▶n. a helmet worn by a motorcyclist to protect the head.

crash·ing /'kraSHiNG/ ▶adj. informal complete; total: *a crashing bore.* ∎ **crash·ing·ly** adv.

crash-land ▶v. (of an aircraft) land roughly in an emergency.

crash·wor·thi·ness /'kraSH,wərTHēnis/ ▶n. the degree to which a vehicle will protect its occupants from the effects of a crash. ∎ **crash·wor·thy** /'kraSH,wərTHē/ adj.

crass /kras/ ▶adj. very thoughtless and stupid. ∎ **crass·ly** adv. **crass·ness** n.

-crat ▶comb.form referring to a member or supporter of a particular form of government or rule: *democrat.*

crate /krāt/ ▶n. **1** a slatted wooden case for transporting goods. **2** a square container divided into small individual units for holding bottles. **3** informal an old and ramshackle vehicle. ▶v. pack something in a crate for transportation.

cra·ter /'krātər/ ▶n. **1** a large hollow forming the mouth of a volcano. **2** a large bowl-shaped hollow caused by an explosion or the impact of a meteorite. ▶v. form a crater or craters in the ground or a planet.

-cratic ▶comb.form relating to a particular kind of government or rule: *democratic.*

cra·vat /krə'vat/ ▶n. a short, wide strip of fabric worn by men around the neck and tucked inside an open-necked shirt.

crave /krāv/ ▶v. **1** feel a powerful desire for something. **2** old use ask for: *I must crave your indulgence.*

cra·ven /'krāvən/ ▶adj. lacking in courage; cowardly. ∎ **cra·ven·ly** adv.

crav·ing /'krāviNG/ ▶n. a powerful desire for something.

craw /krô/ ▶ n. dated the crop (part of the throat) of a bird.
– PHRASES **stick in one's craw** see STICK².

craw·fish /'krô,fiSH/ ▶ n. (pl. same or **crawfishes**) a crayfish.

crawl /krôl/ ▶ v. **1** move forward on the hands and knees or with the body close to the ground. **2** (of an insect or small animal) move slowly along a surface. **3** move along very slowly: *the traffic was crawling along.* **4** (**be crawling with**) be unpleasantly covered or crowded with: *the place was crawling with soldiers.* **5** informal behave in an excessively friendly or submissive way to win someone's favor. ▶ n. **1** an act of crawling. **2** a very slow speed. **3** a swimming stroke involving alternate overarm movements and rapid kicks of the legs.
– PHRASES **make one's skin crawl** cause one to feel fear or disgust (likened to something crawling on the skin).

crawl·er /'krôlər/ ▶ n. Computing a program that searches the World Wide Web, typically in order to create an index of data.

cray·fish /'krā,fiSH/ ▶ n. (pl. same or **crayfishes**) a freshwater or sea shellfish resembling a small lobster.

cray·on /'krā,än, 'krāən/ ▶ n. a stick of colored chalk or wax, used for drawing. ▶ v. draw something with a crayon or crayons.

craze /krāz/ ▶ n. a widespread but short-lived enthusiasm for something. ▶ v. (**be crazed**) (of a surface) be covered with a network of fine cracks. ■ **cra·zing** n.

crazed /krāzd/ ▶ adj. (often in combination) behaving in an uncontrolled or insane way: *drug-crazed kids.*

cra·zy /'krāzē/ ▶ adj. (**crazier, craziest**) **1** insane, especially in a wild way. **2** very enthusiastic: *I'm crazy about Cindy.* **3** foolish or absurd: *it was a crazy idea.* ▶ n. (pl. **crazies**) informal an insane person. ■ **cra·zi·ly** adv. **cra·zi·ness** n.
– PHRASES **like crazy** to a great degree.

creak /krēk/ ▶ v. **1** make or move with a scraping or squeaking sound. **2** show weakness under strain: *the system is creaking at the seams.* ▶ n. a scraping or squeaking sound. ■ **creak·y** adj. (**creakier, creakiest**).

cream /krēm/ ▶ n. **1** the thick fatty liquid that rises to the top when milk is left to stand. **2** a food containing cream or having a creamy consistency. **3** a thick liquid cosmetic or medical substance that is applied to the skin. **4** the very best of a group: *the cream of American society.* **5** a very pale yellow or off-white color. ▶ v. **1** mash a cooked vegetable with milk or cream. **2** work butter to form a smooth soft paste. **3** defeat someone heavily, especially in a sports contest.

cream cheese ▶ n. soft, rich cheese made from unskimmed milk and cream.

cream·er /'krēmər/ ▶ n. **1** a cream or milk substitute for adding to coffee or tea. **2** a small pitcher for cream.

cream·er·y /'krēm(ə)rē/ ▶ n. (pl. **creameries**) a place where butter and cheese are made.

cream of tar·tar ▶ n. an acidic compound produced during the fermentation of wine and used chiefly in baking powder.

cream puff ▶ n. a cake made of puff pastry filled with cream.

cream·y /'krēmē/ ▶ adj. (**creamier, creamiest**) resembling or containing a lot of cream.

■ **cream·i·ly** adv. **cream·i·ness** n.

crease /krēs/ ▶ n. **1** a line or ridge produced by folding, pressing, or crushing. **2** a wrinkle or furrow in the skin. ▶ v. **1** make or become crumpled or wrinkled. **2** (of a bullet) graze someone or something, causing little damage.

cre·ate /krē'āt/ ▶ v. **1** bring something into existence. **2** cause to happen: *divorce creates problems for children.* **3** appoint to a noble title or rank: *he was created a baronet.*

cre·a·tine /'krēə,tēn, 'krēətn/ ▶ n. a compound formed in protein metabolism and involved in the supply of energy for contraction of the muscles.

cre·a·tion /krē'āsHən/ ▶ n. **1** the action of bringing something into existence. **2** a thing that has been made or invented, especially something showing artistic talent. **3** (**the Creation**) the creating of the universe, regarded as an act of God. **4** (**Creation**) literary the universe.

cre·a·tion·ism /krē'āsHə,nizəm/ ▶ n. the belief that the universe and living creatures were created by God in accordance with the account given in the Old Testament. ■ **cre·a·tion·ist** n. & adj.

cre·a·tive /krē'ātiv/ ▶ adj. **1** involving the use of the imagination or original ideas in order to create something. **2** having good imagination or original ideas. ■ **cre·a·tive·ly** adv. **cre·a·tive·ness** n. **cre·a·tiv·i·ty** /,krē-ā'tivitē/ n.

cre·a·tive ac·count·ing ▶ n. informal the exploitation of loopholes in financial regulation to gain advantage or to present figures in a misleadingly favorable light.

cre·a·tor /krē'ātər/ ▶ n. **1** a person or thing that creates something. **2** (**the Creator**) God.

crea·ture /'krēCHər/ ▶ n. **1** a living being, in particular an animal as distinct from a person. **2** a person viewed in a particular way: *you heartless creature!*

crea·ture com·forts ▶ pl.n. things that contribute to a comfortable life, such as good food and accommodations.

crèche /kresH/ ▶ n. a model or tableau representing the scene of Jesus Christ's birth, typically displayed at Christmas.

cred /kred/ ▶ n. informal short for CREDIBILITY (sense 2).

cred·al /'krēdl/ (also **creedal**) ▶ adj. relating to a statement of Christian or other religious belief.

cre·dence /'krēdns/ ▶ n. **1** belief in something as true: *he gave no credence to the witness's statement.* **2** the likelihood of something being true; plausibility.

cre·den·tial /krə'denCHəl/ ▶ n. (usu. **credentials**) **1** a qualification, achievement, or quality that gives an indication of a person's suitability for something: *her academic credentials cannot be doubted.* **2** a document proving a person's identity or qualifications. **3** a letter of introduction given by a government to an ambassador before a new posting.

cred·i·bil·i·ty /,kredə'bilitē/ ▶ n. **1** the quality of being trusted or believable. **2** (also **street credibility**) acceptability among fashionable young urban people.

cred·i·bil·i·ty gap ▶ n. an apparent difference between what is said or promised and what happens or is true.

cred·i·ble /'kredəbəl/ ▶ adj. able to be believed; convincing. ■ **cred·i·bly** adv.

cred·it /'kredit/ ▶ n. **1** an arrangement in which a store or other business enables a customer to pay at a later date for goods or services supplied: *we supply quality cars on credit.* **2** money borrowed or lent under a credit arrangement. **3** public acknowledgment or praise for an achievement or quality. **4** a source of pride: *the fans are a credit to the club.* **5** a written acknowledgment of a contributor's role displayed at the beginning or end of a movie or television program. **6** an entry in an account recording a sum received. **7** a unit of study counting toward a degree or diploma.
▶ v. (**credits, crediting, credited**) **1** believe that someone has done something or has a particular quality: *he is credited with coining the phrase.* **2** add an amount of money to an account.
– PHRASES **do someone credit** make someone worthy of praise or respect.

cred·it·a·ble /'kreditəbəl/ ▶ adj. deserving public acknowledgment and praise. ■ **cred·it·a·bly** /-blē/ adv.

cred·it card ▶ n. a plastic card allowing the holder to buy things on credit.

cred·i·tor /'kreditər/ ▶ n. a person or company to whom money is owing.

cred·it un·ion ▶ n. a nonprofit cooperative whose members can borrow money at low interest rates.

cred·it·worth·y /'kredit,wərTHē/ ▶ adj. considered suitable to receive financial credit. ■ **cred·it·wor·thi·ness** n.

cre·do /'krēdō, 'krādō/ ▶ n. (pl. **credos**) a statement of a person's beliefs or aims.

cred·u·lous /'krejələs/ ▶ adj. excessively ready to believe things; gullible. ■ **cre·du·li·ty** /krə'd(y)ōōlitē/ n. **cred·u·lous·ly** adv.

Cree /krē/ ▶ n. (pl. same or **Crees**) a member of an American Indian people of central Canada.

creed /krēd/ ▶ n. **1** a system of religious belief; a faith. **2** a statement of beliefs or principles: *nationalism is his creed.*

creed·al /'krēdl/ ▶ adj. variant spelling of CREDAL.

creek /krēk/ ▶ n. **1** a small waterway such as an inlet in a shoreline. **2** a stream or minor tributary of a river.
– PHRASES **up the creek** informal in severe difficulty or trouble.

creel /krēl/ ▶ n. a large basket for carrying fish.

creep /krēp/ ▶ v. (past and past part. **crept**) **1** move slowly and carefully to avoid being noticed. **2** progress or develop gradually: *errors crept into his game.* **3** (as adj. **creeping**) (of a plant) growing along the ground or other surface. ▶ n. **1** informal a contemptible person, especially one who behaves in a servile way to win favor. **2** slow and gradual movement or progress.
– PHRASES **give someone the creeps** informal make someone feel disgust or fear.

creep·er /'krēpər/ ▶ n. a plant that grows along the ground or another surface.

creep·y /'krēpē/ ▶ adj. (**creepier, creepiest**) informal causing fear or unease. ■ **creep·i·ly** adv. **creep·i·ness** n.

creep·y-crawl·y /'krôlē/ ▶ n. (pl. **creepy-crawlies**) informal a spider, worm, or other small creature.

cre·ma /'krämə/ ▶ n. a frothy film that forms on the top of freshly made espresso.

cre·mate /'krē,māt, kri'māt/ ▶ v. dispose of a corpse by burning it to ashes. ■ **cre·ma·tion** /kri'māSHən/ n.

cre·ma·to·ri·um /,krēmə'tôrēəm, ,krem-/ ▶ n. (pl. **crematoria** /-'tôrēə/ or **crematoriums**) a building where the dead are cremated.

crème brû·lée /,krem broō'lā/ ▶ n. (pl. **crèmes brûlées** pronunc. same, or **crème brûlées** /broō'lāz/) a dessert of custard topped with caramelized sugar.

crème car·a·mel /,krem karə'mel, 'karə,mel/ ▶ n. (pl. **crèmes caramel** pronunc. same, or **crème caramels**) a custard dessert made with whipped cream and eggs and topped with caramel.

crème de la crème /,krem də lə 'krem/ ▶ n. the best person or thing of a particular kind.

crème de menthe /,krēm də 'menTH, ,krēm də 'mint/ ▶ n. a green peppermint-flavored liqueur.

crème fraiche /,krem 'fresh/ ▶ n. a type of thick cream with buttermilk, sour cream, or yogurt.

cren·el·lat·ed /'krenl,ātid/ (also **crenelated**) ▶ adj. (of a building) having battlements.

cren·el·la·tions /,krenl'āSHənz/ ▶ pl.n. battlements.

Cre·ole /'krē,ōl/ ▶ n. **1** a person of mixed European and black descent. **2** a descendant of European settlers in the Caribbean or Central or South America. **3** a white descendant of French settlers in Louisiana. **4** a language formed from a combination of a European language and another language, especially an African language.

cre·o·sote /'krēə,sōt/ ▶ n. a dark brown oil used as a wood preservative. ▶ v. treat something with creosote.

crepe /krāp/ (also **crepe**) ▶ n. **1** a light, thin fabric with a wrinkled surface. **2** hard-wearing wrinkled rubber used for the soles of shoes. **3** /krāp, krep/a thin pancake. ■ **crêp·ey** (also **crêpy**) adj.

crêpe de Chine /,krāp də 'shēn/ ▶ n. a fine crêpe fabric of silk or a similar material.

crepe pa·per ▶ n. thin, crinkled paper used for making decorations.

crêpe Su·zette /,krāp soō'zet/ ▶ n. (pl. **crêpes Suzette** pronunc. same) a thin sweet pancake flamed briefly in alcohol at the table before being served.

crept /krept/ ▶ past and past participle of CREEP.

cre·pus·cu·lar /krə'pəskyələr/ ▶ adj. chiefly literary resembling or relating to twilight.

cre·scen·do /krə'shendō/ ▶ n. **1** (pl. **crescendos** or **crescendi** /-dē/) a gradual increase in loudness in a piece of music. **2** the loudest or climactic point: *the shrieks of laughter reached a crescendo.* ▶ adv. & adj. Music gradually becoming louder. ▶ v. (**crescendoes, crescendoing, crescendoed**) increase in loudness or intensity.

cres·cent /'kresənt/ ▶ n. the form of the waxing or waning moon, seen as a narrow curved shape tapering to a point at each end.

cress /kres/ ▶ n. a plant with pungent, edible leaves, some kinds of which are used in salads.

crest /krest/ ▶ n. **1** a tuft or growth of feathers, fur, or skin on the head of a bird or other animal. **2** a plume of feathers on a helmet. **3** the top of a ridge, wave, etc. **4** a distinctive heraldic design representing a family or organization. ▶ v. **1** reach the top of: *he finally crested the hill.* **2** (as adj. **crested**) having a crest.

crest·fal·len /'krest,fôlən/ ▶ adj. sad and disappointed.

/kri'māSHən/ n.

Cre·ta·ceous /krəˈtāsнəs/ ▶adj. relating to the last period of the Mesozoic era (about 146 to 65 million years ago), at the end of which dinosaurs and many other organisms died out.

Cre·tan /ˈkrētn/ ▶n. a person from the Greek island of Crete. ▶adj. relating to Crete.

cre·tin /ˈkrētn/ ▶n. 1 a stupid person. 2 Medicine, dated a person who is deformed and has learning difficulties because of a congenital lack of thyroid hormone. ■ **cre·tin·ism** /-ˌizəm/ n.

cre·tin·ous /ˈkrētnəs/ ▶adj. very stupid.

cre·tonne /ˈkrēˌtän, kriˈtän/ ▶n. a heavy cotton fabric, typically with a floral pattern, used for upholstery.

Creutz·feldt–Ja·kob dis·ease /ˈkroitsˌfelt ˈyäkôb/ ▶n. a fatal disease that affects nerve cells in the brain, one form of which (**new variant Creutzfeldt–Jakob disease**) is possibly linked to BSE.

cre·vasse /krəˈvas/ ▶n. a deep open crack in a glacier or ice field.

crev·ice /ˈkrevəs/ ▶n. a narrow opening or crack in a rock or wall.

crew /krōō/ ▶n. (treated as sing. or pl.) 1 a group of people who work on and operate a ship, boat, aircraft, or train. 2 a group of such people excluding the officers. 3 informal, often derogatory a group of people associated in some way. ▶v. act as a member of a crew on a ship, boat, aircraft, etc.

crew cut ▶n. a very short haircut for men and boys.

crew·el /ˈkrōōəl/ ▶n. a thin, loosely twisted worsted yarn used for tapestry and embroidery.

crew neck ▶n. a close-fitting round neckline.

crib /krib/ ▶n. 1 a child's bed. 2 a rack for animal fodder; a manger. 3 informal a translation of a text for use by students, especially in a surreptitious way. 4 informal a house or apartment. 5 short for CRIBBAGE. ▶v. (**cribs**, **cribbing**, **cribbed**) informal copy another person's work dishonestly or without acknowledgment.

crib·bage /ˈkribij/ ▶n. a card game for two players, the objective of which is to play cards whose value reaches exactly 15 or 31.

crib death ▶n. the unexplained death of a baby in its sleep.

crick /krik/ ▶n. a painful stiff feeling in the neck or back. ▶v. twist or strain one's neck or back, causing painful stiffness.

crick·et[1] /ˈkrikit/ ▶n. an open-air game played by two teams of eleven players with a ball, bats, and wickets, the batsmen attempting to score runs by hitting the ball and running between the wickets. ■ **crick·et·er** n. **crick·et·ing** adj.
– PHRASES **not cricket** Brit. informal not fair or honorable.

crick·et[2] ▶n. an insect like a grasshopper but with shorter legs, the male of which produces a shrill chirping sound.

cri de cœur /ˌkrē də ˈkər/ ▶n. (pl. **cris de cœur** pronunc. same) a passionate appeal or complaint.

cried /krīd/ ▶ past and past participle of CRY.

cri·er /ˈkrīər/ ▶n. 1 an officer who makes public announcements in a court of law. 2 short for TOWN CRIER.

crime /krīm/ ▶n. 1 an act or activity that is illegal and can be punished by law. 2 such acts or activities considered as a whole: *the victims of violent crime.* 3 something seen as immoral or shameful: *such a war would be a crime against*

humanity.

crim·i·nal /ˈkrimənl/ ▶n. a person who has committed a crime. ▶adj. 1 relating to crime or a crime. 2 informal disgraceful and shocking: *a criminal waste of taxpayers' money.* ■ **crim·i·nal·i·ty** /ˌkriməˈnalitē/ n. **crim·i·nal·ly** adv.

crim·i·nal·ize /ˈkrimənlˌīz/ ▶v. 1 make an activity illegal. 2 turn someone into a criminal by making their activities illegal. ■ **crim·i·nal·i·za·tion** /ˌkrimənl-əˈzāsнən/ n.

crim·i·nol·o·gy /ˌkriməˈnäləjē/ ▶n. the scientific study of crime and criminals. ■ **crim·i·nol·o·gist** n.

crimp /krimp/ ▶v. 1 press something into small folds or ridges. 2 make curls or waves in a person's hair by pressing it with a curling iron or a similar device. ■ **crimp·er** n.

crim·son /ˈkrimzən/ ▶n. a rich deep red color. ▶v. (of a person's face) become flushed, especially through embarrassment.

cringe /krinj/ ▶v. (**cringes**, **cringing**, **cringed**) 1 shrink back or cower in fear or in a submissive way. 2 have a sudden feeling of embarrassment or disgust.

crin·kle /ˈkriNGkəl/ ▶v. form small creases or wrinkles. ▶n. a small crease or wrinkle. ■ **crin·kly** adj.

crin·o·line /ˈkrinl-in/ ▶n. a stiffened or hooped petticoat formerly worn to give a long skirt a very full and rounded shape.

cripes /krīps/ ▶exclam. informal an expression of surprise.

crip·ple /ˈkripəl/ ▶n. old use or offensive a person who is unable to walk or move properly through disability or injury. ▶v. 1 make someone unable to move or walk properly. 2 severely damage or weaken something: *families crippled by mounting debts.*

USAGE
As a noun, the word **cripple** is often regarded as offensive and should be avoided. Terms such as 'disabled person' are preferable.

cri·sis /ˈkrīsis/ ▶n. (pl. **crises**) 1 a time of extreme difficulty or danger: *the current economic crisis.* 2 the time when a problem or difficult situation is at its worst point.

crisp /krisp/ ▶adj. 1 firm, dry, and brittle. 2 (of the weather) cool, fresh, and invigorating. 3 (of a person's way of speaking) brisk and decisive. ▶n. a dessert of fruit baked with a crunchy topping of brown sugar, butter, and flour. ▶v. give food a crisp surface by cooking it in an oven or under a broiler. ■ **crisp·ly** adv. **crisp·ness** n.

crisp·bread /ˈkrispˌbred/ ▶n. a thin, crisp cracker made from crushed rye or wheat.

crisp·y /ˈkrispē/ ▶adj. (**crispier**, **crispiest**) firm and brittle; crisp.

criss·cross /ˈkrisˌkrôs/ ▶n. a pattern of intersecting lines. ▶v. 1 form a crisscross pattern on a place. 2 move or travel around a place by going back and forth repeatedly.

cri·te·ri·on /krīˈti(ə)rēən/ ▶n. (pl. **criteria** /-ˈti(ə)rēə/) a principle or standard by which something may be judged or decided.

USAGE
The singular form is **criterion** and the plural form is **criteria**. Do not use **criteria** as if it were a singular noun: say *a further criterion needs to be considered* not *a further criteria needs to be considered.*

crit·ic /'kritik/ ▶ n. **1** a person who expresses disapproval of someone or something. **2** a person who reviews literary or artistic works.

crit·i·cal /'kritikəl/ ▶ adj. **1** expressing disapproving comments or judgments: *the judge was very critical of him.* **2** expressing or involving an assessment of a literary or artistic work. **3** at a point of danger or crisis: *the floods were rising and the situation was critical.* **4** extremely ill and at risk of death. **5** having a decisive importance in the success or failure of something; crucial: *confidence has been the critical factor in their success.* **6** Mathematics & Physics relating to a point of transition from one state to another. **7** (of a nuclear reactor or fuel) maintaining a chain reaction that can sustain itself. ■ **crit·i·cal·ly** adv.

crit·i·cal mass ▶ n. **1** Physics the minimum amount of fissile material needed to maintain a nuclear chain reaction. **2** the minimum amount of resources required to start a venture or keep it going.

crit·i·cism /'kritə,sizəm/ ▶ n. **1** the expression of disapproval of someone or something. **2** the assessment of literary or artistic works.

crit·i·cize /'kritə,sīz/ ▶ v. **1** express disapproval of someone or something. **2** assess a literary or artistic work.

cri·tique /kri'tēk/ ▶ n. a detailed analysis and assessment of something. ▶ v. (**critiques, critiquing, critiqued**) analyze and assess something in detail.

crit·ter /'kritər/ ▶ n. informal or dialect a living creature.

croak /krōk/ ▶ n. a characteristic deep hoarse sound made by a frog or a crow. ▶ v. **1** utter a croak. **2** informal die. ■ **croak·y** adj.

croak·er /'krōkər/ ▶ n. another name for DRUM².

Cro·a·tian /krō'āsHən/ ▶ n. (also **Croat** /'krō,at, 'krō,ät, krōt/) **1** a person from Croatia. **2** the language of the Croatians, almost identical to Serbian but written in the Roman alphabet. ▶ adj. relating to Croatia or Croatian.

croc /kräk/ ▶ n. informal a crocodile.

cro·chet /krō'sHā/ ▶ n. a handicraft in which yarn is looped into a fabric of connected stitches by means of a hooked needle. ▶ v. (**crochets** /krō'sHāz/, **crocheting** /-'sHāiNG/, **crocheted** /-'sHād/) make a garment or piece of fabric in this way.

crock¹ /kräk/ ▶ n. **1** an earthenware pot or jar. **2** (also vulgar slang **crock of shit**) a thing that is considered to be complete nonsense.

crock² ▶ n. **1** an earthenware pot or jar. **2** an item of crockery.

crock·er·y /'kräkərē/ ▶ n. plates, dishes, cups, and similar items made of earthenware or china.

croc·o·dile /'kräkə,dīl/ ▶ n. a large predatory tropical reptile living partly in water, with long jaws and a long tail.

croc·o·dile tears ▶ pl.n. insincere tears or expressions of sorrow.

cro·cus /'krōkəs/ ▶ n. (pl. **crocuses**) a small spring-flowering plant with bright yellow, purple, or white flowers.

Croe·sus /'krēsəs/ ▶ n. a very wealthy person.

croft /krôft/ Brit. ▶ n. a small rented farm in Scotland or northern England. ▶ v. farm land as a croft or crofts. ■ **croft·er** n.

Crohn's dis·ease /'krōnz/ ▶ n. a disease of the

intestines, especially the colon and ileum.

crois·sant /k(r)wä'sänt, -'sän/ ▶ n. a crescent-shaped roll made of sweet flaky dough.

Cro-Mag·non /krō 'magnən, 'manyən/ ▶ n. the earliest form of modern human in Europe, appearing *c.* 35,000 years ago.

crone /krōn/ ▶ n. an ugly old woman.

cro·ny /'krōnē/ ▶ n. (pl. **cronies**) informal, often derogatory a person's close friend or companion.

cro·ny·ism /'krōnē,izəm/ (also **croneyism**) ▶ n. derogatory the practice of appointing friends and associates to positions of authority, especially when they are not suitably qualified.

crook /krook/ ▶ n. **1** a shepherd's hooked staff. **2** a bishop's crozier. **3** a bend, especially at the elbow in a person's arm. **4** informal a criminal or dishonest person. ▶ v. bend a finger or leg. ▶ adj. Austral./NZ informal **1** bad or unwell. **2** dishonest or illegal.

crook·ed /'krookəd/ ▶ adj. **1** bent or twisted out of shape or position. **2** informal dishonest or illegal. ■ **crook·ed·ly** adv. **crook·ed·ness** n.

croon /kroon/ ▶ v. hum, sing, or speak in a soft, low voice. ■ **croon·er** n.

crop /kräp/ ▶ n. **1** a plant, especially a cereal, fruit, or vegetable, grown for food or other use. **2** an amount of a crop harvested at one time. **3** an amount of people or things appearing at one time: *this new crop of indie bands.* **4** a very short hairstyle. **5** a riding crop. **6** a pouch in a bird's throat where food is stored or prepared for digestion. ▶ v. (**crops, cropping, cropped**) **1** cut something very short. **2** (of an animal) bite off and eat the tops of plants. **3** (**crop up**) appear or happen unexpectedly: *his name cropped up in the conversation.* **4** harvest a crop from an area. **5** sow or plant land with plants that will produce a crop.

crop cir·cle ▶ n. an area of crops that has been flattened in the form of a circle or other pattern by unexplained means.

crop dust·ing ▶ n. the spraying of powdered insecticide or fertilizer on crops from the air.

crop·per /'kräpər/ ▶ n. a plant that yields a particular crop.
– PHRASES **come a cropper** informal **1** fall over heavily. **2** experience a defeat or disaster.

crop top (also **cropped top**) ▶ n. a woman's casual garment for the upper body, cut short so that it reveals the stomach.

cro·quet /krō'kā/ ▶ n. a game played on a lawn, in which wooden balls are driven through a series of hoops with a mallet.

cro·quette /krō'ket/ ▶ n. a small cake or roll of chopped vegetables, meat, or fish, fried in breadcrumbs.

cro·sier ▶ n. variant spelling of CROZIER.

cross /krôs/ ▶ n. **1** a mark, object, or figure formed by two short intersecting lines or pieces (+ or ×). **2** an upright post with a bar fixed across it, as used in ancient times for crucifixion. **3** (**the Cross**) the cross on which Christ was crucified. **4** a cross-shaped medal awarded for bravery or showing rank in some orders of knighthood. **5** a thing that is unavoidable and has to be endured: *she's just a cross we have to bear.* **6** an animal or plant resulting from cross-breeding; a hybrid. **7** (**a cross between**) a mixture of two things: *a cross between a bar and a restaurant.* **8** (in soccer) a pass of the ball across the field toward the center close to one's opponents' goal.

▶ v. **1** go or extend across or to the other side of: *she crossed the street and walked down the hill.* **2** pass in an opposite or different direction; intersect. **3** place crosswise: *Michelle crossed her legs.* **4** draw a line or lines across something. **5** Soccer pass the ball across the field toward the center when attacking. **6** cause an animal of one species, breed, or variety to interbreed with one of another. **7** oppose or stand in the way of: *no one dared to cross him.* ▶ adj. annoyed. ■ **cross·ly** adv. **cross·ness** n.

– PHRASES **at cross purposes** misunderstanding one another. **cross one's fingers** put one finger across another as a sign of hoping for good luck. **cross my heart (and hope to die)** used to emphasize the truthfulness and sincerity of what one is saying. **cross something off** delete an item from a list. **cross oneself** make the sign of the Cross in front of one's chest as a sign of Christian reverence or to call on God for protection. **cross something out/through** delete a word or phrase by drawing a line through it. **cross swords** have an argument or dispute. **get one's wires (or lines) crossed** have a misunderstanding.

cross·bar /'krôs,bär/ ▶ n. **1** (in sports) a horizontal bar between the two upright posts of a goal. **2** a bar between the handlebars and saddle on a bicycle.

cross·bill /'krôs,bil/ ▶ n. a finch with a beak whose upper and lower parts are crossed, enabling it to extract seeds from the cones of conifers.

cross·bor·der ▶ adj. passing, occurring, or performed across a border between two countries.

cross·bow /'krôs,bō/ ▶ n. a medieval bow fixed across a wooden support, having a groove for the bolt and a mechanism for drawing and releasing the string.

cross·breed /'krôs,brēd/ ▶ n. an animal or plant produced by crossing two different species, breeds, or varieties. ▶ v. produce an animal or plant in this way.

cross-check ▶ v. check figures or information by using an alternative source or method.

cross-con·tam·i·na·tion ▶ n. the process by which bacteria or other microorganisms are unintentionally transferred from one substance or object to another. ■ **cross-con·tam·i·nate** v.

cross-coun·try ▶ adj. **1** across fields or countryside, rather than keeping to roads or tracks. **2** across a region or country, in particular not keeping to main or direct routes. ▶ n. the sport of cross-country running, riding, skiing, or driving.

cross-cul·tur·al ▶ adj. of or relating to different cultures or comparison between them.

cross·cur·rent /'krôs,kərənt/ ▶ n. **1** a current in a river or sea that flows across another. **2** a situation or tendency marked by conflict with another: *political crosscurrents.*

cross·cut /'krôs,kət/ ▶ v. **1** cut wood or stone across its main grain or axis. **2** alternate one sequence with another when editing a movie.

cross·dres·sing ▶ n. the practice of wearing clothing usually worn by the opposite sex.

crosse /krôs/ ▶ n. the stick used in lacrosse.

cross-ex·am·ine ▶ v. question a witness called by the other party in a court of law to challenge or extend the testimony that they have already

given. ■ **cross-ex·am·i·na·tion** n.

cross-eyed ▶ adj. having one or both eyes turned inward toward the nose, either temporarily or as a permanent condition.

cross-fer·ti·lize ▶ v. fertilize a plant using pollen from another plant of the same species. ■ **cross-fer·ti·li·za·tion** n.

cross·fire /'krôs,fīr/ ▶ n. gunfire from two or more directions passing through the same area.

cross-grained ▶ adj. **1** (of timber) having a grain that runs across the regular grain. **2** stubbornly uncooperative or bad-tempered.

cross·hairs /'krôs,he(ə)rz/ ▶ pl.n. a pair of fine wires crossing at right angles at the focus of an optical instrument or gunsight.

cross·hatch /'krôs,haCH/ ▶ v. shade an area with many intersecting parallel lines.

cross·ing /'krôsiNG/ ▶ n. **1** a place where things, especially roads or railroad lines, cross. **2** a place at which one may safely cross a street or railroad track. **3** a journey across water in a ship.

cross-leg·ged /'leg(ə)d/ ▶ adj. & adv. (of a seated person) with the legs crossed at the ankles and the knees bent outward.

cross·o·ver /'krôs,ōvər/ ▶ n. **1** a point or place of crossing from one side to the other. **2** the production of work in a new style or combination of styles, especially in popular music: *a rock-funk crossover.*

cross-own·er·ship ▶ n. the ownership by one corporation of different companies with related interests or commercial aims.

cross·piece /'krôs,pēs/ ▶ n. a beam or bar fixed or placed across something else.

cross-pol·li·nate ▶ v. pollinate a flower or plant with pollen from another flower or plant.

cross-post ▶ v. send a message to more than one Internet newsgroup at the same time. ▶ n. a message that has been cross-posted.

cross-ques·tion ▶ v. question someone in great detail.

cross ref·er·ence ▶ n. a reference to another text or part of a text, given to provide further information. ■ **cross-re·fer** v.

cross·roads /'krôs,rōdz/ ▶ n. an intersection of two or more roads.

cross sec·tion ▶ n. **1** a surface exposed by making a straight cut through a solid object at right angles to its length. **2** a typical or representative sample of a larger group: *a cross-section of society.*

cross stitch ▶ n. an embroidery stitch formed of two stitches crossing each other.

cross·talk /'krôs,tôk/ ▶ n. **1** unwanted transfer of signals between communication channels. **2** witty conversation.

cross·walk /'krôs,wôk/ ▶ n. a pedestrian crossing.

cross·wind /'krôs,wind/ ▶ n. a wind blowing across one's direction of travel.

cross·wise /'krôs,wīz/ (also **crossways**) ▶ adv. **1** in the form of a cross. **2** diagonally.

cross·word /'krôs,wərd/ ▶ n. a puzzle consisting of a grid of squares and blanks into which words crossing vertically and horizontally are written according to clues.

crotch /kräCH/ ▶ n. **1** the part of the human body between the legs where they join the torso. **2** a fork in a tree, road, or river.

crotch·et·y /'kräCHətē/ ▶ adj. irritable.

crouch /krouch/ ▶ v. bend the knees and bring the upper body forward and down. ▶ n. a crouching position.

croup[1] /kr00p/ ▶ n. inflammation of the throat in children, causing coughing and breathing difficulties.

croup[2] ▶ n. the rump or hindquarters of a horse.

croup·i·er /'kr00pē,ā, -pēər/ ▶ n. the person in charge of a gambling table, gathering in and paying out money or tokens.

crou·ton /'kr00,tän, kr00'tän/ ▶ n. a small piece of fried or toasted bread served with soup or used as a garnish.

crow[1] /krō/ ▶ n. a large bird with glossy black plumage, a heavy bill, and a harsh call.
– PHRASES **as the crow flies** in a straight line across country.

crow[2] ▶ v. (past **crowed**) 1 (of a cock) make its characteristic loud cry. 2 express pride or triumph in a tone of gloating satisfaction. ▶ n. the cry of a cock.

crow·bar /'krō,bär/ ▶ n. an iron bar with a flattened end, used as a lever.

crowd /kroud/ ▶ n. 1 a large number of people gathered together. 2 informal, often derogatory a group of people with a shared interest or quality: *a day at the beach with the sailing crowd*. ▶ v. 1 (of a number of people) fill a space almost completely. 2 move or come together as a crowd: *passengers crowded into the train*. 3 move or stand too close to someone. 4 (**crowd someone/thing out**) keep someone or something out by taking their place.

crowd·ed /'kroudid/ ▶ adj. (of a place) filled almost completely by a large number of people.

crowd-pleas·er ▶ n. a person or thing with great popular appeal.

crow·foot /'krō,fŏŏt/ ▶ n. (pl. **crowfoots**) a water plant with white or yellow flowers.

crown /kroun/ ▶ n. 1 a circular ornamental headdress worn by a monarch as a symbol of authority. 2 (**the Crown**) the monarchy or reigning monarch. 3 a wreath of leaves or flowers worn as an emblem of victory. 4 an award or distinction gained by a victory or achievement: *the world championship crown*. 5 the top or highest part of something such as a person's head or a hat. 6 the part of a tooth projecting from the gum. 7 an artificial replacement or covering for the upper part of a tooth. 8 a former British coin worth five shillings (or 25 pence). ▶ v. 1 ceremonially place a crown on the head of someone to invest them as a monarch. 2 rest on or form the top of: *a simple altar crowned by a wooden cross*. 3 be the triumphant conclusion of: *the victory that crowned his career*. 4 fit a crown to a tooth. 5 informal hit someone on the head.

Crown Col·o·ny ▶ n. a British colony controlled by the Crown.

Crown jew·els ▶ pl.n. the crown and other jewelry worn or carried by the sovereign on state occasions.

crown prince ▶ n. (in some countries) a male heir to a throne.

crown prin·cess ▶ n. 1 the wife of a crown prince. 2 (in some countries) a female heir to a throne.

crow's feet ▶ pl.n. wrinkles at the outer corner of a person's eye.

crow's nest ▶ n. a platform for a lookout at the masthead of a ship.

cro·zier /'krōzhər/ (also **crosier**) ▶ n. a hooked staff carried by a bishop.

CRT ▶ abbr. cathode ray tube.

cru·cial /'kr00shəl/ ▶ adj. of great importance, especially in the success or failure of something: *negotiations were at a crucial stage*. ■ **cru·cial·ly** adv.

cru·ci·ate lig·a·ment /'kr00sh(ē)ət, -sHē,āt/ ▶ n. either of a pair of ligaments in the knee that cross each other and connect the femur (thigh bone) to the tibia (shinbone).

cru·ci·ble /'kr00səbəl/ ▶ n. 1 a container in which metals or other substances may be melted or subjected to very high temperatures. 2 a situation in which people or things are severely tested, often interacting to produce something new: *a relationship forged in the crucible of war*.

cru·cif·er·ous /kr00'sifərəs/ ▶ adj. (of a plant) belonging to the cabbage family, with four equal petals arranged in a cross.

cru·ci·fix /'kr00sə,fiks/ ▶ n. a representation of a cross with a figure of Jesus on it.

cru·ci·fix·ion /,kr00sə'fiksHən/ ▶ n. 1 the execution of a person by crucifying them. 2 (**the Crucifixion**) the killing of Jesus in this way.

cru·ci·form /'kr00sə,fôrm/ ▶ adj. having the shape of a cross.

cru·ci·fy /'kr00sə,fī/ ▶ v. (**crucifies, crucifying, crucified**) 1 put someone to death by nailing or binding them to a cross. 2 informal criticize someone severely.

crud /krəd/ ▶ n. informal 1 an unpleasantly dirty or messy substance. 2 nonsense. ■ **crud·dy** adj.

crude /kr00d/ ▶ adj. 1 in a natural or raw state; not yet processed or refined: *crude oil*. 2 simple or makeshift: *crude stone tools*. 3 likely to be only approximately accurate: *a crude index of economic progress*. 4 offensively coarse or vulgar. ▶ n. natural petroleum. ■ **crude·ly** adv. **crude·ness** n. **cru·di·ty** /'kr00ditē/ n.

cru·di·tés /,kr00də'tā/ ▶ pl.n. mixed raw vegetables served with a sauce into which they may be dipped.

cru·el /'kr00əl/ ▶ adj. (**crueler, cruelest**) 1 taking pleasure in the pain or suffering of others. 2 causing pain or suffering. ■ **cru·el·ly** adv.

cru·el·ty /'kr00əltē/ ▶ n. (pl. **cruelties**) cruel behavior or attitudes.

cru·et /'kr00ət/ ▶ n. a small container or set of containers for salt, pepper, oil, or vinegar for use at a dining table.

cruise /kr00z/ ▶ v. 1 sail, travel, or move slowly around without a definite destination, especially for pleasure. 2 travel smoothly at a moderate or economical speed. 3 easily achieve an objective: *the home team cruised to a 7–2 victory*. 4 informal wander about in search of a sexual partner. ▶ n. a voyage on a ship taken as a vacation and usually calling in at several places.

cruise con·trol ▶ n. a device in a motor vehicle that maintains a selected constant speed without requiring the driver to use the accelerator pedal.

cruise mis·sile ▶ n. a low-flying missile that is guided to its target by an on-board computer.

cruis·er /'kr00zər/ ▶ n. 1 a fast warship larger than a destroyer and less heavily armed than a battleship. 2 a yacht or motorboat with passenger accommodations.

crumb /krəm/ ▶ n. **1** a small fragment of bread, cake, or cookie. **2** a very small amount: *there was only one crumb of comfort.*

crum·ble /'krəmbəl/ ▶ v. **1** break or fall apart into small fragments. **2** gradually disintegrate or fail: *the party's fragile unity began to crumble.* ▶ n. a baked dessert made with fruit and a crumbly pastry topping.

crum·bly /'krəmblē/ ▶ adj. easily breaking into small fragments.

crum·my /'krəmē/ (also **crumby**) ▶ adj. (**crummier, crummiest**) informal bad, unpleasant, or of poor quality.

crum·pet /'krəmpət/ ▶ n. a thick, flat cake with a soft, open texture, eaten toasted and buttered.

crum·ple /'krəmpəl/ ▶ v. **1** crush something so that it becomes creased and wrinkled. **2** suddenly fall or collapse: *she crumpled to the floor.*

crum·ple zone ▶ n. a part of a motor vehicle designed to crumple easily in a crash and absorb the main force of an impact.

crunch /krənCH/ ▶ v. **1** crush something hard or brittle with the teeth, making a grinding sound. **2** make or move with a grinding sound: *the snow crunched as we walked.* ▶ n. **1** a crunching sound. **2** (**the crunch**) informal a crucial moment or situation. **3** a sit-up.

crunch·y /'krənCHē/ ▶ adj. (**crunchier, crunchiest**) making a crunching noise when bitten or crushed. ■ **crunch·i·ness** n.

cru·sade /krōō'sād/ ▶ n. **1** any of a series of medieval military expeditions made by Europeans to recover the Holy Land from the Muslims. **2** an energetic organized campaign with a political, social, or religious aim: *a crusade against crime.* ▶ v. (often as adj. **crusading**) lead or take part in a crusade. ■ **cru·sad·er** n.

crush /krəSH/ ▶ v. **1** press or squeeze forcefully so as to injure, squash, or break up: *the car was crushed under a truck.* **2** violently subdue or defeat: *troops were used to crush the rebellion.* **3** make someone feel extremely disappointed or embarrassed. ▶ n. **1** a crowd of people pressed closely together. **2** informal a strong, usually short-lived feeling of love for someone; an infatuation. **3** a drink made from the juice of crushed fruit. ■ **crush·a·ble** adj. **crush·er** n.

crushed vel·vet ▶ n. a type of velvet that has its nap pointing in different directions in irregular patches.

crust /krəst/ ▶ n. **1** the tough outer part of a loaf of bread. **2** a hardened layer or coating on something soft. **3** a layer of pastry covering a pie. **4** the outermost layer of rock of which a planet consists, especially the part of the earth above the mantle. **5** a deposit formed in wine or port aged in the bottle. ▶ v. form into or cover with a crust.

crus·ta·cean /krə'stāSHən/ ▶ n. an animal with a hard outer shell, usually living in water, such as a crab, lobster, or shrimp.

crust·y /'krəstē/ ▶ adj. (**crustier, crustiest**) **1** having or consisting of a crust. **2** (of an old person) easily irritated. ■ **crust·i·ness** n.

crutch /krəCH/ ▶ n. **1** a long stick with a crosspiece at the top, used as a support by a person who is lame. **2** a person or thing used for support or reassurance. **3** the crotch of the body or a garment.

crux /krəks, krŏŏks/ ▶ n. (**the crux**) the most important or difficult part of an issue or problem: *the crux of the matter is whether compensation should be paid.*

cry /krī/ ▶ v. (**cries, crying, cried**) **1** shed tears. **2** shout or scream loudly. **3** (of a bird or other animal) make a loud distinctive call. **4** (**cry out for**) be in great need of: *a system that is crying out for fundamental change.* ▶ n. (pl. **cries**) **1** a period of shedding tears. **2** a loud shout or scream. **3** a distinctive call made by a bird or other animal.

cry·ba·by /'krī,bābē/ ▶ n. (pl. **crybabies**) a person who cries frequently or readily.

cry·ing /'krī-iNG/ ▶ adj. very great: *it'd be a crying shame if the local bar disappeared.*

cry·o·gen·ics /,krīə'jeniks/ ▶ pl.n. (treated as sing.) **1** the branch of physics concerned with the production and effects of very low temperatures. **2** another term for CRYONICS. ■ **cry·o·gen·ic** adj.

cry·on·ics /krī'äniks/ ▶ pl.n. (treated as sing.) the deep-freezing of the bodies of people who have died of an incurable disease, in the hope of a future cure. ■ **cry·on·ic** adj.

cry·o·sur·ger·y /,krīō'sərjərē/ ▶ n. a type of surgery using instruments that freeze and destroy diseased or unwanted tissue.

crypt /kript/ ▶ n. an underground room or vault beneath a church, used as a chapel or burial place.

cryp·tic /'kriptik/ ▶ adj. **1** mysterious or obscure in meaning: *a cryptic message.* **2** (of a crossword) having difficult clues that indicate the solutions indirectly. **3** Zoology referring to coloration or markings that camouflage an animal in its natural environment. ■ **cryp·ti·cal·ly** /-ik(ə)lē/ adv.

cryp·to·gram /'kriptə,gram/ ▶ n. a text written in code.

cryp·tog·ra·phy /krip'tägrəfē/ ▶ n. the art of writing or solving codes. ■ **cryp·tog·ra·pher** n. **cryp·to·graph·ic** /,kriptə'grafik/ adj.

cryp·tol·o·gy /krip'täləjē/ ▶ n. the study of codes, or the art of writing and solving them. ■ **cryp·to·log·i·cal** /,kriptə'läjikəl/ adj. **cryp·tol·o·gist** n.

cryp·to·spor·i·di·um /,kriptəspə'ridēəm/ ▶ n. (pl. **cryptosporidia** /,kriptəspə'ridēə/) a single-celled parasite found in the intestines of many animals, where it sometimes causes disease.

crys·tal /'kristl/ ▶ n. **1** a clear transparent mineral, especially quartz. **2** a piece of a solid substance with a regular internal structure with symmetrically arranged plane faces. **3** very clear glass. ▶ adj. clear and transparent: *the crystal waters of the lake.*

crys·tal ball ▶ n. a solid globe of glass or rock crystal, used for predicting the future.

crys·tal·line /'kristl-in, -tl-,īn, -tl-,ēn/ ▶ adj. **1** having the structure and form of a crystal. **2** literary very clear.

crys·tal·lize /'kristə,līz/ ▶ v. **1** form crystals. **2** make or become definite and clear: *writing can help to crystallize your thoughts.* **3** (as adj. **crystallized**) (of fruit) coated with and preserved in sugar. ■ **crys·tal·li·za·tion** /,kristələ'zāSHən/ n.

crys·tal·log·ra·phy /,kristə'lägrəfē/ ▶ n. the branch of science concerned with the structure and properties of crystals. ■ **crys·tal·log·ra·pher** n. **crys·tal·lo·graph·ic** /-lə'grafik/ adj.

crys·tal meth /meTH/ ▶ n. the crystalline, smokable form of methamphetamine, produced only for illicit use.

Cs ▶ symbol the chemical element cesium.

c/s ▶ abbr. cycles per second.

C-sec·tion ▶ n. short for CESAREAN SECTION.

CS gas ▶ n. a powerful form of tear gas used in the control of riots.

CST ▶ abbr. Central Standard Time.

CT ▶ abbr. **1** computerized (or computed) tomography. **2** Connecticut.

ct ▶ abbr. **1** carat. **2** cent.

CTS ▶ abbr. carpal tunnel syndrome.

Cu ▶ symbol the chemical element copper.

cu. ▶ abbr. cubic.

cub /kəb/ ▶ n. **1** the young of a fox, bear, lion, or other carnivorous mammal. **2** (also **Cub Scout**) a member of the junior branch of the Boy Scouts of America, for boys aged about 7 to 10. ▶ v. (**cubs, cubbing, cubbed**) **1** give birth to cubs. **2** hunt fox cubs.

Cu·ban /'kyōōbən/ ▶ n. a person from Cuba. ▶ adj. relating to Cuba.

cub·by /'kəbē/ ▶ n. (pl. **cubbies**) a cubbyhole.

cub·by·hole /'kəbē,hōl/ ▶ n. a small enclosed space or room.

cube /kyōōb/ ▶ n. **1** a symmetrical three-dimensional shape with six equal square faces. **2** the product of a number multiplied by itself twice. ▶ v. **1** find the cube of a number. **2** cut food into small cube-shaped pieces.

cube root ▶ n. the number that, when multiplied by itself twice, produces a particular number.

cu·bic /'kyōōbik/ ▶ adj. **1** having the shape of a cube. **2** referring to a volume equal to that of a cube whose edge is a given unit of length: *a cubic meter*. **3** involving the cube of a number. ■ **cu·bi·cal** adj.

cu·bi·cle /'kyōōbikəl/ ▶ n. a small area of a room that is partitioned off for privacy.

cub·ism /'kyōō,bizəm/ ▶ n. an early 20th-century style of painting in which objects are represented as being made up of geometric shapes. ■ **cub·ist** n. & adj.

cu·bit /'kyōōbit/ ▶ n. an ancient measure of length, approximately equal to the length of a forearm.

cu·boid /'kyōō,boid/ ▶ adj. having the shape of a cube. ▶ n. a solid that has six rectangular faces at right angles to each other.

cub re·port·er ▶ n. informal a young or inexperienced newspaper reporter.

cuck·old /'kəkəld, -ōld/ ▶ n. a man whose wife has committed adultery. ▶ v. make a married man a cuckold. ■ **cuck·old·ry** n.

cuck·oo /'kōōkōō, 'kŏŏkōō/ ▶ n. a gray or brown bird known for the two-note call of the male and for the habit of laying its eggs in the nests of other birds. ▶ adj. informal crazy.

cuck·oo clock ▶ n. a clock with a mechanical cuckoo that pops out on the hour making a sound like a cuckoo's call.

cuck·oo spit ▶ n. whitish froth found in compact masses on leaves and plant stems, produced by the larvae of certain insects.

cu·cum·ber /'kyōō,kəmbər/ ▶ n. a long green-skinned fruit with watery flesh, eaten raw in salads.

cud /kəd/ ▶ n. partly digested food returned from the first stomach of cattle or similar animals to the mouth for further chewing.

– PHRASES **chew the cud** think or talk in a thoughtful way.

cud·dle /'kədl/ ▶ v. **1** hold someone close in one's arms as a way of showing love or affection. **2** (often **cuddle up to**) lie or sit close to someone. ▶ n. an affectionate hug.

cud·dly /'kədlē, 'kədl-ē/ ▶ adj. (**cuddlier, cuddliest**) pleasantly soft or plump.

cudg·el /'kəjəl/ ▶ n. a short thick stick used as a weapon. ▶ v. (**cudgels, cudgeling, cudgeled**) beat someone with a cudgel.

– PHRASES **take up the cudgels** start to defend or support someone or something strongly.

cue[1] /kyōō/ ▶ n. **1** a signal to an actor to enter or to begin their speech or performance. **2** an action or event that is a signal for someone to do something: *he took her words as a cue to leave*. **3** a facility for playing through an audio or video recording very quickly until a desired point is reached. ▶ v. (**cues, cueing** or **cuing, cued**) **1** give someone a cue. **2** set a piece of audio or video equipment so that it is ready to play a particular part of a recording.

– PHRASES **on cue** at the right moment.

cue[2] (also **cue stick**) ▶ n. a long tapering wooden rod for striking the ball in snooker, billiards, or pool. ▶ v. (**cues, cueing** or **cuing, cued**) use a cue to strike the ball.

cue ball ▶ n. the ball that is to be struck with the cue in pool, snooker, billiards, etc.

cue card ▶ n. a card held beside a camera for a television broadcaster to read from while appearing to look into the camera.

cuff[1] /kəf/ ▶ n. **1** the end part of a sleeve, where the material is turned back or a separate band is sewn on. **2** the turned-up end of a trouser leg. **3** (**cuffs**) informal handcuffs.

– PHRASES **off the cuff** informal without previous thought or preparation.

cuff[2] ▶ v. hit someone with an open hand, especially on the head. ▶ n. a blow given with an open hand.

cuff·link /'kəf,liNGk/ ▶ n. a device for fastening together the sides of a shirt cuff.

cui·rass /kwi'ras, kyŏŏr'as/ ▶ n. historical a piece of armor covering the chest and the back.

cui·sine /kwi'zēn/ ▶ n. a style or method of cooking, especially as characteristic of a particular country or region: *traditional French cuisine*.

cul-de-sac /'kəl di ,sak/ ▶ n. (pl. **cul-de-sacs** or **culs-de-sac** pronunc. same) a street or passage closed at one end.

cu·li·nar·y /'kələ,nerē, 'kyōōlə-/ ▶ adj. of or for cooking.

cull /kəl/ ▶ v. **1** slaughter a selected number of a certain kind of animal in order to reduce its population. **2** select or obtain from a large quantity or a variety of sources: *data culled from a number of websites*. ▶ n. a selective slaughter of a certain kind of animal: *a seal cull*.

cul·mi·nate /'kəlmə,nāt/ ▶ v. reach a climax or point of highest development: *the protests culminated in a mass rally at the town hall*. ■ **cul·mi·na·tion** /,kəlmə'nāshən/ n.

cu·lottes /'k(y)ōō,läts, k(y)ōō'läts/ ▶ pl.n. women's knee-length shorts, cut with very full legs to resemble a skirt.

cul·pa·ble /'kəlpəbəl/ ▶ adj. deserving blame.

■ **cul·pa·bil·i·ty** /ˌkəlpəˈbilitē/ n. **cul·pa·bly** /-blē/ adv.

cul·prit /ˈkəlprət, ˈkəlˌprit/ ▶ n. a person who is responsible for a crime or offense.

cult /kəlt/ ▶ n. **1** a system of religious worship directed toward a particular figure or object. **2** a small religious group regarded by others as strange or as having too great a control over its members. **3** (often before another noun) something popular or fashionable among a particular group of people: *a cult film.* ■ **cult·ish** adj. **cult·ist** n.

cul·ti·var /ˈkəltəˌvär/ ▶ n. a plant variety that has been produced by selective breeding.

cul·ti·vate /ˈkəltəˌvāt/ ▶ v. **1** prepare and use land for crops or gardening. **2** grow plants or crops. **3** try to develop or gain a quality or skill: *he cultivated an air of sophistication.* **4** try to win the friendship or support of someone. **5** (as adj. **cultivated**) refined and well educated. ■ **cul·ti·va·ble** /-vəbəl/ adj. **cul·ti·vat·a·ble** /-ˌvātəbəl/ adj. **cul·ti·va·tion** /ˌkəltəˈvāsHən/ n.

cul·ti·va·tor /ˈkəltəˌvātər/ ▶ n. a mechanical implement for breaking up the ground.

cul·tur·al /ˈkəlcHərəl/ ▶ adj. **1** relating to the culture of a society. **2** relating to the arts and to intellectual achievements. ■ **cul·tur·al·ly** adv.

cul·ture /ˈkəlcHər/ ▶ n. **1** the arts and other instances of human intellectual achievement regarded as a whole. **2** a refined understanding or appreciation of this. **3** the art, customs, ideas, and social behavior of a nation, people, or group: *Afro-Caribbean culture.* **4** a preparation of cells or bacteria grown in an artificial medium for scientific study, or the process of growing such cells or bacteria. **5** the growing of plants. ▶ v. grow cells or bacteria for scientific study.

cul·tured /ˈkəlcHərd/ ▶ adj. **1** well educated and able to appreciate art, literature, music, etc. **2** (of a pearl) formed around a foreign body inserted into an oyster.

cul·ture shock ▶ n. a feeling of disorientation experienced when someone suddenly comes into contact with an unfamiliar culture or way of life.

cul·ture vul·ture ▶ n. informal a person who is very interested in the arts.

cul·vert /ˈkəlvərt/ ▶ n. a tunnel carrying a stream or open drain under a road or railroad.

cum /ko͝om, kəm/ ▶ prep. combined with; also used as: *a study-cum-bedroom.*

cum·ber·some /ˈkəmbərsəm/ ▶ adj. **1** large and heavy and so difficult to carry or use. **2** complicated and inefficient or time-consuming: *NATO's cumbersome decision-making processes.*

cum·brous /ˈkəmbrəs/ ▶ adj. literary cumbersome.

cum·in /ˈkəmən, ˈk(y)o͞o-/ (also **cummin**) ▶ n. the seeds of a plant of the parsley family, used as a spice in cooking.

cum·mer·bund /ˈkəmərˌbənd/ ▶ n. a sash worn around the waist, especially as part of a man's formal evening suit.

cum·quat /ˈkəmˌkwät/ ▶ n. variant spelling of KUMQUAT.

cu·mu·late /ˈkyo͞omyəˌlāt/ ▶ v. accumulate or be accumulated. ■ **cu·mu·la·tion** /ˌkyo͞omyəˈlāsHən/ n.

cu·mu·la·tive /ˈkyo͞omyələtiv, -ˌlātiv/ ▶ adj. increasing or increased in amount, strength, or effect by successive additions: *the cumulative effect of human activities on the environment.* ■ **cu·mu·la·tive·ly** adv.

cu·mu·lo·nim·bus /ˌkyo͞omyələˈnimbəs/ ▶ n. (pl. **cumulonimbi** /-ˈnimbī, -bē/) cloud forming a towering mass with a flat base, as in thunderstorms.

cu·mu·lus /ˈkyo͞omyələs/ ▶ n. (pl. **cumuli** /-ˌlī, -lē/) cloud forming rounded masses heaped on each other above a flat base.

cu·ne·i·form /kyo͞oˈnēəˌfôrm, ˈkyo͞on(ē)ə-/ ▶ adj. relating to the wedge-shaped characters used in the ancient writing systems of Mesopotamia, Persia, and Ugarit. ▶ n. cuneiform writing.

cun·ni·lin·gus /ˌkənlˈiNGgəs/ ▶ n. stimulation of a woman's genitals using the tongue or lips.

cun·ning /ˈkəniNG/ ▶ adj. **1** skilled in deceiving people to achieve one's aims. **2** ingenious; clever. ▶ n. the ability to achieve things by using deception or cleverness. ■ **cun·ning·ly** adv.

cunt /kənt/ ▶ n. vulgar slang **1** a woman's genitals. **2** an unpleasant or stupid person.

cup /kəp/ ▶ n. **1** a small bowl-shaped container with a handle for drinking from. **2** a cup-shaped trophy with a stem and two handles, awarded as a prize in a contest. **3** a sports contest in which the winner is awarded a cup. **4** a measure of capacity used in cooking, equal to half a US pint (0.237 liter). **5** either of the two parts of a bra shaped to contain or support one breast. **6** a mixed drink made from wine or cider and fruit juice. ▶ v. (**cups**, **cupping**, **cupped**) **1** form one's hand or hands into the curved shape of a cup. **2** place one's curved hand or hands around something.

– PHRASES **in one's cups** informal drunk. **not one's cup of tea** informal not what one likes or is interested in.

cup·board /ˈkəbərd/ ▶ n. a piece of furniture or small recess with a door and usually shelves, used for storage.

cup·cake /ˈkəpˌkāk/ ▶ n. a small iced cake baked in a cup-shaped container.

cup·ful /ˈkəpˌfo͝ol/ ▶ n. **1** the amount held by a cup. **2** (in cooking) the amount a measuring cup will hold: *add two cupfuls of flour.*

Cu·pid /ˈkyo͞opəd/ ▶ n. **1** Roman Mythology the god of love. **2** (also **cupid**) a picture or statue of a naked winged baby boy with a bow and arrow.

cu·pid·i·ty /kyo͞oˈpiditē/ ▶ n. greed for money or possessions.

Cu·pid's bow ▶ n. a pronounced double curve at the top edge of a person's upper lip.

cu·po·la /ˈkyo͞opələ/ ▶ n. **1** a small rounded dome on or forming a roof. **2** a gun turret.

cu·pro·nick·el /ˌk(y)o͞oprōˈnikəl/ ▶ n. an alloy of copper and nickel, especially as used in "silver" coins.

cur /kər/ ▶ n. **1** an aggressive mongrel dog. **2** informal a despicable man.

cu·ra·çao /ˌk(y)o͝orəˈsō, -ˈsou/ ▶ n. (pl. **curaçaos**) a liqueur flavored with bitter oranges.

cu·ra·re /k(y)o͞oˈrärē/ ▶ n. a paralyzing poison obtained from South American plants.

cu·rate[1] /ˈkyo͞orət, -ˌrāt/ ▶ n. a member of the clergy who assists a parish priest.

cu·rate[2] /ˈkyo͞oˌrāt/ ▶ v. select, organize, and look after the items in a collection or exhibition. ■ **cu·ra·tion** /kyəˈrāsHən/ n.

cur·a·tive /ˈkyo͞orətiv/ ▶ adj. able to cure disease. ▶ n. something that is able to cure disease.

cu·ra·tor /'kyŏŏr,ātər, kyŏŏ'rātər, 'kyŏŏrətər/
▶ n. a keeper of a museum or other collection.
■ **cu·ra·to·ri·al** /,kyŏŏrə'tôrēəl/ **adj.**

curb /kərb/ ▶ v. control or put a limit on: *the new
law aims to curb fraud.* ▶ n. **1** a stone or concrete
edging to a sidewalk or raised path. **2** a control
or limit on something. **3** a type of bit with a strap
or chain attached that passes under a horse's
lower jaw.

curb·side /'kərb,sīd/ ▶ n. the side of a road or
sidewalk that is nearer to the curb.

curb·stone /'kərb,stōn/ ▶ n. a long, narrow stone
or concrete block, laid end to end with others to
form a curb.

curd /kərd/ (also **curds**) ▶ n. a soft, white
substance formed when milk coagulates, used to
make cheese.

cur·dle /'kərdl/ ▶ v. (of a liquid) separate into
solid and liquid parts.

cure /kyŏŏr/ ▶ v. **1** make a person who is ill well
again. **2** end a disease or condition or solve a
problem. **3** preserve meat, fish, etc., by salting,
drying, or smoking. ▶ n. **1** something that cures
a disease or solves a problem. **2** the healing of a
person who is unwell. **3** a Christian minister's
area of responsibility. ■ **cur·a·ble** **adj.** **cur·er** n.

cure-all ▶ n. a remedy that will supposedly cure
any ailment or problem.

cu·ret·tage /,kyŏŏrə'täzH/ ▶ n. the use of a
curette, especially to scrape material from the
lining of the uterus.

cu·rette /kyŏŏ'ret/ ▶ n. a small surgical
instrument used to scrape away material,
especially from the uterus.

cur·few /'kər,fyŏŏ/ ▶ n. **1** a regulation ordering
people to remain indoors between specified
hours, typically at night. **2** the time at which a
curfew begins.

Cu·ri·a /'kyŏŏrēə/ ▶ n. the papal court at the
Vatican, by which the Roman Catholic Church is
governed. ■ **Cu·ri·al** **adj.**

cu·rie /kyŏŏ'rē, 'kyŏŏrē/ ▶ n. (pl. **curies**) a unit
of radioactivity, corresponding to 3.7 × 10¹⁰
disintegrations per second.

cu·ri·o /'kyŏŏrē,ō/ ▶ n. (pl. **curios**) an object that is
interesting because it is rare or unusual.

cu·ri·os·i·ty /,kyŏŏrē'äsitē/ ▶ n. (pl. **curiosities**)
1 a strong desire to know or learn something.
2 an unusual or interesting object or fact.

cu·ri·ous /'kyŏŏrēəs/ ▶ adj. **1** eager to know
or learn something. **2** strange; unusual.
■ **cu·ri·ous·ly** adv.

cu·ri·um /'kyŏŏrēəm/ ▶ n. a radioactive metallic
chemical element made by high-energy atomic
collisions.

curl /kərl/ ▶ v. **1** form or cause to form a curved
or spiral shape: *her fingers curled around the
microphone.* **2** (**curl up**) sit or lie with the
knees drawn up. **3** move in a spiral or curved
course. **4** play at the game of curling. ▶ n. a thing
forming a spiral or coil, especially a lock of hair.
■ **curl·y** adj. (**curlier**, **curliest**).
– PHRASES **make someone's hair curl** informal
shock or horrify someone.

curl·er /'kərlər/ ▶ n. **1** a roller or clasp around
which a lock of hair is wrapped to curl it. **2** a
player in the game of curling.

cur·lew /'kər,lŏŏ, 'kərl,yŏŏ/ ▶ n. (pl. same or
curlews) a large brown wading bird with a long
bill that curves downward.

curl·i·cue /'kərlē,kyŏŏ/ ▶ n. a decorative curl or
twist.

curl·ing /'kərliNG/ ▶ n. a game played on ice, in
which large circular flat stones are slid across the
surface toward a mark.

curl·ing i·ron ▶ pl.n. a device incorporating a
heated rod around which hair can be wound so
as to curl it.

cur·mudg·eon /kər'məjən/ ▶ n. a bad-tempered
or surly person. ■ **cur·mudg·eon·ly** adj.

cur·rant /'kərənt, 'kə-rənt/ ▶ n. **1** a dried fruit
made from a small seedless variety of grape. **2** a
shrub producing small edible black, red, or white
berries.

cur·ren·cy /'kərənsē, 'kə-rənsē/ ▶ n. (pl.
currencies) **1** a system of money in general use
in a country. **2** the fact or quality or period of
being accepted or in use: *this minority view has
now gained currency.*

cur·rent /'kərənt, 'kə-rənt/ ▶ adj. **1** happening
or being used or done now: *current events.* **2** in
common or general use: *the other meaning of
the word is still current.* ▶ n. **1** a body of water
or air moving in a definite direction through
a surrounding body of water or air. **2** a flow of
electrically charged particles.

> **USAGE**
> Do not confuse **current** with **currant**. **Current**
> means 'happening now' (*current events*) or 'a flow
> of water, air, or electricity' (*strong ocean currents*),
> whereas **currant** means 'a dried grape.'

cur·rent as·sets ▶ pl.n. cash and other assets that
are expected to be converted to cash within a
year. Compare with FIXED ASSETS.

cur·rent·ly /'kərəntlē, 'kə-rəntlē / ▶ adv. at the
present time.

cur·ric·u·lum /kə'rikyələm/ ▶ n. (pl. **curricula** /-lə/
or **curriculums**) the subjects comprising a course
of study in a school or college. ■ **cur·ric·u·lar**
/-lər/ adj.

cur·ric·u·lum vi·tae /kə'rik(y)ələm 'vē,tī, 'vītē/
▶ n. (pl. **curricula vitae** /kə'rik(y)ələ/) a résumé.

cur·ry¹ /'kərē, 'kə-rē/ ▶ n. (pl. **curries**) a dish of
meat, vegetables, or fish, cooked in a hot, spicy
sauce of Indian origin. ▶ v. (**curries, currying,
curried**) prepare or flavor food with a spicy
sauce.

cur·ry² ▶ v. (**curries, currying, curried**) **1** groom
a horse with a curry comb. **2** historical treat tanned
leather to improve its properties.
– PHRASES **curry favor** try to gain favor by
flattery and servile behavior.

cur·ry comb ▶ n. a hand-held device with
serrated ridges, used for grooming horses.

cur·ry pow·der ▶ n. a mixture of finely ground
spices, such as turmeric and coriander, used for
making curry.

curse /kərs/ ▶ n. **1** an appeal to a supernatural
power to harm someone or something. **2** a cause
of harm or misery: *the disease became the curse
of cotton workers.* **3** an offensive word or phrase
used to express anger or annoyance. ▶ v. **1** use
a curse against someone. **2** (**be cursed with**)
be continually affected by something bad: *I'm
cursed with a slow metabolism.* **3** say offensive
words; swear.

curs·ed /'kərsid, kərst/ ▶ adj. informal, dated used to
express annoyance or irritation.

cur·sive /'kərsiv/ ▶ adj. (of writing) written with
the characters joined.

cur·sor /ˈkərsər/ ▶ n. **1** a movable indicator on a computer screen identifying the point that will be affected by input from the user. **2** the sliding part engraved with a hairline used to locate points on a slide rule.

cur·so·ry /ˈkərsərē/ ▶ adj. hasty and therefore not thorough. ■ **cur·so·ri·ly** /ˈkərsərəlē/ adv.

curt /kərt/ ▶ adj. so brief or abrupt as to be rude. ■ **curt·ly** adv. **curt·ness** n.

cur·tail /kərˈtāl/ ▶ v. limit or cut short: *we would not wish to curtail freedom of speech.* ■ **cur·tail·ment** n.

cur·tain /ˈkərtn/ ▶ n. **1** a piece of material suspended at the top to form a screen, hung at a window in pairs or between the stage and auditorium of a theater. **2** (**the curtain**) the rise or fall of a stage curtain between acts or scenes. **3** (**curtains**) informal a disastrous outcome. ▶ v. provide or screen something with a curtain or curtains.

cur·tain call ▶ n. the appearance of one or more performers on stage after a performance to acknowledge the audience's applause.

cur·tain-rais·er ▶ n. an event happening just before a longer or more important one.

cur·tain wall ▶ n. **1** a fortified wall around a medieval castle, typically one linking towers together. **2** a wall that encloses the space within a building but does not support the roof.

curt·sy /ˈkərtsē/ (also **curtsey**) ▶ n. (pl. **curtsies** or **curtseys**) a woman's or girl's respectful greeting, made by bending the knees with one foot in front of the other. ▶ v. (**curtsies, curtsying, curtsied**; also **curtseys, curtseying, curtseyed**) perform a curtsy.

cur·va·ceous /kərˈvāSHəs/ ▶ adj. (especially of a woman or a woman's figure) having an attractively curved shape.

cur·va·ture /ˈkərvəCHər, -ˌCHŏŏr/ ▶ n. the fact of being curved or the degree to which something is curved: *at that level the curvature of the earth is visible.*

curve /kərv/ ▶ n. **1** a line or outline that gradually bends. **2** a line on a graph showing how one quantity varies with respect to another. ▶ v. form or move in a curve: *the path curved around the house.*

cur·vi·lin·e·ar /ˌkərvəˈlinēər/ ▶ adj. contained by or consisting of a curved line or lines.

curv·y /ˈkərvē/ ▶ adj. (**curvier, curviest**) **1** having many curves. **2** informal (of a woman's figure) curvaceous. ■ **curv·i·ness** n.

cush·ion /ˈkŏŏSHən/ ▶ n. **1** a bag of cloth stuffed with soft material, used as a comfortable support for sitting or leaning on. **2** a means of protection against impact or something unpleasant. **3** the elastic lining of the sides of a billiard table, from which the ball rebounds. ▶ v. **1** soften the effect of an impact on someone or something. **2** lessen the adverse effects of: *he presented her with a gift to cushion the shock.*

cush·y /ˈkŏŏSHē/ ▶ adj. (**cushier, cushiest**) informal (of a task or situation) easy and undemanding.

cusp /kəsp/ ▶ n. **1** a pointed end where two curves meet, such as each of the ends of a crescent moon. **2** a cone-shaped projection on a tooth. **3** the initial point of an astrological sign or house. **4** a point of transition between two different states: *those on the cusp of adulthood.* ■ **cusped** adj.

cuss /kəs/ informal ▶ n. an annoying or stubborn person or animal. ▶ v. swear or curse.

cuss·ed /ˈkəsəd/ ▶ adj. informal awkward; annoying. ■ **cuss·ed·ness** n.

cuss word ▶ n. a swear word.

cus·tard /ˈkəstərd/ ▶ n. a boiled or baked dessert made with milk, eggs, and sugar.

cus·tard ap·ple ▶ n. a large fleshy, mainly tropical fruit with a sweet yellow pulp.

cus·tard pie ▶ n. an open pie containing cold set custard, or a similar container of foam, as thrown in slapstick comedy.

cus·to·di·an /kəsˈtōdēən/ ▶ n. **1** a person who has responsibility for or looks after something. **2** a janitor.

cus·to·dy /ˈkəstədē/ ▶ n. **1** protective care of someone or something. **2** Law parental responsibility, especially as allocated to one of two parents who are getting divorced. **3** imprisonment, especially while waiting for trial. ■ **cus·to·di·al** /ˌkəˈstōdēəl/ adj.

cus·tom /ˈkəstəm/ ▶ n. **1** a traditional way of behaving or doing something that is specific to a particular society, place, or time. **2** a thing that a person often does; a habit: *it was my custom to nap for an hour every day.*

cus·tom·ar·y /ˈkəstəˌmerē/ ▶ adj. in accordance with custom; usual. ■ **cus·tom·ar·i·ly** adv.

cus·tom·er /ˈkəstəmər/ ▶ n. **1** a person who buys goods or services from a store or business. **2** a person of a specified kind that one has to deal with: *he's a tough customer.*

cus·tom house (also **customs house**) ▶ n. chiefly historical the office at a port or frontier where customs duty is collected.

cus·tom·ize /ˈkəstəˌmīz/ ▶ v. modify to suit a particular person or task: *food manufacturers customize products for restaurant chains.* ■ **cus·tom·iz·a·ble** adj. **cus·tom·i·za·tion** /ˌkəstəməˈzāSHən/ n.

cus·tom-made (also **custom-built**) ▶ adj. made to a particular customer's order.

cus·toms /ˈkəstəmz/ ▶ pl.n. **1** the duties charged by a government on imported goods. **2** the official department that administers and collects such duties.

cut /kət/ ▶ v. (**cuts, cutting, cut**) **1** make an opening, incision, or wound in something with a sharp implement. **2** make, shorten, remove, or divide with a sharp implement: *I cut his photo out of the paper.* **3** (as adj. **cut**) make or design a garment in a particular way: *an impeccably cut suit.* **4** reduce the amount or quantity of something. **5** end or interrupt the provision of a supply. **6** go across or through: *is it illegal to cut across a highway on foot?* **7** stop filming or recording. **8** move to another shot in a movie. **9** make a sound recording. **10** divide a deck of playing cards by lifting a portion from the top. **11** mix an illegal drug with another substance. ▶ n. **1** an act of cutting. **2** a result of cutting: *a cut on his jaw.* **3** a reduction in amount or size. **4** the style in which a garment or the hair is cut: *the elegant cut of his jacket.* **5** a piece of meat cut from a carcass. **6** informal a share of profits. **7** a version of a movie after editing: *the director's cut.* – PHRASES **be cut from the same cloth** be of the same nature. **be cut out for** (or **to be**) informal have exactly the right qualities for a particular role. **a cut above** informal noticeably better than. **cut and dried** (of a situation) completely settled. **cut and paste** (on a word processor or computer) move an item from one part of a file to another. **cut and run** informal hastily leave a difficult situation rather than deal with it. **cut and thrust** a spirited and rapid interchange of views. **cut both ways 1** (of a point) serve both sides of an argument. **2** have both good and bad effects. **cut corners** do something with a lack of thoroughness to save time or money. **cut someone dead** completely ignore someone. **cut in 1** interrupt someone. **2** pull in too closely in front of another vehicle after overtaking. **3** move ahead of one's proper place in a line of people. **4** (of a machine) begin operating automatically. **cut someone in** informal include someone in a deal and give them a share of the profits. **cut it out** informal stop it. **cut the mustard** informal reach the required standard. **cut no ice** informal have no influence or effect. **cut someone/thing off 1** block the usual means of access to a place. **2** deprive someone of a supply of power, water, etc. **3** break a telephone connection with someone. **4** disinherit someone. **cut out** (of an engine) suddenly stop operating. **cut someone out** exclude someone. **cut one's teeth** gain initial experience of an activity. **cut a tooth** (of a baby) have a tooth appear through the gum. **cut someone up** informal (of a driver) overtake someone and pull in too closely. **make the cut** reach a certain standard, especially one that allows you into the final round of a competition.

cu·ta·ne·ous /kyooʹtānēəs/ ▶ adj. relating to or affecting the skin.

cut·a·way /ʹkətə,wā/ ▶ adj. **1** (of a coat or jacket) having the front cut away below the waist. **2** (of a diagram of an object) having some external parts left out to reveal the interior.

cut·back /ʹkət,bak/ ▶ n. a reduction, especially in expenditure.

cute /kyoot/ ▶ adj. **1** attractive in a charming or sweet way. **2** informal sexually attractive. **3** informal clever; shrewd. ■ **cute·ly** adv. **cute·ness** n.

cute·sy /ʹkyootsē/ ▶ adj. informal excessively charming or sweet.

cut glass ▶ n. glass with decorative patterns cut into it.

cu·ti·cle /ʹkyootikəl/ ▶ n. **1** the dead skin at the base of a fingernail or toenail. **2** the outer cellular layer of a hair. **3** the epidermis of the body.

cut·ie /ʹkyootē/ ▶ n. an attractive or endearing person.

cut·lass /ʹkətləs/ ▶ n. a short sword with a slightly curved blade, formerly used by sailors.

cut·ler /ʹkətlər/ ▶ n. a person who makes or sells cutlery.

cut·ler·y /ʹkətlərē/ ▶ n. knives, forks, and spoons used for eating or serving food.

cut·let /ʹkətlət/ ▶ n. **1** a portion of sliced meat, coated in breadcrumbs and served either grilled or fried. **2** a flat cake of chopped meat, covered in breadcrumbs and shaped like a veal chop.

cut·off /ʹkət,ôf/ ▶ n. **1** (usu. before another noun) a point or level marking a limit: *May 21 is the official cutoff date.* **2** a device for interrupting a power or fuel supply. **3** (**cutoffs**) shorts made by cutting off the legs of a pair of jeans.

cut·out /ʹkət,out/ ▶ n. **1** a shape cut out of board or paper. **2** a hole cut for decoration or for something to be inserted. **3** a device that automatically breaks an electric circuit for safety.

cut·purse /ʹkət,pərs/ ▶ n. old use a pickpocket.

cut·rate (also **cut·price**) ▶ adj. for sale at a reduced price; cheap.

cut·ter /ʹkətər/ ▶ n. **1** a person or thing that cuts something. **2** a light, fast patrol boat or sailboat.

cut·throat /ʹkət,тнrōt/ ▶ adj. fierce and ruthless: *an unforgiving, cutthroat business.* ▶ n. dated a murderer or other violent criminal.

cut·ting /ʹkətiNG/ ▶ n. **1** a piece cut off from something, such as a piece cut from a plant for propagation. **2** an open passage dug out through higher ground for a railroad, road, or canal. ▶ adj. **1** capable of cutting. **2** (of a remark) hurtful. ■ **cut·ting·ly** adv.

cut·ting edge ▶ n. the latest or most advanced stage; the forefront. ▶ adj. (**cutting-edge**) innovative; pioneering.

cut·tle·fish /ʹkətl,fiSH/ ▶ n. (pl. same or **cuttlefishes**) a squidlike marine mollusk that squirts out a black liquid when attacked.

cut up ▶ adj. informal (of a person) very distressed: *his girlfriend is dying and he's really cut up about it.* ▶ n. **1** a film or sound recording made by cutting and editing material from preexisting recordings. **2** (**cutup**) informal a person who is fond of making jokes or playing pranks.

cut·worm /ʹkət,wərm/ ▶ n. a moth caterpillar that lives in the upper layers of the soil and eats through the stems of young plants at ground level.

cu·vée /k(y)ooʹvā/ ▶ n. a type, blend, or batch of wine, especially champagne.

cuz /kəz/ ▶ conj. informal short for BECAUSE.

CV ▶ abbr. curriculum vitae.

CVS ▶ abbr. chorionic villus sampling, a test made in early pregnancy to detect fetal abnormalities.

cwm /koom/ ▶ n. (chiefly in Wales) a steep-sided hollow at the head of a valley or on a mountainside.

cwt ▶ abbr. hundredweight.

cy·an /ʹsī,an, ʹsīən/ ▶ n. a greenish-blue color that is one of the primary colors.

cy·a·nide /ʹsīə,nīd/ ▶ n. a highly poisonous compound containing a metal combined with carbon and nitrogen atoms.

cy·a·no·bac·te·ri·a /,sīənōbakʹtirēə, sī,anō-/ ▶ pl.n. microorganisms that are related to bacteria but capable of photosynthesis; blue-green algae.

cy·a·no·co·bal·a·min /,sīənō,kōʹbaləmin, sī,anō-/ ▶ n. vitamin B_{12}, found in liver, fish, and eggs, a deficiency of which can cause pernicious anemia.

cy·a·no·gen /sīʹanəjən/ ▶ n. a highly poisonous gas.

cy·a·no·sis /,sīəʹnōsəs/ ▶ n. a bluish discoloration of the skin due to poor circulation or inadequate oxygenation of the blood. ■ **cy·a·not·ic** /,sīəʹnätik/ adj.

cyber- ▶ comb.form relating to information technology, the Internet, and virtual reality: *cyberspace.*

cy·ber·ca·fe /,sībərkaʹfā/ ▶ n. a cafe where customers can also use computer terminals and access the Internet.

cy·ber·crime /ʹsībər,krīm/ ▶ n. criminal activities carried out by means of computers or the Internet. ■ **cy·ber·crim·i·nal** /ʹsībər,krimənl/ n.

cy·ber·net·ics /,sībərʹnetiks/ ▶ pl.n. (treated as sing.) the science of communications and automatic control systems in both machines and living things. ■ **cy·ber·net·ic** adj.

cy·ber·punk /'sībər,pəNGk/ ▸ n. a type of science fiction set in a lawless subculture of an oppressive society dominated by computer technology.

cy·ber·space /'sībər,spās/ ▸ n. the hypothetical environment in which communication over computer networks occurs.

cy·ber·squat·ting /'sībər,skwätiNG/ ▸ n. the practice of registering an Internet domain name that a company or organization may later want for itself, in the hope of selling it back to them at a profit. ■ **cy·ber·squat·ter** n.

cy·ber·stalk·ing /'sībər,stôkiNG/ ▸ n. the repeated use of electronic communications to harass or frighten someone, for example by sending threatening emails. ■ **cy·ber·stalk·er** n.

cy·ber·ter·ror·ism /,sībər'terə,rizəm/ ▸ n. the use of computers to cause severe disruption or widespread fear in the attempt to achieve a political aim. ■ **cy·ber·ter·ror·ist** n.

cy·borg /'sī,bôrg/ ▸ n. (in science fiction) a person having mechanical elements built into the body to extend their normal physical abilities.

cy·brid /'sī,brid/ ▸ n. Microbiology a hybrid cell produced artificially by the fusion of two cells, one of which lacks a nucleus.

cy·cad /'sīkad, 'sī,kad/ ▸ n. a tall, cone-bearing, palmlike plant of warm regions.

cy·cla·men /'sīkləmən, 'sik-/ ▸ n. (pl. same or **cyclamens**) a plant having pink, red, or white flowers with backward-curving petals.

cy·cle /'sīkəl/ ▸ n. 1 a series of events that are regularly repeated in the same order: *the cycle of growth and harvest.* 2 a complete sequence of changes associated with a recurring phenomenon such as an alternating electric current. 3 a bicycle. 4 a series of musical or literary works composed around a particular theme. ▸ v. 1 ride a bicycle. 2 follow a repeated sequence of events: *on the laptop this message cycles every few seconds.*

cy·clic /'sīklik, 'sik-/ ▸ adj. 1 occurring in cycles: *the cyclic rotation of the earth and moon.* 2 having a molecular structure containing one or more closed rings of atoms. ■ **cy·cli·cal** adj. **cy·cli·cal·ly** /-ik(ə)lē/ adv.

cy·clist /'sīk(ə)list/ ▸ n. a person who rides a bicycle.

cy·clone /'sī,klōn/ ▸ n. 1 a system of winds rotating inward to an area of low barometric pressure; a depression. 2 a tropical storm. ■ **cy·clon·ic** /sī'klänik/ adj.

cy·clo·pe·an /,sīklə'pēən, sī'klōpēən/ ▸ adj. 1 relating to or resembling a Cyclops. 2 made with massive irregular stone blocks: *cyclopean walls.*

cy·clo·pe·di·a /,sīklə'pēdēə/ (also **cyclopaedia**) ▸ n. (in book titles) an encyclopedia.

Cy·clops /'sī,kläps/ ▸ n. (pl. same) Greek Mythology a member of a race of savage giants with only one eye.

cy·clo·tron /'sīklə,trän/ ▸ n. a piece of equipment for accelerating charged atomic and subatomic particles by making them move spirally in a magnetic field.

cyg·net /'signət/ ▸ n. a young swan.

cyl·in·der /'siləndər/ ▸ n. 1 a three-dimensional shape with straight parallel sides and a circular or oval cross section. 2 a piston chamber in a steam or internal combustion engine. 3 a cylindrical container for liquefied gas under pressure.

cyl·in·der head ▸ n. the end cover of a cylinder in an internal combustion engine, against which the piston compresses the cylinder's contents.

cy·lin·dri·cal /sə'lindrikəl/ ▸ adj. having the shape of a cylinder. ■ **cy·lin·dri·cal·ly** /sə'lindrik(ə)lē/ adv.

cym·bal /'simbəl/ ▸ n. a musical instrument consisting of a slightly concave round brass plate that is either struck against another one or hit with a stick.

cyme /sīm/ ▸ n. a flower cluster with a central stem bearing a single flower on the end that develops first. Compare with RACEME.

Cym·ric /'kəmrik/ ▸ adj. (of language or culture) Welsh. ▸ n. the Welsh language.

cyn·ic /'sinik/ ▸ n. 1 a person who believes that people are motivated purely by self-interest. 2 a person who raises doubts about something; a skeptic. 3 (**Cynic**) (in ancient Greece) a member of a school of philosophers who despised wealth and pleasure. ■ **cyn·i·cism** n.

cyn·i·cal /'sinikəl/ ▸ adj. 1 believing that people always act from selfish motives. 2 proceeding from self-interest, regardless of accepted standards: *a cynical disregard for safety.* 3 doubtful; skeptical: *young people are very cynical about advertising.* 4 contemptuous; mocking. ■ **cyn·i·cal·ly** adv.

cy·no·sure /'sīnə,sHŏŏr, 'sin-/ ▸ n. a person or thing that is the center of attention or admiration.

cy·pher ▸ n. variant spelling of CIPHER.

cy·press /'sīprəs/ ▸ n. an evergreen coniferous tree with small dark green leaves.

Cyp·ri·ot /'siprēət, -,ät/ ▸ n. 1 a person from Cyprus. 2 the dialect of Greek used in Cyprus. ▸ adj. relating to Cyprus.

Cy·ril·lic /sə'rilik/ ▸ adj. referring to the alphabet used for Russian, Ukrainian, Bulgarian, Serbian, and some other Slavic languages. ▸ n. the Cyrillic alphabet.

cyst /sist/ ▸ n. 1 a thin-walled abnormal sac or cavity in the body, containing fluid. 2 a sac or bladder containing liquid in an animal or plant.

cys·tic /'sistik/ ▸ adj. 1 relating to cysts. 2 relating to the urinary bladder or the gallbladder.

cys·tic fi·bro·sis ▸ n. an inherited disease in which the production of abnormally thick mucus leads to the blockage of the pancreatic ducts, intestines, and bronchi.

cys·ti·tis /sis'tītis/ ▸ n. inflammation of the urinary bladder, typically caused by infection and accompanied by frequent painful urination.

cy·tol·o·gy /sī'täləjē/ ▸ n. the branch of biology concerned with the structure and function of plant and animal cells. ■ **cy·to·log·i·cal** /,sītl'äjikəl/ adj. **cy·tol·o·gist** n.

cy·to·meg·a·lo·vi·rus /,sītə,megəlō'vīrəs/ ▸ n. a kind of herpesvirus that usually produces very mild symptoms in an infected person but may cause severe neurological damage in people with weakened immune systems and in the newborn.

cy·to·plasm /'sītə,plazəm/ ▸ n. the material or protoplasm within a living cell, excluding the nucleus. ■ **cy·to·plas·mic** /,sītə'plazmik/ adj.

czar /zär, (t)sär/ (etc.) ▸ n. 1 variant spelling of

TSAR. 2 a person with great authority or power in a particular area: *the government's new drug czar.*

Czech /cHek/ ▶ n. **1** a person from the Czech Republic or (formerly) Czechoslovakia. **2** the Slavic language spoken in the Czech Republic. ▶ adj. relating to the Czech Republic.

Czech·o·slo·vak /ˌcHekəˈslōˌväk, -ˌvak/ (also **Czechoslovakian** /ˌcHekəsləˈväkēən, -ˈvakēən/) ▶ n. a person from the former country of Czechoslovakia, now divided between the Czech Republic and Slovakia. ▶ adj. relating to the former country of Czechoslovakia.

D¹ (also **d**) ▶ n. (pl. **Ds** or **D's**) **1** the fourth letter of the alphabet. **2** referring to the fourth item in a set. **3** Music the second note of the scale of C major. **4** the Roman numeral for 500.

D² ▶ abbr. **1** Democrat or Democratic. **2** depth (in the sense of the dimension of an object from front to back). **3** (with a numeral) dimension(s) or dimensional. **4** a dry cell battery of a size commonly used in flashlights and portable televisions. **5** (in tables of sports results) drawn.

d ▶ abbr. **1** (in genealogies) daughter. **2** deci-. **3** (in travel timetables) departs. **4** (**d.**) died (used to indicate a date of death).

'd ▶ contr. **1** had. **2** would.

DA ▶ abbr. district attorney.

D/A ▶ abbr. Electronics digital to analog.

DAB ▶ abbr. digital audio broadcasting.

dab¹ /dab/ ▶ v. (**dabs, dabbing, dabbed**) **1** press something lightly with a cloth or sponge. **2** apply a substance with light quick strokes. ▶ n. a small amount of a substance lightly applied.

dab² ▶ n. a small North Atlantic flatfish.

dab·ble /'dabəl/ ▶ v. **1** move one's hands or feet around gently in water. **2** take part in an activity in a casual way: *I was a vegetarian and dabbled in yoga.* ■ **dab·bler** n.

dab hand ▶ n. Brit. informal a person who is very skilled in a particular activity.

da ca·po /dä 'käpō/ ▶ adv. & adj. Music repeat or repeated from the beginning.

dace /dās/ ▶ n. (pl. same) a small freshwater fish related to the carp.

da·cha /'däcHə/ ▶ n. (in Russia) a country house or cottage, used as a vacation home.

dachs·hund /'däksənd, 'däks,hŏŏnt/ ▶ n. a breed of dog with a long body and very short legs.

da·coit /də'koit/ ▶ n. a member of a band of armed robbers in India or Myanmar (Burma).

Da·cron /'dā,krän, 'dak,rän/ ▶ n. trademark a synthetic polyester (polyethylene terephthalate) with tough, elastic properties, used as a textile fabric.

dac·tyl /'daktl/ ▶ n. Poetry a metrical foot consisting of one stressed syllable followed by two unstressed syllables. ■ **dac·tyl·ic** /dak'tilik/ adj.

dad /dad/ ▶ n. informal one's father.

Da·da /'dädä/ ▶ n. an early 20th-century movement in the arts that mocked conventions and emphasized the illogical and absurd.
■ **Da·da·ism** /-,izəm/ n. **Da·da·ist** n. & adj.

dad·dy /'dadē/ ▶ n. (pl. **daddies**) informal one's father.

dad·dy long·legs /'laNG,legz/ ▶ n. (pl. same) an arachnid with a globular body and long thin legs, typically living in leaf litter and on tree trunks.

da·do /'dädō/ ▶ n. (pl. **dados**) **1** the lower part of the wall of a room, when decorated differently

from the upper part. **2** Architecture the part of a pedestal between the base and the cornice.

dae·mon /'dēmən/ ▶ n. old-fashioned spelling of **DEMON**. ■ **dae·mon·ic** /di'mänik/ adj.

daf·fo·dil /'dafə,dil/ ▶ n. a plant bearing bright yellow flowers with a long trumpet-shaped center.

daf·fy /'dafē/ ▶ adj. (**daffier, daffiest**) informal silly or mildly eccentric. ■ **daf·fi·ness** n.

daft /daft/ ▶ adj. informal silly; foolish.

dag·ger /'dagər/ ▶ n. **1** a short pointed knife, used as a weapon. **2** another term for **OBELUS**.
– PHRASES **be at daggers drawn** (of two people) be bitterly hostile toward each other. **look daggers at** glare angrily at.

da·go /'dägō/ ▶ n. (pl. **dagos** or **dagoes**) informal, offensive a Spanish, Portuguese, or Italian-speaking person.

da·guerre·o·type /də'ge(ə)rə,tīp/ (also **daguerrotype**) ▶ n. an early type of photograph produced by means of a silver-coated copper plate and mercury vapor.

dahl·ia /'dalyə, 'däl-/ ▶ n. a garden plant with brightly colored single or double flowers.

dai·kon /'dī,kän, -kən/ ▶ n. a radish with a large slender white root that is typically eaten cooked, especially in Eastern cuisine.

dai·ly /'dālē/ ▶ adj. done, happening, or produced every day or every weekday. ▶ adv. every day. ▶ n. (pl. **dailies**) informal a newspaper published every day except Sunday.

dain·ty /'däntē/ ▶ adj. (**daintier, daintiest**) delicately small and pretty: *dainty white snowdrops.* ▶ n. (pl. **dainties**) a small appetizing item of food. ■ **dain·ti·ly** adv. **dain·ti·ness** n.

dai·qui·ri /'dakərē, 'dīkə-/ ▶ n. (pl. **daiquiris**) a cocktail containing rum and lime juice.

dair·y /'de(ə)rē/ ▶ n. (pl. **dairies**) a building where milk and milk products are processed and distributed. ▶ adj. **1** made from milk. **2** involved in milk production. ■ **dair·y·ing** n.

dair·y·maid /'de(ə)rē,mād/ ▶ n. old use a woman employed in a dairy.

dair·y·man /'de(ə)rēmən, -,man/ ▶ n. (pl. **dairymen**) a man who works in a dairy or who sells dairy products.

da·is /'dāis, 'dī-/ ▶ n. a low platform for a lectern or throne.

dai·sy /'dāzē/ ▶ n. (pl. **daisies**) a small plant having flowers with a yellow center and white petals.

dai·sy chain ▶ n. a string of daisies threaded together by their stems.

dai·sy wheel ▶ n. a spoked disk carrying printing characters, used in word processors and typewriters.

dal /däl/ (also **dhal**) ▶ n. (in Indian cooking) split legumes.

Da·lai La·ma /ˈdälī ˈlämə/ ▶ n. the spiritual head of Tibetan Buddhism.

dale /dāl/ ▶ n. a valley, especially in northern England.

dal·li·ance /ˈdalēəns, ˈdalyəns/ ▶ n. 1 a casual romantic or sexual relationship. 2 a brief or casual involvement with something: *his dalliance with the far right.*

dal·ly /ˈdalē/ ▶ v. (**dallies, dallying, dallied**) 1 act or move slowly. 2 (**dally with**) have a casual sexual relationship with someone. 3 (**dally with**) take a casual interest in: *I dallied with the idea of asking her friend to come, too.*

Dal·ma·tian /dalˈmāsHən/ ▶ n. a breed of large dog with short white hair and dark spots.

dam¹ /dam/ ▶ n. a barrier built across a river to hold back water, in order to form a reservoir or prevent flooding. ▶ v. (**dams, damming, dammed**) build a dam across a river.

dam² ▶ n. the female parent of certain mammals, especially horses.

dam·age /ˈdamij/ ▶ n. 1 physical harm that affects the value, functioning, or usefulness of something. 2 harmful effects: *the damage to his reputation was considerable.* 3 (**damages**) financial compensation for a loss or injury. ▶ v. cause harm to; have a bad effect on: *some industrial solvents can damage people's health.*
– PHRASES **what's the damage?** informal, humorous what does it cost?

dam·ag·ing /ˈdamijiNG/ ▶ adj. harmful or undesirable.

dam·a·scened /ˈdamə,sēnd, ,damə'sēnd/ ▶ adj. 1 (of iron or steel) given a wavy pattern by hammer-welding and repeated heating and forging. 2 (of metal) inlaid with gold or silver.

dam·ask /ˈdaməsk/ ▶ n. a rich heavy fabric with a pattern woven into it. ▶ adj. literary pink or light red.

dame /dām/ ▶ n. 1 (**Dame**) (in the UK) the title of a woman awarded a knighthood, equivalent to *Sir.* 2 informal a woman.

dam·mit /ˈdamit/ ▶ exclam. used to express anger and frustration.

damn /dam/ ▶ v. 1 curse someone or something. 2 criticize strongly: *a company spokesman damned the plan as financially unsound.* 3 (**be damned**) (in Christian belief) be condemned by God to eternal punishment in hell. 4 (**be damned**) be doomed to misfortune or failure. ▶ exclam. informal expressing anger or frustration. ▶ adj. informal used to emphasize anger or frustration.
– PHRASES **damn someone/thing with faint praise** praise someone or something so unenthusiastically as to suggest condemnation. **not be worth a damn** informal have no value.

dam·na·ble /ˈdamnəbəl/ ▶ adj. very bad or unpleasant. ■ **dam·na·bly** /-blē/ adv.

dam·na·tion /damˈnāsHən/ ▶ n. condemnation to eternal punishment in hell. ▶ exclam. expressing anger or frustration.

damned /damd/ ▶ adj. used to emphasize anger or frustration.
– PHRASES **do** (or **try**) **one's damnedest** do (or try) one's utmost.

damn·ing /ˈdamiNG/ ▶ adj. strongly suggestive of guilt: *damning evidence.*

damp /damp/ ▶ adj. slightly wet. ▶ n. moisture in the air, on a surface, or in a solid substance.

▶ v. 1 make something damp. 2 (**damp something down**) control or restrain a feeling or situation. 3 (**damp something down**) make a fire burn less strongly by reducing its air supply. 4 reduce or stop the vibration of the strings of a musical instrument. ■ **damp·ish** adj. **damp·ly** adv. **damp·ness** n.

damp·en /ˈdampən/ ▶ v. 1 make something damp. 2 make less strong or intense: *nothing could dampen her enthusiasm.* ■ **damp·en·er** n.

damp·er /ˈdampər/ ▶ n. 1 a pad for silencing a piano string. 2 a device for reducing vibration or oscillation. 3 a movable metal plate used to regulate the air flow in a flue or chimney.
– PHRASES **put a damper on** informal have a subduing or restraining effect on.

dam·sel /ˈdamzəl/ ▶ n. old use or humorous a young unmarried woman.

dam·sel·fly /ˈdamzəl,flī/ ▶ n. (pl. **damselflies**) a slender insect related to the dragonflies.

dam·son /ˈdamzən, -sən/ ▶ n. a small purple-black plumlike fruit.

dan /dan/ ▶ n. 1 any of ten degrees of advanced proficiency in judo or karate. 2 a person who has achieved a dan.

dance /dans/ ▶ v. 1 move rhythmically to music. 2 move in a quick and lively way: *midges danced over the stream.* ▶ n. 1 a series of steps and movements that match the rhythm of a piece of music. 2 an act of dancing. 3 a social gathering at which people dance. 4 (also **dance music**) pop music for dancing to in clubs. ■ **danc·er** n. **danc·ing** n.
– PHRASES **dance attendance on** try hard to please someone.

dance hall ▶ n. 1 a large public hall or building where people pay to enter and dance. 2 (**dancehall**) a style of dance music derived from reggae.

D and C ▶ abbr. dilatation and curettage.

dan·de·li·on /ˈdandl,īən/ ▶ n. a weed with large bright yellow flowers followed by rounded heads of seeds with downy tufts.

dan·der /ˈdandər/ ▶ n. (in phrase **get/have one's dander up**) informal lose one's temper.

dan·di·fied /ˈdandi,fīd/ ▶ adj. (of a man) excessively concerned about his clothes and appearance.

dan·dle /ˈdandl/ ▶ v. gently bounce a young child on one's knees or in one's arms.

dan·druff /ˈdandrəf/ ▶ n. flakes of dead skin on a person's scalp and in the hair.

D & X ▶ abbr. dilation and extraction, a method of performing late-term abortions.

dan·dy /ˈdandē/ ▶ n. (pl. **dandies**) a man who is excessively concerned with having a stylish and fashionable appearance. ▶ adj. (**dandier, dandiest**) informal excellent. ■ **dan·dy·ish** adj.

Dane /dān/ ▶ n. a person from Denmark.

dan·ger /ˈdānjər/ ▶ n. 1 the possibility of suffering harm: *her life was in danger.* 2 a cause of harm. 3 the possibility of something unpleasant or undesirable happening: *there's no danger of putting on weight in that restaurant.*
– PHRASES **in danger of** likely to incur or to suffer from. **out of danger** (of a person who has suffered a serious injury or illness) not expected to die.

dan·ger·ous /ˈdānjərəs/ ▶ adj. 1 able or likely to cause harm: *dangerous chemicals like DDT.*

2 likely to cause problems. ■ **dan·ger·ous·ly** adv. **dan·ger·ous·ness** n.

dan·gle /'daNGgəl/ ▶ v. **1** hang so as to swing freely. **2** offer something attractive to someone to persuade them to do something: *one firm is dangling a grand prize of a Porsche for referrals.* ■ **dan·gler** n. **dan·gly** adj.

dan·gling par·ti·ci·ple /'daNGg(ə)liNG/ ▶ n. Grammar a participle intended to refer to a noun that is not actually present.

> **USAGE**
> A **dangling participle** is one that is left 'hanging' because it does not relate to the noun it should. For example, in the sentence *arriving at the station, the sun came out,* the word *arriving* is a dangling participle, because the sentence reads grammatically as if it is **the sun** (the subject of the sentence) that is **arriving**. This is incorrect in standard English.

Dan·ish /'dānish/ ▶ adj. relating to Denmark or the Danes. ▶ n. the language of Denmark.

Dan·ish blue ▶ n. a strong-flavored blue-veined white cheese.

Dan·ish pas·try ▶ n. a pastry of sweetened yeast dough topped with icing and filled with fruit, cheese, or nuts.

dank /daNGk/ ▶ adj. damp and cold.

daph·ni·a /'dafnēə/ ▶ n. (pl. same) a minute semitransparent freshwater crustacean.

dap·per /'dapər/ ▶ adj. (of a man) neat in dress and appearance.

dap·ple /'dapəl/ ▶ v. mark with spots or small patches: *a forest clearing dappled with sunlight.* ▶ n. a patch of color or light.

dap·ple gray ▶ adj. (of a horse) gray or white with darker ringlike markings.

DAR ▶ abbr. Daughters of the American Revolution.

dare /de(ə)r/ ▶ v. (3rd sing. present usu. **dare** before an expressed or implied infinitive without 'to') **1** have the courage to do something. **2** challenge to do something: *he ran his first marathon because his grandchildren dared him to.* ▶ n. a challenge, especially to prove courage.
– PHRASES **how dare you** used to express indignation. **I dare say** (or **daresay** /ˌde(ə)r'sā/) it is probable.

dare·dev·il /'de(ə)rˌdevəl/ ▶ n. a person who enjoys doing dangerous things.

dar·ing /'de(ə)riNG/ ▶ adj. **1** willing to do dangerous or risky things; bold. **2** involving risk or danger. **3** boldly unconventional: *daring, see-through evening gowns.* ▶ n. adventurous courage; boldness. ■ **dar·ing·ly** adv.

Dar·jee·ling /'där'jēliNG/ ▶ n. a high-quality tea grown in northern India.

dark /därk/ ▶ adj. **1** with little or no light. **2** of a deep color: *dark green.* **3** (of skin, hair, or eyes) brown or black. **4** unpleasant or gloomy: *the dark days of the war.* **5** evil. **6** mysterious: *a dark secret.* **7** (**darkest**) humorous most remote or uncivilized. ▶ n. **1** (**the dark**) the absence of light. **2** nightfall. ■ **dark·ish** adj. **dark·ly** adv. **dark·ness** n.
– PHRASES **in the dark** in a state of ignorance. **a shot** (or **stab**) **in the dark** a wild guess.

Dark Ag·es ▶ pl.n. **1** the period in Europe between the fall of the Roman Empire and the Middle Ages, *c.*500–1100, regarded as lacking culture and knowledge. **2** a period characterized by a lack of knowledge or progress: *the dark ages of computing.*

dark·en /'därkən/ ▶ v. **1** make or become darker. **2** become unhappy or angry.
– PHRASES **never darken someone's door** keep away from someone's home.

dark horse ▶ n. a competitor or candidate who has little chance of winning or who wins unexpectedly.

dark·ling /'därkliNG/ ▶ adj. literary **1** characterized by darkness. **2** growing darker.

dark mat·ter ▶ n. Astronomy nonluminous material believed to exist in space.

dark·net /'därkˌnet/ ▶ n. Computing a computer network with restricted access that is used chiefly for illegal peer-to-peer file sharing.

dark·room /'därkˌrōōm, -ˌrŏŏm/ ▶ n. a room for developing photographs, from which normal light is excluded.

dar·ling /'därliNG/ ▶ n. **1** used as an affectionate form of address. **2** a lovable person. **3** a person popular with a particular group: *she is the darling of the media.* ▶ adj. **1** beloved. **2** pretty; charming.

darm·stadt·i·um /därm'statēəm, -'sнtät-/ ▶ n. a radioactive chemical element produced artificially.

darn[1] /därn/ ▶ v. mend knitted material by interweaving yarn across it. ■ **darn·ing** n.

darn[2] ▶ v., adj., & exclam. informal euphemism for DAMN.

darned /därnd/ ▶ adj. informal euphemism for DAMNED.

dart /därt/ ▶ n. **1** a small pointed missile thrown or fired as a weapon. **2** a small pointed missile used in the game of darts. **3** (**darts**) (usu. treated as sing.) an indoor game in which darts are thrown at a dartboard. **4** a sudden rapid movement. **5** a tapered tuck in a garment. ▶ v. move suddenly or rapidly.

dart·board /'därtˌbôrd/ ▶ n. a circular board used as a target in the game of darts.

Dar·win·ism /'därwəˌnizəm/ ▶ n. the theory of the evolution of species by natural selection, put forward by the English natural historian Charles Darwin. ■ **Dar·win·i·an** /där'winēən/ n. & adj. **Dar·win·ist** n. & adj.

dash /dasн/ ▶ v. **1** run or travel in a great hurry. **2** strike or throw something with great force. **3** destroy or frustrate: *his political hopes were dashed.* **4** (**dash something off**) write something hurriedly. ▶ n. **1** an act of dashing. **2** a small amount added: *whiskey with a dash of soda.* **3** a horizontal stroke in writing, marking a pause or omission. **4** the longer of the signals used in Morse code. **5** a combination of style, enthusiasm, and confidence.

dash·board /'dasн,bôrd/ ▶ n. the panel of instruments and controls facing the driver of a vehicle.

da·shi·ki /də'sнēkē/ ▶ n. (pl. **dashikis**) a loose, brightly colored shirt, originally from West Africa.

dash·ing /'dasнiNG/ ▶ adj. (of a man) attractive, adventurous, and confident. ■ **dash·ing·ly** adv.

das·tard·ly /'dastərdlē/ ▶ adj. dated or humorous wicked and cruel.

DAT /dat/ ▶ abbr. digital audiotape.

da·ta /'datə, 'dātə/ ▶ n. **1** facts and statistics used for reference or analysis. **2** the quantities, characters, or symbols on which operations are performed by a computer.

USAGE

The word **data** is the plural of Latin **datum**, and in scientific use it is usually treated as a plural noun, taking a plural verb (e.g. *the data were classified*). In everyday use, however, **data** is often treated as a singular, and sentences such as *data was collected over a number of years* are now generally accepted.

da·ta·bank /'datə,baNGk, 'dā-/ ▶ n. a large store of data in a computer.

da·ta·base /'datə,bās, 'dā-/ ▶ n. a structured set of data held in a computer.

dat·a·ble /'dātəbəl/ (also **dateable**) ▶ adj. 1 able to be dated to a particular time. 2 (of a person) suitable as a companion on a date.

da·ta cap·ture ▶ n. the action of gathering data and putting it into a form accessible by computer.

da·ta proc·ess·ing ▶ n. any operation performed on data, especially by a computer.

da·ta pro·tec·tion ▶ n. 1 protection of the integrity of digitally stored data. 2 legal control over access to data stored in computers.

date[1] /dāt/ ▶ n. 1 the day of the month or year as specified by a number. 2 a day or year when a particular event occurred or will occur. 3 a social or romantic appointment. 4 a musical or theatrical performance, especially as part of a tour. ▶ v. 1 establish the date of something. 2 write or print the date on something. 3 (**date from** or **date back to**) start or originate at a particular time in the past. 4 (as adj. **dated**) old-fashioned. 5 informal go on a date or regular dates with someone.
– PHRASES **to date** until now.

date[2] ▶ n. 1 a sweet, dark brown, oval fruit with a hard stone, usually eaten dried. 2 (also **date palm**) a tall palm tree that bears this fruit, native to western Asia and North Africa.

date·a·ble ▶ adj. variant spelling of DATABLE.

date·book /'dāt,bŏŏk/ ▶ n. a book with spaces for each day of the year in which one notes appointments or important information.

date·line /'dāt,līn/ ▶ n. a line at the head of a dispatch or newspaper article showing the date and place of writing.

date rape ▶ n. rape by a person with whom the victim has gone on a date.

dat·ing a·gen·cy ▶ n. a service that arranges introductions for people seeking romantic partners or friends.

da·tive /'dātiv/ ▶ n. (in Latin, Greek, German, etc.) the grammatical case of nouns and pronouns that indicates an indirect object or the person or thing affected by a verb.

da·tum /'dātəm, 'datəm/ ▶ n. (pl. **data** /'datə, 'dātə/) a piece of information.

da·tu·ra /də't(y)ŏŏrə/ ▶ n. a North American plant whose flowers contain toxic or narcotic substances.

daub /dôb/ ▶ v. 1 carelessly coat or smear something with a thick substance. 2 spread a thick substance on a surface. ▶ n. 1 plaster, clay, or a similar substance, especially when mixed with straw and applied to laths or wattles to form a wall. 2 a patch or smear of a thick substance. 3 a painting done without much skill.

daugh·ter /'dôtər, 'dä-/ ▶ n. 1 a girl or woman in relation to her parents. 2 a female descendant.
 daugh·ter·ly adj.

daugh·ter·board /'dôtər,bôrd, 'dä-/ (also **daughtercard** /'dôtər,kärd, 'dä-/) ▶ n. a small printed circuit board that attaches to a larger one.

daugh·ter-in-law ▶ n. (pl. **daughters-in-law**) the wife of one's son.

daunt /dônt, dänt/ ▶ v. (usu. **be daunted**) make someone feel intimidated or apprehensive.
 daunt·ing adj.

daunt·less /'dôntlis, 'dänt-/ ▶ adj. fearless and determined.

dau·phin /'dôfin/ ▶ n. historical the eldest son of a king of France.

dav·en·port /'davən,pôrt/ ▶ n. a large upholstered sofa, typically able to be converted into a bed.

da·vit /'davit, 'dā-/ ▶ n. a small crane on a ship, especially one of a pair for lowering a lifeboat.

Da·vy Jones's lock·er /,dāvē 'jōnz(əz)/ ▶ n. informal the bottom of the sea, regarded as the grave of people who drown.

daw·dle /'dôdl/ ▶ v. move slowly; take one's time.
 daw·dler n.

dawn /dôn, dän/ ▶ n. 1 the first appearance of light in the sky in the morning. 2 the beginning of something: *the dawn of civilization*. ▶ v. 1 (of a day) begin. 2 come into existence: *a new era had dawned*. 3 (**dawn on**) become obvious to: *the truth began to dawn on him*.

dawn cho·rus ▶ n. the early-morning singing of birds.

day /dā/ ▶ n. 1 a period of twenty-four hours, reckoned from midnight to midnight and corresponding to a rotation of the earth on its axis. 2 the time between sunrise and sunset. 3 (usu. **days**) a particular period of the past. 4 (**the day**) the present time or the time in question. 5 (**one's day**) the youthful or successful period of one's life. ▶ adj. working or done during the day: *my day job*.
– PHRASES **any day** informal at any time or under any circumstances. **call it a day** decide to stop doing something. **day by day** gradually and steadily. **day in, day out** continuously or repeatedly over a long period. **day-to-day** 1 happening on a daily basis. 2 involving the usual tasks or routines of every day: *the day-to-day running of the company*. **that will be the day** informal that is very unlikely. **these days** at present.

day·bed /'dā,bed/ ▶ n. a couch that can be made into a bed.

day·break /'dā,brāk/ ▶ n. dawn.

day care cen·ter ▶ n. a place providing daytime care for children or for elderly or disabled people.

day·dream /'dā,drēm/ ▶ n. a series of pleasant thoughts that distract one's attention from the present. ▶ v. have a daydream. ■ **day·dream·er** n.

Day-Glo /'dā ,glō/ ▶ n. trademark a fluorescent paint or other coloring.

day·light /'dā,līt/ ▶ n. 1 the natural light of the day. 2 dawn. 3 visible distance between one person or thing and another.
– PHRASES —— **the living daylights out of someone** do a particular thing to someone very strongly or severely: *you scared the living daylights out of me*.

day·light sav·ing time ▶ n. time as adjusted to achieve longer evening daylight by setting the clocks an hour ahead of the standard time.

day off ▶ n. (pl. **days off**) a day's vacation from work or school.

day·pack /'dā‚pak/ ▶ n. a small backpack.

day school ▶ n. a school for students who live at home.

day·time /'dā‚tīm/ ▶ n. 1 the time between sunrise and sunset. 2 the period of time corresponding to normal working hours.

day trip ▶ n. a journey or excursion completed in one day. ■ **day trip·per** n.

daze /dāz/ ▶ v. make someone feel stunned or bewildered. ▶ n. a state of stunned confusion or bewilderment. ■ **daz·ed·ly** /'dāzidlē/ adv.

daz·zle /'dazəl/ ▶ v. 1 (of a bright light) blind someone temporarily. 2 impress someone greatly: *I was dazzled by the beauty of the exhibition*. ▶ n. blinding brightness. ■ **daz·zle·ment** n. **daz·zler** n. **daz·zling** adj.

Db ▶ symbol the chemical element dubnium.

dB ▶ abbr. decibel(s).

DBS ▶ abbr. 1 direct broadcasting by satellite. 2 direct-broadcast satellite.

DC ▶ abbr. 1 direct current. 2 District of Columbia.

DD ▶ abbr. Doctor of Divinity.

D-Day ▶ n. 1 the day (June 6, 1944) in World War II on which Allied forces invaded northern France. 2 the day on which something important is to begin.

DDR ▶ abbr. historical German Democratic Republic.

DDT ▶ abbr. dichlorodiphenyltrichloroethane, a compound used as an insecticide but now banned in many countries.

DE ▶ abbr. Delaware.

de- ▶ prefix forming or added to verbs or their derivatives. 1 down; away: *deduct*. 2 completely: *denude*. 3 referring to removal or reversal: *de-ice*.

dea·con /'dēkən/ ▶ n. 1 (in Catholic, Anglican, and Orthodox Churches) a minister ranking below a priest. 2 (in some Protestant Churches) a lay officer assisting a minister.

dea·con·ess /'dēkənis/ ▶ n. a woman with duties similar to those of a deacon.

de·ac·ti·vate /dē'aktəvāt/ ▶ v. make something inactive by disconnecting or destroying it. ■ **de·ac·ti·va·tion** /dē‚aktə'vāsHən/ n.

dead /ded/ ▶ adj. 1 no longer alive. 2 (of a part of the body) numb. 3 displaying no emotion. 4 no longer relevant or important. 5 without activity or excitement. 6 (of equipment) not working. 7 complete; absolute: *dead silence*. ▶ adv. 1 completely; exactly: *dead on time*. 2 straight; directly: *dead ahead*. ■ **dead·ness** n. – PHRASES **dead and buried** over; finished. **dead meat** informal in trouble: *if anyone finds out, you're dead meat*. **the dead of night** the quietest, darkest part of the night. **the dead of winter** the coldest part of winter. **dead to the world** informal fast asleep. **from the dead** from being dead; from death.

dead·beat /'ded‚bēt/ ▶ adj. (**dead beat**) informal completely exhausted. ▶ n. informal 1 a lazy or disreputable person. 2 a person who tries to evade paying a debt.

dead·bolt /'ded‚bōlt/ ▶ n. a bolt secured by turning a knob or key, rather than by spring action.

dead duck ▶ n. informal an unsuccessful or useless person or thing.

dead·en /'dedn/ ▶ v. 1 make a noise or sensation

less intense. 2 make something numb.

dead end ▶ n. 1 an end people of a road or passage from which no exit is possible. 2 a situation in which no further progress can be made.

dead hand ▶ n. an undesirable and long-lasting influence.

dead·head /'ded‚hed/ ▶ n. 1 (**Deadhead**) a fan and follower of the rock group The Grateful Dead. 2 a passenger or member of an audience with a free ticket. ▶ v. remove dead flowerheads from a plant.

dead heat ▶ n. a result in a race in which two or more competitors finish at exactly the same time.

dead let·ter ▶ n. a law or treaty that has not been repealed but is no longer applied.

dead·line /'ded‚līn/ ▶ n. the latest time or date by which something should be completed.

dead·lock /'ded‚läk/ ▶ n. a situation in which no progress can be made. ▶ v. (**be deadlocked**) be in a situation in which no progress can be made.

dead loss ▶ n. an unproductive or useless person or thing.

dead·ly /'dedlē/ ▶ adj. (**deadlier, deadliest**) 1 causing or able to cause death. 2 complete; total: *they were deadly enemies*. 3 extremely accurate or effective: *her deadly aim with a tennis ball*. 4 informal extremely boring. ▶ adv. 1 in a way that resembles or suggests death: *her skin was deadly pale*. 2 extremely: *he was deadly serious*. ■ **dead·li·ness** n.

dead·ly night·shade ▶ n. a poisonous bushy plant with drooping purple flowers and round black fruit.

dead·ly sin ▶ n. (in Christian tradition) a sin regarded as leading to damnation.

dead·pan /'ded‚pan/ ▶ adj. (of a person's expression) not showing any emotion.

dead reck·on·ing ▶ n. the calculation of one's position, especially at sea, by estimating the direction and distance traveled.

dead ring·er ▶ n. a person or thing that looks very like another.

dead·weight /'ded‚wāt/ ▶ n. 1 the weight of a person or thing without the strength or ability to move themselves. 2 the total weight of cargo, stores, etc., that a ship can carry.

dead·wood /'ded‚wo͝od/ ▶ n. useless or unproductive people or things.

dead zone ▶ n. 1 a place or period in which nothing happens. 2 a place where it is not possible to receive a cell-phone or radio signal.

deaf /def/ ▶ adj. 1 wholly or partially unable to hear. 2 (**deaf to**) unwilling to listen or respond to: *she was deaf to all advice*. ■ **deaf·ness** n. – PHRASES **fall on deaf ears** be ignored. **turn a deaf ear** refuse to listen or respond.

deaf·en /'defən/ ▶ v. 1 make someone deaf. 2 (as adj. **deafening**) extremely loud. ■ **deaf·en·ing·ly** /'defəniNGlē/ adv.

deaf mute ▶ n. a person who is deaf and unable to speak.

USAGE
As the noun **deaf mute** may be regarded as offensive, it is advisable to use terms such as **profoundly deaf** instead.

deal[1] /dēl/ ▶ n. 1 an agreement between two or more parties for their mutual benefit. 2 a particular form of treatment given or received:

working mothers get a bad deal. **3** the process
of distributing cards in a card game. ▶ **v.** (past
and past part. **dealt** /delt/) **1** (**deal something
out**) distribute something. **2** (usu. **deal in**) buy
and sell a product or commodity commercially.
3 buy and sell illegal drugs. **4** distribute cards to
players for a game or round.
– PHRASES **a big deal** informal an important
thing. **deal someone or something a blow**
hit or be harmful to someone or something.
deal with 1 do business with. **2** take action
to put something right. **3** cope with: *a way of
helping people deal with loss.* **4** have something
as a subject. **a good** (or **great**) **deal 1** a large
amount. **2** to a considerable extent: *a good deal
better.* **3** an attractive price; a bargain: *she gave
me a good deal on her old car.* **a square deal** a fair
bargain or treatment.

deal² ▶ n. fir or pine wood (as a building
material).

deal·er /'dēlər/ ▶ n. **1** a person who buys and
sells goods. **2** a person who sells illegal drugs.
3 a player who deals cards in a card game.
■ **deal·er·ship** /-ˌSHip/ n.

dealer plates ▶ pl.n. temporary license plates
used by car dealers or manufacturers on
unlicensed cars.

dealt /delt/ ▶ past participle of DEAL¹.

dean /dēn/ ▶ n. **1** the head of the governing body
of a cathedral. **2** the head of a university faculty
or department or of a medical school. **3** a college
official who is responsible for the discipline and
welfare of students.

dean·er·y /'dēnərē/ ▶ n. (pl. **deaneries**) the
official house of a dean.

dear /di(ə)r/ ▶ adj. **1** regarded with deep
affection. **2** used in the polite introduction
to a letter. **3** chiefly Brit. expensive. ▶ n. **1** a
lovable person. **2** used as an affectionate
form of address. ▶ adv. chiefly Brit. at a high cost.
▶ exclam. used in expressions of surprise or dismay.

dear·ly /'di(ə)rlē/ ▶ adv. **1** very much. **2** at great
cost.

dearth /dərTH/ ▶ n. a lack or inadequate amount
of something: *a dearth of reliable information.*

death /deTH/ ▶ n. **1** the action or fact of
dying. **2** an instance of a person or an animal
dying. **3** the state of being dead. **4** the end
of something: *the death of communism.*
■ **death·less** adj.
– PHRASES **at death's door** so ill that one may
die. **catch one's death** (**of cold**) informal catch a
severe cold. **die a death** fail or come to an end.
do something to death do something so often
that it becomes boring. **like death warmed over**
informal extremely tired or ill. **put someone to
death** execute someone. **to death 1** until dead.
2 used for emphasis: *I'm sick to death of him.*

death·bed /'deTH,bed/ ▶ n. the bed where
someone is dying or has died.

death camp ▶ n. a prison camp in which many
people die or are put to death.

death cer·tif·i·cate ▶ n. an official statement,
signed by a doctor, giving details of a person's
death.

death knell ▶ n. an event that signals the end of
something.

death·ly /'deTHlē/ ▶ adj. (**deathlier, deathliest**)
suggesting death: *a deathly silence.*

death mask ▶ n. a plaster cast of a person's face,
made just after their death.

death pen·al·ty ▶ n. punishment by execution.

death rate ▶ n. the number of deaths per one
thousand people per year.

death rat·tle ▶ n. a gurgling sound in a dying
person's throat.

death row /'rō/ ▶ n. a prison block for people
sentenced to death.

death toll ▶ n. the number of deaths resulting
from a particular cause.

death trap ▶ n. a dangerous building, vehicle,
etc.

death-watch bee·tle ▶ n. a beetle whose larvae
bore into dead wood and timbers.

death wish ▶ n. an unconscious desire for one's
own death.

deb /deb/ ▶ n. informal a debutante.

de·ba·cle /di'bakəl, -'bäkəl/ ▶ n. a complete
failure or disaster.

de·bar /dē'bär/ ▶ v. (**debars, debarring,
debarred**) officially prohibit someone from
doing something. ■ **de·bar·ment** n.

de·bark /dē'bärk/ ▶ v. leave a ship or aircraft.

de·base /di'bās/ ▶ v. lower the quality, value,
or character of someone or something.
■ **de·base·ment** n.

de·bat·a·ble /di'bātəbəl/ ▶ adj. open to discussion
or argument.

de·bate /di'bāt/ ▶ n. **1** a formal discussion
in a public meeting or lawmaking body, in
which opposing arguments are presented.
2 an argument. ▶ v. **1** discuss or argue about
something. **2** consider a course of action:
she debated whether or not to go for a swim.
■ **de·bat·er** n.
– PHRASES **under debate** being discussed.

de·bauched /di'bôCHt/ ▶ adj. overindulging
in sex, alcohol, or drugs. ■ **de·bauch·er·y**
/di'bôCHərē/ n.

de·ben·ture /di'benCHər/ ▶ n. an unsecured
loan certificate issued by a company, backed by
general credit rather than by specified assets.

de·bil·i·tate /di'bili,tāt, dē-/ ▶ v. severely weaken
someone or something. ■ **de·bil·i·ta·tion**
/di,bili'tāSHən/ n.

de·bil·i·ty /di'bilitē/ ▶ n. (pl. **debilities**) physical
weakness.

deb·it /'debit/ ▶ n. **1** an entry in an account
recording a sum owed. **2** a payment made or
owed. ▶ v. (**debits, debiting, debited**) (of a
bank) remove money from a customer's account.

deb·it card ▶ n. a card allowing the holder
to remove money from a bank account
electronically when making a purchase.

deb·o·nair /,debə'ne(ə)r/ ▶ adj. (of a man)
confident, stylish, and charming.

de·bouch /di'bouCH, -'bōōSH/ ▶ v. emerge
from a confined space into a wide, open area.
■ **de·bouch·ment** n.

de·brief /dē'brēf/ ▶ v. question someone in detail
about a completed mission. ■ **de·brief·ing** n.

de·bris /də'brē, ,dā-/ ▶ n. **1** scattered pieces of
trash or the remains of something that has been
destroyed. **2** loose broken pieces of rock.

debt /det/ ▶ n. **1** a sum of money owed. **2** the state
of owing money: *he got into debt.* **3** a feeling of
gratitude for a favor or service.

debt of hon·or ▶ n. a debt whose repayment is
not legally binding but depends on a sense of
moral obligation.

debt·or /'detər/ ▶ n. a person who owes money.

de·bug /dēˈbəg/ ▶v. (**debugs, debugging, debugged**) remove errors from computer hardware or software. ■ **de·bug·ger** n.

de·bunk /dēˈbəNGk/ ▶v. show that a widely held belief or opinion is false or exaggerated. ■ **de·bunk·er** n.

de·burr /dēˈbər/ (also **debur**) ▶v. (**deburrs, deburring, deburred**) smooth the rough edges of an object.

de·but /dāˈbyoo/ ▶n. 1 a person's first appearance or performance in a capacity or role. 2 dated the first appearance of a debutante in society. ▶adj. referring to the first recording or publication of a singer or writer: *her debut album.* ▶v. perform in public for the first time.

deb·u·tant /ˈdebyoōˌtänt, ˈdebyə-/ ▶n. a person making a debut.

deb·u·tante /ˈdebyoōˌtänt, ˈdebyə-/ ▶n. a young upper-class woman making her first appearance in society.

Dec. ▶abbr. December.

dec·ade /ˈdekād/ ▶n. a period of ten years.

dec·a·dent /ˈdekədənt/ ▶adj. 1 having low moral standards and interested only in pleasure and enjoyment. 2 luxuriously self-indulgent: *a decadent soak in a scented bath.* ■ **dec·a·dence** n. **dec·a·dent·ly** adv.

de·caf /ˈdēˌkaf/ ▶n. informal decaffeinated coffee.

de·caf·fein·a·ted /dēˈkafəˌnātəd/ ▶adj. (of tea or coffee) having had most or all of its caffeine removed.

dec·a·gon /ˈdekəˌgän/ ▶n. a plane figure with ten straight sides and angles.

dec·a·he·dron /ˌdekəˈhēdrən/ ▶n. (pl. **decahedra** /-drə/ or **decahedrons**) a solid figure with ten plane faces.

de·cal /ˈdēkal/ ▶n. a design on prepared paper for transferring onto glass, porcelain, etc.

de·cal·ci·fied /dēˈkalsəˌfīd/ ▶adj. (of rock or bone) containing a reduced quantity of calcium salts. ■ **de·cal·ci·fi·ca·tion** /dēˌkalsəfiˈkāsHən/ n.

dec·a·li·ter /ˈdekəˌlētər/ ▶n. a metric unit of capacity, equal to 10 liters.

Dec·a·logue /ˈdekəˌlôg, -ˌläg/ ▶n. the Ten Commandments.

de·camp /diˈkamp/ ▶v. leave suddenly or secretly.

de·cant /diˈkant/ ▶v. 1 pour something from one container into another to separate liquid from sediment. 2 figurative empty out; move as if by pouring.

de·cant·er /diˈkantər/ ▶n. a glass container with a stopper into which wine or liquor is decanted.

de·cap·i·tate /diˈkapiˌtāt/ ▶v. kill someone by cutting off their head. ■ **de·cap·i·ta·tion** /diˌkapiˈtāsHən/ n.

dec·a·pod /ˈdekəˌpäd/ ▶n. a crustacean with five pairs of walking legs, such as a shrimp.

de·car·bon·ize /dēˈkärbəˌnīz/ ▶v. remove carbon deposits from an engine.

de·cath·lon /diˈkaTH(ə)ˌlän/ ▶n. a track-and-field event in which each competitor takes part in the same ten events. ■ **de·cath·lete** /-ˈkaTH(ə)ˌlēt/ n.

de·cay /diˈkā/ ▶v. 1 rot as a result of the action of bacteria and fungi. 2 become progressively worse; deteriorate. 3 Physics (of a radioactive substance, particle, etc.) undergo change to a different form by emitting radiation. ▶n. 1 the state or process of decaying. 2 rotten matter or tissue.

de·cease /diˈsēs/ ▶n. formal or Law death.

de·ceased /diˈsēst/ formal or Law ▶n. (**the deceased**) the recently dead person in question. ▶adj. recently dead.

de·ce·dent /diˈsēdnt/ ▶n. Law a person who has died: *questions concerning the decedent's intentions.*

de·ceit /diˈsēt/ ▶n. behavior intended to make someone believe something that is not true.

de·ceit·ful /diˈsētfəl/ ▶adj. deliberately behaving in a way that makes others believe things that are not true. ■ **de·ceit·ful·ly** adv. **de·ceit·ful·ness** n.

de·ceive /diˈsēv/ ▶v. 1 deliberately make someone believe something that is not true. 2 (of a thing) give a mistaken impression: *don't be deceived by the book's title.* ■ **de·ceiv·er** n.

de·cel·er·ate /dēˈseləˌrāt/ ▶v. begin to move more slowly. ■ **de·cel·er·a·tion** /-ˌseləˈrāsHən/ n.

De·cem·ber /diˈsembər/ ▶n. the twelfth month of the year.

de·cen·cy /ˈdēsənsē/ ▶n. (pl. **decencies**) 1 behavior that follows generally accepted standards of morality or respectability. 2 (**decencies**) standards of acceptable behavior.

de·cen·ni·al /diˈsenēəl/ ▶adj. lasting for or happening every ten years.

de·cent /ˈdēsənt/ ▶adj. 1 following generally accepted standards of morality or respectability. 2 of an acceptable standard. 3 informal kind or generous. ■ **de·cent·ly** adv.

de·cen·tral·ize /dēˈsentrəˌlīz/ ▶v. transfer authority from central to local government. ■ **de·cen·tral·i·za·tion** /dēˌsentrəliˈzāsHən/ n.

de·cep·tion /diˈsepsHən/ ▶n. 1 the action of deceiving someone. 2 a thing that deceives others into believing something that is not true.

de·cep·tive /diˈseptiv/ ▶adj. giving an impression different from the true one; misleading.

de·cep·tive·ly /diˈseptivlē/ ▶adv. 1 to a lesser extent than appears the case. 2 to a greater extent than appears the case.

> **USAGE**
> **Deceptively** can mean both one thing and also its complete opposite. A *deceptively smooth surface* is one that appears smooth but in fact is not smooth at all, while a *deceptively spacious room* is one that does not look spacious but is in fact **more** spacious than it appears. To avoid confusion, it is often better to reword a sentence rather than use **deceptively**.

deci- ▶comb.form one tenth: *deciliter.*

dec·i·bel /ˈdesəˌbel, -bəl/ ▶n. a unit of measurement expressing the intensity of a sound or the power of an electrical signal.

de·cide /diˈsīd/ ▶v. 1 consider something carefully and make a judgment or choice: *she decided to stay at home.* 2 settle an issue or contest: *the game was decided by a penalty shot.* 3 give a judgment concerning a legal case. ■ **de·cid·a·ble** adj. **de·cid·ing** adj.

de·cid·ed /diˈsīdid/ ▶adj. definite; clear: *a decided improvement.* ■ **de·cid·ed·ly** adv.

de·cid·u·ous /diˈsijoōəs/ ▶adj. 1 (of a tree or shrub) shedding its leaves annually. Contrasted with **EVERGREEN**. 2 (of teeth or horns) shed after a time.

dec·i·li·ter /ˈdesəˌlētər/ (Brit. **decilitre**) ▶n. a metric unit of capacity, equal to one tenth of a liter.

dec·i·mal /ˈdes(ə)məl/ ▶adj. relating to a system

of numbers based on the number ten. ▶ n. a fractional number in the decimal system, written with figures to the right of a decimal point.

dec·i·mal·ize /'desəmə,līz/ ▶ v. convert a system of coinage or weights and measures to a decimal system. ■ **dec·i·mal·i·za·tion** /,des(ə)mələ'zāsHən/ n.

dec·i·mal place ▶ n. the position of a digit to the right of a decimal point.

dec·i·mal point ▶ n. a dot placed after the figure representing units in a decimal fraction.

dec·i·mate /'desə,māt/ ▶ v. **1** kill or destroy a large proportion of a group. **2** drastically reduce the strength of something. ■ **dec·i·ma·tion** /,desə'māsHən/ n.

> **USAGE**
> The earliest sense of **decimate** was 'kill one in every ten of a group,' a reference to the ancient Roman practice of killing one in every ten of a group of soldiers as a collective punishment. This has been more or less totally superseded by the sense 'kill or destroy a large proportion of a group,' although some people argue that this later sense is wrong.

dec·i·me·ter /'desə,mētər/ (Brit. **decimetre**) ▶ n. a metric unit of length, equal to one tenth of a meter.

de·ci·pher /di'sīfər/ ▶ v. **1** convert something written in code into normal language. **2** succeed in understanding or interpreting something: *his handwriting was difficult to decipher.* ■ **de·ci·pher·a·ble** adj. **de·ci·pher·ment** n.

de·ci·sion /di'siZHən/ ▶ n. **1** a choice or judgment made after considering something. **2** the action or process of deciding. **3** decisiveness.

de·ci·sive /di'sīsiv/ ▶ adj. **1** having great importance for the final result of a situation: *a decisive battle.* **2** able to make decisions quickly. ■ **de·ci·sive·ly** adv. **de·ci·sive·ness** n.

deck /dek/ ▶ n. **1** a floor of a ship, especially the upper level. **2** a floor or platform resembling a ship's deck, especially one attached to a house. **3** a set of playing cards. **4** a component in sound-reproduction equipment, incorporating a player or recorder for discs or tapes. ▶ v. **1** decorate or dress someone or something brightly or attractively: *the Morris dancers were decked out in rustic costume.* **2** informal knock someone to the ground with a punch.
– PHRASES **hit the deck** informal fall to the ground.

deck chair ▶ n. a folding chair with a wooden frame and a canvas seat.

deck·hand /'dek,hand/ ▶ n. a member of a ship's crew performing cleaning or manual work.

deck·ing /'dekiNG/ ▶ n. material used in making a deck.

deck·le /'dekəl/ ▶ n. a continuous belt on either side in a paper-making machine, used for controlling the size of paper produced.

de·claim /di'klām/ ▶ v. speak or recite something in an emphatic or dramatic way. ■ **de·clam·a·to·ry** /-'klamə,tôrē/ adj.

dec·la·ma·tion /,deklə'māsHən/ ▶ n. the action of declaiming something.

dec·la·ra·tion /,deklə'rāsHən/ ▶ n. **1** a formal statement or announcement. **2** an act of declaring something.

de·clar·a·tive /di'kle(ə)rətiv, -'klar-/ ▶ adj. **1** making a declaration: *a declarative statement.* **2** (of a sentence or phrase) taking the

form of a simple statement.

de·clare /di'kle(ə)r/ ▶ v. **1** announce something solemnly or officially. **2** (**declare oneself**) reveal one's intentions or identity. **3** (as adj. **declared**) having stated something openly: *a declared atheist.* **4** acknowledge that one has income or goods on which tax or duty should be paid.

dé·clas·sé /,däklä'sā/ (also **déclassée**) ▶ adj. having fallen in social status.

de·clas·si·fy /dē'klasə,fī/ ▶ v. (**declassifies, declassifying, declassified**) officially declare information or documents to be no longer secret. ■ **de·clas·si·fi·ca·tion** /dē,klasəfi'kāsHən/ n.

de·clen·sion /di'klensHən/ ▶ n. the changes in the form of a noun, pronoun, or adjective that identify its grammatical case, number, and gender.

dec·li·na·tion /,deklə'nāsHən/ ▶ n. **1** Astronomy the position of a point in the sky equivalent to latitude on the earth. **2** the angular deviation of a compass needle from true north.

de·cline /di'klīn/ ▶ v. **1** become smaller, weaker, or worse: *the breeding population has declined in recent years.* **2** politely refuse to accept or do something: *he declined to comment on the rumors.* **3** (especially of the sun) move downward. **4** Grammar form a noun, pronoun, or adjective according to case, number, and gender. ▶ n. a gradual and continuous loss of strength, numbers, or value.

de·cliv·i·ty /di'klivitē/ ▶ n. (pl. **declivities**) a downward slope.

de·clut·ter /dē'klətər/ ▶ v. remove superfluous or unnecessary articles from a house, room, etc.

dec·o /'dekō/ ▶ n. short for ART DECO.

de·coc·tion /di'käksHən/ ▶ n. a concentrated liquid produced by heating or boiling a substance.

de·code /di'kōd/ ▶ v. **1** convert a coded message into intelligible language. **2** convert audio or video signals from analog to digital. ■ **de·cod·er** n.

dé·colle·tage /dā,kälə'täzH ,dekələ-/ ▶ n. **1** a low neckline on a woman's dress or top. **2** a woman's cleavage or breasts as revealed by such a neckline.

dé·colle·té /dā,kälə'tā, ,dekələ-/ ▶ adj. having a low neckline. ▶ n. a décolletage.

de·col·o·nize /dē'kälə,nīz/ ▶ v. withdraw from a colony, leaving it independent. ■ **de·col·o·ni·za·tion** /-,kälənə'zāsHən/ n.

de·com·mis·sion /,dēkə'misHən/ ▶ v. **1** take a ship out of service. **2** dismantle a nuclear reactor or weapon and make it safe.

de·com·pose /,dēkəm'pōz/ ▶ v. **1** (of organic matter) decay. **2** (of a substance) break down into its component elements. ■ **de·com·po·si·tion** /dē,kämpə'zisHən/ n.

de·com·press /,dēkəm'pres/ ▶ v. **1** expand compressed computer data to its normal size. **2** reduce the air pressure on a person who has been experiencing high pressure while deep-sea diving. ■ **de·com·pres·sor** n.

de·com·pres·sion /,dēkəm'presHən/ ▶ n. **1** reduction in air pressure. **2** a gradual reduction of air pressure on a person who has been experiencing high pressure while deep-sea diving. **3** the process of decompressing computer data.

de·com·pres·sion cham·ber ▶ n. a small room in which the air pressure can be varied, used to allow deep-sea divers to adjust to normal air pressure.

de·com·pres·sion sick·ness ▶ n. a serious condition that results when too rapid decompression causes nitrogen bubbles to form in the tissues of the body.

de·con·ges·tant /ˌdēkənˈjestənt/ ▶ n. a medicine taken to relieve a stuffy nose.

de·con·struct /ˌdēkənˈstrəkt/ ▶ v. 1 analyze something by the method of deconstruction. 2 reduce something to its constituent parts in order to reinterpret it. ▪ **de·con·struc·tive** adj.

de·con·struc·tion /ˌdēkənˈstrəksнən/ ▶ n. a method of literary and cultural analysis that states that something has many different meanings and emphasizes the role of the subject in the production of meaning. ▪ **de·con·struc·tion·ism** /-ˌnizəm/ n. **de·con·struc·tion·ist** /-ist/ adj. & n.

de·con·tam·i·nate /ˌdēkənˈtaməˌnāt/ ▶ v. remove dangerous substances from an area or object. ▪ **de·con·tam·i·na·tion** /-ˌtaməˈnāsнən/ n.

de·con·tex·tu·al·ize /ˌdēkənˈteksснōōəˌlīz/ ▶ v. consider something separately from its context. ▪ **de·con·tex·tu·al·i·za·tion** /-ˌteksснōōələˈzāsнən/ n.

de·cor /dāˈkôr, diˈ-/ ▶ n. the furnishing and decoration of a room.

dec·o·rate /ˈdekəˌrāt/ ▶ v. 1 make something more attractive by putting extra items in or on it: *the square was decorated with colored lights.* 2 apply paint, wallpaper, etc., to a room or building. 3 give an award or medal to someone.

dec·o·ra·tion /ˌdekəˈrāsнən/ ▶ n. 1 the process or art of decorating something. 2 an object or pattern that makes something look more attractive. 3 the way in which something is decorated. 4 a medal or award conferred as an honor.

dec·o·ra·tive /ˈdek(ə)rətiv, ˈdekəˌrātiv/ ▶ adj. 1 making something look more attractive: *decorative motifs.* 2 relating to decoration. ▪ **dec·o·ra·tive·ly** adv.

dec·o·ra·tor /ˈdekəˌrātər/ ▶ n. a person whose job it is to design the interior of someone's home, by choosing colors, materials, and furnishings.

dec·o·rous /ˈdekərəs, diˈkôrəs/ ▶ adj. in keeping with good taste; polite and restrained. ▪ **dec·o·rous·ly** adv. **dec·o·rous·ness** n.

de·co·rum /diˈkôrəm/ ▶ n. polite and socially acceptable behavior.

de·cou·page /ˌdākōōˈpäzн/ ▶ n. the decoration of a surface with paper cutouts.

de·cou·ple /dēˈkəpəl/ ▶ v. separate or disengage one thing from another.

de·coy ▶ n. /ˈdēˌkoi/ 1 a real or imitation bird or mammal used by hunters to lure game. 2 a person or thing used to mislead someone or lure them into a trap. ▶ v. /diˈkoi/ lure a person or animal by means of a decoy.

de·crease ▶ v. /diˈkrēs/ make or become smaller or fewer in size, amount, or strength. ▶ n. /ˈdēˌkrēs, diˈkrēs/ 1 an instance of decreasing. 2 the process of decreasing.

de·cree /diˈkrē/ ▶ n. 1 an official order from a ruler or government that has the force of law. 2 a judgment or decision made by certain courts of law. ▶ v. (**decrees, decreeing, decreed**) order something by decree.

dec·re·ment /ˈdekrəmənt/ ▶ n. 1 a reduction or diminution: *a decrement in sympathetic nervous activity.* 2 an amount by which something is reduced or diminished: *10 mg weekly decrements.* ▶ v. chiefly Computing cause a discrete reduction in a numerical quantity: *the instruction decrements the accumulator by one.*

de·crep·it /diˈkrepit/ ▶ adj. 1 worn out or ruined because of age or neglect. 2 elderly and infirm. ▪ **de·crep·i·tude** /-ˌt(y)ōōd/ n.

de·crim·i·nal·ize /dēˈkriminlˌīz/ ▶ v. change the law so that something is no longer illegal or a criminal offense. ▪ **de·crim·i·nal·i·za·tion** /-ˌkriminlˌi·ˈzāsнən/ n.

de·cry /diˈkrī/ ▶ v. (**decries, decrying, decried**) express strong public disapproval of something.

de·crypt /diˈkript/ ▶ v. make a coded or unclear message intelligible. ▪ **de·cryp·tion** n.

ded·i·cate /ˈdediˌkāt/ ▶ v. 1 devote time or effort to a particular task, activity, or purpose: *Joan has dedicated her life to animals.* 2 address a book to a person as a sign of respect or affection. 3 hold an official ceremony to mark the fact that something has been built to honor a particular deity, saint, etc.: *the temple is dedicated to Krishna.* ▪ **ded·i·ca·tee** /ˌdedikāˈtē/ n. **ded·i·ca·tor** n. **ded·i·ca·to·ry** /-kəˌtôrē/ adj.

ded·i·cat·ed /ˈdediˌkātid/ ▶ adj. 1 devoting much time or effort to a particular task, activity, or purpose: *a dedicated musician.* 2 used or designed for one particular purpose only: *a dedicated high-speed rail link.*

ded·i·ca·tion /ˌdediˈkāsнən/ ▶ n. 1 the quality of devoting much time or effort to a particular task, activity, or purpose. 2 the action of dedicating a church or other building to a particular deity or saint. 3 the words with which a book is dedicated to someone.

de·duce /diˈd(y)ōōs/ ▶ v. form an opinion or conclusion on the basis of the information or evidence available. ▪ **de·duc·i·ble** /-səbəl/ adj.

de·duct /diˈdəkt/ ▶ v. subtract an amount from a total: *the tax is deducted from your earnings.*

de·duct·i·ble /diˈdəktəbəl/ ▶ adj. able to be deducted, especially from taxable income. ▪ **de·duct·i·bil·i·ty** /-ˌdəktəˈbilitē/ n.

de·duc·tion /diˈdəksнən/ ▶ n. 1 the action of deducting an amount from a total. 2 an amount that is or may be deducted. 3 a method of reasoning in which a general rule or principle is used to draw a particular conclusion. ▪ **de·duc·tive** /diˈdəktiv/ adj.

deed /dēd/ ▶ n. 1 an action that is performed deliberately. 2 a legal document that is signed and delivered, especially one relating to property ownership or legal rights.

dee·jay /ˈdēˌjā/ ▶ n. informal a DJ.

deem /dēm/ ▶ v. formal regard or consider something in a particular way: *the event was deemed a great success.*

de·em·pha·size /dēˈemfəˌsīz/ ▶ v. reduce the importance or prominence given to something.

deep /dēp/ ▶ adj. 1 extending far down or in from the top or surface. 2 extending a particular distance from the top, surface, or outer edge. 3 (of sound) low in pitch and full in tone. 4 (of color) dark: *a deep blue.* 5 very intense or extreme: *a deep sleep.* 6 difficult to understand. 7 (in ball games) far down or across the field. ▶ n. 1 (**the deep**) literary the sea. 2 (usu. **deeps**) a deep part of the sea. ▶ adv. far down or in; deeply.

■ **deep·ness** n.

– PHRASES **go off the deep end** informal give way suddenly to an outburst of emotion. **in deep water** informal in trouble or difficulty. **jump** (or **be thrown**) **in at the deep end** informal face a difficult situation without much experience.

deep-dyed ▶ adj. informal complete: *a deep-dyed conservative.*

deep·en /'dēpən/ ▶ v. make or become deeper.

deep freeze ▶ n. (also **deep freezer**) a freezer.
▶ v. (**deep-freeze**) freeze or store food in a deep freeze.

deep-fry ▶ v. fry food in enough fat or oil to cover it completely.

deep·ly /'dēplē/ ▶ adv. **1** far down or in. **2** intensely.

deep-root·ed ▶ adj. **1** firmly embedded in thought, behavior, or culture, and so having a persistent influence: *deep-rooted concern about declining values.* **2** (of a plant) having roots that extend well down into the soil.

deep-seat·ed (also **deep-rooted**) ▶ adj. firmly established.

deep space ▶ n. outer space.

deep-vein throm·bo·sis ▶ n. thrombosis in a vein lying deep below the skin, especially in the legs.

deer /di(ə)r/ ▶ n. (pl. same) a hoofed animal, the male of which usually has antlers.

deer·skin /'di(ə)r,skin/ ▶ n. leather made from the skin of a deer.

deer·stalk·er /'di(ə)r,stôkər/ ▶ n. a soft cloth cap, originally worn for hunting, with ear flaps that can be tied together over the top.

de·es·ca·late /dē'eskə,lāt/ ▶ v. reduce the intensity of a conflict or crisis. ■ **de·es·ca·la·tion** n.

de·face /di'fās/ ▶ v. deliberately spoil the appearance of something. ■ **de·face·ment** n.

de fac·to /di 'faktō, dā/ ▶ adv. existing in fact, whether legally recognized or not. Compare with DE JURE. ▶ adj. existing in fact but not necessarily legally recognized: *a de facto one-party system.*

de·fal·ca·tion /,dēfal'kāshən, -fôl-/ ▶ v. formal the stealing or misuse of funds placed in one's trust or under one's control.

de·fame /di'fām/ ▶ v. say or write something that damages the reputation of someone or something. ■ **def·a·ma·tion** /,defə'māshən/ n. **de·fam·a·to·ry** /-'famə,tôrē/ adj.

de·fault /di'fôlt/ ▶ n. **1** failure to fulfill an obligation, especially to repay a loan or appear in a court of law. **2** a previously selected option adopted by a computer program or other mechanism when no alternative is specified.
▶ v. **1** fail to fulfill an obligation, especially to repay a loan or to appear in court. **2** (**default to**) go back automatically to a previously selected option. ■ **de·fault·er** n.
– PHRASES **by default** because of a lack of opposition or positive action. **in default of** in the absence of.

de·feat /di'fēt/ ▶ v. **1** win a victory over a person, team, army, etc. **2** prevent someone from achieving an aim or prevent an aim from being achieved. **3** reject or block a proposal or motion. ▶ n. an instance of defeating someone or something or the state of being defeated.

de·feat·ist /di'fētist/ ▶ n. a person who gives in to failure too readily or who expects to fail. ▶ adj. accepting failure too readily; expecting to fail. ■ **de·feat·ism** /-tizəm/ n.

def·e·cate /'defi,kāt/ ▶ v. expel waste matter from the bowels. ■ **def·e·ca·tion** /,defi'kāshən/ n.

de·fect[1] /'dē,fekt/ ▶ n. a fault or imperfection.

de·fect[2] /di'fekt/ ▶ v. abandon one's country or cause in favor of an opposing one. ■ **de·fec·tion** /di'fekshən/ n. **de·fec·tor** /-tər/ n.

de·fec·tive /di'fektiv/ ▶ adj. imperfect or faulty. ■ **de·fec·tive·ly** adv. **de·fec·tive·ness** n.

de·fend /di'fend/ ▶ v. **1** protect someone or something from harm or danger. **2** act as the lawyer for the party being accused or sued in a lawsuit. **3** attempt to justify: *he defended his decision to fire the strikers.* **4** compete to hold on to a title or seat in a contest or election. **5** (in sports) protect one's goal rather than attempt to score against one's opponents. ■ **de·fend·a·ble** adj. **de·fend·er** n.

de·fend·ant /di'fendənt/ ▶ n. a person sued or accused in a court of law. Compare with PLAINTIFF.

de·fen·es·tra·tion /dē,fenə'strāshən/ ▶ n. formal or humorous the action of throwing someone out of a window. ■ **de·fen·es·trate** /-'fenə,strāt/ v.

de·fense /di'fens, 'dē,fens/ (Brit. **defence**) ▶ n. **1** the action of defending something against attack. **2** military measures or resources for protecting a country. **3** (**defenses**) fortifications against attack. **4** the attempted justification of something: *the government's defense of the police action.* **5** the case presented by or on behalf of the party being accused or sued in a lawsuit. **6** (**the defense**) the counsel for the defendant in a lawsuit. **7** (in sports) the action of defending one's goal, or the players on a team who perform this role.

de·fense·less /di'fenslis/ ▶ adj. without defense or protection; completely vulnerable.

de·fense·man /di'fensmən/ ▶ n. (pl. **defensemen**) (mainly in ice hockey and lacrosse) a player in a defensive position.

de·fense mech·an·ism ▶ n. **1** an automatic reaction of the body against disease-causing organisms. **2** a mental process (e.g., repression or projection) initiated, typically unconsciously, to avoid conscious conflict or anxiety.

de·fen·si·ble /di'fensəbəl/ ▶ adj. **1** able to be justified by reasoning or argument. **2** able to be defended or protected.

de·fen·sive /di'fensiv/ ▶ adj. **1** used or intended to defend or protect: *troops in defensive positions.* **2** very anxious to defend oneself against or avoid criticism. ■ **de·fen·sive·ly** adv. **de·fen·sive·ness** n.
– PHRASES **on the defensive** expecting or resisting criticism or attack.

de·fer[1] /di'fər/ ▶ v. (**defers, deferring, deferred**) put something off until a later time. ■ **de·fer·ment** n. **de·fer·ral** /-'fərəl/ n.

de·fer[2] ▶ v. (**defers, deferring, deferred**) (**defer to**) give in to or agree to accept: *he deferred to Tim's superior knowledge.*

def·er·ence /'defərəns/ ▶ n. polite respect shown toward someone or something.

def·er·en·tial /,defə'renchəl/ ▶ adj. showing polite respect. ■ **def·er·en·tial·ly** adv.

de·fi·ance /di'fīəns/ ▶ n. open refusal to obey someone or something.

de·fi·ant /di'fīənt/ ▶ adj. openly refusing to obey someone or something. ■ **de·fi·ant·ly** adv.

de·fib·ril·la·tion /dē,fibrə'lāshən/ ▶ n. Medicine the administration of a controlled electric shock to the heart to stop fibrillation of the muscles and allow the normal rhythm to be resumed. ■ **de·fib·ril·late** /dē'fibrə,lāt/ v. **de·fib·ril·la·tor** /dē'fibrə,lātər/ n.

de·fi·cien·cy /di'fishənsē/ ▶ n. (pl. **deficiencies**) **1** a lack or shortage of something. **2** a failing or shortcoming.

de·fi·cien·cy dis·ease ▶ n. a disease caused by the lack of some essential element in the diet, usually a particular vitamin or mineral.

de·fi·cient /di'fishənt/ ▶ adj. **1** not having enough of a particular quality or ingredient: *a diet deficient in vitamin A.* **2** inadequate in amount or quality: *the documentary evidence is deficient.*

def·i·cit /'defəsit/ ▶ n. **1** the amount by which something, especially a sum of money, falls short. **2** an excess of money spent over money earned.

de·file¹ /di'fīl/ ▶ v. **1** make something dirty or polluted. **2** treat something holy with a lack of respect. ■ **de·file·ment** n. **de·fil·er** n.

de·file² /di'fīl, 'dē,fīl/ ▶ n. a steep-sided narrow gorge or passage (originally one requiring troops to march in single file).

de·fine /di'fīn/ ▶ v. **1** state or describe the exact nature or scope of: *the contract will seek to define the client's obligations.* **2** give the meaning of a word or phrase. **3** mark out the limits or outline of something. ■ **de·fin·a·ble** adj.

def·i·nite /'defənit/ ▶ adj. **1** clearly stated or decided; not vague or doubtful: *a definite answer.* **2** known to be true or real: *we have no definite proof.* **3** (of a person) certain about something. **4** having exact and measurable physical limits. ■ **def·i·nite·ness** n.

def·i·nite ar·ti·cle ▶ n. Grammar the word *the.*

def·i·nite·ly /'defənitlē/ ▶ adv. without doubt; certainly.

def·i·ni·tion /,defə'nishən/ ▶ n. **1** a statement of the exact meaning of a word or the nature or scope of something. **2** the action of defining something. **3** the degree of sharpness in outline of an object or image. ■ **def·i·ni·tion·al** adj.
– PHRASES **by definition** by its very nature.

de·fin·i·tive /di'finitiv/ ▶ adj. **1** (of a conclusion or agreement) final and not able to be changed. **2** (of a book or other text) the most accurate and trusted of its kind. ■ **de·fin·i·tive·ly** adv.

de·flate /di'flāt/ ▶ v. **1** let air or gas out of a tire, balloon, etc. **2** make someone feel suddenly gloomy or discouraged. **3** reduce price levels in an economy. ■ **de·fla·tor** n.

de·fla·tion /di'flāshən/ ▶ n. **1** the action or process of deflating or being deflated. **2** reduction of the general level of prices in an economy. ■ **de·fla·tion·ar·y** /di'flāshə,nerē/ adj.

de·flect /di'flekt/ ▶ v. **1** turn aside from a straight course. **2** prevent something undesirable from being aimed at one: *the mayor has sought to deflect criticism over the issue.* **3** prevent someone from following an intended course of action. ■ **de·flec·tion** /di'flekshən/ n. **de·flec·tive** adj. **de·flec·tor** n.

de·flow·er /dē'flou(-ə)r/ ▶ v. dated or literary have sex with a woman who is a virgin.

de·fo·li·ant /dē'fōlēənt/ ▶ n. a chemical used to remove the leaves from trees and plants.

de·fo·li·ate /dē'fōlē,āt/ ▶ v. remove leaves from trees or plants. ■ **de·fo·li·a·tion** /dē,fōlē'āshən/ n.

de·for·est /dē'fôrist, -'fär-/ ▶ v. clear an area of forest or trees. ■ **de·for·est·a·tion**
/dē,fôrə'stāshən, -,fär-/ n.

de·form /di'fôrm/ ▶ v. change or spoil the usual shape of someone or something. ■ **de·form·a·ble** adj. **de·for·ma·tion** /,dēfôr'māshən, ,defər-/ n. **de·formed** adj.

de·form·i·ty /di'fôrmitē/ ▶ n. (pl. **deformities**) **1** a deformed part, especially of the body. **2** the state of being deformed.

de·frag·ment /,dēfrag'ment/ ▶ v. Computing reduce the fragmentation of a file or set of files by concatenating parts stored in separate locations on a disk. ■ **de·frag·men·ta·tion** /dē,fragmən'tāshən, -,men-/ n. **de·frag·ment·er** n.

de·fraud /di'frôd/ ▶ v. illegally obtain money from someone by deception.

de·fray /di'frā/ ▶ v. provide money to pay an expense.

de·frock /dē'fräk/ ▶ v. officially remove a member of the Christian clergy from their job because of wrongdoing.

de·frost /di'frôst/ ▶ v. **1** free a freezer or refrigerator of ice. **2** thaw frozen food.

deft /deft/ ▶ adj. **1** quick and neatly skillful: *deft athletic moves.* **2** showing cleverness and skill: *a deft comedy.* ■ **deft·ly** adv. **deft·ness** n.

de·funct /di'fəNGkt/ ▶ adj. no longer existing or functioning.

de·fuse /di'fyōōz/ ▶ v. **1** make a situation less tense or dangerous. **2** remove the fuse from an explosive device so as to prevent it from exploding.

> **USAGE**
> **Defuse** and **diffuse** are often confused. **Defuse** means 'make a situation less tense or dangerous' (*talks were held to defuse the crisis*), while **diffuse** means 'spread over a wide area' (*this early language probably diffused across the world*).

de·fy /di'fī/ ▶ v. (**defies, defying, defied**) **1** openly resist or refuse to obey someone or something. **2** be of such a kind that something is almost impossible: *his actions defy belief.* **3** challenge someone to do or prove something. ■ **de·fi·er** n.

dé·ga·gé /,dāgä'zHā/ ▶ adj. literary not concerned with or involved in something.

de·gen·er·ate ▶ v. /di'jenə,rāt/ become worse; deteriorate: *the meeting threatened to degenerate into a brawl.* ▶ adj. /di'jenərit/ having very low moral standards. ▶ n. /di'jenərit/ a person with very low moral standards. ■ **de·gen·er·a·cy** /-rəsē/ n. **de·gen·er·a·tion** /di,jenə'rāshən/ n.

de·gen·er·a·tive /di'jenərətiv, -ə,rātiv/ ▶ adj. (of a disease) becoming progressively worse, with loss of function in the organs or tissues.

de·glaze /dē'glāz/ ▶ v. add liquid to the cooking juices and meat sediments in a pan to make a gravy or sauce.

deg·ra·da·tion /,degrə'dāshən/ ▶ n. **1** the state of being degraded or humiliated. **2** the process of being broken down or made worse.

de·grade /di'grād/ ▶ v. **1** cause someone to suffer a loss of dignity or self-respect: *viewers want to see reality TV that degrades participants.* **2** lower the quality of something. **3** cause something to break down or deteriorate chemically. ■ **de·grad·a·ble** adj. **deg·ra·da·tive** /'degrə,dātiv/ adj.

de·grad·ing /di'grādiNG/ ▶ adj. causing a loss of self-respect; humiliating.

de·gree /di'grē/ ▶ n. **1** the amount, level, or

extent to which something happens or is present: *a degree of caution is wise.* **2** a unit of measurement of angles, equivalent to one ninetieth of a right angle. **3** a unit in a scale of temperature, intensity, hardness, etc. **4** an academic rank awarded by a college or university after examination or completion of a course. **5** each of a set of grades used to classify burns or criminal offenses: *second-degree murder.* **6** old use social or official rank.
– PHRASES **by degrees** gradually. **to a degree** to some extent.

de·gree day ▶ n. a unit used to determine the heating requirements of buildings, representing a fall of one degree below a specified average outdoor temperature (usually 18°C or 65°F) for one day.

de·hisce /diˈhis/ ▶ v. technical (especially of a seed case) gape or burst open. ■ **de·his·cence** /-ˈhisəns/ n. **de·his·cent** /-ˈhisənt/ adj.

de·hu·man·ize /dēˈ(h)yo͞oməˌnīz/ ▶ v. deprive someone of good human qualities such as compassion or kindness. ■ **de·hu·man·i·za·tion** /dē,(h)yo͞oməniˈzāsʜən/ n.

de·hu·mid·i·fy /ˌdē(h)yo͞oˈmidəˌfī/ ▶ v. (**dehumidifies, dehumidifying, dehumidified**) remove moisture from the air or a gas. ■ **de·hu·mid·i·fi·ca·tion** /-midəfiˈkāsʜən/ n. **de·hu·mid·i·fi·er** n.

de·hy·drate /dēˈhīdrāt/ ▶ v. **1** cause someone to lose a large amount of water from their body. **2** remove water from food in order to preserve it. ■ **de·hy·dra·tion** /ˌdēhīˈdrāsʜən/ n.

de·ice /dēˈīs/ ▶ v. remove ice from something. ■ **de·ic·er** n.

de·i·fy /ˈdēəˌfī/ ▶ v. (**deifies, deifying, deified**) worship or treat someone as a god. ■ **de·i·fi·ca·tion** /ˌdēəfiˈkāsʜən/ n.

deign /dān/ ▶ v. do something that one considers to be beneath one's dignity: *celebrities often don't deign to talk to the masses.*

de·in·dus·tri·al·i·za·tion /dē-inˌdəstrēəliˈzāsʜən/ ▶ n. the reduction of industrial activity in a region or economy.

de·ism /ˈdēizəm/ ▶ n. belief in the existence of an all-powerful creator who does not intervene in the universe. Compare with THEISM. ■ **de·ist** n. **de·is·tic** /dēˈistik/ adj.

de·i·ty /ˈdēitē/ ▶ n. (pl. **deities**) **1** a god or goddess. **2** the state or quality of being a god or goddess.

dé·jà vu /ˌdāzʜä ˈvo͞o/ ▶ n. a feeling of having already experienced the present situation.

de·ject·ed /diˈjektəd/ ▶ adj. sad and dispirited. ■ **de·ject·ed·ly** adv.

de·jec·tion /diˈjeksʜən/ ▶ n. sadness or low spirits.

de ju·re /di ˈjo͝orē, dā ˈjo͝orā/ ▶ adv. according to rightful entitlement; by right. Often contrasted with DE FACTO. ▶ adj. existing by legal right; rightful.

de·lay /diˈlā/ ▶ v. **1** make or be late or slow. **2** put off to a later time; postpone: *ministers agreed to delay their decision.* ▶ n. **1** a period of time by which someone or something is delayed. **2** the action of delaying someone or something.

de·lec·ta·ble /diˈlektəbəl/ ▶ adj. delicious or delightful. ■ **de·lec·ta·bly** /-blē/ adv.

de·lec·ta·tion /ˌdēlekˈtāsʜən/ ▶ n. formal, chiefly humorous pleasure and delight.

del·e·gate ▶ n. /ˈdeligit/ **1** a person sent to represent others, in particular at a conference.

2 a member of a committee. ▶ v. /ˈdeləˌgāt/ **1** give a task or responsibility to a less senior person. **2** authorize someone to act as a representative. ■ **del·e·ga·tor** /-ˌgātər/ n.

del·e·ga·tion /ˌdeliˈgāsʜən/ ▶ n. **1** a group of delegates or representatives. **2** the action of giving one's work or responsibilities to someone else.

de·lete /diˈlēt/ ▶ v. **1** remove or cross out written or printed matter. **2** remove data from a computer's memory. ■ **de·le·tion** /diˈlēsʜən/ n.

del·e·te·ri·ous /ˌdeliˈti(ə)rēəs/ ▶ adj. formal causing harm or damage.

delft /delft/ ▶ n. glazed earthenware, typically with blue decoration on a white background.

del·i /ˈdelē/ ▶ n. (pl. **delis**) informal a delicatessen.

de·lib·er·ate ▶ adj. /diˈlibərit/ **1** done on purpose; intentional. **2** careful and unhurried: *a conscientious and deliberate worker.* ▶ v. /-ˌrāt/ consider carefully and for a long time: *I deliberated over the menu.* ■ **de·lib·er·ate·ly** /-ritlē/ adv. **de·lib·er·ate·ness** /-ritnis/ n.

de·lib·er·a·tion /diˌlibəˈrāsʜən/ ▶ n. **1** long and careful consideration. **2** carefulness and lack of haste.

de·lib·er·a·tive /diˈlibərətiv, -əˌrātiv/ ▶ adj. relating to consideration or discussion.

del·i·ca·cy /ˈdelikəsē/ ▶ n. (pl. **delicacies**) **1** fineness or intricacy: *the delicacy of the palace's architecture.* **2** lack of robustness; fragility. **3** discretion and tact. **4** a delicious or expensive food.

del·i·cate /ˈdelikit/ ▶ adj. **1** very fine or intricate in texture or structure: *a delicate lace shawl.* **2** easily broken or damaged; fragile. **3** tending to become ill easily. **4** requiring or showing tact, sensitivity, or skill: *a delicate issue.* **5** (of a color or flavor) subtle and pleasant. ■ **del·i·cate·ly** adv.

del·i·ca·tes·sen /ˌdelikəˈtesən/ ▶ n. a store selling cooked meats, cheeses, and unusual or foreign prepared foods.

De·li·cious /diˈlisʜəs/ ▶ n. a red or yellow variety of eating apple with a sweet flavor and a slightly elongated shape.

de·li·cious /diˈlisʜəs/ ▶ adj. **1** very pleasant to the taste. **2** giving great pleasure; delightful: *a delicious irony.* ■ **de·li·cious·ly** adv. **de·li·cious·ness** n.

de·light /diˈlīt/ ▶ v. **1** please someone greatly. **2** (**delight in**) take great pleasure in doing something. ▶ n. **1** great pleasure. **2** a cause of great pleasure: *the illustrations are a delight.*

de·light·ed /diˈlītid/ ▶ adj. feeling or showing great pleasure. ■ **de·light·ed·ly** adv.

de·light·ful /diˈlītfəl/ ▶ adj. causing delight; very pleasing. ■ **de·light·ful·ly** adv.

de·lim·it /diˈlimit/ ▶ v. (**delimits, delimiting, delimited**) determine the limits or boundaries of something. ■ **de·lim·i·ta·tion** /-ˌlimiˈtāsʜən/ n. **de·lim·it·er** n.

de·lin·e·ate /diˈlinēˌāt/ ▶ v. describe or indicate something precisely. ■ **de·lin·e·a·tion** /-ˌlinēˈāsʜən/ n.

de·link /dēˈliNGk/ ▶ v. break the connection between two things: *In 1971, the United States government delinked the dollar from gold.*

de·lin·quen·cy /diˈliNGkwənsē/ ▶ n. (pl. **delinquencies**) **1** minor crime, especially that committed by young people. **2** formal neglect of one's duty.

de·lin·quent /diˈliNGkwənt/ ▶ adj. **1** (especially

of young people) tending to commit crime.
2 formal failing in one's duty. ▸ n. a person who tends to commit crime.

del·i·ques·cent /ˌdeliˈkwesənt/ ▸ adj. technical or literary becoming or having a tendency to become liquid. ■ **del·i·ques·cence** n. **del·i·quesce** /ˌdeliˈkwes/ v.

de·lir·i·ous /diˈli(ə)rēəs/ ▸ adj. **1** in a very disturbed mental state; affected by delirium. **2** very excited or happy. ■ **de·lir·i·ous·ly** adv.

de·lir·i·um /diˈli(ə)rēəm/ ▸ n. a highly disturbed state of mind characterized by restlessness, illusions, and incoherent thought and speech.

de·lir·i·um tre·mens /diˈli(ə)rēəm ˈtrēmənz/ ▸ n. a condition in which alcoholics who are trying to give up alcohol experience tremors and hallucinations.

de·liv·er /diˈlivər/ ▸ v. **1** bring and hand over something to the person who is to receive it. **2** provide something promised or expected: *the complex delivers all the usual attractions.* **3** state or present in a formal way: *he delivered a lecture on endangered species.* **4** launch or aim a blow or attack. **5** save or set someone free from something. **6** assist in the birth of a baby. **7** (also **be delivered of**) give birth to a baby. ■ **de·liv·er·a·ble** /diˈlivərəbəl/ adj. **de·liv·er·er** n.
– PHRASES **deliver the goods** informal provide what is promised or expected.

de·liv·er·ance /diˈlivərəns/ ▸ n. **1** the action of being rescued or set free. **2** a formal or authoritative statement.

de·liv·er·y /diˈlivərē/ ▸ n. (pl. **deliveries**) **1** the action of delivering something. **2** the process of giving birth. **3** an act of throwing or bowling a ball, or striking a blow. **4** the way or style of giving a speech: *her delivery was stilted.*

dell /del/ ▸ n. literary a small valley.

Del·phic /ˈdelfik/ ▸ adj. deliberately ambiguous or hard to understand: *Delphic utterances.*

del·phin·i·um /delˈfinēəm/ ▸ n. (pl. **delphiniums**) a garden plant having tall spikes of blue flowers.

del·ta /ˈdeltə/ ▸ n. **1** a triangular area of land at the mouth of a river where it splits into several channels. **2** the fourth letter of the Greek alphabet (Δ, δ), represented as 'd.'

del·ta wing ▸ n. a single triangular swept-back wing on some aircraft.

del·toid /ˈdeltoid/ ▸ n. (also **deltoid muscle**) a thick triangular muscle covering the shoulder joint. ▸ adj. technical triangular.

de·lude /diˈlo͞od/ ▸ v. persuade someone to believe something that is not true. ■ **de·lud·ed** adj.

del·uge /ˈdel(y)o͞oj/ ▸ n. **1** a severe flood or very heavy fall of rain. **2** a great quantity of something arriving at the same time: *a deluge of angry letters.* ▸ v. **1** overwhelm with a great quantity of something: *they've been deluged with unwanted emails.* **2** flood a place.

de·lu·sion /diˈlo͞oZHən/ ▸ n. a false belief or impression about oneself or one's situation: *I must get over this delusion that I know how to type.* ■ **de·lu·sion·al** /-ZHənl/ adj. **de·lu·sive** /diˈlo͞osiv/ adj. **de·lu·so·ry** /diˈlo͞osərē, -zərē/ adj.

de·luxe /diˈləks/ ▸ adj. of a higher quality and more expensive than usual.

delve /delv/ ▸ v. **1** reach inside a receptacle and search for something. **2** investigate something in depth: *any financial company can delve into my private life.* **3** old use dig or excavate.

de·mag·net·ize /dēˈmagniˌtīz/ ▸ v. remove magnetic properties from something. ■ **de·mag·net·i·za·tion** /-ˌmagnitəˈzāSHən/ n.

dem·a·gogue ▸ n. /ˈdeməˌgäg/ a political leader who appeals to the desires and prejudices of the general public. ■ **dem·a·gog·ic** /ˌdeməˈgäjik, -ˈgägik, -ˈgōjik/ adj. **dem·a·gog·uer·y** /ˈdeməˌgägərē/ n. **dem·a·go·gy** /ˈdeməˌgäjē, -ˌgōjē/ n.

de·mand /diˈmand/ ▸ n. **1** a very firm and forceful request. **2** (**demands**) things that are urgent, necessary, or difficult: *the physical and mental demands of climbing.* **3** the desire of consumers for a particular product or service: *a surge in demand for strong ales.* ▸ v. **1** ask or ask for in a firm or forceful way. **2** need a quality, skill, action, etc.: *it was a difficult job that demanded their attention.*
– PHRASES **in demand** sought after. **on demand** as soon as or whenever required.

de·mand·ing /diˈmandiNG/ ▸ adj. requiring much skill or effort.

de·mar·cate /diˈmärˌkāt, ˈdēˌmärˌkāt/ ▸ v. set the boundaries or limits of something.

de·mar·ca·tion /ˌdēmärˈkāSHən/ ▸ n. **1** the action of fixing boundaries. **2** a dividing line.

de·ma·te·ri·al·ize /ˌdēməˈti(ə)rēəˌlīz/ ▸ v. become no longer physically present; disappear. ■ **de·ma·te·ri·al·i·za·tion** /-ˌti(ə)rēələˈzāSHən/ n.

de·mean /diˈmēn/ ▸ v. **1** cause a loss of dignity or respect for: *much reality TV demeans people for the sake of ratings.* **2** (**demean oneself**) do something that is beneath one's dignity. ■ **de·mean·ing** adj.

de·mean·or /diˈmēnər/ (Brit. **demeanour**) ▸ n. a person's outward behavior or bearing.

de·ment·ed /diˈmentid/ ▸ adj. **1** suffering from dementia. **2** informal wild and irrational. ■ **de·ment·ed·ly** adv.

de·men·tia /diˈmenSHə/ ▸ n. a mental disorder marked by memory failures, personality changes, and impaired reasoning.

dem·e·ra·ra su·gar /ˌdeməˈre(ə)rə, -ˈrärə/ ▸ n. Brit. light brown cane sugar.

de·mer·it /diˈmerit/ ▸ n. a mark awarded against someone for a fault or offense.

de·mer·sal /diˈmərsəl/ ▸ adj. living close to the seabed.

de·mesne /diˈmān/ ▸ n. **1** historical land attached to a manor. **2** old use a region or domain.

demi- ▸ prefix **1** half: *demisemiquaver.* **2** partially; lesser: *demigod.*

dem·i·god /ˈdemēˌgäd/ (or **demigoddess**) ▸ n. a partly divine or lesser god (or goddess).

dem·i·john /ˈdemēˌjän/ ▸ n. a bulbous narrow-necked bottle holding from 3 to 10 gallons of liquid.

de·mil·i·ta·rize /dēˈmilitəˌrīz/ ▸ v. remove all military forces from an area. ■ **de·mil·i·ta·ri·za·tion** /-ˌmilitərəˈzāSHən/ n.

dem·i·monde /ˈdemēˌmänd/ ▸ n. a group of people on the fringes of respectable society.

de·mise /diˈmīz/ ▸ n. **1** a person's death. **2** the end or failure of something.

dem·o /ˈdemō/ informal ▸ n. (pl. **demos**) a demonstration recording or piece of software. ▸ v. (**demos, demoing, demoed**) demonstrate software or equipment.

de·mo·bi·lize /dēˈmōbəˌlīz/ ▸ v. take troops out of active service. ■ **de·mo·bi·li·za·tion**

/-ˌmōbəliˈzāsHən/ n.

de·moc·ra·cy /diˈmäkrəsē/ ▶ n. (pl. **democracies**) **1** a form of government in which the people can vote for representatives to govern the country on their behalf. **2** a country governed by elected representatives. **3** control of a group by the majority of its members.

dem·o·crat /ˈdeməˌkrat/ ▶ n. **1** a supporter of democracy. **2** (**Democrat**) a member of the Democratic Party.

dem·o·crat·ic /ˌdeməˈkratik/ ▶ adj. **1** relating to or supporting democracy. **2** based on the principle that all members of society are equal. **3** (**Democratic**) relating to the Democratic Party. ■ **dem·o·crat·i·cal·ly** /-ik(ə)lē/ adv.

Dem·o·crat·ic Par·ty ▶ n. one of the two main US political parties (the other being the Republican Party), which follows a program tending to promote a strong central government and expansive social programs.

de·moc·ra·tize /diˈmäkrəˌtīz/ ▶ v. introduce a democratic system or principles to something. ■ **de·moc·ra·ti·za·tion** /-ˌmäkrətəˈzāsHən/ n.

de·mod·u·late /dēˈmäjəˌlāt/ ▶ v. Electronics extract or separate a modulating signal from its carrier. ■ **de·mod·u·la·tion** /-ˌmäjəˈlāsHən/ n. **de·mod·u·la·tor** n.

dem·o·graph·ic /ˌdeməˈgrafik/ ▶ adj. relating to the structure of populations. ▶ n. a particular sector of a population: *the drink is popular with a young demographic.* ■ **dem·o·graph·i·cal·ly** /-ik(ə)lē/ adv.

de·mog·ra·phy /diˈmägrəfē/ ▶ n. the study of the structure of human populations using statistics of births, deaths, etc. ■ **de·mog·ra·pher** n.

dem·oi·selle /ˌdem(w)əˈzel/ ▶ n. old use a young woman.

de·mol·ish /diˈmälisH/ ▶ v. **1** pull or knock down a building. **2** prove wrong or put an end to: *the authors demolish a number of old myths.* **3** informal overwhelmingly defeat someone. **4** humorous eat up food quickly.

dem·o·li·tion /ˌdeməˈlisHən/ ▶ n. the action of demolishing something.

de·mon /ˈdēmən/ ▶ n. **1** an evil spirit or devil. **2** often humorous an evil or destructive person or thing. ▶ adj. forceful or skillful: *she's a demon cook.*

de·mon·e·tize ▶ v. make a coin or currency no longer valid as money. ■ **de·mon·e·ti·za·tion** /-ˌmänitəˈzāsHən/ n.

de·mo·ni·ac /diˈmōnēˌak/ ▶ adj. relating to or resembling a demon or demons; demonic. ■ **de·mo·ni·a·cal** /ˌdēməˈnīəkəl/ adj.

de·mon·ic /diˈmänik/ ▶ adj. relating to or resembling demons or evil spirits. ■ **de·mon·i·cal·ly** /-ik(ə)lē/ adv.

de·mon·ize /ˈdeməˌnīz/ ▶ v. portray as wicked or threatening: *he aims to demonize smokers and make them social outcasts.* ■ **de·mon·i·za·tion** /ˌdēməniˈzāsHən/ n.

de·mon·ol·o·gy /ˌdēməˈnäləjē/ ▶ n. **1** the study of demons or belief in demons. **2** a set of beliefs about a group regarded as harmful or unwelcome.

de·mon·stra·ble /diˈmänstrəbəl/ ▶ adj. clearly apparent or able to be logically proved. ■ **de·mon·stra·bly** /-blē/ adv.

dem·on·strate /ˈdemənˌstrāt/ ▶ v. **1** clearly show something by giving proof or evidence: *these results demonstrate our continued*

strong performance. **2** show and explain how something works or is done. **3** reveal a feeling or quality by one's actions. **4** take part in a public demonstration.

dem·on·stra·tion /ˌdemənˈstrāsHən/ ▶ n. **1** the action of demonstrating or showing something. **2** a public meeting or march protesting against something or expressing views on an issue.

de·mon·stra·tive /diˈmänstrətiv/ ▶ adj. **1** tending to show one's feelings openly. **2** serving to show or prove something. **3** Grammar (of a determiner or pronoun) indicating the person or thing referred to (e.g., *this, that, those*). ■ **de·mon·stra·tive·ly** adv.

dem·on·stra·tor /ˈdemənˌstrātər/ ▶ n. **1** a person who takes part in a public protest meeting or march. **2** a person who shows how a particular piece of equipment works or how a skill or craft is performed. **3** a piece of merchandise that can be tested by potential buyers.

de·mor·al·ize /diˈmôrəˌlīz/ ▶ v. cause someone to lose confidence or hope. ■ **de·mor·al·i·za·tion** /-ˌmôrələˈzāsHən/ n. **de·mor·al·ized** adj. **de·mor·al·iz·ing** adj.

de·mote /diˈmōt/ ▶ v. move someone to a lower rank or position. ■ **de·mo·tion** /diˈmōsHən/ n.

de·mot·ic /diˈmätik/ ▶ adj. (of language) used by ordinary people; colloquial. ▶ n. ordinary colloquial speech.

de·mo·ti·vate /dēˈmōtəˌvāt/ ▶ v. make someone less eager to work or make an effort. ■ **de·mo·tiv·a·tion** /dēˌmōtəˈvāsHən/ n.

de·mount·a·ble /dēˈmountəbəl/ ▶ adj. able to be dismantled or removed and readily reassembled or repositioned.

de·mur /diˈmər/ ▶ v. (**demurs, demurring, demurred**) raise objections or show reluctance. ■ **de·mur·ral** n.
– PHRASES **without demur** without objecting or hesitating: *they accepted without demur.*

de·mure /diˈmyo͝or/ ▶ adj. (**demurer, demurest**) (of a woman) reserved, modest, and shy. ■ **de·mure·ly** adv. **de·mure·ness** n.

de·mu·tu·al·ize /dēˈmyo͞ocho͞owəˌlīz/ ▶ v. change a mutual organization such as a savings and loan association to one of a different kind.

de·mys·ti·fy /dēˈmistəˌfī/ ▶ v. (**demystifies, demystifying, demystified**) make a subject easier to understand. ■ **de·mys·ti·fi·ca·tion** /-ˌmistəfiˈkāsHən/ n.

de·my·thol·o·gize /ˌdēmiˈTHäləˌjīz/ ▶ v. reinterpret a subject so that it is free of mythical elements.

den /den/ ▶ n. **1** a wild animal's lair or home. **2** informal a small, comfortable room in a house where a person can relax or pursue an activity in private. **3** a place where people meet to do something wrong or forbidden: *a den of vice.*

de·nar·i·us /diˈne(ə)rēəs/ ▶ n. (pl. **denarii** /-ˈne(ə)rēˌī/) an ancient Roman silver coin.

de·na·tion·al·ize /dēˈnasHənlˌīz/ ▶ v. transfer a nationalized industry or organization to private ownership. ■ **de·na·tion·al·i·za·tion** /-ˌnasHənləˈzāsHən/ n.

de·na·ture /dēˈnāCHər/ ▶ v. **1** alter the natural qualities of: *the scrambler denatured her voice.* **2** make alcohol unfit for drinking by adding poisonous or foul-tasting substances. ■ **de·na·tur·a·tion** /dēˌnāCHəˈrāsHən/ n.

den·drite /ˈdendrīt/ ▶ n. a short extension of a nerve cell that conducts impulses to the cell body. ■ **den·drit·ic** /den'dritik/ **adj.**

den·gue /'deɴɢgē, -gā/ (also **dengue fever**) ▶ n. a tropical disease transmitted by mosquitoes, causing sudden fever and acute pains in the joints.

de·ni·a·ble /di'nīəbəl/ ▶ adj. able to be denied. ■ **de·ni·a·bil·i·ty** /-,nīə'bilitē/ n.

de·ni·al /di'nīəl/ ▶ n. 1 a statement that something is not true. 2 the action of denying something. 3 refusal to accept that something unpleasant or distressing is true: *Tim was initially in denial of his illness.*

de·ni·er /'denēər/ ▶ n. a unit by which the fineness of yarn is measured.

den·i·grate /'deni,grāt/ ▶ v. criticize someone or something in an unfair way. ■ **den·i·gra·tion** /,deni'grāsHən/ n. **den·i·gra·tor** n.

den·im /'denəm/ ▶ n. 1 a hard-wearing cotton twill fabric. 2 (**denims**) jeans or other clothes made of denim.

den·i·zen /'denəzən/ ▶ n. formal or humorous an inhabitant or occupant of a particular place.

de·nom·i·nate /di'nämə,nāt/ ▶ v. 1 formal give a name to: *he has denominated her 'Little Mother.'* 2 (**be denominated**) (of sums of money) be expressed in a specified unit of money.

de·nom·i·na·tion /di,nämə'nāsHən/ ▶ n. 1 a recognized branch of a church or religion. 2 the face value of a bill, coin, postage stamp, etc. 3 formal a name.

de·nom·i·na·tion·al /di',nämə'nāsHənl/ ▶ adj. relating to a particular branch of a church or religion. ■ **de·nom·i·na·tion·al·ism** /-,izəm/ n.

de·nom·i·na·tor /di'nämə,nātər/ ▶ n. Mathematics the number below the line in a fraction; a divisor.

de·note /di'nōt/ ▶ v. 1 be a sign of or indicate something. 2 (of a word or phrase) have as a main or literal meaning (e.g., the word *mother* denotes 'a woman who is a parent'). ■ **de·no·ta·tion** /,dēnō'tāsHən/ n.

de·noue·ment /,dānō͞o'mäN/ (also **dénouement**) ▶ n. the final part of a play, movie, or story, in which matters are explained or resolved.

de·nounce /di'nouns/ ▶ v. publicly declare someone or something to be wrong or evil. ■ **de·nounce·ment** n.

de no·vo /dā 'nōvō, di/ ▶ adv. & adj. starting from the beginning; anew.

dense /dens/ ▶ adj. 1 containing many people or things crowded closely together: *dense jungle.* 2 having a thick or closely packed texture: *dense rye bread.* 3 informal stupid. ■ **dense·ly** adv. **dense·ness** n.

den·si·ty /'densitē/ ▶ n. (pl. **densities**) 1 the degree to which a substance is dense; mass per unit volume. 2 the quantity of people or things in a particular area: *areas of low population density.*

dent /dent/ ▶ n. a slight hollow in a surface made by a blow or pressure. ▶ v. 1 mark something with a dent. 2 have an adverse effect on something.

den·tal /'dentl/ ▶ adj. 1 relating to the teeth or to dentistry. 2 Phonetics (of a consonant) pronounced with the tip of the tongue against the upper front teeth (as *th*) or the ridge containing the sockets of the upper teeth (as *n, d, t*). ■ **den·tal·ly** adv.

den·tate /'den,tāt/ ▶ adj. technical having a toothlike or serrated edge.

den·ti·frice /'dentəfris/ ▶ n. a paste or powder for cleaning the teeth.

den·til /'dentl, -til/ ▶ n. Architecture one of a series of small rectangular blocks used as a decoration under the molding of a cornice.

den·tine /'den,tēn/ (also **dentin** /'dentn/) ▶ n. hard dense bony tissue forming the bulk of a tooth.

den·tist /'dentist/ ▶ n. a person who is qualified to treat the diseases and conditions that affect the teeth and gums. ■ **den·tist·ry** n.

den·ti·tion /den'tisHən/ ▶ n. the arrangement or condition of the teeth in a particular species.

den·ture /'dencHər/ ▶ n. a removable plate or frame holding one or more false teeth.

de·nude /di'n(y)o͞od/ ▶ v. strip of covering; make bare: *the land is denuded of trees.* ■ **den·u·da·tion** /,den(y)o͞o'dāsHən/ n.

de·nun·ci·a·tion /di,nənsē'āsHən/ ▶ n. public condemnation of someone or something. ■ **de·nun·ci·a·to·ry** /-'nənsēə,tôrē/ adj.

Den·ver boot ▶ n. a clamp placed by the police on the wheel of an illegally parked vehicle to make it immobile.

de·ny /di'nī/ ▶ v. (**denies, denying, denied**) 1 state that something is not true. 2 refuse to admit or accept: *they denied all knowledge of the ship's sinking.* 3 refuse to give something requested or desired to someone. 4 (**deny oneself**) go without something that one desires.

de·o·dor·ant /dē'ōdərənt/ ▶ n. a substance that removes or conceals bodily smells.

de·o·dor·ize /dē'ōdə,rīz/ ▶ v. remove or conceal an unpleasant smell in a place. ■ **de·o·dor·iz·er** n.

de·ox·y·gen·a·ted /dē'äksijə,nātid/ ▶ adj. having had the oxygen removed. ■ **de·ox·y·gen·a·tion** /-,äksijə'nāsHən/ n.

de·ox·y·ri·bo·nu·cle·ic ac·id /dē,äksē,rībōn(y)o͞o'klēik/ ▶ n. see DNA.

de·part /di'pärt/ ▶ v. 1 leave, especially to start a journey. 2 (**depart from**) do something different from a usual course of action.

de·part·ed /di'pärtid/ ▶ adj. dead; deceased.

de·part·ment /di'pärtmənt/ ▶ n. 1 a division of a business, government, or other large organization, dealing with a specific area of activity. 2 an administrative district, especially in France. 3 (**one's department**) informal an area of special skill or responsibility: *Tiling the floor? That's your department.* ■ **de·part·men·tal** /di,pärt'mentl, ,dēpärt-/ adj. **de·part·men·tal·ly** /di,pärt'mentlē, ,dēpärt-/ adv.

de·part·ment store ▶ n. a large store stocking many types of goods in different departments.

de·par·ture /di'pärCHər/ ▶ n. 1 the action of leaving. 2 a change from a usual course of action.

de·pend /di'pend/ ▶ v. (**depend on**) 1 be controlled or determined by: *differences in earnings depended on a variety of factors.* 2 rely on someone or something.

de·pend·a·ble /di'pendəbəl/ ▶ adj. trustworthy and reliable. ■ **de·pend·a·bil·i·ty** /-,pendə'bilitē/ n. **de·pend·a·bly** /-blē/ adv.

de·pend·en·cy /di'pendənsē/ ▶ n. (pl. **dependencies**) 1 a country or province controlled by another. 2 the state of being dependent on someone or something.

de·pend·ent /di'pendənt/ ▶ adj. 1 (**dependent on**) determined or influenced by: *benefits will be dependent on length of service.* 2 relying

on someone or something for support.
3 (**dependent on**) unable to do without
something. ▶ n. (Brit. **dependant**) a person who
relies on another, especially a family member,
for financial support. ■ **de·pend·ence** n.
de·pend·ent·ly adv.

de·per·son·al·ize /dē'pərsənə,līz/ ▶ v. deprive
someone or something of human characteristics
or individuality. ■ **de·per·son·al·i·za·tion**
/dē,pərsənələ'zāsʜən/ n.

de·pict /di'pikt/ ▶ v. **1** represent someone or
something by a drawing, painting, or other
art form. **2** describe something in words.
■ **de·pic·tion** n.

dep·i·late /'depə,lāt/ ▶ v. remove the hair from
someone. ■ **dep·i·la·tion** /,depə'lāsʜən/ n.
dep·i·la·tor /'depə,lātər/ n.

de·pil·a·to·ry /di'pilə,tôrē/ ▶ adj. used to remove
unwanted hair. ▶ n. (pl. **depilatories**) a cream or
lotion for removing unwanted hair.

de·plane /dē'plān/ ▶ v. disembark from an
aircraft.

de·plete /di'plēt/ ▶ v. reduce the number or
quantity of: *fish stocks are severely depleted.*
■ **de·plet·er** n. **de·ple·tion** /-'plēsʜən/ n.

de·plet·ed u·ra·ni·um ▶ n. uranium from which
most of the fissile isotope uranium-235 has been
removed.

de·plor·a·ble /di'plôrəbəl/ ▶ adj. deserving strong
condemnation; shockingly bad. ■ **de·plor·a·bly**
adv.

de·plore /di'plôr/ ▶ v. feel or express strong
disapproval of something.

de·ploy /di'ploi/ ▶ v. **1** bring or move troops
into position for military action. **2** bring into
effective action: *the FBI began to deploy an
Internet monitoring system.* ■ **de·ploy·a·ble** adj.
de·ploy·ment n.

de·po·lit·i·cize /,dēpə'liti,sīz/ ▶ v. remove
something from political activity or influence.
■ **de·po·lit·i·ci·za·tion** /-,litisə'zāsʜən/ n.

de·po·nent /di'pōnənt/ ▶ n. Law a person who
gives a sworn statement to be used as evidence.

de·pop·u·late /dē'päpyə,lāt/ ▶ v. substantially
reduce the population of an area.
■ **de·pop·u·la·tion** /-,päpyə'lāsʜən/ n.

de·port /di'pôrt/ ▶ v. **1** expel a foreigner or
immigrant from a country. **2** (**deport oneself**)
old use behave in a specified way. ■ **de·por·ta·tion**
/,dēpôr'tāsʜən/ n. **de·por·tee** /,dēpôr'tē/ n.

de·port·ment /di'pôrtmənt/ ▶ n. **1** the way a
person stands and walks. **2** a person's behavior
or manners.

de·pose /di'pōz/ ▶ v. **1** remove someone from
office suddenly and forcefully. **2** Law give
evidence under oath, especially in writing.

de·pos·it /di'päzit/ ▶ n. **1** a sum of money paid
into a bank account. **2** a sum payable as a first
installment of a larger payment. **3** a returnable
sum paid on the rental of something, to cover
possible loss or damage. **4** a layer of a substance
that has accumulated or been laid down: *mineral
deposits.* **5** the action of depositing something.
▶ v. (**deposits, depositing, deposited**) **1** put
down in a specific place: *he deposited her at
the station.* **2** put something in a place for
safekeeping. **3** pay a sum of money as a deposit.
4 (of water or another natural agency) lay down
matter as a layer or covering. ■ **de·pos·i·tor** n.

de·pos·i·tar·y /di'päzi,terē/ (also **depository**)
▶ n. (pl. **depositaries**) a person to whom

something is given for safekeeping.

dep·o·si·tion /,depə'zisʜən/ ▶ n. **1** the action of
removing someone from office. **2** Law a sworn
statement to be used as evidence. **3** the action of
depositing something.

de·pos·i·tor·y /di'päzi,tôrē/ ▶ n. (pl. **depositories**)
1 a place where things are stored. **2** variant
spelling of DEPOSITARY.

de·pot /'dēpō, 'de-/ ▶ n. **1** a place for the storage
of large quantities of goods. **2** a place where
buses, trains, or other vehicles are housed and
maintained. **3** a railroad or bus station.

de·prave /di'prāv/ ▶ v. make someone immoral or
wicked. ■ **de·prav·i·ty** /di'pravitē/ n.

de·praved /di'prāvd/ ▶ adj. morally corrupt.

dep·re·cate /'depri,kāt/ ▶ v. **1** express
disapproval of someone or something. **2** another
term for DEPRECIATE (sense 2). ■ **dep·re·ca·tion**
/,deprə'kāsʜən/ n. **dep·re·ca·to·ry** /'deprikə,tôrē/
adj.

de·pre·ci·ate /di'prēsʜē,āt/ ▶ v. **1** reduce in value
over time: *avoid buying new cars that depreciate
quickly.* **2** criticize or dismiss something as
unimportant. ■ **de·pre·ci·a·ble** /di'prēsʜ(ē)əbəl/
adj. **de·pre·ci·a·tion** /di,prēsʜē'āsʜən/ n.

dep·re·da·tion /,deprə'dāsʜən/ ▶ n. an act that
causes harm or damage: *the protection of crops
from the depredations of birds.*

de·press /di'pres/ ▶ v. **1** make someone feel very
unhappy or dispirited. **2** reduce the level of
activity in a system. **3** push or pull something
down. ■ **de·press·ing** adj. **de·press·ing·ly** adv.

de·pres·sant /di'presənt/ ▶ adj. reducing activity
in bodily processes. ▶ n. a drug or other agent
that reduces activity in bodily processes.

de·pressed /di'prest/ ▶ adj. **1** very unhappy and
dispirited. **2** suffering from clinical depression.
3 suffering from economic recession: *depressed
rural areas.*

de·pres·sion /di'presʜən/ ▶ n. **1** severe
unhappiness and dejection. **2** a medical
condition in which a person experiences severe
feelings of hopelessness and inadequacy. **3** a
long and severe recession in an economy or
market. **4** the action of lowering or depressing
something. **5** a sunken place or hollow. **6** an area
of low atmospheric pressure that may bring rain.

de·pres·sive /di'presiv/ ▶ adj. tending to cause
depression. ▶ n. a person who tends to suffer
from depression.

de·pres·sur·ize /dē'presʜə,rīz/ ▶ v. release the
pressure inside a compartment or container.
■ **de·pres·sur·i·za·tion** /-,presʜərə'zāsʜən/ n.

dep·ri·va·tion /,deprə'vāsʜən/ ▶ n. **1** hardship
resulting from the lack of basic necessities. **2** the
lack or denial of something necessary: *sleep
deprivation.*

de·prive /di'prīv/ ▶ v. prevent from having or
using something: *the city was deprived of its
water supply.*

de·prived /di'prīvd/ ▶ adj. suffering a harmful
lack of basic material and cultural necessities.

Dept ▶ abbr. Department.

depth /depʜ/ ▶ n. **1** the distance from the top
or surface down or from the front to back of
something. **2** the quality of being intense,
extreme, or complex. **3** extensive and detailed
treatment or knowledge: *third-year courses go
into more depth.* **4** (**the depths**) the deepest,
lowest, or inmost part: *the depths to which
morality has sunk.* ■ **depth·less** adj.

– PHRASES **out of one's depth** in a situation beyond one's ability to cope.

depth charge ▶ n. an explosive charge designed to explode under water, used for attacking submarines.

dep·u·ta·tion /ˌdepyəˈtāSHən/ ▶ n. a group of people who are appointed to act on behalf of a larger group.

de·pute ▶ v. /diˈpyo͞ot/ appoint someone to perform a task for which one is responsible.

dep·u·tize /ˈdepyəˌtīz/ ▶ v. **1** make someone a deputy. **2** temporarily act on behalf of someone else: *you will be required to deputize for the manager in her absence.*

dep·u·ty /ˈdepyətē/ ▶ n. (pl. **deputies**) **1** a person appointed to undertake the duties of a more senior person in that person's absence. **2** a parliamentary representative in certain countries.

de·rac·i·nat·ed /diˈrasəˌnātid/ ▶ adj. displaced from one's environment. ■ **de·rac·i·na·tion** /-ˌrasəˈnāSHən/ n.

de·rail /dēˈrāl/ ▶ v. **1** cause a train to leave the tracks. **2** obstruct a process by diverting it from its intended course. ■ **de·rail·ment** n.

de·rail·leur /diˈrālər/ ▶ n. a bicycle gear that works by lifting the chain from one sprocket wheel to another.

de·range /diˈrānj/ ▶ v. **1** (usu as adj. **deranged**) make someone insane. **2** throw something into disorder. ■ **de·range·ment** n.

Der·by /ˈdərbē/ ▶ n. (pl. **Derbies**) **1** an annual race at Epsom Downs in England for three-year-old horses, founded by the 12th Earl of Derby. **2** a similar race elsewhere: *the Kentucky Derby.* **3** (**derby**) a bowler hat.

de·reg·u·late /dēˈregyəˌlāt/ ▶ v. remove regulations from something. ■ **de·reg·u·la·tion** /-ˌregyəˈlāSHən/ n. **de·reg·u·la·to·ry** /-ləˌtôrē/ adj.

der·e·lict /ˈderəˌlikt/ ▶ adj. **1** in a very poor condition as a result of disuse and neglect. **2** shamefully negligent. ▶ n. a person without a home, job, or possessions.

der·e·lic·tion /ˌderəˈlikSHən/ ▶ n. **1** the state of having been abandoned and become dilapidated. **2** (**dereliction of duty**) shameful failure to fulfill one's obligations.

de·ride /diˈrīd/ ▶ v. express contempt for someone or something; ridicule.

de ri·gueur /də riˈgər, rēˈgœr/ ▶ adj. considered necessary for acceptance in fashionable society.

de·ri·sion /diˈrizHən/ ▶ n. contemptuous ridicule or mockery.

de·ri·sive /diˈrīsiv/ ▶ adj. expressing contempt or ridicule. ■ **de·ri·sive·ly** adv.

de·ri·so·ry /diˈrīsərē, -ˈrī-/ ▶ adj. **1** ridiculously small or inadequate: *a derisory pay rise.* **2** expressing derision; derisive.

der·i·va·tion /ˌderəˈvāSHən/ ▶ n. **1** the action of obtaining something from a source or origin. **2** the formation of a word from another word. ■ **der·i·va·tion·al** adj.

de·riv·a·tive /diˈrivətiv/ ▶ adj. imitative of the work of another artist, writer, etc., and regarded as unoriginal. ▶ n. **1** something that is based on or derived from something else: *the new drug is just a derivative of an old antibiotic.* **2** Mathematics an expression representing the rate of change of one quantity in relation to another.

de·rive /diˈrīv/ ▶ v. **1** (**derive something from**) obtain or get something from: *they derived great comfort from this assurance.* **2** (**derive**

something **from**) base something on a modification of something else. **3** (**derive from**) originate or develop from: *the word may derive from Old English.* ■ **de·riv·a·ble** adj.

der·ma·ti·tis /ˌdərməˈtītis/ ▶ n. inflammation of the skin as a result of irritation or an allergic reaction.

der·ma·tol·o·gy /ˌdərməˈtäləjē/ ▶ n. the branch of medicine concerned with skin disorders. ■ **der·ma·to·log·i·cal** /-ˌmətlˈäjikəl/ adj. **der·ma·to·log·i·cal·ly** /-ˌmətlˈäjik(ə)lē/ adv. **der·ma·tol·o·gist** /-jist/ n.

der·mis /ˈdərmis/ ▶ n. the thick layer of the skin below the epidermis, consisting of living tissue. ■ **der·mal** /-məl/ adj.

der·nier cri /ˈdernyā ˈkrē/ ▶ n. the very latest fashion: *she's wearing the dernier cri in bohemian chic.*

der·o·gate /ˈderəˌgāt/ ▶ v. formal **1** (**derogate from**) cause something to seem less valuable or important; detract from. **2** (**derogate from**) deviate from an agreement or rule: *one country derogated from the Rome Convention.* **3** be critical of someone or something. ■ **der·o·ga·tion** /ˌderəˈgāSHən/ n.

de·rog·a·to·ry /diˈrägəˌtôrē/ ▶ adj. showing a critical or disrespectful attitude. ■ **de·rog·a·to·ri·ly** /-ˌtôrəlē/ adv.

der·rick /ˈderik/ ▶ n. **1** a kind of crane with a movable pivoted arm. **2** the framework over an oil well, holding the drilling machinery.

der·ri·ère /ˌderēˈe(ə)r/ ▶ n. euphemistic or humorous a person's buttocks.

der·ring-do /ˌderiNGˈdo͞o/ ▶ n. dated or humorous action displaying heroic courage.

der·ris /ˈderis/ ▶ n. an insecticide made from the powdered roots of a tropical plant.

der·vish /ˈdərviSH/ ▶ n. a member of a Muslim (specifically Sufi) religious group vowed to poverty, some orders of which are known for their wild rituals.

de·sal·i·nate /dēˈsaləˌnāt/ ▶ v. remove salt from seawater. ■ **de·sal·i·na·tion** /-ˌsaləˈnāSHən/ n.

des·cant /ˈdesˌkant/ ▶ n. an independent treble melody sung or played above a basic melody.

des·cant re·cord·er ▶ n. Music the most common size of recorder, with a range of two octaves above the C above middle C.

de·scend /diˈsend/ ▶ v. **1** move down or downward. **2** slope or lead downward. **3** (**descend to**) act in a shameful way that is below one's usual standards: *she began to despise herself for having descended to self-pity.* **4** (**descend on**) make a sudden attack on or unwelcome visit to someone or something. **5** (**be descended from**) have someone as an ancestor. **6** pass by inheritance: *his lands descended to his eldest son.* ■ **de·scend·ent** adj. **de·scend·er** n.

de·scend·ant /diˈsendənt/ ▶ n. **1** a person, animal, or plant that is descended from a particular ancestor. **2** something that has developed from an earlier version of something: *the instrument is a descendant of the lute.*

de·scent /diˈsent/ ▶ n. **1** the action of descending. **2** a downward slope. **3** a person's origin or nationality.

de·scribe /diˈskrīb/ ▶ v. **1** give a detailed account in words of someone or something. **2** mark out or draw a geometrical figure. ■ **de·scrib·a·ble** adj. **de·scrib·er** n.

de·scrip·tion /di'skripsHən/ ▶n. 1 a spoken or written account. 2 the action of describing someone or something. 3 a sort, kind, or class: *people of any description.*

de·scrip·tive /di'skriptiv/ ▶adj. 1 describing someone or something; giving a description. 2 describing something in an objective and nonjudgmental way. ■ **de·scrip·tive·ly** adv.

de·scrip·tor /di'skriptər/ ▶n. 1 a word or expression used to describe or identify something. 2 Computing a piece of stored data that indicates how other data is stored.

de·scry /di'skrī/ ▶v. (**descries, descrying, descried**) literary catch sight of someone or something.

des·e·crate /'desi,krāt/ ▶v. treat something sacred with violent disrespect. ■ **des·e·cra·tion** /,desi'krāsHən/ n. **des·e·cra·tor** /-,krātər/ n.

de·seg·re·gate /dē'segri,gāt/ ▶v. end a policy of racial segregation in a school or similar institution. ■ **de·seg·re·ga·tion** /dē,segri'gāsHən/ n.

de·se·lect /,dēsə'lekt/ ▶v. turn off a selected feature on a list of options on a computer menu. ■ **de·se·lec·tion** /-'leksHən/ n.

de·sen·si·tize /dē'sensi,tīz/ ▶v. 1 make something less sensitive. 2 make someone less likely to be shocked or distressed by cruelty or suffering. ■ **de·sen·si·ti·za·tion** /dē,sensitə'zāsHən/ n.

de·sert¹ /də'zərt/ ▶v. 1 leave in a disloyal or treacherous way; abandon: *her husband deserted her long ago.* 2 (usu. as adj. **deserted**) leave a place, causing it to appear empty. 3 illegally leave the armed forces. ■ **de·ser·tion** /-'zərsHən/ n.

de·sert² /'dezərt/ ▶n. 1 a waterless area of land with little or no water, typically covered with sand. 2 a situation or area considered dull and uninteresting: *a cultural desert.* ▶adj. (of a place) like a desert.

de·sert·er /də'zərtər/ ▶n. a member of the armed forces who deserts.

de·sert·i·fi·ca·tion /di,zərtəfi'kāsHən/ ▶n. the process by which fertile land becomes desert.

des·ert is·land /'dezərt/ ▶n. a remote, uninhabited tropical island.

de·serts /də'zərts/ ▶pl.n. (usu. in phrase **get** or **receive one's just deserts**) the reward or punishment that a person deserves.

de·serve /də'zərv/ ▶v. do something or show qualities worthy of a reward or punishment: *Amanda deserves a lot of credit.* ■ **de·serv·ed·ly** /-vidlē/ adv.

de·serv·ing /də'zərving/ ▶adj. worthy of favorable treatment or assistance.

de·sex /dē'seks/ ▶v. 1 deprive someone of sexual qualities. 2 castrate or spay an animal.

dés·ha·bil·lé /,dezə'bēlā, -'bēä/ (also **dishabille** /,disə'bēl/) ▶n. the state of being only partly clothed.

des·ic·cate /'desi,kāt/ ▶v. (usu. as adj. **desiccated**) remove the moisture from something. ■ **des·ic·ca·tion** /-'kāsHən/ n.

de·sid·er·a·tum /di,sidə'rätəm, -'rātəm, -,zidə-/ ▶n. (pl. **desiderata** /-tə/) something that is needed or wanted.

de·sign /də'zīn/ ▶n. 1 a plan or drawing produced to show the appearance and workings of something before it is made. 2 the art or action of producing a design. 3 a decorative pattern. 4 underlying purpose or planning: *the appearance of design in the universe.*

▶v. 1 produce a design for something. 2 plan or intend for a purpose: *the reforms were designed to stimulate economic growth.*
– PHRASES **by design** on purpose; intentionally. **have designs on** aim to obtain something.

des·ig·nate ▶v. /'dezig,nāt/ 1 officially give a specified status or name to: *most of the waste is designated as hazardous.* 2 appoint someone to a specified position. ▶adj. /-nit, -,nāt/ (after a noun) appointed to a post but not yet having taken it up: *the Director designate.* ■ **des·ig·na·tor** /-,nātər/ n.

des·ig·nat·ed driv·er ▶n. a person who abstains from alcohol in order to drive others home safely.

des·ig·nat·ed hit·ter ▶n. Baseball a nonfielding player named before the start of a game to be in the batting order, typically in place of the pitcher.

des·ig·na·tion /,dezig'nāsHən/ ▶n. 1 the action of designating or choosing someone or something. 2 an official title or description.

de·sign·ed·ly /də'zīnidlē/ ▶adv. on purpose; intentionally.

de·sign·er /də'zīnər/ ▶n. a person who designs things. ▶adj. made by a famous fashion designer: *designer jeans.*

de·sign·er ba·by ▶n. a baby whose genetic makeup has been selected in order to remove a particular defect, or to ensure that a specified gene is present.

de·sign·er drug ▶n. a synthetic analog of an illegal drug, especially one devised to circumvent drug laws.

de·sign·ing /də'zīning/ ▶adj. acting in a calculating, deceitful way.

de·sir·a·ble /də'zī(ə)rəbəl/ ▶adj. 1 wished for being attractive, useful, or necessary: *it is desirable to have a rechargeable battery.* 2 sexually attractive. ■ **de·sir·a·bil·i·ty** /-,zī(ə)rə'bilitē/ n. **de·sir·a·bly** adv.

de·sire /də'zī(ə)r/ ▶n. 1 a strong feeling of wanting to have something or wishing for something to happen: *the desire for fame.* 2 strong sexual feeling or appetite. ▶v. 1 strongly wish for or want something. 2 want someone sexually.

de·sir·ous /di'zīrəs/ ▶adj. strongly wishing to have: *the pope was desirous of peace.*

de·sist /di'sist/ ▶v. stop doing something; cease.

desk /desk/ ▶n. 1 a piece of furniture with a flat or sloping surface, for writing or other work. 2 a counter in a hotel, bank, or airport. 3 a specified section of a news organization: *the sports desk.*

de·skill /dē'skil/ ▶v. reduce the level of skill required to carry out a job.

desk·top /'desk,täp/ ▶n. 1 a microcomputer suitable for use at an ordinary desk. 2 the working area of a computer screen regarded as representing the working surface of a desk.

desk·top pub·lish·ing ▶n. the production of high-quality printed matter by means of a printer linked to a computer, with special software.

des·o·late ▶adj. /'desəlit/ 1 (of a place) empty and bleak. 2 very unhappy or lonely. ▶v. /'desə,lāt/ make someone very unhappy. ■ **des·o·la·tion** /,desə'lāsHən/ n.

de·spair /di'spe(ə)r/ ▶n. the complete loss or absence of hope. ▶v. lose or be without hope: *he despaired of finding a good restaurant.*

– PHRASES **be the despair of** cause someone to lose hope.

des·patch ▶ v. & n. variant spelling of DISPATCH.

des·per·a·do /ˌdespəˈrädō/ ▶ n. (pl. **desperadoes** or **desperados**) a desperate or reckless criminal.

des·per·ate /ˈdespərit/ ▶ adj. **1** full of despair; completely without hope. **2** extremely bad or serious: *a desperate shortage.* **3** having a great need or desire for something: *I'm desperate for a drink.* **4** violent or dangerous. ■ **des·per·ate·ly** adv.

des·per·a·tion /ˌdespəˈrāshən/ ▶ n. a state of despair, especially as resulting in extreme behavior.

des·pi·ca·ble /diˈspikəbəl/ ▶ adj. deserving hatred and contempt. ■ **des·pi·ca·bly** /-blē/ adv.

de·spise /diˈspīz/ ▶ v. feel hatred or disgust for someone or something. ■ **de·spis·er** n.

de·spite /diˈspīt/ ▶ prep. in spite of.

de·spoil /diˈspoil/ ▶ v. literary steal valuable possessions from a place. ■ **de·spoil·er** n.

de·spo·li·a·tion /-ˌspōlēˈāshən/ n.

de·spond·ent /diˈspändənt/ ▶ adj. in low spirits from loss of hope or courage. ■ **de·spond·en·cy** n. **de·spond·ent·ly** adv.

des·pot /ˈdespət/ ▶ n. a ruler with total power, especially one who uses it in a cruel way. ■ **des·pot·ic** /diˈspätik/ adj. **des·pot·ism** /ˈdespəˌtizəm/ n.

des·sert /diˈzərt/ ▶ n. the sweet dish eaten at the end of a meal.

des·sert wine ▶ n. a sweet wine drunk with or following dessert.

de·sta·bi·lize /dēˈstābəˌlīz/ ▶ v. upset the stability of something. ■ **de·sta·bi·li·za·tion** /-ˌstābələˈzāshən/ n.

des·ti·na·tion /ˌdestəˈnāshən/ ▶ n. the place to which someone or something is going or being sent.

des·tine /ˈdestin/ ▶ v. (**be destined**) **1** be intended for or certain to do something: *he was destined to be an engineer.* **2** be bound for a particular destination.

des·ti·ny /ˈdestinē/ ▶ n. (pl. **destinies**) **1** the events that will happen to a person or thing in the future: *we share a common destiny.* **2** the power believed to control the future; fate.

des·ti·tute /ˈdestiˌt(y)o͞ot/ ▶ adj. very poor and lacking the means to provide for oneself. ■ **des·ti·tu·tion** /ˌdestiˈt(y)o͞oshən/ n.

de·stroy /diˈstroi/ ▶ v. **1** end the existence of something by attacking or damaging it. **2** kill an animal in a quick and painless way.

de·stroy·er /diˈstroiər/ ▶ n. **1** a person or thing that destroys something. **2** a small, fast warship.

de·struct·i·ble /diˈstraktəbəl/ ▶ adj. able to be destroyed.

de·struc·tion /diˈstrakshən/ ▶ n. **1** the action of destroying something or the state of being destroyed. **2** a cause of someone's ruin: *gambling was his destruction.*

de·struc·tive /diˈstraktiv/ ▶ adj. **1** causing severe damage or destruction. **2** negative and unhelpful: *destructive criticism.* ■ **de·struc·tive·ly** adv. **de·struc·tive·ness** n.

des·ue·tude /ˈdeswiˌt(y)o͞od/ ▶ n. formal a state of disuse.

des·ul·to·ry /ˈdesəlˌtôrē/ ▶ adj. **1** lacking purpose or enthusiasm. **2** going from one subject to another in a half-hearted way: *a desultory*

conversation. ■ **des·ul·to·ri·ly** /-ˌtôrəlē/ adv.

de·tach /diˈtaCH/ ▶ v. **1** disconnect something and remove it. **2** (**detach oneself from**) leave or distance oneself from a group or situation. **3** (**be detached**) (of a group of soldiers) be sent on a separate mission. ■ **de·tach·a·ble** adj.

de·tached /diˈtaCHt/ ▶ adj. **1** separate or disconnected. **2** (of a house) not joined to another on either side. **3** not involved; objective: *a detached, cynical reporter.*

de·tach·ment /diˈtaCHmənt/ ▶ n. **1** the state of being objective or aloof. **2** a group of troops, ships, etc., sent on a separate mission. **3** the action of detaching something.

de·tail /diˈtāl, ˈdētāl/ ▶ n. **1** a small individual item or fact. **2** small items or facts as a whole: *attention to detail.* **3** a small part of a picture reproduced separately for close study. **4** a small detachment of troops or police officers given a special duty. ▶ v. **1** give full information about something. **2** select someone to undertake a particular task.

– PHRASES **in detail** as regards every aspect; fully.

de·tailed /diˈtāld, ˈdēˌtāld/ ▶ adj. having many details.

de·tail·ing /ˈdētāliNG/ ▶ n. small decorative features on a building, garment, or work of art.

de·tain /diˈtān/ ▶ v. **1** prevent someone from proceeding; delay. **2** keep someone in official custody. ■ **de·tain·er** n. **de·tain·ment** n.

de·tain·ee /diˌtāˈnē, ˌdētāˈnē/ ▶ n. a person held in custody, especially for political reasons.

de·tect /diˈtekt/ ▶ v. **1** discover the presence or existence of something. **2** notice something very slight: *I detected a hint of nervousness in him.* **3** discover or investigate a crime. ■ **de·tect·a·ble** adj. **de·tect·a·bly** /-əblē/ adv. **de·tec·tion** /diˈtekshən/ n.

de·tec·tive /diˈtektiv/ ▶ n. a person, especially a police officer, whose occupation is to investigate crimes.

de·tec·tor /diˈtektər/ ▶ n. a device designed to discover the presence of something and to send out a signal.

dé·tente /dāˈtänt/ ▶ n. the easing of hostility or strained relations between countries.

de·ten·tion /diˈtenshən/ ▶ n. **1** the state of being detained in official custody. **2** the punishment of being kept in school after hours.

de·ten·tion cen·ter ▶ n. an institution where people are held in detention for short periods, in particular illegal immigrants, refugees, people awaiting trial or sentence, or youthful offenders.

de·ter /diˈtər/ ▶ v. (**deters, deterring, deterred**) **1** discourage from doing something, especially by fear of the consequences: *the record heat didn't deter her from her daily run.* **2** prevent something from happening.

de·ter·gent /diˈtərjənt/ ▶ n. a liquid or powder for removing dirt and grease from clothes, dishes, etc.

de·te·ri·o·rate /diˈti(ə)rēəˌrāt/ ▶ v. become gradually worse. ■ **de·te·ri·o·ra·tion** /-ˌti(ə)rēəˈrāshən/ n.

de·ter·mi·nant /diˈtərmənənt/ ▶ n. **1** a factor that decisively affects the nature or outcome of something: *genetics may be the most important determinant of your weight.* **2** Mathematics a quantity obtained by adding products of the elements of a square matrix according to a given rule.

de·ter·mi·nate /də'tərmənit/ ▶ adj. having fixed and definite limits. ■ **de·ter·mi·na·cy** /-minəsē/ n.

de·ter·mi·na·tion /di,tərmə'nāsHən/ ▶ n. 1 the quality of being determined; firmness of purpose. 2 the action of establishing or deciding something.

de·ter·mine /di'tərmin/ ▶ v. 1 cause to happen in a particular way or to have a particular nature: *it is biological age that determines our looks.* 2 firmly decide to do something. 3 establish something by research or calculation. ■ **de·ter·mi·na·ble** /di'tərminəbəl/ adj.

de·ter·mined /di'tərmind/ ▶ adj. having firmness of purpose; resolute. ■ **de·ter·mined·ly** adv.

de·ter·min·er /di'tərminər/ ▶ n. 1 a person or thing that determines or decides something. 2 Grammar a word that comes before a noun to show how the noun is being used, for example *a, the, every.*

de·ter·min·ism /di'tərmə,nizəm/ ▶ n. the belief that people are not free to do as they wish because their lives are determined by factors outside their control. ■ **de·ter·min·ist** n. & adj. **de·ter·min·is·tic** /-,tərmə'nistik/ adj.

de·ter·rent /di'tərənt/ ▶ n. a thing that discourages or is intended to discourage someone from doing something. ▶ adj. able or intended to deter. ■ **de·ter·rence** n.

de·test /di'test/ ▶ v. dislike someone or something intensely.

de·test·a·ble /di'testəbəl/ ▶ adj. deserving intense dislike.

de·tes·ta·tion /,dēte'stāsHən/ ▶ n. intense dislike.

de·throne /dē'THrōn/ ▶ v. 1 remove a monarch from power. 2 remove someone from a position of authority or dominance. ■ **de·throne·ment** n.

det·o·nate /'detn,āt/ ▶ v. explode or cause to explode. ■ **det·o·na·tion** /,detn'āsHən/ n.

det·o·na·tor /'detn,ātər/ ▶ n. a device or charge used to detonate an explosive.

de·tour /'dē,tŏŏr/ ▶ n. a long or roundabout route taken to avoid something or to visit something along the way. ▶ v. take a detour.

de·tox /'dētäks/ informal ▶ n. detoxification. ▶ v. detoxify.

de·tox·i·fy /dē'täksə,fī/ ▶ v. (**detoxifies, detoxifying, detoxified**) 1 remove harmful or toxic substances from something. 2 abstain or help to abstain from alcohol or drugs until the bloodstream is free of toxins. ■ **de·tox·i·fi·ca·tion** /dē,täksəfi'kāsHən/ n. **de·tox·i·fi·er** n.

de·tract /di'trakt/ ▶ v. (**detract from**) cause something to seem less valuable or impressive. ■ **de·trac·tion** /-'traksHən/ n.

de·trac·tor /di'traktər/ ▶ n. a person who is critical of someone or something.

de·train /dē'trān/ ▶ v. leave a train.

det·ri·ment /'detrəmənt/ ▶ n. harm or damage: *she fasted to the detriment of her health.* ■ **det·ri·men·tal** /,detrə'mentl/ adj. **det·ri·men·tal·ly** adv.

de·tri·tus /di'trītəs/ ▶ n. debris or waste material. ■ **de·tri·tal** /-təl/ adj.

de·tu·mes·cence /,dēt(y)ōō'mesəns/ ▶ n. the process of subsiding from a state of swelling or sexual arousal. ■ **de·tu·mes·cent** adj.

de·tune /dē't(y)ōōn/ ▶ v. 1 cause a musical instrument to become out of tune. 2 reduce the performance of a motor vehicle or engine by adjustment.

deuce¹ /d(y)ōōs/ ▶ n. 1 Tennis the score of 40 all in a game, at which two consecutive points are needed to win the game. 2 the number two on dice or playing cards.

deuce² ▶ n. (**the deuce**) informal used as a euphemism for 'devil' in exclamations or for emphasis.

de·us ex ma·chi·na /'dāəs eks 'mäkənə, -'mak-/ ▶ n. an unexpected event that saves a seemingly hopeless situation.

deu·te·ri·um /d(y)ōō'ti(ə)rēəm/ ▶ n. Chemistry a stable isotope of hydrogen with a mass approximately twice that of the usual isotope.

Deutsch·mark /'doich,märk/ ▶ n. (until the introduction of the euro in 2002) the basic unit of money of Germany.

de·val·ue /dē'valyōō/ ▶ v. (**devalues, devaluing, devalued**) 1 reduce the worth of: *people seem to devalue my achievement.* 2 reduce the official value of a currency in relation to other currencies. ■ **de·val·u·a·tion** /,dēvalyōō'āsHən/ n.

dev·as·tate /'devə,stāt/ ▶ v. 1 destroy or ruin something. 2 (**be devastated**) be overwhelmed with shock or grief. ■ **dev·as·ta·tion** /,devə'stāsHən/ n. **dev·as·ta·tor** n.

dev·as·tat·ing /'devə,stātiNG/ ▶ adj. 1 highly destructive. 2 very distressing or shocking. 3 informal very impressive or attractive. ■ **dev·as·tat·ing·ly** adv.

de·vel·op /di'veləp/ ▶ v. (**develops, developing, developed**) 1 become or make larger or more advanced. 2 start to exist, experience, or possess: *he developed a passionate interest in fitness.* 3 convert land to a new purpose, especially by constructing buildings. 4 treat a photographic film with chemicals to make a visible image. ■ **de·vel·op·a·ble** /di'veləpəbəl/ adj. **de·vel·op·er** n.

de·vel·op·ing coun·try ▶ n. a poor agricultural country that is seeking to become more advanced economically and socially.

de·vel·op·ment /di'veləpmənt/ ▶ n. 1 the action of developing or the state of being developed: *she traces the development of the novel.* 2 a new product or idea. 3 a new stage in a changing situation. 4 an area with new buildings on it. ■ **de·vel·op·men·tal** /di,veləp'mentl/ adj. **de·vel·op·men·tal·ly** adv.

de·vi·ant /'dēvēənt/ ▶ adj. departing from normal standards, especially in social or sexual behavior. ▶ n. a person who departs from normal standards. ■ **de·vi·ance** /'dēvēəns/ n. **de·vi·an·cy** /-ənsē/ n.

de·vi·ate /'dēvē,āt/ ▶ v. depart from an established course or from normal standards: *the vet deviated from an accepted standard of care.* ■ **de·vi·a·tion** /,dēvē'āsHən/ n.

de·vice /di'vīs/ ▶ n. 1 a piece of mechanical or electronic equipment made for a particular purpose. 2 a plan or method with a particular aim: *a clever marketing device.* 3 a drawing or design. – PHRASES **leave someone to their own devices** leave someone to do as they wish.

dev·il /'devəl/ ▶ n. 1 (**the Devil**) (in Christian and Jewish belief) the most powerful evil spirit. 2 an evil spirit. 3 a very wicked or cruel person. 4 a mischievous person. 5 informal a person with specified characteristics: *the poor devil.* 6 (**the devil**) expressing surprise or annoyance. – PHRASES **between the devil and the deep blue sea** caught in a dilemma. **devil-may-care**

cheerful and reckless. **the devil to pay** serious trouble to be dealt with. **like the devil** with great speed or energy. **speak** (or **talk**) **of the devil** said when a person appears just after being mentioned.

dev·iled /'devəld/ ▶ adj. cooked with hot seasoning.

dev·il·ish /'devəlisн/ ▶ adj. **1** evil and cruel. **2** mischievous: *a devilish grin.* **3** very difficult to deal with. ▶ adv. informal, dated very: *a devilish clever guy.* ■ **dev·il·ish·ly** adv. **dev·il·ish·ness** n.

dev·il·ment /'devəlmənt/ ▶ n. reckless mischief.

dev·il·ry /'devəlrē/ ▶ n. **1** wicked activity. **2** reckless mischief.

dev·il's ad·vo·cate ▶ n. a person who expresses an unpopular opinion in order to provoke debate.

de·vi·ous /'dēvēəs/ ▶ adj. **1** skillful in using underhanded tactics. **2** (of a route or journey) indirect. ■ **de·vi·ous·ly** adv. **de·vi·ous·ness** n.

de·vise /di'vīz/ ▶ v. plan or invent a complex procedure or device. ■ **de·vis·er** n.

de·vi·tal·ize /dē'vītl‚īz/ ▶ v. deprive someone or something of strength and energy. ■ **de·vi·tal·i·za·tion** /dē‚vītlə'zāsнən/ n.

de·void /di'void/ ▶ adj. (**devoid of**) completely lacking in: *the dancers were devoid of glamour.*

dev·o·lu·tion /‚devə'loosнən/ ▶ n. the transfer of power by central government to local or regional governments. ■ **dev·o·lu·tion·ar·y** /-‚nerē/ adj. **dev·o·lu·tion·ist** /-ist/ n.

de·volve /di'välv/ ▶ v. **1** transfer power to a lower level, especially from central to regional government. **2** (**devolve on/upon/to**) (of duties or responsibility) pass to a deputy or successor.

De·vo·ni·an /di'vōnēən/ ▶ adj. Geology relating to the fourth period of the Paleozoic era (about 409 to 363 million years ago), when the first amphibians appeared.

de·vo·ré /də'vôrā/ ▶ n. a velvet fabric with a pattern formed by burning the pile away with acid.

de·vote /di'vōt/ ▶ v. (**devote something to**) give time or resources to a person or activity.

de·vot·ed /di'vōtid/ ▶ adj. very loving or loyal. ■ **de·vot·ed·ly** adv.

dev·o·tee /‚devə'tē, -'tā/ ▶ n. **1** a person who is very enthusiastic about someone or something. **2** a person with a strong belief in a particular religion or god.

de·vo·tion /di'vōsнən/ ▶ n. **1** great love or loyalty. **2** religious worship. **3** (**devotions**) prayers or religious observances. ■ **de·vo·tion·al** adj.

de·vour /di'vou(ə)r/ ▶ v. **1** eat food greedily. **2** (of fire or a similar force) destroy something completely. **3** read something quickly and eagerly. ■ **de·vour·er** n.

de·vout /di'vout/ ▶ adj. **1** deeply religious. **2** earnestly sincere: *my devout hope.* ■ **de·vout·ly** adv.

dew /d(y)oo/ ▶ n. tiny drops of moisture that form on cool surfaces at night when water vapor in the air condenses.

dew·ber·ry /'d(y)oo‚berē/ ▶ n. (pl. **dewberries**) the edible blue-black fruit of a trailing bramble.

dew·drop /'d(y)oo‚dräp/ ▶ n. a drop of dew.

Dew·ey dec·i·mal clas·si·fi·ca·tion /'d(y)oo-ē/ ▶ n. a decimal system of library classification that uses a three-figure code from 000 to 999 to represent the major branches of knowledge.

dew·lap /'d(y)oo‚lap/ ▶ n. a fold of loose skin hanging from the neck or throat of an animal such as a cow.

dew point ▶ n. the atmospheric temperature (varying according to pressure and humidity) below which water droplets begin to condense and dew can form.

dew·y /'d(y)ooē/ ▶ adj. wet with dew.

dew·y-eyed ▶ adj. naive or sentimental: *dewy-eyed liberals.*

dex·ter /'dekstər/ ▶ adj. Heraldry on or toward the bearer's right-hand side of a coat of arms. The opposite of SINISTER.

dex·ter·i·ty /dek'steritē/ ▶ n. **1** skill in performing tasks with the hands. **2** the ability to do something skillfully: *mental dexterity.*

dex·ter·ous /'dekst(ə)rəs/ (also **dextrous** /'dekstrəs/) ▶ adj. showing skill; adroit. ■ **dex·ter·ous·ly** adv.

dex·trose /'dekstrōs/ ▶ n. a naturally occurring form of glucose.

DH ▶ abbr. **1** Doctor of Humanities. **2** Baseball designated hitter.

dhar·ma /'därmə/ ▶ n. (in Indian religion) the eternal law of the universe.

dho·bi /'dōbē/ ▶ n. (pl. **dhobis**) (in the Indian subcontinent) a person whose occupation is washing clothes.

dho·ti /'dōtē/ ▶ n. (pl. **dhotis**) a piece of cloth tied around the waist and covering most of the legs, worn by some Indian men.

dhow /dou/ ▶ n. a ship with a lateen sail or sails, used in the Arabian region.

di- ▶ comb.form twice; two-; double: *dioxide.*

dia. ▶ abbr. diameter.

di·a·be·tes /‚dīə'bētēz, -tis/ ▶ n. a disorder of the metabolism in which a lack of the hormone insulin results in a failure to absorb sugar and starch properly.

di·a·bet·ic /‚dīə'betik/ ▶ adj. having or relating to diabetes. ▶ n. a person with diabetes.

di·a·bol·i·cal /‚dīə'bälikəl/ ▶ adj. (also **diabolic**) relating to or like the Devil, especially in being evil. ■ **di·a·bol·i·cal·ly** /-ik(ə)lē/ adv.

di·ab·o·lism /dī'abə‚lizəm/ ▶ n. worship of the Devil. ■ **di·ab·o·list** n.

di·ac·o·nal /dī'akənl/ ▶ adj. (in the Christian Church) relating to a deacon or deacons.

di·ac·o·nate /dī'akənit, -‚nāt/ ▶ n. **1** (in the Christian Church) the position of deacon. **2** a group of deacons.

di·a·crit·ic /‚dīə'kritik/ ▶ n. a sign, such as an accent, written above or below a letter to indicate a difference in pronunciation from the same letter when unmarked. ■ **di·a·crit·i·cal** adj.

di·a·dem /'dīə‚dem/ ▶ n. a jeweled crown or headband worn as a symbol of royalty.

di·ag·nose /‚dīəg'nōs/ ▶ v. **1** identify the nature of an illness or problem by examining the symptoms. **2** identify the medical condition of someone. ■ **di·ag·nos·a·ble** adj.

di·ag·no·sis /‚dīəg'nōsis/ ▶ n. (pl. **diagnoses**) the identification of the nature of an illness or other problem by examination of the symptoms.

di·ag·nos·tic /‚dīəg'nästik/ ▶ adj. relating to the diagnosis of illness or other problems. ▶ n. **1** a distinctive symptom or characteristic. **2** (**diagnostics**) (treated as sing. or pl.) the practice or techniques of diagnosis. ■ **di·ag·nos·ti·cal·ly**

/-ik(ə)lē/ adv. **di·ag·nos·ti·cian** /-,näs'tisHən/ n.

di·ag·o·nal /dī'agənl/ ▸ adj. 1 (of a straight line) joining two opposite corners of a rectangle, square, or other shape. 2 (of a line) straight and at an angle; slanting. ▸ n. a diagonal line. ■ **di·ag·o·nal·ly** adv.

di·a·gram /'dīə,gram/ ▸ n. a simplified drawing showing the appearance or structure of something. ■ **di·a·gram·mat·ic** /,dīəgrə'matik/ adj. **di·a·gram·mat·i·cal·ly** /,dīəgrə'matik(ə)lē/ adv.

di·al /'dī(ə)l/ ▸ n. 1 a disk marked to show the time on a clock or to indicate a measurement by means of a pointer. 2 a disc with numbered holes on a telephone, turned to make a call. 3 a disc turned to select a setting on a radio, washing machine, etc. ▸ v. (**dials, dialing, dialed**) call a telephone number by turning a dial or using a keypad. ■ **di·al·er** n.

di·a·lect /'dīə,lekt/ ▸ n. a form of a language that is used in a specific region or by a specific social group: *Yorkshire dialect.* ■ **di·a·lec·tal** /,dīə'lektəl/ adj.

di·a·lec·tic /,dīə'lektik/ (also **dialectics**) ▸ n. (usu. treated as sing.) Philosophy 1 the investigation of the truth of opposing opinions by logical discussion. 2 the existence of opposing social forces, concepts, etc.: *union leaders have been hidebound by the dialectic of class war.* ■ **di·a·lec·ti·cal** /,dīə'lektikəl/ adj. **di·a·lec·ti·cal·ly** /-ik(ə)lē/ adv.

di·a·log box /'dīə,läg, -,lôg/ ▸ n. a small area on a computer screen in which the user is prompted to provide information or select commands.

di·a·log·ic /,dīə'läjik/ ▸ adj. relating to or in the form of dialogue. ■ **di·a·log·i·cal** adj.

di·a·logue /'dīə,läg, -,lôg/ (also **dialog**) ▸ n. 1 conversation between two or more people as a feature of a book, play, movie, etc. 2 a discussion intended to explore a subject or resolve a problem.

di·al tone ▸ n. a sound produced by a telephone that indicates that a caller may start to dial.

di·al-up ▸ adj. (of a computer system or service) used remotely via a telephone line.

di·al·y·sis /dī'aləsis/ ▸ n. (pl. **dialyses** /-sēz/) 1 Chemistry the separation of particles in a liquid on the basis of differences in their ability to pass through a membrane. 2 the purification of blood by dialysis, as a substitute for the normal function of the kidney.

di·a·man·té /,dēəmän'tā/ ▸ adj. decorated with glass cut to resemble diamonds.

di·am·e·ter /dī'amitər/ ▸ n. a straight line passing from side to side through the center of a circle or sphere.

di·a·met·ri·cal /,dīə'metrikəl/ (also **diametric**) ▸ adj. 1 (of opposites) completely different: *he's the diametrical opposite of Gabriel.* 2 relating to a diameter. ■ **di·a·met·ri·cal·ly** adv.

dia·mond /'dī(ə)mənd/ ▸ n. 1 a precious stone consisting of a clear and colorless crystalline form of pure carbon, the hardest naturally occurring substance. 2 a figure with four straight sides of equal length forming two opposite acute angles and two opposite obtuse angles; a rhombus. 3 a baseball field. 4 (**diamonds**) one of the four suits in a deck of playing cards.
– PHRASES **diamond in the rough 1** an uncut diamond. **2** a good or kind person who is not very polite, stylish, or well educated.

dia·mond·back /'dī(ə)mənd,bak/ ▸ n. 1 (also

diamondback rattlesnake) a large, common North American rattlesnake with diamond-shaped markings. 2 (also **diamondback terrapin**) another term for TERRAPIN (sense 1).

dia·mond ju·bi·lee ▸ n. the sixtieth anniversary of a notable event.

di·a·mor·phine /,dīə'môrfēn/ ▸ n. technical heroin.

di·an·thus /dī'anTHəs/ ▸ n. (pl. **dianthuses**) a flowering plant of a group that includes the pinks and carnations.

di·a·pa·son /,dīə'pāzən, -sən/ ▸ n. an organ stop sounding a main set of pipes.

dia·per /'dī(ə)pər/ ▸ n. a piece of material wrapped around a baby's bottom and between its legs to absorb and retain urine and feces.

di·aph·a·nous /dī'afənəs/ ▸ adj. light, delicate, and translucent.

di·a·phragm /'dīə,fram/ ▸ n. 1 a muscular partition separating the thorax from the abdomen in mammals. 2 a taut flexible membrane in mechanical or acoustic systems. 3 a thin contraceptive cap fitting over the neck of the uterus. 4 a device for varying the effective aperture of the lens in a camera or other optical system. ■ **di·a·phrag·mat·ic** /,dīəfrag'matik/ adj.

di·a·rist /'dīərist/ ▸ n. a person who writes a diary.

di·ar·rhe·a /,dīə'rēə/ (Brit. **diarrhoea**) ▸ n. an illness in which there are frequent discharges of liquid feces from the bowels. ■ **di·ar·rhe·al** adj.

di·a·ry /'dīərē/ ▸ n. (pl. **diaries**) 1 a book in which one keeps a daily record of events and experiences. 2 a book marked with each day's date, in which to note appointments.

di·as·po·ra /dī'aspərə/ ▸ n. 1 (**the diaspora**) the dispersion of the Jews beyond Israel, chiefly in the 8th to 6th centuries BC. 2 the dispersion of any people from their original homeland.

di·as·to·le /dī'astl-ē/ ▸ n. the phase of the heartbeat when the heart muscle relaxes and the chambers fill with blood. Often contrasted with SYSTOLE. ■ **di·as·tol·ic** /,dīə'stälik/ adj.

di·a·tom /'dīə,täm/ ▸ n. a single-celled alga that has a cell wall of silica. ■ **di·a·to·ma·ceous** /,dīətə'māsHəs/ adj.

di·a·tom·ic /,dīə'tämik/ ▸ adj. Chemistry consisting of two atoms.

di·a·ton·ic /,dīə'tänik/ ▸ adj. Music involving only the notes of the major or minor scale, without additional sharps, flats, etc.

di·a·tribe /'dīə,trīb/ ▸ n. a harsh and forceful verbal attack.

di·az·e·pam /dī'azə,pam/ ▸ n. a tranquilizing drug used to relieve anxiety. Also called VALIUM(trademark).

dib·ble /'dibəl/ ▸ n. a pointed hand tool for making holes in the ground for seeds or young plants.

dibs /dibz/ (also **first dibs**) ▸ pl.n. informal a pre-emptive claim or right: *strategists will get first dibs on plumbing the data.*

dice /dīs/ ▸ n. (pl. same; sing. also **die** /dī/) a small cube with faces bearing from one to six spots, used in games of chance. See also DIE². ▸ v. 1 cut food into small cubes. 2 (**dice with**) take great risks with: *he enjoyed dicing with death.*

dic·ey /'dīsē/ ▸ adj. (**dicier, diciest**) informal unpredictable and potentially dangerous.

di·chot·o·my /dī'kätəmē/ ▸ n. (pl. **dichotomies**) a separation between two things that are opposed or different: *the dichotomy between good and evil.*

■ **di·chot·o·mous** adj.

dick[1] /dik/ ▶ n. vulgar slang a penis.

dick[2] ▶ n. informal, dated a detective.

dick·ens /'dikənz/ ▶ n. informal used to express annoyance or surprise: *what the dickens is going on?*

Dick·en·si·an /di'kenzēən/ ▶ adj. like the novels of Charles Dickens, especially in terms of the poverty that they portray.

dick·er /'dikər/ ▶ v. 1 engage in petty argument or bargaining: *she advised him not to dicker over the extra fee.* 2 treat something casually or irresponsibly; toy with something.

dick·ey /'dikē/ (also **dicky**) ▶ n. (pl. **dickies** or **dickeys**) informal a false shirt front.

dick·head /'dik‚hed/ ▶ n. vulgar slang a stupid or ridiculous man.

di·cot·y·le·don /dī‚kätl'ēdn/ ▶ n. a plant with an embryo bearing two cotyledons (leaves growing from a germinating seed).

dic·ta /'diktə/ ▶ plural of DICTUM.

dic·tate ▶ v. /'dik‚tāt/ 1 state or order something authoritatively. 2 control or influence: *choice is often dictated by availability.* 3 say or read aloud words to be typed or written down. ▶ n. /‚dik'tāt/ an order or principle that must be obeyed: *those who follow the dictates of fashion.* ■ **dic·ta·tion** /dik'tāsʜən/ n.

dic·ta·tor /'dik‚tātər/ ▶ n. a ruler with total power over a country.

dic·ta·to·ri·al /‚diktə'tôrēəl/ ▶ adj. 1 relating to or controlled by a dictator. 2 insisting on total obedience; domineering. ■ **dic·ta·to·ri·al·ly** adv.

dic·ta·tor·ship /'dik‚tātər‚sʜip, ‚diktātər-/ ▶ n. 1 government by a dictator. 2 a country governed by a dictator.

dic·tion /'diksʜən/ ▶ n. 1 the choice and use of words in speech or writing. 2 a person's way of pronouncing words.

dic·tion·ar·y /'diksʜə‚nerē/ ▶ n. (pl. **dictionaries**) a book that lists the words of a language and gives their meaning, or their equivalent in a different language.

dic·tum /'diktəm/ ▶ n. (pl. **dicta** /-tə/ or **dictums**) 1 a formal or authoritative statement. 2 a short statement that expresses a general truth.

did /did/ ▶ past of DO[1].

di·dac·tic /dī'daktik/ ▶ adj. intended to teach or give moral guidance: *a didactic religious novel.* ■ **di·dac·ti·cal·ly** /-ik(ə)lē/ adv. **di·dac·ti·cism** /-tə‚sizəm/ n.

did·dle /'didl/ ▶ v. 1 informal cheat or swindle someone. 2 informal pass time aimlessly or unproductively. 3 vulgar slang have sexual intercourse with (someone).

didg·er·i·doo /‚dijərē'doo/ ▶ n. an Australian Aboriginal wind instrument in the form of a long wooden tube, blown to produce a deep resonant sound.

did·n't /'didnt/ ▶ contr. did not.

didst /didst/ ▶ old-fashioned second person singular past of DO[1].

die[1] /dī/ ▶ v. (**dies, dying, died**) 1 stop living. 2 (**die out**) become extinct. 3 become less loud or strong: *the storm had died down by now.* 4 (**be dying for/to do**) informal be very eager to have or to do something.

– PHRASES **die hard** change very slowly: *old habits die hard.* **never say die** do not give up hope. **to die for** informal extremely good or desirable.

die[2] ▶ n. 1 singular form of DICE. 2 (pl. **dies**) a device for cutting or molding metal or for stamping a design onto coins or medals.

– PHRASES **the die is cast** an event has happened that cannot be changed.

die·back /'dī‚bak/ ▶ n. a condition in which a tree or shrub begins to die from the tip of its leaves or roots backward.

die-cast ▶ adj. (of a metal object) formed by pouring molten metal into a mold.

die·hard /'dī‚härd/ ▶ n. a person who strongly supports something in spite of opposition or changing circumstances.

di·e·lec·tric /‚dīə'lektrik/ Physics ▶ adj. that does not conduct electricity; insulating. ▶ n. an insulator.

die-off ▶ n. the death of a significant proportion of a population: *mass die-offs of staghorn and elkhorn corals.*

di·er·e·sis /dī'erəsis/ ▶ n. (pl. **diereses** /-sēz/) a mark (¨) placed over a vowel to indicate that it is sounded separately, as in *naïve.*

die·sel /'dēzəl/ ▶ n. 1 an internal combustion engine in which the heat of compressed air is used to ignite the fuel. 2 (also **diesel oil**) a form of petroleum used to fuel diesel engines.

di·et[1] /'dī-it/ ▶ n. 1 the kinds of food that a person or animal usually eats. 2 a limited range or amount of food, eaten in order to lose weight or for medical reasons. ▶ v. (**diets, dieting, dieted**) eat a limited range or amount of food to lose weight. ▶ adj. (of food or drink) having a reduced fat or sugar content. ■ **die·tar·y** /'dī-i‚terē/ adj. **di·et·er** n.

di·et[2] ▶ n. 1 a lawmaking assembly in certain countries. 2 historical a regular meeting of the states of a confederation.

di·e·tet·ics /‚dī-i'tetiks/ ▶ pl.n. (treated as sing.) the branch of knowledge concerned with the diet and its effects on health. ■ **di·e·tet·ic** adj.

di·e·ti·tian /‚dī-i'tishən/ (also **dietician**) ▶ n. an expert on diet and nutrition.

diff /dif/ ▶ n. informal 1 difference. 2 different.

dif·fer /'difər/ ▶ v. 1 be unlike or dissimilar. 2 disagree with someone.

– PHRASES **beg to differ** politely disagree.

dif·fer·ence /'dif(ə)rəns/ ▶ n. 1 a way in which people or things are not the same. 2 the state of being unlike: *there's little difference between the two main parties.* 3 a disagreement or quarrel. 4 the remainder left after one value is subtracted from another.

dif·fer·ent /'dif(ə)rənt/ ▶ adj. 1 not the same as another or each other. 2 separate: *he was arrested on two different occasions.* 3 informal new and unusual. ■ **dif·fer·ent·ly** adv. **dif·fer·ent·ness** n.

USAGE

In general, **different from** is the construction most often used in the US and Britain, although **different than** (used almost exclusively in North America) is also used, especially in speech. **Different to** is common in Britain, but sounds strange to American ears.

dif·fer·en·ti·a·ble /‚difə'rensʜəbəl/ ▶ adj. able to be distinguished or differentiated. ■ **dif·fer·en·ti·a·bil·i·ty** /-‚rensʜə'bilitē/ n.

dif·fer·en·tial /‚difə'rencʜəl/ ▶ adj. relating to or depending on a difference; varying according to circumstances: *intense competition has not eliminated differential pricing.*

▶ **n. 1** a difference in amount. **2** Mathematics an infinitesimal difference between successive values of a variable. **3** a gear allowing a vehicle's driven wheels to revolve at different speeds in cornering. ■ **dif·fer·en·tial·ly** adv.

dif·fer·en·tial cal·cu·lus ▶ n. Mathematics the part of calculus concerned with the derivatives of functions.

dif·fer·en·tial e·qua·tion ▶ n. an equation involving derivatives of a function or functions.

dif·fer·en·ti·ate /ˌdifəˈrenSHēˌāt/ ▶ v. **1** recognize or identify as different; distinguish: *children can differentiate the past from the present.* **2** cause something to appear different or distinct. **3** Mathematics transform a function into its derivative. ■ **dif·fer·en·ti·a·tion** /-ˌrenSHēˈāSHən/ n. **dif·fer·en·ti·a·tor** /-ˌātər/ n.

dif·fi·cult /ˈdifikəlt/ ▶ adj. **1** needing much effort or skill to do or understand: *I had a difficult decision to make.* **2** causing or full of problems: *a difficult economic climate.* **3** not easy to please or satisfy; awkward.

dif·fi·cul·ty /ˈdifikəltē/ ▶ n. (pl. **difficulties**) **1** the state of being difficult. **2** a problem. **3** a difficult or dangerous situation: *he went for a swim but got into difficulties.*

dif·fi·dent /ˈdifidənt/ ▶ adj. modest or shy because of a lack of self-confidence. ■ **dif·fi·dence** n. **dif·fi·dent·ly** adv.

dif·frac·tion /diˈfrakSHən/ ▶ n. Physics the process by which a beam of light or other system of waves is spread out as a result of passing through a narrow opening or across an edge. ■ **dif·fract** /diˈfrakt/ v. **dif·frac·tive** /-tiv/ adj.

dif·fuse ▶ v. /diˈfyo͞oz/ **1** spread over a wide area: *this early language probably diffused across the world.* **2** Physics (of a gas or liquid) intermingle with another substance by movement.
▶ adj. /diˈfyo͞os/ **1** spread out over a large area; not concentrated. **2** not clear or concise. ■ **dif·fuse·ly** /-ˈfyo͞oslē/ adv. **dif·fus·er** /diˈfyo͞ozər/ (also **diffusor**) n.

USAGE
On the difference between **diffuse** and **defuse**, see the note at **DEFUSE**.

dif·fu·sion /diˈfyo͞oZHən/ ▶ n. **1** the action of spreading over a wide area. **2** Physics the intermingling of substances by the natural movement of their particles. ▶ adj. (of a range of garments) produced for the mass market by a fashion designer: *a revamped diffusion line.* ■ **dif·fu·sive** /-siv/ adj.

dig /dig/ ▶ v. (**digs**, **digging**; past and past part. **dug**) **1** break up and turn over or move earth. **2** make a hole by digging. **3** remove from the ground by digging: *workmen dug the cable up.* **4** push or poke sharply: *he dug his hands in his pockets.* **5** (**dig into/through**) search or rummage in something. **6** (**dig something out/up**) discover facts. **7** (**dig in**) begin eating heartily. **8** informal, dated like or appreciate. ▶ n. **1** an act of digging. **2** an archaeological excavation. **3** a sharp push or poke. **4** informal a mocking or critical remark. **5** (**digs**) informal lodgings.
– PHRASES **dig in one's heels** stubbornly refuse to compromise.

di·ge·ra·ti /dijəˈrätē/ ▶ pl.n. informal people with expertise in information technology.

di·gest ▶ v. /diˈjest, dī-/ **1** break down food in

the stomach and intestines into substances that can be absorbed by the body. **2** reflect on and absorb information. ▶ n. /ˈdīˌjest/ a compilation or summary of material or information. ■ **di·gest·er** n.

di·gest·i·ble /diˈjestəbəl, dī-/ ▶ adj. **1** (of food) able to be digested. **2** (of information) easy to understand. ■ **di·gest·i·bil·i·ty** /-ˌjestəˈbilitē/ n.

di·ges·tif /ˌdējesˈtēf/ ▶ n. a drink taken before or after a meal in order to help digestion.

di·ges·tion /diˈjesCHən, dī-/ ▶ n. **1** the process of digesting food. **2** a person's capacity to digest food.

di·ges·tive /diˈjestiv, dī-/ ▶ adj. relating to the digestion of food. ▶ n. a food or medicine that aids the digestion of food.

dig·ger /ˈdigər/ ▶ n. a person, animal, or large machine that digs earth.

dig·i·cam /ˈdijiˌkam/ ▶ n. a digital camera.

dig·it /ˈdijit/ ▶ n. **1** any of the numerals from 0 to 9. **2** a finger or thumb.

dig·it·al /ˈdijitl/ ▶ adj. **1** relating to information represented as a series of binary digits, as in a computer. **2** relating to computer technology: *the digital revolution.* **3** (of a clock or watch) showing the time by displaying numbers electronically. **4** relating to a finger or fingers. ■ **dig·it·al·ly** adv.

dig·it·al au·di·o·tape ▶ n. magnetic tape on which sound is recorded digitally.

dig·it·al cam·er·a ▶ n. a camera that produces digital images that can be stored in a computer and displayed on screen.

dig·it·al di·vide ▶ n. the gulf between those who have ready access to computers and the Internet, and those who do not.

dig·i·tal·is /ˌdijiˈtalis/ ▶ n. a drug prepared from foxglove leaves, containing substances that stimulate the heart muscle.

dig·i·tal·ize ▶ v. another term for DIGITIZE. ■ **dig·i·tal·i·za·tion** /ˌdijitl-əˈzāSHən/ n.

dig·it·al sig·na·ture ▶ n. a digital code that is attached to an electronically transmitted document to verify its contents and the sender's identity.

dig·i·tize /ˈdijiˌtīz/ ▶ v. convert pictures or sound into a digital form that can be processed by a computer. ■ **dig·i·ti·za·tion** /ˌdijitəˈzāSHən/ n. **dig·i·tiz·er** n.

dig·ni·fied /ˈdigniˌfīd/ ▶ adj. having a serious manner that is worthy of respect.

dig·ni·fy /ˈdignəˌfī/ ▶ v. (**dignifies, dignifying, dignified**) make something seem impressive or worthy of respect.

dig·ni·tar·y /ˈdigniˌterē/ ▶ n. (pl. **dignitaries**) a high-ranking person.

dig·ni·ty /ˈdignitē/ ▶ n. (pl. **dignities**) **1** the state of being worthy of respect: *the dignity of labor.* **2** a calm or serious manner. **3** a sense of self-respect.

di·graph /ˈdīˌgraf/ ▶ n. a combination of two letters representing one sound, as in *ph* and *ey*.

di·gress /dīˈgres/ ▶ v. leave the main subject temporarily in speech or writing. ■ **di·gres·sion** /-ˈgreSHən/ n. **di·gres·sive** /-ˈgresiv/ adj.

di·he·dral /dīˈhēdrəl/ ▶ adj. having or contained by two plane faces.

dike¹ /dīk/ (also **dyke**) ▶ n. **1** an embankment built to prevent flooding from the sea. **2** an earthwork serving as a boundary or defense:

Offa's Dike. **3** a ditch or watercourse. **4** Geology an intrusion of igneous rock cutting across existing strata. Compare with SILL.

dike² ▶ n. variant spelling of DYKE².

dik·tat /dik'tät/ ▶ n. a decree imposed by someone in power without popular consent.

di·lap·i·dat·ed /di'lapiˌdātid/ ▶ adj. in a state of disrepair or ruin. ■ **di·lap·i·da·tion** /diˌlapi'dāsʜən/ n.

dil·a·ta·tion /ˌdilə'tāsʜən, ˌdī-/ ▶ n. Medicine & Physiology the action of widening a vessel or opening in the body.

di·late /'dīˌlāt, dī'lāt/ ▶ v. **1** make or become wider, larger, or more open: *her eyes dilated with horror.* **2** (**dilate on**) speak or write at length on a subject. ■ **di·la·tion** /dī'lāsʜən/ n. **di·la·tor** /'dīˌlātər, dī'lātər/ n.

dil·a·to·ry /'diləˌtôrē/ ▶ adj. **1** slow to act. **2** intended to cause delay: *dilatory tactics.* ■ **dil·a·to·ri·ness** n.

dil·do /'dildō/ ▶ n. (pl. **dildos** or **dildoes**) an object shaped like an erect penis, used for sexual stimulation.

di·lem·ma /di'lemə/ ▶ n. **1** a situation in which a difficult choice has to be made between alternatives that are equally undesirable. **2** informal a difficult situation or problem.

dil·et·tante /ˌdili'tänt/ ▶ n. (pl. **dilettanti** /-'täntē/ or **dilettantes**) a person who dabbles in a subject for enjoyment but without serious study. ■ **dil·et·tan·tish** adj. **dil·et·tant·ism** /-ˌtizəm/ n.

dil·i·gent /'dilədʒənt/ ▶ adj. careful and conscientious in carrying out a task or duties. ■ **dil·i·gence** n. **dil·i·gent·ly** adv.

dill /dil/ ▶ n. an herb, the leaves and seeds of which are used in cooking or for medicinal purposes.

dil·ly-dal·ly /'dilē/ ▶ v. (**dilly-dallies, dilly-dallying, dilly-dallied**) informal dawdle or be indecisive.

di·lute /di'lōōt, dī-/ ▶ v. **1** make a liquid thinner or weaker by adding water or another solvent. **2** make weaker by modifying or adding other elements: *they rejected any attempt to dilute the law.* ▶ adj. **1** (of a liquid) made thinner or weaker by the addition of a solvent. **2** Chemistry (of a solution) having a relatively low concentration of solute. ■ **di·lut·er** n. **di·lu·tion** /di'lōōsʜən, dī-/ n. **di·lu·tive** /-'lōōtiv/ adj.

dim /dim/ ▶ adj. (**dimmer, dimmest**) **1** not bright or well lit: *the dim corridors of the building.* **2** made difficult to see by darkness or distance: *dim shapes of men passed to and fro.* **3** (of the eyes) not able to see clearly. **4** not clearly remembered. **5** informal stupid or slow to understand. ▶ v. (**dims, dimming, dimmed**) make or become dim. ■ **dim·ly** adv. **dimm·a·ble** adj. **dim·ness** n.
– PHRASES **take a dim view of** regard with disapproval.

dime /dīm/ ▶ n. a ten-cent coin.

di·men·sion /di'mensʜən/ ▶ n. **1** a measurable extent, such as length, breadth, or height. **2** an aspect or feature: *the story has an international dimension.* ■ **di·men·sion·al** /-sʜənl/ adj. **di·men·sion·al·ly** /-sʜənl-ē/ adv.

di·mer /'dīmər/ ▶ n. Chemistry a molecule consisting of two identical molecules linked together.

di·min·ish /di'minisʜ/ ▶ v. **1** become or make smaller, weaker, or less. **2** cause to seem less impressive or valuable: *the trial has aged and*

diminished him.

di·min·u·en·do /diˌminyōō'endō/ ▶ adv. & adj. Music with a decrease in loudness. ▶ n. Music a decrease in loudness.

dim·i·nu·tion /ˌdimə'n(y)ōōsʜən/ ▶ n. a reduction in the size, extent, or importance of something.

di·min·u·tive /di'minyətiv/ ▶ adj. **1** very or unusually small. **2** (of a word, name, or suffix) implying smallness (e.g., *-let* in *booklet*). ▶ n. a shortened form of a name, typically used informally.

dim·i·ty /'dimitē/ ▶ n. a sheer cotton fabric woven with raised stripes or checks.

dim·mer /'dimər/ (also **dimmer switch**) ▶ n. a device for varying the brightness of an electric light.

di·mor·phic /dī'môrfik/ ▶ adj. chiefly Biology occurring in or representing two distinct forms. ■ **di·mor·phism** /-fizəm/ n.

dim·ple /'dimpəl/ ▶ n. **1** a small depression formed in the fleshy part of the cheeks when one smiles. **2** a slight depression in the surface of an object. ▶ v. produce a dimple or dimples on something. ■ **dim·ply** adj.

dim sum /'dim 'səm/ ▶ n. a Chinese dish of small dumplings containing various fillings.

dim·wit /'dimˌwit/ ▶ n. informal a stupid or silly person. ■ **dim·wit·ted** adj.

DIN /din/ ▶ n. any of a series of international technical standards, used especially for electrical connections and film speeds.

din /din/ ▶ n. a prolonged loud and unpleasant noise. ▶ v. (**dins, dinning, dinned**) (**din something into**) put information into someone's mind by constant repetition.

di·nar /di'när/ ▶ n. **1** the basic unit of money of Bosnia and Serbia. **2** the basic unit of money of certain countries of the Middle East and North Africa.

dine /dīn/ ▶ v. **1** eat dinner. **2** (**dine out on**) regularly entertain friends with an interesting or amusing story.

din·er /'dīnər/ ▶ n. **1** a person eating a meal, especially in a restaurant. **2** a dining car on a train. **3** a small roadside restaurant.

di·nette /dī'net/ ▶ n. **1** a small room or part of a room used for eating meals. **2** a set of table and chairs for such an area.

ding¹ /diNG/ ▶ v. make a metallic ringing sound.

ding² informal ▶ n. a mark or dent on the bodywork of a car, boat, or other vehicle. ▶ v. **1** dent something. **2** hit someone, especially on the head. **3** criticize, injure, or penalize someone.

ding·bat /'diNGˌbat/ ▶ n. informal a stupid or eccentric person.

ding-dong /'diNG ˌdôNG/ ▶ n. informal a silly or foolish person.

din·ghy /'diNGē/ ▶ n. (pl. **dinghies**) a small open boat for recreation or racing.

din·go /'diNGgō/ ▶ n. (pl. **dingoes** or **dingos**) a wild or semi-domesticated Australian dog with a sandy-colored coat.

din·gy /'dinjē/ ▶ adj. (**dingier, dingiest**) gloomy and drab. ■ **din·gi·ly** adv. **din·gi·ness** n.

din·ing car ▶ n. a railroad car equipped as a restaurant.

din·ing room ▶ n. a room in a house or hotel in which meals are eaten.

dink·y /'diNGkē/ ▸ adj. (**dinkier, dinkiest**) informal attractively small and neat.

din·ner /'dinər/ ▸ n. 1 the main meal of the day, taken either around midday or in the evening. 2 a formal evening meal.

din·ner jack·et ▸ n. a man's short jacket without tails, worn with a bow tie for formal evening occasions.

di·no·saur /'dīnə,sôr/ ▸ n. 1 an extinct reptile of the Mesozoic era, often reaching an enormous size. 2 a thing that is outdated or has become obsolete.

dint /dint/ ▸ n. a dent or hollow in a surface. – PHRASES **by dint of** by means of.

di·o·cese /'dīəsis, -,sēz, -,sēs/ ▸ n. (pl. **dioceses** /'dīəsēz/) (in the Christian Church) a district for which a bishop is responsible. ∎ **di·oc·e·san** /dī'äsisən/ adj.

di·ode /'dī,ōd/ ▸ n. 1 a semiconductor device with two terminals, typically allowing the flow of current in one direction only. 2 a thermionic valve with two electrodes.

di·oe·cious /dī'ēsHəs/ ▸ adj. (of a plant or invertebrate animal) having the male and female reproductive organs in separate individuals. Compare with MONOECIOUS.

Di·o·ny·sian /,dīə'nisHən, -'niseˉən, -'nīseˉən/ (also **Dionysiac** /-'nisē,ak, -'nīsē-/) ▸ adj. 1 relating to Dionysus, the Greek god of fertility and wine, associated with ecstatic religious rites. 2 wild and uninhibited.

di·op·ter /dī'äptər/ ▸ n. a unit of refractive power, equal to the reciprocal of the focal length (in meters) of a given lens.

di·op·tric /dī'äptrik/ ▸ adj. relating to the refraction of light. ∎ **di·op·trics** pl.n.

di·o·ram·a /,dīə'ramə, -'rä-/ ▸ n. 1 a model representing a scene with three-dimensional figures against a painted background. 2 chiefly historical a scenic painting, viewed through a peephole, in which changes in color and direction of illumination simulate changes in the weather and time of day.

di·o·rite /'dīə,rīt/ ▸ n. a speckled, coarse-grained igneous rock.

di·ox·ide /dī'äk,sīd/ ▸ n. Chemistry an oxide with two atoms of oxygen to one of a metal or other element.

di·ox·in /dī'äksin/ ▸ n. a highly toxic organic compound produced as a byproduct in some manufacturing processes.

dip /dip/ ▸ v. (**dips, dipping, dipped**) 1 (**dip something in/into**) put or lower something briefly in or into liquid. 2 sink, drop, or slope downward: *the sun had dipped below the horizon.* 3 (of a level or amount) temporarily become lower or smaller. 4 move something briefly downward. 5 (**dip into**) reach into a bag or container to take something out. 6 (**dip into**) spend from one's financial resources. ▸ n. 1 an act of dipping. 2 a thick sauce in which pieces of food are dipped before eating. 3 a brief swim. 4 a brief downward slope followed by an upward one.

Dip. ▸ abbr. diploma.

diph·the·ri·a /dif'THi(ə)rēə, dip-/ ▸ n. a serious contagious disease causing inflammation of the mucous membranes, especially in the throat.

diph·thong /'dif,THäNG, 'dip-, -,THôNG/ ▸ n. a sound formed by the combination of two vowels in a single syllable (as in *coin*).

di·plod·o·cus /di'plädəkəs/ ▸ n. a huge plant-eating dinosaur of the late Jurassic period, with a long slender neck and tail.

dip·loid /'dip,loid/ ▸ adj. (of a cell or nucleus) containing two complete sets of chromosomes, one from each parent. Compare with HAPLOID.

di·plo·ma /di'plōmə/ ▸ n. a certificate awarded by a school or college for successfully completing a course of study.

di·plo·ma·cy /di'plōməsē/ ▸ n. 1 the profession, activity, or skill of managing international relations. 2 skill and tact in dealing with people.

dip·lo·mat /'diplə,mat/ ▸ n. an official representing a country abroad.

dip·lo·mat·ic /,diplə'matik/ ▸ adj. 1 relating to diplomacy. 2 dealing with people in a tactful way. ∎ **dip·lo·mat·i·cal·ly** /-ik(ə)lē/ adv.

dip·lo·mat·ic im·mu·ni·ty ▸ n. exemption from certain laws granted to diplomats by the country in which they are working.

dip·lo·mat·ic pouch ▸ n. a container in which official mail is sent to or from an embassy, and which is not subject to customs inspection.

di·pole /'dī,pōl/ ▸ n. 1 Physics a pair of equal and oppositely charged or magnetized poles separated by a distance. 2 an aerial consisting of a horizontal metal rod with a connecting wire at its center. ∎ **di·po·lar** /dī'pōlər/ adj.

dip·per /'dipər/ ▸ n. 1 a songbird that dives into fast-flowing streams to feed. 2 a ladle.

dip·py /'dipē/ ▸ adj. (**dippier, dippiest**) informal foolish or eccentric.

dip·so·ma·ni·a /,dipsə'mānēə/ ▸ n. alcoholism. ∎ **dip·so·ma·ni·ac** /-nē,ak/ n.

dip·stick /'dip,stik/ ▸ n. a rod for measuring the depth of a liquid, especially oil in an engine.

dip·tych /'diptik/ ▸ n. a painting on two hinged wooden panels, typically forming an altarpiece.

dire /dīr/ ▸ adj. 1 very serious or urgent. 2 (of a threat or warning) portending disaster.

di·rect /di'rekt, dī-/ ▸ adj. 1 going from one place to another without changing direction or stopping. 2 with nothing or no one in between: *I had no direct contact with Mr. Clark.* 3 straightforward; frank. 4 clear; unambiguous. 5 (of descent) proceeding in continuous succession from parent to child. ▸ adv. in a direct way or by a direct route. ▸ v. 1 aim something toward: *he directed his criticism at the media.* 2 control or manage something. 3 supervise and control a movie, play, or other production. 4 tell or show someone the way. 5 give an order to someone. ∎ **di·rect·ness** n.

di·rect ac·tion ▸ n. the use of strikes or other public forms of protest rather than negotiation to achieve one's aims.

di·rect cur·rent ▸ n. an electric current flowing in one direction only. Compare with ALTERNATING CURRENT.

di·rec·tion /di'reksHən, dī-/ ▸ n. 1 a course along which someone or something moves, or which leads to a destination. 2 a point to or from which a person or thing moves or faces: *a house with views in all directions.* 3 the management or guidance of someone or something. 4 aim or purpose: *his lack of direction in life.* 5 (**directions**) instructions on how to reach a destination or how to do something. ∎ **di·rec·tion·less** adj.

di·rec·tion·al /di'reksHənl/ ▸ adj. 1 relating to or indicating direction. 2 operating or sending radio signals in one direction only: *a directional microphone.*

di·rec·tive /di'rektiv/ ▶ n. an official or authoritative instruction.

di·rect·ly /di'rektlē/ ▶ adv. **1** in a direct way. **2** exactly in a specified position: *the house directly opposite.* **3** immediately; at once.

di·rect mail ▶ n. advertising material mailed to prospective customers without their having asked for it.

di·rect ob·ject ▶ n. a noun phrase that refers to a person or thing that is directly affected by the action of a transitive verb (e.g., *the dog* in *she fed the dog*).

di·rec·tor /di'rektər/ ▶ n. **1** a person who is in charge of a department, organization, or activity. **2** a member of the managing board of a business. **3** a person who directs a movie, play, etc. ■ **di·rec·to·ri·al** /di‚rek'tôrēəl, ‚dīrek-/ adj. **di·rec·tor·ship** /-‚SHip/ n.

di·rec·to·rate /di'rektərit/ ▶ n. **1** the board of directors of a company. **2** a section of a government department in charge of a particular activity.

di·rec·tor gen·er·al ▶ n. (pl. **directors general**) the chief executive of a large governmental, multinational, or private organization.

di·rec·to·ry /di'rektərē/ ▶ n. (pl. **directories**) **1** a book listing individuals or organizations with details such as addresses and telephone numbers. **2** a computer file listing other files.

di·rect speech ▶ n. the reporting of speech by repeating the actual words of a speaker, for example *'I'm going', she said.* Contrasted with REPORTED SPEECH.

di·rect tax ▶ n. a tax, such as income tax, that is charged on the income or profits of the person who pays it.

dirge /dərj/ ▶ n. **1** a lament for the dead, especially one forming part of a funeral rite. **2** a mournful song or piece of music.

dir·ham /də'ram/ ▶ n. the basic unit of money of Morocco and the United Arab Emirates.

dir·i·gi·ble /'dirijəbəl, də'rijə-/ ▶ n. an airship.

di·ri·gisme /'diri‚ZHizəm, ‚diri'ZHizəm, ‚dērē'ZHēsm(ə)/ ▶ n. government control of economic and social matters. ■ **di·ri·giste** /‚diri'ZHēst, ‚dirē-/ adj.

dirk /dərk/ ▶ n. a short dagger of a kind formerly carried by Scottish Highlanders.

dirn·dl /'dərndl/ ▶ n. **1** (also **dirndl skirt**) a full, wide skirt gathered into a tight waistband. **2** a woman's dress with a dirndl skirt and a close-fitting bodice.

dirt /dərt/ ▶ n. **1** a substance that makes something unclean. **2** soil or earth. **3** informal excrement. **4** informal scandalous or damaging information.

dirt·bag /'dərt‚bag/ ▶ n. informal a physically or morally repulsive person.

dirt bike ▶ n. a motorcycle designed for use on rough terrain, especially in scrambling.

dirt cheap ▶ adj. & adv. informal very cheap.

dirt poor ▶ adj. & adv. very poor.

dirt track ▶ n. a racing track made of earth or rolled cinders.

dirt·y /'dərtē/ ▶ adj. (**dirtier**, **dirtiest**) **1** covered or marked with dirt; not clean. **2** concerned with sex in a lewd or obscene way: *dirty jokes.* **3** dishonest; dishonorable. **4** (of weather)

rough and unpleasant. **5** (of a nuclear weapon) producing considerable radioactive fallout. ▶ v. (**dirties**, **dirtying**, **dirtied**) make someone or something dirty. ■ **dirt·i·ly** adv. **dirt·i·ness** n. – PHRASES **do the dirty on** Brit. informal cheat or betray someone. **play dirty** informal act in a dishonest or unfair way.

dirt·y bomb ▶ n. a conventional bomb that contains radioactive material.

dirt·y look ▶ n. informal a look expressing disapproval, disgust, or anger.

dirt·y trick ▶ n. **1** a dishonest or unkind act. **2** (**dirty tricks**) underhanded political or commercial activity designed to discredit an opponent or competitor.

dirt·y word ▶ n. a thing regarded with dislike: *capitalism is a dirty word for some young people.*

dirt·y work ▶ n. unpleasant or dishonest activities that are delegated to someone else.

dis /dis/ (also **diss**) ▶ v. (**disses**, **dissing**, **dissed**) informal act or speak in a disrespectful way toward.

dis- ▶ prefix **1** expressing negation: *disadvantage.* **2** expressing reversal or absence: *dishonor.* **3** expressing removal or separation: *disperse.*

dis·a·bil·i·ty /‚disə'bilitē/ ▶ n. (pl. **disabilities**) **1** a physical or mental condition that limits a person's movements, senses, or activities. **2** a disadvantage.

dis·a·ble /dis'ābəl/ ▶ v. **1** (of a disease, injury, or accident) limit someone in their movements, senses, or activities. **2** put something out of action. ■ **dis·a·ble·ment** n.

dis·a·bled /dis'ābəld/ ▶ adj. having a physical or mental disability.

> USAGE
> **Disabled** is the standard term for people with physical or mental disabilities, and should be used instead of terms such as **crippled** or **handicapped**, which often cause offense.

dis·a·buse /‚disə'byōōz/ ▶ v. persuade someone that an idea or belief is mistaken: *Greg soon disabused her of this idea.*

di·sac·cha·ride /dī'sakə‚rīd/ ▶ n. a sugar whose molecule can be broken down to give two simple sugar molecules.

dis·ad·van·tage /‚disəd'vantij/ ▶ n. something that causes a problem or that makes success or progress less likely: *women are at a disadvantage in competing for jobs with men.* ▶ v. **1** put someone in an unfavorable position. **2** (as adj. **disadvantaged**) having less money and fewer opportunities than the rest of society. ■ **dis·ad·van·ta·geous** /dis‚advən'tājəs/ adj.

dis·af·fect·ed /‚disə'fektid/ ▶ adj. discontented through having lost one's feelings of loyalty. ■ **dis·af·fec·tion** /‚disə'feksHən/ n.

dis·a·gree /‚disə'grē/ ▶ v. (**disagrees**, **disagreeing**, **disagreed**) **1** have a different opinion. **2** fail to correspond or be consistent: *results that disagree with the findings reported so far.* **3** (**disagree with**) make someone slightly ill. ■ **dis·a·gree·ment** n.

dis·a·gree·a·ble /‚disə'grēəbəl/ ▶ adj. **1** not pleasant or enjoyable. **2** unfriendly and bad-tempered. ■ **dis·a·gree·a·bly** adv.

dis·al·low /‚disə'lou/ ▶ v. declare something to be invalid. ■ **dis·al·low·ance** n.

dis·am·big·u·ate /‚disam'bigyōō‚āt/ ▶ v. remove uncertainty of meaning from something with more than one possible meaning.

■ **dis·am·big·u·a·tion** /-ˌbigyōō'āsHən/ *n.*

dis·ap·pear /ˌdisə'pi(ə)r/ ▶ *v.* **1** cease to be visible. **2** cease to exist. **3** be lost or impossible to find. ■ **dis·ap·pear·ance** *n.*

dis·ap·point /ˌdisə'point/ ▶ *v.* **1** fail to fulfill someone's hopes. **2** prevent hopes from becoming a reality. ■ **dis·ap·point·ing** *adj.* **dis·ap·point·ing·ly** *adv.*

dis·ap·point·ed /ˌdisə'pointid/ ▶ *adj.* sad or displeased because one's hopes have not been fulfilled. ■ **dis·ap·point·ed·ly** *adv.*

dis·ap·point·ment /ˌdisə'pointmənt/ ▶ *n.* **1** sadness or displeasure caused by the failure of one's hopes to be fulfilled. **2** a cause of disappointment.

dis·ap·pro·ba·tion /ˌdisˌaprə'bāsHən/ ▶ *n.* formal strong disapproval.

dis·ap·prove /ˌdisə'prōōv/ ▶ *v.* think that someone or something is wrong or bad. ■ **dis·ap·prov·al** *n.* **dis·ap·prov·ing** *adj.*

dis·arm /dis'ärm/ ▶ *v.* **1** take a weapon or weapons away from a person, force, or country. **2** win over a hostile or suspicious person: *her political skills will disarm critics.* **3** remove the fuse from a bomb.

dis·ar·ma·ment /dis'ärməmənt/ ▶ *n.* the reduction or withdrawal of military forces and weapons.

dis·arm·ing /dis'ärming/ ▶ *adj.* removing suspicion or hostility, especially through charm. ■ **dis·arm·ing·ly** *adv.*

dis·ar·range /ˌdisə'rānj/ ▶ *v.* make something untidy or disordered.

dis·ar·ray /ˌdisə'rā/ ▶ *n.* a state of disorder or untidiness.

dis·as·sem·ble /ˌdisə'sembəl/ ▶ *v.* take something to pieces. ■ **dis·as·sem·bly** *n.*

dis·as·so·ci·ate /ˌdisə'sōsHēˌāt, -'sōsē-/ ▶ *v.* another term for **DISSOCIATE**. ■ **dis·as·so·ci·a·tion** /ˌdisəˌsōsHē'āsHən, -ˌsōsē-/ *n.*

dis·as·ter /di'zastər/ ▶ *n.* **1** a sudden accident or a natural catastrophe that causes great damage or loss of life. **2** an event or situation causing ruin or failure: *the deteriorating dollar is a disaster for the economy.*

dis·as·trous /di'zastrəs/ ▶ *adj.* **1** causing great damage. **2** informal highly unsuccessful. ■ **dis·as·trous·ly** *adv.*

dis·a·vow /ˌdisə'vou/ ▶ *v.* deny any responsibility or support for something. ■ **dis·a·vow·al** *n.*

dis·band /dis'band/ ▶ *v.* stop or cause to stop operating as an organized group.

dis·bar /dis'bär/ ▶ *v.* (**disbars, disbarring, disbarred**) expel a lawyer from the Bar. ■ **dis·bar·ment** /-mənt/ *n.*

dis·be·lief /ˌdisbə'lēf/ ▶ *n.* **1** inability or refusal to accept that something is true or real. **2** lack of faith.

dis·be·lieve /ˌdisbə'lēv/ ▶ *v.* **1** be unable to believe someone or something. **2** have no religious faith. ■ **dis·be·liev·er** *n.*

dis·burse /dis'bərs/ ▶ *v.* pay out money from a fund. ■ **dis·burse·ment** *n.*

disc ▶ *n.* variant spelling of **DISK**.

dis·card ▶ *v.* /dis'kärd/ get rid of something as useless or unwanted. ▶ *n.* /'disˌkärd/ a discarded item.

disc brake ▶ *n.* a type of vehicle brake employing the friction of pads against a disk attached to the wheel.

dis·cern /di'sərn/ ▶ *v.* **1** recognize or find something out. **2** see or hear someone or something with difficulty. ■ **dis·cern·i·ble** *adj.*

dis·cern·ing /di'sərning/ ▶ *adj.* having or showing good judgment. ■ **dis·cern·ment** *n.*

dis·charge ▶ *v.* /dis'CHärj/ **1** officially tell someone that they can or must leave: *he was discharged from the Air Force.* **2** cause a liquid, gas, or other substance to flow out. **3** fire a gun or missile. **4** do all that is required to fulfill a responsibility. **5** release someone from a contract or obligation. **6** Physics release or neutralize the electric charge of a battery or electric field. ▶ *n.* /'disˌCHärj/ **1** the action of discharging someone or something. **2** a substance that has been discharged. **3** a flow of electricity through the air or other gas. ■ **dis·charg·er** /dis'CHärjər/ *n.*

dis·ci·ple /di'sīpəl/ ▶ *n.* **1** a follower of Jesus during his life, especially one of the twelve Apostles. **2** a follower or student of a teacher, leader, or philosopher. ■ **dis·ci·ple·ship** /di'sīpəlˌsHip/ *n.*

dis·ci·pli·nar·i·an /ˌdisəplə'nerēən/ ▶ *n.* a person who enforces firm discipline.

dis·ci·pline /'disəplin/ ▶ *n.* **1** the training of people to obey rules or a code of behavior. **2** controlled behavior resulting from such training: *he was able to maintain discipline among his men.* **3** an activity providing mental or physical training: *kung fu is a discipline open to all.* **4** a branch of academic study. ▶ *v.* **1** train someone to be obedient or self-controlled by punishment or imposing rules. **2** formally punish someone for an offense. **3** (as adj. **disciplined**) behaving in a controlled way. ■ **dis·ci·pli·nar·y** /'disəpləˌnerē/ *adj.*

disc jock·ey ▶ *n.* (also **disk jockey**) full form of DJ.

dis·claim /dis'klām/ ▶ *v.* **1** deny responsibility for or knowledge of something. **2** Law renounce a legal claim to a property or title.

dis·claim·er /dis'klāmər/ ▶ *n.* a statement denying responsibility for something.

dis·close /dis'klōz/ ▶ *v.* **1** make secret or new information known. **2** allow something hidden to be seen.

dis·clo·sure /dis'klōzHər/ ▶ *n.* **1** the disclosing of new or secret information. **2** a fact that is made known.

dis·co /'diskō/ ▶ *n.* (pl. **discos**) **1** a club or party at which people dance to pop music. **2** (also **disco music**) soul-influenced, melodic pop music.

dis·cog·ra·phy /dis'kägrəfē/ ▶ *n.* (pl. **discographies**) **1** a descriptive catalog of musical recordings. **2** the study of musical recordings and compilation of descriptive catalogs.

dis·coid /'disˌkoid/ ▶ *adj.* technical shaped like a disk. ■ **dis·coi·dal** /dis'koidl/ *adj.*

dis·col·or /dis'kələr/ ▶ *v.* change to a different, less attractive color. ■ **dis·col·or·a·tion** /-ˌkələ'rāsHən/ *n.*

dis·com·bob·u·late /ˌdiskəm'bäbyəˌlāt/ ▶ *v.* humorous disconcert or confuse someone.

dis·com·fit /dis'kəmfit/ ▶ *v.* (**discomfits, discomfiting, discomfited**) make someone uneasy or embarrassed. ■ **dis·com·fi·ture** /dis'kəmfiˌCHŏŏr/ *n.*

dis·com·fort /dis'kəmfərt/ ▶ *n.* **1** slight pain. **2** slight anxiety or embarrassment. ▶ *v.* cause discomfort to someone.

dis·com·mode /ˌdiskəˈmōd/ ▸ v. formal cause someone trouble or inconvenience.

dis·com·pose /ˌdiskəmˈpōz/ ▸ v. disturb or agitate someone. ■ **dis·com·po·sure** /-ˈpōzHər/ n.

dis·con·cert /ˌdiskənˈsərt/ ▸ v. disturb the composure of; unsettle: *troops are disconcerted by the anti-war protests.* ■ **dis·con·cert·ed** adj. **dis·con·cert·ing** adj.

dis·con·nect /ˌdiskəˈnekt/ ▸ v. 1 break the connection between two things. 2 detach an electrical device from a power supply. ■ **dis·con·nec·tion** /-ˈneksHən/ n.

dis·con·nect·ed /ˌdiskəˈnektid/ ▸ adj. (of speech, writing, or thought) lacking a logical sequence.

dis·con·so·late /disˈkänsəlit/ ▸ adj. very unhappy and unable to be comforted. ■ **dis·con·so·late·ly** adv.

dis·con·tent /ˌdiskənˈtent/ ▸ n. lack of contentment or satisfaction. ■ **dis·con·tent·ed** adj. **dis·con·tent·ment** n.

dis·con·tin·ue /ˌdiskənˈtinyo͞o/ ▸ v. (**discontinues**, **discontinuing**, **discontinued**) stop doing, providing, or making something. ■ **dis·con·tin·u·a·tion** /-ˌtinyo͞oˈäsHən/ n.

dis·con·tin·u·ous /ˌdiskənˈtinyo͞oəs/ ▸ adj. having intervals or gaps; not continuous. ■ **dis·con·ti·nu·i·ty** /ˌdiskäntnˈ(y)o͞oitē/ n. (pl. **discontinuities**).

dis·cord /ˈdiskôrd/ ▸ n. 1 lack of agreement or harmony: *financial difficulties can lead to marital discord.* 2 lack of harmony between musical notes sounding together.

dis·cord·ant /disˈkôrdnt/ ▸ adj. 1 not in harmony or agreement: *discordant opinions.* 2 (of a sound) harsh and unpleasant. ■ **dis·cord·ance** /-dns/ n.

dis·co·theque /ˈdiskəˌtek/ ▸ n. full form of DISCO (sense 1).

dis·count ▸ n. /ˈdiskount/ a deduction from the usual cost of something. ▸ v. /ˈdiskount, disˈkount/ 1 deduct a discount from the usual price of something. 2 regard something as unworthy of consideration because it seems improbable. ■ **dis·count·er** n.

dis·coun·te·nance /disˈkountn-əns/ ▸ v. 1 refuse to approve something. 2 unsettle someone.

dis·cour·age /disˈkərij, -ˈkə-rij/ ▸ v. 1 cause someone to lose confidence or enthusiasm. 2 try to persuade someone not to do something: *we want to discourage children from smoking.* ■ **dis·cour·age·ment** n. **dis·cour·ag·ing** adj.

dis·course ▸ n. /ˈdisˌkôrs/ 1 written or spoken communication or debate. 2 a formal written or verbal discussion of a topic. ▸ v. /disˈkôrs/ speak or write about a topic with authority.

dis·cour·te·ous /disˈkərtēəs/ ▸ adj. rude and lacking consideration for others. ■ **dis·cour·te·ous·ly** adv.

dis·cour·te·sy /disˈkərtəsē/ ▸ n. (pl. **discourtesies**) 1 rude and inconsiderate behavior. 2 a rude and inconsiderate act or remark.

dis·cov·er /disˈkəvər/ ▸ v. 1 find someone or something unexpectedly or during a search. 2 become aware of a fact or situation. 3 be the first to find or observe a place, substance, or scientific phenomenon. ■ **dis·cov·er·a·ble** adj. **dis·cov·er·er** n.

dis·cov·er·y /disˈkəvərē/ ▸ n. (pl. **discoveries**) 1 the action of discovering something. 2 a person or thing discovered.

dis·cred·it /disˈkredit/ ▸ v. (**discredits**, **discrediting**, **discredited**) 1 damage a person's good reputation. 2 make an idea or account seem false or unreliable. ▸ n. loss or lack of respect for someone. ■ **dis·cred·it·a·ble** /disˈkreditəbəl/ adj.

dis·creet /disˈkrēt/ ▸ adj. (**discreeter**, **discreetest**) careful to keep something secret or to avoid undue attention. ■ **dis·creet·ly** adv.

> **USAGE**
> **Discrete** and **discreet** are often confused. **Discreet** means 'careful to keep something secret or to avoid attention' (*we made some discreet inquiries*), while **discrete** means 'separate' (*products are organized in discrete batches*).

dis·crep·an·cy /disˈkrepənsē/ ▸ n. (pl. **discrepancies**) a difference between facts that should be the same. ■ **dis·crep·ant** /-pənt/ adj.

dis·crete /disˈkrēt/ ▸ adj. separate and distinct. ■ **dis·crete·ly** adv. **dis·crete·ness** n.

dis·cre·tion /disˈkresHən/ ▸ n. 1 the quality of being careful not to reveal information or give offense. 2 the freedom to decide what should be done in a particular situation: *you will be offered bribes, which you may accept or decline at your discretion.*

dis·cre·tion·ar·y /disˈkresHəˌnerē/ ▸ adj. done or used according to a person's judgment.

dis·crim·i·nate /disˈkriməˌnāt/ ▸ v. 1 recognize a difference: *babies can discriminate between different facial expressions.* 2 treat different categories of people unfairly on the grounds of race, sex, or age. ■ **dis·crim·i·na·tive** /disˈkriməˌnātiv/ adj. **dis·crim·i·na·tor** /disˈkriməˌnātər/ n.

dis·crim·i·nat·ing /disˈkriməˌnātiNG/ ▸ adj. having or showing good taste or judgment.

dis·crim·i·na·tion /disˌkriməˈnāsHən/ ▸ n. 1 unfair treatment of different categories of people on the grounds of race, sex, or age. 2 recognition of the difference between one thing and another. 3 good judgment or taste.

dis·crim·i·na·to·ry /disˈkrimənəˌtôrē/ ▸ adj. showing discrimination or prejudice.

dis·cur·sive /disˈkərsiv/ ▸ adj. 1 wandering from subject to subject. 2 relating to discourse. ■ **dis·cur·sive·ly** adv. **dis·cur·sive·ness** n.

dis·cus /ˈdiskəs/ ▸ n. (pl. **discuses**) a heavy disk thrown in athletic contests.

dis·cuss /disˈkəs/ ▸ v. 1 talk about something so as to reach a decision. 2 talk or write about a topic in detail. ■ **dis·cuss·a·ble** adj.

dis·cus·sant /disˈkəsənt/ ▸ n. a person who takes part in a discussion, especially a prearranged one.

dis·cus·sion /disˈkəsHən/ ▸ n. 1 the action of discussing something. 2 a debate about or a detailed written treatment of a topic.

dis·cus·sion board ▸ n. Computing another term for MESSAGE BOARD.

dis·dain /disˈdān/ ▸ n. the feeling that someone or something does not deserve one's consideration or respect. ▸ v. consider to be unworthy of respect: *people disdained the go-getters of eighties Wall Street.*

dis·dain·ful /disˈdānfəl/ ▸ adj. showing contempt or lack of respect. ■ **dis·dain·ful·ly** adv.

dis·ease /diˈzēz/ ▸ n. a disorder in a human, animal, or plant, caused by infection, diet, or faulty functioning of a process. ■ **dis·eased** adj.

dis·e·con·o·my /ˌdisiˈkänəmē/ ▸ n. (pl.

diseconomies) an economic disadvantage such as an increase in cost arising from an increase in the size of an organization.

dis·em·bark /ˌdisemˈbärk/ ▶ v. leave a ship, aircraft, or train. ■ **dis·em·bar·ka·tion** /disˌembärˈkāshən/ n.

dis·em·bod·ied /ˌdisemˈbädēd/ ▶ adj. **1** separated from or existing without the body. **2** (of a sound) coming from a person who cannot be seen. ■ **dis·em·bod·i·ment** n.

dis·em·bow·el /ˌdisemˈbouəl/ ▶ v. (**disembowels, disemboweling, disemboweled**) cut open and remove the internal organs of someone or something. ■ **dis·em·bow·el·ment** n.

dis·em·pow·er /ˌdisemˈpouər/ ▶ v. make someone less powerful or confident. ■ **dis·em·pow·er·ment** n.

dis·en·chant /ˌdisenˈchant/ ▶ v. make someone disillusioned. ■ **dis·en·chant·ment** n.

dis·en·fran·chise /ˌdisenˈfranchīz/ ▶ v. deprive someone of a right, especially the right to vote. ■ **dis·en·fran·chise·ment** n.

dis·en·gage /ˌdisenˈgāj/ ▶ v. **1** release or detach: *he disengaged his arm from hers.* **2** remove troops from an area of conflict. **3** (as adj. **disengaged**) emotionally detached; uninvolved. ■ **dis·en·gage·ment** n.

dis·en·tan·gle /ˌdisenˈtaNGgəl/ ▶ v. free someone or something from something they are entangled with.

dis·e·qui·lib·ri·um /disˌēkwəˈlibrēəm/ ▶ n. a loss or lack of equilibrium or stability, especially in relation to supply, demand, and prices.

dis·es·tab·lish /ˌdisiˈstablish/ ▶ v. deprive a national Church of its official status. ■ **dis·es·tab·lish·ment** n.

dis·es·teem /ˌdisiˈstēm/ ▶ n. lack of respect or admiration. ▶ v. formal have a low opinion of someone or something.

dis·fa·vor /disˈfāvər/ ▶ n. **1** disapproval or dislike. **2** the state of being disliked.

dis·fig·ure /disˈfigyər/ ▶ v. spoil the appearance of someone or something. ■ **dis·fig·u·ra·tion** /-ˌfigyəˈrāshən/ n. **dis·fig·ure·ment** n.

dis·gorge /disˈgôrj/ ▶ v. **1** pour out; discharge: *a bus disgorged a load of tourists.* **2** vomit food.

dis·grace /disˈgrās/ ▶ n. **1** loss of the respect of others as the result of unacceptable behavior: *he left office in disgrace.* **2** a shamefully bad person or thing. ▶ v. bring disgrace to someone or something.

dis·grace·ful /disˈgrāsfəl/ ▶ adj. shockingly unacceptable. ■ **dis·grace·ful·ly** adv.

dis·grun·tled /disˈgrəntld/ ▶ adj. angry or dissatisfied. ■ **dis·grun·tle·ment** n.

dis·guise /disˈgīz/ ▶ v. **1** change the appearance or nature of someone or something so as to prevent recognition: *a reporter disguised himself as a delivery man.* **2** hide a feeling or situation. ▶ n. **1** a means of concealing one's identity. **2** the state of being disguised: *the troops were rebels in disguise.*

dis·gust /disˈgəst/ ▶ n. revulsion or strong disapproval. ▶ v. cause someone to feel revulsion or strong disapproval. ■ **dis·gust·ed** adj. **dis·gust·ed·ly** adv.

dis·gust·ing /disˈgəstiNG/ ▶ adj. arousing revulsion or strong disapproval. ■ **dis·gust·ing·ly** adv. **dis·gust·ing·ness** n.

dish /dish/ ▶ n. **1** a shallow container for cooking or serving food. **2** a particular kind of food served as part of a meal: *Thai dishes.* **3** (**the dishes**) all the crockery and utensils used for a meal. **4** a shallow, concave container: *a soap dish.* **5** informal an attractive person. ▶ v. **1** (**dish something out/up**) put food on a plate or plates before a meal. **2** (**dish something out**) distribute in a casual or indiscriminate way: *the company dished out free tickets to all its employees.*
– PHRASES **dish the dirt** informal reveal or spread scandal.

dis·har·mo·ny /disˈhärmənē/ ▶ n. lack of harmony; disagreement or discord. ■ **dis·har·mo·ni·ous** /-ˌhärˈmōnēəs/ adj.

dish·cloth /ˈdishˌklôth/ (also **dishrag** /ˈdishˌrag/) ▶ n. a cloth for washing dishes.

dis·heart·en /disˈhärtn/ ▶ v. make someone lose hope or confidence. ■ **dis·heart·en·ing** adj.

di·shev·eled /diˈshevəld/ ▶ adj. (of a person's hair, clothes, or appearance) unkempt; disordered. ■ **di·shev·el·ment** n.

dis·hon·est /disˈänist/ ▶ adj. not honest, trustworthy, or sincere. ■ **dis·hon·est·ly** adv. **dis·hon·es·ty** n. (pl. **dishonesties**).

dis·hon·or /disˈänər/ (Brit. **dishonour**) ▶ n. a state of shame or disgrace. ▶ v. **1** bring shame or disgrace to someone or something. **2** fail to honor an agreement or check.

dis·hon·or·a·ble /disˈänərəbəl/ ▶ adj. bringing shame or disgrace. ■ **dis·hon·or·ably** /-blē/ adv.

dis·hon·or·a·ble dis·charge ▶ n. dismissal from the armed forces as a result of criminal or morally unacceptable actions.

dish tow·el ▶ n. a cloth for drying washed dishes, glasses, and utensils.

dish·wash·er /ˈdishˌwôshər, -ˌwäsh-/ ▶ n. a machine for washing dishes automatically.

dish·wa·ter /ˈdishˌwôtər, -ˌwätər/ ▶ n. **1** dirty water in which dishes have been washed. **2** insipid drink: *I sipped the barely brown dishwater he passed off as coffee.*

dish·y /ˈdishē/ ▶ adj. (**dishier, dishiest**) informal, chiefly Brit. sexually attractive.

dis·il·lu·sion /ˌdisəˈlōōzhən/ ▶ n. disappointment from discovering that one's beliefs are mistaken or unrealistic. ▶ v. make someone realize that a belief is mistaken or unrealistic. ■ **dis·il·lu·sioned** adj. **dis·il·lu·sion·ment** /ˌdisəˈlōōzhənmənt/ n.

dis·in·cen·tive /ˌdisinˈsentiv/ ▶ n. a factor that discourages a particular action: *falling house prices are a disincentive to development.*

dis·in·cli·na·tion /disˌinkləˈnāshən, disˌiNGklə-/ ▶ n. a reluctance to do something.

dis·in·clined /ˌdisinˈklīnd/ ▶ adj. reluctant; unwilling.

dis·in·fect /ˌdisinˈfekt/ ▶ v. clean something with a disinfectant in order to destroy bacteria. ■ **dis·in·fec·tion** /-ˈfeksHən/ n.

dis·in·fect·ant /ˌdisinˈfektənt/ ▶ n. a chemical liquid that destroys bacteria.

dis·in·for·ma·tion /disˌinfərˈmāsHən/ ▶ n. information that is intended to mislead.

dis·in·gen·u·ous /ˌdisinˈjenyōōəs/ ▶ adj. not candid or sincere, especially in pretending ignorance about something. ■ **dis·in·gen·u·ous·ly** adv. **dis·in·gen·u·ous·ness** n.

dis·in·her·it /ˌdisinˈherit/ ▶ v. (**disinherits, disinheriting, disinherited**) prevent a person who was one's heir from inheriting one's property.

dis·in·te·grate /dis'intə,grāt/ ▶ v. **1** break up into small parts as a result of impact or decay. **2** become weaker or less united and gradually fail: *I'm afraid that our family is disintegrating.* ■ **dis·in·te·gra·tion** /dis,intə'grāshən/ n. **dis·in·te·gra·tor** /-,grātər/ n.

dis·in·ter /,disin'tər/ ▶ v. (**disinters, disinterring, disinterred**) dig up something buried.

dis·in·ter·est /dis'int(ə)rist/ ▶ n. **1** the state of being impartial. **2** lack of interest.

dis·in·ter·est·ed /dis'intə,restid, -tristid/ ▶ adj. **1** not influenced by personal feelings; impartial. **2** not interested in someone or something. ■ **dis·in·ter·est·ed·ly** adv. **dis·in·ter·est·ed·ness** n.

> **USAGE**
> Strictly speaking, **disinterested** should only be used to mean 'impartial' (*the judgments of disinterested outsiders are likely to be more useful*) and should not be used to mean 'not interested' (in other words, the same as **uninterested**). The second meaning is very common, but should be avoided as it is not accepted by everyone.

dis·in·ter·me·di·a·tion /,disintər,mēdē'āshən/ ▶ n. reduction in the use of intermediaries between producers and consumers, e.g., by investing directly in the securities market rather than through a bank. ■ **dis·in·ter·me·di·ate** /-,intər'mēdēāt/ v.

dis·in·vest /,disin'vest/ ▶ v. withdraw or reduce an investment. ■ **dis·in·vest·ment** n.

dis·joint·ed /dis'jointid/ ▶ adj. not coherent or connected: *a disjointed, scrappy game.*

dis·junc·tion /dis'jəNGkshən/ ▶ n. a difference or lack of agreement between things expected to be similar.

dis·junc·tive /dis'jəNGktiv/ ▶ adj. lacking connection or consistency.

disk /disk/ (also **disc**) ▶ n. **1** a flat, thin, circular object. **2** an information storage device for a computer, on which data is stored either magnetically or optically. **3** (**disc**) a layer of cartilage separating vertebrae in the spine. **4** (**disc**) dated a phonograph record.

disk drive ▶ n. a device that allows a computer to read from and write to computer disks.

disk·ette /dis'ket/ ▶ n. another term for FLOPPY.

disk jockey ▶ n. variant spelling of DISC JOCKEY.

dis·like /dis'līk/ ▶ v. feel distaste for or hostility toward someone or something. ▶ n. **1** a feeling of distaste or hostility. **2** a thing that is disliked. ■ **dis·lik·a·ble** (also **dislikeable**) adj.

dis·lo·cate /dis'lōkāt, 'dislō,kāt/ ▶ v. **1** displace a bone from its proper position in a joint. **2** disrupt something. ■ **dis·lo·ca·tion** /,dislō'kāshən/ n.

dis·lodge /dis'läj/ ▶ v. remove something from a fixed position. ■ **dis·lodge·ment** n.

dis·loy·al /dis'loiəl/ ▶ adj. not loyal or faithful to someone or something. ■ **dis·loy·al·ly** adv. **dis·loy·al·ty** /-tē/ n.

dis·mal /'dizməl/ ▶ adj. **1** causing or showing gloom or depression. **2** informal disgracefully bad. ■ **dis·mal·ly** adv.

dis·man·tle /dis'mantl/ ▶ v. take something to pieces. ■ **dis·man·tle·ment** n. **dis·man·tler** /-t(ə)lər/ n.

dis·mast /dis'mast/ ▶ v. break or force down the mast or masts of a ship.

dis·may /dis'mā/ ▶ n. concern and distress resulting from an unpleasant surprise. ▶ v. make someone concerned and upset.

dis·mem·ber /dis'membər/ ▶ v. **1** cut off the limbs of a person or animal. **2** divide up a territory or organization. ■ **dis·mem·bered** adj. **dis·mem·ber·ment** n.

dis·miss /dis'mis/ ▶ v. **1** order or allow someone to leave. **2** order an employee to leave a job. **3** treat as unworthy of serious consideration: *his comments were dismissed as a joke by the minister.* **4** refuse to allow a legal case to continue. ■ **dis·miss·a·ble** (also **dismissible**) adj. **dis·miss·al** n.

dis·mis·sive /dis'misiv/ ▶ adj. suggesting that something is unworthy of serious consideration. ■ **dis·mis·sive·ly** adv.

dis·mount /dis'mount/ ▶ v. get off or down from a horse or bicycle.

dis·o·be·di·ent /,disə'bēdēənt/ ▶ adj. failing or refusing to obey rules or someone in authority. ■ **dis·o·be·di·ence** n. **dis·o·be·di·ent·ly** adv.

dis·o·bey /,disə'bā/ ▶ v. fail or refuse to obey an order, rule, or person in authority.

dis·o·blig·ing /,disə'blījiNG/ ▶ adj. unwilling to help or cooperate.

dis·or·der /dis'ôrdər/ ▶ n. **1** a lack of order; confusion. **2** the breakdown of peaceful and law-abiding behavior. **3** an illness that disrupts normal physical or mental functions: *a skin disorder.* ▶ v. (usu. as adj. **disordered**) bring disorder to: *a disordered room.*

dis·or·der·ly /dis'ôrdərlē/ ▶ adj. **1** not organized or tidy. **2** involving a breakdown of peaceful and law-abiding behavior. ■ **dis·or·der·li·ness** n.

dis·or·gan·ized /dis'ôrgə,nīzd/ ▶ adj. **1** not properly planned and controlled. **2** not able to plan one's activities efficiently. ■ **dis·or·gan·i·za·tion** /-,ôrgənə'zāshən/ n.

dis·o·ri·ent /dis'ôrē,ent/ ▶ v. cause someone to lose their sense of direction or feel confused. ■ **dis·o·ri·en·ta·tion** /dis,ôrēən'tāshən/ n.

dis·o·ri·en·tate /dis'ôrēən,tāt/ ▶ v. another term for DISORIENT.

dis·own /dis'ōn/ ▶ v. refuse to have anything further to do with someone.

dis·par·age /di'sparij/ ▶ v. suggest that someone or something is worthless or unimportant. ■ **dis·par·age·ment** n. **dis·par·ag·ing** adj.

dis·pa·rate /'dispərit, di'sparit/ ▶ adj. **1** very different from one another: *no small feat, blending such disparate languages into one.* **2** containing elements very different from one another: *a culturally disparate country.*

dis·par·i·ty /di'sparitē/ ▶ n. (pl. **disparities**) a great difference.

dis·pas·sion·ate /dis'pashənit/ ▶ adj. not influenced by strong emotion; rational and impartial. ■ **dis·pas·sion** n. **dis·pas·sion·ate·ly** adv.

dis·patch /dis'pach/ ▶ v. **1** send someone or something to a destination or for a purpose. **2** deal with a task or opponent quickly and efficiently. **3** kill someone or something. ▶ n. **1** the action of dispatching someone or something. **2** an official report on government or military affairs. **3** a report sent to a newspaper by a journalist working abroad. **4** promptness and efficiency: *officials believed the problem would be resolved with dispatch.* ■ **dis·patch·er** n.

dis·pel /dis'pel/ ▶ v. (**dispels, dispelling,**

dispelled) make a doubt, feeling, or belief disappear.

dis·pen·sa·ble /dis'pensəbəl/ ▶ adj. able to be replaced or done without.

dis·pen·sa·ry /dis'pensərē/ ▶ n. (pl. **dispensaries**) a room where medicines are prepared and provided.

dis·pen·sa·tion /ˌdispən'sāsHən, -pen-/ ▶ n. 1 permission to be exempt from a rule or usual requirement. 2 the religious or political system of a particular time: *the capitalist dispensation.* 3 the action of dispensing something. ■ **dis·pen·sa·tion·al** adj.

dis·pense /dis'pens/ ▶ v. 1 distribute or supply something to a number of people. 2 (of a pharmacist) supply medicine according to a doctor's prescription. 3 (**dispense with**) get rid of or manage without: *we intend to dispense with a central heating system.* ■ **dis·pens·er** n.

dis·per·sal /dis'pərsəl/ ▶ n. 1 the spreading of things or people over a wide area. 2 the action of causing a group to go in different directions.

dis·per·sant /dis'pərsənt/ ▶ n. a liquid or gas used to disperse small particles in a medium.

dis·perse /dis'pərs/ ▶ v. 1 spread something over a wide area. 2 go in different directions: *the crowd dispersed.* 3 Physics divide light into constituents of different wavelengths.

■ **dis·pers·er** n. **dis·pers·i·ble** adj. **dis·per·sive** adj.

dis·per·sion /dis'pərzHən, -sHən/ ▶ n. the action of dispersing people or things or the state of being dispersed.

dis·pir·it /di'spirit/ ▶ v. cause someone to lose enthusiasm or hope. ■ **dis·pir·it·ed·ly** adv. **dis·pir·it·ing** adj.

dis·place /dis'plās/ ▶ v. 1 move something from its proper or usual position. 2 take over the position or role of: *drama, having been displaced by soap operas a couple of years ago, is back.* 3 (especially of war or natural disaster) force someone to leave their home.

dis·placed per·son ▶ n. a person who is forced to leave their home country because of war, persecution, or natural disaster; a refugee.

dis·place·ment /dis'plāsmənt/ ▶ n. 1 the action of displacing someone or something. 2 the amount by which something is moved from its position. 3 the volume or weight of water displaced by a floating ship, used as a measure of the ship's size.

dis·play /dis'plā/ ▶ v. 1 put something on show in a noticeable and attractive way. 2 clearly show a quality, emotion, or skill. 3 show data or an image on a screen. ▶ n. 1 a show or other event for public entertainment. 2 an act of showing something: *a public display of affection.* 3 objects, data, or images that are displayed. 4 an electronic device for displaying data.

dis·please /dis'plēz/ ▶ v. annoy or upset someone. ■ **dis·pleased** adj. **dis·pleas·ing** adj.

dis·pleas·ure /dis'plezHər/ ▶ n. a feeling of annoyance or dissatisfaction.

dis·port /dis'pôrt/ ▶ v. (**disport oneself**) old use enjoy oneself unrestrainedly; frolic.

dis·pos·a·ble /dis'pōzəbəl/ ▶ adj. 1 (of an article) intended to be used once and then thrown away. 2 (of financial assets) available to be used when required. ▶ n. a disposable article.

■ **dis·pos·a·bil·i·ty** /-ˌpōzə'bilitē/ n.

dis·pos·a·ble in·come ▶ n. income remaining after deduction of taxes and other compulsory charges, available to be spent or saved as one wishes.

dis·pos·al /dis'pōzəl/ ▶ n. the action of disposing or getting rid of something.

– PHRASES **at one's disposal** available for one to use whenever or however one wishes.

dis·pose /dis'pōz/ ▶ v. 1 (**dispose of**) get rid of something by throwing it away or by giving or selling it to someone. 2 (**dispose of**) overcome a rival, problem, or threat. 3 (usu. **be disposed to**) make someone likely to do or think something: *I am not disposed to argue about it.* 4 (as adj. **disposed**) having a specified attitude: *he was never favorably disposed toward Hitler.* 5 arrange people or things in a particular way. ■ **dis·pos·er** n.

dis·po·si·tion /ˌdispə'zisHən/ ▶ n. 1 a person's natural qualities of mind and character. 2 an inclination or tendency to do something. 3 the way in which people or things are arranged.

dis·pos·sess /ˌdispə'zes/ ▶ v. deprive someone of land or property. ■ **dis·pos·ses·sion** n.

dis·proof /dis'prōōf/ ▶ n. evidence that something is untrue.

dis·pro·por·tion /ˌdisprə'pôrsHən/ ▶ n. a state of inequality between two things.

■ **dis·pro·por·tion·al** adj. **dis·pro·por·tion·al·ly** adv.

dis·pro·por·tion·ate /ˌdisprə'pôrsHənit/ ▶ adj. too large or too small in comparison with something else. ■ **dis·pro·por·tion·ate·ly** adv.

dis·prove /dis'prōōv/ ▶ v. prove that something is false.

dis·put·a·ble /dis'pyōōtəbəl/ ▶ adj. open to question.

dis·pu·ta·tion /ˌdispyōō'tāsHən/ ▶ n. debate or argument.

dis·pu·ta·tious /ˌdispyōō'tāsHəs/ ▶ adj. fond of having arguments.

dis·pute /dis'pyōōt/ ▶ v. 1 argue about something. 2 question whether a statement or fact is true or valid. 3 compete for: *the two drivers crashed while disputing the lead.* ▶ n. 1 an argument or disagreement. 2 a disagreement between management and employees that leads to industrial action. ■ **dis·pu·tant** /-'pyōōtnt/ n.

dis·qual·i·fy /dis'kwälə,fī/ ▶ v. (**disqualifies, disqualifying, disqualified**) prevent someone from performing an activity or taking up a job because they have broken a law or rule or are unsuitable: *he was disqualified from being a company director.* ■ **dis·qual·i·fi·ca·tion** /dis,kwäləfi'kāsHən/ n.

dis·qui·et /dis'kwī-it/ ▶ n. a feeling of worry or unease. ▶ v. make someone worried or uneasy. ■ **dis·qui·et·ing** adj. **dis·qui·e·tude** /dis'kwī-i,t(y)ōōd/ n.

dis·qui·si·tion /ˌdiskwə'zisHən/ ▶ n. a long or complex discussion of a topic in speech or writing.

dis·re·gard /ˌdisri'gärd/ ▶ v. fail to consider or pay attention to someone or something. ▶ n. lack of attention or consideration: *they have shown utter disregard for customers.*

dis·re·pair /ˌdisri'pe(ə)r/ ▶ n. poor condition due to neglect.

dis·rep·u·ta·ble /dis'repyətəbəl/ ▶ adj. not respectable in appearance or character.

dis·re·pute /ˌdisrə'pyōōt/ ▶ n. the state of having a bad reputation: *he was accused of bringing football into disrepute.*

dis·re·spect /ˌdisriˈspekt/ ▶ n. lack of respect or courtesy. ▶ v. informal show a lack of respect for someone or something. ■ **dis·re·spect·ful** adj. **dis·re·spect·ful·ly** adv.

dis·robe /disˈrōb/ ▶ v. take off one's clothes.

dis·rupt /disˈrəpt/ ▶ v. interrupt the normal operation of an activity or process. ■ **dis·rupt·er** (also **disruptor**) n. **dis·rup·tion** /-ˈrəpsHən/ n.

dis·rup·tive /disˈrəptiv/ ▶ adj. disturbing or interrupting the normal operation of something.

diss ▶ v. variant spelling of DIS.

dis·sat·is·fac·tion /disˌsatisˈfaksHən/ ▶ n. lack of satisfaction.

dis·sat·is·fied /disˈsatisˌfīd/ ▶ adj. not content or happy.

dis·sect /diˈsekt, dī-/ ▶ v. **1** methodically cut up a body or plant in order to study its internal parts. **2** analyze something in great detail. **3** (as adj. **dissected**) technical divided into separate parts. ■ **dis·sec·tion** n. **dis·sec·tor** n.

dis·sem·ble /diˈsembəl/ ▶ v. hide or disguise one's true motives or feelings. ■ **dis·sem·bler** n.

dis·sem·i·nate /diˈseməˌnāt/ ▶ v. spread something, especially information, widely. ■ **dis·sem·i·na·tion** /-ˌseməˈnāsHən/ n. **dis·sem·i·na·tor** n.

dis·sen·sion /diˈsensHən/ ▶ n. disagreement that causes trouble within a group.

dis·sent /diˈsent/ ▶ v. **1** express disagreement with an official or widely held view. **2** disagree with the doctrine of an established or orthodox church. ▶ n. disagreement with an official or widely held view.

dis·sent·er /diˈsentər/ ▶ n. **1** a person who disagrees with a widely held view. **2** (**Dissenter**) Brit. historical a member of a nonestablished Church; a Nonconformist.

dis·ser·ta·tion /ˌdisərˈtāsHən/ ▶ n. a long essay, especially one written for a university degree.

dis·serv·ice /disˈsərvis/ ▶ n. a harmful action.

dis·si·dent /ˈdisidənt/ ▶ n. a person who opposes official policy. ▶ adj. opposing official policy. ■ **dis·si·dence** /ˈdisidəns/ n.

dis·sim·i·lar /disˈsimilər/ ▶ adj. not similar; different: *two seemingly dissimilar ideas*. ■ **dis·sim·i·lar·i·ty** /-ˌsiməˈlaritē/ n.

dis·sim·u·late /diˈsimyəˌlāt/ ▶ v. hide or disguise one's thoughts or feelings. ■ **dis·sim·u·la·tion** /-ˌsimyəˈlāsHən/ n.

dis·si·pate /ˈdisəˌpāt/ ▶ v. **1** disperse or disappear: *his anger seemed to dissipate*. **2** waste money, energy, or resources. ■ **dis·si·pa·tive** /-ˌpātiv/ adj. **dis·si·pa·tor** n.

dis·si·pat·ed /ˈdisəˌpātid/ ▶ adj. indulging excessively in sex, drinking alcohol, and similar activities.

dis·si·pa·tion /ˌdisəˈpāsHən/ ▶ n. **1** dissipated living. **2** the action of dissipating something.

dis·so·ci·ate /diˈsōsHēˌāt, -ˈsōsē-/ ▶ v. **1** disconnect or separate something from something else. **2** (**dissociate oneself from**) declare that one is not connected with someone or something. ■ **dis·so·ci·a·tion** /diˌsōsēˈāsHən/ n. **dis·so·ci·a·tive** /-ˌātiv, -sHətiv/ adj.

dis·sol·u·ble /diˈsälyəbəl/ ▶ adj. able to be dissolved, loosened, or disconnected.

dis·so·lute /ˈdisəˌlōōt/ ▶ adj. indulging in immoral activities.

dis·so·lu·tion /ˌdisəˈlōōsHən/ ▶ n. **1** the formal closing down or ending of an official body or agreement. **2** the action of dissolving or decomposing. **3** immoral living.

dis·solve /diˈzälv/ ▶ v. **1** (of a solid) disperse into a liquid so as to form a solution. **2** close down, dismiss, or end an assembly or agreement. **3** (**dissolve into/in**) give way to strong emotion. ■ **dis·solv·a·ble** adj.

dis·so·nant /ˈdisənənt/ ▶ adj. lacking harmony; discordant. ■ **dis·so·nance** n.

dis·suade /diˈswād/ ▶ v. (**dissuade someone from**) persuade or advise someone not to do something. ■ **dis·sua·sion** /-ˈswāZHən/ n. **dis·sua·sive** /-ˈswāsiv/ adj.

dis·taff /ˈdistaf/ ▶ n. a stick or spindle onto which wool or flax is wound for spinning.
– PHRASES **the distaff side** the female side of a family.

dis·tal /ˈdistl/ ▶ adj. chiefly Anatomy situated away from the center of the body or from the point of attachment. The opposite of PROXIMAL. ■ **dis·tal·ly** adv.

dis·tance /ˈdistəns/ ▶ n. **1** the length of the space between two points. **2** the state of being distant or remote: *they are separated by decades and by distance*. **3** a far-off point or place. **4** an interval of time. **5** the full length or time of a race or other contest. ▶ v. **1** make someone or something far off or remote. **2** (**distance oneself from**) declare that one is not connected with someone or something.

dis·tance learn·ing ▶ n. a method of studying in which lectures are broadcast and lessons are conducted by correspondence or over the Internet.

dis·tant /ˈdistənt/ ▶ adj. **1** far away in space or time. **2** at a specified distance: *the town lay half a mile distant*. **3** far apart in resemblance or relationship: *a distant acquaintance*. **4** aloof or reserved. ■ **dis·tant·ly** adv.

dis·taste /disˈtāst/ ▶ n. dislike or mild hostility.

dis·taste·ful /disˈtāstfəl/ ▶ adj. unpleasant or disagreeable. ■ **dis·taste·ful·ly** adv. **dis·taste·ful·ness** n.

dis·tem·per /disˈtempər/ ▶ n. **1** a kind of paint made of powdered pigment mixed with glue or size, used on walls. **2** a disease affecting dogs, causing fever and coughing. ▶ v. paint something with distemper.

dis·tend /disˈtend/ ▶ v. swell because of internal pressure. ■ **dis·tend·ed** adj. **dis·ten·si·bil·i·ty** /-ˌtensəˈbilitē/ n. **dis·ten·si·ble** /-ˈtensəbəl/ adj. **dis·ten·sion** /-ˈtensHən/ n.

dis·till /disˈtil/ (Brit. **distil**) ▶ v. **1** purify a liquid by heating it so that it vaporizes, then cooling and condensing the vapor and collecting the resulting liquid. **2** make liquor by distilling. **3** extract the most important aspects of: *he distilled their comments into two-page summaries*. ■ **dis·til·la·tion** /ˌdistəˈlāsHən/ n. **dis·till·er** n.

dis·til·late /ˈdistilit, -ˌlāt/ ▶ n. a substance formed by distillation.

dis·till·er·y /disˈtilərē/ ▶ n. (pl. **distilleries**) a place where liquor is manufactured.

dis·tinct /disˈtiNGkt/ ▶ adj. **1** recognizably different. **2** able to be perceived clearly by the senses: *a distinct smell of vinegar*. ■ **dis·tinct·ly** adv. **dis·tinct·ness** n.

dis·tinc·tion /disˈtiNGksHən/ ▶ n. **1** a noticeable difference or contrast. **2** the separation of people or things into different groups. **3** outstanding excellence. **4** a special honor or recognition.

dis·tinc·tive /dis'tiNGktiv/ ▶ adj. characteristic of a person or thing, so making it different from others: *a coffee with a distinctive caramel flavor.* ■ **dis·tinc·tive·ly** adv. **dis·tinc·tive·ness** n.

dis·tin·guish /dis'tiNGgwish/ ▶ v. **1** recognize or treat someone or something as different. **2** manage to see or hear something barely perceptible. **3** be a distinctive characteristic of: *what distinguishes sports from games?* **4** (**distinguish oneself**) do something very well. ■ **dis·tin·guish·a·ble** adj.

dis·tin·guished /dis'tiNGgwisht/ ▶ adj. **1** very successful and greatly respected. **2** dignified in appearance.

dis·tort /dis'tôrt/ ▶ v. **1** pull or twist something out of shape. **2** give a misleading account of something. **3** change the form of an electrical signal or sound wave during transmission or amplification. ■ **dis·tort·ed** adj. **dis·tor·tion** /-'tôrsHən/ n.

dis·tract /dis'trakt/ ▶ v. **1** prevent someone from concentrating on something. **2** divert attention from something. ■ **dis·tract·ed** adj. **dis·tract·ing** adj.

dis·trac·tion /dis'traksHən/ ▶ n. **1** a thing that distracts someone's attention. **2** an activity that provides entertainment. **3** mental agitation: *he loved her to distraction.*

dis·trait /dis'trā/ ▶ adj. distracted; absentminded.

dis·traught /dis'trôt/ ▶ adj. very worried and upset.

dis·tress /dis'tres/ ▶ n. **1** great anxiety, sorrow, or difficulty. **2** the state of a ship or aircraft when in danger or difficulty. **3** a state of physical strain, especially difficulty in breathing. ▶ v. **1** make someone very worried or upset. **2** give furniture or clothing artificial marks of age and wear. ■ **dis·tressed** adj. **dis·tress·ful** adj. **dis·tress·ing** adj.

dis·trib·u·tar·y /dis'tribyōō,terē/ ▶ n. (pl. **distributaries**) a branch of a river that does not return to the main stream after leaving it, as in a delta.

dis·trib·ute /dis'tribyōōt/ ▶ v. **1** hand out or give shares of something to a number of people. **2** (**be distributed**) be spread over an area. **3** supply goods to retailers. ■ **dis·trib·ut·a·ble** adj.

dis·tri·bu·tion /,distrə'byōōsHən/ ▶ n. **1** the action of distributing something. **2** the way in which something is shared among a group or spread over an area: *the uneven distribution of wealth.* ■ **dis·tri·bu·tion·al** adj.

dis·tri·bu·tive /dis'tribyətiv/ ▶ adj. relating to distribution or things that are distributed.

dis·trib·u·tor /dis'tribyətər/ ▶ n. **1** an agent who supplies goods to retailers. **2** a device in a gasoline engine for passing electric current to each spark plug in turn.

dis·trict /'distrikt/ ▶ n. an area of a town or region, regarded as a unit for administrative purposes or because of a particular feature: *the central business district.* ▶ v. divide into districts.

dis·trict at·tor·ney ▶ n. a public official who acts as prosecutor for the government in a particular district.

dis·tro /'distrō/ ▶ n. Computing **1** a distribution, especially of Linux software or of webzines. **2** a particular distributable or distributed version of Linux software.

dis·trust /dis'trəst/ ▶ n. the feeling that someone or something cannot be relied on. ▶ v. have little trust in someone or something. ■ **dis·trust·ful** adj. **dis·trust·ful·ly** adv.

dis·turb /dis'tərb/ ▶ v. **1** interfere with the normal arrangement or functioning of something. **2** interrupt the sleep, relaxation, or privacy of someone. **3** make someone anxious. ■ **dis·turb·ing** adj.

dis·tur·bance /dis'tərbəns/ ▶ n. **1** the interruption or disruption of a settled or normal condition: *precautions can be taken to minimize wildlife disturbance.* **2** a breakdown of peaceful behavior; a riot.

dis·turbed /dis'tərbd/ ▶ adj. having emotional or psychological problems.

di·sul·fide /dī'səl,fīd/ ▶ n. Chemistry a sulfide containing two atoms of sulfur in its molecule or empirical formula.

dis·un·ion /dis'yōōnyən/ ▶ n. the breaking up of something such as a federation.

dis·u·nit·ed /,disyōō'nītid/ ▶ adj. lacking unity or agreement. ■ **dis·u·ni·ty** /dis'yōōnitē/ n.

dis·use /dis'yōōs/ ▶ n. the state of not being used. ■ **dis·used** /dis'yōōzd/ adj.

di·syl·la·ble /dī'siləbəl, di-/ ▶ n. Poetry a word or metrical foot consisting of two syllables. ■ **di·syl·lab·ic** /,dīsi'labik, di-/ adj.

ditch /dicH/ ▶ n. a narrow channel dug to hold or carry water. ▶ v. **1** informal abandon or get rid of: *she had recently been ditched by her boyfriend.* **2** (with reference to an aircraft) bring or come down in a forced landing on the sea. **3** provide a place with a ditch.

dith·er /'diTHər/ ▶ v. be indecisive. ▶ n. informal a state of agitation or indecision. ■ **dith·er·er** n. **dith·er·y** adj.

dith·y·ramb /'diTHə,ram/ ▶ n. (in ancient Greece) an ecstatic choral hymn dedicated to the god Dionysus. ■ **dith·y·ram·bic** /,diTHə'rambik/ adj.

dit·to /'ditō/ ▶ n. **1** the same thing again (used in lists and often indicated by a ditto mark). **2** (also **ditto mark**) a symbol consisting of two apostrophes (") placed under an item to be repeated.

dit·ty /'ditē/ ▶ n. (pl. **ditties**) a short simple song.

ditz /dits/ ▶ n. informal a scatterbrained person.

dit·zy /'ditsē/ (also **ditsy**) ▶ adj. informal silly or scatterbrained. ■ **dit·zi·ness** n.

di·u·ret·ic /,dīyə'retik/ ▶ adj. causing an increase in the flow of urine. ▶ n. a diuretic drug.

di·ur·nal /dī'ərnl/ ▶ adj. **1** of or during the daytime. **2** daily; of each day. ■ **di·ur·nal·ly** adv.

di·va /'dēvə/ ▶ n. **1** a famous female opera singer. **2** a haughty, spoiled woman.

Di·va·li ▶ n. variant spelling of DIWALI.

di·van /di'van, 'dī,van/ ▶ n. a long, low sofa without a back or arms.

dive /dīv/ ▶ v. (past and past part. **dived** or **dove** /dōv/) **1** plunge head first and with arms outstretched into water. **2** go to a deeper level in water. **3** swim under water using breathing equipment. **4** plunge steeply downward through the air. **5** move quickly or suddenly: *he dived into the bushes.* ▶ n. **1** an act of diving. **2** informal a disreputable nightclub or bar.

dive-bomb ▶ v. **1** bomb a target while diving steeply in an aircraft. **2** (of a bird or flying insect) attack something by swooping down on it. ■ **dive-bomb·er** n.

div·er /'dīvər/ ▶ n. **1** a person who dives under water as a sport or as part of their work. **2** a large diving waterbird with a straight pointed bill.

di·verge /dī'vərj, dī-/ ▶ v. **1** (of a road or route) separate from another route and go in a different direction. **2** (of opinions, theories, etc.) be different from one another. **3** (**diverge from**) depart from a particular pattern or standard: *individuals may well diverge from the norm.* ■ **di·ver·gence** n. **di·verg·ing** adj.

di·ver·gent /dī'vərjənt, dī-/ ▶ adj. different.

di·vers /'dīvərz/ ▶ adj. old use or literary of many different kinds.

di·verse /dī'vərs, dī-/ ▶ adj. widely varied: *people from diverse backgrounds.* ■ **di·verse·ly** adv.

di·ver·si·fy /dī'vərsi,fī, dī-/ ▶ v. (**diversifies**, **diversifying**, **diversified**) **1** make or become more varied. **2** (of a company) enlarge or vary its range of products or field of operation. ■ **di·ver·si·fi·ca·tion** /-,vərsifi'kāsHən/ n.

di·ver·sion /dī'vərzHən, dī-/ ▶ n. **1** an instance of diverting something. **2** something intended to distract attention: *a raid was carried out at the airfield to create a diversion.* **3** a pastime or pleasant activity. ■ **di·ver·sion·ar·y** /-,nerē/ adj.

di·ver·si·ty /dī'vərsitē, dī-/ ▶ n. (pl. **diversities**) **1** the state of being varied. **2** a variety of things.

di·vert /dī'vərt, dī-/ ▶ v. **1** change the direction or course of: *traffic was diverted from the highway.* **2** distract someone or their attention. **3** amuse or entertain someone. ■ **di·vert·ing** adj.

di·ver·tic·u·li·tis /,dīvər,tikyə'lītis/ ▶ n. inflammation of a diverticulum in the alimentary tract, causing abdominal pain and diarrhea or constipation.

di·ver·tic·u·lum /,dīvər'tikyələm/ ▶ n. (pl. **diverticula** /-lə/) an abnormal sac or pouch formed in the wall of the alimentary tract.

di·ver·ti·men·to /di,vərtə'mentō/ ▶ n. (pl. **divertimenti** /-'mentē/ or **divertimentos**) a light and entertaining piece of music.

di·ver·tisse·ment /dī'vərtismənt/ ▶ n. a minor entertainment.

di·vest /dī'vest, dī-/ ▶ v. **1** (**divest someone/ thing of**) deprive someone or something of: *he was divested of his property.* **2** (**divest oneself of**) remove or get rid of: *he divested himself of his jacket.*

di·vide /dī'vīd/ ▶ v. **1** separate something into parts. **2** share something out: *the house was sold and the money divided between us.* **3** cause disagreement between people or groups: *the issue has divided the community.* **4** form a boundary between two areas. **5** find how many times a number contains another. **6** (of a lawmaking assembly) separate into two groups for voting. ▶ n. a wide difference between two groups: *the North–South divide.*

div·i·dend /'divi,dend/ ▶ n. **1** a sum of money that is divided among a number of people, such as the part of a company's profits paid to its shareholders. **2** (**dividends**) benefits gained from something: *the policy would pay dividends in the future.* **3** Mathematics a number to be divided by another number.

di·vid·er /dī'vīdər/ ▶ n. **1** a screen or piece of furniture that divides a room into two separate parts. **2** (**dividers**) a measuring compass.

div·i·na·tion /,divə'nāsHən/ ▶ n. the use of supernatural means to find out about the future or the unknown. ■ **di·vin·a·to·ry** /dī'vinə,tôrē/ adj.

di·vine¹ /dī'vīn/ ▶ adj. (**diviner, divinest**) **1** relating to, from, or like God or a god. **2** informal excellent. ▶ n. **1** dated a priest, religious leader, or theologian. **2** (**the Divine**) providence or God. ■ **di·vine·ly** adv.

di·vine² ▶ v. **1** discover something by guesswork or intuition. **2** have supernatural insight into the future. **3** search for underground water or minerals using a pointer that is supposedly moved by unseen influences. ■ **di·vin·er** n.

div·ing bell ▶ n. an open-bottomed chamber supplied with air, in which a person can be let down under water.

div·ing board ▶ n. a board projecting over a swimming pool or other body of water, from which people dive or jump in.

div·ing suit ▶ n. a watertight suit, typically with a helmet and an air supply, worn for working or exploring deep under water.

di·vin·ing rod ▶ n. a forked stick or rod supposed to move when held over ground in which water or minerals can be found.

di·vin·i·ty /dī'vinitē/ ▶ n. (pl. **divinities**) **1** the state or quality of being divine. **2** a god or goddess. **3** (**the Divinity**) God. **4** the study of religion; theology.

di·vis·i·ble /dī'vizəbəl/ ▶ adj. **1** capable of being divided. **2** (of a number) containing another number a number of times without a remainder. ■ **di·vis·i·bil·i·ty** /-,vizə'bilitē/ n.

di·vi·sion /dī'vizHən/ ▶ n. **1** the action of dividing something or the state of being divided. **2** each of the parts into which something is divided. **3** a major unit or section of an organization. **4** a number of teams or players grouped together in a sport for competitive purposes. **5** a partition that divides two groups or things. ■ **di·vi·sion·al** /dī'vizHənl/ adj.

di·vi·sion sign ▶ n. the sign ÷, placed between two numbers showing that the first is to be divided by the second, as in $6 ÷ 3 = 2$.

di·vi·sive /dī'vīsiv/ ▶ adj. causing disagreement or hostility between people or groups. ■ **di·vi·sive·ness** n.

di·vi·sor /dī'vīzər/ ▶ n. Mathematics a number by which another number is to be divided.

di·vorce /dī'vôrs/ ▶ n. the legal ending of a marriage. ▶ v. **1** legally end one's marriage with one's husband or wife. **2** (**divorce someone/ thing from**) detach or separate someone or something from: *religion cannot be divorced from morality.*

di·vor·cée /divôr'sā, -'sē/ ▶ n. a divorced woman.

div·ot /'divət/ ▶ n. a piece of turf cut out of the ground, especially by a golf club in making a stroke.

di·vulge /dī'vəlj, dī-/ ▶ v. reveal information that is meant to be private or secret.

div·vy /'divē/ ▶ v. (**divvies, divvying, divvied**) informal divide up and share.

Di·wa·li /di'wälē/ (also **Divali**) ▶ n. a Hindu festival held in October and November and celebrated with lights.

Dix·ie /'diksē/ ▶ n. an informal name for the southern states of the US.

Dix·ie·land /'diksē,land/ ▶ n. a kind of jazz with a strong two-beat rhythm.

diz·zy /'dizē/ ▶ adj. (**dizzier, dizziest**) **1** having a sensation of spinning around and losing one's balance. **2** informal (of a woman) silly but attractive. ▶ v. (**dizzies, dizzying, dizzied**) make someone feel unsteady, confused, or amazed. ■ **diz·zi·ly** adv. **diz·zi·ness** n.

DJ /'dēˌjā/ ▶ n. **1** a person who introduces and plays recorded pop music on the radio or at a nightclub or private party; a disc jockey. **2** a person who uses samples of recorded music to make techno or rap music. ▶ v. (**DJ's, DJ'ing, DJ'd**) perform as a DJ.

djel·la·ba /jə'läbə/ (also **djellabah** or **jellaba**) ▶ n. a loose woolen hooded cloak of a kind traditionally worn by Arabs.

Dji·bou·ti·an /jə'bōōtēən/ ▶ n. a person from Djibouti, a country on the northeast coast of Africa. ▶ adj. relating to Djibouti.

djinn /jin/ ▶ n. (pl. same or **djinns**) (in Arabian and Muslim mythology) an intelligent spirit able to appear in human or animal form.

DL ▶ abbr. **1** Football defensive lineman. **2** disabled list.

dl ▶ abbr. deciliter(s).

DM (also **D-mark**) ▶ abbr. Deutschmark.

dm ▶ abbr. decimeter(s).

DMA ▶ abbr. Computing direct memory access.

DMZ ▶ abbr. demilitarized zone, an area from which warring parties agree to remove their military forces.

DNA ▶ n. deoxyribonucleic acid, a substance carrying genetic information that is present in the cell nuclei of nearly all living organisms.

DNA fin·ger·print·ing (also **DNA profiling**) ▶ n. another term for GENETIC FINGERPRINTING.

do[1] /dōō/ ▶ v. (**does** /dəz/; past **did** /did/; past part. **done** /dən/) **1** carry out or complete an action, duty, or task. **2** act or progress in a particular way: *the team did well.* **3** work on something to bring it to a required state: *she's doing her hair.* **4** have a particular result or effect on: *the walk will do me good.* **5** work at for a living or take as one's subject of study: *what does she do?* **6** make or provide something. **7** be suitable or acceptable: *he'll do.* **8** (**be/have done with**) stop being concerned about someone or something. ▶ auxiliary v. **1** used before a verb in questions and negative statements. **2** used to refer back to a verb already mentioned: *he looks better than he did before.* **3** used in commands, or to give emphasis to a positive verb: *do sit down.* ▶ n. (pl. **dos** or **do's**) **1** informal a party or other social event. **2** informal a hairdo. ■ **do·a·ble** /'dōōəbəl/ (informal) adj. **do·er** n.

– PHRASES **can/could do with** would find useful or would like. **do away with** informal put an end to; kill. **do for 1** informal defeat, ruin, or kill. **2** be good enough for. **do someone in** informal kill someone. **dos and don'ts** rules of behavior. **do time** informal spend a period of time in prison. **do something up 1** fasten or wrap something. **2** informal renovate or redecorate a building or room.

do[2] /dō/ ▶ n. Music the first note of a major scale, coming before 're.'

DOA ▶ abbr. dead on arrival, used to describe a person who is declared dead immediately upon arrival at a hospital.

Do·ber·man /'dōbərmən/ (also **Dobermann** or **Doberman pinscher** /'pinsHər/) ▶ n. a large breed of dog with powerful jaws, typically black with tan markings.

doc /däk/ ▶ abbr. informal doctor.

do·cent /'dōsənt/ ▶ n. **1** (in certain colleges and universities) a member of the teaching staff

immediately below professor in rank. **2** a guide in a museum, art gallery, or zoo.

doc·ile /'däsəl/ ▶ adj. willing to accept control or instruction; submissive. ■ **doc·ile·ly** adv. **do·cil·i·ty** /dä'silitē/ n.

dock[1] /däk/ ▶ n. **1** a structure extending alongshore or out from the shore into a body of water, to which boats may be moored. **2** an enclosed area of water in a port for the loading, unloading, and repair of ships. **3** (also **loading dock**) a platform for loading trucks or freight trains. ▶ v. **1** (with reference to a ship) come or bring into a dock. **2** (of a spacecraft) join with a space station or another spacecraft in space. **3** attach a piece of equipment to another.

dock[2] ▶ n. the enclosure in a criminal court where a defendant stands or sits.

dock[3] ▶ n. a weed with broad leaves, popularly used to relieve nettle stings.

dock[4] ▶ v. **1** deduct money or a point in a game. **2** cut an animal's tail short.

dock·er /'däkər/ ▶ n. another term for LONGSHOREMAN.

dock·et /'däkit/ ▶ n. **1** a calendar or list of cases awaiting action in a court. **2** a document or label listing the contents of a package or delivery. ▶ v. (**dockets, docketing, docketed**) **1** enter (a case) in a court calendar. **2** mark a package with a label or document listing the contents.

dock·ing sta·tion ▶ n. a device to which a portable computer is connected so that it can be used like a desktop computer.

dock·side /'däkˌsīd/ ▶ n. the area immediately next to a dock.

dock·yard /'däkˌyärd/ ▶ n. an area with docks and equipment for repairing and maintaining ships.

doc·tor /'däktər/ ▶ n. **1** a person who is qualified to practice medicine. **2** (**Doctor**) a person who holds the highest university degree. ▶ v. **1** change something in order to deceive other people: *the technical data had been doctored.* **2** add a harmful or strong ingredient to food or drink.

– PHRASES **be what the doctor ordered** informal be beneficial or desirable.

doc·tor·al /'däktərəl/ ▶ adj. relating to a doctorate.

doc·tor·ate /'däktərit/ ▶ n. the highest degree awarded by a graduate school or other educational institution.

Doc·tor of Phi·los·o·phy ▶ n. a person holding a doctorate in any subject except law, medicine, or sometimes theology.

doc·tri·naire /ˌdäktrə'ner/ ▶ adj. very strict in applying beliefs or principles.

doc·trine /'däktrin/ ▶ n. a set of beliefs or principles held and taught by a Church, political party, or other group. ■ **doc·tri·nal** /'däktrənl/ adj. **doc·tri·nal·ly** adv.

doc·u·dra·ma /'däkyəˌdrämə/ ▶ n. a television movie based on a dramatized version of real events.

doc·u·ment ▶ n. /'däkyəmənt/ a piece of written, printed, or electronic matter that provides information or evidence. ▶ v. /'däkyəˌment/ record something in written, photographic, or other form.

doc·u·men·ta·ry /ˌdäkyə'mentərē/ ▶ n. (pl. **documentaries**) a movie or television or radio program giving a factual account of something, using film, photographs, and sound recordings of real events. ▶ adj. consisting of documents and other material providing a factual account of something: *documentary evidence.*

doc·u·men·ta·tion /ˌdäkyəmenˈtāsHən/ ▶ n. **1** documents providing official information or evidence. **2** written specifications or instructions.

dod·der /ˈdädər/ ▶ v. be slow and unsteady. ■ **dod·der·er** n. **dod·der·ing** adj. **dod·der·y** adj.

dod·dle /ˈdädl/ ▶ n. Brit. informal a very easy task.

do·dec·a·gon /dōˈdekəˌgän/ ▶ n. a plane figure with twelve straight sides and angles.

do·dec·a·he·dron /dōˌdekəˈhēdrən/ ▶ n. (pl. **dodecahedra** /-drə/ or **dodecahedrons**) a three-dimensional shape having twelve plane faces.

dodge /däj/ ▶ v. **1** avoid someone or something by making a sudden quick movement. **2** cunningly avoid doing or paying something. ▶ n. **1** an act of dodging someone or something. **2** informal a cunning trick, especially one used to avoid something.

dodg·er /ˈdäjər/ ▶ n. informal a person who avoids doing or paying something: *a tax dodger.*

dodg·y /ˈdäjē/ ▶ adj. (**dodgier, dodgiest**) Brit. informal **1** dishonest. **2** risky. **3** not working well or in good condition.

do·do /ˈdōdō/ ▶ n. (pl. **dodos** or **dodoes**) **1** a large extinct flightless bird formerly found on Mauritius. **2** informal an old-fashioned or ineffective person or thing.

DOE ▶ abbr. Department of Energy.

doe /dō/ ▶ n. **1** a female deer or reindeer. **2** a female hare, rabbit, rat, ferret, or kangaroo.

doe-eyed ▶ adj. having large, gentle, dark eyes.

do·er /ˈdōər/ ▶ n. **1** the person who does something: *the doer of the action.* **2** a person who acts rather than merely talking or thinking.

does /dəz/ ▶ third person singular present of DO¹.

does·n't /ˈdəzənt/ ▶ contr. does not.

doff /däf, dôf/ ▶ v. remove an item of clothing, especially a hat.

dog /dôg/ ▶ n. **1** a domesticated carnivorous mammal kept as a pet or used for work or hunting. **2** any member of the dog family, which includes the wolf, fox, coyote, jackal, and other species. **3** the male of an animal of the dog family. **4** informal, derogatory a woman regarded as unattractive. **5** dated a person of a particular kind: *you lucky dog!* ▶ v. (**dogs, dogging, dogged**) **1** follow someone closely and persistently. **2** cause continual trouble for: *he was dogged by ill health in later years.*
– PHRASES **dog eat dog** used to describe an extremely competitive situation in which people are willing to harm each other in order to succeed. **go to the dogs** informal get into a very bad state.

dog col·lar ▶ n. informal a clerical collar.

dog days ▶ pl.n. chiefly literary the hottest period of the year (formerly calculated from the first time Sirius, the Dog Star, rose at the same time as the sun).

doge /dōj/ ▶ n. historical the chief magistrate of Venice or Genoa.

dog-eared ▶ adj. having worn or battered corners.

dog·fight /ˈdôgˌfīt/ ▶ n. **1** a close combat between military aircraft. **2** a ferocious struggle or fight. ■ **dog·fight·ing** n.

dog·fish /ˈdôgˌfisH/ ▶ n. (pl. same or **dogfishes**)

a small shark with a long tail, living close to the seabed.

dog·ged /ˈdôgid/ ▶ adj. very persistent. ■ **dog·ged·ly** adv. **dog·ged·ness** n.

dog·ger·el /ˈdôgərəl, ˈdäg-/ ▶ n. badly written poetry, often intended to be amusing.

dog·gie ▶ n. variant spelling of DOGGY.

dog·gone /ˈdôgˈgôn/ ▶ adj. informal used to express surprise, annoyance, or pleasure.

dog·gy /ˈdôgē/ ▶ adj. **1** relating to or like a dog. **2** fond of dogs. ▶ n. (also **doggie**) (pl. **doggies**) a child's word for a dog.

dog·gy bag ▶ n. a bag used to take home food left uneaten after a meal in a restaurant.

dog·house /ˈdôgˌhous/ ▶ n. a dog's kennel.
– PHRASES **in the doghouse** informal having annoyed or displeased someone.

dog·leg /ˈdôgˌleg/ ▶ n. **1** a sharp bend in a road. **2** Golf a hole at which the player cannot aim directly at the green from the tee.

dog·ma /ˈdôgmə/ ▶ n. a principle or set of principles laid down by an authority and intended to be accepted without question.

dog·mat·ic /dôgˈmatik/ ▶ adj. forcefully putting forward one's own beliefs or opinions and unwilling to accept those of other people. ■ **dog·mat·i·cal·ly** /-ik(ə)lē/ adv. **dog·ma·tism** /ˈdôgməˌtizəm/ n. **dog·ma·tist** n.

do-good·er /ˈdōōˌgoŏdər/ ▶ n. a well-meaning but unrealistic or interfering person.

dog pad·dle ▶ n. a simple swimming stroke resembling that of a dog. ▶ v. (**dog-paddle**) swim using this stroke.

dog·sled /ˈdôgˌsled/ ▶ n. a sled designed to be pulled by dogs.

Dog Star ▶ n. Sirius, the brightest star in the sky.

dog tag ▶ n. **1** a metal tag attached to a dog's collar, typically giving its name and owner's address. **2** informal a soldier's metal identity tag, worn on a chain around the neck.

dog-tired ▶ adj. extremely tired.

dog·wood /ˈdôgˌwoŏd/ ▶ n. a flowering shrub or small tree with hard wood, red stems, and colorful berries.

doh ▶ exclam. variant spelling of DUH.

doi·ly /ˈdoilē/ ▶ n. (pl. **doilies**) a small ornamental mat made of lace or paper.

do·ing /ˈdōōiNG/ ▶ n. **1** (also **doings**) a person's actions or activities. **2** effort: *it would take some doing to calm him down.*

do-it-your·self ▶ adj. (of work, especially building, painting, or decorating) done or to be done by an amateur at home.

do·jo /ˈdōˌjō/ ▶ n. (pl. **dojos**) a place in which judo and other martial arts are practiced.

Dol·by /ˈdōlbē, ˈdôl-/ ▶ n. trademark **1** a noise-reduction system used in tape recording. **2** an electronic system providing stereophonic sound for movie theaters and televisions.

dol·ce vi·ta /ˌdōlcHä ˈvētə/ ▶ n. a life of pleasure and luxury.

dol·drums /ˈdōldrəmz, ˈdäl-, ˈdôl-/ ▶ pl.n. (**the doldrums**) **1** a state of inactivity or depression. **2** a region of the Atlantic Ocean with calms, sudden storms, and unpredictable winds.

dole /dōl/ ▶ n. (often in phrase **on the dole**) registered as unemployed and receiving benefits from the government. ▶ v. (**dole something out**) distribute something.

dole·ful /ˈdōlfəl/ ▶ adj. **1** sorrowful. **2** causing unhappiness or misfortune. ■ **dole·ful·ly** adv.

dol·er·ite /'dälə,rīt/ ▶ n. a dark igneous rock.

doll /däl/ ▶ n. **1** a small model of a human figure, used as a child's toy. **2** informal an attractive young woman. ▶ v. (**doll oneself up**) informal dress oneself smartly and attractively.

dol·lar /'dälər/ ▶ n. the basic unit of money of the US, Canada, Australia, and various other countries.

dol·lar sign (also **dollar mark**) ▶ n. the sign $, representing a dollar.

doll·house /'däl,hous/ ▶ n. a miniature toy house for dolls.

dol·lop /'däləp/ informal ▶ n. a shapeless mass or lump, especially of soft food. ▶ v. (**dollops, dolloping, dolloped**) add or serve out soft food in a casual or careless way.

dol·ly /'dälē/ ▶ n. (pl. **dollies**) **1** a child's word for a doll. **2** informal, dated an attractive young woman. **3** a small platform on wheels for holding or moving heavy objects.

dol·ma·des /dôl'mäᴛʜes/ ▶ pl.n. (sing. **dolma** /'dôlmə/) a Greek and Turkish dish of spiced rice and meat wrapped in vine or cabbage leaves.

dol·man sleeve /'dōlmən/ ▶ n. a loose sleeve cut in one piece with the body of a garment.

dol·men /'dōlmən, 'däl-/ ▶ n. a megalithic tomb with a large flat stone laid on upright ones.

do·lo·mite /'dälə,mīt, 'dō-/ ▶ n. a mineral or rock consisting chiefly of a carbonate of calcium and magnesium. ■ **dol·o·mit·ic** /,dälə'mitik/ adj.

do·lor /'dōlər/ ▶ n. literary a state of great sorrow or distress.

dol·or·ous /'dōlərəs/ ▶ adj. literary feeling great sorrow or distress.

dol·phin /'dälfin, 'dôl-/ ▶ n. a small whale with a beaklike snout and a curved fin on the back.

dol·phi·nar·i·um /,dälfi'ne(ə)rēəm, ,dôl-/ ▶ n. (pl. **dolphinariums** or **dolphinaria**) an aquarium in which dolphins are kept and trained for public entertainment.

dolt /dōlt/ ▶ n. a stupid person. ■ **dolt·ish** adj.

do·main /dō'mān/ ▶ n. **1** an area controlled by a ruler or government. **2** an area of activity or knowledge. **3** a subset of the Internet with addresses all having the same suffix.

dome /dōm/ ▶ n. **1** a rounded vault forming the roof of a building, typically with a circular base. **2** a sports stadium or other building with a domed roof. ■ **domed** adj.

do·mes·tic /də'mestik/ ▶ adj. **1** relating to a home or family. **2** of or for use in the home. **3** fond of family life and running a home. **4** (of an animal) tame and kept by humans. **5** existing or occurring within a country; not foreign. ▶ n. a person employed to do household tasks. ■ **do·mes·ti·cal·ly** /-ik(ə)lē/ adv.

do·mes·ti·cate /də'mesti,kāt/ ▶ v. **1** tame an animal and keep it as a pet or for farm produce. **2** make someone fond of and good at family life and running a home. **3** grow a plant for food. ■ **do·mes·ti·ca·tion** /-,mesti'kāsʜən/ n.

do·mes·tic·i·ty /,dōme'stisitē/ ▶ n. home or family life.

do·mes·tic part·ner·ship ▶ n. (in some US states) a legally recognized union of a couple who have not been joined in a traditional marriage and whose status may or may not be that of a civil union.

do·mes·tic sci·ence ▶ n. dated home economics.

dom·i·cile /'dämə,sīl, 'dō-, 'däməsəl/ ▶ n. formal or Law **1** the country in which a person lives permanently. **2** a person's home. ▶ v. (**be domiciled**) formal or Law be living in a particular place.

dom·i·cil·i·ar·y /,dämə'silē,erē, ,dō-/ ▶ adj. concerned with or occurring in someone's home.

dom·i·nant /'dämənənt/ ▶ adj. **1** most important, powerful, or influential. **2** (of a gene) appearing in offspring even if a contrary gene is also inherited. Compare with RECESSIVE. ■ **dom·i·nance** n. **dom·i·nant·ly** adv.

dom·i·nate /'dämə,nāt/ ▶ v. **1** have power or influence over: *the economy is dominated by multinational corporations.* **2** be the most important or noticeable person or thing in: *he dominated the race from start to finish.* **3** be the tallest or largest thing in a place. ■ **dom·i·na·tion** /,dämə'nāsʜən/ n. **dom·i·na·tor** n.

dom·i·na·trix /,dämə'nätriks/ ▶ n. (pl. **dominatrices** /-trə,sēz/ or **dominatrixes**) a dominating woman, especially in sadomasochistic practices.

dom·i·neer·ing /,dämə'ni(ə)riNG/ ▶ adj. arrogant and overbearing.

Do·min·i·can[1] /də'minikən/ ▶ n. a member of an order of friars founded by St. Dominic, or of a similar religious order for women. ▶ adj. relating to St. Dominic or the Dominicans.

Do·min·i·can[2] ▶ n. a person from the Dominican Republic in the Caribbean. ▶ adj. relating to the Dominican Republic.

Do·min·i·can[3] ▶ adj. of or relating to the island of Dominica or its people.

do·min·ion /də'minyən/ ▶ n. **1** supreme power or control. **2** the territory of a sovereign or government. **3** (**Dominion**) historical a self-governing territory of the British Commonwealth.

dom·i·no /'dämə,nō/ ▶ n. (pl. **dominoes**) **1** any of 28 small oblong pieces marked with 0–6 dots in each half. **2** (**dominoes**) (treated as sing.) the game played with these pieces.

dom·i·no ef·fect ▶ n. a situation in which one event appears to cause a series of similar events to happen elsewhere.

don[1] /dän/ ▶ n. **1** a university teacher, especially a senior member of a college at Oxford or Cambridge. **2** informal a high-ranking member of the Mafia.

don[2] ▶ v. (**dons, donning, donned**) put on an item of clothing.

do·nate /'dōnāt, dō'nāt/ ▶ v. **1** give money, clothes, etc., to a charity or good cause. **2** allow blood or an organ to be removed from one's body for transfusion or transplantation. ■ **do·na·tor** n.

do·na·tion /dō'nāsʜən/ ▶ n. **1** something that is given to a charity. **2** the act of donating something.

done /dən/ past participle of **DO**[1] ▶ adj. **1** (of food) cooked thoroughly. **2** no longer happening or existing. **3** informal socially acceptable: *the done thing.* ▶ exclam. (in response to an offer) I accept! – PHRASES **done for** informal in serious trouble. **done in** informal extremely tired.

don·gle /'dänGgəl, 'dôNG-/ ▶ n. an electronic device that must be attached to a computer in order for protected software to be used.

don·jon /'dänjən, 'dôn-/ ▶ n. the strongest or central tower of a castle.

Don Juan /,dän '(h)wän/ ▶ n. a man who seduces

many women.

don·key /'dôNGkē, 'däNG-/ ▶ n. (pl. **donkeys**) **1** a domesticated mammal of the horse family with long ears and a braying call. **2** informal a foolish person.
– PHRASES **donkey's years** informal a very long time.

don·nish /'dänisH/ ▶ adj. like a college don; concerned with scholarly rather than practical matters.

do·nor /'dōnər/ ▶ n. **1** a person who donates something. **2** a substance, molecule, etc., that provides electrons for a physical or chemical process.

do·nor card ▶ n. a card consenting to the use of one's organs for transplant surgery in the event of one's death.

don't /dōnt/ ▶ contr. do not.

do·nut /'dō,nət/ (also **doughnut**) ▶ n. a small fried cake or ring of sweetened dough.

doo·dad /'dōō,dad/ ▶ n. informal **1** an object whose name is not known or has been forgotten. **2** a fancy article or trivial ornament: *there were crystal doodads all over the place.*

doo·dle /'dōōdl/ ▶ v. draw or scribble absentmindedly. ▶ n. a drawing made absentmindedly. ■ **doo·dler** n.

doo·dle·bug /'dōōdl,bəg/ ▶ n. informal a V-1 flying bomb used by Germany in World War II.

doom /dōōm/ ▶ n. death, destruction, or another terrible fate. ▶ v. (**be doomed**) be fated to fail or be destroyed: *the marriage was doomed from the start.* ■ **doom·y** adj.

doom·say·er /'dōōm,sāər/ ▶ n. a person who predicts disaster, especially in politics or economics. ■ **doom·say·ing** n.

dooms·day /'dōōmz,dā/ ▶ n. **1** the last day of the world's existence. **2** (in religious belief) the day of the Last Judgment.

door /dôr/ ▶ n. **1** a movable barrier at the entrance to a building, room, or vehicle, or in the framework of a cupboard. **2** the distance from one building in a row to another: *he lived two doors away.*
– PHRASES **lay something at someone's door** blame someone for something. **out of doors** in or into the open air.

door·bell /'dôr,bel/ ▶ n. a bell in a building that can be rung by visitors outside.

do-or-die /'dōō ər 'dī/ ▶ adj. showing or requiring a great determination to succeed.

door·keep·er /'dôr,kēpər/ ▶ n. a person on duty at the entrance to a building.

door·knob /'dôr,näb/ ▶ n. a rounded door handle.

door·man /'dôr,man, -mən/ ▶ n. (pl. **doormen**) a man who is on duty at the entrance to a large building.

door·mat /'dôr,mat/ ▶ n. **1** a mat placed in a doorway for wiping the shoes. **2** informal a person who allows others to control them or treat them badly.

door·nail /'dôr,nāl/ ▶ n. (in phrase **dead as a doornail**) dead (used for emphasis).

door prize ▶ n. a prize awarded by lottery to the holder of a ticket purchased or distributed at a dance, party, or other function.

door·step /'dôr,step/ ▶ n. a step leading up to the outer door of a house.
– PHRASES **on one's** (or **the**) **doorstep** situated very close by.

door·stop /'dôr,stäp/ (also **doorstopper**) ▶ n. an object that keeps a door open or in place.

door·way /'dôr,wā/ ▶ n. an entrance with a door.

doo-wop /'dōō ,wäp/ ▶ n. a style of pop music involving close harmony vocals and nonsense phrases.

doo·zy /'dōōzē/ ▶ n. (pl. **doozies**) informal something outstanding or unique of its kind.

do·pa·mine /'dōpə,mēn/ ▶ n. a compound that exists in the body as a neurotransmitter and from which other substances including adrenaline are formed.

dope /dōp/ ▶ n. **1** informal an illegal drug, especially marijuana or heroin. **2** a drug used to improve the performance of an athlete, racehorse, or greyhound. **3** informal a stupid person. **4** informal information. ▶ v. **1** give a drug to a racehorse, greyhound, or athlete to improve their performance. **2** (**be doped up**) informal be heavily under the influence of drugs.

dope·y /'dōpē/ (also **dopy**) ▶ adj. (**dopier**, **dopiest**) informal **1** in a semiconscious state from sleep or a drug. **2** stupid. ■ **dop·i·ly** adv. **dop·i·ness** n.

dop·pel·gäng·er /'däpəl,gaNGər/ ▶ n. a ghost or double of a living person.

Dop·pler ef·fect /'däplər/ ▶ n. Physics an increase (or decrease) in the apparent frequency of sound, light, or other waves as the source and the observer move toward (or away from) each other.

do·ra·do /də'rädō/ ▶ n. (pl. **dorados**) a large brightly colored edible fish of warm seas.

Dor·ic /'dôrik, 'där-/ ▶ adj. relating to a classical order of architecture characterized by a fluted column with a square slab on top.

dork /dôrk/ ▶ n. informal a stupid person.

dorm /dôrm/ ▶ n. informal a dormitory.

dor·mant /'dôrmənt/ ▶ adj. **1** (of an animal) in or as if in a deep sleep. **2** (of a plant or bud) alive but not growing. **3** (of a volcano) temporarily inactive. ■ **dor·man·cy** n.

dor·mer /'dôrmər/ (also **dormer window**) ▶ n. a window set vertically into a sloping roof.

dor·mi·to·ry /'dôrmi,tôrē/ ▶ n. (pl. **dormitories**) a bedroom for a number of people in an institution.

dor·mouse /'dôr,mous/ ▶ n. (pl. **dormice**) a small mouselike rodent with a bushy tail.

dor·sal /'dôrsəl/ ▶ adj. technical on or relating to the upper side or back. Compare with VENTRAL. ■ **dor·sal·ly** adv.

do·ry[1] /'dôrē/ ▶ n. (pl. **dories**) a narrow sea fish with a large mouth.

do·ry[2] ▶ n. (pl. **dories**) a small flat-bottomed rowboat with a high bow and stern, originally used for fishing in New England.

DOS /dôs/ ▶ abbr. Computing disk operating system.

DoS ▶ abbr. Computing denial of service.

dos·age /'dōsij/ ▶ n. the size of a dose of medicine or radiation.

dose /dōs/ ▶ n. **1** a quantity of a medicine or drug taken at one time. **2** an amount of radiation received or absorbed at one time. **3** informal a sexually transmitted infection. ▶ v. give someone a medicine or drug.

do·sha /'dōsHə/ ▶ n. (in Ayurvedic medicine) each of three energies believed to circulate in the body and control its activity.

do-si-do /'dō sē 'dō/ ▶ n. (pl. **do-si-dos**) (in country dancing) a figure in which two dancers pass around each other back to back.

do·sim·e·ter /dō'simitər/ ▶ n. a device used to measure an absorbed dose of radiation. ∎ **do·sim·e·try** n.

dos·si·er /'dôsē,ā, 'däs-/ ▶ n. a collection of documents about a person or subject.

dost /dəst/ ▶ old-fashioned second person singular present of DO¹.

DOT ▶ abbr. Department of Transportation.

dot /dät/ ▶ n. **1** a small round mark or spot. **2** the shorter signal of the two used in Morse code. **3** Music a dot used to indicate the lengthening of a note or rest by half, or to indicate staccato. ▶ v. (**dots, dotting, dotted**) **1** mark something with a dot or dots. **2** scatter something over an area: *the meadow was dotted with buttercups and daisies.*
– PHRASES **dot the i's and cross the t's** informal ensure that all details are correct. **on the dot** informal exactly on time.

dot·age /'dōtij/ ▶ n. the period of life in which a person is old and weak.

do·tard /'dōtərd/ ▶ n. an old person, especially one who is weak or senile.

dot-com (also **dot.com**) ▶ n. a company that conducts its business on the Internet.

dote /dōt/ ▶ v. (**dote on**) be extremely and uncritically fond of: *she's a flirt but he dotes on her.* ∎ **dot·ing** adj.

doth /dəTH/ ▶ old-fashioned third person singular present of DO¹.

dot ma·trix ▶ n. a grid of dots that are filled selectively to produce an image on a screen or on paper.

dot-org (also **dot.org**) ▶ n. a nonprofit organization that conducts its business on the Internet.

dot·ted line ▶ n. a line made up of dots or dashes (often used in reference to the space left for a signature on a contract).

dot·ter·el /'dätərəl/ ▶ n. (pl. same or **dotterels**) a small migratory plover (bird).

dot·ty /'dätē/ ▶ slightly mad or eccentric. ∎ **dot·ti·ly** adv. **dot·ti·ness** n.

dou·ble /'dəbəl/ ▶ adj. **1** consisting of two equal, identical, or similar parts or things. **2** having twice the usual size, quantity, or strength: *a double brandy.* **3** designed to be used by two people. **4** having two different roles or interpretations: *she began a double life.* **5** (of a flower) having more than one circle of petals. ▶ adv. twice the amount or extent. ▶ n. **1** a thing that is twice as large as usual or is made up of two parts. **2** a person who looks exactly like another. **3** (**doubles**) a game involving sides made up of two players. **4** Baseball a hit that allows the batter to reach second base safely. ▶ pron. an amount twice as large as usual. ▶ v. **1** make or become double. **2** fold or bend over on itself. **3** (**double up**) bend over or curl up with pain or laughter. **4** (**double as**) be used in or play another, different role: *a pocket-sized computer that doubles as a cell phone.* **5** (**double back**) go back in the direction one has come. ∎ **dou·ble·ness** n. **dou·bler** n. **dou·bly** adv.
– PHRASES **at the double** very fast.

dou·ble a·gent ▶ n. an agent who pretends to act as a spy for one country while in fact acting for its enemy.

dou·ble-bar·reled ▶ adj. **1** (of a gun) having two

barrels. **2** having two parts or aspects: *a double-barreled strategy for reducing crime.* **3** more than usually forceful, impressive, or sensational: *John Woo's double-barreled action sequences.*

dou·ble bass /bās/ ▶ n. the largest and lowest-pitched instrument of the violin family.

dou·ble bill ▶ n. a program of entertainment with two main items.

dou·ble bind ▶ n. a dilemma.

dou·ble-blind ▶ adj. (of a test or trial) in which information that may influence the behavior of the tester or subject is withheld.

dou·ble boil·er ▶ n. a saucepan with an upper compartment heated by boiling water in the lower one.

dou·ble bond ▶ n. a chemical bond in which two pairs of electrons are shared between two atoms.

dou·ble-breast·ed ▶ adj. (of a jacket or coat) having a large overlap at the front and two rows of buttons.

dou·ble-check ▶ v. check something again to make certain.

dou·ble chin ▶ n. a roll of flesh below a person's chin.

dou·ble-cross ▶ v. betray a person one is supposedly helping.

dou·ble-deal·ing ▶ n. deceitful behavior. ▶ adj. acting deceitfully.

dou·ble-deck·er ▶ n. a vehicle with two floors, one on top of the other.

dou·ble-dig·it ▶ adj. (of a number, variable, or percentage) between 10 and 99: *double-digit inflation.*

dou·ble Dutch ▶ n. a jump-rope game played with two ropes swung in opposite directions.

dou·ble-edged ▶ adj. **1** (of a blade) having two cutting edges. **2** having two contrasting aspects or possible outcomes.

dou·ble en·ten·dre /'dōōb(ə)l än'tändrə/ ▶ n. (pl. **double entendres** pronunc. same) a word or phrase with two possible meanings, one of which is usually risqué or indecent.

dou·ble-en·try ▶ adj. relating to a system of bookkeeping in which each transaction is entered as a debit in one account and a credit in another.

dou·ble ex·po·sure ▶ n. the repeated exposure of a photographic plate or film.

dou·ble fault ▶ n. Tennis an instance of two consecutive faults in serving, resulting in the loss of a point.

Dou·ble Glouces·ter ▶ n. a hard cheese originally made in Gloucestershire, England.

dou·ble·head·er /,dəbəl'hedər/ ▶ n. **1** a sporting event in which two games are played in succession at the same venue. **2** a train pulled by two locomotives.

dou·ble he·lix ▶ n. a pair of parallel helices intertwined about a common axis, especially that in the structure of DNA.

dou·ble jeop·ard·y ▶ n. Law the prosecution or punishment of a person twice for the same offense.

dou·ble-joint·ed ▶ adj. (of a person) having unusually flexible joints.

dou·ble neg·a·tive ▶ n. Grammar a negative statement containing two negative elements (e.g., *didn't say nothing*), regarded as incorrect in standard English.

dou·ble-park ▶ v. park a vehicle alongside one that is already parked.

dou·ble play ▶ n. Baseball a defensive play in which two players are put out.

dou·ble pneu·mo·nia ▶ n. pneumonia affecting both lungs.

dou·ble·speak /'dəbəl,spēk/ ▶ n. language that is deliberately unclear or ambiguous.

dou·ble stand·ard ▶ n. a rule or principle applied unfairly in different ways to different people.

dou·blet /'dəblət/ ▶ n. 1 a man's short close-fitting padded jacket, worn from the 14th to the 17th century. 2 a pair of similar things.

dou·ble take ▶ n. a second reaction to something unexpected, immediately after one's first reaction.

dou·ble·think /'dəbəl,THiNGk/ ▶ n. the acceptance of conflicting opinions or beliefs at the same time.

dou·ble time ▶ n. a rate of pay equal to double the standard rate.

dou·ble vi·sion ▶ n. the perception of two overlapping images of a single scene.

dou·ble wham·my ▶ n. informal a blow or setback consisting of two separate elements.

dou·bloon /də'blo͞on/ ▶ n. historical a Spanish gold coin.

doubt /dout/ ▶ n. a feeling of uncertainty.
▶ v. 1 feel uncertain about something: *I doubt if he makes much money.* 2 disbelieve or mistrust: *I have no reason to doubt him.* ■ **doubt·er** n. **doubt·ing** adj.
– PHRASES **no doubt 1** certainly. **2** probably.

doubt·ful /'doutfəl/ ▶ adj. 1 feeling uncertain. 2 not known with certainty: *the fire was of doubtful origin.* 3 unlikely: *it's doubtful whether the council will be able to recover the money.* ■ **doubt·ful·ly** adv.

doubt·ing Thom·as /'täməs/ ▶ n. a person who refuses to believe something without proof.

doubt·less /'doutlis/ ▶ adv. very probably. ■ **doubt·less·ly** adv.

douche /do͞osH/ ▶ n. 1 a shower of water. 2 a jet of liquid applied to part of the body for cleansing or medicinal purposes. 3 a device for washing out the vagina as a contraceptive measure.
▶ v. spray or clean someone or something with water.

dough /dō/ ▶ n. 1 a thick mixture of flour and liquid, for baking into bread or pastry. 2 informal money. ■ **dough·y** adj.

dough·ty /'doutē/ ▶ adj. (**doughtier, doughtiest**) brave and determined.

Doug·las fir /'dəgləs/ ▶ n. a tall, slender conifer valued for its wood.

dour /do͞or, dou(ə)r/ ▶ adj. very severe, stern, or gloomy. ■ **dour·ly** adv. **dour·ness** n.

douse /dous/ (also **dowse**) ▶ v. 1 drench something with liquid. 2 extinguish a fire or light.

dove[1] /dəv/ ▶ n. 1 a stocky bird with a small head, short legs, and a cooing voice, very similar to but generally smaller than a pigeon. 2 (in politics) a person who favors a policy of peace and negotiation. ■ **dov·ish** (also **doveish**) adj.

dove[2] /dōv/ ▶ past and past participle of DIVE.

dove·cote /'dəv,kōt/ (also **dovecot**) ▶ n. a shelter with nest holes for domesticated pigeons.

dove·tail /'dəv,tāl/ ▶ v. 1 fit together easily or conveniently: *flights that dovetail with the working day.* 2 join things by means of a dovetail joint. ▶ n. a wedge-shaped joint formed by interlocking two pieces of wood.

dow·a·ger /'douəjər/ ▶ n. 1 a widow who holds a title or property that belonged to her late husband. 2 a dignified elderly woman.

dow·dy /'doudē/ ▶ adj. (**dowdier, dowdiest**) (especially of a woman) unfashionable and dull in appearance. ■ **dow·di·ly** adv. **dow·di·ness** n.

dow·el /'douəl/ ▶ n. a headless peg used for holding components. ▶ v. (**dowels, doweling, doweled**) fasten things with a dowel.

dow·el·ing /'douəliNG/ ▶ n. cylindrical rods that are cut into dowels.

dow·er /'dou(-ə)r/ ▶ n. 1 a widow's share for life of her husband's estate. 2 old use a dowry.

Dow Jones In·dus·tri·al Av·er·age /'dou 'jōnz/ ▶ n. an index of figures indicating the relative price of shares on the New York Stock Exchange.

down[1] /doun/ ▶ adv. 1 toward or in a lower place or position. 2 to or at a lower level or value. 3 in or into a weaker or worse position, mood, or condition. 4 to a smaller amount or size, or a simpler or more basic state. 5 away from a central place or the north. 6 from an earlier to a later point in time or order. 7 in or into writing. 8 (of a computer system) out of action. ▶ prep. 1 from a higher to a lower point of. 2 at a point farther along the course of. 3 along the course or extent of. 4 informal at or to a place. ▶ adj. 1 directed or moving toward a lower place or position. 2 unhappy. 3 (of a computer system) out of action. ▶ v. informal 1 knock or bring someone or something to the ground. 2 consume a drink.
– PHRASES **be down on** informal dislike or feel hostile toward someone. **be down to 1** be caused by. 2 be left with: *I'm down to my last few pounds.* **down in the mouth** informal unhappy. **down on one's luck** informal having a period of bad luck.

down[2] ▶ n. fine, soft feathers or hairs.

down[3] ▶ n. 1 a gently rolling hill. 2 (**the Downs**) ridges of undulating chalk and limestone hills in southern England.

down and out ▶ adj. homeless and having no money; destitute. ▶ n. (**down-and-out**) a destitute person.

down-at-the-heels ▶ adj. shabby because of a lack of money.

down·beat /'doun,bēt/ ▶ adj. 1 pessimistic or gloomy. 2 relaxed and understated. ▶ n. Music an accented beat, usually the first of the bar.

down·cast /'doun,kast/ ▶ adj. 1 (of a person's eyes) looking downward. 2 feeling sad or depressed.

down·draft /'doun,draft/ ▶ n. a downward current or draft of air, especially one down a chimney into a room.

down·er /'dounər/ ▶ n. informal 1 a depressant or tranquilizing drug. 2 a sad or depressing experience.

down·fall /'doun,fôl/ ▶ n. a loss of power, wealth, or status.

down·field /'doun'fēld/ ▶ adv. (in sports) in or to a position nearer to the opponents' end of a field.

down·force /'doun,fôrs/ ▶ n. a force acting on a moving vehicle having the effect of pressing it down toward the ground, giving it increased stability.

down·grade /'doun,grād/ ▶ v. reduce someone or something to a lower grade, rank, or level of importance.

down·heart·ed /'doun'härtid/ ▶ adj. feeling sad or discouraged.

down·hill /'doun'hil/ ▶ adv. & adj. **1** toward the bottom of a slope. **2** into a steadily worsening situation: *his career was rapidly going downhill.*

down·link /'doun,liNGk/ ▶ n. a telecommunications link for signals coming to the earth from a satellite, spacecraft, or aircraft.

down·load /'doun,lōd/ ▶ v. copy data from one computer system to another or to a disk. ▶ n. **1** a downloaded computer file. **2** the process of downloading data. ■ **down·load·a·ble** adj.

down·mar·ket /'doun,märkit/ ▶ adj. & adv. cheaper and of low quality or status.

down pay·ment ▶ n. an initial payment made when buying something on credit.

down·play /'doun,plā/ ▶ v. make something appear less important than it really is.

down·pour /'doun,pôr/ ▶ n. a heavy fall of rain.

down·right /'doun,rīt/ ▶ adj. utter; complete: *a downright lie.* ▶ adv. extremely: *he was downright rude.*

down·riv·er /'doun'rivər/ ▶ adv. & adj. toward or situated at a point nearer the mouth of a river.

down·scale /'doun,skāl/ ▶ v. reduce the size or extent of something. ▶ adj. downmarket.

down·shift /'doun,SHift/ ▶ v. adopt a simpler and less stressful lifestyle.

down·side /'doun,sīd/ ▶ n. the negative aspect of something.

down·size /'doun,sīz/ ▶ v. reduce the number of staff employed by a company in order to cut costs.

down·spout /'doun,spout/ ▶ n. a pipe to carry rainwater from a roof to a drain or to ground level.

down·stage /'doun'stāj/ ▶ adj. & adv. at or toward the front of a stage.

down·stairs /'doun'ste(ə)rz/ ▶ adv. & adj. down a flight of stairs; on or to a lower floor. ▶ n. the ground floor or lower floors of a building.

down·state /'doun'stāt/ ▶ adj. & adv. of, in, or to the southern part of a state.

down·stream /'doun'strēm/ ▶ adv. & adj. situated or moving in the direction in which a stream or river flows.

Down syn·drome /dounz/ (also **Down's syndrome**) ▶ n. a medical disorder caused by a genetic defect, causing intellectual impairment and physical abnormalities.

down·tem·po /'doun,tempō/ ▶ adj. (of music) played at a slow tempo.

down·time /'doun,tīm/ ▶ n. time during which a computer or other machine is out of action.

down-to-earth ▶ adj. practical and realistic.

down·town /'doun'toun/ ▶ adj. & adv. of, in, or toward the central area or main business area of a city. ▶ n. a downtown area. ■ **down·town·er** n.

down·trend /'doun,trend/ ▶ n. a downward tendency, especially in economic matters: *a downtrend in the share price.*

down·trod·den /'doun,trädn/ ▶ adj. treated badly by people in power and lacking the energy or ability to resist.

down·turn /'doun,tərn/ ▶ n. a decline in economic or other activity.

down un·der informal (also **Down Under**) ▶ adv. in or to Australia or New Zealand. ▶ n. Australia and New Zealand.

down·ward /'dounwərd/ ▶ adv. (also **downwards**) toward a lower point or level. ▶ adj. moving toward a lower level. ■ **down·ward·ly** adv.

down·wind /'doun'wind/ ▶ adv. & adj. in the direction in which the wind is blowing.

down·y /'dounē/ ▶ adj. (**downier, downiest**) covered with fine soft hair or feathers.

dow·ry /'dou(ə)rē/ ▶ n. (pl. **dowries**) property or money brought by a bride to her husband on their marriage.

dowse¹ /douz/ ▶ v. search for underground water or minerals with a pointer that is supposedly moved by unseen influences. ■ **dows·er** n.

dowse² /dous/ ▶ v. variant spelling of DOUSE.

dox·ol·o·gy /däk'säləjē/ ▶ n. (pl. **doxologies**) a set form of prayer praising God.

doy·en /doi'en, 'doi,en/ ▶ n. (fem. **doyenne** /doi'en/) the most respected or prominent person in a particular group or profession: *the doyenne of American poetry.*

doz. ▶ abbr. dozen.

doze /dōz/ ▶ v. sleep lightly. ▶ n. a short light sleep.

doz·en /'dəzən/ ▶ n. (pl. same) **1** a group or set of twelve. **2** informal a lot. ■ **doz·enth** /'dəzənTH/ adj.

do·zy /'dōzē/ ▶ adj. (**dozier, doziest**) feeling drowsy and lazy. ■ **do·zi·ly** adv. **do·zi·ness** n.

DP ▶ abbr. **1** data processing. **2** Baseball double play.

DPT ▶ abbr. diphtheria, pertussis (whooping cough), and tetanus, a combined vaccine given to small children.

Dr. ▶ abbr. (as a title) Doctor.

dr. ▶ abbr. **1** drachma(s). **2** dram(s).

drab /drab/ ▶ adj. (**drabber, drabbest**) lacking brightness or interest; dull and dreary. ▶ n. a dull light brown color. ■ **drab·ly** adv. **drab·ness** n.

drach·ma /'dräkmə/ ▶ n. (pl. **drachmas** or **drachmae** /-mē/) **1** (until the introduction of the euro in 2002) the basic unit of money of Greece. **2** a silver coin of ancient Greece.

dra·co·ni·an /drə'kōnēən, drā-/ ▶ adj. (of laws or punishments) extremely harsh or severe.

draft /draft/ ▶ n. **1** a preliminary version of a piece of writing. **2** a plan or sketch. **3** (**the draft**) compulsory recruitment for military service. **4** (Brit. **draught**) a current of cool air in a room or confined space. **5** (Brit. **draught**) a written order requesting a bank to pay a specified sum of money. **6** (Brit. **draught**) a single act of drinking or breathing in. **7** (Brit. **draught**) the depth of water needed to float a particular ship. ▶ v. **1** prepare a preliminary version of a piece of writing. **2** select a person or group and send them somewhere for a purpose: *volunteers were drafted to help with crowd control.* **3** conscript someone for military service. ▶ adj. (Brit. **draught**) **1** (of beer) served from a cask rather than from a bottle or can. **2** (of an animal) used for pulling heavy loads. ■ **draft·er** n.

draft·ee /draf'tē/ ▶ n. a person conscripted for military service.

drafts·man /'draftsmən/ (or **draftswoman** /'drafts,woŏmən/) ▶ n. (pl. **draftsmen** or **draftswomen**) **1** a person who makes detailed technical plans or drawings. **2** an artist skilled in drawing. **3** a person who drafts legal documents. ■ **drafts·man·ship** /-,SHip/ n.

draft·y /'draftē/ (Brit. **draughty**) ▶ adj. (**draftier**, **draftiest**) (of a room, space, etc.) uncomfortable because drafts of cold air are blowing through it.

drag /drag/ ▶ v. (**drags**, **dragging**, **dragged**) **1** pull something along forcefully, roughly, or with difficulty. **2** trail along the ground. **3** take someone somewhere, despite their reluctance. **4** move an image across a computer screen using a mouse. **5** (of time) pass slowly. **6** (**drag something out**) prolong something unnecessarily. **7** (**drag something up**) informal deliberately mention something unwelcome. **8** search the bottom of an area of water with grapnels or nets. **9** (**drag on**) informal inhale the smoke from a cigarette. ▶ n. **1** informal a boring or tiresome person or thing. **2** informal an act of inhaling smoke from a cigarette. **3** the action of dragging. **4** the force exerted by air or water to slow down a moving object.
– PHRASES **drag one's feet 1** walk wearily or with difficulty. **2** be slow or reluctant to act. **in drag** (of a man) wearing women's clothes.

drag·gle /'dragəl/ ▶ v. **1** make something dirty or wet by trailing it on the ground. **2** hang untidily.

drag·net /'drag,net/ ▶ n. **1** a net drawn through water or across ground to trap fish or game. **2** a systematic search for criminals.

drag·o·man /'dragəmən/ ▶ n. (pl. **dragomans** or **dragomen**) an interpreter or guide in a country speaking Arabic, Turkish, or Persian.

drag·on /'dragən/ ▶ n. **1** a mythical monster like a giant reptile, typically able to breathe out fire. **2** derogatory a fierce and intimidating woman.

drag·on·fly /'dragən,flī/ ▶ n. (pl. **dragonflies**) a fast-flying long-bodied insect with two pairs of large transparent wings.

dra·goon /drə'goŏn/ ▶ n. **1** a member of any of several British cavalry regiments. **2** historical a mounted infantryman armed with a rifle or musket. ▶ v. force or persuade someone to do something: *she had been dragooned into helping with the housework.*

drag queen ▶ n. informal a man who dresses up in very flamboyant or showy women's clothes.

drag race ▶ n. a short race between two cars to see which can accelerate fastest from a standstill. ■ **drag rac·er** n. **drag rac·ing** n.

drag·ster /'dragstər/ ▶ n. a car used in drag races.

drain /drān/ ▶ v. **1** make the liquid in something run out: *we drained the swimming pool.* **2** (of liquid) flow away from, out of, or into something: *the river drains into the Pacific.* **3** become dry as liquid runs off. **4** deprive of strength or vitality: *she felt drained of energy.* **5** cause a resource to be lost or used up: *my mother's hospital bills are draining my income.* **6** drink the entire contents of a glass, cup, etc. ▶ n. **1** a channel or pipe carrying off surplus liquid. **2** a thing that uses up a resource or one's strength.
– PHRASES **go down the drain** informal be totally wasted.

drain·age /'drānij/ ▶ n. **1** the action or process of draining something. **2** a system of drains.

drain·board /'drān,bôrd/ ▶ n. a sloping grooved surface next to a sink, on which dishes are left to drain.

drain·er /'drānər/ ▶ n. **1** a rack used to hold draining dishes. **2** a drainboard.

drain·pipe /'drān,pīp/ ▶ n. a pipe for carrying off rainwater from a building.

drake /drāk/ ▶ n. a male duck.

DRAM /'dē,ram/ ▶ n. Electronics a memory chip that depends upon an applied voltage to keep the stored data.

dram /dram/ ▶ n. **1** historical a unit of weight equivalent to one eighth of an ounce. **2** (also **fluid dram**) historical a liquid measure equivalent to one eighth of a fluid ounce. **3** chiefly Scottish a small drink of liquor.

dra·ma /'drämə/ ▶ n. **1** a play. **2** plays as a literary genre. **3** an exciting series of events.

dra·mat·ic /drə'matik/ ▶ adj. **1** relating to drama. **2** sudden and striking: *a dramatic increase in the prison population.* **3** exciting or impressive. **4** intended to create an effect; theatrical: *he flung out his arms in a dramatic gesture.* ■ **dra·mat·i·cal·ly** /-ik(ə)lē/ adv.

dra·mat·ics /drə'matiks/ ▶ pl.n. **1** the study or practice of acting in and producing plays. **2** theatrically exaggerated behavior.

dram·a·tis per·so·nae /'drämətis pər'sōnē/ ▶ pl.n. the characters of a play or novel.

dram·a·tist /'drämə,tist/ ▶ n. a person who writes plays.

dram·a·tize /'drämə,tīz/ ▶ v. **1** present a novel, event, etc., as a play or movie. **2** exaggerate the excitement or seriousness of something. ■ **dram·a·ti·za·tion** /,dräməti'zāSHən/ n.

dram·a·turge /'drämə,tərj/ (also **dramaturg**) ▶ n. **1** a dramatist. **2** a literary editor on the staff of a theater who consults with authors and edits texts.

dram·a·tur·gy /'drämə,tərjē/ ▶ n. the theory and practice of writing plays. ■ **dram·a·tur·gi·cal** /,drämə'tərjikəl/ adj.

Dram·bu·ie /dram'boŏē/ ▶ n. trademark a sweet Scotch whiskey liqueur.

dra·me·dy /'drämədē/ (pl. **dramedies**) ▶ n. a television program or movie containing both dramatic and comedic elements.

drank /draNGk/ ▶ past of DRINK.

drape /drāp/ ▶ v. arrange cloth or clothing loosely on or around something. ▶ n. **1** (**drapes**) long curtains. **2** the way in which a garment or fabric hangs.

drap·er /'drāpər/ ▶ n. Brit. dated a person who sells fabrics.

dra·per·y /'drāpərē/ ▶ n. (pl. **draperies**) cloth, curtains, or clothing hanging in loose folds.

dras·tic /'drastik/ ▶ adj. having a strong or far-reaching effect. ■ **dras·ti·cal·ly** /-ik(ə)lē/ adv.

drat /drat/ ▶ exclam. used to express mild annoyance. ■ **drat·ted** adj.

draught /'draft/ ▶ n. & adj. British spelling of certain senses of DRAFT.

draughts /'draf(t)s/ ▶ n. British term for the game of checkers (see CHECKER²).

Dra·vid·i·an /drə'vidēən/ ▶ n. **1** a family of languages spoken in southern India and Sri Lanka, including Tamil and Kannada. **2** a member of any of the peoples speaking these languages. ▶ adj. relating to Dravidian or Dravidians.

draw /drô/ ▸ v. (past **drew**; past part. **drawn**)
1 produce a picture, diagram, etc., by making lines and marks on paper. **2** pull or drag a vehicle so as to make it follow behind. **3** pull or move in a particular direction: *the train drew out of the station.* **4** pull curtains shut or open. **5** arrive at a point in time: *the campaign drew to a close.* **6** take something from a container or receptacle: *he drew his gun.* **7** get or take something from a source: *he draws inspiration from ordinary scenes and places.* **8** take in a breath. **9** be the cause of a particular response: *his action drew fierce criticism.* **10** attract someone to a place or an event. **11** persuade someone to reveal or do something: *he refused to be drawn into the argument.* **12** reach a conclusion. **13** finish a contest or game with an even score. ▸ n. **1** an act of selecting names at random, for prizes, sporting events, etc. **2** a game or match that ends with the scores even. **3** a person or thing that is very attractive or interesting. **4** an act of inhaling smoke from a cigarette.
– PHRASES **draw someone's fire** attract hostile criticism away from a more important target. **draw the line at** refuse to do or tolerate something. **draw on 1** (of a period of time) pass by and approach its end. **2** suck smoke from a cigarette or pipe. **draw someone/thing out 1** make something last longer. **2** persuade someone to be more talkative. **draw up** come to a halt. **draw something up** prepare a plan or document.

USAGE
On the confusion of **draw** and **drawer**, see the note at DRAWER.

draw·back /'drô,bak/ ▸ n. a disadvantage or problem.

draw·bridge /'drô,brij/ ▸ n. a bridge that is hinged at one end so that it can be raised.

draw·er /'drô(ə)r/ ▸ n. **1** a storage compartment made to slide horizontally in and out of a desk or chest. **2** (**drawers**) dated or humorous underpants. **3** a person who draws something. **4** the person who writes a check.

USAGE
The word **drawer**, which mainly means 'a sliding storage compartment,' is often spelled incorrectly as **draw** (which, as a noun, chiefly means 'an even score at the end of a game,' as in *the match ended in a draw*).

draw·ing /'drô-iNG/ ▸ n. **1** a picture or diagram made with a pencil, pen, or crayon rather than paint. **2** the art or skill of making drawings.

draw·ing board ▸ n. a board on which paper can be spread for artists or designers to work on.
– PHRASES **back to the drawing board** a plan has failed and a new one is needed.

draw·ing room ▸ n. a room in a large private house in which guests are received.

drawl /drôl/ ▸ v. speak in a slow, lazy way with prolonged vowel sounds. ▸ n. a drawling accent.

drawn /drôn/ past participle of DRAW
▸ adj. looking strained from illness or exhaustion.

drawn-out ▸ adj. lasting longer than is necessary.

draw·string /'drô,striNG/ ▸ n. a string in the seam of a garment or bag that can be pulled to tighten or close it.

dray /drā/ ▸ n. a low vehicle or cart without sides, for delivering barrels or other heavy loads.

dread /dred/ ▸ v. anticipate something with great anxiety or fear. ▸ n. great anxiety or fear.
▸ adj. greatly feared; dreadful: *the dread disease.*
■ **dread·ed** adj.

dread·ful /'dredfəl/ ▸ adj. **1** extremely bad or serious. **2** used for emphasis: *I'm a dreadful hoarder.* ■ **dread·ful·ly** adv.

dread·locks /'dred,läks/ ▸ pl. n. a Rastafarian hairstyle in which the hair is twisted into tight braids or ringlets. ■ **dread·locked** adj.

dread·nought /'dred,nôt/ ▸ n. historical a type of battleship of the early 20th century, equipped entirely with large-caliber guns.

dream /drēm/ ▸ n. **1** a series of thoughts, images, and sensations occurring in a person's mind during sleep. **2** a long-held ambition or ideal: *his childhood dream of climbing Everest.* **3** informal a wonderful or perfect person or thing. ▸ v. (past and past part. **dreamed** or **dreamt** /dremt/)
1 experience dreams during sleep. **2** indulge in daydreams or fantasies. **3** think of as being possible: *I never dreamed she'd take offense.*
4 (**dream something up**) imagine or invent something. ■ **dream·er** n. **dream·less** adj.
– PHRASES **like a dream** informal very easily or successfully.

dream·boat /'drēm,bōt/ ▸ n. informal a very attractive person, especially a man.

dream·land /'drēm,land/ ▸ n. **1** sleep regarded as a world of dreams. **2** an imagined and unrealistically ideal world: *there was always in the Cotton Club a certain dreamland aspect.*

dream·scape /'drēm,skāp/ ▸ n. a scene with the strangeness characteristic of dreams.

dream·y /'drēmē/ ▸ adj. (**dreamier, dreamiest**)
1 tending to daydream, or giving the impression that someone is daydreaming: *she had a dreamy look in her eyes.* **2** having a magical or pleasantly unreal quality. ■ **dream·i·ly** adv. **dream·i·ness** n.

drear·y /'dri(ə)rē/ ▸ adj. (**drearier, dreariest**) dull, bleak, and depressing. ■ **drear·i·ly** adv. **drear·i·ness** n.

dreck /drek/ ▸ n. informal rubbish.

dredge[1] /drej/ ▸ v. **1** clean out the bed of a harbor, river, etc., with a dredge. **2** bring something up from a river or seabed with a dredge. **3** (**dredge something up**) mention something unwelcome or unpleasant that has been forgotten. ▸ n. a piece of equipment for bringing up objects or mud from a river or seabed by scooping or dragging. ■ **dredg·er** n.

dredge[2] ▸ v. sprinkle food with sugar or another powdered substance.

dregs /dregz/ ▸ pl. n. **1** the last drops of a liquid left in a container, together with any sediment. **2** the most worthless parts: *the dregs of society.*

drench /drenCH/ ▸ v. **1** wet someone or something thoroughly. **2** (often as adj. **drenched**) cover with large amounts of something: *a sun-drenched clearing.* ▸ n. a dose of medicine given to an animal.

Dres·den chi·na /'drezdən/ ▸ n. porcelain with elaborate decoration and delicate colorings, made originally at Dresden in Germany.

dress /dres/ ▸ v. **1** (also **get dressed**) put on one's clothes. **2** put clothes on someone else. **3** wear clothes in a particular way or of a particular type: *she dresses well.* **4** decorate or arrange something in an artistic or attractive way. **5** clean, treat, or apply a dressing to a wound. **6** clean and prepare food for cooking or eating. **7** add a dressing to a salad. **8** apply fertilizer to an area of ground or a plant. **9** treat or smooth the surface of leather, fabric, or stone. ▶ n. **1** a one-piece garment for a woman or girl that covers the body and extends down over the legs. **2** clothing of a particular kind: *evening dress.* ▶ adj. (of clothing) formal or ceremonial: *a dress suit.*

– PHRASES **dress down** informal wear informal clothes. **dressed to kill** informal wearing glamorous clothes intended to create a striking impression. **dress up** dress in smart or formal clothes, or in a special costume.

dres·sage /drə'säzH/ ▶ n. the art of training horses to perform a set of controlled movements at the rider's command.

dress cir·cle ▶ n. the first level of seats above the ground floor in a theater.

dress code ▶ n. a set of rules specifying the required manner of dress at a school, office, club, restaurant, etc.

dres·ser[1] /'dresər/ ▶ n. **1** a sideboard with shelves above for storing and displaying dishes. **2** a chest of drawers.

dres·ser[2] ▶ n. **1** a person who dresses in a particular way: *a snappy dresser.* **2** a person who looks after theatrical costumes.

dress·ing /'dresiNG/ ▶ n. **1** (also **salad dressing**) a sauce for salads, usually consisting of oil and vinegar with herbs or other flavorings. **2** stuffing. **3** a piece of material placed on a wound to protect it. **4** a layer of fertilizer spread over land.

dress·ing-down ▶ n. informal a severe reprimand.

dress·ing gown ▶ n. a long, loose robe worn after getting out of bed or having a bath or shower.

dress·ing room ▶ n. **1** a room in which actors or other performers change clothes. **2** a small room attached to a bedroom for storing clothes.

dress·ing ta·ble ▶ n. a table with a mirror and drawers, used while dressing or applying makeup.

dress·mak·er /'dres,mākər/ ▶ n. a person who makes women's clothes. ■ **dress·mak·ing** n.

dress re·hears·al ▶ n. a final rehearsal in which everything is done as it would be in a real performance.

dress shirt ▶ n. a man's white shirt worn with a bow tie and a dinner jacket on formal occasions.

dress·y /'dresē/ ▶ adj. (**dressier**, **dressiest**) (of clothes) suitable for a festive or formal occasion.

drew /drōō/ ▶ past of DRAW.

drib·ble /'dribəl/ ▶ v. **1** (of a liquid) fall slowly in drops or a thin stream. **2** allow saliva to run from the mouth. **3** (in sports) take the ball forward with slight touches or (in basketball) by continuous bouncing. ▶ n. **1** a thin stream of liquid. **2** (in sports) an act of dribbling. ■ **drib·bler** n. **drib·bly** adj.

dribs and drabs /'dribz ənd 'drabz/ ▶ pl.n. (in phrase **in dribs and drabs**) informal in small amounts over a period of time.

dried /drīd/ ▶ past and past participle of DRY.

dri·er[1] /'drīər/ ▶ n. variant spelling of DRYER.

dri·er[2] ▶ adj. comparative of DRY.

drift /drift/ ▶ v. **1** be carried slowly by a current of air or water. **2** walk or move slowly or casually. **3** (of snow, leaves, etc.) be blown into heaps by the wind. ▶ n. **1** a continuous slow movement from one place to another: *the population drift from rural areas to cities.* **2** the general intention or meaning of someone's remarks: *he got her*

drift. 3 a large mass of snow, leaves, etc., piled up by the wind. **4** movement away from an intended course or direction of currents or winds. **5** Geology deposits left by retreating ice sheets.

drift·er /'driftər/ ▶ n. **1** a person who is continually moving from place to place, without any fixed home or job. **2** a fishing boat equipped with a drift net.

drift net ▶ n. a large fishing net kept upright by weights at the bottom and floats at the top and allowed to drift in the sea.

drift·wood /'drift,wŏŏd/ ▶ n. pieces of wood floating on the sea or washed ashore.

drill[1] /dril/ ▶ n. **1** a tool or machine used for boring holes. **2** training in military exercises. **3** instruction by means of repeated exercises. **4** (**the drill**) informal the correct procedure. ▶ v. **1** bore a hole with a drill. **2** subject someone to military training or other intensive instruction. **3** Computing (**drill down**) access data that is in a lower level of a hierarchically structured database. ■ **drill·er** n.

drill[2] ▶ n. **1** a machine that makes small furrows, sows seed in them, and then covers the sown seed. **2** a small furrow made by such a machine. ▶ v. sow seed with a drill.

drill[3] ▶ n. a strong cotton or linen fabric woven with parallel diagonal lines.

drill·ing rig ▶ n. a large structure with equipment for drilling an oil well.

drill press ▶ n. a machine tool for drilling holes, set on a fixed stand.

drill ser·geant ▶ n. a noncommissioned officer who trains soldiers in basic military skills.

dri·ly /'drīlē/ (also **dryly**) ▶ adv. in a matter-of-fact or ironically humorous way.

drink /driNGk/ ▶ v. (past **drank**; past part. **drunk**) **1** take a liquid into the mouth and swallow. **2** consume alcohol, especially regularly or in large amounts. **3** (**drink something in**) watch or listen eagerly to something. ▶ n. **1** a liquid for drinking. **2** a quantity of liquid swallowed at one time. **3** alcohol or an alcoholic drink. ■ **drink·a·ble** adj. **drink·er** n.

– PHRASES **drink someone's health** (or **drink to someone**) express good wishes for someone by raising one's glass and drinking a small amount.

drink·ing foun·tain ▶ n. a device producing a small jet of water for drinking.

drip /drip/ ▶ v. (**drips**, **dripping**, **dripped**) fall or let fall in small drops of liquid. ▶ n. **1** a small drop of a liquid. **2** a piece of equipment that slowly passes fluid, nutrients, or drugs into a patient's body through a vein. **3** informal a weak and ineffectual person.

drip-dry ▶ adj. (of an item of clothing) able to dry without forming creases if hung up when wet.

drip-feed ▶ v. supply a patient with fluid through a drip.

drip·ping /'dripiNG/ ▶ n. (**drippings**) fat that has melted and dripped from roasting meat. ▶ adj. extremely wet.

drip·py /'dripē/ ▶ adj. (**drippier**, **drippiest**) informal weak, ineffectual, or very sentimental. ■ **drip·pi·ly** adv. **drip·pi·ness** n.

drive /drīv/ ▶ v. (past **drove** /drōv/; past part. **driven**) **1** operate and control a motor vehicle. **2** carry someone or something in a motor vehicle. **3** propel or carry along: *the storm drove the vessel onto the rocks.* **4** urge animals or people to move. **5** make someone act in a particular

way: *depression drove him to attempt suicide.*
6 provide the energy to keep an engine or machine in motion. **7** Golf hit a ball from the tee. ▶ **n. 1** a trip or journey in a car. **2** (also **driveway**) a short private road leading to a house. **3** an inborn desire or urge: *his sex drive.* **4** an organized effort to achieve a particular purpose: *a sales drive.* **5** determination and ambition. **6** the transmission of power to machinery or to the wheels of a vehicle. **7** Golf a shot from the tee. ■ **driv·a·ble** (also **driveable**) adj.
– PHRASES **what someone is driving at** the point that someone is trying to make.

drive-by ▶ adj. **1** (of a shooting or other act) carried out from a passing vehicle: *a drive-by shooting.* **2** informal superficial or casual: *drive-by journalism.* **3** informal (of a medical procedure in a hospital or clinic) involving a brief duration of on-site care for the patient. **4** informal referring to a facility that performs such procedures as a customary practice: *drive-by clinics.*

drive-in ▶ adj. (of a movie theater, restaurant, etc.) that one can visit without leaving one's car.

driv·el /ˈdrivəl/ ▶ n. silly nonsense.

driv·en /ˈdrivən/ ▶ past participle of DRIVE.

driv·er /ˈdrīvər/ ▶ n. **1** a person or thing that drives something. **2** a flat-faced golf club used for hitting the ball from the tee.
– PHRASES **in the driver's seat** in control.

driv·er's li·cense ▶ n. an official document permitting a person to drive a motor vehicle.

drive·shaft /ˈdrīvˌSHaft/ ▶ n. a rotating shaft that transmits torque in an engine.

drive·train /ˈdrīvˌtrān/ ▶ n. the system in a motor vehicle that connects the transmission to the drive axles.

drive·way /ˈdrīvˌwā/ ▶ n. a short road leading from a public road to a house or garage.

driv·ing /ˈdrīviNG/ ▶ adj. **1** having a controlling influence: *the driving force behind the plan.* **2** being blown by the wind with great force: *driving rain.*

driv·ing range ▶ n. an area where golfers can practice drives.

driz·zle /ˈdrizəl/ ▶ n. light rain falling in very fine drops. ▶ v. **1** (**it drizzles, it is drizzling, it drizzled**) rain lightly. **2** pour a thin stream of a liquid ingredient over food. ■ **driz·zly** adj.

DRM ▶ abbr. digital rights management; the protection of the interests of owners of copyright on digitally stored data, or technology that facilitates this.

drogue /drōg/ ▶ n. a device towed behind a boat or aircraft to reduce speed or improve stability, or as a target for gunnery practice.

droid /droid/ ▶ n. (in science fiction) a robot.

droit de sei·gneur /ˌdrwä də sān'yər/ ▶ n. the alleged right of a medieval feudal lord to have sex with a vassal's bride on her wedding night.

droll /drōl/ ▶ adj. amusing in a strange or unexpected way. ■ **droll·er·y** /ˈdrōlərē/ n. **drol·ly** adv.

drom·e·dar·y /ˈdräməˌderē/ ▶ n. (pl. **dromedaries**) an Arabian camel, with one hump.

drone /drōn/ ▶ v. **1** make a continuous low humming sound. **2** (**drone on**) speak at length in a boring way. ▶ n. **1** a low continuous humming sound. **2** a pipe (especially in a set of bagpipes) or string used to sound a continuous low-pitched note. **3** a male bee that does no work in a colony but can fertilize a queen. **4** a lazy person. **5** a

remote-controlled aircraft with no pilot.

drool /drōol/ ▶ v. **1** drop saliva uncontrollably from the mouth. **2** (often **drool over**) informal show great pleasure or desire. ▶ n. saliva falling from the mouth.

droop /drōop/ ▶ v. **1** bend or hang downward limply. **2** sag down as a result of tiredness or low spirits: *the corners of his mouth drooped.* ▶ n. an act of drooping.

droop·y /ˈdrōopē/ ▶ adj. (**droopier, droopiest**) **1** hanging down limply; drooping. **2** not having much strength or spirit. ■ **droop·i·ly** adv. **droop·i·ness** n.

drop /dräp/ ▶ v. (**drops, dropping, dropped**) **1** fall or cause to fall. **2** sink to the ground. **3** make or become lower, weaker, or less: *he dropped his speed.* **4** abandon or discontinue: *the charges against him were dropped.* **5** (often **drop someone off**) set down or unload a passenger or goods. **6** informal collapse from exhaustion. **7** lose a point, game, etc. **8** mention something casually. ▶ n. **1** a small round or pear-shaped amount of liquid. **2** an instance of falling or dropping. **3** a small drink, especially of alcohol. **4** an abrupt fall or slope. **5** a small candy.
– PHRASES **at the drop of a hat** informal without hesitation; immediately. **drop back/behind** fall back or get left behind. **drop by/in** pay someone a brief or casual visit. **drop dead** die suddenly and unexpectedly. **drop one's guard** stop being defensive or self-protective. **a drop in the bucket** a very small amount compared with what is needed. **drop someone a line** informal send someone a note or letter. **drop off** fall asleep. **drop out 1** stop participating in something. **2** start living an unconventional lifestyle.

drop cloth ▶ n. a sheet for covering furniture or flooring to protect it from dust or while decorating.

drop-dead ▶ adv. informal used to emphasize attractiveness: *drop-dead gorgeous.*

drop goal ▶ n. Rugby a goal scored by a drop kick of the ball over the crossbar.

drop han·dle·bars ▶ pl.n. handlebars with the handles bent below the rest of the bar, used especially on racing cycles.

drop-in ▶ n. **1** visited or visiting on an informal basis without making appointments: *a drop-in center for addicts.* **2** (of an object such as a chair seat) designed to drop into position.

drop kick ▶ n. (formerly, in football) a kick for a field goal or conversion made by dropping the ball and kicking it as it bounces.

drop·let /ˈdräplit/ ▶ n. a very small drop of a liquid.

drop-off ▶ n. a decline or decrease.

drop·out /ˈdräpˌout/ ▶ n. a person who has abandoned a course of study or rejected conventional society to pursue an alternative lifestyle.

drop·per /ˈdräpər/ ▶ n. a short glass tube with a rubber bulb at one end, for measuring out drops of liquid.

drop·pings /ˈdräpiNGz/ ▶ pl.n. the excrement of animals.

drop shot ▶ n. (in tennis or squash) a softly hit shot that drops abruptly to the ground.

drop·sy /ˈdräpsē/ ▶ n. old-fashioned or less technical term for EDEMA. ■ **drop·si·cal** /ˈdräpsikəl/ adj.

drop waist ▶ n. a style of waistline with the seam

positioned at the hips rather than the waist.

drop zone ▶ n. an area into which troops or supplies are dropped by parachute.

dro·soph·i·la /drəˈsäfələ/ ▶ n. a fruit fly of a kind widely used in genetic research.

dross /drôs, dräs/ ▶ n. **1** rubbish. **2** scum on the surface of molten metal.

drought /drout/ ▶ n. a very long period of abnormally low rainfall, leading to a shortage of water.

drove[1] /drōv/ ▶ past of DRIVE.

drove[2] ▶ n. **1** a flock of animals being driven. **2** a large number of people doing the same thing: *tourists arrived in droves.*

dro·ver /drōvər/ ▶ n. historical a person who drove sheep or cattle to market.

drown /droun/ ▶ v. **1** die as a result of submersion in water, or kill someone in this way. **2** flood an area. **3** (usu. **drown someone/thing out**) make someone or something impossible to hear by making a very loud noise.
– PHRASES **drown one's sorrows** forget one's problems by getting drunk.

drowse /drouz/ ▶ v. be half asleep; doze.

drow·sy /ˈdrouzē/ ▶ adj. (**drowsier, drowsiest**) sleepy. ■ **drow·si·ly** adv. **drow·si·ness** n.

drub·bing /ˈdrəbiNG/ ▶ n. **1** a beating. **2** informal a resounding defeat in a match or contest. ■ **drub** v.

drudge /drəj/ ▶ n. a person made to do hard, menial, or dull work.

drudg·er·y /ˈdrəjərē/ ▶ n. hard, menial, or dull work.

drug /drəg/ ▶ n. **1** a substance used in the treatment or prevention of disease or infection. **2** an illegal substance taken for its narcotic or stimulant effects. ▶ v. (**drugs, drugging, drugged**) give someone a drug, especially in order to make them unconscious.

drug·gie /ˈdrəgē/ ▶ n. informal a drug addict.

drug·gist /ˈdrəgist/ ▶ n. a pharmacist or a seller of medicinal drugs.

drug·store /ˈdrəgˌstôr/ ▶ n. a pharmacy that also sells toiletries and other articles.

Dru·id /ˈdrōoid/ ▶ n. a priest in the ancient Celtic religion. ■ **Dru·id·ic** /drōoˈidik/ adj. **Dru·id·i·cal** /drōoˈidikəl/ adj. **Dru·id·ism** /-ˌizəm/ n.

drum[1] /drəm/ ▶ n. **1** a percussion instrument with a skin stretched across a rounded frame, sounded by being struck with sticks or the hands. **2** a sound made by or resembling that of a drum. **3** a cylindrical container or part. ▶ v. (**drums, drumming, drummed**) **1** play on a drum. **2** make a continuous rhythmic noise. **3** (**drum something into**) teach someone something by repeating it many times. **4** (**drum something up**) try to get business or support from people. **5** (**drum someone out**) expel someone from somewhere in disgrace.

drum[2] ▶ n. any of several fish, many edible, that make a drumming sound by vibrating the swim bladder, found mainly in estuarine and shallow coastal waters.

drum and bass /bäs/ ▶ n. a type of dance music consisting largely of electronic drums and bass.

drum·beat /ˈdrəmˌbēt/ ▶ n. a stroke or pattern of strokes on a drum.

drum·head /ˈdrəmˌhed/ ▶ n. the membrane or skin of a drum.

drum kit ▶ n. a set of drums, cymbals, and other percussion instruments.

drum·lin /ˈdrəmlin/ ▶ n. Geology a mound or small hill consisting of compacted boulder clay.

drum ma·jor ▶ n. **1** a noncommissioned officer commanding regimental drummers. **2** the male leader of a marching band, who twirls a baton.

drum ma·jor·ette ▶ n. the female leader of a marching band, who twirls a baton.

drum·mer /ˈdrəmər/ ▶ n. a person who plays a drum or drums.

drum roll ▶ n. a rapid succession of drumbeats.

drum·stick /ˈdrəmˌstik/ ▶ n. **1** a stick used for beating a drum. **2** the lower cut of the leg of a cooked chicken or similar bird.

drunk /drəNGk/ past part. of DRINK ▶ adj. affected by alcohol to such an extent that one is not in control of oneself. ▶ n. a person who is drunk or who often drinks too much.

drunk·ard /ˈdrəNGkərd/ ▶ n. a person who is often drunk.

drunk driv·ing ▶ n. the crime of driving a vehicle with too much alcohol in the blood.

drunk·en /ˈdrəNGkən/ ▶ adj. **1** drunk. **2** caused by or showing the effects of drink: *a drunken stupor.* ■ **drunk·en·ly** adv. **drunk·en·ness** n.

drupe /drōop/ ▶ n. Botany a fleshy fruit with thin skin and a central stone, e.g., a plum or olive.

dry /drī/ ▶ adj. (**drier, driest**) **1** free from moisture or liquid. **2** not producing or yielding water, oil, or milk. **3** without grease or other lubrication. **4** serious and boring. **5** (of humor) subtle and expressed in a matter-of-fact way. **6** (of wine) not sweet. **7** not allowing the sale or drinking of alcohol. ▶ v. (**dries, drying, dried**) **1** make or become dry. **2** preserve something by evaporating the moisture from it. **3** (**dry up**) (of a supply or flow) decrease and stop. **4** (**dry up**) informal stop talking. **5** (**dry out**) informal overcome one's addiction to alcohol. ■ **dry·ness** n.

dry·ad /ˈdrīˌad, -əd/ ▶ n. (in folklore and classical mythology) a nymph living in a tree or forest.

dry cell (also **dry battery**) ▶ n. an electric cell (or battery) in which the electrolyte is absorbed in a solid to form a paste.

dry-clean ▶ v. clean a garment with a chemical solvent rather than water.

dry dock ▶ n. a dock that can be drained of water to allow a ship's hull to be repaired.

dry·er /ˈdrīər/ (also **drier**) ▶ n. a machine or device for drying something, especially the hair or laundry.

dry fly ▶ n. an artificial fishing fly that floats lightly on the water.

dry goods ▶ n. fabric, thread, clothing, and related merchandise, especially as distinct from hardware and groceries.

dry ice ▶ n. **1** solid carbon dioxide. **2** white mist produced with this as a theatrical effect.

dry·ly /ˈdrīlē/ ▶ adv. variant spelling of DRILY.

dry rot ▶ n. a fungus causing wood to decay in conditions where there is poor ventilation.

dry run ▶ n. a rehearsal of a performance or procedure.

dry·suit /ˈdrīˌsōot/ ▶ n. a waterproof rubber suit for water sports, under which warm clothes can be worn.

Ds ▶ symbol the chemical element darmstadtium.

DSc ▶ abbr. Doctor of Science.

DSL ▶ abbr. digital subscriber line, a method of routing digital data on copper telephone wires, allowing high-speed Internet access and simultaneous use of the line for voice transmission.

DSP ▸ abbr. digital signal processor or processing.

DST ▸ abbr. daylight saving time.

DTD ▸ abbr. document type definition; a template that sets out the format and tag structure of an XML or SGML-compliant document.

DTP ▸ abbr. desktop publishing.

DTs ▸ pl.n. informal delirium tremens.

du·al /'d(y)o͞oəl/ ▸ adj. consisting of two parts, elements, or aspects. ■ **du·al·i·ty** /d(y)o͞o'alitē/ n. **du·al·ly** adv.

du·al·ism /'d(y)o͞oə,lizəm/ ▸ n. **1** division into two opposed or contrasted aspects, such as good and evil or mind and matter. **2** the quality or state of having two parts, elements, or aspects. ■ **du·al·ist** n. & adj. **du·al·is·tic** /,d(y)o͞oə'listik/ adj.

dub[1] /dəb/ ▸ v. (**dubs, dubbing, dubbed**) **1** give someone an unofficial name or nickname. **2** knight someone by touching their shoulder with a sword in a special ceremony.

dub[2] ▸ v. (**dubs, dubbing, dubbed**) **1** provide a movie with a soundtrack in a different language from the original. **2** add sound effects or music to a movie or a recording. **3** make a copy of a recording. ▸ n. **1** an act of dubbing sound effects or music. **2** a style of popular music originating from the remixing of recorded music (especially reggae).

du·bi·ous /'d(y)o͞obēəs/ ▸ adj. **1** hesitating or doubtful. **2** probably not honest; morally suspect: *dubious sales methods.* **3** of questionable value: *he has the dubious distinction of being Hollywood's top gossip columnist.* ■ **du·bi·ous·ly** adv. **du·bi·ous·ness** n.

dub·ni·um /'dəbnēəm/ ▸ n. a very unstable chemical element made by high-energy atomic collisions.

Du·bon·net /,d(y)o͞obə'nā/ ▸ n. trademark a sweet red vermouth made in France.

du·cal /'d(y)o͞okəl/ ▸ adj. relating to a duke or dukedom.

duc·at /'dəkət/ ▸ n. a former European gold coin.

duch·ess /'dəCHis/ ▸ n. **1** the wife or widow of a duke. **2** a woman holding a rank equivalent to duke.

duch·y /'dəCHē/ ▸ n. (pl. **duchies**) the territory of a duke or duchess.

duck[1] /dək/ ▸ n. (pl. same or **ducks**) **1** a waterbird with a broad blunt bill, short legs, and webbed feet. **2** a female duck. Contrasted with **DRAKE**.

– PHRASES **like water off a duck's back** (of a critical remark) having no effect.

duck[2] ▸ v. **1** lower the head or body quickly to avoid being hit or seen. **2** push someone under water. **3** informal avoid an unwelcome duty. ▸ n. a quick lowering of the head. ■ **duck·er** n.

duck[3] ▸ n. a strong untwilled linen or cotton fabric, used chiefly for casual or work clothes and sails.

duck-billed plat·y·pus ▸ n. see **PLATYPUS**.

duck·boards /'dək,bôrdz/ ▸ pl.n. wooden slats joined together to form a path over muddy ground.

duck·ling /'dəkliNG/ ▸ n. a young duck.

duck·weed /'dək,wēd/ ▸ n. a tiny flowering plant that floats in large quantities on still water.

duck·y /'dəkē/ ▸ adj. informal excellent; delightful.

duct /dəkt/ ▸ n. **1** a tube or passageway in a

building or machine for air, cables, etc. **2** a tube in the body through which tears or other fluids pass. ▸ v. convey something through a duct. ■ **duct·ing** n.

duc·tile /'dəktl, -,tīl/ ▸ adj. (of a metal) able to be drawn out into a thin wire. ■ **duc·til·i·ty** /dək'tilitē/ n.

duct tape ▸ n. strong cloth-backed waterproof adhesive tape.

duct·work /'dəkt,wərk/ ▸ n. a system or network of ducts.

dud /dəd/ informal ▸ n. **1** a thing that fails to work properly. **2** (**duds**) clothes. ▸ adj. failing to work or meet a standard.

dude /do͞od/ ▸ n. informal **1** a man. **2** a stylish man.

dude ranch ▸ n. (in the western US) a cattle ranch converted to a vacation center for tourists.

dudg·eon /'dəjən/ ▸ n. (in phrase **in high dudgeon**) feeling resentful or angry.

due /d(y)o͞o/ ▸ adj. **1** expected at or planned for a certain time: *the baby's due in June.* **2** owed or deserving something: *he was due for a raise.* **3** needing to be paid; owing. **4** required as a legal or moral duty. **5** proper: *driving without due care and attention.* ▸ n. **1** (**one's due/dues**) a person's right. **2** (**dues**) fees. ▸ adv. (of a point of the compass) directly.

– PHRASES **due to 1** caused by. **2** because of. **give someone their due** be fair to someone. **in due course** at the appropriate time.

> USAGE
>
> Some people think that you should not use **due to** to mean 'because of' for the reason that **due** is an adjective and should not be used as a preposition. However, this use is now common and acceptable in standard English.

du·el /'d(y)o͞oəl/ ▸ n. **1** historical a prearranged contest with deadly weapons between two people to settle a point of honor. **2** a contest between two parties. ▸ v. (**duels, dueling, dueled**) fight a duel. ■ **du·el·ist** n.

du·en·na /d(y)o͞o'enə/ ▸ n. an older woman acting as a governess and chaperone to girls in a Spanish family.

due proc·ess ▸ n. fair treatment through the normal judicial system, especially as a citizen's entitlement.

du·et /d(y)o͞o'et/ ▸ n. **1** a performance by two singers, instrumentalists, or dancers. **2** a musical composition for two performers. ▸ v. (**duets, duetting, duetted**) perform a duet.

duff[1] /dəf/ ▸ n. decaying vegetable matter covering the ground under trees.

duff[2] ▸ n. informal a person's buttocks: *I did not get where I am today by sitting on my duff.*

duf·fel /'dəfəl/ (also **duffle**) ▸ n. **1** a coarse woolen cloth with a thick nap. **2** a duffel bag.

duf·fel bag ▸ n. a cylindrical canvas bag closed by a drawstring.

duf·fer /'dəfər/ ▸ n. informal an incompetent or stupid person, especially an elderly one.

dug[1] /dəg/ ▸ past and past participle of **DIG**.

dug[2] ▸ n. the udder, teat, or nipple of a female animal.

du·gong /'do͞ogäNG, -gôNG/ ▸ n. (pl. same or **dugongs**) a sea cow (mammal) found in the Indian Ocean.

dug·out /'dəg,out/ ▸ n. **1** a trench that is roofed over as a shelter for troops. **2** a low shelter at the side of a sports field for a team's coaches and substitutes. **3** (also **dugout canoe**) a canoe made from a hollowed tree trunk.

duh /də, dŏŏ/ ▶ **exclam.** informal used to comment on an action perceived as foolish or stupid: *I left the keys in the ignition—duh!*

dui·ker /'dīkər/ ▶ **n.** (pl. same or **duikers**) a small African antelope.

du jour /də ZHŏŏr, ˌd(y)ŏŏ/ ▶ **adj.** informal enjoying great but probably short-lived popularity: *black comedy is the genre du jour.*

duke /d(y)ŏŏk/ ▶ **n. 1** a man holding the highest hereditary title in Britain and some other countries. **2** chiefly historical (in parts of Europe) a male ruler of a small independent state. ■ **duke·dom** n.

dul·cet /'dəlsit/ ▶ **adj.** often ironic (of a sound) sweet and soothing.

dul·ci·mer /'dəlsəmər/ ▶ **n.** (also **hammered dulcimer**) a musical instrument with strings that are struck with hand-held hammers.

dull /dəl/ ▶ **adj. 1** not interesting or exciting: *a very dull book.* **2** lacking brightness; not shiny. **3** (of the weather) overcast. **4** slow to understand; rather stupid. **5** not clearly felt or heard: *a dull pain in his jaw.* ▶ **v.** make or become dull. ■ **dull·ness** n. **dul·ly** adv.

dull·ard /'dələrd/ ▶ **n.** a slow or stupid person.

dulse /dəls/ ▶ **n.** a dark red edible seaweed with flattened fronds.

du·ly /'d(y)ŏŏlē/ ▶ **adv.** in accordance with what is required, appropriate, or expected.

dumb /dəm/ ▶ **adj. 1** offensive unable to speak; lacking the power of speech. **2** temporarily unable or unwilling to speak. **3** informal stupid. **4** (of a computer terminal) having no independent processing capability. ▶ **v.** (**dumb something down**) informal make something less intellectually challenging so as to appeal to a wider audience. ■ **dumb·ly** adv. **dumb·ness** n.

> **USAGE**
> Avoid **dumb** in the sense meaning 'not able to speak,' as it is likely to cause offense; use alternatives such as **speech-impaired**.

dumb·bell /'dəmˌbel/ ▶ **n. 1** a short bar with a weight at each end, used for exercise or muscle-building. **2** informal a stupid person.

dumb·found /'dəmˌfound/ (also **dumfound**) ▶ **v.** greatly astonish someone.

dum·bo /'dəmbō/ ▶ **n.** (pl. **dumbos**) informal a stupid person.

dumb·struck /'dəmˌstrək/ ▶ **adj.** so shocked or surprised as to be unable to speak.

dumb·wait·er /'dəmˌwātər/ ▶ **n.** a small elevator for carrying food and dishes between floors.

dum·dum /'dəmˌdəm/ (also **dumdum bullet**) ▶ **n.** a kind of soft-nosed bullet that expands on impact.

dum·my /'dəmē/ ▶ **n.** (pl. **dummies**) **1** a model of a human being. **2** an object designed to resemble and act as a substitute for the real one. **3** (in sports) a pretended pass or kick. **4** informal a stupid person. ▶ **v.** (**dummies, dummying, dummied**) create a prototype of a book or page.

dump /dəmp/ ▶ **n. 1** a site where garbage or waste is left. **2** a heap of garbage left at a dump. **3** informal an unpleasant or dreary place. **4** informal an act of defecation. **5** an act of dumping stored computer data. ▶ **v. 1** get rid of garbage or

something unwanted. **2** put something down heavily or carelessly. **3** informal abandon someone. **4** copy stored computer data to a different location. **5** send goods to a foreign market for sale at a low price.
– PHRASES **dump on** informal abuse or criticize (someone).

dump·ling /'dəmpliNG/ ▶ **n. 1** a small savory ball of dough boiled in water or in a stew. **2** a pastry consisting of fruit enclosed in a sweet dough and baked.

dumps /dəmps/ ▶ **pl.n.** (in phrase (**down**) **in the dumps**) informal depressed or unhappy.

dump·ster /'dəmpstər/ (also **Dumpster** trademark) ▶ **n.** a large trash receptacle designed to be hoisted and emptied into a truck.

dump truck ▶ **n.** a truck with a body that tilts or opens at the back for unloading.

dump·y /'dəmpē/ ▶ **adj.** (**dumpier, dumpiest**) short and stout.

dun[1] /dən/ ▶ **n.** a dull grayish-brown color.

dun[2] ▶ **v.** (**duns, dunning, dunned**) persistently demand that someone repays a debt.

dunce /dəns/ ▶ **n.** a person who is slow at learning.

dunce cap ▶ **n.** a paper cone formerly put on the head of a dunce at school as a mark of disgrace.

dun·der·head /'dəndərˌhed/ ▶ **n.** informal a stupid person. ■ **dun·der·head·ed** adj.

dune /d(y)ŏŏn/ ▶ **n.** a mound or ridge of sand formed by the wind, especially on the coast or in a desert.

dung /dəNG/ ▶ **n.** manure.

dun·ga·rees /ˌdəNGgə'rēz/ ▶ **pl.n.** blue jeans or overalls.

dung bee·tle ▶ **n.** a beetle whose larvae feed on dung, especially a scarab.

dun·geon /'dənjən/ ▶ **n.** a strong underground prison cell, especially in a castle.

dung·hill /'dəNGˌhil/ ▶ **n.** a heap of dung or refuse.

dunk /dəNGk/ ▶ **v. 1** dip food into a drink or soup before eating it. **2** immerse someone or something in water.

dun·lin /'dənlin/ ▶ **n.** (pl. same or **dunlins**) a sandpiper with a downcurved bill and reddish-brown upper parts.

dun·no /də'nō/ ▶ **contr.** informal (I) do not know.

du·o /'d(y)ŏŏ-ō/ ▶ **n.** (pl. **duos**) **1** a pair of people or things, especially in music or entertainment. **2** Music a duet.

du·o·dec·i·mal /ˌd(y)ŏŏə'desəməl, ˌd(y)ŏŏ-ō-/ ▶ **adj.** relating to a system of counting that has twelve as a base.

du·o·de·num /ˌd(y)ŏŏə'dēnəm, d(y)ŏŏ'ädn-əm/ ▶ **n.** (pl. **duodenums**) the first part of the small intestine immediately beyond the stomach. ■ **du·o·de·nal** /-'dēnl, -'ädnəl/ adj.

du·o·logue /'d(y)ŏŏəˌläg, -ˌlôg/ ▶ **n.** a play or part of a play with speaking roles for only two actors.

du·op·o·ly /d(y)ŏŏ'äpəlē/ ▶ **n.** (pl. **duopolies**) a situation in which two suppliers dominate a market.

dupe /d(y)ŏŏp/ ▶ **v.** deceive or trick someone. ▶ **n.** a person who has been deceived or tricked.

du·ple /'d(y)ŏŏpəl/ ▶ **adj.** (of musical rhythm) based on two main beats to the measure.

du·plex /'d(y)ŏŏpleks/ ▶ **n. 1** a residential

building divided into two apartments. **2** an apartment on two floors. ▸ adj. having two parts.

du·pli·cate ▸ adj. /'d(y) o͞oplәkit/ **1** exactly like something else. **2** having two corresponding parts. ▸ n. /'d(y)o͞oplәkit/ one of two or more identical things. ▸ v. /'d(y)o͞oplә,kāt/ **1** make or be an exact copy of something. **2** multiply something by two. **3** do something again unnecessarily. ▪ **du·pli·ca·tion** /,d(y)o͞oplә'kāshәn/.

du·pli·ca·tor /'d(y)o͞oplә,kātәr/ ▸ n. a machine for copying something.

du·plic·i·ty /d(y)o͞o'plisitē/ ▸ n. dishonest behavior that is intended to deceive someone. ▪ **du·plic·i·tous** adj.

du·ra·ble /'d(y)o͞orәbәl/ ▸ adj. **1** hard-wearing. **2** (of goods) not for immediate consumption and so able to be kept. ▪ **du·ra·bil·i·ty** /,d(y)o͞orә'bilitē/ n. **du·ra·bly** adv.

du·ra·ble goods ▸ pl. n. goods not for immediate consumption and able to be kept for a period of time.

du·ra ma·ter /'d(y)o͞orә 'mātәr, 'mä-/ ▸ n. the tough outermost membrane enveloping the brain and spinal cord.

du·ra·tion /d(y)o͞or'āshәn/ ▸ n. the time during which something continues: *a flight of over eight hours' duration.* – PHRASES **for the duration 1** until the end of something. **2** informal for a very long time.

du·ress /d(y)o͞o'res/ ▸ n. threats or violence used to force a person into doing something: *confessions extracted under duress.*

du·ri·an /'do͞orēәn, -rē,än/ ▸ n. a tropical Asian fruit with a fetid smell but pleasant taste.

dur·ing /'d(y)o͞oriNG/ ▸ prep. **1** throughout the course of a period of time. **2** at a particular point in the course of: *he met the prime minister during his first visit to the country.*

du·rum wheat /'d(y)o͞orәm/ ▸ n. a kind of hard wheat, yielding flour from which pasta is made.

dusk /dәsk/ ▸ n. the darker stage of twilight.

dusk·y /'dәskē/ ▸ adj. (**duskier, duskiest**) **1** dark or soft in color. **2** literary poorly lit; dim. ▪ **dusk·i·ly** adv. **dusk·i·ness** n.

dust /dәst/ ▸ n. **1** fine, dry powder consisting of tiny particles of earth or waste matter. **2** any material in the form of tiny particles: *coal dust.* ▸ v. **1** remove dust from the surface of something. **2** cover something lightly with a powdered substance. **3** (**dust something off**) bring something out for use again after a long period of neglect. – PHRASES **when the dust settles** when things quiet down.

dust bowl ▸ n. a dry area where vegetation has been lost and soil reduced to dust and eroded.

dust cov·er ▸ n. a dust jacket or drop cloth.

dust dev·il ▸ n. a small whirlwind or air vortex over land, visible as a column of dust and debris.

dust·er /'dәstәr/ ▸ n. a cloth for dusting furniture.

dust jack·et ▸ n. a removable paper cover on a book.

dust·pan /'dәst,pan/ ▸ n. a flat hand-held container into which dust and waste can be swept.

dust storm ▸ n. a strong wind carrying clouds of fine dust and sand.

dust-up ▸ n. informal a fight or quarrel.

dust·y /'dәstē/ ▸ adj. (**dustier, dustiest**) **1** covered

with or resembling dust. **2** (of a color) dull or muted. **3** staid and uninteresting: *the society has banished its dusty, fusty, middle-aged-male image.* ▪ **dust·i·ly** adv. **dust·i·ness** n.

Dutch /dәcH/ ▸ adj. relating to the Netherlands or its language. ▸ n. the language of the Netherlands. – PHRASES **go Dutch** share the cost of a meal equally.

Dutch auc·tion ▸ n. a method of selling in which the price is reduced until a buyer is found.

Dutch cap ▸ n. a woman's lace cap with triangular flaps on each side, worn as part of Dutch traditional dress.

Dutch cour·age ▸ n. confidence gained from drinking alcohol.

Dutch elm dis·ease ▸ n. a disease of elm trees, caused by a fungus.

Dutch·man /'dәcHmәn/ (or **Dutchwoman** /'dәcH,wo͞omәn/) ▸ n. (pl. **Dutchmen** or **Dutchwomen**) a person from the Netherlands, or a person of Dutch descent.

Dutch ov·en ▸ n. a covered earthenware or cast-iron pot used for slow cooking.

Dutch un·cle ▸ n. informal a person giving firm but benevolent advice.

du·ti·a·ble /'d(y)o͞otēәbәl/ ▸ adj. (of goods) on which customs or other duties have to be paid.

dut·i·ful /'d(y)o͞otәfәl/ ▸ adj. **1** doing one's duty in an obedient way. **2** done because of a feeling of obligation rather than enthusiasm: *dutiful applause greeted his speech.* ▪ **du·ti·ful·ly** adv.

du·ty /'d(y)o͞otē/ ▸ n. (pl. **duties**) **1** something one has to do because it is morally right or legally necessary: *it's my duty to uphold the law.* **2** a task required as part of one's job. **3** a payment charged on the import, export, manufacture, or sale of goods. – PHRASES **on** (or **off**) **duty** doing (or not doing) one's regular work.

du·ty-bound ▸ adj. morally or legally obliged to do something.

du·ty-free ▸ adj. & adv. (of goods) exempt from payment of duty.

du·vet /,d(y)o͞o'vā/ ▸ n. a soft, thick quilt used instead of an upper sheet and blankets.

DVD ▸ abbr. a high-density videodisc.

DVD-R ▸ abbr. DVD recordable, a DVD that can be recorded on once only.

DVD-ROM ▸ abbr. DVD read-only memory, a DVD used in a computer for displaying data.

DVD-RW (also **DVD-RAM**) ▸ abbr. DVD rewritable (or random-access memory), a DVD on which recordings can be made and erased a number of times.

DVM ▸ abbr. Doctor of Veterinary Medicine.

dwarf /dwôrf/ ▸ n. (pl. **dwarfs** or **dwarves** /dwôrvz/) **1** a member of a mythical race of short, stocky humanlike creatures. **2** a person who is unusually small. **3** (also **dwarf star**) a star of relatively small size and low luminosity. ▸ adj. (of an animal or plant) much smaller than is usual for its type or species. ▸ v. cause to seem small in comparison: *the church is dwarfed by cranes.* ▪ **dwarf·ish** adj.

USAGE
Although the use of **dwarf** to mean 'an unusually small person' is normally considered offensive, there is no term that has been established as an acceptable general alternative.

dwarf·ism /'d(w)ôrfizəm/ ▶ n. unusually low stature or small size.

dweeb /dwēb/ ▶ n. informal a boring, studious, or socially inept person.

dwell /dwel/ ▶ v. (past and past part. **dwelt** or **dwelled**) 1 formal live in or at a place. 2 (**dwell on**) think, speak, or write at length about something. ■ **dwell·er** n.

dwell·ing /'dweliNG/ (also **dwelling place**) ▶ n. formal a house or other place where someone lives.

dwin·dle /'dwindl/ ▶ v. gradually become smaller or weaker: *a weekly audience that's dwindled to less than one million.*

Dy ▶ symbol the chemical element dysprosium.

dy·ad /'dīad/ ▶ n. technical something consisting of two elements or parts. ■ **dy·ad·ic** /dī'adik/ adj.

dye /dī/ ▶ n. a natural or synthetic substance used to color something. ▶ v. (**dyes**, **dyeing**, **dyed**) color something with dye. ■ **dy·er** n.
 – PHRASES **dyed in the wool** having firm beliefs that will never change.

dye·stuff /'dī,stəf/ ▶ n. a substance that is used as a dye or that yields a dye.

dy·ing /'dī-iNG/ ▶ present participle of DIE¹.

dyke¹ /dīk/ (also **dike**) ▶ n. variant spelling of DIKE¹.

dyke² (also **dike**) ▶ n. informal a lesbian. ■ **dyke·y** adj.

dy·nam·ic /dī'namik/ ▶ adj. 1 (of a process or system) constantly changing or progressing: *the dynamic market in Latin America.* 2 full of energy and new ideas. 3 Physics relating to forces producing motion. Often contrasted with STATIC. ▶ n. a force that stimulates change or progress: *evaluation is part of the basic dynamic of the project.* ■ **dy·nam·i·cal** adj. **dy·nam·i·cal·ly** /-ik(ə)lē/ adv.

dy·nam·ic range ▶ n. the range of sound intensity that occurs in a piece of music or that can be handled by a piece of equipment.

dy·nam·ics /dī'namiks/ ▶ pl.n. 1 (treated as sing.) the branch of mechanics concerned with the motion of bodies under the action of forces. 2 the forces that stimulate change or progress within a system or process. 3 the varying levels of volume of sound in a musical performance.

dy·na·mism /'dīnə,mizəm/ ▶ n. the quality of being full of energy, vigor, or enthusiasm: *the prosperity and dynamism of Barcelona.*

dy·na·mite /'dīnə,mīt/ ▶ n. 1 a high explosive made of nitroglycerine. 2 informal a very impressive or potentially dangerous person or thing: *that policy is political dynamite.* ▶ v. blow something up with dynamite.

dy·na·mo /'dīnə,mō/ ▶ n. (pl. **dynamos**) 1 a machine for converting mechanical energy into electrical energy. 2 informal an extremely energetic person.

dy·na·mom·e·ter /,dīnə'mämitər/ ▶ n. an instrument that measures the power output of an engine.

dy·nast /'dī,nast, -nəst/ ▶ n. a member of a dynasty, especially a hereditary ruler.

dy·nas·ty /'dīnəstē/ ▶ n. (pl. **dynasties**) 1 a series of rulers of a country who belong to the same family. 2 a succession of prominent people from the same family. ■ **dy·nas·tic** /dī'nastik/ adj. **dy·nas·ti·cal·ly** /dī'nastik(ə)lē/ adv.

dyne /dīn/ ▶ n. Physics force required to give a mass of one gram an acceleration of one centimeter per second every second.

dys- ▶ comb.form bad; difficult (used especially in medical terms): *dyspepsia.*

dys·en·ter·y /'disən,terē/ ▶ n. a disease in which the intestines are infected, resulting in severe diarrhea.

dys·func·tion·al /dis'fəNGkshənl/ ▶ adj. 1 not operating normally or properly. 2 unable to deal adequately with normal relationships between people. ■ **dys·func·tion** n. **dys·func·tion·al·ly** adv.

dys·lex·i·a /dis'leksēə/ ▶ n. a disorder involving difficulty in learning to read or interpret words, letters, and other symbols. ■ **dys·lex·ic** /-'leksik/ adj. & n.

dys·men·or·rhe·a /,dismenə'rēə/ ▶ n. Medicine painful menstruation.

dys·mor·phi·a /dis'môrfēə/ ▶ n. Medicine deformity or abnormality in the shape or size of a part of the body. ■ **dys·mor·phic** /dis'môrfik/ adj.

dys·pep·sia /dis'pepsēə, -'pepsнə/ ▶ n. indigestion.

dys·pep·tic /dis'peptik/ ▶ adj. 1 relating to or having dyspepsia (indigestion). 2 irritable; bad-tempered.

dys·pha·sia /dis'fāzнə/ ▶ n. a disorder marked by difficulty in using language coherently, due to brain disease or damage. ■ **dys·pha·sic** /-'fāzik/ adj.

dys·pho·ri·a /dis'fôrēə/ ▶ n. a state of unease or general dissatisfaction. ■ **dys·phor·ic** /-'fôrik/ adj.

dys·pla·sia /dis'plāzнə/ ▶ n. the enlargement of an organ or tissue by the proliferation of abnormal cells. ■ **dys·plas·tic** /dis'plastik/ adj.

dys·prax·i·a /dis'praksēə/ ▶ n. a disorder of the brain in childhood resulting in poor physical coordination.

dys·pro·si·um /dis'prōzēəm/ ▶ n. a soft silvery-white metallic chemical element of the lanthanide series.

dys·to·pi·a /dis'tōpēə/ ▶ n. an imaginary place or society in which everything is bad. ■ **dys·to·pi·an** adj. & n.

dys·tro·phy /'distrəfē/ ▶ n. a disorder in which an organ or tissue of the body wastes away. See also MUSCULAR DYSTROPHY. ■ **dys·troph·ic** /dis'träfik/ adj.

Ee

E¹ (also **e**) ▸ n. (pl. **Es** or **E's**) **1** the fifth letter of the alphabet. **2** referring to the fifth item in a set. **3** Music the third note of the scale of C major.

E² ▸ abbr. **1** East or Eastern. **2** informal the drug Ecstasy or a tablet of Ecstasy. **3** Physics energy.

e¹ ▸ symbol **1** (€) euro or euros. **2** (*e*) Mathematics the transcendental number that is the base of natural logarithms, approximately equal to 2.71828.

e² /ē/ ▸ n. (pl. **e's**) an email system, message, or messages. ▸ v. (**e's e'ing e'd**) **1** send an email to someone: *e me to make an offer.* **2** send (a message) by email.

e- ▸ prefix referring to the use of electronic data transfer, especially through the Internet.

ea. ▸ abbr. each.

each /ēCH/ ▸ determiner & pron. every one of two or more people or things, regarded separately. ▸ adv. to, for, or by every one of a group.

each oth·er ▸ pron. the other one or ones.

ea·ger /'ēgər/ ▸ adj. **1** strongly wanting to do or have: *I was eager to help.* **2** keenly expectant or interested. ■ **ea·ger·ly** adv. **ea·ger·ness** n.

ea·gle /'ēgəl/ ▸ n. a large keen-sighted bird of prey with long broad wings and a large hooked bill. ■ **ea·glet** n.

ea·gle-eyed ▸ adj. sharp-sighted and very observant.

ea·gle owl ▸ n. a very large owl with ear tufts and a deep hoot.

ear¹ /i(ə)r/ ▸ n. **1** the organ of hearing and balance in humans and other vertebrates, especially the external part of this. **2** an ability to recognize and appreciate music or language. **3** willingness to listen: *she offers a sympathetic ear to worried pet owners.* ■ **eared** adj.
– PHRASES **be all ears** informal be listening eagerly. **one's ears are burning** one is subconsciously aware of being talked about. **have someone's ear** have access to and influence with someone. **have** (or **keep**) **an ear to the ground** be well informed about events and trends. **be out on one's ear** informal be abruptly dismissed from a job. **up to one's ears** in informal very busy with.

ear² ▸ n. the seed-bearing head of a cereal plant.

ear·ache /'i(ə)r,āk/ ▸ n. pain inside the ear.

ear·drum /'i(ə)r,drəm/ ▸ n. the membrane of the middle ear, which vibrates in response to sound waves.

ear·ful /'i(ə)r,fŏŏl/ ▸ n. informal a prolonged amount of talking, typically an angry reprimand.

ear·hole /'i(ə)r,hōl/ ▸ n. the external opening of the ear.

earl /ərl/ ▸ n. a British nobleman ranking above a viscount and below a marquess. ■ **earl·dom** n.

Earl Grey ▸ n. a kind of China tea flavored with bergamot.

ear·lobe /'i(ə)r,lōb/ ▸ n. see LOBE.

ear·ly /'ərlē/ ▸ adj. (**earlier, earliest**) & adv. **1** before the usual or expected time. **2** belonging or happening at the beginning of a particular period or sequence: *he's in his early fifties.* ■ **ear·li·ness** n.
– PHRASES **at the earliest** not before the time or date specified. **early bird** humorous a person who gets up or arrives early. **early** (or **earlier**) **on** at an early (or earlier) stage.

Ear·ly Eng·lish ▸ adj. referring to a style of English Gothic architecture typical of the late 12th and 13th centuries, marked by pointed arches and narrow pointed windows.

ear·ly mu·sic ▸ n. medieval, Renaissance, and early baroque music, especially as revived and played on period instruments.

ear·mark /'i(ə)r,märk/ ▸ v. set aside for a particular purpose: *the government has earmarked $15 million to fight hackers.* ▸ n. **1** an identifying feature. **2** an identifying mark on the ear of a domesticated animal.

ear·muffs /'i(ə)r,məfs/ ▸ pl.n. a pair of soft fabric coverings, connected by a band, worn over the ears to protect them from cold or noise.

earn /ərn/ ▸ v. **1** obtain money in return for work or services. **2** receive deservedly for one's behavior or achievements: *he earned a master's degree in English.* **3** (of capital invested) gain money as interest or profit. ■ **earn·er** n.

earned in·come /ərnd/ ▸ n. money derived from paid work as opposed to profit from investments.

ear·nest¹ /'ərnist/ ▸ adj. very serious and sincere. ■ **ear·nest·ly** adv. **ear·nest·ness** n.
– PHRASES **in earnest 1** with greater effort or intensity than before. **2** sincere and serious about one's intentions.

ear·nest² ▸ n. a sign or promise of what is to come.

earn·ings /'ərniNGz/ ▸ pl.n. money or income earned.

ear·phone /'i(ə)r,fōn/ ▸ n. an electrical device worn on the ear to listen to radio or recorded sound.

ear·piece /'i(ə)r,pēs/ ▸ n. the part of a telephone, radio receiver, or other device that is applied to the ear during use.

ear-pierc·ing ▸ adj. loud and shrill. ▸ n. the piercing of the lobes or edges of the ears to allow earrings to be worn.

ear·plug /'i(ə)r,pləg/ ▸ n. a piece of wax, absorbent cotton, or rubber placed in the ear as protection against noise or water.

ear·ring /'i(ə)r,(r)iNG/ ▸ n. a piece of jewelry worn on the lobe or edge of the ear.

ear·shot /'i(ə)r,sHät/ ▸ n. the range or distance over which one can hear or be heard.

ear-split·ting ▸adj. very loud.

earth /ərTH/ ▸n. **1** (also **Earth**) the planet on which we live. **2** the substance of the land surface; soil. **3** the underground lair of a badger or fox. ■ **earth·ward** /'ərTHwərd/ adj. & adv. **earth·wards** adv.
– PHRASES **come** (or **bring**) **back** (**down**) **to earth** return to reality. **on earth** used for emphasis: *what on earth are you doing?*

earth·bound /'ərTH,bound/ ▸adj. **1** confined to the earth or to material things. **2** moving toward the earth.

earth·en /'ərTHən/ ▸adj. **1** made of compressed earth. **2** (of a pot) made of baked or fired clay.

earth·en·ware /'ərTHən,wer/ ▸n. pottery made of fired clay.

earth·ling /'ərTHliNG/ ▸n. (in science fiction) an inhabitant of the earth.

earth·ly /'ərTHlē/ ▸adj. **1** relating to the earth or human life. **2** worldly rather than spiritual. **3** informal used for emphasis: *there was no earthly reason to rush.* ■ **earth·li·ness** n.

earth·quake /'ərTH,kwāk/ ▸n. a sudden violent shaking of the ground, caused by movements within the earth's crust.

earth sci·en·ces ▸pl.n. the branches of science concerned with the physical composition of the earth and its atmosphere.

earth-shat·ter·ing ▸adj. informal very important or shocking.

earth·work /'ərTH,wərk/ ▸n. a large artificial bank of soil, especially one made as a defense in ancient times.

earth·worm /'ərTH,wərm/ ▸n. a burrowing worm that lives in the soil.

earth·y /'ərTHē/ ▸adj. (**earthier, earthiest**) **1** resembling or suggestive of soil: *an earthy smell.* **2** direct and uninhibited about sex or bodily functions. ■ **earth·i·ly** adv. **earth·i·ness** n.

ear trum·pet ▸n. a trumpet-shaped device formerly used as a hearing aid.

ear·wax /'i(ə)r,waks/ ▸n. the protective yellow waxy substance produced in the passage of the outer ear.

ear·wig /'i(ə)r,wig/ ▸n. a small insect with a pair of pincers at its rear end.

ease /ēz/ ▸n. **1** lack of difficulty or effort: *he beat his opponent with ease.* **2** freedom from worries or problems. ▸v. **1** make something less serious or severe. **2** (**ease off/up**) become less intense or unpleasant: *the gale eased off a bit.* **3** move carefully or gradually. **4** (of share prices, interest rates, etc.) decrease in value or amount. ■ **ease·ful** adj. (literary).
– PHRASES **at ease** Military in a relaxed attitude with the feet apart and the hands behind the back.

ea·sel /'ēzəl/ ▸n. a wooden frame on legs for holding an artist's work in progress.

ease·ment /'ēzmənt/ ▸n. Law a right to cross or otherwise use someone else's land for a specified purpose.

eas·i·ly /'ēz(ə)lē/ ▸adv. **1** without difficulty or effort. **2** without doubt; definitely. **3** very probably.

east /ēst/ ▸n. (**the east**) **1** the direction in which the sun rises at the equinoxes, on the right-hand side of a person facing north. **2** the eastern part of a place. **3** (**the East**) the regions or countries lying to the east of Europe, especially

China, Japan, and India. **4** (**the East**) the former communist states of eastern Europe. ▸adj. **1** lying toward, near, or facing the east. **2** (of a wind) blowing from the east. ▸adv. to or toward the east. ■ **east·bound** /'ēs(t),bound/ adj. & adv.

Eas·ter /'ēstər/ (also **Easter Day** or **Easter Sunday**) ▸n. the Christian festival celebrating the resurrection of Jesus.

Eas·ter egg ▸n. a chocolate egg or decorated hard-boiled egg given as a gift at Easter.

east·er·ly /'ēstərlē/ ▸adj. & adv. **1** facing or moving toward the east. **2** (of a wind) blowing from the east. ▸n. (pl. **easterlies**) a wind blowing from the east.

east·ern /'ēstərn/ ▸adj. **1** situated in, directed toward, or facing the east. **2** (**Eastern**) relating to or characteristic of the regions to the east of Europe. ■ **east·ern·most** /'ēstərn,mōst/ adj.

east·ern·er /'ēstərnər/ ▸n. a person from the east of a region or country.

East·ern time ▸n. the standard time in a zone including the eastern states of the US and parts of Canada.

east-north·east ▸n. the direction midway between east and northeast.

east-south·east ▸n. the direction midway between east and southeast.

east·ward /'ēs(t)wərd/ ▸adj. in an easterly direction. ▸adv. (also **eastwards**) toward the east. ■ **east·ward·ly** adj. & adv.

eas·y /'ēzē/ ▸adj. (**easier, easiest**) **1** achieved without great effort; not difficult. **2** free from worry or problems: *the easy life of the rich.* **3** not anxious or awkward. **4** informal, derogatory (of a woman) very willing to have sex. ▸exclam. be careful! ■ **eas·i·ness** n.
– PHRASES **easy on the eye** (or **ear**) informal pleasant to look at (or listen to). **go** (or **be**) **easy on** informal **1** do not be too harsh with someone. **2** do not use too much of something. **take it easy** do something in a leisurely way; relax.

eas·y chair ▸n. a large, comfortable armchair.

eas·y·go·ing /'ēzē,gōiNG/ ▸adj. relaxed and open-minded.

eas·y lis·ten·ing ▸n. popular music that is tuneful and undemanding.

eas·y street ▸n. informal a state of financial security.

eat /ēt/ ▸v. (past **ate** /āt/; past part. **eaten** /'ētn/) **1** put food into the mouth and chew and swallow it. **2** (**eat out** or **in**) have a meal in a restaurant (or at home). **3** (**eat something away**) gradually erode or destroy something. **4** (**eat into**) use up a part of: *my loan payments are eating into my savings.* **5** (**eat something up**) use resources in very large quantities. ▸n. (**eats**) informal light food or snacks. ■ **eat·er** n.
– PHRASES **eat one's heart out** long for something that cannot be achieved. **eat one's words** admit that one was wrong. **what's eating you** (or **him** etc.)? informal what is worrying or annoying you (or him etc.)?

eat·a·ble /'ētəbəl/ ▸adj. fit to be eaten as food. ▸n. (**eatables**) items of food.

eat·er·y /'ētərē/ ▸n. (pl. **eateries**) informal a restaurant or cafe.

eat·ing ap·ple ▸n. an apple suitable for eating raw.

eau de co·logne /,ō də kə'lōn/ ▸n. (pl. **eaux de cologne** pronunc. same) a toilet water with a strong scent.

eau de toi·lette /ˌō də twä'let/ ▶ n. (pl. **eaux de toilette** pronunc. same) a dilute form of perfume; toilet water.

eau de vie /ˌō də 'vē/ ▶ n. (pl. **eaux de vie** pronunc. same) brandy.

eaves /ēvz/ ▶ pl.n. the part of a roof that meets or overhangs the walls of a building.

eaves·drop /'ēvzˌdräp/ ▶ v. (**eavesdrops, eavesdropping, eavesdropped**) secretly listen to a conversation. ■ **eaves·drop·per** n.

ebb /eb/ ▶ n. the movement of the tide out to sea. ▶ v. **1** (of tidewater) move away from the land; recede. **2** gradually become less or weaker: *my confidence ebbed away.*
– PHRASES **at a low ebb** in a weakened or depressed state.

Eb·o·la fe·ver /ē'bōlə/ ▶ n. an infectious, generally fatal disease caused by a virus and marked by fever and severe internal bleeding.

E·bon·ics /ē'bäniks/ ▶ n. (treated as sing.) American black English regarded as a language in its own right rather than as a dialect of standard English.

eb·on·ite /'ebəˌnīt/ ▶ n. another term for VULCANITE.

eb·on·ized /'ebəˌnīzd/ ▶ adj. (of furniture) made to look like ebony.

eb·on·y /'ebənē/ ▶ n. **1** heavy blackish or very dark brown wood from a tree of tropical and warm regions. **2** a very dark brown or black color.

e-book /'ēˌbo͝ok/ ▶ n. an electronic version of a printed book that can be read on a personal computer or special hand-held device.

e·bul·lient /i'bo͝olyənt, i'bəlyənt/ ▶ adj. cheerful and full of energy. ■ **e·bul·lience** n. **e·bul·lient·ly** adv.

e-busi·ness ▶ n. **1** an online business. **2** another term for E-COMMERCE.

EC ▶ abbr. **1** European Commission. **2** European Community.

ec·cen·tric /ik'sentrik/ ▶ adj. **1** unconventional and slightly strange. **2** technical not placed centrally or not having its axis placed centrally. ▶ n. a person who is unconventional and slightly strange. ■ **ec·cen·tri·cal·ly** adv.

ec·cen·tric·i·ty /ˌeksen'trisitē/ ▶ n. (pl. **eccentricities**) **1** the quality of being unconventional and slightly strange. **2** an eccentric act or habit.

ec·cle·si·al /i'klēzēəl/ ▶ adj. formal relating to a Christian Church or denomination.

ec·cle·si·as·tic /iˌklēzē'astik/ formal ▶ n. a member of the Christian clergy. ▶ adj. ecclesiastical.

ec·cle·si·as·ti·cal /iˌklēzē'astikəl/ ▶ adj. relating to the Christian Church or its clergy. ■ **ec·cle·si·as·ti·cal·ly** adv.

ec·cle·si·ol·o·gy /iˌklēzē'äləjē/ ▶ n. **1** the study of churches, especially church architecture. **2** theology as applied to the nature and structure of the Christian Church. ■ **ec·cle·si·o·log·i·cal** /iˌklēzēə'läjikəl/ adj. **ec·cle·si·ol·o·gist** /-jist/ n.

ECG ▶ abbr. electrocardiogram or electrocardiograph.

ech·e·lon /'esHəˌlän/ ▶ n. **1** a level or rank in an organization, profession, or society. **2** a formation of troops, ships, aircraft, or vehicles in parallel rows with the end of each row projecting further than the one in front.

e·chid·na /ə'kidnə/ ▶ n. (pl. **echidnas**) a spiny egg-laying mammal native to Australia and New Guinea.

ech·i·na·cea /ˌekə'nāsHə/ ▶ n. a North American plant used in herbal medicine.

echi·no·derm /i'kīnəˌdərm, 'ekənəˌdərm/ ▶ n. a marine invertebrate (sea creature) of a large group that includes starfishes and sea urchins.

ech·o /'ekō/ ▶ n. (pl. **echoes**) **1** a sound caused by the reflection of sound waves from a surface back to the listener. **2** a reflected radio or radar beam. **3** something suggestive of or similar to something else: *his early work shows echoes of Manet and Whistler.* ▶ v. (**echoes, echoing, echoed**) **1** (of a sound) reverberate or be repeated after the original sound has stopped. **2** be suggestive of or similar to: *his political opinions echoed his father's.* **3** repeat someone's words or opinions. ■ **ech·o·ey** adj.

ech·o·car·di·og·ra·phy /ˌekōˌkärdē'ägrəfē/ ▶ n. the use of ultrasound waves to investigate the action of the heart. ■ **ech·o·car·di·o·gram** /ˌekō'kärdēəˌgram/ n. **ech·o·car·di·o·graph** /ˌekō'kärdēəˌgraf/ n. **ech·o·car·di·o·graph·ic** /-ˌkärdēə'grafik/ adj.

ech·o cham·ber ▶ n. an enclosed space for producing echoes.

e·cho·ic /e'kō-ik/ ▶ adj. **1** relating to or like an echo. **2** representing a sound by imitation; onomatopoeic.

ech·o·lo·ca·tion /ˌekōlō'kāsHən/ ▶ n. the location of objects by reflected sound, in particular as used by animals such as dolphins and bats.

ech·o sound·er ▶ n. a device for determining the depth of the seabed or detecting objects in water by measuring the time taken for echoes to return to the listener.

echt /ekt/ ▶ adj. authentic and typical.

e·clair /ā'kler, i'kler/ (also **éclair**) ▶ n. a log-shaped pastry filled with cream and topped with chocolate icing.

ec·lamp·si·a /i'klam(p)sēə/ ▶ n. Medicine a condition in which a pregnant woman with high blood pressure experiences convulsions. ■ **ec·lamp·tic** /i'klam(p)tik/ adj.

é·clat /ā'klä/ ▶ n. brilliant or successful effect: *a few of the men landed with the same éclat as their leader.*

ec·lec·tic /i'klektik/ ▶ adj. using ideas from a wide variety of sources: *he thrived on an eclectic diet of classical and jazz.* ▶ n. a person whose ideas or tastes are derived from a wide variety of sources. ■ **ec·lec·ti·cal·ly** adv. **ec·lec·ti·cism** /i'klekti,sizəm/ n.

e·clipse /i'klips/ ▶ n. **1** an occasion when one planet, the moon, etc., passes between another and the observer, or in front of a planet's source of light. **2** a sudden loss of significance or power. ▶ v. **1** (of a planet, the moon, etc.) obscure the light coming from or shining on another. **2** make less significant or powerful: *he was one of the composers whose fame has been eclipsed by Mozart.*

e·clip·tic /i'kliptik/ ▶ n. Astronomy a great circle on the celestial sphere representing the sun's apparent circular path among the stars during the year.

eco- ▶ comb.form representing ECOLOGY.

ec·o-friend·ly /'ēkō-/ ▶ adj. not harmful to the environment.

ec·o·la·bel·ing /ˌekōˈlābəliNG, ˈēkō-/ ▶ n. the use of labels to identify products that meet recognized environmental standards. ■ **ec·o·la·bel** n.

E. co·li /ē ˈkōlī/ ▶ n. the bacterium *Escherichia coli*, found in the intestines of humans and other animals, some strains of which can cause severe food poisoning.

e·co·log·i·cal foot·print ▶ n. the sum of an individual's or other entity's impact on the environment, based on consumption and pollution.

e·col·o·gy /iˈkäləjē/ ▶ n. the branch of biology concerned with the relations of organisms to one another and to their surroundings. ■ **ec·o·log·i·cal** /ˌekəˈläjikəl, ˌēkə-/ adj. **ec·o·log·i·cal·ly** /ˌekəˈläjik(ə)lē, ˌēkə-/ adv. **e·col·o·gist** /-jist/ n.

e·com·merce (also **e-business**) ▶ n. commercial transactions conducted on the Internet.

e·con·o·met·rics /iˌkänəˈmetriks/ ▶ pl.n. (treated as sing.) the branch of economics concerned with the use of statistical methods in describing economic systems. ■ **e·con·o·met·ric** adj. **e·con·o·me·tri·cian** /iˌkänəməˈtrishən/ n.

ec·o·nom·ic /ˌekəˈnämik, ˌēkə-/ ▶ adj. 1 relating to economics or the economy of a country or region. 2 profitable, or concerned with profitability: *organizations must become larger if they are to remain economic.* 3 sparing in the use of resources or money.

ec·o·nom·i·cal /ˌekəˈnämikəl, ˌēkə-/ ▶ adj. 1 giving good value or return in relation to the resources used or money spent: *a small, economical car.* 2 careful not to waste resources or money. ■ **ec·o·nom·i·cal·ly** /ˌekəˈnämik(ə)lē, ˌēkə-/ adv. – PHRASES **economical with the truth** euphemistic lying or deliberately withholding information.

ec·o·nom·ic mi·grant ▶ n. a person who travels from one country to another to improve their standard of living.

ec·o·nom·ics /ˌekəˈnämiks, ˌēkə-/ ▶ pl.n. (often treated as sing.) the branch of knowledge concerned with the production, consumption, and transfer of wealth.

e·con·o·mist /iˈkänəmist/ ▶ n. an expert in economics.

e·con·o·mize /iˈkänəˌmīz/ ▶ v. spend less; reduce one's expenses.

e·con·o·my /iˈkänəmē/ ▶ n. (pl. **economies**) 1 the state of a country or region in terms of the production and consumption of goods and services and the supply of money. 2 the careful use of resources so as to avoid waste: *the outboard engine increases fuel economy.* 3 a financial saving. 4 (also **economy class**) the cheapest class of air or rail travel. ▶ adj. offering good value for money: *an economy pack.* – PHRASES **economy of scale** a proportionate saving in costs gained by an increased level of production.

ec·o·re·gion /ˈekōˌrējən, ˈēkō-/ ▶ n. a major ecosystem defined by distinctive geography and receiving uniform solar radiation and moisture.

ec·o·sphere /ˈekōˌsfi(ə)r, ˈēkō-/ ▶ n. a region in which life exists or could exist; the biosphere.

ec·o·sys·tem /ˈekōˌsistəm, ˈēkō-/ ▶ n. a biological community of interacting animals and plants and their environment.

ec·o·tour·ism /ˌekōˈto͞orizəm, ˌēkō-/ ▶ n. tourism directed toward unspoiled natural environments and intended to support conservation efforts. ■ **ec·o·tour** n. **ec·o·tour·ist** n.

ec·o·war·ri·or /ˈekō-/ ▶ n. informal a person involved in protest activities aimed at protecting the environment.

ec·ru /ˈekro͞o/ ▶ n. a light cream or beige color.

ec·sta·sy /ˈekstəsē/ ▶ n. (pl. **ecstasies**) 1 an overwhelming feeling of happiness or joyful excitement. 2 (**Ecstasy**) an illegal amphetamine-based drug. 3 old use an emotional or religious frenzy or trance.

ec·stat·ic /ekˈstatik/ ▶ adj. very happy or excited. ▶ n. a person who is subject to mystical experiences. ■ **ec·stat·i·cal·ly** adv.

ECT ▶ abbr. electroconvulsive therapy.

ec·to·morph /ˈektəˌmôrf/ ▶ n. Physiology a person with a lean and delicate body build. Compare with ENDOMORPH and MESOMORPH.

ec·top·ic preg·nan·cy /ekˈtäpik/ ▶ n. a pregnancy in which the fetus develops outside the uterus, typically in a Fallopian tube.

ec·to·plasm /ˈektəˌplazəm/ ▶ n. a substance that supposedly comes out of the body of a medium during a trance. ■ **ec·to·plas·mic** /ˌektəˈplazmik/ adj.

Ec·ua·dor·e·an /ˌekwəˈdôrēən/ (also **Ecuadorian**) ▶ n. a person from Ecuador. ▶ adj. relating to Ecuador.

ec·u·men·i·cal /ˌekyəˈmenikəl/ ▶ adj. 1 representing a number of different Christian Churches. 2 promoting unity among the world's Christian Churches. ■ **ec·u·men·i·cal·ly** adv.

ec·u·me·nism /ˈekyəməˌnizəm, eˈkyo͞omə-/ ▶ n. the aim of promoting unity among the world's Christian Churches.

ec·ze·ma /ˈegzəmə, ˈeksə-, igˈzēmə/ ▶ n. a condition in which patches of skin become rough and inflamed, causing itching and bleeding.

ed. ▶ abbr. 1 edited by. 2 edition. 3 editor. 4 education.

E·dam /ˈēdəm/ ▶ n. a round yellow cheese with a red wax coating.

ed·a·ma·me /ˌedəˈmämä/ ▶ n. a dish of green soybeans boiled or steamed in their pods.

ed·dy /ˈedē/ ▶ n. (pl. **eddies**) a circular movement of water causing a small whirlpool. ▶ v. (**eddies**, **eddying**, **eddied**) (of water, air, smoke, etc.) move in a circular way.

e·del·weiss /ˈādlˌwīs, -ˌvīs/ ▶ n. a mountain plant with small flowers and gray-green leaves.

e·de·ma /iˈdēmə/ (Brit. **oedema**) ▶ n. an excess of watery fluid in the cavities or tissues of the body.

E·den /ˈēdn/ ▶ n. 1 (also **Garden of Eden**) the place where Adam and Eve lived in the biblical story of the Creation. 2 a place or state of great happiness or unspoiled beauty. ■ **E·den·ic** /iˈdenik/ adj.

e·den·tate /ēˈdenˌtāt/ ▶ n. a mammal of a group that has no incisor or canine teeth, including the anteaters and sloths.

edge /ej/ ▶ n. 1 the outside limit of an object, area, or surface. 2 the sharpened side of a blade. 3 the line along which two surfaces of a solid meet. 4 a slight advantage over close rivals: *Europe is losing its competitive edge.* 5 an intense or striking quality: *the chef has a fiery edge to her cooking.* ▶ v. 1 provide something with an edge or border. 2 move carefully or furtively: *I tried to edge away from her.* ■ **edged** adj. **edg·er** n.

– PHRASES **on edge** tense, nervous, or irritable. **set someone's teeth on edge** (especially of a sound) cause intense discomfort or irritation to someone.

edge·wise /'ej,wīz/ (also **edgeways** /-,wāz/) ▶ adv. with the edge uppermost or toward the viewer.
– PHRASES **get a word in edgewise** manage to break into a lively conversation or monologue.

edg·ing /'ejiNG/ ▶ n. something forming an edge or border.

edg·y /'ejē/ ▶ adj. (**edgier, edgiest**) **1** tense, nervous, or irritable. **2** informal avant-garde and unconventional. ■ **edg·i·ly** adv. **edg·i·ness** n.

EDI ▶ abbr. electronic data interchange.

ed·i·ble /'edəbəl/ ▶ adj. fit to be eaten. ▶ n. (**edibles**) items of food. ■ **ed·i·bil·i·ty** /,edə'bilitē/ n.

e·dict /'ēdikt/ ▶ n. an official order or proclamation.

ed·i·fice /'edəfis/ ▶ n. formal **1** a large, imposing building. **2** a complex system: *the edifice of economic reform degenerated into corruption.*

ed·i·fy /'edə,fī/ ▶ v. (**edifies, edifying, edified**) give educational or morally improving instruction to someone. ■ **ed·i·fi·ca·tion** /,edəfi'kāsHən/ n. **ed·i·fy·ing** /'edə,fī-iNG/ adj.

ed·it /'edit/ ▶ v. (**edits, editing, edited**) **1** prepare written material for publication by correcting, shortening, or improving it. **2** prepare material for a movie or a radio or television program. **3** change online text on a computer or word processor. **4** be editor of a newspaper or magazine. ▶ n. a change made as a result of editing. ■ **ed·it·a·ble** /'editəbəl/ adj.

e·di·tion /i'disHən/ ▶ n. **1** a particular form or version of a published written work. **2** the total number of copies of a book, newspaper, etc., issued at one time. **3** a particular instance of a regular radio or television program.

ed·i·tor /'editər/ ▶ n. **1** a person who is in charge of a newspaper, magazine, or multiauthor book. **2** a person who commissions or prepares written or recorded material for publication or broadcasting. ■ **ed·i·tor·ship** n.

ed·i·to·ri·al /,edi'tôrēəl/ ▶ adj. relating to the commissioning or preparing of material for publication. ▶ n. a newspaper article giving an opinion on a topical issue. ■ **ed·i·to·ri·al·ist** n. **ed·i·to·ri·al·ly** adv.

ed·i·to·ri·al·ize /,edi'tôrēə,līz/ ▶ v. (of a newspaper or editor) express opinions rather than just report news.

EDP ▶ abbr. electronic data processing.

EDT ▶ abbr. Eastern Daylight Time.

ed·u·cate /'ejə,kāt/ ▶ v. **1** give intellectual and moral instruction to someone. **2** give someone information on a particular subject: *a campaign to educate consumers about food safety.* **3** (as adj. **educated**) showing or having had a good education: *a polished, educated girl.* ■ **ed·u·ca·ble** /-kəbəl/ adj. **ed·u·ca·tive** /-,kātiv/ adj. **ed·u·ca·tor** /-,kātər/ n.

ed·u·cat·ed guess ▶ n. a guess based on knowledge and experience.

ed·u·ca·tion /,ejə'kāsHən/ ▶ n. **1** the process of teaching or learning. **2** the theory and practice of teaching. **3** information about or training in a particular subject: *health education.* **4** (**an education**) an enlightening experience: *traveling has been quite an education for this*

former teacher. ■ **ed·u·ca·tion·al** /,ejə'kāsHənl/ adj. **ed·u·ca·tion·al·ist** n. **ed·u·ca·tion·al·ly** adv. **ed·u·ca·tion·ist** n.

Ed·ward·i·an /ed'wôrdēən, -'wär-/ ▶ adj. relating to the reign of King Edward VII (1901–10). ▶ n. a person who lived during the Edwardian period.

EEC ▶ abbr. European Economic Community.

EEG ▶ abbr. electroencephalogram or electroencephalograph.

eel /ēl/ ▶ n. a snakelike fish with a very long, thin body and small fins. ■ **eel-like** /-,līk/ adj. **eel·y** adj.

EEOC ▶ abbr. Equal Employment Opportunity Commission.

e'er /e(ə)r/ ▶ adv. literary form of EVER.

ee·rie /'i(ə)rē/ ▶ adj. (**eerier, eeriest**) strange and frightening. ■ **ee·ri·ly** adv. **ee·ri·ness** n.

ef·face /i'fās/ ▶ v. **1** cause to disappear: *nothing could efface the bitter memory.* **2** (**efface oneself**) make oneself appear unimportant. **3** erase a mark from a surface. ■ **ef·face·ment** n.

ef·fect /i'fekt/ ▶ n. **1** a change that is a result of an action or other cause. **2** the state of being or becoming operative: *the agreement took effect in 2004.* **3** the extent to which something succeeds: *wind power can be used to great effect.* **4** (**effects**) personal belongings. **5** (**effects**) the lighting, sound, or scenery used in a play or movie. **6** Physics a physical phenomenon, typically named after its discoverer. ▶ v. bring about: *the senator effected many policy changes.*
– PHRASES **for effect** in order to impress people. **in effect** in practice, even if not formally acknowledged.

> USAGE
> On the confusion of **effect** and **affect**, see the note at AFFECT[1].

ef·fec·tive /i'fektiv/ ▶ adj. **1** producing a desired or intended result. **2** (of a law or policy) operative. **3** existing in fact, though not formally acknowledged as such: *he remains in effective control of the military.* ■ **ef·fec·tive·ly** adv. **ef·fec·tive·ness** n.

ef·fec·tu·al /i'fekcHOOəl/ ▶ adj. **1** producing an intended result; effective. **2** (of a legal document) valid or binding. ■ **ef·fec·tu·al·ly** adv.

ef·fem·i·nate /i'femənət/ ▶ adj. (of a man) having characteristics regarded as typical of a woman. ■ **ef·fem·i·na·cy** /i'femənəsē/ n. **ef·fem·i·nate·ly** adv.

ef·fen·di /i'fendē/ ▶ n. (pl. **effendis**) a man of high education or social standing in an eastern Mediterranean or Arab country.

ef·fer·ves·cent /,efər'vesənt/ ▶ adj. **1** (of a liquid) giving off bubbles; fizzy. **2** lively and enthusiastic. ■ **ef·fer·vesce** /,efər'ves/ v. **ef·fer·ves·cence** n.

ef·fete /i'fēt/ ▶ adj. **1** no longer effective; weak. **2** (of a man) affected or effeminate. ■ **ef·fete·ly** adv. **ef·fete·ness** n.

ef·fi·ca·cious /,efi'kāsHəs/ ▶ adj. successful in producing an intended effect; effective. ■ **ef·fi·ca·cious·ly** adv.

ef·fi·ca·cy /'efikəsē/ ▶ n. the ability to produce an intended result.

ef·fi·cien·cy /i'fisHənsē/ ▶ n. (pl. **efficiencies**) **1** the quality of being efficient. **2** a means of using resources in a less wasteful way: *the company will seek to maximize cost efficiencies.*

ef·fi·cien·cy a·part·ment (also **efficiency**) ▶ n. an apartment in which one room typically contains the kitchen, living, and sleeping quarters, with a separate bathroom.

ef·fi·cient /i'fishənt/ ▶ adj. working well with minimum waste of money or effort. ■ **ef·fi·cient·ly** adv.

ef·fi·gy /'efijē/ ▶ n. (pl. **effigies**) a sculpture or model of a person.

ef·flo·res·cence /,eflə'resəns/ ▶ n. **1** literary a very high stage of development: *an efflorescence of art.* **2** the crystallization of salts on a surface such as brick. ■ **ef·flo·res·cent** adj.

ef·flu·ent /'eflooənt/ ▶ n. liquid waste or sewage discharged into a river or the sea.

ef·flu·vi·um /i'flooveəm/ ▶ n. (pl. **effluvia** /-vēə/) an unpleasant or harmful smell or discharge.

ef·fort /'efərt/ ▶ n. **1** a vigorous or determined attempt to do something. **2** physical or mental vigor: *he put considerable effort into achieving this goal.* ■ **ef·fort·ful** adj.

ef·fort·less /'efərtlis/ ▶ adj. done or achieved without effort; natural and easy. ■ **ef·fort·less·ly** adv. **ef·fort·less·ness** n.

ef·fron·ter·y /i'frəntərē/ ▶ n. insolent or disrespectful behavior.

ef·ful·gent /i'fooljənt, i'fəl-/ ▶ adj. literary shining brightly. ■ **ef·ful·gence** n.

ef·fu·sion /i'fyoozнən/ ▶ n. **1** a discharge of something, especially a liquid. **2** an unrestrained expression of feelings in speech or writing: *effusions of patriotic bigotry.*

ef·fu·sive /i'fyoosiv/ ▶ adj. expressing gratitude or approval in an unrestrained way. ■ **ef·fu·sive·ly** adv. **ef·fu·sive·ness** n.

e-fit /'ē ,fit/ ▶ n. an electronic picture of a person's face made from photographs of separate facial features, created by a computer program.

EFL ▶ abbr. English as a foreign language.

e.g. ▶ abbr. for example.

e·gal·i·tar·i·an /i,galə'terēən/ ▶ adj. believing in or based on the principle that all people are equal and deserve equal rights and opportunities. ▶ n. a person who supports the principle of equality for all. ■ **e·gal·i·tar·i·an·ism** n.

egg¹ /eg/ ▶ n. **1** an oval or round object laid by a female bird, reptile, fish, or invertebrate and containing an ovum that can develop into a new organism. **2** an infertile egg of a chicken, used for food. **3** the cell in female humans and animals that is capable of producing young; an ovum. **4** informal, dated a person of a specified kind: *he's a good egg.* ■ **egg·y** adj.
– PHRASES **kill the goose that lays the golden eggs** destroy a reliable and valuable source of income. **with egg on one's face** informal appearing foolish or ridiculous.

egg² ▶ v. (**egg someone on**) urge or encourage someone to do something foolish or risky.

egg·beat·er /'eg,bētər/ ▶ n. **1** a kitchen utensil used for beating ingredients such as eggs or cream. **2** informal a helicopter.

egg·head /'eg,hed/ ▶ n. informal, derogatory a very intelligent or studious person.

egg·nog /'eg,näg, -,nôg/ ▶ n. a drink consisting of eggs, cream, and flavorings, often with alcohol.

egg·plant /'eg,plant/ ▶ n. the dark purple, egg-shaped fruit of a plant of the nightshade family.

egg·shell /'eg,shel/ ▶ n. the thin, brittle outer layer of an egg. ▶ adj. **1** (of china) very thin and delicate. **2** referring to a paint that dries with a slight sheen.

egg white ▶ n. the clear substance around the yolk of an egg that turns white when cooked or beaten.

e·go /'ēgō/ ▶ n. (pl. **egos**) **1** a person's sense of their own worth and importance: *staying fit is a great boost to the ego.* **2** the part of the mind that is responsible for the interpretation of reality and a sense of personal identity. Compare with ID and SUPEREGO.

e·go·cen·tric /,ēgō'sentrik/ ▶ adj. thinking only of oneself; self-centered. ■ **e·go·cen·tric·al·ly** /-(ə)lē/ adv. **e·go·cen·tric·i·ty** /,ēgōsen'trisitē/ n. **e·go·cen·trism** /,ēgō'sentrizəm/ n.

e·go·ism /'ēgō,izəm/ ▶ n. another term for EGOTISM. ■ **e·go·ist** n. **e·go·is·tic** /-'istik/ adj.

e·go·ma·ni·a /,ēgō'mānēə/ ▶ n. obsessive self-centeredness. ■ **e·go·ma·ni·ac** /-nē,ak/ n. **e·go·ma·ni·a·cal** /-mə'nīəkəl/ adj.

e·go·tism /'ēgə,tizəm/ ▶ n. the quality of being excessively conceited or self-centered. ■ **e·go·tist** n. **e·go·tis·tic** /,ēgə'tistik/ adj. **e·go·tis·ti·cal** /,ēgə'tistikəl/ adj.

e·go trip ▶ n. informal something that a person does to feel self-important.

e·gre·gious /i'grējəs/ ▶ adj. outstandingly bad; shocking. ■ **e·gre·gious·ly** adv. **e·gre·gious·ness** n.

e·gress /'ē,gres/ ▶ n. formal **1** the action of going out of or leaving a place. **2** a way out.

e·gret /'ēgrit, 'ē,gret, 'egrit/ ▶ n. a heron with mainly white plumage, having long plumes in the breeding season.

E·gyp·tian /i'jipshən/ ▶ n. **1** a person from Egypt. **2** the language used in ancient Egypt. ▶ adj. relating to Egypt.

E·gyp·tol·o·gy /,ējip'täləjē/ ▶ n. the study of the language, history, and culture of ancient Egypt. ■ **E·gyp·to·log·i·cal** /,ijiptə'läjikəl/ adj. **E·gyp·tol·o·gist** n.

eh /ā, e/ ▶ exclam. used to ask for something to be repeated or explained or to elicit agreement.

Eid /ēd/ (also **Id**) ▶ n. **1** (in full **Eid ul-Fitr** /ēd ool 'fētr/) the Muslim festival marking the end of the fast of Ramadan. **2** (in full **Eid ul-Adha** /ēd ool 'ädə/) the festival marking the culmination of the annual pilgrimage to Mecca.

ei·der /'īdər/ (also **eider duck**) ▶ n. (pl. same or **eiders**) a northern sea duck, the male of which has mainly black-and-white plumage.

ei·der·down /'īdər,doun/ ▶ n. **1** the down from a female eider duck. **2** chiefly Brit. a quilt or comforter filled with down (originally from the female eider duck) or another soft material.

ei·det·ic /ī'detik/ ▶ adj. relating to mental images that are unusually vivid and detailed.

eight /āt/ ▶ cardinal number **1** one more than seven; 8. (Roman numeral: **viii** or **VIII**.) **2** an eight-oared rowing shell or its crew.
– PHRASES **pieces of eight** historical Spanish dollars, equivalent to eight reals.

eight·een /ā'tēn, 'ā,tēn/ ▶ cardinal number one more than seventeen; 18. (Roman numeral: **xviii** or **XVIII**.) ■ **eight·eenth** /ā'tēnтн, 'ā,tēnтн/ ordinal number.

eight·een-wheel·er ▶ n. a large tractor-trailer with eighteen wheels.

eighth /'ā(t)тн/ ▶ ordinal number **1** that is number eight in a sequence; 8th. **2** (**an eighth** or **one eighth**) each of eight equal parts into which something is divided.

eighth note ▶ n. a musical note having the value of half a quarter note, shown by a solid dot with a hooked stem.

eight·y /'ātē/ ▶ cardinal number (pl. **eighties**) ten less than ninety; 80. (Roman numeral: **lxxx** or **LXXX**.) ■ **eight·i·eth** /'ātēiTH/ ordinal number.

eigh·ty-six /,ātē 'siks/ (also **86**) informal ▶ n. someone regarded as undesirable as a restaurant or bar patron. ▶ v. **1** refuse to serve someone: *he got 86ed from a reservation casino.* **2** reject, discard, or cancel.

ein·stein·i·um /īn'stīnēəm/ ▶ n. an unstable radioactive chemical element made by high-energy atomic collisions.

eis·tedd·fod /ī'steTH,väd/ ▶ n. (pl. **eisteddfods** or **eisteddfodau** /-'vädī/) a competitive festival of music and poetry in Wales.

ei·ther /'ēTHər, 'ĪTHər/ ▶ conj. & adv. **1** used before the first of two alternatives specified (the other being introduced by 'or'). **2** (adv.) used to indicate a similarity or link with a statement just made: *You don't like him, do you? I don't either.* **3** for that matter; moreover. ▶ determiner & pron. **1** one or the other of two people or things. **2** each of two.

> **USAGE**
>
> In good English, it is important that **either** and **or** are correctly placed so that the structures following each word balance each other. For example, it is better to say *I'm going to buy either a new camera or a new video* rather than *I'm either going to buy a new camera or a video.*

e·jac·u·late ▶ v. /i'jakyə,lāt/ **1** (of a man or male animal) eject semen from the penis at the moment of orgasm. **2** dated say something suddenly. ▶ n. /-,lit/ semen that has been ejaculated. ■ **e·jac·u·la·tion** /i,jakyə'lāsHən/ n. **e·jac·u·la·tor** /i'jakyə,lātər/ n. **e·jac·u·la·to·ry** /-lə,tôrē/ adj.

e·ject /i'jekt/ ▶ v. **1** force or throw something out violently or suddenly. **2** make someone leave a place or post. **3** (of a pilot) escape from an aircraft by means of an ejection seat. ■ **e·jec·tion** /i'jeksHən/ n. **e·jec·tor** /i'jektər/ n.

e·jec·tion seat (also **ejector seat**) ▶ n. an aircraft seat that can throw its occupant from the craft in an emergency.

eke /ēk/ ▶ v. (**eke something out**) **1** make a living with difficulty. **2** make something last longer by using it sparingly: *retired folk hunting for bargains to eke out their social security money.*

EKG ▶ abbr. **1** electrocardiogram. **2** electrocardiograph. **3** electrocardiography.

el /el/ ▶ n. **1** (**the El**) an elevated railroad or section of railroad, especially in Chicago. **2** a train running on such a railroad.

e·lab·o·rate ▶ adj. /i'lab(ə)rit/ involving many carefully arranged parts; detailed and complicated. ▶ v. /i'labə,rāt/ **1** develop or present a theory or policy in detail. **2** (**elaborate on**) add more detail to something already said. ■ **e·lab·o·rate·ly** adv. **e·lab·o·ra·tion** /i,labə'rāsHən/ n. **e·lab·o·ra·tive** /-,rātiv/ adj.

é·lan /ā'län, ā'lan/ (also **elan**) ▶ n. energy and stylishness: *he played the march with great élan.*

e·land /'ēlənd/ ▶ n. a large African antelope with spiral horns.

e·lapse /i'laps/ ▶ v. (of time) pass.

e·las·tic /i'lastik/ ▶ adj. **1** able to return to normal size or shape after being stretched or squeezed. **2** flexible and adaptable: *the definition of ethnicity is elastic.* ▶ n. cord, tape, or fabric that returns to its original length or shape after being stretched. ■ **e·las·ti·cal·ly** /-(ə)lē/ adv. **e·las·tic·i·ty** /i,la'stisitē, ē,la-/ n. **e·las·ti·cize** /i'lastə,sīz/ v.

e·las·tic band ▶ n. a rubber band.

e·las·ti·cized /i'lastə,sīzd/ ▶ adj. (of a garment or material) made elastic with rubber thread or tape.

e·las·tin /i'lastin/ ▶ n. an elastic, fibrous protein found in connective body tissue.

e·las·to·mer /i'lastəmər/ ▶ n. a natural or synthetic polymer with elastic properties, e.g., rubber. ■ **e·las·to·mer·ic** /i,lastə'merik/ adj.

e·lat·ed /i'lātid/ ▶ adj. very happy and excited.

e·la·tion /i'lāsHən/ ▶ n. great happiness and excitement.

el·bow /'el,bō/ ▶ n. **1** the joint between the forearm and the upper arm. **2** a piece of piping or something similar bent through an angle. ▶ v. **1** hit or push someone with one's elbow. **2** (often **elbow one's way**) move by pushing past people with one's elbows. – PHRASES **up to one's elbows in** deeply involved in something.

el·bow grease ▶ n. informal hard physical work, especially vigorous cleaning.

el·bow room ▶ n. informal adequate space to move or work in.

eld·er[1] /'eldər/ ▶ adj. (of one or more out of a group of people) of a greater age. ▶ n. **1** (**one's elder**) a person older than oneself. **2** a leader or senior figure in a community. **3** an official or minister in certain Protestant Churches.

eld·er[2] ▶ n. a small tree or shrub with white flowers and bluish-black or red berries.

el·der·ber·ry /'eldər,berē/ ▶ n. (pl. **elderberries**) the berry of the elder, used for making jelly or wine.

el·der·flow·er /'eldər,flou(-ə)r/ ▶ n. the flower of the elder, used to make wines and cordials.

eld·er·ly /'eldərlē/ ▶ adj. old or aging.

eld·er states·man ▶ n. an experienced and respected politician or other public figure.

eld·est /'eldəst/ ▶ adj. (of one out of a group of people) oldest.

El Do·ra·do /,el də'rädō/ (also **eldorado**) ▶ n. (pl. **El Dorados**) a place of great abundance and wealth.

el·e·cam·pane /,elikam'pān/ ▶ n. a plant with yellow daisylike flowers and bitter roots that are used in herbal medicine.

e·lect /i'lekt/ ▶ v. **1** choose someone to hold public office or another position by voting. **2** choose to do something: *the manager elected to leave him out of the project.* ▶ adj. **1** (of a person) chosen or singled out. **2** (**-elect**) elected to a position but not yet in office: *the president-elect.* ■ **e·lect·a·bil·i·ty** /i,lektə'bilitē/ n. **e·lect·a·ble** adj.

e·lec·tion /i'leksHən/ ▶ n. **1** a formal process by which a person is elected, especially to a public office. **2** the action of electing someone.

e·lec·tion·eer·ing /i,leksHə'ni(ə)riNG/ ▶ n. the action of campaigning to be elected to a political position.

e·lec·tive /i'lektiv/ ▶ adj. **1** relating to or appointed by election. **2** (of a course of study, medical treatment, etc.) chosen by the person concerned; not compulsory.

e·lec·tor /i'lektər, -ˌtôr/ ▶ n. **1** a person who has the right to vote in an election. **2** a member of the electoral college. **3** (**Elector**) historical a German prince entitled to take part in the election of the Holy Roman Emperor.

e·lec·tor·al /i'lektərəl/ ▶ adj. relating to elections or electors. ■ **e·lec·tor·al·ly** adv.

e·lec·tor·al col·lege ▶ n. a group of people chosen to represent the members of a political party in the election of a leader.

e·lec·tor·ate /i'lektərət/ ▶ n. **1** the group of people in a country or area who are entitled to vote in an election. **2** historical the office or territories of a German elector.

e·lec·tric /i'lektrik/ ▶ adj. **1** relating to, worked by, or producing electricity. **2** very exciting or intense: *the atmosphere was electric.*

e·lec·tri·cal /i'lektrikəl/ ▶ adj. relating to, operating by, or producing electricity. ■ **e·lec·tri·cal·ly** adv.

e·lec·tri·cal storm ▶ n. a thunderstorm or other violent disturbance of the electrical condition of the atmosphere.

e·lec·tric blan·ket ▶ n. an electrically wired blanket used for heating a bed.

e·lec·tric blue ▶ n. a steely or brilliant light blue.

e·lec·tric chair ▶ n. a chair in which convicted criminals are executed by electrocution.

e·lec·tric eel ▶ n. a large eel-like freshwater fish of South America, which uses pulses of electricity to kill its prey.

e·lec·tric fence ▶ n. a fence through which an electric current can be passed, giving an electric shock to any person or animal touching it.

e·lec·tric gui·tar ▶ n. a guitar with a built-in pickup that converts sound vibrations into electrical signals for amplification.

e·lec·tri·cian /ilek'trisHən, ˌēlek-/ ▶ n. a person who installs and maintains electrical equipment.

e·lec·tric·i·ty /ilek'trisitē, ˌēlek-/ ▶ n. **1** a form of energy resulting from the existence of charged particles (such as electrons), either statically as a buildup of charge or dynamically as a current. **2** the supply of electric current to a building. **3** great excitement or intense emotion: *the atmosphere was charged with sexual electricity.*

e·lec·tric shock ▶ n. a sudden discharge of electricity through a part of the body.

e·lec·tri·fy /i'lektrəˌfī/ ▶ v. (**electrifies, electrifying, electrified**) **1** pass an electric current through something. **2** convert a machine or system to the use of electrical power. **3** (as adj. **electrifying**) very exciting or impressive: *an electrifying performance.* ■ **e·lec·tri·fi·ca·tion** /iˌlektrəfi'kāSHən/ n.

e·lec·tro /i'lektrō/ ▶ n. a style of dance music with a fast beat and synthesized backing track.

e·lec·tro·car·di·og·ra·phy /iˌlektrōˌkärdē'ägrəfē/ ▶ n. the measurement and recording of activity in the heart using electrodes placed on the skin. ■ **e·lec·tro·car·di·o·gram** /iˌlektrō'kärdēəˌgram/ n. **e·lec·tro·car·di·o·graph** /iˌlektrō'kärdiəˌgraf/ n. **e·lec·tro·car·di·o·graph·ic** /-ˌkärdiə'grafik/ adj.

e·lec·tro·con·vul·sive /iˌlektrōkən'vəlsiv/ ▶ adj. relating to the treatment of mental illness by applying electric shocks to the brain.

e·lec·tro·cute /i'lektrəˌkyōōt/ ▶ v. injure or kill

someone by electric shock. ■ **e·lec·tro·cu·tion** /iˌlektrə'kyōōSHən/ n.

e·lec·trode /i'lektrōd/ ▶ n. a conductor through which electricity enters or leaves something.

e·lec·tro·dy·nam·ics /iˌlektrōdī'namiks/ ▶ pl.n. (usu. treated as sing.) the branch of mechanics concerned with the interaction of electric currents with magnetic or electric fields. ■ **e·lec·tro·dy·nam·ic** adj.

e·lec·tro·en·ceph·a·log·ra·phy /iˌlektrōən ˌsefə'lägrəfē/ ▶ n. the measurement and recording of electrical activity in the brain. ■ **e·lec·tro·en·ceph·a·lo·gram** /iˌlektrōən'sefələˌgram/ n. **e·lec·tro·en·ceph·a·lo·graph** /iˌlektrōən'sefələˌgraf/ n.

e·lec·trol·y·sis /ilek'träləsis, ˌēlek-/ ▶ n. **1** chemical decomposition produced by passing an electric current through a conducting liquid. **2** the removal of hair roots or blemishes on the skin by means of an electric current. ■ **e·lec·tro·lyt·ic** /iˌlektrə'litik/ adj.

e·lec·tro·lyte /i'lektrəˌlīt/ ▶ n. **1** a liquid or gel that contains ions and can be decomposed by electrolysis, e.g., that present in a battery. **2** (usu. **electrolytes**) the ions, such as sodium and potassium, in cells, blood, or other organic matter.

e·lec·tro·mag·net /iˌlektrō'magnit/ ▶ n. a metal core made into a magnet by the passage of electric current through a surrounding coil.

e·lec·tro·mag·net·ic /iˌlektrōmag'netik/ ▶ adj. relating to the interrelation of electric currents or fields and magnetic fields. ■ **e·lec·tro·mag·net·i·cal·ly** /-(ə)lē/ adv. **e·lec·tro·mag·net·ism** /iˌlektrō'magnəˌtizəm/ n.

e·lec·tro·mag·net·ic ra·di·a·tion ▶ n. a kind of radiation including visible light, radio waves, gamma rays, and X-rays, in which electric and magnetic fields vary simultaneously.

e·lec·tro·me·chan·i·cal /iˌlektrōmə'kanikəl/ ▶ adj. referring to a mechanical device that is electrically operated.

e·lec·tro·mo·tive /iˌlektrə'mōtiv/ ▶ adj. tending to produce an electric current.

e·lec·tro·mo·tive force ▶ n. a difference in potential that tends to give rise to an electric current.

e·lec·tron /i'lekˌträn/ ▶ n. Physics a stable negatively charged subatomic particle found in all atoms and acting as the primary carrier of electricity in solids.

e·lec·tron·ic /ilek'tränik, ˌēlek-/ ▶ adj. **1** having components such as microchips and transistors that control and direct electric currents. **2** relating to electrons or electronics. **3** relating to or carried out by means of a computer or other electronic device: *electronic shopping.* ■ **e·lec·tron·i·cal·ly** /-(ə)lē/ adv.

e·lec·tron·i·ca /ilek'tränikə, ˌēlek-/ ▶ n. a style of popular electronic music deriving from techno and rave.

e·lec·tron·ic pub·lish·ing ▶ n. the issuing of written material as electronic files rather than on paper.

e·lec·tron·ics /ilek'träniks, ˌēlek-/ ▶ pl.n. **1** (usu. treated as sing.) the branch of physics and technology concerned with the design of circuits using transistors and microchips, and with the behavior and movement of electrons. **2** (treated as pl.) circuits or devices using transistors, microchips, etc.

e·lec·tron mi·cro·scope ▶ n. a microscope with

high magnification and resolution, employing electron beams in place of light.

e·lec·tro·pho·re·sis /i͵lektrəfə'rēsis/ ▶ n. the movement of charged particles in a fluid or gel under the influence of an electric field. ∎ **e·lec·tro·pho·ret·ic** /-'retik/ adj.

e·lec·tro·plate /i'lektrə͵plāt/ ▶ v. coat a metal object with another metal using electrolysis. ▶ n. electroplated articles.

e·lec·tro·scope /i'lektrə͵skōp/ ▶ n. an instrument for detecting and measuring electric charge.

e·lec·tro·shock /i'lektrə͵sнäk/ ▶ adj. another term for ELECTROCONVULSIVE.

e·lec·tro·stat·ic /i͵lektrə'statik/ ▶ adj. relating to stationary electric charges or fields as opposed to electric currents. ∎ **e·lec·tro·stat·ic·al·ly** adv. **e·lec·tro·stat·ics** pl.n.

e·lec·tro·sur·ger·y /i͵lektrō'sərjərē/ ▶ n. surgery using a high-frequency electric current to cut tissue. ∎ **e·lec·tro·sur·gi·cal** /-'sərjikəl/ adj.

e·lec·tro·ther·a·py /i͵lektrō'тнerəpē/ ▶ n. the use of electric currents passed through the body to treat paralysis and other disorders.

e·lec·trum /i'lektrəm/ ▶ n. an alloy of gold with at least 20 percent of silver, used for jewelry.

el·e·gant /'eləgənt/ ▶ adj. **1** graceful and stylish. **2** pleasingly clever but simple: *an unbelievably elegant theory of everything.* ∎ **el·e·gance** n. **el·e·gant·ly** adv.

el·e·gi·ac /͵elə'jīək, e'lējē͵ak/ ▶ adj. **1** relating to or characteristic of an elegy. **2** sad; mournful: *the elegiac, bittersweet tone of the narrator's voice.* ∎ **el·e·gi·a·cal·ly** /͵elə'jīək(ə)lē/ adv.

el·e·gy /'eləjē/ ▶ n. (pl. **elegies**) a mournful poem, typically a lament for someone who has died.

el·e·ment /'eləmənt/ ▶ n. **1** an essential or typical part: *there are four elements to the proposal.* **2** (also **chemical element**) each of more than one hundred substances that cannot be chemically changed or broken down. **3** any of the four substances (earth, water, air, and fire) formerly believed to be the basic constituents of all matter. **4** a small amount: *an element of danger.* **5** a distinct group within a larger group: *right-wing elements in the army.* **6** (**the elements**) rain and other bad weather. **7** a part in an electric device consisting of a wire through which an electric current is passed to provide heat.
– PHRASES **in one's element** in a situation in which one feels happy or relaxed.

el·e·men·tal /͵elə'mentl/ ▶ adj. **1** forming an essential or typical feature; fundamental: *the sauces are made from a few elemental ingredients.* **2** relating to or resembling the powerful forces of nature: *elemental hatred.* **3** relating to a chemical element.

el·e·men·ta·ry /͵elə'ment(ə)rē/ ▶ adj. **1** relating to the most basic aspects of a subject. **2** straightforward and simple to understand: *elementary tasks.* **3** Chemistry not able to be decomposed into elements or other primary constituents. ∎ **el·e·men·tar·i·ly** /-rəlē/ adv.

el·e·men·ta·ry par·ti·cle ▶ n. any of various fundamental subatomic particles, including those that are the smallest and most basic constituents of matter (leptons and quarks) or are combinations of these, and those that transmit one of the four fundamental interactions in nature (gravitational, electromagnetic, strong, and weak).

el·e·men·ta·ry school ▶ n. a primary school for the first four to eight grades, and usually including kindergarten.

el·e·phant /'eləfənt/ ▶ n. (pl. same or **elephants**) a very large mammal with a trunk, curved tusks, and large ears, native to Africa and southern Asia.

el·e·phan·ti·a·sis /͵eləfən'tīəsis/ ▶ n. a medical condition in which a limb becomes hugely enlarged, typically caused by a type of parasitic worm.

el·e·phan·tine /͵elə'fantēn, -͵tīn, 'eləfən͵tēn, -͵tīn/ ▶ adj. typical of or like an elephant, especially in being large or clumsy.

el·e·vate /'elə͵vāt/ ▶ v. **1** lift something to a higher position. **2** raise to a higher level or status: *the prize elevated her to the front rank of writers.*

el·e·vat·ed /'elə͵vātid/ ▶ adj. having a high intellectual or moral level.

el·e·va·tion /͵elə'vāsнən/ ▶ n. **1** the action of elevating someone or something: *his elevation to superstar status.* **2** the height of a place above sea level. **3** the angle of something with the horizontal. **4** a particular side of a building, or a scale drawing of this. ∎ **el·e·va·tion·al** adj.

el·e·va·tor /'elə͵vātər/ ▶ n. a platform or compartment for raising and lowering people or things to different floors of a building.

el·ev·en /i'levən/ ▶ cardinal number **1** one more than ten; 11. (Roman numeral: **xi** or **XI**.) **2** a sports team of eleven players. ∎ **e·lev·en·fold** /-͵fōld/ adj. & adv.

el·ev·enth /i'levənтн/ ▶ ordinal number **1** that is number eleven in a sequence; 11th. **2** (**an eleventh**/**one eleventh**) each of eleven equal parts into which something is divided.
– PHRASES **the eleventh hour** the latest possible moment.

elf /elf/ ▶ n. (pl. **elves** /elvz/) a supernatural creature of folk tales, represented as a small human figure with pointed ears. ∎ **elf·ish** adj. **elv·en** /'elvən/ adj. (literary) **elv·ish** /'elvisн/ adj.

elf·in /'elfən/ ▶ adj. like an elf, especially in being small and delicate.

e·lic·it /i'lisit/ ▶ v. (**elicits, eliciting, elicited**) draw out or produce a response or reaction: *my alternative parenting choices have often elicited criticism.* ∎ **e·lic·i·ta·tion** /i͵lisi'tāsнən/ n. **e·lic·i·tor** /-tər/ n.

e·lide /i'līd/ ▶ v. **1** omit a sound or syllable when speaking. **2** join or merge things together.

el·i·gi·ble /'eləjəbəl/ ▶ adj. **1** meeting the conditions to do or receive something: *you may be eligible for a refund.* **2** desirable or suitable as a wife or husband. ∎ **el·i·gi·bil·i·ty** /͵eləjə'bilitē/ n.

e·lim·i·nate /i'limə͵nāt/ ▶ v. **1** completely remove or get rid of something. **2** exclude from consideration or further participation: *the team was eliminated from the competition.* ∎ **e·lim·i·na·tion** /i͵limə'nāsнən/ n. **e·lim·i·na·tor** /-͵nātər/ n.

e·li·sion /i'lizнən/ ▶ n. **1** the omission of a sound or syllable in speech. **2** the action of joining or merging things.

e·lite /ə'lēt, ā'lēt/ (also **élite**) ▶ n. a group of people regarded as the best in a particular society or organization: *China's educated elite.*

e·lit·ism /ə'lē͵tizəm, ā'lē-/ ▶ n. **1** the belief that a society or system should be run by a group of people regarded as superior to others. **2** the superior attitude or behavior associated with an elite: *the elitism that weakened our education system for a century.* ■ **e·lit·ist** adj. & n.

e·lix·ir /i'liksər/ ▶n. a magical potion, especially one supposedly able to make people live forever.

E·liz·a·be·than /i,lizə'bēᴛнən/ ▶adj. relating to or typical of the reign of Queen Elizabeth I (1558–1603). ▶n. a person alive during the reign of Queen Elizabeth I.

elk /elk/ ▶n. **1** (pl. same or **elks**) a large North American red deer; a wapiti. **2** (pl. same or **elks**) British term for **moose**. **3** (**Elk**) a member of the the Benevolent and Protective Order of Elks, a charitable fraternal organization.

el·lipse /i'lips/ ▶n. a regular oval shape resulting when a cone is cut by an oblique plane that does not intersect the base.

el·lip·sis /i'lipsis/ ▶n. (pl. **ellipses** /-sēz/) **1** the omission of words from speech or writing. **2** a set of dots indicating such an omission.

el·lip·soid /i'lipsoid/ ▶n. a symmetrical three-dimensional figure with a circular cross-section when viewed along one axis and elliptical cross-sections when viewed along the other axes. ■ **el·lip·soi·dal** /ilip'soidl, ,elip-/ adj.

el·lip·tic /i'liptik/ ▶adj. relating to or having the shape of an ellipse. ■ **el·lip·tic·i·ty** /i,lip'tisitē, ,elip-/ n.

el·lip·ti·cal /i'liptikəl/ ▶adj. **1** (of speech or writing) having a word or words deliberately omitted: *a superficial, elliptical narrative.* **2** another term for **elliptic**. ■ **el·lip·ti·cal·ly** /-(ə)lē/ adv.

elm /elm/ ▶n. a tall deciduous tree with serrated leaves.

El Ni·ño /el 'nēnyō/ ▶n. (pl. **El Niños**) an irregular and complex cycle of climatic changes including unusually warm water off northern Peru and Ecuador.

el·o·cu·tion /,elə'kyo͞osнən/ ▶n. the skill of speaking clearly and pronouncing words distinctly. ■ **el·o·cu·tion·ist** n.

e·lon·gate /i'lôNG,gāt, i'läNG-/ ▶v. (usu. as adj. **elongated**) make or become longer: *polar bears have elongated snouts.* ■ **e·lon·ga·tion** /i,lôNG'gāsнən, ē,lôNG-, i,läNG-, ē,läNG-/ n.

e·lope /i'lōp/ ▶v. run away secretly in order to get married. ■ **e·lope·ment** n.

el·o·quence /'eləkwəns/ ▶n. fluent or persuasive speaking or writing.

el·o·quent /'eləkwənt/ ▶adj. **1** fluent or persuasive in speaking or writing. **2** clearly expressing something: *an art that is eloquent of America's cultural diversity.* ■ **el·o·quent·ly** adv.

else /els/ ▶adv. **1** in addition; besides. **2** different; instead.
– PHRASES **or else 1** used to introduce the second of two alternatives. **2** used as a threat or warning: *she'd better shape up, or else.*

else·where /'els,(h)wer/ ▶adv. in, at, or to another place or other places. ▶pron. another place.

ELT ▶abbr. English language teaching.

e·lu·ci·date /i'lōōsi,dāt/ ▶v. make something easier to understand. ■ **e·lu·ci·da·tion** /i,lōōsi'dāsнən/ n.

e·lude /i'lōōd/ ▶v. **1** cleverly escape from or avoid someone or something. **2** fail to be understood or achieved by: *the logic of this eluded her.*

e·lu·sive /i'lōōsiv/ ▶adj. difficult to find, catch, or achieve: *the elusive golden moon bear.* ■ **e·lu·sive·ly** adv. **e·lu·sive·ness** n.

el·ver /'elvər/ ▶n. a young eel.

elves /elvz/ ▶ plural of **elf**.

E·ly·sian /i'lizнən, i'lē-/ ▶adj. relating to or like paradise.

EM ▶abbr. **1** electromagnetic. **2** emergency medicine.

em /em/ ▶n. Printing **1** a unit for measuring the width of printed matter, equal to the height of the type size being used. **2** a unit of measurement equal to twelve points.

'em /əm/ ▶contr. informal them: *let 'em know who's boss.*

e·ma·ci·at·ed /i'māsнē,ātid/ ▶adj. abnormally thin and weak. ■ **e·ma·ci·a·tion** /i,māsнē'āsнən/ n.

e-mail /'ē ,māl/ ▶n. **1** a message sent electronically from one computer user to another or others via a network. **2** the system of sending emails. ▶v. mail someone or send a message using email. ■ **e·mail·er** n.

em·a·nate /'emə,nāt/ ▶v. **1** (**emanate from**) come or spread out from a source. **2** give out: *he emanated compassion.*

em·a·na·tion /,emə'nāsнən/ ▶n. **1** something that emanates or comes from a source. **2** the action of coming from a source.

e·man·ci·pate /i'mansə,pāt/ ▶v. **1** set someone free, especially from legal, social, or political restrictions. **2** free someone from slavery. ■ **e·man·ci·pa·tion** /i,mansə'pāsнən/ n. **e·man·ci·pa·to·ry** /-pə,tôrē/ adj.

e·mas·cu·late /i'maskyə,lāt/ ▶v. **1** make weaker or less effective: *the world wars emasculated British power.* **2** deprive a man of his male role or identity. ■ **e·mas·cu·la·tion** /i,maskyə'lāsнən/ n.

em·balm /em'bä(l)m/ ▶v. preserve a corpse from decay, usually by injection of a preservative. ■ **em·balm·er** n.

em·bank·ment /em'baNGkmənt/ ▶n. **1** a wall or bank built to prevent flooding by a river. **2** a bank of earth or stone built to carry a road or railroad over low ground.

em·bar·go /em'bärgō/ ▶n. (pl. **embargoes**) an official ban, especially on trade or other commercial activity with a particular country. ▶v. (**embargoes, embargoing, embargoed**) ban something officially.

em·bark /em'bärk/ ▶v. **1** go on board a ship or aircraft. **2** (**embark on**) begin a new project or course of action. ■ **em·bar·ka·tion** /,embär'kāsнən/ n.

em·bar·ras de ri·chesses /äɴbä'rä də rē'sнɛs/ ▶n. more resources than one knows what to do with.

em·bar·rass /em'barəs/ ▶v. **1** make someone feel awkward, self-conscious, or ashamed. **2** (**be embarrassed**) be put in financial difficulties. ■ **em·bar·rassed** adj. **em·bar·rass·ing** adj.

em·bar·rass·ment /-mənt/ ▶n. **1** a feeling of self-consciousness, shame, or awkwardness. **2** a cause of self-consciousness, shame, or awkwardness: *her extreme views might be an embarrassment to the movement.*

em·bas·sy /-/ ▶n. (pl. **embassies**) **1** the official home or offices of an ambassador. **2** chiefly historical a deputation or mission sent by one country to another.

em·bat·tled /em'batld/ ▶adj. **1** troubled by many

difficulties: *the embattled chancellor.* **2** prepared for war because surrounded by enemy forces. **3** (of a building) having battlements.

em·bed /em'bed/ (also **imbed**) ► v. (**embeds, embedding, embedded**) **1** fix something firmly and deeply in a surrounding mass. **2** cause an idea or feeling to be firmly lodged in a culture or someone's mind: *this myth is embedded in the national consciousness.* **3** attach a journalist to a military unit during a conflict.

em·bel·lish /em'belish/ ► v. **1** make something more attractive; decorate. **2** add extra, often exaggerated, details to a story to make it more interesting. ■ **em·bel·lish·ment** n.

em·ber /'embər/ ► n. a small piece of burning wood or coal in a dying fire.

em·bez·zle /em'bezəl/ ► v. steal money placed in one's trust or under one's control. ■ **em·bez·zle·ment** n. **em·bez·zler** n.

em·bit·ter /em'bitər/ ► v. (usu. as adj. **embittered**) make someone bitter or resentful.

em·bla·zon /em'blāzn/ ► v. **1** display a design on something in a noticeable way: *T-shirts emblazoned with the names of baseball teams.* **2** depict a heraldic device on something.

em·blem /'embləm/ ► n. **1** a heraldic design or symbol as a distinctive badge of a nation, organization, or family. **2** a symbol representing a quality or idea: *the bards wore white, as an emblem of peace.*

em·blem·at·ic /,emblə'matik/ ► adj. representing a particular quality or idea: *Mill was an emblematic figure of his age.*

em·bod·i·ment /em'bädēmənt, im-/ ► n. **1** a physical or visible form of an idea or quality: *dance was the embodiment of cultural tradition.* **2** the representation of something in a physical or visible form.

em·bod·y /em'bädē/ ► v. (**embodies, embodying, embodied**) **1** give a physical or visible form to an idea or quality. **2** include or contain as a constituent part: *the changes in law embodied in the Civil Rights Act.*

em·bold·en /em'bōldən/ ► v. give courage or confidence to someone.

em·bo·lism /'embə,lizəm/ ► n. obstruction of an artery, typically by a clot of blood or an air bubble.

em·bo·lus /'embələs/ ► n. (pl. **emboli** /-,lī, -,lē/) a blood clot, air bubble, fatty deposit, or other object obstructing a blood vessel. ■ **em·bol·ic** /em'bälik/ adj.

em·bon·point /,äNbôN'pwaN/ ► n. plumpness, especially of a woman's bosom.

em·boss /em'bôs, -'bäs/ ► v. carve or mold a raised design on a surface. ■ **em·boss·er** n.

em·brace /em'brās/ ► v. **1** hold someone closely in one's arms, especially to show affection. **2** include or contain something. **3** accept or support a belief or change willingly. ► n. an act of embracing someone. ■ **em·brace·a·ble** adj.

em·bra·sure /em'brāzHər/ ► n. **1** an opening or recess around a window or door forming an enlargement of the area from the inside. **2** an opening in a wall or parapet, used for shooting through.

em·bro·ca·tion /,embrə'kāsHən/ ► n. a liquid medication rubbed on the body to relieve pain from strains.

em·broi·der /em'broidər/ ► v. **1** sew decorative needlework patterns on something. **2** add

false or exaggerated details to a story. ■ **em·broi·der·er** n.

em·broi·der·y /em'broid(ə)rē/ ► n. (pl. **embroideries**) **1** the art or pastime of embroidering. **2** embroidered cloth.

em·broil /em'broil/ ► v. involve someone deeply in a conflict or difficult situation.

em·bry·o /'embrē,ō/ ► n. (pl. **embryos**) **1** an unborn animal in the process of development, especially an unborn human being in the first eight weeks from fertilization of the egg. Compare with FETUS. **2** the part of a seed that develops into a new plant. **3** something at an early stage of development.

em·bry·ol·o·gy /,embrē'äləjē/ ► n. the branch of biology and medicine concerned with the study of embryos. ■ **em·bry·o·log·i·cal** /,embrēə'läjikəl/ adj. **em·bry·ol·o·gist** /-jist/ n.

em·bry·on·ic /,embrē'änik/ ► adj. **1** relating to an embryo. **2** in an early stage of development: *the plan is still in its embryonic stages.*

em·cee /,em'sē/ informal ► n. a master of ceremonies. ► v. (**emcees, emceeing, emceed**) act as master of ceremonies at a public entertainment or large social occasion.

e·mend /i'mend/ ► v. correct and revise written material. ■ **e·men·da·tion** /,ēmən'dāsHən, ,emən-/ n.

em·er·ald /'em(ə)rəld/ ► n. **1** a bright green precious stone that is a variety of beryl. **2** a bright green color.

e·merge /i'mərj/ ► v. **1** become gradually visible. **2** begin to exist or become apparent: *the jogging boom emerged during the 1970s.* **3** (of facts) become known. **4** recover from or survive a difficult period. ■ **e·mer·gence** n.

e·mer·gen·cy /i'mərjənsē/ ► n. (pl. **emergencies**) **1** a serious, unexpected, and often dangerous situation requiring immediate action. **2** the emergency room in a hospital. ► adj. arising from or used in an emergency: *an emergency exit.*

e·mer·gen·cy room ► n. the department of a hospital that provides immediate treatment for acute illnesses and trauma.

e·mer·gent /i'mərjənt/ ► adj. in the process of coming into being: *a newly emergent middle class.*

e·mer·i·tus /i'merətəs/ ► adj. having retired but allowed to keep a title as an honor: *an emeritus professor.*

em·er·y /'em(ə)rē/ ► n. a grayish-black form of the mineral corundum used in powdered form for smoothing and polishing.

em·er·y board ► n. a strip of thin wood or cardboard coated with emery or another abrasive and used as a nail file.

e·met·ic /i'metik/ ► adj. (of a substance) causing vomiting. ► n. a substance that causes vomiting.

EMF ► abbr. **1** electromagnetic field(s). **2** (**emf**) electromotive force.

em·i·grant /'emigrənt/ ► n. a person who emigrates to another country.

em·i·grate /'emi,grāt/ ► v. leave one's own country in order to settle permanently in another. ■ **em·i·gra·tion** /,emi'grāsHən/ n.

é·mi·gré /'emə,grā/ ► n. a person who has emigrated to another country, especially for political reasons.

em·i·nence /'emənəns/ ► n. **1** the quality of being highly accomplished and respected within a particular area of activity. **2** an important or distinguished person. **3** (**His/Your Eminence**) a title given to a Roman Catholic cardinal. **4** literary a piece of rising ground.

em·i·nent /'emənənt/ ▸ adj. **1** respected; distinguished. **2** outstanding or obvious: *the eminent reasonableness of their claim*. ■ **em·i·nent·ly** adv.

em·i·nent do·main ▸ n. Law the right of a government to take over private property for public use, with payment of compensation.

e·mir /ə'mi(ə)r/ (also **amir** pronunc. same) ▸ n. a title of various Muslim (mainly Arab) rulers.

e·mir·ate /ə'mi(ə)r‚āt, ə'mi(ə)rit, 'emərit/ ▸ n. the rank, lands, or reign of an emir.

em·is·sar·y /'emə‚serē/ ▸ n. (pl. **emissaries**) a person sent as a diplomatic representative on a special mission.

e·mis·sion /i'mishən/ ▸ n. **1** the action of emitting something, especially heat, light, gas, or radiation. **2** a substance that is emitted.

e·mis·sions tra·ding ▸ n. a system by which countries and organizations receive permits to produce a specified amount of carbon dioxide and other greenhouse gases, which they may trade with others.

e·mit /i'mit/ ▸ v. (**emits, emitting, emitted**) **1** discharge or give out gas, radiation, etc. **2** make a sound. ■ **e·mit·ter** n.

Em·men·tal /'emən‚täl/ (also **Emmenthal** pronunc. same) ▸ n. a hard Swiss cheese with holes in it, similar to Gruyère.

Em·my /'emē/ ▸ n. (pl. **Emmys**) a statuette awarded annually to an outstanding television program or performer.

e·mo /'ēmō/ ▸ n. **1** a style of popular music derived from hardcore punk music and characterized by emotional, usually introspective lyrics. **2** the subculture or style associated with this music.

e·mol·lient /i'mälyənt/ ▸ adj. **1** softening or soothing the skin. **2** attempting to avoid conflict; calming. ▸ n. a substance that softens the skin.

e·mol·u·ment /i'mälyəmənt/ ▸ n. formal a salary, fee, or benefit from employment.

e·mote /i'mōt/ ▸ v. show emotion in an exaggerated way: *he failed to cry, or at least emote, when his mother died.*

e·mo·ti·con /i'mōtə‚kän/ ▸ n. a representation of a facial expression such as a smile, formed with keyboard characters and used in email or texting to show the writer's feelings.

e·mo·tion /i'mōshən/ ▸ n. **1** a strong feeling, such as joy or anger. **2** instinctive feeling as distinguished from reasoning or knowledge. ■ **e·mo·tion·less** adj.

e·mo·tion·al /i'mōshənəl/ ▸ adj. **1** relating to a person's emotions. **2** showing intense feeling: *an emotional speech.* **3** easily affected by or openly displaying emotion: *I'm emotional, sensitive, and shy.* ■ **e·mo·tion·al·ism** /-‚izəm/ n. **e·mo·tion·al·ize** /-‚līz/ v. **e·mo·tion·al·ly** adv.

e·mo·tive /i'mōtiv/ ▸ adj. arousing intense feeling. ■ **e·mo·tive·ly** adv.

USAGE
Emotive and **emotional** have similar meanings but they are not exactly the same. **Emotive** means 'arousing intense feeling' (*hunting is a highly emotive issue*), while **emotional** tends to mean 'showing intense feeling' (*an emotional speech*).

em·pa·na·da /empə'nädə/ ▸ n. a Spanish or Latin American pastry turnover with a savory filling.

em·pan·el /em'panl/ ▸ v. variant spelling of IMPANEL.

em·pa·thize /'empə‚THīz/ ▸ v. understand and share the feelings of another.

em·pa·thy /'empəTHē/ ▸ n. the ability to understand and share the feelings of another person. ■ **em·pa·thet·ic** /‚empə'THetik/ adj. **em·path·ic** /em'paTHik/ adj.

USAGE
Do not confuse **empathy** and **sympathy**. **Empathy** means 'the ability to understand and share the feelings of another person' (*the artist developed a considerable empathy with his elderly subject*), whereas **sympathy** means 'the feeling of being sorry for someone who is unhappy or in difficulty' (*they had great sympathy for the flood victims*).

em·per·or /'emp(ə)rər/ ▸ n. the ruler of an empire.

em·per·or pen·guin ▸ n. the largest kind of penguin, which breeds in the Antarctic and has a yellow patch on each side of the head.

em·pha·sis /'emfəsis/ ▸ n. (pl. **emphases** /-‚sēz/) **1** special importance, value, or prominence given to something: *management is placing greater emphasis on improving productivity.* **2** stress given to a word or words in speaking.

em·pha·size /'emfə‚sīz/ ▸ v. give special importance or prominence to something.

em·phat·ic /em'fatik/ ▸ adj. **1** showing or giving emphasis. **2** definite and clear: *an emphatic win.* ■ **em·phat·i·cal·ly** /em'fatik(ə)lē/ adv.

em·phy·se·ma /‚emfə'sēmə, -'zēmə/ (also **pulmonary emphysema**) ▸ n. a condition in which the air sacs of the lungs are damaged and enlarged, causing breathlessness. ■ **em·phy·sem·a·tous** /‚emfə'semətəs, -'sēmə-, -'zemə-, -'zēmə-/ adj.

em·pire /'em‚pī(ə)r/ ▸ n. **1** a large group of states ruled over by a single monarch or ruling authority. **2** a large commercial organization under the control of one person or group: *an entertainment empire.* **3** (usu. **Empire**) (of a dress) having a low neck and high waistline, a style popular during the First Empire (1804–15) in France.'

em·pir·i·cal /em'pirikəl/ (also **empiric** /em'pirik/) ▸ adj. based on observation or experience rather than theory or logic: *empirical studies of seed dispersal.* ■ **em·pir·i·cal·ly** adv.

em·pir·i·cism /em'pirə‚sizəm/ ▸ n. the theory that all knowledge is derived from experience and observation. ■ **em·pir·i·cist** n. & adj.

em·place·ment /em'plāsmənt/ ▸ n. a structure or platform on which a gun is placed for firing.

em·ploy /em'ploi/ ▸ v. **1** give work to someone and pay them for it. **2** make use of: *the methods they employed to collect the data.* **3** keep someone occupied. ■ **em·ploy·a·bil·i·ty** /em‚ploi-ə'bilitē/ n. **em·ploy·a·ble** adj.
– PHRASES **in the employ of** employed by.

em·ploy·ee /em'ploi-ē, ‚emploi'ē/ ▸ n. a person employed for wages or a salary.

em·ploy·er /em'ploi-ər/ ▸ n. a person or organization that employs people.

em·ploy·ment /em'ploimənt/ ▸ n. **1** the action of employing someone or something. **2** the state of having paid work: *a fall in the numbers* *in full-time employment.* **3** a person's work or profession.

em·po·ri·um /em'pôrēəm/ ▶ n. (pl. **emporia** /-'pôrēə/ or **emporiums**) a large store selling a wide variety of goods.

em·pow·er /em'pou(-ə)r/ ▶ v. **1** give authority or power to someone. **2** make someone stronger or more confident. ■ **em·pow·er·ment** n.

em·press /'empris/ ▶ n. **1** a female emperor. **2** the wife or widow of an emperor.

emp·ty /'em(p)tē/ ▶ adj. (**emptier, emptiest**) **1** containing nothing; not filled or occupied. **2** not likely to be fulfilled: *an empty threat.* **3** having no meaning or purpose: *an empty life going nowhere.* ▶ v. (**empties, emptying, emptied**) **1** remove the contents from a container. **2** (of a place, vehicle, or container) become empty: *the bus emptied in a flash.* **3** (of a river) flow into the sea or a lake. ▶ n. (pl. **empties**) informal a bottle or glass left empty of its contents. ■ **emp·ti·ly** adv. **emp·ti·ness** n.

emp·ty-hand·ed ▶ adj. having failed to obtain or achieve what one wanted.

emp·ty-head·ed ▶ adj. unintelligent and foolish.

emp·ty nest·er ▶ n. informal a parent whose children have grown up and left home.

em·py·re·an /em'pirēən, ,empə'rēən/ ▶ n. (**the empyrean**) literary heaven or the sky.

EMS ▶ abbr. **1** emergency medical service. **2** European Monetary System.

EMT ▶ abbr. emergency medical technician.

EMU ▶ abbr. Economic and Monetary Union.

e·mu /'ēm(y)ōō/ ▶ n. a large flightless fast-running Australian bird similar to an ostrich.

em·u·late /'emyə,lāt/ ▶ v. **1** try to do as well as or better than a person or an achievement. **2** Computing reproduce the function or action of (a different computer or software system). ■ **em·u·la·tion** /,emyə'lāshən/ n. **em·u·la·tor** /-,lātər/ n.

e·mul·si·fi·er /i'məlsə,fī(ə)r/ ▶ n. a substance that stabilizes an emulsion, especially an additive used to stabilize processed foods.

e·mul·si·fy /i'məlsə,fī/ ▶ v. (**emulsifies, emulsifying, emulsified**) make into or become an emulsion. ■ **e·mul·si·fi·a·ble** /-,fīəbəl/ adj. **e·mul·si·fi·ca·tion** /i,məlsəfi'kāshən/ n.

e·mul·sion /i'məlshən/ ▶ n. **1** a liquid in which particles of one liquid are evenly dispersed in the other. **2** a type of matte paint for walls. **3** a light-sensitive coating for photographic films and plates, containing crystals of a silver compound dispersed in a medium such as gelatin.

en /en/ ▶ n. Printing a unit of measurement equal to half an em.

en·a·ble /en'ābəl/ ▶ v. **1** provide someone with the ability or means to do something. **2** make something possible. **3** chiefly Computing make a device or system operational. **4** (as adj. **-enabled**) adapted for use with the specified application or system: *WAP-enabled cell phones.* ■ **en·a·ble·ment** n. **en·a·bler** n.

en·act /en'akt/ ▶ v. **1** make a bill or other proposal law. **2** act out a role or play. ■ **en·ac·tor** n.

en·act·ment /en'aktmənt/ ▶ n. **1** the process of enacting something. **2** a law that has been passed.

e·nam·el /i'naməl/ ▶ n. **1** a colored shiny substance applied to metal, glass, or pottery

for decoration or protection. **2** the hard glossy substance that covers the crown of a tooth. **3** a paint that dries to give a smooth, hard coat. ▶ v. (**enamels, enameling, enameled**) (usu. as adj. **enameled**) coat or decorate something with enamel. ■ **e·nam·el·er** n.

en·am·or /i'namər/ (chiefly Brit. **enamour**) ▶ v. (**be enamored of/with/by**) be filled with love or admiration for: *half the village are enamored of her.*

en bloc /än 'bläk/ ▶ adv. all together or all at once.

en·camp /en'kamp/ ▶ v. settle in or establish a camp.

en·camp·ment /en'kampmənt/ ▶ n. **1** a place where a camp is set up. **2** the process of setting up a camp.

en·cap·su·late /en'kaps(y)ə,lāt/ ▶ v. **1** express clearly and in few words: *can you encapsulate the idea in two sentences?* **2** enclose something in or as if in a capsule. ■ **en·cap·su·la·tion** /en,kaps(y)ə'lāshən/ n.

en·case /en'kās/ ▶ v. enclose or cover something in a case or close-fitting surround. ■ **en·case·ment** n.

en·caus·tic /en'kôstik/ ▶ adj. (in painting and ceramics) decorated with colored clays or pigments mixed with hot wax, which are burned in as an inlay. ▶ n. the art or process of encaustic painting.

en·ceph·a·li·tis /en,sefə'lītis/ ▶ n. inflammation of the brain. ■ **en·ceph·a·lit·ic** /-'litik/ adj.

en·ceph·a·log·ra·phy /en,sefə'lägrəfē/ ▶ n. any of various techniques for recording the structure or electrical activity of the brain. ■ **en·ceph·a·lo·gram** /en'sefələ,gram/ n.

en·ceph·a·lo·my·e·li·tis /en,sefələ,mīə'lītis/ ▶ n. inflammation of the brain and spinal cord, typically caused by acute infection with a virus.

en·ceph·a·lop·a·thy /en,sefə'läpəthē/ ▶ n. (pl. **encephalopathies**) a disease in which the functioning of the brain is affected, especially by viral infection or toxins in the blood.

en·chant /en'CHant/ ▶ v. **1** fill someone with delight. **2** put someone under a spell. ■ **en·chant·er** n. **en·chant·ment** n. **en·chant·ress** /en'CHantris/ n.

en·chant·ing /en'CHanting/ ▶ adj. delightfully charming or attractive. ■ **en·chant·ing·ly** adv.

en·chi·la·da /,enCHə'lädə/ ▶ n. a tortilla filled with meat or cheese and served with chili sauce. – PHRASES **the whole enchilada** informal the whole situation; everything.

en·ci·pher /en'sīfər/ ▶ v. convert something into a coded form. ■ **en·ci·pher·ment** n.

en·cir·cle /en'sərkəl/ ▶ v. surround or form a circle around someone or something. ■ **en·cir·cle·ment** n.

encl. (also **enc.**) ▶ abbr. **1** enclosed. **2** enclosure.

en·clave /'en,klāv, 'äNG-/ ▶ n. **1** a small territory surrounded by a larger territory whose inhabitants are of a different nationality or culture. **2** a group that is different from those surrounding it: *the engineering department is a male enclave.*

en·close /en'klōz/ ▶ v. **1** surround or close off on all sides: *breakwaters enclosed the harbor.* **2** (**enclose something in/within**) place an object inside a container. **3** place another document or an object in an envelope together with a letter.

en·clo·sure /en'klōzHər/ ▶ n. **1** an area that

is enclosed by a fence, wall, or other barrier. **2** a document or object placed in an envelope together with a letter.

en·code /en'kōd/ ▶ v. convert something into a coded form. ■ **en·cod·er** n.

en·co·mi·um /en'kōmēəm/ ▶ n. (pl. **encomiums** or **encomia** /-mēə/) formal a speech or piece of writing praising someone or something.

en·com·pass /en'kəmpəs/ ▶ v. **1** include a wide range or number of things. **2** surround or cover: *the estate encompasses twelve acres.*

en·core /'än,kôr/ ▶ n. a repeated or additional performance of an item at the end of a concert, as called for by an audience. ▶ exclam. again! (as called by an audience at the end of a concert).

en·coun·ter /en'koun(t)ər/ ▶ v. **1** unexpectedly be faced with something difficult. **2** unexpectedly meet someone. ▶ n. **1** an unexpected or casual meeting. **2** a confrontation or difficult struggle: *his close encounter with death.*

en·cour·age /en'kərij, -'kə-rij/ ▶ v. **1** give support, confidence, or hope to someone. **2** help an activity, belief, etc., to develop. ■ **en·cour·ag·er** n. **en·cour·ag·ing** adj.

en·cour·age·ment /en'kərijmənt, -'kə-rijmənt/ ▶ n. **1** the action of encouraging someone to do something. **2** something that encourages someone: *his success served as an encouragement to younger artists.*

en·croach /en'krōCH/ ▶ v. **1** (**encroach on**) gradually intrude on a person's territory, rights, etc. **2** advance gradually beyond expected or acceptable limits: *the sea has encroached all around the coast.* ■ **en·croach·ment** n.

en croute /än 'krōōt/ ▶ adj. & adv. in a pastry crust.

en·crust /en'krəst/ ▶ v. cover something with a hard surface layer. ■ **en·crus·ta·tion** /,enkrəs'tāsHən/ n.

en·crypt /en'kript/ ▶ v. convert something into code. ■ **en·cryp·tion** /-'kripsHən/ n.

en·cum·ber /en'kəmbər/ ▶ v. prevent from moving or acting freely: *they were encumbered with cameras, tape recorders, and other gadgets.*

en·cum·brance /en'kəmbrəns/ ▶ n. **1** something that prevents freedom of action or movement. **2** Law a mortgage or other claim on property or assets.

en·cyc·li·cal /en'siklikəl/ ▶ n. a letter sent by the pope to all bishops of the Roman Catholic Church.

en·cy·clo·pe·di·a /en,sīklə'pēdēə/ ▶ n. a book or set of books giving information on many subjects or on many aspects of one subject, typically arranged alphabetically.

en·cy·clo·pe·dic /en,sīklə'pēdik/ ▶ adj. **1** having detailed information on a wide variety of subjects: *an encyclopedic knowledge of food.* **2** relating to encyclopedias or information suitable for an encyclopedia.

en·cy·clo·pe·dist /en,sīklə'pēdist/ ▶ n. a person who writes, edits, or contributes to an encyclopedia.

end /end/ ▶ n. **1** the final part of something. **2** the furthest part of something. **3** the stopping of a state or situation: *they called for an end to violence.* **4** a person's death or downfall. **5** a goal or desired result. **6** a part or share of an activity: *your end of the deal.* **7** a small piece that is left after use. **8** the part of an athletic field or court defended by one team or player.

▶ v. **1** come or bring to an end; finish. **2** (**end in**) have something as its result: *the match ended in a draw.* **3** (**end up**) eventually reach or come to a particular state or place.
– PHRASES **be the end** informal be the limit of what one can tolerate. **end it all** commit suicide. **the end of one's rope** having no patience or energy left. **in the end** eventually. **keep** (or **hold**) **one's end up** informal perform well in a demanding situation. **make** (**both**) **ends meet** earn just enough money to live on. **no end** informal very much. **no end of** informal a vast number or amount of. **on end 1** continuously. **2** upright.

en·dan·ger /en'dānjər/ ▶ v. put someone or something in danger. ■ **en·dan·ger·ment** n.

en·dan·gered /en'dānjərd/ ▶ adj. in danger of becoming extinct.

en·dear /en'di(ə)r/ ▶ v. make someone popular or well liked: *her personality endeared her to everyone.*

en·dear·ing /en'di(ə)riNG/ ▶ adj. inspiring affection. ■ **en·dear·ing·ly** adv.

en·dear·ment /en'di(ə)rmənt/ ▶ n. **1** a word or phrase expressing love or affection. **2** love or affection.

en·deav·or /en'devər/ ▶ v. try hard to do or achieve something. ▶ n. **1** a serious attempt to achieve something. **2** serious and prolonged effort: *the museum's treasures spanned forty thousand years of human endeavor.*

en·dem·ic /en'demik/ ▶ adj. **1** (of a disease or condition) regularly found among particular people or in a certain area. **2** (of a plant or animal) native or restricted to a certain area. ■ **en·de·mism** /'endə,mizəm/ n.

end·game /'en(d),gām/ ▶ n. the final stage of a game such as chess or bridge, when few pieces or cards remain.

end·ing /'endiNG/ ▶ n. an end or final part.

en·dive /'en,dīv, 'än,dēv/ ▶ n. **1** a plant with bitter curly or smooth leaves, eaten in salads. **2** (also **Belgian endive**) a chicory crown.

end·less /'en(d)ləs/ ▶ adj. **1** seeming to have no limits in size or amount: *the possibilities are endless.* **2** continuing indefinitely: *video screens showing endless catwalk shows.* **3** (of a belt, chain, or tape) having the ends joined to allow for continuous action. ■ **end·less·ly** adv. **end·less·ness** n.

end·most /'en(d),mōst/ ▶ adj. nearest to the end.

endo- ▶ comb.form internal; within: *endoderm.*

en·do·crine /'endəkrin/ ▶ adj. (of a gland) producing hormones or other products directly into the blood.

en·do·cri·nol·o·gy /,endəkrə'näləjē/ ▶ n. the branch of physiology and medicine concerned with endocrine glands and hormones. ■ **en·do·cri·nol·o·gist** n.

en·dog·e·nous /en'däjənəs/ ▶ adj. technical relating to an internal cause or origin. Often contrasted with EXOGENOUS. ■ **en·dog·e·nous·ly** adv.

en·do·me·tri·o·sis /,endō,mētrē'ōsis/ ▶ n. a condition in which tissue from the mucous membrane lining the uterus appears outside it, causing pelvic pain.

en·do·me·tri·um /,endō'mētrēəm/ ▶ n. the mucous membrane lining the uterus. ■ **en·do·me·tri·al** adj.

en·do·morph /'endə,môrf/ ▶ n. Physiology a person with a soft round body build and a high proportion of fat tissue. Compare with

ECTOMORPH and MESOMORPH.

en·dor·phin /enˈdôrfin/ ▶ n. any of a group of chemical compounds produced in the body that have a painkilling effect.

en·dorse /enˈdôrs/ ▶ v. **1** declare one's public approval of someone or something. **2** sign a check on the back to specify another person as the payee or to accept responsibility for paying it. ■ **en·dors·a·ble** adj. **en·dors·er** n.

en·dorse·ment /enˈdôrsmənt/ ▶ n. **1** a declaration of approval: *the president's endorsement of the plan.* **2** the action of endorsing a check or bill of exchange.

en·do·scope /ˈendəˌskōp/ ▶ n. an instrument that can be introduced into the body to view its internal parts. ■ **en·do·scop·ic** /ˌendəˈskäpik/ adj. **en·do·scop·i·cal·ly** /ˌendəˈskäpik(ə)lē/ adv. **en·dos·co·py** /enˈdäskəpē/ n.

en·do·skel·e·ton /ˌendōˈskelitn/ ▶ n. an internal skeleton, such as that of vertebrates.

en·do·sperm /ˈendəˌspərm/ ▶ n. the part of a seed that acts as a food store for the developing plant embryo.

en·do·ther·mic /ˌendəˈTHərmik/ ▶ adj. (of a chemical reaction) accompanied by the absorption of heat.

en·dow /enˈdou/ ▶ v. **1** provide a person or institution with an income or property, especially by a bequest in a will. **2** provide with a quality, ability, or feature: *these singers are endowed with magnificent voices.* **3** establish a university post, annual prize, etc., by donating funds.

en·dow·ment /enˈdoumənt/ ▶ n. **1** money given to a college or other institution to provide it with an income. **2** a natural quality or ability. ▶ adj. referring to a form of life insurance involving payment of a fixed sum to the insured person on a specified date, or to their estate should they die before this date.

end·pa·per /ˈen(d)ˌpāpər/ ▶ n. a leaf of paper at the beginning or end of a book, fixed to the inside of the cover.

end·point /ˈen(d)ˌpoint/ (also **end point**) ▶ n. the final stage of a period or process.

en·due /enˈd(y)o͞o/ ▶ v. (**endues, enduing, endued**) literary (usu. **be endued with**) provide someone or something with a quality or ability.

en·dur·ance /enˈd(y)o͞orəns/ ▶ n. **1** the ability to endure something unpleasant and prolonged. **2** the capacity of something to withstand prolonged wear and tear.

en·dure /enˈd(y)o͞or/ ▶ v. **1** suffer something unpleasant and prolonged patiently. **2** remain in existence. ■ **en·dur·a·ble** adj.

end-us·er ▶ n. the person who uses a particular product.

end·ways /ˈen(d)ˌwāz/ (also **endwise**) ▶ adv. with the end facing upward, forward, or toward the viewer.

ENE ▶ abbr. east-northeast.

en·e·ma /ˈenəmə/ ▶ n. a medical procedure in which fluid is injected into the rectum, especially to empty it.

en·e·my /ˈenəmē/ ▶ n. (pl. **enemies**) **1** a person who is actively opposed or hostile to someone or something. **2** (**the enemy**) (treated as sing. or pl.) a hostile nation or its armed forces in wartime. **3** a thing that damages or opposes something: *boredom is the great enemy of happiness.*

en·er·get·ic /ˌenərˈjetik/ ▶ adj. showing or involving great energy or activity. ■ **en·er·get·i·cal·ly** adv.

en·er·gy /ˈenərjē/ ▶ n. (pl. **energies**) **1** the strength and vitality required to keep active: *she had boundless energy and a zest for life.* **2** (**energies**) the physical and mental effort that is put into something. **3** power derived from physical or chemical resources to provide light and heat or to work machines. **4** Physics the capacity of matter and radiation to perform work. ■ **en·er·gize** /ˈenərˌjīz/ v.

en·er·vate /ˈenərˌvāt/ ▶ v. make someone feel drained of energy. ■ **en·er·va·tion** /ˌenərˈvāSHən/ n.

en·fant ter·ri·ble /äNˌfäN teˈrēbl(ə)/ ▶ n. (pl. **enfants terribles** pronunc. same) a person who behaves in an unconventional or controversial way.

en·fee·ble /enˈfēbəl/ ▶ v. weaken someone or something. ■ **en·fee·ble·ment** n.

en·fi·lade /ˈenfəˌlād, -ˌläd/ ▶ n. a volley of gunfire directed along a line of soldiers from end to end. ▶ v. direct a volley of gunfire along a line of soldiers.

en·fold /enˈfōld/ ▶ v. surround or envelop someone or something.

en·force /enˈfôrs/ ▶ v. **1** make sure that a law, rule, or duty is obeyed or fulfilled. **2** (often as adj. **enforced**) force or require something to happen: *months of enforced idleness.* ■ **en·force·a·ble** adj. **en·force·ment** n. **en·forc·er** n.

en·fran·chise /enˈfranˌCHīz/ ▶ v. **1** give the right to vote to someone. **2** historical free a slave. ■ **en·fran·chise·ment** n.

en·gage /enˈgāj/ ▶ v. **1** attract or involve someone's interest or attention. **2** (**engage in/with**) participate or become involved in: *he was engaged in a lively conversation with the barber.* **3** employ someone. **4** promise to do something. **5** enter into combat with an enemy force. **6** (of a part of a machine or engine) move into position so as to come into operation.

en·gaged /enˈgājd/ ▶ adj. **1** busy; occupied. **2** having formally agreed to marry. **3** Brit. (of a telephone line) unavailable because already in use; busy.

en·gage·ment /enˈgājmənt/ ▶ n. **1** a formal agreement to get married. **2** an appointment. **3** the state of being involved in something. **4** a battle between armed forces.

en·gag·ing /enˈgājiNG/ ▶ adj. charming and attractive. ■ **en·gag·ing·ly** adv.

en·gen·der /enˈjendər/ ▶ v. give rise to a feeling, situation, or condition.

en·gine /ˈenjən/ ▶ n. **1** a machine with moving parts that converts power into motion. **2** a railroad locomotive. **3** historical a mechanical device, especially one used in warfare: *a siege engine.* ■ **en·gine·less** adj.

en·gi·neer /ˌenjəˈni(ə)r/ ▶ n. **1** a person who designs, builds, or maintains engines, machines, or structures. **2** a person who controls an engine, especially on an aircraft or ship. **3** a person who cleverly plans something. ▶ v. **1** design and build a machine or structure. **2** cleverly plan something: *she engineered another meeting with him.*

en·gi·neer·ing /ˌenjəˈni(ə)riNG/ ▶ n. **1** the branch of science and technology concerned with the design, building, and use of engines, machines, and structures. **2** an area of study or activity concerned with development in a particular area: *software engineering.*

Eng·lish /'ɪNG(g)lɪsH/ ▶ n. the language of England, now used in many varieties throughout the world. ▶ adj. relating to England.
■ **Eng·lish·ness** n.

Eng·lish break·fast ▶ n. a substantial cooked breakfast, typically including bacon and eggs.

Eng·lish·man /'ɪNG(g)lɪsH,mən/ (or **Englishwoman** /'ɪNG(g)lɪsH,wŏŏmən/) ▶ n. (pl. **Englishmen** or **Englishwomen**) a person from England.

Eng·lish muf·fin ▶ n. a flat, circular, spongy bread roll made from yeast dough and eaten split, toasted, and buttered.

en·gorge /en'gôrj/ ▶ v. (often as adj. **engorged**) swell or cause to swell with blood, water, etc.
■ **en·gorge·ment** n.

en·grained /en'grānd/ ▶ adj. variant spelling of INGRAINED.

en·grave /en'grāv/ ▶ v. **1** cut or carve words or a design on a hard surface. **2** cut a design as lines on a metal plate for printing. **3** (**be engraved on** or **in**) be permanently fixed in one's mind.
■ **en·grav·er** n.

en·grav·ing /en'grāvɪNG/ ▶ n. **1** a print made from an engraved plate, block, or other surface. **2** the process or art of cutting or carving a design on a hard surface.

en·gross /en'grōs/ ▶ v. involve or occupy someone completely: *he was engrossed in a computer game.* ■ **en·gross·ing** adj.

en·gulf /en'gəlf/ ▶ v. **1** (of a natural force) sweep over something so as to completely surround or cover it. **2** (of a feeling) powerfully affect or overwhelm someone. ■ **en·gulf·ment** n.

en·hance /en'hans/ ▶ v. increase the quality, value, or extent of: *the system is intended to enhance the user's online shopping experience.*
■ **en·hance·ment** n. **en·hanc·er** n.

e·nig·ma /i'nigmə/ ▶ n. a person or thing that is mysterious or difficult to understand.

en·ig·mat·ic /,enig'matik/ ▶ adj. difficult to understand; mysterious: *an enigmatic smile.*
■ **en·ig·mat·i·cal** adj. **en·ig·mat·i·cal·ly** /-(ə)lē/ adv.

en·join /en'join/ ▶ v. **1** instruct or urge someone to do something. **2** (**enjoin someone from**) Law prohibit someone from performing an action by an injunction.

en·joy /en'joi/ ▶ v. **1** take pleasure in an activity or occasion. **2** (**enjoy oneself**) have a pleasant time. **3** possess and benefit from: *these professions enjoy high status.*

en·joy·a·ble /en'joi-əbəl/ ▶ adj. giving delight or pleasure. ■ **en·joy·a·bil·i·ty** /en,joi-ə'bilitē/ n. **en·joy·a·bly** adv.

en·joy·ment /en'joimənt/ ▶ n. **1** the state or process of taking pleasure in something: *the weather didn't mar our enjoyment of the trip.* **2** a thing that gives pleasure. **3** the fact of having and benefiting from something.

en·large /en'lärj/ ▶ v. **1** make or become bigger. **2** (**enlarge on**) speak or write about something in greater detail. ■ **en·larg·er** n.

en·large·ment /en'lärjmənt/ ▶ n. **1** the action of enlarging something or the state of being enlarged. **2** a photograph that is larger than the original negative or than an earlier print.

en·light·en /en'lītn/ ▶ v. **1** give someone greater knowledge and understanding about something.

2 (as adj. **enlightened**) rational, tolerant, and well informed.

en·light·en·ment /en'lītnmənt/ ▶ n. **1** the gaining of knowledge and understanding.
2 (**the Enlightenment**) a European intellectual movement of the late 17th and 18th centuries emphasizing reason and individualism rather than tradition.

en·list /en'list/ ▶ v. **1** enroll or be enrolled in the armed services. **2** ask for someone's help in doing something. ■ **en·list·ee** /,enlist'ē/ n. **en·list·ment** n.

en·list·ed man ▶ n. a member of the armed forces below the rank of officer.

en·liv·en /en'līvən/ ▶ v. **1** make more interesting or appealing: *the vegetables are enlivened by a spicy coconut sauce.* **2** make someone more cheerful or lively.

en masse /än 'mas/ ▶ adv. all together.

en·mesh /en'mesH/ ▶ v. (usu. **be enmeshed in**) entangle someone or something.

en·mi·ty /'enmitē/ ▶ n. (pl. **enmities**) the state of being an enemy; hostility.

en·no·ble /en'nōbəl/ ▶ v. **1** give someone a noble rank or title. **2** give greater dignity to: *ennoble the mind and uplift the spirit.* ■ **en·no·ble·ment** n.

en·nui /än'wē/ ▶ n. listlessness and dissatisfaction arising from boredom.

e·nol·o·gy /ē'näləjē/ ▶ n. the study of wines.
■ **e·no·log·i·cal** /,ēnə'läjikəl/ adj. **e·nol·o·gist** /-jist/ n.

e·nor·mi·ty /i'nôrmitē/ ▶ n. (pl. **enormities**) **1** (**the enormity of**) the extreme seriousness or extent of something bad. **2** great size or scale: *he shook his head at the enormity of the task.* **3** a serious crime or sin.

USAGE
The earliest meaning of **enormity** was 'a crime' and some people therefore object to its use in modern English in another way of saying **immensity** (as in *the enormity of the task*). However, this use is now broadly accepted in standard English.

e·nor·mous /i'nôrməs/ ▶ adj. very large; huge.
■ **e·nor·mous·ly** adv. **e·nor·mous·ness** n.

e·nough /i'nəf/ ▶ determiner & pron. as much or as many as is necessary or desirable. ▶ adv. **1** to the required degree or extent. **2** to a moderate degree.
– PHRASES **enough is enough** no more will be tolerated.

en pas·sant /,än pä'sänt, än pä'sän/ ▶ adv. by the way; in passing.

en·quire, etc. /en'kwīr/ ▶ v. chiefly British spelling of INQUIRE, etc.

en·rage /en'rāj/ ▶ v. make someone very angry.

en·rap·ture /en'rapcHər/ ▶ v. give great pleasure to someone. ■ **en·rapt** /en'rapt/ adj.

en·rich /en'rɪcH/ ▶ v. **1** improve the quality or value of: *photography has enriched my life.* **2** make someone wealthy or wealthier.
■ **en·rich·ment** n.

en·riched u·ra·ni·um ▶ n. uranium containing an increased proportion of the fissile isotope U-235, making it more explosive.

en·roll /en'rōl/ (Brit. **enrol**) ▶ v. officially register or recruit someone as a member or student.

en·roll·ment /en'rōlmənt/ (Brit. **enrolment**)
▶ n. **1** the action of enrolling or being enrolled.

2 the number of people enrolled.

en·route /än 'rōōt, en, äN/ ▶ adv. on the way.

en·sconce /en'skäns/ ▶ v. settle in a comfortable, safe, or secret place: *he was ensconced in a conference room.*

en·sem·ble /än'sämbəl/ ▶ n. **1** a group of musicians, actors, or dancers who perform together. **2** a group of items viewed as a whole, in particular a set of clothes worn together. **3** a musical passage for a whole choir or group of instruments.

en·shrine /en'sHrīn/ ▶ v. **1** preserve a right, tradition, or idea in a form that ensures it will be respected: *the train operators claim that their subsidy is enshrined in European law.* **2** place a holy or precious object in an appropriate place or container. ■ **en·shrine·ment** n.

en·shroud /en'sHroud/ ▶ v. literary envelop something completely and hide it from view.

en·sign /'ensən, 'en,sīn/ ▶ n. **1** a flag, especially a military or naval one indicating nationality. **2** the lowest rank of commissioned officer in the US Navy and Coast Guard, above chief warrant officer and below lieutenant.

en·slave /en'slāv/ ▶ v. **1** make someone a slave. **2** make someone completely dominated by something. ■ **en·slave·ment** n. **en·slav·er** n.

en·snare /en'sner/ ▶ v. put someone in a difficult situation or under the control of another: *fraud ensnares the poor.*

en·sue /en'sōō/ ▶ v. (**ensues, ensuing, ensued**) happen afterward or as a result: *once the auction starts, pandemonium ensues.*

en·sure /en'sHŏŏr/ ▶ v. **1** make certain that something will occur or be so. **2** (**ensure against**) make sure that a problem does not occur.

> **USAGE**
> On the difference between **ensure** and **insure**, see the note at **INSURE**.

ENT ▶ abbr. ear, nose, and throat (as a department in a hospital).

en·tab·la·ture /en'tabləCHər, -,CHŏŏr/ ▶ n. Architecture the upper part of a classical building supported by columns, comprising the architrave, frieze, and cornice.

en·tail /en'tāl/ ▶ v. **1** involve something as an unavoidable part or consequence: *any major surgery entails a certain degree of risk.* **2** Law limit the inheritance of property over a number of generations so that ownership remains within a family or group. ■ **en·tail·ment** n.

en·tan·gle /en'taNGgəl/ ▶ v. (usu. **be entangled in/with**) **1** make something tangled. **2** involve someone in a complicated situation.

en·tan·gle·ment /en'taNGgəlmənt/ ▶ n. **1** a complicated or compromising relationship or situation. **2** a barrier, typically made of stakes and barbed wire, placed to impede enemy soldiers or vehicles.

en·tente /än'tänt/ (also **entente cordiale** /kôr'dyäl/) ▶ n. a friendly understanding or informal alliance between countries.

en·ter /'entər/ ▶ v. **1** come or go into a place. **2** (often **enter into**) begin to be involved in or do something: *the firm entered into talks to join the consortium.* **3** join an institution or profession. **4** register as a participant in a competition, exam, etc. **5** (**enter into**) undertake to be bound by an agreement. **6** write or key

information in a book, computer, etc.

en·ter·ic /en'terik/ ▶ adj. relating to or occurring in the intestines.

en·ter·i·tis /,entə'rītis/ ▶ n. inflammation of the small intestine, usually accompanied by diarrhea.

en·ter·o·vi·rus /,entərō'vīrəs/ ▶ n. any of a group of RNA viruses (including those causing polio and hepatitis A) that typically occur in the gastrointestinal tract, sometimes spreading to the central nervous system or other parts of the body.

en·ter·prise /'entər,prīz/ ▶ n. **1** a large project. **2** a business or company. **3** initiative and resourcefulness: *their success was thanks to a mixture of talent and enterprise.*

en·ter·pris·ing /'entər,prīziNG/ ▶ adj. showing initiative and resourcefulness. ■ **en·ter·pris·ing·ly** adv.

en·ter·tain /,entər'tān/ ▶ v. **1** provide someone with amusement or enjoyment. **2** receive someone as a guest and give them food and drink. **3** give consideration to: *I entertained little hope of success.*

en·ter·tain·er /,entər'tānər/ ▶ n. a person, such as a singer or comedian, whose job is to entertain others.

en·ter·tain·ing /,entər'tāniNG/ ▶ adj. providing amusement or enjoyment. ■ **en·ter·tain·ing·ly** adv.

en·ter·tain·ment /,entər'tānmənt/ ▶ n. **1** the provision of amusement or enjoyment. **2** an event or performance designed to entertain people.

en·thrall /en'THrôl/ ▶ v. fascinate someone and hold their attention. ■ **en·thrall·ment** n.

en·throne /en'THrōn/ ▶ v. mark the new reign or period of office of a monarch or bishop by a ceremony in which they sit on a throne. ■ **en·throne·ment** n.

en·thuse /en'THōōz/ ▶ v. **1** express great enthusiasm for something: *they enthused over my new look.* **2** make someone interested and enthusiastic.

en·thu·si·asm /en'THōōzē,azəm/ ▶ n. **1** great enjoyment, interest, or approval. **2** something that arouses enthusiasm.

en·thu·si·ast /en'THōōzē,ast/ ▶ n. a person who is full of enthusiasm for something.

en·thu·si·as·tic /en,THōōzē'astik/ ▶ adj. having or showing great enjoyment, interest, or approval. ■ **en·thu·si·as·ti·cal·ly** adv.

en·tice /en'tīs/ ▶ v. persuade someone to do something by offering something pleasant or beneficial. ■ **en·tice·ment** n. **en·tic·ing** adj.

en·tire /en'tīr/ ▶ adj. including everything, everyone, or every part; whole.

en·tire·ly /en'tīrlē/ ▶ adv. wholly; completely.

en·tire·ty /en'tī(ə)rtē, -'tīritē/ ▶ n. (**the entirety**) the whole of something: *the ambition to acquaint oneself with the entirety of science.* – PHRASES **in its entirety** as a whole.

en·ti·tle /en'tītl/ ▶ v. **1** give someone a right to do or receive: *employees are normally entitled to severance pay.* **2** give a title to a book, play, etc.

en·ti·tle·ment /en'tītlmənt/ ▶ n. **1** the fact of having a right to something: *full entitlement to fees and maintenance should be offered.* **2** the amount to which a person has a right: *many have* *exhausted their welfare entitlements.*

en·ti·tle·ment pro·gram ▶ n. a government program that guarantees certain benefits to a particular group or segment of the population.

en·ti·ty /'entitē/ ▶ n. (pl. **entities**) a thing that has its own distinct and independent existence.

en·tomb /en'tōom/ ▶ v. **1** place a dead body in a tomb. **2** bury in or under something: *the miners were entombed in a tunnel all night.*
■ **en·tomb·ment** n.

en·to·mol·o·gy /,entə'mäləjē/ ▶ n. the branch of zoology concerned with the study of insects. ■ **en·to·mo·log·i·cal** /-mə'läjikəl/ adj. **en·to·mol·o·gist** n.

en·tou·rage /,äntoo'räzн/ ▶ n. a group of people who accompany an important person.

en·tr'acte /'än,trakt, än'trakt/ ▶ n. **1** an interval between two acts of a play or opera. **2** a piece of music or a dance performed during such an interval.

en·trails /'entrālz, 'entrəlz/ ▶ pl.n. a person's or animal's intestines or internal organs.

en·train /en'trān/ ▶ v. formal board a train.

en·trance¹ /'entrəns/ ▶ n. **1** an opening through which one may enter a place. **2** an act of entering. **3** the right, means, or opportunity to enter: *he studied at home to gain entrance to Stanford University.*

en·trance² /en'trans/ ▶ v. **1** fill someone with wonder and delight. **2** cast a spell on someone.
■ **en·trance·ment** n. **en·tranc·ing** adj.

en·trant /'entrənt/ ▶ n. a person who enters, joins, or takes part in something.

en·trap /en'trap/ ▶ v. (**entraps, entrapping, entrapped**) **1** catch someone or something in a trap. **2** (of a police officer) trick someone into committing a crime in order to have them prosecuted. ■ **en·trap·ment** n.

en·treat /en'trēt/ ▶ v. ask someone to do something in an earnest or emotional way.

en·treat·y /en'trētē/ ▶ n. (pl. **entreaties**) an earnest or emotional request.

en·tre·chat /,äntrə'sнä/ ▶ n. Ballet a vertical jump during which the dancer repeatedly crosses the feet and beats them together.

en·tre·côte /'äntrə,kōt/ ▶ n. a boned steak cut off the sirloin.

en·trée /'än,trā, än'trā/ ▶ n. **1** the main course of a meal. **2** the right to enter a place or social group: *their veneer of respectability gave them an entrée to the business community.*

en·trench /en'trencн/ ▶ v. **1** establish something so firmly that change is difficult: *prejudice is entrenched in our society.* **2** establish a military force in trenches or other fortified positions.
■ **en·trench·ment** n.

en·tre·pôt /'äntrə,pō/ ▶ n. a port or other place that acts as a center for import and export.

en·tre·pre·neur /,äntrəprə'noŏr, -'nər/ ▶ n. a person who sets up a business or businesses, taking financial risks in the hope of profit. ■ **en·tre·pre·neur·i·al** adj. **en·tre·pre·neur·i·al·ism** n. **en·tre·pre·neur·i·al·ly** adv. **en·tre·pre·neur·ism** n.

en·tro·py /'entrəpē/ ▶ n. Physics a quantity expressing how much of a system's thermal energy is unavailable for conversion into mechanical work. ■ **en·tro·pic** /en'träpik/ adj.

en·trust /en'trəst/ ▶ v. **1** (**entrust someone with**) give a responsibility to someone.

2 (**entrust something to**) put something into someone's care.

en·try /'entrē/ ▶ n. (pl. **entries**) **1** an act of entering. **2** an entrance, such as a door. **3** the right, means, or opportunity to enter: *she was refused entry to the meeting.* **4** an item recorded in a list, diary, ledger, or reference book. **5** a person who enters a competition.

en·try-lev·el ▶ adj. suitable for a beginner or first-time user.

en·try·way /'entrē,wā/ ▶ n. a way in to somewhere or something; an entrance.

en·twine /en'twīn/ ▶ v. wind or twist things together.

e·nu·mer·ate /i'n(y)ōomə,rāt/ ▶ v. **1** mention a number of things one by one. **2** formal count people or things. ■ **e·nu·mer·a·ble** /i'n(y)ōomərəbəl/ adj. **e·nu·mer·a·tion** /i,n(y)ōomə'räsнən/ n.

e·nu·mer·a·tor /i'n(y)ōomə,rātər/ ▶ n. a person employed in taking a census of the population.

e·nun·ci·ate /i'nənsē,āt/ ▶ v. **1** say or pronounce something clearly. **2** set out a policy or theory precisely. ■ **e·nun·ci·a·tion** /i,nənsē'āsнən/ n.

en·u·re·sis /,enyə'rēsis/ ▶ n. involuntary urination, especially by children at night.

en·vel·op /en'veləp/ ▶ v. (**envelops, enveloping, enveloped**) wrap up, cover, or surround completely: *we were enveloped in fog and rain.*
■ **en·vel·op·ment** n.

en·vel·ope /'envə,lōp, 'änvə-/ ▶ n. **1** a flat paper container with a sealable flap, used to enclose a letter or document. **2** a structure or layer that covers or encloses something.
– PHRASES **push the envelope** informal approach or extend the limits of what is possible.

en·vi·a·ble /'envēəbəl/ ▶ adj. arousing or likely to arouse envy; desirable: *he has an enviable record of success.* ■ **en·vi·a·bly** adv.

en·vi·ous /'envēəs/ ▶ adj. feeling or showing envy. ■ **en·vi·ous·ly** adv.

en·vi·ron·ment /en'vīrənmənt, -'vī(ə)rn-/ ▶ n. **1** the surroundings or conditions in which a person, animal, or plant lives or operates. **2** (**the environment**) the natural world, especially as affected by human activity. **3** the overall structure within which a computer, user, or program operates. ■ **en·vi·ron·men·tal** /en,vīrən'men(t)l, -,vī(ə)rn-/ adj. **en·vi·ron·men·tal·ly** adv.

en·vi·ron·men·tal·ist /en,vīrən'men(t)l-ist, -,vī(ə)rn-/ ▶ n. a person who is concerned about protecting the environment. ■ **en·vi·ron·men·tal·ism** n.

en·vi·rons /en'vīrənz, -'vī(ə)rnz/ ▶ pl.n. the area surrounding a place.

en·vis·age /en'vizij/ ▶ v. **1** think of something as a possible or desirable future event. **2** form a mental picture of something.

en·vi·sion /en'vizнən/ ▶ v. imagine something as a future possibility.

en·voy /'en,voi, 'än,voi/ ▶ n. **1** a messenger or representative, especially one on a diplomatic mission. **2** (also **envoy extraordinary**) a diplomat ranking below ambassador and above chargé d'affaires.

en·vy /'envē/ ▶ n. (pl. **envies**) **1** discontented longing aroused by someone else's possessions, qualities, or luck. **2** (**the envy of**) a person or thing that arouses envy: *you can have a barbecue that will be the envy of your neighbors.*

▶ v. (**envies, envying, envied**) long to have something that belongs to someone else.

en·wrap /en'rap/ ▶ v. (**enwraps, enwrapping, enwrapped**) cover or envelop someone or something.

en·zyme /'enzīm/ ▶ n. a substance produced by a living organism that acts as a catalyst to bring about a specific biochemical reaction. ■ **en·zy·mat·ic** /ˌenzə'matik/ adj. **en·zy·mic** /en'zīmik, -'zimik/ adj.

E·o·cene /'ēə,sēn/ ▶ adj. Geology relating to the second epoch of the Tertiary period (56.5 to 35.4 million years ago), when the first horses and whales appeared.

e·on /'ēən, 'ē,än/ (also chiefly Brit. **aeon**) ▶ n. 1 an indefinite and very long period of time: *they'd left eons ago.* 2 a major division of geological time, subdivided into eras.

EP ▶ abbr. 1 (of a record or compact disc) extended-play. 2 European Parliament.

ep- ▶ prefix variant spelling of EPI- shortened before a vowel or *h.*

EPA ▶ abbr. Environmental Protection Agency.

épa·ter /ā'pätā/ ▶ v. (in phrase **épater les bourgeois**) shock people regarded as conventional or complacent.

ep·au·let /'epə,let, ˌepə'let/ (also **epaulette**) ▶ n. an ornamental shoulder piece on a military uniform.

é·pée /ˌe'pā/ ▶ n. a sharp-pointed dueling sword, used, with the end blunted, in fencing.

e·phed·rine /ə'fedrin, 'efə,drēn/ ▶ n. a drug that causes constriction of the blood vessels and widening of the bronchial passages, used to relieve asthma and hay fever.

e·phem·er·a /ə'fem(ə)rə/ ▶ pl.n. items of short-lived interest or usefulness, especially those later valued by collectors.

e·phem·er·al /ə'fem(ə)rəl/ ▶ adj. lasting or living for a very short time. ■ **e·phem·er·al·i·ty** /ə,femə'ralitē/ n. **e·phem·er·al·ly** adv.

epi- (also **ep-** before a vowel or *h*) ▶ prefix 1 upon: *epigraph.* 2 above: *epidermis.*

ep·ic /'epik/ ▶ n. 1 a long poem describing the adventures of heroic or legendary figures or the history of a nation. 2 a long movie or book portraying heroic adventures or covering a long period of time. ▶ adj. 1 relating to an epic. 2 grand or heroic in scale: *an epic journey around the world.* ■ **ep·i·cal** adj. **ep·i·cal·ly** /-(ə)lē/ adv.

ep·i·cene /'epi,sēn/ ▶ adj. 1 having characteristics of both sexes or no characteristics of either sex. 2 effeminate.

ep·i·cen·ter /'epi,sentər/ (Brit. **epicentre**) ▶ n. the point on the earth's surface directly above the origin of an earthquake. Compare with FOCUS.

ep·i·cure /'epi,kyoōr/ ▶ n. a person who takes particular pleasure in fine food and drink.

Ep·i·cu·re·an /ˌepikyə'rēən, ˌepi'kyoōrēən/ ▶ n. 1 a follower of the ancient Greek philosopher Epicurus, who taught that pleasure, particularly mental pleasure, was the highest good. 2 (**epicurean**) an epicure. ▶ adj. 1 relating to Epicurus or his ideas. 2 (**epicurean**) relating to or suitable for an epicure. ■ **Ep·i·cu·re·an·ism** /ˌepəkyə'rēə,nizəm, -'kyoōrēə-/ n.

ep·i·cy·cle /'epi,sīkəl/ ▶ n. Geometry a small circle whose center moves around the circumference of a larger one. ■ **ep·i·cy·clic** /ˌepi'sīklik, 'epi-/ adj.

ep·i·dem·ic /ˌepi'demik/ ▶ n. 1 a widespread occurrence of an infectious disease in a community at a particular time. 2 a widespread outbreak of something undesirable: *an epidemic of violent crime.* ▶ adj. relating to or like an epidemic.

ep·i·de·mi·ol·o·gy /ˌepi,dēmē'äləjē/ ▶ n. the study of the spread and control of diseases. ■ **ep·i·de·mi·o·log·i·cal** /-ə'läjikəl/ adj. **ep·i·de·mi·ol·o·gist** n.

ep·i·der·mis /ˌepi'dərmis/ ▶ n. 1 the surface layer of an animal's skin, overlying the dermis. 2 the outer layer of tissue in a plant. ■ **ep·i·der·mal** /-'dərməl/ adj.

ep·i·did·y·mis /ˌepi'didəməs/ ▶ n. (pl. **epididymides** /-'didə,mi,dēz, -di'dimi,dēz/) a highly convoluted duct behind the testis, along which sperm passes to the vas deferens. ■ **ep·i·did·y·mal** /-məl/ adj.

ep·i·du·ral /ˌepi'd(y)oōrəl/ ▶ n. an anesthetic delivered into the space around the dura mater (outermost membrane) of the spinal cord, used especially in childbirth. ▶ adj. on or around the outermost membrane of the spinal cord.

ep·i·glot·tis /ˌepi'glätəs/ ▶ n. a flap of cartilage behind the root of the tongue, which descends during swallowing to cover the opening of the windpipe.

ep·i·gone /'epi,gōn/ ▶ n. literary a follower or imitator of a distinguished artist, philosopher, musician, etc.

ep·i·gram /'epi,gram/ ▶ n. 1 a concise and witty saying or remark. 2 a short witty poem. ■ **ep·i·gram·mat·ic** /ˌepigrə'matik/ adj.

ep·i·graph /'epi,graf/ ▶ n. 1 an inscription on a building, statue, or coin. 2 a short quotation introducing a book or chapter.

ep·i·la·tion /ˌepə'lāshən/ ▶ n. the removal of hair by the roots. ■ **ep·i·la·tor** /'epə,lātər/ n.

ep·i·lep·sy /'epə,lepsē/ ▶ n. a disorder of the nervous system causing periodic loss of consciousness or convulsions. ■ **ep·i·lep·tic** /ˌepə'leptik/ adj. & n.

ep·i·logue /'epə,lôg, -,läg/ (also **epilog**) ▶ n. a section or speech at the end of a book or play that comments on or acts as a conclusion to what has happened.

ep·i·neph·rine /ˌepi'nefrin/ ▶ n. another term for ADRENALINE.

e·piph·a·ny /i'pifənē/ ▶ n. (pl. **epiphanies**) 1 (**Epiphany**) the occasion on which Jesus appeared to the Magi (Gospel of Matthew, chapter 2). 2 (**Epiphany**) the festival commemorating this, on January 6. 3 a moment of sudden and great revelation or understanding. ■ **ep·i·phan·ic** /ˌepə'fanik/ adj.

ep·i·phyte /'epə,fīt/ ▶ n. a plant that grows on a tree or other plant but is not a parasite. ■ **ep·i·phyt·ic** /ˌepə'fitik/ adj.

e·pis·co·pa·cy /i'piskəpəsē/ ▶ n. (pl. **episcopacies**) 1 the government of a Church by bishops. 2 (**the episcopacy**) the bishops of a region or Church as a group.

e·pis·co·pal /i'piskəpəl/ ▶ adj. 1 relating to a bishop or bishops. 2 (of a Church) governed by or having bishops. ■ **e·pis·co·pal·ly** adv.

E·pis·co·pal Church ▶ n. the Anglican Church in Scotland and the US, with elected bishops.

e·pis·co·pa·lian /i,piskə'pālēən/ ▶ adj. 1 relating to the government of a Church by bishops. 2 of or belonging to an episcopal Church. ▶ n. 1 a supporter of the government of a Church by bishops. 2 (**Episcopalian**) a member of the Episcopal Church. ▪ **e·pis·co·pa·lian·ism** n.

e·pis·co·pate /i'piskəpət, -ˌpāt/ ▶ n. 1 the position or period of office of a bishop. 2 (**the episcopate**) the bishops of a Church or region as a group.

e·pi·si·ot·o·my /iˌpēzēˈätəmē/ ▶ n. (pl. **episiotomies**) a surgical cut that may be made at the opening of the vagina during childbirth to make a difficult delivery easier.

ep·i·sode /'epiˌsōd/ ▶ n. 1 an event or a sequence of events. 2 each of the separate installments into which a serialized story or program is divided.

ep·i·sod·ic /ˌepəˈsädik/ ▶ adj. 1 made up of a series of separate events. 2 occurring at irregular intervals. ▪ **ep·i·sod·i·cal·ly** /-(ə)lē/ adv.

e·pis·te·mol·o·gy /iˌpistəˈmäləjē/ ▶ n. the branch of philosophy that deals with knowledge. ▪ **ep·i·ste·mic** /ˌepəˈstemik, -ˈstē-/ adj. **e·pis·te·mo·log·i·cal** /-məˈläjikəl/ adj. **e·pis·te·mol·o·gist** /-jist/ n.

e·pis·tle /i'pisəl/ ▶ n. 1 formal or humorous a letter. 2 (**Epistle**) a book of the New Testament in the form of a letter from an Apostle.

e·pis·to·lar·y /i'pistəˌlerē/ ▶ adj. 1 relating to the writing of letters. 2 (of a literary work) in the form of letters.

ep·i·taph /'epiˌtaf/ ▶ n. 1 words written in memory of a person who has died, especially as an inscription on a tombstone. 2 something that is a reminder of a person, time, or event: *the story makes a sorry epitaph to a great career.*

ep·i·the·li·um /ˌepəˈTHēlēəm/ ▶ n. (pl. **epithelia** /-lēə/) the thin tissue forming the outer layer of the body's surface and lining the alimentary canal and other hollow structures. ▪ **ep·i·the·li·al** /-lēəl/ adj.

ep·i·thet /'epəˌTHet/ ▶ n. 1 a word or phrase expressing a characteristic quality of the person or thing mentioned. 2 such a word or phrase used as an insult: *she constantly hurls racist epithets at him.*

e·pit·o·me /i'pitəmē/ ▶ n. (**the epitome of**) a perfect example of a quality or type: *she was the epitome of a well-bred New Englander.*

e·pit·o·mize /i'pitəˌmīz/ ▶ v. be a perfect example of: *the patriotic spirit was epitomized by the poetry of Rupert Brooke.*

ep·och /'epək/ ▶ n. 1 a long period of time marked by particular events or characteristics: *the Victorian epoch.* 2 the beginning of a period of history. 3 Geology a division of time that is a subdivision of a period and is itself subdivided into ages. ▪ **ep·och·al** /'epəkəl/ adj.

ep·och-mak·ing ▶ adj. very important and likely to have a great effect on a particular period of time.

ep·o·nym /'epəˌnim/ ▶ n. 1 a word that comes from the name of a person. 2 a person after whom a discovery, invention, place, etc., is named.

e·pon·y·mous /əˈpänəməs/ ▶ adj. 1 (of a person) giving their name to something. 2 (of a thing) named after a particular person or group.

ep·ox·ide /e'päkˌsīd/ ▶ n. an organic compound whose molecule contains a three-membered ring involving an oxygen atom and two carbon atoms.

ep·ox·y /i'päksē/ (also **epoxy resin**) ▶ n. (pl. **epoxies**) an adhesive, plastic, paint, etc., made from synthetic polymers containing epoxide groups.

EPROM /'ēˌpräm/ ▶ n. Computing a read-only

memory whose contents can be erased and reprogrammed using special means.

Ep·som salts /'epsəm/ ▶ pl.n. crystals of magnesium sulfate, used as a laxative.

EQ ▶ abbr. 1 educational quotient. 2 emotional quotient.

eq·ua·ble /'ekwəbəl/ ▶ adj. 1 calm and even-tempered. 2 not varying greatly: *an equable climate.* ▪ **eq·ua·bil·i·ty** /ˌekwəˈbilitē/ n. **eq·ua·bly** /-blē/ adv.

e·qual /'ēkwəl/ ▶ adj. 1 being the same in quantity, size, degree, value, or status. 2 evenly or fairly balanced: *an equal contest.* 3 (**equal to**) having the ability or resources to meet a challenge. ▶ n. a person or thing that is equal to another. ▶ v. (**equals, equaling, equaled**) 1 be equal or equivalent to something. 2 match or rival: *he equaled the championship record.*

e·qual·i·ty /i'kwälitē/ ▶ n. the state of being equal.

e·qual·ize /'ēkwəˌlīz/ ▶ v. make or become equal. ▪ **e·qual·i·za·tion** /ˌēkwəliˈzāsHən/ n.

e·qual·iz·er /'ēkwəˌlīzər/ ▶ n. a thing that has an equalizing effect.

e·qual·ly /'ēkwəlē/ ▶ adv. 1 in an equal way or to an equal extent: *all children should be treated equally.* 2 in amounts or parts that are equal.

USAGE

The expression **equally as**, as in *follow-up discussion is equally as important* should be avoided: just use **equally** or **as** on its own.

---

e·qual op·por·tu·ni·ty ▶ n. the policy of treating employees and others without discrimination, especially on the basis of their sex, race, or age: *an equal opportunity employer.*

e·quals sign (also **equal sign**) ▶ n. the symbol =.

e·qua·nim·i·ty /ˌēkwəˈnimitē, ˌekwə-/ ▶ n. calmness of temper; composure. ▪ **e·quan·i·mous** /i'kwänəməs/ adj.

e·quate /i'kwāt/ ▶ v. 1 consider one thing as equal or equivalent to another: *customers equate their name with quality.* 2 make two or more things the same or equal to each other: *we must equate supply and demand.*

e·qua·tion /i'kwāzHən/ ▶ n. 1 Mathematics a statement that the values of two mathematical expressions are equal (indicated by the sign =). 2 Chemistry a formula representing the changes that occur in a chemical reaction. 3 the process of equating one thing with another.

e·qua·tor /i'kwātər/ ▶ n. an imaginary line around the earth at equal distances from the poles, dividing the earth into northern and southern hemispheres.

e·qua·to·ri·al /ˌekwəˈtôrēəl/ ▶ adj. relating to, at, or near the equator. ▪ **e·qua·to·ri·al·ly** adv.

eq·uer·ry /'ekwərē, əˈkwerē/ ▶ n. (pl. **equerries**) 1 a male officer of the British royal household acting as an attendant to a member of the royal family. 2 historical an officer of a prince's or nobleman's household who was responsible for the stables.

e·ques·tri·an /i'kwestrēən/ ▶ adj. 1 relating to horse riding. 2 depicting or representing a person on horseback: *an equestrian statue.* ▶ n. (fem. **equestrienne** /iˌkwestrēˈen/) a person who rides a horse.

e·ques·tri·an·ism /i'kwestrēəˌnizəm/ ▶ n. the skill or sport of horse riding.

equi- ▶ comb.form equal; equally: *equidistant.*

e·qui·dis·tant /ˌēkwi'distənt, ˌekwi-/ ▸ adj. at equal distances. ■ **e·qui·dis·tance** n.

e·qui·lat·er·al /ˌēkwə'latərəl, ˌekwə-/ ▸ adj. (of a triangle) having all sides the same length.

e·qui·lib·ri·um /ˌēkwə'librēəm, ˌekwə-/ n. (pl. **equilibria** /-'librēə/) **1** a state in which opposing forces or influences are balanced. **2** the state of being physically balanced. **3** a calm state of mind.

e·quine /'ekwīn, 'ē,kwīn/ ▸ adj. **1** relating to horses or other members of the horse family. **2** resembling a horse. ▸ n. a horse or other member of the horse family.

e·qui·noc·tial /ˌēkwə'näksнəl, ˌekwə-/ ▸ adj. **1** relating to or at the time of the equinox. **2** at or near the equator.

e·qui·nox /'ekwə,näks, 'ēkwə-/ ▸ n. the time or date (twice each year, about September 22 and March 20) at which the sun crosses the celestial equator and when day and night are of equal length.

e·quip /i'kwip/ ▸ v. (**equips, equipping, equipped**) **1** supply with the items needed for a purpose: *all bedrooms are equipped with a color TV.* **2** prepare someone for a situation, activity, or task: *a course that equips students with the skills needed to enter the profession.*

eq·ui·page /'ekwəpij/ ▸ n. **1** old use equipment. **2** historical a carriage and horses with attendants.

e·quip·ment /i'kwipmənt/ ▸ n. **1** the items needed for a particular purpose. **2** the process of supplying these items.

e·qui·poise /'ekwə,poiz/ ▸ n. a state of balance between different forces or interests.

eq·ui·ta·ble /'ekwitəbəl/ ▸ adj. treating everyone fairly and equally. ■ **eq·ui·ta·bly** /-əblē/ adv.

eq·ui·ta·tion /ˌekwi'tāsнən/ ▸ n. formal the art and practice of horse riding.

eq·ui·ty /'ekwitē/ ▸ n. (pl. **equities**) **1** the quality of being fair and impartial. **2** Law a branch of law that developed alongside common law and is concerned with fairness and justice. **3** the value of a mortgaged property after all the charges and debts secured against it have been paid. **4** the value of the shares issued by a company. **5** (**equities**) stocks and shares that do not pay a fixed amount of interest.

e·quiv·a·lent /i'kwivələnt/ ▸ adj. (often **equivalent to**) **1** equal in value, amount, function, meaning, etc. **2** having the same or a similar effect. ▸ n. a person or thing that is equivalent to another. ■ **e·quiv·a·lence** n. **e·quiv·a·len·cy** /i'kwivələnsē/ n. **e·quiv·a·lent·ly** adv.

e·quiv·o·cal /i'kwivəkəl/ ▸ adj. unclear in meaning or intention; ambiguous. ■ **e·quiv·o·cal·ly** adv.

e·quiv·o·cate /i'kwivə,kāt/ ▸ v. use ambiguous or evasive language. ■ **e·quiv·o·ca·tion** /i,kwivə'kāsнən/ n.

ER ▸ abbr. **1** emergency room. **2** Queen Elizabeth.

Er ▸ symbol the chemical element erbium.

er /ə, ər/ ▸ exclam. expressing hesitation: *Er, I'm not sure.*

ERA ▸ abbr. **1** Baseball earned run average. **2** Equal Rights Amendment.

e·ra /'i(ə)rə, 'erə/ ▸ n. **1** a long and distinct period of history. **2** Geology a major division of time that is a subdivision of an eon and is itself subdivided into periods.

e·rad·i·cate /i'radi,kāt/ ▸ v. remove or destroy something completely. ■ **e·rad·i·ca·tion** /i,radi'kāsнən/ n. **e·rad·i·ca·tor** n.

e·rase /i'rās/ ▸ v. **1** rub something out. **2** remove all traces of something. ■ **e·ras·a·ble** /-əbəl/ adj. **e·ra·sure** /i'rāsнər/ n.

e·ras·er /i'rāsər/ ▸ n. a piece of rubber or plastic used to rub out something written.

er·bi·um /'ərbēəm/ ▸ n. a soft silvery-white metallic chemical element of the lanthanide series.

ere /e(ə)r/ ▸ prep. & conj. literary or old use before (in time).

e·rect /i'rekt/ ▸ adj. **1** rigidly upright or straight. **2** (of a body part) enlarged and rigid, especially in sexual excitement. ▸ v. **1** construct a building, wall, etc. **2** create or establish: *the party that erected the welfare state.* ■ **e·rect·ly** adv. **e·rect·ness** n. **e·rec·tor** n.

e·rec·tile /i'rektl, -,tīl/ ▸ adj. able to become erect.

e·rec·tile dys·func·tion ▸ n. inability of a man to maintain an erection sufficient for satisfying sexual activity.

e·rec·tion /i'reksнən/ ▸ n. **1** the action of erecting a structure or object. **2** a building or other upright structure. **3** an erect state of the penis.

er·e·mite /'erə,mīt/ ▸ n. a Christian hermit. ■ **er·e·mit·ic** /,erə'mitik/ adj. **er·e·mit·i·cal** /,erə'mitikəl/ adj.

erg /ərg/ ▸ n. Physics a unit of work or energy.

er·go /'ərgō, 'ergō/ ▸ adv. therefore.

er·go·nom·ic /ˌərgə'nämik/ ▸ adj. **1** relating to ergonomics. **2** designed to improve people's efficiency in their working environment. ■ **er·go·nom·ic·al·ly** adv.

er·go·nom·ics /ˌərgə'nämiks/ ▸ pl.n. (treated as sing.) the study of people's efficiency in their working environment.

er·got /'ərgət, -,gät/ ▸ n. a disease of rye and other cereals, caused by a fungus.

er·i·ca /'erikə/ ▸ n. a plant of a large genus including the heaths.

er·i·ca·ceous /,eri'kāsнəs/ ▸ adj. relating to plants of the heather family.

Er·in /'erən/ ▸ n. old use or literary Ireland.

Er·i·tre·an /,erə'trēən, -'trāən/ ▸ n. a person from the nation of Eritrea in NE Africa. ▸ adj. relating to Eritrea.

ERM ▸ abbr. Exchange Rate Mechanism.

er·mine /'ərmən/ ▸ n. (pl. same or **ermines**) **1** a stoat. **2** the white winter fur of the stoat, used for trimming the ceremonial robes of judges or members of the nobility.

e·rode /i'rōd/ ▸ v. **1** gradually wear or be worn away. **2** gradually destroy or weaken: *the country's manufacturing base has been severely eroded.*

e·rog·e·nous /i'räjənəs/ ▸ adj. (of a part of the body) sensitive to sexual stimulation.

e·ro·sion /i'rōzнən/ ▸ n. the process of eroding something or the result of being eroded. ■ **e·ro·sion·al** adj. **e·ro·sive** /i'rōsiv/ adj.

e·rot·ic /i'rätik/ ▸ adj. relating to or arousing sexual desire or excitement. ■ **e·rot·i·cal·ly** adv.

e·rot·i·ca /i'rätikə/ ▸ pl.n. (treated as sing. or pl.) erotic literature or art.

e·rot·i·cism /i'räti,sizəm/ ▸ n. **1** the quality of being erotic. **2** sexual desire or excitement.

e·rot·i·cize /i'rätə,sīz/ ▸ v. give something the

quality of being able to arouse sexual desire or excitement. ■ **e·rot·i·ci·za·tion** /i,rätəsə'zāsHən/ n.

e·ro·to·ma·ni·a /i,rätə'mānēə, -,rōtə-/ ▶ n. **1** excessive sexual desire. **2** a delusion in which a person believes that another person is in love with them. ■ **e·ro·to·ma·ni·ac** /-'mānē,ak/ n.

err /ər, er/ ▶ v. **1** make a mistake. **2** (often as adj. **erring**) do wrong: *her erring husband.*
– PHRASES **err on the side of** display more rather than less of a particular quality in one's actions: *they erred on the side of caution.*

er·rand /'erənd/ ▶ n. a short journey made to deliver or collect something, especially on someone else's behalf.

er·rant /'erənt/ ▶ adj. **1** formal or humorous straying from the accepted course or standards. **2** old use or literary traveling in search of adventure. ■ **er·rant·ry** n.

er·rat·ic /i'ratik/ ▶ adj. not happening at regular times or following a regular pattern; unpredictable: *her behavior was becoming erratic.* ■ **er·rat·i·cal·ly** adv.

er·ra·tum /i'rätəm, -'rä-, -'rat-/ ▶ n. (pl. **errata** /-tə/) an error in printing or writing, especially as noted in a list added to a book or published in a subsequent edition of a newspaper or journal.

er·ro·ne·ous /i'rōnēəs/ ▶ adj. wrong; incorrect. ■ **er·ro·ne·ous·ly** adv.

er·ror /'erər/ ▶ n. **1** a mistake. **2** the state of being wrong in behavior or judgment: *the crash was caused by human error.* **3** technical the amount by which something is inaccurate in a calculation or measurement.

er·satz /'er,säts, -,zäts, er'zäts/ ▶ adj. **1** (of a product) made or used as a poor-quality substitute for something else. **2** not real or genuine: *ersatz emotion.*

Erse /ərs/ ▶ n. the Scottish or Irish Gaelic language.

erst·while /'ərst,(h)wīl/ ▶ adj. former. ▶ adv. old use formerly.

e·ruc·ta·tion /i,rək'tāsHən/ ▶ n. formal a belch.

er·u·dite /'er(y)ə,dīt/ ▶ adj. having or showing knowledge or learning. ■ **er·u·di·tion** /'er(y)ōō,disHən/ n.

e·rupt /i'rəpt/ ▶ v. **1** (of a volcano) forcefully eject lava, rocks, ash, or gases. **2** break out suddenly: *fierce fighting erupted.* **3** give way to feelings in a sudden and noisy way: *the crowd erupted into applause.* **4** (of a spot, rash, etc.) suddenly appear on the skin. ■ **e·rup·tive** adj.

e·rup·tion /i'rəpsHən/ ▶ n. an act or instance of erupting.

er·y·sip·e·las /,erə'sipələs/ ▶ n. a skin disease causing large raised red patches on the face and legs.

er·y·the·ma /,erə'THēmə/ ▶ n. reddening of the skin, usually in patches, as a result of injury or irritation causing dilatation of the blood capillaries. ■ **er·y·the·mal** /-məl/ adj. **er·y·them·a·tous** /-'THemətəs, -'THēmətəs/ adj.

e·ryth·ro·cyte /i'riTHrə,sīt/ ▶ n. a blood cell that contains hemoglobin and transports oxygen to the tissues; a red blood cell.

Es ▶ symbol the chemical element einsteinium.

es·ca·late /'eskə,lāt/ ▶ v. **1** increase rapidly: *costs started to escalate.* **2** become more intense or serious: *the crisis escalated.* ■ **es·ca·la·tion** /,eskə'lāsHən/ n.

es·ca·la·tor /'eskə,lātər/ ▶ n. a moving staircase consisting of a circulating belt of steps driven by a motor.

es·ca·lope /,eskə'lōp, i'skäləp, -'skal-/ ▶ n. a thin slice of meat, especially veal, coated in breadcrumbs and fried.

es·ca·pade /'eskə,pād/ ▶ n. an incident involving daring and adventure.

es·cape /i'skāp/ ▶ v. **1** break free from imprisonment or control. **2** elude or get free from someone. **3** succeed in avoiding something dangerous or undesirable: *she narrowly escaped death.* **4** fail to be noticed or remembered by: *his name escapes me.* **5** (of gas, liquid, or heat) leak from a container. ▶ n. **1** an act of escaping. **2** a means of escaping. **3** (also **escape key**) Computing a key that interrupts the current operation. ■ **es·cap·ee** /i,skā'pē, ,eskā'pē/ n. **es·cap·er** n.

es·cape clause ▶ n. a clause in a contract that specifies the conditions under which a party can be freed from an obligation.

es·cape·ment /i'skāpmənt/ ▶ n. **1** a mechanism that connects and regulates the moving parts in a clock or watch. **2** the part of the mechanism in a piano that enables the hammer to fall back as soon as it has struck the string. **3** a mechanism in a typewriter that shifts the carriage a small fixed amount to the left after a key is pressed and released.

es·cap·ism /i'skāp,izəm/ ▶ n. the habit of trying to distract oneself from unpleasant realities by engaging in fantasy or forms of entertainment. ■ **es·cap·ist** n. & adj.

es·cap·ol·o·gist /i,skā'päləjist, ,eskā-/ ▶ n. an entertainer who specializes in breaking free from ropes, handcuffs, and chains. ■ **es·cap·ol·o·gy** n.

es·car·got /,eskär'gō/ ▶ n. a snail, especially as an item on a menu.

es·carp·ment /i'skärpmənt/ ▶ n. a long, steep slope at the edge of a plateau or separating areas of land at different heights.

es·cha·tol·o·gy /,eskə'täləjē/ ▶ n. the part of theology concerned with death, judgment, and destiny. ■ **es·cha·to·log·i·cal** /e,skatl'äjikəl, ,eskətl-/ adj.

es·cheat /es'CHēt/ ▶ n. chiefly historical the return of property to the government, or (in feudal law) to a lord, if the owner should die without legal heirs.

es·chew /es'CHōō/ ▶ v. deliberately avoid doing or being involved in something. ■ **es·chew·al** n.

es·cort ▶ n. /'es,kôrt/ **1** a person, vehicle, or group accompanying another in order to protect or guard them or as a mark of rank. **2** a person who accompanies a member of the opposite sex to a social event. **3** euphemistic a prostitute. ▶ v. /i'skôrt/ accompany a person, vehicle, or group somewhere: *he escorted her back to her hotel.*

es·cri·toire /,eskri'twär/ ▶ n. a small writing desk with drawers and compartments.

es·crow /'eskrō/ ▶ n. Law a bond, deed, or other document kept by a third party and taking effect only when a specified condition has been fulfilled: *the board holds funds in escrow.*

es·cutch·eon /i'skəCHən/ ▶ n. **1** a shield or emblem bearing a coat of arms. **2** a flat piece of metal framing a keyhole, door handle, or light switch.
– PHRASES **a blot on one's escutcheon** something that damages one's reputation or

character.

ESE ▸ abbr. east-southeast.

-ese ▸ suffix forming adjectives and nouns.
1 referring to an inhabitant or language of a country or city: *Chinese.* **2** often derogatory (especially with reference to language) referring to character or style: *journalese.*

es·ker /'eskər/ ▸ n. Geology a long winding ridge of sediment deposited by meltwater from a retreating glacier or ice sheet.

Es·ki·mo /'eskə,mō/ ▸ n. (pl. same or **Eskimos**) **1** a member of a people inhabiting northern Canada, Alaska, Greenland, and eastern Siberia. **2** either of the two main languages of the Eskimo (Inuit and Yupik). ▸ adj. relating to the Eskimos or their languages.

> **USAGE**
> The word **Eskimo** is now regarded by some people as offensive and the peoples inhabiting the regions of northern Canada and parts of Greenland and Alaska prefer to call themselves **Inuit**. The term **Eskimo**, however, is the only term that covers both the Inuit and the Yupik (peoples of Siberia, the Aleutian Islands, and Alaska), and is still widely used.

ESL ▸ abbr. English as a second language.

ESN ▸ abbr. electronic serial number.

ESOL /'ē,säl/ ▸ abbr. English for speakers of other languages.

e·soph·a·gus /i'säfəgəs/ ▸ n. (pl. **esophagi** /-,gī, -,jī/) the muscular tube that connects the throat to the stomach. ■ **e·soph·a·ge·al** /i,säfə'jēəl/ adj.

es·o·ter·ic /,esə'terik/ ▸ adj. intended for or understood by only a small number of people who have a specialized knowledge of something. ■ **es·o·ter·i·cal·ly** adv.

es·o·ter·i·ca /,esə'terikə/ ▸ pl.n. subjects or publications understood by or intended for people with a specialized knowledge of something.

ESP ▸ abbr. extrasensory perception.

es·pa·drille /'espə,dril/ ▸ n. a light canvas shoe with a sole made of rope or rubber molded to look like rope.

es·pal·ier /i'spalyər, -yā/ ▸ n. a fruit tree or ornamental shrub whose branches are trained to grow flat against a wall.

es·par·to /i'spärtō/ (also **esparto grass**) ▸ n. (pl. **espartos**) a coarse grass native to Spain and North Africa, used to make ropes, wickerwork, and paper.

es·pe·cial /i'spesHəl/ ▸ adj. **1** notable; special: *the interior carvings are of especial interest.* **2** for or belonging chiefly to one person or thing.

es·pe·cial·ly /i'spesHəlē/ ▸ adv. **1** used to single out one person or thing over all others: *both of them were nervous, especially Geoffrey.* **2** to a great extent; very much: *he didn't especially like dancing.*

> **USAGE**
> Although similar in meaning, the words **especially** and **specially** are not interchangeable. In the broadest terms both can mean 'particularly' (a song written especially for Jonathan or a song written specially for Jonathan). However, in sentences such as both of them were nervous, especially Geoffrey, where **especially** means 'in particular, chiefly,' **specially** is informal and should not be used in written English.

Es·pe·ran·to /,espə'räntō/ ▸ n. an artificial language invented in 1887 as an international means of communication. ■ **Es·pe·ran·tist** /-'tist/ n.

es·pi·o·nage /'espēə,näzн, -,näj/ ▸ n. the practice of spying or of using spies.

es·pla·nade /'esplə,näd, -,näd/ ▸ n. a long, open, level area, typically beside the sea, along which people may walk for pleasure.

es·pous·al /i'spouzəl, -səl/ ▸ n. an act of adopting or supporting a cause, belief, or way of life: *his espousal of unorthodox religious views.*

es·pouse /i'spouz/ ▸ v. adopt or support a cause, belief, or way of life.

es·pres·so /e'spresō/ (also **expresso** /ik'spresō/) ▸ n. (pl. **espressos**) strong black coffee made by forcing steam through ground coffee beans.

es·prit /e'sprē/ ▸ n. liveliness.

es·prit de corps /e,sprē də 'kôr/ ▸ n. a feeling of pride and loyalty uniting the members of a group.

es·py /i'spī/ ▸ v. (**espies, espying, espied**) literary catch sight of someone or something.

Esq. ▸ abbr. Esquire.

-esque ▸ suffix (forming adjectives) in the style of: *Kafkaesque.*

es·quire /'eskwīr, i'skwīr/ ▸ n. **1** (**Esquire**) a title added to a lawyer's surname. **2** historical a young nobleman who acted as an attendant to a knight.

-ess ▸ suffix forming nouns referring to females: *abbess.*

> **USAGE**
> In modern English, many people regard feminine forms such as **poetess** or **authoress** as old-fashioned or sexist. It is therefore often better to use the gender-neutral base form instead (e.g. she's a famous author).

es·say ▸ n. /'esā/ **1** a piece of writing on a particular subject. **2** formal an attempt or effort. ▸ v. /e'sā/ formal attempt: *Donald essayed a smile.* ■ **es·say·ist** /'esā-ist/ n.

es·sence /'esəns/ ▸ n. **1** the basic or most important feature of something, which determines its character: *conflict is the essence of drama.* **2** an extract obtained from a plant or other substance and used for flavoring or perfume. – PHRASES **in essence** basically; fundamentally. **of the essence** very important.

es·sen·tial /i'sencHəl/ ▸ adj. **1** absolutely necessary. **2** central to the nature of something; fundamental: *the essential weakness of the plaintiff's case.* ▸ n. (**essentials**) **1** things that are absolutely necessary. **2** the fundamental elements of something: *the essentials of democracy.* ■ **es·sen·tial·ly** adv.

es·sen·tial oil ▸ n. a natural oil extracted from a plant.

EST ▸ abbr. Eastern Standard Time.

est. ▸ abbr. **1** established. **2** estimated.

es·tab·lish /i'stablisн/ ▸ v. **1** set something up on a firm or permanent basis. **2** bring about contact or communication with a person, group, or country: *the two countries established diplomatic relations.* **3** make something accepted or recognized by other people: *he had established his reputation as a journalist.* **4** discover the facts of a situation or find something out for certain: *investigators are trying to establish the cause of the fire.* **5** (as adj. **established**) recognized by the government as the national Church or religion.

es·tab·lish·ment /i'stablishmənt/ ► n. **1** the action of establishing something or the state of being established. **2** a business organization, institution, or household. **3** (**the Establishment**) a group in a society who have power and influence in matters of policy or opinion, and who are seen as being opposed to change.

es·tab·lish·men·tar·i·an /i,stablishmən'terēən/ ► adj. supporting the principle of an established Church. ► n. a person who supports the principle of an established Church.

es·tate /i'stāt/ ► n. **1** a property consisting of a large house and extensive grounds. **2** a property where crops such as coffee or rubber are cultivated or where wine is produced. **3** all the money and property owned by a person at the time of their death. **4** old use or literary a particular state, period, or condition in life: *the holy estate of matrimony*.

es·teem /i'stēm/ ► n. respect and admiration. ► v. **1** respect and admire: *he was esteemed as a philosopher*. **2** formal consider: *I should esteem it an honor if you would allow me to escort you*.

es·ter /'estər/ ► n. an organic chemical compound formed by a reaction between an acid and an alcohol.

es·thet·ic, etc. ► adj. variant spelling of AESTHETIC, etc.

es·ti·ma·ble /'estəməbəl/ ► adj. worthy of great respect. ■ **es·ti·ma·bly** /-blē/ adv.

es·ti·mate ► v. /'estə,māt/ roughly calculate the value, number, or amount of something: *the contract is estimated to be worth about $1 million*. ► n. /'estəmit/ **1** an approximate calculation of the value, number, or amount of something. **2** a written statement indicating the likely price that will be charged for a particular piece of work. **3** a judgment or opinion. ■ **es·ti·ma·tion** /,estə'māshən/ n.

es·ti·ma·tor /'estə,mātər/ ► n. **1** a person who estimates the price, value, number, quantity, or extent of something. **2** Statistics a quantity used or evaluated as an estimate of the value of a parameter.

Es·to·ni·an /e'stōnēən/ ► n. a person from Estonia. ► adj. relating to Estonia.

es·top·pel /e'stäpəl/ ► n. Law the principle that precludes a person from asserting something contrary to what is implied by a previous action or statement of that person or by a previous pertinent judicial determination.

es·tra·di·ol /,estrə'dīōl, -,äl/ (Brit. **oestradiol**) ► n. a major estrogen produced in the ovaries.

es·tranged /i'strānjd/ ► adj. **1** no longer on friendly terms with someone: *she was estranged from her daughter*. **2** (of a husband or wife) no longer living with their spouse. ■ **es·trange·ment** n.

es·tro·gen /'estrəjən/ (Brit. **oestrogen**) ► n. any of a group of hormones that produce and maintain female physical and sexual characteristics.

es·trus /'estrəs/ (Brit. **oestrus**) ► n. a regularly occurring period of time during which many female mammals are fertile and sexually receptive to males.

es·tu·ar·y /'eschoō,erē/ ► n. (pl. **estuaries**) the mouth of a large river, where it enters the sea and becomes affected by the tides. ■ **es·tu·a·rine** /'eschoōə,rīn, -ə,rēn/ adj.

ET ► abbr. **1** (in North America) Eastern time. **2** extraterrestrial.

ETA¹ ► abbr. estimated time of arrival.

ETA² /'etə/ ► abbr. a Basque separatist movement in Spain.

e-tail·er ► n. a retailer who sells goods via electronic transactions on the Internet.

et al. /,et 'al, ,et 'äl/ ► abbr. and others.

etc. ► abbr. et cetera.

et cet·er·a /et 'setərə, 'setrə/ (also **etcetera**) ► adv. and other similar things; and so on.

etch /ech/ ► v. **1** engrave metal, glass, or stone by drawing on a protective coating with a needle, and then covering it with acid to attack the exposed parts. **2** cut a text or design on a surface: *her initials were etched on the table*. **3** (**be etched**) be clearly visible: *exhaustion was etched on his face*. **4** (**be etched on/in**) be fixed permanently in someone's mind: *the date would be etched on his memory for the rest of his life*. ■ **etch·er** n.

etch·ing /'eching/ ► n. **1** the art or process of etching. **2** a print produced by etching.

ETD ► abbr. estimated time of departure.

e·ter·nal /i'tərnl/ ► adj. **1** lasting or existing forever. **2** valid for all time: *eternal truths*. ■ **e·ter·nal·ly** adv.
– PHRASES **eternal triangle** a relationship between three people involving sexual rivalry.

e·ter·ni·ty /i'tərnitē/ ► n. (pl. **eternities**) **1** unending time. **2** Theology endless life after death. **3** (**an eternity**) informal an undesirably long period of time.

eth·ane /'eTH,ān/ ► n. a flammable hydrocarbon gas present in petroleum and natural gas.

eth·a·nol /'eTHə,nôl, -,näl/ ► n. chemical name for ALCOHOL (sense 1).

e·ther /'ēTHər/ ► n. **1** a highly flammable liquid used as an anesthetic and as a solvent. **2** (also **aether**) chiefly literary the sky or the upper regions of air. ■ **e·ther·ic** /i'THerik, i'THi(ə)rik/ adj.

e·the·re·al /i'THi(ə)rēəl/ ► adj. **1** extremely delicate and light. **2** heavenly or spiritual. ■ **e·the·re·al·i·ty** /i,THi(ə)rē'alitē/ n. **e·the·re·al·ly** adv.

E·ther·net /'ēTHər,net/ ► n. a system for connecting a number of computer systems to form a local area network.

eth·ic /'eTHik/ ► n. a set of moral principles or rules of behavior: *the Puritan work ethic*.

eth·i·cal /'eTHikəl/ ► adj. **1** relating to moral principles or the branch of knowledge concerned with these. **2** morally correct. ■ **eth·i·cal·ly** adv.

eth·ics /'eTHiks/ ► pl. n. **1** the moral principles that govern a person's behavior or the way in which an activity is conducted. **2** the branch of knowledge concerned with moral principles. ■ **eth·i·cist** /'eTHisist/ n.

E·thi·o·pi·an /,ēTHē'ōpēən/ ► n. a person from Ethiopia. ► adj. relating to Ethiopia.

eth·nic /'eTHnik/ ► adj. **1** relating to a group of people who have a common national or cultural tradition. **2** referring to origin by birth rather than by present nationality: *ethnic Albanians*. **3** belonging to or characteristic of a non-Western cultural tradition: *ethnic music*. ■ **eth·ni·cal·ly** /-(ə)lē/ adv. **eth·nic·i·ty** /eTH'nisitē/ n.

eth·nic cleans·ing ► n. the mass expulsion or killing of members of an ethnic or religious group in an area by those of another group.

eth·no·cen·tric /ˌeᴛнnōˈsentrik/
▶ adj. assessing other cultures according to
the particular values or characteristics of
one's own. ■ **eth·no·cen·tri·cal·ly** /-(ə)lē/
adv. **eth·no·cen·tric·i·ty** /-ˌsen'trisitē/ n.
eth·no·cen·trism /-ˌtrizəm/ n.

eth·nog·ra·phy /eᴛнˈnägrəfē/ ▶ n. the
scientific description of peoples and cultures.
■ **eth·nog·ra·pher** n. **eth·no·graph·ic**
/ˌeᴛнnəˈgrafik/ adj.

eth·nol·o·gy /eᴛнˈnäləjē/ ▶ n. the study of
the characteristics of different peoples and
the differences and relationships between
them. ■ **eth·no·log·i·cal** /ˌeᴛнnəˈläjikəl/ adj.
eth·nol·o·gist n.

e·thol·o·gy /ēˈᴛнäləjē/ ▶ n. **1** the science of
animal behavior. **2** the study of human behavior
from a biological perspective. ■ **e·tho·log·i·cal**
/ˌēᴛнəˈläjikəl/ adj. **e·thol·o·gist** n.

e·thos /ˈēᴛнäs/ ▶ n. the characteristic spirit and
attitudes of a culture, era, or community.

eth·yl /ˈeᴛнəl/ ▶ n. the radical −C₂H₅, present in
alcohol and ethane.

eth·yl al·co·hol ▶ n. another term for ALCOHOL
(sense 1).

eth·yl·ene /ˈeᴛнəˌlēn/ ▶ n. a flammable
hydrocarbon gas present in natural gas and coal
gas.

eth·yl·ene gly·col ▶ n. a colorless viscous
alcohol used as an antifreeze and in the
manufacture of polyesters.

e·ti·o·lat·ed /ˈētēəˌlātid/ ▶ adj. (of a plant) pale
and weak due to a lack of light.

e·ti·ol·o·gy /ˌētēˈäləjē/ ▶ n. **1** Medicine the cause of
a disease or condition. **2** the investigation of a
cause or a reason. ■ **e·ti·o·log·i·cal** /ˌētēəˈläjikəl/
adj.

et·i·quette /ˈetikit, -ˌket/ ▶ n. the customary
rules of polite or correct behavior in a society or
among members of a profession.

E·trus·can /iˈtrəskən/ ▶ n. **1** a person from
Etruria, an ancient nation state of west-central
Italy that was at its height c. 500 BC. **2** the
language of Etruria. ▶ adj. relating to Etruria.

et seq. /et sek/ ▶ adv. and what follows (used in
page references).

-ette ▶ suffix forming nouns referring to. **1** small
size: kitchenette. **2** an imitation or substitute:
leatherette. **3** female gender: suffragette.

é·tude /āˈt(y)ōōd/ ▶ n. a short musical
composition or exercise.

et·y·mol·o·gy /ˌetəˈmäləjē/ ▶ n. (pl. **etymologies**)
an account of the origins and the developments
in meaning of a word. ■ **et·y·mo·log·i·cal**
/-məˈläjikəl/ adj. **et·y·mo·log·i·cal·ly**
/-məˈläjik(ə)lē/ adv. **et·y·mol·o·gist** n.

EU ▶ abbr. European Union.

Eu ▶ symbol the chemical element europium.

eu·ca·lyp·tus /ˌyōōkəˈliptəs/ (also **eucalypt**
/ˈyōōkəˌlipt/) ▶ n. (pl. **eucalyptuses**) **1** an
evergreen Australasian tree valued for its wood,
oil, gum, and resin. **2** the oil from eucalyptus
leaves, used for its medicinal properties.

eu·car·y·ote ▶ n. variant spelling of EUKARYOTE.

Eu·cha·rist /ˈyōōkərist/ ▶ n. **1** the Christian
ceremony commemorating the Last Supper,
in which consecrated bread and wine are
consumed. **2** the consecrated bread and wine
used in this ceremony, especially the bread.

■ **Eu·cha·ris·tic** /ˌyōōkəˈristik/ adj.

eu·chre /ˈyōōkər/ ▶ n. a card game played with
the thirty-two highest cards, the aim being to
win at least three of the five tricks played.

Eu·clid·e·an /yōōˈklidēən/ ▶ adj. (of systems of
geometry) based on the principles of the Greek
mathematician Euclid (c. 300 BC).

eu·gen·ics /yōōˈjeniks/ ▶ pl.n. the science of
improving a population by controlled breeding,
in such a way as to increase the occurrence of
desirable mental and physical characteristics.
■ **eu·gen·ic** adj. **eu·gen·i·cist** /-ˈjenisist/ n. & adj.

eu·kar·y·ote /yōōˈkarēˌōt, -ēət/ (also **eucaryote**)
▶ n. Biology an organism whose genetic material
is DNA in the form of chromosomes contained
within a distinct nucleus (i.e., all living
organisms other than bacteria). Compare with
PROKARYOTE.

eu·lo·gize /ˈyōōləˌjīz/ ▶ v. praise someone
or something highly. ■ **eu·lo·gist** /-jist/ n.
eu·lo·gis·tic /ˌyōōləˈjistik/ adj.

eu·lo·gy /ˈyōōləjē/ ▶ n. (pl. **eulogies**) a speech
or piece of writing that praises someone or
something highly, typically someone who has
just died.

eu·nuch /ˈyōōnək/ ▶ n. a man who has been
castrated.

eu·phe·mism /ˈyōōfəˌmizəm/ ▶ n. (when
referring to something unpleasant or
embarrassing) a mild or less direct word
used rather than one that is blunt or may
be considered offensive. ■ **eu·phe·mis·tic**
/ˌyōōfəˈmistik/ adj. **eu·phe·mis·ti·cal·ly** /-(ə)lē/
adv.

eu·pho·ni·ous /yōōˈfōnēəs/ ▶ adj. sounding
pleasant. ■ **eu·pho·ni·ous·ly** adv.

eu·pho·ni·um /yōōˈfōnēəm/ ▶ n. a brass musical
instrument resembling a small tuba.

eu·pho·ny /ˈyōōfənē/ ▶ n. the quality of having a
pleasant sound.

eu·phor·bi·a /yōōˈfôrbēə/ ▶ n. a plant of a large
genus that includes the spurges.

eu·pho·ri·a /yōōˈfôrēə/ ▶ n. a feeling of intense
happiness. ■ **eu·phor·ic** /yōōˈfôrik, -ˈfär-/ adj.
eu·phor·i·cal·ly /yōōˈfôrik(ə)lē, -ˈfär-/ adv.

Eur·a·sian /yōōˈräzhən/ ▶ adj. **1** of mixed
European (or European-American) and Asian
parentage. **2** relating to Eurasia (the landmass
of Europe and Asia together). ▶ n. a person of
Eurasian parentage.

eu·re·ka /yōōˈrēkə, yə-/ ▶ exclam. a cry of joy
or satisfaction when one finds or discovers
something.

Eu·ro /ˈyərō, ˈyōōrō/ ▶ adj. informal European,
especially concerned with the European Union.

eu·ro /ˈyərō, ˈyōōrō/ ▶ n. (pl. **euros**) a basic unit
of money of twelve member countries of the
European Union.

Eu·ro·cen·tric /ˌyərōˈsentrik, ˌyōōrō-/
▶ adj. regarding European culture as the most
important; chiefly concerned with Europe.
■ **Eu·ro·cen·trism** /-ˈsen,trizəm/ n.

Eu·ro·crat /ˈyərəˌkrat, ˈyōōrə-/ ▶ n. informal, chiefly
derogatory a bureaucrat in the administration of the
European Union.

Eu·ro·dol·lar /ˈyərōˌdälər, ˈyōōrō-/ ▶ n. a US
dollar held in Europe or elsewhere outside the
US.

Eu·ro·land /ˈyərōˌland, ˈyōōrō-/ (also **Eurozone**
/ˈyərəˌzōn, ˈyōōrō-/) ▶ n. the economic region

formed by those member countries of the European Union that have adopted the euro.

Eu·ro·pe·an /ˌyərəˈpēən, ˌyŏŏrə-/ ▶ n. **1** a person from Europe. **2** a person of European parentage. ▶ adj. relating to Europe or the European Union. ■ **Eu·ro·pe·an·ism** /-ˌnizəm/ n. **Eu·ro·pe·an·ize** /ˌyərəˈpēəˌnīz, ˌyŏŏrə-/ v.

Eu·ro·pe·an Un·ion ▶ n. an economic and political association of certain European countries, with free trade between member countries.

eu·ro·pi·um /yəˈrōpēəm/ ▶ n. a soft silvery-white metallic element of the lanthanide series.

Eu·ro·pop /ˈyŏŏrōˌpop/ ▶ n. pop music from continental Europe with simple tunes and words, often sung in English.

Eu·ro·trash /ˈyərōˌtrash, ˈyŏŏrō-/ ▶ n. informal rich European socialites, especially those living in the US.

Eu·sta·chian tube /yŏŏˈstāsн(ē)ən, -kēən/ ▶ n. a narrow passage leading from the pharynx to the cavity of the middle ear that equalizes the pressure on each side of the eardrum.

eu·tha·na·sia /ˌyŏŏтнəˈnāzнə/ ▶ n. the painless killing of a patient who has an incurable disease or who is in an irreversible coma.

eu·troph·ic /yŏŏˈträfik, -trō-/ ▶ adj. (of a lake or other body of water) rich in nutrients and so supporting a dense plant population, the decomposition of which kills animal life by depriving it of oxygen.

EVA ▶ abbr. **1** ethyl vinyl acetate. **2** (in space) extravehicular activity.

e·vac·u·ate /iˈvakyəˌwāt/ ▶ v. **1** remove someone from a place of danger to a safer place. **2** leave a dangerous place. **3** technical remove the contents from a container. **4** empty the bowels. ■ **e·vac·u·a·tion** /iˌvakyŏŏˈāsнən/ n.

e·vac·u·ee /iˌvakyŏŏˈē/ ▶ n. a person evacuated from a place of danger.

e·vade /iˈvād/ ▶ v. **1** escape or avoid someone or something, especially by cunning. **2** avoid dealing with or discussing: *don't try to evade the issue.* **3** avoid paying tax or duty, especially by illegitimate means. ■ **e·vad·er** n.

e·val·u·ate /iˈvalyŏŏˌāt/ ▶ v. **1** form an idea of the amount or value of something. **2** Mathematics find a numerical expression or equivalent for a formula, function, or equation. ■ **e·val·u·a·tion** /iˌvalyŏŏˈāsнən/ n. **e·val·u·a·tive** /-yŏŏˌātiv, -ətiv/ adj. **e·val·u·a·tor** /-yŏŏˌātər/ n.

ev·a·nes·cent /ˌevəˈnesənt/ ▶ adj. chiefly literary quickly fading from sight, memory, or existence. ■ **ev·a·nesce** /ˌevəˈnes/ v. **ev·a·nes·cence** n.

e·van·gel·i·cal /ˌivanˈjelikəl/ ▶ adj. **1** relating to a tradition within Protestant Christianity emphasizing the authority of the Bible and salvation through personal faith in Jesus. **2** relating to the teaching of the gospel or Christianity. **3** passionate in supporting something. ▶ n. a member of the evangelical tradition in the Christian Church. ■ **e·van·gel·i·cal·ism** /-izəm/ n. **e·van·gel·i·cal·ly** adv.

e·van·ge·list /iˈvanjəlist/ ▶ n. **1** a person who tries to convert others to Christianity. **2** the writer of one of the four Gospels. **3** a passionate supporter of something. ■ **e·van·ge·lism** /iˈvanjəˌlizəm/ n. **e·van·ge·lis·tic** /iˌvanjəˈlistik/ adj.

e·van·ge·lize /iˈvanjəˌlīz/ ▶ v. **1** convert or try to

convert someone to Christianity. **2** preach the gospel. ■ **e·van·ge·li·za·tion** /iˌvanjəliˈzāsнən/ n.

e·vap·o·rate /iˈvapəˌrāt/ ▶ v. **1** turn from liquid into vapor. **2** cease to exist: *my patience evaporated.* ■ **e·vap·o·ra·tion** /iˌvapəˈrāsнən/ n. **e·vap·o·ra·tive** /iˈvapəˌrātiv/ adj. **e·vap·o·ra·tor** /-ˌrātər/ n.

e·vap·o·rat·ed milk ▶ n. thick milk that has had some of the liquid removed by evaporation.

e·va·sion /iˈvāzнən/ ▶ n. **1** the action of evading or avoiding something. **2** a statement that avoids dealing with something.

e·va·sive /iˈvāsiv/ ▶ adj. **1** avoiding a direct answer to a question. **2** intended to avoid or escape: *evasive action.* ■ **e·va·sive·ly** adv. **e·va·sive·ness** n.

eve /ēv/ ▶ n. **1** the day or period of time immediately before an event. **2** literary evening.

e·ven[1] /ˈēvən/ ▶ adj. **1** flat and smooth; level. **2** equal in number, amount, or value. **3** not varying much in speed, quality, etc.; regular: *just bike at an even pace.* **4** equally balanced: *the match was even.* **5** (of a person's temper) placid; calm. **6** (of a number) able to be divided by two without a remainder. ▶ v. make or become even. ▶ adv. used for emphasis: *he knows even less than I do.* ■ **e·ven·ly** adv. **e·ven·ness** n. – PHRASES **even as** at the very same time as. **even if** despite the possibility that. **even now** (or **then**) **1** in spite of what has (or had) happened. **2** at this (or that) very moment. **even so** nevertheless. **even though** despite the fact that.

e·ven[2] ▶ n. old use or literary evening.

e·ven-hand·ed /ˈēvənˈhandid/ ▶ adj. fair and impartial. ■ **e·ven-hand·ed·ly** adv. **e·ven-hand·ed·ness** n.

eve·ning /ˈēvniNG/ ▶ n. the period of time at the end of the day.

eve·ning prim·rose ▶ n. a plant with pale yellow flowers that open in the evening, used for a medicinal oil.

eve·ning star ▶ n. (**the evening star**) the planet Venus, seen shining in the western sky after sunset.

e·ven mon·ey ▶ n. (in betting) odds offering an equal chance of winning or losing.

e·ven·song /ˈēvənˌsôNG, ˈevənˌsäNG/ ▶ n. (especially in the Anglican Church) a service of evening prayers, psalms, and canticles.

e·vent /iˈvent/ ▶ n. **1** a thing that happens or takes place. **2** a public or social occasion. **3** each of several contests making up a sports competition. ■ **e·vent·less** adj. – PHRASES **in any event** (or **at all events**) whatever happens or may have happened. **in the event of/that** if the specified thing happens.

e·vent·ful /iˈventfəl/ ▶ adj. marked by interesting or exciting events.

e·vent ho·ri·zon ▶ n. Astronomy a hypothetical boundary around a black hole beyond which no light or other radiation can escape.

e·ven·tide /ˈēvənˌtīd/ ▶ n. old use or literary evening.

e·vent·ing /iˈventiNG/ ▶ n. a riding competition in which competitors must take part in each of several contests. ■ **e·vent·er** n.

e·ven·tu·al /iˈvenchŏŏəl/ ▶ adj. occurring at the end of a process or period of time: *he was optimistic about the eventual outcome of the talks.* ■ **e·ven·tu·al·ly** adv.

e·ven·tu·al·i·ty /i,venchŏŏ'alitē/ ▶ n. (pl. **eventualities**) a possible event or outcome.

e·ven·tu·ate /i'venchŏŏ,āt/ ▶ v. formal **1** occur as a result. **2** (**eventuate in**) lead to something as a result.

ev·er /'evər/ ▶ adv. **1** at any time. **2** used in comparisons and questions for emphasis: *I felt better than ever.* **3** at all times; always. **4** increasingly: *having to borrow ever larger sums.*
– PHRASES **ever so** informal very.

ev·er·green /'evər,grēn/ ▶ adj. **1** (of a plant) retaining green leaves throughout the year. Contrasted with DECIDUOUS. **2** having a lasting freshness or appeal: *the timeless quality of our evergreen brand.* ▶ n. an evergreen plant.

ev·er·last·ing /,evər'lastiNG/ ▶ adj. lasting forever or a very long time. ■ **ev·er·last·ing·ly** adv.

ev·er·more /,evər'môr/ ▶ adv. literary always; forever.

eve·ry /'evrē/ ▶ determiner **1** used to refer to all the members of a set without exception. **2** indicating how often something happens: *every thirty minutes.* **3** all possible: *every effort was made.*
– PHRASES **every bit as** (in comparisons) equally as. **every other** each alternate in a series.

eve·ry·bod·y /'evrē,bädē, -,bədē/ ▶ pron. every person.

eve·ry·day /'evrē,dā/ ▶ adj. **1** daily. **2** ordinary; commonplace.

Eve·ry·man /'evrē,man/ ▶ n. an ordinary or typical person.

eve·ry·one /'evrē,wən/ ▶ pron. every person.

eve·ry one ▶ pron. each one.

eve·ry·thing /'evrē,THiNG/ ▶ pron. **1** all things, or all the things of a group or class. **2** the most important thing or aspect: *money isn't everything.*

eve·ry·where /'evrē,(h)wer/ ▶ adv. **1** in or to all places. **2** in many places; very common: *sandwich bars are everywhere.*

e·vict /i'vikt/ ▶ v. legally force someone to leave a building or piece of land. ■ **e·vic·tion** /i'viksHən/ n.

ev·i·dence /'evədəns/ ▶ n. **1** information or signs indicating whether something is true or valid. **2** information used to establish facts in a legal investigation or acceptable as testimony in a court of law. ▶ v. be or show evidence of: *the city's economic growth is evidenced by the creation of new jobs.*
– PHRASES **in evidence** noticeable; conspicuous.

ev·i·dent /'evədənt/ ▶ adj. clear or obvious. ■ **ev·i·dent·ly** adv.

ev·i·den·tial /,evi'denchəl/ ▶ adj. formal relating to or providing evidence.

ev·i·den·tia·ry /,evi'densHərē/ ▶ adj. chiefly Law another term for EVIDENTIAL.

e·vil /'ēvəl/ ▶ adj. **1** very immoral, cruel, and wicked. **2** associated with the devil: *evil spirits.* **3** very unpleasant: *an evil smell.* ▶ n. **1** extreme wickedness. **2** something harmful or undesirable: *the evil of censorship.* ■ **e·vil·ly** adv. **e·vil·ness** n.
– PHRASES **the evil eye** a gaze superstitiously believed to cause harm.

e·vil·do·er /'ēvəl,dŏŏər/ ▶ n. a person who does evil things.

e·vince /i'vins/ ▶ v. formal reveal the presence of a quality or feeling.

e·vis·cer·ate /i'visə,rāt/ ▶ v. formal disembowel someone or something. ■ **e·vis·cer·a·tion** /i,visə'rāsHən/ n.

e·voc·a·tive /i'väkətiv/ ▶ adj. bringing strong images, memories, or feelings to mind: *wonderfully evocative family snapshots.*

e·voke /i'vōk/ ▶ v. **1** bring to the mind: *he said the race evoked memories of his own days as a top athlete.* **2** obtain a response. ■ **ev·o·ca·tion** /,ēvō'kāsHən, ,evə-/ n.

ev·o·lu·tion /,evə'lŏŏsHən/ ▶ n. **1** the process by which different kinds of living organism are believed to have developed from earlier forms. **2** the gradual development of something. ■ **ev·o·lu·tion·ar·i·ly** /,evə,lŏŏsHə'ne(ə)rəlē/ adv. **ev·o·lu·tion·ar·y** /-,nerē/ adj.

ev·o·lu·tion·ist /,evə'lŏŏsHənist/ ▶ n. a person who believes in the theories of evolution and natural selection. ■ **ev·o·lu·tion·ism** /-,nizəm/ n.

e·volve /i'välv/ ▶ v. **1** develop gradually: *over the years, the business evolved into the one he runs today.* **2** (of an organism) develop from earlier forms by evolution.

ewe /yŏŏ/ ▶ n. a female sheep.

ew·er /'yŏŏər/ ▶ n. a large jug with a wide mouth.

ex¹ /eks/ ▶ prep. without; excluding.

ex² ▶ n. informal a former husband, wife, or other partner in a relationship.

ex- (also **e-**; **ef-** before *f*) ▶ prefix **1** out: *exclude.* **2** upward: *extol.* **3** thoroughly: *excruciating.* **4** giving rise to: *exasperate.* **5** former: *ex-husband.*

ex·ac·er·bate /ig'zasər,bāt/ ▶ v. make something bad worse. ■ **ex·ac·er·ba·tion** /ig,zasər'bāsHən/ n.

ex·act /ig'zakt/ ▶ adj. **1** correct in every detail: *an exact replica.* **2** not approximate; precise: *the exact time of the solstice.* **3** accurate and careful about minor details. ▶ v. **1** demand and obtain something from someone. **2** take revenge on someone. ■ **ex·act·ness** n.

ex·act·ing /ig'zaktiNG/ ▶ adj. demanding a great deal of effort or skill.

ex·ac·tion /ig'zaksHən/ ▶ n. formal **1** the action of exacting or demanding a payment. **2** a sum of money demanded.

ex·ac·ti·tude /ig'zaktə,t(y)ŏŏd/ ▶ n. the quality of being exact.

ex·act·ly /ig'zak(t)lē/ ▶ adv. **1** used to emphasize the accuracy of something: *she stayed for exactly two weeks in each state.* **2** used to confirm or agree with what has just been said.

ex·ag·ger·ate /ig'zajə,rāt/ ▶ v. **1** make something seem larger, better, or worse than it really is. **2** (as adj. **exaggerated**) enlarged or altered beyond normal proportions. ■ **ex·ag·ger·at·ed·ly** adv. **ex·ag·ger·a·tion** /ig,zajə'rāsHən/ n.

ex·alt /ig'zôlt/ ▶ v. **1** praise someone or something highly. **2** raise someone to a higher rank or position.

ex·al·ta·tion /,egzôl'tāsHən, ,eksôl-/ ▶ n. **1** extreme happiness. **2** the action of praising or elevating someone or something.

ex·alt·ed /ig'zôltid, eg-/ ▶ adj. **1** at a high level: *the exalted rank of inspector.* **2** (of an idea) noble; lofty.

ex·am /ig'zam/ ▶ n. **1** short for EXAMINATION (sense 2). **2** a medical test: *an eye exam.*

ex·am·i·na·tion /ig,zamə'nāsHən/ ▶ n. **1** a detailed inspection or investigation. **2** a formal test of knowledge or ability in a subject or skill. **3** the action of examining someone or something.

ex·am·ine /ig'zamən/ ▸ v. **1** inspect someone or something closely to determine their nature or condition. **2** test someone's knowledge or ability. **3** Law formally question a defendant or witness in court. ■ **ex·am·i·nee** /ig,zamə'nē/ n. **ex·am·in·er** n.

ex·am·ple /ig'zampəl/ ▸ n. **1** a thing that is typical of its kind or that illustrates a general rule. **2** a person or thing regarded in terms of their suitability to be imitated.
– PHRASES **for example** used to introduce something chosen as a typical case. **make an example of** punish someone as a warning to others.

ex·as·per·ate /ig'zaspə,rāt/ ▸ v. irritate someone intensely. ■ **ex·as·per·at·ed** adj. **ex·as·per·at·ing** adj. **ex·as·per·a·tion** /ig,zaspə'rāshən/ n.

ex ca·the·dra /,eks kə'THēdrə/ ▸ adv. & adj. with the full authority of office (especially that of the pope).

ex·ca·vate /'ekskə,vāt/ ▸ v. **1** make a hole or channel by digging. **2** carefully remove earth from an area in order to find buried remains. **3** dig out objects or material from the ground. ■ **ex·ca·va·tion** /,ekskə'vāshən/ n. **ex·ca·va·tor** /'ekskə,vātər/ n.

ex·ceed /ik'sēd/ ▸ v. **1** be greater in number or size than: *our sales should exceed $2.1 billion.* **2** go beyond what is stipulated by a set limit. **3** be better than something; surpass.

ex·ceed·ing·ly /ik'sēdiNGlē/ ▸ adv. extremely; very.

ex·cel /ik'sel/ ▸ v. (**excels, excelling, excelled**) be exceptionally good at an activity or subject.

ex·cel·lence /'eksələns/ ▸ n. the quality of being excellent.

Ex·cel·len·cy /'eksələnsē/ ▸ n. (pl. **Excellencies**) (**His, Your**, etc. **Excellency**) a title or form of address for certain high officials of state, especially ambassadors, or of the Roman Catholic Church.

ex·cel·lent /'eksələnt/ ▸ adj. extremely good; outstanding.

ex·cept /ik'sept/ ▸ prep. not including; other than. ▸ conj. used before a statement that is not included in one just made. ▸ v. exclude from a category or group: *present company excepted.*

USAGE
On the confusion of **except** and **accept**, see the note at ACCEPT.

ex·cept·ing /ik'septiNG/ ▸ prep. except for; apart from.

ex·cep·tion /ik'sepshən/ ▸ n. a person or thing that is not included in a general statement or that does not follow a rule.
– PHRASES **take exception to** object strongly to something.

ex·cep·tion·a·ble /ik'sepshənəbəl/ ▸ adj. formal open to objection; causing disapproval or offense.

ex·cep·tion·al /ik'sepshənəl/ ▸ adj. **1** unusually good. **2** unusual; not typical: *the drug could only be used in exceptional circumstances.* ■ **ex·cep·tion·al·ly** adv.

ex·cerpt ▸ n. /'ek,sərpt/ a short extract from a movie or piece of music or writing. ▸ v. /ik'sərpt/ take a short extract from a piece of writing.

ex·cess ▸ n. /ik'ses, 'ekses/ **1** an amount that is

more than necessary, permitted, or desirable. **2** extreme behavior, especially in eating or drinking too much: *bouts of alcoholic excess.* **3** (**excesses**) unacceptable or illegal behavior. ▸ adj. exceeding a permitted or desirable amount.

ex·cess bag·gage ▸ n. luggage weighing more than the limit allowed on an aircraft, liable to an extra charge.

ex·ces·sive /ik'sesiv/ ▸ adj. more than is necessary, normal, or desirable. ■ **ex·ces·sive·ly** adv. **ex·ces·sive·ness** n.

ex·change /iks'CHānj/ ▸ n. **1** an act of giving something and receiving something else in return. **2** a short conversation or argument. **3** the changing of money to its equivalent in another currency. **4** a building or institution in which commodities are traded. **5** a set of equipment that connects telephone lines during a call. ▸ v. give something and receive something else in return. ■ **ex·change·a·ble** adj. **ex·chang·er** n.

ex·change rate ▸ n. the value at which one currency may be exchanged for another.

ex·cheq·uer /eks'CHekər, iks-/ ▸ n. **1** a royal or national treasury. **2** (**Exchequer**) (in the UK) the account at the Bank of England into which public money is paid.

ex·cise¹ /'ek,sīz/ ▸ n. a tax charged on certain goods, such as alcohol, and licenses for certain activities.

ex·cise² /ik'sīz/ ▸ v. **1** cut something out surgically. **2** remove a section from a piece of writing or music. ■ **ex·ci·sion** /-'sizhən/ n.

ex·cit·a·ble /ik'sītəbəl/ ▸ adj. easily excited. ■ **ex·cit·a·bil·i·ty** /ik,sītə'bilitē/ n. **ex·cit·a·bly** /-əblē/ adv.

ex·cite /ik'sīt/ ▸ v. **1** make someone feel very enthusiastic and eager. **2** arouse someone sexually. **3** give rise to: *the new sauces are exciting particular interest.* **4** increase the energy or activity in a physical or biological system. ■ **ex·ci·ta·tion** /ek,sī'tāshən/ n. **ex·cit·a·to·ry** /ik'sītə,tôrē/ (chiefly Physiology) adj. **ex·cit·ed** adj.

ex·cite·ment /ik'sītmənt/ ▸ n. **1** a feeling of great enthusiasm and eagerness. **2** something that arouses great enthusiasm and eagerness. **3** sexual arousal.

ex·cit·ing /ik'sītiNG/ ▸ adj. causing great enthusiasm and eagerness. ■ **ex·cit·ing·ly** adv.

ex·claim /ik'sklām/ ▸ v. cry out suddenly, especially in surprise, anger, or pain.

ex·cla·ma·tion /,ek:sklə'māshən/ ▸ n. a sudden cry or remark. ■ **ex·clam·a·to·ry** /ik'sklamə,tôrē/ adj.

ex·cla·ma·tion point (also **exclamation mark**) ▸ n. a punctuation mark (!) indicating an exclamation.

ex·clude /ik'sklo͞od/ ▸ v. **1** prevent someone from entering or participating in something. **2** deliberately leave out when considering or doing something: *this information was excluded from the judicial investigation.* ■ **ex·clud·a·ble** adj. **ex·clud·er** n.

ex·clud·ing /ik'sklo͞odiNG/ ▸ prep. not taking someone or something into account; except.

ex·clu·sion /ik'sklo͞ozhən/ ▸ n. the action of excluding someone or something from something. ■ **ex·clu·sion·ar·y** /-,nerē/ adj.

ex·clu·sive /ik'sklo͞osiv/ ▸ adj. **1** restricted to the person, group, or area concerned: *the problem isn't exclusive to Atlanta.* **2** high-class and expensive; select. **3** not including other things. **4** unable to exist or be true if something else exists or is true: *when it comes to hedges, fast growing and low maintenance are mutually exclusive.* **5** (of a story) not published or broadcast elsewhere. ►**n.** a story published or broadcast by only one source. ■ **ex·clu·sive·ly** adv. **ex·clu·sive·ness** n. **ex·clu·siv·i·ty** /ˌekskloo'sivitē/ n.

ex·com·mu·ni·cate /ˌekskə'myooniˌkāt/ ►**v.** officially ban someone from the sacraments and services of the Christian Church. ■ **ex·com·mu·ni·ca·tion** /ˌekskəˌmyooni'kāshən/ n.

ex·con ►**n.** informal an ex-convict; a former prisoner.

ex·co·ri·ate /ik'skôrēˌāt/ ►**v. 1** formal criticize someone severely. **2** Medicine damage or remove part of the surface of the skin. ■ **ex·co·ri·a·tion** /ikˌskôrē'āshən/ n.

ex·cre·ment /'ekskrəmənt/ ►**n.** waste matter emptied from the bowels; feces. ■ **ex·cre·men·tal** /ˌekskrə'men(t)l/ adj.

ex·cres·cence /ik'skresəns/ ►**n. 1** an abnormal growth protruding from a body or plant. **2** an unattractive object or feature.

ex·cre·ta /ik'skrētə/ ►**n.** waste discharged from the body, especially feces and urine.

ex·crete /ik'skrēt/ ►**v.** discharge a waste substance from the body. ■ **ex·cre·tion** /ik'skrēshən/ n. **ex·cre·to·ry** /'ekskriˌtôrē/ adj.

ex·cru·ci·at·ing /ik'skrooshēˌātiNG/ ►**adj. 1** intensely painful. **2** very embarrassing, awkward, or tedious. ■ **ex·cru·ci·at·ing·ly** adv.

ex·cul·pate /'ekskəlˌpāt/ ►**v.** formal show or declare that someone is not guilty of wrongdoing. ■ **ex·cul·pa·tion** /ˌekskəl'pāshən/ n. **ex·cul·pa·to·ry** /ˌeks'kəlpəˌtôrē/ adj.

ex·cur·sion /ik'skərzhən/ ►**n.** a short journey or trip, especially one taken for leisure. ■ **ex·cur·sion·ist** n.

ex·cur·sus /ek'skərsəs/ ►**n.** (pl. same or **excursuses**) a detailed discussion of a particular point in a book.

ex·cuse ►**v.** /ik'skyooz/ **1** try to find reasons for a fault or offense; try to justify: *she did nothing to hide or excuse his cruelty.* **2** forgive a minor fault or a person committing one: *sit down—excuse the mess.* **3** release someone from a duty or requirement. **4** allow someone to leave a room or gathering. **5** (**excuse oneself**) say politely that one is leaving. ►**n.** /ik'skyoos/ **1** a reason given to justify a fault or offense. **2** something said to conceal the real reason for an action. **3** (**an excuse for**) informal a poor or inadequate example of: *you pathetic excuse for a human being!* ■ **ex·cus·a·ble** /-zəbəl/ adj. **ex·cus·a·bly** /-zəblē/ adv.
– PHRASES **excuse me 1** a polite apology. **2** used to ask someone to repeat what they have just said.

ex·ec /eg'zek/ ►**n.** informal an executive (businessperson): *top execs.*

ex·e·cra·ble /'eksikrəbəl/ ►**adj.** extremely bad or unpleasant. ■ **ex·e·cra·bly** /-blē/ adv.

ex·e·crate /'eksiˌkrāt/ ►**v.** feel or express great hatred for someone or something. ■ **ex·e·cra·tion** /ˌeksi'krāshən/ n.

ex·e·cut·a·ble /'eksiˌkyootəbəl/ Computing ►**adj.** (of a file or program) able to be run by a computer. ►**n.** an executable file or program.

ex·e·cute /'eksiˌkyoot/ ►**v. 1** put a plan, order,

or course of action into effect: *the companies have executed a five-year agreement.* **2** perform a skillful action or maneuver. **3** carry out a sentence of death on a condemned person. **4** make a legal document valid by signing or sealing it. **5** carry out a judicial sentence, the terms of a will, or other order. **6** run a computer file or program.

ex·e·cu·tion /ˌeksi'kyooshən/ ►**n. 1** the carrying out of a plan, order, or course of action. **2** the killing of a condemned person. **3** the way in which something is produced or carried out.

ex·e·cu·tion·er /ˌeksi'kyoosh(ə)nər/ ►**n.** an official who executes condemned criminals.

ex·ec·u·tive /ig'zekyətiv, eg-/ ►**n. 1** a senior manager in a business. **2** a decision-making committee or other group in an organization. **3** (**the executive**) the branch of a government responsible for putting decisions or laws into effect. ►**adj.** having the power to put plans, actions, or laws into effect.

ex·ec·u·tor /ig'zekyətər/ ►**n.** a person appointed by someone to carry out the terms of their will.

ex·ec·u·trix /ig'zekyə,triks/ ►**n.** (pl. **executrices** /-,trisēz/ or **executrixes**) a female executor of a will.

ex·e·ge·sis /ˌeksi'jēsis/ ►**n.** (pl. **exegeses** /-sēz/) critical explanation of a written work, especially of the Bible. ■ **ex·e·get·i·cal** /-'jetikəl/ adj.

ex·e·gete /'eksəˌjēt/ ►**n.** a person who interprets a written work, especially the Bible.

ex·em·plar /ig'zemplər, -ˌplär/ ►**n.** a person or thing serving as a typical example or appropriate model.

ex·em·pla·ry /ig'zemplərē/ ►**adj. 1** providing a good example to others; very good. **2** (of a punishment) serving as a warning.

ex·em·pli·fy /ig'zempləˌfī/ ►**v.** (**exemplifies**, **exemplifying**, **exemplified**) be or give a typical example of: *the best dry sherry is exemplified by the fino of Jerez.* ■ **ex·em·pli·fi·ca·tion** /igˌzempləfi'kāshən/ n.

ex·empt /ig'zem(p)t/ ►**adj.** free from an obligation or requirement imposed on others: *since he is only 13, he is exempt from prosecution.* ►**v.** make someone exempt from something.

ex·emp·tion /ig'zem(p)shən/ ►**n. 1** the process of exempting or state of being exempt from something: *exemption from antitrust laws.* **2** (also **personal exemption**) an amount of money that can be earned or received free of tax.

ex·er·cise /'eksərˌsīz/ ►**n. 1** physical activity carried out for the sake of health and fitness. **2** an activity carried out for a specific purpose: *a public relations exercise.* **3** a task set to practice or test a skill. **4** (**exercises**) military drills or training maneuvers. **5** the application of a power, right, or process: *the exercise of authority.* ►**v. 1** use or apply a power, right, or quality: *the industry has exercised restraint so far.* **2** do physical activity. **3** worry or perplex someone. ■ **ex·er·cis·a·ble** /-əbəl/ adj. **ex·er·cis·er** n.

ex·er·cise ball ►**n.** a lightweight, inflated plastic ball 18–36 inches (45–91 cm) across, used in exercises for fitness and physiotherapy.

ex·er·cise bike ►**n.** a stationary piece of exercise equipment resembling an ordinary bicycle.

ex·ert /ig'zərt/ ►**v. 1** apply or bring to bear a force, influence, or quality. **2** (**exert oneself**) make a physical or mental effort.

ex·er·tion /igˈzərsʜən/ ▸ n. **1** physical or mental effort. **2** the application of a force, influence, or quality.

ex·e·unt /ˈekseˌənt, ˈekseˌo͞ont/ ▸ v. (as a stage direction) (actors) leave the stage.

ex·fo·li·ate /eksˈfōlēˌāt/ ▸ v. **1** (of a material) be shed from a surface in scales or layers. **2** wash or rub part of the body with a granular substance to remove dead skin cells. ■ **ex·fo·li·ant** /eksˈfōlēənt/ n. **ex·fo·li·a·tion** /eksˌfōlēˈāsʜən/ n. **ex·fo·li·a·tor** /-ˌātər/ n.

ex gra·ti·a /eks ˈgrāsʜēə/ ▸ adv. & adj. (of payment) given as a gift or favor rather than because of any legal requirement.

ex·hale /eksˈhāl, ˈeksˌhāl/ ▸ v. **1** breathe out. **2** give off vapor or fumes. ■ **ex·ha·la·tion** /ˌeks(h)əˈlāsʜən/ n.

ex·haust /igˈzôst/ ▸ v. **1** tire someone out. **2** use up all of: *the company exhausted these funds in six months.* **3** explore a subject or possibilities so fully that there is nothing left to be said or discovered. **4** expel gas or steam from an engine or other machine. ▸ n. **1** waste gases or air expelled from an engine or other machine. **2** the system through which waste gases are expelled. ■ **ex·haust·er** n. **ex·haust·i·ble** adj. **ex·haust·ing** adj.

ex·haus·tion /igˈzôscʜən/ ▸ n. **1** a state of extreme tiredness. **2** the action of using something up.

ex·haus·tive /igˈzôstiv/ ▸ adj. covering all aspects fully. ■ **ex·haus·tive·ly** adv. **ex·haus·tive·ness** n.

ex·hib·it /igˈzibit/ ▸ v. **1** publicly display an item in an art gallery or museum. **2** show a quality: *he exhibited great humility.* ▸ n. **1** an object or collection of objects on display in an art gallery or museum. **2** Law a document or other object produced in a court as evidence. ■ **ex·hib·i·tor** n.

ex·hi·bi·tion /ˌeksəˈbisʜən/ ▸ n. **1** a public display of items in an art gallery or museum. **2** a display or demonstration of a skill or quality.
– PHRASES **make an exhibition of oneself** behave very foolishly in public.

ex·hi·bi·tion·ism /ˌeksəˈbisʜəˌnizəm/ ▸ n. **1** behavior that is intended to attract attention to oneself. **2** a mental condition in which a person feels an urge to display their genitals in public. ■ **ex·hi·bi·tion·ist** n. **ex·hi·bi·tion·is·tic** /-ˌbisʜəˈnistik/ adj.

ex·hil·a·rate /igˈziləˌrāt/ ▸ v. make someone feel very happy or full of energy. ■ **ex·hil·a·rat·ing** adj. **ex·hil·a·ra·tion** /igˌziləˈrāsʜən/ n.

ex·hort /igˈzôrt/ ▸ v. strongly urge someone to do something. ■ **ex·hor·ta·tion** /ˌegzôrˈtāsʜən, ˌeksôr-/ n.

ex·hume /igˈz(y)o͞om, eksˈ(y)o͞om/ ▸ v. dig out something buried, especially a corpse from the ground. ■ **ex·hu·ma·tion** /ˌegz(y)o͞oˈmāsʜən, ˌeks(h)yo͞o-/ n.

ex·i·gen·cy /ˈeksijənsē, igˈzijənsē/ ▸ n. (pl. **exigencies**) an urgent need or demand: *the exigencies of contemporary life.*

ex·i·gent /ˈeksijənt/ ▸ adj. pressing; demanding.

ex·ig·u·ous /igˈzigyo͞oəs, ikˈsig-/ ▸ adj. formal very small.

ex·ile /ˈegˌzīl, ˈekˌsīl/ ▸ n. **1** the state of being barred from one's native country. **2** a person who lives in exile. ▸ v. expel and bar someone from their native country.

ex·ist /igˈzist/ ▸ v. **1** be real; be present in a place or situation: *his supporters say the deal never existed.* **2** be alive; live.

ex·ist·ence /igˈzistəns/ ▸ n. **1** the fact or state of existing. **2** a way of living: *a rural existence.*

ex·ist·ent /igˈzistənt/ ▸ adj. existing.

ex·is·ten·tial /ˌegziˈstencʜəl/ ▸ adj. **1** relating to existence. **2** concerned with existentialism. ■ **ex·is·ten·tial·ly** adv.

ex·is·ten·tial·ism /ˌegziˈstencʜəˌlizəm/ ▸ n. a philosophical theory that emphasizes that human beings are free agents, responsible for their own actions. ■ **ex·is·ten·tial·ist** n. & adj.

ex·it /ˈegzit, ˈeksit/ ▸ n. **1** a way out of a building, room, or passenger vehicle. **2** an act of leaving. **3** a place for traffic to leave a major road or roundabout. ▸ v. (**exits, exiting, exited**) **1** go out of or leave a place. **2** terminate a computer process or program.

ex·it poll ▸ n. a poll of people leaving a polling station, asking how they voted.

ex ni·hi·lo /ˈeks ˈnē(h)əlō, ˈnī(h)əlō/ ▸ adv. formal out of nothing: *he created a paradise ex nihilo.*

exo- ▸ prefix external; from outside: *exoskeleton.*

ex·o·bi·ol·o·gy /ˌeksōbīˈäləjē/ ▸ n. the branch of science concerned with the possibility and likely nature of life on other planets or in space. ■ **ex·o·bi·ol·o·gist** n.

ex·o·crine /ˈeksəˌkrin, ˈeksəˌkrēn/ ▸ adj. (of a gland) producing hormones or other products through ducts rather than directly into the blood.

ex·o·dus /ˈeksədəs/ ▸ n. a mass departure of people.

ex of·fi·ci·o /ˈeks əˈfisʜēō/ ▸ adv. & adj. by virtue of one's position or status.

ex·og·e·nous /ekˈsäjənəs/ ▸ adj. technical relating to an external cause or origin. Often contrasted with ENDOGENOUS. ■ **ex·og·e·nous·ly** adv.

ex·on·er·ate /igˈzänəˌrāt/ ▸ v. officially state that someone has not done something wrong or illegal. ■ **ex·on·er·a·tion** /igˌzänəˈrāsʜən/ n.

ex·o·plan·et /ˈeksōˌplanit/ ▸ n. a planet that orbits a star outside the solar system: *most of the 100 known exoplanets are comparable in mass to Jupiter.*

ex·or·bi·tant /igˈzôrbitənt/ ▸ adj. (of a price or amount charged) unreasonably high. ■ **ex·or·bi·tant·ly** adv.

ex·or·cise /ˈeksôrˌsīz, ˈeksər-/ (or **exorcize**) ▸ v. drive out a supposed evil spirit from a person or place. ■ **ex·or·cism** /ˈeksôrˌsizəm, ˈeksər-/ n. **ex·or·cist** /ˈeksôrˌsist, ˈeksər-/ n.

ex·o·skel·e·ton /ˈeksōˈskelitn/ ▸ n. the rigid external covering of the body in insects and some other invertebrate animals.

ex·o·ther·mic /ˌeksəˈTHərmik/ ▸ adj. (of a chemical reaction) accompanied by the release of heat.

ex·ot·ic /igˈzätik/ ▸ adj. **1** originating in or typical of a distant foreign country. **2** strikingly colorful or unusual: *youths with exotic haircuts.* ▸ n. an exotic plant or animal. ■ **ex·ot·i·cal·ly** /-(ə)lē/ adv. **ex·ot·i·cism** /igˈzätəˌsizəm/ n.

ex·ot·i·ca /igˈzätikə/ ▸ pl.n. unusual and interesting objects: *Hawaiian exotica.*

ex·ot·ic danc·er ▸ n. a striptease dancer.

ex·pand /ikˈspand/ ▸ v. **1** make or become larger or more extensive. **2** (**expand on**) give more details about something. ■ **ex·pand·a·bil·i·ty** /ikˌspandəˈbilitē/ n. **ex·pand·a·ble** adj. **ex·pand·er** n.

ex·pand·ed /ik'spandid/ ▸adj. **1** (of a material) having a light cellular structure. **2** relatively broad in shape.

ex·panse /ik'spans/ ▸n. a wide continuous area of something: *a vast expanse of sand dunes.*

ex·pan·sion /ik'spanSHən/ ▸n. **1** the action of becoming larger or more extensive. **2** the political strategy of extending a state's territory by encroaching on that of other nations.
■ **ex·pan·sion·ar·y** /ik'spanSHə,nerē/ adj.

ex·pan·sion card (also **expansion board**) ▸n. a circuit board that can be inserted in a computer to give extra facilities or memory.

ex·pan·sion·ism /ik'spanSHə,nizəm/ ▸n. the policy of extending a state's territory by encroaching on that of other nations.
■ **ex·pan·sion·ist** n. & adj.

ex·pan·sive /ik'spansiv/ ▸adj. **1** covering a wide area; extensive. **2** relaxed, friendly, and communicative. ■ **ex·pan·sive·ly** adv.
ex·pan·sive·ness n.

ex par·te /eks 'pärtē/ ▸ adj. & adv. Law with respect to or in the interests of one side only.

ex·pat /eks'pat/▸ n. & adj. informal short for EXPATRIATE.

ex·pa·ti·ate /ik'spāSHē,āt/ ▸v. speak or write at length or in detail: *professors shuffling forth to expatiate on the American dream.*
■ **ex·pa·ti·a·tion** /ik,spāSHē'āSHən/ n.

ex·pa·tri·ate /eks'pātrēit/ ▸n. a person who lives outside their native country. ▸adj. living outside one's native country. ■ **ex·pa·tri·a·tion** /eks,pātrē'āSHən/ n.

ex·pect /ik'spekt/ ▸v. **1** regard something as likely to happen. **2** regard someone as likely to do or be something. **3** believe that someone will arrive soon. **4** require or demand something because it is appropriate or a person's duty: *Picasso quickly mastered the style that was expected of a fashionable portrait painter.* **5** (**be expecting**) informal be pregnant. ■ **ex·pect·a·ble** adj.

ex·pect·an·cy /ik'spektənsē/ ▸n. (pl. **expectancies**) **1** hope or anticipation that something will happen. **2** something expected: *a life expectancy of 22 to 25 years.*

ex·pect·ant /ik'spektənt/ ▸adj. **1** hoping or anticipating that something is about to happen. **2** (of a woman) pregnant. **3** (of a man) about to become a father. ■ **ex·pect·ant·ly** adv.

ex·pec·ta·tion /,ekspek'tāSHən/ ▸n. **1** belief that something will happen or be the case. **2** a thing that is expected to happen.

ex·pec·to·rant /ik'spektərənt/ ▸n. a medicine that helps to bring up phlegm from the air passages, used to treat coughs.

ex·pec·to·rate /ik'spektə,rāt/ ▸v. cough or spit out phlegm from the throat or lungs.
■ **ex·pec·to·ra·tion** /ik,spektə'rāSHən/ n.

ex·pe·di·ent /ik'spēdēənt/ ▸adj. **1** convenient and practical although not always fair or right: *either side could break the agreement if it were expedient to do so.* **2** suitable or appropriate.
▸n. a means of achieving an end. ■ **ex·pe·di·ence** n. **ex·pe·di·en·cy** n. **ex·pe·di·ent·ly** adv.

ex·pe·dite /'ekspə,dīt/ ▸v. make an action or process happen sooner or be accomplished more quickly. ■ **ex·pe·dit·er** (also **expediter**) n.

ex·pe·di·tion /,ekspə'diSHən/ ▸n. **1** a journey undertaken by a group of people with a particular purpose. **2** formal promptness or speed in doing something. ■ **ex·pe·di·tion·ar·y**

/,ekspə'diSHə,nerē/ adj.

ex·pe·di·tious /,ekspə'diSHəs/ ▸adj. quick and efficient. ■ **ex·pe·di·tious·ly** adv.

ex·pel /ik'spel/ ▸v. (**expels, expelling, expelled**) **1** force someone to leave a school, organization, or place. **2** force something out, especially from the body. ■ **ex·pel·la·ble** adj. **ex·pel·lee** /,ekspel'lē/ n.

ex·pend /ik'spend/ ▸v. spend or use up a resource.

ex·pend·a·ble /ik'spendəbəl/ ▸adj. able to be sacrificed or abandoned because of little significance when compared to an overall purpose. ■ **ex·pend·a·bil·i·ty** /ik,spendə'bilitē/ n.

ex·pend·i·ture /ik'spendiCHər/ ▸n. **1** the action of spending funds. **2** the amount of money spent. **3** the use of energy or other resources.

ex·pense /ik'spens/ ▸n. **1** the cost of something. **2** (**expenses**) specific costs spent in carrying out a job or task. **3** something on which money must be spent: *tolls are a daily expense.*
– PHRASES **at the expense of 1** paid for by someone. **2** so as to harm something.

ex·pense ac·count ▸n. an arrangement under which money spent in the course of business is later repaid by one's employer.

ex·pen·sive /ik'spensiv/ ▸adj. costing a lot of money. ■ **ex·pen·sive·ly** adv. **ex·pen·sive·ness** n.

ex·pe·ri·ence /ik'spi(ə)rēəns/ ▸n. **1** practical contact with and observation of facts or events. **2** knowledge or skill gained over time. **3** an event that leaves an impression on one: *a frightening experience.* ▸v. **1** encounter or undergo an event or situation. **2** feel an emotion.

ex·pe·ri·enced /ik'spi(ə)rēənst/ ▸adj. having knowledge or skill in a particular field gained over time.

ex·pe·ri·en·tial /ek,spi(ə)rē'enCHəl/ ▸adj. involving or based on experience and observation. ■ **ex·pe·ri·en·tial·ly** adv.

ex·per·i·ment /ik'sperəmənt/ ▸n. **1** a scientific procedure undertaken to make a discovery, test a theory, or demonstrate a fact. **2** a new idea or method that is tried out without being sure of the outcome: *the previous experiment in democracy ended in disaster.* ▸v. **1** perform a scientific experiment. **2** try out new ideas or methods. ■ **ex·per·i·men·ta·tion** /ik,sperəmən'tāSHən/ n. **ex·per·i·ment·er** n.

ex·per·i·men·tal /ik,sperə'men(t)l/ ▸adj. **1** based on new ideas and not yet fully tested or established: *an experimental drug.* **2** relating to scientific experiments. **3** (of art, music, etc.) departing from established conventions; innovative. ■ **ex·per·i·men·tal·ism** /-izəm/ n. **ex·per·i·men·tal·ist** /-ist/ n. **ex·per·i·men·tal·ly** adv.

ex·pert /'ek,spərt/ ▸n. a person who has great knowledge or skill in a particular area. ▸adj. having or involving great knowledge or skill. ■ **ex·pert·ly** adv.

ex·per·tise /,ekspər'tēz, -'tēs/ ▸n. great skill or knowledge in a particular field.

ex·pi·ate /'ekspē,āt/ ▸v. make amends for guilt or wrongdoing. ■ **ex·pi·a·tion** /,ekspē'āSHən/ n. **ex·pi·a·to·ry** /'ekspēə,tôrē/ adj.

ex·pi·ra·tion /,ekspə'rāSHən/ ▸n. the ending of the fixed period for which a contract is valid: *the expiration of the lease.*

ex·pire /ik'spīr/ ▸v. **1** (of a document or agreement) come to the end of its period of validity. **2** (of a period of time) come to an end. **3** (of a person) die. **4** technical breathe out air from the lungs. ■ **ex·pir·a·to·ry** /ik'spīrə,tôrē/ adj.

ex·plain /ik'splān/ ▶v. **1** make something clear by giving a detailed description. **2** give a reason or justification for: *Cassie found it necessary to explain her black eye.* **3** (**explain oneself**) justify one's motives or behavior. **4** (**explain something away**) make something seem less embarrassing by giving an excuse or reason for it. ■ **ex·plain·a·ble** adj. **ex·plain·er** n.

ex·pla·na·tion /,eksplə'nāsHən/ ▶n. **1** a statement or description that makes something clear. **2** a reason or justification for an action or belief.

ex·plan·a·to·ry /ik'splanə,tôrē/ ▶adj. intended to explain something. ■ **ex·plan·a·to·ri·ly** /ik,splanə'tôrəlē/ adv.

ex·ple·tive /'eksplitiv/ ▶n. an oath or swear word.

ex·pli·ca·ble /ek'splikəbəl, 'eksplik-/ ▶adj. able to be explained or understood.

ex·pli·cate /'ekspli,kāt/ ▶v. analyze and explain an idea or literary work in detail. ■ **ex·pli·ca·tion** /,ekspli'kāsHən/ n. **ex·pli·ca·tor** /-,kātər/ n.

ex·plic·it /ik'splisit/ ▶adj. **1** clear and detailed, with no room for confusion or doubt. **2** describing or showing sexual activity in a direct and detailed way. ■ **ex·plic·it·ly** adv. **ex·plic·it·ness** n.

ex·plode /ik'splōd/ ▶v. **1** burst or shatter violently as a result of the release of internal energy. **2** suddenly express an emotion. **3** increase suddenly in number or extent: *the herbal medicine market has exploded.* **4** show a belief or theory to be false. **5** (as adj. **exploded**) (of a diagram) showing parts of something in the normal relative positions but slightly separated from each other. ■ **ex·plod·er** n.

ex·ploit ▶v. /ik'sploit/ **1** make use of a person or situation in an unfair way, so as to gain advantage for oneself: *people desperate to lose weight were being exploited by unscrupulous salesmen.* **2** make good use of a resource. ▶n. /'ek,sploit/ a bold or daring act. ■ **ex·ploit·a·ble** adj. **ex·ploi·ta·tion** /,eksploi'tāsHən/ n. **ex·ploit·er** /ik'sploitər/ n.

ex·ploit·a·tive /ik'sploitətiv/ (also **exploitive** /ik'sploitiv/) ▶adj. treating someone unfairly so as to make money or gain an advantage.

ex·plore /ik'splôr/ ▶v. **1** travel through an unfamiliar area in order to learn about it. **2** inquire into or examine in detail: *she explored the possibility of going back to school.* **3** examine something by touch. ■ **ex·plo·ra·tion** /,eksplə'rāsHən/ n. **ex·plor·a·to·ry** /ik'splôrə,tôrē/ adj. **ex·plor·er** n.

ex·plo·sion /ik'splōzHən/ ▶n. **1** an act of exploding. **2** a sudden increase in amount or extent: *an explosion in information technology.*

ex·plo·sive /ik'splōsiv/ ▶adj. **1** able or likely to explode. **2** likely to cause an outburst of anger or controversy. **3** (of an increase) sudden and dramatic. ▶n. a substance that can be made to explode. ■ **ex·plo·sive·ly** adv. **ex·plo·sive·ness** n.

ex·po /'ekspō/ ▶n. (pl. **expos**) a large exhibition.

ex·po·nent /ik'spōnənt/ ▶n. **1** a person who promotes an idea or theory. **2** a person who does a particular thing skillfully. **3** Mathematics a raised figure beside a number indicating how many times that number is to be multiplied by itself (e.g., 3 in $2^3 = 2 \times 2 \times 2$).

ex·po·nen·tial /,ekspə'nencHəl/ ▶adj. **1** (of an increase) becoming more and more rapid. **2** relating to or expressed by a mathematical exponent. ■ **ex·po·nen·tial·ly** adv.

ex·port ▶v. /ik'spôrt, 'ekspôrt/ **1** send goods or services to another country for sale. **2** spread or introduce ideas or customs to another country. ▶n. /'ek,spôrt/ **1** an article or service sold abroad. **2** the sale of goods or services to other countries. ■ **ex·port·a·ble** /ik'spôrtəbəl/ adj. **ex·por·ta·tion** /,ekspôr'tāsHən/ n. **ex·port·er** n.

ex·pose /ik'spōz/ ▶v. **1** make something visible by uncovering it. **2** reveal the true nature of: *he has been exposed as a liar.* **3** (**expose someone to**) make someone vulnerable to possible harm or risk. **4** (as adj. **exposed**) unprotected from the weather. **5** (**expose oneself**) publicly and indecently display one's genitals. **6** subject photographic film to light. ■ **ex·pos·er** n.

ex·po·sé /,ekspō'zā/ ▶n. a report in the media that reveals something shocking.

ex·po·si·tion /,ekspə'zisHən/ ▶n. **1** a detailed description and explanation of a theory. **2** a large public exhibition of art or trade goods. **3** Music the part of a movement in which the principal themes are first presented. ■ **ex·po·si·tion·al** adj.

ex·pos·i·tor /ik'späzitər/ ▶n. a person who explains complicated ideas or theories. ■ **ex·pos·i·to·ry** /ik'späzi,tôrē/ adj.

ex post fac·to /,eks pōst 'faktō/ ▶adj. & adv. formal with retrospective action or effect.

ex·pos·tu·late /ik'späscHə,lāt/ ▶v. express strong disapproval or disagreement. ■ **ex·pos·tu·la·tion** /ik,späscHə'lāsHən/ n.

ex·po·sure /ik'spōzHər/ ▶n. **1** the state of being exposed to something harmful: *a few simple practices can reduce exposure to bacteria.* **2** a physical condition resulting from being exposed to severe weather conditions. **3** the revelation of something secret. **4** the publicizing of information or an event. **5** the quantity of light reaching a photographic film, as determined by shutter speed and lens aperture.

ex·pound /ik'spound/ ▶v. present and explain a theory or idea in detail. ■ **ex·pound·er** n.

ex·press[1] /ik'spres/ ▶v. **1** convey a thought or feeling in words or by gestures and behavior. **2** squeeze out liquid or air. **3** Mathematics represent something by a figure, symbol, or formula. ■ **ex·press·i·ble** adj.

ex·press[2] ▶adj. **1** operating at high speed. **2** (of a delivery service) using a special messenger. ▶adv. by express train or delivery service. ▶n. **1** (also **express train**) a train that stops at few stations and so travels quickly. **2** a special delivery service. ▶v. send something by express messenger or delivery.

ex·press[3] ▶adj. **1** stated clearly and openly: *it was his express wish that the event should continue.* **2** specifically identified to the exclusion of anything else: *the league was formed with the express purpose of raising the level of soccer.* ■ **ex·press·ly** adv.

ex·pres·sion /ik'spresHən/ ▶n. **1** the action of expressing thoughts or feelings. **2** a look on someone's face that conveys a particular feeling: *a sad expression.* **3** a word or phrase expressing an idea. **4** Mathematics a collection of symbols expressing a quantity. ■ **ex·pres·sion·less** adj.

ex·pres·sion·ism /ik'spresHə,nizəm/ ▶n. a

style in art, music, or drama in which the artist or writer seeks to express the inner world of emotion rather than external reality. ■ **ex·pres·sion·ist** n. & adj. **ex·pres·sion·is·tic** /ik͵spreshə'nistik/ adj.

ex·pres·sive /ik'spresiv/ ▶ adj. **1** effectively conveying thought or feeling. **2** (**expressive of**) conveying a quality or idea. ■ **ex·pres·sive·ly** adv. **ex·pres·sive·ness** n. **ex·pres·siv·i·ty** /͵ekspre'sivitē/ n.

ex·press·way /ik'spres͵wā/ ▶ n. a highway designed for fast traffic, with a dividing strip between the traffic in opposite directions and two or more lanes in each direction.

ex·pro·pri·ate /͵eks'prōprē͵āt/ ▶ v. (of the government) take property from its owner for public use or benefit. ■ **ex·pro·pri·a·tion** /͵eks͵prōprē'āshən/ n. **ex·pro·pri·a·tor** n.

ex·pul·sion /ik'spəlshən/ ▶ n. the action of expelling someone or something. ■ **ex·pul·sive** /ik'spəlsiv/ adj.

ex·punge /ik'spənj/ ▶ v. completely remove something undesirable or unpleasant.

ex·pur·gate /'ekspər͵gāt/ ▶ v. remove matter regarded as obscene or unsuitable from a piece of writing. ■ **ex·pur·ga·tion** /͵ekspər'gāshən/ n. **ex·pur·ga·tor** n.

ex·quis·ite /ek'skwizit, 'ekskwizit/ ▶ adj. **1** very beautiful and delicate. **2** highly refined: *exquisite taste.* **3** intensely felt: *the exquisite pain of love.* ■ **ex·quis·ite·ly** adv. **ex·quis·ite·ness** n.

ex·tant /'ekstənt, ek'stant/ ▶ adj. still in existence.

ex·tem·po·ra·ne·ous /ik͵stempə'rānēəs/ ▶ adj. another term for EXTEMPORARY. ■ **ex·tem·po·ra·ne·ous·ly** adv.

ex·tem·po·rar·y /ik'stempə͵rerē/ ▶ adj. spoken or done without preparation.

ex·tem·po·re /ik'stempərē/ ▶ adj. & adv. spoken or done without preparation.

ex·tem·po·rize /ik'stempə͵rīz/ ▶ v. compose or perform something without preparation; improvise. ■ **ex·tem·po·ri·za·tion** /ik͵stempəri'zāshən/ n.

ex·tend /ik'stend/ ▶ v. **1** make something larger or longer in space or time. **2** occupy a specified area or continue for a specified distance: *the damage extended 40 meters either side of the store.* **3** offer or give: *he extended a warm welcome to new members.* **4** stretch out the body or a limb. **5** strain or exert someone to the utmost. ■ **ex·tend·a·ble** /-əbəl/ adj. **ex·tend·er** n. **ex·tend·i·ble** /-əbəl/ adj. **ex·ten·si·bil·i·ty** /ik͵stensə'bilitē/ n. **ex·ten·si·ble** /-'stensəbəl/ adj.

ex·tend·ed fam·i·ly ▶ n. a family that extends beyond the parents and children to include grandparents and other relatives.

ex·ten·sion /ik'stenshən/ ▶ n. **1** the action of extending something. **2** a part added to a building to enlarge it. **3** an additional period of time allowed for something. **4** an extra telephone on the same line as the main one. **5** (**extensions**) lengths of long artificial hair woven into a person's own hair. **6** (also **extension cord**) an additional length of electric cable that can be plugged into a fixed socket and has another socket on the end. ■ **ex·ten·sion·al** adj.

ex·ten·sive /ik'stensiv/ ▶ adj. **1** covering a large area. **2** large in amount or scale: *an extensive collection of antiques.* **3** (of agriculture)

obtaining a relatively small crop from a large area with a minimum of capital and labor. ■ **ex·ten·sive·ly** adv. **ex·ten·sive·ness** n.

ex·ten·sor /ik'stensər, -͵sôr/ ▶ n. a muscle whose contraction extends a limb or other part of the body.

ex·tent /ik'stent/ ▶ n. **1** the area covered by something. **2** the size or scale of something: *they have no idea of the extent of the problem.* **3** the degree to which something is the case: *all couples edit the truth to some extent.*

ex·ten·u·at·ing /ik'stenyōō͵āting/ ▶ adj. showing reasons why an offense should be treated less seriously: *hunger and poverty are not treated by the courts as extenuating circumstances.* ■ **ex·ten·u·a·tion** /ik͵stenyōō'āshən/ n.

ex·te·ri·or /ik'sti(ə)rēər/ ▶ adj. relating to, forming, or on the outside of something. ▶ n. the outer surface or structure of something. ■ **ex·te·ri·or·ly** adv.

ex·ter·mi·nate /ik'stərmə͵nāt/ ▶ v. destroy someone or something completely. ■ **ex·ter·mi·na·tion** /ik͵stərmə'nāshən/ n. **ex·ter·mi·na·tor** n.

ex·ter·nal /ik'stərnl/ ▶ adj. **1** belonging to or forming the outside of something. **2** coming from a source outside the person or thing affected: *many external factors can influence the incidence of cancer.* **3** relating to another country or institution. ▶ n. (**externals**) the outward features of something. ■ **ex·ter·nal·ly** adv.

ex·ter·nal ear ▶ n. the parts of the ear outside the eardrum, especially the pinna.

ex·ter·nal·ize /ik'stərnə͵līz/ ▶ v. **1** express a thought or feeling in words or actions. **2** give external existence or physical form to something. ■ **ex·ter·nal·i·za·tion** /ik͵stərnəli'zāshən/ n.

ex·tinct /ik'stiNG(k)t/ ▶ adj. **1** (of a species or other large group) having no living members. **2** no longer in existence. **3** (of a volcano) not having erupted in recorded history.

ex·tinc·tion /ik'stiNG(k)shən/ ▶ n. the state of being or process of becoming extinct.

ex·tin·guish /ik'stiNGgwish/ ▶ v. **1** put out a fire or light. **2** put an end to: *no human life should be extinguished for the benefit of another.* **3** cancel a debt by full payment. ■ **ex·tin·guish·er** n.

ex·tir·pate /'ekstər͵pāt/ ▶ v. completely destroy something. ■ **ex·tir·pa·tion** /͵ekstər'pāshən/ n.

ex·tol /ik'stōl/ ▶ v. (**extols, extolling, extolled**) praise someone or something enthusiastically.

ex·tort /ik'stôrt/ ▶ v. obtain something by force, threats, or other unfair means. ■ **ex·tor·tion** /ik'stôrshən/ n. **ex·tor·tion·ist** /ik'stôrshənist/ n.

ex·tor·tion·ate /ik'stôrshənit/ ▶ adj. (of a price) much too high. ■ **ex·tor·tion·ate·ly** adv.

ex·tra /'ekstrə/ ▶ adj. added to an existing or usual amount or number. ▶ adv. **1** to a greater extent than usual. **2** in addition. ▶ n. **1** an item in addition to what is usual or necessary, for which an extra charge is made. **2** a person taking part in a crowd scene in a movie or play.

extra- ▶ prefix **1** outside; beyond: *extramarital.* **2** beyond the scope of: *extracurricular.*

ex·tract ▶ v. /ik'strakt/ **1** remove something with care or effort. **2** obtain a substance or resource from something by a special method. **3** obtain something from someone unwilling to give it: *in the Middle Ages, they would torture people to extract a false confession.* **4** select a passage from a written work, movie, or piece of music for quotation, performance, or reproduction. ▶ n. /'ek,strakt/ **1** a short passage taken from a written work, movie, or piece of music. **2** the concentrated form of the active ingredient of a substance: *vanilla extract.* ■ **ex·tract·a·ble** adj. **ex·trac·tive** adj.

ex·trac·tion /ik'straksHən/ ▶ n. **1** the action of extracting something. **2** the ethnic origin of someone's family: *a woman of Polish extraction.*

ex·trac·tor /ik'straktər/ ▶ n. a machine or device used to extract something. ▶ adj. referring to a fan used for removing unpleasant smells and stale air from a room.

ex·tra·cur·ric·u·lar /,ekstrəkə'rikyələr/ ▶ adj. (of an activity at a school or college) done in addition to the normal curriculum.

ex·tra·dite /'ekstrə,dīt/ ▶ v. hand over a person accused or convicted of a crime in another state or a foreign country to the legal authority of that state or country. ■ **ex·tra·di·tion** /,ekstrə'disHən/ n.

ex·tra·mar·i·tal /,ekstrə'maritl/ ▶ adj. occurring outside marriage.

ex·tra·mu·ral /,ekstrə'myŏŏrəl/ ▶ adj. **1** outside the boundaries of a town or city. **2** Brit. (of a course of study) arranged for people who are not full-time members of a university or other educational establishment. ■ **ex·tra·mu·ral·ly** adv.

ex·tra·ne·ous /ik'strānēəs/ ▶ adj. **1** unrelated to the subject; irrelevant. **2** of external origin. ■ **ex·tra·ne·ous·ly** adv.

ex·tra·net /'ekstrə,net/ ▶ n. an intranet that can be partially accessed by authorized outside users, enabling organizations to exchange data in a secure way.

ex·tra·or·di·naire /,ekstrə,ôrdn'er/ ▶ adj. outstanding in a particular area: *a gardener extraordinaire.*

ex·traor·di·nar·y /ik'strôrdn,erē, ,ekstrə'ôrdn-/ ▶ adj. **1** very unusual or remarkable. **2** (of a meeting) specially arranged rather than being one of a regular series. **3** (of an official) specially employed: *Ambassador Extraordinary.* ■ **ex·traor·di·nar·i·ly** /-,erəlē/ adv. **ex·traor·di·nar·i·ness** n.

ex·traor·di·nar·y ren·di·tion ▶ n. another term for RENDITION (sense 3).

ex·trap·o·late /ik'strapə,lāt/ ▶ v. **1** use a fact or conclusion that is valid for one situation and apply it to a different or larger one. **2** extend a graph by inferring unknown values from trends in the known data. ■ **ex·trap·o·la·tion** /ik,strapə'lāsHən/ n. **ex·trap·o·la·tive** /-,lātiv/ adj.

ex·tra·sen·so·ry per·cep·tion /,ekstrə'sensərē/ ▶ n. the supposed faculty of perceiving things by means other than the known senses, e.g., by telepathy, precognition, or clairvoyance.

ex·tra·ter·res·tri·al /,ekstrətə'restrēəl/ ▶ adj. relating to things beyond the earth or its atmosphere. ▶ n. a fictional being from outer space.

ex·trav·a·gant /ik'stravəgənt/ ▶ adj. **1** lacking restraint in spending money or using resources. **2** costing a great deal. **3** exceeding what is reasonable or appropriate: *extravagant claims about the product.* ■ **ex·trav·a·gance** n. **ex·trav·a·gant·ly** adv.

ex·trav·a·gan·za /ik,stravə'ganzə/ ▶ n. an elaborate and spectacular entertainment.

ex·tra·ve·hic·u·lar /,ekstrəvē'hikyələr/ ▶ adj. referring to activity performed in space outside a spacecraft.

ex·tra vir·gin ▶ adj. (of olive oil) of a particularly fine grade, made from the first pressing of the olives.

ex·treme /ik'strēm/ ▶ adj. **1** to the highest degree; very great. **2** highly unusual; exceptional: *in extreme cases the soldier may be discharged.* **3** very severe or serious. **4** not moderate, especially politically. **5** furthest from the center or a given point: *the extreme north of Scotland.* **6** (of a sport) performed in a dangerous environment. ▶ n. **1** either of two things that are as different from each other as possible. **2** the most extreme degree: *extremes of temperature.* ■ **ex·treme·ly** adv.

ex·treme unc·tion ▶ n. (in the Roman Catholic Church) a former name for the sacrament of anointing of the sick, especially when administered to the dying.

ex·trem·ist /ik'strēmist/ ▶ n. a person who holds extreme political or religious views. ■ **ex·trem·ism** /-,mizəm/ n.

ex·trem·i·ty /ik'stremitē/ ▶ n. (pl. **extremities**) **1** the furthest point or limit. **2** (**extremities**) the hands and feet. **3** severity or seriousness: *the extremity of the violence.* **4** extreme difficulty or hardship.

ex·tri·cate /'ekstri,kāt/ ▶ v. free from a difficult or restrictive situation or place: *the company has to extricate itself from its current financial mess.* ■ **ex·tri·ca·tion** /,ekstri'kāsHən/ n.

ex·trin·sic /ik'strinzik, -sik/ ▶ adj. coming or operating from outside; not part of the essential nature of something: *extrinsic environmental influences.* ■ **ex·trin·si·cal·ly** adv.

ex·tro·vert /'ekstrə,vərt/ ▶ n. **1** an outgoing, socially confident person. **2** Psychology a person predominantly concerned with external things or objective considerations. ▶ adj. relating to or typical of an extrovert. ■ **ex·tro·ver·sion** /,ekstrə'vərzHən/ n. **ex·tro·vert·ed** adj.

ex·trude /ik'strood/ ▶ v. **1** thrust or force something out. **2** shape a material such as metal or plastic by forcing it through a die. ■ **ex·tru·sion** /ik'strooZHən/ n.

ex·tru·sive /ik'stroosiv/ ▶ adj. (of rock) that has been forced out at the earth's surface as lava or other volcanic deposits.

ex·u·ber·ant /ig'zoobərənt/ ▶ adj. **1** lively and cheerful. **2** literary growing profusely. ■ **ex·u·ber·ance** n. **ex·u·ber·ant·ly** adv.

ex·ude /ig'zood/ ▶ v. **1** (of liquid or a smell) discharge or be discharged slowly and steadily. **2** clearly display an emotion or quality: *silk skirts exuding elegance.* ■ **ex·u·da·tion** /,eksyoo'dāsHən, ,eksə-/ n.

ex·ult /ig'zəlt/ ▶ v. show or feel triumphant elation. ■ **ex·ul·ta·tion** /,eksəl'tāsHən, ,egzəl-/ n.

ex·ult·ant /ig'zəltnt/ ▶ adj. triumphantly happy. ■ **ex·ult·an·cy** n. **ex·ult·ant·ly** adv.

ex-vo·to /eks 'vōtō/ ▶ n. (pl. **ex-votos**) an offering given in order to fulfill a vow.

eye /ī/ ▶ n. **1** the organ of sight in humans and animals. **2** the small hole in a needle through which the thread is passed. **3** a small metal loop into which a hook is fitted as a fastener on a garment. **4** a person's opinion or feelings: *to European eyes, the city seems overcrowded.*

5 an eyelike marking on an animal or bird. **6** a round, dark spot on a potato from which a new shoot grows. **7** the calm region at the center of a storm. ▶ v. (**eyes, eyeing** or **eying, eyed**) look at someone or something closely or with interest.
– PHRASES **be all eyes** be watching eagerly and attentively. **an eye for an eye and a tooth for a tooth** doing the same thing in return is the appropriate way to deal with an offense or crime. **give someone the eye** informal look at someone with sexual interest. **have an eye for** be able to recognize and judge something wisely. **have one's eye on** aim to acquire something. **have** (or **keep**) **one's eye on** keep someone under careful observation. **have** (or **with**) **an eye to** have (or having) as one's objective. **have eyes in the back of one's head** know what is going on around one even when one cannot see it. **keep an eye out** (or **open**) look out for something. **make eyes at** look at someone with sexual interest. **one in the eye for** a disappointment or setback for someone. **open someone's eyes** cause someone to realize something. **see eye to eye** be in full agreement. **a twinkle** (or **gleam**) **in someone's eye** something that is as yet no more than an idea or dream. **up to one's eyes** informal very busy. **with one's eyes open** fully aware of possible difficulties.

eye·ball /ˈīˌbôl/ ▶ n. the round part of the eye of a vertebrate, within the eyelids and socket.
▶ v. informal stare at someone or something closely.
– PHRASES **eyeball to eyeball** face to face with someone, especially in an aggressive way.

eye·brow /ˈīˌbrou/ ▶ n. the strip of hair growing on the ridge above a person's eye socket.
– PHRASES **raise one's eyebrows** (or **an eyebrow**) show surprise or mild disapproval.

eye-catch·ing ▶ adj. immediately appealing or noticeable.

eye con·tact ▶ n. the act of looking directly into one another's eyes: *make eye contact with your interviewers.*

eye·ful /ˈīˌfo͝ol/ ▶ n. informal **1** a long steady look. **2** an eye-catching person or thing.

eye·glass /ˈīˌglas/ ▶ n. **1** a single lens for correcting or assisting poor eyesight, especially a monocle. **2** (**eyeglasses**) another term for GLASSES.

eye·hole /ˈīˌhōl/ ▶ n. a hole to look through, especially in a curtain or mask.

eye·lash /ˈīˌlaSH/ ▶ n. each of the short hairs growing on the edges of the eyelids.

eye·let /ˈīlit/ ▶ n. **1** a small round hole made in leather or cloth, used for threading a lace, string, or rope through. **2** a metal ring reinforcing an eyelet.

eye·lid /ˈīˌlid/ ▶ n. each of the upper and lower folds of skin that cover the eye when closed.

eye·lin·er /ˈīˌlīnər/ ▶ n. a cosmetic applied as a line around the eyes.

eye-o·pen·er ▶ n. informal an event or situation that proves to be unexpectedly revealing.

eye·patch /ˈīˌpaCH/ ▶ n. a patch worn to protect an injured eye.

eye·piece /ˈīˌpēs/ ▶ n. the lens that is closest to the eye in a microscope or other optical instrument.

eye-pop·ping ▶ adj. informal astonishingly large or blatant.

eye·shade /ˈīˌSHād/ ▶ n. a translucent visor used to protect the eyes from strong light.

eye·shad·ow /ˈīˌSHadō/ ▶ n. a colored cosmetic applied to the eyelids or to the skin around the eyes.

eye·shot /ˈīˌSHät/ ▶ n. the distance for which one can see: *he is within eyeshot.*

eye·sight /ˈīˌsīt/ ▶ n. a person's ability to see.

eye sock·et ▶ n. the cavity in the skull that encloses an eyeball with its surrounding muscles.

eye·sore /ˈīˌsôr/ ▶ n. a very ugly thing.

eye·tooth /ˈīˌto͞oTH/ ▶ n. a canine tooth, especially one in the upper jaw.
– PHRASES **give one's eyeteeth for** (or **to be**) do anything in order to have or be something: *I'd give my eyeteeth for a new car.*

eye track·ing ▶ n. a technology that monitors eye movements as a means of detecting abnormalities or of studying how people interact with text or online documents.

eye·wash /ˈīˌwôSH, -ˌwäSH/ ▶ n. **1** liquid for cleansing a person's eye. **2** informal nonsense.

eye·wear /ˈīˌwer/ ▶ n. things worn on the eyes, such as spectacles and contact lenses.

eye·wit·ness /ˈīˌwitnəs/ ▶ n. a person who has seen something happen and can give a first-hand description of it.

eyr·ie /ˈe(ə)rē, ˈi(ə)rē/ ▶ n. variant spelling of AERIE.

Ff

F¹ (also **f**) ▶ n. (pl. **Fs** or **F's**) **1** the sixth letter of the alphabet. **2** Music the fourth note of the scale of C major.

F² ▶ abbr. **1** Fahrenheit. **2** farad(s). **3** female. **4** franc(s). ▶ symbol **1** the chemical element fluorine. **2** Physics force.

f ▶ abbr. **1** Grammar feminine. **2** (in textual references) folio. **3** Music forte. **4** (in racing results) furlong(s). ▶ symbol **1** focal length. **2** Electronics frequency.

fa /fä/ ▶ n. Music the fourth note of a major scale, coming after 'mi' and before 'sol.'

FAA ▶ abbr. Federal Aviation Administration.

fab /fab/ ▶ adj. informal fabulous; wonderful.

Fa·bi·an /'fābēən/ ▶ n. a member or supporter of the Fabian Society, an organization that aims to establish socialism in a gradual way that does not involve revolution. ▶ adj. **1** relating to the Fabians. **2** using cautious delaying tactics to wear out an enemy. ■ **Fa·bi·an·ism** /-ˌnizəm/ n. **Fa·bi·an·ist** /-ist/ n.

fa·ble /'fābəl/ ▶ n. **1** a short story with a moral, typically featuring animals as characters. **2** a myth or legend. **3** a false statement; a nonfactual account.

fa·bled /'fābəld/ ▶ adj. **1** famous: *a fabled guitarist*. **2** mythical or imaginary: *a fabled beast*.

fab·ric /'fabrik/ ▶ n. **1** material produced by weaving or knitting textile fibers; cloth. **2** the walls, floor, and roof of a building. **3** the essential structure of a system or organization: *the fabric of society*.

fab·ri·cate /'fabrəˌkāt/ ▶ v. **1** invent something, typically in order to deceive other people: *police officers had fabricated evidence to secure convictions*. **2** construct or manufacture an industrial product. ■ **fab·ri·ca·tion** /ˌfabrə'kāSHən/ n. **fab·ri·ca·tor** /-ˌkātər/ n.

fab·ric soft·en·er ▶ n. liquid used to soften clothes when they are being washed.

fab·u·list /'fabyəlist/ ▶ n. **1** a person who composes fables. **2** a liar.

fab·u·lous /'fabyələs/ ▶ adj. **1** very great; extraordinary: *his fabulous wealth*. **2** informal wonderful. **3** mythical. ■ **fab·u·lous·ly** adv. **fab·u·lous·ness** n.

fa·cade /fə'säd/ (also **façade**) ▶ n. **1** the face of a building, especially the front. **2** a deceptive outward appearance: *her facade of bravery crumbled and she burst into tears*.

face /fās/ ▶ n. **1** the front part of a person's head from the forehead to the chin, or the corresponding part in an animal. **2** an expression on someone's face. **3** the front or main surface of something. **4** a vertical or sloping side of a mountain or cliff. **5** an aspect: *the unacceptable face of social drinking*. ▶ v. **1** be positioned with the face or front toward or in a particular

direction: *the house faces due east*. **2** confront and deal with or accept: *I had to face the fact that I might never have a child*. **3** have a difficult event or situation ahead of one: *the president is facing a political crisis*. **4** (**face off**) get ready to argue or fight with someone. **5** cover the surface of something with a layer of a different material. ■ **faced** adj.

– PHRASES **face the music** be confronted with the unpleasant results of one's actions. **face to face** close together and looking directly at one another. **get out of someone's face** stop harassing or annoying someone. **in the face of** when confronted with something. **in one's face** directly at or against one: *she slammed the door in my face*. **lose** (or **save**) **face** suffer (or avoid) humiliation. **make a face** produce an expression on one's face that shows dislike, disgust, or amusement. **on the face of it** apparently. **to someone's face** used to refer to remarks made openly and directly to someone.

face card ▶ n. a playing card that is a king, queen, or jack of a suit.

face-cloth /'fās,klôTH/ ▶ n. a washcloth used specifically for one's face.

face-down /ˌfās'doun/ ▶ adv. & adj. with the face, front, or upper part downward: *all of the papers were laid facedown on the table*.

face·less /'fāsləs/ ▶ adj. **1** (of a person) remote and impersonal: *faceless bureaucrats*. **2** (of a place) having no distinguishing characteristics or identity.

face·lift /'fāslift/ ▶ n. **1** a surgical operation to remove unwanted wrinkles by tightening the skin of the face. **2** a procedure carried out to improve the appearance of something.

face mask ▶ n. **1** a protective mask covering the face or part of the face. **2** (also **facial mask**) a cosmetic preparation spread over the face to improve the skin.

face-off ▶ n. **1** a direct confrontation. **2** Ice Hockey the start of play.

face·plate /'fāsplāt/ ▶ n. **1** a protective or decorative cover for a piece of equipment or an electrical fitting. **2** the transparent window of a diver's or astronaut's helmet.

face-sav·ing ▶ adj. preserving one's reputation or dignity.

fac·et /'fasət/ ▶ n. **1** one of the sides of a cut gemstone. **2** an aspect: *every facet of our business*. ■ **fac·et·ed** adj.

face time ▶ n. **1** time spent in face-to-face contact with someone: *we need to sit down for some face time, just you and me*. **2** time spent being filmed or photographed by the media: *the authors all wanted face time at our events*.

fa·ce·tious /fə'sēSHəs/ ▶ adj. showing inappropriate humor or trying to be amusing at an inappropriate time. ■ **fa·ce·tious·ly** adv. **fa·ce·tious·ness** n.

face val·ue ▶ n. the value printed or depicted on a coin, postage stamp, etc.
– PHRASES **take something at face value** accept or believe that something is what it appears to be.

fa·cial /'fāsHəl/ ▶ adj. relating to or affecting the face. ▶ n. a beauty treatment for the face. ■ **fa·cial·ly** adv.

fa·cial mask ▶ n. another term for FACE MASK (sense 2).

fa·cial tis·sue ▶ n. a tissue that is used to blow one's nose, contain a sneeze, etc.

fa·ci·es /'fā,sHēz, 'fāsHē,ēz/ ▶ n. **1** Medicine the facial expression of a person that is typical of a particular disease or condition. **2** Geology the character of a rock expressed by its formation, composition, and fossil content.

fac·ile /'fasəl/ ▶ adj. **1** (of an idea, remark, etc.) simplistic and lacking careful thought. **2** (of success) easily achieved.

fa·cil·i·tate /fə'sili,tāt/ ▶ v. make something easy or easier. ■ **fa·cil·i·ta·tion** /fə,sili'tāsHən/ n. **fa·cil·i·ta·tive** /-,tātiv/ adj.

fa·cil·i·ta·tor /fə'sili,tātər/ ▶ n. someone or something that helps to produce a result, especially by directing or leading an activity: *a support group facilitator.*

fa·cil·i·ty /fə'silətē/ ▶ n. (pl. **facilities**) **1** a building, service, or piece of equipment provided for a particular purpose. **2** a natural ability to do something well and easily.

fac·ing /'fāsiNG/ ▶ n. **1** a piece of material attached to the edge of a garment at the neck, armhole, etc., and turned inside, used to strengthen the edge. **2** an outer layer covering the surface of a wall. ▶ adj. positioned so as to face something.

fac·sim·i·le /fak'siməlē/ ▶ n. an exact copy, especially of written or printed material.

fact /fakt/ ▶ n. **1** a thing that is definitely known to be true. **2** (**facts**) information used as evidence or as part of a report.
– PHRASES **before** (or **after**) **the fact** Law before (or after) the committing of a crime. **facts and figures** precise details. **a fact of life** something that must be accepted, even if unpleasant. **the facts of life** information about sex and reproduction. **the face of the matter** the truth. **in** (**point of**) **fact** in reality.

fact-find·ing ▶ adj. having the purpose of discovering and establishing facts about something: *a fact-finding investigation.*

fac·tion¹ /'faksHən/ ▶ n. a small group within a larger one whose members disagree with some of the beliefs of the larger group. ■ **fac·tion·al** adj. **fac·tion·al·ism** /-l,izəm/ n.

fac·tion² ▶ n. a type of literature or cinema in which real events are used as a basis for a fictional story or dramatization.

fac·tious /'faksHəs/ ▶ adj. relating to or causing disagreement.

fac·ti·tious /fak'tisHəs/ ▶ adj. not genuine; made up.

fac·toid /'fak,toid/ ▶ n. **1** a piece of unreliable information that is repeated so often that it becomes accepted as fact. **2** a brief or trivial piece of information.

fac·tor /'faktər/ ▶ n. **1** a circumstance, fact, or influence that contributes to a result: *ill health*

was an important factor in his decision to retire early. **2** Mathematics a number or quantity that when multiplied with another produces a given number or expression. **3** a level on a scale of measurement: *sunblock with a protection factor of 15.* **4** any of a number of substances in the blood that are involved in clotting. **5** a gene that determines a hereditary characteristic. **6** an agent who buys and sells goods on commission. **7** Finance a business that buys another firm's invoices at a discount and then collects the money due from them for itself. ▶ v. (**factor something in/out**) include (or exclude) something as relevant when making a decision.

fac·tor VIII /,faktər 'āt/ (also **factor eight**) ▶ n. a blood protein involved in the clotting of blood, a lack of which causes one of the main forms of hemophilia.

fac·to·ri·al /fak'tôrēəl/ Mathematics ▶ n. the product of an integer and all the integers below it, e.g., $4 \times 3 \times 2 \times 1$ (*factorial 4*, denoted by *4!* and equal to 24). ▶ adj. relating to a factor or factorial.

fac·tor·ize /'faktə,rīz/ ▶ v. Mathematics break down or be able to be broken down into factors. ■ **fac·tor·i·za·tion** /,faktərə'zāsHən/ n.

fac·to·ry /'fakt(ə)rē/ ▶ n. (pl. **factories**) a building where goods are manufactured or assembled chiefly by machine.

fac·to·ry farm·ing ▶ n. a system of rearing poultry, pigs, or cattle indoors under strictly controlled conditions.

fac·to·ry floor ▶ n. the workers in a company or industry, rather than the management.

fac·to·ry out·let ▶ n. a store in which goods, especially surplus stock, are sold directly by the manufacturers at a discount.

fac·to·ry ship ▶ n. a fishing vessel with facilities for immediate processing of the catch on board.

fac·to·tum /fak'tōtəm/ ▶ n. (pl. **factotums**) an employee who does all kinds of work.

fac·tu·al /'fakCHŌōəl/ ▶ adj. based on or concerned with fact or facts. ■ **fac·tu·al·ly** adv.

fac·ul·ta·tive /'fakəl,tātiv/ ▶ adj. **1** Biology adopting a particular mode of life in response to conditions: *facultative biennials.* **2** occurring optionally in response to circumstances, rather than by nature: *evidence that mountain birds make facultative altitudinal movements.*

fac·ul·ty /'fakəltē/ ▶ n. (pl. **faculties**) **1** a basic mental or physical power: *the faculty of sight.* **2** an ability: *his faculty for taking the initiative.* **3** (treated as sing. or pl.) the teaching or research staff of a college or university. **4** a group of university departments concerned with a particular area of knowledge.

fad /fad/ ▶ n. a temporary widespread enthusiasm for something; a craze. ■ **fad·dish** adj. **fad·dism** /-,izəm/ n. **fad·dist** n.

fade /fād/ ▶ v. **1** gradually grow faint and disappear. **2** lose or cause to lose color. **3** (of a movie or video image or recorded sound) become more or less clear or loud. ▶ n. an act of fading.

fade-in ▶ n. a gradual increase in sound volume or in the visibility of a filmed scene.

fade-out ▶ n. a gradual decrease, until disappearance, in sound volume or in the visibility of a filmed scene.

fad·er /'fādər/ ▶ n. a device for varying the volume of sound in a movie or video recording, or the intensity of light.

fa·do /ˈfäˌT͟Hoo/ ▶n. (pl. **fados**) a type of popular Portuguese song, usually with a sad theme.

fae·ces, etc. ▶pl.n. British spelling of FECES, etc.

fa·er·ie /ˈferē/ (also **faery**) ▶n. old use or literary **1** a fairy. **2** fairyland.

Faer·o·ese /ˌfe(ə)rōˈēz/ (also chiefly Brit. **Faroese**) ▶n. (pl. same) **1** a person from the Faeroe Islands. **2** the language of the Faeroe Islands.

fag¹ /fag/ ▶n. informal, derogatory a male homosexual. ■ **fag·gy** adj.

fag² ▶n. Brit. informal a cigarette.

fag³ Brit. ▶n. **1** informal a tiring or unwelcome task. **2** an underclassman at a private school who does minor chores for an older student. ▶v. (**fags, fagging, fagged**) **1** (of a private-school student) act as a fag. **2** (as adj. **fagged out**) informal exhausted. **3** informal work hard.

fag·got /ˈfagət/ ▶n. **1** informal, derogatory a male homosexual. **2** British spelling of FAGOT. ■ **fag·got·y** adj.

fag·ot /ˈfagət/ (Brit. **faggot**) ▶n. a bundle of sticks bound together as fuel.

fag·ot·ing /ˈfagətiNG/ (Brit. **faggoting**) ▶n. embroidery in which threads are fastened together in bundles.

Fahr. ▶abbr. Fahrenheit.

Fahr·en·heit /ˈfarənˌhīt/ ▶adj. relating to a scale of temperature on which water freezes at 32° and boils at 212°.

fa·ience /fīˈäns, fā-/ ▶n. a type of glazed ceramic earthenware.

fail /fāl/ ▶v. **1** be unsuccessful in achieving something. **2** be unable to meet the standards set by a test. **3** neglect to do something: *she failed to keep the appointment.* **4** not happen in the way expected: *chaos has failed to materialize.* **5** stop working properly. **6** become weaker or less good: *his sight was failing.* **7** let someone down: *her courage failed her.* **8** go out of business. ▶n. a mark that is not high enough to pass an exam or test.
– PHRASES **never fail to do something** used to indicate that something invariably happens: *such comments never fail to annoy him.* **without fail** whatever happens.

failed /fāld/ ▶adj. **1** not having achieved an intended goal or result: *failed negotiations.* **2** no longer operating or functional: *a failed backup system.*

fail·ing /ˈfāliNG/ ▶n. a weakness in a person's character. ▶prep. if not.

fail·o·ver /ˈfālˌōvər/ ▶n. Computers the capability to switch automatically to a backup system in the event of a failure, or the process of doing this.

fail-safe ▶adj. **1** causing machinery to return to a safe condition if a breakdown occurs. **2** unlikely or unable to fail.

fail·ure /ˈfālyər/ ▶n. **1** lack of success. **2** an unsuccessful person or thing. **3** an instance of not doing something that is expected: *their failure to comply with the rules.* **4** an instance of something not functioning properly.

fain /fān/ old use ▶adv. gladly. ▶adj. willing or obliged to do something.

faint /fānt/ ▶adj. **1** not clearly seen, heard, or smelled. **2** (of a hope, chance, or idea) slight. **3** close to losing consciousness. ▶v. briefly lose consciousness because of an inadequate supply of oxygen to the brain. ▶n. a sudden loss of consciousness. ■ **faint·ly** adv. **faint·ness** n.

USAGE
Do not confuse **faint** with **feint**. Faint means 'not clearly seen, heard, or smelled' (*the faint murmur of voices*) or 'lose consciousness', whereas **feint** means 'a pretended attacking movement' or 'make a pretended attacking movement.'

faint-heart·ed ▶adj. timid.

fair¹ /fe(ə)r/ ▶adj. **1** treating people equally. **2** just or appropriate in the circumstances. **3** considerable in size or amount: *I do a fair bit of business traveling.* **4** moderately good. **5** (of hair or complexion) light; blond. **6** (of weather) fine and dry. **7** old use beautiful. ▶adv. **1** in a fair way. **2** dialect very: *she'll be fair delighted to see you.* ■ **fair·ness** n.
– PHRASES **fair and square 1** with absolute accuracy. **2** honestly and straightforwardly. **fair enough** used to admit that something is reasonable or acceptable. **the fair sex** (also **the fairer sex**) dated or humorous women. **no fair** informal unfair: *ooh, he brought his posse ... no fair.*

fair² ▶n. **1** a gathering of sideshows, rides, and other amusements for public entertainment. **2** an event at which people, businesses, etc., display and sell goods. **3** an exhibition held to promote particular products.

fair cop·y ▶n. a copy of written or printed matter produced after final corrections have been made.

fair game ▶n. a person or thing regarded as a reasonable target for criticism or exploitation.

fair·ground /ˈfe(ə)rˌground/ ▶n. an outdoor area where a fair is held.

Fair Isle ▶n. a traditional multicolored geometric design used in woolen knitwear.

fair·ly /ˈfe(ə)rlē/ ▶adv. **1** with justice. **2** moderately. **3** actually (used for emphasis): *he fairly snarled at her.*

fair-mind·ed ▶adj. judging things in a fair and impartial way.

fair play ▶n. respect for the rules or equal treatment for all.

fair trade ▶n. trade in which fair prices are paid to producers in developing countries.

fair use ▶n. legally defined limits on the right to reproduce or cite copyrighted material without obtaining permission.

fair·way /ˈfe(ə)rˌwā/ ▶n. **1** the part of a golf course between a tee and a green. **2** a channel in a river or harbor that can be used by shipping.

fair-weath·er friend ▶n. a person whose friendship cannot be relied on in times of difficulty.

fair·y /ˈfe(ə)rē/ ▶n. (pl. **fairies**) **1** a small imaginary being of human form that has magical powers. **2** informal, derogatory a male homosexual.

fair·y god·moth·er ▶n. a female character in fairy tales who brings unexpected good fortune to the hero or heroine.

fair·y·land /ˈfe(ə)rēˌland/ ▶n. the imaginary home of fairies.

fair·y ring ▶n. a ring of dark grass caused by the growth of certain fungi, once believed to have been made by fairies dancing.

fair·y tale ▶n. **1** a children's story about magical and imaginary beings and lands. **2** an untrue account. ▶adj. magical, idealized, or perfect: *a fairy-tale romance.*

fait ac·com·pli /ˌfet əkämˈplē, ˌfāt/ ▶n. a thing that has been done or decided and cannot now be altered.

faith /fāTH/ ▶ n. **1** complete trust or confidence in someone or something. **2** strong belief in a religion. **3** a system of religious belief.

faith-based ▶ adj. affiliated with or based on an organized religion: *faith-based nonprofit organizations.*

faith-ful /'fāTHfəl/ ▶ adj. **1** remaining loyal. **2** remaining sexually loyal to a lover or to a husband or wife. **3** true to the facts or the original: *a faithful copy.* ▶ n. (**the faithful**) those who are faithful to a particular religion or political party. ■ **faith-ful-ly** adv. **faith-ful-ness** n.

faith heal-ing ▶ n. a method of treating a sick person through the power of religious faith and prayer, rather than by medical means.

faith-less /'fāTHlis/ ▶ adj. **1** disloyal, especially to a lover or spouse. **2** without religious faith. ■ **faith-less-ness** n.

fa-ji-tas /fə'hētəz/ ▶ pl.n. a Mexican dish consisting of strips of spiced meat with vegetables and cheese, wrapped in a soft tortilla.

fake /fāk/ ▶ adj. not genuine. ▶ n. a person or thing that is not genuine. ▶ v. **1** make something that seems genuine in order to deceive other people: *she faked her spouse's signature.* **2** pretend to have a particular feeling or illness. **3** (**fake someone out**) deceive someone: *later we'll learn some moves to help you fake out your opponent.* ■ **fak-er** n. **fak-er-y** n.

fa-kir /fə'ki(ə)r, 'fākər/ ▶ n. a Muslim (or, loosely, a Hindu) holy man who lives on charitable donations.

fa-la-fel /fə'läfəl/ (also **felafel**) ▶ n. a Middle Eastern dish of spiced mashed chickpeas formed into balls and deep-fried.

fal-con /'falkən, 'fôl-/ ▶ n. a fast-flying bird of prey with long pointed wings.

fal-con-er /'falkənər, 'fôl-/ ▶ n. someone who keeps, trains, or hunts with birds of prey.

fal-con-ry /'falkənrē, 'fôl-/ ▶ n. the skill of keeping birds of prey and training them to hunt.

fall /fôl/ ▶ v. (past **fell**; past part. **fallen**) **1** move downward quickly and without control. **2** collapse to the ground. **3** (**fall off**) become detached and drop to the ground. **4** hang or slope down: *the land fell away in a steep bank.* **5** (of someone's face) show dismay or disappointment. **6** decrease: *the level of unemployment is falling.* **7** become: *she fell silent.* **8** occur: *her birthday fell on a Sunday.* **9** be captured or defeated in a battle or contest. **10** (**fall to**) become someone's duty. ▶ n. **1** an act of falling. **2** a thing that falls or has fallen. **3** a waterfall. **4** a decrease. **5** a defeat or downfall. **6** autumn.
– PHRASES **fall apart** (or **to pieces**) **1** break up, come apart, or disintegrate: *their marriage is likely to fall apart.* **2** (of a person) lose one's capacity to cope: *he fell apart when his mother died.* **fall back** retreat. **fall behind 1** fail to keep up with one's competitors. **2** fail to keep a commitment to repay: *borrowers falling behind with their mortgage payments.* **fall back on** turn to something in difficulty. **fall for** informal **1** fall in love with. **2** be deceived by. **fall foul of** come into conflict with. **fall in** (or **into**) **line** do what one is told or what other people do. **fall into place** begin to make sense. **fall in with 1** meet someone by chance and become involved with them. **2** agree to something. **fall on 1** attack someone fiercely or unexpectedly. **2** be someone's duty. **fall out** have an argument. **fall short** (**of**) **1** (of a missile) fail to reach its

target. **2** fail to reach a required standard. **fall through** (of a plan, project, etc.) not happen or be completed.

fal-la-cious /fə'lāshəs/ ▶ adj. based on a mistaken belief; wrong: *a fallacious argument.*

fal-la-cy /'faləsē/ ▶ n. (pl. **fallacies**) **1** a mistaken belief. **2** a mistake in reasoning that makes an argument invalid.

fall-back /'fôl,bak/ ▶ n. an alternative plan for use in an emergency.

fall-en /'fôlən/ past participle of FALL ▶ adj. **1** dated (of a woman) regarded as having lost her honor as a result of an extramarital sexual relationship. **2** killed in battle.

fall-en an-gel ▶ n. (in Christian, Jewish, and Muslim tradition) an angel who rebelled against God and was cast out of heaven.

fall guy ▶ n. informal a person who is blamed for something that is not their fault; a scapegoat.

fal-li-ble /'faləbəl/ ▶ adj. capable of making mistakes or being wrong. ■ **fal-li-bil-i-ty** /,falə'bilətē/ n.

fall-ing-out ▶ n. a quarrel.

fall-ing star ▶ n. a meteor or shooting star.

fall line ▶ n. the line of steepest descent down a slope, as for skiing or a watercourse.

fall-off /'fôl,ôf/ ▶ n. a decrease.

Fal-lo-pi-an tube /fə'lōpēən/ ▶ n. (in a female mammal) either of a pair of tubes along which eggs travel from the ovaries to the uterus.

fall-out /'fôl,out/ ▶ n. **1** radioactive particles spread over a wide area after a nuclear explosion. **2** the bad results of a situation or action: *the political fallout from his decision.*

fal-low¹ /'falō/ ▶ adj. **1** (of farmland) plowed but left for a period of time without being planted with crops. **2** (of a period of time) when nothing is done or achieved.

fal-low² ▶ n. a pale brown or reddish yellow color.

fal-low deer ▶ n. a small Eurasian deer with a white-spotted reddish-brown coat in summer.

false /fôls/ ▶ adj. **1** not correct or true; wrong. **2** invalid or illegal: *false imprisonment.* **3** not genuine; artificial: *false eyelashes.* **4** based on something that is not true or correct: *a false sense of security.* **5** literary (of a person) not faithful. ■ **false-ly** adv. **false-ness** n. **fal-si-ty** /'fôlsətē/ n.

false a-larm ▶ n. a warning given about something that does not happen.

false col-or ▶ n. representation in color other than the natural one in order to enhance visible information: *false-color infrared images.*

false dawn ▶ n. **1** a transient light that precedes the rising of the sun by about two or three hours. **2** a promising situation that comes to nothing.

false e-con-o-my ▶ n. an apparent financial saving that in fact leads to greater expenditure.

false front ▶ n. a facade or appearance that is intended to deceive: *I was ready to put on a false front and be civil to my parents.*

false-hood /'fôls,hŏŏd/ ▶ n. **1** the state of being untrue. **2** a lie.

false mem-o-ry ▶ n. an apparent memory of an event, especially one of childhood sexual abuse, that did not actually happen, sometimes arising from techniques used in psychoanalysis.

false move ▶ n. an unwise action that could have dangerous consequences.

false neg·a·tive ▶ n. an incorrect test result indicating the absence of a condition that is in fact present.

false pos·i·tive ▶ n. an incorrect test result indicating the presence of a condition that is in fact absent.

false pre·tens·es ▶ pl.n. behavior intended to deceive other people.

false start ▶ n. **1** an occasion when a competitor in a race starts before the official signal has been given, so that the race has to be started again. **2** an unsuccessful attempt to begin something.

false step ▶ n. **1** a slip or stumble. **2** a mistake.

fal·set·to /fôl'setō/ ▶ n. (pl. **falsettos**) a high-pitched voice above a person's natural range, used by male singers.

fals·ies /'fôlsēz/ ▶ pl.n. pads in women's clothing used to increase the apparent size of the breasts.

fal·si·fy /'fôlsə,fī/ ▶ v. (**falsifies, falsifying, falsified**) alter information or evidence so as to mislead others. ■ **fal·si·fi·able** /,fôlsə'fīəbəl/ adj. **fal·si·fi·ca·tion** /,fôlsəfə'kāsHən/ n.

fal·ter /'fôltər/ ▶ v. **1** lose strength or momentum. **2** move or speak hesitantly. ■ **fal·ter·ing** adj.

fame /fām/ ▶ n. the state of being famous.

famed /fāmd/ ▶ adj. famous; well known.

fa·mil·iar /fə'milyər/ ▶ adj. **1** well known as a result of long or close association: *a familiar figure*. **2** frequently encountered; common: *the situation was all too familiar*. **3** (**familiar with**) having a good knowledge of: *we're familiar with the terrain of northwest Minnesota*. **4** friendly. **5** more friendly or informal than is appropriate. ▶ n. **1** (also **familiar spirit**) a spirit supposedly attending and obeying a witch. **2** a close friend or associate. ■ **fa·mil·iar·i·ty** /fə,milē'aritē, -,mil'yar-/ n. (pl. **familiarities**) **fa·mil·iar·ly** adv.

fa·mil·iar·ize /fə'milyə,rīz/ ▶ v. (**familiarize someone with**) give someone better knowledge or understanding of something. ■ **fa·mil·iar·i·za·tion** /fə,milyərə'zāsHən/ n.

fam·i·ly /'fam(ə)lē/ ▶ n. (pl. **families**) **1** a group consisting of parents and their children living together as a unit. **2** a group of people related by blood or marriage. **3** the children of a person or couple. **4** all the descendants of a common ancestor: *the house has been in the family for 300 years.* **5** a group of things that are alike in some way. **6** Biology a main category into which animals and plants are divided, ranking above genus and below order. ▶ adj. designed to be suitable for children as well as adults: *family entertainment.* ■ **fa·mil·ial** /fə'milēəl, -'milyəl/ adj.
– PHRASES **in the family way** informal pregnant.

fam·i·ly name ▶ n. a surname.

fam·i·ly plan·ning ▶ n. the control of the number of children in a family by means of contraception.

fam·i·ly prac·tice ▶ n. the branch of medicine designed to provide basic health care to all the members of a family. ■ **fam·i·ly prac·ti·tion·er** n.

fam·i·ly room ▶ n. a room in a house where family members relax and enjoy recreation.

fam·i·ly tree ▶ n. a diagram showing the relationship between people in several generations of a family.

fam·i·ly val·ues ▶ pl.n. values supposedly characteristic of a traditional family unit, typically those of high moral standards and discipline.

fam·ine /'famən/ ▶ n. a severe shortage of food.

fam·ished /'famisHt/ ▶ adj. informal extremely hungry.

fa·mous /'fāməs/ ▶ adj. **1** known about by many people. **2** informal magnificent.

fa·mous·ly /'fāməslē/ ▶ adv. **1** as is widely known: *they have famously reclusive lifestyles.* **2** excellently: *we got along famously.*

fan[1] /fan/ ▶ n. **1** a device with rotating blades that creates a current of air for cooling or ventilation. **2** a hand-held device that is waved so as to cool the user. ▶ v. (**fans, fanning, fanned**) **1** wave something so as to drive a current of air toward someone or something. **2** (of an air current) increase the strength of a fire. **3** make a belief or emotion stronger: *newspapers fanned national tensions.* **4** (**fan out**) spread out from a central point to cover a wide area.

fan[2] ▶ n. a person who has a strong interest in or admiration for a particular sport, art form, famous person, etc. ■ **fan·dom** n.

fa·nat·ic /fə'natik/ ▶ n. **1** a person who holds extreme or dangerous religious or political opinions. **2** informal a person with an obsessive enthusiasm for a pastime or hobby. ■ **fa·nat·i·cal** adj. **fa·nat·i·cal·ly** adv. **fa·nat·i·cism** /fə'natə,sizəm/ n.

fan belt ▶ n. a belt driving the fan that cools the radiator of a motor vehicle.

fan·boy /'fan,boi/ (or **fangirl** /'fan,gərl/) ▶ n. informal, derogatory an obsessive male (or female) fan, usually of movies, comic books, or science fiction.

fan·ci·er /'fansēər/ ▶ n. a person who has a special interest in or breeds a particular animal.

fan·ci·ful /'fansəfəl/ ▶ adj. **1** overimaginative and unrealistic. **2** existing only in the imagination. **3** highly ornamental or imaginative in design. ■ **fan·ci·ful·ly** /-f(ə)lē/ adv. **fan·ci·ful·ness** n.

fan club ▶ n. an organized group of fans of a famous person or team.

fan·cy /'fansē/ ▶ adj. (**fancier, fanciest**) **1** elaborate or highly decorated. **2** sophisticated or expensive: *a fancy Italian restaurant.* ▶ v. (**fancies, fancying, fancied**) **1** informal find someone sexually attractive: *I think Sid fancies your sister.* **2** informal want or want to do: *do you fancy some dessert?* **3** (**fancy oneself**) informal have an unduly high opinion of oneself, or of one's ability in a particular area: *she fancies herself a gourmet cook.* **4** used to express surprise: *fancy that!* ▶ n. (pl. **fancies**) **1** a superficial or brief feeling of attraction. **2** the power of imagining things. **3** something that is imagined. ■ **fan·ci·ly** /'fansəlē/ adv. **fan·ci·ness** n.
– PHRASES **take** (or **catch**) **someone's fancy** appeal to someone. **take a fancy to** become fond of someone or something.

fan·cy-free ▶ adj. not emotionally involved with anyone.

fan·dan·go /fan'danggō/ ▶ n. (pl. **fandangoes** or **fandangos**) **1** a lively Spanish dance for two people. **2** a foolish or frivolous act or thing.

fan·fare /'fan,fer/ ▶ n. **1** a short ceremonial tune or flourish played on brass instruments. **2** great media attention surrounding the introduction of something.

fan·fic /'fan,fik/ ▶ n. short for FAN FICTION.

fan fic·tion ▶ n. a genre of amateur writing based on characters and events from mass entertainment or popular culture.

fang /fanG, fānG/ ▶ n. **1** a large sharp tooth,

especially a canine tooth of a dog or wolf. **2** a tooth with which a snake injects poison. **3** the biting mouthpart of a spider. ■ **fanged** adj.

fan·girl ▶ n. see **FANBOY**.

fan·light /'fan,līt/ ▶ n. a small semicircular window over a door or another window.

fan·ny /'fanē/ ▶ n. (pl. **fannies**) **1** informal a person's buttocks. **2** Brit. vulgar slang a woman's genitals.

fan·ny pack ▶ n. a small pouch worn around the waist and used for storing valuables and small items.

fan·tab·u·lous /fan'tabyələs/ ▶ adj. informal excellent; wonderful.

fan·tail /'fan,tāl/ ▶ n. **1** a fan-shaped tail or end of something. **2** a domestic pigeon of a broad-tailed variety. ■ **fan-tailed** adj.

fan·ta·sia /fan'tāzhə, fantə'zēə/ ▶ n. **1** a musical composition that does not follow a conventional form. **2** a musical composition based on several familiar tunes.

fan·ta·size /'fantə,sīz/ ▶ v. daydream about desirable but unlikely situations or events: *she fantasized about living on a boat in the Caribbean.* ■ **fan·ta·sist** n.

fan·tas·tic /fan'tastik/ ▶ adj. **1** hard to believe or unlikely to happen: *fantastic schemes.* **2** informal very good, attractive, or large. ■ **fan·tas·ti·cal** adj. **fan·tas·ti·cal·ly** /-(ə)lē/ adv.

fan·ta·sy /'fantəsē/ ▶ n. (pl. **fantasies**) **1** the imagining of unlikely or impossible things. **2** a daydream about a situation or event that is desirable but unlikely to happen. **3** a type of imaginative fiction involving magic and adventure.

fan·zine /'fan,zēn, fan'zēn/ ▶ n. a magazine for fans of a particular team, performer, activity, etc.

FAQ /fak/ ▶ abbr. frequently asked questions.

far /fär/ ▶ adv. (**farther**, **farthest** or **further**, **furthest**) **1** at, to, or by a great distance. **2** over a long time. **3** by a great deal. ▶ adj. **1** situated at a great distance. **2** distant from the center. **3** more distant than another object of the same kind: *the far corner.*
– PHRASES **as far as 1** to the extent that. **2** for a great enough distance to reach: *I decided to walk as far as the reservoir.* **be a far cry from** be very different from. **by far** by a great amount. **far and away** by a very large amount. **far and wide** over a large area. **far gone 1** in a bad or worsening state. **2** advanced in time. **go far 1** achieve a great deal. **2** be worth or amount to much. **go too far** go beyond what is reasonable or acceptable. (**in**) **so far as** to the extent that.

far·ad /'farəd, -,ad/ ▶ n. the SI unit of electrical capacitance.

far·a·day /'farə,dā/ ▶ n. a unit of electrical charge equal to 96,485 coulombs.

far·a·way /'färə,wā/ ▶ adj. **1** distant in space or time. **2** seeming remote from one's present situation; dreamy: *a faraway look.*

farce /färs/ ▶ n. **1** a comic play involving ridiculously improbable situations and events. **2** this type of humor or performance. **3** an absurd or ridiculous event: *the debate turned into a drunken farce.*

far·ci·cal /'färsikəl/ ▶ adj. absurd or ridiculous. ■ **far·ci·cal·ly** adv.

fare /fer/ ▶ n. **1** the money a passenger on public transportation has to pay. **2** a passenger in a taxi. **3** a range of food. ▶ v. perform in a particular

way: *the party fared badly in the April elections.*

Far East ▶ n. China, Japan, and other countries of east Asia. ■ **Far East·ern** adj.

fare·well /fer'wel/ ▶ exclam. goodbye. ▶ n. an act of parting or of marking someone's departure.

far-fetched ▶ adj. very difficult to believe.

far-flung ▶ adj. distant or remote.

far·i·na·ceous /,farə'nāshəs/ ▶ adj. **1** made of flour or meal. **2** containing or resembling starch; starchy.

farm /färm/ ▶ n. **1** an area of land and its buildings used for growing crops and rearing animals. **2** a place for breeding or growing something: *a fish farm.* ▶ v. **1** make one's living by growing crops or keeping livestock. **2** (**farm something out**) send out or subcontract work to others. ■ **farm·ing** n.

farm·er /'färmər/ ▶ n. a person who owns or manages a farm.

farm·hand /'färm,hand/ ▶ n. a worker on a farm.

farm·house /'färm,hous/ ▶ n. a house attached to a farm.

farm·land /'färm,land/ ▶ n. (also **farmlands**) land used for farming.

farm·stead /'färm,sted/ ▶ n. a farm and its buildings.

farm·yard /'färm,yärd/ ▶ n. a yard or small area of land surrounded by or next to farm buildings.

far·o /'ferō/ ▶ n. a gambling card game in which players bet on the order in which the cards will appear.

Far·o·ese /,fe(ə)rō'ēz, -'ēs/ ▶ n. & adj. chiefly British spelling of **FAEROESE**.

far-off ▶ adj. distant in time or space.

far out ▶ adj. **1** unconventional. **2** informal excellent.

far·ra·go /fə'rägō, -'rā-/ ▶ n. (pl. **farragoes**) a confused mixture.

far-reach·ing ▶ adj. having many important effects or implications.

far·ri·er /'farēər/ ▶ n. a smith who shoes horses. ■ **far·ri·er·y** n.

far·row /'farō/ ▶ n. a litter of pigs. ▶ v. (of a sow) give birth to piglets.

far-see·ing ▶ adj. having foresight; farsighted.

Far·si /'färsē/ ▶ n. the modern form of the Persian language, spoken in Iran.

far·sight·ed /'fär,sītid, -'sītid/ ▶ adj. **1** unable to see things clearly if they are relatively close to the eyes. **2** having or showing an awareness of what may happen in the future: *a farsighted exit strategy is very much a factor for both candidates.*

fart /färt/ informal ▶ v. **1** emit wind from the anus. **2** (**fart around/about**) waste time on silly or unimportant things. ▶ n. **1** an emission of wind from the anus. **2** a boring or unpleasant person.

far·ther /'fär<u>TH</u>ər/ ▶ adv. & adj. variant form of **FURTHER**.

> **USAGE**
> On the difference in use between **farther** and **further**, see the note at **FURTHER**.

farth·est /'fär<u>TH</u>ist/ ▶ adj. & adv. variant form of **FURTHEST**.

far·thing /'fär<u>TH</u>iNG/ ▶ n. **1** a former coin of the UK, equal to a quarter of an old penny. **2** chiefly Brit. the least possible amount: *she didn't care a farthing.*

far·thin·gale /'fär<u>TH</u>iNG,gāl/ ▶ n. historical a hooped petticoat or circular pad of fabric around the hips, formerly worn under women's skirts to extend and shape them.

Far West ▶ n. the region of North America west of the Rocky Mountains.

fas·ces /'fasˌēz/ ▶ pl.n. historical a bundle of rods with a projecting ax blade, used as a symbol of a magistrate's power in ancient Rome.

fas·ci·a /'fasʜ(ē)ə, 'fā-/ (also chiefly Brit. **facia**) ▶ n. 1 a board covering the ends of rafters or other fittings. 2 a detachable covering for the front of a cellular phone. 3 (in classical architecture) a long flat surface between moldings on an architrave. 4 Brit. the dashboard of a motor vehicle.

fas·ci·cle /'fasikəl/ ▶ n. 1 Anatomy & Biology a bundle of fibrous or stringy structures. 2 a separately published installment of a book or other printed work.

fas·ci·nate /'fasəˌnāt/ ▶ v. attract or interest someone very much. ■ **fas·ci·nat·ing** adj. **fas·ci·nat·ing·ly** adv.

fas·ci·na·tion /ˌfasəˈnāsʜən/ ▶ n. 1 the state of being very attracted to and interested in someone or something. 2 the power of something to attract or interest someone.

> **USAGE**
> Be careful to distinguish between the expressions **fascination with** and **fascination for**. A person has a **fascination with** something they are very interested in (*her fascination with the British royal family*), whereas something interesting holds a **fascination for** a person (*circuses have a fascination for children*).

fas·cism /'fasʜˌizəm/ ▶ n. 1 a right-wing system of government characterized by extreme nationalistic beliefs and strict obedience to a leader or the state. 2 extreme right-wing or intolerant views or practices. ■ **fas·cist** n. & adj. **fa·scis·tic** /fa'sʜistik/ adj.

fash·ion /'fasʜən/ ▶ n. 1 a style of clothing, hair, behavior, etc., that is currently popular. 2 the production and marketing of new styles of clothing and cosmetics. 3 a way of doing something: *they strolled across in a leisurely fashion.* ▶ v. form or make something: *a bench fashioned out of a fallen tree trunk.*
– PHRASES **after a fashion** to a certain extent but not perfectly. **in** (or **out of**) **fashion** fashionable (or unfashionable).

fash·ion·a·ble /'fasʜ(ə)nəbəl/ ▶ adj. in or influenced by a style that is currently popular. ■ **fash·ion·a·bil·i·ty** /ˌfasʜ(ə)nə'bilətē/ n. **fash·ion·a·bly** adv.

fash·ion·is·ta /ˌfasʜə'nēstə/ ▶ n. informal 1 a designer at a leading fashion house. 2 a devoted follower of fashion.

fast[1] /fast/ ▶ adj. 1 moving or capable of moving at high speed. 2 taking place or acting rapidly. 3 (of a clock or watch) ahead of the correct time. 4 firmly fixed or attached. 5 (of a dye) not fading in light or when washed. 6 (of photographic film) needing only a short exposure. 7 involving or engaging in exciting or immoral activities. ▶ adv. 1 at high speed. 2 within a short time. 3 firmly or securely.
– PHRASES **fast asleep** in a deep sleep. **pull a fast one** informal try to gain an unfair advantage.

fast[2] ▶ v. go without food or drink, especially for religious or medical reasons. ▶ n. an act or period of fasting.

fast·back /'fas(t)ˌbak/ ▶ n. a car with a rear that slopes continuously from the roof to the bumper.

fast·ball /'fas(t)ˌbôl/ ▶ n. a baseball pitch thrown at or near a pitcher's top speed, usually faster than 90 mph.

fast breed·er ▶ n. a nuclear reactor using high-speed neutrons.

fas·ten /'fasən/ ▶ v. 1 close or do up securely. 2 fix or hold something in place. 3 (**fasten on**) pick out and concentrate on something: *critics fastened on two sections of the report.* ■ **fas·ten·er** n. **fas·ten·ing** n.

fast food ▶ n. easily prepared food sold in snack bars and restaurants as a quick meal.

fast for·ward ▶ n. on a player of recorded media, a control for moving the content forward rapidly. ▶ v. (**fast-forward**) move the content of recorded media forward with this control.

fas·tid·i·ous /fas'tidēəs/ ▶ adj. 1 very careful about accuracy and detail. 2 very concerned about cleanliness. ■ **fas·tid·i·ous·ly** adv. **fas·tid·i·ous·ness** n.

fast lane ▶ n. 1 a highway lane for fast-moving traffic. 2 a hectic or highly pressured lifestyle: *Hong Kong's high-rise corporate fast lane.*

fast·ness /'fas(t)nəs/ ▶ n. 1 a secure place well protected by natural features. 2 the ability of a dye to maintain its color.

fast-talk ▶ v. informal pressure someone into doing something by using rapid or misleading speech.

fast track ▶ n. a rapid way of achieving something. ▶ v. (**fast-track**) speed up the development or progress of something.

fat /fat/ ▶ n. 1 a natural oily substance found in animal bodies, deposited under the skin or around certain organs. 2 such a substance, or a similar one made from plants, used in cooking. 3 Chemistry any of a group of organic compounds of glycerol and acids that form the main constituents of animal and vegetable fat. ▶ adj. (**fatter, fattest**) 1 (of a person or animal) having much excess fat. 2 (of food) containing much fat. 3 informal large or substantial: *fat profits.* 4 informal very little: *fat chance.* ■ **fat·ness** n. **fat·tish** adj.
– PHRASES **live off the fat of the land** have the best of everything.

fa·tal /'fātl/ ▶ adj. 1 causing death. 2 leading to failure or disaster: *a fatal mistake.* ■ **fa·tal·ly** adv.

fa·tal·ism /'fātlˌizəm/ ▶ n. 1 the belief that all events are decided in advance by a supernatural power and that humans have no control over them. 2 an attitude characterized by the belief that nothing can be done to prevent something from happening. ■ **fa·tal·ist** n. **fa·tal·is·tic** /ˌfātl'istik/ adj.

fa·tal·i·ty /fā'talətē, fə-/ ▶ n. (pl. **fatalities**) an occurrence of death by accident, in war, or from disease.

fat burn·er ▶ n. an over-the-counter drug that claims to burn calories by increasing the body's metabolism.

fat cat ▶ n. derogatory a wealthy and powerful business executive or politician.

fate /fāt/ ▶ n. 1 the development of events outside a person's control, regarded as decided in advance by a supernatural power. 2 the outcome of a situation for someone or something: *after his show was canceled, his wife's* *series suffered the same fate.* **3** (**the Fates**) Greek & Roman Mythology the three goddesses (Clotho, Lachesis, and Atropos) who controlled the lives of humans. ▶ v. (**be fated**) be destined to happen or act in a particular way: *it was as if they were fated to meet again.*

fate·ful /ˈfātfəl/ ▶ adj. having far-reaching and usually disastrous consequences. ∎ **fate·ful·ly** adv.

fat·head /ˈfatˌhed/ ▶ n. informal a stupid person.

fa·ther /ˈfäT͟Hər/ ▶ n. **1** a male parent. **2** an important male figure in the origin and early history of something: *Jung was one of the fathers of modern psychoanalysis.* **3** literary a male ancestor. **4** (often as a title or form of address) a priest. **5** (**the Father**) (in Christian belief) God. ▶ v. be the father of someone. ∎ **fa·ther·hood** n. **fa·ther·less** adj.

Fa·ther Christ·mas ▶ n. a British name for SANTA CLAUS.

fa·ther-in-law ▶ n. (pl. **fathers-in-law**) the father of one's husband or wife.

fa·ther·land /ˈfäT͟Hərˌland/ ▶ n. a person's native country.

fa·ther·ly /ˈfäT͟Hərlē/ ▶ adj. like a father, especially in being protective and affectionate. ∎ **fa·ther·li·ness** n.

Fa·ther's Day ▶ n. a day of the year on which fathers are honored with gifts and greetings cards (usually the third Sunday in June).

fath·om /ˈfaT͟Həm/ ▶ n. a unit of length equal to six feet (1.8 meters), used in measuring the depth of water. ▶ v. **1** understand or find an explanation for: *he couldn't fathom why she was so anxious.* **2** measure the depth of water. ∎ **fath·om·a·ble** adj. **fath·om·less** adj.

fa·tigue /fəˈtēg/ ▶ n. **1** extreme tiredness. **2** brittleness in metal or other materials caused by repeated stress. **3** (**fatigues**) loose-fitting clothing of a sort worn by soldiers. **4** (also **fatigue duty**) a menial nonmilitary task assigned to a soldier. ▶ v. (**fatigues, fatiguing, fatigued**) make someone extremely tired.

fat·so /ˈfatsō/ ▶ n. (pl. **fatsos**) informal, derogatory a fat person.

fat·ten /ˈfatn/ ▶ v. make or become fat or fatter.

fat·ty /ˈfatē/ ▶ adj. (**fattier, fattiest**) **1** containing a large amount of fat. **2** Medicine involving abnormal amounts of fat being deposited in a part of the body: *fatty degeneration of the arteries.* ▶ n. (pl. **fatties**) informal, derogatory a fat person. ∎ **fat·ti·ness** n.

fat·ty ac·id ▶ n. an organic acid whose molecule contains a hydrocarbon chain.

fat·u·ous /ˈfaCHo͞oəs/ ▶ adj. silly and pointless. ∎ **fat·u·ous·ly** adv. **fat·u·ous·ness** n.

fat·wa /ˈfätwä/ ▶ n. an authoritative ruling on a point of Islamic law.

fau·cet /ˈfôsit, ˈfäs-/ ▶ n. a device for controlling a flow of liquid or gas from a pipe or container; a tap.

fault /fôlt/ ▶ n. **1** an unattractive or unsatisfactory feature; a defect or mistake. **2** responsibility for an accident or misfortune: *it's not my fault he's in this mess.* **3** (in tennis) a service that breaks the rules. **4** an extended break in the continuity of layers of rock formation, caused by movement of the earth's crust. ▶ v. criticize someone or something for being unsatisfactory: *her colleagues could not fault her dedication to the job.* ∎ **fault·less** adj. **fault·less·ly** adv.

– PHRASES **at fault 1** responsible for an undesirable situation or event; in the wrong: *we recover compensation from the person at fault.* **2** mistaken or defective: *he suspected that his calculator was at fault.* **find fault** make a criticism or objection. —— **to a fault** to an excessive extent: *he was generous to a fault.*

fault line /ˈfôlt ˌlīn/ ▶ n. **1** the intersection of a geological fault with the earth's surface. **2** an undesirable or unbridgeable division: *the fault lines separating cultural politics and historical interpretation.*

fault·y /ˈfôltē/ ▶ adj. (**faultier, faultiest**) **1** not working or made correctly. **2** (of thinking or reasoning) containing mistakes.

faun /fôn/ ▶ n. Roman Mythology a lustful god of woods and fields, represented as a man with a goat's horns, ears, legs, and tail.

fau·na /ˈfônə, ˈfänə/ ▶ n. (pl. **faunas**) the animals of a particular region, habitat, or period of time. Compare with FLORA. ∎ **fau·nal** adj.

Faus·ti·an /ˈfoustēən/ ▶ adj. relating to the German astronomer Johann Faust, who was reputed to have sold his soul to the Devil.

Fauve /fōv/ ▶ n. a member of a group of early 20th-century French artists who painted in very bright colors. ∎ **Fauv·ism** n. **Fauv·ist** n. & adj.

faux /fō/ ▶ adj. made in imitation; artificial.

faux pas /fō ˈpä, fō ˈpä/ ▶ n. (pl. same) an embarrassing blunder in a social situation.

fa·va bean /ˈfävə ˌbēn/ ▶ n. another term for BROAD BEAN.

fave /fāv/ ▶ n. & adj. informal short for FAVORITE.

fa·vor /ˈfāvər/ (Brit. **favour**) ▶ n. **1** approval or liking: *training is looked upon with favor by many employers.* **2** an act of kindness beyond what is due or usual: *I've come to ask you a favor.* **3** special treatment given to one person at the expense of another. **4** a small gift or souvenir: *they gave out personalized pens as party favors.* **5** old use a thing such as a badge that is worn as a mark of favor or support. ▶ v. **1** regard with approval or liking: *these politicians favor raising taxes.* **2** give unfairly preferential treatment to: *critics say the new regulations favor the worst polluters.* **3** work to someone's or something's advantage: *the soil and climate here don't favor tall trees.* **4** informal look like a parent or other relative. **5** (**favor someone with**) give someone something they wish for.

– PHRASES **in favor** meeting with approval: *they were not in favor with the party.* **in someone's favor** to someone's advantage: *events were moving in his favor.* **in favor of** to be replaced by: *will today's teenage athletes drop soccer in favor of basketball, tennis, or golf?*

fa·vor·a·ble /ˈfāv(ə)rəbəl/ ▶ adj. **1** expressing approval or agreement: *a favorable response.* **2** advantageous or helpful: *favorable economic conditions.* **3** suggesting a good outcome: *a favorable prognosis.* ∎ **fa·vor·a·bly** adv.

fa·vor·ite /ˈfāv(ə)rət/ ▶ adj. preferred to all others of the same kind. ▶ n. **1** a favorite person or thing. **2** the competitor thought most likely to win.

fa·vor·ite son ▶ n. **1** a famous man who is particularly admired in his native area: *a brilliant idea from Toledo's favorite son.* **2** a person supported as a presidential candidate by delegates from the candidate's home state.

fa·vor·it·ism /ˈfāv(ə)rəˌtizəm/ ▶ n. the unfair favoring of one person or group at the expense of another.

favour, etc. ▶ n. & v. British spelling of FAVOR, etc.

fawn¹ /fôn, fän/ ▶ n. **1** a young deer in its first year. **2** a light brown color.

fawn² ▶ v. **1** try to please someone by flattering them or paying them too much attention. **2** (of a dog) show extreme devotion, especially by rubbing against someone. ■ **fawn·ing** adj.

fax /faks/ ▶ n. **1** an exact copy of a document made by electronic scanning and sent by telecommunications links. **2** the making or sending of documents in this way. **3** (also **fax machine**) a machine for sending and receiving such documents. ▶ v. **1** send a document by fax. **2** contact someone by fax.

faze /fāz/ ▶ v. informal disconcert or unsettle someone.

FBI ▶ abbr. Federal Bureau of Investigation.

FCC ▶ abbr. Federal Communications Commission.

FDA ▶ abbr. Food and Drug Administration.

FDIC ▶ abbr. Federal Deposit Insurance Corporation, a body that underwrites most private bank deposits.

FDR ▶ abbr. Franklin Delano Roosevelt.

Fe ▶ symbol the chemical element iron.

fe·al·ty /ˈfēltē/ ▶ n. historical the loyalty sworn to a feudal lord by a tenant or vassal.

fear /fi(ə)r/ ▶ n. **1** an unpleasant emotion caused by the threat of danger, pain, or harm. **2** the likelihood of something unwelcome happening: *she observed them without fear of attracting attention.* ▶ v. **1** be afraid of someone or something. **2** (**fear for**) be anxious about: *she feared for her son's safety.*

fear·ful /ˈfi(ə)rfəl/ ▶ adj. **1** showing or causing fear. **2** informal very great. ■ **fear·ful·ly** adv. **fear·ful·ness** n.

fear·less /ˈfi(ə)rlis/ ▶ adj. without fear; brave. ■ **fear·less·ly** adv. **fear·less·ness** n.

fear·some /ˈfi(ə)rsəm/ ▶ adj. frightening, especially in appearance. ■ **fear·some·ly** adv.

fea·si·ble /ˈfēzəbəl/ ▶ adj. **1** able to be done easily. **2** likely; probable. ■ **fea·si·bil·i·ty** /ˌfēzəˈbilətē/ n. **fea·si·bly** adv.

> **USAGE**
> Some people object to the use of **feasible** to mean 'likely' or 'probable' (as in *the most feasible explanation*). This sense has been in the language for centuries, however, and is generally considered to be acceptable.

feast /fēst/ ▶ n. **1** a large meal, especially one marking a special occasion. **2** an annual religious celebration. **3** a day dedicated to a particular saint. ▶ v. **1** have a feast. **2** (**feast on**) eat large quantities of something.
– PHRASES **feast one's eyes on** gaze at someone or something with pleasure. **feast or famine** either too much of something or too little.

feast day ▶ n. a day on which an annual Christian celebration is held.

feat /fēt/ ▶ n. an achievement requiring great courage, skill, or strength.

feath·er /ˈfeT͟Hər/ ▶ n. any of the flat structures growing from a bird's skin, consisting of a partly hollow horny shaft fringed with fine strands. ▶ v. **1** turn an oar so that the blade passes through the air edgeways. **2** (as adj. **feathered**) covered or decorated with feathers. ■ **feath·er·y** adj.
– PHRASES **a feather in one's cap** an achievement to be proud of. **feather one's nest** make oneself richer, usually at someone else's expense.

feath·er·bed /ˈfeT͟Hərˌbed/ ▶ n. a bed with a mattress stuffed with feathers. ▶ v. provide someone or something with very favorable economic or working conditions.

feath·er·brained /ˈfeT͟Hərˌbrānd/ ▶ adj. silly or absentminded.

feath·er·ing /ˈfeT͟HəriNG/ ▶ n. **1** a bird's plumage. **2** the feathers of an arrow. **3** featherlike markings.

feath·er·light /ˈfeT͟Hərˌlīt/ ▶ adj. extremely light: *feather-light fabrics.*

feath·er·weight /ˈfeT͟Hərˌwāt/ ▶ n. **1** a weight in boxing between bantamweight and lightweight. **2** a person or thing of little or no importance.

fea·ture /ˈfēCHər/ ▶ n. **1** a distinctive element or aspect: *the town has many interesting features.* **2** a part of the face, such as the mouth or nose. **3** a newspaper or magazine article or a broadcast program devoted to a particular topic. **4** (also **feature film**) a full-length movie forming the main item in a movie theater program. ▶ v. **1** have as a feature: *the hotel features a swimming pool and spacious gardens.* **2** have as an important actor or participant. **3** have an important or notable part in: *floral designs feature prominently in Persian rugs.* ■ **fea·tured** adj.

fea·ture-length /ˈfēCHərˌleNG(k)TH/ ▶ adj. about the same length as a typical movie: *a feature-length documentary.*

fea·ture·less /ˈfēCHərlis/ ▶ adj. lacking in distinguishing or interesting characteristics: *featureless suburban wasteland.*

Feb. ▶ abbr. February.

fe·brile /ˈfebˌrīl, ˈfēˌbrīl/ ▶ adj. **1** having or showing the symptoms of a fever. **2** overactive and excitable: *Poe's febrile imagination.*

Feb·ru·ar·y /ˈfeb(y)o͞oˌerē, ˈfebro͞o-/ ▶ n. (pl. **Februaries**) the second month of the year.

fe·ces /ˈfēsēz/ (Brit. **faeces**) ▶ pl.n. waste matter remaining after food has been digested, passed out of the body through the anus. ■ **fe·cal** /ˈfēkl/ adj.

feck·less /ˈfekləs/ ▶ adj. irresponsible and lacking strength of character. ■ **feck·less·ly** adv. **feck·less·ness** n.

fe·cund /ˈfekənd, ˈfē-/ ▶ adj. **1** very fertile: *a lush and fecund garden.* **2** producing many new and creative ideas: *these were her most fecund years.* ■ **fe·cun·di·ty** /feˈkəndətē, fiˈkən-/ n.

Fed /fed/ ▶ n. informal a federal official, especially an FBI agent.

fed /fed/ ▶ past and past participle of FEED.

Fe·da·yeen /ˌfedäˈēn, -dīˈēn/ ▶ pl.n. an Arab or Muslim commando force, especially one operating against Israel or against occupying forces in Iraq.

fed·er·al /ˈfed(ə)rəl/ ▶ adj. **1** relating to a system of government in which several states unite under a central authority but remain independent in internal affairs. **2** relating to the central government of a federation: *federal laws.* **3** (**Federal**) US historical relating to the Northern States in the Civil War. ■ **fed·er·al·ly** adv.

fed·er·al case ▶ n. **1** a criminal case under the jurisdiction of a federal court. **2** a matter of great concern or with dire consequences: *I'm not trying to make a federal case out of this but you've got to do something.*

fed·er·al·ism /ˈfed(ə)rəˌlizəm/ ▶ n. the federal principle or system of government. ■ **fed·er·al·ist** n. & adj.

Fed·er·al Re·serve ▶ n. the banking authority that has the functions of a central bank.

fed·er·ate /ˈfedəˌrāt/ ▶ v. (of a number of states or organizations) unite on a federal basis.

fed·er·a·tion /ˌfedəˈrāshən/ ▶ n. 1 a group of states that have a central government but are independent in internal affairs. 2 an organization within which smaller divisions have some internal independence.

Fed·Ex /ˌfedeks/ (also **Fedex**) ▶ v. trademark send by courier, especially Federal Express: *the tape was FedExed to New York on Friday.*

fe·do·ra /fəˈdôrə/ ▶ n. a soft felt hat with a curled brim and the crown creased lengthways.

fed up ▶ adj. informal annoyed or bored.

fee /fē/ ▶ n. 1 a payment given for professional advice or services. 2 a sum of money paid in order to join an organization, gain admission to somewhere, etc.

fee·ble /ˈfēbəl/ ▶ adj. (**feebler**, **feeblest**) 1 lacking physical or mental strength. 2 not convincing or impressive: *a feeble excuse.* ■ **fee·ble·ness** n. **fee·bly** adv.

fee·ble-mind·ed ▶ adj. 1 foolish; stupid. 2 dated having less than average intelligence.

feed /fēd/ ▶ v. (past and past part. **fed** /fed/) 1 give food to a person or animal. 2 provide enough food for: *she needed money to feed and clothe her family.* 3 eat: *slugs and snails feed at night.* 4 supply with material, power, water, etc.: *a lake fed by waterfalls.* 5 pass something gradually through a confined space. 6 prompt an actor with a line. ▶ n. 1 an act of feeding or of being fed. 2 food for domestic animals. 3 a device or pipe for supplying material to a machine. 4 the supply of raw material to a machine or device. 5 a broadcast distributed by a satellite or network from a central source to a large number of radio or television stations.

feed·back /ˈfēdˌbak/ ▶ n. 1 comments about a product or a person's performance, used as a basis for improvement. 2 the return of a fraction of the output of an amplifier, microphone, or other device to the input of the same device, causing distortion or a whistling sound.

feed·er /ˈfēdər/ ▶ n. 1 a person or animal that eats a particular food or in a particular way. 2 a thing that feeds or supplies something. 3 a road or rail route linking outlying districts with a main system.

feed·ing fren·zy ▶ n. 1 an aggressive group attack on prey by a number of sharks or piranhas. 2 an episode of frantic and unscrupulous competition for something, especially on the part of journalists covering a sensational story.

feed·lot /ˈfēdˌlät/ ▶ n. an enclosed area where livestock are fed and fattened for market.

feed·stock /ˈfēdˌstäk/ ▶ n. raw material used to supply a machine or industrial process.

fee-for-serv·ice ▶ adj. (of professional and especially medical services) charging a set fee for every service provided: *clinicians will be permitted to bill on a fee-for-service basis.*

feel /fēl/ ▶ v. (past and past part. **felt** /felt/) 1 notice, be aware of, or examine by touch or through physical sensation: *she felt her hand on his shoulder.* 2 give a sensation of a particular quality when touched: *his hair felt rough.* 3 experience an emotion or sensation: *I felt angry and upset.* 4 be affected by: *investors who have felt the effects of the recession.* 5 have a belief, attitude, or impression: *I felt that he hated me.* 6 (**feel up to**) have the strength or energy to do something. ▶ n. 1 an act of feeling. 2 the sense of touch. 3 a sensation given by something when touched. 4 an impression given by something: *a cafe with a European feel.*
– PHRASES **feel free** (**to do something**) have no hesitation or shyness (often used as an invitation or for reassurance): *feel free to say what you like.* **feel like** (**doing**) **something** be inclined to have or do: *I feel like celebrating.* **get a feel for** become familiar with something. **have a feel for** have a sensitive appreciation or understanding of something.

feel·er /ˈfēlər/ ▶ n. 1 an animal organ such as an antenna that is used for testing things by touch. 2 a tentative proposal intended to find out someone's attitude or opinion.

feel-good ▶ adj. informal causing a feeling of happiness and well-being: *a feel-good movie.*

feel·ing /ˈfēliNG/ ▶ n. 1 an emotional state or reaction. 2 (**feelings**) the emotional side of a person's character: *I don't want to hurt her feelings.* 3 strong emotion. 4 the capacity to experience the sense of touch: *she lost all feeling in her leg.* 5 the sensation of touching or being touched: *the feeling of silk next to your skin.* 6 a belief or opinion. 7 (**feeling for**) a sensitivity to or intuitive understanding of something: *he had a feeling for poetry.* ▶ adj. showing emotion or sensitivity. ■ **feel·ing·ly** adv.

fee sim·ple ▶ n. (pl. **fees simple**) Law a permanent and absolute tenure in land with freedom to dispose of it at will.

feet /fēt/ ▶ plural of FOOT.

feet first ▶ adj. & adv. 1 without hesitation or preparation: *the show requires the audience to jump in feet first.* 2 after death; as a corpse: *everyone told me they were going to carry me out feet first.*

feh /fe/ ▶ exclam. conveying disapproval, displeasure, or disgust: *the greatest writer in the English language? Feh!*

feign /fān/ ▶ v. pretend to feel or have: *he feigned surprise.*

feint /fānt/ ▶ n. a deceptive or pretended attacking movement in boxing or fencing. ▶ v. make a feint.

> **USAGE**
> On the confusion of **feint** and **faint**, see the note at FAINT.

feist·y /ˈfīstē/ ▶ adj. (**feistier**, **feistiest**) lively and spirited. ■ **feist·i·ly** adv. **feist·i·ness** n.

fe·la·fel ▶ n. variant spelling of FALAFEL.

feld·spar /ˈfel(d)ˌspär/ (also **felspar**) ▶ n. a mineral forming igneous rocks, consisting chiefly of aluminum silicates.

fe·lic·i·ta·tions /fəˌlisəˈtāshənz/ ▶ pl.n. formal congratulations.

fe·lic·i·tous /fəˈlisətəs/ ▶ adj. well chosen or appropriate: *a felicitous phrase.* ■ **fe·lic·i·tous·ly** adv.

fe·lic·i·ty /fəˈlisətē/ ▶ n. (pl. **felicities**) 1 great happiness. **2** the ability to express oneself in an appropriate way. **3** an appropriate or well-chosen feature of a work of literature: *his reviews shimmer with verbal felicities.*

fe·line /'fēˌlīn/ ▶ adj. relating to or resembling a cat or cats. ▶ n. a cat or other animal of the cat family.

fell[1] /fel/ ▶ past of FALL.

fell[2] ▶ v. **1** cut down a tree. **2** knock someone down. **3** stitch down the edge of a seam to lie flat.

fell[3] ▶ adj. literary very evil or fierce.
– PHRASES **in one fell swoop** all in one go.

fel·la·ti·o /fə'lāsʜ(ē)ˌō/ ▶ n. stimulation of a man's penis with the mouth. ■ **fel·late** v.

fell·er[1] /'felər/ ▶ n. nonstandard spelling of FELLOW.

fell·er[2] ▶ n. a person who cuts down trees.

fel·low /'felō/ ▶ n. **1** a man or boy. **2** a person in the same situation or associated with another: *they raised money for their fellows in need.* **3** a thing of the same kind as another. **4** a member of a learned society. **5** (also **research fellow**) a graduate receiving funds for a period of research. **6** Brit. a member of the governing body of certain colleges. ▶ adj. sharing a particular activity, situation, or condition: *a fellow sufferer.*

fel·low feel·ing ▶ n. sympathy based on shared experiences.

fel·low·ship /'felōˌsʜip/ ▶ n. **1** friendliness and companionship based on shared interests. **2** a group of people meeting to pursue a shared interest or aim. **3** the position of a fellow of a college or society.

fel·low trav·el·er ▶ n. **1** a person who is sympathetic with a group's aims and policies without being a member of it: *journalists who are regarded as fellow travelers of the administration.* **2** chiefly historical a person who sympathizes with the Communist Party but is not a member of it. ■ **fel·low trav·el·ing** adj.

fel·on /'felən/ ▶ n. a person who has committed a felony.

fel·o·ny /'felənē/ ▶ n. (pl. **felonies**) a crime regarded as more serious than a misdemeanor. ■ **fe·lo·ni·ous** /fə'lōnēəs/ adj. **fe·lo·ni·ous·ly** adv.

felt[1] /felt/ ▶ n. cloth made by rolling and pressing wool, which causes the fibers to mat together. ▶ v. **1** mat together or become matted. **2** (as adj. **felted**) covered with felt.

felt[2] ▶ past and past participle of FEEL.

felt-tip pen (also **felt-tipped pen**) ▶ n. a pen with a writing point made of felt or tightly packed fibers.

fe·luc·ca /fə'lookə, -'ləkə/ ▶ n. a small boat propelled by oars or sails, used especially on the Nile.

FEMA /'fēmə/ ▶ abbr. Federal Emergency Management Agency.

fe·male /'fēˌmāl/ ▶ adj. **1** referring to the sex that can bear offspring or produce eggs. **2** relating to or typical of women or female animals. **3** (of a plant or flower) having a pistil but no stamens. **4** (of a fitting) manufactured hollow so that a corresponding male part can be inserted. ▶ n. a female person, animal, or plant. ■ **fe·male·ness** n.

fem·i·nine /'femənin/ ▶ adj. **1** having qualities traditionally associated with women, especially delicacy and prettiness. **2** relating to women; female. **3** Grammar (of a gender of nouns and adjectives in certain languages) treated as

female. ■ **fem·i·nine·ly** adv. **fem·i·nin·i·ty** /ˌfemə'ninətē/ n.

fem·i·nism /'feməˌnizəm/ ▶ n. a movement or theory supporting women's rights on the grounds of equality of the sexes. ■ **fem·i·nist** n. & adj.

fem·i·nize /'feməˌnīz/ ▶ v. make something more feminine or female. ■ **fem·i·ni·za·tion** /ˌfemənə'zāsʜən/ n.

femme fa·tale /ˌfem fə'tal, fə'täl/ ▶ n. (pl. **femmes fatales** pronunc. same) an attractive and seductive woman.

femto- ▶ comb.form referring to a factor of one quadrillionth (10^{-15}): *femtojoule.*

fe·mur /'fēmər/ ▶ n. (pl. **femurs** or **femora** /'femərə/) the bone of the thigh. ■ **fem·o·ral** /'femərəl/ adj.

fen[1] /fen/ ▶ n. a low and marshy or frequently flooded area of land. ■ **fen·ny** adj.

fen[2] ▶ n. (pl. same) a unit of money of China, equal to one hundredth of a yuan.

fence /fens/ ▶ n. **1** a barrier enclosing an area, typically consisting of posts connected by wire, wood, etc. **2** a large upright obstacle in steeplechasing, show jumping, or cross-country races. **3** informal a dealer in stolen goods. **4** a guard or guide on a plane or other tool. ▶ v. **1** surround or protect something with a fence. **2** (**fence something in/off**) enclose or separate with a fence for protection or to prevent escape: *everything is fenced in to keep out the wolves.* **3** informal deal in stolen goods. **4** practice the sport of fencing. ■ **fenc·er** n.
– PHRASES **side of the fence** either of the opposing positions involved in a conflict: *whatever side of the fence you are on, the issue is here to stay.* **sit on the fence** avoid making a decision.

fenc·ing /'fensiNG/ ▶ n. **1** the sport of fighting with blunted swords in order to score points. **2** a series of fences. **3** material for making fences.

fend /fend/ ▶ v. **1** (**fend for oneself**) look after and provide for oneself. **2** (**fend someone/thing off**) defend oneself from an attack or attacker.

fend·er /'fendər/ ▶ n. **1** the mudguard or area around the wheel well of a vehicle. **2** a low frame around a fireplace to keep in falling coals. **3** a cushioning device hung over a ship's side to protect it against impact.

fen·es·tra·tion /ˌfenə'strāsʜən/ ▶ n. Architecture the arrangement of windows in a building.

feng shui /'fəNG 'sʜwē, -sʜwā/ ▶ n. an ancient Chinese system of designing buildings and positioning objects inside buildings to ensure a favorable flow of energy.

fen·nel /'fenl/ ▶ n. a plant whose leaves and seeds are used as an herb, and whose base is eaten as a vegetable.

fen·ta·nyl /'fentənil, 'fentn-il/ ▶ n. a fast-acting narcotic analgesic and sedative that is sometimes abused for its heroinlike effect.

fen·u·greek /'fenyəˌgrēk/ ▶ n. a white-flowered plant with seeds that are used as a spice.

fe·ral /'fi(ə)rəl, 'ferəl/ ▶ adj. **1** (of an animal or plant) wild, especially after having been domesticated. **2** resembling a wild animal.

fer·ma·ta /fer'mätə, fər-/ ▶ n. Music a pause of unspecified length on a note or rest, or the mark (⌢) that designates this.

fer·ment ▶ v. /fər'ment/ **1** undergo or cause to undergo fermentation. **2** stir up disorder.

▶ n. /'fərment/ a state of unrest or excitement, especially among a large group of people: *the creative ferment of postwar Britain.* ■ **fer·ment·a·ble** /fər'mentəbəl/ adj. **fer·ment·er** /fər'mentər/ n.

fer·men·ta·tion /ˌfərmən'tāsHən/ ▶ n. the chemical breakdown of a substance by bacteria, yeasts, or other microorganisms, such as when sugar is converted into alcohol. ■ **fer·ment·a·tive** /fər'men(t)ətiv/ adj.

fer·mi·on /'fermē,än, 'fər-/ ▶ n. Physics a subatomic particle, such as a nucleon, that has a spin of a half integer.

fer·mi·um /'fermēəm, 'fər-/ ▶ n. an unstable radioactive chemical element made by high-energy atomic collisions.

fern /fərn/ ▶ n. (pl. same or **ferns**) a flowerless plant that has feathery or leafy fronds and reproduces by spores. ■ **fern·er·y** n. (pl. **ferneries**) **fern·y** adj.

fe·ro·cious /fə'rōsHəs/ ▶ adj. **1** savagely fierce, cruel, or violent. **2** informal very great; extreme. ■ **fe·ro·cious·ly** adv. **fe·roc·i·ty** /fə'räsətē/ n.

-ferous (usu. **-iferous**) ▶ comb.form having or containing a specified thing: *Carboniferous.*

fer·ret /'ferət/ ▶ n. **1** a domesticated albino or brown polecat, used, especially in Europe, for catching rabbits. **2** informal a search. ▶ v. (**ferrets**, **ferreting, ferreted**) **1** search for something in a place or container. **2** (**ferret something out**) discover something by determined searching. **3** (usu. as n. **ferreting**) hunt with ferrets. ■ **fer·ret·er** n. **fer·ret·y** adj.

fer·ric /'ferik/ ▶ adj. Chemistry relating to iron with a valence of three.

Fer·ris wheel /'feris/ ▶ n. a fairground ride consisting of a giant vertical revolving wheel with passenger cars suspended on its outer edge.

fer·ro·e·lec·tric /ˌferō-i'lektrik/ ▶ adj. displaying permanent electric polarization that varies in strength with the applied electric field. ■ **fer·ro·e·lec·tric·i·ty** /ˌferō-i,lek'trisətē/ n.

fer·ro·mag·net·ic /ˌferō,mag'netik/ ▶ adj. Physics having the ability to become magnetic and to retain magnetic properties, as iron and some other metals do. ■ **fer·ro·mag·ne·tism** /ˌferō'magnə,tizəm/ n.

fer·rous /'ferəs/ ▶ adj. **1** (of metals) containing iron. **2** Chemistry relating to iron with a valence of two.

fer·rule /'ferəl/ ▶ n. a metal ring or cap used to strengthen the end of a handle, stick, or tube.

fer·ry /'ferē/ ▶ n. (pl. **ferries**) a boat or ship for carrying passengers and goods, especially as a regular service. ▶ v. (**ferries, ferrying, ferried**) carry someone or something by ferry or other transport. ■ **fer·ry·man** n. (pl. **ferrymen**)

fer·tile /'fərtl/ ▶ adj. **1** (of soil or land) producing or capable of producing abundant vegetation or crops. **2** (of a person, animal, or plant) able to conceive young or produce seed. **3** producing new and inventive ideas: *a fertile imagination.* ■ **fer·til·i·ty** /fər'tilitē/ n.

fer·ti·lize /'fərtl,īz/ ▶ v. **1** introduce sperm or pollen into an egg, female animal, or plant to develop a new individual. **2** add fertilizer to soil or land. ■ **fer·til·i·za·tion** /ˌfərtl-i'zāsHən/ n.

fer·ti·liz·er /'fərtl,īzər/ ▶ n. a chemical or natural substance added to soil to increase its fertility.

fer·vent /'fərvənt/ ▶ adj. intensely passionate. ■ **fer·ven·cy** n. **fer·vent·ly** adv.

fer·vid /'fərvid/ ▶ adj. intensely or excessively enthusiastic. ■ **fer·vid·ly** adv.

fer·vor /'fərvər/ (Brit. **fervour**) ▶ n. intense and passionate feeling: *the party swept to power on a tide of patriotic fervor.*

fes·cue /'feskyōō/ ▶ n. a narrow-leaved grass, some kinds of which are used for pasture and fodder.

fess /fes/ ▶ v. informal (**fess up**) confess; own up: *he fessed up about his relationship to Lawrence.*

-fest ▶ comb.form informal in nouns referring to a festival or large gathering of a specified kind: *a media-fest.*

fes·tal /'festəl/ ▶ adj. relating to a festival; festive.

fes·ter /'festər/ ▶ v. **1** (of a wound or sore) become septic. **2** (of food or rubbish) become rotten. **3** (of a negative feeling or problem) become worse or more intense: *hate can breed and fester for centuries.*

fes·ti·val /'festəvəl/ ▶ n. **1** a day or period of celebration, typically for religious reasons. **2** an organized series of concerts, movies, etc.

fes·tive /'festiv/ ▶ adj. **1** relating to a festival. **2** typical of a festival or celebration; happy. ■ **fes·tive·ly** adv.

fes·tiv·i·ty /fe'stivətē/ ▶ n. (pl. **festivities**) **1** joyful celebration. **2** (**festivities**) activities or events celebrating a special occasion.

fes·toon /fes'tōōn/ ▶ v. decorate something with chains of flowers, lights, etc. ▶ n. a decorative chain of flowers, leaves, or ribbons, hung in a curve.

fet·a /'fetə/ (also **feta cheese**) ▶ n. a salty Greek cheese made from the milk of sheep or goats.

fe·tal /'fētl/ ▶ adj. **1** relating to a fetus. **2** (of a posture) typical of a fetus, with the limbs folded in front of the body.

fetch /fecH/ ▶ v. **1** go for and bring back someone or something. **2** sell for a particular price: *the old ax fetched $50 at auction.* ■ **fetch·er** n.

fetch·ing /'fecHiNG/ ▶ adj. attractive: *a fetching black miniskirt.* ■ **fetch·ing·ly** adv.

fete /fāt, fet/ (also **fête**) ▶ n. a celebration or festival. ▶ v. praise, welcome, or entertain publicly: *in New York, she was feted like royalty.*

fet·id /'fetid/ ▶ adj. smelling very unpleasant.

fet·ish /'fetisH/ ▶ n. **1** an object worshiped for its supposed magical powers. **2** a form of sexual desire in which sexual pleasure is gained from an object, part of the body, or activity. **3** something that a person is obsessively devoted to: *a fetish for detail.* ■ **fet·ish·ism** n. **fet·ish·ist** n. **fet·ish·is·tic** /ˌfeti'sHistik/ adj.

fet·ish·ize /'feti,sHīz/ ▶ v. **1** make something the object of a sexual fetish. **2** have an excessive and irrational commitment to: *an author who fetishizes privacy.* ■ **fet·ish·i·za·tion** /ˌfetisHi'zāsHən/ n.

fet·lock /'fet,läk/ ▶ n. a joint of a horse's leg between the knee and the hoof.

fe·tor /'fētər/ ▶ n. a strong, foul smell.

fet·ter /'fetər/ ▶ v. **1** restrict the freedom of: *like most schools, it just rolls on, fettered by routine.* **2** restrain someone with chains or shackles. ▶ n. (**fetters**) restraints or controls. **2** a chain or shackle placed around a prisoner's ankles.

fet·tle /'fetl/ ▶ n. condition: *I was in fine fettle.*

fet·tuc·ci·ne /ˌfetə'cHēnē/ ▶ pl.n. pasta made in ribbons.

fe·tus /'fētəs/ ▶ n. (pl. **fetuses**) an unborn

mammal, in particular an unborn human more than eight weeks after conception.

feud /fyood/ ► n. **1** a prolonged and bitter dispute. **2** a state of prolonged hostility and violence between two groups. ► v. take part in a feud.

feu·dal /'fyoodl/ ► adj. relating to feudalism.

feu·dal·ism /'fyoodl,izəm/ ► n. the social system in medieval Europe, in which the nobility held lands in exchange for military service, and those at a lower level in society worked and fought for the nobles in exchange for land and protection.

fe·ver /'fēvər/ ► n. **1** an abnormally high body temperature, usually accompanied by shivering, headache, and in severe instances, delirium. **2** great excitement or agitation: *World Cup fever.* ■ **fe·ver·ish** adj. **fe·ver·ish·ly** adv. **fe·ver·ish·ness** n.

fe·vered /'fēvərd/ ► adj. **1** having or showing the symptoms of fever. **2** nervously excited or agitated: *the fevered chants of the crowd.*

fe·ver·few /'fēvər,fyoo/ ► n. an aromatic plant with feathery leaves and daisylike flowers, used as an herbal remedy for headaches.

fe·ver pitch ► n. a state of extreme excitement.

few /fyoo/ ► determiner, pron., & adj. **1** (**a few**) a small number of. **2** not many. ► n. (**the few**) a select minority of people.

– PHRASES **every few** once in every small group of (typically units of time): *she visits every few weeks.* **few and far between** scarce. **no fewer than** a surprisingly large number of. **quite a few** a fairly large number.

USAGE

Many people use the words **fewer** and **less** incorrectly. The rule is that **fewer** should be used with plural nouns, as in *eat fewer cookies* or *there are fewer people here today.* Use **less** with nouns referring to things that cannot be counted, as in *a job with less money.* It is wrong to use **less** with a plural noun (*less cookies, less people*).

---

fey /fā/ ► adj. **1** unworldly and vague. **2** able to see into the future; clairvoyant.

fez /fez/ ► n. (pl. **fezzes**) a flat-topped conical red hat, worn by men in some Muslim countries.

ff ► abbr. Music fortissimo.

ff. ► abbr. **1** folios. **2** following pages.

FHA ► abbr. Federal Housing Administration.

fi·an·cé /,fē,än'sā, fē'änsā/ ► n. (fem. **fiancée** pronunc. same) a person to whom another is engaged to be married.

fi·as·co /fē'askō/ ► n. (pl. **fiascos**) a ridiculous or humiliating failure.

fi·at /'fēat, 'fē,ät/ ► n. an official order or authorization.

fib /fib/ ► n. a trivial lie. ► v. (**fibs, fibbing, fibbed**) tell a fib. ■ **fib·ber** n.

fi·ber /'fībər/ (Brit. **fibre**) ► n. **1** a thread or strand from which a plant or animal tissue, mineral substance, or textile is formed. **2** a substance formed of fibers. **3** substances in vegetables, fruit, and some other foods, that are difficult to digest and therefore help the passage of food through the body. **4** strength of character: *a lack of moral fiber.*

fiber·board /'fībər,bôrd/ ► n. a building material made of wood fibers compressed into boards.

fi·ber·glass /'fībər,glas/ ► n. **1** a reinforced plastic material composed of glass fibers embedded in a resin matrix. **2** a textile fabric made from woven glass fibers.

fi·ber op·tics ► pl.n. (treated as sing.) the use of

thin flexible transparent fibers to transmit light signals, chiefly for telecommunications or for internal inspection of the body. ■ **fi·ber-op·tic** adj.

Fi·bo·nac·ci se·ries /,fēbə'näcHē 'si(ə)rēz/ ► n. Mathematics a series of numbers in which each number (**Fibonacci number**) is the sum of the two preceding numbers (e.g., the series 1, 1, 2, 3, 5, 8, etc.).

fibre, etc. ► n. British spelling of FIBER, etc.

fi·bril /'fībrəl, 'fib-/ ► n. technical a small or slender fiber.

fi·bril·late /'fibrə,lāt/ ► v. (of a muscle, especially in the heart) make a quivering movement due to uncoordinated contraction of the individual fibers. ■ **fi·bril·la·tion** /,fibrə'lāsHən/ n.

fi·brin /'fībrən/ ► n. an insoluble protein formed as a fibrous mesh during the clotting of blood.

fi·brin·o·gen /fī'brinəjən/ ► n. a soluble protein present in blood plasma, from which fibrin is produced.

fi·bro·blast /'fībrə,blast, 'fib-/ ► n. a cell in connective tissue that produces collagen and other fibers.

fi·broid /'fī,broid/ ► adj. relating to fibers or fibrous tissue. ► n. a noncancerous tumor of fibrous tissues, typically developing in the wall of the uterus.

fi·bro·my·al·gia /,fībrōmī'alj(ē)ə/ ► n. a chronic disorder characterized by musculoskeletal pain, fatigue, and tenderness in localized areas.

fi·bro·sis /fī'brōsəs/ ► n. the thickening and scarring of connective tissue, usually as a result of injury. ■ **fi·brot·ic** /fī'brätik/ adj.

fi·brous /'fībrəs/ ► adj. consisting of or characterized by fibers.

fib·u·la /'fibyələ/ ► n. (pl. **fibulae** /'fibyəlē, -,lī/ or **fibulas**) the outer of the two bones between the knee and the ankle, parallel with the tibia.

FICA /'fīkə/ ► abbr. Federal Insurance Contributions Act, the law the governs deductions from salary and wages to fund Social Security.

fick·le /'fikəl/ ► adj. changeable, especially as regards one's loyalties. ■ **fick·le·ness** n.

fic·tion /'fiksHən/ ► n. **1** literary works in prose describing imaginary events and people. **2** something that is invented or untrue: *keeping up the fiction that they were happily married.* **3** a false belief or statement, accepted as true for the sake of convenience. ■ **fic·tion·al** adj. **fic·tion·al·ly** adv. **fic·tion·ist** n.

fic·tion·al·ize /'fiksHənə,līz/ ► v. make a true story into a fictional one.

fic·ti·tious /fik'tisHəs/ ► adj. **1** imaginary or invented; not real or true. **2** referring to the characters and events found in fiction.

fic·tive /'fiktiv/ ► adj. created by the imagination. ■ **fic·tive·ness** n.

fi·cus /'fīkəs/ ► n. (pl. same) a tree, shrub, or plant of the fig family, especially a potted one.

fid·dle /'fidl/ ► n. informal **1** a violin. **2** chiefly Brit. an act of fraud or cheating. ► v. **1** touch or fidget with something restlessly or nervously. **2** informal falsify figures, data, or records. **3** informal play the violin. ■ **fid·dler** n.

– PHRASES **fit as a fiddle** in very good health. **play second fiddle to** take a subordinate role to someone or something.

fid·dle-fad·dle /'fidl ,fadl/ ► n. trivial matters; nonsense.

fid·dler crab ▶ n. a small amphibious crab, the males of which have one greatly enlarged claw.

fid·dle·sticks /'fidl,stiks/ ▶ exclam. informal, dated nonsense.

fi·del·i·ty /fə'delətē/ ▶ n. 1 continuing faithfulness to a person, cause, or belief. 2 the degree of exactness with which something is copied or reproduced.

fidg·et /'fijit/ ▶ v. (**fidgets, fidgeting, fidgeted**) make small movements through nervousness or impatience. ▶ n. 1 a person who fidgets. 2 (**the fidgets**) mental or physical restlessness. ■ **fidg·et·y** adj.

fi·du·ci·ar·y /fə'dŌŌSHē,erē, -SHərē/ Law ▶ adj. involving trust, especially with regard to the relationship between a trustee and a beneficiary. ▶ n. (pl. **fiduciaries**) a trustee.

fie /fī/ ▶ exclam. old use used to express disgust or outrage.

fief /fēf/ ▶ n. 1 historical an estate of land held on condition of feudal service. 2 a person's area of operation or control. ■ **fief·dom** /'fēfdəm/ n.

field /fēld/ ▶ n. 1 an area of open land, especially one planted with crops, or a pasture. 2 a piece of land used for a sport or game. 3 a subject of study or area of activity: *experts in the field of design.* 4 a region or space with a particular property: *a magnetic field.* 5 a range within which objects are visible from a particular viewpoint or through a piece of equipment: *the webcam's field of view.* 6 (**the field**) all the participants in a contest or sport. 7 a scene of a battle or a military campaign. ▶ v. 1 chiefly Baseball attempt to catch or stop the ball and return it after it has been hit. 2 select someone to play in a game or to run in an election. 3 deal with a difficult question, problem, etc. ▶ adj. 1 carried out or working in the natural environment, rather than in a laboratory or office: *a field operation.* 2 (of military equipment) light and mobile for use. ■ **field·er** n.
– PHRASES **in the field 1** (of troops) engaged in combat or maneuvers. 2 engaged in practical work in the natural environment. **play the field** informal have a series of casual sexual relationships.

field corn ▶ n. corn that is grown as livestock feed or for processing as a market grain, in contrast to sweet corn.

field day ▶ n. an opportunity for action or success, especially at the expense of others: *he's having a field day bossing people around.*

field·er's choice ▶ n. Baseball a play in which the fielding team's decision to put out another player allows the batter to reach first base safely.

field e·vents ▶ pl.n. track-and-field contests other than races, such as throwing and jumping events.

field glass·es ▶ pl.n. binoculars for outdoor use.

field goal ▶ n. 1 Football a goal scored by a placekick, scoring three points. 2 Basketball a basket scored while the clock is running and the ball is in play.

field guide ▶ n. a book for the identification of birds, flowers, minerals, or other things in their natural environment.

field hock·ey ▶ n. hockey played on a field, as opposed to ice hockey.

field hos·pi·tal ▶ n. a temporary hospital set up near a battlefield.

field·ing /'fēldiNG/ ▶ n. 1 Baseball & Cricket the activity or skills involved in being a fielder. 2 Military the deployment of personnel or materiel: *the fielding of a software bridging capability.*

field mar·shal ▶ n. the highest rank of army officer in the UK and several other countries.

field mouse ▶ n. a common dark brown mouse with a long tail and large eyes.

field mush·room ▶ n. the common edible mushroom.

field of·fi·cer (also **field-grade officer**) ▶ n. a major, lieutenant colonel, or colonel.

field of vi·sion ▶ n. the entire area that a person or animal is able to see when their eyes are fixed in one position.

field test ▶ n. (also **field trial**) a test carried out in the environment in which a product is to be used. ▶ v. (**field-test**) test a product in the environment in which it is to be used.

field trip ▶ n. an expedition made by students or research workers to study something at first hand.

field·work /'fēld,wərk/ ▶ n. practical work conducted by a researcher in the field rather than in a laboratory or office.

fiend /fēnd/ ▶ n. 1 an evil spirit or demon. 2 a very wicked or cruel person. 3 informal a person who is very interested in something: *an exercise fiend.*

fiend·ish /'fēndiSH/ ▶ adj. 1 very cruel or unpleasant. 2 informal very complex. ■ **fiend·ish·ly** adv.

fierce /fi(ə)rs/ ▶ adj. 1 violent or aggressive; ferocious. 2 intense or powerful: *her fierce determination never to lose the new order in her life.* ■ **fierce·ly** adv. **fierce·ness** n.

fier·y /'fi(ə)rē/ ▶ adj. (**fierier, fieriest**) 1 resembling or consisting of fire. 2 quick-tempered or passionate. ■ **fier·i·ly** adv. **fier·i·ness** n.

fi·es·ta /fē'estə/ ▶ n. 1 (in Spanish-speaking regions) a religious festival. 2 an event marked by festivities or celebration.

FIFA /'fēfə/ ▶ abbr. Fédération Internationale de Football Association, the international governing body of soccer.

fife /fīf/ ▶ n. a small shrill flute played in military bands.

FIFO /'fī,fō/ ▶ abbr. first in first out (chiefly with reference to methods of stock valuation or data storage). Compare with **LIFO**.

fif·teen /fif'tēn, 'fif,tēn/ ▶ cardinal number 1 one more than fourteen; 15. (Roman numeral: **xv** or **XV**.) 2 a team of fifteen players, especially in rugby. ■ **fif·teenth** ordinal number.

fifth /fi(f)TH/ ▶ ordinal number 1 that is number five in a sequence; 5th. 2 (**a fifth/one fifth**) each of five equal parts into which something is divided. 3 a musical interval spanning five consecutive notes in a scale, in particular (also **perfect fifth**) an interval of three whole steps and a half step. ■ **fifth·ly** adv.
– PHRASES **take** (or **plead**) **the fifth** exercise the right guaranteed by the Fifth Amendment to the Constitution to refuse to answer questions in order to avoid incriminating oneself.

fifth col·umn ▶ n. a group within a country at war who are working for its enemies. ■ **fifth col·umn·ist** n.

fifth wheel ▶ n. 1 a superfluous person or thing: *she had said that he wouldn't be a fifth wheel on this trip.* 2 a coupling between a trailer and the vehicle that pulls it.

fif·ty /'fiftē/ ▶ cardinal number (pl. **fifties**) ten less than sixty; 50. (Roman numeral: **l** or **L**.)

■ **fif·ti·eth** ordinal number.

fif·ty-fif·ty ▶ adj. & adv. with equal shares or chances.

fig /fig/ ▶ n. a soft pear-shaped fruit with sweet flesh and many small seeds.
– PHRASES **not give** (or **care**) **a fig** not care at all.

fig. ▶ abbr. figure: see fig. 7a.

fight /fīt/ ▶ v. (past and past part. **fought** /fôt/) **1** take part in a violent struggle involving physical force or weapons. **2** take part in a war or contest. **3** (**fight back**) counterattack or retaliate in a fight, struggle, or contest. **4** (**fight someone/thing off**) defend oneself against an attack by someone or something. **5** quarrel or argue. **6** struggle to overcome, end, or prevent: *he came to power with a pledge to fight corruption.* **7** try very hard to obtain or do something: *doctors fought to save her life.* ▶ n. **1** an act of fighting. **2** a vigorous struggle or campaign.
– PHRASES **fight fire with fire** use the weapons or tactics of one's opponent, even if one finds them distasteful. **fight it out** settle a dispute by fighting or competing aggressively: *they fought it out in court.* **fight one's way** move forward with difficulty.

fight·er /ˈfītər/ ▶ n. **1** a person or animal that fights. **2** a fast military aircraft designed for attacking other aircraft.

fight·ing chance ▶ n. a possibility of success if great effort is made.

fig leaf ▶ n. a leaf of a fig tree, used to conceal the genitals of naked people in paintings and sculpture.

fig·ment /ˈfigmənt/ ▶ n. a thing that exists only in a person's imagination.

fig·ur·al /ˈfigyərəl/ ▶ adj. another term for FIGURATIVE.

fig·u·ra·tion /ˌfigyəˈrāSHən/ ▶ n. **1** decoration using designs. **2** the representation of people or things in art as they appear in real life. **3** Music use of elaborate counterpoint.

fig·ur·a·tive /ˈfigyərətiv/ ▶ adj. **1** not using words in their literal sense; metaphorical. **2** (of art) representing people or things as they appear in real life. ■ **fig·ur·a·tive·ly** adv.

fig·ure /ˈfigyər/ ▶ n. **1** a number or numerical symbol. **2** an amount of money. **3** a person's bodily shape, especially that of a woman. **4** an important or distinctive person: *he became something of a cult figure.* **5** an artistic representation of a person or animal. **6** a geometrical shape defined by one or more lines. **7** a diagram or illustrative drawing. **8** a short succession of musical notes from which longer passages are developed. ▶ v. **1** play a significant part in something. **2** (**figure someone/thing out**) understand someone or something. **3** calculate an amount arithmetically. **4** informal, think or consider: *I figured I was safe here.* **5** (**figure on**) informal expect something to happen or be the case.

fig·ure eight ▶ n. an object or movement having the shape of the number eight.

fig·ure·head /ˈfigyərˌhed/ ▶ n. **1** a person who is leader in name only, lacking real power. **2** a carved bust or full-length figure set at the prow of an old-fashioned sailing ship.

fig·ure of speech ▶ n. a word or phrase used in a nonliteral sense to create a particular effect in speech or writing.

fig·ure skat·ing ▶ n. a type of ice skating in which the skater combines a number of movements including steps, jumps, and turns.

fig·ur·ine /ˌfigyəˈrēn/ ▶ n. a small statue of a person.

Fi·ji·an /ˌfējēən, fiˈjēən/ ▶ n. a person from Fiji. ▶ adj. relating to Fiji.

fil·a·ment /ˈfiləmənt/ ▶ n. **1** a slender threadlike object or fiber. **2** a metal wire in an electric light bulb, which glows white-hot when an electric current is passed through it. **3** Botany the slender part of a stamen that supports the anther. ■ **fil·a·men·ta·ry** /ˌfiləˈmentərē/ adj. **fil·a·men·tous** /ˌfiləˈmentəs/ adj.

fil·a·ri·a·sis /ˌfiləˈrīəsəs/ ▶ n. a disease caused by infestation with parasitic worms, transmitted by biting flies and mosquitoes in the tropics.

fil·bert /ˈfilbərt/ ▶ n. a cultivated hazelnut.

filch /filCH/ ▶ v. informal steal something small.

file¹ /fīl/ ▶ n. **1** a folder or box for keeping loose papers together and in order. **2** Computing a collection of data or programs stored under a single identifying name. **3** a line of people or things one behind another. **4** Military a small detachment of troops. ▶ v. **1** place a document in a file. **2** officially place a legal document, application, or charge on record. **3** walk one behind the other.

file² ▶ n. a tool with a roughened surface or surfaces, used for smoothing or shaping a hard material. ▶ v. smooth or shape something with a file.

fi·lé /fiˈlā, ˈfēlā/ ▶ n. powdered sassafras leaves used to flavor or thicken soup, especially gumbo.

file·name /ˈfīlˌnām/ ▶ n. an identifying name given to a computer file.

file-shar·ing ▶ n. the practice of or ability to transmit files from one computer to another over a network or the Internet: *file-sharing software.*

fi·let /fiˈlā, ˈfīlā/ ▶ n. & v. variant spelling of FILLET in all culinary senses.

fi·let mi·gnon /fiˈlā mēnˈyōn/ ▶ n. a small, tender cut of beef from the end of the tenderloin.

fil·i·al /ˈfilēəl, ˈfilyəl/ ▶ adj. relating to or due from a son or daughter: *no one can accuse me of neglecting my filial duty.*

fil·i·bus·ter /ˈfiləˌbəstər/ ▶ n. prolonged speaking that obstructs progress in a lawmaking assembly. ▶ v. obstruct the progress of legislation by prolonged speaking.

fil·i·gree /ˈfiləˌgrē/ (also **filagree**) ▶ n. delicate ornamental work of fine gold, silver, or copper wire. ■ **fil·i·greed** adj.

fil·ings /ˈfīliNGz/ ▶ pl.n. small particles rubbed off by a file.

Fil·i·pi·no /ˌfiləˈpēnō/ ▶ n. (pl. **Filipinos**; fem. **Filipina**, pl. **Filipinas**) **1** a person from the Philippines. **2** the national language of the Philippines. ▶ adj. relating to Filipinos or their language.

fill /fil/ ▶ v. **1** make or become full: *his wardrobe is filled with designer clothes.* **2** block up a hole or gap. **3** be an overwhelming presence in: *the smell of garlic filled the air.* **4** cause someone to experience a feeling. **5** satisfy a need. **6** occupy a period of time. **7** hold and perform the duties of a position or role. ▶ n. (**one's fill**) as much as one wants or can bear.
– PHRASES **fill in** act as a substitute. **fill someone in** give someone information. **fill out** put on weight. **fill something out** (or **in**) complete

a form by adding information. **fill someone's shoes** (or **boots**) informal take over someone's role and fulfill it satisfactorily.

fill·er¹ /'filər/ ▸ n. 1 something used to fill a gap or cavity, or to increase bulk. 2 an item serving only to fill space or time in a broadcast, conversation, etc.

fill·er² ▸ n. (pl. same) a unit of money of Hungary, equal to one hundredth of a forint.

fil·let /'filit/ ▸ n. 1 a boneless piece of meat from near the loins or ribs of an animal. 2 a boned side of a fish. 3 a band or ribbon binding the hair. 4 Architecture a narrow flat band separating two moldings. ▸ v. (**fillets, filleting, filleted**) 1 remove the bones from a fish. 2 cut meat or fish into boneless strips.

fill·ing /'filiNG/ ▸ n. 1 a quantity of material that fills or is used to fill something. 2 a piece of material used to fill a cavity in a tooth. ▸ adj. (of food) leaving one feeling pleasantly full.

fill·ing sta·tion ▸ n. a gas station.

fil·lip /'filəp/ ▸ n. a stimulus or boost: *the latest initiative will bring a fillip to the area's economy.*

fil·ly /'filē/ ▸ n. (pl. **fillies**) 1 a young female horse, especially one less than four years old. 2 humorous a lively girl or young woman.

film /film/ ▸ n. 1 a thin, flexible strip of plastic or other material coated with a light-sensitive substance, used in a camera to produce photos or motion pictures. 2 a movie; a motion picture. 3 motion pictures considered as an art or industry. 4 material in the form of a very thin flexible sheet. 5 a thin layer covering a surface. ▸ v. 1 make a movie of a story, event, etc.; capture an event or performance on film. 2 become covered with a thin layer of something.

film·ic /'filmik/ ▸ adj. relating to movies or cinematography.

film·mak·er /'film,mākər/ ▸ n. a person who directs or produces movies. ■ **film·mak·ing** n.

film noir /,film 'nwär/ ▸ n. a style of movie marked by a mood of pessimism, fatalism, and menace.

film·og·ra·phy /fil'mägrəfē/ ▸ n. (pl. **filmographies**) a list of movies or television projects by one director or actor, or on one subject.

film stock ▸ n. photographic or cinematic film that has not been exposed or processed.

film·strip /'film,strip/ ▸ n. a series of transparencies in a strip for projection.

film·y /'filmē/ ▸ adj. (**filmier, filmiest**) 1 thin and translucent: *a flowing robe of filmy chiffon.* 2 covered with a thin film.

fi·lo /'fēlō/ (also **phyllo**) ▸ n. a kind of flaky pastry in the form of very thin sheets.

fi·lo·vi·rus /'fēlō,vīrəs, 'fī-/ ▸ n. an RNA virus of a group that causes certain severe fevers characterized by hemorrhages.

fils /fēs/ ▸ n. used after a French surname to distinguish a son from a father of the same name.

fil·ter /'filtər/ ▸ n. 1 a device or substance that allows liquid or gas to pass through it, but holds back any solid particles. 2 a screen, plate, or layer that absorbs some of the light passing through it. 3 a piece of computer software that processes data before passing it to another application, for example to remove unwanted material. ▸ v. 1 pass something through a filter. 2 move gradually in or out of somewhere: *the sun*

filtered through the window. 3 (of information) gradually become known. ■ **fil·ter·a·ble** adj.

fil·tra·tion /fil'trāsHən/ n.

fil·ter-feed·ing ▸ adj. (of an aquatic animal) feeding by filtering out plankton or nutrients suspended in the water.

fil·ter tip ▸ n. a filter attached to a cigarette for removing impurities from the inhaled smoke.

filth /filTH/ ▸ n. 1 disgusting dirt. 2 obscene and offensive language or printed material.

filth·y /'filTHē/ ▸ adj. (**filthier, filthiest**) 1 disgustingly dirty. 2 obscene and offensive. 3 informal very unpleasant or disagreeable: *filthy weather.* ▸ adv. informal extremely: *she's filthy rich.* ■ **filth·i·ly** adv. **filth·i·ness** n.

fil·trate /'fil,trāt/ ▸ n. a liquid that has passed through a filter.

fin /fin/ ▸ n. 1 a flattened part that projects from the body of a fish or other aquatic animal, used for propelling, steering, and balancing. 2 an underwater swimmer's flipper. 3 a projection on an aircraft, rocket, or car, for providing aerodynamic stability. ■ **finned** adj.

fin. ▸ abbr. 1 finance. 2 financial. 3 finish.

fi·na·gle /fə'nāgəl/ ▸ v. informal obtain something in a dishonest or devious way. ■ **fi·na·gler** n.

fi·nal /'fīnl/ ▸ adj. 1 coming at the end; last. 2 allowing no further doubt or dispute: *the decision of the judges is final.* ▸ n. 1 the last game in a tournament, which will decide the overall winner. 2 (**finals**) a series of games forming the final stage of a competition. 3 an exam at the end of a term, academic year, or particular class.

fi·nal cut ▸ n. the final edited version of a filmed production or sound recording.

fi·na·le /fə'nalē, -'nälē/ ▸ n. the last part of a piece of music, a performance, or a public event.

fi·nal·ist /'fīnl-ist/ ▸ n. a person or team competing in a final or finals.

fi·nal·i·ty /fī'nalətē, fi-/ ▸ n. (pl. **finalities**) the fact or quality of being final and unable to be changed.

fi·nal·ize /'fīnl,īz/ ▸ v. complete or decide on a final version of a plan or agreement. ■ **fi·nal·i·za·tion** /,fīnl-ə'zāsHən/ n.

fi·nal·ly /'fīn(ə)lē/ ▸ adv. 1 after a long time and much difficulty or delay. 2 as a final point in a series.

fi·nal so·lu·tion ▸ n. the Nazi policy (1941–45) of exterminating Jews.

fi·nance /'fīnans, fə'nans/ ▸ n. 1 the management of large amounts of money by governments or large organizations. 2 funds to support an enterprise. 3 (**finances**) the money available to a country, state, organization, or person. ▸ v. provide funding for a person or enterprise.

fi·nance com·pa·ny ▸ n. a company concerned primarily with providing money, as for short-term loans.

fi·nan·cial /fə'nancHəl, fī-/ ▸ adj. relating to finance. ■ **fi·nan·cial·ly** adv.

fi·nan·cial plan·ner ▸ n. someone who is employed to manage savings and investments.

fi·nan·cial year ▸ n. British term for FISCAL YEAR.

fin·an·cier /,finən'si(ə)r, fə'nan,si(ə)r/ ▸ n. a person who manages the finances of governments or other large organizations.

finch /finCH/ ▸ n. a songbird of a large group

including the canary and goldfinch, most of which have short stubby bills.

find /fīnd/ ▸ v. (past and past part. **found**) **1** discover someone or something by chance or by searching. **2** recognize or discover to be present or to be the case: *vitamin B12 is found in dairy products.* **3** confirm something by research or calculation. **4** reach or arrive at a state or point by a natural or normal process. **5** Law (of a court) officially declare to be the case: *he was found guilty of fraud.* **6** (**find against** or **for**) Law (of a court) make a decision against (or in favor of) someone. ▸ n. a valuable or interesting discovery. ■ **find·a·ble** adj.
– PHRASES **find favor** be liked or prove acceptable: *the ballet did not find favor with the public.* **find someone out** discover that someone has lied or been dishonest. **find something out** discover information or a fact.

find·er /'fīndər/ ▸ n. **1** a person who finds someone or something. **2** a small telescope attached to a large one, used to locate an object for observation. **3** a viewfinder in a camera.

fin de siè·cle /ˌfan də sēˈäkl(ə)/ ▸ adj. relating to or typical of the end of a century, especially the 19th century.

find·ing /'fīndiNG/ ▸ n. a conclusion reached as a result of an inquiry, investigation, or trial.

fine[1] /fīn/ ▸ adj. **1** of very high quality. **2** satisfactory. **3** healthy and feeling well. **4** (of the weather) bright and clear. **5** very thin: *fine hair.* **6** of delicate or intricate workmanship. **7** difficult to distinguish because precise or subtle: *the ear makes fine distinctions between different noises.* ▸ adv. informal in a satisfactory or pleasing way. ▸ v. **1** (usu. **fine down**) make or become thinner. **2** clarify beer or wine by causing the precipitation of sediment. ■ **fine·ly** adv. **fine·ness** n.
– PHRASES **the finer points** the more complex or detailed aspects: *he went on to discuss the finer points of his work.*

fine[2] ▸ n. a sum of money imposed as a punishment by a court of law or other authority. ▸ v. punish someone by a fine.

fine art ▸ n. art intended to appeal mainly or solely to the sense of beauty, such as painting.
– PHRASES **have something down to a fine art** achieve a high level of skill in something through experience.

fine print ▸ n. another term for SMALL PRINT.

fin·er·y /'fīnərē/ ▸ n. showy clothes or decoration.

fines herbes /ˌfēn'(z)erb/ ▸ pl.n. mixed herbs used in cooking.

fi·nesse /fə'nes/ ▸ n. **1** impressive delicacy and skill: *his acting showed considerable dignity and finesse.* **2** subtle skill in handling people or situations. **3** (in bridge and whist) an attempt to win a trick with a card that is not a certain winner. ▸ v. **1** do something with great subtlety and skill. **2** slyly attempt to avoid blame when dealing with a situation.

fine-tooth comb (also **fine-toothed comb**) ▸ n. (in phrase **with a fine-tooth comb**) with a very thorough search or analysis.

fine-tune ▸ v. make small adjustments to something in order to achieve the best performance.

fin·ger /'fiNGgər/ ▸ n. **1** each of the four slender jointed parts attached to either hand (or five, if the thumb is included). **2** a measure of liquor in a glass, based on the breadth of a finger. **3** a long, narrow object. ▸ v. **1** touch or feel someone or something with the fingers. **2** informal inform on someone. **3** Music play a passage with a particular sequence of positions of the fingers. ■ **fin·gered** adj. **fin·ger·less** adj.
– PHRASES **have a finger in every pie** be involved in a large number of activities. **have** (or **keep**) **one's finger on the pulse of something** be aware of the latest trends and developments of something: *she keeps her finger on the pulse of the fashion scene.* **lay a finger on** touch someone with the intention of harming them. **put one's finger on** identify something exactly.

fin·ger·board /'fiNGgər,bôrd/ ▸ n. a flat strip on the neck of a stringed instrument, against which the strings are pressed in order to vary the pitch.

fin·ger bowl ▸ n. a small bowl holding water for rinsing the fingers at a meal.

fin·ger food ▸ n. food that can conveniently be eaten with the fingers.

fin·ger·ing /'fiNGgəriNG/ ▸ n. a way or technique of using the fingers to play a musical instrument.

fin·ger·mark /'fiNGgər,märk/ ▸ n. a mark left on a surface by a dirty or greasy finger.

fin·ger·nail /'fiNGgər,nāl/ ▸ n. the nail on the upper surface of the tip of each finger.

fin·ger paint ▸ n. thick paint designed to be applied with the fingers, used by young children.

fin·ger·pick /'fiNGgər,pik/ ▸ v. play a guitar or similar instrument using the fingernails or plectrums worn on the fingertips.

fin·ger·print /'fiNGgər,print/ ▸ n. a mark made on a surface by a person's fingertip, useful for identification. ▸ v. record a person's fingerprints.

fin·ger·tip /'fiNGgər,tip/ ▸ n. the tip of a finger. ▸ adj. using or operated by the fingers: *fingertip controls.*
– PHRASES **at one's fingertips** (especially of information) readily available.

fin·i·al /'finēəl/ ▸ n. **1** a distinctive section or ornament at the highest point of a roof, pinnacle, or similar structure. **2** an ornament at the top, end, or corner of an object.

fin·ick·y /'finikē/ ▸ adj. **1** fussy about one's requirements: *a finicky eater.* **2** excessively detailed or elaborate. ■ **fin·ick·i·ness** n.

fin·is /'finis, fi'nē/ ▸ n. the end (printed at the end of a book or shown at the end of a movie).

fin·ish /'finiSH/ ▸ v. **1** bring or come to an end. **2** consume the whole or the remainder of food or drink. **3** (**finish with**) have no more need or desire for someone or something. **4** reach the end of a race or other competition. **5** complete the manufacture or decoration of something by giving it an attractive surface appearance. ▸ n. **1** an end or final stage. **2** the place at which a race or competition ends. **3** the way in which a manufactured article is finished: *nylon with a shiny finish.* ■ **fin·ish·er** n.
– PHRASES **finish someone off** kill or comprehensively defeat someone. **finish up 1** complete an action or process: *the electrician should finish up by Friday.* **2** end by doing something or being in a particular position: *we finished up tired and humiliated.*

fin·ish·ing school ▸ n. a private school where girls are taught how to behave correctly in fashionable society.

fin·ish·ing touch ▸ n. a final detail that completes and improves a piece of work.

fi·nite /ˈfīnīt/ ▸ adj. limited in size or extent.
■ **fi·nite·ly** adv. **fi·nite·ness** n.

fi·ni·to /fəˈnētō/ ▸ adj. informal finished: *his door closed, and that was it—the end, finito.*

fink /fiNGk/ informal ▸ n. an unpleasant or contemptible person, especially one who acts as an informant. ▸ v. (**fink on**) inform on to the authorities: *it turns out that Wally's been finking on us for years.*

Finn /fin/ ▸ n. a person from Finland.

Finn·ish /ˈfiniSH/ ▸ n. the language of the Finns. ▸ adj. relating to the Finns or their language.

fiord ▸ n. variant spelling of **FJORD**.

fir /fər/ ▸ n. an evergreen coniferous tree with upright cones and flat needle-shaped leaves.

fire /fīr/ ▸ n. **1** the state of burning, in which substances combine chemically with oxygen from the air and give out bright light, heat, and smoke. **2** an instance of burning in which something is destroyed. **3** wood or coal burned in a hearth or stove for heating or cooking. **4** passionate emotion or enthusiasm. **5** the firing of guns. **6** strong criticism: *we took a lot of fire for our initial tax proposal.* ▸ v. **1** shoot a bullet or projectile from a gun or other weapon. **2** direct a rapid succession of questions or statements toward someone. **3** informal dismiss someone from a job. **4** stimulate: *this personal testimony fired the girls' imagination.* **5** (**fire someone up**) fill someone with enthusiasm. **6** supply a furnace, power station, etc., with fuel. **7** bake or dry pottery or bricks in a kiln. **8** old use set fire to something.
– PHRASES **catch fire** begin to burn. **fire away** informal go ahead. **firing on all cylinders** functioning at a peak level. **light a fire under someone** stimulate someone to work or act more quickly or enthusiastically. **on fire 1** burning. **2** very excited. **set fire to** (or **set something on fire**) cause something to burn. **set the world on fire** do something remarkable or sensational. **under fire 1** being shot at. **2** being strongly criticized.

fire a·larm ▸ n. a device making a loud noise that gives warning of a fire.

fire ant ▸ n. a tropical American ant that has a painful and sometimes dangerous sting.

fire·arm /ˈfī(ə)r,ärm/ ▸ n. a rifle, pistol, or other portable gun.

fire·ball /ˈfīr,bôl/ ▸ n. **1** a ball of flame or fire. **2** a large bright meteor. **3** an energetic or hot-tempered person.

fire·bomb /ˈfīr,bäm/ ▸ n. a bomb designed to cause a fire. ▸ v. attack something with a firebomb.

fire·brand /ˈfīr,brand/ ▸ n. a passionate supporter of a particular cause.

fire·break /ˈfīr,brāk/ ▸ n. an obstacle that prevents fire from spreading, especially a strip of open space in a forest.

fire·brick /ˈfīr,brik/ ▸ n. a brick capable of withstanding intense heat, used especially to line furnaces and fireplaces.

fire com·pa·ny ▸ n. another term for FIRE DEPARTMENT.

fire·crack·er /ˈfīr,krakər/ ▸ n. a firework that explodes with a loud bang.

fire·damp /ˈfīr,damp/ ▸ n. a gas, chiefly methane, that forms an explosive mixture with air in coal mines.

fire de·part·ment ▸ n. the department of a local or municipal authority in charge of preventing and fighting fires.

fire door ▸ n. **1** a fire-resistant door to prevent the spread of fire. **2** a door to the outside of a building, used as an emergency exit.

fire drill ▸ n. a practice of the emergency procedures to be used in case of fire.

fire-eat·er ▸ n. an entertainer who appears to eat fire.

fire en·gine ▸ n. a vehicle carrying firefighters and their equipment.

fire es·cape ▸ n. a staircase or ladder used for escaping from a burning building.

fire ex·tin·guish·er ▸ n. a portable device that discharges a jet of liquid, foam, or gas to extinguish a fire.

fire·fight /ˈfīr,fīt/ ▸ n. Military a battle using guns rather than bombs or other weapons.

fire·fight·er /ˈfīr,fītər/ ▸ n. a person whose job is to extinguish fires.

fire·fly /ˈfīr,flī/ ▸ n. (pl. **fireflies**) a kind of beetle that glows in the dark.

fire·house /ˈfīr,hous/ ▸ n. a fire station.

fire i·rons ▸ pl.n. tools for tending a domestic fire, especially tongs, a poker, and a shovel.

fire·light /ˈfīr,līt/ ▸ n. light from a fire in a fireplace.

fire·man /ˈfīrmən/ ▸ n. (pl. **firemen**) a firefighter.

fire·place /ˈfīr,plās/ ▸ n. a partially enclosed space at the base of a chimney for a domestic fire.

fire·pow·er /ˈfīr,pou(-ə)r/ ▸ n. the destructive capacity of guns, missiles, or a military force.

fire·proof /ˈfīr,prōof/ ▸ adj. able to withstand fire or great heat.

fire sale ▸ n. **1** a sale of merchandise, sometimes damaged, from a business that has suffered a fire. **2** a sale of merchandise or assets from a seller facing bankruptcy.

fire·side /ˈfīr,sīd/ ▸ n. the part of a room around a fireplace.

fire·side chat ▸ n. an informal and intimate conversation.

fire sta·tion ▸ n. a facility at which a fire department houses its fire engines and other equipment.

fire·storm /ˈfīr,stôrm/ ▸ n. a very intense and destructive fire, fanned by strong currents of air drawn in from the surrounding area.

fire·trap /ˈfīr,trap/ ▸ n. a building without any or enough fire exits.

fire·wall /ˈfīr,wôl/ ▸ n. **1** a wall or partition designed to stop the spread of fire. **2** a part of a computer system or network that blocks unauthorized access to a network while allowing outward communication.

fire·wa·ter /ˈfīr,wôtər, -,wätər/ ▸ n. humorous or dated strong alcohol.

Fire·Wire /ˈfī(ə)r,wī(ə)r/ ▸ n. trademark a technology that allows high-speed data exchange between computers or between devices and computers.

fire·wood /ˈfīr,wŏŏd/ ▸ n. wood that is burned as fuel.

fire·work /ˈfīr,wərk/ ▸ n. **1** a device containing chemicals that burn or explode when it is ignited, producing spectacular colored lights and loud noises. **2** (**fireworks**) an outburst of anger or a display of great skill or energy.

fir·ing line ▶ n. **1** the front line of troops in a battle. **2** a position where one is likely to be criticized or blamed: *the chief executive is in the firing line again.*

fir·ing squad ▶ n. a group of soldiers appointed to shoot a condemned person.

fir·kin /ˈfərkən/ ▶ n. chiefly historical a small cask used chiefly for liquids, butter, or fish.

firm¹ /fərm/ ▶ adj. **1** having a surface or structure that does not give way or sink under pressure. **2** solidly in place and stable. **3** having steady power or strength: *a firm grip.* **4** showing determination and strength of character. **5** fixed or definite: *she had no firm plans.* ▶ v. **1** make something firm. **2** (often **firm something up**) make an agreement or plan explicit and definite. ▶ adv. in a determined way: *he vowed to stand firm.* ■ **firm·ly** adv. **firm·ness** n.
– PHRASES **a firm hand** strict discipline or control.

firm² ▶ n. a business organization.

fir·ma·ment /ˈfərməmənt/ ▶ n. literary the heavens; the sky.

firm·ware /ˈfərmˌwer/ ▶ n. Computing software permanently programmed into a read-only memory.

first /fərst/ ▶ ordinal number **1** coming before all others in time or order; 1st. **2** before doing something else. **3** before all others in position, rank, or importance. **4** informal something never previously achieved or occurring.
– PHRASES **at first** at the beginning. **of the first order** (or **magnitude**) of the highest quality or degree: *a soprano of the first order.*

first aid ▶ n. emergency medical help given to a sick or injured person until full treatment is available. ■ **first-aid·er** n.

first base ▶ n. Baseball the base that is the first destination of a runner.
– PHRASES **get to first base** informal succeed in the first step of an undertaking.

first·born /ˈfərstˌbôrn/ ▶ n. the first child to be born to someone.

first class ▶ n. **1** a set of people or things grouped together as the best. **2** the best accommodations in an aircraft, train, or ship. ▶ adj. **& adv. 1** relating to the first class; of the best quality: *a first-class Thai restaurant.* **2** of or relating to a class of mail given priority: *send it out first class.*

first-de·gree ▶ adj. **1** (of burns) affecting only the surface of the skin and causing reddening. **2** Law (of crime, especially murder) in the most serious category.

first·hand /ˈfərstˈhand/ ▶ adj. **& adv.** from the original source or personal experience; direct: *firsthand knowledge.*
– PHRASES **at first hand** directly or from personal experience.

first la·dy ▶ n. the wife of the president of the US or other head of state.

first-line ▶ adj. of first resort: *first-line drugs for HIV exposure.*

first·ly /ˈfərstlē/ ▶ adv. in the first place; first.

first mate ▶ n. the officer second in command to the master of a merchant ship.

first name ▶ n. a personal name given to someone at birth or baptism and used before a family name.
– PHRASES **be on a first-name basis** have a friendly and informal relationship.

First Na·tion ▶ n. (in Canada) any of several

indigenous American Indian and Inuit communities that enjoy official status.

first of·fend·er ▶ n. a person who is convicted of a criminal offense for the first time.

first of·fi·cer ▶ n. **1** the first mate on a merchant ship. **2** the second in command to the captain on an aircraft.

first per·son ▶ n. the form of a pronoun or verb used to refer to oneself, or to a group including oneself.

first prin·ci·ples ▶ pl.n. the basic or fundamental concepts or assumptions on which a theory, system, or method is based.

first-rate ▶ adj. of the best class, quality, or condition; excellent.

first re·fus·al ▶ n. the privilege of deciding whether to accept or reject something before it is offered to others.

first re·spond·er ▶ n. someone designated or trained to respond to an emergency: *the department is extending its smallpox vaccination program to first responders.*

first run ▶ n. the period when a movie, play, or television program is first shown or performed: *this series was great during the first run and it is even better now.* ■ **first-run** adj.

first strike ▶ n. an opening attack with nuclear weapons.

first string ▶ n. **1** the best players on a sports team, who normally play the most. **2** the outstanding people or things in a group: *these aren't the first string of gangster movies.*

First World ▶ n. the industrialized capitalist countries of western Europe, North America, Japan, Australia, and New Zealand.

firth /fərTH/ ▶ n. a narrow inlet of the sea.

fis·cal /ˈfiskəl/ ▶ adj. **1** relating to financial matters. **2** relating to the income received by a government, especially as raised through taxes. ■ **fis·cal·ly** adv.

fis·cal year ▶ n. a year as reckoned for taxing or accounting purposes.

fish¹ /fiSH/ ▶ n. (pl. same or **fishes**) **1** a cold-blooded animal with a backbone, gills, and fins, living in water. **2** the flesh of fish as food. **3** informal a person who is slightly strange: *he's an odd fish.* ▶ v. **1** catch fish with a net or hook and line. **2** (**fish something out**) pull or take something out of water or a container. **3** grope or feel for something hidden. **4** (**fish for**) try to get a response or information by indirect means: *I wasn't fishing for compliments.* ■ **fish·a·ble** adj. **fish·ing** n.
– PHRASES **a big fish** an important person. **a cold fish** a person who is unfriendly or shows little emotion. **a fish out of water** a person who feels out of place in their surroundings. **have other** (or **bigger**) **fish to fry** have more important matters to deal with.

> USAGE
> The normal plural of **fish** is **fish** (*he caught two huge fish*), but the older form **fishes** is still used when referring to different kinds of fish: *freshwater fishes of Pennsylvania.*

fish² ▶ n. **1** (also **fishplate**) a flat piece fixed across a joint to strengthen or connect it, e.g., in railroad track. **2** a long curved piece of wood lashed to a ship's damaged mast or spar as a temporary repair.

fish and chips ▶ n. batter-fried fish fillets served

with french fries.

fish·bowl /'fisʜ‚bōl/ ▸ n. a round glass bowl for keeping pet fish in.

fish·cake /'fisʜ‚kāk/ ▸ n. a patty of shredded fish and mashed potato.

fish·er /'fisʜər/ ▸ n. old use a fisherman.

fish·er·man /'fisʜərmən/ ▸ n. (pl. **fishermen**) a person who catches fish for a living or for sport.

fish·er·y /'fisʜərē/ ▸ n. (pl. **fisheries**) **1** a place where fish are reared, or caught in large numbers. **2** the occupation or industry of catching or rearing fish.

fish·eye /'fisʜ‚ī/ ▸ n. a very wide-angle lens with a field of vision covering up to 180°, the scale being reduced toward the edges.

fish·hook /'fisʜ‚ho͝ok/ ▸ n. a hook, typically barbed and baited, for catching fish.

fish·ing line ▸ n. a long thread of silk or nylon attached to a baited hook and used for catching fish.

fish·ing rod ▸ n. a long, tapering rod to which a fishing line is attached.

fish·meal /'fisʜ‚mēl/ ▸ n. ground dried fish used as fertilizer or animal feed.

fish·mon·ger /'fisʜ‚mənɢɡər, -‚mänɢɡər/ ▸ n. a person or store that sells fish for food.

fish·net /'fisʜ‚net/ ▸ n. an open mesh fabric resembling a fishing net.

fish·plate /'fisʜ‚plāt/ ▸ n. another term for FISH².

fish sauce ▸ n. a Thai and Vietnamese sauce used as a flavoring or condiment, prepared from fermented anchovies and salt.

fish·stick /'fisʜ‚stik/ ▸ n. a small oblong piece of flaked or ground fish coated in batter or breadcrumbs.

fish story ▸ n. an incredible or far-fetched story.

fish·tail /'fisʜ‚tāl/ ▸ n. a thing that is forked like a fish's tail. ▸ v. (of a vehicle) travel with its rear end sliding uncontrollably from side to side.

fish·wife /'fisʜ‚wīf/ ▸ n. (pl. **fishwives** /-‚wīvz/) a woman with a loud, harsh voice.

fish·y /'fisʜē/ ▸ adj. (**fishier**, **fishiest**) **1** referring to or resembling a fish or fish. **2** informal causing feelings of doubt or suspicion.

fis·sile /'fisəl, 'fis‚īl/ ▸ adj. **1** (of an atom or element) able to undergo nuclear fission. **2** (chiefly of rock) easily split.

fis·sion /'fisʜən, 'fizʜən/ ▸ n. **1** the action of splitting into two or more parts. **2** a reaction in which an atomic nucleus splits in two, releasing much energy. **3** Biology reproduction by means of a cell dividing into two or more new cells. ▸ v. (of atoms) undergo fission. ■ **fis·sion·a·ble** adj.

fis·sure /'fisʜər/ ▸ n. a long, narrow crack. ▸ v. split; crack.

fist /fist/ ▸ n. a person's hand when the fingers are bent in toward the palm and held there tightly. ■ **fist·ed** adj. **fist·ful** /'fist‚fo͝ol/ n.

fist·fight /'fist‚fīt/ ▸ n. a fight with bare fists.

fist·i·cuffs /'fisti‚kəfs/ ▸ pl.n. fighting with the fists.

fis·tu·la /'fisᴄʜələ/ ▸ n. (pl. **fistulas** or **fistulae** /'fisᴄʜəlē/) an abnormal or surgically made passage between a hollow or tubular organ and the body surface, or between two hollow or tubular organs.

fit¹ /fit/ ▸ adj. (**fitter**, **fittest**) **1** of a suitable quality, standard, or type: *food fit for human consumption.* **2** having the necessary qualities or skills to do something competently. **3** in good health, especially through regular physical exercise. ▸ v. (**fits, fitting, fitted** or **fit**) **1** be of the right shape and size for someone or something. **2** be of the right size, shape, or number to occupy a position or place: *we can all fit in her car.* **3** fix something into place. **4** (often **be fitted with**) provide something with a component or article. **5** join together to form a whole. **6** be suitable for; match: *the punishment should fit the crime.* **7** make someone suitable for a role or task: *a business degree fits the student for a professional career.* **8** (usu. **be fitted for**) try clothing on someone in order to make or alter it to the correct size. ▸ n. the way in which something fits. ■ **fit·ly** adv. **fit·ness** n.

– PHRASES **fit in** be compatible with other members of a group or in harmony with other elements of a situation. **fit someone/thing in** (or **into**) manage to find time to see someone or do something. **fit someone/thing out** (or **up**) provide someone or something with necessary items. **see fit** consider it correct or acceptable.

fit² ▸ n. **1** a sudden attack of an illness, such as epilepsy, in which a person makes violent, uncontrolled movements and often loses consciousness. **2** a sudden short period of coughing, laughter, etc. **3** a sudden burst of intense feeling: *a fit of jealous rage.*

– PHRASES **in** (or **by**) **fits and starts** with irregular bursts of activity.

fit·ful /'fitfəl/ ▸ adj. not continuous, regular, or steady: *a few hours' fitful sleep.* ■ **fit·ful·ly** adv. **fit·ful·ness** n.

fit·ted /'fitid/ ▸ adj. **1** made to fill a space or to cover something closely. **2** chiefly Brit. (of a room) equipped with matching units of furniture.

fit·ter /'fitər/ ▸ n. **1** a person who puts together or installs machinery, engine parts, or other equipment: *a pipe fitter.* **2** a person who supervises the cutting, fitting, or alteration of clothes or shoes.

fit·ting /'fitinɢ/ ▸ n. **1** a small part attached to a piece of furniture or equipment. **2** an occasion when one tries on a garment that is being made or altered. ▸ adj. appropriate; right or proper. ■ **fit·ting·ly** adv.

fit·ting room ▸ n. a room in a store where one can try on clothes before buying them.

five /fīv/ ▸ cardinal number one more than four; 5. (Roman numeral: **v** or **V**.) ■ **five·fold** /'fīv‚fōld/ adj. & adv.

five o'clock shad·ow ▸ n. a slight growth of beard visible on a man's chin several hours after he has shaved.

fiv·er /'fīvər/ informal ▸ n. **1** a five-dollar bill. **2** Brit. a five-pound note.

five-spice ▸ n. a blend of five powdered spices, typically fennel seeds, cinnamon, cloves, star anise, and peppercorns, used in Chinese cooking.

five-star ▸ adj. **1** (especially of a hotel or restaurant) denoting the highest class or quality: *a five-star luxury resort.* **2** (in the armed forces) referring to the highest military rank, awarded only in wartime: *a five-star general.*

fix /fiks/ ▸ v. **1** attach or position something securely. **2** (**fix on**) direct or be directed unwaveringly toward: *her gaze fixed on Jess.* **3** decide or settle on: *no date has yet been fixed.* **4** make unchanging or permanent: *the rate of interest is fixed for two years.* **5** repair something.

6 make arrangements for something. **7** (**be fixing to do something**) informal be intending or planning to do something: *you're fixing to get into trouble.* **8** informal influence the outcome of something in an underhanded way. **9** informal provide someone with food or drink: *I'll fix you a sandwich.* ▶ n. informal **1** a difficult or awkward situation. **2** a dose of a narcotic drug to which one is addicted. **3** an act of fixing something. ■ **fix·a·ble** adj.
– PHRASES **fix someone up** informal **1** provide someone with something: *they'll fix him up with a room.* **2** arrange for someone to meet a possible romantic partner. **fix something up** arrange or organize something. **get a fix on** find out the position, nature, or facts of.

fix·ate /'fik,sāt/ ▶ v. (**fixate on** or **be fixated on**) be obsessively interested in someone or something.

fix·a·tion /fik'sāsHən/ ▶ n. **1** an obsessive interest in someone or something. **2** the process by which some plants and microorganisms combine chemically with nitrogen or carbon dioxide in the air to form solid compounds.

fix·a·tive /'fiksətiv/ ▶ n. a substance used to fix, protect, or stabilize something.

fixed /fikst/ ▶ adj. **1** fastened securely in position. **2** not changing or able to be changed. **3** (of contests) with the outcome dishonestly arranged in advance: *charges of fixed games on the front pages.* **4** (**fixed for**) informal situated in terms of: *how are you fixed for cash?* ■ **fix·ed·ly** /'fiksidlē/ adv.

fixed as·sets ▶ pl.n. assets that are bought for long-term use and are not likely to be converted quickly into cash, such as land, buildings, and equipment. Compare with CURRENT ASSETS.

fixed-in·come ▶ adj. **1** Finance (of investments) paying a constant rate of return: *fixed-income mutual funds.* **2** having an income that does not increase: *fixed-income seniors.*

fixed-wing ▶ adj. (of aircraft) of the conventional type as opposed to those with rotating wings, such as helicopters.

fix·er /'fiksər/ ▶ n. **1** a person who arranges or manipulates something, especially in an illicit or devious way: *alleged price fixers who avoided arrest.* **2** a substance used for fixing a photographic image.

fix·ings /'fiksiNGz/ ▶ pl.n. the ingredients necessary to prepare a dish or meal.

fix·i·ty /'fiksitē/ ▶ n. the state of being unchanging or permanent.

fix·ture /'fiksCHər/ ▶ n. **1** a piece of equipment or furniture that is fixed in position in a building or vehicle. **2** (**fixtures**) articles attached to a house or land and considered legally part of it so that they normally remain in place when an owner moves. **3** informal a person or thing that has become firmly established in a particular place.

fizz /fiz/ ▶ v. **1** (of a liquid) produce bubbles of gas and make a hissing sound. **2** make a buzzing or crackling sound. ▶ n. **1** the quality of being fizzy. **2** informal a fizzy drink, especially sparkling wine. **3** liveliness.

fiz·zle /'fizəl/ ▶ v. **1** make a feeble hissing or spluttering sound. **2** (**fizzle out**) gradually become less successful; end in a disappointing way.

fizz·y /'fizē/ ▶ adj. (**fizzier, fizziest**) (of a drink) containing bubbles of gas. ■ **fizz·i·ness** n.

fjord /fē'ôrd, fyôrd/ (also **fiord**) ▶ n. a long, narrow, deep inlet of the sea between high cliffs, found especially in Norway.

FL ▶ abbr. Florida.

fl. ▶ abbr. **1** floruit. **2** fluid.

Fla. ▶ abbr. Florida.

flab /flab/ ▶ n. informal soft, loose excess flesh on a person's body.

flab·ber·gast /'flabər,gast/ ▶ v. (usu. as adj. **flabbergasted**) informal surprise someone greatly.

flab·by /'flabē/ ▶ adj. (**flabbier, flabbiest**) **1** (of a part of a person's body) soft, loose, and fleshy. **2** lacking force, strength, or tight control; not impressive or effective: *a flabby script.* ■ **flab·bi·ness** n.

flac·cid /'fla(k)səd/ ▶ adj. soft and limp. ■ **flac·cid·i·ty** /fla(k)'sidətē/ n.

flack ▶ n. variant spelling of FLAK.

flag[1] /flag/ ▶ n. **1** an oblong piece of cloth that, usually attached to a pole, is displayed as a symbol of a country or organization or as a signal. **2** a device or symbol resembling a flag, used as a marker. ▶ v. (**flags, flagging, flagged**) **1** mark something for attention. **2** direct or alert someone by waving a flag or using hand signals. **3** (**flag someone down**) signal to a driver to stop.
– PHRASES **fly the flag 1** (of a ship) be registered in a particular country and sail under its flag. **2** represent one's country or show that one is a member of a party or organization.

flag[2] ▶ n. a flagstone. ■ **flagged** adj.

flag[3] ▶ n. a plant of the iris family, with long sword-shaped leaves.

flag[4] ▶ v. (**flags, flagging, flagged**) **1** become tired or less enthusiastic. **2** (as adj. **flagging**) becoming weaker or less dynamic: *the country's flagging economy.*

Flag Day ▶ n. June 14, the anniversary of the adoption of the official US flag in 1777.

flag·el·late[1] /'flajə,lāt/ ▶ v. whip someone, either as a form of religious punishment or for sexual pleasure. ■ **flag·el·la·tion** /,flajə'lāsHən/ n.

flag·el·late[2] /'flajələt, -,lāt/ ▶ adj. (of a single-celled organism) having one or more flagella used for swimming.

fla·gel·lum /,flə'jeləm/ ▶ n. (pl. **flagella** /-'jelə/) Biology a long, thin projection that enables many single-celled organisms to swim.

flag foot·ball ▶ n. a form of football in which pulling a strip of plastic (a flag) from a ball carrier's loosely attached belt is the equivalent of tackling.

flag·on /'flagən/ ▶ n. a large bottle or other container in which wine, cider, or beer is sold or served.

flag·pole /'flag,pōl/ ▶ n. a pole used for flying a flag.

fla·grant /'flāgrənt/ ▶ adj. very obvious and unashamed: *a flagrant violation of the law.* ■ **fla·grant·ly** adv.

flag·ship /'flag,sHip/ ▶ n. **1** the ship in a fleet that carries the commanding admiral. **2** the best or most important thing owned or produced by an organization.

flag·staff /'flag,staf/ ▶ n. a flagpole.

flag·stone /'flag,stōn/ ▶ n. a flat square or rectangular stone slab, used for paving.

flag stop ▶ n. a bus stop at which the bus halts only if requested by a passenger or if signaled.

flag-wav·ing ▸ n. a display of extreme patriotism.

flail /flāl/ ▸ v. **1** swing or wave one's arms or legs wildly. **2** (usu. **flail around/about**) struggle to move while swinging one's arms and legs wildly. ▸ n. a tool or machine with a swinging action, used for threshing.

flair /fler/ ▸ n. **1** a natural ability or talent. **2** stylishness.

> USAGE
> On the confusion of **flair** with **flare**, see the note at **FLARE**.

flak /flak/ (also **flack**) ▸ n. **1** antiaircraft fire. **2** strong criticism.

flake[1] /flāk/ ▸ n. a small, flat, very thin piece of something. ▸ v. **1** come away from a surface in flakes. **2** separate something into flakes.

flake[2] ▸ v. (**flake out**) informal fall asleep or drop from exhaustion.

flak jack·et ▸ n. a sleeveless jacket made of heavy fabric reinforced with metal, worn as protection against bullets and shrapnel.

flak·y /'flākē/ ▸ adj. (**flakier, flakiest**) **1** breaking or separating easily into flakes. **2** informal unconventional or eccentric. ■ **flak·i·ness** n.

flam·bé /fläm'bā/ ▸ adj. (after a noun) (of food) covered with liquor and set alight briefly: *steak flambé.* ▸ v. (**flambés, flambéing, flambéed** /-'bād/) cover food with liquor and set it alight briefly.

flam·beau /'flam,bō/ ▸ n. (pl. **flambeaus** or **flambeaux** /-,bōz/) **1** a flaming torch. **2** a branched candlestick.

flam·boy·ant /flam'boiənt/ ▸ adj. **1** confident and lively in a way that attracts the attention of other people. **2** brightly colored or highly decorated. ■ **flam·boy·ance** n. **flam·boy·ant·ly** adv.

flame /flām/ ▸ n. **1** a hot glowing body of ignited gas produced by something on fire. **2** a brilliant orange-red color. ▸ v. **1** give off flames. **2** set something alight. **3** (of a strong emotion) appear suddenly and fiercely. **4** (of a person's face) become red with embarrassment or anger. **5** informal send an abusive email message to someone.
– PHRASES **burst into flame** (or **flames**) suddenly begin to burn fiercely: *the grass looked ready to burst into flame.* **old flame** informal a former lover.

fla·men·co /flə'meNGkō/ ▸ n. a style of Spanish guitar music accompanied by singing and dancing.

flame·proof /'flām,proof/ ▸ adj. **1** (of fabric) treated so as to be nonflammable. **2** (of cookware) able to be used either in an oven or on a stovetop.

flame·throw·er /'flām,THrōər/ ▸ n. a weapon that sprays out burning fuel.

flam·ing /'flāmiNG/ ▸ adj. **1** sending out flames. **2** very hot. **3** full of passion: *the ache of flaming desire.* **4** full of anger: *their flaming disputes.* **5** informal expressing annoyance: *that flaming dog!*

fla·min·go /flə'miNGgō/ ▸ n. (pl. **flamingos** or **flamingoes**) a wading bird with mainly pink or scarlet plumage and a long neck and legs.

flam·ma·ble /'flaməbəl/ ▸ adj. easily set on fire. ■ **flam·ma·bil·i·ty** /,flamə'bilətē/ n.

> USAGE
> For advice on the words **flammable** and **inflammable**, see the note at **INFLAMMABLE**.

flan /flan/ ▸ n. **1** a custard with a caramel topping. **2** a baked dish consisting of an open-topped pastry case with a savory or sweet filling.

flange /flanj/ ▸ n. a projecting flat rim on an object for strengthening it or attaching it to something. ■ **flanged** adj.

flank /flaNGk/ ▸ n. **1** the side of a person's or animal's body between the ribs and the hip. **2** the side of something such as a building or mountain. **3** the left or right side of a group of people. ▸ v. be situated on each or on one side of: *the road is flanked by avenues of trees.*

flank·er /'flaNGkər/ ▸ n. **1** Rugby a wing forward. **2** Military a fortification to the side of a force or position.

flan·nel /'flanl/ ▸ n. **1** a kind of soft-woven woolen or cotton fabric. **2** (**flannels**) trousers made of woolen flannel.

flap /flap/ ▸ v. (**flaps, flapping, flapped**) move or be moved up and down or from side to side. ▸ n. **1** a piece of something attached on one side only, that covers an opening. **2** a hinged or sliding section of an aircraft wing, used to control upward movement. **3** a single flapping movement. **4** informal a state of worry or panic. ■ **flap·py** adj.

flap·jack /'flap,jak/ ▸ n. a pancake.

flap·per /'flapər/ ▸ n. informal (in the 1920s) a fashionable and unconventional young woman.

flare /fle(ə)r/ ▸ n. **1** a sudden brief burst of flame or light. **2** a device producing a very bright flame as a signal or marker. **3** a gradual widening toward the hem of a garment. ▸ v. **1** burn or shine with a sudden intensity. **2** (usu. **flare up**) suddenly start or become stronger or more violent: *rioting flared up in other towns and cities.* **3** (**flare up**) suddenly become angry. **4** gradually become wider at one end.

> USAGE
> Do not confuse **flare** with **flair**: **flare** means 'burn' or 'gradually become wider,' whereas **flair** means 'a natural ability or talent.' Trousers whose legs widen from the knees down are **flared**, not **flaired**.

flare-up ▸ n. a sudden outburst, especially of violence or an undesirable medical symptom: *a flare-up between the two countries.*

flash /flash/ ▸ v. **1** shine or cause to shine with a bright but brief or irregular light. **2** move or pass swiftly: *the scenery flashed by.* **3** display or be displayed briefly or repeatedly: *a message flashed up on the screen.* **4** informal display something in an obvious way so as to impress people: *they flash their money around.* **5** informal (of a man) show the genitals in public. ▸ n. **1** a sudden brief burst of bright light. **2** a camera attachment that produces a flash of light, for taking photographs in poor light. **3** a sudden or brief occurrence: *a flash of inspiration.* **4** a bright patch of color. ▸ adj. informal stylish or expensive in a way designed to attract attention and impress people; flashy.
– PHRASES **flash in the pan** a sudden but brief success. **in a flash** very quickly.

flash·back /'flash,bak/ ▸ n. **1** a scene in a movie or novel set in a time earlier than the main story. **2** a sudden vivid memory of a past event.

flash·bulb /'flash,bəlb/ ▸ n. a light bulb for one-time use that flashes in order to illuminate a photographic subject.

flash·card /'flasH,kärd/ ▶ n. a card containing a small amount of clearly displayed information, held up for students to see, as an aid to learning.

flash drive ▶ n. a removable data storage device containing flash memory that has no moving parts.

flash·er /'flasHər/ ▶ n. **1** a device or signal in which a light flashes on and off. **2** informal a person, especially a man, who exposes his genitals in public.

flash flood ▶ n. a sudden local flood resulting from extreme rainfall.

flash-for·ward ▶ n. a narrative device, used especially in movies, in which the action jumps to a future scene or development : *a flash-forward set in a mental clinic.* ▶ v. jump to future time in a narrative.

flash·ing /'flasHiNG/ ▶ n. a strip of metal used to seal the junction of a roof with another surface.

flash·light /'flasH,līt/ ▶ n. **1** a battery-operated portable light. **2** a light giving an intense flash, used for photographing at night or indoors.

flash mem·o·ry ▶ n. Computing memory that retains data in the absence of a power supply.

flash·point /'flasH,point/ ▶ n. **1** a point or place at which anger or violence flares up. **2** Chemistry the temperature at which a flammable compound gives off enough vapor to ignite in air.

flash·y /'flasHē/ ▶ adj. (**flashier, flashiest**) stylish or expensive in a way designed to attract attention and impress other people. ■ **flash·i·ly** adv. **flash·i·ness** n.

flask /flask/ ▶ n. **1** a conical or round bottle with a narrow neck. **2** chiefly Brit. a thermos. **3** a hip flask. **4** Brit. a lead-lined container for radioactive nuclear waste.

flat[1] /flat/ ▶ adj. (**flatter, flattest**) **1** having a level and even surface. **2** not sloping; horizontal. **3** with a level surface and little height or depth: *a flat cap.* **4** (of shoes) without high heels. **5** flat-chested. **6** without liveliness or interest: *a flat voice.* **7** (of a carbonated drink) no longer fizzy. **8** (of something kept inflated) having lost some or all of its air. **9** (of a fee, charge, or price) unvarying; fixed. **10** (of a negative statement) definite and firm: *a flat denial.* **11** (of musical sound) below true or normal pitch. **12** (after a noun) (of a note or key) lower by a half step than a particular note or key: *E flat.* ▶ adv. **1** in or to a horizontal position. **2** so as to become level and even. **3** informal completely; absolutely: *she turned him down flat.* **4** emphasizing the speed of an action: *in ten minutes flat.* ▶ n. **1** the flat part of something. **2** (**flats**) an area of low level ground, especially near water. **3** informal a flat tire. **4** an upright section of stage scenery. **5** a musical note that is a semitone lower than the corresponding one of natural pitch, indicated by the sign ♭. ■ **flat·ly** adv. **flat·ness** n. **flat·tish** adj.
– PHRASES **fall flat** fail to produce the intended effect. **flat out** as fast or as hard as possible.

flat[2] ▶ n. chiefly Brit. an apartment.

flat·bed /'flat,bed/ ▶ adj. referring to a vehicle whose body consists of an open platform without raised sides or ends, used for carrying loads. ▶ n. **1** a flatbed vehicle, or its open platform. **2** Computing a scanner or other device that keeps paper flat during use.

flat·bread /'flat,bred/ ▶ n. an unleavened bread.

flat·chest·ed ▶ adj. (of a woman) having small breasts.

flat feet ▶ pl. n. feet with arches that are lower than usual.

flat·fish /'flat,fisH/ ▶ n. (pl. same or **flatfishes**) a sea fish, such as a flounder or sole, that swims on its side with both eyes on the upper side of its flattened body.

flat·foot·ed ▶ adj. **1** having flat feet. **2** informal clumsy.

flat·i·ron /'flat,īərn/ ▶ n. historical an iron heated on a hotplate or fire.

flat·line /'flat,līn/ ▶ v. informal die. ■ **flat·lin·er** n.

flat·ten /'flatn/ ▶ v. **1** make or become flat or flatter. **2** informal knock someone down. ■ **flat·ten·er** n.

flat·ter /'flatər/ ▶ v. **1** praise or compliment someone excessively or insincerely. **2** (**be flattered**) feel honored and pleased. **3** (**flatter oneself**) believe something good about oneself, especially something that has no basis in reality. **4** (of clothing or a color) make someone appear attractive. **5** (often as adj. **flattering**) paint or draw someone so that they appear more attractive than in reality. ■ **flat·ter·er** n.

flat·ter·y /'flatərē/ ▶ n. (pl. **flatteries**) excessive or insincere praise.

flat·top /'flat,täp/ ▶ n. **1** a short haircut in which hair on top of the head is trimmed to a level plane. **2** informal an aircraft carrier.

flat·u·lent /'flacHələnt/ ▶ adj. suffering from a buildup of gas in the intestines or stomach. ■ **flat·u·lence** n.

fla·tus /'flātəs/ ▶ n. Medicine gas from the stomach or intestines, especially when voided through the rectum.

flat·ware /'flat,we(ə)r/ ▶ n. **1** eating utensils such as knives, forks, and spoons. **2** relatively flat dishes such as plates and saucers.

flat·worm /'flat,wərm/ ▶ n. a type of worm, such as a tapeworm, with a flattened body that lacks blood vessels.

flaunt /flônt, flänt/ ▶ v. display something proudly or in a way intended to attract attention.

USAGE
Be careful not to confuse **flaunt** with **flout**. **Flaunt** means 'display something in a way intended to attract attention' (*some students like to flaunt their wealth*), while **flout** means 'openly fail to follow a rule or convention' (*the tendency of some athletes to flout regulations*).

flau·tist /'flôtist, 'flou-/ ▶ n. another term for FLUTIST.

fla·vo·noid /'flāvə,noid/ ▶ n. any of a group of naturally occurring chemical compounds including several white or yellow plant pigments.

fla·vor /'flāvər/ (Brit. **flavour**) ▶ n. **1** the distinctive taste of a food or drink. **2** a particular quality or atmosphere: *the resort has a distinctly Italian flavor.* ▶ v. alter or add to the taste of food or drink by adding a particular ingredient: *cottage cheese flavored with chives.* ■ **fla·vor·ful** adj. **fla·vor·less** adj. **fla·vor·some** adj.
– PHRASES **flavor of the month** a person or thing that is currently popular.

fla·vor·ing /'flāvəriNG/ ▶ n. a substance used to add to or alter the flavor of a food or drink.

flavour, etc. ▶ n. British spelling of FLAVOR, etc.

flaw /flô/ ▶ n. **1** a mark or flaw that spoils something. **2** a fundamental weakness or mistake. ▶ v. (usu. as adj. **flawed**) spoil or

weaken: *a flawed genius*. ■ **flaw·less adj.**
flaw·less·ly adv.

flax /flaks/ ▶ n. **1** a blue-flowered plant that is
grown for its seed (flaxseed or linseed) and for
thread made from its stalks. **2** thread made from
flax, used to make linen.

flax·en /'flaksən/ ▶ adj. literary (of hair) pale yellow.

flax·seed /'flak(s),sēd/ ▶ n. the seeds of the flax
plant used as a nutritional supplement rich in
omega-3 fatty acids, and (especially when called
LINSEED) as the source of linseed oil.

flay /flā/ ▶ v. **1** strip the skin from a body or
carcass. **2** whip or beat someone so hard that
some of their skin is removed. **3** criticize
someone harshly.

flea /flē/ ▶ n. a small wingless jumping insect that
feeds on the blood of mammals and birds.
– PHRASES **a flea in one's ear** a sharp reprimand.

flea-bit·ten ▶ adj. **1** bitten by or infested with
fleas. **2** shabby or run-down.

flea col·lar ▶ n. an insecticide-treated collar for a
pet dog or cat.

flea mar·ket ▶ n. an indoor or outdoor market
selling the secondhand goods of various vendors
at low prices.

fleck /flek/ ▶ n. **1** a very small patch of color or
light. **2** a small particle: *flecks of dust*. ▶ v. mark
or dot with small areas of a particular color or
small pieces of something: *her brown hair was
flecked with gray*.

fled /fled/ ▶ past and past participle of FLEE.

fledge /flej/ ▶ v. **1** (of a young bird) develop wing
feathers that are large enough for flight. **2** (as adj.
fledged) having just taken on a particular role: *a
newly fledged Detective Inspector*.

fledg·ling /'flejliNG/ (also **fledgeling**) ▶ n. a
young bird that has just developed wing feathers
that are large enough for flight. ▶ adj. new and
inexperienced: *a fledgling democracy*.

flee /flē/ ▶ v. (**flees, fleeing**; past and past part. **fled**
/fled/) run away.

fleece /flēs/ ▶ n. **1** the wool coat of a sheep.
2 a soft, warm fabric with a texture similar
to sheep's wool, or a jacket made from this.
▶ v. informal swindle someone by charging them
too much money. ■ **fleec·y adj.**

fleet¹ /flēt/ ▶ n. **1** a group of ships sailing
together. **2** (**the fleet**) a country's navy. **3** a
number of vehicles or aircraft operating
together.

fleet² ▶ adj. fast and nimble. ■ **fleet·ness n.**
– PHRASES **fleet of foot** able to walk or move
swiftly.

fleet³ ▶ v. literary move or pass quickly.

Fleet Ad·mi·ral ▶ n. an admiral of the highest
rank in the US Navy.

fleet·ing /'flētiNG/ ▶ adj. lasting for a very short
time. ■ **fleet·ing·ly adv.**

Flem·ing /'flemiNG/ ▶ n. **1** a Flemish person. **2** a
member of the Flemish-speaking people living in
northern and western Belgium.

Flem·ish /'flemiSH/ ▶ n. **1** (**the Flemish**) the
people of Flanders, a region divided between
Belgium, France, and the Netherlands. **2** the
Dutch language as spoken in Flanders.
▶ adj. relating to the Flemish people or language.

flesh /fleSH/ ▶ n. **1** the soft substance in the body
consisting of muscle tissue and fat. **2** the edible
soft part of a fruit or vegetable. **3** (**the flesh**) the
physical aspects and needs of the human body:

pleasures of the flesh. ▶ v. (**flesh something
out**) give more information or details about
something: *the governor fleshed out his economic
philosophy*.
– PHRASES **flesh and blood 1** a close relative;
one's family. **2** used to emphasize people's
physical and emotional reality, often in contrast
to something abstract, spiritual, or mechanical:
*an embodiment of feminine ideals rather than a
flesh and blood woman*. **in the flesh** in person or
(of a thing) in its actual state. **make someone's
flesh crawl** make someone feel fear, horror, or
disgust.

flesh-col·ored ▶ adj. of the color of European
people's skin: *wildly undulating flesh-colored
clay tiles*.

flesh·ly /'fleSHlē/ ▶ adj. (**fleshlier, fleshliest**)
relating to the body and its needs.

flesh·pots /'fleSH,päts/ ▶ pl.n. places where people
can satisfy their sexual desires.

flesh wound ▶ n. a wound that breaks the skin
but does not damage bones or vital organs.

flesh·y /'fleSHē/ ▶ adj. (**fleshier, fleshiest**)
1 having a lot of flesh; plump. **2** (of leaves
or fruit) soft and thick. **3** resembling flesh.
■ **flesh·i·ness n.**

fleur-de-lis /,flər dl'ē, ,floor-/ (also **fleur-
de-lys**) ▶ n. (pl. **fleurs-de-lis** pronunc. same) a
representation of a lily made up of three petals
bound together near their bases.

flew /floo/ ▶ past of FLY¹.

flex /fleks/ ▶ v. **1** bend a limb or joint. **2** tighten
a muscle. **3** warp or bend and then return to the
proper shape.

flex-fu·el ▶ adj. referring to a motor vehicle that
will run on gasoline, ethanol, or the two in
any combination: *flex-fuel subcompacts have
captured 20% of Brazil's new car market*.

flex·i·ble /'fleksəbəl/ ▶ adj. **1** capable of bending
easily without breaking. **2** able to change or be
changed in response to different circumstances.
■ **flex·i·bil·i·ty** /,fleksə'bilətē/ n. **flex·i·bly** /-blē/
adv.

flex·ion /'flekSHən/ (also **flection**) ▶ n. the action
of bending or the condition of being bent.

flex·or /'flek,sor, -,sôr/ ▶ n. a muscle whose
contraction bends a limb or other part of the
body.

flex·time /'fleks,tīm/ ▶ n. a system by which
employees work an agreed total number of hours
but have some flexibility as to when they start
and finish work each day.

flick /flik/ ▶ v. **1** make a sudden sharp movement.
2 hit or remove something with a flick of the
fingers: *she flicked some ash off her sleeve*.
3 (**flick through**) look quickly through a book
or a collection of papers. ▶ n. **1** a sudden sharp
movement up and down or from side to side.
2 the sudden release of a finger or thumb held
bent against another finger. **3** informal a movie.

flick·er¹ /'flikər/ ▶ v. **1** shine or burn unsteadily.
2 (of a feeling) be felt or shown briefly. **3** make
small, quick movements. ▶ n. **1** a flickering
movement or light. **2** a brief feeling or
indication of emotion: *a flicker of alarm*.

flick·er² ▶ n. any of several colorful North
American woodpeckers that are often ground
feeders.

fli·er /'flīər/ ▶ n. variant spelling of FLYER.

flight /flīt/ ▶ n. **1** the action or process of flying.
2 a journey made in an aircraft or in space. **3** the

path of something through the air. **4** the action of running away: *the enemy were in flight.* **5** a very imaginative idea or story: *a flight of fancy.* **6** a flock of birds flying together. **7** a series of steps between floors or levels. **8** a unit of about six aircraft operating together. **9** the tail of an arrow or dart.
– PHRASES **take flight 1** (of a bird) take off and fly. **2** run away.

flight at·tend·ant ▶ n. a steward or stewardess on an aircraft.

flight deck ▶ n. **1** the cockpit of a large aircraft. **2** the deck of an aircraft carrier, used as a runway.

flight feath·er ▶ n. any of the large feathers in a bird's wing that support it during flight.

flight·less /'flītlis/ ▶ adj. (of a bird or insect) naturally unable to fly.

flight path ▶ n. the route taken by an aircraft or spacecraft.

flight re·cord·er ▶ n. an electronic device in an aircraft that records technical details during a flight, used in the event of an accident to discover its cause.

flight·y /'flītē/ ▶ adj. (**flightier, flightiest**) irresponsible and uninterested in serious things. ■ **flight·i·ness** n.

flim·flam /'flim‚flam/ ▶ n. informal **1** insincere and unconvincing talk. **2** a confidence trick.

flim·sy /'flimzē/ ▶ adj. (**flimsier, flimsiest**) **1** weak and fragile. **2** (of clothing) light and thin. **3** unconvincing: *a flimsy excuse.* ■ **flim·si·ly** adv. **flim·si·ness** n.

flinch /flincH/ ▶ v. **1** make a quick, nervous movement as an instinctive reaction to fear or pain. **2** (**flinch from**) avoid something through fear or anxiety.

fling /fliNG/ ▶ v. (past and past part. **flung** /floNG/) **1** throw something forcefully. **2** move or go suddenly and forcefully: *he flung out his arm.* **3** (**fling oneself into**) take part in an activity or enterprise with great enthusiasm. **4** (**fling something on/off**) put on or take off clothes carelessly and rapidly. ▶ n. **1** a short period of enjoyment or wild behavior. **2** a short sexual relationship. **3** a Highland fling.

flint /flint/ ▶ n. **1** a hard gray rock consisting of nearly pure silica. **2** a piece of this rock. **3** a piece of flint or a metal alloy, used to produce a spark in a cigarette lighter.

flint·lock /'flint‚läk/ ▶ n. an old-fashioned type of gun fired by a spark from a flint.

flint·y /'flintē/ ▶ adj. (**flintier, flintiest**) **1** relating to, containing, or resembling flint. **2** stern and showing no emotion: *a flinty stare.* ■ **flint·i·ly** adv. **flint·i·ness** n.

flip /flip/ ▶ v. (**flips, flipping, flipped**) **1** turn over with a sudden, quick movement: *the plane flipped over.* **2** press a button or switch in order to turn a machine or device on or off. **3** move or toss something with a quick action. **4** (**flip through**) look through a book, magazine, etc. **5** (also **flip one's lid**) informal suddenly become very angry or lose one's self-control. ▶ n. a flipping action or movement. ▶ adj. not serious or respectful.

flip chart ▶ n. a very large pad of paper bound so that pages can be turned over at the top, used on a stand at presentations.

flip-flop ▶ n. a light sandal with a thong that passes between the big and second toes.

flip·pant /'flipənt/ ▶ adj. not treating something with the appropriate seriousness or respect. ■ **flip·pan·cy** /'flipənsē/ n. **flip·pant·ly** adv.

flip·per /'flipər/ ▶ n. **1** a broad, flat limb without fingers, used for swimming by sea animals such as seals and turtles. **2** each of a pair of flat rubber attachments worn on the feet for underwater swimming. **3** a pivoted arm in a pinball machine.

flip·ping /'flipiNG/ ▶ adj. Brit. informal used for emphasis or to express mild annoyance.

flip side ▶ n. informal **1** the reverse or less pleasant aspect of a situation. **2** dated the B-side of a pop single record.

flirt /flərt/ ▶ v. **1** behave as if one finds another person sexually attractive but without intending to have a relationship with them. **2** (**flirt with**) show a casual interest in an idea or activity. **3** (**flirt with**) deliberately behave in such a way as to risk danger or death. ▶ n. a person who likes to flirt. ■ **flir·ta·tion** /-'tāsHən/ n. **flirt·y** (**flirtier, flirtiest**) adj.

flir·ta·tious /‚flər'tāsHəs/ ▶ adj. liking to flirt with people. ■ **flir·ta·tious·ly** adv.

flit /flit/ ▶ v. (**flits, flitting, flitted**) move swiftly and lightly.

flit·ter /'flitər/ ▶ v. move quickly here and there.

float /flōt/ ▶ v. **1** rest on the surface of a liquid without sinking. **2** move slowly, hover, or be suspended in a liquid or the air: *clouds floated across the sky.* **3** put forward an idea as a suggestion or to test other people's reactions. **4** (as adj. **floating**) not settled or living permanently in one place: *the region's floating population.* **5** offer the shares of a company for sale on the stock market for the first time. **6** allow a currency to have a variable rate of exchange against other currencies. **7** provide funds to begin an enterprise with the expectation of being paid back with the enterprise's first proceeds: *would you float us the cash to stock our hotdog cart?* ▶ n. **1** a lightweight object or device designed to float on water. **2** a small floating object attached to a fishing line that moves when a fish bites. **3** a platform mounted on a truck and carrying a display in a procession. **4** a sum of money used for change at the beginning of a period of selling in a store, stall, etc. **5** a soft drink with a scoop of ice cream floating in it. **6** a hand tool with a rectangular blade used for smoothing plaster. ■ **float·er** n.

float·a·tion ▶ n. variant spelling of FLOTATION.

float·ing-point ▶ adj. Computing referring to a method of encoding numbers as two sequences of bits, one representing the number's significant digits and the other an exponent.

float·ing rib ▶ n. any of the lower ribs that are not attached directly to the breastbone.

float·plane /'flōt‚plān/ ▶ n. a seaplane.

float·y /'flōtē/ ▶ adj. giving the impression of floating, or of being able to float: *this floaty pale dress that swirls around her legs.*

floc·cu·lent /'fläkyələnt/ ▶ adj. having or resembling tufts of wool.

flock¹ /fläk/ ▶ n. **1** a number of birds moving or resting together. **2** a number of domestic animals, especially sheep, that are kept together. **3** (**a flock/flocks**) a large number or crowd: *a flock of children.* **4** a Christian congregation under the charge of a particular minister. ▶ v. gather or move in a flock or crowd: *tourists flocked to the area.*

flock² ▶ n. a soft material for stuffing cushions

and quilts, made of wool refuse or torn-up cloth.

floe /flō/ ▶ n. a sheet of floating ice.

flog /fläg/ ▶ v. (**flogs, flogging, flogged**) **1** beat someone with a whip or stick as a punishment. **2** informal talk about or promote something repeatedly or at excessive length: *the issue has been flogged to death already.* ■ **flog·ger** n.

flood /fləd/ ▶ n. **1** an overflow of a large amount of water over dry land. **2** (**the Flood**) the flood described in the Bible, brought by God because of the wickedness of the human race. **3** an overwhelming quantity of things or people appearing at once: *a flood of refugees.* **4** an outpouring of tears or emotion. **5** the rising of the tide. ▶ v. **1** cover or become covered with water in a flood. **2** (of a river) become swollen and overflow its banks. **3** (usu. **be flooded out**) drive someone out of their home or business with a flood: *most of the families who have been flooded out will receive compensation.* **4** arrive in very large numbers: *letters of support and sympathy flooded in.* **5** fill completely: *she flooded the room with light.* **6** overfill the carburetor of an engine with fuel, causing the engine to fail to start.

flood·gate /ˈfləd,gāt/ ▶ n. **1** a gate that can be opened or closed to control a flow of water, especially the lower gate of a lock. **2** (**the floodgates**) controls or restraints holding something back: *the case could open the floodgates for thousands of similar claims.*

flood·light /ˈfləd,līt/ ▶ n. a large, powerful light used to illuminate a stage, sports field, etc. ▶ v. (past and past part. **floodlit** /ˈfləd,lit/) (usu. as adj. **floodlit**) light up a stage, sports field, etc., with floodlights.

flood·plain /ˈfləd,plān/ ▶ n. an area of low-lying ground next to a river that regularly becomes flooded.

flood tide ▶ n. an incoming tide.

floor /flôr/ ▶ n. **1** the lower surface of a room. **2** a story of a building. **3** the bottom of the sea, a cave, etc. **4** a minimum level of prices or wages. **5** (**the floor**) the part of a lawmaking body in which members sit and from which they speak. **6** (**the floor**) the right to speak in a debate: *other speakers have the floor.* ▶ v. **1** provide a room with a floor. **2** informal knock someone to the ground. **3** informal completely baffle someone. ■ **floor·ing** n.

floor·board /ˈflôr,bôrd/ ▶ n. a long plank making up part of a wooden floor.

floor ex·er·cise ▶ n. **1** a routine of gymnastic exercises performed without the use of any apparatus. **2** any fitness exercise performed on the floor, without special equipment.

floor lamp ▶ n. a tall lamp designed to stand on the floor.

floor man·ag·er ▶ n. **1** an employee in a large store who supervises salespeople. **2** the stage manager of a television production.

floor plan ▶ n. a scale diagram of the arrangement of rooms in one story of a building.

floor sam·ple ▶ n. an article of merchandise that has been displayed in a store and is offered for sale at a reduced price.

floor show ▶ n. an entertainment presented on the floor of a nightclub or restaurant.

floo·zy /ˈflōōzē/ (also **floozie**) ▶ n. (pl. **floozies**) informal, chiefly humorous a girl or woman who has a reputation for promiscuity.

flop /fläp/ ▶ v. (**flops, flopping, flopped**) **1** hang or swing loosely. **2** sit or lie down heavily and clumsily. **3** informal fail totally. ▶ n. **1** a heavy, clumsy fall. **2** informal a total failure.

-flop ▶ comb.form Computing floating-point operations per second.

flop·house /ˈfläp,hous/ ▶ n. informal a place providing cheap accommodations for homeless people.

flop·py /ˈfläpē/ ▶ adj. (**floppier, floppiest**) not firm or rigid; flopping or hanging loosely. ▶ n. (pl. **floppies**) (also **floppy disk**) Computing a flexible removable magnetic disk used for storing data.

flo·ra /ˈflôrə/ ▶ n. (pl. **floras**) **1** the plants of a particular region, habitat, or period of time. Compare with FAUNA. **2** the bacteria found naturally in the intestines.

flo·ral /ˈflôrəl/ ▶ adj. relating to or decorated with flowers. ■ **flo·ral·ly** adv.

Flor·en·tine /ˈflôrən,tēn, -tīn/ ▶ adj. **1** relating to the city of Florence in Italy. **2** (**florentine**) (after a noun) (of food) served on top of or prepared with spinach: *chicken florentine.* ▶ n. **1** a person from Florence. **2** a cookie consisting mainly of nuts and preserved fruit, coated on one side with chocolate.

flo·res·cence /flôrˈesəns, fləˈres-/ ▶ n. the process of flowering.

flo·ret /ˈflôrət/ ▶ n. **1** one of the small flowers making up a composite flowerhead. **2** one of the flowering stems making up a head of cauliflower or broccoli.

flo·ri·bun·da /ˌflôrəˈbəndə/ ▶ n. a plant, especially a rose, that bears dense clusters of flowers.

flo·ri·cul·ture /ˈflôri,kəlCHər/ ▶ n. the growing of flowers.

flor·id /ˈflôrid, ˈflär-/ ▶ adj. **1** having a red or flushed complexion. **2** too elaborate or ornate: *florid prose.* ■ **flor·id·ly** adv.

flor·in /ˈflôrən, ˈflär-/ ▶ n. **1** a former British coin worth two shillings. **2** an English gold coin of the 14th century. **3** a guilder, a former coin of the Netherlands.

flo·rist /ˈflôrist/ ▶ n. a person who sells and arranges cut flowers. ■ **flo·rist·ry** n.

flo·ru·it /ˈflôr(y)ōoit/ ▶ v. used to indicate when a historical figure lived, worked, or was most active.

floss /flôs, fläs/ ▶ n. **1** (also **dental floss**) a soft thread used to clean between the teeth. **2** untwisted silk threads used in embroidery. **3** the rough silk enveloping a silkworm's cocoon. ▶ v. clean between one's teeth with dental floss. ■ **floss·y** adj.

flo·ta·tion /flōˈtāsHən/ (also **floatation**) ▶ n. **1** the action of floating. **2** the process of offering a company's shares for sale on the stock market for the first time.

flo·til·la /flōˈtilə/ ▶ n. a small fleet of ships or boats.

flot·sam /ˈflätsəm/ ▶ n. wreckage found floating on the sea.

– PHRASES **flotsam and jetsam** useless or discarded objects.

flounce¹ /flouns/ ▶ v. move in a way that draws attention to oneself in order to emphasize one's impatience or annoyance. ▶ n. an exaggerated action expressing annoyance or impatience.

flounce² ▶ n. a wide ornamental strip of material gathered and sewn to a skirt or dress; a frill. ■ **flounced** adj. **flounc·y** adj.

floun·der¹ /'floundər/ ▶ v. **1** stagger clumsily in mud or water. **2** have trouble doing or understanding something.

> **USAGE**
> On the confusion of **flounder** and **founder**, see the note at **FOUNDER³**.

floun·der² ▶ n. a small flatfish of shallow coastal waters.

flour /'flou(ə)r/ ▶ n. a powder produced by grinding grain, used to make bread, cakes, and pastry. ▶ v. sprinkle something with flour. ■ **flour·y** adj.

flour·ish /'flərish/ ▶ v. **1** grow or develop in a healthy or vigorous way. **2** be working or at the height of one's career during a particular period. **3** wave something around dramatically. ▶ n. **1** an exaggerated gesture or movement, made especially to attract attention. **2** an ornamental flowing curve in handwriting. **3** a fanfare played by brass instruments.

flout /flout/ ▶ v. openly fail to follow a rule, law, or convention.

> **USAGE**
> On the confusion of **flout** and **flaunt**, see the note at **FLAUNT**.

flow /flō/ ▶ v. **1** move steadily and continuously in a current or stream. **2** move steadily and freely: *people flowed into the courtyard.* **3** (of the sea or a tidal river) move toward the land; rise. **4** (**flow from**) result from; be caused by: *there are certain advantages that may flow from that decision.* ▶ n. **1** the action of flowing. **2** a steady, continuous stream: *the flow of traffic.* **3** the rise of a tide or a river.
– PHRASES **go with the flow** informal be relaxed and accept a situation, rather than trying to alter or control it.

flow chart (also **flow diagram**) ▶ n. a diagram showing a sequence of operations or functions making up a complex process or computer program.

flow·er /'flou(-ə)r/ ▶ n. **1** the part of a plant from which the seed or fruit develops, usually having brightly colored petals. **2** (often in phrase **in flower**) the state or period in which a plant's flowers have developed and opened. **3** (**the flower of**) the best of a group: *the flower of Ireland's youth.* ▶ v. **1** produce flowers. **2** develop richly and fully: *a musical form that flowered in the nineteenth century.*

flow·ered /'flou(-ə)rd/ ▶ adj. decorated with patterns of flowers.

flow·er girl ▶ n. **1** a young girl attending the bridge at a wedding. **2** historical a woman or girl who sells flowers, especially in the street.

flow·er head ▶ n. a compact mass of flowers at the top of a stem, especially a flat cluster of florets.

flow·er·pot /'flou(-ə)r,pät/ ▶ n. an earthenware or plastic container in which to grow a plant.

flow·er pow·er ▶ n. the promotion by hippies of peace and love as means of changing the world.

flow·er·y /'flou(-ə)rē/ ▶ adj. **1** full of, decorated with, or resembling flowers. **2** (of speech or writing) elaborate.

flow·ing /'flōing/ ▶ adj. **1** (especially of long hair or clothing) hanging or draping loosely and gracefully. **2** (of a line or contour) smoothly continuous: *the flowing curves of the lawn.* **3** (of language, movement, or style) graceful and fluent. ■ **flow·ing·ly** adv.

flown /flōn/ ▶ past participle of **FLY¹**.

fl. oz. ▶ abbr. fluid ounce.

flu /flōō/ ▶ n. influenza.

flub /fləb/ informal ▶ v. (**flubs, flubbing, flubbed**) botch or bungle: *she flubbed her lines.* ▶ n. a thing badly or clumsily done; a blunder.

fluc·tu·ate /'fləkchōō,āt/ ▶ v. rise and fall irregularly in number or amount: *her weight has fluctuated between 112 and 154 pounds.* ■ **fluc·tu·a·tion** /,fləkchōō'āshən/ n.

flue /flōō/ ▶ n. **1** a duct in a chimney for smoke and waste gases. **2** a pipe or passage for conveying heat.

flu·ent /'flōōənt/ ▶ adj. **1** speaking or writing in an articulate and natural way. **2** (of a language) used easily and accurately. **3** smoothly graceful and easy: *a runner in fluent motion.* ■ **flu·en·cy** n. **flu·ent·ly** adv.

fluff /fləf/ ▶ n. **1** soft fibers gathered in small light clumps. **2** the soft fur or feathers of a young mammal or bird. **3** informal a mistake. ▶ v. **1** (usu. **fluff something up/out**) make something fuller and softer by shaking or patting. **2** informal fail to accomplish properly: *he fluffed his only line.*

fluff·y /'fləfē/ ▶ adj. (**fluffier, fluffiest**) **1** resembling or covered with fluff. **2** (of food) light in texture. **3** informal frivolous, silly, or vague: *fluffy game shows.* ■ **fluff·i·ness** n.

flu·gel·horn /'flōōgəl,hôrn/ ▶ n. a brass musical instrument like a cornet but with a fuller tone.

flu·id /'flōōid/ ▶ n. a substance, such as a liquid or gas, that has no fixed shape and yields easily to external pressure. ▶ adj. **1** able to flow easily. **2** not settled or stable: *today's fluid social environment.* **3** (of movement) smoothly elegant or graceful. ■ **flu·id·i·ty** /flōō'idətē/ n. **flu·id·ly** adv.

flu·id ounce ▶ n. **1** a unit of capacity equal to one sixteenth of a pint (approximately 0.03 liter). **2** Brit. a unit of capacity equal to one twentieth of a pint (approximately 0.028 liter).

fluke¹ /flōōk/ ▶ n. a lucky chance occurrence. ■ **fluk·y** (also **flukey**) adj. (**flukier, flukiest**)

fluke² ▶ n. a parasitic flatworm that typically has suckers and hooks for attachment to the host.

fluke³ ▶ n. **1** a broad triangular plate on the arm of an anchor. **2** either of the lobes of a whale's tail.

flume /flōōm/ ▶ n. **1** an artificial channel for water. **2** a water slide at a swimming pool or amusement park.

flum·mer·y /'fləmərē/ ▶ n. empty talk; nonsense.

flum·mox /'fləməks/ ▶ v. informal baffle or bewilder someone.

flung /fləng/ ▶ past and past participle of **FLING**.

flunk /fləngk/ ▶ v. informal **1** fail an exam. **2** (**flunk out**) (of a student) leave or be dismissed from school or college as a result of failing to reach the required standard.

flun·ky /'fləngkē/ (also **flunkey**) ▶ n. (pl. **flunkies** or **flunkeys**) **1** chiefly derogatory a person who performs menial tasks. **2** chiefly historical a uniformed manservant or footman.

fluo·resce /flōō(ə)'res, flôr'es/ ▶ v. shine or glow brightly due to fluorescence.

fluo·res·cence /flŏŏ(ə)'resəns, flôr'esəns/
▸ n. 1 light given out by a substance when it is exposed to radiation such as that of ultraviolet light or X-rays. 2 the property of giving out light in this way.

fluo·res·cent /ˌflŏŏ(ə)'resənt, flôr'esənt/
▸ adj. 1 having or showing fluorescence. 2 (of lighting) based on fluorescence from a substance illuminated by ultraviolet light. 3 vividly colorful.

fluor·i·date /'flŏŏrə,dāt, 'flôr-/ ▸ v. add traces of fluorides to something. ■ **fluor·i·da·tion** /ˌflŏŏrə'dāsHən, ˌflôr-/ n.

fluor·ide /'flŏŏrˌīd, 'flôr-/ ▸ n. 1 a compound of fluorine with another element or group. 2 a fluorine-containing salt added to water supplies or toothpaste to reduce tooth decay.

fluor·i·nate /'flŏŏrə,nāt, 'flôr-/ ▸ v. 1 introduce fluorine into a compound. 2 another term for **FLUORIDATE**. ■ **fluor·i·na·tion** /ˌflŏŏrə'nāsHən, ˌflôr-/ n.

fluor·ine /'flŏŏrˌēn, flôr-/ ▸ n. a poisonous, extremely reactive, pale yellow gaseous chemical element.

fluo·rite /'flŏŏrˌīt, flôr-/ ▸ n. a mineral form of calcium fluoride.

fluor·o·car·bon /ˌflŏŏrō'kärbən, ˌflôrō-/ ▸ n. a compound formed by replacing one or more of the hydrogen atoms in a hydrocarbon with fluorine atoms. Fluorocarbons are widely used in lubricants, cleaners, and aerosols.

fluor·o·quin·o·lone /ˌflŏŏrō'kwinlˌōn, ˌflôrō-/ ▸ n. any of a class of therapeutic antibiotics that are active against a range of bacteria associated with human and animal diseases. Their use in livestock has sparked concerns about the spread of bacteria resistant to them in humans.

fluor·o·scope /'flŏŏrə,skōp, 'flôr-/ ▸ n. an instrument used for viewing X-ray images without taking and developing X-ray photographs. ■ **fluor·o·scop·ic** /ˌflŏŏrə'skäpik, ˌflôr-/ adj. **fluo·ros·co·py** /flŏŏr'äskəpē, flôr-/ n.

flu·or·spar /'flŏŏr,spär, 'flôr-/ ▸ n. another term for **FLUORITE**.

flur·ried /'flərēd, 'flə-rēd/ ▸ adj. agitated, confused, or anxious.

flur·ry /'flərē, 'flə-rē/ ▸ n. (pl. **flurries**) 1 a small swirling mass of snow, leaves, etc., moved by a gust of wind. 2 a sudden short spell of activity or excitement. 3 a number of things arriving suddenly and at the same time: *a flurry of emails.*

flush[1] /fləsH/ ▸ v. 1 (of a person's skin or face) become red and hot, typically through illness or emotion. 2 (**be flushed with**) be excited or very pleased by: *flushed with success, I was getting into my stride.* 3 clean something by passing large quantities of water through it. 4 remove or dispose of something by flushing with water. 5 force a person or animal out of hiding: *their task was to flush out the rebels.* ▸ n. 1 a reddening of the face or skin. 2 a sudden rush of intense emotion. 3 a period of freshness and vigor: *the first flush of youth.* 4 an act of flushing something with water. ■ **flush·er** n.

flush[2] ▸ adj. (usu. **flush with**) 1 completely level with another surface. 2 *informal* having plenty of something, especially money.

flush[3] ▸ n. (in poker) a hand of cards all of the same suit.

flus·ter /'fləstər/ ▸ v. (often as adj. **flustered**) make someone agitated or confused. ▸ n. a

flustered state.

flute /flŏŏt/ ▸ n. 1 a high-pitched wind instrument consisting of a tube with holes along it. 2 a tall, narrow wine glass. 3 Architecture an ornamental vertical groove in a column. ▸ v. speak in a melodious way.

flut·ed /'flŏŏtid/ ▸ adj. (of an object) having a series of decorative grooves.

flut·ing /'flŏŏtiNG/ ▸ n. 1 a sound reminiscent of that of a flute: *the silvery fluting of a blackbird.* 2 a groove or set of grooves forming a surface decoration.

flut·ist /'flŏŏtist/ ▸ n. a flute player.

flut·ter /'flətər/ ▸ v. 1 fly unsteadily by flapping the wings quickly and lightly. 2 move with a light irregular motion: *flags fluttered in the breeze.* 3 (of a pulse or heartbeat) beat irregularly. ▸ n. 1 an act of fluttering. 2 a state of nervous excitement. 3 Electronics rapid variation in the pitch or amplitude of a signal, especially of recorded sound. Compare with **wow**[2]. ■ **flut·ter·y** adj.

flut·y /'flŏŏtē/ (also **flutey**) ▸ adj. (**flutier, flutiest**) reminiscent of the sound of a flute: *a high, fluty voice.*

flu·vi·al /'flŏŏvēəl/ ▸ adj. chiefly Geology relating to or found in a river.

flux /fləks/ ▸ n. 1 continuous change: *urban life is in a constant state of flux.* 2 technical the action of flowing. 3 Medicine an abnormal discharge from or within the body. 4 Physics the total amount of radiation, or of electric or magnetic field lines, passing through an area. 5 a substance mixed with a solid to lower the melting point, used in soldering or smelting.

fly[1] /flī/ ▸ v. (**flies, flying, flew** /flŏŏ/; past part. **flown** /flōn/) 1 (of a winged creature or aircraft) move through the air. 2 control the flight of an aircraft. 3 carry or accomplish in an aircraft: *by June 22, the squadron had flown 207 sorties.* 4 go or move quickly: *his fingers flew across the keyboard.* 5 move or be thrown quickly through the air. 6 wave or flutter in the wind. 7 (of a flag) be displayed on a flagpole. 8 (**fly at**) attack someone verbally or physically. 9 old use run away; flee. ▸ n. (pl. **flies**) 1 an opening at the crotch of a pair of pants, closed with a zipper or buttons. 2 a flap of material covering the opening of a tent. 3 (**the flies**) the space over the stage in a theater. ■ **fly·a·ble** adj.
– PHRASES **fly in the face of** oppose or be the opposite of what is usual or expected. **fly off the handle** informal lose one's temper suddenly.

fly[2] ▸ n. (pl. **flies**) 1 a flying insect with a single pair of transparent wings and sucking or piercing mouthparts. 2 used in names of other flying insects, e.g., *dragonfly.* 3 a fishing bait consisting of a natural or artificial flying insect.
– PHRASES **a fly in the ointment** a minor irritation that spoils the enjoyment of something. **fly on the wall** an unnoticed observer.

fly·a·way /'flīə,wā/ ▸ adj. (of hair) fine and difficult to control.

fly·by /'flī,bī/ ▸ n. (pl. **flybys**) a flight past a point, especially the close approach of a spacecraft to a planet or moon for observation.

fly-by-night ▸ adj. unreliable or untrustworthy, especially in financial matters.

fly-by-wire ▸ adj. referring to a semiautomatic computer-regulated system for controlling an aircraft or spacecraft.

fly·catch·er /'flī,kaCHər, -,keCHər/ ▸ n. a perching bird that catches flying insects.

fly·er /'flīər/ (also **flier**) ▸ n. **1** a person or thing that flies. **2** informal a fast-moving person or thing. **3** a small leaflet advertising an event or product. **4** a flying start.

fly-fish·ing ▸ n. the sport of fishing using a rod and an artificial fly as bait.

fly·ing /'flī-iNG/ ▸ adj. **1** able to move through the air. **2** hasty; brief: *a flying visit.*
– PHRASES **with flying colors** very well; with particular merit.

fly·ing but·tress ▸ n. Architecture a buttress slanting from a separate column, typically forming an arch with the wall it supports.

fly·ing fish ▸ n. a fish of warm seas that leaps out of the water and uses its winglike pectoral fins to glide for some distance.

fly·ing sau·cer ▸ n. a disk-shaped flying craft supposedly piloted by aliens.

fly·ing squir·rel ▸ n. a small tree squirrel that has skin joining the fore and hind limbs for gliding from tree to tree.

fly·ing start ▸ n. **1** a start of a race in which the competitors are already moving at speed as they pass the starting point. **2** a good beginning giving an advantage over competitors.

fly·leaf /'flī,lēf/ ▸ n. (pl. **flyleaves** /-,lēvz/) a blank page at the beginning or end of a book.

fly·o·ver /'flī,ōvər/ ▸ n. **1** a low flight by one or more aircraft over a specific location. **2** a ceremonial flight of aircraft past a person or place. **3** Brit. an overpass.

fly·pa·per /'flī,pāpər/ ▸ n. sticky, poison-treated strips of paper that are hung indoors to catch and kill flies.

fly·sheet /'flī,SHēt/ ▸ n. a fabric cover pitched over a tent to give extra protection against bad weather.

fly swat·ter ▸ n. an implement used for swatting insects, typically a square of plastic mesh attached to a wire handle.

fly·way /'flī,wā/ ▸ n. a route regularly used by large numbers of migrating birds.

fly·weight /'flī,wāt/ ▸ n. a weight in boxing and other sports intermediate between light flyweight and bantamweight.

fly·wheel /'flī,(h)wēl/ ▸ n. a heavy wheel in a machine that is used to increase momentum and thereby provide greater stability or a reserve of available power.

FM ▸ abbr. frequency modulation: *FM radio.*

Fm ▸ symbol the chemical element fermium.

fm ▸ abbr. **1** fathom(s). **2** femtometer.

fmr. ▸ abbr. former.

f-num·ber ▸ n. the ratio of the focal length of a camera lens to the diameter of the aperture being used for a particular shot.

FOAF (also **FOF**) ▸ abbr. friend of a friend.

foal /fōl/ ▸ n. a young horse or related animal. ▸ v. (of a mare) give birth to a foal.

foam /fōm/ ▸ n. **1** a mass of small bubbles formed on or in liquid. **2** a liquid substance containing many small bubbles: *shaving foam.* **3** (also **foam rubber**) a lightweight form of rubber or plastic made by solidifying foam. ▸ v. form or produce foam. ∎ **foam·y** adj.
– PHRASES **foam at the mouth** informal be very angry.

FOB ▸ abbr. **1** Military forward operating base.

2 Commerce (preceding a geographic location) free on board; indicating the point at which shipping charges are applicable.

fob¹ /fäb/ ▸ n. **1** a chain attached to a watch for carrying in a vest or waistband pocket. **2** (also **fob pocket**) a small pocket for carrying a watch. **3** a tab on a key ring.

fob² ▸ v. (**fobs, fobbing, fobbed**) **1** (**fob someone off**) try to deceive someone into accepting excuses or something inferior. **2** (**fob something off on**) give something inferior to someone.

fo·cac·cia /fō'käCH(ē)ə/ ▸ n. a type of flat Italian bread made with olive oil and flavored with herbs.

fo·cal /'fōkəl/ ▸ adj. relating to a focus, especially the focus of a lens. ∎ **fo·cal·ly** adv.

fo·cal length ▸ n. the distance between the center of a lens or curved mirror and its focus.

fo·cal point ▸ n. **1** the point at which rays or waves from a lens or mirror meet, or the point from which rays or waves going in different directions appear to proceed. **2** the center of interest or activity: *a fireplace serves as the focal point of any room.*

fo'c'·sle /'fōksəl/ ▸ n. variant spelling of FORECASTLE.

fo·cus /'fōkəs/ ▸ n. (pl. **focuses** or **foci** /'fō,sī, -,kī/) **1** the center of interest or activity. **2** the state or quality of having or producing a clear, well-defined image: *his face is out of focus.* **3** the point at which an object must be situated in order for a lens or mirror to produce a clear image of it. **4** a focal point. **5** the point of origin of an earthquake. Compare with EPICENTER. **6** Geometry a fixed point with reference to which an ellipse, parabola, or other curve is drawn. ▸ v. (**focuses, focusing, focused** or **focusses, focussing, focussed**) **1** (of a person or their eyes) adapt to the prevailing level of light and become able to see clearly. **2** (**focus on**) pay particular attention to: *I was able to focus on a single project.* **3** adjust the focus of a telescope, camera, etc. **4** (of rays or waves) meet or cause to meet at a single point. ∎ **fo·cus·er** n.

fo·cus group ▸ n. a group of people assembled to assess a new product, political campaign, etc.

fod·der /'fädər/ ▸ n. **1** food for cattle and other livestock. **2** people or things regarded only as material to satisfy a need: *young people ending up as factory fodder.*

foe /fō/ ▸ n. formal or literary an enemy or opponent.

fog /fôg, fäg/ ▸ n. **1** a thick cloud of tiny water droplets suspended in the atmosphere at or near the earth's surface that restricts visibility. **2** a state or cause of confusion. **3** Photography cloudiness obscuring the image on a developed negative or print. ▸ v. (**fogs, fogging, fogged**) **1** cover or become covered with steam. **2** bewilder or confuse: *the sedative still fogged Jack's mind.* **3** Photography make a film, negative, or print cloudy.

fog bank ▸ n. a dense mass of fog, especially at sea.

fog·bound /'fôg,bound, 'fäg-/ ▸ adj. surrounded or hidden by fog.

fo·gey /'fōgē/ (also **fogy**) ▸ n. (pl. **fogeys** or **fogies**) a very old-fashioned or conservative person. ∎ **fo·gey·ish** adj. **fo·gey·ism** n.

fog·gy /'fôgē, 'fägē/ ▸ adj. (**foggier, foggiest**) **1** full of fog. **2** confused or unclear: *my memories*

of the event are foggy.
- PHRASES **not have the foggiest (idea)** informal have no idea at all.

fog·horn /ˈfôgˌhôrn, ˈfäg-/ ▶n. a device making a loud, deep sound as a warning to ships in fog.

fo·gy /ˈfōgē/ ▶n. variant spelling of FOGEY.

FOIA ▶abbr. Freedom of Information Act.

foi·ble /ˈfoibəl/ ▶n. a minor weakness or eccentricity.

foie gras /fwä ˈgrä/ (also **pâté de foie gras** /ˈpätā də fwä ˌgrä/) ▶n. a pâté made from the liver of a fattened goose.

foil¹ /foil/ ▶v. 1 prevent something wrong or undesirable from succeeding. 2 prevent someone from doing something.

foil² ▶n. 1 metal hammered or rolled into a thin, flexible sheet. 2 a person or thing that contrasts with and so emphasizes the qualities of another: *silver foliage provides the perfect foil for bright flower colors.*

foil³ ▶n. a light, blunt-edged fencing sword with a button on its point.

foist /foist/ ▶v. (**foist someone/thing on**) impose an unwelcome person or thing on: *electricity privatization was foisted on the public.*

fold¹ /fōld/ ▶v. 1 bend something over on itself so that one part of it covers another. 2 (often as adj. **folding**) be able to be folded into a flatter shape. 3 cover or wrap something in a flexible material. 4 affectionately hold someone in one's arms. 5 informal (of a company) go out of business. 6 (**fold something in/into**) mix an ingredient gently with another ingredient. ▶n. 1 a folded part or thing: *drooping folds of skin.* 2 a line or crease produced by folding. 3 chiefly Brit. a slight hill or hollow. 4 Geology a bend or curvature of strata. ■ **fold·a·ble** adj.
- PHRASES **fold one's arms** cross one's arms over one's chest. **fold one's hands** bring or hold one's hands together.

fold² ▶n. 1 a pen or enclosure for sheep. 2 (**the fold**) a group with shared aims and values: *Welcome back to the fold, Brother Ben.*

-fold ▶suffix forming adjectives and adverbs from cardinal numbers. 1 in an amount multiplied by: *threefold.* 2 consisting of a specified number of parts: *twofold.*

fold·a·way /ˈfōldəˌwā/ ▶adj. designed to be folded up for easy storage or transport.

fold·er /ˈfōldər/ ▶n. 1 a folding cover or holder for storing loose papers. 2 Computing a directory containing related files.

fol·de·rol /ˈfäldəˌräl, ˈfōldəˌrôl/ ▶n. trivial or nonsensical fuss.

fold·out /ˈfōlˌdout/ ▶n. (of a page, a furniture part, or a bed) designed to be opened out for use and then folded away: *a foldout map.* ▶n. a page or piece of furniture designed in such a way.

fo·li·age /ˈfōl(ē)ij/ ▶n. the leaves of a plant.

fo·li·ar /ˈfōlēər/ ▶adj. technical relating to leaves.

fo·li·ate /ˈfōlēət, -ˌāt/ ▶adj. decorated with leaves or a leaflike pattern.

fo·lic ac·id /ˈfōlik, ˈfä-/ ▶n. a vitamin of the B complex found especially in leafy green vegetables, liver, and kidneys.

fo·lie à deux /fōˌlē ä ˈdœ/ ▶n. (pl. **folies à deux**) delusion or mental illness shared by two people in a close relationship.

fo·li·o /ˈfōlēˌō/ ▶n. (pl. **folios**) 1 a sheet of paper folded once to form two leaves (four pages) of a book. 2 a book made up of such sheets. 3 an individual leaf of paper numbered on the front side only. 4 the page number in a printed book.

folk /fōk/ ▶pl.n. 1 (also **folks**) informal people in general. 2 (**one's folks**) one's family, especially one's parents. 3 (also **folk music**) traditional music of unknown authorship, passed on by word of mouth. ▶adj. originating from the beliefs, culture, and customs of ordinary people: *folk wisdom.* ■ **folk·ish** adj.
- PHRASES **just (plain) folks** ordinary, down-to-earth, unpretentious people.

folk art ▶n. art created by people who have no academic training in art or who are not publicly identified as artists. Folk art typically reflects cultural traditions and values.

folk dance ▶n. a traditional dance of a particular people or area.

folk et·y·mol·o·gy ▶n. 1 a popular but mistaken account of the origin of a word or phrase. 2 the process by which the form of an unfamiliar or foreign word is adapted to a more familiar form through popular use.

folk·ie /ˈfōkē/ ▶n. informal a singer, player, or fan of folk music.

folk·lore /ˈfōkˌlôr/ ▶n. the traditional beliefs, stories, and customs of a community, passed on by word of mouth. ■ **folk·lor·ic** /-ˌlôrik/ adj. **folk·lor·ist** n.

folk med·i·cine ▶n. treatment of disease or injury based on tradition rather than on modern scientific practice, and typically using simple, locally available remedies.

folk sing·er ▶n. a singer of folk songs.

folk·son·o·my /ˌfōkˈsänəmē/ ▶n. the activity of sorting information into categories derived from the consensus of the information users, or the result of this.

folk·sy /ˈfōksē/ ▶adj. (**folksier, folksiest**) traditional and homey, especially in an artificial way: *his carefully cultivated, folksy image.* ■ **folk·si·ness** n.

folk tale ▶n. a traditional story originally passed on by word of mouth.

fol·li·cle /ˈfälikəl/ ▶n. a small cavity in the body, especially one in which the root of a hair develops. ■ **fol·lic·u·lar** /fəˈlikyələr/ adj.

fol·low /ˈfälō/ ▶v. 1 move or travel behind someone or something. 2 go after someone so as to observe them. 3 go along a route or path. 4 come after in time or order: *the six years that followed his death.* 5 (also **follow on from**) happen as a result of something else. 6 be a logical consequence. 7 act according to an instruction or example. 8 accept someone as a guide, example, or leader of a movement. 9 take an interest in or pay close attention to: *supporters who have followed the team through thick and thin.* 10 understand someone or something. 11 practice or undertake a career or course of action. 12 (**follow something through**) continue an action or task to its conclusion. 13 (**follow something up**) pursue or investigate something further.
- PHRASES **follow one's nose 1** trust one's instincts. 2 go straight ahead. **follow suit 1** do the same as someone else. 2 (in card games) play a card of the suit led.

fol·low·er /ˈfälō-ər/ ▶n. 1 a supporter, fan, or disciple. 2 a person who follows someone or something. ■ **fol·low·er·ship** n.

fol·low·ing /'fälō-ɪNG/ ▶ prep. coming after or as a result of. ▶ n. a group of supporters or admirers. ▶ adj. next in time or order.

fol·low-through ▶ n. the continuing of an action or task to its conclusion.

fol·low-up ▶ n. **1** an activity carried out to monitor or further develop earlier work. **2** a work that follows or builds on an earlier work.

fol·ly /'fälē/ ▶ n. (pl. **follies**) **1** lack of good sense; foolishness. **2** a foolish act or idea. **3** an ornamental building with no practical purpose, built in a park or large landscaped yard.

fo·ment /'fō,ment, fō'ment/ ▶ v. stir up trouble or violence. ■ **fo·men·ta·tion** /,fōmen'tāshən, -mən-/ n.

fond /fänd/ ▶ adj. **1** (**fond of**) feeling affection for someone or having a liking for something. **2** affectionate; loving: *fond memories of our childhood.* **3** (of a hope or belief) not likely to be fulfilled; foolishly optimistic. ■ **fond·ly** adv. **fond·ness** n.

fon·dant /'fändənt/ ▶ n. **1** a thick paste made of sugar and water, used in making candy and cake icing. **2** a candy made of fondant.

fon·dle /'fändl/ ▶ v. stroke or caress someone lovingly or erotically. ▶ n. an act of fondling. ■ **fon·dler** n.

fon·due /fän'd(y)oo/ ▶ n. a dish in which small pieces of food are dipped into melted cheese, a hot sauce, or hot oil.

font[1] /fänt/ ▶ n. a large stone bowl in a church that holds the water used in baptism.

font[2] (Brit. also **fount**) ▶ n. Printing a set of type of a particular face and size.

fon·ta·nel /,fäntn'el/ (Brit. **fontanelle**) ▶ n. a soft area between the bones of the skull in a baby or fetus, where the sutures are not yet fully formed.

fon·ti·na /fän'tēnə/ ▶ n. a pale yellow Italian cheese.

food /food/ ▶ n. any nutritious substance that people or animals eat or drink or that plants absorb to maintain life and growth.
– PHRASES **food for thought** something that merits serious consideration.

food chain ▶ n. a series of organisms each dependent on the next as a source of food.

food court ▶ n. an area, typically in a shopping mall, where fast food outlets and tables and chairs are located.

food·ie /'foodē/ (also **foody**) ▶ n. (pl. **foodies**) informal a person with a strong interest in food; a gourmet.

food poi·son·ing ▶ n. illness caused by bacteria or other toxins in food, typically with vomiting and diarrhea.

food proc·es·sor ▶ n. **1** an electric kitchen appliance used for chopping, mixing, or puréeing foods. **2** a company that converts agricultural products into processed foods.

food·stuff /'food,stəf/ ▶ n. a substance suitable to be eaten as food.

food sup·ple·ment ▶ n. a substance ingested to remedy a real or perceived deficiency in a person's diet.

fool /fool/ ▶ n. **1** a person who acts unwisely. **2** historical a jester or clown. ▶ v. **1** trick or deceive someone. **2** (**fool around**) act in a joking or silly way. **3** (**fool around**) engage in casual or extramarital sex. ■ **fool·er·y** n.

– PHRASES **make a fool of 1** trick or deceive someone so that they look foolish. **2** (**make a fool of oneself**) behave in an incompetent or inappropriate way.

fool·har·dy /'fool,härdē/ ▶ adj. bold in a reckless way. ■ **fool·har·di·ly** /-,härdl-ē/ adv. **fool·har·di·ness** n.

fool·ish /'foolish/ ▶ adj. lacking good sense or judgment; silly or unwise. ■ **fool·ish·ly** adv. **fool·ish·ness** n.

fool·proof /'fool,proof/ ▶ adj. incapable of going wrong or being misused.

fool's gold ▶ n. a brassy yellow mineral that can be mistaken for gold, especially pyrite.

foot /foot/ ▶ n. (pl. **feet**) **1** the part of the leg below the ankle, on which a person walks. **2** the base or bottom of something vertical. **3** the end of a bed where the occupant's feet normally rest. **4** a unit of length equal to 12 inches (30.48 cm). **5** Poetry a group of syllables making up a basic unit of meter. ▶ v. informal **1** pay a bill. **2** (**foot it**) go somewhere on foot. ■ **foot·less** adj.

– PHRASES **feet of clay** a flaw or weakness in a person otherwise admired. **get** (or **start**) **off on the right** (or **wrong**) **foot** make a good (or bad) start. **have** (or **keep**) **one's feet on the ground** be (or remain) practical and sensible. **have** (or **get**) **a foot in the door** have (or gain) a first introduction to a profession or organization. **have one foot in the grave** humorous be very old or ill. **land** (or **fall**) **on one's feet** have good luck or success. **on** (or **by**) **foot** walking rather than using transport. **put one's best foot forward** begin with as much effort and determination as possible. **put one's foot down** informal be firm when faced with opposition or disobedience. **put one's foot in one's mouth** informal say or do something tactless or embarrassing. **under one's feet** in one's way. **under foot** on the ground.

foot·age /'footij/ ▶ n. **1** a length of film made for movies or television. **2** size or length measured in feet.

foot-and-mouth dis·ease ▶ n. a disease caused by a virus in cattle and sheep, causing ulcers on the hoofs and around the mouth.

foot·ball /'foot,bôl/ ▶ n. **1** a team game played in North America with an oval ball on a field marked out as a gridiron. **2** a large inflated oval ball used in football. **3** (in the UK) soccer. **4** (in the UK) a soccer ball.

foot·board /'foot,bôrd/ ▶ n. **1** an upright panel forming the foot of a bed. **2** a board acting as a step up to a vehicle such a train.

foot·bridge /'foot,brij/ ▶ n. a bridge for pedestrians.

foot·er /'footər/ ▶ n. **1** a person or thing of a specified number of feet in length or height: *a six-footer.* **2** a line of writing appearing at the foot of each page of a book or document.

foot·fall /'foot,fôl/ ▶ n. the sound of a footstep or footsteps.

foot·hill /'foot,hil/ ▶ n. a low hill at the base of a mountain or mountain range.

foot·hold /'foot,hōld/ ▶ n. **1** a secure position from which further progress may be made: *the company has failed to gain a foothold in Japan.* **2** a place where one can place a foot to give secure support while climbing.

foot·ing /'footɪNG/ ▶ n. **1** (**one's footing**) a secure grip with one's feet. **2** the basis on which something is established or operates: *we are on*

equal footing with our competitors in the market.
3 the foundations of a wall.

foot·lights /'foŏt,līts/ ▶ pl.n. a row of spotlights along the front of a stage at the level of the actors' feet.

foot·lock·er /'foŏt,läkər/ ▶ n. a small trunk or chest, typically the width of a single bed.

foot·loose /'foŏt,loōs/ ▶ adj. free to go where one likes and do as one pleases.

foot·man /'foŏtmən/ ▶ n. (pl. **footmen**) a uniformed servant whose duties include admitting visitors.

foot·note /'foŏt,nōt/ ▶ n. an additional piece of information printed at the bottom of a page.

foot·path /'foŏt,paTH/ ▶ n. a path for people to walk along.

foot·plate /'foŏt,plāt/ ▶ n. a platform for placing one or both feet on a piece of machinery or equipment.

foot·print /'foŏt,print/ ▶ n. the mark left by a foot or shoe on a surface or the ground.

foot·rest /'foŏt,rest/ ▶ n. a support for the feet, used when sitting.

foot·sie /'foŏtsē/ ▶ n. (in phrase **play footsie** (or **footsies**)) informal touch someone's feet lightly with one's own as a playful expression of romantic interest.

foot sol·dier ▶ n. **1** a soldier who fights on foot. **2** a low-ranking person who nevertheless does valuable work.

foot·sore /'foŏt,sôr/ ▶ adj. having sore feet from much walking.

foot·step /'foŏt,step/ ▶ n. a step taken in walking, especially as heard by another person.
– PHRASES **follow** (or **tread**) **in someone's footsteps** do as another person did before.

foot·stool /'foŏt,stoōl/ ▶ n. a low stool for resting the feet on when sitting.

foot·tap·ping ▶ adj. having a strong rhythmical musical beat.

foot·wear /'foŏt,wer/ ▶ n. shoes, boots, and other coverings for the feet.

foot·work /'foŏt,wərk/ ▶ n. the way in which one moves one's feet in dancing and sport.

fop /fäp/ ▶ n. a man who is excessively concerned with his clothes and appearance. ■ **fop·per·y** n. **fop·pish** adj.

for /fôr, fər/ ▶ prep. **1** affecting or relating to. **2** in favor of. **3** on behalf of. **4** because of. **5** so as to get, have, or do. **6** in the direction of. **7** over a distance or during a period of time. **8** in exchange for or in place of. **9** in relation to the expected norm of: *she was tall for her age.* **10** indicating an occasion in a series. ▶ conj. literary because; since.
– PHRASES **be in for it** informal be about to be punished or get into trouble.

fo·ra /'fôrə/ ▶ plural of **forum** (sense 2).

for·age /'fôrij, 'fär-/ ▶ v. **1** search for food. **2** search for something: *she foraged in her pocket for a tissue.* ▶ n. food for horses and cattle. ■ **for·ag·er** n.

fo·ra·men /fə'rāmən/ ▶ n. (pl. **foramina** /-'ramənə/) Anatomy an opening, hole, or passage, especially in a bone.

for·ay /'fôr,ā, 'fär,ā/ ▶ n. **1** a sudden attack or raid into enemy territory. **2** a spirited attempt to become involved in a new activity: *this is the firm's first foray into cookbook publishing.* ▶ v. attempt a new activity. ■ **for·ay·er** n.

for·bade /fər'bad, fôr-, -'bād/ (also **forbad** /fər'bad, fôr-/) ▶ past of **forbid**.

for·bear[1] /fər'ber, fôr-/ ▶ v. (past **forbore** /fər'bôr, fôr-/; past part. **forborne** /fər'bôrn, fôr-/) stop oneself from doing something.

> **USAGE**
> Do not confuse **forbear** with **forebear**. **Forbear** means 'stop oneself from doing something' (*he doesn't forbear to write about the bad times*), while **forebear** (which is also sometimes spelled **forbear**) means 'an ancestor' (*our Stone Age forebears*).

for·bear[2] ▶ n. variant spelling of **forebear**.

for·bear·ance /fôr'berəns, fər-/ ▶ n. the quality of being patient and tolerant toward others.

for·bear·ing /fôr'beriNG, fər-/ ▶ adj. patient and restrained.

for·bid /fər'bid, fôr-/ ▶ v. (**forbids**, **forbidding**, **forbade** /-'bad, -'bād/ or **forbad** /-'bad/; past part. **forbidden**) **1** refuse to allow something. **2** order someone not to do something.
– PHRASES **forbidden fruit** a thing that is desired all the more because it is not allowed.

for·bid·ding /fər'bidiNG, fôr-/ ▶ adj. appearing unfriendly or threatening. ■ **for·bid·ding·ly** adv.

for·bore /fər'bôr, fôr-/ ▶ past of **forbear**[1].

for·borne /fər'bôrn, fôr-/ ▶ past participle of **forbear**[1].

force /fôrs/ ▶ n. **1** physical strength or energy accompanying action or movement: *we had to lean against the force of the wind.* **2** strong pressure on someone to do something backed by the use or threat of violence. **3** influence or power: *the force of public opinion.* **4** a person or thing having power or influence. **5** an organized group of military personnel, police, or workers. **6** Physics an influence that changes the motion of a body or produces motion or stress in a stationary body. ▶ v. **1** make a way through or into something by force. **2** push into a specified position using force: *thieves tried to force open the cash register.* **3** achieve something by effort. **4** make someone do something against their will. **5** (**force something on**) impose something on: *the new technology is being forced on retailers by the banks.* **6** make a plant develop or mature more quickly than normal. ■ **forc·er** n.
– PHRASES **force someone's hand** make someone do something. **in force 1** in great strength or numbers. **2** (**in/into force**) in or into effect.

forced land·ing ▶ n. the abrupt landing of an aircraft in an emergency.

force-feed ▶ v. force someone to eat food.

force field ▶ n. **1** another term for **field** (sense 4 of the noun): *a classical molecular mechanical force field.* **2** (chiefly in science fiction and paranormal literature) an area of space in which a particular exotic force exerts its effects.

force·ful /'fôrsfəl/ ▶ adj. powerful, assertive, or vigorous. ■ **force·ful·ly** adv. **force·ful·ness** n.

force ma·jeure /ˌfôrs mä'ZHər/ ▶ n. **1** Law unforeseeable circumstances that prevent someone from fulfilling a contract. **2** superior strength.

force·meat /'fôrs,mēt/ ▶ n. a mixture of chopped and seasoned meat or vegetables used as a stuffing or garnish.

for·ceps /'fôrsəps, -,seps/ ▶ pl.n. **1** a pair of pincers used in surgery or in a laboratory. **2** a large surgical instrument with broad blades, used to assist in the delivery of a baby.

for·ci·ble /ˈfôrsəbəl/ ▸ adj. done by force.
■ **for·ci·bly** adv.

ford /fôrd/ ▸ n. a shallow place in a river or stream where it can be crossed. ▸ v. cross a river or stream at a ford. ■ **ford·a·ble** adj.

fore /fôr/ ▸ adj. situated or placed in front.
▸ n. the front part of something, especially a ship. ▸ exclam. called out as a warning to people in the path of a golf ball.
– PHRASES **to the fore** in or to a prominent or leading position.

fore- ▸ comb.form **1** before; in advance: *foreshorten.*
2 in or at the front of: *forecourt.*

fore and aft ▸ adj. **1** backward and forward.
2 (of a ship's sail or rigging) set lengthwise, not on the yards.

fore·arm[1] /ˈfôrˌärm/ ▸ n. the part of a person's arm from the elbow to the wrist.

fore·arm[2] /fôrˈärm/ ▸ v. (**be forearmed**) be prepared in advance for danger or attack.

fore·bear /ˈfôrˌber/ (also **forbear**) ▸ n. an ancestor.

> **USAGE**
> **Forebear** (meaning 'an ancestor') can also be spelled **forbear** and is often confused with the verb **forbear**. See the note at FORBEAR[1].

fore·bode /fôrˈbōd/ ▸ v. old use act as an advance warning of something bad.

fore·bod·ing /fôrˈbōdiNG/ ▸ n. a feeling that something bad is going to happen.
▸ adj. suggesting that something bad is going to happen.

fore·brain /ˈfôrˌbrān/ ▸ n. the front part of the brain.

fore·cast /ˈfôrˌkast/ ▸ v. (past and past part. **forecast** or **forecasted**) predict or estimate a future event or trend. ▸ n. a prediction or estimate, especially of the weather or a financial trend.
■ **fore·cast·er** n.

fore·cas·tle /ˈfōksəl, ˈfôrˌkasəl/ (also **fo'c's'le**) ▸ n. the front part of a ship below the deck.

fore·close /fôrˈklōz/ ▸ v. **1** take possession of a mortgaged property when a person fails to keep up with their mortgage payments. **2** rule out or prevent a course of action. ■ **fore·clo·sure** /fôrˈklōzнər/ n.

fore·court /ˈfôrˌkôrt/ ▸ n. **1** an open area in front of a large building. **2** the part of a tennis court between the service line and the net.

fore·doom /fôrˈdo͞om/ ▸ v. (**be foredoomed**) literary be condemned beforehand to certain failure.

fore·fa·ther /ˈfôrˌfäтнər/ (or **foremother** /ˈfôrˌməтнər/) ▸ n. an ancestor.

fore·fin·ger /ˈfôrˌfiNGgər/ ▸ n. the finger next to the thumb.

fore·foot /ˈfôrˌfo͝ot/ ▸ n. (pl. **forefeet**) each of the two front feet of a four-footed animal.

fore·front /ˈfôrˌfrənt/ ▸ n. the leading position or place: *he has always been at the forefront of research.*

fore·gath·er /fôrˈgaтнər/ (also **forgather**) ▸ v. formal assemble or gather together.

fore·go[1] ▸ v. variant spelling of FORGO.

fore·go[2] /fôrˈgō/ ▸ v. (**foregoes, foregoing**, **forewent** /fôrˈwent/; past part. **foregone** /ˈfôrˌgôn/) old use come before someone or something in place or time.

fore·go·ing /fôrˈgōiNG/ ▸ adj. previously mentioned.

fore·gone /ˈfôrˌgôn/ ▸ past participle of FOREGO[1], FOREGO[2].
– PHRASES **a foregone conclusion** an easily predictable result.

fore·ground /ˈfôrˌground/ ▸ n. **1** the part of a view or picture nearest to the observer. **2** the most prominent or important position. ▸ v. make something the most important feature.

fore·hand /ˈfôrˌhand/ ▸ n. (in tennis and other racket sports) a stroke played with the palm of the hand facing in the direction of the stroke.

fore·head /ˈfôrəd, ˈfôrˌhed/ ▸ n. the part of the face above the eyebrows.

for·eign /ˈfôrən, ˈfär-/ ▸ adj. **1** relating to or typical of a country or language other than one's own. **2** dealing with or involving other countries. **3** coming or introduced from outside: *the difficulty of introducing foreign genes into plants.* **4** (**foreign to**) not familiar to or typical of: *aisles of food and cosmetics entirely foreign to the average consumer.* ■ **for·eign·ness** n.

for·eign bod·y ▸ n. an unwanted object that has entered the body from outside.

for·eign·er /ˈfôrənər, ˈfär-/ ▸ n. **1** a person from a foreign country. **2** informal a stranger or outsider.

for·eign ex·change ▸ n. the currency of other countries.

For·eign Le·gion ▸ n. a military formation of the French army composed chiefly of non-Frenchmen.

for·eign min·is·ter ▸ n. a government minister in charge of relations with foreign countries.

fore·knowl·edge /fôrˈnäləj/ ▸ n. awareness of something before it happens or exists.

fore·land /ˈfôrlənd/ ▸ n. **1** an area of land in front of a particular feature. **2** a piece of land that juts out into the sea; a promontory.

fore·leg /ˈfôrˌleg/ ▸ n. either of the front legs of a four-footed animal.

fore·limb /ˈfôrˌlim/ ▸ n. either of the front limbs of an animal.

fore·lock /ˈfôrˌläk/ ▸ n. a lock of hair growing just above the forehead.

fore·man /ˈfôrmən/ (or **forewoman** /ˈfôrˌwo͝omən/) ▸ n. (pl. **foremen** or **forewomen**) **1** a worker who supervises other workers. **2** (in a court of law) a leader of a jury, who speaks on its behalf.

fore·mast /ˈfôrˌmast, -məst/ ▸ n. the mast of a ship nearest the bow.

fore·most /ˈfôrˌmōst/ ▸ adj. highest in rank, importance, or position. ▸ adv. in the first place.

fore·name /ˈfôrˌnām/ ▸ n. another term for FIRST NAME.

fore·noon /ˈfôrˌno͞on/ ▸ n. the morning.

fo·ren·sic /fəˈrenzik, -sik/ ▸ adj. **1** relating to the use of scientific methods to investigate crime. **2** relating to courts of law. ▸ n. (**forensics**) forensic tests or techniques. ■ **fo·ren·si·cal·ly** adv.

fo·ren·sic med·i·cine ▸ n. the application of medical knowledge to the investigation of crime, particularly in establishing the causes of injury or death.

fore·or·dain /ˌfôrôrˈdān/ ▸ v. (of God or fate) appoint or determine something beforehand.

fore·paw /ˈfôrˌpô/ ▸ n. either of the front paws of a quadruped.

fore·play /ˈfôrˌplā/ ► n. sexual activity that precedes intercourse.

fore·run·ner /ˈfôrˌrənər/ ► n. a person or thing that comes before and influences someone or something else.

fore·sail /ˈfôrˌsāl, -səl/ ► n. the main sail on a foremast.

fore·see /fôrˈsē/ ► v. (**foresees, foreseeing, foresaw** /fôrˈsô/; past part. **foreseen**) be aware of something beforehand; predict. ■ **fore·see·a·ble** adj. **fore·see·a·bly** adv.

fore·shad·ow /fôrˈsHadō/ ► v. be a warning or indication of: *changes have begun that could foreshadow a new workplace situation.*

fore·shore /ˈfôrˌsHôr/ ► n. the part of a shore between high- and low-water marks, or between the water and cultivated or developed land.

fore·short·en /fôrˈsHôrtn/ ► v. 1 depict an object or view as being closer or shallower than in reality, so as to convey an effect of perspective. 2 reduce something in time or scale.

fore·sight /ˈfôrˌsīt/ ► n. 1 the ability to predict and prepare for future events and needs. 2 the front sight of a gun. ■ **fore·sight·ed** /ˈfôrˌsītid/ adj.

fore·skin /ˈfôrˌskin/ ► n. the retractable roll of skin covering the end of the penis.

for·est /ˈfôrəst, ˈfär-/ ► n. 1 a large area covered with trees and undergrowth. 2 a mass of vertical or tangled objects: *a forest of pillars.* ► v. (usu. as adj. **forested**) plant land with trees. ■ **for·est·a·tion** /ˌfôrəˈstāsHən, ˌfär-/ n.

fore·stall /fôrˈstôl/ ► v. 1 prevent or delay something anticipated by taking action before it happens: *he forestalled the Board's plans by obtaining an injunction.* 2 prevent someone from doing something by anticipating what they are going to do.

for·est·er /ˈfôrəstər/ ► n. a person in charge of a forest or skilled in forestry.

for·est·ry /ˈfôrəstrē, ˈfär-/ ► n. the science or practice of planting, managing, and caring for forests.

fore·taste /ˈfôrˌtāst/ ► n. a sample of something that is to come: *it had been an exceptionally warm day, a foretaste of heatwaves to come.*

fore·tell /fôrˈtel/ ► v. (past and past part. **foretold** /fôrˈtōld/) predict the future.

fore·thought /ˈfôrˌтнôt/ ► n. careful consideration of what will be necessary or may happen in the future.

fore·to·ken /ˈfôrˌtōkən/ ► v. literary be a sign of a future event.

fore·told /fôrˈtōld/ ► past and past participle of FORETELL.

for·ev·er /fəˈrevər, fô-/ ► adv. 1 (also **for ever**) for all future time. 2 a very long time. 3 continually; all the time.

fore·warn /fôrˈwôrn/ ► v. warn someone of a possible future danger or problem.

fore·went /fôrˈwent/ ► past of FOREGO¹, FOREGO².

fore·wing /ˈfôrˌwiNG/ ► n. either of the two front wings of a four-winged insect.

fore·word /ˈfôrˌwərd/ ► n. a short introduction to a book.

forex /ˈfôˌreks/ ► abbr. foreign exchange.

for·feit /ˈfôrfit/ ► v. (**forfeits, forfeiting, forfeited**) 1 lose or be deprived of property or a right as a penalty for a fault or mistake. 2 lose or give up as a necessary result: *she had forfeited*

her studies after marriage. ► n. 1 a penalty for a fault or mistake. 2 Law a right, privilege, or item of property lost as a result of wrongdoing. ► adj. lost as a penalty for wrongdoing. ■ **for·fei·ture** /ˈfôrfəcHər/ n.

for·fend /fôrˈfend/ ► v. (in phrase **heaven forfend**) used to express dismay or horror at the thought of something happening: *Invite him back? Heaven forfend!*

for·gath·er /fôrˈgaTHər/ ► v. variant spelling of FOREGATHER.

for·gave /fərˈgāv/ ► past of FORGIVE.

forge¹ /fôrj/ ► v. 1 make or shape a metal object by heating and hammering the metal. 2 create something strong or successful: *the two women forged a close bond.* 3 produce a fraudulent copy or imitation of a banknote, work of art, signature, etc. ► n. 1 a blacksmith's workshop. 2 a furnace or hearth for melting or refining metal. ■ **forg·er** n.

forge² ► v. 1 move forward gradually or steadily. 2 (**forge ahead**) make progress.

for·ger·y /ˈfôrjərē/ ► n. (pl. **forgeries**) 1 the action of forging a banknote, work of art, etc. 2 a forged or copied item.

for·get /fərˈget/ ► v. (**forgets, forgetting, forgot** /fərˈgät/; past part. **forgotten** /fərˈgätn/ or **forgot**) 1 fail to remember something. 2 accidentally fail to do something. 3 deliberately cease to think of someone or something. 4 (**forget oneself**) fail to behave in an appropriate way. ■ **for·get·ta·ble** adj.

for·get·ful /fərˈgetfəl/ ► adj. apt or likely not to remember. ■ **for·get·ful·ly** adv. **for·get·ful·ness** n.

for·get-me-not ► n. a low-growing plant with bright blue flowers.

for·give /fərˈgiv/ ► v. (past **forgave** /fərˈgāv/; past part. **forgiven**) 1 stop feeling angry or resentful toward someone for an offense or mistake. 2 no longer feel angry about or wish to punish an offense, flaw, or mistake. ■ **for·giv·a·ble** adj.

for·give·ness /fərˈgivnəs/ ► n. the action of forgiving or the state of being forgiven.

for·giv·ing /fərˈgiviNG/ ► adj. 1 ready and willing to forgive: *Taylor was in a forgiving mood.* 2 tolerant: *these flooring planks are more forgiving of heavy traffic than real wood.*

for·go /fôrˈgō/ (also **forego**) ► v. (**forgoes, forgoing, forwent** /fôrˈwent/; past part. **forgone** /ˈfôrˌgôn/) go without something desirable.

for·got /fərˈgät/ ► past and past participle of FORGET.

for·got·ten /fərˈgätn/ ► past participle of FORGET.

for·int /ˈfôrˌint/ ► n. the basic unit of money of Hungary.

fork /fôrk/ ► n. 1 a small implement with two or more prongs used for lifting or holding food. 2 a farm or garden tool with prongs, used for digging or lifting. 3 each of a pair of supports in which a bicycle or motorcycle wheel revolves. 4 the point where a road, path, or river divides into two parts. 5 either of the parts where a road, path, or river divides. ► v. 1 divide into two parts. 2 take one route or the other at a fork. 3 dig or lift something with a fork. 4 (**fork something out/over/up**) informal pay money for something, especially reluctantly.

forked /fôrkt/ ► adj. having a divided or pronged end.

fork·lift /ˈfôrkˌlift/ ► n. (also **forklift truck**) a

vehicle with a pronged device in front for lifting and carrying heavy loads.

for·lorn /fər'lôrn, fôr-/ ▶ adj. **1** pitifully sad and lonely. **2** unlikely to succeed or be fulfilled: *a forlorn attempt to escape*. ■ **for·lorn·ly** adv. **for·lorn·ness** n.
– PHRASES **forlorn hope** a persistent hope that is unlikely to be fulfilled.

form /fôrm/ ▶ n. **1** the visible shape or arrangement of something. **2** a particular way in which a thing exists or appears: *a press release in the form of an eight-page booklet*. **3** a type of something. **4** a printed document with blank spaces for information to be inserted. **5** the state of an athlete with regard to their current standard of play: *illness has affected her form*. **6** details of previous performances by a racehorse or greyhound. **7** a person's mood and state of health: *she was in good form*. **8** the usual or correct method or procedure. ▶ v. **1** bring together parts to create something. **2** go to make up: *the ideas that form the basis of the book*. **3** establish or develop something. **4** make or be made into a certain form: *form the dough into balls*. ■ **form·a·ble** adj. **form·less** adj.
– PHRASES **in form** playing or performing well. **off** (or **out of**) **form** not playing or performing well.

for·mal /'fôrməl/ ▶ adj. **1** suitable for or referring to an official or important occasion: *formal evening wear*. **2** officially recognized: *a formal complaint*. **3** having a recognized form, structure, or set of rules: *he had little formal education*. **4** (of language) characterized by more elaborate grammatical structures and conservative vocabulary. **5** concerned with outward form rather than content. ■ **for·mal·ly** adv.

form·al·de·hyde /fôr'maldə,hīd, fər-/ ▶ n. a colorless pungent gas, used in solution as a preservative for biological specimens.

for·ma·lin /'fôrməlin/ ▶ n. a solution of formaldehyde in water.

for·mal·ism /'fôrmə,lizəm/ ▶ n. (in art, music, literature, etc.) concern or excessive concern with rules and outward form rather than the content of something. ■ **for·mal·ist** n.

for·mal·i·ty /fôr'malətē/ ▶ n. (pl. **formalities**) **1** a thing done to follow convention or rules: *a statutory declaration that all the formalities have been complied with*. **2** correct and formal behavior. **3** (**a formality**) a thing done or occurring as a matter of course.

for·mal·ize /'fôrmə,līz/ ▶ v. **1** give something legal or official status. **2** give something a definite form or shape. ■ **for·mal·i·za·tion** /,fôrməli'zāsHən/ n.

for·mat /'fôr,mat/ ▶ n. **1** the way in which something is arranged or presented. **2** the shape, size, and presentation of a book, document, etc. **3** the medium in which a sound recording is made available: *LP and CD formats*. **4** Computing a defined structure for the processing, storage, or display of data. ▶ v. (**formats, formatting, formatted**) (especially in computing) arrange or put something into a particular format.

for·ma·tion /fôr'māsHən/ ▶ n. **1** the action of forming or the process of being formed. **2** a structure or arrangement: *strange rock formations*. **3** a formal arrangement of aircraft in flight or troops. ■ **for·ma·tion·al** adj.

for·ma·tive /'fôrmətiv/ ▶ adj. having an important influence on the development of someone or something: *his formative years in Victorian Scotland*. ■ **for·ma·tive·ly** adv.

form·er[1] /'fôrmər/ ▶ adj. **1** having previously been: *her former husband*. **2** relating to or occurring in the past. **3** (**the former**) referring to the first of two things mentioned.

form·er[2] ▶ n. a person or thing that forms something.

for·mer·ly /'fôrmərlē/ ▶ adv. in the past.

For·mi·ca /fôr'mīkə, fər-/ ▶ n. trademark a hard plastic laminate used for countertops, cupboard doors, etc.

for·mic ac·id /'fôrmik/ ▶ n. an acid present in the fluid produced by some ants.

for·mi·da·ble /'fôrmədəbəl, fôr'midəbəl, fər'mid-/ ▶ adj. inspiring fear or respect through being impressively large, powerful, or capable. ■ **for·mi·da·bly** adv.

form let·ter ▶ n. a standardized letter to deal with frequently occurring matters.

for·mu·la /'fôrmyələ/ ▶ n. (pl. **formulae** /-,lē, -,lī/ (in senses 1 and 2) or **formulas**) **1** a mathematical relationship or rule expressed in symbols. **2** (also **chemical formula**) a set of chemical symbols showing the elements present in a compound and their relative proportions. **3** a method for achieving something: *at ZDC, we stick to our proven formula for success*. **4** a fixed form of words used in a particular situation. **5** a list of ingredients with which something is made. **6** a baby's liquid food preparation based on cow's milk or soy protein. **7** a classification of race car: *Formula One*.

for·mu·la·ic /,fôrmyə'lāik/ ▶ adj. **1** made up of or containing a set form of words. **2** following a rule or style too closely: *the lyrics are dry and formulaic*. ■ **for·mu·la·i·cal·ly** adv.

for·mu·lar·y /'fôrmyə,lerē/ ▶ n. (pl. **formularies**) **1** an official list giving details of prescribable medicines. **2** a collection of set forms for use in religious ceremonies.

for·mu·late /'fôrmyə,lāt/ ▶ v. **1** create or prepare something methodically. **2** express an idea in a concise or systematic way. ■ **for·mu·la·tor** n.

for·mu·la·tion /,fôrmyə'lāsHən/ ▶ n. **1** the action of creating or preparing something. **2** a mixture prepared according to a formula.

for·ni·cate /'fôrni,kāt/ ▶ v. formal or humorous have sexual intercourse with someone one is not married to. ■ **for·ni·ca·tion** /,fôrni'kāsHən/ n. **for·ni·ca·tor** n.

for·sake /fər'sāk, fôr-/ ▶ v. (past **forsook** /-'sŏŏk/; past part. **forsaken**) chiefly literary **1** abandon someone. **2** give up something valued or pleasant.

for·sooth /fər'sŏŏTH/ ▶ adv. old use or humorous indeed.

for·swear /fôr'swe(ə)r/ ▶ v. (past **forswore** /fôr'swôr/; past part. **forsworn** /fôr'swôrn/) formal agree to give up or do without something.

for·syth·i·a /fər'siTHēə/ ▶ n. a shrub whose bright yellow flowers appear in early spring before its leaves.

fort /fôrt/ ▶ n. a building constructed to defend a place against attack.
– PHRASES **hold** (**down**) **the fort** take responsibility for something while someone is away.

for·te[1] /'fôr,tā, fôrt/ ▶ n. a thing at which someone excels: *photo sessions are not his forte*.

for·te[2] ▶ adv. & adj. Music loud or loudly.

for·te·pi·an·o /ˌfôrtāpēˈanō, -pēˈänō/ ▶ n. (pl. **fortepianos**) a piano, especially one of the kind made in the 18th and early 19th centuries.

forth /fôrᴛʜ/ ▶ adv. formal or literary **1** out and away from a starting point. **2** so as to be revealed. **3** onward in time.
– PHRASES **and so forth** and so on.

forth·com·ing /fôrᴛʜˈkəmiNG, ˈfôrᴛʜˌkəmiNG/ ▶ adj. **1** about to happen or appear. **2** ready or made available when required: *help was not forthcoming.* **3** willing to reveal information.

forth·right /ˈfôrᴛʜˌrīt/ ▶ adj. direct and outspoken. ■ **forth·right·ly** adv. **forth·right·ness** n.

forth·with /fôrᴛʜˈwiᴛʜ/ ▶ adv. without delay.

for·ti·fi·ca·tion /ˌfôrtəˌfəˈkāSHən/ ▶ n. **1** a defensive wall or other structure built to strengthen a place against attack. **2** the action of fortifying something.

for·ti·fy /ˈfôrtəˌfī/ ▶ v. (**fortifies, fortifying, fortified**) **1** provide a place with defensive structures as protection against attack. **2** encourage or strengthen someone. **3** add liquor to wine to make port, sherry, etc. **4** make food more nutritious by adding vitamins. ■ **for·ti·fi·er** n.

for·tis·si·mo /fôrˈtisəˌmō/ ▶ adv. & adj. Music very loud or loudly.

for·ti·tude /ˈfôrtəˌtōōd/ ▶ n. courage and strength in bearing pain or trouble.

fort·night /ˈfôrtˌnīt/ ▶ n. chiefly Brit. a period of two weeks. ■ **fort·night·ly** adj. & adv.

For·tran /ˈfôrˌtran/ ▶ n. a high-level computer programming language used especially for scientific applications.

for·tress /ˈfôrtrəs/ ▶ n. a fort or a strongly fortified town.

for·tu·i·tous /fôrˈtōōətəs/ ▶ adj. **1** happening by chance rather than intention. **2** happening by a lucky chance; fortunate. ■ **for·tu·i·tous·ly** adv. **for·tu·i·tous·ness** n. **for·tu·i·ty** n. (pl. **fortuities**).

for·tu·nate /ˈfôrCHənət/ ▶ adj. **1** having or happening by good luck; lucky. **2** favorable; advantageous: *in the fortunate position of being headhunted to join a major firm.*

for·tu·nate·ly /ˈfôrCHənətlē/ ▶ adv. it is fortunate that.

for·tune /ˈfôrCHən/ ▶ n. **1** chance as a force affecting people's lives. **2** luck, especially good luck. **3** (**fortunes**) the success or failure of a person or enterprise. **4** a large amount of money or assets.
– PHRASES **a small fortune** informal a large amount of money. **tell someone's fortune** predict a person's future by palmistry or similar methods.

for·tune cook·ie ▶ n. a thin folded cookie containing a slip of paper with a prediction or aphorism written on it, served in Chinese restaurants.

for·tune-tell·er ▶ n. a person who predicts what will happen in people's lives. ■ **for·tune-tell·ing** n.

for·ty /ˈfôrtē/ ▶ cardinal number (pl. **forties**) ten less than fifty; 40. (Roman numeral: **xl** or **XL**.) ■ **for·ti·eth** ordinal number.
– PHRASES **forty winks** informal a short daytime sleep.

for·ty-five ▶ n. a phonograph record played at 45 rpm.

fo·rum /ˈfôrəm/ ▶ n. (pl. **forums**) **1** a meeting or medium for an exchange of views. **2** (pl. **fora** /ˈfôrə/) (in ancient Roman cities) a public square or marketplace used for judicial and other business.

for·ward /ˈfôrwərd/ ▶ adv. (also **forwards**) **1** in the direction that one is facing or traveling. **2** onward so as to make progress. **3** ahead in time. **4** in or near the front of a ship or aircraft. ▶ adj. **1** toward the direction that one is facing or traveling. **2** relating to the future. **3** bold or overfamiliar. **4** progressing toward a successful conclusion: *the decision is a forward step.* **5** situated in or near the front of a ship or aircraft. ▶ n. an attacking player in soccer, hockey, or other sports. ▶ v. **1** send a letter or email on to a further address. **2** send a document or goods. **3** help something to develop or progress. ■ **for·ward·er** n. **for·ward·ly** adv. **for·ward·ness** n.

for·ward-look·ing (also **forward-thinking**) ▶ adj. favoring innovation; progressive.

for·went /fôrˈwent/ ▶ past of FORGO.

fos·sil /ˈfäsəl/ ▶ n. **1** the remains or impression of a prehistoric plant or animal that have become hardened into rock. **2** humorous an old or outdated person or thing.

fos·sil fu·el ▶ n. a natural fuel such as coal or gas, formed in the geological past from the remains of animals and plants.

fos·sil·ize /ˈfäsəˌlīz/ ▶ v. preserve an animal or plant so that it becomes a fossil. ■ **fos·sil·i·za·tion** /ˌfäsəliˈzāSHən/ n.

fos·ter /ˈfôstər, ˈfäs-/ ▶ v. **1** promote the development of: *they hope the visit will foster improved relations between the two countries.* **2** bring up a child that is not one's own by birth. ■ **fos·ter·age** n. **fos·ter·er** n.

fought /fôt/ ▶ past and past participle of FIGHT.

foul /foul/ ▶ adj. **1** having a very unpleasant smell or taste; disgusting. **2** very unpleasant: *he was in a foul mood.* **3** wicked or obscene. **4** not allowed by the rules of a sport. **5** polluted or contaminated. ▶ n. (in sports) a piece of play that is not allowed by the rules. ▶ v. **1** make something foul or polluted. **2** (of an animal) dirty something with excrement. **3** (in sports) commit a foul against an opponent. **4** (**foul out**) Basketball be put out of the game for exceeding the permitted number of fouls. **5** (**foul out**) Baseball (of a batter) be made out by hitting a foul ball that is caught by an opposing player. **6** (**foul something up**) make a mistake with or spoil something. **7** cause a cable or anchor to become entangled or jammed. ■ **foul·ly** adv. **foul·ness** n.

fou·lard /fōōˈlärd/ ▶ n. a thin, soft material of silk or silk and cotton.

foul ball ▶ n. Baseball a ball struck so that it falls or will fall outside the lines extending from home plate past first and third bases.

foul-mouthed ▶ adj. using bad language.

foul play ▶ n. **1** unfair play in a game or sport. **2** criminal or violent activity, especially murder.

foul-up ▶ n. a problem caused by a stupid mistake.

found[1] /found/ ▶ past and past participle of FIND.

found[2] ▶ v. **1** establish an institution or organization. **2** (**be founded on**) be based on a particular principle or idea.

found[3] ▶ v. **1** melt and mold metal. **2** fuse materials to make glass. **3** make an object by melting and molding metal.

foun·da·tion /foun'dāsʜən/ ▸ n. **1** the lowest load-bearing part of a building, typically below ground level. **2** a basis for something: *the Chinese laid the scientific foundation for many modern discoveries.* **3** justification or reason: *there was no foundation for the claim.* **4** an institution or organization. **5** the establishment of an institution or organization. **6** a cream or powder applied to the face as a base for other makeup. ■ **foun·da·tion·al** adj.

foun·da·tion stone ▸ n. a stone laid at a ceremony to celebrate the laying of a building's foundation.

found·er¹ /'foundər/ ▸ n. a person who founds an institution or settlement.

found·er² ▸ n. the owner or operator of a foundry.

found·er³ ▸ v. **1** (of a plan or undertaking) fail; come to nothing. **2** (of a ship) fill with water and sink. **3** (of a horse) stumble or fall.

> **USAGE**
> The words **founder** and **flounder** are often confused. **Founder** chiefly means 'fail' (*a proposed merger between the two airlines foundered last year*), while **flounder** means 'have trouble doing or understanding something' (*the school was floundering in confusion about its role in the world*).

found·ing fa·ther ▸ n. **1** a person who starts or helps start a movement or institution. **2** (**Founding Father**) a member of the convention that drew up the US Constitution in 1787.

found·ling /'foundliNG/ ▸ n. a young child who has been abandoned by its parents and is found and cared for by others.

found ob·ject ▸ n. an object found or picked up at random and considered aesthetically pleasing.

found·ry /'foundrē/ ▸ n. (pl. **foundries**) a workshop or factory for casting metal.

fount¹ /fänt, fount/ ▸ n. **1** a source of a desirable quality: *he was a fount of wisdom.* **2** literary a spring or fountain.

fount² ▸ n. Brit. variant spelling of FONT².

foun·tain /'fountn/ ▸ n. **1** an ornamental structure in a pool or lake from which a jet of water is pumped into the air. **2** a source of something desirable: *Susan is a fountain of knowledge about the area.* **3** literary a natural spring of water. ▸ v. spurt or cascade like a fountain.

foun·tain·head /'fountn,hed/ ▸ n. an original source of something.

foun·tain pen ▸ n. a pen with a container from which ink flows continuously to the nib.

four /fôr/ ▸ cardinal number one more than three; 4. (Roman numeral: **iv** or **IV**.) ■ **four·fold** adj. & adv.

four-by-four (also **4 × 4**) ▸ n. a vehicle with four-wheel drive.

four-di·men·sion·al ▸ adj. having the three dimensions of space (length, breadth, and depth) plus time.

4H (also **Four-H**) ▸ n. a government-sponsored organization with many local branches that teaches agricultural and practical skills to children in rural areas.

four-leaf clo·ver ▸ n. **1** a clover leaf with four leaflets instead of the usual three, thought to bring good luck. **2** a stylized representation of this.

four-let·ter word ▸ n. any of several short words referring to sex or excretion, regarded as rude or offensive.

four-post·er (also **four-poster bed**) ▸ n. a bed with a post at each corner, sometimes supporting a canopy.

four-score /'fôr'skôr/ ▸ cardinal number old use eighty.

four·some /'fôrsəm/ ▸ n. a group of four people.

four-square ▸ adj. **1** (of a building) having a square shape and solid appearance. **2** firm and resolute. ▸ adv. in a firm and resolute way: *the senator had come out four-square in favor of the line-item veto.*

four-stroke ▸ adj. (of an internal-combustion engine) having a cycle of four strokes (intake, compression, combustion, and exhaust).

four·teen /,fôr'tēn, 'fôr,tēn/ ▸ cardinal number one more than thirteen; 14. (Roman numeral: **xiv** or **XIV.**) ■ **four·teenth** ordinal number.

fourth /fôrth/ ▸ ordinal number **1** that is number four in a sequence; 4th. **2** (**a fourth/one fourth**) a quarter: *a fourth of the pizza is gone.* **3** Music an interval spanning four consecutive notes in a diatonic scale. ■ **fourth·ly** adv.

fourth di·men·sion ▸ n. time regarded as a dimension comparable to the three linear dimensions.

fourth es·tate ▸ n. journalism; the press.

Fourth of Ju·ly ▸ n. another term for INDEPENDENCE DAY.

4WD ▸ abbr. four-wheel drive.

four-wheel drive ▸ n. a transmission system that provides power directly to all four wheels of a vehicle.

fowl /foul/ ▸ n. (pl. same or **fowls**) **1** (also **domestic fowl**) a domesticated bird kept for its eggs or flesh; a cock or hen. **2** any domesticated bird, e.g., a turkey. **3** birds as a group, especially as the quarry of hunters. ■ **fowl·er** n. **fowl·ing** n.

fox /fäks/ ▸ n. **1** an animal of the dog family with a pointed muzzle and bushy tail. **2** informal a cunning or sly person. **3** informal a sexually attractive woman. ▸ v. informal baffle or deceive someone.

fox·glove /'fäks,gləv/ ▸ n. a tall plant with pinkish-purple or white bell-shaped flowers growing up the stem.

fox·hole /'fäks,hōl/ ▸ n. a hole in the ground used by troops as a shelter against enemy fire or as a firing point.

fox·hound /'fäks,hound/ ▸ n. a breed of dog with smooth hair and drooping ears, trained to hunt foxes in packs.

fox hunt·ing ▸ n. the sport of hunting a fox across country with a pack of hounds, carried out by people on foot and horseback.

fox·tail /'fäks,tāl/ ▸ n. a common meadow grass that has soft brushlike flowering spikes.

fox·trot /'fäks,trät/ ▸ n. a ballroom dance with alternation of slow and quick steps.

fox·y /'fäksē/ ▸ adj. (**foxier**, **foxiest**) **1** resembling a fox. **2** cunning or sly. **3** informal (of a woman) sexually attractive. ■ **fox·i·ly** adv. **fox·i·ness** n.

foy·er /'foiər, 'foi,ā/ ▸ n. a large entrance hall in a hotel or theater.

Fr. ▸ abbr. Father (as a courtesy title of priests).

fr. ▸ abbr. franc(s).

fra·cas /'fräkəs, 'frak-/ ▸ n. (pl. **fracases**) a noisy disturbance or quarrel.

frac·tal /ˈfraktəl/ ▶ n. Mathematics a curve or geometrical figure, each part of which has the same statistical character as the whole.

frac·tion /ˈfraksHən/ ▶ n. 1 a numerical quantity that is not a whole number (e.g., ½, 0.5). 2 a very small part, amount, or proportion. 3 Chemistry each of the parts of a mixture, with different boiling points, which may be separated by distillation.

frac·tion·al /ˈfraksHənl/ ▶ adj. 1 relating to or expressed as a fraction. 2 very small in amount. ■ **frac·tion·al·ly** adv.

frac·tious /ˈfraksHəs/ ▶ adj. 1 easily irritated. 2 difficult to control. ■ **frac·tious·ly** adv. **frac·tious·ness** n.

frac·ture /ˈfrakCHər/ ▶ n. 1 a crack or break, especially in a bone or layer of rock. 2 the cracking or breaking of a hard object or material. ▶ v. 1 break or cause to break. 2 (of a group) split up or fragment.

frag·ile /ˈfrajəl, -ˌjīl/ ▶ adj. 1 easily broken, damaged, or destroyed. 2 (of a person) not strong; delicate. ■ **fra·gil·i·ty** /frəˈjilitē/ n.

frag·ile X syn·drome ▶ n. an inherited condition characterized by an X chromosome that is abnormally susceptible to damage, especially by folic acid deficiency. Affected individuals tend to be mentally handicapped.

frag·ment ▶ n. /ˈfragmənt/ 1 a small part broken off or detached. 2 an isolated or incomplete part: *a fragment of conversation.* ▶ v. /ˈfragˌment, ˈfragˈment/ break into fragments.

frag·men·tar·y /ˈfragmənˌterē/ ▶ adj. consisting of small disconnected or incomplete parts. ■ **frag·men·tar·i·ly** /ˌfragmənˈterəlē/ adv.

frag·men·ta·tion /ˌfragmənˈtāsHən/ ▶ n. the process of breaking or the state of being broken into fragments.

fra·grance /ˈfrāgrəns/ ▶ n. 1 a pleasant, sweet smell. 2 a perfume or aftershave. ■ **fra·granced** adj.

fra·grant /ˈfrāgrənt/ ▶ adj. having a pleasant, sweet smell. ■ **fra·grant·ly** adv.

frail /frāl/ ▶ adj. 1 (of a person) weak and delicate. 2 easily damaged or broken. ■ **frail·ness** n.

frail·ty /ˈfrāltē/ ▶ n. (pl. **frailties**) 1 the condition of being frail or weak. 2 weakness in a person's character or morals.

frame /frām/ ▶ n. 1 a rigid structure surrounding a picture, door, etc. 2 (**frames**) a metal or plastic structure holding the lenses of a pair of glasses. 3 the rigid supporting structure of a vehicle, building, or other object. 4 a person's body with reference to its size or build: *her slim frame.* 5 the underlying structure of a system, concept, or written work: *the novels rested on a frame of moral truth.* 6 a single complete picture in a series forming a movie, television, or video film. 7 another term for RACK¹ (sense 3 of the noun). 8 a round of play in bowling. ▶ v. 1 place a picture in a frame. 2 surround so as to create an attractive image: *short hair cut to frame the face.* 3 formulate or develop a plan or system. 4 informal produce false evidence against an innocent person to make them appear guilty of a crime. ■ **framed** adj. **frame·less** adj. **fram·er** n. – PHRASES **frame of mind** a particular mood. **frame of reference** a set of values according to which judgments can be made.

frame-up ▶ n. informal a conspiracy to incriminate someone falsely.

frame·work /ˈfrāmˌwərk/ ▶ n. a supporting or underlying structure.

franc /fraNGk/ ▶ n. the basic unit of money of France, Belgium, Switzerland, Luxembourg, and several other countries (replaced in France, Belgium, and Luxembourg by the euro in 2002).

fran·chise /ˈfranˌCHīz/ ▶ n. 1 formal permission granted by a government or company to a person or group enabling them to sell certain products or provide a service. 2 a business or service run under a franchise. 3 the right to vote in public elections. ▶ v. 1 grant a franchise to someone. 2 grant a franchise for goods or a service. ■ **fran·chi·see** /ˌfranCHīˈzē/ n. **fran·chis·er** (also **franchisor**) /ˌfranCHəˈzôr/ n.

Fran·cis·can /franˈsiskən/ ▶ n. a monk or nun of a Christian religious order following the precepts of the Italian monk St. Francis of Assisi. ▶ adj. relating to St. Francis or the Franciscans.

fran·ci·um /ˈfransēəm/ ▶ n. an unstable radioactive chemical element of the alkali-metal group.

Franco- (also **franco-**) ▶ comb.form 1 French; French and ...: *francophone | Franco-American.* 2 relating to France: *Francophile.*

Fran·co·phile /ˈfraNGkəˌfil/ ▶ n. a person who is fond of or greatly admires France or the French.

fran·co·phone /ˈfraNGkəˌfōn/ ▶ adj. French-speaking. ▶ n. a French-speaking person.

fran·gi·ble /ˈfranjəbəl/ ▶ adj. literary or technical fragile; brittle.

fran·gi·pan·i /ˌfranjəˈpanē, -ˈpänē/ ▶ n. (pl. **frangipanis**) 1 a tropical American tree or shrub with fragrant white, pink, or yellow flowers. 2 perfume obtained from the frangipani plant.

Frank /fraNGk/ ▶ n. a member of a Germanic people that conquered Gaul in the 6th century. ■ **Frank·ish** adj. & n.

frank¹ /fraNGk/ ▶ adj. 1 honest and direct, especially when dealing with unpleasant matters. 2 open or undisguised: *he looked at her with frank admiration.* ■ **frank·ness** n.

frank² ▶ v. stamp an official mark on a letter or parcel to indicate that postage has been paid or does not need to be paid. ▶ n. a franking mark on a letter or parcel.

Frank·en·food /ˈfraNGkənˌfo͝od/ ▶ n. informal, derogatory a genetically modified food.

Frank·en·stein /ˈfraNGkənˌstīn/ (also **Frankenstein's monster**) ▶ n. a thing that becomes terrifying or destructive to its maker.

frank·furt·er /ˈfraNGkˌfərtər/ ▶ n. a seasoned smoked sausage made of beef and pork.

frank·in·cense /ˈfraNGkənˌsens/ ▶ n. an aromatic resinous substance obtained from an African tree and burned as incense.

frank·ly /ˈfraNGklē/ ▶ adv. 1 in an honest and direct way. 2 to be frank.

fran·tic /ˈfrantik/ ▶ adj. 1 distraught with fear, anxiety, or other emotion. 2 done in a hurried and chaotic way: *frantic efforts to put out the fires.* ■ **fran·ti·cal·ly** adv. **fran·tic·ness** n.

frap·pé /fraˈpā/ ▶ adj. (of a drink) iced or chilled. ▶ n. 1 a drink served with ice or frozen to a slushy consistency. 2 (**frappe** /frap/) a milkshake, especially one made with ice cream.

fra·ter·nal /frəˈtərnl/ ▶ adj. 1 relating to or like a brother; brotherly. 2 relating to a fraternity. 3 (of twins) developed from separate ova (female reproductive cells) and therefore not identical. ■ **fra·ter·nal·ly** adv.

fra·ter·ni·ty /frəˈtərnətē/ ▶ n. (pl. **fraternities**) **1** a male students' society in a college or university. **2** a group of people sharing the same profession or interests: *the medical fraternity.* **3** friendship and shared support within a group.

frat·er·nize /ˈfratərˌnīz/ ▶ v. (usu. **fraternize with**) be on friendly terms, especially with someone whom one is not supposed to be friendly with. ■ **frat·er·ni·za·tion** /ˌfratərniˈzāSHən/ n.

frat·ri·cide /ˈfratrəˌsīd/ ▶ n. **1** the killing of one's brother or sister. **2** the accidental killing of one's own forces in war. ■ **frat·ri·cid·al** /ˌfratrəˈsīdl/ adj.

Frau /frou/ ▶ n. a title or form of address for a married or widowed German woman.

fraud /frôd/ ▶ n. **1** the crime of deceiving someone to gain money or personal advantage. **2** a person who deceives others into believing that he or she has certain qualities or abilities.

fraud·u·lent /ˈfrôjələnt/ ▶ adj. **1** done by or involving fraud. **2** intended to deceive. ■ **fraud·u·lence** n. **fraud·u·lent·ly** adv.

fraught /frôt/ ▶ adj. **1** (**fraught with**) filled with something undesirable. **2** causing or feeling anxiety or stress.

Fräu·lein /ˈfroiˌlīn/ ▶ n. a title or form of address for an unmarried German woman.

fray[1] /frā/ ▶ v. **1** (of a fabric, rope, or cord) unravel or become worn at the edge. **2** (of a person's nerves or temper) show the effects of strain.

fray[2] ▶ n. (**the fray**) **1** a very competitive or demanding situation: *with new manufacturers entering the fray, the competition is certain to intensify.* **2** a battle or fight.

fraz·zle /ˈfrazəl/ informal ▶ v. **1** (as adj. **frazzled**) completely exhausted. **2** make something shrivel up with burning. ▶ n. (**a frazzle**) **1** an exhausted state. **2** a burned state.

freak /frēk/ ▶ n. **1** informal a person who is obsessed with a particular activity or interest: *a fitness freak.* **2** a very unusual and unexpected event. **3** (also **freak of nature**) a person, animal, or plant with a physical abnormality. **4** informal a person regarded as strange because of their unusual appearance or behavior. ▶ adj. very unusual and unexpected: *a freak accident.* ▶ v. (usu. **freak out**) informal react or cause to react in a wild, shocked, or excited way. ■ **freak·ish** adj.

freak show ▶ n. **1** a sideshow at a fair, featuring abnormally developed people or animals. **2** an unusual or grotesque event viewed for pleasure, especially when it is in bad taste: *his latest film is a fabulous freak show.*

freak·y /ˈfrēkē/ ▶ adj. (**freakier, freakiest**) informal very odd or strange. ■ **freak·i·ly** adv. **freak·i·ness** n.

freck·le /ˈfrekəl/ ▶ n. a small light brown spot on the skin. ▶ v. cover or become covered with freckles. ■ **freck·ly** /ˈfrekl-ē, ˈfreklē/ adj.

free /frē/ ▶ adj. (**freer, freest**) **1** able to do what one wants; not under the control of anyone else. **2** not confined, obstructed, or fixed: *they set the birds free.* **3** not having or not filled with things to do: *I spent my free time shopping.* **4** not occupied or in use. **5** (**free of/from**) not containing or affected by something undesirable. **6** available without charge. **7** (usu. **free with**) using or spending something without restraint. **8** behaving or speaking without restraint. **9** (of art, music, etc.) not following the normal conventions. **10** (of a translation) conveying the general meaning; not literal. ▶ adv. without cost or payment. ▶ v. (**frees, freeing, freed**) **1** make someone or something free. **2** make something available for a purpose. ■ **free·ness** n.

– PHRASES **free and easy** informal and relaxed. **a free hand** freedom to act completely as one wishes. **a free ride** a situation in which someone benefits without making a fair contribution. **the free world** the noncommunist countries of the world, as formerly opposed to the Soviet bloc.

-free ▶ comb.form free of or from: *tax-free.*

free a·gent ▶ n. **1** a person who can act without restrictions imposed by others. **2** an athlete who is not bound by a contract and can join another team.

free-as·so·ci·ate ▶ v. allow the mind to supply whatever word, thought, or image is suggested by one previously mentioned or noted: *people then start to free-associate and shout out ideas.* ■ **free as·so·ci·a·tion** n.

free·base /ˈfrēˌbās/ ▶ n. cocaine that has been purified by heating with ether, taken by inhaling the fumes or smoking the residue. ▶ v. take cocaine in this way.

free·bie /ˈfrēbē/ ▶ n. informal a thing given free of charge.

free·board /ˈfrēˌbôrd/ ▶ n. the height of a ship's side between the waterline and the deck.

free·boot·er /ˈfrēˌbootər/ ▶ n. a person who behaves in an illegal way for their own advantage. ■ **free·boot·ing** adj.

free·born /ˈfrēˌbôrn/ ▶ adj. not born in slavery.

freed·man /ˈfrēdmən, -ˌman/ ▶ n. (pl. **freedmen**) historical an emancipated slave.

free·dom /ˈfrēdəm/ ▶ n. **1** the power or right to act, speak, or think as one wants. **2** the state of being free: *clothing that allows maximum freedom of movement.* **3** (**freedom from**) the state of not being subject to or affected by something undesirable. **4** unrestricted use of something: *the dog had the freedom of the house.*

free·dom fight·er ▶ n. a person who takes part in a struggle to achieve political freedom.

free en·ter·prise ▶ n. an economic system in which private businesses compete with each other with little state control.

free fall ▶ n. **1** downward movement under the force of gravity. **2** a rapid decline that cannot be stopped: *the euro was in free fall.* ▶ v. (**free-fall**) fall rapidly.

free-for-all ▶ n. a disorganized or unrestricted situation or event in which everyone may take part.

free-form ▶ adj. not in a regular or formal structure.

free·hand /ˈfrēˌhand/ ▶ adj. & adv. done by hand without the aid of instruments such as rulers.

free·hold /ˈfrēˌhōld/ ▶ n. chiefly Brit. permanent and absolute ownership of land or property with the freedom to sell it when one wishes. ■ **free·hold·er** n.

free kick ▶ n. (in soccer and rugby) an unimpeded kick of the stationary ball awarded when the opposing team has broken the rules.

free·lance /ˈfrēˌlans/ ▶ adj. self-employed and hired to work for different companies on particular assignments. ▶ adv. earning one's living as a freelance. ▶ n. (also **freelancer**) a freelance worker. ▶ v. earn one's living as a freelance.

free·load·er /ˈfrēˌlōdər/ ▶ n. informal a person who

takes advantage of others' generosity without giving anything in return. ■ **free·load** /ˈfrēˌlōd/ v.

free love ▶ n. dated the practice of having sexual relationships freely, without being faithful to one partner.

free·ly /ˈfrēlē/ ▶ adv. **1** not under the control of someone else. **2** without restriction or restraint: *a world where people cannot speak freely.* **3** in abundant amounts. **4** willingly and readily.

free·man /ˈfrēmən/ ▶ n. (pl. **freemen**) **1** a person who is entitled to full political and civil rights. **2** historical a person who is not a slave or serf.

free mar·ket ▶ n. an economic system in which prices are determined by supply and demand rather than controlled by a government.

Free·ma·son /ˈfrēˌmāsən/ ▶ n. a member of an international order whose members help each other and hold secret ceremonies. ■ **Free·ma·son·ry** n.

fre·er /ˈfrēər/ ▶ adj. comparative of FREE.

free rad·i·cal ▶ n. a highly reactive molecule with one odd electron not paired up in a chemical bond.

free-range ▶ adj. (of livestock or their produce) kept or produced in natural conditions, where the animals may move around freely.

free·sia /ˈfrēzHə/ ▶ n. a small plant with fragrant, colorful, tubular flowers, native to southern Africa.

free speech ▶ n. the right to express any opinions without censorship.

free spir·it ▶ n. an independent or uninhibited person: *they raised their children to be free spirits.*

fre·est /ˈfrēəst/ ▶ adj. superlative of FREE.

free·stand·ing /ˈfrēˈstandiNG/ ▶ adj. not attached to or supported by another structure.

free·style /ˈfrēˌstīl/ ▶ n. (usu. before another noun) a contest, race, or type of sport in which there are few restrictions on the style or technique that competitors employ. ▶ v. perform or compete in an unrestricted or improvised fashion. ■ **free·styl·er** n.

free·think·er /ˈfrēˈᴛʜiNGkər/ ▶ n. a person who questions or rejects accepted opinions, especially those concerning religious belief.

free throw ▶ n. Basketball an unimpeded attempt at a basket (worth one point) awarded to a player following a foul or other infringement.

free trade ▶ n. international trade left to its natural course without tariffs or other restrictions.

free verse ▶ n. poetry that does not rhyme or have a regular rhythm.

free·ware /ˈfrēˌwe(ə)r/ ▶ n. software that is available free of charge.

free·way /ˈfrēˌwā/ ▶ n. an express highway, especially one with controlled access.

free·wheel /ˈfrēˌ(h)wēl/ ▶ v. **1** ride on a bicycle without using the pedals. **2** (as adj. **freewheeling**) not concerned with rules or the results of one's actions. ▶ n. a bicycle wheel that is able to revolve freely when no power is being applied to the pedals. ■ **free·wheel·er** n.

free will ▶ n. the power to act according to one's own wishes.

freeze /frēz/ ▶ v. (past **froze** /frōz/; past part. **frozen** /ˈfrōzən/) **1** (with reference to a liquid) turn to or be turned into ice or another solid as a result of extreme cold. **2** block or become blocked or

rigid with ice. **3** be or make very cold. **4** store something at a very low temperature in order to preserve it. **5** become suddenly motionless with fear or shock. **6** hold at a fixed level or in a fixed state: *the Act has given the police powers to freeze the assets of suspects.* **7** (of a computer screen) suddenly become locked. **8** (**freeze someone out**) informal make someone feel left out by being hostile or cold toward them. ▶ n. **1** an act of holding something at a fixed level or in a fixed state. **2** a period of very cold weather. ■ **freeze·a·ble** adj.

freeze-dry ▶ v. preserve something by rapidly freezing it and then removing the ice in a vacuum.

freeze-frame ▶ n. **1** a single frame forming a motionless image from a film or videotape. **2** the facility or process of stopping a film or videotape to obtain a freeze-frame.

freez·er /ˈfrēzər/ ▶ n. a refrigerated cabinet or room for preserving food at very low temperatures.

freeze-up ▶ n. **1** an instance of something freezing: *gas line freeze-up.* **2** a period when freezing temperatures prevail: *areas where they hunt seals after freeze-up.*

freez·ing /ˈfrēziNG/ ▶ adj. **1** below 32°F (0°C). **2** very cold. **3** (of fog or rain) consisting of droplets that freeze rapidly on contact with a surface. ▶ n. the freezing point of water (32°F/0°C).

freez·ing point ▶ n. the temperature at which a liquid turns into a solid when cooled.

freight /frāt/ ▶ n. **1** transport of goods in bulk by truck, train, ship, or aircraft. **2** goods transported by freight. ▶ v. **1** transport goods by freight. **2** (**be freighted with**) be laden or burdened with: *each word was freighted with anger.*

freight car ▶ n. a railroad car for carrying freight.

freight·er /ˈfrātər/ ▶ n. a large ship or aircraft designed to carry freight.

French /frenCH/ ▶ adj. relating to France or its people or language. ▶ n. the language of France, also used in parts of Belgium, Switzerland, Canada, and elsewhere. ■ **French·ness** n.
– PHRASES **excuse** (or **pardon**) **my French** informal used to apologize for swearing.

French bread ▶ n. white bread in a long, crisp loaf.

French Ca·na·di·an ▶ n. a Canadian whose native language is French. ▶ adj. relating to French Canadians.

French chalk ▶ n. a kind of steatite (talc) used for marking cloth and removing grease.

French dress·ing ▶ n. a salad dressing of vinegar, oil, and seasonings.

French fries ▶ pl. n. potato cut into strips and deep-fried.

French horn ▶ n. a brass instrument with a coiled tube, valves, and a wide bell.

French·i·fy /ˈfrenCHiˌfī/ ▶ v. (**Frenchifies, Frenchifying, Frenchified**) often derogatory make someone or something French in form or character.

French kiss ▶ n. a kiss with contact between tongues. ■ **French kiss·ing** n.

French·man /ˈfrenCHmən/ (or **Frenchwoman**) ▶ n. (pl. **Frenchmen** or **Frenchwomen**) a person who is French by birth or descent.

French toast ▶ n. bread coated in egg and milk and fried.

French win·dow ▸ n. each of a pair of casement windows extending to the floor in an outside wall, serving as a window and door.

French·wom·an /ˈfrenCHˌwoŏmən/ ▸ n. (pl. **Frenchwomen**) a female who is French by birth or descent.

fre·net·ic /frəˈnetik/ ▸ adj. fast and energetic in a disorganized or uncontrolled way. ■ **fre·net·i·cal·ly** adv. **fre·net·i·cism** /frəˈnetiˌsizəm/ n.

fren·zy /ˈfrenzē/ ▸ n. (pl. **frenzies**) a state or period of uncontrolled excitement or wild behavior. ■ **fren·zied** adj. **fren·zied·ly** adv.

Fre·on /ˈfrēˌän/ ▸ n. trademark an aerosol propellant, refrigerant, or organic solvent consisting of one or more of a group of chlorofluorocarbons and related compounds.

fre·quen·cy /ˈfrēkwənsē/ ▸ n. (pl. **frequencies**) 1 the rate at which something occurs in a given period or sample: *the lightning strikes seemed to increase in frequency.* 2 the fact or state of being frequent. 3 the number of cycles per second of a sound, light, or radio wave. 4 the particular waveband at which radio signals are broadcast or transmitted.

fre·quen·cy mod·u·la·tion ▸ n. the varying of the frequency of a wave, used as a means of broadcasting an audio signal by radio.

fre·quent ▸ adj. /ˈfrēkwənt/ 1 occurring or done many times at short intervals. 2 doing something often; regular: *he was a frequent visitor to Paris.* ▸ v. /frēˈkwent/ visit a place often or regularly. ■ **fre·quent·er** /frēˈkwentər-/ n. **fre·quent·ly** /ˈfrēkwəntlē/ adv.

fre·quen·ta·tive /frēˈkwentətiv/ ▸ adj. Grammar (of a verb or verbal form) expressing frequent repetition or intensity of action.

fres·co /ˈfreskō/ ▸ n. (pl. **frescoes** or **frescos**) a painting done on wet plaster on a wall or ceiling, in which the colors become fixed as the plaster dries. ■ **fres·coed** adj.

fresh /freSH/ ▸ adj. 1 not previously known or used; new or different: *a fresh approach to treating problem skin.* 2 (of food) recently made or picked; not frozen or preserved. 3 recently created and so not impaired: *the memory was fresh in their minds.* 4 (**fresh from/out of**) (of a person) having just had a particular experience or come from a particular place: *we were fresh out of art school.* 5 pleasantly clean and cool: *fresh air.* 6 (of the wind) cool and fairly strong. 7 (of water) not salty. 8 full of energy. 9 informal too familiar toward someone, especially in a sexual way. ▸ adv. newly; recently. ■ **fresh·ly** adv. **fresh·ness** n.

fresh·en /ˈfreSHən/ ▸ v. 1 make or become fresh. 2 top off a drink. 3 (of wind) become stronger and colder. ■ **fresh·en·er** n.

fresh·et /ˈfreSHət/ ▸ n. 1 the flood of a river from heavy rain or melted snow. 2 a rush of fresh water flowing into the sea.

fresh·man /ˈfreSHmən/ ▸ n. (pl. **freshmen**) a first-year student at a high school, college, or university.

fresh·wa·ter /ˈfreSHˌwôtər, -ˌwätər/ ▸ adj. relating to or found in fresh water; not of the sea.

fret¹ /fret/ ▸ v. (**frets, fretting, fretted**) 1 be constantly or visibly anxious. 2 gradually wear away something. ▸ n. chiefly Brit. a state of anxiety.

fret² ▸ n. each of a sequence of ridges on the fingerboard of some stringed instruments, used for fixing the positions of the fingers. ▸ v. (**frets, fretting, fretted**) provide a stringed instrument with frets.

fret³ ▸ n. an ornamental design of vertical and horizontal lines. ▸ v. (**frets, fretting, fretted**) decorate something with fretwork.

fret·ful /ˈfretfəl/ ▸ adj. anxious or upset. ■ **fret·ful·ly** adv. **fret·ful·ness** n.

fret·saw /ˈfretˌsô/ ▸ n. a saw with a narrow blade for cutting designs in thin wood or metal.

fret·work /ˈfretˌwərk/ ▸ n. decorative patterns cut in wood with a fretsaw.

Freud·i·an /ˈfroidēən/ ▸ adj. 1 relating to or influenced by the Austrian psychotherapist Sigmund Freud and his methods of psychoanalysis. 2 able to be analyzed in terms of unconscious thoughts or desires: *a Freudian slip.* ▸ n. a follower of Freud or his methods. ■ **Freud·i·an·ism** /-ˌnizəm/ n.

Fri. ▸ abbr. Friday.

fri·a·ble /ˈfrīəbəl/ ▸ adj. easily crumbled. ■ **fri·a·bil·i·ty** /ˌfrīəˈbilətē/ n.

fri·ar /ˈfrīər/ ▸ n. a member of certain religious orders of men.

fri·ar·y /ˈfrīərē/ ▸ n. (pl. **friaries**) a building or community occupied by friars.

fric·as·see /ˈfrikəˌsē, ˌfrikəˈsē/ ▸ n. a dish of stewed or fried pieces of meat served in a thick white sauce. ■ **fric·as·seed** adj.

fric·a·tive /ˈfrikətiv/ ▸ adj. referring to a type of consonant (e.g., *f*) made by the friction of breath in a narrow opening.

fric·tion /ˈfriksHən/ ▸ n. 1 the resistance that one surface or object encounters when moving over another. 2 the action of one surface or object rubbing against another. 3 conflict or disagreement: *a number of issues are causing friction between the two countries.* ■ **fric·tion·al** adj. **fric·tion·less** adj.

Fri·day /ˈfrīdā, -dē/ ▸ n. the day of the week before Saturday and following Thursday.

fridge /frij/ ▸ n. a refrigerator.

fried /frīd/ ▸ past and past participle of **FRY¹**.

friend /frend/ ▸ n. 1 a person that one likes and knows well. 2 a person who supports a particular cause or organization. 3 (**Friend**) a Quaker. ■ **friend·less** adj. **friend·ship** n.

– PHRASES **friend of the court** another term for AMICUS.

friend·ly /ˈfrendlē/ ▸ adj. (**friendlier, friendliest**) 1 kind and pleasant. 2 on good terms; not hostile. 3 (in combination) not harmful to a specified thing: *environment-friendly.* 4 Military relating to or allied with one's own forces: *two soldiers were killed by friendly fire.* ■ **friend·li·ly** adv. **friend·li·ness** n.

friend·ly fire ▸ n. another term for FRATRICIDE (sense 2).

frieze /frēz/ ▸ n. 1 a broad horizontal band of sculpted or painted decoration. 2 Architecture the part of an entablature between the architrave and the cornice.

frig·ate /ˈfrigit/ ▸ n. a warship with a mixed armament, generally lighter than a destroyer.

frig·ate bird ▸ n. a tropical seabird with a deeply forked tail and a long hooked bill.

fright /frīt/ ▸ n. 1 a sudden intense feeling of fear. 2 a shock.

– PHRASES **look a fright** informal look ridiculous or very disheveled. **take fright** suddenly become frightened.

fright·en /ˈfrītn/ ▸ v. **1** make someone afraid. **2** (**frighten someone/thing off**) make someone or something too afraid to do something. ■ **fright·ened** adj. **fright·en·er** n. **fright·en·ing** adj. **fright·en·ing·ly** adv.

fright·ful /ˈfrītfəl/ ▸ adj. **1** very unpleasant, serious, or shocking. **2** informal terrible; awful. ■ **fright·ful·ly** adv. **fright·ful·ness** n.

fright wig ▸ n. a wig with the hair arranged sticking out, as worn by a clown.

frig·id /ˈfrijid/ ▸ adj. **1** very cold. **2** (especially of a woman) unable to be sexually aroused. **3** stiff or formal in style: *the house is no frigid art museum.* ■ **fri·gid·i·ty** /frəˈjidətē/ n. **frig·id·ly** adv.

fri·jo·les /frēˈhōlēz/ ▸ pl.n. (in Mexican cooking) beans.

frill /fril/ ▸ n. **1** a strip of gathered or pleated material used as a decorative edging. **2** a frill-like fringe of feathers, hair, skin, etc., on a bird or other animal. **3** (**frills**) unnecessary extra features: *a comfortable room with no frills.* ■ **frilled** adj. **frill·y** adj.

fringe /frinj/ ▸ n. **1** a border of threads, tassels, or twists, used to edge clothing or material. **2** chiefly Brit. the front part of someone's hair, cut so as to hang over the forehead; bangs. **3** a natural border of hair or fibers in an animal or plant. **4** an outer part or edge of an area, group, or activity: *loners living on the fringes of society.* ▸ adj. not part of the mainstream; unconventional: *fringe theater.* ▸ v. provide with or form a fringe: *the sea is fringed by palm trees.* ■ **fring·ing** n. **fring·y** adj.

fringe ben·e·fit ▸ n. an additional benefit, especially one given to an employee.

frip·per·y /ˈfripərē/ ▸ n. (pl. **fripperies**) **1** showy or unnecessary ornament. **2** a frivolous or trivial thing.

fris·bee /ˈfrizbē/ ▸ n. trademark a plastic disk designed for skimming through the air as an outdoor game.

Fri·sian /ˈfriznən, ˈfrē-/ ▸ n. **1** a person from Frisia or Friesland in the Netherlands. **2** the Germanic language spoken in northern parts of the Netherlands and adjacent islands. ▸ adj. relating to Frisia or Friesland.

frisk /frisk/ ▸ v. **1** pass the hands over someone in a search for hidden weapons or drugs. **2** skip or move playfully; frolic.

frisk·y /ˈfriskē/ ▸ adj. (**friskier, friskiest**) playful and full of energy.

fris·son /frēˈsôN/ ▸ n. a sudden strong feeling of excitement or fear; a thrill.

frit·il·lar·y /ˈfritl̩ˌerē/ ▸ n. (pl. **fritillaries**) **1** a plant with hanging bell-like flowers. **2** a butterfly with orange-brown wings checkered with black.

frit·ta·ta /frēˈtätə/ ▸ n. an Italian dish made with fried beaten eggs, resembling a Spanish omelet.

frit·ter¹ /ˈfritər/ ▸ v. (**fritter something away**) waste time, money, or energy on trivial matters.

frit·ter² ▸ n. a piece of fruit, vegetable, or meat that is coated in batter and deep-fried.

fritz /frits/ ▸ n. (in phrase **go** or **be on the fritz**) informal (of a machine) stop working properly.

friv·o·lous /ˈfrivələs/ ▸ adj. **1** not having any serious purpose or value. **2** (of a person) not serious or responsible. ■ **fri·vol·i·ty** /friˈvälətē/ n. **friv·o·lous·ly** adv.

frizz /friz/ ▸ v. (of hair) form into a mass of tight curls. ▸ n. a mass of tightly curled hair.

friz·zle¹ /ˈfrizəl/ ▸ v. fry something until crisp or burned.

friz·zle² ▸ v. form hair into tight curls.

friz·zy /ˈfrizē/ ▸ adj. (**frizzier, frizziest**) formed of a mass of small, tight curls. ■ **friz·zi·ness** n.

fro /frō/ ▸ adv. see TO AND FRO at TO.

frock /fräk/ ▸ n. **1** chiefly Brit. a dress. **2** a loose outer garment, especially a long gown worn by monks or priests.

frock coat ▸ n. a man's double-breasted, long-skirted coat, now worn chiefly on formal occasions.

frog¹ /frôg, fräg/ ▸ n. **1** a tailless amphibian with a short squat body and very long hind legs for leaping. **2** (**Frog**) informal, derogatory a French person. ■ **frog·gy** adj.
– PHRASES **have a frog in one's throat** informal find it hard to speak because of hoarseness.

frog² ▸ n. **1** a thing used to hold or fasten something. **2** an ornamental coat fastener consisting of a spindle-shaped button and a loop.

frog³ ▸ n. an elastic horny pad in the sole of a horse's hoof.

frog·man /ˈfrôgˌman, ˈfräg-, -mən/ ▸ n. (pl. **frogmen**) a diver equipped with a rubber suit, flippers, and breathing equipment.

frog·march /ˈfrôgˌmärCH, ˈfräg-/ ▸ v. force someone to walk forward with their arms pinned from behind.

frol·ic /ˈfrälik/ ▸ v. (**frolics, frolicking, frolicked**) play or move around in a cheerful and lively way. ▸ n. a lively or playful act or activity. ■ **frol·ick·er** n.

frol·ic·some /ˈfräliksəm/ ▸ adj. lively and playful.

from /frəm/ ▸ prep. **1** indicating the point at which a journey, process, or action starts. **2** indicating the source of something. **3** indicating the starting point of a range. **4** indicating separation, removal, or prevention. **5** indicating a cause. **6** indicating a difference.
– PHRASES **from time to time** occasionally.

frond /fränd/ ▸ n. the leaf or leaflike part of a palm, fern, or similar plant.

front /frənt/ ▸ n. **1** the side or part of an object that presents itself to view or that is normally seen first. **2** the position directly ahead. **3** the forward-facing part of a person's body. **4** any face of a building, especially that of the main entrance: *the west front of the cathedral.* **5** the furthest position that an armed force has reached. **6** Meteorology the forward edge of an advancing mass of air. **7** a particular situation or area of activity: *good news on the job front.* **8** an organized political group. **9** a deceptive appearance or way of behaving: *I put on a brave front.* **10** a person or organization serving as a cover for secret or illegal activities. **11** boldness and confidence. ▸ adj. of or at the front. ▸ v. **1** have the front facing toward something. **2** place or be placed at the front of something. **3** provide something with a front or facing. **4** lead or be prominent in: *the group is fronted by two girl singers.* **5** present or host a television or radio program. **6** act as a front for secret or illegal activity. ■ **front·ward** adj. & adv. **front·wards** adv.
– PHRASES **in front of** in the presence of. **out front 1** at or to the front; in front: *two station wagons stopped out front.* **2** in the auditorium of a theater. **up front 1** at or near the front: *the floor plan has an open living area up front.* **2** in

advance: *every fee must be paid up front.* **3** open and direct; frank: *I vowed to be up front with her.*

front·age /'frəntij/ ▶ n. **1** the facade of a building. **2** a piece of land adjoining a street or waterway.

front·age road ▶ n. a subsidiary road running parallel to a main road or highway and giving access to houses and businesses. Also called SERVICE ROAD.

fron·tal /'frəntl/ ▶ adj. **1** relating to or at the front. **2** relating to the forehead or front part of the skull. ■ **fron·tal·ly** adv.

fron·tal lobe ▶ n. each of the paired lobes of the brain lying immediately behind the forehead.

front and cen·ter ▶ adv. prominently; at the forefront: *trade negotiators put this issue front and center.*

front burn·er ▶ n. the focus of attention: *a revamp of the 1872 Mining Law is next up on the front burner.*

front court ▶ n. **1** the part of a basketball court where each team tries to score against its opponent. **2** the players on a team who usually play closest to the other team's basket when trying to score.

front desk ▶ n. the main desk at a hotel or motel, for checking in or out and handling requests from guests.

front-end ▶ adj. **1** informal (of money) paid or charged at the beginning of a transaction. **2** Computing (of a device or program) directly accessed by the user and allowing access to further devices or programs.

fron·tier /ˌfrən'ti(ə)r/ ▶ n. **1** a border separating two countries. **2** the extreme limit of settled land beyond which lies wilderness. **3** the limit of knowledge or achievement in a particular area: *fundamental problems at the frontiers of cosmology.*

fron·tiers·man /ˌfrən'ti(ə)rzmən/ (or **frontierswoman** /ˌfrən'ti(ə)rzˌwʊmən/) ▶ n. (pl. **frontiersmen** or **frontierswomen** /ˌfrən'ti(ə)rzˌwimin/) a man (or woman) living in the region of a frontier.

fron·tis·piece /'frəntisˌpēs/ ▶ n. an illustration facing the title page of a book.

front line ▶ n. **1** the part of an army that is closest to the enemy. **2** the most important position in an area of activity: *we're on the front line of world theater.*

front·man /'frəntˌman, -mən/ ▶ n. (pl. **frontmen**) **1** the leader of a band. **2** a person who represents an illegal organization to give it an appearance of legitimacy.

front of·fice ▶ n. the management or administrative officers of a business or other organization.

front-page ▶ adj. **1** appearing on the first page of a newspaper or similar publication and containing important or remarkable news: *they ran a front-page story headlined "White-Collar Chic.".* **2** worthy of being printed on the first page of a newspaper, etc.: *dishonest research has become front-page news.*

front run·ner ▶ n. the leading contestant in a race or other competition.

front-wheel drive ▶ n. a transmission system that provides power to the front wheels of a motor vehicle.

frosh /fräsH/ ▶ n. informal freshman or freshmen: *I went to private school for my frosh and*

sophomore year.

frost /frôst/ ▶ n. **1** a deposit of white ice crystals formed on surfaces when the temperature falls below freezing. **2** a period of cold weather when frost forms. ▶ v. **1** cover or be covered with frost. **2** decorate a cake, cupcake, etc., with icing. **3** tint hair strands to lighten the color of isolated strands.

frost·bite /'frôs(t)ˌbīt/ ▶ n. injury to body tissues, especially the nose, fingers, or toes, caused by exposure to extreme cold. ■ **frost·bit·ten** /'frôs(t)ˌbitn/ adj.

frost·ed /'frôstid/ ▶ adj. **1** covered with frost. **2** (of glass) having a textured surface so that it is difficult to see through. **3** (of food) decorated with icing. **4** (of hair) having isolated strands tinted a light color.

frost·ing /'frôstiNG/ ▶ n. **1** icing. **2** a roughened matte finish on otherwise shiny material such as glass or steel.

frost·y /'frôstē/ ▶ adj. (**frostier**, **frostiest**) **1** (of the weather) very cold with frost forming on surfaces. **2** cold and unfriendly. ■ **frost·i·ly** adv. **frost·i·ness** n.

froth /frôtH/ ▶ n. **1** a mass of small bubbles in liquid. **2** worthless or superficial talk, ideas, or activities: *the network has to explain the substance rather than the froth of politics.* ▶ v. **1** form or produce froth. **2** be very angry or agitated.

froth·y /'frôtHē, -tHē/ ▶ adj. (**frothier**, **frothiest**) **1** full of or covered with a mass of small bubbles. **2** light and entertaining but of little substance: *lots of frothy interviews.* ■ **froth·i·ly** adv. **froth·i·ness** n.

frou-frou /'frooˌfroo/ ▶ n. (usu. before another noun) frills or other ornamentation: *a little frou-frou skirt.*

frown /froun/ ▶ v. **1** furrow one's brows to show disapproval, displeasure, or concentration. **2** (**frown on**) disapprove of: *casual sex is still frowned upon.* ▶ n. an act of frowning.

frowz·y /'frouzē/ (also **frowsy**) ▶ adj. scruffy, dingy, and neglected in appearance.

froze /frōz/ ▶ past of FREEZE.

fro·zen /'frōzən/ ▶ past participle of FREEZE.

fruc·ti·fy /'frəktəˌfī/ ▶ v. (**fructifies**, **fructifying**, **fructified**) formal **1** make or become fruitful. **2** bear fruit.

fruc·tose /'frəkˌtōs, 'frook-, -ˌtōz/ ▶ n. a simple sugar found chiefly in honey and fruit.

fru·gal /'froogəl/ ▶ adj. **1** using only as much money or food as is necessary: *a frugal way of life.* **2** (of a meal) simple, plain, and costing little. ■ **fru·gal·i·ty** /froo'galətē/ n. **fru·gal·ly** adv.

fru·gi·vore /'froojiˌvôr/ ▶ n. an animal that feeds on fruit. ■ **fru·giv·o·rous** /froo'jivərəs/ adj.

fruit /froot/ ▶ n. **1** the sweet and fleshy product of a tree or other plant that contains seed and can be eaten as food. **2** Botany the seed-bearing structure of a plant, e.g., an acorn. **3** the result or reward of work or activity: *the state is encouraging people to enjoy the fruits of their labor.* **4** informal, derogatory a male homosexual. ▶ v. (of a plant) produce fruit.

fruit·ar·i·an /froo'te(ə)rēən/ ▶ n. a person who eats only fruit. ■ **fruit·ar·i·an·ism** n.

fruit bat ▶ n. a large bat that feeds chiefly on fruit or nectar.

fruit·cake /'frootˌkāk/ ▶ n. **1** a dense cake containing dried fruits and nuts. **2** informal an eccentric or mad person.

fruit cock·tail ▶ n. a chopped fruit salad, often sold in cans.

fruit fly ▶ n. a small fly that feeds on fruit in both its adult and larval stages.

fruit·ful /'frōōtfəl/ ▶ adj. 1 producing much fruit; fertile. 2 producing good results: *fruitful research.* ■ **fruit·ful·ly** adv. **fruit·ful·ness** n.

fruit·ing bod·y ▶ n. the spore-producing organ of a fungus, often seen as a toadstool.

fru·i·tion /frōō'ishən/ ▶ n. 1 the fulfillment of a plan or project. 2 literary the state or action of producing fruit.

fruit·less /'frōōtləs/ ▶ adj. 1 failing to achieve the desired results; unproductive: *a fruitless search for contentment.* 2 not producing fruit. ■ **fruit·less·ly** adv. **fruit·less·ness** n.

fruit sal·ad ▶ n. a mixture of different types of chopped fruit.

fruit·y /'frōōtē/ ▶ adj. (**fruitier, fruitiest**) 1 relating to, resembling, or containing fruit. 2 (of a voice) deep and rich. 3 informal, derogatory relating to or associated with homosexuals. ■ **fruit·i·ness** n.

frump /frəmp/ ▶ n. an unattractive woman who wears dowdy old-fashioned clothes. ■ **frump·y** adj.

frus·trate /'frəs,trāt/ ▶ v. 1 prevent a plan or action from progressing or succeeding. 2 prevent someone from doing or achieving something. 3 make someone annoyed or dissatisfied as a result of being unable to do something. ■ **frus·trat·ed** adj. **frus·trat·ing** adj.

frus·tra·tion /frə'strāshən/ ▶ n. 1 the feeling of being upset or annoyed as a result of being unable to do something. 2 a cause of dissatisfaction or annoyance: *the frustrations of travel.* 3 the prevention of the progress, success, or fulfillment of something.

fry¹ /frī/ ▶ v. (**fries, frying, fried**) 1 cook or be cooked in hot fat or oil. 2 informal (of a person) burn or overheat. ▶ n. (pl. **fries**) 1 a fried dish or meal: *we'll have one burger and two fish fries.* 2 a gathering where fried food is served: *Friday night is the Rotary fish fry.* 3 (**fries**) French fries.

fry² ▶ pl.n. young fish, especially when newly hatched.

fry·er /'frīər/ ▶ n. 1 a large, deep container for frying food. 2 a small young chicken suitable for frying.

fry·ing pan (also **frypan** /'frī,pan/) ▶ n. a shallow pan with a long handle, used for frying food.
– PHRASES **out of the frying pan into the fire** from a bad situation to one that is worse.

FSBO ▶ abbr. for sale by owner; relating to sales of private homes by their owners: *visit our home buying page to see FSBO homes for sale.*

FSH ▶ abbr. follicle-stimulating hormone, a hormone that promotes the formation of ova or sperm.

f-stop ▶ n. a camera setting corresponding to a particular f-number.

FT ▶ abbr. 1 full-time. 2 Basketball free throw.

Ft. ▶ abbr. Fort: *Ft. Lauderdale.*

ft. ▶ abbr. foot or feet.

FTC ▶ abbr. Federal Trade Commission.

FTP ▶ abbr. Computing file transfer protocol, a standard for the exchange of program and data files across a network.

fu·bar /'fōō,bär/ ▶ adj. out of working order; seriously, perhaps irreparably, damaged: *the clock in the hall is fubar.*

fuch·sia /'fyōōshə/ ▶ n. 1 an ornamental shrub with drooping tubular flowers that are typically of two different colors. 2 a vivid purplish-red color.

fuck /fək/ vulgar slang ▶ v. 1 have sexual intercourse with someone. 2 damage or ruin something. ▶ n. an act of sexual intercourse. ▶ exclam. a strong expression of annoyance or contempt.
– PHRASES **fuck off** go away. **fuck someone/thing up** 1 damage someone emotionally. 2 do something badly.

fuck-up ▶ n. vulgar slang 1 a mess or botched job: *near misses, complete misses, and total fuck-ups.* 2 someone who regularly botches things: *I was a C-student fuck-up.*

fud·dled /'fədld/ ▶ adj. confused or stupefied, especially with alcohol: *my head was aching and my brain seemed fuddled.*

fud·dy-dud·dy /'fədē ,dədē/ ▶ n. (pl. **fuddy-duddies**) informal a person who is old-fashioned and who often disapproves of modern ideas, behavior, etc.

fudge /fəj/ ▶ n. 1 a soft candy made from sugar, butter, and milk or cream. 2 an attempt to fudge an issue. ▶ v. 1 present or deal with an issue in a vague way, especially to conceal the truth or mislead people. 2 manipulate facts or figures so as to present a more desirable picture.

fueh·rer ▶ n. variant spelling of FÜHRER.

fu·el /'fyōōəl/ ▶ n. 1 material such as coal, gas, or oil that is burned to produce heat or power. 2 food, drink, or drugs as a source of energy. 3 something that stirs up argument or strong emotion. ▶ v. (**fuels, fueling, fueled**) 1 supply something with fuel. 2 stir up or strengthen: *the slide in share prices fueled demands for government intervention.*

fu·el cell ▶ n. a cell producing an electric current directly from a chemical reaction.

fu·el in·jec·tion ▶ n. the direct introduction of fuel under pressure into the combustion units of an internal-combustion engine, as a way of improving a car's performance.

fuel rod ▶ n. a rod-shaped fuel element in a nuclear reactor.

fu·gal /'fyōōgəl/ ▶ adj. relating to a fugue.

fu·gi·tive /'fyōōjətiv/ ▶ n. a person who has escaped from captivity or is in hiding. ▶ adj. quick to disappear; fleeting: *a fugitive glimpse.*

fugue /fyōōg/ ▶ n. 1 a musical composition in which a short melody or phrase is introduced by one part and successively taken up by others. 2 Psychiatry a period during which someone loses their memory or sense of identity and may leave their home or usual surroundings.

füh·rer /'fyōōrər/ (also **fuehrer**) ▶ n. the title used by Hitler as leader of Germany.

ful·crum /'fōōlkrəm, 'fəl-/ ▶ n. (pl. **fulcra** /-krə/ or **fulcrums**) the point on which a lever turns or is supported.

ful·fill /fōōl'fil/ (Brit. **fulfil**) ▶ v. 1 achieve or realize something desired, promised, or predicted: *I fulfilled a childhood dream when I became champion.* 2 satisfy or meet a requirement or condition. 3 (**fulfill oneself**) gain happiness or satisfaction by fully developing one's abilities. ■ **ful·filled** adj. **ful·fill·ing** adj.

ful·fill·ment /fōōl'filmənt/ (Brit. **fulfilment**) ▶ n. 1 a feeling of satisfaction or happiness as a result of fully developing one's abilities. **2** the action of fulfilling something.

full /fŏŏl/ ▸ adj. **1** containing or holding as much or as many as possible; having no empty space. **2** (**full of**) having a large number or quantity of something. **3** not lacking or omitting anything; complete: *I don't know the full story.* **4** (**full of**) unable to stop talking or thinking about: *they had their photographs taken and he was full of it.* **5** plump or rounded. **6** (of flavor, sound, or color) strong or rich. ▸ adv. **1** straight; directly. **2** very.
– PHRASES **full of oneself** very self-satisfied and proud of oneself. **full on 1** running at or providing maximum power or capacity. **2** so as to make a direct impact. **3** (**full-on**) informal unrestrained: *hours of full-on fun.* **full speed** (or **steam**) **ahead** proceeding with as much speed or energy as possible. **full up** filled to capacity. **in full 1** with nothing omitted: *your life story in full.* **2** to the full amount due: *their relocation costs would be paid in full.* **3** to the utmost; completely: *the textbooks have failed to exploit in full the opportunities offered.*

full·back /'fŏŏl,bak/ ▸ n. **1** Football an offensive player in the backfield. **2** a defender who plays at the side in a game such as soccer or field hockey.

full-blood·ed ▸ adj. wholehearted and enthusiastic.

full-blown ▸ adj. fully developed.

full-bod·ied ▸ adj. rich and satisfying in flavor or sound.

full bore ▸ adv. at full speed or maximum capacity. ▸ adj. referring to firearms with a relatively large caliber.

full-court press ▸ n. **1** Basketball a defensive tactic in which members of a team cover their opponents throughout the court and not just near their own basket. **2** an instance of aggressive pressure: *if the president were to mount a full-court press for the space station.*

full·er·ene /,fŏŏlə'rēn/ ▸ n. Chemistry a form of carbon having a molecule consisting of atoms joined together in a hollow structure.

ful·ler's earth /'fŏŏlərz/ ▸ n. a type of clay used to treat cloth during manufacture.

full-fledged ▸ adj. **1** completely developed or established; of full status: *a full-fledged police detective.* **2** (of a bird) having fully developed wing feathers and able to fly.

full-fron·tal ▸ adj. fully exposing the front of the body, especially the genitals.

full-grown ▸ adj. having reached maturity: *full-grown wheat.*

full house ▸ n. **1** a theater or meeting that is filled to capacity. **2** a poker hand with three of a kind and a pair. **3** a winning card at bingo in which all the numbers have been successfully marked off.

full-length ▸ adj. **1** of the standard length: *a full-length Disney cartoon.* **2** (of a garment or curtain) extending to, or almost to, the ground. **3** (of a mirror or portrait) showing the whole human figure. ▸ adv. (usu. **full length**) (of a person) with the body lying stretched out and flat: *Lucy flung herself full length on the floor.*

full moon ▸ n. the phase of the moon in which its whole disk is illuminated.

full·ness /'fŏŏlnəs/ ▸ n. **1** the state of being full. **2** richness or abundance.
– PHRASES **in the fullness of time** after a due

length of time has passed.

full-scale ▸ adj. **1** (of a model or representation) of the same size as the thing represented. **2** as complete and thorough as possible: *a full-scale search of the area.*

full stop ▸ n. Brit. another term for PERIOD (sense 4 of the noun).

full-time ▸ adj. using the whole of a person's available working time. ▸ adv. on a full-time basis. ■ **full-tim·er** n.

ful·ly /'fŏŏlē/ ▸ adv. **1** completely or entirely. **2** no less or fewer than: *fully 65 percent.*

ful·ly fledged ▸ adj. British term for FULL-FLEDGED.

ful·mar /'fŏŏlmər, -,mär/ ▸ n. a large gray and white northern seabird.

ful·mi·nate /'fŏŏlmə,nāt, 'fəl-/ ▸ v. protest strongly about something. ■ **ful·mi·na·tion** /,fŏŏlmə'nāsнən, -fəl-/ n.

ful·some /'fŏŏlsəm/ ▸ adj. **1** excessively complimentary or flattering. **2** of large size or quantity; generous or plentiful: *fulsome details.* ■ **ful·some·ly** adv. **ful·some·ness** n.

> USAGE
> Although the earliest sense of **fulsome** was 'plentiful,' this meaning was replaced by the negative sense 'excessively flattering' and is now generally thought to be incorrect. The word is often heard in phrases such as **fulsome praise**, however, where the speaker just means that the praise is abundant rather than excessively flattering.

fu·ma·role /'fyŏŏmə,rōl/ ▸ n. an opening in or near a volcano, through which hot sulfurous gases emerge.

fum·ble /'fəmbəl/ ▸ v. **1** use the hands clumsily while doing or handling something. **2** (of the hands) do or handle something clumsily. **3** (**fumble around/about**) move around clumsily using the hands to find one's way. **4** express oneself or deal with something clumsily or nervously. **5** (in ball games) fail to catch or field the ball cleanly. ▸ n. an act of fumbling. ■ **fum·bler** n. **fum·bling** adj.

fume /fyŏŏm/ ▸ n. a gas or vapor that smells strongly or is dangerous to inhale. ▸ v. **1** send out fumes. **2** feel extremely angry. ■ **fum·ing** adj.

fu·mi·gate /'fyŏŏmə,gāt/ ▸ v. use the fumes of certain chemicals to disinfect a contaminated area. ■ **fu·mi·gant** /-gənt/ n. **fu·mi·ga·tion** /,fyŏŏmə'gāsнən/ n. **fu·mi·ga·tor** /-,gātər/ n.

fun /fən/ ▸ n. **1** lighthearted enjoyment. **2** a source of this: *exercise can be great fun.* **3** playfulness: *she's full of fun.* ▸ adj. informal enjoyable.
– PHRASES **make fun of** tease or laugh at in a mocking way.

func·tion /'fəNGksнən/ ▸ n. **1** an activity that is natural to or the purpose of a person or thing. **2** a large or formal social event or ceremony. **3** a computer operation corresponding to a single instruction from the user. **4** Mathematics a relation or expression involving one or more variables. ▸ v. **1** work or operate in a proper or particular way. **2** (**function as**) fulfill the purpose or task of: *the building functions as a youth center.*

func·tion·al /'fəNGksнənl/ ▸ adj. **1** relating to or having a function. **2** designed to be practical and useful, rather than attractive. **3** working or operating. **4** (of a disease) affecting the

operation rather than the structure of an organ.
■ **func·tion·al·ly** adv.

func·tion·al·ism /'fəNGkSHənl,izəm/ ▶ n. the theory that the design of an object should be governed by its use rather than an attractive appearance. ■ **func·tion·al·ist** n. & adj.

func·tion·al·i·ty /,fəNGkSHə'nalətē/ ▶ n. 1 the quality of being functional. 2 the range of operations that can be run on a computer or other electronic system.

func·tion·ar·y /'fəNGkSHə,nerē/ ▶ n. (pl. **functionaries**) an official.

func·tion key ▶ n. a key on a computer keyboard that can be assigned a particular function or operation.

fund /fənd/ ▶ n. 1 a sum of money saved or made available for a purpose. 2 (**funds**) financial resources. 3 a large stock of something.
▶ v. provide money for something: *a project funded by the Arts Council.* ■ **fund·er** n. **fund·ing** n.

fun·da·ment /'fəndəmənt/ ▶ n. 1 the foundation or basis of something. 2 humorous a person's buttocks.

fun·da·men·tal /,fəndə'mentl/ ▶ adj. of central importance: *a fundamental difference of opinion.* ▶ n. a central or basic rule or principle. ■ **fun·da·men·tal·ly** adv.

fun·da·men·tal·ism /,fəndə'mentl,izəm/ ▶ n. 1 a form of Protestant Christianity that promotes the belief that everything written in the Bible is literally true. 2 the strict following of the basic underlying doctrines of any religion or ideology. ■ **fun·da·men·tal·ist** n. & adj.

fund-rais·er ▶ n. 1 a person who raises money for an organization or cause. 2 an event held to raise money for an organization or cause. ■ **fund-rais·ing** n.

fu·ner·al /'fyōōn(ə)rəl/ ▶ n. a ceremony held shortly after a person's death, usually including the person's burial or cremation.
– PHRASES **it's your funeral** informal said to warn someone that the consequences of an unwise act are their own responsibility.

fu·ner·al di·rec·tor ▶ n. a person whose business is preparing dead bodies for burial or cremation and making arrangements for funerals.

fu·ner·al home (also **funeral parlor**) ▶ n. an establishment where people who have died are prepared for burial or cremation.

fu·ner·ar·y /'fyōōnə,rerē/ ▶ adj. relating to a funeral or to other rites in which people who have died are commemorated.

fu·ne·re·al /fyə'ni(ə)rēəl, fyōō-/ ▶ adj. having the somber quality or atmosphere appropriate to a funeral.

fun·gi /'fənjī, -,gī/ ▶ plural of FUNGUS.

fun·gi·cide /'fənjə,sīd, 'fəNGgə-/ ▶ n. a chemical that destroys fungus. ■ **fun·gi·cid·al** /,fənjə'sīdl, ,fəNGgə-/ adj.

fun·gus /'fəNGgəs/ ▶ n. (pl. fungi /-jī, -gī/) a spore-producing organism, such as a mushroom, that has no leaves or flowers and grows on other plants or on decaying matter. ■ **fun·gal** /'fəNGgəl/ adj. **fun·goid** /'fəNG,goid/ adj.

fu·nic·u·lar /fyōō'nikyələr/ ▶ adj. (of a railroad on a steep slope) operated by cables attached to cars that balance each other while one goes up and the other goes down. ▶ n. a funicular railroad.

funk¹ /fōōNGk, fəNGk/ informal ▶ n. (also **blue funk**) 1 a state of depression: *falling into a deep funk.*

2 chiefly Brit. a state of panic or fear.

funk² ▶ n. a style of popular dance music of US black origin, having a strong rhythm.

funk·y /'fəNGkē/ ▶ adj. (**funkier, funkiest**) informal 1 (of music) having a strong dance rhythm. 2 unconventionally modern and stylish. 3 strongly musty: *a funky smell.* ■ **funk·i·ly** adv. **funk·i·ness** n.

fun·nel /'fənl/ ▶ n. 1 a utensil that is wide at the top and narrow at the bottom, used for guiding liquid or powder into a small opening. 2 a metal chimney on a ship or steam engine. ▶ v. (**funnels, funneling, funneled**) guide or move through a funnel or narrow space: *the wind was funneling through the gorge.*

fun·nel cloud ▶ n. a rotating, funnel-shaped cloud forming the core of a tornado or waterspout.

fun·ny /'fənē/ ▶ adj. (**funnier, funniest**) 1 causing laughter or amusement. 2 strange; peculiar. 3 suspicious: *there's something funny going on.* 4 informal slightly unwell. ■ **fun·ni·ly** adv.

fun·ny bone ▶ n. informal the part of the elbow over which a sensitive nerve passes.

fun·ny busi·ness ▶ n. deceptive, disobedient, or lecherous behavior: *funny business in the fund industry.*

fun·ny farm ▶ n. informal, derogatory a psychiatric hospital.

fun run ▶ n. informal an uncompetitive run for sponsored runners, held in support of a charity.

fur /fər/ ▶ n. 1 the short, soft hair of certain animals. 2 the skin of an animal with fur on it, used in making clothes. 3 a coat made from fur. 4 a coating formed on the tongue as a symptom of sickness. ■ **furred** adj.
– PHRASES **the fur will fly** informal there will be a dramatic argument.

fur·be·low /'fərbə,lō/ ▶ n. 1 a strip of gathered or pleated material attached to a skirt or petticoat. 2 (**furbelows**) showy ornaments or trimmings.

fur·bish /'fərbisH/ ▶ v. (usu. as adj. **furbished**) give a fresh look to (something old or shabby); renovate: *the newly furbished church.*

fu·ri·ous /'fyōōrēəs/ ▶ adj. 1 extremely angry. 2 full of energy, intensity, or anger: *he strode off at a furious pace.* ■ **fu·ri·ous·ly** adv.

furl /fərl/ ▶ v. roll or fold something up neatly and securely. ■ **furled** adj.

fur·long /'fər,lôNG, -,läNG/ ▶ n. an eighth of a mile, 220 yards.

fur·lough /'fərlō/ ▶ n. leave of absence, especially from military duty.

fur·nace /'fərnəs/ ▶ n. 1 an enclosed chamber in which material can be heated to very high temperatures. 2 a very hot place.

fur·nish /'fərnisH/ ▶ v. 1 provide a room or building with furniture and fittings. 2 (**furnish someone with**) supply someone with equipment or information: *she was able to furnish me with details of the incident.* 3 be a source of something. ■ **fur·nished** adj. **fur·nish·er** n.

fur·nish·ing /'fərnisHiNG/ ▶ n. 1 (**furnishings**) furniture and fittings in a room or building. 2 (as adj.) referring to fabrics used for curtains or upholstery: *furnishing fabrics.*

fur·ni·ture /'fərnicHər/ ▶ n. 1 the movable articles that are used to make a room or building suitable for living or working in, such as tables, chairs, or desks. 2 the small accessories or fittings that are required or desired for a particular task or function: *pendants, finials, and other decorative furniture.*

fu·ror /'fyŏŏr,ôr, -ər/ (Brit. **furore** /,fyŏŏ'rôrē/) ▶ n. an outbreak of public anger or excitement.

fur·ri·er /'fərēər/ ▶ n. a person who prepares or deals in furs.

fur·row /'fərō, 'fə-rō/ ▶ n. **1** a long, narrow trench made in the ground by a plow. **2** a rut or groove. **3** a deep wrinkle on a person's face. ▶ v. **1** make a furrow in the ground or the surface of something. **2** (of a person's forehead) become wrinkled: *his brow furrowed in concentration.*

fur·ry /'fərē/ ▶ adj. (**furrier, furriest**) covered with or like fur. ■ **fur·ri·ness** n.

fur seal ▶ n. a seal whose thick underside fur is used commercially as sealskin.

fur·ther /'fərTHər/ used as comparative of FAR ▶ adv. (also **farther** /'färTHər/) **1** at, to, or by a greater distance. **2** over a greater expanse of space or time. **3** beyond the point already reached. **4** at or to a more advanced or desirable stage. **5** in addition; also. ▶ adj. **1** (also **farther**) more distant in space. **2** additional. ▶ v. help the progress or development of something.
– PHRASES **not go any further** (of a secret) not be told to anyone else. **until further notice** used to indicate that a situation will not change until another announcement is made: *the museum is closed to the public until further notice.*

> **USAGE**
> Is there any difference between **further** and **farther**? When talking about distance, either form can be used: *she moved further down the train* and *she moved farther down the train* are both correct. However you should use **further** when you mean 'beyond or in addition to what has already been done' (*have you anything further to say?*) or 'additional' (*phone for further information*).

fur·ther·ance /'fərTHərəns/ ▶ n. the action of helping a scheme or plan to progress.

fur·ther·more /'fərTHər,môr/ ▶ adv. in addition; besides.

fur·ther·most /'fərTHər,mōst/ (also **farthermost** /'färTHər,mōst/) ▶ adj. at the greatest distance from something.

fur·thest /'fərTHist/ (also **farthest** /'färTHist/) used as superlative of FAR ▶ adj. **1** situated at the greatest distance. **2** covering the greatest area or distance. ▶ adv. **1** at or by the greatest distance. **2** over the greatest distance or area. **3** to the most extreme or advanced point.

fur·tive /'fərtiv/ ▶ adj. done in a secretive or guilty way. ■ **fur·tive·ly** adv. **fur·tive·ness** n.

fu·ry /'fyŏŏrē/ ▶ n. (pl. **furies**) **1** extreme anger. **2** extreme strength or violence: *the fury of the storm.* **3** (**Furies**) Greek Mythology three goddesses who punished wrongdoers.

fuse[1] /fyŏŏz/ ▶ v. **1** join or blend to form a single entity. **2** melt a material or object with intense heat, so as to join it with something else. **3** provide a circuit or electrical appliance with a fuse. ▶ n. a safety device consisting of a strip of wire that melts and breaks an electric circuit if the current exceeds a safe level.

fuse[2] (also **fuze**) ▶ n. **1** a length of material along which a small flame moves to explode a bomb or firework. **2** a device in a bomb that controls the timing of the explosion. ▶ v. fit a fuse to a bomb.

fuse box ▶ n. a box or board containing the fuses for electrical circuits in a building.

fu·se·lage /'fyŏŏsə,läzн, -zə-/ ▶ n. the main body of an aircraft.

fu·si·ble /'fyŏŏzəbəl/ ▶ adj. able to be fused or melted easily.

fu·sil·lade /'fyŏŏsə,läd, -,läd/ ▶ n. a series of shots fired at the same time or in rapid succession.

fu·sion /'fyŏŏzнən/ ▶ n. **1** the process or result of fusing things to form a single entity. **2** a reaction in which light atomic nuclei fuse to form a heavier nucleus, releasing much energy. **3** popular music that is a mixture of different styles, especially jazz and rock. ▶ adj. referring to food or cooking that combines elements of both eastern and western cuisine.

fuss /fəs/ ▶ n. **1** a display of unnecessary or excessive excitement or activity. **2** a protest or complaint. ▶ v. **1** show unnecessary or excessive concern about something. **2** pay too much attention to someone: *his mother fussed over him all the time.*

fuss·pot /'fəs,pät/ ▶ n. informal a fussy person.

fuss·y /'fəsē/ ▶ adj. (**fussier, fussiest**) **1** too concerned about one's requirements and therefore hard to please. **2** full of unnecessary detail or decoration. ■ **fuss·i·ly** adv. **fuss·i·ness** n.

fus·tian /'fəscнən/ ▶ n. a thick, hard-wearing twilled cloth.

fus·ty /'fəstē/ ▶ adj. (**fustier, fustiest**) **1** smelling stale and damp or stuffy. **2** old-fashioned. ■ **fus·ti·ness** n.

fu·tile /'fyŏŏtl, -,til/ ▶ adj. producing no useful results; pointless. ■ **fu·tile·ly** adv. **fu·til·i·ty** /'fyŏŏ'tilətē/

fu·ton /'fŏŏ,tän/ ▶ n. **1** a Japanese padded mattress with no springs, able to rolled up when not in use. **2** a type of low wooden sofa bed with such a mattress.

fu·ture /'fyŏŏcнər/ ▶ n. **1** (**the future**) time that is still to come. **2** events or conditions occurring or existing in time still to come. **3** a prospect of success or happiness: *I might have a future as an artist.* **4** Grammar the tense of verbs expressing events that have not yet happened. **5** (**futures**) contracts for assets bought at agreed prices but delivered and paid for later. ▶ adj. **1** existing or occurring in the future. **2** planned or destined to hold a particular position: *his future wife.* **3** Grammar (of a tense) expressing an event yet to happen.
– PHRASES **in the future** from now on.

fu·ture per·fect ▶ n. Grammar a tense of verbs expressing an action expected to be completed in the future, in English exemplified by *will have done.*

fu·ture shock ▶ n. a state of distress or disorientation caused by rapid social or technological change.

fu·tur·ism /'fyŏŏcнə,rizəm/ ▶ n. **1** concern with events and trends of the future or that anticipate the future. **2** (**Futurism**) an early 20th-century artistic movement that strongly rejected traditional artistic forms and embraced modern technology. ■ **fu·tur·ist, Fu·tur·ist** adj. & n.

fu·tur·is·tic /,fyŏŏcнə'ristik/ ▶ adj. **1** having or involving very modern technology or design. **2** (of a movie or book) set in the future. ■ **fu·tur·is·ti·cal·ly** adv.

fu·tu·ri·ty /fyŏŏ'tŏŏrətē, -'cнŏŏrətē/ ▶ n. (pl. **futurities**) **1** the future time. **2** a future event.

fuze /fyŏŏz/ ▶ n. variant spelling of FUSE[2].

fuzz[1] /fəz/ ▶ n. a frizzy mass of hair or fiber. ▶ v. make or become fuzzy.

fuzz² ▶ n. (**the fuzz**) informal the police.

fuzz·y /ˈfəzē/ ▶ adj. (**fuzzier**, **fuzziest**) **1** having a frizzy texture or appearance. **2** indistinct or vague: *a fuzzy picture*. ■ **fuzz·i·ly** adv. **fuzz·i·ness** n.

fuzz·y log·ic ▶ n. a form of logic in which predicates can have fractional values rather than simply being true or false.

F-word ▶ n. euphemistic the word 'fuck.'

FX ▶ abbr. visual or sound effects.

FYI ▶ abbr. for your information.

Gg

G¹ (also **g**) ▶ n. (pl. **Gs** or **G's**) **1** the seventh letter of the alphabet. **2** referring to the next item after F in a set. **3** Music the fifth note in the scale of C major.

G² ▶ abbr. **1** giga- (10⁹). **2** informal grand (a thousand dollars). **3** the force exerted by the earth's gravitational field. ▶ symbol referring to movies that are suitable for audiences of all ages.

g ▶ abbr. **1** Chemistry gas. **2** gram(s). ▶ symbol Physics the acceleration due to gravity (9.81 m/s⁻²).

G8 ▶ abbr. Group of Eight, a group of eight industrial nations whose heads of government meet regularly.

GA ▶ abbr. Georgia.

Ga ▶ symbol the chemical element gallium.

gab /gab/ ▶ v. (**gabs, gabbing, gabbed**) informal talk at length.
– PHRASES **the gift of the gab** the ability to speak fluently and persuasively.

gab·ar·dine /'gabər,dēn/ ▶ n. a smooth, hard-wearing worsted or cotton cloth, used especially for making raincoats.

gab·ble /'gabəl/ ▶ v. talk rapidly and in a way that is hard to understand. ▶ n. rapid, unintelligible talk. ■ **gab·bler** n.

gab·by /'gabē/ ▶ adj. (**gabbier, gabbiest**) informal excessively or annoying talkative.

gab·er·dine /'gabər,dēn/ ▶ n. variant spelling of GABARDINE.

gab·fest /'gab,fest/ ▶ n. informal **1** a conference or other gathering with prolonged talking: *these summits are merely empty gabfests.* **2** a lengthy conversation.

ga·ble /'gābəl/ ▶ n. **1** the triangular upper part of a wall at the end of a ridged roof. **2** a gable-shaped canopy over a window or door. ■ **ga·bled** adj.

Gab·o·nese /,gabə'nēz, -'nēs/ ▶ n. (pl. same) a person from Gabon, a country in West Africa. ▶ adj. relating to Gabon.

gad /gad/ ▶ v. (**gads, gadding, gadded**) (**gad about/around**) informal enjoy oneself by visiting many different places or traveling from one place to another.

gad·a·bout /'gadə,bout/ ▶ n. informal a person who is always traveling from one place to another enjoying themselves.

gad·fly /'gad,flī/ ▶ n. (pl. **gadflies**) **1** a large fly that bites livestock. **2** an annoying person.

gadg·et /'gajit/ ▶ n. a small mechanical device or tool. ■ **gadg·et·ry** n.

gad·o·lin·i·um /,gadl'inēəm/ ▶ n. a soft silvery-white metallic chemical element of the lanthanide series.

gad·wall /'gad,wôl/ ▶ n. a brownish-gray freshwater duck that is found across Eurasia and North America.

gad·zooks /,gad'zŏŏks/ ▶ exclam. old use expressing surprise or annoyance.

Gael /gāl/ ▶ n. a Gaelic-speaking person.

Gael·ic /'gālik/ ▶ n. **1** (also **Scottish Gaelic**) a Celtic language spoken in western Scotland, brought from Ireland in the 5th and 6th centuries AD. **2** (also **Irish Gaelic**) the Celtic language of Ireland; Irish. ▶ adj. relating to the Celtic languages and their speakers.

gaff /gaf/ ▶ n. **1** a stick with a hook or barbed spear, for landing large fish. **2** Sailing a spar to which the head of a fore-and-aft sail is bent.

gaffe /gaf/ ▶ n. an embarrassing blunder or mistake.

gaf·fer /'gafər/ ▶ n. **1** the chief electrician in a movie or television production unit. **2** informal an old man.

gag¹ /gag/ ▶ n. **1** a piece of cloth put in or over a person's mouth to prevent them from speaking. **2** a restriction on free speech. ▶ v. (**gags, gagging, gagged**) **1** put a gag on someone. **2** prevent someone from speaking freely. **3** choke or retch.

gag² ▶ n. a joke or funny story.

ga·ga /'gä,gä/ ▶ adj. informal rambling in speech or thought, especially as a result of old age.

gage¹ /gāj/ ▶ n. old use **1** a valued object given as a guarantee of someone's good faith. **2** a glove or other object thrown down as a challenge to fight.

gage² ▶ n. & v. variant spelling of GAUGE.

gag·gle /'gagəl/ ▶ n. **1** a flock of geese. **2** informal a noisy group of people: *a gaggle of children.*

gag order ▶ n. a judge's order that a case may not be discussed in public.

gag rule ▶ n. a regulation or directive that prohibits discussion of a particular matter: *York violated the gag rule at the expense of his own job.*

Gai·a /'gīə/ ▶ n. the earth viewed as a vast self-regulating organism.

gai·e·ty /'gāitē/ ▶ n. (pl. **gaieties**) **1** the state or quality of being lighthearted and cheerful. **2** lively celebrations or festivities.

gail·lar·di·a /gə'lärdēə/ ▶ n. a plant of the daisy family cultivated for its bright red and yellow flowers.

gai·ly /'gālē/ ▶ adv. **1** in a lighthearted and cheerful way. **2** without thinking of the consequences of one's actions. **3** with a bright appearance.

gain /gān/ ▶ v. **1** obtain or secure: *troops gained control of the town.* **2** reach or arrive at a place. **3** (**gain on**) come closer to a person or thing being chased. **4** increase the amount or rate of weight or speed. **5** increase in value. **6** (**gain in**) improve or progress in some way: *she has gained in confidence.* **7** benefit: *both of them stood to gain from the relationship.* **8** (of a clock or watch) become fast. ▶ n. **1** a thing that is gained. **2** an increase in wealth or resources. ■ **gain·er** n.

gain·ful /'gānfəl/ ▶ adj. (of employment) useful and for which one is paid. ■ **gain·ful·ly** adv.

gain·say /,gān'sā, 'gān,sā/ ▶ v. (past and past part. **gainsaid**) formal deny or contradict a fact or statement.

gait /gāt/ ▶ n. **1** a person's way of walking. **2** the pattern of steps of a horse or dog at a particular speed.

gait·er /'gātər/ ▶ n. **1** a covering of cloth or leather for the ankle and lower leg. **2** a shoe or overshoe extending to the ankle or above. ■ **gait·ered** adj.

gal /gal/ ▶ n. informal a girl or young woman.

gal. ▶ abbr. gallon(s).

ga·la /'gālə, 'galə/ ▶ n. a social occasion with special entertainments: (as adj.) *a gala affair.*

ga·lac·tic /gə'laktik/ ▶ adj. relating to a galaxy or galaxies. ■ **ga·lac·tic·al·ly** adv.

ga·lan·gal /gə'laNGgəl/ (also **galingale** /'galin,gāl/) ▶ n. an Asian plant of the ginger family, used in cooking and herbal medicine.

gal·ax·y /'galəksē/ ▶ n. (pl. **galaxies**) **1** a system of millions or billions of stars held together by gravitational attraction. **2** (**the Galaxy**) the galaxy of which the solar system is a part; the Milky Way. **3** a large and impressive group of people or things: *a galaxy of celebrities.*

gale /gāl/ ▶ n. **1** a very strong wind. **2** an outburst of laughter.

ga·le·na /gə'lēnə/ ▶ n. a metallic gray or black mineral consisting of lead sulfide.

ga·lette /gə'let/ ▶ n. **1** a round, flat, crusty cake. **2** a buckwheat pancake or crepe with a sweet or savory filling.

Gal·i·le·an[1] /,galə'lēən/ ▶ adj. relating to the Italian astronomer and physicist Galileo Galilei.

Gal·i·le·an[2] ▶ n. a person from Galilee, the region of ancient Palestine associated with the ministry of Jesus and now part of Israel. ▶ adj. relating to Galilee.

gall[1] /gôl/ ▶ n. bold and disrespectful behavior: *she had the gall to ask him for money.*

gall[2] ▶ n. **1** annoyance or resentment. **2** a sore on the skin made by rubbing. ▶ v. **1** make someone feel annoyed or resentful. **2** make the skin sore by rubbing. ■ **gall·ing** adj.

gall[3] ▶ n. an abnormal growth on plants and trees, caused by the presence of insect larvae, mites, or fungi.

gall. ▶ abbr. gallon(s).

gal·lant ▶ adj. **1** /'galənt/ brave or heroic. **2** /gə'lant, -'länt/ (of a man) polite and charming to women. ▶ n. /gə'lant, -'länt, 'galənt/ a man who is charmingly attentive to women. ■ **gal·lant·ly** adv.

gal·lant·ry /'galəntrē/ ▶ n. (pl. **gallantries**) **1** courageous behavior. **2** polite attention paid by men to women.

gall·blad·der /'gôl,bladər/ ▶ n. a small sac-shaped organ beneath the liver, in which bile is stored.

gal·le·on /'galēən, 'galyən/ ▶ n. historical a large square-rigged sailing ship with three or more decks and masts.

gal·le·ri·a /,galə'rēə/ ▶ n. a long covered passageway, typically lined with stores and other businesses.

gal·ler·y /'galərē/ ▶ n. (pl. **galleries**) **1** a room or building in which works of art are displayed. **2** a

balcony or upper floor projecting from a back or side wall inside a hall or church. **3** the highest balcony in a theater, having the least expensive seats. **4** a long room or passage forming a portico or colonnade. **5** a horizontal underground passage in a mine. ■ **gal·ler·ied** adj.

– PHRASES **play to the gallery** do something intended to win approval or make oneself popular.

gal·ley /'galē/ ▶ n. (pl. **galleys**) **1** historical a low, flat ship with one or more sails and up to three banks of oars, often manned by slaves or criminals. **2** a narrow kitchen in a ship or aircraft. **3** (also **galley proof**) a printer's proof in the form of long single-column strips.

gal·liard /'galyərd/ ▶ n. historical a lively dance in triple time for two people.

Gal·lic /'galik/ ▶ adj. **1** relating to or characteristic of France or the French. **2** relating to the Gauls. ■ **Gal·li·cize** v.

gal·lic ac·id ▶ n. an organic acid extracted from tannins that has antioxidant properties.

Gal·li·cism /'gali,sizəm/ ▶ n. a French word or phrase adopted in another language.

gal·li·mau·fry /,galə'môfrē/ ▶ n. a jumble or mixture.

gal·li·na·ceous /,galə'nāshəs/ ▶ adj. relating to the order of birds that includes domestic poultry and game birds such as grouse, partridges, and pheasants.

gal·li·um /'galēəm/ ▶ n. a soft silvery-white metallic chemical element that melts just above normal room temperature.

gal·li·um ar·sen·ide ▶ n. a metallic compound that is used to make light-emitting diodes, integrated circuits, and some other computer components.

gal·li·vant /'galə,vant/ ▶ v. informal go from place to place enjoying oneself.

gal·lon /'galən/ ▶ n. **1** a unit of volume for measuring liquids, equal to four quarts (or eight pints): in the US, equivalent to 3.79 liters; in Britain (also **imperial gallon**), equivalent to 4.55 liters. **2** (**gallons**) informal large quantities of something.

gal·lop /'galəp/ ▶ n. **1** the fastest pace of a horse, with all the feet off the ground together in each stride. **2** a ride on a horse at a gallop. ▶ v. (**gallops, galloping, galloped**) **1** go at the pace of a gallop. **2** move or progress very rapidly.

gal·lows /'galōz/ ▶ pl.n. (usu. treated as sing.) **1** a structure consisting of two uprights and a crosspiece, used for hanging a person. **2** (**the gallows**) execution by hanging.

gal·lows hu·mor ▶ n. grim and ironical humor in a desperate or hopeless situation.

gall·stone /'gôl,stōn/ ▶ n. a small hard mass formed abnormally in the gallbladder or bile ducts, causing pain and obstruction.

Gal·lup poll /'galəp/ ▶ n. trademark an assessment of public opinion by questioning a representative sample of the population, used in forecasting voting results in an election.

gall wasp ▶ n. a small winged antlike insect, the female of which lays eggs in plant tissue that cause a gall to form when the larvae hatch.

ga·loot /gə'lo͞ot/ ▶ n. informal a clumsy or stupid person.

ga·lore /gə'lôr/ ▶ adj. in large quantities: *there were prizes galore.*

ga·losh /gə'läsн/ ▶ n. (usu. **galoshes**) a

waterproof rubber overshoe.

ga·lumph /gəˈləmf/ ▶ v. informal move in a clumsy, heavy, or noisy way.

gal·van·ic /galˈvanik/ ▶ adj. **1** relating to or involving electric currents produced by chemical action. **2** sudden and dramatic. ■ **gal·van·i·cal·ly** adv.

gal·va·nize /ˈgalvəˌnīz/ ▶ v. **1** make someone do something by shocking or exciting them: *a bang on the door galvanized her into action.* **2** (as adj. **galvanized**) (of iron or steel) coated with a protective layer of zinc. ■ **gal·va·ni·za·tion** /ˌgalvəniˈzāsHən/ n.

gal·va·nom·e·ter /ˌgalvəˈnämitər/ ▶ n. an instrument for detecting and measuring small electric currents.

Gam·bi·an /ˈgambēən/ ▶ n. a person from Gambia, a country in West Africa. ▶ adj. relating to Gambia.

gam·bit /ˈgambit/ ▶ n. **1** an opening action or remark intended to gain someone an advantage. **2** (in chess) an opening move in which a player makes a sacrifice for the sake of some compensating advantage.

gam·ble /ˈgambəl/ ▶ v. **1** play games of chance for money. **2** bet a sum of money. **3** take risky action in the hope of a successful result: *they are gambling on a turnaround in the company's fortunes.* ▶ n. a risky undertaking. ■ **gam·bler** n.

gam·bol /ˈgambəl/ ▶ v. (**gambols, gamboling, gamboled**) run or jump about playfully. ▶ n. an act of gamboling.

game¹ /gām/ ▶ n. **1** an activity taken part in for amusement. **2** a form of competitive activity or sport played according to rules. **3** a complete period of play, ending in a final result. **4** a single portion of play, forming a scoring unit within a game. **5** (**games**) a meeting for sporting contests. **6** the equipment used in playing a board game, computer game, etc. **7** informal a type of activity or business: *he was in the restaurant game.* **8** a secret plan or trick. **9** wild mammals or birds hunted for sport or food. ▶ adj. eager and willing to do something new or challenging: *they were game for anything.* ▶ v. play at games of chance for money. ■ **game·ly** adv. **game·ness** n. **game·ster** n.

– PHRASES **ahead of the game** ahead of one's competitors. **beat someone at their own game** use someone's own methods to outdo them. **the game is up** the deception or crime is revealed and so cannot succeed. **the only game in town** the best, the most important, or the only thing worth considering. **play the game** behave in a fair or honorable way. **play games** behave or conduct business in a way that lacks due seriousness or respect: *don't play games with me!*

game² ▶ adj. dated (of a person's leg) lame.

game bird ▶ n. **1** a bird shot for sport or food. **2** a bird of a large group that includes pheasants, grouse, quails, guineafowl, etc.

game·cock /ˈgāmˌkäk/ ▶ n. a rooster bred and trained for cockfighting.

game fish ▶ n. (pl. same) a fish caught by anglers for sport, especially (in fresh water) salmon and trout and (in the sea) marlins, sharks, bass, and mackerel.

game·keep·er /ˈgāmˌkēpər/ ▶ n. a person employed to breed and protect game for a large estate.

gam·e·lan /ˈgaməˌlan/ ▶ n. a traditional

instrumental group in Java and Bali, including many bronze percussion instruments.

game plan ▶ n. a plan for success in sports, politics, or business: *he's revised his game plan to make sure he stays in charge.*

game point ▶ n. (in tennis and other sports) a point that if won by a player or side will also win them the game.

gam·er /ˈgāmər/ ▶ n. **1** a participant in a computer or role-playing game. **2** (especially in sports) a person known for consistently making a strong effort regardless of challenging or adverse conditions.

game show ▶ n. a television program in which people compete to win prizes.

games·man·ship /ˈgāmzmənˌsHip/ ▶ n. the art of winning games by using tactics to make one's opponent less confident. ■ **games·man** n.

gam·ete /ˈgamēt, gəˈmēt/ ▶ n. a cell that is able to unite with another of the opposite sex in sexual reproduction to form a zygote.

game the·o·ry ▶ n. the mathematical study of strategies for dealing with competitive situations where the outcome of a participant's choice of action depends critically on the actions of other participants.

ga·me·to·cyte /gəˈmētəˌsīt/ ▶ n. Biology a cell that divides by meiosis to form a spermatozoon or an ovum.

gam·e·to·gen·e·sis /gəˌmētəˈjenəsis/ ▶ n. Biology the formation of gametes from gametocytes.

ga·me·to·phyte /gəˈmētəˌfīt/ ▶ n. Botany the sexual form of a plant in the alternation of generations.

game warden ▶ n. a person, often a government employee, who oversees hunting and wildlife in a particular area.

gam·ey ▶ adj. variant spelling of GAMY.

gam·ine /ˈgamēn/ ▶ adj. (of a girl) attractively boyish in appearance. ▶ n. a girl who is attractively boyish in appearance.

gam·ma /ˈgamə/ ▶ n. the third letter of the Greek alphabet (Γ, γ), represented as 'g.' ▶ adj. relating to gamma rays.

gam·ma glob·u·lin /ˈgläbyələn/ ▶ n. a mixture of blood proteins, mainly immunoglobulins, often given to boost immunity.

gam·ma rays (also **gamma radiation**) ▶ pl. n. penetrating electromagnetic radiation of shorter wavelength than X-rays.

gam·ut /ˈgamət/ ▶ n. **1** the complete range or scope of something: *the whole gamut of human emotion.* **2** a complete scale of musical notes; the range of a voice or instrument. **3** historical a musical scale consisting of seven overlapping scales, containing all the recognized notes used in medieval music.

– PHRASES **run the gamut** experience, display, or perform the complete range of something: *they ran the gamut of electronic dance music.*

gam·y /ˈgāmē/ (also **gamey**) ▶ adj. (**gamier, gamiest**) (of meat) having the strong flavor or smell of game when it is slightly decomposed and so ready to cook. ■ **gam·i·ness** n.

gan·der /ˈgandər/ ▶ n. **1** a male goose. **2** informal a look or glance.

gang /gaNG/ ▶ n. **1** an organized group of criminals or rowdy young people. **2** informal a group of people who regularly meet and do things together. **3** an organized group of people doing manual work. **4** a set of switches, sockets, or other devices grouped together. ▶ v. **1** (**gang together**) form a group or gang. **2** (**gang up**) join together to oppose or intimidate someone: *the other children ganged up on him.*

gang·bang /'gaNG,baNG/ ▶ n. informal **1** a gang rape. **2** a sexual orgy. **3** an instance of violence involving members of a criminal gang.
■ **gang·bang·er** n.

gang·bust·ers /'gaNG,bəstər/ ▶ pl.n. (in phrase **go** (or **like**) **gangbusters**) informal used to refer to great energy, speed, or success: *four-wheel-drive sales are going gangbusters.*

gang·land /'gaNG,land/ ▶ n. the world of criminal gangs.

gan·gli·on /'gaNGglēən/ ▶ n. (pl. **ganglia** /-glēə/ or **ganglions**) Anatomy & Medicine **1** a structure containing a number of nerve cells, often forming a swelling on a nerve fiber. **2** a mass of gray matter within the central nervous system. **3** an abnormal but harmless swelling on the sheath of a tendon. ■ **gan·gli·on·ic** /,gaNGglē'änik/ adj.

gan·gly /'gaNGglē/ (also **gangling**) ▶ adj. (**ganglier, gangliest**) informal long or tall, thin, and awkward in movement: *a doe and a gangling half-grown fawn burst out of the trees.*

gang·plank /'gaNG,plaNGk/ ▶ n. a movable plank used to board or leave a ship or boat.

gang rape ▶ n. the rape of one person by a group of other people.

gan·grene /'gaNGgrēn, gaNG'grēn/ ▶ n. the death and decomposition of body tissue, caused by an obstructed blood supply or bacterial infection.
■ **gan·gre·nous** /'gaNGgrənəs/ adj.

gang·sta /'gaNGstə/ ▶ n. **1** informal a member of a street gang. **2** (also **gangsta rap**) a type of rap music featuring aggressive lyrics, often with reference to gang violence.

gang·ster /'gaNGstər/ ▶ n. a member of an organized gang of violent criminals.
■ **gang·ster·ism** n.

gang·way /'gaNG,wā/ ▶ n. **1** a movable bridge linking a ship to the shore. **2** a raised platform or walkway providing a passage. **3** Brit. a passage between rows of seats in an auditorium, aircraft, etc.

gan·ja /'gänjə/ ▶ n. marijuana.

gan·net /'ganit/ ▶ n. **1** a large seabird with mainly white plumage. **2** Brit. informal a greedy person.

gan·try /'gantrē/ ▶ n. (pl. **gantries**) a bridgelike overhead structure supporting equipment such as a crane or railroad signals.

gaol ▶ n. Brit. variant spelling of JAIL.

gap /gap/ ▶ n. **1** a break or hole in an object or between two objects. **2** a space, interval, or break. ■ **gap·py** adj.

gape /gāp/ ▶ v. **1** stare with one's mouth open wide in amazement or wonder. **2** (often as adj. **gaping**) be or become wide open: *a gaping wound.* ▶ n. **1** an open-mouthed stare. **2** a wide opening.

ga·rage /gə'räzн, -'räj/ ▶ n. **1** a building in which a car or other motor vehicle is kept. **2** an establishment that provides services and repairs for motor vehicles. **3** (also **garage rock**) a form of unpolished pop music incorporating elements of rock, blues, and soul. ▶ v. put or keep a motor vehicle in a garage.

ga·rage sale ▶ n. a sale of unwanted goods held in or outside of a garage; a yard sale.

ga·ram ma·sa·la /,gärəm mə'sälə/ ▶ n. a spice mixture used in Indian cooking.

garb /gärb/ ▶ n. clothing of a particular kind: *women in riding garb.* ▶ v. dress in distinctive clothes: *a motorcyclist garbed in black leather.*

gar·bage /'gärbij/ ▶ n. **1** domestic rubbish or waste. **2** something worthless or meaningless.

gar·bage can ▶ n. a container, typically plastic or metal, for household refuse.

gar·bage dis·pos·al ▶ n. an electric device fitted to the waste pipe of a kitchen sink for grinding up food waste.

gar·ban·zo /gär'bänzō/ (also **garbanzo bean**) ▶ n. (pl. **garbanzos**) another term for CHICKPEA.

gar·ble /'gärbəl/ ▶ v. reproduce a message or transmission in a confused and distorted way.
■ **gar·bler** n.

gar·çon /gär'sôN/ ▶ n. a waiter in a French restaurant.

gar·den /'gärdn/ ▶ n. **1** a piece of cultivated land for growing flowers or vegetables. **2** (**gardens**) ornamental grounds laid out for public enjoyment. ▶ v. cultivate or work in a garden.
■ **gar·den·er** n.

gar·den a·part·ment ▶ n. a ground-floor apartment with a door opening onto a yard or garden.

gar·den cen·ter ▶ n. a place where plants and gardening equipment are sold.

gar·de·nia /gär'dēnyə/ ▶ n. a tree or shrub of warm climates, with large fragrant white or yellow flowers.

gar·den par·ty ▶ n. a social event held on a lawn or in a garden.

gar·den-va·ri·e·ty ▶ adj. of the usual or ordinary type; commonplace.

gar·fish /'gär,fisн/ ▶ n. any of a number of long, slender freshwater fish with beaklike jaws and sharply pointed teeth.

gar·gan·tu·an /gär'gancнŌŌən/ ▶ adj. very large; enormous.

gar·gle /'gärgəl/ ▶ v. wash one's mouth and throat with a liquid that is kept in motion by breathing through it. ▶ n. **1** a liquid used for gargling. **2** an act of gargling.

gar·goyle /'gär,goil/ ▶ n. a spout in the form of a grotesque carved face or figure, set below the roof of a building to carry rainwater away.

gar·ish /'gärisн/ ▶ adj. unpleasantly bright and showy; lurid. ■ **gar·ish·ly** adv. **gar·ish·ness** n.

gar·land /'gärlənd/ ▶ n. a wreath of flowers and leaves, worn on the head or hung as a decoration. ▶ v. decorate someone or something with a garland.

gar·lic /'gärlik/ ▶ n. the bulb of a plant of the onion family, having a strong taste and smell and used as a flavoring in cooking. ■ **gar·lick·y** adj.

gar·lic mus·tard ▶ n. a European mustard plant that grows wild in the eastern US and that has both medicinal and culinary uses.

gar·ment /'gärmənt/ ▶ n. an item of clothing.

gar·ner /'gärnər/ ▶ v. gather or collect: *the series has garnered more than thirty-five awards.*

gar·net /'gärnit/ ▶ n. a deep red semiprecious stone.

gar·nish /'gärnisн/ ▶ v. **1** decorate food with a small amount of another food: *pheasant breast garnished with truffles.* **2** Law order that money or wages be seized to settle a debt. ▶ n. a small amount of food used to decorate other food.

gar·nish·ee /ˌgärniˈsHē/ ▶ n. someone who is served with a garnishment.

gar·nish·ment /ˈgärnisHmənt/ ▶ n. Law a court order directing that money or wages of a third party be seized to satisfy a debt.

gar·ret /ˈgarit/ ▶ n. a top-floor or attic room.

gar·ri·son /ˈgarəsən/ ▶ n. a group of troops stationed in a fortress or town to defend it. ▶ v. provide a place with a garrison.

gar·rote /gəˈrät, -ˈrōt/ (also **garotte**; **garrotte**) ▶ v. strangle someone with a wire or cord. ▶ n. a wire, cord, or other implement used to strangle someone.

gar·ru·lous /ˈgar(y)ələs/ ▶ adj. excessively talkative. ■ **gar·ru·li·ty** /gəˈrōōlitē/ n. **gar·ru·lous·ly** adv.

gar·ter /ˈgärtər/ ▶ n. **1** a band worn around the leg to keep up a stocking or sock. **2** a suspender for a sock or stocking.

gar·ter snake ▶ n. **1** a common harmless North American snake with longitudinal stripes. **2** a venomous burrowing African snake, typically dark with lighter bands.

gas /gas/ ▶ n. (pl. **gases** or **gasses**) **1** an airlike fluid substance that expands freely to fill any space available. **2** a flammable gas used as a fuel. **3** a gas used as an anesthetic. **4** gasoline. **5** (**a gas**) informal an entertaining or amusing person or thing. **6** Mining an explosive mixture of firedamp with air. ▶ v. (**gases**, **gassing**, **gassed**) **1** harm or kill someone or something with gas. **2** informal talk excessively about trivial things. ■ **gas·ser** n.

gas·bag /ˈgasˌbag/ ▶ n. informal a person who talks excessively about trivial things.

gas cham·ber ▶ n. an airtight room that can be filled with poisonous gas to kill people or animals.

gas·e·ous /ˈgasēəs, ˈgasHəs/ ▶ adj. relating to or having the characteristics of a gas.

gas guz·zler ▶ n. informal a car with high fuel consumption.

gash /gasH/ ▶ n. a long, deep cut or wound. ▶ v. make a gash in something.

gas·ket /ˈgaskit/ ▶ n. a sheet or ring of rubber or other material sealing the junction between two surfaces in an engine or other device.

gas·light /ˈgasˌlīt/ ▶ n. light from a lamp that uses a jet of burning gas. ■ **gas·lit** /-ˌlit/ adj.

gas mask ▶ n. a protective mask used to cover the face as a defense against poison gas.

gas·o·hol /ˈgasəˌhôl, -ˌhäl/ ▶ n. a mixture of gasoline and ethanol used as fuel for internal-combustion engines.

gas·o·line /ˌgasəˈlēn, ˈgasəlēn/ ▶ n. a light fuel oil obtained by distilling petroleum and used in internal-combustion engines.

gas·om·e·ter /gasˈämitər/ ▶ n. a large tank in which gas is stored before being distributed to consumers.

gasp /gasp/ ▶ v. **1** take a quick breath with the mouth open, from pain, breathlessness, or astonishment. **2** (**gasp for**) struggle for air by gasping. ▶ n. a sudden quick breath.
– PHRASES **the last gasp** the point of exhaustion, death, or completion.

gas sta·tion ▶ n. a service station, especially one without repair facilities.

gas·sy /ˈgasē/ ▶ adj. (**gassier**, **gassiest**) resembling or full of gas.

gas·tric /ˈgastrik/ ▶ adj. relating to the stomach.

gas·tric juice ▶ n. an acid fluid produced by the stomach glands, which helps digestion.

gas·tri·tis /gaˈstrītis/ ▶ n. inflammation of the lining of the stomach.

gas·tro·en·ter·i·tis /ˌgastrōˌentəˈrītis/ ▶ n. inflammation of the stomach and intestines, causing diarrhea and vomiting.

gas·tro·en·ter·ol·o·gy /ˌgastrōˌentəˈräləjē/ ▶ n. the branch of medicine that deals with disorders of the stomach and intestines. ■ **gas·tro·en·te·rol·o·gist** n.

gas·tro·nome /ˈgastrəˌnōm/ ▶ n. a gourmet.

gas·tron·o·my /gaˈstränəmē/ ▶ n. the practice or art of choosing, preparing, and eating good food. ■ **gas·tro·nom·ic** /ˌgastrəˈnämik/ adj.

gas·tro·pod /ˈgastrəˌpäd/ ▶ n. Zoology any of a large class of mollusks including snails, slugs, and whelks.

gas·works /ˈgasˌwərks/ ▶ pl.n. (treated as sing.) a place where gas is manufactured and processed.

gat /gat/ ▶ n. informal, dated a revolver or pistol.

gate /gāt/ ▶ n. **1** a hinged barrier used to close an opening in a wall, fence, or hedge. **2** an exit from an airport building to an aircraft. **3** a hinged or sliding barrier for controlling the flow of water on a waterway. **4** the number of people who pay to attend a sports event. **5** an electric circuit with an output that depends on the combination of several inputs. ■ **gat·ed** adj.

-gate ▶ comb.form in nouns referring to a scandal, especially one involving a cover-up: *Irangate*.

ga·teau /gäˈtō, ga-/ ▶ n. (pl. **gateaus** or **gateaux** /-ˈtōz/) a rich cake with layers of cream or fruit.

gate-crash ▶ v. enter a party without an invitation or ticket. ■ **gate-crash·er** n.

gat·ed com·mu·ni·ty ▶ n. a residential area, typically fenced in, that has a guarded entrance for vehicular and pedestrian traffic.

gate·fold /ˈgātˌfōld/ ▶ n. an oversized folded page in a book or magazine, intended to be opened out for reading.

gate·house /ˈgātˌhous/ ▶ n. **1** a house standing by the gateway to a country estate. **2** historical a room over a city or palace gate, often used as a prison.

gate·keep·er /ˈgātˌkēpər/ ▶ n. an attendant at a gate.

gate·keep·ing /ˈgātˌkēpiNG/ ▶ n. **1** the activity of controlling, and usually limiting, general access to something: *her agent will be practicing a little more gatekeeping.* **2** Computing a service that controls access to files, computers, networks, etc.

gate·leg ta·ble /ˈgātˌleg/ ▶ n. a table with hinged legs that may be swung out from the center to support folding leaves.

gate·post /ˈgātˌpōst/ ▶ n. a post on which a gate is hinged or against which it shuts.

gate·way /ˈgātˌwā/ ▶ n. **1** an opening in a wall or fence that can be closed by a gate. **2** (**gateway to**) a means of entering somewhere or achieving something: *college education is a gateway to the middle class.* **3** a device used to connect two different computer networks, especially a connection to the Internet.

gate·way drug ▶ n. a habit-forming drug that may lead to the use of more seriously addictive drugs.

gath·er /ˈgaT͟Hər/ ▶ v. **1** come or bring together; assemble or collect. **2** increase in speed, force, etc. **3** understand something to be the case as a result of information or evidence: *I gather he's resigned.* **4** collect plants or fruits for food. **5** harvest a crop. **6** draw together or toward oneself: *she gathered the child in her arms.* **7** pull fabric together in a series of folds by drawing thread through it. ▶ n. (**gathers**) a part of a garment that is gathered. ■ **gath·er·er** n.

gath·er·ing /ˈgaT͟HəriNG/ ▶ n. a group of people assembled for a purpose.

Gat·ling gun /ˈgatliNG/ ▶ n. historical a rapid-fire, crank-driven machine gun with a cylindrical cluster of several barrels.

ga·tor /ˈgātər/ ▶ n. informal an alligator.

GATT /gat/ ▶ abbr. General Agreement on Tariffs and Trade.

gauche /gōsH/ ▶ adj. unsophisticated and awkward when dealing with others. ■ **gauche·ly** adv. **gauche·ness** n.

gau·che·rie /ˌgōsHəˈrē/ ▶ n. awkward or unsophisticated ways.

gau·cho /ˈgouCHō/ ▶ n. (pl. **gauchos**) a cowboy from the South American plains.

gaud·y /ˈgôdē/ ▶ adj. (**gaudier, gaudiest**) tastelessly bright or showy: *gaudy multicolored shorts.* ■ **gaud·i·ly** adv. **gaud·i·ness** n.

gauge /gāj/ (chiefly technical also **gage**) ▶ n. **1** an instrument that measures and gives a visual display of the amount, level, or contents of something. **2** the thickness, size, or capacity of a wire, tube, bullet, etc., especially as a standard measure. **3** the distance between the rails of a railroad track. ▶ v. **1** judge or assess a situation or mood: *it is difficult to gauge his true feelings.* **2** estimate or determine the amount or level of something. **3** measure the dimensions of an object with a gauge. ■ **gaug·er** n.

Gaul /gôl/ ▶ n. a person from the ancient European region of Gaul.

Gaul·ish /ˈgôlisH/ ▶ n. the Celtic language of the ancient Gauls. ▶ adj. relating to the ancient Gauls.

Gaull·ist /ˈgô‚list/ ▶ n. a supporter of the principles and policies of the French statesman Charles de Gaulle, characterized chiefly by conservatism and nationalism. ▶ adj. relating to Gaullists or Gaullism. ■ **Gaull·ism** /ˈgô‚lizəm/ n.

gaunt /gônt/ ▶ adj. **1** lean and haggard, especially through suffering or age. **2** (of a place) grim or desolate. ■ **gaunt·ly** adv. **gaunt·ness** n.

gaunt·let[1] /ˈgôntlit, ˈgänt-/ ▶ n. **1** a strong glove with a long, loose wrist. **2** a leather glove with steel plates, worn as part of medieval armor. – PHRASES **take up** (or **throw down**) **the gauntlet** accept (or issue) a challenge.

gaunt·let[2] ▶ n. (in phrase **run the gauntlet**) **1** go through an intimidating crowd or experience in order to reach a goal. **2** historical undergo the military punishment of receiving blows while running between two rows of men with sticks.

gauss /gous/ ▶ n. (pl. same or **gausses**) a unit of magnetic flux density, equal to one ten-thousandth of a tesla.

Gauss·i·an dis·tri·bu·tion /ˈgousēən/ ▶ n. another term for NORMAL DISTRIBUTION.

gauze /gôz/ ▶ n. **1** a thin transparent fabric. **2** thin, loosely woven cloth used for dressing wounds. **3** (also **wire gauze**) a fine wire mesh. ■ **gauz·y** adj.

gave /gāv/ ▶ past of GIVE.

gav·el /ˈgavəl/ ▶ n. a small hammer with which an auctioneer, judge, or chair of a meeting hits a surface to call for attention or order.

gav·el-to-gav·el ▶ adj. (of media coverage of an event or trial) from beginning to end and all-inclusive: *C-SPAN plans gavel-to-gavel coverage from the convention floor.*

ga·votte /gəˈvät/ ▶ n. a medium-paced French dance, popular in the 18th century.

gawk /gôk/ ▶ v. stare in a stupid or rude way. ▶ n. an awkward or shy person. ■ **gawk·er** n.

gawk·y /ˈgôkē/ ▶ adj. nervously awkward and ungainly. ■ **gawk·i·ly** adv. **gawk·i·ness** n.

gawp /gôp/ ▶ v. informal stare in a stupid or rude way. ■ **gawp·er** n.

gay /gā/ ▶ adj. (**gayer, gayest**) **1** (especially of a man) homosexual. **2** relating to homosexuals. **3** dated lighthearted and carefree. **4** dated brightly colored; showy. ▶ n. a homosexual person, especially a man. ■ **gay·ness** n.

gay·dar /ˈgāˌdär/ ▶ n. informal the supposed ability of homosexuals to recognize one another by interpreting very slight indications.

ga·za·ni·a /gəˈzānēə/ ▶ n. a tropical herbaceous plant of the daisy family, with flowers that are typically orange or yellow.

gaze /gāz/ ▶ v. look steadily and intently. ▶ n. a steady intent look. ■ **gaz·er** n.

ga·ze·bo /gəˈzēbō/ ▶ n. (pl. **gazebos**) a freestanding roofed structure with a wide view of the surrounding area, found typically in parks and backyards.

ga·zelle /gəˈzel/ ▶ n. a small antelope with curved horns and white underparts.

ga·zette /gəˈzet/ ▶ n. a journal or newspaper, especially the official journal of an organization.

gaz·et·teer /ˌgaziˈti(ə)r/ ▶ n. a list of place names published as a book or part of a book.

ga·zil·lion /gəˈzilyən/ ▶ cardinal number informal a very large number or quantity.

gaz·pa·cho /gäˈspäCHō/ ▶ n. (pl. **gazpachos**) a cold Spanish soup made chiefly from tomatoes and peppers.

GB ▶ abbr. **1** Great Britain. **2** (also **Gb**) Computing gigabyte(s) or gigabit(s).

Gd ▶ symbol the chemical element gadolinium.

GDP ▶ abbr. gross domestic product.

GDR ▶ abbr. historical German Democratic Republic.

Ge ▶ symbol the chemical element germanium.

gear /gi(ə)r/ ▶ n. **1** (**gears**) a set of toothed wheels that connect the engine to the wheels of a vehicle and work together to alter its speed. **2** a particular setting of gears in a vehicle: *I never left third gear.* **3** informal equipment, possessions, or clothing. ▶ v. **1** design or adjust gears to give a particular speed or power output. **2** adapt something for a particular purpose or group: *an activity program geared to senior citizens.* **3** (**gear** (**someone/thing**) **up**) prepare to do something, or prepare someone to do something: *we're gearing up to expand out of California.* – PHRASES **in** (or **out of**) **gear** with a gear (or no gear) engaged.

gear·box /ˈgi(ə)r‚bäks/ ▶ n. a set of gears with its casing, especially in a motor vehicle; the transmission.

gear·ing /ˈgi(ə)riNG/ ▶ n. **1** the set or arrangement of gears in a machine. **2** British term for LEVERAGE (sense 3).

gear·shift /ˈgi(ə)r‚sHift/ (also **shift lever**) ▶ n. a lever used to engage or change gears in a motor vehicle.

gear·wheel /'gi(ə)r,(h)wēl/ ▶ n. **1** a toothed wheel in a set of gears. **2** (on a bicycle) a cogwheel driven directly by the chain.

geck·o /'gekō/ ▶ n. (pl. **geckos** or **geckoes**) a lizard of warm regions, with adhesive pads on the feet.

GED ▶ abbr. general equivalency degree (or diploma).

gee¹ /jē/ (also **gee whiz** /'jē '(h)wiz/) ▶ exclam. informal a mild expression of surprise, enthusiasm, or sympathy.

gee² ▶ exclam. (**gee up**) a command to a horse to go faster.

gee·gaw /'gēgô/ ▶ n. a showy object, especially one that is useless or worthless: *overpriced geegaws to hang in their kitchen.*

geek /gēk/ ▶ n. informal **1** a person who is unfashionable or awkward in the company of other people. **2** an obsessive enthusiast: *a computer geek.* ■ **geek·dom** n. **geek·y** adj. (**geekier, geekiest**)

geese /gēs/ ▶ plural of GOOSE.

geez ▶ exclam. variant spelling of JEEZ.

gee·zer /'gēzər/ ▶ n. informal, derogatory an old man.

ge·fil·te fish /gə'filtə/ ▶ n. a dish fishcakes boiled in broth and served chilled.

Gei·ger count·er /'gīgər/ ▶ n. a device for measuring radioactivity.

gei·sha /'gāsʜə, 'gē-/ ▶ n. (pl. same or **geishas**) a Japanese hostess trained to entertain men with conversation, dance, and song.

gel¹ /jel/ ▶ n. **1** a jellylike substance, especially one used in cosmetic or medicinal products. **2** Chemistry a semisolid suspension of a solid dispersed in a liquid. ▶ v. (**gels, gelling, gelled**) **1** Chemistry form into a gel. **2** smooth or style the hair with gel.

gel² (also **jell**) ▶ v. **1** (of jelly or a similar substance) set or become firmer. **2** take definite form or begin to work well: *we had new players and it took some time for the team to gel.*

gel·a·tin /'jelətn/ ▶ n. a clear water-soluble protein obtained from animal bones, used in food preparation, photographic processing, and glue.

ge·lat·i·nous /jə'latn-əs/ ▶ adj. **1** having a jellylike consistency. **2** of or like the protein gelatin.

ge·la·to /jə'lätō/ ▶ n. an Italian-style ice cream.

gel·cap /'jel,kap/ ▶ n. a gelatin capsule containing liquid medication or other substance to be taken orally.

geld /geld/ ▶ v. castrate a male animal.

geld·ing /'geldiɴɢ/ ▶ n. a castrated male horse.

gel·ig·nite /'jelig,nīt/ ▶ n. a high explosive made from nitroglycerine and nitrocellulose in a base of wood pulp and sodium.

gel pen ▶ n. a pen that uses a gel-based ink, combining the permanence of oil-based ink and the smooth glide of water-based ink.

gem /jem/ ▶ n. **1** a precious or semiprecious stone, especially one that has been cut and polished. **2** an outstanding person or thing: *a gem of a book.*

gem·i·nate /'jemənit/ ▶ adj. Phonetics (of a consonant sound) doubled.

Gem·i·ni /'jemə,nī, -,nē/ ▶ n. **1** a constellation and the third sign of the zodiac (the Twins), which the sun enters about May 21. **2** (**a Gemini**) a person born when the sun is in this sign. ■ **Gem·i·ni·an** /-,nīən/ n. & adj.

gems·bok /'gemz,bäk/ ▶ n. a large African antelope with black-and-white head markings and long straight horns.

gem·stone /'jem,stōn/ ▶ n. a gem used in a piece of jewelry.

-gen ▶ comb.form referring to a substance that produces something: *allergen.*

gen·darme /'zʜändärm/ ▶ n. a paramilitary police officer in French-speaking countries.

gen·dar·me·rie /zʜän'därmərē/ ▶ n. **1** the headquarters of a force of gendarmes. **2** a force of gendarmes.

gen·der /'jendər/ ▶ n. **1** Grammar a class (usually masculine, feminine, common, or neuter) into which nouns and pronouns are placed in some languages. **2** the state of being male or female (with reference to social or cultural differences). **3** the members of one or the other sex. ■ **gen·dered** adj.

> **USAGE**
>
> The words **gender** and **sex** both have the sense 'the state of being male or female,' but they are used in different ways: **sex** usually refers to biological differences, while **gender** tends to refer to cultural or social ones.

gen·der gap ▶ n. a discrepancy in opportunities, status, attitudes, etc., between men and women.

gen·der-neu·tral ▶ adj. **1** involving, directed at, or designed for use by both sexes equally: *gender-neutral bathrooms.* **2** (of language) not specific to one sex; referring to a person of either sex: *the need for a gender-neutral pronoun.*

gene /jēn/ ▶ n. a distinct sequence of DNA forming part of a chromosome, by which offspring inherit characteristics from a parent. ■ **gen·ic** /'jenik/ adj.

ge·ne·al·o·gy /,jēnē'äləjē, -'al-/ ▶ n. (pl. **genealogies**) **1** a line of descent traced continuously from an ancestor. **2** the study of lines of descent. ■ **ge·ne·a·log·i·cal** /,jēnēə'läjikəl/ adj. **ge·ne·al·o·gist** n.

gene-al·tered ▶ adj. (especially in journalism) genetically modified: *the much ballyhooed, vine-ripened, gene-altered, rot-resistant tomato.*

gene pool ▶ n. the stock of different genes in a particular species of animal or plant.

gen·er·a /'jenərə/ ▶ plural of GENUS.

gen·er·al /'jenərəl/ ▶ adj. **1** affecting or concerning all or most people or things; not specialized or limited: *books of general interest.* **2** involving only the main features or elements; not detailed. **3** chief or principal: *the general manager.* ▶ n. **1** a commander of an army, or an army officer ranking above lieutenant general. **2** short for BRIGADIER GENERAL, LIEUTENANT GENERAL, or MAJOR GENERAL.

–PHRASES **in general 1** usually; mainly. **2** as a whole.

gen·er·al an·es·the·tic ▶ n. an anesthetic that affects the whole body and causes a loss of consciousness.

gen·er·al de·liv·er·y ▶ n. mail delivery to a post office for collection by the addressee.

gen·er·al e·lec·tion ▶ n. **1** a regular election of candidates for office, as opposed to a primary election. **2** a regular election for state or national offices.

gen·er·al·is·si·mo /,jenərə'lisə,mō/ ▶ n. (pl. **generalissimos**) the commander of a combined military force consisting of army, navy, and air force units.

gen·er·al·ist /ˈjenərəlist/ ▶ n. a person who is competent in several different fields or activities.

gen·er·al·i·ty /ˌjenəˈralitē/ ▶ n. (pl. **generalities**) 1 a statement or principle that is general rather than specific: *you're talking in generalities.* 2 the quality or state of being general. 3 (**the generality**) the majority.

gen·er·al·ize /ˈjenərəˌlīz/ ▶ v. 1 make a general or broad statement based on specific cases: *you cannot generalize about the actions of one set of employees.* 2 make something more common or more widely applicable. 3 (as adj. **generalized**) (of a disease) affecting much or all of the body; not localized. ■ **gen·er·al·iz·a·ble** adj. **gen·er·al·i·za·tion** /ˌjenərəliˈzāsHən/ n.

gen·er·al·ly /ˈjenərəlē/ ▶ adv. 1 in most cases. 2 without regard to details or exceptions. 3 by or to most people; widely.

gen·er·al prac·ti·tion·er ▶ n. a doctor who provides primary health care to patients of any age. ■ **gen·er·al prac·tice** n.

gen·er·al-pur·pose ▶ adj. having a range of potential uses or functions.

gen·er·al·ship /ˈjenərəlˌSHip/ ▶ n. the skill and practice of exercising military command.

gen·er·al staff ▶ n. the staff assisting a military commander.

gen·er·al store ▶ n. a store, typically in a rural area, that carries a wide variety of merchandise such as food, housewares, hardware, and dry goods, without being divided into departments.

gen·er·al strike ▶ n. a strike of workers in all or most industries.

gen·er·ate /ˈjenəˌrāt/ ▶ v. create or produce: *the article generated much reader interest.*

gen·er·a·tion /ˌjenəˈrāSHən/ ▶ n. 1 all of the people born and living at about the same time: *he was one of the cleverest entrepreneurs of his generation.* 2 the average period (about thirty years) in which children grow up and have children of their own. 3 a set of members of a family regarded as a single stage in descent. 4 a group of people of similar age involved in an activity: *a new generation of actors.* 5 a stage in the development of a product: *the next generation of cell phones.* 6 the production or creation of something. ■ **gen·er·a·tion·al** adj.

gen·er·a·tion gap ▶ n. a difference in attitudes between people of different generations, leading to lack of understanding.

Gen·er·a·tion X ▶ n. the generation born between the mid 1960s and the mid 1970s, typically seen as lacking a sense of direction and feeling that they have no role in society. ■ **Gen·er·a·tion X·er** n.

gen·er·a·tive /ˈjenərətiv, -ˌrātiv/ ▶ adj. capable of production or reproduction.

gen·er·a·tor /ˈjenəˌrātər/ ▶ n. 1 a person or thing that generates something. 2 a dynamo or similar machine for converting mechanical energy into electricity.

ge·ner·ic /jəˈnerik/ ▶ adj. 1 referring to a class, group, or genus; not specific: *Indians are fond of saag (a generic term for leafy greens).* 2 (of goods) having no brand name. ■ **ge·ner·i·cal·ly** adv.

gen·er·os·i·ty /ˌjenəˈräsitē/ ▶ n. 1 the quality of being kind and generous. 2 the fact of being plentiful or large: *diners cannot complain about the generosity of portions.*

gen·er·ous /ˈjenərəs/ ▶ adj. 1 freely giving more than is necessary or expected. 2 kind toward others. 3 larger or more plentiful than is usual: *a generous helping of rice.* ■ **gen·er·ous·ly** adv.

gen·e·sis /ˈjenəsis/ ▶ n. 1 the origin of something. 2 (**Genesis**) the first book of the Bible, which includes the story of the creation of the world.

gene ther·a·py ▶ n. the introduction of normal genes into cells in place of missing or defective ones in order to correct genetic disorders.

ge·net·ic /jəˈnetik/ ▶ adj. 1 relating to genes or heredity. 2 relating to genetics. 3 relating to the origin of something. ■ **ge·net·i·cal** adj. **ge·net·i·cal·ly** adv.

ge·net·i·cal·ly mod·i·fied /jəˈnetik(ə)lē ˈmädəˌfīd/ ▶ adj. (of a plant or animal) containing genetic material that has been artificially altered so as to produce a desired characteristic.

ge·net·ic blue·print ▶ n. (not in technical use) a genomic map: *determining the genetic blueprints for all malaria parasites.*

ge·net·ic code ▶ n. the means by which DNA and RNA molecules carry genetic information.

ge·net·ic en·gi·neer·ing ▶ n. the deliberate modification of a plant or animal by altering its genetic material.

ge·net·ic fin·ger·print·ing ▶ n. the analysis of DNA from samples of body tissues or fluids in order to identify individuals.

ge·net·ics /jəˈnetiks/ ▶ pl.n. (treated as sing.) the study of the way in which inherited characteristics are passed from one generation to another. ■ **ge·net·i·cist** n.

ge·net·ic screen·ing ▶ n. the screening, especially by DNA analysis, of a population or individual for genetic susceptibility to particular disorders and diseases.

ge·net·ic test·ing ▶ n. the sequencing of human DNA to discover genetic differences, anomalies, or mutations that may prove pathological: *genetic testing for Huntington's disease.*

ge·ni·al /ˈjēnyəl, -nēəl/ ▶ adj. friendly and cheerful. ■ **ge·ni·al·i·ty** /ˌjēnēˈalitē/ n. **gen·ial·ly** adv.

-genic ▶ comb. form 1 producing or produced by: *carcinogenic.* 2 well suited to: *photogenic.*

ge·nie /ˈjēnē/ ▶ n. (pl. **genii** /-nēˌī/ or **genies**) (in Arabian folklore) a spirit, especially one capable of granting wishes when summoned.

ge·ni·i /ˈjēnēˌī/ ▶ plural of GENIE.

gen·i·tal /ˈjenitl/ ▶ adj. referring to human or animal reproductive organs. ▶ n. (**genitals**) a person or animal's external reproductive organs. ■ **gen·i·tal·ly** adv.

gen·i·ta·li·a /ˌjeniˈtālēə, -ˈtālyə/ ▶ pl.n. formal or technical a person or animal's genitals.

gen·i·tive /ˈjenitiv/ ▶ n. the grammatical case of a word that is used to show possession or close association.

ge·ni·to·u·ri·nar·y /ˌjenitōˈyo͝orəˌnerē/ ▶ adj. relating to the genital and urinary organs.

gen·ius /ˈjēnyəs/ ▶ n. (pl. **geniuses**) 1 exceptional intellectual power or other natural ability: *a painter of genius.* 2 an exceptionally intelligent or able person. 3 the prevalent character of a nation, period, etc.

gen·o·cide /ˈjenəˌsīd/ ▶ n. the deliberate killing of a very large number of people from a particular ethnic group or nation. ■ **gen·o·cid·al** /ˌjenəˈsīdl/ adj.

ge·nome /'jē,nōm/ ▶ n. **1** the full set of the chromosomes of an animal, plant, or other life form. **2** the complete set of genetic material present in an animal, plant, or other life form.

ge·no·mics /jē'nōmiks, -'näm-/ ▶ pl.n. the branch of biology concerned with the structure, function, evolution, and mapping of genomes. ■ **ge·no·mic** adj.

gen·o·type /'jenə,tīp, 'jē-/ ▶ n. the genetic makeup of an individual animal, plant, or other life form. ■ **gen·o·typ·ic** adj.

gen·re /'zнänrə/ ▶ n. a style or category of art or literature. ▶ adj. referring to a style of painting showing scenes from ordinary life.

gent /jent/ ▶ n. informal **1** a gentleman. **2** (**the Gents**) Brit. a men's restroom.

gen·teel /jen'tēl/ ▶ adj. polite and refined in an affected or exaggerated way. ■ **gen·teel·ly** adv.

gen·tian /'jenснən/ ▶ n. a plant of temperate and mountainous regions with violet or blue trumpet-shaped flowers.

Gen·tile /'jentīl/ ▶ adj. not Jewish. ▶ n. a person who is not Jewish.

gen·til·i·ty /jen'tilitē/ ▶ n. polite and refined behavior, especially as typical of a high social class: *the ideal of Victorian gentility was to distance oneself from the taint of commerce.*

gen·tle /'jentl/ ▶ adj. (**gentler, gentlest**) **1** mild or kind; not rough or violent: *a gentle and loving mother.* **2** not harsh or severe. **3** old use noble or courteous. ■ **gen·tle·ness** n. **gen·tly** adv.

gent·le·folk /'jentl,fōk/ ▶ pl.n. old use people of noble birth or good social position.

gen·tle·man /'jentlmən/ ▶ n. (pl. **gentlemen**) **1** a courteous or honorable man. **2** a man of good social position. **3** (in polite or formal use) a man. ■ **gen·tle·man·ly** adj.

gen·tle·man's a·gree·ment ▶ n. an arrangement based on trust rather than on a legal contract.

gen·tle·wom·an /'jentl,wŏomən/ ▶ n. (pl. **gentlewomen**) old use a woman of noble birth or good social position.

gen·tri·fy /'jentrə,fī/ ▶ v. (**gentrifies, gentrifying, gentrified**) renovate or improve a house or district so that it is in keeping with middle-class taste. ■ **gen·tri·fi·ca·tion** /,jentrəfi'kāsнən/ n. **gen·tri·fi·er** n.

gen·try /'jentrē/ ▶ n. (**the gentry**) people of good social position.

gen·u·flect /'jenyə,flekt/ ▶ v. lower the body briefly by bending one knee to the ground in worship or as a sign of respect. ■ **gen·u·flec·tion** /,jenyə'fleksнən/ n.

gen·u·ine /'jenyŏoin/ ▶ adj. **1** truly what it is said to be; authentic: *a genuine leather handbag.* **2** able to be trusted; sincere. ■ **gen·u·ine·ly** adv. **gen·u·ine·ness** n.

ge·nus /'jēnəs/ ▶ n. (pl. **genera** /'jenərə/) **1** a category in the classification of animals and plants that ranks above species and below family, shown by a capitalized Latin name, e.g., *Leo.* **2** a class of things that have common characteristics.

Gen-X /'jen 'eks/ ▶ n. short for GENERATION X. ■ **Gen-X·er** /'jen 'eksər/ n.

geo- ▶ comb.form relating to the earth: *geology.*

ge·o·cen·tric /,jēō'sentrik/ ▶ adj. **1** having the earth as the center, as in former astronomical systems. Compare with HELIOCENTRIC. **2** Astronomy measured from or considered in relation to the center of the earth.

ge·o·chem·is·try /,jēō'keməstrē/ ▶ n. the study of the chemical composition of the earth and its constituent materials.

ge·ode /'jēōd/ ▶ n. **1** a small cavity in rock lined with crystals or other mineral matter. **2** a rock containing such a cavity.

ge·o·des·ic /,jēə'desik, -'dē-/ ▶ adj. **1** referring to the shortest possible line between two points on a sphere or other curved surface. **2** (of a dome) constructed from struts that follow geodesic lines and form an open framework of triangles and polygons.

ge·od·e·sy /jē'ädəsē/ ▶ n. the branch of mathematics concerned with the shape and area of the earth. ■ **ge·od·e·sist** n.

ge·o·det·ic /,jēə'detik/ ▶ adj. relating to geodesy, especially as applied to land surveying.

ge·og·ra·phy /jē'ägrəfē/ ▶ n. **1** the study of the physical features of the earth and of human activity as it relates to these. **2** the way in which the physical features of a place are arranged: *the rugged geography of British Columbia.* ■ **ge·og·ra·pher** n. **ge·o·graph·ic** /,jēə'grafik/ **ge·o·graph·i·cal** /,jēə'grafikəl/ adj. **ge·o·graph·i·cal·ly** /,jēə'grafik(ə)lē/ adv.

ge·ol·o·gy /jē'äləjē/ ▶ n. **1** the science that deals with the physical structure and substance of the earth. **2** the geological features of a district. ■ **ge·o·log·ic** /,jēə'läjik/ adj. **ge·o·log·i·cal** /,jēə'läjikəl/ adj. **ge·o·log·i·cal·ly** /,jēə'läjik(ə)lē/ adv. **ge·ol·o·gist** n.

ge·o·man·cy /'jēə,mansē/ ▶ n. the art of siting buildings so as to encourage good fortune. ■ **ge·o·man·cer** n. **ge·o·man·tic** /,jēə'mantik/ adj.

ge·o·met·ric /,jēə'metrik/ ▶ adj. **1** relating to geometry. **2** (of a design) consisting of regular lines and shapes. ■ **ge·o·met·ri·cal** adj. **ge·o·met·ri·cal·ly** adv.

ge·o·met·ric mean ▶ n. the central number in a geometric progression (e.g., 9 in 3, 9, 27).

ge·o·met·ric pro·gres·sion (also **geometric series**) ▶ n. a sequence of numbers with a constant ratio between each number and the one before (e.g., 1, 3, 9, 27, 81, in which each number in the sequence is multiplied by 3 to create the next number).

ge·om·e·try /jē'ämətrē/ ▶ n. (pl. **geometries**) **1** the branch of mathematics concerned with the properties and relations of points, lines, surfaces, and solids. **2** the shape and relative arrangement of the parts of something. ■ **ge·om·e·tri·cian** /,jēəmə'trisнən/ n.

ge·o·mor·phol·o·gy /,jēō,môr'fäləjē/ ▶ n. the study of the physical features of the surface of the earth and their relation to its geological structures. ■ **ge·o·mor·pho·log·i·cal** /-,môrfə'läjikəl/ adj. **ge·o·mor·phol·o·gist** n.

ge·o·phys·ics /,jēō'fiziks/ ▶ pl.n. (treated as sing.) the physics of the earth. ■ **ge·o·phys·i·cal** adj. **ge·o·phys·i·cist** n.

ge·o·po·lit·i·cal /,jēōpə'litikəl/ ▶ adj. relating to politics, especially concerning international relations, as influenced by geographical factors. ■ **ge·o·pol·i·tics** /,jēō'pälə,tiks/ n.

geor·gette /jôr'jet/ ▶ n. a thin silk or crêpe dress material.

Geor·gian[1] /'jôrjən/ ▶ adj. **1** relating to or characteristic of the reigns of the British Kings George I–IV (1714–1830). **2** relating to British neoclassical architecture of this period.

Geor·gian² ▶ n. **1** a person from the country of Georgia. **2** the official language of Georgia. ▶ adj. relating to Georgians or Georgian.

Geor·gian³ ▶ adj. relating to the US state of Georgia. ▶ n. a person from Georgia.

ge·o·sta·tion·ar·y /ˌjēō'stāshəˌnerē/ ▶ adj. (of an artificial satellite) orbiting in such a way that it appears to be stationary above a fixed point on the earth's surface.

ge·o·stra·te·gic /ˌjēōstrə'tējik/ ▶ adj. relating to the strategy required in dealing with international political problems.

ge·o·ther·mal /ˌjēō'THərməl/ ▶ adj. relating to or produced by the internal heat of the earth.

ge·ra·ni·um /jə'rānēəm/ ▶ n. **1** a garden plant with red, pink, or white flowers; a pelargonium. **2** a plant or small shrub of a genus that comprises the cranesbills.

ger·ber·a /'gərbərə/ ▶ n. a tropical plant of the daisy family, with large brightly colored flowers.

ger·bil /'jərbəl/ ▶ n. a mouselike desert rodent, often kept as a pet.

ger·i·at·ric /ˌjerē'atrik/ ▶ adj. **1** relating to old people. **2** informal very old or out of date; decrepit. ▶ n. an old person, especially one receiving special care.

> **USAGE**
> **Geriatric** is the normal term used to refer to the health care of old people (a *geriatric ward*). When used outside such situations, it carries overtones of being decrepit and can be offensive if used with reference to people.

ger·i·at·rics /ˌjerē'atriks/ ▶ pl.n. (treated as sing. or pl.) the branch of medicine or social science concerned with the health and care of old people. ■ **ger·i·a·tri·cian** /ˌjerēə'trishən/ n.

germ /jərm/ ▶ n. **1** a microorganism, especially one that causes disease. **2** a portion of an organism capable of developing into a new one or part of one. **3** an initial stage from which something may develop: *the germ of an idea.*

Ger·man /'jərmən/ ▶ n. **1** a person from Germany. **2** the language of Germany, Austria, and parts of Switzerland. ▶ adj. relating to Germany or German. ■ **Ger·man·ize** v.

ger·mane /jər'mān/ ▶ adj. relevant to a subject under consideration: *considerations germane to a foreign policy decision.*

Ger·man·ic /jər'manik/ ▶ adj. **1** referring to the language family that includes English, German, Dutch, Frisian, and the Scandinavian languages. **2** referring to the peoples of ancient northern and western Europe speaking such languages. **3** characteristic of Germans or Germany. ▶ n. **1** the Germanic languages. **2** the ancient language from which the Germanic languages developed.

ger·ma·ni·um /jər'mānēəm/ ▶ n. a shiny gray chemical element with semiconducting properties.

Ger·man mea·sles ▶ pl.n. (usu. treated as sing.) another term for RUBELLA.

Ger·man shep·herd ▶ n. a large breed of dog often used as guard dogs or for police work; an Alsatian.

germ cell ▶ n. Biology a cell that is able to unite with another of the opposite sex in sexual reproduction; a gamete.

ger·mi·cide /'jərməˌsīd/ ▶ n. a substance that destroys harmful microorganisms.

■ **ger·mi·cid·al** /ˌjərmə'sīdl/ adj.

ger·mi·nal /'jərmənl/ ▶ adj. **1** relating to a germ cell or embryo. **2** in the earliest stage of development: *a germinal idea.* **3** providing material for future development.

ger·mi·nate /'jərməˌnāt/ ▶ v. (of a seed or spore) begin to grow and put out shoots after a period of being dormant. ■ **ger·mi·na·tion** /ˌjərmə'nāshən/ n.

germ war·fare ▶ n. the use of disease-spreading microorganisms as a military weapon.

ger·on·tol·o·gy /ˌjeran'täləjē/ ▶ n. the scientific study of old age and old people. ■ **ge·ron·to·log·i·cal** /jə,räntl'äjikəl/ adj. **ger·on·tol·o·gist** n.

ger·ry·man·der /'jerēˌmandər/ ▶ v. alter the boundaries of a constituency so as to favor one political party in an election.

ger·und /'jerənd/ ▶ n. Grammar a verb form that functions as a noun, in English ending in *-ing* (e.g., *asking* in *do you mind my asking you?*).

ges·so /'jesō/ ▶ n. a hard compound of plaster of Paris or whiting in size, used in sculpture.

ge·stalt /gə'sHtält, -'sHtôlt/ ▶ n. Psychology an organized whole that is perceived as more than the sum of its parts.

Ge·sta·po /gə'stäpō/ ▶ n. the German secret police under Nazi rule.

ges·ta·tion /je'stāshən/ ▶ n. **1** the process of developing in the uterus between conception and birth. **2** the development of something over a period of time: *the gestation of a musical can take months.* ■ **ges·tate** /'je,stāt/ v. **ges·ta·tion·al** /-sHənl/ adj.

ges·tic·u·late /je'stikyəˌlāt/ ▶ v. gesture dramatically instead of speaking or to emphasize one's words. ■ **ges·tic·u·la·tion** /je,stikyə'lāsHən/ n.

ges·ture /'jescHər/ ▶ n. **1** a movement of part of the body to express an idea or meaning. **2** an action performed to convey one's feelings or intentions: *the prisoners were released as a gesture of goodwill.* **3** an action performed for show in the knowledge that it will have no effect. ▶ v. make a gesture. ■ **ges·tur·al** adj.

ge·sund·heit /gə'zo͞ontīt/ ▶ exclam. used to wish good health to someone who has just sneezed.

get /get/ ▶ v. (**gets, getting, got** /gät/; past part. **got, gotten** /'gätn/) **1** come to have or hold something. **2** succeed in obtaining, achieving, or experiencing something. **3** experience or suffer something. **4** pick up, fetch, or deal with something. **5** reach a particular state or condition: *she'd gotten thinner.* **6** move to or from a specified position or place. **7** persuade someone to do something. **8** begin to be or do something, especially gradually or by chance: *we got talking.* **9** catch or thwart someone. **10** travel by or catch a form of transport. **11** informal punish, injure, or kill someone. **12** used with past participle to form the passive: *the field got flooded.* ■ **get·ta·ble** adj. **get·ter** n.

– PHRASES **be out to get someone** be determined to punish or harm someone: *they think we are the bad guys and out to get them.* **get something across** manage to communicate an idea clearly. **get along** have a harmonious or friendly relationship: *they seem to get along pretty well.* **get around 1** persuade someone to do or allow something. **2** deal successfully with a problem. **get around to** find the time to deal with a task. **get at 1** reach or gain access to somewhere. **2** informal imply something:

what are you getting at? **3** informal discover or determine something: *Purcell's statement gets at the heart of the issue.* **get away** escape or leave. **get away with** escape blame or punishment for something. **get back at** take revenge on someone. **get by** manage with difficulty to live. **get down to** begin to do or give serious attention to something. **get in on** become involved in (a profitable or exciting activity). **get it on** informal have sexual intercourse. **get off** informal escape a punishment. **get off on** informal be excited or aroused by (something): *some guys get off on that kind of attention.* **get off** vulgar slang have an orgasm. **get on 1** make progress with a task. **2 (be getting on)** informal be old or comparatively old. **get over** recover from an illness or an unpleasant experience. **get something over** manage to communicate something. **get something over with** deal with an unpleasant but necessary task promptly. **get through 1** pass or endure a difficult experience or period. **2** use up a large amount or number of something. **3** make contact by telephone. **4** succeed in communicating with someone. **get to** informal annoy or upset someone. **get together** gather socially or to cooperate. **get up** rise from bed after sleeping. **get up to** be involved in something.

get·a·way /'getə,wā/ ▶ n. **1** an escape, especially after committing a crime. **2** a short vacation.

get-go ▶ n. informal the very beginning: *it was a terrific marriage right from the get-go.*

get-to·geth·er ▶ n. an informal social gathering.

get·up /'getəp/ ▶ n. informal an outfit, especially an unusual one: *our Halloween getups were really scary.*

gey·ser /'gīzər/ ▶ n. a hot spring in which water intermittently boils, sending a tall column of water and steam into the air.

Gha·na·ian /gə'nāən, gə'nīən/ ▶ n. a person from Ghana. ▶ adj. relating to Ghana.

ghast·ly /'gastlē/ ▶ adj. **(ghastlier, ghastliest) 1** causing great horror or fear. **2** informal very unpleasant. **3** very white. ■ **ghast·li·ness** n.

ghat /gôt, gät/ ▶ n. **1** (in the Indian subcontinent) a flight of steps leading down to a river. **2** (in the Indian subcontinent) a mountain pass.

GHB ▶ abbr. (sodium) gamma-hydroxybutyrate, a designer drug with anesthetic properties.

ghee /gē/ ▶ n. clarified butter used in Indian cooking.

gher·kin /'gərkin/ ▶ n. a small pickled cucumber.

ghet·to /'getō/ ▶ n. (pl. **ghettos** or **ghettoes**) **1** a part of a city occupied by people of a particular race, nationality, or ethnic group. **2** historical the Jewish quarter in a city.

ghet·to blast·er ▶ n. informal a large portable radio and cassette or CD player.

ghet·to·ize /'getō,īz/ ▶ v. put in an isolated or segregated place, group, or situation: *they were black and quickly ghettoized in northern cities.* ■ **ghet·to·i·za·tion** /,getō-i'zāsHən/ n.

ghost /gōst/ ▶ n. **1** an apparition of a dead person that is believed to appear to the living. **2** a faint trace: *the ghost of a smile.* ▶ v. act as ghostwriter of a book.
– PHRASES **give up the ghost** die or stop functioning.

ghost·ing /'gōstiNG/ ▶ n. the appearance of a secondary image on a television or other display screen.

ghost·ly /'gōstlē/ ▶ adj. **(ghostlier, ghostliest)** relating to or like a ghost; eerie.

ghost town ▶ n. a town with few or no remaining inhabitants.

ghost·writ·er /'gōst,rītər/ ▶ n. a person employed to write material for another person who is the named author. ■ **ghost·write** v.

ghoul /gōōl/ ▶ n. **1** an evil spirit, especially one supposed to rob graves and feed on dead bodies. **2** a person with an unhealthy interest in death or disaster. ■ **ghoul·ish** adj. **ghoul·ish·ly** adv. **ghoul·ish·ness** n.

GHQ ▶ abbr. General Headquarters.

GHz (also **gHz**) ▶ abbr. gigahertz.

GI ▶ n. **1** (pl. **GIs**) a private in the Army. **2** glycemic index.

gi·ant /'jīant/ ▶ n. **1** an imaginary or mythical being of human form but superhuman size. **2** an unusually tall or large person or thing. **3** a star of relatively great size and luminosity. ▶ adj. very large; gigantic. ■ **gi·ant·ess** n.

gi·ant-kill·er ▶ n. a person or team that defeats a much more powerful opponent. ■ **gi·ant-kill·ing** n.

gib·ber /'jibər/ ▶ v. speak rapidly and in a way that is difficult to understand.

gib·ber·ish /'jibərisH/ ▶ n. speech or writing that is meaningless or difficult to understand.

gib·bet /'jibit/ ▶ n. historical **1** a gallows. **2** an upright post with an arm on which the bodies of executed criminals were left hanging.

gib·bon /'gibən/ ▶ n. a small ape with long, powerful arms, native to the forests of SE Asia.

gib·bous /'gibəs/ ▶ adj. (of the moon) having the illuminated part greater than a semicircle and less than a circle.

gibe /jīb/ (also **jibe**) ▶ n. an insulting or mocking remark. ▶ v. make insulting or mocking remarks.

gib·lets /'jiblits/ ▶ pl.n. the liver, heart, gizzard, and neck of a chicken or other fowl.

gid·dy /'gidē/ ▶ adj. **(giddier, giddiest) 1** having or causing a sensation of spinning and losing one's balance; dizzy. **2** excitable and not interested in serious things. ■ **gid·di·ly** adv. **gid·di·ness** n.

gid·dy-up /,gidē 'əp/ ▶ exclam. said to make a horse start moving or go faster.

GIF /jif/ ▶ n. Computing **1** a format for image files. **2** a file in this format.

gift /gift/ ▶ n. **1** a thing given willingly to someone without payment; a present. **2** a natural ability or talent: *she has a gift for math.* **3** informal a very easy task. ▶ v. **1** give something as a gift. **2 (gift someone with)** provide someone with an ability or talent. **3** (as adj. **gifted)** having exceptional talent or ability. ■ **gift·ed·ness** n.
– PHRASES **look a gift horse in the mouth** find fault with something that has been received as a gift or favor.

gift cer·tif·i·cate ▶ n. a voucher that can be exchanged for merchandise in a store, given as a present.

gift wrap ▶ n. decorative paper for wrapping gifts. ▶ v. **(gift-wrap)** wrap a gift in decorative paper.

gig¹ /gig/ informal ▶ n. **1** a live performance by a musician or other performer. **2** a task or assignment: *spotting whales seemed like a great gig.* ▶ v. **(gigs, gigging, gigged)** perform a gig or gigs.

gig² ▸ n. chiefly historical a light two-wheeled carriage pulled by one horse.

gig³ ▸ n. informal short for GIGABYTE.

giga- ▸ comb.form **1** referring to a factor of one billion (10⁹): *gigawatt.* **2** Computing referring to a factor of 2³⁰.

gig·a·bit /ˈɡiɡəˌbit, ˈjiɡ-/ ▸ n. a unit of information stored in a computer equal to one billion (10⁹) or (strictly) 2³⁰ bits.

gig·a·byte /ˈɡiɡəˌbīt, ˈjiɡ-/ ▸ n. a unit of information stored in a computer equal to one billion (10⁹) or (strictly) 2³⁰ bytes.

gig·a·flop /ˈɡiɡəˌfläp/ ▸ n. Computing a unit of computing speed equal to one billion floating-point operations per second.

gig·a·hertz /ˈɡiɡəˌhərts, ˈjiɡ-/ ▸ n. a unit of frequency equivalent to one billion hertz.

gi·gan·tic /jīˈɡantik/ ▸ adj. very great in size or extent. ■ **gi·gan·ti·cal·ly** adv.

gi·gan·tism /jīˈɡantizəm/ ▸ n. chiefly Biology unusual or abnormal largeness.

gig·a·watt /ˈɡiɡəˌwät, ˈjiɡ-/ ▸ n. a unit of power equal to one billion watts.

gig·gle /ˈɡiɡəl/ ▸ v. laugh lightly in a nervous or silly way. ▸ n. a nervous or silly laugh. ■ **gig·gler** n. **gig·gly** adj.

gig·o·lo /ˈjiɡəˌlō/ ▸ n. (pl. **gigolos**) a young man paid by an older woman to be her escort or lover.

gigue /zнēg/ ▸ n. Music a lively piece of music in the style of a dance, typically of the Renaissance or baroque period.

Gi·la mon·ster /ˈhēlə/ ▸ n. a venomous lizard native to the Southwest and Mexico.

gild /ɡild/ ▸ v. **1** cover something thinly with gold. **2** (as adj. **gilded**) wealthy and privileged: *gilded youth.* ■ **gild·er** n. **gild·ing** n.
– PHRASES **gild the lily** try to improve what is already beautiful or excellent.

gill¹ /ɡil/ ▸ n. **1** the breathing organ of fish and some amphibians. **2** the vertical plates on the underside of mushrooms and many toadstools. ▸ v. gut or clean a fish. ■ **gilled** adj.
– PHRASES **to the gills** until completely full.

gill² /jil/ ▸ n. a unit of measure for liquids, equal to a quarter of a pint.

gilt /ɡilt/ ▸ adj. covered thinly with gold leaf or gold paint. ▸ n. gold leaf or gold paint applied in a thin layer to a surface.

gim·bal /ˈɡimbəl, ˈjim-/ (also **gimbals**) ▸ n. a device for keeping an instrument such as a compass horizontal in a moving vessel or aircraft.

gim·crack /ˈjim,krak/ ▸ adj. showy but flimsy or poorly made. ▸ n. a cheap and showy ornament. ■ **gim·crack·er·y** /-krakərē/ n.

gim·let /ˈɡimlit/ ▸ n. a small T-shaped tool with a screw-tip for boring holes.

gim·mick /ˈɡimik/ ▸ n. something intended to attract attention rather than fulfill a useful purpose. ■ **gim·mick·ry** n. **gim·mick·y** adj.

gimp /ɡimp/ ▸ n. informal, often offensive **1** a physically handicapped person. **2** a limp. **3** a feeble or contemptible person. ■ **gimp·y** adj.

gin¹ /jin/ ▸ n. **1** a clear alcoholic spirit distilled from grain or malt and flavored with juniper berries. **2** (also **gin rummy**) a form of the card game rummy.

gin² ▸ n. **1** a machine for separating cotton from its seeds. **2** a trap for catching small game.

gin and ton·ic ▸ n. a cocktail made with gin and

tonic water, and usually a slice of lime.

gin·ger /ˈjinjər/ ▸ n. **1** a hot spice made from the rhizome of a SE Asian plant. **2** a light reddish-yellow color. ▸ v. **1** (**ginger someone/thing up**) make someone or something more lively or exciting. **2** flavor something with ginger. ■ **gin·ger·y** adj.

gin·ger ale ▸ n. a carbonated soft drink flavored with ginger.

gin·ger·bread /ˈjinjər,bred/ ▸ n. **1** cake made with molasses and flavored with ginger. **2** fancy decoration, especially on the facade of a building.

gin·ger·ly /ˈjinjərlē/ ▸ adv. in a careful or cautious way.

gin·ger snap ▸ n. a hard, ginger-flavored cookie.

ging·ham /ˈɡiNɡəm/ ▸ n. lightweight cotton cloth with a check pattern.

gin·gi·vi·tis /ˌjinjəˈvītis/ ▸ n. inflammation of the gums.

gink·go /ˈɡiNɡkō/ (also **gingko**) ▸ n. (pl. **ginkgos** or **ginkgoes**) a Chinese tree with fan-shaped leaves and yellow flowers.

gi·nor·mous /jiˈnôrməs, jī-/ ▸ adj. informal very large.

gin·seng /ˈjinseNɡ/ ▸ n. the tuber of an east Asian and North American plant, believed to have medicinal properties.

gip·sy ▸ n. variant spelling of GYPSY.

gi·raffe /jəˈraf/ ▸ n. (pl. same or **giraffes**) a large African mammal with a very long neck and legs, the tallest living animal.

gird /ɡərd/ ▸ v. (past and past part. **girded** or **girt** /ɡərt/) literary encircle or secure something with a belt or band.
– PHRASES **gird (up) one's loins** prepare and strengthen oneself for something difficult.

gird·er /ˈɡərdər/ ▸ n. a large metal beam used in building bridges and large buildings.

gir·dle /ˈɡərdl/ ▸ n. **1** a belt or cord worn around the waist. **2** a woman's elasticized corset extending from waist to thigh. ▸ v. encircle something with a girdle or belt.

girl /ɡərl/ ▸ n. **1** a female child. **2** a young woman. **3** a person's girlfriend. ■ **girl·hood** n. **girl·ish** adj. **girl·ish·ly** adv.

girl·friend /ˈɡərl,frend/ ▸ n. **1** a person's regular female companion in a romantic or sexual relationship. **2** a woman's female friend.

girl·ie /ˈɡərlē/ (also **girly**) ▸ adj. **1** often derogatory typical of or resembling a girl. **2** depicting nude or partially nude young women in erotic poses: *girlie magazines.* ▸ n. (pl. **girlies**) informal a girl or young woman.

Girl Scout ▸ n. a member of the Girl Scouts of America.

girt /ɡərt/ ▸ past participle of GIRD.

girth /ɡərTH/ ▸ n. **1** the measurement around the middle of something. **2** a band attached to a saddle and fastened around a horse's belly.

GIS ▸ abbr. geographic information system, a software application for storing and manipulating geographic information.

gist /jist/ ▸ n. the main or general meaning of a speech or piece of writing.

Git·mo /ˈɡit,mō/ ▸ n. informal the US naval base or detention facility at Guantánamo Bay, Cuba.

give /ɡiv/ ▸ v. (**gives, giving, gave** /ɡāv/; past part. **given**) **1** cause someone to receive or have something. **2** cause to experience or suffer: *he* *gives me the creeps.* **3** carry out an action or make a sound. **4** present an appearance or impression. **5** state or put forward information. **6** alter in shape under pressure rather than resist or break. **7** concede that someone deserves something. ▶ n. the capacity of something to bend under pressure. ■ **giv·er** n.

– PHRASES **give and take** willingness on both sides of a relationship to make concessions. **give something away** reveal something secret. **give the game away** accidentally reveal something secret. **give in** stop fighting or arguing. **give or take** informal to within a specified amount. **give out** stop operating. **give something off/out** produce and send out a smell, heat, etc. **give rise to** cause something to happen. **give up** stop making an effort and accept that one has failed. **give someone up** hand over a wanted person. **give something up** stop doing, eating, or drinking something regularly.

give·a·way /ˈgivəˌwā/ ▶ n. informal **1** something that reveals the truth about something: *the shape of the parcel was a dead giveaway.* **2** something given free, especially for promotional purposes.

giv·en /ˈgivən/ past participle of GIVE ▶ adj. **1** specified or stated. **2** (**given to**) inclined to. ▶ prep. taking into account. ▶ n. an established fact or situation.

giv·en name ▶ n. another term for FIRST NAME.

giz·mo /ˈgizmō/ ▶ n. (pl. **gizmos**) informal a clever device; a gadget.

giz·zard /ˈgizərd/ ▶ n. a muscular, thick-walled part of a bird's stomach for grinding food.

gla·brous /ˈglābrəs/ ▶ adj. technical free from hair or down; smooth.

gla·cé /glaˈsā/ ▶ adj. (of fruit) preserved in sugar.

gla·cial /ˈglāSHəl/ ▶ adj. **1** relating to ice, especially in the form of glaciers. **2** very cold or unfriendly. ■ **gla·cial·ly** adv.

gla·cial pe·ri·od ▶ n. an ice age.

gla·ci·at·ed /ˈglāSHēˌātid/ ▶ adj. covered or having been covered by glaciers or ice sheets.

gla·ci·a·tion /ˌglāSHēˈāSHən/ ▶ n. **1** the state or result of being covered by glaciers or ice sheets. **2** an ice age.

gla·cier /ˈglāSHər/ ▶ n. a slowly moving mass of ice formed by the accumulation of snow on mountains or near the poles.

glad /glad/ ▶ adj. (**gladder, gladdest**) **1** feeling pleasure or happiness. **2** grateful: *I'm glad for the second chance.* **3** causing happiness. ■ **glad·ly** adv. **glad·ness** n.

glad·den /ˈgladn/ ▶ v. make someone glad.

glade /glād/ ▶ n. an open space in a forest or other wooded area.

glad-hand ▶ v. (especially of a politician) greet or welcome someone warmly. ■ **glad-hand·er** n.

glad·i·a·tor /ˈgladēˌātər/ ▶ n. (in ancient Rome) a man trained to fight with weapons against other men or wild animals in an arena. ■ **glad·i·a·to·ri·al** /ˌgladēəˈtôrēəl/ adj.

glad·i·o·lus /ˌgladēˈōləs/ ▶ n. (pl. **gladioli** /-lī/) a plant with sword-shaped leaves and tall stems of brightly colored flowers.

glad rags ▶ pl. n. informal clothes for a party or special occasion.

Glad·stone bag /ˈgladˌstōn/ ▶ n. a bag having two equal compartments joined by a hinge.

glam /glam/ informal ▶ adj. glamorous. ▶ v. (**glams, glamming, glammed**) (**glam someone up**)

make someone look glamorous.

glam·or·ize /ˈglaməˌrīz/ ▶ v. make something, especially something bad, seem attractive or desirable. ■ **glam·or·i·za·tion** /ˌglaməriˈzāSHən/ n.

glam·or·ous /ˈglamərəs/ ▶ adj. excitingly attractive and appealing. ■ **glam·or·ous·ly** adv.

glam·our /ˈglamər/ (also **glamor**) ▶ n. an attractive and exciting quality. ▶ adj. referring to photography or publications that feature a culture of beauty and excitement: *a glamour model.*

glance /glans/ ▶ v. **1** take a brief or hurried look. **2** hit something and bounce off at an angle. ▶ n. a brief or hurried look. ■ **glanc·ing** adj.

gland /gland/ ▶ n. **1** an organ of the body that produces particular chemical substances. **2** a lymph node.

glan·du·lar /ˈglanjələr/ ▶ adj. relating to or affecting a gland or glands.

glans /glanz/ ▶ n. (pl. **glandes** /ˈglandēz/) the rounded part forming the end of the penis or clitoris.

glare /gle(ə)r/ ▶ v. **1** stare in an angry way. **2** shine with a dazzling light. **3** (as adj. **glaring**) highly obvious: *a glaring error.* ▶ n. **1** an angry stare. **2** dazzling light. **3** overwhelming public attention: *his visit will be conducted in the full glare of publicity.* ■ **glar·ing·ly** adv. **glar·y** adj.

glas·nost /ˈglazˌnōst, ˈglas-, ˈgläz-, ˈgläs-/ ▶ n. (in the former Soviet Union) the policy or practice of more open government.

glass /glas/ ▶ n. **1** a hard, brittle, transparent substance made by fusing sand with soda and lime. **2** a drinking container made of glass. **3** chiefly Brit. a mirror. **4** a lens or optical instrument, in particular a monocle or a magnifying lens. ▶ v. cover or enclose something with glass. ■ **glass·ful** n. **glass·ware** n.

glass block (also **glass brick**) ▶ n. a block of tempered glass used as a construction material, or these collectively: *a wide swath of glass block from the tub platform to the ceiling.*

glass·blow·ing /ˈglasˌblō-iNG/ ▶ n. the craft of making glassware by blowing semimolten glass through a long tube. ■ **glass·blow·er** n.

glass ceil·ing ▶ n. a situation in which certain groups, especially women and minorities, find that progress in a profession is blocked although there are no official barriers to advancement.

glass·es /ˈglasiz/ ▶ pl. n. a pair of lenses set in a frame that rests on the nose and ears, used to correct defective eyesight.

glass·y /ˈglasē/ ▶ adj. (**glassier, glassiest**) **1** resembling glass. **2** (of a person's eyes or expression) showing no interest or liveliness. ■ **glass·i·ly** adv.

Glas·we·gian /glazˈwējən, -jēən, glas-/ ▶ n. a person from Glasgow, Scotland. ▶ adj. relating to Glasgow, Scotland.

glau·co·ma /glôˈkōmə/ ▶ n. a condition of increased pressure within the eyeball, causing gradual loss of sight.

glau·cous /ˈglôkəs/ ▶ adj. technical or literary **1** dull grayish-green or blue in color. **2** covered with a powdery bloom like that on grapes.

glaze /glāz/ ▶ v. **1** fit panes of glass into a window frame or similar structure. **2** enclose or cover something with glass. **3** cover something with a glaze. **4** lose brightness and liveliness: *transactions complex enough to make an* *accountant's eyes glaze over.* ▶ n. **1** a glasslike substance fused onto the surface of pottery to form an impervious decorative coating. **2** a liquid such as milk or beaten egg, used to form a shiny coating on food. **3** Art a thin topcoat of transparent paint used to modify the tone of an underlying color. ■ **glaz·ing** n.

gla·zier /ˈglāzhər/ ▶ n. a person whose profession is fitting glass into windows and doors.

GLBT ▶ abbr. gay, lesbian, bisexual, and transgendered: *a planned GLBT cable channel.*

gleam /glēm/ ▶ v. shine brightly, especially with reflected light. ▶ n. **1** a faint or brief light. **2** a brief or faint sign of a quality or emotion: *there was a gleam of mischief in her eyes.* ■ **gleam·ing** adj.

– PHRASES **a gleam in someone's eye** see EYE.

glean /glēn/ ▶ v. **1** collect information or objects gradually from various sources. **2** historical gather leftover grain after a harvest. ■ **glean·er** n.

glean·ings /ˈglēniNGz/ ▶ pl.n. things gathered from various sources.

glee /glē/ ▶ n. **1** great delight. **2** a song for men's voices in three or more parts.

glee club ▶ n. an amateur choir or chorus.

glee·ful /ˈglēfəl/ ▶ adj. very happy, especially in a gloating way. ■ **glee·ful·ly** adv.

glen /glen/ ▶ n. a narrow valley.

glib /glib/ ▶ adj. (**glibber, glibbest**) using words easily, but without much thought or sincerity. ■ **glib·ly** adv. **glib·ness** n.

glide /glīd/ ▶ v. **1** move with a smooth, quiet, continuous motion. **2** fly without power or in a glider. ▶ n. an instance of gliding. ■ **glid·ing** n.

glid·er /ˈglīdər/ ▶ n. a light aircraft designed to fly without using an engine.

glim·mer /ˈglimər/ ▶ v. shine faintly with a wavering light. ▶ n. **1** a faint or wavering light. **2** a faint sign of a feeling or quality: *a glimmer of hope.* ■ **glim·mer·ing** adj. & n.

glimpse /glimps/ ▶ n. a brief or partial view. ▶ v. see someone or something briefly or partially.

glint /glint/ ▶ v. give out or reflect small flashes of light. ▶ n. **1** a small flash of reflected light. **2** an expression of an emotion in a person's eyes: *the unmistakable glint of interest in her eye.*

glis·san·do /gliˈsändō/ ▶ n. (pl. **glissandi** /-dē/ or **glissandos**) Music a continuous slide upward or downward between two notes.

glis·ten /ˈglisən/ ▶ v. (of something wet or oily) shine or sparkle. ▶ n. a sparkling light reflected from something wet or oily.

glis·ter /ˈglistər/ literary ▶ v. sparkle; glitter. ▶ n. a sparkle.

glitch /glicH/ ▶ n. informal **1** a sudden fault or failure of equipment. **2** an unexpected setback in a plan.

glit·ter /ˈglitər/ ▶ v. **1** shine with a bright, shimmering reflected light. **2** (as adj. **glittering**) impressively successful or glamorous: *a glittering career.* ▶ n. **1** bright, shimmering reflected light. **2** tiny pieces of sparkling material used for decoration. **3** an attractive but superficial quality: *a stylist's life is not all glitter and glamour.* ■ **glit·ter·y** adj.

glit·te·ra·ti /ˌglitəˈrätē/ ▶ pl.n. informal fashionable people involved in show business or other glamorous activity.

glitz /glits/ ▶ n. informal showy but superficial display. ■ **glitz·y** adj.

glitz·y /ˈglitsē/ ▶ adj. (**glitzier, glitziest**) informal ostentatiously attractive (often used to suggest superficial glamor): *I wanted something glitzy to wear to the launch party.* ■ **glitz·i·ly** /-səlē/ adv. **glitz·i·ness** n.

gloam·ing /ˈglōmiNG/ ▶ n. (**the gloaming**) literary twilight; dusk.

gloat /glōt/ ▶ v. be smug or pleased about one's own success or another person's misfortune. ■ **gloat·er** n. **gloat·ing** adj. & n.

glob /gläb/ ▶ n. informal a lump of a semiliquid substance.

glob·al /ˈglōbəl/ ▶ adj. **1** relating to the whole world; worldwide. **2** relating to or including the whole of something, or of a group of things. **3** Computing operating or applying through the whole of a file or program. ■ **glob·al·ly** adv.

glob·al·ism /ˈglōbəˌlizəm/ ▶ n. the operation or planning of economic and foreign policy on a global basis. ■ **glob·al·ist** /ˈglōbəlist/ n. & adj.

glob·al·i·za·tion /ˌglōbəliˈzāsHən/ ▶ n. the process by which businesses start operating on a global scale. ■ **glob·al·ize** /ˈglōbəˌlīz/ v.

glob·al vil·lage ▶ n. the world considered as a single community linked by telecommunications.

glob·al warm·ing ▶ n. the gradual increase in the overall temperature of the earth's atmosphere due to the greenhouse effect caused by increased levels of pollutants.

globe /glōb/ ▶ n. **1** a spherical or rounded object. **2** (**the globe**) the earth. **3** a spherical representation of the earth. ■ **glo·bose** /ˈglōbōs/ adj.

globe·trot·ter /ˈglōbˌträtər/ ▶ n. informal a person who travels widely. ■ **globe·trot·ting** /ˈglōbˌträtiNG/ n. & adj.

glob·u·lar /ˈgläbyələr/ ▶ adj. **1** globe-shaped; spherical. **2** composed of globules.

glob·ule /ˈgläbyōōl/ ▶ n. a small round particle of a substance; a drop.

glob·u·lin /ˈgläbyəlin/ ▶ n. any of a group of simple proteins found in blood serum.

glock·en·spiel /ˈgläkənˌspēl, -ˌsHpēl/ ▶ n. a musical percussion instrument containing tuned metal pieces that are struck with small hammers.

glom /gläm/ ▶ v. (**gloms, glomming, glommed**) informal **1** become stuck or joined: *muddy leaves will glom onto your tires.* **2** steal: *he was about to glom my wallet.*

gloom /glōōm/ ▶ n. **1** partial or total darkness. **2** a state of depression or despondency.

– PHRASES **gloom and doom** see DOOM.

gloom·y /ˈglōōmē/ ▶ adj. (**gloomier, gloomiest**) **1** dark or poorly lit. **2** causing or feeling depression or despondency: *despite the gloomy forecasts, a political crisis looks unlikely.* ■ **gloom·i·ly** adv. **gloom·i·ness** n.

glop /gläp/ ▶ n. informal sloppy or sticky semifluid matter. ■ **glop·py** adj.

glo·ri·fy /ˈglôrəˌfī/ ▶ v. (**glorifies, glorifying, glorified**) **1** represent something as admirable, especially undeservedly. **2** (as adj. **glorified**) made to appear more important or special than is the case: *he was nothing more than a glorified janitor.* **3** praise and worship God. ■ **glo·ri·fi·ca·tion** /ˌglôrəfiˈkāsHən/ n.

glo·ri·ous /ˈglôrēəs/ ▶ adj. **1** having or bringing glory: *his glorious career with the quartet is coming to an end.* **2** very beautiful or impressive. **3** very enjoyable. ■ **glo·ri·ous·ly** adv. **glo·ri·ous·ness** n.

glo·ry /'glôrē/ ▶ n. (pl. **glories**) **1** great fame or honor won by notable achievements: *he began his pursuit of Olympic glory with the 100 meters.* **2** magnificence; great beauty. **3** a very beautiful or impressive thing. **4** worship and thanksgiving offered to God. ▶ v. (**glory in**) take great pride or pleasure in: *he gloried in the power of public office.*
– PHRASES **in (all) one's glory** in a state of great happiness or radiance.

glo·ry hole ▶ n. **1** a funnel-shaped surface excavation from which ore is mined. **2** informal a hole in a wall through which fellatio or male masturbation is conducted secretly. **3** dated, informal an untidy room or cupboard used for storage.

gloss[1] /gläs, glôs/ ▶ n. **1** the shine on a smooth surface. **2** (also **gloss paint**) a type of paint that dries to a shiny surface. **3** an attractive appearance that conceals something ordinary or unpleasant: *the gloss of suburban life.* ▶ v. **1** apply a glossy substance to something. **2** (**gloss over**) try to conceal or pass over something by mentioning it briefly or misleadingly.

gloss[2] ▶ n. a translation or explanation of a word, phrase, or passage. ▶ v. provide a translation or explanation of a word, phrase, or passage.

glos·sa·ry /'gläsərē, 'glô-/ ▶ n. (pl. **glossaries**) an alphabetical list of words relating to a specific subject, dialect, or written work, with explanations.

gloss·y /'gläsē, 'glô-/ ▶ adj. (**glossier, glossiest**) **1** shiny and smooth. **2** superficially attractive and stylish. ▶ n. (pl. **glossies**) informal a magazine printed on glossy paper with many color photographs. ■ **gloss·i·ly** adv. **gloss·i·ness** n.

glot·tal /'glätl/ ▶ adj. relating to the glottis (part of the larynx).

glot·tal stop ▶ n. a speech sound made by opening and closing the glottis, sometimes used instead of a properly sounded *t*.

glot·tis /'glätis/ ▶ n. the part of the larynx consisting of the vocal cords and the slitlike opening between them.

glove /gləv/ ▶ n. **1** a covering for the hand with separate parts for each finger and the thumb. **2** a padded protective covering for the hand used in boxing and other sports. ■ **gloved** adj.
– PHRASES **fit like a glove** (of clothes) fit exactly. **the gloves are** (or **come**) **off** used to indicate that something will be done in an uncompromising and perhaps brutal way: *they had begun a civil campaign, but now the gloves are off.*

glove com·part·ment (also **globebox**) ▶ n. a small storage compartment in the dashboard of a motor vehicle.

glow /glō/ ▶ v. **1** give out a steady light without flame. **2** especially of one's complexion, look or feel warm or healthy: *she was glowing with excitement.* **3** look very pleased or happy. ▶ n. **1** a steady light. **2** a feeling or appearance of warmth or health. **3** a strong feeling of pleasure or well-being: *a glow of pride.*

glow·er /'glouər/ ▶ v. have an angry or sullen expression. ▶ n. an angry or sullen look.

glow·ing /'glōiNG/ ▶ adj. expressing great praise: *a glowing report.* ■ **glow·ing·ly** adv.

glow-worm ▶ n. a type of beetle, the wingless female of which glows to attract males.

glox·in·i·a /gläk'sinēə/ ▶ n. a tropical American

---

plant with large, velvety, bell-shaped flowers.

glu·cose /'glōōkōs/ ▶ n. a simple sugar that is an important energy source in living organisms.

glue /glōō/ ▶ n. an adhesive substance used for sticking objects or materials together.
▶ v. (**glues, gluing** or **glueing, glued**) **1** fasten or join things with glue. **2** (**be glued to**) informal be paying very close attention to something. ■ **glue·y** adj.

glue-sniff·ing ▶ n. the practice of inhaling intoxicating fumes from certain types of glue.

glug /gləg/ informal ▶ v. (**glugs, glugging, glugged**) pour or drink liquid with a hollow gurgling sound. ▶ n. a hollow gurgling sound. ■ **glug·ga·ble** adj.

glum /gləm/ ▶ adj. (**glummer, glummest**) sad or dejected. ■ **glum·ly** adv.

glut /glət/ ▶ n. an excessively abundant supply. ▶ v. (**gluts, glutting, glutted**) supply or fill something to excess.

glu·ten /'glōōtn/ ▶ n. a substance containing a number of proteins that is found in wheat and other cereal grains.

glu·te·us /'glōōtēəs/ ▶ n. (pl. **glutei** /-tē,ī/) any of three muscles in each buttock that move the thigh. ■ **glu·te·al** /-tēəl/ adj.

glu·ti·nous /'glōōtn-əs/ ▶ adj. **1** like glue in texture; sticky. **2** excessively sentimental; sickly: *glutinous ballads.*

glut·ton /'glətn/ ▶ n. **1** an excessively greedy eater. **2** a person who is very eager for something difficult or challenging: *I was a glutton for punishment.* ■ **glut·ton·ous** adj.

glut·ton·y /'glətn-ē/ ▶ n. the habit or fact of eating excessively.

gly·ce·mic in·dex /glī'sēmik/ ▶ n. a scale that ranks foods from 1 to 100 based on their effect on blood-sugar levels.

glyc·er·in /'glisərin/ (Brit. **glycerine** /-rin, -,rēn, ,glisə'rēn/) ▶ n. another term for GLYCEROL.

glyc·er·ol /'glisə,rôl, -,räl/ ▶ n. a colorless, sweet liquid formed as a byproduct in soap manufacture, used in making cosmetics, explosives, and antifreeze.

gly·cine /'glīsēn/ ▶ n. Biochemistry the simplest naturally occurring amino acid. It is a constituent of most proteins.

gly·co·gen /'glīkəjən/ ▶ n. a substance deposited in bodily tissues as a store of glucose.

gly·col /'glīkôl, -kōl/ ▶ n. short for ETHYLENE GLYCOL.

gly·col·y·sis /glī'käləsis/ ▶ n. the breakdown of glucose by enzymes, releasing energy.

gly·co·side /'glīkə,sīd/ ▶ n. a compound formed from a simple sugar and another compound by replacement of a hydroxyl group in the sugar molecule.

glyph /glif/ ▶ n. **1** a hieroglyphic character. **2** Architecture an ornamental carved groove, as on a Greek frieze. **3** Computing a small graphic symbol.

GM ▶ abbr. **1** general manager. **2** genetically modified.

gm ▶ abbr. gram(s).

G-man ▶ n. informal an FBI agent.

GMO ▶ abbr. genetically modified organism.

GMT ▶ abbr. Greenwich Mean Time.

gnarled /närld/ ▶ adj. knobbly, rough, and twisted, especially with age.

gnarl·y /'närlē/ ▶ adj. (**gnarlier, gnarliest**)

1 gnarled. **2** informal dangerous, challenging, or unpleasant. **3** informal extremely amazing or excellent.

gnash /nasн/ ▶v. grind one's teeth together, especially as a sign of anger.

gnat /nat/ ▶n. a small two-winged fly resembling a mosquito.

gnaw /nô/ ▶v. **1** bite at or nibble something persistently. **2** cause persistent anxiety or pain: *his conscience gnawed at him.*

gneiss /nīs/ ▶n. a metamorphic rock with a banded or layered structure, typically consisting of feldspar, quartz, and mica.

gnoc·chi /'näkē/ ▶pl.n. (in Italian cooking) small dumplings made from potato, semolina, or flour.

gnome /nōm/ ▶n. **1** an imaginary creature like a tiny man, supposed to guard the earth's treasures underground. **2** a small garden ornament in the form of a bearded man with a pointed hat. ■ **gnom·ish** adj.

gno·mic /'nōmik/ ▶adj. clever but often difficult to understand: *I had to have the gnomic response interpreted for me.* ■ **gno·mi·cal·ly** adv.

gno·sis /'nōsis/ ▶n. knowledge of spiritual mysteries.

Gnos·ti·cism /'nästə,sizəm/ ▶n. a heretical movement of the 2nd-century Christian Church, teaching that mystical knowledge (gnosis) of the supreme divine being enables the human spirit to be redeemed. ■ **Gnos·tic** /'nästik/ adj. & n.

GNP ▶abbr. gross national product.

gnu /n(y)ōō/ ▶n. a large African antelope with a long head and a beard and mane.

go[1] ▶v. (**goes**, **going**, **went** /went/; past part. **gone** /gôn, gän/) **1** move to or from a place. **2** pass into or be in a specified state: *my mind went blank.* **3** (often **go into**) start an activity or course of action: *I'll go skiing | she went into business.* **4** engage in an activity on a regular basis. **5** lie or extend in a certain direction. **6** come to an end; cease to exist. **7** disappear or be used up. **8** (of time) pass. **9** pass time in a particular way: *they went for months without talking.* **10** have a particular outcome. **11** (**be going to be/do**) used to express a future tense. **12** function or operate. **13** be matching. **14** be acceptable or permitted: *anything goes.* **15** fit into or be regularly kept in a particular place. **16** make a specified sound. **17** informal say. **18** (**go by/under**) be known or called by a specified name. ▶n. (pl. **goes**) informal **1** an attempt: *give it a go.* **2** a turn to do or use something. **3** a single item, action, or spell of activity: *the remedies cost up to five bucks a go.* **4** spirit or energy.

– PHRASES **go about** begin or carry on with an activity. **go along with** agree to something. **go around 1** be sufficient to supply everybody present. **2** circulate or be communicated within a group: *there's a rumor going around.* **go at** energetically attack or tackle something. **go back** (of two people) have known each other for a specified, usually long period of time: *Victor and I go back longer than I care to admit.* **go back on** fail to keep a promise. **go down 1** be defeated in a contest. **2** obtain a specified reaction: *the show went down well.* **go for 1** decide on something. **2** attempt to gain something. **3** attack someone. **go in for** like or regularly take part in something. **going!, gone!** an auctioneer's announcement that bidding is closing or closed. **go into 1** investigate or inquire into something. **2** (of a whole number)

be capable of dividing another, typically without a remainder. **go off 1** (of a bomb or gun) explode or fire. **2** informal begin to dislike someone or something. **go on 1** continue or persevere. **2** take place. **go out 1** stop shining or burning. **2** (of the tide) ebb. **3** carry on a regular romantic relationship with someone. **go over** examine or check the details of something. **go through 1** undergo a difficult experience. **2** examine something carefully. **3** informal use up or spend something. **go under** become bankrupt. **go with 1** give one's consent or agreement to (a person or their views). **2** have a romantic relationship with (someone). **go without** suffer lack or hardship. **have——going for one** informal ——is in one's favor. **make a go of** informal be successful in something. **on the go** informal very active or busy. **to go** (of food or drink from a restaurant or cafe) to be eaten or drunk off the premises.

USAGE
For information on the use of **go** followed by **and** (as in *I must go and change*), see the note at **AND**.

go[2] ▶n. a Japanese board game of territorial possession and capture.

goad /gōd/ ▶v. **1** keep annoying or criticizing someone until they react. **2** urge cattle on with a goad. ▶n. **1** a thing that stimulates someone into action. **2** a spiked stick used for driving cattle.

go-a·head informal ▶n. (**the go-ahead**) permission to proceed. ▶adj. enterprising and ambitious.

goal /gōl/ ▶n. **1** (in soccer, football, etc.) a pair of posts linked by a crossbar and forming a space into or over which the ball has to be sent to score. **2** an instance of sending the ball into or over a goal. **3** an aim or desired result: *my goal is to make movies.* ■ **goal·less** adj.

goal·ie /'gōlē/ ▶n. informal a goalkeeper.

goal·keep·er /'gōl,kēpər/ ▶n. a player in soccer or field hockey whose role is to stop the ball from entering the goal.

goal kick ▶n. Soccer a free kick taken by the defending side after attackers send the ball over the end line outside the goal.

goal line ▶n. in field sports, a line on which the goal is placed or which acts as the boundary beyond which a try or touchdown is scored.

goal·post /'gōl,pōst/ ▶n. either of the two upright posts of a goal.
– PHRASES **move the goalposts** unfairly alter the conditions or rules of something while it is still happening.

goal·scor·er /'gōl,skôrər/ ▶n. a player who scores a goal. ■ **goal·scor·ing** adj.

goal·tend·er /'gōl,tendər/ ▶n. a goalkeeper, especially in hockey.

go-a·round ▶n. **1** an instance of an activity or pattern that occurs repeatedly: *this is the third go-around for clearance talks.* **2** Aviation a circular flight pattern following an abandoned landing attempt.

goat /gōt/ ▶n. **1** a hardy domesticated mammal that has backward-curving horns and (in the male) a beard. **2** a wild mammal related to the goat, such as the ibex. **3** informal a lecherous man. ■ **goat·ish** adj. **goat·y** adj.
– PHRASES **get someone's goat** informal irritate someone.

goat-an·te·lope ▶n. a mammal of a group including the chamois, with characteristics of both goats and antelopes.

goat·ee /gōˈtē/ ▸ n. a small pointed beard like that of a goat. ■ **goat·eed** adj.

goat·herd /ˈgōtˌhərd/ ▸ n. a person who looks after goats.

goat·skin /ˈgōtˌskin/ ▸ n. leather made from the skin of a goat.

gob¹ /gäb/ informal ▸ n. **1** a lump of a slimy or thick semiliquid substance. **2** (**gobs of**) a lot of: *he wants to make gobs of money selling DVDs.*

gob² ▸ n. Brit. informal a person's mouth.

gob·ble¹ /ˈgäbəl/ ▸ v. **1** eat hurriedly and noisily. **2** use a large amount of something very quickly: *impractical ventures gobbled up the rock star's cash.* ■ **gob·bler** n.

gob·ble² ▸ v. (of a male turkey) make a swallowing sound in the throat. ■ **gob·bler** n.

gob·ble·dy·gook /ˈgäbəldēˌgook, -ˌgook/ (also **gobbledegook**) ▸ n. informal language that is difficult to understand because of excessive use of technical terms.

go-be·tween ▸ n. an intermediary or negotiator.

gob·let /ˈgäblit/ ▸ n. a drinking glass with a foot and a stem.

gob·lin /ˈgäblin/ ▸ n. (in folklore and fairy tales) a small, ugly, mischievous creature.

go·by /ˈgōbē/ ▸ n. (pl. **gobies**) a small sea fish, typically with a sucker on the underside.

go-cart ▸ n. variant spelling of GO-KART.

God /gäd/ ▸ n. **1** (in Christianity and other religions that believe in only one God) the creator and supreme ruler of the universe. **2** (**god**) a superhuman being or spirit worshiped as having power over nature and human life. **3** (**god**) a greatly admired or influential person. **4** (**the gods**) informal the gallery in a theater. ▸ exclam. used to express surprise, anger, etc., or for emphasis. ■ **god·hood** n. **god·like** adj. – PHRASES **God the Father,** (**the**) **Son, and** (**the**) **Holy Ghost** (in Christian doctrine) the persons of the Trinity. **God's gift** chiefly ironic the best possible person for someone: *he thought he was God's gift to women.*

god·child /ˈgädˌCHīld/ ▸ n. (pl. **godchildren** /-ˌCHildrən/) a person in relation to a godparent.

god·damn /ˈgädˈdam/ (also **goddam** or **goddamned**) ▸ adj., adv., & n. informal used for emphasis, especially to express anger or frustration: (as adj.) *this goddamn weather* | (as n.) *I don't give a goddamn what you do!*

god·daugh·ter /ˈgädˌdôtər/ ▸ n. a female godchild.

god·dess /ˈgädis/ ▸ n. **1** a female god. **2** a woman who is greatly admired, especially for her beauty.

go·de·tia /gəˈdēsHə/ ▸ n. a North American plant with showy lilac to red flowers.

god·fa·ther /ˈgädˌfäTHər/ ▸ n. **1** a male godparent. **2** a male leader of a Mafia family.

God-fear·ing ▸ adj. earnestly religious.

god·for·sak·en /ˈgädfərˌsākən/ ▸ adj. (of a place) unattractive, remote, or depressing.

God-giv·en ▸ adj. **1** received from God: *the God-given power to work miracles.* **2** possessed without question, as if by divine authority: *the union man's God-given right to strike.*

god·head /ˈgädˌhed/ ▸ n. **1** (**the Godhead**) God. **2** divine nature.

god·less /ˈgädlis/ ▸ adj. **1** not believing in a god or God. **2** wicked; very bad.

god·ly /ˈgädlē/ ▸ adj. (**godlier, godliest**) devoutly religious; pious. ■ **god·li·ness** n.

god·moth·er /ˈgädˌməTHər/ ▸ n. a female godparent.

god·par·ent /ˈgädˌpe(ə)rənt, -ˌpar-/ ▸ n. a person who presents a child at baptism and promises to take responsibility for their religious education.

god·send /ˈgädˌsend/ ▸ n. something very helpful or welcome at a particular time.

god·son /ˈgädˌsən/ ▸ n. a male godchild.

God·speed /ˈgädˈspēd/ ▸ exclam. dated an expression of good wishes to a person starting a journey.

god·wit /ˈgädwit/ ▸ n. a large long-legged wading bird with a long bill.

go·er /ˈgōər/ ▸ n. (often in combination) a person who regularly attends a specified place or event: *a theatergoer.*

goes /gōs/ ▸ third person singular present of GO¹.

go·fer /ˈgōfər/ (also **gopher**) ▸ n. informal a person who runs errands.

go-get·ter ▸ n. informal an energetic and very enterprising person. ■ **go-get·ting** adj.

gog·gle /ˈgägəl/ ▸ v. **1** look with wide open eyes. **2** (of the eyes) protrude or open wide. ▸ n. (**goggles**) close-fitting protective glasses with side shields.

gog·gle-eyed ▸ adj. having wide-open eyes, especially through astonishment.

go-go ▸ adj. referring to an unrestrained and erotic style of dancing to pop music.

go·ing /ˈgōiNG/ ▸ n. **1** the condition of the ground as regards its suitability for horse racing or walking. **2** conditions for, or progress in, an activity or enterprise: *the company sold its advertising airtime for $500 million, good going in a recession.* ▸ adj. (of a price) usual or current.

go·ing con·cern ▸ n. a thriving business.

go·ing-o·ver ▸ n. informal **1** a thorough cleaning or inspection. **2** an attack or heavy defeat.

go·ings-on ▸ pl.n. informal suspect or unusual activities.

goi·ter /ˈgoitər/ (Brit. **goitre**) ▸ n. a swelling of the neck resulting from enlargement of the thyroid gland. ■ **goi·trous** /ˈgoitrəs/ adj.

go-kart (also **go-cart**) ▸ n. a small race car with a lightweight body.

gold /gōld/ ▸ n. **1** a yellow precious metal, used in jewelry and decoration and to guarantee the value of currencies. **2** a deep yellow or yellow-brown color. **3** coins or articles made of gold.

gold card ▸ n. a credit card that provides benefits not available on a standard card.

gold-dig·ger ▸ n. informal a woman who forms relationships with men purely for financial gain.

gold disc ▸ n. a framed golden replica of a compact disc awarded to a recording artist or group for sales exceeding a specified figure.

gold dust ▸ n. fine particles of gold.

gold·en /ˈgōldən/ ▸ adj. **1** made of or resembling gold. **2** (of a period) very happy and prosperous. **3** excellent: *a golden opportunity.* **4** (of celebrations) marking the fiftieth anniversary: *their golden wedding anniversary.* ■ **gold·en·ly** adv.

gold·en age ▸ n. the period when something is most successful: *the golden age of musical theater.*

gold·en boy (or **golden girl**) ▶ n. informal a very popular or successful young person.

Gold·en De·li·cious ▶ n. a variety of eating apple with a greenish-yellow skin.

gold·en ea·gle ▶ n. a large eagle with yellow-tipped head feathers.

Gold·en Fleece ▶ n. **1** Mythology the fleece of a golden ram, guarded by an unsleeping dragon. **2** a goal that is highly desirable but difficult to achieve.

gold·en goose ▶ n. a continuing source of wealth or profit that may be exhausted if it is misused.

gold·en hand·cuffs ▶ pl.n. informal benefits provided by an employer to discourage an employee from working elsewhere.

gold·en hand·shake ▶ n. informal a payment given to someone who is laid off or retires early.

gold·en old·ie ▶ n. informal an old song or movie that is still well known and popular.

gold·en re·triev·er ▶ n. a breed of retriever with a thick golden-colored coat.

gold·en·rod /'gōldən,räd/ ▶ n. a plant with tall spikes of small bright yellow flowers.

gold·en rule ▶ n. a basic principle that should always be followed.

gold·en·seal /'gōldən,sēl/ ▶ n. a woodland plant of the buttercup family whose bright yellow root has medicinal and antibacterial properties.

gold·field /'gōld,fēld/ ▶ n. a district in which gold is found as a mineral.

gold·finch /'gōld,fincH/ ▶ n. a gregarious finch with bright yellow plumage.

gold·fish /'gōld,fish/ ▶ n. (pl. same or **goldfishes**) a small reddish-golden carp popular in ponds and aquariums.

gold·fish bowl ▶ n. **1** a spherical glass container for goldfish. **2** a place or situation lacking privacy.

gold leaf ▶ n. gold beaten into a very thin sheet, used in gilding.

gold med·al ▶ n. a medal made of or colored gold, awarded for first place in a competition.

gold mine ▶ n. **1** a place where gold is mined. **2** a source of wealth or resources.

gold plate ▶ n. **1** a thin layer of gold applied as a coating to another metal. **2** dishes, flatware, etc., made of or plated with gold.

gold rush ▶ n. a rapid movement of people to a newly discovered goldfield.

gold·smith /'gōld,smiTH/ ▶ n. a person who makes gold articles.

gold stand·ard ▶ n. historical the system by which the value of a currency was defined in terms of gold.

go·lem /'gōləm/ ▶ n. (in Jewish legend) a clay figure brought to life by magic.

golf /gälf, gôlf/ ▶ n. a game played on an outdoor course, the aim of which is to strike a small hard ball with a club into a series of small holes with the fewest possible strokes. ▶ v. (usu. as n. **golfing**) play golf. ■ **golf·er** n.

golf club ▶ n. **1** a club used to hit the ball in golf, with a heavy wooden or metal head and a slender shaft. **2** a membership organization for golf players, or its premises.

golf course ▶ n. a course on which golf is played, typically consisting of 18 holes.

Go·li·ath /gə'līəTH/ ▶ n. a person or thing of enormous size or strength.

gol·li·wog /'gälē,wäg/ ▶ n. dated a soft doll with a black face and fuzzy hair.

gol·ly /'gälē/ ▶ exclam. informal used to express surprise or delight.

go·nad /'gōnad/ ▶ n. a bodily organ that produces gametes; a testis or ovary. ■ **go·nad·al** /gō'nadl/ adj.

gon·do·la /'gändələ, gän'dōlə/ ▶ n. **1** a flat-bottomed boat used on Venetian canals, having a high point at each end and worked by one oar at the stern. **2** a cabin on a ski lift, or suspended from an airship or balloon.

gon·do·lier /,gändl'i(ə)r/ ▶ n. a person who propels and steers a gondola.

gone /gôn/ past participle of **GO**¹. ▶ adj. **1** no longer present, available, or in existence. **2** informal having reached a specified time in a pregnancy: *she's four months gone.*

gon·er /'gônər/ ▶ n. informal a person or thing that is doomed or cannot be saved.

gong /gäNG, gôNG/ ▶ n. a metal disk with a turned rim, giving a resonant note when struck.

gon·na /'gônə, 'gənə/ ▶ contr. informal going to: *we're gonna win this game.*

gon·or·rhe·a /,gänə'rēə/ (Brit. **gonorrhoea**) ▶ n. a sexually transmitted disease causing discharge from the urethra or vagina.

goo /gōō/ ▶ n. informal a sticky or slimy substance.

goo·ber /'gōōbər/ ▶ n. informal **1** a dimwitted person; a yokel. **2** (also **goober pea**) a peanut.

good /gōōd/ ▶ adj. (**better** /'betər/, **best** /best/) **1** having the required qualities; of a high standard. **2** morally right, polite, or obedient. **3** enjoyable, pleasant, or satisfying. **4** appropriate or suitable. **5** (**good for**) beneficial to. **6** thorough: *have a good look around.* **7** at least: *a good 20 years ago.* ▶ n. **1** behavior that is right or acceptable. **2** something beneficial: *he resigned for the good of the country.* **3** (**goods**) products or possessions.

– PHRASES **as good as** very nearly. **be —— to the good** have a specified net profit or advantage. **come up with** (or **deliver**) **the goods** informal do what is expected or required. **do someone good** be beneficial to someone. **for good** forever. **good and ——** informal used as an intensifier before an adjective or adverb: *it'll be good and dark by then.* **the Good Book** the Bible. **good for you!** well done! **a good word** words recommending or defending a person. **in good time 1** with no risk of being late. **2** (also **all in good time**) in due course but without haste. **make something good** (or **make good on something**) **1** compensate for loss, damage, or expense. **2** fulfill a promise or claim.

good·bye /,gōōd'bī/ (also **goodby**) ▶ exclam. used to express good wishes when parting or ending a conversation. ▶ n. (pl. **goodbyes**; also **goodbys**) an instance of saying 'goodbye'; a parting.

good faith ▶ n. honesty or sincerity of intention.

good-for-noth·ing ▶ adj. worthless and lazy. ▶ n. a worthless and lazy person.

Good Fri·day ▶ n. the Friday before Easter Sunday, on which the Crucifixion of Jesus is commemorated in the Christian Church.

good-heart·ed ▶ adj. kind and well meaning.

good-hu·mored ▶ adj. friendly or cheerful.

good·ie ▶ n. variant spelling of **GOODY**.

good-look·ing ▶ adj. physically attractive.

good·ly /ˈgŏŏdlē/ ▸adj. (**goodlier, goodliest**) considerable in size or quantity.

good-na·tured ▸adj. kind and unselfish.

good·ness /ˈgŏŏdnis/ ▸n. 1 the quality of being good. 2 the nutritious element of food. ▸exclam. expressing surprise, anger, etc.

good night ▸exclam. expressing good wishes on parting at night or before going to bed.

good old boy ▸n. informal, often derogatory 1 a member of a network of men that has controlling influence in some sphere. 2 a Southern white male regarded as typical in being somewhat unsophisticated.

goods and chat·tels ▸pl.n. all kinds of personal possessions.

good-sized ▸adj. adequately or generously large: *the text is supplied in good-sized clear print.*

good-tem·pered ▸adj. not easily angered.

good-time ▸adj. interested in pleasure more than anything else.

good·will /ˌgŏŏdˈwil/ ▸n. 1 friendly or helpful feelings or attitude. 2 the established reputation of a business regarded as an asset and calculated as part of its value when it is sold.

good·y /ˈgŏŏdē/ ▸n. (also **goodie**) (pl. **goodies**) informal something attractive or desirable, especially something tasty to eat. ▸exclam. expressing childish delight.

good·y bag ▸n. a bag containing a selection of desirable items, especially one given to party guests as they leave or to customers as a promotional offer.

good·y-good·y informal ▸n. a person who behaves well so as to impress other people. ▸adj. virtuous in a smug or showy way.

good·y two-shoes ▸n. another term for GOODY-GOODY.

goo·ey /ˈgŏŏē/ ▸adj. (**gooier, gooiest**) informal 1 soft and sticky. 2 excessively sentimental: *gooey nostalgia.* ■ **goo·ey·ness** n.

goof /gŏŏf/ informal ▸n. 1 a mistake. 2 a foolish or stupid person. ▸v. 1 fool around. 2 make a mistake. 3 (**goof off**) evade a duty.

goof·ball /ˈgŏŏf,bôl/ ▸n. informal 1 a naive, silly, or stupid person. 2 a narcotic pill, especially a barbiturate.

goof·y /ˈgŏŏfē/ ▸adj. (**goofier, goofiest**) informal 1 foolish; harmlessly eccentric. 2 (in surfing, snowboarding, etc.) having the right leg in front of the left on the board. ■ **goof·i·ly** adv. **goof·i·ness** n.

goo·gle /ˈgŏŏgəl/ ▸v. 1 use an Internet search engine, especially Google: *she spent the afternoon googling aimlessly.* 2 search for the name of someone or something on the Internet in order to find information about them.

gook[1] /gŏŏk/ ▸n. informal, offensive a person of SE Asian descent.

gook[2] /gŏŏk, gək/ ▸n. informal a sloppy wet or viscous substance: *all that gook she kept putting on her hair.*

goon /gŏŏn/ ▸n. informal 1 a foolish or eccentric person. 2 a thug.

goose /gŏŏs/ ▸n. (pl. **geese**) 1 a large waterbird with a long neck and webbed feet. 2 a female goose. 3 informal a foolish person. ▸v. informal poke someone between the buttocks.

goose·ber·ry /ˈgŏŏs,berē/ ▸n. (pl. **gooseberries**) a round edible yellowish-green berry with a hairy skin.

goose·bumps /ˈgŏŏs,bəmps/ ▸pl.n. a state of the skin in which small bumps appear and hairs are erect, resulting from cold, emotion, or fear.

goose·flesh /ˈgŏŏs,flesh/ ▸n. another term for GOOSEBUMPS.

goose step ▸n. a military marching step in which the legs are not bent at the knee. ▸v. (**goose-step**) march with the legs kept straight.

GOP ▸abbr. Grand Old Party (the Republican Party).

go·pher /ˈgōfər/ ▸n. 1 (also **pocket gopher**) a burrowing American rodent with pouches on its cheeks. 2 variant spelling of GOFER.

Gor·di·an knot /ˈgôrdēən/ ▸n. (in phrase **cut the Gordian knot**) solve a difficult problem in a direct or forceful way.

gore[1] /gôr/ ▸n. blood that has been shed, especially as a result of violence.

gore[2] ▸v. (of an animal such as a bull) pierce or stab someone with a horn or tusk.

gore[3] ▸n. a triangular or tapering piece of material used in making a garment, sail, or umbrella. ■ **gored** adj.

gorge /gôrj/ ▸n. a steep, narrow valley or ravine. ▸v. eat a large amount greedily. ■ **gorg·er** n.
– PHRASES **one's gorge rises** one is sickened or disgusted.

gor·geous /ˈgôrjəs/ ▸adj. 1 beautiful; very attractive. 2 informal very pleasant. ■ **gor·geous·ly** adv. **gor·geous·ness** n.

gor·get /ˈgôrjit/ ▸n. historical an article of clothing or piece of armor covering the throat. 2 a patch of color on the throat of a bird.

Gor·gon /ˈgôrgən/ (also **gorgon**) ▸n. 1 Greek Mythology each of three sisters with snakes for hair, who had the power to turn anyone who looked at them to stone. 2 a fierce or repulsive woman.

Gor·gon·zo·la /ˌgôrgənˈzōlə/ ▸n. a rich, strong-flavored Italian cheese with bluish-green veins.

go·ril·la /gəˈrilə/ ▸n. 1 a powerfully built great ape of central Africa, the largest living primate. 2 informal a heavily built aggressive-looking man.

gorse /gôrs/ ▸n. a yellow-flowered shrub with thin prickly leaves.

gor·y /ˈgôrē/ ▸adj. (**gorier, goriest**) 1 involving violence and bloodshed. 2 covered in blood. ■ **gor·i·ness** n.
– PHRASES **the gory details** humorous explicit details.

gosh /gäsh/ ▸exclam. informal used to express surprise or for emphasis.

gos·hawk /ˈgäs,hôk/ ▸n. a short-winged hawk resembling a large sparrowhawk.

gos·ling /ˈgäzliNG/ ▸n. a young goose.

gos·pel /ˈgäspəl/ ▸n. 1 the teachings of Jesus. 2 (**Gospel**) the record of Jesus's life and teaching in the first four books of the New Testament. 3 (**Gospel**) each of the first four books of the New Testament. 4 (also **gospel truth**) something absolutely true. 5 (also **gospel music**) a style of black American evangelical religious singing.

gos·sa·mer /ˈgäsəmər/ ▸n. a fine, filmy substance consisting of cobwebs spun by small spiders. ▸adj. very fine and insubstantial.

gos·sip /ˈgäsəp/ ▸n. 1 casual conversation or unproven reports about other people. 2 chiefly derogatory a person who likes talking about other people's private lives. ▸v. (**gossips, gossiping, gossiped**) engage in gossip. ■ **gos·sip·er** n.

gos·sip·y adj.

gos·sip col·umn ▶ n. a section of a newspaper devoted to gossip about well-known people.

got /gät/ ▶ past and past participle of GET.

Goth /gäᴛʜ/ ▶ n. **1** a member of a Germanic people that invaded the Roman Empire between the 3rd and 5th centuries. **2** (also **goth**) a young person of a group favoring black clothing and a style of rock music having apocalyptic or mystical lyrics.

Goth·ic /'gäᴛʜik/ ▶ adj. **1** relating to the style of architecture prevalent in western Europe in the 12th–16th centuries, characterized by pointed arches and elaborate tracery. **2** very gloomy or horrifying. **3** (of lettering) derived from the angular style of handwriting with broad vertical downstrokes used in medieval western Europe. **4** relating to the ancient Goths. ▶ n. **1** Gothic architecture. **2** the extinct language of the Goths.

goth·ic nov·el ▶ n. an English type of fiction popular in the 18th to early 19th centuries, characterized by an atmosphere of mystery and horror.

go-to ▶ adj. informal (usually of people representing some resource) of first resort: *he's Hollywood's go-to guy when a trained bear is needed.*

got·ta /'gätə/ ▶ contr. informal have got to: *you gotta be careful.*

got·ten /'gätn/ ▶ past participle of GET.

gouache /gwäsʜ, gōō'äsʜ/ ▶ n. **1** a method of painting using watercolors thickened with a type of glue. **2** watercolors thickened with a type of glue.

Gou·da /'gōōdə/ ▶ n. a flat round Dutch cheese with a yellow rind.

gouge /gouj/ ▶ v. **1** make a rough hole or groove in a surface. **2** (**gouge something out**) cut or force something out roughly or brutally. ▶ n. **1** a chisel with a concave blade. **2** a hole or groove made by gouging. ■ **goug·er** n.

gou·lash /'gōō,läsʜ/ ▶ n. a Hungarian stew of meat and vegetables, flavored with paprika.

gou·ra·mi /gōō'rämē/ ▶ n. (pl. same or **gouramis**) an Asian fish of a large group including many kinds popular in aquariums.

gourd /gôrd, gōōrd/ ▶ n. **1** the large hard-skinned fleshy fruit of a climbing or trailing plant. **2** a container made from the hollowed and dried skin of a gourd.

gour·mand /gōōr'mänd/ ▶ n. **1** a person who enjoys eating, sometimes to excess. **2** a person who is knowledgeable about good food; a gourmet.

gour·man·dize /'gōōrmən,dīz/ ▶ v. eat good food, especially to excess.

gour·met /,gôr'mā, ,gōōr-/ ▶ n. a person who is knowledgeable about good food. ▶ adj. (of food or a meal) high quality.

gout /gout/ ▶ n. **1** a disease that causes the joints to swell and become painful. **2** literary a drop or spot. ■ **gout·y** adj.

gov. ▶ abbr. **1** government. **2** governor.

gov·ern /'gəvərn/ ▶ v. **1** conduct the policy and affairs of a country, state, organization, or people. **2** control or influence: *the wines are governed by strict regulations.* **3** Grammar (of a word) require that another word or group of words be in a particular case. ■ **gov·ern·a·bil·i·ty** /,gəvərnə'bilitē/ n. **gov·ern·a·ble** adj.

gov·ern·ance /'gəvərnəns/ ▶ n. the action or style of governing something.

gov·ern·ess /'gəvərnis/ ▶ n. a woman employed to teach children in a private household.

gov·ern·ing bod·y ▶ n. a group of people who govern an institution such as a school in partnership with the managers.

gov·ern·ment /'gəvər(n)mənt/ ▶ n. **1** (treated as sing. or pl.) the group of people who govern a nation or state. **2** the system by which a nation, state, or community is governed. **3** the action or way of governing a nation, state, or organization: *he believed in strong government.* ■ **gov·ern·men·tal** /,gəvər(n)'mentl/ adj.

gov·er·nor /'gəvə(r)nər/ ▶ n. **1** the elected executive head of a US state. **2** an official appointed to govern a town or region. **3** the representative of the British Crown in a colony or in a Commonwealth country that regards the British monarch as head of state. **4** a member of a governing body. **5** Brit. informal a person's employer or manager. ■ **gov·er·nor·ship** /-,sʜip/ n.

Gov·er·nor Gen·er·al ▶ n. (pl. **Governors General**) the chief representative of the British Crown in a Commonwealth country of which the British monarch is head of state.

govt. ▶ abbr. government.

gown /goun/ ▶ n. **1** a long dress worn on formal occasions. **2** a protective garment worn in a hospital by surgical staff or patients. **3** a loose cloak indicating a person's profession or status, worn by a judge, academic, or university student. **4** the members of a university as distinct from the residents of a town. ▶ v. (**be gowned**) be dressed in a gown.

goy /goi/ ▶ n. (pl. **goyim** /'goi-im/ or **goys**) informal, derogatory a Jewish word for a non-Jew. ■ **goy·ish** adj.

GP ▶ abbr. **1** general practitioner. **2** Grand Prix.

GPA ▶ abbr. grade point average.

GPO ▶ abbr. **1** government printing office. **2** general post office. **3** group purchasing organization.

GPRS ▶ abbr. general packet radio services, a technology for radio transmission of small packets of data, especially between cell phones and the Internet.

GPS ▶ abbr. Global Positioning System (a satellite navigational system).

gr. ▶ abbr. **1** grain(s). **2** gram(s). **3** gross.

grab /grab/ ▶ v. (**grabs, grabbing, grabbed**) **1** seize someone or something suddenly and roughly. **2** informal obtain quickly or when an opportunity arises: *get into town early to grab a parking space.* **3** informal impress: *how does that grab you?* ▶ n. **1** a quick sudden attempt to seize something. **2** a mechanical device for moving loads. ■ **grab·ber** n.
– PHRASES **up for grabs** informal available.

grab bag ▶ n. **1** an eclectic or miscellaneous assortment: *financing a grab bag of more than 20 right-wing front groups.* **2** a container from which a person takes a wrapped item at random, not knowing the contents.

grab·by /'grabē/ ▶ adj. informal **1** having or showing a selfish desire for something; greedy. **2** attracting attention; arousing people's interest: *a grabby angle on a news story.*

grace /grās/ ▶ n. **1** elegance of movement. **2** polite good will: *she had the grace to look sheepish.* **3** (**graces**) attractive qualities or behavior. **4** (in Christian belief) the free and unearned favor of God. **5** a person's favor. **6** a period officially allowed for an obligation to be met: *the sport has three years' grace before the ban comes into force.* **7** a short prayer of thanks said before or after a meal. **8** (**His**, **Her**, or **Your Grace**) used as forms of description or address for a duke, duchess, or archbishop. ▶ v. **1** bring honor to something by one's presence. **2** make more attractive: *a fresh wreath graced an upstairs window.*

– PHRASES **the** (**Three**) **Graces** Greek Mythology three beautiful goddesses believed to personify charm, grace, and beauty. **with good** (or **bad**) **grace** in a willing (or reluctant) way.

grace·ful /'grāsfəl/ ▶ adj. having or showing grace or elegance. ■ **grace·ful·ly** adv. **grace·ful·ness** n.

grace·less /'grāslis/ ▶ adj. lacking grace, elegance, or charm. ■ **grace·less·ly** adv. **grace·less·ness** n.

grace note ▶ n. Music an extra note added to ornament a melody.

gra·cious /'grāsнəs/ ▶ adj. **1** polite, kind, and pleasant. **2** elegant in a way associated with upper-class status or wealth: *magazines devoted to gracious living.* **3** (in Christian belief) showing God's grace. ▶ exclam. expressing polite surprise. ■ **gra·cious·ly** adv. **gra·cious·ness** n.

grack·le /'grakəl/ ▶ n. a songbird of the American blackbird family with glossy black plumage.

grad /grad/ ▶ n. informal term for GRADUATE.

gra·da·tion /grā'dāsнən/ ▶ n. **1** a scale of successive changes, stages, or degrees. **2** a stage in a such a scale. ■ **gra·da·tion·al** adj.

grade /grād/ ▶ n. **1** a specified level of rank, quality, proficiency, or value: *the worst grade of coffee.* **2** a mark indicating the quality of a student's work. **3** a class in a school comprising children grouped according to age or ability. **4** the steepness of a road or hill; gradient. ▶ v. **1** arrange people or things in groups according to quality, size, ability, etc.: *caviar is graded according to the size of its grains.* **2** pass gradually from one level to another. **3** reduce a road to an easier gradient.

– PHRASES **make the grade** informal succeed.

grade cross·ing ▶ n. a place where a railroad and a road cross at the same level.

grade point av·er·age ▶ n. (abbr.: **GPA**) an indication of a student's academic achievement arrived at by averaging grades where A=4, B=3, C=2, and D=1.

grad·er /'grādər/ ▶ n. **1** a person or thing that grades: *a certified beef grader.* **2** a wheeled machine for leveling the ground or making roads. **3** (in combination) a student in a specified grade in school: *a fifth grader.*

grade school ▶ n. elementary school.

gra·di·ent /'grādēənt/ ▶ n. **1** a sloping part of a road or railroad. **2** the degree to which the ground slopes. **3** a change in the magnitude of a property (e.g., temperature) observed in passing from one point or moment to another.

grad·u·al /'grajōōəl/ ▶ adj. **1** taking place in stages over an extended period. **2** (of a slope) not steep. ■ **grad·u·al·ly** adv. **grad·u·al·ness** n.

grad·u·al·ism /'grajōōˌlizəm/ ▶ n. a policy or theory of gradual rather than sudden change. ■ **grad·u·al·ist** n.

grad·u·ate ▶ n. /'grajōōit/ a person who has been awarded a high-school diploma, a college degree, or a certificate of training. ▶ v. /'grajōōˌāt/ **1** successfully complete high school, a college

degree program, or a course of training. **2** (**graduate to**) move up to something more advanced. **3** arrange or mark out something in a scale in gradations. **4** change gradually.

grad·u·ate school ▶ n. a division of a university offering advanced programs beyond the bachelor's degree.

grad·u·a·tion /ˌgrajōō'āsнən/ ▶ n. **1** the receiving or conferring of an academic degree or diploma. **2** the ceremony at which degrees are conferred. **3** the action of dividing into degrees or other proportionate divisions on a graduated scale. **4** a mark on a container or instrument indicating a degree of quantity.

graf·fi·ti /grə'fētē/ ▶ pl.n. (treated as sing. or pl.) writing or drawings on a surface in a public place. ▶ v. write or draw graffiti on a surface. ■ **graf·fi·tist** n.

graft[1] /graft/ ▶ n. **1** a shoot or twig inserted into a slit on the trunk or stem of a living plant, from which it receives sap. **2** a piece of living body tissue that is transplanted surgically to replace diseased or damaged tissue. **3** an operation in which tissue is transplanted. ▶ v. **1** insert or transplant something as a graft. **2** add or attach to something else, especially inappropriately: *plate glass windows had been grafted onto an eighteenth-century building.*

graft[2] informal ▶ n. bribery and other corrupt measures adopted to gain power or money in politics or business. ■ **graft·er** n.

Grail /grāl/ (also **Holy Grail**) ▶ n. (in medieval legend) the cup or platter used by Jesus at the Last Supper, especially as the object of quests by knights.

grain /grān/ ▶ n. **1** wheat or other cultivated cereal used as food. **2** a single seed or fruit of a cereal. **3** a small hard particle of a substance such as sand. **4** the smallest unit of weight in the troy and avoirdupois systems. **5** the smallest possible amount: *there wasn't a grain of truth in the rumors.* **6** the lengthwise arrangement of fibers, particles, or layers in wood, paper, rock, etc. ■ **grained** adj.

– PHRASES **against the grain** contrary to one's nature or instinct.

grain·y /'grānē/ ▶ adj. (**grainier**, **grainiest**) **1** consisting of grains; granular. **2** (of a photograph) showing visible grains of emulsion. ■ **grain·i·ness** n.

gram[1] /gram/ (Brit. also **gramme**) ▶ n. a metric unit of mass equal to one thousandth of a kilogram.

gram[2] ▶ n. informal grandmother.

gram·mar /'gramər/ ▶ n. **1** the whole structure of a language, including the rules for the way words are formed and their relationship to each other in a sentence. **2** knowledge and use of the rules or principles of grammar: *bad grammar.* **3** a book on grammar.

gram·mar·i·an /grə'me(ə)rēən/ ▶ n. a person who studies and writes about grammar.

gram·mar school ▶ n. **1** another term for ELEMENTARY SCHOOL. **2** (in the UK, especially formerly) a state secondary school that admits students on the basis of their ability.

gram·mat·i·cal /grə'matikəl/ ▶ adj. relating to or following the rules of grammar. ■ **gram·mat·i·cal·i·ty** /-ˌmati'kalitē/ n. **gram·mat·i·cal·ly** adv.

Gram·my /'gramē/ ▶ n. (pl. **Grammys** or

Grammies) an annual award given by the American National Academy of Recording Arts and Sciences for achievement in the music industry.

gram·o·phone /'grămə,fōn/ ▶ n. dated, chiefly Brit. a record player.

gram·pus /'grampəs/ ▶ n. (pl. **grampuses**) a killer whale or other dolphinlike sea animal.

gra·na·ry /'grānərē, 'gran-/ ▶ n. (pl. **granaries**) 1 a storehouse for threshed grain. 2 a region growing large quantities of cereal.

grand /grand/ ▶ adj. 1 magnificent and impressive. 2 large or ambitious in scope or scale: *a grand plan for converting dying neighborhoods into thriving communities.* 3 of the highest importance or rank. 4 dignified, noble, or proud. 5 informal excellent. 6 (in combination) (in names of family relationships) referring to one generation removed in ascent or descent: *a grand-niece.* ▶ n. 1 (pl. same) informal a thousand dollars or pounds. 2 a grand piano. ■ **grand·ly** adv. **grand·ness** n.

grand·child /'grand,CHīld/ ▶ n. (pl. **grandchildren** /'grand,CHildrən/) a child of one's son or daughter.

grand·dad /'gran,dad/ (also **grandad**, **grandaddy**) ▶ n. informal one's grandfather.

grand·daugh·ter /'gran,dôtər/ ▶ n. a daughter of one's son or daughter.

grand duke ▶ n. 1 (in Europe, especially formerly) a prince or nobleman ruling over a small independent country. 2 historical a son (or grandson) of a Russian tsar.

grande dame /'gran 'dam, 'grän 'däm/ ▶ n. a woman who is influential within a particular area of activity.

gran·dee /gran'dē/ ▶ n. 1 a Spanish or Portuguese nobleman of the highest rank. 2 a high-ranking or eminent man.

gran·deur /'granjər, 'gran,dyŏŏr/ ▶ n. 1 the quality of being grand and impressive: *the wild grandeur of the mountains.* 2 high rank or social importance.

grand·fa·ther /'gran(d),fäTHər/ ▶ n. 1 the father of one's father or mother. 2 a founder or originator of something. ▶ v. exempt from a new law or regulation: *smokers who worked here before the ban have been grandfathered.*

grand·fa·ther clause ▶ n. a clause exempting certain classes of people or things from the requirements of a new piece of legislation.

grand·fa·ther clock ▶ n. a clock in a tall freestanding wooden case, driven by weights.

Grand Gui·gnol /grän gēn'yôl/ ▶ n. dramatic entertainment of a sensational or horrific nature.

gran·di·flo·ra /,grandə'flôrə/ ▶ adj. (of a cultivated plant) bearing large flowers.

gran·dil·o·quent /gran'dilәkwənt/ ▶ adj. using long or difficult words in order to impress. ■ **gran·dil·o·quence** n. **gran·dil·o·quent·ly** adv.

gran·di·ose /'grandē,ōs, ,grandē'ōs/ ▶ adj. very large or ambitious, especially in a way that is intended to impress: *the city was built on a vast and grandiose scale.* ■ **gran·di·ose·ly** adv. **gran·di·os·i·ty** /,grandē'äsitē/ n.

grand ju·ry ▶ n. Law a jury selected to examine the validity of an accusation prior to trial.

grand lar·ce·ny ▶ n. Law theft of personal property having a value above a legally specified amount.

grand·ma /'gran(d),mä, 'gram-/ ▶ n. informal one's grandmother.

grand mal /,gran(d) 'mäl, 'mal/ ▶ n. a serious form of epilepsy with muscle spasms and prolonged loss of consciousness. Compare with PETIT MAL.

grand mas·ter ▶ n. 1 (also **grandmaster**) a chess player of the highest class. 2 (**Grand Master**) the head of an order of chivalry or of Freemasons.

grand·moth·er /'gran(d),məTHər/ ▶ n. the mother of one's father or mother.

grand op·er·a ▶ n. an opera on a serious theme in which the entire libretto (including dialogue) is sung.

grand·pa /'gran(d),pä, 'gram-/ ▶ n. informal one's grandfather.

grand·par·ent /'gran(d),pe(ə)rənt, -,par-/ ▶ n. a grandmother or grandfather.

grand pi·an·o ▶ n. a large full-toned piano that has the body, strings, and soundboard arranged horizontally and is supported by three legs.

Grand Prix /,grän 'prē, ,gran/ ▶ n. (pl. **Grands Prix** pronunc. same) a race forming part of an auto-racing or motorcycling world championship.

grand slam ▶ n. 1 the winning of each of a group of major championships or matches in a particular sport in the same year. 2 Bridge the bidding and winning of all thirteen tricks.

grand·son /'gran(d),sən/ ▶ n. the son of one's son or daughter.

grand·stand /'gran(d),stand/ ▶ n. the main spectator area at a racetrack or sports arena. ▶ v. (usu. as n. **grandstanding**) derogatory seek to attract applause or favorable attention from spectators or the media.

grand to·tal ▶ n. the final amount after everything is added up.

grand tour ▶ n. 1 historical a cultural tour of Europe formerly undertaken by upper-class young men. 2 a guided tour of a building, exhibit, or institution.

grange /grānj/ ▶ n. 1 (**the Grange**) in the US, a farmers' association that sponsors community activities and political lobbying. 2 Brit. a country house with farm buildings attached. 3 old use a barn.

gran·ite /'granit/ ▶ n. a very hard rock consisting mainly of quartz, mica, and feldspar. ■ **gra·nit·ic** /grə'nitik/ adj.

gran·ny /'granē/ (also **grannie**) ▶ n. (pl. **grannies**) informal one's grandmother.

gran·ny knot ▶ n. a square knot with the ends crossed the wrong way and therefore liable to slip.

Gran·ny Smith ▶ n. a bright green variety of apple with crisp, tart flesh.

gra·no·la /grə'nōlə/ ▶ n. a kind of breakfast cereal or snack food consisting typically of rolled oats, honey, nuts, and dried fruits.

grant /grant/ ▶ v. 1 agree to give something to someone or allow them to do something. 2 give something formally or legally to: *someone with a fear of torture would be granted asylum.* 3 admit to someone that something is true. ▶ n. 1 a sum of money given by a government or public body for a particular purpose. 2 the action of granting something. ■ **gran·tee** /gran'tē/ n. **gran·tor** /gran'tôr, 'grantər/ (also **granter**) n.
– PHRASES **take someone/thing for granted**

1 fail to appreciate someone or something as a result of overfamiliarity. **2** assume that something is true.

grant·ed /'grantid/ ▶ adv. admittedly; it is true. ▶ conj. **(granted that)** even assuming that.

gran·u·lar /'granyələr/ ▶ adj. **1** resembling or consisting of granules. **2** having a roughened surface. ■ **gran·u·lar·i·ty** /ˌgranyə'laritē/ n.

gran·u·lat·ed /'granyəˌlātid/ ▶ adj. **1** in the form of granules. **2** technical having a roughened surface. ■ **gran·u·la·tion** /ˌgranyə'lāsHən/ n.

gran·ule /'granyōōl/ ▶ n. a small hard particle of a substance.

grape /grāp/ ▶ n. a green, purple, or black berry growing in clusters on a vine, eaten as fruit and used in making wine. ■ **grap·ey** adj.

grape·fruit /'grāpˌfrōōt/ ▶ n. (pl. same) a large round yellow citrus fruit with a slightly bitter taste.

grape hy·a·cinth ▶ n. a small plant with clusters of small globular blue flowers.

grape·shot /'grāpˌsHät/ ▶ n. historical ammunition consisting of a number of small iron balls fired together from a cannon.

grape·vine /'grāpˌvīn/ ▶ n. **1** a vine bearing grapes. **2** (**the grapevine**) informal the spreading of information through rumor and informal conversation: *I heard on the grapevine that he'd been very impressive.*

graph /graf/ ▶ n. a diagram showing the relation between two or more sets of numbers or quantities, typically plotted along a pair of lines at right angles.

-graph ▶ comb.form **1** referring to something written or drawn in a specified way: *autograph.* **2** referring to an instrument that records something: *seismograph.*

graph·ic /'grafik/ ▶ adj. **1** relating to visual art, especially involving drawing, engraving, or lettering. **2** giving vividly explicit detail: *graphic descriptions of sexual practices.* **3** in the form of a graph. ▶ n. a visual image displayed on a computer screen or stored as data.

graph·i·cal /'grafikəl/ ▶ adj. **1** relating to or in the form of a graph. **2** relating to visual art or computer graphics. ■ **graph·i·cal·ly** adv.

graph·ic arts ▶ pl.n. visual arts based on the use of line and tone rather than three-dimensional work or the use of color.

graph·ic de·sign ▶ n. the art of combining words and pictures in advertisements, magazines, or books.

graph·ic nov·el ▶ n. a novel in comic-strip format.

graph·ics /'grafiks/ ▶ pl.n. (usu. treated as sing.) the use of drawings, designs, or pictures to illustrate books, magazines, etc.

graph·ite /'graˌfīt/ ▶ n. a gray form of carbon used as pencil lead and as a solid lubricant in machinery. ■ **gra·phit·ic** /grə'fitik/ adj.

graph·ol·o·gy /gra'fäləjē/ ▶ n. the study of handwriting, especially as used to analyze a person's character. ■ **graph·o·log·i·cal** /ˌgrafə'läjikəl/ adj. **graph·ol·o·gist** n.

graph pa·per ▶ n. paper printed with a network of small squares, used for drawing graphs or other diagrams.

-graphy ▶ comb.form forming nouns referring to: **1** a descriptive science: *geography.* **2** a technique of producing images: *radiography.* **3** a style of

writing or drawing: *calligraphy.* **4** writing about a specified subject: *hagiography.* **5** a written or printed list: *filmography.* ■ **-graphic** comb.form.

grap·nel /'grapnəl/ ▶ n. a device with iron claws, attached to a rope and used for dragging or grasping.

grap·ple /'grapəl/ ▶ v. **1** take a firm hold of someone and struggle to overcome them. **2** (**grapple with**) struggle to deal with or understand: *Europe is grappling with a fuel crisis.* ■ **grap·pler** n.

grasp /grasp/ ▶ v. **1** seize and hold someone or something firmly. **2** take an opportunity eagerly. **3** understand something fully. ▶ n. **1** a firm grip. **2** a person's capacity to achieve or understand something: *the top job was within her grasp.* ■ **grasp·a·ble** adj. **grasp·er** n.

grasp·ing /'graspiNG/ ▶ adj. greedy for wealth.

grass /gras/ ▶ n. **1** vegetation consisting of short plants with long, narrow leaves. **2** ground covered with grass. **3** informal marijuana. **4** Brit. informal a police informer. ▶ v. **1** cover an area with grass. **2** (often **grass on**) Brit. informal inform the police of someone's criminal activity.
– PHRASES **not let the grass grow under one's feet** not delay in taking action. **put someone/ thing out to grass 1** put an animal out to graze. **2** informal force someone to retire.

grass·hop·per /'grasˌhäpər/ ▶ n. an insect with long hind legs that are used for jumping and for producing a chirping sound.

grass·land /'grasˌland/ ▶ n. (also **grasslands**) a large area of grass-covered land, especially one used for grazing.

grass roots ▶ pl.n. the most basic level of an activity or organization.

grass wid·ow ▶ n. a woman whose husband is away often or for a long time.

grass·y /'grasē/ ▶ adj. (**grassier, grassiest**) covered with or resembling grass.

grate¹ /grāt/ ▶ v. **1** shred food by rubbing it on a grater. **2** make an unpleasant scraping sound. **3** have an irritating effect: *the fly's buzzing grated on my nerves.*

grate² ▶ n. **1** a metal frame for holding fuel in a fireplace. **2** the recess of a fireplace.

grate·ful /'grātfəl/ ▶ adj. feeling or showing one's appreciation of something that has been done for one. ■ **grate·ful·ly** adv.

grat·er /'grātər/ ▶ n. a device having a surface covered with sharp-edged holes, used for grating food.

grat·i·fi·ca·tion /ˌgratəfi'kāsHən/ ▶ n. **1** pleasure, especially when gained from the satisfaction of a desire: *a thirst for sexual gratification.* **2** a source of pleasure.

grat·i·fy /'gratəˌfī/ ▶ v. (**gratifies, gratifying, gratified**) **1** give pleasure or satisfaction to: *he was gratified that they liked the book.* **2** indulge or satisfy a desire.

grat·in /'grätn, 'gratn/ ▶ n. a casserole with a light browned crust of breadcrumbs or melted cheese.

grat·ing¹ /'grātiNG/ ▶ adj. **1** sounding harsh and unpleasant. **2** irritating: *his grating confrontational personality.* ■ **grat·ing·ly** adv.

grat·ing² ▶ n. a framework of parallel or crossed bars that covers an opening.

grat·is /'gratis/ ▶ adv. & adj. free of charge.

grat·i·tude /'gratəˌt(y)ōōd/ ▶ n. the quality of being grateful; appreciation of kindness.

gra·tu·i·tous /grə't(y)o͞oitəs/ ▸ adj. 1 having no justifiable reason or purpose: *studios were under pressure to tone down gratuitous violence.* 2 free of charge. ■ **gra·tu·i·tous·ly** adv.

gra·tu·i·ty /grə't(y)o͞oitē/ ▸ n. (pl. **gratuities**) formal a sum of money given to someone who has provided a service; a tip.

grave[1] /grāv/ ▸ n. 1 a hole dug in the ground for a coffin or a corpse. 2 (**the grave**) death.
– PHRASES **dig one's own grave** do something foolish that causes one's downfall. **turn in one's grave** (of a dead person) be likely to have been angry or distressed about something had they been alive.

grave[2] ▸ adj. 1 giving cause for alarm or concern: *he was in grave danger.* 2 solemn or serious: *her face was grave.* ■ **grave·ly** adv.

grave[3] ▸ v. (past part. **graven** or **graved**) 1 literary fix something firmly in the mind. 2 old use engrave something on a surface.

grave ac·cent /grāv, grāv/ ▸ n. a mark (`) placed over a vowel in some languages to indicate a change in its sound quality.

grave·dig·ger /'grāv,digər/ ▸ n. a person who digs graves.

grav·el /'gravəl/ ▸ n. a loose mixture of small stones and coarse sand, used for paths and roads. ▸ v. (**gravels, graveling, graveled**) cover something with gravel.

grav·el·ly /'gravəlē/ ▸ adj. 1 resembling, containing, or consisting of gravel. 2 (of a voice) deep and rough-sounding.

grav·en im·age ▸ n. a carved figure of a god used as an idol.

grav·er /'grāvər/ ▸ n. an engraving tool.

Graves' dis·ease ▸ n. a swelling of the neck and protrusion of the eyes resulting from hyperthyroidism.

grave·stone /'grāv,stōn/ ▸ n. an inscribed headstone marking a grave.

grave·yard /'grāv,yärd/ ▸ n. a burial ground, especially one beside a church.

grave·yard shift ▸ n. a work shift that runs from midnight to 8 a.m.

gra·vim·e·ter /grə'vimitər/ ▸ n. an instrument for measuring the force of gravity at different places.

grav·i·met·ric /,gravə'metrik/ ▸ adj. 1 relating to the measurement of weight. 2 relating to the measurement of gravity.

grav·i·tas /'gravi,täs/ ▸ n. a dignified and serious manner.

grav·i·tate /'gravi,tāt/ ▸ v. 1 be drawn toward a place, person, or thing: *his children gravitated toward careers in music.* 2 Physics move, or tend to move, toward a center of gravity.

grav·i·ta·tion /,gravi'tāSHən/ ▸ n. 1 movement, or a tendency to move, toward a center of gravity. 2 Physics gravity. ■ **grav·i·ta·tion·al** adj. **grav·i·ta·tion·al·ly** adv.

grav·i·ty /'gravitē/ ▸ n. 1 the force that attracts a body toward the center of the earth, or toward any other physical body having mass. 2 extreme importance or seriousness: *the gravity of environmental crimes.* 3 a solemn or serious manner.

grav·lax /'gräv,läks/ ▸ n. a Scandinavian dish of dry-cured salmon marinated in herbs.

gra·vure /grə'vyo͝or/ ▸ n. short for PHOTOGRAVURE.

gra·vy /'grāvē/ ▸ n. (pl. **gravies**) a sauce made by adding stock, flour, and seasoning to the fat and juices that come out of meat during cooking.

gra·vy boat ▸ n. a long, narrow vessel used for serving gravy.

gra·vy train ▸ n. informal a situation in which someone can easily make a lot of money.

gray /grā/ (also chiefly Brit. **grey**) ▸ adj. 1 of a color between black and white, as of ashes or lead. 2 (of hair) turning gray or white with age. 3 (of the weather) cloudy and dull; without sun. 4 dull and nondescript: *gray, faceless men.* 5 not accounted for in official statistics: *the gray economy.* ▸ n. gray color. ▸ v. (especially of hair) become gray. ■ **gray·ish** adj. **gray·ness** n.

gray a·re·a ▸ n. an area of activity that does not easily fit into an existing category and is difficult to deal with.

gray·beard /'grā,bi(ə)rd/ ▸ n. humorous an old man.

gray·ling /'grāliNG/ ▸ n. an edible silvery-gray freshwater fish with horizontal violet stripes.

gray mat·ter ▸ n. 1 the darker tissue of the brain and spinal cord. 2 informal intelligence.

gray seal ▸ n. a large North Atlantic seal with a spotted grayish coat.

gray squir·rel ▸ n. a tree squirrel with mainly gray fur, native to eastern North America and introduced elsewhere.

gray wa·ter ▸ n. Ecology the relatively clean wastewater from baths, sinks, washing machines, and kitchen appliances.

graze[1] /grāz/ ▸ v. 1 (of cattle, sheep, etc.) eat grass in a field. 2 informal eat frequent snacks at irregular intervals. ■ **graz·er** n.

graze[2] ▸ v. 1 scrape and break the skin on part of the body. 2 touch something lightly in passing. ▸ n. a slight injury caused by grazing the skin.

graz·ing /'grāziNG/ ▸ n. grassland suitable for use as pasture.

GRE ▸ abbr. Graduate Record Examination, a set of tests usually required of applicants to US graduate schools in fields other than business, law, and medicine.

grease /grēs/ ▸ n. 1 a thick oily substance, especially one used to lubricate machinery. 2 animal fat used or produced in cooking. ▸ v. smear or lubricate something with grease.
– PHRASES **grease the palm of** informal bribe someone. **like greased lightning** informal very rapidly.

grease gun ▸ n. a device for pumping grease under pressure to a particular point.

grease mon·key ▸ n. derogatory or humorous an auto mechanic.

grease·paint /'grēs,pānt/ ▸ n. a waxy substance used as makeup by actors.

greas·er /'grēsər, -zər/ ▸ n. 1 informal a rough young man, especially one who greases back his hair and who consorts with a tough group. 2 an auto mechanic or an unskilled engineer on a ship.

greas·y /'grēsē, -zē/ ▸ adj. (**greasier, greasiest**) 1 covered with or resembling grease. 2 polite or friendly in a way that seems excessive and insincere. ■ **greas·i·ly** adv. **greas·i·ness** n.

greas·y spoon ▸ n. informal a shabby cafe serving inexpensive fried meals.

great /grāt/ ▸ adj. 1 much higher than average in amount, extent, or intensity. 2 much higher than average in ability, quality, or importance: *a great Italian composer.* 3 informal excellent. 4 used to emphasize a description: *I was a great* *fan of Hank's.* **5** (**Greater**) referring to an area that includes the center of a city and a large urban area around it: *Greater Los Angeles.* **6** (in combination) (in names of family relationships) referring to one degree further removed upward or downward: *a great-aunt.* ▶ n. a famous and successful person. ▶ adv. informal very well. ■ **great·ness** n.

great ape ▶ n. a large ape of a family closely related to humans, including the gorilla and chimpanzees.

great-aunt ▶ n. an aunt of one's father or mother.

Great Dane ▶ n. a very large and powerful dog with short hair.

great di·vide ▶ n. **1** a distinction regarded as significant that is difficult to ignore or overcome: *the great divide between workers and management.* **2** an event, date, or place regarded as a point of significant and irrevocable change or difference: *to our parents the war was the great divide.*

great horned owl ▶ n. a large owl found throughout North and South America, with hornlike ear tufts.

great·ly /ˈgrātlē/ ▶ adv. very much.

great-neph·ew ▶ n. a son of one's nephew or niece.

great-niece ▶ n. a daughter of one's nephew or niece.

great room ▶ n. a large room in a modern house that combines features of a living room with those of a dining room or family room.

great-un·cle ▶ n. an uncle of one's mother or father.

Great War ▶ n. World War I.

greave /grēv/ ▶ n. historical a piece of armor for the shin.

grebe /grēb/ ▶ n. a diving waterbird with a long neck and a very short tail.

Gre·cian /ˈgrēsʜən/ ▶ adj. relating to ancient Greece, especially its architecture.

Greco- (also **Graeco-**) ▶ comb. form Greek; Greek and ...: *Graeco-Roman.*

greed /grēd/ ▶ n. **1** a strong and selfish desire for possessions, wealth, or power. **2** a desire to eat more food than is necessary.

greed·y /ˈgrēdē/ ▶ adj. (**greedier**, **greediest**) **1** having an excessive desire for food. **2** having or showing a strong and selfish desire for wealth or power: *people driven from their land by greedy developers.* ■ **greed·i·ly** adv. **greed·i·ness** n.

Greek /grēk/ ▶ n. **1** a person from Greece. **2** the ancient or modern language of Greece. ▶ adj. relating to Greece.
– PHRASES **it's all Greek to me** informal I can't understand it at all.

green /grēn/ ▶ adj. **1** of the color between blue and yellow in the spectrum; colored like grass. **2** covered with grass or other vegetation. **3** (**Green**) concerned with or supporting protection of the environment. **4** (of a plant or fruit) young or unripe. **5** inexperienced or naive. **6** in an untreated or original state; not cured, seasoned, etc. ▶ n. **1** green color or material. **2** a piece of common grassy land, especially in the center of a town or village. **3** an area of smooth, very short grass immediately surrounding a hole on a golf course. **4** (**greens**) green vegetables. **5** (**Green**) a member or supporter of an environmentalist group or party. ▶ v. **1** make or become green. **2** make something less harmful to the environment. ■ **green·ish** adj. **green·ness** n.
– PHRASES **the green-eyed monster** jealousy personified.

green au·dit ▶ n. an assessment of a business as regards its observance of practices that seek to minimize harm to the environment.

green·back /ˈgrēn,bak/ ▶ n. informal a dollar.

green bean ▶ n. the immature pod of any of various bean plants, eaten as a vegetable.

green belt ▶ n. an area of open land around a city, on which building is restricted.

Green Be·ret ▶ n. informal a member of the US Army Special Forces, or a British commando.

green card ▶ n. a permit that allows a foreign national to live and work permanently in the US.

green·er·y /ˈgrēnərē/ ▶ n. green foliage or vegetation.

green·field /ˈgrēn,fēld/ ▶ adj. (of a site) previously undeveloped or built on.

green·fly /ˈgrēn,flī/ ▶ n. (pl. **greenflies**) a green aphid.

green·gage /ˈgrēn,gāj/ ▶ n. a small greenish plum.

green·gro·cer /ˈgrēn,grōsər/ ▶ n. chiefly Brit. a person who sells fruit and vegetables. ■ **green·gro·cer·y** n.

green·horn /ˈgrēn,hôrn/ ▶ n. informal an inexperienced or naive person.

green·house /ˈgrēn,hous/ ▶ n. a glass building in which plants that need protection from cold weather are grown.

green·house ef·fect ▶ n. the trapping of the sun's warmth in a planet's lower atmosphere, because visible radiation from the sun passes through the atmosphere more readily than infrared radiation coming from the planet's surface.

green·house gas ▶ n. a gas, such as carbon dioxide, that contributes to the greenhouse effect by absorbing infrared radiation.

Green·land·er /ˈgrēn,landər/ ▶ n. a person from Greenland.

green light ▶ n. **1** a green traffic light giving permission to proceed. **2** permission to go ahead with a project.

green on·ion ▶ n. a small immature onion with a long green stem, eaten chiefly in salads; a scallion.

green pep·per ▶ n. an unripe sweet pepper, green in color and eaten as a vegetable.

green rev·o·lu·tion ▶ n. a large increase in crop production in developing countries achieved by the use of artificial fertilizers, pesticides, and high-yield crop varieties.

green room ▶ n. a room in a theater or studio in which performers can relax when they are not performing.

greens·keep·er /ˈgrēnz,kēpər/ ▶ n. a person employed to look after a golf course.

green·stone /ˈgrēn,stōn/ ▶ n. **1** a greenish igneous rock containing feldspar and hornblende. **2** chiefly NZ a variety of jade.

green stuff ▶ n. informal money: *the company's green stuff piled up to some $60 billion.*

green tea ▶ n. tea made from unfermented leaves, produced mainly in China and Japan.

green thumb ▶ n. a natural talent for growing plants.

Green·wich Mean Time ▶ n. the time measured at the Greenwich meridian, used as the standard time in a zone that includes the British Isles.

Green·wich me·rid·i·an ▶ n. the meridian of zero longitude, passing through Greenwich, England.

green·wood /ˈgrēnˌwood/ ▶ n. old use woods or forest in leaf, especially as a refuge for medieval outlaws.

greet /grēt/ ▶ v. **1** give a word or sign of welcome when meeting someone. **2** react to or acknowledge in a particular way. **3** (of a sight or sound) become apparent to a person arriving somewhere. ■ **greet·er** n.

greet·ing /ˈgrētiNG/ ▶ n. **1** a word or sign of welcome when meeting someone. **2** (usu. **greetings**) a formal expression of good wishes.

greet·ing card ▶ n. a decorative card sent to express good wishes on a particular occasion.

gre·gar·i·ous /griˈge(ə)rēəs/ ▶ adj. **1** fond of company; sociable. **2** (of animals) living in flocks, herds, or colonies. ■ **gre·gar·i·ous·ly** adv. **gre·gar·i·ous·ness** n.

Gre·go·ri·an cal·en·dar /grəˈgôrēən/ ▶ n. the modified form of the Julian calendar introduced in 1582 by Pope Gregory XIII, and still used today.

Gre·go·ri·an chant /grəˈgôrēən/ ▶ n. medieval church plainsong.

grem·lin /ˈgremlin/ ▶ n. a mischievous creature regarded as responsible for unexplained mechanical or electrical faults.

gre·nade /grəˈnād/ ▶ n. a small bomb thrown by hand or launched mechanically.

Gre·na·di·an /grəˈnādēən/ ▶ n. a person from the Caribbean country of Grenada. ▶ adj. relating to Grenada.

gren·a·dier /ˌgrenəˈdi(ə)r/ ▶ n. **1** historical a soldier armed with grenades. **2** (**Grenadiers** or **Grenadier Guards**) (in the UK) the first regiment of the royal household infantry.

gren·a·dine /ˈgrenəˌdēn, ˌgrenəˈdēn/ ▶ n. a sweet syrup made in France from pomegranates.

grew /grōō/ ▶ past of GROW.

grey, etc. ▶ adj. chiefly British spelling of GRAY, etc.

grey·hound /ˈgrāˌhound/ ▶ n. a swift, slender breed of dog used in racing.

grid /grid/ ▶ n. **1** a framework of bars that are parallel or cross each other. **2** a network of lines that cross each other to form a series of squares or rectangles. **3** a network of cables or pipes for distributing power, especially high-voltage electricity. **4** a pattern of lines marking the starting places on an auto-racing track.

grid·dle /ˈgridl/ ▶ n. a heavy, flat iron plate that is heated and used for cooking food. ▶ v. cook food on a griddle.

grid·i·ron /ˈgridˌīərn/ ▶ n. **1** a frame of parallel metal bars used for grilling meat or fish over an open fire. **2** a grid pattern, especially of streets. **3** a football field, marked with regularly spaced parallel lines.

grid·lock /ˈgridˌläk/ ▶ n. a traffic jam affecting a whole network of intersecting streets. ■ **grid·locked** adj.

grief /grēf/ ▶ n. **1** intense sorrow, especially caused by someone's death. **2** informal trouble or annoyance.
– PHRASES **come to grief** have an accident; meet

with disaster.

griev·ance /ˈgrēvəns/ ▶ n. a real or imagined cause for complaint.

grieve /grēv/ ▶ v. **1** feel intense sorrow, especially as a result of someone's death. **2** cause great distress to someone. ■ **griev·er** n.

griev·ous /ˈgrēvəs/ ▶ adj. formal (of something bad) very severe or serious: *the loss of his father was a grievous blow.* ■ **griev·ous·ly** adv.

grif·fin /ˈgrifin/ (also **gryphon** /ˈgrifən/ or **griffon** /ˈgrifən/) ▶ n. a mythical creature with the head and wings of an eagle and the body of a lion.

grif·fon /ˈgrifən/ ▶ n. **1** a dog of a small terrierlike breed. **2** a large vulture with pale brown plumage.

grift /grift/ ▶ v. engage in petty swindling. ▶ n. a petty swindle. ■ **grift·er** n.

grill /gril/ ▶ n. **1** a metal framework used for cooking food on an open fire; gridiron. **2** a restaurant serving grilled food: *the bar and grill on Polk Street.* **3** a dish of food cooked using a grill. **4** variant form of GRILLE. **5** Brit. the broiling unit of an oven; broiler. ▶ v. **1** cook food using a grill. **2** informal question someone in a relentless or aggressive way.

grille /gril/ (also **grill**) ▶ n. a grating or screen of metal bars or wires.

grim /grim/ ▶ adj. (**grimmer**, **grimmest**) **1** very serious or gloomy; forbidding. **2** horrifying, depressing, or worrying: *the grim realities of warfare.* ■ **grim·ly** adv. **grim·ness** n.

grim·ace /ˈgriməs, griˈmās/ ▶ n. a twisted expression on a person's face, expressing disgust, pain, or wry amusement. ▶ v. make a grimace.

grime /grīm/ ▶ n. dirt ingrained on a surface. ▶ v. make something black or dirty with grime. ■ **grim·y** adj. (**grimier**, **grimiest**)

Grim Reap·er ▶ n. a personification of death in the form of a cloaked skeleton wielding a large scythe.

grin /grin/ ▶ v. (**grins**, **grinning**, **grinned**) smile broadly. ▶ n. a broad smile.
– PHRASES **grin and bear it** suffer pain or misfortune without complaining.

Grinch /grinCH/ ▶ n. informal a spoilsport or killjoy.

grind /grīnd/ ▶ v. (past and past part. **ground**) **1** reduce something to small particles or powder by crushing it. **2** make something sharp or smooth by rubbing it against a hard or abrasive surface or tool. **3** rub together or move gratingly. **4** (**grind someone down**) weaken someone by treating them harshly over a long period of time. **5** (**grind something out**) produce something slowly and laboriously. **6** (as adj. **grinding**) (of a difficult situation) oppressive and seemingly endless: *grinding poverty.* **7** informal (of a dancer) rotate the hips. ▶ n. hard, dull work: *the daily grind.* ■ **grind·ing·ly** adv.
– PHRASES **grind to a halt** (or **come to a grinding halt**) slow down gradually and then stop completely.

grind·er /ˈgrīndər/ ▶ n. **1** a machine or tool that grinds: *a meat grinder.* **2** a person employed to grind something. **3** a tooth, especially a molar. **4** a submarine sandwich.

grind·stone /ˈgrīndˌstōn/ ▶ n. **1** a thick revolving disk of abrasive material used for sharpening or polishing metal objects. **2** a millstone.
– PHRASES **keep one's nose to the grindstone** work hard and continuously.

grin·go /'griNGgō/ ▶ n. (pl. **gringos**) informal, derogatory (in Latin America) a white English-speaking person.

grip /grip/ ▶ v. (**grips, gripping, gripped**) 1 take and keep a firm hold of something. 2 affect deeply: *she was gripped by a feeling of panic.* 3 (often as adj. **gripping**) hold someone's attention or interest: *a gripping drama.* ▶ n. 1 a firm hold. 2 an understanding of something. 3 a part or attachment by which something is held in the hand. 4 old use a traveling bag. 5 a member of a camera crew responsible for moving and setting up equipment. ■ **grip·per** n.
– PHRASES **come** (or **get**) **to grips with** begin to deal with or understand. **in the grip of** dominated or affected by something undesirable or adverse: *people caught in the grip of a drug problem.* **lose one's grip** become unable to understand or control one's situation.

gripe /grīp/ ▶ v. 1 informal complain or grumble. 2 (as adj. **griping**) (of pain in the stomach or intestines) sudden and acute. ▶ n. 1 informal a minor complaint. 2 pain in the stomach or intestines; colic.

gris·ly /'grizlē/ ▶ adj. (**grislier, grisliest**) causing horror or disgust. ■ **gris·li·ness** n.

> **USAGE**
> **Grisly** and **grizzly** are often confused. **Grisly** means 'causing horror or disgust,' as in a *grisly murder*, whereas a **grizzly** is a kind of large North American bear.

grist /grist/ ▶ n. 1 grain that is ground to make flour. 2 malt crushed to make mash for brewing.
– PHRASES **grist for the mill** useful experience or knowledge.

gris·tle /'grisəl/ ▶ n. tough inedible cartilage in meat. ■ **gris·tly** adj.

grit /grit/ ▶ n. 1 small loose particles of stone or sand. 2 (also **gritstone** /'grit,stōn/) a coarse sandstone. 3 courage and determination. ■ **grit·ter** n.
– PHRASES **grit one's teeth** 1 clench one's teeth. 2 be determined to do or continue to do something difficult or unpleasant.

grits /grits/ ▶ pl.n. a dish of coarsely ground corn kernels boiled with water or milk.

grit·ty /'gritē/ ▶ adj. (**grittier, grittiest**) 1 containing or covered with grit. 2 showing courage and determination. 3 showing something unpleasant as it really is; uncompromising: *a gritty prison drama.* ■ **grit·ti·ly** adv. **grit·ti·ness** n.

griz·zled /'grizəld/ ▶ adj. having gray or gray-streaked hair.

griz·zly /'grizlē/ (also **grizzly bear**) ▶ n. (pl. **grizzlies**) a large variety of brown bear often having white-tipped fur, native to western North America.

> **USAGE**
> On the confusion of **grizzly** and **grisly**, see the note at **GRISLY**.

groan /grōn/ ▶ v. 1 make a deep sound of pain or despair. 2 make a low creaking sound when pressure or weight is applied. 3 (**groan under**) be weighed down by: *a table groaning under an assortment of richly spiced dishes.* ▶ n. a groaning sound. ■ **groan·er** n.

gro·cer /'grōsər/ ▶ n. a person who sells food and small household items.

gro·cer·y /'grōs(ə)rē/ ▶ n. (pl. **groceries**) 1 a grocer's store or business. 2 (**groceries**) items of food sold in a grocer's store or supermarket.

grog /gräg/ ▶ n. 1 liquor (originally rum) mixed with water. 2 informal alcoholic drink.

grog·gy /'grägē/ ▶ adj. (**groggier, groggiest**) feeling dazed, weak, or unsteady. ■ **grog·gi·ly** adv. **grog·gi·ness** n.

groin¹ /groin/ ▶ n. 1 the area between the abdomen and the thigh on either side of the body. 2 the region of the genitals. 3 Architecture a curved edge formed by two intersecting roof arches.

groin² ▶ n. a low wall or barrier built out into the sea from a beach to prevent the beach from shifting or being eroded.

grom·met /'grämit/ ▶ n. a protective eyelet in a hole that a rope or cable passes through.

groom /grōōm, grŏŏm/ ▶ v. 1 brush and clean a horse's or dog's coat. 2 (often as adj. **groomed**) keep oneself neat and tidy in appearance: *a beautifully groomed woman.* 3 prepare or train someone for a particular purpose or activity: *she had been groomed to take over her father's business.* 4 (of a pedophile) prepare a child for a meeting, especially via an Internet chat room. ▶ n. 1 a person employed to take care of horses. 2 a bridegroom.

groove /grōōv/ ▶ n. 1 a long, narrow cut in a hard material. 2 a spiral track cut in a phonograph record, into which the stylus fits. 3 an established routine or habit. 4 informal a rhythmic pattern in popular or jazz music. ▶ v. 1 make a groove or grooves in something. 2 informal dance to or play pop or jazz music. ■ **grooved** adj. **groov·er** n.
– PHRASES **in** (or **into**) **the groove** 1 informal performing consistently well or confidently: *it might take me a couple of races to get back into the groove.* 2 indulging in relaxed and spontaneous enjoyment: *the music swings and gets people in the groove.*

groov·y /'grōōvē/ ▶ adj. (**groovier, grooviest**) informal, dated or humorous fashionable and exciting. ■ **groov·i·ly** adv. **groov·i·ness** n.

grope /grōp/ ▶ v. 1 feel about uncertainly with one's hands. 2 informal fondle someone for sexual pleasure, especially against their will. ▶ n. informal an act of groping someone. ■ **grop·er** n.

gros·beak /'grōs,bēk/ ▶ n. a songbird with a stout conical bill and brightly colored plumage.

gros·grain /'grō,grān/ ▶ n. a heavy ribbed fabric, typically of silk or rayon.

gros point /'grō ,point/ ▶ n. a type of needlepoint embroidery consisting of stitches crossing two or more threads of the canvas in each direction.

gross /grōs/ ▶ adj. 1 unattractively large. 2 very obvious and unacceptable: *gross misconduct.* 3 informal very unpleasant; repulsive. 4 rude or vulgar. 5 (of income, profit, or interest) without deduction of tax or other contributions. Often contrasted with NET². 6 (of weight) including contents or other variable items. ▶ adv. without tax or other contributions having been deducted. ▶ v. 1 produce or earn an amount of money as gross profit or income. 2 (**gross someone out**) informal disgust someone. ▶ n. 1 (pl. same) an amount equal to twelve dozen; 144. 2 (pl. **grosses**) a gross profit or income. ■ **gross·ly** adv. **gross·ness** n.

gross do·mes·tic prod·uct ▶ n. the total value of goods produced and services provided within a country during one year.

gross na·tion·al prod·uct ▶ n. the total value of goods produced and services provided by a country during one year, equal to the gross domestic product plus the net income from foreign investments.

gro·tesque /grō'tesk/ ▶ adj. **1** comically or repulsively ugly or distorted. **2** shocking or offensive: *a grotesque waste of money.* ▶ n. **1** a grotesque figure or image. **2** a style of decorative painting or sculpture in which human and animal forms are interwoven with flowers and foliage. ■ **gro·tesque·ly** adv. **gro·tesque·ness** n.

gro·tes·quer·ie /grō'teskərē/ ▶ n. (pl. **grotesqueries**) the quality of being grotesque, or things that are grotesque.

grot·to /'grätō/ ▶ n. (pl. **grottoes** or **grottos**) a small picturesque cave, especially an artificial one in a park or garden.

grot·ty /'grätē/ ▶ adj. (**grottier, grottiest**) Brit. informal **1** unpleasant and of poor quality. **2** unwell. ■ **grot·ti·ness** n.

grouch /grouCH/ informal ▶ n. **1** a person who is often grumpy. **2** a complaint or grumble. ▶ v. complain; grumble.

grouch·y /'grouCHē/ ▶ adj. (**grouchier, grouchiest**) irritable and bad-tempered; grumpy. ■ **grouch·i·ly** adv.

ground[1] /ground/ ▶ n. **1** the solid surface of the earth. **2** land or soil of a particular kind: *marshy ground.* **3** an area of land or sea with a particular use: *fishing grounds.* **4** (**grounds**) an area of enclosed land surrounding a large house. **5** (**grounds**) reasons for doing or believing something. **6** a prepared surface to which paint or other decoration is applied. **7** (**grounds**) small pieces of solid matter in a liquid, especially coffee, that settle at the bottom. ▶ v. **1** ban or prevent a pilot or aircraft from flying. **2** run a ship aground. **3** (**be grounded in/on**) have as a firm theoretical or practical basis: *an area of research grounded in classical physics.* **4** informal (of a parent) refuse to allow a child to go out socially, as a punishment.
– PHRASES **be thick** (or **thin**) **on the ground** exist in large (or small) numbers or amounts. **break new ground** achieve or create something new. **gain ground** become more popular or accepted. **get off the ground** start happening or functioning successfully. **give** (or **lose**) **ground** retreat or lose one's advantage. **go to ground** (of a fox or other animal) enter its burrow. **hold** (or **stand**) **one's ground** not retreat or lose one's advantage. **on the ground** in a place where real, practical work is done.

ground[2] ▶ past and past participle of **GRIND**.

ground ball (also **grounder**) ▶ n. Baseball a hit ball that travels along the ground.

ground·break·ing /'ground,brāking/ ▶ adj. involving completely new methods or discoveries.

ground con·trol ▶ n. (treated as sing. or pl.) the personnel and equipment that monitor and direct the flight and landing of aircraft or spacecraft.

ground cov·er ▶ n. low-growing, spreading plants that help to prevent weeds or stabilize soil.

ground floor ▶ n. the floor of a building at ground level.

ground glass ▶ n. **1** glass with a smooth ground surface that makes it nontransparent. **2** glass ground into an abrasive powder.

ground·hog /'ground,häg/, -,hôg/ ▶ n. another term for WOODCHUCK.

ground·ing /'grounding/ ▶ n. basic training or instruction in a subject.

ground·less /'ground-lis/ ▶ adj. not based on any good reason.

ground rules ▶ pl.n. basic principles controlling the way in which something is done.

ground·sel /'groun(d)səl/ ▶ n. a plant of the daisy family with small yellow flowers.

grounds·keep·er /'groun(d)z,kēpər/ (Brit. **groundsman**) ▶ n. a person who maintains a sports field, a park, or the grounds of a school or other institution.

ground speed ▶ n. an aircraft's speed relative to the ground.

ground squir·rel ▶ n. a burrowing squirrel of a large group including the chipmunks.

ground·swell /'groun(d),swel/ ▶ n. a buildup of opinion in a large section of the population.

ground·wa·ter /'ground,wôtər, -,wätər/ ▶ n. water held underground in the soil or in rock.

ground·work /'ground,wərk/ ▶ n. preliminary or basic work.

ground ze·ro ▶ n. **1** the point on the earth's surface directly below an exploding nuclear bomb. **2** informal a starting point or base for an activity: *his favorite phase was ground zero, when ideas would fly around.* **3** (**Ground Zero**) the site of the former World Trade Center in New York City, since the terrorist attacks of September 11, 2001.

group /grōōp/ ▶ n. (treated as sing. or pl.) **1** a number of people or things located, gathered, or classed together. **2** a number of musicians who play popular music together. **3** a division of an air force. **4** Chemistry a set of elements occupying a column in the periodic table and having broadly similar properties. **5** Chemistry a combination of atoms having a recognizable identity in a number of compounds. ▶ v. place in or form a group or groups: *sofas and chairs were grouped around a low table.*

group dy·nam·ics ▶ pl.n. (also treated as sing.) Psychology the processes involved when people in a group interact with each other, or the study of these.

group·er /'grōōpər/ ▶ n. a large heavy-bodied fish found in warm seas.

group home ▶ n. a home where a small number of unrelated people requiring support or supervision, such as the mentally ill, can live together.

group·ie /'grōōpē/ ▶ n. informal a person who follows a pop group or celebrity, often in the hope of a sexual relationship with them.

group·ing /'grōōping/ ▶ n. a group of people with a shared interest or aim, especially within a larger organization.

group ther·a·py ▶ n. a form of psychiatric therapy in which patients meet to discuss their problems.

grouse[1] /grous/ ▶ n. (pl. same) a medium-sized game bird with a plump body and feathered legs.

grouse[2] ▶ v. complain or grumble. ▶ n. a grumble or complaint.

grout /grout/ ▶ n. a mortar or paste for filling

crevices, especially the gaps between wall or floor tiles. ▶ v. fill in crevices with grout.

grove /grōv/ ▶ n. a small wood, orchard, or group of trees.

grov·el /'grävəl, 'grə-/ ▶ v. (**grovels, groveling, groveled**) 1 crouch or crawl on the ground. 2 act in a very humble way in an attempt to gain forgiveness or favorable treatment. ■ **grov·el·er** n.

grow /grō/ ▶ v. (past **grew**; past part. **grown**) 1 (of a living thing) undergo natural development by increasing in size and changing physically. 2 (of a plant) germinate and develop. 3 become larger or greater over a period of time; increase. 4 become gradually or increasingly: *we grew braver.* 5 (**grow up**) become an adult. 6 (**grow on**) become gradually more appealing to: *the tune grows on you.* 7 (**grow out of**) become too large to wear a garment. 8 (**grow out of**) become too mature to continue to do something: *she had long since grown out of her disco phase.*

grow·er /'grōər/ ▶ n. 1 someone who grows a particular type of crop: *tomato growers.* 2 a plant that grows in a specified way.

grow·ing pains ▶ pl.n. 1 pains that can occur in the limbs of young children. 2 difficulties experienced in the early stages of an enterprise.

growl /groul/ ▶ v. 1 (especially of a dog) make a low sound of hostility in the throat. 2 say something in a low, angry voice. 3 make a low rumbling sound. ▶ n. a growling sound.

growl·er /'groulər/ ▶ n. 1 a person or thing that growls. 2 a small iceberg.

grown /grōn/ ▶ past participle of **grow**.

grown-up ▶ adj. adult. ▶ n. informal an adult.

growth /grōTH/ ▶ n. 1 the process of growing. 2 something that has grown or is growing. 3 a tumor or other abnormal formation.

growth hor·mone ▶ n. a hormone that stimulates growth in animal or plant cells.

growth in·dus·try ▶ n. an industry that is developing particularly rapidly.

growth ring ▶ n. a concentric layer of wood, shell, or bone developed during a regular period of growth.

growth stock ▶ n. a company stock that tends to increase in capital value rather than yield high income.

grub /grəb/ ▶ n. 1 the larva of an insect, especially a beetle. 2 informal food. ▶ v. (**grubs, grubbing, grubbed**) 1 dig shallowly in soil. 2 (**grub something up**) dig something up. 3 search clumsily and unmethodically: *I began grubbing around in the wastebasket.* ■ **grub·ber** n.

grub·by /'grəbē/ ▶ adj. (**grubbier, grubbiest**) 1 dirty; grimy. 2 involving activities that are dishonest or immoral: *a grubby affair.* ■ **grub·bi·ness** n.

grudge /grəj/ ▶ n. a long-lasting feeling of resentment or dislike: *he held a grudge against his former boss.* ▶ v. 1 be resentfully unwilling to give or allow something: *he grudged the money spent on her.* 2 feel resentful that someone has achieved something: *I don't grudge him his moment of triumph.*

grudg·ing /'grəjiNG/ ▶ adj. given or allowed only reluctantly or resentfully: *a grudging apology.*

gru·el /'grōōəl/ ▶ n. a thin liquid food of oatmeal boiled in milk or water.

gruel·ing /'grōōəliNG/ ▶ adj. extremely tiring and demanding. ■ **gruel·ing·ly** adv.

grue·some /'grōōsəm/ ▶ adj. causing disgust or horror. ■ **grue·some·ly** adv. **grue·some·ness** n.

gruff /grəf/ ▶ adj. 1 (of a person's voice) rough and low in pitch. 2 abrupt or unfriendly in manner. ■ **gruff·ly** adv. **gruff·ness** n.

grum·ble /'grəmbəl/ ▶ v. 1 complain in a bad-tempered but muted way. 2 make a low rumbling sound. ▶ n. a complaint. ■ **grum·bler** n.

grump /grəmp/ ▶ n. informal 1 a grumpy person. 2 a period of sulking.

grump·y /'grəmpē/ ▶ adj. (**grumpier, grumpiest**) bad-tempered and sulky. ■ **grump·i·ly** adv. **grump·i·ness** n.

grunge /grənj/ ▶ n. 1 a style of rock music with a loud, harsh guitar sound. 2 a casual, deliberately untidy style of fashion including loose, layered clothing and ripped jeans. 3 informal grime; dirt. ■ **grun·gy** adj.

grunt /grənt/ ▶ v. 1 (of an animal, especially a pig) make a low, short guttural sound. 2 make a low sound as a result of physical effort or to show agreement. ▶ n. a grunting sound. ■ **grunt·er** n.

Gru·yère /grōō'yer, grē-/ ▶ n. a Swiss cheese with a firm texture.

gryph·on ▶ n. variant spelling of **griffin**.

GSA ▶ abbr. 1 General Services Administration, a federal department that manages supplies, properties, and services for all other departments. 2 Girl Scouts of America.

GSM ▶ abbr. Global System (or Standard) for Mobile.

G-spot ▶ n. an area of the wall of the vagina believed to be very sensitive to sexual stimulation.

GST ▶ abbr. generation-skipping tax.

G-string ▶ n. a skimpy undergarment covering the genitals, consisting of a narrow strip of cloth attached to a waistband.

G-suit ▶ n. a garment lined with pressurized air pouches, worn by fighter pilots and astronauts to enable them to withstand high gravitational forces.

GT ▶ n. a high-performance car.

GTi ▶ n. a GT car with a fuel-injection engine.

gua·ca·mo·le /ˌgwäkə'mōlē/ ▶ n. a dish of mashed avocado mixed with chili peppers, tomatoes, and other ingredients.

guai·a·cum /'gwīəkəm/ ▶ n. an evergreen tree of the Caribbean and tropical America, formerly important for its hard, heavy, oily wood.

gua·nine /'gwänēn/ ▶ n. Biochemistry a purine derivative that is one of the four constituent bases of nucleic acids.

gua·no /'gwänō/ ▶ n. the excrement of seabirds, used as a fertilizer.

gua·ra·na /gwä'ränə/ ▶ n. a substance prepared from the seeds of a Brazilian shrub, believed to have medicinal properties.

Gua·ra·ni /ˌgwärə'nē/ ▶ n. (pl. same) 1 a member of an American Indian people of Paraguay and adjacent regions. 2 the language of the Guarani. 3 (**guarani**) the basic unit of money of Paraguay.

guar·an·tee /ˌgarən'tē/ ▶ n. 1 an assurance that certain conditions will be fulfilled or that certain things will be done. 2 an assurance that a product will remain in working order for a particular length of time. 3 something that makes an outcome certain: *a degree is no* guarantee of a fast-track career. **4** money or a valuable item given or promised as an assurance that something will be done. **5** variant spelling of GUARANTY. ▶v. (**guarantees, guaranteeing, guaranteed**) **1** provide a guarantee for something: *the company guarantees to refund your money.* **2** promise with certainty: *no one can guarantee a profit on stocks and shares.* **3** provide financial security for something.

guar·an·tor /ˌgarən'tôr, 'garəntər/ ▶n. a person or organization that gives or acts as a guarantee.

guar·an·ty /'garən,tē/ (also **guarantee**) ▶n. (pl. **guaranties**) **1** a formal pledge to pay another person's debt or to perform another person's obligation in the case of default. **2** a thing serving as security for a pledge.

guard /gärd/ ▶v. **1** watch over someone or something in order to protect or control them. **2** protect against damage or harm: *the company fiercely guarded its independence.* **3** (**guard against**) take precautions against: *farmers must guard against sudden changes in the market.* ▶n. **1** a person, especially a soldier, assigned to protect a person or to control access to somewhere. **2** (treated as sing. or pl.) a body of soldiers guarding a place or person. **3** a prison employee who guards the inmates. **4** a defensive posture taken up in a fight. **5** a state of looking out for possible dangers or difficulties: *he let his guard slip.* **6** a device worn or fitted on something to prevent injury or damage: *a retractable blade guard.*
– PHRASES **on** (or **off**) **guard** prepared (or unprepared) for a surprise or difficulty. **under guard** being guarded.

guard·ed /'gärdid/ ▶adj. cautious and having possible reservations: *the proposals were given a guarded welcome.* ■ **guard·ed·ly** adv.

guard·house /'gärd,hous/ (also **guardroom** /'gärd,rōōm, -,rŏŏm/) ▶n. a building for soldiers guarding the entrance to a military camp or for the detention of military prisoners.

guard·i·an /'gärdēən/ ▶n. **1** a person who defends or protects something. **2** a person legally responsible for someone unable to manage their own affairs, especially a child whose parents have died. ■ **guard·i·an·ship** n.

guard·i·an an·gel ▶n. a spirit believed to watch over and protect a person or place.

guard of hon·or ▶n. another term for HONOR GUARD.

guard·rail /'gärd,rāl/ ▶n. **1** a rail that prevents people from falling off or being hit by something. **2** a strong fence at the side of a road or traffic lane to prevent vehicles from leaving it.

guards·man /'gärdzmən/ ▶n. (pl. **guardsmen**) a member of the US National Guard.

guar gum /gwär/ ▶n. a gum used in the food and paper industries, obtained from the seeds of an African and Asian bean plant.

Gua·te·ma·lan /ˌgwätə'mälən/ ▶n. a person from Guatemala in Central America. ▶adj. relating to Guatemala.

gua·va /'gwävə/ ▶n. a tropical American fruit with pink juicy flesh.

gu·ber·na·to·ri·al /ˌgōōbərnə'tôrēəl/ ▶adj. relating to a governor, particularly of a US state.

gudg·eon[1] /'gəjən/ ▶n. a small freshwater fish often used as bait by anglers.

gudg·eon[2] ▶n. **1** a pivot or spindle on which

something swings or rotates. **2** the tubular part of a hinge into which the pin fits. **3** a socket at the stern of a boat, into which the rudder is fitted. **4** a pin holding two blocks of stone together.

guel·der rose /'geldər/ ▶n. a shrub with heads of fragrant creamy-white flowers followed by translucent red berries.

Guern·sey /'gərnzē/ ▶n. (pl. **Guernseys**) **1** a breed of dairy cattle from Guernsey in the Channel Islands, noted for producing rich, creamy milk. **2** (**guernsey**) a thick sweater made from oiled wool.

guer·ril·la /gə'rilə/ (also **guerilla**) ▶n. a member of a small independent group fighting against the government or regular forces.

guess /ges/ ▶v. **1** estimate or suppose something without having enough information to be sure of being right. **2** correctly estimate: *she's guessed where we're going.* **3** (**I guess**) informal I suppose: *I guess I'd better tell you.* ▶n. an estimate or conclusion formed by guessing. ■ **guess·er** n.

guess·ti·mate (also **guestimate**) informal ▶n. /'gestəmit/ an estimate based on a mixture of guesswork and calculation. ▶v. /'gestə,māt/ estimate something by using a mixture of guesswork and calculation.

guess·work /'ges,wərk/ ▶n. the process or results of guessing.

guest /gest/ ▶n. **1** a person invited to visit someone's home or to a social occasion. **2** a person invited to take part in a broadcast or entertainment. **3** a person staying at a hotel or guest house. ▶v. appear as a guest in a broadcast or entertainment.
– PHRASES **guest of honor** the most important guest at an occasion.

guest·book /'gest,bŏŏk/ ▶n. **1** a book in which visitors to a public building or private home write their names and addresses, and sometimes remarks. **2** a Web page where visitors to a site may leave their names and comments.

guest house ▶n. **1** a small, separate house on the grounds of a larger house, used for accommodating overnight guests. **2** a private house offering accommodations to paying guests.

guest room ▶n. **1** a room in a private home for accommodating guests. **2** a hotel room.

guest work·er ▶n. a person with temporary permission to work in another country.

guff /gəf/ ▶n. informal ridiculous talk or ideas; nonsense.

guf·faw /gə'fô/ ▶n. a loud, deep laugh. ▶v. give a loud, deep laugh.

guid·ance /'gīdns/ ▶n. **1** advice or information aimed at solving a problem or difficulty. **2** the directing of the movement or position of something.

guide /gīd/ ▶n. **1** a person who advises or shows the way to other people. **2** something that helps a person make a decision or form an opinion: *your resting pulse rate is a rough guide to your physical condition.* **3** a book providing information on a subject. **4** a structure or marking that directs the movement or positioning of something. ▶v. **1** show someone the way to a place. **2** direct the positioning or movement of something. **3** (as adj. **guided**) directed by remote control or internal equipment: *a guided missile.* **4** direct or influence the behavior or development of: *his entire life was guided by his religious beliefs.*

guide·book /'gīd,boŏk/ ▸ n. a book containing information about a place for visitors or tourists.

guide dog ▸ n. a dog that has been trained to lead a blind person.

guide·line /'gīd,līn/ ▸ n. a general rule, principle, or piece of advice.

guild /gild/ ▸ n. 1 a medieval association of craftsmen or merchants. 2 an association of people who do the same work or have the same interests or aims.

guild·er /'gildər/ ▸ n. (pl. same or **guilders**) 1 (until the introduction of the euro in 2002) the basic unit of money of the Netherlands. 2 historical a gold or silver coin formerly used in the Netherlands, Germany, and Austria.

guild·hall /'gild,hôl/ ▸ n. 1 the meeting place of a guild or corporation. 2 Brit. a town hall.

guile /gīl/ ▸ n. clever but dishonest or devious behavior. ■ **guile·ful** adj.

guile·less /'gīllis/ ▸ adj. innocent, honest, and sincere. ■ **guile·less·ly** adv.

guil·le·mot /'gilə,mät/ ▸ n. an auk with a narrow pointed bill, nesting on cliff ledges.

guil·lo·tine /'gilə,tēn, 'gēə-/ ▸ n. 1 a machine with a heavy blade that slides down a frame, used for beheading people. 2 a device with a descending or sliding blade used for cutting paper or sheet metal. ▸ v. execute someone with a guillotine.

guilt /gilt/ ▸ n. 1 the fact of having committed an offense or crime. 2 a feeling of having done something wrong.

guilt·less /'giltlis/ ▸ adj. having no guilt; innocent. ■ **guilt·less·ly** adv.

guilt trip ▸ n. informal a feeling of guilt about something, especially when this feeling is self-indulgent or deliberately provoked by another person.

guilt·y /'giltē/ ▸ adj. (**guiltier, guiltiest**) 1 responsible for a particular wrongdoing, fault, or mistake: *he was found guilty of manslaughter.* 2 having or showing a feeling of guilt: *a guilty conscience.* ■ **guilt·i·ly** adv. **guilt·i·ness** n.

guin·ea /'ginē/ ▸ n. a former British gold coin with a value of 21 shillings (now £1.05).

guin·ea fowl ▸ n. (pl. same) a large African game bird with slate-colored, white-spotted plumage.

guin·ea pig ▸ n. 1 a tailless South American rodent, often kept as a pet. 2 a person or thing used in an experiment.

guise /gīz/ ▸ n. an outward form, appearance, or way of presenting someone or something: *the country has carried on whaling under the guise of scientific research.*

gui·tar /gi'tär/ ▸ n. a stringed musical instrument with six (or occasionally twelve) strings, played by plucking or strumming with the fingers or a plectrum. ■ **gui·tar·ist** n.

Gu·ja·ra·ti /,goŏjə'rätē/ (also **Gujerati**) ▸ n. (pl. **Gujaratis**) 1 a person from the Indian state of Gujarat. 2 the language of the Gujaratis. ▸ adj. relating to the Gujaratis or their language.

Gu·lag /'goŏläg/ ▸ n. (**the Gulag**) a system of harsh labor camps maintained in the Soviet Union 1930–1955.

gulch /gəlCH/ ▸ n. a narrow, steep-sided ravine.

gulf /gəlf/ ▸ n. 1 a deep inlet of the sea almost surrounded by land, with a narrow mouth. 2 a deep ravine. 3 a substantial difference between two people, ideas, or situations: *the gulf between rich and poor.*

Gulf War syn·drome ▸ n. an unexplained medical condition affecting some veterans of the 1991 Gulf War, characterized by fatigue, chronic headaches, and skin and breathing disorders.

gull[1] /gəl/ ▸ n. a long-winged seabird having white plumage with a gray or black back.

gull[2] ▸ v. fool or deceive someone. ▸ n. a person who is fooled or deceived.

Gul·lah /'gələ/ ▸ n. (pl. same or **Gullahs**) 1 a member of a black people living on the coast of South Carolina and nearby islands. 2 the Creole language of the Gullah, having an English base with West African elements.

gul·let /'gəlit/ ▸ n. the passage by which food passes from the mouth to the stomach; the esophagus.

gul·li·ble /'gələbəl/ ▸ adj. easily persuaded to believe something. ■ **gul·li·bil·i·ty** /,gələ'bilitē/ n.

gull-wing ▸ adj. (of a door on a car or aircraft) opening upward.

gul·ly /'gəlē/ (also **gulley**) ▸ n. (pl. **gullies, gulleys**) 1 a ravine or deep channel caused by the action of running water. 2 a gutter or drain.

gulp /gəlp/ ▸ v. 1 swallow drink or food quickly or in large mouthfuls. 2 swallow with difficulty as a result of strong emotion: *she gulped, trying hard to stop crying.* ▸ n. 1 an act of gulping. 2 a large mouthful of liquid drunk quickly.

gum[1] /gəm/ ▸ n. 1 a thick sticky substance produced by some trees and shrubs. 2 glue used for sticking paper or other light materials together. 3 chewing gum or bubble gum. ▸ v. (**gums, gumming, gummed**) 1 cover or fasten something with gum or glue. 2 (**gum something up**) clog up a mechanism and prevent it from working properly.

gum[2] ▸ n. the firm area of flesh around the roots of the teeth in the upper or lower jaw.

gum ar·a·bic ▸ n. a gum produced by some kinds of acacia tree, and used as glue and in incense.

gum·bo /'gəmbō/ ▸ n. (pl. **gumbos**) (in Cajun cooking) a spicy chicken or seafood soup thickened with okra, filé, or roux.

gum·drop /'gəm,dräp/ ▸ n. a firm, jellylike candy.

gum·my[1] /'gəmē/ ▸ adj. (**gummier, gummiest**) sticky.

gum·my[2] ▸ adj. (**gummier, gummiest**) toothless: *a gummy grin.*

gum·my[3] ▸ n. (pl. **gummies**) a candy made to imitate a gummy bear but in another shape, such as a shark or a heart.

gum·my bear ▸ n. a small chewy translucent candy made in the shape of a bear.

gump·tion /'gəmpsHən/ ▸ n. informal initiative and resourcefulness.

gum·shoe /'gəm,sHoŏ/ ▸ n. informal, dated a detective.

gum tree ▸ n. a tree that produces gum, especially a eucalyptus.

gun /gən/ ▸ n. 1 a weapon incorporating a metal tube from which bullets or shells are propelled by explosive force. 2 a device using pressure to send out a substance or object: *a grease gun.* 3 a gunman: *a hired gun.* ▸ v. (**guns, gunning, gunned**) 1 (**gun someone down**) shoot someone with a gun. 2 (**be gunning for**) be actively looking for an opportunity to blame or attack someone. 3 make a vehicle's engine operate at excessive speed.

– PHRASES **go great guns** informal proceed forcefully or successfully. **jump the gun** informal act before the proper or appropriate time. **stick to one's guns** informal refuse to compromise or change. **under the gun** informal under great pressure: *manufacturers are under the gun to offer green alternatives.*

gun·boat /ˈgənˌbōt/ ▶ n. a small ship armed with guns.

gun·boat di·plo·ma·cy ▶ n. foreign policy supported by the use or threat of military force.

gun·cot·ton /ˈgənˌkätn/ ▶ n. an explosive made by steeping cotton or wood pulp in a mixture of nitric and sulfuric acids.

gun dog ▶ n. a dog trained to retrieve game that has been shot.

gun·fight /ˈgənˌfīt/ ▶ n. a fight involving an exchange of gunfire. ■ **gun·fight·er** n.

gun·fire /ˈgənˌfī(ə)r/ ▶ n. the repeated firing of a gun or guns.

gung-ho /ˈgəNG ˈhō/ ▶ adj. too eager to take part in fighting or warfare.

gunk /gəNGk/ ▶ n. informal an unpleasantly sticky or messy substance.

gun·man /ˈgənmən/ ▶ n. (pl. **gunmen**) a man who uses a gun to commit a crime or terrorist act.

gun·met·al /ˈgənˌmetl/ ▶ n. **1** a gray corrosion-resistant form of bronze containing zinc. **2** a dull bluish-gray color.

gun·nel /ˈgənl/ ▶ n. variant spelling of GUNWALE.

gun·ner /ˈgənər/ ▶ n. a person, especially in military service, who operates a gun.

gun·ner·y /ˈgənərē/ ▶ n. the design, manufacture, or firing of heavy guns.

gun·ner·y ser·geant ▶ n. a noncommissioned officer in the US Marine Corps ranking above staff sergeant and below master sergeant.

gun·ny /ˈgənē/ ▶ n. coarse fabric, typically made from jute fiber and used for making sacks.

gun·play /ˈgənˌplā/ ▶ n. the use of guns.

gun·point /ˈgənˌpoint/ ▶ n. (in phrase **at gunpoint**) while threatening someone or being threatened with a gun.

gun·pow·der /ˈgənˌpoudər/ ▶ n. an explosive consisting of a powdered mixture of saltpeter, sulfur, and charcoal.

gun·run·ner /ˈgənˌrənər/ ▶ n. a person involved in the illegal sale or importing of firearms. ■ **gun·run·ning** n.

gun·ship /ˈgənˌSHip/ ▶ n. a heavily armed helicopter.

gun·shot /ˈgənˌSHät/ ▶ n. a shot fired from a gun.

gun-shy ▶ adj. (especially of a hunting dog) alarmed at the sound of a gun.

gun·sight /ˈgənˌsīt/ ▶ n. a device on a gun enabling it to be aimed accurately.

gun·sling·er /ˈgənˌsliNGər/ ▶ n. informal a person who carries a gun.

gun·smith /ˈgənˌsmiTH/ ▶ n. a person who makes and sells small firearms.

gun·wale /ˈgənl/ (also **gunnel**) ▶ n. the upper edge or planking of the side of a boat. – PHRASES **to the gunwales** informal so as to be almost overflowing.

gup·py /ˈgəpē/ ▶ n. (pl. **guppies**) a small freshwater fish native to tropical America, popular in aquariums.

gur·gle /ˈgərgəl/ ▶ v. make a hollow bubbling sound. ▶ n. a gurgling sound.

Gur·kha /ˈgo͝orkə/ ▶ n. **1** a member of any of several Nepalese peoples noted for their ability as soldiers. **2** a member of a regiment in the British army established for Nepalese recruits.

gur·ney /ˈgərnē/ ▶ n. (pl. **gurneys**) a stretcher on wheels for transporting hospital patients.

gu·ru /ˈgo͝oro͞o, go͞oˈro͞o/ ▶ n. **1** a Hindu spiritual teacher. **2** each of the ten first leaders of the Sikh religion. **3** an influential teacher or expert on a particular subject: *a management guru.*

gush /gəSH/ ▶ v. **1** flow in a strong, fast stream. **2** express approval in a very enthusiastic way. ▶ n. a strong, fast stream. ■ **gush·ing** adj.

gush·er /ˈgəSHər/ ▶ n. an oil well from which oil gushes without being pumped.

gush·y /ˈgəSHē/ ▶ adj. (**gushier**, **gushiest**) expressing approval in a very enthusiastic way.

gus·set /ˈgəsit/ ▶ n. **1** a piece of material sewn into a garment to strengthen or enlarge a part of it. **2** a bracket strengthening an angle of a structure.

gust /gəst/ ▶ n. **1** a brief, strong rush of wind. **2** a sudden burst of rain, sound, etc. ▶ v. blow in gusts.

gus·to /ˈgəstō/ ▶ n. enthusiasm and energy.

gust·y /ˈgəstē/ ▶ adj. (**gustier**, **gustiest**) **1** characterized by or blowing in gusts: *a gusty morning.* **2** having or showing gusto: *gusty female vocals.* ■ **gust·i·ly** /ˈgəstəlē/ adv. **gust·i·ness** n.

gut /gət/ ▶ n. **1** the stomach or intestine. **2** (**guts**) internal organs that have been removed or exposed. **3** (**guts**) the internal parts or essence of something. **4** (**guts**) informal courage and determination. **5** fiber from the intestines of animals, used for violin or racket strings. ▶ v. (**guts**, **gutting**, **gutted**) **1** take out the internal organs of a fish or other animal before cooking it. **2** remove or destroy the internal parts of: *the building was gutted by fire.* ▶ adj. informal instinctive: *a gut feeling.* – PHRASES **bust a gut** informal **1** make a strenuous effort: *a problem that nobody's going to bust a gut trying to solve.* **2** laugh uncontrollably.

gut·less /ˈgətləs/ ▶ adj. informal lacking courage or determination. ■ **gut·less·ness** n.

guts·y /ˈgətsē/ ▶ adj. (**gutsier**, **gutsiest**) informal **1** showing courage and determination. **2** (of food or drink) having a strong flavor. ■ **guts·i·ness** n.

gut·ta-per·cha /ˌgətə ˈpərCHə/ ▶ n. a hard, tough substance resembling rubber, obtained from certain Malaysian trees.

gut·ter /ˈgətər/ ▶ n. **1** a shallow trough beneath the edge of a roof, or a channel at the side of a street, for carrying off rainwater. **2** (**the gutter**) a very poor or squalid environment. ▶ v. (of a flame) flicker and burn unsteadily.

gut·ter·snipe /ˈgətərˌsnīp/ ▶ n. a scruffy, badly behaved child who spends most of their time on the street.

gut·tur·al /ˈgətərəl/ ▶ adj. **1** (of a speech sound) produced in the throat and harsh-sounding. **2** (of a way of speaking) characterized by guttural sounds. ■ **gut·tur·al·ly** adv.

gut-wrench·ing /ˈadj. informal extremely upsetting or unpleasant: *gut-wrenching violence.*

guy[1] /gī/ ▶ n. **1** informal a man. **2** (**guys**) informal people of either sex. ▶ v. make fun of someone.

guy[2] ▶ n. a rope or line fixed to the ground to secure a tent.

Guy·a·nese /ˌgīəˈnēz, -ˈnēs/ ▶ n. (pl. same) a person from Guyana, a country on the NE coast of South America. ▶ adj. relating to Guyana.

guz·zle /ˈgəzəl/ ▶ v. eat or drink something greedily. ■ **guz·zler** n.

gybe ▶ v. & n. British spelling of JIBE².

gym /jim/ ▶ n. **1** a gymnasium. **2** a private club with facilities for improving or maintaining physical fitness. **3** gymnastics.

gym bag ▶ n. a bag for holding sports equipment and clothing.

gym·kha·na /jimˈkänə/ ▶ n. an event consisting of a series of competitions on horseback, typically for children.

gym·na·si·um /jimˈnāzēəm/ ▶ n. (pl. **gymnasiums** or **gymnasia** /-zēə/) a hall or building equipped for gymnastics, games, and other physical exercise.

gym·nast /ˈjimnist/ ▶ n. a person trained in gymnastics.

gym·nas·tics /jimˈnastiks/ ▶ pl.n. (also treated as sing.) exercises involving physical agility, flexibility, and coordination. ■ **gym·nas·tic** adj.

gym·no·sperm /ˈjimnəˌspərm/ ▶ n. a plant of a large group that have seeds that are not protected by an ovary or fruit, such as conifers.

gy·ne·col·o·gy /ˌgīnəˈkäləjē, ˌjinə-/ (Brit. **gynaecology**) ▶ n. the branch of medicine concerned with conditions and diseases specific to women and girls, especially those affecting the reproductive system. ■ **gyn·e·co·log·i·cal** /-kəˈläjikəl/ adj. **gyn·e·co·log·i·cal·ly** /-kəˈläjik(ə)lē/ adv. **gy·ne·col·o·gist** n.

gyn·e·co·mas·ti·a /ˌgīnəkōˈmastēə/ ▶ n. Medicine enlargement of a man's breasts, usually due to hormone imbalance or hormone therapy.

gyp /jip/ ▶ v. (**gyps, gypping, gypped**) informal cheat or swindle someone.

gyp·sum /ˈjipsəm/ ▶ n. a soft white or gray mineral used to make plaster of Paris and in the building industry.

gyp·sy /ˈjipsē/ (also **gipsy**) ▶ n. (pl. **gypsies**) **1** a member of a traveling people with dark skin and hair who speak a langauge (Romany) related to Hindi. **2** someone with an unconventional or transient lifestyle. ▶ adj. (of a business or merchant) nonunion or unlicensed: *gypsy trucking firms*. ■ **gyp·sy·ish** adj.

gyp·sy moth ▶ n. a European moth, introduced to the US in the 19th century, whose caterpillar feeds on tree foliage and can be a serious pest.

gy·rate /ˈjīrāt/ ▶ v. **1** move in a circle or spiral. **2** dance by rotating the hips in a suggestive way. ■ **gy·ra·tion** n. **gy·ra·tor** n. **gy·ra·to·ry** adj.

gyre /jīr/ ▶ v. literary whirl. ▶ n. a spiral or vortex.

gyr·fal·con /ˈjərˌfalkən, -ˌfôl-/ ▶ n. a large arctic falcon, with mainly gray or white plumage.

gy·ro¹ /ˈjīrō/ ▶ n. (pl. **gyros**) a gyroscope or gyrocompass.

gy·ro² /ˈyērō, ˈzʜirō/ ▶ n. (pl. **gyros**) a sandwich made with slices of spiced meat cooked on a spit, served with salad in pita bread.

gy·ro·com·pass /ˈjīrōˌkəmpəs/ ▶ n. a compass in which the direction of true north is maintained by a gyroscope rather than magnetism.

gy·ro·scope /ˈjīrəˌskōp/ ▶ n. a device used to provide stability or maintain a fixed direction, consisting of a wheel or disk spinning rapidly about an axis that is itself free to alter in direction. ■ **gy·ro·scop·ic** adj.

H¹ /ācʜ/ (also **h**) ▶ n. (pl. **Hs** or **H's**) the eighth letter of the alphabet.

H² ▶ abbr. **1** (of a pencil lead) hard. **2** height. **3** Physics henry(s). ▶ symbol the chemical element hydrogen.

h ▶ abbr. **1** (in measuring the height of horses) hand(s). **2** hour(s).

ha¹ ▶ abbr. hectare(s).

ha² /hä/ (also **hah**) ▶ exclam. used to express surprise, suspicion, triumph, or some other emotion.

ha·be·as cor·pus /ˈhābēəs ˈkôrpəs/ ▶ n. Law a writ requiring that a person who has been arrested be brought before a judge or into court, to decide whether their detention is lawful.

hab·er·dash·er /ˈhabərˌdasʜər/ ▶ n. a person who sells men's clothing. ■ **hab·er·dash·er·y** n.

hab·it /ˈhabit/ ▶ n. **1** something that a person does regularly. **2** informal an addiction to a drug. **3** a long, loose garment worn by a monk or nun.

hab·it·a·ble /ˈhabitəbəl/ ▶ adj. of a good enough condition to live in. ■ **hab·it·a·bil·i·ty** n.

hab·i·tat /ˈhabiˌtat/ ▶ n. the natural home or environment of an animal or plant.

hab·i·ta·tion /ˌhabiˈtāsʜən/ ▶ n. **1** the fact of living somewhere. **2** formal a house or home.

hab·it-form·ing ▶ adj. (of a drug) addictive.

ha·bit·u·al /həˈbicʜōōəl/ ▶ adj. **1** done regularly and in a way that is difficult to stop: *her father's habitual complaints.* **2** regular; usual: *his habitual dress.* ■ **ha·bit·u·al·ly** adv.

ha·bit·u·ate /həˈbicʜōōˌāt/ ▶ v. make or become used to something. ■ **ha·bit·u·a·tion** n.

ha·bit·u·é /həˈbicʜōōˌā/ ▶ n. a person who regularly goes to a particular place.

há·ček /ˈhaˌchek/ ▶ n. a mark (ˇ) placed over a letter to alter the sound in Slavic and other languages.

ha·ci·en·da /ˌhäsēˈendə/ ▶ n. (in Spanish-speaking countries) a large estate with a house.

hack¹ /hak/ ▶ v. **1** cut something with rough or heavy blows. **2** kick something wildly or roughly. **3** use a computer to gain unauthorized access to data in another system. **4** (**hack it**) informal manage; cope. ▶ n. a rough cut or blow. ■ **hack·a·ble** adj. **hack·er** n.

hack² ▶ n. **1** a writer, especially a journalist, who produces mediocre or unoriginal work. **2** a horse for ordinary riding, or one that can be hired. **3** a ride on a horse. **4** a taxicab. ▶ v. ride a horse. ■ **hack·er·y** n.

hack·ing cough ▶ n. a dry, frequent cough.

hack·le /ˈhakəl/ ▶ n. **1** (**hackles**) hairs along an animal's back that rise when it is angry or alarmed. **2** a long, narrow feather on the neck or lower back of a domestic rooster or other bird.

– PHRASES **make someone's hackles rise** make someone angry or indignant.

hack·ney /ˈhaknē/ ▶ n. (pl. **hackneys**) chiefly historical **1** a horse with a high-stepping trot, used in harness. **2** a horse-drawn vehicle kept for hire.

hack·neyed /ˈhaknēd/ ▶ adj. (of a phrase or idea) unoriginal and used too often.

hack·saw /ˈhakˌsô/ ▶ n. a saw with a narrow blade set in a frame, used for cutting metal.

had /had/ ▶ past and past participle of **HAVE**.

had·dock /ˈhadək/ ▶ n. (pl. same) a silvery-gray edible fish of North Atlantic coastal waters.

Ha·des /ˈhādēz/ ▶ n. **1** Greek Mythology the underworld; the home of the spirits of the dead. **2** informal hell.

Ha·dith /həˈdēтʜ/ ▶ n. (pl. same or **Hadiths**) a collection of Islamic traditions containing sayings of the prophet Muhammad.

had·n't /ˈhadnt/ ▶ contr. had not.

had·ron /ˈhadˌrän/ ▶ n. Physics a subatomic particle of a type that is held in atomic nuclei, such as a baryon or meson.

hadst /hadst/ ▶ old-fashioned second person singular past of **HAVE**.

haf·ni·um /ˈhafnēəm/ ▶ n. a hard silver-gray metal resembling zirconium.

haft /haft/ ▶ n. the handle of a knife, ax, or spear.

hag /hag/ ▶ n. **1** an ugly old woman. **2** a witch.

hag·fish /ˈhagˌfisʜ/ ▶ n. (pl. same or **hagfishes**) a primitive jawless sea fish with a slimy eel-like body and a rasping tongue used for feeding on dead or dying fish.

hag·gard /ˈhagərd/ ▶ adj. looking exhausted and ill.

hag·gis /ˈhagis/ ▶ n. (pl. same) a Scottish dish consisting of seasoned sheep's or calf's offal mixed with suet and oatmeal, boiled in a bag traditionally made from the animal's stomach.

hag·gle /ˈhagəl/ ▶ v. argue or negotiate with someone about the price of something. ■ **hag·gler** n.

hag·i·og·ra·phy /ˌhagēˈägrəfē, ˌhāgē-/ ▶ n. **1** literature concerned with the lives of saints. **2** a biography that idealizes its subject. ■ **hag·i·og·ra·pher** n. **hag·i·o·graph·ic** /ˌhagēəˈgrafik, ˌhāgē-/ adj. **hag·i·o·graph·i·cal** /ˌhagēəˈgrafəkəl, ˌhāgē-/ adj.

hah ▶ exclam. another spelling of **HA²**.

ha-ha /ˈhä ˌhä, ˌhä ˈhä/ ▶ n. a ditch with a wall on its inner side below ground level, forming a boundary to a park or garden without interrupting the view.

hai·ku /ˈhīˌkōō, ˌhīˈkōō/ ▶ n. (pl. same or **haikus**) a Japanese poem of seventeen syllables, in three lines of five, seven, and five.

hail¹ /hāl/ ▶ n. **1** pellets of frozen rain falling in showers. **2** a large number of things hurled

forcefully through the air: *a hail of missiles.*
▶v. (**it hails, it is hailing, it hailed**) hail falls.

hail² ▶v. **1** call out to someone to attract attention. **2** describe enthusiastically: *he was hailed as a literary genius.* **3** (**hail from**) have one's home or origins in: *she hails from the Midwest.* ▶exclam. old use expressing greeting or praise.

Hail Mar·y ▶n. (pl. **Hail Marys**) a prayer to the Virgin Mary used chiefly by Roman Catholics.

hail·stone /ˈhālˌstōn/ ▶n. a pellet of hail.

hail·storm /ˈhālˌstôrm/ ▶n. a storm of heavy hail.

hair /he(ə)r/ ▶n. **1** any of the fine threadlike strands growing from the skin of mammals and other animals, or from the outer layer of a plant. **2** strands of hair collectively, especially on a person's head. ■ **hair·less** adj.
– PHRASES **hair of the dog** informal an alcoholic drink taken to cure a hangover. **a hair's breadth** a very small margin. **let one's hair down** informal enjoy oneself in an uninhibited way. **make someone's hair stand on end** alarm someone. **split hairs** make small and unnecessary distinctions.

hair·ball /ˈhe(ə)rˌbôl/ ▶n. a ball of hair that collects in the stomach of an animal as a result of the animal licking its coat.

hair·band /ˈhe(ə)rˌband/ ▶n. a band worn over the top of the head and behind the ears to keep the hair off the face.

hair·brush /ˈhe(ə)rˌbrəsʜ/ ▶n. a brush for smoothing one's hair.

hair·cut /ˈheərˌkət/ ▶n. **1** the style in which someone's hair is cut. **2** an act of cutting someone's hair.

hair·do /ˈhe(ə)rˌdōō/ ▶n. (pl. **hairdos**) informal the style of a person's hair.

hair·dress·er /ˈhe(ə)rˌdresər/ ▶n. a person who cuts and styles hair. ■ **hair·dress·ing** n.

hair·dry·er /ˈhe(ə)rˌdrīər/ (also **hairdrier**) ▶n. an electrical device for drying the hair with warm air.

hair·line /ˈhe(ə)rˌlīn/ ▶n. the edge of a person's hair. ▶adj. very thin or fine: *a hairline fracture.*

hair·net /ˈhe(ə)rˌnet/ ▶n. a small piece of fine net used to hold the hair in place.

hair·piece /ˈhe(ə)rˌpēs/ ▶n. a patch or bunch of false hair used to add to a person's natural hair.

hair·pin /ˈhe(ə)rˌpin/ ▶n. a U-shaped pin for fastening the hair.

hair·pin turn ▶n. a sharp U-shaped bend in a road.

hair·rais·ing ▶adj. extremely alarming or frightening.

hair shirt ▶n. a shirt made of stiff cloth woven from horsehair, formerly worn as a penance for having done wrong.

hair·split·ting ▶n. the making of small and unnecessary distinctions.

hair·spray /ˈhe(ə)rˌsprā/ ▶n. a solution sprayed on hair to keep it in place.

hair·spring /ˈhe(ə)rˌspriNG/ ▶n. a flat coiled spring that regulates the timekeeping in some clocks and watches.

hair·style /ˈhe(ə)rˌstīl/ ▶n. a way in which someone's hair is cut or arranged. ■ **hair·styl·ing** n. **hair·styl·ist** n.

hair trig·ger ▶n. a firearm trigger set for release at the slightest pressure. ▶adj. (**hair-trigger**)

liable to change suddenly and violently.

hair·y /ˈhe(ə)rē/ ▶adj. (**hairier, hairiest**) **1** covered with or resembling hair. **2** informal dangerous or frightening: *a hairy mountain road.* ■ **hair·i·ness** n.

Hai·tian /ˈhāsʜən/ ▶n. a person from Haiti. ▶adj. relating to Haiti.

haj·i /ˈhajē/ (also **hajji**) ▶n. (pl. **hajis**) a Muslim who has been to Mecca as a pilgrim.

hajj /haj/ (also **haj**) ▶n. the pilgrimage to Mecca that all Muslims are expected to make at least once if they can afford to do so.

hake /hāk/ ▶n. (pl. same or **hakes**) a long-bodied edible fish with strong teeth.

ha·lal /həˈläl, həˈlal/ ▶adj. (of meat) prepared as prescribed by Muslim law.

hal·berd /ˈhalbərd, ˈhôl-/ (also **halbert**) ▶n. historical a combined spear and battle-ax.

hal·cy·on /ˈhalsēən/ ▶adj. (of a past time) idyllically happy and peaceful: *halcyon days.*

hale¹ /hāl/ ▶adj. (of an old person) strong and healthy.

hale² ▶v. old use haul.

half /haf/ ▶n. (pl. **halves** /havz/) **1** either of two equal or matching parts into which something is or can be divided. **2** either of two equal periods into which a sports game or performance is divided. **3** a halfback. ▶predeterminer & pron. an amount equal to a half. ▶adj. forming a half. ▶adv. **1** to the extent of half. **2** partly: *half-cooked.*
– PHRASES **go halves** share the cost of something equally. **half a chance** informal the slightest opportunity. **half past one** (**two**, etc.) thirty minutes after one (two, etc.) o'clock. **not half 1** not nearly. **2** informal not at all. **too —— by half** excessively ——: *he's too charming by half.*

half-and-half ▶adv. & adj. in equal parts. ▶n. a mixture of milk and cream.

half-assed ▶adj. vulgar slang done without much skill or effort.

half·back /ˈhafˌbak/ ▶n. **1** Football an offensive back usually positioned behind the quarterback and to the side of the fullback. **2** a usually defensive player in a ball game such as soccer or field hockey whose position is between the forwards and the fullbacks.

half-baked ▶adj. informal not well planned or considered.

half blood ▶n. **1** offensive another term for HALF-BREED. **2** dated the relationship between people having one parent in common. **3** dated a person related to another in this way.

half-breed ▶n. offensive a person whose parents are of different races, especially an American Indian and a person of white European ancestry.

half-broth·er (or **half-sister**) ▶n. a brother (or sister) with whom one has only one parent in common.

half-caste ▶n. offensive a person whose parents are of different races.

half-cock ▶n. the partly raised position of the cock of a gun. ■ **half-cocked** adj.
– PHRASES **at half-cock** when only partly ready.

half dol·lar ▶n. a US or Canadian coin worth fifty cents.

half-doz·en (also **half a dozen**) ▶n. a group of six.

half-har·dy ▶adj. (of a plant) able to grow

outdoors except in severe frost.

half-heart·ed ▶ adj. without enthusiasm or energy. ■ **half-heart·ed·ly** adv. **half-heart·ed·ness** n.

half hitch ▶ n. a knot formed by making a loop in a rope and passing one end through it.

half hour ▶ n. **1** (also **half an hour**) a period of thirty minutes. **2** a point in time thirty minutes after the beginning of an hour of the clock. ■ **half-hour·ly** adj. & adv.

half-life ▶ n. the time taken for the radioactivity of a substance to fall to half its original value.

half-light ▶ n. dim light, such as that at dusk.

half-mast ▶ n. the position of a flag that is being flown some way below the top of its staff as a mark of respect for a recent death.

half meas·ures ▶ pl.n. actions or policies that are not forceful or decisive enough.

half-moon ▶ n. **1** the moon when only half its surface is visible from the earth. **2** a semicircular or crescent-shaped object.

half nel·son ▶ n. see NELSON.

half note ▶ n. a musical note having the time value of two quarter notes or half a whole note, represented by a ring with a stem.

half step ▶ n. the smallest interval used in classical Western music, equal to a twelfth of an octave or half a tone; a semitone.

half-tim·bered ▶ adj. having walls with a timber frame and a brick or plaster filling.

half-time /'haf,tīm/ ▶ n. a short interval between two halves of a game or contest.

half·tone /'haf,tōn/ ▶ n. a reproduction of a photographic image in which the different shades are produced by dots of varying sizes.

half-track ▶ n. a vehicle with wheels at the front and caterpillar tracks at the rear.

half-truth ▶ n. a statement that is only partly true.

half-vol·ley ▶ n. (in tennis and soccer) a strike or kick of the ball immediately after it bounces.

half·way /'haf'wā/ ▶ adv. & adj. **1** at or to a point equal in distance between two others. **2** (as adv.) to some extent: *halfway decent.*
– PHRASES **meet someone halfway** compromise; concede some points in order to gain others.

half·way house ▶ n. **1** the halfway point in a process. **2** a place where drug addicts, discharged prisoners, or psychiatric patients can stay for a short time to prepare themselves for a return to normal life.

half·wit /'haf,wit/ ▶ n. informal a stupid person. ■ **half-wit·ted** adj.

hal·i·but /'haləbət/ ▶ n. (pl. same) a large edible marine flatfish.

hal·ide /'ha,līd, 'hā-/ ▶ n. a chemical compound formed from a halogen and another element or group: *silver halide.*

hal·i·to·sis /,hali'tōsəs/ ▶ n. unpleasant-smelling breath.

hall /hôl/ ▶ n. **1** an area in a building into which rooms open; a corridor. **2** the room or space just inside the front entrance of a house. **3** a large room for meetings, concerts, etc. **4** (also **residence hall**) a college or university building in which students live. **5** Brit. a large country house. **6** the main living room of a medieval house.

hal·le·lu·jah /,halə'lōōyə/ (also **alleluia** /,alə'lōōyə/) ▶ exclam. God be praised.

hall·mark /'hôl,märk/ ▶ n. **1** an official mark stamped on articles made of gold, silver, or platinum as a guarantee of their purity. **2** a distinctive feature of something: *tiny bubbles are the hallmark of fine champagne.* ▶ v. stamp an object with a hallmark.

hal·lo /hə'lō/ ▶ exclam. variant spelling of HELLO.

Hall of Fame ▶ n. an establishment commemorating the achievements of a group of people, especially athletes.

hal·loo /hə'lōō/ ▶ exclam. **1** used to attract someone's attention. **2** used to encourage dogs during a hunt.

hal·lowed /'halōd/ ▶ adj. **1** made holy: *a hallowed shrine.* **2** greatly honored and respected: *the hallowed ground of Fenway Park.*

Hal·low·een /,halə'wēn, ,hälə-, -ō'ēn/ (also **Hallowe'en**) ▶ n. the night of October 31, the eve of All Saints' Day.

hal·lu·ci·nate /hə'lōōsən,āt/ ▶ v. experience a seemingly real perception of something not actually present. ■ **hal·lu·ci·na·tion** /hə,lōōsən'āshən/ n.

hal·lu·ci·na·to·ry /hə'lōōsənə,tôrē/ ▶ adj. resembling or causing hallucinations: *hallucinatory drugs.*

hal·lu·ci·no·gen /hə'lōōsənə,jən/ ▶ n. a drug causing hallucinations. ■ **hal·lu·ci·no·gen·ic** adj.

hall·way /'hôl,wā/ ▶ n. another term for HALL (sense 2).

ha·lo /'hālō/ ▶ n. (pl. **haloes** or **halos**) **1** (in a painting) a circle of light surrounding the head of a holy person. **2** a circle of light around the sun or moon, refracted through ice crystals in the atmosphere. ▶ v. (**haloes, haloing, haloed**) surround someone or something with a halo, or with something resembling a halo.

hal·o·gen /'haləjən/ ▶ n. any of the nonmetallic chemical elements fluorine, chlorine, bromine, iodine, and astatine. ▶ adj. using a filament surrounded by iodine vapor or that of another halogen: *a halogen bulb.*

hal·on /'hā,län/ ▶ n. any of a number of gaseous compounds of carbon with halogens, used in fire extinguishers.

halt¹ /hôlt/ ▶ v. bring or come to an abrupt stop. ▶ n. a stopping of movement or activity.
– PHRASES **call a halt** stop something: *he decided to call a halt to all further discussions.*

halt² ▶ adj. old use lame or limping.

halt·er /'hôltər/ ▶ n. **1** a rope or strap placed around the head of an animal and used to lead or tether it. **2** old use a noose for hanging a person. **3** a strap by which the bodice of a sleeveless dress or top is fastened or held behind the neck, leaving the shoulders and back bare. **4** a top with such a neck. ▶ v. put a halter on an animal.

hal·ter neck ▶ n. (also **halter top**) a style of woman's top that is fastened behind the neck, leaving the shoulders, upper back, and arms bare.

halt·ing /'hôltiNG/ ▶ adj. slow and hesitant. ■ **halt·ing·ly** adv.

hal·vah /'hälvä/ (also **halva**) ▶ n. a Middle Eastern confection made of sesame flour and honey.

halve /hav, häv/ ▶ v. **1** divide something into two parts of equal size. **2** reduce or be reduced by half: *pre-tax profits halved to $5 million.*

halves /havz, hävz/ ▶ plural of HALF.

hal·yard /'halyərd/ ▶ n. a rope used for raising and lowering a sail, yard, or flag on a ship.

ham[1] /ham/ ▶ n. **1** meat from the upper part of a pig's leg that has been salted and dried or smoked. **2** (**hams**) the back of the thigh or the thighs and buttocks.

ham[2] ▶ n. **1** a bad actor, especially one who overacts. **2** (also **radio ham**) informal an amateur radio operator. ▶ v. (**hams, hamming, hammed**) informal overact.

ham·a·dry·ad /ˌhamə'drīəd/ ▶ n. (in classical mythology) a nymph who lives in a tree and dies when the tree dies.

ham·burg·er /'ham,bərgər/ ▶ n. a small patty of ground beef, fried, broiled, or grilled and typically served on a bun or roll.

ham-fist·ed /'ham ,fistid/ (also **ham-handed**) ▶ adj. informal clumsy; awkward.

ham·let /'hamlit/ ▶ n. a small village or settlement.

ham·mam /ha'mäm, hə'mäm/ ▶ n. a Turkish bath.

ham·mer /'hamər/ ▶ n. **1** a tool consisting of a heavy metal head mounted at the end of a handle, used for breaking things and driving in nails. **2** an auctioneer's mallet, tapped to indicate a sale. **3** a part of a mechanism that hits another, e.g., one exploding the charge in a gun. **4** a heavy metal ball attached to a wire for throwing in an athletic contest. ▶ v. **1** hit something repeatedly. **2** (**hammer away**) work hard and persistently. **3** (**hammer something in/into**) make something stick in someone's mind by constant repetition: *a story that has been hammered into her since childhood.* **4** (**hammer something out**) laboriously work out the details of a plan or agreement. **5** informal utterly defeat a person or team in a contest.
– PHRASES **come** (or **go**) **under the hammer** be sold at an auction. **hammer and tongs** informal with great energy or enthusiasm.

ham·mer and sick·le ▶ n. the symbols of the industrial worker and the peasant used as the emblem of the former Soviet Union and of international communism.

ham·mer drill ▶ n. a power drill that delivers a rapid succession of blows.

ham·mer·head /'hamər,hed/ ▶ n. a shark with flattened extensions on either side of the head.

ham·mer·lock /'hamər,läk/ ▶ n. an armlock in which a person's arm is bent up behind their back.

ham·mer·toe /'hamər,tō/ ▶ n. a toe that is bent permanently downward, typically as a result of pressure from footwear.

ham·mock /'hamək/ ▶ n. a wide strip of canvas or rope mesh suspended at both ends, used as a bed.

Ham·mond or·gan /'hamənd/ ▶ n. trademark a type of electronic organ.

ham·my /'hamē/ ▶ adj. (**hammier, hammiest**) informal (of acting) exaggerated or overly theatrical.

ham·per[1] /'hampər/ ▶ n. **1** a large basket with a lid, used for laundry. **2** a basket with a handle and a hinged lid, used for food, cutlery, etc., on a picnic.

hamper[2] ▶ v. slow down or prevent the movement or progress of: *their work is hampered by lack of funds.*

ham·ster /'hamstər/ ▶ n. a burrowing rodent with a short tail and large cheek pouches, native to Europe and North Asia, often kept as a pet.

ham·string /'ham,striNG/ ▶ n. **1** any of five tendons at the back of a person's knee. **2** the large tendon at the back of the hind leg of a horse or other four-legged animal. ▶ v. (past and past part. **hamstrung**) **1** cripple a person or animal by cutting their hamstrings. **2** prevent someone or something from taking action or making progress.

Han /han/ ▶ n. **1** the Chinese dynasty that ruled almost continuously from 206 BC until AD 220. **2** the dominant ethnic group in China.

hand /hand/ ▶ n. **1** the end part of the arm beyond the wrist. **2** a pointer on a clock or watch indicating the passing of units of time. **3** (**hands**) a person's power or control: *taking the law into their own hands.* **4** an active role: *he had a big hand in organizing the event.* **5** help in doing something: *do you need a hand?* **6** a person who does physical work, especially in a factory, on a farm, or on board a ship. **7** informal a round of applause. **8** the set of cards dealt to a player in a card game. **9** a person's handwriting or workmanship. **10** a unit of measurement of a horse's height, equal to 4 inches (10.16 cm). **11** dated a promise of marriage made by or on behalf of a woman. ▶ v. **1** give something to someone. **2** (**hand something down**) pass something to a successor or descendant. **3** (**hand something in**) give something to a person in authority for their attention. **4** (**hand something out**) distribute something among a group. ▶ adj. **1** operated by or held in the hand: *hand luggage.* **2** done or made manually: *hand signals.*
– PHRASES **at hand** easy to reach; near. **by hand** by a person and not a machine. **get** (or **keep**) **one's hand in** become (or remain) practiced in something. **hand in glove** in close association. **hand in hand** closely associated or connected. (**from**) **hand to mouth** satisfying only one's immediate needs; with no money in reserve. **hands down** easily and decisively. **in hand 1** in progress or receiving attention. **2** ready for use if required. **in safe hands** protected by someone trustworthy. **make** (or **lose** or **spend**) **money hand over fist** informal make (or lose or spend) money very rapidly. **on hand** present and available. **on someone's hands 1** as someone's responsibility. **2** at someone's disposal: *he has time on his hands.* **on the one** (or **the other**) **hand** used to present factors for (and against) something. **out of hand 1** not under control. **2** without taking time to think: *the proposal was rejected out of hand.* **to hand** within easy reach. **turn one's hand to** do something that is different from one's usual occupation.

hand·bag /'han(d),bag/ ▶ n. a woman's purse.

hand·ball /'han(d),bôl/ ▶ n. **1** a game similar to squash, in which the ball is hit with the hand in a walled court. **2** Soccer unlawful touching of the ball with the hand or arm.

hand·bell /'han(d),bel/ ▶ n. a small bell, especially one of a set tuned to a range of notes and played by a group of people.

hand·bill /'han(d),bil/ ▶ n. a small printed advertisement or other notice distributed by hand.

hand·book /'han(d),bo͝ok/ ▶ n. a book giving

basic information or instructions.

hand·brake /'han(d),brāk/ ▶ n. **1** the emergency or parking brake on a motor vehicle. **2** a brake operated by hand, as on a bicycle.

hand·cart /'han(d),kärt/ ▶ n. a small cart pushed or drawn by hand.

hand·clap /'han(d),klap/ ▶ n. a clapping of the hands.

hand·craft·ed /'han(d),kraftid/ ▶ adj. made skillfully by hand.

hand·cuff /'han(d),kəf/ ▶ n. (**handcuffs**) a pair of lockable linked metal rings for securing a prisoner's wrists. ▶ v. put handcuffs on someone.

hand·ful /'han(d),fŏŏl/ ▶ n. (pl. **handfuls**) **1** a quantity that fills the hand. **2** a small number or amount. **3** informal a person who is difficult to deal with or control.

hand gre·nade ▶ n. a hand-thrown grenade.

hand·grip /'han(d),grip/ ▶ n. **1** a handle for holding onto something. **2** a grasp with the hand, especially considered in terms of its strength, as in a handshake.

hand·gun /'han(d),gən/ ▶ n. a gun designed for use with one hand.

hand·held /'hand,held/ ▶ adj. designed to be held in the hand: *a handheld metal detector*.

hand·hold /'hand,hōld/ ▶ n. something for a hand to grip on.

hand·i·cap /'handē,kap/ ▶ n. **1** a condition that restricts a person's ability to function physically, mentally, or socially. **2** something that makes progress or success difficult: *not being able to drive was something of a handicap*. **3** a disadvantage placed on a superior competitor in a sport in order to make the chances more equal, such as the extra weight given to a racehorse on the basis of its previous performance. **4** the number of strokes by which a golfer normally exceeds par for a course. ▶ v. (**handicaps, handicapping, handicapped**) make it difficult for someone or something to progress or succeed: *the industry was handicapped by an acute manpower shortage*.

hand·i·capped /'handē,kapt/ ▶ adj. (of a person) having a condition that restricts their ability to function physically, mentally, or socially.

USAGE

Until quite recently the word **handicapped** was the standard term used to refer to people with physical and mental disabilities. For a brief period in the second half of the 20th century, it looked as if **handicapped** would be replaced by **disabled**, but both words are now acceptable and interchangeable in standard American English, and neither word has been overtaken by newer coinages such as **differently abled** or **physically** (or **mentally**) **challenged**.

---

hand·i·craft /'handē,kraft/ ▶ n. **1** an activity involving the making of decorative objects by hand. **2** decorative objects made by hand.

hand·i·work /'handē,wərk/ ▶ n. **1** (**one's handiwork**) something that one has made or done. **2** the making of things by hand.

hand·ker·chief /'haNGkərchif, -CHēf/ ▶ n. (pl. **handkerchiefs** or **handkerchieves** /'haNGkərchivz, -CHēvz/) a square of cotton or other material for wiping one's nose.

han·dle /'handl/ ▶ v. **1** feel or manipulate something with the hands. **2** deal or cope with a situation, person, or problem: *he handled the interview confidently*. **3** control or manage something commercially. **4** (**handle oneself**) behave oneself in a particular way. **5** (of a vehicle) respond in a particular way when being driven: *the new model does not handle well*. ▶ n. **1** the part by which a thing is held, carried, or controlled. **2** a way of understanding, controlling, or approaching a person or situation: *they seem unable to get a handle on the problem*. **3** informal the name of a person or place. ■ **han·dled** adj. **hand·ling** n.

han·dle·bar /'handl,bär/ (also **handlebars**) ▶ n. the steering bar of a bicycle or motorcycle.

han·dle·bar mus·tache ▶ n. a wide, thick mustache with the ends curving slightly upward.

han·dler /'handlər/ ▶ n. **1** a person who handles a particular type of article: *baggage handlers*. **2** a person who trains or has charge of an animal. **3** a person who trains or manages another person.

hand·made /'han(d)'mād/ ▶ adj. made by hand rather than machine.

hand·maid·en /'han(d),mādn/ ▶ n. **1** old use a female servant. **2** a subservient partner or element: *shipping is the handmaiden of commerce and industry*.

hand-me-down ▶ n. a garment or other item that has been passed on from another person.

hand·off /'hand,ôf, -,äf/ ▶ n. **1** a transfer of power, control, or responsibility. **2** Football an exchange made by handing the ball to a teammate.

hand·out /'hand,out/ ▶ n. **1** an amount of money or other aid given to a person or organization. **2** a piece of printed information provided free of charge, especially to accompany a lecture.

hand·o·ver /'hand,ōvər/ ▶ n. an act of handing something over.

hand·pick ▶ v. select someone or something carefully.

hand·print /'hand,print/ ▶ n. the mark left by the impression of a hand.

hand·rail /'han(d),rāl/ ▶ n. a rail fixed to posts or a wall for people to hold onto for support.

hand·saw /'han(d),sô/ ▶ n. a wood saw worked by one hand.

hand·set /'han(d),set/ ▶ n. **1** the part of a telephone that is held up to speak into and listen to. **2** a hand-held control device for a piece of electronic equipment.

hands-free ▶ adj. (especially of a telephone) designed to be operated without using the hands.

hand·shake /'han(d),SHāk/ ▶ n. an act of shaking a person's hand. ■ **hand·shak·ing** n.

hands-off ▶ adj. not involving or requiring direct control or intervention: *her hands-off management style*.

hand·some /'hansəm/ ▶ adj. (**handsomer, handsomest**) **1** (of a man) good-looking. **2** (of a woman) striking and strong-featured rather than conventionally pretty. **3** (of a thing) well made and of obvious quality. **4** (of an amount) large: *a handsome profit*. ■ **hand·some·ly** adv. **hand·some·ness** n.

hands-on ▶ adj. involving or offering active participation.

hand·spring /'hand,spriNG/ ▶ n. a jump through the air onto one's hands followed by another onto one's feet.

hand·stand /'hand,stand/ ▸ n. an act of balancing upside down on one's hands.

hand-to-hand ▸ adj. (of fighting) at close quarters and involving physical contact between the opponents.

hand·work /'hand,wərk/ ▸ n. work done with the hands: *the transition from handwork to machine production.* ■ **hand·worked** adj.

hand·wo·ven /'hand'wōvən/ ▸ adj. made on a hand-operated loom.

hand·writ·ing /'han(d),rītiNG/ ▸ n. 1 writing with a pen or pencil rather than by typing or printing. 2 a person's particular style of writing. – PHRASES **the handwriting** (or **writing**) **is on the wall** there are clear signs that something unpleasant or unwelcome is going to happen.

hand·writ·ten /'han(d),ritn/ ▸ adj. written with a pen or pencil.

hand·y /'handē/ ▸ adj. (**handier, handiest**) 1 convenient to handle or use; useful. 2 in a convenient place or position. 3 skillful with one's hands. ■ **hand·i·ly** adv. **hand·i·ness** n.

hand·y·man /'handē,man/ ▸ n. (pl. **handymen**) a person employed to do renovations or domestic repairs.

hang /haNG/ ▸ v. (past and past part. **hung** except in sense 2) 1 suspend or be suspended from above with the lower part not attached. 2 (past and past part. **hanged**) kill someone by suspending them from a rope tied around the neck (used as a form of capital punishment). 3 attach something so as to allow free movement about the point of attachment (such as a hinge): *hanging a door.* 4 (of fabric or a garment) fall or drape in a particular way. 5 attach meat or game to a hook and leave it until it is ready to cook. 6 paste wallpaper to a wall. 7 remain static in the air: *a cloud of smoke hung over the city.* 8 (of something bad or unwelcome) be oppressively present or imminent: *a sense of dread hung over him.* ▸ n. the way in which something hangs or is hung. – PHRASES **get the hang of** informal learn how to operate or do something. **hang around 1** wait around; loiter. 2 (**hang around with**) associate with someone. **hang back** remain behind. **hang fire** delay taking action. **hang on 1** hold tightly. 2 informal wait for a short time. 3 be dependent on: *so much hangs on exam results.* 4 listen closely to something. **hang out** informal spend time relaxing or enjoying oneself. **hang tough** informal be or remain inflexible or firmly resolved. **hang up** end a telephone conversation by cutting the connection.

> **USAGE**
> **Hang** has two past tense and past participle forms: **hanged** and **hung**. Use **hung** in general situations (*they hung out the washing*), but use **hanged** to refer to execution of someone by hanging (*the prisoner was hanged*).

hang·ar /'haNGər/ ▸ n. a large building in which aircraft are kept.

hang·dog /'haNG,dôg, -,däg/ ▸ adj. having a dejected or guilty appearance; shamefaced.

hang·er /'haNGər/ ▸ n. 1 a person who hangs something. 2 (also **coat hanger**) a curved frame of wood, plastic, or metal with a hook at the top, for hanging clothes from a rail.

hang·er-on ▸ n. (pl. **hangers-on**) someone who tries to associate with a rich or powerful person

in order to benefit from the relationship.

hang glid·er ▸ n. an unpowered flying device for a single person, consisting of a frame with fabric stretched over it from which the operator is suspended. ■ **hang-glide** v. **hang-glid·ing** n.

hang·ing /'haNGiNG/ ▸ n. 1 the practice of hanging condemned criminals as a form of capital punishment. 2 a decorative piece of fabric hung on the wall of a room or around a bed. ▸ adj. suspended in the air.

hang·man /'haNGmən, -,man/ ▸ n. (pl. **hangmen**) an executioner who hangs condemned people.

hang·nail /'haNG,nāl/ ▸ n. a piece of torn skin at the root of a fingernail.

hang·out /'haNG,out/ ▸ n. informal a place where someone spends a great deal of time.

hang·o·ver /'haNG,ōvər/ ▸ n. 1 a severe headache or other aftereffects caused by drinking too much alcohol. 2 a custom, feeling, etc., that has survived from the past: *this feeling of insecurity was a hangover from her schooldays.*

hang-up ▸ n. informal an emotional problem or inhibition.

hank /haNGk/ ▸ n. a coil or length of wool, hair, or other material.

hank·er /'haNGkər/ ▸ v. (**hanker after/for/to do**) feel a desire for or to do: *she hankered after a traditional white wedding.*

han·ky /'haNGkē/ (also **hankie**) ▸ n. (pl. **hankies**) informal a handkerchief.

han·ky-pan·ky /'paNGkē/ ▸ n. informal behavior considered to be slightly improper.

Han·o·ve·ri·an /,hanə've(ə)rēən/ ▸ adj. relating to the royal house of Hanover, who ruled as monarchs in Britain from 1714 to 1901.

Han·sard /'hansərd/ ▸ n. the official word-for-word record of debates in the British, Canadian, Australian, New Zealand, or South African parliament.

Han·sen's dis·ease /'hansənz/ ▸ n. another term for LEPROSY.

han·som /'hansəm/ (also **hansom cab**) ▸ n. historical a two-wheeled horse-drawn cab for two passengers, with the driver seated behind.

han·ta·vi·rus /'hantə,vīrəs/ ▸ n. one of several viruses, carried by rodents, that can cause disease in all humans.

Ha·nuk·kah /'KHänəkə, 'hänəkə/ (also **Chanukkah**) ▸ n. an eight-day Jewish festival of lights held in December, commemorating the rededication of the Jewish Temple in Jerusalem.

hap·haz·ard /,hap'hazərd/ ▸ adj. having no particular order or plan; disorganized. ■ **hap·haz·ard·ly** adv.

hap·less /'haplis/ ▸ adj. unlucky; unfortunate. ■ **hap·less·ly** adv.

hap·loid /'hap,loid/ ▸ adj. (of a cell or nucleus) containing a single set of unpaired chromosomes. Compare with DIPLOID.

hap·pen /'hapən/ ▸ v. 1 take place; occur. 2 come about by chance: *it just so happened that she turned up that afternoon.* 3 (**happen on**) come across something by chance: *I happened on a street with a few restaurants.* 4 chance to do something or come about. 5 (**happen to**) be experienced by: *the same thing happened to me.* 6 (**happen to**) become of: *I don't care what happens to the money.* – PHRASES **as it happens** actually; as a matter of fact.

hap·pen·ing /'hap(ə)niNG/ ▶ n. an event or occurrence. ▶ adj. informal fashionable.

hap·pen·stance /'hapən,stans/ ▶ n. coincidence.

hap·py /'hapē/ ▶ adj. (**happier, happiest**) 1 feeling or showing pleasure or contentment. 2 willing to do something. 3 fortunate and convenient: *a happy coincidence.* 4 (in combination) informal inclined to use a particular thing too readily or at random: *trigger-happy.* ■ **hap·pi·ly** adv. **hap·pi·ness** n.

hap·py-go-luck·y ▶ adj. cheerfully unconcerned about the future.

hap·py hour ▶ n. a period of the day when drinks are sold at reduced prices in a bar or restaurant.

hap·py hunt·ing ground ▶ n. a place where success or enjoyment can be found.

hap·py me·di·um ▶ n. a satisfactory compromise.

hap·tic /'haptik/ ▶ adj. technical relating to the sense of touch.

ha·ra·ki·ri /,härə 'ki(ə)rē, ,harə-, ,harē 'karē/ ▶ n. a method of ritual suicide involving cutting open the stomach with a sword, formerly practiced in Japan by samurai.

ha·ram /'he(ə)rəm, 'harəm/ ▶ adj. forbidden by Islamic law.

ha·rangue /hə'raNG/ ▶ v. address a person or group in a loud and aggressive or critical way. ▶ n. a forceful and aggressive or critical speech.

ha·rass /hə'ras, 'harəs/ ▶ v. 1 torment someone by putting constant pressure on them or by saying or doing unpleasant things to them: *he had been harassed by the police.* 2 (as adj. **harassed**) feeling tired or tense as a result of too many demands made on one: *harassed parents.* 3 make repeated small-scale attacks on an enemy in order to wear down their resistance. ■ **ha·rass·er** n. **ha·rass·ment** n.

har·bin·ger /'härbənjər/ ▶ n. a person or thing that announces or signals the approach of something: *this plant is the first harbinger of spring.*

har·bor /'härbər/ (Brit. **harbour**) ▶ n. a place on the coast where ships may moor in shelter. ▶ v. 1 keep a thought or feeling secretly in one's mind. 2 give a refuge or shelter to someone or something. 3 carry the germs of a disease.

hard /härd/ ▶ adj. 1 solid, firm, and rigid; not easily broken, bent, or pierced. 2 requiring or showing a great deal of endurance or effort; difficult. 3 (of a person) not showing any signs of weakness; tough. 4 done with a great deal of force or strength: *a hard whack.* 5 harsh or unpleasant to the senses: *the hard light of morning.* 6 (of information or a subject of study) concerned with precise facts that can be proved. 7 (of drink) strongly alcoholic. 8 (of a drug) very addictive. 9 (of pornography) very obscene and explicit. 10 referring to an extreme faction within a political party: *the hard left.* 11 (of water) containing mineral salts. ▶ adv. 1 with a great deal of effort or force. 2 so as to be solid or firm. 3 to the fullest extent possible. ■ **hard·ish** adj. **hard·ness** n.

– PHRASES **be hard put** find it very difficult. **hard and fast** (of a rule or distinction) fixed and definitive. **hard at it** informal busily working. **hard feelings** feelings of resentment. **hard luck** used to express sympathy or commiserations. **hard of hearing** not able to hear well. **hard on** following

soon after. **hard up** informal short of money. **the hard way** through suffering or learning from the unpleasant consequences of mistakes: *his reputation was earned the hard way.* **play hard to get** informal deliberately adopt an uninterested attitude.

hard·back /'härd,bak/ ▶ n. a book bound in stiff covers.

hard·ball /'härd,bôl/ ▶ n. 1 baseball, especially as contrasted with softball. 2 informal uncompromising and ruthless methods or dealings, especially in politics: *the leadership played hardball to win the vote.*

hard-bit·ten ▶ adj. tough and cynical.

hard·board /'härd,bôrd/ ▶ n. stiff board made of compressed and treated wood pulp.

hard-boiled ▶ adj. 1 (of an egg) boiled until solid. 2 (of a person) tough and cynical.

hard cash ▶ n. coins and bills as opposed to other forms of payment.

hard cop·y ▶ n. a printed version on paper of data held in a computer.

hard core ▶ n. 1 the most committed or uncompromising members of a group. 2 very explicit pornography. 3 (usu. **hardcore**) a type of rock or dance music that is experimental, loud, and played aggressively.

hard·cov·er /'härd,kəvər/ ▶ n. another term for HARDBACK.

hard disk (also **hard drive**) ▶ n. Computing a rigid nonremovable magnetic disk with a large data storage capacity.

hard drive ▶ n. Computing a self-contained storage device containing a read-write mechanism plus one or more hard disks, inside a sealed unit.

hard·en /'härdn/ ▶ v. 1 make or become hard or harder. 2 (as adj. **hardened**) fixed in a bad habit or way of life: *hardened criminals.* ■ **hard·en·er** n.

hard hat ▶ n. 1 a rigid protective helmet, as worn at construction sites. 2 informal a worker who wears a hard hat.

hard·head·ed /'härd,hedid/ ▶ adj. tough and realistic.

hard-heart·ed ▶ adj. unsympathetic or uncaring.

hard-hit·ting ▶ adj. uncompromisingly direct and honest.

har·di·hood /'härdē,hood/ ▶ n. dated boldness; daring.

hard la·bor ▶ n. a type of punishment that takes the form of heavy physical work.

hard line ▶ n. a strict and uncompromising policy or attitude: *he takes a hard line on most moral issues.* ▶ adj. uncompromising; strict. ■ **hard·lin·er** n.

hard·ly /'härdlē/ ▶ adv. 1 almost no; almost not; almost none: *there was hardly any wind.* 2 no or not. 3 only with great difficulty. 4 only a very short time before: *the party had hardly started when the police arrived.*

hard-nosed ▶ adj. informal realistic and tough-minded.

hard-on ▶ n. vulgar slang an erection of the penis.

hard pal·ate ▶ n. the bony front part of the roof of the mouth.

hard·pan /'härd,pan/ ▶ n. a hardened layer, occurring in or below the soil, that resists penetration by water and plant roots.

hard-pressed ▶ adj. in difficulties or under

pressure: *she'd be hard-pressed to find anyone else who'd put up with her.*

hard rock ▶ n. very loud rock music with a heavy beat.

hard·scape /'härd,skāp/ ▶ n. the nonliving or constructed fixtures of a planned outdoor area.

hard·scrab·ble /'härd,skrabəl/ ▶ adj. **1** returning little in exchange for great effort: *her uncle's hardscrabble peanut farm.* **2** characterized by chronic poverty and hardship: *a hardscrabble coal town in the mountains.*

hard sell ▶ n. a policy or technique of aggressive selling or advertising.

hard·ship /'härd,SHip/ ▶ n. severe suffering or difficulty.

hard·tack /'härd,tak/ ▶ n. old use hard dry bread or biscuit, especially as rations for sailors or soldiers.

hard·top /'härd,täp/ ▶ n. a motor vehicle with a rigid roof that in some cases is detachable.

hard·ware /'härd,we(ə)r/ ▶ n. **1** tools and other items used in the home and in activities such as gardening. **2** the machines, wiring, and other physical components of a computer. **3** heavy military equipment such as tanks and missiles.

hard·wear·ing ▶ adj. able to stand much wear.

hard-wired ▶ adj. Electronics involving permanently connected circuits rather than software.

hard·wood /'härd,wŏŏd/ ▶ n. the wood from broad-leaved trees as opposed to that of conifers.

har·dy /'härdē/ ▶ adj. (**hardier**, **hardiest**) **1** capable of enduring difficult conditions; robust. **2** (of a plant) able to survive outside during winter. ■ **har·di·ness** n.

hare /he(ə)r/ ▶ n. a fast-running, long-eared mammal resembling a large rabbit, with very long hind legs.

hare·bell /'he(ə)r,bel/ ▶ n. a plant with pale blue bell-shaped flowers.

hare·brained /'he(ə)r,brānd/ ▶ adj. foolish and unlikely to succeed: *steer clear of harebrained schemes.*

Ha·re Krish·na /,härē 'krisHnə, ,harē/ ▶ n. a member of a religious sect based on the worship of the Hindu god Krishna.

hare·lip /'he(ə)r,lip/ ▶ n. offensive term for CLEFT LIP.

> **USAGE**
> The word **harelip** can cause offense and should be avoided; use **cleft lip** instead.

har·em /'he(ə)rəm, 'har-/ ▶ n. **1** the separate part of a Muslim household reserved for women. **2** the wives and concubines of a polygamous Muslim man.

har·i·cot /'hari,kō/ ▶ n. a round white variety of French bean.

ha·ris·sa /hə'rēsə/ ▶ n. a hot sauce or paste used in North African cuisine, made from chili peppers, paprika, and olive oil.

hark /härk/ ▶ v. **1** literary listen. **2** (**hark back to**) recall or remind one of something in the past.

hark·en ▶ v. variant spelling of HEARKEN.

har·le·quin /'härlik(w)ən/ ▶ n. (**Harlequin**) a character in traditional pantomime, wearing a mask and a diamond-patterned costume. ▶ adj. in varied colors; variegated.

har·lot /'härlət/ ▶ n. old use a prostitute or promiscuous woman. ■ **har·lot·ry** n.

harm /härm/ ▶ n. **1** physical injury to a person. **2** damage done to something. **3** an adverse effect: *there was no harm in looking, was there?* ▶ v. **1** physically injure someone. **2** damage or have an adverse effect on: *when we use products that waste energy, we harm the environment.*

harm·ful /'härmfəl/ ▶ adj. causing or likely to cause harm. ■ **harm·ful·ly** adv. **harm·ful·ness** n.

harm·less /'härmlis/ ▶ adj. not able or likely to cause harm. ■ **harm·less·ly** adv. **harm·less·ness** n.

har·mon·ic /här'mänik/ ▶ adj. **1** relating to or characterized by harmony. **2** Music relating to a harmonic. ▶ n. Music a tone produced by vibration of a string in any of certain fractions (half, third, etc.) of its length. ■ **har·mon·i·cal·ly** adv.

har·mon·i·ca /här'mänikə/ ▶ n. a small rectangular wind instrument with a row of metal reeds that produce different notes.

har·mo·ni·ous /här'mōnēəs/ ▶ adj. **1** tuneful; not discordant. **2** arranged in a pleasing way so that each part goes well with the others: *dishes providing a harmonious blend of color, flavor, and aroma.* **3** free from disagreement or conflict. ■ **har·mo·ni·ous·ly** adv. **har·mo·ni·ous·ness** n.

har·mo·ni·um /här'mōnēəm/ ▶ n. a keyboard instrument in which the notes are produced by air driven through metal reeds by foot-operated bellows.

har·mo·nize /'härmə,nīz/ ▶ v. **1** add notes to a melody to produce harmony. **2** sing or play in harmony. **3** make or be harmonious or in agreement: *unsweetened coconut harmonizes well with many Indian dishes.* **4** make things consistent with each other. ■ **har·mo·ni·za·tion** /,härmənə'zāsHən/ n. **har·mo·niz·er** n.

har·mo·ny /'härmənē/ ▶ n. (pl. **harmonies**) **1** the combination of musical notes sounded at the same time to produce a pleasing effect. **2** a pleasing quality when things are arranged together well. **3** a state of agreement and peaceful existence: *images of racial harmony.*

har·ness /'härnis/ ▶ n. **1** a set of straps and fittings by which a horse or other animal is fastened to a cart, plow, etc., and is controlled by its driver. **2** an arrangement of straps for fastening something such as a parachute to a person's body or for restraining a young child. ▶ v. **1** fit a horse or other animal with a harness. **2** control and use so as to achieve or produce something: *we will harness new technology to keep the police ahead of the criminals.* – PHRASES **in harness** in the routine of daily work.

harp /härp/ ▶ n. a musical instrument consisting of a frame supporting a series of parallel strings of different lengths, played by plucking with the fingers. ▶ v. (**harp on**) keep talking or writing about something in a boring way. ■ **harp·ist** n.

har·poon /,här'pōōn/ ▶ n. a barbed spearlike missile attached to a long rope and thrown by hand or fired from a gun, used for catching whales and other large sea creatures. ▶ v. spear something with a harpoon. ■ **har·poon·er** n.

harp seal ▶ n. a slender North Atlantic seal that typically has a dark harp-shaped mark on its gray back.

harp·si·chord /'härpsi,kôrd/ ▶ n. a keyboard instrument similar in shape to a grand piano, with horizontal strings plucked by points of quill, leather, or plastic operated by pressing the keys. ■ **harp·si·chord·ist** n.

har·py /'härpē/ ▶ n. (pl. **harpies**) **1** Greek & Roman Mythology a monster with a woman's head and body and a bird's wings and claws. **2** an unpleasant woman.

har·que·bus /'(h)ärk(w)əbəs/ (also **arquebus**) ▶ n. a former type of portable gun supported on a tripod or a forked rest.

har·ri·dan /'haridn/ ▶ n. a bossy or aggressive old woman.

har·ri·er[1] /'harēər/ ▶ n. a long-winged, slender bird of prey.

har·ri·er[2] ▶ n. a hound of a breed used for hunting hares.

har·row /'harō/ ▶ n. an implement consisting of a heavy frame set with teeth that is dragged over plowed land to break up or spread the soil. ▶ v. **1** use a harrow to break up soil. **2** (as adj. **harrowing**) very distressing.

har·rumph /hə'rəmf/ ▶ v. **1** clear the throat noisily. **2** grumpily express disapproval.

har·ry /'harē/ ▶ v. (**harries, harrying, harried**) **1** carry out repeated attacks on an enemy. **2** harass someone continuously.

harsh /härsh/ ▶ adj. **1** unpleasantly rough or intense to the senses: *a harsh white light*. **2** cruel or severe. **3** (of climate or conditions) difficult to survive in; hostile. ■ **harsh·en** v. **harsh·ly** adv. **harsh·ness** n.

hart /härt/ ▶ n. an adult male deer, especially a red deer over five years old.

har·te·beest /'härt(ə),bēst/ ▶ n. a large African antelope with a long head and sloping back.

har·um-scar·um /'he(ə)rəm 'ske(ə)rəm/ ▶ adj. reckless or impetuous.

har·vest /'härvist/ ▶ n. **1** the process or period of gathering in crops. **2** the season's yield or crop. ▶ v. gather a crop as a harvest. ■ **har·vest·a·ble** adj. **har·vest·er** n.

har·vest·man /'härvəstmən/ ▶ n. (pl. **harvestmen**) another term for DADDY LONGLEGS.

har·vest moon ▶ n. the full moon that is seen closest to the time of the autumnal equinox.

har·vest mouse ▶ n. a small mouse that nests among the stalks of growing grains.

has /haz/ ▶ third person singular present of HAVE.

has-been ▶ n. informal a person or thing that is outdated or no longer significant.

hash[1] /hash/ ▶ n. a dish of diced cooked meat reheated with potatoes. ▶ v. **1** make (meat or other food) into a hash. **2** (**hash something out**) come to agreement on something after much discussion. – PHRASES **make a hash of** informal make a mess of something. **settle someone's hash** informal deal with someone in a forceful and decisive way.

hash[2] ▶ n. informal hashish.

hash[3] (also **hash mark, hash sign**) ▶ n. the symbol #.

hash browns ▶ pl.n. a dish of chopped and fried cooked potatoes.

hash·ish /'ha,shēsh/ ▶ n. an extract of the cannabis plant.

Ha·sid /KHä'sēd, 'KHäsid, 'häsid/ (also **Chasid, Chassid,** or **Hassid**) ▶ n. (pl. **Hasidim** /,KHäsē'dēm, hä'sēdim/) a follower of Hasidism, a mystical Jewish movement founded in the eighteenth century and represented today by fundamentalist communities in Israel and New York. ■ **Ha·sid·ic** /KHä'sedik, hä'sēdik/ adj.

Has·i·dism /'hasi,dizəm/ n.

has·n't /'haznt/ ▶ contr. has not.

hasp /hasp/ ▶ n. a hinged metal plate that forms part of a fastening for a door or lid and is fitted over a metal loop and secured by a pin or padlock.

Has·sid ▶ n. variant spelling of HASID.

has·si·um /'hasēəm/ ▶ n. a very unstable chemical element made by high-energy atomic collisions.

has·sle /'hasəl/ informal ▶ n. **1** annoying inconvenience. **2** a situation of conflict or disagreement: *she didn't want to get into a hassle with her dad over money*. ▶ v. harass or pester someone.

has·sock /'hasək/ ▶ n. **1** a thick, firmly padded cushion, in particular a footstool. **2** a firm clump of grass or matted vegetation in marshy ground.

hast /hast/ ▶ old-fashioned second person singular present of HAVE.

haste /hāst/ ▶ n. speed or urgency in doing something: *the note was clearly written in haste*.

has·ten /'hāsən/ ▶ v. **1** be quick to do something; move quickly. **2** make something happen sooner than expected.

hast·y /'hāstē/ ▶ adj. (**hastier, hastiest**) **1** done with speed or urgency. **2** acting too quickly and without much thought: *the medics were a little hasty in predicting an early death for him*. ■ **hast·i·ly** adv. **hast·i·ness** n.

hat /hat/ ▶ n. a shaped covering for the head, typically with a brim and a crown. ■ **hat·ful** n. **hat·less** adj. **hat·ted** adj. – PHRASES **keep something under one's hat** keep something a secret. **pass the hat** collect contributions of money. **take one's hat off to someone** used to express admiration or praise for someone. **talk through one's hat** informal talk foolishly or ignorantly. **throw one's hat in the ring** express willingness to take up a challenge, especially to enter a political race.

hat·band /'hat,band/ ▶ n. a decorative ribbon around a hat, just above the brim.

hatch[1] /hach/ ▶ n. **1** a small opening in a floor, wall, or roof allowing access from one area to another. **2** a door in an aircraft, spacecraft, or submarine. **3** an opening in the deck of a boat or ship.

hatch[2] ▶ v. **1** (of a young bird, fish, or reptile) emerge or cause to emerge from its egg. **2** (of an egg) open and produce a young animal. **3** think up a plot or plan. ▶ n. a newly hatched brood.

hatch·back /'hach,bak/ ▶ n. a car with a door across the full width at the back end that opens upward.

hatch·er·y /'hachərē/ ▶ n. (pl. **hatcheries**) an establishment where fish or poultry eggs are hatched.

hatch·et /'hachit/ ▶ n. a small ax with a short handle. – PHRASES **bury the hatchet** end a quarrel or conflict.

hatch·et job ▶ n. informal a fierce spoken or written attack.

hatch·et man ▶ n. informal a person employed to carry out unpleasant tasks on behalf of someone else.

hatch·ling /'hachling/ ▶ n. a newly hatched young animal.

hatch·way /'hach,wā/ ▶ n. an opening or hatch,

especially in a ship's deck.

hate /hāt/ ▶ v. feel intense dislike for someone or something. ▶ n. intense dislike. ▶ adj. (of a hostile act) motivated by intense dislike or prejudice: *a hate crime.* ■ **hat·er** n.

hate·ful /'hātfəl/ ▶ adj. arousing or deserving hate; very unpleasant. ■ **hate·ful·ly** adv. **hate·ful·ness** n.

hath /haTH/ ▶ old-fashioned third person singular present of HAVE.

hath·a yo·ga /'häTHə/ ▶ n. a system of physical exercises and breathing control used in yoga.

ha·tred /'hātrid/ ▶ n. intense dislike or ill will.

hat·ter /'hatər/ ▶ n. a person who makes and sells hats.
– PHRASES **(as) mad as a hatter** informal completely insane.

hat trick ▶ n. three successes of the same kind, especially (in ice hockey or soccer) three goals scored by the same player in a game.

haugh·ty /'hôtē/ ▶ adj. (**haughtier, haughtiest**) behaving in an arrogant and superior way toward others. ■ **haugh·ti·ly** adv. **haugh·ti·ness** n.

haul /hôl/ ▶ v. **1** pull or drag something with effort. **2** transport something in a truck or cart. ▶ n. **1** a quantity of something obtained, especially illegally: *they escaped with a haul of antiques.* **2** a number of fish caught at one time. **3** a distance to be traveled: *the thirty-mile haul to Boston.* ■ **haul·er** n.

haul·age /'hôlij/ ▶ n. the commercial transport of goods.

haunch /hônCH, hänCH/ ▶ n. **1** the buttock and thigh of a human or animal. **2** the leg and loin of an animal, as food.

haunt /hônt, hänt/ ▶ v. **1** (of a ghost) appear regularly in a place. **2** (of a person) visit a place often. **3** be persistently and disturbingly present in the mind: *both men are haunted by memories of death.* ▶ n. a place frequented by a specified person: *the bar was a favorite haunt of artists.* ■ **haunt·er** n.

haunt·ed /'hôntid, 'hän-/ ▶ adj. **1** (of a place) frequented by a ghost. **2** having or showing signs of great distress.

haunt·ing /'hônting, 'hän-/ ▶ adj. beautiful or sad in a way that is hard to forget: *the haunting sound of the flutes.* ■ **haunt·ing·ly** adv.

haute cou·ture /ˌōt ˌko͞o'to͝or/ ▶ n. the designing and making of high-quality clothes by leading fashion houses.

haute cui·sine /ˌōt ˌkwə'zēn/ ▶ n. high-quality cooking in the traditional French style.

hau·teur /hō'tər/ ▶ n. proud haughtiness of manner.

Ha·va·na /hə'vanə/ ▶ n. a cigar made in Cuba or from Cuban tobacco.

have /hav/ ▶ v. (**has, having, had**) **1** possess, own, or hold something. **2** experience: *I had difficulty keeping awake.* **3** be able to make use of something. **4** (**have to**) be obliged to; must. **5** perform a particular action: *he had a look around.* **6** show a personal quality or characteristic. **7** suffer from an illness or disability. **8** cause to be or be done: *she had dinner ready.* **9** place, hold, or keep something in a particular position. **10** receive something from someone. **11** take or invite someone into one's home. **12** eat or drink something. **13** (**not have**) refuse to allow or accept something. **14** (**be**

had) informal be cheated or deceived. ▶ auxiliary v. used with a past participle to form the perfect, pluperfect, and future perfect tenses, and the conditional mood.
– PHRASES **have had it** informal be beyond repair or revival. **have (got) it in for someone** informal behave in a hostile way toward someone. **have (got) nothing on** informal **1** be not nearly as good as (someone or something), especially in a particular respect: *bright though his three sons were, they had nothing on Sally.* **2 have nothing (or something) on someone** know nothing (or something) discreditable or incriminating about someone: *I am not worried—they've got nothing on me.* **have it out** informal attempt to settle a dispute by confrontation. **the haves and the have-nots** informal people with plenty of money and those who are poor.

> **USAGE**
>
> Be careful not to write **of** when you mean **have** or **'ve**: *I could've told you that,* not *I could of told you that.* The mistake occurs because the pronunciation of **have** can sound the same as that of **of,** so that the words are confused when they are written down.

ha·ven /'hāvən/ ▶ n. **1** a place of safety. **2** a harbor or small port.

have·n't /'havənt/ ▶ contr. have not.

hav·er·sack /'havərˌsak/ ▶ n. a small, sturdy bag carried on the back or over the shoulder, especially by soldiers and hikers.

hav·oc /'havək/ ▶ n. **1** widespread destruction. **2** great confusion or disorder.
– PHRASES **play havoc with** completely disrupt something.

haw[1] /hô/ ▶ n. the red fruit of the hawthorn.

haw[2] ▶ v. See HEM AND HAW at HEM[2].

Ha·wai·ian /hə'wīən, -'woi-ən/ ▶ n. **1** a person from Hawaii. **2** the language of Hawaii. ▶ adj. relating to Hawaii.

Ha·wai·ian shirt ▶ n. a brightly colored and gaily patterned shirt.

hawk[1] /hôk/ ▶ n. **1** a fast-flying bird of prey with broad rounded wings and a long tail. **2** any bird of prey used in falconry. **3** a person who advocates aggressive policies in foreign affairs. ▶ v. hunt game with a trained hawk. ■ **hawk·ish** adj.

hawk[2] ▶ v. offer goods for sale in the street.

hawk[3] ▶ v. **1** clear the throat noisily. **2** (**hawk something up**) bring phlegm up from the throat.

hawk·er /'hôkər/ ▶ n. a person who travels around selling goods.

haw·ser /'hôzər/ ▶ n. a thick rope or cable for mooring or towing a ship.

haw·thorn /'hô,THôrn/ ▶ n. a thorny shrub or tree with white, pink, or red blossoms and small dark red fruits (haws).

hay /hā/ ▶ n. grass that has been mown and dried for use as fodder. ■ **hay·ing** n.
– PHRASES **hit the hay** informal go to bed. **make hay (while the sun shines)** make good use of an opportunity while it lasts.

hay fe·ver ▶ n. an allergy to pollen or dust, causing sneezing and watery eyes.

hay·loft /'hā,lôft/ ▶ n. a loft over a stable or in a barn used for storing hay or straw.

hay·mak·er /'hā,mākər/ ▶ n. **1** a person involved in making hay. **2** informal derogatory, a forceful blow. ■ **hay·mak·ing** n.

hay·seed /'hā,sēd/ ▶ n. informal, derogatory a simple, unsophisticated country person.

hay·stack /'hā,stak/ ▶ n. a large packed pile of hay.

hay·wire /'hā,wīr/ ▶ adj. informal out of control: *everybody's weather is going haywire.*

haz·ard /'hazərd/ ▶ n. **1** a danger or risk of danger: *many people view fast food as a health hazard.* **2** an obstacle, such as a bunker, on a golf course. **3** literary chance; probability. ▶ v. **1** say something in a tentative way. **2** put something at risk of being lost.

haz·ard lights ▶ pl.n. flashing indicator lights on a vehicle, used to warn that the vehicle is stationary or unexpectedly slow.

haz·ard·ous /'hazərdəs/ ▶ adj. risky; dangerous. ■ **haz·ard·ous·ly** adv.

haz·ard pay ▶ n. extra payment for working under dangerous conditions.

haze[1] /hāz/ ▶ n. **1** a thin mist typically caused by fine particles of dust, pollutants, or water vapor. **2** a state of mental confusion: *I went to bed in an alcoholic haze.* ▶ v. **1** cover or conceal with a haze. **2** to force (a new or potential recruit to the miliary, a college fraternity, etc.) to perform strenuous, humiliating, or dangerous tasks.

haze[2] ▶ v. force a new or potential recruit to the military, a college fraternity, etc., to perform strenuous, humiliating, or dangerous tasks: *rookies were mercilessly hazed.*

ha·zel /'hāzəl/ ▶ n. **1** a shrub or small tree bearing catkins in spring and edible nuts in autumn. **2** a reddish-brown or greenish-brown color, especially of someone's eyes.

ha·zel·nut /'hāzəl,nət/ ▶ n. the round brown edible nut of the hazel.

ha·zy /'hāzē/ ▶ adj. (**hazier**, **haziest**) **1** covered by a haze. **2** vague, unclear, or confused: *those days are a hazy memory.* ■ **ha·zi·ly** adv. **ha·zi·ness** n.

H-bomb ▶ n. short for HYDROGEN BOMB.

HDL ▶ abbr. high-density lipoprotein.

HD radio ▶ n. **1** trademark a technology for broadcasting terrestrial radio signals digitally that permits multicasting in traditional radio bandwidths. **2** a radio capable of receiving these signals.

HDTV ▶ abbr. high-definition television.

He ▶ symbol the chemical element helium.

he /hē/ ▶ pron. (third person sing.) **1** used to refer to a man, boy, or male animal previously mentioned or easily identified. **2** used to refer to a person or animal of unspecified sex. ▶ n. a male; a man.

> USAGE
> Until recently, **he** was used to refer to both males and females when a person's sex was not specified; this is now regarded as outdated and sexist. One solution is to use **he or she**, but this can be awkward if used repeatedly. An alternative is to use **they**, especially where it occurs after an indefinite pronoun such as **everyone** or **someone** (as in *everyone needs to feel that they matter*): this is becoming more and more accepted both in speech and in writing.

head /hed/ ▶ n. **1** the upper part of the body, containing the brain, mouth, and sense organs. **2** a person in charge of something. **3** the front, forward, or upper part or end of something. **4** a person considered as a unit: *they paid fifty dollars a head.* **5** (treated as pl.) a specified number of animals: *seventy head of cattle.* **6** a compact mass of leaves or flowers at the top of a stem. **7** the cutting or operational end of a tool or mechanism. **8** a part of a computer or a tape or video recorder that transfers information to and from a tape or disk. **9** the source of a river or stream. **10** the foam on top of a glass of beer. **11** (**heads**) the side of a coin bearing the image of a head. **12** pressure of water or steam in an engine or other confined space: *a good head of steam.* **13** informal a toilet, especially on a boat or ship. ▶ adj. chief; principal. ▶ v. **1** be or act as the head of: *the foreign policy team is headed by an academic.* **2** (also **be headed**) move in a specified direction: *I headed for the exit.* **3** give a title or heading to something. **4** (**head someone/thing off**) intercept someone or something and force them to turn aside. **5** Soccer shoot or pass the ball with the head. ■ **head·ed** adj. **head·less** adj.

– PHRASES **come to a head** reach a crisis. **go to someone's head 1** (of alcohol) make someone slightly drunk. **2** (of success) make someone conceited. **head first 1** with the head in front of the rest of the body. **2** without thinking beforehand. **a head for** a talent for or an ability to cope with something: *a head for heights.* —— **one's head off** informal talk, laugh, shout, etc., unrestrainedly. **head over heels 1** turning over completely in forward motion. **2** madly in love. **a head start** an advantage granted or gained at the beginning. **keep** (or **lose**) **one's head** remain (or fail to remain) calm. **keep one's head above water** avoid falling into debt or difficulty. **make heads or tails of** understand something at all. **off the top of one's head** without careful thought. **out of one's head** crazy. **over someone's head 1** (also **above someone's head**) beyond someone's ability to understand. **2** without consulting someone. **turn someone's head** make someone conceited.

head·ache /'hed,āk/ ▶ n. **1** a continuous pain in the head. **2** informal a cause of worry or trouble. ■ **head·ach·y** adj.

head·band /'hed,band/ ▶ n. a band of fabric worn around the head as a decoration or to keep the hair off the face.

head·bang·er /'hed,baNGər/ ▶ n. informal a fan or performer of heavy metal music.

head·board /'hed,bôrd/ ▶ n. an upright panel at the head of a bed.

head·butt /'hed,bət/ ▶ v. attack someone by hitting them hard with the head. ▶ n. an act of headbutting.

head·case /'hed,kās/ ▶ n. informal a mentally ill or unstable person.

head count ▶ n. a count of the number of people present or available.

head·dress /'hed,dres/ ▶ n. an ornamental covering for the head.

head·er /'hedər/ ▶ n. **1** Soccer a shot or pass made with the head. **2** informal a headlong fall or dive. **3** a line of writing at the top of each page of a book or document. **4** (also **header tank**) a raised tank of water maintaining pressure in a plumbing system. **5** a brick or stone laid at right angles to the face of a wall.

head·gear /'hed,gi(ə)r/ ▶ n. **1** hats and other items worn on the head. **2** orthodontic equipment worn on the head and attached to braces on the teeth.

head·hunt /'hed,hənt/ ▸ v. **1** approach someone already employed elsewhere to fill a vacant position. **2** (as n. **headhunting**) the practice among some societies of collecting the heads of dead enemies as trophies. ▪ **head·hunt·er** n.

head·ing /'hediNG/ ▸ n. **1** a title at the top of a page or section of a book. **2** a direction or bearing. **3** the top of a curtain extending above the hooks or wire by which it is suspended.

head·land /'hedlənd, 'hed,land/ ▸ n. a narrow piece of land projecting into the sea.

head·light /'hed,līt/ (also **headlamp** /'hed,lamp/) ▸ n. a powerful light at the front of a motor vehicle or railroad engine.

head·line /'hed,līn/ ▸ n. **1** a heading at the top of an article or page in a newspaper or magazine. **2** (**the headlines**) a summary of the most important items of news. ▸ v. **1** provide an article with a headline. **2** appear as the star performer at a concert.

head·lin·er /'hed,līnər/ ▸ n. a performer or act that is promoted as the star attraction on a program or advertisement.

head·lock /'hed,läk/ ▸ n. a method of restraining someone by holding an arm firmly around their head.

head·long /'hed,lôNG, -,läNG/ ▸ adv. & adj. **1** with the head first. **2** in a rush.

head·man /'hedmən/ ▸ n. (pl. **headmen**) the leader of a tribe.

head·mas·ter /'hed,mastər/ (or **headmistress**) ▸ n. the man (or woman) in change of a school, especially a private school; the principal.

head of state ▸ n. a president, monarch, or other official leader of a country, who may also be the head of government.

head·on ▸ adj. & adv. **1** with or involving the front of a vehicle. **2** with or involving direct confrontation.

head·phones /'hed,fōnz/ ▸ pl.n. a pair of earphones joined by a band placed over the head.

head·piece /'hed,pēs/ ▸ n. a device worn on the head.

head·quar·ter /'hed,kwôrtər/ ▸ v. (**be headquartered**) have headquarters at a specified place.

head·quar·ters /'hed,kwôrtərz/ ▸ n. (treated as sing. or pl.) **1** the managerial and administrative center of an organization. **2** the premises occupied by a military commander and the commander's staff.

head·rest /'hed,rest/ ▸ n. a padded support for the head on the back of a seat.

head·room /'hed,rōōm, -,rŏŏm/ ▸ n. the space between the top of a vehicle or a person's head and the ceiling or other structure above.

head·scarf /'hed,skärf/ ▸ n. (pl. **headscarves** /-,skärvz/) a square of fabric worn as a covering for the head.

head·set /'hed,set/ ▸ n. a set of headphones with a microphone attached.

head·ship /'hed,SHip/ ▸ n. the position of leader: *the rising rate of female headship.*

head·shrink·er /'hed,SHriNGkər/ ▸ n. informal a psychiatrist, psychologist, or psychotherapist.

head·stone /'hed,stōn/ ▸ n. an inscribed stone slab set up at the head of a grave.

head·strong /'hed,strôNG/ ▸ adj. determined to do things in one's own way, regardless of advice

to the contrary.

heads-up ▸ n. informal an advance warning of something: *I had a heads-up on what would happen.*

head-to-head ▸ adj. & adv. involving two parties confronting each other in a dispute or contest.

head-turn·ing ▸ adj. very noticeable or attractive.

head·wa·ters /'hed,wôtərz, -,wätərz/ ▸ pl.n. the tributary streams of a river close to or forming its source.

head·way /'hed,wā/ ▸ n. (in phrase **make headway**) make progress.

head·wind /'hed,wind/ ▸ n. a wind blowing from directly in front.

head·word /'hed,wərd/ ▸ n. a word that begins a separate entry in a reference book such as a dictionary.

head·y /'hedē/ ▸ adj. (**headier, headiest**) **1** exciting or exhilarating: *the heady days following the election.* **2** (of alcohol) intoxicating. ▪ **head·i·ly** adv.

heal /hēl/ ▸ v. **1** make or become sound or healthy again. **2** put right an undesirable situation. ▪ **heal·er** n.

health /helTH/ ▸ n. **1** the state of being free from illness or injury. **2** a person's mental or physical condition.

health·care /'helTH,ke(ə)r/ ▸ n. the maintenance and improvement of physical and mental health through the provision of medical services.

health cen·ter ▸ n. an establishment housing local medical services.

health club ▸ n. a private club with exercise facilities and health and beauty treatments.

health food ▸ n. food that is thought to be good for one's health.

health·ful /'helTHfəl/ ▸ adj. good for one's health. ▪ **health·ful·ly** adv. **health·ful·ness** n.

health tour·ism ▸ n. the practice of traveling abroad in order to receive medical treatment.

health·y /'helTHē/ ▸ adj. (**healthier, healthiest**) **1** having or promoting good health. **2** normal, sensible, or desirable. **3** of a very satisfactory size or amount: *a healthy profit.* ▪ **health·i·ly** adv. **health·i·ness** n.

heap /hēp/ ▸ n. **1** a pile of a substance or of a number of objects. **2** informal a large amount or number: *we have heaps of room.* **3** informal an old vehicle in bad condition. ▸ v. **1** put in or form a heap. **2** (**heap something with**) load something with a large amount of something. **3** (**heap something on**) give much praise, abuse, etc., to: *the press heaped abuse on him.*

hear /hi(ə)r/ ▸ v. (past and past part. **heard** /hərd/) **1** perceive a sound with the ear. **2** be told about something. **3** (**have heard of**) be aware of the existence of: *nobody had heard of my college.* **4** (**hear from**) receive a letter or phone call from someone. **5** listen to someone or something. **6** listen to and judge a case or person bringing a case in a court of law. ▪ **hear·a·ble** adj. **hear·er** n.
– PHRASES **hear! hear!** used to express full agreement with something in a speech. **will** (or **would**) **not hear of** will (or would) not allow or agree to.

hear·ing /'hi(ə)riNG/ ▸ n. **1** the faculty of perceiving sounds. **2** the range within which sounds may be heard; earshot. **3** an opportunity to state one's case: *a fair hearing.* **4** an act of listening to evidence before an official or in a court of law.

hear·ing aid ▸ n. a small amplifying device worn in or on the ear by a partially deaf person.

hark·en /'härkən/ (also **harken**) ▸ v. (usu. **hearken to**) old use listen.

hear·say /'hi(ə)r,sā/ ▸ n. information received from others that cannot be proved.

hearse /hərs/ ▸ n. a vehicle for carrying the coffin at a funeral.

heart /härt/ ▸ n. **1** the hollow muscular organ in the chest that pumps the blood around the body. **2** the central, innermost, or vital part: *the heart of the city.* **3** a person's capacity for feeling love or compassion. **4** mood or feeling: *a change of heart.* **5** courage or enthusiasm. **6** a shape representing a heart with two equal curves meeting at a point at the bottom and a cusp at the top. **7** (**hearts**) one of the four suits in a deck of playing cards.
– PHRASES **after one's own heart** sharing one's tastes. **at heart** in one's real nature, in contrast to how one may appear. **break someone's heart** overwhelm someone with sadness. **by heart** from memory. **close** (or **dear**) **to one's heart** very important to one. **from the** (or **the bottom of one's**) **heart** in a very sincere way. **have a heart of gold** have a very kind nature. **have the heart to do something** be insensitive enough to do something. **have one's heart in one's mouth** be very alarmed or apprehensive. **in one's heart of hearts** in one's innermost feelings. **tug** (or **pull**) **at one's heartstrings** arouse strong feelings of love or pity. **take something to heart** be very upset by criticism. **wear one's heart on one's sleeve** show one's feelings openly.

heart·ache /'härt,āk/ ▸ n. distress or grief.

heart at·tack ▸ n. a sudden occurrence of coronary thrombosis.

heart·beat /'härt,bēt/ ▸ n. a pulsation of the heart.
– PHRASES **a heartbeat away** very close.

heart·break /'härt,brāk/ ▸ n. overwhelming distress. ■ **heart·break·ing** adj. **heart·bro·ken** /'härt,brōkən/ adj.

heart·break·er /'härt,brākər/ ▸ n. **1** a person who is very attractive but who is irresponsible in emotional relationships. **2** a story or event that causes overwhelming distress.

heart·burn /'härt,bərn/ ▸ n. a form of indigestion felt as a burning sensation in the chest, caused by acid regurgitation into the esophagus.

heart·en /'härtn/ ▸ v. make more cheerful or confident: *he was heartened by the increase in party membership.* ■ **heart·en·ing** adj.

heart fail·ure ▸ n. severe failure of the heart to function properly, especially as a cause of death.

heart·felt /'härt,felt/ ▸ adj. deeply and strongly felt.

hearth /härTH/ ▸ n. the floor or area in front of a fireplace.

hearth·rug /'härTH,rəg/ ▸ n. a rug laid in front of a fireplace.

heart·i·ly /'härtl-ē/ ▸ adv. **1** in a hearty way. **2** very: *I'm heartily sick of them.*

heart·land /'härt,land/ ▸ n. **1** the central or most important part of a country or area. **2** the central part of the US; the Midwest.

heart·less /'härtlis/ ▸ adj. lacking any pity for

others; very unkind or unfeeling. ■ **heart·less·ly** adv. **heart·less·ness** n.

heart·rend·ing ▸ adj. very sad or distressing.

heart·sick /'härt,sik/ (also **heartsore** /'härt,sôr/) ▸ adj. literary despondent from grief or loss of love.

heart·stop·ping ▸ adj. very exciting.

heart·throb /'härt,THräb/ ▸ n. informal a man, typically a celebrity, whose good looks excite romantic feelings.

heart-to-heart ▸ adj. (of a conversation) intimate and personal.

heart·warm·ing /'härt,wôrmiNG/ ▸ adj. emotionally rewarding or uplifting.

heart·wood /'härt,wŏŏd/ ▸ n. the dense inner part of a tree trunk, yielding the hardest timber.

heart·y /'härtē/ ▸ adj. (**heartier, heartiest**) **1** enthusiastic and friendly. **2** cheerful and full of energy: *a big bluff hearty man.* **3** (of a feeling or opinion) deeply felt. **4** (of a meal) wholesome and filling. ■ **heart·i·ness** n.

heat /hēt/ ▸ n. **1** the quality of being hot; high temperature. **2** heat as a form of energy arising from the random movement of molecules. **3** a source or level of heat for cooking. **4** intensity of feeling: *an attempt to take some heat out of the debate.* **5** (**the heat**) informal great pressure to do or achieve something: *the heat is on.* **6** a preliminary round in a race or contest.
▸ v. **1** make or become hot or warm. **2** (**heat up**) become more intense and exciting. **3** (as adj. **heated**) passionate: *a heated argument.* ■ **heat·ed·ly** adv.
– PHRASES **in the heat of the moment** while temporarily angry or excited and without stopping to think. **in heat** (of a female mammal) in a sexual state of readiness for mating.

heat·er /'hētər/ ▸ n. a device for warming something.

heat ex·haus·tion ▸ n. a condition caused by prolonged exposure to heat during activity and characterized by weakness, profuse sweating, dizziness, and nausea.

heath /hēTH/ ▸ n. **1** an area of open uncultivated land, especially in Britain, covered with heather, gorse, and coarse grasses. **2** a dwarf shrub with small pink or purple bell-shaped flowers, found on heaths and moors.

heath·en /'hēTHən/ ▸ n. derogatory a person who does not belong to a widely held religion (especially Christianity, Judaism, or Islam) as regarded by people who do. ▸ adj. relating to heathens. ■ **heath·en·ish** adj. **heath·en·ism** n.

heath·er /'heTHər/ ▸ n. a dwarf shrub with purple flowers, found on moors and heaths. ■ **heath·er·y** adj.

heath·land /'hēTH,land/ ▸ n. an extensive area of heath.

heat·ing /'hētiNG/ ▸ n. equipment or devices used to provide heat, especially to a building.

heat·proof /'hēt,prŏŏf/ ▸ adj. able to resist great heat.

heat-seek·ing ▸ adj. (of a missile) able to detect and home in on heat produced by a target.

heat·stroke /'hēt,strōk/ ▸ n. a feverish condition caused by failure of the body's temperature-regulating mechanism when exposed to very high temperatures.

heat wave ▸ n. a prolonged period of unusually hot weather.

heave /hēv/ ▶ v. (past and past part. **heaved** or Nautical **hove** /hōv/) **1** lift, haul, or throw something heavy with great effort. **2** rise and fall rhythmically or spasmodically: *his shoulders heaved as he wept.* **3** produce a sigh noisily. **4** try to vomit. **5** (**heave to**) (of a ship) come to a stop. ▶ n. an act of heaving something. ■ **heav·er** n.

– PHRASES **heave in sight** (or **into view**) (especially of a ship) come into view.

heave-ho ▶ n. (**the heave-ho**) informal dismissal from a job or contest.

heav·en /ˈhevən/ ▶ n. **1** (in various religions) the place where God or the gods live and where good people go after death. **2** (**the heavens**) literary the sky. **3** a place or state of great happiness. **4** (also **heavens**) used in exclamations as a substitute for 'God.' ■ **heav·en·ward** adj. & adv. **heav·en·wards** adv.

– PHRASES **the heavens open** it suddenly starts to rain very heavily. **in seventh heaven** very happy; ecstatic.

heav·en·ly /ˈhevənlē/ ▶ adj. **1** relating to heaven; divine. **2** relating to the sky. **3** informal very pleasant; wonderful.

heav·en·ly bod·y ▶ n. a planet, star, or other object in space.

heav·en-sent ▶ adj. happening unexpectedly and at a very favorable time.

heav·y /ˈhevē/ ▶ adj. (**heavier**, **heaviest**) **1** weighing a great deal. **2** very dense, thick, or substantial: *heavy gray clouds.* **3** of more than the usual size, amount, or force: *heavy traffic.* **4** striking or falling with force: *he felt a heavy blow on his shoulder.* **5** needing much physical effort. **6** not delicate or graceful. **7** serious or difficult to understand: *a heavy discussion.* **8** informal full of anger or other strong emotion and difficult to deal with: *things were getting heavy.* **9** (of music, especially rock) having a strong bass component and a forceful rhythm. **10** (of ground) muddy or full of clay. ▶ n. (pl. **heavies**) informal a large, strong man, especially one hired for protection. ■ **heav·i·ly** adv. **heav·i·ness** n.

heav·y-du·ty ▶ adj. designed to withstand a great deal of use or wear.

heav·y go·ing ▶ n. a person or situation that is difficult or boring.

heav·y-hand·ed ▶ adj. clumsy, insensitive, or overly forceful.

heav·y-heart·ed ▶ adj. depressed or melancholy.

heav·y hit·ter (also **big hitter**) ▶ n. informal an important or powerful person.

heav·y hy·dro·gen ▶ n. another term for DEUTERIUM.

heav·y in·dus·try ▶ n. the manufacture of large, heavy articles and materials in bulk.

heav·y met·al ▶ n. **1** a type of very loud harsh-sounding rock music with a strong beat. **2** a metal of relatively high density, or of high relative atomic weight.

heav·y pet·ting ▶ n. sexual activity between two people that stops short of intercourse.

heav·y·set /ˈhevēˌset/ ▶ adj. (of a person) broad and strongly built.

heav·y wa·ter ▶ n. water in which the hydrogen in the molecules is partly or wholly replaced by the isotope deuterium, used especially in nuclear reactors.

heav·y·weight /ˈhevēˌwāt/ ▶ n. **1** a weight in boxing and other sports, typically the heaviest

category. **2** informal an influential person. ▶ adj. **1** of above-average weight. **2** informal serious or influential: *heavyweight news coverage.*

He·bra·ic /hēˈbrāik/ ▶ adj. relating to Hebrew or the Hebrew people.

He·brew /ˈhēbrōō/ ▶ n. **1** a member of an ancient people living in what is now Israel and Palestine, whose scriptures and traditions form the basis of the Jewish religion. **2** the language of the Hebrews, in its ancient or modern form.

heck /hek/ ▶ exclam. used for emphasis, or to express surprise, annoyance, etc.

heck·le /ˈhekəl/ ▶ v. interrupt a public speaker with derisive comments or abuse. ■ **heck·ler** n.

hec·tare /ˈhekˌte(ə)r/ ▶ n. a metric unit of square measure, equal to 10,000 square meters (2.471 acres).

hec·tic /ˈhektik/ ▶ adj. full of frantic activity. ■ **hec·ti·cal·ly** adv.

hec·tor /ˈhektər/ ▶ v. talk to someone in a bullying way. ■ **hec·tor·ing** adj.

he'd /hēd/ ▶ contr. **1** he had. **2** he would.

hedge /hej/ ▶ n. **1** a fence or boundary formed by closely growing bushes. **2** a way of protecting oneself against financial loss or another adverse situation: *a hedge against inflation.* ▶ v. **1** surround something with a hedge. **2** avoid making a definite statement or commitment. **3** protect an investor or investment against loss by making compensating contracts or transactions. ■ **hedg·er** n.

– PHRASES **hedge one's bets** avoid committing oneself when faced with a difficult choice.

hedge fund ▶ n. a limited partnership of investors that uses high-risk methods in hopes of realizing large capital gains.

hedge·hog /ˈhejˌhôg, -ˌhäg/ ▶ n. a small mammal with a spiny coat, able to roll itself into a ball for defense.

hedge·row /ˈhejˌrō/ ▶ n. a hedge of wild bushes and occasional trees bordering a road or field.

he·don·ism /ˈhēdnˌizəm/ ▶ n. behavior based on the belief that pleasure is the most important thing in life. ■ **he·don·ist** n. **he·don·is·tic** /ˌhēdnˈistik/ adj.

hee·bie-jee·bies /ˈhēbē ˈjēbēz/ ▶ pl.n. (**the heebie-jeebies**) informal a state of nervous fear or anxiety.

heed /hēd/ ▶ v. pay attention to someone or something. ■ **heed·ful** adj.

– PHRASES **pay** (or **take**) **heed** pay careful attention.

heed·less /ˈhēdlis/ ▶ adj. showing a reckless lack of care or attention. ■ **heed·less·ly** adv. **heed·less·ness** n.

hee-haw /ˈhē ˌhô/ ▶ n. the loud, harsh cry of a donkey or mule. ▶ v. make the loud, harsh cry of a donkey or mule.

heel[1] /hēl/ ▶ n. **1** the back part of the foot below the ankle. **2** the part of a shoe or boot supporting the heel. **3** the part of the palm of the hand next to the wrist. **4** informal, dated an inconsiderate or untrustworthy man. ▶ exclam. a command to a dog to walk close behind its owner. ▶ v. fit a new heel on a shoe or boot. ■ **heeled** adj.

– PHRASES **at** (or **on**) **the heels of** following closely after someone or something. **bring someone to heel** bring someone under control. **cool one's heels** be kept waiting. **take to one's heels** run away. **kick up one's heels** have a lively, enjoyable time.

heel² ▸ v. (of a ship) lean over owing to the pressure of wind or an uneven load.

heel·ball /ˈhēlˌbôl/ ▸ n. a mixture of hard wax and lampblack used by shoemakers for polishing or in brass rubbing.

heft /heft/ ▸ v. **1** lift or carry something heavy. **2** lift or hold something to test its weight. ▸ n. **1** the weight of someone or something. **2** ability or influence.

heft·y /ˈheftē/ ▸ adj. (**heftier, heftiest**) **1** large and heavy. **2** (of a number or amount) considerable: *she could face a hefty fine.* ■ **heft·i·ly** adv.

He·ge·li·an /həˈgālēən/ ▸ adj. relating to the German philosopher Georg Hegel or his philosophy. ▸ n. a follower of Hegel. ■ **He·ge·li·an·ism** /həˈgālēəˌnizəm/ n.

he·gem·o·ny /həˈjemənē, ˈhejəˌmōnē/ ▸ n. dominance of one social group or country over others. ■ **heg·e·mon·ic** /ˌhegəˈmänik/ adj.

He·gi·ra /hiˈjīrə, ˈhejərə/ (also **Hejira** or **Hijra**) ▸ n. **1** Muhammad's departure from Mecca to Medina in AD 622, marking the consolidation of the first Muslim community. **2** the Muslim era reckoned from this date.

heif·er /ˈhefər/ ▸ n. a young female cow that has not had a calf.

height /hīt/ ▸ n. **1** the measurement of someone or something from head to foot or from base to top. **2** the distance of something above ground or sea level. **3** the quality of being tall or high. **4** a high place. **5** the most intense part or period: *the height of the attack.* **6** an extreme example: *it would be the height of bad manners not to attend the wedding.*

height·en /ˈhītn/ ▸ v. **1** make or become more intense. **2** make something higher.

Heim·lich ma·neu·ver /ˈhīmlik, ˈhīmlikH/ ▸ n. a first-aid procedure for dislodging an obstruction from a person's windpipe, in which a sudden strong pressure is applied on the abdomen between the navel and the rib cage.

hei·nous /ˈhānəs/ ▸ adj. very wicked: *a heinous crime.* ■ **hei·nous·ly** adv. **hei·nous·ness** n.

heir /e(ə)r/ ▸ n. **1** a person who is legally entitled to the property or rank of another on that person's death. **2** a person who continues the work of a predecessor. ■ **heir·less** adj. **heir·ship** n.

heir ap·par·ent ▸ n. (pl. **heirs apparent**) **1** an heir whose rights cannot be taken away by the birth of another heir. **2** a person who is most likely to take on the job or role of another.

heir·ess /ˈe(ə)ris/ ▸ n. a female heir, especially to vast wealth.

heir·loom /ˈe(ə)rˌlo͞om/ ▸ n. a valuable object that has belonged to a family for several generations.

heir pre·sump·tive ▸ n. (pl. **heirs presumptive**) an heir whose rights may be taken away by the birth of another heir.

heist /hīst/ informal ▸ n. a robbery. ▸ v. steal something.

He·ji·ra ▸ n. variant spelling of **HEGIRA**.

held /held/ ▸ past and past participle of **HOLD¹**.

hel·i·cal /ˈhelikəl, ˈhē-/ ▸ adj. having the shape or form of a helix; spiral. ■ **hel·i·cal·ly** adv.

hel·i·ces /ˈhelēˌsēz/ ▸ plural of **HELIX**.

hel·i·cop·ter /ˈheliˌkäptər/ ▸ n. a type of aircraft powered by one or two sets of horizontally

revolving rotors.

he·li·o·cen·tric /ˌhēlēōˈsentrik/ ▸ adj. **1** having the sun as the center, as in the accepted astronomical model of the solar system. Compare with **GEOCENTRIC**. **2** Astronomy measured from or considered in relation to the center of the sun.

he·li·o·graph /ˈhēlēəˌgraf/ ▸ n. **1** a device that reflects sunlight in flashes from a movable mirror, used to send signals. **2** a message sent using a heliograph. ■ **he·li·o·graph·ic** /ˌhēlēəˈgrafik/ adj.

he·li·o·sphere /ˈhēlēəˌsfi(ə)r/ ▸ n. the region of space, including the solar system, in which the solar wind has a significant influence. ■ **he·li·o·spher·ic** /ˌhēlēəˈsferik, -ˈsfi(ə)rik/ adj.

he·li·o·trope /ˈhēlēəˌtrōp/ ▸ n. a plant of the borage family with fragrant purple or blue flowers.

hel·i·pad /ˈheləˌpad/ ▸ n. a landing and takeoff area for helicopters.

hel·i·port /ˈheliˌpôrt/ ▸ n. an airport or landing place for helicopters.

hel·i·ski·ing /ˈheliˌskē-iNG/ ▸ n. skiing in which the skier is taken up the mountain by helicopter.

he·li·um /ˈhēlēəm/ ▸ n. a light colorless gas that does not burn.

he·lix /ˈhēliks/ ▸ n. (pl. **helices** /-ləˌsēz/) an object with a three-dimensional spiral shape like that of a wire wound in a single layer around a cylinder or cone.

hell /hel/ ▸ n. **1** (in various religions) a place of evil and everlasting suffering to which the wicked are sent after death. **2** a state or place of great suffering. ▸ exclam. used to express annoyance or surprise or for emphasis. ■ **hell·ward** adv. & adj.
– PHRASES **all hell breaks loose** informal suddenly there is chaos. **come hell or high water** whatever difficulties may occur. **for the hell of it** informal just for fun. **give someone hell** informal reprimand someone severely. **hell for leather** as fast as possible. **like hell** informal very fast, much, hard, etc. **not a hope in hell** informal no chance at all. **until hell freezes over** forever.

he'll /hēl/ ▸ contr. he shall or he will.

hell·bent ▸ adj. determined to achieve something at all costs.

hell·cat /ˈhelˌkat/ ▸ n. a spiteful, violent woman.

hel·le·bore /ˈheləˌbôr/ ▸ n. a poisonous winter-flowering plant with large white, green, or purplish flowers.

Hel·lene /ˈhelēn/ ▸ n. a Greek.

Hel·len·ic /heˈlenik/ ▸ adj. **1** Greek. **2** relating to ancient Greek culture between *c.* 1050 BC and *c.* 300 BC. ▸ n. the Greek language.

Hel·len·ism /ˈheləˌnizəm/ ▸ n. **1** the national character or culture of Greece, especially ancient Greece. **2** the study or imitation of ancient Greek culture. ■ **Hel·len·ist** n. **Hel·len·ize** v.

Hel·len·is·tic /ˌheləˈnistik/ ▸ adj. relating to ancient Greek culture from the death of Alexander the Great (323 BC) to the defeat of Cleopatra and Mark Antony by Octavian in 31 BC.

hell·fire /ˈhelˌfīr/ ▸ n. the fire said to exist in hell.

hell·hole /ˈhelˌhōl/ ▸ n. a very unpleasant place.

hell·hound /ˈhelˌhound/ ▸ n. a demon in the form of a dog.

hell·ish /ˈhelisH/ ▸ adj. **1** relating to or like hell.

2 informal extremely difficult or unpleasant.
■ **hell·ish·ly** adv. **hell·ish·ness** n.

hel·lo /hə'lō, he'lō, 'helō/ (also **hallo** or **hullo**) ▶ exclam. **1** used as a greeting or to attract someone's attention. **2** (often pronounced with a prolonged final vowel) expressing sarcasm or anger: *hello! were you even listening?*

hell·rais·er /'hel,rāzər/ ▶ n. a person who causes trouble by violent, drunken, or outrageous behavior.

Hell's An·gel ▶ n. a member of a gang of male motorcycle enthusiasts, originally known for their lawless behavior.

helm /helm/ ▶ n. **1** a tiller or wheel for steering a ship or boat. **2** (**the helm**) a position of leadership. ▶ v. **1** steer a boat or ship. **2** manage the running of something.

hel·met /'helmit/ ▶ n. a hard or padded protective hat. ■ **hel·met·ed** adj.

helms·man /'helmzmən/ ▶ n. (pl. **helmsmen**) a person who steers a ship or boat.

hel·ot /'helət/ ▶ n. **1** (in part of ancient Greece) a member of a class of people having a status in between slaves and citizens. **2** a serf or slave.

help /help/ ▶ v. **1** make it easier for someone to do something. **2** improve a situation or problem. **3** (**help someone to**) serve someone with food or drink. **4** (**help oneself**) take something without asking permission. **5** (**can/could not help**) cannot or could not stop oneself doing: *he couldn't help laughing.* ▶ n. **1** the action of helping someone. **2** a person or thing that helps someone. **3** a person employed to do household tasks. ■ **help·er** n.

help·er cell ▶ n. a T cell that influences or controls the differentiation or activity of other cells of the immune system.

help·ful /'helpfəl/ ▶ adj. **1** giving or ready to give help. **2** useful. ■ **help·ful·ly** adv. **help·ful·ness** n.

help·ing /'helpiNG/ ▶ n. a portion of food served to one person at one time.

help·less /'helplis/ ▶ adj. **1** unable to defend oneself or to act without help. **2** uncontrollable: *helpless laughter.* ■ **help·less·ly** adv. **help·less·ness** n.

help·line /'help,līn/ ▶ n. a telephone service providing help with problems.

help·mate /'help,māt/ (also **helpmeet** /-,mēt/) ▶ n. a helpful companion or partner.

hel·ter-skel·ter /'heltər 'skeltər/ ▶ adj. & adv. in a hasty and confused or disorganized way. ▶ n. disorder; confusion.

hem¹ /'hem/ ▶ n. the edge of a piece of cloth or item of clothing that has been turned under and stitched down. ▶ v. (**hems, hemming, hemmed**) **1** make a hem on a piece of cloth or item of clothing). **2** (**hem someone/thing in**) surround someone or something and restrict their space or movement.

hem² ▶ exclam. expressing the sound made when coughing or clearing the throat to attract attention or show hesitation.

– PHRASES **hem and haw** hesitate; be indecisive.

he-man ▶ n. informal a very well-built, masculine man.

he·ma·tite /'hēmə,tīt/ ▶ n. a reddish-black mineral consisting of iron oxide.

he·ma·tol·o·gy /,hēmə'täləjē/ ▶ n. the branch of medicine concerned with the study and treatment of the blood. ■ **he·ma·to·log·i·cal** /-tə'läjikəl/ adj. **he·ma·tol·o·gist** n.

he·ma·to·ma /,hēmə'tōmə/ ▶ n. a solid swelling of clotted blood within the tissues.

hemi- ▶ prefix half: *hemisphere.*

hem·i·ple·gi·a /,hemə'plēj(ē)ə/ ▶ n. paralysis of one side of the body. ■ **hem·i·ple·gic** n. & adj.

hem·i·sphere /'hemə,sfi(ə)r/ ▶ n. **1** a half of a sphere. **2** a half of the earth, usually as divided into northern and southern halves by the equator, or into western and eastern halves by an imaginary line passing through the North and South Poles. **3** (also **cerebral hemisphere**) each of the two parts of the cerebrum (the main part of the brain) of a vertebrate. ■ **hem·i·spher·ic** /,hemə'sfi(ə)rik, -'sferik/ adj. **hem·i·spher·i·cal** /,hemə'sfi(ə)rikəl, -'sferikəl/ adj.

hem·line /'hem,līn/ ▶ n. the level of the lower edge of a garment such as a skirt or coat.

hem·lock /'hem,läk/ ▶ n. **1** a very poisonous plant of the parsley family, with fernlike leaves and small white flowers. **2** a poison obtained from this plant.

he·mo·glo·bin /'hēmə,glōbin/ ▶ n. a red protein containing iron, responsible for transporting oxygen in the blood.

he·mo·lyt·ic /,hēmə'litik/ ▶ adj. relating to or involving the rupture or destruction of red blood cells: *hemolytic anemia.*

he·mo·phil·i·a /,hēmə'filēə/ ▶ n. a medical condition in which the ability of the blood to clot is greatly reduced, causing severe bleeding from even a slight injury.

he·mo·phil·i·ac /,hēmə'filē,ak/ ▶ n. a person with hemophilia.

hem·or·rhage /'hem(ə)rij/ ▶ n. **1** a severe loss of blood from a ruptured blood vessel. **2** a damaging loss of valuable people or resources: *the continuing hemorrhage of doctors.* ▶ v. **1** bleed heavily from a ruptured blood vessel. **2** use or spend something valuable in large amounts: *the business was hemorrhaging cash.*

hem·or·rhoid /'hem(ə),roid/ ▶ n. a swollen vein or group of veins (piles) in the region of the anus.

he·mo·sta·sis /,hēmə'stāsəs, heme-/ ▶ n. the stopping of a flow of blood. ■ **he·mo·stat·ic** /-'statik/ adj.

hemp /hemp/ ▶ n. **1** the cannabis plant. **2** the fiber of the cannabis plant, extracted from the stem and used to make rope, strong fabrics, paper, etc. **3** marijuana.

hen /hen/ ▶ n. **1** a female bird, especially of a domestic fowl. **2** (**hens**) domestic fowls of either sex.

hen·bane /'hen,bān/ ▶ n. a poisonous plant of the nightshade family, with sticky hairy leaves and an unpleasant smell.

hence /hens/ ▶ adv. **1** as a consequence; for this reason. **2** from now; in the future: *two years hence.* **3** (also **from hence**) old use from here.

hence·forth /'hens,fôrth/ (also **henceforward**) ▶ adv. from this or that time on.

hench·man /'henCHmən/ ▶ n. (pl. **henchmen**) **1** chiefly derogatory a faithful supporter or assistant, especially one prepared to engage in criminal or dishonest activities. **2** historical a squire or page attending a prince or nobleman.

henge /henj/ ▶ n. a prehistoric monument consisting of a circle of stone or wooden uprights.

hen·na /'henə/ ▸ n. a reddish-brown dye made from the powdered leaves of a tropical shrub, used especially to color the hair and decorate the body. ▸ v. (**hennas, hennaing, hennaed**) dye the hair with henna.

hen par·ty ▸ n. informal a social gathering for women only.

hen·peck /'hen,pek/ ▸ v. (usu. as adj. **henpecked**) (of a woman) continually criticize and nag (her husband or other male partner).

hen·ry /'henrē/ ▸ n. (pl. **henries** or **henrys**) Physics the SI unit of inductance.

hep¹ /hep/ ▸ adj. old-fashioned term for **HIP³**.

hep² ▸ n. informal short for **HEPATITIS**: *hep C.*

hep·a·rin /'hepərin/ ▸ n. a compound found in the liver and other tissues that prevents blood clotting or coagulating, used in the treatment of thrombosis.

he·pat·ic /hə'patik/ ▸ adj. relating to the liver.

hep·a·ti·tis /,hepə'titis/ ▸ n. a disease in which the liver becomes inflamed, causing jaundice and other symptoms, mainly spread by a series of viruses (**hepatitis A**, **B**, and **C**) transmitted in blood or food.

hep·cat /'hep,kat/ ▸ n. informal, dated a stylish or fashionable person.

hepta- ▸ comb.form seven; having seven: *heptathlon.*

hep·ta·gon /'heptə,gän/ ▸ n. a plane figure with seven straight sides and angles.

hep·tath·lon /hep'taTHˌlän/ ▸ n. an athletic contest for women that consists of seven separate events. ■ **hep·tath·lete** n.

her /hər/ ▸ pron. (third person sing.) **1** used as the object of a verb or preposition to refer to a female person or animal previously mentioned. **2** referring to a ship, country, or other thing regarded as female. ▸ **possessive determiner 1** belonging to or associated with a female person or animal previously mentioned. **2** (**Her**) used in titles: *Her Royal Highness.*

her·ald /'herəld/ ▸ n. **1** an official employed to oversee matters concerning state ceremonies and the use of coats of arms. **2** historical a person who carried official messages, made proclamations, and oversaw tournaments. **3** a person or thing viewed as a sign that something is about to happen: *daffodils are the herald of spring.* ▸ v. **1** be a sign that something is about to happen: *the speech heralded a change in policy.* **2** describe in enthusiastic terms: *he was heralded as the next Sinatra.*

he·ral·dic /hə'raldik/ ▸ adj. relating to heraldry. ■ **he·ral·di·cal·ly** adv.

her·ald·ry /'herəldrē/ ▸ n. the system by which coats of arms are drawn up, described, and regulated.

herb /(h)ərb/ ▸ n. **1** any plant whose leaves, seeds, or flowers are used for flavoring food or in medicine. **2** Botany any seed-bearing plant that does not have a woody stem and dies down to the ground after flowering. ■ **herb·y** adj.

her·ba·ceous /(h)ər'bāSHəs/ ▸ adj. relating to herbs (in the botanical sense).

her·ba·ceous bor·der ▸ n. a garden border consisting mainly of flowering plants that live for several years.

herb·age /'(h)ərbij/ ▸ n. herbaceous plants, especially grass used for grazing.

herb·al /'(h)ərbəl/ ▸ adj. relating to or made from

herbs. ▸ n. a book that describes herbs and their culinary and medicinal properties.

her·bal·ism /'(h)ərbə,lizəm/ ▸ n. the study or practice of using herbs for medicinal or therapeutic purposes.

herb·al·ist /'(h)ərbəlist/ ▸ n. a person who practices herbalism, or one who grows or sells herbs for medicinal purposes.

her·bar·i·um /(h)ər'be(ə)rēəm/ ▸ n. (pl. **herbaria** /-'be(ə)rēə/) a collection of dried plants organized in a systematic way.

herbed /(h)ərbd/ ▸ adj. cooked or flavored with herbs.

herb·i·cide /'(h)ərbə,sīd/ ▸ n. a poisonous substance used to destroy unwanted plants.

her·bi·vore /'(h)ərbə,vôr/ ▸ n. an animal that feeds on plants. ■ **her·biv·o·rous** /(h)ər'biv(ə)rəs/ adj.

Her·cu·le·an /,hərkyə'lēən, hər'kyōōlēən/ ▸ adj. requiring great strength or effort: *a Herculean task.*

herd /hərd/ ▸ n. **1** a large group of animals, especially hoofed mammals, that live or are kept together. **2** derogatory a large group of people: *herds of tourists.* ▸ v. **1** move in a particular direction. **2** keep or look after livestock. ■ **herd·er** n.

herd in·stinct ▸ n. an inclination or natural tendency to behave or think like the majority of a group.

herds·man /'hərdzmən/ ▸ n. (pl. **herdsmen**) the owner or keeper of a herd of domesticated animals.

here /hi(ə)r/ ▸ adv. **1** in, at, or to this place or position. **2** (usu. **here is/are**) used when introducing or handing over something or someone. **3** used when indicating a time, point, or situation that has arrived or is happening. ▸ exclam. used to attract someone's attention. – PHRASES **here and now** at the present time. **here and there** in various places. **here's to** used to wish someone health or success before drinking. **neither here nor there** of no importance or relevance.

here·a·bouts /'hirə,bouts/ (also **hereabout**) ▸ adv. near this place.

here·af·ter /hi(ə)r'aftər/ ▸ adv. formal **1** from now on or at some time in the future. **2** after death. ▸ n. (**the hereafter**) life after death.

here·by /,hi(ə)r'bī, 'hi(ə)r,bī/ ▸ adv. formal as a result of this.

he·red·i·tar·y /hə'redi,terē/ ▸ adj. **1** passed on by or relating to inheritance. **2** (of a characteristic or disease) able to be passed on genetically from parents to their offspring. ■ **he·red·i·tar·i·ly** /hə,redi'te(ə)rəlē/ adv.

he·red·i·ty /hə'reditē/ ▸ n. **1** the passing on of physical or mental characteristics genetically from one generation to another. **2** the inheriting of a title, office, or right.

Her·e·ford /'hərfərd, 'herə-/ ▸ n. an animal of a breed of red and white beef cattle.

here·in /,hi(ə)r'in/ ▸ adv. formal in this document, book, or matter.

here·in·af·ter /,hi(ə)r'in'aftər/ ▸ adv. formal further on in this document.

here·of /,hi(ə)r'əv/ ▸ adv. formal of this document.

her·e·sy /'herəsē/ ▸ n. (pl. **heresies**) **1** belief or opinion that goes against traditional religious doctrine. **2** opinion that differs greatly from what is generally accepted.

her·e·tic /ˈherətɪk/ ▸ n. **1** a person who holds beliefs or opinions that go against traditional religious doctrine. **2** a person whose opinion differs greatly from that which is generally accepted. ■ **he·ret·i·cal** /həˈretɪkəl/ adj. **he·ret·i·cal·ly** adv.

here·to /ˌhi(ə)rˈtoo/ ▸ adv. formal to this matter or document.

here·to·fore /ˈhi(ə)rtəˌfôr/ ▸ adv. formal before now.

here·un·der /ˌhi(ə)rˈəndər/ ▸ adv. formal **1** as provided for under the terms of this document. **2** further on in this document.

here·up·on /ˌhi(ə)rəˈpän/ ▸ adv. old use after or as a result of this.

here·with /ˌhirˈwiTH, -ˈwiTH/ ▸ adv. formal with this letter or document.

her·it·a·ble /ˈheritəbəl/ ▸ adj. able to be inherited. ■ **her·it·a·bil·i·ty** /ˌheritəˈbilitē/ n. **her·it·a·bly** adv.

her·it·age /ˈheritij/ ▸ n. **1** property that is or may be inherited; an inheritance. **2** valued things such as historic buildings that have been passed down from previous generations. ▸ adj. (of a plant variety) not hybridized with another; old-fashioned: *heritage roses*.

her·maph·ro·dite /hərˈmafrədīt/ ▸ n. **1** a person or animal with both male and female sex organs or characteristics. **2** Botany a plant having stamens and pistils in the same flower. ■ **her·maph·ro·dit·ic** /-ˌmafrəˈditik/ adj. **her·maph·ro·dit·ism** /-diˌtizəm/ n.

her·me·neu·tic /ˌhərməˈn(y)ootik/ ▸ adj. relating to interpretation, especially of the Bible or literary texts. ■ **her·me·neu·ti·cal** adj.

her·me·neu·tics /ˌhərməˈn(y)ootiks/ ▸ pl.n. (usu. treated as sing.) the branch of knowledge that deals with interpretation, especially of the Bible or literary texts.

her·met·ic /hərˈmetik/ ▸ adj. **1** (of a seal or closure) complete and airtight. **2** insulated or protected from outside influences: *a hermetic society*. ■ **her·met·i·cal·ly** adv.

her·mit /ˈhərmit/ ▸ n. **1** a person living in solitude for religious reasons. **2** a person who prefers to live alone. ■ **her·mit·ic** /hərˈmitik/ adj.

her·mit·age /ˈhərmitij/ ▸ n. the home of a hermit, especially when small and remote.

her·mit crab ▸ n. a crab with a soft abdomen that lives in shells cast off by other shellfish.

her·ni·a /ˈhərnēə/ ▸ n. (pl. **hernias**) a condition in which part of an organ (typically the intestine) protrudes through the wall of the cavity containing it. ■ **her·ni·a·ted** /ˈhərnēˌātid/ adj. **her·ni·a·tion** /hərnēˈāsHən/ n.

he·ro /ˈhi(ə)rō/ ▸ n. (pl. **heroes**) **1** a person who is admired for their courage or outstanding achievements. **2** the chief male character in a book, play, or movie. **3** (in mythology and folklore) a person of superhuman qualities. **4** a submarine sandwich.

he·ro·ic /həˈrōik/ ▸ adj. **1** relating to or like a hero or heroine; very brave. **2** grand or ambitious in size or intention: *this is filmmaking on a heroic scale*. ▸ n. (**heroics**) brave or dramatic behavior or talk. ■ **he·ro·i·cal·ly** adv.

her·o·in /ˈherō-in/ ▸ n. a highly addictive painkilling drug obtained from morphine.

her·o·ine /ˈherō-in/ ▸ n. **1** a woman admired for her courage or outstanding achievements. **2** the

chief female character in a book, play, or movie.

her·o·ism /ˈherōˌizəm/ ▸ n. great bravery.

her·on /ˈherən/ ▸ n. a large fish-eating wading bird with long legs, a long neck, and a long pointed bill.

her·on·ry /ˈherənrē/ ▸ n. (pl. **heronries**) a breeding colony of herons, typically in a group of trees.

hero wor·ship ▸ n. extreme admiration for someone. ▸ v. (**hero-worship**) admire someone very much.

her·pes /ˈhərpēz/ ▸ n. a disease caused by a virus, affecting the skin (often with blisters) or the nervous system. ■ **her·pet·ic** /hərˈpetik/ adj.

her·pes sim·plex ▸ n. a form of herpes that may produce cold sores, genital inflammation, or conjunctivitis.

her·pes·vi·rus /ˈhərpēzˌvīrəs/ ▸ n. any of a group of viruses causing herpes and other diseases.

her·pes zos·ter /ˈzästər/ ▸ n. **1** medical name for SHINGLES. **2** a herpesvirus that causes shingles and chicken pox.

her·pe·tol·o·gy /ˌhərpəˈtäləjē/ ▸ n. the branch of zoology concerned with reptiles and amphibians. ■ **her·pe·to·log·i·cal** /-təˈläjəkəl/ adj. **her·pe·tol·o·gist** n.

Herr /he(ə)r/ ▸ n. a title or form of address for a German-speaking man, corresponding to *Mr.*

her·ring /ˈhering/ ▸ n. an edible silvery fish that is found in shoals in coastal waters.

her·ring·bone /ˈheringˌbōn/ ▸ n. a zigzag pattern consisting of columns of short parallel lines, with all the lines in one column sloping one way and all the lines in the next column sloping the other way.

her·ring gull ▸ n. a common northern gull with gray black-tipped wings.

hers /hərz/ ▸ possessive pron. used to refer to a thing or things belonging to or associated with a female person or animal previously mentioned.

> **USAGE**
> There is no apostrophe: the spelling should be **hers** not *her's*.

her·self /hərˈself/ ▸ pron. (third person sing.) **1** (reflexive) used as the object of a verb or preposition to refer to a female person or animal previously mentioned as the subject of the clause. **2** (emphatic) she or her personally.

hertz /hərts/ ▸ n. (pl. same) the SI unit of frequency, equal to one cycle per second.

he's /hēz/ ▸ contr. **1** he is. **2** he has.

hes·i·tant /ˈhezitənt/ ▸ adj. slow to act or speak as a result of indecision or reluctance. ■ **hes·i·tance** n. **hes·i·tan·cy** n. **hes·i·tant·ly** adv.

hes·i·tate /ˈheziˌtāt/ ▸ v. **1** pause indecisively. **2** be reluctant to do something: *please do not hesitate to contact me*. ■ **hes·i·ta·tion** /ˌheziˈtāsHən/ n.

het·er·o /ˈhetərō/ ▸ n. & adj. informal short for HETEROSEXUAL.

hetero- ▸ comb.form other; different: *heterosexual*.

het·er·o·cy·clic /ˌhetərōˈsīklik, -ˈsiklik/ ▸ adj. referring to a chemical compound whose molecule contains a ring of atoms of at least two elements (one of which is generally carbon).

het·er·o·dox /ˈhetərəˌdäks/ ▸ adj. not following the usual or accepted standards or beliefs. ■ **het·er·o·dox·y** n.

het·er·o·ge·ne·ous /ˌhetərəˈjēnēəs/ ▸ adj. consisting of many different kinds of people or things; varied: *a heterogeneous collection.* ■ **het·er·o·ge·ne·i·ty** /-jəˈnēətē/ n. **het·er·o·ge·ne·ous·ly** adv.

het·er·ol·o·gous /ˌhetəˈräləgəs/ ▸ adj. chiefly Biology not homologous. ■ **het·er·ol·o·gy** /-ˈräləjē/ n.

het·er·o·mor·phic /ˌhetərəˈmôrfik/ ▸ adj. Biology occurring in two or more forms, especially at different stages in the life cycle. ■ **het·er·o·morph** /ˈhetərəˌmôrf/ n.

het·er·o·sex·ism /ˌhetərōˈsekˌsizəm/ ▸ n. discrimination or prejudice against homosexuals on the assumption that heterosexuality is the norm. ■ **het·er·o·sex·ist** adj.

het·er·o·sex·u·al /ˌhetərōˈsekshoōəl/ ▸ adj. **1** sexually attracted to the opposite sex. **2** (of a sexual relationship) between a man and a woman. ▸ n. a heterosexual person. ■ **het·er·o·sex·u·al·i·ty** /-ˌseksHoōˈalitē/ n. **het·er·o·sex·u·al·ly** adv.

het up /ˌhet ˈəp/ ▸ adj. informal angry and agitated.

heu·ris·tic /hyoōˈristik/ ▸ adj. **1** allowing a person to discover or learn something for themselves. **2** Computing proceeding to a solution by trial and error or by rules that are only loosely defined. ▸ n. **1** (**heuristics**) (usu. treated as sing.) the study and use of heuristic techniques. **2** a heuristic process or method. ■ **heu·ris·ti·cal·ly** adv.

hew /hyoō/ ▸ v. (past part. **hewn** /hyoōn/ or **hewed**) **1** chop or cut wood, coal, etc., with an ax, pick, or other tool. **2** (**be hewn**) be cut or formed from a hard material: *a seat hewn out of a fallen tree trunk.* **3** (**hew to**) conform or adhere to.

hex¹ /heks/ ▸ v. cast a spell on someone. ▸ n. **1** a magic spell. **2** a witch.

hex² ▸ adj. short for HEXADECIMAL.

hexa- (also **hex-** before a vowel) ▸ comb.form six; having six: *hexagon.*

hex·a·dec·i·mal /ˌheksəˈdes(ə)məl/ ▸ adj. Computing relating to or using a system of numerical notation that has 16 rather than 10 as its base.

hex·a·gon /ˈheksəˌgän/ ▸ n. a plane figure with six straight sides and angles. ■ **hex·ag·o·nal** /hekˈsagənl/ adj.

hex·a·gram /ˈheksəˌgram/ ▸ n. a six-pointed star formed by two intersecting equilateral triangles.

hex·a·he·dron /ˌheksəˈhēdrən/ ▸ n. (pl. **hexahedra** or **hexahedrons**) a solid figure with six plane faces. ■ **hex·a·he·dral** adj.

hex·am·e·ter /hekˈsamitər/ ▸ n. a line of verse consisting of six metrical feet.

hex·ane /ˈhekˌsān/ ▸ n. a colorless liquid hydrocarbon of the alkane series, commonly used as a solvent.

hex·a·va·lent /ˌheksəˈvālənt/ ▸ adj. Chemistry having a valence of six.

hey /hā/ ▸ exclam. used to attract attention or to express surprise, interest, annoyance, etc.

hey·day /ˈhāˌdā/ ▸ n. (**one's heyday**) the period of someone's or something's greatest success, popularity, activity, etc.: *the paper has lost millions of readers since its heyday in 1964.*

HF ▸ abbr. Physics high frequency.

Hf ▸ symbol the chemical element hafnium.

Hg ▸ symbol the chemical element mercury.

HHS ▸ abbr. (Department of) Health and Human Services.

HI ▸ abbr. Hawaii.

hi /hī/ ▸ exclam. informal used as a friendly greeting.

hi·a·tal her·ni·a (also **hiatus hernia**) ▸ n. a condition in which an organ (usually the stomach) protrudes through the diaphragm at the opening for the esophagus.

hi·a·tus /hīˈātəs/ ▸ n. (pl. **hiatuses**) a pause or gap in a series, sequence, or process: *there was a brief hiatus in the war.*

Hib /hib/ ▸ n. a bacterium that causes meningitis in very young children or babies.

hi·ba·chi /həˈbächē/ ▸ n. (pl. **hibachis**) a portable apparatus for grilling foods over charcoal.

hi·ber·nate /ˈhībərˌnāt/ ▸ v. (of an animal) spend the winter in a state like deep sleep. ■ **hi·ber·na·tion** /ˌhībərˈnāsHən/ n. **hi·ber·na·tor** n.

Hi·ber·ni·an /hīˈbərnēən/ ▸ adj. Irish (now chiefly used in names). ▸ n. an Irish person (now chiefly used in names).

hi·bis·cus /hīˈbiskəs/ ▸ n. a plant of the mallow family with large brightly colored flowers.

hic·cup /ˈhikəp/ (also **hiccough** pronunc. same) ▸ n. **1** a gulping sound in the throat caused by an involuntary spasm of the diaphragm and respiratory organs. **2** a minor difficulty or setback. ▸ v. (**hiccups, hiccuping, hiccuped**) make the sound of a hiccup or series of hiccups. ■ **hic·cup·y** adj.

hick /hik/ ▸ n. informal an unsophisticated person from the country.

hick·ey /ˈhikē/ ▸ n. (pl. **hickeys**) informal a temporary red mark on the skin caused by biting or sucking during sexual play.

hick·o·ry /ˈhik(ə)rē/ ▸ n. **1** a tree found in chiefly in North America with tough, heavy wood and edible nuts. **2** a stick made of hickory wood.

hid /hid/ ▸ past of HIDE¹.

hid·den /ˈhidn/ ▸ past participle of HIDE¹. ■ **hid·den·ness** n.

hid·den a·gen·da ▸ n. a secret motive or plan.

hide¹ /hīd/ ▸ v. (past **hid** /hid/; past part. **hidden** /ˈhidn/) **1** put or keep out of sight: *I hid the key under a flowerpot.* **2** conceal oneself. **3** keep something secret.
– PHRASES **hide one's light under a bushel** keep quiet about one's talents or accomplishments.

hide² ▸ n. the skin of an animal, especially when made into leather.
– PHRASES **neither hide nor hair of** not the slightest trace of.

hide-and-seek ▸ n. a children's game in which one player tries to find other players who have hidden themselves.

hide·a·way /ˈhīdəˌwā/ ▸ n. a place where one can hide or be alone. ▸ adj. designed to be concealed when not in use: *a hideaway bed.*

hide·bound /ˈhīdˌbound/ ▸ adj. unwilling or unable to abandon old-fashioned ideas or customs in favor of new ways of thinking.

hid·e·ous /ˈhidēəs/ ▸ adj. **1** extremely ugly. **2** extremely unpleasant. ■ **hid·e·ous·ly** adv. **hid·e·ous·ness** n.

hide·out /ˈhīdˌout/ ▸ n. a hiding place, especially one used by someone who has broken the law.

hid·ey-hole /ˈhīdēˌhōl/ (also **hidy-hole**) ▸ n. informal a hiding place.

hid·ing¹ /ˈhīdiNG/ ▸ n. **1** a physical beating. **2** informal a severe defeat.

hid·ing² ▸ n. the action of hiding or the state of being hidden: *he had gone into hiding.*

hie /hī/ ▸ v. (**hies, hieing** or **hying, hied**) old use
go quickly.

hi·er·ar·chi·cal /ˌhī(ə)'rärkikəl/ ▸ adj. arranged
in order of rank or status. ■ **hi·er·ar·chi·cal·ly** adv.

hi·er·ar·chy /'hī(ə)ˌrärkē/ ▸ n. (pl. **hierarchies**)
1 a system in which people are ranked one above
the other according to their status or authority.
2 a classification of things according to their
relative importance.

hi·er·at·ic /ˌhī(ə)'ratik/ ▸ adj. relating to priests.

hi·er·o·glyph /'hī(ə)rəˌglif/ ▸ n. a picture of an
object representing a word, syllable, or sound,
especially as found in the ancient Egyptian
writing system.

hi·er·o·glyph·ic /ˌhī(ə)rə'glifik/
▸ n. (**hieroglyphics**) writing consisting of
hieroglyphs. ▸ adj. relating to or written in
hieroglyphs.

hi·er·o·phant /'hī(ə)rəˌfant/ ▸ n. a person,
especially a priest, who interprets sacred
mysteries or other things that are very difficult
to understand. ■ **hi·er·o·phan·tic** adj.

hi-fi /'hī 'fī/ informal ▸ adj. relating to the
reproduction of high-fidelity sound. ▸ n. (pl.
hi-fis) a set of equipment for reproducing high-
fidelity sound.

hig·gle·dy-pig·gle·dy /'higəldē 'pigəldē/
▸ adv. & adj. in confusion or disorder.

high /hī/ ▸ adj. **1** extending far upward. **2** of
a specified height. **3** far above ground or sea
level. **4** great or greater than normal in amount,
value, size, or intensity: *high blood pressure.*
5 (of a period or movement) at its peak: *high
summer.* **6** great in rank or status; important.
7 culturally or morally superior: *a man with
high ideals.* **8** (of a sound or note) at or near the
top of a musical scale; not deep or low. **9** informal
under the influence of drugs or alcohol. **10** (of
food) strong-smelling because beginning to go
bad. **11** (of game) slightly decomposed and so
ready to cook. ▸ n. **1** a high point, level, or figure.
2 an area of high atmospheric pressure. **3** informal
a state of intense happiness. ▸ adv. **1** at or to
a considerable or specified height. **2** at a high
price. **3** (of a sound) at or to a high pitch.
– PHRASES **from on high 1** from a very high
place. **2** from remote high authority or heaven.
high and dry 1 stranded by the sea as it retreats.
2 in a very difficult position. **high and low**
in many different places. **high and mighty**
informal arrogant. **the high ground** a position of
superiority. **it is high time that** —— it is past
the time when something should have happened
or been done. **on one's high horse** informal
behaving arrogantly or pompously. **run high**
1 (of a river) be full and close to overflowing,
with a strong current. **2** (of feelings) be intense.

high altar ▸ n. the chief altar of a church.

high·ball /'hīˌbôl/ ▸ n. a drink consisting of
whiskey and a mixer such as soda or ginger ale,
served in a tall glass with ice.

high beam ▸ n. **1** the brightest setting of
a vehicle's headlights. **2** (**high beams**) the
headlights of a vehicle when set on high beam:
the glare from his high beams.

high-born ▸ adj. having noble parents.

high·brow /'hīˌbrou/ ▸ adj. often derogatory
concerned with serious artistic or cultural ideas;
intellectual or refined. ▸ n. a person of this type.

high chair ▸ n. a small chair with long legs for a
baby or small child, fitted with a tray and used
at mealtimes.

High Church ▸ n. a tradition within the Anglican
Church that emphasizes the importance of ritual
and the authority of bishops and priests.

high-class ▸ adj. of a high standard, quality, or
social class.

high com·mand ▸ n. the commander-in-chief
and associated senior staff of an army, navy, or
air force.

high com·mis·sion ▸ n. an embassy of
one Commonwealth country in another.
■ **high com·mis·sion·er** n.

high court ▸ n. **1** a supreme court of justice.
2 the US Supreme Court.

high-end ▸ adj. referring to the most expensive
of a range of products.

high·er ed·u·ca·tion ▸ n. education beyond
high school, especially at a college or university.

high ex·plo·sive ▸ n. a powerful chemical
explosive of the kind used in shells and bombs.

high-fa·lu·tin /ˌhīfə'lootn/ ▸ adj. informal grand or
self-important in a pompous or pretentious way.

high fash·ion ▸ n. another term for HAUTE
COUTURE.

high fi·del·i·ty ▸ n. the reproduction of sound
with little distortion.

high fi·nance ▸ n. financial transactions
involving large sums of money.

high five ▸ n. informal a gesture of celebration or
greeting in which two people slap each other's
palms with their arms raised.

high·fli·er /'hīflīər/ ▸ n. **1** someone who very
successful, especially academically or in
business. **2** a stock that trades at a high price or
that has risen sharply.

high-flown ▸ adj. (especially of language)
extravagant or intended to impress.

high fre·quen·cy ▸ n. (in radio) a frequency of
3–30 megahertz.

high gear ▸ n. a gear that makes a wheeled
vehicle move fast.

High Ger·man ▸ n. the standard literary and
spoken form of German, originally used in the
highlands in the south of Germany.

high-grade ▸ adj. **1** of very good quality. **2** (of
a medical condition) of a more serious kind;
major: *a high-grade tumor.*

high-hand·ed ▸ adj. using one's authority
forcefully and without considering the feelings
of other people.

high-hat ▸ n. **1** a snobbish or supercilious person.
2 variant spelling of HI-HAT. ▸ adj. snobbish or
supercilious.

high-im·pact ▸ adj. (of physical exercises,
especially aerobics) placing a great deal of stress
on the body.

high jinks /jiNGks/ ▸ pl. n. high-spirited fun.

high jump ▸ n. (**the high jump**) an athletic
event in which competitors jump as high as
possible over a bar that is raised after each
round. ■ **high jump·er** n.

high·land /'hīlənd/ ▸ n. (also **highlands**) **1** an
area of high or mountainous land. **2** (**the
Highlands**) the mountainous northern part of
Scotland. ■ **high·land·er** n.

High·land fling ▸ n. an energetic solo Scottish
dance consisting of a series of complex steps.

high-lev·el ▸ adj. **1** involving senior people;

of relatively high importance: *high-level negotiations.* **2** (of a computer programming language) having instructions resembling an existing language such as English, making it relatively easy to use.

high life ▶ n. an extravagant social life as enjoyed by wealthy people.

high·light /'hī,līt/ ▶ n. **1** an outstanding part of an event or period of time: *that season was the highlight of his career.* **2** a bright or reflective area in a painting, picture, or design. **3** (**highlights**) bright tints in the hair, produced by bleaching or dyeing. ▶ v. **1** draw attention to: *the issues highlighted by the report.* **2** mark something with a highlighter. **3** create highlights in hair.

high·light·er /'hī,lītər/ ▶ n. **1** a broad felt-tipped pen used to overlay transparent fluorescent color on a part of a text or illustration. **2** a cosmetic used to emphasize the cheekbones or other facial features.

high·ly /'hīlē/ ▶ adv. **1** to a high degree or level. **2** favorably.

high-main·te·nance ▶ adj. **1** needing a lot of work to keep in good condition: *high-maintenance bricks and mortar.* **2** informal (of a person or relationship) demanding a lot of attention.

High Mass ▶ n. a Roman Catholic mass with full ritual procedure, including music and incense.

high-mind·ed ▶ adj. having strong moral principles.

high·ness /'hīnis/ ▶ n. **1** (**His, Her, Your Highness**) a title given to a person of royal rank, or used in addressing them. **2** the quality of being high: *the highness of her cheekbones.*

high-oc·tane ▶ adj. **1** (of gasoline) having a high octane number and therefore allowing an engine to run smoothly. **2** powerful or dynamic: *a high-octane career.*

high-pitched ▶ adj. (of a sound) high in pitch.

high-pow·ered ▶ adj. informal (of a person) dynamic and forceful.

high-pres·sure ▶ adj. **1** involving a high degree of activity and exertion; stressful: *a high-pressure career.* **2** (of a salesperson or sales pitch) employing a high degree of coercion; insistent. **3** involving or using much physical force: *high-pressure jets of water.* **4** referring to a condition of the atmosphere with the pressure above average.

high priest ▶ n. **1** a chief priest of a non-Christian religion. **2** (also **high priestess**) the leader of a cult or movement.

high-pro·file ▶ adj. attracting much attention or publicity: *a high-profile court case.*

high re·lief ▶ n. see RELIEF (sense 8).

high-rise ▶ adj. (of a building) having many stories. ▶ n. a building with many stories.

high road ▶ n. a morally superior approach toward something: *she took the high road and refused to engage in negative campaigning.*

high roll·er ▶ n. informal a person who gambles or spends large sums of money.

high school ▶ n. a secondary school that typically comprises grades 9 through 12.

high seas ▶ pl.n. (**the high seas**) the open ocean, especially the areas that are not under the control of any one country.

high sea·son ▶ n. the most popular time of year for a vacation, when prices are highest.

high sher·iff ▶ n. see SHERIFF.

high so·ci·e·ty ▶ n. see SOCIETY (sense 3).

high spir·its ▶ pl.n. lively and cheerful behavior or mood. ■ **high-spir·it·ed** adj.

high spot ▶ n. the most enjoyable part of an experience or period of time.

high street Brit. ▶ n. the main street of a town. ▶ adj. (**high-street**) catering to the needs of the ordinary public: *high-street fashion.*

high-strung ▶ adj. very nervous and easily upset.

high·tail /'hī,tāl/ ▶ v. informal move or travel fast.

high tea ▶ n. Brit. a meal eaten in the late afternoon or early evening, typically consisting of a cooked dish and tea.

high-tech /'hī 'tek/ (also **hi-tech**) ▶ adj. **1** using, needing, or involved in high technology. **2** (of architecture and interior design) functional in style and using materials such as steel, plastic, and glass.

high tech·nol·o·gy ▶ n. advanced technological development, especially in electronics.

high-ten·sile ▶ adj. (of metal) very strong under tension.

high tide (also **high water**) ▶ n. **1** the state of the tide when at its highest level. **2** the highest point of something: *the high tide of nationalism.*

high-top ▶ adj. referring to a sneaker with a laced upper that extends above the ankle. ▶ n. (**high-tops**) a pair of such shoes.

high trea·son ▶ n. see TREASON.

high-wa·ter mark ▶ n. the level reached by the sea at high tide, or by a lake or river during a flood.

high·way /'hī,wā/ ▶ n. **1** a main road, especially one connecting major towns or cities. **2** (chiefly in official use) a public road.

high·way·man /'hī,wāmən/ ▶ n. (pl. **highwaymen**) historical a man, typically on horseback, who held up and robbed travelers.

high wire ▶ n. a high tightrope. ▶ adj. requiring great skill or judgment.

hi-hat (also **high-hat**) ▶ n. a pair of foot-operated cymbals forming part of a drum kit.

hi·jab /hi'jäb/ ▶ n. a head covering worn in public by some Muslim women.

hi·jack /'hī,jak/ ▶ v. **1** illegally seize control of an aircraft, ship, vehicle, etc., while it is traveling somewhere. **2** take over something and use it for a new purpose: *the organization had been hijacked by extremists.* ▶ n. an instance of hijacking an aircraft, ship, etc. ■ **hi·jack·er** n.

Hij·ra /'hijrə/ ▶ n. variant spelling of HEGIRA.

hike /hīk/ ▶ n. **1** a long walk, especially in the country or wilderness. **2** a sharp increase, especially in price. **3** informal a long distance. ▶ v. **1** go on a hike. **2** pull or lift up clothing. **3** increase a price sharply. ■ **hik·er** n.

hi·lar·i·ous /hə'le(ə)rēəs/ ▶ adj. extremely funny. ■ **hi·lar·i·ous·ly** adv.

hi·lar·i·ty /hə'le(ə)ritē/ ▶ n. a state of great amusement causing loud laughter.

hill /hil/ ▶ n. a naturally raised area of land, not as high or craggy as a mountain.
– PHRASES **over the hill** informal old and past one's prime.

hill·bil·ly /'hil,bilē/ ▶ n. (pl. **hillbillies**) informal, chiefly derogatory an unsophisticated country person.

hill·ock /'hilək/ ▶ n. a small hill or mound.
■ **hill·ock·y** adj.

hill·side /'hil,sīd/ ▶ n. the sloping side of a hill.

hill sta·tion ▶ n. a town in the low mountains of the Indian subcontinent, popular as a vacation-resort during the hot season.

hill·top /'hil,täp/ ▶ n. the summit of a hill.

hill·y /'hilē/ ▶ adj. (**hillier, hilliest**) having many hills. ■ **hill·i·ness** n.

hilt /hilt/ ▶ n. the handle of a sword, dagger, or knife.
– PHRASES **to the hilt** completely.

him /him/ ▶ pron. (third person sing.) used as the object of a verb or preposition to refer to a male person or animal previously mentioned.

> USAGE
> Why is it often said that you should say *I could never be as good as he* rather than *I could never be as good as him*? For a discussion of this issue, see the note at PERSONAL PRONOUN.

Him·a·la·yan /,himə'lāən/ ▶ adj. relating to the Himalayas, a mountain system in southern Asia.

him·self /him'self/ ▶ pron. (third person sing.)
1 (reflexive) used as the object of a verb or preposition to refer to a male person or animal previously mentioned as the subject of the clause. 2 (emphatic) he or him personally.

hind¹ /hīnd/ ▶ adj. situated at the back.

hind² ▶ n. a female deer.

hind·er¹ /'hindər/ ▶ v. delay or impede someone or something.

hind·er² /'hīndər/ ▶ adj. situated at or toward the back.

Hin·di /'hindē/ ▶ n. a language of northern India derived from Sanskrit. ▶ adj. relating to Hindi.

hind·limb /'hīn(d),lim/ ▶ n. either of the two back limbs of an animal.

hind·most /'hīn(d),mōst/ ▶ adj. farthest back.

hind·quar·ters /'hīn(d),kwôrtərz/ ▶ pl.n. the hind legs and adjoining parts of a four-legged animal.

hin·drance /'hindrəns/ ▶ n. a thing that delays or impedes someone or something.

hind·sight /'hīn(d),sīt/ ▶ n. understanding of a situation or event after it has happened.

Hin·du /'hindoo/ ▶ n. (pl. **Hindus**) a follower of Hinduism. ▶ adj. relating to Hinduism.

Hin·du·ism /'hindoo,izəm/ ▶ n. a major religious and cultural tradition of the Indian subcontinent, including belief in reincarnation and the worship of a large number of gods and goddesses. ■ **Hin·du·ize** v.

Hin·du·sta·ni /,hindoo'stänē/ ▶ n. a group of languages and dialects spoken in NW India that includes Hindi and Urdu.

hind·wing /'hīn(d),wiNG/ ▶ n. either of the two back wings of a four-winged insect.

hinge /hinj/ ▶ n. a movable joint or mechanism by which a door, gate, or lid opens and closes or that connects linked objects. ▶ v. (**hinges, hinging, hinged**) 1 attach or join something with a hinge. 2 (**hinge on**) depend entirely on: *the city's future is likely to hinge on the election.*

hin·ny /'hinē/ ▶ n. (pl. **hinnies**) the offspring of a female donkey and a male horse.

hint /hint/ ▶ n. 1 a slight or indirect indication. 2 a very small trace of something. 3 a small item of practical information. ▶ v. 1 indicate

something indirectly. 2 (**hint at**) be a slight indication of: *a sound that hinted at deep power.*

hin·ter·land /'hintər,land/ (also **hinterlands**) ▶ n. 1 the remote areas of a country, away from the coast and major rivers. 2 the area around or beyond a major town or port.

hip¹ /hip/ ▶ n. a projection of the pelvis and upper thigh bone on each side of the body. ■ **hipped** adj.
– PHRASES **be joined at the hip** informal (of two people) be inseparable.

hip² ▶ n. the fruit of a rose.

hip³ ▶ adj. (**hipper, hippest**) informal 1 very fashionable. 2 (**hip to**) aware of or informed about something. ■ **hip·ness** n.

hip⁴ ▶ exclam. introducing a communal cheer: *hip, hip, hooray!*

hip·bone /'hip,bōn/ ▶ n. a large bone forming the main part of the pelvis on each side of the body.

hip flask ▶ n. a small flask for liquor, carried in a hip pocket.

hip-hop ▶ n. a style of pop music of US black and Hispanic origin, featuring rap with an electronic backing. ■ **hip-hop·per** n.

hip·pie /'hipē/ ▶ n. variant spelling of HIPPY.

hip·po /'hipō/ ▶ n. (pl. same or **hippos**) informal a hippopotamus.

Hip·po·crat·ic oath /'hipə'kratik/ ▶ n. an oath formerly taken by medical doctors to observe a code of professional behavior (parts of which are still used in some medical schools).

hip·po·drome /'hipə,drōm/ ▶ n. 1 an arena for equestrian or other sporting events. 2 (in ancient Greece or Rome) a course for chariot or horse races.

hip·po·pot·a·mus /,hipə'pätəməs/ ▶ n. (pl. **hippopotamuses** or **hippopotami** /-,mī, -,mē/) a large African mammal with a thick skin and massive jaws, living partly on land and partly in water.

hip·py /'hipē/ (also **hippie**) ▶ n. (pl. **hippies**) (especially in the 1960s) a young person, typically having long hair, who advocates peace and free love and dresses unconventionally.
■ **hip·pie·dom** n. **hip·py·ish** adj.

hip·ster /'hipstər/ ▶ n. informal a person who follows the latest trends and fashions.

hip·sters /'hipstərz/ ▶ pl.n. pants with a waistline at the hips; hip-huggers.

hire /hīr/ ▶ v. 1 appoint someone as an employee. 2 employ someone for a short time to do a particular job. 3 (**hire oneself out**) make oneself available for temporary employment. ▶ n. 1 the action of hiring someone or something. 2 a recently recruited employee. ■ **hire·a·ble** adj. **hir·er** n.
– PHRASES **for hire** available to be hired.

hire·ling /'hīrliNG/ ▶ n. chiefly derogatory a person who is willing to undertake any kind of work provided that they are paid.

hir·sute /'hər,soot, hər'soot, 'hi(ə)r,soot/ ▶ adj. having a great deal of hair on the face or body; hairy. ■ **hir·sute·ness** n.

his /hiz/ ▶ possessive determiner 1 belonging to or associated with a male person or animal previously mentioned. 2 (**His**) used in titles: *His Honor.* ▶ possessive pron. used to refer to a thing belonging to or associated with a male person or animal previously mentioned.

His·pan·ic /hi'spanik/ ▶ adj. relating to Spain or to Spanish-speaking countries, especially those of Latin America. ▶ n. a Spanish-speaking person, especially one of Latin American descent, living in the US. ■ **His·pan·i·cize** /hi'spani,sīz/ v.

> **USAGE**
> In the US, **Hispanic** is the standard accepted term when referring to Spanish-speaking people living in the US. Other, more specific terms such as **Latino** and **Chicano** are also used where occasion demands.

hiss /his/ ▶ v. **1** make a sharp sound like that made when pronouncing the letter *s*, often as a sign of disapproval or mockery. **2** whisper something in an urgent or angry way. ▶ n. **1** a hissing sound. **2** electrical interference at audio frequencies.

his·ta·mine /'histə,mēn, -,min/ ▶ n. a compound that is released by cells in response to injury and in allergic reactions.

his·to·gram /'histə,gram/ ▶ n. Statistics a diagram consisting of rectangles whose height is proportional to the frequency of a variable and whose width is equal to the class interval.

his·tol·o·gy /hi'stäləjē/ ▶ n. the branch of biology concerned with the microscopic structure of tissues. ■ **his·to·log·i·cal** /,histə'läjikəl/ adj. **his·tol·o·gist** n.

his·to·pa·thol·o·gy /,histōpə'ᴛʜäləjē/ ▶ n. the branch of medicine concerned with the changes in tissues caused by disease. ■ **his·to·path·o·log·i·cal** /,histō,paᴛʜə'läjikəl/ adj. **his·to·pa·thol·o·gist** n.

his·to·ri·an /hi'stôrēən/ ▶ n. an expert in history.

his·tor·ic /hi'stôrik, -'stär-/ ▶ adj. **1** famous or important in history, or likely to be so in the future: *a historic occasion.* **2** Grammar (of a tense) used in describing past events.

> **USAGE**
> **Historic** and **historical** do not have the same meaning. **Historic** means 'famous or important in history' (*a historic occasion*), whereas **historical** chiefly means 'relating to history' (*historical evidence*).

his·tor·i·cal /hi'stôrikəl, -'stär-/ ▶ adj. **1** relating to history: *historical evidence.* **2** belonging to or set in the past. **3** (of the study of a subject) based on an analysis of its development over a period. ■ **his·tor·i·cal·ly** adv.

his·tor·i·cism /hi'stôrə,sizəm, -'stär-/ ▶ n. **1** the theory that social and cultural developments are determined by history. **2** excessive regard for past styles of art and architecture. ■ **his·tor·i·cist** n. **his·tor·i·cize** v.

his·to·ric·i·ty /,histə'risitē/ ▶ n. historical authenticity.

his·tor·ic pres·ent /'prezənt/ ▶ n. Grammar the present tense used instead of the past in vivid narrative or informal speech.

his·to·ri·og·ra·phy /hi,stôrē'ägrəfē, -,stär-/ ▶ n. **1** the study of the writing of history and of written histories. **2** the writing of history. ■ **his·to·ri·og·ra·pher** n. **his·to·ri·o·graph·ic** /-ə'grafik/ adj. **his·to·ri·o·graph·i·cal** /-ə'grafikəl/ adj.

his·to·ry /'hist(ə)rē/ ▶ n. (pl. **histories**) **1** the study of past events. **2** the past considered as a whole. **3** the past events connected with someone or something: *a patient with a complicated medical history.* **4** a continuous record of past events or trends.
– PHRASES **be history** informal be dismissed or

dead; be finished.

his·tri·on·ic /,histrē'änik/ ▶ adj. **1** excessively theatrical or dramatic. **2** formal relating to actors or acting. ▶ n. (**histrionics**) exaggerated behavior designed to attract attention. ■ **his·tri·on·i·cal·ly** adv.

hit /hit/ ▶ v. (**hits**, **hitting**, **hit**) **1** strike someone or something with the hand or a tool, bat, weapon, etc. **2** come into contact with someone or something quickly and forcefully. **3** strike a target. **4** cause harm or distress to: *the area was badly hit by layoffs.* **5** (**hit out**) make a strongly worded criticism or attack. **6** be suddenly realized by: *it hit me that I was successful.* **7** (**hit on**) informal suddenly discover or think of something. **8** (**hit on**) informal make sexual advances toward. **9** informal reach or arrive at a place, level, or figure. ▶ n. **1** an instance of hitting or being hit. **2** a successful movie, pop record, etc. **3** Computing an instance of identifying an item of data that matches the requirements of a search. **4** an instance of a particular website being accessed by a user. **5** informal a murder carried out by a criminal organization. **6** informal a dose of an addictive drug. ■ **hit·ter** n.
– PHRASES **hit-and-miss** done or occurring at random. **hit-and-run** (of a road accident) from which the driver responsible leaves rapidly without helping the other people involved. **hit someone below the belt 1** Boxing give one's opponent an illegal low blow. **2** behave unfairly toward someone. **hit the ground running** informal start something new with energy and enthusiasm. **hit it off** informal be naturally well suited. **hit the nail on the head** find exactly the right answer. **hit-or-miss** as likely to be unsuccessful as successful. **hit the road** (or **trail**) informal set out on a journey.

hitch /hicʜ/ ▶ v. **1** move something into a different position with a jerk: *she hitched up her skirt and ran.* **2** fasten or tether an animal with a rope. **3** informal travel or obtain a lift by hitch-hiking. ▶ n. **1** a temporary difficulty. **2** a temporary knot used to fasten one thing to another.
– PHRASES **get hitched** informal get married.

hitch·er /'hicʜər/ ▶ n. a hitch-hiker.

hitch·hike /'hicʜ,hīk/ ▶ v. travel by getting free rides in passing vehicles: *he dropped out in 1976 and hitchhiked west.* ■ **hitch·hik·er** n.

hi-tech ▶ adj. variant spelling of HIGH-TECH.

hith·er /'hiᴛʜər/ ▶ adv. old use to or toward this place.
– PHRASES **hith·er and thith·er** (also **hither and yon**) to and fro.

hith·er·to /'hiᴛʜər,too͞, ,hiᴛʜər'too͞/ ▶ adv. until the point in time under discussion.

Hit·ler·i·an /hit'le(ə)rēən/ ▶ adj. relating to or characteristic of the Austrian-born Nazi leader and Chancellor of Germany, Adolf Hitler.

hit list ▶ n. a list of people to be killed for criminal or political reasons.

hit man ▶ n. informal a hired assassin.

hit pa·rade ▶ n. dated a list of popular things, especially of best-selling songs.

Hit·tite /'hitīt/ ▶ n. **1** a member of an ancient people who established an empire in the western peninsula of Asia and Syria *c.* 1700–1200 BC. **2** the language of the Hittites. ▶ adj. relating to the Hittites.

HIV ▶ abbr. human immunodeficiency virus (the

virus that causes AIDS).

hive /hīv/ ▸ n. **1** a beehive. **2** a place full of people working hard. ▸ v. place bees in a hive.

hives /hīvz/ ▸ pl.n. (treated as sing. or pl.) a very itchy rash of round, red weals on the skin, caused by an allergic reaction.

HIV-pos·i·tive ▸ adj. having had a positive result in a blood test for HIV.

HK ▸ abbr. Hong Kong.

hl ▸ abbr. hectoliter(s).

HMO ▸ abbr. health maintenance organization; an organization to which subscribers pay a predetermined fee in return for a range of medical services.

HMS ▸ abbr. Her or His Majesty's Ship.

Ho ▸ symbol the chemical element holmium.

ho¹ /hō/ ▸ n. (pl. **hos** or **hoes**) informal **1** a prostitute. **2** derogatory a woman.

ho² /hō/ ▸ exclam. **1** an expression of surprise, admiration, triumph, or derision. **2** used as the second element of various exclamations: *heave ho!* **3** used to call for attention: *ho there!*

hoa·gie /'hōgē/ ▸ n. another term for **SUBMARINE SANDWICH**.

hoard /hôrd/ ▸ n. **1** a secret store of money or valuables. **2** a store of useful information. ▸ v. gradually collect something and store it away. ■ **hoard·er** n.

> **USAGE**
> **Hoard** and **horde** are sometimes confused. A **hoard** is 'a secret store' (*a hoard of treasure*), while **horde** is a word showing disapproval when talking about 'a large group of people' (*hordes of greedy shareholders*).

hoar·frost /'hôr,frôst, -,fräst/ ▸ n. a grayish-white, feathery deposit of frost.

hoarse /hôrs/ ▸ adj. (of a voice) rough and harsh. ■ **hoarse·ly** adv. **hoarse·en** v. **hoarse·ness** n.

hoar·y /'hôrē/ ▸ adj. (**hoarier, hoariest**) **1** old and having gray or white hair. **2** old and unoriginal: *a hoary old adage.* ■ **hoar·i·ly** adv. **hoar·i·ness** n.

hoax /hōks/ ▸ n. a humorous or cruel trick. ▸ v. deceive someone with a hoax. ■ **hoax·er** n.

hob·bit /'häbit/ ▸ n. a member of an imaginary race similar to humans, of small size and with hairy feet.

hob·ble /'häbəl/ ▸ v. **1** walk awkwardly, typically because of pain. **2** strap together the legs of a horse or other animal to prevent it from straying. ▸ n. an awkward way of walking. ■ **hob·bler** n.

hob·by /'häbē/ ▸ n. (pl. **hobbies**) a leisure activity that a person does regularly for pleasure.

hob·by·horse /'häbē,hôrs/ ▸ n. **1** a child's toy consisting of a stick with a model of a horse's head at one end. **2** a rocking horse. **3** a person's favorite topic of conversation.

hob·by·ist /'häbēist/ ▸ n. a person with a particular hobby.

hob·gob·lin /'häb,gäblən/ ▸ n. a mischievous imp.

hob·nail /'häb,nāl/ ▸ n. a short heavy-headed nail used to reinforce the soles of boots. ■ **hob·nailed** adj.

hob·nob /'häb,näb/ ▸ v. (**hobnobs, hobnobbing, hobnobbed**) informal spend time socially with rich or important people.

ho·bo /'hō,bō/ ▸ n. (pl. **hoboes** or **hobos**) a homeless person; a tramp.

Hob·son's choice /'häbsənz/ ▸ n. a choice of taking what is offered or nothing at all.

hock¹ /häk/ ▸ n. **1** the joint in the hind leg of a four-legged animal, between the knee and the fetlock. **2** a knuckle of pork or ham.

hock² ▸ v. informal pawn an object. – PHRASES **in hock 1** having been pawned. **2** in debt.

hock·ey /'häkē/ ▸ n. **1** short for ICE HOCKEY. **2** short for FIELD HOCKEY.

ho·cus-po·cus /,hōkəs'pōkəs/ ▸ n. **1** meaningless talk used to deceive someone. **2** a form of words used by a conjuror.

hod /häd/ ▸ n. **1** a builder's V-shaped open trough attached to a short pole, used for carrying bricks. **2** a coal scuttle.

hodge·podge /'häj,päj/ ▸ n. a confused mixture.

Hodg·kin's dis·ease /'häjkinz/ ▸ n. a cancerous disease causing enlargement of the lymph nodes, liver, and spleen.

hoe /hō/ ▸ n. a long-handled gardening tool with a thin metal blade, used mainly for weeding. ▸ v. (**hoes, hoeing, hoed**) use a hoe to turn earth or cut through weeds. ■ **ho·er** n.

hoe·down /'hō,doun/ ▸ n. a gathering for lively folk dancing.

hog /hôg, häg/ ▸ n. **1** a castrated male pig reared for slaughter. **2** informal a greedy person. ▸ v. (**hogs, hogging, hogged**) informal take or use most or all of something selfishly. ■ **hog·ger** n. **hog·gish** adj. – PHRASES **go (the) whole hog** informal do something completely or thoroughly.

ho·gan /'hō,gän, -gən/ ▸ n. a traditional Navajo hut of logs and earth.

hog·back /'hôg,bak, 'häg-/ (also **hog's back**) ▸ n. a long steep hill or mountain ridge.

hogs·head /'hôgz,hed, 'hägz-/ ▸ n. **1** a large cask. **2** a measure of liquid volume for wine or beer.

hog-tie ▸ v. **1** secure by fastening together the hands and feet of a person, or all four feet of an animal. **2** impede or hinder greatly.

hog·wash /'hôg,wôsh, 'häg,wäsh/ ▸ n. informal nonsense.

hog·weed /'hôg,wēd, 'häg-/ ▸ n. a large white-flowered weed of the parsley family.

ho-hum /'hō 'həm/ ▸ exclam. used to express boredom or resignation. ▸ adj. boring: *a ho-hum script.*

hoi pol·loi /'hoi pə,loi/ ▸ pl.n. derogatory the ordinary people.

hoi·sin sauce /'hoisin, hoi'sin/ ▸ n. a sweet, spicy, dark red sauce made from soybeans, used in Chinese cooking.

hoist /hoist/ ▸ v. **1** raise something by means of ropes and pulleys. **2** haul or lift something up. ▸ n. **1** an act of hoisting something. **2** a device for hoisting something. ■ **hoist·er** n.

hoi·ty-toi·ty /'hoitē 'toitē/ ▸ adj. snobbish or haughty.

hok·ey /'hōkē/ ▸ adj. (**hokier, hokiest**) informal excessively sentimental or artificial.

ho·kum /'hōkəm/ ▸ n. informal **1** nonsense; rubbish. **2** unoriginal or sentimental material in a movie, book, etc.

hold¹ /hōld/ ▸ v. (past and past part. **held** /held/) **1** grasp, carry, or support someone or something. **2** contain or be able to contain: *the tank held twenty-four gallons.* **3** have, own, or occupy

something. **4** keep or detain someone. **5** stay or keep at a certain value or level: *MCI shares held at 99 cents.* **6** have a belief or opinion. **7** (**hold someone/thing in**) regard someone or something in a particular way: *the speed limit is held in contempt by many drivers.* **8** (**hold someone to**) make someone keep a promise. **9** continue to follow a course. **10** arrange and take part in a meeting or conversation. **11** informal refrain from adding or using something: *a strawberry margarita, but hold the tequila.*
▶ n. **1** an act or way of grasping someone or something. **2** a handhold. **3** a degree of power or control: *Tom had some kind of hold over his father.*
– PHRASES **get hold of 1** grasp something. **2** informal find or contact someone. **hold something against someone** continue to feel resentful for something that someone has done. **hold back** hesitate. **hold something down** informal succeed in keeping a job. **hold fast 1** remain tightly secured. **2** continue to believe in a principle. **hold forth** talk at length. **hold good** (or **true**) remain true or valid. **hold it** informal wait or stop doing something. **hold off** (of bad weather) fail to occur. **hold someone/thing off 1** resist an attacker or challenge. **2** postpone an action or decision. **hold on 1** wait; stop. **2** keep going in difficult circumstances. **hold out 1** resist difficult circumstances. **2** continue to be enough. **hold out for** continue to demand something. **hold something over 1** postpone something. **2** use a piece of information to intimidate (someone). **hold up** remain strong. **hold someone/thing up 1** delay someone or something. **2** rob someone using the threat of violence. **3** present someone or something as an example. **no holds barred** without rules or restrictions. **on hold** waiting to be dealt with or connected by telephone. **take hold** start to have an effect.

hold² ▶ n. a storage space in the lower part of a ship or aircraft.

hold·er /ˈhōldər/ ▶ n. **1** a device or implement for holding something: *a cigarette holder.* **2** a person who holds something: *holders of two American hostages | a US passport holder.* **3** the possessor of a trophy, championship, or record: *the record holder in the 100-yard dash.*

hold·ing /ˈhōldiNG/ ▶ n. **1** an area of land held by lease. **2** (**holdings**) stocks and other financial assets owned by a person or organization.

hold·ing com·pa·ny ▶ n. a company created to buy shares in other companies, which it then controls.

hold·ing pat·tern ▶ n. **1** the flight path maintained by an aircraft awaiting permission to land. **2** a state or period of no progress or change.

hold·o·ver /ˈhōldˌōvər/ ▶ n. a person or thing surviving from an earlier time, especially someone surviving in office or remaining on a sports team.

hold·up /ˈhōldˌəp/ ▶ n. **1** a cause of delay. **2** a robbery carried out with the threat of violence.

hole /hōl/ ▶ n. **1** a hollow space in a solid object or surface. **2** an opening or gap in or passing through something. **3** (in golf) a hollow in the ground into which the ball must be hit. **4** informal an awkward or unpleasant place or situation.
▶ v. **1** make a hole or holes in something. **2** Golf hit the ball into a hole. **3** (**hole up**) informal hide

oneself. ■ **hol·ey** adj.
– PHRASES **hole in one** (pl. **holes in one**) Golf a shot that enters the hole from the tee. **in the hole** informal in debt: *$50,000 in the hole.* **make a hole in** use a large amount of something.

hole in the heart ▶ n. an abnormal opening present from birth in the wall between the chambers of the heart, resulting in inadequate circulation of oxygenated blood.

hole-in-the-wall ▶ n. informal a small dingy place, especially a bar or restaurant.

Ho·li /ˈhōlē/ ▶ n. a Hindu spring festival celebrated in honor of Krishna.

hol·i·day /ˈhäləˌdā/ ▶ n. **1** a day of national or religious celebration when no work is done. **2** chiefly Brit. a vacation.

ho·li·er-than-thou ▶ adj. offensively certain that one is morally superior to others.

ho·li·ness /ˈhōlēnis/ ▶ n. **1** the state of being holy. **2** (**His/Your Holiness**) the title of the Pope, Orthodox patriarchs, and the Dalai Lama.

ho·lism /ˈhōlˌizəm/ ▶ n. Medicine the treating of the whole person, taking into account mental and social factors, rather than just the symptoms of a disease. ■ **ho·lis·tic** /hōˈlistik/ adj.

hol·lan·daise sauce /ˈhälənˌdāz/ ▶ n. a creamy sauce made of butter, egg yolks, and vinegar.

hol·ler /ˈhälər/ informal ▶ v. give a loud shout.
▶ n. a loud shout.

hol·low /ˈhälō/ ▶ adj. **1** having a hole or empty space inside. **2** curving inward; concave: *hollow cheeks.* **3** (of a sound) echoing. **4** worthless or insincere: *hollow election promises.* ▶ n. **1** a hole or depression. **2** a small valley. ▶ v. **1** form by making a hole: *the pond was hollowed out by hand.* **2** make a depression in. ■ **hol·low·ly** adv. **hol·low·ness** n.

hol·ly /ˈhälē/ ▶ n. an evergreen shrub with prickly dark green leaves and red berries.

hol·ly·hock /ˈhälēˌhäk/ ▶ n. a tall plant of the mallow family, with large showy flowers.

hol·mi·um /ˈhōlmēəm/ ▶ n. a soft silvery-white metallic element.

hol·o·caust /ˈhäləˌkôst, ˈhōlə-/ ▶ n. **1** destruction or killing on a mass scale. **2** (**the Holocaust**) the mass murder of Jews under the German Nazi regime in World War II.

Hol·o·cene /ˈhäləˌsēn, ˈhōlə-/ ▶ adj. Geology relating to the present epoch (from about 10,000 years ago, following the Pleistocene).

hol·o·gram /ˈhäləˌgram, ˈhōlə-/ ▶ n. a photographic image formed in such a way that it looks three-dimensional when it is lit up. ■ **hol·o·graph·ic** adj. **hol·og·ra·phy** n.

hol·o·graph /ˈhäləˌgraf, ˈhōlə-/ ▶ n. a manuscript handwritten by its author.

hol·ster /ˈhōlstər/ ▶ n. a holder for carrying a handgun, worn on a belt or under the arm.
▶ v. put a gun into its holster.

ho·ly /ˈhōlē/ ▶ adj. (**holier, holiest**) **1** dedicated to God or a religious purpose. **2** morally and spiritually excellent.

ho·ly day ▶ n. a religious festival.

Ho·ly Fa·ther ▶ n. the Pope.

ho·ly or·ders ▶ pl.n. see ORDER (sense 10 of the noun).

Ho·ly Roll·er (also **holy roller**) ▶ n. informal, derogatory a member of an evangelical Christian group that expresses religious fervor by frenzied excitement or trances.

Ho·ly Ro·man Em·pire ▶ n. the western part of the Roman Empire, as revived by Charlemagne in 800.

Ho·ly See ▶ n. the office of Pope, or people associated with the Pope in governing the Roman Catholic Church.

Ho·ly Spir·it (or **Holy Ghost**) ▶ n. (in Christianity) the third person of the Trinity; God as spiritually active in the world.

ho·ly war ▶ n. a war waged in support of a religious cause.

ho·ly wa·ter ▶ n. water blessed by a priest and used in religious ceremonies and rituals.

Ho·ly Week ▶ n. the week before Easter.

Ho·ly Writ ▶ n. sacred writings as a whole, especially the Bible.

hom·age /'(h)ämij/ ▶ n. honor or respect shown publicly to someone: *they paid homage to the local boy who became president.*

hom·bre /'ämbrā, -brē/ ▶ n. informal a man, especially one of a particular type: *their quarterback is one tough hombre.*

hom·burg /'hämbərg/ ▶ n. a man's felt hat having a narrow curled brim and a lengthwise indentation in the crown.

home /hōm/ ▶ n. 1 the place where someone lives. 2 an institution for people needing professional care. 3 a place where something flourishes or from which it originated: *Barcelona became the home of Modernism.* 4 the finishing point in a race. 5 (in games) the place where a player is free from attack. ▶ adj. 1 relating to the home. 2 made, done, or intended for use in the home. 3 relating to someone's own country. 4 (in team sports) referring to a team's own ground. ▶ adv. 1 to or at someone's home. 2 to the end of something: *a couple more questions and you're home.* 3 to the intended or correct position: *he slid the bolt home noisily.* ▶ v. 1 (of an animal) return by instinct to its territory. 2 (**home in on**) move or be aimed toward a target or destination.
– PHRASES **at home** 1 comfortable and at ease. 2 ready to receive visitors. **bring something home to** make someone realize the significance of something. **close to home** (of a remark) uncomfortably accurate. **home free** having successfully achieved or being within sight of achieving one's objective: *at 7-0 they should have been home free.*

home·bod·y /'hōm,bädē/ ▶ n. (pl. **homebodies**) informal a person who likes to stay at home, especially one who is perceived as unadventurous.

home·boy /'hōm,boi/ (or **homegirl** /'hōm,gərl/) ▶ n. informal 1 a person from one's own town or neighborhood. 2 (especially among urban black people) a member of a peer group or gang.

home brew ▶ n. beer or other alcoholic drink brewed at home.

home·buy·er /'hōm,bīər/ ▶ n. a person who buys a house or condominium.

home·com·ing /'hōm,kəmiNG/ ▶ n. an instance of returning home.

home ec /'hōm 'ek/ ▶ n. informal short for HOME ECONOMICS.

home ec·o·nom·ics ▶ pl.n. (often treated as sing.) the study of cookery and household management.

home front ▶ n. the civilian population and activities of a nation whose armed forces are engaged in a foreign war.

home fur·nish·ings ▶ pl.n. curtains, chair coverings, and other cloth items used to decorate a room.

home·grown /'hōm'grōn/ ▶ adj. grown or produced in one's own garden or country.

home·land /'hōm,land/ ▶ n. 1 a person's native land. 2 a self-governing state occupied by a particular people: *they are fighting for a Kurd homeland.* 3 historical any of ten partially self-governing areas in South Africa assigned to particular African peoples.

home·less /'hōmlis/ ▶ adj. not having anywhere to live. ■ **home·less·ness** n.

home·ly /'hōmlē/ ▶ adj. (**homelier**, **homeliest**) (of a person) unattractive. ■ **home·li·ness** n.

home·made /'hō(m)'mād/ ▶ adj. made at home.

home·mak·er /'hōm,mākər/ ▶ n. a person who manages a home.

home mov·ie ▶ n. a movie made at home or without professional equipment or expertise, especially one featuring one's own activities.

Home Of·fice ▶ n. the British government department dealing with law and order, immigration, etc., in England and Wales.

ho·me·o·path /'hōmēə,paTH/ ▶ n. a person who practices homeopathy.

ho·me·op·a·thy /,hōmē'äpəTHē/ ▶ n. a system of complementary medicine in which disease is treated by minute doses of natural substances that would normally produce symptoms of the disease. ■ **ho·me·o·path·ic** adj. /'hōmēə,paTHik/.

ho·me·o·sta·sis /,hōmēə'stāsis/ ▶ n. the tendency of the body to keep its own temperature, blood pressure, etc., at a constant level. ■ **ho·me·o·stat·ic** /-'statik/ adj.

home·own·er /'hōm,ōnər/ ▶ n. a person who owns their own home.

home page ▶ n. a person's or organization's introductory document on the Internet.

home plate ▶ n. a five-sided rubber mat next to which a baseball batter stands and over which the pitcher must throw the ball for a strike.

ho·mer /'hōmər/ Baseball, informal ▶ n. a home run. ▶ v. hit a home run.

Ho·mer·ic /hō'merik/ ▶ adj. relating to the ancient Greek poet Homer or to the epic poems that he is thought to have written.

home·room /'hōm,rōōm, -,rŏŏm/ ▶ n. a classroom in which fixed groups of students gather, usually daily, for school administrative purposes.

home rule ▶ n. the government of a place by its own citizens.

home run ▶ n. Baseball a hit that allows the batter to make a complete circuit of the bases.

home·school·er /'hōm'skōōlər/ ▶ pl.n. 1 a child who is educated at home by their parents. 2 a parent who educates their child or children at home.

home·school·ing /'hōm'skōōliNG/ ▶ n. the education of children at home by their parents. ■ **home·school** v.

Home Sec·re·tar·y ▶ n. (in the UK) the foreign minister; the counterpart of the US secretary of state.

home·sick /'hōm,sik/ ▶ adj. missing one's home during a time away from it.

home·spun /'hōm,spən/ ▶ adj. 1 simple and unsophisticated. 2 (of cloth or yarn) made or spun at home. ▶ n. homespun cloth.

home·stead /'hōm,sted/ ▶ n. a farmhouse with surrounding land and outbuildings. ■ **home·stead·er** n. **home·stead·ing** n.

home stretch ▶ n. the final stretch of a racetrack, or the final stage of a process: *when vacation shopping reaches its home stretch.*

home truth ▶ n. an unpleasant fact about oneself, pointed out by someone else.

home·ward /'hōmwərd/ ▶ adv. (also **homewards**) toward home. ▶ adj. going or leading toward home.

home·work /'hōm,wərk/ ▶ n. 1 school work that a student is required to do at home. 2 preparation for an event or situation. 3 paid work done in one's own home. ■ **home·work·er** n.

home·wreck·er /'hōm,rekər/ ▶ n. informal someone who is blamed for the breakup of a marriage or family, such as an adulterous partner.

hom·ey /'hōmē/ (also **homy**) ▶ adj. (**homier, homiest**) 1 comfortable and cozy. 2 unsophisticated. ▶ n. variant of HOMIE.

hom·i·cide /'hämə,sīd, 'hōmə-/ ▶ n. the killing of another person. ■ **hom·i·cid·al** /,hämə'sīdl, ,hōmə-/ adj.

hom·ie /'hōmē/ (also **homey**) ▶ n. (pl. **homies** or **homeys**) informal a homeboy or homegirl.

hom·i·let·ic /,hämə'letik/ ▶ adj. relating to or like a homily; morally uplifting.

hom·i·ly /'häməlē/ ▶ n. (pl. **homilies**) 1 a talk on a religious subject that is intended to be spiritually uplifting. 2 a tedious talk on a moral issue. ■ **hom·i·list** n.

hom·ing /'hōmiNG/ ▶ adj. 1 (of a pigeon or other animal) able to return home from a great distance. 2 (of a weapon) able to find and hit a target electronically.

hom·i·nid /'hämə,nid/ ▶ n. a member of a family of primates that includes humans and their fossil ancestors.

hom·i·noid /'hämə,noid/ ▶ n. Zoology a primate of a group that includes humans, their fossil ancestors, and the great apes.

hom·i·ny /'hämənē/ ▶ n. coarsely ground corn used to make grits.

ho·mo /'hōmō/ informal, chiefly derogatory ▶ n. (pl. **homos**) a homosexual man. ▶ adj. homosexual.

homo- ▶ comb.form 1 same: *homogeneous.* 2 relating to homosexual love: *homoerotic.*

ho·mo·e·rot·ic /,hōmō-i'rätik/ ▶ adj. concerning or arousing sexual desire centered on a person of the same sex. ■ **ho·mo·e·rot·i·cism** /-,sizəm/ n.

ho·mo·ge·ne·ous /,hōmə'jēnēəs/ ▶ adj. 1 of the same kind; alike. 2 consisting of parts all of the same kind: *a homogeneous society.* ■ **ho·mo·ge·ne·i·ty** /,hōməjə'nēitē, ,hämə-/ n. **ho·mo·ge·ne·ous·ly** adv. **ho·mo·ge·ne·ous·ness** n.

ho·mog·e·nize /hə'mäjə,nīz/ ▶ v. 1 treat milk so that the particles of fat are broken down and the cream does not separate. 2 make different things more similar or uniform. ■ **ho·mog·e·ni·za·tion** /hə,mäjənī'zāsHən/ n. **ho·mog·e·niz·er** n.

hom·o·graph /'hämə,graf, 'hōmə-/ ▶ n. each of two or more words having the same spelling but different meanings and origins (e.g., BOW¹ and BOW² in this dictionary).

ho·mol·o·gous /hō'mäləgəs, hə-/ ▶ adj. 1 having a similar relative position or structure; corresponding. 2 Biology (of organs) similar in

position, structure, and evolutionary origin. ■ **ho·mol·o·gize** /hō'mälə,jīz, hə-/ v. **ho·mol·o·gy** /hō'mäləjē, hə-/ n.

ho·mo·logue /'hōmə,lôg, -,läg/ (also **homolog**) ▶ n. technical a thing that has the same relative position or structure as another.

hom·o·nym /'hämə,nim, 'hōmə-/ ▶ n. each of two or more words having the same spelling or pronunciation but different meanings and origins (e.g., CAN¹ and CAN² in this dictionary). ■ **ho·mon·y·mous** /hō'mänəməs/ adj.

ho·mo·pho·bi·a /,hōmə'fōbēə/ ▶ n. an extreme and irrational hatred or fear of homosexuality and homosexuals. ■ **ho·mo·phobe** /'hōmə,fōb/ n. **ho·mo·pho·bic** /-'fōbik/ adj.

ho·mo·phone /'hämə,fōn, 'hōmə-/ ▶ n. each of two or more words having the same pronunciation but different meanings, origins, or spelling (e.g., *new* and *knew*).

ho·mop·ter·an /hō'mäptərən/ ▶ n. any of a group of insects, including aphids and cicadas, in which the forewings are uniform in texture.

Ho·mo sa·pi·ens /'hōmō 'sāpēənz/ ▶ n. the primate species to which modern humans belong.

ho·mo·sex·u·al /,hōmə'seksHōōəl/ ▶ adj. feeling or involving sexual attraction to people of one's own sex. ▶ n. a homosexual person. ■ **ho·mo·sex·u·al·i·ty** /-,seksHōō'alitē/ n. **ho·mo·sex·u·al·ly** adv.

ho·mun·cu·lus /hə'məNGkyələs, hō-/ ▶ n. (pl. **homunculi** /-,lī/) a very small human or humanlike creature.

hom·y ▶ adj. variant spelling of HOMEY.

hon /hən/ ▶ n. informal short for HONEY (sense 2).

Hon. ▶ abbr. 1 (in official job titles) Honorary. 2 (in titles of judges and, in the UK, nobility and members of parliament) Honorable.

hon·cho /'hänchō/ ▶ n. (pl. **honchos**) informal a leader.

Hon·du·ran /hän'd(y)ŏŏrən/ ▶ n. a person from Honduras, a country in Central America. ▶ adj. relating to Honduras.

hone /hōn/ ▶ v. 1 make better or more efficient: *she honed her singing skills.* 2 sharpen a tool with a whetstone.

hon·est /'änist/ ▶ adj. 1 truthful and sincere. 2 fairly earned through hard work: *an honest living.* 3 simple and unpretentious. ▶ adv. informal genuinely; really.

hon·est·ly /'änistlē/ ▶ adv. 1 in an honest way. 2 really (used for emphasis).

hon·est-to-God ▶ adj. informal genuine; real.

hon·est-to-good·ness ▶ adj. genuine and straightforward.

hon·es·ty /'änistē/ ▶ n. 1 the quality of being honest and sincere: *they spoke with honesty about their fears.* 2 a plant of the mustard family with round, flat translucent seed pods.

hon·ey /'hənē/ ▶ n. (pl. **honeys**) 1 a sweet, sticky yellowish-brown fluid made by bees from flower nectar. 2 darling; sweetheart. 3 informal an excellent example of something: *it's a honey of a car.* 4 informal an attractive girl.

hon·ey·bee /'hənē,bē/ ▶ n. the common bee.

hon·ey·comb /'hənē,kōm/ ▶ n. 1 a structure of six-sided cells of wax, made by bees to store honey and eggs. 2 a structure resembling a bee's honeycomb. ▶ v. fill an area with cavities or tunnels.

hon·ey·dew /'hənē,d(y)ōō/ ▸ n. a sweet, sticky substance produced by aphids (small insects) feeding on the sap of plants.

hon·ey·dew mel·on ▸ n. a variety of melon with pale skin and sweet green flesh.

hon·eyed /'hənēd/ ▸ adj. 1 containing or coated with honey. 2 soothing and soft: *honeyed words.* 3 having a warm yellow color.

hon·ey·moon /'hənē,mōōn/ ▸ n. 1 a vacation taken by a newly married couple. 2 an initial period of enthusiasm or goodwill. ▸ v. go on a honeymoon. ■ **hon·ey·moon·er** n.

hon·ey·pot /'hənē,pät/ ▸ n. a place to which many people are attracted.

hon·ey·suck·le /'hənē,səkəl/ ▸ n. a climbing shrub with fragrant yellow and pink flowers.

hon·ey·trap /'hənē,trap/ ▸ n. a plan in which an attractive person entices another person into revealing information or doing something unwise.

honk /hängk, hôngk/ ▸ n. 1 the cry of a goose. 2 the sound of a car horn. ▸ v. make a honk.

hon·ky /'hängkē, 'hông-/ ▸ n. (pl. **honkies**) informal, derogatory (among black people) a white person.

hon·ky-tonk /'hängkē ,tängk, 'hôngkē ,tôngk/ ▸ n. informal 1 a cheap or disreputable bar or club. 2 ragtime piano music.

hon·or /'änər/ (Brit. **honour**) ▸ n. 1 great respect. 2 a clear sense of what is morally right. 3 something that is a privilege and a pleasure: *he had the honor of introducing the president.* 4 a person or thing that brings credit to something. 5 an award or title given as a reward for achievement. 6 (**honors**) a course of degree studies more specialized than for an ordinary program. 7 (**honors**) a special distinction for academic achievement. 8 (**His, Your,** etc. **Honor**) a title of respect for a judge or mayor. 9 dated a woman's chastity. 10 Bridge an ace, king, queen, or jack. ▸ v. 1 regard someone or something with great respect. 2 pay public respect to: *talented writers were honored at a special ceremony.* 3 fulfill a duty or keep an agreement.

hon·or·a·ble /'änərəbəl/ ▸ adj. 1 bringing or worthy of honor. 2 (**Honorable**) a title indicating eminence or distinction, given especially to judges and certain high officials. ■ **hon·or·a·bly** adv.

hon·or·a·ble men·tion ▸ n. a commendation for a candidate in an exam or competition who is not awarded a prize.

hon·o·rar·i·um /,änə're(ə)rēəm/ ▸ n. (pl. **honorariums** or **honoraria** /-'re(ə)rēə/) a voluntary payment for professional services that are offered without charge.

hon·or·ar·y /'änə,rerē/ ▸ adj. 1 (of a title or position) given as an honor. 2 (of a person) holding such a title or position: *an honorary member of the club.*

hon·or guard ▸ n. a group of soldiers ceremonially welcoming an important visitor or escorting a casket in a funeral.

hon·or·if·ic /,änə'rifik/ ▸ adj. given as a mark of respect.

hon·or roll ▸ n. a list of people who have attained an honor, especially a list of students who have earned excellent grades.

hon·or sys·tem ▸ n. a system of payment or examination that relies solely on the honesty of the people concerned.

hon·our, etc. ▸ n. & v. British spelling of **HONOR,** etc.

hooch /hōōch/ (also **hootch**) ▸ n. informal strong alcoholic drink, especially inferior or illicit whiskey.

hood[1] /hōōd/ ▸ n. 1 a covering for the head and neck with an opening for the face. 2 the metal part covering the engine of a vehicle. 3 a protective canopy. ▸ v. put a hood on or over someone. ■ **hood·ed** adj.

hood[2] ▸ n. informal a gangster or violent criminal.

hood[3] ▸ n. informal a neighborhood.

-hood ▸ suffix forming nouns referring to. 1 a condition or quality: *womanhood.* 2 a collection or group: *brotherhood.*

hood·ie /'hōōdē/ ▸ n. a hooded garment, especially a sweatshirt.

hood·lum /'hōōdləm, 'hōōd-/ ▸ n. a gangster or other violent criminal.

hoo·doo /'hōō,dōō/ ▸ n. 1 a run or cause of bad luck. 2 voodoo. ▸ v. (**hoodoos, hoodooing, hoodooed**) bring bad luck to someone or something.

hood·wink /'hōōd,wingk/ ▸ v. deceive or trick someone.

hood·y /'hōōdē/ (also **hoodie**) ▸ n. (pl. **hoodies**) a hooded sweatshirt or other top.

hoo·ey /'hōōē/ ▸ n. informal nonsense.

hoof /hōōf, hōōf/ ▸ n. (pl. **hoofs** or **hooves** /hōōvz, hōōvz/) the horny part of the foot of a horse, cow, etc. ■ **hoofed** adj.
  – PHRASES **hoof it** informal 1 go on foot. 2 dance. **on the hoof** informal 1 without great thought or preparation. 2 (of livestock) not yet slaughtered.

hoof·er /'hōōfər, 'hōōfər/ ▸ n. informal a professional dancer.

hoo-ha /'hōō ,hä/ ▸ n. informal a commotion or fuss.

hook /hōōk/ ▸ n. 1 a piece of curved metal or other material for catching hold of things or hanging things on. 2 a short swinging punch made with the elbow bent and rigid. 3 a thing designed to catch people's attention. 4 a catchy passage in a song. ▸ v. 1 attach or fasten something with a hook. 2 bend into a curved shape: *he hooked his thumbs in his belt.* 3 catch a fish with a hook. 4 (**be hooked**) informal be very interested or addicted. 5 (in golf) hit the ball in a curving path.
  – PHRASES **by hook or by crook** by any possible means. **hook, line, and sinker** completely. **hook up 1** link to electronic equipment. 2 meet or join another person or people. **off the hook 1** informal no longer in trouble. 2 (of a telephone receiver) not on its rest.

hook·ah /'hōōkə, 'hōōkə/ ▸ n. an oriental tobacco pipe with a long, flexible tube that draws the smoke through water in a bowl.

hook and eye ▸ n. a small metal hook and loop used to fasten a garment.

hooked /hōōkt/ ▸ adj. 1 having or resembling a hook or hooks. 2 informal captivated or addicted.

hook·er /'hōōkər/ ▸ n. informal a prostitute.

hook·up /'hōōk,əp/ ▸ n. 1 a connection to electricity, a utility, a communications system, etc. 2 informal a relationship initiated for a purpose, especially sex: *a date tomorrow night with my hookup from last week.*

hook·worm /'hōōk,wərm/ ▸ n. a parasitic worm

with hooklike mouthparts that can infest the intestines.

hook·y /'hŏŏkē/ (also **hookey**) ▶ n. (in phrase **play hooky**) informal stay away from school or work without permission or explanation.

hoo·li·gan /'hŏŏləgin/ ▶ n. a violent young troublemaker. ■ **hoo·li·gan·ism** n.

hoop /hŏŏp/ ▶ n. 1 a circular band of a rigid material. 2 a large ring used as a toy or for circus performers to jump through. 3 the round metal rim from which a basketball net is suspended. 4 (**hoops**) informal the game of basketball: *the UNC quarterback might not return to hoops.* ▶ v. bind or surround with hoops. ■ **hooped** adj.

hoop·la /'hŏŏ,plä, 'hŏŏp,lä/ ▶ n. informal excitement surrounding an event or situation.

hoo·poe /'hŏŏ,pō, -,pōō/ ▶ n. a salmon-pink bird with a long bill, a large crest, and black-and-white wings and tail.

hoop·ster /'hŏŏpstər/ ▶ n. informal a basketball player.

hoo·ray /hə'rā, hŏŏ-/ ▶ exclam. hurrah.

hoot /hŏŏt/ ▶ n. 1 a low sound made by owls or a similar sound made by a horn, siren, etc. 2 a shout of scorn or disapproval. 3 an outburst of laughter. 4 (**a hoot**) informal a very amusing person or thing. ▶ v. make or cause to make a hoot.
– PHRASES **not care** (or **give**) **a hoot** (or **two hoots**) informal not care at all.

hootch /hŏŏcH/ ▶ n. variant spelling of HOOCH.

hoot·en·an·ny /'hŏŏtn,anē/ ▶ n. (pl. **hootenannies**) informal an informal gathering with country or folk music and sometimes dancing.

hoot·er /'hŏŏtər/ ▶ n. informal 1 a person's nose. 2 (**hooters**) a woman's breasts.

hooves /hŏŏvz, hŏŏvz/ ▶ plural of HOOF.

hop¹ /häp/ ▶ v. (**hops, hopping, hopped**) 1 jump along on one foot. 2 (of a bird or animal) jump along with two or all feet at once. 3 jump over or off something. 4 informal move or go somewhere quickly: *hop in then and we'll be off.* ▶ n. 1 a hopping movement. 2 a short journey or distance. 3 an informal dance.
– PHRASES **hopping mad** informal very angry.

hop² ▶ n. a climbing plant whose dried flowers (**hops**) are used in brewing to give beer a bitter flavor. ■ **hop·py** adj.

hope /hōp/ ▶ n. 1 a feeling of expectation and desire for something to happen. 2 a cause or source of hope: *her only hope is surgery.* ▶ v. 1 expect and want something to happen. 2 intend if possible to do something. ■ **hop·er** n.

hope chest ▶ n. a chest containing household linen and clothing stored by a woman in preparation for her marriage.

hope·ful /'hōpfəl/ ▶ adj. feeling or inspiring hope. ▶ n. a person likely or hoping to succeed. ■ **hope·ful·ness** n.

hope·ful·ly /'hōpfəlē/ ▶ adv. 1 in a hopeful way. 2 it is to be hoped that.

> USAGE
> The traditional sense of **hopefully** is 'in a hopeful way.' The newer use, meaning 'it is to be hoped that' (as in *hopefully, it should be finished next year*) is now the most common, although some people still think that it is incorrect.

hope·less /'hōplis/ ▶ adj. 1 feeling or causing despair. 2 very bad or incompetent.

■ **hope·less·ly** adv. **hope·less·ness** n.

Ho·pi /'hōpē/ ▶ n. (pl. same or **Hopis**) 1 a member of an American Indian people living chiefly in NE Arizona. 2 the language of the Hopi.

hop·per /'häpər/ ▶ n. 1 a container that tapers downward and discharges its contents at the bottom. 2 a person or thing that hops.

hop·scotch /'häp,skäcH/ ▶ n. a children's game of hopping into and over squares marked on the ground to retrieve a marker.

horde /hôrd/ ▶ n. 1 chiefly derogatory a large group of people. 2 an army or tribe of nomadic warriors.

> USAGE
> On the confusion of **horde** and **hoard**, see the note at HOARD.

hore·hound /'hôr,hound/ ▶ n. a plant of the mint family, traditionally used as a medicinal herb.

ho·ri·zon /hə'rīzən/ ▶ n. 1 the line at which the earth's surface and the sky appear to meet. 2 the limit of a person's knowledge, experience, or interest: *she wanted to leave home and broaden her horizons.*
– PHRASES **on the horizon** about to happen; imminent.

hor·i·zon·tal /,hôrə'zän(t)l/ ▶ adj. parallel to the plane of the horizon; at right angles to the vertical. ▶ n. a horizontal line, plane, or structure. ■ **hor·i·zon·tal·i·ty** /-,zän'talitē/ n. **hor·i·zon·tal·ly** adv.

hor·i·zon·tal sta·bi·liz·er ▶ n. a horizontal airfoil at the tail of an aircraft.

hor·mone /'hôr,mōn/ ▶ n. a substance produced by a living thing and carried by blood or sap to regulate the action of specific cells or tissues. ■ **hor·mo·nal** /hôr'mōnl/ adj.

hor·mone re·place·ment ther·a·py ▶ n. treatment with certain hormones to make symptoms of menopause or osteoporosis less severe.

horn /hôrn/ ▶ n. 1 a hard bony outgrowth, often curved and pointed, found in pairs on the heads of cattle, sheep, and other animals. 2 the substance of which horns are composed. 3 a brass wind instrument, conical in shape or wound into a spiral. 4 an instrument sounding a signal. 5 a pointed projection or object. ■ **horned** adj.
– PHRASES **blow one's own horn** talk boastfully about one's achievements. **draw** (or **pull**) **in one's horns** become less assertive or ambitious. **horn in** informal interfere or intrude. **on the horns of a dilemma** faced with a decision involving equally unfavorable alternatives.

horn·beam /'hôrn,bēm/ ▶ n. a deciduous tree with hard pale wood.

horn·bill /'hôrn,bil/ ▶ n. a tropical bird with a hornlike structure on its large curved bill.

horn·blende /'hôrn,blend/ ▶ n. a dark brown, black, or green mineral present in many rocks.

hor·net /'hôrnit/ ▶ n. a kind of large wasp, typically red and yellow or red and black.
– PHRASES **stir up a hornets' nest** cause a situation full of difficulties or angry feelings.

horn of plen·ty ▶ n. a cornucopia.

horn·pipe /'hôrn,pīp/ ▶ n. 1 a lively solo dance traditionally performed by sailors. 2 a piece of music for such a dance.

horn-rimmed ▶ adj. (of glasses) having rims made of horn or a similar substance.

horn·y /'hôrnē/ ▶ adj. (**hornier, horniest**) 1 made of or resembling horn. 2 hard and rough. 3 informal sexually aroused or arousing. ■ **horn·i·ness** n.

ho·rol·o·gy /hə'räləjē/ ▶ n. 1 the study and measurement of time. 2 the art of making clocks and watches. ■ **hor·o·log·i·cal** /ˌhôrə'läjikəl/ adj. **ho·rol·o·gist** n.

hor·o·scope /'hôrəˌskōp, 'härə-/ ▶ n. a forecast of a person's future based on the relative positions of the stars and planets at the time of that person's birth.

hor·ren·dous /hə'rendəs, hô-/ ▶ adj. highly unpleasant or horrifying. ■ **hor·ren·dous·ly** adv.

hor·ri·ble /'hôrəbəl, 'här-/ ▶ adj. 1 causing or likely to cause horror. 2 very unpleasant. ■ **hor·ri·bly** adv.

hor·rid /'hôrid, 'här-/ ▶ adj. 1 causing horror. 2 very unpleasant. ■ **hor·rid·ly** adv. **hor·rid·ness** n.

hor·ri·fic /hô'rifik, hə-/ ▶ adj. causing horror. ■ **hor·rif·i·cal·ly** adv.

hor·ri·fy /'hôrəˌfī, 'här-/ ▶ v. (**horrifies, horrifying, horrified**) fill someone with horror. ■ **hor·ri·fied** adj. **hor·ri·fy·ing** adj.

hor·ror /'hôrər, 'här-/ ▶ n. 1 an intense feeling of fear, shock, or disgust. 2 a cause of horror. 3 intense dislike: *he had a horror of modernity.* 4 informal a badly behaved or mischievous child.

hors de com·bat /ˌôr də käm'bä/ ▶ adj. out of action due to injury or damage.

hors d'oeuvre /ôr 'dərv, 'dœvrə/ ▶ n. (pl. same or **hors d'oeuvres** pronunc. same or /'dərvz/) a savory appetizer.

horse /hôrs/ ▶ n. 1 a large four-legged mammal with a flowing mane and tail, used for riding and for pulling heavy loads. 2 an adult male horse, as opposed to a mare or colt. 3 (treated as sing. or pl.) cavalry. 4 a structure on which something is mounted or supported: *a clothes horse.* ▶ v. (**horse around**) informal fool around.
– PHRASES **from the horse's mouth** from the person directly concerned in the matter. **hold one's horses** informal wait a moment.

horse·back /'hôrsˌbak/ ▶ n. (in phrase **on horseback**) & adj. mounted on a horse.

horse chest·nut ▶ n. 1 a large deciduous tree producing nuts enclosed in a spiny case. 2 the fruit or seed of this tree.

horse·flesh /'hôrsˌflesн/ ▶ n. horses considered as a group.

horse·fly /'hôrsˌflī/ ▶ n. (pl. **horseflies**) a large fly that bites horses and other large mammals.

horse·hair /'hôrsˌhe(ə)r/ ▶ n. hair from the mane or tail of a horse, used in furniture for padding.

horse lat·i·tudes ▶ pl.n. a belt of calm air and sea occurring in both the northern and southern hemispheres between the trade winds and the westerlies.

horse laugh ▶ n. a loud, coarse laugh.

horse·man /'hôrsmən/ (or **horsewoman** /'hôrsˌwo͝omən/) ▶ n. (pl. **horsemen** or **horsewomen** /'hôrsˌwimin/) a rider on horseback, especially a skilled one. ■ **horse·man·ship** n.

horse·play /'hôrsˌplā/ ▶ n. rough, boisterous play.

horse·pow·er /'hôrsˌpou(-ə)r/ ▶ n. (pl. same) an imperial unit of power equal to 550 foot-pounds per second (about 750 watts), especially as a measurement of engine power.

horse race ▶ n. 1 a race between two or more horses ridden by jockeys. 2 a very close contest: *the election was still a horse race.* ■ **horse rac·ing** n.

horse·rad·ish /'hôrsˌradisн/ ▶ n. a plant of the mustard family grown for its strong-tasting root, which is often made into a sauce.

horse sense ▶ n. informal common sense.

horse·shoe /'hôr(s)ˌsнo͞o/ ▶ n. 1 a U-shaped iron band attached to the base of a horse's hoof. 2 (**horseshoes**) (treated as sing.) a game in which horseshoes are thrown at a stake in the ground.

horse·tail /'hôrsˌtāl/ ▶ n. a flowerless plant with a jointed stem and narrow leaves.

horse·trad·ing ▶ n. informal hard and shrewd bargaining.

horse·whip /'hôrsˌ(h)wip/ ▶ n. a long whip used for driving and controlling horses. ▶ v. (**horsewhips, horsewhipping, horsewhipped**) beat someone or something with a horsewhip.

hors·ey /'hôrsē/ (also **horsy**) ▶ adj. (**horsier, horsiest**) 1 relating to or resembling a horse. 2 very interested in horses or horse racing.

horst /hôrst/ ▶ n. Geology a raised elongated block of the earth's crust lying between two faults.

hor·ta·to·ry /'hôrtəˌtôrē/ ▶ adj. formal strongly urging someone to do something.

hor·ti·cul·ture /'hôrtiˌkəlcнər/ ▶ n. the art or practice of garden cultivation and management. ■ **hor·ti·cul·tur·al** /ˌhôrti'kəlcнərəl/ adj. **hor·ti·cul·tur·ist** (also **horticulturalist**) n.

ho·san·na /hō'zanə, -'zä-/ (also **hosannah**) ▶ n. & exclam. a biblical cry of praise or joy.

hose /hōz/ ▶ n. 1 a flexible tube conveying water. 2 (treated as pl.) stockings, socks, and tights. ▶ v. water or spray something with a hose.

ho·sier·y /'hōzнərē/ ▶ n. stockings, socks, and tights.

hos·pice /'häspis/ ▶ n. 1 a home providing care for people who are sick or terminally ill. 2 old use a lodging for travelers, especially one run by a religious order.

hos·pi·ta·ble /hä'spitəbəl, 'häspitəbəl/ ▶ adj. 1 friendly and welcoming to guests or strangers. 2 (of an environment) pleasant and favorable for living in. ■ **hos·pi·ta·bly** adv.

hos·pi·tal /'häˌspitl/ ▶ n. an institution providing medical and surgical treatment and nursing care for sick or injured people.

hos·pi·tal·i·ty /ˌhäspi'talitē/ ▶ n. the friendly and generous treatment of guests or strangers.

hos·pi·tal·ize /'häspitlˌīz/ ▶ v. admit someone to a hospital for treatment. ■ **hos·pi·tal·i·za·tion** /ˌhäspitl-li'zāsнən/ n.

Host /hōst/ ▶ n. (**the Host**) the bread consecrated in the Christian Eucharist (Holy Communion).

host¹ /hōst/ ▶ n. 1 a person who receives or entertains guests. 2 the presenter of a television or radio program. 3 a place or organization that holds and organizes an event to which others are invited. 4 a computer that mediates multiple access to databases or provides other services to a network. 5 an animal or plant on or in which a parasite lives. ▶ v. act as host at an event or for a television or radio program.

host² ▶ n. (**a host/hosts of**) a large number of people or things.

hos·ta /'hōstə, 'hästə/ ▶ n. a shade-tolerant plant with ornamental foliage.

hos·tage /'hästij/ ▶ n. a person held prisoner in an attempt to make others give in to a demand.
– PHRASES **a hostage to fortune** an act or remark regarded as unwise because it invites trouble in the future.

hos·tel /'hästl/ ▶ n. an establishment that provides cheap food and lodging for a particular group of people.

host·ess /'hōstis/ ▶ n. **1** a female host. **2** a woman employed at a restaurant to welcome and seat customers.

hos·tile /'hästl, 'hä,stīl/ ▶ adj. **1** showing or feeling dislike or opposition. **2** relating to a military enemy. **3** (of a takeover bid) opposed by the company to be bought. ■ **hos·tile·ly** adv.

hos·til·i·ty /hä'stilitē/ ▶ n. (pl. **hostilities**) **1** hostile behavior. **2** (**hostilities**) acts of warfare: *a cessation of hostilities.*

hot /hät/ ▶ adj. (**hotter**, **hottest**) **1** having a high temperature. **2** feeling or producing an uncomfortable sensation of heat. **3** feeling or showing anger, lust, or other strong emotion. **4** informal currently popular, fashionable, or interesting: *they know the hottest dance moves.* **5** informal very knowledgeable or skillful: *she's very hot on local history.* **6** (**hot on**) informal strict about something. **7** informal (of goods) stolen. ■ **hot·ly** adv. **hot·ness** n.
– PHRASES **have the hots for** informal be sexually attracted to someone. **hot under the collar** informal angry or resentful. **in hot water** informal in trouble. **make it** (or **things**) **hot for** informal stir up trouble for someone.

hot air ▶ n. informal empty or boastful talk.

hot-air bal·loon ▶ n. another term for **BALLOON** (sense 2 of the noun).

hot·bed /'hät,bed/ ▶ n. **1** an environment where a particular activity happens or flourishes: *the country was a hotbed of revolt.* **2** a bed of earth heated by fermenting manure, for raising or forcing plants.

hot-blood·ed ▶ adj. lustful; passionate.

hot but·ton ▶ adj. informal arousing passionate emotions or debate: *a hot-button issue.*

hot·cake /'hät,kāk/ ▶ n. a pancake.
– PHRASES **like hotcakes** quickly and in great quantity, especially because of popularity: *his latest CD is selling like hotcakes.*

hot dog ▶ n. **1** a hot sausage served in a long, soft roll. **2** a person who shows off, especially a skier or surfer. ▶ v. (**hotdog**) (**hotdogs**, **hotdogging**, **hotdogged**) informal perform stunts.

ho·tel /hō'tel/ ▶ n. an establishment providing accommodations and meals for travelers and tourists.

ho·te·lier /,ōtel'yā, hōtl'i(ə)r/ ▶ n. a person who owns or manages a hotel.

hot flash ▶ n. a sudden feeling of heat in the skin or face, often as a symptom of menopause.

hot·foot /'hät,fŏŏt/ ▶ adv. in eager haste.
▶ v. (**hotfoot it**) hurry eagerly.

hot·head /'hät,hed/ ▶ n. a rash or quick-tempered person. ■ **hot-head·ed** adj.

hot·house /'hät,hous/ ▶ n. **1** a heated greenhouse. **2** an environment that encourages rapid growth or development. ▶ v. educate a child to a higher level than is usual for their age.

hot key ▶ n. Computing a key or combination of keys providing quick access to a function within a program.

hot·line /'hät,līn/ ▶ n. a direct telephone line set up for a specific purpose.

hot mon·ey ▶ n. capital that is frequently transferred between financial institutions in an attempt to maximize interest or profit.

hot pants ▶ pl.n. women's tight, brief shorts.

hot plate ▶ n. a flat heated metal or ceramic surface used for cooking food or keeping it hot.

hot po·ta·to ▶ n. informal a controversial issue that is difficult to deal with.

hot rod ▶ n. a motor vehicle that has been specially modified to give it extra power and speed. ▶ v. (**hot-rod**) **1** modify a vehicle or other device to make it faster or more powerful. **2** drive a hot rod. ■ **hot-rod·der** n.

hot seat ▶ n. (**the hot seat**) informal **1** the position of a person who carries full responsibility for something. **2** the electric chair.

hot·shot /'hät,sHät/ ▶ n. informal an important or exceptionally able person.

hot spot ▶ n. **1** a place of significant activity or danger. **2** a small area with a high temperature in comparison to its surroundings. **3** (also **wireless hot spot**) a place in a public building with a signal that allows wireless connection to the Internet.

hot spring ▶ n. a spring of naturally hot water, typically heated by subterranean volcanic activity.

hot stuff ▶ n. informal **1** a person or thing of outstanding talent or interest. **2** a sexually exciting person, book, etc.

hot-tem·pered ▶ adj. easily angered.

Hot·ten·tot /'hätn,tät/ ▶ n. & adj. offensive formerly used to refer to the Khoikhoi peoples of South Africa and Namibia.

hot tick·et ▶ n. informal a person or thing that is in great demand.

hot·tie /'hätē/ (also **hotty**) ▶ n. informal a sexually attractive person.

hot tub ▶ n. a large tub filled with hot bubbling water, used for recreation or therapy.

hot-wa·ter bot·tle (also **hot-water bag**) ▶ n. a rubber container that is filled with hot water and used for warming a bed or part of the body.

hot-wire ▶ v. informal start the engine of a vehicle by bypassing the ignition switch.

Hou·di·ni /hŏŏ'dēnē/ ▶ n. a person skilled at escaping from difficult situations.

hound /hound/ ▶ n. a dog of a breed used for hunting. ▶ v. harass or pursue relentlessly: *she was hounded by the media.*

hounds·tooth /'houn(d)z,tŏŏTH/ ▶ n. a large checked pattern with notched corners.

hour /ou(ə)r/ ▶ n. **1** a period of 60 minutes, one of the twenty-four equal parts that a day is divided into. **2** a time of day specified as an exact number of hours from midnight or midday. **3** a period set aside for a particular purpose or activity: *leisure hours.* **4** a point in time: *the store is half-full even at this hour.*
– PHRASES **on the hour** at an exact hour, or on each hour, of the day or night.

hour·glass /'ou(ə)r,glas/ ▶ n. a device with two connected glass bulbs containing sand that takes an hour to fall from the upper to the lower bulb. ▶ adj. shaped like an hourglass: *her hourglass figure.*

hou·ri /'hŏŏrē/ ▶ n. (pl. **houris**) a beautiful young

woman, especially one of the virgin companions of the faithful in the Muslim Paradise.

hour·ly /'ou(ə)rlē/ ▸ adj. **1** done or occurring every hour. **2** calculated hour by hour. ▸ adv. **1** every hour. **2** by the hour.

house ▸ n. /hous/ **1** a building for people to live in. **2** a building devoted to a particular activity or purpose: *a house of prayer.* **3** a firm or institution: *a fashion house.* **4** a religious community that occupies a particular building. **5** a residential hall at a school or college. **6** a lawmaking assembly. **7** a dynasty: *the House of Stewart.* **8** (also **house music**) a style of fast electronic dance music. **9** Astrology one of twelve divisions of the celestial sphere. ▸ adj. /hous/ **1** (of an animal or plant) kept in or infesting buildings. **2** relating to resident medical staff at a hospital. **3** relating to a firm, institution, or society: *a house journal.* ▸ v. /houz/ **1** provide someone with shelter or accommodations. **2** provide space for: *the museum houses a collection of Roman sculpture.* **3** enclose or encase something. ■ **house·ful** /'hous,fŏŏl/ n.
– PHRASES **like a house on fire** (or **afire**) informal vigorously, excellently. **keep house** run a household. **on the house** at the management's expense. **put one's house in order** make necessary reforms.

house ar·rest ▸ n. the state of being kept as a prisoner in one's own house.

house·boat /'hous,bōt/ ▸ n. a boat that is equipped for use as a home.

house·bound /'hous,bound/ ▸ adj. unable to leave one's house, often due to illness or old age.

house·boy /'hous,boi/ ▸ n. a boy or man employed to undertake domestic duties.

house·break /'hous,brāk/ (past. **housebroke** /'hous,brōk/; past participle **housebroken** /'hous,brōkən/) ▸ v. **1** train a pet to urinate and defecate outside the house or only in a special place. **2** informal or humorous teach someone good manners or neatness.

house·break·ing /'hous,brākiNG/ ▸ n. the action of breaking into a building to commit a crime. ■ **house·break·er** n.

house·coat /'hous,kōt/ ▸ n. a woman's long, loose robe for casual wear around the house.

house·dress /'hous,dres/ ▸ n. a simple, usually washable, dress suitable for wearing while doing housework.

house·fly /'hous,flī/ ▸ n. (pl. **houseflies**) a common small fly often found in and around houses.

house·hold /'hous,(h)ōld/ ▸ n. a house and its occupants regarded as a unit. ■ **house·hold·er** n.

house·hold name (also **household word**) ▸ n. a famous person or thing.

house·hunt·ing ▸ n. the process of seeking a house to buy or rent. ■ **house·hunt·er** n.

house hus·band ▸ n. a man who lives with a partner and carries out the household duties traditionally done by a housewife.

house·keep·er /'hous,kēpər/ ▸ n. a person, typically a woman, employed to manage a household.

house·keep·ing /'hous,kēpiNG/ ▸ n. **1** the management of a household. **2** the department in a hotel, etc. that oversees its cleaning, linen, and glassware. **3** operations such as record-keeping and maintenance in an organization or a

computer that support its real work.

house lights ▸ pl.n. the lights in the area of a theater where the audience sits.

house·maid /'hous,mād/ ▸ n. a female employee who cleans rooms.

house mar·tin ▸ n. a black-and-white bird of the swallow family, nesting on buildings.

house·mas·ter /'hous,mastər/ (or **housemistress**) ▸ n. chiefly Brit. a teacher in charge of a house at a boarding school.

house·mate /'hous,māt/ ▸ n. a person with whom one shares a house.

house mouse ▸ n. a grayish-brown mouse found abundantly as a scavenger in houses.

House of Com·mons ▸ n. the part of Parliament in the UK whose members are elected by voters.

House of Lords ▸ n. **1** the part of Parliament in the UK whose members are peers and bishops and are not elected by voters. **2** a committee of specially qualified members of the House of Lords, appointed as the ultimate judicial appeal court of England and Wales.

House of Rep·re·sent·a·tives ▸ n. the lower house of the US Congress.

house·plant /'hous,plant/ ▸ n. a plant grown indoors.

house·proud ▸ adj. very concerned with the cleanliness and appearance of one's home.

house·sit ▸ v. live in and look after a house while its owner is away. ■ **house·sit·ter** n.

house spar·row ▸ n. a common brown and gray sparrow that nests in the eaves and roofs of houses.

house style ▸ n. a company's preferred manner of presentation and layout of written material.

house-to-house ▸ adj. & adv. performed at or taken to each house in turn.

house-train ▸ v. train a pet to urinate and defecate outside the house.

house·wares /'hous,we(ə)rz/ ▸ n. kitchen utensils and similar household items.

house·warm·ing /'hous,wôrmiNG/ ▸ n. a party celebrating a move to a new home.

house·wife /'hous,wīf/ ▸ n. (pl. **housewives** /-,wīvz/) a married woman whose main occupation is caring for her family and running the household. ■ **house·wife·ly** adj. **house·wif·er·y** /-,wīfərē/ n.

house·work /'hous,wərk/ ▸ n. cleaning and other work done in running a home.

hous·ing /'houziNG/ ▸ n. **1** houses and apartments as a whole. **2** the provision of accommodations. **3** a rigid casing for a piece of equipment.

HOV ▸ abbr. high-occupancy vehicle.

hove /hōv/ Nautical ▸ past tense of HEAVE.

hov·el /'həvəl, 'hävəl/ ▸ n. a small squalid or run-down dwelling.

hov·er /'həvər/ ▸ v. **1** remain in one place in the air. **2** linger close at hand in an uncertain way. **3** remain near a particular level or between two states: *the temperature hovered around ten degrees.* ▸ n. an act of hovering. ■ **hov·er·er** n.

hov·er·craft /'həvər,kraft/ ▸ n. (pl. same) a vehicle or craft that travels over land or water on a cushion of air.

how /hou/ ▸ adv. **1** in what way or by what means. **2** in what condition or health. **3** to what extent or degree. **4** the way in which.

– PHRASES **how about?** would you like? **how do you do?** said when meeting a person for the first time in a formal situation. **how many** what number. **how much** what amount or price. **how's that for——?** isn't that a remarkable instance of——?

how·dah /'houdə/ ▶ n. a seat for riding on the back of an elephant or camel, usually having a canopy.

how·dy /'houdē/ ▶ exclam. an informal friendly greeting.

how·ev·er /hou'evər/ ▶ adv. **1** used to introduce a statement that contrasts with a previous one. **2** in whatever way or to whatever extent.

how·itz·er /'houətsər/ ▶ n. a short gun for firing shells at a steep angle.

howl /houl/ ▶ n. **1** a long wailing cry made by an animal. **2** a loud cry of pain, amusement, etc. ▶ v. make a howling sound.

howl·er /'houlər/ ▶ n. informal a stupid mistake.

howl·ing /'houliNG/ ▶ adj. informal great: *the meal was a howling success.*

how·so·ev·er /ˌhousō'evər/ formal or old use ▶ adv. to whatever extent. ▶ conj. in whatever way.

h.p. (also **HP**) ▶ abbr. **1** high pressure. **2** horsepower.

HQ ▶ abbr. headquarters.

HR ▶ abbr. **1** House of Representatives. **2** human resources.

hr. ▶ abbr. hour(s).

HRH ▶ abbr. Brit. Her (or His) Royal Highness.

HRT ▶ abbr. hormone replacement therapy.

Hs ▶ symbol the chemical element hassium.

HTML ▶ abbr. Computing Hypertext Markup Language.

HTTP ▶ abbr. Computing Hypertext Transfer (or Transport) Protocol.

hub /həb/ ▶ n. **1** the central part of a wheel, rotating on or with the axle. **2** the center of an activity, region, or network.

hub·bub /'həbəb/ ▶ n. **1** a loud, confused noise caused by a crowd. **2** a busy, noisy situation.

hub·by /'həbē/ ▶ n. (pl. **hubbies**) informal a husband.

hub·cap /'həbˌkap/ ▶ n. a cover for the hub of a motor vehicle's wheel.

hu·bris /'(h)yōōbris/ ▶ n. excessive pride or self-confidence. ■ **hu·bris·tic** adj.

huck·ster /'həkstər/ ▶ n. **1** a person who sells small items, either door-to-door or from a stall. **2** a person who uses aggressive selling techniques. ■ **huck·ster·ism** n.

HUD /həd/ ▶ abbr. (Department of) Housing and Urban Development.

hud·dle /'hədl/ ▶ v. **1** crowd together. **2** curl one's body into a small space. ▶ n. a number of people or things grouped closely together.

hue /(h)yōō/ ▶ n. **1** a color or shade. **2** technical the quality of a color, dependent on its dominant wavelength, by virtue of which it is discernible as red, green, etc. **3** an aspect: *men of all political hues.*

hue and cry ▶ n. clamor or public outcry.

huff /həf/ ▶ v. (often in phrase **huff and puff**) **1** breathe out noisily. **2** show one's annoyance in an obvious way. ▶ n. a fit of petty annoyance.

huff·y /'həfē/ ▶ adj. (**huffier, huffiest**) easily offended. ■ **huff·i·ly** adv. **huff·i·ness** n.

hug /həg/ ▶ v. (**hugs, hugging, hugged**) **1** hold

someone or something tightly in one's arms or against one's body. **2** keep close to: *a few craft hugged the shore.* ▶ n. an act of hugging. ■ **hug·ga·ble** adj. **hug·ger** n.

huge /(h)yōōj/ ▶ adj. very large; enormous. ■ **huge·ly** adv. **huge·ness** n.

Hu·gue·not /'hyōōgəˌnät/ ▶ n. a French Protestant of the 16th–17th centuries.

huh /hə/ ▶ exclam. used to express scorn or surprise, or in questions to invite agreement.

hu·la /'hōōlə/ (also **hula-hula**) ▶ n. a dance performed by Hawaiian women, in which the dancers sway their hips.

hu·la hoop (also trademark **Hula-Hoop**) ▶ n. a large hoop spun around the body by gyrating the hips.

hulk /həlk/ ▶ n. **1** an old ship stripped of fittings and permanently moored. **2** a large or clumsy person or thing.

hulk·ing /'həlkiNG/ ▶ adj. informal very large or clumsy.

hull¹ /həl/ ▶ n. the main body of a ship or other vessel.

hull² ▶ n. **1** the outer covering of a fruit or seed. **2** the cluster of leaves and stalk on a strawberry or raspberry. ▶ v. remove the hulls from (fruit, seeds, or grain).

hul·la·ba·loo /'hələbəˌlōō, ˌhələbə'lōō/ ▶ n. informal a commotion or uproar.

hul·lo /hə'lō/ ▶ exclam. variant spelling of HELLO.

hum /həm/ ▶ v. (**hums, humming, hummed**) **1** make a low continuous sound like that of a bee. **2** sing with closed lips. **3** informal be in a very busy state. ▶ n. a low continuous sound. ■ **hum·ma·ble** adj. **hum·mer** n.

hu·man /'(h)yōōmən/ ▶ adj. **1** relating to or characteristic of human beings. **2** showing the better qualities of human beings, such as kindness. ▶ n. (also **human being**) a person. ■ **hu·man·ly** adv. **hu·man·ness** n.

hu·mane /(h)yōō'mān/ ▶ adj. **1** kind or considerate toward people or animals. **2** formal (of a branch of learning) intended to civilize people. ■ **hu·mane·ly** adv. **hu·mane·ness** n.

Hu·mane So·ci·e·ty ▶ n. trademark a nonprofit organization that attempts to prevent cruelty to animals and often operates animal shelters.

hu·man in·ter·est ▶ n. the aspect of a news story that interests people because it describes other people's experiences or emotions.

hu·man·ism /'(h)yōōməˌnizəm/ ▶ n. **1** a system of thought that regards people as capable of using their intelligence to live their lives, rather than relying on religious belief. **2** a Renaissance cultural movement that revived interest in ancient Greek and Roman thought. ■ **hu·man·ist** n. & adj. **hu·man·is·tic** /ˌ(h)yōōmə'nistik/ adj.

hu·man·i·tar·i·an /(h)yōōˌmaniˈte(ə)rēən/ ▶ adj. concerned with or seeking to improve human welfare: *humanitarian aid.* ▶ n. a humanitarian person. ■ **hu·man·i·tar·i·an·ism** n.

USAGE
Sentences such as *this is the worst humanitarian disaster this country has seen* show a loose use of **humanitarian** to mean 'human.' This use is especially common in journalism but is best avoided in careful writing.

hu·man·i·ty /(h)yōō'manitē/ ▶ n. (pl. **humanities**) **1** human beings as a whole. **2** the condition of being human. **3** sympathy and kindness toward other people. **4** (**humanities**) studies concerned with human culture, such as literature, art, or history.

hu·man·ize /'(h)yōōmə,nīz/ ▶ v. **1** make something more pleasant or suitable for people. **2** give a human character to something. ∎ **hu·man·i·za·tion** /,hyōōməni'zāshən/ n.

hu·man·kind /'(h)yōōmən,kīnd/ ▶ n. human beings as a whole.

hu·man na·ture ▶ n. the general characteristics and feelings shared by all people.

hu·man·oid /'(h)yōōmə,noid/ ▶ adj. resembling a human in appearance or character. ▶ n. a being resembling a human.

hu·man re·sourc·es ▶ pl.n. **1** the collective personnel of a business or organization. **2** the department of a business or organization that deals with the administration, management, and training of personnel.

hu·man rights ▶ pl.n. basic rights to which every person is entitled, such as freedom.

hum·ble /'hembəl/ ▶ adj. (**humbler, humblest**) **1** having or showing a modest or low estimate of one's own importance. **2** of low rank. **3** not large or special: *a small, humble chalet.* ▶ v. make someone feel less important or proud. ∎ **hum·bly** adv.

– PHRASES **eat humble pie** make a humble apology and accept humiliation.

hum·bug /'həm,bəg/ ▶ n. **1** false or misleading talk or behavior. **2** a person who is not sincere or honest. ∎ **hum·bug·ger·y** n.

hum·ding·er /'həm'diNGər/ ▶ n. informal a remarkable or outstanding person or thing.

hum·drum /'həm,drəm/ ▶ adj. lacking excitement or variety; dull.

hu·mec·tant /(h)yōō'mektənt/ ▶ adj. retaining or preserving moisture. ▶ n. a substance used to reduce the loss of moisture.

hu·mer·us /'(h)yōōmərəs/ ▶ n. (pl. **humeri** /-mə,rī/) the bone of the upper arm, between the shoulder and the elbow. ∎ **hu·mer·al** adj.

hu·mid /'(h)yōōmid/ ▶ adj. (of the air or weather) damp and warm. ∎ **hu·mid·ly** adv.

hu·mid·i·fi·er /(h)yōō'midə,fī(ə)r/ ▶ n. a device that increases indoor atmospheric moisture.

hu·mid·i·fy /(h)yōō'midə,fī/ ▶ v. (**humidifies, humidifying, humidified**) (often as adj. **humidified**) increase the level of moisture in air. ∎ **hu·mid·i·fi·ca·tion** /-,midəfi'kāshən/ n.

hu·mid·i·ty /(h)yōō'miditē/ ▶ n. **1** the state or quality of being humid. **2** a measure of the amount of water vapor in the atmosphere or a gas.

hu·mi·dor /'(h)yōōmi,dôr/ ▶ n. an airtight container for keeping cigars or tobacco moist.

hu·mil·i·ate /(h)yōō'milē,āt/ ▶ v. make someone feel ashamed or foolish in front of another. ∎ **hu·mil·i·a·ting** adj. **hu·mil·i·a·tion** /-,milē'āshən/ n. **hu·mil·i·a·tor** n.

hu·mil·i·ty /(h)yōō'militē/ ▶ n. the quality of having a modest view of one's importance.

hum·ming·bird /'həmiNG,bərd/ ▶ n. a small long-billed tropical American bird able to hover by beating its wings extremely fast.

hum·mock /'həmək/ ▶ n. a small hill or mound. ∎ **hum·mock·y** adj.

hum·mus /'hŏŏməs, 'həm-/ ▶ n. a thick Middle Eastern dip made from chickpeas puréed with olive oil and garlic.

hu·mon·gous /(h)yōō'mäNGgəs, -'məNG-/ (also **humungous**) ▶ adj. informal very large; enormous.

hu·mor /'(h)yōōmər/ (Brit. **humour**) ▶ n. **1** the quality of being amusing. **2** a state of mind: *her good humor vanished.* **3** (also **cardinal humor**) each of four fluids of the body that were formerly believed to determine a person's physical and mental qualities. ▶ v. agree with someone's wishes so as to keep the person in a good mood. ∎ **hu·mor·less** adj.

– PHRASES **out of humor** in a bad mood.

hu·mor·ist /'(h)yōōmərist/ ▶ n. a writer or speaker who is known for being amusing.

hu·mor·ous /'(h)yōōmərəs/ ▶ adj. **1** causing amusement. **2** having or showing a sense of humor. ∎ **hu·mor·ous·ly** adv. **hu·mor·ous·ness** n.

humour, etc. ▶ n. British spelling of HUMOR, etc.

hump /həmp/ ▶ n. **1** a rounded raised mass of earth or land. **2** a rounded part projecting from the back of a camel or other animal or as an abnormality on a person's back. ▶ v. **1** informal lift or carry something heavy with difficulty. **2** (as adj. **humped**) having a hump. **3** vulgar slang have sex with someone. ∎ **hump·less** adj. **hump·y** adj.

– PHRASES **over the hump** informal past the most difficult part of something.

hump·back /'həmp,bak/ ▶ n. **1** (also **humpback whale**) a baleen whale that has a hump and long white flippers. **2** another term for HUNCHBACK. ∎ **hump·backed** adj.

hu·mun·gous ▶ adj. variant spelling of HUMONGOUS.

hu·mus /'(h)yōōməs/ ▶ n. the organic component of soil, formed from dead and dying leaves and other plant material.

Hum·vee /'həm'vē/ ▶ n. trademark a modern, multipurpose military vehicle.

Hun /hən/ ▶ n. **1** a member of an Asiatic people who invaded Europe in the 4th–5th centuries. **2** informal, derogatory a German (especially during World Wars I and II).

hunch /hənCH/ ▶ v. raise one's shoulders and bend the top of one's body forward. ▶ n. a belief that something is true, based on a feeling rather than evidence.

hunch·back /'hənCH,bak/ ▶ n. offensive a person with a hump on his or her back. ∎ **hunch·backed** adj.

hun·dred /'həndrid/ ▶ cardinal number **1** ten more than ninety; 100. (Roman numeral: **c** or **C.**) **2** (**hundreds**) informal an unspecified large number. **3** (**the —— hundreds**) the years of a specified century: *the early nineteen hundreds.* **4** used to express whole hours in the twenty-four-hour system. ∎ **hun·dred·fold** adj. & adv. **hun·dredth** ordinal number.

– PHRASES **a** (or **one**) **hundred percent 1** entirely. **2** informal completely fit and healthy. **3** informal maximum effort and commitment.

hun·dred·weight /'həndrid,wāt/ ▶ n. (pl. same or **hundredweights**) **1** (also **short hundredweight**) a unit of weight equal to 100 lb (about 45.4 kg). **2** (also **metric hundredweight**) a unit of weight equal to 50 kg. **3** (also **long hundredweight**) Brit. a unit of weight equal to 112 lb (about 50.8 kg).

hung /həNG/ past and past participle of HANG. ▶ adj. **1** (of a jury) unable to agree on a verdict. **2** (of an elected body in the UK and Canada) having no political party with an overall majority. **3** (**hung up about/on**) informal have an obsession or problem about.

Hun·gar·i·an /həNG'ge(ə)rēən/ ▶ n. **1** a person from Hungary. **2** the official language of Hungary. ▶ adj. relating to Hungary.

hun·ger /'həNGgər/ ▶ n. **1** a feeling of discomfort and a need to eat, caused by a lack of food. **2** a strong desire: *his hunger for money.* ▶ v. (**hunger after/for**) have a strong desire for someone or something.

hun·ger strike ▶ n. a prolonged refusal to eat, carried out as a protest.

hung·o·ver /'həNGg'ōvər/ (also **hung over**) ▶ adj. suffering from a hangover.

hun·gry /'həNGgrē/ ▶ adj. (**hungrier, hungriest**) **1** feeling or showing hunger. **2** having a strong desire: *a party hungry for power.* ■ **hun·gri·ly** adv. **hun·gri·ness** n.

hunk /həNGk/ ▶ n. **1** a large piece cut or broken from something larger. **2** informal a strong, sexually attractive man. ■ **hunk·y** (**hunkier, hunkiest**) adj.

hunk·er /'həNGkər/ ▶ v. **1** squat or crouch down low. **2** (**hunker down**) approach a task seriously.

hun·kers /'həNGkərz/ ▶ pl.n. informal a person's haunches.

hunk·y-do·ry /'həNGkē 'dôrē/ ▶ adj. informal fine; going well.

hunt /hənt/ ▶ v. **1** chase and kill a wild animal for sport or food. **2** try to find by thorough searching: *he desperately hunted for a new job.* **3** (**hunt someone down**) chase and capture someone. **4** (as adj. **hunted**) appearing alarmed or harassed. ▶ n. **1** an act of hunting. **2** a group of people who meet regularly to hunt animals as a sport. ■ **hunt·ing** n.

hunt·er /'hən(t)ər/ ▶ n. **1** a person or animal that hunts. **2** a breed of horse developed for stamina in fox hunting. ■ **hunt·ress** /'həntris/ n.

hunt·er-gath·er·er ▶ n. a member of a nomadic people who live chiefly by hunting, fishing, and harvesting wild food.

hunt·ing ground ▶ n. a place where people are likely to find what they are looking for.

Hun·ting·ton's dis·ease ▶ n. a hereditary disease marked by degeneration of brain cells, causing chorea (disorder of the nervous system) and progressive dementia.

hunts·man /'həntsmən/ ▶ n. (pl. **huntsmen**) **1** a person who hunts. **2** an official in charge of hounds during a fox hunt.

hur·dle /'hərdl/ ▶ n. **1** one of a series of upright frames that athletes in a race must jump over. **2** (**hurdles**) a hurdle race. **3** a problem or difficulty that must be overcome: *the project must still clear several hurdles before work can start.* ▶ v. **1** run in a hurdle race. **2** jump over a hurdle or other obstacle while running. ■ **hur·dler** n.

hur·dy-gur·dy /'hərdē ,gərdē/ ▶ n. (pl. **hurdy-gurdies**) **1** a musical instrument with a droning sound played by turning a handle, with keys worked by the other hand. **2** informal a barrel organ.

hurl /hərl/ ▶ v. **1** throw someone or something with great force. **2** shout abuse or insults.

hurl·ing /'hərliNG/ ▶ n. an Irish game resembling hockey, played with a shorter stick.

hurl·y-burl·y /'hərlē 'bərlē/ ▶ n. busy and noisy activity.

hur·rah /hŏŏ'rä, hə-/ (also **hooray, hurray**)

▶ exclam. used to express joy or approval.

hur·ri·cane /'həri,kān, 'hə-ri-/ ▶ n. a severe storm with a violent wind, in particular a tropical cyclone in the Caribbean.

hur·ri·cane lamp ▶ n. an oil lamp in which the flame is protected from the wind by a glass chimney.

hur·ry /'hərē, 'hə-rē/ ▶ v. (**hurries, hurrying, hurried**) **1** move or act quickly. **2** do quickly or too quickly: *guided tours tend to be hurried.* ▶ n. **1** great speed or urgency in doing something. **2** a need for speed or haste; urgency: *relax, what's the hurry?* ■ **hur·ried** adj. **hur·ried·ly** adv.

– PHRASES **in a hurry** informal easily; readily: *you won't forget that in a hurry.*

hurt /hərt/ ▶ v. (past and past part. **hurt**) **1** cause pain or injury to someone. **2** feel pain. **3** upset or distress someone. ▶ n. **1** injury or pain. **2** unhappiness or distress.

hurt·ful /'hərtfəl/ ▶ adj. causing mental pain or distress. ■ **hurt·ful·ly** adv.

hur·tle /'hərtl/ ▶ v. move at great speed, especially in an uncontrolled way.

hus·band /'həzbənd/ ▶ n. a married man considered in relation to his wife. ▶ v. use resources economically.

hus·band·man /'həzbəndmən/ ▶ n. (pl. **husbandmen**) old use a farmer.

hus·band·ry /'həzbəndrē/ ▶ n. **1** the care, cultivation, and breeding of crops and animals; farming. **2** management and careful use of resources.

hush /həSH/ ▶ v. **1** make or become quiet. **2** (**hush something up**) prevent something from becoming public. ▶ n. a silence.

hush-hush ▶ adj. informal highly secret or confidential.

hush mon·ey ▶ n. informal money paid to someone to prevent them from revealing information.

hush pup·py ▶ n. a small deep-fried ball of cornmeal batter.

husk /həsk/ ▶ n. the dry outer covering of some fruits or seeds. ▶ v. remove the husk or husks from fruit or seeds.

husk·y¹ /'həskē/ ▶ adj. (**huskier, huskiest**) **1** sounding low-pitched and slightly hoarse: *her deliciously husky voice.* **2** big and strong. ■ **husk·i·ly** adv. **husk·i·ness** n.

husky² ▶ n. (pl. **huskies**) a powerful dog of a breed with a thick double coat, used in the Arctic for pulling sleds.

hus·sar /hə'zär/ ▶ n. a soldier in a light cavalry regiment that adopted a dress uniform modeled on that of the Hungarian light horsemen of the 15th century.

hus·sy /'həsē, 'həzē/ ▶ n. (pl. **hussies**) an immoral or impudent girl or woman.

hust·ings /'həstiNGz/ ▶ n. (treated as pl. or sing.) (**the hustings**) the political meetings and other campaigning that take place before an election.

hus·tle /'həsəl/ ▶ v. **1** push roughly; jostle. **2** (**hustle someone into**) pressure someone into doing something without time for consideration. **3** informal obtain something dishonestly or by aggressive methods. **4** informal work as a prostitute. ▶ n. busy movement and activity: *the hustle and bustle of the big city.*

hus·tler /'həslər/ ▶ n. informal **1** an aggressively

enterprising person; a go-getter. **2** an enterprising and often dishonest person, especially one trying to sell something. **3** an expert player, especially at pool or billiards, who pretends to be less skillful than they are and lures or challenges less skilled, especially amateur, players into games in order to win money from them. **4** a female prostitute. **5** a male prostitute, especially for homosexual clients.

hut /hət/ ▶ n. a small simple house or shelter.

hutch /həCH/ ▶ n. **1** a box with a wire mesh front, used for keeping rabbits or other small domesticated animals. **2** a cupboard or dresser typically with open shelves above.

Hu·tu /ˈho͞oto͞o/ ▶ n. (pl. same or **Hutus** or **Bahutu** /bəˈho͞oto͞o/) a member of a people forming the majority population in Rwanda and Burundi.

huz·zah /həˈzä/ ▶ exclam. old use or ironic used to express approval or delight.

HVAC ▶ abbr. heating, ventilation, and air conditioning.

hwy ▶ abbr. highway.

hy·a·cinth /ˈhīəˌsinTH/ ▶ n. a plant with fragrant bell-shaped flowers.

hy·a·line /ˈhīəlin, -ˌlīn/ ▶ adj. Anatomy & Zoology having a glassy, translucent appearance: *hyaline cartilage.*

hy·brid /ˈhībrid/ ▶ n. **1** the offspring of two plants or animals of different species or varieties, such as a mule. **2** a thing made by combining two different elements: *tae-bo, a hybrid of aerobics and Thai kick-boxing.* ■ **hy·brid·i·ty** /hīˈbriditē/ n.

hy·brid car ▶ n. a car with a gasoline engine and an electric motor, each of which can propel it.

hy·brid·ize /ˈhībriˌdīz/ ▶ v. breed individuals of two different species or varieties to produce hybrids. ■ **hy·brid·i·za·tion** /ˌhībrədiˈzāsHən/ n.

hy·dra /ˈhīdrə/ ▶ n. a minute freshwater invertebrate animal with a tubular body and a ring of tentacles around the mouth.

hy·dran·gea /hīˈdrānjə/ ▶ n. a shrub with large white, blue, or pink clusters of flowers.

hy·drant /ˈhīdrənt/ ▶ n. an upright water pipe with a nozzle to which a fire hose can be attached.

hy·drate ▶ n. /ˈhīˌdrāt/ a compound in which water molecules are chemically bound to another compound or an element. ▶ v. /ˈhīˈdrāt/ cause something to absorb or combine with water. ■ **hy·dra·tion** /hīˈdrāsHən/ n.

hy·drau·lic /hīˈdrôlik/ ▶ adj. relating to or operated by a liquid moving in a confined space under pressure. ■ **hy·drau·li·cal·ly** adv.

hy·drau·lics /hīˈdrôliks/ ▶ pl.n. (usu. treated as sing.) the branch of science concerned with the use of liquids moving under pressure to provide mechanical force.

hy·dra·zine /ˈhīdrəˌzēn/ ▶ n. Chemistry a colorless volatile alkaline liquid with powerful reducing properties, used in chemical synthesis and rocket fuels.

hy·dride /ˈhīˌdrīd/ ▶ n. Chemistry a compound of hydrogen with a metal.

hy·dro /ˈhīdrō/ ▶ n. (pl. **hydros**) **1** a hydroelectric power plant. **2** hydroelectricity.

hydro- (also **hydr-**) ▶ comb.form **1** relating to water or fluid: *hydraulic.* **2** combined with hydrogen:

hydrocarbon.

hy·dro·car·bon /ˈhīdrəˌkärbən/ ▶ n. a compound of hydrogen and carbon, such as those that are the chief components of petroleum and natural gas.

hy·dro·ceph·a·lus /ˌhīdrōˈsefələs/ ▶ n. a condition in which fluid accumulates in the brain. ■ **hy·dro·ce·phal·ic** /ˌhīdrōsəˈfalik/ adj. **hy·dro·ceph·a·ly** n.

hy·dro·chlo·ric ac·id /ˌhīdrəˈklôrik/ ▶ n. a corrosive acid containing hydrogen and chlorine.

hy·dro·chlo·ride /ˌhīdrəˈklôˌrīd/ ▶ n. a compound of an organic base with hydrochloric acid.

hy·dro·cor·ti·sone /ˌhīdrəˈkôrtiˌzōn/ ▶ n. a steroid hormone used to treat inflammation and rheumatism.

hy·dro·cy·an·ic ac·id /ˌhīdrōsīˈanik/ ▶ n. a highly poisonous acidic solution of hydrogen cyanide.

hy·dro·dy·nam·ics /ˌhīdrōdīˈnamiks/ ▶ pl.n. (treated as sing.) the branch of science concerned with the forces acting on or exerted by fluids (especially liquids). ■ **hy·dro·dy·nam·ic** adj. **hy·dro·dy·nam·i·cal·ly** adv.

hy·dro·e·lec·tric /ˌhīdrōəˈlektrik/ ▶ adj. relating to the generation of electricity using flowing water to drive a turbine that powers a generator. ■ **hy·dro·e·lec·tric·i·ty** /-əlekˈtrisitē/ n.

hy·dro·foil /ˈhīdrəˌfoil/ ▶ n. **1** a boat fitted with structures (known as foils) that lift the hull clear of the water to increase speed. **2** each of the foils of a hydrofoil.

hy·dro·gel /ˈhīdrəˌjel/ ▶ n. a gel in which the liquid component is water.

hy·dro·gen /ˈhīdrəjən/ ▶ n. a colorless, odorless, highly flammable gas that is the lightest of the chemical elements.

hy·dro·gen·ate /ˈhīdrəjəˌnāt, hīˈdräjənāt/ ▶ v. combine a substance with hydrogen. ■ **hy·dro·gen·a·tion** /ˌhīdrəjəˈnāsHən, hīˌdräjə-/ n.

hy·dro·gen bomb ▶ n. a nuclear bomb whose destructive power comes from the fusion of isotopes of hydrogen (deuterium and tritium).

hy·dro·gen per·ox·ide ▶ n. a colorless liquid used in some disinfectants and bleaches.

hy·dro·gen sul·fide ▶ n. a colorless poisonous gas with a smell of rotten eggs, made by the action of acids on sulfides.

hy·drog·ra·phy /hīˈdrägrəfē/ ▶ n. the science of surveying and charting seas, lakes, and rivers. ■ **hy·drog·ra·pher** n. **hy·dro·graph·ic** /ˌhīdrəˈgrafik/ adj.

hy·drol·o·gy /hīˈdräləjē/ ▶ n. the branch of science concerned with the properties and distribution of water on the earth's surface. ■ **hy·dro·log·ic** /ˌhīdrəˈläjik/ adj. **hy·dro·log·i·cal** /ˌhīdrəˈläjikəl/ adj. **hy·drol·o·gist** n.

hy·drol·y·sis /hīˈdräləsis/ ▶ n. Chemistry the chemical breakdown of a compound due to reaction with water. ■ **hy·dro·lyt·ic** /ˌhīdrəˈlitik/ adj.

hy·dro·lyze /ˈhīdrəˌlīz/ (Brit **hydrolyse**) ▶ v. break down a compound by chemical reaction with water.

hy·drom·e·ter /hīˈdrämitər/ ▶ n. an instrument for measuring the density of liquids.

hy·drop·a·thy /hīˈdräpəTHē/ ▶ n. the treatment of illness through the use of water, either internally or by external means such as steam baths. ■ **hy·dro·path·ic** /ˌhīdrəˈpaTHik/ adj.

hy·dro·phil·ic /ˌhīdrəˈfilik/ ▶ adj. having a tendency to mix with or dissolve in water.

hy·dro·pho·bi·a /ˌhīdrəˈfōbēə/ ▶ n. 1 extreme fear of water, especially as a symptom of rabies. 2 rabies.

hy·dro·pho·bic /ˌhīdrəˈfōbik/ ▶ adj. 1 tending to repel or fail to mix with water. 2 relating to or suffering from hydrophobia.

hy·dro·phone /ˈhīdrəˌfōn/ ▶ n. a microphone that detects sound waves under water.

hy·dro·plane /ˈhīdrəˌplān/ ▶ n. 1 a light, fast motorboat designed to skim over the surface of water. 2 a finlike attachment that enables a moving submarine to rise or fall in the water. 3 a seaplane. ▶ v. another term for AQUAPLANE.

hy·dro·pon·ics /ˌhīdrəˈpäniks/ ▶ pl.n. (treated as sing.) the growing of plants in sand, gravel, or liquid, with added nutrients but without soil. ■ **hy·dro·pon·ic** adj. **hy·dro·pon·i·cal·ly** adv.

hy·dro·sphere /ˈhīdrəˌsfir/ ▶ n. the seas, lakes, and other waters of the earth's surface, considered as a group.

hy·dro·stat·ic /ˌhīdrəˈstatik/ ▶ adj. relating to the pressure and other characteristics of liquid that is not in motion. ■ **hy·dro·stat·ics** pl.n.

hy·dro·ther·a·py /ˌhīdrəˈTHerəpē/ ▶ n. 1 the use of exercises in a pool to treat conditions such as arthritis. 2 another term for HYDROPATHY.

hy·dro·ther·mal /ˌhīdrəˈTHərməl/ ▶ adj. relating to the action of heated water in the earth's crust. ■ **hy·dro·ther·mal·ly** adv.

hy·dro·ther·mal vent ▶ n. an opening in the sea floor out of which heated mineral-rich water flows.

hy·drous /ˈhīdrəs/ ▶ adj. containing water.

hy·drox·ide /hīˈdräkˌsīd/ ▶ n. a compound containing OH negative ions together with a metallic element.

hy·drox·yl /hīˈdräksəl/ ▶ n. Chemistry the radical –OH, present in alcohols and many other organic compounds.

hy·dro·zo·an /ˌhīdrəˈzōən/ ▶ n. a small marine or freshwater animal related to jellyfish and corals and belonging to a group that includes hydras and the Portuguese man-of-war. ▶ adj. relating to the hydrozoans.

hy·e·na /hīˈēnə/ ▶ n. a doglike carnivorous African mammal with an erect mane.

hy·giene /ˈhīˌjēn/ ▶ n. conditions or practices that help to prevent illness or disease, especially the keeping of oneself and one's surroundings clean.

hy·gi·en·ic /hīˈjenik, -ˈjē-/ ▶ adj. clean and free of the organisms that spread disease. ■ **hy·gi·en·i·cal·ly** adv.

hy·gien·ist /hīˈjenəst, -jē-/ ▶ n. a person working with a dentist who specializes in scaling and polishing teeth and giving advice on oral hygiene.

hy·grom·e·ter /hīˈgrämitər/ ▶ n. an instrument for measuring humidity.

hy·gro·scop·ic /ˌhīgrəˈskäpik/ ▶ adj. tending to absorb moisture from the air.

hy·ing /ˈhī-iNG/ ▶ present participle of HIE.

hy·men /ˈhīmən/ ▶ n. a membrane that partially closes the opening of the vagina and is usually broken on the first occasion a woman or girl has sex.

hy·me·nop·ter·an /ˌhīməˈnäptərən/ ▶ n. an

insect having four transparent wings, belonging to a large group that includes the bees, wasps, and ants. ■ **hy·me·nop·ter·ous** /-tərəs/ adj.

hymn /him/ ▶ n. a religious song of praise, especially a Christian song in praise of God. ▶ v. praise or celebrate something.

hym·nal /ˈhimnəl/ ▶ n. a book of hymns.

hym·no·dy /ˈhimnədē/ ▶ n. the singing or composing of hymns.

hy·oid /ˈhīˌoid/ ▶ n. a U-shaped bone in the neck that supports the tongue. ▶ adj. relating to this bone.

hype[1] /hīp/ informal ▶ n. extravagant or excessive publicity or sales promotion. ▶ v. publicize something in an excessive or extravagant way.

hype[2] ▶ v. (**be hyped up**) informal be stimulated or very excited.

hy·per /ˈhīpər/ ▶ adj. informal full of nervous energy; hyperactive.

hyper- ▶ prefix 1 over; beyond; above: *hypersonic.* 2 excessively; above normal: *hyperactive.*

hy·per·ac·tive /ˌhīpərˈaktiv/ ▶ adj. abnormally or extremely active. ■ **hy·per·ac·tiv·i·ty** /-ˌakˈtivitē/ n.

hy·per·bar·ic /ˌhīpərˈbarik/ ▶ adj. relating to or involving a gas at a pressure greater than normal.

hy·per·bo·la /hīˈpərbələ/ ▶ n. (pl. **hyperbolas** or **hyperbolae** /-lē/) a symmetrical curve formed when a cone is cut by a plane nearly parallel to the cone's axis.

hy·per·bo·le /hīˈpərbəlē/ ▶ n. a way of speaking or writing that deliberately exaggerates things for effect.

hy·per·bol·ic /ˌhīpərˈbälik/ ▶ adj. 1 (of language) deliberately exaggerated. 2 relating to a hyperbola. ■ **hy·per·bol·i·cal·ly** adv.

hy·per·crit·i·cal /ˌhīpərˈkritikəl/ ▶ adj. excessively and unreasonably critical.

hy·per·drive /ˈhīpərˌdrīv/ ▶ n. (in science fiction) a supposed propulsion system for travel in hyperspace.

hy·per·e·mi·a /ˌhīpəˈrēmēə/ ▶ n. an excess of blood in the vessels supplying an organ or other part of the body. ■ **hy·per·e·mic** /-ˈrēmik/ adj.

hy·per·gly·ce·mi·a /ˌhīpərglīˈsēmēə/ (Brit. **hyperglycaemia**) ▶ n. an excess of glucose in the bloodstream, often associated with the common form of diabetes. ■ **hy·per·gly·ce·mic** adj.

hy·per·i·cin /hīˈperəsin/ ▶ n. a substance found in the leaves and flowers of St. John's wort, believed to have properties similar to those of antidepressant drugs.

hy·per·i·cum /hīˈperikəm/ ▶ n. a yellow-flowered plant of a family that includes St. John's wort.

hy·per·in·fla·tion /ˌhīpərinˈflāSHən/ ▶ n. inflation of prices or wages occurring at a very high rate.

hy·per·ki·net·ic /ˌhīpərkəˈnetik/ ▶ adj. 1 frenetic; hyperactive. 2 relating to mental disorders marked by hyperactivity and inability to concentrate.

hy·per·link /ˈhīpərˌliNGk/ ▶ n. Computing a link from a hypertext document to another location, activated by clicking on a highlighted word or image.

hy·per·mar·ket /ˈhīpərˌmärkit/ ▶ n. Brit. a very large supermarket.

hy·per·me·di·a /ˌhīpərˈmēdēə/ ▶ n. Computing an

extension to hypertext providing multimedia facilities, such as sound and video.

hy·per·re·al /ˌhīpə(r)'rēəl/ ▶ adj. 1 exaggerated in comparison to reality. 2 (of art) extremely realistic.

hy·per·sen·si·tive /ˌhīpər'sensitiv/ ▶ adj. abnormally or excessively sensitive.

hy·per·son·ic /ˌhīpər'sänik/ ▶ adj. 1 relating to speeds of more than five times the speed of sound (Mach 5). 2 relating to sound frequencies above about a billion hertz.

hy·per·space /'hīpər,spās/ ▶ n. 1 space of more than three dimensions. 2 (in science fiction) a notional space–time continuum in which it is possible to travel faster than light.

hy·per·ten·sion /ˌhīpər'tenshən/ ▶ n. abnormally high blood pressure. ■ **hy·per·ten·sive** /-'tensiv/ adj.

hy·per·text /'hīpər,tekst/ ▶ n. Computing a software system allowing users to move quickly between related documents or sections of text.

hy·per·ther·mi·a /ˌhīpər'ᴛʜərmēə/ ▶ n. the condition of having an abnormally high body temperature.

hy·per·thy·roid·ism /ˌhīpər'ᴛʜīroi,dizəm/ ▶ n. overactivity of the thyroid gland, resulting in an increased rate of metabolism. ■ **hy·per·thy·roid** adj.

hy·per·ton·ic /ˌhīpər'tänik/ ▶ adj. 1 having a higher osmotic pressure than a particular fluid, typically a body fluid or intracellular fluid. 2 having abnormally high muscle tone.

hy·per·tro·phy /hī'pərtrəfē/ ▶ n. abnormal enlargement of an organ or tissue resulting from an increase in size of its cells. ■ **hy·per·troph·ic** /ˌhīpər'träfik, -'trō-/ adj. **hy·per·troph·ied** /-trəfēd/ adj.

hy·per·ven·ti·late /ˌhīpər'ventl,āt/ ▶ v. 1 breathe at an abnormally rapid rate. 2 be or become overexcited. ■ **hy·per·ven·ti·la·tion** /-,ventl'āshən/ n.

hy·pha /'hīfə/ ▶ n. (pl. **hyphae** /-fē/) Botany each of the filaments that make up the mycelium of a fungus.

hy·phen /'hīfən/ ▶ n. the sign (-) used to join words to show that they have a combined meaning or that they are grammatically linked, or to divide a word into parts between one part and the next.

> **USAGE**
> When phrasal verbs such as **build up** and **catch up** are made into nouns, they are written either as one word (a *buildup of pressure*) or with a hyphen (*we're always playing catch-up*). However, a normal phrasal verb should not have a hyphen: *continue to build up your pension.*

hy·phen·ate /'hīfə,nāt/ ▶ v. write words with a hyphen. ■ **hy·phen·a·tion** /'hīfə,nāshən/ n.

hyp·na·gog·ic /ˌhipnə'gäjik, -'gō-/ (also **hypnogogic**) ▶ adj. relating to the state immediately before sleep. ■ **hyp·na·gog·i·a** n.

hyp·no·sis /hip'nōsis/ ▶ n. the practice of causing a person to enter a state of consciousness in which they lose the power of voluntary action and respond readily to suggestions or commands.

hyp·no·ther·a·py /ˌhipnō'ᴛʜerəpē/ ▶ n. the use of hypnosis to treat physical or mental problems. ■ **hyp·no·ther·a·pist** n.

hyp·not·ic /hip'nätik/ ▶ adj. 1 producing or relating to hypnosis. 2 causing one to feel very relaxed or drowsy. 3 (of a drug) causing sleep. ■ **hyp·not·i·cal·ly** adv.

hyp·no·tism /'hipnə,tizəm/ ▶ n. the study or practice of hypnosis. ■ **hyp·no·tist** n.

hyp·no·tize /'hipnə,tīz/ ▶ v. put someone into a state of hypnosis.

hy·po /'hīpō/ ▶ n. 1 the chemical sodium thiosulfate used as a photographic fixer. 2 (pl. **hypos**) informal a hypodermic needle or syringe.

hypo- (also **hyp-**) ▶ prefix 1 under: *hypodermic.* 2 below normal: *hypoglycemia.*

hy·po·al·ler·gen·ic /ˌhīpō,alər'jenik/ ▶ adj. unlikely to cause an allergic reaction.

hy·po·chlo·rous ac·id /ˌhīpə'klôrəs/ ▶ n. a weak acid with oxidizing properties formed when chlorine dissolves in cold water, used in bleaching and water treatment. ■ **hy·po·chlo·rite** /-,rīt/ n.

hy·po·chon·dri·a /ˌhīpə'kändrēə/ ▶ n. excessive anxiety about one's health.

hy·po·chon·dri·ac /ˌhīpə'kändrē,ak/ ▶ n. a person who is excessively worried about their health.

hy·poc·ri·sy /hi'päkrisē/ ▶ n. (pl. **hypocrisies**) the practice of claiming to have higher moral standards than is the case.

hyp·o·crite /'hipə,krit/ ▶ n. a person who claims to have higher moral standards than is the case. ■ **hyp·o·crit·i·cal** adj. **hyp·o·crit·i·cal·ly** adv.

hy·po·der·mic /ˌhīpə'dərmik/ ▶ adj. 1 (of a needle or syringe) used to inject a drug or other substance beneath the skin. 2 relating to the region immediately beneath the skin. ▶ n. a hypodermic syringe or injection. ■ **hy·po·der·mi·cal·ly** adv.

hy·po·gly·ce·mi·a /ˌhīpōglī'sēmēə/ (Brit. **hypoglycaemia**) ▶ n. lack of glucose in the bloodstream. ■ **hy·po·gly·ce·mic** adj.

hy·po·ma·ni·a /ˌhīpə'mānēə/ ▶ n. a mild form of mania, marked by elation and hyperactivity. ■ **hy·po·man·ic** /-'manik/ adj.

hy·po·ten·sion /ˌhīpə'tenshən/ ▶ n. abnormally low blood pressure. ■ **hy·po·ten·sive** adj.

hy·pot·e·nuse /hī'pätn,(y)ōōs/ ▶ n. the longest side of a right triangle, opposite the right angle.

hy·po·thal·a·mus /ˌhīpə'ᴛʜaləməs/ ▶ n. (pl. **hypothalami** /-,mī/) a region of the front part of the brain below the thalamus, controlling body temperature, thirst, and hunger, and involved in sleep and emotional activity. ■ **hy·po·tha·lam·ic** /ˌhīpō,ᴛʜə'lamik/ adj.

hy·po·ther·mi·a /ˌhīpə'ᴛʜərmēə/ ▶ n. the condition of having an abnormally low body temperature.

hy·poth·e·sis /hī'päᴛʜəsis/ ▶ n. (pl. **hypotheses** /-,sēz/) a proposed explanation of something made on the basis of limited evidence, used as a starting point for further investigation.

hy·poth·e·size /hī'päᴛʜə,sīz/ ▶ v. put forward an explanation as a hypothesis.

hy·po·thet·i·cal /ˌhīpə'ᴛʜetikəl/ ▶ adj. based on an assumption or imagined situation rather than fact. ■ **hy·po·thet·i·cal·ly** adv.

hy·po·thy·roid·ism /ˌhīpō'ᴛʜīroi,dizəm/ ▶ n. abnormally low activity of the thyroid gland, resulting in retarded growth and mental development. ■ **hy·po·thy·roid** adj.

hy·pox·i·a /hī'päksēə/ ▶ n. a situation in which not enough oxygen reaches the body tissues. ■ **hy·pox·ic** adj.

hy·rax /'hī,raks/ ▶ n. a small mammal with a short tail, found in Africa and Arabia.

hys·sop /'hisəp/ ▶ n. a small bushy plant whose bitter minty leaves are used in cooking and herbal medicine.

hys·ter·ec·to·my /,histə'rektəmē/ ▶ n. (pl. **hysterectomies**) a surgical operation to remove all or part of the uterus.

hys·te·ri·a /hi'sterēə, -'sti(ə)rēə/ ▶ n. 1 extreme or uncontrollable emotion or excitement: a note of hysteria crept into his voice. 2 dated a psychological disorder involving a change in self-awareness or the conversion of psychological stress into physical symptoms.

hys·ter·ic /hi'sterik/ ▶ n. 1 (**hysterics**) wildly emotional behavior. 2 (**hysterics**) informal uncontrollable laughter. 3 a person suffering from hysteria.

hys·ter·i·cal /hi'sterikəl/ ▶ adj. 1 in a state of uncontrolled excitement or other strong emotion. 2 informal very funny. ■ **hys·ter·i·cal·ly** adv.

Hz ▶ abbr. hertz.

I¹ (also **i**) ▶ **n.** (pl. **Is** or **I's**) **1** the ninth letter of the alphabet. **2** the Roman numeral for one.

I² /ī/ ▶ **pron.** (first person sing.) used by a speaker to refer to himself or herself.

I³ ▶ **abbr. 1** (preceding a highway number) Interstate. **2** (**I.**) Island(s) or Isle(s). ▶ **symbol** the chemical element iodine.

IA ▶ **abbr.** Iowa.

IAEA ▶ **abbr.** International Atomic Energy Agency.

i·amb /ˈīamb/ ▶ **n.** Poetry a metrical foot consisting of one short (or unstressed) syllable followed by one long (or stressed) syllable.

i·am·bic /īˈambik/ Poetry ▶ **adj.** (of poetry or poetic metre) using iambuses. ▶ **n.** (**iambics**) verse using iambuses.

IAQ ▶ **abbr.** indoor air quality.

i·at·ro·gen·ic /ī,atrəˈjenik/ ▶ **adj.** (of illness) caused by medical treatment.

I-beam ▶ **n.** a girder that has the shape of a capital I when viewed in section.

I·be·ri·an /īˈbi(ə)rēən/ ▶ **adj.** relating to Iberia (the peninsula that consists of modern Spain and Portugal). ▶ **n.** a person from Iberia.

i·bex /ˈī,beks/ ▶ **n.** (pl. **ibexes**) a wild mountain goat with long curved horns.

IBF ▶ **abbr.** International Boxing Federation.

ib·id. /ˈibid/ ▶ **adv.** in the same source (referring to the work cited in the previous note).

i·bis /ˈībis/ ▶ **n.** (pl. same or **ibises**) a large wading bird with a long downcurved bill, a long neck, and long legs.

IBS ▶ **abbr.** irritable bowel syndrome.

i·bu·pro·fen /ˌībyōōˈprōfən/ ▶ **n.** a synthetic compound used as a painkiller and to reduce inflammation.

IC ▶ **abbr.** integrated circuit.

ICBM ▶ **abbr.** intercontinental ballistic missile.

ICC ▶ **abbr. 1** Interstate Commerce Commission. **2** International Criminal Court.

ICE ▶ **abbr. 1** Immigration and Customs Enforcement. **2** in case of emergency; referring to a program in which cell phone users store their emergency contact information in their phone's address book.

ice /īs/ ▶ **n. 1** frozen water, a brittle transparent crystalline solid. **2** a frozen mixture of fruit juice or flavored water and sugar. ▶ **v. 1** decorate something with icing. **2** (usu. **ice up/over**) become covered or blocked with ice. ■ **iced adj.**
– PHRASES **break the ice** start the conversation at the beginning of a social gathering so as to make people feel more relaxed. **on ice 1** (of wine, food, or biological material) kept chilled by being surrounded by ice. **2** (especially of a plan or proposal) held in reserve for future

consideration: *the recommendation was put on ice.* **3** (of an entertainment) performed by skaters: *Cinderella on Ice.* **on thin ice** in a precarious or risky situation.

ice age ▶ **n.** a period when ice covered much of the earth's surface, in particular during the Pleistocene period.

ice·berg /ˈīs,bərg/ ▶ **n.** a large mass of ice floating in the sea.
– PHRASES **the tip of the iceberg** the small noticeable part of a much larger situation or problem.

ice·berg let·tuce ▶ **n.** a kind of lettuce having a closely packed round head of crisp pale leaves.

ice·box /ˈīs,bäks/ ▶ **n. 1** a chilled container for keeping food cold. **2** dated a refrigerator.

ice·break·er /ˈīs,brākər/ ▶ **n.** a ship designed for breaking a channel through ice.

ice cap ▶ **n.** a permanent covering of ice over a large area, especially at the North and South Poles.

ice cream ▶ **n.** a semi-soft frozen dessert made with sweetened and flavored milk fat.

ice cream cone ▶ **n. 1** a cone-shaped wafer for holding ice cream. **2** ice cream served in such a cone.

ice danc·ing ▶ **n.** a form of ice skating involving choreographed dance moves performed by skaters in pairs.

iced tea ▶ **n.** a chilled drink of black tea served in a glass.

ice field ▶ **n.** a large flat expanse of floating ice, especially in Polar regions.

ice fish·ing ▶ **n.** fishing through holes drilled in the ice on a lake or reservoir. ■ **ice-fish v.**

ice floe ▶ **n.** see FLOE.

ice hock·ey ▶ **n.** a form of hockey played on an ice rink between two teams of six skaters.

Ice·land·er /ˈīsləndər/ ▶ **n.** a person from Iceland.

Ice·lan·dic /īsˈlandik/ ▶ **n.** the language of Iceland. ▶ **adj.** relating to Iceland or its language.

ice pack ▶ **n.** a bag filled with ice and held against part of the body to reduce swelling or lower temperature.

ice pick ▶ **n.** a small pick used by climbers or for breaking ice.

ice skate ▶ **n.** a boot with a blade attached to the sole, used for skating on ice. ▶ **v.** skate on ice as a sport or pastime. ■ **ice skat·er n. ice skat·ing n.**

I Ching /ˈē ˈCHiNG, ˈjiNG/ ▶ **n.** an ancient Chinese manual for foretelling the future.

ich·thy·ol·o·gy /ˌikTHēˈäləjē/ ▶ **n.** the branch of zoology concerned with fish. ■ **ich·thy·o·log·i·cal** /-əˈläjikəl/ adj. **ich·thy·ol·o·gist n.**

ich·thy·o·saur /ˈikTHēə,sôr/ (also **ichthyosaurus**

/ˌikтнēə'sôrəs/) ► n. a fossil marine reptile with a long pointed head, four flippers, and a vertical tail.

i·ci·cle /'īsikəl/ ► n. a hanging, tapering piece of ice formed when dripping water freezes.

ic·ing /'īsiNG/ ► n. a mixture of sugar with liquid or butter and often flavoring, used as a coating for cakes or cookies. – PHRASES **the icing on the cake** an additional thing that makes something already good even better.

ick·y /'ikē/ ► adj. (**ickier, ickiest**) informal **1** unpleasantly sticky. **2** distastefully sentimental. **3** nasty or repulsive.

i·con /'ī,kän/ ► n. **1** (also **ikon**) (in the Orthodox Church) a painting of Jesus or another holy figure, typically on wood, that is itself treated as holy and used as an aid to prayer. **2** a person or thing admired as a symbol of a particular idea, quality, time, etc.: *an iron-jawed icon of American manhood*. **3** a small symbol on a computer screen that represents a program, option, or window.

i·con·ic /ī'känik/ ► adj. referring to someone or something regarded as a symbol of a particular idea, quality, period, etc.: *he became an iconic figure for directors around the world*. ■ **i·con·i·cal·ly** adv.

i·con·o·clast /ī'känə,klast/ ► n. **1** a person who attacks cherished beliefs or established values and practices. **2** (in the past) a person who destroyed images used in religious worship. ■ **i·con·o·clasm** n. **i·con·o·clas·tic** /ī,känə'klastik/ adj.

i·co·nog·ra·phy /,īkə'nägrəfē/ ► n. (pl. **iconographies**) **1** the use or study of images or symbols in visual arts. **2** the images or symbols associated with a person or movement. **3** the illustration of a subject by drawings or figures. ■ **i·co·nog·ra·pher** n. **i·con·o·graph·ic** /ī,känə'grafik/ adj.

i·co·nol·o·gy /,īkə'näləjē/ ► n. **1** the study of visual imagery and its symbolism and interpretation, especially in social or political terms. **2** symbolism: *the iconology of a work of art*. ■ **i·con·o·log·i·cal** /ī,känə'läjikəl/ adj.

i·co·nos·ta·sis /,īkə'nästəsis/ ► n. (pl. **iconostases** /-,sēz/) a screen bearing icons, separating the sanctuary of many Eastern churches from the nave.

i·co·sa·he·dron /ī,kōsə'hēdrən, ī,käsə-/ ► n. (pl. **icosahedra** /-drə/ or **icosahedrons**) a three-dimensional shape with twenty plane faces. ■ **i·co·sa·he·dral** /-drəl/ adj.

ICT ► abbr. information and computing technology.

ICU ► abbr. intensive care unit.

i·cy /'īsē/ ► adj. (**icier, iciest**) **1** covered with or consisting of ice. **2** very cold: *an icy wind*. **3** very unfriendly or hostile: *her voice was icy*. ■ **i·ci·ly** adv. **i·ci·ness** n.

ID ► abbr. **1** identification or identity. **2** Idaho.

id /id/ ► n. Psychoanalysis the part of the unconscious mind consisting of a person's basic inherited instincts, needs, and feelings. Compare with EGO and SUPEREGO.

id. ► abbr. idem.

I'd /īd/ ► contr. **1** I had. **2** I should or I would.

IDE ► abbr. Computing Integrated Drive Electronics, a standard for interfacing computers and their peripherals.

i·de·a /ī'dēə/ ► n. **1** a thought or suggestion about a possible course of action. **2** a mental impression: *shop around to get an idea of what things cost*. **3** a belief: *nineteenth-century ideas about drinking*. **4** (**the idea**) the aim or purpose: *the idea was to bring people into bookstores*.

i·de·al /ī'dē(ə)l/ ► adj. **1** most suitable; perfect: *an ideal opportunity to brush up on her French*. **2** desirable or perfect but existing only in the imagination: *in an ideal world, we might have made a different decision*. ► n. **1** a person or thing regarded as perfect. **2** a principle or standard that is worth trying to achieve: *tolerance and freedom, the liberal ideals*. ■ **i·de·al·ly** adv.

i·de·al gas ► n. Chemistry a hypothetical gas whose molecules occupy negligible space and have no interactions, and that consequently obeys the gas laws exactly.

i·de·al·ism /ī'dē(ə),lizəm/ ► n. **1** the belief that ideals can be achieved, even when this is unrealistic. **2** (in art or literature) the representation of things as perfect or better than in reality. ■ **i·de·al·ist** n. **i·de·al·is·tic** /ī,dē(ə)'listik/ adj. **i·de·al·is·ti·cal·ly** /ī,dē(ə)'listik(ə)lē/ adv.

i·de·al·ize /ī'dē(ə),līz/ ► v. (often as adj. **idealized**) regard or represent as perfect or better than in reality: *her idealized account of their life together*. ■ **i·de·al·i·za·tion** /ī,dē(ə)li'zāsHən/ n.

i·de·a·tion /,īdē'āsHən/ ► n. Psychology the formation of ideas or concepts: *paranoid ideation*. ■ **i·de·a·tion·al** /-sHənl/ adj. **i·de·a·tion·al·ly** adv.

i·dée fixe /ē,dā 'fēks/ ► n. (pl. **idées fixes** pronunc. same) an idea that dominates someone's mind; an obsession.

i·dem /'ī,dem, 'idem/ ► adv. used in quotations to indicate an author or word that has just been mentioned.

i·den·ti·cal /ī'dentikəl/ ► adj. **1** exactly alike or the same: *four girls in identical green outfits*. **2** (of twins) developed from a single fertilized ovum, and therefore of the same sex and very similar in appearance. ■ **i·den·ti·cal·ly** adv.

i·den·ti·fi·ca·tion /ī,dentəfi'kāsHən/ ► n. **1** the action of identifying someone or something or the fact of being identified. **2** an official document or other proof of one's identity.

i·den·ti·fy /ī'dentə,fī/ ► v. (**identifies, identifying, identified**) **1** prove or recognize who or what a person or thing is: *he couldn't identify his attackers*. **2** recognize something as being worthy of attention: *a system that ensures that the student's needs are identified*. **3** (**identify with**) feel that one understands or shares the feelings of another person. **4** (**identify with**) associate someone or something closely with: *the policy was closely identified with the prime minister*. ■ **i·den·ti·fi·a·ble** adj. **i·den·ti·fi·a·bly** adv. **i·den·ti·fi·er** n.

i·den·ti·ty /ī'dentitē/ ► n. (pl. **identities**) **1** the fact of being who or what a person or thing is: *he knows the identity of the bombers*. **2** the characteristics determining who or what a person or thing is and distinguishing them from others: *a sense of national identity*. **3** a close similarity or feeling of understanding.

i·den·ti·ty cri·sis ► n. Psychiatry a period of uncertainty and confusion in which a person's sense of identity becomes insecure, typically due to a change in their expected aims or role in society.

i·den·ti·ty theft ► n. the fraudulent use of another person's name and other personal information in order to obtain money or goods.

id·e·o·gram /'idēə,gram, 'īdēə-/ (also **ideograph**

/'īdēˌgraf, 'īdēə-/ ▶ n. a character used in a writing system to symbolize the idea of a thing rather than the sounds used to say it (e.g., a numeral).

i·de·o·logue /'īdēəˌlôg, -ˌläg, 'idēə-/ ▶ n. a person who follows a system of ideas and principles in a strict and inflexible way.

i·de·ol·o·gy /ˌīdē'äləjē, ˌidē-/ ▶ n. (pl. **ideologies**) 1 a system of ideas and principles forming the basis of an economic or political theory. 2 the set of beliefs held by a particular social group: *bourgeois ideology*. ■ **i·de·o·log·i·cal** /-ə'läjikəl/ adj. ■ **i·de·o·log·i·cal·ly** /-ə'läjik(ə)lē/ adv. **i·de·ol·o·gist** n.

ides /īdz/ ▶ pl.n. (in the ancient Roman calendar) a day falling roughly in the middle of each month, from which other dates were calculated.

id·i·o·cy /'idēəsē/ ▶ n. (pl. **idiocies**) extremely stupid behavior.

id·i·o·lect /'idēəˌlekt/ ▶ n. the way that a particular person uses language.

id·i·om /'idēəm/ ▶ n. 1 a group of words whose meaning is different from the meanings of the individual words (e.g., *rain cats and dogs*). 2 a form of language and grammar used by particular people at a particular time or place. 3 a style of expression in music or art that is characteristic of a particular group or place: *a restrained classical idiom*.

id·i·o·mat·ic /ˌidēə'matik/ ▶ adj. using or relating to expressions that are natural to a native speaker: *he spoke fluent, idiomatic English*. ■ **id·i·o·mat·i·cal·ly** adv.

id·i·o·path·ic /ˌidēə'paᴛʜik/ ▶ adj. relating to any disease or condition that arises spontaneously or for which the cause is unknown.

id·i·o·syn·cra·sy /ˌidēə'siNGkrəsē/ ▶ n. (pl. **idiosyncrasies**) 1 a distinctive or unusual way of behaving or thinking peculiar to a particular person. 2 a distinctive characteristic of something: *the idiosyncrasies of the prison system*.

id·i·o·syn·crat·ic /ˌidēəsiNG'kratik, ˌidē-ō-/ ▶ adj. peculiar or distinctively individual: *her idiosyncratic diet*. ■ **id·i·o·syn·crat·i·cal·ly** adv.

id·i·ot /'idēət/ ▶ n. 1 informal a stupid person. 2 old use a mentally disabled person.

id·i·ot·ic /ˌidē'ätik/ ▶ adj. very stupid or foolish. ■ **id·i·ot·i·cal·ly** adv.

id·i·ot sa·vant ▶ n. (pl. **idiot savants** or **idiots savants** pronunc. same) a person who has a mental disability or learning difficulties but is gifted in a particular way, such as the ability to perform feats of memory.

i·dle /'īdl/ ▶ adj. 1 tending to avoid work; lazy. 2 not working or not in use. 3 having no purpose or effect: *she did not make idle threats*. ▶ v. 1 spend time doing nothing. 2 (of an engine) run slowly while out of gear. ■ **i·dle·ness** n. **i·dler** n. **i·dly** adv.

i·dol /'īdl/ ▶ n. 1 a statue or picture of a god that is itself worshiped. 2 a person who is greatly admired: *a soccer idol*.

i·dol·a·try /ī'dälətrē/ ▶ n. 1 the practice of worshiping statues or pictures of a god or gods. 2 extreme admiration or devotion. ■ **i·dol·a·ter** n. **i·dol·a·trous** adj.

i·dol·ize /'īdlˌīz/ ▶ v. admire or love someone greatly or excessively. ■ **i·dol·i·za·tion** /ˌīdl-i'zāsHən/ n.

i·dyll /'īdl/ ▶ n. 1 a very happy or peaceful period

or situation. 2 a short poem or piece of writing describing a picturesque country scene or incident.

i·dyl·lic /ī'dilik/ ▶ adj. extremely happy, peaceful, or picturesque. ■ **i·dyl·li·cal·ly** adv.

i.e. ▶ abbr. that is to say.

IEEE /ˌī ˌtripəl'ē/ ▶ abbr. Institute of Electrical and Electronics Engineers.

if /if/ ▶ conj. 1 on the condition or in the event that. 2 despite the possibility or fact that. 3 whether. 4 every time that; whenever. 5 expressing a polite request or tentative opinion. 6 expressing surprise or regret. ▶ n. a situation that is not certain: *there are so many ifs and buts in the policy*.
– PHRASES **if anything** used to suggest tentatively that something may be the case (often the opposite of something previously implied): *I haven't made much of this—if anything, I've played it down*. **if so** if that is the case.

USAGE
If and **whether** are more or less interchangeable in sentences like *I'll see if he left an address* and *I'll see whether he left an address*, although **whether** is more formal and more suitable for written use.

if·fy /'ifē/ ▶ adj. (**iffier, iffiest**) informal 1 uncertain. 2 seeming bad or wrong in some way.

ig·loo /'iglōō/ ▶ n. a dome-shaped Eskimo house, typically built from blocks of solid snow.

ig·ne·ous /'ignēəs/ ▶ adj. Geology (of rock) formed when molten rock cools and solidifies.

ig·nite /ig'nīt/ ▶ v. 1 catch fire or set on fire. 2 provoke or stir up: *the words ignited new fury in him*. ■ **ig·ni·ter** n.

ig·ni·tion /ig'nisHən/ ▶ n. 1 the action of catching fire or setting something on fire. 2 the process of starting the combustion of fuel in the cylinders of an internal-combustion engine. 3 the mechanism for bringing this about.

ig·no·ble /ig'nōbəl/ ▶ adj. (**ignobler, ignoblest**) 1 not good or honest; dishonorable. 2 of humble origin or social status. ■ **ig·no·bly** adv.

ig·no·min·i·ous /ˌignə'minēəs/ ▶ adj. deserving or causing public disgrace or shame: *an ignominious defeat*. ■ **ig·no·min·i·ous·ly** adv.

ig·no·min·y /'ignəˌminē, ig'näminē/ ▶ n. public shame or disgrace.

ig·no·ra·mus /ˌignə'rāməs, -'raməs/ ▶ n. (pl. **ignoramuses**) an ignorant or stupid person.

ig·no·rance /'ignərəns/ ▶ n. lack of knowledge or information.

ig·no·rant /'ignərənt/ ▶ adj. 1 lacking knowledge or education. 2 (often **ignorant of**) not informed about or aware of a particular subject or fact: *I was ignorant of the effects of radiotherapy*. 3 informal not polite; rude. ■ **ig·no·rant·ly** adv.

ig·nore /ig'nôr/ ▶ v. 1 deliberately take no notice of: *I shouted to her but she ignored me*. 2 fail to consider something important.

i·gua·na /i'gwänə/ ▶ n. a large tropical American lizard with a spiny crest along the back.

i·ke·ba·na /ˌikə'bänə, ˌēke-/ ▶ n. the art of Japanese flower arrangement.

i·kon ▶ n. variant spelling of ICON (sense 1).

IL ▶ abbr. Illinois.

il·e·um /'ilēəm/ ▶ n. (pl. **ilea** /'ilēə/) the third and lowest part of the small intestine, between the jejunum and the cecum. ■ **il·e·al** /-əl/ adj.

il·i·ac /ˈilēˌak/ ▸ adj. relating to the ilium or the nearby regions of the lower body.

il·i·um /ˈilēəm/ ▸ n. (pl. **ilia** /ˈilēə/) the large broad bone forming the upper part of each half of the pelvis.

ilk /ilk/ ▸ n. a type: *fascists, racists, and others of that ilk.*

ill /il/ ▸ adj. **1** not in good health; unwell. **2** bad, harmful, or unfavorable: *she suffered no ill effects.* ▸ adv. **1** badly, wrongly, or imperfectly: *ill-chosen.* **2** only with difficulty: *she could ill afford the cost.* ▸ n. **1** a problem or misfortune: *the ills of society.* **2** evil or harm.
– PHRASES **ill at ease** uncomfortable or embarrassed. **speak** (or **think**) **ill of** say (or think) something critical about.

Ill. ▸ abbr. Illinois.

I'll /īl/ ▸ contr. I shall; I will.

ill-ad·vised ▸ adj. unwise or badly thought out.

ill-bred ▸ adj. badly brought up or rude.

ill-con·ceived ▸ adj. not carefully planned or considered.

il·le·gal /i(l)ˈlēgəl/ ▸ adj. against the law.
■ **il·le·gal·i·ty** n. (pl. **illegalities**) **il·le·gal·ly** adv.

> **USAGE**
> **Illegal** and **unlawful** have slightly different meanings. An illegal act is against the law, but an **unlawful** one only goes against the rules that apply in a particular situation. For example, handball in soccer is **unlawful**, but not **illegal**.

il·leg·i·ble /i(l)ˈlejəbəl/ ▸ adj. not clear enough to be read. ■ **il·leg·i·bil·i·ty** n. **il·leg·i·bly** adv.

il·le·git·i·mate /ˌi(l)ləˈjitəmit/ ▸ adj. **1** not allowed by law or a particular set of rules: *the strike was condemned as illegitimate.* **2** (of a child) having parents who are not married to each other. ■ **il·le·git·i·ma·cy** n. **il·le·git·i·mate·ly** adv.

ill-equipped ▸ adj. not having the necessary equipment or resources.

ill-fat·ed ▸ adj. destined to fail or have bad luck.

ill-found·ed ▸ adj. not based on fact or reliable evidence.

ill-got·ten ▸ adj. acquired by illegal or unfair means.

il·lib·er·al /i(l)ˈlib(ə)rəl/ ▸ adj. restricting freedom of thought or behavior.

il·lic·it /i(l)ˈlisit/ ▸ adj. forbidden by law, rules, or accepted standards: *an illicit relationship.* ■ **il·lic·it·ly** adv.

il·lim·it·a·ble /i(l)ˈlimitəbəl/ ▸ adj. having no limits or end. ■ **il·lim·it·a·bly** adv.

il·lit·er·ate /i(l)ˈlitərit/ ▸ adj. **1** unable to read or write. **2** having no knowledge of a particular subject or activity: *voters who are politically illiterate.* ■ **il·lit·er·a·cy** /-əsē/ n.
– PHRASES **functionally illiterate** lacking the literacy necessary for coping with most jobs and many everyday situations.

ill-judged ▸ adj. lacking careful thought; unwise.

ill-man·nered ▸ adj. having bad manners; rude.

ill-na·tured ▸ adj. bad-tempered and sullen.

ill·ness /ˈilnis/ ▸ n. a disease or period of sickness.

il·log·i·cal /i(l)ˈläjikəl/ ▸ adj. not sensible or based on sound reasoning. ■ **il·log·i·cal·i·ty** n. (pl. **illogicalities**) **il·log·i·cal·ly** adv.

ill-starred ▸ adj. unlucky.

ill-tem·pered ▸ adj. irritable or surly.

ill-treat ▸ v. treat someone or something cruelly.
■ **ill-treat·ment** n.

il·lu·mi·nate /iˈlo͞oməˌnāt/ ▸ v. **1** light something up. **2** (usu. as adj. **illuminating**) help to clarify or explain something: *a most illuminating discussion.* **3** decorate a page or initial letter in a manuscript with gold, silver, or colored designs.
■ **il·lu·mi·na·tor** n.

il·lu·mi·na·ti /iˌlo͞oməˈnätē/ ▸ pl.n. people claiming to possess special knowledge or understanding.

il·lu·mi·na·tion /iˌlo͞oməˈnāSHən/ ▸ n. **1** lighting or light. **2** (**illuminations**) a display of lights on a building or other structure. **3** understanding or enlightenment: *he had moments of intense spiritual illumination.*

il·lu·mine /iˈlo͞omən/ ▸ v. literary light something up.

ill-use /ˈil ˈyo͞oz/ ▸ v. treat someone badly.

il·lu·sion /iˈlo͞oZHən/ ▸ n. **1** a false or unreal idea or belief: *he had no illusions about her.* **2** something that seems to exist but does not, or that seems to be something it is not: *he uses color to give an illusion of space.*

il·lu·sion·ist /iˈlo͞oZHənist/ ▸ n. a magician or conjuror.

il·lu·sive /iˈlo͞osiv/ ▸ adj. chiefly literary deceptive; illusory.

il·lu·so·ry /iˈlo͞osərē, -zərē/ ▸ adj. apparently real but not actually so. ■ **il·lu·so·ri·ly** adv.

il·lus·trate /ˈiləˌstrāt/ ▸ v. **1** provide a book, magazine, etc., with pictures. **2** make something clear by using examples, charts, or pictures. **3** act as an example of: *the World Cup illustrated what high standards our players must achieve.*
■ **il·lus·tra·tor** n.

il·lus·tra·tion /ˌiləˈstrāSHən/ ▸ n. **1** a picture illustrating a book, magazine, etc. **2** the action of illustrating something. **3** an example that proves something or helps to explain it: *the case provides a good illustration of the legal problems.*

il·lus·tra·tive /iˈləstrətiv, ˈiləˌstrātiv/ ▸ adj. **1** serving as an example or explanation. **2** relating to pictorial illustration. ■ **il·lus·tra·tive·ly** adv.

il·lus·tri·ous /iˈləstrēəs/ ▸ adj. famous and admired for past achievements.

ill will ▸ n. hostility or animosity toward someone.

IM ▸ abbr. Computing **1** instant message. **2** instant messaging.

im- ▸ prefix variant spelling of IN-¹, IN-² before *b*, *m*, *p* (as in *imbibe, immodest, impart*).

I'm /īm/ ▸ contr. I am.

im·age /ˈimij/ ▸ n. **1** a likeness of a person or thing in the form of a picture or statue. **2** a picture of someone or something seen on a television or computer screen, through a lens, or as a reflection. **3** the impression that a person, organization, or product presents to the public: *the band's squeaky-clean image.* **4** a picture in the mind. **5** a person or thing that closely resembles another: *he's the image of his father.* **6** a simile or metaphor. ▸ v. make or form an image of someone or something. ■ **im·age·less** adj.

im·ag·er /ˈimijər/ ▸ n. an electronic or other device that records images.

im·age·ry /ˈimij(ə)rē/ ▸ n. **1** language using similes and metaphors that produces images in the mind. **2** visual symbolism. **3** visual images

im·ag·i·na·ble /i'maj(ə)nəbəl/ ▶ adj. possible to be thought of or believed. ■ **i·mag·i·na·bly** adv.

im·ag·i·nar·y /i'majə,nerē/ ▶ adj. **1** existing only in the imagination. **2** Mathematics expressed in terms of the square root of −1 (represented by *i* or *j*): *imaginary numbers.*

im·ag·i·na·tion /i,majə'nāsHən/ ▶ n. **1** the faculty or action of forming ideas or images in the mind: *her story captured the public's imagination.* **2** the ability of the mind to be creative or resourceful.

im·ag·i·na·tive /i'maj(ə)nətiv/ ▶ adj. having or showing creativity or inventiveness. ■ **i·mag·i·na·tive·ly** adv. **i·mag·i·na·tive·ness** n.

im·ag·ine /i'majən/ ▶ v. **1** form a mental image of someone or something. **2** believe that something unreal exists. **3** suppose or assume: *we imagined that Mabel would move away after Ned died.* ■ **i·mag·in·er** n.

im·ag·ing /'imijiNG/ ▶ n. the process or activity of creating images of physical objects using digitizing equipment: *diagnostic imaging of the brain.*

im·ag·in·ings /i'majəniNGz/ ▶ pl.n. thoughts or fantasies.

im·ag·ism /'imə,jizəm/ ▶ n. a movement in early 20th-century English and American poetry that aimed to achieve clarity of expression through the use of precise images. ■ **im·ag·ist** n.

i·ma·go /i'māgō, i'mä-/ ▶ n. (pl. **imagos** or **imagines** /i'māgə,nēz/) the final and fully developed adult stage of an insect.

i·mam /i'mäm/ ▶ n. **1** the person who leads prayers in a mosque. (**Imam**) a title of various Muslim leaders. ■ **i·mam·ate** /-,māt/ n.

IMAX /'ī,maks/ ▶ n. trademark a technique of wide-screen cinematography that produces an image approximately ten times larger than that from standard 35 mm film.

im·bal·ance /im'baləns/ ▶ n. a lack of proportion or balance.

im·be·cile /'imbəsəl, -,sil/ ▶ n. informal a stupid person. ▶ adj. stupid; idiotic. ■ **im·be·cil·ic** /,imbə'silik/ adj. **im·be·cil·i·ty** /,imbə'silitē/ (pl. **imbecilities**) n.

im·bed ▶ v. variant spelling of EMBED.

im·bibe /im'bīb/ ▶ v. **1** formal or humorous drink alcohol. **2** literary absorb ideas or knowledge. ■ **im·bib·er** n.

im·bro·glio /im'brōlyō/ ▶ n. (pl. **imbroglios**) a very confused or complicated situation.

im·bue /im'byōō/ ▶ v. (**imbues, imbuing, imbued**) fill with a feeling or quality: *we were imbued with a sense of purpose.*

IMF ▶ abbr. International Monetary Fund.

im·i·tate /'imi,tāt/ ▶ v. **1** follow someone or something as a model. **2** copy a person's speech or behavior, especially to amuse people. **3** make a copy of or simulate something. ■ **im·i·ta·ble** /'imitəbəl/ adj. **im·i·ta·tor** n.

im·i·ta·tion /,imi'tāsHən/ ▶ n. **1** a copy. **2** the action of imitating someone or something.

im·i·ta·tive /'imi,tātiv/ ▶ adj. **1** following a model or example. **2** (of a word) reproducing a natural sound (e.g., fizz); onomatopoeic. ■ **im·i·ta·tive·ly** adv.

im·mac·u·late /i'makyəlit/ ▶ adj. **1** completely clean, neat, or tidy. **2** free from flaws or mistakes: *an immaculate safety record.* ■ **im·mac·u·la·cy** n. **im·mac·u·late·ly** adv.

Im·mac·u·late Con·cep·tion ▶ n. (in the Roman Catholic Church) the doctrine that the Virgin Mary was free of the sin common to all human beings from the moment she was conceived.

im·ma·nent /'imənənt/ ▶ adj. **1** present as a natural part of something; inherent: *love is a force immanent in the world.* **2** (of God) permanently present throughout the universe. ■ **im·ma·nence** n.

im·ma·te·ri·al /,i(m)mə'ti(ə)rēəl/ ▶ adj. **1** unimportant under the circumstances; irrelevant. **2** spiritual rather than physical. ■ **im·ma·te·ri·al·i·ty** /-,ti(ə)rē'alitē/ n.

im·ma·ture /,imə'cHŏŏr, -'t(y)ŏŏr/ ▶ adj. **1** not fully developed. **2** lacking the emotional or intellectual development of an adult or mature person; childish. ■ **im·ma·ture·ly** adv. **im·ma·tu·ri·ty** n.

im·meas·ur·a·ble /i'mezHərəbəl/ ▶ adj. too large or extreme to measure. ■ **im·meas·ur·a·bly** adv.

im·me·di·a·cy /i'mēdēəsē/ ▶ n. **1** the quality of providing direct and instant involvement with something: *the immediacy of television images.* **2** lack of delay; speed.

im·me·di·ate /i'mēdē-it/ ▶ adj. **1** occurring or done at once. **2** most urgent: *the immediate concern was how to avoid taxes.* **3** nearest in time, space, or relationship. **4** direct: *a coronary was the immediate cause of death.*

im·me·di·ate·ly /i'mēdē-itlē/ ▶ adv. **1** at once. **2** very close in time, space, or relationship.

im·me·mo·ri·al /,i(m)mə'môrēəl/ ▶ adj. existing from before what can be remembered or found in records: *they had lived there from time immemorial.* ■ **im·me·mo·ri·al·ly** adv.

im·mense /i'mens/ ▶ adj. very large or great. ■ **im·men·si·ty** n.

im·mense·ly /i'menslē/ ▶ adv. to a great extent; extremely.

im·merse /i'mərs/ ▶ v. **1** dip or submerge someone or something in a liquid. **2** (**immerse oneself** or **be immersed**) involve oneself deeply in an activity or interest.

im·mer·sion /i'mərzHən, -sHən/ ▶ n. **1** the action of immersing someone or something in a liquid. **2** deep involvement in an interest or activity.

im·mer·sive /i'mərsiv/ ▶ adj. (of a computer display) generating a three-dimensional image that appears to surround the user.

im·mi·grant /'imigrənt/ ▶ n. a person who comes to live permanently in a foreign country.

im·mi·grate /'imi,grāt/ ▶ v. come to live permanently in a foreign country: *the Mennonites immigrated to western Canada in the 1870s.* ■ **im·mi·gra·tion** /,imi'grāsHən/ n.

im·mi·nent /'imənənt/ ▶ adj. about to happen. ■ **im·mi·nence** n. **im·mi·nent·ly** adv.

im·mis·ci·ble /i(m)'misəbəl/ ▶ adj. (of liquids) not forming a homogeneous mixture when mixed.

im·mo·bile /i(m)'mōbəl, -bēl, -bīl/ ▶ adj. **1** not moving; motionless. **2** unable to move or be moved. ■ **im·mo·bil·i·ty** /,i(m)mō'bilitē/ n.

im·mo·bi·lize /i(m)'mōbə,līz/ ▶ v. prevent someone or something from moving or operating as normal. ■ **im·mo·bi·li·za·tion** /-,mōbəli'zāsHən/ n. **im·mo·bi·li·zer** n.

im·mod·er·ate /i(m)'mädərit/ ▶ adj. not sensible or restrained; excessive. ■ **im·mod·er·ate·ly** adv.

im·mod·est /i(m)ˈmädist/ ▶ adj. **1** tending to be boastful. **2** tending to show off one's body. ■ **im·mod·est·ly** adv. **im·mod·es·ty** n.

im·mo·late /ˈiməˌlāt/ ▶ v. kill or offer something as a sacrifice, especially by burning. ■ **im·mo·la·tion** /iməˈlāshən/ n.

im·mor·al /i(m)ˈmôrəl, -ˈmärəl/ ▶ adj. not following accepted standards of morality. ■ **im·mor·al·i·ty** /iməˈralitē, imô-/ n. (pl. **immoralities**) **im·mor·al·ly** adv.

> **USAGE**
> On the difference between **immoral** and **amoral**, see the note at **AMORAL**.

im·mor·tal /i(m)ˈmôrtl/ ▶ adj. **1** living forever. **2** deserving to be remembered forever: *an immortal children's book*. ▶ n. **1** an immortal being, especially a Greek or Roman god. **2** a person who will remain famous for a long time. ■ **im·mor·tal·i·ty** /ˌi(m)ˌmôrˈtalitē/ n.

im·mor·tal·ize /i(m)ˈmôrtlˌīz/ ▶ v. cause someone or something to be remembered for a very long time.

im·mov·a·ble /i(m)ˈmoōvəbəl/ ▶ adj. **1** not able to be moved. **2** not able to be changed or persuaded: *an immovable truth*. **3** Law (of property) consisting of land, buildings, or other permanent items. ■ **im·mov·a·bly** adv.

im·mune /iˈmyoōn/ ▶ adj. **1** having a natural resistance to a particular infection. **2** relating to such resistance: *the immune system*. **3** not affected or influenced by something: *no one is immune to her charm*. **4** protected or exempt from a duty or penalty.

im·mune re·sponse ▶ n. the reaction of the cells and fluids of the body to the presence of an antigen (harmful substance).

im·mune sys·tem ▶ n. the organs and processes of the body that provide resistance to infection and toxins.

im·mu·ni·ty /iˈmyoōnitē/ ▶ n. (pl. **immunities**) **1** the ability of an organism to resist a particular infection: *immunity to rubella*. **2** exemption from a duty or penalty: *the rebels were given immunity from prosecution*.

im·mu·nize /ˈimyəˌnīz/ ▶ v. make a person or animal immune to infection, typically by inoculation. ■ **im·mu·ni·za·tion** /imyəniˈzāshən/ n.

im·mu·no·de·fi·cien·cy /ˌimyənōdəˈfishənsē, iˌmyoō-/ ▶ n. failure of the immune system to protect the body from infection.

im·mu·no·glob·u·lin /ˌimyənōˈgläbyələn, iˌmyoō-/ ▶ n. a protein produced in the blood that functions as an antibody.

im·mu·nol·o·gy /ˌimyəˈnäləjē/ ▶ n. the branch of medicine and biology concerned with immunity to infection. ■ **im·mu·no·log·ic** /imyənəˈläjik, iˌmyoō-/ adj. **im·mu·no·log·i·cal** /imyənəˈläjikəl, iˌmyoō-/ adj. **im·mu·nol·o·gist** n.

im·mu·no·sup·pres·sion /ˌimyənōsəˈpreshən, iˌmyoō-/ ▶ n. prevention of a person's natural response to infection, especially as induced to help the survival of an organ after a transplant operation. ■ **im·mu·no·sup·pres·sant** n. **im·mu·no·sup·pressed** adj.

im·mu·no·ther·a·py /ˌimyənōˈтнerəpē, iˌmyoō-/ ▶ n. the prevention or treatment of disease with substances that stimulate the body's resistance to infection.

im·mure /iˈmyoōr/ ▶ v. confine or imprison someone.

im·mu·ta·ble /iˈmyoōtəbəl/ ▶ adj. not changing or able to be changed. ■ **im·mu·ta·bil·i·ty** /iˌmyoōtəˈbilitē/ n. **im·mu·ta·bly** adv.

i-Mode /ˈī ˌmōd/ ▶ n. a technology that allows data to be transferred to and from Internet sites via cell phones.

imp /imp/ ▶ n. **1** a small, mischievous devil. **2** a mischievous child.

im·pact ▶ n. /ˈimˌpakt/ **1** an act of one object hitting another. **2** a marked effect or influence: *man's impact on the environment*. ▶ v. /imˈpakt/ **1** hit another object. **2** have a strong effect: *high interest rates have impacted on retail spending*. **3** press something firmly into something else. ■ **im·pact·ful** /imˈpaktfəl/ adj. **im·pac·tor** /imˈpaktər/ n.

im·pact·ed /imˈpaktid/ ▶ adj. (of a tooth) wedged between another tooth and the jaw. ■ **im·pac·tion** n.

im·pair /imˈpe(ə)r/ ▶ v. **1** weaken or damage something. **2** (as adj. **impaired**) having a disability of a specified kind: *hearing-impaired*. ■ **im·pair·ment** n.

im·pal·a /imˈpalə, -ˈpälə/ ▶ n. (pl. same) an antelope of southern and East Africa, with lyre-shaped horns.

im·pale /imˈpāl/ ▶ v. pierce someone or something with a sharp object. ■ **im·pale·ment** n. **im·pal·er** n.

im·pal·pa·ble /imˈpalpəbəl/ ▶ adj. **1** unable to be felt by touch. **2** not easily understood. ■ **im·pal·pa·bly** adv.

im·pan·el /imˈpanl/ (also **empanel**) ▶ v. (**impanels, impaneling, impaneled**) enroll a jury or enroll someone onto a jury. ■ **im·pan·el·ment** n.

im·part /imˈpärt/ ▶ v. **1** communicate information. **2** give a quality: *the mushrooms impart a woody flavor to the salad*.

im·par·tial /imˈpärshəl/ ▶ adj. treating everyone equally; not biased. ■ **im·par·ti·al·i·ty** /-ˌpärshēˈalitē/ n. **im·par·tial·ly** adv.

im·pass·a·ble /imˈpasəbəl/ ▶ adj. impossible to travel along or over. ■ **im·pass·a·bil·i·ty** /-ˌpasəˈbilitē/ n.

im·passe /ˈimˌpas, imˈpas/ ▶ n. a situation in which progress is impossible; a deadlock.

im·pas·sioned /imˈpashənd/ ▶ adj. filled with or showing great emotion.

im·pas·sive /imˈpasiv/ ▶ adj. not feeling or showing emotion. ■ **im·pas·sive·ly** adv. **im·pas·siv·i·ty** /impəˈsivitē/ n.

im·pas·to /imˈpastō, -ˈpästō/ ▶ n. the process or technique of laying on paint thickly so that it stands out from a surface.

im·pa·tiens /imˈpāshənz/ ▶ n. a plant of the balsam family, with abundant red, pink, or white flowers.

im·pa·tient /imˈpāshənt/ ▶ adj. **1** lacking patience or tolerance. **2** restlessly eager: *they were impatient for change*. ■ **im·pa·tience** n. **im·pa·tient·ly** adv.

im·peach /imˈpēch/ ▶ v. **1** charge the holder of a public office with misconduct. **2** question the validity or worth of something. ■ **im·peach·a·ble** adj. **im·peach·ment** n.

im·pec·ca·ble /imˈpekəbəl/ ▶ adj. without any faults or mistakes; perfect. ■ **im·pec·ca·bil·i·ty** /-ˌpekəˈbilitē/ n. **im·pec·ca·bly** adv.

im·pe·cu·ni·ous /ˌimpəˈkyoōnēəs/ ▶ adj. having little or no money. ■ **im·pe·cu·ni·os·i·ty** /-ˌkyoōnēˈäsitē/ n.

im·ped·ance /im'pēdns/ ▶ n. the total resistance of an electric circuit to the flow of alternating current.

im·pede /im'pēd/ ▶ v. delay or block the progress or action of: *matters that would impede progress.*

im·ped·i·ment /im'pedəmənt/ ▶ n. **1** a hindrance or obstruction. **2** (also **speech impediment**) a defect in a person's speech, such as a lisp or stammer.

im·pel /im'pel/ ▶ v. (**impels, impelling, impelled**) **1** drive or urge someone to do something. **2** drive someone or something forward. ■ **im·pel·ler** n.

im·pend·ing /im'pending/ ▶ adj. (especially of something bad or important) be about to happen: *a sense of impending danger.*

im·pen·e·tra·ble /im'penetrəbəl/ ▶ adj. **1** impossible to get through or into. **2** impossible to understand. ■ **im·pen·e·tra·bil·i·ty** /-ˌpenətrə'bilitē/ n. **im·pen·e·tra·bly** adv.

im·pen·i·tent /im'penitnt/ ▶ adj. not feeling shame or regret. ■ **im·pen·i·tence** n. **im·pen·i·tent·ly** adv.

im·per·a·tive /im'perətiv/ ▶ adj. **1** vitally important; essential. **2** giving an authoritative command. **3** Grammar (of a mood of a verb) expressing a command, as in *Come here!* ▶ n. an essential or urgent thing. ■ **im·per·a·tive·ly** adv.

im·per·cep·ti·ble /ˌimpər'septəbəl/ ▶ adj. too slight or gradual to be seen, heard, or felt. ■ **im·per·cep·ti·bly** adv.

im·per·fect /im'pərfikt/ ▶ adj. **1** faulty or incomplete. **2** Grammar (of a tense) referring to a past action in progress but not completed at the time in question. ■ **im·per·fect·ly** adv.

im·per·fec·tion /ˌimpər'feksHən/ ▶ n. **1** a fault, blemish, or undesirable feature. **2** the state of being faulty or incomplete.

im·pe·ri·al /im'pi(ə)rēəl/ ▶ adj. **1** relating to an empire or an emperor. **2** typical of an emperor; majestic. **3** (of weights and measures) based on a nonmetric system formerly used for all measures in the UK, and still used for some. ■ **im·pe·ri·al·ly** adv.

im·pe·ri·al·ism /im'pi(ə)rēəˌlizəm/ ▶ n. a policy of extending a country's power and influence through establishing colonies or by military force. ■ **im·pe·ri·al·ist** /im'pi(ə)rēəlist/ n. & adj. **im·pe·ri·al·is·tic** /im'pi(ə)rēə'listik/ adj.

im·per·il /im'perəl/ ▶ v. (**imperils, imperiled, imperiling**) put someone or something in danger. ■ **im·per·il·ment** n.

im·pe·ri·ous /im'pi(ə)rēəs/ ▶ adj. expecting to be obeyed without question; arrogant and domineering. ■ **im·pe·ri·ous·ly** adv. **im·pe·ri·ous·ness** n.

im·per·ish·a·ble /im'perisHəbəl/ ▶ adj. lasting forever. ■ **im·per·ish·a·bly** adv.

im·per·ma·nent /im'pərmənənt/ ▶ adj. not lasting or unchanging. ■ **im·per·ma·nence** n. **im·per·ma·nent·ly** adv.

im·per·me·a·ble /im'pərmēəbəl/ ▶ adj. not allowing fluid to pass through. ■ **im·per·me·a·bil·i·ty** /-ˌpərmēə'bilitē/ n.

im·per·mis·si·ble /ˌimpər'misəbəl/ ▶ adj. not permitted or allowed.

im·per·son·al /im'pərsənl/ ▶ adj. **1** not influenced by or involving personal feelings. **2** lacking human qualities; cold or anonymous: *an impersonal high-rise.* **3** Grammar (of a verb) used only with *it* as a subject (as in *it is snowing*). ■ **im·per·son·al·i·ty** /-ˌpərsə'nalitē/ n. **im·per·son·al·ly** adv.

im·per·son·ate /im'pərsəˌnāt/ ▶ v. pretend to be another person to entertain or deceive people. ■ **im·per·son·a·tion** /-ˌpərsə'nāsHən/ n. **im·per·son·a·tor** n.

im·per·ti·nent /im'pərtn-ənt/ ▶ adj. **1** not showing proper respect. **2** formal not relevant or pertinent. ■ **im·per·ti·nence** n. **im·per·ti·nent·ly** adv.

im·per·turb·a·bie /ˌimpər'tərbəbəl/ ▶ adj. not easily upset or excited. ■ **im·per·turb·a·bil·i·ty** /-tərbə'bilitē/ n. **im·per·turb·a·bly** adv.

im·per·vi·ous /im'pərvēəs/ ▶ adj. **1** not allowing fluid to pass through. **2** (**impervious to**) unable to be affected by: *he worked, apparently impervious to the heat.* ■ **im·per·vi·ous·ly** adv. **im·per·vi·ous·ness** n.

im·pet·u·ous /im'pecHŏōəs/ ▶ adj. acting or done quickly and without thought or care. ■ **im·pet·u·os·i·ty** /-ˌpecHŏō'äsitē/ n. **im·pet·u·ous·ly** adv. **im·pet·u·ous·ness** n.

im·pe·tus /'impitəs/ ▶ n. **1** the force or energy with which a body moves. **2** something that makes a process happen or happen more quickly: *the main impetus for change has been the enforcement of legislation.*

im·pi·e·ty /im'pī-itē/ ▶ n. lack of religious respect or reverence.

im·pinge /im'pinj/ ▶ v. (**impinges, impinging, impinged**) **1** have an effect: *these laws clearly impinge on freedom of speech.* **2** advance over an area belonging to another; encroach. ■ **im·pinge·ment** n.

im·pi·ous /'impēəs, im'pī-/ ▶ adj. not showing respect or reverence. ■ **im·pi·ous·ly** adv.

imp·ish /'impisH/ ▶ adj. inclined to do naughty things for fun; mischievous. ■ **imp·ish·ly** adv. **imp·ish·ness** n.

im·plac·a·ble /im'plakəbəl/ ▶ adj. **1** unwilling to stop opposing someone or something: *an implacable enemy of the arts.* **2** unable to be stopped; relentless. ■ **im·plac·a·bil·i·ty** /-ˌplakə'bilitē/ n. **im·plac·a·bly** adv.

im·plant ▶ v. /im'plant/ **1** insert tissue or an artificial object into the body for medical purposes. **2** establish an idea in the mind. **3** (of a fertilized egg) become attached to the wall of the uterus. ▶ n. /'im,plant/ a thing that has been implanted. ■ **im·plan·ta·tion** /ˌimplan'tāsHən/ n.

im·plant·a·ble /im'plantəbəl/ ▶ adj. capable of or designed for being implanted in living tissue: *an implantable defibrillator.*

im·plau·si·ble /im'plôzəbəl/ ▶ adj. not seeming reasonable or probable. ■ **im·plau·si·bil·i·ty** /-ˌplôzə'bilitē/ n. **im·plau·si·bly** adv.

im·ple·ment ▶ n. /'impləmənt/ a tool, utensil, or other piece of equipment that is used for a particular purpose. ▶ v. /-ˌment/ put a decision, plan, or agreement into effect. ■ **im·ple·men·ta·tion** /ˌimpləmən'tāsHən/ n. **im·ple·ment·er** /-ˌmentər/ n.

im·pli·cate /'impli,kāt/ ▶ v. **1** show someone to be involved in a crime. **2** (**be implicated in**) bear some of the responsibility for: *he was implicated in the bombing of the hotel.* **3** convey a meaning indirectly; imply something. ■ **im·pli·ca·tive** /'impli,kātiv, im'plikətiv/ adj.

im·pli·ca·tion /ˌimpli'kāsHən/ ▶ n. **1** the conclusion that can be drawn from something although it is not stated directly. **2** a likely consequence of something. **3** the state of being involved in something. ■ **im·pli·ca·tion·al** adj.

im·plic·it /im'plisit/ ▶ adj. **1** suggested though not directly stated. **2** (**implicit in**) always to be found in: *the problems implicit in all social theory*. **3** with no qualification or question: *an implicit faith*. ■ **im·plic·it·ly** adv. **im·plic·it·ness** n.

im·plode /im'plōd/ ▶ v. collapse violently inward. ■ **im·plo·sion** n. **im·plo·sive** adj.

im·plore /im'plôr/ ▶ v. beg someone earnestly or desperately to do something. ■ **im·plor·ing·ly** adv.

im·ply /im'plī/ ▶ v. (**implies**, **implying**, **implied**) **1** suggest something rather than state it directly. **2** suggest something as a likely consequence: *the forecast traffic increase implied more pollution*.

> **USAGE**
> The words **imply** and **infer** can describe the same situation, but from different points of view. If a person **implies** something, as in *he implied that the General was a traitor*, it means that they are suggesting something but not saying it directly. If you **infer** something from what has been said, as in *we inferred from his words that the General was a traitor*, this means that you come to the conclusion that this is what they really mean.

im·po·lite /ˌimpə'līt/ ▶ adj. not having or showing good manners. ■ **im·po·lite·ly** adv. **im·po·lite·ness** n.

im·pol·i·tic /im'päliˌtik/ ▶ adj. not wise or prudent.

im·pon·der·a·ble /im'pändərəbəl/ ▶ adj. difficult or impossible to assess. ▶ n. a factor that is difficult or impossible to assess.

im·port /im'pôrt/ ▶ v. **1** bring goods or services into a country from abroad. **2** transfer data into a computer file or document. ▶ n. **1** an article or service imported from abroad. **2** the action of importing goods or services. **3** the implied meaning of something. **4** importance. ■ **im·port·a·ble** adj. **im·por·ta·tion** /ˌimpôr'tāshən/ n. **im·port·er** n.

im·por·tant /im'pôrtnt/ ▶ adj. **1** of great significance or value. **2** having great authority or influence: *important modern writers*. ■ **im·por·tance** n. **im·por·tant·ly** adv.

im·por·tu·nate /im'pôrchənit/ ▶ adj. very persistent. ■ **im·por·tu·nate·ly** adv. **im·por·tu·ni·ty** /ˌimpôr't(y)oŏnitē/ n. (pl. **importunities**).

im·por·tune /ˌimpôr't(y)oŏn, im'pôrchən/ ▶ v. harass someone with persistent requests.

im·pose /im'pōz/ ▶ v. **1** introduce something that must be obeyed or done: *they plan to impose a tax on fuel*. **2** force something to be accepted. **3** take unreasonable advantage of someone: *she had imposed on Mark's kindness*. **4** (**impose oneself**) exert firm control over something: *the director was unable to impose himself on the production*.

im·pos·ing /im'pōziNG/ ▶ adj. grand and impressive. ■ **im·pos·ing·ly** adv.

im·po·si·tion /ˌimpə'zishən/ ▶ n. **1** the action of introducing something that must be obeyed or done. **2** something that has been imposed; an unwelcome demand or burden.

im·pos·si·ble /im'päsəbəl/ ▶ adj. **1** not able to occur, exist, or be done: *I was in an impossible situation*. **2** very difficult to deal with. ■ **im·pos·si·bil·i·ty** /im,päsə'bilitē/ n. (pl. **impossibilities**) **im·pos·si·bly** adv.

im·pos·tor /im'pästər/ (also **imposter**) ▶ n. a person who pretends to be someone else in order to deceive or defraud others.

im·pos·ture /im'päschər/ ▶ n. an act of pretending to be someone else in order to deceive others.

im·po·tent /'impətnt/ ▶ adj. **1** unable to take effective action; powerless. **2** (of a man) unable to achieve an erection or orgasm. ■ **im·po·tence** n. **im·po·ten·cy** n. **im·po·tent·ly** adv.

im·pound /im'pound/ ▶ v. **1** seize and take legal possession of something. **2** shut up domestic animals in an enclosure. **3** (of a dam) hold back water. ■ **im·pound·ment** n.

im·pov·er·ish /im'päv(ə)rish/ ▶ v. (often as adj. **impoverished**) **1** make a person or area poor. **2** make worse in quality: *impoverished soil*. ■ **im·pov·er·ish·ment** n.

im·prac·ti·ca·ble /im'praktikəbəl/ ▶ adj. impossible to be done in practice: *it was impracticable to widen the road here*. ■ **im·prac·ti·ca·bil·i·ty** /-ˌpraktikə'bilitē/ n. **im·prac·ti·ca·bly** adv.

im·prac·ti·cal /im'praktikəl/ ▶ adj. not adapted for use or action; not sensible: *impractical high heels*. ■ **im·prac·ti·cal·i·ty** /-ˌprakti'kalitē/ n. **im·prac·ti·cal·ly** adv.

im·pre·ca·tion /ˌimpri'kāshən/ ▶ n. formal a spoken curse.

im·pre·cise /ˌimpri'sīs/ ▶ adj. not exact or detailed. ■ **im·pre·cise·ly** adv. **im·pre·ci·sion** /-'sizhən/ n.

im·preg·na·ble /im'preg-nəbəl/ ▶ adj. **1** unable to be captured or broken into. **2** unable to be overcome: *Dallas forged an impregnable lead*. ■ **im·preg·na·bil·i·ty** /-ˌpregnə'bilitē/ n. **im·preg·na·bly** adv.

im·preg·nate /im'pregˌnāt/ ▶ v. **1** soak or saturate something with a substance. **2** fill with a feeling or quality: *an atmosphere impregnated with tension*. **3** make someone pregnant. ■ **im·preg·na·tion** /ˌimpreg'nāshən/ n.

im·pre·sa·ri·o /ˌimprə'särēˌō, -'se(ə)r-/ ▶ n. (pl. **impresarios**) a person who organizes and often finances theatrical or musical productions.

im·press ▶ v. /im'pres/ **1** make someone feel admiration and respect. **2** (**impress something on**) emphasize the importance of something to someone. **3** make a mark or design on something using a stamp or seal. ▶ n. /'im,pres/ **1** an act of impressing a mark. **2** a mark made by pressure. **3** a person's characteristic quality: *his desire to put his own impress on the films he made*.

im·pres·sion /im'preshən/ ▶ n. **1** an idea, feeling, or opinion. **2** an effect produced on someone: *his quick wit made a good impression*. **3** an imitation of a person or thing, done to entertain. **4** a mark impressed on a surface. **5** the printing of a number of copies of a publication for issue at one time. **6** a particular printed version of a book, especially one reprinted with no or only minor alteration.

im·pres·sion·a·ble /im'presh(ə)nəbəl/ ▶ adj. easily influenced. ■ **im·pres·sion·a·bil·i·ty** /-ˌpresh(ə)nə'bilitē/ n.

Im·pres·sion·ism /im'preshə,nizəm/ ▶ n. a style or movement in painting concerned with showing the visual impression of a particular moment, especially the shifting effects of light. ■ **Im·pres·sion·ist** /im'preshənist/ n. & adj.

im·pres·sion·ist /im'preshənist/ ▶ n. an

entertainer who impersonates famous people.

im·pres·sion·is·tic /im,presHə'nistik/ ▶ adj. **1** based on personal impressions or reactions. **2** (**Impressionistic**) in the style of Impressionism. ■ **im·pres·sion·is·ti·cal·ly** adv.

im·pres·sive /im'presiv/ ▶ adj. arousing admiration through size, quality, or skill. ■ **im·pres·sive·ly** adv. **im·pres·sive·ness** n.

im·pri·ma·tur /,imprə'mätər, -'mātər/ ▶ n. **1** a person's authoritative approval. **2** an official license issued by the Roman Catholic Church to print a religious book.

im·print ▶ v. /im'print/ **1** make a mark on an object by pressure. **2** make an impression or effect on: *he'd always have this ghastly image imprinted on his mind.* ▶ n. /'imprint/ **1** a mark made by pressure. **2** a printer's or publisher's name and other details in a publication. **3** a brand name under which books are published.

im·pris·on /im'prizən/ ▶ v. put or keep someone in prison. ■ **im·pris·on·ment** n.

im·prob·a·ble /im'präbəbəl/ ▶ adj. not likely to be true or to happen. ■ **im·prob·a·bil·i·ty** /-,präbə'bilitē/ n. (pl. **improbabilities**) **im·prob·a·bly** adv.

im·promp·tu /im'präm(p),t(y)oō/ ▶ adj. & adv. done without being planned or rehearsed. ▶ n. (pl. **impromptus**) a short piece of instrumental music, especially a solo, similar to an improvisation.

im·prop·er /im'präpər/ ▶ adj. **1** not following accepted standards of behavior. **2** not modest or decent. ■ **im·prop·er·ly** adv.

im·prop·er frac·tion ▶ n. a fraction in which the numerator is greater than the denominator, such as ⁵⁄₄

im·pro·pri·e·ty /,imprə'prī-itē/ ▶ n. (pl. **improprieties**) behavior that fails to conform to standards of morality or honesty.

im·prove /im'proōv/ ▶ v. **1** make or become better: (as adj. **improved**) *improved road and rail links.* **2** (**improve on**) achieve or produce something better than something else. **3** (as adj. **improving**) giving moral or intellectual benefit. ■ **im·prov·a·bil·i·ty** /im,proōvə'bilitē/ n. **im·prov·a·ble** adj. **im·prov·er** n.

im·prove·ment /im'proōvmənt/ ▶ n. **1** the action of making or becoming better. **2** a thing that improves something or is better than something else: *home improvements.*

im·prov·i·dent /im'prävidənt/ ▶ adj. not providing for future needs. ■ **im·prov·i·dence** n. **im·prov·i·dent·ly** adv.

im·prov·i·sa·tion /im,prävi'zāsHən/ ▶ n. **1** the action of improvising something. **2** a piece of music, drama, or verse created without preparation. ■ **im·prov·i·sa·tion·al** adj.

im·pro·vise /'imprə,vīz/ ▶ v. **1** create and perform music, drama, or verse without preparation. **2** make something from whatever is available. ■ **im·pro·vi·sa·to·ry** /im'prävizə,tôrē/ adj. **im·pro·vis·er** n.

im·pru·dent /im'proōdnt/ ▶ adj. not thinking about the results of an action; rash. ■ **im·pru·dence** n. **im·pru·dent·ly** adv.

im·pu·dent /'impyəd(ə)nt/ ▶ adj. not showing proper respect to someone; impertinent. ■ **im·pu·dence** n. **im·pu·dent·ly** adv.

im·pugn /im'pyoōn/ ▶ v. express doubts about the honesty or validity of a fact or statement.

im·pulse /'im,pəls/ ▶ n. **1** a sudden strong urge

to act, without thinking about the results. **2** something that causes something to happen; an impetus: *the impulse for the book came from personal experience.* **3** a pulse of electrical energy. **4** Physics a force acting briefly on a body and producing a change of momentum.

im·pul·sion /im'pəlsHən/ ▶ n. **1** a strong urge to do something. **2** the influence behind an action or process.

im·pul·sive /im'pəlsiv/ ▶ adj. acting or done without thinking ahead. ■ **im·pul·sive·ly** adv. **im·pul·sive·ness** n. **im·pul·siv·i·ty** /,im,pəl'sivitē/ n.

im·pu·ni·ty /im'pyoōnitē/ ▶ n. freedom from punishment or from the harmful results of an action: *rebels crossed the border with impunity.*

im·pure /im'pyoōr/ ▶ adj. **1** mixed with unwanted substances. **2** morally wrong, especially in sexual matters.

im·pu·ri·ty /im'pyoōritē/ ▶ n. (pl. **impurities**) **1** the quality or state of being impure. **2** a substance that spoils the purity of something.

im·pute /im'pyoōt/ ▶ v. believe that something undesirable has been done or caused by someone or something: *the crimes imputed to the prince.* ■ **im·put·a·ble** adj. **im·pu·ta·tion** /,impyə'tāsHən/ n.

IN ▶ abbr. Indiana.

In ▶ symbol the chemical element indium.

in /in/ ▶ prep. **1** so as to be enclosed, surrounded, or inside. **2** expressing a period of time during which an event takes place. **3** expressing the length of time before an event is expected to happen. **4** expressing a state, condition, or quality. **5** expressing inclusion or involvement. **6** indicating the means of expression used: *put it in writing.* **7** indicating a person's occupation or profession. **8** expressing a value as a proportion of a whole: *ten cents in the dollar.* ▶ adv. **1** expressing movement that results in being inside or surrounded. **2** expressing the state of being enclosed or surrounded. **3** present at one's home or office. **4** expressing arrival at a destination. **5** (of the tide) rising or at its highest level. ▶ adj. informal fashionable.
– PHRASES **be in for** be going to experience something, especially something unpleasant. **in on** knowing a secret. **in that** for the reason that. **in with** informal enjoying friendly relations with. **the ins and outs** informal all the details.

in. ▶ abbr. inch(es).

in-¹ ▶ prefix **1** (added to adjectives) not: *infertile.* **2** (added to nouns) without; a lack of: *inaction.*

in-² ▶ prefix in; into; toward; within: *influx.*

in·a·bil·i·ty /,inə'bilitē/ ▶ n. the state of being unable to do something.

in ab·sen·tia /,in əb'sensн(ē)ə/ ▶ adv. while not present.

in·ac·ces·si·ble /,inak'sesəbəl/ ▶ adj. **1** unable to be reached or used. **2** difficult to understand or appreciate. **3** (of a person) not open to advances; unapproachable. ■ **in·ac·ces·si·bil·i·ty** /,inaksesə'bilətē/ n. **in·ac·ces·si·bly** adv.

in·ac·cu·rate /,in'akyərit/ ▶ adj. not accurate or correct. ■ **in·ac·cu·ra·cy** n. (pl. **inaccuracies**) **in·ac·cu·rate·ly** adv.

in·ac·tion /in'aksHən/ ▶ n. lack of action where some action is expected or appropriate.

in·ac·ti·vate /in'aktə,vāt/ ▶ v. make something inactive or inoperative. ■ **in·ac·ti·va·tion** /-,aktə'vāsHən/ n.

in·ac·tive /in'aktiv/ ▶ adj. not active or working. ■ **in·ac·tiv·i·ty** /ˌinak'tivitē/ n.

in·ad·e·quate /ˌin'adikwit/ ▶ adj. **1** not enough or not good enough: *inadequate funding.* **2** unable to deal with a situation or with life. ■ **in·ad·e·qua·cy** /-kwəsē/ n. (pl. **inadequacies**) **in·ad·e·quate·ly** adv.

in·ad·mis·si·ble /ˌinəd'misəbəl/ ▶ adj. **1** (especially of evidence in court) not accepted as valid. **2** not to be allowed. ■ **in·ad·mis·si·bil·i·ty** /ˌinəd,misə'bilitē/ n.

in·ad·vert·ent /ˌinəd'vərtnt/ ▶ adj. not deliberate or intentional. ■ **in·ad·vert·ence** n. **in·ad·vert·ent·ly** adv.

in·ad·vis·a·ble /ˌinəd'vīzəbəl/ ▶ adj. likely to have undesirable results; unwise. ■ **in·ad·vis·a·bil·i·ty** /ˌinəd,vīzə'bilitē/ n.

in·al·ien·a·ble /in'ālēənəbəl/ ▶ adj. unable to be taken away from or given away by the possessor: *inalienable rights.* ■ **in·al·ien·a·bly** adv.

in·ane /i'nān/ ▶ adj. lacking sense or meaning; silly. ■ **in·ane·ly** adv. **in·an·i·ty** /i'nanitē/ n. (pl. **inanities**).

in·an·i·mate /in'anəmit/ ▶ adj. not alive: *inanimate objects like stones.*

in·ap·pli·ca·ble /in'aplikəbəl, ˌinə'plik-/ ▶ adj. not relevant or appropriate. ■ **in·ap·pli·ca·bil·i·ty** /-,aplikə'bilitē/ n.

in·ap·pro·pri·ate /ˌinə'prōprē-it/ ▶ adj. not suitable or appropriate. ■ **in·ap·pro·pri·ate·ly** adv. **in·ap·pro·pri·ate·ness** n.

in·apt /in'apt/ ▶ adj. not suitable or appropriate. ■ **in·apt·ly** adv.

in·ar·gu·a·ble /ˌin'ärgyōōəbəl/ ▶ adj. not subject to debate or argument: *an inarguable fact.* ■ **in·ar·gu·a·bly** adv.

in·ar·tic·u·late /ˌinär'tikyəlit/ ▶ adj. **1** unable to express one's ideas or feelings clearly or easily. **2** not expressed in words. ■ **in·ar·tic·u·la·cy** n. **in·ar·tic·u·late·ly** adv. **in·ar·tic·u·late·ness** n.

in·as·much /ˌinəz'məCH/ ▶ adv. (**inasmuch as**) **1** to the extent that. **2** considering that; since.

in·at·ten·tive /ˌinə'tentiv/ ▶ adj. not paying attention. ■ **in·at·ten·tion** n. **in·at·ten·tive·ly** adv. **in·at·ten·tive·ness** n.

in·au·di·ble /in'ôdəbəl/ ▶ adj. unable to be heard. ■ **in·au·di·bil·i·ty** /ˌinôdə'bilitē/ n. **in·au·di·bly** adv.

in·au·gu·ral /in'ôg(y)ərəl/ ▶ adj. marking the beginning of an organization or period of office.

in·au·gu·rate /in'ôg(y)ə,rāt/ ▶ v. **1** introduce a new system, project, or period. **2** admit someone formally to a position or office. **3** mark the opening of an organization or the first public use of a service with a special ceremony. ■ **in·au·gu·ra·tion** /-ôg(y)ə'rāsHən/ n. **in·au·gu·ra·tor** n.

in·aus·pi·cious /ˌinô'spisHəs/ ▶ adj. not likely to lead to success; unpromising. ■ **in·aus·pi·cious·ly** adv. **in·aus·pi·cious·ness** n.

in·au·then·tic /ˌinô'THentik/ ▶ adj. not authentic, genuine, or sincere. ■ **in·au·then·tic·i·ty** /-ôTHən'tisitē/ n.

in-be·tween ▶ adj. informal situated somewhere between two extremes or recognized categories; intermediate: *I am not unconscious, but in some in-between state.* ▶ n. an intermediate thing: *successes, failures and in-betweens.*

in·board /'in,bôrd/ ▶ adv. & adj. within or toward the center of a ship, aircraft, or vehicle.

in·born /'in'bôrn/ ▶ adj. existing from birth.

in·bound /'in,bound/ ▶ adj. & adv. traveling back toward an original point of departure.

in-box ▶ n. the window on a computer screen in which received emails are displayed.

in·bred /'in,bred/ ▶ adj. **1** produced by breeding from closely related people or animals. **2** existing from birth; inborn.

in·breed /'in,brēd/ ▶ v. (past and past part. **inbred** /'in,bred/) (often as n. **inbreeding**) breed from closely related people or animals.

in·built /'in,bilt/ ▶ adj. present as an original or essential part: *his inbuilt sense of direction.*

Inc. /iNGk/ ▶ abbr. Incorporated.

In·ca /'iNGkə/ ▶ n. **1** a member of a South American Indian people living in the central Andes before the Spanish conquest in the early 1530s. **2** the supreme ruler of the Incas. ■ **In·can** adj.

in·cal·cu·la·ble /in'kalkyələbəl, iNG-/ ▶ adj. **1** too great to be calculated or estimated. **2** not able to be calculated or estimated. ■ **in·cal·cu·la·bil·i·ty** /-,kalkyələ'bilitē/ n. **in·cal·cu·la·bly** adv.

in cam·er·a ▶ adv. see CAMERA.

in·can·des·cent /ˌinkən'desənt/ ▶ adj. **1** glowing as a result of being heated. **2** (of an electric light) containing a filament that glows white-hot when heated by a current passed through it. **3** informal very angry. ■ **in·can·des·cence** n. **in·can·des·cent·ly** adv.

in·can·ta·tion /ˌinkan'tāsHən/ ▶ n. words said as a magic spell or charm. ■ **in·can·ta·to·ry** /in'kantə,tôrē/ adj.

in·ca·pa·ble /ˌin'kāpəbəl/ ▶ adj. **1** (**incapable of**) lacking the ability or required quality to do something. **2** unable to behave rationally or take care of oneself. ■ **in·ca·pa·bil·i·ty** /ˌin,kāpə'bilitē/ n.

in·ca·pac·i·tate /ˌinkə'pasi,tāt/ ▶ v. prevent someone from functioning in a normal way. ■ **in·ca·pac·i·tant** n. **in·ca·pac·i·ta·tion** /-,pasi'tāsHən/ n.

in·ca·pac·i·ty /ˌinkə'pasitē/ ▶ n. (pl. **incapacities**) **1** inability to do something or to function normally. **2** legal disqualification.

in·car·cer·ate /in'kärsə,rāt/ ▶ v. imprison or confine someone. ■ **in·car·cer·a·tion** /-,kärsə'rāsHən/ n.

in·car·nate ▶ adj. /in'kärnit, -,nāt/ **1** (of a god or spirit) in human form. **2** represented in physical form: *she was beauty incarnate.* ▶ v. /'inkär,nāt/ **1** be the living embodiment of a quality. **2** embody or represent a god or spirit in human form.

in·car·na·tion /ˌinkär'nāsHən/ ▶ n. **1** a physical embodiment of a god, spirit, or quality: *they regarded the dictator as the incarnation of evil.* **2** (**the Incarnation**) (in Christian belief) the embodiment of God the Son in human flesh as Jesus. **3** (with reference to reincarnation) each of a series of earthly lifetimes or forms.

in·cau·tious /in'kôsHəs/ ▶ adj. not concerned about potential problems or risks. ■ **in·cau·tion** n. **in·cau·tious·ly** adv.

in·cen·di·ar·y /in'sendē,erē/ ▶ adj. **1** (of a bomb) designed to cause fires. **2** tending to stir up conflict. ▶ n. (pl. **incendiaries**) a bomb designed to cause fires. ■ **in·cen·di·a·rism** /-,dēə,rizəm/ n.

in·cense¹ /'in,sens/ ▶ n. a gum, spice, or other substance that is burned for the sweet smell it produces. ▶ v. perfume with incense.

in·cense² /in'sens/ ▶ v. make someone very angry.

in·cen·tive /in'sentiv/ ▶ n. a thing that motivates or encourages someone to do something.

in·cen·tiv·ize /in'sentə,vīz/ ▶ v. provide with an incentive for doing something: *this is likely to incentivize management to find savings.*

in·cep·tion /in'sepSHən/ ▶ n. the establishment or starting point of an institution or activity.

in·cer·ti·tude /in'sərti,t(y) o͞od/ ▶ n. a state of uncertainty.

in·ces·sant /in'sesənt/ ▶ adj. continuing without stopping. ■ **in·ces·sant·ly** adv.

in·cest /'in,sest/ ▶ n. sexual intercourse between people classed as being too closely related to marry each other.

in·ces·tu·ous /in'sesCHo͞oəs/ ▶ adj. **1** involving sex between people who are too closely related to marry each other. **2** excessively close and resistant to outside influence: *a small, incestuous legal community.* ■ **in·ces·tu·ous·ly** adv.

inch /inCH/ ▶ n. **1** a unit of length equal to one twelfth of a foot (2.54 cm). **2** a quantity of rainfall that would cover a horizontal surface to a depth of one inch. **3** a very small amount or distance: *don't yield an inch.* ▶ v. move along slowly and carefully.
– PHRASES **every inch 1** the whole area or distance. **2** entirely; very much so. (**to**) **within an inch of** almost to the point of; very close to.

in·cho·ate /in'kō-it, -āt/ ▶ adj. just begun and so not fully formed or developed. ■ **in·cho·ate·ly** adv.

inch·worm /'inCH,wərm/ ▶ n. a caterpillar that moves forward by arching and straightening its body.

in·ci·dence /'insidəns/ ▶ n. **1** the occurrence, rate, or frequency of something undesirable: *an increased incidence of cancer.* **2** Physics the intersection of a line or ray with a surface.

in·ci·dent /'insidənt/ ▶ n. **1** an instance of something happening; an event. **2** a violent event, such as an attack. **3** the occurrence of dangerous or exciting events: *the plane landed without incident.* ▶ adj. **1** (**incident to**) resulting from. **2** (of light or other radiation) falling on a surface. **3** Physics relating to the intersection of a line or ray with a surface.

in·ci·den·tal /,insi'dentl/ ▶ adj. **1** occurring in connection with or as a result of something else: *the risks incidental to a firefighter's job.* **2** occurring as a minor accompaniment to something else: *incidental expenses.* ▶ n. an incidental detail or expense.

in·ci·den·tal·ly /,insi'dent(ə)lē/ ▶ adv. **1** by the way. **2** in an incidental way.

in·ci·den·tal mu·sic ▶ n. music used in a movie or play as a background.

in·cin·er·ate /in'sinə,rāt/ ▶ v. destroy something by burning. ■ **in·cin·er·a·tion** /-,sinə'rāsHən/ n.

in·cin·er·a·tor /in'sinə,rātər/ ▶ n. a device for burning waste material.

in·cip·i·ent /in'sipēənt/ ▶ adj. beginning to happen or develop. ■ **in·cip·i·ent·ly** adv.

in·cise /in'sīz/ ▶ v. **1** make a cut or cuts in a surface. **2** cut a mark or decoration into a surface.

in·ci·sion /in'sizHən/ ▶ n. **1** a cut made as part of a surgical operation. **2** the action of cutting into something.

in·ci·sive /in'sīsiv/ ▶ adj. **1** showing or having clear thought and sharp insight: *incisive*

questions. **2** (of an action) quick and direct. ■ **in·ci·sive·ly** adv. **in·ci·sive·ness** n.

in·ci·sor /in'sīzər/ ▶ n. a narrow-edged tooth at the front of the mouth, adapted for cutting.

in·cite /in'sīt/ ▶ v. **1** encourage or stir up violent or unlawful behavior. **2** urge someone to act in a violent or unlawful way. ■ **in·cite·ment** n. **in·cit·er** n.

in·ci·vil·i·ty /,insə'vilətē/ ▶ n. (pl. **incivilities**) rude or offensive speech or behavior.

in·clem·ent /in'klemənt/ ▶ adj. (of the weather) unpleasantly cold or wet. ■ **in·clem·en·cy** n. (pl. **inclemencies**).

in·cli·na·tion /,inklə'nāsHən, ,iNGklə-/ ▶ n. **1** a person's natural tendency to act or feel in a particular way: *Jack was a scientist by inclination.* **2** (**inclination for/to/toward**) an interest in or liking for something. **3** a slope or slant. **4** the angle at which a straight line or plane slopes away from another.

in·cline ▶ v. /in'klīn/ **1** tend or be willing to think or do: *I was inclined to accept her offer.* **2** (**be inclined**) have a specified tendency or talent: *Sam was mathematically inclined.* **3** lean or turn away from the vertical or horizontal. **4** bend the head forward and downward. ▶ n. /'in,klīn/ an inclined surface or plane; a slope.

in·clined plane ▶ n. a plane inclined at an angle to the horizontal, used to make it easier to raise a load.

in·clude /in'klo͞od/ ▶ v. **1** have or contain something as part of a whole: *the price includes bed and breakfast.* **2** make or treat someone or something as part of a whole or group.

in·clud·ing /in'klo͞odiNG/ ▶ prep. containing someone or something as part of a whole or group.

in·clu·sion /in'klo͞ozHən/ ▶ n. **1** the action of including or the state of being included. **2** a person or thing that is included.

in·clu·sion·a·ry /in'klo͞ozHə,nerē/ ▶ adj. designed for or accommodating people who differ in age, income, race, or some other quality: *inclusionary membership policies.*

in·clu·sive /in'klo͞osiv/ ▶ adj. **1** including all the expected or required services or items. **2** (**inclusive of**) containing a specified element as part of a whole. **3** (after a noun) including the limits stated: *the ages of 55 to 59 inclusive.* **4** not excluding any section of society or any party: *an inclusive peace process.* ■ **in·clu·sive·ly** adv. **in·clu·sive·ness** n.

in·cog·ni·to /,inkäg'nētō, in'kägni,tō/ ▶ adj. & adv. having one's true identity concealed. ▶ n. (pl. **incognitos**) a false identity.

in·co·her·ent /,inkō'hi(ə)rənt, -iNG-, -'her-/ ▶ adj. **1** (of language or a speaker) difficult to understand. **2** not logical or well organized. ■ **in·co·her·ence** n. **in·co·her·en·cy** n. (pl. **incoherencies**) **in·co·her·ent·ly** adv.

in·come /'in,kəm, 'iNG-/ ▶ n. money received during a particular period for work or from investments.

in·come tax ▶ n. tax levied directly on personal income.

in·com·ing /'in,kəmiNG/ ▶ adj. **1** coming in. **2** (of an official or administration) having just been elected or appointed to succeed another. ▶ n. (**incomings**) revenue; income.

in·com·men·su·ra·ble /,inkə'mensərəbəl, -sHər-/ ▶ adj. **1** not able to be judged or measured by the same standards. **2** Mathematics (of numbers) in a ratio that cannot be expressed by means of integers.

in·com·men·su·rate /ˌinkəˈmensərit, -SHə-/ ▸adj. **1** (**incommensurate with**) not in keeping or in proportion with something. **2** another term for **INCOMMENSURABLE** (sense 1).

in·com·mode /ˌinkəˈmōd/ ▸v. formal cause inconvenience to someone.

in·com·mo·di·ous /ˌinkəˈmōdēəs/ ▸adj. formal or dated causing inconvenience or discomfort.

in·com·mu·ni·ca·ble /ˌinkəˈmyoōnikəbəl/ ▸adj. not able to be communicated to others.

in·com·mu·ni·ca·do /ˌinkəˌmyoōniˈkädō/ ▸adj. & adv. not able to communicate with other people.

in·com·pa·ra·ble /inˈkämp(ə)rəbəl/ ▸adj. so strong or impressive that nothing can be compared to it: *the furnishings are of incomparable beauty.* ■ **in·com·pa·ra·bly** adv.

in·com·pat·i·ble /ˌinkəmˈpatəbəl, ˌiNG-/ ▸adj. **1** (of two things) not able to exist or be used together. **2** (of two people) not able to live or work together without disagreeing. ■ **in·com·pat·i·bil·i·ty** /-ˌpatəˈbilitē/ n. (pl. **incompatibilities**).

in·com·pe·tent /inˈkämpətənt, iNG-/ ▸adj. **1** not sufficiently skillful to do something successfully. **2** Law not qualified to act in a particular capacity. ▸n. an incompetent person. ■ **in·com·pe·tence** n. **in·com·pe·ten·cy** n. **in·com·pe·tent·ly** adv.

in·com·plete /ˌinkəmˈplēt, ˌiNG-/ ▸adj. not finished or having all the necessary parts. ■ **in·com·plete·ly** adv. **in·com·plete·ness** n. **in·com·ple·tion** n.

in·com·pre·hen·si·ble /ˌinkämprəˈhensəbəl, inˌkäm-/ ▸adj. not able to be understood. ■ **in·com·pre·hen·si·bil·i·ty** /inˌkämprəhensəˈbilitē/ n. **in·com·pre·hen·si·bly** adv. **in·com·pre·hen·sion** /ˌinkämprəˈhensHən, inˌkäm-/ n.

in·con·ceiv·a·ble /ˌinkənˈsēvəbəl/ ▸adj. not able to be imagined or grasped mentally. ■ **in·con·ceiv·a·bly** adv.

in·con·clu·sive /ˌinkənˈkloōsiv, ˌiNG-/ ▸adj. not leading to a firm conclusion or result. ■ **in·con·clu·sive·ly** adv. **in·con·clu·sive·ness** n.

in·con·gru·ent /inˈkäNGgroōənt, ˌinkənˈgroō-/ ▸adj. out of place; incongruous. ■ **in·con·gru·ent·ly** adv.

in·con·gru·ous /inˈkäNGgroōəs/ ▸adj. out of place or not appropriate in a particular situation. ■ **in·con·gru·i·ty** /ˌinkənˈgroō-itē, ˌiNG-, -käNG-/ n. (pl. **incongruities**) **in·con·gru·ous·ly** adv.

in·con·se·quen·tial /inˌkänsəˈkwencHəl/ ▸adj. not important or significant. ■ **in·con·se·quen·ti·al·i·ty** /-ˌkwencHēˈalitē/ n. **in·con·se·quen·tial·ly** adv.

in·con·sid·er·a·ble /ˌinkənˈsidərəbəl/ ▸adj. small in size, amount, extent, etc.: *a not inconsiderable number.*

in·con·sid·er·ate /ˌinkənˈsidərit/ ▸adj. thoughtlessly causing hurt or inconvenience to others. ■ **in·con·sid·er·ate·ly** adv. **in·con·sid·er·ate·ness** n.

in·con·sist·ent /ˌinkənˈsistənt/ ▸adj. **1** having parts or elements that differ from or contradict each other. **2** (**inconsistent with**) not in keeping with. ■ **in·con·sist·en·cy** n. (pl. **inconsistencies**) **in·con·sist·ent·ly** adv.

in·con·sol·a·ble /ˌinkənˈsōləbəl/ ▸adj. not able to be comforted or consoled. ■ **in·con·sol·a·bly** adv.

in·con·spic·u·ous /ˌinkənˈspikyoōəs/ ▸adj. not clearly visible or noticeable. ■ **in·con·spic·u·ous·ly** adv. **in·con·spic·u·ous·ness** n.

in·con·stant /inˈkänstənt/ ▸adj. frequently changing; variable or irregular. ■ **in·con·stan·cy** n.

in·con·test·a·ble /ˌinkənˈtestəbəl/ ▸adj. not able to be disputed. ■ **in·con·test·a·bly** adv.

in·con·ti·nent /inˈkäntənənt, -ˈkäntn-ənt/ ▸adj. **1** unable to control when one urinates or defecates. **2** lacking self-control. ■ **in·con·ti·nence** n. **in·con·ti·nent·ly** adv.

in·con·tro·vert·i·ble /inˌkäntrəˈvərtəbəl/ ▸adj. not able to be denied or disputed. ■ **in·con·tro·vert·i·bly** adv.

in·con·ven·ience /ˌinkənˈvēn-yəns/ ▸n. the state of being slightly troublesome or difficult. ▸v. cause someone slight trouble or difficulty.

in·con·ven·ient /ˌinkənˈvēn-yənt/ ▸adj. causing trouble, difficulties, or discomfort. ■ **in·con·ven·ient·ly** adv.

in·cor·po·rate /inˈkôrpəˌrāt/ ▸v. **1** take in or contain as part of a whole: *some schemes incorporated all these variations.* **2** combine ingredients into one substance. **3** (often as adj. **incorporated**) form a company or other organization as a legal corporation. ■ **in·cor·po·ra·tion** /-ˌkôrpəˈrāsHən/ n. **in·cor·po·ra·tive** /inˈkôrpəˌrātiv/ adj. **in·cor·po·ra·tor** n.

in·cor·po·re·al /ˌinkôrˈpôrēəl/ ▸adj. not having a physical body or form.

in·cor·rect /ˌinkəˈrekt/ ▸adj. **1** not true or factually accurate; wrong: *the doctor gave you incorrect advice.* **2** not following accepted standards or rules. ■ **in·cor·rect·ly** adv. **in·cor·rect·ness** n.

in·cor·ri·gi·ble /inˈkôrijəbəl, -ˈkär-/ ▸adj. not able to be changed or reformed: *he's an incorrigible liar.* ■ **in·cor·ri·gi·bil·i·ty** /-ˌkôrijəˈbilitē, -ˌkär-/ n. **in·cor·ri·gi·bly** adv.

in·cor·rupt·i·ble /ˌinkəˈrəptəbəl/ ▸adj. **1** not able to be corrupted, especially by taking bribes. **2** not subject to death or decay; everlasting. ■ **in·cor·rupt·i·bil·i·ty** /-ˌrəptəˈbilitē/ n.

in·crease ▸v. /inˈkrēs/ become or make greater in size, amount, or intensity: *car use is increasing at an alarming rate.* ▸n. /ˈinˌkrēs/ an instance of growing or making greater. ■ **in·creas·ing** adj. **in·creas·ing·ly** adv.

– PHRASES **on the increase** becoming greater, more common, or more frequent.

in·cred·i·ble /inˈkredəbəl/ ▸adj. **1** impossible or hard to believe. **2** informal very good. ■ **in·cred·i·bil·i·ty** /-ˌkredəˈbilitē/ n. **in·cred·i·bly** adv.

in·cred·u·lous /inˈkrejələs/ ▸adj. unwilling or unable to believe something. ■ **in·cre·du·li·ty** /ˌinkrəˈd(y)oōlitē/ n. **in·cred·u·lous·ly** adv.

in·cre·ment /ˈiNGkrəmənt, ˈin-/ ▸n. an increase or addition, especially one of a series on a fixed scale. ■ **in·cre·men·tal** adj. **in·cre·men·tal·ly** adv.

in·crim·i·nate /inˈkriməˌnāt/ ▸v. make someone appear guilty of a crime or wrongdoing: (as adj. **incriminating**) *incriminating evidence.* ■ **in·crim·i·na·tion** /-ˌkriməˈnāsHən/ n. **in·crim·i·na·to·ry** /-ˌkriməˌtôrē/ adj.

in-crowd ▸n. (**the in-crowd**) informal a small group of people perceived by others to be particularly fashionable or popular.

in·cu·bate /ˈinkyəˌbāt, ˈiNG-/ ▸v. **1** (of a bird)

sit on eggs to keep them warm and hatch them. **2** keep bacteria, cells, etc., at a suitable temperature so that they develop. **3** (of an infectious disease) develop slowly without noticeable signs. ■ **in·cu·ba·tion** /ˌinkyəˈbāSHən, ˌiNG-/ n.

in·cu·ba·tor /ˈinkyəˌbātər, ˈiNG-/ ▶ n. **1** a machine used to hatch eggs or grow microorganisms under controlled conditions. **2** an enclosed machine providing a controlled and protective environment for the care of premature babies.

in·cu·bus /ˈiNGkyəbəs, ˈin-/ ▶ n. (pl. **incubi** /-ˌbī/) **1** a male demon believed to have sex with sleeping women. **2** literary a cause of difficulty or anxiety.

in·cul·cate /inˈkəlˌkāt, ˈinkəl-/ ▶ v. fix an idea in someone's mind by constantly repeating it. ■ **in·cul·ca·tion** /ˌinkəlˈkāSHən/ n.

in·cum·ben·cy /inˈkəmbənsē/ ▶ n. (pl. **incumbencies**) the period during which an office is held.

in·cum·bent /inˈkəmbənt/ ▶ adj. **1** (**incumbent on**) necessary for someone as a duty. **2** currently holding an office or post. ▶ n. **1** the holder of an office or post. **2** (in the Christian Church) the holder of a benefice.

in·cur /inˈkər, iNG-/ ▶ v. (**incurs, incurring, incurred**) do something that results in one experiencing something unpleasant or unwelcome: *he incurred the crowd's anger.*

in·cur·a·ble /ˌinˈkyo͝orəbəl/ ▶ adj. **1** not able to be cured. **2** not able to be changed: *he's an incurable romantic.* ▶ n. an incurable person. ■ **in·cur·a·bly** adv.

in·cu·ri·ous /inˈkyo͝orēəs/ ▶ adj. not eager to know something; lacking curiosity. ■ **in·cu·ri·os·i·ty** /-ˌkyo͝orēˈäsitē/ n. **in·cu·ri·ous·ly** adv.

in·cur·sion /inˈkərzHən/ ▶ n. a sudden or brief invasion or attack.

Ind. ▶ abbr. **1** (often of politicians) Independent. **2** Indian. **3** Indiana.

in·debt·ed /inˈdetid/ ▶ adj. **1** owing gratitude to someone: *Alex obviously feels indebted to his rescuer.* **2** owing money. ■ **in·debt·ed·ness** n.

in·de·cent /inˈdēsənt/ ▶ adj. **1** not following accepted standards of behavior in relation to sexual matters. **2** not appropriate in the circumstances: *he was buried with indecent haste.* ■ **in·de·cen·cy** n. (pl. **indecencies**) **in·de·cent·ly** adv.

in·de·cent as·sault ▶ n. sexual assault that does not involve rape.

in·de·cent ex·po·sure ▶ n. the crime of intentionally showing one's genitals in public.

in·de·ci·pher·a·ble /ˌindiˈsīfərəbəl/ ▶ adj. not able to be read or understood.

in·de·ci·sive /ˌindiˈsīsiv/ ▶ adj. **1** not able to make decisions quickly. **2** not settling an issue: *an indecisive battle.* ■ **in·de·ci·sion** /ˌindiˈsizHən/ n. **in·de·ci·sive·ly** adv. **in·de·ci·sive·ness** n.

in·dec·o·rous /ˌinˈdekərəs, ˌindiˈkôrəs/ ▶ adj. not in keeping with good taste and propriety; improper.

in·deed /inˈdēd/ ▶ adv. **1** used to emphasize a statement or answer. **2** used to introduce a further and stronger or more surprising point.

in·de·fat·i·ga·ble /ˌindiˈfatigəbəl/ ▶ adj. never tiring or stopping. ■ **in·de·fat·i·ga·bly** adv.

in·de·fen·si·ble /ˌindiˈfensəbəl/ ▶ adj. not able to

be justified or defended. ■ **in·de·fen·si·bly** adv.

in·de·fin·a·ble /ˌindəˈfīnəbəl/ ▶ adj. not able to be defined or described exactly. ■ **in·de·fin·a·bly** /-blē/ adv.

in·def·i·nite /inˈdefənit/ ▶ adj. **1** not clearly expressed or defined; vague. **2** lasting for an unknown or unstated length of time. ■ **in·def·i·nite·ly** adv. **in·def·i·nite·ness** n.

in·def·i·nite ar·ti·cle ▶ n. Grammar the words *a* or *an.*

in·def·i·nite pro·noun ▶ n. Grammar a pronoun that does not refer to any person or thing in particular, e.g., *anything, everyone.*

in·del·i·ble /inˈdeləbəl/ ▶ adj. **1** unable to be forgotten: *the beauty of the valley made an indelible impression on him.* **2** (of ink or a mark) unable to be removed. ■ **in·del·i·bly** adv.

in·del·i·cate /inˈdelikit/ ▶ adj. **1** lacking sensitive understanding or tact. **2** slightly indecent. ■ **in·del·i·ca·cy** n. **in·del·i·cate·ly** adv.

in·dem·ni·fy /inˈdemnəˌfī/ ▶ v. (**indemnifies, indemnifying, indemnified**) **1** compensate someone for harm or loss. **2** protect or insure someone against legal responsibility for their actions. ■ **in·dem·ni·fi·ca·tion** /-ˌdemnəfiˈkāSHən/ n. **in·dem·ni·fi·er** n.

in·dem·ni·ty /inˈdemnitē/ ▶ n. (pl. **indemnities**) **1** security or protection against a loss. **2** security against or exemption from legal responsibility for one's actions. **3** a sum of money paid to compensate for damage or loss, especially by a country defeated in war.

in·dent ▶ v. /inˈdent/ **1** form hollows, dents, or notches in something. **2** begin a line of writing further from the margin than the other lines. ▶ n. /inˈdent, ˈinˌdent/ a space left by indenting writing. ■ **in·dent·er** (also **indentor**) n.

in·den·ta·tion /ˌindenˈtāSHən/ ▶ n. **1** a deep recess or notch on an edge or surface. **2** the action of indenting something, especially a line of writing.

in·den·ture /inˈdenCHər/ ▶ n. **1** a formal agreement or contract, such as one formerly binding an apprentice to work for an employer. **2** historical a contract by which a person agreed to work for a set period for a landowner in a British colony in exchange for passage to the colony. ▶ v. chiefly historical bind someone by an indenture as an apprentice or laborer. ■ **in·den·ture·ship** n.

in·de·pend·ence /ˌindəˈpendəns/ ▶ n. the fact or state of being independent.

In·de·pend·ence Day ▶ n. a national holiday on July 4 celebrating the anniversary of the adoption of the Declaration of Independence in 1776.

in·de·pend·ent /ˌindəˈpendənt/ ▶ adj. **1** free from outside control or influence: *you should take independent advice.* **2** (of a country) self-governing. **3** having or earning enough money to support oneself. **4** not connected with another person or thing; separate. **5** (of broadcasting, a school, etc.) not supported by public funds. ▶ n. an independent person or organization. ■ **in·de·pend·en·cy** n. **in·de·pend·ent·ly** adv.

in-depth ▶ adj. comprehensive and thorough.

in·de·scrib·a·ble /ˌindiˈskrībəbəl/ ▶ adj. too unusual, extreme, or vague to be adequately described. ■ **in·de·scrib·a·bly** adv.

in·de·struct·i·ble /ˌindiˈstrəktəbəl/ ▶ adj. not able to be destroyed. ■ **in·de·struct·i·bil·i·ty** /-ˌstrəktəˈbilitē/ n. **in·de·struct·i·bly** adv.

in·de·ter·mi·na·ble /ˌindi'tərmənəbəl/ ▶ adj. not able to be determined.

in·de·ter·mi·nate /ˌindi'tərmənit/ ▶ adj. **1** not exactly known, established, or defined: *a woman of indeterminate age*. **2** Mathematics (of a quantity) having no definite or definable value.

in·dex /'in,deks/ ▶ n. (pl. **indexes** or especially in technical use **indices** /-də,sēz/) **1** an alphabetical list of names or subjects with references to the places in a book where they occur. **2** an alphabetical list or catalogue of books or documents. **3** a sign or measure of something: *doers was an index of social class*. **4** a number representing the relative value or magnitude of something in terms of a standard: *a price index*. **5** Mathematics an exponent or other superscript or subscript number appended to a quantity. ▶ v. **1** record items in or provide something with an index. **2** link the value of prices, wages, etc., automatically to the value of a price index. ■ **in·dex·a·ble** adj. **in·dex·a·tion** /ˌindek'sāshən/ n. **in·dex·er** n.

in·dex fin·ger ▶ n. the forefinger.

In·di·a ink ▶ n. deep black ink used especially in drawing and technical graphics.

In·di·an /'indēən/ ▶ n. **1** a person from India. **2** dated an American Indian. ▶ adj. **1** relating to India. **2** dated relating to American Indians. ■ **In·di·an·ize** v. **In·di·an·ness** n.

USAGE
Do not use the outdated terms **Indian** or **Red Indian** to refer to American native peoples; use **American Indian** or **Native American** instead.

In·di·an sum·mer ▶ n. a period of dry, warm weather occurring in late autumn.

in·di·cate /'indi,kāt/ ▶ v. **1** point out or show something. **2** be a sign of: *sales indicate a growing market for such art*. **3** mention something briefly or indirectly. **4** (**be indicated**) be necessary or recommended: *treatment for shock may be indicated*. **5** Brit. (of a driver) use a turn signal.

in·di·ca·tion /ˌindi'kāshən/ ▶ n. **1** a sign or piece of information that indicates something: *early indications of success*. **2** a reading given by a gauge or meter. **3** a symptom that suggests certain medical treatment is necessary: *heavy bleeding is a common indication for hysterectomy*.

in·dic·a·tive /in'dikətiv/ ▶ adj. **1** acting as a sign: *having recurrent dreams is not necessarily indicative of any psychological problem*. **2** Grammar (of a form of a verb) expressing a simple statement of fact (e.g., *she left*). ▶ n. Grammar an indicative verb.

in·di·ca·tor /'indi,kātər/ ▶ n. **1** a thing that shows a state or level: *car ownership as an indicator of affluence*. **2** a gauge or meter that gives particular information: *a speed indicator*. **3** a chemical compound that changes color at a specific pH value or in the presence of a particular substance, and can be used to monitor a chemical change.

in·di·ces /'indi,sēz/ ▶ plural of **INDEX**.

in·dict /in'dīt/ ▶ v. formally accuse someone of or charge them with a crime.

in·dict·a·ble /in'dītəbəl/ ▶ adj. (of an offense) making the person who commits it liable to be charged with a crime that warrants a trial by jury.

in·dict·ment /in'dītmənt/ ▶ n. Law a formal charge or accusation of a crime. **2** an indication that a system or situation is bad and deserves to be condemned: *these escalating crime figures are an indictment of our society*.

in·die /'indē/ ▶ adj. informal (of a pop group or record label) not belonging or linked to a major record company.

in·dif·fer·ent /in'dif(ə)rənt/ ▶ adj. **1** having no particular interest in or feelings about something. **2** not particularly good; mediocre. ■ **in·dif·fer·ence** n. **in·dif·fer·ent·ly** adv.

in·dig·e·nize /in'dijə,nīz/ ▶ v. bring something under the control or influence of native people. ■ **in·dig·e·ni·za·tion** /-,dijəni'zāshən/ n.

in·dig·e·nous /in'dijənəs/ ▶ adj. originating or occurring naturally in a particular place; native.

in·di·gent /'indijənt/ ▶ adj. very poor. ▶ n. a person who is very poor. ■ **in·di·gence** n.

in·di·gest·i·ble /ˌindi'jestəbəl/ ▶ adj. **1** difficult or impossible to digest. **2** difficult to read or understand. ■ **in·di·gest·i·bil·i·ty** /-,jestə'bilitē/ n. **in·di·gest·i·bly** adv.

in·di·ges·tion /ˌindi'jeschən, -dī-/ ▶ n. pain or discomfort in the stomach caused by difficulty in digesting food.

in·dig·nant /in'dignənt/ ▶ adj. feeling or showing offense and annoyance. ■ **in·dig·nant·ly** adv.

in·dig·na·tion /ˌindig'nāshən/ ▶ n. annoyance caused by what is seen as unfair treatment.

in·dig·ni·ty /in'dignitē/ ▶ n. (pl. **indignities**) treatment or circumstances that cause one to feel ashamed or embarrassed.

in·di·go /'indi,gō/ ▶ n. (pl. **indigos**) **1** a dark blue dye obtained from a tropical plant. **2** a dark blue color.

in·di·rect /ˌində'rekt/ ▶ adj. **1** not direct: *an indirect route*. **2** (of taxation) charged on goods and services rather than income or profits. **3** (of costs) arising from the regular expenses involved in running a business or from subsidiary work. ■ **in·di·rec·tion** n. **in·di·rect·ly** adv. **in·di·rect·ness** n.

in·di·rect ob·ject ▶ n. Grammar a person or thing that is affected by the action of a transitive verb but is not the main object (e.g., *him* in *give him the book*).

in·di·rect speech ▶ n. another term for **REPORTED SPEECH**.

in·dis·cern·i·ble /ˌindi'sərnəbəl/ ▶ adj. impossible to see or distinguish clearly.

in·dis·ci·pline /in'disəplin/ ▶ n. disorderly or uncontrolled behavior.

in·dis·creet /ˌindi'skrēt/ ▶ adj. too ready to reveal things that should remain secret or private. ■ **in·dis·creet·ly** adv.

in·dis·cre·tion /ˌindi'skreshən/ ▶ n. behavior or an act or remark that is indiscreet or shows a lack of good judgment.

in·dis·crim·i·nate /ˌindi'skrimənit/ ▶ adj. done or acting at random or without careful judgment. ■ **in·dis·crim·i·nate·ly** adv.

in·dis·pen·sa·ble /ˌindi'spensəbəl/ ▶ adj. absolutely necessary. ■ **in·dis·pen·sa·bil·i·ty** /-,spensə'bilitē/ n.

in·dis·posed /ˌindi'spōzd/ ▶ adj. **1** slightly unwell. **2** unwilling to do something.

in·dis·po·si·tion /ˌindispə'zishən/ ▶ n. a slight illness.

in·dis·put·a·ble /ˌindis'pyo͞otəbəl/ ▶ adj. unable to be challenged or denied. ■ **in·dis·put·a·bil·i·ty**

in·dis·sol·u·ble /ˌindiˈsälyəbəl/ ▸ adj. unable to be destroyed; lasting.

in·dis·tinct /ˌindisˈtiNGkt/ ▸ adj. not clear or sharply defined. ■ **in·dis·tinct·ly** adv. **in·dis·tinct·ness** n.

in·dis·tin·guish·a·ble /indisˈtiNGgwiSHəbəl/ ▸ adj. not able to be identified as different or distinct. ■ **in·dis·tin·guish·a·bly** /-blē/ adv.

in·di·um /ˈindēəm/ ▸ n. a soft silvery-white metallic chemical element resembling zinc, used in some alloys and semiconductor devices.

in·di·vid·u·al /ˌindəˈvijəwəl/ ▸ adj. **1** single; separate. **2** relating to or for one particular person: *the individual needs of the children.* **3** striking or unusual; original: *a highly individual musical style.* ▸ n. **1** a single person or item as distinct from a group. **2** a person of a particular kind: *a selfish individual.* **3** a person who is unusual or different from other people.

in·di·vid·u·al·ism /ˌindəˈvijōōəˌlizəm/ ▸ n. **1** independence and self-reliance. **2** a social theory that favors the idea that individual people should have freedom of action rather than be controlled by society or the government. ■ **in·di·vid·u·al·ist** n. & adj. **in·di·vid·u·al·is·tic** /-ˌvijōōəˈlistik/ adj.

in·di·vid·u·al·i·ty /ˌindəˌvijəˈwalitē/ ▸ n. the quality or character of a person or thing that makes them different from others.

in·di·vid·u·al·ize /ˌindəˈvijōōəˌlīz/ ▸ v. make or alter something in such a way as to suit the needs or wishes of a particular person.

in·di·vid·u·al·ly /ˌindəˈvijəwəlē/ ▸ adv. **1** one by one; singly; separately: *individually wrapped cheese slices.* **2** in a distinctive manner: *each sign is individually designed and crafted.* **3** personally; in an individual capacity: *partnerships and individually owned companies.*

in·di·vid·u·ate /ˌindəˈvijōōˌāt/ ▸ v. distinguish someone or something from other people or things of the same kind. ■ **in·di·vid·u·a·tion** /-ˌvijōōˈāSHən/ n.

in·di·vis·i·ble /ˌindiˈvizəbəl/ ▸ adj. **1** unable to be divided or separated. **2** (of a number) unable to be divided by another number exactly without leaving a remainder. ■ **in·di·vis·i·bil·i·ty** /ˌindivizəˈbilitē/ n. **in·di·vis·i·bly** adv.

in·doc·tri·nate /inˈdäktrəˌnāt/ ▸ v. make someone accept a set of beliefs, without allowing them to consider any alternatives. ■ **in·doc·tri·na·tion** /-ˌdäktrəˈnāSHən/ n.

In·do-Eu·ro·pe·an /ˌindō-/ ▸ n. **1** the family of languages spoken over the greater part of Europe and Asia as far as northern India. **2** a person who speaks an Indo-European language. ▸ adj. relating to Indo-European languages.

in·do·lent /ˈindələnt/ ▸ adj. wanting to avoid activity or exertion; lazy. ■ **in·do·lence** n. **in·do·lent·ly** adv.

in·dom·i·ta·ble /inˈdämitəbəl/ ▸ adj. impossible to subdue or defeat. ■ **in·dom·i·ta·bil·i·ty** /-ˌdämitəˈbilitē/ n. **in·dom·i·ta·bly** adv.

In·do·ne·sian /ˌindəˈnēzHən/ ▸ n. **1** a person from Indonesia. **2** the group of languages spoken in Indonesia. ▸ adj. relating to Indonesia.

in·door /ˈinˌdôr/ ▸ adj. situated, done, or used inside a building or under cover.

in·doors /inˈdôrz/ ▸ adv. into or within a building. ▸ n. the area or space inside a building.

in·drawn /ˈinˌdrôn/ ▸ adj. **1** (of breath) taken in.

2 (of a person) shy and introspective.

in·du·bi·ta·ble /inˈd(y)ōōbitəbəl/ ▸ adj. formal impossible to doubt; unquestionable. ■ **in·du·bi·ta·bly** adv.

in·duce /inˈd(y)ōōs/ ▸ v. **1** persuade or influence someone to do something. **2** bring about or cause: *herbs to induce sleep.* **3** cause a pregnant woman to go into labor by the use of drugs or other artificial means. **4** produce an electric charge or current or a magnetic state by induction. ■ **in·duc·er** n. **in·duc·i·ble** adj.

in·duce·ment /inˈd(y)ōōsmənt/ ▸ n. **1** a thing that persuades or influences someone to do something. **2** a bribe.

in·duct /inˈdəkt/ ▸ v. **1** formally admit someone to an organization or establish them in a position. **2** enlist someone for military service. ■ **in·duc·tee** n. /ˌindəkˈtē/.

in·duc·tance /inˈdəktəns/ ▸ n. Physics the property of an electric conductor or circuit that causes an electromotive force to be generated by a change in the current flowing.

in·duc·tion /inˈdəkSHən/ ▸ n. **1** the action or process of introducing someone to an organization or establishing them in a position. **2** the action or process of inducing something. **3** a method of reasoning in which a general rule or conclusion is drawn from particular facts or examples. **4** the production of an electric or magnetic state in an object by bringing an electrified or magnetized object close to it (without touching it). **5** the drawing of the fuel mixture into the cylinders of an internal-combustion engine.

in·duc·tive /inˈdəktiv/ ▸ adj. **1** using a method of reasoning that draws general conclusions from particular facts or examples. **2** relating to electric or magnetic induction. **3** Physics possessing inductance. ■ **in·duc·tive·ly** adv.

in·dulge /inˈdəlj/ ▸ v. **1** (**indulge in**) allow oneself to enjoy the pleasure of something: *we indulged in an ice cream sundae.* **2** satisfy a desire or interest: *she was able to indulge a growing passion for literature.* **3** allow someone to do or have whatever they wish.

in·dul·gence /inˈdəljəns/ ▸ n. **1** the action of allowing oneself to do something pleasurable. **2** a thing that is indulged in; a luxury. **3** a willingness to tolerate someone's faults. **4** an extension of the time in which a bill or debt has to be paid. **5** chiefly historical (in the Roman Catholic Church) the setting aside or cancellation by the Pope of the punishment still due for sins after absolution.

in·dul·gent /inˈdəljənt/ ▸ adj. **1** readily indulging someone or overlooking their faults. **2** self-indulgent. ■ **in·dul·gent·ly** adv.

in·dus·tri·al /inˈdəstrēəl/ ▸ adj. relating to or used in industry, or having many industries. ▸ n. (**industrials**) industrial companies or traded investments in them. ■ **in·dus·tri·al·ly** adv.

in·dus·tri·al·ism /inˈdəstrēəˌlizəm/ ▸ n. a social or economic system based on manufacturing industries.

in·dus·tri·al·ist /inˈdəstrēəlist/ ▸ n. a person who owns or controls a manufacturing business.

in·dus·tri·al·ize /inˈdəstrēəˌlīz/ ▸ v. (often as adj. **industrialized**) develop industries in a country or region on a wide scale. ■ **in·dus·tri·al·i·za·tion** /inˌdəstrēəliˈzāSHən/ n.

in·dus·tri·al park ▸ n. an area of land developed

as a site for factories and other industrial use.

in·dus·tri·al re·la·tions ▸ pl.n. the relations between management and workers in industry.

in·dus·tri·al-strength ▸ adj. very strong or powerful.

in·dus·tri·ous /inˈdəstrēəs/ ▸ adj. hard-working. ■ **in·dus·tri·ous·ly** adv. **in·dus·tri·ous·ness** n.

in·dus·try /ˈindəstrē/ ▸ n. (pl. **industries**) **1** economic activity concerned with the processing of raw materials and manufacture of goods in factories. **2** a particular branch of economic or commercial activity: *the tourist industry.* **3** hard work.

In·dy /ˈindē/ ▸ n. a form of auto racing in which specially constructed cars are driven around a banked, regular, typically oval circuit, which allows for exceptionally high speeds.

in·e·bri·ate ▸ v. /iˈnēbrēˌāt/ (usu. as adj. **inebriated**) make someone drunk. ▸ adj. /-brē-it/ drunk. ■ **in·e·bri·a·tion** /iˌnēbrēˈāshən/ n.

in·ed·i·ble /inˈedəbəl/ ▸ adj. not fit for eating.

in·ef·fa·ble /inˈefəbəl/ ▸ adj. **1** too great or extreme to be expressed in words: *the ineffable beauty of the Everglades.* **2** too sacred to be spoken. ■ **in·ef·fa·bil·i·ty** /-efəˈbilitē/ n. **in·ef·fa·bly** adv.

in·ef·fec·tive /ˌiniˈfektiv/ ▸ adj. not producing any or the desired effect. ■ **in·ef·fec·tive·ly** adv. **in·ef·fec·tive·ness** n.

in·ef·fec·tu·al /ˌiniˈfekchōōəl/ ▸ adj. **1** not producing any or the desired effect. **2** lacking the necessary forcefulness in a role or situation. ■ **in·ef·fec·tu·al·ly** adv.

in·ef·fi·cient /ˌiniˈfishənt/ ▸ adj. failing to make the best use of time or resources. ■ **in·ef·fi·cien·cy** n. **in·ef·fi·cient·ly** adv.

in·e·las·tic /iniˈlastik/ ▸ adj. (of a material) not elastic. ■ **in·e·las·tic·al·ly** adv. **in·e·las·tic·i·ty** /iniˌlaˈstisitē, inēˌla-/ n.

in·el·e·gant /inˈeligənt/ ▸ adj. not elegant or graceful. ■ **in·el·e·gance** n. **in·el·e·gant·ly** adv.

in·el·i·gi·ble /inˈeləjəbəl/ ▸ adj. not eligible. ■ **in·el·i·gi·bil·i·ty** /inˈeləjəˈbilitē/ n.

in·e·luc·ta·ble /ˌiniˈləktəbəl/ ▸ adj. unable to be resisted or avoided; inescapable. ■ **in·e·luc·ta·bly** adv.

in·ept /iˈnept/ ▸ adj. awkward or clumsy; incompetent. ■ **in·ept·i·tude** /-tiˌt(y)ōōd/ n. **in·ept·ly** adv. **in·ept·ness** n.

in·e·qual·i·ty /ˌiniˈkwälitē/ ▸ n. (pl. **inequalities**) lack of equality.

in·eq·ui·ta·ble /inˈekwitəbəl/ ▸ adj. unfair; unjust. ■ **in·eq·ui·ta·bly** adv.

in·eq·ui·ty /inˈekwitē/ ▸ n. (pl. **inequities**) lack of fairness or justice.

in·e·rad·i·ca·ble /ˌinəˈradikəbəl/ ▸ adj. unable to be destroyed or removed. ■ **in·e·rad·i·ca·bly** adv.

in·ert /iˈnərt/ ▸ adj. **1** lacking the ability or strength to move. **2** without active chemical properties. ■ **in·ert·ly** adv. **in·ert·ness** n.

in·ert gas ▸ n. another term for NOBLE GAS.

in·er·tia /iˈnərshə/ ▸ n. **1** lack of desire or ability to move or change. **2** Physics a property of matter by which it continues in its existing state of rest or continues moving in a straight line, unless changed by an external force. ■ **in·er·tial** adj.

in·es·cap·a·ble /ˌiniˈskāpəbəl/ ▸ adj. unable to be avoided or denied. ■ **in·es·cap·a·bil·i·ty** /-ˌskāpəˈbilitē/ n. **in·es·cap·a·bly** adv.

in·es·sen·tial /ˌiniˈsenchəl/ ▸ adj. not absolutely necessary. ▸ n. an inessential thing.

in·es·ti·ma·ble /inˈestəməbəl/ ▸ adj. too great to be measured. ■ **in·es·ti·ma·bly** adv.

in·ev·i·ta·ble /inˈevitəbəl/ ▸ adj. certain to happen; unavoidable. ▸ n. (**the inevitable**) a situation that is unavoidable. ■ **in·ev·i·ta·bil·i·ty** /-ˌevitəˈbilitē/ n. **in·ev·i·ta·bly** adv.

in·ex·act /ˌinigˈzakt/ ▸ adj. not quite accurate. ■ **in·ex·ac·ti·tude** /ˌinigˈzaktəˌt(y)ōōd/ n. **in·ex·act·ly** adv. **in·ex·act·ness** n.

in·ex·cus·a·ble /ˌinikˈskyōōzəbəl/ ▸ adj. too bad to be justified or tolerated. ■ **in·ex·cus·a·bly** adv.

in·ex·haust·i·ble /ˌinigˈzôstəbəl/ ▸ adj. (of an amount or supply of something) available in unlimited quantities. ■ **in·ex·haust·i·bly** adv.

in·ex·o·ra·ble /inˈeksərəbəl/ ▸ adj. **1** impossible to stop or prevent: *the inexorable march of new technology.* **2** (of a person) impossible to persuade; unrelenting. ■ **in·ex·o·ra·bil·i·ty** /-ˌeksərəˈbilitē/ n. **in·ex·o·ra·bly** adv.

in·ex·pen·sive /ˌinikˈspensiv/ ▸ adj. not costing a great deal; cheap. ■ **in·ex·pen·sive·ly** adv. **in·ex·pen·sive·ness** n.

in·ex·pe·ri·ence /ˌinikˈspi(ə)rēəns/ ▸ n. lack of experience. ■ **in·ex·pe·ri·enced** adj.

in·ex·pert /inˈekspərt/ ▸ adj. lacking skill or knowledge in a particular field. ■ **in·ex·pert·ly** adv.

in·ex·pli·ca·ble /ˌinekˈsplikəbəl, inˈeksplikəbəl/ ▸ adj. unable to be explained or accounted for. ■ **in·ex·pli·ca·bil·i·ty** /ˈinekˌsplikəˈbilitē/ n. **in·ex·pli·ca·bly** adv.

in·ex·press·i·ble /ˌinikˈspresəbəl/ ▸ adj. (of a feeling) too strong to be described or expressed in words. ■ **in·ex·press·i·bly** adv.

in·ex·pres·sive /ˌinikˈspresiv/ ▸ adj. showing no expression. ■ **in·ex·pres·sive·ly** adv. **in·ex·pres·sive·ness** n.

in·ex·tin·guish·a·ble /ˌinikˈstiNGgwishəbəl/ ▸ adj. unable to be extinguished.

in ex·tre·mis /ˌin ekˈstrāmēs, ikˈstrēmis/ ▸ adv. **1** in an extremely difficult situation. **2** at the point of death.

in·ex·tri·ca·ble /ˌinikˈstrikəbəl, inˈekstri-/ ▸ adj. impossible to disentangle or separate: *the past and the present are inextricable.* ■ **in·ex·tri·ca·bly** adv.

in·fal·li·bil·i·ty /inˌfaləˈbilitē/ ▸ n. **1** the quality of being infallible; the inability to be wrong. **2** (also **papal infallibility**) (in the Roman Catholic Church) the doctrine that in specified circumstances the pope is incapable of error in pronouncing dogma.

in·fal·li·ble /inˈfaləbəl/ ▸ adj. **1** incapable of making mistakes or being wrong. **2** never failing; always effective. ■ **in·fal·li·bly** adv.

in·fa·mous /ˈinfəməs/ ▸ adj. **1** well known for some bad quality or deed. **2** morally bad; wicked. ■ **in·fa·mous·ly** adv.

in·fa·my /ˈinfəmē/ ▸ n. (pl. **infamies**) **1** the state of being known for something bad. **2** a wicked act.

in·fan·cy /ˈinfənsē/ ▸ n. **1** the state or period of being a baby or very young child. **2** the early stage in the development or growth of something: *opinion polls were in their infancy.*

in·fant /ˈinfənt/ ▸ n. a baby or very young child.

in·fan·ta /inˈfantə/ ▸ n. historical a daughter of the king or queen of Spain or Portugal.

in·fan·ti·cide /inˈfantiˌsīd/ ▸ n. the killing of a

baby or very young child.

in·fan·tile /'infən,tīl, 'infənt-il/ ▶ adj. 1 relating to or affecting babies and very young children. 2 derogatory childish.

in·fan·til·ism /'infəntl,izəm, in'fan-/ ▶ n. 1 childish behavior. 2 Psychology a condition in which characteristics or behavior of babies or very young children persist into adult life.

in·fan·try /'infəntrē/ ▶ n. soldiers who fight on foot. ■ **in·fan·try·man** n. (pl. **infantrymen**).

in·farct /'in,färkt/ ▶ n. Medicine a small area of dead tissue resulting from a failure of the blood supply. ■ **in·farc·tion** /in'färksHən/ n.

in·fat·u·ate /in'faCHŌŌ,āt/ ▶ v. (**be infatuated with**) have an intense but usually short-lived passion for someone. ■ **in·fat·u·a·tion** /-,faCHŌŌ'āsHən/ n.

in·fect /in'fekt/ ▶ v. 1 affect a person, part of the body, etc., with an organism that causes disease. 2 contaminate something.

in·fec·tion /in'feksHən/ ▶ n. 1 the process of infecting someone or something or the state of being infected. 2 an infectious disease.

in·fec·tious /in'feksHəs/ ▶ adj. 1 (of a disease or disease-causing organism) liable to be transmitted through the environment. 2 (of a person or animal) likely to spread infection. 3 likely to spread to or influence other people: *her enthusiasm is infectious.* ■ **in·fec·tious·ly** adv. **in·fec·tious·ness** n.

in·fec·tious mon·o·nu·cle·o·sis ▶ n. an infectious disease caused by a virus, resulting in swollen lymph glands and long-term lack of energy.

in·fec·tive /in'fektiv/ ▶ adj. capable of causing infection.

in·fe·lic·i·tous /,infə'lisitəs/ ▶ adj. unfortunate; inappropriate. ■ **in·fe·lic·i·tous·ly** adv.

in·fe·lic·i·ty /,infə'lisitē/ ▶ n. (pl. **infelicities**) 1 an inappropriate remark or action. 2 old use unhappiness or misfortune.

in·fer /in'fər/ ▶ v. (**infers, inferring, inferred**) work something out from evidence and reasoning rather than from direct statements. ■ **in·fer·a·ble** (also **inferrable**) adj.

> **USAGE**
> On the use of **imply** and **infer**, see the note at IMPLY.

in·fer·ence /'inf(ə)rəns/ ▶ n. 1 a conclusion reached on the basis of evidence and reasoning. 2 the process of reaching a conclusion in this way. ■ **in·fer·en·tial** /,infə'renCHəl/ adj.

in·fe·ri·or /in'fi(ə)rēər/ ▶ adj. 1 lower in rank, status, or quality. 2 of low standard or quality. 3 chiefly Anatomy low or lower in position. 4 (of a letter or symbol) written or printed below the line. ▶ n. a person lower than another in rank, status, or ability. ■ **in·fe·ri·or·i·ty** /in,fi(ə)rē'ôritē, -'äritē/ n.

in·fe·ri·or·i·ty com·plex ▶ n. a feeling that one is of lower status or has less ability than other people, resulting in aggressive or withdrawn behavior.

in·fer·nal /in'fərnl/ ▶ adj. 1 relating to hell or the underworld. 2 informal very annoying: *an infernal nuisance.* ■ **in·fer·nal·ly** adv.

in·fer·no /in'fərnō/ ▶ n. (pl. **infernos**) 1 a large uncontrollable fire. 2 (**Inferno**) hell.

in·fer·tile /in'fərtl/ ▶ adj. 1 unable to have children or (of an animal) bear young. 2 (of

land) unable to produce crops or vegetation. ■ **in·fer·til·i·ty** /,infər'tilitē/ n.

in·fest /in'fest/ ▶ v. (of insects or organisms) be present in large numbers, typically so as to cause damage or disease. ■ **in·fes·ta·tion** /,infe'stāsHən/ n.

in·fi·del /'infədl, -,del/ ▶ n. chiefly old use a person who has no religion or whose religion is not that of the majority.

in·fi·del·i·ty /,infi'delitē/ ▶ n. (pl. **infidelities**) 1 the action or state of being sexually unfaithful. 2 lack of religious faith.

in·fight·ing /'in,fītiNG/ ▶ n. conflict within a group or organization.

in·fill /'in,fil/ ▶ n. (also **infilling**) material or buildings used to fill a space or hole. ▶ v. fill or block up a space or hole.

in·fil·trate /'infil,trāt, in'fil-/ ▶ v. 1 enter or gain access to an organization or place in a gradual and surreptitious way. 2 pass slowly into or through something. ■ **in·fil·tra·tion** /,infil'trāsHən/ n. **in·fil·tra·tor** n.

in·fi·nite /'infənit/ ▶ adj. 1 without limits and impossible to measure or calculate: *the infinite number of stars in the universe.* 2 very great in amount or degree: *he bathed the wound with infinite care.* ■ **in·fi·nite·ly** adv. **in·fin·i·tude** /in'fini,t(y)ŌŌd/ n.

in·fin·i·tes·i·mal /,infini'tes(ə)məl/ ▶ adj. extremely small. ■ **in·fin·i·tes·i·mal·ly** adv.

in·fin·i·tive /in'finitiv/ ▶ n. the basic form of a verb, often occurring in English with the word *to*, as in *to see, to ask.* ■ **in·fin·i·ti·val** /-fini'tīvəl/ adj.

in·fin·i·ty /in'finitē/ ▶ n. (pl. **infinities**) 1 the state or quality of having no limit and being impossible to measure or calculate. 2 a very great number or amount. 3 Mathematics a number greater than any assignable quantity or countable number (symbol ∞).

in·firm /in'fərm/ ▶ adj. physically weak.

in·fir·ma·ry /in'fərm(ə)rē/ ▶ n. (pl. **infirmaries**) a hospital or place set aside for the care of sick or injured people.

in·fir·mi·ty /in'fərmitē/ ▶ n. (pl. **infirmities**) physical or mental weakness.

in fla·gran·te de·lic·to /,in flə'grāntä də'liktō, flə'grantē/ ▶ adv. in the very act of doing something wrong, especially having illicit sex.

in·flame /in'flām/ ▶ v. 1 make something stronger or worse: *comments that inflamed what was already a sensitive situation.* 2 arouse strong feelings in someone. 3 cause inflammation in a part of the body.

in·flam·ma·ble /in'flaməbəl/ ▶ adj. easily set on fire. ■ **in·flam·ma·bil·i·ty** /-,flamə'bilitē/ n.

> **USAGE**
> The words **inflammable** and **flammable** both mean 'easily set on fire.' It is, however, safer to use **flammable** to avoid ambiguity, as the *in-* part of **inflammable** can give the impression that the word means 'nonflammable.'

in·flam·ma·tion /,inflə'māsHən/ ▶ n. a condition in which an area of the skin or body becomes reddened, swollen, hot, and often painful, especially as a reaction to injury or infection.

in·flam·ma·to·ry /in'flamə,tôrē/ ▶ adj. 1 relating to or causing inflammation. 2 arousing or intended to arouse angry or violent feelings.

in·flat·a·ble /in'flātəbəl/ ▶ adj. capable of being

inflated. ▶n. a plastic or rubber object that is inflated before use.

in·flate /in'flāt/ ▶v. **1** expand something by filling it with air or gas. **2** increase something by a large or excessive amount. **3** (as adj. **inflated**) exaggerated: *an inflated view of her own importance.* **4** bring about inflation of a currency or in an economy.

in·fla·tion /in'flāSHən/ ▶n. **1** the action of inflating something. **2** a general increase in prices and fall in the value of money. ■ **in·fla·tion·ar·y** adj. **in·fla·tion·ist** /-nist/ n. & adj.

in·flect /in'flekt/ ▶v. **1** Grammar (of a word) change by inflection. **2** vary the intonation or pitch of the voice.

in·flec·tion /in'flekSHən/ ▶n. **1** Grammar a change in the form of a word (typically the ending) to show a grammatical function or quality such as tense, mood, person, number, case, and gender. **2** a variation in intonation or pitch of the voice. **3** chiefly Mathematics a change of curvature from convex to concave. ■ **in·flec·tion·al** adj.

in·flex·i·ble /in'fleksəbəl/ ▶adj. **1** not able to be altered or adapted. **2** unwilling to change or compromise. **3** not able to be bent; stiff. ■ **in·flex·i·bil·i·ty** /-,fleksə'bilitē/ n. **in·flex·i·bly** adv.

in·flict /in'flikt/ ▶v. (**inflict something on**) **1** cause someone to suffer something unpleasant: *they inflicted serious injuries on the other men.* **2** impose something unwelcome on someone: *she is wrong to inflict her beliefs on everyone else.* ■ **in·flic·tion** n.

in·flight /'in,flīt/ ▶adj. occurring or provided during an aircraft flight: *inflight entertainment.*

in·flo·res·cence /,inflô'resəns, -flə-/ ▶n. **1** the complete flowerhead of a plant, including stems, stalks, bracts, and flowers. **2** the process of flowering.

in·flow /'in,flō/ ▶n. **1** the movement of liquid or air into a place. **2** the movement of a lot of money, people, or things into a place.

in·flu·ence /'inflōōəns/ ▶n. **1** the power or ability to have an effect on someone's beliefs or actions. **2** a person or thing with the power or ability to do this. **3** the power arising out of one's status, contacts, or wealth. ▶v. have an effect on: *feminist ideas have influenced the lawmakers.* ■ **in·flu·enc·er** n.
– PHRASES **under the influence** informal affected by alcohol or drugs.

in·flu·en·tial /,inflōō'enCHəl/ ▶adj. having great influence. ■ **in·flu·en·tial·ly** adv.

in·flu·en·za /,inflōō'enzə/ ▶n. a highly contagious infection of the nose, throat, and lungs, spread by a virus and causing fever, severe aching, and catarrh.

in·flux /'in,fləks/ ▶n. **1** the arrival or entry of large numbers of people or things. **2** an inflow of water into a river, lake, or the sea.

in·fo /'infō/ ▶n. informal information.

in·fo·mer·cial /'infō,mərSHəl/ ▶n. a long television advertisement that gives a great deal of information about a product in a supposedly objective way.

in·form /in'fôrm/ ▶v. **1** give facts or information to someone. **2** (**inform on**) give information about someone's involvement in a crime to the police. **3** have an important influence on; determine the nature of: *religion informs every*

aspect of their lives.

in·for·mal /in'fôrməl/ ▶adj. **1** relaxed, friendly, or unofficial. **2** (of clothes) suitable for everyday wear; casual. **3** referring to the language of everyday speech and writing, rather than that used in official and formal situations. ■ **in·for·mal·i·ty** /,infôr'malitē/ n. **in·for·mal·ly** adv.

in·form·ant /in'fôrmənt/ ▶n. **1** a person who gives information to someone else. **2** an informer.

in·for·mat·ics /,infər'matiks/ ▶pl.n. (treated as sing.) Computing the science of processing data for storage and retrieval.

in·for·ma·tion /,infər'māSHən/ ▶n. **1** facts or knowledge provided or learned. **2** what is conveyed or represented by a particular arrangement or sequence of things: *genetically transmitted information.* ■ **in·for·ma·tion·al** adj. **in·for·ma·tion·al·ly** adv.

in·for·ma·tion sci·ence ▶n. Computing the study of processes for storing and retrieving information.

in·for·ma·tion su·per·high·way ▶n. an extensive electronic network such as the Internet, used for the rapid transfer of information in digital form.

in·for·ma·tion tech·nol·o·gy ▶n. the study or use of systems such as computers and telecommunications for storing, retrieving, and sending information.

in·for·ma·tive /in'fôrmətiv/ ▶adj. providing useful information. ■ **in·for·ma·tive·ly** adv.

in·formed /in'fôrmd/ ▶adj. **1** having or showing knowledge: *an informed readership.* **2** (of a decision or judgment) based on an understanding of the facts.

in·form·er /in'fôrmər/ ▶n. a person who informs on another person to the police or other authority.

in·fo·tain·ment /,infō'tānmənt/ ▶n. broadcast programs that present news and serious subjects in an entertaining way.

infra- ▶prefix below: *infrasonic.*

in·frac·tion /in'frakSHən/ ▶n. a breaking of a law, agreement, or set of rules.

in·fra dig /,infrə 'dig/ ▶adj. informal beneath one's dignity.

in·fra·or·der /'infrə,ôrdər/ ▶n. Biology a taxonomic category that ranks below a suborder.

in·fra·red /,infrə'red/ ▶n. electromagnetic radiation having a wavelength just greater than that of red light but less than that of microwaves, emitted particularly by heated objects. ▶adj. relating to such radiation.

in·fra·son·ic /,infrə'sänik/ ▶adj. relating or referring to sound waves with a frequency below the range that can be heard by the human ear.

in·fra·sound /'infrə,sound/ ▶n. infrasonic sound waves.

in·fra·struc·ture /'infrə,strəkCHər/ ▶n. the basic physical and organizational structures (e.g., buildings, roads, and power supplies) needed for a society or enterprise to function. ■ **in·fra·struc·tur·al** /,infrə'strəkCHərəl/ adj.

in·fre·quent /in'frēkwənt/ ▶adj. not occurring often; rare. ■ **in·fre·quen·cy** n. **in·fre·quent·ly** adv.

in·fringe /in'frinj/ ▶v. **1** break the terms of a law, agreement, etc. **2** limit or restrict someone's rights: *such widespread surveillance could infringe on personal liberties.* ■ **in·fringe·ment** n. **in·fring·er** n.

in·fu·ri·ate /in'fyoŏorē,āt/ ▶ v. make someone very irritated or angry. ■ **in·fu·ri·at·ing** adj.

in·fuse /in'fyooz/ ▶ v. **1** fill something with a quality: *a play infused with humor.* **2** soak tea, herbs, etc., to extract the flavor or healing properties. **3** Medicine allow a liquid to flow into a vein or tissue. ■ **in·fus·er** n.

in·fu·sion /in'fyoŏozнən/ ▶ n. **1** a drink or remedy prepared by soaking tea or herbs. **2** a new or additional element introduced into something: *the company needs a serious infusion of cash.* **3** the action of infusing something.

in·gen·ious /in'jēnyəs/ ▶ adj. clever, original, and inventive. ■ **in·gen·ious·ly** adv.

in·gé·nue /'änjə,noō, 'änzн–/ ▶ n. an innocent or unsophisticated young woman.

in·ge·nu·i·ty /,injə'n(y)oŏitē/ ▶ n. the quality of being clever, original, and inventive.

in·gen·u·ous /in'jenyooəs/ ▶ adj. innocent and unsuspecting. ■ **in·gen·u·ous·ly** adv. **in·gen·u·ous·ness** n.

in·gest /in'jest/ ▶ v. take food or drink into the body by swallowing or absorbing it. ■ **in·ges·tion** n.

in·glo·ri·ous /in'glôrēəs/ ▶ adj. causing shame; dishonorable.

in·go·ing /'in,gōiNG/ ▶ adj. going toward or into.

in·got /'iNGgət/ ▶ n. a rectangular block of steel, gold, or other metal.

in·grain /in'grān/ ▶ v. firmly fix or establish (a habit, belief, or attitude) in a person. ▶ adj. /'in,grān/ (of a textile) composed of fibers that have been dyed different colors before being woven.

in·grained /in'grānd/ (also **engrained**) ▶ adj. **1** (of a habit or attitude) firmly established and hard to change. **2** (of dirt) deeply embedded.

in·grate /'in,grāt/ formal or literary ▶ n. an ungrateful person. ▶ adj. ungrateful.

in·gra·ti·ate /in'grāsнē,āt/ ▶ v. (**ingratiate oneself**) try to gain favor with someone by flattering or trying to please them. ■ **in·gra·ti·at·ing** adj. **in·gra·ti·a·tion** /-,grāsнē'āsнən/ n.

in·grat·i·tude /in'grati,t(y)oōd/ ▶ n. a lack of gratitude for something that has been done for one.

in·gre·di·ent /in'grēdēənt, iNG–/ ▶ n. **1** any of the substances that are combined to make a particular dish. **2** one of the parts or elements of something: *their romance had all the ingredients of a fairy tale.*

in·gress /'in,gres/ ▶ n. **1** the action of entering or coming in. **2** a place or means of access.

in·group ▶ n. an exclusive, typically small, group of people with a shared interest or identity: *an in-group of scholars involved in sociological debates.*

in·grown /'in,grōn/ (also **ingrowing** /'in,grōiNG/) ▶ adj. (of a toenail) growing inward into the flesh of the toe.

in·gui·nal /'iNGgwənəl/ ▶ adj. relating to the groin.

in·hab·it /in'habit/ ▶ v. (**inhabits, inhabiting, inhabited**) live in or occupy a place. ■ **in·hab·it·a·ble** adj.

in·hab·it·ant /in'habitnt/ ▶ n. a person or animal that lives in or occupies a place.

in·hal·ant /in'hālənt/ ▶ n. a medicine that is inhaled.

in·hale /in'hāl/ ▶ v. breathe in air, gas, smoke, etc. ■ **in·ha·la·tion** /,inhə'lāsнən/ n.

in·hal·er /in'hālər/ ▶ n. a portable device used for inhaling a medicine.

in·here /in'hi(ə)r/ ▶ v. (**inhere in/within**) formal be an essential or permanent part of something.

in·her·ent /in'hi(ə)rənt, -'her–/ ▶ adj. existing in someone or something as a permanent or essential part or quality: *the risks inherent in our business.* ■ **in·her·ent·ly** adv.

in·her·it /in'herit/ ▶ v. (**inherits, inheriting, inherited**) **1** receive money, property, or a title as an heir at the death of the previous holder. **2** have a quality or characteristic that one's parents or ancestors also possessed: *she inherited her mother's strong-willed nature.* **3** receive or be left with a situation, object, etc., from a predecessor or former owner. ■ **in·her·it·a·ble** adj. **in·her·i·tor** n.

in·her·it·ance /in'heritəns/ ▶ n. **1** money, property, or a title received on the death of the previous owner. **2** the action of inheriting something.

in·her·it·ance tax ▶ n. tax levied on property and money acquired by inheritance.

in·hib·it /in'hibit/ ▶ v. (**inhibits, inhibiting, inhibited**) **1** hinder or restrict an action or process: *cold inhibits plant growth.* **2** make someone unable to act in a relaxed and natural way. ■ **in·hib·it·ed** adj.

in·hi·bi·tion /,in(h)i'bisнən/ ▶ n. **1** a feeling that makes someone unable to act in a relaxed and natural way. **2** the action of inhibiting something.

in·hib·i·tor /in'hibitər/ ▶ n. a substance that slows down or prevents a particular chemical reaction or other process. ■ **in·hib·i·to·ry** adj.

in·hos·pi·ta·ble /,inhä'spitəbəl, in'häs–/ ▶ adj. **1** (of an environment) harsh and difficult to live in. **2** unwelcoming.

in·house ▶ adj. & adv. within an organization.

in·hu·man /in'(h)yoōmən/ ▶ adj. **1** lacking good human qualities; cruel or brutal. **2** not human in nature or character. ■ **in·hu·man·ly** adv.

in·hu·mane /,in(h)yoō'mān/ ▶ adj. showing no compassion for the misery or suffering of other people; cruel. ■ **in·hu·mane·ly** adv.

in·hu·man·i·ty /,in(h)yoō'manitē/ ▶ n. (pl. **inhumanities**) cruel or brutal behavior.

in·im·i·cal /i'nimikəl/ ▶ adj. harmful or unfavorable: *the policy was inimical to America's real interests.* ■ **in·im·i·cal·ly** adv.

in·im·i·ta·ble /i'nimitəbəl/ ▶ adj. impossible to imitate; unique. ■ **in·im·i·ta·bly** adv.

in·iq·ui·ty /i'nikwitē/ ▶ n. (pl. **iniquities**) highly unfair or immoral behavior. ■ **in·iq·ui·tous** adj.

in·i·tial /i'nisнəl/ ▶ adj. existing or occurring at the beginning: *our initial impression was favorable.* ▶ n. the first letter of a name or word. ▶ v. (**initials, initialing, initialed**) mark a document with one's initials as a sign of approval or authorization. ■ **in·i·tial·ly** adv.

in·i·tial·ism /i'nisнə,lizəm/ ▶ n. an abbreviation consisting of initial letters pronounced separately (e.g., *CPU*).

in·i·tial·ize /i'nisнə,līz/ ▶ v. Computing **1** (often **be initialized to**) set to the value or put in the condition appropriate to the start of an operation: *the counter is initialized to one.* **2** format (a computer disk). ■ **in·i·tial·i·za·tion** /i͟ˌnisHəli'zāsHən/ n.

in·i·ti·ate ▶ v. /i'nisHē͟ˌāt/ **1** cause a process or action to begin. **2** admit someone into a society or group with a formal ceremony or ritual. **3** (**initiate someone into**) introduce someone to a new activity or skill: *they were initiated into the mysteries of mathematics.* ▶ n. /i'nisHēit/ a person who has been initiated into a society, group, or new activity. ■ **in·i·ti·a·tion** /i͟ˌnisHē'āsHən/ n. **in·i·ti·a·tor** /i'nisHē͟ˌātər/ n. **in·i·ti·a·to·ry** /-əˌtôrē/ adj.

in·i·ti·a·tive /i'nisH(ē)ətiv/ ▶ n. **1** the ability to act independently and with a fresh approach. **2** the power or opportunity to act before others do: *we have lost the initiative.* **3** a new development or fresh approach to a problem: *a new initiative against car theft.*
– PHRASES **on one's own initiative** without being prompted by other people. **take** (or **seize**) **the initiative** be the first to take action in a particular situation: *antiglobalization groups have seized the initiative in the dispute.*

in·ject /in'jekt/ ▶ v. **1** introduce a drug or other substance into the body with a syringe: *the doctor injected a painkilling drug.* **2** administer a drug or medicine to a person or animal with a syringe: *he injected himself with adrenaline.* **3** introduce something under pressure into a passage, cavity, or solid material. **4** introduce a new or different element into something: *she tried to inject scorn into her tone.* ■ **in·ject·a·ble** adj. & n. **in·jec·tor** n.

in·jec·tion /in'jeksHən/ ▶ n. **1** an act of giving a person or animal a drug using a syringe. **2** a substance that is injected. **3** a large sum of additional money used to help a situation, business, etc.

in·joke ▶ n. a joke that is shared exclusively by a small group.

in·ju·di·cious /ˌinjōō'disHəs/ ▶ adj. showing poor judgment; unwise. ■ **in·ju·di·cious·ly** adv.

in·junc·tion /in'jəNG(k)sHən/ ▶ n. **1** an order made by a court of law stating that a person must or must not do something. **2** an authoritative warning. ■ **in·junc·tive** /-'jəNG(k)tiv/ adj.

in·jure /'injər/ ▶ v. **1** do physical harm to someone or something. **2** harm or damage: *a company's reputation could be injured by a libel suit.*

in·jured /'injərd/ ▶ adj. **1** physically harmed. **2** offended or upset: *his injured pride.*

in·ju·ri·ous /in'jŏŏrēəs/ ▶ adj. **1** causing or likely to cause harm or damage. **2** (of language) libelous.

in·ju·ry /'injərē/ ▶ n. (pl. **injuries**) **1** an instance of being physically harmed. **2** the fact of being injured; harm or damage.

in·jus·tice /in'jəstis/ ▶ n. **1** lack of justice or fairness. **2** an unjust act or occurrence.

ink /iNGk/ ▶ n. **1** a colored fluid used for writing, drawing, or printing. **2** a black liquid squirted by a cuttlefish, octopus, or squid to confuse a predator. ▶ v. **1** write or mark words or a design with ink. **2** cover metal type or a stamp with ink before printing.

ink·jet print·er /'iNGkˌjet/ ▶ n. a printer in which the characters are formed by minute jets of ink.

ink·ling /'iNGkliNG/ ▶ n. a slight suspicion; a hint.

ink·well /'iNGkˌwel/ ▶ n. historical a container for ink, usually fitted into a hole in a desk.

ink·y /'iNGkē/ ▶ adj. (**inkier, inkiest**) **1** as dark as ink. **2** stained with ink.

in·laid /'inˌlād/ ▶ past and past participle of INLAY.

in·land /'inˌland, -lənd/ ▶ adj. & adv. **1** in or into the interior of a country. **2** (as adj.) chiefly Brit. carried on within a country; domestic: *inland trade.* ▶ n. the interior of a country or region. ■ **in·land·er** n.

in·law ▶ n. a relative by marriage. ▶ comb.form related by marriage: *father-in-law.*

in·lay /ˌin'lā/ ▶ v. (past and past part. **inlaid**) decorate an object by embedding pieces of a different material in its surface. ▶ n. /'inˌlā/ **1** inlaid decoration. **2** a material or substance used for inlaying. **3** a filling shaped to fit a cavity in a tooth.

in·let /'inˌlet, -lit/ ▶ n. **1** a small arm of the sea, a lake, or a river. **2** a place or means of entry: *an air inlet.* **3** (in tailoring and dressmaking) an inserted piece of material.

inline (also **in-line**) ▶ adj. **1** having parts arranged in a line. **2** forming an integral part of a continuous sequence of operations or machines.

inline skate (also **in-line skate**) ▶ n. a roller skate in which the wheels are fixed in a single line along the sole of the boot. ■ **in·line skat·er** n. **in·line skat·ing** n.

in lo·co pa·ren·tis /in ˌlōkō pə'rentis/ ▶ adv. & adj. (of a teacher or other adult) in the place of a parent; as a guardian.

in·mate /'inˌmāt/ ▶ n. a person living in an institution such as a prison or hospital.

in me·mo·ri·am /ˌin mə'môrēəm/ ▶ prep. in memory of a dead person.

in·most /'inˌmōst/ ▶ adj. closest to the center; innermost.

inn /in/ ▶ n. an establishment that provides food, drink, and accommodations, especially for travelers.

in·nards /'inərdz/ ▶ pl.n. informal **1** internal organs; entrails. **2** the internal workings of a device or machine.

in·nate /i'nāt/ ▶ adj. inborn; natural. ■ **in·nate·ly** adv. **in·nate·ness** n.

in·ner /'inər/ ▶ adj. **1** situated inside; close to the center. **2** mental or spiritual: *inner strength.* **3** private; not expressed. ▶ n. an inner part.

in·ner cit·y ▶ n. an area in or near the center of a city, especially when associated with social and economic problems.

in·ner ear ▶ n. the part of the ear embedded in the temporal bone, consisting of the semicircular canals and the cochlea.

in·ner·most /'inərˌmōst/ ▶ adj. **1** furthest in; closest to the center. **2** (of thoughts) most private and deeply felt.

in·ner tube ▶ n. a separate inflatable tube inside a tire.

in·ning /'iniNG/ ▶ n. Baseball each division of a game during which both sides have a turn at batting.

in·nings /'iniNGz/ ▶ n. (pl. same) (treated as sing.) Cricket each of the divisions of a game during which one side has a turn at batting.

inn·keep·er /'inˌkēpər/ ▶ n. chiefly old use a person who runs an inn.

in·no·cent /'inəsənt/ ▶ adj. **1** not guilty of a crime or offense. **2** having had little experience of life, especially of sexual matters. **3** not directly involved in an event yet suffering its consequences: *an innocent bystander.* **4** not intended to cause offense: *an innocent remark.* **5** (**innocent of**) without experience or knowledge of something: *a man innocent of war's cruelties.* ▶ n. an innocent person. ■ **in·no·cence** n. **in·no·cent·ly** adv.

in·noc·u·ous /i'näkyōəs/ ▶ adj. not harmful or offensive. ■ **in·noc·u·ous·ly** adv.

in·no·vate /'inə,vāt/ ▶ v. introduce new methods, ideas, or products. ■ **in·no·va·tor** n. **in·no·va·to·ry** /-və,tôrē/ adj.

in·no·va·tion /,inə'vāsHən/ ▶ n. **1** the action of introducing new methods, ideas, or products. **2** a new method, idea, or product.

in·no·va·tive /'inə,vātiv/ ▶ adj. **1** featuring new ideas or methods; advanced and original: *innovative designs.* **2** (of a person) original and creative in their thinking.

in·nu·en·do /,inyōō'endō/ ▶ n. (pl. **innuendoes** or **innuendos**) a remark that makes an indirect reference to something, typically something rude or unpleasant.

in·nu·mer·a·ble /i'n(y)ōōmərəbəl/ ▶ adj. too many to be counted.

in·nu·mer·ate /i'n(y)ōōmərit/ ▶ adj. without a basic knowledge of mathematics and arithmetic. ■ **in·nu·mer·a·cy** /-rəsē/ n.

in·oc·u·late /i'näkyə,lāt/ ▶ v. **1** another term for **VACCINATE**. **2** introduce cells or microorganisms into a substance in which they can be grown. ■ **in·oc·u·la·tion** /i,näkyə'lāsHən/ n. **in·oc·u·la·tor** n.

in·of·fen·sive /,inə'fensiv/ ▶ adj. not objectionable or harmful. ■ **in·of·fen·sive·ly** adv. **in·of·fen·sive·ness** n.

in·op·er·a·ble /in'äp(ə)rəbəl/ ▶ adj. **1** not able to be safely treated or removed by a surgical operation: *an inoperable brain tumor.* **2** not able to be used. **3** impractical; unworkable.

in·op·er·a·tive /in'äp(ə)rətiv/ ▶ adj. not working or taking effect.

in·op·por·tune /,in,äpər't(y)ōōn/ ▶ adj. happening at an inconvenient time.

in·or·di·nate /i'nôrdn-it/ ▶ adj. unusually large; excessive. ■ **in·or·di·nate·ly** adv.

in·or·gan·ic /,inôr'ganik/ ▶ adj. **1** not consisting of or coming from living matter. **2** Chemistry relating or referring to compounds that do not contain carbon. ■ **in·or·gan·i·cal·ly** adv.

in·pa·tient /'in,pāsHənt/ ▶ n. a patient who stays in a hospital while receiving treatment.

in·put /'in,pŏŏt/ ▶ n. **1** what is put or taken in or operated on by any process or system. **2** a person's contribution: *I'd value your input.* **3** energy supplied to a device or system; an electrical signal. **4** a place or device from which electricity, data, etc., enters a system. ▶ v. (**inputs, inputting**; past and past part. **input** or **inputted**) put data into a computer. ■ **in·put·ter** n.

in·quest /'in,kwest, 'iNG-/ ▶ n. **1** a judicial inquiry to find out the facts relating to a particular incident. **2** an inquiry by a coroner's court into the cause of a death.

in·quire /in'kwīr/ (also chiefly Brit. **enquire**) ▶ v. **1** ask someone for information. **2** (**inquire after**) ask about someone's health or situation. **3** (**inquire into**) investigate something. ■ **in·quir·er** n.

in·quir·ing /in'kwīriNG/ ▶ adj. **1** interested in learning new things: *an open, inquiring mind.*

2 (of a look) expressing a wish for information. ■ **in·quir·ing·ly** adv.

in·quir·y /in'kwī(ə)rē, 'in,kwī(ə)rē, 'inkwərē/ ▶ n. (pl. **inquiries**) **1** an act of asking for information. **2** an official investigation.

in·qui·si·tion /,inkwi'zisHən, ,iNG-/ ▶ n. **1** a period of long and intensive questioning or investigation. **2** the verdict of an official inquiry.

in·quis·i·tive /in'kwizitiv, iNG-/ ▶ adj. **1** eager to learn things. **2** too curious about other people's affairs; prying. ■ **in·quis·i·tive·ly** adv. **in·quis·i·tive·ness** n.

in·quis·i·tor /in'kwizitər/ ▶ n. a person conducting a long, intensive, or relentless period of questioning or investigation. ■ **in·quis·i·to·ri·al** /in,kwizi'tôrēəl/ adj.

in re ▶ prep. in the legal case of; with regard to: *in re Mancet's Estate.*

in·road /'in,rōd/ ▶ n. (usu. in phrase **make inroads in/into**) a gradual entry into or effect on a place or situation: *the firm is beginning to make inroads into the US market.*

in·rush /'in,rəsH/ ▶ n. a sudden inward rush or flow. ■ **in·rush·ing** adj. & n.

INS ▶ abbr. Immigration and Naturalization Service, a former federal agency that was absorbed into Immigration and Customs Enforcement.

in·sa·lu·bri·ous /,insə'lōōbrēəs/ ▶ adj. not clean or well kept; seedy or squalid.

in·sane /in'sān/ ▶ adj. **1** seriously mentally ill. **2** extremely foolish; irrational. ■ **in·sane·ly** adv. **in·san·i·ty** /in'sanitē/ n. (pl. **insanities**).

in·sa·tia·ble /in'sāsHəbəl/ ▶ adj. impossible to satisfy. ■ **in·sa·tia·bil·i·ty** /-,sāsHə'bilitē/ n. **in·sa·tia·bly** adv.

in·scribe /in'skrīb/ ▶ v. **1** write or carve words or symbols on a surface. **2** write a dedication to someone in a book. **3** Geometry draw a figure within another so that their boundaries touch but do not intersect.

in·scrip·tion /in'skripsHən/ ▶ n. **1** words or symbols inscribed on a monument, in a book, etc. **2** the action of inscribing something. ■ **in·scrip·tion·al** adj.

in·scru·ta·ble /in'skrōōtəbəl/ ▶ adj. impossible to understand or interpret. ■ **in·scru·ta·bil·i·ty** /-,skrōōtə'bilitē/ n. **in·scru·ta·bly** adv.

in·seam /'in,sēm/ ▶ n. the seam in a pair of pants from the crotch to the bottom of the leg, or the length of this.

in·sect /'in,sekt/ ▶ n. a small invertebrate animal with a body divided into three segments (head, thorax, and abdomen), six legs, two antennae, and usually one or two pairs of wings.

in·sec·ti·cide /in'sekti,sīd/ ▶ n. a substance used for killing insects. ■ **in·sec·ti·cid·al** /-,sekti'sīdl/ adj.

in·sec·tile /in'sektl, -,tīl/ ▶ adj. resembling an insect.

in·sec·ti·vore /in'sektə,vôr/ ▶ n. **1** an animal that feeds on insects and other invertebrates. **2** Zoology a mammal of an order that includes the shrews, moles, and hedgehogs. ■ **in·sec·tiv·o·rous** /,in,sek'tivərəs/ adj.

in·se·cure /,insi'kyŏŏr/ ▶ adj. **1** not confident or self-assured. **2** not firm or firmly fixed. **3** (of a place) easily broken into; not protected. ■ **in·se·cure·ly** adv. **in·se·cu·ri·ty** n. (pl. **insecurities**).

in·sem·i·nate /in'semə,nāt/ ▶ v. introduce semen into the vagina of a woman or a female animal. ■ **in·sem·i·na·tion** /-,semə'nāsʜən/ n. ■ **in·sem·i·na·tor** n.

in·sen·sate /in'sen,sāt, -sit/ ▶ adj. **1** lacking physical sensation. **2** lacking sympathy for other people; unfeeling. **3** completely lacking sense or reason.

in·sen·si·ble /in'sensəbəl/ ▶ adj. **1** unconscious. **2** numb; without feeling. **3** (**insensible of/to**) unaware of or indifferent to something. **4** too small or gradual to be noticed. ■ **in·sen·si·bly** adv. **in·sen·si·bil·i·ty** /in,sensə'bilitē/ n.

in·sen·si·tive /in'sensitiv/ ▶ adj. **1** showing or having no concern for the feelings of other people. **2** not able to feel something physically: *she was remarkably insensitive to pain.* **3** not aware of or able to respond to something: *politicians had been insensitive to local issues.* ■ **in·sen·si·tive·ly** adv. **in·sen·si·tiv·i·ty** /-,sensi'tivitē/ n.

in·sen·ti·ent /in'sensʜ(ē)ənt/ ▶ adj. incapable of feeling; inanimate. ■ **in·sen·ti·ence** n.

in·sep·a·ra·ble /in'sep(ə)rəbəl/ ▶ adj. **1** unable to be separated or treated separately. **2** very friendly and close. ■ **in·sep·a·ra·bil·i·ty** /-,sep(ə)rə'bilitē/ n. **in·sep·a·ra·bly** adv.

in·sert ▶ v. /in'sərt/ **1** place or fit something into something else: *she inserted her key into the lock.* **2** include text in a piece of writing. ▶ n. /'in,sərt/ **1** a loose page or section in a magazine. **2** an ornamental section of cloth inserted into a garment. **3** a shot inserted in a film or video. ■ **in·sert·a·ble** adj. **in·sert·er** n.

in·ser·tion /in'sərsʜən/ ▶ n. **1** the action of inserting something. **2** a change or new item inserted in a piece of writing. **3** each appearance of an advertisement in a newspaper or magazine.

in·serv·ice ▶ adj. (of training) intended to take place during the course of employment.

in·set ▶ n. /'in,set/ **1** a thing inserted; an insert. **2** a small picture or map inserted within the border of a larger one. ▶ v. /in'set/ (**insets**, **insetting**; past and past part. **inset** or **insetted**) **1** put something in as an inset. **2** decorate something with an inset: *tables inset with ceramic tiles.*

in·shore /'in'sʜôr/ ▶ adj. **1** at sea but close to the shore. **2** operating at sea but near the coast. ▶ adv. toward or closer to the shore.

in·side ▶ n. /'in'sīd/ **1** the inner side, surface, or part of something. **2** (**insides**) informal the stomach and bowels. **3** the part of a road furthest from the center. **4** the side of a curve where the edge is shorter. ▶ adj. /,in'sīd, 'in,sīd/ **1** situated on or in, or coming from, the inside. **2** (in some sports) referring to positions nearer to the center of the field. **3** known or done by someone within an organization: *inside information.* ▶ prep. & adv. /,in'sīd/ **1** situated or moving within. **2** within a person's body or mind. **3** indoors. **4** informal in prison. **5** (in some sports) closer to the center of the field than. **6** in less than the period of time specified.
– PHRASES **inside of** informal **1** within: *something inside of me wanted to believe him.* **2** in less than (the period of time specified): *rerigging a ship for a voyage inside of a week.* **on the inside** informal in a position in which one can get private information.

in·side job ▶ n. informal a crime committed by or with the help of a person associated with the place where it occurred.

in·side out ▶ adv. with the inner surface turned outward.
– PHRASES **know something inside out** know something very thoroughly. **turn something inside out 1** turn the inner surface of something outward. **2** change something utterly: *it is not so easy to turn your whole life inside out.*

in·sid·er /in'sīdər/ ▶ n. a person within an organization, especially someone who has information unavailable to people outside it.

in·sid·er trad·ing ▶ n. the illegal practice of trading on the stock exchange with the benefit of confidential information.

in·side track ▶ n. **1** the inner, shorter track of a racetrack. **2** a position of advantage: *he always had the inside track for the starring role.*

in·sid·i·ous /in'sidēəs/ ▶ adj. proceeding or spreading gradually or without being noticed, but causing serious harm. ■ **in·sid·i·ous·ly** adv. **in·sid·i·ous·ness** n.

in·sight /'in,sīt/ ▶ n. **1** the ability to see and understand the truth about someone or something. **2** an understanding of the nature of someone or something: *a fascinating insight into the town's industrial heritage.* ■ **in·sight·ful** /in'sītfəl/ adj. **in·sight·ful·ly** adv. /in'sītfəlē/

in·sig·ni·a /in'signēə/ ▶ n. (pl. same or **insignias**) a badge or emblem of someone's rank, position, or membership in a group or organization.

in·sig·nif·i·cant /,insig'nifikənt/ ▶ adj. having little or no importance or value. ■ **in·sig·nif·i·cance** n. **in·sig·nif·i·cant·ly** adv.

in·sin·cere /,insin'si(ə)r/ ▶ adj. not expressing one's true feelings. ■ **in·sin·cere·ly** adv. **in·sin·cer·i·ty** /-'seritē/ n. (pl. **insincerities**)

in·sin·u·ate /in'sinyə,wāt/ ▶ v. **1** suggest or hint at something bad in an indirect and unpleasant way. **2** (**insinuate oneself into**) maneuver oneself gradually into a favorable position: *he insinuated himself into the president's confidence.* ■ **in·sin·u·at·ing** adj.

in·sin·u·a·tion /in,sinyo͞o'āsʜən/ ▶ n. an unpleasant hint or suggestion.

in·sip·id /in'sipid/ ▶ adj. **1** lacking flavor. **2** not interesting or exciting. ■ **in·si·pid·i·ty** /,insə'piditē/ n. **in·sip·id·ly** adv.

in·sist /in'sist/ ▶ v. **1** demand or state something forcefully, without accepting refusal. **2** (**insist on**) persist in doing something.

in·sist·ent /in'sistənt/ ▶ adj. **1** demanding something and not allowing refusal: *she was very insistent that I call her.* **2** repeated and demanding attention. ■ **in·sist·ence** n. **in·sis·tent·ly** adv.

in si·tu /,in 'sīto͞o, 'sē-/ ▶ adv. & adj. in the original or appropriate position.

in·so·bri·e·ty /,insə'brī-itē/ ▶ n. drunkenness.

in·so·far /,insō'fär/ ▶ adv. (**insofar as**) to the extent that: *his philosophy spoke of personal problems only insofar as they illustrated general ones.*

in·sole /'in,sōl/ ▶ n. **1** a removable sole worn inside a shoe for warmth or to improve the fit. **2** the fixed inner sole of a boot or shoe.

in·so·lent /'insələnt/ ▶ adj. rude and disrespectful. ■ **in·so·lence** n. **in·so·lent·ly** adv.

in·sol·u·ble /in'sälyəbəl/ ▶ adj. **1** impossible to solve. **2** (of a substance) unable to be dissolved. ■ **in·sol·u·bil·i·ty** /-,sälyə'bilitē/ n.

in·sol·vent /in'sälvənt/ ▶ adj. not having enough money to pay debts owed. ■ **in·sol·ven·cy** n.

in·som·ni·a /in'sämnēə/ ▶ n. the condition of being unable to sleep. ■ **in·som·ni·ac** /-nē,ak/ n. & adj.

in·so·much /,insō'məcH/ ▶ adv. (**insomuch that/as**) to the extent that.

in·sou·ci·ant /in'sōōsēənt, ,ANSōō'syän/ ▶ adj. casually unconcerned. ■ **in·sou·ci·ance** n. **in·sou·ci·ant·ly** /in'sōōsēəntlē/ adv.

in·spect /in'spekt/ ▶ v. 1 look at someone or something closely. 2 examine someone or something to ensure that they reach an official standard. ■ **in·spec·tion** n.

in·spec·tor /in'spektər/ ▶ n. 1 an official who ensures that regulations are obeyed. 2 a police officer ranking below a superintendent or police chief. ■ **in·spec·to·rate** n. **in·spec·to·ri·al** /,inspek'tōrēəl/ adj. **in·spec·tor·ship** n.

in·spi·ra·tion /,inspə'rāsHən/ ▶ n. 1 the process of being filled with a feeling or with the urge to do something: *the Rocky Mountains have provided inspiration for many artists.* 2 a person or thing that inspires other people. 3 a sudden clever idea. 4 the process of breathing in. ■ **in·spi·ra·tion·al** adj.

in·spire /in'spīr/ ▶ v. 1 give someone the desire, enthusiasm, or confidence to do something. 2 create a feeling in a person. 3 give rise to: *the film was successful enough to inspire a sequel.* 4 breathe in air; inhale. ■ **in·spir·a·to·ry** /in'spīrə,tôrē/ adj. **in·spir·er** n. **in·spir·ing** adj.

in·spired /in'spīrd/ ▶ adj. 1 displaying creativity or excellence. 2 (of air or another substance) that has been breathed in.

inst. ▶ abbr. institution; institute.

in·sta·bil·i·ty /,instə'bilitē/ ▶ n. (pl. **instabilities**) lack of stability.

in·stall /in'stôl/ ▶ v. 1 place or fix equipment in position ready for use. 2 establish someone in a new place or role. ■ **in·stall·er** n.

in·stal·la·tion /,instə'lāsHən/ ▶ n. 1 the action of installing or establishing someone or something. 2 a large piece of equipment installed for use. 3 a military or industrial establishment. 4 an art exhibit constructed within a gallery.

in·stall·ment /in'stôlmənt/ (Brit **instalment**) ▶ n. 1 a sum of money due as one of several payments made over a period of time. 2 one of several parts of something published or broadcast at intervals.

in·stance /'instəns/ ▶ n. 1 an example or single occurrence of something. 2 a particular case: *she hired a writer, in this instance a novelist.* ▶ v. give something as an example.
– PHRASES **for instance** as an example. **in the first instance** in the first stage of a series of actions.

in·stant /'instənt/ ▶ adj. 1 happening immediately. 2 (of food) processed to allow quick preparation. 3 dated urgent; pressing. ▶ n. 1 a precise moment of time. 2 a very short time. ■ **in·stant·ly** adv.

in·stan·ta·ne·ous /,instən'tānēəs/ ▶ adj. occurring or done immediately. ■ **in·stan·ta·ne·i·ty** /in,stantn'ē-itē/ n. **in·stan·ta·ne·ous·ly** adv.

in·stan·ti·ate /in'stancHē,āt/ ▶ v. represent something by a particular instance or example. ■ **in·stan·ti·a·tion** /-,stancHē'āsHən/ n.

in·stant mes·sag·ing ▶ n. the exchange of typed messages between computer users in real time via the Internet. ■ **in·stant mes·sage** n.

in·stant re·play ▶ n. an immediate playback of part of a television broadcast, typically one in slow motion showing an incident in a sports event.

in·stead /in'sted/ ▶ adv. 1 as an alternative or substitute. 2 (**instead of**) in place of.

in·step /'in,step/ ▶ n. the part of a person's foot between the ball and the ankle.

in·sti·gate /'insti,gāt/ ▶ v. 1 cause something to happen or begin: *they instigated legal proceedings.* 2 (**instigate someone to/to do**) encourage someone to do something, especially something bad. ■ **in·sti·ga·tion** /,insti'gāsHən/ n. **in·sti·ga·tor** n.

in·still /in'stil/ ▶ v. 1 gradually establish an idea or attitude in someone's mind: *her mother instilled in Harriet a love for cooking.* 2 put a liquid into something in drops. ■ **in·stil·la·tion** /,instə'lāsHən/ n.

in·stinct /'in,stiNGkt/ ▶ n. 1 an inborn tendency to behave in a certain way. 2 a natural ability or skill. 3 a feeling based on intuition rather than facts or reasoning. ■ **in·stinc·tu·al** /ins'tiNGkcHōōəl/ adj.

in·stinc·tive /in'stiNG(k)tiv/ ▶ adj. based on instinct rather than conscious thought or training. ■ **in·stinc·tive·ly** adv.

in·sti·tute /'insti,t(y)ōōt/ ▶ n. an organization for the promotion of science, education, culture, or a particular profession. ▶ v. 1 begin or establish a scheme, policy, legal proceedings, etc. 2 appoint someone to a position, especially as a cleric.

in·sti·tu·tion /,insti't(y)ōōsHən/ ▶ n. 1 an important organization such as a university, bank, hospital, or church. 2 an organization providing residential care for people with special needs. 3 an established law or custom. 4 informal a well-established and familiar person or thing. 5 the establishment or introduction of something.

in·sti·tu·tion·al /,insti't(y)ōōsHənl/ ▶ adj. 1 relating to an institution. 2 typical of an institution, especially in being impersonal or unimaginative. ■ **in·sti·tu·tion·al·ism** /-,izəm/ n. **in·sti·tu·tion·al·ly** adv.

in·sti·tu·tion·al·ize /,insti't(y)ōōsHənl,īz/ ▶ v. 1 establish as an accepted part of an organization or culture: *claims that racism is institutionalized in education.* 2 place someone in a residential institution. 3 (**be/become institutionalized**) be or become apathetic and dependent after a long period in a residential institution. ■ **in·sti·tu·tion·al·i·za·tion** /,insti,t(y)ōōsHənl-i'zāsHən/ n.

in·struct /in'strəkt/ ▶ v. 1 tell or order someone to do something. 2 teach someone a subject or skill. 3 inform someone of a fact or situation.

in·struc·tion /in'strəksHən/ ▶ n. 1 an act of telling someone to do something; an order. 2 (**instructions**) detailed information about how something should be done. 3 teaching or education. 4 a code in a computer program that defines and carries out an operation. ■ **in·struc·tion·al** adj.

in·struc·tive /in'strəktiv/ ▶ adj. useful and informative. ■ **in·struc·tive·ly** adv.

in·struc·tor /in'strəktər/ ▶ n. 1 a teacher. 2 a college or university teacher ranking below assistant professor.

in·stru·ment /ˈinstrəmənt/ ▸ n. **1** a tool or implement, especially for precision work. **2** a measuring device, especially in a vehicle or aircraft. **3** (also **musical instrument**) a device for producing musical sounds. **4** a means of pursuing an aim: *her car is the instrument of her freedom.* **5** a person who is exploited by another. **6** a formal or legal document.

in·stru·men·tal /ˌinstrəˈmentl/ ▸ adj. **1** serving as a means of achieving something. **2** (of music) performed on instruments. **3** relating to an implement or measuring device. ▸ n. a piece of music performed by instruments, with no vocals. ■ **in·stru·men·tal·i·ty** /ˌinstrəmənˈtalitē, -men-/ n. **in·stru·men·tal·ly** adv.

in·stru·men·tal·ist /ˌinstrəˈmentl-ist/ ▸ n. a player of a musical instrument.

in·stru·men·ta·tion /ˌinstrəmənˈtāSHən, -men-/ ▸ n. **1** the instruments used in a piece of music. **2** the arrangement of a piece of music for particular instruments. **3** measuring instruments as a group.

in·stru·ment pan·el ▸ n. a surface in front of a driver's or pilot's seat where the vehicle's or aircraft's instruments are situated.

in·sub·or·di·nate /ˌinsəˈbôrdn-it/ ▸ adj. disobedient to orders or authority. ■ **in·sub·or·di·na·tion** /-ˌbôrdnˈāSHən/ n.

in·sub·stan·tial /ˌinsəbˈstanCHəl/ ▸ adj. lacking strength and solidity. ■ **in·sub·stan·ti·al·i·ty** /-ˌstanCHēˈalitē/ n. **in·sub·stan·tial·ly** adv.

in·suf·fer·a·ble /inˈsəf(ə)rəbəl/ ▸ adj. **1** too extreme to bear; intolerable. **2** unbearably arrogant or conceited. ■ **in·suf·fer·a·bly** adv.

in·suf·fi·cient /ˌinsəˈfiSHənt/ ▸ adj. not enough for a purpose. ■ **in·suf·fi·cien·cy** /ˌinsəˈfiSHənsē/ n. **in·suf·fi·cient·ly** adv.

in·su·lar /ˈins(y)ələr/ ▸ adj. **1** ignorant of or uninterested in cultures, ideas, or peoples outside one's own experience. **2** relating to an island. ■ **in·su·lar·i·ty** /ˌins(y)əˈlaritē/ n.

in·su·late /ˈins(y)əˌlāt/ ▸ v. **1** place material between one thing and another to prevent loss of heat or intrusion of sound. **2** cover something with nonconducting material to prevent the passage of electricity. **3** protect someone from something unpleasant. ■ **in·su·la·tor** n.

in·su·la·tion /ˌins(y)əˈlāSHən/ ▸ n. **1** material used to insulate something. **2** the action of insulating or state of being insulated: *his comparative insulation from the world.*

in·su·lin /ˈinsələn/ ▸ n. a hormone produced in the pancreas that regulates glucose levels in the blood, and the lack of which causes diabetes.

in·sult ▸ v. /inˈsəlt/ speak to or treat someone with disrespect or abuse. ▸ n. /ˈinˌsəlt/ **1** a disrespectful or abusive remark or action. **2** a thing so worthless as to be offensive: *the pay offer is an absolute insult.* ■ **in·sult·ing·ly** adv.

in·su·per·a·ble /inˈso͞op(ə)rəbəl/ ▸ adj. impossible to overcome. ■ **in·su·per·a·bly** adv.

in·sup·port·a·ble /ˌinsəˈpôrtəbəl/ ▸ adj. **1** unable to be supported or justified. **2** unable to be endured; intolerable. ■ **in·sup·port·a·bly** adv.

in·sur·ance /inˈSHo͝orəns/ ▸ n. **1** an arrangement by which a company or the government guarantees to provide compensation for loss, damage, illness, or death in return for payment of a specified premium. **2** money paid as compensation under an insurance policy. **3** a

thing providing protection against a possible event: *jackets hung on their chairs, insurance against the air conditioning.*

in·sur·ance pol·i·cy ▸ n. a contract of insurance.

in·sure /inˈSHo͝or/ ▸ v. **1** arrange for compensation in the event of damage to or loss of property, or a death, in exchange for regular payments to a company. **2** (**insure someone against**) protect someone against a possible event. **3** another term for ENSURE. ■ **in·sur·a·ble** adj.

in·sured /inˈSHo͝ord/ ▸ adj. covered by insurance: *an insured risk.* ▸ n. (**the insured**) (pl. same) a person or organization covered by insurance.

in·sur·er /inˈSHo͝orər/ ▸ n. a company that provides insurance.

in·sur·gent /inˈsərjənt/ ▸ n. a rebel or revolutionary. ▸ adj. relating to rebels. ■ **in·sur·gence** n. **in·sur·gen·cy** n. (pl. **insurgencies**)

in·sur·mount·a·ble /ˌinsərˈmountəbəl/ ▸ adj. too great to be overcome. ■ **in·sur·mount·a·bly** adv.

in·sur·rec·tion /ˌinsəˈrekSHən/ ▸ n. a violent uprising against authority. ■ **in·sur·rec·tion·ar·y** adj. **in·sur·rec·tion·ist** n. & adj.

in·sus·cep·ti·ble /ˌinsəˈseptəbəl/ ▸ adj. not likely to be affected by something. ■ **in·sus·cep·ti·bil·i·ty** /ˌinsəˌseptəˈbilitē/ n.

in·tact /inˈtakt/ ▸ adj. not damaged in any way. ■ **in·tact·ness** n.

in·tact fam·i·ly ▸ n. a nuclear family in which membership has remained constant, without divorce or other divisive factors.

in·ta·glio /inˈtalyō, -ˈtäl-/ ▸ n. (pl. **intaglios**) **1** an incised or engraved design. **2** a gem with an incised design.

in·take /ˈinˌtāk/ ▸ n. **1** an amount or quantity taken in. **2** an act of taking something in. **3** a place or structure through which something is taken in.

in·tan·gi·ble /inˈtanjəbəl/ ▸ adj. **1** unable to be touched; not physical: *the intangible gift of joy.* **2** vague and abstract. ▸ n. an abstract or intangible thing. ■ **in·tan·gi·bil·i·ty** /-ˌtanjəˈbilitē/ n. **in·tan·gi·bly** adv.

in·te·ger /ˈintijər/ ▸ n. a whole number.

in·te·gral ▸ adj. /ˈintigrəl, inˈteg-/ **1** necessary to make a whole complete; fundamental: *games are an integral part of the curriculum.* **2** included as part of a whole. **3** forming a whole; complete. **4** Mathematics relating to an integer or integers. ▸ n. /ˈintigrəl/ Mathematics a function of which a given function is the derivative, and which may express the area under the curve of a graph of the function. ■ **in·te·gral·ly** adv.

in·te·gral cal·cu·lus ▸ n. Mathematics the part of calculus concerned with the integrals of functions.

in·te·grate ▸ v. /ˈintiˌgrāt/ **1** combine or be combined to form a whole: *transport planning should be integrated with energy policy.* **2** make or become accepted as a member of a social group. **3** Mathematics find the integral of a function. ■ **in·te·gra·ble** /-grəbəl/ adj. **in·te·gra·tive** /-ˌgrātiv/ adj. **in·te·gra·tor** n.

in·te·grat·ed cir·cuit ▸ n. an electronic circuit on a small piece of semiconducting material, performing the same function as a larger circuit of separate components.

in·te·gra·tion /ˌinti'grāsHən/ ▸ n. **1** the action of combining things to form a whole. **2** the mixing of peoples or groups who were previously segregated. ■ **in·te·gra·tion·ist** n.

in·teg·ri·ty /in'tegritē/ ▸ n. **1** the quality of being honest and having strong moral principles. **2** the state of being whole or unified. **3** the quality of being sound in construction.

in·teg·u·ment /in'tegyəmənt/ ▸ n. a tough outer protective layer, especially of an animal or plant. ■ **in·teg·u·men·ta·ry** /-ˌtegyə'mentərē/ adj.

in·tel·lect /'intlˌekt/ ▸ n. **1** the faculty of using the mind to think logically and understand things. **2** an intelligent person.

in·tel·lec·tu·al /ˌintl'ekcHᴏᴏəl/ ▸ adj. **1** having a highly developed ability to think logically and understand things. **2** relating or appealing to the intellect. ▸ n. a person with a highly developed intellect. ■ **in·tel·lec·tu·al·ly** adv.

in·tel·lec·tu·al·ism /ˌintl'ekcHᴏᴏəˌlizəm/ ▸ n. the use of the intellect at the expense of the emotions. ■ **in·tel·lec·tu·al·ist** n.

in·tel·lec·tu·al·ize /ˌintl'ekcHᴏᴏəˌlīz/ ▸ v. **1** make something seem rational or logical. **2** talk or write in a logical or intellectual way.

in·tel·lec·tu·al prop·er·ty ▸ n. Law intangible property that is the result of creativity, e.g., patents or copyrights.

in·tel·li·gence /in'telijəns/ ▸ n. **1** the ability to gain and apply knowledge and skills. **2** the collection of secret information of military or political value. **3** secret information collected about an enemy or competitor.

in·tel·li·gence quo·tient ▸ n. a number representing a person's reasoning ability, compared to the statistical norm, 100 being average.

in·tel·li·gent /in'telijənt/ ▸ adj. **1** having intelligence, especially of a high level. **2** (of a device) able to vary its state or action in response to varying situations and past experience. **3** (of a computer terminal) having its own processing capability. ■ **in·tel·li·gent·ly** adv.

in·tel·li·gent de·sign ▸ n. a theory that life, or the universe, cannot have arisen by chance and was designed and created by some intelligent entity.

in·tel·li·gent·si·a /in,teli'jentsēə/ ▸ n. (treated as sing. or pl.) intellectuals or highly educated people as a class.

in·tel·li·gi·ble /in'telijəbəl/ ▸ adj. able to be understood. ■ **in·tel·li·gi·bil·i·ty** /-,telijə'bilitē/ n. **in·tel·li·gi·bly** adv.

in·tem·per·ate /in'temp(ə)rit/ ▸ adj. **1** lacking self-control. **2** characterized by excessive drinking of alcohol. ■ **in·tem·per·ance** n. **in·tem·per·ate·ly** adv.

in·tend /in'tend/ ▸ v. **1** have a course of action as one's aim or plan. **2** plan that something should be, do, or mean something: *the book was intended as a satire.* **3** (**intend for/to do**) design or plan something for a particular purpose. **4** (**be intended for**) be meant for the use of someone.

■ **in·tend·er** n.

in·tend·ed /in'tendid/ ▸ adj. planned or meant. ▸ n. (**one's intended**) informal one's fiancé(e).

in·tense /in'tens/ ▸ adj. **1** very great in force, degree, or strength: *the job demands intense concentration.* **2** very earnest or serious. ■ **in·tense·ly** adv. **in·tense·ness** n.

in·ten·si·fi·er /in'tensə,fīər/ ▸ n. **1** a thing that makes something more intense. **2** Grammar an adverb used to give force or emphasis (e.g., *really* in *my feet are really cold*).

in·ten·si·fy /in'tensə,fī/ ▸ v. (**intensifies, intensifying, intensified**) increase in degree, force, or strength: *the war has intensified.* ■ **in·ten·si·fi·ca·tion** /in'tensəfi'kāsHən/ n.

in·ten·si·ty /in'tensitē/ ▸ n. (pl. **intensities**) **1** the quality of being great in force, degree, or strength: *the pain grew in intensity.* **2** chiefly Physics the measurable amount of a property, such as force or brightness.

in·ten·sive /in'tensiv/ ▸ adj. **1** concentrated on a single subject or into a short time: *an intensive course in Arabic.* **2** (of agriculture) aiming to achieve maximum production within a limited area. **3** (in combination) concentrating on or making much use of something: *labor-intensive methods.* ■ **in·ten·sive·ly** adv. **in·ten·sive·ness** n.

in·ten·sive care ▸ n. special medical treatment given to a dangerously ill patient.

in·tent /in'tent/ ▸ n. something intended; a plan or intention. ▸ adj. **1** (**intent on**) determined to do something. **2** (**intent on**) concentrating hard on something. **3** showing earnest and eager attention. ■ **in·tent·ly** adv. **in·tent·ness** n.

– PHRASES **to** (or **for**) **all intents and purposes** in all important respects. **with intent** Law with the intention of committing a crime.

in·ten·tion /in'tencHən/ ▸ n. **1** an aim or plan. **2** (**one's intentions**) a man's plans in respect to marriage. ■ **in·ten·tioned** adj.

in·ten·tion·al /in'tencHənl/ ▸ adj. done on purpose; deliberate. ■ **in·ten·tion·al·i·ty** /in,tencHə'nalitē/ n. **in·ten·tion·al·ly** adv.

in·ter /in'tər/ ▸ v. (**inters, interring, interred**) place a corpse in a grave or tomb.

inter- ▸ prefix **1** between; among: *interbreed.* **2** so as to affect both; mutually: *interaction.*

in·ter·act /ˌintər'akt/ ▸ v. (of two people or things) act so as to affect each other. ■ **in·ter·ac·tion** n.

in·ter·ac·tive /ˌintər'aktiv/ ▸ adj. **1** influencing each other. **2** (of a computer or other electronic device) allowing a two-way flow of information between it and a user. ■ **in·ter·ac·tive·ly** adv. **in·ter·ac·tiv·i·ty** /-ak'tivitē/ n.

in·ter a·li·a /'intər 'ālēə, 'älēə/ ▸ adv. among other things.

in·ter·breed /ˌintər'brēd/ ▸ v. (past and past part. **interbred**) breed or cause to breed with an animal of a different race or species.

in·ter·ca·lar·y /in'tərkə,lerē, ˌintər'kalərē/ ▸ adj. **1** (of a day or a month) inserted in the calendar to harmonize it with the solar year, e.g., February 29 in leap years. **2** inserted between or among other things: *elaborate intercalary notes and footnotes.*

in·ter·cede /ˌintər'sēd/ ▸ v. intervene on behalf of someone.

in·ter·cel·lu·lar /ˌintər'selyələr/ ▸ adj. located or occurring between cells.

in·ter·cept ▸ v. /ˌintər'sept/ stop a person, vehicle,

or communication so as to prevent them from continuing to a destination. ▸ n. /ˈintərˌsept/ **1** an act of intercepting someone or something. **2** Mathematics the point at which a line cuts the axis of a graph. ■ **in·ter·cep·tion** /ˌintərˈsepsHən/ n. **in·ter·cep·tor** /ˌintərˈseptər/ n.

in·ter·ces·sion /ˌintərˈsesHən/ ▸ n. **1** the action of intervening on behalf of someone. **2** the saying of a prayer on behalf of another person. ■ **in·ter·ces·sor** n. **in·ter·ces·so·ry** adj.

in·ter·change ▸ v. /ˌintərˈCHānj/ **1** exchange things with each other. **2** put each of two things in the other's place. ▸ n. /ˈintərˌCHānj/ **1** the action of exchanging people or things. **2** an exchange of words. **3** a road junction on several levels so that traffic streams do not intersect.

in·ter·change·a·ble /ˌintərˈCHānjəbəl/ ▸ adj. **1** (of things) able to be interchanged. **2** very similar: *interchangeable disco divas.* ■ **in·ter·change·a·bil·i·ty** /ˌintərˌCHānjəˈbilitē/ n. **in·ter·change·a·bly** adv.

in·ter·cit·y /ˈintərˌsitē/ ▸ adj. existing or traveling between cities.

in·ter·com /ˈintərˌkäm/ ▸ n. an electrical device allowing one-way or two-way communication.

in·ter·com·mu·ni·cat·ing /ˌintərkəˈmyōōni ˌkātiNG/ ▸ adj. (of two rooms) having a shared connecting door.

in·ter·com·mu·ni·ca·tion /ˌintərkəˌmyōōniˈkā sHən/ ▸ n. the process of communicating between people or groups.

in·ter·con·nect /ˌintərkəˈnekt/ ▸ v. connect with each other. ■ **in·ter·con·nec·tion** n.

in·ter·con·ti·nen·tal /ˌintərˌkäntnˈentl/ ▸ adj. relating to or traveling between continents.

in·ter·cool·er /ˌintərˈkōōlər/ ▸ n. a device for cooling gas between successive compressions, especially in a supercharged engine. ■ **in·ter·cool** v.

in·ter·course /ˈintərˌkôrs/ ▸ n. **1** communication or dealings between people. **2** sexual intercourse.

in·ter·crop /ˌintərˈkräp/ ▸ v. (**intercrops, intercropped, intercropped**) (often as n. **intercropping** /ˈintərˌkräpiNG/) grow a crop among plants of a different kind.

in·ter·cut /ˌintərˈkət/ ▸ v. (**intercuts, intercutting, intercut**) alternate scenes with contrasting scenes in a movie.

in·ter·de·nom·i·na·tion·al /ˌintərdiˌnämə ˈnāsHənl/ ▸ adj. relating to more than one religious denomination.

in·ter·de·part·men·tal /ˌintərdiˌpärtˈmentl, -ˌdēpärt-/ ▸ adj. relating to more than one department.

in·ter·de·pend·ent /ˌintərdiˈpendənt/ ▸ adj. dependent on each other. ■ **in·ter·de·pend·ence** n. **in·ter·de·pend·en·cy** n.

in·ter·dict ▸ n. /ˈintərˌdikt/ **1** an authoritative order forbidding something. **2** (in the Roman Catholic Church) a sentence barring a person or place from ecclesiastical functions and privileges. ▸ v. /ˌintərˈdikt/ prohibit or forbid something. ■ **in·ter·dic·tion** /ˌintərˈdiksHən/ n.

in·ter·dis·ci·pli·nar·y /ˌintərˈdisəpliˌnerē/ ▸ adj. relating to more than one branch of knowledge.

in·ter·est /ˈint(ə)rist/ ▸ n. **1** the state of wanting to know about something or someone. **2** the quality of arousing curiosity or holding the attention: *a tale full of interest.* **3** a subject that

one enjoys doing or studying. **4** money paid for the use of money that is lent. **5** a person's advantage or benefit. **6** a share, right, or stake in property or a financial undertaking. **7** a group in politics or business having a common concern. ▸ v. **1** arouse someone's curiosity or attention. **2** (**interest someone in**) persuade someone to do or obtain something. **3** (as adj. **interested**) involved in something and so not impartial: *interested parties.* ■ **in·ter·est·ed·ly** adv.
– PHRASES **in the interests** (or **interest**) **of** **something** for the benefit of: *in the interests of security we are keeping the information confidential.* **of interest** interesting: *much of it is of interest to historians.*

in·ter·est·ing /ˈint(ə)ristiNG, ˈintəˌrestiNG/ ▸ adj. arousing curiosity or interest. ■ **in·ter·est·ing·ly** adv.

in·ter·face /ˈintərˌfās/ ▸ n. **1** a point where two things meet and interact. **2** a device or program enabling a user to communicate with a computer, or for connecting two items of hardware or software. **3** chiefly Physics a surface forming a boundary between two portions of matter or space. ▸ v. (**interface with**) **1** interact with another person, system, etc. **2** Computing connect with something by an interface.

in·ter·fac·ing /ˈintərˌfāsiNG/ ▸ n. an extra layer of material or an adhesive stiffener, applied to the facing of a garment to add support.

in·ter·faith /ˈintərˌfāTH/ ▸ adj. relating to or between different religions.

in·ter·fere /ˌintərˈfi(ə)r/ ▸ v. **1** (**interfere with**) prevent something from continuing or being carried out properly. **2** (**interfere with**) handle or adjust something without permission. **3** become involved in something without being asked or required to do so: *she tried not to interfere in her children's lives.* **4** Physics (of waves of the same wavelength) interact to produce interference. ■ **in·ter·fer·er** n. **in·ter·fer·ing** adj.

in·ter·fer·ence /ˌintərˈfi(ə)rəns/ ▸ n. **1** the action of interfering with someone or something. **2** disturbance to radio signals caused by unwanted signals from other sources. **3** Physics the combination of waves of the same wavelength from two or more sources, producing a new wave pattern. ■ **in·ter·fer·en·tial** /-fəˈrenCHəl/ adj.

in·ter·fer·on /ˌintərˈfi(ə)rˌän/ ▸ n. a protein released by animal cells that prevents a virus from reproducing.

in·ter·fuse /ˌintərˈfyōōz/ ▸ v. literary join or mix things together. ■ **in·ter·fu·sion** n.

in·ter·ga·lac·tic /ˌintərgəˈlaktik/ ▸ adj. relating to or situated between galaxies.

in·ter·gla·cial /ˌintərˈglāsHəl/ ▸ adj. Geology relating to a period of milder climate between two glacial periods.

in·ter·gov·ern·men·tal /ˌintərˌgəvər(n)ˈmentl/ ▸ adj. relating to or conducted between governments.

in·ter·im /ˈintərəm/ ▸ n. (**the interim**) the time between two events. ▸ adj. in or for the time between two events; provisional.

in·te·ri·or /inˈti(ə)rēər/ ▸ adj. **1** situated within or inside something; inner. **2** remote from the coast or frontier; inland. **3** relating to a country's internal affairs. **4** within the mind or soul: *an interior monologue.* ▸ n. **1** the interior part of a building, country, etc. **2** the internal affairs of a country. ■ **in·te·ri·or·ize** v. **in·te·ri·or·ly** adv.

in·te·ri·or dec·o·ra·tion ▸ n. the decoration of

the interior of a building or room, with regard for color combination and artistic effect.

in·te·ri·or de·sign ▶ n. the design, decoration, and furnishings of the interior of a room or building.

in·te·ri·or·i·ty /inˌti(ə)rēˈôritē, -ˈär-/ ▶ n. the quality of being interior or inward.

in·ter·ject /ˌintərˈjekt/ ▶ v. say something suddenly as an interruption.

in·ter·jec·tion /ˌintərˈjeksHən/ ▶ n. an exclamation or interruption.

in·ter·lace /ˌintərˈlās/ ▶ v. **1** cross or be crossed together; interweave. **2** (**interlace something with**) mingle or intersperse something with: *discussion interlaced with mathematics.*

in·ter·lard /ˌintərˈlärd/ ▶ v. (**interlard something with**) intersperse speech or writing with contrasting words and phrases.

in·ter·leave /ˌintərˈlēv/ ▶ v. **1** place something between the layers of something else. **2** insert blank leaves between the pages of a book.

in·ter·li·brar·y loan /ˌintərˈlībrerē/ ▶ n. a system in which one library borrows a book from another library for the use of an individual.

in·ter·line /ˌintərˈlīn/ ▶ v. put an extra lining in a garment or curtain.

in·ter·lin·e·ar /ˌintərˈlinēər/ ▶ adj. written between the lines of another piece of writing.

in·ter·link /ˌintərˈliNGk/ ▶ v. join or connect things together. ■ **in·ter·link·age** n.

in·ter·lock /ˌintərˈläk/ ▶ v. (of two or more things) engage with each other by overlapping or fitting together. ▶ n. **1** a device for connecting or coordinating the function of components. **2** (also **interlock fabric**) a fabric with closely interlocking stitches allowing it to stretch.

in·ter·loc·u·tor /ˌintərˈläkyətər/ ▶ n. formal a person who takes part in a conversation. ■ **in·ter·lo·cu·tion** /-ləˈkyōōsHən/ n.

in·ter·loc·u·to·ry /ˌintərˈläkyəˌtôrē/ ▶ adj. Law (of a decree or judgment) given provisionally during the course of a legal action.

in·ter·lop·er /ˈintərˌlōpər, ˌintərˈlōpər/ ▶ n. a person who is present in a place or situation where they are not wanted or do not belong.

in·ter·lude /ˈintərˌlōōd/ ▶ n. **1** a period of time or activity that contrasts with what goes before or after it: *a romantic interlude.* **2** a pause between the acts of a play. **3** a piece of music played between other pieces or between the verses of a hymn.

in·ter·mar·ry /ˌintərˈmarē/ ▶ v. (**intermarries, intermarrying, intermarried**) (of people of different races, castes, or religions) marry each other. ■ **in·ter·mar·riage** n.

in·ter·me·di·ar·y /ˌintərˈmēdēˌerē/ ▶ n. (pl. **intermediaries**) a person who acts as a link between people in order to try to bring about an agreement. ▶ adj. intermediate.

in·ter·me·di·ate /ˌintərˈmēdē-it/ ▶ adj. **1** coming between two things in time, place, or character: *an intermediate stage of development.* **2** having a level of knowledge or skill between basic and advanced. ▶ n. a thing coming between other things in time, place, or character. ■ **in·ter·me·di·a·cy** n. **in·ter·me·di·a·tion** /-ˌmēdēˈāsHən/ n.

in·ter·ment /inˈtərmənt/ ▶ n. the burial of a corpse in a grave or tomb.

in·ter·mez·zo /ˌintərˈmetsō/ ▶ n. (pl. **intermezzi** /-ˈmetsē/ or **intermezzos**) **1** a short connecting instrumental movement in an opera or other musical work. **2** a short piece for a solo instrument. **3** a light dramatic or other performance between the acts of a play.

in·ter·mi·na·ble /inˈtərmənəbəl/ ▶ adj. endless or seemingly endless. ■ **in·ter·mi·na·bly** adv.

in·ter·min·gle /ˌintərˈmiNGgəl/ ▶ v. mix or mingle together.

in·ter·mis·sion /ˌintərˈmisHən/ ▶ n. **1** a pause or break. **2** an interval between parts of a play or movie.

in·ter·mit·tent /ˌintərˈmitnt/ ▶ adj. occurring at irregular intervals: *intermittent rain.* ■ **in·ter·mit·ten·cy** n. **in·ter·mit·tent·ly** adv.

in·ter·mix /ˌintərˈmiks/ ▶ v. mix together. ■ **in·ter·mix·a·ble** adj. **in·ter·mix·ture** n.

in·ter·mod·al /ˌintərˈmodl/ ▶ adj. involving two or more different modes of transport.

in·ter·mo·lec·u·lar /ˌintərməˈlekyələr/ ▶ adj. existing or occurring between molecules.

in·tern ▶ v. /inˈtərn/ confine someone as a prisoner. ▶ n. /ˈinˌtərn/ **1** a recent medical graduate receiving supervised training in a hospital and acting as an assistant physician or surgeon. **2** a student or trainee who does a job to gain work experience. ■ **in·tern·ment** /inˈtərnmənt/ n. **in·tern·ship** /-ˌsHip/ n.

in·ter·nal /inˈtərnl/ ▶ adj. **1** relating to or situated on the inside. **2** inside the body. **3** relating to affairs and activities within a country. **4** existing or used within an organization. **5** in one's mind or soul. ▶ n. (**internals**) inner parts or features. ■ **in·ter·nal·i·ty** /ˌintərˈnalitē/ n. **in·ter·nal·ly** adv.

in·ter·nal com·bus·tion en·gine ▶ n. an engine in which power is generated by the expansion of hot gases from the burning of fuel with air inside the engine.

in·ter·nal ex·ile ▶ n. banishment from a part of one's own country as a punishment.

in·ter·nal·ize /inˈtərnlˌīz/ ▶ v. unconsciously make an attitude or belief part of one's behavior. ■ **in·ter·nal·i·za·tion** /inˌtərnl-iˈzāsHən/ n.

in·ter·nal mar·ket ▶ n. **1** another term for SINGLE MARKET. **2** a system within an organization whereby departments buy each other's services.

in·ter·nal med·i·cine ▶ n. a branch of medicine specializing in the diagnosis and nonsurgical treatment of diseases.

in·ter·na·tion·al /ˌintərˈnasHənl/ ▶ adj. **1** existing or occurring between nations. **2** agreed on or used by all or many nations. ■ **in·ter·na·tion·al·i·ty** /-ˌnasHəˈnalitē/ n. **in·ter·na·tion·al·ly** adv.

In·ter·na·tion·al Date Line ▶ n. an imaginary North–South line through the Pacific Ocean, chiefly along the meridian furthest from Greenwich, to the east of which the date is a day earlier than it is to the west.

in·ter·na·tion·al·ism /ˌintərˈnasHənlˌizəm/ ▶ n. the belief in or promotion of cooperation and understanding between nations. ■ **in·ter·na·tion·al·ist** n.

in·ter·na·tion·al·ize /ˌintərˈnasHənlˌīz/ ▶ v. make something international in scope or nature. ■ **in·ter·na·tion·al·i·za·tion** /-ˌnasHənl-iˈzāsHən/ n.

in·ter·na·tion·al law ▶ n. a set of rules established by custom or treaty and recognized by nations as binding in their relations with one another.

international style ▶ n. a style of 20th-century architecture characterized by the use of steel and reinforced concrete, simple lines, and strict geometric forms.

in·ter·ne·cine /,intər'nesēn, -'nēsēn, -sin/ ▶ adj. **1** destructive to both sides in a conflict. **2** relating to conflict within a group: *internecine rivalries.*

in·tern·ee /,intər'nē/ ▶ n. a prisoner.

In·ter·net /'intər,net/ ▶ n. a global computer network providing a variety of information and communication facilities.

in·ter·op·er·a·ble /,intər'äp(ə)rəbəl/ ▶ adj. (of computer systems or software) able to exchange and make use of information. ■ **in·ter·op·er·a·bil·i·ty** /-,äp(ə)rə'bilitē/ n.

in·ter·pen·e·trate /,intər'peni,trāt/ ▶ v. (of different things) mix or merge together. ■ **in·ter·pen·e·tra·tion** /-,peni'trāsHən/ n.

in·ter·per·son·al /,intər'pərsənəl/ ▶ adj. relating to relationships between people. ■ **in·ter·per·son·al·ly** adv.

in·ter·phase /'intər,fāz/ ▶ n. Biology the resting phase between successive mitotic divisions of a cell, or between the first and second divisions of meiosis.

in·ter·plan·e·tar·y /,intər'plani,terē/ ▶ adj. situated or traveling between planets.

in·ter·play /'intər,plā/ ▶ n. the way in which things interact: *the painting has a dramatic interplay of light and shade.*

In·ter·pol /'intər,pōl/ ▶ n. an international organization that coordinates investigations made by the police forces of member countries into international crimes.

in·ter·po·late /in'tərpə,lāt/ ▶ v. **1** insert something different or additional into something else. **2** add a remark to a conversation. **3** Mathematics insert an intermediate term into a series by estimating it from surrounding known values. ■ **in·ter·po·la·tion** /-,tərpə'lāsHən/ n. **in·ter·po·la·tor** n.

in·ter·pose /,intər'pōz/ ▶ v. **1** insert between one thing and another: *she interposed herself between the newcomers.* **2** intervene between parties. **3** say something as an interruption. ■ **in·ter·po·si·tion** /,intərpə'zisHən/ n.

in·ter·pret /in'tərprit/ ▶ v. (**interprets, interpreting, interpreted**) **1** explain the meaning of something. **2** translate aloud the words of a person speaking a different language. **3** understand as having a particular meaning: *he interpreted her silence as indifference.* **4** perform a creative work in a way that conveys one's understanding of the creator's ideas. ■ **in·ter·pret·a·ble** adj. **in·ter·pre·ta·tive** (also **interpretive**) adj.

in·ter·pre·ta·tion /in,tərpri'tāsHən/ ▶ n. **1** the action of explaining the meaning of something. **2** an explanation. **3** the way in which a performer expresses a creative work. ■ **in·ter·pre·ta·tion·al** adj.

in·ter·pret·er /in'tərpritər/ ▶ n. a person who interprets foreign speech aloud as it is spoken.

in·ter·ra·cial /,intər'rāsHəl/ ▶ adj. existing between or involving different races. ■ **in·ter·ra·cial·ly** adv.

in·ter·reg·num /,intər'regnəm/ ▶ n. (pl. **interregnums**) a period between reigns or political regimes when normal government is suspended.

in·ter·re·late /,intərə'lāt/ ▶ v. relate or connect to one other. ■ **in·ter·re·lat·ed·ness** n. **in·ter·re·la·tion** n. **in·ter·re·la·tion·ship** n.

in·ter·ro·gate /in'terə,gāt/ ▶ v. ask someone questions in a detailed or aggressive way. ■ **in·ter·ro·ga·tion** /in,terə'gāsHən/ n. **in·ter·ro·ga·tor** n.

in·ter·rog·a·tive /,intə'rägətiv/ ▶ adj. **1** expressing a question: *a hard, interrogative stare.* **2** Grammar used in questions. ▶ n. a word used in questions, e.g., *how* or *what.* ■ **in·ter·rog·a·tive·ly** adv.

in·ter·rog·a·to·ry /,intə'rägə,tôrē/ ▶ adj. expressing a question; questioning.

in·ter·rupt /,intə'rəpt/ ▶ v. **1** stop the continuous progress of something. **2** stop a person who is speaking or saying or doing something. **3** break the continuity of a line, surface, or view. ■ **in·ter·rupt·er** (also **interruptor**) n. **in·ter·rupt·i·ble** adj. **in·ter·rup·tive** adj.

in·ter·rup·tion /,intə'rəpsHən/ ▶ n. **1** an act, remark, or period that stops the progress of something. **2** the action of interrupting someone or something.

in·ter·sect /,intər'sekt/ ▶ v. **1** divide something by passing or lying across it. **2** (of lines, roads, etc.) cross or cut each other.

in·ter·sec·tion /,intər'seksHən/ ▶ n. **1** a point at which roads intersect or cross each other. **2** a point or line common to lines or surfaces that intersect. ■ **in·ter·sec·tion·al** adj.

in·ter·sex /'intər,seks/ ▶ n. the condition of having both male and female sex organs or characteristics.

in·ter·sex·u·al /,intər'seksHŌŌəl/ ▶ adj. **1** existing or occurring between the sexes. **2** relating to the condition of having both male and female sex organs or characteristics; hermaphroditic. ■ **in·ter·sex·u·al·i·ty** /-,seksHŌŌ'alitē/ n.

in·ter·space /'intər,spās/ ▶ n. a space between objects. ▶ v. /,intər'spās/ (usu. **be interspaced**) put or occupy a space between: *five pearls interspaced with diamonds.*

in·ter·sperse /,intər'spərs/ ▶ v. scatter or place things among or between other things. ■ **in·ter·sper·sion** n.

in·ter·state /'intər,stāt/ ▶ adj. existing or carried on between states. ▶ n. one of a system of highways extending across the US.

in·ter·stel·lar /,intər'stelər/ ▶ adj. occurring or situated between stars.

in·ter·stice /in'tərstis/ ▶ n. (pl. **interstices** /-sti,sēz/) a small space between things.

in·ter·sti·tial /,intər'stisHəl/ ▶ adj. relating to or found in small spaces between things. ■ **in·ter·sti·tial·ly** adv.

in·ter·tex·tu·al·i·ty /,intər,teksCHŌŌ'alitē/ ▶ n. the relationship between pieces of writing. ■ **in·ter·tex·tu·al** /-'teksCHŌŌəl/ adj.

in·ter·trib·al /,intər'trībəl/ ▶ adj. existing or occurring between different tribes.

in·ter·twine /,intər'twīn/ ▶ v. twist or twine together.

in·ter·val /'intərvəl/ ▶ n. **1** a period of time between two events. **2** a pause in activity, especially (Brit.) a pause between parts of a performance or a sports match. **3** a space or gap between things: *the path is marked with rocks at intervals.* **4** the difference in pitch between two sounds.

in·ter·vene /,intər'vēn/ ▶ v. **1** come between

people or things so as to prevent or alter a situation: *he intervened in the dispute.* **2** (usu. as adj. **intervening**) occur or be between events or things. ■ **in·ter·ven·er** (also **intervenor**) n.

in·ter·ven·tion /ˌintər'vensHən/ ▶ n. **1** the action of intervening between people or things to influence or control a situation. **2** action taken to improve a medical disorder. ■ **in·ter·ven·tion·al** adj.

in·ter·ven·tion·ist /ˌintər'vensHənist/ ▶ adj. favoring intervention to influence or control a situation. ▶ n. a person who favors intervening to influence or control a situation. ■ **in·ter·ven·tion·ism** n.

in·ter·view /'intər,vyōō/ ▶ n. **1** an occasion on which a journalist or broadcaster puts questions to a person. **2** a formal meeting at which a person is asked questions to assess their suitability for a job or college admission. **3** a session of formal questioning of a person by the police. ▶ v. hold an interview with someone. ■ **in·ter·view·ee** /ˌintər,vyōō'ē/ n. **in·ter·view·er** n.

in·ter·war /ˌintər'wôr/ ▶ adj. existing in the period between two wars, especially the two world wars.

in·ter·weave /ˌintər'wēv/ ▶ v. (past **interwove** /ˌintər'wōv/; past part. **interwoven** /ˌintər'wōvən/) weave or become woven together.

in·tes·tate /in'testāt, -tit/ ▶ adj. not having made a will before dying. ■ **in·tes·ta·cy** /-təsē/ n.

in·tes·tine /in'testən/ (also **intestines**) ▶ n. the long tubular organ leading from the end of the stomach to the anus. ■ **in·tes·ti·nal** /in'testənəl/ adj.

in·ti·fa·da /ˌintə'fädə/ ▶ n. the Palestinian uprising against Israeli occupation of the West Bank and Gaza Strip, beginning in 1987.

in·ti·ma·cy /'intəməsē/ ▶ n. (pl. **intimacies**) **1** close familiarity or friendship. **2** a familiar or private act or remark.

in·ti·mate¹ /'intəmit/ ▶ adj. **1** close and friendly: *they're on intimate terms.* **2** private and personal. **3** euphemistic having a sexual relationship. **4** involving very close connection: *her intimate involvement with the community.* **5** (of knowledge) detailed. **6** having a relaxed and cozy atmosphere. ▶ n. a very close friend. ■ **in·ti·mate·ly** adv.

in·ti·mate² /'intə,māt/ ▶ v. state something, especially in an indirect way. ■ **in·ti·ma·tion** /ˌintə'māsHən/ n.

in·tim·i·date /in'timi,dāt/ ▶ v. frighten someone, especially so as to force them into doing something. ■ **in·tim·i·da·tion** /-ˌtimi'dāsHən/ n. **in·tim·i·da·tor** /-'timi,dātər/ n. **in·tim·i·da·to·ry** /-ˌtimidə,tôrē/ adj.

in·to /'intōō/ ▶ prep. **1** expressing movement or direction to a point on or within. **2** expressing a change of state or the result of an action. **3** so as to turn toward. **4** about or concerning. **5** expressing division. **6** informal very interested in.

in·tol·er·a·ble /in'tälərəbəl/ ▶ adj. unable to be endured. ■ **in·tol·er·a·bly** adv.

in·tol·er·ant /in'tälərənt/ ▶ adj. not tolerant of views or behavior that differ from one's own. ■ **in·tol·er·ance** n. **in·tol·er·ant·ly** adv.

in·to·na·tion /ˌintə'nāsHən, -tō-/ ▶ n. **1** the rise and fall of the voice in speaking. **2** the action of saying something with little rise and fall of the voice. **3** accuracy of musical pitch. ■ **in·to·na·tion·al** adj.

in·tone /in'tōn/ ▶ v. say or recite something with little rise and fall of the pitch of the voice.

in to·to /ˌin 'tōtō/ ▶ adv. as a whole.

in·tox·i·cant /in'täksikənt/ ▶ n. a substance that causes someone to lose their self-control.

in·tox·i·cate /in'täksikāt/ ▶ v. **1** (of alcoholic drink or a drug) cause someone to lose their self-control. **2** excite or exhilarate someone. ■ **in·tox·i·ca·tion** /-ˌtäksi'kāsHən/ n.

intra- ▶ prefix (added to adjectives) on the inside; within: *intramural.*

in·trac·ta·ble /in'traktəbəl/ ▶ adj. **1** hard to solve or deal with. **2** (of a person) stubborn. ■ **in·trac·ta·bil·i·ty** /-ˌtraktə'bilitē/ n. **in·trac·ta·bly** adv.

in·tra·mu·ral /ˌintrə'myōōrəl/ ▶ adj. **1** situated or done within a building. **2** taking place within a single educational institution.

in·tra·net /'intrə,net/ ▶ n. a private communications network created with Internet software.

in·tran·si·gent /in'transijənt, -zi-/ ▶ adj. refusing to change one's views. ▶ n. a person who refuses to change their views. ■ **in·tran·si·gence** n. **in·tran·si·gen·cy** n. **in·tran·si·gent·ly** adv.

in·tran·si·tive /in'transitiv, -zi-/ ▶ adj. Grammar (of a verb) not taking a direct object, e.g., *die* in *he died suddenly.* The opposite of TRANSITIVE. ■ **in·tran·si·tive·ly** adv. **in·tran·si·tiv·i·ty** /-,transi'tivitē, -zi-/ n.

in·tra·u·ter·ine /ˌintrə'yōōtərin, -rīn/ ▶ adj. within the uterus.

in·tra·u·ter·ine de·vice ▶ n. a contraceptive device fitted inside the uterus, which prevents the implantation of fertilized eggs.

in·tra·ve·nous /ˌintrə'vēnəs/ ▶ adj. within or into a vein or veins. ■ **in·tra·ve·nous·ly** adv.

in·trep·id /in'trepid/ ▶ adj. not afraid of danger or difficulty; brave or bold. ■ **in·tre·pid·i·ty** /ˌintrə'piditē/ n. **in·trep·id·ly** adv.

in·tri·ca·cy /'intrikəsē/ ▶ n. (pl. **intricacies**) **1** the quality of being complicated or detailed. **2** (**intricacies**) complicated details.

in·tri·cate /'intrikit/ ▶ adj. very complicated or detailed. ■ **in·tri·cate·ly** adv.

in·trigue ▶ v. /in'trēg/ (**intrigues**, **intriguing**, **intrigued**) **1** arouse someone's curiosity or interest. **2** plot something illegal or harmful. ▶ n. /'in,trēg/ **1** the plotting of something illegal or harmful. **2** a secret love affair. ■ **in·tri·guer** n. **in·tri·guing** adj. **in·tri·guing·ly** adv. *the album is intriguingly titled The Revenge of the Goldfish.*

in·trin·sic /in'trinzik, -sik/ ▶ adj. belonging to the basic nature of someone or something; essential: *the club was an intrinsic part of New York nightlife.* ■ **in·trin·si·cal·ly** adv.

in·tro /'intrō/ ▶ n. (pl. **intros**) informal an introduction.

intro- ▶ prefix into; inward: *introvert.*

in·tro·duce /ˌintrə'd(y)ōōs/ ▶ v. **1** bring something into use or operation for the first time. **2** present someone by name to another. **3** (**introduce something to**) cause someone to learn about a subject or experience an activity for the first time. **4** insert something. **5** occur at the start of: *a horn solo introduces the symphony.* **6** provide an opening announcement for a television or radio program. **7** present new legislation for debate in a lawmaking assembly. ■ **in·tro·duc·er** n.

in·tro·duc·tion /ˌintrəˈdəkSHən/ ▶ n. **1** the action of introducing someone or something. **2** a thing newly brought in. **3** an act of introducing one person to another. **4** a thing that introduces another, such as a section at the beginning of a book. **5** a book or course of study intended for people who are beginning to study a subject. **6** a person's first experience of a subject or activity.

in·tro·duc·to·ry /ˌintrəˈdəktərē/ ▶ adj. serving as an introduction; basic or preliminary.

in·tro·it /ˈinˌtrō-it, -ˌtroit/ ▶ n. (in the Christian Church) a psalm or antiphon sung or said while the priest approaches the altar for Holy Communion.

in·tro·spec·tion /ˌintrəˈspekSHən/ ▶ n. the examination of one's own thoughts or feelings. ■ **in·tro·spec·tive** adj. **in·tro·spec·tive·ly** adv.

in·tro·vert /ˈintrəˌvərt/ ▶ n. a shy, quiet person who is mainly concerned with their own thoughts and feelings. ▶ adj. another term for INTROVERTED. ■ **in·tro·ver·sion** n.

in·tro·vert·ed /ˈintrəˌvərtid/ ▶ adj. **1** relating to an introvert. **2** (of a community, company, or other group) concerned principally with its own affairs.

in·trude /inˈtro͞od/ ▶ v. **1** enter a place or situation where one is unwelcome or uninvited. **2** interrupt and disturb: *the noise began to intrude into her thoughts.*

in·trud·er /inˈtro͞odər/ ▶ n. a person who intrudes, especially one who enters a building with criminal intent.

in·tru·sion /inˈtro͞ozHən/ ▶ n. **1** the action of entering a place or situation where one is unwelcome or uninvited. **2** a thing that intrudes.

in·tru·sive /inˈtro͞osiv/ ▶ adj. **1** unwelcome or uninvited and causing disturbance or annoyance: *an intrusive question.* **2** (of igneous rock) that has been forced when molten into cracks in neighboring rocks. ■ **in·tru·sive·ly** adv. **in·tru·sive·ness** n.

in·tu·it /inˈt(y)o͞o-it/ ▶ v. (past and past part. **intuited**) understand or work something out by intuition.

in·tu·i·tion /ˌint(y)o͞oˈisHən/ ▶ n. the ability to understand or know something immediately, without conscious reasoning.

in·tu·i·tive /inˈt(y)o͞oitiv/ ▶ adj. **1** based on what one feels to be true; instinctive. **2** (chiefly of computer software) easy to use and understand. ■ **in·tu·i·tive·ly** adv. **in·tu·i·tive·ness** n.

In·u·it /ˈin(y)o͞o-it/ ▶ n. **1** (pl. same or **Inuits**) a member of a people of northern Canada and parts of Greenland and Alaska. **2** the language of the Inuit.

> **USAGE**
> For an explanation of the terms **Inuit** and **Eskimo**, see the note at ESKIMO.

I·nuk·ti·tut /iˈn(y)o͞oktiˌto͞ot/ ▶ n. the Inuit language.

in·un·date /ˈinənˌdāt/ ▶ v. **1** overwhelm with things to be dealt with: *we've been inundated with complaints.* **2** flood something. ■ **in·un·da·tion** /ˌinənˈdāSHən/ n.

in·ure /iˈn(y)o͝or/ ▶ v. (**be inured to**) become used to something, especially something unpleasant.

in u·ter·o /in ˈyo͞otərō/ ▶ adv. & adj. in a woman's uterus; before birth.

in·vade /inˈvād/ ▶ v. **1** (of an armed force) enter a country so as to conquer or occupy it. **2** enter

somewhere in large numbers. **3** intrude on: *his privacy was being invaded.* **4** (of a parasite or disease) spread into the body. ■ **in·vad·er** n.

in·va·lid[1] /ˈinvəlid/ ▶ n. a person made weak or disabled by illness or injury. ■ **in·va·lid·ism** /-ˌizəm/ n.

in·va·lid[2] /inˈvalid/ ▶ adj. **1** not valid or officially recognized. **2** not true because based on incorrect information or faulty reasoning. ■ **in·val·id·ly** adv.

in·val·i·date /inˈvaliˌdāt/ ▶ v. **1** make or prove an argument or theory to be incorrect or faulty. **2** make an official document or procedure no longer legally valid. ■ **in·val·i·da·tion** /-ˌvaliˈdāSHən/ n.

in·va·lid·i·ty /ˌinvəˈliditē/ ▶ n. the fact of being invalid.

in·val·u·a·ble /inˈvalyo͞oəbəl/ ▶ adj. very valuable. ■ **in·val·u·a·bly** adv.

in·var·i·a·ble /inˈve(ə)rēəbəl/ ▶ adj. **1** never changing. **2** Mathematics (of a quantity) constant. ■ **in·var·i·a·bil·i·ty** /-ˌve(ə)rēəˈbilitē/ n.

in·var·i·a·bly /inˈve(ə)rēəblē/ ▶ adv. in every case or on every occasion; always.

in·va·sion /inˈvāzHən/ ▶ n. **1** an instance of invading a country. **2** the arrival of a large number of people or things. **3** an intrusion: *random drug testing is an invasion of privacy.*

in·va·sive /inˈvāsiv/ ▶ adj. **1** tending to invade or intrude: *invasive grasses.* **2** (of medical procedures) involving the introduction of instruments or other objects into the body.

in·vec·tive /inˈvektiv/ ▶ n. strongly abusive or critical language.

in·veigh /inˈvā/ ▶ v. (**inveigh against**) speak or write about someone with great hostility.

in·vei·gle /inˈvāgəl/ ▶ v. persuade someone to do something by deception or flattery: *he can inveigle any woman into bed in minutes.*

in·vent /inˈvent/ ▶ v. **1** create or design a new device or process. **2** make up a false story, name, etc. ■ **in·ven·tor** n.

in·ven·tion /inˈvensHən/ ▶ n. **1** the action of inventing something. **2** a newly created device or process. **3** a false story. **4** a person's creative ability.

in·ven·tive /inˈventiv/ ▶ adj. having or showing creativity or original thought. ■ **in·ven·tive·ly** adv. **in·ven·tive·ness** n.

in·ven·to·ry /ˈinvənˌtôrē/ ▶ n. (pl. **inventories**) **1** a complete list of items such as goods in stock or the contents of a building. **2** a quantity of goods in stock. ▶ v. (**inventories**, **inventorying**, **inventoried**) make an inventory of items.

in·verse /ˈinvərs, inˈvərs/ ▶ adj. opposite in position, direction, order, or effect. ▶ n. **1** a thing that is the opposite or reverse of another. **2** Mathematics a reciprocal quantity. ■ **in·verse·ly** adv.

in·verse pro·por·tion (also **inverse ratio**) ▶ n. a relation between two quantities such that one increases in proportion as the other decreases.

in·ver·sion /inˈvərzHən/ ▶ n. **1** the action of inverting something or the state of being inverted. **2** (also **temperature** or **thermal inversion**) a reversal of the normal decrease of air temperature with altitude, or of water temperature with depth. ■ **in·ver·sive** /-ˈvərsiv/ adj.

in·vert /inˈvərt/ ▶ v. put something upside down or in the opposite position, order, or arrangement. ■ **in·vert·er** n. **in·vert·i·ble** adj.

in·ver·te·brate /in'vərtəbrit, -ˌbrāt/ ▶ n. an animal having no backbone, such as a mollusk. ▶ adj. relating to invertebrates.

in·vest /in'vest/ ▶ v. **1** put money into financial schemes, shares, or property with the expectation of making a profit. **2** devote time or energy to an undertaking with the expectation of a worthwhile result. **3** (**invest in**) informal buy something whose usefulness will repay the cost. **4** (**invest someone/thing with**) provide someone or something with a quality: *these weapons are invested with an almost mystical value by collectors.* **5** formally appoint someone to a rank or office. ■ **in·vest·a·ble** adj. **in·ves·tor** n.

in·ves·ti·gate /in'vestiˌgāt/ ▶ v. **1** carry out a systematic or formal inquiry into an incident or allegation so as to establish the truth. **2** carry out research into a subject. **3** make a search or systematic inquiry. ■ **in·ves·ti·ga·tor** n. **in·ves·ti·ga·to·ry** /-gəˌtôrē/ adj.

in·ves·ti·ga·tion /inˌvestiˈgāsHən/ ▶ n. **1** the action of investigating something or someone. **2** a formal inquiry or systematic study.

in·ves·ti·ga·tive /in'vestiˌgātiv/ ▶ adj. **1** relating to investigation or research. **2** (of journalism or a journalist) investigating and seeking to expose dishonesty or injustice.

in·ves·ti·ture /in'vestiCHər, -ˌCHŏŏr/ ▶ n. **1** the action of formally investing a person with honors or rank. **2** a ceremony at which this takes place.

in·vest·ment /in'ves(t)mənt/ ▶ n. **1** the action of investing money in something for profit. **2** a thing worth buying because it may be profitable or useful in the future.

in·vest·ment bank ▶ n. a bank that deals in securities and provides services for large investors. ■ **in·vest·ment bank·er** n. **in·vest·ment bank·ing** n.

in·vet·er·ate /in'vetərit/ ▶ adj. **1** having a long-standing and firmly established habit or interest: *an inveterate gambler.* **2** (of a feeling or habit) firmly established. ■ **in·vet·er·a·cy** n. **in·vet·er·ate·ly** adv.

in·vid·i·ous /in'vidēəs/ ▶ adj. unacceptable, unfair, and likely to arouse resentment or anger in others. ■ **in·vid·i·ous·ly** adv. **in·vid·i·ous·ness** n.

in·vig·or·ate /in'vigəˌrāt/ ▶ v. give strength or energy to someone or something. ■ **in·vig·or·at·ing** adj. **in·vig·or·a·tion** /inˌvigə'rāsHən/ n.

in·vin·ci·ble /in'vinsəbəl/ ▶ adj. too powerful to be defeated or overcome. ■ **in·vin·ci·bil·i·ty** /-ˌvinsə'bilitē/ n. **in·vin·ci·bly** adv.

in·vi·o·la·ble /in'vīələbəl/ ▶ adj. never to be broken, infringed or violated: *inviolable rules.* ■ **in·vi·o·la·bil·i·ty** /inˌvīələ'bilitē/ n. **in·vi·o·la·bly** adv.

in·vi·o·late /in'vīəlit/ ▶ adj. that is or should be free from injury or attack.

in·vis·i·ble /in'vizəbəl/ ▶ adj. **1** unable to be seen, either by nature or because hidden. **2** relating to earnings that a country makes from the sale of services rather than tangible commodities. ■ **in·vis·i·bil·i·ty** /-ˌvizə'bilitē/ n. **in·vis·i·bly** adv.

in·vi·ta·tion /ˌinvi'tāsHən/ ▶ n. **1** a written or spoken request inviting someone to go somewhere or to do something. **2** the action of inviting someone to go somewhere or to do something. **3** a situation or action that is likely to result in a particular outcome: *his tactics were an invitation to disaster.*

in·vite ▶ v. /in'vīt/ **1** ask someone in a friendly or formal way to go somewhere or to do something. **2** request something formally or politely. **3** tend to result in a particular outcome. ▶ n. /'inˌvīt/ informal an invitation. ■ **in·vi·tee** /ˌinvī'tē/ n. **in·vit·er** n.

in·vit·ing /in'vītiNG/ ▶ adj. tempting or attractive. ■ **in·vit·ing·ly** adv.

in vi·tro /in 'vē̩trō/ ▶ adj. & adv. (of biological processes) taking place in a test tube or elsewhere outside a living organism.

in vi·vo /in 'vēvō/ ▶ adv. & adj. (of biological processes) taking place in a living organism.

in·vo·ca·tion /ˌinvə'kāsHən/ ▶ n. **1** the action of appealing to someone or something as an authority or in support of an argument. **2** an appeal to a god or spirit.

in·voice /'inˌvois/ ▶ n. a list of goods or services provided, with a statement of the sum due. ▶ v. send an invoice to someone for goods or services.

in·voke /in'vōk/ ▶ v. **1** appeal to someone or something as an authority or in support of an argument. **2** call on a god or spirit in prayer or as a witness. **3** call earnestly for something. **4** give rise to: *how could she explain the accident without invoking his wrath?*

in·vol·un·tar·y /in'välənˌterē/ ▶ adj. **1** done without conscious control. **2** (especially of muscles or nerves) involved in processes that are not consciously controlled. **3** done against someone's will. ■ **in·vol·un·tar·i·ly** /inˌvälən'te(ə)rəlē, -'välənˌter-/ adv.

in·vo·lut·ed /'invəˌlŏŏtid/ ▶ adj. formal complicated or intricate.

in·volve /in'välv/ ▶ v. **1** (of a situation or event) include something as a necessary part or result. **2** cause to experience or participate in an activity or situation: *his car was stolen and involved in a crash.* **3** (**be/get involved**) be or become occupied or engrossed in something. **4** (**be involved**) be in a romantic relationship with someone. ■ **in·volve·ment** n.

in·volved /in'välvd/ ▶ adj. difficult to understand; complicated.

in·vul·ner·a·ble /in'vəlnərəbəl/ ▶ adj. impossible to harm or damage. ■ **in·vul·ner·a·bil·i·ty** /-ˌvəlnərə'bilitē/ n. **in·vul·ner·a·bly** adv.

-in-wait·ing ▶ comb.form **1** referring to a position as attendant to a royal person: *lady-in-waiting.* **2** awaiting a turn or about to happen: *a political administration-in-waiting.*

in·ward /'inwərd/ ▶ adj. **1** directed or proceeding toward the inside. **2** mental or spiritual. ▶ adv. (also **inwards**) **1** toward the inside. **2** into or toward the mind or spirit. ■ **in·ward·ly** adv. **in·ward·ness** n.

in-your-face ▶ adj. informal blatantly aggressive or provocative.

I/O ▶ abbr. Electronics input-output.

IOC ▶ abbr. International Olympic Committee.

i·o·dide /'īəˌdīd/ ▶ n. a compound of iodine with another element or group.

i·o·dine /'īəˌdīn/ ▶ n. **1** a black crystalline nonmetallic chemical element of the halogen group. **2** an antiseptic solution of iodine in alcohol.

i·o·dized /'īəˌdīzd/ ▶ adj. impregnated with iodine: *iodized salt.*

i·on /' īən, 'ī,än/ ▸ n. an atom or molecule with a net electric charge through loss or gain of electrons, either positive (a **cation**) or negative (an **anion**).

i·on ex·change ▸ n. the exchange of ions of the same charge between an insoluble solid and a solution in contact with it, used in water-softening and other purification processes.

I·o·ni·an /ī'ōnēən/ ▸ n. a person from the Ionian Islands, a chain of islands off the western coast of mainland Greece. ▸ adj. relating to the Ionians or the Ionian Islands.

I·on·ic /ī'änik/ ▸ adj. relating to a classical order of architecture characterized by a column with scroll shapes on the top.

i·on·ic /ī'änik/ ▸ adj. **1** relating to ions. **2** (of a chemical bond) formed by the attraction of ions with opposite charges. Often contrasted with COVALENT. ▪ **i·on·i·cal·ly** adv.

i·on·ize /'īə,nīz/ ▸ v. convert an atom, molecule, or substance into an ion or ions, typically by removing one or more electrons. ▪ **i·on·iz·a·ble** adj. **i·on·i·za·tion** /,īəni'zāsнən/ n.

i·on·iz·er /'īə,nīzər/ ▸ n. a device that produces ions, especially one used to improve the quality of the air in a room.

i·on·o·sphere /ī'änə,sfi(ə)r/ ▸ n. the layer of the atmosphere above the mesosphere that contains a high concentration of ions and electrons and is able to reflect radio waves. ▪ **i·on·o·spher·ic** /ī,änə'sfi(ə)rik, -'sfer-/ adj.

i·o·ta /ī'ōtə/ ▸ n. **1** the ninth letter of the Greek alphabet (I, ι), represented as 'i.' **2** an extremely small amount: *it won't make an iota of difference.*

IOU ▸ n. a signed document acknowledging a debt.

IP ▸ abbr. Computing Internet Protocol.

IPA ▸ abbr. International Phonetic Alphabet.

ip·e·cac /'ipikak/ ▸ n. the dried rhizome of a South American shrub, or a drug prepared from this, used as an emetic and expectorant.

IPO ▸ abbr. initial public offering, the first issue of a company's shares to the public, used as a means of raising startup or expansion capital.

iPod /'ī,päd/ ▸ n. trademark a type of personal digital audio player.

ip·so fac·to /'ipsō 'faktō/ ▸ adv. by that very fact or act.

IQ ▸ abbr. intelligence quotient.

IR ▸ abbr. infrared.

Ir ▸ symbol the chemical element iridium.

IRA /'īrə/ ▸ abbr. individual retirement account.

I·ra·ni·an /i'rānēən, i'rä-/ ▸ n. a person from Iran. ▸ adj. relating to Iran.

I·ra·qi /i'räkē, i'rakē/ ▸ n. (pl. **Iraqis**) **1** a person from Iraq. **2** the form of Arabic spoken in Iraq. ▸ adj. relating to Iraq.

i·ras·ci·ble /i'rasəbəl/ ▸ adj. hot-tempered; irritable. ▪ **i·ras·ci·bil·i·ty** /i,rasə'bilitē/ n. **i·ras·ci·bly** adv.

i·rate /ī'rāt/ ▸ adj. very angry. ▪ **i·rate·ly** adv.

IRC ▸ abbr. Computing Internet Relay Chat.

ire /ī(ə)r/ ▸ n. chiefly literary anger.

i·ren·ic /ī'renik, ī'rē-/ ▸ adj. formal intended or intending to maintain or bring about peace.

ir·i·des·cent /,iri'desənt/ ▸ adj. showing bright colors that seem to change when seen from different angles. ▪ **ir·i·des·cence** n.

ir·i·des·cent·ly adv.

i·rid·i·um /i'ridēəm/ ▸ n. a hard, dense silvery-white metallic element.

ir·i·dol·o·gy /,iri'däləjē/ ▸ n. (in alternative medicine) a method of diagnosing illnesses or conditions by examining the iris of the eye. ▪ **ir·i·dol·o·gist** n.

i·ris /'īris/ ▸ n. **1** a colored ring-shaped membrane behind the cornea of the eye, with the pupil in the center. **2** a plant with sword-shaped leaves and purple or yellow flowers.

I·rish /'īrisн/ ▸ n. (also **Irish Gaelic**) the Celtic language of Ireland. ▸ adj. relating to Ireland or Irish. ▪ **I·rish·man** n. (pl. **Irishmen**) **I·rish·ness** n. **I·rish·wom·an** n. (pl. **Irishwomen**)

I·rish cof·fee ▸ n. coffee mixed with a dash of Irish whiskey and served with cream on top.

I·rish set·ter ▸ n. a breed of setter (dog) with a long, silky dark red coat and a long feathered tail.

I·rish wolf·hound ▸ n. a large grayish hound with a rough coat.

irk /ərk/ ▸ v. irritate or annoy someone.

irk·some /'ərksəm/ ▸ adj. irritating or annoying. ▪ **irk·some·ly** adv.

i·ron /'īərn/ ▸ n. **1** a strong, hard magnetic silvery-gray metal, used in construction and manufacturing. **2** a tool made of iron. **3** a hand-held implement with a flat heated steel base, used to smooth clothes. **4** a golf club used for hitting the ball at a high angle. **5** (**irons**) handcuffs or chains used as a restraint. ▸ v. **1** smooth clothes with an iron. **2** (**iron something out**) settle a difficulty or problem. – PHRASES **have many** (or **other**) **irons in the fire** have a range of options or be involved in several activities.

I·ron Age ▸ n. the period that followed the Bronze Age, when weapons and tools came to be made of iron.

i·ron·clad /'īərn,klad/ ▸ adj. **1** covered or protected with iron. **2** impossible to weaken or change: *an ironclad guarantee.*

Iron Cur·tain ▸ n. (**the Iron Curtain**) a barrier regarded as separating the former Soviet bloc and the West before the decline of communism in eastern Europe.

iron fist ▸ n. (also **iron hand**) harsh and strictly enforced control: *touting the need for Uncle Sam's iron fist.*

i·ron·ic /ī'ränik/ ▸ adj. **1** expressing an idea with words that usually mean the opposite in order to be humorous or emphasize a point. **2** happening in the opposite way to what is expected. ▪ **i·ron·i·cal** adj. **i·ron·i·cal·ly** adv.

i·ron·ing /'īərninG/ ▸ n. clothes that need to be or have just been ironed.

i·ron·ing board ▸ n. a long, narrow board with folding legs, on which clothes are ironed.

i·ro·nist /'īrənist, 'īərnist/ ▸ n. a person who uses irony. ▪ **i·ro·nize** v.

i·ron lung ▸ n. a rigid case fitted over a patient's body, used to provide artificial respiration by means of mechanical pumps.

i·ron maid·en ▸ n. a former instrument of torture consisting of a coffin-shaped box lined with iron spikes.

i·ron man ▸ n. **1** an exceptionally strong man. **2** a sporting contest involving several events and requiring a great deal of stamina.

i·ron·stone /'Īərn‚stōn/ ▶n. **1** sedimentary rock containing iron compounds. **2** a kind of dense opaque stoneware.

i·ron·wood /'Īərn‚wŏŏd/ ▶n. any of a number of trees that produce very hard timber, including the hornbeam.

i·ron·work /'Īərn‚wərk/ ▶n. things made of iron.

i·ron·works /'Īərn‚wərks/ ▶n. a place where iron is smelted or iron goods are made.

i·ro·ny /'Īrənē, 'īərnē/ ▶n. (pl. **ironies**) **1** the expression of meaning through the use of words that normally mean the opposite, typically in order to be humorous or emphasize a point. **2** a situation that is the opposite to what is expected.

Ir·o·quois /'irə‚kwoi/ ▶n. (pl. same) a member of a former group of six American Indian peoples who lived mainly in southern Ontario and Quebec and northern New York State.

ir·ra·di·ate /i'rādē‚āt/ ▶v. **1** expose someone or something to radiation. **2** shine light on something, or appear to do so: *happiness filled her, irradiating her whole face.* ■ **ir·ra·di·a·tion** /i‚rādē'āsHən/ n.

ir·ra·tion·al /i'rasHənl/ ▶adj. not logical or reasonable. ■ **ir·ra·tion·al·i·ty** /i‚rasHə'nalitē/ n. **ir·ra·tion·al·ly** adv.

ir·rec·on·cil·a·ble /i‚rekən'sīləbəl, i'rekən‚sī-/ ▶adj. **1** incompatible: *the two points of view were irreconcilable.* **2** not able to be resolved: *irreconcilable differences.* ■ **ir·rec·on·cil·a·bly** adv.

ir·re·cov·er·a·ble /i‚ri'kəvərəbəl/ ▶adj. not able to be recovered or remedied. ■ **ir·re·cov·er·a·bly** adv.

ir·re·deem·a·ble /i‚ri'dēməbəl/ ▶adj. not able to be saved, improved, or corrected. ■ **ir·re·deem·a·bly** adv.

ir·re·den·tist /i‚ri'dentist/ ▶n. a person believing that territory formerly belonging to their own country should be restored to it. ■ **ir·re·den·tism** /-‚tizəm/ n.

ir·re·duc·i·ble /i‚ri'd(y)ōōsəbəl/ ▶adj. not able to be reduced or simplified. ■ **ir·re·duc·i·bly** adv.

ir·ref·u·ta·ble /i‚rə'fyōōtəbəl, i'refyə-/ ▶adj. impossible to deny or disprove. ■ **ir·ref·u·ta·bly** adv.

ir·re·gard·less /i‚ri'gärdlis/ ▶adj. & adv. informal regardless.

ir·reg·u·lar /i'regyələr/ ▶adj. **1** not even or regular in shape, arrangement, or occurrence: *an irregular heartbeat.* **2** contrary to the rules or to that which is normal or established: *irregular financial dealings.* **3** (of troops) not belonging to regular army units. **4** Grammar (of a word) having inflections that do not conform to the usual rules. ▶n. a member of an irregular military force. ■ **ir·reg·u·lar·i·ty** /i‚regyə'laritē/ n. (pl. **irregularities**) **ir·reg·u·lar·ly** adv.

ir·rel·e·vant /i'reləvənt/ ▶adj. not relevant to the subject or matter in question. ■ **ir·rel·e·vance** n. **ir·rel·e·van·cy** n. (pl. **irrelevancies**) **ir·rel·e·vant·ly** adv.

ir·re·li·gious /‚iri'lijəs/ ▶adj. without religious belief, or showing no respect for religion. ■ **ir·re·li·gion** n.

ir·re·me·di·a·ble /i‚ri'mēdēəbəl/ ▶adj. impossible to remedy. ■ **ir·re·me·di·a·bly** adv.

ir·re·mov·a·ble /i‚ri'mōōvəbəl/ ▶adj. not able to be removed.

ir·rep·a·ra·ble /i'rep(ə)rəbəl/ ▶adj. impossible to repair or put right: *irreparable brain damage.* ■ **ir·rep·a·ra·bly** adv.

ir·re·place·a·ble /‚iri'plāsəbəl/ ▶adj. impossible to replace if lost or damaged.

ir·re·press·i·ble /‚iri'presəbəl/ ▶adj. not able to be controlled or restrained. ■ **ir·re·press·i·bly** adv.

ir·re·proach·a·ble /‚iri'prōchəbəl/ ▶adj. not able to be criticized; faultless. ■ **ir·re·proach·a·bly** adv.

ir·re·sist·i·ble /‚iri'zistəbəl/ ▶adj. too tempting or powerful to be resisted. ■ **ir·re·sist·i·bly** adv.

ir·res·o·lute /i(r)'rezə‚lōōt/ ▶adj. uncertain. ■ **ir·res·o·lute·ly** adv. **ir·res·o·lu·tion** /-‚rezə'lōōsHən/ n.

ir·re·solv·a·ble /‚iri'zälvəbəl/ ▶adj. impossible to solve.

ir·re·spec·tive /‚iri'spektiv/ ▶adj. (**irrespective of**) regardless of.

ir·re·spon·si·ble /‚iri'spänsəbəl/ ▶adj. not showing a proper sense of responsibility. ■ **ir·re·spon·si·bil·i·ty** /-‚spänsə'bilitē/ n. **ir·re·spon·si·bly** adv.

ir·re·triev·a·ble /‚iri'trēvəbəl/ ▶adj. not able to be improved or put right. ■ **ir·re·triev·a·bly** adv.

ir·rev·er·ent /i'rev(ə)rənt/ ▶adj. disrespectful. ■ **ir·rev·er·ence** n. **ir·rev·er·ent·ly** adv.

ir·re·vers·i·ble /‚iri'vərsəbəl/ ▶adj. impossible to be reversed or altered. ■ **ir·re·vers·i·bil·i·ty** /-‚vərsə'bilitē/ n. **ir·re·vers·i·bly** adv.

ir·rev·o·ca·ble /i'revəkəbəl/ ▶adj. not able to be changed, reversed, or recovered: *an irrevocable decision.* ■ **ir·rev·o·ca·bil·i·ty** /i‚revəkə'bilitē/ n. **ir·rev·o·ca·bly** adv.

ir·ri·gate /'irigāt/ ▶v. **1** supply water to land or crops by means of channels. **2** Medicine apply a flow of water or medication to an organ or wound. ■ **ir·ri·ga·ble** /-gəbəl/ adj. **ir·ri·ga·tion** /‚iri'gāsHən/ n. **ir·ri·ga·tor** /-‚gātər/ n.

ir·ri·ta·ble /'iritəbəl/ ▶adj. **1** easily annoyed or angered. **2** Medicine abnormally sensitive. ■ **ir·ri·ta·bil·i·ty** /‚iritə'bilitē/ n. **ir·ri·ta·bly** adv.

ir·ri·ta·ble bow·el syn·drome ▶n. a condition involving recurrent abdominal pain and diarrhea or constipation.

ir·ri·tant /'iritənt/ ▶n. **1** a substance that irritates part of the body. **2** a source of continual annoyance. ▶adj. causing irritation to the body.

ir·ri·tate /'iri‚tāt/ ▶v. **1** make someone annoyed or angry. **2** cause inflammation in a part of the body. ■ **ir·ri·tat·ing** adj. **ir·ri·tat·ing·ly** adv. **ir·ri·ta·tion** /‚iri'tāsHən/ n.

ir·rup·tion /i'rəpsHən/ ▶n. a sudden forcible entry. ■ **ir·rupt** /i'rəpt/ v. **ir·rup·tive** /i'rəptiv/ adj.

IRS ▶abbr. Internal Revenue Service.

is /iz/ ▶ third person singular present of BE.

ISA ▶abbr. Computing industry standard architecture.

ISBN ▶abbr. international standard book number.

is·che·mi·a /is'kēmēə/ ▶n. an inadequate blood supply to a part of the body, especially the heart muscles. ■ **is·che·mic** adj.

ISDN ▶abbr. integrated services digital network, a telecommunications network through which sound, images, and data can be transmitted as digitized signals.

-ise ▶suffix chiefly British variant spelling of -IZE.

> **USAGE**
> For advice on the use of **-ise** or **-ize**, see the note at **-IZE**.

i·sin·glass /ˈīzənˌglas, ˈīziNG-/ ▸ n. a kind of gelatin obtained from fish.

Is·lam /isˈläm, iz-/ ▸ n. 1 the religion of the Muslims, based on belief in one God and regarded by them to have been revealed through Muhammad as the Prophet of Allah. 2 the Muslim world. ∎ **Is·lam·i·za·tion** /isˌlämiˈzāsHən, iz-/ n. **Is·lam·ize** /ˈisləˌmīz, ˈiz-/ v.

Is·lam·ic /isˈlämik/ ▸ adj. relating to Islam. ∎ **Is·lam·i·cize** /isˈlämiˌsīz, iz-/ v.

Is·lam·ism /ˈisləˌmizəm, ˈiz-/ ▸ n. Islamic extremism or fundamentalism. ∎ **Is·lam·ist** /ˈisləˌmist, ˈiz-/ (also **Islamicist** /isˈlämiˌsist, iz-/) n. & adj.

Is·lam·o·pho·bi·a /isˌläməˈfōbēə, iz-/ ▸ n. a hatred or fear of Islam or Muslims.

is·land /ˈīlənd/ ▸ n. 1 a piece of land surrounded by water. 2 a thing that is isolated, detached, or surrounded: *the last island of democracy in this country.* ∎ **is·land·er** n.

isle /īl/ ▸ n. literary (except in place names) an island.

is·let /ˈīlət/ ▸ n. a small island.

is·lets of Lang·er·hans /ˈlaNGərˌhanz, ˈläNGərˌhäns/ ▸ pl.n. groups of cells in the pancreas that produce insulin.

ism /ˈizəm/ ▸ n. informal, chiefly derogatory a distinctive system, philosophy, or ideology.

is·n't /ˈizənt/ ▸ contr. is not.

ISO ▸ abbr. 1 International Organization for Standardization. 2 (in personal ads) in search of.

i·so·bar /ˈīsəˌbär/ ▸ n. a line on a map connecting points having the same atmospheric pressure. ∎ **i·so·bar·ic** /ˌīsəˈbarik, -ˈbär-/ adj.

i·so·late /ˈīsəˌlāt/ ▸ v. 1 place someone or something apart or alone. 2 Chemistry & Biology obtain or extract a compound, microorganism, etc., in a pure form. 3 cut off the electrical or other connection to something. ▸ n. /ˈīsəˌlit/ an isolated person or thing. ∎ **i·so·la·tor** n.

i·so·lat·ed /ˈīsəˌlātid/ ▸ adj. 1 remote; lonely: *isolated villages.* 2 single; exceptional: *isolated incidents of unrest.*

i·so·la·tion /ˌīsəˈlāsHən/ ▸ n. the process of isolating someone or something or the fact of being isolated.
– PHRASES **in isolation** without relation to others; separately.

i·so·la·tion·ism /ˌīsəˈlāsHəˌnizəm/ ▸ n. a policy of remaining apart in the political affairs of other countries. ∎ **i·so·la·tion·ist** n.

i·so·mer /ˈīsəmər/ ▸ n. 1 Chemistry each of two or more compounds with the same formula but a different arrangement of atoms and different properties. 2 Physics each of two or more atomic nuclei with the same atomic number and mass number but different energy states. ∎ **i·so·mer·ic** /ˌīsəˈmerik/ adj. **i·som·er·ism** /īˈsäməˌrizəm/ n. **i·som·er·ize** /īˈsäməˌrīz/ v.

i·so·met·ric /ˌīsəˈmetrik/ ▸ adj. 1 having equal dimensions. 2 Physiology involving an increase in muscle tension but no contraction of the muscle. 3 (of perspective drawing) having the three main dimensions represented by axes 120° apart. ∎ **i·so·met·ri·cal·ly** adv. **i·som·e·try** /īˈsämitrē/ n.

i·so·met·rics /ˌīsəˈmetriks/ ▸ pl.n. a system of physical exercises in which muscles are made to act against each other or against a fixed object.

i·so·mor·phic /ˌīsəˈmôrfik/ ▸ adj. having a similar form and relationship. ∎ **i·so·mor·phism** n. **i·so·morph·ous** adj.

i·sos·ce·les /īˈsäsəˌlēz/ ▸ adj. (of a triangle) having two sides of equal length.

i·so·therm /ˈīsəˌTHərm/ ▸ n. a line on a map or diagram connecting points having the same temperature. ∎ **i·so·ther·mal** /ˌīsəˈTHərməl/ adj. & n.

i·so·ton·ic /ˌīsəˈtänik/ ▸ adj. 1 Physiology (of a muscle action) taking place with normal contraction. 2 (of a drink) containing essential salts and minerals in the same concentration as normally found in the body.

i·so·tope /ˈīsəˌtōp/ ▸ n. Chemistry each of two or more forms of the same element that contain equal numbers of protons but different numbers of neutrons in their nuclei. ∎ **i·so·top·ic** /ˌīsəˈtäpik/ adj.

i·so·trop·ic /ˌīsəˈträpik, -ˈtrōpik/ ▸ adj. Physics having the same size or properties when measured in different directions.

ISP ▸ abbr. Internet service provider.

Is·rae·li /izˈrālē/ ▸ n. (pl. **Israelis**) a person from Israel. ▸ adj. relating to the modern country of Israel.

Is·ra·el·ite /ˈizrēəˌlīt/ ▸ n. a member of the ancient Hebrew nation.

is·sei /ˈē(s)ˌsā/ ▸ n. (pl. same) a Japanese immigrant to North America. Compare with NISEI and SANSEI.

is·sue /ˈisHōō/ ▸ n. 1 an important topic or problem to be discussed or resolved: *environmental issues.* 2 (**issues**) personal problems or difficulties. 3 the action of supplying or distributing something. 4 each of a regular series of publications. 5 formal or Law children of one's own. ▸ v. (**issues, issuing, issued**) 1 supply or distribute something. 2 formally send out or make known: *the minister issued a statement.* 3 (**issue from**) come, go, or flow out from: *exotic smells issued from a nearby building.* ∎ **is·su·ance** /-əns/ n. **is·su·er** n.
– PHRASES **at issue** under discussion. **make an issue of** treat something too seriously or as a problem. **take issue with** disagree with or challenge.

isth·mus /ˈisməs/ ▸ n. (pl. **isthmuses**) a narrow strip of land with sea on either side, linking two larger areas of land.

IT ▸ abbr. information technology.

it /it/ ▸ pron. (third person sing.) 1 used to refer to a thing previously mentioned or easily identified. 2 referring to an animal or child of unspecified sex. 3 used to identify a person: *it's me.* 4 used as a subject in statements about time, distance, or weather: *it is raining.* 5 used to refer to something specified later in the sentence: *it is impossible to get there today.* 6 used to refer to the situation or circumstances: *if it's convenient.* 7 exactly what is needed or desired.

It. ▸ abbr. 1 Italian. 2 Italy.

I·tal·ian /iˈtalyən/ ▸ n. 1 a person from Italy. 2 the language of Italy, descended from Latin. ▸ adj. relating to Italy or Italian. ∎ **I·tal·ian·ize** /iˈtalyəˌnīz/ v.

I·tal·ian·ate /iˈtalyəˌnāt/ ▸ adj. Italian in character or appearance.

Italian ice ▸ n. a frozen dessert consisting of fruit juice or purée in a sugar syrup.

i·tal·ic /iˈtalik, īˈtal-/ ▸ adj. referring to the sloping typeface used especially for emphasis and in foreign words. ▸ n. (also **italics**) an italic typeface or letter.

i·tal·i·cize /iˈtaliˌsīz, īˈtal-/ ▶ v. print or format text in italics.

itch /iCH/ ▶ n. **1** an uncomfortable sensation that causes a desire to scratch the skin. **2** informal an impatient desire. ▶ v. **1** have an itch. **2** informal feel an impatient desire to do something: *he was itching to get outside.*

itch·y /ˈiCHē/ ▶ adj. (**itchier**, **itchiest**) having or causing an itch. ■ **itch·i·ness** n.
– PHRASES **have itchy feet** informal have a strong urge to travel.

it'd /ˈitid/ ▶ contr. **1** it had. **2** it would.

i·tem /ˈītəm/ ▶ n. an individual article or unit: *an item of clothing.*
– PHRASES **be an item** informal (of a couple) be in a romantic or sexual relationship.

i·tem·ize /ˈītəˌmīz/ ▶ v. **1** present something as a list of individual items or parts. **2** identify various deductions on one's tax return in order to get credit for them: *you can take the deduction even if you don't itemize.*

it·er·ate /ˈitəˌrāt/ ▶ v. **1** do or say something repeatedly. **2** make repeated use of a mathematical or computational procedure, applying it each time to the result of the previous application. ■ **it·er·a·tion** /ˌitəˈrāsHən/ n. **it·er·a·tive** /ˈitəˌrātiv, -rətiv/ adj.

i·tin·er·ant /īˈtinərənt, iˈtin-/ ▶ adj. traveling from place to place. ▶ n. an itinerant person.

i·tin·er·ar·y /īˈtinəˌrerē, iˈtin-/ ▶ n. (pl. **itineraries**) a planned route or journey.

-itis ▶ suffix forming names of diseases that cause inflammation: *cystitis.*

it'll /ˈitl/ ▶ contr. **1** it shall. **2** it will.

its /its/ ▶ possessive determiner **1** belonging to or associated with a thing previously mentioned or easily identified. **2** belonging to or associated with a child or animal of unspecified sex.

> **USAGE**
> A common error in writing is to confuse the possessive **its** (as in *turn the camera on its side*) with the form **it's** (short for either **it is** or **it has**, as in *it's my fault; it's been a hot day*).

it's /its/ ▶ contr. **1** it is. **2** it has.

it·self /itˈself/ ▶ pron. (third person sing.) **1** (reflexive) used to refer to something previously mentioned as the subject of the clause: *his horse hurt itself.* **2** (emphatic) used to emphasize a particular thing or animal mentioned: *she wanted him more than life itself.*

– PHRASES **in itself** viewed in its essential qualities.

it·ty-bit·ty /ˈitē ˈbitē/ (also **itsy-bitsy** /ˈitsē ˈbitsē/) ▶ adj. informal very small; tiny.

IUD ▶ abbr. intrauterine device.

IV ▶ abbr. intravenous or intravenously.

I've /īv/ ▶ contr. I have.

IVF ▶ abbr. in vitro fertilization.

i·vied /ˈīvēd/ ▶ adj. covered in ivy.

I·vies /ˈīvēz/ ▶ pl.n. the Ivy League schools collectively, or other schools perceived as being of equal stature.

I·vo·ri·an /īˈvôrēən/ ▶ n. a person from the Ivory Coast, a country in West Africa. ▶ adj. relating to the Ivory Coast.

i·vo·ry /ˈīvərē/ ▶ n. (pl. **ivories**) **1** a hard creamy-white substance that forms the main part of the tusks of an elephant or walrus. **2** the creamy-white color of ivory. **3** (**the ivories**) informal the keys of a piano.

i·vo·ry tow·er ▶ n. a privileged or secluded existence in which someone does not have to face the normal difficulties of life.

i·vy /ˈīvē/ ▶ n. (pl. **ivies**) a woody evergreen climbing plant, typically with shiny five-pointed leaves.

I·vy League ▶ n. a group of long-established and prestigious universities in the eastern US.

I·yen·gar /ēˈyenGgär/ ▶ n. a type of yoga focusing on the correct alignment of the body, making use of straps, wooden blocks, and other objects to help achieve the correct postures.

-ize ▶ suffix forming verbs meaning: **1** make or become: *privatize.* **2** cause to resemble: *Americanize.* **3** treat in a specified way: *pasteurize.* **4** treat or cause to combine with a specified substance: *carbonize.* **5** perform or subject someone to a specified practice: *hospitalize.*

> **USAGE**
> Many verbs that end in **-ize** can also end in **-ise**, especially in British English. However, there are a small number of verbs that must always be spelled with **-ise** at the end. This is either because **-ise** forms part of a larger word element, such as *-mise* in **compromise**, or because the verb corresponds to a noun that has **-s-** in the stem, such as **televise** (from *television*).

Jj

J¹ (also **j**) ▶ n. (pl. **Js** or **J's**) the tenth letter of the alphabet.

J² ▶ abbr. **1** (in card games) jack. **2** Physics joule(s).

jab /jab/ ▶ v. (**jabs, jabbing, jabbed**) poke someone or something roughly or quickly with a sharp or pointed object. ▶ n. **1** a quick, sharp poke or blow. **2** informal an injection, especially a vaccination.

jab·ber /ˈjabər/ ▶ v. talk rapidly and excitedly. ▶ n. rapid, excited talk.

ja·bot /ᴢнaˈbō, jaˈ-/ ▶ n. an ornamental ruffle on the front of a shirt or blouse.

jac·a·ran·da /ˌjakəˈrandə/ ▶ n. a tropical American tree with blue trumpet-shaped flowers and sweet-smelling wood.

jack¹ /jak/ ▶ n. **1** a device for lifting heavy objects, especially one for raising the axle of a motor vehicle off the ground. **2** a playing card with a picture of a soldier, page, or knave on it, normally ranking next below a queen. **3** a phone jack. **4** the small white ball at which players aim in lawn bowling. **5** a small metal piece used in games of tossing and catching. **6** (**jacks**) a game played by tossing and catching jacks. **7** a small national flag flown at the bow of a vessel in harbor. **8** the male of various animals, e.g., the donkey. **9** used in names of animals and plants that are smaller than similar kinds, e.g., **jack pine.** ▶ v. **1** (**jack something up**) raise something with a jack. **2** (**jack something up**) informal increase something by a considerable amount: *the hotels have jacked up their prices.* **3** (**jack off**) vulgar slang masturbate.
– PHRASES **jack of all trades (and master of none)** a person who can do many different types of work (but has special skill in none). **not know jack** informal be ignorant: *you don't have to know jack about music to be a producer.*

jack² ▶ v. informal steal something.

jack·al /ˈjakəl/ ▶ n. a wild dog that feeds on the decaying flesh of dead animals, found in Africa and southern Asia.

jack·ass /ˈjakˌas/ ▶ n. **1** a stupid person. **2** a male ass or donkey.

jack·boot /ˈjakˌboōt/ ▶ n. a large leather military boot reaching to the knee. ■ **jack·boot·ed** adj.

jack·daw /ˈjakˌdô/ ▶ n. a small gray-headed Eurasian crow, noted for its inquisitiveness.

jack·et /ˈjakit/ ▶ n. **1** an outer garment extending to the waist or hips, with sleeves. **2** an outer covering placed around something for protection or insulation. **3** the skin of a potato. ▶ v. (**jackets, jacketing, jacketed**) cover something with a jacket.

Jack Frost ▶ n. frost represented as a human being.

jack·fruit /ˈjakˌfroōt/ ▶ n. the very large edible fruit of an Asian tree.

jack·ham·mer /ˈjakˌhamər/ ▶ n. a portable pneumatic hammer or drill. ▶ v. beat or hammer something heavily or loudly and repeatedly.

jack-in-the-box ▶ n. a toy consisting of a box containing a figure on a spring that pops up when the lid is opened.

jack-in-the-pul·pit ▶ n. a woodland plant having a purple or green spadix that is followed by bright red berries.

jack·knife /ˈjakˌnīf/ ▶ n. (pl. **jackknives**) **1** a large knife with a folding blade. **2** a dive in which the body is bent at the waist and then straightened. ▶ v. (**jackknifes, jackknifing, jackknifed**) **1** move one's body into a bent or doubled-up position. **2** (of a tractor-trailer or other articulated vehicle) bend into a V-shape in an uncontrolled skidding movement. **3** (of a diver) perform a jackknife.

jack-o'-lan·tern /ˈjak ə ˌlantərn/ ▶ n. a lantern made from a hollowed-out pumpkin in which holes are cut to represent facial features, made especially for Halloween.

jack pine ▶ n. a small, hardy North American pine with short needles.

jack·pot /ˈjakˌpät/ ▶ n. a large cash prize in a game or lottery.
– PHRASES **hit the jackpot** informal have great or unexpected success.

jack·rab·bit /ˈjakˌrabət/ ▶ n. a hare found in open country in western North American.

Jack Rus·sell /ˈrəsəl/ (also **Jack Russell terrier**) ▶ n. a small breed of terrier with short legs.

Jac·o·be·an /ˌjakəˈbēən/ ▶ adj. relating to or characteristic of the reign of James I of England (1603–1625). ▶ n. a person who lived in the Jacobean period.

Jac·o·bite /ˈjakəˌbīt/ ▶ n. a supporter of the deposed James II and his descendants in their claim to the British throne after the Revolution of 1688. ■ **Jac·o·bit·ism** /-bīˌtizəm/ n.

Ja·cob's lad·der ▶ n. a plant with blue or white flowers and slender pointed leaves formed in ladderlike rows.

jac·quard /ˈjaˌkärd, jəˈkärd/ ▶ n. **1** a piece of equipment consisting of perforated cards, fitted to a loom for weaving patterned and brocaded fabrics. **2** a fabric made on a jacquard loom.

ja·cuz·zi /jəˈkoōzē/ ▶ n. (pl. **jacuzzis**) trademark a large bath with jets of water that massage the body.

jade¹ /jād/ ▶ n. **1** a hard bluish, green stone used for ornaments and jewelry. **2** a light, bluish green color.

jade² ▶ n. old use **1** a bad-tempered or disreputable woman. **2** an old or worn-out horse.

jad·ed /ˈjādid/ ▶ adj. tired or lacking enthusiasm

after having had too much of something.

jade·ite /ˈjādˌīt/ ▶ n. a green, blue, or white form of jade.

JAG ▶ abbr. judge advocate general.

jag¹ /jag/ ▶ v. (**jags, jagging, jagged**) stab, pierce, or prick something. ▶ n. a sharp projection. ∎ **jag·gy** adj.

jag² ▶ n. informal a period of unrestrained activity or emotion: *a crying jag.*

jag·ged /ˈjagid/ ▶ adj. with rough, sharp points sticking out. ∎ **jag·ged·ly** adv. **jag·ged·ness** n.

jag·uar /ˈjagˌwär/ ▶ n. a large, heavily built cat that has a yellowish-brown coat with black spots, found mainly in Central and South America.

Jah /jä, yä/ ▶ n. the Rastafarian name for God.

jai a·lai /ˈhī (ə)ˌlī/ ▶ n. a game in which a ball is thrown using a long curved wicker basket.

jail /jāl/ (Brit. also **gaol**) ▶ n. a place for holding people accused or convicted of a crime. ▶ v. put someone in jail.

jail·bait /ˈjālˌbāt/ ▶ n. informal a young woman, or young women as a group, regarded as sexually attractive but under the legal age of consent.

jail·bird /ˈjālˌbərd/ ▶ n. informal a person who is or has repeatedly been in prison.

jail·break /ˈjālˌbrāk/ ▶ n. an escape from jail.

jail·er /ˈjālər/ ▶ n. **1** a person in charge of a jail or its prisoners. **2** someone who forcibly confines someone else.

jail·house /ˈjālˌhous/ ▶ n. a prison.

Jain /jān/ ▶ n. a follower of Jainism. ▶ adj. relating to Jainism.

Jain·ism /ˈjāˌnizəm/ ▶ n. an Indian religion characterized by nonviolence and strict self-discipline.

jake /jāk/ ▶ adj. informal all right; satisfactory.

ja·la·pe·ño /ˌhäləˈpānyō, -ˈpē-/ ▶ n. (pl. **jalapeños**) a very hot green chili pepper.

ja·lop·y /jəˈläpē/ ▶ n. (pl. **jalopies**) informal a dilapidated old car.

jal·ou·sie /ˈjaləˌsē/ ▶ n. a blind or shutter made of a row of angled slats.

jam¹ /jam/ ▶ v. (**jams, jamming, jammed**) **1** squeeze or pack tightly into a space: *four of us were jammed in one compartment.* **2** push something roughly and forcibly into position: *he jammed his hat on.* **3** crowd onto a road or area so as to block it. **4** become or make unable to function due to a part becoming stuck: *the photocopier jammed.* **5** (**jam something on**) apply something forcibly: *he jammed on the brakes.* **6** make a radio transmission unintelligible by causing interference. **7** informal improvise with other musicians. ▶ n. **1** an instance of something jamming or becoming stuck. **2** informal an awkward situation. **3** informal an improvised performance by a group of musicians. ∎ **jam·mer** n.

jam² ▶ n. a thick spread made from sweetened fruit.

Ja·mai·can /jəˈmākən/ ▶ n. a person from Jamaica. ▶ adj. relating to Jamaica.

jamb /jam/ ▶ n. a side post of a doorway, window, or fireplace.

jam·ba·lay·a /ˌjəmbəˈlīə/ ▶ n. a Cajun dish of rice with shrimp, chicken, and vegetables.

jam·bo·ree /ˌjambəˈrē/ ▶ n. **1** a lavish or noisy celebration or party. **2** a large rally of Boy Scouts

or Girl Scouts.

jam-packed ▶ adj. informal extremely crowded or full to capacity.

Jan. ▶ abbr. January.

Jane Doe /ˈjān ˈdō/ ▶ n. an anonymous female party in a legal action or an unidentified woman.

jan·gle /ˈjaNGgəl/ ▶ v. **1** make or cause to make a ringing metallic sound. **2** (of a person's nerves) be set on edge. ▶ n. a ringing metallic sound. ∎ **jan·gly** adj.

jan·is·sar·y /ˈjaniˌserē/ ▶ n. (pl. **janissaries**) historical a Turkish infantryman in the Sultan's guard.

jan·i·tor /ˈjanitər/ ▶ n. a caretaker of a building; a custodian. ∎ **jan·i·to·ri·al** /ˌjaniˈtôrēəl/ adj.

Jan·u·ar·y /ˈjanyōōˌerē/ ▶ n. (pl. **Januaries**) the first month of the year.

Jap /jap/ ▶ n. & adj. informal, offensive short for JAPANESE.

ja·pan /jəˈpan/ ▶ n. a black glossy varnish originating in Japan. ▶ v. (**japans, japanning, japanned**) varnish something with japan.

Jap·a·nese /ˌjapəˈnēz, -ˈnēs/ ▶ n. (pl. same) **1** a person from Japan. **2** the language of Japan. ▶ adj. relating to Japan.

Jap·a·nese bee·tle ▶ n. a metallic green and copper beetle that is a garden pest in both its adult and larval stages.

jape /jāp/ ▶ n. dated a practical joke.

ja·pon·i·ca /jəˈpänikə/ ▶ n. an Asian shrub of the rose family, with bright red flowers.

jar¹ /jär/ ▶ n. a wide-mouthed cylindrical container made of glass or pottery.

jar² ▶ v. (**jars, jarring, jarred**) **1** send a painful or uncomfortable shock through a part of the body. **2** strike against something with an unpleasant vibration or jolt. **3** have an unpleasant or annoying effect: *a laugh that jarred on the ears.* **4** conflict or clash with something: *the play's symbolism jarred with the realism of its setting.* ▶ n. an instance of jarring. ∎ **jar·ring** adj.

jar·di·nière /ˌjärdnˈi(ə)r, ˌzʜärdnˈye(ə)r/ ▶ n. **1** an ornamental pot or stand for displaying plants. **2** a garnish of mixed vegetables.

jar·gon /ˈjärgən/ ▶ n. words or expressions used by a particular group that are difficult for other people to understand. ∎ **jar·gon·is·tic** /ˌjärgəˈnistik/ adj. **jar·gon·ize** v.

jas·mine /ˈjazmən/ ▶ n. a shrub or climbing plant with sweet-smelling white, pink, or yellow flowers.

jas·per /ˈjaspər/ ▶ n. an opaque reddish-brown variety of quartz.

jaun·dice /ˈjôndis/ ▶ n. **1** yellowing of the skin or whites of the eyes, caused especially by a liver disorder. **2** bitterness or resentment. ∎ **jaun·diced** adj.

jaunt /jônt/ ▶ n. a short trip for pleasure.

jaun·ty /ˈjôntē/ ▶ adj. (**jauntier, jauntiest**) having a lively and self-confident manner. ∎ **jaun·ti·ly** adv. **jaun·ti·ness** n.

Ja·va /ˈjävə, ˈjavə/ ▶ n. trademark a computer programming language designed to work across different computer systems.

Ja·van /ˈjävən, ˈjavən/ ▶ n. a person from the Indonesian island of Java. ▶ adj. relating to Java.

Jav·a·nese /ˌjävəˈnēz, -ˈnēs/ ▶ n. (pl. same) **1** a person from Java. **2** the language of central Java. ▶ adj. relating to Java.

jave·lin /ˈjav(ə)lən/ ▶ n. a long, light spear

thrown in a competitive sport or as a weapon.

jaw /jô/ ▸ n. **1** each of the upper and lower bony structures in vertebrates forming the framework of the mouth and containing the teeth. **2** (**jaws**) the grasping, biting, or crushing mouthparts of an invertebrate. **3** (**jaws**) the gripping parts of a tool such as a wrench or vice. ▸ v. informal talk or gossip at length.

jaw·bone /'jô,bōn/ ▸ n. a bone of the jaw, especially that of the lower jaw.

jaw-drop·ping ▸ adj. informal amazing.

jaw·line /'jô,līn/ ▸ n. the contour of the lower edge of a person's jaw.

jay /jā/ ▸ n. a noisy bird of the crow family with boldly patterned plumage.

jay·walk /'jā,wôk/ ▸ v. walk across a street in violation of pedestrian laws, especially where there is no crosswalk or at an intersection when the traffic has the right of way. ■ **jay·walk·er** n.

jazz /jaz/ ▸ n. a type of music of black American origin, typically instrumental and characterized by improvisation. ▸ v. (**jazz something up**) make something more lively or attractive.
− PHRASES **and all that jazz** informal and other similar things.

jazz·y /'jazē/ ▸ adj. (**jazzier, jazziest**) **1** relating to or like jazz. **2** bright, colorful, and showy.

jct. ▸ abbr. junction.

jeal·ous /'jeləs/ ▸ adj. **1** envious of someone else's achievements or advantages. **2** having a resentful suspicion that one's partner is sexually attracted to or involved with someone else: *a jealous husband.* **3** very protective of one's rights or possessions: *they kept a jealous eye over their interests.* ■ **jeal·ous·ly** adv. **jeal·ous·y** n. (pl. **jealousies**).

jeans /jēnz/ ▸ pl.n. casual pants made of denim.

jeep /jēp/ ▸ n. trademark a sturdy motor vehicle with four-wheel drive.

jee·pers /'jēpərz/ ▸ exclam. used to express surprise or alarm.

jeer /ji(ə)r/ ▸ v. make rude and mocking remarks to someone. ▸ n. a rude and mocking remark.

jeez /jēz/ ▸ exclam. a mild expression used to show surprise or annoyance.

je·had ▸ n. variant spelling of JIHAD.

Je·ho·vah /jə'hōvə/ ▸ n. a form of the Hebrew name of God.

Je·ho·vah's Wit·ness ▸ n. a member of a Christian sect that denies many traditional Christian doctrines and preaches that Jesus will return to earth at the Last Judgment.

je·june /ji'jōōn/ ▸ adj. **1** naive and simplistic. **2** (of ideas or writings) dull.

je·ju·num /ji'jōōnəm/ ▸ n. the part of the small intestine between the duodenum and ileum.

Jek·yll /'jekəl/ ▸ n. (in phrase **a Jekyll and Hyde**) a person who displays alternately good and evil personalities.

jell /jel/ ▸ v. variant spelling of GEL².

jel·la·ba /jə'läbə/ ▸ n. variant spelling of DJELLABA.

jel·lied /'jelēd/ ▸ adj. (of food) set in a jelly.

jell·o /'jelō/ (also trademark **Jell-O**) ▸ n. a fruit-flavored gelatin dessert made up from a powder.

Jell·o shot ▸ n. an alcoholic beverage consisting of liquor incorporated into sweetened gelatin dessert and chilled in a small container.

jel·ly /'jelē/ ▸ n. (pl. **jellies**) **1** a sweet semisolid spread made from fruit juice and sugar boiled to

a thick consistency. **2** a substance with a similar semisolid consistency: *the eggs are encased in an amber-colored jelly.* **3** a gumdrop or other candy made with gelatin.

jel·ly bean ▸ n. a bean-shaped candy with a jellylike center and a firm sugar coating.

jel·ly·fish /'jelē,fish/ ▸ n. (pl. same or **jellyfishes**) a sea animal with a soft bell- or saucer-shaped body that has stinging tentacles around the edge.

jel·ly roll ▸ n. a cylindrical cake made from a flat sponge cake spread with a filling such as jam and rolled up.

jen·ny /'jenē/ ▸ n. (pl. **jennies**) a female donkey or ass.

jeop·ard·ize /'jepər,dīz/ ▸ v. put someone or something into a situation where there is a risk of loss, harm, or failure.

jeop·ard·y /'jepərdē/ ▸ n. danger of loss, harm, or failure.

jer·bo·a /jər'bōə/ ▸ n. a rodent with very long hind legs found in deserts from North Africa to central Asia.

jer·e·mi·ad /jerə'mīəd, -,ad/ ▸ n. a long, mournful complaint.

jerk¹ /jərk/ ▸ n. **1** a quick, sharp, sudden movement. **2** informal a stupid person. ▸ v. **1** move or raise something with a jerk. **2** (**jerk someone around**) informal deal with someone dishonestly or unfairly. ■ **jerk·er** n.

jerk² ▸ v. prepare pork or chicken by marinating it in spices and barbecuing it over a wood fire. ▸ n. meat that has been marinated and barbecued over a wood fire.

jer·kin /'jərkin/ ▸ n. a sleeveless jacket.

jerk·y¹ /'jərkē/ ▸ adj. (**jerkier, jerkiest**) moving in abrupt stops and starts. ■ **jerk·i·ly** adv. **jerk·i·ness** n.

jerk·y² ▸ n. meat that has been cured by being cut into long, thin strips and dried.

jer·o·bo·am /jerə'bōəm/ ▸ n. a wine bottle with a capacity four times larger than that of an ordinary bottle.

Jer·ry /'jerē/ ▸ n. (pl. **Jerries**) informal, derogatory a German.

jer·ry-built ▸ adj. badly or hastily built. ■ **jer·ry-build·er** n.

jer·sey /'jərzē/ ▸ n. (pl. **jerseys**) **1** a knitted garment with long sleeves. **2** a distinctive shirt worn by a player in certain sports. **3** a soft knitted fabric. **4** (**Jersey**) an animal of a breed of light brown dairy cattle.

Je·ru·sa·lem ar·ti·choke /jə'rōōs(ə)ləm, -'rōōz-/ ▸ n. a knobbly root vegetable with white flesh.

jest /jest/ ▸ n. a joke. ▸ v. speak or act in a joking way.

jest·er /'jestər/ ▸ n. historical a professional joker or "fool" at a medieval court.

Jes·u·it /'jezhōōit, 'jez(y)ōō-/ ▸ n. a member of the Society of Jesus, a Roman Catholic order of priests founded by St. Ignatius Loyola.

Jes·u·it·i·cal /jezhōō'itikəl, jez(y)ōō-/ ▸ adj. **1** relating to the Jesuits. **2** using evasive language, in a way once associated with Jesuits.

Je·sus /'jēzəs/ (also **Jesus Christ**) ▸ n. the central figure of the Christian religion, believed by Christians to be the Messiah and the Son of God. ▸ exclam. informal expressing irritation, dismay, or surprise.

jet¹ /jet/ ▸ n. **1** a rapid stream of liquid or gas forced out of a small opening. **2** an aircraft powered by jet engines. ▶ v. (**jets, jetting, jetted**) **1** spurt out in a jet. **2** travel by jet aircraft.

jet² ▶ n. **1** a hard black semiprecious mineral. **2** (also **jet black**) a glossy black color.

je·té /zhə'tā/ ▶ n. Ballet a spring from one foot to the other, with the following leg extended backward while in the air.

jet en·gine ▶ n. an aircraft engine that provides force for forward movement by ejecting a high-speed jet of gas obtained by burning fuel in air.

jet·foil /'jet,foil/ ▶ n. a type of passenger-carrying hydrofoil.

jet lag ▶ n. extreme tiredness and other effects felt by a person after a long flight across different time zones. ■ **jet-lagged** adj.

jet·lin·er /'jet,līnər/ ▶ n. a large jet aircraft that carries passengers.

jet pro·pul·sion ▶ n. propulsion by the backward ejection of a high-speed jet of gas or liquid.

jet·sam /'jetsəm/ ▶ n. unwanted material or goods that have been thrown overboard from a ship and washed ashore.

jet set ▶ n. (**the jet set**) informal fashionable and wealthy people who frequently travel abroad for pleasure. ■ **jet-set·ter** n. **jet-set·ting** adj.

jet ski ▶ n. trademark a small jet-propelled vehicle that skims across the surface of water and is ridden in a similar way to a motorcycle. ■ **jet-ski·er** n. **jet-ski·ing** n.

jet stream ▶ n. any of several narrow bands of very strong predominantly westerly air currents encircling the globe several miles above the earth.

jet·ti·son /'jetisən, -zən/ ▶ v. **1** throw or drop something from an aircraft or ship. **2** abandon or discard an unwanted person or thing.

jet·ty /'jetē/ ▶ n. (pl. **jetties**) **1** a landing stage or small pier for boats. **2** a construction built out into the water to protect a harbor, riverbank, or coastline.

jeu·nesse do·rée /zhə,nes dô'rā/ ▶ n. fashionable, wealthy, and stylish young people.

Jew /jōō/ ▶ n. a member of the people whose traditional religion is Judaism and who trace their origins to the ancient Hebrew people of Israel.

jew·el /'jōōəl/ ▶ n. **1** a precious stone. **2** (**jewels**) pieces of jewelry. **3** a hard precious stone used as a bearing in a watch or other device. **4** a highly valued person or thing: *she was a jewel of a nurse.* ■ **jew·eled** adj.
– PHRASES **the jewel in the crown** the most valuable or successful part of something.

jew·el box ▶ n. a storage box for a compact disc.

jew·el·er /'jōō(ə)lər/ (Brit. **jeweller**) ▶ n. a person who makes or sells jewelry.

jew·el·ry /'jōō(ə)lrē/ (Brit. **jewellery**) ▶ n. personal ornaments such as necklaces, rings, or bracelets.

Jew·ess /'jōō-is/ ▶ n. usu. offensive a Jewish woman or girl.

Jew·ish /'jōō-ish/ ▶ adj. relating to Jews or Judaism. ■ **Jew·ish·ness** n.

Jew·ish New Year ▶ n. another term for ROSH HASHANAH.

Jew·ry /'jōōrē/ ▶ n. Jews as a group.

Jew's harp ▶ n. a small musical instrument like a U-shaped harp, held between the teeth and struck with a finger.

Je·ze·bel /'jezə,bel, -bəl/ ▶ n. a shameless or immoral woman.

jiao /jyou/ ▶ n. (pl. same) a unit of money of China, equal to one tenth of a yuan.

jib /jib/ ▶ n. **1** Sailing a triangular sail set in front of the mast. **2** the projecting arm of a crane.

jibe¹ /jīb/ ▶ n. & v. variant spelling of GIBE.

jibe² (Brit. **gybe**) Sailing ▶ v. **1** change course by swinging the sail across a following wind. **2** (of a sail or boom) swing across the wind. ▶ n. an act of jibing.

jibe³ ▶ v. (usu. **jibe with**) informal be in accordance or agree with something.

jif·fy /'jifē/ (also **jiff**) ▶ n. informal a moment.

jig /jig/ ▶ n. **1** a lively dance with leaping movements. **2** a device that holds a piece of work and guides the tool operating on it. ▶ v. (**jigs, jigging, jigged**) **1** move up and down jerkily. **2** dance a jig.

jig·ger¹ /'jigər/ ▶ n. **1** a machine or vehicle with a part that rocks or moves to and fro. **2** a measure of liquor or wine. ▶ v. informal rearrange or tamper with something.

jig·ger² ▶ n. variant spelling of CHIGGER.

jig·gle /'jigəl/ ▶ v. move lightly and quickly from side to side or up and down. ▶ n. an instance of jiggling. ■ **jig·gly** adj.

jig·gy /'jigē/ ▶ adj. informal **1** uninhibited, especially in a sexual way. **2** trembling or nervous, especially as the result of drug withdrawal.

jig·saw /'jig,sô/ ▶ n. **1** a puzzle consisting of a picture printed on cardboard or wood and cut into many interlocking shapes that have to be fitted together. **2** a machine saw with a fine blade enabling it to cut curved lines.

ji·had /ji'häd/ (also **jehad**) ▶ n. (in Islam) a war or struggle against unbelievers. ■ **ji·had·ist** n.

ji·had·i /ji'hädē/ (also **jehadi**) ▶ n. (pl. **jihadis**) a person involved in a jihad.

jilt /jilt/ ▶ v. abruptly break off a relationship with a lover.

Jim Crow /'jim 'krō/ ▶ n. **1** the former practice of segregating black people in the US. **2** offensive a black person. ■ **Jim Crow·ism** n.

jim·my /'jimē/ (also Brit. **jemmy** /'jemē/) ▶ n. (pl. **jimmies**) a short crowbar, used especially by burglars. ▶ v. (**jimmies, jimmying, jimmied**) informal force open a window or door with a jimmy.

jim·son weed /'jimsən/ ▶ n. a strong-smelling poisonous plant with large, trumpet-shaped white flowers and toothed leaves.

jin·gle /'jiNGgəl/ ▶ n. **1** a light ringing sound such as that made by metal objects being shaken together. **2** a short, easily remembered slogan, verse, or tune. ▶ v. make a light ringing sound. ■ **jin·gler** n. **jin·gly** adj.

jin·go·ism /'jiNGgō,izəm/ ▶ n. chiefly derogatory extreme patriotism in the form of aggressive foreign policy. ■ **jin·go·ist** n. **jin·go·is·tic** /,jiNGgō'istik/ adj.

jink /jiNGk/ ▶ v. change direction suddenly and nimbly. ▶ n. a sudden quick change of direction.

jinn /jin/ (also **djinn**) ▶ n. (pl. same or **jinns**) (in Arabian and Muslim mythology) an intelligent spirit able to appear in human or animal form.

jinx /jiNGks/ ▶ n. a person or thing that brings bad luck. ▶ v. bring bad luck to someone or something.

jir·ga /'jərgə/ ▶ n. (in Afghanistan) a tribal council.

jit·ter /'jitər/ informal ▶ n. **1** (**the jitters**) a feeling of

extreme nervousness. **2** slight irregular variation in an electrical signal. ▸ v. act nervously.
■ **jit·ter·i·ness** n. **jit·ter·y** adj.

jit·ter·bug /'jitər,bəg/ ▸ n. a fast dance performed to swing music, popular in the 1940s.
▸ v. (**jitterbugs, jitterbugging, jitterbugged**) dance the jitterbug.

jiu·jit·su ▸ n. variant spelling of JUJITSU.

jive /jīv/ ▸ n. a style of lively dance popular in the 1940s and 1950s, performed to swing music or rock and roll. ▸ v. dance the jive. ■ **jiv·er** n.

job /jōb/ ▸ n. **1** a paid position of regular employment. **2** a task or piece of work. **3** informal a crime, especially a robbery. **4** informal a procedure to improve the appearance of something: *a nose job.* ▸ v. (**jobs, jobbing, jobbed**) (usu. as adj. **jobbing**) do casual or occasional work.
– PHRASES **do the job** informal achieve the required result: *a piece of board will do the job.* **do a job on someone** informal do something that harms or defeats an opponent.

job·ber /'jäbər/ ▸ n. **1** a person who does casual or occasional work. **2** informal a professional wrestler who frequently loses a match.

job·less /'jäbləs/ ▸ adj. without a paid job.
■ **job·less·ness** n.

job lot ▸ n. a batch of articles sold or bought at one time, especially at a discount.

job-share ▸ v. (of two part-time employees) share a single full-time job. ▸ n. an arrangement in which two part-time employees share a full-time job. ■ **job-shar·er** n.

jock /jäk/ ▸ n. informal **1** an enthusiast or participant in a particular sport or other activity. **2** a disk jockey. **3** a young man who is socially adept and physically fit but not very intelligent. **4** a pilot.

jock·ey /'jäkē/ ▸ n. (pl. **jockeys**) a professional rider in horse races. ▸ v. (**jockeys, jockeying, jockeyed**) struggle to gain or achieve something: *drivers are constantly jockeying for position.*

jock·strap /'jäk,strap/ ▸ n. a support or pouch worn to protect a man's genitals, especially in sports.

jo·cose /jō'kōs/ ▸ adj. formal playful or humorous.
■ **jo·cose·ly** adv. **jo·cos·i·ty** /-'käsitē/ n. (pl. **jocosities**).

joc·u·lar /'jäkyələr/ ▸ adj. humorous or amusing.
■ **joc·u·lar·i·ty** /jäkyə'laritē/ n. **joc·u·lar·ly** adv.

joc·und /'jäkənd, 'jō-/ ▸ adj. formal cheerful and lighthearted.

jodh·purs /'jädpərz/ ▸ pl.n. trousers worn for horse riding that are close-fitting below the knee.

Joe Blow ▸ n. informal a name for a hypothetical average man.

jog /jäg/ ▸ v. (**jogs, jogging, jogged**) **1** run at a steady, gentle pace, especially for exercise. **2** (**jog along/on**) continue in a steady, uneventful way. **3** knock something slightly. ▸ n. **1** a spell of jogging. **2** a gentle running pace. **3** a slight push or knock. ■ **jog·ger** n.
– PHRASES **jog someone's memory** make someone remember something.

jog·gle /'jägəl/ ▸ v. move with repeated small jerks.

john /jän/ ▸ n. informal **1** a toilet. **2** a prostitute's client.

John Bull ▸ n. a character representing England or the typical Englishman.

John Doe ▸ n. an anonymous male party in a legal action or an unidentified man.

John Do·ry /'dôrē/ ▸ n. (pl. **John Dories**) an edible dory (fish) of the eastern Atlantic and Mediterranean, with a black oval mark on each side.

John Han·cock ▸ n. informal a person's signature: *put your John Hancock right here.*

john·ny·come·late·ly ▸ n. informal a newcomer to or late starter at a place or area of activity.

joie de vi·vre /,zʜwä də 'vēvrə/ ▸ n. lively enjoyment of life.

join /join/ ▸ v. **1** link or become linked to. **2** unite to form a whole: *they joined up with local environmentalists.* **3** become a member or employee of an organization. **4** (also **join in**) take part in an activity. **5** meet or go somewhere with someone. **6** (**join up**) become a member of the armed forces. ▸ n. a place where things are connected or fastened together. ■ **join·a·ble** adj.
– PHRASES **join forces** combine efforts.

join·er /'joinər/ ▸ n. **1** informal a person who readily joins groups or campaigns. **2** dated a person who constructs the wooden parts of a building.

joint /joint/ ▸ n. **1** a point at which parts are joined. **2** a structure in the body by which two bones are fitted together. **3** the part of a plant stem from which a leaf or branch grows. **4** Brit. a large piece of meat; a roast. **5** informal a place for eating, drinking, or entertainment: *a burger joint.* **6** informal a marijuana cigarette. ▸ adj. **1** shared, held, or made by two or more people: *a joint account.* **2** sharing in an achievement or activity. ▸ v. **1** (usu. as adj. **jointed**) provide or fasten something with joints. **2** cut beef, fowl, etc., at the joint, creating separate pieces for roasting, frying, etc. ■ **joint·ly** adv.
– PHRASES **out of joint 1** (of a joint of the body) dislocated. **2** in a state of disorder.

Joint Chiefs of Staff ▸ n. the chiefs of the Army and Air Force, the commandant of the Marine Corps, and the chief of Naval Operations.

joint·er /'jointər/ ▸ n. a plane for preparing a wooden edge for joining to another.

joint-stock ▸ adj. relating to joint ownership by shareholders.

joist /joist/ ▸ n. a length of lumber or steel supporting the floor or ceiling of a building.

jo·jo·ba /hō'hōbə/ ▸ n. an oil extracted from the seeds of a North American shrub, used in cosmetics.

joke /jōk/ ▸ n. **1** a thing that someone says to cause amusement or laughter. **2** a trick played for fun. **3** informal a ridiculously inadequate person or thing: *public transportation is a joke.* ▸ v. make jokes. ■ **jok·ey** (also **joky**) adj. **jok·ing·ly** adv.
– PHRASES **the joke is on someone** informal someone looks foolish, especially after trying to make someone else look so.

jok·er /'jōkər/ ▸ n. **1** a person who is fond of joking. **2** informal a foolish or ridiculous person. **3** a playing card with the figure of a jester, used as a wild card.
– PHRASES **the joker in the deck** a person or factor likely to have an unpredictable effect.

jol·li·fi·ca·tion /jäləfi'kāsʜən/ ▸ n. lively celebration with others; merrymaking.

jol·li·ty /'jälitē/ ▸ n. (pl. **jollities**) **1** lively and cheerful activity. **2** the quality of being cheerful.

jol·ly¹ /'jälē/ ▸ adj. (**jollier, jolliest**) **1** happy and cheerful. **2** lively and entertaining. ▸ v. (**jollies**,

jollying, jollied) informal encourage in a friendly way: *he jollied her along.* ► adv. Brit. informal very. ■ **jol·li·ly** adv. **jol·li·ness** n.

– PHRASES **get one's jollies** informal have fun or find pleasure.

jol·ly² (also **jolly boat**) ► n. (pl. **jollies**) a ship's boat that is smaller than a cutter.

Jol·ly Rog·er /ˈjälē ˈräjər/ ► n. a pirate's flag with a white skull and crossbones on a black background.

jolt /jōlt/ ► v. **1** push or shake someone or something abruptly and roughly. **2** shock someone into taking action. ► n. **1** a sudden or violent movement. **2** a surprise or shock.

jon·quil /ˈjänkwəl/ ► n. a narcissus with small sweet-smelling yellow flowers.

Jor·da·ni·an /jôrˈdänēən/ ► n. a person from Jordan. ► adj. relating to Jordan.

josh /jäsʜ/ ► v. informal tease someone playfully. ■ **josh·er** n.

Josh·u·a tree /ˈjäsʜo͞oə/ ► n. a tall branching yucca of SW North America, with clusters of spiky leaves.

jos·tle /ˈjäsəl/ ► v. **1** push or bump against someone roughly. **2** (**jostle for**) struggle or compete forcefully for: *they jostled for control of the company.*

jot /jät/ ► v. (**jots, jotting, jotted**) write something quickly. ► n. a very small amount: *his rich voice has not lost a jot of its power.*

jot·tings /ˈjätiNGZ/ ► pl.n. brief, sketchy, or incomplete notes or drawings.

joule /jo͞ol/ ► n. the unit of work or energy in the SI system.

jounce /jouns/ ► v. jolt or bounce.

jour·nal /ˈjərnl/ ► n. **1** a newspaper or magazine dealing with a particular subject. **2** a diary or daily record. ► v. (**journals, journaling, journaled**) write in a journal or diary.

jour·nal·ese /ˌjərnlˈēz/ ► n. informal an unoriginal and poor writing style supposedly typical of journalists.

jour·nal·ism /ˈjərnlˌizəm/ ► n. the activity or profession of being a journalist.

jour·nal·ist /ˈjərnl-ist/ ► n. a person who writes for newspapers or magazines or prepares news or features to be broadcast on radio or television. ■ **jour·nal·is·tic** /ˌjərnlˈistik/ adj.

jour·ney /ˈjərnē/ ► n. (pl. **journeys**) an act of traveling from one place to another. ► v. (**journeys, journeying, journeyed**) travel somewhere. ■ **jour·ney·er** n.

jour·ney·man /ˈjərnēmən/ ► n. (pl. **journeymen**) **1** a skilled worker who is employed by another. **2** a worker or athlete who is reliable but not outstanding.

joust /joust/ ► v. **1** (of a medieval knight) fight an opponent on horseback with lances. **2** (usu. as n. **jousting**) compete for superiority with someone: *he ignored Sam's verbal jousting.* ► n. a medieval contest in which knights on horseback fought with lances. ■ **joust·er** n.

Jove /jōv/ ► n. (in phrase **by Jove**) dated used for emphasis or to indicate surprise.

jo·vi·al /ˈjōvēəl/ ► adj. cheerful and friendly. ■ **jo·vi·al·i·ty** /ˌjōvēˈalitē/ n. **jo·vi·al·ly** adv.

Jo·vi·an /ˈjōvēən/ ► adj. **1** relating to the planet Jupiter or the class of giant planets to which Jupiter belongs. **2** (in Roman mythology) relating to the god Jove (or Jupiter). ► n. a

hypothetical or fictional inhabitant of the planet Jupiter.

jowl /joul/ ► n. **1** the lower part of a person's cheek, especially when fleshy. **2** the cheek of a pig used as meat: *hog jowls and collard greens.* **3** the loose skin at the throat of cattle. ■ **jowl·y** adj.

joy /joi/ ► n. **1** great pleasure and happiness. **2** a cause of great pleasure and happiness.

joy·ful /ˈjoifəl/ ► adj. feeling or causing great pleasure or happiness. ■ **joy·ful·ly** adv. **joy·ful·ness** n.

joy·less /ˈjoiləs/ ► adj. not giving or feeling any pleasure or satisfaction; grim or dismal.

joy·ous /ˈjoiəs/ ► adj. chiefly literary full of happiness and joy. ■ **joy·ous·ly** adv. **joy·ous·ness** n.

joy·ride /ˈjoiˌrīd/ ► n. informal **1** a fast ride in a stolen vehicle. **2** a ride for enjoyment. ■ **joy·rid·er** n. **joy·rid·ing** n.

joy·stick /ˈjoiˌstik/ ► n. informal **1** the control column of an aircraft. **2** a lever for controlling the movement of an image on a computer screen.

JP ► abbr. Justice of the Peace.

JPEG /ˈjāˌpeg/ ► n. Computing a format for compressing images.

Jr. ► abbr. junior (in names): *George Smith, Jr.*

ju·bi·lant /ˈjo͞obələnt/ ► adj. happy and triumphant. ■ **ju·bi·lant·ly** adv.

ju·bi·la·tion /ˌjo͞obəˈlāsʜən/ ► n. a feeling of great happiness and triumph.

ju·bi·lee /ˈjo͞obəˌlē, ˌjo͞obəˈlē/ ► n. a special anniversary, especially one celebrating twenty-five or fifty years of something.

Judaeo- ► comb.form chiefly British spelling of JUDEO-.

Ju·da·ic /jo͞oˈdāik/ ► adj. relating to Judaism or the ancient Jews.

Ju·da·ism /ˈjo͞odē,izəm, -dā-/ ► n. the religion of the Jews, based on the Old Testament and the Talmud. ■ **Ju·da·ist** n.

Ju·da·ize /ˈjo͞odē,īz, -dā-/ ► v. make someone or something Jewish. ■ **Ju·da·i·za·tion** n.

Ju·das /ˈjo͞odəs/ ► n. a person who betrays a friend.

jud·der /ˈjədər/ ► v. chiefly Brit. shake rapidly and forcefully. ■ **jud·der·y** adj.

Judeo- (also Brit. **Judaeo-**) ► comb.form Jewish; Jewish and ...: *Judeo-Christian.*

judge /jəj/ ► n. **1** a public officer appointed or elected to decide cases in a court of law. **2** a person who decides the results of a competition. **3** a person with the necessary knowledge or skill to give an opinion. ► v. **1** form an opinion about: *a work should be judged on its own merits.* **2** give a verdict on a case or person in a court of law. **3** decide the results of a competition. ■ **judge·ship** /-,sʜip/ n.

judg·ment /ˈjəjmənt/ (also chiefly Brit. **judgement**) ► n. **1** the ability to make considered decisions or form sensible opinions: *an error of judgment.* **2** an opinion or conclusion. **3** a decision of a court of law or judge.

– PHRASES **against one's better judgment** opposite to what one feels to be wise. **sit in judgment** assume the right to judge or criticize someone.

judg·men·tal /jəjˈmentl/ (also chiefly Brit. **judgemental**) ► adj. **1** relating to the use of judgment. **2** excessively critical. ■ **judg·men·tal·ly** adv.

judg·ment call ► n. **1** a ruling by a sports

official that is based on observation and may be appealed. **2** any subjective observation or judgment.

Judg·ment Day ▶ n. the time of the Last Judgment; the end of the world.

ju·di·ca·ture /ˈjo͞odikəˌCHo͝or, -ˌkāCHər/ ▶ n. **1** the administration of a national or state justice system. **2** (**the judicature**) judges as a group.

ju·di·cial /jo͞oˈdisHəl/ ▶ adj. relating to a court of law or judge. ■ **ju·di·cial·ly** adv.

> **USAGE**
> On the difference between **judicial** and **judicious**, see the note at JUDICIOUS.

ju·di·ci·ar·y /jo͞oˈdisHēˌerē, -ˈdisHərē/ ▶ n. (pl. **judiciaries**) (usu. **the judiciary**) the system of judges of a country or state.

ju·di·cious /jo͞oˈdisHəs/ ▶ adj. having or done with good judgment; sensible. ■ **ju·di·cious·ly** adv. **ju·di·cious·ness** n.

> **USAGE**
> **Judicious** and **judicial** do not mean the same thing. **Judicious** means 'having or done with good judgment, sensible' (*the judicious use of public investment*), whereas **judicial** means 'relating to a court of law or judge' (*the judicial system*).

ju·do /ˈjo͞odō/ ▶ n. a sport of unarmed combat using holds and leverage to unbalance the opponent.

jug /jəg/ ▶ n. **1** a large container for liquids, with a handle and a narrow mouth. **2** (**jugs**) vulgar slang a woman's breasts. **3** (**the jug**) informal prison.

jug band ▶ n. a group of jazz, blues, or folk musicians using simple or improvised instruments such as jugs and washboards.

jug·ger·naut /ˈjəgərˌnôt/ ▶ n. a huge, powerful, and overwhelming force or institution: *you can't fight the juggernaut of bureaucracy.*

jug·gle /ˈjəgəl/ ▶ v. **1** continuously throw up and catch a number of objects so as to keep at least one in the air at any time. **2** manage to deal with several activities at the same time. **3** organize or manipulate facts to as to present them in the most effective or favorable way. ■ **jug·gler** n.

jug·u·lar /ˈjəgyələr/ ▶ adj. relating to the neck or throat. ▶ n. (also **jugular vein**) any of several large veins in the neck, carrying blood from the head.
− PHRASES **go for the jugular** attack an opponent's weakest point in an aggressive way.

juice /jo͞os/ ▶ n. **1** the liquid present in fruit or vegetables, often made into a drink. **2** (**juices**) fluid produced by the stomach. **3** (**juices**) liquid coming from meat or other food in cooking. **4** informal fuel or electrical energy. **5** (**juices**) informal a person's creative abilities. ▶ v. **1** extract the juice from fruit or vegetables. **2** (**juice something up**) informal liven something up: *juice up the plot with some love interest.*

juic·er /ˈjo͞osər/ ▶ n. a device for extracting juice from fruit and vegetables.

juic·y /ˈjo͞osē/ ▶ adj. (**juicier, juiciest**) **1** full of juice. **2** informal interestingly scandalous: *a juicy bit of gossip.* **3** informal likely to be rewarding or profitable: *juicy projects.* ■ **juic·i·ly** adv. **juic·i·ness** n.

ju·jit·su /jo͞oˈjitso͞o/ (also **jiujitsu**) ▶ n. a Japanese system of unarmed combat and physical training.

ju·ju /ˈjo͞oˌjo͞o/ ▶ n. **1** a charm or fetish, especially as used by some West African peoples.

2 supernatural power believed to be possessed by a charm or fetish.

ju·jube /ˈjo͞oˌjo͞ob/ ▶ n. **1** an edible berrylike fruit of a shrub, formerly eaten as a cough cure. **2** a jujube-flavored lozenge or candy.

juke·box /ˈjo͞okˌbäks/ ▶ n. a machine that plays a selected musical recording when a coin is inserted.

Jul. ▶ abbr. July.

ju·lep /ˈjo͞oləp/ ▶ n. **1** a sweet drink made from sugar syrup. **2** short for MINT JULEP.

Jul·ian cal·en·dar /ˈjo͞olyən, -lēən/ ▶ n. a calendar introduced by the Roman general Julius Caesar, in which the year consisted of 365 days, every fourth year having 366 (replaced by the Gregorian calendar).

ju·li·enne /ˌjo͞olēˈen/ ▶ n. a portion of food cut into short, thin strips. ▶ v. cut food into short, thin strips.

Ju·ly /jo͞oˈlī/ ▶ n. (pl. **Julys**) the seventh month of the year.

jum·ble /ˈjəmbəl/ ▶ n. an untidy collection of things. ▶ v. mix things up in a confused way.

jum·bo /ˈjəmbō/ informal ▶ n. (pl. **jumbos**) **1** a very large person or thing. **2** (also **jumbo jet**) a very large airliner. ▶ adj. very large.

jump /jəmp/ ▶ v. **1** push oneself off the ground using the muscles in one's legs and feet. **2** move over, onto, or down from somewhere by jumping. **3** move suddenly and quickly: *I jumped to my feet.* **4** make an uncontrolled movement in surprise. **5** (**jump at/on**) accept an opportunity or offer eagerly. **6** (**jump on**) informal attack or criticize someone suddenly. **7** pass abruptly from one subject or state to another. **8** rise suddenly and by a large amount: *prices jumped two percent in two weeks.* **9** (**be jumping**) informal (of a place) be very lively. ▶ n. **1** an act of jumping. **2** a large or sudden change or increase. **3** an obstacle to be jumped by a horse.
− PHRASES **get** (or **have**) **the jump on someone** informal get (or have) an advantage over someone as a result of one's prompt action. **jump down someone's throat** informal respond to someone in a sudden and angry way. **jump out** have a strong visual or mental impact; be very striking: *advertising posters that really jump out at you.* **jump ship** (of a sailor) leave a ship without permission. **jump through hoops** go through a complicated procedure in order to achieve something. **one jump ahead** one stage ahead of a rival.

jump cut ▶ n. (in movies or television) an abrupt transition from one scene to another.

jumped-up ▶ adj. informal considering oneself to be more important than one really is.

jump·er¹ /ˈjəmpər/ ▶ n. **1** a collarless sleeveless dress, usually worn over a blouse. **2** Brit. a sweater.

jump·er² ▶ n. a person or animal that jumps.

jump·er ca·ble ▶ n. each of a pair of cables fitted with clips at either end, used for recharging a battery in a motor vehicle by connecting it to the battery in another.

jump jet ▶ n. a jet aircraft that can take off and land vertically.

jump-off ▶ n. a deciding round in a show jumping competition.

jump rope ▶ n. a length of rope used for jumping by swinging it over the head and under the feet.

jump-start ▶ v. **1** start a car with a dead battery

by using jumper cables or by a sudden release of the clutch while it is being pushed. **2** give impetus to something that is progressing slowly or has stopped. ▶n. an act of jump-starting something.

jump·suit /'jəm(p),sŏŏt/ ▶n. a one-piece garment incorporating a pair of pants and a sleeved top.

jump·y /'jəmpē/ ▶adj. (**jumpier, jumpiest**) informal **1** anxious and uneasy. **2** stopping and starting abruptly. ■ **jump·i·ly** adv. **jump·i·ness** n.

Jun. ▶abbr. June.

jun·co /'jəNGkō/ ▶n. (pl. **juncos**) a small North American songbird related to the buntings, with mainly gray and brown plumage.

junc·tion /'jəNGkshən/ ▶n. **1** a point where two or more things meet or are joined. **2** a place where roads or railroad lines meet. **3** the action of joining things or the state of being joined.

junc·tion box ▶n. a box containing a junction of electric wires or cables.

junc·ture /'jəNGkchər/ ▶n. **1** a particular point in time. **2** a place where things join.

June /jŏŏn/ ▶n. the sixth month of the year.

June bug ▶n. a large brown scarab beetle that appears in late spring and early summer.

June·teenth /jŏŏn'tēnTH/ ▶n. a festival held annually on June 19 by some African Americans to commemorate emancipation from slavery in Texas on that day in 1865.

Jung·i·an /'yŏŏNGgēən/ ▶adj. relating to the Swiss psychologist Carl Jung or his work. ▶n. a follower of Jung or his work.

jun·gle /'jəNGgəl/ ▶n. **1** an area of land with dense forest and tangled vegetation, typically in the tropics. **2** a very complex or competitive situation: *a jungle of competing technologies.* **3** a style of dance music with very fast electronic drum tracks and slower synthesized bass lines. ■ **jun·gly** adj.
– PHRASES **the law of the jungle** the principle that people who are strongest and most selfish will be most successful.

jun·gle gym ▶n. a structure of connected bars or rope for children to climb on.

jun·glist /'jəNGglist/ ▶n. a performer or fan of jungle music. ▶adj. of or relating to jungle music.

jun·ior /'jŏŏnyər/ ▶adj. **1** relating to young or younger people. **2** relating to students in the third year of a four-year course at college or high school. **3** (after a name) referring to the younger of two people with the same name in a family. **4** low or lower in rank or status: *a junior officer.* ▶n. **1** a person who is a specified number of years younger than someone else: *he's five years her junior.* **2** a student in the third year at college or high school. **3** (in sports) a young competitor, typically under the age of 16 or 18. **4** a person with low rank or status.

jun·ior col·lege ▶n. a two-year college offering complete courses of training or preparation for completion at a four-year college.

jun·ior high school ▶n. a school intermediate between an elementary school and a high school.

ju·ni·per /'jŏŏnəpər/ ▶n. an evergreen shrub or small tree with berries that are used to flavor gin.

junk¹ /jəNGk/ ▶n. informal **1** useless or worthless articles or material; rubbish. **2** heroin. ▶v. informal get rid of something regarded as worthless or useless.

junk² ▶n. a flat-bottomed sailboat used in China and the East Indies.

junk bond ▶n. a high-yielding high-risk security, typically issued to finance a takeover.

junk DNA ▶n. genomic DNA that does not encode proteins and whose function is not well understood.

jun·ket /'jəNGkit/ ▶n. **1** informal an extravagant trip enjoyed by officials at public expense. **2** a dish of sweetened curds of milk. ▶v. (**junkets, junketing, junketed**) informal take part in an extravagant trip at public expense.

junk food ▶n. preprepared food with little nutritional value.

junk·ie /'jəNGkē/ (also **junky**) ▶n. informal **1** a drug addict. **2** a person with an obsessive interest in or enthusiasm for something: *a media junkie.*

junk mail ▶n. informal unsolicited advertising or promotional material received through the mail or email.

junk·y /'jəNGkē/ ▶adj. useless or of little value: *her junky blue car.* ▶n. (pl. **junkies**) variant spelling of JUNKIE.

junk·yard /'jəNGk,yärd/ ▶n. a place where scrap is collected before being discarded, reused, or recycled.

Ju·no·esque /jŏŏnō'esk/ ▶adj. (of a woman) tall and shapely.

jun·ta /'hŏŏntə, 'jəntə/ ▶n. a military or political group that rules a country after taking power by force.

Ju·pi·ter /'jŏŏpitər/ ▶n. the largest planet in the solar system, fifth in order from the sun.

Ju·ras·sic /jə'rasik/ ▶adj. Geology relating to the second period of the Mesozoic era (about 208 to 146 million years ago), when large reptiles were dominant and the first birds appeared.

ju·rid·i·cal /jŏŏ'ridikəl/ ▶adj. Law relating to judicial proceedings and the law. ■ **ju·rid·i·cal·ly** adv.

ju·ris·dic·tion /jŏŏris'dikshən/ ▶n. **1** the official power to make legal decisions and judgments: *the Arizona court had no jurisdiction over the defendants.* **2** the area or sphere of activity over which the legal authority of a court or other institution extends. **3** a system of courts of law. ■ **ju·ris·dic·tion·al** adj.

ju·ris·pru·dence /jŏŏris'prŏŏdns/ ▶n. **1** the theory or philosophy of law. **2** a legal system. ■ **ju·ris·pru·den·tial** /-prŏŏ'denchəl/ adj.

ju·rist /'jŏŏrist/ ▶n. **1** a lawyer or a judge. **2** an expert in law. ■ **ju·ris·tic** /jŏŏ'ristik/ adj.

ju·ror /'jŏŏrər, -ôr/ ▶n. a member of a jury.

ju·ry /'jŏŏrē/ ▶n. (pl. **juries**) **1** a group of people (typically twelve) sworn to give a verdict in a legal case on the basis of evidence given in court. **2** a group of people judging a competition.
– PHRASES **the jury is out** a decision has not yet been reached.

ju·ry-rigged ▶adj. **1** (of a ship) having makeshift rigging. **2** makeshift; improvised. ■ **ju·ry-rig** v.

jus /zhŏŏ(s), jŏŏs/ ▶n. (especially in French cuisine) a thin gravy or sauce made from meat juices.

just /jəst/ ▶adj. **1** morally right and fair. **2** appropriate or deserved: *we got our just deserts.* **3** (of an opinion) well founded; justifiable. ▶adv. **1** exactly. **2** exactly or nearly at this or that moment. **3** very recently. **4** by a small amount. **5** simply; only. ■ **just·ly** adv. **just·ness** n.

– PHRASES **just in case** as a precaution. **just so 1** arranged or done very carefully. **2** formal expressing agreement.

jus·tice /ˈjəstis/ ▶ n. **1** behavior or treatment that is morally right and fair. **2** the quality of being right and fair: *the justice of his case.* **3** the administration of law in a way that is fair and morally right. **4** a judge or magistrate.

– PHRASES **bring someone to justice** arrest and try someone in court for a crime. **do oneself justice** perform as well as one is able. **do someone/thing justice** treat someone or something with due fairness.

jus·tice of the peace ▶ n. a magistrate appointed to hear minor cases, perform marriages, grant licenses, etc., in a town, county, or other local district.

jus·ti·ci·a·ble /jəˈstisH(ē)əbəl/ ▶ adj. Law subject to trial in a court of law.

jus·ti·fi·a·ble /ˈjəstəˌfīəbəl, jəstəˈfī-/ ▶ adj. able to be shown to be right or reasonable: *the paper takes justifiable pride in its political coverage.* ■ **jus·ti·fi·a·bil·i·ty** /ˌjəstəˌfīəˈbilitē/ n. **jus·ti·fi·a·bly** adv.

jus·ti·fi·ca·tion /ˌjəstəfiˈkāsHən/ ▶ n. **1** the action of justifying something. **2** good reason for something that exists or has been done: *there's no justification for the job losses.*

jus·ti·fy /ˈjəstəˌfī/ ▶ v. (**justifies, justifying, justified**) **1** prove something to be right or reasonable. **2** be a good reason for: *the*

situation was grave enough to justify further investigation. **3** adjust written words so that the lines of type form straight edges at both sides. ■ **jus·tif·i·ca·to·ry** /jəˈstifəkəˌtôrē, ˌjəstəfiˈkātôrē/ adj. **jus·ti·fi·er** n.

jut /jət/ ▶ v. (**juts, jutting, jutted**) extend out, over, or beyond the main body or line of something.

Jute /jōōt/ ▶ n. a member of a Germanic people that settled in southern Britain in the 5th century. ■ **Jut·ish** adj.

jute /jōōt/ ▶ n. rough fiber made from the stems of a tropical plant, used for making rope or sacking.

ju·ve·nile /ˈjōōvəˌnīl, -vənl/ ▶ adj. **1** relating to young people or animals. **2** childish; immature. ▶ n. **1** a young person or animal. **2** Law a person below the age at which ordinary criminal prosecution is possible (18 in most countries). ■ **ju·ve·nil·i·ty** /ˌjōōvəˈnilitē/ n.

ju·ve·nile de·lin·quen·cy ▶ n. the regular committing of criminal acts by a young person. ■ **ju·ve·nile de·lin·quent** n.

ju·ve·nil·i·a /ˌjōōvəˈnilēə/ ▶ pl.n. works produced by an author or artist when young.

jux·ta·pose /ˈjəkstəˌpōz, jəkstəˈpōz/ ▶ v. place things close together, especially so as to show a contrast: *a world of obscene extravagance juxtaposed with abject poverty.* ■ **jux·ta·po·si·tion** /ˌjəkstəpəˈzisHən/ n.

Kk

K¹ (also **k**) ▶ n. (pl. **Ks** or **K's**) the eleventh letter of the alphabet.

K² ▶ abbr. **1** kelvin(s). **2** Computing kilobyte(s). **3** kilometer(s). **4** (in card games and chess) king. **5** Köchel (catalogue of Mozart's works). **6** informal thousand. ▶ symbol the chemical element potassium.

k ▶ abbr. kilo-.

Kab·ba·lah /'kabələ, kə'bä-/ (also **Kabbala**, **Cabbala, Cabala**, or **Qabalah**) ▶ n. the ancient Jewish tradition of mystical interpretation of the Bible. ■ **Kab·ba·lism** /'kabə,lizəm/ n. **Kab·ba·list** /-list/ n. **Kab·ba·lis·tic** /,kabə'listik/ adj.

ka·bob ▶ n. variant spelling of **KEBAB**.

ka·bu·ki /kə'bōōkē/ ▶ n. a form of traditional Japanese drama performed by men, with stylized song, mime, and dance.

ka·ching /kə'cHiNG/ ▶ n. used to represent the sound of a cash register, especially with reference to making money.

Kad·dish /'kädisH/ ▶ n. **1** an ancient Jewish prayer sequence recited in the synagogue service. **2** a form of the Kaddish recited for the dead.

Kaf·fir /'kafər/ ▶ n. offensive, chiefly S. African a black African.

> **USAGE**
> The word **Kaffir** is a racially abusive and offensive term, and in South Africa its use is actionable.

kaf·fi·yeh /kə'fē(y)ə/ ▶ n. variant spelling of **KEFFIYEH**.

Kaf·ka·esque /,käfkə'esk/ ▶ adj. relating to the Czech novelist Franz Kafka or his nightmarish fictional world.

kaf·tan /'kaftən, -,tan/ (also **caftan**) ▶ n. **1** a woman's long, loose dress. **2** a man's long belted tunic, worn in the Near East.

ka·hu·na /kə'hōōnə/ ▶ n. informal an important person.

kai·se·ki /kī'sekē/ ▶ n. a style of traditional Japanese cuisine in which a series of very small, intricate dishes are prepared; a meal served in this style.

kai·ser /'kīzər/ ▶ n. historical the German Emperor, the Emperor of Austria, or the head of the Holy Roman Empire.

kal·an·cho·e /,kalən'kō-ē, kə'laNGkō-ē/ ▶ n. a tropical succulent plant with clusters of tubular flowers.

Ka·lash·ni·kov /kə'läsHnə,kôf, -,kôv/ ▶ n. a type of rifle or submachine gun made in Russia.

kale /kāl/ (also **kail**) ▶ n. a variety of cabbage with large dark-green leaves and a loosely packed head.

ka·lei·do·scope /kə'līdə,skōp/ ▶ n. **1** a toy consisting of a tube containing mirrors and pieces of colored glass or paper, whose reflections produce changing patterns when the tube is rotated. **2** a constantly changing pattern: *the dancers moved in a kaleidoscope of color.* ■ **ka·lei·do·scop·ic** /-,līdə'skäpik/ adj.

kal·ends ▶ pl.n. variant spelling of **CALENDS**.

Ka·ma Su·tra /'kämə 'sōōtrə/ ▶ n. an ancient Sanskrit work on the art of love and sexual technique.

ka·mi·ka·ze /,kämi'käzē/ ▶ n. (in World War II) a Japanese aircraft loaded with explosives and making a deliberate suicidal crash on an enemy target. ▶ adj. reckless or potentially self-destructive.

kan·ga·roo /,kaNGgə'rōō/ ▶ n. a large Australian marsupial with a long, powerful tail and strong hind legs that enable it to travel by leaping.

kan·ga·roo court ▶ n. an unofficial court formed by a group of people to try someone regarded as guilty of an offense.

kan·ga·roo rat ▶ n. a seed-eating, hopping rodent with large cheek pouches and long hind legs, found from Canada to Mexico.

Kant·i·an /'käntēən/ ▶ adj. relating to the German philosopher Immanuel Kant or his philosophy. ▶ n. a follower of Kant's philosophy. ■ **Kant·i·an·ism** n.

ka·o·lin /'kāəlin/ ▶ n. a fine soft white clay, used for making china and in medicine.

ka·pok /'kā,päk/ ▶ n. a cottonlike substance that grows around the seeds of a tropical tree, used as stuffing for cushions, soft toys, etc.

Ka·po·si's sar·co·ma /kə'pōsēz sär'kōmə, 'kapə,sēz, 'käpō,sHez/ ▶ n. a form of cancer involving multiple tumors of the lymph nodes or skin, occurring chiefly in people with depressed immune systems, for example, as a result of AIDS.

ka·put /kə'pŏŏt, kä-/ ▶ adj. informal broken and useless.

kar·a·bi·ner /,karə'bēnər/ (also **carabiner**) ▶ n. a coupling link with a safety closure, used by rock climbers.

kar·a·kul /'karəkəl/ (also **caracul**) ▶ n. **1** a breed of Asian sheep with a dark curled fleece when young. **2** cloth or fur made from or resembling the fleece of the karakul.

kar·a·o·ke /,karē'ōkē/ ▶ n. a form of entertainment in which people sing popular songs over prerecorded backing tracks.

kar·at /'karət/ (chiefly Brit. also **carat**) ▶ n. a measure of the purity of gold, pure gold being 24 karats.

ka·ra·te /kə'rätē/ ▶ n. an oriental system of unarmed combat using the hands and feet to deliver and block blows.

kar·ma /'kärmə/ ▶ n. **1** (in Hinduism and Buddhism) the sum of a person's actions in this and previous lives, viewed as affecting their fate in this or future existences. **2** informal good or bad luck, viewed as resulting from one's actions. ■ **kar·mic** adj.

karst /kärst/ ▶ n. Geology a limestone region with underground streams and many cavities in the rock. ■ **kars·tic** adj.

kart /kärt/ ▶ n. a small race car with a tubular frame, no suspension, and a rear-mounted engine. ■ **kart·ing** n.

kas·bah /'käzbä/ (also **casbah**) ▶ n. a fortress in the old part of a North African city, and the narrow streets that surround it.

Kash·mir·i /ˌkashˈmi(ə)rē, ˌkazн-/ ▶ n. (pl. **Kashmiris**) **1** a person from Kashmir. **2** the language of Kashmir. ▶ adj. relating to Kashmir.

ka·ta /'kätə/ ▶ n. **1** a system of individual training exercises for practitioners of karate and other martial arts. **2** (pl. same or **katas**) an individual exercise of this kind.

ka·ta·na /kə'tänə/ ▶ n. a long, single-edged sword used by samurai.

ka·ty·did /'kātēˌdid/ ▶ n. a large North American insect related to the grasshoppers, the male of which makes a sound that resembles its name.

ka·va /'kävə/ ▶ n. a Polynesian drink that causes drowsiness, made from the crushed roots of a plant of the pepper family.

kay·ak /'kīˌak/ ▶ n. a canoe made of a light frame with a watertight covering. ▶ v. (**kayaks, kayaking, kayaked**) travel in a kayak. ■ **kay·ak·er** n.

ka·zoo /kə'zōō/ ▶ n. a musical instrument consisting of a pipe with a hole in it, over which is a membrane that produces a buzzing sound when the player hums into it.

KB (also **Kb**) ▶ abbr. kilobyte(s).

KC ▶ abbr. **1** Kansas City. **2** Kennel Club. **3** Knights of Columbus.

kcal ▶ abbr. kilocalorie(s).

ke·a /kēə/ ▶ n. a New Zealand parrot with a long, narrow bill and mainly olive-green plumage.

ke·bab /kə'bäb/ (also **kabob**) ▶ n. a dish of pieces of meat, fish, or vegetables roasted or grilled on a skewer or spit.

kedge /kej/ ▶ v. move a boat by hauling in a hawser attached at a distance to an anchor. ▶ n. a small anchor used for kedging a boat.

keel /kēl/ ▶ n. a lengthwise structure along the base of a ship, often extended downward to increase stability. ▶ v. (**keel over**) **1** fall over; collapse. **2** (of a boat or ship) turn over on its side; capsize.

keel·boat /'kēlˌbōt/ ▶ n. **1** a yacht built with a permanent keel rather than a centerboard. **2** a large, flat freight boat used on rivers.

keel·haul /'kēlˌhôl/ ▶ v. **1** humorous punish or reprimand someone severely. **2** historical punish someone by dragging them through the water under the keel of a ship.

keel·son /'kēlsən/ (also **kelson**) ▶ n. a structure running the length of a ship, that fastens the timbers or plates of the floor to the keel.

keen¹ /kēn/ ▶ adj. **1** eager and enthusiastic. **2** (**keen on**) interested in: *the school was very keen on sports.* **3** (of a blade) sharp. **4** (of a sense) highly developed. **5** quick to understand things: *her keen intellect.* **6** (of the air or wind) extremely cold. ■ **keen·ly** adv. **keen·ness** n.

keen² ▶ v. **1** wail in grief for a dead person. **2** make an eerie wailing sound. ▶ n. an Irish funeral song accompanied with wailing as a lament for the dead.

keep /kēp/ ▶ v. (past and past part. **kept** /kept/) **1** continue to have something. **2** continue in a specified condition, position, or activity: *I should have kept quiet, but I blundered on.* **3** save or retain something for use in the future. **4** store something in a regular place. **5** do something promised, agreed, or necessary: *I have to go and keep another appointment soon.* **6** (of food) remain in good condition. **7** make a note about something. **8** write in a diary. **9** make someone late. **10** provide accommodations and food for someone. **11** own and look after an animal. **12** (as adj. **kept**) (of a woman) supported financially in return for sex. ▶ n. **1** food, clothes, and other essentials for living. **2** the strongest or central tower of a castle.

– PHRASES **for keeps** informal permanently. **keep from** avoid doing something. **keep someone from** prevent someone from doing something. **keep something from** cause something to remain a secret from someone. **keep on** continue to do something. **keep someone/thing on** continue to use or employ someone or something. **keep to 1** avoid leaving a path, road, or place. **2** stay on schedule or to the point being discussed. **3** fulfill a promise. **keep up** move at the same rate as someone or something else. **keep someone up** continue a course of action. **keep up with 1** be aware of current events. **2** continue to be in contact with someone. **keep up with the Joneses** try hard not to be outdone by one's neighbors or friends.

keep·er /'kēpər/ ▶ n. **1** a person who manages or looks after something or someone. **2** a goalkeeper. **3** an object that protects or secures another. **4** informal a thing worth keeping.

keep·ing /'kēpiNG/ ▶ n. (in phrase **in** or **out of keeping with**) harmonious or suitable (or inharmonious or unsuitable) in a particular situation: *the cuisine is in keeping with the hotel's Edwardian character.*

keep·sake /'kēpˌsāk/ ▶ n. a small item kept in memory of the person who gave it or originally owned it.

kef·fi·yeh /kə'fē(y)ə/ (also **kaffiyeh**) ▶ n. a headdress worn by Arab men, consisting of a square of fabric fastened by a band around the head.

keg /keg/ ▶ n. a small barrel. ▶ adj. (of beer) supplied in a keg, to which carbon dioxide has been added.

keis·ter /'kēstər/ (also **keester**) ▶ n. **1** informal a person's buttocks. **2** dated a suitcase, bag, or box for carrying belongings or goods.

ke·loid /'kēˌloid/ ▶ n. an area of fibrous tissue formed at the site of a scar or injury.

kelp /kelp/ ▶ n. a very large brown seaweed with broad fronds divided into strips.

kel·pie /'kelpē/ ▶ n. a water spirit of Scottish folklore, typically taking the form of a horse.

kel·vin /'kelvən/ ▶ n. the SI base unit of thermodynamic temperature, equal to one degree Celsius.

Kel·vin scale ▶ n. the scale of temperature with absolute zero as zero and the freezing point of water as 273.15 kelvins.

ken /ken/ ▶ n. (**one's ken**) one's range of knowledge or understanding. ▶ v. (**kens, kenning**; past and past part. **kenned** or **kent** /kent/) Scottish & N. English **1** know someone or something.

2 recognize someone or something.

ken·do /'ken,dō/ ▶ n. a Japanese form of fencing with two-handed bamboo swords.

ken·nel /'kenl/ ▶ n. 1 a small shelter for a dog. 2 (**kennels**) (treated as sing. or pl.) a boarding or breeding establishment for dogs. ▶ v. (**kennels**, **kenneling**, **kenneled**) put or keep a dog in a kennel or kennels.

kent /kent/ ▶ past and past participle of KEN.

Ken·yan /'kenyən, 'kēnyən/ ▶ n. a person from Kenya. ▶ adj. relating to Kenya.

kep·i /'kāpē, 'kepē/ ▶ n. (pl. **kepis**) a French military cap with a horizontal peak.

kept /kept/ ▶ past and past participle of KEEP.

ker·a·tin /'kerətin/ ▶ n. a fibrous protein forming the main constituent of hair, feathers, hoofs, claws, and horns.

kerb, etc. /kərb/ ▶ n. British spelling of CURB (sense 1 of the noun), etc.

ker·chief /'kərchəf, -,chēf/ ▶ n. 1 a piece of fabric used to cover the head. 2 dated a handkerchief.

kerf /kərf/ ▶ n. 1 a slit made by cutting with a saw. 2 the cut end of a felled tree.

ker·nel /'kərnl/ ▶ n. 1 the softer part of a nut, seed, or fruit stone contained within its hard shell. 2 the seed and hard husk of a cereal, especially wheat. 3 the central or most important part of something: *there is a kernel of truth in what he asserted.*

ker·o·sene /'kerə,sēn, 'kar-, ,kerə'sēn, ,kar-/ ▶ n. a light fuel oil, used in jet engines and domestic heaters and lamps.

kes·trel /'kestrəl/ ▶ n. a small falcon that hovers with rapidly beating wings while searching for prey.

ke·ta·mine /'ketə,mēn, -min/ ▶ n. a medical drug used as an anesthetic and painkiller and also illegally as a hallucinogen.

ketch /kech/ ▶ n. a type of two-masted sailboat.

ketch·up /'kechəp/ (also **catsup**) ▶ n. a spicy sauce made chiefly from tomatoes and vinegar.

ke·tone /'kē,tōn/ ▶ n. any of a class of organic chemical compounds including acetone.

ke·to·sis /kē'tōsis/ ▶ n. the condition of having raised levels of ketones in the body, associated with abnormal fat metabolism and diabetes mellitus. ■ **ke·tot·ic** /-'tätik/ adj.

ket·tle /'ketl/ ▶ n. a metal or plastic container with a lid, spout, and handle, used for boiling water.
– PHRASES **a different kettle of fish** informal something completely different from the one just mentioned. **the pot calling the kettle black** used to say that a person is criticizing someone for faults that they have themselves. **a fine** (or **pretty**) **kettle of fish** informal an awkward situation.

ket·tle·drum /'ketl,drəm/ ▶ n. a large drum shaped like a bowl, with adjustable pitch.

keV ▶ abbr. kiloelectronvolt(s).

Kev·lar /'kevlär/ ▶ n. trademark a very strong synthetic fiber used to reinforce tires, helmets, and bulletproof vests.

key¹ /kē/ ▶ n. (pl. **keys**) 1 a small piece of shaped metal that is inserted into a lock and turned to open or close it. 2 an instrument for grasping and turning a screw, peg, or nut. 3 a lever pressed down by the finger in playing an instrument such as the organ, piano, or flute. 4 each of several buttons on a panel for operating a typewriter or computer terminal. 5 a means of achieving or understanding something: *discipline seems to be the key to her success.* 6 an explanatory list of symbols used in a map or table. 7 a word or system for solving a code. 8 a group of musical notes based on a particular note and comprising a scale. ▶ adj. vitally important: *he was a key figure in the civil war.*
▶ v. (**keys, keying, keyed**) 1 enter or operate on data by means of a computer keyboard. 2 (**be keyed up**) be nervous, tense, or excited. 3 (**key something to**) make something suitable for or in harmony with: *courses keyed to the needs of health professionals.*

key² /kē/ ▶ n. a low-lying island or reef in the Caribbean or off the coast of Florida.

key·board /'kē,bôrd/ ▶ n. 1 a panel of keys for use with a computer or typewriter. 2 a set of keys on a piano or similar musical instrument. 3 an electronic musical instrument with keys arranged as on a piano. ▶ v. enter data by means of a keyboard. ■ **key·board·er** n.

key card (also **card key**) ▶ n. a small plastic card that can be used instead of a door key, containing magnetically encoded data.

key grip ▶ n. the person in a film crew who is in charge of the camera equipment.

key·hole /'kē,hōl/ ▶ n. a hole in a lock into which the key is inserted.

Keynes·i·an /'kānzēən/ ▶ adj. relating to the theories of the English economist John Maynard Keynes, who believed that government spending on public works is necessary to stimulate the economy and provide employment.
■ **Keynes·i·an·ism** n.

key·note /'kē,nōt/ ▶ n. 1 a central theme: *individuality was the keynote of the Nineties.* 2 the note on which a musical key is based. ▶ adj. (of a speech) setting out the central theme of a conference.

key·pad /'kē,pad/ ▶ n. a small keyboard or set of buttons for operating a portable electronic device or telephone.

key·punch /'kē,pənch/ ▶ n. a device for transferring data by means of punched holes or notches on a series of cards or paper tape.

key ring ▶ n. a metal ring for holding keys together in a bunch.

key sig·na·ture ▶ n. Music a combination of sharps or flats after the clef at the beginning of each stave, indicating the key of a composition.

key·stone /'kē,stōn/ ▶ n. 1 the central part of a policy or system: *he has made tax cuts the keystone of his domestic policy.* 2 a central stone at the summit of an arch, locking the whole together.

key·stroke /'kē,strōk/ ▶ n. a single pressing of a key on a keyboard.

key·word /'kē,wərd/ ▶ n. 1 a word or idea of great significance: *homes and jobs are the keywords in the campaign.* 2 a word used in a computer system to indicate the content of a document. 3 a significant word mentioned in an index.

kg ▶ abbr. kilogram(s).

kha·ki /'kakē/ ▶ n. (pl. **khakis**) 1 a cotton or wool fabric of a dull brownish-yellow color, used especially in military clothing. 2 a dull greenish- or yellowish-brown color. 3 (**khakis**) clothing, especially pants, of this fabric and color.

Khal·sa /ˈkälsə/ ▶ n. the company of fully initiated Sikhs to which devout orthodox Sikhs are ritually admitted at puberty.

khan /kän/ ▶ n. a title given to rulers and officials in central Asia, Afghanistan, and some other Muslim countries. ■ **khan·ate** n.

khat /kät/ ▶ n. the leaves of an Arabian shrub, which are chewed (or drunk as an infusion) as a stimulant.

kheer /ki(ə)r/ ▶ n. an Indian dessert consisting of rice and sugar boiled in milk or coconut milk, often flavored with cardamom and ground nuts.

Khmer /kəˈme(ə)r, kme(ə)r/ ▶ n. (pl. same or **Khmers**) 1 a person from Cambodia. 2 the official language of Cambodia.

Khoi·khoi /ˈkoiˌkoi/ (also **Khoi**) ▶ n. (pl. same) a member of a group of peoples of South Africa and Namibia.

kHz ▶ abbr. kilohertz.

kib·ble /ˈkibəl/ ▶ n. ground meal shaped into pellets, especially for pet food.

kib·butz /kiˈbo͝ots/ ▶ n. (pl. **kibbutzim** /ˌkiˌbo͝otˈsēm/) a farming settlement in Israel in which work is shared by the whole community.

kib·butz·nik /kiˈbo͝otsnik/ ▶ n. a member of a kibbutz.

kib·itz /ˈkibits/ ▶ v. informal 1 look on and offer unwelcome advice, especially at a card game. 2 speak informally; chat. ■ **kib·itz·er** n.

ki·bosh /kəˈbäsh, ˈkīˌbäsh/ (also **kybosh**) ▶ n. (in phrase **put the kibosh on**) informal put a decisive end to: *he put the kibosh on the deal.*

kick /kik/ ▶ v. 1 hit or propel someone or something forcibly with the foot. 2 strike out with the foot or feet. 3 informal succeed in giving up a habit or addiction. 4 (of a gun) recoil when fired. ▶ n. 1 an instance of kicking. 2 informal a thrill of pleasurable excitement: *rich kids turning to crime just for kicks.* 3 informal the strong stimulating effect of alcohol or a drug.
– PHRASES **kick against** resist or disagree with something. **kick around** (or **about**) lie unwanted or unused. **kick someone around** treat someone roughly or without respect. **kick something around** discuss an idea informally. **kick the bucket** informal die. **kick in** come into effect or operation. **a kick in the teeth** informal a serious setback. **kick off** 1 (of a football or soccer game) be started or resumed by a player kicking the ball from the center spot. 2 (also **kick something off**) begin or cause something to begin. **kick oneself** be annoyed with oneself. **kick someone out** informal expel or dismiss someone.

kick-ass ▶ adj. informal forceful, vigorous, and aggressive: *he's a kick-ass guy who takes no prisoners.*

kick·back /ˈkikˌbak/ ▶ n. 1 a sudden forceful recoil. 2 informal an underhanded payment made to someone in return for help in arranging a business or political deal.

kick-box·ing ▶ n. a form of martial art that combines boxing with elements of karate, in particular kicking with bare feet.

kick·er /ˈkikər/ ▶ n. 1 the player in a team who scores by kicking or who kicks to gain positional advantage. 2 informal an unexpected and often unpleasant discovery or turn of events. 3 an extra clause in a contract.

kick·ing /ˈkikiNG/ ▶ adj. informal (especially of music) lively and exciting.

kick·off /ˈkikˌôf/ ▶ n. 1 the start or resumption of a soccer match, with a kick from the center spot. 2 informal the start of an event or activity.

kick-pleat ▶ n. an inverted pleat in a narrow skirt to allow freedom of movement.

kick·stand /ˈkikˌstand/ ▶ n. a rod attached to a bicycle or motorcycle that may be kicked into a vertical position to support the vehicle when it is stationary.

kick-start ▶ v. 1 start a motorcycle engine with a downward thrust of a pedal. 2 provide an impetus to start or boost a process: *the government could kick-start the economy by cutting interest rates.* ▶ n. 1 an act of kick-starting something. 2 a device to kick-start an engine.

kid[1] /kid/ ▶ n. 1 informal a child or young person. 2 a young goat.
– PHRASES **handle** (or **treat**) **someone/thing with kid gloves** deal with someone or something very carefully. **kids' stuff** informal something that is easy or simple to do.

kid[2] ▶ v. (**kids**, **kidding**, **kidded**) informal 1 fool someone into believing something. 2 (**kid around**) behave in a silly way.

kid broth·er (or **kid sister**) ▶ n. informal a younger brother (or sister).

kid·die /ˈkidē/ (also **kiddy**) ▶ n. (pl. **kiddies**) informal a young child.

kid·do /ˈkidō/ ▶ n. (pl. **kiddos** or **kiddoes**) informal used as a friendly or slightly condescending form of address.

kid·dush /ˈkidəSH, kēˈdoͦoSH/ ▶ n. a Jewish ceremony of prayer and blessing over wine, performed at a meal preceding the Sabbath or a holy day.

kid·nap /ˈkidˌnap/ ▶ v. (**kidnaps**, **kidnapping**, **kidnapped;** also **kidnaps**, **kidnaping**, **kidnaped**) take someone by force and keep them captive, typically to obtain a ransom for their release. ▶ n. an instance of kidnapping someone. ■ **kid·nap·per** n.

kid·ney /ˈkidnē/ ▶ n. (pl. **kidneys**) 1 each of a pair of organs in the abdominal cavity that remove waste products from the blood and excrete urine. 2 the kidney of a sheep, ox, or pig as food.

kid·ney bean ▶ n. a dark red kidney-shaped bean, eaten as a vegetable.

kid·ney ma·chine ▶ n. a machine that performs the functions of a person's kidney when one or both organs are damaged.

kid·ney stone ▶ n. a hard mass formed in the kidneys, typically consisting of insoluble calcium compounds.

kiel·ba·sa /kilˈbäsə, kēl-/ ▶ n. a highly seasoned Polish sausage, typically containing garlic.

kif /kif/ (also **kef** /kef/) ▶ n. a substance, especially powdered resin from the cannabis plant, smoked to produce a drowsy state.

ki·lim /kēˈlēm, ˈkiləm/ (also **kelim**) ▶ n. a carpet or rug woven without a pile, made in Turkey, Kurdistan, and neighboring areas.

kill /kil/ ▶ v. 1 cause the death of someone or something. 2 put an end to or defeat something. 3 informal overwhelm someone with an emotion: *the suspense is killing me.* 4 informal cause pain or distress to someone. 5 pass time, typically while waiting for an event. ▶ n. 1 an act of killing, especially of one animal by another. 2 an animal or animals killed by a hunter or another animal.
– PHRASES **be in at the kill** be present at or

benefit from the successful completion of an enterprise.

kill·deer /ˈkilˌdi(ə)r/ (also **killdeer plover**) ▶ n. a widespread American plover with a plaintive call that resembles its name.

kill·er /ˈkilər/ ▶ n. **1** a person or thing that kills. **2** informal a very impressive or difficult thing. **3** informal a hilarious joke.

kill·er whale ▶ n. a large toothed whale with black-and-white markings and a prominent fin on its back.

kil·li·fish /ˈkilēˌfiSH/ ▶ n. (pl. same or **killifishes**) a small, brightly colored fish of fresh or brackish water.

kill·ing /ˈkiliNG/ ▶ n. an act of causing death. ▶ adj. informal exhausting or unbearable. – PHRASES **make a killing** make a great deal of money out of something.

kill·ing field ▶ n. a place where many people have been killed, especially during a war.

kill·joy /ˈkilˌjoi/ ▶ n. a person who spoils the enjoyment of others by behaving very seriously or disapprovingly.

kiln /kiln, kil/ ▶ n. a furnace or oven for burning, baking, or drying pottery, bricks, or lime.

ki·lo /ˈkēlō/ ▶ n. (pl. **kilos**) a kilogram.

kilo- ▶ comb.form referring to a factor of one thousand (10^3): *kilometer.*

kil·o·byte /ˈkiləˌbīt/ ▶ n. a unit of information stored in a computer equal to 1,024 bytes.

kil·o·cal·o·rie /ˈkiləˌkalərē/ ▶ n. a unit of energy of one thousand calories (equal to one large calorie).

kil·o·gram /ˈkiləˌgram/ ▶ n. the SI unit of mass, equal to 1,000 grams (approximately 2.205 lb).

kil·o·hertz /ˈkiləˌhərts/ ▶ n. a measure of frequency equivalent to 1,000 cycles per second.

kil·o·joule /ˈkiləˌjo͞ol, ˈkiləˌjoul/ ▶ n. 1,000 joules, especially as a measure of the energy value of foods.

kil·o·li·ter /ˈkiləˌlētər/ ▶ n. 1,000 liters (equivalent to 220 imperial gallons).

kil·o·me·ter /kiˈlämitər, ˈkiləˌmētər/ (Brit. **kilometre**) ▶ n. a metric unit of measurement equal to 1,000 meters (approximately 0.62 miles). ■ **kil·o·met·ric** /ˌkiləˈmetrik/ adj.

kil·o·ton /ˈkiləˌtən/ ▶ n. a unit of explosive power equivalent to 1,000 tons of TNT.

kil·o·volt /ˈkiləˌvōlt/ ▶ n. 1,000 volts.

kil·o·watt /ˈkiləˌwät/ ▶ n. 1,000 watts.

kil·o·watt-hour ▶ n. a measure of electrical energy equivalent to a power consumption of one thousand watts for one hour.

kilt /kilt/ ▶ n. a knee-length skirt of pleated tartan cloth, traditionally worn by men as part of Scottish Highland dress. ▶ v. (usu. as adj. **kilted**) arrange a garment or material in pleats. ■ **kilt·ed** adj.

kil·ter /ˈkiltər/ ▶ n. (in phrase **out of kilter**) out of harmony or balance.

kim·chi /ˈkimCHē/ ▶ n. a Korean dish of spicy pickled cabbage.

ki·mo·no /kəˈmōnō, -nə/ ▶ n. (pl. **kimonos**) a long, loose Japanese robe having wide sleeves and tied with a sash.

kin /kin/ ▶ n. (treated as pl.) one's family and relations. ▶ adj. (of a person) related.

kind¹ /kīnd/ ▶ n. **1** a group or type of people or things with similar characteristics: *all kinds*

of music. **2** character; nature: *language makes humans different in kind from other animals.* **3** (in the Christian Church) each of the elements (bread and wine) consumed during Holy Communion.

– PHRASES **in kind 1** in the same way. **2** (of payment) in goods or services as opposed to money. **kind of** informal rather. **of a kind** only partly deserving the name. **one of a kind** unique. **two** (or **three, four,** etc.) **of a kind** the same or very similar.

> USAGE
> When using **kind** to refer to a plural noun, it is incorrect to say *these kind of questions are not relevant* (that is, to have kind in the singular): you should use *kinds* instead (*these kinds of questions are not relevant*).

kind² ▶ adj. caring, friendly, and generous.

kind·a /ˈkīndə/ informal ▶ contr. kind of: *I think it's kinda funny.*

kin·der·gar·ten /ˈkindərˌgärtn, -ˌgärdn/ ▶ n. a school that prepares children for first grade. ■ **kin·der·gar·ten·er** /-ˌgärtnər, -ˌgärd-/ (also **kindergartner**) n.

kind-heart·ed ▶ adj. having a kind and sympathetic nature. ■ **kind-heart·ed·ly** adv. **kind-heart·ed·ness** n.

kin·dle /ˈkindl/ ▶ v. **1** light a flame or set something on fire. **2** arouse an emotion or reaction: *his enthusiasm for politics was kindled by his wife.*

kin·dling /ˈkindliNG/ ▶ n. small sticks or twigs used for lighting fires.

kind·ly /ˈkīn(d)lē/ ▶ adv. **1** in a kind way. **2** please (used in a polite request). ▶ adj. (**kindlier, kindliest**) kind; warm-hearted. ■ **kind·li·ness** n. – PHRASES **not take kindly to** not welcome or be pleased by something.

kind·ness /ˈkīn(d)nis/ ▶ n. **1** the quality of being caring, friendly, and generous. **2** a kind act.

kin·dred /ˈkindrid/ ▶ n. **1** (treated as pl.) one's family and relations. **2** relationship by blood. ▶ adj. having similar qualities: *books on kindred subjects.*

kin·dred spir·it ▶ n. a person whose interests or attitudes are similar to one's own.

kine /kīn/ ▶ pl.n. old use cows as a group; cattle.

kin·e·mat·ics /ˌkinəˈmatiks/ ▶ pl.n. (treated as sing.) the branch of mechanics concerned with the motion of objects without reference to the forces that cause the motion. ■ **kin·e·mat·ic** adj.

ki·ne·si·ol·o·gy /kəˌnēsēˈäləjē, -zē-/ ▶ n. the study of the mechanics of body movements.

ki·ne·sis /kəˈnēsis/ ▶ n. technical movement; motion.

ki·net·ic /kəˈnetik/ ▶ adj. **1** relating to or resulting from motion. **2** (of a work of art) depending on movement for its effect. ■ **ki·net·i·cal·ly** adv.

ki·net·ic en·er·gy ▶ n. Physics energy that a body possesses as a result of being in motion. Compare with POTENTIAL ENERGY.

ki·net·ics /kəˈnetiks/ ▶ pl.n. (treated as sing.) **1** the branch of chemistry concerned with the rates of chemical reactions. **2** Physics another term for DYNAMICS (sense 1).

ki·ne·to·scope /kəˈnetəˌskōp, -ˈnē-/ ▶ n. an early motion-picture device in which the images were viewed through a peephole.

kin·folk /ˈkinˌfōk/ (also **kinsfolk**) ▶ pl.n. a person's family and other blood relations.

king /kiNG/ ▶ n. **1** the male ruler of an independent country, especially one who inherits the position by birth. **2** the best or most important person or thing in an area of activity or group: *India's king of fruits, the mango.* **3** a playing card bearing a picture of a king, ranking next below an ace. **4** the most important chess piece, which the opponent has to checkmate in order to win. **5** a piece in checkers with extra capacity for moving, made by crowning an ordinary piece that has reached the opponent's baseline. ■ **king·ly** adj. **king·ship** n.

king·bird /ˈkiNGˌbərd/ ▶ n. a large American tyrant flycatcher, typically with a gray head and back and yellowish or white underparts.

King Charles span·iel ▶ n. a small breed of spaniel with a white, black, and tan coat.

king co·bra ▶ n. a brownish cobra native to the Indian subcontinent, the largest of all venomous snakes.

king·dom /ˈkiNGdəm/ ▶ n. **1** a country, state, or territory ruled by a king or queen. **2** an area associated with or dominated by a particular person or thing: *the world they came upon was far from being a kingdom of brotherly love.* **3** the spiritual reign or authority of God. **4** each of the three divisions (animal, vegetable, and mineral) in which natural objects are classified.
– PHRASES **to kingdom come** informal into the next world.

king·fish·er /ˈkiNGˌfishər/ ▶ n. a colorful bird with a long sharp beak that dives to catch fish in rivers and ponds.

King James Bi·ble (also **King James Version**) ▶ n. another name for AUTHORIZED VERSION.

king·let /ˈkiNGlit/ ▶ n. a very small greenish bird with a bright orange or yellow crown.

king·mak·er /ˈkiNGˌmākər/ ▶ n. a person who uses their political influence to bring a leader to power.

king of beasts ▶ n. the lion.

King of Kings ▶ n. (in the Christian Church) God.

king·pin /ˈkiNGˌpin/ ▶ n. **1** a main or large bolt in a central position. **2** a vertical bolt used as a pivot. **3** a person or thing that is essential to the success of an organization or operation.

king post ▶ n. an upright post in the center of a roof truss, extending from the tie beam to the apex of the truss.

king-sized (also **king-size**) ▶ adj. of a larger size than normal; very large.

kink /kiNGk/ ▶ n. **1** a sharp twist or curve in something that is otherwise straight. **2** a flaw or obstacle in a plan or operation. **3** a quirk in a person's character. ▶ v. form a kink in something.

kin·ka·jou /ˈkiNGkəˌjo͞o/ ▶ n. a mammal with a tail that can grasp things, found in the tropical forests of Central and South America.

kink·y /ˈkiNGkē/ ▶ adj. (**kinkier, kinkiest**) **1** informal relating to or liking unusual sexual activities. **2** having kinks or twists. ■ **kink·i·ly** adv. **kink·i·ness** n.

kins·folk /ˈkinzˌfōk/ ▶ pl.n. another term for KINFOLK.

kin·ship /ˈkinˌship/ ▶ n. **1** family or blood relationship. **2** a sharing of characteristics or origins: *they felt a kinship with architects.*

kins·man /ˈkinzmən/ (or **kinswoman**) ▶ n. (pl. **kinsmen** or **kinswomen**) one of a person's blood relations.

ki·osk /ˈkēˌäsk/ ▶ n. a small open-fronted cubicle from which newspapers, refreshments, or tickets

are sold.

kip·per /ˈkipər/ ▶ n. a herring that has been split open, salted, and dried or smoked. ▶ v. cure a herring by splitting it open and salting and drying or smoking it.

kirk /kərk/ ▶ n. Scottish & N. English **1** a church. **2** (**the Kirk** or **the Kirk of Scotland**) the Church of Scotland.

kirsch /ki(ə)rsh/ ▶ n. brandy distilled from the fermented juice of cherries.

kir·tle /ˈkərtl/ ▶ n. old use **1** a woman's gown or outer petticoat. **2** a man's tunic or coat.

kis·met /ˈkizmit, -ˌmet/ ▶ n. destiny or fate.

kiss /kis/ ▶ v. **1** touch or caress someone with the lips as a sign of love, affection, or greeting. **2** Billiards (of a ball) lightly touch another ball. ▶ n. a touch or caress with the lips. ■ **kiss·a·ble** adj.
– PHRASES **kiss of death** an action that ensures that an enterprise will fail. **kiss of life 1** mouth-to-mouth resuscitation. **2** something that revives a failing enterprise. **kiss of peace** a ceremonial kiss given as a sign of unity, especially during the Christian Eucharist (Holy Communion).

kiss·er /ˈkisər/ ▶ n. **1** a person who kisses someone. **2** informal a person's mouth.

kiss·ing cous·in ▶ n. a relative known well enough to greet with a kiss.

kiss·o·gram /ˈkisəˌgram/ ▶ n. a novelty greeting delivered by a person who accompanies it with a kiss.

kiss·y /ˈkisē/ ▶ adj. informal involving or fond of kissing; amorous.

Ki·swa·hi·li /ˌkiswäˈhēlē/ ▶ n. another term for SWAHILI.

kit¹ /kit/ ▶ n. **1** a set of articles or equipment for a specific purpose. **2** a set of all the parts needed to assemble something.

kit² ▶ n. the young of certain animals, e.g., the beaver, ferret, and mink.

kit bag ▶ n. a long cylindrical canvas bag for carrying a soldier's possessions.

kitch·en /ˈkichən/ ▶ n. **1** a room where food is prepared and cooked. **2** a set of cabinets and appliances installed in a kitchen.

kitch·en cab·i·net ▶ n. informal a group of unofficial political advisers considered to be too influential.

kitch·en·ette /ˌkichəˈnet/ ▶ n. a small kitchen or part of a room equipped as a kitchen.

kitch·en gar·den ▶ n. a garden where vegetables and fruit are grown for household use.

kitch·en-sink ▶ adj. (of drama) dealing with working-class life in a very realistic way.

kitch·en·ware /ˈkichənˌwe(ə)r/ ▶ n. kitchen utensils.

kite /kīt/ ▶ n. **1** a toy consisting of a light frame with thin material stretched over it, flown in the wind at the end of a long string. **2** a long-winged bird of prey with a forked tail and a soaring flight. **3** Geometry a quadrilateral figure having two pairs of equal sides next to each other. ▶ v. **1** (usu. as n. **kiting**) fly a kite. **2** informal write or use a check fraudulently.

kite·surf·ing /ˈkītˌsərfiNG/ (also **kiteboarding**) ▶ n. the sport of riding on a surfboard while harnessed or holding onto a specially designed kite, using the wind for propulsion.

kith /kiTH/ ▶ n. (in phrase **kith and kin**) one's family and other relations.

kitsch /kich/ ▶ n. art, objects, or design

considered to be tastelessly showy or sentimental. ■ **kitsch·i·ness** n. **kitsch·y** adj.

kit·ten /'kitn/ ▶ n. **1** a young cat. **2** the young of certain other animals, such as the rabbit and beaver. ▶ v. give birth to kittens.
– PHRASES **have kittens** informal be very nervous or upset.

kit·ten heel ▶ n. a type of low stiletto heel.

kit·ten·ish /'kitn-isH/ ▶ adj. playful, lively, or flirtatious. ■ **kit·ten·ish·ly** adv.

kit·ti·wake /'kitē,wāk/ ▶ n. a small gull that nests in colonies on sea cliffs and has a loud call that resembles its name.

kit·ty¹ /'kitē/ ▶ n. (pl. **kitties**) **1** a fund of money for use by a group of people. **2** a pool of money in some card games.

kit·ty² ▶ n. (pl. **kitties**) a pet name for a cat.

kit·ty-cor·ner ▶ adj. & adv. another term for CATER-CORNERED.

ki·wi /'kēwē/ ▶ n. (pl. **kiwis**) **1** a flightless, tailless New Zealand bird with hairlike feathers and a long downcurved bill. **2** (**Kiwi**) informal a New Zealander.

ki·wi fruit ▶ n. (pl. same) the fruit of an Asian climbing plant, with a thin hairy skin, green flesh, and black seeds.

kJ ▶ abbr. kilojoule(s).

KKK ▶ abbr. Ku Klux Klan.

Klans·man /'klanzmən/ (or **Klanswoman** /'klanz'wŏŏmən/) ▶ n. (pl. **Klansmen** or **Klanswomen**) a member of the Ku Klux Klan, an extremist right-wing secret society in the US.

klax·on /'klaksən/ ▶ n. trademark an electric horn or similar loud warning device.

klep·to·ma·ni·a /,kleptə'mānēə, -'mānyə/ ▶ n. a recurrent urge to steal things. ■ **klep·to·ma·ni·ac** n. & adj.

klieg light /klēg/ ▶ n. a powerful electric lamp used in filming.

klip·spring·er /'klip,sprinɡər/ ▶ n. a small antelope native to rocky regions of southern Africa.

kludge /klŏŏj/ ▶ n. informal something hastily or badly put together.

klutz /kləts/ ▶ n. informal a clumsy, awkward, or foolish person. ■ **klutz·y** adj.

km ▶ abbr. kilometer(s).

knack /nak/ ▶ n. **1** a skill at performing a task. **2** a tendency to do something: *he had the knack of falling asleep anywhere.*

knap·sack /'nap,sak/ ▶ n. a small rucksack used by soldiers and hikers.

knap·weed /'nap,wēd/ ▶ n. a plant with purple thistlelike flowerheads.

knave /nāv/ ▶ n. **1** old use a dishonest or unscrupulous man. **2** (in cards) a jack. ■ **knav·er·y** n. **knav·ish** adj.

knead /nēd/ ▶ v. **1** work dough or clay with the hands. **2** massage a part of the body by squeezing and pressing it.

knee /nē/ ▶ n. **1** the joint between the thigh and the lower leg. **2** the upper surface of a person's thigh when in a sitting position. ▶ v. (**knees, kneeing, kneed**) hit someone with the knee.
– PHRASES **bring someone to their knees** defeat someone or force them to submit.

knee·cap /'nē,kap/ ▶ n. the convex bone in front of the knee joint. ▶ v. (**kneecaps, kneecapping, kneecapped**) shoot someone in the knee or leg as a punishment.

knee-high ▶ n. (usu. **knee-highs**) a sock or nylon stocking with an elasticized top that reaches the knee.

knee-jerk ▶ n. an involuntary kick caused by a blow on the tendon just below the knee. ▶ adj. automatic and unthinking: *a knee-jerk reaction.*

kneel /nēl/ ▶ v. (past and past part. **knelt** /nelt/ or also **kneeled**) fall or rest on a knee or the knees.

kneel·er /'nēlər/ ▶ n. a cushion or bench for kneeling on.

knell /nel/ literary ▶ n. the sound of a bell, especially when rung solemnly for a death or funeral. ▶ v. (of a bell) ring solemnly.

knelt /nelt/ ▶ past and past participle of KNEEL.

knew /n(y)ŏŏ/ ▶ past of KNOW.

knick·er·bock·ers /'nikər,bäkərz/ ▶ pl.n. short loose-fitting trousers gathered in at or just below the knee.

knick·ers /'nikərz/ ▶ pl.n. **1** knickerbockers. **2** Brit. a woman's or girl's underpants.

knick-knack /'nik,nak/ ▶ n. a small ornament, usually one of little value.

knife /nīf/ ▶ n. (pl. **knives** /nīvz/) **1** a cutting instrument consisting of a blade fixed into a handle. **2** a cutting blade on a machine. ▶ v. stab someone with a knife.
– PHRASES **at knifepoint** /'nīf,point/ under threat of injury from a knife.

knife-edge ▶ n. the cutting edge of a knife.
– PHRASES **on a knife-edge** in a very tense or dangerous situation: *investors could be living on a knife-edge for the next twelve months.*

knife pleat ▶ n. a sharp, narrow pleat on a skirt.

knight /nīt/ ▶ n. **1** (in the Middle Ages) a man raised to military rank after serving his sovereign or lord as a page and squire. **2** (in the UK) a man awarded a nonhereditary title by the sovereign and entitled to use 'Sir' in front of his name. **3** a chess piece, typically shaped like a horse's head, that moves by jumping to the opposite corner of a rectangle two squares by three. ▶ v. give a man the title of knight. ■ **knight·ly** adj.
– PHRASES **knight in shining armor** a gallant man who helps a woman in a difficult situation.

knight er·rant ▶ n. a medieval knight who wandered in search of opportunities to perform acts of chivalry and courage.

knight·hood /'nīt,hŏŏd/ ▶ n. the title, rank, or status of a knight.

knit /nit/ ▶ v. (**knits, knitting**; past and past part. **knitted** or (especially in sense 3) **knit**) **1** make a garment by interlocking loops of yarn with knitting needles or on a machine. **2** make a plain stitch in knitting. **3** unite or join together: *their two clans are knit together by common traditions.* **4** tighten one's eyebrows in a frown. ▶ n. (**knits**) knitted garments. ■ **knit·ter** n. **knit·ting** n.

knit·ting nee·dle ▶ n. a long, thin, pointed rod used as part of a pair for hand knitting.

knit·wear /'nit,we(ə)r/ ▶ n. knitted garments.

knives /nīvz/ ▶ plural of KNIFE.

knob /näb/ ▶ n. **1** a rounded lump or ball at the end or on the surface of something. **2** a ball-shaped handle on a door or drawer. **3** a round control switch on a machine. **4** a small lump of something: *a knob of butter.* **5** vulgar slang a man's penis. ■ **knobbed** adj. **knob·by** adj.

knock /näk/ ▶v. **1** strike a surface noisily to attract attention. **2** collide forcefully with someone or something. **3** strike someone or something so that they move or fall. **4** make a hole, dent, etc., in something by striking it. **5** informal criticize someone or something. **6** (of an engine) make a thumping or rattling noise.
▶n. **1** a sudden short sound caused by a blow. **2** a blow or collision. **3** a setback.
– PHRASES **knock around** (or **about**) informal **1** travel or spend time without a specific purpose. **2** happen to be present. **knock something back** informal consume a drink quickly. **knock something down** informal **1** reduce the price of an article. **2** (at an auction) confirm a sale to a bidder by a knock with a hammer. **knock it off** informal stop doing something. **knock off** informal stop work. **knock something off** informal produce a piece of work quickly and easily. **knock someone out 1** make someone unconscious. **2** informal astonish or greatly impress someone. **3** eliminate a competitor in a knockout competition. **knock someone up** vulgar slang make a woman pregnant. **the school of hard knocks** painful or difficult but useful life experiences.

knock·a·bout /'näkə,bout/ ▶adj. (of comedy) rough and slapstick.

knock·down /'näk,doun/ ▶adj. **1** informal (of a price) very low. **2** (of furniture) easily dismantled.

knock·er /'näkər/ ▶n. **1** a hinged object fixed to a door and rapped by visitors to attract attention. **2** informal a person who continually finds fault. **3** (**knockers**) informal a woman's breasts.

knock-kneed ▶adj. having legs that curve inward at the knee.

knock·off /'näk,ôf/ ▶n. informal a copy or imitation of a product.

knock·out /'näk,out/ ▶n. **1** an act of making someone unconscious. **2** informal an extremely attractive or impressive person or thing.

knoll /nōl/ ▶n. a small hill or mound.

knot /nät/ ▶n. **1** a fastening made by looping a piece of string, rope, etc., on itself and tightening it. **2** a tangled mass in hair, wool, or other fibers. **3** a hard mass in wood at the point where the trunk and a branch join. **4** a hard lump of tissue in the body. **5** a small group of people: *a knot of spectators.* **6** a unit of speed equivalent to one nautical mile per hour, used of ships, aircraft, or winds. ▶v. (**knots, knotting, knotted**) **1** fasten something with a knot: *scarves were knotted loosely around their throats.* **2** make something tangled. **3** cause a muscle to become tense and hard. **4** (of the stomach) tighten as a result of tension.
– PHRASES **tie someone** (**up**) **in knots** informal completely confuse someone. **tie the knot** informal get married.

knot gar·den ▶n. a formal garden laid out in a complex design.

knot·grass /'nät,gras/ ▶n. a common plant with jointed creeping stems and small pink flowers.

knot·hole /'nät,hōl/ ▶n. a hole in a piece of wood where a knot has fallen out.

knot·ty /'nätē/ ▶adj. (**knottier, knottiest**) **1** full of knots. **2** extremely difficult or complex: *a knotty problem.*

knot·weed /'nät,wēd/ ▶n. knotgrass or a related plant.

know /nō/ ▶v. (past **knew** /n(y)ōō/; past part.

known /nōn/) **1** be aware of something through observation, inquiry, or information. **2** be absolutely sure of something. **3** be familiar or friendly with someone. **4** have a good command of a subject or language. **5** have personal experience of: *a man who had known better times.* **6** (usu. **be known as**) think of as having a particular characteristic, or give a particular name or title to: *the boss was universally known as 'Sir.'* **7** old use have sex with someone. ■ **know·a·ble** adj.
– PHRASES **be in the know** informal be aware of something known only to a few people. **know no bounds** have no limits. **know one's own mind** be decisive and certain. **know the ropes** have experience of the correct way of doing something. **know what's what** informal be experienced and competent in a particular area.

know-how ▶n. practical knowledge or skill.

know·ing /'nōiNG/ ▶adj. **1** suggesting that one has secret knowledge: *a knowing smile.* **2** chiefly derogatory experienced or shrewd. ■ **know·ing·ly** adv. **know·ing·ness** n.
– PHRASES **there is no knowing** no one can tell whether something is the case.

knowl·edge /'nälij/ ▶n. **1** information and skills gained through experience or education. **2** the total of what is known. **3** awareness of or familiarity with a fact or situation: *he denied all knowledge of the incident.*
– PHRASES **to** (**the best of**) **my knowledge 1** so far as I know. **2** as I know for certain.

knowl·edge·a·ble /'nälijəbəl/ (also **knowledgable**) ▶adj. intelligent and well informed. ■ **know·ledge·a·bly** adv.

knowl·edge base ▶n. **1** a store of information or data that is available to draw on. **2** the underlying set of facts and rules that a computer system has available to solve a problem.

knowl·edge work·er ▶n. a person whose job involves handling or using information.

known /nōn/ past participle of **KNOW**.
▶adj. **1** recognized, familiar, or within the scope of knowledge: *a subject little known to English readers.* **2** publicly acknowledged to be: *a known criminal.* **3** Mathematics (of a quantity or variable) having a value that can be stated.

know-noth·ing ▶n. an ignorant person.

knuck·le /'nəkəl/ ▶n. **1** each of the joints of a finger. **2** a knee-joint of a four-legged animal, or the part joining the leg to the foot. **3** a cut of meat consisting of the knuckle of a four-legged animal. ▶v. rub or press something with the knuckles.
– PHRASES **knuckle down 1** apply oneself seriously to a task. **2** (also **knuckle under**) submit to someone's authority. **rap someone on the knuckles** rebuke or criticize someone.

knuck·le·ball /'nəkəl,bôl/ (also **knuckler**) ▶n. Baseball a slow pitch that has virtually no spin and moves erratically, typically made using the knuckles of the first joints of the index and middle fingers.

knuck·le·dust·er /'nəkəl,dəstər/ ▶n. a metal fitting worn over the knuckles in fighting to increase the effect of blows.

knuck·le·head /'nəkəl,hed/ ▶n. informal a stupid person.

knuck·le sand·wich ▶n. informal a punch in the mouth.

knurl /nərl/ ▶n. a small projecting knob or ridge. ■ **knurled** adj.

KO /ˌkāˈō/ ▸ n. a knockout in a boxing match.
▸ v. (**KO's**, **KO'ing**, **KO'd**) knock someone out in a boxing match.

ko·a·la /kōˈälə/ ▸ n. a bearlike tree-dwelling Australian marsupial that has thick gray fur and feeds on eucalyptus leaves.

ko·an /ˈkōˌän/ ▸ n. (in Zen Buddhism) a paradox or puzzle that cannot be understood or answered in conventional terms, requiring a learner to abandon ordinary ways of understanding in order to move toward enlightenment.

kof·ta /ˈkôftə/ ▸ n. (pl. same or **koftas**) (in Middle Eastern and Indian cooking) a spiced meatball.

kohl /kōl/ ▸ n. a black powder used as eye makeup.

kohl·ra·bi /kōlˈräbē/ ▸ n. (pl. **kohlrabies**) a variety of cabbage with an edible turniplike stem.

koi /koi/ ▸ n. (pl. same) a large common Japanese carp.

ko·la /ˈkōlə/ ▸ n. variant spelling of COLA (sense 2).

kol·khoz /kəlˈkôz, -ˈKHôz/ ▸ n. (pl. same or **kolkhozes**) a collective farm in the former Soviet Union.

Ko·mo·do drag·on /kəˈmōdō/ ▸ n. a very large lizard native to Komodo and neighboring Indonesian islands.

kook /kŏŏk/ ▸ n. informal a mad or eccentric person. ∎ **kook·y** adj. (**kookier**, **kookiest**)

kook·a·bur·ra /ˈkŏŏkəˌbərə/ ▸ n. a very large, noisy Australasian kingfisher that feeds on reptiles and birds.

ko·pek /ˈkōpek/ (also **copeck** or **kopeck**) ▸ n. a unit of money of Russia and some other countries of the former Soviet Union, equal to one hundredth of a ruble.

ko·ra /ˈkôrə/ ▸ n. a West African musical instrument shaped like a lute and played like a harp.

Ko·ran /kəˈrän, kô-, ˈkôrän/ (also **Quran** or **Qur'an**) ▸ n. the sacred book of Islam, believed to be the word of God as dictated to Muhammad and written down in Arabic. ∎ **Ko·ran·ic** /-ˈränik/ adj.

Ko·re·an /kəˈrēən, kô-/ ▸ n. 1 a person from Korea. 2 the language of Korea. ▸ adj. relating to Korea.

kor·ma /ˈkôrmə/ ▸ n. a mild Indian curry of meat or fish marinated in yogurt or curds.

ko·sher /ˈkōsHər/ ▸ adj. 1 (of food) prepared according to the requirements of Jewish law. 2 informal genuine and legitimate.

Ko·so·var /ˈkôsəˌvär, ˈkäs-/ ▸ n. a person from Kosovo. ∎ **Ko·so·van** /ˈkôsəˌvən, ˈkäs-/ n. & adj.

kow·tow /ˈkouˈtou/ ▸ v. 1 be excessively meek and obedient in one's behavior toward someone: *she didn't have to kowtow to a boss.* 2 historical kneel and touch the ground with the forehead as a gesture of deference or submission, as part of Chinese custom.

KP ▸ abbr. kitchen police, designating the US military personnel assigned to kitchen duties, or the assignment itself.

kph ▸ abbr. kilometers per hour.

Kr ▸ symbol the chemical element krypton.

kraal /kräl/ S. African ▸ n. 1 a traditional African village of huts. 2 an enclosure for sheep and cattle.

kraft /kraft/ (also **kraft paper**) ▸ n. a kind of strong, smooth brown wrapping paper.

kra·ken /ˈkräkən/ ▸ n. a mythical sea monster said to appear off the coast of Norway.

Kraut /krout/ ▸ n. informal, offensive a German.

krem·lin /ˈkremlin/ ▸ n. 1 a citadel within a Russian town. 2 (**the Kremlin**) the citadel in Moscow, housing the Russian government.

krill /kril/ ▸ pl.n. small shrimplike crustaceans that are the main food of baleen whales.

kris /krēs/ ▸ n. a Malay or Indonesian dagger with a wavy-edged blade.

kro·na /ˈkrōnə/ ▸ n. 1 (pl. **kronor** pronunc. same) the basic unit of money of Sweden. 2 (pl. **kronur** pronunc. same) the basic unit of money of Iceland.

kro·ne /ˈkrōnə/ ▸ n. (pl. **kroner** pronunc. same) the basic unit of money of Denmark and Norway.

kru·ger·rand /ˈkrŏŏgəˌrand/ (also **Kruger** /ˈkrŏŏgər, ˈkrʏər/) ▸ n. a South African gold coin bearing a portrait of President Kruger.

kryp·ton /ˈkripˌtän/ ▸ n. an inert gaseous chemical element, present in trace amounts in the air.

KS ▸ abbr. Kansas.

Kshat·ri·ya /k(ə)ˈsHätrēə/ ▸ n. a member of the second-highest Hindu caste, that of the military.

kt ▸ abbr. knot(s).

ku·dos /ˈk(y)ŏŏˌdōs, -ˌdōz, -ˌdäs/ ▸ n. praise, admiration, and respect.

> **USAGE**
> Despite appearances, **kudos** is not a plural word. The use of it as if it were a plural, as in *he received many kudos for his work*, is wrong (the correct use is *he received much kudos for his work*).

ku·du /ˈkŏŏdōō/ ▸ n. (pl. same or **kudus**) a striped African antelope, the male of which has long spirally curved horns.

Ku Klux Klan /ˈkŏŏ ˌkləks ˈklan/ ▸ n. an extremist right-wing secret society in the US whose members believe in the supremacy of white people.

kuk·ri /ˈkŏŏkrē/ ▸ n. (pl. **kukris**) a curved knife that broadens toward the point, used by Gurkhas.

ku·lak /ˈkŏŏˌlak, -ˈläk/ ▸ n. historical a peasant in Russia wealthy enough to own a farm and hire workers.

küm·mel /ˈkiməl/ ▸ n. a sweet liqueur flavored with caraway and cumin seeds.

kum·quat /ˈkəmˌkwät/ (also **cumquat**) ▸ n. an East Asian fruit like a small orange, with an edible sweet rind and acid pulp.

kun·da·li·ni /ˌkŏŏndlˈēnē/ ▸ n. (in yoga) latent female energy believed to lie coiled at the base of the spine.

kung fu /ˈkəNG ˈfŏŏ, ˈkŏŏNG/ ▸ n. a Chinese martial art resembling karate.

Kurd /kərd/ ▸ n. a member of a mainly Islamic people living in Kurdistan, an area composed of parts of Turkey, Iraq, Iran, Syria, Armenia, and Azerbaijan.

Kurd·ish /ˈkərdisH/ ▸ n. the Iranian language of the Kurds. ▸ adj. relating to the Kurds.

kur·ta /ˈkərtə/ ▸ n. a loose collarless shirt worn by people from the Indian subcontinent.

Ku·wai·ti /kəˈwātē/ ▸ n. (pl. **Kuwaitis**) a person from Kuwait. ▸ adj. relating to Kuwait.

kV ▸ abbr. kilovolt(s).

kvetch /k(ə)vecʜ, kfecʜ/ informal ▶ n. **1** a person who complains a great deal. **2** a complaint. ▶ v. complain.

kW ▶ abbr. kilowatt(s).

Kwan·zaa /ˈkwänzə/ ▶ n. a secular festival observed by many African Americans from December 26 to January 1 as a celebration of their cultural heritage and traditional values.

kwash·i·or·kor /ˌkwäsʜēˈôrkôr, -kər/ ▶ n. a form of malnutrition caused by a lack of protein in the diet, typically affecting young children in certain parts of Africa.

kWh ▶ abbr. kilowatt-hour(s).

KY ▶ abbr. Kentucky.

Kyr·i·e /ˈki(ə)rē͞ā/ (also **Kyrie eleison** /iˈlā-iˌsän, -sən/) ▶ n. (in the Christian Church) a short repeated appeal to God used in many set forms of public worship.

L¹ (also **l**) ▶ n. (pl. **Ls** or **L's**) **1** the twelfth letter of the alphabet. **2** the Roman numeral for 50.

L² ▶ abbr. **1** (**L.**) Lake, Loch, or Lough. **2** large (as a clothes size). **3** (in tables of sports results) lost.

l ▶ abbr. **1** left. **2** (in horse racing) length(s). **3** (**l.**) line. **4** liter(s). ▶ symbol (in mathematical formulas) length.

£ /pound(z)/ ▶ symbol pound(s).

LA ▶ abbr. **1** Los Angeles. **2** Louisiana.

La ▶ symbol the chemical element lanthanum.

la /lä/ ▶ n. Music the sixth note of a major scale, coming after 'sol' and before 'ti.'

Lab /lab/ ▶ abbr. a Labrador retriever.

lab /lab/ ▶ n. informal a laboratory.

la·bel /'lābəl/ ▶ n. **1** a small piece of paper, fabric, etc., attached to an object and giving information about it. **2** the name or trademark of a fashion company. **3** a company that produces recorded music. **4** a classifying name given to a person or thing: *young women who dislike the feminist label.* ▶ v. (**labels, labeling, labeled**) **1** attach a label to something. **2** place someone or something in a category: *he was labeled as an anarchist.*

la·bi·a /'lābēə/ ▶ pl. n. (sing. **labium** /'lābēəm/) the inner and outer folds of the vulva (the female external genitals).

la·bi·al /'lābēəl/ ▶ adj. **1** chiefly Anatomy & Biology relating to the labia or lips. **2** Phonetics (of a consonant) produced with the lips partially or completely closed (e.g., *p* or *w*), or (of a vowel) produced with rounded lips (e.g., *oo*).

la·bile /'lā,bīl, -bəl/ ▶ adj. **1** technical liable to change; easily altered. **2** Chemistry easily broken down or displaced.

la·bi·um /'lābēəm/ ▶ n. singular of **LABIA**.

la·bor /'lābər/ (Brit. **labour**) ▶ n. **1** work, especially hard physical work. **2** workers as a group. **3** the process of childbirth. ▶ v. **1** work hard. **2** work at an unskilled manual job. **3** try hard to do something in the face of difficulty: *biologists have labored for years to develop hardier crops.* **4** move with difficulty. **5** (**labor under**) believe something that is not true: *you've been laboring under a misapprehension.*

– PHRASES **a labor of love** a task done for pleasure, not reward. **labor the point** repeat or emphasize something that has already been said and understood.

lab·o·ra·to·ry /'labrə,tôrē/ ▶ n. (pl. **laboratories**) a room or building for scientific experiments, research, or teaching, or for the manufacture of drugs or chemicals.

la·bor camp ▶ n. a prison camp in which punishment takes the form of heavy manual work.

La·bor Day ▶ n. a public holiday held in honor of working people in some countries on May 1, or (in the US and Canada) on the first Monday in September.

la·bored /'lābərd/ ▶ adj. **1** done with great difficulty: *labored breathing.* **2** not natural or spontaneous: *a rather labored joke.*

la·bor·er /'lāb(ə)rər/ ▶ n. a person doing unskilled manual work.

la·bor force ▶ n. the members of a population who are able to work.

la·bor-in·ten·sive ▶ adj. needing a large workforce or a large amount of work in relation to what is produced.

la·bo·ri·ous /lə'bôrēəs/ ▶ adj. **1** requiring considerable time and effort. **2** showing obvious signs of effort: *a slow, laborious speech.* ■ **la·bo·ri·ous·ly** adv.

la·bor-sav·ing ▶ adj. designed to reduce the amount of work needed to carry out a task.

la·bor un·ion ▶ n. an organized association of workers formed to protect and further their rights and interests.

la·bour, etc. ▶ n. British spelling of **LABOR**, etc.

La·bour Par·ty ▶ n. a British political party formed to represent the interests of ordinary working people.

Lab·ra·dor /'labrə,dôr/ (also **Labrador retriever**) ▶ n. a breed of retriever with a black or yellow coat, used also as a guide dog.

la·bur·num /lə'bərnəm/ ▶ n. a small hardwood tree with hanging clusters of yellow flowers followed by pods of poisonous seeds.

lab·y·rinth /'lab(ə),rinTH/ ▶ n. **1** a complicated irregular network of passages or paths. **2** an intricate and confusing arrangement: *the labyrinth of immigration laws.* **3** a complex bony structure in the inner ear that contains the organs of hearing and balance. ■ **lab·y·rin·thine** /,labə'rin,THēn, -'rinTHin, -'rinTHin, -'rin,THīn/ adj.

lac /lak/ ▶ n. a resinous substance produced by an Asian insect (the **lac insect**), used to make varnish, shellac, etc.

lace /lās/ ▶ n. **1** a delicate open fabric of cotton or silk made by looping, twisting, or knitting thread in patterns. **2** a cord or leather strip used to fasten a shoe or garment. ▶ v. **1** fasten a shoe or garment with a lace or laces. **2** twist or tangle things together. **3** add an ingredient, especially alcohol, to a drink or dish to improve the flavor or to make it stronger: *coffee laced with brandy.*

lac·er·ate /'lasə,rāt/ ▶ v. tear or cut the flesh or skin. ■ **lac·er·a·tion** /,lasə'rāsнən/ n.

lace·wing /'lās,wiNG/ ▶ n. a delicate insect with large, clear membranous wings.

lach·ry·mal /'lakrəməl/ (also **lacrimal** or **lacrymal**) ▶ adj. **1** formal or literary connected with weeping or tears. **2** Physiology & Anatomy concerned with the production of tears.

lach·ry·mose /'lakrə‚mōs, -‚mōz/ ▶ adj. formal or literary **1** tending to cry easily; tearful. **2** causing tears; sad.

lac·ing /'lāsiNG/ ▶ n. **1** a laced fastening of a shoe or garment. **2** a dash of liquor added to a drink.

lack /lak/ ▶ n. the state of being without or not having enough of something: *the lack of funds available for research.* ▶ v. (also **lack for**) be without or without enough of: *he lacked imagination.*

lack·a·dai·si·cal /‚lakə'dāzikəl/ ▶ adj. lacking enthusiasm and thoroughness. ■ **lack·a·dai·si·cal·ly** adv.

lack·ey /'lakē/ ▶ n. (pl. **lackeys**) **1** a servant. **2** a person who is too willing to serve or obey others.

lack·ing /'lakiNG/ ▶ adj. missing or not having enough of something: *she was shy and lacking in confidence.*

lack·lus·ter /'lak‚ləstər/ ▶ adj. **1** lacking energy or inspiration: *a lackluster performance.* **2** (of the hair or eyes) not shining.

la·con·ic /lə'känik/ ▶ adj. using very few words: *his laconic reply suggested a lack of interest in the subject.* ■ **la·con·i·cal·ly** /-(ə)lē/ adv.

lac·quer /'lakər/ ▶ n. **1** a varnish made of shellac or of synthetic substances. **2** the sap of an East Asian tree (the **lacquer tree**) used as a varnish. **3** a chemical substance sprayed on hair to keep it in place. ▶ v. (often as adj. **lacquered**) coat with lacquer. ■ **lac·quered** adj.

lac·ri·mal ▶ adj. variant spelling of LACHRYMAL.

la·crosse /lə'krôs, -'kräs/ ▶ n. a team game, originally played by North American Indians, in which a ball is thrown, carried, and caught with a long-handled stick that has a net at one end.

lac·ry·mal ▶ adj. variant spelling of LACHRYMAL.

lac·tate[1] /‚lak'tāt/ ▶ v. (of a female mammal) produce milk.

lac·tate[2] /'lak‚tāt/ ▶ n. Chemistry a salt or ester of lactic acid.

lac·ta·tion /lak'tāsHən/ ▶ n. **1** the producing of milk by the mammary glands. **2** the process of suckling a baby or young animal.

lac·tic /'laktik/ ▶ adj. relating to or obtained from milk.

lac·tic ac·id ▶ n. an organic acid present in sour milk and produced in the muscles during strenuous exercise.

lac·tose /'lak‚tōs, -‚tōz/ ▶ n. Chemistry a compound sugar present in milk.

lac·to·veg·e·tar·i·an /'laktō-/ ▶ n. a person who eats only dairy products and vegetables.

la·cu·na /lə'k(y)o͞onə/ ▶ n. (pl. **lacunae** /-nī, -nē/ or **lacunas**) a gap or missing portion: *there are a few lacunae in the historical record.*

la·cus·trine /lə'kəstrin/ ▶ adj. technical or literary relating to lakes.

lac·y /'lāsē/ ▶ adj. (**lacier, laciest**) made of, resembling, or trimmed with lace.

lad /lad/ ▶ n. a boy or young man.

lad·der /'ladər/ ▶ n. **1** a structure consisting of a series of bars or steps between two uprights, used for climbing up or down. **2** a series of stages by which progress can be made: *the career ladder.* **3** Brit. a run in a pair of tights or stockings.

lad·der·back ▶ n. an upright chair with a back resembling a ladder.

lad·die /'ladē/ ▶ n. informal, chiefly Scottish a boy or young man.

lad·en /'lādn/ ▶ adj. loaded or weighed down.

la·di·da /‚lä dē 'dä/ (also **lah-di-dah**) ▶ adj. informal pretentious or snobbish.

la·dies /'lādēz/ ▶ plural of LADY.

la·dies' man (also **lady's man**) ▶ n. informal a man who enjoys spending time and flirting with women.

la·dies' room ▶ n. a women's restroom in a public building.

La·di·no /lə'dēnō/ ▶ n. (pl. **Ladinos**) **1** the language of some Sephardic Jews, based on medieval Spanish. **2** (in Latin America) a person of mixed race or a Spanish-speaking white person.

la·dle /'lādl/ ▶ n. a large long-handled spoon with a cup-shaped bowl, for serving soup, stew, or sauce. ▶ v. **1** serve or transfer soup or sauce with a ladle. **2** (**ladle something out**) distribute something in large amounts. ■ **la·dle·ful** /-‚fo͞ol/ n.

la·dy /'lādē/ ▶ n. (pl. **ladies**) **1** (in polite or formal use) a woman. **2** a woman of high social position. **3** (**Lady**) (in the UK) a title used by peeresses, female relatives of peers, the wives and widows of knights, etc. **4** a polite and well-educated woman. **5** (**the Ladies**) a women's public toilet. – PHRASES **My Lady** a polite form of address to certain noblewomen.

la·dy·bug /'lādē‚bəg/ (also **ladybird** /'lādē‚bərd/) ▶ n. a small beetle having a red or yellow back with black spots.

La·dy chap·el ▶ n. a chapel dedicated to the Virgin Mary in a church or cathedral.

La·dy Day ▶ n. the Christian feast of the Annunciation, March 25.

la·dy·fin·ger /'lādē‚fiNGgər/ ▶ n. a small finger-shaped sponge cake.

la·dy-in-wait·ing ▶ n. (pl. **ladies-in-waiting**) a woman who attends a queen or princess.

la·dy·kill·er /'lādē‚kilər/ ▶ n. informal a charming man who habitually seduces women.

la·dy·like /'lādē‚līk/ ▶ adj. appropriate for or typical of a well-mannered woman or girl.

la·dy of the night ▶ n. euphemistic a prostitute.

La·dy·ship /'lādē‚sHip/ ▶ n. (**Her/Your Ladyship**) a respectful way of referring to or addressing a woman who has a title.

la·dy's maid ▶ n. chiefly historical a maid who attended to the personal needs of her mistress.

la·dy's man ▶ n. variant spelling of LADIES' MAN.

la·dy's man·tle ▶ n. a plant with greenish flowers, formerly used in herbal medicine.

la·dy's slip·per ▶ n. an orchid whose flower has a pouch- or slipper-shaped lip.

lag[1] /lag/ ▶ v. (**lags, lagging, lagged**) move or develop more slowly than another or others: *the country was lagging behind its European competitors.* ▶ n. (also **time lag**) a period of time between two events; a delay.

lag[2] ▶ v. (**lags, lagging, lagged**) cover a water tank, pipes, etc., with material designed to prevent heat loss.

la·ger /'lägər/ ▶ n. a light effervescent beer.

lag·gard /'lagərd/ ▶ n. a person who falls behind others. ▶ adj. slower than desired or expected.

lag·ging /'lagiNG/ ▶ n. material providing heat insulation for a water tank, pipes, etc.

la·goon /lə'gōon/ ▸ n. **1** a stretch of salt water separated from the sea by a low sandbank or coral reef. **2** a small freshwater lake near a larger lake or river.

lah ▸ n. Music variant spelling of LA.

lah-di-dah ▸ n. variant spelling of LA-DI-DA.

la·i·cize /'lāə,sīz/ ▸ v. formal withdraw clerical or ecclesiastical character or status from someone or something. ■ **la·i·cism** /-,sizəm/ n. **la·i·ci·za·tion** /,lāəsə'zāsHən/ n.

laid /lād/ ▸ past and past participle of LAY[1].

laid-back ▸ adj. informal relaxed and easygoing.

lain /lān/ ▸ past participle of LIE[1].

lair /le(ə)r/ ▸ n. **1** a wild animal's resting place. **2** a person's hiding place or den.

laird /le(ə)rd/ ▸ n. (in Scotland) a person who owns a large estate.

lais·sez-faire /,lesā 'fe(ə)r, ,lezā/ ▸ n. a policy of allowing things to take their course without interfering, especially nonintervention by governments in the workings of the free market.

la·i·ty /'lāətē/ ▸ n. (**the laity**) people who are not members of the clergy.

lake[1] /lāk/ ▸ n. **1** a large area of water surrounded by land. **2** a pool of liquid. ■ **lake·side** /'lāk,sīd/ n.

lake[2] ▸ n. a purplish-red pigment, originally made with lac.

lakh /läk, lak/ ▸ n. Indian a hundred thousand.

lam[1] /lam/ ▸ v. (**lams, lamming, lammed**) (often **lam into**) informal hit someone or something hard or repeatedly.

lam[2] ▸ n. (in phrase **on the lam**) informal in the process of running away or escaping.

la·ma /'lämə/ ▸ n. **1** a title given to a spiritual leader in Tibetan Buddhism as a mark of respect. **2** a Tibetan or Mongolian Buddhist monk.

La·marck·ism /lə'mär,kizəm/ ▸ n. the theory of evolution proposed by the French naturalist Jean Baptiste de Lamarck (1744–1829), based on the proposition that characteristics acquired by an animal or plant in order to survive can be passed on to its offspring. ■ **La·marck·i·an** /lə'märkēən/ n. & adj.

la·ma·ser·y /'lämə,serē/ ▸ n. (pl. **lamaseries**) a monastery of lamas.

lamb /lam/ ▸ n. **1** a young sheep. **2** a mild-mannered, gentle, or innocent person. ▸ v. **1** (of a ewe) give birth to lambs. **2** tend ewes during the period when lambs are born. ■ **lamb·ing** n. – PHRASES **the Lamb of God** a title of Jesus.

lam·ba·da /lam'bädə/ ▸ n. a fast Brazilian dance that couples perform in close physical contact.

lam·baste /lam'bāst, -'bast/ (also **lambast** /-'bast/) ▸ v. criticize someone or something harshly.

lam·bent /'lambənt/ ▸ adj. literary glowing or flickering with a soft radiance.

Lam·bru·sco /lam'brōoskō, -'brōos-/ ▸ n. a sparkling red or white wine made from grapes grown in the Emilia-Romagna region of northern Italy.

lambs·wool /'lamz,wŏol/ ▸ n. soft, fine wool from lambs, used to make knitted garments.

lame /lām/ ▸ adj. **1** walking with difficulty as the result of an injury or illness affecting the leg or foot. **2** (of an explanation or excuse) unconvincingly feeble. **3** dull and uninspiring: *a lame, predictable storyline.* ▸ v. make a person or animal lame. ■ **lame·ly** adv. **lame·ness** n.

la·mé /la'mā, lä-/ ▸ n. fabric with interwoven gold or silver threads.

lame·brain /'lām,brān/ ▸ adj. informal a stupid person.

lame duck ▸ n. **1** an ineffectual or unsuccessful person or thing. **2** a president or administration in the final period of office, after a successor has been elected.

la·mel·la /lə'melə/ ▸ n. (pl. **lamellae** /-'melē, -'melī/) technical a thin layer, membrane, or plate of tissue, especially in bone. ■ **la·mel·lar** /-'melər/ adj. **la·mel·late** /'laməlit, lə'melit, 'lamə,lāt/ adj.

la·ment /lə'ment/ ▸ n. **1** a passionate expression of grief. **2** a song, piece of music, or poem expressing grief or regret. ▸ v. **1** mourn a person's death. **2** (as adj. **the lamented** or **the late lamented**) a conventional way of referring to a dead person. **3** express regret or disappointment about something: *he lamented the modernization of the old buildings.* ■ **lam·en·ta·tion** /,lamən'tāsHən/ n.

lam·en·ta·ble /'laməntəbəl, lə'mentəbəl/ ▸ adj. **1** (of circumstances or conditions) very bad: *the industry is in a lamentable state.* **2** (of an event or attitude) regrettable: *her prejudice showed lamentable immaturity.* ■ **la·men·ta·bly** /-əblē/ adv.

lam·i·na /'lamənə/ ▸ n. (pl. **laminae** /-,nē, -,nī/) technical a thin layer, plate, or scale of sedimentary rock, organic tissue, or other material. ■ **lam·i·nar** /'lamənər/ adj.

lam·i·nate ▸ v. /'lamə,nāt/ **1** cover a flat surface with a layer of protective material. **2** manufacture something by sticking layers of material together. **3** split into layers or leaves. **4** beat or roll metal into thin plates. ▸ n. /-nit, -,nāt/ a laminated structure or material. ▸ adj. /-nit, -,nāt/ consisting or made of many layers of material stuck together. ■ **lam·i·na·tion** /,lamə'nāsHən/ n.

Lam·mas /'laməs/ (also **Lammas Day**) ▸ n. the first day of August, formerly observed as a harvest festival.

lam·mer·gei·er /'lamər,gīər/ (also **lammergeyer**) ▸ n. a long-winged, long-tailed vulture, noted for dropping bones to break them and get at the marrow.

lamp /lamp/ ▸ n. **1** an electric, oil, or gas device for giving light. **2** an electrical device producing ultraviolet or other radiation, especially for therapeutic purposes.

lamp·black /'lamp,blak/ ▸ n. a black pigment made from soot.

lamp·light /'lamp,līt/ ▸ n. the light cast by a lamp. ■ **lamp·lit** /-,lit/ adj.

lam·poon /lam'pōon/ ▸ v. publicly ridicule or mock someone or something. ▸ n. a speech or piece of writing that ridicules or mocks someone or something.

lamp·post /'lam(p),pōst/ ▸ n. a tall pole with a light at the top, used to light a street.

lam·prey /'lamprē/ ▸ n. (pl. **lampreys**) an eel-like jawless fish that has a sucker mouth with horny teeth and a rasping tongue.

lamp·shade /'lamp,sHād/ ▸ n. a cover for a lamp, used to soften or direct its light.

LAN /lan/ ▸ abbr. Computing local area network.

lance /lans/ ▸ n. **1** a long weapon with a wooden shaft and a pointed steel head, formerly used by a horseman in charging. **2** a metal pipe supplying a jet of oxygen to a furnace or to make a very hot flame for cutting. ▸ v. **1** prick or cut open an abscess or boil with a lancet or other sharp instrument. **2** pierce something.

lance·let /'lanslit/ ▸ n. a small invertebrate marine animal.

lan·ce·o·late /'lansēəlit, -ˌlāt/ ▸ adj. technical having a narrow oval shape tapering to a point at each end.

lanc·er /'lansər/ ▸ n. a soldier of a cavalry regiment armed or formerly armed with lances.

lan·cet /'lansit/ ▸ n. a small, broad, two-edged surgical knife with a sharp point.

lan·cet win·dow ▸ n. a slender window with a pointed arch, especially in a medieval church.

land /land/ ▸ n. **1** the part of the earth's surface that is not covered by water. **2** an area of ground in terms of its ownership or use: *the land north of town.* **3** (**the land**) ground or soil as a basis for agriculture. **4** a country or state. ▸ v. **1** go ashore. **2** put someone or something on land from a boat. **3** come down to the ground, or bring an aircraft or spacecraft to the ground. **4** bring a fish to land with a net or rod. **5** informal succeed in obtaining or achieving something desirable: *she landed a contract with a major film studio.* **6** (**land up**) reach a place or destination. **7** (**land up with**) end up with an unwelcome situation. **8** (**land someone in**) informal put in someone in a difficult situation: *his exploits landed him in trouble.* **9** (**land someone with**) inflict something unwelcome on someone: *the mistake landed the company with a massive bill.* **10** informal inflict a blow on someone. ■ **land·less** adj.
– PHRASES **how the land lies** what the situation is. **the land of Nod** humorous a state of sleep.

lan·dau /'lanˌdou/ ▸ n. historical a four-wheeled enclosed horse-drawn carriage.

land bridge ▸ n. an area of land formerly connecting two landmasses that are now separate.

land·ed /'landid/ ▸ adj. **1** owning much land, especially through inheritance. **2** consisting of or relating to land owned through inheritance.

land·er /'landər/ ▸ n. a spacecraft designed to land on the surface of a planet or moon.

land·fall /'lan(d)ˌfôl/ ▸ n. **1** an arrival at land on a sea or air journey. **2** a collapse of a mass of land. **3** the contact of a hurricane with a landmass.

land·fill /'lan(d)ˌfil/ ▸ n. **1** the disposal of waste material by burying it. **2** waste material that has been buried. **3** an area filled in by this process.

land·form /'lan(d)ˌfôrm/ ▸ n. a natural feature of the earth's surface.

land·hold·er /'landˌhōldər/ ▸ n. a landowner.

land·ing /'landiNG/ ▸ n. **1** a level area at the top of a staircase or between flights of stairs. **2** the action of coming to land or bringing something to land. **3** a place where people and goods can be landed from a boat.

land·ing craft ▸ n. a boat specially designed for putting troops and military equipment ashore on a beach.

land·ing gear ▸ n. the undercarriage of an aircraft.

land·ing stage ▸ n. a platform onto which passengers or cargo can be landed from a boat.

land·la·dy /'lan(d)ˌlādē/ ▸ n. (pl. **landladies**) **1** a woman who rents out land or property. **2** a woman who owns or runs an inn, boardinghouse, or similar establishment.

land·line /'lan(d)ˌlīn/ ▸ n. a conventional telecommunications connection by cable laid across land.

land·locked /'lan(d)ˌläkt/ ▸ adj. almost or entirely surrounded by land: *a landlocked country.*

land·lord /'lan(d)ˌlôrd/ ▸ n. **1** a man (in legal use also a woman) who rents out land or property. **2** a man who owns or runs an inn, boardinghouse, or similar establishment.

land·lord·ism /'lan(d)lôrˌdizəm/ ▸ n. the system whereby land or property is owned by landlords to whom tenants pay a fixed rent.

land·lub·ber /'lan(d)ˌləbər/ ▸ n. informal a person who is not used to the sea or sailing.

land·mark /'lan(d)ˌmärk/ ▸ n. **1** an object or feature of a landscape or town that is easily seen and recognized from a distance. **2** an event, discovery, or change marking an important stage or turning point: *a landmark in civil aviation technology.*

land·mass /'lan(d)ˌmas/ ▸ n. a continent or other large body of land.

land·mine /'lan(d)ˌmīn/ ▸ n. an explosive mine laid on or just under the surface of the ground.

land·own·er /'lanˌdōnər/ ▸ n. a person who owns land. ■ **land·own·er·ship** /'landōnərˌSHip/ n. **land·own·ing** adj. & n.

land·scape /'lan(d)ˌskāp/ ▸ n. **1** all the visible features of an area of land. **2** a picture of an area of countryside. **3** the distinctive features of an area of intellectual activity: *the political landscape.* ▸ v. improve the appearance of a piece of land by changing its contours, planting trees and shrubs, etc. ■ adj. referring to a format for printed material that is wider than it is high. Compare with PORTRAIT. ■ **land·scap·er** n. **land·scap·ist** /-ˌskäpist/ n.

land·scape ar·chi·tec·ture ▸ n. the art and practice of designing the outdoor environment, especially so as to make parks or gardens harmonize with buildings or roads.

land·scape gar·den·ing ▸ n. the art and practice of laying out grounds in a way that is ornamental or that imitates natural scenery.

land·side /'lan(d)ˌsīd/ ▸ n. the area of an airport terminal to which the general public has unrestricted access.

land·slide /'lan(d)ˌslīd/ ▸ n. **1** the sliding down of a mass of earth or rock from a mountain or cliff. **2** an overwhelming majority of votes for one party in an election.

lands·man /'lan(d)zmən/ ▸ n. (pl. **landsmen**) a person unfamiliar with the sea or sailing.

land·ward /'lan(d)wərd/ ▸ adv. (also **landwards**) toward land. ▸ adj. facing toward land as opposed to sea.

lane /lān/ ▸ n. **1** a narrow road, especially in a rural area. **2** a division of a road intended to separate single lines of traffic according to speed or direction. **3** each of a number of parallel strips of track or water for competitors in a race. **4** a route or course regularly followed by ships and aircraft.

lan·gous·tine /'laNGgəˌstēn/ ▸ n. a small European lobster.

lan·guage /'laNGgwij/ ▸ n. **1** the method of human communication, either spoken or written, consisting of the use of words in a structured and conventional way. **2** the system of communication used by a particular community or country. **3** a particular style of speaking or writing: *legal language.* **4** the manner or style of a piece of writing or speech. **5** a system of symbols and rules for writing computer programs.

lan·guid /ˈlaNGgwid/ ▶ adj. **1** relaxed and not inclined to exert oneself physically. **2** weak or faint from illness or tiredness. ■ **lan·guid·ly** adv.

lan·guish /ˈlaNGgwiSH/ ▶ v. **1** grow weak or feeble. **2** be kept in an unpleasant place or situation: *he was languishing in jail.*

lan·guor /ˈlaNG(g)ər/ ▶ n. tiredness or inactivity, especially when pleasurable. ■ **lan·guor·ous** /-g(ə)rəs, ˈlaNGgərəs/ adj. **lan·guor·ous·ly** /-g(ə)rəslē, ˈlaNGgərəslē/ adv.

La Ni·ña /lä ˈnēnyə/ ▶ n. an occasional cooling of the water in the equatorial Pacific, which is associated with widespread weather changes complementary to those of El Niño.

lank /laNGk/ ▶ adj. **1** (of hair) long, limp, and straight. **2** lanky.

lank·y /ˈlaNGkē/ ▶ adj. (**lankier, lankiest**) awkwardly thin and tall. ■ **lank·i·ness** n.

lan·o·lin /ˈlanl-in/ ▶ n. a fatty substance found naturally on sheep's wool and used as a base for ointments.

lan·tern /ˈlantərn/ ▶ n. **1** a lamp enclosed in a metal frame with glass panels. **2** the light chamber at the top of a lighthouse. **3** a square, curved, or polygonal structure on the top of a dome or a room, with glass or open sides.

lan·tern-jawed ▶ adj. having long, thin jaws.

lan·tern slide ▶ n. historical a photographic slide for use in a magic lantern.

lan·tha·nide /ˈlanTHəˌnīd/ ▶ n. any of the series of fifteen rare-earth elements from lanthanum to lutetium in the periodic table.

lan·tha·num /ˈlanTHənəm/ ▶ n. a silvery-white rare-earth metallic chemical element.

lan·yard /ˈlanyərd/ (also **laniard**) ▶ n. **1** a rope used to adjust the tension in a ship's rigging. **2** a cord passed around the neck, shoulder, or wrist for holding a whistle or similar object.

La·o·tian /lāˈōSHən/ ▶ n. a person from the country of Laos in SE Asia. ▶ adj. relating to Laos.

lap¹ /lap/ ▶ n. the flat area between the waist and knees of a seated person.
– PHRASES **in someone's lap** as someone's responsibility. **in the lap of luxury** in conditions of great comfort and wealth.

lap² ▶ n. **1** one circuit of a track or racetrack. **2** a part of a journey or other undertaking: *the last lap of their four-day tour.* **3** an overlapping or projecting part. **4** a single turn of rope, thread, or cable around a drum or reel. ▶ v. (**laps, lapping, lapped**) **1** overtake a competitor in a race to become one or more laps ahead. **2** (**lap someone/thing in**) literary enfold someone or something protectively in something soft: *he was lapped in blankets.*

lap³ ▶ v. (**laps, lapping, lapped**) **1** (of an animal) take up liquid with the tongue. **2** (**lap something up**) accept something with obvious pleasure: *she's lapping up all the attention.* **3** (of water) wash against something with a gentle rippling sound: *a sun-kissed island lapped by an azure sea.* ▶ n. the action of water lapping.

lap·a·ros·co·py /ˌlapəˈräskəpē/ ▶ n. (pl. **laparoscopies**) a surgical procedure in which a fiber-optic instrument is inserted through the wall of the abdomen to enable the internal organs to be viewed. ■ **lap·a·ro·scope**

/ˈlap(ə)rəˌskōp/ n. **lap·a·ro·scop·ic** /ˌlap(ə)rəˈskäpik/ adj.

lap·a·rot·o·my /ˌlapəˈrätəmē/ ▶ n. (pl. **laparotomies**) a surgical incision into the abdomen, to make a diagnosis or in preparation for major surgery.

lap danc·ing ▶ n. erotic dancing in which the dancer performs a striptease near to or on the lap of a paying customer. ■ **lap dance** n. **lap danc·er** n.

lap·dog /ˈlapˌdôg, -ˌdäg/ ▶ n. **1** a small pampered pet dog. **2** a person who is completely under the influence of another.

la·pel /ləˈpel/ ▶ n. the part on each side of a coat or jacket immediately below the collar that is folded back against the front opening.

lap·i·dar·y /ˈlapəˌderē/ ▶ adj. **1** relating to the engraving, cutting, or polishing of stones and gems. **2** (of language) elegant and concise. ▶ n. (pl. **lapidaries**) a person who cuts, polishes, or engraves stones and gems.

lap·is laz·u·li /ˈlapis ˈlazyəˌlī, ˈlazhəˌlī, ˈlazyəlē/ (also **lapis**) ▶ n. **1** a bright blue rock used in jewelery. **2** the pigment ultramarine, originally made by crushing lapis lazuli.

lap joint ▶ n. a joint between shafts, rails, etc., made by halving the thickness of each part at the joint and fitting them together.

Lap·land·er /ˈlapˌlandər, -ləndər/ ▶ n. a person from Lapland, a region in northern Europe.

Lapp /lap/ ▶ n. **1** a member of a people of the extreme north of Scandinavia. **2** the language of the Lapps.

> **USAGE**
> Although the term **Lapp** is still widely used and is the most familiar term to many people, the people themselves prefer to be called **Sami**.

lap·pet /ˈlapit/ ▶ n. **1** a fold or hanging piece of flesh in some animals. **2** a loose or overlapping part of a garment.

lapse /laps/ ▶ n. **1** a brief failure of concentration, memory, or judgment. **2** a decline from previously high standards: *his lapse into petty crime.* **3** a period of time between two events. **4** Law the termination of a right or privilege through disuse or failure to follow the appropriate procedures. ▶ v. **1** (of a right, privilege, or agreement) become invalid because it is not used, claimed, or renewed. **2** (usu. as adj. **lapsed**) stop following the rules and practices of a religion or doctrine: *a lapsed Catholic.* **3** (**lapse into**) pass gradually into a different, often worse state or condition: *the country lapsed into chaos.*

lap·top /ˈlapˌtäp/ ▶ n. a portable microcomputer suitable for use while traveling.

lap·wing /ˈlapˌwiNG/ ▶ n. a large crested plover (bird) with a dark green back, black-and-white head, and a loud call.

lar·board /ˈlärˌbôrd, -bərd/ ▶ n. Nautical old-fashioned term for PORT³.

lar·ce·ny /ˈlärs(ə)nē/ ▶ n. (pl. **larcenies**) theft of personal property. ■ **lar·ce·nous** /-nəs/ adj.

larch /lärCH/ ▶ n. a northern coniferous tree with bunches of deciduous bright green needles and tough wood.

lard /lärd/ ▶ n. fat from the abdomen of a pig, prepared for use in cooking. ▶ v. **1** insert strips of fat or bacon in meat before cooking. **2** add many obscure or technical expressions to talk or writing: *his conversation is larded with references* *to Coleridge.*

lard·er /ˈlärdər/ ▶ n. a room or large cupboard for storing food.

lar·don /ˈlärdn/ ▶ n. (also **lardoon**) a chunk or strip of bacon inserted in meat before it is cooked.

lard·y /ˈlärdē/ ▶ adj. informal (of a person) fat.

large /lärj/ ▶ adj. **1** of great or relatively great size, extent, or capacity. **2** of wide range or scope: *we can afford to take a larger view of the situation.* ■ **large·ness** n. **larg·ish** adj.
– PHRASES **at large 1** escaped or not yet captured. **2** as a whole: *society at large.*

large in·tes·tine ▶ n. the part of the alimentary canal that consists of the cecum, colon, and rectum collectively.

large·ly /ˈlärjlē/ ▶ adv. on the whole; mostly.

large-scale ▶ adj. involving large numbers or a large area; extensive.

lar·gesse /lärˈzHes, -ˈjes/ (also **largess**) ▶ n. **1** generosity. **2** money or gifts given generously.

lar·go /ˈlärˌgō/ ▶ adv. & adj. Music in a slow tempo and dignified style.

lar·i·at /ˈlarēət/ ▶ n. a rope used as a lasso or for tethering animals.

lark[1] /lärk/ ▶ n. a brown songbird that sings while in flight.

lark[2] informal ▶ n. an amusing adventure or escapade. ▶ v. enjoy oneself by behaving in a playful and mischievous way.

lark·spur /ˈlärkˌspər/ ▶ n. a Mediterranean plant resembling a delphinium.

lar·va /ˈlärvə/ ▶ n. (pl. **larvae** /-vē, -ˌvī/) the immature form of an insect or other animal that undergoes metamorphosis, e.g., a caterpillar or tadpole. ■ **lar·val** /-vəl/ adj.

la·ryn·ge·al /ləˈrinj(ē)əl, ˌlarənˈjēəl/ ▶ adj. relating to the larynx.

lar·yn·gi·tis /ˌlarənˈjītis/ ▶ n. inflammation of the larynx.

lar·ynx /ˈlariNGks, ˈler-/ ▶ n. (pl. **larynxes** or **larynges** /ləˈrinˌjēz/) the hollow muscular organ forming an air passage to the lungs and containing the vocal cords.

la·sa·gna /ləˈzänyə/ (also **lasagne**) ▶ n. **1** pasta in the form of sheets or wide strips. **2** an Italian dish consisting of lasagna baked with meat or vegetables and a cheese sauce.

las·civ·i·ous /ləˈsivēəs/ ▶ adj. feeling or showing obvious sexual desire. ■ **las·civ·i·ous·ly** adv. **las·civ·i·ous·ness** n.

la·ser /ˈlāzər/ ▶ n. a device that produces a beam of light of a type used for surgery, compact discs, and holograms.

la·ser·disc /ˈlāzərˌdisk/ ▶ n. a disc resembling a large compact disc, used for high-quality video and for interactive multimedia.

la·ser print·er ▶ n. a computer printer in which a laser is used to form a pattern of electrically charged dots on a light-sensitive drum, which attracts toner.

lash /lasH/ ▶ v. **1** beat a person or animal with a whip or stick. **2** beat forcefully against: *waves lashed the coast.* **3** (**lash out**) attack someone or something verbally or physically. **4** (of an animal) move its tail quickly and violently. **5** fasten something securely with a cord or rope. ▶ n. **1** a sharp blow or stroke with a whip or stick. **2** the flexible leather part of a whip. **3** an eyelash.

lash·ing /ˈlasHiNG/ ▶ n. **1** a whipping or beating. **2** a cord used to fasten something securely.

LASIK /ˈlāzik/ ▶ n. eye surgery to correct vision in which a laser reshapes the inner cornea.

lass /las/ (also **lassie**) ▶ n. chiefly Scottish & N. English a girl or young woman.

las·si /ˈlasē/ ▶ n. a sweet or savory Indian drink made from a yogurt or buttermilk base with water.

las·si·tude /ˈlasəˌt(y)ood/ ▶ n. physical or mental weariness; lack of energy.

las·so /ˈlasō, ˈlasoo, laˈsoo/ ▶ n. (pl. **lassos** or **lassoes**) a rope with a noose at one end, used especially in North America for catching cattle or horses. ▶ v. (**lassoes, lassoing, lassoed**) catch an animal with a lasso.

last[1] /last/ ▶ adj. **1** coming after all others in time or order. **2** most recent in time: *last year.* **3** immediately preceding something in order: *their last album.* **4** lowest in importance or rank. **5** (**the last**) the least likely or suitable. **6** only remaining: *it's our last hope.* ▶ adv. **1** on the last occasion before the present: *she was last seen on Friday evening.* **2** (in combination) after all others in order: *the last-named film.* **3** (in stating numbered points) lastly. ▶ n. (pl. same) **1** the last person or thing. **2** (**the last of**) the only remaining part of.
– PHRASES **at last** (or **at long last**) in the end; after much delay. **the last minute** the latest possible time before an event. **the last word 1** a final statement on a subject. **2** the most modern or advanced example of something: *the hotel is the last word in luxury.* **to the last** up to the last moment of a person's life.

last[2] ▶ v. **1** continue for a specified period of time. **2** remain operating or usable for a considerable or specified length of time: *the car is built to last.* **3** (of provisions or resources) be enough for someone for a specified period of time: *there was only enough food to last them three months.* **4** (often **last something out**) manage to survive or endure something.

last[3] ▶ n. a shaped stand used by a shoemaker for shaping or repairing a shoe or boot.

last-ditch ▶ adj. referring to a final desperate attempt to achieve something.

last-gasp ▶ adj. done or happening at the last possible moment.

last·ing /ˈlastiNG/ ▶ adj. enduring or able to endure for a long time: *a lasting impression.*

Last Judg·ment ▶ n. the judgment of humankind expected in some religions to take place at the end of the world.

last·ly /ˈlastlē/ ▶ adv. as a final point; last.

last name ▶ n. a person's surname.

last rites ▶ pl.n. (in the Christian Church) a religious ceremony performed for and in the presence of a person who is about to die.

Last Sup·per ▶ n. the meal eaten by Jesus and his disciples on the night before the Crucifixion.

last trump ▶ n. the trumpet blast that in some religions is thought will wake the dead on Judgment Day.

lat. ▶ abbr. latitude.

latch /lacH/ ▶ n. **1** a bar with a catch and lever used for fastening a door or gate. **2** a spring lock for an outer door that catches when the door is closed and can only be opened from the outside with a key. ▶ v. fasten a door or gate with a latch.
– PHRASES **latch onto** informal **1** join someone and

remain with them as a constant and usually unwelcome companion. **2** take up an idea or trend enthusiastically: *Californians had a reputation for latching onto fads.* **3** understand the meaning of something.

latch·key /'lacн,kē/ ▶ n. (pl. **latchkeys**) a key of a house's outer door.

latch·key child ▶ n. a child who is alone at home after school until a parent returns from work.

late /lāt/ ▶ adj. **1** acting, arriving, or happening after the proper or usual time. **2** belonging or taking place far on in a particular time or period: *a woman in her late fifties.* **3** far on in the day or night. **4** (**the/one's late**) (of a person) no longer alive: *his late wife.* **5** (**latest**) of most recent date or origin. ▶ adv. **1** after the proper or usual time. **2** toward the end of a period. **3** far on in the day or night. **4** (**later**) at a time in the near future; afterward. **5** (**late of**) formerly but not now living or working in a place. ▶ n. (**the latest**) the most recent news or fashion. ■ **late·ness** n. **lat·ish** (also **lateish**) adj. & adv.
– PHRASES **at the latest** no later than the time specified. **of late** recently.

late·com·er /'lāt,kəmər/ ▶ n. a person who arrives late.

la·teen /lə'tēn, la-/ ▶ n. **1** (also **lateen sail**) a triangular sail on a long yard at an angle of 45° to the mast. **2** a ship rigged with such a sail.

late·ly /'lātlē/ ▶ adv. recently; not long ago.

la·tent /'lātnt/ ▶ adj. existing but not yet developed, apparent, or active: *her latent talent.* ■ **la·ten·cy** n. **la·tent·ly** adv.

la·tent heat ▶ n. Physics the heat required to convert a solid into a liquid or vapor, or a liquid into a vapor, without change of temperature.

la·tent im·age ▶ n. an image on exposed photographic film that has not yet been made visible by developing.

lat·er·al /'latərəl, 'latrəl/ ▶ adj. relating to, toward, or from the side or sides. ▶ n. a lateral part, especially a shoot or branch growing out from the side of a stem. ■ **lat·er·al·ly** adv.

lat·er·ite /'latə,rīt/ ▶ n. a reddish clayey topsoil found in tropical regions, sometimes used to make roads.

la·tex /'lā,teks/ ▶ n. **1** a milky fluid found in many plants, notably the rubber tree, that coagulates on exposure to the air. **2** a synthetic product resembling latex, used to make paints, coatings, etc.

lath /laтн/ ▶ n. (pl. **laths**) a thin, flat strip of wood, especially one of a series forming a foundation for the plaster of a wall.

lathe /lāтн/ ▶ n. a machine for shaping wood or metal by means of a rotating drive that turns the piece being worked on against changeable cutting tools.

lath·er /'laтнər/ ▶ n. **1** a frothy white mass of bubbles produced by soap when mixed with water. **2** heavy sweat visible on a horse's coat as a white foam. **3** (**a lather**) informal a state of agitation or nervous excitement. ▶ v. **1** form a lather. **2** rub something with soap until a lather is produced. **3** spread a substance thickly or liberally: *we lathered butter on our toast.*

la·thi /'lätē/ ▶ n. (pl. **lathis**) (in the Indian subcontinent) a long metal-bound bamboo stick used as a weapon, especially by police.

Lat·in /'latn/ ▶ n. **1** the language of ancient Rome and its empire. **2** a person from a

country whose language developed from Latin. ▶ adj. **1** relating to the Latin language. **2** relating to countries using languages that developed from Latin, especially Latin America. **3** relating to the Western or Roman Catholic Church. ■ **Lat·in·ism** /-,izəm/ n. **Lat·in·ist** /-ist/ n. **La·tin·i·ty** /lə'tinitə, la-/ n.

La·ti·na /lə'tēnə, la-/ ▶ n. fem. of LATINO.

Lat·in A·mer·i·can ▶ adj. relating to the parts of the American continent where Spanish or Portuguese is the main national language. ▶ n. a person from Latin America.

Lat·in·ate /'latn,āt/ ▶ adj. (of language) having the character of Latin.

Lat·in·ize /'latn,īz/ ▶ v. give a Latin or Latinate form to a word. ■ **Lat·in·i·za·tion** n.

La·ti·no /lə'tēnō, la-/ ▶ n. (pl. **Latinos**; fem. **Latina**, pl. **Latinas**) a Latin American inhabitant of the US. ▶ adj. relating to Latinos or Latinas.

lat·i·tude /'latə,t(y)ōōd/ ▶ n. **1** the angular distance of a place north or south of the equator. **2** (**latitudes**) regions with reference to their temperature and distance from the equator: *northern latitudes.* **3** scope for freedom of action or thought: *journalists have considerable latitude in criticizing public figures.* ■ **lat·i·tu·di·nal** /,latə't(y)ōōdn-əl/ adj. **lat·i·tu·di·nal·ly** /,latə't(y)ōōdn-əlē/ adv.

lat·i·tu·di·nar·i·an /,latə,t(y)ōōdn'erēən/ ▶ adj. liberal in religious views. ▶ n. a person with a liberal religious outlook. ■ **lat·i·tu·di·nar·i·an·ism** /-,nizəm/ n.

la·trine /lə'trēn/ ▶ n. a communal toilet in a camp or barracks.

lat·te /'lä,tā/ (also **caffè latte** /ka'fä, kə-/) ▶ n. a drink of frothy steamed milk with a shot of espresso coffee.

lat·ter /'latər/ ▶ adj. **1** nearer to the end than to the beginning. **2** recent: *in latter years.* **3** (**the latter**) referring to the second or second-mentioned of two people or things.

lat·ter-day ▶ adj. modern or contemporary, especially when resembling a person or thing of the past: *a latter-day Noah.*

Lat·ter-Day Saints ▶ pl.n. the Mormons' name for themselves.

lat·ter·ly /'latərlē/ ▶ adv. **1** recently. **2** in the later stages of a period of time.

lat·tice /'latis/ ▶ n. **1** a structure or pattern consisting of strips crossing each other with square or diamond-shaped spaces left between. **2** a regular repeated three-dimensional arrangement of atoms, ions, or molecules in a metal or other crystalline solid. ■ **lat·ticed** adj. **lat·tice·work** /'latis,wərk/ n.

Lat·vi·an /'latvēən/ ▶ n. **1** a person from Latvia. **2** the language of Latvia. ▶ adj. relating to Latvia.

laud /lôd/ ▶ v. formal praise someone or something highly. ■ **lau·da·tion** /lô'dāsнən/ n.

laud·a·ble /'lôdəbəl/ ▶ adj. deserving praise. ■ **laud·a·bly** /-blē/ adv.

lau·da·num /'lôdn-əm, 'lôdnəm/ ▶ n. a solution prepared from opium and formerly used as a painkiller.

laud·a·to·ry /'lôdə,tôrē/ ▶ adj. expressing praise.

laugh /laf/ ▶ v. **1** make the sounds that express lively amusement. **2** (**laugh at**) make fun of. **3** (**laugh something off**) dismiss something by treating it light-heartedly. **4** (**be laughing**) informal be in a fortunate or successful position. ▶ n. **1** an act of laughing. **2** (**a laugh**) informal a

cause of laughter. ■ **laugh·er** n.
– PHRASES **have the last laugh** be eventually proved right or at an advantage. **laugh someone/thing out of court** dismiss someone or something as being obviously ridiculous. **laugh up one's sleeve** be secretly amused.

laugh·a·ble /'lafəbəl/ ▶ adj. so ridiculous as to be amusing. ■ **laugh·a·bly** /-blē/ adv.

laugh·ing gas ▶ n. nontechnical term for NITROUS OXIDE.

laugh·ing·stock /'lafɪNGˌstäk/ ▶ n. a person who is ridiculed by everyone.

laugh·ter /'laftər/ ▶ n. the action or sound of laughing.

laugh track ▶ n. recorded laughter added to a comedy show, especially a television situation comedy.

launch[1] /lônCH, länCH/ ▶ v. **1** move a boat or ship from land into the water. **2** send a rocket or missile on its course. **3** hurl or move forcefully: *I launched myself out of bed.* **4** begin an enterprise or introduce a new product. **5** (**launch into**) begin something energetically and enthusiastically. ▶ n. **1** an act of launching something. **2** an occasion at which a new product or publication is introduced to the public.

launch[2] ▶ n. a large motorboat, used especially for short trips.

launch·er /'lônCHər, 'län-/ ▶ n. a structure that holds a rocket or missile during launching.

launch pad (also **launching pad**) ▶ n. the area on which a rocket stands for launching, typically a platform with a supporting structure.

laun·der /'lôndər, 'län-/ ▶ v. **1** wash and iron clothes or linen. **2** informal pass illegally obtained money through legitimate businesses or foreign banks to conceal its origins. ■ **laun·der·er** n.

laun·dress /'lôndrəs, 'län-/ ▶ n. dated a woman employed to launder clothes and linen.

laun·dro·mat /'lôndrəˌmat, 'län-/ ▶ n. trademark an establishment with coin-operated washing machines and dryers for public use.

laun·dry /ˌlôndrē, 'län-/ ▶ n. (pl. **laundries**) **1** clothes and linen that need to be washed or that have been newly washed. **2** a room or building where clothes and linen are washed and ironed.

laun·dry bas·ket ▶ n. a basket for dirty clothing.

laun·dry list ▶ n. a long or exhaustive list.

lau·re·ate /'lôrē-it, 'lär-/ ▶ n. **1** a person given an award for outstanding creative or intellectual achievement. **2** a Poet Laureate. ■ **lau·re·ate·ship** /-ˌSHip/ n.

lau·rel /'lôrəl, 'lär-/ ▶ n. **1** an evergreen shrub or small tree with dark green glossy leaves. **2** (**laurels**) a crown woven from bay leaves and awarded as a sign of victory or mark of honor in classical times. **3** (**laurels**) honor or praise for an achievement.
– PHRASES **rest on one's laurels** be so satisfied with what one has already achieved that one makes no further effort.

la·va /'lävə, 'lavə/ ▶ n. hot molten or semifluid rock that erupts from a volcano or fissure, or solid rock formed when this cools.

la·vage /lə'väzH, 'lavij/ ▶ n. the process of washing out a body cavity, such as the colon or stomach.

la·va lamp ▶ n. a transparent electric lamp containing a viscous liquid in which a suspended waxy substance rises and falls in constantly

changing shapes.

lav·a·to·ry /'lavəˌtôrē/ ▶ n. (pl. **lavatories**) a bathroom.

lave /lāv/ ▶ v. literary wash something.

lav·en·der /'lavəndər/ ▶ n. **1** a small evergreen shrub with narrow strong-smelling leaves and bluish-purple flowers. **2** a pale bluish-purple color.

lav·en·der wa·ter ▶ n. a perfume made from distilled lavender.

la·ver /'lāvər/ (also **purple laver**) ▶ n. an edible seaweed with thin reddish-purple and green fronds.

lav·ish /'laviSH/ ▶ adj. **1** very rich, elaborate, or luxurious. **2** giving or given in large amounts: *lavish funding from abroad.* ▶ v. give in abundant or extravagant quantities: *he lavished money and attention on the family.* ■ **lav·ish·ly** adv. **lav·ish·ness** n.

law /lô/ ▶ n. **1** a rule or system of rules recognized by a country or community as regulating the actions of its members and enforced by the imposition of penalties. **2** such rules as a subject of study or as the basis of the legal profession. **3** statute law and the common law as distinct from equity. **4** a rule that controls correct behavior in a sport. **5** a statement of the fact that a particular natural or scientific phenomenon always occurs if certain conditions are present. **6** something that has binding force or effect: *his word was law.* **7** (**the law**) informal the police.
– PHRASES **be a law unto oneself** behave in an unconventional or unpredictable way. **lay down the law** issue instructions in a domineering way. **take the law into one's own hands** illegally punish someone according to one's own ideas of justice.

law·a·bid·ing ▶ adj. obedient to the laws of society.

law·break·er /'lôˌbrākər/ ▶ n. a person who breaks the law.

law court ▶ n. a court of law.

law·ful /'lôfəl/ ▶ adj. following, permitted by, or recognized by the law or a set of rules. ■ **law·ful·ly** adv. **law·ful·ness** n.

law·giv·er /'lôˌgivər/ ▶ n. a person who draws up and enacts laws.

law·less /'lôləs/ ▶ adj. not governed by or obedient to laws. ■ **law·less·ly** adv. **law·less·ness** n.

law·mak·er /'lôˌmākər/ ▶ n. a member of a government who draws up laws. ■ **law·mak·ing** /-ˌmākiNG/ adj. & n.

law·man /'lôˌmən, -man/ ▶ n. (pl. **lawmen**) a law-enforcement officer, especially a sheriff.

lawn[1] /lôn/ ▶ n. an area of mown grass in a yard, garden, or park.

lawn[2] ▶ n. a fine linen or cotton fabric.

lawn bowl·ing (Brit. **bowls**) ▶ n. a game played with wooden bowls, the object of which is to roll one's bowl as close as possible to a small white ball (the jack).

lawn·mow·er /'lônˌmōər/ ▶ n. a machine for cutting the grass on a lawn.

lawn ten·nis ▶ n. dated or formal tennis.

law of av·er·ag·es ▶ n. the supposed principle that future events are likely to turn out so that they balance any past events.

law of na·ture ▶ n. another term for NATURAL LAW.

law·ren·ci·um /lôˈrensēəm/ ▸ n. a very unstable chemical element made by high-energy collisions.

law·suit /ˈlôˌso͞ot/ ▸ n. a claim or dispute brought to a court of law to be decided.

law·yer /ˈloi-ər, ˈlôyər/ ▸ n. a person who practices or studies law; an attorney or a counselor. ■ **law·yer·ing** n. **law·yer·ly** adj.

lax /laks/ ▸ adj. 1 not strict, severe, or careful enough: *lax security arrangements.* 2 (of limbs or muscles) relaxed. ■ **lax·i·ty** n. **lax·ly** adv. **lax·ness** n.

lax·a·tive /ˈlaksətiv/ ▸ n. a medicine that causes a person to empty their bowels. ▸ adj. causing the bowels to empty.

lay¹ /lā/ ▸ v. (past and past part. **laid** /lād/) 1 put something down gently or carefully. 2 put something down and set it in position for use. 3 assign or place: *they tried to lay the blame on others.* 4 (**lay something before**) present material for consideration and action to someone. 5 (of a female bird, reptile, etc.) produce an egg from inside the body. 6 stake an amount of money in a bet. 7 cause a ghost to stop appearing. 8 (**get laid**) vulgar slang have sex. ▸ n. 1 the general appearance of an area of land. 2 the position or direction in which something lies. 3 vulgar slang a sexual partner or act of sex.
– PHRASES **lay claim to** claim that one has a right to something or possesses a skill or quality. **lay something down 1** formulate and enforce a rule or principle. 2 build up a deposit of a substance. 3 store wine in a cellar. 4 pay or bet money. **lay something in/up** build up a stock in case of need. **lay into** informal attack someone violently. **the lay of the land 1** the features of an area. 2 the current situation. **lay off** informal give something up. **lay someone off** discharge a worker because of a shortage of work. **lay something on thick** (or **with a trowel**) informal greatly exaggerate or overemphasize something. **lay someone open** expose someone to the risk of something. **lay someone out** prepare someone for burial after death. **lay something out 1** construct or arrange buildings or gardens according to a plan. 2 arrange and present material for printing and publication. 3 informal spend a sum of money. **lay something to rest 1** bury a body in a grave. 2 put an end to fear, anxiety, etc. **lay someone up** put someone out of action through illness or injury.

> **USAGE**
> The words **lay** and **lie** are often used incorrectly. **Lay** generally means 'put something down' (*they are going to lay the carpet*), whereas **lie** means 'be in a horizontal position to rest' (*why don't you lie down?*). The past tense and past participle of **lay** is **laid** (*they laid the carpet*); the past tense of **lie** is **lay** (*he lay on the floor*) and the past participle is **lain** (*she had lain awake for hours*).

lay² ▸ adj. 1 not belonging to the clergy. 2 not having professional qualifications or expert knowledge in a particular subject.

lay³ ▸ n. 1 a short lyric or narrative poem intended to be sung. 2 literary a song.

lay⁴ ▸ past of LIE¹.

lay·a·bout /ˈlāəˌbout/ ▸ n. derogatory a person who does little or no work.

lay·a·way /ˈlāəˌwā/ ▸ n. (also **layaway plan**) a system of paying a deposit to secure an item for later purchase: *she picked up a coat she had on layaway.*

lay broth·er (or **lay sister**) ▸ n. a person who has taken the vows of a religious order but is not ordained and is employed in ancillary or manual work.

lay·er /ˈlāər/ ▸ n. 1 a sheet or thickness of material, typically one of several, covering a surface. 2 (in combination) a person or thing that lays something: *a cable-layer.* 3 a shoot fastened down to take root while attached to the parent plant. ▸ v. (often as adj. **layered**) arrange or cut something in a layer or layers.

lay·ette /lāˈet/ ▸ n. a set of clothing and bedclothes for a newborn child.

lay·man /ˈlāmən/ (or **laywoman** /ˈlāˌwo͝omən/ or **layperson** /ˈlāˌpərsən/) ▸ n. (pl. **laymen**, **laywomen**, **laypersons**, or **laypeople** /ˈlāˌpēpəl/) 1 a member of a Church who is not a priest or minister. 2 a person without professional or specialized knowledge in a particular subject.

lay·off /ˈlāˌôf, -ˌäf/ ▸ n. 1 an instance of discharging a worker or workers because of a shortage of work. 2 a temporary break from an activity.

lay·out /ˈlāˌout/ ▸ n. 1 the way in which something, especially a page, is laid out. 2 a thing set out in a particular way.

lay·o·ver /ˈlāˌōvər/ ▸ n. a rest or wait before a further stage in a journey.

lay read·er ▸ n. (in the Anglican Church) a layperson authorized to preach and to conduct some services but not to celebrate the Holy Communion.

lay·up /ˈlāəp/ ▸ n. Basketball a one-handed shot made from near the basket, especially one that rebounds off the backboard.

lay·wom·an /ˈlāˌwo͝omən/ ▸ n. see LAYMAN.

laze /lāz/ ▸ v. spend time relaxing or doing very little. ▸ n. a spell of lazing.

la·zy /ˈlāzē/ ▸ adj. (**lazier**, **laziest**) 1 unwilling to work or use energy. 2 showing a lack of effort or care: *a lazy investigation.* ■ **la·zi·ly** adv. **la·zi·ness** n.

la·zy·bones /ˈlāzēˌbōnz/ ▸ n. (pl. same) informal a lazy person.

la·zy eye ▸ n. an eye with poor vision due to underuse, especially the unused eye in a squint.

lb. ▸ abbr. pound(s) (in weight).

l.c. ▸ abbr. 1 in the passage cited. 2 lower case.

LCD ▸ abbr. 1 Electronics & Computing liquid crystal display. 2 Mathematics lowest (or least) common denominator.

LCM ▸ abbr. Mathematics lowest (or least) common multiple.

ld. ▸ abbr. 1 lead. 2 load.

LDS ▸ abbr. Latter-Day Saints.

lea /lē/ ▸ n. literary an open area of grassy land.

leach /lēCH/ ▸ v. (of a soluble substance) drain away from soil or other material by the action of water passing through it.

lead¹ /lēd/ ▸ v. (past and past part. **led** /led/) 1 draw, guide, or take a person or animal with one. 2 be a route or means of access: *the street led into the square.* 3 (**lead (up) to**) result in. 4 influence to do or believe something: *that may lead them to reconsider.* 5 be in charge of other people. 6 be in first place in a competition or contest. 7 be best in an area of activity: *these companies lead the way in new technological developments.*

8 have a particular way of life. 9 (often **lead** (**off**) **with**) begin with a particular action or item. 10 (**lead up to**) come before: *the weeks leading up to the election.* 11 (**lead someone on**) deceive someone into believing that one is attracted to them. 12 (in card games) play the first card in a trick or round of play. ▶ n. 1 an example for others to follow: *others followed our lead.* 2 (**the lead**) first place in a competition or contest. 3 an amount by which a competitor is ahead of the others: *a one-goal lead.* 4 the chief part in a play or movie. 5 a clue to be followed in solving a problem. 6 a strap or cord for restraining and guiding a dog. 7 a wire conveying electric current from a source to an appliance, or connecting two points of a circuit together. ▶ adj. 1 playing the chief part in a musical group: *the lead singer.* 2 referring to the main item in a newspaper, magazine, or broadcast: *the lead article.*
– PHRASES **lead someone down the garden path** *informal* give someone misleading clues or signals.

lead² /led/ ▶ n. 1 a heavy bluish-gray soft metallic element. 2 graphite used as the part of a pencil that makes a mark. 3 (**leads**) lead frames holding the glass of a lattice or stained-glass window. 4 *Nautical* a lump of lead suspended on a line to determine the depth of water. 5 *Printing* a blank space between lines of print.

lead crys·tal /led/ (also **lead glass**) ▶ n. glass containing a substantial proportion of lead oxide, making it more refractive.

lead·ed /ˈledid/ ▶ adj. 1 framed, covered, or weighted with lead. 2 (of gasoline) containing lead.

lead·en /ˈlednˌ/ ▶ adj. 1 dull, heavy, or slow: *he hoped sleep would loosen his leaden legs.* 2 dull gray in color. ■ **lead·en·ly** adv.

lead·er /ˈlēdər/ ▶ n. 1 a person or thing that leads. 2 a person or thing that is the most successful or advanced in a particular area. 3 the principal player in a music group. 4 a short strip of nonfunctioning material at each end of a reel of film or recording tape for connection to the spool. ■ **lead·er·less** adj. **lead·er·ship** /ˈlēdərˌSHip/ n.

lead·er board ▶ n. a scoreboard showing the names and current scores of the leading competitors, especially in a golf match.

lead-in /ˈlēd ˌin/ ▶ n. an introduction to something.

lead·ing /ˈlēdiNG/ ▶ adj. most important or in first place.

lead·ing edge ▶ n. the forefront of technological development.

lead·ing light ▶ n. a person who is prominent or influential in a particular field or organization.

lead·ing ques·tion ▶ n. a question that prompts the desired answer.

lead-off /ˈled/ ▶ adj. 1 (of an action) beginning a series or a process: *the album's lead-off track.* 2 (**leadoff**) *Baseball* referring to the first batter in a lineup or of an inning.

lead time /lēd/ ▶ n. the time between the beginning and completion of a production process.

lead-up /ˈlēd/ ▶ n. an event or sequence that leads up to something else.

leaf /lēf/ ▶ n. (pl. **leaves**) 1 a flat, typically green structure that grows from the stem of a plant. 2 the state of having leaves: *the trees were in leaf.* 3 a single sheet of paper, especially in a book; a page. 4 gold, silver, or other metal in the form of very thin foil. 5 a hinged or detachable part, especially of a table. ▶ v. 1 (of a plant) put out new leaves. 2 (**leaf through**) turn over pages or papers, reading them quickly or casually. ■ **leaf·age** n. **leaf·less** adj.
– PHRASES **turn over a new leaf** start to act or behave in a better way.

leaf·let /ˈlēflit/ ▶ n. 1 a printed sheet of paper containing information or advertising and usually distributed free. 2 a small leaf, especially a component of a compound leaf. ▶ v. (**leaflets, leafleting, leafleted**) distribute leaflets to people or an area.

leaf lit·ter ▶ n. another term for LITTER (sense 6 of the noun).

leaf mold ▶ n. soil consisting chiefly of decayed leaves.

leaf·y /ˈlēfē/ ▶ adj. (**leafier, leafiest**) 1 having many leaves. 2 full of trees and shrubs: *a leafy avenue.* ■ **leaf·i·ness** n.

league¹ /lēg/ ▶ n. 1 a collection of people, countries, or groups that combine to help each other or promote something. 2 a group of sports clubs that play each other over a period for a championship. 3 a class of quality or excellence: *the two men were not in the same league.* ▶ v. (**leagues, leaguing, leagued**) join in a league or alliance.
– PHRASES **in league** (of people) conspiring with each other.

league² ▶ n. a former measure of distance, usually about three miles.

leak /lēk/ ▶ v. 1 (of a container or covering) accidentally allow contents to escape or enter through a hole or crack. 2 (of liquid, gas, etc.) escape or enter accidentally through a hole or crack. 3 deliberately disclose secret information. ▶ n. 1 a hole or crack through which contents leak. 2 an instance of leaking. ■ **leak·age** n. **leak·er** n. **leak·y** adj.
– PHRASES **have** (or **take**) **a leak** *informal* urinate.

lean¹ /lēn/ ▶ v. (past and past part. **leaned** /lēnd/ or chiefly Brit. **leant** /lent/) 1 be in or move into a sloping position. 2 (**lean against/on**) slope and rest against. 3 (**lean on**) rely on someone for support. 4 (**lean to/toward**) favor a point of view. 5 (**lean on**) *informal* intimidate someone into doing something. ▶ n. an instance of leaning or sloping.

lean² ▶ adj. 1 (of a person) having no unwanted fat; thin. 2 (of meat) containing little fat. 3 (of a period of time) difficult because money or food is scarce: *the lean years of the Depression.* 4 (of an industry or organization) efficient and with no waste. 5 (of a vaporized fuel mixture) having a high proportion of air. ▶ n. the lean part of meat. ■ **lean·ness** n.

lean·ing /ˈlēniNG/ ▶ n. a tendency or preference: *communist leanings.*

lean-to ▶ n. (pl. **lean-tos**) a building sharing a wall with a larger building and having a roof that leans against that wall.

leap /lēp/ ▶ v. (past or past part. **leaped** /lēpt/ or **leapt** /lept/) 1 jump high, far, or across something. 2 move quickly and suddenly: *Ann leapt to her feet.* 3 (**leap at**) accept something eagerly. 4 (especially of a price or amount) increase dramatically. 5 (**leap out**) be immediately noticeable. ▶ n. 1 an instance of leaping. 2 a sudden change or increase. ■ **leap·er** n.

– PHRASES **a leap in the dark** a daring step or enterprise with an unpredictable outcome. **by** (or **in**) **leaps and bounds** with very rapid progress.

leap·frog /'lēp,frôg, -,fräg/ ▶ n. a game in which players in turn vault with parted legs over others who are bending down. ▶ v. (**leapfrogs, leapfrogging, leapfrogged**) **1** vault over someone in the game of leapfrog. **2** reach a leading position by overtaking others or omitting a stage in a process: *the firm has leapfrogged over all its rivals.*

leap year ▶ n. a year, occurring once every four years, that has 366 days (February 29 being the additional day).

learn /lərn/ ▶ v. (past and past part. **learned** /lərnd/ or chiefly Brit. **learnt** /lərnt/) **1** gain knowledge of or skill in something through study or experience or by being taught. **2** become aware of something by information or from observation. **3** memorize something. **4** old use or informal teach someone. ■ **learn·a·ble** adj. **learn·er** n.

learn·ed /'lərnid/ ▶ adj. having or showing much knowledge gained by studying.

learn·ing /'lərniNG/ ▶ n. knowledge or skills gained through study or by being taught.

learn·ing curve ▶ n. the rate of a person's progress in gaining experience or new skills.

learn·ing dis·a·bil·i·ty ▶ n. difficulty in gaining knowledge and skills to the level expected of one's age. ■ **learn·ing-dis·a·bled** adj.

> USAGE
> The term **learning disability** covers general conditions such as Down syndrome as well as more specific conditions such as dyslexia. It is considered less discriminatory and more positive than terms such as **mental handicap**, especially in official situations.

lease /lēs/ ▶ n. a contract by which one party conveys land, property, services, etc., to another for a specified time, in return for payment. ▶ v. rent something on lease.

– PHRASES **a new lease on life** a substantially improved chance to lead a happy or successful life.

lease·hold /'lēs,hōld/ ▶ n. **1** the holding of property by a lease. **2** a piece of land or property held by a lease. ■ **lease·hold·er** n.

leash /lēsh/ ▶ n. a strap or cord for restraining and guiding a dog. ▶ v. put a leash on a dog.

least /lēst/ ▶ determiner & pron. (usu. **the least**) smallest in amount, extent, or significance. ▶ adv. to the smallest extent or degree.

– PHRASES **at least 1** not less than. **2** if nothing else. **3** anyway. **at the least** (or **very least**) **1** not less than. **2** taking the most pessimistic view. **not in the least** not at all. **not least** in particular.

least·ways /'lēst,wāz/ (also **leastwise**) ▶ adv. dialect or informal at least.

leath·er /'leTHər/ ▶ n. **1** a material made from the skin of an animal by tanning or a similar process. **2** a piece of leather as a polishing cloth. **3** (**leathers**) leather clothes worn by a motorcyclist. ▶ adj. referring to people, especially homosexuals, who wear leather clothing and accessories as a sign of rough masculinity: *leather bar.* ▶ v. **1** (as adj. **leathered**) covered with leather. **2** informal beat with a leather strap.

leath·er·back /'leTHər,bak/ (also **leatherback turtle**) ▶ n. a very large black turtle with a thick leathery shell, living chiefly in tropical seas.

leath·er·ette /,leTHə'ret/ ▶ n. imitation leather.

leath·ern /'leTHərn/ ▶ adj. old use made of leather.

leath·er·y /'leTH(ə)rē/ ▶ adj. having a tough, hard texture like leather. ■ **leath·er·i·ness** n.

leave[1] /lēv/ ▶ v. (past and past part. **left** /left/) **1** go away from someone or something. **2** stop living at, attending, or working for: *he left home at 16.* **3** allow something to remain; go away without taking something. **4** (**be left**) remain to be used or dealt with: *drink left from the wedding.* **5** cause to be in a particular state or position: *leave the door open.* **6** let someone do something without help or interference. **7** (**leave something to**) let someone deal with or be responsible for something. **8** deposit something to be collected or dealt with. **9** have someone as a surviving relative after one's death. **10** give something to someone in a will. ■ **leav·er** n.

– PHRASES **leave someone/thing be** informal avoid disturbing or interfering with someone or something. **leave off** stop doing something. **leave someone/thing out** fail to include someone or something.

leave[2] ▶ n. **1** (also **leave of absence**) time when one has permission to be absent from work or duty. **2** formal permission: *seeking leave to appeal.*

– PHRASES **take one's leave** formal say goodbye.

leav·en /'levən/ ▶ n. **1** a substance, typically yeast, added to dough to make it ferment and rise. **2** an influence or quality that modifies or improves something: *John's humor was the leaven of his charm.* ▶ v. **1** (usu. as adj. **leavened**) make dough or bread ferment and rise by adding yeast or another leaven. **2** make an addition to improve something: *the debate was leavened by humor.*

leaves /lēvz/ ▶ plural of LEAF.

leave-tak·ing ▶ n. an act of saying goodbye.

leav·ings /'lēviNGz/ ▶ pl.n. things that have been left as worthless.

Leb·a·nese /,lebə'nēz, -'nēs/ ▶ n. (pl. same) a person from Lebanon. ▶ adj. relating to Lebanon.

Le·bens·raum /'lābəns,roum, -bənz-/ ▶ n. territory that a state or nation believes is needed for its natural development.

lech·er /'lecHər/ ▶ n. a lecherous man. ■ **lech·er·y** n.

lech·er·ous /'lecH(ə)rəs/ ▶ adj. having or showing excessive or offensive sexual desire. ■ **lech·er·ous·ly** adv. **lech·er·ous·ness** n.

lec·i·thin /'lesəthin/ ▶ n. a substance found in egg yolk and other animal and plant tissues, often used as an emulsifier in food processing.

lec·tern /'lektərn/ ▶ n. a tall stand with a sloping top used to support a book or papers from which a speaker can read while standing up.

lec·tion·ar·y /'leksHə,nerē/ ▶ n. (pl. **lectionaries**) a list or book of portions of the Bible to be read at church services.

lec·ture /'lekcHər/ ▶ n. **1** an educational talk to an audience, especially one of students in a university. **2** a lengthy reprimand or warning. ▶ v. **1** give an educational talk or talks. **2** criticize or reprimand someone.

lec·tur·er /'lekcHərər/ ▶ n. a person who gives lectures, such as a teacher at a college or university.

lec·ture·ship /'lekcHər,sHip/ ▶ n. a post as a lecturer.

LED ▶ abbr. light-emitting diode, a semiconductor diode that glows when a voltage is applied.

led /led/ ▶ past and past participle of LEAD[1].

le·der·ho·sen /ˈlādərˌhōzən/ ▶ pl. n. leather shorts with suspenders, traditionally worn by men in the Alps.

ledge /lej/ ▶ n. **1** a narrow horizontal surface projecting from a wall, cliff, or other vertical surface. **2** an underwater ridge, especially one of rocks near the seashore.

ledg·er /ˈlejər/ ▶ n. a book in which financial accounts are kept.

ledg·er line (also **leger line**) ▶ n. Music a short line added for notes above or below the range of a staff.

lee /lē/ ▶ n. **1** (also **lee side**) the side of something sheltered from the wind. Contrasted with WEATHER. **2** shelter from wind or weather given by an object.

leech¹ /lēch/ ▶ n. **1** a worm that sucks the blood of animals or people, used in medicine for bloodletting. **2** a person who lives off others.

leech² ▶ n. old use a doctor or healer.

leek /lēk/ ▶ n. a vegetable related to the onion, with flat overlapping leaves forming an elongated cylindrical bulb.

leer /li(ə)r/ ▶ v. look or gaze in a lustful or unpleasant way. ▶ n. a lustful or unpleasant look.

leer·y /ˈli(ə)rē/ ▶ adj. (**leerier, leeriest**) informal cautious or wary: *a city leery of gang violence.* ■ **leer·i·ness** n.

lees /lēz/ ▶ pl. n. the sediment of wine in the bottom of the barrel.

lee shore ▶ n. a shore lying on the side of a ship that is sheltered from the wind (and onto which the ship could be blown).

lee·ward /ˈlēwərd, ˈlo͞oərd/ ▶ adj. & adv. on or toward the side sheltered from the wind or toward which the wind is blowing. Contrasted with WINDWARD. ▶ n. the leeward side.

lee·way /ˈlēˌwā/ ▶ n. **1** the amount of freedom to move or act that is available: *we have a lot of leeway in how we do our jobs.* **2** the sideways drift of a ship to leeward of the desired course.

left¹ /left/ ▶ adj. **1** on, toward, or relating to the side of a person or thing that is to the west when the person or thing is facing north. **2** relating to a left-wing person or group. ▶ adv. on or to the left side. ▶ n. **1** (**the left**) the left-hand part, side, or direction. **2** a left turn. **3** a person's left fist, or a blow given with it. **4** (often **the Left**) (treated as sing. or pl.) a group or party with radical, reforming, or socialist views. ■ **left·ish** adj. **left·most** /ˈlef(t)ˌmōst/ adj. **left·ward** /ˈleftwərd/ adj. & adv. **left·wards** adv.

– PHRASES **have two left feet** be clumsy or awkward.

left² ▶ past and past participle of LEAVE¹.

left field ▶ n. **1** Baseball the part of the outfield to the left of center field from the perspective of home plate. **2** Baseball the position of the defensive player stationed in left field. **3** informal a surprising or unconventional position or direction. **4** a position of ignorance or confusion: *he's so far out in left field he doesn't know what's going on.*

left hand ▶ n. the region or direction on the left side of someone or something. ▶ adj. **1** on or toward the left side. **2** done with or using the left hand.

left-hand·ed ▶ adj. **1** (of a person) using the left hand more naturally than the right. **2** done with the left hand. **3** turning to the left; toward the left. **4** (of a screw) advanced by turning

counterclockwise.

left-hand·er ▶ n. **1** a left-handed person. **2** a blow struck with a person's left hand.

left·ie ▶ n. variant spelling of LEFTY.

left·ism /ˈleftˌtizəm/ ▶ n. the political views or policies of the Left. ■ **left·ist** /ˈleftist/ n. & adj.

left·o·ver /ˈleftˌōvər/ ▶ n. (**leftovers**) something, especially food, remaining after the rest has been used. ▶ adj. remaining; surplus.

left wing ▶ n. **1** the radical, liberal, or socialist section of a political party or system. **2** the left side of a sports team on the field or of an army. ■ **left-wing·er** n.

left·y /ˈleftē/ (also **leftie**) ▶ n. (pl. **lefties**) informal **1** a left-wing person. **2** a left-handed person.

leg /leg/ ▶ n. **1** each of the limbs on which a person or animal moves and stands. **2** a long, thin support or prop, especially of a chair or table. **3** a section of a journey, process, or race. **4** (in sports) each of two games constituting a round of a competition. **5** (**legs**) informal sustained popularity or success: *some books have legs, others don't.* ■ **leg·ged** adj.

– PHRASES **not have a leg to stand on** be unable to justify one's arguments or actions. **on one's** (or **its**) **last legs** near the end of life, usefulness, or existence.

leg·a·cy /ˈlegəsē/ ▶ n. (pl. **legacies**) **1** an amount of money or property left to someone in a will. **2** a situation that exists because of a past event or action: *all the ills in the country are the legacy of military rule.* ▶ adj. (of computer hardware or software) that has been superseded but is difficult to replace because of its wide use.

le·gal /ˈlēgəl/ ▶ adj. **1** relating to or required by the law. **2** permitted by law. ■ **le·gal·ly** adv.

le·gal age ▶ n. the age at which a person takes on the rights and responsibilities of an adult.

le·gal aid ▶ n. payment from public funds given to people who cannot afford to pay for legal advice or proceedings.

le·gal·ese /ˌlēgəˈlēz, -ˈlēs/ ▶ n. informal the formal and technical language of legal documents.

le·gal·ism /ˈlēgəˌlizəm/ ▶ n. the practice of keeping strictly to the law. ■ **le·gal·ist** n. & adj. **le·gal·is·tic** /ˌlēgəˈlistik/ adj.

le·gal·i·ty /ləˈgalətē/ ▶ n. (pl. **legalities**) **1** the quality or state of being legal. **2** (**legalities**) rules and duties imposed by law.

le·gal·ize /ˈlēgəˌlīz/ ▶ v. make something that was illegal allowed by the law. ■ **le·gal·i·za·tion** /ˌlēgələˈzāSHən, -ˌlīˈzā-/ n.

le·gal sep·a·ra·tion ▶ n. an arrangement by which a husband and wife remain married but live apart, following a court order.

le·gal ten·der ▶ n. coins or banknotes that must be accepted if offered in payment of a debt.

leg·ate /ˈlegit/ ▶ n. a member of the clergy who represents the Pope.

leg·a·tee /ˌlegəˈtē/ ▶ n. a person who receives a legacy.

le·ga·tion /liˈgāSHən/ ▶ n. **1** a diplomatic minister and their staff. **2** the official residence of a diplomat.

le·ga·to /liˈgätō/ ▶ adv. & adj. Music in a smooth, flowing way.

leg·end /ˈlejənd/ ▶ n. **1** a traditional story about the past that may or may not have a factual basis. **2** a very famous person: *a screen legend.* **3** an inscription or explanatory wording. ▶ adj. very well known: *his speed and ferocity in attack were legend.*

leg·end·ar·y /'lejən,derē/ ▶ adj. **1** relating to or based on traditional stories about the past. **2** remarkable enough to be famous: *France's legendary chefs.* ■ **leg·end·ar·i·ly** /-,derəlē, ,lejən'de(ə)r-/ adv.

leg·er·de·main /,lejərdə'mān, 'lejərdə,mān/ ▶ n. **1** skillful use of the hands when performing conjuring tricks. **2** deception; trickery.

le·ger line ▶ n. variant spelling of LEDGER LINE.

leg·gings /'legiNGz/ ▶ pl.n. **1** tight-fitting stretch pants worn by women and children. **2** protective coverings for the legs.

leg·gy /'legē/ ▶ adj. (**leggier, leggiest**) **1** long-legged. **2** (of a plant) having a long and straggly stem or stems.

leg·i·ble /'lejəbəl/ ▶ adj. (of handwriting or print) clear enough to read. ■ **leg·i·bil·i·ty** /,lejə'bilətē/ n. **leg·i·bly** adv.

le·gion /'lējən/ ▶ n. **1** a division of 3,000–6,000 men in the ancient Roman army. **2** (**a legion/legions of**) a vast number of people or things. ▶ adj. great in number: *her fans are legion.*

le·gion·ar·y /'lējə,nerē/ ▶ n. (pl. **legionaries**) a soldier in an ancient Roman legion.

le·gion·naire /,lējə'ner/ ▶ n. **1** a member of the Foreign Legion. **2** a member of a national association for former servicemen and servicewomen.

le·gion·naires' dis·ease ▶ n. a form of pneumonia spread chiefly in water droplets through air conditioning systems.

leg i·ron ▶ n. a metal band or chain placed around a prisoner's ankle as a restraint.

leg·is·late /'lejə,slāt/ ▶ v. make laws.

leg·is·la·tion /,lejə'slāSHən/ ▶ n. laws as a whole.

leg·is·la·tive /'lejə,slātiv/ ▶ adj. **1** having the power to make laws. **2** relating to laws or a lawmaking body. ■ **leg·is·la·tive·ly** adv.

leg·is·la·tor /'lejə,slātər/ ▶ n. a person who makes laws; a member of a legislature.

leg·is·la·ture /'lejə,slāCHər/ ▶ n. the lawmaking body of a country or state.

le·git·i·mate ▶ adj. /li'jitəmit/ **1** in accordance with the law or rules. **2** (of a child) born of parents lawfully married to each other. **3** able to be defended or justified: *a legitimate excuse for being late.* **4** (of a sovereign) having a title based on strict hereditary right. ▶ v. /-,māt/ make something lawful. ■ **le·git·i·ma·cy** /-məsē/ n. **le·git·i·mate·ly** /-mitlē/ adv. **le·git·i·ma·tion** /li,jitə'māSHən/ n.

le·git·i·mize /li'jitə,mīz/ ▶ v. make something lawful or legitimate. ■ **le·git·i·mi·za·tion** /li,jitəmə'zāSHən/ n.

Le·go /'legō/ ▶ n. trademark a toy consisting of interlocking plastic building blocks.

leg·room /'leg,rōōm, -,rŏŏm/ ▶ n. space in which a seated person can put their legs.

leg·ume /'leg,yōōm, lə'gyōōm/ ▶ n. **1** a plant of the pea family grown as a crop. **2** a seed, pod, or other edible part of a plant of the pea family.

le·gu·mi·nous /li'gyōōmənəs/ ▶ adj. relating to plants of the pea family, typically having seeds in pods and root nodules containing nitrogen-fixing bacteria.

leg-up ▶ n. **1** an act of helping someone to mount a horse or high object. **2** a boost to improve one's position.

leg warm·ers ▶ pl.n. a pair of knitted garments covering the legs from ankle to knee or thigh.

leg·work /'leg,wərk/ ▶ n. work that involves tiring or boring travel from place to place.

lei /lā/ ▶ n. a Polynesian garland of flowers.

leish·man·i·a·sis /,lēSHmə'nīəsəs/ ▶ n. a tropical and subtropical disease transmitted by the bite of sandflies.

lei·sure /'lēzhər, 'lezhər/ ▶ n. time spent in or free for relaxation or enjoyment. ■ **lei·sured** adj.

– PHRASES **at leisure 1** not occupied; free. **2** in an unhurried way. **at one's leisure** when convenient.

lei·sure·ly /'lēzhərlē, 'lezhər-/ ▶ adj. relaxed and unhurried. ▶ adv. without hurry. ■ **lei·sure·li·ness** n.

lei·sure·wear /'lēzhər,we(ə)r, 'lezhər-/ ▶ n. casual clothes worn for leisure activities.

leit·mo·tif /'lītmō,tēf/ (also **leitmotiv** pronunc. same) ▶ n. a recurring theme in a musical or literary work.

lem·ming /'lemiNG/ ▶ n. **1** a short-tailed Arctic rodent that periodically migrates in large numbers. **2** a person who unthinkingly joins a mass movement, especially a rush to destruction.

lem·on /'lemən/ ▶ n. **1** a pale yellow oval citrus fruit with thick skin and acidic juice. **2** a drink made from or flavored with lemon juice. **3** a pale yellow color. **4** informal an unsatisfactory or disappointing person or thing, especially an automobile. ■ **lem·on·y** adj.

lem·on·ade /,lemə'nād, 'lemə,nād/ ▶ n. a sweetened drink made from lemon juice or lemon flavoring and sweetened water.

lem·on balm ▶ n. a bushy lemon-scented herb of the mint family.

lem·on grass ▶ n. a tropical grass that yields an oil that smells of lemon, used in Asian cooking.

le·mur /'lēmər/ ▶ n. a primate with a pointed snout and a long tail that lives in trees in Madagascar.

lend /lend/ ▶ v. (past and past part. **lent** /lent/) **1** allow someone to use something on the understanding that it will be returned. **2** allow someone to use a sum of money under an agreement to pay it back later, typically with interest. **3** contribute or add a quality to: *the smile lent his face a boyish charm.* **4** (**lend itself to**) (of a thing) be suitable for something. ■ **lend·er** n.

– PHRASES **lend an ear** listen sympathetically or attentively.

lend·ing li·brar·y ▶ n. a public library from which books may be borrowed for a limited time.

length /leNG(k)TH, lenTH/ ▶ n. **1** the measurement or extent of something from end to end. **2** the amount of time occupied by something: *schools have reduced the length of summer vacation.* **3** the quality of being long. **4** the full distance that a thing extends for. **5** the extent of a garment downward when worn. **6** the length of a horse or boat as a measure of the lead in a race. **7** a stretch or piece of something. **8** a degree to which a course of action is taken: *they go to great lengths to avoid the press.*

– PHRASES **at length 1** in detail; fully. **2** after a

long time.

length·en /'leŋ(k)thən, 'lenthən/ ▶ v. make or become longer.

length·ways /'leŋ(k)th,wāz, 'lenth-/ ▶ adv. lengthwise.

length·wise /'leŋ(k)th,wīz, 'lenth-/ ▶ adv. in a direction parallel with the length of something. ▶ adj. lying or moving lengthwise.

length·y /'leŋ(k)thē, 'lenthē/ ▶ adj. (**lengthier, lengthiest**) very or excessively long in time or extent. ■ **length·i·ly** adv.

le·ni·ent /'lēnēənt, 'lēnyənt/ ▶ adj. not as strict or severe as expected: *a lenient one-year sentence.* ■ **le·ni·ence** n. **le·ni·en·cy** n. **le·ni·ent·ly** adv.

Le·nin·ism /'lenə,nizəm/ ▶ n. Marxism as interpreted and applied by the Soviet premier Vladimir Ilich Lenin. ■ **Le·nin·ist** n. & adj.

lens /lenz/ ▶ n. 1 a piece of glass or other transparent material with one or both sides curved for concentrating or dispersing light rays. 2 the light-gathering device of a camera, containing a group of compound lenses. 3 the transparent structure behind the iris in the eye, by which light is focused onto the retina.

lens·man /'lenzmən, -,man/ ▶ n. (pl. **lensmen**) a professional photographer or cameraman.

Lent /lent/ ▶ n. (in the Christian Church) the period preceding Easter, during which some people give up food or other things that they enjoy.

lent /lent/ ▶ past and past participle of LEND.

Lent·en /'lent(ə)n/ ▶ adj. relating to Lent.

len·tic·u·lar /len'tikyələr/ ▶ adj. 1 shaped like a lentil, especially by having two curved surfaces. 2 relating to the lens of the eye.

len·ti·go /len'tīgō, -'tē-/ ▶ n. (pl. **lentigines** /-'tijə,nēz/) a small brown patch on the skin, typically found in elderly people.

len·til /'lent(ə)l/ ▶ n. a pulse (edible seed) that is dried and then soaked and cooked before eating.

len·to /'lentō/ ▶ adv. & adj. Music slow or slowly.

Le·o /'lēō/ ▶ n. 1 a constellation and the fifth sign of the zodiac (the Lion), which the sun enters about July 23. 2 (**a Leo**) a person born when the sun is in this sign.

le·o·nine /'lēə,nīn/ ▶ adj. relating to or resembling a lion or lions.

leop·ard /'lepərd/ ▶ n. (fem. **leopardess**) a large solitary cat with a black-spotted fawn or brown coat, found in the forests of Africa and southern Asia.

le·o·tard /'lēə,tärd/ ▶ n. a close-fitting, stretchy one-piece garment covering the body to the top of the thighs, worn for dance, gymnastics, and exercise.

lep·er /'lepər/ ▶ n. 1 a person with leprosy. 2 a person who is rejected or avoided by others: *the story suggested she was a social leper.*

Lep·i·dop·ter·a /,lepə'däptərə/ ▶ pl.n. an order of insects comprising the butterflies and moths. ■ **lep·i·dop·ter·an** adj. & n. **lep·i·dop·ter·ist** /,lepə'däptərist/ n. **lep·i·dop·ter·ous** /-'tərəs/ adj.

lep·re·chaun /'leprə,kän, -,kôn/ ▶ n. (in Irish folklore) a small, mischievous sprite.

lep·ro·sy /'leprəsē/ ▶ n. a contagious disease that causes discoloration and lumps on the skin and, in severe cases, disfigurement and deformities.

lep·rous /'leprəs/ ▶ adj. referring to or suffering from leprosy.

lep·ton /'leptän/ ▶ n. Physics a subatomic particle of

a type that is not held in atomic nuclei, such as an electron or neutrino.

les·bi·an /'lezbēən/ ▶ n. a woman who is sexually attracted to other women. ▶ adj. referring to lesbians or homosexuality in women. ■ **les·bi·an·ism** /-,nizəm/ n.

lese-maj·es·ty /,lez 'majəstē, ,lēz/ (also **lèse-majesté** /,lez ,mäjə'stä/) ▶ n. 1 the insulting of a monarch; treason. 2 arrogant or disrespectful behavior.

le·sion /'lēzhən/ ▶ n. an area in an organ or tissue that has been damaged through injury or disease; a wound.

less /les/ ▶ determiner & pron. 1 a smaller amount of; not as much. 2 fewer in number. ▶ adv. to a smaller extent; not so much. ▶ prep. minus.
– PHRASES **less is more** used to express the view that a minimalist approach is more effective.

USAGE
On the difference in use between **less** and **fewer**, see the note at FEW.

les·see /le'sē/ ▶ n. a person who holds the lease of a property.

less·en /'lesən/ ▶ v. make or become less; diminish.

less·er /'lesər/ ▶ adj. not so great, large, or important as the other or the rest.

less·er-known ▶ adj. not as well or widely known as others of the same kind.

les·son /'lesən/ ▶ n. 1 a period of learning or teaching. 2 a thing learned by teaching or experience. 3 a thing that acts as a warning or encouragement. 4 a passage from the Bible read aloud during a church service.

les·sor /'les,ôr, le'sôr/ ▶ n. a person who leases a property to another.

lest /lest/ ▶ conj. formal 1 to p1.40 avoid the risk of. 2 because of the possibility of.

USAGE
The word **lest** takes the *subjunctive* mood of a verb, meaning that the correct use is *she was worrying lest he be attacked* (not … *lest he was attacked*). See SUBJUNCTIVE.

let[1] /let/ ▶ v. (**lets, letting, let**) 1 allow someone to do something or something to happen. 2 used to express an intention, proposal, or instruction: *let's have a drink.* 3 chiefly Brit. rent out a room or other property. 4 used to express an assumption on which a theory or calculation is to be based: *let x = 10.* ■ **let·ting** n.
– PHRASES **let alone** not to mention. **let someone down** fail to support or help someone. **let fly** attack someone. **let someone/thing go** 1 allow a person or animal to go free. 2 release one's grip on someone or something. **let oneself go** 1 act in an uninhibited way. 2 become careless in one's habits or appearance. **let someone off** 1 refrain from punishing someone. 2 excuse someone from a task or duty. **let something off** cause a gun, firework, or bomb to fire or explode. **let on** informal reveal information. **let something out** 1 make a sound or cry. 2 make a piece of clothing looser or larger. **let up** informal become less intense.

let[2] ▶ n. (in racket sports) a situation in which a point is not counted and is played for again.
– PHRASES **without let or hindrance** formal without obstruction; freely.

let·down /'let,doun/ ▶ n. a disappointment.

le·thal /ˈlēTHəl/ ▶ adj. **1** able or enough to cause death. **2** very harmful or destructive. ■ **le·thal·i·ty** /lēˈTHalətē/ n. **le·thal·ly** adv.

leth·ar·gy /ˈleTHərjē/ ▶ n. a lack of energy and enthusiasm. ■ **le·thar·gic** /ləˈTHärjik/ adj. **le·thar·gi·cal·ly** /ləˈTHäjik(ə)lē/ adv.

let's /lets/ ▶ contr. let us.

let·ter /ˈletər/ ▶ n. **1** a symbol representing one or more of the sounds used in speech; any of the symbols of an alphabet. **2** a written, typed, or printed communication, sent by mail or messenger. **3** the precise terms of a statement or requirement: *adherence to the letter of the law.* **4** (**letters**) literature. ▶ v. carve or write letters on something. ■ **let·ter·ing** n.
– PHRASES **to the letter** precisely or exactly.

let·ter bomb ▶ n. an explosive device hidden in a small package, which explodes when the package is opened.

let·ter car·ri·er ▶ n. a mail carrier.

let·ter·head /ˈletərˌhed/ ▶ n. a printed heading on stationery, stating the sender's name and address.

let·ter of cred·it ▶ n. a letter issued by one bank to another to serve as a guarantee for payments made to a specified person.

let·ter o·pen·er ▶ n. a blunt knife or other device used for opening envelopes.

let·ter·press /ˈletərˌpres/ ▶ n. printing from a hard, raised image under pressure, using viscous ink.

let·tuce /ˈletis/ ▶ n. a cultivated plant with edible leaves that are eaten in salads.

let·up ▶ n. informal a brief time when something becomes less intense, difficult, or tiring.

leu·cine /ˈlo͞oˌsēn, -sin/ ▶ n. a hydrophobic amino acid that is a constituent of most proteins and an essential nutrient in the diet of vertebrates.

leu·ke·mi·a /lo͞oˈkēmēə/ (Brit. **leukaemia**) ▶ n. a serious disease in which increased numbers of immature or abnormal white cells are produced, stopping the production of normal blood cells. ■ **leu·ke·mic** /-ˈkēmik/ adj.

leu·ko·cyte /ˈlo͞okəˌsīt/ (also Brit. **leucocyte**) ▶ n. a colorless cell that circulates in the blood and body fluids and acts against foreign substances and disease; a white blood cell.

Le·vant /ləˈvant, ləˈvänt/ ▶ n. (**the Levant**) historical the eastern part of the Mediterranean. ■ **Le·van·tine** /ˈlevənˌtīn, -ˌtēn, ləˈvantin/ n. & adj.

lev·ee[1] /ˈlevē/ ▶ n. **1** an embankment built to prevent a river from overflowing. **2** a ridge of sediment deposited naturally alongside a river. **3** a landing place; a quay.

lev·ee[2] ▶ n. old use a formal reception of visitors or guests.

lev·el /ˈlevəl/ ▶ n. **1** a position or stage on a scale of quantity, extent, rank, or quality: *a high level of unemployment.* **2** a horizontal line or surface. **3** a height or distance from the ground or another base point: *storms caused river levels to rise.* **4** a floor of a multistory building. **5** a flat area of land. **6** (also **spirit level**) a device consisting of a sealed glass tube partially filled with a liquid, containing an air bubble whose position reveals whether a surface is perfectly level or plumb. **7** an instrument giving a line

parallel to the plane of the horizon for testing whether things are horizontal. ▶ adj. **1** having a flat, horizontal surface. **2** having the same height, position, or value as someone or something else: *her face was level with his own.* **3** calm and steady. ▶ v. (**levels, leveling, leveled**) **1** make or become level or flat. **2** make or become equal or similar. **3** aim or direct a weapon, criticism, or accusation. **4** (**level with**) informal be frank or honest with someone. ■ **lev·el·ly** adv. **lev·el·ness** n.
– PHRASES **a level playing field** a situation in which everyone has an equal chance of succeeding. **on the level** informal honest; truthful.

lev·el·er /ˈlev(ə)lər/ ▶ n. **1** a person or thing that levels something. **2** a situation or activity in which distinctions of class, age, or ability do not matter: *he valued the sport because it was a great leveler.*

lev·el·head·ed /ˈlevəlˈhedid/ ▶ adj. calm and sensible. ■ **lev·el·head·ed·ly** adv. **lev·el·head·ed·ness** n.

lev·er /ˈlevər, ˈlēvər/ ▶ n. **1** a rigid bar resting on a pivot, used to move a load with one end when pressure is applied to the other. **2** an arm or handle that is moved to operate a mechanism. ▶ v. **1** lift or move something with a lever. **2** move with effort: *she levered herself up.*

lev·er·age /ˈlev(ə)rij, ˈlēv(ə)rij/ ▶ n. **1** the exertion of force by means of a lever. **2** the power to influence: *states trying to regain their former leverage.* **3** the ratio of a company's loan capital (debt) to the value of its common stock (equity).

lev·er·aged buy·out ▶ n. the purchase of a controlling share in a company by its management, using capital borrowed from outside the company.

lev·er·et /ˈlev(ə)rit/ ▶ n. a young hare in its first year.

le·vi·a·than /ləˈvīəTHən/ ▶ n. **1** a very large or powerful thing. **2** (in biblical use) a sea monster.

lev·i·tate /ˈlevəˌtāt/ ▶ v. rise or cause to rise and hover in the air. ■ **lev·i·ta·tion** /ˌlevəˈtāSHən/ n.

lev·i·ty /ˈlevətē/ ▶ n. the treatment of a serious matter with humor or lack of respect.

le·vy /ˈlevē/ ▶ v. (**levies, levying, levied**) **1** impose a tax, fee, or fine. **2** old use enlist someone for military service. ▶ n. (pl. **levies**) **1** an act of imposing a tax, fee, or fine: *a levy on energy-intensive industries.* **2** a sum of money raised by a tax, fee, or fine. **3** old use a body of enlisted troops.

lewd /lo͞od/ ▶ adj. crude and offensive in a sexual way. ■ **lewd·ly** adv. **lewd·ness** n.

lex·i·cal /ˈleksikəl/ ▶ adj. **1** relating to the words of a language. **2** relating to a lexicon or dictionary. ■ **lex·i·cal·ly** adv.

lex·i·cog·ra·phy /ˌleksəˈkägrəfē/ ▶ n. the practice of compiling dictionaries. ■ **lex·i·cog·ra·pher** n. **lex·i·co·graph·ic** /-kəˈgrafik/ adj.

lex·i·con /ˈleksiˌkän, -kən/ ▶ n. **1** the vocabulary of a person, language, or subject area. **2** a dictionary.

ley /lā/ (also **ley line**) ▶ n. a supposed straight line connecting ancient sites, believed by some people to be associated with lines of energy and other paranormal phenomena.

LF ▶ abbr. low frequency.

LI ▶ abbr. Long Island.

Li ▶ symbol the chemical element lithium.

li·a·bil·i·ty /ˌlīəˈbilətē/ ▶ n. (pl. **liabilities**) **1** the state of being legally responsible for something. **2** a thing for which someone is legally responsible, especially a debt. **3** a person or thing likely to cause embarrassment or difficulty: *the party has become a liability to green politics.*

li·a·ble /ˈlī(ə)bəl/ ▶ adj. **1** responsible by law. **2** (**liable to**) legally required to do something. **3** (**liable to do**) likely to do, be, or experience: *areas liable to flooding.*

li·aise /lēˈāz/ ▶ v. **1** cooperate on a matter of shared concern. **2** (**liaise between**) act as a link to assist communication between people.

li·ai·son /ˈlēəˌzän, lēˈā-/ ▶ n. **1** communication or cooperation between people or organizations. **2** a sexual relationship, especially a secret one.

li·ai·son of·fi·cer ▶ n. a person who is employed to form a working relationship between two organizations to their mutual benefit.

li·a·na /lēˈänə, -ˈanə/ (also **liane** /-ˈän, -ˈan/) ▶ n. a woody climbing plant that hangs from trees, especially in tropical rainforests.

li·ar /ˈlīər/ ▶ n. a person who tells lies.

lib /lib/ ▶ n. informal (in the names of political movements) the liberation of a specified group: *women's lib.* ■ **lib·ber** n.

li·ba·tion /līˈbāsHən/ ▶ n. **1** a drink poured out as an offering to a god. **2** humorous an alcoholic drink.

li·bel /ˈlībəl/ ▶ n. **1** the crime of publishing a false statement that is damaging to a person's reputation. Compare with SLANDER. **2** a published false statement that damages a person's reputation. ▶ v. (**libels, libeling, libeled**) publish a false and damaging statement about someone. ■ **li·bel·ous** adj.

lib·er·al /ˈlib(ə)rəl/ ▶ adj. **1** willing to respect and accept behavior or opinions different from one's own. **2** (of a society, law, etc.) favorable to individual rights and freedoms. **3** (in politics favoring individual liberty, free trade, and moderate reform. **4** (**Liberal**) relating to Liberals or a Liberal Party. **5** (of an interpretation) broadly understood; not strictly literal. **6** (given, used, or giving in generous amounts: *liberal amounts of wine were consumed.* **7** (of education) concerned with broadening general knowledge and experience. ▶ n. **1** a person of liberal views. **2** (**Liberal**) a supporter or member of a Liberal Party. ■ **lib·er·al·ism** /-ˌlizəm/ n. **lib·er·al·i·ty** /ˌlibəˈralətē/ n. **lib·er·al·ly** adv.

lib·er·al arts ▶ pl.n. academic subjects such as literature, philosophy, mathematics, and social and physical sciences as distinct from professional and technical subjects.

lib·er·al·ize /ˈlib(ə)rəˌlīz/ ▶ v. remove or loosen restrictions on something, typically an economic or political system. ■ **lib·er·al·i·za·tion** /ˌlib(ə)rələˈzāsHən, -ˌlīˈzā-/ n.

lib·er·ate /ˈlibəˌrāt/ ▶ v. **1** set someone free, especially from imprisonment or oppression. **2** (as adj. **liberated**) free from social conventions, especially with regard to sexual roles. ■ **lib·er·a·tion** /ˌlibəˈrāsHən/ n. **lib·er·a·tion·ist** /ˌlibəˈrāsHənist/ n. **lib·er·a·tor** /-ˌrātər/ n. **lib·er·a·tor·y** /ˈlibərəˌtôrē/ adj.

lib·er·a·tion the·ol·o·gy ▶ n. a movement in Christian belief that attempts to address the problems of poverty and social injustice.

Li·be·ri·an /līˈbi(ə)rēən/ ▶ n. a person from Liberia, a country in in West Africa. ▶ adj. relating to Liberia.

lib·er·tar·i·an /ˌlibərˈte(ə)rēən/ ▶ n. a person who believes that the government should intervene only minimally in the lives of its citizens. ■ **lib·er·tar·i·an·ism** /ˌlibərˈte(ə)rēəˌnizəm/ n.

lib·er·tine /ˈlibərˌtēn/ ▶ n. a man who behaves without moral principles, especially in sexual matters. ■ **lib·er·tin·ism** /-ˌnizəm/ n.

lib·er·ty /ˈlibərtē/ ▶ n. (pl. **liberties**) **1** the state of being free; freedom. **2** a right or privilege. **3** the power or scope to act as one pleases: *he's not at liberty to discuss his real work.* **4** informal a disrespectful remark or action.
– PHRASES **take liberties with 1** behave in an excessively familiar way toward someone. **2** treat something without strict faithfulness to the facts or to an original. **take the liberty** do something without first asking permission.

li·bid·i·nous /ləˈbidn-əs/ ▶ adj. having or showing a strong sex drive.

li·bi·do /ləˈbēdō/ ▶ n. (pl. **libidos**) sexual desire. ■ **li·bid·i·nal** /-ˈbidn-əl/ adj.

Li·bra /ˈlēbrə, ˈlī-/ ▶ n. **1** a constellation and the seventh sign of the zodiac (the Scales), which the sun enters about September 23. **2** (**a Libra**) a person born when the sun is in this sign. ■ **Li·bran** n. & adj.

li·brar·i·an /līˈbre(ə)rēən/ ▶ n. a person in charge of or assisting in a library. ■ **li·brar·i·an·ship** /-ˌsHip/ n.

li·brar·y /ˈlīˌbrerē, -brərē/ ▶ n. (pl. **libraries**) **1** a building or room containing a collection of books and periodicals for use by the public or the members of an institution. **2** a private collection of books. **3** an organized collection of movies, recorded music, etc., kept for research or borrowing. **4** (also **software library**) a collection of computer programs and software packages made generally available.

li·bret·to /ləˈbretō/ ▶ n. (pl. **libretti** /-ˈbretē/ or **librettos**) the text of an opera or other long vocal work. ■ **li·bret·tist** n.

Lib·y·an /ˈlibēən/ ▶ n. a person from Libya. ▶ adj. relating to Libya.

lice /līs/ ▶ plural of LOUSE.

li·cense /ˈlīsəns/ ▶ n. (Brit. **licence**) **1** a permit from an authority to own, use, or do something. **2** freedom to behave without restraint: *the government has given the army too much license.* **3** the freedom of writer or artist to deviate from facts or accepted rules. ▶ v. (Brit. also **licence**) **1** grant a license to someone. **2** authorize or permit something. ■ **li·cens·a·ble** adj. **li·cens·er** (also **licensor**) n.

li·cen·see /ˌlīsənˈsē/ ▶ n. the holder of a license, especially to sell alcoholic drinks.

li·cense plate ▶ n. a sign showing a unique series of letters or numbers, fixed to a vehicle to indicate that it has been registered with the government.

li·cen·sure /ˈlīsənsHər, -ˌsHŏŏr/ ▶ n. the granting or regulation of licenses, as for professionals.

li·cen·ti·ate /līˈsensH(ē)it/ ▶ n. **1** the holder of a certificate of competence to practice a particular profession. **2** (in certain colleges and universities) a degree between that of bachelor and master or doctor. ■ **li·cen·ti·ate·ship** /-ˌsHip/ n.

li·cen·tious /lī'sensʜəs/ ▶ adj. promiscuous and unprincipled in sexual matters. ■ **li·cen·tious·ly** adv. **li·cen·tious·ness** n.

li·chen /'līkən/ ▶ n. a simple plant consisting of a fungus living in close association with an alga, typically growing on rocks, walls, and trees. ■ **li·chened** adj.

lic·it /'lisit/ ▶ adj. formal not forbidden; lawful.

lick /lik/ ▶ v. **1** pass the tongue over something in order to taste, moisten, or clean it. **2** move lightly and quickly: *the flames licked around the wood.* **3** informal overcome someone decisively. ▶ n. **1** an act of licking. **2** informal a small amount or quick application of something: *a lick of paint.* **3** informal a short phrase or solo in jazz or popular music. – PHRASES **at a lick** informal at a fast pace. **a lick and a promise** informal a hasty performance of a task, especially of cleaning something. **lick someone's boots** (or vulgar slang **ass**) be excessively flattering or servile toward someone.

lick·ing /'likiNG/ ▶ n. informal a severe defeat or beating.

lic·o·rice /'lik(ə)risʜ, -ris/ ▶ n. a chewy black substance made from the juice of a root and used in making candies and medicine.

lid /lid/ ▶ n. **1** a removable or hinged cover for the top of a container. **2** an eyelid. ■ **lid·ded** adj. **lid·less** adj.

li·do /'lēdō/ (also **lido deck**) ▶ n. (pl. **lidos**) a deck on a cruise ship where swimming pools are located.

lie[1] /lī/ ▶ v. (**lies, lying** /'lī-iNG/, **lay** /lā/; past part. **lain** /lān/) **1** be in or take up a horizontal or resting position on a supporting surface. **2** be or remain in a particular state: *many buildings were lying empty.* **3** be situated in a specified position or direction. **4** be found: *the solution lies in a return to traditional values.* ▶ n. the way, direction, or position in which something lies or comes to rest. – PHRASES **let something lie** take no action on a problematic matter. **lie in state** (of the corpse of a person of national importance) be laid in a public place of honor before burial. **lie low** keep out of sight; avoid attention. **lie with** old use have sex with. **take something lying down** accept an insult or reprimand without protest.

> **USAGE**
> For the correct use of **lay** and **lie**, see the note at **LAY**[1].

lie[2] ▶ n. **1** a deliberately false statement. **2** a situation involving deception or based on a mistaken impression. ▶ v. (**lies, lying** /'lī-iNG/, **lied**) **1** tell a lie or lies. **2** present a false impression: *the camera cannot lie.* – PHRASES **give the lie to** show that something assumed to be true is not true.

Lieb·frau·milch /'lēb,frou,milCH, 'lēp-, -,milk, -,milkH/ ▶ n. a light white wine from the Rhine region.

lied /lēd, lēt/ ▶ n. (pl. **lieder** /'lēdər/) a type of German song, typically for solo voice with piano accompaniment.

lie de·tec·tor ▶ n. a device for determining whether a person is telling the truth.

lie-down ▶ n. chiefly Brit. a short rest on a bed or sofa.

lief /lēf/ ▶ adv. (**as lief**) old use as happily.

liege /lēj, lēzʜ/ ▶ n. historical **1** (also **liege lord**) a

lord or sovereign under the feudal system. **2** a person who served a lord in the feudal system.

lien /'lē(ə)n/ ▶ n. Law a right to keep the property of another person until a debt owed by that person is paid.

lieu /lōō/ ▶ n. (in phrase **in lieu**) instead: *rum was used by local merchants in lieu of cash.*

Lieut. ▶ abbr. lieutenant.

lieu·ten·ant /lōō'tenənt/ ▶ n. **1** a person who acts as a deputy or substitute for a superior. **2** a rank of officer in the Navy or Coast Guard. ■ **lieu·ten·an·cy** /-'tenənsē/ n. (pl. **lieutenancies**).

lieu·ten·ant colo·nel ▶ n. a rank of officer in the Army, Air Force, or Marine Corps above major and below colonel.

lieu·ten·ant com·man·der ▶ n. a rank of officer in the Navy or Coast Guard, above lieutenant and below commander.

lieu·ten·ant gen·er·al ▶ n. a high rank of officer in the Army, Air Force, or Marine Corps above major general and below general.

lieu·ten·ant gov·er·nor ▶ n. a deputy state governor.

life /līf/ ▶ n. (pl. **lives** /līvz/) **1** the condition that distinguishes animals and plants from inorganic matter, including the ability to grow, breathe, and reproduce. **2** the existence of an individual human being or animal. **3** a particular type or aspect of people's existence: *school life.* **4** living things and their activity. **5** the period during which something continues to exist, function, or be valid. **6** vitality or energy. **7** informal a sentence of imprisonment for life. **8** a biography. ▶ adj. (in art) based on a living rather than an imagined form: *a life drawing.* – PHRASES **as large as** (or **larger than**) **life** informal noticeably present. **not on your life** informal definitely not. **take one's life in one's hands** risk being killed.

life·belt /'līf,belt/ ▶ n. a life preserver in the shape of a belt.

life·blood /'līf,bləd/ ▶ n. a vital factor or force: *intelligence is the lifeblood of antiterrorist operations.*

life·boat /'līf,bōt/ ▶ n. **1** a type of boat launched from land to rescue people at sea. **2** a small boat kept on a ship for use in an emergency.

life·bu·oy /'līf,bōō-ē, -,boi/ ▶ n. a life preserver, especially one in the shape of a ring.

life cy·cle ▶ n. the series of changes in the life of an organism.

life ex·pec·tan·cy ▶ n. the period that a person may expect to live.

life force ▶ n. the force that gives something its vitality or strength.

life form ▶ n. any living thing.

life·guard /'līf,gärd/ ▶ n. a person employed to rescue swimmers who get into difficulty at a beach or swimming pool.

life in·sur·ance ▶ n. insurance that pays out a sum of money either on the death of the insured person or after a set period.

life jack·et ▶ n. a sleeveless inflatable jacket for keeping a person afloat in water.

life·less /'līflis/ ▶ adj. **1** dead or apparently dead. **2** not containing living things. **3** lacking vitality or excitement. ■ **life·less·ly** adv. **life·less·ness** n.

life·like /'līf,līk/ ▶ adj. very similar to the person or thing represented.

life·line /'līf,līn/ ▶ n. **1** a thing on which someone or something depends or that provides a means of escape: *visitors are a lifeline for lonely elderly people*. **2** a rope thrown to rescue someone in water or used by sailors to secure themselves to a boat. **3** (in palmistry) a line on the palm of a person's hand, regarded as indicating how long they will live.

life·long /ˈlīfˌlôNG, -ˌläNG/ ▶ adj. lasting in a particular state throughout a person's life.

life part·ner ▶ n. a romantic partner to whom one has made a lifetime commitment.

life pre·serv·er ▶ n. a device made of buoyant or inflatable material, such as a life jacket or lifebelt, to keep someone afloat in water.

lif·er /ˈlīfər/ ▶ n. informal a person serving a life sentence in prison.

life raft ▶ n. an inflatable raft for use in an emergency at sea.

life·sav·er /ˈlīfˌsāvər/ ▶ n. **1** informal a thing that saves someone from serious difficulty. **2** a ring-shaped life preserver.

life sci·enc·es ▶ pl.n. the sciences concerned with the study of living organisms, including biology, botany, and zoology.

life sen·tence ▶ n. a punishment of life imprisonment.

life-size (also **life-sized**) ▶ adj. of the same size as the person or thing represented.

life-skill ▶ n. (often plural) a skill required for everyday life.

life·span /ˈlīfˌspan/ ▶ n. the length of time for which a person or animal lives or a thing functions.

life·style /ˈlīfˌstīl/ ▶ n. the way in which someone lives.

life sup·port ▶ n. the maintenance of a patient's vital functions following an injury or serious illness.

life-threat·en·ing ▶ adj. potentially fatal.

life·time /ˈlīfˌtīm/ ▶ n. **1** the length of time that a person lives or a thing lasts. **2** informal a very long time.

life·work /ˈlīfˈwərk/ ▶ n. the entire or principal work, labor, or task of a person's lifetime.

LIFO /ˈlīfō/ ▶ abbr. last in first out (chiefly with reference to methods of stock valuation or data storage). Compare with **FIFO**.

lift /lift/ ▶ v. **1** raise or be raised to a higher position or level. **2** pick someone or something up and move them to a different position. **3** formally remove or end a legal restriction, decision, or ban. **4** (**lift off**) (of an aircraft, spacecraft, or rocket) take off, especially vertically. **5** informal steal something. ▶ n. **1** an act of lifting. **2** a free ride in another person's vehicle. **3** a device for carrying people up or down a mountain. **4** a feeling of increased cheerfulness: *winning the match has given everyone a lift*. **5** upward force exerted by the air on an airfoil. **6** Brit. an elevator. ■ **lift·a·ble** adj. **lift·er** n.
– PHRASES **not lift a finger** refuse to make the slightest effort.

lift·off /ˈliftˌôf, -ˌäf/ ▶ n. the vertical takeoff of a spacecraft, rocket, or aircraft.

lig·a·ment /ˈligəmənt/ ▶ n. **1** a short band of tough, flexible fibrous tissue that connects two bones or cartilages or holds together a joint. **2** a fold of membrane that supports a body organ and keeps it in position. ■ **lig·a·men·tous** /ˌligəˈmentəs/ adj.

li·ga·ture /ˈligəCHər, -ˌCHo͝or/ ▶ n. **1** a thing used for tying something tightly, especially a cord used in surgery to tie up a bleeding artery. **2** Music a slur or tie. **3** Printing a character consisting of two or more joined letters, e.g., æ. ▶ v. bind or connect something with a ligature.

light¹ /līt/ ▶ n. **1** the natural form of energy that makes things visible; electromagnetic radiation from about 390 to 740 nm in wavelength. **2** a source of illumination such as a lamp. **3** (**lights**) traffic lights. **4** a device producing a flame or spark. **5** an expression in someone's eyes. **6** understanding: *light dawned in her eyes*. **7** an area that is brighter or paler than its surroundings. **8** a window or section of a window. ▶ v. (past **lit**; past part. **lit** or **lighted**) **1** provide something with light. **2** ignite or be ignited. ▶ adj. **1** having a considerable amount of natural light. **2** (of a color) pale. ■ **light·less** adj. **light·ness** n.
– PHRASES **bring** (or **come**) **to light** make (or become) widely known or evident. **in a —— light** in the way specified. **in** (**the**) **light of** taking something into consideration. **light at the end of the tunnel** an indication that a period of difficulty is ending. **the light of day** general public attention. **light up 1** become illuminated. **2** become lively or happy. **light something up** ignite a cigarette, pipe, or cigar before smoking it. **see the light** understand or realize something. **throw** (or **cast** or **shed**) **light on** help to explain something by providing further information.

light² ▶ adj. **1** not heavy or heavy enough. **2** not strongly or heavily built or made. **3** relatively low in density, amount, or intensity: *traffic was light*. **4** carrying or suitable for small loads. **5** gentle or delicate. **6** not serious or challenging: *light entertainment*. **7** (of sleep or a sleeper) easily disturbed. **8** easily done. **9** cheerful or carefree. ■ **light·ish** adj. **light·ly** adv. **light·ness** n.
– PHRASES **make light of** treat something as unimportant. **make light work of** accomplish something quickly and easily.

light³ ▶ v. (past and past part. **lit** /lit/ or **lighted**) (**light on**) come upon or discover someone or something by chance.

light bulb ▶ n. a glass bulb containing inert gas, inserted into a lamp or ceiling socket, that provides light when an electric current is passed through it.

light cream ▶ n. thin cream with a relatively low fat content.

light·en /ˈlītn/ ▶ v. **1** make or become lighter in weight. **2** make or become less serious.

light·en² ▶ v. make or become brighter.

light·er¹ /ˈlītər/ ▶ n. a device producing a small flame, used to light cigarettes.

light·er² ▶ n. a flat-bottomed barge used to transfer goods to and from ships in harbor.

light-fin·gered ▶ adj. informal prone to steal.

light-foot·ed ▶ adj. fast and nimble on one's feet.

light·head·ed /ˈlītˈhedid/ ▶ adj. dizzy and slightly faint.

light·heart·ed /ˈlītˈhärtid/ ▶ adj. **1** amusing and entertaining. **2** cheerful or carefree. ■ **light·heart·ed·ly** adv.

light·house /ˈlītˌhous/ ▶ n. a tower or other structure containing a light to warn ships at sea.

light in·dus·try ▶ n. the manufacture of small or light articles.

light·ing /'lītiNG/ ▶ n. **1** equipment for producing light. **2** the arrangement or effect of lights.

light me·ter ▶ n. an instrument measuring the intensity of light, used when taking photographs.

light·ning /'lītniNG/ ▶ n. a high-voltage electrical discharge between a cloud and the ground or within a cloud, accompanied by a bright flash. ▶ adj. very quick: *lightning speed.*

> **USAGE**
> Do not confuse **lightning** with **lightening**.
> **Lightning** means 'a high-voltage electrical discharge and bright flash in the sky' (*thunder and lightning*) or 'very quick,' whereas **lightening** is part of the verb **lighten** and means 'getting lighter' (*the sea was lightening from black to gray*).

light·ning bug ▶ n. another term for **FIREFLY**.

light·ning rod ▶ n. a metal rod or wire fixed in a high and exposed place to divert lightning into the ground.

light pen ▶ n. **1** a hand-held penlike photosensitive device used for passing information to a computer. **2** a hand-held device for reading bar codes.

light pol·lu·tion ▶ n. excessive brightening of the night sky by street lights and other artificial sources.

light·ship /'lītˌSHip/ ▶ n. an anchored boat with a light to warn ships at sea.

light·weight /'lītˌwāt/ ▶ n. **1** a weight in boxing and other sports between featherweight and welterweight. **2** informal a person of little importance. ▶ adj. **1** of thin material or build. **2** lacking seriousness or importance: *lightweight magazine essays.*

light year ▶ n. Astronomy a unit of distance equivalent to the distance that light travels in one year, 9.4607 × 10¹² km (nearly 6 trillion miles).

lig·ne·ous /'lignēəs/ ▶ adj. consisting of or resembling wood.

lig·nin /'lignin/ ▶ n. a complex organic substance found in the cell walls of many plants, making them rigid and woody.

lig·nite /'ligˌnīt/ ▶ n. a type of soft brownish coal.

lik·a·ble /'līkəbəl/ (also **likeable**) ▶ adj. pleasant; easy to like. ■ **lik·a·bly** /-blē/ adv.

like¹ /līk/ ▶ prep. **1** similar to. **2** in the same way as. **3** in a way appropriate to. **4** in this way. **5** such as. **6** used to ask about the nature of someone or something. ▶ conj. informal **1** in the same way that. **2** as if. ▶ n. **1** a similar person or thing. **2** (**the like**) things of the same kind. ▶ adj. having similar characteristics.
– PHRASES **like so** informal in this way.

> **USAGE**
> When writing formal English, do not use **like** to mean 'as if', as in *he's behaving like he owns the place*; use **as if** or **as though** instead.

like² ▶ v. **1** find someone or something pleasant or satisfactory. **2** wish for or want something. ▶ n. (**likes**) the things one likes.

like·li·hood /'līklēˌho͝od/ ▶ n. the state or fact of being likely or probable.

like·ly /'līklē/ ▶ adj. (**likelier, likeliest**) **1** such as well might be the case; probable. **2** apparently suitable; promising. ▶ adv. probably.
– PHRASES **a likely story!** used to express disbelief. **not likely!** informal certainly not.

like-mind·ed ▶ adj. having similar tastes or opinions.

lik·en /'līkən/ ▶ v. (**liken someone/thing to**) point out that someone or something is similar to; compare: *he likened the election to a job interview.*

like·ness /'līknis/ ▶ n. **1** the fact of being alike; resemblance. **2** outward appearance: *humans are made in God's likeness.* **3** a portrait or other representation of a person.

like·wise /'līkˌwīz/ ▶ adv. **1** also; moreover. **2** in a similar way.

lik·ing /'līkiNG/ ▶ n. **1** a regard or fondness for someone or something. **2** a person's taste: *the coffee was just to his liking.*

li·lac /'līˌläk, -ˌlak, -lək/ ▶ n. **1** a shrub or small tree with fragrant violet, pink, or white blossoms. **2** a pale pinkish-violet color.

Lil·li·pu·tian /ˌlilə'pyo͞oSHən/ ▶ adj. very small or unimportant. ▶ n. a very small or unimportant person or thing.

lilt /lilt/ ▶ n. **1** a characteristic rising and falling of the voice when speaking. **2** a gentle rhythm in a tune. ▶ v. speak, sing, or sound with a lilt.

lil·y /'lilē/ ▶ n. (pl. **lilies**) a plant with large trumpet-shaped flowers on a tall, slender stem.

lil·y-liv·ered ▶ adj. weak and cowardly.

lil·y of the val·ley ▶ n. a plant of the lily family, with broad leaves and small white bell-shaped flowers.

lil·y pad ▶ n. a leaf of a water lily.

lil·y-white ▶ adj. **1** pure white. **2** totally innocent or pure.

li·ma bean /'līmə/ ▶ n. an edible flat whitish bean.

limb¹ /lim/ ▶ n. **1** an arm, leg, or wing. **2** a large branch of a tree. **3** a projecting part of a structure, object, or natural feature. ■ **limb·less** adj.
– PHRASES **out on a limb** in a position where one is not supported by anyone else.

limb² ▶ n. Astronomy a specified edge of the disk of the sun, moon, or other celestial object.

lim·ber¹ /'limbər/ ▶ v. (**limber up**) warm up in preparation for exercise or activity. ▶ adj. supple; flexible.

lim·ber² ▶ n. the detachable front part of a gun carriage.

lim·bic sys·tem /'limbik/ ▶ n. a complex system of nerves and networks in the brain, controlling the basic emotions and drives such as fear and hunger.

lim·bo¹ /'limbō/ ▶ n. **1** (in some Christian beliefs) the place between heaven and hell where the souls of people who have not been baptized go when they die. **2** (pl. **limbos**) an uncertain period of waiting for a decision.

lim·bo² ▶ n. (pl. **limbos**) a West Indian dance in which the dancer bends backward to pass under a horizontal bar that is progressively lowered toward the ground. ▶ v. (**limbos, limboing, limboed**) dance the limbo.

lime¹ /līm/ ▶ n. **1** a product obtained from burning chalk or limestone, used in agriculture to improve certain soils or in traditional building to make mortar and plaster. **2** any salt or alkali containing calcium. ▶ v. treat soil or water with lime. ■ **lim·y** adj.

lime² ▶ n. **1** a rounded green citrus fruit similar to a lemon. **2** a bright light green color. **3** a drink made from lime juice.

lime³ (also **lime tree**) ▶ n. a deciduous tree with

heart-shaped leaves and yellowish blossoms.

lime·ade /ˌlīmˈād, ˈlīmˌād/ ▶ n. a drink made from lime juice sweetened with sugar.

lime·kiln /ˈlīmˌkil(n)/ ▶ n. a kiln for burning limestone to produce quicklime.

lime·light /ˈlīmˌlīt/ ▶ n. **1 (the limelight)** the focus of public attention. **2** an intense white light produced by heating lime, formerly used in theaters.

lim·er·ick /ˈlim(ə)rik/ ▶ n. a humorous five-line poem with a rhyme scheme *aabba*.

lime·stone /ˈlīmˌstōn/ ▶ n. a hard sedimentary rock composed mainly of calcium carbonate.

Lim·ey /ˈlīmē/ ▶ n. (pl. **Limeys**) informal, often derogatory a British person.

lim·i·nal /ˈlimənl/ ▶ adj. technical **1** relating to a transitional or initial stage. **2** at or on a boundary or threshold. ■ **lim·i·nal·i·ty** /ˌliməˈnalətē/ n.

lim·it /ˈlimit/ ▶ n. **1** a point beyond which something does not or may not pass. **2** a restriction on the size or amount of something that is allowed or possible: *an age limit.* **3** the furthest extent of one's endurance. ▶ v. (**limits, limiting, limited**) set a limit on; restrict: *try to limit the amount you drink.* ■ **lim·it·er** n.
– PHRASES **be the limit** informal be very annoying. **off limits** out of bounds. **within limits** up to a point.

lim·i·ta·tion /ˌliməˈtāSHən/ ▶ n. **1** a rule or condition that limits someone or something; a restriction. **2** a fault or failing. **3** the act of limiting something.

lim·it·ed /ˈlimitid/ ▶ adj. **1** restricted in size, amount, extent, or ability. **2** (of a monarchy or government) operating under limitations of power set down in a constitution.

lim·it·ed li·a·bil·i·ty ▶ n. the condition of being legally responsible for the debts of a company only to the extent of the value of one's shares when they were issued.

lim·it·less /ˈlimitlis/ ▶ adj. without a limit; very large or extensive: *limitless possibilities.* ■ **lim·it·less·ly** adv. **lim·it·less·ness** n.

limn /lim/ ▶ v. literary depict or describe someone or something in painting or words. ■ **lim·ner** /ˈlim(n)ər/ n.

lim·o /ˈlimō/ ▶ n. (pl. **limos**) informal a limousine.

lim·ou·sine /ˈliməˌzēn, ˌliməˈzēn/ ▶ n. a large, luxurious car.

limp¹ /limp/ ▶ v. **1** walk with difficulty because of an injured leg or foot. **2** (of a damaged ship or aircraft) move with difficulty. ▶ n. a walk hampered by an injury.

limp² ▶ adj. **1** not stiff or firm. **2** lacking energy or vigor. ■ **limp·ly** adv. **limp·ness** n.

lim·pet /ˈlimpit/ ▶ n. a marine shellfish with a conical shell and a muscular foot for clinging tightly to rocks.

lim·pet mine ▶ n. a mine that attaches magnetically to a ship's hull and explodes after a certain time.

lim·pid /ˈlimpid/ ▶ adj. **1** (of a liquid or the eyes) clear. **2** (especially of writing or music) clear or melodious. ■ **lim·pid·i·ty** /limˈpidətē/ n. **lim·pid·ly** adv.

limp-wrist·ed ▶ adj. informal weak, feeble, or effeminate.

linch·pin /ˈlinCHˌpin/ (also **lynchpin**) ▶ n. **1** a vital or essential person or thing. **2** a pin through the end of an axle to keep a wheel in position.

lin·dane /ˈlinˌdān/ ▶ n. a synthetic insecticide, now restricted in use due to its persistence in the environment.

lin·den /ˈlindən/ ▶ n. a basswood or lime tree.

line¹ /līn/ ▶ n. **1** a long, narrow mark or band. **2** a row or series of people or things. **3** a row of written or printed words. **4** a direction, course, or channel. **5** a telephone connection. **6** a railroad track or route. **7** a limit or boundary: *the issue cut across class lines.* **8** a range of products. **9** an area of activity: *the stresses unique to their line of work.* **10** a wrinkle in the skin. **11** a shape or outline. **12** a length of cord, wire, etc. **13** a connected series of military defenses facing an enemy force. **14** (also **line of battle**) an arrangement of troops for action in battle. **15** informal a remark intended to achieve a purpose: *he saved his best lines for single women.* **16** (**lines**) the words of an actor's part. ▶ v. **1** stand or be positioned at intervals along a route. **2** (**line someone/thing up**) arrange people or things in a row. **3** (**line someone/thing up**) have someone or something prepared. **4** (as adj. **lined**) marked or covered with lines.
– PHRASES **come** (or **bring**) **into line** conform (or cause to conform) with something. **in line** under control. **in line for** likely to receive something. **in** (or **out of**) **line with** in (or not in) alignment or accordance with something. **lay it on the line** speak frankly. **line of fire** the expected path of gunfire or a missile. **on the line** at serious risk. **out of line** informal behaving inappropriately or badly.

line² ▶ v. cover the inner surface of something with a layer of different material.
– PHRASES **line one's pocket** make money, especially by dishonest means.

lin·e·age /ˈlinē-ij/ ▶ n. a person's ancestry or pedigree.

lin·e·al /ˈlinēəl/ ▶ adj. **1** in a direct line of descent or ancestry. **2** consisting of lines; linear. ■ **lin·e·al·ly** adv.

lin·e·a·ment /ˈlin(ē)əmənt/ ▶ n. (usu. **lineaments**) literary a distinctive feature of the face.

lin·e·ar /ˈlinēər/ ▶ adj. **1** arranged in or extending along a straight line. **2** consisting of lines. **3** progressing in a series of stages: *a linear narrative.* **4** involving one dimension only. **5** Mathematics able to be represented by a straight line on a graph. ■ **lin·e·ar·i·ty** /ˌlinēˈaritē/ n. **lin·e·ar·ly** adv.

lin·e·ar e·qua·tion ▶ n. an equation between two variables that gives a straight line when plotted on a graph.

lin·e·a·tion /ˌlinēˈāSHən/ ▶ n. **1** a line or linear marking. **2** the action of drawing lines or marking with lines.

line·back·er /ˈlīnˌbakər/ ▶ n. Football a defensive player normally positioned behind the line of scrimmage, but in front of the safeties.

line danc·ing ▶ n. a type of country and western dancing in which a line of dancers follow a choreographed pattern of steps. ■ **line dance** n. **line danc·er** n.

line draw·ing ▶ n. a drawing based on the use of line rather than shading.

line drive ▶ n. Baseball a powerfully hit ball that travels in the air and relatively close to and parallel with the ground.

line·man /ˈlīnmən/ ▶ n. (pl. **linemen**) **1** a person employed to lay and maintain railroad tracks. **2** a person employed to repair and maintain telephone or power lines. **3** Football a player normally positioned on the line of scrimmage.

line man·ag·er ▸ n. chiefly Brit. a manager to whom an employee is directly responsible. ■ **line man·age·ment** n.

lin·en /'linin/ ▸ n. **1** cloth woven from flax. **2** articles such as sheets or clothes that were traditionally made of linen.

line-out ▸ n. an electrical connection that carries output from a video or audio device.

lin·er[1] /'līnər/ ▸ n. **1** a large passenger ship. **2** a cosmetic for outlining or accentuating the eyes or lips.

lin·er[2] ▸ n. a lining of a garment, container, etc.

lin·er note ▸ n. (usu. **liner notes**) the printed text supplied with a compact disc or on the sleeve of a phonograph record.

lines·man /'līnzmən/ ▸ n. (pl. **linesmen**) (in sports) an official who assists the referee or umpire in deciding whether the ball is out of play.

line·up /'līn,əp/ ▸ n. **1** a group of people or things assembled for a purpose. **2** the schedule of television programs for a particular period. **3** a group of people assembled so that an eyewitness may identify a suspect for a crime from among them.

lin·gam /'liNGgəm/ ▸ n. Hinduism a phallus or phallic object as a symbol of Shiva, the god of reproduction.

lin·ger /'liNGgər/ ▸ v. **1** be slow or reluctant to leave. **2** (**linger over**) spend a long time over something. **3** be slow to fade, disappear, or die: *the tradition seems to linger on.* ■ **lin·ger·er** n.

lin·ge·rie /ˌlänzHə'rā, -jə-/ ▸ n. women's underwear and nightclothes.

lin·go /'liNGgō/ ▸ n. (pl. **lingos** or **lingoes**) informal **1** a foreign language. **2** the jargon of a particular subject or group.

lin·gua fran·ca /'liNGgwə 'fraNGkə/ ▸ n. (pl. **lingua francas**) a language used as a common language between speakers whose native languages are different.

lin·gual /'liNGgwəl/ ▸ adj. technical **1** relating to the tongue. **2** relating to speech or language. ■ **lin·gual·ly** adv.

lin·gui·ne /liNG'gwēnē/ ▸ pl.n. small ribbons of pasta.

lin·guist /'liNGgwist/ ▸ n. **1** a person skilled in foreign languages. **2** a person who studies linguistics.

lin·guis·tic /liNG'gwistik/ ▸ adj. relating to language or linguistics. ■ **lin·guis·ti·cal·ly** /tik(ə)lē/ adv.

lin·guis·tics /liNG'gwistiks/ ▸ pl.n. (treated as sing.) the scientific study of language and its structure.

lin·i·ment /'linəmənt/ ▸ n. an ointment rubbed on the body to relieve pain or bruising.

lin·ing /'līniNG/ ▸ n. a layer of different material covering or attached to the inside of something.

link /liNGk/ ▸ n. **1** a relationship or connection between people or things. **2** something that enables people to communicate with each other. **3** a means of contact or transport between two places. **4** a code or instruction connecting one part of a computer program, website, etc., to another. **5** a loop in a chain. ▸ v. make, form,

or suggest a link with or between: *a network of routes linking towns and villages.* ■ **link·er** n.

link·age /'liNGkij/ ▸ n. **1** the action of linking people or things. **2** a system of links.

links /liNGks/ (also **golf links**) ▸ pl.n. (treated as sing. or pl.) a golf course.

link-up /'liNGk,əp/ ▸ n. **1** an instance of people or things linking. **2** a connection enabling people or machines to communicate with each other.

Lin·nae·an /li'nēən, -'nāən/ (also **Linnean**) ▸ adj. relating to the Swedish botanist Linnaeus (Latinized name of Carl von Linné) or his classification of animals and plants.

lin·net /'linit/ ▸ n. a mainly brown and gray finch with a reddish breast and forehead.

li·no·cut /'līnō,kət/ ▸ n. a design carved in relief on a block of linoleum, used for printing.

lin·o·le·ic ac·id /ˌlinə'lēik, -'lā-, lə'nōlēik/ ▸ n. a polyunsaturated fatty acid present in linseed oil and other oils and essential in the diet.

li·no·le·um /lə'nōlēəm/ ▸ n. a floor covering consisting of a canvas backing thickly coated with a preparation of linseed oil and powdered cork.

lin·seed /'lin,sēd/ ▸ n. the seeds of the flax plant.

lin·seed oil ▸ n. oil extracted from linseed, used especially in paint and varnish.

lint /lint/ ▸ n. **1** short, fine fibers that separate from cloth or yarn during processing. **2** a fabric with a raised nap on one side, used for dressing wounds. ■ **lint·y** adj.

lin·tel /'lintl/ ▸ n. a horizontal support across the top of a door or window. ■ **lin·teled** adj.

Lin·ux /'linəks/ ▸ n. trademark an open-source version of the UNIX computer operating system.

li·on /'līən/ ▸ n. (fem. **lioness**) **1** a large tawny cat of Africa and NW India, the male of which has a shaggy mane. **2** a brave, strong, or fierce person. **3** (also **literary lion**) a famous author. – PHRASES **the lion's share** the largest part of something.

li·on·heart·ed /'līən,härtid/ ▸ adj. brave and determined.

li·on·ize /'līə,nīz/ ▸ v. treat someone as a celebrity. ■ **li·on·i·za·tion** /ˌlīənə'zāsHən/ n.

lip /lip/ ▸ n. **1** either of the two fleshy parts forming the edges of the mouth opening. **2** the edge of a hollow container or an opening. **3** informal disrespectful talk. ■ **lip·less** adj. **lipped** adj. – PHRASES **bite one's lip** stop oneself from saying something or laughing. **pass one's lips** be eaten, drunk, or spoken. **pay lip service** to express superficial respect or support for something.

li·pase /'lip,ās, 'lī,pās/ ▸ n. an enzyme produced by the pancreas that promotes the breakdown of fats.

lip balm ▸ n. a preparation to prevent or relieve sore or chapped lips.

lip·gloss /'lip,gläs, -,glôs/ (also **lip gloss**) ▸ n. a glossy cosmetic applied to the lips.

lip·id /'lipid/ ▸ n. any of a class of fats that are insoluble in water and include many natural oils, waxes, and steroids.

lip·o·pro·tein /ˌlipə'prō,tēn, ˌlī-/ ▸ n. a soluble protein that transports lipids (a type of fat) in the blood.

lip·o·some /'lipə,sōm, 'lī-/ ▸ n. a tiny artificial container of insoluble fat enclosing a water droplet, used to carry drugs into body tissues.

lip·o·suc·tion /'lipō,səksHən, 'lī-/ ▶ n. a technique in cosmetic surgery for removing excess fat from under the skin by suction.

lip·py /'lipē/ informal ▶ adj. (**lippier, lippiest**) disrespectful; impertinent.

lip-read /,rēd/ ▶ v. understand speech from watching a speaker's lip movements. ■ **lip-read·er** n.

lip·stick /'lip,stik/ ▶ n. colored cosmetic applied to the lips from a small solid stick.

lip-sync /,siNGk/ (also **lip-synch**) ▶ v. (of an actor or singer) move the lips silently in time to prerecorded music or speech.

liq·ue·fy /'likwə,fī/ ▶ v. (**liquefies, liquefying, liquefied**) make or become liquid. ■ **liq·ue·fac·tion** /,likwə'faksHən/ n.

li·queur /li'kər, -'k(y)ŏŏr/ ▶ n. a strong, sweet flavored alcoholic liquor.

liq·uid /'likwid/ ▶ n. a substance that flows freely but remains at constant volume, such as water or oil. ▶ adj. **1** relating to or in the form of a liquid. **2** clear, like water: *liquid dark eyes.* **3** (of a sound) pure and flowing. **4** (of assets) held in or easily converted into cash. ■ **liq·uid·ly** adv. **liq·uid·ness** n.

liq·ui·date /'likwə,dāt/ ▶ v. **1** close a business and sell what it owns in order to pay its debts. **2** sell something in order to get money. **3** pay off a debt. **4** informal kill someone. ■ **liq·ui·da·tion** /,likwə'dāsHən/ n. **liq·ui·da·tor** n.

liq·uid crys·tal dis·play ▶ n. an electronic visual display in which the application of an electric current to a liquid crystal layer makes it opaque.

liq·uid·i·ty /li'kwidətē/ ▶ n. the availability of liquid assets to a market or company.

liq·ui·fy /'likwə,fī/ ▶ v. variant spelling of **LIQUEFY**.

liq·uor /'likər/ ▶ n. **1** alcoholic drink, especially distilled spirits. **2** liquid that has been produced in or used for cooking.

li·ra /'li(ə)rə/ ▶ n. **1** (pl. **lire** /'li(ə)rā, -rə/) (until the introduction of the euro in 2002) the basic monetary unit of Italy. **2** (pl. **lira**) the basic unit of money of Turkey.

-lish ▶ suffix forming nouns referring to a blend of a language with English, as used by native speakers of the first language: *Spanglish.*

lisle /līl/ ▶ n. a fine, smooth cotton thread formerly used for stockings.

lisp /lisp/ ▶ n. a speech defect in which *s* is pronounced like *th* in *thick* and *z* is pronounced like *th* in *this.* ▶ v. speak with a lisp. ■ **lisp·er** n.

lis·some /'lisəm/ (also **lissom**) ▶ adj. slim, supple, and graceful. ■ **lis·some·ness** n.

list¹ /list/ ▶ n. **1** a number of connected items or names written one below or one after the other. **2** a selvage of a piece of fabric. **3** (**lists**) historical a fence of stakes enclosing an area for a tournament. ▶ v. **1** make a list of people or things. **2** include someone or something in a list. – PHRASES **enter the lists** issue or accept a challenge.

list² ▶ v. (of a ship) lean over to one side. ▶ n. an instance of leaning to one side.

lis·ten /'lisən/ ▶ v. **1** give one's attention to a sound. **2** (**listen for** or **listen out for**) make an effort to hear something. **3** (**listen in**) listen to a private conversation. **4** respond to advice or a request: *politicians should listen to popular*

opinion. ▶ n. an act of listening. ■ **lis·ten·er** n.

lis·ten·a·ble /'lisənəbəl/ ▶ adj. easy or pleasant to listen to. ■ **lis·ten·a·bil·i·ty** /,lis(ə)nə'bilitē/ n.

lis·ten·ing post ▶ n. a station for intercepting electronic communications.

lis·te·ri·a /li'stirēə/ ▶ n. a type of bacterium that infects humans and other animals through contaminated food.

lis·te·ri·o·sis /li,sti(ə)rē'ōsis/ ▶ n. disease caused by infection with listeria, which can resemble influenza or meningitis and may cause miscarriage.

list·ing /'listiNG/ ▶ n. **1** a list or catalog. **2** an entry in a list.

list·less /'lis(t)lis/ ▶ adj. lacking energy or enthusiasm. ■ **list·less·ly** adv. **list·less·ness** n.

list price ▶ n. the price of an article as listed by the manufacturer.

lit¹ /lit/ ▶ past and past participle of **LIGHT¹, LIGHT³**.

lit² ▶ n. short for **LITERATURE**: *chick lit.*

lit·a·ny /'litn-ē/ ▶ n. (pl. **litanies**) **1** a series of prayers in church services, usually recited by the clergy and responded to by the people. **2** a long and boring list of complaints, reasons, etc.

li·tchi /'lēcHē/ ▶ n. variant spelling of **LYCHEE**.

lite /līt/ ▶ adj. **1** relating to low-fat or low-sugar versions of food or drink products. **2** (often in combination) informal referring to a simplified or less challenging version of something: *schmaltzy reggae-lite.*

li·ter /'lētər/ (Brit. **litre**) ▶ n. a metric unit of capacity equal to 1,000 cubic centimeters (about 2.1 pints).

lit·er·a·cy /'lit(ə)rəsē/ ▶ n. **1** the ability to read and write. **2** ability or knowledge in a particular area: *computer literacy.*

lit·er·al /'lit(ə)rəl/ ▶ adj. **1** using or interpreting words in their usual or most basic sense. **2** (of a translation) representing the exact words of the original text. **3** informal absolute (used for emphasis): *fifteen years of literal hell.* ■ **lit·er·al·ness** n.

lit·er·al·ism /'lit(ə)rə,lizəm/ ▶ n. the interpretation of words in their usual or most basic sense. ■ **lit·er·al·ist** n. **lit·er·al·is·tic** /,lit(ə)rə'listik/ adj.

lit·er·al·ly /'lit(ə)rəlē/ ▶ adv. **1** in a literal way or sense. **2** informal used for emphasis rather than being actually true: *we were literally killing ourselves laughing.*

lit·er·ar·y /'litə,rerē/ ▶ adj. **1** concerning the writing, study, or content of literature. **2** (of language) typical of or suitable for works of literature or formal writing. ■ **lit·er·ar·i·ness** n.

lit·er·ar·y crit·i·cism ▶ n. the art or practice of judging the qualities and character of works of literature.

lit·er·ate /'litərit/ ▶ adj. **1** able to read and write. **2** knowledgeable in a particular field: *computer literate.*

lit·e·ra·ti /,litə'rätē/ ▶ pl.n. educated people who are interested in literature.

lit·er·a·ture /'lit(ə)rəcHər, -,cHŏŏr, -,t(y)ŏŏr/ ▶ n. **1** written works such as novels, plays, and poems that are regarded as having artistic merit. **2** books and writings on a particular subject. **3** leaflets and other material giving information or advice.

lithe /līTH/ ▶ adj. slim, supple, and graceful. ■ **lithe·ly** adv. **lithe·ness** n.

lith·i·um /ˈliTHēəm/ ▶ n. **1** a light, soft, silver-white metallic chemical element. **2** a lithium salt used as a drug in the treatment of manic-depressive illness or depression.

lith·o /ˈliTHō/ informal ▶ n. (pl. **lithos**) short for LITHOGRAPHY or LITHOGRAPH. ▶ adj. short for LITHOGRAPHIC. ▶ v. (**lithoes, lithoing, lithoed**) short for LITHOGRAPH.

lith·o·graph /ˈliTHəˌgraf/ ▶ n. a print made by lithography. ▶ v. print text or pictures by lithography. ■ **lith·o·graph·ic** /ˌliTHəˈgrafik/ adj.

li·thog·ra·phy /liˈTHägrəfē/ ▶ n. the process of printing from a flat metal (formerly stone) surface treated so as to repel the ink except where it is required for printing. ■ **li·thog·ra·pher** n.

li·thol·o·gy /liˈTHäləjē/ ▶ n. the study of the physical characteristics of rocks. ■ **lith·o·log·i·cal** /ˌliTHəˈläjikəl/ adj.

lith·o·sphere /ˈliTHəˌsfi(ə)r/ ▶ n. the rigid outer part of the earth, consisting of the crust and upper mantle. ■ **lith·o·spher·ic** /ˌliTHəˈsferik, -ˈsfi(ə)r-/ adj.

Lith·u·a·ni·an /ˌliTHəˈwānēən/ ▶ n. **1** a person from Lithuania. **2** the language of Lithuania. ▶ adj. relating to Lithuania.

lit·i·gant /ˈlitəgənt/ ▶ n. a person involved in a dispute or claim being heard in a court of law.

lit·i·gate /ˈlitəˌgāt/ ▶ v. take a dispute or claim to a court of law. ■ **lit·i·ga·tion** /ˌlitəˈgāSHən/ n. **lit·i·ga·tor** n.

li·ti·gious /ləˈtijəs/ ▶ adj. having a tendency to take legal action to settle disputes. ■ **li·ti·gious·ness** n.

lit·mus /ˈlitməs/ ▶ n. a dye obtained from certain lichens that is red under acid conditions and blue under alkaline conditions.

lit·mus pa·per ▶ n. paper stained with litmus, used as a test for acids or alkalis.

lit·mus test ▶ n. a reliable test of the truth or value of something.

li·to·tes /ˈlītəˌtēz, ˈlit-, līˈtōtēz/ ▶ n. ironical understatement in which something is expressed by the negative of its opposite (e.g., *I'm not unhappy about that* for *I'm happy about that*).

li·tre ▶ n. British spelling of LITER.

LittD ▶ abbr. Doctor of Letters.

lit·ter /ˈlitər/ ▶ n. **1** small items of trash left lying in a public place. **2** an untidy collection of things. **3** a number of young born to an animal at one time. **4** (also **cat litter**) absorbent material lining a tray where a cat can urinate and defecate indoors. **5** straw or other plant matter used as animal bedding. **6** (also **leaf litter**) decomposing leaves and other matter forming a layer on top of soil. **7** historical a vehicle containing a bed or seat enclosed by curtains and carried by men or animals. **8** a stretcher for carrying a sick or wounded person. ▶ v. make a place or area untidy with scattered articles: *clothes and newspapers littered the floor.*

lit·ter·bug /ˈlitərˌbəg/ ▶ n. informal a person who carelessly drops litter in public places.

lit·tle /ˈlitl/ ▶ adj. **1** small in size, amount, or degree. **2** (of a person) young or younger: *my little brother.* **3** short in time or distance. **4** relatively unimportant. ▶ determiner & pron. **1** (**a little**) a small amount of something. **2** (**a little**) a short time or distance. **3** not much. ▶ adv. (**less, least**) **1** (**a little**) to a small extent. **2** hardly or not at all. ■ **lit·tle·ness** n. – PHRASES **little by little** gradually.

lit·tle fin·ger ▶ n. the smallest finger, at the outer side of the hand. – PHRASES **twist** (or **wind** or **wrap**) **someone around one's little finger** be able to make someone do whatever one wants.

Lit·tle League ▶ n. youth baseball or softball for children up to age 12. ■ **Lit·tle Lea·guer** n.

lit·tle peo·ple ▶ pl.n. **1** people of very small stature. **2** the ordinary people of a country or organization. **3** fairies or leprechauns.

lit·to·ral /ˈlitərəl/ ▶ adj. relating to the shore of the sea or a lake. ▶ n. a region lying along a shore.

li·tur·gi·cal /liˈtərjikəl/ ▶ adj. relating to liturgy or public worship. ■ **li·tur·gi·cal·ly** adv. **lit·ur·gist** /ˈlitərjist/ n.

lit·ur·gy /ˈlitərjē/ ▶ n. (pl. **liturgies**) a set form of public worship used in the Christian Church.

liv·a·ble /ˈlivəbəl/ ▶ adj. **1** worth living. **2** fit to live in. **3** (**livable with**) informal easy to live with. ■ **liv·a·bil·i·ty** /ˌlivəˈbilətē/ n.

live[1] /liv/ ▶ v. **1** remain alive. **2** be alive at a particular time. **3** spend one's life in a particular way or under particular circumstances: *they are living in fear.* **4** make one's home in a particular place or with a particular person. **5** (**live in/out**) have one's home at (or away from) the place where one works or studies. **6** supply oneself with the means of staying alive: *they live by hunting and fishing.* **7** (**live for**) regard something as the most important aspect of one's life: *he lived for his painting.* **8** survive in someone's mind: *her name lived on.* – PHRASES **live something down** succeed in making other people forget something embarrassing or regrettable. **live it up** informal lead a very enjoyable life, usually by being extravagant and having an exciting social life. **live off** (or **on**) **1** depend on someone or something as a source of income or support. **2** eat as a major part of one's diet. **live rough** live outdoors as a result of being homeless. **live together** (of a couple not married to each other) share a home and have a sexual relationship. **live up to** fulfill expectations, a commitment, etc.: *the president lived up to his promise.* **live with 1** share a home and have a sexual relationship with a person to whom one is not married. **2** accept or tolerate something unpleasant.

live[2] /līv/ ▶ adj. **1** living. **2** (of a musical performance) played in front of an audience. **3** (of a broadcast) transmitted at the time it occurs; not recorded. **4** of current or continuing interest and importance: *a live issue.* **5** (of a wire or device) connected to a source of electric current. **6** containing or using explosive that has not been detonated: *live ammunition.* **7** (of coals) burning. **8** (of yogurt) containing the living microorganisms by which it is formed. ▶ adv. at the time of something's occurrence or performance: *the match will be televised live.*

live·a·ble ▶ adj. variant spelling of LIVABLE.

live·bear·ing /ˈlīvˌbe(ə)riNG/ ▶ adj. bearing live young rather than laying eggs. ■ **live·bear·er** /ˈlīvˌbe(ə)rər/ n.

lived-in /ˈlivd ˌin/ ▶ adj. (of a room or building) showing comforting signs of wear and habitation.

live-in /ˈliv ˌin/ ▶ adj. **1** (of a domestic employee) living in an employer's house. **2** living with someone as their sexual partner: *his live-in girlfriend.* **3** (of a course of study, treatment, etc.) residential.

live·li·hood /ˈlīvlēˌho͝od/ ▶ n. a means of earning money in order to live.

live·long /ˈlivˌlông, -ˌläNG/ ▶ adj. literary (of a period of time) entire: *all this livelong day.*

live·ly /ˈlīvlē/ ▶ adj. (**livelier**, **liveliest**) **1** full of life and energy. **2** (of a place) full of activity. **3** intellectually stimulating: *a lively debate.* **4** mentally quick and active: *her lively mind.* ■ **live·li·ness** n.
– PHRASES **look lively** informal move more quickly and energetically.

liv·en /ˈlīvən/ ▶ v. (**liven someone/thing up** or **liven up**) make or become more lively or interesting.

liv·er¹ /ˈlivər/ ▶ n. **1** a large organ in the abdomen that produces bile and neutralizes toxins. **2** the flesh of an animal's liver as food.

liv·er² ▶ n. a person who lives in a particular way: *a clean liver.*

liv·er spot ▶ n. a small brown spot on the skin.

liv·er·wort /ˈlivərˌwərt, -ˌwôrt/ ▶ n. a small flowerless green plant that grows in moist habitats.

liv·er·y /ˈliv(ə)rē/ ▶ n. (pl. **liveries**) **1** a special uniform worn by an official or a servant such as a footman. **2** a distinctive design and color scheme used on the vehicles or products of a company. ■ **liv·er·ied** adj.
– PHRASES **at livery** (of a horse) kept for the owner and fed and cared for at a fixed charge.

liv·er·y sta·ble ▶ n. a stable where horses are kept at livery or may be hired out.

lives /līvz/ ▶ plural of LIFE.

live·stock /ˈlīvˌstäk/ ▶ n. farm animals.

live wire /līv/ ▶ n. informal an energetic and lively person.

liv·id /ˈlivid/ ▶ adj. **1** informal furiously angry. **2** dark bluish-gray in color. ■ **li·vid·i·ty** /ləˈvidətē/ n.

liv·ing /ˈliviNG/ ▶ n. **1** a way or style of life: *the benefits of country living.* **2** an income that is enough to live on, or the means of earning it.
▶ adj. **1** alive. **2** (of a place) for living rather than working in: *living quarters.* **3** (of a language) still spoken and used.
– PHRASES **in** (or **within**) **living memory** within or during a time that is remembered by people still alive. **the living image of** an exact copy or likeness of someone.

liv·ing room ▶ n. a room in a house for general everyday use.

liv·ing wage ▶ n. a wage that is high enough to enable someone to maintain a normal standard of living.

liv·ing will ▶ n. a written statement giving details of a person's wishes regarding their future medical treatment should they become unable to give informed consent.

liz·ard /ˈlizərd/ ▶ n. a four-legged reptile with a long body and tail and a rough, scaly, or spiny skin.

ll. ▶ abbr. (in textual references) lines.

'll ▶ contr. shall; will.

lla·ma /ˈlämə/ ▶ n. a domesticated animal of the camel family found in the Andes, used for carrying loads and valued for its soft woolly fleece.

lm ▶ abbr. lumen(s).

ln ▶ abbr. Mathematics natural logarithm.

LNB ▶ abbr. low noise blocker, a circuit on a satellite dish that selects the required signal from the transmission.

LNG ▶ abbr. liquefied natural gas.

lo /lō/ ▶ exclam. old use used to draw attention to an interesting event.
– PHRASES **lo and behold** used to present a new scene or situation.

loach /lōCH/ ▶ n. a small freshwater fish with several long, thin growths (barbels) near the mouth.

load /lōd/ ▶ n. **1** a heavy or bulky thing being or about to be carried. **2** the total number or amount carried in a vehicle or container. **3** a weight or source of pressure. **4** (**a load/loads of**) informal a large quantity or amount of something. **5** the amount of work to be done by a person or machine. **6** the amount of power supplied by a source. **7** a burden of responsibility, worry, or grief: *their offer took a load off my mind.* ▶ v. **1** put a load or large quantity of something on or in a vehicle or container. **2** insert something into a device so that it will operate. **3** put ammunition into a firearm. **4** transfer data or a program into a computer's memory. **5** bias something so that a particular outcome is likely: *the odds were loaded against them before the match.* ■ **load·er** n.
– PHRASES **get a load of** informal take a look at (used to draw attention to someone or something). **load the dice against** (or **in favor of**) put someone or something at a disadvantage (or an advantage).

load·ed /ˈlōdid/ ▶ adj. **1** carrying a load. **2** (of dice) weighted so that they will always fall in the same way when thrown. **3** having an underlying meaning or implication: *a loaded question.* **4** informal wealthy. **5** informal drunk.

load fac·tor ▶ n. the ratio of the average or actual amount of some quantity and the maximum possible or permissible.

load·ing /ˈlōdiNG/ ▶ n. **1** the application of a load to something. **2** the amount of load applied. **3** an increase in an insurance premium due to a factor that increases the risk involved.

load·mas·ter /ˈlōdˌmastər/ ▶ n. the member of an aircraft's crew responsible for the cargo.

load·stone ▶ n. variant spelling of LODESTONE.

loaf¹ /lōf/ ▶ n. (pl. **loaves** /lōvz/) a quantity of bread that is shaped and baked in one piece.

loaf² ▶ v. spend time in an idle or aimless way.

loaf·er /ˈlōfər/ ▶ n. **1** a person who spends their time in an idle or aimless way. **2** trademark a casual leather shoe with a flat heel.

loam /lōm/ ▶ n. **1** a fertile soil of clay and sand containing humus. **2** a paste of clay and water with sand and chopped straw, used in making bricks and plastering walls. ■ **loam·y** adj.

loan /lōn/ ▶ n. **1** a thing that is borrowed, especially a sum of money that is expected to be paid back with interest. **2** the action of lending something. ▶ v. give something as a loan.
– PHRASES **on loan** being borrowed.

loan shark ▶ n. informal a moneylender who charges extremely high rates of interest.

loath /lōTH, lōTH/ (also **loth**) ▶ adj. reluctant; unwilling.

USAGE
Do not confuse **loath** and **loathe**. **Loath** is an adjective meaning 'reluctant or unwilling' (*I was loath to leave*), whereas **loathe** is a verb meaning 'feel hatred or disgust for' (*she loathed him on sight*).

loathe /lōтн/ ▶ v. feel hatred or disgust for someone or something.

loath·some /'lōтнsəm, 'lōтн-/ ▶ adj. causing hatred or disgust.

loaves /lōvz/ ▶ plural of LOAF¹.

lob /läb/ ▶ v. (**lobs, lobbing, lobbed**) throw or hit something in a high arc. ▶ n. (in tennis) a ball lobbed over an opponent or a stroke producing this result.

lo·bar /'lō,bär, -bər/ ▶ adj. relating to or affecting a lobe, especially a lobe of a lung.

lo·bate /'lō,bāt/ ▶ adj. having a lobe or lobes.

lob·by /'läbē/ ▶ n. (pl. **lobbies**) 1 a room out of which one or more other rooms or corridors lead, typically one near the entrance of a public building. 2 a group of people trying to influence politicians on a particular issue: *members of the anti-abortion lobby.* 3 an organized attempt by members of the public to influence politicians. ▶ v. (**lobbies, lobbying, lobbied**) try to influence a politician on an issue. ■ **lob·by·ist** n.

lobe /lōb/ ▶ n. 1 a roundish projection or division of something. 2 (also **ear lobe**) the rounded fleshy part at the lower edge of the outer ear. 3 a major division of an organ such as the brain. ■ **lobed** adj.

lo·bel·ia /lō'bēlēə, -'bēlyə/ ▶ n. a garden plant with blue or scarlet flowers.

lo·bot·o·mize /lə'bätə,mīz/ ▶ v. perform a lobotomy on someone.

lo·bot·o·my /lə'bätəmē/ ▶ n. (pl. **lobotomies**) a surgical operation involving cutting into part of the brain, formerly used to treat mental illness.

lob·ster /'läbstər/ ▶ n. 1 a large edible shellfish with large pincers. 2 the flesh of this animal as food.

lob·ster pot ▶ n. a basketlike trap in which lobsters are caught.

lob·ster ther·mi·dor /'тнərmə,dôr/ ▶ n. a dish of lobster cooked in a cream sauce, returned to its shell, sprinkled with cheese, and browned under the broiler.

lo·cal /'lōkəl/ ▶ adj. 1 relating to a particular area or to the area in which a person lives: *the local post office.* 2 (in technical use) relating to a particular region or part: *a local infection.* 3 Computing referring to a device that can be accessed without the use of a network. ▶ n. a person who lives in a particular area. ■ **lo·cal·ly** adv.

lo·cal an·es·thet·ic ▶ n. an anesthetic that affects only a part of the body.

lo·cal ar·e·a net·work ▶ n. a computer network that links devices within a building or group of adjacent buildings.

lo·cale /lō'kal/ ▶ n. a place where something happens or is set.

lo·cal gov·ern·ment ▶ n. the administration of a particular town, county, or district, with representatives elected by people who live there.

lo·cal·i·ty /lō'kalətē/ ▶ n. (pl. **localities**) 1 an area or neighborhood. 2 the position or site of something.

lo·cal·ize /'lōkə,līz/ ▶ v. 1 (often as adj. **localized**) restrict or assign something to a particular place: *a localized infection.* 2 make something local in character: *a more localized news service.* ■ **lo·cal·iz·a·ble** adj. **lo·cal·i·za·tion** /,lōkələ'zāshən/ n. **lo·cal·iz·er** n.

lo·cal time ▶ n. time as reckoned in a particular region or time zone.

lo·cate /'lō,kāt, lō'kāt/ ▶ v. 1 discover the exact place or position of: *engineers were working to locate the fault.* 2 (**be located**) be situated in a particular place. ■ **lo·cat·a·ble** adj. **lo·ca·tor** n.

lo·ca·tion /lō'kāshən/ ▶ n. 1 a particular place or position. 2 the action of locating someone or something. 3 an actual place in which a movie or television broadcast is made, outside a studio. ■ **lo·ca·tion·al** adj.

loc. cit. /'läk 'sit/ ▶ abbr. in the passage already quoted.

loch /läk, läкн/ ▶ n. Scottish 1 a lake. 2 a narrow strip of sea, almost surrounded by land.

lo·ci /'lō,sī, -,sē, -,kē, -,kī/ ▶ plural of LOCUS.

lo·ci clas·si·ci /'lō,sī 'klasə,sī, 'lō,sē 'klasə,sē, 'lō,kē 'klasi,kē, 'lō,kī 'klasi,kī/ ▶ plural of LOCUS CLASSICUS.

lock¹ /läk/ ▶ n. 1 a mechanism for keeping a door or container fastened, operated by a key. 2 a similar device used to prevent the operation of a vehicle or other machine. 3 a short section of a canal or river with gates and sluices at each end that can be opened or closed to change the water level, used for raising and lowering boats. 4 informal a person or thing that is certain to succeed; a certainty. 5 (in wrestling and martial arts) a hold that prevents an opponent from moving a limb. 6 old use a mechanism for exploding the charge of a gun. ▶ v. 1 fasten or secure something with a lock. 2 (**lock something up**) shut and secure a building by fastening its doors with locks. 3 enclose or shut in by locking a door, fastening a lid, etc.: *the prisoners are locked in overnight.* 4 (**lock someone up**/**away**) imprison someone. 5 make or become fixed in one position or unable to move: *the brakes locked.* 6 (**be locked in**) be deeply involved in a difficult situation: *they were locked in a legal battle.* 7 (**lock on to**) locate and then track a target by radar or similar means. ■ **lock·a·ble** adj.

– PHRASES **lock horns** become involved in a conflict or dispute. **lock, stock, and barrel** including everything.

lock² ▶ n. 1 a section of a person's hair that coils or hangs in a piece. 2 (**locks**) literary a person's hair.

lock·down /'läk,doun/ ▶ n. the confining of prisoners to their cells.

lock·er /'läkər/ ▶ n. a small lockable cupboard or compartment in which belongings may be left temporarily.

lock·er room ▶ n. a changing room containing rows of lockers, especially in schools or gymnasiums.

lock·et /'läkit/ ▶ n. a small ornamental case worn on a chain around a person's neck, used to hold an item of sentimental value such as a tiny photograph or a lock of hair.

lock·in ▶ n. an arrangement that obliges a person or company to negotiate or trade only with a specific company.

lock·jaw /'läk,jô/ ▶ n. spasm of the jaw muscles, causing the mouth to remain tightly closed, typically as a symptom of tetanus.

lock·nut /'läk,nət/ ▶ n. 1 a nut screwed down on another to keep it tight. 2 a nut designed so that, once tightened, it cannot be accidentally loosened.

lock·out /'läk,out/ ▶ n. a situation in which an employer refuses to allow employees to enter their place of work until certain terms are agreed to.

lock·smith /'läk,smiTH/ ▶ n. a person who makes and repairs locks.

lock·step /'läk,step/ ▶ n. 1 a way for a body of people to march with each as close as possible to the one in front. 2 close imitation of another's actions: *they raised prices in lockstep with those of foreign competitors.*

lock·up /'läk,əp/ ▶ n. 1 a makeshift jail. 2 the action of becoming fixed or immovable.

lo·co /,lōkō/ ▶ adj. informal crazy.

lo·co·mo·tion /,lōkə'mōsHən/ ▶ n. movement or the ability to move from one place to another.

lo·co·mo·tive /,lōkə'mōtiv/ ▶ n. a powered rail vehicle used for pulling trains. ▶ adj. relating to locomotion.

lo·co·mo·tor /,lōkə'mōtər/ (also **locomotory**) ▶ adj. chiefly Biology relating to locomotion.

lo·co·weed /'lōkō,wēd/ ▶ n. 1 a plant of the pea family that, if eaten by livestock, can cause a brain disorder marked by unpredictable behavior and loss of coordination. 2 informal cannabis.

lo·cus /'lōkəs/ ▶ n. (pl. **loci** /'lō,sī, -,sē, -,kē, -,kī/) 1 technical a particular position, point, or place. 2 Mathematics a curve or other figure formed by all the points satisfying a particular condition.

lo·cus clas·si·cus /'lōkəs 'klasikəs/ ▶ n. (pl. **loci classici** /'lō,sī 'klasə,sī, 'lō,sē 'klasə,sē, 'lō,kē 'klasi,kē, 'lō,kī 'klasi,kī/) the best known or most authoritative passage on a particular subject.

lo·cust /'lōkəst/ ▶ n. a large tropical grasshopper that migrates in vast swarms and is very destructive to vegetation.

lo·cu·tion /lō'kyōsHən/ ▶ n. 1 a word or phrase. 2 a person's particular style of speech.

lode /lōd/ ▶ n. a vein of metal ore in the earth.

lo·den /'lōdn/ ▶ n. 1 a thick waterproof woolen cloth. 2 the dark green color in which such cloth is often made.

lode·star /'lōd,stär/ ▶ n. a star that is used to guide the course of a ship, especially the Pole Star.

lode·stone /'lōd,stōn/ (also **loadstone**) ▶ n. 1 a piece of magnetite or other naturally magnetic mineral, able to be used as a magnet. 2 a person or thing that is a focus of attention or attraction.

lodge /läj/ ▶ n. 1 a small house at the gates of a large house with grounds, occupied by a gatekeeper or other employee. 2 a small country house occupied by people engaged in hunting and shooting. 3 a branch or meeting place of an organization such as the Freemasons. 4 a beaver's den. 5 an American Indian tent or other dwelling. ▶ v. 1 formally present a complaint, appeal, etc., to the proper authorities. 2 make or become firmly fixed or embedded in a place: *he had a bullet lodged in his skull.* 3 rent accommodations in another person's house. 4 provide someone with rented accommodations. 5 (**lodge something in/with**) leave money or a valuable item in a place or with a person for safekeeping.

lodge·ment /'läjmənt/ ▶ n. 1 chiefly literary a place in which a person or thing is lodged. 2 the depositing of money in a particular bank or account.

lodge·pole pine /'läjipōl/ ▶ n. a straight-trunked pine tree traditionally used by some American Indians to construct lodges.

lodg·er /'läjər/ ▶ n. a person who pays rent to live in a property with the owner.

lodg·ing /'läjiNG/ ▶ n. 1 temporary accommodations. 2 (**lodgings**) a rented room or rooms, usually in the same house as the owner.

lo·ess /les, ləs, 'lō,es/ ▶ n. a loosely compacted fine soil originally deposited by the wind.

lo-fi /'lō 'fī/ (also **low-fi**) ▶ adj. relating to or using sound reproduction of a lower quality than hi-fi.

loft /lôft, läft/ ▶ n. 1 a room or storage space directly under the roof of a house or other building. 2 a large, open living area in a converted warehouse or other large building. 3 a gallery in a church or hall. 4 a shelter with nest holes for pigeons. 5 Golf upward movement given to the ball in a stroke. 6 the thickness of an insulating material such as that in a sleeping bag. ▶ v. kick, hit, or throw a ball or missile high into the air.

loft·y /'lôftē, 'läf-/ ▶ adj. (**loftier, loftiest**) 1 tall and impressive. 2 morally good or admirable; noble: *lofty ideals.* 3 haughty and aloof. ■ **loft·i·ly** adv. **loft·i·ness** n.

log¹ /lôg, läg/ ▶ n. 1 a part of the trunk or a large branch of a tree that has fallen or been cut off. 2 (also **logbook**) an official record of events during the voyage of a ship or aircraft. 3 a piece of equipment for measuring the speed of a ship, originally one consisting of a float attached to a knotted line. ▶ v. (**logs, logging, logged**) 1 enter information in an official record: *customs officials logged the contents of every ship.* 2 achieve a certain distance, speed, or time. 3 (**log in/on** or **out/off**) go through the procedures to begin (or finish) using a computer. 4 cut down an area of forest to use the wood commercially. ■ **log·ger** n. **log·ging** n.

log² ▶ n. short for LOGARITHM.

loge /lōzH/ ▶ n. a private box or enclosure in a theater. a mid-priced seating section in a stadium, often the back portion of a lower tier.

lo·gan·ber·ry /'lōgən,berē/ ▶ n. (pl. **loganberries**) an edible soft red fruit, similar to a raspberry.

log·a·rithm /'lôgə,riTHəm, 'lägə-/ ▶ n. one of a series of numbers, representing the power to which a fixed number (the base) must be raised to produce a given number, used to simplify calculations. ■ **log·a·rith·mic** /,lôgə'riTHmik, ,lägə-/ adj.

log·book /'lôg,bŏŏk, 'läg-/ ▶ n. a log of a ship or aircraft.

log·ger·head /'lôgər,hed, 'lägər-/ ▶ n. (also **loggerhead turtle**) a large-headed reddish-brown turtle of warm seas.

– PHRASES **at loggerheads** engaged in strong dispute or disagreement.

log·gia /'lōj(ē)ə, 'lō-/ ▶ n. a gallery or room with one or more open sides, especially with one side open to a garden.

log·ic /'läjik/ ▶ n. 1 the science of reasoning. 2 good or valid reasoning: *the logic of the argument is faulty.* 3 an underlying system or set of principles used in preparing a computer or electronic device to perform a particular task. ■ **lo·gi·cian** /lə'jisHən, lō-/ n.

log·i·cal /'läjikəl/ ▶ adj. 1 relating to or following the rules of logic. 2 capable of or showing rational thought. 3 expected or sensible under the circumstances: *the polar expedition* *is a logical extension of his Arctic travels.* ■ **log·i·cal·ly** adv.

log·ic bomb ► n. Computing a set of instructions secretly incorporated into a program so that if a particular condition is satisfied they will be carried out, usually with harmful effects.

log·in /'lôg,in, 'läg-/ (also **logon**) ► n. an act of logging in to a computer, or the password needed to do so.

lo·gis·tics /lə'jistiks, lō-/ ► pl.n. (treated as sing. or pl.) **1** the detailed coordination of a large and complex project or event. **2** the commercial activity of transporting goods to customers. ■ **lo·gis·tic** adj. **lo·gis·ti·cal** adj. **lo·gis·ti·cal·ly** adv.

log·jam /'lôg,jam, 'läg-/ ► n. **1** a situation that seems unable to be settled; deadlock. **2** a backlog.

lo·go /'lō,gō/ ► n. (pl. **logos**) a design or symbol adopted by an organization to identify its products.

log·roll·ing /'lôg,rōliNG, 'läg-/ ► n. **1** informal the practice of exchanging favors, especially in politics. **2** a sport in which two contestants stand on a floating log and try to knock each other off by spinning it with their feet. ■ **log·roll·er** n.

loin /loin/ ► n. **1** the part of the body on both sides of the spine between the lowest ribs and the hipbones. **2** a cut of meat from the back or sides of an animal, near the tail. **3** (**loins**) literary a person's sexual organs.

loin·cloth /'loin,klôтн, -,kläтн/ ► n. a piece of cloth wrapped around the hips, worn by men in some hot countries as their only garment.

loi·ter /'loitər/ ► v. stand around without any obvious purpose. ■ **loi·ter·er** n.

Lo·li·ta /lō'lētə/ ► n. (**a Lolita**) a sexually precocious young girl.

loll /läl/ ► v. **1** sit, lie, or stand in a lazy, relaxed way. **2** hang loosely: *he let his head loll back.*

lol·la·pa·loo·za /,läləpə'lōōzə/ ► n. informal a very impressive or attractive person or thing.

lol·li·pop /'läle,päp/ ► n. a flat, rounded candy on the end of a stick.

lol·ly·gag /'lälē,gag/ ► v. (**lollygags, lollygagging, lollygagged**) informal spend time in an aimless way.

Lom·bard /'läm,bärd, -bərd/ ► n. **1** a member of a Germanic people who invaded Italy in the 6th century. **2** a person from Lombardy in northern Italy. ■ **Lom·bar·dic** /läm'bärdik/ adj.

lone /lōn/ ► adj. **1** having no companions; solitary. **2** lacking the support of other people: *I am by no means a lone voice.* **3** literary (of a place) remote and rarely visited.

lone·ly /'lōnlē/ ► adj. (**lonelier, loneliest**) **1** sad because one has no friends or company. **2** spent without company: *long, lonely hours.* **3** (of a place) remote and rarely visited. ■ **lone·li·ness** n.

lone·ly hearts ► pl.n. people looking for a lover or friend through the personal columns of a newspaper.

lon·er /'lōnər/ ► n. a person who prefers to be alone.

lone·some /'lōnsəm/ ► adj. lonely.

long¹ /lôNG, läNG/ ► adj. (**longer** /'lôNGgər, 'läNG-/, **longest** /'lôNGgist, 'läNG-/) **1** of a great distance or duration. **2** having a particular length, distance, or duration: *the ship will be 150 yards long.* **3** relatively great in extent: *a long list.* **4** (of a ball in sports) traveling a great

distance, or further than expected. **5** Phonetics (of a vowel) pronounced in a way that takes longer than a short vowel in the same position (e.g., in standard American English the vowel /ōō/ in *food*). **6** (of odds in betting) reflecting a low level of probability. **7** (**long on**) informal well supplied with something: *an industry that's long on ideas but short on cash.* ► n. a long time. ► adv. (**longer, longest**) **1** for a long time. **2** at a distant time: *long ago.* **3** throughout a particular period of time: *all day long.* **4** (with reference to the ball in sports) at, to, or over a great distance. ■ **long·ish** /'lôNGgish, 'läNG-/ adj.

– PHRASES **as** (or **so**) **long as 1** during the whole time that. **2** provided that. **in the long run** (or **term**) eventually. **the long and the short of it** all that can or need be said. **long in the tooth** rather old.

long² ► v. (**long for/to do**) have a strong wish for or to do something.

long. ► abbr. longitude.

long·board /'lôNG,bôrd, 'läNG-/ ► n. a type of long surfboard.

long·boat /'lôNG,bōt, 'läNG-/ ► n. **1** historical a large boat that could be launched from a sailing ship. **2** another term for LONGSHIP.

long·bow /'lôNG,bō, 'läNG-/ ► n. historical a large bow drawn by hand and shooting a long feathered arrow.

long-dis·tance ► adj. **1** traveling or operating between distant places. **2** Athletics referring to a race distance of 6 miles or 10,000 meters (6 miles 376 yds), or longer. ► adv. between distant places.

long di·vi·sion ► n. the process of dividing one number by another with the calculations written down.

long-drawn (also **long-drawn-out**) ► adj. lasting a very long time, or too long.

longe /lənj/ ► n. variant of LUNGE².

lon·gev·i·ty /lôn'jevətē, län-/ ► n. long life.

long face ► n. an unhappy or disappointed expression.

long·hand /'lôNG,hand, 'läNG-/ ► n. ordinary handwriting (as opposed to shorthand, typing, or printing).

long haul ► n. **1** a relatively long distance in terms of travel or the transport of goods. **2** a lengthy and difficult task.

long·horn /'lôNG,hôrn, 'läNG-/ ► n. a breed of cattle with long horns.

long·house /'lôNG,hous, 'läNG-/ ► n. a large communal house in parts of Malaysia and Indonesia or among some North American Indians.

long·ing /'lôNGiNG/ ► n. a strong wish to do or have something. ► adj. having or showing a strong wish to do or have something: *a longing look.* ■ **long·ing·ly** adv.

lon·gi·tude /'länji,t(y)ōōd, 'lôn-/ ► n. the distance of a place east or west of the Greenwich meridian, measured in degrees.

lon·gi·tu·di·nal /,länjə't(y)ōōdn-əl, ,lôn-/ ► adj. **1** running lengthwise. **2** relating to the distance of a place east or west of the Greenwich meridian. ■ **lon·gi·tu·di·nal·ly** adv.

long johns /jänz/ ► pl.n. informal underwear with closely fitted legs reaching to the ankles.

long jump ► n. (**the long jump**) an athletic event in which competitors jump as far as possible along the ground in one leap. ■ **long jump·er** n.

long·leaf pine /ˈlôNGˌlēf, ˈläNG-/ ▶ n. a large pine tree with very long needles and cones, formerly an important source of turpentine.

long-life ▶ adj. (of perishable goods) treated so as to stay fresh for longer than usual.

long·line /ˈlôNGˌlīn, ˈläNG-/ ▶ n. a deep-sea fishing line with a large number of hooks attached to it.

long-lived /livd/ ▶ adj. living or lasting a long time.

long-play·ing ▶ adj. (of a record) 12 inches (about 30 cm) in diameter and designed to rotate at 33⅓ revolutions per minute.

long-range ▶ adj. **1** able to be used or be effective over long distances. **2** relating to a period of time far into the future.

long·ship /ˈlôNGˌSHip, ˈläNG-/ ▶ n. a long, narrow warship with oars and a sail, used by the Vikings.

long·shore /ˈlôNGˌSHôr, ˈläNG-/ ▶ adj. relating to or moving along the seashore.

long·shore·man /ˌlôNGˈSHôrmən, ˌläNG-/ ▶ n. (pl. **longshoremen**) a person employed to load and unload ships.

long shot ▶ n. an attempt or guess that has only the slightest chance of succeeding or being accurate.
– PHRASES **not by a long shot** informal not at all.

long-stand·ing ▶ adj. having existed for a long time.

long-suf·fer·ing ▶ adj. bearing problems or annoying behavior patiently.

long suit ▶ n. **1** (in bridge or whist) a situation in which a player holds several cards of one suit in a hand. **2** an outstanding personal quality or achievement: *tact was not his long suit.*

long-term ▶ adj. occurring over or relating to a long period of time: *the long-term effects of smoking.*

lon·gueur /lôNGˈgər, läNG-/ ▶ n. a tedious period of time or passage in a book or piece of music.

long un·der·wear ▶ n. a warm, close-fitting undergarment with ankle-length legs and often long sleeves.

long wave ▶ n. **1** a radio wave of a wavelength above one kilometer (and a frequency below 300 kilohertz). **2** broadcasting using radio waves of 1 to 10 kilometers wavelength.

long·ways /ˈlôNGˌwāz, ˈläNG-/ ▶ adv. lengthwise.

long-wind·ed /ˈwindid/ ▶ adj. lengthy and boring.

loo /lo͞o/ ▶ n. Brit. informal a toilet.

loo·fah /ˈlo͞ofə/ ▶ n. a long, rough, fibrous object used like a bath sponge, consisting of the dried inner parts of a tropical fruit.

look /lo͝ok/ ▶ v. **1** direct one's gaze in a particular direction. **2** have the appearance or give the impression of being: *he looked unhappy.* **3** face in a particular direction: *the rooms look out over the harbor.* ▶ n. **1** an act of looking at someone or something. **2** an expression of a feeling or thought by looking at someone: *he gave me a funny look.* **3** the appearance of someone or something: *the contemporary look of the city skyline.* **4** (**looks**) a person's facial appearance. **5** a style or fashion: *Italian designers unveiled their latest looks.* ▶ exclam. (also **look here!**) used to call attention to what one is going to say.
– PHRASES **look after** take care of. **look at 1** think of something in a particular way. **2** examine a matter and consider what action to take. **look down on** (also **look down one's nose**

at) regard someone or something with a feeling of superiority. **look for** attempt to find. **look in** make a short visit. **look into** investigate. **look lively** (or **sharp**) informal be quick; get moving. **look on** watch without getting involved. **look out** be alert for possible trouble or danger. **look to 1** rely on someone to do something. **2** hope or expect to do something. **look up** improve. **look something up** search for and find a piece of information in a reference work. **look someone up** informal visit or contact someone. **look up to** have a great deal of respect for.

look·a·like /ˈlo͝okəˌlīk/ ▶ n. a person or thing that looks very similar to another.

look·er /ˈlo͝okər/ ▶ n. **1** a person with a particular appearance: *she's not a bad looker.* **2** informal a very attractive person.

look·ing glass ▶ n. a mirror.

look·out /ˈlo͝okˌout/ ▶ n. **1** a place from which to keep watch. **2** a person stationed to keep watch for danger or trouble. **3** (**one's lookout**) informal one's own responsibility or problem: *if they let him in that's their lookout.*
– PHRASES **be on the lookout** (or **keep a lookout**) **for 1** be alert to possible danger or trouble. **2** keep searching for something.

look-see ▶ n. informal a brief look or inspection.

look·up /ˈlo͝okˌəp/ ▶ n. systematic retrieval of electronic information.

loom¹ /lo͞om/ ▶ n. a piece of equipment for weaving fabric.

loom² ▶ v. **1** appear as a vague shape, especially one that is large or threatening: *vehicles loomed out of the darkness.* **2** (of an unwelcome event) seem about to happen: *there is a crisis looming.*

loon¹ /lo͞on/ ▶ n. informal a silly or foolish person.

loon² ▶ n. another term for DIVER (sense 2).

loon·y /ˈlo͞onē/ informal ▶ n. (pl. **loonies**) a crazy or silly person. ▶ adj. (**loonier, looniest**) crazy or silly. ■ **loon·i·ness** n.

loon·y bin ▶ n. informal, derogatory an institution for people with mental illnesses.

loop /lo͞op/ ▶ n. **1** a shape produced by a curve that bends around and crosses itself. **2** an endless strip of tape or film allowing sounds or images to be continuously repeated. **3** a complete circuit for an electric current. **4** Computing a programmed sequence of instructions that is repeated until or while a particular condition is satisfied. ▶ v. **1** form into a loop or loops: *she looped her arms around his neck.* **2** follow a course that forms a loop or loops.
– PHRASES **in** (or **out of**) **the loop** informal aware (or unaware) of information known to only a privileged few. **loop the loop** (of an aircraft) fly in a vertical circle.

loop·er /ˈlo͞opər/ ▶ n. **1** another term for INCHWORM. **2** Baseball a fly ball that becomes a hit by dropping out of the reach of the infielders.

loop·hole /ˈlo͞opˌ(h)ōl/ ▶ n. an inexact wording or omission in a law or contract that enables someone to avoid doing something.

loop·y /ˈlo͞opē/ ▶ adj. (**loopier, loopiest**) informal crazy or silly. ■ **loop·i·ness** n.

loose /lo͞os/ ▶ adj. **1** not firmly or tightly fixed in place. **2** not held, tied, or packaged together. **3** not tied up or shut in: *the bull was loose in the field.* **4** (of a garment) not fitting tightly or closely. **5** not dense or compact in structure. **6** relaxed: *her loose, easy stride.* **7** not strict;

inexact: *a loose interpretation.* **8** careless and indiscreet: *loose talk.* **9** dated promiscuous or immoral. **10** (of the ball in a game) in play but not in any player's possession. ▶v. **1** release someone or something. **2** relax one's grip. **3** (usu. **loose something off**) fire a shot, bullet, etc. ■ **loose·ly** adv. **loose·ness** n.
– PHRASES **on the loose** having escaped from prison or confinement.

> USAGE
> Do not confuse **loose** and **lose**; **loose** means 'not fixed in place or tied up' (*a loose tooth*), while **lose** means 'have something taken away' (*she might lose her job*) or 'become unable to find someone or something'.

loose can·non ▶n. an unpredictable person who may cause unintentional harm or damage.

loose end ▶n. a detail that is not yet settled or explained.
– PHRASES **be at loose ends** have nothing specific to do.

loose-leaf ▶adj. (of a folder) having pages that can be taken out and put in separately.

loos·en /'lōōsən/ ▶v. **1** make or become loose. **2** (**loosen up**) warm up in preparation for an activity. ■ **loos·en·er** n.
– PHRASES **loosen someone's tongue** make someone talk freely.

loose·strife /'lōō(s)ˌstrīf/ ▶n. a waterside plant with a tall upright spike of purple or yellow flowers.

loos·ey-goos·ey /'lōōsē 'gōōsē/ ▶adj. informal **1** not tense; relaxed or comfortable. **2** lacking in definition, care, or precision.

loot /lōōt/ ▶n. **1** goods stolen from empty buildings during a war or riot. **2** goods stolen by a thief. **3** informal money. ▶v. steal goods from empty buildings during a war or riot. ■ **loot·er** n.

lop /läp/ ▶v. (**lops, lopping, lopped**) **1** cut off a branch or limb from a tree or body. **2** informal make something smaller or less by a particular amount: *the new highway lops an hour off commuting time.* ■ **lop·per** n.

lope /lōp/ ▶v. run with a long bounding stride. ▶n. a long bounding stride.

lop-eared ▶adj. (of an animal) having drooping ears. ■ **lop ears** pl.n.

lop·sid·ed /'läpˌsīdid/ ▶adj. with one side lower or smaller than the other. ■ **lop·sid·ed·ly** adv. **lop·sid·ed·ness** n.

lo·qua·cious /lō'kwāshəs/ ▶adj. talkative. ■ **lo·quac·i·ty** /'ləkwasətē/ n.

lo·quat /'lōˌkwät/ ▶n. a small egg-shaped yellow fruit from an East Asian tree.

lord /lôrd/ ▶n. **1** (in the UK) a man of noble rank. **2** (**Lord**) (in the UK) a title given formally to a baron, less formally to a marquess, earl, or viscount, and as a courtesy title to a younger son of a duke or marquess. **3** (**the Lords**) (in the UK) the House of Lords, or its members. **4** a master or ruler. **5** (**Lord**) a name for God or Jesus. ▶exclam. (**Lord**) used in exclamations expressing surprise or worry, or for emphasis. ▶v. (**lord it over**) act in an arrogant and bullying way toward someone.
– PHRASES **the Lord's Day** Sunday. **the Lord's Prayer** the prayer taught by Jesus to his disciples, beginning 'Our Father.'

lord·ly /'lôrdlē/ ▶adj. (**lordlier, lordliest**)

characteristic of or suitable for a lord. ■ **lord·li·ness** n.

lord·ship /'lôrdˌSHip/ ▶n. **1** (**His/Your Lordship**) (in the UK) a form of address to a judge, bishop, or nobleman. **2** supreme power or rule.

lore /lôr/ ▶n. a body of traditions and knowledge relating to a particular subject: *farming lore.*

lor·gnette /lôrn'yet/ (also **lorgnettes**) ▶n. a pair of glasses or opera glasses held by a long handle at one side.

lor·i·keet /'lôrəˌkēt, 'lär-/ ▶n. a small bird of the lory family, found chiefly in New Guinea.

lo·ris /'lôris/ ▶n. (pl. **lorises**) a small, slow-moving primate that lives in thick vegetation in South Asia.

lor·ry /'lôrē, 'lärē/ ▶n. (pl. **lorries**) Brit. a large, heavy motor vehicle for transporting goods or troops; a truck.

lo·ry /'lôrē/ ▶n. (pl. **lories**) a small Australasian or SE Asian parrot.

lose /lōōz/ ▶v. (past and past part. **lost** /lôst, läst/) **1** no longer have or keep: *I've lost my appetite.* **2** have something taken away: *she was upset about losing her job.* **3** become unable to find something or someone. **4** fail to win a game or contest. **5** earn less money than one is spending. **6** waste or fail to take advantage of: *he may have lost his chance.* **7** (**be lost**) be destroyed or killed. **8** escape from a pursuer. **9** (**lose oneself in/be lost in**) be or become deeply absorbed in: *he had been lost in thought.* **10** (of a watch or clock) become slow by a particular amount of time.
– PHRASES **lose face** become less well respected. **lose heart** become discouraged. **lose it** informal lose control of one's temper or emotions. **lose out** not get a full chance or opportunity. **lose one's** (or **the**) **way** become lost.

> USAGE
> On the confusion of **lose** and **loose**, see the note at LOOSE.

los·er /'lōōzər/ ▶n. **1** a person or thing that loses or has lost a game or contest. **2** informal a person who is generally unsuccessful in life.

los·ing bat·tle ▶n. a struggle in which failure seems certain.

loss /lôs, läs/ ▶n. **1** the fact or process of losing something or someone. **2** a person, thing, or amount lost. **3** the feeling of grief after losing a valued person or thing. **4** a person or thing that is badly missed when lost.
– PHRASES **at a loss 1** uncertain or puzzled. **2** making less money than is spent in operating or producing something.

loss-lead·er ▶n. a product sold at a loss to attract customers.

lost /lôst, läst/ past and past participle of LOSE. ▶adj. unable to find one's way; not knowing where one is.
– PHRASES **be lost for words** be so surprised or upset that one cannot think what to say. **be lost on** fail to be noticed or understood by: *the irony is lost on him.*

lost cause ▶n. a person or thing that can no longer hope to succeed or be improved.

lost gen·er·a·tion ▶n. the generation reaching maturity during and just after World War I, many of whose men were killed during those years.

lot /lät/ ▶ pron. *informal* **1** (**a lot** or **lots**) a large number or amount of something. **2** (**the lot**) the whole number or amount. ▶ adv. (**a lot** or **lots**) *informal* a great deal. ▶ n. **1** (treated as *sing.* or *pl.*) *informal* a particular group or set of people or things: *you lot think you're so clever.* **2** an item or set of items for sale at an auction. **3** a method of deciding something by choosing an item at random, especially one piece of paper from a number of pieces. **4** a person's destiny, luck, or situation in life: *many housewives are not happy with their lot.* **5** an area of land: *a parking lot.*
– PHRASES **draw** (or **cast**) **lots** decide something by choosing one piece of paper from a number of other pieces. **fall to someone's lot** become someone's task or responsibility. **throw in one's lot with** decide to join a person or group and share their fate.

> **USAGE**
> Although **a lot of** and **lots of** are very common in speech, they still have an informal feel and it is better to avoid them in formal English; use alternatives such as **many** or **a large number** instead.
> The correct spelling is **a lot**; do not spell it as one word (*alot*).

lo-tech ▶ adj. variant spelling of LOW-TECH.
loth ▶ adj. variant spelling of LOATH.
Lo·thar·i·o /lōˈTHe(ə)rēˌō, -ˈTHär-/ ▶ n. (pl. **Lotharios**) a man who has many casual sexual relationships with women; a womanizer.
lo·tion /ˈlōshən/ ▶ n. a thick creamy liquid applied to the skin as a medicine or cosmetic.
lot·ter·y /ˈlätərē/ ▶ n. (pl. **lotteries**) **1** a means of raising money by selling numbered tickets and giving prizes to the holders of numbers drawn at random. **2** something whose success is governed by chance: *the Grand Prix was made a lottery by heavy rain.*
lot·to /ˈlätō/ ▶ n. (pl. **lottos**) **1** a children's game similar to bingo, using illustrated counters or cards. **2** a lottery.
lo·tus /ˈlōtəs/ ▶ n. **1** a kind of large water lily. **2** (in Greek mythology) a legendary fruit that causes dreamy forgetfulness and an unwillingness to leave.
lo·tus-eat·er ▶ n. a person who indulges in pleasure and luxury rather than dealing with practical concerns.
lo·tus po·si·tion ▶ n. a cross-legged position for meditation, with the feet resting on the thighs.
louche /lōōsh/ ▶ adj. having a bad reputation but still attractive: *a louche rock star.*
loud /loud/ ▶ adj. **1** producing or capable of producing much noise. **2** expressed forcefully: *the bold decision to introduce change despite loud protests from all.* **3** very bright and tasteless: *a loud checked suit.* ▶ adv. with much noise. ■ **loud·en** v. **loud·ly** adv. **loud·ness** n.
– PHRASES **out loud** so as to be heard; aloud.
loud·mouth /ˈloudˌmouTH/ ▶ n. *informal* a person who talks too much or makes tactless remarks.
loud·speak·er /ˈloudˌspēkər/ ▶ n. a device that converts electrical impulses into sound.
lough /läk, läKH/ ▶ n. (in Ireland) a loch.
lounge /lounj/ ▶ v. lie, sit, or stand in a relaxed or lazy way. ▶ n. **1** a room in a hotel, theater, or airport in which to relax or wait. **2** a couch or sofa, especially a backless one having a headrest at one end.
lounge liz·ard ▶ n. *informal* an idle man who spends

his time among rich and fashionable people.
loung·er /ˈlounjər/ ▶ n. a person who spends their time in a lazy or relaxed way.
loupe /lōōp/ ▶ n. a small magnifying glass used by jewelers and watchmakers.
lour ▶ v. variant spelling of LOWER³.
louse /lous/ ▶ n. **1** (pl. **lice** /līs/) a small wingless insect that lives as a parasite on humans, animals, and plants. **2** (pl. **louses**) *informal* an unpleasant person. ▶ v. (**louse something up**) *informal* spoil something.
lous·y /ˈlouzē/ ▶ adj. (**lousier, lousiest**) **1** *informal* very poor or bad. **2** infested with lice. **3** (**lousy with**) *informal* full of or teeming with something undesirable. ■ **lous·i·ly** /-zəlē/ adv. **lous·i·ness** n.
lout /lout/ ▶ n. a rough or aggressive man or boy. ■ **lout·ish** adj.
lou·ver /ˈlōōvər/ (also **louvre**) ▶ n. each of a set of slanting slats fixed at intervals in a door, shutter, or cover to allow air or light through. ■ **lou·vered** adj.
lov·a·ble /ˈləvəbəl/ (also **loveable**) ▶ adj. inspiring love or affection. ■ **lov·a·ble·ness** n. **lov·a·bly** /-blē/ adv.
lov·age /ˈləvij/ ▶ n. a large white-flowered plant used as an herb in cooking.
love /ləv/ ▶ n. **1** a strong feeling of affection. **2** strong affection linked with sexual attraction. **3** a great interest and pleasure in something. **4** a person or thing that one loves: *she was the love of his life.* **5** (in tennis, squash, etc.) a score of zero. ▶ v. **1** feel love for someone. **2** like or enjoy something very much. **3** (as adj. **loving**) showing love or great care. ■ **love·less** adj. **lov·ing·ly** adv.
– PHRASES **make love 1** have sex. **2** (**make love to**) *dated* pay romantic attention to someone. **there's no love lost between** the people mentioned dislike each other.
love·a·ble /ˈləvəbəl/ ▶ adj. variant spelling of LOVABLE.
love af·fair ▶ n. **1** a romantic or sexual relationship between two people who are not married to each other. **2** an intense enthusiasm for something.
love·bird /ˈləvˌbərd/ ▶ n. **1** a very small African or Madagascan parrot that shows affection for its mate. **2** (**lovebirds**) *informal* an openly affectionate couple.
love bite ▶ n. a hickey.
love child ▶ n. a child born to parents who are not married to each other.
love han·dles ▶ pl.n. *informal* excess fat at a person's waistline.
love-in ▶ n. *informal* (especially among hippies in the 1960s) a gathering at which people are encouraged to express friendship and physical attraction.
love-in-a-mist ▶ n. a plant whose blue flowers are surrounded by threadlike green bracts (modified leaves).
love life ▶ n. the part of a person's life concerning their relationships with lovers.
love·lorn /ˈləvˌlôrn/ ▶ adj. unhappy because one loves someone who does not feel the same in return.
love·ly /ˈləvlē/ ▶ adj. (**lovelier, loveliest**) **1** very beautiful. **2** very pleasant. ▶ n. (pl. **lovelies**) *informal* a beautiful woman or girl. ■ **love·li·ness** n.
love·mak·ing /ˈləvˌmāking/ ▶ n. sexual intercourse and other sexual activity.
love nest ▶ n. *informal* a private place where two

lovers spend time together.

lov·er /ˈləvər/ ▶ n. **1** a person in a sexual or romantic relationship with someone. **2** a person who enjoys a specified thing: *a music lover.*

love seat ▶ n. a small sofa for two people.

love·sick /ˈləvˌsik/ ▶ adj. in love, or missing the person one loves, so much that one is unable to act normally. ■ **love·sick·ness** n.

love·y-dove·y /ˈləvē ˈdəvē/ ▶ adj. informal very affectionate or romantic.

lov·ing cup ▶ n. a two-handled cup passed around at banquets.

low[1] /lō/ ▶ adj. **1** not high or tall; of less than average height. **2** not far above the ground, horizon, or sea level. **3** below average in amount, extent, or intensity. **4** ranking below others in importance: *training was given low priority.* **5** lacking quality; inferior. **6** (of a sound) deep or quiet. **7** unfavorable: *she had a low opinion of herself.* **8** depressed or lacking energy. **9** lacking moral principles; unscrupulous or dishonest. ▶ n. **1** a low point, level, or figure. **2** an area of low atmospheric pressure. ▶ adv. **1** in or into a low position or state. **2** quietly or at a low pitch. ■ **low·ish** adj. **low·ness** n.

low[2] ▶ v. (of a cow) moo. ▶ n. a moo.

low·ball /ˈlōˌbôl/ informal ▶ adj. (of an estimate, bid, etc.) deceptively or unrealistically low. ▶ v. offer a deceptively or unrealistically low estimate or bid to.

low beam ▶ n. a vehicle headlight providing short-range illumination.

low·brow /ˈlōˌbrou/ ▶ adj. chiefly derogatory not intellectual or interested in culture.

Low Church ▶ n. a tradition within the Anglican Church that places relatively little emphasis on ritual and the authority of bishops and priests.

low com·e·dy ▶ n. comedy bordering on farce.

low·down /ˈlōˌdoun/ informal ▶ adj. unfair or dishonest. ▶ n. (**the lowdown**) the true or most important facts about something.

low-end ▶ adj. referring to the less expensive products in a range.

low·er[1] /ˈlōər/ ▶ adj. comparative of **Low**[1]. **1** less high in position, importance, or amount. **2** (of a geological period or formation) older (and hence forming more deeply buried strata): *the Lower Cretaceous.* **3** (in place names) situated to the south. ■ **low·er·most** /-ˌmōst/ adj.

low·er[2] ▶ v. **1** move someone or something downward. **2** make or become less in amount, intensity, or value: *I lowered my voice to a whisper.* **3** (**lower oneself**) behave in a way that is humiliating.

low·er[3] /ˈlou(ə)r/ (also **lour**) ▶ v. **1** (of the sky) look dark and threatening. **2** look angry or sullen; scowl.

low·er·case /ˈlōərˌkās/ ▶ n. small letters as opposed to capitals.

low·er class /ˈlōər/ (also **lower classes**) ▶ n. the working class.

low·er court /ˈlōər/ ▶ n. Law a court whose decisions may be overruled by another on appeal.

low·er house /ˈlōər/ (also **lower chamber**) ▶ n. **1** one of two houses (often the larger) in a bicameral legislature or parliament and typically having the primary responsibility for legislation. **2** (often **the House**) the House of Representatives (of the US or of a US state).

3 (**the Lower House**) (in the UK) the House of Commons.

low·est com·mon de·nom·i·na·tor /lōist/ ▶ n. **1** Mathematics the lowest common multiple of the denominators of several fractions. **2** derogatory the level of the least discriminating audience or other group.

low·est com·mon mul·ti·ple /lōist/ ▶ n. Mathematics the lowest quantity that is a multiple of two or more given quantities.

low-fi ▶ adj. variant spelling of **LO-FI**.

low fre·quen·cy ▶ n. (in radio) a frequency of 30–300 kilohertz.

low gear ▶ n. a gear that causes a vehicle to move slowly.

Low Ger·man ▶ n. a German dialect spoken in much of northern Germany.

low-grade ▶ adj. **1** of low quality or strength. **2** (of a medical condition) of a less serious kind; minor: *a low-grade fever.*

low-hang·ing fruit ▶ n. informal a thing that can be won or obtained with little effort.

low-im·pact /ˈimˌpakt/ ▶ adj. **1** (of physical exercises) putting little stress on the body. **2** having relatively little effect on the environment.

low-key (also **low-keyed**) ▶ adj. not elaborate, showy, or intensive; restrained.

low·land /ˈlōlənd, -ˌland/ ▶ n. **1** low-lying country. **2** (**the Lowlands**) the part of Scotland lying south and east of the Highlands. ■ **low·land·er** n.

low-lev·el ▶ adj. **1** of relatively little importance. **2** (of a computer programming language) similar to machine code in form.

low-life /ˈlōˌlīf/ ▶ n. (pl. **lowlifes**) **1** dishonest or immoral people or activities. **2** informal a dishonest or immoral person.

low·light /ˈlōˌlīt/ ▶ n. **1** (**lowlights**) darker dyed streaks in the hair. **2** informal a disappointing or dull event or feature.

low·ly /ˈlōlē/ ▶ adj. (**lowlier, lowliest**) low in status or importance. ▶ adv. to a low degree: *lowly paid workers.* ■ **low·li·ness** n.

low-ly·ing ▶ adj. (of land) not far above sea level.

low-pro·file ▶ adj. avoiding attention or publicity: *a low-profile campaign.*

low re·lief ▶ n. see **RELIEF** (sense 8).

low-rise ▶ adj. **1** (of a building) having few stories. **2** (of trousers) cut so as to fit low on the hips rather than on the waist.

low sea·son ▶ n. the least popular time of year for a vacation, when prices are lowest.

low-slung ▶ adj. **1** lower in height or closer to the ground than usual. **2** (of clothes) cut to fit low on the hips rather than the waist.

low spir·its ▶ pl. n. a feeling of sadness and gloom.

low-tech /ˈlō ˈtek/ (also **lo-tech**) ▶ adj. using or needing only low technology: *low-tech solar heating systems.*

low tech·nol·o·gy ▶ n. less advanced technological development or equipment.

low tide (also **low water**) ▶ n. the state of the tide when at its lowest level.

low-wa·ter mark ▶ n. the level reached by the sea at low tide.

lox /läks/ ▶ n. smoked salmon.

loy·al /ˈloiəl/ ▶ adj. showing firm and constant

support for a person, an organization, or one's country. ■ **loy·al·ly** adv.

loy·al·ist /'lɔiəlist/ ▸ n. **1** a person who remains loyal to the established ruler or government. **2** (**Loyalist**) a colonist of the American Revolutionary period who supported the British. ■ **loy·al·ism** /-ˌlizəm/ n.

loy·al·ty /'lɔiəltē/ ▸ n. (pl. **loyalties**) **1** the state of being loyal or faithful to a person, an organization, or one's country. **2** a strong feeling of support or commitment: *arguments with in-laws can cause divided loyalties.*

loz·enge /'läzənj/ ▸ n. **1** a small tablet of medicine that is sucked to soothe a sore throat. **2** a diamond shape; a rhombus.

LP ▸ abbr. long-playing (phonograph record).

LPG ▸ abbr. liquefied petroleum gas.

LPN ▸ abbr. Licensed Practical Nurse.

Lr ▸ symbol the chemical element lawrencium.

LSAT /'elˌsat/ ▸ abbr. Law School Admission Test.

LSD ▸ n. lysergic acid diethylamide, a powerful drug that causes hallucinations.

Lt ▸ abbr. Lieutenant.

Ltd ▸ abbr. Brit. (after a company name) Limited.

Lu ▸ symbol the chemical element lutetium.

lub·ber /'ləbər/ ▸ n. old use or dialect a big, clumsy person. ■ **lub·ber·ly** adj. & adv.

lube /lōōb/ informal ▸ n. a lubricant. ▸ v. lubricate something.

lu·bri·cant /'lōōbrəkənt/ ▸ n. a substance for lubricating machinery or part of the body.

lu·bri·cate /'lōōbrəˌkāt/ ▸ v. apply a substance such as oil or grease to machinery or part of the body to allow smooth movement. ■ **lu·bri·ca·tion** /ˌlōōbrə'kāsHən/ n. **lu·bri·ca·tor** n.

lu·bri·cious /lōō'brisHəs/ ▸ adj. referring to sexual matters in a crude or offensive way. ■ **lu·bri·cious·ly** adv. **lu·bric·i·ty** /-'brisitē/ n.

lu·cent /'lōōsənt/ ▸ adj. literary glowing with or giving off light; shining. ■ **lu·cen·cy** n.

lu·cid /'lōōsid/ ▸ adj. **1** easy to understand; clear: *a lucid account.* **2** showing an ability to think clearly. **3** literary bright or luminous. ■ **lu·cid·i·ty** /lōō'siditē/ n. **lu·cid·ly** adv.

Lu·ci·fer /'lōōsəfər/ ▸ n. **1** the Devil. **2** (**lucifer**) old use a match.

luck /lək/ ▸ n. **1** good things that happen by chance: *it was just luck that the first goal went in.* **2** chance considered as a force that causes success or failure: *we both had bad luck and lost five thousand dollars.* ▸ v. informal (**luck into/onto**) find or obtain something by good luck. – PHRASES **no such luck** informal unfortunately not. **try one's luck** attempt something risky.

luck·i·ly /'ləkəlē/ ▸ adv. it is fortunate that.

luck·less /'ləkləs/ ▸ adj. having bad luck; unfortunate.

luck·y /'ləkē/ ▸ adj. (**luckier, luckiest**) having, bringing, or resulting from good luck: *seven's my lucky number.*

lu·cra·tive /'lōōkrətiv/ ▸ adj. producing a great deal of profit; profitable. ■ **lu·cra·tive·ly** adv.

lu·cre /'lōōkər/ ▸ n. literary money, especially when gained in an underhanded or dishonorable way.

lu·cu·bra·tion /ˌlōōk(y)ə'brāsHən/ ▸ n. literary a scholarly or pedantic piece of writing.

Lud·dite /'lədˌīt/ ▸ n. **1** often derogatory a person opposed to industrialization or new technology.

2 a member of any of the bands of English workers who opposed mechanization and destroyed machinery in the early 19th century. ■ **Lud·dism** /-ˌizəm/ n. **Lud·dit·ism** /-ˌīt,izəm/ n.

lu·dic /'lōōdik/ ▸ adj. formal spontaneous; playful.

lu·di·crous /'lōōdəkrəs/ ▸ adj. absurd; ridiculous. ■ **lu·di·crous·ly** adv. **lu·di·crous·ness** n.

luff /ləf/ ▸ v. steer a sailing ship nearer the wind.

Luft·waf·fe /'lōōftˌwäfə, -ˌväfə/ ▸ n. the German air force until the end of World War II.

lug[1] /ləg/ ▸ v. (**lugs, lugging, lugged**) carry or drag a heavy object with great effort.

lug[2] ▸ n. **1** a projection on an object by which it may be carried or fixed in place. **2** an uncouth, aggressive man.

luge /lōōzH/ ▸ n. a light toboggan ridden in a sitting or lying position.

Lu·ger /'lōōgər/ ▸ n. trademark a type of German automatic pistol.

lug·gage /'ləgij/ ▸ n. suitcases or other bags for a traveler's belongings.

lug·ger /'ləgər/ ▸ n. a small ship with two or three masts and a four-sided sail on each.

lug nut ▸ n. a large rounded nut used especially to attach a vehicle wheel to its axle.

lu·gu·bri·ous /lə'g(y)ōōbrēəs/ ▸ adj. sad and dismal; mournful. ■ **lu·gu·bri·ous·ly** adv. **lu·gu·bri·ous·ness** n.

lug·worm /'ləgˌwərm/ ▸ n. a worm that lives in muddy sand, used as fishing bait.

luke·warm /'lōōkˌwôrm/ ▸ adj. **1** only slightly warm. **2** not enthusiastic or interested: *a lukewarm response.*

lull /ləl/ ▸ v. **1** calm someone or send them to sleep with soothing sounds or movements. **2** make someone feel secure or confident, even if they are at risk. **3** (of noise or a storm) become quiet or calm. ▸ n. a temporary period of quiet or inactivity.

lull·a·by /'lələˌbī/ ▸ n. (pl. **lullabies**) a soothing song sung to send a child to sleep.

lum·ba·go /ˌləm'bāgō/ ▸ n. pain in the lower back.

lum·bar /'ləmbər, -ˌbär/ ▸ adj. relating to the lower back.

lumbar punc·ture ▸ n. Medicine the taking of spinal fluid from the lower back through a hollow needle, usually for diagnosis.

lum·ber[1] /'ləmbər/ ▸ v. move in a slow, heavy, awkward way.

lum·ber[2] ▸ n. partly prepared timber. ▸ v. cut and prepare forest timber for transport and sale.

lum·ber·jack /'ləmbərˌjak/ (also **lumberman** /'ləmbərˌmən/) ▸ n. a person who fells trees, cuts them into logs, or transports them.

lum·ber·jack shirt ▸ n. a shirt of brushed cotton or flannel, typically with a check pattern.

lum·ber·yard /'ləmbərˌyärd/ ▸ n. a place that sells lumber and other building materials.

lu·men /'lōōmən/ ▸ n. Physics the SI unit of flux of light.

lu·mi·naire /ˌlōōmə'ner/ ▸ n. a complete electric light unit.

lu·mi·nance /'lōōmənəns/ ▸ n. **1** the component of a television signal that carries information on the brightness of the image. **2** Physics the intensity of light emitted from a surface per unit area in a given direction.

lu·mi·nar·y /'lōōməˌnerē/ ▸ n. (pl. **luminaries**) **1** a person who is influential or famous within an area of activity: *culinary luminaries.* **2** old use the sun or moon.

lu·mi·nesce /ˌlo͞oməˈnes/ ▶ v. produce light by luminescence.

lu·mi·nes·cence /ˌlo͞oməˈnesəns/ ▶ n. the production of light by a substance that has not been heated, as in fluorescence. ■ **lu·mi·nes·cent** adj.

lu·mi·nos·i·ty /ˌlo͞oməˈnäsətē/ ▶ n. (pl. **luminosities**) the quality of being bright or shining.

lu·mi·nous /ˈlo͞omənəs/ ▶ adj. **1** bright or shining, especially in the dark. **2** Physics relating to visible light. ■ **lu·mi·nous·ly** adv.

lum·mox /ˈləməks/ ▶ n. informal a clumsy, stupid person.

lump¹ /ləmp/ ▶ n. **1** an irregular mass or piece of something hard or solid. **2** a swelling under the skin. **3** informal a heavy, clumsy, or slow-witted person. ▶ v. treat as alike, regardless of details: *Hong Kong and Bangkok tend to be lumped together in vacation brochures.*
– PHRASES **a lump in the throat** a feeling of tightness in the throat caused by strong emotion.

lump² ▶ v. (**lump it**) informal accept or put up with something whether one likes it or not.

lump·ec·to·my /ˌləmˈpektəmē/ ▶ n. (pl. **lumpectomies**) a surgical operation in which a lump, typically a tumor, is removed from the breast.

lum·pen /ˈləmpən, ˈlo͞om-/ ▶ adj. **1** lumpy and misshapen. **2** uncultured and stupid.

lum·pen·pro·le·tar·i·at /ˈləmpənˌprōləˈte(ə)rēət, ˈlo͞om-/ ▶ n. (in Marxism) the lower orders of society who are not interested in politics or revolutionary advancement.

lump·fish /ˈləmpˌfiSH/ ▶ n. (pl. same or **lumpfishes**) a North Atlantic fish with edible roe.

lump·ish /ˈləmpiSH/ ▶ adj. **1** stupid or slow-witted. **2** roughly or clumsily formed. ■ **lump·ish·ly** adv. **lump·ish·ness** n.

lump sum ▶ n. a single payment made at one time, as opposed to several installments.

lump·y /ˈləmpē/ ▶ adj. (**lumpier, lumpiest**) full of or covered with lumps. ■ **lump·i·ly** adv. **lump·i·ness** n.

lu·na·cy /ˈlo͞onəsē/ ▶ n. (pl. **lunacies**) **1** insanity (not in technical use). **2** great foolishness.

lu·nar /ˈlo͞onər/ ▶ adj. relating to, determined by, or resembling the moon.

lu·nar e·clipse ▶ n. an eclipse in which the moon passes into the earth's shadow.

lu·nar month ▶ n. **1** a month measured between successive new moons (roughly 29½ days). **2** (in general use) four weeks.

lu·na·tic /ˈlo͞onəˌtik/ ▶ n. **1** a person who is mentally ill (not in technical use). **2** a very foolish person.

lu·na·tic a·sy·lum ▶ n. dated a psychiatric hospital.

lu·na·tic fringe ▶ n. a small section within a group, having extreme or eccentric views.

lunch /lənCH/ ▶ n. a meal eaten in the middle of the day. ▶ v. eat lunch. ■ **lunch·er** n.
– PHRASES **out to lunch** informal unbalanced or crazy.

lunch·eon /ˈlənCHən/ ▶ n. formal lunch.

lunch·meat /ˈlənCHˌmēt/ ▶ n. meat sold in slices for sandwiches; cold cuts.

lunch·time /ˈlənCHˌtīm/ ▶ n. the time when lunch is eaten.

lu·nette /lo͞oˈnet/ ▶ n. **1** an arched window or other aperture in a domed ceiling. **2** a crescent-shaped or semicircular alcove containing a painting or statue.

lung /ləNG/ ▶ n. each of the pair of organs within the ribcage of humans and most vertebrates, into which air is drawn in breathing. ■ **lunged** adj. **lung·ful** /-ˌfo͝ol/ n.

lunge¹ /lənj/ ▶ n. **1** a sudden forward movement of the body. **2** a thrust in fencing, in which the leading leg is bent while the back leg remains straightened. ▶ v. (**lunges, lunging** or **lungeing, lunged**) make a sudden forward movement or thrust.

lunge² /lənj/ (also **longe** pronunc. same) ▶ n. a long rein on which a horse is made to move in a circle around its trainer.

lung·fish /ˈləNGˌfiSH/ ▶ n. (pl. same or **lungfishes**) a freshwater fish with one or two sacs that function as lungs, enabling it to breathe air and live dormant in mud to survive drought.

lun·gi /ˈlo͞oNGgē/ ▶ n. (pl. **lungis**) an item of clothing like a sarong, wrapped around the waist and extending to the ankles, worn in India and Burma (Myanmar).

lunk /ləNGk/ (also **lunkhead**) ▶ n. informal a slow-witted person.

lu·pine¹ /ˈlo͞opin/ ▶ n. a plant with a tall stem bearing many small colorful flowers.

lu·pine² /ˈlo͞oˌpīn/ ▶ adj. relating to or like a wolf or wolves.

lu·pus /ˈlo͞opəs/ ▶ n. an ulcerous skin disease, especially **lupus vulgaris** (/ˌvəlˈge(ə)ris/) that is due to direct infection with tuberculosis.

lu·pus er·y·the·ma·to·sus /ˌerəˌTHēməˈtōsəs/ ▶ n. an inflammatory disease causing scaly red patches on the skin.

lurch¹ /lərCH/ ▶ v. make a sudden unsteady movement; stagger. ▶ n. a sudden unsteady movement.

lurch² ▶ n. (in phrase **leave someone in the lurch**) leave someone in a difficult situation without assistance or support.

lure /lo͝or/ ▶ v. tempt someone to do something or to go somewhere. ▶ n. **1** the attractive or tempting qualities of a person or thing: *the lure of the city.* **2** a type of bait used in fishing or hunting. **3** a bunch of feathers with a piece of meat attached to a long string, which a falconer swings around their head to recall a hawk.

lur·ex /ˈlo͝orˌeks/ ▶ n. trademark yarn or fabric incorporating a glittering metallic thread.

lu·rid /ˈlo͝orid/ ▶ adj. **1** unpleasantly vivid in color. **2** deliberately shocking or sensational: *lurid accounts of murders.* ■ **lu·rid·ly** adv. **lu·rid·ness** n.

lurk /lərk/ ▶ v. **1** wait in hiding so as to attack someone or something. **2** be present in an underlying or hidden way: *danger lurks beneath the surface.*

lurk·er /ˈlərkər/ ▶ n. a person who visits an Internet bulletin board or chat room but does not participate.

lus·cious /ˈləSHəs/ ▶ adj. **1** having a pleasingly rich, sweet taste. **2** very pleasing to the senses: *luscious harmonies.* **3** (of a woman) sexually attractive. ■ **lus·cious·ly** adv. **lus·cious·ness** n.

lush¹ /ləsн/ ▶adj. 1 (of vegetation) growing thickly. 2 rich and pleasing to the senses: *the album's lush production.* 3 informal sexually attractive. ■ **lush·ly** adv. **lush·ness** n.

lush² ▶n. informal a drunkard.

lust /ləst/ ▶n. 1 strong sexual desire. 2 a passionate desire for something: *a lust for power.* ▶v. (usu. **lust for/after**) feel strong desire for someone or something.

lus·ter /'ləstər/ (Brit. **lustre**) ▶n. 1 a soft sheen or glow. 2 prestige or distinction: *a celebrity player will add luster to the lineup.* 3 a thin metallic coating used to give an iridescent glaze to ceramics. ■ **lus·tered** adj. **lus·ter·less** adj.

lust·ful /'ləs(t)fəl/ ▶adj. filled with strong sexual desire. ■ **lust·ful·ly** adv. **lust·ful·ness** n.

lus·trous /'ləstrəs/ ▶adj. having a soft glow or sheen. ■ **lus·trous·ly** adv. **lus·trous·ness** n.

lust·y /'ləstē/ ▶adj. (**lustier, lustiest**) healthy and strong; vigorous. ■ **lust·i·ly** adv. **lust·i·ness** n.

lute /lōōt/ ▶n. a stringed instrument with a long neck and a rounded body with a flat front, played by plucking.

lu·te·nist /'lōōtn·ist, 'lōōtnist/ (also **lutanist**) ▶n. a lute player.

lu·te·ti·um /lōō'tēsн(ē)əm/ ▶n. a rare silvery-white metallic chemical element of the lanthanide series.

Lu·ther·an /'lōōтн(ə)rən/ ▶n. a member of the Lutheran Church, a Protestant Church based on the beliefs and teachings of the German theologian Martin Luther. ▶adj. relating to the teachings of Martin Luther or to the Lutheran Church. ■ **Lu·ther·an·ism** /-,nizəm/ n.

lu·thi·er /'lōōtēər/ ▶n. a maker of stringed instruments.

lux /ləks/ ▶n. (pl. same) the SI unit of illumination.

luxe /ləks, lōōks/ ▶n. luxury.

lux·u·ri·ant /,ləg'zнōōrēənt, ,lək'sнōōr-/ ▶adj. 1 (of vegetation or hair) growing thickly and strongly. 2 rich and pleasing to the senses: *the novel's luxuriant prose.* ■ **lux·u·ri·ance** n. **lux·u·ri·ant·ly** adv.

lux·u·ri·ate /,ləg'zнōōrē,āt, ,lək'sнōōr-/ ▶v. (**luxuriate in**) take pleasure in something enjoyable.

lux·u·ri·ous /,ləg'zнōōrēəs, ,lək'sнōōr-/ ▶adj. 1 very elegant, comfortable, and expensive. 2 giving sensual pleasure: *long, luxurious baths.* ■ **lux·u·ri·ous·ly** adv. **lux·u·ri·ous·ness** n.

lux·u·ry /'ləksн(ə)rē, 'ləgzн(ə)-/ ▶n. (pl. **luxuries**) 1 a state of great comfort and elegance, especially when involving great expense. 2 an item that is expensive and enjoyable but not essential. ▶adj. expensive and elegant; luxurious: *a luxury yacht.*

LW ▶abbr. long wave.

lx ▶abbr. Physics lux.

ly·can·thrope /'līkən,тнrōp/ ▶n. a werewolf.

ly·can·thro·py /lī'kanтнrəpē/ ▶n. the mythical transformation of a person into a wolf. ■ **ly·can·throp·ic** /,līkən'тнräpik/ adj.

ly·chee /'lēcнē/ (also **litchi**) ▶n. a small round fruit with sweet white flesh, a large stone, and thin rough skin.

lych·gate /'licн,gāt/ ▶n. a roofed gateway to a churchyard.

ly·co·pene /'līkə,pēn/ ▶n. a red pigment related to carotene and present in tomatoes and many berries and fruits.

Ly·cra /'līkrə/ ▶n. trademark a synthetic elastic fiber or fabric used for close-fitting clothing.

lye /lī/ ▶n. a strongly alkaline solution, especially of potassium hydroxide, used for washing or cleaning.

ly·ing¹ /'lī·iNG/ ▶ present participle of **LIE**¹.

ly·ing² ▶ present participle of **LIE**².

Lyme dis·ease /līm/ ▶n. a form of arthritis caused by bacteria that are transmitted by ticks.

lymph /limf/ ▶n. a colorless fluid containing white blood cells that bathes the tissues of the body.

lym·phat·ic /lim'fatik/ ▶adj. relating to lymph or its production. ▶n. a structure like a vein that conveys lymph in the body.

lym·phat·ic sys·tem ▶n. the network of vessels through which lymph drains from the body tissues into the blood.

lymph node (also **lymph gland**) ▶n. each of a number of small swellings in the body's lymphatic system where lymph is filtered and lymphocytes are formed.

lym·pho·cyte /'limfə,sīt/ ▶n. a form of small leukocyte (white blood cell) with a single round nucleus, occurring especially in the lymphatic system.

lym·pho·ma /lim'fōmə/ ▶n. (pl. **lymphomas**) cancer of the lymph nodes.

lynch /lincн/ ▶v. (of a group) kill someone for an alleged crime without a legal trial, especially by hanging. ■ **lynch·er** n.

lynch·pin /'lincн,pin/ ▶n. variant spelling of LINCHPIN.

lynx /liNGks/ ▶n. a wild cat with a short tail and tufted ears.

lynx-eyed ▶adj. keen-sighted.

ly·on·naise /,līə'nāz/ ▶adj. (especially of sliced potatoes) cooked with onions or with a white wine and onion sauce.

lyre /līr/ ▶n. a stringed instrument like a small U-shaped harp with strings fixed to a crossbar, used especially in ancient Greece.

lyre·bird /'līr,bərd/ ▶n. a large Australian songbird, the male of which has a long lyre-shaped tail.

lyr·ic /'lirik/ ▶n. 1 (also **lyrics**) the words of a song. 2 a fairly short poem expressing the writer's emotions or mood. ▶adj. 1 (of poetry) expressing the writer's emotions or mood, usually briefly. 2 (of a singing voice) light.

lyr·i·cal /'lirikəl/ ▶adj. 1 (of literature, art, or music) expressing the writer's emotions in an imaginative and pleasing way. 2 (of poetry) expressing the writer's emotions or mood; lyric. 3 relating to the words of a popular song. ■ **lyr·i·cal·ly** adv.

– PHRASES **wax lyrical** talk in a very enthusiastic and unrestrained way.

lyr·i·cism /'lirə,sizəm/ ▶n. the expression of emotion in literature or music in an imaginative and pleasing way.

lyr·i·cist /'lirəsist/ ▶n. a person who writes the words to popular songs.

ly·ser·gic ac·id /lī'sərjik, li-/ ▶n. a substance prepared from natural ergot alkaloids or synthetically, from which the drug LSD can be made.

Reference Section

1.
US Presidents

Name	Life dates	Party	Term in office
1. George Washington	1732–1799	Federalist	1789–1797
2. John Adams	1735–1826	Federalist	1797–1801
3. Thomas Jefferson	1743–1826	Democratic-Republican	1801–1809
4. James Madison	1751–1836	Democratic-Republican	1809–1817
5. James Monroe	1758–1831	Democratic-Republican	1817–1825
6. John Quincy Adams	1767–1848	Democratic-Republican	1825–1829
7. Andrew Jackson	1767–1845	Democrat	1829–1837
8. Martin Van Buren	1782–1862	Democrat	1837–1841
9. William Henry Harrison	1773–1841	Whig	1841
10. John Tyler	1790–1862	Whig	1841–1845
11. James Knox Polk	1795–1849	Democrat	1845–1849
12. Zachary Taylor	1784–1850	Whig	1849–1850
13. Millard Fillmore	1800–1874	Whig	1850–1853
14. Franklin Pierce	1804–1869	Democrat	1853–1857
15. James Buchanan	1791–1868	Democrat	1857–1861
16. Abraham Lincoln	1809–1865	Republican	1861–1865
17. Andrew Johnson	1808–1875	Democrat	1865–1869
18. Ulysses Simpson Grant	1822–1885	Republican	1869–1877
19. Rutherford Birchard Hayes	1822–1893	Republican	1877–1881
20. James Abram Garfield	1831–1881	Republican	1881
21. Chester Alan Arthur	1830–1886	Republican	1881–1885
22. (Stephen) Grover Cleveland	1837–1908	Democrat	1885–1889
23. Benjamin Harrison	1833–1901	Republican	1889–1893
24. (Stephen) Grover Cleveland	1837–1908	Democrat	1893–1897
25. William McKinley	1843–1901	Republican	1897–1901
26. Theodore Roosevelt	1858–1919	Republican	1901–1909
27. William Howard Taft	1857–1930	Republican	1909–1913
28. (Thomas) Woodrow Wilson	1856–1924	Democrat	1913–1921
29. Warren Gamaliel Harding	1865–1923	Republican	1921–1923
30. (John) Calvin Coolidge	1872–1933	Republican	1923–1929
31. Herbert Clark Hoover	1874–1964	Republican	1929–1933
32. Franklin Delano Roosevelt	1882–1945	Democrat	1933–1945
33. Harry S Truman	1884–1972	Democrat	1945–1953
34. Dwight David Eisenhower	1890–1969	Republican	1953–1961
35. John Fitzgerald Kennedy	1917–1963	Democrat	1961–1963
36. Lyndon Baines Johnson	1908–1973	Democrat	1963–1969
37. Richard Milhous Nixon	1913–1994	Republican	1969–1974

Name	Life dates	Party	Term in office
38. Gerald Rudolph Ford	1913–2006	Republican	1974–1977
39. James Earl Carter, Jr.	1924–	Democrat	1977–1981
40. Ronald Wilson Reagan	1911–2004	Republican	1981–1989
41. George Herbert Walker Bush	1924–	Republican	1989–1993
42. William Jefferson Clinton	1946–	Democrat	1993–2001
43. George Walker Bush	1946–	Republican	2001–2009

2.
US States

State	Abbreviations		Capital
	traditional	postal	
Alabama	Ala.	AL	Montgomery
Alaska	Alas.	AK	Juneau
Arizona	Ariz.	AZ	Phoenix
Arkansas	Ark.	AR	Little Rock
California	Calif.	CA	Sacramento
Colorado	Colo.	CO	Denver
Connecticut	Conn.	CT	Hartford
Delaware	Del.	DE	Dover
Florida	Fla.	FL	Tallahassee
Georgia	Ga.	GA	Atlanta
Hawaii	—	HI	Honolulu
Idaho	Ida.	ID	Boise
Illinois	Ill.	IL	Springfield
Indiana	Ind.	IN	Indianapolis
Iowa	Ia.	IA	Des Moines
Kansas	Kan.	KS	Topeka
Kentucky	Ky.	KY	Frankfort
Louisiana	La.	LA	Baton Rouge
Maine	Me.	ME	Augusta
Maryland	Md.	MD	Annapolis
Massachusetts	Mass.	MA	Boston
Michigan	Mich.	MI	Lansing
Minnesota	Minn.	MN	St. Paul
Mississippi	Miss.	MS	Jackson
Missouri	Mo.	MO	Jefferson City
Montana	Mont.	MT	Helena
Nebraska	Nebr.	NE	Lincoln
Nevada	Nev.	NV	Carson City
New Hampshire	N.H.	NH	Concord
New Jersey	N.J.	NJ	Trenton
New Mexico	N. Mex.	NM	Santa Fe
New York	N.Y.	NY	Albany
North Carolina	N.C.	NC	Raleigh
North Dakota	N. Dak.	ND	Bismarck
Ohio	—	OH	Columbus
Oklahoma	Okla.	OK	Oklahoma City

State	Abbreviations		Capital
	traditional	postal	
Oregon	Ore.	OR	Salem
Pennsylvania	Pa.	PA	Harrisburg
Rhode Island	R.I.	RI	Providence
South Carolina	S.C.	SC	Columbia
South Dakota	S. Dak.	SD	Pierre
Tennessee	Tenn.	TN	Nashville
Texas	Tex.	TX	Austin
Utah	—	UT	Salt Lake City
Vermont	Vt.	VT	Montpelier
Virginia	Va.	VA	Richmond
Washington	Wash.	WA	Olympia
West Virginia	W. Va.	WV	Charleston
Wisconsin	Wis.	WI	Madison
Wyoming	Wyo.	WY	Cheyenne

3.
Countries of the World

Country	Capital	Continent/Area	Nationality
Afghanistan	Kabul	Asia	Afghan
Albania	Tirana	Europe	Albanian
Algeria	Algiers	Africa	Algerian
Andorra	Andorra la Vella	Europe	Andorran
Angola	Luanda	Africa	Angolan
Antigua and Barbuda	St. John's	North America	Antiguan, Barbudan
Argentina	Buenos Aires	South America	Argentinian, Argentine
Armenia	Yerevan	Europe	Armenian
Australia	Canberra	Australia	Australian
Austria	Vienna	Europe	Austrian
Azerbaijan	Baku	Europe	Azerbaijani
Bahamas,The	Nassau	North America	Bahamian
Bahrain	Manama	Asia	Bahraini
Bangladesh	Dhaka	Asia	Bangladeshi
Barbados	Bridgetown	North America	Barbadian
Belarus	Minsk	Europe	Belorussian, Belarussian, *or* Belarusian
Belgium	Brussels	Europe	Belgian
Belize	Belmopan	North America	Belizean
Benin	Porto Novo	Africa	Beninese
Bhutan	Thimphu	Asia	Bhutanese
Bolivia	La Paz; Sucre	South America	Bolivian
Bosnia and Herzegovina	Sarajevo	Europe	Bosnian, Herzegovinian
Botswana	Gaborone	Africa	Motswana, *sing.*, Batswana, *pl.*
Brazil	Brasilia	South America	Brazilian
Brunei	Bandar Seri Begawan	Asia	Bruneian
Bulgaria	Sofia	Europe	Bulgarian
Burkina Faso	Ouagadougou	Africa	Burkinese
Burma (Myanmar)	Rangoon (Yangon); Nay Pyi Taw	Asia	Burmese
Burundi	Bujumbura	Africa	Burundian, *n.*; Burundi, *adj.*

Country	Capital	Continent/Area	Nationality
Cambodia	Phnom Penh	Asia	Cambodian
Cameroon	Yaoundé	Africa	Cameroonian
Canada	Ottawa	North America	Canadian
Cape Verde	Praia	Africa	Cape Verdean
Central African Republic	Bangui	Africa	Central African
Chad	N'Djamena	Africa	Chadian
Chile	Santiago	South America	Chilean
China	Beijing	Asia	Chinese
Colombia	Bogotá	South America	Colombian
Comoros	Moroni	Africa	Comoran
Congo, Democratic Republic of the (*formerly* Zaire)	Kinshasa	Africa	Congolese
Congo, Republic of the	Brazzaville	Africa	Congolese, *n.*; Congolese *or* Congo, *adj.*
Costa Rica	San José	North America	Costa Rican
Côte d'Ivoire	Yamoussoukro	Africa	Ivorian
Croatia	Zagreb	Europe	Croat, *n.*; Croatian, *adj.*
Cuba	Havana	North America	Cuban
Cyprus	Nicosia	Europe	Cypriot
Czech Republic	Prague	Europe	Czech
Denmark	Copenhagen	Europe	Dane, *n.*; Danish, *adj.*
Djibouti	Djibouti	Africa	Djiboutian
Dominica	Roseau	North America	Dominican
Dominican Republic	Santo Domingo	North America	Dominican
Ecuador	Quito	South America	Ecuadorean
Egypt	Cairo	Africa	Egyptian
El Salvador	San Salvador	North America	Salvadoran
Equatorial Guinea	Malabo	Africa	Equatorial Guinean *or* Equatoguinean
Eritrea	Asmara	Africa	Eritrean
Estonia	Tallinn	Europe	Estonian
Ethiopia	Addis Ababa	Africa	Ethiopian
Fiji	Suva	Oceania	Fijian
Finland	Helsinki	Europe	Finn, *n.*; Finnish, *adj.*
France	Paris	Europe	French
Gabon	Libreville	Africa	Gabonese
Gambia	Banjul	Africa	Gambian
Georgia	Tbilisi	Europe	Georgian
Germany	Berlin	Europe	German
Ghana	Accra	Africa	Ghanaian
Greece	Athens	Europe	Greek

Country	Capital	Continent/Area	Nationality
Grenada	St. George's	North America	Grenadian
Guatemala	Guatemala City	North America	Guatemalan
Guinea	Conakry	Africa	Guinean
Guinea-Bissau	Bissau	Africa	Guinea-Bissauan
Guyana	Georgetown	South America	Guyanese
Haiti	Port-au-Prince	North America	Haitian
Holy See	Vatican City	Europe	
Honduras	Tegucigalpa	North America	Honduran
Hungary	Budapest	Europe	Hungarian
Iceland	Reykjavik	Europe	Icelander, *n.*; Icelandic, *adj.*
India	New Delhi	Asia	Indian
Indonesia	Djakarta	Asia	Indonesian
Iran	Tehran	Asia	Iranian
Iraq	Baghdad	Asia	Iraqi
Ireland, Republic of	Dublin	Europe	Irish
Israel	Jerusalem	Asia	Israeli
Italy	Rome	Europe	Italian
Jamaica	Kingston	North America	Jamaican
Japan	Tokyo	Asia	Japanese
Jordan	Amman	Asia	Jordanian
Kazakhstan	Astana	Asia	Kazakhstani
Kenya	Nairobi	Africa	Kenyan
Kiribati	Tarawa	Oceania	I-Kiribati
Korea, North (*see* North Korea)			
Korea, South (*see* South Korea)			
Kuwait	Kuwait City	Asia	Kuwaiti
Kyrgyzstan	Bishkek	Asia	Kyrgyz
Laos	Vientiane	Asia	Lao *or* Laotian
Latvia	Riga	Europe	Latvian
Lebanon	Beirut	Asia	Lebanese
Lesotho	Maseru	Africa	Mosotho, *sing.*; Basotho, *pl.*; Basotho, *adj.*
Liberia	Monrovia	Africa	Liberian
Libya	Tripoli	Africa	Libyan
Liechtenstein	Vaduz	Europe	Liechtensteiner, *n.*; Liechtenstein, *adj.*
Lithuania	Vilnius	Europe	Lithuanian
Luxembourg	Luxembourg	Europe	Luxembourger, *n.*; Luxembourg, *adj.*
Macedonia	Skopje	Europe	Macedonian
Madagascar	Antananarivo	Africa	Malagasy

Country	Capital	Continent/Area	Nationality
Malawi	Lilongwe	Africa	Malawian
Malaysia	Kuala Lumpur	Asia	Malaysian
Maldives	Male	Asia	Maldivian
Mali	Bamako	Africa	Malian
Malta	Valletta	Europe	Maltese
Marshall Islands	Majuro	Oceania	Marshallese
Mauritania	Nouakchott	Africa	Mauritanian
Mauritius	Port Louis	Africa	Mauritian
Mexico	Mexico City	North America	Mexican
Micronesia	Kolonia	Oceania	Micronesian
Moldova	Chişinău	Europe	Moldovan
Monaco	Monaco	Europe	Monacan *or* Monegasque
Mongolia	Ulaanbaatar	Asia	Mongolian
Montenegro	Podgorica	Europe	Montenegrin
Morocco	Rabat	Africa	Moroccan
Mozambique	Maputo	Africa	Mozambican
Myanmar (*see* Burma)			
Namibia	Windhoek	Africa	Namibian
Nauru	Yaren District	Oceania	Nauruan
Nepal	Kathmandu	Asia	Nepalese
Netherlands	Amsterdam; The Hague	Europe	Dutchman *or* Dutchwoman, *n.*; Dutch, *adj.*
New Zealand	Wellington	Oceania	New Zealander, *n.*; New Zealand, *adj.*
Nicaragua	Managua	North America	Nicaraguan
Niger	Niamey	Africa	Nigerien
Nigeria	Abuja	Africa	Nigerian
North Korea	Pyongyang	Asia	North Korean
Norway	Oslo	Europe	Norwegian
Oman	Muscat	Asia	Omani
Pakistan	Islamabad	Asia	Pakistani
Palau	Koror	Oceania	Palauan
Panama	Panama City	North America	Panamanian
Papua New Guinea	Port Moresby	Oceania	Papua New Guinean
Paraguay	Asunción	South America	Paraguayan
Peru	Lima	South America	Peruvian
Philippines	Manila	Asia	Filipino, *n.*; Philippine, *adj.*
Poland	Warsaw	Europe	Pole, *n.*; Polish, *adj.*
Portugal	Lisbon	Europe	Portuguese
Qatar	Doha	Asia	Qatari
Romania	Bucharest	Europe	Romanian
Russia	Moscow	Europe & Asia	Russian

Country	Capital	Continent/Area	Nationality
Rwanda	Kigali	Africa	Rwandan, Rwandese
Saint Kitts and Nevis	Basseterre	North America	Kittsian; Nevisian
Saint Lucia	Castries	North America	St. Lucian
Saint Vincent and the Grenadines	Kingstown	North America	St. Vincentian *or* Vincentian
Samoa (*formerly* Western Samoa)	Apia	Oceania	Samoan
San Marino	San Marino	Europe	Sammarinese
São Tomé and Príncipe	São Tomé	Africa	Sao Tomean
Saudi Arabia	Riyadh	Asia	Saudi *or* Saudi Arabian
Senegal	Dakar	Africa	Senegalese
Serbia	Belgrade	Europe	Serbian
Seychelles	Victoria	Indian Ocean	Seychellois, *n.*; Seychelles, *adj.*
Sierra Leone	Freetown	Africa	Sierra Leonean
Singapore	Singapore	Asia	Singaporean, *n.*; Singapore, *adj.*
Slovakia	Bratislava	Europe	Slovak
Slovenia	Ljubljana	Europe	Slovene, *n.*; Slovenian, *adj.*
Solomon Islands	Honiara	Oceania	Solomon Islander
Somalia	Mogadishu	Africa	Somali
South Africa	Pretoria; Cape Town	Africa	South African
South Korea	Seoul	Asia	South Korean
Spain	Madrid	Europe	Spanish
Sri Lanka	Colombo	Asia	Sri Lankan
Sudan	Khartoum	Africa	Sudanese
Suriname	Paramaribo	South America	Surinamer, *n.*; Surinamese, *adj.*
Swaziland	Mbabane	Africa	Swazi
Sweden	Stockholm	Europe	Swede, *n.*; Swedish, *adj.*
Switzerland	Berne	Europe	Swiss
Syria	Damascus	Asia	Syrian
Taiwan	Taipei	Asia	Taiwanese
Tajikistan	Dushanbe	Asia	Tajik
Tanzania	Dodoma	Africa	Tanzanian
Thailand	Bangkok	Asia	Thai
Timor-Leste	Dili	Asia	Timor-Lestean
Togo	Lomé	Africa	Togolese
Tonga	Nuku'alofa	Oceania	Tongan
Trinidad and Tobago	Port-of-Spain	South America	Trinidadian; Tobagonian
Tunisia	Tunis	Africa	Tunisian
Turkey	Ankara	Asia & Europe	Turk, *n.*; Turkish, *adj.*
Turkmenistan	Ashgabat	Asia	Turkmen

Country	Capital	Continent/Area	Nationality
Tuvalu	Funafuti	Oceania	Tuvaluan
Uganda	Kampala	Africa	Ugandan
Ukraine	Kiev	Europe	Ukrainian
United Arab Emirates	Abu Dhabi	Africa	Emirati *or* Emirian
United Kingdom	London	Europe	Briton, *n.*; British, *collective pl. & adj.*
United States of America	Washington, DC	North America	American
Uruguay	Montevideo	South America	Uruguayan
Uzbekistan	Tashkent	Asia	Uzbek
Vanuatu	Vila	Oceania	Ni-Vanuatu
Venezuela	Caracas	South America	Venezuelan
Vietnam	Hanoi	Asia	Vietnamese
Western Samoa (*see* Samoa)			
Yemen	Sana'a	Asia	Yemeni
Zaire (*see* Congo)			
Zambia	Lusaka	Africa	Zambian
Zimbabwe	Harare	Africa	Zimbabwean

4.
Standard Weights and Measures with Metric Equivalents and Conversions

Equivalents

Length

1 inch	= 2.54 centimeters
1 foot = 12 inches	= 0.3048 meter
1 yard = 3 feet = 36 inches	= 0.9144 meter
1 (statute) mile = 1,760 yards = 5,280 feet	= 1.609 kilometers

Area

1 sq. inch	= 6.45 sq. centimeters
1 sq. foot = 144 sq. inches	= 9.29 sq. decimeters
1 sq. yard = 9 sq. feet	= 0.836 sq. meter
1 acre = 4,840 sq. yards	= 0.405 hectare
1 sq. mile = 640 acres	= 259 hectares

Volume

CUBIC

1 cu. inch	= 16.4 cu. centimeters
1 cu. foot = 1,728 cu. inches	= 0.0283 cu. meter
1 cu. yard = 27 cu. feet	= 0.765 cu. meter

DRY

1 pint = 33.60 cu. inches	= 0.550 liter
1 quart = 2 pints	= 1.101 liters
1 peck = 8 quarts	= 8.81 liters
1 bushel = 4 pecks	= 35.3 liters

LIQUID

1 fluid ounce	= 29.573 milliliters
1 gill = 4 fluid ounces	= 118.294 milliliters
1 pint = 16 fluid ounces = 28.88 cu. inches	= 0.473 liter
1 quart = 2 pints	= 0.946 liter
1 gallon = 4 quarts	= 3.785 liters

Avoirdupois Weight

1 grain	= 0.065 gram
1 dram	= 1.772 grams
1 ounce = 16 drams	= 28.35 grams
1 pound = 16 ounces = 7,000 grains	= 0.4536 kilogram (0.45359237 exactly)
1 stone (British) = 14 pounds	= 6.35 kilograms
1 ton = 2,000 pounds	
1 hundredweight (US) = 100 pounds	
20 hundredweight (US) = 2,000 pounds	

Conversions

Standard	Multiply by	To get metric
LENGTH		
inches	2.5	centimeters
feet	30	centimeters
yards	0.9	meters
miles	1.6	kilometers
AREA		
square inches	6.5	square centimeters
square feet	0.09	square meters
square yards	0.8	square meters
square miles	2.6	square kilometers
acres	0.4	hectares
VOLUME		
cubic feet	0.03	cubic meters
cubic yards	0.76	cubic meters
teaspoons	5	milliliters
tablespoons	15	milliliters
cubic inches	16	milliliters
fluid ounces	30	milliliters
cups	0.24	liters
pints	0.47	liters
quarts	0.95	liters
gallons	3.8	liters
WEIGHT		
ounces	28	grams
pounds	0.45	kilograms
short tons	0.9	metric tons
TEMPERATURE		
degrees Fahrenheit	subtract 32, then multiply by 5/9	degrees Celsius

5.
Metric Weights and Measures with Standard Equivalents and Conversions

Equivalents

Length

1 millimeter (mm)	= 0.039 inch
1 centimeter (cm) = 10 millimeters	= 0.394 inch
1 decimeter (dm) = 10 centimeters	= 3.94 inches
1 meter (m) = 10 decimeters	= 1.094 yards
1 decameter = 10 meters	= 10.94 yards
1 hectometer = 100 meters	= 109.4 yards
1 kilometer (km) = 1,000 meters	= 0.6214 mile

Area

1 sq. centimeter	= 0.155 sq. inch
1 sq. meter = 10,000 sq. centimeters	= 1.196 sq. yards
1 are = 100 sq. meters	= 119.6 sq. yards
1 hectare = 100 ares	= 2.471 acres
1 sq. kilometer = 100 hectares	= 0.386 sq. mile

Volume

CUBIC

1 cu. centimeter	= 0.061 cu. inch
1 cu. meter = 1,000,000 cu. centimeters	= 1.308 cu. yards

CAPACITY

1 milliliter (ml)	= 0.034 fluid ounce
1 centiliter (cl) = 10 milliliters	= 0.34 fluid ounce
1 deciliter (dl) = 10 centiliters	= 3.38 fluid ounces
1 liter (l) = 10 deciliters	= 1.06 quarts
1 decaliter = 10 liters	= 2.64 gallons
1 hectoliter = 100 liters	= 2.75 bushels

Weight

1 milligram (mg)	= 0.015 grain
1 centigram = 10 milligrams	= 0.154 grain
1 decigram (dg) = 10 centigrams	= 1.543 grains
1 gram (g) = 10 decigrams	= 15.43 grains
1 decagram = 10 grams	= 5.64 drams
1 hectogram = 100 grams	= 3.527 ounces
1 kilogram (kg) = 1,000 grams	= 2.205 pounds
1 ton (metric ton) = 1,000 kilograms	= 0.984 (long) ton

Conversions

Metric	Multiply by	To get standard
LENGTH		
millimeters	0.04	inches
centimeters	0.4	inches
meters	3.3	feet
meters	1.1	yards
kilometers	0.6	miles
AREA		
square centimeters	0.16	square inches
square meters	1.2	square yards
square kilometers	0.4	square miles
hectares	2.5	acres
VOLUME		
cubic meters	35	cubic feet
cubic meters	1.3	cubic yards
milliliters	0.03	fluid ounces
milliliters	0.06	cubic inches
liters	2.1	pints
liters	1.06	quarts
liters	0.26	gallons
WEIGHT		
grams	0.035	ounces
kilograms	2.2	pounds
metric tons	1.1	short tons
TEMPERATURE		
degrees Celsius	9/5, then add 32	degrees Fahrenheit

6.
Chemical Elements

Element	Symbol	Atomic Number	Element	Symbol	Atomic Number
actinium	Ac	89	germanium	Ge	32
aluminum	Al	13	gold	Au	79
americium	Am	95	hafnium	Hf	72
antimony	Sb	51	hassium	Hs	108
argon	Ar	18	helium	He	2
arsenic	As	33	holmium	Ho	67
astatine	At	85	hydrogen	H	1
barium	Ba	56	indium	In	49
berkelium	Bk	97	iodine	I	53
beryllium	Be	4	iridium	Ir	77
bismuth	Bi	83	iron	Fe	26
bohrium	Bh	107	krypton	Kr	36
boron	B	5	lanthanum	La	57
bromine	Br	35	lawrencium	Lr	103
cadmium	Cd	48	lead	Pb	82
calcium	Ca	20	lithium	Li	3
californium	Cf	98	lutetium	Lu	71
carbon	C	6	magnesium	Mg	12
cerium	Ce	58	manganese	Mn	25
cesium	Cs	55	meitnerium	Mt	109
chlorine	Cl	17	mendelevium	Md	101
chromium	Cr	24	mercury	Hg	80
cobalt	Co	27	molybdenum	Mo	42
copper	Cu	29	neodymium	Nd	60
curium	Cm	96	neon	Ne	10
darmstadtium	Ds	110	neptunium	Np	93
dubnium	Db	105	nickel	Ni	28
dysprosium	Dy	66	niobium	Nb	41
einsteinium	Es	99	nitrogen	N	7
erbium	Er	68	nobelium	No	102
europium	Eu	63	osmium	Os	76
fermium	Fm	100	oxygen	O	8
fluorine	F	9	palladium	Pd	46
francium	Fr	87	phosphorus	P	15
gadolinium	Gd	64	platinum	Pt	78
gallium	Ga	31	plutonium	Pu	94

Element	Symbol	Atomic Number
polonium	Po	84
potassium	K	19
praseodymium	Pr	59
promethium	Pm	61
protactinium	Pa	91
radium	Ra	88
radon	Rn	86
rhenium	Re	75
rhodium	Rh	45
rubidium	Rb	37
ruthenium	Ru	44
rutherfordium	Rf	104
samarium	Sm	62
scandium	Sc	21
seaborgium	Sg	106
selenium	Se	34
silicon	Si	14
silver	Ag	47
sodium	Na	11
strontium	Sr	38

Element	Symbol	Atomic Number
sulfur	S	16
tantalum	Ta	73
technetium	Tc	43
tellurium	Te	52
terbium	Tb	65
thallium	Tl	81
thorium	Th	90
thulium	Tm	69
tin	Sn	50
titanium	Ti	22
tungsten (or wolfram)	W	74
uranium	U	92
vanadium	V	23
xenon	Xe	54
ytterbium	Yb	70
yttrium	Y	39
zinc	Zn	30
zirconium	Zr	40

Mm

M[1] (also **m**) ▶ n. (pl. **Ms** or **M's**) **1** the thirteenth letter of the alphabet. **2** the Roman numeral for 1,000.

M[2] ▶ abbr. **1** male. **2** medium. **3** mega-. **4** Monsieur. **5** motorway.

m ▶ abbr. **1** married. **2** masculine. **3** Physics mass. **4** Chemistry meta-. **5** meter(s). **6** mile(s). **7** milli-. **8** million(s). **9** minute(s).

MA ▶ abbr. **1** Massachusetts. **2** Master of Arts.

ma /mä/ ▶ n. informal a person's mother.

ma'am /mam/ ▶ n. a term of respectful or polite address used for a woman; madam.

ma·ca·bre /məˈkäbrə, -ˈkäb/ ▶ adj. disturbing and horrifying because concerned with death or injury.

mac·ad·am /məˈkadəm/ ▶ n. broken stone used with tar or bitumen for surfacing roads and paths.

mac·a·da·mi·a /ˌmakəˈdāmēə/ ▶ n. the round edible nut of an Australian tree.

ma·caque /məˈkäk, -ˈkak/ ▶ n. a medium-sized monkey with a long face and cheek pouches for holding food.

mac·a·ro·ni /ˌmakəˈrōnē/ ▶ n. **1** pasta in the form of narrow curved tubes. **2** (pl. **macaronies**) an 18th-century British dandy who imitated continental fashions.

mac·a·roon /ˌmakəˈrōon/ ▶ n. a light cookie made with egg white and ground almonds or coconut.

ma·caw /məˈkô/ ▶ n. a large brightly colored parrot with a long tail, native to Central and South America.

Mc·Car·thy·ism /məˈkärTHēˌizəm/ ▶ n. a campaign against alleged communists in the US government and other organizations carried out under Senator Joseph McCarthy from 1950–54. ■ **Mc·Car·thy·ite** /-THēˌīt/ adj. & n.

mac·chi·a·to /ˌmäkēˈätō/ ▶ n. espresso coffee with a dash of frothy steamed milk.

Mc·Coy /məˈkoi/ ▶ n. (in phrase **the real McCoy**) informal the real thing.

Mace /mās/ ▶ n. trademark an irritant chemical used in an aerosol to disable attackers.

mace[1] /mās/ ▶ n. **1** a ceremonial staff carried as a symbol of authority by certain officials. **2** historical a heavy club with a spiked metal head.

mace[2] ▶ n. a spice consisting of the dried outer covering of the nutmeg.

Mac·e·do·ni·an /ˌmasəˈdōnēən/ ▶ n. a person from the republic of Macedonia (formerly part of Yugoslavia), ancient Macedonia, or the modern Greek region of Macedonia. ▶ adj. relating to Macedonia.

mac·er·ate /ˈmasəˌrāt/ ▶ v. soften or break up food by soaking in a liquid. ■ **mac·er·a·tion** /ˌmasəˈrāSHən/ n.

Mc·Guf·fin /məˈgəfin/ ▶ n. an object or device in a movie or a book that serves merely as a trigger for the plot.

Mach /mäk, mäKH/ ▶ n. used with a numeral (as **Mach 1, Mach 2**, etc.) to indicate the speed of sound, twice the speed of sound, etc.

ma·chet·e /məˈSHetē/ ▶ n. a broad, heavy knife used as an implement or weapon.

Mach·i·a·vel·li·an /ˌmakēəˈvelēən, ˌmäk-/ ▶ adj. cunning, scheming, and unscrupulous.

ma·chic·o·la·tion /məˌCHikəˈlāSHən/ ▶ n. (in medieval fortifications) an opening between the supports of a projecting structure, through which stones or burning objects could be dropped on attackers. ■ **ma·chic·o·lat·ed** /məˈCHikəˌlātid/ adj.

ma·chin·a·ble /məˈSHēnəbəl/ ▶ adj. (of a material) able to be worked by a machine tool. ■ **ma·chin·a·bil·i·ty** /məˌSHēnəˈbilətē/ n.

mach·i·na·tions /ˌmakəˈnāSHənz, ˌmaSHə-/ ▶ pl.n. secret plots; scheming.

ma·chine /məˈSHēn/ ▶ n. **1** a device using mechanical power and having several parts, for performing a particular task. **2** a well-organized group of influential people: *the council's publicity machine*. ▶ v. make or operate on something with a machine.

ma·chine code (also **machine language**) ▶ n. a computer programming language consisting of instructions that a computer can respond to directly.

ma·chine gun ▶ n. an automatic gun that fires bullets in rapid succession for as long as the trigger is pressed. ▶ v. (**machine-gun**) shoot someone with a machine gun.

ma·chine-read·a·ble ▶ adj. in a form that a computer can process.

ma·chin·er·y /məˈSHēn(ə)rē/ ▶ n. **1** machines as a whole, or the components of a machine. **2** an organized system or structure: *the machinery of the state*.

ma·chine tool ▶ n. a fixed power tool for cutting or shaping metal, wood, etc.

ma·chine trans·la·tion ▶ n. translation carried out by a computer.

ma·chin·ist /məˈSHēnist/ ▶ n. a person who operates a machine or who makes machinery.

ma·chis·mo /məˈCHēzmō, -ˈkēz-/ ▶ n. strong or aggressive masculine pride.

ma·cho /ˈmäCHō, ˈmaCHō/ ▶ adj. showing aggressive pride in one's masculinity.

mack·er·el /ˈmak(ə)rəl/ ▶ n. an edible sea fish with a greenish-blue back.

mack·in·tosh /ˈmakənˌtäSH/ (also **macintosh**) ▶ n. Brit. a full-length waterproof coat.

mac·ra·mé /ˈmakrəˌmā/ ▶ n. the craft of knotting cord or string in patterns to make decorative articles.

mac·ro /'makrō/ ▶ n. (pl. **macros**) Computing a single instruction that expands automatically into a set of instructions to perform a particular task.

macro- ▶ comb.form large; large-scale: *macroeconomics.*

mac·ro·bi·ot·ic /ˌmakrōbī'ätik/ ▶ adj. (of diet) consisting of unprocessed organic foods, based on Buddhist principles of the balance of yin and yang.

mac·ro·car·pa /'makrəˌkärpə/ ▶ n. a Californian cypress tree with a large spreading crown of horizontal branches.

mac·ro·cosm /'makrəˌkäzəm/ ▶ n. the whole of a complex structure (such as the world) contrasted with a small or representative part of it (a microcosm). ■ **mac·ro·cos·mic** /ˌmakrə'käzmik/ adj.

mac·ro·ec·o·nom·ics /'makrōˌekə'nämiks, -ˌēkə-/ ▶ pl.n. (treated as sing.) the branch of economics concerned with large-scale economic factors, such as interest rates.

mac·ro lens ▶ n. a camera lens suitable for taking photographs unusually close to the subject.

mac·ro·mol·e·cule /ˌmakrō'mäləˌkyōōl/ ▶ n. a molecule containing a very large number of atoms, such as a protein. ■ **mac·ro·mo·lec·u·lar** /-mə'lekyələr/ adj.

ma·cron /'māˌkrän, 'mak-, 'mākrən/ ▶ n. a written or printed mark (¯) used to indicate a long vowel in some languages, or a stressed vowel in verse.

mac·ro·phage /'makrəˌfāj/ ▶ n. a large phagocytic cell found in stationary form in the tissues or as a mobile white blood cell, especially at sites of infection.

mac·ro·scop·ic /ˌmakrə'skäpik/ ▶ adj. **1** visible to the naked eye; not microscopic. **2** relating to large-scale or general analysis.

mac·u·la /'makyələ/ (also **macule** /'makˌyōōl/) ▶ n. (pl. **maculae** /-ˌlē, -ˌlī/) Medicine an area of skin discoloration.

ma·cum·ba /mə'kōōmbə/ ▶ n. a religion of African origin practiced in Brazil, using sorcery, ritual dance, and fetishes.

mad /mad/ ▶ adj. (**madder, maddest**) **1** mentally ill. **2** very foolish; not sensible. **3** impulsive, confused, or frenzied: *it was a mad dash to get away.* **4** informal very enthusiastic about something. **5** informal very angry. **6** (of a dog) having rabies. ■ **mad·ly** adv. **mad·ness** n.

Mad·a·gas·can /ˌmadə'gaskən/ ▶ n. a person from Madagascar. ▶ adj. relating to Madagascar.

mad·am /'madəm/ ▶ n. **1** a polite form of address for a woman. **2** a woman who runs a brothel.

Mad·ame /mə'däm, -'dam/ ▶ n. (pl. **Mesdames** /mā'däm, -'dam/) a title or form of address for a French-speaking woman.

mad·cap /'madˌkap/ ▶ adj. foolish or reckless.

mad cow dis·ease ▶ n. informal term for **BSE**.

MADD /mad/ ▶ abbr. Mothers Against Drunk Driving.

mad·den /'madn/ ▶ v. **1** drive someone insane. **2** make someone very annoyed.

mad·der /'madər/ ▶ n. a red dye or pigment obtained from the roots of a plant.

mad·ding /'madiNG/ ▶ adj. literary acting madly; frenzied: *far from the madding crowd.*

made /mād/ ▶ past and past participle of **MAKE**.

Ma·dei·ra /mə'di(ə)rə, mə'de(ə)rə/ ▶ n. a strong sweet white wine from the island of Madeira in the Atlantic Ocean.

mad·e·leine /'madl-ən, ˌmadl-'än/ ▶ n. a small rich sponge cake.

Mad·e·moi·selle /ˌmad(ə)m(w)ə'zel, mam'zel/ ▶ n. (pl. **Mesdemoiselles** /ˌmād(ə)m(w)ə'zel(z)/) a title or form of address for an unmarried French-speaking woman.

made to meas·ure ▶ adj. specially made to fit a particular person or thing: *made-to-measure curtains.*

made-up ▶ adj. **1** wearing makeup. **2** invented; untrue.

mad·house /'madˌhous/ ▶ n. **1** informal a scene of great confusion or uproar. **2** historical an institution for the mentally ill.

mad·man /'madˌman, -mən/ (or **madwoman**) ▶ n. (pl. **madmen** or **madwomen**) **1** a person who is mentally ill. **2** a foolish or reckless person.

Ma·don·na /mə'dänə/ ▶ n. (**the Madonna**) the Virgin Mary.

mad·ras /'madrəs, mə'dras, mə'dräs/ ▶ n. **1** a colorful striped or checked cotton fabric. **2** a hot spiced curry dish.

mad·ri·gal /'madrigəl/ ▶ n. a 16th- or 17th-century song for several voices without instrumental accompaniment.

mael·strom /'mālˌsträm, -strəm/ ▶ n. **1** a powerful whirlpool. **2** a state or situation of confused movement or turmoil: *they were caught up in a maelstrom of change.*

mae·nad /'mēˌnad/ ▶ n. (in ancient Greece) a female follower of the god Bacchus, associated with frenzied rites.

maes·tro /'mīstrō/ ▶ n. (pl. **maestri** /'mīstrē/ or **maestros**) **1** a distinguished male conductor or performer of classical music. **2** a distinguished man in any area of activity.

Ma·fi·a /'mäfēə/ ▶ n. **1** (**the Mafia**) an international criminal organization originating in Sicily. **2** (**mafia**) a powerful group who secretly influence matters: *the top tennis mafia.*

Ma·fi·o·so /ˌmäfē'ōsō, -zō/ ▶ n. (pl. **Mafiosi** /-sē, -zē/) a member of the Mafia.

mag /mag/ ▶ n. informal a magazine (periodical).

mag·a·zine /ˌmagə'zēn, 'magəˌzēn/ ▶ n. **1** a periodical publication containing articles and illustrations. **2** a regular television or radio program dealing with a variety of items. **3** a chamber holding cartridges to be fed automatically to the breech of a gun. **4** a store for arms, ammunition, and explosives.

mage /māj/ ▶ n. old use or literary a magician or learned person.

ma·gen·ta /mə'jentə/ ▶ n. a light reddish-purple color.

mag·got /'magət/ ▶ n. a soft-bodied legless larva of a fly or other insect, found in decaying matter.

ma·gi /'mājī/ ▶ plural of **MAGUS**.

mag·ic /'majik/ ▶ n. **1** the power of apparently using mysterious or supernatural forces to make things happen. **2** conjuring tricks performed to entertain. **3** a mysterious and fascinating quality: *the magic of the theater.* **4** informal exceptional skill or talent. ▶ adj. apparently having supernatural powers. ▶ v. (**magics, magicking, magicked**) do or create by or as if by magic: *they magicked their island out of sight.*

mag·i·cal /'majikəl/ ▶ adj. **1** relating to or using magic. **2** very pleasant or enjoyable. ■ **mag·i·cal·ly** adv.

mag·ic car·pet ▶ n. (especially in Arabian stories) a carpet that is able to transport people through the air.

ma·gi·cian /mə'jishən/ ▶ n. **1** a person with magic powers. **2** a conjuror.

mag·ic lan·tern ▶ n. an early form of projector for showing photographic slides.

mag·ic mush·room ▶ n. informal a toadstool that causes hallucinations if eaten.

mag·ic re·al·ism (also **magical realism**) ▶ n. a type of literature in which realistic narrative is combined with surreal elements of dream or fantasy.

mag·is·te·ri·al /ˌmajəˈsti(ə)rēəl/ ▶ adj. **1** having or showing great authority: *a magisterial volume.* **2** relating to a magistrate. ■ **mag·is·te·ri·al·ly** adv.

mag·is·tra·cy /ˈmajəstrəsē/ ▶ n. (pl. **magistracies**) **1** the position or authority of a magistrate. **2** magistrates as a group.

mag·is·trate /ˈmajəˌstrāt/ ▶ n. an official who administers the law, especially one with authority to judge minor cases and hold preliminary hearings.

mag·lev /ˈmagˌlev/ ▶ n. a transport system in which trains glide above a track, supported by magnetic repulsion.

mag·ma /ˈmagmə/ ▶ n. very hot fluid or semifluid material within the earth's crust from which lava and other igneous rock is formed by cooling.

Mag·na Car·ta /ˌmagnə ˈkärtə/ ▶ n. a charter of liberty and political rights signed by King John of England in 1215.

mag·nan·i·mous /magˈnanəməs/ ▶ adj. generous or forgiving, especially toward a rival or less powerful person. ■ **mag·na·nim·i·ty** /ˌmagnəˈnimətē/ n. **mag·nan·i·mous·ly** adv.

mag·nate /ˈmagˌnāt, ˈmagnət/ ▶ n. a wealthy and influential businessman or businesswoman.

mag·ne·sia /magˈnēzhə, -ˈnēshə/ ▶ n. a compound of magnesium used to reduce stomach acid and as a laxative.

mag·ne·si·um /magˈnēzēəm, -zhəm/ ▶ n. a silvery-white metallic element that burns with a brilliant white flame.

mag·net /ˈmagnət/ ▶ n. **1** a piece of iron or other material that can attract iron-containing objects and that points north and south when suspended. **2** a person or thing that has a powerful attraction: *the beach is a magnet for sun-worshipers.*

mag·net·ic /magˈnetik/ ▶ adj. **1** having the property of magnetism. **2** very attractive. ■ **mag·net·i·cal·ly** adv.

mag·net·ic field ▶ n. a region around a magnet within which the force of magnetism acts.

mag·net·ic mine ▶ n. a mine that detonates when it comes near a magnetized body such as a ship or tank.

mag·net·ic north ▶ n. the direction in which the north end of a compass needle will point in response to the earth's magnetic field.

mag·net·ic pole ▶ n. each of the points near the geographical North and South Poles, indicated by the needle of a magnetic compass.

mag·net·ic res·o·nance im·ag·ing ▶ n. a technique for producing images of bodily organs by measuring the response of the atomic nuclei of body tissues to high-frequency radio waves when placed in a strong magnetic field.

mag·net·ic storm ▶ n. a disturbance of the magnetic field of the earth.

mag·net·ic tape ▶ n. tape used in recording sound, pictures, or computer data.

mag·net·ism /ˈmagnəˌtizəm/ ▶ n. **1** the property displayed by magnets and produced by the motion of electric charges, which results in objects being attracted or pushed away. **2** the ability to attract and charm people.

mag·net·ite /ˈmagnəˌtīt/ ▶ n. a gray-black magnetic mineral that is an important form of iron ore.

mag·net·ize /ˈmagnəˌtīz/ ▶ v. give magnetic properties to something.

mag·ne·to /magˈnētō/ ▶ n. (pl. **magnetos**) a small electric generator containing a permanent magnet and used to provided high-voltage pulses, especially (formerly) in the ignition systems of internal-combustion engines.

mag·ne·tom·e·ter /ˌmagnəˈtämətər/ ▶ n. an instrument used for measuring magnetic forces, especially the earth's magnetism.

mag·ne·tron /ˈmagnəˌträn/ ▶ n. an electron tube for amplifying or generating microwaves, with the flow of electrons controlled by an external magnetic field.

mag·net school ▶ n. a public school offering special instruction and programs not available elsewhere.

Mag·nif·i·cat /magˈnifiˌkät, mänˈyifi-/ ▶ n. the hymn of the Virgin Mary (Gospel of Luke, chapter 1), sung as a regular part of a Christian service.

mag·ni·fi·ca·tion /ˌmagnəfiˈkāshən/ ▶ n. **1** the action of magnifying something with a lens or microscope. **2** the degree to which something can be made to appear larger by means of a lens or microscope.

mag·nif·i·cence /magˈnifəsəns/ ▶ n. the quality of being very impressive or attractive: *the magnificence of nature.*

mag·nif·i·cent /magˈnifəsənt/ ▶ adj. **1** very beautiful, impressive, or elaborate. **2** very good; excellent. ■ **mag·nif·i·cent·ly** adv.

mag·nif·i·co /magˈnifiˌkō/ ▶ n. (pl. **magnificoes**) informal an important or powerful person.

mag·ni·fy /ˈmagnəˌfī/ ▶ v. (**magnifies**, **magnifying**, **magnified**) **1** make something appear larger than it is, especially with a lens or microscope. **2** intensify or increase: *that way we can magnify our efforts.* **3** old use praise someone or something highly. ■ **mag·ni·fi·er** n.

mag·ni·fy·ing glass ▶ n. a lens that produces an enlarged image, used to examine small or finely detailed things.

mag·nil·o·quent /magˈniləkwənt/ ▶ adj. formal using language that is excessively elaborate or pompous.

mag·ni·tude /ˈmagnəˌtoōd/ ▶ n. **1** great size, extent, or importance: *events of tragic magnitude.* **2** the size of something. **3** the degree of brightness of a star.

mag·no·lia /magˈnōlyə/ ▶ n. a tree or shrub with large creamy-pink or -white waxy flowers.

mag·nox /ˈmagˌnäks/ ▶ n. a magnesium-based alloy used to enclose uranium fuel elements in some nuclear reactors.

mag·num /ˈmagnəm/ ▶ n. (pl. **magnums**) **1** a wine bottle of twice the standard size, normally 1½ liters. **2** trademark a gun designed to fire cartridges that are more powerful than its caliber would suggest.

mag·num o·pus /ˈmagnəm ˈōpəs/ ▶ n. a work of art, music, or literature that is the most important that a person has produced.

mag·pie /'mag,pī/ ▸ n. **1** a black and white bird with a long tail and a noisy cry. **2** a person who obsessively collects unimportant things.

ma·gus /'māgəs/ ▸ n. (pl. **magi** /'mā,jī/) **1** a priest of ancient Persia. **2** a sorcerer. **3** (**the Magi**) the three wise men from the East who brought gifts to the infant Jesus.

Mag·yar /'mag,yär/ ▸ n. **1** a member of the predominant people in Hungary. **2** the Hungarian language.

ma·ha·ra·ja /,mähə'räjə, -'räzнə/ (also **maharajah**) ▸ n. historical an Indian prince.

ma·ha·ra·ni /,mähə'ränē/ ▸ n. historical a maharaja's wife or widow.

Ma·ha·ri·shi /,mähə'rēsнē, mə'härəsнē/ ▸ n. a great Hindu wise man or spiritual leader.

ma·hat·ma /mə'hätmə, -'hatmə/ ▸ n. (in the Indian subcontinent) a holy or wise person regarded with love and respect.

Ma·ha·ya·na /,mähə'yänə/ ▸ n. one of the two major traditions of Buddhism (the other being Theravada), practiced especially in China, Tibet, Japan, and Korea.

Ma·hi·can /mə'hēkən/ (also **Mohican** /mō'hēkən/) ▸ n. **1** a member of an American Indian people formerly inhabiting the Upper Hudson Valley in New York. **2** the Algonquian language of this people. ▸ adj. relating to the Mahicans.

ma·hi·ma·hi /,mähē'mähē/ ▸ n. an edible marine fish of warm seas, with silver and bright blue or green coloration.

mah-jongg /mä 'zнäng, -zнông/ (also **mah-jong**) ▸ n. a Chinese game played with 136 or 144 small rectangular tiles.

ma·hog·a·ny /mə'hägənē/ ▸ n. **1** hard reddish-brown wood from a tropical tree, used for furniture. **2** a rich reddish-brown color.

ma·hout /mə'hout/ ▸ n. (in the Indian subcontinent and SE Asia) a person who works with and rides an elephant.

maid /mād/ ▸ n. **1** a female domestic servant. **2** old use a girl or young woman.

maid·en /'mādn/ ▸ n. old use an unmarried girl or young woman, especially a virgin. ▸ adj. **1** (of an older woman) unmarried. **2** first of its kind: *a maiden voyage.*

maid·en·hair fern /'mādn,he(ə)r/ ▸ n. a fern with fine stems and delicate fronds.

maid·en·head /'mādn,hed/ ▸ n. old use **1** a girl's or woman's virginity. **2** the hymen.

maid·en name ▸ n. the surname of a married woman before her marriage.

maid of hon·or ▸ n. **1** a principal bridesmaid. **2** an unmarried noblewoman attending a queen or princess.

maid·serv·ant /'mād,sərvənt/ ▸ n. dated a female servant.

mail¹ /māl/ ▸ n. **1** letters and packages sent by the postal system. **2** the postal system. **3** email. ▸ v. **1** send a letter or package using the postal system. **2** send email to someone.

mail² ▸ n. historical flexible armor made of metal rings or plates.

mail·bag /'māl,bag/ ▸ n. a large sack or bag for carrying mail.

mail·box /'māl,bäks/ ▸ n. **1** a box for mail at the entrance to a person's house. **2** a public box into which mail is placed for collection. **3** a computer file in which emails are stored.

mail car·ri·er ▸ n. a person who is employed to deliver and collect letters and parcels.

mail·er /'mālər/ ▸ n. **1** the sender of a letter or package by mail. **2** a container for conveying items by mail, typically a padded envelope or protective tube. **3** a computer program that sends email.

mail·ing /'māling/ ▸ n. an item of advertising mailed to a large number of people.

mail·ing list ▸ n. a list of the names and addresses of people to whom advertising matter or information may be mailed regularly.

mail·man /'māl,man/ ▸ n. (pl. **mailmen**) a person who is employed to deliver and collect letters and packages.

mail or·der ▸ n. the selling of goods by mail.

maim /mām/ ▸ v. injure someone so that part of the body is permanently damaged.

main /mān/ ▸ adj. chief in size or importance. ▸ n. **1** a principal water or gas pipe or electricity cable. **2** (**the main**) old use or literary the open ocean.
– PHRASES **in the main** on the whole.

main·board /'mān,bôrd/ ▸ n. another term for MOTHERBOARD.

main brace ▸ n. the rope attached to the main yard (spar) of a sailing ship.

main clause ▸ n. Grammar a clause that can form a complete sentence standing alone, having a subject and a verb.

main course ▸ n. the most substantial course of a meal.

main drag ▸ n. informal the main street of a town.

main·frame /'mān,frām/ ▸ n. a large high-speed computer, especially one supporting numerous workstations.

main·land /'mānlənd, -,land/ ▸ n. the main area of land of a country, not including islands and separate territories.

main line ▸ n. **1** a chief railroad line. **2** informal a principal vein as a site for a drug injection. ▸ v. (**mainline**) informal inject a drug into a vein.

main·ly /'mānlē/ ▸ adv. for the most part; chiefly.

main man ▸ n. informal a close and trusted friend.

main·mast /'mān,mast/ ▸ n. the principal mast of a ship.

main·sail /'mānsəl, -,sāl/ ▸ n. the chief sail of a ship, especially the lowest sail on the mainmast of a square-rigged ship.

main·spring /'mān,spring/ ▸ n. **1** the most influential or important part: *faith was the mainspring of her life.* **2** the chief spring in a watch, clock, etc.

main·stay /'mān,stā/ ▸ n. **1** a thing on which something else is based or depends: *cotton is the mainstay of the economy.* **2** a rope or wire that extends from the top of the mainmast of a sailing ship to the foot of the mast nearest the front.

main·stream /'mān,strēm/ ▸ n. the ideas, attitudes, or activities that are shared by most people. ▸ adj. belonging to or typical of the mainstream. ▸ v. bring into the mainstream: *vegetarianism has been mainstreamed.*

main street ▸ n. **1** the principal street of a town. **2** (**Main Street**) used in reference to the materialism, mediocrity, or parochialism regarded as typical of small-town life.

main·tain /mān'tān/ ▸ v. **1** cause to continue in the same state or at the same level: *she maintained close links with India.* **2** keep a building, machine, or road in good condition by checking or repairing it regularly. **3** provide enough money to support someone. **4** strongly state that something is the case: *he has always maintained his innocence.* ■ **main·tain·a·bil·i·ty** /ˌmānˌtānəˈbilətē/ n. **main·tain·a·ble** adj. **main·tain·er** n.

main·te·nance /ˈmānt(ə)nəns, ˈmāntn-əns/ ▶ n. **1** the process of keeping something in the same state or in good condition. **2** Brit. the provision of financial support for a former husband or wife after divorce.

ma·iol·i·ca /mīˈäləkə/ ▶ n. fine Italian earthenware with colored decoration on an opaque white glaze.

maî·tre d'hô·tel /ˌmātrə dōˈtel, ˌmetrə/ (also **maître d'** /ˌmātrə ˈdē, ˌmātär/) ▶ n. (pl. **maîtres d'hôtel** (pronunc. same) or **maître d's**) the head waiter of a restaurant.

maize /māz/ ▶ n. technical or chiefly British term for CORN¹ (sense 1).

ma·jes·tic /məˈjestik/ ▶ adj. impressively grand or beautiful. ■ **ma·jes·ti·cal·ly** adv.

maj·es·ty /ˈmajəstē/ ▶ n. (pl. **majesties**) **1** impressive grandeur or beauty. **2** royal power. **3** (**His**, **Your**, etc. **Majesty**) a title given to a sovereign or their wife or widow.

ma·jol·i·ca /məˈjälikə/ ▶ n. a kind of earthenware imitating Italian maiolica.

ma·jor /ˈmājər/ ▶ adj. **1** important, serious, or significant. **2** greater or more important; main: *he got the major share of the profit.* **3** (of a musical scale) having intervals of a half step between the third and fourth, and seventh and eighth notes. Contrasted with MINOR. ▶ n. **1** a rank of officer in the US Army, Marine Corps, and Air Force, above captain and below lieutenant colonel. **2** Music a major key, interval, or scale. **3** a student's main subject or course. **4** a student specializing in a specified subject. ▶ v. (**major in**) specialize in a particular subject at a college or university.

Ma·jor·can /məˈjôrkən, mäˈyôrkən/ ▶ n. a person from Majorca. ▶ adj. relating to Majorca.

ma·jor-do·mo /ˌmājər ˈdōmō/ ▶ n. (pl. **major-domos**) the chief steward of a large household.

ma·jor gen·er·al ▶ n. a rank of officer in the US Army, Air Force, and Marine Corps, above brigadier general and below lieutenant general.

ma·jor·i·tar·i·an /məˌjôriˈte(ə)rēən, -ˌjär-/ ▶ adj. governed by or believing in decision by a majority.

ma·jor·i·ty /məˈjôrətē, -ˈjär-/ ▶ n. (pl. **majorities**) **1** the greater number. **2** the number by which votes for one candidate in an election are more than those for all other candidates combined. **3** the age when a person is legally a full adult, usually 18 or 21.

USAGE
The main meaning of **majority** is 'the greater number' and it should be used with plural nouns: *the majority of cases.* It is not good English to use **majority** with nouns that do not take a plural to mean 'the greatest part', as in *she ate the majority of the meal.*

ma·jor·i·ty rule ▶ n. the principle that the greater number of people should exercise greater power.

ma·jor league ▶ n. **1** the highest-level professional league or leagues in a sport, such as the American and National Leagues of baseball.

2 the highest attainable level in any endeavor or activity: *major-league corporations.*

ma·jus·cule /ˈmajəsˌkyo͞ol/ ▶ n. a capital letter.

make /māk/ ▶ v. (past and past part. **made** /mād/) **1** form something by putting parts together or combining substances. **2** cause or bring about something. **3** force someone to do something. **4** (**make something into**) alter something so that it forms something else. **5** add up to: *one and one makes two.* **6** estimate, decide, or calculate something. **7** gain or earn money or profit. **8** be suitable for: *this fern makes a good house plant.* **9** manage to arrive at or achieve something. **10** prepare to go in a particular direction or do a particular thing: *I made toward the car.* **11** (**make it**) become successful. **12** arrange bedclothes tidily on a bed ready for use. ▶ n. the manufacturer or trade name of a product.

– PHRASES **have** (**got**) **it made** informal be in a position where success is certain. **make away with** steal something. **make do** manage with the limited means available. **make for 1** move toward. **2** tend to result in. **3** (**be made for**) be very suitable for. **make it up to** compensate someone for unfair treatment. **make something of 1** give attention or importance to. **2** understand the meaning of. **make off** leave hurriedly. **make off with** steal something. **make or break** be the factor that decides whether something will succeed or fail. **make someone/thing out 1** manage with difficulty to see, hear, or understand someone or something. **2** pretend to be or do something. **3** draw up a list or document. **make out** informal **1** make progress; get on. **2** engage in sexual activity. **make someone over** give someone a new image with cosmetics, hairstyling, and clothes. **make something over 1** transfer the possession of something. **2** redesign or refit something: *Anna helped to make over our website.* **make sail** spread a sail or sails, especially to begin a voyage. **make time** find the time to do something. **make up** become friendly again after a quarrel. **make someone up** apply cosmetics to someone. **make something up 1** put something together from parts or ingredients. **2** invent a story. **3** (also **make up for**) compensate for something. **make up one's mind** make a decision. **make way** allow room for someone or something else. **on the make** informal **1** trying to make money or gain an advantage. **2** looking for a sexual partner.

make-be·lieve ▶ n. a state of fantasy or pretense. ▶ adj. imitating something real; pretend.

make-do ▶ adj. makeshift or temporary.

make·o·ver /ˈmākˌōvər/ ▶ n. a complete transformation of the appearance of someone or something.

mak·er /ˈmākər/ ▶ n. **1** a person or thing that makes something. **2** (**our**, **the**, etc. **Maker**) God. – PHRASES **meet one's Maker** chiefly humorous die.

make·shift /ˈmākˌSHift/ ▶ adj. acting as a temporary substitute or measure.

make·up /ˈmākˌəp/ ▶ n. **1** cosmetics applied to the face. **2** the way in which something is formed or put together: *the makeup of the rock.* **3** the arrangement of written matter, illustrations, etc., on a printed page.

make·weight /ˈmākˌwāt/ ▶ n. **1** an unimportant person or thing that is only included to complete something. **2** something added to make up a required weight.

mak·ing /ˈmākiNG/ ▶ n. **1** (in phrase **be the making of**) bring about the success of.

2 (makings) the necessary qualities: *she had the makings of a great teacher.*

ma·ko /'mākō, 'mäkō/ ▶ n. (pl. **makos**) a large shark with a deep blue back and white underparts.

mal- ▶ comb.form **1** bad; badly: *malodorous.* **2** wrong or incorrectly: *malfunction.* **3** not: *maladroit.*

mal·a·chite /'malə,kīt/ ▶ n. a bright green mineral that contains copper.

mal·ad·just·ed /,malə'jəstid/ ▶ adj. failing to cope with normal social situations.

mal·ad·min·is·tra·tion /,maləd'minə'strāshən/ ▶ n. formal dishonest or inefficient management or administration. ■ **mal·ad·min·is·ter** /,maləd'ministər/ v.

mal·a·droit /,malə'droit/ ▶ adj. inefficient or clumsy.

mal·a·dy /'malədē/ ▶ n. (pl. **maladies**) literary a disease or illness.

Mal·a·gas·y /,malə'gasē/ ▶ n. (pl. same or **Malagasies**) **1** a person from Madagascar. **2** the language of Madagascar.

ma·laise /mə'lāz, -'lez/ ▶ n. a general feeling of unease, bad health, or low spirits.

mal·a·mute /'malə,myōōt/ ▶ n. a powerful dog of a breed with a thick, gray coat, bred by the Inuit and used to pull sleds.

mal·a·prop·ism /'malə,präpizəm/ (also **malaprop** /'malə,präp/) ▶ n. the mistaken use of a word in place of a similar-sounding one (e.g., 'dance a *flamingo*' instead of *flamenco*).

ma·lar·i·a /mə'le(ə)rēə/ ▶ n. a disease that causes recurrent attacks of fever, caused by a parasite that is transmitted by mosquitoes. ■ **ma·lar·i·al** adj.

ma·lar·key /mə'lärkē/ ▶ n. informal nonsense.

mal·a·thi·on /,malə'тнī,än/ ▶ n. a synthetic insecticide containing phosphorus.

Ma·la·wi·an /mə'läwēən/ ▶ n. a person from Malawi in south central Africa. ▶ adj. relating to Malawi.

Ma·lay /mə'lā, 'mā,lā/ ▶ n. **1** a member of a people inhabiting Malaysia and Indonesia. **2** the language of the Malays. ▶ adj. relating to the Malays or their language.

Ma·lay·an /mə'lāən/ ▶ n. another term for MALAY. ▶ adj. relating to Malays or Malaya (now part of Malaysia).

Ma·lay·sian /mə'lāzhən/ ▶ n. a person from Malaysia. ▶ adj. relating to Malaysia.

mal·con·tent /,malkən'tent, 'malkən,tent/ ▶ n. a person who is dissatisfied and rebellious.

Mal·div·i·an /môl'divēən, mäl-/ ▶ n. a person from the Maldives, a country consisting of a chain of islands in the Indian Ocean. ▶ adj. relating to the Maldives.

male /māl/ ▶ adj. **1** relating to the sex that can fertilize or inseminate the female to give rise to offspring. **2** relating to or typical of men: *a deep male voice.* **3** (of a plant or flower) having stamens but not functional pistils. **4** (of a fitting) manufactured to fit inside a corresponding female part. ▶ n. a male person, animal, or plant. ■ **male·ness** n.

mal·e·dic·tion /,malə'dikshən/ ▶ n. a curse.

mal·e·fac·tor /'malə,faktər/ ▶ n. formal a criminal or other wrongdoer.

ma·lef·ic /mə'lefik/ ▶ adj. literary causing harm or destruction. ■ **ma·lef·i·cent** /-'lefəsənt/ adj.

ma·lev·o·lent /mə'levələnt/ ▶ adj. wishing evil to others. ■ **ma·lev·o·lence** n. **ma·lev·o·lent·ly** adv.

mal·fea·sance /mal'fēzəns/ ▶ n. Law wrongdoing, especially by a public official.

mal·for·ma·tion /,malfôr'māshən, -fər-/ ▶ n. **1** a part of the body that is not formed correctly. **2** the state of being abnormally shaped or formed. ■ **mal·formed** /mal'fôrmd/ adj.

mal·func·tion /mal'fəngkshən/ ▶ v. (of equipment or machinery) fail to function normally. ▶ n. a failure to function normally.

Ma·li·an /'mälēən/ ▶ n. a person from Mali, a country in West Africa. ▶ adj. relating to Mali.

mal·ice /'maləs/ ▶ n. the desire to harm someone.

mal·ice a·fore·thought ▶ n. Law the intention to kill or harm, which distinguishes murder from unlawful killing.

ma·li·cious /mə'lishəs/ ▶ adj. intending or intended to do harm: *his talent for malicious gossip.* ■ **ma·li·cious·ly** adv. **ma·li·cious·ness** n.

ma·lign /mə'līn/ ▶ adj. harmful or evil. ▶ v. criticize someone in a spiteful way. ■ **ma·lig·ni·ty** /-'lignətē/ n. **ma·lign·ly** adv.

ma·lig·nan·cy /mə'lignənsē/ ▶ n. (pl. **malignancies**) **1** the presence of a malignant tumor; cancer. **2** a cancerous growth. **3** the quality of being harmful or evil.

ma·lig·nant /mə'lignənt/ ▶ adj. **1** harmful or evil. **2** (of a tumor) tending to grow uncontrollably or to recur after removal; cancerous.

ma·lin·ger /mə'linggər/ ▶ v. pretend to be ill in order to avoid duty or work. ■ **ma·lin·ger·er** n.

mall /môl/ ▶ n. **1** a large enclosed pedestrian shopping area. **2** a sheltered walk or promenade.

mal·lard /'malərd/ ▶ n. a wild duck, the male of which has a dark green head and white collar.

mal·le·a·ble /'malyəbəl, 'malēə-/ ▶ adj. **1** able to be hammered or pressed into shape without breaking or cracking. **2** easily influenced: *a malleable youth.* ■ **mal·le·a·bil·i·ty** /,malyə'bilitē, ,malēə-/ n.

mal·let /'malət/ ▶ n. **1** a hammer with a large wooden head. **2** a long-handled wooden stick with a head like a hammer, for hitting a croquet or polo ball.

mal·low /'malō/ ▶ n. a plant with pink or purple flowers.

malm·sey /'mä(l)mzē/ ▶ n. a very sweet Madeira wine.

mal·nour·ished /mal'nərisht, -'nə-risht/ ▶ adj. suffering from lack of food or of the right foods. ■ **mal·nourish·ment** /-'nərishmənt/ n.

mal·nu·tri·tion /,malnōō'trishən/ ▶ n. the state of not having enough food or not eating enough of the right foods.

mal·oc·clu·sion /,malə'klōōzhən/ ▶ n. imperfect positioning of the teeth when the jaws are closed.

mal·o·dor·ous /mal'ōdərəs/ ▶ adj. smelling very unpleasant.

mal·prac·tice /mal'praktəs/ ▶ n. illegal, corrupt, or negligent professional behavior.

malt /môlt/ ▶ n. barley or other grain that has been soaked in water, allowed to sprout, and dried, used for brewing or distilling. ▶ v. **1** convert grain into malt. **2** (as adj. **malted**) mixed with malt or a malt extract.

Mal·tese /môl'tēz/ ▶ n. (pl. same) a person from Malta. ▶ adj. relating to Malta.

Mal·tese cross ▶ n. a cross with arms of equal

length that broaden from the center and have their ends indented in a shallow V-shape.

Mal·thu·sian /mal'TH(y)o͞oZHən, môl-/ ▸ adj. relating to the theory of the English economist Thomas Malthus that, if unchecked, the population tends to increase at a greater rate than its food supplies. ▸ n. a person who supports this theory.

malt liq·uor ▸ n. alcoholic liquor made from malt by fermentation rather than distillation; beer with a relatively high alcohol content.

malt·ose /'môl,tōs, -,tōz/ ▸ n. a sugar produced by the breakdown of starch, e.g., by enzymes found in malt and saliva.

mal·treat /mal'trēt/ ▸ v. treat a person or animal badly or cruelly. ▪ **mal·treat·ment** n.

malt whis·key ▸ n. whiskey made only from malted barley.

mal·ver·sa·tion /ˌmalvər'sāSHən/ ▸ n. formal corrupt behavior by a person in public office.

mal·ware /'mal,we(ə)r/ ▸ n. software that is intended to damage or disable computers and computer systems.

mam /mäm/ ▸ n. informal a term of respectful or polite address used for a woman; ma'am.

ma·ma /'mämə/ (also **mamma**) ▸ n. 1 one's mother. 2 informal a mature woman: *she is one hot mama.*

mam·ba /'mämbə/ ▸ n. a large, highly venomous African snake.

mam·bo /'mämbō/ ▸ n. (pl. **mambos**) a Latin American dance similar to the rumba.

mam·mal /'mamǝl/ ▸ n. a warm-blooded vertebrate animal that has hair or fur, produces milk, and (typically) bears live young. ▪ **mam·ma·li·an** /mǝ'mālēǝn/ adj.

mam·ma·ry /'mamǝrē/ ▸ adj. relating to the breasts or other milk-producing organs of mammals: *a mammary gland.* ▸ n. (pl. **mammaries**) informal a breast.

mam·mo·gram /'mamǝ,gram/ ▸ n. an image obtained by mammography.

mam·mog·ra·phy /ma'mägrǝfē/ ▸ n. a technique using X-rays to diagnose and locate tumors of the breasts.

Mam·mon /'mamǝn/ ▸ n. wealth regarded as an evil influence or false object of worship.

mam·moth /'mamǝTH/ ▸ n. a large extinct form of elephant with a hairy coat and long curved tusks. ▸ adj. huge; enormous.

mam·my /'mamē/ ▸ n. (pl. **mammies**) informal 1 a child's name for their mother. 2 offensive (formerly in the South) a black nursemaid or nanny in charge of white children.

man /man/ ▸ n. (pl. **men**) 1 an adult human male. 2 a male member of a workforce, team, etc. 3 a husband or lover. 4 a person. 5 human beings in general: *places untouched by man.* 6 a piece or token used in a board game. ▸ v. (**mans, manning, manned**) provide a place or machine with the personnel to run, operate, or defend it. ▸ exclam. informal used for emphasis or to express surprise, admiration, or delight.
– PHRASES **man about town** a fashionable and sociable man. **the man in the street** the average man. **man of the cloth** a clergyman. **man of letters** a male scholar or author. **man to man** in a direct and frank way between two men. **to a man** with no exceptions.

-man ▸ comb.form forming nouns referring to:
1 a man of a specified nationality or origin: *Frenchman.* 2 a person belonging to a specified group or having a specified occupation or role: *chairman.* 3 a ship of a specified kind: *merchantman.*

man·a·cle /'manikǝl/ ▸ n. a metal band or chain fastened around a person's hands or ankles to restrict their movement. ▸ v. restrict someone with a manacle or manacles.

man·age /'manij/ ▸ v. 1 be in charge of people or an organization. 2 control the use of money, time, or other resources. 3 succeed in doing or dealing with: *she eventually managed to buy a house.* 4 succeed or cope despite difficulties. 5 be free to attend an appointment. ▪ **man·ag·ing** adj.

man·age·a·ble /'manijǝbǝl/ ▸ adj. able to be dealt with or controlled without difficulty.

man·aged care ▸ n. a system of health care in which patients visit only certain doctors and hospitals, and in which the cost of treatment is monitored by a managing company.

man·age·ment /'manijmǝnt/ ▸ n. 1 the process of managing people or things. 2 the managers of an organization.

man·age·ment ac·count·ing ▸ n. the provision of financial data and advice to a company for use in the organization and development of its business. ▪ **man·age·ment ac·count·ant** n.

man·ag·er /'manijǝr/ ▸ n. 1 a person who manages an organization, a group of staff, or a sports team. 2 a person in charge of the business affairs of an athlete, actor, or performer. ▪ **man·a·ge·ri·al** /ˌmanǝ'ji(ǝ)rēǝl/ adj. **man·ag·er·ship** /-ˌSHip/ n.

man-at-arms ▸ n. old use a soldier.

man·a·tee /'manǝ,tē/ ▸ n. a large mammal that lives in the sea near tropical Atlantic coasts.

Man·che·go /man'CHāgō/ ▸ n. a Spanish cheese traditionally made with sheep's milk.

Man·chu /'man,CHo͞o, man'CHo͞o/ ▸ n. a member of a people originally living in Manchuria in NE China, who formed the last imperial dynasty of China (1644–1912).

man·da·la /'mandǝlǝ, 'mǝn-/ ▸ n. an intricate circular design symbolizing the universe in Hinduism and Buddhism.

man·da·mus /man'dāmǝs/ ▸ n. a writ issued as a command to an inferior court or ordering a person to perform a public or statutory duty.

man·da·rin /'mandǝrǝn/ ▸ n. 1 (**Mandarin**) the official form of the Chinese language. 2 a high-ranking official in the former imperial Chinese civil service. **3** a powerful official or senior bureaucrat. **4** a small citrus fruit with a loose yellow-orange skin.

man·da·rin col·lar ▶ n. a close-fitting upright collar.

man·da·rin duck ▶ n. a small East Asian duck, the male of which has an orange ruff and sail-like feathers on each side of the body.

man·date ▶ n. /'man,dāt/ **1** an official order or authorization. **2** the authority to carry out a policy, regarded as given by voters to the winner of an election: *a government with a popular mandate*. **3** historical a commission from the League of Nations (the forerunner of the UN) to a member nation to administer a territory. ▶ v. /,man'dāt/ authorize someone to do something.

man·da·to·ry /'mandə,tôrē/ ▶ adj. required by law or mandate; compulsory. ■ **man·da·to·ri·ly** /-,tôrəlē/ adv.

man·di·ble /'mandəbəl/ ▶ n. **1** the lower jawbone in a mammal or fish. **2** either of the upper and lower parts of a bird's beak. **3** either half of the crushing organ in an insect's mouthparts.

man·do·lin /,mandə'lin, 'mandələn/ ▶ n. **1** a musical instrument resembling a lute, having paired metal strings plucked with a plectrum. **2** (also **mandoline** pronunc. same) a kitchen implement consisting of a frame with adjustable blades, for slicing vegetables. ■ **man·do·lin·ist** /-'linist/ n.

man·drake /'man,drāk/ ▶ n. a plant with a forked fleshy root supposedly resembling the human form, used in herbal medicine and magic.

man·drel /'mandrəl/ ▶ n. **1** a shaft or spindle in a lathe to which work is fixed while being turned. **2** a cylindrical rod around which metal or other material is forged or shaped.

man·drill /'mandrəl/ ▶ n. a large West African baboon with a red and blue face, the male having a blue rump.

mane /mān/ ▶ n. **1** a growth of long hair on the neck of a horse, lion, or other mammal. **2** a person's long flowing hair.

man·eat·er ▶ n. **1** an animal that can kill and eat people. **2** informal a dominant woman who has many sexual partners. ■ **man·eat·ing** adj.

ma·nège /ma'nezH, mə-,-näzH/ ▶ n. **1** a riding school. **2** the movements in which a horse is trained in a riding school.

ma·neu·ver /mə'n(y)ōōvər/ (Brit. **manoeuvre**) ▶ n. **1** a movement or series of moves requiring skill and care. **2** a carefully planned scheme or action. **3** (**maneuvers**) a large-scale military exercise. ▶ v. **1** move skillfully or carefully. **2** carefully manipulate someone or something in order to achieve an aim.

ma·neu·ver·a·ble /mə'n(y)ōōvərəbəl/ ▶ adj. (of a boat or aircraft) able to be maneuvered easily. ■ **ma·neu·ver·a·bil·i·ty** /mə,nōōvərə'bilətē/ n.

man·ful /'manfəl/ ▶ adj. brave and determined. ■ **man·ful·ly** adv.

man·ga /'maNG,ga, 'män-/ ▶ n. Japanese cartoons, comic books, and animated films with a science-fiction or fantasy theme.

man·ga·bey /'maNGgə,bā/ ▶ n. a long-tailed monkey from West and central Africa.

man·ga·nese /'maNGgə,nēz, -,nēs/ ▶ n. a hard gray metallic element used in special steels and magnetic alloys.

ma·nge /mānj/ ▶ n. a skin disease in some

animals that is caused by mites and results in severe itching and hair loss.

man·gel-wur·zel /'maNGgəl 'wərzəl/ ▶ n. another term for **MANGOLD**.

man·ger /'mānjər/ ▶ n. a long trough from which horses or cattle feed.

man·gle[1] /'maNGgəl/ ▶ v. **1** destroy or severely damage something by tearing or crushing. **2** spoil or do something badly: *he was mangling Bach on the piano*.

man·gle[2] ▶ n. a large machine for ironing sheets, usually when they are damp, using heated rollers.

man·go /'maNGgō/ ▶ n. (pl. **mangoes** or **mangos**) an oval tropical fruit with yellow flesh.

man·gold /'maNGgōld/ ▶ n. a variety of beet with a large root, grown as feed for farm animals.

man·go·steen /'maNGgə,stēn/ ▶ n. a tropical fruit with juicy white flesh inside a thick reddish-brown rind.

man·grove /'man,grōv, 'maNG-/ ▶ n. a tropical tree or shrub found in tropical coastal swamps, with tangled roots that grow above ground.

man·gy /'mānjē/ ▶ adj. (**mangier**, **mangiest**) **1** having mange. **2** in poor condition; shabby.

man·han·dle /'man,handl/ ▶ v. **1** move a heavy object with effort. **2** drag or push someone roughly.

man·hat·tan /man'hatn, mən-/ ▶ n. a cocktail made of vermouth and whiskey.

man·hole /'man,hōl/ ▶ n. a covered opening allowing access to a sewer or other underground structure.

man·hood /'man,hŏŏd/ ▶ n. **1** the state or period of being a man. **2** the men of a country or society. **3** the qualities traditionally associated with men, such as strength and sexual potency.

man-hour ▶ n. an hour regarded in terms of the amount of work that can be done by one person within this period.

man·hunt /'man,hənt/ ▶ n. an organized search for a suspect, criminal, or escaped prisoner.

ma·ni·a /'mānēə/ ▶ n. **1** mental illness characterized by an overactive imagination and excited activity. **2** an excessive enthusiasm; an obsession.

-mania ▶ comb.form **1** referring to a specified type of mental abnormality or obsession: *kleptomania*. **2** referring to extreme enthusiasm: *Beatlemania*. ■ **-maniac** comb.form.

ma·ni·ac /'mānē,ak/ ▶ n. **1** a person who behaves in an extremely wild or violent way. **2** informal a person with an extreme enthusiasm for something. ■ **ma·ni·a·cal** /mə'nīəkəl/ adj. **ma·ni·a·cal·ly** /mə'nīək(ə)lē/ adv.

man·ic /'manik/ ▶ adj. **1** relating to a mental illness characterized by an overactive imagination and excited activity. **2** showing wild excitement and energy: *a manic grin*. ■ **man·i·cal·ly** /-(ə)lē/ adv.

man·ic de·pres·sion ▶ n. a mental disorder marked by alternating periods of excited activity and depression. ■ **man·ic-de·pres·sive** adj. & n.

Man·i·chae·an /,manə'kēən/ (also **Manichean**) ▶ adj. **1** chiefly historical relating to Manichaeism. **2** relating to a contrast or conflict between opposites. ■ **Man·i·chae·an·ism** /-'kēə,nizəm/ n.

Man·i·chae·ism /'manə,kēizəm/ (also **Manicheism**) ▶ n. a religious system with Christian, Gnostic, and pagan elements, founded in Persia in the 3rd century by Manes and based on a belief in an ancient conflict between light and darkness.

man·i·cure /'mani,kyŏŏr/ ► n. a cosmetic treatment of the hands and nails. ► v. 1 give a manicure to a person or the hands. 2 (as adj. **manicured**) (of a lawn or garden) neatly trimmed and maintained. ■ **man·i·cur·ist** /'mani,kyŏŏrist/ n.

man·i·fest¹ /'manə,fest/ ► adj. clear and obvious. ► v. 1 show or display: *she manifested signs of severe depression.* 2 (of an illness or disorder) become apparent. 3 (of a ghost) appear. ■ **man·i·fest·ly** adv.

man·i·fest² ► n. 1 a document listing a ship's contents, cargo, crew, and passengers. 2 a list of passengers or cargo in an aircraft.

man·i·fes·ta·tion /,manəfə'stāsHən, -,fes'tāsHən/ ► n. 1 a sign that something exists or is happening: *graffiti was a manifestation of bored youth.* 2 an appearance of a god or spirit in physical form.

Man·i·fest Des·ti·ny ► n. the 19th-century doctrine or belief that US expansion throughout the American continents was both justified and inevitable.

man·i·fes·to /,manə'festō/ ► n. (pl. **manifestos**) a public declaration of the policy and aims of a political party or other group.

man·i·fold /'manə,fōld/ ► adj. 1 many and various. 2 having many different forms or aspects. ► n. a pipe with several openings that connect to other parts, especially one in an internal combustion engine conveying air and fuel from the carburetor to the cylinders or leading from the cylinders to the exhaust pipe.

man·i·kin /'manikən/ (also **mannikin**) ► n. 1 a very small person. 2 a jointed model of the human body.

Ma·nil·a /mə'nilə/ (also **Manilla**) ► n. 1 strong brown paper, originally made from a Philippine plant. 2 a cigar or cheroot made in Manila.

man·i·oc /'manē,äk/ ► n. another term for CASSAVA.

ma·nip·u·late /mə'nipyə,lāt/ ► v. 1 handle or control a tool, device, etc., in a skillful way. 2 control or influence someone in a clever or underhanded way. 3 alter or present information so as to mislead someone. 4 examine or treat part of the body by feeling or moving it with the hand. ■ **ma·nip·u·la·ble** /-ləbəl/ adj. **ma·nip·u·la·tion** /mə,nipyə'lāsHən/ n. **ma·nip·u·la·tor** /-,lātər/ n.

ma·nip·u·la·tive /mə'nipyələtiv, -,lātiv/ ► adj. 1 controlling a person or situation in a clever or underhanded way. 2 relating to manipulation of an object or part of the body.

man·kind /,man'kīnd, 'man,kīnd/ ► n. human beings as a whole; the human race.

man·ly /'manlē/ ► adj. (**manlier**, **manliest**) 1 having qualities traditionally associated with men, such as courage and strength. 2 suitable for a man: *manly sports.* ■ **man·li·ness** n.

man-made ► adj. made or caused by human beings.

man·na /'manə/ ► n. 1 (in the Bible) the substance miraculously supplied as food to the Israelites in the wilderness (Book of Exodus, chapter 16). 2 something unexpected and very welcome or beneficial.

manned /mand/ ► adj. having a human crew.

man·ne·quin /'manikən/ ► n. 1 a dummy used to display clothes in a store window. 2 dated a fashion model.

man·ner /'manər/ ► n. 1 a way in which something is done or happens. 2 a person's outward behavior or attitude toward other people: *his relaxed, easy manner.* 3 (**manners**) polite social behavior. 4 a style in literature or art. 5 literary a kind or sort.
– PHRASES **all manner of** many different kinds of. **in a manner of speaking** in some sense. **to the manner born** naturally at ease in a particular job or situation.

man·nered /'manərd/ ► adj. 1 behaving in a specified way: *well-mannered.* 2 (of behavior, art, literary style, etc.) marked by distinctive or exaggerated features intended to be impressive.

man·ner·ism /'manə,rizəm/ ► n. 1 a habitual gesture or way of speaking or behaving. 2 the use of a very distinctive style in art, literature, or music. 3 (**Mannerism**) a style of 16th-century Italian art characterized by distortions in scale and perspective. ■ **man·ner·ist** n. & adj.

man·ner·ly /'manərlē/ ► adj. well-mannered; polite.

man·ni·kin /'manikən/ ► n. variant spelling of MANIKIN.

man·nish /'manisH/ ► adj. (of a woman) looking or behaving like a man.

man-of-war (also **man-o'-war** /,manə'wôr/) ► n. historical an armed sailing ship.

ma·nom·e·ter /mə'nämətər/ ► n. an instrument for measuring the pressure of fluids.

man·or /'manər/ ► n. 1 a large country house with lands. 2 (in medieval times) an area of land controlled by a lord. ■ **ma·no·ri·al** /mə'nôrēəl/ adj.

manoeuvre ► n. & v. British spelling of MANEUVER.

man·pow·er /'man,pouər/ ► n. the number of people working or available for work or service.

man·qué /mäNG'kā/ ► adj. having never become what one might have been; unfulfilled: *an actor manqué.*

man·sard /'man,särd, -sərd/ ► n. a roof with four sides, in each of which the lower part of the slope is steeper than the upper part.

manse /mans/ ► n. 1 a house provided for a minister of certain Christian churches, especially the Scottish Presbyterian Church. 2 a large, stately house; a mansion.

man·serv·ant /'man,sərvənt/ ► n. (pl. **menservants**) a male servant.

man·sion /'mansHən/ ► n. a large, impressive house.

man-sized ► adj. 1 of the size of a human being. 2 large enough to occupy, suit, or satisfy a man: *a man-sized breakfast.* 3 formidable: *a man-sized job.*

man·slaugh·ter /'man,slôtər/ ► n. the crime of killing a person without intending to do so.

man·ta /'mantə/ ► n. (also **manta ray**) a very large ray (fish) of tropical seas.

man·tel /'mantl/ ► n. (also **mantle**) ► n. a mantelpiece or mantelshelf.

man·tel·piece /'mantl,pēs/ ► n. 1 a structure surrounding a fireplace. 2 a mantelshelf.

man·tel·shelf /'mantl,sHelf/ ► n. a shelf forming the top of a mantelpiece.

man·til·la /man'tē(y)ə, -'tilə/ ► n. (in Spain) a lace or silk scarf traditionally worn by women over the hair and shoulders.

man·tis /'mantis/ (also **praying mantis**)
▶ n. (pl. same or **mantises**) a slender insect with a triangular head, typically waiting motionless for prey with its forelegs folded like hands in prayer.

man·tle /'mantl/ ▶ n. **1** a woman's loose sleeveless cloak or shawl. **2** a covering layer of something: *a mantle of snow.* **3** (also **gas mantle**) a mesh cover fixed around a gas jet to give a glowing light when heated. **4** an important role or responsibility that passes from one person to another. **5** the region of the earth's interior between the crust and the core, consisting of hot, dense silicate rock. ▶ v. literary cover or envelop something.

man·tra /'mantrə, 'män-/ ▶ n. **1** (originally in Hinduism and Buddhism) a word or sound repeated to help concentration while meditating. **2** a Vedic hymn. **3** a frequently repeated statement or slogan.

man·trap /'man,trap/ ▶ n. a trap for catching people.

man·u·al /'manyə(wə)l/ ▶ adj. **1** relating to or operated with the hands: *a manual typewriter.* **2** using or working with the hands: *a manual worker.* ▶ n. **1** a book giving instructions or information. **2** an organ keyboard played with the hands, not the feet. ■ **man·u·al·ly** adv.

man·u·fac·to·ry /,manyə'fakt(ə)rē/ ▶ n. (pl. **manufactories**) old use a factory.

man·u·fac·ture /,manyə'fakchər/ ▶ v. **1** make something on a large scale using machinery. **2** make up evidence or a story. ▶ n. the process of making goods on a large scale using machinery. ■ **man·u·fac·tur·er** n.

man·u·mit /,manyə'mit/ ▶ v. (**manumits**, **manumitting**, **manumitted**) historical free someone from slavery. ■ **man·u·mis·sion** /-'mishən/ n.

ma·nure /mə'n(y)o͝or/ ▶ n. animal dung used for fertilizing land. ▶ v. spread manure on land.

man·u·script /'manyə,skript/ ▶ n. **1** a handwritten book, document, or piece of music. **2** an author's handwritten or typed work, submitted for printing and publication.

Manx /maNGks/ ▶ n. the Celtic language formerly spoken on the Isle of Man, still used for some ceremonial purposes. ▶ adj. relating to the Isle of Man.

Manx cat ▶ n. a breed of cat without a tail.

man·y /'menē/ ▶ determiner, pron., & adj. (**more**, **most**) a large number of people or things. ▶ n. (**the many**) the majority of people.

man·za·nil·la /,manzə'nē(y)ə, -'nilə/ ▶ n. a pale, very dry Spanish sherry.

ma·ña·na /mən'yänə/ ▶ adv. tomorrow, or at some time in the future.

Mao·ism /'mou,izəm/ ▶ n. the communist policies and theories of the former Chinese head of state Mao Zedong. ■ **Mao·ist** n. & adj.

Ma·o·ri /'mourē/ ▶ n. (pl. same or **Maoris**) **1** a member of the aboriginal people of New Zealand. **2** the Polynesian language of the Maori.

map /map/ ▶ n. **1** a flat diagram of an area of land or sea showing physical features, cities, roads, etc. **2** a diagram or collection of data showing the arrangement, distribution, or sequence of something. ▶ v. (**maps**, **mapping**, **mapped**) **1** represent or record something on a map. **2** (**map something out**) plan something in detail.

– PHRASES **off the map** very distant or remote. **put someone/thing on the map** make someone or something famous.

ma·ple /'māpəl/ ▶ n. a tree or shrub with five-pointed leaves, winged fruits, and syrupy sap.

ma·ple leaf ▶ n. the leaf of the maple, used as the Canadian national emblem.

ma·ple syr·up ▶ n. sugary syrup produced from the sap of a maple tree.

ma·quette /ma'ket/ ▶ n. a small model or sketch made by a sculptor as a basis for a larger work.

ma·quis /mä'kē/ ▶ n. (pl. same) **1** (**the Maquis**) the French resistance movement during the German occupation of France in World War II. **2** dense evergreen vegetation characteristic of coastal regions in the Mediterranean.

mar /mär/ ▶ v. (**mars, marring, marred**) damage or spoil: *violence marred a number of New Year celebrations.*

Mar. ▶ abbr. March.

mar·a·bou /'marə,bōo/ ▶ n. **1** an African stork with a massive bill and large neck pouch. **2** down feathers from the marabou used as trimming for hats or clothing.

ma·rac·a /mə'räkə/ ▶ n. a hollow gourd or gourd-shaped container filled with small beans, stones, etc., shaken as a musical instrument.

mar·a·schi·no /,marə'sHē,nō, -'skē-/ ▶ n. (pl. **maraschinos**) a strong, sweet liqueur made from a kind of cherry.

mar·a·schi·no cher·ry ▶ n. a cherry preserved in maraschino.

mar·a·thon /'marə,THän/ ▶ n. **1** a long-distance running race, strictly one of 26 miles 385 yards (42.195 km). **2** a long and very difficult task.

ma·raud /mə'rôd/ ▶ v. go about in search of goods to steal or people to attack. ■ **ma·raud·er** n.

mar·ble /'märbəl/ ▶ n. **1** a hard form of limestone, typically with streaks of color running through it, that may be polished and used in sculpture and building. **2** a small ball of colored glass used as a toy. **3** (**marbles**) (treated as sing.) a game in which marbles are rolled along the ground. **4** (**one's marbles**) informal one's mental faculties. ▶ v. stain or streak something so that it looks like marble. ■ **mar·bled** adj.

mar·bling /'märbəliNG/ ▶ n. **1** coloring or marking that resembles marble. **2** streaks of fat in lean meat.

marc /märk/ ▶ n. **1** the skins and other remains from grapes that have been pressed for winemaking. **2** an alcoholic spirit distilled from this.

mar·ca·site /'märkə,sīt/ ▶ n. **1** a semiprecious stone consisting of iron pyrites. **2** a piece of polished metal cut as a gem.

March /märcH/ ▶ n. the third month of the year.

march /märcH/ ▶ v. **1** walk in time with other people and with regular paces, like a soldier. **2** proceed quickly and with determination. **3** force someone to walk somewhere quickly. **4** take part in an organized procession to make a protest. ▶ n. **1** an act of marching. **2** a procession organized as a protest. **3** a piece of music written to accompany marching. ■ **march·er** n.

– PHRASES **on the march 1** engaged in marching. **2** making progress.

March·es /'märcHiz/ ▶ pl.n. an area of land on the border between two countries or territories.

march·ing or·ders ▸n. **1** instructions for troops to depart. **2** informal a dismissal from a place, job, etc.

mar·chio·ness /'märsH(ə)nəs/ ▸n. **1** the wife or widow of a marquess. **2** a woman holding the rank of marquess in her own right.

Mar·di Gras /'märdē ˌgrä/ ▸n. a carnival held in some countries on Shrove Tuesday.

mare¹ /me(ə)r/ ▸n. the female of a horse or related animal.

ma·re² /'märā/ ▸n. (pl. **maria** /'märēə/) a large plain of volcanic rock on the surface of the moon.

mare's nest ▸n. **1** a complicated situation. **2** a discovery that turns out to be illusory or worthless.

mare's tail ▸n. **1** a water plant with whorls of narrow leaves around a tall thick stem. **2** (**mare's tails**) long straight streaks of cirrus cloud.

mar·ga·rine /'märjərən/ ▸n. a butter substitute made from vegetable oils or animal fats.

mar·ga·ri·ta /ˌmärgə'rētə/ ▸n. a cocktail made with tequila and lemon or lime juice.

mar·gin /'märjən/ ▸n. **1** an edge or border. **2** the blank border on each side of the print on a page. **3** an amount by which something is won. **4** an amount included or allowed for so as to ensure success or safety: *there was no margin for error.* **5** the furthest reach or limit: *the margins of acceptability.*

mar·gin·al /'märjənl/ ▸adj. **1** relating to or situated on an edge or border. **2** of minor importance. **3** (of a decision or distinction) very narrow. ■ **mar·gin·al·i·ty** /ˌmärjə'nalətē/ n.

mar·gi·na·li·a /ˌmärjə'nālēə/ ▸pl.n. notes written or printed in the margin of a book or manuscript.

mar·gin·al·ize /'märjənəˌlīz/ ▸v. treat a person, group, or idea as unimportant. ■ **mar·gin·al·i·za·tion** /ˌmärjənələ'zāsHən/ n.

mar·gin·al·ly /'märjənəlē/ ▸adv. to only a limited extent.

mar·grave /'märˌgrāv/ ▸n. historical the hereditary title of some princes of the Holy Roman Empire.

mar·gue·rite /ˌmärg(y)ə'rēt/ ▸n. another term for OXEYE DAISY.

ma·ri·a /'märēə/ ▸ plural of MARE².

ma·ri·a·chi /ˌmärē'äCHē/ ▸n. (pl. **mariachis**) a musician performing traditional Mexican folk music.

mar·i·gold /'mariˌgōld/ ▸n. a plant of the daisy family with yellow or orange flowers.

ma·ri·jua·na /ˌmarə'(h)wänə/ ▸n. cannabis.

ma·rim·ba /mə'rimbə/ ▸n. a deep-toned xylophone of African origin.

ma·ri·na /mə'rēnə/ ▸n. a purpose-built harbor with moorings for yachts and small boats.

mar·i·nade ▸n. /ˌmarə'nād/ a mixture of oil, vinegar, and spices, in which meat, fish, or other food is soaked before cooking in order to flavor or soften it. ▸v. also /'marəˌnād/ another term for MARINATE.

ma·ri·na·ra /ˌmarə'narə, ˌmärə'närə/ ▸n. (in Italian cooking) a sauce made from tomatoes, onions, and herbs.

mar·i·nate /'marəˌnāt/ ▸v. soak meat, fish, or other food in a marinade. ■ **mar·i·na·tion** /ˌmarə'nāsHən/ n.

ma·rine /mə'rēn/ ▸adj. **1** relating to the sea. **2** relating to shipping or a navy. ▸n. a member of a body of troops trained to serve on land or sea, in particular a member of the US Marine Corps.

mar·i·ner /'marənər/ ▸n. formal or literary a sailor.

mar·i·on·ette /ˌmarēə'net/ ▸n. a puppet worked by strings.

mar·i·tal /'maritl/ ▸adj. relating to marriage or the relations between husband and wife. ■ **mar·i·tal·ly** adv.

mar·i·time /'mariˌtīm/ ▸adj. **1** relating to shipping or other activity taking place at sea. **2** living or found in or near the sea. **3** (of a climate) moist and mild owing to the influence of the sea.

mar·jo·ram /'märjərəm/ ▸n. a plant of the mint family whose sweet-scented leaves are used as an herb in cooking.

mark¹ /märk/ ▸n. **1** a small area on a surface having a different color from its surroundings. **2** something that indicates position or acts as a pointer. **3** a line, figure, or symbol made to identify or record something. **4** a sign or indication of a quality or feeling: *a mark of respect.* **5** a characteristic feature of something: *it is the mark of a civilized society to treat its elderly members well.* **6** a level or stage: *unemployment had passed the two million mark.* **7** a grade awarded for a piece of work. **8** a particular model or type of a vehicle or machine. ▸v. **1** make a mark on something. **2** write a word or symbol on an object to identify it. **3** indicate the position of something. **4** (**mark someone/thing out**) distinguish someone or something from other people or things: *his sword marked him out as an officer.* **5** indicate or acknowledge a significant event: *a ceremony was held to mark the occasion.* **6** (**mark something up** or **down**) increase or reduce the price of an item. **7** assess a written work and give it a mark. **8** notice or pay careful attention to something.
– PHRASES **be quick off the mark** be fast in responding. **make its** (or **one's** or **a**) **mark** have a lasting or significant effect. **mark time 1** (of troops) march on the spot without moving forward. **2** pass one's time in routine activities while waiting for something to happen. **near** (or **close**) **to the mark** almost accurate. **off** (or **wide of**) **the mark** wrong or inaccurate. **on your mark(s)** be ready to start (used to instruct competitors in a race). **up to the mark** up to the required standard.

mark² ▸n. (until the introduction of the euro in 2002) the basic unit of money of Germany.

mark·down /'märkˌdoun/ ▸n. a reduction in price.

marked /märkt/ ▸adj. **1** having a visible mark or other identifying feature. **2** clearly noticeable: *a marked increase in sales.* **3** singled out as a target for attack: *a marked man.* ■ **mark·ed·ly** /'märkədlē/ adv.

mark·er /'märkər/ ▸n. **1** an object used to indicate a position, place, or route. **2** a pen with a broad felt tip. **3** (in soccer) a player who guards an opponent. **4** a person who marks a test or exam.

mar·ket /'märkit/ ▸n. **1** a regular gathering for the buying and selling of food, livestock, or other goods. **2** an outdoor space or hall where people offer goods for sale. **3** a particular area of commercial or competitive activity: *the export market.* **4** demand for a particular

product or service: *the rapidly growing market for Internet software.* ▶v. (**markets, marketing, marketed**) advertise or promote something. ■ **mar·ket·a·ble** /'märkitəbəl/ adj. **mar·ket·er** n.
– PHRASES **on the market** available for sale.

mar·ket·eer /ˌmärkə'ti(ə)r/ ▶n. **1** a person who sells products or services in a market. **2** a person who is in favor of a particular system of trade: *a free marketeer.*

mar·ket·ing /'märkitiNG/ ▶n. the promotion and selling of products or services.

mar·ket·mak·er ▶n. Stock Exchange a dealer in securities or other assets who undertakes to buy or sell at specified prices at all times.

mar·ket·place /'märkət,plās/ ▶n. **1** an open space where a market is held. **2** a competitive or commercial area of activity: *the global marketplace.*

mar·ket re·search ▶n. the activity of gathering information about consumers' needs and preferences.

mar·ket town ▶n. a town of moderate size where a regular market is held.

mar·ket val·ue ▶n. the amount for which something can be sold in an open market.

mark·ing /'märkiNG/ ▶n. **1** an identifying mark. **2** (also **markings**) a pattern of marks on an animal's fur, feathers, or skin.

marks·man /'märksmən/ ▶n. (pl. **marksmen**) a person skilled in shooting. ■ **marks·man·ship** /-ˌSHip/ n.

mark·up /'mär,kəp/ ▶n. **1** the amount added to the price of goods to cover overhead and profit. **2** a set of codes given to different elements of a body of computer data to indicate their relationship to the rest of the data.

marl[1] /märl/ ▶n. rock or soil consisting of clay and lime, formerly used as fertilizer.

marl[2] ▶n. a yarn or fabric with differently colored threads.

mar·lin /'märlən/ ▶n. a large edible fish of warm seas, with a pointed snout.

mar·lin·spike /'märlən,spīk/ (also **marlinespike**) ▶n. a pointed metal tool used by sailors to separate strands of rope or wire.

mar·ma·lade /'märmə,lād/ ▶n. a preserve made from citrus fruit, especially bitter oranges.

mar·mo·re·al /mär'môrēəl/ ▶adj. literary made of or resembling marble.

mar·mo·set /'märmə,set, -,zet/ ▶n. a small tropical American monkey with a silky coat and a long tail.

mar·mot /'märmət/ ▶n. a heavily built burrowing rodent.

Mar·o·nite /'me(ə)rə,nīt/ ▶n. a member of a Christian sect living chiefly in Lebanon.

ma·roon[1] /mə'rōōn/ ▶n. a dark brownish-red color.

ma·roon[2] ▶v. leave someone alone in a remote or inaccessible place.

marque /märk/ ▶n. a make of car, as distinct from a specific model.

mar·quee /mär'kē/ ▶n. a rooflike projection over the entrance to a theater, hotel, or other building.

mar·quess /'märkwəs/ ▶n. a British nobleman ranking above an earl and below a duke.

mar·que·try /'märkətrē/ ▶n. inlaid work made from small pieces of colored wood, used to decorate furniture.

mar·quis /mär'kē, 'märkwəs/ ▶n. **1** (in some European countries) a nobleman ranking above a count and below a duke. **2** variant spelling of MARQUESS.

mar·quise /mär'kēz/ ▶n. **1** the wife or widow of a marquis, or a woman holding the rank of marquis in her own right. **2** a ring set with a pointed oval gem or cluster of gems.

mar·riage /'marij/ ▶n. **1** the formal union of a man and a woman, by which they become husband and wife. **2** a combination of two or more elements: *her music is a marriage of funk, jazz, and hip-hop.*

mar·riage·a·ble /'marijəbəl/ ▶adj. suitable for marriage, especially in terms of age.

mar·ried /'marēd/ ▶adj. united by marriage. ▶n. (**marrieds**) married people.

mar·row /'marō/ ▶n. (also **bone marrow**) a soft fatty substance in the cavities of bones, in which blood cells are produced.
– PHRASES **to the marrow** to one's innermost being.

mar·row·bone /'marō,bōn/ ▶n. a bone containing edible marrow.

mar·ry /'marē/ ▶v. (**marries, marrying, married**) **1** take someone as one's wife or husband in marriage. **2** join two people in marriage. **3** (**marry into**) become a member of a family by marriage. **4** join two things together in a harmonious way: *the show marries poetry with art.*

Mars /märz/ ▶n. a small planet of the solar system, fourth in order from the sun and the nearest to the earth.

Mar·sa·la /mär'sälə/ ▶n. a dark, sweet fortified dessert wine made in Sicily.

marsh /märSH/ ▶n. an area of low-lying land that is flooded in wet seasons or at high tide and typically remains waterlogged. ■ **marsh·y** adj.

mar·shal /'märSHəl/ ▶n. **1** an officer of the highest rank in the armed forces of some countries. **2** a federal or municipal law-enforcement officer. **3** an official responsible for supervising public events. ▶v. (**marshals, marshaling, marshaled**) **1** assemble a group of people, especially soldiers, in an orderly way. **2** bring facts, information, etc., together in an organized way. **3** direct the movement of an aircraft on the ground at an airport.

Marsh Ar·ab ▶n. a member of a semi-nomadic Arab people living in marshland in southern Iraq.

marsh gas ▶n. gas, mainly methane, produced by decaying matter in marshes.

marsh·land /'märSH,land/ ▶n. (also **marshlands**) land consisting of marshes.

marsh·mal·low /'märSH,melō, -,malō/ ▶n. a spongy confection made from a mixture of sugar, egg white, and gelatin.

marsh mal·low ▶n. a tall pink-flowered plant growing in marshes, whose roots were formerly used to make marshmallow.

marsh mar·i·gold ▶n. a plant with large yellow flowers that grows in damp ground and shallow water.

mar·su·pi·al /mär'sōōpēəl/ ▶n. a mammal, such as a kangaroo, whose young are born before they are fully developed and are carried and suckled in a pouch on the mother's belly.

mart /märt/ ▸ n. **1** a store. **2** a market.

mar·ten /ˈmärtn/ ▸ n. a weasel-like forest mammal that is hunted for fur in some countries.

mar·tial /ˈmärsнəl/ ▸ adj. relating to or appropriate to war; warlike. ■ **mar·tial·ly** adv.

mar·tial arts ▸ pl.n. various sports or skills that originated mainly in Japan, Korea, and China as forms of self-defense or attack, such as judo, karate, and kung fu.

mar·tial law ▸ n. government by the military forces of a country, during which ordinary laws are suspended.

Mar·tian /ˈmärsнən/ ▸ n. a supposed inhabitant of the planet Mars. ▸ adj. relating to Mars.

mar·tin /ˈmärtn/ ▸ n. used in names of small short-tailed swallows, e.g., **house martin**.

mar·ti·net /ˌmärtnˈet/ ▸ n. a person who enforces strict discipline.

mar·tin·gale /ˈmärtnˌgāl/ ▸ n. a strap or set of straps running from the noseband or reins to the girth of a horse, used to prevent the horse from raising its head too high.

mar·ti·ni /märˈtēnē/ ▸ n. a cocktail made from gin and dry vermouth.

Mar·ti·niq·uan /ˌmärtnˈēkən/ (also **Martinican**) ▸ n. a person from Martinique, a French island in the Lesser Antilles. ▸ adj. relating to Martinique.

mar·tyr /ˈmärtər/ ▸ n. **1** a person who is killed because of their religious or political beliefs. **2** a person who exaggerates their difficulties in order to obtain sympathy. ▸ v. make someone a martyr. ■ **mar·tyr·dom** /ˈmärtərdəm/ n.

mar·tyr·ol·o·gy /ˌmärtəˈräləjē/ ▸ n. (pl. **martyrologies**) **1** the study of martyrs. **2** a list of martyrs.

mar·vel /ˈmärvəl/ ▸ v. (**marvels, marveling, marveled**) be filled with wonder: *she marveled at the beauty of the scenery.* ▸ n. a person or thing that causes a feeling of wonder.

mar·vel·ous /ˈmärv(ə)ləs/ (Brit. **marvellous**) ▸ adj. **1** causing great wonder; extraordinary. **2** extremely good or pleasing. ■ **mar·vel·ous·ly** adv.

Marx·ism /ˈmärkˌsizəm/ ▸ n. the political and economic theories of Karl Marx and Friedrich Engels, later developed by their followers as the basis for communism. ■ **Marx·i·an** /-sēən/ n. & adj. **Marx·ist** n. & adj.

mar·zi·pan /ˈmärzəˌpan, ˈmärtsə-/ ▸ n. a sweet paste of ground almonds, sugar, and egg whites, used to coat cakes or to make confectionery.

Ma·sai /ˈmäˌsī, mäˈsī/ (also **Maasai**) ▸ n. (pl. same or **Masais**) a member of a pastoral people living in Tanzania and Kenya.

ma·sa·la /məˈsälə/ ▸ n. a mixture of spices ground into a paste or powder and used in Indian cooking.

mas·car·a /maˈskarə/ ▸ n. a cosmetic for darkening and thickening the eyelashes.

mas·car·po·ne /ˌmäskärˈpōn(e)/ ▸ n. a soft, mild Italian cream cheese.

mas·cot /ˈmasˌkät, -kət/ ▸ n. a person, animal, or object that is identified with a person, group, team, etc., and supposed to bring good luck.

mas·cu·line /ˈmaskyələn/ ▸ adj. **1** having the qualities or appearance traditionally associated with men. **2** relating to men; male. **3** Grammar (of a gender of nouns and adjectives in certain languages) treated as male. ■ **mas·cu·lin·i·ty** /ˌmaskyəˈlinitē/ n.

ma·ser /ˈmāzər/ ▸ n. a form of laser generating a beam of microwaves.

MASH /mash/ ▸ abbr. mobile army surgical hospital.

mash /mash/ ▸ v. **1** crush or beat something to a soft mass. **2** (in brewing) mix powdered malt with hot water to form wort. ▸ n. **1** a soft mass made by crushing a substance into a pulp. **2** bran mixed with hot water, given as a food to horses. **3** (in brewing) a mixture of powdered malt and hot water that is left standing until the sugars dissolve to form the wort. **4** Brit. informal mashed potatoes.

mashed potatoes ▸ pl.n. a dish of potatoes that have been boiled until soft, then mashed, usually with butter and milk.

mash-up ▸ n. **1** a recording created by digitally combining and synchronizing instrumental tracks with vocal tracks from two or more different songs: *a mash-up of Madonna's "Ray of Light" and the Sex Pistols.* **2** a video or Web-based product made by combining content or functionality from more than one source.

mask /mask/ ▸ n. **1** a covering for all or part of the face, worn as a disguise, for protection or hygiene, or for theatrical effect. **2** a device used to filter inhaled air or to supply gas for breathing. **3** a likeness of a person's face molded or sculpted in clay or wax. **4** a face pack. ▸ v. **1** cover someone's face or part of their face with a mask. **2** conceal or disguise: *brandy did not mask the bitter taste.* **3** cover an object or surface so as to protect it during painting or similar work. ■ **masked** adj.

masked ball ▸ n. a ball at which participants wear masks to conceal their faces.

mask·ing tape ▸ n. adhesive tape used in painting to cover areas on which paint is not wanted.

mas·och·ism /ˈmasəˌkizəm, ˈmaz-/ ▸ n. the tendency to enjoy one's own pain or humiliation. ■ **mas·och·ist** n. **mas·och·is·tic** /ˌmasəˈkistik, ˌmaz-/ adj.

ma·son /ˈmāsən/ ▸ n. **1** a builder and worker in stone. **2** (**Mason**) a Freemason.

Ma·son–Dix·on line /ˈdiksən/ (also **Mason and Dixon line**) ▸ n. the boundary between Maryland and Pennsylvania, taken as the northern limit of the slave-owning states before the abolition of slavery.

Ma·son·ic /məˈsänik/ ▸ adj. relating to Freemasons.

ma·son jar ▸ n. a wide-mouthed glass jar with an airtight screw top, used for preserving fruit and vegetables.

ma·son·ry /ˈmāsənrē/ ▸ n. **1** stonework. **2** (**Masonry**) Freemasonry.

masque /mask/ ▸ n. a form of dramatic entertainment popular in the 16th and 17th centuries, consisting of dancing and acting performed by players wearing masks.

mas·quer·ade /ˌmaskəˈrād/ ▸ n. **1** an attempt to hide the truth or one's real feelings. **2** a masked ball. ▸ v. **1** pretend to be someone that one is not. **2** be disguised or passed off as something else: *the idle gossip that masquerades as news.*

Mass /mas/ ▸ n. **1** the Christian service of the Eucharist or Holy Communion, especially in the Roman Catholic Church. **2** a musical setting of parts of the liturgy used in the Mass.

mass /mas/ ▸ n. **1** a body of matter with no

definite shape. **2** a large number of people or objects gathered together. **3** (**the masses**) the ordinary people. **4** (**the mass of**) the majority of. **5** (**a mass of**) a large amount of. **6** Physics the quantity of matter that a body contains, as measured by its acceleration under a given force or by the force exerted on it by a gravitational field. ▶ **adj.** done by or affecting large numbers of people or things: *a mass exodus.* ▶ **v.** gather together into a single body or mass: *both countries began massing troops in the region.*

mas·sa·cre /ˈmasikər/ ▶ **n. 1** a brutal slaughter of a large number of people. **2** informal a very heavy defeat. ▶ **v. 1** brutally kill a large number of people. **2** informal inflict a heavy defeat on an opponent.

mas·sage /məˈsäzH, -ˈsäj/ ▶ **n.** the rubbing and kneading of parts of the body with the hands to relieve tension or pain. ▶ **v. 1** give someone a massage. **2** manipulate figures to give a more acceptable result.

mas·sage par·lor ▶ **n. 1** a place where one can pay to have a massage. **2** euphemistic a brothel.

mas·seur /maˈsər, mə-/ ▶ **n.** (fem. **masseuse** /maˈsōōs, mə-, maˈsœz/) a person who provides massage professionally.

mas·sif /maˈsēf/ ▶ **n.** a compact group of mountains.

mas·sive /ˈmasiv/ ▶ **adj. 1** large and heavy or solid. **2** exceptionally large, intense, or severe: *a massive heart attack.* **3** forming a solid or continuous mass. ■ **mas·sive·ly** adv. **mas·sive·ness** n.

mass-mar·ket ▶ **adj.** (of goods) produced in large quantities for many people.

mass me·di·a ▶ **n.** television, radio, and newspapers considered as a group; the media.

mass noun ▶ **n.** Grammar a noun referring to something that cannot be counted, in English usually a noun that has no plural form and is not used with *a* or *an*, e.g., *luggage, happiness.* Contrasted with **COUNT NOUN**.

mass num·ber ▶ **n.** Physics the total number of protons and neutrons in a nucleus.

mass-pro·duce /prəˈdōōs/ ▶ **v.** produce goods in large quantities, using machinery. ■ **mass pro·duc·tion** n.

mast¹ /mast/ ▶ **n. 1** a tall upright post or spar on a boat, generally carrying a sail or sails. **2** any tall upright post, especially a flagpole or a television or radio transmitter.

mast² ▶ **n.** the fruit of beech and other forest trees, especially as food for pigs.

mas·tec·to·my /maˈstektəmē/ ▶ **n.** (pl. **mastectomies**) a surgical operation to remove all or part of a breast.

mas·ter /ˈmastər/ ▶ **n. 1** a man in a position of authority, control, or ownership. **2** a person who is skilled in a particular art or activity: *a master of disguise.* **3** chiefly Brit. the head of a college or school. **4** a person who holds a second or further degree from a university. **5** an original movie, recording, or document from which copies can be made. **6** (**Master**) a title placed before a boy's name. ▶ **adj. 1** (of an artist) having great skill or expertise: *a master painter.* **2** skilled in a particular profession and able to teach others: *a master builder.* **3** main; principal: *the master bedroom.* ▶ **v. 1** gain complete knowledge of or skill in a subject, technique, etc. **2** gain control of: *I managed to master my fears.* **3** make a master copy of a movie or record.

mas·ter-at-arms ▶ **n.** a warrant officer responsible for police duties on board a ship.

mas·ter·class /ˈmastərˌklas/ ▶ **n.** a class, especially in music, given to students by an expert in the field.

mas·ter·ful /ˈmastərfəl/ ▶ **adj. 1** powerful and able to control others. **2** performed or performing very skillfully. ■ **mas·ter·ful·ly** adv.

mas·ter key ▶ **n.** a key that opens several locks, each of which also has its own key.

mas·ter·ly /ˈmastərlē/ ▶ **adj.** performed or performing very skillfully.

mas·ter·mind /ˈmastərˌmīnd/ ▶ **n. 1** a person who is extremely intelligent. **2** a person who plans and directs a complex scheme or enterprise. ▶ **v.** plan and direct a complex scheme or enterprise.

mas·ter of cer·e·mo·nies ▶ **n.** a person in charge of procedure at a state occasion, formal event, or entertainment, who introduces the speakers or performers.

mas·ter·piece /ˈmastərˌpēs/ ▶ **n.** a work of outstanding skill.

mas·ter ser·geant ▶ **n.** a high-ranking noncommissioned officer in the US armed forces.

mas·ter stroke /ˈmastərˌstrōk/ ▶ **n.** an outstandingly skillful or clever move.

mas·ter·work /ˈmastərˌwərk/ ▶ **n.** a masterpiece.

mas·ter·y /ˈmast(ə)rē/ ▶ **n. 1** complete knowledge or command of a subject or skill. **2** control or superiority: *man's mastery over nature.*

mast·head /ˈmastˌhed/ ▶ **n. 1** the highest part of a ship's mast. **2** the name of a newspaper or magazine printed at the top of the first page. **3** a list of staff, owner, advertising rates, etc., in a newspaper or magazine.

mas·tic /ˈmastik/ ▶ **n. 1** an aromatic gum from the bark of a Mediterranean tree, used in making varnish and chewing gum and as a flavoring. **2** a puttylike waterproof substance used as a filler and sealant in building.

mas·ti·cate /ˈmastiˌkāt/ ▶ **v.** chew food. ■ **mas·ti·ca·tion** /ˌmastiˈkāsHən/ n.

mas·tiff /ˈmastif/ ▶ **n.** a dog of a large, strong breed with drooping ears and lips.

mas·ti·tis /maˈstītis/ ▶ **n.** inflammation of the mammary gland in the breast or udder.

mas·to·don /ˈmastəˌdän/ ▶ **n.** a large extinct elephantlike mammal.

mas·toid /ˈmasˌtoid/ (also **mastoid process**) ▶ **n.** a conical projection of the temporal bone behind the ear, to which neck muscles are attached, and that has air spaces linked to the middle ear.

mas·tur·bate /ˈmastərˌbāt/ ▶ **v.** stimulate one's genitals with one's hand for sexual pleasure. ■ **mas·tur·ba·tion** /ˌmastərˈbāsHən/ n. **mas·tur·ba·tor** n. **mas·tur·ba·to·ry** /-bəˌtôrē/ adj.

mat /mat/ ▶ **n. 1** a thick piece of material placed on the floor to protect it from dirt or as a decoration. **2** a piece of thick material for landing on in gymnastics or similar sports. **3** a small piece of material placed on a surface to protect it from the heat or moisture of an object placed on it. **4** a thick, untidy layer of hairy or woolly material.

mat·a·dor /ˈmatəˌdôr/ ▶ **n.** a bullfighter whose task is to kill the bull.

match¹ /macH/ ▶ **n. 1** a contest in which people or teams compete against each other. **2** a person or thing that can compete with another as an equal in quality or strength. **3** an exact equivalent. **4** a pair of things that are very similar or combine together well. **5** a potential husband or wife. **6** a marriage. ▶v. **1** correspond in appearance; combine together well: *the jacket and pants do not match.* **2** be equal to someone or something in quality or strength. **3** place one person or group in competition with another.

match² ▶n. **1** a short, thin stick tipped with a mixture that ignites when rubbed against a rough surface. **2** historical a piece of wick or cord used for lighting gunpowder.

match·book /'macH,bŏŏk/ ▶n. a small cardboard folder of matches with a striking surface on one side.

match·box /'macH,bäks/ ▶n. a small box in which matches are sold.

match·less /'macHləs/ ▶adj. so good that no one or nothing is an equal.

match·lock /'macH,läk/ ▶n. historical a type of gun with a lock in which a piece of wick or cord was placed for igniting the powder.

match·mak·er /'macH,mākər/ ▶n. a person who tries to bring about marriages or relationships between other people.

match play ▶n. Golf a play in which the score is reckoned by the number of holes won. Compare with STROKE PLAY.

match point ▶n. (in tennis and some other sports) a point that, if won by one of the players will also win them the match.

match·stick /'macH,stik/ ▶n. the stem of a match.

match·up /'macHəp/ ▶n. **1** a contest between athletes or sports teams. **2** a pairing or combining of people or things for some purpose.

mate¹ /māt/ ▶n. **1** the sexual partner of an animal. **2** informal a person's spouse or other sexual partner. **3** one of a matched pair: *I've got one glove without a mate.* **4** (in combination) a fellow member or occupant: *his teammates.* **5** an officer on a merchant ship below the master. **6** Brit. informal a friend or companion. **7** chiefly Brit. an assistant to a skilled worker. ▶v. **1** (of animals or birds) come together for breeding. **2** join or connect two things.

mate² ▶n. & v. Chess short for CHECKMATE.

ma·té /'mä,tā/ (also **yerba maté** /'yerbə, 'yər-/) ▶n. an infusion of the bitter, caffeine-rich leaves of a South American shrub.

ma·ter /'mātər/ ▶n. Brit. informal, dated mother.

ma·ter·fa·mil·i·as /,mātərfə'mīlēəs, ,mātər-/ ▶n. (pl. **matresfamilias** /,mä,trās-, ,mātərz-/) the female head of a family or household.

ma·te·ri·al /mə'ti(ə)rēəl/ ▶n. **1** the substance from which something is or can be made. **2** items needed for doing or creating something. **3** cloth or fabric. ▶adj. **1** consisting of or referring to physical objects rather than the mind or spirit: *the material world.* **2** essential or relevant: *evidence material to the case.* ■ **ma·te·ri·al·i·ty** /mə,ti(ə)rē'alitē/ n. **ma·te·ri·al·ly** adv.

ma·te·ri·al·ism /mə'ti(ə)rē,lizəm/ ▶n. **1** a tendency to consider material possessions and physical comfort as more important than spiritual values. **2** Philosophy the doctrine that nothing exists except matter. ■ **ma·te·ri·al·ist** n. & adj. **ma·te·ri·al·is·tic** /mə,ti(ə)rēə'listik/ adj.

ma·te·ri·al·ize /mə'ti(ə)rē,līz/ ▶v. **1** become fact; happen: *the hoped-for investment boom did*

not materialize. **2** appear. ■ **ma·te·ri·al·i·za·tion** /mə,ti(ə)rēələ'zāsHən/ n.

ma·te·ri·el /mə,ti(ə)rē'el/ ▶n. military materials and equipment.

ma·ter·nal /mə'tərnl/ ▶adj. **1** relating to or characteristic of a mother. **2** related through the mother's side of the family. ■ **ma·ter·nal·ly** adv.

ma·ter·ni·ty /mə'tərnətē/ ▶n. motherhood. ▶adj. relating to the period during pregnancy and shortly after childbirth: *maternity clothes.*

math /maTH/ ▶n. mathematics.

math·e·mat·ics /maTH(ə)'matiks/ ▶pl.n. (usu. treated as sing.) the branch of science concerned with number, quantity, and space, either as abstract ideas (**pure mathematics**) or as applied to physics, engineering, and other subjects (**applied mathematics**). ■ **math·e·mat·i·cal** /,maTH(ə)'matikəl/ adj. **math·e·mat·i·cal·ly** /-ik(ə)lē/ adv. **math·e·ma·ti·cian** /,maTH(ə)mə'tisHən/ n.

mat·i·nee /,matn'ā/ ▶n. an afternoon performance in a theater or movie theater.

mat·i·nee i·dol ▶n. informal, dated a handsome actor admired chiefly by women.

mat·ins /'matnz/ ▶n. a service of morning prayer, especially in the Anglican Church.

ma·tri·arch /'mātrē,ärk/ ▶n. **1** a woman who is the head of a family or tribe. **2** a powerful older woman. ■ **ma·tri·ar·chal** /,mātrē'ärkəl/ adj.

ma·tri·ar·chy /'mātrē,ärkē/ ▶n. **1** a form of social organization in which the mother or eldest female is the head of the family. **2** a society in which women hold most or all of the power.

ma·tri·ces ▶ plural of MATRIX.

mat·ri·cide /'matrə,sīd, 'mā-/ ▶n. **1** the killing of one's mother. **2** a person who kills their mother. ■ **mat·ri·cid·al** /,matrə'sīdl, ,mā-/ adj.

ma·tric·u·late /mə'trikyə,lāt/ ▶v. enroll or be enrolled at a college or university. ■ **ma·tric·u·la·tion** /mə,trikyə'lāsHən/ n.

mat·ri·lin·e·al /,matrə'linēəl, ,mā-/ ▶adj. based on relationship with the mother or the female line of descent. ■ **mat·ri·lin·e·al·ly** adv.

mat·ri·mo·ny /'matrə,mōnē/ ▶n. the state of being married, or the ceremony of marriage. ■ **mat·ri·mo·ni·al** /,matrə'mōnēəl/ adj.

ma·trix /'mātriks/ ▶n. (pl. **matrices** /'mātrisēz/ or **matrixes**) **1** an environment or material in which something develops. **2** a mold in which something is cast or shaped. **3** Mathematics a rectangular arrangement of quantities in rows and columns that is manipulated according to particular rules. **4** a gridlike array of elements; a lattice. **5** a mass of rock in which gems, crystals, or fossils are embedded.

ma·tron /'mātrən/ ▶n. **1** a dignified or sedate married woman. **2** a female prison officer. ■ **ma·tron·ly** adj.

ma·tron of hon·or ▶n. a married woman attending the bride at a wedding.

matte /mat/ (also **matt**) ▶adj. (of a surface, paint, etc.) not shiny: *matte white paint.* ▶n. **1** a matte color, paint, or finish. **2** a sheet of cardboard placed on the back of a picture, as a mount or to form a border.

mat·ted /'matid/ ▶adj. (of hair or fur) tangled into a thick mass.

mat·ter /'matər/ ▶n. **1** physical substance or

material in general, as distinct from mind and spirit; (in physics) that which occupies space and possesses mass. **2** a subject or situation under consideration: *complicated financial matters.* **3** (**the matter**) the reason for a problem: *what's the matter?* **4** written or printed material. **5** Law something to be tried or proved in court; a case. ▶ v. be important or significant: *it doesn't matter what she thinks.*
– PHRASES **as a matter of fact** in reality; in fact. **in the matter of** regarding. **a matter of 1** no more than a particular period of time: *they were shown on in a matter of minutes.* **2** a question of. **a matter of course** the natural or expected thing. **no matter 1** regardless of. **2** it is of no importance.

mat·ter-of-fact ▶ adj. unemotional and practical.

mat·ting /'mating/ ▶ n. material used for mats, especially coarse fabric woven from a natural fiber.

mat·tock /'matək/ ▶ n. an agricultural tool similar to a pickax, but with one arm of the head curved like an adze and the other like a chisel edge.

mat·tress /'matrəs/ ▶ n. a fabric case filled with soft, firm, or springy material used for sleeping on.

mat·u·ra·tion /ˌmaCHə'rāSHən/ ▶ n. **1** the action or process of maturing. **2** the formation of pus in a boil, abscess, etc.

ma·ture /mə'CHŏŏr, -'t(y)ŏŏr/ ▶ adj. **1** fully grown or physically developed; adult. **2** like an adult in mental or emotional development. **3** (of thought or planning) careful and thorough. **4** (of certain foods or drinks) ready for consumption. **5** due for payment. ▶ v. **1** become mature. **2** (of an insurance policy) reach the end of its term and so become payable. ■ **ma·ture·ly** adv.

ma·tu·ri·ty /mə'CHŏŏritē, mə't(y)ŏŏr-/ ▶ n. **1** the state, fact, or period of being mature. **2** the time when an insurance policy reaches the end of its term and so becomes payable.

ma·tu·ti·nal /mə't(y)ŏŏtn-əl, ˌmaCHə'tīnl/ ▶ adj. formal relating to or happening in the morning.

mat·zo /'mätsə/ (also **matzoh**) ▶ n. (pl. **matzos**) a crisp cracker of unleavened bread, traditionally eaten by Jews during Passover.

maud·lin /'môdlin/ ▶ adj. sentimental in a tearful or self-pitying way.

maul /môl/ ▶ v. **1** (of an animal) wound a person or other animal by scratching and tearing. **2** handle or treat someone or something savagely or roughly. ▶ n. a tool with a heavy head and a handle, used for crushing, ramming, and driving wedges; a beetle.

maun·der /'môndər/ ▶ v. talk or act in a rambling or aimless way.

Maun·dy Thurs·day /'môndē/ ▶ n. the Thursday before Easter, observed in the Christian Church as a commemoration of the Last Supper.

Mau·ri·ta·ni·an /ˌmôri'tānēən, -'tänyən/ ▶ n. a person from Mauritania, a country in West Africa. ▶ adj. relating to Mauritania.

Mau·ri·tian /mô'riSHən/ ▶ n. a person from the island of Mauritius in the Indian Ocean. ▶ adj. relating to Mauritius.

mau·so·le·um /ˌmôzə'lēəm, ˌmôsə-/ ▶ n. (pl. **mausolea** /-'lēə/ or **mausoleums**) a building containing a tomb or tombs.

mauve /mōv, môv/ ▶ n. a pale purple color.

ma·ven /'māvən/ ▶ n. informal an expert or connoisseur.

mav·er·ick /'mav(ə)rik/ ▶ n. **1** an unconventional or independent-minded person. **2** an unbranded calf or yearling.

maw /mô/ ▶ n. the jaws or throat, especially of a voracious animal.

mawk·ish /'môkiSH/ ▶ adj. expressing emotion in an exaggerated or embarrassing way: *a mawkish ode to parenthood.*

max /maks/ ▶ n. & adj. short for maximum.

max·i /'maksē/ ▶ n. (pl. **maxis**) a skirt or coat reaching to the ankle.

max·il·la /mak'silə/ ▶ n. (pl. **maxillae** /mak'silē, -'sil,ī/) **1** the bone of the upper jaw. **2** (in an insect or other arthropod) each of a pair of chewing mouthparts. ■ **max·il·lar·y** /'maksə,lerē/ adj.

max·im /'maksim/ ▶ n. a short statement expressing a general truth or rule of behavior.

max·i·mize /'maksə,mīz/ ▶ v. **1** make as great or large as possible: *the company is aiming to maximize profits.* **2** make the best use of something. ■ **max·i·mi·za·tion** /ˌmaksəmə'zāSHən/ n. **max·i·miz·er** n.

max·i·mum /'maksəməm/ ▶ n. (pl. **maxima** or **maximums**) the greatest amount, size, or intensity possible or achieved. ▶ adj. greatest in amount, size, or intensity. ■ **max·i·mal** adj.

max·well /'maks,wel, -wəl/ ▶ n. a unit used in measuring the strength of a magnetic field.

May /mā/ ▶ n. **1** the fifth month of the year. **2** (**may**) the hawthorn or its blossom.

may /mā/ ▶ modal v. (3rd sing. present **may;** past **might**) **1** expressing possibility. **2** expressing permission. **3** expressing a wish or hope.
– PHRASES **be that as it may** nevertheless.

USAGE
For an explanation of the difference in use between **may** and **can**, see the note at CAN.

Ma·ya /'mīə/ ▶ n. (pl. same or **Mayas**) a member of a Central American people whose civilization died out *c.* 900 AD. ■ **Ma·yan** adj. & n.

ma·ya /'mīə, 'mäyə/ ▶ n. **1** (in Hinduism) the supernatural power wielded by gods and demons to produce illusions, or the power by which the universe becomes manifest. **2** (in Hinduism and Buddhism) the illusion or appearance of the phenomenal world.

may·ap·ple /'mā,apəl/ ▶ n. an herbaceous plant of the barberry family with large, deeply divided leaves, bearing a yellow, egg-shaped edible fruit in May, long used medicinally.

may·be /'mābē/ ▶ adv. perhaps; possibly.

May·day /'mā,dā/ ▶ n. an international radio distress signal used by ships and aircraft.

May Day ▶ n. May 1, celebrated as a springtime festival or as a holiday in honor of workers.

may·fly /'mā,flī/ ▶ n. (pl. **mayflies**) an insect with transparent wings that lives as an adult for only a very short time.

may·hap /'mā,hap/ ▶ adv. old use perhaps; possibly.

may·hem /'mā,hem/ ▶ n. violent disorder; chaos.

may·n't /'mā(ə)nt/ ▶ contr. may not.

may·on·naise /'māə,nāz, ˌmāə'nāz/ ▶ n. a thick creamy dressing made from egg yolks, oil, and vinegar.

may·or /'māər/ ▶ n. the elected head of a city, town, or other municipality. ■ **may·or·al** /mā'ôrəl, 'māərəl/ adj. **may·or·ship** /-,SHip/ n.

may·or·al·ty /'māərəltē/ ▶ n. (pl. **mayoralties**) the position or term of office of a mayor.

may·or·ess /'māərəs/ ▶ n. **1** the wife of a mayor. **2** a woman elected as mayor.

may·pole /'mā,pōl/ ▶ n. a decorated pole with long ribbons attached to the top, traditionally used for dancing around on May Day.

maze /māz/ ▶ n. **1** a network of paths and walls or hedges, designed as a puzzle, through which one has to find a way. **2** a confusing mass of information.

ma·zur·ka /mə'zərkə, -'zŏōr-/ ▶ n. a lively Polish dance in triple time.

MB ▶ abbr. **1** Bachelor of Medicine. **2** Manitoba. **3** (also **Mb**) Computing megabyte(s).

MBA ▶ abbr. Master of Business Administration.

MBO ▶ abbr. management buyout.

MC ▶ abbr. **1** Master of Ceremonies. **2** Member of Congress. ▶ n. a person who provides entertainment at a club or party by instructing the DJ and performing rap music. ▶ v. (**MC's, MC'ing, MC'd**) perform as an MC.

MCC ▶ abbr. Metropolitan Community Church.

m-com·merce ▶ n. commercial dealings carried out electronically by cell phone.

MD ▶ abbr. **1** Doctor of Medicine. **2** Maryland.

Md ▶ symbol the chemical element mendelevium.

MDMA ▶ abbr. methylenedioxymethamphetamine, the drug Ecstasy.

MDT ▶ abbr. Mountain Daylight Time.

me /mē/ ▶ pron. (first person sing.) used as the object of a verb or preposition or after 'than,' 'as,' or the verb 'to be,' to refer to the speaker himself or herself.

> USAGE
> The pronoun **me** should be used as the object of a verb or preposition, as in *John hates me*. It is wrong to use **me** as the subject of a verb, as in *John and me went to the store*; in this case **I** should be used instead. See PERSONAL PRONOUN.

me·a cul·pa /,māə 'kŏŏl,pə, -,pä/ ▶ exclam. an acknowledgment that one is wrong or at fault.

mead[1] /mēd/ ▶ n. an alcoholic drink of fermented honey and water.

mead[2] ▶ n. literary a meadow.

mead·ow /'medō/ ▶ n. **1** an area of grassland, especially one used for hay. **2** a piece of low ground near a river.

mead·ow·sweet /'medō,swēt, 'medə-/ ▶ n. a tall meadow plant with heads of creamy white fragrant flowers.

mea·ger /'mēgər/ ▶ adj. lacking in quantity or quality: *a meager diet of bread and beans.* ■ **mea·ger·ness** n.

meal[1] /mēl/ ▶ n. **1** any of the regular daily occasions when food is eaten. **2** the food eaten during a meal.

meal[2] ▶ n. the edible part of any grain or seed ground to a powder, used to make flour or to feed animals.

meal tick·et ▶ n. a person or thing that is exploited as a source of money.

meal·time /'mēl,tīm/ ▶ n. the time at which a meal is eaten.

meal·y /'mēlē/ ▶ adj. (**mealier, mealiest**) **1** relating to or containing ground grain or seeds. **2** pale in color.

meal·y·bug /'mēlē,bəg/ ▶ n. a sap-sucking scale insect that is coated with a white powdery wax and that can be a serious pest.

meal·y-mouthed /'mēlē 'moutḥd, -,moutḥt/ ▶ adj. reluctant to speak frankly.

mean[1] /mēn/ ▶ v. (past and past part. **meant** /ment/) **1** intend to express or refer to something. **2** (of a word) have something as its explanation in the same language or its equivalent in another language. **3** intend to do or be the case: *they mean no harm.* **4** have something as a result. **5** intend or design for a particular purpose: *the coat was meant for a much larger person.* **6** be of specified importance to someone.
– PHRASES **mean business** be in earnest. **mean well** have good intentions, but not always carry them out.

mean[2] ▶ adj. **1** unwilling to give or share things; not generous. **2** unkind or unfair. **3** vicious or aggressive. **4** poor in quality and appearance: *her home was mean and small.* **5** dated coming from a low social class. **6** informal excellent. ■ **mean·ly** adv. **mean·ness** n.

mean[3] ▶ n. **1** the average value of a set of quantities. **2** something in the middle of two extremes. ▶ adj. **1** calculated as a mean; average. **2** equally far from two extremes.

me·an·der /mē'andər/ ▶ v. **1** (of a river or road) follow a winding course. **2** wander or progress in a leisurely or aimless way. ▶ n. a bend of a river that curves back on itself.

mean·ie /'mēnē/ (also **meany**) ▶ n. informal a mean or small-minded person.

mean·ing /'mēninG/ ▶ n. **1** what is meant by a word, idea, or action. **2** a sense of purpose.

mean·ing·ful /'mēninGfəl/ ▶ adj. **1** having meaning. **2** important or worthwhile. **3** expressing something without words: *they exchanged meaningful glances.* ■ **mean·ing·ful·ly** adv. **mean·ing·ful·ness** n.

mean·ing·less /'mēninGlis/ ▶ adj. having no meaning or significance. ■ **mean·ing·less·ly** adv. **mean·ing·less·ness** n.

means /mēnz/ ▶ pl.n. (also treated as sing.) **1** an action or method for achieving a result: *language is a means of communication.* **2** a person's financial resources; income.
– PHRASES **by all means** of course. **by means of** by using. **by no means** certainly not. **a man (or woman) of means** a rich man (or woman). **a means to an end** a thing that is not valued in itself but is useful in achieving an aim.

means test ▶ n. an official investigation into a person's finances to determine whether they qualify for a welfare payment or other public funds. ▶ v. (**means-test**) base (a welfare payment, etc.) on a means test.

meant /ment/ ▶ past and past participle of MEAN[1].

mean·time /'mēn,tīm/ ▶ adv. (also **in the meantime**) in the period of time between two events; meanwhile.

mean·while /'mēn,(h)wīl/ ▶ adv. **1** (also **in the meanwhile**) in the period of time between two events. **2** at the same time.

mea·sles /'mēzəlz/ ▶ pl.n. (treated as sing.) an infectious disease spread by a virus, causing fever and a red rash.

mea·sly /'mēzlē/ ▶ adj. (**measlier, measliest**) informal ridiculously small or few.

meas·ure /'mezHər/ ▶ v. **1** determine the size,

amount, or degree of something by comparing it with a standard unit. **2** be of a specified size. **3** (**measure something out**) take an exact quantity of something. **4** assess the importance or value of: *it is hard to measure teaching ability.* **5** (**measure up**) reach the required standard. ▶ n. **1** a means of achieving a purpose: *cost-cutting measures.* **2** a standard unit used to express size, amount, or degree. **3** a measuring device marked with standard units of size, amount, or degree. **4** (**a measure of**) a certain amount or degree of. **5** (**a measure of**) an indication of the extent or quality of. **6** a proposal for a law. **7** (**measures**) a group of rock strata: *coal measures.* **8** any of the sections, typically of equal time value, into which a musical composition is divided. ■ **meas·ur·a·ble** /ˈmezh(ə)rəbəl/ adj. **meas·ur·a·bly** adv. **meas·ur·er** n.

– PHRASES **for good measure** as an amount or item that is additional to what is strictly required. **take** (or **get** or **have**) **the measure of** understand the character or abilities of.

meas·ured /ˈmezhərd/ ▶ adj. **1** slow and regular in rhythm. **2** (of language) carefully considered.

meas·ure·less /ˈmezhərlis/ ▶ adj. literary having no limits.

meas·ure·ment /ˈmezhərmənt/ ▶ n. **1** the action of measuring. **2** an amount, size, or extent found by measuring. **3** a standard unit used in measuring.

meas·ur·ing cup /ˈmezh(ə)riNG/ ▶ n. a cup marked in graded amounts, used for measuring ingredients in cooking.

meat /mēt/ ▶ n. **1** the flesh of an animal as food. **2** the chief part: *let's get to the meat of the matter.*

meat·ball /ˈmēt,bôl/ ▶ n. a ball of ground or chopped meat.

meat loaf ▶ n. ground or chopped meat baked in the shape of a loaf.

meat·pack·ing /ˈmēt,pakiNG/ ▶ n. the business of slaughtering animals and processing the meat for sale as food.

meat·y /ˈmētē/ ▶ adj. (**meatier**, **meatiest**) **1** resembling or full of meat. **2** fleshy or muscular. **3** full of substance or interest: *a meaty, scholarly book.* ■ **meat·i·ness** n.

Mec·ca /ˈmekə/ ▶ n. a place that attracts many people: *the area is a Mecca for skiers.*

me·chan·ic /məˈkanik/ ▶ n. a skilled worker who repairs and maintains machinery.

me·chan·i·cal /məˈkanikəl/ ▶ adj. **1** relating to or operated by a machine or machinery. **2** done without thought; automatic. **3** relating to physical forces or motion. ■ **me·chan·i·cal·ly** adv.

me·chan·i·cal draw·ing ▶ n. a scale drawing done with precision instruments.

me·chan·i·cal en·gi·neer·ing ▶ n. the branch of engineering concerned with the design, construction, and use of machines.

me·chan·ics /məˈkaniks/ ▶ pl.n. **1** (treated as sing.) the branch of study concerned with motion and forces producing motion. **2** machinery or working parts. **3** the practical aspects of something: *the mechanics of cello-playing.*

mech·an·ism /ˈmekə,nizəm/ ▶ n. **1** a piece of machinery. **2** the way in which something works or is brought about.

mech·a·nis·tic /,mekəˈnistik/ ▶ adj. relating to the theory that all natural processes can be explained in purely physical terms.

mech·a·nize /ˈmekə,nīz/ ▶ v. equip a process or place with machines or automatic devices. ■ **mech·a·ni·za·tion** /,mekənəˈzāsHən/ n.

me·co·ni·um /miˈkōnēəm/ ▶ n. the dark green substance forming the first feces of a newborn infant.

MEd /,em 'ed/ ▶ abbr. Master of Education.

med. ▶ abbr. **1** medium. **2** (**med**) informal medical: *med school.*

me·da·ka /məˈdäkə/ ▶ n. a small Japanese freshwater fish of variable color that is bred for aquariums and scientific studies.

med·al /ˈmedl/ ▶ n. a metal disk with an inscription or design, awarded for achievement or to mark an event.

med·al·ist /ˈmedl-ist/ (Brit. **medallist**) ▶ n. a person awarded a medal.

me·dal·lion /məˈdalyən/ ▶ n. **1** a piece of jewelry in the shape of a medal, worn as a pendant. **2** a decorative oval or circular painting, panel, or design. **3** a small flat round or oval cut of meat or fish.

Med·al of Hon·or (also **Congressional Medal of Honor**) ▶ n. the highest US military decoration, awarded by Congress to a member of the armed forces for gallantry and bravery in combat at the risk of life above and beyond the call of duty.

med·dle /ˈmedl/ ▶ v. interfere in something that is not one's concern. ■ **med·dler** n. **med·dle·some** /ˈmedlsəm/ adj.

me·di·a /ˈmēdēə/ ▶ n. **1** television, radio, and newspapers as the means of mass communication. **2** plural of MEDIUM.

USAGE

The word **media** comes from the Latin plural of **medium**. In the normal sense 'television, radio, and newspapers,' it often behaves as a collective noun (one referring to a group of people or things, such as **staff**), and can correctly be used with either a singular or a plural verb: *the media was informed or the media were informed.*

---

me·di·ae·val ▶ adj. variant spelling of MEDIEVAL.

me·di·al /ˈmēdēəl/ ▶ adj. situated in the middle. ■ **me·di·al·ly** adv.

me·di·an /ˈmēdēən/ ▶ adj. **1** technical situated in the middle. **2** having a value in the middle of a series of values arranged in order of magnitude. ▶ n. **1** a median value. **2** Geometry a straight line drawn from one of the angles of a triangle to the middle of the opposite side. **3** (also **median strip**) a strip of land between the lanes of opposing traffic on a divided highway.

me·di·ate /ˈmēdē,āt/ ▶ v. **1** try to settle a dispute between other people or groups. **2** formal be a means of conveying or influencing: *the meaning of poems is mediated by the language employed.* ■ **me·di·a·tion** /,mēdēˈāsHən/ n. **me·di·a·tor** n.

med·ic /ˈmedik/ ▶ n. a military medical corpsman who dispenses first aid at combat sites.

Med·i·caid /ˈmedi,kād/ ▶ n. a federal system of health insurance for people requiring financial assistance.

med·i·cal /ˈmedikəl/ ▶ adj. relating to the science or practice of medicine. ■ **med·i·cal·ly** adv.

med·i·cal cer·ti·fi·cate ▶ n. a doctor's certificate confirming that a person is either unfit or fit to work.

med·i·cal ex·am·in·er ▶ n. a physician employed by a local authority to conduct autopsies and determine causes of death.

med·i·cal of·fi·cer ▶ n. a doctor serving in the armed forces, in a prison, or in a public health service.

me·dic·a·ment /məˈdikəmənt, ˈmedikəˌment/ ▶ n. a medicine.

Med·i·care /ˈmediˌke(ə)r/ ▶ n. a federal system of health insurance for people over 65 years of age and for certain younger people with disabilities.

med·i·cate /ˈmediˌkāt/ ▶ v. **1** give medicine or a drug to someone. **2** (as adj. **medicated**) containing a medicinal substance.

med·i·ca·tion /ˌmedəˈkāSHən/ ▶ n. **1** a medicine or drug. **2** treatment with medicines.

me·dic·i·nal /məˈdisənl/ ▶ adj. **1** having healing properties. **2** relating to medicines.
■ **me·dic·i·nal·ly** adv.

med·i·cine /ˈmedisən/ ▶ n. **1** the science or practice of the treatment and prevention of disease. **2** a drug or other substance taken by mouth in order to treat or prevent disease.

med·i·cine ball ▶ n. a large, heavy solid ball thrown and caught for exercise.

med·i·cine man ▶ n. (especially among North American Indians) a person believed to have magical powers of healing.

med·i·co /ˈmediˌkō/ ▶ n. (pl. **medicos**) a doctor or medical student.

me·di·e·val /ˌmed(ē)ˈēvəl, ˌmēd-, ˌmid-/ (also **mediaeval**) ▶ adj. **1** relating to the Middle Ages. **2** informal outdated, primitive, or unsophisticated: *a country that is medieval in outlook.*
■ **me·di·e·val·ize** v. **me·di·e·val·ly** adv.

me·di·e·val·ist /ˌmed(ē)ˈēvəlist, ˌmēd-/ (also **mediaevalist**) ▶ n. a scholar of medieval history or literature.

me·di·na /məˈdēnə/ ▶ n. the old quarter of a North African town.

me·di·o·cre /ˌmēdēˈōkər/ ▶ adj. of only average quality; not very good.

me·di·oc·ri·ty /ˌmēdēˈäkrətē/ ▶ n. (pl. **mediocrities**) **1** the state of being average in quality. **2** a person of average ability and lacking originality.

med·i·tate /ˈmedəˌtāt/ ▶ v. **1** focus one's mind for a time for spiritual purposes or for relaxation. **2** (**meditate on/about**) think carefully about.

med·i·ta·tion /ˌmedəˈtāSHən/ ▶ n. **1** the action or practice of meditating. **2** a speech or piece of writing expressing considered thoughts on a subject.

med·i·ta·tive /ˈmedəˌtātiv/ ▶ adj. involving or absorbed in focused thought or deep reflection.
■ **med·i·ta·tive·ly** adv.

Med·i·ter·ra·ne·an /ˌmedətəˈrānēən/ ▶ adj. relating to the Mediterranean Sea or the countries around it.

Med·i·ter·ra·ne·an cli·mate ▶ n. a climate that has warm, wet winters and calm, hot, dry summers, characteristic of the Mediterranean region and parts of California, South Africa, and SW Australia.

me·di·um /ˈmēdēəm/ ▶ n. (pl. **media** or **mediums**) **1** a means by which something is expressed, communicated, or achieved: *using the latest technology as a medium for job creation.* **2** a substance through which a force or other influence is transmitted. **3** a form of storage for computer software, such as magnetic tape or disks. **4** a liquid with which pigments are

mixed to make paint. **5** (pl. **mediums**) a person claiming to be able to communicate between the dead and the living. **6** the middle state between two extremes. **7** the substance in which an organism lives or is grown for scientific study. ▶ adj. between two extremes; average.

med·lar /ˈmedlər/ ▶ n. a small brown applelike fruit.

med·ley /ˈmedlē/ ▶ n. (pl. **medleys**) **1** a varied mixture. **2** a collection of musical items performed as a continuous piece.

Mé·doc /māˈdôk, -ˈdäk/ ▶ n. (pl. same or **Médocs**) a red wine produced in the Médoc area of SW France.

me·dul·la /məˈdələ/ ▶ n. **1** a distinct inner region of a body organ or tissue. **2** the soft internal tissue of a plant.

me·dul·la ob·lon·ga·ta /ˌäˌblôNGˈgätə/ ▶ n. the part of the spinal cord extending into the brain.

me·du·sa /məˈd(y)ōōsə, -zə/ ▶ n. (pl. **medusae** /-sē, -sī, -zē, -zī/ or **medusas**) the free-swimming stage in the life cycle of a jellyfish or related organism.

meek /mēk/ ▶ adj. quiet, gentle, and submissive.
■ **meek·ly** adv. **meek·ness** n.

meer·kat /ˈmi(ə)rˌkat/ ▶ n. a small southern African mongoose.

meer·schaum /ˈmi(ə)rˌSHôm, -SHəm/ ▶ n. **1** a soft white claylike material. **2** a tobacco pipe with a bowl made from meerschaum.

meet¹ /mēt/ ▶ v. (past and past part. **met** /met/) **1** come together with someone at the same place and time. **2** see or be introduced to someone for the first time. **3** touch or join: *the wall curved to meet the ceiling.* **4** experience a situation. **5** (**meet with**) receive a reaction. **6** fulfill or satisfy a need or requirement. ▶ n. an organized event at which a number of races or other sporting contests are held.

meet² ▶ adj. old use suitable or proper.

meet·ing /ˈmētiNG/ ▶ n. **1** an organized gathering of people for a discussion or other purpose. **2** a situation in which people meet by chance or arrangement.

meet·ing·house /ˈmētiNGˌhous/ ▶ n. **1** a Quaker place of worship. **2** historical a Protestant place of worship.

meg·a /ˈmegə/ ▶ adj. informal **1** very large. **2** of great significance or importance.

meg·a- ▶ comb.form **1** large: *megalith.* **2** referring to a factor of one million (10^6): *megabyte.*

meg·a·bucks /ˈmegəˌbəks/ ▶ pl.n. informal a huge sum of money.

meg·a·byte /ˈmegəˌbīt/ ▶ n. a unit of information stored in a computer equal to one million or (strictly) 1,048,576 bytes.

meg·a·flop /ˈmegəˌfläp/ ▶ n. Computing a unit of computing speed equal to one million or (strictly) 1,048,576 floating-point operations per second.

meg·a·hertz /ˈmegəˌhərts/ ▶ n. (pl. same) a unit of frequency equal to one million hertz.

meg·a·lith /ˈmegəˌliTH/ ▶ n. a large stone that forms a prehistoric monument or part of one.
■ **meg·a·lith·ic** /ˌmegəˈliTHik/ adj.

meg·a·lo·ma·ni·a /ˌmegəlōˈmānēə/ ▶ n. **1** the false belief that one is very powerful or important. **2** a strong desire for power.
■ **meg·a·lo·ma·ni·ac** /ˌmegəlōˈmānēˌak/ n. & adj.

meg·a·lop·o·lis /ˌmegəˈläpələs/ ▶ n. a very large, densely populated city.

meg·a·phone /'megə,fōn/ ▸ n. a large cone-shaped device for amplifying the voice.

meg·a·pix·el /'megə,piksəl/ ▸ n. Computing a unit of graphic resolution equivalent to 2^{20} or (strictly) 1,048,576 pixels.

meg·a·pode /'megə,pōd/ ▸ n. a large Australasian or SE Asian bird that lives on the ground and builds a mound of plant debris to incubate its eggs.

meg·a·star /'megə,stär/ ▸ n. informal a very famous entertainer or athlete.

meg·a·ton /'megə,tən/ ▸ n. a unit of explosive power equivalent to one million tons of TNT.

meg·a·volt /'megə,vōlt/ ▸ n. one million volts.

meg·a·watt /'megə,wät/ ▸ n. a unit of power equal to one million watts.

mei·o·sis /mī'ōsəs/ ▸ n. (pl. **meioses** /-sēz/) Biology the division of a cell that results in four cells, each with half the number of chromosomes of the original cell. Compare with MITOSIS.
■ **mei·ot·ic** /mī'ätik/ adj.

Meis·sen /'mīsən/ ▸ n. fine porcelain produced at Meissen in Germany since 1710.

-meister ▸ comb.form referring to a person who is skilled or prominent in a particular area of activity: a media-meister.

meit·ner·i·um /mīt'ni(ə)rēəm/ ▸ n. a very unstable chemical element made by high-energy atomic collisions.

mel·a·mine /'melə,mēn/ ▸ n. a hard, heat-resistant plastic used to coat surfaces.

mel·an·cho·li·a /,melən'kōlēə/ ▸ n. dated severe depression.

mel·an·chol·y /'melən,kälē/ ▸ n. deep and long-lasting sadness. ▸ adj. feeling or causing sadness.
■ **mel·an·chol·ic** /,melən'kälik/ adj.

Mel·a·ne·sian /,melə'nēZHən/ ▸ adj. relating to the islands that make up Melanesia in the western Pacific. ▸ n. a person from Melanesia.

me·lange /mā'länj/ ▸ n. a varied mixture.

mel·a·nin /'melənin/ ▸ n. a dark pigment in the hair and skin, responsible for tanning of skin exposed to sunlight.

mel·a·no·ma /,melə'nōmə/ ▸ n. a form of skin cancer that develops in melanin-forming cells.

mel·a·to·nin /,melə'tōnin/ ▸ n. a hormone secreted by the pineal gland that inhibits melanin formation and is involved in regulating various physiological cycles.

Mel·ba toast /'melbə/ ▸ n. very thin crisp toast.

meld /meld/ ▸ v. combine something with something else.

me·lee /'mā,lā, mā'lā/ ▸ n. 1 a confused fight. 2 a confused crowd of people.

mel·lif·lu·ous /mə'liflōōəs/ ▸ adj. pleasingly smooth and musical to hear. ■ **mel·lif·lu·ous·ly** adv. **mel·lif·lu·ous·ness** n.

mel·lo·tron /'melə,trän/ ▸ n. an electronic keyboard instrument in which each key controls the playback of a single prerecorded musical sound.

mel·low /'melō/ ▸ adj. 1 pleasantly smooth or soft in sound, taste, or color. 2 relaxed and good-humored. ▸ v. make or become mellow.

me·lo·de·on /mə'lōdēən/ ▸ n. 1 a small accordion. 2 a small organ similar to the harmonium.

me·lod·ic /mə'lädik/ ▸ adj. 1 relating to melody. 2 pleasant-sounding. ■ **me·lod·i·cal·ly** /-(ə)lē/ adv.

me·lo·di·ous /mə'lōdēəs/ ▸ adj. pleasant-sounding; tuneful.

mel·o·dra·ma /'melə,drämə/ ▸ n. 1 a play full of exciting events and with exaggerated characters and emotions. 2 exaggerated or extreme behavior or events.

mel·o·dra·mat·ic /,melədrə'matik/ ▸ adj. overdramatic or exaggerated: he flung the door open with a melodramatic flourish. ■ **mel·o·dra·mat·i·cal·ly** /-ik(ə)lē/ adv.

mel·o·dy /'melədē/ ▸ n. (pl. **melodies**) 1 a sequence of notes that is musically satisfying; a tune. 2 the arrangement of musical notes to form a tune. 3 the main part in harmonized music.

mel·on /'melən/ ▸ n. a large round fruit with sweet pulpy flesh and many seeds.

melt /melt/ ▸ v. 1 make or become liquid by heating. 2 gradually disappear or disperse: most of the crowd had melted away. 3 become or make more tender or loving.

melt·down /'melt,doun/ ▸ n. 1 a disastrous collapse: the coming economic meltdown. 2 an accident in a nuclear reactor in which the fuel overheats and melts the reactor core.

melt·ing point ▸ n. the temperature at which a solid will melt.

melt·ing pot ▸ n. a place where different peoples, ideas, or styles are mixed together.

melt·wa·ter /'melt,wôtər, -,wätər/ (also **meltwaters**) ▸ n. water formed by the melting of snow and ice.

mem·ber /'membər/ ▸ n. 1 a person or organization belonging to a group or society. 2 a part of a complex structure. 3 old use a part of the body, especially a limb. 4 the penis.

mem·ber·ship /'membər,SHip/ ▸ n. 1 the fact of being a member of a group. 2 the members or the number of members in a group.

mem·brane /'mem,brān/ ▸ n. 1 a skinlike structure that lines, connects, or covers a cell or part of the body. 2 a thin pliable sheet of material forming a barrier or lining. ■ **mem·bra·ne·ous** /mem'brānēəs/ adj. **mem·bra·nous** /'membrənəs, mem'brānəs/ adj.

me·men·to /mə'men,tō/ ▸ n. (pl. **mementos** or **mementoes**) an object kept as a reminder of a person or event.

me·men·to mo·ri /mə'men,tō 'môrē/ ▸ n. (pl. same) an object kept as a reminder that death is inevitable.

mem·o /'memō/ ▸ n. (pl. **memos**) a memorandum.

mem·oir /'mem,wär, -,wôr/ ▸ n. 1 a historical account or biography written from personal knowledge. 2 (**memoirs**) an account written by a public figure of their life and experiences.

mem·o·ra·bil·i·a /,mem(ə)rə'bilēə/ ▸ pl.n. objects kept or collected because of their associations with memorable people or events.

mem·o·ra·ble /'mem(ə)rəbəl/ ▸ adj. worth remembering or easily remembered. ■ **mem·o·ra·bly** adv.

mem·o·ran·dum /,memə'randəm/ ▸ n. (pl. **memoranda** /-də/ or **memorandums**) 1 a note sent from one person to another in an organization. 2 a formal record or report.

me·mo·ri·al /mə'môrēəl/ ▸ n. an object or structure established in memory of a person or event. ▸ adj. in memory of someone. ■ **me·mo·ri·al·ist** /mə'môrēəlist/ n.

me·mo·ri·al·ize /məˈmôrēəˌlīz/ v.

Me·mo·ri·al Day ▶ n. a day on which people who died in active military service are remembered, officially observed in the US on the last Monday in May.

mem·o·rize /ˈməməˌrīz/ ▶ v. learn something by heart.

mem·o·ry /ˈmem(ə)rē/ ▶ n. (pl. **memories**) 1 the faculty by which the mind stores and remembers information. 2 a person or thing remembered. 3 the length of time over which people's memory extends. 4 a computer's equipment or capacity for storing information.
– PHRASES **in memory of** so as to honor and remind people of a dead person.

Mem·o·ry Stick ▶ n. trademark a small electronic device for storing data or transferring it to or from a computer, digital camera, etc.

mem·sa·hib /ˈmemˌsä(h)ib, -ˌsäb/ ▶ n. dated (in the Indian subcontinent) a respectful form of address for a married white woman.

men /men/ ▶ plural of MAN.

men·ace /ˈmenəs/ ▶ n. 1 a dangerous or harmful person or thing. 2 a threatening quality. ▶ v. put someone or something at risk; threaten. ■ **men·ac·ing** adj.

mé·nage à trois /māˈnäzн ä ˈt(r)wä, mə-/ ▶ n. an arrangement in which a married couple and the lover of one of them live together.

me·nag·er·ie /məˈnajərē, -ˈnazн-/ ▶ n. a collection of wild animals kept in captivity for showing to the public.

men·a·qui·none /ˌmenəˈkwinˌōn, -ˈkwīˌnōn/ ▶ n. a member of the vitamin K group, a compound produced by bacteria in the intestines, essential for blood clotting.

mend /mend/ ▶ v. 1 restore something to its correct or working condition. 2 improve an unpleasant situation. ▶ n. a repair in a material. ■ **mend·a·ble** adj. **mend·er** n.
– PHRASES **mend fences** resolve a disagreement with someone. **on the mend** improving in health or condition.

men·da·cious /menˈdāshəs/ ▶ adj. lying; untruthful. ■ **men·da·cious·ly** adv. **men·dac·i·ty** /menˈdasitē/ n.

men·de·le·vi·um /ˌmendəˈlēvēəm, -ˈlā-/ ▶ n. a very unstable chemical element made by high-energy collisions.

Men·de·li·an /menˈdēlēən/ ▶ adj. relating to the theory of heredity based on characteristics transmitted as genes, as developed by the Austrian botanist G. J. Mendel. ■ **Men·del·ism** /ˈmendlˌizəm/ n.

men·di·cant /ˈmendikənt/ ▶ adj. 1 living by begging. 2 (of a religious order) originally dependent on charitable donations. ▶ n. 1 a beggar. 2 a member of a mendicant religious order.

men·folk /ˈmenˌfōk/ ▶ pl.n. the men of a family or community.

men·ha·den /menˈhādn, mən-/ ▶ n. a large deep-bodied fish of the herring family found along the east coast of North America and used to make fish meal and fertilizer.

men·hir /ˈmenˌhi(ə)r/ ▶ n. a tall upright stone erected as a monument in prehistoric times.

me·ni·al /ˈmēnēəl/ ▶ adj. (of work) of low status and requiring little skill. ▶ n. a person with a menial job.

me·nin·ges /məˈninjēz/ ▶ pl.n. (sing. **meninx** /ˈmēninɡks, ˈmen-/) the three membranes that enclose the brain and spinal cord.

men·in·gi·tis /ˌmenənˈjītis/ ▶ n. a serious disease in which the meninges around the brain and spinal cord become inflamed owing to infection with a bacterium or virus.

me·nis·cus /məˈniskəs/ ▶ n. (pl. **menisci** /-kē, -kī/) 1 Physics the curved upper surface of a liquid in a tube. 2 a thin lens that curves outward on one side and inward on the other.

Men·non·ite /ˈmenəˌnīt/ ▶ n. a member of a Protestant sect that emphasizes adult baptism and rejects church organization, military service, and public office.

men·o·pause /ˈmenəˌpôz/ ▶ n. the ending of menstruation or the stage in a woman's life (typically between 45 and 50) when this occurs. ■ **men·o·pau·sal** /ˌmenəˈpôzəl/ adj.

me·nor·ah /məˈnôrə/ ▶ n. a candelabrum used in Jewish worship, typically with eight branches.

men·ses /ˈmenˌsēz/ ▶ pl.n. blood discharged from the uterus at menstruation.

men·stru·al /ˈmenstr(ōō)əl/ ▶ adj. relating to menstruation.

men·stru·ate /ˈmenstrəˌwāt, ˈmenˌstrāt/ ▶ v. (of a woman) discharge blood from the lining of the uterus each month.

men·stru·a·tion /ˌmenstrōōˈāshən, menˈstrā-/ ▶ n. the process in a woman of discharging blood from the lining of the uterus each month from puberty until menopause, except during pregnancy.

men·su·ra·tion /ˌmenshəˈrāshən, ˌmensə-/ ▶ n. 1 the measurement of something. 2 the part of geometry concerned with measuring lengths, areas, and volumes.

mens·wear /ˈmenzˌwe(ə)r/ ▶ n. clothes for men.

men·tal /ˈmentl/ ▶ adj. 1 relating to or done by the mind. 2 relating to disorders or illnesses of the mind. 3 informal insane. ■ **men·tal·ly** adv.

> **USAGE**
> The use of **mental** in sense 2 (as in **mental problems**) is now regarded as old-fashioned, even offensive, and has been largely replaced by **psychiatric**.

men·tal age ▶ n. a person's mental ability expressed as the age at which an average person reaches the same ability.

men·tal block ▶ n. an inability to remember or do something.

men·tal·i·ty /menˈtalitē/ ▶ n. (pl. **mentalities**) a typical way of thinking of a person or group.

men·tal·ly hand·i·capped ▶ adj. having underdeveloped intellectual ability that prevents one from functioning normally in society.

men·thol /ˈmenˌтнôl, -ˌтнäl/ ▶ n. a minty substance found chiefly in peppermint oil, used as a flavoring and in decongestants. ■ **men·tho·lat·ed** /ˈmenтнəˌlātid/ adj.

men·tion /ˈmenchən/ ▶ v. 1 refer to something briefly. 2 refer to someone as being noteworthy: *he is regularly mentioned as a possible Cabinet member.* ▶ n. 1 a reference to someone or something. 2 a formal acknowledgment of something noteworthy.

men·tor /ˈmenˌtôr, -tər/ ▶ n. 1 an experienced and trusted adviser. 2 an experienced person in an organization or educational institution who trains and advises new employees or students.

▶ v. to advise or train someone, especially a younger colleague.

men·u /'menyōō/ ▶ n. **1** a list of dishes available in a restaurant. **2** the food to be served at a meal. **3** a list of commands or options displayed on a computer screen.

me·ow /mē'ou/ ▶ n. the characteristic cry of a cat. ▶ v. make a meow.

Meph·is·to·phe·li·an /mə,fistə'fēlēən, ,mefəstə-/ (also **Mephistophelean**) ▶ adj. literary wicked or evil.

me·phit·ic /mə'fitik/ ▶ adj. literary smelling very unpleasant.

mer·can·tile /'mərkən,tēl, -,tīl/ ▶ adj. relating to trade or commerce.

mer·can·til·ism /'mərkənti,lizəm, -,tē-, -,tī-/ ▶ n. belief in the benefits of profitable trading; commercialism.

Mer·ca·tor pro·jec·tion /mər'kātər/ ▶ n. a world map projection made onto a cylinder in such a way that all parallels of latitude have the same length as the equator.

mer·ce·nar·y /'mərsə,nerē/ ▶ adj. motivated chiefly by the desire to make money. ▶ n. (pl. **mercenaries**) a professional soldier hired to serve in a foreign army.

mer·cer·ized /'mərsə,rīzd/ ▶ adj. (of cotton) chemically treated to make it strong and shiny.

mer·chan·dise ▶ n. /'mərchən,dīz, -,dīs/ goods for sale. ▶ v. /'mərchən,dīz/ (or **merchandize**) promote the sale of goods. ■ **mer·chan·dis·er** /-,dīzər/ n.

mer·chan·dis·ing /'mərchən,dīziNG/ ▶ n. **1** products used to promote a particular movie, pop music group, etc. **2** the promotion of goods in stores and other retail outlets.

mer·chant /'mərchənt/ ▶ n. **1** a wholesale trader. **2** a retail trader. **3** informal, derogatory a person fond of a particular activity: *a speed merchant.* ▶ adj. (of sailors or shipping) involved with commerce.

mer·chant·a·ble /'mərchəntəbəl/ ▶ adj. suitable for sale.

mer·chant·man /'mərchəntmən/ ▶ n. (pl. **merchantmen**) a ship carrying merchandise.

mer·chant ma·rine ▶ n. a country's commercial shipping.

mer·ci·ful /'mərsifəl/ ▶ adj. **1** showing compassion and forgiveness. **2** giving relief from suffering: *her death was a merciful release.*

mer·ci·ful·ly /'mərsif(ə)lē/ ▶ adv. **1** in a merciful way. **2** to one's great relief; fortunately.

mer·ci·less /'mərsiləs/ ▶ adj. showing no mercy. ■ **mer·ci·less·ly** adv. **mer·ci·less·ness** n.

mer·cu·ri·al /mər,kyŏŏrēəl/ ▶ adj. **1** tending to change mood suddenly. **2** relating to the element mercury.

Mer·cu·ry /'mərkyərē/ ▶ n. a small planet that is the closest to the sun in the solar system. ■ **Mer·cu·ri·an** /mər'kyŏŏrēən/ adj.

mer·cu·ry /'mərkyərē/ ▶ n. a heavy silvery-white liquid metallic element used in some thermometers and barometers. ■ **mer·cu·ric** /mər,kyŏŏrik/ adj. **mer·cu·rous** /'mərkyərəs/ adj.

mer·cy /'mərsē/ ▶ n. (pl. **mercies**) **1** compassion or forgiveness shown toward someone in one's power to punish or harm. **2** something to be grateful for. ▶ adj. done from a desire to relieve suffering: *a mercy killing.* ▶ exclam. old use used to express surprise or fear.
– PHRASES **at the mercy of** completely in the power of.

mere[1] /mi(ə)r/ ▶ adj. **1** that is nothing more than what is specified: *questions that cannot be answered by mere mortals.* **2** (**the merest**) the smallest or slightest.

mere[2] ▶ n. literary (except in place names) a lake or pond.

mere·ly /'mi(ə)rlē/ ▶ adv. just; only.

me·ren·gue /mə'reNGgā/ ▶ n. **1** a Caribbean style of dance music typically in duple and triple time. **2** a dance style associated with merengue, with alternating long and short stiff-legged steps.

mer·e·tri·cious /,merə'trishəs/ ▶ adj. appearing attractive but having no real value.

mer·gan·ser /mər'gansər/ ▶ n. a fish-eating diving duck with a long, thin, jagged, and hooked bill.

merge /mərj/ ▶ v. **1** combine or be combined into a whole: *the two banks merged.* **2** blend gradually into something else.

merg·er /'mərjər/ ▶ n. a merging of two things, especially companies, into one.

mer·guez /mər'gez/ ▶ n. (pl. same) a spicy beef and lamb sausage colored with red peppers, originally made in North Africa.

me·rid·i·an /mə'ridēən/ ▶ n. **1** a circle of constant longitude passing through a given place on the earth's surface and the poles. **2** any of twelve pathways in the body, believed by practitioners of Chinese medicine to be a channel for vital energy.

me·rid·i·o·nal /mə'ridēənəl/ ▶ adj. **1** relating to the south, especially southern Europe. **2** relating to a meridian.

me·ringue /mə'raNG/ ▶ n. **1** beaten egg whites and sugar baked until crisp. **2** a small cake made of meringue.

me·ri·no /mə'rēnō/ ▶ n. (pl. **merinos**) **1** a breed of sheep with long, fine wool. **2** a soft woolen or wool-and-cotton material.

mer·i·stem /'merə,stem/ ▶ n. a region of plant tissue consisting of actively dividing cells.

mer·it /'merit/ ▶ n. **1** the quality of being particularly good; excellence. **2** a good point or quality. ▶ v. (**merits**, **meriting**, **merited**) deserve or be worthy of: *offenses regarded as serious enough to merit dismissal.*

mer·i·toc·ra·cy /,meri'täkrəsē/ ▶ n. (pl. **meritocracies**) a society in which power is held by the people with the greatest ability. ■ **mer·i·to·crat** /'meritə,krat/ n. **mer·i·to·crat·ic** /,meritə'kratik/ adj.

mer·i·to·ri·ous /,meri,tôrēəs/ ▶ adj. deserving reward or praise.

mer·lin /'mərlən/ ▶ n. a small dark falcon.

Mer·lot /'mər'lō/ ▶ n. a red wine made from a variety of grape originally from the Bordeaux region of France.

mer·maid /'mər,mād/ ▶ n. a mythical sea creature with a woman's head and trunk and a fish's tail.

mer·man /'mərmən/ ▶ n. (pl. **mermen**) a mythical sea creature with the head and torso of a man and a fish's tail.

mer·ri·ment /'merēmənt/ ▶ n. cheerfulness and fun.

mer·ry /'merē/ ▶ adj. (**merrier**, **merriest**) cheerful and lively. ■ **mer·ri·ly** adv. **mer·ri·ness** n.
– PHRASES **make merry** enjoy oneself with other people by dancing and drinking.

mer·ry-go-round ▶ n. **1** a revolving machine with model horses or cars on which people ride for amusement. **2** a continuous cycle of activities or events.

mer·ry·mak·ing /'merē,mākiNG/ ▶ n. cheerful celebration and fun.

me·sa /'māsə/ ▶ n. an isolated flat-topped hill with steep sides.

mé·sal·li·ance /,māzə'līəns, ,mā,zal'yäNs/ ▶ n. a marriage to a person of a lower social class.

mes·cal /me'skal, mə-/ ▶ n. **1** an intoxicating liquor distilled from a type of agave (plant). **2** a peyote cactus.

mes·ca·line /'meskəlin, -,lēn/ (also **mescalin** /'meskəlin/) ▶ n. a drug that causes hallucinations, made from the peyote cactus.

Mes·dames /mā'däm/ ▶ plural of **MADAME.**

Mes·de·moi·selles /'mādəm(w)ə,zel, 'mād,mwä,zel/ ▶ plural of **MADEMOISELLE.**

mesh /meSH/ ▶ n. **1** material made of a network of wire or thread. **2** the spacing of the strands of a net. **3** a complex or constricting situation: *people caught in the mesh of history.* ▶ v. **1** become entangled or entwined. **2** (**mesh with**) be in harmony with. **3** (of a gearwheel) lock together with another.

mes·mer·ic /mez'merik/ ▶ adj. completely capturing a person's attention so that they become unaware of their surroundings; hypnotic. ■ **mes·mer·i·cal·ly** adv.

mes·mer·ism /'mezmə,rizəm/ ▶ n. historical a therapeutic technique involving hypnotism. ■ **mes·mer·ist** n.

mes·mer·ize /'mezmə,rīz/ ▶ v. capture a person's attention completely.

Mes·o·lith·ic /,mezə'liTHik, ,mē-/ ▶ adj. Geology relating to the middle part of the Stone Age, between the end of the glacial period and the beginnings of agriculture.

mes·o·morph /'mezə,môrf, 'mē-/ ▶ n. Physiology a person with a compact and muscular body build. Compare with **ECTOMORPH** and **ENDOMORPH.**

me·son /'mez,än, 'mā,zän, 'mē,zän/ ▶ n. Physics a subatomic particle that is intermediate in mass between an electron and a proton.

Mes·o·po·ta·mi·an /,mesəpə'tāmēən/ ▶ adj. relating to Mesopotamia, an ancient region of what is now Iraq. ▶ n. a person from Mesopotamia.

mes·o·sphere /'mezə,sfi(ə)r, 'mē-/ ▶ n. the region of the earth's atmosphere above the stratosphere and below the thermosphere.

mes·o·the·li·o·ma /'mezə,THēlē'ōmə, ,mē-/ ▶ n. a cancer affecting the lining of the chest or abdomen, associated mainly with exposure to asbestos.

Mes·o·zo·ic /'mezə'zōik, ,mē-/ ▶ adj. relating to the era between the Palaeozoic and Cenozoic eras, about 245 to 65 million years ago, with evidence of the first mammals, birds, and flowering plants.

mes·quite /mə'skēt/ ▶ n. a spiny tree of the southwestern US and Mexico, yielding wood, medicinal products, and edible pods.

mess /mes/ ▶ n. **1** a dirty or untidy state. **2** a state of confusion or difficulty. **3** euphemistic a dog's or cat's excrement. **4** a place providing meals and recreational facilities for members of the armed forces. **5** a portion of semisolid food. ▶ v. **1** make something untidy or dirty. **2** (**mess about/around**) behave in a silly or playful way. **3** (**mess someone up**) informal cause someone problems. **4** (**mess something up**) informal handle something badly. **5** (**mess with**) informal meddle

with. **6** eat in an armed forces' mess.

mes·sage /'mesij/ ▶ n. **1** a spoken, written, or electronic communication. **2** a significant point or central theme of a novel, speech, etc. ▶ v. send a message to someone, especially by email.

– PHRASES **get the message** informal understand what is meant. **on** (or **off**) **message** (of a politician) following (or not following) the official party line.

mes·sage board ▶ n. a website where people can post and read messages, usually on a specific topic or area of interest.

Mes·sei·gneurs /,māsān'yər(z)/ ▶ plural of **MONSEIGNEUR.**

mes·sen·ger /'mesənjər/ ▶ n. a person who carries a message.

mes·sen·ger RNA ▶ n. the form of RNA in which genetic information transcribed from DNA is transferred to a ribosome.

mess hall ▶ n. a room or building where groups of people, especially soldiers, eat together.

mes·si·ah /mə'sīə/ ▶ n. **1** (**the Messiah**) the person sent by God to save the Jewish people, as prophesied in the Hebrew Bible (the Old Testament). **2** (**the Messiah**) Jesus regarded by Christians as the Messiah of the Hebrew prophecies. **3** a leader regarded as a savior of a country, group, etc.

mes·si·an·ic /,mesē'anik/ ▶ adj. **1** relating to the Messiah. **2** passionate or fervent: *messianic zeal.* ■ **mes·si·a·nism** /'mesēə,nizəm, mə'sīə-/ n.

Mes·sieurs /məs'yœ(r)(z), mās-, mə'si(ə)r(z)/ ▶ plural of **MONSIEUR.**

Mes·srs. /'mesərz/ ▶ plural of **MR.**

mess·y /'mesē/ ▶ adj. (**messier**, **messiest**) **1** untidy or dirty. **2** confused and difficult to deal with. ■ **mess·i·ly** adv. **mess·i·ness** n.

mes·ti·zo /me'stēzō/ ▶ n. (pl. **mestizos**; fem. **mestiza** /mə'stēzə/, pl. **mestizas**) a Latin American of mixed race, especially one of Spanish and American Indian parentage.

met /met/ ▶ past and past participle of **MEET¹.**

met. ▶ abbr. **1** meteorology. **2** metropolitan.

meta- (also **met-** before a vowel or h) ▶ comb.form **1** referring to a change of position or condition: *metamorphosis.* **2** referring to position behind, after, or beyond: *metacarpus.* **3** referring to something of a higher or second-order kind: *metalanguage.*

me·tab·o·lism /mə'tabə,lizəm/ ▶ n. the chemical processes in a living organism by which food is used for tissue growth or energy production. ■ **met·a·bol·ic** /,metə'bälik/ adj.

me·tab·o·lite /mə'tabə,līt/ ▶ n. a substance formed in or necessary for metabolism.

me·tab·o·lize /mə'tabə,līz/ ▶ v. (of the body or an organ) process a substance by metabolism.

met·a·car·pus /,metə,kärpəs/ ▶ n. (pl. **metacarpi** /-pē, -,pī/) the group of five bones of the hand between the wrist and the fingers. ■ **met·a·car·pal** adj. & n.

met·al /'metl/ ▶ n. **1** a solid material that is typically hard, shiny, and able to be shaped and that can conduct electricity and heat, e.g., iron, copper, and gold. **2** heavy metal or similar rock music.

met·a·lan·guage /'metə,laNG(g)wij/ ▶ n. a form of language used to describe or analyze another language.

met·al de·tec·tor ▶ n. an electronic device that gives a signal when it is close to metal.

met·al·ize /'metl,īz/ ▶ v. **1** coat something with a layer of metal. **2** make something metallic.

me·tal·lic /mə'talik/ ▶ adj. **1** relating to or resembling metal. **2** (of sound) sharp and ringing. ■ **me·tal·li·cal·ly** /-ik(ə)lē/ adv.

met·al·log·ra·phy /,metl'ägrəfē/ ▶ n. the descriptive science of the structure and properties of metals. ■ **me·tal·lo·graph·ic** /'metl-ə'grafik/ adj.

met·al·lur·gy /'metl,ərjē/ ▶ n. the scientific study of the properties, production, and purification of metals. ■ **met·al·lur·gi·cal** adj. **met·al·lur·gist** n.

met·al·work /'metl,wərk/ ▶ n. **1** the art of making things from metal. **2** objects made from metal.

met·a·mor·phic /'metə'môrfik/ ▶ adj. (of rock) having been changed by heat, pressure, or other natural agencies. ■ **met·a·mor·phism** /'metə'môr,fizəm/ n.

met·a·mor·phose /,metə'môr,fōz, -,fōs/ ▶ v. **1** (of an insect or amphibian) undergo metamorphosis. **2** change completely in form or nature.

met·a·mor·pho·sis /,metə'môrfəsəs/ ▶ n. (pl. **metamorphoses** /-fə,sēz/) **1** the transformation of an insect or amphibian from an immature form or larva to an adult form in distinct stages. **2** a change in form or nature.

met·a·phor /'metə,fôr, -fər/ ▶ n. **1** a figure of speech in which a word or phrase is used of something to which it does not literally apply (e.g., *the long arm of the law*). **2** a thing seen as symbolic of something else.

met·a·phor·i·cal /,metə'fôrikəl/ (also **metaphoric** /,metə'fôrik/) ▶ adj. relating to or making use of metaphors. ■ **met·a·phor·i·cal·ly** /,metə'fôrik(ə)lē/ adv.

met·a·phys·ic /,metə'fizik/ ▶ n. a system of metaphysics.

met·a·phys·i·cal /,metə'fizikəl/ ▶ adj. **1** relating to metaphysics. **2** beyond physical matter: *the metaphysical battle between Good and Evil.* **3** referring to a group of 17th-century English poets (in particular John Donne, George Herbert, Andrew Marvell, and Henry Vaughan) known for their complex imagery. ■ **met·a·phys·i·cal·ly** adv.

met·a·phys·ics /,metə'fiziks/ ▶ pl.n. (usu. treated as sing.) **1** philosophy concerned with abstract ideas such as the nature of existence or of truth and knowledge. **2** abstract theory with no basis in reality. ■ **met·a·phy·si·cian** /-fə'zisнən/ n.

me·tas·ta·sis /mə'tastəsəs/ ▶ n. (pl. **metastases** /-,sēz/) the development of secondary tumors elsewhere in the body from the primary site of cancer.

met·a·tar·sal /,metə'tärsəl/ ▶ n. any of the bones of the foot.

met·a·tar·sus /,metə'tärsəs/ ▶ n. (pl. **metatarsi** /-tärsē, -tärsī/) the group of bones in the foot, between the ankle and the toes.

met·a·zo·an /,metə'zōən/ ▶ n. an animal other than a protozoan or sponge.

mete /mēt/ ▶ v. (**mete something out**) deal out justice, punishment, etc., to someone.

me·te·or /'mētēər, -ē,ôr/ ▶ n. a small body of matter from outer space that glows as a result of friction with the earth's atmosphere and appears as a shooting star.

me·te·or·ic /,mētē'ôrik/ ▶ adj. **1** relating to meteors or meteorites. **2** (of change or development) very rapid: *her meteoric rise to the top of her profession.*

me·te·or·ite /'mētēə,rīt/ ▶ n. a piece of rock or metal that has fallen to the earth from space.

me·te·or·oid /'mētēə,roid/ ▶ n. a small body that would become a meteor if it entered the earth's atmosphere.

me·te·or·ol·o·gy /,mētēə'räləjē/ ▶ n. the study of atmospheric processes and conditions, especially for weather forecasting. ■ **me·te·or·o·log·i·cal** /-rə'läjikəl/ adj. **me·te·or·ol·o·gist** n.

me·ter[1] /'mētər/ ▶ n. a device that measures and records the quantity, degree, or rate of something. ▶ v. measure the quantity, degree, or rate of something with a meter.

me·ter[2] /'mētər/ (Brit. **metre**) ▶ n. the basic unit of length in the metric system, equal to 100 centimeters (approx. 39.37 inches).

me·ter[3] (Brit. **metre**) ▶ n. **1** the rhythm of a piece of poetry, determined by the number and length of feet in a line. **2** the basic pulse and rhythm of a piece of music.

-meter ▶ comb.form **1** in names of measuring instruments: *thermometer.* **2** in nouns referring to lines of poetry with a specified number of metrical feet: *hexameter.*

meth /meTH/ ▶ n. informal **1** short for CRYSTAL METH. **2** short for METHADONE.

meth·a·done /'meTHə,dōn/ ▶ n. a powerful painkiller, used as a substitute for morphine and heroin in the treatment of addiction.

meth·am·phet·a·mine /,meTHam'fetə,mēn, -min/ ▶ n. a drug related to amphetamine, used illegally as a stimulant.

meth·ane /'meTH,ān/ ▶ n. a colorless, odorless flammable gas that is the main constituent of natural gas.

meth·a·nol /'meTHə,nôl, -,nōl/ ▶ n. a poisonous flammable alcohol, used to make methylated spirit.

meth·e·drine /'meTHə,drēn, -drin/ ▶ n. trademark another term for METHAMPHETAMINE.

me·thinks /mi'THiNGks/ ▶ v. (past **methought**) old use or humorous it seems to me.

meth·od /'meTHəd/ ▶ n. **1** a way of doing something. **2** the quality of being well organized and systematic in one's thinking and behavior.

meth·od act·ing ▶ n. an acting technique in which an actor tries to identify completely with a character's emotions.

me·thod·i·cal /mə'THädikəl/ (also **methodic**) ▶ adj. well organized and systematic. ■ **me·thod·i·cal·ly** /-ik(ə)lē/ adv.

Meth·od·ist /'meTHədəst/ ▶ n. a member of a Christian Protestant denomination originating in the 18th century and based on the ideas of Charles and John Wesley. ▶ adj. relating to Methodists or their beliefs. ■ **Meth·od·ism** /-,dizəm/ n.

meth·od·ol·o·gy /,meTHə'däləjē/ ▶ n. (pl. **methodologies**) a system of methods used in a particular activity or area of study. ■ **meth·od·o·log·i·cal** /-də'läjikəl/ adj.

me·thought /mi'THôt/ ▶ past of METHINKS.

Me·thu·se·lah /mə'TH(y)ōōz(ə)lə/ ▶ n. **1** humorous a very old person. **2** (**methuselah**) a wine bottle of eight times the standard size.

meth·yl /'meTHəl/ ▶ n. Chemistry the radical $-CH_3$, derived from methane.

meth·yl al·co·hol ▶ n. methanol.

meth·yl·ate /'meᴛʜə,lāt/ ▸ v. **1** mix or impregnate something with methanol or methylated spirit. **2** Chemistry introduce a methyl group into a molecule or compound. ■ **meth·yl·a·tion** /,meᴛʜə'lāsʜən/ n.

me·tic·u·lous /mə'tikyələs/ ▸ adj. very careful and precise. ■ **me·tic·u·lous·ly** adv. **me·tic·u·lous·ness** n.

mé·tier /me'tyā, 'me,tyā/ ▸ n. **1** a profession or occupation. **2** an occupation or activity that someone is good at.

met·o·nym /'metə,nim/ ▸ n. a word or phrase used as a substitute for something with which it is closely associated, e.g., *Washington* for the US government. ■ **met·o·nym·ic** /,metə'nimik/ adj. **me·ton·y·my** /mə'tänəmē/ n.

me-too ▸ adj. informal **1** (of a product) designed to imitate or compete with another that has already been successful: *me-too drugs*. **2** (of a person or course of action) adopting the views or policies of another person, especially a competitor.

me·tre /'mētər/ ▸ n. British spelling of METER², METER³.

met·ric /'metrik/ ▸ adj. relating to or using the metric system.

met·ri·cal /'metrikəl/ ▸ adj. **1** relating to or composed in poetic meter. **2** relating to or involving measurement. ■ **met·ri·cal·ly** /-ik(ə)lē/ adv.

met·ric sys·tem ▸ n. the decimal measuring system based on the meter, liter, and gram as units of length, capacity, and weight or mass.

met·ric ton (also **tonne**) ▸ n. a unit of weight equal to 1,000 kilograms (2,205 lb).

met·ro /'metrō/ ▸ n. (pl. **metros**) an underground railroad system in a city, especially Paris.

met·ro·nome /'metrə,nōm/ ▸ n. a musicians' device that marks time at a selected rate by giving a regular tick. ■ **met·ro·nom·ic** /,metrə'nämik/ adj.

me·trop·o·lis /mə'träp(ə)ləs/ ▸ n. the main city of a country or region.

met·ro·pol·i·tan /,metrə'pälitn/ ▸ adj. **1** relating to a large or capital city. **2** relating to the parent country of a colony. **3** Christian Church relating to a metropolitan. ▸ n. **1** a person living in a large or capital city. **2** Christian Church a bishop having authority over the bishops of a province.

met·ro·sex·ual /,metrō'seksʜōōəl/ ▸ n. informal a heterosexual urban man who enjoys shopping, fashion, and similar interests usually associated with women or homosexual men.

met·tle /'metl/ ▸ n. spirit and strength in the face of difficulty.
– PHRASES **be on one's mettle** be ready to show one's ability or courage.

meu·nière /mœn'yer/ ▸ adj. (after a noun) cooked or served in lightly browned butter with lemon juice and parsley: *sole meunière*.

mew /myōō/ ▸ v. (of a cat or gull) make a characteristic high-pitched crying noise. ▸ n. a high-pitched crying noise.

mewl /myōōl/ ▸ v. **1** cry feebly. **2** make a high-pitched crying noise.

mews /myōōz/ ▸ n. (pl. same) Brit. a row of houses or apartments converted from stables in a small street or square.

Mex·i·can /'meksəkən/ ▸ n. a person from Mexico. ▸ adj. relating to Mexico.

me·ze /me'ze/ (also **mezze**) ▸ n. (pl. same or

mezes) (in Turkish, Greek, and Middle Eastern cooking) a selection of hot and cold hors d'oeuvres.

me·zu·zah /mə'zōōzə/ ▸ n. a parchment inscribed with religious texts and attached in a case to the doorpost of a Jewish house as a sign of faith.

mez·za·nine /'mezə,nēn, ,mezə'nēn/ ▸ n. **1** a low story between two others, typically between the ground and second floors of a building. **2** the lowest balcony of a theater or the front rows of the balcony.

mez·zo /'metsō, 'medzō/ (also **mezzo-soprano**) ▸ n. (pl. **mezzos**) a female singer with a voice pitched between soprano and contralto.

mez·zo·tint /'metsō,tint, 'medzō-/ ▸ n. a print made from an engraved metal plate, the surface of which has been scraped and polished to give areas of shade and light respectively.

MF ▸ abbr. medium frequency.

mfg. ▸ abbr. manufacturing.

mfr. ▸ abbr. manufacturer.

Mg ▸ symbol the chemical element magnesium.

mg ▸ abbr. milligram(s).

Mgr. ▸ abbr. **1** (**mgr.**) manager. **2** Monseigneur. **3** Monsignor.

MHR ▸ abbr. (in the US and Australia) Member of the House of Representatives.

MHz ▸ abbr. megahertz.

MI ▸ abbr. Michigan.

mi /mē/ ▸ n. Music the third note of a major scale, coming after 're' and before 'fa.'

mi. ▸ abbr. mile(s).

MIA ▸ abbr. missing in action.

mi·as·ma /mī'azmə, mē-/ ▸ n. literary **1** an unpleasant or unhealthy smell or vapor. **2** an oppressive or unpleasant atmosphere: *a miasma of despair*.

mic /mīk/ ▸ n. informal a microphone.

mi·ca /'mīkə/ ▸ n. a mineral found as minute shiny scales in granite and other rocks.

mice /mīs/ ▸ plural of MOUSE.

Mich·ael·mas /'mikəlməs/ ▸ n. the day of the Christian festival of St. Michael, September 29.

mick·ey /'mikē/ ▸ n. informal a Mickey Finn, or the drug used to make a Mickey Finn: *did you slip him a mickey?*

Mick·ey Finn /'mikē 'fin/ ▸ n. informal a drink to which a drug has been secretly added.

Mick·ey Mouse /,mikē 'mous/ ▸ adj. informal trivial or not of high quality.

Mic·mac /'mik,mak/ ▸ n. (pl. same or **Micmacs**) a member of an American Indian people living in the Maritime Provinces of Canada.

mi·cro /'mīkrō/ ▸ n. (pl. **micros**) a microcomputer or microprocessor. ▸ adj. extremely small or small-scale.

micro- ▸ comb.form **1** very small or of reduced size: *microchip*. **2** referring to a factor of one millionth (10⁻⁶): *microfarad*.

mi·cro·a·nal·y·sis /,mīkrōə'naləsəs/ ▸ n. the analysis of chemical compounds using a sample of a few milligrams.

mi·crobe /'mī,krōb/ ▸ n. a microorganism, especially a bacterium causing disease. ■ **mi·cro·bi·al** /mī'krōbēəl/ adj.

mi·cro·bi·ol·o·gy /,mīkrō,bī'äləjē/ ▸ n. the scientific study of microorganisms.

mi·cro·brew·er·y /,mīkrō'brōōərē/ ▸ n. (pl. **microbreweries**) a brewery producing limited quantities of beer. ■ **mi·cro·brew·er** n.

mi·cro·burst /'mīkrō,bərst/ ▸ n. a sudden, powerful, localized downdraft.

mi·cro·chip /'mīkrō,CHip/ ▸ n. a tiny wafer of silicon or similar material used to make an integrated circuit. ▸ v. (**microchips, microchipping, microchipped**) implant a microchip under the skin of a cat or dog so that they can be identified.

mi·cro·cir·cuit /'mīkrō,sərkət/ ▸ n. a minute electric circuit, especially an integrated circuit.

mi·cro·cli·mate /'mīkrō,klīmət/ ▸ n. the climate of a very small or restricted area.

mi·cro·code /'mīkrə,kōd/ ▸ n. a very low-level set of instructions controlling the operation of a computer.

mi·cro·com·pu·ter /'mīkrōkəm,pyōōtər/ ▸ n. a small computer with a microprocessor as its central processor.

mi·cro·cosm /'mīkrə,käzəm/ ▸ n. a thing seen as a miniature representation of something much larger: *the city's population is a microcosm of modern Malaysia.* ■ **mi·cro·cos·mic** /,mīkrə'käzmik/ adj.

mi·cro·derm·a·bra·sion /,mīkrō,dərmə'brāzHən/ ▸ n. a cosmetic treatment in which the face is sprayed with granular crystals to remove dead skin cells.

mi·cro·dot /'mīkrə,dät/ ▸ n. **1** a photograph, especially of a printed document, reduced to a very small size. **2** informal a tiny tablet of LSD.

mi·cro·ec·o·nom·ics /,mīkrō,ekə'nämiks, -,ēkə-/ ▸ pl.n. (treated as sing.) the part of economics concerned with single factors and the effects of individual decisions.

mi·cro·e·lec·tron·ics /,mīkrōi,lek'träniks/ ▸ pl.n. (usu. treated as sing.) the design, manufacture, and use of microchips and microcircuits.

mi·cro·fi·ber /'mīkrō,fībər/ ▸ n. a very fine synthetic yarn.

mi·cro·fiche /'mīkr,fēsH/ ▸ n. a flat piece of film containing greatly reduced photographs of the pages of a newspaper, catalog, or other document.

mi·cro·film /'mīkrə,film/ ▸ n. a length of film containing greatly reduced photographs of a newspaper, catalog, or other document.

mi·cro·gram /'mīkrə,gram/ ▸ n. one millionth of a gram.

mi·cro·graph /'mīkrə,graf/ ▸ n. a photograph taken using a microscope.

mi·cro·grav·i·ty /,mīkrō'gravətē/ ▸ n. very weak gravity, as in an orbiting spacecraft.

mi·cro·li·ter /,mīkrō'lētər/ ▸ n. one millionth of a liter.

mi·cro·man·age /,mīkrō'manij/ ▸ v. control every part, however small, of an enterprise or activity. ■ **mi·cro·man·age·ment** n.

mi·crom·e·ter /mī'krämətər/ ▸ n. **1** a gauge that measures small distances or thicknesses. **2** one millionth of a meter.

mi·cron /'mī,krän/ ▸ n. one millionth of a meter.

Mi·cro·ne·sian /,mīkrə'nēzHən/ ▸ n. a person from Micronesia, an island group in the western Pacific. ▸ adj. relating to Micronesia.

mi·cro·nu·tri·ent /,mīkrō'n(y)ōōtrēənt/ ▸ n. a chemical element or substance required in trace amounts by living things.

mi·cro·or·gan·ism /,mīkrō'ôrgə,nizəm/ ▸ n. a microscopic organism, especially a bacterium

or virus.

mi·cro·pay·ment /'mīkrō,pāmənt/ ▸ n. a very small payment made each time a user accesses an Internet page or service.

mi·cro·phone /'mīkrə,fōn/ ▸ n. a device for converting sound waves into electrical energy, which can then be amplified, transmitted, or recorded.

mi·cro·proc·es·sor /,mīkrō'präsesər, -'prō,sesər/ ▸ n. an integrated circuit that can perform the role of a central processing unit of a computer.

mi·cro·scope /'mīkrə,skōp/ ▸ n. an instrument used in scientific study for magnifying very small objects.

mi·cro·scop·ic /,mīkrə'skäpik/ ▸ adj. **1** so small as to be visible only with a microscope. **2** very small. **3** relating to a microscope. ■ **mi·cro·scop·i·cal·ly** /-ik(ə)lē/ adv.

mi·cros·co·py /mī'kräskəpē/ ▸ n. the use of a microscope.

mi·cro·sec·ond /'mīkrō,sekənd/ ▸ n. one millionth of a second.

mi·cro·struc·ture /,mīkrō'strəkCHər/ ▸ n. the fine structure in a material that can be made visible and examined with a microscope.

mi·cro·sur·ger·y /,mīkrō'sərjərē/ ▸ n. intricate surgery performed using very small instruments and a microscope.

mi·cro·wave /'mīkrə,wāv/ ▸ n. **1** an electromagnetic wave with a wavelength in the range 0.001–0.3 m, shorter than that of a normal radio wave but longer than those of infrared radiation. **2** (also **microwave oven**) an oven that uses microwaves to cook or heat food. ▸ v. cook food in a microwave oven.

mic·tu·rate /'mikCHə,rāt/ ▸ v. formal urinate. ■ **mic·tu·ri·tion** /,mikCHə'risHən/ n.

mid /mid/ ▸ adj. relating to or in the middle part of a range. ▸ prep. literary in the middle of; amid.

mid- ▸ comb.form **1** referring to the middle of: *midsection.* **2** in the middle; medium; half: *midway.*

mid·air /'mid'e(ə)r/ ▸ n. a part of the air above ground level: *he caught Murray's keys in midair.*

Mi·das touch /'mīdəs/ ▸ n. the ability to make money out of anything one does.

mid·brain /'mid,brān/ ▸ n. a small central part of the brainstem, developing from the middle of the embryonic brain.

mid·day /'mid'dā/ ▸ n. the middle of the day; noon.

mid·den /'midn/ ▸ n. a dunghill or refuse heap.

mid·dle /'midl/ ▸ adj. **1** at an equal distance from the edges or ends of something; central. **2** intermediate in rank, quality, or ability. ▸ n. **1** a middle point or position. **2** informal a person's waist and stomach.

mid·dle age ▸ n. the period after early adulthood and before old age, about 45 to 60. ■ **mid·dle-aged** adj.

Mid·dle Ag·es ▸ pl.n. the period of European history from the fall of the Roman Empire in the West (5th century) to the fall of Constantinople (1453), or, more narrowly, from c. 1000 to 1453.

Mid·dle A·mer·i·ca ▸ n. the conservative middle classes of the US, characterized as living in the Midwest.

mid·dle·brow /'midl'brou/ ▸ adj. informal needing or involving only a moderate level of intellectual effort.

mid·dle C ▸ n. the C near the middle of the piano keyboard, written on the first ledger line below the treble staff or the first ledger line above the bass staff.

mid·dle class ▸ n. the social group made up of business and professional people, between the upper and working classes.

mid·dle dis·tance ▸ n. **1** the part of a real or painted landscape between the foreground and the background. **2** Athletics a race distance between 800 and 5,000 meters.

mid·dle ear ▸ n. the air-filled central cavity of the ear, behind the eardrum.

Mid·dle East ▸ n. an area of SW Asia and northern Africa, stretching from the Mediterranean to Pakistan, in particular Iran, Iraq, Israel, Jordan, Lebanon, and Syria. ■ **Mid·dle East·ern** adj.

Mid·dle Eng·lish ▸ n. the English language from c. 1150 to c. 1470.

mid·dle ground ▸ n. an area of compromise or possible agreement between two opposing positions or groups.

mid·dle·man /'midl,man/ ▸ n. (pl. **middlemen**) **1** a person who buys goods from producers and sells them to retailers or consumers. **2** a person who arranges business or political deals between other people.

mid·dle name ▸ n. a person's name placed after the first name and before the surname.

mid·dle-of-the-road ▸ adj. **1** (of views) not extreme; moderate. **2** (of music) popular with a wide range of people but rather bland or unadventurous.

mid·dle school ▸ n. a school for children in the sixth, seventh, and eighth grades.

mid·dle·weight /'midl,wāt/ ▸ n. a weight in boxing and other sports intermediate between welterweight and light heavyweight.

mid·dling /'midliNG, 'midlin/ ▸ adj. moderate or average. ▸ adv. informal fairly or moderately.

mid·field /'mid,fēld, mid'fēld/ ▸ n. **1** (chiefly in soccer) the central part of the field. **2** the players who play in a central position between attack and defense. ■ **mid·field·er** n.

midge /mij/ ▸ n. a small two-winged fly that forms swarms near water, of which many kinds feed on blood.

mid·get /'mijit/ ▸ n. a very small person or thing. ▸ adj. very small: *a midget submarine*.

MIDI /'midē/ ▸ n. a standard for interconnecting electronic musical instruments and computers.

mid·i /'mi'dē/ ▸ n. (pl. **midis**) a woman's calf-length skirt, dress, or coat.

midi- ▸ comb.form of medium size or length.

mid·land /'midlənd/ ▸ n. **1** the middle part of a country. **2** (**the Midlands**) the inland counties of central England. ▸ adj. (also **midlands**) relating to or in the middle part of a country or the Midlands. ■ **mid·land·er** n.

mid·life /mid'līf/ ▸ n. the central period of a person's life, between around 45 and 60 years old.

mid·life cri·sis ▸ n. an emotional crisis of identity and self-confidence that can occur in early middle age.

mid·line /'mid,līn/ ▸ n. a median line or plane of bilateral symmetry, especially in an organism. ▸ adj. in the middle range of a product line, in terms of expense or features.

mid·night /'mid,nīt/ ▸ n. twelve o'clock at night; the middle of the night.

mid·night blue ▸ n. a very dark blue.

mid·night sun ▸ n. the sun when seen at midnight during the summer within either the Arctic or Antarctic Circle.

mid·point /'mid,point/ ▸ n. **1** a point halfway through a period or process. **2** the exact middle point of something.

mid·rib /'mid,rib/ ▸ n. a large strengthened vein running down the center of a leaf.

mid·riff /'mid,rif/ ▸ n. the front of the body between the chest and the waist.

mid·sec·tion /'mid,seksHən/ ▸ n. the middle part of something.

mid·ship /'mid,sHip/ ▸ n. the middle part of a ship or boat.

mid·ship·man /'mid,sHipmən, mid'sHip-/ ▸ n. (pl. **midshipmen**) **1** a cadet in the US Navy. **2** a rank of officer in the British Royal Navy above cadet and below sub lieutenant.

mid·ships /'mid,sHips/ ▸ adv. & adj. another term for AMIDSHIPS.

midst /midst, mitst/ old use or literary ▸ prep. in the middle of. ▸ n. the middle point or part. – PHRASES **in our** (or **your** or **their**) **midst** among us (or you or them).

mid·stream /'mid'strēm/ ▸ n. the middle of a stream or river. – PHRASES **in midstream** in the middle of doing something.

mid·sum·mer /'mid'səmər/ ▸ n. **1** the middle part of summer. **2** the summer solstice.

mid·term /'mid,tərm/ ▸ n. the middle of a period of office, an academic term, or a pregnancy.

mid·town /'mid,toun/ ▸ n. the central part of a city between the downtown and uptown areas.

mid·way /'mid,wā, -'wā/ ▸ adv. & adj. in or toward the middle.

mid·week /'mid,wēk/ ▸ n. the middle of the week. ▸ adj. & adv. in the middle of the week.

Mid·west /'mid'west/ ▸ n. the region of northern states of the US from Ohio west to the Rocky Mountains. ■ **Mid·west·ern** adj. **Mid·west·ern·er** n.

mid·wife /'mid,wīf/ ▸ n. (pl. **midwives** /'mid,wīvz/) a person who is trained to help women in childbirth. ■ **mid·wife·ry** /mid'wīf(ə)rē, -'wīf(ə)rē/ n.

mid·win·ter /'mid'wintər/ ▸ n. **1** the middle part of winter. **2** the winter solstice.

mien /mēn/ ▸ n. a person's look or manner.

mi·fep·ri·stone /,mifə'pris,tōn/ ▸ n. a synthetic steroid that inhibits the action of progesterone, given orally in early pregnancy to induce abortion.

miffed /mifd/ ▸ adj. informal offended or irritated.

might¹ /mīt/ ▸ modal v. (3rd sing. present **might**) past of MAY. **1** used to express possibility or make a suggestion. **2** used politely or tentatively in questions and requests.

might² ▸ n. great power or strength. – PHRASES **with all one's might** using all one's power or strength.

might·n't /'mītnt/ ▸ contr. might not.

might·y /'mītē/ ▸ adj. (**mightier**, **mightiest**) **1** very powerful or strong. **2** informal very large. ▸ adv. informal extremely. ■ **might·i·ly** adv. **might·i·ness** n.

mi·gnon·ette /ˌminyə'net/ ▸ n. a plant with spikes of small fragrant greenish flowers.

mi·graine /'mī,grān/ ▸ n. a throbbing headache, typically affecting one side of the head and often accompanied by nausea and disturbed vision.

mi·grant /'mīgrənt/ ▸ n. 1 a person who moves from one place to another to find work. 2 an animal that migrates. ▸ adj. tending to migrate or having migrated: *migrant workers.*

mi·grate /'mī,grāt/ ▸ v. 1 (of an animal) move from one habitat to another according to the seasons. 2 move to settle in a new area in order to find work. 3 Computing change or transfer from one system to another. ▪ **mi·gra·tion** /mī'grāsHən/ n. **mi·gra·to·ry** /'mīgrə,tôrē/ adj.

mih·rab /'mi(ə)rəb/ ▸ n. a niche in the wall of a mosque at the point nearest to Mecca, toward which the congregation faces to pray.

mi·ka·do /mi'kädō/ ▸ n. historical a title given to the emperor of Japan.

mike /mīk/ ▸ n. informal a microphone.

mil /mil/ ▸ abbr. informal millions.

mi·la·dy /mə'lādē, mī-/ ▸ n. historical or humorous used to address or refer to an English noblewoman.

mil·age ▸ n. variant spelling of MILEAGE.

milch /milk, milcH/ ▸ adj. (of a domestic mammal) giving or kept for milk.

milch cow ▸ n. a source of easy profit.

mild /mīld/ ▸ adj. 1 not severe, harsh, or extreme: *mild criticism.* 2 (of weather) fairly warm. 3 not sharp or strong in flavor. 4 gentle and calm: *his mild manner.* ▪ **mild·ly** adv. **mild·ness** n.

mil·dew /'mil,d(y)oo/ ▸ n. a coating of minute fungi that grows on plants or on materials such as paper or leather when they are damp. ▪ **mil·dewed** adj.

mild steel ▸ n. strong, tough steel containing a small percentage of carbon.

mile /mīl/ ▸ n. 1 (also **statute mile**) a unit of length equal to 5,280 feet (approximately 1.609 kilometers). 2 (**miles**) informal a very long way. ▸ adv. (**miles**) informal by a great amount or a long way: *the second tape is miles better.* – PHRASES **be miles away** informal be lost in thought. **go the extra mile** try particularly hard to achieve something. **stand** (or **stick**) **out a mile** informal be very obvious or noticeable.

mile·age /'mīlij/ (also **milage**) ▸ n. 1 a number of miles traveled or covered. 2 informal actual or potential benefit or advantage: *she got plenty of mileage out of the rumor.*

mile·post /'mīl,pōst/ ▸ n. 1 a milestone. 2 a post one mile from the finishing post of a race.

mil·er /'mīlər/ ▸ n. informal a person or horse trained to run races of a mile.

mile·stone /'mīl,stōn/ ▸ n. 1 a stone set up beside a road to mark the distance in miles to a particular place. 2 an event marking a significant new development or stage.

mil·foil /'mil,foil/ ▸ n. 1 another term for YARROW. 2 a water plant with whorls of submerged leaves.

mi·lieu /mil'yoō, -'yə(r)/ ▸ n. (pl. **milieux** pronunc. same, or **milieus** /mil'yoōz, -'yə(r)z/) a person's social environment: *his working-class milieu.*

mil·i·tant /'milətənt/ ▸ adj. prepared to take aggressive action in support of a political or social cause. ▸ n. a militant person. ▪ **mil·i·tan·cy** n. **mil·i·tant·ly** adv.

mil·i·tar·i·a /ˌmili'te(ə)rēə/ ▸ pl.n. military articles of historical interest.

mil·i·ta·rism /'milətə,rizəm/ ▸ n. the belief that a country should maintain and readily use strong armed forces. ▪ **mil·i·ta·rist** n. & adj. **mil·i·ta·ris·tic** /ˌmilətə'ristik/ adj.

mil·i·ta·rize /'milətə,rīz/ ▸ v. (often as adj. **militarized**) 1 supply a place with soldiers and other military resources. 2 make something military in nature or similar to an army: *militarized police forces.* ▪ **mil·i·ta·ri·za·tion** /ˌmilətərə'zāsHən/ n.

mil·i·tar·y /'milə,terē/ ▸ adj. relating to or characteristic of soldiers or armed forces. ▸ n. (**the military**) the armed forces of a country. ▪ **mil·i·tar·i·ly** /ˌmilə'te(ə)rəlē/ adv.

mil·i·tar·y hon·ors ▸ pl.n. ceremonies performed by troops as a mark of respect at the burial of a member of the armed forces.

mil·i·tar·y-in·dus·tri·al com·plex ▸ n. a country's military establishment and arms industries, regarded as a strong influence on government.

mil·i·tar·y po·lice ▸ n. a military body responsible for policing and disciplinary duties in the armed forces.

mil·i·tate /'milə,tāt/ ▸ v. (**militate against**) be a powerful or decisive factor in preventing something: *these differences will militate against the two communities coming together.*

USAGE
On the confusion between **militate** and **mitigate**, see the note at MITIGATE.

---

mi·li·tia /mə'lisHə/ ▸ n. 1 a military force made up of civilians, used to supplement a regular army in an emergency. 2 a rebel force opposing a regular army. ▪ **mi·li·tia·man** /mə'lisHəmən/ n. (pl. **militiamen**)

milk /milk/ ▸ n. 1 an opaque white fluid produced by female mammals to feed their young. 2 the milk of cows as a food and drink for humans. 3 the milklike juice of certain plants, such as the coconut. ▸ v. 1 draw milk from a cow or other animal. 2 exploit or defraud by taking small amounts of money over a period of time: *he had milked his grandmother of all her money.* 3 take full advantage of a situation.

milk choc·o·late ▸ n. solid chocolate that has been made with milk.

milk fe·ver ▸ n. an acute illness in cows or other female animals that have just produced young.

milk·maid /'milk,mād/ ▸ n. (in the past) a girl or woman who worked in a dairy.

milk·man /'milkmən, -,man/ ▸ n. (pl. **milkmen**) a man who delivers milk to houses.

milk run ▸ n. informal a routine, uneventful journey, especially by aircraft.

milk·shake /'milk,sHāk/ ▸ n. a cold drink made from milk blended with ice cream and a flavoring such as a syrup or fruit.

milk·sop /'milk,säp/ ▸ n. a timid and indecisive person.

milk this·tle ▸ n. a thistle with a solitary purple flower and glossy leaves, used in herbal medicine.

milk tooth ▸ n. a temporary tooth in a child or young mammal.

milk·weed /'milk,wēd/ ▸ n. an herbaceous American plant that attracts butterflies and produces a milky sap.

milk·y /'milkē/ ▸ adj. (**milkier, milkiest**) 1 containing milk. 2 having a soft white color or clouded appearance. ■ **milk·i·ly** adv. **milk·i·ness** n.

Milk·y Way ▶ n. the galaxy of which our solar system is a part, visible at night as a faint band of light crossing the sky.

mill[1] /mil/ ▶ n. **1** a building equipped with machinery for grinding grain into flour. **2** a device or piece of machinery for grinding solid substances, such as peppercorns. **3** a building fitted with machinery for a manufacturing process: *a steel mill.* ▶ v. **1** grind something in a mill. **2** cut or shape metal with a rotating tool. **3** (usu. as adj. **milled**) produce regular ribbed markings on the edge of a coin. **4** (**mill around/about**) move around in a confused mass.
– PHRASES **go** (or **put someone**) **through the mill** undergo (or make someone undergo) an unpleasant experience.

mill[2] ▶ n. a monetary unit used only in calculations, worth one thousandth of a dollar.

mille·feuille /ˌmēlˈfœy(ə), fəˈwē/ ▶ n. a cake consisting of thin layers of puff pastry and such fillings as whipped cream, custard, or fruit.

mil·le·nar·i·an /ˌmiləˈne(ə)rēən/ ▶ adj. relating to or believing in Christian millenarianism. ▶ n. a person who believes in millenarianism.

mil·le·nar·i·an·ism /ˌmiləˈne(ə)rēəˌnizəm/ ▶ n. the belief in a future thousand-year age of blessedness, beginning with or culminating in the Second Coming of Jesus. ■ **mil·le·nar·i·an·ist** n. & adj.

mil·le·nar·y /ˈmiləˌnerē/ ▶ n. (pl. **millenaries**) **1** a period of a thousand years. **2** a thousandth anniversary. ▶ adj. consisting of a thousand.

mil·len·ni·al /miˈlenēəl/ ▶ adj. relating to a millennium.

mil·len·ni·al·ism /məˈlenēəˌlizəm/ ▶ n. another term for MILLENARIANISM. ■ **mil·len·ni·al·ist** n. & adj.

mil·len·ni·um /məˈlenēəm/ ▶ n. (pl. **millennia** or **millenniums**) **1** a period of a thousand years, especially when calculated from the traditional date of the birth of Jesus. **2** (**the millennium**) the point at which one period of a thousand years ends and another begins. **3** (**the millennium**) Christian Theology the prophesied forthcoming thousand-year reign of Jesus. **4** an anniversary of a thousand years.

> **USAGE**
> The correct spelling is **millennium**, with a double
> **l** and a double **n**. The spelling with one **n** is a
> common mistake, arising from confusion with
> other similar words such as **millenarian**, correctly
> spelled with only one **n**.

mil·len·ni·um bug ▶ n. an inability in older computing software to deal correctly with dates of January 1, 2000 or later.

mill·er /ˈmilər/ ▶ n. a person who owns or works in a grain mill.

mil·let /ˈmilit/ ▶ n. a cereal that bears a large crop of small seeds, used to make flour or alcoholic drinks.

milli- ▶ comb.form a thousand, especially a factor of one thousandth (10^{-3}): *milligram.*

mil·liard /ˈmilˌyärd, -yərd/ ▶ n. Brit., dated one thousand million; a billion.

mil·li·bar /ˈmiləˌbär/ ▶ n. one thousandth of a bar, a unit of atmospheric pressure equivalent to 100 pascals.

mil·li·gram /ˈmiləˌgram/ ▶ n. one thousandth of a gram.

mil·li·li·ter /ˈmiləˌlētər/ ▶ n. one thousandth of a liter.

mil·li·me·ter /ˈmiləˌmētər/ ▶ n. one thousandth of a meter.

mil·li·ner /ˈmilənər/ ▶ n. a person who makes or sells women's hats. ■ **mil·li·ner·y** /ˈmiləˌnerē/ n.

mil·lion /ˈmilyən/ ▶ cardinal number (pl. **millions** or (with numeral or quantifying word) same) **1** the number equivalent to a thousand multiplied by a thousand; 1,000,000 or 10^6. **2** (also **millions**) informal a very large number or amount. ■ **mil·lionth** /-yənTH/ ordinal number.

mil·lion·aire /ˌmilyəˈne(ə)r, ˈmilyəˌne(ə)r/ ▶ n. (fem. **millionairess** /ˌmilyəˈne(ə)rəs/) a person whose money and property are worth one million dollars or more.

mil·li·pede /ˈmiləˌpēd/ ▶ n. a small invertebrate animal with a long body composed of many segments, most of which have two pairs of legs.

mil·li·sec·ond /ˈmiləˌsekənd/ ▶ n. one thousandth of a second.

mill·pond /ˈmilˌpänd/ ▶ n. an artificial pool providing a head of water to power a watermill.

mill·stone /ˈmilˌstōn/ ▶ n. **1** each of a pair of circular stones used for grinding grain. **2** a heavy and inescapable responsibility.

mill wheel ▶ n. a wheel used to drive a watermill.

mi·lo /ˈmīlō/ ▶ n. a drought-resistant variety of sorghum, an important cereal in the central US.

mi·lord /məˈlôrd, mī-/ ▶ n. historical or humorous used to address or refer to an English nobleman.

milque·toast /ˈmilkˌtōst/ ▶ n. a timid or submissive person.

milt /milt/ ▶ n. **1** the semen of a male fish. **2** the reproductive gland of a male fish.

MIME /mīm, 'em 'ī 'em 'ē/ ▶ n. Computing multipurpose Internet mail extensions, a standard for formatting files such as text, graphics, and audio, so they can be sent over the Internet and seen or played by a Web browser or email application.

mime /mīm/ ▶ n. **1** the use of silent gestures and facial expressions to tell a story or convey a feeling, especially as a form of theatrical performance. **2** a performer of mime. ▶ v. use mime to act out a story or convey a feeling.

mim·e·o·graph /ˈmimēəˌgraf/ ▶ n. a duplicating machine that produces copies from a stencil, now superseded by the photocopier.

mi·me·sis /məˈmēsis, mī-/ ▶ n. **1** imitation of reality in art and literature. **2** the quality of resembling another animal or plant.

mi·met·ic /miˈmetik/ ▶ adj. **1** imitating reality in art or literature. **2** resembling another animal or plant.

mim·ic /ˈmimik/ ▶ v. (**mimics, mimicking, mimicked**) **1** imitate someone in order to make fun of them or to entertain others. **2** (of an animal or plant) take on the appearance of another for protection. **3** imitate or copy something. ▶ n. a person skilled in mimicking others.

mim·ic·ry /ˈmimək rē/ ▶ n. **1** imitation of someone or something. **2** the close external resemblance of an animal or plant to another.

mi·mo·sa /miˈmōsə, mī-, -zə/ ▶ n. **1** an acacia tree with delicate fernlike leaves and yellow flowers. **2** a plant of a genus that includes the SENSITIVE PLANT. **3** a drink of champagne and orange juice.

min. ▸abbr. **1** minimum. **2** minute(s).

min·a·ret /ˌminəˈret/ ▸n. a slender tower of a mosque, with a balcony from which Muslims are called to prayer.

min·a·to·ry /ˈminəˌtôrē, ˈmī-/ ▸adj. formal threatening.

mince /mins/ ▸v. **1** cut up meat into very small pieces. **2** walk in an affected way with short, quick steps and swinging hips. ▸n. something minced, especially mincemeat. ■ **minc·er** n.
– PHRASES **not mince (one's) words** speak in a direct way.

mince·meat /ˈminsˌmēt/ ▸n. a mixture of currants, raisins, apples, candied citrus peel, sugar, spices, and suet.
– PHRASES **make mincemeat of** informal defeat someone decisively.

mind /mīnd/ ▸n. **1** a person's faculty of consciousness and thought. **2** a person's ability to reason or remember things. **3** a person's attention or will. **4** an intelligent person.
▸v. **1** be distressed or annoyed by someone or something. **2** feel concern about something. **3** take care with or watch out for: *mind your head on that cupboard!* **4** take care of someone or something temporarily.
– PHRASES **be of two minds** be unable to decide between alternatives. **give someone a piece of one's mind** informal rebuke someone. **have a (good) mind to do** be inclined to do. **in one's mind's eye** in one's imagination. **mind one's Ps & Qs** be careful to be polite and avoid giving offense. **never mind 1** do not be concerned or distressed. **2** let alone. **out of one's mind** not thinking sensibly; crazy. **put one in mind of** remind one of. **to my mind** in my opinion.

mind-bend·ing ▸adj. informal altering one's state of mind.

mind-blow·ing ▸adj. informal overwhelmingly impressive.

mind-bog·gling ▸adj. informal overwhelming; startling.

mind·ed /ˈmīndid/ ▸adj. (often in combination) inclined to think in a particular way: *liberal-minded.*

mind·er /ˈmīndər/ ▸n. a person employed to look after someone or something.

mind·ful /ˈmīndfəl/ ▸adj. (mindful of/that) aware of or recognizing that.

mind game ▸n. a series of actions intended to unsettle someone or to gain an advantage over them.

mind·less /ˈmīn(d)lis/ ▸adj. **1** acting or done without justification and with no concern for the consequences. **2** (mindless of) not thinking of or concerned about. **3** (of an activity) simple and repetitive. ■ **mind·less·ly** adv. **mind·less·ness** n.

mind read·er ▸n. a person who can supposedly discern what another person is thinking.

mind·set /ˈmīndˌset/ ▸n. a person's established set of attitudes.

mine¹ /mīn/ ▸possessive pron. referring to a thing or things belonging to or associated with the speaker.

mine² ▸n. **1** a hole or passage dug in the earth for extracting coal or other minerals. **2** an abundant source: *the book is a mine of information.* **3** a type of bomb placed on or in the ground or water

that detonates on contact. ▸v. **1** extract coal and other minerals from a mine. **2** lay explosive mines on or in the ground or water. **3** exploit a source of information or skill: *his body of work should be mined for its fresh ideas.*

mine·field /ˈmīnˌfēld/ ▸n. **1** an area planted with explosive mines. **2** a subject or situation presenting hidden risks.

min·er /ˈmīnər/ ▸n. a person who works in a mine.

min·er·al /ˈmin(ə)rəl/ ▸n. **1** a solid inorganic substance that occurs naturally, such as copper. **2** an inorganic substance needed by the human body for good health, such as calcium. **3** a substance obtained by mining.

min·er·al·o·gy /ˌminəˈräləjē, -ˈral-/ ▸n. the scientific study of minerals. ■ **min·er·al·og·i·cal** /ˌmin(ə)rəˈläjikəl/ adj. **min·er·al·o·gist** n.

min·er·al oil ▸n. a product produced by distilling petroleum, used as a lubricant or laxative.

min·er·al wa·ter ▸n. water that naturally contains some dissolved salts.

mine·shaft /ˈmīnˌSHaft/ ▸n. a deep, narrow shaft that gives access to a mine.

min·e·stro·ne /ˌminəˈstrōnē/ ▸n. an Italian soup containing vegetables and pasta.

mine·sweep·er /ˈmīnˌswēpər/ ▸n. a warship equipped for detecting and removing tethered explosive mines.

Ming /miNG/ ▸adj. (of Chinese porcelain) made during the Ming dynasty (1368–1644), having vivid colors and elaborate designs.

min·gle /ˈmiNGgəl/ ▸v. **1** mix together. **2** move around and chat at a social function.

min·i /ˈminē/ ▸adj. referring to a very small version of something. ▸n. (pl. **minis**) a very short skirt or dress.

mini- ▸comb.form very small of its kind; miniature: *minibus.*

min·i·a·ture /ˈmin(ē)əCHər, -ˌCHo͝or/ ▸adj. much smaller than normal in size. ▸n. **1** a thing that is much smaller than normal. **2** a very small and highly detailed portrait. ■ **min·i·a·tur·ize** /ˈmin(ē)əCHəˌrīz/ v.

min·i·a·tur·ist /ˈmin(ē)əˌCHo͝orist, -CHərist/ ▸n. an artist who paints miniatures.

min·i·bar /ˈminēˌbär/ ▸n. a refrigerator in a hotel room containing a selection of drinks.

min·i·bus /ˈminēˌbəs/ ▸n. a small bus for about ten to fifteen passengers.

min·i·cam /ˈminēˌkam/ ▸n. a hand-held video camera.

min·i·com·pu·ter /ˈminēkəmˌpyo͞otər/ ▸n. a computer of medium power, more than a microcomputer but less than a mainframe.

min·i·disc /ˈminēˌdisk/ ▸n. a disc similar to a small CD but able to record sound or data as well as play it back.

min·i·dress /ˈminēˌdres/ ▸n. a very short dress.

min·im /ˈminim/ ▸n. one sixtieth of a fluid dram, about one drop of liquid.

min·i·ma /ˈminəmə/ ▸ plural of MINIMUM.

min·i·mal /ˈminəməl/ ▸adj. **1** of a minimum amount, quantity, or degree. **2** (of art) using simple forms or structures. **3** (of music) characterized by the repetition and gradual alteration of short phrases. ■ **min·i·mal·ly** adv.

min·i·mal·ist /'minəməlist/ ▶ adj. **1** relating to minimal art or music. **2** deliberately simple or basic in design. ▶ n. a person who creates minimal art or music. ■ **min·i·mal·ism** /'minəmə,lizəm/ n.

min·i·me ▶ n. informal a person who closely resembles a smaller or younger version of another.

min·i·mize /'minə,mīz/ ▶ v. **1** reduce something to the smallest possible amount or degree. **2** represent something as less important than it really is. ■ **min·i·mi·za·tion** /,minəmə'zāsHən/ n. **min·i·miz·er** n.

min·i·mum /'minəməm/ ▶ n. (pl. **minima** or **minimums**) the least or smallest amount, extent, or intensity possible or recorded: *they checked passports with the minimum of fuss.* ▶ adj. smallest or lowest in amount, extent, or intensity.

min·i·mum wage ▶ n. the lowest wage permitted by law or by agreement.

min·ion /'minyən/ ▶ n. a lowly employee or assistant of a powerful person.

min·i·pill ▶ n. a contraceptive pill containing progestin and not estrogen.

min·i·se·ries /'minē,si(ə)rēz/ ▶ n. a television drama shown in a small number of episodes.

min·i·skirt /'minē,skərt/ ▶ n. a very short skirt. ■ **min·i·skirt·ed** adj.

min·is·ter /'minəstər/ ▶ n. **1** a head of a government department. **2** a member of the clergy, especially in the Presbyterian and Nonconformist Churches. **3** a diplomat, usually ranking below an ambassador, representing a country or sovereign in a foreign country. ▶ v. **1** (**minister to**) attend to the needs of. **2** act as a minister of religion.

min·is·te·ri·al /,minə'sti(ə)rēəl/ ▶ adj. relating to a minister or ministers. ■ **min·is·te·ri·al·ly** adv.

min·is·tra·tions /,minə'strāsHənz/ ▶ pl.n. **1** formal or humorous the provision of help or care. **2** the services of a minister of religion. ■ **min·is·trant** /'minəstrənt/ n.

min·is·try /'minəstrē/ ▶ n. (pl. **ministries**) **1** a government department headed by a minister. **2** a period of government under one minister. **3** the work or office of a minister of religion.

min·i·van /'minē,van/ (also trademark **Mini Van**) ▶ n. a small van fitted with seats for passengers.

mink /miNGk/ ▶ n. a small stoatlike mammal farmed for its fur.

min·ke /'miNGkē/ ▶ n. a small rorqual whale with a dark gray back and white underparts.

min·now /'minō/ ▶ n. **1** a small freshwater fish of the carp family. **2** a minor or unimportant person.

Mi·no·an /mə'nōən, mī-/ ▶ adj. relating to a Bronze Age civilization centered on Crete (*c.* 3000–1050 BC).

mi·nor /'mīnər/ ▶ adj. **1** lesser in importance, seriousness, or significance: *minor alterations.* **2** (of a musical scale) having intervals of a half step between the second and third, and (usually) the fifth and sixth, and the seventh and eighth notes. Contrasted with **MAJOR.** ▶ n. **1** a person under the age of full legal responsibility. **2** Music a minor key, interval, or scale. **3** a student's subsidiary subject or area of concentration. ▶ v. (**minor in**) study a subsidiary subject in college.

Mi·nor·can /mə'nôrkən/ ▶ n. a person from Minorca. ▶ adj. relating to Minorca.

mi·nor·i·ty /mə'nôrətē/ ▶ n. (pl. **minorities**) **1** the smaller number or part. **2** a relatively small group of people differing from the majority in race, religion, etc. **3** the state of being under the age of full legal responsibility.

mi·nor·i·ty lead·er ▶ n. the head of the minority party in a legislative body, especially the US Senate or House of Representatives.

mi·nor league ▶ n. **1** a league below the level of the major league in a particular professional sport, especially baseball. **2** (as adj.) of lesser power or significance: *a minor-league villain.* ■ **mi·nor lea·guer** n.

Min·o·taur /'minə,tôr, 'mī-/ ▶ n. Greek Mythology a creature who was half-man and half-bull, kept in a labyrinth on Crete by King Minos.

min·ox·i·dil /mə'näksə,dil/ ▶ n. a synthetic drug used in the treatment of hypertension and in lotions to promote hair growth.

min·strel /'minstrəl/ ▶ n. a medieval singer or musician.

min·strel·sy /'minstrəlsē/ ▶ n. the activity of performing as a minstrel.

mint[1] /mint/ ▶ n. **1** a plant used as an herb in cooking. **2** the flavor of mint, especially peppermint or spearmint. **3** a peppermint or spearmint candy or breath freshener. ■ **mint·y** adj.

mint[2] ▶ n. **1** a place where coins are made. **2** (**a mint**) informal a large sum of money. ▶ adj. as new; in perfect condition. ▶ v. **1** make a coin by stamping metal. **2** produce something for the first time.

mint ju·lep ▶ n. a cocktail made with bourbon, crushed ice, sugar, and fresh mint.

min·u·et /,minyoō'et/ ▶ n. a slow ballroom dance in triple time, popular in the 18th century.

mi·nus /'mīnəs/ ▶ prep. **1** with the subtraction of. **2** (of temperature) falling below zero by: *minus 32° Fahrenheit.* **3** informal lacking: *he was minus a finger.* ▶ adj. **1** (before a number) below zero; negative. **2** (after a grade) slightly below: *C-minus.* **3** having a negative electric charge. ▶ n. **1** (also **minus sign**) the symbol –, indicating subtraction or a negative value. **2** informal a disadvantage.

mi·nus·cule /'minə,skyoōl, min'əs,kyoōl/ ▶ adj. very small. ▶ n. a lowercase letter.

USAGE

The correct spelling is **minuscule**, not *miniscule*, although the latter form is extremely common.

---

mi·nute[1] /'minit/ ▶ n. **1** a period of time equal to sixty seconds or a sixtieth of an hour. **2** (**a minute**) informal a very short time. **3** (also **arc minute** or **minute of arc**) a measurement of an angle equal to one sixtieth of a degree. – PHRASES **up to the minute** up to date.

mi·nute[2] /mī'n(y)oōt, mə-/ ▶ adj. (**minutest**) **1** very small. **2** very detailed or thorough: *he made a minute examination of the area.* ■ **mi·nute·ly** adv. **mi·nute·ness** n.

mi·nute[3] /'minit/ ▶ n. **1** (**minutes**) a written summary of the points discussed at a meeting. **2** an official written message. ▶ v. record the points discussed at a meeting.

min·ute·man /'minət,man/ ▶ n. (pl. **minutemen**) historical (during the American Revolution) an American militiaman who volunteered to be ready for service at a minute's notice.

min·ute steak /'minit/ ▶ n. a thin slice of steak cooked very quickly.

mi·nu·ti·ae /mə'n(y)ooshē,ē, -shē,ī/ ▸ pl.n. small or precise details.

minx /miNGks/ ▸ n. chiefly humorous an impudent, cunning, or flirtatious girl or young woman. ■ **minx·y** adj.

Mi·o·cene /'mīə,sēn/ ▸ adj. Geology relating to the fourth epoch of the Tertiary period (23.3 to 5.2 million years ago), when the first apes appeared.

mi·ra·bi·le dic·tu /mə'räbə,lā 'diktoo, mə'rabələ/ ▸ adv. wonderful to relate.

mir·a·cle /'mirikəl/ ▸ n. **1** an extraordinary and welcome event believed to be the work of God or a saint. **2** a remarkable and welcome event: *it was a miracle that more people hadn't been killed.* **3** an outstanding example or achievement.

mir·a·cle play ▸ n. a mystery play.

mi·rac·u·lous /mə'rakyələs/ ▸ adj. like a miracle; very surprising and welcome. ■ **mi·rac·u·lous·ly** adv.

mi·rage /mə'räzh/ ▸ n. **1** an optical illusion caused by the refraction of light by heated air, in which a sheet of water seems to appear in a desert or on a hot road. **2** something that seems real or possible but is not in fact so: *such promised happiness is only a mirage.*

mire /mīr/ ▸ n. **1** a stretch of swampy or boggy ground. **2** a difficult situation from which it is hard to escape. ▸ v. (**be mired**) **1** become stuck in mud. **2** become involved in a difficult situation.

mire·poix /mi(ə)r'pwä/ ▸ n. a mixture of chopped sautéed vegetables used in various sauces.

mir·ror /'mirər/ ▸ n. **1** a piece of glass coated with metal that reflects a clear image. **2** something that accurately represents something else. ▸ v. **1** reflect someone or something. **2** correspond to: *the expansion in the Far East has been mirrored in the loss of investment to Eastern Europe.*

mir·ror·ball /'mirər,bôl/ ▸ n. a revolving ball covered with small mirrored facets, used to provide lighting effects at discos.

mir·ror im·age ▸ n. an image that is identical in form to another but has the structure reversed, as if seen in a mirror.

mir·ror site ▸ n. an Internet site that stores contents copied from another site.

mirth /mərTH/ ▸ n. amusement, especially as expressed in laughter. ■ **mirth·ful** adj.

mirth·less /'mərTHlis/ ▸ adj. (of a smile or laugh) lacking real amusement. ■ **mirth·less·ly** adv.

MIRV /mərv/ ▸ abbr. multiple independently targeted re-entry vehicle, an intercontinental nuclear missile with several independent warheads.

mir·y /'mīrē/ ▸ adj. very muddy or boggy.

MIS ▸ abbr. Computing management information system; a computerized information-processing system designed to support the activities of company or organizational management.

mis- ▸ prefix **1** (added to verbs and their derivatives) wrongly, badly, or unsuitably: *mismanage.* **2** (added to some nouns) expressing a negative sense: *misadventure.*

mis·ad·ven·ture /,misəd'venchər/ ▸ n. an unfortunate incident; a mishap.

mis·a·ligned /,misə'līnd/ ▸ adj. incorrectly aligned. ■ **mis·a·lign·ment** /,misə'līnmənt/ n.

mis·al·li·ance /,misə'līəns/ ▸ n. an unsuitable or unhappy alliance or marriage.

mis·an·thrope /'misən,THrōp, 'miz/ ▸ n. a person who dislikes and avoids other people. ■ **mis·an·throp·ic** /,misən'THrapik/ adj. **mis·an·thro·py** /mi'sanTHrəpē/ n.

mis·ap·ply /,misə'plī/ ▸ v. (**misapplies, misapplying, misapplied**) use something for the wrong purpose or in the wrong way. ■ **mis·ap·pli·ca·tion** /-,aplə'kāshən/ n.

mis·ap·pre·hen·sion /,mis,apri'henshən/ ▸ n. a mistaken belief.

mis·ap·pro·pri·ate /,misə'prōprē,āt/ ▸ v. dishonestly take something for one's own use. ■ **mis·ap·pro·pri·a·tion** /-,prōprē'āshən/ n.

mis·be·got·ten /,misbə'gätn/ ▸ adj. **1** badly designed or planned. **2** old use (of a child) illegitimate.

mis·be·have /,misbi'hāv/ ▸ v. behave badly. ■ **mis·be·hav·ior** /-'hāvyər/ n.

misc. ▸ abbr. miscellaneous.

mis·cal·cu·late /mis'kalkyə,lāt/ ▸ v. calculate or assess something wrongly. ■ **mis·cal·cu·la·tion** /,mis,kalkyə'lāshən/ n.

mis·call /mis'kôl/ ▸ v. call something by a wrong or inappropriate name.

mis·car·riage /mis'karij, 'mis,karij/ ▸ n. **1** the early and unplanned expulsion of a fetus from the womb, before it is able to survive independently. **2** an unsuccessful outcome; a failure.

mis·car·riage of jus·tice ▸ n. a failure of a court or judicial system to achieve justice.

mis·car·ry /mis'karē, 'mis,karē/ ▸ v. (**miscarries, miscarrying, miscarried**) **1** (of a pregnant woman) have a miscarriage. **2** (of a plan) fail to achieve an intended result.

mis·cast /mis'kast/ ▸ v. (**be miscast**) (of an actor) be given an unsuitable role.

mis·ceg·e·na·tion /mi,sejə'nāshən, ,misəjə-/ ▸ n. the interbreeding of people of different races.

mis·cel·la·ne·a /,misə'lānēə/ ▸ pl.n. different items collected together.

mis·cel·la·ne·ous /,misə'lānēəs/ ▸ adj. **1** (of a number of things or people) of various types. **2** composed of different kinds: *a miscellaneous collection of problems.* ■ **mis·cel·la·ne·ous·ly** adv.

mis·cel·la·ny /'misə,lānē/ ▸ n. (pl. **miscellanies**) a collection of different things.

mis·chance /mis'chans/ ▸ n. bad luck.

mis·chief /'mischif/ ▸ n. **1** playful misbehavior. **2** harm or trouble caused by someone or something.

mis·chie·vous /'mischivəs/ ▸ adj. **1** misbehaving or fond of misbehaving in a playful way. **2** intended to cause trouble. ■ **mis·chie·vous·ly** adv. **mis·chie·vous·ness** n.

mis·ci·ble /'misəbəl/ ▸ adj. (of liquids) capable of being mixed together.

mis·com·mu·ni·ca·tion /,miskə,myoonə'kāshən/ ▸ n. failure to communicate properly.

mis·con·ceive /,miskən'sēv/ ▸ v. **1** fail to understand something correctly. **2** (**be misconceived**) be badly judged or planned.

mis·con·cep·tion /,miskən'sepshən/ ▸ n. a false or mistaken idea or belief.

mis·con·duct /mis'kän,dəkt/ ▸ n. unacceptable or improper behavior, especially by a professional person.

mis·con·struc·tion /,miskən'strəkshən/ ▸ n. the action of misinterpreting something.

mis·con·strue /ˌmiskən'strōō/
▶ v. (**misconstrues, misconstruing, misconstrued**) interpret something wrongly.

mis·count /mis'kount/ ▶ v. count something incorrectly.

mis·cre·ant /'miskrēənt/ ▶ n. a person who has done something wrong or unlawful.

mis·cue /mis'kyōō/ ▶ v. (**miscues, miscueing** or **miscuing, miscued**) (in billiards) fail to cue the ball properly. ▶ n. an act of miscueing the ball.

mis·deed /mis'dēd/ ▶ n. a wrong or unlawful act.

mis·de·mean·or /'misdiˌmēnər/ (Brit. **misdemeanour**) ▶ n. 1 a minor wrongdoing. 2 Law (in the US and formerly in the UK) an offense regarded as less serious than a felony.

mis·di·ag·nose /mis'dī-igˌnōs, -ˌnōz/ ▶ v. make an incorrect diagnosis of an illness. ■ **mis·di·ag·no·sis** /ˌmisˌdī-ig'nōsəs/ n.

mis·di·al /ˌmis'dī(ə)l/ ▶ v. (**misdials, misdialing, misdialed**) dial a telephone number incorrectly.

mis·di·rect /ˌmisdə'rekt, -dī-/ ▶ v. direct or instruct someone wrongly. ■ **mis·di·rec·tion** /-'rekshən/ n.

mise en scène /ˌmēz ˌän 'sen/ ▶ n. 1 the arrangement of scenery and stage props in a play. 2 the setting of an event.

mi·ser /'mīzər/ ▶ n. a person who hoards wealth and spends as little as possible.

mis·er·a·ble /'miz(ə)rəbəl/ ▶ adj. 1 deeply unhappy or depressed. 2 causing unhappiness or discomfort. 3 gloomy and humorless. 4 too small; inadequate: *all they pay me is a miserable $10,000 a year.* ■ **mis·er·a·ble·ness** n. **mis·er·a·bly** adv.

mis·er·i·cord /mə'zeriˌkôrd/ ▶ n. a ledge projecting from the underside of a hinged seat in a choir stall in a church, giving support to someone standing when the seat is folded up.

mi·ser·ly /'mīzərlē/ ▶ adj. 1 unwilling to spend money; stingy. 2 (of a quantity) too small; inadequate. ■ **mis·er·li·ness** n.

mis·er·y /'miz(ə)rē/ ▶ n. (pl. **miseries**) 1 great unhappiness or distress. 2 a cause of misery.

mis·fire /mis'fīr/ ▶ v. 1 (of a gun) fail to fire properly. 2 (of an internal combustion engine) fail to ignite the fuel correctly. 3 fail to produce the intended result: *he didn't know that his plan had misfired.*

mis·fit /'misˌfit/ ▶ n. a person whose behavior or attitude sets them apart from others.

mis·for·tune /mis'fôrchən/ ▶ n. 1 bad luck. 2 an unfortunate event.

mis·giv·ings /mis'giviNGz/ ▶ pl.n. feelings of doubt or anxiety about what might happen.

mis·gov·ern /mis'gəvərn/ ▶ v. govern a country unfairly or poorly.

mis·guid·ed /mis'gīdid/ ▶ adj. showing poor judgment or reasoning.

mis·han·dle /mis'handəl/ ▶ v. handle or deal with something unwisely or wrongly.

mis·hap /'misˌhap/ ▶ n. an unlucky accident.

mis·hear /mis'hi(ə)r/ ▶ v. (past and past part. **misheard**) fail to hear (a person or their words) correctly.

mis·hit /ˌmis'hit/ ▶ v. (**mishits, mishitting, mishit**) hit or kick a ball badly.

mish·mash /'mishˌmash, -ˌmäsh/ ▶ n. a confused mixture.

mis·i·den·ti·fy /ˌmisī'dentəˌfī/
▶ v. (**misidentifies, misidentifying, misidentified**) identify someone or something incorrectly. ■ **mis·i·den·ti·fi·ca·tion** /-ī,dentəfə'kāshən/ n.

mis·in·form /ˌmisin'fôrm/ ▶ v. give someone false or inaccurate information. ■ **mis·in·for·ma·tion** /ˌmisinfər'māshən/ n.

mis·in·ter·pret /ˌmisin'tərprət/
▶ v. (**misinterprets, misinterpreting, misinterpreted**) interpret something wrongly. ■ **mis·in·ter·pre·ta·tion** /-in,tərprə'tāshən/ n.

mis·judge /ˌmis'jəj/ ▶ v. 1 form an incorrect opinion of someone or something. 2 estimate wrongly: *the horse misjudged the fence and Joe was thrown off.* ■ **mis·judge·ment** (also **misjudgment**) n.

mis·lay /mis'lā/ ▶ v. (past and past part. **mislaid**) lose an object by temporarily forgetting where one has left it.

mis·lead /mis'lēd/ ▶ v. (past and past part. **misled** /mis'led/) give someone inaccurate or false information. ■ **mis·lead·ing** adj.

mis·man·age /mis'manij/ ▶ v. manage something badly or wrongly. ■ **mis·man·age·ment** n.

mis·match /'mis,mach/ ▶ n. a failure to correspond or match: *a huge mismatch between supply and demand.* ▶ v. match people or things unsuitably or incorrectly.

mis·name /mis'nām/ ▶ v. give a wrong or inappropriate name to someone or something.

mis·no·mer /mis'nōmər/ ▶ n. 1 an inaccurate or misleading name. 2 the wrong use of a name or term.

mi·so /'mēsō/ ▶ n. a paste made from fermented soy beans and barley or rice malt, used in Japanese cooking.

mi·sog·y·nist /mə'säjənist/ ▶ n. a man who hates women. ■ **mi·sog·y·nis·tic** /mə,säjə'nistik/ adj.

mi·sog·y·ny /mə'säjənē/ ▶ n. hatred of women.

mis·place /mis'plās/ ▶ v. put something in the wrong place.

mis·placed /mis'plāst/ ▶ adj. 1 not appropriate in the circumstances. 2 (of a feeling) directed to an inappropriate person or thing: *a misplaced faith in the ability of scientists.*

mis·play ▶ v. /mis'plā/ 1 play a ball or card wrongly or badly. 2 err by misjudgment. ▶ n. an instance of playing a ball or card badly.

mis·print /mis,print/ ▶ n. an error in a printed work. ▶ v. print something incorrectly.

mis·pro·nounce /ˌmisprə'nouns/ ▶ v. pronounce something wrongly. ■ **mis·pro·nun·ci·a·tion** /-prə,nənsē'āshən/ n.

mis·quote /mis'kwōt/ ▶ v. quote someone or something inaccurately. ■ **mis·quo·ta·tion** /ˌmiskwō'tāshən/ n.

mis·read /mis'rēd/ ▶ v. (past and past part. **misread** /mis'red/) read or interpret something wrongly.

mis·rep·re·sent /ˌmis,repri'zent/ ▶ v. give a false or misleading account of someone or something. ■ **mis·rep·re·sen·ta·tion** /mis,reprəzən'tāshən/ n.

mis·rule /mis'rōōl/ ▶ n. 1 unfair or inefficient government of a country. 2 disruption of peace; disorder. ▶ v. govern a country badly.

miss¹ /mis/ ▶ v. 1 fail to hit, reach, or come into contact with something aimed at. 2 fail to notice, hear, or understand: *she had shrewd eyes that missed nothing.* 3 omit someone or something. 4 fail to attend or take advantage of something. 5 avoid someone or something. 6 be too late

for a passenger vehicle, etc. **7** notice or feel the loss or absence of: *he missed all his old friends.* ▶ **n. 1** a failure to hit, catch, or reach something. **2** an unsuccessful movie or recording.
− PHRASES **give something a miss** Brit. informal decide not to do or have something. **miss the boat** informal be too slow to take advantage of something.

miss² ▶ **n. 1** (**Miss**) a title used before the name of an unmarried woman or girl. **2** a girl or young woman.

mis·sal /'misəl/ ▶ **n.** a book that contains the set forms of worship used in the Catholic Mass.

mis·shap·en /mis'sнаpən/ ▶ **adj.** not having the normal or natural shape.

mis·sile /'misəl/ ▶ **n. 1** an object that is forcibly propelled at a target. **2** an explosive weapon that is self-propelled or directed by remote control.

miss·ing /'misiNG/ ▶ **adj. 1** absent and unable to be found. **2** not present when expected or supposed to be.

miss·ing link ▶ **n.** a supposed fossil form believed to be a link between humans and apes.

mis·sion /'misHən/ ▶ **n. 1** an important assignment, typically involving travel abroad. **2** an organization involved in a long-term assignment abroad. **3** a military or scientific operation or expedition. **4** the work carried out by a religious organization to spread its faith. **5** an aim or task that a person feels to be their duty: *he made it his mission to foster talent.*

mis·sion·ar·y /'misHə,nerē/ ▶ **n.** (pl. **missionaries**) a person sent on a religious mission. ▶ **adj.** relating to a missionary or religious mission.

mis·sion creep ▶ **n.** a gradual shift in objectives during a military campaign, often resulting in a longer involvement than was planned.

mis·sion state·ment ▶ **n.** a formal summary of the aims and values of an organization.

mis·sis ▶ **n.** variant spelling of MISSUS.

mis·sive /'misiv/ ▶ **n.** formal a letter.

mis·spell /mis'spel/ ▶ **v.** (past and past part. **misspelt** or **misspelled**) spell a word wrongly.

mis·spend /mis'spend/ ▶ **v.** (past and past part. **misspent**) spend time or money foolishly or wastefully.

mis·state /mis'stāt/ ▶ **v.** state something wrongly or inaccurately. ■ **mis·state·ment** n.

mis·step /mis'step, 'mis,step/ ▶ **n.** a badly judged step.

mis·sus /'misəz, -əs/ (also **missis**) ▶ **n.** (**the missus**) informal or humorous a person's wife.

miss·y /'misē/ ▶ **n.** (pl. **missies**) an affectionate or scornful form of address to a young girl.

mist /mist/ ▶ **n. 1** a cloud of tiny water droplets in the atmosphere that limits visibility to a lesser extent than fog. **2** a condensed vapor settling on a surface. ▶ **v.** cover or become covered with mist.

mis·take /mə'stāk/ ▶ **n. 1** a thing that is incorrect. **2** an error of judgment. ▶ **v.** (past **mistook** /mə'stʊk/; past part. **mistaken**) **1** be wrong about: *I mistook the nature of our relationship.* **2** (**mistake someone/thing for**) confuse someone or something with.

mis·tak·en /mə'stākən/ ▶ **adj. 1** wrong in one's opinion or judgment. **2** based on a misunderstanding or faulty judgment. ■ **mis·tak·en·ly** adv.

mis·ter /'mistər/ ▶ **n. 1** variant form of MR. **2** informal a form of address to a man.

mis·time /mis'tīm/ ▶ **v.** choose an inappropriate moment to do or say something.

mis·tle·toe /'misəl,tō/ ▶ **n.** a plant that grows as a parasite on trees and bears white berries in winter.

mis·took /mə'stʊk/ ▶ past of MISTAKE.

mis·tral /'mistrəl, mi'sträl/ ▶ **n.** a strong, cold northwesterly wind that blows through the Rhône valley and southern France.

mis·trans·late /,mis,tranz'lāt, -,trans'lāt/ ▶ **v.** translate something incorrectly. ■ **mis·trans·la·tion** /-'lāsHən/ n.

mis·treat /mis'trēt/ ▶ **v.** treat a person or animal badly or unfairly. ■ **mis·treat·ment** n.

mis·tress /'mistris/ ▶ **n. 1** a woman who controls or owns something. **2** a woman skilled in a particular subject or activity: *she's a mistress of the sound bite.* **3** a woman in a sexual relationship with a man who is married to someone else. **4** (**Mistress**) old use Mrs.

mis·tri·al /'mis,trī(ə)l/ ▶ **n.** a trial that is made invalid through an error in the proceedings.

mis·trust /mis'trəst/ ▶ **v.** have no trust in someone or something. ▶ **n.** lack of trust. ■ **mis·trust·ful** /,mis'trəstfəl/ adj.

mist·y /'mistē/ ▶ **adj.** (**mistier, mistiest**) **1** full of or covered with mist. **2** not clear or distinct: *a few misty memories.* ■ **mist·i·ly** adv. **mist·i·ness** n.

mis·un·der·stand /,mis,əndər'stand/ ▶ **v.** (past and past part. **misunderstood**) fail to understand someone or something correctly.

mis·un·der·stand·ing /,mis,əndər'standiNG/ ▶ **n. 1** a failure to understand something correctly. **2** a disagreement with someone.

mis·use ▶ **v.** /mis'yōoz, 'mis,yōoz/ **1** use something wrongly. **2** treat someone badly or unfairly. ▶ **n.** /,mis'yōos, 'mis,yōos/ the action of misusing something.

mite¹ /mīt/ ▶ **n.** a very tiny creature like a spider, several kinds of which live as parasites on animals or plants.

mite² ▶ **n. 1** a small child or animal. **2** a very small amount. ▶ **adv.** (**a mite**) informal slightly.

mi·ter /'mītər/ (Brit **mitre**) ▶ **n. 1** a tall headdress that tapers to a point at front and back, worn by bishops and senior abbots. **2** a joint made between two pieces of wood cut at an angle so as to form a corner of 90°. ▶ **v.** join pieces of wood by means of a miter.

mit·i·gate /'mitə,gāt/ ▶ **v. 1** make something bad less severe or serious. **2** (as adj. **mitigating**) (of a fact or circumstance) lessening the seriousness of or blame attached to an action. ■ **mit·i·ga·tion** /,mitə'gāsHən/ n.

> **USAGE**
> Do not confuse **mitigate** and **militate**. **Mitigate** means 'make something bad less severe' (*drainage schemes helped to mitigate the problem*), while **militate** is used with **against** to mean 'be a powerful factor in preventing' (*laws that militate against personal freedom*).

mi·to·chon·dri·on /,mītə'kändrēən/ ▶ **n.** (pl. **mitochondria** /-drēə/) Biology a structure found in large numbers in most cells, in which respiration and energy production occur. ■ **mi·to·chon·dri·al** /-drēəl/ adj.

mi·to·sis /mī'tōsəs/ ▶ **n.** (pl. **mitoses** /-sēz/) Biology the division of a cell that results in two daughter cells, each with the same number and kind of chromosomes as the original cell. Compare with MEIOSIS.

mi·tre /'mītər/ ► n. & v. British spelling of MITER.

mitt /mit/ ► n. **1** a mitten. **2** Baseball a glove worn by the catcher and first baseman. **3** a fingerless glove. **4** informal a person's hand.

mit·ten /'mitn/ ► n. a glove having a single section for all four fingers, with a separate section for the thumb.

mitz·vah /'mitsvə/ ► n. (pl. **mitzvoth** /'mits,vōt, -,vōs/) Judaism **1** a precept or commandment. **2** a good deed done from religious duty.

mix /miks/ ► v. **1** combine or be combined to form a whole. **2** make something by combining ingredients. **3** (**mix something up**) spoil the order or arrangement of a group of things. **4** (**mix someone/thing up**) confuse a person or thing with another. **5** combine signals or soundtracks into one to produce a recording. **6** enjoy meeting other people socially. ► n. **1** a mixture. **2** the proportion of different people or things making up a mixture. **3** a version of a sound recording mixed in a different way from the original.
– PHRASES **be mixed up in** (or **with**) be involved in dishonest or underhanded activity.

mixed /mikst/ ► adj. **1** consisting of different kinds, qualities or elements. **2** relating to or intended for both men and women.

mixed bag ► n. a varied assortment of things or people.

mixed bless·ing ► n. a thing that has both advantages and disadvantages.

mixed e·con·o·my ► n. an economic system combining private and public enterprise.

mixed farming ► n. farming of both crops and livestock.

mixed grill ► n. a dish of various grilled meats, mushrooms, and tomatoes.

mixed mar·riage ► n. a marriage between people of different races or religions.

mixed met·a·phor ► n. a combination of metaphors that produces a ridiculous effect (e.g., *this tower of strength will forge ahead*).

mixed-up ► adj. informal suffering from psychological or emotional problems.

mix·er /'miksər/ ► n. **1** a device for mixing things. **2** a person considered in terms of their ability to mix socially. **3** a social gathering. **4** a soft drink that can be mixed with alcohol.

mix·ol·o·gist /mik'säləjist/ ► n. informal a person who is skilled at mixing cocktails and other drinks. ■ **mix·ol·o·gy** n.

mix·ture /'mikscHər/ ► n. **1** a substance made by mixing other substances together. **2** (**a mixture of**) a combination of different things in which each part is distinct: *the area is a bizarre mixture of ancient and modern.* **3** a combination of two or more substances that mix together without any chemical reaction occurring.

mix-up ► n. informal a confusion or misunderstanding.

mi·zu·na /mə'zōōnə/ ► n. a Japanese plant of the rape family, with leaves that are eaten in salads.

miz·zen /'mizən/ (also **mizzenmast** /'mizən,mast/) ► n. the mast behind a ship's mainmast.

ml ► abbr. **1** mile or miles. **2** milliliter or milliliters.

MLA ► abbr. Modern Language Association.

Mlle ► abbr. (pl. **Mlles**) Mademoiselle.

MLS ► abbr. **1** Master of Library Science. **2** Multiple Listing Service, an organization that holds computerized listings of US real estate offered for sale. **3** Major League Soccer.

mm ► abbr. millimeter or millimeters.

Mme ► abbr. (pl. **Mmes**) Madame.

MMR ► abbr. measles, mumps, and rubella (a vaccination given to children).

MMS ► abbr. Multimedia Messaging Service, a system that enables cell phones to send and receive color pictures and sound clips as well as text messages.

MN ► abbr. Minnesota.

Mn ► symbol the chemical element manganese.

mne·mon·ic /nə'mänik/ ► n. a pattern of letters or words that helps one to remember something. ► adj. helping or designed to help the memory.

MO ► abbr. **1** Medical Officer. **2** Missouri. **3** modus operandi. **4** money order.

Mo ► symbol the chemical element molybdenum.

mo·a /'mōə/ ► n. a large extinct flightless bird resembling the emu, formerly found in New Zealand.

moan /mōn/ ► n. **1** a low mournful sound, usually expressing suffering. **2** informal a minor complaint. ► v. **1** make a moan. **2** complain or grumble. ■ **moan·er** n.

moat /mōt/ ► n. a deep, wide ditch filled with water, surrounding and protecting a castle. ■ **moat·ed** adj.

mob /mäb/ ► n. **1** a disorderly crowd of people. **2** (**the Mob**) the Mafia. **3** (**the mob**) derogatory the ordinary people. ► v. (**mobs, mobbing, mobbed**) crowd around someone or into somewhere in an unruly way.

mo·bile /'mōbəl, 'mō,bēl, 'mō,bīl/ ► adj. **1** able to move or be moved freely or easily. **2** (of a store or other service) set up in a vehicle so as to travel around. **3** able or willing to move between occupations, homes, or social classes. **4** (of the features of the face) readily changing expression. ► n. **1** /'mō,bēl/ a decorative structure hung so as to turn freely in the air. **2** /'mōbīl/ chiefly Brit. a cell phone.
– PHRASES **upwardly** (or **downwardly**) **mobile** moving to a higher (or lower) social class.

mo·bile home ► n. a large camper used as permanent living accommodations.

mo·bile phone ► n. a cell phone.

mo·bil·i·ty /mō'bilətē/ ► n. the ability to move or be moved freely and easily.

mo·bi·lize /'mōbə,līz/ ► v. **1** prepare and organize troops for active service. **2** organize people or resources for a particular task. ■ **mo·bi·li·za·tion** /,mōbələ'zāsHən/ n.

Mö·bi·us strip /'mōbēəs/ ► n. a surface with one continuous side formed by joining the ends of a rectangular strip after twisting one end through 180°.

mo·blog /'mō,bläg/ ► n. a weblog whose content originates from cell phones and other portable wireless devices.

mob·ster /'mäbstər/ ► n. informal a gangster.

moc·ca·sin /'mäkəsən/ ► n. a soft leather shoe with the sole turned up and sewn to the upper, originally worn by North American Indians.

mo·cha /'mōkə/ ► n. **1** a fine-quality coffee. **2** a drink or flavoring made with mocha and chocolate.

mo·chac·ci·no /ˌmōkəˈcHēnō/ ▶ n. (pl. **mochaccinos**) a cappuccino containing chocolate syrup or flavoring.

mock /mäk/ ▶ v. **1** tease or laugh at someone scornfully. **2** imitate someone in an unkind way. **3** (**mock something up**) make a replica or imitation of something. ▶ adj. **1** not authentic or real: *a mock-Georgian house.* **2** (of an exam, battle, etc.) arranged for training or practice. ■ **mock·er** n. **mock·ing·ly** adv.

mock·er·y /ˈmäk(ə)rē/ ▶ n. (pl. **mockeries**) **1** scornful teasing; ridicule. **2** an absurd or worthless version of something: *the contents of the bowl were a mockery of food.*
– PHRASES **make a mockery of** make something seem foolish or absurd.

mock-he·ro·ic ▶ adj. imitating the grandiose style of heroic literature in order to mock an ordinary subject.

mock·ing·bird /ˈmäkiNGˌbərd/ ▶ n. a long-tailed American songbird, noted for its mimicry of the calls of other birds.

mock or·ange ▶ n. a bushy shrub with white flowers whose perfume resembles that of orange blossom.

mock-up ▶ n. a model of a machine or structure that is used for teaching or testing.

mod /mäd/ ▶ n. Brit. (especially in the 1960s) a young person of a group who wore stylish clothes and rode motor scooters. ▶ adj. informal modern.

mod·al /ˈmōdl/ ▶ adj. **1** relating to the way in which something is done. **2** Grammar relating to the mood of a verb. **3** (of music) using melodies or harmonies based on modes other than the ordinary major and minor scales. ■ **mo·dal·i·ty** /mōˈdalitē/ n. (pl. **modalities**) **mod·al·ly** adv.

mod·al verb ▶ n. Grammar an auxiliary verb that expresses necessity or possibility, e.g., *must, shall, will.*

mod·ding /ˈmädiNG/ ▶ n. informal the activity of modifying hardware or software to perform in a way desired by the user but not envisioned or permitted by the manufacturer. ■ **mod·der** n.

mode /mōd/ ▶ n. **1** a way in which something occurs or is done: *his preferred mode of travel was a kayak.* **2** a style or fashion in clothes, art, etc. **3** a set of musical notes forming a scale and from which melodies and harmonies are constructed. **4** Statistics the value that occurs most frequently in a given set of data.

mod·el /ˈmädl/ ▶ n. **1** a three-dimensional copy of a person or thing, typically on a smaller scale. **2** something used as an example. **3** an excellent example of a quality: *she was a model of self-control.* **4** a person employed to display clothes by wearing them. **5** a person employed to pose for an artist or photographer. **6** a particular design or version of a product. **7** a simplified mathematical description of a system or process, used to assist calculations and predictions.
▶ v. (**models, modeling, modeled**) **1** make or shape a figure in clay, wax, etc. **2** (**model something on**) use something as an example to follow. **3** display clothes by wearing them. **4** work as an artist's or photographer's model. **5** make a mathematical model of something. **6** (in drawing or painting) make something appear three-dimensional. ■ **mod·el·er** n.

mod·el home ▶ n. a house in a newly built development that is furnished and decorated to

be shown to prospective buyers.

mod·el house (also **model home**) ▶ n. a new house, especially a prefabricated one or one on the site of a new development, that is furnished and decorated to be shown to possible buyers.

mo·dem /ˈmōdəm, ˈmōˌdem/ ▶ n. a device for converting digital and analog signals, especially to enable a computer to be connected to a telephone line.

mod·er·ate ▶ adj. /ˈmäd(ə)rət/ **1** average in amount, intensity, or degree: *we walked at a moderate pace.* **2** (of a political position) not radical or extreme. ▶ n. /ˈmäd(ə)rət/ a person with moderate political views. ▶ v. /ˈmädəˌrāt/ **1** make or become less extreme or intense. **2** be in charge of a decision-making body or a debate. **3** monitor an Internet bulletin board or chat room for inappropriate or offensive content. ■ **mod·er·ate·ly** adv.

mod·er·a·tion /ˌmädəˈrāsHən/ ▶ n. **1** the avoidance of extremes in one's actions or opinions. **2** the action of making something less intense or extreme.

mod·e·ra·to /ˌmädəˈrätō/ ▶ adv. & adj. Music at a moderate pace.

mod·er·a·tor /ˈmädəˌrātər/ ▶ n. **1** a person who helps people to settle a dispute. **2** a person who presides over a debate.

mod·ern /ˈmädərn/ ▶ adj. **1** relating to the present or to recent times. **2** having or using the most up-to-date techniques or equipment. **3** (in the arts) marked by a significant departure from traditional styles and values. ▶ n. a person who believes in a departure from traditional styles or values. ■ **mo·der·ni·ty** /mäˈdərnitē, mə-, -ˈder-/ n. **mod·ern·ly** adv. **mod·ern·ness** n.

mod·ern·ism /ˈmädərˌnizəm/ ▶ n. **1** modern ideas, methods, or styles. **2** a movement in the arts that aims to depart significantly from traditional styles or ideas. ■ **mod·ern·ist** /ˈmädərnist/ n. & adj. **mod·ern·is·tic** /ˌmädərˈnistik/ adj.

mod·ern·ize /ˈmädərˌnīz/ ▶ v. bring something up to date with modern equipment, techniques, or ideas. ■ **mod·ern·i·za·tion** /ˌmädərnəˈzāsHən/ n. **mod·ern·iz·er** n.

mod·est /ˈmädəst/ ▶ adj. **1** viewing one's abilities or achievements in a humble way. **2** relatively moderate, limited, or small: *drink modest amounts of alcohol.* **3** not showing off the body. ■ **mod·est·ly** adv.

mod·es·ty /ˈmädəstē/ ▶ n. the quality or state of being humble, decent, or moderate.

mod·i·cum /ˈmädikəm, ˈmōd-/ ▶ n. a small quantity of something.

mod·i·fi·ca·tion /ˌmädəfəˈkāsHən/ ▶ n. **1** the action of modifying something. **2** a change made.

mod·i·fi·er /ˈmädəˌfī(ə)r/ ▶ n. **1** a person or thing that modifies something. **2** Grammar a word that qualifies the sense of a noun (e.g., *good* and *family* in *a good family house*).

mod·i·fy /ˈmädəˌfī/ ▶ v. (**modifies, modifying, modified**) make partial or minor changes to something.

mod·ish /ˈmōdisH/ ▶ adj. currently fashionable. ■ **mod·ish·ly** adv. **mod·ish·ness** n.

mo·diste /mōˈdēst/ ▶ n. dated a fashionable milliner or dressmaker.

mod·u·lar /ˈmäjələr/ ▶ adj. **1** made up of separate units. **2** Mathematics relating to a modulus.

■ **mod·u·lar·i·ty** /ˌmäjəˈle(ə)ritē/ n.

mod·u·late /ˈmäjəˌlāt/ ▶ v. **1** control or regulate something. **2** vary the strength, tone, or pitch of the voice. **3** adjust the amplitude or frequency of an oscillation or signal. **4** Music change from one key to another. ■ **mod·u·la·tion** /ˌmäjəˈlāsʜən/ n. **mod·u·la·tor** n.

mod·ule /ˈmäjōol/ ▶ n. **1** each of a set of parts or units that can be used to make a more complex structure. **2** each of a set of independent units of study forming part of a course. **3** an independent self-contained unit of a spacecraft.

mod·u·lus /ˈmäjələs/ ▶ n. (pl. **moduli** /-ˌlī, -ˌlē/) **1** Mathematics the magnitude of a number irrespective of whether it is positive or negative. **2** Physics a constant factor relating a physical effect to the force producing it.

mo·dus op·e·ran·di /ˈmōdəs ˌäpəˈrandē, -ˌdī/ ▶ n. (pl. **modi operandi** /ˈmōdē, ˈmōdī/) a way of operating or doing something.

mo·dus vi·ven·di /ˈmōdəs vəˈvendē, -ˌdī/ ▶ n. (pl. **modi vivendi** /ˈmōdē, ˈmōdī/) an arrangement allowing differing or conflicting groups to exist together peacefully.

Mo·gul /ˈmōgəl/ (also **Moghul** or **Mughal** pronunc. same) ▶ n. **1** a member of the Muslim dynasty of Mongol origin that ruled much of India in the 16th–19th centuries. **2** (**mogul**) an important or powerful person.

mo·gul /ˈmōgəl/ ▶ n. a bump on a ski slope formed by the repeated turns of skiers over the same path.

mo·hair /ˈmōˌhe(ə)r/ ▶ n. a yarn or fabric made from the hair of the angora goat.

Mo·ham·me·dan /mooˈhamid(ə)n, mō-/ ▶ n. & adj. variant spelling of **MUHAMMADAN**.

Mo·hawk /ˈmōˌhôk/ ▶ n. (pl. same or **Mohawks**) **1** a member of an American Indian people originally inhabiting parts of what is now upper New York State. **2** the Iroquoian language of this people. **3** a hairstyle with the head shaved except for a strip of hair, typically standing erect, from the middle of the forehead to the back of the neck. ▶ adj. relating to the Mohawks or their language.

Mo·he·gan /mōˈhēgən/ ▶ n. **1** a member of an American Indian people formerly inhabiting western parts of Connecticut and Massachusetts. **2** the Algonquian language of this people. ▶ adj. relating to the Mohegans or their language.

Mo·hi·can /mōˈhēkən/ ▶ adj. & n. old-fashioned variant of **MAHICAN** or **MOHEGAN**.

moi /mwä/ ▶ pron. humorous me.

moi·e·ty /ˈmoiətē/ ▶ n. (pl. **moieties**) formal or technical each of two parts into which a thing is or can be divided.

moi·re /môˈrā, mwä-, mwär/ (also **moiré** /mwäˈrā, mô-/) ▶ n. silk fabric treated to give it an appearance like that of rippled water.

moist /moist/ ▶ adj. slightly wet; damp. ■ **moist·ly** adv. **moist·ness** n.

mois·ten /ˈmoisən/ ▶ v. make or become slightly wet.

mois·ture /ˈmoisᴄʜər/ ▶ n. tiny drops of water or other liquid in the air, in a substance, or condensed on a surface.

mois·tur·ize /ˈmoisᴄʜəˌrīz/ ▶ v. make something, especially the skin, less dry. ■ **mois·tur·iz·er** n.

mo·ji·to /mōˈhētō/ ▶ n. a cocktail originating in Cuba and consisting of white rum, lime or lemon juice, sugar, fresh mint, ice, and club soda.

mo·jo /ˈmōjō/ ▶ n. (pl. **mojos**) **1** a magic charm or spell. **2** power or influence.

mol /mōl/ ▶ n. Chemistry short for **MOLE⁴**.

mo·lar¹ /ˈmōlər/ ▶ n. a grinding tooth at the back of a mammal's mouth.

mo·lar² ▶ adj. Chemistry **1** relating to one mole of a substance. **2** (of a solution) containing one mole of solute per liter of solvent.

mo·las·ses /məˈlasəz/ ▶ n. **1** a thick dark brown liquid obtained from raw sugar. **2** a paler, sweeter version of this used as a table syrup and in baking.

mold¹ /mōld/ (Brit. **mould**) ▶ n. **1** a hollow container used to give shape to molten or hot liquid material when it cools and hardens. **2** a gelatin dessert or mousse. **3** a distinctive type, style, or character: *he's a leader in the mold of Winston Churchill.* ▶ v. **1** form an object out of a soft substance. **2** influence the development of something.
– PHRASES **break the mold** end a restrictive pattern of events or behavior by doing things differently.

mold² (Brit. **mould**) ▶ n. a furry growth of minute fungi occurring in moist warm conditions on organic matter.

mold³ (Brit. **mould**) ▶ n. soft loose earth, especially when rich in organic matter.

Mol·da·vi·an /mälˈdāvēən, mô-/ ▶ n. a person from Moldavia, a former principality of SE Europe. ▶ adj. relating to Moldavia.

mold·board /ˈmōldˌbôrd/ ▶ n. the blade or plate in a plow that turns the earth over.

mold·er /ˈmōldər/ (Brit. **moulder**) ▶ v. slowly decay.

mold·ing /ˈmōldiNG/ (Brit. **moulding**) ▶ n. a shaped strip of wood, stone, or plaster as a decorative architectural feature.

Mol·do·van /məlˈdōvən, mäl-, môl/ ▶ n. a person from Moldova, a country in SE Europe. ▶ adj. relating to Moldova.

mold·y /ˈmōldē/ ▶ adj. (**moldier, moldiest**) **1** covered with or smelling of mold. **2** informal old-fashioned. ■ **mold·i·ness** n.

mo·le¹ /mōl/ ▶ n. **1** a small burrowing mammal with dark velvety fur, a long muzzle, and very small eyes. **2** a spy who manages to gain an important position within the security defenses of a country. **3** someone within an organization who secretly passes on confidential information to another organization or country.

mole² ▶ n. a small dark brown mark on the skin where there is a high concentration of melanin.

mole³ ▶ n. **1** a large solid structure acting as a pier, breakwater, or causeway. **2** a harbor formed by a mole.

mole⁴ ▶ n. Chemistry the SI unit of amount of substance.

mo·le⁵ /ˈmōlā/ ▶ n. a highly spiced Mexican sauce made chiefly from chili peppers and chocolate, served with meat.

mo·lec·u·lar /məˈlekyələr/ ▶ adj. relating to or consisting of molecules.

mo·lec·u·lar bi·ol·o·gy ▶ n. the branch of biology concerned with the macromolecules (e.g., proteins and DNA) essential to life.

mo·lec·u·lar weight ▶ n. another term for **RELATIVE MOLECULAR MASS**.

mol·e·cule /ˈmäləˌkyōol/ ▶ n. a group of atoms chemically bonded together, representing the smallest fundamental unit of a compound that can take part in a chemical reaction.

mole·hill /'mōl,hil/ ▶ n. a small mound of earth thrown up by a burrowing mole.
– PHRASES **make a mountain out of a molehill** exaggerate the importance of a small problem.

mole·skin /'mōl,skin/ ▶ n. **1** the skin of a mole used as fur. **2** a thick cotton fabric with a soft pile surface.

mo·lest /mə'lest/ ▶ v. **1** assault or abuse someone sexually. **2** dated pester or harass someone in a hostile way. ■ **mo·les·ta·tion** /,mō,le-, ,mōlə'stāsHən/ n. **mo·lest·er** n.

moll /mäl/ ▶ n. informal **1** a gangster's girlfriend. **2** dated a prostitute.

mol·li·fy /'mälə,fī/ ▶ v. (**mollifies, mollifying, mollified**) make someone feel less angry or anxious. ■ **mol·li·fi·ca·tion** /,mäləfə'kāsHən/ n.

mol·lusk /'mäləsk/ (Brit. **mollusc**) ▶ n. an invertebrate animal of a large group including snails, slugs, and mussels, with a soft unsegmented body and often an external shell. ■ **mol·lus·kan** /mə'ləs,kən/ adj.

mol·ly /'mälē/ (also **mollie**) ▶ n. (pl. **mollies**) a small fish that is bred for aquariums in many colors, especially black.

mol·ly·cod·dle /'mälē,kädl/ ▶ v. treat someone in an indulgent or overprotective way.

Mo·lo·tov cock·tail /'mälə,tôf, -,tôv, 'mōlə-/ ▶ n. a simple incendiary device thrown by hand, consisting of a bottle of flammable liquid ignited by means of a wick.

molt /mōlt/ (Brit. **moult**) ▶ v. shed old feathers, hair, or skin, to make way for a new growth. ▶ n. a period of molting.

mol·ten /'mōltn/ ▶ adj. (especially of metal, rock, or glass) liquefied by heat.

mol·to /'mōl,tō, 'môl-/ ▶ adv. Music very.

mo·lyb·de·num /mə'libdənəm/ ▶ n. a brittle silver-gray metallic element used in some steels and other alloys.

mom /mäm/ ▶ n. informal one's mother.

mom-and-pop ▶ adj. informal referring to a small store or business of a type often run by a married couple: *a little mom-and-pop diner.*

mo·ment /'mōmənt/ ▶ n. **1** a brief period of time. **2** an exact point in time. **3** formal importance: *the issues were of little moment.* **4** Physics a turning effect produced by a force on an object, expressed as the product of the force and the distance from its line of action to a given point.
– PHRASES **have one's** (or **its**) **moments** be very good at times. **moment of truth** a time when a person or thing is tested or a crisis has to be faced. **of the moment** currently popular, famous, or important.

mo·men·tar·i·ly /,mōmən'te(ə)rəlē/ ▶ adv. **1** for a very short time. **2** very soon.

mo·men·tar·y /'mōmən,terē/ ▶ adj. very brief or short-lived.

mo·men·tous /mō'men(t)əs, mə'-/ ▶ adj. very important or significant: *a momentous decision.* ■ **mo·men·tous·ly** adv. **mo·men·tous·ness** n.

mo·men·tum /mō'mentəm, mə-/ ▶ n. (pl. **momenta** /mō'mentə, mə-/) **1** the force gained by a moving object. **2** the driving force caused by the development of something: *the investigation gathered momentum.* **3** Physics the quantity of motion of a moving body, equal to the product of its mass and velocity.

mom·ma ▶ n. variant spelling of MAMA.

mom·my /'mämē/ ▶ n. (pl. **mommies**) informal one's mother.

Mon. ▶ abbr. Monday.

mon·ad /'mō,nad/ ▶ n. technical a single unit; the number one.

mon·arch /'mänərk, 'män,ärk/ ▶ n. **1** a king, queen, or emperor who rules a country or empire. **2** a large orange and black butterfly. ■ **mo·nar·chi·cal** /mə'närkikəl/ adj.

mon·ar·chism /'mänər,kizəm, 'män,är-/ ▶ n. support for the principle that a monarch should rule a country. ■ **mon·ar·chist** n. & adj.

mon·ar·chy /'mänərkē, 'män,är-/ ▶ n. (pl. **monarchies**) **1** rule by a monarch. **2** a country ruled by a monarch.

mon·as·ter·y /'mänə,sterē/ ▶ n. (pl. **monasteries**) a community of monks living under religious vows.

mo·nas·tic /mə'nastik/ ▶ adj. **1** relating to monks or nuns or their communities. **2** resembling monks or their way of life, especially in being simple, plain, or solitary. ■ **mo·nas·ti·cal·ly** /-ik(ə)lē/ adv. **mo·nas·ti·cism** /-tə,sizəm/ n.

Mon·day /'məndā, -dē/ ▶ n. the day of the week before Tuesday and following Sunday.

Mon·é·gasque /,mänə'gäsk, -'gask/ ▶ n. a person from Monaco. ▶ adj. relating to Monaco.

mon·e·ta·rism /'mänitə,rizəm, 'mən-/ ▶ n. the theory that inflation is best controlled by limiting the supply of money circulating in an economy. ■ **mon·e·ta·rist** n. & adj.

mon·e·tar·y /'mänə,terē, 'mən-/ ▶ adj. relating to money or currency. ■ **mon·e·tar·i·ly** /-,te(ə)rəlē/ adv.

mon·e·tize /'mänə,tīz/ ▶ v. **1** convert something into currency. **2** (as adj. **monetized**) (of a society) adapted to the use of money. ■ **mon·e·ti·za·tion** /,mänətə'zäsHən, ,mänə,tī'zäsHən/ n.

mon·ey /'mənē/ ▶ n. **1** a means of payment in the form of coins and bills. **2** the assets, property, etc., owned by someone or something: *the college is very short of money.* **3** payment or profit: *he's making a lot of money.* **4** (**moneys** or **monies**) formal sums of money.
– PHRASES **for my money** informal in my opinion. **put one's money where one's mouth is** informal take action to support one's statements.

mon·ey·bags /'mənē,bagz/ ▶ n. informal a wealthy person.

mon·eyed /'mənēd/ (also **monied**) ▶ adj. having much money; wealthy.

mon·ey-grub·bing ▶ adj. informal greedily concerned with making money.

mon·ey·lend·er /'mənē,lendər/ ▶ n. a person whose business is lending money, usually at a high rate of interest.

mon·ey·mak·er /'mənē,mākər/ ▶ n. a person or thing that earns a lot of money. ■ **mon·ey·mak·ing** n. & adj.

mon·ey mar·ket ▶ n. the trade in short-term loans between banks and other financial institutions.

mon·ey or·der ▶ n. a printed order for payment of a specified sum, issued by a bank or post office.

mon·ey sup·ply ▶ n. the total amount of money in circulation or in existence in a country.

-monger ▶ comb.form **1** referring to someone who trades in a particular thing: *fishmonger.* **2** chiefly derogatory referring to a person engaging in a particular activity: *rumor-monger*.

Mon·gol /'mäNGgəl/ ▶ n. a person from Mongolia.

> **USAGE**
> The use of the term **mongol** or **mongoloid** to refer to a person with Down syndrome is now unacceptable and considered offensive.

Mon·go·li·an /män'gōlēən, mäNG-/ ▶ n. **1** a person from Mongolia. **2** the language of Mongolia. ▶ adj. relating to Mongolia.

Mon·gol·oid /'mäNGgə,loid/ ▶ adj. **1** relating to the division of humankind that includes the peoples native to east Asia, SE Asia, and Arctic North America. **2** (**mongoloid**) offensive affected with Down syndrome.

> **USAGE**
> The term **Mongoloid** is associated with outdated ideas about racial types; it is potentially offensive and best avoided.

mon·goose /'män,gōos, 'mäNG-/ ▶ n. (pl. **mongooses**) a small carnivorous mammal with a long body and tail, native to Africa and Asia.

mon·grel /'mäNGgrəl, 'məNG-/ ▶ n. a dog of a mixed breed.

mon·ied ▶ adj. variant spelling of MONEYED.

mon·ies /'mənēz/ ▶ plural of MONEY, used in financial contexts.

mon·i·ker /'mänikər/ (also **monicker**) ▶ n. informal a name. ■ **mon·i·kered** adj.

mon·ism /'män,izəm, 'mō,nizəm/ ▶ n. Philosophy a theory or doctrine that denies the existence of a distinction between things such as matter and mind. ■ **mon·ist** n. & adj.

mon·i·tor /'mänətər/ ▶ n. **1** a person or device that monitors something. **2** a display screen used to view a picture from a particular camera or an image generated by a computer. **3** a loudspeaker used by performers to hear what is being played or recorded. **4** a student with disciplinary or other special duties during school hours. **5** (also **monitor lizard**) a large tropical lizard. ▶ v. keep someone or something under observation, especially so as to regulate or record their activity or progress.

monk /məNGk/ ▶ n. a man belonging to a religious community, typically one living under vows of poverty, chastity, and obedience. ■ **monk·ish** adj.

mon·key /'məNGkē/ ▶ n. (pl. **monkeys**) **1** a primate that typically has a long tail and lives in trees in tropical countries. **2** a mischievous child. ▶ v. (**monkeys, monkeying, monkeyed**) **1** (**monkey around/about**) behave in a silly or playful way. **2** (**monkey with**) tamper with something.
– PHRASES **make a monkey of** (or **out of**) make a fool of.

mon·key busi·ness ▶ n. informal mischievous or underhanded behavior.

mon·key puz·zle ▶ n. a coniferous tree with branches covered in spirals of tough spiny leaves.

mon·key suit ▶ n. informal a man's evening dress or formal suit.

mon·key wrench ▶ n. an adjustable wrench with large jaws.

monk·fish /'məNGk,fish/ ▶ n. (pl. same or **monkfishes**) an anglerfish, especially when used as food.

monks·hood /'məNGks,hŏŏd/ ▶ n. a poisonous plant with blue or purple flowers.

mon·o¹ /'mänō/ ▶ adj. **1** (of sound reproduction) using only one transmission channel. **2** monochrome. ▶ n. **1** sound reproduction that uses only one transmission channel. **2** monochrome color reproduction.

mon·o² ▶ n. short for INFECTIOUS MONONUCLEOSIS.

mono- (also **mon-** before a vowel) ▶ comb.form **1** one; single: *monochromatic*. **2** (forming names of chemical compounds) containing one atom or group of a specified kind.

mon·o·bas·ic /,mänō'bāsik/ ▶ adj. Chemistry (of an acid) having one replaceable hydrogen atom.

mon·o·chro·mat·ic /,mänəkrō'matik/ ▶ adj. **1** containing only one color. **2** (of light or other radiation) of a single wavelength or frequency.

mon·o·chrome /'mänə,krōm/ ▶ n. representation or reproduction of images in black and white or in varying tones of one color. ▶ adj. consisting of or displaying images in black and white or in varying tones of one color.

mon·o·cle /'mänikəl/ ▶ n. a single lens worn to improve sight in one eye.

mon·o·clo·nal /,mänə'klōnl/ ▶ adj. Biology relating to a clone or line of clones produced from a single individual or cell.

mon·o·coque /'mänə,kōk, -,käk/ ▶ n. an aircraft or vehicle structure in which the chassis and the body are built as a single piece.

mon·o·cot·y·le·don /,mänə,kätl'ēdn/ ▶ n. a flowering plant whose seeds have a single cotyledon (seed leaf).

mo·noc·u·lar /mə'näkyələr, mä-/ ▶ adj. with, for, or using one eye.

mon·o·cul·ture /'mänə,kəlchər/ ▶ n. the cultivation of a single crop in a particular area.

mon·o·dy /'mänədē/ ▶ n. (pl. **monodies**) **1** an ode sung by a single actor in a Greek tragedy. **2** music with only one melodic line.

mo·noe·cious /mə'nēshəs/ ▶ adj. (of a plant or invertebrate animal) having both the male and female reproductive organs in the same individual. Compare with DIOECIOUS.

mon·o·fil·a·ment /,mänə'filəmənt/ ▶ n. a single strand of a synthetic fiber such as nylon.

mo·nog·a·my /mə'nägəmē/ ▶ n. the state of having only one husband, wife, or sexual partner at any one time. ■ **mo·nog·a·mist** n. **mo·nog·a·mous** adj.

mon·o·glot /'mänə,glät/ ▶ adj. using or speaking only one language.

mon·o·gram /'mänə,gram/ ▶ n. a motif of two or more interwoven letters, typically a person's initials. ■ **mon·o·grammed** adj.

mon·o·graph /'mänə,graf/ ▶ n. a scholarly written study of a single subject.
■ **mon·o·graph·ic** /,mänə'grafik/ adj.

mon·o·hull /'mänō,həl/ ▶ n. a boat with only one hull, as opposed to a catamaran or multihull.

mon·o·lin·gual /,mänə'liNGg(yə)wəl/ ▶ adj. speaking or expressed in only one language.

mon·o·lith /'mänəliTH/ ▶ n. **1** a large single upright block of stone, especially a pillar or monument. **2** a very large organization or institution that is seen as impersonal and slow to change.

mon·o·lith·ic /,mänə'liTHik/ ▶ adj. **1** formed of a single large block of stone. **2** (of an organization or institution) large, impersonal, and slow to change.

mon·o·logue /'mänə,lôg, -,läg/ ▶ n. **1** a long speech

by one actor in a play or movie. **2** a long, boring speech by one person during a conversation.

mon·o·ma·ni·a /ˌmänəˈmānēə/ ▶ n. an obsessive preoccupation with one thing. ■ **mon·o·ma·ni·ac** /-ˈmānēˌak/ n.

mon·o·mer /ˈmänəmər/ ▶ n. a molecule that can be linked to other identical molecules to form a polymer.

mon·o·nu·cle·o·sis /ˌmänōˌn(y)ōōklēˈōsəs/ ▶ n. short for INFECTIOUS MONONUCLEOSIS.

mon·o·phon·ic /ˌmänəˈfänik/ ▶ adj. full form of MONO¹ (sense 1 of the adjective).

mon·o·plane /ˈmänəˌplān/ ▶ n. an aircraft with one pair of wings.

mo·nop·o·list /məˈnäpəlist/ ▶ n. a person or organization that has exclusive control of the supply of a particular product or service. ■ **mo·nop·o·lis·tic** /məˌnäpəˈlistik/ adj.

mo·nop·o·lize /məˈnäpəˌlīz/ ▶ v. dominate or take control of: *bigger teams monopolize the most profitable TV deals.* ■ **mo·nop·o·li·za·tion** /məˌnäpələˈzāsHən/ n.

mo·nop·o·ly /məˈnäpəlē/ ▶ n. (pl. **monopolies**) **1** the exclusive possession or control of the supply of a product or service. **2** an organization having a monopoly, or a product or service controlled by one. **3** exclusive possession or control of something: *men don't have a monopoly on unrequited love.*

mon·o·rail /ˈmänəˌrāl/ ▶ n. a railroad in which the track consists of a single rail.

mon·o·sac·cha·ride /ˌmänəˈsakəˌrīd/ ▶ n. a sugar (e.g., glucose) that cannot be broken down to give a simpler sugar.

mon·o·so·di·um glu·ta·mate /ˌmänəˌsōdēəm ˈglōōtəˌmāt/ ▶ n. a compound used to add flavor to food.

mon·o·syl·lab·ic /ˌmänəsəˈlabik/ ▶ adj. **1** consisting of one syllable. **2** saying only brief words, or saying very little.

mon·o·syl·la·ble /ˌmänəˈsiləbəl, ˈmänəˌsil-/ ▶ n. a word of one syllable.

mon·o·the·ism /ˈmänəˌTHēˌizəm/ ▶ n. the belief that there is a single god. ■ **mon·o·the·ist** n. & adj. **mon·o·the·is·tic** /ˌmänəTHēˈistik/ adj.

mon·o·tone /ˈmänəˌtōn/ ▶ n. a continuing sound, especially of someone's voice, that is unchanging in pitch.

mon·ot·o·nous /məˈnätn-əs/ ▶ adj. **1** boring because of lack of change or variety: *a monotonous job.* **2** (of a sound) lacking variation of tone or pitch. ■ **mon·ot·o·nous·ly** adv. **mo·not·o·ny** /məˈnätn-ē/ n.

mon·o·treme /ˈmänəˌtrēm/ ▶ n. a mammal that possesses a cloaca and lays eggs, i.e., a platypus or echidna.

mon·o·un·sat·u·rat·ed /ˌmänōˌənˈsaCHəˌrātid/ ▶ adj. referring to fats whose molecules are saturated except for one multiple bond, believed to be healthier in the diet than polyunsaturated fats.

mon·ox·ide /məˈnäkˌsīd/ ▶ n. an oxide containing one atom of oxygen.

Mon·roe Doc·trine /mənˈrō/ ▶ n. a principle of US policy, originated by President James Monroe in 1823, that any intervention by external powers in the politics of the Americas is a potentially hostile act against the US.

Mon·sei·gneur /ˌmōⁿsānˈyər/ ▶ n. (pl. **Messeigneurs** /ˌmāsānˈyər(z)/) a title or form of address for a French-speaking prince, cardinal, archbishop, or bishop.

Mon·sieur /məˈsyœ(r), məˈsyər/ ▶ n. (pl. **Messieurs** /məˈsyœ(r)(z), mā-, məˈsyər(z)/) a title or form of address for a French-speaking man, corresponding to *Mr.* or *sir.*

Mon·si·gnor /mänˈsēnyər, mən-/ ▶ n. (pl. **Monsignori** /ˌmänsēnˈyôrē/) the title of various senior Roman Catholic priests and officials.

mon·soon /mänˈsōōn, ˈmänˌsōōn/ ▶ n. **1** a seasonal wind in the region of the Indian subcontinent and SE Asia, bringing rain when blowing from the southwest. **2** the rainy season (typically May to September) accompanying the monsoon. ■ **mon·soon·al** adj.

mons pu·bis /ˈmänz ˈpyōōbis/ ▶ n. the rounded mass of fatty tissue lying over the joint of the pubic bones.

mon·ster /ˈmänstər/ ▶ n. **1** a large, ugly, and frightening imaginary creature. **2** a very cruel or wicked person. ▶ adj. informal extraordinarily large: *a monster 36-lb. carp.*

mon·strance /ˈmänstrəns/ ▶ n. (in the Roman Catholic Church) a container in which the consecrated Host is displayed for veneration.

mon·stros·i·ty /mänˈsträsətē/ ▶ n. (pl. **monstrosities**) **1** a very large and ugly building or other object. **2** a thing that is evil.

mon·strous /ˈmänstrəs/ ▶ adj. **1** very large and ugly or frightening. **2** very evil or wrong: *a monstrous crime.* **3** extraordinarily large: *a monstrous tidal wave.* ■ **mon·strous·ly** adv.

mons Ve·ne·ris /ˈmänz ˈvenərəs/ ▶ n. (in women) the mons pubis.

mon·tage /mänˈtäzH, mōn-, mōN-/ ▶ n. **1** the technique of putting together separate photos or sections of filmed or videotaped images to form a composite whole. **2** a composite picture, video, etc., resulting from this.

mon·tane /mänˈtān, ˈmänˌtān/ ▶ adj. relating to or inhabiting mountainous country.

Mon·te·ne·grin /ˌmäntəˈnegrən/ ▶ n. a person from Montenegro, a republic in the Balkans. ▶ adj. relating to Montenegro.

Mon·tes·so·ri /ˌmäntəˈsôrē/ ▶ n. a system of education that aims to develop a child's natural interests and activities rather than use formal teaching methods.

month /mənTH/ ▶ n. **1** each of the twelve named periods into which a year is divided. **2** a period of time between the same dates in successive calendar months. **3** a period of 28 days or four weeks.

month·ly /ˈmənTHlē/ ▶ adj. done, produced, or happening once a month. ▶ adv. once a month. ▶ n. (pl. **monthlies**) a magazine published once a month.

mon·ty /ˈmäntē/ ▶ n. (**the full monty**) Brit. informal the full amount expected, desired, or possible.

mon·u·ment /ˈmänyəmənt/ ▶ n. **1** a statue or structure built to commemorate a person or event. **2** a structure or site of historical importance. **3** a lasting and memorable example of something: *the house is a monument to timeless elegance.*

mon·u·men·tal /ˌmänyəˈmentl/ ▶ adj. **1** very large or impressive: *a monumental achievement.* **2** acting as a monument. ■ **mon·u·men·tal·i·ty** /ˌmänyəˌmenˈtalətē/ n. **mon·u·men·tal·ly** adv.

moo /mo͞o/ ▸ v. (**moos, mooing, mooed**) (of a cow) make a long, deep sound. ▸ n. (pl. **moos**) the long, deep sound made by a cow.

mooch /mo͞och/ ▸ v. **1** ask for or obtain something without paying for it. **2** informal (**mooch around/about**) stand or walk around in a bored or listless way.

mood /mo͞od/ ▸ n. **1** a temporary state of mind. **2** an angry, irritable, or sulky state of mind: *she's in a mood.* **3** the atmosphere or overall tone of something: *the mood of modern times.* **4** Grammar a form or category of a verb expressing a fact, command, question, wish, or condition.

mood sta·bil·iz·er ▸ n. a drug used in the treatment of mental disorders that are characterized by unstable mood shifts.

mood swing ▸ n. an abrupt and apparently unaccountable change of mood.

mood·y /ˈmo͞odē/ ▸ adj. (**moodier, moodiest**) **1** tending to become bad-tempered or sulky. **2** giving a sad or mysterious impression. ∎ **mood·i·ly** adv. **mood·i·ness** n.

moo·lah /ˈmo͞oˌlä/ ▸ n. informal money.

moo·li /ˈmo͞oˌlē/ ▸ n. a variety of large white slender radish.

moon /mo͞on/ ▸ n. **1** (also **Moon**) the natural satellite of the earth, orbiting it every 28 days and shining by reflected light from the sun. **2** a natural satellite of any planet. **3** literary or humorous a month. ▸ v. **1** (usu. **moon around/about**) behave in a listless or dreamy way. **2** informal expose one's buttocks to someone as an insult or joke.
– PHRASES **over the moon** informal delighted.

moon·beam /ˈmo͞onˌbēm/ ▸ n. a ray of moonlight.

moon boot ▸ n. a thickly padded boot with a fabric or plastic outer surface.

moon-faced ▸ adj. having a round face.

Moon·ie /ˈmo͞onē/ ▸ n. informal, often derogatory a member of the Unification Church.

moon·light /ˈmo͞onˌlīt/ ▸ n. the light of the moon. ▸ v. (past and past part. **moonlighted**) informal have a second job, especially at night, in addition to one's regular employment. ∎ **moon·light·er** n. **moon·lit** adj.

moon·scape /ˈmo͞onˌskāp/ ▸ n. a rocky and barren landscape resembling the moon's surface.

moon·shine /ˈmo͞onˌSHīn/ ▸ n. informal **1** foolish talk or ideas. **2** liquor that has been made illicitly or smuggled.

moon·stone /ˈmo͞onˌstōn/ ▸ n. a pearly white semiprecious form of the mineral feldspar.

moon·struck /ˈmo͞onˌstrək/ ▸ adj. unable to think or act normally, especially as a result of being in love.

moon·walk /ˈmo͞onˌwôk/ ▸ v. **1** walk on the moon. **2** move or dance in a way reminiscent of the weightless movement of walking on the moon.

moon·y /ˈmo͞onē/ ▸ adj. (**moonier, mooniest**) dreamy, especially as a result of being in love.

Moor /mo͝or/ ▸ n. a member of a Muslim people of NW Africa. ∎ **Moor·ish** adj.

moor[1] /mo͝or/ ▸ n. chiefly Brit. a stretch of open uncultivated upland.

moor[2] ▸ v. secure a boat by attaching it by cable or rope to the shore or to an anchor.

moor·hen /ˈmo͝orˌhen/ ▸ n. a water bird with blackish plumage and a red and yellow bill.

moor·ing /ˈmo͝oriNG/ (also **moorings**) ▸ n. **1** a place where a boat is moored. **2** the ropes, chains, or anchors by which a boat is moored.

moor·land /ˈmo͝o(ə)rlənd, -ˌland/ ▸ n. (also **moorlands**) chiefly Brit. an extensive area of moor.

moose /mo͞os/ ▸ n. (pl. same) a large northern deer with broad antlers and a growth of skin hanging from the neck.

moot /mo͞ot/ ▸ adj. debatable or uncertain: *a moot point.* ▸ v. raise a question or topic for discussion: *the scheme was first mooted last October.* ▸ n. a mock trial examining a hypothetical case.

mop /mäp/ ▸ n. **1** a bundle of thick loose strings or a sponge attached to a handle, used for wiping floors. **2** a thick mass of untidy hair. ▸ v. (**mops, mopping, mopped**) **1** clean or soak up liquid from something by wiping: *she mopped the floor.* **2** (**mop something up**) complete or put an end to something by dealing with the remaining parts: *troops mopped up the last pockets of resistance.*

mope /mōp/ ▸ v. be listless and gloomy.

mo·ped /ˈmōˌped/ ▸ n. a light motorcycle with an engine capacity below 50 cc.

mop·pet /ˈmäpət/ ▸ n. informal an endearing small child.

mop·top /ˈmäpˌtäp/ ▸ n. a man's hairstyle in the form of a long shaggy bob.

MOR ▸ abbr. (of music) middle-of-the-road.

mo·raine /məˈrān/ ▸ n. a mass of rocks and sediment carried down and deposited by a glacier.

mor·al /ˈmôrəl, ˈmär-/ ▸ adj. **1** concerned with the principles of right and wrong behavior. **2** based on or following the code of behavior that is considered socially right or acceptable: *they have a moral obligation to pay the money back.* **3** psychological rather than physical or practical: *moral support.* ▸ n. **1** a lesson about right or wrong that can be learned from a story or experience. **2** (**morals**) standards of behavior, or principles of right and wrong. ∎ **mor·al·ly** adv.

mo·rale /məˈral/ ▸ n. the level of a person's or group's confidence or enthusiasm at a particular time: *the extra pay is aimed at boosting morale.*

mor·al·ism /ˈmôrəˌlizəm, ˈmär-/ ▸ n. the practice of moralizing, especially showing a tendency to make judgments about others' morality.

mor·al·ist /ˈmôrəlist/ ▸ n. **1** a teacher or student of morality. **2** a person with a tendency to moralize. ∎ **mor·al·is·tic** /ˌmôrəˈlistik/ adj.

mo·ral·i·ty /məˈralətē, mô-/ ▸ n. (pl. **moralities**) **1** principles concerning the distinction between right and wrong or good and bad behavior. **2** a particular system of values and moral principles. **3** the extent to which an action is right or wrong.

mo·ral·i·ty play ▸ n. a kind of play, popular in the 15th and 16th centuries, that presents a lesson about right and wrong behavior, in which characters represent qualities such as good or evil.

mor·al·ize /ˈmôrəˌlīz, ˈmär-/ ▸ v. comment on issues of right or wrong behavior, especially in a disapproving way. ∎ **mor·al·iz·er** n.

mor·al ma·jor·i·ty ▸ n. **1** the part of society in favor of strict moral standards. **2** (**Moral Majority**) a right-wing Christian movement in the US.

mor·al phi·los·o·phy ▸ n. the branch of philosophy concerned with ethics.

mor·al vic·to·ry ▶ n. a situation in which one's ideas or principles are shown to be fair or justified, even if one has not achieved one's aim.

mo·rass /məˈras, môˈ-/ ▶ n. **1** an area of muddy or boggy ground. **2** a complicated or confused situation: *a morass of lies.*

mor·a·to·ri·um /ˌmôrəˈtôrēəm, ˌmär-/ ▶ n. (pl. **moratoriums** or **moratoria** /-ˈtôrēə/) **1** a temporary ban on an activity. **2** a legal authorization to debtors to postpone payment.

Mo·ra·vi·an /məˈrāvēən/ ▶ n. **1** a person from Moravia in the Czech Republic. **2** a member of a Protestant Church founded by emigrants from Moravia. ▶ adj. relating to Moravia or the Moravian Church.

mo·ray /ˈmôrˌā, məˈrā/ (also **moray eel**) ▶ n. an eellike predatory fish of warm seas.

mor·bid /ˈmôrbəd/ ▶ adj. **1** having or showing an unhealthy interest in unpleasant subjects, especially death and disease. **2** Medicine relating to or indicating disease. ■ **mor·bid·i·ty** /môrˈbidətē/ n. **mor·bid·ly** adv.

mor·dant /ˈmôrdnt/ ▶ adj. (especially of humor) sharply sarcastic. ▶ n. **1** a substance that combines with a dye, used to fix it in a material. **2** a corrosive liquid used to etch the lines on a printing plate.

more /môr/ ▶ determiner & pron. a greater or additional amount or degree. ▶ adv. **1** forming the comparative of adjectives and adverbs. **2** to a greater extent. **3** again. **4** (**more than**) extremely: *I'm more than happy to oblige.*
– PHRASES **more or less 1** to a certain extent. **2** approximately. **no more 1** nothing or no further. **2** (**be no more**) no longer exist.

> **USAGE**
> Do not use **more** with an adjective that is already in a comparative (**-er**) form (as in *more better, more hungrier*); the correct use is *better* or *hungrier* (or *more hungry*).

mo·rel /məˈrel, môˈ-/ ▶ n. an edible fungus having a brown oval or pointed cap with an irregular honeycombed surface.

mo·rel·lo /məˈrelō/ ▶ n. (pl. **morellos**) a kind of sour dark cherry used in cooking.

more·o·ver /môrˈōvər/ ▶ adv. in addition to what has been said; besides.

mo·res /ˈmôrˌāz/ ▶ pl. n. the customs and conventions of a community.

mor·ga·nat·ic /ˌmôrgəˈnatik/ ▶ adj. (of a marriage) between a man of high rank and a woman of low rank who keeps her former status, their children having no claim to the father's possessions or title.

morgue /môrg/ ▶ n. **1** a mortuary. **2** informal a newspaper's archive, or a collection of cuttings, photographs, or other reference material.

mor·i·bund /ˈmôrəˌbənd, ˈmär-/ ▶ adj. **1** at the point of death. **2** in decline or lacking vitality or effectiveness: *the country's moribund economy.*

Mor·mon /ˈmôrmən/ ▶ n. a member of the Church of Jesus Christ of Latter-Day Saints, a religion founded in the US in 1830 by Joseph Smith Jr. ■ **Mor·mon·ism** /-ˌnizəm/ n.

morn /môrn/ ▶ n. literary morning.

mor·nay /môrˈnā/ ▶ adj. referring to or served in a cheese-flavored white sauce: *cauliflower mornay.*

morn·ing /ˈmôrniNG/ ▶ n. **1** the period of time between midnight and noon, especially from sunrise to noon. **2** sunrise. ▶ adv. (**mornings**) informal every morning.

morn·ing-af·ter pill ▶ n. a contraceptive pill that is effective up to about seventy-two hours after having sex.

morn·ing glo·ry ▶ n. a climbing plant of the convolvulus family with trumpet-shaped flowers.

morn·ing sick·ness ▶ n. nausea occurring during early pregnancy.

morn·ing star ▶ n. the planet Venus when visible in the east before sunrise.

Mo·roc·can /məˈräkən/ ▶ n. a person from Morocco in North Africa. ▶ adj. relating to Morocco.

mo·roc·co /məˈräkō/ ▶ n. fine flexible leather made (originally in Morocco) from goatskins.

mo·ron /ˈmôrˌän/ ▶ n. informal a stupid person. ■ **mo·ron·ic** /məˈränik, môˈ-/ adj.

mo·rose /məˈrōs, môˈ-/ ▶ adj. sullen and bad-tempered. ■ **mo·rose·ly** adv. **mo·rose·ness** n.

morph /môrf/ ▶ v. (in computer animation) change smoothly and gradually from one image to another.

mor·pheme /ˈmôrˌfēm/ ▶ n. Linguistics the smallest unit of meaning into which a word can be divided (e.g., *in, come, -ing,* forming *incoming*).

mor·phine /ˈmôrˌfēn/ ▶ n. a drug obtained from opium and used medicinally to relieve pain.

mor·phol·o·gy /môrˈfäləjē/ ▶ n. (pl. **morphologies**) **1** the branch of biology concerned with the forms and structures of living organisms. **2** the study of the forms of words. **3** the form, shape, or structure of something. ■ **mor·pho·log·i·cal** /ˌmôrfəˈläjikəl/ adj. **mor·phol·o·gist** n.

mor·ris danc·ing /ˈmôris, ˈmär-/ ▶ n. traditional English folk dancing performed outdoors by groups of dancers wearing costumes with small bells attached and carrying handkerchiefs or sticks.

mor·row /ˈmôrō, ˈmärō/ ▶ n. (**the morrow**) old use or literary the following day.

Morse code /ˈmôrs/ ▶ n. an alphabet or code in which letters are represented by combinations of long and short signals of light or sound.

mor·sel /ˈmôrsəl/ ▶ n. a small piece of food.

mor·ta·del·la /ˌmôrtəˈdelə/ ▶ n. a type of smooth-textured Italian sausage containing pieces of fat.

mor·tal /ˈmôrtl/ ▶ adj. **1** having to die at some time. **2** causing death: *a mortal wound.* **3** (of fear, pain, etc.) intense. **4** (of conflict or an enemy) lasting until death; never to be reconciled. **5** informal conceivable or imaginable: *every mortal thing.* **6** Christian Theology (of a sin) that deprives the soul of God's grace. Often contrasted with VENIAL. ▶ n. a human being. ■ **mor·tal·ly** adv.

mor·tal·i·ty /môrˈtalətē/ ▶ n. **1** the state of having to die at some time. **2** death, especially on a large scale. **3** (also **mortality rate**) the number of deaths in a particular area or period, or from a particular cause.

mor·tar /ˈmôrtər/ ▶ n. **1** a mixture of lime with cement, sand, and water, used to hold bricks or stones together. **2** a cup-shaped container in which substances are crushed or ground with a pestle. **3** a short cannon for firing shells at high angles. ▶ v. **1** join bricks or stones together with mortar. **2** attack someone or something with shells fired from a mortar.

mor·tar·board /ˈmôrtərˌbôrd/ ▶ n. **1** a hat with a stiff, flat square top and a tassel, worn as part of formal academic dress. **2** a small square board held horizontally by a handle on the underside, used for holding mortar.

mort·gage /ˈmôrgij/ ▶ n. **1** a legal agreement by which a person takes out a loan using property as security (usually a house that is being purchased). **2** an amount of money borrowed in a mortgage. ▶ v. give a bank the right to hold a person's house as security for the loan borrowed from them.

mort·ga·gee /ˌmôrgəˈjē/ ▶ n. the lender in a mortgage.

mort·ga·gor /ˌmôrgiˈjôr, ˈmôrgijər/ ▶ n. the borrower in a mortgage.

mor·ti·cian /môrˈtishən/ ▶ n. an undertaker.

mor·ti·fy /ˈmôrtəˌfī/ ▶ v. (**mortifies, mortifying, mortified**) **1** make someone feel embarrassed or humiliated. **2** use self-discipline to control one's physical desires. **3** (of flesh) become gangrenous. ■ **mor·ti·fi·ca·tion** /ˌmôrtəfəˈkāshən/ n. **mor·ti·fy·ing** adj.

mor·tise /ˈmôrtis/ (also **mortice**) ▶ n. a hole or recess designed to receive a corresponding projection (a tenon) so that the two are held together. ▶ v. **1** join two things together using a mortise and tenon. **2** cut a mortise in something.

mor·tise lock ▶ n. a lock set into the framework of a door in a recess or mortise.

mor·tu·ar·y /ˈmôrCHo͞oˌerē/ ▶ n. (pl. **mortuaries**) a room or building in which dead bodies are kept until burial or cremation. ▶ adj. relating to burial or tombs.

Mo·sa·ic /mōˈzā-ik/ ▶ adj. relating to or associated with the biblical prophet Moses.

mo·sa·ic /mōˈzā-ik/ ▶ n. a picture or pattern produced by arranging together small pieces of stone, tile, or glass of different colors. ■ **mo·sa·i·cist** /ˈmōˈzāəsist/ n.

Mo·selle /mōˈzel/ (also **Mosel**) ▶ n. a light medium-dry white wine from the valley of the Moselle River.

mo·sey /ˈmōzē/ ▶ v. (**moseys, moseying, moseyed**) informal walk or move in a leisurely way.

mosh /mäsh/ ▶ v. informal dance to rock music in a violent way that involves jumping up and down and deliberately colliding with other dancers.

mosh pit ▶ n. informal an area where moshing occurs, especially in front of the stage at a rock concert.

Mos·lem /ˈmäzləm, ˈmäs-/ ▶ n. & adj. variant spelling of MUSLIM.

mosque /mäsk/ ▶ n. a Muslim place of worship.

mos·qui·to /məˈskētō/ ▶ n. (pl. **mosquitoes**) a small fly, some kinds of which transmit diseases through the bite of the female.

mos·qui·to net ▶ n. a fine net hung across a door or window or around a bed to keep mosquitoes away.

moss /môs/ ▶ n. a small flowerless spreading green plant that grows in damp habitats and reproduces by means of spores. ■ **moss·y** adj.

most /mōst/ ▶ determiner & pron. **1** greatest in amount or degree. **2** the majority of. ▶ adv. **1** to the greatest extent. **2** forming the superlative of adjectives and adverbs. **3** very.
– PHRASES **at (the) most** not more than. **for the most part** in most cases; usually. **make the most of** use something to the best advantage.

most·ly /ˈmōstlē/ ▶ adv. **1** on the whole; mainly. **2** usually.

mote /mōt/ ▶ n. a speck.

mo·tel /mōˈtel/ ▶ n. a roadside hotel for motorists.

mo·tet /mōˈtet/ ▶ n. a short piece of sacred choral music.

moth /môTH/ ▶ n. an insect resembling a butterfly but holding its wings flat when at rest and mainly active at night.

moth·ball /ˈmôTHˌbôl/ ▶ n. a small ball of a strong-smelling substance such as naphthalene, placed among stored clothes to keep clothes moths away. ▶ v. put something into storage or on hold for an indefinite period: *plans to invest in four superstores have been mothballed.*

moth-eat·en /ˈmôTH ˌētn/ ▶ adj. damaged or apparently damaged by clothes moths; shabby or threadbare.

moth·er /ˈməTHər/ ▶ n. **1** a female parent. **2** (**Mother**) (especially as a title or form of address) the head of a female religious community. **3** informal an extreme or very large example of something: *the mother of all traffic jams.* ▶ v. **1** bring up a child with care and affection. **2** look after someone kindly and protectively. ■ **moth·er·hood** /-ˌho͝od/ n. **moth·er·less** adj.

moth·er·board /ˈməTHərˌbôrd/ (also **mainboard** /ˈmānˌbôrd/) ▶ n. a printed circuit board containing the main components of a microcomputer.

moth·er coun·try ▶ n. a country in relation to its colonies.

Moth·er Goose ▶ n. the fictitious creator of a collection of nursery rhymes that was first published in London in the 1760s.

moth·er-in-law ▶ n. (pl. **mothers-in-law**) the mother of one's husband or wife.

moth·er·land /ˈməTHərˌland/ ▶ n. a person's native country.

moth·er lode ▶ n. a principal vein of an ore or mineral.

moth·er·ly /ˈməTHərlē/ ▶ adj. relating to or like a mother, especially in being caring, protective, and kind. ■ **moth·er·li·ness** n.

Moth·er Na·ture ▶ n. nature personified as a creative and controlling force.

moth·er-of-pearl ▶ n. a smooth pearly substance lining the shells of oysters and certain other mollusks.

Moth·er's Day ▶ n. a day of the year on which children honor their mothers (in Britain Mothering Sunday, and in North America and South Africa the second Sunday in May).

moth·er ship ▶ n. a large spacecraft or ship from which smaller craft are launched or maintained.

Moth·er Su·pe·ri·or ▶ n. the head of a community of nuns.

moth·er tongue ▶ n. a person's native language.

mo·tif /mōˈtēf/ ▶ n. **1** a single or repeated image forming a design. **2** a theme that is repeated in an artistic, musical, or literary work.

mo·tile /ˈmōtl, ˈmōˌtīl/ ▶ adj. (of cells and single-celled organisms) capable of motion. ■ **mo·til·i·ty** /mōˈtilətē/ n.

mo·tion /ˈmōshən/ ▶ n. **1** the action of moving. **2** a movement or gesture. **3** a formal proposal put to a lawmaking body or committee. ▶ v. direct someone by making a gesture: *he*

motioned her toward the sofa. ■ **mo·tion·less** adj.
– PHRASES **go through the motions** do something with little effort or care.

mo·tion pic·ture ▶ n. a movie.

mo·tion sick·ness ▶ n. nausea caused by motion, especially by traveling in a motor vehicle, boat, or airplane.

mo·ti·vate /ˈmōtəˌvāt/ ▶ v. **1** give someone a motive for doing something: *he was motivated by the desire for profit.* **2** stimulate someone's interest: *it is the teacher's job to motivate the child at school.* ■ **mo·ti·va·tor** /-ˌvātər/ n.

mo·ti·va·tion /ˌmōtəˈvāSHən/ ▶ n. **1** the reason or reasons behind someone's actions or behavior. **2** desire or willingness to do something; enthusiasm. ■ **mo·ti·va·tion·al** /-SHənl/ adj.

mo·tive /ˈmōtiv/ ▶ n. a factor influencing a person to act in a particular way. ▶ adj. producing physical or mechanical motion. ■ **mo·tive·less** adj.

mo·tive pow·er ▶ n. the energy used to drive machinery.

mot juste /ˌmō ˈZHYST/ ▶ n. (pl. **mots justes** pronunc. same) (**the mot juste**) the most appropriate word or expression.

mot·ley /ˈmätlē/ ▶ adj. made up of a variety of very different people or things: *a motley collection of cars.* ▶ n. a varied mixture.

mo·to·cross /ˈmōtōˌkrôs, -ˌkräs/ ▶ n. cross-country racing on motorcycles.

mo·tor /ˈmōtər/ ▶ n. a machine that supplies the power to drive a vehicle or other device. ▶ adj. **1** relating to motor vehicles. **2** giving or producing motion or action. **3** relating to muscular movement or the nerves activating it. ▶ v. travel in a car.

mo·tor·bike /ˈmōtərˌbīk/ ▶ n. a motorcycle.

mo·tor·boat /ˈmōtərˌbōt/ ▶ n. a boat powered by a motor.

mo·tor·cade /ˈmōtərˌkād/ ▶ n. a procession of motor vehicles.

mo·tor·car /ˈmōtərˌkär/ ▶ n. dated or Brit. an automobile.

mo·tor·cy·cle /ˈmōtərˌsīkəl/ ▶ n. a two-wheeled vehicle that is powered by a motor and has no pedals. ■ **mo·tor·cy·cling** /-ˌsīk(ə)liNG/ n. **mo·tor·cy·clist** /-ˌsīk(ə)list/ n.

mo·tor home ▶ n. a motor vehicle equipped like a trailer for living in, with kitchen facilities, beds, etc.

mo·tor·ist /ˈmōtərist/ ▶ n. the driver of a car.

mo·tor·ize /ˈmōtəˌrīz/ ▶ v. (usu. as adj. **motorized**) **1** equip a vehicle or device with a motor to operate or propel it. **2** equip troops with motor transport. ■ **mo·tor·i·za·tion** /ˌmōtərəˈzāSHən/ n.

mo·tor·man /ˈmōtərˌmən/ ▶ n. (pl. **motormen**) the driver of a subway train or streetcar.

mo·tor·mouth /ˈmōtərˌmouTH/ ▶ n. informal a person who talks rapidly and continuously.

mo·tor neu·ron di·sease ▶ n. a disease in which the nerve cells carrying messages to the muscles from the brain gradually deteriorate, causing muscle loss and eventual death.

mo·tor pool ▶ n. a group of vehicles maintained by the government or military for use by personnel.

mo·tor rac·ing ▶ n. the sport of racing in specially developed fast cars.

mo·tor ve·hi·cle ▶ n. a road vehicle powered by an internal combustion engine.

mo·tor·way /ˈmōtərˌwā/ ▶ n. Brit. a road designed for fast traffic; an expressway.

mot·tle /ˈmätl/ ▶ v. (usu. as adj. **mottled**) mark something with patches of a different color. ▶ n. a patch of color.

mot·to /ˈmätō/ ▶ n. (pl. **mottoes** or **mottos**) a short sentence or phrase expressing a belief or aim of a person or group.

moue /mo͞o/ ▶ n. a pout.

mould, etc. /mōld/ ▶ n. & v. British spelling of MOLD¹, MOLD², MOLD³, etc.

mould·er /ˈmōldər/ ▶ v. & n. British spelling of MOLDER.

mould·ing /ˈmōldiNG/ ▶ n. British spelling of MOLDING.

mound /mound/ ▶ n. **1** a raised rounded mass of earth or other material. **2** a small hill. **3** a large pile or quantity of something. ▶ v. heap something up into a rounded pile.

mount¹ /mount/ ▶ v. **1** climb up or onto something. **2** get up on an animal or bicycle to ride it. **3** (**be mounted**) be on horseback. **4** increase in size, number, or intensity: *the costs mount when you buy a home.* **5** organize and begin a course of action. **6** put or fix something in place or on a support. **7** set in or attach a picture to a backing. ▶ n. **1** (also **mounting**) something on which an object is mounted for support or display. **2** a horse used for riding. ■ **mount·a·ble** adj.
– PHRASES **mount guard** keep watch.

mount² ▶ n. old use or in place names a mountain or hill.

moun·tain /ˈmountn/ ▶ n. **1** a very high, steep hill. **2** a large pile or quantity.
– PHRASES **move mountains** achieve spectacular and apparently impossible results.

moun·tain ash ▶ n. a rowan tree.

moun·tain bike ▶ n. a sturdy bicycle having multiple gears and broad tires with deep treads.

moun·tain·eer·ing /ˌmountn'i(ə)riNG/ ▶ n. the sport or activity of climbing mountains. ■ **moun·tain·eer** n.

moun·tain goat ▶ n. a goat that lives on mountains, known for its agility.

moun·tain lau·rel ▶ n. a North American evergreen tree that bears clusters of white or pink flowers.

moun·tain li·on ▶ n. a cougar.

moun·tain·ous /ˈmountn-əs/ ▶ adj. **1** having many mountains. **2** huge; enormous. ■ **moun·tain·ous·ly** adv.

moun·tain sick·ness ▶ n. altitude sickness.

moun·tain·side /ˈmountnˌsīd/ ▶ n. the sloping surface of a mountain.

Moun·tain time ▶ n. the standard time in a zone including the Rocky Mountain areas of the US and Canada.

moun·te·bank /ˈmountiˌbaNGk/ ▶ n. a person who deceives others.

Moun·tie /ˈmountē/ ▶ n. informal a member of the Royal Canadian Mounted Police.

mount·ing /ˈmountiNG/ ▶ n. **1** a backing, setting, or support for something. **2** the action of mounting something.

mourn /môrn/ ▶ v. **1** feel deep sorrow following the death of someone. **2** feel regret or sadness about the loss of something.

mourn·er /ˈmôrnər/ ▶ n. a person who attends a funeral as a relative or friend of the dead person.

mourn·ful /ˈmôrnfəl/ ▶ adj. feeling, showing, or causing sadness or grief. ■ **mourn·ful·ly** adv. **mourn·ful·ness** n.

mourn·ing /ˈmôrniNG/ ▶ n. **1** the expression of deep sorrow for someone who has died. **2** black clothes worn during a period of mourning.

mourn·ing dove ▶ n. a North and Central American dove with a long tail, a gray-brown back, and a plaintive call.

mouse /mous/ ▶ n. (pl. **mice**) **1** a small rodent with a pointed snout and a long thin tail. **2** a timid and quiet person. **3** (pl. also **mouses**) a small hand-held device that controls cursor movements on a computer screen. ▶ v. **1** hunt for or catch mice. **2** informal use a mouse to move a cursor on a computer screen. ■ **mous·er** n.

mouse pad (also **mousepad**) ▶ n. a piece of rigid or slightly resilient material on which a computer mouse is moved.

mouse·trap /ˈmous,trap/ ▶ n. a trap for catching mice, traditionally baited with cheese.

mous·sa·ka /mōōˈsäkə/ ▶ n. a Greek dish of ground lamb layered with eggplant and tomatoes and topped with a cheese sauce.

mousse /mōōs/ ▶ n. **1** a light sweet or savory dish made with whipped cream and beaten egg white. **2** a foamy substance for styling the hair or applying to the skin.

mousse·line /ˌmōōsəˈlēn, -ˈslēn/ ▶ n. **1** a fine fabric similar to muslin. **2** a light sweet or savory mousse.

mous·tache ▶ n. variant spelling of MUSTACHE.

mous·y /ˈmousē, -zē/ (also **mousey**) ▶ adj. (**mousier**, **mousiest**) **1** (of hair) light brown. **2** timid and quiet.

mouth /mouTH/ ▶ n. **1** the opening in the body through which food is taken and sounds are made. **2** an opening or entrance of a structure, container, etc. **3** the place where a river enters the sea. **4** informal impudent or excessive talk. ▶ v. **1** move the lips as if to form words. **2** say something in an insincere way. **3** (**mouth off**) informal express one's opinions in an unpleasantly loud or assertive way.

mouth·feel /ˈmouTH,fēl/ ▶ n. the physical sensations in the mouth produced by a particular food.

mouth·ful /ˈmouTH,fŏŏl/ ▶ n. **1** a quantity of food or drink that fills or can be put in the mouth. **2** a long or complicated word or phrase.

mouth or·gan ▶ n. a harmonica.

mouth·part /ˈmouTH,pärt/ ▶ n. any of the projecting parts surrounding the mouth of an insect or similar creature and adapted for feeding.

mouth·piece /ˈmouTH,pēs/ ▶ n. **1** a part of a musical instrument, telephone, or breathing apparatus that is designed to be put in or against the mouth. **2** chiefly derogatory a person or publication that expresses the views of another person or an organization.

mouth-to-mouth ▶ adj. (of artificial respiration) in which a person breathes into someone's lungs through their mouth.

mouth·wash /ˈmouTH,wôsh, -,wäsh/ ▶ n. an antiseptic liquid for rinsing the mouth or gargling.

mouth·wa·ter·ing /ˈmouTH,wôtəriNG, -,wätəriNG/ ▶ adj. **1** smelling or looking delicious. **2** very attractive or tempting.

mouth·y /ˈmouTHē, ˈmouTHē/ ▶ adj. (**mouthier**, **mouthiest**) informal inclined to talk a lot, especially in an impudent way.

mov·a·ble /ˈmōōvəbəl/ (also **moveable**) ▶ adj. **1** capable of being moved. **2** (of a religious festival) occurring on a different date each year.

move /mōōv/ ▶ v. **1** go or cause to go in a specified direction or way. **2** change or cause to change position. **3** change one's home or place of work. **4** change from one state or activity to another. **5** take or cause to take action. **6** make progress: *aircraft design has moved forward a long way*. **7** arouse sympathy, sadness, or other feelings in: *he was genuinely moved by the tragedy*. **8** propose something for discussion and resolution at a meeting or lawmaking assembly. ▶ n. **1** an instance of moving. **2** an action taken toward achieving a purpose: *my next move is to talk to Mark*. **3** a player's turn during a board game.

– PHRASES **get a move on** informal hurry up. **make a move** take action. **move in** (or **out**) start (or cease) living or working in a place.

move·ment /ˈmōōvmənt/ ▶ n. **1** an act or the process of moving. **2** a group of people who share the same aims or ideas: *the women's movement*. **3** a trend or development. **4** (**movements**) a person's activities during a particular period of time. **5** a main division of a musical work. **6** the moving parts of a mechanism, especially a clock or watch.

mov·er /ˈmōōvər/ ▶ n. **1** a person whose job is to remove and transport furniture from one building, especially a house, to another. **2** a person who instigates or organizes something: *a key mover in making this a successful conference*.

mov·ie /ˈmōōvē/ ▶ n. **1** a motion picture. **2** (**the movies**) a movie theater.

mov·ie·go·er /ˈmōōvē,gōər/ ▶ n. a person who goes to the movies, especially regularly. ■ **mov·ie·go·ing** /-,gō-iNG/ n. & adj.

mov·ing /ˈmōōviNG/ ▶ adj. **1** in motion. **2** arousing sadness or sympathy. ■ **mov·ing·ly** adv.

mov·ing side·walk ▶ n. a moving walkway, typically at an airport.

mow /mō/ ▶ v. (past part. **mowed** or **mown**) **1** cut down grass or a cereal crop. **2** (**mow someone down**) kill someone by gunfire or by knocking them down with a motor vehicle. ■ **mow·er** n.

mox·ie /ˈmäksē/ ▶ n. informal force of character, determination, or nerve.

Mo·zam·bi·can /ˌmōzamˈbēkən/ ▶ n. a person from Mozambique. ▶ adj. relating to Mozambique.

moz·za·rel·la /ˌmätsəˈrelə/ ▶ n. a firm white Italian cheese made from buffalo's or cow's milk.

MP ▶ abbr. **1** Member of Parliament. **2** military police.

MPAA ▶ abbr. Motion Picture Association of America.

mpg ▶ abbr. miles per gallon.

mph ▶ abbr. miles per hour.

MP3 ▶ n. a means of compressing a sound sequence into a very small file, used as a way of downloading audio files from the Internet.

MPV ▶ abbr. multi-purpose vehicle.

Mr. /ˈmistər/ ▶ n. **1** a title used before a man's surname or full name. **2** a title used to address the male holder of an office.

MRE ▸ abbr. meal ready to eat, a precooked and prepackaged meal used by military personnel.

MRI ▸ abbr. magnetic resonance imaging.

Mrs. /'misəz, 'miz-, -əs/ ▸ n. a title used before a married woman's surname or full name.

MRSA /'mərsə/ ▸ abbr. methicillin-resistant *Staphylococcus aureus*, a bacterium with antibiotic resistance that is common in hospitals and some other public places.

Mrs. Grun·dy /'grəndē/ ▸ n. a person with very conventional standards of proper moral behavior.

MS ▸ abbr. **1** manuscript. **2** Mississippi. **3** multiple sclerosis.

Ms. /miz/ ▸ n. a title used before the surname or full name of a married or unmarried woman (a neutral alternative to **Mrs.** or **Miss**).

MSc ▸ abbr. Master of Science.

MS-DOS /,em ,es 'däs, dôs/ ▸ abbr. Computing, trademark Microsoft disk operating system.

MSG ▸ abbr. monosodium glutamate.

Msgr ▸ abbr. **1** Monseigneur. **2** Monsignor.

MSRP ▸ abbr. manufacturer's suggested retail price.

MST ▸ abbr. Mountain Standard Time.

MT ▸ abbr. Montana.

Mt. ▸ abbr. (in place names) Mount. ▸ symbol the chemical element meitnerium.

much /məCH/ ▸ determiner & pron. (**more**, **most**) a large amount. ▸ adv. **1** to a great extent; a great deal. **2** often.
– PHRASES **a bit much** informal rather excessive or unreasonable. (**as**) **much as** even though. **not much of a** not a good example of: *I'm not much of a gardener*. **so much the better** (or **worse**) that is even better (or worse). **too much** too difficult or exhausting to tolerate.

mu·ci·lage /'myōōs(ə)lij/ ▸ n. **1** a thick bodily fluid. **2** a thick or sticky solution extracted from plants, used in medicines and adhesives. ■ **mu·ci·lag·i·nous** /,myōōsə'lajənəs/ adj.

muck /mək/ ▸ n. **1** dirt or waste matter. **2** manure. **3** informal, chiefly Brit. something unpleasant or worthless. ▸ v. **1** (**muck something up**) informal spoil something. **2** (**muck around with**) informal interfere with. **3** (**muck something out**) remove manure from a stable.

muck·rak·ing /'mək,rākiNG/ ▸ n. the searching out and publicizing of scandal about famous people.

muck·y /'məkē/ ▸ adj. (**muckier**, **muckiest**) covered with muck; dirty.

mu·co·sa /myōō'kōzə/ ▸ n. (pl. **mucosae** /-zē, -,zī/) a mucous membrane.

mu·cous /'myōōkəs/ ▸ adj. relating to or covered with mucus.

mu·cous mem·brane ▸ n. a tissue that produces mucus, lining many body cavities and tubular organs.

mu·cus /'myōōkəs/ ▸ n. a slimy substance produced by the mucous membranes and glands of animals for lubrication, protection, etc.

mud /məd/ ▸ n. **1** wet earth that is soft and sticky. **2** damaging information or allegations.
– PHRASES **drag someone through the mud** slander or criticize someone publicly. **someone's name is mud** informal someone is in disgrace or unpopular.

mud·bank /'məd,baNGk/ ▸ n. a bank of mud on the bed of a river or the bottom of the sea.

mud·bath /'məd,baTH/ ▸ n. **1** a very muddy place. **2** a bath in the mud of mineral springs, taken to relieve rheumatic complaints.

mud·dle /'mədl/ ▸ v. **1** bring something into a disordered or confusing state. **2** confuse someone. **3** (**muddle something up**) confuse two or more things with each other. **4** (**muddle through**) cope fairly well. ▸ n. a confused or disordered state. ■ **mud·dled** adj.

mud·dle-head·ed ▸ adj. disorganized or confused.

mud·dy /'mədē/ ▸ adj. (**muddier**, **muddiest**) **1** covered in or full of mud. **2** not bright or clear. ▸ v. (**muddies**, **muddying**, **muddied**) **1** make something muddy. **2** make something difficult to understand.

mud·flap /'mədflap/ ▸ n. a flap hung behind the wheel of a vehicle to protect against mud and stones thrown up from the road.

mud·flat /'məd,flat/ ▸ n. a stretch of muddy land left uncovered at low tide.

mud·guard /'məd,gärd/ ▸ n. a curved strip fitted over a wheel of a bicycle or motorcycle to protect against water and dirt thrown up from the road.

mud·pup·py /'məd,pəpē/ ▸ n. a large aquatic salamander of the eastern US, reaching sexual maturity while retaining an immature body form with feathery external gills.

mud·slide /'məd,slīd/ ▸ n. a mass of mud and other earthy material that is falling or has fallen down a slope.

mud·sling·ing ▸ n. informal the use of insults and accusations to damage an opponent's reputation.

mues·li /'m(y)ōōzlē/ ▸ n. (pl. **mueslis**) a breakfast cereal consisting of oats, dried fruit, and nuts.

mu·ez·zin /m(y)ōō'ezən, 'mōōəzən/ ▸ n. a man who calls Muslims to prayer from the minaret of a mosque.

muff[1] /məf/ ▸ n. a short tube made of fur or other warm material into which the hands are placed for warmth.

muff[2] informal ▸ v. handle something clumsily or badly.

muf·fin /'məfən/ ▸ n. **1** a small spongy cake with a rounded top. **2** short for ENGLISH MUFFIN.

muf·fle /'məfəl/ ▸ v. **1** wrap or cover someone or something for warmth. **2** make a sound quieter or less distinct by covering its source.

muf·fler /'məf(ə)lər/ ▸ n. **1** a scarf worn around the neck and face. **2** a device for deadening the sound of a drum or other instrument. **3** a silencer for a motor vehicle exhaust.

muf·ti[1] /'məftē/ ▸ n. (pl. **muftis**) a Muslim legal expert empowered to give rulings on religious matters.

mufti[2] ▸ n. dated civilian clothes when worn by a person who wears a uniform for their job.

mug /məg/ ▸ n. **1** a large cylindrical cup with a handle. **2** informal a person's face. ▸ v. (**mugs**, **mugging**, **mugged**) **1** attack and rob someone in a public place. **2** informal make faces in front of an audience or a camera. ■ **mug·ger** n.
– PHRASES **a mug's game** informal an activity likely to be unsuccessful or dangerous.

mug·gy /'məgē/ ▸ adj. (**muggier**, **muggiest**) (of the weather) unpleasantly warm and humid.

Mu·ghal /'mŏŏgəl/ ▸ n. variant spelling of MOGUL.

mug·shot /'məg,SHät/ ▸ n. informal a photograph of a person's face made for an official purpose, especially police records.

mug·wort /'məg,wərt, -,wôrt/ ▸ n. a plant with aromatic leaves that are dark green above and whitish below.

Mu·ham·mad·an /mŏ'hämədən, mə-, 'ham-/ (also **Mohammedan**) ▸ n. & adj. old-fashioned term for MUSLIM (not favored by Muslims).

mu·ja·he·din /,mŏŏjəhi'dēn/ (also **mujaheddin**, **mujahideen**) ▸ pl.n. Islamic guerrilla fighters.

muk·luk /'mək,lək/ ▸ n. a high, soft sealskin boot worn in the American Arctic.

mu·lat·to /m(y)ŏŏ'lätō, -'lätō/ ▸ n. (pl. **mulattoes** or **mulattos**) offensive a person with one white and one black parent.

mul·ber·ry /'məl,berē/ ▸ n. (pl. **mulberries**) 1 a dark red or white fruit resembling the loganberry. 2 a dark red or purple color.

mulch /məlCH/ ▸ n. a mass of leaves, bark, or compost spread around or over a plant for protection or to enrich the soil. ▸ v. cover soil or the base of a plant with mulch.

mule[1] /myŏŏl/ ▸ n. 1 the offspring of a male donkey and a female horse, typically sterile. 2 informal a courier for illegal drugs. 3 historical a kind of spinning machine producing yarn on spindles.

mule[2] ▸ n. a slipper or light shoe without a back.

mu·le·teer /,myŏŏlə'tir/ ▸ n. a person who drives mules.

mul·ish /'myŏŏlisH/ ▸ adj. stubborn (like a mule).

mull[1] /məl/ ▸ v. (**mull something over**) think about something at length.

mull[2] ▸ v. (usu as adj. **mulled**) warm a beverage, especially wine or cider, and add sugar and spices to it.

mull[3] ▸ n. a thin, soft, plain muslin, used in bookbinding for joining the spine of a book to its cover.

mul·lah /'mələ, 'mŏŏlə, 'mŏŏlä/ ▸ n. a Muslim who is learned in Islamic theology and sacred law.

mul·lein /'mələn/ ▸ n. a plant with woolly leaves and tall spikes of yellow flowers.

mul·let /'mələt/ ▸ n. any of various sea fish that are caught for food.

mul·li·ga·taw·ny /,məligə'tônē, -'tänē/ ▸ n. a spicy meat soup originally made in India.

mul·lion /'məlyən/ ▸ n. a vertical bar between the panes of glass in a window. ■ **mul·lioned** adj.

multi- ▸ comb.form more than one; many: *multicultural*.

mul·ti·cast /'məlti,kast, ,məlti'kast/ ▸ v. (past and past part. **multicast**) send data across a computer network to several users at the same time. ▸ n. a set of multicast data.

mul·ti·col·ored /,məlti'kələrd, ,məltī-/ (also **multicolor**) ▸ adj. having many colors.

mul·ti·cul·tur·al /,məltē'kəlCH(ə)rəl, ,məltī-/ ▸ adj. relating to or made up of several cultural or ethnic groups. ■ **mul·ti·cul·tur·al·ism** n. **mul·ti·cul·tur·al·ist** n. & adj.

mul·ti·dis·ci·pli·nar·y /,məlti'disəpli'nerē, ,məltī-/ ▸ adj. involving several academic disciplines or professional specializations.

mul·ti·fac·et·ed /,məlti'fasətəd, ,məltī-/ ▸ adj. having many facets or aspects.

mul·ti·far·i·ous /,məlt(ə)'fe(ə)rēəs/ ▸ adj. having many different kinds; very varied: *multifarious talents.*

mul·ti·form /'məlti,fôrm/ ▸ adj. existing in many forms or kinds.

mul·ti·hull /'məlti,həl, 'məltī-/ ▸ n. a boat with two or more, especially three, hulls.

mul·ti·lat·er·al /,məlti'latərəl/ ▸ adj. involving three or more participants, especially governments. ■ **mul·ti·lat·er·al·ism** /-,lizəm/ n. **mul·ti·lat·er·al·ly** adv.

mul·ti·lay·ered /'məlti'lāərd, 'məltī-/ ▸ adj. consisting of several or many layers.

mul·ti·lin·gual /,məltē'linɡg(yə)wəl, ,məltī-/ ▸ adj. in or using several languages.

mul·ti·me·di·a /'məlti'mēdēə, 'məltī-/ ▸ adj. using more than one medium of expression or communication. ▸ n. a system for linking sound and images to text on a computer screen.

mul·ti·mil·lion /'məlti'milyən, 'məltī-/ ▸ adj. consisting of several million of a currency.

mul·ti·mil·lion·aire /,məlti,milyə'ner, ,məltī-/ ▸ n. a person with assets worth several million dollars.

mul·ti·na·tion·al /,məlti'nasHənl, ,məltī-/ ▸ adj. 1 involving several countries or nationalities. 2 operating in several countries. ▸ n. a company operating in several countries. ■ **mul·ti·na·tion·al·ly** adv.

mul·ti·pack /'məlti,pak, 'məltī-/ ▸ n. a package containing a number of similar or identical products.

mul·ti·par·ty /'məlti'pärtē, 'məltī-/ ▸ adj. relating to or involving several political parties.

mul·ti·ple /'məltəpəl/ ▸ adj. 1 having or involving several or many people or things: *multiple occupancy.* 2 (of a disease or injury) affecting several parts of the body. ▸ n. a number that may be divided by another a certain number of times without a remainder.

mul·ti·ple-choice ▸ adj. (of a question on an exam) accompanied by several possible answers, from which the candidate must choose the correct one.

mul·ti·ple scle·ro·sis ▸ n. see SCLEROSIS.

mul·ti·plex /'məltə,pleks/ ▸ n. a movie theater having several separate screens within one building. ▸ adj. 1 consisting of many elements in a complex relationship. 2 involving simultaneous transmission of several messages along a single channel of communication.

mul·ti·pli·cand /,məltəpli'kand/ ▸ n. a quantity that is to be multiplied by another (the multiplier).

mul·ti·pli·ca·tion /,məltəplə'kāsHən/ ▸ n. 1 the process of multiplying. 2 Mathematics the process of combining matrices, vectors, or other quantities under specific rules to obtain their product.

mul·ti·pli·ca·tion sign ▸ n. the sign ×, used to indicate that one quantity is to be multiplied by another.

mul·ti·pli·ca·tion ta·ble ▸ n. a list of multiples of a particular number, typically from 1 to 12.

mul·ti·plic·i·ty /,məltə'plisətē/ ▸ n. (pl. **multiplicities**) a large number or variety.

mul·ti·pli·er /'məltə,plīər/ ▸ n. 1 a quantity by which a given number (the multiplicand) is to be multiplied. **2** a device for increasing the intensity of an electric current, force, etc., to a measurable level.

mul·ti·ply[1] /'məltə‚plī/ ▸ v. (**multiplies, multiplying, multiplied**) **1** add a number to itself a specified number of times. **2** increase in number or quantity: *the problems facing the industry have multiplied alarmingly.* **3** (of an organism) increase in number by reproducing.

mul·ti·ply[2] /'məltəplē/ ▸ adv. in different ways or respects.

mul·ti·proc·ess·ing /‚məlti'präsesiNG, ‚məltī-, -'präsəsiNG/ (also **multiprogramming** /‚məlti'prōgramiNG, ‚məltī-/) ▸ n. the execution of more than one program or task by a computer at the same time.

mul·ti·proc·es·sor /‚məlti'präsesər, -'präsəsər/ ▸ n. a computer with more than one central processor.

mul·ti·pur·pose /‚məltē'pərpəs, ‚məltī-/ ▸ adj. having several purposes.

mul·ti·ra·cial /‚məlti'rāshəl, ‚məl‚tī-/ ▸ adj. relating to or involving people of many races.

mul·ti·stage /'məlti‚stāj, ‚məltī-/ ▸ adj. **1** consisting of or involving several stages or processes. **2** (of a rocket) having at least two sections that contain their own motor and are jettisoned as their fuel runs out.

mul·ti·sto·ry /'məlti‚stôrē, ‚məltī-/ ▸ adj. (of a building) having several stories.

mul·ti·task /'məlti‚task, 'məltī-/ ▸ v. (usu. as n. **multitasking**) **1** (of a computer) execute more than one program or task at the same time. **2** (of a person) deal with more than one task at the same time. ■ **mul·ti·task·er** n.

mul·ti·track /'məlti‚trak, 'məltī-/ ▸ adj. relating to or made by the mixing of several separately recorded tracks of sound.

mul·ti·tude /'məltə‚t(y)ōōd/ ▸ n. **1** a large number of people or things. **2** (**the multitude**) ordinary people.

mul·ti·tu·di·nous /‚məltə't(y)ōōdn-əs/ ▸ adj. **1** very large in number. **2** consisting of many parts or elements.

mul·ti·us·er /'məltē'yōōzər, 'məltī-/ ▸ adj. **1** (of a computer system) able to be used by a number of people simultaneously. **2** referring to a computer game in which several players interact simultaneously using the Internet or other communications.

mul·ti·va·lent /‚məlti'vālənt, ‚məltī-/ ▸ adj. having many interpretations, uses, or values.

mul·ti·verse /'məlti‚vərs/ ▸ n. a hypothetical space or realm consisting of a number of universes, of which our own universe is only one.

mum[1] /məm/ ▸ n. informal, chiefly Brit. one's mother.

mum[2] ▸ adj. (in phrase **keep mum**) informal say nothing so as not to reveal a secret.
– PHRASES **mum's the word** do not reveal a secret.

mum[3] ▸ n. a cultivated chrysanthemum.

mum·ble /'məmbəl/ ▸ v. say something indistinctly and quietly. ▸ n. something said quietly and indistinctly.

mum·bo-jum·bo /'məmbō 'jəmbō/ ▸ n. informal language or a ceremony that seems complicated but has no real meaning.

mum·mer /'məmər/ ▸ n. an actor in a traditional English folk play.

mum·mer·y /'məmərē/ ▸ n. (pl. **mummeries**) **1** a performance of a traditional English folk play. **2** ridiculous or excessive ceremonial procedures.

mum·mi·fy /'məmə‚fī/ ▸ v. (**mummifies, mummifying, mummified**) **1** (especially in ancient Egypt) preserve a body by embalming and wrapping it. **2** dry up a body and so preserve it. ■ **mum·mi·fi·ca·tion** /‚məməfi'kāshən/ n.

mum·my[1] /'məmē/ ▸ n. (pl. **mummies**) informal, chiefly Brit. one's mother.

mum·my[2] ▸ n. (pl. **mummies**) (especially in ancient Egypt) a body that has been preserved for burial by embalming and wrapping in cloth.

mumps /məmps/ ▸ pl.n. (treated as sing.) an infectious disease spread by a virus, causing swelling of the salivary glands at the sides of the face.

munch /mənCH/ ▸ v. eat food with a steady and noticeable chewing action.

Mun·chau·sen's syn·drome /'mōōn‚CHouzənz, 'mən-/ ▸ n. a mental disorder in which a person pretends to be severely ill so as to obtain medical attention.

munch·ies /'mənCHēz/ ▸ pl.n. informal **1** snacks or small items of food. **2** (**the munchies**) a sudden strong desire for food.

mun·dane /‚mən'dān/ ▸ adj. **1** lacking interest or excitement: *his mundane, humdrum existence.* **2** relating to the physical world rather than a heavenly or spiritual one. ■ **mun·dane·ly** adv. **mun·dan·i·ty** /-'dānətē/ n.

mung bean /məNG/ ▸ n. a small round green bean grown in the tropics, chiefly as a source of bean sprouts.

mu·nic·i·pal /myōō'nisəpəl, myə-/ ▸ adj. relating to a town or city or its governing body. ■ **mu·nic·i·pal·ly** adv.

mu·nic·i·pal·i·ty /myōō‚nisə'palətē, myə-/ ▸ n. (pl. **municipalities**) a town or city that has local government.

mu·nif·i·cent /myōō'nifəsənt, myə-/ ▸ adj. very generous. ■ **mu·nif·i·cence** n. **mu·nif·i·cent·ly** adv.

mu·ni·ments /'myōōnəmənts/ ▸ pl.n. Law title deeds or other documents proving a person's right of ownership of land.

mu·ni·tions /myōō'nishənz, myə-/ ▸ pl.n. military weapons, ammunition, equipment, and stores.

munt·jac /'mənt‚jak/ ▸ n. a small SE Asian deer with a doglike bark and small tusks.

mu·on /'myōō‚än/ ▸ n. Physics an unstable subatomic particle of the same class as an electron, but with a mass around 200 times greater.

mu·ral /'myōōrəl/ ▸ n. a picture or design painted directly on a wall. ▸ adj. relating to or resembling a wall.

mur·der /'mərdər/ ▸ n. **1** the unlawful and deliberate killing of one person by another. **2** informal a very difficult or unpleasant situation or experience. ▸ v. **1** kill someone unlawfully and deliberately. **2** informal spoil by lack of skill: *couples were shuffling around to a band murdering Beatles songs.* ■ **mur·der·er** n. **mur·der·ess** n.
– PHRASES **get away with murder** informal succeed in doing whatever one chooses without being punished. **scream bloody murder** informal protest

strongly and noisily.

mur·der·ous /ˈmərdərəs/ ▸ adj. **1** capable of or involving murder or extreme violence. **2** informal very difficult or unpleasant. ■ **mur·der·ous·ly** adv. **mur·der·ous·ness** n.

murk /mərk/ ▸ n. darkness or fog causing poor visibility.

murk·y /ˈmərkē/ ▸ adj. (**murkier**, **murkiest**) **1** dark and gloomy. **2** (of water) dirty or cloudy. **3** unclear so as to conceal dishonesty or immorality: *a Congressman with a murky past.* ■ **murk·i·ly** adv. **murk·i·ness** n.

mur·mur /ˈmərmər/ ▸ v. **1** say something quietly. **2** make a low continuous sound. **3** complain in a subdued way. ▸ n. **1** something that is said quietly. **2** a low continuous background noise. **3** a complaint: *she paid for the meal without a murmur.* **4** a recurring sound heard in the heart through a stethoscope and usually indicating disease or damage.

Mur·phy's Law /ˈmərfēz/ ▸ n. a supposed law of nature, to the effect that anything that can go wrong will go wrong.

mur·rain /ˈmərən/ ▸ n. **1** an infectious disease affecting cattle. **2** old use a plague or crop blight.

Mus·ca·det /ˌməskəˈdā, -ˈde/ ▸ n. a dry white wine from the Loire region of France.

mus·cat /ˈməsˌkat, -ˌkat/ ▸ n. **1** a variety of grape with a musky scent. **2** a sweet or fortified white wine made from muscat grapes.

mus·ca·tel /ˌməskəˈtel/ ▸ n. a sweet wine made from muscat grapes.

mus·cle /ˈməsəl/ ▸ n. **1** a band of tissue in the body that is able to contract so as to move or hold the position of a part of the body. **2** power, influence, or strength: *the plan is designed to increase Japan's financial muscle.* ▸ v. (**muscle in/into**) informal interfere in another's affairs. ■ **mus·cly** /ˈməs(ə)lē/ adj.

> **USAGE**
> Do not confuse **muscle** with **mussel**. **Muscle** means 'the tissue that moves a body part' (*tone up your thigh muscles*), whereas a **mussel** is a kind of shellfish.

mus·cle-bound ▸ adj. having overdeveloped muscles.

mus·cle·man /ˈməsəlˌman/ ▸ n. (pl. **musclemen**) a large, strong man, especially a bodyguard or hired thug.

mus·co·va·do /ˌməskəˈvädō, -ˈvädō/ ▸ n. unrefined sugar made from sugarcane.

Mus·co·vite /ˈməskəˌvīt/ ▸ n. a person from Moscow. ▸ adj. relating to Moscow.

Mus·co·vy /ˈməskəvē/ ▸ n. old use Russia.

mus·cu·lar /ˈməskyələr/ ▸ adj. **1** relating to the muscles. **2** having well-developed muscles. ■ **mus·cu·lar·i·ty** /ˌməskyəˈle(ə)ritē/ n. **mus·cu·lar·ly** adv.

mus·cu·lar dys·tro·phy ▸ n. an inherited condition in which the muscles gradually become weaker and waste away.

mus·cu·la·ture /ˈməskyələchər, -ˌchŏŏr/ ▸ n. the muscular system or arrangement of muscles in a body or an organ.

mus·cu·lo·skel·e·tal /ˌməskyəlōˈskeletl/ ▸ adj. relating to or referring to the musculature and skeleton together.

muse[1] /myōōz/ ▸ n. **1** (**Muse**) (in Greek and Roman mythology) each of nine goddesses who encouraged the arts and sciences. **2** a woman, or a force personified as one, who is the inspiration for a creative artist.

muse[2] ▸ v. **1** be absorbed in thought. **2** say something to oneself in a thoughtful way.

mu·se·um /myōōˈzēəm/ ▸ n. a building in which important or interesting objects are stored and exhibited.

mu·se·um piece ▸ n. an old-fashioned or useless person or object.

mush[1] /məsh/ ▸ n. **1** a soft, wet mass. **2** excessive sentimentality. ▸ v. crush or mash something to form a soft, wet mass.

mush[2] ▸ exclam. a command urging on dogs that pull a dog sled.

mush·room /ˈməshˌrŏŏm, -ˌrŏŏm/ ▸ n. **1** a spore-producing body of a fungus, typically having the form of a domed cap at the top of a stalk and often edible. **2** a pale pinkish-brown color. ▸ v. increase or develop rapidly.

mush·room cloud ▸ n. a mushroom-shaped cloud of dust and debris formed after a nuclear explosion.

mush·y /ˈməshē/ ▸ adj. (**mushier**, **mushiest**) **1** soft and pulpy. **2** excessively sentimental. ■ **mush·i·ness** n.

mu·sic /ˈmyōōzik/ ▸ n. **1** the art of combining vocal or instrumental sounds in a pleasing way. **2** the sound so produced. **3** the written or printed signs representing such sound. – PHRASES **music to one's ears** something very pleasant to hear or learn.

mu·si·cal /ˈmyōōzikəl/ ▸ adj. **1** relating to or accompanied by music. **2** fond of or skilled in music. **3** pleasant-sounding. ▸ n. a play or movie in which singing and dancing play an essential part. ■ **mu·si·cal·i·ty** /ˌmyōōziˈkalətē/ n. **mu·si·cal·ly** adv.

mu·si·cal chairs ▸ pl.n. (treated as sing.) **1** a party game in which players compete for a decreasing number of chairs when the accompanying music is stopped. **2** informal a situation in which people frequently exchange jobs or positions.

mu·sic box ▸ n. a small box that plays a tune when the lid is opened.

mu·sic hall ▸ n. **1** a form of vaudeville entertainment popular in Britain from about 1850 to 1918. **2** a theater where musical events are staged.

mu·si·cian /myōōˈzishən/ ▸ n. a person who plays a musical instrument or composes music. ■ **mu·si·cian·ly** adj. **mu·si·cian·ship** /-ˌship/ n.

mu·si·col·o·gy /ˌmyōōziˈkäləjē/ ▸ n. the study of music as an academic subject. ■ **mu·si·co·log·i·cal** /-kəˈläjikəl/ adj. **mu·si·col·o·gist** /-jist/ n.

musk /məsk/ ▸ n. a strong-smelling substance produced by the male musk deer, used in making perfume. ■ **musk·i·ness** n. **musk·y** adj.

musk deer ▸ n. a small East Asian deer, the male of which produces musk.

mus·keg /ˈməsˌkeg/ ▸ n. a North American swamp or bog formed by an accumulation of decayed vegetation and sphagnum moss.

mus·ket /ˈməskit/ ▸ n. historical a light gun with a long barrel, typically fired from the shoulder.

mus·ket·eer /ˌməskəˈti(ə)r/ ▸ n. historical **1** a soldier armed with a musket. **2** a member of the household troops of the French king in the 17th and 18th centuries.

mus·ket·ry /ˈməskətrē/ ▶ n. **1** musket fire. **2** soldiers armed with muskets. **3** the art or technique of handling a musket.

musk ox ▶ n. a large heavily built goat-antelope with a thick shaggy coat, native to the tundra of North America and Greenland.

musk·rat /ˈməˌskrat/ ▶ n. a large North American rodent with a musky smell that lives partly in water and is valued for its fur.

Mus·lim /ˈməzləm, ˈmŏŏz-/ (also **Moslem**) ▶ n. a follower of Islam. ▶ adj. relating to Muslims or Islam.

mus·lin /ˈməzlən/ ▶ n. a lightweight cotton cloth in a plain weave.

muss /məs/ ▶ v. informal make something untidy or messy.

mus·sel /ˈməsəl/ ▶ n. an edible shellfish with a dark brown or purplish-black shell, found in the sea or in fresh water.

> **USAGE**
> On the confusion of **mussel** with **muscle**, see the note at MUSCLE.

must¹ /məst/ ▶ modal v. (past **had to** or in reported speech **must**) **1** be obliged to; should. **2** used to insist on something. **3** expressing an opinion about something that is very likely. ▶ n. informal something that should be done or bought.

must² ▶ n. grape juice before or during fermentation.

must- ▶ comb.form used to form adjectives referring to things that are essential or highly recommended: *a must-read book.*

mus·tache /ˈməsˌtash, məˈstash/ (also **moustache**) ▶ n. a strip of hair left to grow above a man's upper lip. ■ **mus·tached** adj.

mus·tang /ˈməsˌtaNG/ ▶ n. a small wild horse of the southwestern US.

mus·tard /ˈməstərd/ ▶ n. **1** a hot-tasting yellow or brown paste made from the crushed seeds of a plant, eaten with meat. **2** a brownish-yellow color.

mus·tard gas ▶ n. a liquid whose vapor causes severe irritation and blistering, used in chemical weapons.

mus·ter /ˈməstər/ ▶ v. **1** achieve a feeling, attitude, or reaction: *with all the courage I could muster, I came to my decision.* **2** bring troops together, especially for inspection or military action. **3** (of people) gather together. ▶ n. a formal gathering of troops.
– PHRASES **pass muster** be accepted as satisfactory.

must-have informal ▶ adj. essential or highly desirable. ▶ n. an essential or highly desirable item.

must·n't /ˈməsənt/ ▶ contr. must not.

must-see ▶ n. informal something that should or must be seen, especially a remarkable sight or entertainment.

mus·ty /ˈməstē/ ▶ adj. (**mustier, mustiest**) **1** having a stale or moldy smell or taste. **2** not fresh or original; outdated. ■ **mus·ti·ness** n.

mu·ta·ble /ˈmyōōtəbəl/ ▶ adj. liable to change; changeable. ■ **mu·ta·bil·i·ty** /ˌmyōōtəˈbilətē/ n.

mu·ta·gen /ˈmyōōtəjən/ ▶ n. a substance that causes genetic mutation.

mu·tant /ˈmyōōtnt/ ▶ adj. resulting from or showing the effect of a change in genetic structure. ▶ n. an organism that has undergone a change in genetic structure.

mu·tate /ˈmyōōˌtāt/ ▶ v. change in form or nature; undergo mutation.

mu·ta·tion /myōōˈtāshən/ ▶ n. **1** a change in form or structure. **2** a change in the structure of a gene that results in a variant form and may be transmitted to subsequent generations. **3** a distinct form resulting from a change in genetic structure. ■ **mu·ta·tion·al** adj.

mu·ta·tis mu·tan·dis /m(y)ōōˈtätəs m(y)ōōˈtändəs, -ˈtätəs, -ˈtandəs/ ▶ adv. (used when comparing two or more cases) making necessary alterations while not affecting the main point.

mute /myōōt/ ▶ adj. **1** not speaking or temporarily speechless. **2** lacking the power of speech. **3** (of a letter in a word) not pronounced. ▶ n. **1** dated a person who is unable to speak. **2** a clamp placed over the bridge of a stringed instrument to deaden the resonance of the strings. **3** a pad or cone placed in the opening of a wind instrument. ▶ v. **1** deaden or muffle the sound of something. **2** reduce the strength or intensity of: *his sharp wit was muted by good nature.* **3** (as adj. **muted**) (of color or lighting) not bright; subdued. ■ **mute·ly** adv. **mute·ness** n.

> **USAGE**
> To describe a person without the power of speech as **mute** (especially as in **deaf mute**) is today likely to cause offense. Since there are no accepted alternative terms in general use, the solution may be to use a longer description, such as *she is both deaf and unable to speak.*

mute swan ▶ n. the commonest Eurasian swan, having an orange-red bill with a black knob at the base.

mu·ti·late /ˈmyōōtlˌāt/ ▶ v. **1** cause a severe and disfiguring injury to someone. **2** cause serious damage to something. ■ **mu·ti·la·tion** /ˌmyōōtlˈāshən/ n. **mu·ti·la·tor** n.

mu·ti·neer /ˌmyōōtnˈi(ə)r/ ▶ n. a person who refuses to obey a person in authority.

mu·ti·nous /ˈmyōōtn-əs/ ▶ adj. tending to mutiny or be disobedient; rebellious. ■ **mu·ti·nous·ly** adv.

mu·ti·ny /ˈmyōōtn-ē/ ▶ n. (pl. **mutinies**) an open rebellion against authority, especially by soldiers or sailors against their officers. ▶ v. (**mutinies, mutinying, mutinied**) refuse to obey a person in authority.

mutt /mət/ ▶ n. informal **1** a dog, especially a mongrel. **2** dated a stupid or incompetent person.

mut·ter /ˈmətər/ ▶ v. **1** say something in a very quiet voice. **2** talk or grumble in secret or in private. ▶ n. something said very quietly.

mut·ton /ˈmətn/ ▶ n. the flesh of mature sheep used as food.

mut·ton-chops /ˈmətnˌCHäps/ (also **muttonchop sideburns**) ▶ pl.n. sideburns that are narrow at the top and broad and rounded at the bottom.

mut·ton-head /ˈmətnˌhed/ ▶ n. informal, old use or dated a stupid person.

mu·tu·al /ˈmyōōCHŏŏəl/ ▶ adj. **1** experienced or done by two or more people equally: *a partnership based on mutual respect.* **2** (of two or more people) having the same specified relationship to each other. **3** shared by two or more people: *a mutual friend.* **4** (of an insurance company or other organization) owned by its members and dividing its profits between them. ■ **mu·tu·al·i·ty** /ˌmyōōCHŏŏˈalitē/ n. **mu·tu·al·ly** adv.

mu·tu·al fund ▶ n. an investment program funded by shareholders that trades in diversified holdings and is professionally managed.

muu-muu /'moo,moo/ ▶ n. a loose, brightly colored dress as traditionally worn by Hawaiian women.

mu·zak /'myoo,zak/ ▶ n. trademark recorded light background music played in public places.

muz·zle /'məzəl/ ▶ n. **1** the projecting part of an animal's face, including the nose and mouth. **2** a guard fitted over an animal's muzzle to stop it biting or feeding. **3** the open end of the barrel of a firearm. ▶ v. **1** put a guard over an animal's muzzle. **2** prevent someone from expressing their opinions freely.

muz·zy /'məzē/ ▶ adj. (**muzzier, muzziest**) **1** dazed or confused. **2** blurred or indistinct: *a slightly muzzy picture.* ■ **muz·zi·ly** adv. **muz·zi·ness** n.

MVP ▶ abbr. most valuable player, an award given in various sports to the best player on a team or in a league.

MW ▶ abbr. **1** medium wave. **2** megawatt(s).

my /mī/ ▶ possessive determiner **1** belonging to or associated with the speaker. **2** used in various expressions of surprise.

my·al·gi·a /mī'alj(ē)ə/ ▶ n. pain in a muscle or group of muscles. ■ **my·al·gic** /-jik/ adj.

my·ce·li·um /mī'sēlēəm/ ▶ n. (pl. **mycelia**) Botany a network of fine white filaments (hyphae) making up the main part of a fungus, usually invisible above ground.

My·ce·nae·an /,mīsə'nēən, mī'sēnēən/ ▶ adj. relating to a late Bronze Age civilization in Greece represented by archaeological discoveries at Mycenae and other ancient cities of the Peloponnese.

my·col·o·gy /mī'käləjē/ ▶ n. the scientific study of fungi. ■ **my·co·log·i·cal** /,mīkə'läjikəl/ adj. **my·col·o·gist** /-jist/ n.

my·e·lin /'mīələn/ ▶ n. a whitish fatty substance forming a sheath around many nerve fibers.

my·e·loid /'mīə,loid/ ▶ adj. relating to bone marrow or the spinal cord.

my·e·lo·ma /,mīə'lōmə/ ▶ n. (pl. **myelomas**) a malignant tumor of the bone marrow.

my·nah /'mīnə/ (also **mynah bird**) ▶ n. a southern Asian or Australasian starling with a loud call, some kinds of which can mimic human speech.

my·o·car·di·al in·farc·tion ▶ n. a heart attack.

my·o·car·di·um /,mīə'kärdēəm/ ▶ n. the muscular tissue of the heart. ■ **my·o·car·di·al** /-dēəl/ adj.

my·o·pi·a /mī'ōpēə/ ▶ n. **1** nearsightedness. **2** failure or inability to foresee the future consequences of an action, decision, etc. ■ **my·op·ic** /mī'äpik/ adj.

myr·i·ad /'mirēəd/ ▶ n. **1** (also **myriads**) a countless or very great number of people or things: *myriads of insects danced around the light.* **2** (in classical times) a unit of ten thousand. ▶ adj. countless: *the myriad lights of the city.*

myr·i·a·pod /'mirēə,päd/ ▶ n. a centipede, millipede, or other insect having a long body with numerous leg-bearing segments.

myr·mi·don /'mərmə,dän, -mədən/ ▶ n. a follower

or subordinate of a powerful person, especially one who is willing to engage in dishonest activities.

myrrh /mər/ ▶ n. a sweet-smelling resin obtained from certain trees and used in perfumes, medicines, and incense.

myr·tle /'mərtl/ ▶ n. an evergreen shrub with glossy leaves and white flowers followed by purple-black berries.

my·self /mī'self, mə-/ ▶ pron. (first person sing.) **1** (reflexive) used by a speaker to refer to himself or herself as the object of a verb or preposition when he or she is the subject of the clause: *I hurt myself.* **2** (emphatic) I or me personally: *I wrote it myself.*

mys·te·ri·ous /mi'sti(ə)rēəs/ ▶ adj. **1** difficult or impossible to understand, explain, or identify: *he vanished in mysterious circumstances.* **2** deliberately not saying much about something that interests other people: *he was rather mysterious about you.* ■ **mys·te·ri·ous·ly** adv. **mys·te·ri·ous·ness** n.

mys·ter·y /'mist(ə)rē/ ▶ n. (pl. **mysteries**) **1** something that is difficult or impossible to understand or explain. **2** the quality of being secret or difficult to explain: *much of her past is shrouded in mystery.* **3** a novel, play, or movie dealing with a puzzling crime. **4** (**mysteries**) the secret rites or ceremonies of an ancient religion. **5** chiefly Christian Theology a religious belief based on divine revelation. **6** an incident in the life of Jesus or of a saint as a focus of devotion in the Roman Catholic Church.

mys·ter·y play ▶ n. a popular medieval play based on biblical stories or the lives of the saints.

mys·tic /'mistik/ ▶ n. a person who devotes their time to prayer and meditation in order to become closer to God and to reach truths beyond human understanding. ▶ adj. mystical.

mys·ti·cal /'mistikəl/ ▶ adj. **1** relating to mystics or mysticism. **2** having a spiritual significance that goes beyond human understanding. **3** inspiring a sense of spiritual mystery, awe, and fascination: *the mystical city of Kathmandu.* ■ **mys·ti·cal·ly** adv.

mys·ti·cism /'mistə,sizəm/ ▶ n. **1** the belief that knowledge of God and truths beyond human understanding can be gained by prayer and meditation. **2** religious or spiritual belief that is not clearly defined.

mys·ti·fy /'mistə,fī/ ▶ v. (**mystifies, mystifying, mystified**) **1** utterly bewilder: *I was mystified by his disappearance.* **2** make something seem obscure or mysterious. ■ **mys·ti·fi·ca·tion** /,mistəfi'kāshən/ n. **mys·ti·fy·ing** adj.

mys·tique /mis'tēk/ ▶ n. **1** a quality of mystery, glamour, and power surrounding a person or thing. **2** an air of secrecy surrounding an activity or subject, making it impressive or baffling to people not involved in it.

myth /mith/ ▶ n. **1** a traditional story about the early history of a people or explaining a natural or social phenomenon, typically involving supernatural beings or events. **2** a widely held but false belief. **3** a fictitious or imaginary person or thing.

myth·i·cal /'mithikəl/ ▶ adj. **1** occurring in or characteristic of myths or folk tales. **2** fictitious or imaginary. ■ **myth·ic** /'mithik/ adj. **myth·i·cal·ly** /-ik(ə)lē/ adv.

myth·o·log·i·cal /,mithə'läjikəl/

▶ **adj.** relating to or found in myths or mythology.
■ **myth·o·log·i·cal·ly** /ˌmiTHə'läjik(ə)lē/ **adv.**

my·thol·o·gize /mi'THäləjīz/ ▶ **v.** make someone or something the subject of a myth.

my·thol·o·gy /mi'THäləjē/ ▶ **n.** (pl. **mythologies**) **1** a collection of myths. **2** a set of widely held but exaggerated or false stories or beliefs. **3** the study of myths. ■ **my·thol·o·gist n.**

myth·o·ma·ni·a /ˌmiTHə'mānēə/ ▶ **n.** an abnormal tendency to exaggerate or tell lies. ■ **myth·o·ma·ni·ac** /-'mānē,ak/ **n. & adj.**

myth·o·poe·ia /ˌmiTHə'pēə/ ▶ **n.** the making of a myth or myths. ■ **myth·o·poe·ic** /-'pēik/ **adj.** **myth·o·po·et·ic** /ˌmiTHəpō'etik/ **adj.**

myx·o·ma·to·sis /mik,sōmə'tōsəs/ ▶ **n.** a highly infectious and usually fatal disease of rabbits, spread by a virus and causing inflammation and discharge around the eyes.

Nn

N¹ (also **n**) ▸ n. (pl. **Ns** or **N's**) the fourteenth letter of the alphabet.

N² ▸ abbr. **1** (used in recording moves in chess) knight. **2** (chiefly in place names) New. **3** Physics newton(s). **4** North or Northern. ▸ symbol the chemical element nitrogen.

n ▸ abbr. **1** nano- (10⁻⁹). **2** Grammar neuter. **3** Grammar noun. ▸ symbol an unspecified or variable number.

'n' (also **'n**) ▸ contr. informal and (e.g., *rock 'n' roll*).

Na ▸ symbol the chemical element sodium.

n/a ▸ abbr. **1** not applicable. **2** not available.

NAACP /ˌen dəbəl ˌā sē 'pē/ ▸ abbr. National Association for the Advancement of Colored People.

naan ▸ n. variant spelling of **NAN**.

nab /nab/ ▸ v. (**nabs, nabbing, nabbed**) informal **1** catch someone doing something wrong. **2** take or grab something suddenly.

na·bob /'nābäb/ ▸ n. **1** historical a Muslim official or governor under the Mogul empire. **2** a very rich or important person.

na·celle /nə'sel/ ▸ n. the streamlined outer casing of an aircraft engine.

na·cho /'näCHŌ/ ▸ n. (pl. **nachos**) a tortilla chip topped with melted cheese, peppers, etc.

na·cre /'nākər/ ▸ n. mother-of-pearl. ■ **na·cre·ous** /-krēəs/ adj.

na·da /'nädə/ ▸ pron. informal nothing.

na·dir /'nādər, 'nädi(ə)r/ ▸ n. **1** the lowest or most unsuccessful point: *the nadir of my career.* **2** Astronomy the point in the sky directly opposite the zenith and below an observer.

NAFTA /'naftə/ (also **Nafta**) ▸ abbr. North American Free Trade Agreement.

nag¹ /nag/ ▸ v. (**nags, nagging, nagged**) **1** constantly ask someone to do something that they are reluctant to do. **2** (often as adj. **nagging**) be persistently painful or worrying to someone: *I was left with nagging doubts.* ▸ n. a persistent feeling of anxiety.

nag² ▸ n. informal, often derogatory a horse, especially one that is old or in poor condition.

Na·hua·tl /'nä,wätl/ ▸ n. (pl. same or **Nahuatls**) **1** a member of a group of peoples native to southern Mexico and Central America, including the Aztecs. **2** the language of the Nahuatl.

nai·ad /'nāad, -əd, nī-/ ▸ n. (in classical mythology) a water nymph.

na·if /nī'ēf, nä-/ ▸ adj. naive. ▸ n. a naive person.

nail /nāl/ ▸ n. **1** a small metal spike with a broadened flat head, hammered in to join things together or to serve as a hook. **2** a thin hard layer covering the upper surface of the tip of the fingers and toes. ▸ v. **1** fasten something with a nail or nails. **2** informal catch someone, especially a suspected criminal. **3** (**nail someone down**) informal force someone to commit themselves to something: *I can't nail her down to a specific date.* **4** (**nail something down**) informal identify something precisely.
– PHRASES **a nail in the coffin** an action or event likely to have a bad or destructive effect on someone or something.

nail-bit·er ▸ n. a situation causing great tension or anxiety.

nail file ▸ n. a small file or emery board for smoothing and shaping the fingernails or toenails.

nail pol·ish (Brit. also **nail varnish**) ▸ n. a glossy colored substance applied to the fingernails or toenails.

na·ive /nī'ēv/ (also **naïve**) ▸ adj. **1** lacking experience, wisdom, or judgment. **2** (of art or an artist) produced in or using a simple, childlike style that deliberately rejects sophisticated techniques. ■ **na·ive·ly** adv.

na·ive·té /ˌnī,ēv(ə)'tā, nī'ēv(ə),tā/ (also **naïveté**) ▸ n. lack of experience, wisdom, or judgment.

na·ked /'nākid/ ▸ adj. **1** without clothes. **2** (of an object) without the usual covering or protection: *a naked light bulb.* **3** not hidden or concealed: *naked aggression.* **4** helpless or vulnerable. ■ **na·ked·ly** adv. **na·ked·ness** n.
– PHRASES **the naked eye** the normal power of the eye, without using a telescope, microscope, or other optical instrument.

nam·by-pam·by /'nambē 'pambē/ ▸ adj. weak and ineffectual.

name /nām/ ▸ n. **1** a word or words by which someone or something is known. **2** a famous person. **3** a reputation, especially a good one: *he made a name for himself in the theater.* ▸ v. **1** give someone or something a name. **2** identify or mention by name: *the dead man has been named by police.* **3** specify a time, place, or sum of money.
– PHRASES **call someone names** insult someone verbally. **have to one's name** have in one's possession. **in all but name** existing in practice but not formally recognized as such. **in someone's name 1** formally registered as belonging to or reserved for someone. **2** on behalf of someone. **in the name of** for the sake of. **name names** mention specific names, especially of people accused of wrongdoing. **the name of the game** informal the main purpose or most important aspect of a situation.

name-call·ing ▸ n. abusive language or insults. ■ **name-call·er** n.

name-check /'nām,CHek/ ▸ n. a public mention of someone's name, especially to express gratitude or for publicity purposes. ▸ v. publicly mention someone's name.

name day ▸ n. the feast day of a saint after whom a person is named.

name·drop·ping ▸ n. the casual mentioning of famous people as if one knows them, so as to impress others.

name·less /'nāmlis/ ▸ adj. **1** having no name. **2** not identified by name; anonymous. **3** too horrific or unpleasant to be described.

name·ly /'nāmlē/ ▸ adv. that is to say.

name·plate /'nām,plāt/ ▸ n. a plate attached to something and bearing the name of the owner, occupier, or the thing itself.

name·sake /'nām,sāk/ ▸ n. a person or thing with the same name as another.

Na·mib·i·an /nə'mibēən/ ▸ n. a person from Namibia, a country in southern Africa. ▸ adj. relating to Namibia.

nan /nän/ (also **naan**) ▸ n. a type of soft, flat Indian bread.

nan·a /'nanə/ (Brit. also **nanna**) ▸ n. informal one's grandmother.

nan·cy /'nan'sē/ (also **nance, nancy boy**) ▸ n. (pl. **nancies**) informal, derogatory an effeminate or homosexual man.

nan·keen /nan'kēn/ ▸ n. a yellowish cotton cloth.

nan·ny /'nanē/ ▸ n. (pl. **nannies**) **1** a woman employed to look after a child in its own home. **2** (also **nanny goat**) a female goat. ▸ v. (**nannies, nannying, nannied**) (usu. as n. **nannying**) **1** work as a nanny. **2** treat someone in an overprotective way.

nan·ny state ▸ n. the government viewed as overprotective or as interfering unduly with personal choice.

nano- ▸ comb.form **1** referring to a factor of one billionth (10^{-9}): *nanosecond*. **2** extremely small; submicroscopic: *nanotechnology*.

nan·o·bot /'nanō,bät/ ▸ n. a submicroscopic self-propelled machine, especially one that has some freedom of action and can reproduce.

nan·o·me·ter /'nanə,mētər/ ▸ n. one billionth of a meter.

nan·o·scale /'nanə,skāl, 'nä-/ ▸ adj. of a size measurable in nanometers or microns.

nan·o·sec·ond /'nanə,sekənd/ ▸ n. one billionth of a second.

nan·o·struc·ture /'nanə,strəkċHər, 'nä-/ ▸ n. a structure, especially a semiconductor device, that has dimensions of a few nanometers.

nan·o·tech·nol·o·gy /,nanə,tek'näləjē, ,nanō-/ ▸ n. technology on an atomic or molecular scale, concerned with dimensions of less than 100 nanometers.

nan·o·tube /'nanə,t(y)ōōb/ ▸ n. Chemistry a cylindrical molecule of a fullerene.

nan·o·wire /'nanə,wī(ə)r, 'nä-/ ▸ n. an extremely thin wire made of semiconducting material, used in miniature transistors and some laser applications.

nap[1] /nap/ ▸ n. a short sleep, especially during the day. ▸ v. (**naps, napping, napped**) have a nap.

nap[2] ▸ n. short raised hairs or threads on the surface of materials such as velvet or suede.

na·palm /'nā,pä(l)m/ ▸ n. a highly flammable jellylike form of gasoline, used in firebombs and flamethrowers.

nape /nāp/ ▸ n. the back of a person's neck.

naph·tha /'nafṛHə, 'nap-/ ▸ n. a flammable oil distilled from coal, shale, or petroleum.

naph·tha·lene /'nafṛHə,lēn, 'nap-/ ▸ n. a white crystalline substance used in mothballs and for chemical manufacture.

nap·kin /'napkin/ ▸ n. **1** a square piece of cloth or paper used at a meal to wipe the fingers or lips and to protect clothes. **2** a sanitary napkin.

Na·po·le·on·ic /nə,pōlē'änik/ ▸ adj. relating to or characteristic of the French emperor Napoleon I or his time.

nap·py /'napē/ ▸ adj. informal, often offensive (of a black person's hair) frizzy.

narc /närk/ ▸ n. informal a federal agent or police officer who enforces laws regarding the sale or use of illicit drugs.

nar·cis·sism /'närsə,sizəm/ ▸ n. excessive interest in or admiration of oneself and one's physical appearance. ■ **nar·cis·sist** /'närsəsist/ n. **nar·cis·sis·tic** /,närsə'sistik/ adj.

nar·cis·sus /när'sisəs/ ▸ n. (pl. **narcissi** /-'sisī, -sē/ or **narcissuses**) a daffodil with a flower that has white or pale outer petals and a shallow orange or yellow center.

nar·co·lep·sy /'närkə,lepsē/ ▸ n. a condition characterized by an extreme tendency to fall asleep whenever in relaxing surroundings. ■ **nar·co·lep·tic** /,närkə'leptik/ adj. & n.

nar·co·sis /när'kōsis/ ▸ n. a state of drowsiness or unconsciousness produced by drugs.

nar·cot·ic /när'kätik/ ▸ n. **1** an addictive drug, especially an illegal one, that affects mood or behavior. **2** Medicine a drug that causes drowsiness or unconsciousness and relieves pain. ▸ adj. relating to narcotics.

nar·rate /'nar,āt/ ▸ v. **1** give an account of something. **2** provide a commentary on a movie, television program, etc. ■ **nar·ra·tion** /na'rāsHən/ n. **nar·ra·tor** /'na,rātər/ n.

nar·ra·tive /'narətiv/ ▸ n. **1** an account of connected events; a story. **2** the part of a fictional work that tells the story, as distinct from the dialogue. ▸ adj. in the form of a narrative or relating to the narration of something. ■ **nar·ra·tive·ly** adv.

nar·row /'narō/ ▸ adj. (**narrower, narrowest**) **1** of small width in comparison to length. **2** limited in extent, amount, or scope: *a narrow range of skills*. **3** only just achieved: *a narrow escape*. ▸ v. **1** become or make narrower. **2** (**narrow something down**) reduce the number of possibilities or options. ▸ n. (**narrows**) a narrow channel connecting two larger areas of water. ■ **nar·row·ly** adv. **nar·row·ness** n.

nar·row·cast /'narō,kast/ ▸ v. (past and past part. **narrowcast** or **narrowcasted**) transmit a television program, especially by cable, to a comparatively small or specialist audience.

nar·row gauge ▸ n. a railroad gauge that is narrower than the standard gauge of 4 ft. 8½ inches (1.435 meters).

nar·row-mind·ed ▸ adj. unwilling to listen to or accept the views of other people.

nar·thex /'närṮHeks/ ▸ n. an antechamber or large porch in a church.

nar·whal /'närwəl/ ▸ n. a small Arctic whale, the male of which has a long spirally twisted tusk.

nar·y /'ne(ə)rē/ ▸ adj. informal or dialect form of NOT.

NASA /'nasə/ ▸ abbr. National Aeronautics and Space Administration.

na·sal /'nāzəl/ ▸ adj. **1** relating to the nose. **2** (of a speech sound) produced by the breath passing through the nose, e.g., *m, n, ng*. **3** (of speech) having an intonation caused by the breath passing through the nose. ▪ **na·sal·ly** adv.

na·sal·ize /'nāzə‚līz/ ▶ v. pronounce something nasally. ▪ **na·sal·i·za·tion** /‚nāzəli'zāsHən/ n.

nas·cent /'nāsənt, 'nasənt/ ▶ adj. just coming into existence and beginning to develop: *the nascent economic recovery.*

NASDAQ /'nazdak/ ▶ abbr. National Association of Securities Dealers Automated Quotations, a computerized system for trading in securities.

nas·tur·tium /na'stərsHəm, nə-/ ▶ n. a trailing garden plant with round leaves and bright orange, yellow, or red flowers.

nas·ty /'nastē/ ▶ adj. (**nastier, nastiest**) **1** unpleasant or disgusting. **2** spiteful, violent, or bad-tempered. **3** dangerous or serious: *a nasty bang on the head.* ▶ n. (pl. **nasties**) informal an unpleasant or harmful person or thing. ▪ **nas·ti·ly** adv. **nas·ti·ness** n.

Nat. ▶ abbr. **1** national. **2** nationalist.

na·tal /'nātl/ ▶ adj. relating to the place or time of one's birth.

na·tion /'nāsHən/ ▶ n. a large group of people sharing the same culture, language, or history, and inhabiting a particular country or territory.

na·tion·al /'nasHənəl/ ▶ adj. **1** relating to or characteristic of a nation. **2** owned, controlled, or financially supported by the federal government. ▶ n. a citizen of a particular country: *French nationals.* ▪ **na·tion·al·ly** adv.

na·tion·al debt ▶ n. the total amount of money that a country's government has borrowed.

Na·tion·al Guard ▶ n. the main reserve military force partly maintained by each state of the United States but also available for federal use.

na·tion·al·ism /'nasHənə‚lizəm/ ▶ n. **1** strong support for and pride in one's own country, often to an extreme degree. **2** belief in political independence for a particular country. ▪ **na·tion·al·ist** /'nasHənəlist/ n. & adj. **na·tion·al·is·tic** /‚nasHənə'listik/ adj.

na·tion·al·i·ty /‚nasHə'nalitē/ ▶ n. (pl. **nationalities**) **1** the status of belonging to a particular nation. **2** an ethnic group forming a part of one or more political nations.

na·tion·al·ize /'nasHənə‚līz/ ▶ v. transfer an industry or business from private to government ownership or control. ▪ **na·tion·al·i·za·tion** /‚nasHənəli'zāsHən/ n.

na·tion·al park ▶ n. an area of natural beauty or environmental importance that is protected by the national government and may be visited by the public.

na·tion·al serv·ice ▶ n. Brit. a period of compulsory service in the armed forces during peacetime.

Na·tion·al So·cial·ism ▶ n. historical the political doctrine of the Nazi Party of Germany.

na·tion state ▶ n. a sovereign state most of whose citizens or subjects are united by factors such as a shared language or culture.

na·tion·wide /'nāsHən'wīd/ ▶ adj. & adv. throughout the whole nation.

na·tive /'nātiv/ ▶ n. **1** a person born in a specified place: *she's a native of Boston.* **2** a local inhabitant. **3** an animal or plant that lives or grows naturally in a place. **4** dated, offensive a non-white original inhabitant of a country as regarded by European colonists or travelers. ▶ adj. **1** associated with a person's place of birth: *her native country.* **2** (of a plant or animal) living

or growing naturally in a place. **3** relating to the original inhabitants of a place. **4** naturally in a person's character: *his native wit.*

> **USAGE**
> In sentences such as *she's a native of Boston* the use of the noun **native** is quite acceptable. When it is used to refer to non-white original inhabitants of a country, however, it has an old-fashioned feel and may cause offense.

Na·tive A·mer·i·can ▶ n. a member of any of the peoples who were the original inhabitants of North and South America and the Caribbean Islands. ▶ adj. relating to Native Americans.

> **USAGE**
> **Native American** is now the accepted term in many contexts. See also **AMERICAN INDIAN**.

na·tive speak·er ▶ n. a person who has spoken the language in question from their earliest childhood.

na·tiv·i·ty /nə'tivitē, nā-/ ▶ n. (pl. **nativities**) **1** old use a person's birth. **2** (**the Nativity**) the birth of Jesus.

na·tiv·i·ty play ▶ n. a play performed at Christmas based on the events surrounding the birth of Jesus.

NATO /'nātō/ (also **Nato**) ▶ abbr. North Atlantic Treaty Organization.

nat·ter /'natər/ informal ▶ v. chat casually. ▶ n. a casual and leisurely conversation.

nat·ty /'natē/ ▶ adj. (**nattier, nattiest**) informal smart and fashionable. ▪ **nat·ti·ly** adv.

nat·u·ral /'nacHərəl/ ▶ adj. **1** existing in or obtained from nature; not made or caused by humans: *natural disasters such as earthquakes.* **2** in accordance with nature; normal or to be expected: *he died of natural causes.* **3** born with a particular skill or quality: *a natural leader.* **4** relaxed and unaffected. **5** (of a parent or child) related by blood. **6** old use illegitimate. **7** Music (of a note) not sharp or flat. ▶ n. **1** a person with an inborn gift or talent for a particular task or activity. **2** an off-white color. **3** Music a natural note or a sign (♮) indicating one. ▪ **nat·u·ral·ness** n.

nat·u·ral gas ▶ n. flammable gas, consisting largely of methane, occurring naturally underground and used as fuel.

nat·u·ral his·to·ry ▶ n. the scientific study of animals or plants, especially as concerned with observation rather than carrying out experiments.

nat·u·ral·ism /'nacHərə‚lizəm/ ▶ n. an artistic or literary movement or style based on the highly detailed and realistic portrayal of daily life.

nat·u·ral·ist /'nacHərəlist/ ▶ n. **1** an expert in or student of natural history. **2** a person who practices naturalism in art or literature.

nat·u·ral·is·tic /‚nacHərə'listik/ ▶ adj. **1** closely imitating real life or nature. **2** based on the theory of naturalism in art or literature. ▪ **nat·u·ral·is·ti·cal·ly** adv.

nat·u·ral·ize /'nacHərə‚līz/ ▶ v. **1** make someone who was not born in a particular country a citizen of that country. **2** establish a plant or animal in a region where it does not occur naturally. **3** alter an adopted foreign word so that it conforms more closely to the language that has adopted it. ▪ **nat·u·ral·i·za·tion** /‚nacHərələ'zāsHən/ n.

nat·u·ral law ▶ n. **1** a body of unchanging

moral principles regarded as common to all human beings and forming a basis for human behavior. **2** an observable law relating to natural phenomena.

nat·u·ral log·a·rithm ▶ n. a logarithm to the base *e* (2.71828 ...).

nat·u·ral·ly /'nacHərəlē/ ▶ adv. **1** in a natural way. **2** of course.

nat·u·ral num·bers ▶ pl. n. the sequence of whole numbers 1, 2, 3, etc., used for counting.

nat·u·ral re·sources ▶ pl. n. naturally occurring substances such as coal or oil.

nat·u·ral sci·ence ▶ n. a branch of science that deals with the physical world, e.g., physics, chemistry, geology, biology.

nat·u·ral se·lec·tion ▶ n. the evolutionary process by which those animals and plants that are better adapted to their environment tend to survive and produce more offspring.

na·ture /'nācHər/ ▶ n. **1** the physical world, including plants, animals, the landscape, and natural phenomena, as opposed to people or things made by people. **2** the inborn qualities or characteristics of a person or thing: *it's not in her nature to listen to advice.* **3** a kind, sort, or class: *topics of a religious nature.* **4** hereditary characteristics as a factor that determines someone's personality. Often contrasted with NURTURE. ■ **na·tured** adj.
– PHRASES **in the nature of things** inevitable or inevitably.

na·ture re·serve ▶ n. an area of land managed so as to preserve its plants, animals, and physical features.

na·ture trail ▶ n. a path through the countryside designed to draw attention to natural features.

na·tur·op·a·thy /,nācHə'räpəthē, ,na-/ ▶ n. a system of alternative medicine involving the treatment or prevention of diseases by diet, exercise, and massage rather than by using drugs. ■ **na·tur·o·path** /'nācHərə,paTH, 'na-/ n. **na·tur·o·path·ic** /,nācHərə'paTHik, ,na-/ adj.

naught /nôt/ ▶ n. the digit O; zero.

naugh·ty /'nôtē, nä-/ ▶ adj. (**naughtier, naughtiest**) **1** (especially of a child) disobedient; badly behaved. **2** informal mildly rude or indecent. ■ **naugh·ti·ly** adv. **naugh·ti·ness** n.

nau·se·a /'nôzēə, -zHə/ ▶ n. **1** a feeling of sickness and being about to vomit. **2** disgust or revulsion.

nau·se·ate /'nôzē,āt, - zHē,āt/ ▶ v. make someone feel sick or disgusted.

nau·seous /'nôsHəs, -zHəs, -zēəs/ ▶ adj. **1** feeling sick. **2** causing a feeling of sickness. ■ **nau·seous·ly** adv.

nau·ti·cal /'nôtikəl/ ▶ adj. relating to sailors or navigation. ■ **nau·ti·cal·ly** /-ik(ə)lē/ adv.

nau·ti·cal mile ▶ n. a unit used in measuring distances at sea, equal to 1,852 meters (approximately 6,076 feet).

nau·ti·lus /'nôtl-əs/ ▶ n. (pl. **nautiluses** or **nautili** /'nôtl-ī/) a swimming mollusk with a spiral shell and many short tentacles around the mouth.

Nav·a·jo /'navə,hō, 'nä-/ (also **Navaho**) ▶ n. (pl. same or **Navajos**) **1** a member of an American Indian people of New Mexico and Arizona. **2** the language of the Navajo.

na·val /'nāvəl/ ▶ adj. relating to a navy or navies.

nave[1] /nāv/ ▶ n. the central part of a church apart from the side aisles, chancel, and transepts.

nave[2] ▶ n. the hub of a wheel.

na·vel /'nāvəl/ ▶ n. the small hollow in the center of a person's belly where the umbilical cord was cut at birth.

na·vel-gaz·ing ▶ n. self-satisfied concentration on oneself or a single issue.

na·vel or·ange ▶ n. a variety of orange having a navel-like hollow at the top containing a small secondary fruit.

nav·i·ga·ble /'navigəbəl/ ▶ adj. **1** wide and deep enough to be used by boats and ships. **2** (of a website) easy to move around in. ■ **nav·i·ga·bil·i·ty** /,navəgə'bilitē/ n.

nav·i·gate /'navi,gāt/ ▶ v. **1** plan and direct the route of a ship, aircraft, or other form of transport. **2** sail or travel over a stretch of water or terrain. **3** guide a ship, boat, or vehicle over a particular route: *she navigated the car safely through the traffic.* **4** move around a website, the Internet, etc.

nav·i·ga·tion /,navi'gāsHən/ ▶ n. **1** the process or activity of navigating. **2** the movement of ships. ■ **nav·i·ga·tion·al** adj.

nav·i·ga·tor /'navi,gātər/ ▶ n. **1** a person who navigates a ship, aircraft, etc. **2** historical a person who explored by sea. **3** a browser program for accessing data on the Internet or another information system.

na·vy /'nāvē/ ▶ n. (pl. **navies**) **1** the branch of a country's armed services that carries out military operations at sea. **2** (also **navy blue**) a dark blue color.

na·vy yard ▶ n. a shipyard where naval vessels are built, repaired, and equipped.

na·wab /nə'wäb/ ▶ n. **1** a native governor during the time of the Mogul empire. **2** a Muslim nobleman or person of high status.

nay /nā/ ▶ adv. **1** or rather: *it will take months, nay years.* **2** old use or dialect no. ▶ n. a negative answer.

nay·say·er /'nā,sāər/ ▶ n. a person who denies or opposes something. ■ **nay·say** /'nā,sā/ v. (past and past participle **naysaid**)

Naz·a·rene /'nazə,rēn/ ▶ n. **1** a native or inhabitant of the town of Nazareth in Israel. **2** (**the Nazarene**) Jesus. **3** a member of an early sect of Jewish Christians. ▶ adj. relating to Nazareth or Nazarenes.

Na·zi /'nätsē, 'nat-/ ▶ n. (pl. **Nazis**) historical a member of the far-right National Socialist German Workers' Party. ■ **Na·zism** /-,izəm/ n.

NB ▶ abbr. **1** New Brunswick. **2** (used to draw attention to what follows) take special notice.

Nb ▶ symbol the chemical element niobium.

NC ▶ abbr. **1** network computer. **2** North Carolina.

NC-17 ▶ symbol no one 17 and under admitted, referring to movies classifed as suitable only for people aged 18 and over.

NCO ▶ abbr. non-commissioned officer.

ND ▶ abbr. North Dakota.

Nd ▶ symbol the chemical element neodymium.

Nde·be·le /,əndə'belä, -'bēlē/ ▶ n. (pl. same or **Ndebeles**) a member of a people of Zimbabwe and NE South Africa.

NE ▶ abbr. **1** Nebraska. **2** northeast or northeastern.

Ne ▶ symbol the chemical element neon.

NEA ▶ abbr. **1** National Education Association. **2** National Endowment for the Arts. **3** Nuclear Energy Agency.

Ne·an·der·thal /nē'andərTHôl/ ▶ n. **1** (also **Neanderthal man**) an extinct human living in ice age Europe between *c.* 120,000 and 35,000 years ago. **2** informal a man who is uncouth or who holds very old-fashioned views.

neap /nēp/ (also **neap tide**) ▸ n. a tide just after the first or third quarters of the moon when there is the least difference between high and low water.

Ne·a·pol·i·tan /ˌnēəˈpälitn/ ▸ n. a person from the Italian city of Naples. ▸ adj. **1** relating to Naples. **2** (of ice cream) made in layers of different colors and flavors.

near /ni(ə)r/ ▸ adv. **1** at or to a short distance in space or time. **2** almost: *a near perfect fit.* ▸ prep. (also **near to**) **1** at or to a short distance in space or time from. **2** close to a state or condition; verging on: *she was near tears.* ▸ adj. **1** at a short distance away in space or time. **2** close to being: *a near disaster.* **3** closely related. **4** located on the side of a vehicle that is normally closest to the curb. ▸ v. approach: *he was nearing retirement.* ■ **near·ness** n.

near·by /ˈni(ə)rˌbī/ ▸ adj. & adv. not far away.

Near East ▸ n. the countries of SW Asia between the Mediterranean and India (including the Middle East). ■ **Near East·ern** adj.

near·ly /ˈni(ə)rlē/ ▸ adv. very close to; almost.
– PHRASES **not nearly** nothing like; far from.

near miss ▸ n. **1** a narrowly avoided collision or accident. **2** a bomb or shot that just misses its target.

near·sight·ed /ˈni(ə)rˌsītəd/ ▸ adj. unable to see things clearly unless they are close to the eyes.

near-term ▸ adj. short-term.

neat /nēt/ ▸ adj. **1** tidy or carefully arranged. **2** done with or showing skill or efficiency: *a neat bit of deduction.* **3** (of a drink of liquor) not diluted or mixed with anything else. **4** informal excellent. ■ **neat·ly** adv. **neat·ness** n.

neat·en /ˈnētn/ ▸ v. make something neat.

neath /nēTH/ ▸ prep. literary beneath.

neat's-foot oil ▸ n. oil obtained by boiling the feet of cattle, used to treat leather.

Neb·u·chad·nez·zar /ˌneb(y)əkə(d)ˈnezər/ ▸ n. a very large wine bottle, equal in capacity to about twenty regular bottles.

neb·u·la /ˈnebyələ/ ▸ n. (pl. **nebulae** /-lē/ or **nebulas**) a cloud of gas or dust in outer space, visible in the night sky either as a bright patch or as a dark silhouette against other glowing matter. ■ **neb·u·lar** /ˈnebyələr/ adj.

neb·u·liz·er /ˈnebyəˌlīzər/ ▸ n. a device for producing a fine spray of liquid, used for inhaling a medicinal drug. ■ **neb·u·lize** v.

neb·u·lous /ˈnebyələs/ ▸ adj. **1** in the form of a cloud or haze; hazy: *a nebulous glow.* **2** not clearly defined; vague: *nebulous concepts.* ■ **neb·u·los·i·ty** /ˌnebyəˈläsitē/ n.

nec·es·sar·i·ly /ˌnesəˈse(ə)rəlē/ ▸ adv. as a necessary result; unavoidably.

nec·es·sar·y /ˈnesəˌserē/ ▸ adj. **1** needing to be done, achieved, or present: *major structural changes are necessary.* **2** that must be; unavoidable: *a necessary consequence.* ▸ n. (**necessaries**) the basic requirements of life, such as food and warmth.

ne·ces·si·tate /nəˈsesəˌtāt/ ▸ v. **1** make necessary: *the rain necessitated a change of plan.* **2** force someone to do something.

ne·ces·si·tous /nəˈsesitəs/ ▸ adj. formal lacking the basic requirements of life; poor.

ne·ces·si·ty /nəˈsesətē/ ▸ n. (pl. **necessities**) **1** the state or fact of being needed or essential. **2** a thing that is essential: *a good book is a necessity when traveling.* **3** a situation that requires a particular course of action: *a system born out of political necessity.*

neck /nek/ ▸ n. **1** the part of the body connecting the head to the rest of the body. **2** a narrow connecting or end part, such as the part of a bottle near the mouth. **3** the part of a violin, guitar, or other instrument that bears the fingerboard. **4** the length of a horse's head and neck as a measure of its lead in a race. ▸ v. informal kiss and caress passionately.
– PHRASES **get it in the neck** Brit. informal be severely criticized or punished. **neck and neck** level in a race or competition. **neck of the woods** informal a particular place. **up to one's neck in** informal heavily or busily involved in something.

neck·band /ˈnekˌband/ ▸ n. a strip of material around the neck of a garment.

neck·er·chief /ˈnekərˌCHif, -ˌCHēf/ ▸ n. a square of cloth worn around the neck.

neck·lace /ˈneklis/ ▸ n. **1** an ornamental chain or string of beads, jewels, or links worn around the neck. **2** (in South Africa) a tire soaked with gasoline, placed around a victim's neck and set alight in order to burn them to death.

neck·line /ˈnekˌlīn/ ▸ n. the edge of a dress or top at or below the neck.

neck·tie /ˈnekˌtī/ ▸ n. a strip of material worn beneath a collar, tied in a knot at the front.

neck·wear /ˈnekˌwe(ə)r/ ▸ n. ties, scarves, and other items worn around the neck.

nec·ro·man·cy /ˈnekrəˌmansē/ ▸ n. **1** prediction of the future by supposedly communicating with the dead. **2** witchcraft or black magic. ■ **nec·ro·man·cer** n. **nec·ro·man·tic** /ˌnekrəˈmantik/ adj.

nec·ro·phil·i·a /ˌnekrəˈfilēə/ ▸ n. sexual intercourse with or attraction toward dead bodies. ■ **nec·ro·phil·i·ac** /-ˈfilēˌak/ n.

nec·ro·pho·bi·a /ˌnekrəˈfōbēə/ ▸ n. extreme or irrational fear of death or dead bodies.

ne·crop·o·lis /neˈkräpəlis/ ▸ n. a cemetery, especially a large ancient one.

nec·rop·sy /ˈnekräpsē/ ▸ n. (pl. **necropsies**) another term for **autopsy**.

ne·cro·sis /neˈkrōsis/ ▸ n. the death of most or all of the cells in an organ or tissue due to disease or injury. ■ **ne·crot·ic** /-ˈkrätik/ adj.

nec·ro·tiz·ing /ˈnekrəˌtīziNG/ ▸ adj. causing or accompanied by necrosis.

nec·tar /ˈnektər/ ▸ n. **1** a sugary fluid produced by flowers to encourage pollination by insects, made into honey by bees. **2** (in Greek and Roman mythology) the drink of the gods. **3** a delicious drink.

nec·tar·ine /ˌnektəˈrēn/ ▸ n. a variety of peach with smooth skin.

née /nā/ ▸ adj. born (used in giving a married woman's maiden name): *Mrs. Hargreaves, née Liddell.*

need /nēd/ ▸ v. **1** want something because it is essential or very important: *I need help.* **2** used to express what should or must be done: *need I say more?* ▸ n. **1** circumstances in which something is necessary or must be done: *he was in need of medical care.* **2** a thing that is wanted or required: *his day-to-day needs.* **3** a state of being poor or in great difficulty: *children in need.*

need·ful /ˈnēdfəl/ ▸ adj. formal necessary.

nee·dle /ˈnēdl/ ▸ n. **1** a very thin pointed piece of metal with a hole or eye for thread at the blunter end, used in sewing. **2** a long thin metal or plastic rod with a pointed end, used in knitting. **3** the pointed hollow end of a hypodermic syringe. **4** a stylus used to play records. **5** a thin pointer on a dial, compass, etc. **6** the thin, sharp, stiff leaf of a fir or pine tree. ▸ v. informal deliberately provoke or annoy someone.

nee·dle·point /ˈnēdl,point/ ▸ n. **1** closely stitched embroidery worked over canvas. **2** lace made by hand using a needle rather than bobbins.

need·less /ˈnēdlis/ ▸ adj. unnecessary; avoidable. ∎ **need·less·ly** adv.
– PHRASES **needless to say** of course.

nee·dle·work /ˈnēdl,wərk/ ▸ n. sewing or embroidery.

need·n't /ˈnēdnt/ ▸ contr. need not.

need·y /ˈnēdē/ ▸ adj. (**needier**, **neediest**) **1** lacking the necessities of life; very poor. **2** insecure and needing emotional support. ∎ **need·i·ness** n.

neem /nēm/ ▸ n. a tropical tree from which wood, oil, medicinal products, and insecticide are obtained.

ne'er /ne(ə)r/ ▸ contr. literary or dialect never.

ne'er-do-well /ˈne(ə)r dōō ,wel/ ▸ n. a person who is lazy and irresponsible.

ne·far·i·ous /niˈfe(ə)rēəs/ ▸ adj. wicked or criminal.

ne·gate /nəˈgāt/ ▸ v. **1** prevent something from having an effect: *alcohol negates the effects of the drug.* **2** deny that something exists.

ne·ga·tion /nəˈgāsHən/ ▸ n. **1** the contradiction or denial of something. **2** the absence or opposite of something: *evil is not merely the negation of goodness.* **3** Mathematics replacement of positive by negative.

neg·a·tive /ˈnegətiv/ ▸ adj. **1** characterized by the absence rather than the presence of particular features: *a negative test result.* **2** expressing or implying denial, disagreement, or refusal. **3** not optimistic, encouraging, or desirable: *his negative attitude.* **4** (of a quantity) less than zero. **5** relating to, containing, or producing the kind of electric charge carried by electrons. **6** (of a photographic image) showing light and shade or colors reversed from those of the original. **7** Grammar stating that something is not the case. ▸ n. **1** a word or statement expressing denial or refusal. **2** a negative photographic image from which positive prints may be made. ∎ **neg·a·tive·ly** adv. **neg·a·tiv·i·ty** /ˌnegəˈtivitē/ n.

neg·a·tive eq·ui·ty ▸ n. a situation in which the market value of a property is less than the outstanding amount of the mortgage secured on it.

ne·glect /niˈglekt/ ▸ v. **1** fail to give proper care or attention to: *she neglected her children.* **2** fail to do something: *he neglected to write to her.* ▸ n. the action of neglecting someone or something, or the state of being neglected.

ne·glect·ful /niˈglektfəl/ ▸ adj. failing to give proper care or attention to someone or something.

neg·li·gee /ˈneglə,zHā/ ▸ n. a woman's dressing gown made of very thin fabric.

neg·li·gence /ˈneglijəns/ ▸ n. **1** failure to take proper care in doing something. **2** Law breach of a duty of care that results in damage.

∎ **neg·li·gent** adj.

neg·li·gi·ble /ˈneglijəbəl/ ▸ adj. so small or unimportant that it is not worth considering. ∎ **neg·li·gi·bly** /-blē/ adv.

ne·go·ti·a·ble /nəˈgōsHəbəl/ ▸ adj. **1** able to be changed as a result of discussion: *the fee may be negotiable.* **2** (of a route) able to be traveled on; passable. **3** (of a document) able to be transferred or given to the legal ownership of another person. ∎ **ne·go·ti·a·bil·i·ty** /nə,gōsHə'bilitē/ n.

ne·go·ti·ate /nəˈgōsHē,āt/ ▸ v. **1** try to reach an agreement or compromise by discussion. **2** obtain or bring about by discussion: *he negotiated a new contract.* **3** find a way over an obstacle or through a difficult path. **4** transfer a check, bill, etc., to the legal ownership of another person. ∎ **ne·go·ti·a·tor** n.

ne·go·ti·a·tion /nə,gōsHē'āsHən/ (also **negotiations**) ▸ n. discussion aimed at reaching an agreement or compromise.

Ne·gress /ˈnēgris/ ▸ n. dated a woman or girl of black African origin.

Ne·gro /ˈnēgrō/ ▸ n. (pl. **Negroes**) a member of a group of black peoples originally native to Africa.

> **USAGE**
> The terms **Negro** and **Negress** are now almost always regarded as offensive; **black** and **African-American** are the preferred terms.

Ne·gro spir·it·u·al ▸ n. see SPIRITUAL.

neigh /nā/ ▸ n. a high whinnying sound made by a horse. ▸ v. make a high whinnying sound.

neigh·bor /ˈnābər/ ▸ n. **1** a person living next door to or very near to another. **2** a person or place next to or near another. ▸ v. (usu. as adj. **neighboring**) be situated next to or very near: *neighboring countries.* ∎ **neigh·bor·ly** adj.

neigh·bor·hood /ˈnābər,hŏŏd/ ▸ n. **1** a district within a town or city. **2** the area surrounding a place, person, or object.
– PHRASES **in the neighborhood of** about; approximately.

neigh·bor·hood watch ▸ n. a program in which local groups of householders watch each other's homes to discourage burglary and other crimes.

nei·ther /ˈnēTHər, ˈnī-/ ▸ determiner & pron. not either. ▸ adv. **1** used to show that a negative statement is true of two things: *I am neither a liberal nor a conservative.* **2** used to show that a negative statement is also true of something else.

nel·ly /ˈnelē/ ▸ n. (pl. **nellies**) informal a silly person.

nel·son /ˈnelsən/ ▸ n. a wrestling hold in which one arm is passed under the opponent's arm from behind and the hand is applied to the neck (**half nelson**), or both arms and hands are applied (**full nelson**).

nem·a·tode /ˈnēmə,tōd/ ▸ n. a worm of a group with slender, unsegmented, cylindrical bodies, such as a roundworm or threadworm.

ne·me·sia /nəˈmēzHə/ ▸ n. a plant related to the snapdragon, grown for its colorful funnel-shaped flowers.

nem·e·sis /ˈneməsis/ ▸ n. (pl. **nemeses** /-,sēz/) **1** the inescapable agent of someone's or something's downfall: *it was in New York that she first met her future husband and ultimately her nemesis.* **2** downfall caused by an unavoidable agent.

neo- ▸ comb.form **1** new: *neonate.* **2** a new or revived form of: *neoclassicism.*

ne·o·clas·si·cal /ˌnēōʹklasikəl/ (also **neoclassic**) ▸ adj. relating to the revival of a classical style in the arts. ■ **ne·o·clas·si·cism** /ˌnēōʹklasiˌsizəm/ n. **ne·o·clas·si·cist** n. & adj.

ne·o·co·lo·ni·al·ism /ˌnēōkəʹlōnēəˌlizəm/ ▸ n. the use of economic, political, or cultural pressures to control or influence other countries. ■ **ne·o·co·lo·ni·al** adj. **ne·o·co·lo·ni·al·ist** n. & adj.

ne·o·con /ˌnēōʹkän/ ▸ adj. neoconservative, especially in advocating democratic capitalism. ▸ n. a neoconservative.

ne·o·con·serv·a·tive /ˌnēōkənʹsərvətiv/ ▸ adj. relating to an approach to politics, economics, etc., that represents a return to a traditional conservative viewpoint, in contrast to more radical or liberal schools of thought. ▸ n. a person with neoconservative views.

ne·o·dym·i·um /ˌnēōʹdimēəm/ ▸ n. a silvery-white metallic element of the lanthanide series.

ne·o·Im·pres·sion·ism ▸ n. an artistic movement that aimed to improve on Impressionism through a systematic approach to form and color. ■ **ne·o·Im·pres·sion·ist** adj. & n.

Ne·o·lith·ic /ˌnēəʹliTHik/ ▸ adj. relating to the later part of the Stone Age, when agriculture was introduced and ground or polished stone weapons and implements were used.

ne·ol·o·gism /nēʹäləˌjizəm/ ▸ n. a newly coined word or expression.

ne·on /ʹnēän/ ▸ n. an inert gas that gives an orange glow when electricity is passed through it, used in fluorescent lighting. ▸ adj. very bright or fluorescent in color: *bold neon colors.*

ne·o·na·tal /ˌnēōʹnātl/ ▸ adj. relating to newborn children. ■ **ne·o·na·tol·o·gy** /ˌnāʹtäləjē/ n.

ne·o·nate /ʹnēəˌnāt/ ▸ n. a newborn child or mammal.

ne·o·Na·zi ▸ n. (pl. **neo-Nazis**) a person with extreme racist or nationalist views. ▸ adj. relating to neo-Nazis. ■ **ne·o·Na·zism** n.

ne·o·pho·bi·a /ˌnēōʹfōbēə/ ▸ n. extreme or irrational fear or dislike of anything new or unfamiliar. ■ **ne·o·pho·bic** /-bik/ adj.

ne·o·phyte /ʹnēəˌfīt/ ▸ n. **1** a person who is new to a subject, skill, or belief. **2** a novice in a religious order, or a newly ordained priest.

ne·o·plasm /ʹnēəˌplazəm/ ▸ n. a new and abnormal growth of tissue in the body, especially a cancerous tumor.

ne·o·prene /ʹnēəˌprēn/ ▸ n. a synthetic substance resembling rubber.

Nep·a·lese /ˌnepəʹlēz, -ʹlēs/ ▸ n. a person from Nepal. ▸ adj. relating to Nepal.

Ne·pal·i /nəʹpôlē, -ʹpälē/ ▸ n. (pl. **Nepalis**) **1** a person from Nepal. **2** the language of Nepal. ▸ adj. relating to Nepal or Nepali.

neph·ew /ʹnefyōō/ ▸ n. a son of a person's brother or sister.

neph·rite /ʹnefrīt/ ▸ n. a pale green or white form of jade.

ne·phri·tis /nəʹfrītis/ ▸ n. inflammation of the kidneys.

ne plus ul·tra /ʹnē ˌpləs ʹältrə, ʹnä ˌplōōs ʹōōltrə/ ▸ n. (**the ne plus ultra**) the perfect example of its kind: *the ne plus ultra of editors.*

nep·o·tism /ʹnepəˌtizəm/ ▸ n. favoritism shown to relatives or friends, especially by giving them jobs. ■ **nep·o·tis·tic** /ˌnepəʹtistik/ adj.

Nep·tune /ʹnept(y)ōōn/ ▸ n. a planet of the solar system, eighth in order from the sun. ■ **Nep·tu·ni·an** /nepʹt(y)ōōnēən/ adj.

nep·tu·ni·um /nepʹt(y)ōōnēəm/ ▸ n. a rare radioactive metallic element produced from uranium.

nerd /nərd/ ▸ n. informal a person who is obsessively interested in something and lacks social skills. ■ **nerd·ish** adj. **nerd·y** adj.

Ne·re·id /ʹni(ə)rēid/ ▸ n. Greek Mythology a sea nymph.

nerve /nərv/ ▸ n. **1** a fiber or bundle of fibers in the body that transmits impulses of sensation between the brain or spinal cord and other parts of the body. **2** (**one's nerve**) steadiness and courage in a demanding situation: *the army's commanders were beginning to lose their nerve.* **3** (**nerves**) a person's mental state; nervousness or anxiety. **4** informal impudent or excessively bold behavior. ▸ v. chiefly Brit. (**nerve oneself**) brace oneself for a demanding situation.
– PHRASES **get on someone's nerves** informal irritate someone.

nerve cell ▸ n. a neuron.

nerve cen·ter ▸ n. **1** the control center of an organization or operation. **2** a group of connected nerve cells performing a particular function.

nerve gas ▸ n. a poisonous gas that attacks the nervous system, causing death or disablement.

nerve·less /ʹnərvlis/ ▸ adj. **1** lacking strength or feeling. **2** not nervous; confident.

nerve·rack·ing (also **nerve-wracking**) ▸ adj. causing stress or anxiety.

nerv·ous /ʹnərvəs/ ▸ adj. **1** easily frightened or worried. **2** apprehensive or anxious: *he's nervous about speaking in public.* **3** relating to the nerves. ■ **ner·vous·ly** adv. **ner·vous·ness** n.

nerv·ous break·down ▸ n. a period of mental illness resulting from severe depression or stress.

nerv·ous sys·tem ▸ n. the network of nerve cells and fibers that transmits nerve impulses between parts of the body.

nerv·ous wreck ▸ n. informal a person suffering from stress or emotional exhaustion.

nerv·y /ʹnərvē/ ▸ adj. (**nervier, nerviest**) bold or impudent. ■ **nerv·i·ly** adv. **nerv·i·ness** n.

-ness ▸ suffix forming nouns referring to: **1** a state or condition: *liveliness.* **2** something in a certain state: *wilderness.*

nest /nest/ ▸ n. **1** a structure made by a bird for laying eggs and sheltering its young. **2** a place where an animal or insect breeds or shelters. **3** a place filled with undesirable people or things: *a nest of spies.* **4** a set of similar objects of graduated sizes, fitting together for storage. ▸ v. **1** (of a bird or animal) use or build a nest. **2** fit an object or objects inside a larger one. **3** (often as adj. **nested**) (especially in computing) place something in a lower position in a hierarchy. ■ **nest·er** n.

nest egg ▸ n. a sum of money saved for the future.

nes·tle /ʹnesəl/ ▸ v. **1** settle comfortably within or against something. **2** (of a place) lie in a sheltered position.

nest·ling /ʹnes(t)liNG/ ▸ n. a bird that is too young to leave the nest.

net¹ /net/ ▶ n. **1** a material made of strands of twine or cord woven or knotted together to form open squares. **2** a piece or structure of net for catching fish, surrounding a goal, etc. **3** a fine fabric with a very open weave. **4** a means of catching or securing someone or something: *passengers and luggage go through several checks to make sure no one slips through the net.* **5** (**the Net**) the Internet. **6** a communications or computer network. ▶ v. (**nets, netting, netted**) **1** catch something in a net. **2** catch or obtain in a skillful way: *customs have netted large caches of drugs.* **3** (in sports) kick or hit (a ball or puck) into the net. **4** cover something with a net.

net² ▶ adj. **1** (of an amount, value, or price) remaining after tax, discounts, or expenses have been deducted. Often contrasted with GROSS. **2** (of a weight) not including that of the packaging. **3** (of an effect or result) remaining after other factors have been taken into account; overall. ▶ v. (**nets, netting, netted**) gain a sum of money as clear profit.

neth·er /'neTHər/ ▶ adj. lower in position. ■ **neth·er·most** /-ˌmōst/ adj.

Neth·er·land·er /'neTHər,landər/ ▶ n. a person from the Netherlands. ■ **Neth·er·land·ish** /'neTHər,landisH/ adj.

neth·er re·gions ▶ pl.n. **1** hell; the underworld. **2** euphemistic a person's genitals and buttocks.

neth·er·world /'neTHər,wərld/ ▶ n. **1** the underworld; hell. **2** an area of activity that is hidden, underhanded, or poorly defined.

net prof·it ▶ n. the actual profit after working expenses have been paid.

ne·tsu·ke /'netsəkē/ ▶ n. (pl. same or **netsukes**) a carved ornament of wood or ivory, formerly worn in Japan to suspend items from the sash of a kimono.

net·ting /'netiNG/ ▶ n. material made of net.

net·tle /'netl/ ▶ n. a plant with jagged leaves covered with stinging hairs. ▶ v. annoy someone. – PHRASES **grasp the nettle** Brit. tackle a difficulty boldly.

net·work /'net,wərk/ ▶ n. **1** an arrangement of horizontal and vertical lines that cross each other. **2** a system of railroads, roads, etc., that connect with each other. **3** a group of broadcasting stations that connect to broadcast a program at the same time. **4** a number of interconnected computers or operations. **5** a group of people who keep in contact to exchange information. ▶ v. interact with other people to exchange information and develop contacts. ■ **net·work·er** n.

neu·ral /'n(y)o͞orəl/ ▶ adj. relating to a nerve or the nervous system. ■ **neu·ral·ly** adv.

neu·ral·gia /n(y)o͞o'raljə/ ▶ n. intense pain along a nerve, especially in the head or face. ■ **neu·ral·gic** /-jik/ adj.

neu·ral net·work (also **neural net**) ▶ n. a computer system modeled on the human brain and nervous system.

neur·as·the·ni·a /,n(y)o͞orəs'THēnēə/ ▶ n. a condition characterized by weariness, headaches, and irritability, associated chiefly with emotional disturbance. ■ **neur·as·then·ic** /-'THenik/ adj. & n.

neu·ri·tis /n(y)o͞o'rītis/ ▶ n. inflammation of a peripheral nerve or nerves.

neuro- ▶ comb.form relating to nerves or the nervous system: *neurosurgery.*

neu·ro·chem·is·try /,n(y)o͞orə'keməstrē/ ▶ n. the branch of biochemistry concerned with the processes occurring in nerve tissue and the nervous system. ■ **neu·ro·chem·i·cal** /-'kemikəl/ adj. **neu·ro·chem·ist** /-'kemist/ n.

neu·ro·lep·tic /,n(y)o͞orə'leptik/ ▶ adj. (of a drug) tending to lower nervous tension by reducing nerve functions.

neu·rol·o·gy /n(y)o͞o'räləjē/ ▶ n. the branch of medicine and biology concerned with the nervous system. ■ **neu·ro·log·ic** /-rə'läjik/ adj. **neu·ro·log·i·cal** /-rə'läjikəl/ adj. **neu·rol·o·gist** n.

neu·ron /'n(y)o͞orän/ (also **neurone** /-rōn/) ▶ n. a specialized cell that transmits nerve impulses. ■ **neu·ron·al** /'n(y)o͞orənl, n(y)o͞o'rōnl/ adj.

neu·ro·sci·ence /,n(y)o͞orō'sīəns/ ▶ n. science that deals with the structure or function of the nervous system and brain. ■ **neu·ro·sci·en·tist** /-'sīəntist/ n.

neu·ro·sis /n(y)o͞o'rōsis/ ▶ n. (pl. **neuroses** /-ˌsēz/) a relatively mild mental disorder involving symptoms such as depression, anxiety, obsessive behavior, or hypochondria.

neu·ro·sur·ger·y /,n(y)o͞orō'sərjərē/ ▶ n. surgery performed on the nervous system. ■ **neu·ro·sur·geon** /'n(y)ərō,sərjən/ n. **neu·ro·sur·gi·cal** /-jikəl/ adj.

neu·rot·ic /n(y)o͞o'rätik/ ▶ adj. **1** having or relating to neurosis. **2** informal abnormally sensitive, anxious, or obsessive. ▶ n. a neurotic person. ■ **neu·rot·i·cal·ly** adv. **neu·rot·i·cism** /-'rätə,sizəm/ n.

neu·ro·tox·in /'n(y)o͞orō,täksin/ ▶ n. a poison that acts on the nervous system.

neu·ro·trans·mit·ter /,n(y)o͞orō'tranzmitər/ ▶ n. a chemical substance released from a nerve fiber and bringing about the transfer of an impulse to another nerve, muscle, etc.

neu·ter /'n(y)o͞otər/ ▶ adj. **1** Grammar (of a noun) not masculine or feminine. **2** (of an animal or plant) having no sexual or reproductive organs. ▶ v. **1** castrate or spay a domestic animal. **2** take away the power of: *their only purpose is to neuter local democracy.*

neu·tral /'n(y)o͞otrəl/ ▶ adj. **1** not supporting either side in a dispute or conflict; impartial. **2** deliberately not expressing or provoking strong feeling: *her tone was neutral, devoid of sentiment.* **3** pale gray, cream, or beige in color. **4** Chemistry neither acid nor alkaline; having a pH of about 7. **5** electrically neither positive nor negative. ▶ n. **1** a country or person that does not take sides in a conflict or dispute. **2** pale gray, cream, or beige. **3** a position of a gear mechanism in which the engine is disconnected from the driven parts. ■ **neu·tral·i·ty** /n(y)o͞o'tralitē/ n. **neu·tral·ly** adv.

neu·tral·ize /'n(y)o͞otrə,līz/ ▶ v. **1** prevent something from having an effect by counteracting it with something else: *never try to neutralize odors with air fresheners.* **2** make an acid or alkaline chemically neutral. **3** euphemistic kill or destroy someone or something. ■ **neu·tral·i·za·tion** /,n(y)o͞otrəli'zāsHən/ n.

neu·tri·no /n(y)o͞o'trēnō/ ▶ n. (pl. **neutrinos**) Physics a subatomic particle with a mass close to zero and no electric charge.

neu·tron /'n(y)o͞oträn/ ▶ n. a subatomic particle of about the same mass as a proton but without an electric charge.

neu·tron bomb ▸ n. a nuclear weapon that produces large numbers of neutrons, destroying life but not property.

neu·tron star ▸ n. a very dense star composed mainly of neutrons.

né·vé /'nā'vā/ ▸ n. compacted or hardened snow, especially as found on the upper part of a glacier.

nev·er /'nevər/ ▸ adv. **1** not ever. **2** not at all. – PHRASES **never-never land** an imaginary perfect place. **well I never!** informal expressing great surprise.

nev·er-end·ing ▸ adj. (especially of something unpleasant) having or seeming to have no end.

nev·er·more /,nevər'môr/ ▸ adv. literary never again.

nev·er·the·less /,nevərTHə'les/ ▸ adv. in spite of that.

ne·vus /'nēvəs/ ▸ n. (pl. **nevi** /-,vī/) a birthmark or a mole on the skin.

new /n(y)ōō/ ▸ adj. **1** not existing before; made, introduced, or discovered recently: *she was signing copies of her new book.* **2** not previously used or owned. **3** obtained or experienced recently: *her new coat.* **4** (**new to/at**) not familiar with or experienced at. **5** better than before; renewed or transformed: *the pills would make him a new man.* ▸ adv. newly. ▪ **new·ness** n.

New Age ▸ n. a movement concerned with alternative approaches to traditional Western culture, religion, medicine, etc.

new·bie /'n(y)ōōbē/ ▸ n. (pl. **newbies**) an inexperienced newcomer.

new·born /'n(y)ōō,bôrn/ ▸ adj. recently born. ▸ n. a newborn child.

new·com·er /'n(y)ōōwəl/ ▸ n. **1** a person who has recently arrived. **2** a person who is new to an activity or situation.

new·el /'n(y)ōōwəl/ ▸ n. **1** (also **newel post**) a post at the top or bottom of a flight of stairs, supporting a handrail. **2** the central supporting pillar of a spiral staircase.

new·fan·gled /'n(y)ōō'faNGgəld, -,faNG-/ ▸ adj. derogatory new and different from what one is used to.

new·found /'n(y)ōō,found/ ▸ adj. recently found or discovered: *his newfound political consciousness.*

New·found·land /,n(y)ōōfənd'land, 'n(y)ōōfəndlənd, -,land/ ▸ n. a dog of a very large breed with a thick, coarse coat.

New Guin·e·an /'ginēən/ ▸ n. a person from New Guinea. ▸ adj. relating to New Guinea.

new·ly /'n(y)ōōlē/ ▸ adv. **1** recently. **2** again; afresh: *confidence for the newly single.*

new·ly·wed /'n(y)ōōlē,wed/ ▸ n. a recently married person.

new man ▸ n. chiefly Brit. a man who rejects traditional male attitudes, often taking on childcare and housework.

new math ▸ pl.n. (usu. treated as sing.) a system of teaching mathematics to children, with emphasis on investigation by them and on set theory.

new moon ▸ n. the phase of the moon when it is invisible from earth or first appears as a slender crescent.

news /n(y)ōōz/ ▸ n. **1** new or important information about recent events. **2** (**the news**) a broadcast or published news report. **3** (**news to**) informal information not previously known to someone.

news a·gen·cy ▸ n. an organization that collects and distributes news items to the media.

news·cast /'n(y)ōōz,kast/ ▸ n. a broadcast news report. ▪ **news·cast·er** n.

news con·fer·ence ▸ n. a press conference.

news·feed /'n(y)ōōz,fēd/ (also **news feed**) ▸ n. **1** a service by which news items are provided on a regular or continuous basis for distribution or broadcasting. **2** a system by which data is transferred or exchanged between central computers to provide newsgroup access to networked users.

news·flash /'n(y)ōōz,flash/ ▸ n. a short broadcast of important news that often interrupts other programs.

news·group /'n(y)ōōz,grōōp/ ▸ n. a group of Internet users who exchange information online on a particular topic.

news·let·ter /'n(y)ōōz,letər/ ▸ n. a bulletin issued periodically to the members of a society or other organization.

news·man /'n(y)ōōz,man/ ▸ n. (pl. **newsmen**) a male reporter or journalist.

news·pa·per /'n(y)ōōz,pāpər/ ▸ n. a daily or weekly publication consisting of folded sheets and containing news, articles, and advertisements.

new·speak /'n(y)ōō,spēk/ ▸ n. deliberately misleading and indirect language, used by politicians.

news·print /'n(y)ōōz,print/ ▸ n. cheap, low-quality printing paper used for newspapers.

news·read·er /'n(y)ōōz,rēdər/ ▸ n. **1** Brit. a person who reads the news on radio or television. **2** a computer program for reading emails posted to newsgroups.

news·reel /'n(y)ōōz,rēl/ ▸ n. a short film of news and current affairs.

news·room /'n(y)ōōz,rōōm, -,rŏŏm/ ▸ n. the area in a newspaper or broadcasting office where news is processed.

news·stand /'n(y)ōōz,stand/ ▸ n. a stand for the sale of newspapers.

New Style ▸ n. the method of calculating dates using the Gregorian calendar.

news·wire /'n(y)ōōz,wīr/ ▸ n. an electronically transmitted news service.

news·wor·thy /'n(y)ōōz,wərTHē/ ▸ adj. important enough to be mentioned as news.

news·y /'n(y)ōōzē/ ▸ adj. informal full of news.

newt /n(y)ōōt/ ▸ n. a small animal with a thin body and a long tail that can live in water or on land.

New Tes·ta·ment ▸ n. the second part of the Christian Bible, recording the life and teachings of Jesus and his earliest followers.

new·ton /'n(y)ōōtn/ ▸ n. Physics the SI unit of force.

New·to·ni·an /n(y)ōō'tōnēən/ ▸ adj. relating to or arising from the work of Sir Isaac Newton; behaving according to the principles of classical physics.

new wave ▸ n. **1** a group of people who introduce new styles and ideas in art, movies, literature, etc. **2** a style of rock music popular in the late 1970s, deriving from punk.

New World ▸ n. North and South America in

contrast to Europe, Asia, and Africa.

new year ▶ n. **1** the calendar year just begun or about to begin. **2** the period immediately before and after December 31.

New Year's Day ▶ n. January 1.

New Year's Eve ▶ n. December 31.

New York as·ter ▶ n. a garden plant with numerous pinkish-lilac daisylike flowers that bloom in autumn.

New York·er /ˌn(y)o͞o ˈyôrkər/ ▶ n. a person from the state or city of New York.

New York min·ute /yôrk/ ▶ n. informal a very short time; a moment.

New Zea·land·er /ˌn(y)o͞o ˈzēləndər/ ▶ n. a person from New Zealand.

next /nekst/ ▶ adj. **1** coming immediately after the present one in time, space, or order. **2** (of a day of the week) nearest (or the nearest but one) after the present. ▶ adv. **1** immediately afterwards. **2** following in the specified order: *Joe was the next oldest after Martin.* ▶ n. the next person or thing.

– PHRASES **next of kin** a person's closest living relative or relatives. **next to 1** beside. **2** following in order or importance. **3** almost. **the next world** (in some religious beliefs) the place where people go after death.

next door ▶ adv. & adj. in or to the next house or room.

nex·us /ˈneksəs/ ▶ n. (pl. same or **nexuses**) **1** a connection or series of connections: *the nexus between birth and privilege.* **2** a connected group. **3** a central or focal point.

NF ▶ abbr. Newfoundland.

NFC ▶ abbr. National Football Conference.

NFL ▶ abbr. National Football League.

NGO ▶ abbr. non-governmental organization.

NH ▶ abbr. New Hampshire.

Ni ▶ symbol the chemical element nickel.

ni·a·cin /ˈnīəsin/ ▶ n. another term for **NICOTINIC ACID**.

nib /nib/ ▶ n. the pointed end part of a pen, which distributes the ink.

nib·ble /ˈnibəl/ ▶ v. **1** take small bites out of something. **2** bite a part of the body gently. **3** gradually reduce: *the fringes of the region have been nibbled away by development.* ▶ n. **1** an instance of nibbling. **2** a small piece of food bitten off. **3** (**nibbles**) informal small savory snacks.

nib·let /ˈniblit/ ▶ n. a small piece of food.

nib·lick /ˈniblik/ ▶ n. Golf, dated an iron with a heavy head, used for playing out of bunkers.

nibs /nibz/ ▶ n. (**his nibs**) informal, dated a mock title used to refer to a man who thinks he is important.

Ni·Cad /ˈnīˌkad/ (also trademark **Nicad**) ▶ n. a battery or cell containing nickel, cadmium, and potassium hydroxide.

Nic·a·ra·guan /nikəˈrägwən/ ▶ n. a person from Nicaragua in Central America. ▶ adj. relating to Nicaragua.

nice /nīs/ ▶ adj. **1** pleasant, or attractive. **2** good-natured; kind. **3** fine or subtle: *a nice distinction.* ■ **nice·ly** adv. **nice·ness** n.

ni·ce·ty /ˈnīsitē/ ▶ n. (pl. **niceties**) **1** a fine detail or distinction: *legal niceties are wasted on him.* **2** a detail of polite social behavior. **3** accuracy or precision.

– PHRASES **to a nicety** precisely.

niche /nicH, nēsH/ ▶ n. **1** a shallow recess,

especially one in a wall to display an ornament. **2** (**one's niche**) a position or role in life that suits someone: *he found his niche as a writer.* **3** a particular group seen as a potential market for a product: *targeting the urban youth niche.*

nick /nik/ ▶ n. a small cut or notch. ▶ v. **1** make a small cut in something. **2** (**nick someone for**) informal cheat someone of something. **3** Brit. informal steal something. **4** Brit. informal arrest someone.

– PHRASES **in the nick of time** only just in time.

nick·el /ˈnikəl/ ▶ n. **1** a silvery-white metallic chemical element resembling iron, used in alloys. **2** a five-cent coin. ▶ v. (**nickels, nickeling, nickeled**) coat something with nickel.

nick·el-and-dime ▶ v. put a financial strain on someone by charging small amounts for many minor services. ▶ adj. of little importance; trivial.

nick·el·o·de·on /ˌnikəˈlōdēən/ ▶ n. informal, dated a jukebox.

nick·el sil·ver ▶ n. an alloy of nickel, zinc, and copper.

nick·el steel ▶ n. stainless steel containing chromium and nickel.

nick·name /ˈnikˌnām/ ▶ n. an informal, often amusing name for a person or thing. ▶ v. give a nickname to someone or something.

ni·co·ti·a·na /niˌkōSHēˈänə, -ˈanə/ ▶ n. an ornamental plant related to tobacco, with tubular sweet-smelling flowers.

nic·o·tine /ˈnikəˌtēn/ ▶ n. a toxic oily liquid found in tobacco.

nic·o·tine patch ▶ n. a patch containing nicotine, worn on the skin by a person trying to give up smoking.

nic·o·tin·ic ac·id /ˌnikəˈtinik, -ˈtēnik/ ▶ n. a vitamin of the B complex, found in milk, wheat germ, meat, and other foods.

nic·ti·tat·ing mem·brane /ˈniktiˌtātiNG/ ▶ n. a whitish membrane forming an inner eyelid in birds, reptiles, and some mammals.

niece /nēs/ ▶ n. a daughter of a person's brother or sister.

ni·el·lo /nēˈelō/ ▶ n. **1** a black compound of sulfur with silver, lead, or copper, used for filling in engraved designs in metals. **2** objects decorated with niello.

Nietz·sche·an /ˈnēCHēən/ ▶ adj. relating to the German philosopher Friedrich Wilhelm Nietzsche.

nif·ty /ˈniftē/ ▶ adj. (**niftier, niftiest**) informal particularly good, effective, or stylish. ■ **nif·ti·ly** /-təlē/ adv.

Ni·ge·ri·an /nīˈjirēən/ ▶ n. a person from Nigeria. ▶ adj. relating to Nigeria.

nig·gard /ˈnigərd/ ▶ n. a miserly person.

nig·gard·ly /ˈnigərdlē/ ▶ adj. not generous; stingy: *I was kept on a niggardly allowance.*

nig·ger /ˈnigər/ ▶ n. offensive a black person.

> **USAGE**
> The word **nigger** is very offensive and should not be used.

nig·gle /ˈnigəl/ ▶ v. **1** worry or annoy someone slightly but persistently. **2** criticize someone in a petty way. ▶ n. a minor worry or criticism. ■ **nig·gling** /ˈnig(ə)liNG/ adj. **nig·gly** /ˈnig(ə)lē/ adj.

nigh /nī/ ▶ adv., prep., & adj. **1** old use or literary near. **2** almost; nearly.

night /nīt/ ▶ n. **1** the time from sunset to sunrise.

2 the darkness of night. **3** an evening until bedtime. **4** literary dusk; nightfall. ▶ adv. (**nights**) informal at night.

night·cap /'nīt,kap/ ▶ n. **1** a hot or alcoholic drink taken at bedtime. **2** historical a cap worn in bed.

night·clothes /'nīt,klō(TH)z/ ▶ pl.n. clothes worn in bed.

night·club /'nīt,kləb/ ▶ n. a club that is open at night, with a bar and music.

night·dress /'nīt,dres/ ▶ n. a nightgown.

night·fall /'nīt,fôl/ ▶ n. dusk.

night·gown /'nīt,goun/ ▶ n. a light, loose garment worn by a woman or girl in bed.

night·ie /'nītē/ ▶ n. informal a nightdress.

night·in·gale /'nītn,gāl, 'nītiNG-/ ▶ n. a small brownish thrush noted for its tuneful song, often heard at night.

night·jar /'nīt,jär/ ▶ n. a gray-brown bird with a distinctive call, active at night.

night·life /'nīt,līf/ ▶ n. social activities or entertainment available at night.

night·light /'nīt,līt/ ▶ n. a lamp or candle providing a dim light during the night.

night·ly /'nītlē/ ▶ adj. **1** happening or done every night. **2** happening or done during the night. ▶ adv. every night.

night·mare /'nīt,me(ə)r/ ▶ n. **1** a frightening or unpleasant dream. **2** a very unpleasant or difficult experience or situation: *acne is every teenager's nightmare.* ■ **night·mar·ish** adj.

night owl ▶ n. informal a person who enjoys staying up late at night.

night school ▶ n. evening classes provided for people who work during the day.

night·shirt /'nīt,SHərt/ ▶ n. a long, loose shirt worn in bed.

night·side /'nīt,sīd/ ▶ n. the side of a planet or moon facing away from the sun and therefore in darkness.

night soil ▶ n. human excrement collected at night from buckets, cesspools, and outhouses.

night·spot /'nīt,spät/ ▶ n. informal a nightclub.

night·stand /'nīt,stand/ (also **night table**) ▶ n. a small, low bedside table, typically with drawers.

night·stick /'nīt,stik/ ▶ n. a police officer's club or billy.

night·time /'nīt,tīm/ ▶ n. the time between evening and morning.

night watch·man ▶ n. (pl. **night watchmen**) a person who guards a building at night.

night·wear /'nīt,we(ə)r/ ▶ n. clothing worn in bed.

NIH ▶ abbr. National Institutes of Health.

ni·hil·ism /'nīə,lizəm, 'nē-/ ▶ n. the rejection of all religious and moral principles, often in the belief that life is meaningless. ■ **ni·hil·ist** n. **ni·hil·is·tic** /,nīə'listik, ,nēə-/ adj.

-nik ▶ suffix (forming nouns) referring to a person associated with a specified thing: *beatnik.*

Nik·kei in·dex /'nēkā/ (also **Nikkei average**) ▶ n. an index of figures indicating the relative price of shares on the Tokyo Stock Exchange.

nil /nil/ ▶ n. nothing; zero. ▶ adj. nonexistent.

nil de·spe·ran·dum /'nil ,despə'rändəm/ ▶ exclam. do not despair.

Ni·lot·ic /nī'lätik/ ▶ adj. relating to the Nile River or to the Nile region of Africa.

nim·ble /'nimbəl/ ▶ adj. (**nimbler, nimblest**) quick and agile in movement or thought. ■ **nim·bly** adv.

nim·bus /'nimbəs/ ▶ n. (pl. **nimbi** /-,bī, ,bē/ or **nimbuses**) **1** a large gray rain cloud. **2** a luminous cloud or a halo surrounding a supernatural being or saint.

Nim·by /'nimbē/ ▶ n. (pl. **Nimbys**) informal a person who objects to the siting of unpleasant developments in their neighborhood. ■ **Nim·by·ism** /-,izəm/ n.

nin·com·poop /'ninkəm,pōōp, 'niNG-/ ▶ n. a foolish or stupid person.

nine /nīn/ ▶ cardinal number one less than ten; 9. (Roman numeral: **ix** or **IX.**)
– PHRASES **to the nines** to a great or elaborate extent: *the women were dressed to the nines.*

nine·teen /nīn'tēn, 'nīn,tēn/ ▶ cardinal number one more than eighteen; 19. (Roman numeral: **xix** or **XIX.**) ■ **nine·teenth** /nīn'tēnTH, 'nīn,tēnTH/ ordinal number.

nine·teenth hole ▶ n. humorous the bar in a golf clubhouse, as reached after a round of eighteen holes.

nine·ty /'nīntē/ ▶ cardinal number (pl. **nineties**) ten less than one hundred; 90. (Roman numeral: **xc** or **XC.**) ■ **nine·ti·eth** /-tēiTH/ ordinal number.

nin·ja /'ninjə/ ▶ n. a person skilled in ninjutsu (the Japanese technique of espionage).

nin·jut·su /nin'jōōtsōō/ ▶ n. the traditional Japanese art of stealth, camouflage, and sabotage, first developed for espionage and now popular as a martial art.

nin·ny /'ninē/ ▶ n. (pl. **ninnies**) informal a foolish and weak person.

ninth /nīnTH/ ▶ ordinal number **1** that is number nine in a sequence; 9th. **2** (**a ninth/one ninth**) each of nine equal parts into which something is divided. **3** a musical interval spanning nine consecutive notes in a scale. ■ **ninth·ly** adv.

ni·o·bi·um /nī'ōbēəm/ ▶ n. a silver-gray metallic chemical element.

nip¹ /nip/ ▶ v. (**nips, nipping, nipped**) **1** pinch or bite someone or something sharply. **2** (of cold or frost) hurt or damage someone or something. ▶ n. **1** a sharp bite or pinch. **2** a feeling of sharp coldness.
– PHRASES **nip something in the bud** stop something at an early stage.

nip² ▶ n. a small quantity or sip of liquor.

nip and tuck ▶ adv. & adj. closely contested; neck and neck. ▶ n. informal a cosmetic surgical operation.

nip·per /'nipər/ ▶ n. **1** informal a child. **2** (**nippers**) pliers, pincers, or a similar tool.

nip·ple /'nipəl/ ▶ n. **1** a small projection in the center of each breast, containing (in females) the outlets of the organs that produce milk. **2** a small projection on a machine from which oil or other fluid is dispensed.

nip·py /'nipē/ ▶ adj. (**nippier, nippiest**) informal **1** (of the weather) chilly. **2** inclined to nip or bite. ■ **nip·pi·ly** adv. **nip·pi·ness** n.

nir·va·na /nər'vänə, nir-/ ▶ n. **1** the ultimate goal of Buddhism, a state in which there is no suffering or desire, and no sense of self. **2** a perfect or very happy state or place: *Toronto is a restaurant-goer's nirvana.*

ni·sei /nē'sā, 'nēsā/ (also **Nisei**) ▶ n. (pl. same or **niseis**) a person born in the US or Canada whose parents were immigrants from Japan. Compare with **issei** and **sansei**.

nit /nit/ ▶ n. informal the egg of a human head louse.

ni·ter /ˈnītər/ ▶ n. potassium nitrate; saltpeter.

nit·pick·ing /ˈnit,pikiNG/ ▶ n. informal fussy fault-finding. ■ **nit·pick** v. **nit·pick·er** n.

ni·trate ▶ n. /ˈnītrāt/ a salt or ester of nitric acid.
▶ v. /ˌnīˈtrāt/ treat a substance with nitric acid.
■ **ni·tra·tion** /nīˈtrāsHən/ n.

ni·tric ac·id /ˈnītrik/ ▶ n. a very corrosive acid.

ni·tride /ˈnītrīd/ ▶ n. a compound of nitrogen with another element or group.

ni·tri·fy /ˈnītrəˌfī/ ▶ v. (**nitrifies, nitrifying, nitrified**) convert ammonia or another nitrogen compound into nitrites or nitrates.
■ **ni·tri·fi·ca·tion** /ˌnītrəfiˈkāSHən/ n.

ni·trite /ˈnītrīt/ ▶ n. a salt or ester of nitrous acid.

nitro- ▶ comb.form relating to or containing nitric acid, nitrates, or nitrogen: *nitroglycerine*.

ni·tro·cel·lu·lose /ˌnītrōˈselyəˌlōs, ˌlōz/ ▶ n. a highly flammable material used to make explosives and celluloid.

ni·tro·gen /ˈnītrəjən/ ▶ n. a colorless, odorless gas forming about 78 percent of the earth's atmosphere. ■ **ni·trog·e·nous** /nīˈträjənəs/ adj.

ni·tro·gen cy·cle ▶ n. the series of processes by which nitrogen from the air is converted into compounds that are deposited in the soil, absorbed by plants, and eaten by animals, then returned to the atmosphere when these organic substances decay.

ni·tro·gen di·ox·ide ▶ n. a reddish-brown poisonous gas formed when many metals dissolve in nitric acid.

ni·tro·gen fix·a·tion ▶ n. the chemical processes by which nitrogen in the atmosphere is absorbed into organic compounds.

ni·tro·gly·ce·rin /ˌnītrōˈglisərin/ (also **nitroglycerine** /ˌnītrōˈglisərēn/) ▶ n. an explosive yellow liquid used in dynamite and in medicine as a vasodilator in the treatment of angina.

ni·trous /ˈnītrəs/ ▶ adj. relating to or containing nitrogen.

ni·trous ac·id ▶ n. a weak acid made by the action of acids on nitrites.

ni·trous ox·ide ▶ n. a gas with a sweetish smell, used as an anesthetic.

nit·ty-grit·ty /ˈnitē ˈgritē/ ▶ n. informal the most important aspects or basic details of a matter.

nit·wit /ˈnitˌwit/ ▶ n. informal a silly or foolish person.

nix /niks/ informal ▶ n. nothing. ▶ v. put an end to or cancel something.

NJ ▶ abbr. New Jersey.

NM ▶ abbr. New Mexico.

nm ▶ abbr. **1** nanometer. **2** (also **n.m.**) nautical mile.

NNE ▶ abbr. north-northeast.

NNW ▶ abbr. north-northwest.

No¹ ▶ n. variant spelling of **NOH**.

No² ▶ symbol the chemical element nobelium.

no /nō/ ▶ determiner **1** not any. **2** quite the opposite of: *he's no fool.* **3** hardly any. ▶ exclam. used to refuse, deny, or disagree with something.
▶ adv. (with comparative) not at all. ▶ n. (pl. **noes**) a vote or decision against something.
– PHRASES **no can do** informal I am unable to do it. **no way** informal certainly not; not at all.

no. ▶ abbr. (pl. **nos**) number.

nob·ble /ˈnäbəl/ ▶ v. Brit. informal **1** try to influence

or thwart by underhanded methods: *an attempt to nobble the jury.* **2** tamper with a racehorse to prevent it from winning a race. **3** stop someone so as to talk to them. **4** steal something.

no·bel·i·um /nōˈbelēəm/ ▶ n. a very unstable chemical element made by high-energy collisions.

No·bel Prize /ˈnōbel/ ▶ n. any of six international prizes awarded annually for outstanding work in physics, chemistry, physiology or medicine, literature, economics, and the promotion of peace.

no·bil·i·ty /nōˈbilitē/ ▶ n. **1** the quality of being noble. **2** the aristocracy.

no·ble /ˈnōbəl/ ▶ adj. (**nobler, noblest**)
1 belonging to the aristocracy. **2** having admirable personal qualities or high moral principles: *fighting for a noble cause.*
3 impressive; magnificent. ▶ n. **1** (especially in former times) a member of the aristocracy. **2** a former English gold coin. ■ **no·bly** adv.

no·ble gas ▶ n. any of the gases helium, neon, argon, krypton, xenon, and radon, which seldom or never combine with other elements to form compounds.

no·ble·man /ˈnōbəlmən/ (or **noblewoman** /ˈnōbəlˌwoomən/) ▶ n. (pl. **noblemen** or **noblewomen**) a man (or woman) who belongs to the aristocracy.

no·ble rot ▶ n. a gray mold deliberately cultivated on grapes in order to perfect certain wines.

no·ble sav·age ▶ n. a representative of primitive mankind as idealized in Romantic literature.

no·blesse ▶ n. (in phrase **noblesse oblige** /nōˈbles ōˈblēzH/) noble or wealthy people should help those who are less fortunate.

no·bod·y /ˈnō,bädē, -bədē/ ▶ pron. no person; no one. ▶ n. (pl. **nobodies**) an unimportant person.

no-brain·er ▶ n. informal something that involves little or no mental effort.

nock /näk/ Archery ▶ n. a notch at either end of a bow or at the end of an arrow, for receiving the string of the bow. ▶ v. fit an arrow to the string of the bow.

noc·tur·nal /näkˈtərnl/ ▶ adj. done, occurring, or active at night. ■ **noc·tur·nal·ly** adv.

noc·turne /ˈnäk,tərn/ ▶ n. a short musical composition of a romantic and dreamy nature.

nod /näd/ ▶ v. (**nods, nodding, nodded**) **1** lower and raise one's head slightly and briefly to show agreement or as a greeting or signal. **2** let one's head fall forward when drowsy or asleep. **3** (**nod off**) informal fall asleep. ▶ n. **1** an act of nodding. **2** a gesture acknowledging something: *a feel-good musical with a nod to pantomime.*
– PHRASES **give someone/thing the nod**
1 approve someone or something. **2** give someone a signal. **a nodding acquaintance** a slight acquaintance.

node /nōd/ ▶ n. technical **1** a point in a network at which lines cross or branch. **2** the part of a plant stem from which one or more leaves grow. **3** a small mass of distinct body tissue. **4** Physics & Mathematics a point at which the amplitude of vibration of a wave is zero. ■ **nod·al** adj.

nod·ule /ˈnäjo͞ol/ ▶ n. **1** a small swelling or cluster of cells in the body. **2** a swelling on a root of a plant of the pea family, containing nitrogen-fixing bacteria. **3** a small rounded lump of matter distinct from its surroundings. ■ **nod·u·lar** adj.

No·el /nōˈel/ ▶ n. Christmas.

no-frills ▶ adj. without unnecessary extras, especially ones for comfort or decoration: *a no-frills airline.*

nog·gin /ˈnägin/ ▶ n. informal **1** a person's head. **2** dated a small quantity of liquor.

no-go ▶ adj. informal **1** not ready or not functioning properly. **2** impossible, hopeless, or forbidden: *no-go zones for cars.* ▶ n. a negative response; no.

no-good ▶ adj. informal (of a person) contemptible; worthless: *a no-good layabout.* ▶ n. a worthless or contemptible person.

Noh /nō/ (also **No**) ▶ n. traditional Japanese masked drama with dance and song.

no-hit·ter ▶ n. Baseball a complete game in which a pitcher yields no hits to the opposing team.

noir /nwär/ ▶ n. a type of crime fiction or movie marked by a mood of cynicism, fatalism, and a lack of moral certainty. ■ **noir·ish** /ˈnwärisн/ adj.

noise /noiz/ ▶ n. **1** a loud or unpleasant sound or series of sounds. **2** (**noises**) conventional remarks without real meaning: *Clarissa made encouraging noises.* **3** disturbances that accompany and interfere with an electrical signal. ■ **noise·less** adj.

noise pol·lu·tion ▶ n. harmful or annoying levels of noise.

noi·sette /nwäˈzet/ ▶ n. **1** a small round piece of meat. **2** a chocolate made with hazelnuts.

noi·some /ˈnoisəm/ ▶ adj. literary **1** having a very unpleasant smell. **2** very unpleasant.

nois·y /ˈnoizē/ ▶ adj. (**noisier, noisiest**) full of or making a lot of noise. ■ **nois·i·ly** adv. **nois·i·ness** n.

nol·lie /ˈnälē/ ▶ n. a skateboarding jump performed without the aid of a takeoff ramp, executed by pressing the foot down on the nose of the board.

no·lo con·ten·de·re /ˌnōlō kənˈtendərē/ ▶ n. (also **nolo**) Law a plea by which a defendant accepts conviction as though a guilty plea had been entered but does not admit guilt.

no·mad /ˈnōˌmad/ ▶ n. a member of a people that travels from place to place to find fresh pasture for its animals. ■ **no·mad·ism** /ˈnōmaˌdizəm/ n.

no·mad·ic /nōˈmadik/ ▶ adj. having the life of a nomad; wandering. ■ **no·mad·i·cal·ly** /nōˈmadiklē/ adv.

no man's land ▶ n. an area between two opposing armies that is not controlled by either.

nom de guerre /ˌnäm də ˈger/ ▶ n. (pl. **noms de guerre** pronunc. same) a name used by a person to engage in combat.

nom de plume /ˌnäm də ˈplo͞om/ ▶ n. (pl. **noms de plume** pronunc. same) a name used by a writer instead of their real name; a pen name.

no·men·cla·ture /ˈnōmənˌklāchər/ ▶ n. **1** a system of names used in a particular field. **2** the selecting of names for things in a particular field. **3** formal a name or term given to someone or something. ■ **no·men·cla·tur·al** /ˌnōmənˈklāchərəl/ adj.

nom·i·nal /ˈnäminəl/ ▶ adj. **1** existing in name but not in reality: *nominal independence under military occupation.* **2** (of a sum of money) very small, but charged or paid as a sign that payment is necessary. **3** Grammar relating to or functioning as a noun. ■ **nom·i·nal·ly** adv.

nom·i·nal·ism /ˈnäminəˌlizəm/ ▶ n. Philosophy the theory that general terms or ideas are mere names without any corresponding reality. Often contrasted with REALISM. ■ **nom·i·nal·ist** n.

nom·i·nal val·ue ▶ n. **1** the value that is stated on a coin, bill, etc. **2** the price of a share, bond, or stock when it was issued, rather than its current market value.

nom·i·nate /ˈnäməˌnāt/ ▶ v. **1** put someone forward as a candidate for election or for an honor or award. **2** appoint someone to a job or position. **3** specify something formally. ■ **nom·i·na·tion** /ˌnäməˈnāsнən/ n. **nom·i·na·tor** n.

nom·i·na·tive /ˈnämənətiv/ ▶ n. the grammatical case used for the subject of a verb.

nom·i·nee /ˌnäməˈnē/ ▶ n. **1** a person who is nominated for an office, award, etc. **2** a person or company in whose name a company, stock, or bond is registered.

non- ▶ prefix expressing negation or absence; not: *nonrecognition.*

USAGE

The prefixes (word beginnings) **non-** and **un-** both mean 'not', but they tend to be used in slightly different ways. **Non-** is more neutral, while **un-** often suggests a particular bias or standpoint. For example, **unnatural** means that something is not natural in a bad way, whereas **nonnatural** simply means 'not natural.'

---

non·a·ge·nar·i·an /ˌnänəjəˈne(ə)rēən, ˌnōnə-/ ▶ n. a person between 90 and 99 years old.

non·a·gon /ˈnänəˌgän/ ▶ n. a plane figure with nine straight sides and nine angles.

non·al·co·hol·ic /ˌnän͵alkəˈhôlik, -ˈhälik/ ▶ adj. (of a drink) not containing alcohol.

non·a·ligned /ˌnänəˈlīnd/ ▶ adj. (of a country during the cold war) not allied to any of the major world powers.

non·al·ler·gen·ic /ˌnänalərˈjenik/ ▶ adj. not causing an allergic reaction.

non·be·ing /nänˈbēiNG/ ▶ n. the state of not being; nonexistence.

non·be·liev·er /ˌnänbəˈlēvər/ ▶ n. a person who does not believe in something, especially one who has no religious faith.

non·bel·lig·er·ent /ˌnänbəˈlijərənt/ ▶ adj. not engaged in a war or conflict.

nonce /näns/ ▶ adj. (of a word or expression) coined for one occasion.
– PHRASES **for the nonce** for the present; temporarily.

non·cha·lant /ˌnänsнəˈlänt/ ▶ adj. casually calm and relaxed. ■ **non·cha·lance** n. **non·cha·lant·ly** adv.

non·com /ˈnänˌkäm/ ▶ n. Military informal a noncommissioned officer.

non·com·bat·ant /ˌnänkəmˈbatnt/ ▶ n. a person who is not engaged in fighting during a war, especially a civilian or an army chaplain or doctor.

non·com·mis·sioned /ˌnänkəˈmisнənd/ ▶ adj. (of a military officer) appointed from the lower ranks rather than holding a commission.

non·com·mit·tal /ˌnänkəˈmitl/ ▶ adj. not expressing an opinion. ■ **non·com·mit·tal·ly** adv.

non·com·pli·ance /ˌnänkəmˈplīəns/ ▶ n. failure to act in accordance with a wish or command: *illegal noncompliance with safety procedures.*

non com·pos men·tis /ˌnän ˈkämpəs ˈmentis/ ▶ adj. mentally unbalanced or insane.

non·con·duc·tor /ˌnänkən'dəktər/ ▶ n. a substance that does not conduct heat or electricity. ■ **non·con·duct·ing** adj.

non·con·form·ist /ˌnänkən'förmist/ ▶ n. **1** a person who does not follow accepted ideas or behavior. **2** (**Nonconformist**) a member of a Protestant Church who does not follow the beliefs of the established Church of England. ▶ adj. not following accepted ideas or behavior. ■ **non·con·form·ism** /-ˌmizəm/ n. **non·con·form·i·ty** /ˌnänkən'förmitē/ n.

non·con·trib·u·to·ry /ˌnänkən'tribyəˌtôrē/ ▶ adj. (of a pension) funded by regular payments by the employer, not the employee.

non·co·op·er·a·tion /ˌnänkōˌäpə'rāsHən/ ▶ n. failure to cooperate, especially as a form of protest.

non·de·nom·i·na·tion·al /ˌnändəˌnämə'nāsHənəl/ ▶ adj. open or acceptable to people of any recognized branch of Christianity.

non·de·script /ˌnändə'skript/ ▶ adj. lacking distinctive or interesting features: *a nondescript suburban apartment block.*

non·drink·er /ˌnän'driNGkər/ ▶ n. a person who does not drink alcohol.

none /nən/ ▶ pron. **1** not any. **2** no one. ▶ adv. (**none the**) (with *comparative*) not at all: *none the wiser.*

> **USAGE**
> When you use **none of** with a plural noun or pronoun (such as *them*), or with a singular noun that refers to a group of people or things, you can correctly use either a singular or plural verb: *none of them is coming* or *none of them are coming; none of the family was present* or *none of the family were present.*

non·en·ti·ty /ˌnän'entitē/ ▶ n. (pl. **nonentities**) an unimportant person or thing.

non·es·sen·tial /ˌnänə'sencHəl/ ▶ adj. not absolutely necessary. ▶ n. a nonessential thing.

no·net /nō'net/ ▶ n. **1** a group of nine people or things. **2** a musical composition for nine voices or instruments.

none·the·less /ˌnənTHə'les/ (also **none the less**) ▶ adv. in spite of that; nevertheless.

non·e·vent /ˌnäni'vent/ ▶ n. an event that is not as interesting or important as it was expected to be.

non·ex·ist·ent /ˌnänig'zistənt/ ▶ adj. not existing or not real or present. ■ **non·ex·ist·ence** n.

non·fer·rous /ˌnän'ferəs/ ▶ adj. (of metal) other than iron or steel.

non·fic·tion /ˌnän'fiksHən/ ▶ n. prose writing that deals with real people, facts, or events. ■ **non·fic·tion·al** adj.

non·flam·ma·ble /ˌnän'flaməbəl/ ▶ adj. not catching fire easily.

> **USAGE**
> The terms **nonflammable** and **noninflammable** both mean 'not catching fire easily.' See the note at **INFLAMMABLE.**

non·func·tion·al /ˌnän'fəNGksHənəl/ ▶ adj. **1** not having a particular function. **2** not in working order.

non·gov·ern·men·tal /ˌnängəvər(n)'mentl/ ▶ adj. not belonging to or associated with any government.

non·in·ter·fer·ence /ˌnänintər'fi(ə)rəns/ ▶ n. failure or refusal to intervene, especially in political matters.

non·in·ter·ven·tion /ˌnänintər'vencHən/ ▶ n. the policy of not becoming involved in the affairs of other countries. ■ **non·in·ter·ven·tion·ist** adj. & n.

non·in·va·sive /ˌnänin'vāsiv/ ▶ adj. (of medical procedures) not involving the introduction of instruments into the body.

non·judg·men·tal /ˌnänjəj'mentl/ ▶ adj. avoiding personal and moral judgments.

non·lin·e·ar /ˌnän'linēər/ ▶ adj. not linear or arranged in a straight line.

non·mem·ber /ˈnänˌmembər/ ▶ n. a person, group, or country that is not a member of a particular organization.

non·met·al /ˌnän'metl/ ▶ n. an element or substance that is not a metal. ■ **non·me·tal·lic** /ˌnänmə'talik/ adj.

non·na·tive ▶ adj. **1** (of a person, animal, or plant) not native to a particular place. **2** (of a speaker) not having spoken the language in question from earliest childhood.

non·nat·u·ral ▶ adj. not produced by or involving natural processes.

non·ne·go·ti·a·ble ▶ adj. **1** not open to discussion or modification. **2** not able to be transferred to the legal ownership of another person.

no-no ▶ n. (pl. **no-nos**) informal a thing that is not possible or acceptable.

no-non·sense ▶ adj. simple and straightforward; sensible.

non·op·er·a·tion·al /ˌnänäpə'rāsHənl/ ▶ adj. **1** not working or in use. **2** not involving active duties.

non·pa·reil /ˌnänpə'rel/ ▶ adj. better than anyone or anything else; unrivaled: *he's a nonpareil storyteller.* ▶ n. a person or thing that is unrivaled in a particular area.

non·par·ti·san /ˌnän'pärtizən/ ▶ adj. not biased or prejudiced in favor of a particular cause or political group.

non·pay·ment /ˌnän'pāmənt/ ▶ n. failure to pay an amount of money that is owed.

non·per·son /ˌnän'pərsən/ ▶ n. a person who is ignored or forgotten.

non·plussed /ˌnän'pləst/ ▶ adj. surprised and confused and not knowing how to react.

non·pro·duc·tive /ˌnänprə'dəktiv/ ▶ adj. not producing or able to produce something. ■ **non·pro·duc·tive·ly** adv.

non·pro·fes·sion·al /ˌnänprə'fesHənəl/ ▶ adj. **1** relating to or holding a job that does not need advanced education or training. **2** engaged in an activity that is not one's main paid job: *nonprofessional actors.* ▶ n. a nonprofessional person.

non·prof·it /ˈnän'präfit/ ▶ adj. not making or intended to make a profit.

non·pro·lif·er·a·tion /ˌnänprəˌlifə'rāsHən/ ▶ n. the prevention of an increase in the number of nuclear weapons that are produced.

non·res·i·dent /ˌnän'rezidənt/ ▶ adj. not living in a particular country or a place of work. ▶ n. a person not living in a particular place.

non·sense /ˈnänˌsens/ ▶ n. **1** words that make no sense. **2** foolish or unacceptable behavior.

3 something that one disagrees with or disapproves of.

non·sen·si·cal /nän'sensikəl/ ▶ adj. making no sense; ridiculous. ■ **non·sen·si·cal·ly** /nän'sensik(ə)lē/ adv.

non se·qui·tur /ˌnän 'sekwitər/ ▶ n. a conclusion that does not logically follow from the previous statement.

non·slip /ˌnän'slip/ ▶ adj. designed to prevent slipping.

non·smok·er /nän'smōkər/ ▶ n. a person who does not smoke tobacco. ■ **non·smok·ing** adj.

non·spe·cif·ic /ˌnänspə'sifik/ ▶ adj. not detailed or exact; general.

non·spe·cif·ic u·re·thri·tis ▶ n. inflammation of the urethra due to infection by organisms other than those that cause gonorrhea.

non·stand·ard /'nän'standərd/ ▶ adj. **1** not average or usual. **2** (of language) not considered correct by most educated speakers.

non·start·er /'nän'stärtər/ ▶ n. **1** a person or animal that fails to take part in a race. **2** informal something that has no chance of succeeding.

non·stick /'nän'stik/ ▶ adj. (of a pan or surface) covered with a substance that prevents food from sticking to it during cooking.

non·stop /'nän'stäp/ ▶ adj. **1** continuing without stopping. **2** having no stops on the way to a destination. ▶ adv. without stopping.

non·tech·ni·cal /nän'teknikəl/ ▶ adj. **1** not relating to or involving science or technology. **2** not using technical terms or requiring specialized knowledge.

non·tox·ic /nän'täksik/ ▶ adj. not poisonous or toxic.

non·u·ni·form /nän'yōōnəˌfôrm/ ▶ adj. not uniform or regular; varying.

non·un·ion /nän'yōōnyən/ ▶ adj. not belonging to or connected with a labor union.

non·ver·bal /nän'vərbəl/ ▶ adj. not involving or using words or speech.

non·vi·o·lent /ˌnän'vīələnt/ ▶ adj. **1** using peaceful means rather than force to bring about political or social change. **2** not involving violence: *nonviolent movies.* ■ **non·vi·o·lence** n.

non·white /ˌnän'(h)wīt/ ▶ adj. (of a person) not white or not of European origin. ▶ n. a nonwhite person.

noo·dle¹ /'nōōdl/ ▶ n. (usu. **noodles**) a very thin, long strip of pasta or a similar flour paste.

noo·dle² ▶ n. informal **1** a silly person. **2** a person's head.

noo·dle³ ▶ v. informal improvise or play casually on a musical instrument.

nook /nŏŏk/ ▶ n. a small corner or other place that is sheltered or hidden.
– PHRASES **every nook and cranny** every part of something.

nook·y /'nŏŏkē/ (also **nookie**) ▶ n. informal sexual activity or intercourse.

noon /nōōn/ ▶ n. twelve o'clock in the day; midday.

noon·day /'nōōnˌdā/ ▶ adj. happening or appearing in the middle of the day.

no one ▶ pron. no person; not a single person.

noon·time /'nōōnˌtīm/ (also literary **noontide** /'nōōnˌtīd/) ▶ n. noon.

noose /nōōs/ ▶ n. a loop with a knot that tightens as the rope or wire is pulled, used to hang people or trap animals.

nope /nōp/ ▶ exclam. informal variant of **NO**.

nor /nôr/ ▶ conj. & adv. and not; and not either.

nor' /nôr/ ▶ abbr. (especially in compounds) north: *nor'west.*

nor·a·dren·a·line /ˌnôrə'drenəlin/ ▶ n. a hormone that functions as a neurotransmitter and is also used as a drug to raise blood pressure.

Nor·dic /'nôrdik/ ▶ adj. **1** relating to Scandinavia, Finland, and Iceland. **2** referring to a tall, blond type of person associated with northern Europe.

Nor·dic ski·ing ▶ n. cross-country skiing and ski jumping.

Nor·dic walk·ing ▶ n. a sport or activity that involves walking across country with the aid of long poles resembling ski poles.

no·ri /'nôrē/ ▶ n. (in Japanese cuisine) seaweed, eaten fresh or dried in sheets.

norm /nôrm/ ▶ n. **1** (**the norm**) the usual or standard thing: *strikes were the norm.* **2** a required or acceptable standard: *the norms of good behavior.*

nor·mal /'nôrməl/ ▶ adj. **1** usual, typical, or expected. **2** technical (of a line) intersecting a given line or surface at right angles. ▶ n. **1** the normal state or condition: *her temperature was above normal.* **2** technical a line at right angles to a given line or surface. ■ **nor·mal·i·ty** /nôr'malitē/ (also **normalcy** /'nôrməlsē/) n. **nor·mal·ly** adv.

nor·mal dis·tri·bu·tion (also **Gaussian distribution**) ▶ n. Statistics a function that represents the distribution of a set of variables as a bell-shaped curve.

nor·mal·ize /'nôrməˌlīz/ ▶ v. bring or return to a normal or standard state. ■ **nor·mal·i·za·tion** /ˌnôrmələ'zāSHən/ n.

Nor·man /'nôrmən/ ▶ n. **1** a member of a people of Normandy in northern France who conquered England in 1066. **2** (also **Norman French**) the form of Old French spoken by the Normans. **3** a person from modern Normandy. ▶ adj. **1** relating to the Normans or Normandy. **2** relating to the style of Romanesque architecture used in Britain under the Normans.

nor·ma·tive /'nôrmətiv/ ▶ adj. formal relating to or setting a standard or norm: *a normative theory of world politics.*

No·ro·vi·rus /'nôrəˌvīrəs/ ▶ n. any of a group of viruses that can cause acute gastroenteritis in humans.

Norse /nôrs/ ▶ n. an ancient or medieval form of Norwegian or a related Scandinavian language. ▶ adj. relating to Norse or ancient or medieval Norway or Scandinavia. ■ **Norse·man** n. (pl. **Norsemen** /'nôrsmən/).

north /nôrTH/ ▶ n. **1** the direction in which a compass needle normally points, on the left-hand side of a person facing east. **2** the northern part of a place. ▶ adj. **1** lying toward, near, or facing the north. **2** (of a wind) blowing from the north. ▶ adv. to or toward the north. ■ **north·bound** /'nôrTHˌbound/ adj. & adv.

North A·mer·i·can ▶ n. a person from North America, especially a citizen of the US or Canada. ▶ adj. relating to North America.

north·east /ˌnôrTH'ēst/ ▶ n. the direction or region halfway between north and east. ▶ adj. **1** lying toward, near, or facing the northeast. **2** (of a wind) from the northeast. ▶ adv. to or toward the northeast. ■ **north·east·ern** /-'ēstərn/ adj.

north·east·er·ly /ˌnôrᴛʜˈēstərlē/ ▶ adj. & adv. in a northeastward position or direction. ▶ n. (pl. **northeasterlies**) a wind blowing from the northeast.

north·east·ward /ˌnôrᴛʜˈēstwərd/ ▶ adv. (also **northeastwards**) toward the northeast. ▶ adj. in, toward, or facing the northeast.

north·er·ly /ˈnôrᴛʜərlē/ ▶ adj. & adv. **1** facing or moving toward the north. **2** (of a wind) blowing from the north. ▶ n. (pl. **northerlies**) a north wind.

north·ern /ˈnôrᴛʜərn/ ▶ adj. **1** situated in, directed toward, or facing the north. **2** (usu. **Northern**) relating to or typical of the north. ◼ **north·ern·most** /-ˌmōst/ adj.

north·ern·er /ˈnôrᴛʜərnər/ ▶ n. a person from the north of a region or country.

north·ern lights ▶ pl.n. the aurora borealis.

north·land /ˈnôrᴛʜlənd, -ˌland/ ▶ n. (also **northlands**) literary the northern part of a country or region.

north-north·east ▶ n. the direction midway between north and northeast.

north-north·west ▶ n. the direction midway between north and northwest.

North Star ▶ n. the Polestar.

north·ward /ˈnôrᴛʜwərd/ ▶ adj. in a northerly direction. ▶ adv. (also **northwards**) toward the north. ◼ **north·ward·ly** adj. & adv.

north·west /ˌnôrᴛʜˈwest/ ▶ n. the direction or region halfway between north and west. ▶ adj. **1** lying toward or facing the northwest. **2** (of a wind) from the northwest. ▶ adv. to or toward the northwest. ◼ **north·west·ern** /-ˈwestərn/ adj.

north·west·er·ly /ˌnôrᴛʜˈwestərlē/ ▶ adj. & adv. in a northwestward position or direction. ▶ n. (pl. **northwesterlies**) a wind blowing from the northwest.

north·west·ward /ˌnôrᴛʜˈwestwərd/ ▶ adv. (also **northwestwards**) toward the northwest. ▶ adj. in, toward, or facing the northwest.

Nor·we·gian /nôrˈwējən/ ▶ n. **1** a person from Norway. **2** the language spoken in Norway. ▶ adj. relating to Norway.

nose /nōz/ ▶ n. **1** the part of the face above the mouth, containing the nostrils and used in breathing and smelling. **2** the front part of an aircraft or other vehicle. **3** the sense of smell. **4** a natural talent for detecting something: *he has a nose for a good script.* **5** the characteristic smell of a wine. **6** an act of looking around somewhere. ▶ v. **1** move slowly forward: *they nosed out of the parking place.* **2** look around or pry into something. **3** (of an animal) thrust its nose against or into something.
– PHRASES **by a nose** (of a victory) by a very narrow margin. **cut off one's nose to spite one's face** do something that is supposed to harm someone else but that also puts oneself at a disadvantage. **keep one's nose clean** informal stay out of trouble. **keep one's nose out of** refrain from interfering in another person's business. **put someone's nose out of joint** informal offend someone or hurt their pride. **turn one's nose up at** informal show distaste or contempt for. **under someone's nose** informal directly in front of someone, typically without being noticed by them.

nose·bleed /ˈnōzˌblēd/ ▶ n. an instance of bleeding from the nose.

nose cone ▶ n. the cone-shaped nose of a rocket or aircraft.

nose·dive /ˈnōzˌdīv/ ▶ n. **1** a sudden dramatic decline: *my fortunes took a nosedive.* **2** a steep downward plunge by an aircraft. ▶ v. **1** fall or decline suddenly: *prices nosedived after the market collapsed.* **2** (of an aircraft) make a nosedive.

no-see-um /nō ˈsē əm/ ▶ n. a minute bloodsucking insect, especially a midge.

nose·gay /ˈnōzˌgā/ ▶ n. a small bunch of flowers.

nos·ey /ˈnōzē/ ▶ adj. variant spelling of **NOSY**.

nosh /näsʜ/ informal ▶ n. food. ▶ v. eat enthusiastically or greedily.

no-show ▶ n. a person who has made a reservation or appointment but neither keeps nor cancels it.

nos·tal·gia /näˈstaljə, nə-/ ▶ n. wistful longing or affection for a happier or better time in the past: *touches of nostalgia for the 70s.* ◼ **nos·tal·gic** /näˈstaljik, nə-/ adj. **nos·tal·gi·cal·ly** /näˈstaljik(ə)lē, nə-/ adv.

nos·tril /ˈnästrəl/ ▶ n. either of two external openings of the nose through which air passes to the lungs.

nos·trum /ˈnästrəm/ ▶ n. **1** a favorite method for improving something: *right-wing nostrums such as cutting public spending.* **2** a medicine that is prepared by an unqualified person and is not effective.

nos·y /ˈnōzē/ (also **nosey**) ▶ adj. (**nosier, nosiest**) informal too inquisitive about other people's business. ◼ **nos·i·ly** adv. **nos·i·ness** n.

not /nät/ ▶ adv. **1** used to form or express a negative. **2** less than: *not ten feet away.*

no·ta·ble /ˈnōtəbəl/ ▶ adj. worthy of attention or notice. ▶ n. a famous or important person.

no·ta·bly /ˈnōtəblē/ ▶ adv. **1** in particular. **2** in a way that is noticeable or remarkable.

no·ta·rize /ˈnōtəˌrīz/ ▶ v. have a signature on a document confirmed as legal by a notary.

no·ta·ry /ˈnōtərē/ (in full **notary public**) ▶ n. (pl. **notaries**) a person who is officially authorized to draw up and witness the signing of contracts and other documents. ◼ **no·tar·i·al** /nōˈterēəl/ adj.

no·ta·tion /nōˈtāsʜən/ ▶ n. **1** a system of written symbols used to represent numbers, amounts, or elements in a subject such as music or mathematics. **2** a note or annotation. ◼ **no·tate** /ˈnō,tāt/ v. **no·ta·tion·al** /-nəl/ adj.

notch /näcʜ/ ▶ n. **1** a V-shaped cut or indentation on an edge or surface. **2** a point or level on a scale: *her opinion of him dropped a few notches.* ▶ v. **1** make notches in something. **2** score or achieve something.

note /nōt/ ▶ n. **1** a brief written record of something, used as an aid to memory. **2** a short written message or document. **3** Brit. a banknote. **4** a single sound of a particular pitch and length made by a musical instrument or voice, or a symbol representing this. **5** a particular quality or tone: *there was a note of scorn in his voice.* **6** a bird's song or call. **7** a basic component of a perfume or flavor. ▶ v. **1** pay attention to or notice something. **2** record something in writing.
– PHRASES **hit** (or **strike**) **the right** (or **wrong**) **note** say or do something in the right (or wrong) way. **of note** important. **take note** pay attention.

note·book /ˈnōtˌbo͝ok/ ▶ n. **1** a small book for writing notes in. **2** a portable computer smaller than a laptop.

not·ed /ˈnōtid/ ▶adj. well known; famous.

note·pad /ˈnōtˌpad/ ▶n. **1** a pad of paper for writing notes on. **2** a pocket-sized personal computer in which text is input by writing with a stylus on the screen.

note·pa·per /ˈnōtˌpāpər/ ▶n. paper for writing letters on.

note·per·fect ▶adj. (of a musical performance or performer) technically perfect.

note·wor·thy /ˈnōtˌwərṯHē/ ▶adj. interesting or significant.

noth·ing /ˈnəṯHiNG/ ▶pron. **1** not anything. **2** something of no importance or concern. **3** naught; no amount. ▶adv. not at all.
– PHRASES **for nothing 1** without payment or charge. **2** to no purpose. **nothing but** only. **nothing doing** informal there is no chance of success. **sweet nothings** words of affection exchanged by lovers.

noth·ing·ness /ˈnəṯHiNGnis/ ▶n. the state of not existing or a state where nothing exists.

no·tice /ˈnōtis/ ▶n. **1** the fact of being aware of or paying attention to something: *his silence did not escape my notice.* **2** information or warning that something is going to happen: *interest rates may change without notice.* **3** a formal statement that someone is going to leave a job or end an agreement. **4** a sheet or placard put on display to give information. **5** a small announcement or advertisement published in a newspaper. **6** a short published review of a new movie, play, or book. ▶v. **1** become aware of: *I noticed the youths behaving suspiciously.* **2** (**be noticed**) be recognized as worthy of attention.
– PHRASES **at short** (or **a moment's**) **notice** with little warning. **take** (**no**) **notice** (**of**) pay (no) attention (to).

no·tice·a·ble /ˈnōtisəbəl/ ▶adj. easily seen; clear or apparent. ■ **no·tice·a·bly** /-blē/ adv.

no·ti·fi·a·ble /ˌnōtəˈfīəbəl/ ▶adj. (of an infectious disease) so serious that it must be reported to the health authorities.

no·ti·fy /ˈnōtəˌfī/ ▶v. (**notifies, notifying, notified**) formally inform someone about something. ■ **no·ti·fi·ca·tion** /ˌnōtəfiˈkāsHən/ n.

no·tion /ˈnōsHən/ ▶n. **1** a concept or belief. **2** a person's understanding of something. **3** an impulse or whim.

no·tion·al /ˈnōsHənəl/ ▶adj. based on an estimate or theory; hypothetical. ■ **no·tion·al·ly** adv.

no·to·ri·e·ty /ˌnōtəˈrīətē/ ▶n. the state of being famous for a bad quality or action.

no·to·ri·ous /nəˈtôrēəs, nō-/ ▶adj. famous for a bad quality or action. ■ **no·to·ri·ous·ly** adv.

not·with·stand·ing /ˌnätwiṯHˈstandiNG, -wiṯH-/ ▶prep. in spite of. ▶adv. nevertheless.

nou·gat /ˈnōōgit/ ▶n. a candy made from sugar or honey, nuts, and egg white.

nought /nôt/ ▶n. variant spelling of NAUGHT.

noun /noun/ ▶n. a word (other than a pronoun) that refers to a person, place, or thing.

nour·ish /ˈnərisH, ˈnə-risH/ ▶v. **1** provide someone or something with the food or other substances necessary for growth and health. **2** keep a feeling or belief in the mind for a long time.

nour·ish·ment /ˈnərisHmənt, ˈnə-risH-/ ▶n. the food or other substances necessary for growth,

health, and good condition. **2** the action of nourishing someone or something.

nou·veau riche /ˈnōōvō ˈrēsH/ ▶n. (treated as pl.) people who have recently become rich and who like to display their wealth in an obvious or tasteless way.

nou·velle cui·sine /nōōˈvel kwiˈzēn/ ▶n. a modern style of cooking that avoids rich foods and emphasizes the presentation of the dishes.

Nov. ▶abbr. November.

no·va /ˈnōvə/ ▶n. (pl. **novae** /-vē, -vī/ or **novas**) a star that suddenly becomes very bright and then slowly returns to normal.

nov·el[1] /ˈnävəl/ ▶n. a story about imaginary people and events, long enough to fill a complete book.

nov·el[2] ▶adj. new in an interesting or unusual way: *a novel approach to architecture.*

nov·el·ette /ˌnävəˈlet/ ▶n. a short novel, especially a romantic novel regarded as poorly written.

nov·el·ist /ˈnävəlist/ ▶n. a person who writes novels. ■ **nov·el·is·tic** /ˌnävəˈlistik/ adj.

nov·el·ize /ˈnävəˌlīz/ ▶v. convert a story, screenplay, or play into a novel. ■ **nov·el·i·za·tion** /ˌnävəliˈzāsHən/ n.

no·vel·la /nōˈvelə/ ▶n. a short novel or long short story.

nov·el·ty /ˈnävəltē/ ▶n. (pl. **novelties**) **1** the quality of being new and unusual: *the novelty of being a married woman wore off.* **2** a new or unfamiliar thing. **3** a small and inexpensive toy or ornament. ▶adj. intended to be amusingly unusual: *a novelty teapot.*

No·vem·ber /nōˈvembər, nə-/ ▶n. the eleventh month of the year.

no·ve·na /nōˈvēnə/ ▶n. (in the Roman Catholic Church) a form of worship consisting of special prayers or services on nine successive days.

nov·ice /ˈnävəs/ ▶n. **1** a person who is new to and lacks experience in a job or situation. **2** a person who has entered a religious order and is under probation, before taking vows. **3** Brit. a racehorse that has not yet won a major prize or reached a qualifying level of performance.

no·vi·ti·ate /nōˈvisH(ē)ət, nə-/ (also **noviciate** pronunc. same) ▶n. **1** the period or state of being a novice in a religious order. **2** a religious novice.

no·vo·caine /ˈnōvəˌkān/ (also trademark **Novocain**) ▶n. another term for PROCAINE.

now /nou/ ▶adv. **1** at the present time. **2** at or from this precise moment. **3** under the present circumstances. ▶conj. as a result of the fact.
– PHRASES **now and again** (or **then**) from time to time.

now·a·days /ˈnouəˌdāz/ ▶adv. at the present time, in contrast with the past.

no·where /ˈnō,(h)we(ə)r/ ▶adv. not anywhere. ▶pron. no place.
– PHRASES **from** (or **out of**) **nowhere** appearing or happening suddenly and unexpectedly. **get** (or **go**) **nowhere** make no progress. **nowhere near** not nearly.

no-win ▶adj. (of a situation) in which success or a favorable outcome is impossible.

nox·ious /ˈnäksHəs/ ▶adj. harmful, poisonous, or very unpleasant.

noz·zle /ˈnäzəl/ ▶n. a spout used to control a jet of liquid or gas.

Np ▶symbol the chemical element neptunium.

NRA ▶ abbr. National Rifle Association.

NRC ▶ abbr. **1** National Research Council. **2** National Response Center. **3** Nuclear Regulatory Commission.

NS ▶ abbr. **1** (in calculating dates) New Style. **2** Nova Scotia.

ns ▶ abbr. nanosecond.

n/s ▶ abbr. (in personal advertisements) nonsmoker; nonsmoking.

NSU ▶ abbr. Medicine nonspecific urethritis.

NSW ▶ abbr. New South Wales.

NT ▶ abbr. **1** National Trust. **2** New Testament. **3** Northern Territory. **4** Northwest Territories.

-n't ▶ contr. not, used with auxiliary verbs (e.g., *can't*).

nth /enтн/ ▶ adj. **1** referring to the last or latest item in a long series. **2** Mathematics referring to an unspecified term in a series.
– PHRASES **to the nth degree** to the utmost.

nu·ance /'n(y)ōō,äns/ ▶ n. a subtle difference in meaning, expression, sound, etc.: *the nuances of facial expression.* ▶ v. (often as adj. **nuanced**) give subtle differences to: *an intricate and nuanced portrait.*

nub /nəb/ ▶ n. **1** (**the nub**) the central point of a matter. **2** a small lump. ■ **nub·by** adj.

Nu·bi·an /'n(y)ōōbēən/ ▶ adj. relating to Nubia, an ancient region corresponding to southern Egypt and northern Sudan. ▶ n. **1** a person from Nubia. **2** the language of the Nubians.

nu·bile /'n(y)ōō,bīl, -bəl/ ▶ adj. (of a girl or young woman) sexually attractive. ■ **nu·bil·i·ty** /n(y)ōō'bilitē/ n.

nu·buck /'n(y)ōō,bək/ ▶ n. leather that has been rubbed on the flesh side of the skin to give a suedelike effect.

nu·cle·ar /'n(y)ōōklēər, -kli(ə)r/ ▶ adj. **1** relating to the nucleus of an atom or cell. **2** using energy released in the fission (splitting) or fusion of atomic nuclei. **3** referring to or involving nuclear weapons.

nu·cle·ar fam·i·ly ▶ n. a couple and their children, regarded as a basic unit of society.

nu·cle·ar fuel ▶ n. a substance that will undergo nuclear fission (splitting) and can be used as a source of nuclear energy.

nu·cle·ar med·i·cine ▶ n. the branch of medicine that deals with the use of radioactive substances in research, diagnosis, and treatment.

nu·cle·ar op·tion ▶ n. the most drastic or extreme response possible.

nu·cle·ar phys·ics ▶ pl.n. (treated as sing.) the science of atomic nuclei and the way in which they interact.

nu·cle·ar pow·er ▶ n. power generated by a nuclear reactor.

nu·cle·ar waste ▶ n. radioactive waste material, especially from the use or reprocessing of nuclear fuel.

nu·cle·ar win·ter ▶ n. a period of abnormal cold and darkness predicted to follow a nuclear war, caused by smoke and dust blocking the sun's rays.

nu·cle·ate ▶ v. /'n(y)ōōklē,āt/ (usu. as adj. **nucleated**) form a nucleus. ▶ adj. /'n(y)ōōklēət, -,āt/ chiefly Biology having a nucleus. ■ **nu·cle·a·tion** /,n(y)ōōklē'āsHən/ n.

nu·cle·i /'n(y)ōōklē,ī/ ▶ plural of NUCLEUS.

nu·cle·ic ac·id /n(y)ōō'klē-ik/ ▶ n. a complex organic substance, especially DNA or RNA, that is present in all living cells.

nu·cle·on /'n(y)ōōklē,än/ ▶ n. a proton or neutron (type of subatomic particle).

nu·cle·o·tide /'n(y)ōōklēə,tīd/ ▶ n. a compound forming the basic structural unit of nucleic acids.

nu·cle·us /'n(y)ōōklēəs/ ▶ n. (pl. **nuclei** /-klē,ī/) **1** the central and most important part of an object or group: *the family is the nucleus of Islamic society.* **2** Physics the positively charged central core of an atom, containing nearly all its mass. **3** Biology a structure present in most cells, containing the genetic material.

nude /n(y)ōōd/ ▶ adj. wearing no clothes. ▶ n. a painting, sculpture, or photograph of a naked human figure. ■ **nu·di·ty** /'n(y)ōōdətē/ n.

nudge /nəj/ ▶ v. **1** prod someone with one's elbow to attract their attention. **2** touch or push something gently. **3** gently encourage someone to do something. ▶ n. a light touch or push.

nud·ist /'n(y)ōōdist/ ▶ n. a person who goes naked wherever possible. ■ **nud·ism** /-,dizəm/ n.

nu·ga·to·ry /'n(y)ōōgə,tôrē/ ▶ adj. formal having no purpose or value.

nug·get /'nəgət/ ▶ n. **1** a small lump of gold or other precious metal found in the earth. **2** a small but valuable fact. **3** a small piece of food, typically battered and fried.

nui·sance /'n(y)ōōsəns/ ▶ n. a cause of inconvenience or annoyance.

nuke /n(y)ōōk/ informal ▶ n. a nuclear weapon. ▶ v. attack or destroy something with nuclear weapons.

null /nəl/ ▶ adj. **1** (in phrase **null and void**) having no legal force; invalid. **2** Mathematics having or associated with the value zero.

nul·li·fy /'nələ,fī/ ▶ v. (**nullifies, nullifying, nullified**) **1** make something legally invalid. **2** cancel out the effect of something. ■ **nul·li·fi·ca·tion** /,nələfə'kāsHən/ n.

nul·li·ty /'nəlitē/ ▶ n. (pl. **nullities**) **1** the state of being legally invalid. **2** an unimportant or worthless thing.

numb /nəm/ ▶ adj. **1** (of a part of the body) having no sensation. **2** lacking the power to feel, think, or react: *the tragic events left us shocked and numb.* ▶ v. make someone or something numb. ■ **numb·ly** adv. **numb·ness** n.

num·ber /'nəmbər/ ▶ n. **1** a quantity or value expressed by a word, symbol, or figure. **2** a quantity or amount: *the exhibition attracted vast numbers of visitors.* **3** (**a number of**) several. **4** a song, dance, or other piece of music. **5** informal an item of clothing regarded with approval: *a little black number.* **6** a grammatical classification of words that depends on whether one or more people or things are being referred to. ▶ v. **1** amount to a specified figure or quantity. **2** give a number to each thing in a series. **3** count things or people. **4** include as a member of a group: *she wanted to be numbered among the more fashionable novelists.*
– PHRASES **by the numbers** following standard operating procedure. **have someone's number** informal understand a person's real motives or character. **someone's days are numbered** someone will not survive for much longer. **someone's number is up** informal someone is finished or certain to die. **without number** too many to count.

num·ber crunch·er ▶ n. informal **1** a computer

or program for performing complicated calculations. **2** often derogatory an accountant, statistician, or other person whose job involves dealing with large amounts of numerical data.

num·ber·less /'nəmbərləs/ ▶ adj. too many to be counted; innumerable.

num·ber one ▶ n. **1** the most important person or thing in a particular area or activity. **2** informal oneself. ▶ adj. most important; top: *a number-one priority.*

numb·skull /'nəm,skəl/ (also **numskull**) ▶ n. informal a stupid or foolish person.

nu·mer·al /'n(y)ŌŌm(ə)rəl/ ▶ n. a figure or symbol representing a number.

nu·mer·ate /'n(y)ŌŌm(ə)rət/ ▶ adj. having a good basic knowledge of arithmetic. ▪ **nu·mer·a·cy** /'n(y)ŌŌm(ə)rəsē/ n.

nu·mer·a·tion /,n(y)ŌŌmə'rāshən/ ▶ n. the action of calculating or giving a number to something.

nu·mer·a·tor /'n(y)ŌŌmə,rātər/ ▶ n. Mathematics the number above the line in a fraction.

nu·mer·i·cal /n(y)ŌŌ'merikəl/ ▶ adj. relating to or expressed as a number or numbers. ▪ **nu·mer·ic** adj. **nu·mer·i·cal·ly** adv.

nu·mer·ol·o·gy /,n(y)ŌŌmə'räləjē/ ▶ n. the study of the supposed magical power of numbers. ▪ **nu·mer·o·log·i·cal** /-rə'läjikəl/ adj. **nu·mer·ol·o·gist** /-jist/ n.

nu·me·ro u·no /'n(y)ŌŌmərō 'ŌŌnō/ ▶ n. (pl. **unos**) informal the best or most important person or thing, especially oneself.

nu·mer·ous /'n(y)ŌŌm(ə)rəs/ ▶ adj. **1** great in number; many. **2** consisting of many members. ▪ **nu·mer·ous·ly** adv.

nu·mi·nous /'n(y)ŌŌmənəs/ ▶ adj. having a strong religious or spiritual quality.

nu·mis·mat·ics /,n(y)ŌŌməz'matiks, -məs-/ ▶ pl.n. (usu. treated as sing.) the study or collection of coins, paper currency, and medals. ▪ **nu·mis·mat·ic** adj. **nu·mis·ma·tist** /n(y)ŌŌ'mizmətist, -'mis-/ n.

num·skull ▶ n. variant spelling of NUMBSKULL.

nun /nən/ ▶ n. a member of a female religious community, typically one who has taken vows of poverty, chastity, and obedience.

nun·ci·o /'nənsē,ō, 'nŌŌn-/ ▶ n. (pl. **nuncios**) (in the Roman Catholic Church) an official representative of the pope in a foreign country.

nun·ner·y /'nən(ə)rē/ ▶ n. (pl. **nunneries**) a convent.

nup·tial /'nəpshəl, -CHəl/ ▶ adj. relating to marriage or weddings. ▶ n. (**nuptials**) a wedding.

nurse /nərs/ ▶ n. **1** a person trained to care for sick or injured people. **2** dated a person employed to look after young children. ▶ v. **1** give medical and other care to a sick or injured person. **2** treat or hold carefully or protectively: *he nursed his small case on his lap.* **3** cling to a belief or feeling for a long time: *she nursed the hope that their relationship would improve.* **4** feed a baby at the breast. ▪ **nurs·ing** n.

nurse·maid /'nərs,mād/ ▶ n. dated a woman or girl employed to look after a young child or children.

nurse prac·ti·tion·er ▶ n. a registered nurse who is trained to treat minor ailments and perform many tasks ordinarily performed by a doctor.

nurs·er·y /'nərs(ə)rē/ ▶ n. (pl. **nurseries**) **1** a room in a house in which young children sleep or

play. **2** a place where young children are cared for during the working day. **3** a place where young plants and trees are grown for sale or for planting elsewhere.

nurs·er·y·man /'nərs(ə)rēmən/ ▶ n. (pl. **nurserymen**) a person who works in or owns a plant or tree nursery.

nurs·er·y rhyme ▶ n. a simple traditional song or poem for children.

nurs·er·y school ▶ n. a school for young children, mainly between the ages of three and five.

nurs·ing home ▶ n. a small private institution providing accommodations and health care for elderly people.

nurs·ling /'nərsliNG/ ▶ n. dated a baby that is being breastfed.

nur·ture /'nərCHər/ ▶ v. **1** care for and protect someone or something while they are growing and developing. **2** have a long-standing hope, belief, or ambition. ▶ n. **1** the action of nurturing someone or something. **2** upbringing, education, and environment as a factor determining someone's personality. Often contrasted with NATURE.

nut /nət/ ▶ n. **1** a fruit consisting of a hard shell around an edible kernel. **2** the hard kernel of such a fruit. **3** a small flat piece of metal or other material, typically square or hexagonal, with a threaded hole through the center for screwing onto a bolt. **4** informal a crazy or eccentric person. **5** informal a person who is extremely interested in or enthusiastic about something: *a football nut.* **6** informal a person's head. **7** a small lump of something hard or solid, especially coal. **8** (**nuts**) vulgar slang a man's testicles. ▪ **nut·ty** adj.

– PHRASES **nuts and bolts** informal the basic practical details of a subject or activity. **a tough** (or **hard**) **nut to crack** informal a difficult problem or an opponent that is hard or overcome.

nut·case /'nət,kās/ ▶ n. informal a mad or foolish person.

nut·crack·er /'nət,krakər/ ▶ n. a device for cracking the shells of nuts.

nut·hatch /'nət,hacH/ ▶ n. a small gray-backed songbird that climbs down tree trunks head first.

nut·meg /'nət,meg/ ▶ n. a spice made from the seed of a tropical tree.

nu·tra·ceu·ti·cal /,n(y)ŌŌtrə'sŌŌtikəl/ ▶ n. a food containing health-giving additives.

nu·tri·a /'n(y)ŌŌtrēə/ ▶ n. the skin or fur of the coypu, a large rodent.

nu·tri·ent /'n(y)ŌŌtrēənt/ ▶ n. a substance that provides nourishment essential for life, growth, and health.

nu·tri·ment /'n(y)ŌŌtrəmənt/ ▶ n. the food or other substances necessary for growth and health.

nu·tri·tion /n(y)ŌŌ'trishən/ ▶ n. **1** the process of taking in and absorbing nutrients. **2** the branch of science concerned with this process. ▪ **nu·tri·tion·al** adj. **nu·tri·tion·ist** n.

nu·tri·tious /n(y)ŌŌ'trishəs/ ▶ adj. (of food) full of nutrients and so helping the body to grow or stay healthy. ▪ **nu·tri·tious·ly** adv.

nu·tri·tive /'n(y)ŌŌtrətiv/ ▶ adj. **1** relating to nutrition. **2** nutritious.

nuts /nəts/ ▶ adj. informal insane.

nut·shell /'nət,shel/ ▶ n. (in phrase **in a nutshell**) in the fewest possible words.

nux vom·i·ca /'nəks 'vämikə/ ▶ n. a southern Asian tree with berrylike fruit and toxic seeds that contain strychnine.

nuz·zle /'nəzəl/ ▶ v. rub or push against gently with the nose and mouth: *the foal nuzzled at its mother.*

NV ▶ abbr. Nevada.

NW ▶ abbr. **1** northwest. **2** northwestern.

N-word ▶ n. euphemistic the word 'nigger.'

NY ▶ abbr. New York.

NYC ▶ abbr. New York City.

ny·lon /'nī,län/ ▶ n. **1** a tough, lightweight synthetic material that can be made into fabric, yarn, and many other products. **2** (**nylons**) nylon stockings or tights.

nymph /nimf/ ▶ n. **1** (in Greek and Roman mythology) a spirit of nature in the form of a beautiful young woman. **2** literary a beautiful young woman. **3** an immature form of an insect such as a dragonfly. ■ **nymph·al** adj.

nymph·et /nim'fet, 'nimfit/ ▶ n. an attractive and sexually mature young girl.

nym·pho /'nim'fō/ ▶ n. (pl. **nymphos**) informal a nymphomaniac.

nym·pho·ma·ni·a /,nimfə'mānēə/ ▶ n. uncontrollable or abnormally strong sexual desire in a woman. ■ **nym·pho·ma·ni·ac** /-'mānē,ak/ n.

NYSE ▶ abbr. New York Stock Exchange.

nys·tag·mus /nə'stagməs/ ▶ n. rapid involuntary movements of the eyes.

NZ ▶ abbr. New Zealand.

Oo

O¹ (also **o**) ▶ n. (pl. **Os** or **O's**) **1** the fifteenth letter of the alphabet. **2** (also **oh**) zero.

O² ▶ symbol the chemical element oxygen.

O³ /ō/ ▶ exclam. **1** old-fashioned spelling of **OH¹**. **2** old use used before a name when addressing someone, as in a prayer or poem: *give peace in our time, O Lord.*

o' /ə, ō/ ▶ prep. short for **OF**, used to represent an informal pronunciation: *a cup o' coffee.*

oaf /ōf/ ▶ n. a stupid, rude, or clumsy man. ■ **oaf·ish** adj.

oak /ōk/ ▶ n. **1** a large tree that produces acorns and a hard wood used for building and furniture. **2** a smoky flavor characteristic of wine that has been aged in oak barrels. ■ **oak·en** (old use) adj. **oak·y** adj.

oak ap·ple ▶ n. a spongy growth that forms on oak trees, caused by wasp larvae.

oa·kum /'ōkəm/ ▶ n. chiefly historical loose fiber obtained by untwisting old rope, used especially to fill in cracks in wooden ships.

oar /ôr/ ▶ n. a pole with a flat blade, used for rowing or steering a boat.
– PHRASES **put in one's oar** informal, chiefly Brit. give an opinion without being asked.

oar·lock /'ôr,läk/ ▶ n. a fitting on the side of a boat for holding an oar.

oars·man /'ôrzmən/ (or **oarswoman**) ▶ n. (pl. **oarsmen** or **oarswomen**) a rower.

OAS ▶ abbr. **ORGANIZATION OF AMERICAN STATES.**

o·a·sis /ō'āsis/ ▶ n. (pl. **oases** /ō'āsēz/) **1** a fertile place in a desert where water rises to ground level. **2** a calm and pleasant area or period in the midst of a difficult or hectic place or situation.

oat /ōt/ ▶ n. **1** a cereal plant grown in cool climates. **2** (**oats**) the edible grain of this plant. ■ **oat·y** adj.
– PHRASES **sow one's wild oats** (especially of a young man) have many casual sexual relationships while young.

oath /ōTH/ ▶ n. (pl. **oaths**) **1** a solemn promise about one's future actions or behavior. **2** a sworn declaration, such as the promise to tell the truth, made in a court of law. **3** a swear word.
– PHRASES **under oath** having sworn to tell the truth, especially in a court of law.

oat·meal /'ōt,mēl/ ▶ n. **1** meal made from ground oats, used in breakfast cereals or other food. **2** a dish of this meal cooked with milk or water.

ob·bli·ga·to /,äblə'gätō/ (also **obligato**) ▶ n. (pl. **obbligatos** or **obbligati** /-'gätē/) an accompanying instrumental part that is necessary to a piece of music and must not be left out of a performance.

ob·du·rate /'äbd(y)ərit/ ▶ adj. stubbornly refusing to change one's mind. ■ **ob·du·ra·cy** /-rəsē/ ■ **ob·du·rate·ly** adv.

o·be·ah /'ōbēə/ ▶ n. a kind of magic or witchcraft practiced especially in the Caribbean.

o·be·di·ent /ō'bēdēənt/ ▶ adj. willing to do what one is told. ■ **o·be·di·ence** n. **o·be·di·ent·ly** adv.

o·bei·sance /ō'bāsəns, ō'bē-/ ▶ n. **1** deferential respect for someone. **2** a gesture expressing this, such as a bow.

ob·e·lisk /'äbə,lisk/ ▶ n. a four-sided stone pillar that tapers to a point, set up as a monument or landmark.

ob·e·lus /'äbələs/ ▶ n. (pl. **obeli** /-,lī/) a symbol (†) used in printed material as a reference mark or to indicate that a person is dead.

o·bese /ō'bēs/ ▶ adj. very fat. ■ **o·be·si·ty** n.

o·bey /ō'bā/ ▶ v. **1** do what one is told to do. **2** carry out an order. **3** behave in accordance with a general principle or natural law.

ob·fus·cate /'äbfə,skāt/ ▶ v. make something hard to understand. ■ **ob·fus·ca·tion** /,äbfə'skāsHən/ n. **ob·fus·ca·to·ry** /'äb'fəskə,tôrē/ adj.

o·bi /'ōbē/ ▶ n. (pl. **obis**) a broad sash worn around the waist of a Japanese kimono.

o·bit /'ōbit, ō'bit/ ▶ n. informal an obituary.

ob·i·ter dic·tum /'ōbitər 'diktəm/ ▶ n. (pl. **dicta** /'diktə/) Law a judge's incidental expression of opinion.

o·bit·u·ar·y /ō'bicHoo,erē/ ▶ n. (pl. **obituaries**) a short biography of a person, published in a newspaper soon after their death.

ob·ject ▶ n. /'äbjəkt/ **1** a physical thing that can be seen and touched. **2** a person or thing to which an action or feeling is directed: *he hated being the object of public attention.* **3** a goal or purpose: *the object of the exercise was to shock the audience.* **4** Grammar a noun or pronoun acted on by a transitive verb or by a preposition. ▶ v. /əb'jekt/ express disapproval or opposition: *residents objected to the noise.* ■ **ob·jec·tor** /əb'jektər/ n.
– PHRASES **no object** not influencing or restricting choices or decisions: *money is no object.*

ob·jec·ti·fy /əb'jektə,fī/ ▶ v. (**objectifies, objectifying, objectified**) **1** express something abstract in a concrete form: *good poetry objectifies feeling.* **2** treat someone merely as an object rather than a person. ■ **ob·jec·ti·fi·ca·tion** /əb,jektəfi'kāsHən/ n.

ob·jec·tion /əb'jeksHən/ ▶ n. an expression of disapproval or opposition.

ob·jec·tion·a·ble /əb'jeksHənəbəl/ ▶ adj. unpleasant or offensive.

ob·jec·tive /əb'jektiv/ ▶ adj. **1** not influenced by personal feelings or opinions: *historians try to be objective.* **2** having actual existence outside the mind: *a matter of objective fact.* **3** Grammar relating to a case of nouns and pronouns used for the object of a transitive verb or a preposition. ▶ n. **1** a goal or aim: *his main objective was to* *combat inflation.* **2** (also **objective lens**) the lens in a telescope or microscope nearest to the object observed. ■ **ob·jec·tive·ly** adv. **ob·jec·tiv·i·ty** /ˌäbjekˈtivitē/ n.

ob·ject les·son ▶ n. a striking practical example of what should or should not be done in a particular situation: *they responded to emergencies in a way that was an object lesson to us all.*

ob·jet d'art /ˌôbzHā ˈdär/ ▶ n. (pl. **objets d'art** pronunc. same) a small decorative or artistic object.

ob·late /ˈäbˌlāt, ˌōˈblāt/ ▶ adj. Geometry (of a sphere-shaped body) flattened at each pole.

ob·la·tion /əˈblāsHən/ ▶ n. **1** a thing presented or offered to a god. **2** Christian Church the presentation of bread and wine to God in the service of Holy Communion.

ob·li·gate /ˈäbliˌgāt/ ▶ v. (**be obligated**) have a moral or legal duty to do something: *the hospital is obligated to provide health care.*

ob·li·ga·tion /ˌäbliˈgāsHən/ ▶ n. **1** something a person must do because it is morally right or legally necessary; a duty or commitment: *I have an obligation to look after her.* **2** the state of having to do something because it is morally right or legally necessary: *they are under no obligation to stick to the scheme.* **3** a feeling of gratitude for a service or favor.

ob·li·ga·to /ˌäbliˈgätō/ ▶ n. variant spelling of **OBBLIGATO.**

o·blig·a·to·ry /əˈbligəˌtôrē/ ▶ adj. required by a law, rule, or custom; compulsory.

o·blige /əˈblīj/ ▶ v. **1** compel someone to do something because it is a law, necessity, or duty: *he was obliged to do military service.* **2** do as someone asks in order to help or please them. **3** (**be obliged**) be indebted or grateful.

o·blig·ing /əˈblījiNG/ ▶ adj. willing to help someone or do as they ask. ■ **o·blig·ing·ly** adv.

o·blique /əˈblēk, ōˈblēk/ ▶ adj. **1** neither parallel nor at right angles; slanting. **2** not explicit or direct: *an oblique reference to the US.* **3** Geometry (of a line, plane figure, or surface) inclined at other than a right angle. ■ **o·blique·ly** adv. **o·blique·ness** n. **o·bliq·ui·ty** /əˈblikwətē/ n.

ob·lit·er·ate /əˈblitəˌrāt/ ▶ v. **1** destroy something completely. **2** completely cover: *clouds obliterated the moon.* ■ **ob·lit·er·a·tion** /əˌblitəˈrāsHən/ n.

ob·liv·i·on /əˈblivēən/ ▶ n. **1** the state of being unaware of what is happening around one. **2** the state of being forgotten: *his name will fade into oblivion.* **3** the state of being completely destroyed.

ob·liv·i·ous /əˈblivēəs/ ▶ adj. not aware of what is happening around one: *he was oblivious to his surroundings.* ■ **ob·liv·i·ous·ly** adv. **ob·liv·i·ous·ness** n.

ob·long /ˈäbˌlôNG, -ˌläNG/ ▶ adj. having a rectangular shape. ▶ n. an oblong object or shape.

ob·lo·quy /ˈäbləkwē/ ▶ n. **1** strong public criticism. **2** disgrace brought about by strong public criticism.

ob·nox·ious /əbˈnäksHəs/ ▶ adj. extremely unpleasant. ■ **ob·nox·ious·ly** adv. **ob·nox·ious·ness** n.

o·boe /ˈōbō/ ▶ n. a woodwind instrument of treble pitch, played with a double reed. ■ **o·bo·ist** n.

ob·scene /əbˈsēn/ ▶ adj. **1** (of the portrayal or description of sexual matters) offensive or disgusting according to accepted standards of

morality or decency. **2** (especially of an amount of money) unacceptably large: *obscene pay increases.* ■ **ob·scene·ly** adv.

ob·scen·i·ty /əbˈsenitē/ ▶ n. (pl. **obscenities**) **1** obscene language or behavior. **2** an obscene act or word.

ob·scu·rant·ism /əbˈskyo͞orənˌtizəm, äb-, ˌäbskyə'ran-/ ▶ n. the practice of deliberately preventing the facts or full details of something from becoming known or understood. ■ **ob·scu·rant·ist** n. & adj.

ob·scure /əbˈskyo͞or/ ▶ adj. (**obscurer, obscurest**) **1** not discovered or known about; uncertain. **2** not well known: *a relatively obscure actor.* **3** not clearly expressed or easily understood: *obscure references to Proust.* **4** hard to see or make out. ▶ v. make something difficult to see or understand. ■ **ob·scu·ra·tion** /ˌäbskyə'rāsHən/ n. **ob·scure·ly** adv.

ob·scu·ri·ty /əbˈskyo͞oritē/ ▶ n. (pl. **obscurities**) **1** the state of being unknown or forgotten. **2** the quality of being hard to understand.

ob·se·quies /ˈäbsəkwēz/ ▶ pl. n. funeral rites.

ob·se·qui·ous /əbˈsēkwēəs/ ▶ adj. trying too hard to please someone; excessively obedient or respectful. ■ **ob·se·qui·ous·ly** adv. **ob·se·qui·ous·ness** n.

ob·serv·ance /əbˈzərvəns/ ▶ n. **1** the obeying of a law or rule, or the following of a custom. **2** (**observances**) acts performed for religious or ceremonial reasons.

ob·serv·ant /əbˈzərvənt/ ▶ adj. **1** quick to notice things. **2** following the rules of a religion.

ob·ser·va·tion /ˌäbzərˈvāsHən/ ▶ n. **1** the action of watching someone or something closely: *he was brought into the hospital for observation.* **2** the ability to notice important or significant details: *she was famous for her powers of observation.* **3** a comment based on something one has seen, heard, or noticed. ■ **ob·ser·va·tion·al** adj.

ob·serv·a·to·ry /əbˈzərvəˌtôrē/ ▶ n. (pl. **observatories**) a building housing a telescope or other scientific equipment for studying natural phenomena such as the stars and the weather.

ob·serve /əbˈzərv/ ▶ v. **1** notice someone or something. **2** watch carefully; monitor: *many patients were observed for long periods.* **3** make a remark. **4** obey a law or rule. **5** celebrate or take part in a festival or ritual. ■ **ob·serv·a·ble** adj. **ob·serv·er** n.

ob·sess /əbˈses/ ▶ v. **1** preoccupy someone to a disturbing extent: *he was obsessed with thoughts of suicide.* **2** be constantly talking or worrying about something.

ob·ses·sion /əbˈsesHən/ ▶ n. **1** the state of being obsessed. **2** a person or thing that someone is unable to stop thinking about: *her career had become an obsession.* ■ **ob·ses·sion·al** adj.

ob·ses·sive /əbˈsesiv/ ▶ adj. **1** thinking continually about someone or something: *he was obsessive about cleanliness.* **2** preoccupying a person's mind to a disturbing extent: *obsessive jealousy.* ■ **ob·ses·sive·ly** /-ˈsesivlē/ adv. **ob·ses·sive·ness** /-ˈsesivnis/ n.

ob·ses·sive–com·pul·sive ▶ adj. relating to a mental condition in which a person feels compelled to carry out certain actions over and over again.

ob·sid·i·an /əbˈsidēən, äb-/ ▶ n. a dark glasslike volcanic rock formed when lava solidifies rapidly without crystallizing.

ob·so·les·cent /ˌäbsəˈlesənt/ ▶ adj. becoming obsolete. ■ **ob·so·les·cence** n.

ob·so·lete /ˌäbsəˈlēt/ ▶ adj. no longer produced or used; out of date.

ob·sta·cle /ˈäbstəkəl/ ▶ n. a thing that blocks one's way or makes it difficult to do or achieve something.

ob·ste·tri·cian /ˌäbstəˈtrishən/ ▶ n. a doctor qualified to practice obstetrics.

ob·stet·rics /əbˈstetriks, äb-/ ▶ pl.n. the branch of medicine and surgery concerned with childbirth. ■ **ob·stet·ric** adj.

ob·sti·nate /ˈäbstənit/ ▶ adj. 1 stubbornly refusing to change one's mind. 2 hard to deal with or overcome: *an obstinate problem.* ■ **ob·sti·na·cy** /-nəsē/ n. **ob·sti·nate·ly** adv.

ob·strep·er·ous /əbˈstrepərəs, äb-/ ▶ adj. noisy and difficult to control. ■ **ob·strep·er·ous·ly** adv. **ob·strep·er·ous·ness** n.

ob·struct /əbˈstrəkt, äb-/ ▶ v. 1 be in the way of; block: *she was obstructing the entrance.* 2 make it difficult to achieve something: *they promised not to obstruct the peace process.* ■ **ob·struc·tor** n.

ob·struc·tion /əbˈstrəkshən, äb-/ ▶ n. 1 an obstacle or blockage. 2 the action of obstructing someone or something.

ob·struc·tion·ism /əbˈstrəkshəˌnizəm, äb-/ ▶ n. the practice of deliberately blocking or delaying the progress of lawmaking or other procedures. ■ **ob·struc·tion·ist** n. & adj.

ob·struc·tive /əbˈstrəktiv, äb-/ ▶ adj. deliberately causing difficulties or delays.

ob·tain /əbˈtān, äb-/ ▶ v. 1 come into possession of; get. 2 formal be established or usual: *the standards that obtain in this school.* ■ **ob·tain·a·ble** adj.

ob·trude /əbˈtrōōd/ ▶ v. 1 become obtrusive. 2 impose or force something on someone.

ob·tru·sive /əbˈtrōōsiv, äb-/ ▶ adj. noticeable in an unwelcome or unpleasant way. ■ **ob·tru·sive·ly** adv. **ob·tru·sive·ness** n.

ob·tuse /əbˈt(y)ōōs, äb-/ ▶ adj. 1 annoyingly insensitive or slow to understand. 2 (of an angle) more than 90° and less than 180°. 3 not sharp or pointed; blunt. ■ **ob·tuse·ly** adv. **ob·tuse·ness** n.

ob·verse /ˈäbˌvərs/ ▶ n. 1 the side of a coin or medal with the head or main design. 2 the opposite or counterpart of a fact or truth.

ob·vi·ate /ˈäbvēˌāt/ ▶ v. remove or prevent a need or difficulty.

ob·vi·ous /ˈäbvēəs/ ▶ adj. easily seen or understood; clear. ■ **ob·vi·ous·ly** adv. **ob·vi·ous·ness** n.

o·ca·ri·na /ˌäkəˈrēnə/ ▶ n. a small egg-shaped wind instrument with holes for the fingers.

Oc·cam's ra·zor /ˈäkəmz/ (also **Ockham's razor**) ▶ n. the principle that in explaining something no more assumptions should be made than are necessary.

oc·ca·sion /əˈkāzhən/ ▶ n. 1 a particular event, or the time at which it takes place. 2 a special event or celebration. 3 a suitable time for doing something: *this is not the occasion for a detailed analysis of the proposals.* 4 formal reason or justification: *we have occasion to rejoice.* ▶ v. formal cause something.

– PHRASES **on occasion** from time to time. **rise to the occasion** perform well in response to a

special situation.

oc·ca·sion·al /əˈkāzhənl/ ▶ adj. 1 occurring infrequently or irregularly. 2 produced on or intended for particular occasions: *occasional verse.* ■ **oc·ca·sion·al·ly** adv.

Oc·ci·dent /ˈäksidənt, -ˌdent/ ▶ n. (**the Occident**) literary the countries of the West.

oc·ci·den·tal /ˌäksəˈdentl/ literary ▶ adj. relating to the countries of the West. ▶ n. (**Occidental**) a person from the West.

oc·ci·put /ˈäksəpət/ ▶ n. Anatomy the back of the head. ■ **oc·cip·i·tal** /äkˈsipitl/ adj.

Oc·ci·tan /ˈäksiˌtan/ ▶ n. the medieval or modern language of Languedoc (southern France), including Provençal.

oc·clude /əˈklōōd/ ▶ v. technical 1 close up or block an opening or passage. 2 (of a tooth) come into contact with another in the opposite jaw.

oc·clud·ed front ▶ n. a weather front produced when a cold front catches up with a warm front, so that the warm air in between them is forced upward.

oc·clu·sion /əˈklōōzhən/ ▶ n. technical the process of blocking something up. ■ **oc·clu·sive** /-siv/ adj.

oc·cult /əˈkəlt/ ▶ n. (**the occult**) supernatural or magical powers, practices, or phenomena. ▶ adj. 1 relating to the occult. 2 beyond ordinary knowledge or experience. 3 Medicine (of blood) abnormally present, but detectable only microscopically or by chemical testing. ■ **oc·cult·ism** /-ˌtizəm/ n. **oc·cult·ist** /-tist/ n.

oc·cu·pan·cy /ˈäkyəpənsē/ ▶ n. 1 the action or fact of occupying a place. 2 the proportion of accommodations occupied or used.

oc·cu·pant /ˈäkyəpənt/ ▶ n. 1 a person who occupies a place at a given time. 2 the holder of a job or office.

oc·cu·pa·tion /ˌäkyəˈpāshən/ ▶ n. 1 a job or profession. 2 a way of spending time. 3 the action of occupying a place or the state of being occupied: *the Roman occupation of Britain.*

oc·cu·pa·tion·al /ˌäkyəˈpāshənl/ ▶ adj. relating to a job or profession: *an occupational disease.* ■ **oc·cu·pa·tion·al·ly** adv.

oc·cu·pa·tion·al haz·ard ▶ n. a risk arising as a consequence of a particular job or profession.

oc·cu·pa·tion·al ther·a·py ▶ n. a form of therapy that emphasizes the performance of activities required in daily life. ■ **oc·cu·pa·tion·al ther·a·pist** n.

oc·cu·py /ˈäkyəˌpī/ ▶ v. (**occupies, occupying, occupied**) 1 live or work in a place. 2 fill or take up a space, time, or position. 3 keep someone busy and active: *he has occupied himself with research.* 4 enter and take control of a place, especially by military force. ■ **oc·cu·pi·er** n.

oc·cur /əˈkər/ ▶ v. (**occurs, occurring, occurred**) 1 happen; take place. 2 be found or present: *radon occurs in rocks such as granite.* 3 (**occur to**) come into someone's mind.

oc·cur·rence /əˈkərəns/ ▶ n. 1 a thing that happens; an incident or event. 2 the fact or frequency of something happening or existing: *the occurrence of cancer increases with age.*

OCD ▶ abbr. obsessive-compulsive disorder.

o·cean /ˈōshən/ ▶ n. 1 a very large expanse of sea, specifically each of the Atlantic, Pacific, Indian, Arctic, and Antarctic Oceans. 2 (**the ocean**) the sea.

o·cea·nar·i·um /ˌōshəˈne(ə)rēəm/ ▶ n. (pl.

oceanariums or **oceanaria** /-'ne(ə)rēə/) a large seawater aquarium.

o·ce·an·ic /ˌōshē'anik/ ▸ adj. relating to the ocean.

o·cea·nog·ra·phy /ˌōshə'nägrəfē/ ▸ n. the branch of science concerned with the study of the sea. ■ **o·cea·nog·ra·pher** n. **o·cea·no·graph·ic** /-nə'grafik/ adj.

oc·e·lot /'äsəˌlät, 'ōsə-/ ▸ n. a medium-sized striped and spotted wild cat, native to South and Central America.

o·cher /'ōkər/ ▸ n. a type of earth that varies in color from light yellow to brown or red, used as a pigment.

Ock·ham's ra·zor ▸ n. variant spelling of OCCAM'S RAZOR.

o'·clock /ə'kläk/ ▸ adv. used to specify the hour when telling the time.

OCR ▸ abbr. optical character recognition.

Oct. ▸ abbr. October.

octa- (also **oct-** before a vowel) ▸ comb.form eight; having eight: *octahedron*.

oc·ta·gon /'äktəˌgän, -gən/ ▸ n. a plane figure with eight straight sides and eight angles. ■ **oc·tag·o·nal** /äk'tagənl/ adj.

oc·ta·he·dron /ˌäktə'hēdrən/ ▸ n. (pl. **octahedra** /-drə/ or **octahedrons**) a three-dimensional shape having eight plane faces, in particular eight equal triangular faces. ■ **oc·ta·he·dral** /-drəl/ adj.

oc·tane /'äktān/ ▸ n. a liquid hydrocarbon obtained in petroleum refining.

oc·tane num·ber (or **octane rating**) ▸ n. a figure indicating the quality of a fuel, based on a comparison with a standard mixture.

oc·tave /'äktəv, 'äkˌtāv/ ▸ n. 1 a series of eight musical notes occupying the interval between (and including) two notes, one having twice or half the pitch of the other. 2 the interval between two such notes, or the notes themselves sounding together. 3 a poem or stanza of eight lines; an octet.

oc·ta·vo /äk'tävō/ ▸ n. (pl. **octavos**) a size of book page that results from folding each printed sheet into eight leaves (sixteen pages).

oc·tet /äk'tet/ ▸ n. 1 a group of eight musicians. 2 a musical composition for eight voices or instruments. 3 a group of eight lines of poetry.

octo- (also **oct-** before a vowel) ▸ comb.form eight; having eight: *octopus*.

Oc·to·ber /äk'tōbər/ ▸ n. the tenth month of the year.

oc·to·ge·nar·i·an /ˌäktəjə'ne(ə)rēən/ ▸ n. a person who is between 80 and 89 years old.

oc·to·pus /'äktəpəs/ ▸ n. (pl. **octopuses**) a sea animal with a soft body and eight long tentacles with suckers. ■ **oc·to·poid** /-ˌpoid/ adj.

> **USAGE**
> The standard plural in English of **octopus** is **octopuses**, but as the word comes from Greek, the Greek plural form **octopodes** is still occasionally used. The plural form **octopi**, formed according to rules for Latin plurals, is incorrect.

oc·to·roon /ˌäktə'rōōn/ ▸ n. dated, often offensive a person who is one-eighth black by descent.

oc·tu·ple /'äktəpəl, -'t(y)ōōpəl/ ▸ adj. 1 consisting of eight parts or things. 2 eight times as many or as much.

oc·tup·let /'äktəplit, -'t(y)ōō-/ ▸ n. each of eight children born at one birth.

oc·u·lar /'äkyələr/ ▸ adj. relating to the eyes or vision.

oc·u·list /'äkyəlist/ ▸ n. dated a person who specializes in the medical treatment of diseases or defects of the eye.

oc·u·lus /'äkyələs/ ▸ n. (pl. **oculi** /-ˌlī, -ˌlē/) Architecture 1 a circular window. 2 an opening at the top of a dome.

OD informal ▸ v. (**OD's, OD'ing, OD'd**) take an overdose of a drug. ▸ n. an overdose.

o·da·lisque /'ōdlˌisk/ ▸ n. historical a female slave or concubine in a harem.

odd /äd/ ▸ adj. 1 unusual or unexpected; strange. 2 (of whole numbers such as 3 and 5) having one left over as a remainder when divided by two. 3 (in combination) in the region of: *fifty-odd years*. 4 occasional: *we have the odd drink together*. 5 spare or available: *an odd five minutes*. 6 separated from a pair or set: *an odd sock*. ■ **odd·ly** adv. **odd·ness** n.
– PHRASES **odd one out** a person or thing differing in some way from the other members of a group or set. **odds and ends** various small items that are not part of a larger set.

odd·ball /'ädˌbôl/ ▸ n. informal a strange or eccentric person.

odd·i·ty /'äditē/ ▸ n. (pl. **oddities**) 1 the quality of being strange. 2 a strange person or thing.

odd·ment /'ädmənt/ ▸ n. an item or piece left over from a larger piece or set.

odds /ädz/ ▸ pl.n. 1 the ratio between the amounts placed as a bet and the money that would be received if the bet was won: *odds of 8–1*. 2 (**the odds**) the chances of something happening or being the case. 3 (**the odds**) the advantage thought to be possessed by one person compared to another; superiority in strength, power, or resources: *she clung to the lead against all the odds*.
– PHRASES **at odds** in conflict or disagreement.

odds-on ▸ adj. 1 (especially of a horse) rated as more likely than evens to win. 2 very likely to happen or succeed.

ode /ōd/ ▸ n. a poem addressed to a person or thing, or celebrating an event.

o·dif·er·ous /ō'difərəs/ ▸ adj. variant spelling of ODORIFEROUS.

o·di·ous /'ōdēəs/ ▸ adj. extremely unpleasant; repulsive. ■ **o·di·ous·ly** adv. **o·di·ous·ness** n.

o·di·um /'ōdēəm/ ▸ n. general or widespread hatred or disgust.

o·dom·e·ter /ō'dämitər/ ▸ n. an instrument for measuring the distance traveled by a vehicle.

o·don·tol·o·gy /ˌōdän'täləjē/ ▸ n. the scientific study of the structure and diseases of teeth. ■ **o·don·tol·o·gist** /-jist/ n.

o·dor /'ōdər/ ▸ n. 1 a distinctive smell. 2 a lingering quality or impression: *an odor of suspicion*. ■ **o·dor·ous** adj. **o·dor·less** adj.

o·dor·ant /'ōdərənt/ ▸ n. a substance used to give a scent or smell to a product.

o·dor·if·er·ous /ˌōdə'rifərəs/ ▸ adj. giving off a smell, especially an unpleasant one.

od·ys·sey /'ädəsē/ ▸ n. (pl. **odysseys**) a long, eventful journey. ■ **od·ys·se·an** /ō'disēən, ädə'sēən/ adj.

OECD ▸ abbr. Organization for Economic Cooperation and Development.

OED ▸ abbr. Oxford English Dictionary.

Oed·i·pus com·plex /'edəpəs, 'ēdə-/ ▸ n. (in the theory of Sigmund Freud) the emotions aroused in a young child by an unconscious sexual desire for the parent of the opposite sex. ■ **Oed·i·pal** adj.

OEM ▶ abbr. original equipment manufacturer.

oe·no·phile /'ēnə‚fīl/ (also **enophile**) ▶ n. a connoisseur of wines.

o'er /ōr/ ▶ adv. & prep. old-fashioned or literary form of OVER.

oeu·vre /'œvrə/ ▶ n. the works of an artist, composer, author, etc., considered as a whole.

of /əv/ ▶ prep. **1** expressing the relationship between a part and a whole. **2** belonging to; coming from. **3** expressing the relationship between a scale or measure and a value. **4** made from. **5** expressing the relationship between a direction and a point of reference. **6** expressing the relationship between a general category and something that belongs to such a category. **7** expressing time in relation to the following hour.

> **USAGE**
> Be careful not to write the word **of** instead of **have** in sentences such as *I could have told you.* For more information, see the note at HAVE.

off /ôf, äf/ ▶ adv. **1** away from the place in question. **2** so as to be removed or separated. **3** starting a journey or race. **4** so as to finish or be discontinued. **5** (of an electrical appliance or power supply) not functioning or so as to stop functioning. **6** having a particular level of wealth: *badly off.* ▶ prep. **1** moving away and often down from. **2** situated or leading in a direction away from. **3** so as to be removed, separated, or absent from. **4** having a temporary dislike of. ▶ adj. **1** unsatisfactory or inadequate: *an off day.* **2** (of food) no longer fresh. **3** located on the side of a vehicle that is normally farthest away from the curb. ▶ v. kill; murder.
– PHRASES **off and on** not regularly or all the time.

> **USAGE**
> The use of **off of** rather than **off** is best avoided in formal written English: you should write *the cup fell off the table* rather than *the cup fell off of the table.*

of·fal /'ôfəl, 'äfəl/ ▶ n. the internal organs of an animal used as food.

off·beat /'ôf‚bēt, 'äf-/ ▶ adj. unconventional; unusual. ▶ n. Music any of the normally unaccented beats in a bar.

off-col·or ▶ adj. slightly indecent or obscene.

of·fend /ə'fend/ ▶ v. **1** make someone feel upset, resentful, or annoyed. **2** be displeasing to: *the smell of cigarette ash offended him.* **3** commit an illegal act. ▪ **of·fend·er** n.

of·fense /ə'fens/ (Brit. **offence**) ▶ n. **1** an act that breaks a law or rule. **2** a feeling of hurt or annoyance: *I didn't mean to give offense.* **3** the action of making a military attack. **4** the attacking players on a team.

of·fen·sive /ə'fensiv/ ▶ adj. **1** making someone feel upset, resentful, or annoyed. **2** involved in an attack, or meant for use in an attack: *an offensive weapon.* **3** relating to the team in possession of the ball or puck in a game. ▶ n. **1** an attacking military campaign. **2** a forceful campaign to achieve something: *the need to launch an offensive against crime.* ▪ **of·fen·sive·ly** adv. **of·fen·sive·ness** n.
– PHRASES **be on the offensive** be ready to act aggressively.

of·fer /'ôfər, 'äfər/ ▶ v. **1** present something for someone to accept or reject as they wish.

2 express willingness to do something for someone: *he offered to fix the gate.* **3** provide: *the hotel offers direct access to a spa and pool.* **4** present something to God or another deity as an act of worship: *a monk offered prayers for their health and happiness.* ▶ n. **1** an expression of readiness to do or give something. **2** an amount of money that someone is willing to pay for something. **3** a specially reduced price.
– PHRASES **open to offers** willing to do or sell something for a reasonable price.

of·fer·ing /'ôf(ə)riNG, äf-/ ▶ n. something that is offered; a gift or contribution.

of·fer·to·ry /'ôfər‚tôrē, 'äfər-/ ▶ n. (pl. **offertories**) Christian Church **1** the offering of the bread and wine in the service of Holy Communion. **2** a collection of money made at a church service.

off·hand /'ôf‚hand, 'äf-/ ▶ adj. offensively casual or cool in manner. ▶ adv. without previous thought or consideration: *I can't think of a better answer offhand.*

of·fice /'ôfis, 'äf-/ ▶ n. **1** a room, set of rooms, or building in which business or clerical work is carried out. **2** a position of authority: *the office of director general.* **3** the holding of an official position: *the president took office in 1980.* **4** (**offices**) services done for other people: *the good offices of the rector.* **5** (also **Divine Office**) Christian Church the services of prayers and psalms said daily by Catholic priests or other clergy.

of·fi·cer /'ôfisər, 'äf-/ ▶ n. **1** a person holding a position of authority in the armed forces. **2** a policeman or policewoman. **3** a person holding a position of authority in the government or a large organization.

of·fi·cial /ə'fiSHəl/ ▶ adj. **1** relating to an authority or public organization and its activities and responsibilities. **2** permitted or done by a person or group in a position of authority: *an official inquiry.* ▶ n. a person holding public office or having official duties. ▪ **of·fi·cial·dom** n. **of·fi·cial·ly** adv.

of·fi·cial·ese /ə‚fiSHə'lēz/ ▶ n. formal or complicated language typical of that used in official documents.

of·fi·ci·ant /ə'fiSHēənt/ ▶ n. a priest or minister who performs a religious service or ceremony.

of·fi·ci·ate /ə'fiSHē‚āt/ ▶ v. **1** act as an official in charge of something, especially a sporting event. **2** perform a religious service or ceremony. ▪ **of·fi·ci·a·tion** /ə‚fiSHē'āSHən/ n. **of·fi·ci·a·tor** n.

of·fi·cious /ə'fiSHəs/ ▶ adj. too ready to assert one's authority or interfere. ▪ **of·fi·cious·ly** adv. **of·fi·cious·ness** n.

off·ing /'ôfiNG, 'äf-/ ▶ n. the more distant part of the sea in view.
– PHRASES **in the offing** likely to happen or appear soon.

off-key ▶ adj. & adv. **1** Music not having the correct tone or pitch. **2** not suitable or appropriate.

off-la·bel ▶ adj. (of the use of a drug) prescribed in a way or for a condition not covered by the original FDA approval: *off-label treatments.*

off-lim·its ▶ adj. out of bounds.

off-line /'ôf‚līn, 'äf-/ ▶ adj. not connected to a computer or external network.

off·load /'ôf‚lōd, 'äf-/ ▶ v. **1** unload a cargo. **2** get rid of something by passing it on to someone else.

off-peak ▶ adj. & adv. at a time when demand is less.

off·print /ˈôfˌprint, ˈäf-/ ▶ n. a printed copy of an article that originally appeared as part of a larger publication.

off-put·ting ▶ adj. unpleasant or disconcerting.

off-ramp ▶ n. an exit road from a main highway.

off-road ▶ adj. (of a vehicle or bicycle) for use on rough terrain rather than on public roads.

off-screen ▶ adj. **1** not appearing on a movie or television screen: *an off-screen narrator.* **2** happening in real life rather than fictionally on-screen: *they were off-screen lovers.*
▶ adv. **1** outside what can be seen on a movie or television screen: *the girl is looking off-screen.* **2** in real life rather than fictionally in a movie or on television: *happy endings rarely happen off-screen.*

off sea·son (also **off-season**) ▶ n. a time of year when people do not take part in a particular activity or when a business is quiet.

off·set /ˈôfˌset, ˈäf-/ ▶ v. (**offsetting**; past and past part. **offset**) **1** counteract something by having an equal and opposite force or effect: *many costs can be offset by productivity savings.* **2** place something out of line. **3** transfer an impression by means of offset printing.
▶ n. **1** a consideration or amount that reduces or balances the effect of an opposite one. **2** the amount by which something is out of line. **3** a side shoot from a plant that can be used for propagation. **4** a method of printing in which ink is transferred from a plate or stone to a rubber surface and from that to the paper.

off·shoot /ˈôfˌSHo͞ot, ˈäf-/ ▶ n. **1** a side shoot on a plant. **2** a thing that develops from something else.

off·shore /ˈôfˈSHôr, ˈäf-/ ▶ adj. & adv. **1** situated at sea some distance from the shore. **2** (of the wind) blowing toward the sea from the land. **3** relating to the business of extracting oil or gas from the seabed. **4** made, situated, or registered abroad. **5** relating to a foreign country.

off·shor·ing /ˈôfˈSHôriNG, ˈäf-/ ▶ n. the practice of basing some of a company's processes or services overseas, to take advantage of lower costs.

off·side /ˈôfˈsīd, ˈäf-/ ▶ adj. & adv. (of a player in games such as soccer, football, or hockey) occupying a position on the field where playing the ball or puck is not allowed. ▶ n. (also **offsides**) **1** the fact of being offside. **2** the right side of a horse.

off-site (also **offsite**) ▶ adj. & adv. taking place or situated away from a particular site or premises.

off·spring /ˈôfˌspriNG, ˈäf-/ ▶ n. (pl. same) a person's child or children, or the young of an animal.

off·stage /ˈôfˈstāj, ˈäf-/ ▶ adj. & adv. (in a theater) not on the stage and so not visible to the audience.

off-white ▶ n. a white color with a gray or yellowish tinge.

oft /ôft, äft/ (also **oft-times**) ▶ adv. old use or literary often.

of·ten /ˈôf(t)ən, ˈäf-/ (also **oftentimes** /ˈôf(t)ənˌtīmz, ˈäf-/) ▶ adv. (**oftener**, **oftenest**) **1** frequently. **2** in many cases.

o·gee /ōˈjē/ ▶ n. Architecture an S-shaped line or molding.

o·gee arch ▶ n. Architecture a pointed arch with two S-shaped curves meeting at the top.

o·gle /ˈōgəl, ä-/ ▶ v. stare at someone in a lecherous way. ■ **o·gler** n.

o·gre /ˈōgər/ ▶ n. (fem. **ogress** /ˈōgris/) **1** (in folklore) a man-eating giant. **2** a cruel or terrifying person. ■ **o·gre·ish** /ˈōg(ə)risH/ (also **ogrish**) adj.

OH ▶ abbr. Ohio.

oh¹ /ō/ ▶ exclam. expressing surprise, disappointment, joy, acknowledgment, etc.

oh² ▶ n. variant spelling of **o¹** (sense 2).

ohm /ōm/ ▶ n. the SI unit of electrical resistance. (Symbol: Ω)

oil /oil/ ▶ n. **1** a thick, sticky liquid obtained from petroleum, used especially as a fuel or lubricant. **2** petroleum. **3** any of various thick liquids that cannot be dissolved in water and are obtained from animals or plants. **4** Chemistry any of a group of organic compounds of glycerol and fatty acids that are liquid at room temperature. **5** (also **oils**) oil paint. ▶ v. lubricate, coat, or treat something with oil.

oil·can /ˈoilˌkan/ ▶ n. a can with a long nozzle used for applying oil to machinery.

oil·cloth /ˈoilˌklôtʜ/ ▶ n. cotton fabric treated with oil to make it waterproof.

oil·er /ˈoilər/ ▶ n. **1** an oil tanker. **2** a person who oils machinery. **3** informal an oil well. **4** (**oilers**) oilskin garments.

oil·field /ˈoilˌfēld/ ▶ n. an area where oil is found beneath the ground or the seabed.

oil paint ▶ n. artists' paint made from ground pigment mixed with linseed or other oil.

oil paint·ing ▶ n. **1** the art of painting in oil paint. **2** a picture painted in oil paint.

oil palm ▶ n. a tropical West African palm whose fruit yields a kind of oil.

oil plat·form ▶ n. a structure positioned on the seabed to provide a stable base above water for drilling and servicing oil wells.

oil rig (or **oil platform**) ▶ n. a structure designed to stand on the seabed to provide a stable base above water for drilling oil wells.

oil·seed /ˈoilˌsēd/ ▶ n. any of various seeds from crops from which oil is obtained, e.g., rape, peanut, or cotton.

oil·skin /ˈoilˌskin/ ▶ n. **1** heavy cotton cloth waterproofed with oil. **2** (**oilskins**) a set of garments made of oilskin.

oil slick ▶ n. a film or layer of oil floating on an area of water.

oil·stone /ˈoilˌstōn/ ▶ n. a fine-grained flat stone used with oil for sharpening chisels, planes, or other tools.

oil well ▶ n. a shaft bored in rock so as to extract oil.

oil·y /ˈoilē/ ▶ adj. (**oilier**, **oiliest**) **1** containing, covered with, or soaked in oil. **2** resembling oil. **3** (of a person) polite or flattering in an insincere and unpleasant way. ■ **oil·i·ness** n.

oink /oiNGk/ ▶ n. the characteristic grunting sound made by a pig. ▶ v. (of a pig) grunt.

oint·ment /ˈointmənt/ ▶ n. a smooth substance that is rubbed on the skin for medicinal purposes.

OJ ▶ abbr. orange juice.

O·jib·wa /ōˈjibˌwä, -wə/ ▶ n. (pl. same or **Ojibwas**) a member of an American Indian people of the area around Lake Superior.

OK¹ /ˈōˈkā/ (also **okay**) informal ▶ exclam. expressing agreement or acceptance. ▶ adj. **1** satisfactory, but not especially good. **2** permissible; allowed. ▶ adv. in a satisfactory way. ▶ n. approval or permission. ▶v. (**OK's**, **OK'ing**, **OK'd**) approve or agree to something.

OK² ▶abbr. Oklahoma.

o·ka·pi /ōˈkäpē/ ▶n. (pl. same or **okapis**) a large African mammal of the giraffe family, having a dark chestnut coat with stripes on the hindquarters and upper legs.

o·kay /ˈōˈkā/ ▶exclam., adj., adv., n., & v. variant spelling of **ok¹**.

o·kra /ˈōkrə/ ▶n. the long seed pods of a tropical plant, eaten as a vegetable.

old /ōld/ ▶adj. (**older**, **oldest**) **1** having lived for a long time. **2** made or built long ago. **3** possessed or used for a long time: *I gave my old clothes away.* **4** long-established or known. **5** former; previous: *they moved back to their old house.* **6** of a specified age. **7** informal expressing affection or contempt. ■ **old·ish** adj. **old·ness** n.
– PHRASES **of old 1** in or belonging to the past. **2** for a long time. **the old days** a period in the past. **the old school** the traditional form or type: *a gentleman of the old school.*

old age ▶n. the later part of normal life.

old boy net·work (also **old boys' network**) ▶n. an informal system through which men use their positions of influence to help others who went to the same school or university.

old coun·try ▶n. (**the old country**) the native country of a person who has gone to live abroad.

olde /ˈōld, ˈōldē/ ▶adj. mock old-fashioned attractively old-fashioned; quaint.

old·en /ˈōldən/ ▶adj. relating to former times.

Old Eng·lish ▶n. the language of the Anglo-Saxons (up to about 1150).

Old Eng·lish sheep·dog ▶n. a large breed of sheepdog with a shaggy blue-gray and white coat.

old-fash·ioned ▶adj. **1** no longer current or modern; outdated. **2** (of a person or their views) favoring traditional styles, ideas, or customs.

Old French ▶n. the French language up to about 1400.

Old Glo·ry ▶n. informal the US national flag.

old-growth ▶adj. (of a tree or forested area) never felled, harvested, or cleared; mature: *old-growth forests.*

old guard ▶n. the long-standing members of a group, who are typically unwilling to accept change.

old hand ▶n. a very experienced person.

old hat ▶n. informal something that is boringly familiar or outdated.

old·ie /ˈōldē/ ▶n. informal an old song, movie, or television program that is still well-known or popular.

old la·dy ▶n. informal a person's mother, wife, or female lover.

old maid ▶n. **1** derogatory a single woman regarded as too old for marriage. **2** a prim and fussy person.

old man ▶n. informal a person's father, husband, or male lover.

old man's beard ▶n. a wild clematis with gray fluffy hairs around the seeds.

old mas·ter ▶n. a great artist of the past, especially of the 13th–17th century in Europe.

Old Norse ▶n. the language of medieval Norway, Iceland, Denmark, and Sweden.

old salt ▶n. informal an experienced sailor.

old·ster /ˈōl(d)stər/ ▶n. informal an older person.

Old Style ▶n. the former method of calculating dates using the Julian calendar.

Old Tes·ta·ment ▶n. the first part of the Christian Bible, comprising the sacred writings of Judaism in thirty-nine books.

old-time ▶adj. relating to or typical of the past.

old-tim·er ▶n. informal a very experienced person.

old wives' tale ▶n. a widely held traditional belief that is now thought to be unscientific or incorrect.

old wom·an ▶n. **1** informal a person's mother, wife, or female lover. **2** derogatory a fussy or timid person.

old-world ▶adj. belonging to or associated with past times; quaint.

Old World ▶n. Europe, Asia, and Africa, regarded as the part of the world known before the discovery of the Americas.

o·lé /ōˈlā/ ▶exclam. bravo!

o·le·ag·i·nous /ˌōlēˈajənəs/ ▶adj. **1** oily or greasy. **2** excessively flattering; obsequious: *oleaginous speeches praising government policies.*

o·le·an·der /ˈōlēˌandər/ ▶n. an evergreen shrub of warm countries with clusters of white, pink, or red flowers.

o·le·o /ˈōlēō/ ▶n. informal margarine.

ol·fac·tion /älˈfaksʜən, ōl-/ ▶n. technical the sense of smell.

ol·fac·to·ry /älˈfakt(ə)rē, ōl-/ ▶adj. relating to the sense of smell.

ol·i·garch /ˈäliˌgärk, ˈōl-/ ▶n. a ruler in a country governed by a small group of people.

ol·i·gar·chy /ˈäliˌgärkē, ˈōli-/ ▶n. (pl. **oligarchies**) **1** a small group of people having control of a country. **2** a country governed by a small group of people. ■ **ol·i·gar·chic** /ˌäliˈgärkik, ˌōli-/ adj.

Ol·i·go·cene /ˈäligōˌsēn/ ▶adj. Geology relating to the third epoch of the Tertiary period (35.4 to 23.3 million years ago), when the first primates appeared.

ol·i·gop·o·ly /ˌäliˈgäpəlē/ ▶n. (pl. **oligopolies**) a state of limited competition, in which a market is shared by a small number of producers or sellers. ■ **ol·i·gop·o·list** n. **ol·i·gop·o·lis·tic** /ˌäliˌgäpəˈlistik/ adj.

ol·ive /ˈäliv/ ▶n. **1** a small oval fruit with a hard pit and bitter flesh, green when unripe and black when ripe. **2** the small evergreen tree that produces olives. **3** (also **olive green**) a grayish-green color. ▶adj. (of a person's complexion) yellowish brown; sallow.

ol·ive branch ▶n. an offer to restore friendly relations.

ol·ive drab ▶n. a dull olive-green color, used in some military uniforms.

ol·ive oil ▶n. an oil obtained from olives, used in cooking and salad dressings.

Ol·mec /ˈälˌmek, ˈōl-/ ▶n. (pl. same or **Olmecs**) **1** a member of a prehistoric people who lived on the Gulf of Mexico. **2** an unrelated people inhabiting this area during the 15th and 16th centuries.

O·lym·pi·ad /ōˈlimpēˌad, əˈlim-/ ▶n. **1** a staging of the Olympic Games. **2** a major international contest in a particular game, sport, or scientific subject.

O·lym·pi·an /ə'limpēən, ō'lim-/ ▶ adj. **1** relating to the Olympic Games. **2** like a god, especially in being powerful or aloof: *an editorial filled with Olympian disdain for the president.* **3** associated with Mount Olympus in Greece, traditional home of the Greek gods. ▶ n. **1** a competitor in the Olympic Games. **2** a person who is greatly admired or superior to others. **3** any of the twelve main Greek gods.

O·lym·pic /ə'limpik, ō'lim-/ ▶ adj. relating to the Olympic Games. ▶ n. (**the Olympics**) the Olympic Games.

O·lym·pic Games ▶ pl. n. **1** a sports festival held every four years in different countries, established in 1896. **2** an ancient Greek festival with athletic, literary, and musical competitions, held every four years at Olympia in Greece.

om /ōm/ ▶ n. Hinduism & Tibetan Buddhism a mystic syllable, considered the most sacred mantra.

O·ma·ni /ō'mänē/ ▶ n. a person from Oman in the Arabian peninsula. ▶ adj. relating to Oman.

OMB ▶ abbr. (in the federal government) Office of Management and Budget.

om·buds·man /'ämbədzmən, -ˌbŏodz-/ ▶ n. (pl. **ombudsmen**) an official appointed to investigate people's complaints against an organization.

o·me·ga /ō'mägə, ō'mē-/ ▶ n. **1** the last letter of the Greek alphabet (Ω, ω), represented as 'o.' **2** (usu. before another noun) the last of a series.

o·me·ga-3 fat·ty ac·id ▶ n. an unsaturated fatty acid of a kind occurring chiefly in fish oils.

om·e·let /'äm(ə)lit/ (also **omelette**) ▶ n. a dish of beaten eggs cooked in a frying pan and folded over, usually with a filling inside.

o·men /'ōmən/ ▶ n. **1** an event regarded as a sign of future good or bad luck. **2** indication of the future: *a bird of evil omen.*

o·mer·tà /ō'me(ə)rtə, ˌōmer'tä/ ▶ n. the Mafia code of silence about criminal activity.

om·i·nous /'ämənəs/ ▶ adj. giving the impression that something bad is going to happen: *the first ominous signs of mental torment soon emerged.* ■ **om·i·nous·ly** adv. **om·i·nous·ness** n.

o·mis·sion /ō'mishən/ ▶ n. **1** the action of leaving something out. **2** something that has been left out or not done. **3** a failure to fulfill a duty.

o·mit /ō'mit/ ▶ v. (**omits, omitting, omitted**) **1** leave out or exclude someone or something. **2** fail to do: *he modestly omits to mention that he was a pole-vault champion.* ■ **o·mis·si·ble** /ō'misəbəl/ adj.

omni- ▶ comb. form **1** all; of all things: *omniscient.* **2** in all ways or places: *omnipresent.*

om·ni·bus /'ämnəˌbəs/ ▶ n. **1** a book containing several works previously published separately. **2** dated a bus.

om·ni·com·pet·ent /ˌämni'kämpətənt/ ▶ adj. able to deal with all matters. ■ **om·ni·com·pet·ence** n.

om·ni·di·rec·tion·al /ˌämniˌdi'reksHənl/ ▶ adj. Telecommunications receiving signals from or transmitting in all directions.

om·nip·o·tent /äm'nipətənt/ ▶ adj. having unlimited or very great power. ■ **om·nip·o·tence** n.

om·ni·pres·ent /ˌämnə'preznt/ ▶ adj. **1** widely or constantly encountered: *omnipresent military checkpoints.* **2** (of God) present everywhere at the same time. ■ **om·ni·pres·ence** n.

om·nis·cient /äm'nishənt/ ▶ adj. knowing everything. ■ **om·nis·cience** n. **om·nis·cient·ly** adv.

om·ni·sex·u·al /ˌämni'seksHōōəl/ ▶ adj. relating to or engaging in sexual activity with all kinds of people.

om·ni·vore /'ämnəˌvôr/ ▶ n. an animal that eats both plants and meat.

om·niv·o·rous /äm'niv(ə)rəs/ ▶ adj. **1** (of an animal) eating both plants and meat. **2** taking in or using whatever is available; not selective: *an omnivorous reader.* ■ **om·niv·o·rous·ly** adv.

ON ▶ abbr. Ontario.

on /än, ôn/ ▶ prep. **1** in contact with and supported by a surface. **2** onto. **3** in the possession of. **4** forming a noticeable part of the surface of: *a scratch on her arm.* **5** about; concerning. **6** as a member of a committee, jury, etc. **7** having the thing mentioned as a target, aim, or focus: *thousands marched on Washington.* **8** stored in or broadcast by. **9** in the course of a journey or while traveling in a vehicle. **10** indicating the day or time of an event. **11** engaged in. **12** regularly taking a drug or medicine. **13** paid for by. **14** added to. ▶ adv. **1** in contact with and supported by a surface. **2** (of clothing) being worn. **3** further forward; with continued movement or action: *I drove on.* **4** (of an entertainment or event) taking place or being presented. **5** (of an electrical appliance or power supply) functioning. **6** on duty or on stage. – PHRASES **on and on** continually; without stopping. **you're on** informal said when accepting a challenge or bet.

on·a·ger /'änəjər/ ▶ n. a wild ass native to northern Iran.

on-air ▶ adj. broadcasting: *his on-air antics helped breathe new life into the series.*

o·nan·ism /'ōnəˌnizəm/ ▶ n. formal **1** masturbation. **2** sexual intercourse in which the penis is withdrawn before ejaculation. ■ **o·nan·ist** n. **o·nan·is·tic** /ˌōnə'nistik/ adj.

once /wəns/ ▶ adv. **1** on one occasion or for one time only. **2** on even one occasion: *he never once complained.* **3** in the past; formerly. ▶ conj. as soon as; when. – PHRASES **all at once** suddenly. **at once 1** immediately. **2** at the same time; simultaneously. **for once** (or **this once**) on this occasion only. **once and for all** (or **once for all**) now and for the last time; finally. **once** (or **every once**) **in a while** occasionally. **once or twice** a few times. **once upon a time** at some time in the past.

once-o·ver ▶ n. informal a rapid inspection, search, or piece of work.

on·co·gene /'äNGkəˌjēn/ ▶ n. a gene that in certain circumstances can transform a cell into a tumor cell. ■ **on·co·gen·ic** /ˌäNGkə'jenik/ adj.

on·col·o·gy /äN'kälojē, äNG-/ ▶ n. the study and treatment of tumors. ■ **on·co·log·i·cal** /ˌäNkə'läjikəl, ˌäNG-/ adj. **on·col·o·gist** n.

on·com·ing /'änˌkəmiNG, 'ôn-/ ▶ adj. approaching from the front; moving toward one.

on·co·pro·tein /ˌäNGkə'prōtē(ə)n/ ▶ n. a protein encoded by an oncogene that can cause the transformation of a cell into a tumor cell if introduced into it.

one /wən/ ▶ cardinal number **1** the lowest cardinal number; 1. (Roman numeral: **i** or **I**.) **2** a single person or thing. **3** single; sole. **4** identical; the same. **5** (before a person's name) a certain. **6** informal a noteworthy example of: *he was one smart-mouthed troublemaker.* ▶ **pron. 1** used to refer to a person or thing previously mentioned or easily identified. **2** a person of a specified kind: *her loved ones.* **3** (third person sing.) used to refer to the speaker, or any person, as representing people in general.

– PHRASES **at one** in agreement or harmony. **be one up on** informal have an advantage over someone. **one and all** everyone. **one and only** unique; single. **one another** each other. **one by one** separately and following each other. **one day** at an unspecified time in the past or future. **one or two** informal a few.

> **USAGE**
> In modern English the use of **one** to mean 'anyone' or 'me and people in general' (*one must try one's best*) is chiefly restricted to formal situations and writing, and can be regarded as pompous or overformal. In informal and spoken contexts the normal alternative is **you** (*you have to do what you can, don't you?*).

one-armed ban·dit ▶ **n.** informal a slot machine operated by pulling a long handle at the side.

one-di·men·sion·al ▶ **adj.** not complex or deep; superficial.

one-horse race ▶ **n.** a contest in which one competitor is clearly better than all the others.

one-horse town ▶ **n.** informal a small town with few and poor facilities.

o·nei·ric /ōˈnīrik/ ▶ **adj.** formal relating to dreams or dreaming.

one-lin·er ▶ **n.** informal a short joke or witty remark.

one-man band ▶ **n. 1** a street entertainer who plays many instruments at the same time. **2** a person who runs a business alone.

one·ness /ˈwən(n)is/ ▶ **n. 1** the state of being unified, whole, or in harmony: *the oneness of man and nature.* **2** the state of being one in number.

one-night stand (also **one-nighter** /ˈnītər/) ▶ **n. 1** informal a sexual relationship lasting only one night. **2** a single performance of a play or show in a particular place.

one-on-one ▶ **n.** informal a face-to-face encounter.

on·er·ous /ˈōnərəs, ˈänərəs/ ▶ **adj.** involving great effort and difficulty: *the onerous task of running a country.*

one·self /wənˈself/ ▶ **pron.** (third person sing.) **1** (reflexive) used as the object of a verb or preposition when this is the same as the subject of the clause and the subject is 'one.' **2** (emphatic) used to emphasize that one does something individually or without help. **3** in one's normal state of body or mind.

one-shot ▶ **adj.** informal achieved with a single attempt or action.

one-sid·ed ▶ **adj. 1** giving only one point of view; biased. **2** (of a contest or conflict) not involving participants of equal ability.

one-stop ▶ **adj.** (of a store or other business) capable of supplying all a customer's needs within a particular range of goods or services: *one-stop shopping.*

one-time ▶ **adj.** former.

one-to-one ▶ **adj. & adv.** referring to a situation in which two people come into direct contact or

opposition. ▶ **n.** informal a face-to-face meeting or conversation.

one-track mind ▶ **n.** informal a mind preoccupied with one subject, especially sex.

one-trick po·ny ▶ **n.** informal a person or thing with only one special feature or talent.

one-two ▶ **n. 1** a pair of punches in quick succession with alternate hands. **2** chiefly Football a move in which a player plays a short pass to a teammate and moves forward to receive an immediate return pass.

one-up·man·ship /wən ˈəpmənˌSHip/ (also **one-upsmanship**) ▶ **n.** informal the technique of gaining an advantage over someone else.

one-way ▶ **adj.** moving or allowing movement in one direction only.

on·go·ing /ˈänˌgōiNG, ˈôn-/ ▶ **adj.** continuing; still in progress.

on·ion /ˈənyən/ ▶ **n.** a vegetable consisting of a bulb with a strong taste and smell. ■ **on·ion·y** adj.

on·line /ˈänlīn, ˈôn-/ ▶ **adj. & adv. 1** controlled by or connected to a computer. **2** available on or carried out via the Internet: *online banking.* **3** in or into operation.

on·look·er /ˈänˌlo͝okər, ˈôn-/ ▶ **n.** a person who watches something without getting involved in it. ■ **on·look·ing** adj.

on·ly /ˈōnlē/ ▶ **adv. 1** and no one or nothing more besides. **2** no longer ago than. **3** not until. **4** with the negative result that: *he turned, only to find his way blocked.* ▶ **adj. 1** alone of its or their kind; single or solitary. **2** alone deserving consideration. ▶ **conj.** informal except that.

– PHRASES **only just 1** by a very small margin. **2** very recently. **only too** —— to an extreme or regrettable extent.

> **USAGE**
> The traditional view is that, to avoid confusion, you should place the adverb **only** next to the word or words whose meaning it restricts: *I have seen him only once* rather than *I have only seen him once.* In practice, people tend to state **only** as early as possible in the sentence, generally just before the main verb, and the result is usually clear.

on·o·mas·tic /ˌänəˈmastik/ ▶ **adj.** relating to the study of the history and origin of proper names. ■ **on·o·mas·tics** n.

on·o·mat·o·poe·ia /ˌänəˌmatəˈpēə, -ˌmätə-/ ▶ **n.** the use or formation of words that sound similar to the noise described (e.g., *cuckoo, sizzle*). ■ **on·o·mat·o·poe·ic** /-ˈpē-ik/ (or **onomatopoetic** /-pōˈetik/) adj. **on·o·mat·o·poe·i·cal·ly** /-ˈpē-ik(ə)lē/ (or **onomatopoetically** /-pōˈetik(ə)lē/) adv.

on-ramp ▶ **n.** a lane for traffic entering a turnpike or highway.

on·rush /ˈänˌrəSH, ˈôn-/ ▶ **n.** a surging rush forward. ■ **on·rush·ing** adj.

on-screen ▶ **adj. & adv. 1** shown or appearing in a movie or television program: *on-screen violence.* **2** making use of or performed using a video screen: *on-screen editing facilities.*

on·set /ˈänˌset, ˈôn-/ ▶ **n.** the beginning of something, especially something unpleasant: *technology is effective in detecting the onset of heart disease.*

on·shore /ˈänˌSHôr, ˈôn-/ ▶ **adj. & adv. 1** situated or occurring on land. **2** (of the wind) blowing from the sea toward the land.

on·side /'än'sīd, 'ôn-/ ▶ adj. & adv. (of a player in soccer, hockey, etc.) occupying a position where playing the ball is allowed.

on-site (also **onsite**) ▶ adj. & adv. taking place or situated on a particular site or premises.

on·slaught /'än,slôt, 'ôn-/ ▶ n. **1** a fierce or destructive attack. **2** an overwhelmingly large quantity of people or things: *the onslaught of cars far exceeds capacity.*

on·stage /'än'stāj, 'ôn-/ ▶ adj. & adv. (in a theater) on the stage and so visible to the audience.

on·to /'än,tōō, 'ôn-/ ▶ prep. moving to a place on: *they went up onto the ridge.*

– PHRASES **be onto** informal **1** be close to discovering that someone has done something wrong. **2** have an idea that is likely to lead to an important discovery.

> **USAGE**
> It is important to maintain a distinction between the preposition **onto** or **on to** and the use of the adverb **on** followed by the preposition **to**: *she climbed onto* (sometimes *on to*) *the roof*, but *let's go on to* (never onto) *the next chapter.*

on·tol·o·gy /än'täləjē/ ▶ n. the branch of philosophy concerned with the nature of being. ■ **on·to·log·i·cal** /,äntə'läjikəl/ adj. **on·tol·o·gist** n.

o·nus /'ōnəs/ ▶ n. a duty or responsibility: *the onus is on you to spot mistakes.*

on·ward /'änwərd, 'ôn-/ ▶ adv. (also **onwards**) **1** in a continuing forward direction; ahead. **2** so as to make progress. ▶ adj. moving forward.

on·yx /'äniks/ ▶ n. a semiprecious variety of agate with different colors in layers.

oo·dles /'ōōdlz/ ▶ pl. n. informal a very great number or amount.

o·o·lite /'ōə,līt/ ▶ n. limestone consisting of rounded granules, each consisting of calcium carbonate surrounding a grain of sand. ■ **o·o·lit·ic** /,ōə'litik/ adj.

oo·long /'ōō,lông, -,läng/ ▶ n. a kind of dark-colored partly fermented China tea.

oom·pah /'ōōm,pä, 'ôōm-/ ▶ n. informal the sound of deep-toned brass instruments in a band.

oomph /ōōmf, ōōmf/ (also **umph**) ▶ n. informal the quality of being exciting, vigorous, or sexually attractive: *add oomph to your personal style.*

oops /ōōps, ōōps/ ▶ exclam. informal used to show recognition of a mistake or minor accident.

ooze /ōōz/ ▶ v. **1** (of a fluid) slowly trickle or seep out. **2** give a powerful impression of: *she oozes sex appeal.* ▶ n. **1** wet mud or slime, especially that found at the bottom of a river, lake, or sea. **2** the sluggish flow of a fluid. ■ **ooz·y** adj.

op /äp/ ▶ n. informal **1** a surgical operation. **2** (**ops**) military operations.

Op. (also **op.**) ▶ abbr. Music (before a number given to each work of a composer) opus.

o·pac·i·ty /ō'pasitē/ ▶ n. **1** the state of being opaque or difficult to see through. **2** the quality of being difficult to understand.

o·pal /'ōpəl/ ▶ n. a semitransparent gemstone in which many small points of shifting color can be seen.

o·pal·es·cent /,ōpə'lesənt/ ▶ adj. showing many small points of shifting color: *opalescent eyes.* ■ **o·pal·es·cence** n.

o·pal·ine /'ōpə,lēn, -,līn/ ▶ adj. showing many

points of shifting color; opalescent.

o·paque /ō'pāk/ ▶ adj. (**opaquer, opaquest**) **1** not able to be seen through; not transparent. **2** difficult or impossible to understand. ■ **o·paque·ly** adv.

op art ▶ n. a form of abstract art that gives the illusion of movement by its use of pattern and color.

op. cit. /'äp ,sit/ ▶ adv. in the work already cited.

OPEC /'ōpek/ ▶ abbr. Organization of the Petroleum Exporting Countries.

op-ed /'äped/ ▶ adj. referring to the page opposite the editorial page in a newspaper, devoted to commentary, feature articles, etc.

o·pen /'ōpən/ ▶ adj. **1** not closed, fastened, or restricted. **2** exposed to view or attack; not covered or protected. **3** (**open to**) likely to suffer from or be affected by: *the system is open to abuse.* **4** spread out, expanded, or unfolded. **5** admitting customers or visitors; available for business. **6** accessible or available. **7** frank and communicative. **8** not disguised or hidden: *his eyes showed open admiration.* **9** not finally decided. **10** (**open to**) making possible: *a message open to different interpretations.* **11** (of a string of a musical instrument) allowed to vibrate along its whole length. **12** (of an electric circuit) having a break in the conducting path. ▶ v. **1** make or become open. **2** formally begin or establish: *he opened his own restaurant.* **3** make something available or more widely known. **4** (**open onto/into**) give access to. **5** (**open up**) become more frank or communicative. **6** break the conducting path of an electric circuit. ▶ n. **1** (**the open**) outdoors or in the countryside. **2** (**Open**) a competition with no restrictions on who may compete. ■ **o·pen·a·ble** adj. **o·pen·ness** n.

– PHRASES **in open court** in a court of law, before the judge and the public. **in** (or **into**) **the open** not concealed or secret. **open-and-shut** not disputed; straightforward. **open up** (or **open fire**) begin shooting.

o·pen air ▶ n. a free or unenclosed space outdoors. ▶ adj. (**open-air**) positioned or taking place out of doors.

o·pen book ▶ n. a person or thing that is easily understood or interpreted.

o·pen-end·ed ▶ adj. having no limit decided in advance.

o·pen en·roll·ment ▶ n. the unrestricted enrollment of students at schools, colleges, or universities of their choice.

o·pen·er /'ōp(ə)nər/ ▶ n. **1** a device for opening something. **2** the first of a series of games, cultural events, etc.

– PHRASES **for openers** informal to start with.

o·pen-hand·ed ▶ adj. **1** (of a blow) delivered with the palm of the hand. **2** giving freely; generous.

o·pen-heart·ed ▶ adj. friendly and kind.

o·pen-heart sur·ger·y ▶ n. surgery in which the heart is exposed and the blood made to bypass it.

o·pen house ▶ n. **1** a place or situation in which all visitors are welcome. **2** a day when members of the public are invited to visit a place or institution to which they do not normally have access.

o·pen·ing /'ōp(ə)niNG/ ▶ n. **1** a space or gap that allows access or passage. **2** a beginning.

3 a ceremony at which a building, show, etc., is declared to be open. **4** an opportunity or available job: *there are few openings for an ex-football player.* ▶ **adj.** coming at the beginning; initial.

o·pen let·ter ▶ **n.** a letter addressed to a particular person but intended for publication in a newspaper or journal.

o·pen·ly /ˈōpənlē/ ▶ **adv.** in a frank, honest, or public way.

o·pen mar·ket ▶ **n.** a situation in which people or companies can trade without restrictions.

o·pen mar·riage ▶ **n.** a marriage in which both partners agree that each may have other sexual partners.

o·pen-mind·ed ▶ **adj.** willing to consider new ideas.

o·pen-necked ▶ **adj.** (of a shirt) worn with the collar unbuttoned and without a tie.

o·pen-pit ▶ **adj.** (of mining) in which coal or ore is extracted from a level near the earth's surface, rather than from shafts.

o·pen-plan ▶ **adj.** (of a room or building) having few or no dividing walls.

o·pen sea·son ▶ **n. 1** the annual period when restrictions on the killing of certain types of wildlife are lifted. **2** a period when all restrictions on a particular activity or product are abandoned or ignored.

o·pen se·cret ▶ **n.** a supposed secret that is in fact known to many people.

o·pen-source ▶ **adj.** referring to computer software for which the original source code is made freely available.

o·pen-toed ▶ **adj.** (of a shoe) not covering the toes.

o·pen·work /ˈōpənˌwərk/ ▶ **n.** ornamental work in cloth, leather, etc., with regular patterns of openings and holes.

o·pe·ra[1] /ˈäp(ə)rə/ ▶ **n. 1** a dramatic work set to music for singers and musicians. **2** a building in which operas are performed.

o·pe·ra[2] ▶ plural of **opus**.

op·er·a·ble /ˈäp(ə)rəbəl/ ▶ **adj. 1** able to be used. **2** able to be treated by a surgical operation.

o·pe·ra buf·fa /ˈäp(ə)rə ˈbo͞ofə, ˌōperä ˈbo͞ofä/ ▶ **n.** (pl. **opere buffe** /ˈäpərä ˈbo͞ofä, ˈōpəˌrä/) a comic opera, especially in Italian.

op·er·a glass·es ▶ **pl.n.** small binoculars for use at the opera or theater.

op·er·a house ▶ **n.** a theater designed for the performance of opera.

op·er·and /ˈäpəˌrand/ ▶ **n.** Mathematics the quantity on which an operation is to be done.

o·pe·ra se·ri·a /ˈäp(ə)rə ˈsi(ə)rēə, ˈōpeˌrä ˈserēˌä/ ▶ **n.** (pl. **opere serie** /ˈäpərä ˈsi(ə)rēä, ˈōpeˌrä ˈserēˌä/) an opera, especially one of the 18th century in Italian, on a serious theme.

op·er·ate /ˈäpəˌrāt/ ▶ **v. 1** (of a machine, process, or system) be in action; function. **2** control a machine, process, or business. **3** (of an organization) carry on its activities in a particular way or from a particular place: *they operate from a New York office.* **4** (of an armed force) carry on military activities in a particular place. **5** be in effect: *a powerful law operates in politics.* **6** perform a surgical operation.

op·er·at·ic /ˌäpəˈratik/ ▶ **adj. 1** relating to opera. **2** melodramatic or exaggerated: *she wrung her hands in operatic despair.* ■ **op·er·at·i·cal·ly** /-ik(ə)lē/ **adv.**

op·er·at·ing prof·it ▶ **n.** a gross profit before expenses are deducted.

op·er·at·ing room ▶ **n.** a room in which surgical operations are performed.

op·er·at·ing sys·tem ▶ **n.** the low-level software that supports a computer's basic functions.

op·er·at·ing ta·ble ▶ **n.** a table on which a patient is placed during a surgical operation.

op·er·a·tion /ˌäpəˈrāshən/ ▶ **n. 1** the action or process of operating: *we have a lot of security measures in operation.* **2** an act of surgery performed on a patient to remove or repair a damaged body part. **3** an organized action involving a number of people: *a rescue operation.* **4** a business organization. **5** Mathematics a process in which a number, quantity, expression, etc., is altered according to formal rules.

op·er·a·tion·al /ˌäpəˈrāshənl/ ▶ **adj. 1** being used or ready for use. **2** relating to the functioning of an organization. ■ **op·er·a·tion·al·ly adv.**

op·er·a·tive /ˈäp(ə)rətiv, ˈäpəˌrātiv/ ▶ **adj. 1** functioning or having effect. **2** (of a word) having the most importance in a phrase. **3** relating to surgery. ▶ **n. 1** a worker. **2** a private detective or secret agent. ■ **op·er·a·tive·ly adv.**

op·er·a·tor /ˈäpəˌrātər/ ▶ **n. 1** a person who operates equipment or a machine. **2** a person who works at the switchboard of a telephone exchange. **3** a person or company that runs a business. **4** informal a person who acts in a clever or manipulative way: *a smooth operator.* **5** a mathematical symbol or function referring to an operation (e.g., ×, +).

op·er·et·ta /ˌäpəˈretə/ ▶ **n.** a short opera on a light or humorous theme.

o·phid·i·an /ōˈfidēən/ ▶ **adj.** literary resembling or typical of a snake: *a soft, ophidian hiss.*

oph·thal·mi·a /äfˈTHalmēə, äp-/ ▶ **n.** inflammation of the eye, especially conjunctivitis.

oph·thal·mic /äfˈTHalmik, äp-/ ▶ **adj.** relating to the eye and its diseases.

oph·thal·mol·o·gy /ˌäfTHə(l)ˈmäləjē, äp-/ ▶ **n.** the study and treatment of disorders and diseases of the eye. ■ **oph·thal·mo·log·i·cal** /-məˈläjikəl/ **adj. oph·thal·mol·o·gist n.**

oph·thal·mo·scope /äfˈTHalməˌskōp, äp-/ ▶ **n.** an instrument for inspecting the retina and other parts of the eye. ■ **oph·thal·mo·scop·ic** /ˌäfTHalmōˈskäpik, äp-/ **adj. oph·thal·mos·co·py** /ˌäfTHəlˈmäskəpē, äp-/ **n.**

o·pi·ate /ˈōpēət, -ˌāt/ ▶ **n. 1** a drug containing or related to opium. **2** something that causes a false sense of contentment: *movies are the opiate of the people.* ▶ **adj.** relating to or containing opium. ■ **o·pi·at·ed adj.**

o·pine /ōˈpīn/ ▶ **v.** formal state something as one's opinion.

o·pin·ion /əˈpinyən/ ▶ **n. 1** a personal view not necessarily based on fact or knowledge. **2** the views of people in general: *public opinion.* **3** an estimate of quality or worth: *he had a high opinion of himself.* **4** a formal statement of advice by an expert or professional.
— PHRASES **a matter of opinion** something not capable of being proven either way.

o·pin·ion·at·ed /əˈpinyəˌnātid/ ▶ **adj.** tending to state one's views forcefully and to be unwilling to change them.

o·pin·ion poll ▶ **n.** the questioning of a small

sample of people in order to assess wider public opinion.

o·pi·oid /'ōpē͡oid/ ▶ n. a compound resembling opium. ▶ adj. relating to opioids.

o·pi·um /'ōpēəm/ ▶ n. an addictive drug prepared from the juice of a poppy, used to alter mood or behavior and in medicine as a painkiller.

o·pos·sum /(ə)'päsəm/ ▶ n. an American marsupial mammal with a tail that it can use for grasping.

opp. ▶ abbr. opposite.

op·po·nent /ə'pōnənt/ ▶ n. 1 a person who opposes or competes with another in a contest, argument, or fight. 2 a person who disagrees with a proposal or practice.

op·por·tune /ˌäpər't(y)ōōn/ ▶ adj. 1 (of a time) especially convenient or appropriate for something: *he chose an opportune moment to get away.* 2 done or occurring at an especially convenient or appropriate time. ■ **op·por·tune·ly** adv.

op·por·tun·ist /ˌäpər't(y)ōōnist/ ▶ n. a person who takes advantage of opportunities when they arise, regardless of whether or not they are right to do so. ▶ adj. taking advantage of opportunities when they arise; opportunistic. ■ **op·por·tun·ism** /-ˌnizəm/ n.

op·por·tun·is·tic /ˌäpərt(y)ōō'nistik/ ▶ adj. 1 taking advantage of opportunities when they arise, especially in a selfish way. 2 (of an infection) occurring when the immune system is depressed. ■ **op·por·tun·is·ti·cal·ly** /-ik(ə)lē/ adv.

op·por·tu·ni·ty /ˌäpər't(y)ōōnitē/ ▶ n. (pl. **opportunities**) 1 a favorable time or set of circumstances for doing something. 2 a chance for employment or promotion: *job opportunities.*

op·pos·a·ble /ə'pōzəbəl/ ▶ adj. (of the thumb of a primate mammal) capable of facing and touching the other digits on the same hand.

op·pose /ə'pōz/ ▶ v. 1 (also **be opposed to**) disagree with and try to prevent or resist: *Ross was rabidly opposed to the plan.* 2 compete with or fight someone. 3 (as adj. **opposed**) (of two or more things) contrasting or conflicting. 4 (as adj. **opposing**) opposite. ■ **op·pos·er** n.

op·po·site /'äpəzit/ ▶ adj. 1 situated on the other or further side; facing. 2 completely different. 3 being the other of a contrasted pair: *the opposite ends of the price range.* 4 (of angles) between opposite sides of the intersection of two lines. ▶ n. a person or thing that is completely different from or the reverse of another. ▶ adv. in an opposite position. ▶ prep. in a position opposite to. ■ **op·po·site·ly** adv.

op·po·site num·ber ▶ n. a person's counterpart in another organization.

op·po·site sex ▶ n. (**the opposite sex**) women in relation to men or vice versa.

op·po·si·tion /ˌäpə'zishən/ ▶ n. 1 resistance or disagreement: *there was considerable opposition to the plan.* 2 a group of opponents. 3 (**the opposition**) the political party that is opposed to the one in office. 4 a contrast or complete opposite. ■ **op·po·si·tion·al** adj. **op·po·si·tion·ist** adj. & n.

op·press /ə'pres/ ▶ v. 1 treat or govern someone in a very harsh and unfair way. 2 make someone feel distressed or anxious. ■ **op·pres·sion** /ə'preshən/ n. **op·pres·sor** n.

op·pres·sive /ə'presiv/ ▶ adj. 1 harsh and demanding strict obedience: *an oppressive*

dictatorship. 2 causing anxiety or distress. 3 (of weather) hot and humid. ■ **op·pres·sive·ly** adv. **op·pres·sive·ness** n.

op·pro·bri·ous /ə'prōbrēəs/ ▶ adj. formal expressing criticism or scorn. ■ **op·pro·bri·ous·ly** adv.

op·pro·bri·um /ə'prōbrēəm/ ▶ n. formal 1 criticism or scorn. 2 public disgrace arising from bad behavior.

opt /äpt/ ▶ v. make a choice: *the couple opted for a traditional marriage.*
– PHRASES **opt out** choose not to participate in something.

op·tic /'äptik/ ▶ adj. relating to the eye or vision.

op·ti·cal /'äptikəl/ ▶ adj. relating to vision, light, or optics. ■ **op·ti·cal·ly** adv.

op·ti·cal char·ac·ter rec·og·ni·tion ▶ n. the identification of printed characters using photoelectric devices and computer software.

op·ti·cal fi·ber ▶ n. a thin glass fiber through which light can be transmitted.

op·ti·cal il·lu·sion ▶ n. a thing that deceives the eye by appearing to be something that it is not.

op·ti·cian /äp'tishən/ ▶ n. a person qualified to make and supply eyeglasses and contact lenses.

op·tic nerve ▶ n. each of the pair of nerves transmitting impulses from the eyes to the brain.

op·tics /'äptiks/ ▶ pl.n. (usu. treated as sing.) the branch of science concerned with vision and the behavior of light.

op·ti·mal /'äptəməl/ ▶ adj. best or most favorable. ■ **op·ti·mal·i·ty** /ˌäptə'malitē/ n. **op·ti·mal·ly** adv.

op·ti·mism /'äptəˌmizəm/ ▶ n. 1 hopefulness and confidence about the future or success of something. 2 Philosophy the belief that this world is the best of all possible worlds. ■ **op·ti·mist** n.

op·ti·mis·tic /ˌäptə'mistik/ ▶ adj. hopeful and confident about the future. ■ **op·ti·mis·ti·cal·ly** /-ik(ə)lē/ adv.

op·ti·mize /'äptəˌmīz/ ▶ v. make the best use of a situation or resource. ■ **op·ti·mi·za·tion** /ˌäptəmə'zāshən/ n. **op·ti·miz·er** n.

op·ti·mum /'äptəməm/ ▶ adj. most likely to lead to a favorable outcome: *the units combine high quality with optimum performance.* ▶ n. (pl. **optima** /-mə/ or **optimums**) the most favorable conditions for growth or success.

op·tion /'äpshən/ ▶ n. 1 a thing that is or may be chosen. 2 the freedom or right to choose: *she was given the option of resigning or being fired.* 3 a right to buy or sell something at a specified price within a set time.
– PHRASES **keep** (or **leave**) **one's options open** not commit oneself.

op·tion·al /'äpshənl/ ▶ adj. available to be chosen but not compulsory. ■ **op·tion·al·i·ty** /ˌäpshə'nalitē/ n. **op·tion·al·ly** adv.

op·tom·e·trist /äp'tämitrist/ ▶ n. a person who practices optometry.

op·tom·e·try /äp'tämitrē/ ▶ n. the occupation of measuring eyesight, prescribing corrective lenses, and detecting eye disease.

opt-out ▶ n. an instance of choosing not to participate in something: *opt-outs from key parts of the treaty.*

op·u·lent /'äpyələnt/ ▶ adj. expensive and luxurious: *opulent furnishings.* ■ **op·u·lence** n. **op·u·lent·ly** adv.

o·pus /'ōpəs/ ▶ n. (pl. **opuses** or **opera** /'äp(ə)rə/)

1 a musical composition or set of compositions. **2** an artistic work.

OR ▶ abbr. Oregon.

or[1] /ôr/ ▶ conj. **1** used to link alternatives. **2** introducing a word that means the same as a preceding word or phrase, or that explains it. **3** otherwise.

or[2] ▶ n. gold or yellow, as a conventional heraldic color.

-or ▶ suffix **1** forming nouns referring to a person or thing performing the action of a verb: *escalator.* **2** forming nouns referring to a state: *terror.*

or·a·cle /'ôrəkəl/ ▶ n. **1** (in ancient Greece or Rome) a priest or priestess who acted as a channel for advice or prophecy from the gods. **2** an authority that is always correct.

o·rac·u·lar /ô'rakyələr/ ▶ adj. **1** relating to an oracle. **2** hard to interpret. **3** having the authority of an oracle.

o·ral /'ôrəl/ ▶ adj. **1** spoken rather than written. **2** relating to the mouth. **3** done or taken by the mouth. ▶ n. a spoken exam or test. ■ **o·ral·ly** adv.

> **USAGE**
> On the confusion of **oral** and **aural**, see the note at **AURAL**.

o·ral his·to·ry ▶ n. the collection and study of historical information spoken by people.

o·ral·ism /'ôrə,lizəm/ ▶ n. the teaching of deaf people to communicate by the use of speech and lip-reading rather than sign language. ■ **o·ral·ist** adj. & n.

or·ange /ô'rinZH, 'är-/ ▶ n. **1** a large round citrus fruit with a tough reddish-yellow rind. **2** a bright reddish-yellow color. ▶ adj. reddish yellow. ■ **or·ang·ey** (also **orangy**) adj.

or·ange·ade /,ôrənj'ād, ,är-/ ▶ n. a soft drink flavored with orange.

or·ange pe·koe /'pē,kō/ ▶ n. a type of black tea made from young leaves.

or·ange rough·y /'rəfē/ ▶ n. a widespread edible fish whose reddish body turns orange after being exposed to air.

or·ange·ry /'ôrənjrē, ,är-/ ▶ n. (pl. **orangeries**) a type of large conservatory where orange trees are grown.

or·ange stick ▶ n. a thin pointed stick for manicuring the fingernails.

o·rang·u·tan /ə'raNG(g)ə,tan/ (also **orangutang** /ô'raNG(g)ə,taNG/) ▶ n. a large ape with long red hair, native to forests in Borneo and Sumatra.

o·rate /ô'rāt, 'ôr,āt/ ▶ v. make a speech, especially a long or pompous one.

o·ra·tion /ô'rāsHən/ ▶ n. a formal speech made on a public occasion.

or·a·tor /'ôrətər, 'är-/ ▶ n. a skillful public speaker. ■ **or·a·to·ri·al** /,ôrə'tôrēəl/ adj.

or·a·to·ri·o /,ôrə'tôrē,ō, ,är-/ ▶ n. (pl. **oratorios**) a large-scale musical work on a religious theme for orchestra and voices.

or·a·to·ry[1] /'ôrə,tôrē, 'är-/ ▶ n. (pl. **oratories**) a small chapel for private worship.

or·a·to·ry[2] ▶ n. powerful and persuasive public speaking. ■ **or·a·tor·i·cal** /,ôrə'tôrikəl/ adj.

orb /ôrb/ ▶ n. **1** a spherical object or shape. **2** a golden globe with a cross on top, carried by a monarch on ceremonial occasions.

or·bit /'ôrbit/ ▶ n. **1** the regularly repeated elliptical course of a planet, moon, spacecraft, etc., around a star or planet. **2** an area of activity or influence: *they brought many friends within the orbit of our lives.* **3** the path of an electron around an atomic nucleus. **4** Anatomy the eye socket. ▶ v. (**orbits, orbiting, orbited**) move in orbit around a star or planet. ■ **or·bit·er** n.

or·bit·al /'ôrbitl/ ▶ adj. relating to an orbit or orbits. ■ **or·bit·al·ly** adv.

or·bit·al sand·er ▶ n. a sander in which the sanding surface has a minute circular motion without rotating relative to the object being worked on.

or·ca /'ôrkə/ ▶ n. a killer whale.

or·chard /'ôrcHərd/ ▶ n. a piece of enclosed land planted with fruit trees.

or·ches·tra /'ôrkistrə, -,kestrə/ ▶ n. **1** (treated as sing. or pl.) a large group of musicians with string, woodwind, brass, and percussion sections. **2** (also **orchestra pit**) the part of a theater where the orchestra plays, typically in front of the stage and on a lower level. **3** the ground floor seats in a theater. **4** the semicircular space in front of an ancient Greek theater stage where the chorus danced and sang. ■ **or·ches·tral** /ôr'kestrəl/ adj. **or·ches·tral·ly** adv.

or·ches·trate /'ôrki,strāt/ ▶ v. **1** adapt a musical composition so that it can be performed by an orchestra. **2** organize a complicated event or situation carefully or secretly: *a nationwide campaign orchestrated by conservationists.* ■ **or·ches·tra·tion** /,ôrkə'strāsHən/ n. **or·ches·tra·tor** /-,strātər/ n.

or·chid /'ôrkid/ ▶ n. a plant of a large family with complex showy flowers. ■ **or·chi·da·ceous** /,ôrki'dāsHəs/ adj.

or·dain /ôr'dān/ ▶ v. **1** make someone a priest or minister. **2** order something officially: *the king ordained that the courts should be revived.* **3** (of God or fate) decide something in advance.

or·deal /ôr'dēl/ ▶ n. **1** a prolonged painful or unpleasant experience. **2** an ancient test of guilt or innocence in which the accused person was subjected to severe pain, survival of which was taken as divine proof of their innocence.

or·der /'ôrdər/ ▶ n. **1** the arrangement of people or things according to a particular sequence or method: *I filed the cards in alphabetical order.* **2** a state in which everything is in its right place. **3** a state in which the laws and rules regulating public behavior are followed: *a breakdown of law and order.* **4** an instruction that must be obeyed; a command. **5** a request for something to be made, supplied, or served. **6** the set procedure followed in a meeting, court of law, or religious service. **7** quality or nature: *poetry of the highest order.* **8** a social class or system. **9** a rank in the Christian ministry. **10** (**orders** or **holy orders**) the rank of an ordained minister of the Church. **11** a society of monks, nuns, or friars living under the same rule. **12** (**Order**) Brit. an institution founded by a king or queen to honor good conduct: *the Order of the Garter.* **13** Biology a main category into which animals and plants are divided that ranks below class and above family. **14** any of the five classical styles of architecture (Doric, Ionic, Corinthian, Tuscan, and Composite). ▶ v. **1** give a command: *she ordered me to leave.* **2** request that something be made, supplied, or served: *I ordered a steak.* **3** arrange something methodically.

– PHRASES **in order 1** in the right condition for operation or use. **2** appropriate in the circumstances. **in order for** (or **that**) so that. **in order to** with the purpose of doing. **of the order of** approximately. **on order** (of goods) requested but not yet received. **the order of the day 1** the current situation. **2** the day's business to be considered in a meeting, etc. **out of order** not working properly or at all.

or·der·ly /'ôrdərlē/ ▶ adj. **1** neatly and methodically arranged. **2** well behaved. ▶ n. (pl. **orderlies**) **1** a hospital worker responsible for cleaning and other nonmedical tasks. **2** a soldier who carries orders or performs minor tasks for an officer. ■ **or·der·li·ness** n.

or·der of mag·ni·tude ▶ n. **1** a level in a system of classifying things by size, typically where each level is higher by a factor of ten. **2** relative size or quantity.

or·di·nal /'ôrdn-əl/ ▶ adj. relating to order in a series.

or·di·nal num·ber ▶ n. a number defining a thing's position in a series, such as 'first' or 'second.'

or·di·nance /'ôrdn-əns/ ▶ n. formal **1** an official order. **2** a religious rite.

or·di·nand /'ôrdn,and/ ▶ n. a person who is training to be ordained as a priest or minister.

or·di·nar·y /'ôrdn,erē/ ▶ adj. **1** having no distinctive features; normal or usual. **2** not interesting or exceptional: *a very ordinary piece of work.* ▶ n. (pl. **ordinaries**) **1** what is commonplace or standard: *a level of skill well above the ordinary.* **2** (**Ordinary**) those parts of a Roman Catholic service, especially the Mass, that do not vary from day to day. **3** a rule or book laying down the order of divine service. **4** Heraldry any of the simplest main emblems or devices used in coats of arms. ■ **or·di·nar·i·ly** adv. **or·di·nar·i·ness** n.
– PHRASES **out of the ordinary** unusual.

or·di·nate /'ôrdnit, -,āt/ ▶ n. Mathematics a straight line from a point on a graph drawn parallel to the vertical axis and meeting the other; the y- coordinate.

or·di·na·tion /,ôrdn'āshən/ ▶ n. the action of ordaining someone as a priest or minister.

ord·nance /'ôrdnəns/ ▶ n. **1** large guns mounted on wheels. **2** military weapons, ammunition, and equipment. **3** a branch of the armed forces dealing with military supplies.

Or·do·vi·cian /,ôrdə'vishən/ ▶ adj. Geology relating to the second period of the Palaeozoic era (about 510 to 439 million years ago), when the first vertebrates appeared.

or·dure /'ôrjər/ ▶ n. excrement or dung.

ore /ôr/ ▶ n. a naturally occurring material from which a metal or valuable mineral can be extracted.

ø·re /'ərə/ ▶ n. (pl. same) a monetary unit of Denmark and Norway, equal to one hundredth of a krone.

ö·re /'ərə/ ▶ n. (pl. same) a monetary unit of Sweden, equal to one hundredth of a krona.

o·reg·a·no /ə'regə,nō/ ▶ n. a sweet-smelling plant whose leaves are used as an herb in cooking.

org. ▶ abbr. **1** organic. **2** organization or organized.

or·gan /'ôrgən/ ▶ n. **1** a part of an animal or plant that is adapted for a particular function, for example the heart or kidneys. **2** a large musical keyboard instrument with rows of pipes

supplied with air from bellows. **3** a smaller keyboard instrument producing similar sounds electronically. **4** a newspaper or journal that puts forward the views of a political party or movement. ■ **or·gan·ist** n.

or·gan·dy /'ôrgəndē/ (also **organdie**) ▶ n. a fine, translucent, stiff cotton muslin.

or·gan·elle /,ôrgə'nel/ ▶ n. Biology a specialized structure within a cell.

or·gan grind·er ▶ n. a street musician who plays a barrel organ.

or·gan·ic /ôr'ganik/ ▶ adj. **1** relating to or obtained from living matter. **2** not involving or produced with artificial chemicals such as fertilizers: *organic farming.* **3** (of a chemical compound) containing carbon and chiefly or ultimately of biological origin. **4** relating to or affecting an organ or organs of the body. **5** (of the parts of a whole) fitting together in a harmonious way. **6** (of development or change) continuous or natural. ▶ n. (usu. **organics**) **1** a food produced by organic farming. **2** an organic compound. ■ **or·gan·i·cal·ly** /-ik(ə)lē/ adv.

or·gan·ism /'ôrgə,nizəm/ ▶ n. **1** an individual animal, plant, or other life form. **2** a whole made up of interdependent parts.

or·gan·i·za·tion /,ôrgəni'zāshən/ ▶ n. **1** an organized group of people with a particular purpose, e.g., a business. **2** the action of organizing something. **3** a systematic arrangement or approach. ■ **or·gan·i·za·tion·al** /-shənl/ adj. **or·gan·i·za·tion·al·ly** /-shən-lē/ adv.

or·gan·ize /'ôrgə,nīz/ ▶ v. **1** arrange something in a systematic way: *the book is organized into nine thematic chapters.* **2** make arrangements or preparations for an event or activity: *social programs are organized by the school.* **3** form people into a labor union or other political group. ■ **or·gan·iz·er** n.

or·ga·no·phos·phate /,ôrgənə'fäs,fāt, ôr,ganō'-/ ▶ n. any of a group of organic compounds whose molecules contain phosphates, especially a pesticide of this kind.

or·gan·za /ôr'ganzə/ ▶ n. a thin, stiff, transparent fabric made of silk or a synthetic yarn.

or·gasm /'ôr,gazəm/ ▶ n. the climax of sexual excitement, when feelings of sexual pleasure are most intense. ▶ v. have an orgasm. ■ **or·gas·mic** /ôr'gazmik/ adj.

or·gi·as·tic /,ôrjē'astik/ ▶ adj. relating to or like an orgy.

or·gy /'ôrjē/ ▶ n. (pl. **orgies**) **1** a wild party involving a great deal of drinking and indiscriminate sexual activity. **2** an instance of engaging in a particular activity to an extreme or excessive degree: *an orgy of spending.*

o·ri·el /'ôrēəl/ ▶ n. a large upper-story bay with a window (an **oriel window**), supported by brackets or projections from the wall.

o·ri·ent ▶ n. /'ôrēənt/ (**the Orient**) literary the countries of the East, especially east Asia. ▶ adj. /'ôrē,ent/ literary oriental. ▶ v. /'ôrē,ent/ **1** align or position something in relation to the points of a compass or other specified positions. **2** (**orient oneself**) find one's position in relation to unfamiliar surroundings. **3** tailor or adapt something to particular needs or circumstances: *magazines oriented to the business community.*

o·ri·en·tal /,ôrē'entl/ ▶ adj. relating to or from the Far East. ▶ n. often offensive a person of Far Eastern descent. ■ **o·ri·en·tal·ism** /,ôrē'en(t)l,izəm/ n.

o·ri·en·tal·ist n. **o·ri·en·tal·ly** adv.

> **USAGE**
> The term **oriental** is now regarded as old-fashioned and potentially offensive as a term referring to people from the Far East. **Asian** and more specific terms such as **East Asian, Chinese,** and **Japanese** are preferred.

o·ri·en·ta·tion /ˌôrēən'tāshən/ ▶n. **1** the action of orienting someone or something. **2** the relative position or direction of something. **3** a person's basic attitude, beliefs, or feelings about something: *a bill outlawing job discrimination on the basis of sexual orientation.* ■ **o·ri·en·ta·tion·al** adj.

o·ri·en·teer·ing /ˌôrian'ti(ə)riNG/ ▶n. a competitive sport in which runners have to find their way across rough country with the aid of a map and compass. ■ **o·ri·en·teer** n. & v.

or·i·fice /'ôrəfis/ ▶n. an opening, particularly one in the body such as a nostril.

o·ri·ga·mi /ˌôrə'gämē/ ▶n. the Japanese art of folding paper into decorative shapes and figures.

or·i·gin /'ôrəjən/ ▶n. **1** the point or place where something begins: *the origin of the universe.* **2** a person's social background or ancestry: *his Italian origins.* **3** Mathematics a fixed point from which coordinates are measured.

o·rig·i·nal /ə'rijənl/ ▶adj. **1** existing from the beginning; first or earliest: *a Tudor fireplace with original oak beams.* **2** produced by an artist, author, etc.; not a copy. **3** new and different from what has been done before; inventive: *an unusual and original idea.* ▶n. the earliest form of something, from which copies can be made. ■ **o·rig·i·nal·ly** adv.

o·rig·i·nal·i·ty /ə,rijə'nalitē/ ▶n. **1** the ability to think independently or creatively. **2** the quality of being new or inventive.

o·rig·i·nal sin ▶n. (in Christian theology) the tendency to be sinful that is thought to be present in all human beings as a consequence of Adam and Eve's disobedience.

o·rig·i·nate /ə'rijə,nāt/ ▶v. **1** begin in a particular place or situation: *the word originated as a marketing term.* **2** create or initiate something. ■ **o·rig·i·na·tion** /ə,rijə'nāshən/ n. **o·rig·i·na·tor** n.

O-ring ▶n. a pliable ring with a circular cross section used to seal joints between pipes, etc.

o·ri·ole /'ôrē,ōl/ ▶n. a brightly colored bird with a musical call.

or·i·son /'ôrisən, -zən, 'är-/ ▶n. literary a prayer.

or·mo·lu /'ôrmə,lōō/ ▶n. a gold-colored alloy of copper, zinc, and tin used in decoration.

or·na·ment /'ôrnəmənt/ ▶n. **1** an object designed to make something look more attractive but usually having no practical purpose. **2** decorative items as a whole. **3** (**ornaments**) Music embellishments made to a melody. ▶v. make something more attractive by adding decorative items: *large rooms ornamented with marble and gilt columns.* ■ **or·na·men·ta·tion** /ˌôrnəmen'tāshən/ n.

or·na·men·tal /ˌôrnə'mentl/ ▶adj. acting or intended as an ornament; decorative. ▶n. a plant grown for its attractive appearance. ■ **or·na·men·tal·ly** adv.

or·nate /ôr'nāt/ ▶adj. elaborately or highly decorated. ■ **or·nate·ly** adv. **or·nate·ness** n.

or·ner·y /'ôrn(ə)rē/ ▶adj. informal bad-tempered.

or·ni·thol·o·gy /ˌôrnə'THäləjē/ ▶n. the scientific study of birds. ■ **or·ni·tho·log·i·cal** /ˌôrniTHə'läjikəl/ adj. **or·ni·thol·o·gist** n.

or·ni·thop·ter /ˌôrnə'THäptər/ ▶n. chiefly historical a flying machine with flapping wings.

o·ro·tund /'ôrə,tənd/ ▶adj. **1** (of a person's voice) resonant and impressive. **2** (of writing or style) pompous.

or·phan /'ôrfən/ ▶n. a child whose parents are dead. ▶v. (**be orphaned**) (of a child) be made an orphan.

or·phan·age /'ôrfənij/ ▶n. a residential institution where orphans are cared for.

or·pi·ment /'ôrpəmənt/ ▶n. a bright yellow mineral formerly used as a dye and artist's pigment.

or·rer·y /'ôrərē/ ▶n. (pl. **orreries**) a clockwork model of the solar system.

or·ris /'ôris/ (also **orris root**) ▶n. a preparation made from the fragrant root of a kind of iris, used in perfumery.

ortho- ▶comb.form **1** straight; rectangular; upright: *orthodontics.* **2** correct: *orthography.*

or·tho·don·tics /ˌôrTHə'däntiks/ ▶pl.n. (treated as sing.) the treatment of irregularities in the teeth and jaws. ■ **or·tho·don·tic** adj. **or·tho·don·tist** /-tist/ n.

or·tho·dox /'ôrTHə,däks/ ▶adj. **1** following traditional or generally accepted beliefs: *orthodox medical treatment.* **2** conventional or normal. **3** (**Orthodox**) relating to Orthodox Judaism or the Orthodox Church.

Or·tho·dox Church ▶n. any of the ancient branches of the Christian Church that originated in eastern Europe and the Middle East and that do not accept the authority of the Pope of Rome.

Or·tho·dox Ju·da·ism ▶n. a branch of Judaism that teaches that the requirements of Jewish law and traditional custom regarding religious and everyday life must be strictly followed.

or·tho·dox·y /'ôrTHə,däksē/ ▶n. (pl. **orthodoxies**) **1** traditional or generally accepted theories, beliefs, or practices. **2** the state of being orthodox. **3** the whole community of Orthodox Jews or Orthodox Christians.

or·thog·ra·phy /ôr'THägrəfē/ ▶n. (pl. **orthographies**) the conventional spelling system of a language. ■ **or·tho·graph·ic** /ˌôrTHə'grafik/ adj.

or·tho·pe·dics /ˌôrTHə'pēdiks/ (Brit. **orthopaedics**) ▶pl.n. (treated as sing.) the branch of medicine concerned with the correction of deformities caused by disease of or damage to bones or joints. ■ **or·tho·pe·dic** adj.

or·thot·ics /ôr'THätiks/ ▶pl.n. (treated as sing.) the branch of medicine concerned with the design and fitting of mechanical devices such as braces or splints. ■ **or·thot·ic** adj. & n.

or·to·lan /'ôrtl-ən/ ▶n. a small songbird formerly eaten as a delicacy.

Or·well·i·an /ôr'welēən/ ▶adj. relating to the work of the British novelist George Orwell, especially the totalitarian government depicted in *Nineteen Eighty-Four.*

o·ryx /'ôriks/ ▶n. a large antelope with long horns, found in arid regions of Africa and Arabia.

OS ▶abbr. **1** (in calculating dates) Old Style. **2** Computing operating system. **3** Ordinary Seaman. **4** (as a size of clothing) outsize.

Os ▸ symbol the chemical element osmium.

Os·car /'äskər/ ▸ n. trademark the nickname for a gold statuette given as an Academy Award.

os·cil·late /'äsə‚lāt/ ▸ v. 1 move or swing back and forth in a regular rhythm. 2 waver between extremes of opinion or emotion: *he was oscillating between fear and bravery.* ■ **os·cil·la·tion** /‚äsə'lāsHən/ n. **os·cil·la·tor** n. **os·cil·la·to·ry** /ə'silə‚tôrē/ adj.

os·cil·lo·scope /ə'silə‚skōp/ ▸ n. a device for showing changes in electrical current as a display on the screen of a cathode ray tube.

OSHA /'ōsHə/ ▸ abbr. Occupational Safety and Health Administration.

o·sier /'ōzHər/ ▸ n. a small willow tree with long flexible shoots used in making baskets.

os·mi·um /'äzmēəm/ ▸ n. a hard, dense silvery-white metallic element.

os·mo·reg·u·la·tion /‚äzmō‚regyə'läsHən/ ▸ n. Biology the control of water content and salt concentration in the body of an organism.

os·mo·sis /äz'mōsis, äs-/ ▸ n. 1 a process by which molecules of a solvent pass through a semipermeable membrane from a less concentrated solution into a more concentrated one. 2 the gradual absorbing of ideas or information. ■ **os·mot·ic** /-mätik/ adj.

os·prey /'äsprā, -prē/ ▸ n. (pl. **ospreys**) a large fish-eating bird of prey with a brown back and white underside.

OSS ▸ abbr. Office of Strategic Services, a US intelligence organization during World War II.

os·se·ous /'äsēəs/ ▸ adj. chiefly Zoology & Medicine consisting of or turned into bone.

os·si·cle /'äsikəl/ ▸ n. a very small bone, especially one of those that transmit sounds within the middle ear.

os·si·fy /'äsə‚fī/ ▸ v. (**ossifies, ossifying, ossified**) 1 turn into bone or bony tissue. 2 (usu. as adj. **ossified**) stop developing: *ossified political institutions.* ■ **os·si·fi·ca·tion** /‚äsəfi'käsHən/ n.

os·su·ar·y /'äsho͞o‚erē, 'äs(y)o͞o-/ ▸ n. (pl. **ossuaries**) a container or room for the bones of dead people.

os·ten·si·ble /ä'stensəbəl, ə'sten-/ ▸ adj. apparently true, but not necessarily so. ■ **os·ten·si·bly** /-blē/ adv.

os·ten·ta·tion /‚ästen'tāsHən/ ▸ n. a showy display of wealth, knowledge, etc., that is intended to impress other people.

os·ten·ta·tious /‚ästən'tāsHəs/ ▸ adj. expensive or showy in a way that is intended to impress other people: *ostentatious gold jewelry.* ■ **os·ten·ta·tious·ly** adv.

osteo- ▸ comb.form relating to the bones: *osteoporosis.*

os·te·o·ar·thri·tis /‚ästēōär'THrītis/ ▸ n. a condition in which cartilage in the joints deteriorates, causing pain and stiffness.

os·te·ol·o·gy /‚ästē'äləjē/ ▸ n. the study of the skeleton and bony structures. ■ **os·te·o·log·i·cal** /‚ästēə'läjikəl/ adj. **os·te·ol·o·gist** n.

os·te·o·my·e·li·tis /‚ästēō‚mīə'lītis/ ▸ n. inflammation of bone or bone marrow.

os·te·op·a·thy /‚ästē'äpəTHē/ ▸ n. a system of complementary medicine involving the manipulation of the bones and muscles. ■ **os·te·o·path** /'ästēə‚paTH/ n. **os·te·o·path·ic** /‚ästēə'paTHik/ adj.

os·te·o·pe·ni·a /‚ästēō'pēnēə/ ▸ n. reduced bone

mass that is less severe than osteoporosis.

os·te·o·po·ro·sis /‚ästēōpə'rōsis/ ▸ n. a medical condition in which the bones become brittle and fragile, typically as a result of hormonal changes, or lack of calcium or vitamin D.

os·ti·na·to /‚ästi'nätō/ ▸ n. (pl. **ostinatos** or **ostinati** /-tē/) a continually repeated musical phrase or rhythm.

os·tler /'äslər/ (also **hostler** /'(h)äslər/) ▸ n. historical a man employed at an inn to look after customers' horses.

os·tra·cize /'ästrə‚sīz/ ▸ v. exclude someone from a society or group; refuse to meet or speak to someone. ■ **os·tra·cism** /-‚sizəm/ n.

os·trich /'ästricH/ ▸ n. 1 a large flightless swift-running African bird with a long neck and long legs. 2 a person who refuses to accept unpleasant truths.

Os·tro·goth /'ästrə‚gäTH/ ▸ n. a member of the eastern branch of the Goths, who conquered Italy in the 5th–6th centuries AD.

OT ▸ abbr. 1 occupational therapist; occupational therapy. 2 Old Testament.

o·ta·ku /ō'täko͞o/ ▸ pl.n. (in Japan) young people who are highly skilled in or obsessed with computer technology to the detriment of their social skills.

OTC ▸ abbr. 1 over the counter. 2 (in the UK) Officers' Training Corps.

oth·er /'əTHər/ ▸ adj. & pron. 1 used to refer to a person or thing that is different from one already mentioned or known: *other people found her difficult.* 2 additional: *one other word of advice.* 3 alternative of two: *the other side of the page.* 4 those not already mentioned. – PHRASES **the other day** (or **night, week**, etc.) a few days (or nights, weeks, etc.) ago.

oth·er half ▸ n. (**one's other half**) informal one's wife, husband, or partner.

oth·er·ness /'əTHərnis/ ▸ n. the quality or fact of being different.

oth·er·wise /'əTHər‚wīz/ ▸ adv. 1 in different circumstances; or else. 2 in other respects. 3 in a different way. 4 alternatively. ▸ adj. in a different state or situation.

oth·er wom·an ▸ n. the mistress of a married man.

oth·er·world·ly ▸ adj. 1 relating to an imaginary or spiritual world. 2 not aware of the realities of life; unworldly.

o·ti·ose /'ōsHē‚ōs, 'ōtē‚ōs/ ▸ adj. serving no practical purpose; pointless.

o·ti·tis /ō'tītis/ ▸ n. inflammation of part of the ear, especially the middle ear (**otitis media**).

ot·ter /'ätər/ ▸ n. a fish-eating mammal with a long body, dense fur, and webbed feet, living partly in water and partly on land.

Ot·to·man /'ätəmən/ ▸ adj. historical 1 relating to the Turkish dynasty of Osman I (Othman I), founded in about 1300. 2 relating to the Ottoman Empire, the Turkish empire ruled by the successors of Osman I. 3 Turkish. ▸ n. (pl. **Ottomans**) a Turk, especially of the Ottoman period.

ot·to·man /'ätəmən/ ▸ n. (pl. **ottomans**) a low upholstered seat without a back or arms that can also be used as a box or chest, the seat being hinged to form a lid.

ou·bli·ette /‚o͞oblē'et/ ▸ n. a secret dungeon that can only be accessed through a trapdoor in its ceiling.

ouch /ouCH/ ▸ **exclam.** used to express pain.

ought /ôt/ ▸ **modal v.** (3rd sing. present and past **ought**) **1** used to indicate duty or correctness. **2** used to indicate something that is probable. **3** used to indicate a desirable or expected state. **4** used to give or ask advice.

> **USAGE**
> The correct way of forming negative sentences with **ought** is *he ought not to have gone.* Uses such as *he didn't ought to have gone* and *he hadn't ought to have gone* are found in dialect but are not acceptable in standard modern English.

ought·n't /ôtnt/ ▸ **contr.** ought not.

Oui·ja board /ˈwējə, -jē/ ▸ **n.** trademark a board with letters, numbers, and other signs around its edge, to which a pointer moves, supposedly in answer to questions at a seance.

ounce /ouns/ ▸ **n. 1** a unit of weight of one sixteenth of a pound avoirdupois (approximately 28 grams). **2** a unit of one twelfth of a pound troy, equal to 480 grains (approximately 31 grams). **3** a very small amount: *a girl without an ounce of ambition.*

our /ou(ə)r, är/ ▸ **possessive determiner 1** belonging to or connected with the speaker and one or more other people. **2** belonging to or associated with people in general. **3** used in formal contexts by a writer, editor, or monarch to refer to something associated with himself or herself.

Our Fa·ther ▸ **n. 1** God. **2** The Lord's Prayer.

Our La·dy ▸ **n.** the Virgin Mary.

Our Lord ▸ **n.** God or Jesus.

ours /ou(ə)rz, ärz/ ▸ **possessive pron.** used to refer to something belonging to or connected with the speaker and one or more other people.

> **USAGE**
> There is no apostrophe: the spelling should be **ours** not *our's.*

our·self /ou(ə)rˈself, är-/ ▸ **pron.** (first person pl.) used instead of 'ourselves,' typically when 'we' refers to people in general.

> **USAGE**
> The standard reflexive pronoun (a word such as 'myself' or 'himself') corresponding to **we** and **us** is **ourselves**, as in *we enjoyed ourselves.* The singular form **ourself** is sometimes used, but it is not widely accepted in standard English.

our·selves /ou(ə)rˈselvz, är-/ ▸ **pron.** (first person pl.) **1** used as the object of a verb or preposition when this is the same as the subject of the clause and the subject is the speaker and one or more other people considered together. **2** (emphatic) we or us personally.

oust /oust/ ▸ **v.** force out of a job or position of power: *three directors have been ousted from the board.*

oust·er /ˈoustər/ ▸ **n.** dismissal or expulsion from a position.

out /out/ ▸ **adv. 1** moving away from a place, especially from one that is enclosed to one that is open. **2** away from one's home or place of work. **3** outdoors. **4** so as to be revealed, heard, or known. **5** at or to an end: *the romance fizzled out.* **6** at a specified distance away from the target. **7** to sea, away from the land. **8** (of the tide) falling or at its lowest level. **9** no longer in prison. **10** (of a light or fire) so as to be extinguished or no longer burning.

▸ **prep.** through to the outside. ▸ **adj. 1** not at home or one's place of work. **2** made public or available. **3** open about one's homosexuality. **4** not possible or worth considering. **5** no longer existing or current. **6** unconscious. **7** mistaken. **8** (of the ball in tennis, squash, etc.) outside the playing area. **9** Baseball no longer batting. ▸ **v.** informal reveal that someone is homosexual.

– PHRASES **out for** intent on having: *he was out for revenge.* **out of 1** from. **2** not having a stock or supply of something. **out to do** trying hard to do something: *they were out to impress.*

> **USAGE**
> It is better to write **out of** rather than simply **out** in sentences such as *he threw it out of the window.*

out- ▸ **prefix 1** to the point of surpassing or going beyond: *outperform.* **2** external; separate; from outside: *outbuildings.* **3** away from: *outpost.*

out·age /ˈoutij/ ▸ **n.** a period when a power supply or other service is not available.

out-and-out ▸ **adj.** in every way; complete: *an out-and-out lie.*

out·back /ˈoutˌbak/ ▸ **n.** (**the outback**) the remote inland area of Australia that has very few inhabitants.

out·bid /ˌoutˈbid/ ▸ **v.** (**outbids, outbidding**; past and past part. **outbid**) bid more for something than someone else.

out·board /ˈoutˌbô(ə)rd/ ▸ **adj. & adv.** on, toward, or near the outside of a ship or aircraft. ▸ **n. 1** an outboard motor. **2** a boat with an outboard motor.

out·board mo·tor ▸ **n.** a portable motor that can be attached to the outside of a boat.

out·bound /ˈoutˈbound/ ▸ **adj. & adv.** traveling from a place rather than arriving in it.

out·break /ˈoutˌbrāk/ ▸ **n.** a sudden or violent occurrence of war, disease, etc.

out·build·ing /ˈoutˌbildiNG/ ▸ **n.** a smaller building near to but separate from a main building.

out·burst /ˈoutˌbərst/ ▸ **n. 1** a sudden release of strong emotion: *an angry outburst from the director.* **2** a sudden violent occurrence of something: *outbursts of fighting.*

out·cast /ˈoutˌkast/ ▸ **n.** a person rejected by their society or social group.

out·class /ˌoutˈklas/ ▸ **v.** be far better than someone or something.

out·come /ˈoutˌkəm/ ▸ **n.** the result or consequence of an action or event: *his remarks did not affect the outcome of the trial.*

out·crop /ˈoutˌkräp/ ▸ **n.** a part of a rock formation that is visible above the surface of the ground.

out·cry /ˈoutˌkrī/ ▸ **n.** (pl. **outcries**) a strong expression of public disapproval.

out·dat·ed /ˌoutˈdātid/ ▸ **adj.** no longer used or fashionable.

out·dis·tance /ˌoutˈdistəns/ ▸ **v.** leave a competitor or pursuer far behind.

out·do /ˌoutˈdoo/ ▸ **v.** (**outdoes** /ˌoutˈdəz/, **outdoing** /ˌoutˈdooiNG/; past **outdid** /ˌoutˈdid/; past part. **outdone** /ˌoutˈdən/) be better than someone else.

out·door /ˈoutˈdôr/ ▸ **adj. 1** done, situated, or used outdoors. **2** fond of being outdoors.

out·doors /ˌoutˈdôrz/ ▸ **adv.** in or into the open air. ▸ **n.** any area outside buildings or shelter.

out·doors·man /ˈoutˈdôrzmən/ ▸ n. (pl. **outdoorsmen**; fem. **outdoorswoman** /-ˌwŏŏmən/ pl. **outdoorswomen**) a person who spends a lot of time outdoors or doing outdoor activities.

out·er /ˈoutər/ ▸ adj. **1** outside; external. **2** further from the center or the inside.

out·er·most /ˈoutərˌmōst/ ▸ adj. furthest from the center.

out·er space ▸ n. the universe beyond the earth's atmosphere.

out·er·wear /ˈoutərˌwe(ə)r/ ▸ n. clothing worn over other clothes, especially outdoors.

out·fall /ˈoutˌfôl/ ▸ n. the place where a river, drain, or sewer empties into the sea, a river, or a lake.

out·field /ˈoutˌfēld/ ▸ n. the outer part of a baseball field.

out·fight /ˌoutˈfīt/ ▸ v. (past and past participle **outfought**) fight better than and beat (an opponent).

out·fit /ˈoutˌfit/ ▸ n. **1** a set of clothes worn together. **2** informal a group of people working together as a business, team, etc. ▸ v. (**outfits**, **outfitting**, **outfitted**) provide someone with a set of clothes, equipment, etc.

out·fit·ter /ˈoutˌfitər/ (also **outfitters**) ▸ n. a store that sells clothing and equipment, especially for outdoor activities.

out·flank /ˌoutˈflaNGk/ ▸ v. **1** move around the side of an enemy, especially so as to attack them from behind. **2** outwit someone.

out·flow /ˈoutˌflō/ ▸ n. a large amount of something that moves or is transferred out of a place.

out·fox /ˌoutˈfäks/ ▸ v. informal defeat someone by being more clever or cunning than they are.

out·gas /ˌoutˈgas/ ▸ v. (**outgases**, **outgassing**, **outgassed**) release or give off a substance as a gas or vapor.

out·go·ing /ˈoutˌgōiNG/ ▸ adj. **1** friendly and confident. **2** leaving a job or position. **3** going out or away from a place.

out·grow /ˌoutˈgrō/ ▸ v. (past **outgrew** /ˌoutˈgrōō/; past part. **outgrown** /ˌoutˈgrōn/) **1** grow too big for something. **2** stop doing or having an interest in something as one matures: *she had outgrown her collection of china kittens.* **3** grow faster or taller than someone or something else.

out·growth /ˈoutˌgrōTH/ ▸ n. **1** something that grows out of something else. **2** a natural development or result.

out·gun /ˌoutˈgən/ ▸ v. (**outguns**, **outgunning**, **outgunned**) have more or better weapons than another person or group.

out·house /ˈoutˌhous/ ▸ n. a small building containing a toilet, typically with no plumbing.

out·ing /ˈoutiNG/ ▸ n. **1** a short trip taken for pleasure. **2** informal an occasion when a competitor takes part in a sporting event, or an actor appears in a movie, play, etc.: *an actress in her first screen outing.* **3** the practice of revealing someone's homosexuality.

out·land·ish /outˈlandiSH/ ▸ adj. extremely unusual or unconventional; bizarre.

out·last /ˌoutˈlast/ ▸ v. last longer than: *the kind of beauty that will outlast youth.*

out·law /ˈoutˌlô/ ▸ n. **1** a person who has broken the law, especially one who has escaped captivity or is in hiding. **2** historical a person who has been deprived of legal rights or protection. ▸ v. **1** make

something illegal: *secondary picketing has been outlawed.* **2** historical deprive someone of legal rights or protection. ■ **out·law·ry** /-ˌlôrē/ n.

out·lay /ˈoutˌlā/ ▸ n. an amount of money spent.

out·let /ˈoutˌlet/ ▸ n. **1** a pipe or hole through which water or gas may escape. **2** a point from which goods are sold or distributed: *a fast-food outlet.* **3** a retail store offering discounted merchandise. **4** a means of expressing one's talents, energy, or emotions: *boxing provided a perfect outlet for his aggression.* **5** the mouth of a river. **6** an electrical output socket.

out·li·er /ˈoutˌlīər/ ▸ n. **1** a thing that is separate or detached from a main body or system. **2** a younger rock formation among older rocks.

out·line /ˈoutˌlīn/ ▸ n. **1** a drawing or diagram showing the shape of an object. **2** the contours or outer edges of an object. **3** a brief description of the main points of something. ▸ v. **1** draw or define the outer edge or shape of something. **2** give a summary of: *she outlined the case briefly.*

out·live /ˌoutˈliv/ ▸ v. live or last longer than someone or something else.

out·look /ˈoutˌlŏŏk/ ▸ n. **1** a person's point of view or attitude to life. **2** a view. **3** what is likely to happen in the future.

out·ly·ing /ˈoutˌlī-iNG/ ▸ adj. situated far from a center.

out·man /ˌoutˈman/ ▸ v. (**outmans, outmanning, outmanned**) (usu. as adj. **outmanned**) **1** outnumber: *the rebels are outmanned.* **2** overpower with skill or physical strength.

out·ma·neu·ver /ˌoutməˈnōōvər/ ▸ v. evade or gain an advantage over an opponent by using skill and cunning.

out·match /ˌoutˈmaCH/ ▸ v. be better than someone or something else.

out·mod·ed /ˌoutˈmōdid/ ▸ adj. old-fashioned.

out·num·ber /ˌoutˈnəmbər/ ▸ v. be more numerous than: *women outnumbered men by three to one.*

out-of-bod·y ex·pe·ri·ence ▸ n. a sensation of being outside one's body, typically of observing oneself from a distance.

out of date ▸ adj. **1** old-fashioned. **2** no longer valid.

out·pace /ˌoutˈpās/ ▸ v. go, rise, or improve faster than someone or something else.

out·pa·tient /ˈoutˌpāSHənt/ ▸ n. a patient who goes to a hospital for treatment without staying overnight.

out·per·form /ˌoutpərˈfôrm/ ▸ v. perform better than someone or something else.

out·place·ment /ˈoutplāsmənt/ ▸ n. the action of helping workers who have been laid off find new employment.

out·play /ˌoutˈplā/ ▸ v. play better than another person or team.

out·post /ˈoutˌpōst/ ▸ n. **1** a small military camp at a distance from the main army. **2** a remote part of a country or empire.

out·pour·ing /ˈoutˌpôriNG/ ▸ n. **1** something that streams out rapidly. **2** an outburst of strong emotion: *an outpouring of grief.*

out·put /ˈoutˌpŏŏt/ ▸ n. **1** the amount of something produced. **2** the process of producing something. **3** the power, energy, etc., supplied by a device or system. **4** Electronics a place where power or information leaves a system. ▸ v. (**outputting**; past and past part. **output** or

outputted) (of a computer) produce data.

out·rage /'out͟rāj/ ▸ n. **1** an extremely strong reaction of anger, shock, or indignation. **2** an extremely cruel, wicked, or shocking act: *some of the worst terrorist outrages.* ▸ v. make someone feel extremely angry, shocked, or indignant.

out·ra·geous /out'rājəs/ ▸ adj. **1** shockingly bad or unacceptable: *an outrageous waste of time and money.* **2** very unusual and slightly shocking: *her outrageous costumes.* ■ **out·ra·geous·ly** adv. **out·ra·geous·ness** n.

out·ran /ˌout'ran/ ▸ past of OUTRUN.

out·rank /ˌout'raNGk/ ▸ v. **1** have a higher rank than someone else. **2** be better or more important than something else.

ou·tré /o͞o'trā/ ▸ adj. unusual and startling.

out·reach /'out͟rēCH/ ▸ n. an organization's involvement with the community, especially in the context of social welfare.

out·rid·er /'out͟rīdər/ ▸ n. a person in a vehicle or on horseback who escorts or guards another vehicle.

out·rig·ger /'out͟rigər/ ▸ n. **1** a spar or framework projecting from or over a boat's side. **2** a float fixed parallel to a canoe or other boat to help keep it stable. **3** a boat fitted with an outrigger.

out·right /'out͟rīt/ ▸ adv. **1** altogether: *unions rejected the offer outright.* **2** in an open and direct way. **3** immediately or instantly. ▸ adj. **1** open and direct: *an outright refusal.* **2** complete and total: *an outright ban.*

out·run /ˌout'rən/ ▸ v. (**outruns, outrunning**; past **outran** /ˌout'ran/; past part. **outrun**) **1** run or travel faster or farther than someone or something else. **2** go beyond or exceed something.

out·sell /ˌout'sel/ ▸ v. (past and past part. **outsold**) be sold in greater quantities than another product.

out·set /'out͟set/ ▸ n. the start or beginning.

out·shine /ˌout'SHīn/ ▸ v. (past and past part. **outshone** /ˌout'SHòn/) **1** shine more brightly than something else. **2** be much better than: *his technical expertise far outshone that of his rivals.*

out·shoot /ˌout'SHo͞ot/ ▸ v. (past and past participle **outshot**) **1** shoot better than (someone else). **2** Sports make or take more shots than (another player or team).

out·side /'out͟sīd/ ▸ n. **1** the external side or surface of something. **2** the external appearance of someone or something. **3** the side of a bend or curve where the edge is longer. ▸ adj. **1** situated on or near the outside. **2** not of or belonging to a particular group, organization, etc.: *outside contractors.* **3** (in soccer, etc.) referring to positions nearer to the sides of the field. ▸ prep. & adv. **1** situated or moving beyond the boundaries of something. **2** (in football, soccer, etc.) closer to the side of the field than. **3** beyond the limits or scope of something. **4** not being a member of a particular group.
– PHRASES **at the outside** at the most. **an outside chance** a remote possibility.

out·side in·ter·est ▸ n. an interest not connected with one's work or studies.

out·sid·er /ˌout'sīdər/ ▸ n. **1** a person who does not belong to a particular group. **2** a competitor thought to have little chance of success.

out·size /ˌout'sīz/ ▸ adj. (also **outsized**) exceptionally large.

out·skirts /'out͟skərts/ ▸ pl.n. the outer parts of a town or city.

out·smart /ˌout'smärt/ ▸ v. defeat or get the better of someone by being clever or cunning.

out·sold /ˌout'sōld/ ▸ past and past participle of OUTSELL.

out·sole /'out͟sōl/ ▸ n. the outer sole of a boot or shoe.

out·source /'out͟sôrs/ ▸ v. **1** obtain goods from an outside supplier. **2** arrange for work to be done outside one's own company.

out·spo·ken /ˌout'spōkən/ ▸ adj. (of a person or alterance) frank and direct. ■ **out·spok·en·ness** n.

out·spread /ˌout'spred/ ▸ adj. extended or stretched out as far as possible.

out·stand·ing /ˌout'standiNG, 'out-/ ▸ adj. **1** exceptionally good. **2** clearly noticeable. **3** not yet dealt with or paid. ■ **out·stand·ing·ly** adv.

out·sta·tion /'out͟stāSHən/ ▸ n. a branch of an organization situated far from its headquarters.

out·stay /ˌout'stā/ ▸ v. stay somewhere for longer than the expected or permitted time.

out·stretched /ˌout'strecHt, ˌout'strecHd/ ▸ adj. extended or stretched out.

out·strip /ˌout'strip/ ▸ v. (**outstrips, outstripping, outstripped**) **1** move faster than and overtake someone or something else. **2** exceed or go beyond: *demand is outstripping supply.* **3** be better than: *the company outstripped its competitors.*

out·ta /'outə/ (also **outa**) ▸ prep. an informal contraction of "out of," used in representing colloquial speech: *we'd better get outta here.*

out·take /'out͟tāk/ ▸ n. a scene or sequence filmed or recorded for a movie or program but not included in the final version.

out·vote /ˌout'vōt/ ▸ v. defeat someone or something by winning a larger number of votes.

out·ward /'outwərd/ ▸ adj. **1** of, on, or from the outside. **2** going out or away from a place. ▸ adv. (also **outwards**) toward the outside. ■ **out·ward·ly** adv.

out·weigh /ˌout'wā/ ▸ v. be heavier, greater, or more significant than: *the advantages greatly outweigh the disadvantages.*

out·wit /ˌout'wit/ ▸ v. (**outwits, outwitting, outwitted**) defeat or gain an advantage over someone as a result of greater cleverness or ingenuity.

out·work /'out͟wərk/ ▸ n. an outer section of a fortification. ■ **out·work·er** n.

ou·zo /'o͞ozō/ ▸ n. an anise-flavored Greek liqueur.

o·va /'ōvə/ ▸ plural of OVUM.

o·val /'ōvəl/ ▸ adj. having a rounded and slightly elongated outline; egg-shaped. ▸ n. **1** an oval object or design. **2** an oval sports field or track.

O·val Of·fice ▸ n. the office of the US president in the White House.

o·var·i·an /ō've(ə)rēən/ ▸ adj. relating to the ovaries.

o·va·ry /'ōv(ə)rē/ ▸ n. (pl. **ovaries**) **1** a female reproductive organ in which eggs or ova are produced. **2** the base of the reproductive organ of a flower, containing one or more ovules.

o·vate /'ō͟vāt/ ▸ adj. oval; egg-shaped.

o·va·tion /ō'vāSHən/ ▸ n. a long and enthusiastic round of applause.

ov·en /'əvən/ ▸ n. **1** an enclosed compartment in which food is cooked or heated. **2** a small furnace or kiln.

ov·en·proof /'əvən,prŏŏf/ ▸ adj. suitable for use in an oven.

ov·en·read·y ▸ adj. (of food) sold as a prepared dish, ready for cooking in an oven.

o·ver /'ōvər/ ▸ prep. **1** extending upward from or above. **2** above so as to cover or protect. **3** expressing movement or a route across. **4** beyond and falling or hanging from. **5** expressing length of time. **6** at a higher level, layer, or intensity than. **7** higher or more than. **8** expressing authority or control. **9** on the subject of. ▸ adv. **1** expressing movement or a route across an area. **2** beyond and falling or hanging from a point. **3** in or to the place indicated. **4** expressing action and result: *the car flipped over.* **5** finished. **6** expressing repetition of a process.
– PHRASES **be over** be no longer affected by something. **over and above** in addition to.

over- ▸ prefix **1** excessively: *overambitious.* **2** completely: *overjoyed.* **3** upper; outer; extra: *overcoat.* **4** over; above: *overcast.*

o·ver·a·chieve /,ōvərə'cHēv/ ▸ v. **1** do better than expected. **2** be excessively dedicated to the achievement of success. ■ **o·ver·a·chieve·ment** n. **o·ver·a·chiev·er** n.

o·ver·act /,ōvər'akt/ ▸ v. act a role in a play or movie in an exaggerated way.

o·ver·ac·tive /,ōvər'aktiv/ ▸ adj. more active than is normal or desirable. ■ **o·ver·ac·tiv·i·ty** /,ōvərak'tivətē/ n.

o·ver·all /'ōvər,äl/ ▸ adj. taking everything into account; total. ▸ adv. taken as a whole. ▸ n. (**overalls**) a garment consisting of pants with a front flap over the chest held up by straps over the shoulders.

o·ver·am·bi·tious /,ōvəram'bisHəs/ ▸ adj. too ambitious.

o·ver·arch /,ōvər'ärcH/ ▸ v. **1** form an arch over something. **2** (as adj. **overarching**) covering or dealing with everything: *a single overarching principle.*

o·ver·arm /'ōvər,ärm/ ▸ adj. & adv. done with the arm moving above the level of the shoulder.

o·ver·ate /,ōvər'et/ ▸ past of OVEREAT.

o·ver·awe /,ōvər'ô/ ▸ v. impress someone so much that they are silent or nervous.

o·ver·bal·ance /,ōvər'baləns/ ▸ v. fall or cause to fall due to loss of balance.

o·ver·bear·ing /,ōvər'be(ə)riNG/ ▸ adj. trying to impose one's views or control other people in a forceful and unpleasant way.

o·ver·bite /'ōvər,bīt/ ▸ n. the overlapping of the lower teeth by the upper.

o·ver·blown /,ōvər'blōn/ ▸ adj. **1** made to seem more important or impressive than is really the case: *an overblown action thriller.* **2** (of a flower) past its prime.

o·ver·board /'ōvər,bôrd/ ▸ adv. from a ship into the water.
– PHRASES **go overboard 1** be very enthusiastic. **2** react in an extreme way.

o·ver·book /,ōvər'bŏŏk/ ▸ v. accept more reservations for a flight or hotel than there is room for.

o·ver·bur·den /,ōvər'bərdn/ ▸ v. give someone or something more work or pressure than it is possible to deal with.

o·ver·came /ōvər'kām/ ▸ past of OVERCOME.

o·ver·ca·pac·i·ty /,ōvərkə'pasitē/ ▸ n. a situation in which an industry or factory cannot sell as much as it is designed to produce.

o·ver·cast /'ōvər,kast, ,ōvər'kast/ ▸ adj. (of the sky or weather) cloudy; dull.

o·ver·cau·tious /,ōvər'kôsHəs/ ▸ adj. excessively cautious.

o·ver·charge /,ōvər'cHärj/ ▸ v. charge someone too high a price for something.

o·ver·class /'ōvər,klas/ ▸ n. often derogatory a privileged, wealthy, or powerful section of society.

o·ver·coat /'ōvər,kōt/ ▸ n. **1** a long warm coat. **2** a top layer of paint or varnish.

o·ver·come /,ōvər'kəm/ ▸ v. (past **overcame** /,ōvər'kām/; past part. **overcome**) **1** succeed in dealing with a problem. **2** defeat an opponent. **3** (of an emotion) overwhelm: *she was overcome with excitement.*

o·ver·com·mit /,ōvərkə'mit/ ▸ v. (**overcommits, overcommitting, overcommitted**) (**overcommit oneself**) undertake to do more than one is capable of doing.

o·ver·com·pen·sate /,ōvər'kämpən,sāt/ ▸ v. do something that is too extreme in an attempt to correct a problem. ■ **o·ver·com·pen·sa·tion** /'ōvər,kämpən'sāsHən/ n.

o·ver·con·fi·dent /,ōvər'känfidənt/ ▸ adj. excessively confident. ■ **o·ver·con·fi·dence** n.

o·ver·cook /,ōvər'kŏŏk/ ▸ v. cook food for too long.

o·ver·crowd·ed /,ōvər'kroudid/ ▸ adj. filled with more people or things than is usual or comfortable. ■ **o·ver·crowd·ing** n.

o·ver·de·ter·mine /,ōvərdi'tərmən/ ▸ v. formal determine or account for something in more than one way or with more conditions than are necessary. ■ **o·ver·de·ter·mi·na·tion** /'ōvərdi,tərmə'nāsHən/ n.

o·ver·de·vel·op /,ōvərdə'veləp/ ▸ v. (**overdevelops, overdeveloping, overdeveloped**) develop something too much. ■ **o·ver·de·vel·op·ment** n.

o·ver·do /,ōvər'dŏŏ/ ▸ v. (**overdoes** /,ōvər'dəz/, **overdoing** /,ōvər'dŏŏiNG/, **overdid** /,ōvər'did/; past part. **overdone** /,ōvər'dən/) **1** do something excessively or in an exaggerated way. **2** use too much of: *I'd overdone the garlic in the curry.* **3** (**overdo it/things**) exhaust oneself. **4** (as adj. **overdone**) overcooked.

o·ver·dose /'ōvər,dōs/ ▸ n. an excessive and dangerous dose of a drug. ▸ v. take an overdose. ■ **o·ver·dos·age** n.

o·ver·draft /'ōvər,draft/ ▸ n. a deficit in a bank account caused by drawing more money than the account holds.

o·ver·dram·a·tize /,ōvər'dramə,tīz, -'dramə-/ ▸ v. react to or portray something in an excessively dramatic way. ■ **o·ver·dra·mat·ic** /-drə'matik/ adj.

o·ver·drawn /,ōvər'drôn/ ▸ adj. **1** (of a bank account) in a state in which more money has been taken out than the account holds. **2** having an overdrawn bank account.

o·ver·dressed /,ōvər'drest, ,ōvər'dresd/ ▸ adj. wearing clothes that are too elaborate or formal for a particular occasion.

o·ver·drive /'ōvər,drīv/ ▸ n. **1** a mechanism in a motor vehicle providing an extra gear above the usual top gear. **2** a state of great or excessive activity: *my heart had gone into overdrive.* ■ **o·ver·driv·en** /'ōvər,drivən/ adj.

o·ver·due /,ōvər'd(y)ŏŏ/ ▸ adj. not having arrived,

happened, or been done at the expected or required time.

o·ver·ea·ger /ˌōvər'ēgər/ ▶ adj. excessively eager.

o·ver·eat /ˌōvər'ēt/ ▶ v. (past **overate** /ˌōvər'āt/; past part. **overeaten**) eat too much.

o·ver·e·lab·o·rate /ˌōvəri'lab(ə)rit/ ▶ adj. excessively elaborate.

o·ver·e·mo·tion·al /ˌōvəri'mōsHənl/ ▶ adj. excessively emotional.

o·ver·em·pha·size /ˌōvər'emfəˌsīz/ ▶ v. place excessive emphasis or importance on something. ■ **o·ver·em·pha·sis** /ˌōvər'emfəˌsis/ n.

o·ver·en·thu·si·as·tic /ˌōvərenˌTHŌŌzē'astik/ ▶ adj. excessively enthusiastic. ■ **o·ver·en·thu·si·asm** /ˌōvərenˌTHŌŌzēˌazəm/ n.

o·ver·es·ti·mate /ˌōvər'estəˌmāt/ ▶ v. estimate as better or greater than in reality: *has the record company overestimated the popularity of these new stars?* ▶ n. an excessively high estimate. ■ **o·ver·es·ti·ma·tion** /ˌōvərˌestə'māsHən/ n.

o·ver·ex·cit·ed /ˌōvərik'sītid/ ▶ adj. too excited to behave sensibly. ■ **o·ver·ex·cit·a·ble** adj. **o·ver·ex·cite·ment** n.

o·ver·ex·ert /ˌōvərig'zərt/ ▶ v. (**overexert oneself**) exhaust oneself by making too much physical effort. ■ **o·ver·ex·er·tion** /ˌōvərig'zərsHən/ n.

o·ver·ex·pose /ˌōvərik'spōz/ ▶ v. 1 subject photographic film to too much light. 2 (as adj. **overexposed**) seen too much on television, in the newspapers, etc. ■ **o·ver·ex·po·sure** /-ik'spōzHər/ n.

o·ver·ex·tend /ˌōvərik'stend/ ▶ v. 1 involve someone in excessive work or financial commitments: *the major chains overextended themselves in the 1980s.* 2 make something too long.

o·ver·fa·mil·iar /ˌōvərfə'milyər/ ▶ adj. 1 too well known. 2 behaving or speaking in an inappropriately informal way. ■ **o·ver·fa·mil·i·ar·i·ty** /-fəˌmilē'aritē/ n.

o·ver·feed /ˌōvər'fēd/ ▶ v. (past and past part. **overfed** /ˌōvər'fed/) feed someone or something too much.

o·ver·fill /ˌōvər'fil/ ▶ v. put more into a container than there is room for.

o·ver·fish /ˌōvər'fisH/ ▶ v. take too many fish from the sea or a river or lake, greatly reducing the stock.

o·ver·flow /ˌōvər'flō/ ▶ v. 1 flow over the brim of a container. 2 be excessively full or crowded. 3 (**overflow with**) be very full of an emotion. ▶ n. 1 the overflowing of a liquid. 2 the people or things that do not fit into a particular space. 3 (also **overflow pipe**) an outlet for excess water.

o·ver·fly /ˌōvər'flī/ ▶ v. (**overflies**; past **overflew**; past participle **overflown**) fly over a place or territory. ■ **o·ver·flight** /'ōvərˌflīt/ n.

o·ver·gar·ment /'ōvərˌgärmənt/ ▶ n. an item of clothing worn over others.

o·ver·gen·er·al·ize /ˌōvər'jen(ə)rəˌlīz/ ▶ v. express something in a way that is too general.

o·ver·gen·er·ous /ˌōvər'jen(ə)rəs/ ▶ adj. excessively generous.

o·ver·graze /ˌōvər'grāz/ ▶ v. graze grassland too heavily.

o·ver·ground /'ōvərˌground/ ▶ adv. & adj. on or above the ground.

o·ver·grown /ˌōvər'grōn/ ▶ adj. 1 covered with plants that have been allowed to grow wild. 2 having grown too large.

o·ver·growth /'ōvərˌgrōTH/ ▶ n. excessive growth of something.

o·ver·hand /'ōvərˌhand/ ▶ adj. & adv. (of a throw or stroke with a racket) made with the hand passing above the level of the shoulder.

o·ver·hang /ˌōvər'haNG/ ▶ v. (past and past part. **overhung** /ˌōvər'həNG/) hang outward over something. ▶ n. a part that hangs outward over something.

o·ver·haul /ˌōvər'hôl/ ▶ v. 1 examine and repair equipment or machinery. 2 analyze and improve a system or process. ▶ n. a thorough examination of machinery or a system, with repairs or changes made if necessary.

o·ver·head /'ōvər'hed/ ▶ adv. above the head. ▶ adj. 1 situated above the head. 2 (of a garage door) opened by being raised and pushed back into a horizontal position. 3 (of a driving mechanism) above the object driven. ▶ n. 1 the regular expenses involved in running a business or organization, such as rent, electricity, wages, etc. 2 a transparency for use with an overhead projector.

o·ver·head pro·jec·tor ▶ n. a device that projects an enlarged image of a transparency by means of an overhead mirror.

o·ver·hear /ˌōvər'hi(ə)r/ ▶ v. (past and past part. **overheard** /ˌōvər'hərd/) hear someone or something accidentally or secretly.

o·ver·heat /ˌōvər'hēt/ ▶ v. 1 make or become too hot. 2 (of a country's economy) show marked inflation when increased demand results in rising prices.

o·ver·hung /ˌōvər'həNG/ ▶ past and past participle of **OVERHANG**.

o·ver·hype /ˌōvər'hīp/ ▶ v. informal make exaggerated claims about the good qualities of a product, idea, or event, in order to get public attention.

o·ver·in·dulge /ˌōvərin'dəlj/ ▶ v. 1 have too much of something enjoyable. 2 give in to someone's wishes too readily. ■ **o·ver·in·dul·gence** n. **o·ver·in·dul·gent** adj.

o·ver·in·flat·ed /ˌōvərin'flātid/ ▶ adj. 1 (of a price or value) excessive. 2 exaggerated: *overinflated claims.* 3 filled with too much air.

o·ver·joyed /ˌōvər'joid/ ▶ adj. very happy.

o·ver·kill /'ōvərˌkil/ ▶ n. too much of something: *the heavy security has raised concerns of overkill.*

o·ver·lad·en /ˌōvər'lādn/ ▶ adj. carrying too large a load.

o·ver·laid /ˌōvər'lād/ ▶ past and past participle of **OVERLAY**[1].

o·ver·lain /ˌōvər'lān/ ▶ past participle of **OVERLIE**.

o·ver·land /'ōvərˌland/ ▶ adj. & adv. by land.

o·ver·lap /ˌōvər'lap/ ▶ v. (**overlaps, overlapping, overlapped**) 1 extend over something so as to partly cover it. 2 (of two events) occur at the same time for part of their duration. 3 cover part of the same area of interest or responsibility: *the union's commitments overlapped with those of NATO.* ▶ n. 1 an overlapping part or amount. 2 a common area of interest or responsibility.

o·ver·large /ˌōvər'lärj/ ▶ adj. too large.

o·ver·lay[1] /ˌōvər'lā/ ▶ v. (past and past part. **overlaid** /ˌōvər'lād/) 1 coat the surface of something. 2 (of a quality or feeling) become more noticeable than a previous one: *the concern in his voice* *was overlaid with annoyance.* ▶ n. /'ōvər‚lā/ **1** a covering. **2** a transparent sheet over artwork or a map, giving additional detail.

o·ver·lay² ▶ past of OVERLIE.

o·ver·leaf /'ōvər‚lēf/ ▶ adv. on the other side of the page.

o·ver·lie /‚ōvər'lī/ ▶ v. (**overlies, overlying** /'ōvər'lī-iNG/, **overlay** /‚ōvər'lā/; past part. **overlain** /‚ōvər'lān/) lie on top of something.

o·ver·load /‚ōvər'lōd/ ▶ v. **1** load something too heavily. **2** put too great a demand on: *the staff is heavily overloaded with work.* ▶ n. an excessive amount.

o·ver·lock /‚ōvər'läk/ ▶ v. prevent fraying of an edge of cloth by oversewing it. ■ **o·ver·lock·er** n.

o·ver·long /'ōvər'lônG, -'länG/ ▶ adj. & adv. too long.

o·ver·look /'ōvər'lŏŏk/ ▶ v. **1** fail to notice: *she's overlooked one important fact.* **2** choose to ignore a fault or wrongdoing. **3** have a view of something from above.

o·ver·lord /'ōvər‚lôrd/ ▶ n. a person who rules or controls many people.

o·ver·ly /'ōvərlē/ ▶ adv. excessively; too.

o·ver·ly·ing /'ōvər'lī-iNG/ ▶ present participle of OVERLIE.

o·ver·man /‚ōvər'man/ ▶ v. (**overmans, overmanning, overmanned**) provide an organization with more employees than necessary.

o·ver·man·tel /'ōvər‚mantl/ ▶ n. an ornamental structure over a mantelpiece.

o·ver·mas·ter /‚ōvər'mastər/ ▶ v. literary overcome someone or something.

o·ver·much /'ōvər'məCH/ ▶ adv., determiner, & pron. too much.

o·ver·night /'ōvər'nīt/ ▶ adv. **1** for the duration of a night. **2** during a night. **3** very quickly. ▶ adj. **1** done, happening, or for use overnight. **2** very quick; instant: *Tom became an overnight celebrity.* ▶ v. **1** stay in a place overnight. **2** ship something for delivery the next day. ■ **o·ver·night·er** n.

o·ver·op·ti·mis·tic /‚ōvər‚optə'mistik/ ▶ adj. having a feeling of optimism about something that is unlikely to be justified.

o·ver·paint /‚ōvər'pānt/ ▶ v. cover something with paint.

o·ver·pass /'ōvər‚pas/ ▶ n. a bridge by which a road or railroad passes over another.

o·ver·pay /‚ōvər'pā/ ▶ v. (past and past part. **overpaid**) pay someone too much. ■ **o·ver·pay·ment** n.

o·ver·play /‚ōvər'plā/ ▶ v. give too much importance or emphasis to something. – PHRASES **overplay one's hand** spoil one's chance of success by being too confident.

o·ver·pop·u·lat·ed /‚ōvər'päpyə‚lātid/ ▶ adj. (of an area or city) having too many people living in it. ■ **o·ver·pop·u·la·tion** /'ōvər‚päpyə'lāsHən/ n.

o·ver·pow·er /‚ōvər'pou(-ə)r/ ▶ v. **1** defeat someone with superior strength. **2** have an overwhelming effect on: *he was overpowered by the fumes.* ■ **o·ver·pow·er·ing** adj.

o·ver·priced /‚ōvər'prīsd/ ▶ adj. too expensive.

o·ver·print ▶ v. /‚ōvər'print/ print additional matter on a stamp or other surface already bearing print: *menus will be overprinted with company logos.*

o·ver·pro·duce /‚ōvərprə'd(y)ōōs/ ▶ v. **1** produce too much of something. **2** record or produce a song or movie in an excessively elaborate way. ■ **o·ver·pro·duc·tion** /-'dəksHən/ n.

o·ver·pro·tec·tive /‚ōvərprə'tektiv/ ▶ adj. excessively protective.

o·ver·qual·i·fied /‚ōvər'kwôlə‚fīd/ ▶ adj. too highly qualified.

o·ver·ran /‚ōvər'ran/ ▶ past of OVERRUN.

o·ver·rate /‚ōvər'rāt/ ▶ v. (often as adj. **overrated**) have too high an opinion of someone or something.

o·ver·reach /‚ōvər'rēCH/ ▶ v. (**overreach oneself**) fail as a result of being too ambitious or trying too hard.

o·ver·re·act /‚ōvər-rē'akt/ ▶ v. react to something more strongly or emotionally than is justified. ■ **o·ver·re·ac·tion** /-rē'aksHən/ n.

o·ver·ride /‚ōvər'rīd/ ▶ v. (past **overrode** /‚ōvər'rōd/; past part. **overridden** /‚ōvər'ridn/) **1** use one's authority to reject or cancel another's decision or order. **2** be more important than: *teachers' professionalism should override personal feelings.* **3** interrupt the action of an automatic device. ▶ n. a device on a machine for overriding an automatic process. ■ **o·ver·rid·ing** adj.

o·ver·ripe /‚ōvər'rīp/ ▶ adj. too ripe.

o·ver·rule /‚ōvər'rōōl/ ▶ v. use one's superior authority to reverse or disallow another's decision or order.

o·ver·run /‚ōvər'rən/ ▶ v. (**overruns, overrunning, overran** /‚ōvər'ran/; past part. **overrun**) **1** spread over or occupy a place in large numbers. **2** go beyond a set time, cost, or limit.

o·ver·seas /'ōvər'sēz/ ▶ adv. in or to a foreign country. ▶ adj. relating to a foreign country.

o·ver·see /‚ōvər'sē/ ▶ v. (**oversees, overseeing, oversaw** /‚ōvər'sô/; past part. **overseen**) supervise a person or their work. ■ **o·ver·se·er** /'ōvər‚si(ə)r, -‚sēər/ n.

o·ver·sell /‚ōvər'sel/ ▶ v. (past and past part. **oversold** /‚ōvər'sōld/) **1** exaggerate the quality or worth of someone or something. **2** sell more of something than is available.

o·ver·sen·si·tive /‚ōvər'sensitiv/ ▶ adj. excessively sensitive. ■ **o·ver·sen·si·tiv·i·ty** n.

o·ver·sexed /‚ōvər'sekst/ ▶ adj. having unusually strong sexual desires.

o·ver·shad·ow /‚ōvər'sHadō/ ▶ v. **1** appear more important or successful than: *he was overshadowed by his brilliant brother.* **2** cast gloom over something. **3** tower above and cast a shadow over something.

o·ver·shirt /'ōvər‚sHərt/ ▶ n. a loose shirt worn over other clothes.

o·ver·shoe /'ōvər‚sHōō/ ▶ n. a protective shoe worn over a normal shoe.

o·ver·shoot /‚ōvər'sHōōt/ ▶ v. (past and past part. **overshot**) **1** accidentally go past an intended stopping or turning point. **2** exceed a financial target or limit.

o·ver·sight /'ōvər‚sīt/ ▶ n. an unintentional failure to notice or do something.

o·ver·sim·pli·fy /‚ōvər'simplə‚fī/ ▶ v. (**oversimplifies, oversimplifying, oversimplified**) simplify something so much that an inaccurate impression is given. ■ **o·ver·sim·pli·fi·ca·tion** /'ōvər‚simpləfi'kāsHən/ n.

o·ver·sized /'ōvər‚sīzd/ (also **oversize**) ▶ adj. bigger than the usual size.

o·ver·skirt /'ōvər‚skərt/ ▶ n. an outer skirt, worn over the skirt of a dress.

o·ver·sleep /ˌōvərˈslēp/ ▶ v. (past and past part. **overslept** /ˌōvərˈslept/) sleep longer or later than one intended.

o·ver·sold /ˌōvərˈsōld/ ▶ past and past participle of OVERSELL.

o·ver·spe·cial·ize /ˌōvərˈspeshəˌlīz/ ▶ v. concentrate too much on one aspect of something. ■ **o·ver·spe·cial·i·za·tion** /ˌōvərˌspeshəliˈzāshən/ n.

o·ver·spend /ˌōvərˈspend/ ▶ v. (past and past part. **overspent**) spend too much.

o·ver·spill /ˈōvərˌspil/ ▶ n. Brit. part of the population of a city or town moving from an overcrowded area to live elsewhere.

o·ver·staffed /ˌōvərˈstaft/ ▶ adj. having more employees than are necessary.

o·ver·state /ˌōvərˈstāt/ ▶ v. state something too strongly; exaggerate something. ■ **o·ver·state·ment** n.

o·ver·stay /ˌōvərˈstā/ ▶ v. stay longer than an allowed or expected time.

o·ver·steer /ˌōvərˈsti(ə)r/ ▶ v. (of a vehicle) turn more sharply than is desirable.

o·ver·step /ˌōvərˈstep/ ▶ v. (**oversteps, overstepping, overstepped**) go beyond a set or accepted limit.
– PHRASES **overstep the mark** behave in an unacceptable way.

o·ver·stim·u·late /ˌōvərˈstimyəˌlāt/ ▶ v. stimulate someone or something excessively. ■ **o·ver·stim·u·la·tion** /ˈōvərˌstimyəˈlāshən/ n.

o·ver·stock /ˌōvərˈstäk/ ▶ v. stock something with more of something than is necessary or required. ▶ n. a supply or quantity that exceeds demand.

o·ver·strain /ˌōvərˈstrān/ ▶ v. place too much strain on someone or something.

o·ver·stress /ˌōvərˈstres/ ▶ v. 1 cause too much stress to someone or something. 2 lay too much emphasis on something.

o·ver·stretch /ˈōvərˌstrechˈ/ ▶ v. 1 make excessive demands on: *classes are large and facilities are overstretched.* 2 stretch something too much.

o·ver·stuffed /ˌōvərˈstaft/ ▶ adj. 1 (of a container) excessively full. 2 (of furniture) covered completely with padded upholstery.

o·ver·sub·scribed /ˌōvərsəbˈskrībd/ ▶ adj. 1 (of something for sale) applied for in greater quantities than are available. 2 chiefly Brit. (of a course, college, etc.) having more applications than available places.

o·ver·sup·ply /ˈōvərsəˌplī/ ▶ n. (pl. **oversupplies**) an excessive supply of something.
▶ v. (**oversupplies, oversupplying, oversupplied**) supply with too much or too many of something: *the country was oversupplied with lawyers.*

o·vert /ōˈvərt, ˈōvərt/ ▶ adj. done or shown openly: *an overt act of aggression.* ■ **o·vert·ly** adv. **o·vert·ness** n.

o·ver·take /ˌōvərˈtāk/ ▶ v. (past **overtook** /ˌōvərˈto͝ok/; past part. **overtaken**) 1 catch up with and pass someone while traveling in the same direction. 2 become greater or more successful than someone or something. 3 suddenly affect: *weariness overtook him.*

o·ver·tax /ˌōvərˈtaks/ ▶ v. 1 make excessive demands on a person's strength or abilities. 2 require people to pay too much tax.

o·ver·throw /ˌōvərˈᴛʜrō/ ▶ v. (past **overthrew** /ˌōvərˈᴛʜro͞o/; past part. **overthrown**) 1 forcibly

remove someone from power. 2 put an end to something through force. ▶ n. the forcible removal of someone from power.

o·ver·time /ˈōvərˌtīm/ ▶ n. 1 time worked in addition to one's normal working hours. 2 extra time played at the end of a game that is tied. ▶ adv. in addition to normal working hours.

o·ver·tired /ˌōvərˈtīrd/ ▶ adj. excessively tired; exhausted.

o·ver·tone /ˈōvərˌtōn/ ▶ n. 1 a subtle additional quality or implication: *the decision had political overtones.* 2 a musical tone that is a part of the harmonic series above a fundamental note and may be heard with it.

o·ver·top /ˌōvərˈtäp/ ▶ v. (**overtops, overtopping, overtopped**) be higher or taller than someone or something.

o·ver·train /ˌōvərˈtrān/ ▶ v. 1 (especially of an athlete) train too hard or for too long. 2 subject to excessive training.

o·ver·ture /ˈōvərCHər, -ˌCHo͝or/ ▶ n. 1 an orchestral piece at the beginning of a musical work. 2 an independent orchestral composition in one movement. 3 (**overtures**) approaches made with the aim of opening negotiations or establishing a relationship: *he began making overtures to merchant banks.* 4 an introduction to something more substantial.

o·ver·turn /ˌōvərˈtərn/ ▶ v. 1 turn over and come to rest upside down. 2 abolish or reverse a decision, system, etc.

o·ver·use ▶ v. /ˌōvərˈyo͞oz/ use something too much. ▶ n. /ˈōvərˈyo͞os/ excessive use.

o·ver·val·ue /ˌōvərˈvalyo͞o/ ▶ v. (**overvalues, overvaluing, overvalued**) 1 overestimate the importance of something. 2 fix the value of something, especially a currency at too high a level. ■ **o·ver·val·u·a·tion** /ˈōvərˌvalyo͞oˈāshən/ n.

o·ver·view /ˈōvərˌvyo͞o/ ▶ n. a general summary or survey.

o·ver·ween·ing /ˈōvərˈwēniNG/ ▶ adj. (especially of a quality) excessive: *overweening pride.*

o·ver·weight /ˈōvərˈwāt/ ▶ adj. above a normal, desirable, or permitted weight.

o·ver·whelm /ˌōvər(h)welm/ ▶ v. 1 have a strong emotional effect on: *she was overwhelmed by guilt.* 2 give someone too much of something. 3 defeat someone or something completely. 4 cover something completely with a huge mass of water. ■ **o·ver·whelm·ing** adj.

o·ver·win·ter /ˈōvərˈwin(t)ər/ ▶ v. 1 spend the winter in a particular place. 2 (of an insect, plant, etc.) survive through the winter.

o·ver·work /ˈōvərˈwərk/ ▶ v. 1 work or cause to work too hard. 2 use a word or idea too much and so make it less effective. ▶ n. excessive work.

o·ver·write /ˌōvərˈrīt/ ▶ v. (past **overwrote** /ˌōvərˈrōt/; past part. **overwritten** /ˌōvərˈritn/) 1 write on top of other writing. 2 destroy computer data by entering new data in its place. 3 write something too elaborately.

o·ver·wrought /ˈōvəˈrôt/ ▶ adj. 1 in a state of nervous excitement or anxiety. 2 (of a piece of writing or a work of art) too elaborate.

o·ver·zeal·ous /ˈōvərˈzeləs/ ▶ adj. excessively enthusiastic.

o·vi·duct /ˈōviˌdəkt/ ▶ n. the tube through which an ovum (female reproductive cell) passes from an ovary.

o·vine /ˈōˌvīn/ ▶ adj. relating to sheep.

o·vip·a·rous /ō'vipərəs/ ▸ adj. (of an animal such as a bird) producing young by means of eggs that are hatched after they have been laid by the parent. Compare with VIVIPAROUS.

o·vi·pos·i·tor /ˌōvə'päzitər/ ▸ n. a tubular organ through which a female insect or fish deposits eggs.

o·void /'ō.void/ ▸ adj. 1 egg-shaped. 2 (of a plane figure) oval. ▸ n. an oval or egg-shaped object or shape.

ov·u·late /'ōvyə.lāt, 'äv-/ ▸ v. (of a woman or female animal) discharge ova (reproductive cells) from the ovary. ∎ **ov·u·la·tion** /ˌōvyə'lāsHən, ˌäv-/ n.

ov·ule /'ōvyōōl, 'äv-/ ▸ n. the part of the ovary of seed plants that becomes the seed after fertilization. ∎ **ov·u·lar** /-lər/ adj.

o·vum /'ōvəm/ ▸ n. (pl. **ova** /'ōvə/) a mature female reproductive cell that can divide to develop into an embryo if fertilized by a male cell.

ow /ou/ ▸ exclam. used to express sudden pain.

owe /ō/ ▸ v. 1 be required to pay money or goods to someone in return for something received. 2 be morally obliged to do or give something to: *you owe me an apology.* 3 (**owe something to**) have something because of: *I owe my life to you.*

ow·ing /'ō-iNG/ ▸ adj. (of money) yet to be paid.
– PHRASES **owing to** because of.

owl /oul/ ▸ n. a bird of prey with large eyes, a hooked beak, and a hooting call, active at night.

owl·et /'oulit/ ▸ n. a young or small owl.

owl·ish /'oulisH/ ▸ adj. 1 like an owl, especially in appearing to be wise or solemn. 2 (of glasses) resembling the large round eyes of an owl. ∎ **owl·ish·ly** adv.

own /ōn/ ▸ adj. & pron. 1 (with a possessive) belonging or relating to the person specified: *I saw it with my own eyes.* 2 done or produced by the person specified. 3 particular to the person or thing specified; individual. ▸ v. 1 possess something. 2 formal admit or acknowledge that something is the case. 3 (**own up**) admit to having done something wrong or embarrassing.
– PHRASES **come into its** (or **one's**) **own** become fully effective. **hold one's own** remain in a strong position in a demanding situation.

own·er /'ōnər/ ▸ n. a person who owns something.

own·er·ship /'ōnər.sHip/ ▸ n. the act, state, or right of possessing something.

own goal ▸ n. (in soccer) a goal scored when a player accidentally hits the ball into their own team's goal.

ox /äks/ ▸ n. (pl. **oxen**) 1 a cow or bull. 2 a castrated bull, used for pulling heavy loads.

ox·al·ic ac·id /äk'salik/ ▸ n. a poisonous acid found in rhubarb leaves and other plants.

ox·bow /'äks.bō/ ▸ n. a loop formed by a horseshoe bend in a river.

ox·bow lake ▸ n. a curved lake formed from a horseshoe bend in a river where the main stream has cut across the neck and no longer flows around the loop of the bend.

Ox·bridge /'äks.brij/ ▸ n. chiefly Brit. Oxford and Cambridge universities regarded together.

ox·en /'äksən/ ▸ plural of ox.

ox·eye dai·sy ▸ n. a daisy that has large white flowers with yellow centers.

ox·ford /'äksfərd/ ▸ n. a type of lace-up shoe with a low heel.

ox·i·dant /'äksidənt/ ▸ n. Chemistry a substance that brings about oxidation.

ox·i·da·tion /ˌäksi'dāsHən/ ▸ n. Chemistry the process of oxidizing or the result of being oxidized. ∎ **ox·i·da·tive** /'äksi.dātiv/ adj.

ox·ide /'äk.sīd/ ▸ n. a compound of oxygen with another element or group.

ox·i·dize /'äksi.dīz/ ▸ v. 1 combine or cause to combine with oxygen. 2 Chemistry cause a substance to undergo a reaction in which electrons are lost to another substance or molecule. The opposite of REDUCE. ∎ **ox·i·di·za·tion** /ˌäksidi'zāsHən/ n. **ox·i·diz·er** n.

ox·tail /'äks.tāl/ ▸ n. the tail of an ox (used in making soup).

ox·y·a·cet·y·lene /ˌäksēə'setl-in, -.ēn/ ▸ adj. (of welding or cutting techniques) using a very hot flame produced by mixing acetylene and oxygen.

ox·y·co·done /ˌäksē'kō.dōn, ˌäksē'kō.dän/ (also trademark **OxyContin** /ˌäksē'käntin/) ▸ n. a synthetic painkilling drug similar to morphine.

ox·y·gen /'äksəjən/ ▸ n. a colorless, odorless, gaseous chemical element, forming about 20 percent of the earth's atmosphere and essential to life.

ox·y·gen·ate /'äksəjə.nāt/ ▸ v. (often as adj. **oxygenated**) supply or enrich with oxygen: *oxygenated blood.* ∎ **ox·y·gen·a·tion** /ˌäksəjə'nāsHən/ n. **ox·y·gen·a·tor** n.

ox·y·gen bar ▸ n. a place where people pay to inhale pure oxygen for its reputedly therapeutic effects.

ox·y·gen mask ▸ n. a mask placed over the nose and mouth and connected to an oxygen supply, used when the body is not able to gain enough oxygen by breathing air.

ox·y·mo·ron /ˌäksə'môr.än/ ▸ n. a figure of speech in which apparently contradictory terms appear together (e.g., *a deafening silence*). ∎ **ox·y·mo·ron·ic** /-mə'ränik/ adj.

ox·y·to·cin /ˌäksə'tōsən/ ▸ n. a hormone released by the pituitary gland that in women causes contraction of the uterus during labor and stimulates the flow of milk into the breasts.

o·yez /'ō'yā, 'ō'yez/ (also **oyes**) ▸ exclam. a call given by a town crier or court official to ask for silence before an announcement.

oys·ter /'oistər/ ▸ n. 1 a shellfish with two hinged oval shells, several kinds of which are farmed for food or pearls. 2 a shade of grayish white.
– PHRASES **the world is your oyster** you have a wide range of opportunities available to you.

oys·ter·catch·er /'oistər.kacHər/ ▸ n. a wading bird with black or black-and-white plumage and a strong orange-red bill, feeding chiefly on shellfish.

oys·ter mush·room ▸ n. an edible fungus with a grayish-brown oval cap.

Oz /äz/ ▸ n. & adj. Brit. & Austral. informal Australia or Australian.

oz. ▸ abbr. ounce(s).

o·zone /'ō.zōn/ ▸ n. a strong-smelling, toxic form of oxygen, formed by electrical discharges or ultraviolet light.

o·zone hole ▸ n. an area of the ozone layer where the ozone is greatly reduced, due to CFCs and other pollutants.

o·zone lay·er ▸ n. a layer in the earth's stratosphere containing a high concentration of ozone, which absorbs most of the ultraviolet radiation reaching the earth from the sun.

P¹ (also **p**) ► n. (pl. **Ps** or **P's**) the sixteenth letter of the alphabet.

P² ► abbr. (on road signs and street plans) parking. ► symbol the chemical element phosphorus.

p ► abbr. **1** page. **2** Brit. penny or pence.

P2P ► abbr. peer-to-peer, an Internet network that enables a group of users to access and copy files from each other's hard drives.

PA ► abbr. **1** Pennsylvania. **2** public address. **3** personal assistant.

Pa ► abbr. pascal(s). ► symbol the chemical element protactinium.

pa /pä/ ► n. informal a person's father.

p.a. ► abbr. per annum.

pab·lum /'pabləm/ (also **pabulum** /'pabyələm/) ► n. literary bland intellectual matter or entertainment: *predictable pop pablum.*

PAC /pak/ ► abbr. **1** Pan-Africanist Congress. **2** political action committee.

pa·ca /'päkə, 'pakə/ ► n. a large South American rodent that has a reddish-brown coat with rows of white spots.

pace¹ /pās/ ► n. **1** a single step taken when walking or running. **2** speed in walking, running, or moving. **3** the speed or rate at which something happens or develops: *the pace of change.* **4** a way in which a horse is trained to run or walk. ► v. **1** walk up and down in a small area, typically as an expression of anxiety. **2** (**pace something out**) measure a distance by walking it and counting the number of steps taken. **3** set the speed or rate at which something happens or develops: *they paced their drinking throughout the week.* **4** lead another runner in a race in order to establish a competitive speed. **5** (**pace oneself**) do something at a controlled and steady rate.
– PHRASES **keep pace with** progress at the same speed as. **put someone through their paces** make someone demonstrate their abilities. **stand** (or **stay**) **the pace** be able to keep up with others.

pace² /'pā,sē, 'pä,CHä/ ► prep. with due respect to someone.

pace·mak·er /'pās,mākər/ ► n. **1** an artificial device for stimulating and regulating the heart muscle. **2** another term for PACESETTER.

pace·set·ter /'pās,setər/ ► n. **1** a runner or other competitor who sets the pace at the beginning of a race or other competition. **2** a person or organization viewed as taking the lead or setting a standard for others: *Alaska is the pacesetter when it comes to salaries for teachers.* ■ **pace·set·ting** adj. & n.

pach·y·derm /'pakə,dərm/ ► n. a very large mammal with thick skin, especially an elephant, rhinoceros, or hippopotamus.

pa·cif·ic /pə'sifik/ ► adj. **1** peaceful or pacifying: *a pacific gesture.* **2** (**Pacific**) relating to the Pacific Ocean. ► n. (**the Pacific**) the Pacific Ocean. ■ **pa·cif·i·cal·ly** /-(ə)lē/ adv.

Pa·cif·ic time ► n. the standard time in a zone including the Pacific coastal region of the US and Canada.

pac·i·fi·er /'pasə,fīər/ ► n. a rubber or plastic nipple for a baby to suck on.

pac·i·fism /'pasə,fizəm/ ► n. the belief that disputes should be settled peacefully and that war and violence are always wrong. ■ **pac·i·fist** n. & adj.

pac·i·fy /'pasə,fī/ ► v. (**pacifies, pacifying, pacified**) **1** make someone less angry or upset. **2** bring peace to a country or groups in conflict. ■ **pa·cif·i·ca·tion** /,pasifi'kāsHən/ n.

pack¹ /pak/ ► n. **1** a cardboard or paper container and the items inside it. **2** a collection of related documents. **3** a group of animals that live and hunt together. **4** chiefly derogatory a group of similar things or people: *the reports were a pack of lies.* **5** (**the pack**) the main body of competitors following the leader in a race. **6** Rugby a team's forwards. **7** (**Pack**) an organized group of Cub Scouts or Brownies. **8** a rucksack. **9** a hot or cold pad of absorbent material, used for treating an injury. ► v. **1** fill a suitcase or bag with clothes and other items needed for travel. **2** place something in a container for transport or storage. **3** be capable of being folded up for transport or storage: *a tent that packs away compactly.* **4** cram a large number of things into something. **5** cover, surround, or fill something. **6** informal carry a gun: *he drove downtown packing an automatic.* ■ **pack·a·ble** adj. **pack·er** n.
– PHRASES **pack a punch 1** be capable of hitting with skill or force. **2** have a powerful effect. **pack something in** informal give up an activity or job. **pack someone off** informal send someone somewhere without much notice. **send someone packing** informal dismiss someone abruptly.

pack² ► v. fill a jury or committee with people likely to support a particular verdict or decision.

pack·age /'pakij/ ► n. **1** an object or group of objects wrapped in paper or packed in a box. **2** the box or bag in which things are packed. **3** (also **package deal**) a set of proposals or terms offered or agreed as a whole. **4** informal a package tour. **5** a collection of related computer programs or sets of instructions. ► v. **1** put something into a box or wrapping. **2** present in a favorable way: *school science is packaged to appeal to boys.* **3** combine various products for sale as one unit. ■ **pack·aged** adj. **pack·ag·er** n.

pack·age tour ► n. a vacation organized by

a travel agent, the price of which includes arrangements for transportation and accommodations.

pack·ag·ing /'pakijiNG/ ▸ n. materials used to wrap or protect goods.

pack an·i·mal ▸ n. **1** an animal used to carry heavy loads. **2** an animal that lives and hunts in a pack.

packed /pakd/ ▸ adj. very crowded.

pack·et /'pakit/ ▸ n. **1** a paper or cardboard container. **2** Computing a block of data transmitted across a network. ▸ v. (**packets, packeting, packeted**) wrap something up in a packet.

pack·et boat ▸ n. dated a boat traveling at regular intervals between two ports, originally carrying mail and later taking passengers.

pack·horse /'pak,hôrs/ ▸ n. a horse used to carry loads.

pack ice ▸ n. a mass of ice floating in the sea, formed by smaller pieces freezing together.

pack·ing /'pakiNG/ ▸ n. material used to protect fragile goods in transit.

pack rat ▸ n. **1** a ratlike rodent that accumulates a mound of sticks and debris in its nest. **2** a person who saves unnecessary objects or hoards things.

pact /pakt/ ▸ n. a formal agreement between people or parties.

pad¹ /'pad/ ▸ n. **1** a thick piece of soft or absorbent material. **2** the fleshy underpart of an animal's foot or of a human finger. **3** a protective guard worn over a part of the body by an athlete. **4** a number of sheets of blank paper fastened together at one edge. **5** a flat-topped structure or area used for helicopter takeoff and landing or for rocket-launching. **6** informal a person's home. ▸ v. (**pads, padding, padded**) **1** fill or cover something with a pad or padding. **2** make a speech or piece of writing longer by adding unnecessary material.

pad² /'pad/ ▸ v. (**pads, padding, padded**) walk with steady steps making a soft, dull sound.

pad·ding /'padiNG/ ▸ n. **1** soft material used to pad or stuff something. **2** unnecessary material added to a speech or piece of writing to make it longer.

pad·dle¹ /'padl/ ▸ n. **1** a short pole with a broad blade at one or both ends, used to move a small boat through the water. **2** an implement or part of a machine shaped like a paddle, used for stirring or mixing. **3** each of the boards fitted around the outside edge of a paddle wheel or mill wheel. ▸ v. **1** move a boat with a paddle or paddles. **2** (of a bird or other animal) swim with short fast strokes. ■ **pad·dler** n.

pad·dle² Brit. ▸ v. walk with bare feet in shallow water. ▸ n. an act of paddling. ■ **pad·dler** n.

pad·dle·boat /'padl,bōt/ ▸ n. a boat powered by steam and propelled by paddle wheels.

pad·dle wheel ▸ n. a large steam-driven wheel with paddles around its edge, attached to the side or stern of a ship and moving the ship as it turns.

pad·dock /'padək/ ▸ n. **1** a small field or enclosure for horses. **2** an enclosure next to a racetrack where horses or cars are displayed before a race.

Pad·dy /'padē/ ▸ n. (pl. **Paddies**) informal, chiefly offensive an Irishman.

pad·dy /'padē/ ▸ n. (pl. **paddies**) **1** (also **paddy field**) a field where rice is grown. **2** rice before threshing or still in the husk.

pad·dy wag·on ▸ n. informal a police van.

pad·lock /'pad,läk/ ▸ n. a detachable lock hanging by a hinged hook on the object fastened. ▸ v. secure something with a padlock.

pa·dre /'pädrā/ ▸ n. informal a chaplain in the armed services.

pa·dro·ne /pə'drōnā, pə'drōnē/ ▸ n. a patron or master, especially a Mafia boss.

pae·an /'pēən/ ▸ n. a song of praise or triumph.

pa·el·la /pä'äyä, pə'elə/ ▸ n. a Spanish dish of rice, saffron, chicken, seafood, and vegetables, cooked in a large shallow pan.

pa·gan /'pā'gən/ ▸ n. a person who holds religious beliefs other than those of the main world religions. ▸ adj. relating to pagans or their beliefs. ■ **pa·gan·ism** /-,nizəm/ n.

page¹ /pāj/ ▸ n. **1** one side of a leaf of a book, magazine, or newspaper, or the material on it. **2** both sides of such a leaf considered as a single unit. **3** a section of data displayed on a computer screen at one time. **4** a particular event considered as part of a longer history: *the vote will form a page in the world's history.* ▸ v. (**page through**) **1** look through the pages of a book, magazine, etc. **2** move through and display information on a computer screen one page at a time.

page² ▸ n. **1** a boy or young man employed in a hotel or club to run errands, open doors, etc. **2** a young boy attending a bride at a wedding. **3** historical a boy who entered the service of a knight while training to be a knight himself. ▸ v. summon someone over a public address system or by means of a pager.

pag·eant /'pajənt/ ▸ n. **1** a public entertainment consisting of a procession of people in elaborate costumes, or an outdoor performance of a historical scene. **2** (also **beauty pageant**) a beauty contest.

pag·eant·ry /'pajəntrē/ ▸ n. elaborate display or ceremony.

page·boy /'pāj,boi/ ▸ n. **1** a page in a hotel or attending a bride at a wedding. **2** a woman's hairstyle consisting of a shoulder-length bob with the ends rolled under.

pag·er /'pājər/ ▸ n. a small radio device that bleeps or vibrates to inform the bearer that someone wishes to contact them or that it has received a short text message.

page-turn·er ▸ n. informal an exciting book. ■ **page-turn·ing** adj.

pag·i·nate /'pajə,nāt/ ▸ n. give numbers to the pages of a book, journal, document, etc. ■ **pag·i·na·tion** /,pajə'nāSHən/ n.

pa·go·da /pə'gōdə/ ▸ n. a Hindu or Buddhist temple, typically having a tower with several tiers.

paid /pād/ ▸ past and past participle of PAY.

paid-up ▸ adj. **1** (of a member of an organization) with all subscriptions paid in full. **2** committed to a cause or group: *a fully paid-up postmodernist.*

pail /pāl/ ▸ n. a bucket.

pain /pān/ ▸ n. **1** a very unpleasant feeling caused by illness or injury. **2** mental suffering or distress. **3** (**pains**) great care or trouble: *she took pains to see that everyone ate well.* **4** (also **pain in the neck** or vulgar slang **pain in the ass**) informal

an annoying or boring person or thing. ▶ v. cause pain to someone.
– PHRASES **on** (or **under**) **pain of** the punishment for wrongdoing being: *we must not, on pain of death, utter a sound.*

> USAGE
> Do not confuse **pain** with **pane**. Pain means 'an unpleasant feeling caused by illness or injury' (*agonizing stomach pains*), whereas **pane** means 'a sheet of glass' (*a window pane*).

pained /pānd/ ▶ adj. showing annoyance or distress: *a pained expression came over his face.*

pain·ful /'pānfəl/ ▶ adj. **1** affected with or causing pain. **2** informal very bad: *their attempts at reggae are painful.* ■ **pain·ful·ly** adv. **pain·ful·ness** n.

pain·kil·ler /'pān,kilər/ ▶ n. a medicine for relieving pain. ■ **pain·kill·ing** adj.

pain·less /'pānləs/ ▶ adj. **1** not causing pain. **2** involving little effort or stress. ■ **pain·less·ly** adv. **pain·less·ness** n.

pains·tak·ing /'pānz,tāking, 'pān,stāking/ ▶ adj. very careful and thorough. ■ **pains·tak·ing·ly** adv.

paint /pānt/ ▶ n. **1** a colored substance that is spread over a surface to give a thin decorative or protective coating. **2** dated cosmetic makeup. ▶ v. **1** apply paint to something. **2** apply a liquid to a surface with a brush. **3** produce a picture with paint. **4** give a description of: *the city isn't as bad as it's painted.*
– PHRASES **be like watching paint dry** be very boring. **paint oneself into a corner** leave oneself no means of escape or room to maneuver. **paint the town red** informal go out and enjoy oneself in a lively way.

paint·ball /'pānt,bôl/ ▶ n. a combat game in which participants shoot capsules of paint at each other with air guns.

paint·box /'pānt,bäks/ ▶ n. a box holding a palette of dry paints for painting pictures.

paint·brush /'pānt,brəsh/ ▶ n. a brush for applying paint.

paint·ed la·dy ▶ n. **1** a butterfly with mainly orange-brown wings and darker markings. **2** a Victorian house, the exterior of which is painted in three or more colors to accentuate the architectural features.

paint·er[1] /'pāntər/ ▶ n. **1** an artist who paints pictures. **2** a person who paints buildings.

paint·er[2] ▶ n. a rope attached to the bow of a boat for tying it to a quay.

paint·er·ly /'pāntərlē/ ▶ adj. **1** relating to or like a painter; artistic. **2** (of a painting) characterized by qualities of color, brushstroke, and texture rather than of line.

paint·ing /'pānting/ ▶ n. **1** the action of painting. **2** a painted picture.

paint·work /'pānt,wərk/ ▶ n. chiefly Brit. painted surfaces in a building or on a vehicle.

pair /pe(ə)r/ ▶ n. **1** a set of two things used together or regarded as a unit. **2** an article consisting of two joined or corresponding parts: *a pair of jeans.* **3** two people or animals that are related or considered together. **4** two opposing members of a parliament who agree to be absent for a particular vote, leaving the relative position of the parties unaffected. ▶ v. **1** join or put together to form a pair: *a cardigan paired with a matching skirt.* (**pair off/up**) form a romantic or sexual relationship.

pai·sa /'pīsä/ ▶ n. (pl. **paise** /-sä/) a unit of money of India, Pakistan, and Nepal, equal to one hundredth of a rupee.

pais·ley /'pāzlē/ ▶ n. an intricate pattern on fabric, consisting of curved shapes resembling feathers.

Pai·ute /'pī(y)ōōt, pī'(y)ōōt/ ▶ n. (pl. same or **Paiutes**) a member of either of two American Indian peoples (the **Southern Paiute** and the **Northern Paiute**) of the western US.

pa·ja·mas /pə'jäməz, -jaməz/ (Brit. **pyjamas**) ▶ pl.n. **1** a set of loose-fitting pants and shirt worn in bed. **2** a loose pair of pants with a drawstring waist, worn by both sexes in some Asian countries.

Pak·i /'pakē/ ▶ n. (pl. **Pakis**) informal, offensive, chiefly Brit. a Pakistani person.

Pak·i·sta·ni /,pakə'stanē, ,päki'stänē/ ▶ n. (pl. **Pakistanis**) a person from Pakistan. ▶ adj. relating to Pakistan.

pa·ko·ra /pə'kôrə/ ▶ n. (in Indian cooking) a piece of battered and deep-fried vegetable or meat.

pal /pal/ informal ▶ n. a friend. ▶ v. (**pals, palling, palled**) (**pal around**) spend time with a friend.

pal·ace /'palis/ ▶ n. a large, impressive building forming the official residence of a sovereign, president, archbishop, etc.

pal·ace coup ▶ n. the nonviolent overthrow of a sovereign or government by senior officials within the ruling group.

pal·a·din /'palədin/ ▶ n. **1** literary a brave, chivalrous knight. **2** historical any of the twelve most famous warriors of Charlemagne's court.

palaeo-, etc. ▶ comb.form British spelling of PALEO-, etc.

pal·an·quin /,palən'kēn/ ▶ n. (in India and the East) a seat with a canopy, carried on poles and used as a form of transport for one passenger.

pal·at·a·ble /'palətəbəl/ ▶ adj. **1** pleasant to taste. **2** pleasant or acceptable to someone. ■ **pal·at·a·bil·i·ty** /,palətə'bilətē/ n.

pal·a·tal /'palətl/ ▶ adj. **1** relating to the palate. **2** Phonetics (of a speech sound) made by placing the blade of the tongue against or near the hard palate (e.g., *y* in *yes*).

pal·ate /'palit/ ▶ n. **1** the roof of the mouth, separating the cavities of the mouth and nose in vertebrates. **2** a person's ability to distinguish between and appreciate different flavors: *a cocktail created for the discerning palates of the international jet set.*

> USAGE
> On the confusion of **palate** with **palette** or **pallet**, see the note at PALLET[2].

pa·la·tial /pə'lāshəl/ ▶ adj. resembling a palace, especially in being impressively spacious or grand. ■ **pa·la·tial·ly** adv.

pa·lat·i·nate /pə'latn,āt, -,it/ ▶ n. historical a territory under the jurisdiction of a palatine official or feudal lord.

pal·a·tine /'palə,tīn/ ▶ adj. chiefly historical **1** (of an official or feudal lord) having local authority that elsewhere belongs only to a king or queen. **2** (of a territory) subject to such authority.

pa·lav·er /pə'lavər, -'läv-/ ▶ n. informal a lengthy or boring fuss about something; an unnecessarily long-drawn-out process.

pa·laz·zo /pə'lätsō/ ▶ n. (pl. **palazzos** or **palazzi** /-'lätsē/) a large, grand building, especially in Italy.

pa·laz·zo pants ▶ pl.n. women's loose wide-legged pants.

pale[1] /pāl/ ▶ adj. **1** of a light shade or color. **2** (of a person's face) having little color, through shock, fear, illness, etc. **3** not very good or impressive: *a pale imitation of the real thing.* ▶ v. **1** become pale in one's face. **2** seem or become less good or important: *his version of the song pales in comparison to the original.* ■ **pale·ly** adv. **pale·ness** n.

pale[2] ▶ n. **1** a wooden stake used with others to form a fence. **2** a boundary or limit. **3** old use or historical an area within set boundaries or subject to a particular jurisdiction.
– PHRASES **beyond the pale** outside the boundaries of acceptable behavior.

pale·face /'pāl,fās/ ▶ n. informal, derogatory a name supposedly used by North American Indians for a white person.

paleo- (Brit. **palaeo-**) ▶ comb.form older or ancient: *Paleolithic.*

Pa·le·o·cene /'pālēə,sēn/ ▶ adj. Geology relating to the earliest epoch of the Tertiary period (about 65 to 56.5 million years ago), a time of rapid development of mammals.

pa·le·og·ra·phy /,pālē'ägrəfē/ ▶ n. the study of ancient writing systems and manuscripts. ■ **pa·le·og·ra·pher** /-fər/ n. **pa·le·o·graph·ic** /,pālēə'grafik/ adj.

Pa·le·o·lith·ic /,pālēə'liTHik/ ▶ adj. Archaeology relating to the early phase of the Stone Age, up to the end of the glacial period.

pa·le·on·tol·o·gy /,pālē,ən'täləjē/ ▶ n. the branch of science concerned with fossil animals and plants. ■ **pa·le·on·to·log·i·cal** /,pālē,äntə'läjikəl/ adj. **pa·le·on·tol·o·gist** /-jist/ n.

Pa·le·o·zo·ic /,pālēə'zōik/ ▶ adj. Geology relating to the era between the Precambrian eon and the Mesozoic era, about 570 to 245 million years ago, which ended with the rise to dominance of the reptiles.

Pal·es·tin·i·an /,palə'stinēən/ ▶ adj. relating to Palestine. ▶ n. a member of the native Arab population of Palestine.

pal·ette /'palit/ ▶ n. **1** a thin board on which an artist lays and mixes paints. **2** the range of colors used by an artist.

> **USAGE**
> On the confusion of **palette**, **palate**, and **pallet**, see the note at PALLET[2].

pal·ette knife ▶ n. a thin steel blade with a handle for mixing paints or for applying or removing paint.

pal·i·mo·ny /'palə,mōnē/ ▶ n. informal financial support given by one member of an unmarried couple to the other after separation.

pal·imp·sest /'palimp,sest/ ▶ n. **1** a parchment or other surface on which writing has been applied over earlier writing that has been erased. **2** something altered or used again but still bearing visible traces of its earlier form: *the house is a palimpsest of the taste of successive owners.*

pal·in·drome /'palin,drōm/ ▶ n. a word or sequence of words that reads the same backward as forward, e.g., *madam.* ■ **pal·in·drom·ic** /,palin'drämik, -'drō-/ adj.

pal·ing /'pāliNG/ ▶ n. **1** a fence made from stakes. **2** a stake used in such a fence.

pal·i·sade /,palə'sād/ ▶ n. a fence of stakes or iron railings forming an enclosure or defense.

pall[1] /pôl/ ▶ n. **1** a cloth spread over a coffin, hearse, or tomb. **2** a dark cloud of smoke or dust. **3** a general atmosphere of gloom or fear: *the murder had cast a pall of terror over the village.*

pall[2] ▶ v. become less appealing or interesting as a result of being too familiar: *the thrill of flouting her father's wishes began to pall.*

Pal·la·di·an /pə'lādēən/ ▶ adj. referring to a neoclassical style of architecture based on that of the Italian architect Andrea Palladio.

pal·la·di·um /pə'lādēəm/ ▶ n. a rare silvery-white metallic element resembling platinum.

pall·bear·er /'pôl,be(ə)rər/ ▶ n. a person helping to carry or escorting a coffin at a funeral.

pal·let[1] /'palit/ ▶ n. a straw mattress or makeshift bed.

pal·let[2] ▶ n. a portable platform on which goods can be moved, stacked, and stored. ■ **pal·let·ize** /'palə,tīz/ v.

> **USAGE**
> Do not confuse **pallet** with **palate** or **palette**. A **pallet** is 'a portable platform for moving goods' or 'a makeshift bed,' **palate** means 'the roof of the mouth' or 'a person's ability to distinguish between different flavors,' and a **palette** is 'an artist's board for mixing paints.'

pal·liasse /,pal'yas, 'pal,yas/ ▶ n. a straw mattress.

pal·li·ate /'palē,āt/ ▶ v. **1** make the symptoms of a disease less severe without curing it. **2** cause something bad to seem less serious: *there is no way to palliate his offense.* ■ **pal·li·a·tion** /,palē'āsHən/ n.

pal·li·a·tive /'palē,ātiv, 'palēətiv/ ▶ adj. **1** (of a medicine or medical care) relieving pain without curing the condition that is causing it. **2** (of an action) intended to make a problem less severe without dealing with its underlying cause. ▶ n. a palliative medicine or remedy.

pal·lid /'palid/ ▶ adj. **1** pale, especially because of poor health. **2** weak or insipid: *a pallid ray of winter sun.*

pal·lor /'palər/ ▶ n. an unhealthy pale appearance.

pal·ly /'palē/ ▶ adj. informal having a close, friendly relationship.

palm[1] /pä(l)m/ ▶ n. **1** (also **palm tree**) an evergreen tree with a crown of very long feathered or fan-shaped leaves, growing in warm regions. **2** a leaf of a palm tree awarded as a prize or viewed as a symbol of victory.

palm[2] ▶ n. the inner surface of the hand between the wrist and fingers. ▶ v. **1** hide a small object in the hand, especially as part of a trick. **2** (**palm something off**) sell or get rid of something dishonestly, especially by misrepresenting its quality or worth. **3** (**palm someone off**) Brit. informal persuade someone to accept something that is unwanted or has little value.
– PHRASES **in the palm of one's hand** under one's control or influence. **read someone's palm** tell someone's fortune by looking at the lines on their palm.

pal·mate /'pal,māt, 'pä(l)-/ ▶ adj. shaped like an open hand with a number of sections resembling fingers: *palmate leaves.*

pal·met·to /pä(l)'metō, pal-/ ▶ n. (pl. **palmettos**) an American palm with large fan-shaped leaves.

palm·is·try /'pä(l)məstrē/ ▶ n. the supposed interpretation of a person's character or prediction of their future by examining their hand. ■ **palm·ist** n.

Palm Sun·day ▸ n. the Sunday before Easter, on which Jesus's entry into Jerusalem is celebrated by processions in which palm tree branches are carried.

palm·top /'pä(l)m,täp/ ▸ n. a computer small and light enough to be held in one hand.

palm·y /'pä(l)mē/ ▸ adj. (**palmier, palmiest**) comfortable and prosperous: *the palmy days of the 1970s.*

pal·o·mi·no /,palə'mēnō/ ▸ n. (pl. **palominos**) a pale golden or tan-colored horse with a white mane and tail.

palp /palp/ ▸ n. each of a pair of long segmented feelers near the mouth of some insects and crustaceans.

pal·pa·ble /'palpəbəl/ ▸ adj. 1 able to be touched or felt. 2 (of a feeling or atmosphere) so intense that one seems to experience it as a physical sensation: *a palpable sense of loss.*
■ **pal·pa·bly** adv.

pal·pate /'pal,pāt/ ▸ v. examine a part of the body by touch, especially for medical purposes.
■ **pal·pa·tion** /pal'pāshən/ n.

pal·pi·tate /'palpi,tāt/ ▸ v. 1 (of the heart) beat rapidly or irregularly. 2 shake or tremble.

pal·pi·ta·tion /,palpi'tāshən/ ▸ n. 1 throbbing or trembling. 2 (**palpitations**) a noticeably rapid, strong, or irregular heartbeat.

pal·sy /'pôlzē/ ▸ n. (pl. **palsies**) dated paralysis, especially when accompanied by involuntary shaking of the limbs. ▸ v. (**be palsied**) suffer from palsy.

pal·try /'pôltrē/ ▸ adj. (**paltrier, paltriest**) 1 (of an amount) very small. 2 petty or trivial.
■ **pal·tri·ness** n.

pam·pas /'pampəz, -pəs/ ▸ n. (treated as sing. or pl.) large treeless plains in South America.

pam·pas grass ▸ n. a tall South American grass with silky flowering plumes.

pam·per /'pampər/ ▸ v. lavish care and attention on someone; spoil someone.

pam·phlet /'pamflit/ ▸ n. a small booklet or leaflet containing information about a particular subject. ▸ v. (**pamphlets, pamphleting, pamphleted**) distribute pamphlets to people.

pam·phlet·eer /,pamfli'ti(ə)r/ ▸ n. a person who writes pamphlets, especially ones that deal with political issues. ■ **pam·phlet·eer·ing** n.

pan¹ /pan/ ▸ n. 1 a metal container for cooking food in. 2 a bowl fitted at either end of a pair of scales. 3 a shallow bowl in which gravel and mud are shaken and washed by people looking for gold. 4 a hollow in the ground in which water collects or in which salt is deposited after evaporation. 5 a part of the lock that held the priming in old types of gun. 6 a steel drum.
▸ v. (**pans, panning, panned**) 1 informal criticize someone or something severely. 2 (**pan out**) informal end up or conclude: *he's happy with the way the deal panned out.* 3 wash gravel in a pan to separate out gold.

pan² ▸ v. (**pans, panning, panned**) swing a video or film camera on a horizontal plane to give a panoramic effect or follow a subject. ▸ n. a panning movement.

pan³ ▸ n. variant spelling of PAAN.

pan- ▸ comb.form including everything or everyone, especially the whole of a continent, people, etc.: *pan-African.*

pan·a·ce·a /,panə'sēə/ ▸ n. a solution or remedy for all difficulties or diseases.

pa·nache /pə'nash, -'näsh/ ▸ n. an impressively confident and stylish way of doing something.

pan·a·ma /'panə,mä, -,mô/ ▸ n. a man's wide-brimmed hat of strawlike material, originally made from the leaves of a tropical palm tree.

Pan·a·ma·ni·an /,panə'mānēən/ ▸ n. a person from Panama. ▸ adj. relating to Panama.

pan·a·tel·a /,panə'telə/ ▸ n. a long thin cigar.

pan·cake /'pan,kāk/ ▸ n. 1 a thin, flat cake of batter, fried and turned in a pan. 2 theatrical makeup consisting of a flat solid layer of compressed powder.

pan·cet·ta /pan'chetə/ ▸ n. Italian cured belly of pork.

pan·chro·mat·ic /,pankrō'matik/ ▸ adj. (of black-and-white photographic film) sensitive to all visible colors of the spectrum.

pan·cre·as /'pangkrēəs, 'pankrēəs/ ▸ n. (pl. **pancreases**) a large gland behind the stomach that produces digestive enzymes and releases them into the duodenum. ■ **pan·cre·at·ic** /-krē'atik/ adj.

pan·cre·a·ti·tis /,pangkrēə'tītis, ,pan-/ ▸ n. inflammation of the pancreas.

pan·da /'pandə/ ▸ n. 1 (also **giant panda**) a large black-and-white bearlike mammal native to bamboo forests in China. 2 (also **red panda**) a raccoonlike Himalayan mammal with thick reddish-brown fur and a bushy tail.

pan·da·nus /pan'dānəs, -'danəs/ ▸ n. a tropical tree or shrub with a twisted stem and long, narrow spiny leaves from which fiber is obtained.

pan·dem·ic /pan'demik/ ▸ adj. (of a disease) widespread over a whole country or large part of the world. ▸ n. an outbreak of such a disease.

pan·de·mo·ni·um /,pandə'mōnēəm/ ▸ n. a state of wild and noisy disorder or confusion; uproar.

pan·der /'pandər/ ▸ v. (**pander to**) satisfy or indulge someone's desires or tastes, especially when these are unreasonable or distasteful: *newspapers are pandering to people's baser instincts.* ▸ n. dated a pimp.

pan·dit /'pandit, 'pən-/ (also **pundit** pronunc. same) ▸ n. a Hindu scholar learned in Sanskrit and Hindu philosophy and religion.

Pan·do·ra's box /pan'dôrəz/ ▸ n. a process that once begun creates many complicated problems.

pane /pān/ ▸ n. 1 a single sheet of glass in a window or door. 2 a sheet or page of stamps.

> USAGE
> On the confusion of **pane** and **pain**, see the note at PAIN.

pa·neer /pə'ni(ə)r/ ▸ n. a type of milk curd cheese used in Indian and Iranian cooking.

pan·e·gyr·ic /,panə'jirik/ ▸ n. a speech or piece of writing in praise of someone or something.

pan·el /'panl/ ▸ n. 1 a distinct, usually rectangular section of a door, vehicle, item of clothing, etc. 2 a flat board on which instruments or controls are fixed. 3 a small group of people brought together to investigate, discuss, or decide on something. 4 a jury, or a list of available jurors.
■ **pan·eled** adj.

pan·el·ing /'panəling/ (Brit. **panelling**) ▸ n. wooden panels as a decorative wall covering.

pan·el·ist /'panəlist/ (Brit. **panellist**) ▸ n. a member of a panel taking part in a game show or discussion.

pan·el truck ▶ n. a small enclosed delivery truck; a van.

pan-fry ▶ v. fry food in a pan in shallow fat.

pang /paNG/ ▶ n. a sudden sharp pain or painful emotion: *pangs of remorse.*

Pan·gloss·i·an /pan'glôsēən, -'gläs-/ ▶ adj. literary unrealistically optimistic.

pan·go·lin /'paNGgəlin, paNG'gōlin/ ▶ n. an insect-eating mammal whose body is covered with horny overlapping scales.

pan·han·dle /'pan,handl/ ▶ n. a narrow strip of territory projecting from the main territory of one state into another. ▶ v. informal beg in the street. ■ **pan·han·dler** n.

pan·ic /'panik/ ▶ n. **1** sudden uncontrollable fear or anxiety. **2** frenzied hurry to do something. ▶ v. (**panics, panicking, panicked**) feel sudden uncontrollable fear or anxiety, or make someone feel this: *the crowd panicked and stampeded for the exit.* ■ **pan·ick·y** adj.

pan·ic at·tack ▶ n. a sudden overwhelming feeling of acute anxiety, making someone unable to function normally.

pan·ic but·ton ▶ n. a button for summoning help in an emergency.

pan·i·cle /'panikəl/ ▶ n. a loose branching cluster of flowers, as in oats.

pan·ic room ▶ n. another term for SAFE ROOM.

pa·ni·ni /pə'nēnē/ ▶ n. (pl. same or **paninis**) a sandwich made with a baguette or with Italian bread, typically toasted.

pan·jan·drum /pan'jandrəm/ ▶ n. a pompous, self-important person in a position of authority.

panne /pan/ (also **panne velvet**) ▶ n. a glossy fabric resembling velvet, with a flattened pile.

pan·nier /'panyər, 'panēər/ ▶ n. **1** a bag or box fitted on either side of the rear wheel of a bicycle or motorcycle. **2** a basket, especially each of a pair carried by a donkey or mule.

pan·o·ply /'panəplē/ ▶ n. a large or impressive collection or display of something.

pan·op·tic /pa'näptik/ ▶ adj. showing or seeing the whole of something at one view.

pan·o·ram·a /,panə'ramə, -'rämə/ ▶ n. **1** an unbroken view of the whole region surrounding an observer. **2** a complete survey of a subject or sequence of events: *a full panorama of 20th-century art.* ■ **pan·o·ram·ic** /-'ramik/ adj. **pan·o·ram·i·cal·ly** /-'ramik(ə)lē/ adv.

pan·pipes /'pan,pīps/ ▶ pl.n. a musical instrument made from a row of short pipes fixed together.

pan·sex·u·al /pan'seksHōōəl/ ▶ adj. another term for OMNISEXUAL.

pan·sy /'panzē/ ▶ n. **1** a plant of the viola family, with brightly colored flowers. **2** informal, derogatory an effeminate or homosexual man.

pant /pant/ ▶ v. **1** breathe with short, quick breaths, typically as a result of physical exertion. **2** (**pant for**) long for something. ▶ n. a short, quick breath.

pan·ta·loons /,pantə'lōōnz/ ▶ pl.n. **1** women's baggy pants gathered at the ankles. **2** historical men's close-fitting breeches fastened below the calf or at the foot.

pan·tech·ni·con /pan'teknikən, -,kän/ ▶ n. Brit. a large van for transporting furniture.

pan·the·ism /'panTHē,izəm/ ▶ n. **1** the belief that God is present in all things in the universe. **2** the worship or tolerance of many gods. ■ **pan·the·ist** n. **pan·the·is·tic** /,panTHē'istik/ adj.

pan·the·on /'panTHē,än, -THēən/ ▶ n. **1** all the gods of a people or religion. **2** an ancient temple dedicated to all the gods. **3** a collection of famous or important people: *the pantheon of powerful Washington journalists.*

pan·ther /'panTHər/ ▶ n. **1** a leopard, especially a black one. **2** a cougar.

pant·ies /'pantēz/ ▶ pl.n. informal underpants worn by women and girls.

pan·tile /'pan,tīl/ ▶ n. a roof tile curved to form an S-shaped section, fitted to overlap its neighbor.

pan·to·graph /'pantə,graf/ ▶ n. **1** an instrument for copying a plan or drawing on a different scale by a system of hinged and jointed rods. **2** a jointed framework conveying a current to an electric train or trolley car from overhead wires.

pan·to·mime /'pantə,mīm/ ▶ n. **1** an entertainment in which performers express meaning through gestures. **2** Brit. a theatrical entertainment involving music, topical jokes, and slapstick comedy, usually produced around Christmas. **3** a ridiculous or confused action or situation.

pan·to·then·ic ac·id /,pantə'THenik/ ▶ n. a vitamin of the B complex, found in rice, bran, and other foods, and essential for the oxidation of fats and carbohydrates.

pan·try /'pantrē/ ▶ n. (pl. **pantries**) a small room or cupboard in which food, dishes, and utensils are kept.

pants /pants/ ▶ pl.n. **1** an outer garment covering the body from the waist to the ankles, with a separate part for each leg; trousers. **2** chiefly Brit. underpants. ▶ adj. (**pant**) relating to pants: *her pant pockets.*
– PHRASES **fly** (or **drive**) **by the seat of one's pants** informal rely on instinct rather than logic or knowledge. **scare** (or **bore**, etc.) **the pants off** informal make someone extremely scared (or bored, etc.). **wear the pants** informal be the dominant partner in a relationship.

pant·suit /'pant,sōōt/ (also **pants suit**) ▶ n. a pair of pants and a matching jacket worn by women.

pant·y·hose /'pantē,hōz/ ▶ pl.n. women's thin nylon tights.

pan·zer /'panzər/ ▶ n. a German armored military unit.

pap /pap/ ▶ n. **1** bland soft or semiliquid food suitable for babies or invalids. **2** books, magazines, television programs, or other forms of entertainment that require no intellectual effort. ■ **pap·py** adj.

pa·pa /'päpə/ ▶ n. one's father.

pa·pa·cy /'pāpəsē/ ▶ n. (pl. **papacies**) the position or period of office of the pope.

pa·pal /'pāpəl/ ▶ adj. relating to the pope or the papacy. ■ **pa·pal·ly** adv.

pa·pa·raz·zo /,päpə'rätsō/ ▶ n. (pl. **paparazzi** /-'rätsē/) a freelance photographer who pursues celebrities to get photographs of them.

pa·paw /pə'pô, 'pôpô/ ▶ n. variant spelling of PAWPAW.

pa·pa·ya /pə'pīə/ ▶ n. a tropical fruit with edible orange flesh and small black seeds.

pa·per /'pāpər/ ▶ n. **1** material manufactured in thin sheets from the pulp of wood or other fibrous substances, used for writing or printing on or as wrapping material. **2** (**papers**) sheets of paper covered with writing or printing; documents. **3** a newspaper. **4** a government

report or policy document. **5** an essay or dissertation. ▶v. **1** cover a wall with wallpaper. **2** (**paper something over**) disguise an awkward problem instead of resolving it. ▶adj. officially recorded but having no real existence or use: *a paper profit.* ■ **pa·per·less** adj. **pa·per·y** adj.
– PHRASES **on paper 1** in writing. **2** in theory rather than in reality.

pa·per·back /'pāpər,bak/ ▶n. a book bound in stiff paper or flexible cardboard.

pa·per·boy /'pāpər,boi/ (or **paper girl** /'pāpər,gərl/) ▶n. a boy (or girl) who delivers newspapers to people's homes.

pa·per clip ▶n. a piece of bent wire or plastic used for holding several sheets of paper together.

pa·per mon·ey ▶n. money in the form of banknotes.

pa·per route ▶n. **1** a job of regularly delivering newspapers. **2** the route taken to do this.

pa·per-thin ▶adj. very thin or insubstantial.

pa·per ti·ger ▶n. a person or thing that appears threatening but is actually weak or ineffectual.

pa·per trail ▶n. the total amount of written evidence of someone's activities.

pa·per·weight /'pāpər,wāt/ ▶n. a small, heavy object for keeping loose papers in place.

pa·per·work /'pāpər,wərk/ ▶n. routine work involving written documents.

pa·pier mâ·ché /,pāpər mə'shā, pä'p(y)ā/ ▶n. a mixture of paper and glue that is easily molded but becomes hard when dry.

pa·pil·la /pə'pilə/ ▶n. (pl. **papillae** /-'pil,ē, -'pil,ī/) a small rounded protuberance on a part of the body or on a plant. ■ **pap·il·lar·y** /'papə,lerē/ adj.

pap·il·lo·ma /,papə'lōmə/ ▶n. (pl. **papillomas** or **papillomata** /-mətə/) a small, usually benign wartlike growth.

pap·il·lon /,päpē'yôn/ ▶n. a breed of toy dog with ears suggesting the form of a butterfly.

pa·pist /'pāpist/ chiefly derogatory ▶n. a Roman Catholic. ■ adj. Roman Catholic.

pa·poose /pa'pōos, pə-/ ▶n. often offensive a young North American Indian child.

pap·ri·ka /pə'prēkə, pa-/ ▶n. a deep orange-red powdered spice made from certain varieties of sweet pepper.

Pap test /pap/ ▶n. a test to detect cancer of the cervix or uterus using a specimen from the neck of the uterus spread on a microscope slide (**Pap smear**).

Pap·u·an /'pāpōōən, 'papyōōən/ ▶n. **1** a person from Papua or Papua New Guinea. **2** a group of languages spoken in Papua New Guinea and neighboring islands. ▶adj. relating to Papua or its languages.

pap·ule /'pap,yōōl/ ▶n. a small pimple or swelling on the skin, often forming part of a rash.

pa·py·rus /pə'pīrəs/ ▶n. (pl. **papyri** /-'pīrī/ or **papyruses**) **1** a material made in ancient Egypt from the stem of a kind of water plant, used for writing or painting on. **2** the plant from which papyrus was obtained.

par /pär/ ▶n. **1** Golf the number of strokes a first-class player should normally require for a particular hole or course. **2** Stock Exchange the face value of a share or other security. ▶v. (**pars, parring, parred**) Golf play a hole in a score equal to par.
– PHRASES **above** (or **below** or **under**) **par** above (or below) the usual or expected level. **on par with** equal to. **par for the course** what is normal or expected in any given circumstances.

par·a[1] /'parə/ ▶n. informal a paratrooper.

par·a[2] /'pärə/ ▶n. (pl. same or **paras**) a unit of money of Bosnia, Montenegro, and Serbia, equal to one hundredth of a dinar.

para- (also **par-**) ▶prefix **1** beside; adjacent to: *parallel.* **2** beyond or distinct from, but comparable to: *paramilitary.*

par·a·ble /'parəbəl/ ▶n. a simple story used to illustrate a moral or spiritual lesson.

pa·rab·o·la /pə'rabələ/ ▶n. (pl. **parabolas** or **parabolae** /-lē, -lī/) a symmetrical open plane curve of the kind formed by the intersection of a cone with a plane parallel to its side. ■ **par·a·bol·ic** /,parə'bälik/ adj.

par·a·chute /'parə,shōōt/ ▶n. a cloth canopy that allows a person or heavy object attached to it to descend slowly through the air when dropped from a high position. ▶v. **1** drop from an aircraft by parachute. **2** chiefly Brit. appoint someone in an emergency or from outside the existing management structure: *he was parachuted in as chief executive in May.* ■ **par·a·chut·ist** n.

pa·rade /pə'rād/ ▶n. **1** a public procession. **2** a formal march or gathering of troops for inspection or display. **3** a series or succession: *the parade of celebrities who troop onto his show.* **4** a boastful or obvious display of something. ▶v. **1** walk, march, or display something in a parade. **2** display something in order to impress other people or attract attention: *he enjoyed being able to parade his knowledge.* **3** (**parade as**) appear to be something that is not the case: *these untruths parading as history.*

pa·rade ground ▶n. a place where troops gather for parade.

par·a·did·dle /'parə,didl/ ▶n. Music a simple drum roll consisting of four even strokes.

par·a·digm /'parə,dīm/ ▶n. a typical example, pattern, or model of something: *society's paradigm of the 'ideal woman.'* ■ **par·a·dig·mat·ic** /,parədig'matik/ adj. **par·a·dig·mat·i·cal·ly** adv.

par·a·digm shift ▶n. a fundamental change in approach or in the assumptions underlying something.

par·a·dise /'parə,dīs/ ▶n. **1** (in some religions) heaven as the place where the good live after death. **2** the Garden of Eden. **3** an ideal or very beautiful place or state: *the surrounding countryside is a walker's paradise.* ■ **par·a·dis·al** /,parə'dīsəl/ adj. **par·a·di·si·a·cal** /,parədi'sīəkəl/ adj.

par·a·dox /'parə,däks/ ▶n. **1** a statement that sounds absurd or seems to contradict itself but may in fact be true. **2** a person or thing that combines contradictory features or qualities. ■ **par·a·dox·i·cal** /,parə'däksikəl/ adj. **par·a·dox·i·cal·ly** adv.

par·af·fin /'parəfin/ ▶n. **1** (also **paraffin wax**) a flammable waxy solid obtained from petroleum or shale and used for sealing and waterproofing and in candles. **2** (also **paraffin oil** or **liquid paraffin**) Brit. a liquid fuel made in a similar way, especially kerosene.

par·a·glid·ing /'parə,glīdiNG/ ▶n. a sport in which a person glides through the air attached to a wide parachute after jumping from or being hauled to a height. ■ **par·a·glide** v. **par·a·glid·er** n.

par·a·gon /'parə,gän, -gən/ ▶ n. a person or thing seen as perfect, or as a perfect example of a particular quality: *he was a paragon of blond male beauty.*

par·a·graph /'parə,graf/ ▶ n. a distinct section of a piece of writing, beginning on a new line and often indented.

par·a·graph mark ▶ n. a symbol (usually ¶) used to mark a new paragraph or as a reference mark.

Par·a·guay·an /,parə'gwīən, -'gwä-/ ▶ n. a person from Paraguay. ▶ adj. relating to Paraguay.

par·a·keet /'parə,kēt/ (also **parrakeet**) ▶ n. a small parrot with mainly green plumage and a long tail.

par·a·le·gal /,parə'lēgəl/ ▶ n. a person trained in certain legal matters but not fully qualified as a lawyer.

par·al·lax /'parə,laks/ ▶ n. 1 the apparent difference in the position of an object when viewed from different positions, e.g., through the viewfinder and the lens of a camera. 2 Astronomy the angular difference in the apparent positions of a star observed from opposite sides of the earth's orbit. ■ **par·al·lac·tic** /,parə'laktik/ adj.

par·al·lel /'parə,lel, -ləl/ ▶ adj. 1 (of lines, planes, or surfaces) side by side and having the same distance continuously between them. 2 occurring or existing at the same time or in a similar way: *a parallel universe.* ▶ n. 1 a person or thing that is similar or comparable to another. 2 a similarity or comparison: *there are interesting parallels between the 1960s and the 1940s.* 3 (also **parallel of latitude**) each of the imaginary parallel circles of latitude on the earth's surface. 4 Printing two parallel lines (‖) used as a reference mark for footnotes. ▶ v. (**parallels**, **paralleling**, **paralleled**) 1 run or lie parallel to something. 2 be similar or corresponding to: *changes in 20th century art have paralleled changes in society.* ■ **par·al·lel·ism** n.
– PHRASES **in parallel 1** taking place at the same time and having some connection. **2** (of electrical components or circuits) connected to common points at each end, so that the current is divided between them.

par·al·lel bars ▶ pl.n. a pair of parallel rails on posts, used in gymnastics.

par·al·lel im·ports ▶ pl.n. goods imported by unlicensed distributors for sale at less than the manufacturer's official retail price.

par·al·lel·o·gram /,parə'lelə,gram/ ▶ n. a plane figure with four straight sides and opposite sides parallel.

Par·a·lym·pics /,parə'limpiks/ ▶ pl.n. (usu. treated as sing.) an international athletic competition for athletes with disabilities. ■ **Par·a·lym·pic** adj.

pa·ral·y·sis /pə'raləsis/ ▶ n. (pl. **paralyses** /-sēz/) 1 the loss of the ability to move part or most of the body. 2 inability to act or function.

par·a·lyt·ic /,parə'litik/ ▶ adj. relating to paralysis. ■ **par·a·lyt·i·cal·ly** adv.

par·a·lyze /'parə,līz/ (Brit. also **paralyse**) ▶ v. 1 cause a person or part of the body to become partly or wholly incapable of movement. 2 prevent someone or something from functioning: *the regional capital was paralyzed by a general strike.*

par·a·me·ci·um /,parə'mēsн(ē)əm, -sēəm/ ▶ n. (pl.

paramecia /,parə'mēsн(ē)ə, -sēə/) a single-celled freshwater animal that has a slipperlike shape.

par·a·med·ic /,parə'medik/ ▶ n. a person who is trained to do medical work, especially emergency first aid, but is not a fully qualified doctor. ■ **par·a·med·i·cal** adj.

pa·ram·e·ter /pə'ramitər/ ▶ n. 1 a limit or boundary that dictates the scope of a particular process or activity: *the parameters within which the media work.* 2 technical a numerical or other measurable factor forming one of a set that defines a system or sets the conditions of its operation. 3 Mathematics a quantity that is fixed for the case in question but may vary in other cases. ■ **par·a·met·ric** /,parə'metrik/ adj. **par·a·met·ri·cal·ly** adv.

par·a·mil·i·tar·y /,parə'mili,terē/ ▶ adj. organized on similar lines to a military force. ▶ n. (pl. **paramilitaries**) a member of a paramilitary organization.

par·a·mount /'parə,mount/ ▶ adj. 1 more important than anything else: *the safety of the staff is paramount.* 2 having supreme power. ■ **par·a·mount·cy** /-sē/ n.

par·a·mour /'parə,mŏŏr/ ▶ n. old use a person's lover, especially the illicit lover of someone who is married.

par·a·noi·a /,parə'noiə/ ▶ n. 1 a mental condition characterized by delusions of persecution, unfounded jealousy, or exaggerated self-importance. 2 unjustified suspicion and mistrust of other people. ■ **par·a·noi·ac** /-'noi-ak, -'noi-ik/ (also **paranoic** /-'noi-ik/) adj. & n. **par·a·noi·a·cal·ly** adv.

par·a·noid /'parə,noid/ ▶ adj. 1 relating to or suffering from paranoia. 2 unreasonably or obsessively anxious, suspicious, or mistrustful: *he was paranoid about being overcharged.*

par·a·nor·mal /,parə'nôrməl/ ▶ adj. beyond the scope of normal scientific understanding. ■ **par·a·nor·mal·ly** adv.

par·a·pet /'parəpit/ ▶ n. 1 a low protective wall along the edge of a roof, bridge, or balcony. 2 a protective wall or bank along the top of a military trench.

par·a·pher·na·lia /,parəfə(r)'nālyə/ ▶ n. (treated as sing. or pl.) miscellaneous items, especially the equipment needed for a particular activity.

par·a·phrase /'parə,frāz/ ▶ v. express the meaning of something written or spoken using different words. ▶ n. a rewording of something written or spoken.

par·a·ple·gi·a /,parə'plēj(ē)ə/ ▶ n. paralysis of the legs and lower body. ■ **par·a·ple·gic** /-jik/ adj. & n.

par·a·psy·chol·o·gy /,parəsī'kälǝjē/ ▶ n. the study of mental phenomena that cannot be explained by scientific knowledge, such as hypnosis or telepathy. ■ **par·a·psy·cho·log·i·cal** /-,sīkə'läjikəl/ adj. **par·a·psy·chol·o·gist** /-jist/ n.

par·a·quat /'parə,kwät/ ▶ n. a poisonous fast-acting weedkiller.

par·a·sail·ing /'parə,sāliNG/ ▶ n. the sport of gliding through the air wearing an open parachute while being towed by a motorboat. ■ **par·a·sail** /'parə,sāl/ n. & v.

par·a·site /'parə,sīt/ ▶ n. 1 an animal or plant that lives in or on another animal or plant from which it obtains food. 2 derogatory a person who lives off or exploits other people. ■ **par·a·sit·ism** /'parəsi,tizəm, -,sī-/ n.

par·a·sit·ic /ˌparəˈsitik/ ▶ adj. **1** (of an animal or plant) living in or on another animal or plant. **2** resulting from infestation by a parasite: *a parasitic disease.* **3** derogatory (of a person) habitually relying on or exploiting other people. ■ **par·a·sit·i·cal** adj. **par·a·sit·i·cal·ly** adv.

par·a·si·tize /ˈparəsɪˌtīz, -sī-/ ▶ v. live in or on another animal or plant as a parasite.

par·a·si·tol·o·gy /ˌparəsɪˈtäləjē, -sī-/ ▶ n. the study of parasitic animals and plants. ■ **par·a·si·tol·o·gist** /-jist/ n.

par·a·sol /ˈparəˌsȯl, -ˌsäl/ ▶ n. a light umbrella used to give shade from the sun.

par·a·sym·pa·thet·ic /ˌparəˌsimpəˈTHetik/ ▶ adj. relating to a system of nerves arising from the brain and the lower end of the spinal cord and supplying the internal organs, blood vessels, and glands.

par·a·thy·roid /ˌparəˈTHĪˌroid/ ▶ n. a gland next to the thyroid that produces a hormone that regulates calcium levels in a person's body.

par·a·troops /ˈparəˌtro͞ops/ ▶ pl.n. troops equipped to be dropped by parachute from aircraft. ■ **par·a·troop·er** n.

par·boil /ˈpärˌboil/ ▶ v. partly cook something by boiling it.

par·cel /ˈpärsəl/ ▶ n. **1** an object or collection of objects wrapped in paper in order to be carried or sent by post. **2** a quantity or amount of something: *a parcel of land.* ▶ v. (**parcels, parceling, parceled**) **1** make something into a parcel by wrapping it. **2** (**parcel something out**) divide something into portions and then share it between people.

parch /pärCH/ ▶ v. **1** make something dry through intense heat. **2** (as adj. **parched**) informal extremely thirsty.

parch·ment /ˈpärCHmənt/ ▶ n. **1** a stiff material made from the skin of a sheep or goat, formerly used for writing on. **2** (also **parchment paper**) stiff translucent paper treated to resemble parchment.

pard·ner ▶ n. variant spelling of PARTNER, used to represent US dialect speech: *howdy, pardner!*

par·don /ˈpärdn/ ▶ n. **1** the action of forgiving someone for a mistake or offense. **2** an official cancellation of the legal consequences of an offense. **3** Christian Church, historical an indulgence. ▶ v. **1** forgive or excuse a person, mistake, or offense. **2** give an offender an official pardon. ▶ exclam. used to ask a speaker to repeat something because one did not hear or understand it. ■ **par·don·a·ble** adj.

par·don·er /ˈpärdn-ər/ ▶ n. historical a person licensed to sell papal pardons or indulgences.

pare /pe(ə)r/ ▶ v. **1** trim something by cutting away its outer edges. **2** (often **pare something away/down**) reduce or diminish something in a number of small successive stages: *the company's domestic operations were pared down.*

par·ent /ˈpe(ə)rənt, ˈpar-/ ▶ n. **1** a father or mother. **2** an animal or plant from which younger ones are derived. **3** an organization that owns or controls a number of smaller organizations. **4** old use a forefather or ancestor. ▶ v. (often as n. **parenting**) be or act as a parent to someone: *institutions cannot provide good parenting.* ■ **pa·ren·tal** /pəˈrentl/ adj. **pa·ren·tal·ly** /pəˈrentl-ē/ adv. **par·ent·hood** /-ˌho͝od/ n.

par·ent·age /ˈpe(ə)rəntij, ˈpar-/ ▶ n. the identity and origins of one's parents.

pa·ren·the·sis /pəˈrenTHəsis/ ▶ n. (pl. **parentheses** /-ˌsēz/) **1** a word or phrase inserted as an explanation or afterthought, in writing usually marked off by parentheses, dashes, or commas. **2** (**parentheses**) a pair of round brackets ( ) used to include such a word or phrase.

par·en·thet·i·cal /ˌparənˈTHetikəl/ (also **parenthetic**) ▶ adj. added as an explanation or afterthought. ■ **par·en·thet·i·cal·ly** adv.

par ex·cel·lence /ˌpär ˌeksəˈläns/ ▶ adj. (after a noun) better or more than all others of the same kind: *a designer par excellence.*

par·fait /pärˈfā/ ▶ n. **1** a rich cold dessert made with whipped cream, eggs, and fruit. **2** a dessert consisting of layers, especially of ice cream, meringue, and fruit, served in a tall glass.

par·he·li·on /pärˈhēlēən, -ˈhēlyən/ ▶ n. (pl. **parhelia** /-ˈhēlēə/) a bright spot in the sky on either side of the sun, formed by the refraction of sunlight through ice crystals high in the atmosphere.

pa·ri·ah /pəˈrīə/ ▶ n. **1** an outcast: *they were treated as social pariahs.* **2** historical a member of a low caste or of no caste in southern India.

pa·ri·e·tal /pəˈrīətəl/ ▶ adj. relating to the walls of a body cavity.

pa·ri·e·tal bone ▶ n. a bone forming the central side and upper back part of each side of the skull.

pa·ri·e·tal lobe ▶ n. either of the paired lobes of the brain at the top of the head.

par·i·mu·tu·el /ˌparə ˈmyo͞oCHo͞oəl/ ▶ n. a form of betting in which gamblers backing the first three places divide the losers' stakes.

par·ings /ˈpe(ə)riNGz/ ▶ pl.n. thin strips pared off from something.

par·ish /ˈpariSH/ ▶ n. **1** (in the Christian Church) a small administrative district with its own church and clergy. **2** (in Louisiana) a territorial division corresponding to a county in other states. **3** (also **civil parish**) Brit. the smallest unit of local government in rural areas.

pa·rish·ion·er /pəˈriSHənər/ ▶ n. a person who lives in a particular church parish.

Pa·ri·sian /pəˈrizHən, -ˈrē-, -ˈrizē-/ ▶ adj. relating to Paris. ▶ n. a person from Paris.

Pa·ri·si·enne /pəˌrēzē·en/ ▶ n. a Parisian girl or woman.

par·i·ty /ˈparitē/ ▶ n. **1** the state of being equal or equivalent: *the euro's slide to parity with the dollar.* **2** Mathematics the fact of being an even or an odd number.

park /pärk/ ▶ n. **1** a large public green area in a town or city, where people go to walk, relax, play games, etc. **2** a large area of land kept in its natural state for public recreational use. **3** an area devoted to a particular purpose: *an industrial park.* **4** chiefly Brit. a large area of woodland and pasture attached to a country house. ▶ v. **1** stop and leave a vehicle somewhere for a period of time. **2** informal leave something in a convenient place until required. **3** (**park oneself**) informal sit down.

par·ka /ˈpärkə/ ▶ n. a large, insulated windproof jacket with a hood.

park·ing ga·rage ▶ n. a multilevel building in which cars or other vehicles are left temporarily.

park·ing lot ▶ n. an area where cars or other vehicles are left temporarily.

park·ing me·ter ▶ n. a machine next to a parking space in a street, into which coins are inserted to pay for parking a vehicle.

park·ing tick·et ▶ n. a notice informing a driver of a fine for parking illegally.

Par·kin·son's dis·ease /'pärkinsənz/ ▶ n. a progressive disease of the brain and nervous system marked by involuntary trembling, muscular rigidity, and slow, imprecise movement. ■ **Par·kin·son·ism** /'pärkinsən,izəm/ n.

Par·kin·son's law ▶ n. the idea that work expands so as to fill the time available for its completion.

park·land /'pärk,land/ (also **parklands**) ▶ n. open land consisting of fields and scattered groups of trees.

park·way /'pärk,wā/ ▶ n. a highway or main road with trees, grass, etc., planted alongside.

par·lance /'pärləns/ ▶ n. a way of using words associated with a particular subject: *medical parlance.*

par·lay /'pär,lā, -lē/ ▶ v. (**parlay something into**) turn an asset, situation, etc., into something much better or more valuable: *a banker who parlayed a sizable inheritance into a financial empire.* ▶ n. a bet placed on a series of events, the winnings and stake from each being placed on the next.

par·ley /'pärlē/ ▶ n. (pl. **parleys**) a meeting between opponents or enemies to discuss terms for a truce. ▶ v. (**parleys, parleying, parleyed**) hold a parley.

par·lia·ment /'pärləmənt/ ▶ n. 1 (**Parliament**) (in the UK) the highest lawmaking body, consisting of the king or queen, the House of Lords, and the House of Commons. 2 a similar body in other countries.

par·lia·men·tar·i·an /,pärləmen'te(ə)rēən/ ▶ n. 1 a member of parliament who is experienced in parliamentary procedures and debates. 2 historical a supporter of Parliament in the English Civil War; a Roundhead. ▶ adj. relating to parliament or parliamentarians.

par·lia·men·ta·ry /,pärlə'mentərē/ ▶ adj. relating to, enacted by, or suitable for a parliament.

par·lor /'pärlər/ (Brit. **parlour**) ▶ n. 1 dated a sitting room. 2 a store or business providing particular goods or services: *an ice-cream parlor.* 3 a room or building equipped for milking cows.

par·lor game ▶ n. an indoor game, especially a word game.

par·lous /'pärləs/ ▶ adj. old use or humorous dangerously uncertain; precarious: *the parlous state of the economy.*

Par·ma ham /'pärmə/ ▶ n. a strongly flavored Italian cured ham, eaten uncooked and thinly sliced.

Par·me·san /'pärmə,zän/ ▶ n. a hard, dry Italian cheese used chiefly in grated form.

pa·ro·chi·al /pə'rōkēəl/ ▶ adj. 1 relating to a parish. 2 having a narrow outlook or range: *parochial attitudes.* ■ **pa·ro·chi·al·ism** /-,izəm/ n.

pa·ro·chi·al school ▶ n. a private school operated and supported by a particular church or parish, especially a Catholic one.

par·o·dy /'parədē/ ▶ n. (pl. **parodies**) 1 a piece of writing or music that deliberately copies the style of another, exaggerating it in order to be funny or ironical. 2 an imitation of something that falls far short of the real thing.

▶ v. (**parodies, parodying, parodied**) produce a parody of something. ■ **pa·rod·ic** /pə'rädik/ adj. **par·o·dist** /-dist/ n.

pa·role /pə'rōl/ ▶ n. 1 the temporary or permanent release of a prisoner before the end of a sentence, on condition that they behave well. 2 historical a prisoner of war's word of honor not to escape or, if released, to return to custody under certain specified conditions. ▶ v. release a prisoner on parole. ■ **pa·rol·ee** /-,rō'lē/ n.

pa·rot·id /pə'rätid/ ▶ adj. relating to a pair of large salivary glands situated just in front of each ear.

par·ox·ysm /'parək,sizəm, pə'räk-/ ▶ n. a sudden attack or outburst: *a paroxysm of weeping.* ■ **par·ox·ys·mal** /,parək'sizməl, pə,räk-/ adj.

par·quet /pär'kā/ ▶ n. flooring composed of wooden blocks arranged in a geometric pattern. ■ **par·quet·ry** /'pärkitrē/ n.

parr /pär/ ▶ n. (pl. same) a young salmon or trout up to two years old.

par·ri·cide /'parə,sīd/ ▶ n. 1 the killing of a parent or other near relative. 2 a person who commits parricide. ■ **par·ri·cid·al** /,parə'sīdl/ adj.

par·rot /'parət/ ▶ n. a mainly tropical bird with brightly colored plumage and a strong hooked bill, some kinds of which are able to mimic human speech. ▶ v. (**parrots, parroting, parroted**) repeat something mechanically.

par·rot·fish /'parət,fiSH/ ▶ n. (pl. same or **parrotfishes**) a brightly colored sea fish with a parrotlike beak.

par·ry /'parē/ ▶ v. (**parries, parrying, parried**) 1 ward off a weapon or attack. 2 say something to avoid answering a question directly. ▶ n. (pl. **parries**) an act of parrying.

parse /pärs/ ▶ v. divide a sentence into parts and describe the grammar of each word or part.

par·sec /'pär,sek/ ▶ n. a unit of astronomical distance equal to about 3.25 light years.

Par·see /'pär'sē, 'pärsē/ ▶ n. a descendant of a group of Zoroastrian Persians who fled to India during the 7th–8th centuries.

par·si·mo·ny /'pärsə,mōnē/ ▶ n. extreme unwillingness to spend money or use resources. ■ **par·si·mo·ni·ous** /,pärsə'mōnēəs/ adj.

pars·ley /'pärslē/ ▶ n. an herb with crinkly or flat leaves, used for seasoning or garnishing food.

pars·nip /'pärsnip/ ▶ n. a long tapering cream-colored root vegetable.

par·son /'pärsən/ ▶ n. 1 dated, informal any member of the clergy, especially a Protestant one. 2 (in the Church of England) a parish priest.

par·son·age /'pärsənij/ ▶ n. a church house provided for a parson.

par·son's nose ▶ n. informal the piece of fatty flesh at the rump of a cooked fowl.

part /pärt/ ▶ n. 1 a piece or section that is combined with others to make up a whole. 2 some but not all of something. 3 a specified fraction of a whole: *a twentieth part.* 4 a role played by an actor or actress. 5 a person's contribution to something: *he played a key part in ending the revolt.* 6 (**parts**) informal a region. 7 a measure allowing comparison between the amounts of different ingredients used in a mixture: *a mix of one part cement to five parts ballast.* 8 a melody or other constituent of harmony given to a particular voice or instrument. 9 a line of scalp revealed by combing the hair away from it on either side. ▶ v. **1** move apart or divide to leave a central space: *her lips parted in a smile.* **2** (also **be parted**) leave someone's company. **3** (**part with**) give up possession of. ▶ adv. partly: *part jazz, part blues.*

– PHRASES **be part and parcel of** be an essential element of. **for my** (or **his, her,** etc.) **part** as far as I am (or he, she, etc., is) concerned. **in part** to some extent. **on the part of** used to say that someone is responsible for something. **part company** go in different directions or end a relationship. **take part** join in an activity. **take the part of** give support to someone in a dispute.

par·take /pär'tāk/ ▶ v. (past **partook** /pär'tŏŏk/; past part. **partaken**) formal **1** (**partake of**) eat or drink something. **2** (**partake in**) participate in an activity.

par·terre /pär'te(ə)r/ ▶ n. a group of flower beds laid out in a formal pattern.

part ex·change ▶ n. Brit. a way of buying something in which one gives an article that one already owns as part of the payment for a more expensive one, paying the balance in money.

par·the·no·gen·e·sis /ˌpärthənō'jenəsis/ ▶ n. Biology reproduction from an ovum without fertilization, especially in some invertebrate animals and lower plants. ■ **par·the·no·ge·net·ic** /-jə'netik/ adj.

Par·thi·an shot /'pärTHēən/ ▶ n. another term for PARTING SHOT.

par·tial /'pärSHəl/ ▶ adj. **1** existing only in part; incomplete. **2** favoring one side in a dispute above the other; biased. **3** (**partial to**) having a liking for. ■ **par·ti·al·i·ty** /ˌpärSHē'alitē/ n. **par·tial·ly** adv.

par·tic·i·pant /pär'tisəpənt/ ▶ n. a person who takes part in something.

par·tic·i·pate /pär'tisəˌpāt/ ▶ v. take part in an activity or event. ■ **par·tic·i·pa·tion** /pärˌtisə'pāSHən/ n. **par·tic·i·pa·tive** /-ˌpātiv, -pətiv/ adj. **par·tic·i·pa·tor** /-ˌpātər/ n. **par·tic·i·pa·to·ry** /-pəˌtôrē/ adj.

par·ti·ci·ple /'pärtəˌsipəl/ ▶ n. Grammar a word formed from a verb and used as an adjective or noun (*burned* as in *burned toast*; *breeding* as in *good breeding*) or used to make compound verb forms (*going* as in *is going*; *been* as in *has been*). ■ **par·ti·cip·i·al** /ˌpärtə'sipēəl/ adj.

par·ti·cle /'pärtikəl/ ▶ n. **1** a minute piece of a substance. **2** Physics a component of the physical world smaller than an atom, e.g., an electron or proton. **3** Grammar an adverb or preposition that has comparatively little meaning, e.g., *in, up, off,* or *over,* used with verbs to make phrasal verbs.

par·ti·cle·board /'pärtikəlˌbôrd/ ▶ n. another term for CHIPBOARD.

par·ti·col·ored /'pärti'kələrd/ ▶ adj. having two or more different colors.

par·tic·u·lar /pə(r)'tikyələr/ ▶ adj. **1** relating to an individual member of a group or class. **2** more than is usual; special: *he had dressed with particular care.* **3** insisting that something should be correct or suitable in every detail; fastidious: *she is very particular about cleanliness.* ▶ n. a detail.

– PHRASES **in particular** especially.

par·tic·u·lar·ism /pə(r)'tikyələˌrizəm/ ▶ n. **1** exclusive attachment to one's own group, party, or nation. **2** the principle of leaving each

state in an empire or federation free to govern itself.

par·tic·u·lar·i·ty /pə(r)ˌtikyə'laritē/ ▶ n. (pl. **particularities**) **1** the quality of being individual. **2** attention to detail in the treatment of something. **3** (**particularities**) small details.

par·tic·u·lar·ize /pə(r)'tikyələˌrīz/ ▶ v. formal treat something individually or in detail. ■ **par·tic·u·lar·i·za·tion** /pə(r)ˌtikyələˌrī'zāSHən/ n.

par·tic·u·lar·ly /pə(r)'tikyələrlē/ ▶ adv. **1** more than is usual; especially or very. **2** in particular; specifically.

par·tic·u·late /pär'tikyəlit, -ˌlāt/ ▶ adj. relating to or in the form of minute particles. ▶ n. (**particulates**) matter in the form of minute particles.

part·ing shot ▶ n. a cutting remark made by someone as they are leaving.

par·ti·san /'pärtəzən/ ▶ n. **1** a strong supporter of a party, cause, or person. **2** a member of an armed group fighting secretly against an occupying force. ▶ adj. prejudiced in favor of a particular cause, party, or person. ■ **par·ti·san·ship** /-ˌSHip/ n.

par·ti·tion /pär'tiSHən, pər-/ ▶ n. **1** a light interior wall or other structure dividing a space into parts. **2** the division of something into parts, especially a country. ▶ v. **1** divide into parts: *an agreement was reached to partition the country.* **2** divide a room with a partition. ■ **par·ti·tion·ist** /-ist/ n.

par·ti·tive /'pärtitiv/ ▶ adj. (of a grammatical construction) indicating that only a part of a whole is referred to (e.g., *a slice of bacon, some of the children*). ▶ n. a noun or pronoun used as the first term in a partitive construction (e.g., *slice, some*).

part·ly /'pärtlē/ ▶ adv. to some extent; not completely.

part·ner /'pärtnər/ ▶ n. **1** a person who takes part in an undertaking with another or others, especially in a business with shared risks and profits. **2** either of two people doing something as a pair. **3** either member of a couple in a marriage or a romantic or sexual relationship. ▶ v. be the partner of someone.

part·ner·ship /'pärtnərˌSHip/ ▶ n. **1** the state of being a partner or partners. **2** an association of two or more people as partners.

part of speech ▶ n. a category in which a word is placed according to its grammatical function, e.g., noun, pronoun, adjective, verb.

par·took /pär'tŏŏk/ ▶ past of PARTAKE.

par·tridge /'pärtrij/ ▶ n. (pl. same or **partridges**) a short-tailed game bird with mainly brown plumage.

part song ▶ n. a song with three or more voice parts, typically without musical accompaniment.

part-time ▶ adj. & adv. for only part of the usual working day or week.

par·tu·ri·ent /pär't(y)ŏŏrēənt/ ▶ adj. technical about to give birth; in labor.

par·tu·ri·tion /ˌpärchŏŏ'riSHən/ ▶ n. formal or technical the action of giving birth; childbirth.

part·way /'pärtˌwā, 'pärt'wā/ ▶ adv. part of the way.

par·ty /'pärtē/ ▶ n. (pl. **parties**) **1** a social gathering of invited guests. **2** a political organization that puts forward candidates for election for local or national office. **3** a group

of people taking part in an activity or trip.
4 a person or group forming one side in an agreement or dispute. **5** informal, dated a person of a particular type: *an old party came in to clean.*
▶ v. (**parties, partying, partied**) informal enjoy oneself by going out socially and typically also drinking and dancing.
– PHRASES **be party** (or **a party**) **to** be involved in.

par·ty line ▶ n. **1** a policy or policies officially adopted by a political party. **2** a telephone line shared by two or more subscribers.

par·ty pol·i·tics ▶ pl.n. (treated as sing. or pl.) politics that relate to political parties rather than to the good of the general public.

par·ty poop·er ▶ n. informal a person who spoils other people's fun.

par·ty wall ▶ n. a wall shared by two adjoining buildings or rooms.

par·ve·nu /ˈpärvə,n(y)o͞o/ ▶ n. chiefly derogatory a person from a humble background who has recently become rich or famous.

par·vo·vi·rus /ˈpärvō,vīrəs/ ▶ n. any of a class of very small viruses causing contagious disease in dogs and other animals.

pas·cal /päˈskäl/ ▶ n. the SI unit of pressure, equal to one newton per square meter.

pas·chal /ˈpaskəl/ ▶ adj. **1** relating to Easter. **2** relating to the Jewish Passover.

pas de deux /ˌpä də ˈdo͞o/ ▶ n. (pl. same) Ballet a dance for a couple.

pa·sha /ˈpäSHə, ˈpaSHə, pəˈSHä/ (also **pacha** pronunc. same) ▶ n. historical the title of a Turkish officer of high rank.

pash·mi·na /pəSHˈmēnə/ ▶ n. a shawl made from fine-quality goat's wool.

Pash·to /ˈpəSHtō/ ▶ n. the official language of Afghanistan, also spoken in northern Pakistan.

pa·so do·ble /ˌpäsō ˈdōblā/ ▶ n. (pl. **paso dobles**) a fast-paced ballroom dance based on a Latin American marching style.

pasque·flow·er /ˈpask,flou(-ə)r/ ▶ n. a spring-flowering plant with purple flowers.

pass[1] /pas/ ▶ v. **1** move or go onward, past, through, or across. **2** change from one state or condition to another: *those who have just passed from middle-aged to elderly.* **3** transfer something to someone. **4** kick, hit, or throw the ball to a teammate. **5** (of time) go by. **6** occupy or spend time. **7** be done or said: *not another word passed between them.* **8** come to an end. **9** be successful in an exam, test, or course. **10** declare something to be satisfactory. **11** approve or put into effect a proposal or law by voting. **12** formally state a judgment or sentence. **13** choose not to do or have something that is offered: *we'll pass on dessert and just have coffee.* **14** discharge urine or feces from the body. ▶ n. **1** an act of passing. **2** a success in an exam. **3** an official document authorizing the holder to go somewhere or use something. **4** (also **a pretty pass**) an undesirable situation: *things came to such a pass that mothers feared for their daughters' safety.* **5** a single scan through a set of computer data or a program.
■ **pass·er** n.
– PHRASES **make a pass at** informal make a sexual approach to someone. **pass as/for** be accepted as. **pass away/on** (of a person) die. **pass something off** lightly dismiss an awkward remark. **pass someone/thing off as** present

someone or something in a way that gives a false impression. **pass out** become unconscious. **pass someone over** ignore someone's claims to be promoted. **pass something over** avoid mentioning or considering something. **pass something up** choose not to take up an opportunity.

pass[2] ▶ n. a route over or through mountains.

pass·a·ble /ˈpasəbəl/ ▶ adj. **1** just good enough to be accepted. **2** (of a route) able to be traveled along or on. ■ **pass·a·bly** adv.

pas·sage /ˈpasij/ ▶ n. **1** the action of passing: *the feeling will fade with the passage of time.* **2** a way through something. **3** a journey by sea or air. **4** the right to pass through somewhere: *a permit for safe passage.* **5** a short section from a written work or musical composition.

pas·sage·way /ˈpasij,wā/ ▶ n. a corridor or other narrow passage between buildings or rooms.

pass·book /ˈpas,bo͝ok/ ▶ n. a book issued by a bank to an account holder, recording amounts deposited and withdrawn.

pas·sé /paˈsā/ ▶ adj. no longer fashionable; out of date.

pas·sen·ger /ˈpasinjər/ ▶ n. a person traveling in a vehicle, ship, or aircraft other than the driver, pilot, or crew.

pas·sen·ger pi·geon ▶ n. an extinct long-tailed North American pigeon, noted for its long migrations in huge flocks.

pass·er·by /ˈpasər,bī/ ▶ n. (pl. **passersby** /ˈpasərz,bī/) a person who happens to be walking past something or someone.

pas·ser·ine /ˈpasərin, -,rīn/ ▶ adj. referring to birds of a large group distinguished by having feet adapted for perching and including all songbirds.

pas·sim /ˈpasim/ ▶ adv. (of references) at various places throughout a written work.

pass·ing /ˈpasiNG/ ▶ adj. **1** done quickly and casually. **2** (of a resemblance or similarity) slight. ▶ n. **1** the end of something. **2** euphemistic a person's death.
– PHRASES **in passing** while doing or saying something else; briefly.

pas·sion /ˈpaSHən/ ▶ n. **1** very strong emotion. **2** intense sexual love. **3** an intense enthusiasm for something: *the English have a passion for gardens.* **4** (**the Passion**) the suffering and death of Jesus. ■ **pas·sion·less** adj.

pas·sion·ate /ˈpaSHənit/ ▶ adj. having or showing intense emotion, sexual love, or enthusiasm: *a passionate belief in freedom.*
■ **pas·sion·ate·ly** adv.

pas·sion·flow·er /ˈpaSHən,flou(-ə)r/ ▶ n. a climbing plant with a flower whose parts are said to suggest objects associated with Jesus's Crucifixion.

pas·sion fruit ▶ n. the edible purple fruit of some species of passionflower.

Pas·sion play ▶ n. a play about Jesus's crucifixion.

pas·sive /ˈpasiv/ ▶ adj. **1** accepting or allowing what happens or what others do, without reacting or resisting: *he takes on a passive role in the story.* **2** Grammar (of verbs) in which the subject undergoes the action of the verb (e.g., *they were killed* as opposed to the active form *he killed them*). **3** (of a circuit or device) containing no source of energy or electromotive force. **4** Chemistry (of a metal) unreactive because of a thin inert surface layer of oxide. ▶ n. a passive form of a verb. ■ **pas·sive·ly** adv. **pas·sive·ness** n. **pas·siv·i·ty** /pa'sivitē/ n.

pas·sive re·sist·ance ▶ n. nonviolent opposition to authority, especially a refusal to cooperate with legal requirements.

pas·sive smok·ing ▶ n. breathing in smoke from other people's cigarettes, cigars, or pipes.

pass·key /'pas,kē/ ▶ n. **1** a key given only to people who are officially allowed access. **2** a master key.

Pass·o·ver /'pas,ōvər/ ▶ n. the major Jewish spring festival, commemorating the liberation of the Israelites from slavery in Egypt.

pass·port /'pas,pôrt/ ▶ n. **1** an official government document certifying the holder's identity and citizenship and entitling them to travel abroad. **2** a thing that enables someone to do or achieve something: *qualifications are a passport to success.*

pass·word /'pas,wərd/ ▶ n. **1** a secret word or phrase used to gain entry to somewhere. **2** a series of letters and/or numbers allowing someone to use a computer system.

past /past/ ▶ adj. **1** gone by in time and no longer existing: *the danger is now past.* **2** belonging to a former time. **3** (of time) occurring before and leading up to the present: *he's been unwell for the past six months.* **4** (of a tense of a verb) expressing an action that has happened or a state that used to exist. ▶ n. **1** a past period or the events in it. **2** a person's or thing's history or earlier life: *the country's colorful past.* **3** a past tense or form of a verb. ▶ prep. **1** beyond in time or space. **2** in front of or from one side to the other of. **3** beyond the scope, limits, or power of: *I was long past caring.* ▶ adv. **1** so as to pass from one side to the other. **2** used to indicate the passage of time.
– PHRASES **not put it past** believe someone to be capable of doing something wrong or rash. **past it** informal, chiefly Brit. too old to be any good at anything.

pas·ta /'pästə/ ▶ n. dough formed into various shapes (e.g., spaghetti, lasagna), cooked as part of a dish or in boiling water.

paste /pāst/ ▶ n. **1** a thick, soft, moist substance. **2** a savory spread: *salmon paste.* **3** a glue made from water and starch. **4** a hard glassy substance used in making imitation gems. ▶ v. **1** coat or stick something with paste. **2** Computing insert a section of data into a document. **3** informal beat or defeat someone severely.

paste·board /'pās(t),bôrd/ ▶ n. thin board made by pasting together sheets of paper.

pas·tel /pa'stel/ ▶ n. **1** a crayon made of powdered pigments bound with gum or resin. **2** a picture drawn with pastels. **3** a pale shade of a color. ▶ adj. (of a color) pale. ■ **pas·tel·ist** (also **pastelist**) n.

pas·tern /'pastərn/ ▶ n. the part of a horse's or other animal's foot between the fetlock and the hoof.

paste·up ▶ n. a document prepared for copying or printing by pasting various sections on a backing.

pas·teur·ize /'pascHə,rīz/ ▶ v. make milk or other food safe to eat by heating it to destroy most of the microorganisms in it. ■ **pas·teur·i·za·tion** /,pascHəri'zāsHən/ n.

pas·tiche /pa'stēsH, pä-/ ▶ n. an artistic work in a style that imitates that of another work, artist, or period. ■ **pas·ti·cheur** /pas'tēsHər/ n.

past·ie /'pāstē/ ▶ n. variant spelling of PASTY.

pas·tille /pa'stēl/ ▶ n. a small candy or lozenge.

pas·time /'pas,tīm/ ▶ n. an activity done regularly for enjoyment; a hobby.

pas·tis /pä'stēs/ ▶ n. (pl. same) an anise-flavored aperitif.

past mas·ter ▶ n. a person who is skilled in an activity.

pas·tor /'pastər/ ▶ n. a minister in charge of a Christian church or congregation.

pas·to·ral /'pastərəl, pas'tôrəl/ ▶ adj. **1** relating to or portraying country life: *the property is located in a beautiful pastoral setting.* **2** relating to the farming or grazing of sheep or cattle. **3** (in the Christian Church) relating to the giving of spiritual guidance by the clergy. ▶ n. a literary work portraying an idealized version of country life. ■ **pas·to·ral·ism** /'pastərə,lizəm/ n.

pas·to·rale /,pastə'räl, -'ral/ ▶ n. (pl. **pastorales** or **pastorali** /-'rälē/) **1** a slow instrumental composition in compound time. **2** a simple musical play with a rural subject.

past par·ti·ci·ple ▶ n. the form of a verb that is used in forming perfect and passive tenses and sometimes as an adjective, e.g., *looked* in *have you looked?*, *lost* in *lost property.*

past per·fect ▶ n. Grammar a tense of verbs expressing an action completed prior to some past point of time, in English exemplified by *he had gone.*

pas·tra·mi /pə'strämē/ ▶ n. highly seasoned smoked beef.

pas·try /'pāstrē/ ▶ n. (pl. **pastries**) **1** a dough of flour, fat, and water, used as a base and covering in baked dishes such as pies. **2** a cake consisting of sweet pastry with a cream, jam, or fruit filling.

pas·tur·age /'pascHərij/ ▶ n. **1** land used for grazing cattle or sheep. **2** the occupation of pasturing cattle or sheep.

pas·ture /'pascHər/ ▶ n. land covered with grass, suitable for grazing cattle or sheep. ▶ v. put animals to graze in a pasture.
– PHRASES **new pastures** (or **pastures new**) somewhere offering new opportunities. **put someone out to pasture** force someone to retire.

past·y¹ /'pastē/ (also **pastie**) ▶ n. (pl. **pasties**) Brit. a folded pastry case filled with meat and vegetables.

past·y² /'pāstē/ ▶ adj. (**pastier, pastiest**) (of a person's skin) unhealthily pale.

pat¹ /pat/ ▶ v. (**pats, patting, patted**) **1** tap someone or something quickly and gently with the flat of the hand. **2** mold or position something with gentle taps. ▶ n. **1** an act of patting. **2** a compact mass of a soft substance.
– PHRASES **a pat on the back** an expression of congratulation or encouragement.

pat² ▶ adj. too quick and easy and not convincing: *there are no pat answers to these questions.*
– PHRASES **have something down pat** have something memorized perfectly.

Pat·a·go·ni·an /,patə'gōnēən/ ▶ n. a person from the South American region of Patagonia. ▶ adj. relating to Patagonia.

patch /pacH/ ▶ n. **1** a piece of material used to mend a hole or strengthen a weak point. **2** a small area that is different from its surroundings. **3** a small plot of land: *a cabbage* *patch.* **4** informal a brief period of time: *she's going through a bad patch.* **5** a shield worn over a sightless or injured eye. **6** an adhesive piece of material containing a drug and worn on the skin so that the drug may be gradually absorbed. **7** a temporary electrical or telephone connection. **8** a small piece of code inserted to correct or improve a computer program. ▶ *v.* **1** mend, strengthen, or protect something with a patch. **2** (**patch someone/thing up**) informal treat an injured person or repair something temporarily. **3** (**patch something up**) informal settle a quarrel or dispute. **4** (**patch something together**) make something hastily. **5** connect someone by a temporary electrical, radio, or telephonic connection. ■ **patch·er** n.

patch·ou·li /pə'chōōlē/ ▶ n. a scented oil obtained from a SE Asian shrub, used in perfumery, insecticides, and medicine.

patch pock·et ▶ n. a pocket made of a separate piece of cloth sewn onto the outside of a garment.

patch test ▶ n. an allergy test in which a range of substances are applied to the skin in light scratches or under a patch.

patch·work /'pach,wərk/ ▶ n. **1** needlework in which small pieces of cloth in different designs are sewn together to form a larger piece of fabric. **2** a thing composed of many different elements: *a patchwork of educational courses.* ■ **patch·worked** adj.

patch·y /'pachē/ ▶ adj. (**patchier, patchiest**) **1** existing or happening in small, isolated areas: *patchy fog.* **2** not complete or even throughout: *his memory of what happened was patchy.* ■ **patch·i·ly** adv. **patch·i·ness** n.

pate /pāt/ ▶ n. old use or humorous a person's head.

pâ·té /'pätā/ ▶ n. a rich savory paste made from finely ground or mashed meat, fish, or other ingredients.

pâ·té de foie gras /'pätā də ,fwä 'grä/ ▶ n. fuller form of FOIE GRAS.

pa·tel·la /pə'telə/ ▶ n. (pl. **patellae** /-lē/) the kneecap. ■ **pa·tel·lar** /-'telər/ adj.

pat·en /'patn/ ▶ n. a plate for holding the bread during the Eucharist (Holy Communion).

pat·ent ▶ n. /'patnt/ a government license giving a person or body the sole right to make, use, or sell an invention for a set period. ▶ adj. **1** easily recognizable; obvious/pātnt, 'pat-/: *she smiled with patent insincerity.* **2** /'patnt/made and marketed under a patent. ▶ v. /'patnt/ obtain a patent for an invention. ■ **pat·ent·a·ble** adj. **pat·ent·ly** /'patntlē, 'pā-/ adv.

pat·ent·ee /,patn'tē/ ▶ n. a person or body that obtains or holds a patent.

pat·ent leath·er ▶ n. glossy varnished leather.

pat·ent med·i·cine ▶ n. a medicine made and sold under a patent and available without prescription.

pa·ter /'pātər, 'pä-, 'pa-/ ▶ n. Brit. informal, dated father.

pa·ter·fa·mil·i·as /,pātərfə'milēəs, ,pä-/ ▶ n. (pl. **patresfamilias** /,pätrēzfə-, ,pä-/) the male head of a family.

pa·ter·nal /pə'tərnl/ ▶ adj. **1** relating to or like a father. **2** related through the father. ■ **pa·ter·nal·ly** adv.

pa·ter·nal·ism /pə'tərnl,izəm/ ▶ n. the policy of people in authority protecting those who are governed or employed by them, but also restricting their freedom or responsibilities.

■ **pa·ter·nal·ist** n. & adj. **pa·ter·nal·is·tic** /-,tərnl'istik/ adj.

pa·ter·ni·ty /pə'ternitē/ ▶ n. **1** the state of being a father. **2** a person's descent from a father.

pa·ter·ni·ty suit ▶ n. a court case held to establish the identity of a child's father.

pa·ter·nos·ter /'pätər,nästər, 'patər-/ ▶ n. (in the Roman Catholic Church) the Lord's Prayer.

path /paTH/ ▶ n. **1** a way or track laid down for walking or made by continual treading. **2** the direction in which a person or thing moves. **3** a course of action: *a chosen career path.*

path. ▶ abbr. **1** pathological. **2** pathology.

path·break·ing ▶ adj. pioneering; innovative.

pa·thet·ic /pə'THetik/ ▶ adj. **1** arousing pity. **2** informal completely inadequate. ■ **pa·thet·i·cal·ly** adv.

pa·thet·ic fal·la·cy ▶ n. (in art and literature) the depiction of inanimate things or animals as having human feelings.

path·find·er /'paTH,fīndər/ ▶ n. a person who goes ahead and discovers or shows others a way.

patho- ▶ comb.form relating to disease: *pathology.*

path·o·gen /'paTHəjən, -,jen/ ▶ n. a microorganism that can cause disease. ■ **path·o·gen·ic** /,paTHə'jenik/ adj.

path·o·log·i·cal /,paTHə'läjikəl/ (US **pathologic**) ▶ adj. **1** relating to or caused by a disease. **2** informal possessing a quality to an extreme or uncontrollable degree: *a pathological liar.* **3** relating to pathology. ■ **path·o·log·i·cal·ly** adv.

pa·thol·o·gy /pə'THäləjē/ ▶ n. **1** the branch of medicine concerned with the causes and effects of diseases. **2** the typical behavior of a disease. ■ **pa·thol·o·gist** n.

pa·thos /'pā,THäs, -,THôs/ ▶ n. a quality that arouses pity or sadness.

path·way /'paTH,wā/ ▶ n. a path or its course.

pa·tience /'pāshəns/ ▶ n. **1** the ability to accept delay, trouble, or suffering without becoming angry or upset. **2** Brit. solitaire (card game).

pa·tient /'pāshənt/ ▶ adj. able to accept delay, trouble, or suffering without becoming angry or upset: *supporters have been patient and understanding.* ▶ n. a person receiving or registered to receive medical treatment. ■ **pa·tient·ly** adv.

pat·i·na /pə'tēnə/ ▶ n. **1** a green or brown film on the surface of old bronze. **2** a sheen on wooden furniture produced by age and polishing. ■ **pat·i·nat·ed** /'patn,ātid/ adj. **pat·i·na·tion** /,patn'āshən/ n.

pat·i·o /'patē,ō/ ▶ n. (pl. **patios**) **1** a paved outdoor area adjoining a house. **2** a roofless inner courtyard in a Spanish or Spanish-American house.

pat·i·o door ▶ n. a large glass sliding door leading to a patio or balcony.

pa·tis·se·rie /pə'tisərē/ ▶ n. **1** a store where pastries and cakes are sold. **2** pastries and cakes.

pat·ois /'pa,twä, 'pä-/ ▶ n. (pl. same) the local dialect of a region, especially one with low status in relation to the standard language of the country.

pa·tres·fa·mil·i·as /,patrēzfə'milēəs, ,pä-/ ▶ plural of PATERFAMILIAS.

pa·tri·arch /'pātrē,ärk/ ▶ n. **1** the male head of a family or tribe. **2** a biblical figure regarded as a father of the human race, such as Abraham, Isaac, or Jacob. **3** a powerful or respected older man. **4** a high-ranking bishop in certain Christian churches. **5** the head of an independent Orthodox Church. ■ **pa·tri·ar·chal** /ˌpātrēˈärkəl/ adj. **pa·tri·arch·ate** /ˈpātrē,ärkit/ n.

pa·tri·arch·y /ˈpātrē,ärkē/ ▶ n. (pl. **patriarchies**) **1** a system of society in which men hold most or all of the power. **2** a form of social organization in which the father or eldest male is the head of the family.

pa·tri·cian /pəˈtrishən/ ▶ n. **1** an aristocrat. **2** a member of the nobility in ancient Rome. ▶ adj. relating to or typical of aristocrats; upperclass.

pat·ri·cide /ˈpatrə,sīd/ ▶ n. **1** the killing of a father by his child. **2** a person who kills their father.

pat·ri·lin·e·al /ˌpatrəˈlinēəl/ ▶ adj. relating to or based on relationship to the father or descent through the male line.

pat·ri·mo·ny /ˈpatrə,mōnē/ ▶ n. (pl. **patrimonies**) **1** property inherited from a person's father or male ancestor. **2** valued things passed down from previous generations; heritage.

pa·tri·ot /ˈpātrēət/ ▶ n. a person who strongly supports their country and is prepared to defend it. ■ **pa·tri·ot·ism** /-,tizəm/ n.

pa·tri·ot·ic /ˌpātrēˈätik/ ▶ adj. devoted to and vigorously supporting one's country. ■ **pa·tri·ot·i·cal·ly** adv.

pa·tris·tic /pəˈtristik/ ▶ adj. relating to the early Christian theologians or their writings.

pa·trol /pəˈtrōl/ ▶ n. **1** a person or group that keeps watch over an area by walking or traveling around it at regular intervals. **2** the action of patrolling an area. **3** a unit of six to eight Scouts or Guides forming part of a troop. ▶ v. (**patrols**, **patrolling**, **patrolled**) keep watch over an area by regularly walking or traveling around it. ■ **pa·trol·ler** n.

pa·trol·man /pəˈtrōlmən/ ▶ n. (pl. **patrolmen**) a patrolling police officer.

pa·tron /ˈpātrən/ ▶ n. **1** a person who gives financial or other support to a person, organization, or cause. **2** a regular customer of a restaurant, hotel, or store. ■ **pa·tron·ess** /ˈpātrənis/ n.

pa·tron·age /ˈpatrənij, ˈpā-/ ▶ n. **1** support given by a patron: *the arts could no longer depend on private patronage.* **2** the system by which a powerful person gives a job or privilege to someone in return for their support. **3** the regular customers attracted by a restaurant, hotel, or store. **4** a patronizing way of behaving.

pa·tron·ize /ˈpātrə,nīz, ˈpa-/ ▶ v. **1** treat someone in a way that suggests they are inferior. **2** be a regular customer of a restaurant, hotel, or store.

pa·tron saint ▶ n. the protecting or guiding saint of a person or place.

pat·ro·nym·ic /ˌpatrəˈnimik/ ▶ n. a name derived from the name of a father or ancestor, e.g., *Johnson, O'Brien.*

pat·sy /ˈpatsē/ ▶ n. (pl. **patsies**) informal a person who is easily taken advantage of.

pat·ten /ˈpatn/ ▶ n. historical a shoe with a raised sole or set on an iron ring, worn to raise the feet above wet ground.

pat·ter¹ /ˈpatər/ ▶ v. **1** make a repeated light tapping sound. **2** run with quick light steps. ▶ n. a repeated light tapping sound.

pat·ter² ▶ n. **1** rapid continuous talk, such as that used by a comedian. **2** the jargon of a group or profession: *the patter of an urban street culture.*

pat·tern /ˈpatərn/ ▶ n. **1** a repeated decorative design. **2** a regular form or order in which a series of things occur: *a change in working patterns.* **3** a model, design, or set of instructions for making something. **4** an example for others to follow. **5** a sample of cloth or wallpaper. ▶ v. **1** decorate something with a pattern. **2** (**pattern something on/after**) use something as a model for something else: *the characters are not patterned on real people.*

pat·ty /ˈpatē/ ▶ n. (pl. **patties**) **1** a small flat cake of minced food, especially meat. **2** a flat, round chocolate-covered mint candy. **3** Brit. a small meat pie or turnover.

pau·ci·ty /ˈpôsitē/ ▶ n. the presence of something in only small or insufficient quantities or amounts: *a paucity of information.*

Pau·line /ˈpô,līn, -,lēn/ ▶ adj. relating to St. Paul.

paunch /pônch, pänch/ ▶ n. a belly or abdomen that is large or sticks out. ■ **paunch·y** adj.

pau·per /ˈpôpər/ ▶ n. **1** a very poor person. **2** historical a person who received public charity. ■ **pau·per·ism** /-,rizəm/ n. **pau·per·ize** /-,rīz/ v.

pause /pôz/ ▶ v. stop temporarily: *he paused for a moment, as if he was going to say more.* ▶ n. **1** a temporary stop in action or speech. **2** a mark (⌒) over a musical note or rest that is to be lengthened by an unspecified amount. – PHRASES **give pause to someone** (or **give someone pause for thought**) cause someone to stop and think before doing something.

pa·vane /pəˈvän/ (also **pavan**) ▶ n. a stately dance in slow duple time, popular in the 16th and 17th centuries.

pave /pāv/ ▶ v. cover a piece of ground with stones, concrete, asphalt, or bricks. ■ **pav·er** n. **pav·ing** n. – PHRASES **pave the way for** create the circumstances to enable something to happen.

pave·ment /ˈpāvmənt/ ▶ n. **1** the hard surface of a road or street. **2** Geology a horizontal expanse of bare rock with cracks or joints. **3** British term for SIDEWALK.

pa·vil·ion /pəˈvilyən/ ▶ n. **1** a summer house or other decorative shelter in a park or large garden. **2** a large tent used at a show or fair. **3** a temporary display stand or other structure at a trade exhibition.

Pav·lov·i·an /pavˈlōvēən, -ˈläv-/ ▶ adj. relating to trained reflexes as described by the Russian physiologist Ivan P. Pavlov, famous for training dogs to respond instantly to various stimuli.

paw /pô/ ▶ n. **1** an animal's foot having claws and pads. **2** informal a person's hand. ▶ v. **1** feel or scrape something with a paw or hoof. **2** informal touch or handle someone or something clumsily or sexually.

pawl /pôl/ ▶ n. a pivoted bar or lever whose free end engages with the teeth of a cogwheel or ratchet, allowing it to move or turn in one direction only.

pawn¹ /pôn/ ▶ n. **1** a chess piece of the smallest size and value. **2** a person used by others for their own purposes.

pawn² ▶ v. place an object with a pawnbroker as security for money lent. – PHRASES **in pawn** (of an object) held as security by a pawnbroker.

pawn·brok·er /ˈpôn,brōkər/ ▶ n. a person licensed to lend money in exchange for an article left with them, which they can sell if the borrower fails to pay the money back.

Paw·nee /pô'nē/ ▸ n. (pl. same or **Pawnees**) a member of an American Indian confederacy now living mainly in Oklahoma.

pawn·shop /'pôn,SHäp/ ▸ n. a pawnbroker's store.

paw·paw /'pôpô/ (also **papaw** /pə'pô, 'pôpô/) ▸ n. **1** a papaya (fruit). **2** an edible yellow fruit from a North American tree related to the custard apple.

pay /pā/ ▸ v. (past and past part. **paid**) **1** give someone money owed to them for work, goods, or as a debt. **2** be profitable or advantageous: *crime doesn't pay*. **3** suffer as a result of an action: *someone's got to pay for all that grief*. **4** give someone attention, respect, or a compliment. **5** call on or visit someone. **6** give what is due or deserved to someone. ▸ n. money paid for work. ■ **pay·er** n.
– PHRASES **in the pay of** employed by. **pay someone back** take revenge on someone. **pay dearly** suffer for wrongdoing or failure. **pay one's last respects** show respect toward a dead person by attending their funeral. **pay off** informal yield good results. **pay someone off 1** dismiss someone with a final payment. **2** pay someone not to do something: *he offered to pay her off to drop the case.* **pay something out** let out a rope by slackening it. **pay through the nose** informal pay much more than a fair price.

pay·a·ble /'pāəbəl/ ▸ adj. **1** that must be paid. **2** able to be paid.

pay·back /'pā,bak/ ▸ n. **1** profit from an investment equal to the initial amount invested. **2** informal an act of revenge.

pay·check /'pā,CHek/ ▸ n. a check for salary or wages made out to an employee.

pay·day /'pā,dā/ ▸ n. a day on which someone is paid their wages.

pay dirt ▸ n. **1** ground containing ore in sufficient quantity to be profitably extracted. **2** informal profit or reward: *the gig pays three hundred bucks a week—looks like I just hit pay dirt.*

pay·ee /pā'ē/ ▸ n. a person to whom money is paid or to be paid.

pay·load /'pā,lōd/ ▸ n. **1** passengers and cargo as the part of a vehicle's load that earns money. **2** an explosive warhead carried by an aircraft or missile. **3** the load carried by a spacecraft.

pay·mas·ter /'pā,mastər/ ▸ n. **1** a person who pays another and therefore controls them. **2** an official who pays troops or workers.

pay·ment /'pāmənt/ ▸ n. **1** the action of paying or the process of being paid. **2** an amount paid.

pay·off /'pā,ôf/ ▸ n. informal **1** a payment, especially as a bribe or on leaving a job. **2** the return on investment or on a bet. **3** a final outcome.

pay·o·la /pā'ōlə/ ▸ n. the practice of bribing someone in return for the unofficial promotion of a product.

pay·out /'pā,out/ ▸ n. a large payment of money.

pay-per-view ▸ n. a television service in which viewers have to pay a fee to watch a particular program.

pay·phone /'pā,fōn/ ▸ n. a public telephone operated by coins or by a credit or prepaid card.

pay·roll /'pā,rōl/ ▸ n. a list of a company's employees and the amount of money they are to be paid.

Pb ▸ symbol the chemical element lead.

pb ▸ abbr. paperback.

PBS ▸ abbr. Public Broadcasting Service.

PC ▸ abbr. **1** personal computer. **2** (also **pc**) politically correct; political correctness.

PCB ▸ abbr. **1** Electronics printed circuit board. **2** Chemistry polychlorinated biphenyl, a poisonous compound formed as waste in some industrial processes.

PCV ▸ abbr. Brit. passenger-carrying vehicle.

PD ▸ abbr. **1** Police Department: *the Chicago PD*. **2** public domain: *PD software*.

Pd ▸ symbol the chemical element palladium.

PDA ▸ abbr. personal digital assistant, a basic palmtop computer.

PDF ▸ n. Computing **1** a file format for capturing and sending electronic documents in exactly the intended format. **2** a file in this format.

PDQ ▸ abbr. informal pretty damn quick.

PDT ▸ abbr. Pacific Daylight Time.

PE ▸ abbr. physical education.

pea /pē/ ▸ n. **1** a round green seed eaten as a vegetable. **2** the climbing plant that has pods containing peas.

peace /pēs/ ▸ n. **1** freedom from noise or anxiety; tranquility. **2** freedom from or the ending of war. **3** (**the peace**) an action such as a handshake, signifying Christian unity and performed during the Eucharist (Holy Communion).
– PHRASES **at peace 1** free from anxiety or distress. **2** euphemistic dead. **hold one's peace** remain silent. **keep the peace** refrain or prevent others from disturbing civil order. **make (one's) peace** re-establish friendly relations with someone.

peace·a·ble /'pēsəbəl/ ▸ adj. **1** inclined to avoid conflict. **2** free from conflict; peaceful. ■ **peace·a·bly** adv.

Peace Corps ▸ n. an organization that enables young people to work as volunteers in developing countries.

peace div·i·dend ▸ n. a sum of public money available for other purposes when spending on defense is reduced.

peace·ful /'pēsfəl/ ▸ adj. **1** free from noise or anxiety: *her peaceful mood vanished.* **2** not involving war or violence. **3** inclined to avoid conflict; peaceable. ■ **peace·ful·ly** adv. **peace·ful·ness** n.

peace·keep·ing /'pēs,kēpiNG/ ▸ n. the practice of using an international military force to maintain a truce. ■ **peace·keep·er** n.

peace·mak·er /'pēs,mākər/ ▸ n. a person who brings about peace. ■ **peace·mak·ing** n.

peace·nik /'pēs,nik/ ▸ n. informal, often derogatory a member of a pacifist movement.

peace of·fer·ing ▸ n. a gift that is given in an attempt to re-establish friendly relations.

peace pipe ▸ n. a tobacco pipe offered and smoked as a token of peace among North American Indians.

peace·time /'pēs,tīm/ ▸ n. a period when a country is not at war.

peach[1] /pēCH/ ▸ n. **1** a round fruit with juicy yellow flesh, downy red and yellow skin, and a stone inside. **2** a pinkish-orange color. **3** informal an exceptionally good or attractive person or thing: *it was another peach of a day.* ■ **peach·y** adj.

peach[2] ▸ v. (**peach on**) informal inform on.

pea·cock /'pē,käk/ ▸ n. a large male bird of the pheasant family, having very long tail feathers with eyelike markings that can be fanned out in display.

pea·cock blue ▸ n. a greenish-blue color like that of a peacock's neck.

pea·fowl /'pē͵foul/ ▸ n. a peacock or peahen.

pea green ▸ n. a bright green color.

pea·hen /'pē͵hen/ ▸ n. a female peafowl, which has mainly brown plumage and a shorter tail than a peacock.

pea jack·et (also **pea coat**) ▸ n. a short double-breasted overcoat of coarse woolen cloth.

peak /pēk/ ▸ n. **1** the pointed top of a mountain. **2** a mountain with a pointed top. **3** the point of highest activity, achievement, intensity, etc.: *he was at his peak as a cricketer.* ▸ v. reach a highest point or maximum. ▸ adj. characterized by maximum activity or demand.

peak·ed /'pē͵kid/ ▸ adj. pale from illness or exhaustion.

peak load ▸ n. the maximum of electrical power demand.

peal /pēl/ ▸ n. **1** a loud ringing of a bell or bells. **2** a loud repeated or resounding sound of thunder or laughter. **3** a set of bells. ▸ v. (of a bell or sound) ring or resound loudly.

pea·nut /'pēnət/ ▸ n. **1** the oval edible seed of a plant native to South America, whose seeds develop in underground pods. **2** (**peanuts**) informal a very small sum of money.

pea·nut but·ter ▸ n. a spread made from ground roasted peanuts.

pear /pe(ə)r/ ▸ n. a yellow or green edible fruit that is narrow at the stalk and widens toward the bottom.

pearl /pərl/ ▸ n. **1** a small, hard, shiny white or bluish-gray ball formed inside the shell of an oyster or other mollusk and having great value as a gem. **2** a highly valued person or thing: *pearls of wisdom.* **3** a very pale bluish-gray or white color.
– PHRASES **cast pearls before swine** offer valuable things to people who do not appreciate them.

pearl bar·ley ▸ n. barley reduced to small round grains by grinding.

pearled /pərld/ ▸ adj. literary decorated with or wearing pearls.

pearl·es·cent /pər'lesənt/ ▸ adj. having a soft glow resembling that of mother-of-pearl.

pearl·y /'pərlē/ ▸ adj. (**pearlier**, **pearliest**) resembling a pearl in luster or color.
▸ n. (**pearlies**) (also **pearly whites**) informal a person's teeth.

Pearl·y Gates ▸ pl.n. informal the gates of heaven.

pear-shaped ▸ adj. having hips that are disproportionately wide in relation to the upper part of the body.

peas·ant /'pezənt/ ▸ n. **1** a poor farmer or farm laborer of low social status. **2** informal an ignorant, rude, or unsophisticated person. ■ **peas·ant·ry** n.

pea·shoot·er /'pē͵sho͞otər/ ▸ n. a toy weapon consisting of a small tube out of which dried peas are blown.

pea soup ▸ n. **1** a thick soup made from dried split peas. **2** informal a thick, yellowish fog.

pea-souper ▸ n. chiefly Brit. a very thick fog.

peat /pēt/ ▸ n. partly decomposed vegetable matter forming a deposit on acidic, boggy ground, dried for use in gardening and as fuel. ■ **peat·y** adj.

peat moss ▸ n. a large moss that grows on boggy ground and decays to form peat deposits, which are used as compost.

peb·ble /'pebəl/ ▸ n. a small stone made smooth and round by the action of water or sand. ■ **peb·bly** adj.

pec /pek/ ▸ n. informal a pectoral muscle.

pe·can /pə'kän, 'pē͵kan/ ▸ n. a smooth pinkish-brown nut with a kernel similar to a walnut, obtained from a tree of the southern US.

pec·ca·dil·lo /͵pekə'dilō/ ▸ n. (pl. **peccadilloes** or **peccadillos**) a minor fault.

pec·ca·ry /'pekərē/ ▸ n. (pl. **peccaries**) a piglike mammal found from the southwestern US to Paraguay.

peck¹ /pek/ ▸ v. **1** (of a bird) strike or bite something with its beak. **2** kiss someone lightly and briefly. **3** (**peck at**) informal eat food without enthusiasm. **4** type something slowly and laboriously. ▸ n. **1** an act of pecking. **2** a quick, light kiss.

peck² ▸ n. a measure of capacity for dry goods, equal to a quarter of a bushel.

peck·er /'pekər/ ▸ n. vulgar slang a penis.
– PHRASES **keep your pecker up** informal, chiefly Brit. remain cheerful.

peck·ing or·der ▸ n. a strict order of importance among members of a group.

peck·ish /'pekish/ ▸ adj. informal, chiefly Brit. hungry.

pec·o·ri·no /͵pekə'rēnō/ ▸ n. an Italian cheese made from ewes' milk.

pec·tin /'pektin/ ▸ n. a soluble jellylike substance present in ripe fruits, used to set jams and jellies.

pec·to·ral /'pektərəl/ ▸ adj. relating to or worn on the breast or chest. ▸ n. a pectoral muscle.

pec·to·ral mus·cle ▸ n. each of four large paired muscles that cover the front of the ribcage.

pec·u·la·tion /͵pekyə'lāshən/ ▸ n. formal embezzlement of public funds.

pe·cu·liar /pə'kyo͞olyər/ ▸ adj. **1** different to what is normal or expected; strange. **2** (**peculiar to**) belonging exclusively to. **3** particular; special: *the peculiar difficulties faced by West African women.* ■ **pe·cu·liar·ly** adv.

pe·cu·li·ar·i·ty /pə͵kyo͞olē'aritē/ ▸ n. (pl. **pecularities**) **1** an unusual or distinctive feature or habit. **2** the state of being strange or odd.

pe·cu·ni·ar·y /pi'kyo͞onē͵erē/ ▸ adj. formal relating to money.

ped·a·gogue /'pedə͵gäg/ ▸ n. formal or humorous a teacher.

ped·a·go·gy /'pedə͵gäjē, -͵gōjē/ ▸ n. the profession or theory of teaching. ■ **ped·a·gog·ic** /͵pedə'gäjik/ (also **pedagogical**) adj.

ped·al¹ /'pedl/ ▸ n. **1** each of a pair of foot-operated levers for powering a bicycle or other vehicle. **2** a foot-operated throttle, brake, or clutch control. **3** a foot-operated lever on a piano, organ, etc., for sustaining or softening the tone. ▸ v. (**pedals, pedaling, pedaled**) work the pedals of a bicycle or other vehicle to move along. ■ **ped·al·er** (Brit. **pedaller**) n.

> **USAGE**
> Do not confuse the words **pedal** and **peddle**. **Pedal** is a noun referring to a foot-operated lever, as on a bicycle; as a verb it means 'work the pedals of a bicycle' (*we pedaled along the road*). **Peddle** is a verb meaning 'sell goods or promote an idea' (*she peddled a ridiculous view of the past*).

ped·al² /ˈpedl/ ▶adj. chiefly Medicine & Zoology relating to the foot or feet.

ped·al push·ers ▶pl.n. women's calf-length pants.

ped·ant /ˈpednt/ ▶n. a person who is excessively concerned with minor detail or with displaying academic learning. ■ **pe·dan·tic** /pəˈdantik/ adj. **pe·dan·ti·cal·ly** /-tik(ə)lē/ adv. **ped·ant·ry** n.

ped·dle /ˈpedl/ ▶v. 1 sell goods by going from place to place. 2 sell an illegal drug or stolen item. 3 promote an idea persistently or widely.

> **USAGE**
> On the confusion between **pedal** and **peddle**, see the note at **PEDAL¹**.

ped·dler /ˈpedlər, ˈpedl-ər/ (also **pedlar**) ▶n. 1 a traveling trader who sells small goods. 2 a person who sells illegal drugs or stolen goods. 3 a person who promotes an idea or view persistently.

ped·er·as·ty /ˈpedəˌrastē/ ▶n. sexual intercourse between a man and a boy. ■ **ped·er·ast** /ˈpedəˌrast/ n. **ped·er·as·tic** /ˌpedəˈrastik/ adj.

ped·es·tal /ˈpedəstl/ ▶n. 1 the base or support on which a statue or column is mounted. 2 the supporting column of a washbasin or toilet pan. – **PHRASES** **put someone on a pedestal** admire someone greatly and uncritically.

pe·des·tri·an /pəˈdestrēən/ ▶n. a person walking rather than traveling in a vehicle. ▶adj. not exciting or interesting: *a pedestrian task.* ■ **pe·des·tri·an·ly** adv.

pe·des·tri·an·ize /pəˈdestrēəˌnīz/ ▶v. make a street or area accessible only to pedestrians. ■ **pe·des·tri·an·i·za·tion** /pəˌdestrēəniˈzāSHən/ n.

pe·di·at·rics /ˌpēdēˈatriks/ (Brit. **paediatrics**) ▶pl.n. (treated as sing.) the branch of medicine concerned with children and their diseases. ■ **pe·di·at·ric** /-ˈatrik/ adj. **pe·di·a·tri·cian** /ˌpēdēəˈtriSHən/ n.

ped·i·cure /ˈpediˌkyo͝or/ ▶n. a cosmetic treatment of the feet and toenails. ■ **ped·i·cur·ist** n.

ped·i·gree /ˈpedəˌgrē/ ▶n. 1 the record of an animal's origins, showing that all the animals from which it is descended are of the same breed. 2 a person's family background or ancestry. 3 the history or origin of a person or thing: *the scheme has a long pedigree.*

ped·i·ment /ˈpedəmənt/ ▶n. the triangular upper part above the entrance to a classical building.

pe·dom·e·ter /pəˈdämitər/ ▶n. an instrument for estimating the distance traveled on foot by recording the number of steps taken.

pe·do·phile /ˈpedəˌfīl, ˌpēdə-/ (Brit. **paedophile**) ▶n. a person who is sexually attracted to children. ■ **pe·do·phil·i·a** /ˌpedəˈfīlēə, ˌpēdə-/ n. **pe·do·phil·i·ac** /-ˈfīlēˌak/ adj. & n.

pe·dun·cle /ˈpēˌdəNGkəl, pəˈdəNGkəl/ ▶n. 1 Botany the stalk carrying a flower or fruit. 2 Zoology a stalklike connecting structure. ■ **pe·dun·cu·late** /pəˈdəNGkyəˌlāt, -lit/ adj.

pee /pē/ informal ▶v. (**pees, peeing, peed**) urinate. ▶n. 1 an act of urinating. 2 urine.

peek /pēk/ ▶v. 1 look quickly or furtively. 2 stick out slightly so as to be just visible: *his socks were so full of holes his toes peeked through.* ▶n. a quick or furtive look.

peek·a·boo /ˈpēkəˌbo͞o/ ▶adj. (of an item of clothing) made of transparent fabric or having a pattern of small holes.

peel /pēl/ ▶v. 1 remove the outer covering or skin from a fruit or vegetable. 2 (of a surface or object) lose parts of its outer layer or covering in small pieces. 3 (**peel something away/off**) remove a thin outer covering. 4 (**peel off**) leave a group by veering away. ▶n. the outer skin or rind of a fruit or vegetable. ■ **peel·a·ble** adj. **peel·ings** pl.n.

peel·er /ˈpēlər/ ▶n. a knife or device for peeling fruit and vegetables.

peen /pēn/ ▶n. the rounded or wedge-shaped end of a hammer head opposite the face.

peep¹ /pēp/ ▶v. 1 look quickly and furtively. 2 (**peep out**) come slowly or partially into view. ▶n. 1 a quick or furtive look. 2 a glimpse of something: *a peep of gold earring.*

peep² ▶n. a weak or brief high-pitched sound. ▶v. make a peep. – **PHRASES** **not a peep** not the slightest sound or complaint.

peep·er /ˈpēpər/ ▶n. 1 a person who looks quickly or furtively. 2 (**peepers**) informal a person's eyes.

peep·hole /ˈpēpˌhōl/ ▶n. a small hole in a door through which callers may be identified.

peep·ing Tom ▶n. a person who gains sexual pleasure from secretly watching people undress or have sex.

peep show ▶n. a form of entertainment in which pictures are viewed through a lens or hole set into a box.

peer¹ /pi(ə)r/ ▶v. 1 look with difficulty or concentration. 2 be just visible: *the towers peer over the roofs.*

peer² ▶n. 1 a member of the nobility in Britain or Ireland, comprising the ranks of duke, marquess, earl, viscount, and baron. 2 a person of the same age, status, or ability as another specified person: *his astute management is better than any of his peers.* – **PHRASES** **without peer** better than all others; unrivaled.

peer·age /ˈpi(ə)rij/ ▶n. 1 the title and rank of peer or peeress. 2 (**the peerage**) peers as a group.

peer·ess /ˈpi(ə)ris/ ▶n. 1 a woman holding the rank of a peer in her own right. 2 the wife or widow of a peer.

peer group ▶n. a group of people of approximately the same age, status, and interests.

peer·less /ˈpi(ə)rlis/ ▶adj. better than all others; unrivaled.

peer-to-peer ▶adj. Computing denoting a network in which each computer can act as a server for the others, allowing shared access to files and peripherals without the need for a central server.

peeve /pēv/ informal ▶v. annoy or irritate someone: *he was peeved at being left out.* ▶n. a cause of annoyance.

peev·ish /ˈpēviSH/ ▶adj. easily annoyed; irritable. ■ **peev·ish·ly** adv. **peev·ish·ness** n.

peg /peg/ ▶n. 1 a short projecting pin or bolt used for hanging things on, securing something in place, or marking a position. 2 Brit. a clothespin. 3 informal a person's leg. ▶v. (**pegs, pegging, pegged**) 1 fix, attach, or mark something with a peg or pegs. 2 fix a price, rate, or amount at a particular level. 3 (**peg away**) informal work hard over a long period. – **PHRASES** **a square peg in a round hole** a person in a situation unsuited to their abilities or character. **take** (or **bring**) **someone down a peg or two** make someone less arrogant.

peg·board /'peg,bôrd/ ▶ n. a board with a regular pattern of small holes for pegs.

peg leg ▶ n. informal an artificial leg.

peign·oir /,pān'wär/ ▶ n. a woman's light bathrobe or negligee.

pe·jo·ra·tive /pə'jôrətiv, 'pejə,rātiv/ ▶ adj. (of a word or phrase) expressing contempt or disapproval. ■ **pe·jo·ra·tive·ly** adv.

Pe·king duck /,pē'kiNG, ,pā-/ ▶ n. a Chinese dish consisting of strips of roast duck served with shredded vegetables and a sweet sauce.

Pe·king·ese (also **Pekinese**) ▶ n. /'pēkə,nēz, -,nēs/ (pl. same) a small dog of a short-legged breed with long hair and a snub nose. ▶ adj. /,pēkiNG'ēz, -'ēs/ relating to Beijing (Peking).

pe·lag·ic /pə'lajik/ ▶ adj. technical 1 relating to the open sea. 2 (chiefly of fish) inhabiting the upper layers of the open sea.

pel·ar·go·ni·um /,pelär'gōnēəm/ ▶ n. a garden plant with red, pink, or white flowers.

pelf /pelf/ ▶ n. literary money, especially when gained dishonestly.

pel·i·can /'pelikən/ ▶ n. a large waterbird with a long bill and a pouch hanging from its throat.

pe·lisse /pə'lēs/ ▶ n. historical a woman's long cloak with armholes or sleeves.

pel·la·gra /pə'lagrə, -'lāgrə, -'lägrə/ ▶ n. a disease that results from a lack of a vitamin, causing inflamed skin, diarrhea, and mental disturbance.

pel·let /'pelit/ ▶ n. 1 a small, rounded, compressed mass of a substance. 2 a piece of small shot or other lightweight bullet. ▶ v. (**pellets, pelleting, pelleted**) form a substance into pellets. ■ **pel·let·ize** /'peli,tīz/ v.

pell-mell /'pel 'mel/▶ adj. & adv. in a confused, rushed, or disorderly way.

pel·lu·cid /pə'lōōsid/ ▶ adj. literary 1 transparent or semitransparent. 2 easily understood: *pellucid answers.*

pe·lo·ta /pə'lōtə/ ▶ n. a Basque or Spanish ball game played in a walled court with basketlike rackets.

pel·o·ton /'pelə,tän/ ▶ n. the main group of cyclists in a race.

pelt¹ /pelt/ ▶ v. 1 hurl missiles at someone or something. 2 (**pelt down**) (chiefly of rain) fall very heavily. 3 run very quickly.
– PHRASES (**at**) **full pelt** Brit. as fast as possible.

pelt² ▶ n. the skin of an animal with the fur, wool, or hair still on it.

pel·vic gir·dle ▶ n. (in vertebrates) the enclosing structure formed by the pelvis.

pel·vis /'pelvis/ ▶ n. (pl. **pelvises** or **pelves** /-vēz/) the large bony frame at the base of the spine to which the lower limbs are attached. ■ **pel·vic** /'pelvik/ adj.

pen¹ /pen/ ▶ n. 1 an instrument for writing or drawing with ink. 2 an electronic device used with a writing surface to enter commands into a computer. ▶ v. (**pens, penning, penned**) write or compose something.

pen² ▶ n. 1 a small enclosure for farm animals. 2 a covered dock for a submarine or other warship. ▶ v. (**pens, penning, penned**) 1 put or keep an animal in a pen. 2 (**pen someone up/in**) confine someone in a restricted space.

pen³ ▶ n. a female swan.

pe·nal /'pēnəl/ ▶ adj. 1 relating to the punishment of offenders under the legal system. 2 chiefly Brit. very severe: *penal rates of interest.*

pe·nal·ize /'pēnəl,īz, 'pē-/ ▶ v. 1 give a penalty or punishment to someone who has broken the law or a rule. 2 make an action punishable by law. 3 put in an unfavorable position: *single people are often penalized by hotels by being charged a supplement.* ■ **pe·nal·i·za·tion** /,pēnəli'zāsHən, ,pē-/ n.

pe·nal ser·vi·tude ▶ n. imprisonment with hard labor.

pen·al·ty /'penltē/ ▶ n. (pl. **penalties**) 1 a punishment for breaking a law, rule, or contract. 2 a disadvantage suffered as a result of an action or situation: *feeling cold is one of the penalties of old age.* 3 a penalty kick or shot.

pen·al·ty ar·e·a (also **penalty box**) ▶ n. Soccer the rectangular area marked out in front of each goal, within which a foul by a defender involves the award of a penalty kick.

pen·al·ty box ▶ n. Ice Hockey an enclosure alongside the rink where players who have been assessed penalties must remain while they serve out their penalties.

pen·al·ty kick ▶ n. 1 Soccer a free shot at the goal awarded to the attacking team after a foul within the penalty area. 2 Rugby a place kick awarded to a team after an offense by an opponent.

pen·ance /'penəns/ ▶ n. 1 punishment inflicted on oneself to show that one is sorry for wrongdoing: *he had done public penance for those hasty words.* 2 (chiefly in the Roman Catholic and Orthodox Church) a religious act in which a person confesses their sins to a priest and is asked to perform a religious duty before being given formal forgiveness. 3 a religious duty that a priest asks a person to do to show repentance for a sin.

pence /pens/ Brit. ▶ plural of PENNY (used for sums of money).

pen·chant /'penchənt/ ▶ n. a strong liking for or tendency to do something: *a penchant for champagne.*

pen·cil /'pensəl/ ▶ n. an instrument for writing or drawing, typically consisting of a thin stick of graphite enclosed in a wooden case. ▶ v. (**pencils, penciling, penciled**) 1 write, draw, or color something with a pencil. 2 (**pencil something in**) arrange or note something down provisionally.

pen·cil push·er ▶ n. informal an office worker who deals with routine paperwork.

pen·cil skirt ▶ n. a very narrow straight skirt.

pend·ant /'pendənt/ ▶ n. 1 a piece of jewelry that hangs from a necklace chain. 2 a light designed to hang from the ceiling. ▶ adj. hanging downward.

pend·ent /'pendənt/ ▶ adj. literary hanging down or overhanging.

pend·ing /'pendiNG/ ▶ adj. 1 awaiting decision or settlement. 2 about to happen. ▶ prep. until something happens.

pen·du·lous /'penjələs, 'pendyə-/ ▶ adj. hanging down; drooping.

pen·du·lum /'penjələm, 'pendyə-/ ▶ n. a weight hung from a fixed point so that it can swing freely, especially one regulating the mechanism of a clock. ■ **pen·du·lar** /-lər/ adj.

pe·ne·plain /'pēnə,plān/ ▶ n. a level land surface produced by erosion over a long period.

pen·e·trate /'peni,trāt/ ▸ v. **1** go into or through something, especially with force or effort. **2** gain access to an organization, place, or system, especially in an underhanded way: *our network had been penetrated by foreign agents.* **3** (of a company) begin to sell its products in a new market or area. **4** understand something complex. **5** (as adj. **penetrating**) (of a sound) clearly heard through or above other sounds. **6** (of a man) insert the penis into the vagina or anus of a sexual partner. ■ **pen·e·tra·ble** /'penitrəbəl/ adj. **pen·e·tra·tive** /'peni,trātiv/ adj. **pen·e·tra·tor** n.

pen·e·tra·tion /,peni'trāsHən/ ▸ n. **1** the action of penetrating. **2** the extent to which a product is recognized and bought by customers in a particular market: *the company achieved remarkable market penetration.* **3** understanding of complex matters.

pen·guin /'peNGgwin, 'peNGwin/ ▸ n. a flightless black and white seabird of the southern hemisphere, with wings used as flippers.

pen·i·cil·lin /,penə'silən/ ▸ n. an antibiotic produced naturally by certain blue molds and now usually made synthetically.

pen·in·su·la /pə'ninsələ/ ▸ n. a long, narrow piece of land projecting out into a sea or lake. ■ **pen·in·su·lar** adj.

pe·nis /'pēnis/ ▸ n. (pl. **penises** or **penes** /-nēz/) the male organ that is used for sexual intercourse and urinating. ■ **pe·nile** /'pēnəl, -nīl/ adj.

pen·i·tent /'penitnt/ ▸ adj. feeling sorrow and regret for having done wrong. ▸ n. a person who repents their sins or does a religious duty required by a priest. ■ **pen·i·tence** n. **pen·i·ten·tial** /,penə'tensHəl/ adj. **pen·i·tent·ly** adv.

pen·i·ten·tia·ry /,penə'tensHərē/ ▸ n. (pl. **penitentiaries**) a prison for people convicted of serious crimes.

pen·knife /'pen,nīf/ ▸ n. (pl. **penknives**) a small knife with a blade that folds into the handle.

pen·light /'pen,līt/ ▸ n. a small flashlight shaped like a pen.

pen·man /'pen,mən/ ▸ n. (pl. **penmen**) **1** a person with a specified ability in handwriting. **2** historical a person employed to write or copy documents; a clerk.

pen·man·ship /'penmən,sHip/ ▸ n. **1** the art or skill of writing by hand. **2** a person's handwriting.

pen name ▸ n. a name used by a writer instead of their real name.

pen·nant /'penənt/ ▸ n. **1** a long, narrow pointed flag, especially one flown by a ship and used for signaling. **2** a flag identifying a sports team, club, etc.

pen·ne /'penā/ ▸ pl.n. pasta in the form of short wide tubes.

pen·ni·less /'penēlis/ ▸ adj. having no money; very poor.

pen·non /'penən/ ▸ n. less common term for **PENNANT**.

Penn·syl·va·nia Dutch (also **Pennsylvania German**) ▸ n. a dialect of High German spoken in parts of Pennsylvania.

Penn·syl·va·nian /,pensəl'vānyən, -'vānēən/ ▸ adj. **1** relating to the state of Pennsylvania. **2** Geology relating to or denoting the later part of the Carboniferous period in North America.

▸ n. a native or inhabitant of Pennsylvania.

pen·ny /'penē/ ▸ n. (pl. **pennies** (for separate coins); **pence** /pens/ (for a sum of money)) **1** a one-cent coin. **2** a British bronze coin worth one hundredth of a pound. **3** a former British coin worth one twelfth of a shilling and 240th of a pound.
– PHRASES **in for a penny, in for a pound** used to say that since one has started something one may as well spend as much time or money as is necessary to complete it. **not a penny** no money at all. **penny wise and pound foolish** economical in small matters but extravagant in large ones.

pen·ny-far·thing ▸ n. chiefly Brit. an early type of bicycle with a very large front wheel and a small rear wheel.

pen·ny-pinch·ing ▸ adj. unwilling to spend money; stingy. ▸ n. unwillingness to spend money; stinginess. ■ **pen·ny-pinch·er** n.

pen·ny·roy·al /'penē,roiəl/ ▸ n. a small-leaved plant of the mint family, used in herbal medicine.

pen·ny stock ▸ n. Stock Exchange a common stock valued at less than one dollar.

pen·ny·wort /'penēwərt, -,wôrt/ ▸ n. a plant with small rounded leaves, growing in crevices or marshy places.

pe·nol·o·gy /pē'näləjē/ ▸ n. the study of the punishment of crime and of prison management. ■ **pe·no·log·i·cal** /,pēnə'läjikəl/ adj. **pe·nol·o·gist** n.

pen pal ▸ n. a person with whom one becomes friendly by exchanging letters.

pen·sée /,pän'sā/ ▸ n. a thought written down in a concise or witty form.

pen·sion¹ /'pensHən/ ▸ n. **1** a regular payment made to retired people and to some widows and disabled people, either by the government or from an investment fund. **2** historical a regular payment made to a favorite of a monarch or to an artist or scholar. ▸ v. (**pension someone off**) dismiss someone from employment and pay them a pension. ■ **pen·sion·a·ble** adj. **pen·sion·er** n.

pen·sion² /pänsē'ôn/ ▸ n. a small hotel or guest house in France and other European countries.

pen·si·o·ne /pänsē'ônā/ ▸ n. (pl. **pensioni** /-'ônē/) a small hotel or guest house in Italy.

pen·sive /'pensiv/ ▸ adj. engaged in deep or serious thought. ■ **pen·sive·ly** adv. **pen·sive·ness** n.

pen·ste·mon /pen'stēmən, 'penstəmən/ ▸ n. a North American plant with snapdragonlike flowers.

pent /pent/ ▸ adj. chiefly literary another term for **PENT-UP**.

penta- ▸ comb.form five; having five: *pentagon.*

pen·ta·cle /'pentəkəl/ ▸ n. a pentagram.

pen·tad /'pen,tad/ ▸ n. a group or set of five.

pen·ta·gon /'pentə,gän/ ▸ n. **1** a plane figure with five straight sides and five angles. **2** (**the Pentagon**) the headquarters of the US Department of Defense, near Washington DC. ■ **pen·tag·o·nal** /pen'tagənəl/ adj.

pen·ta·gram /'pentə,gram/ ▸ n. a five-pointed star drawn using a continuous line, often used as a mystic and magical symbol.

pen·tam·e·ter /pen'tamitər/ ▸ n. a line of verse consisting of five metrical feet.

pen·tan·gle /ˈpenˌtaNGgəl/ ▶ n. a pentagram.

pen·ta·prism /ˈpentəˌprizəm/ ▶ n. a five-sided prism that deviates light from any direction, used chiefly in camera viewfinders.

Pen·ta·teuch /ˈpentəˌt(y)o͞ok/ ▶ n. the first five books of the Old Testament and Hebrew Scriptures (Genesis, Exodus, Leviticus, Numbers, and Deuteronomy).

pen·tath·lon /penˈtaTH(ə)ˌlän/ ▶ n. an athletic contest consisting of five different events for each competitor, in particular (**modern pentathlon**) a contest involving fencing, shooting, swimming, riding, and cross-country running. ■ **pen·tath·lete** /penˈtaTHlēt/ n.

pen·ta·ton·ic /ˌpentəˈtänik/ ▶ adj. relating to or consisting of a musical scale of five notes.

Pen·te·cost /ˈpentəˌkôst, -ˌkäst/ ▶ n. 1 the Christian festival celebrating the coming of the Holy Spirit to the disciples of Jesus after his Ascension. 2 the Jewish festival of Shavuoth, held on the fiftieth day after the second day of Passover.

Pen·te·cos·tal /ˌpentəˈkôstl, -ˈkästl/ ▶ adj. 1 relating to a Christian movement that emphasizes the gifts of the Holy Spirit, such as 'speaking in tongues' and healing of the sick. 2 relating to the Christian festival of Pentecost. ■ **Pen·te·cos·tal·ism** /-ˌizəm/ n. **Pen·te·cos·tal·ist** adj. & n.

pent·house /ˈpentˌhous/ ▶ n. an apartment on the top floor of a tall building.

Pen·to·thal /ˈpentəˌTHôl, -ˌTHäl/ ▶ n. trademark an anesthetic and sedative drug.

pent-up ▶ adj. not expressed or released: *pent-up anger.*

pe·nul·ti·mate /peˈnəltəmit/ ▶ adj. last but one in a series; second to the last.

pe·num·bra /peˈnəmbrə/ ▶ n. (pl. **penumbrae** /-brē, -brī/ or **penumbras**) the partially shaded outer region of the shadow cast by an object. ■ **pe·num·bral** /-brəl/ adj.

pe·nu·ri·ous /pəˈn(y)o͝orēəs/ ▶ adj. formal 1 having no money; very poor. 2 unwilling to spend money; stingy. ■ **pe·nu·ri·ous·ly** adv.

pen·u·ry /ˈpenyərē/ ▶ n. the state of having no money; great poverty.

pe·on /ˈpēˌän, ˈpēən/ ▶ n. an unskilled Spanish-American farm worker.

pe·o·ny /ˈpēənē/ ▶ n. a plant grown for its large white, pink, or red flowers.

peo·ple /ˈpēpəl/ ▶ pl.n. 1 human beings in general or as a whole. 2 (**the people**) the ordinary citizens of a country. 3 (pl. **peoples**) (treated as sing. or pl.) the members of a particular nation, community, or ethnic group. 4 (**one's people**) one's employees or supporters. 5 (**one's people**) dated one's relatives. ▶ v. inhabit a place: *a mountain region peopled by warring clans.*

pep /pep/ informal ▶ v. (**peps, pepping, pepped**) (**pep someone/thing up**) make someone or something more lively or interesting. ▶ n. liveliness or energy. ■ **pep·py** adj.

pep·lum /ˈpepləm/ ▶ n. a short flared strip of fabric attached at the waist of a woman's jacket, dress, or blouse.

pep·per /ˈpepər/ ▶ n. 1 a hot-tasting powder made from peppercorns, used to flavor food. 2 the fruit of a tropical American plant, of which sweet peppers and chili peppers are varieties. ▶ v. 1 season food with pepper. 2 cover or fill with a large amount of scattered items: *the script*

is peppered with four-letter words. 3 hit someone or something repeatedly with small missiles or gunshot. ■ **pep·per·y** adj.

pep·per·corn /ˈpepərˌkôrn/ ▶ n. the dried berry of a climbing vine, used whole as a spice or crushed or ground to make pepper.

pep·per·mint /ˈpepərˌmint/ ▶ n. 1 a plant of the mint family that produces aromatic leaves and oil, used as a flavoring in food. 2 a candy flavored with peppermint oil.

pep·per·o·ni /ˌpepəˈrōnē/ ▶ n. beef and pork sausage seasoned with pepper.

pep·per spray ▶ n. an aerosol spray containing oils obtained from cayenne pepper that irritate the eyes, used to disable an attacker.

pep pill ▶ n. informal a pill containing a stimulant drug.

pep·sin /ˈpepsin/ ▶ n. the chief digestive enzyme in the stomach, which breaks down proteins.

pep talk ▶ n. informal a talk intended to make someone feel braver or more enthusiastic.

pep·tic /ˈpeptik/ ▶ adj. relating to digestion.

pep·tic ul·cer ▶ n. an ulcer in the lining of the stomach or small intestine.

pep·tide /ˈpeptīd/ ▶ n. a chemical compound consisting of two or more linked amino acids.

per /pər/ ▶ prep. 1 for each. 2 by means of. – PHRASES **as per** in accordance with. **as per usual** as usual.

per. ▶ abbr. 1 percentile. 2 period. 3 person.

per- ▶ prefix 1 through; all over: *pervade.* 2 completely; very: *perfect.* 3 Chemistry having the maximum proportion of a particular element in combination: *peroxide.*

per·ad·ven·ture /ˌpərədˈvenCHər, ˌper-/ ▶ adv. old use perhaps. ▶ n. uncertainty or doubt.

per·am·bu·late /pəˈrambyəˌlāt/ ▶ v. formal walk or travel from place to place. ■ **per·am·bu·la·tion** /pəˌrambyəˈlāSHən/ n. **per·am·bu·la·to·ry** /-ləˌtôrē/ adj.

per·am·bu·la·tor /pəˈrambyəˌlātər/ ▶ n. dated, chiefly Brit. a baby carriage.

per an·num /pər ˈanəm/ ▶ adv. for each year.

per·cale /pərˈkāl, -ˈkal/ ▶ n. a closely woven fine cotton fabric.

per cap·i·ta /pər ˈkapitə/ ▶ adv. & adj. for each person.

per·ceive /pərˈsēv/ ▶ v. 1 become aware of something through the senses. 2 come to realize: *her mouth fell open as she perceived the truth.* 3 regard in a particular way: *the couple were perceived as arrogant.* ■ **per·ceiv·a·ble** adj. **per·ceiv·er** n.

per·cent /pərˈsent/ ▶ adv. by a specified amount in or for every hundred. ▶ n. one part in every hundred.

per·cent·age /pərˈsentij/ ▶ n. 1 a rate, number, or amount in each hundred. 2 any proportion or share in relation to a whole: *camera phones are making up a huge percentage of all cell phone sales.* 3 a share in the profits of something, granted as a commission.

per·cen·tile /pərˈsenˌtīl/ ▶ n. Statistics each of 100 equal groups into which a large group of people can be divided, according to their place on a scale measuring a particular value.

per·cept /ˈpərsept/ ▶ n. Philosophy an object of perception; something that is perceived.

per·cep·ti·ble /pərˈseptəbəl/ ▶ adj. able to be seen or noticed: *a perceptible decline in public confidence.* ■ **per·cep·ti·bly** /-blē/ adv.

per·cep·tion /pər'sepsнən/ ▶ n. **1** the ability to see, hear, or become aware of something through the senses. **2** the process of perceiving something. **3** a way of understanding or interpreting something: *the public perception of him seems distorted.* **4** intuitive understanding; insight.

per·cep·tive /pər'septiv/ ▶ adj. having or showing sensitive insight. ■ **per·cep·tive·ly** adv. **per·cep·tive·ness** n.

per·cep·tu·al /pər'sepcʜōōəl/ ▶ adj. relating to the ability to perceive things through the senses. ■ **per·cep·tu·al·ly** adv.

perch¹ /pərcʜ/ ▶ n. **1** an object on which a bird rests or roosts. **2** a high or narrow seat or resting place. ▶ v. **1** sit, rest, or place somewhere. **2** (**be perched**) (of a building) be situated above or on the edge of something. ■ **perch·er** n.

perch² ▶ n. (pl. same or **perches**) a freshwater fish with a spiny fin on its back and dark vertical bars on the body.

per·chance /pər'cʜans/ ▶ adv. old use or literary by some chance; perhaps.

per·che·ron /'pərsʜə,rän, 'pərcʜə-/ ▶ n. a powerful breed of gray or black horse, used for pulling loads.

per·cip·i·ent /pər'sipēənt/ ▶ adj. having a sensitive understanding; perceptive. ■ **per·cip·i·ence** n. **per·cip·i·ent·ly** adv.

per·co·late /'pərkə,lāt/ ▶ v. **1** (of a liquid or gas) filter through a porous surface or substance. **2** (of information or ideas) spread gradually through a group of people: *this attitude is starting to percolate down to the masses.* **3** prepare coffee in a percolator. ■ **per·co·la·tion** /,pərkə'lāsʜən/ n.

per·co·la·tor /'pərkə,lātər/ ▶ n. a machine for making coffee, consisting of a pot in which boiling water is circulated through a small chamber that holds the ground beans.

per·cuss /pər'kəs/ ▶ v. gently tap a part of the body as part of a medical diagnosis.

per·cus·sion /pər'kəsʜən/ ▶ n. **1** musical instruments that are played by being struck or shaken, such as drums or cymbals. **2** the striking of one solid object with or against another. ■ **per·cus·sion·ist** /-ist/ n. **per·cus·sive** /-'kəsiv/ adj.

per·cus·sion cap ▶ n. full form of CAP¹ (sense 6 of the noun).

per di·em /pər 'dēəm/ ▶ adv. & adj. for each day.

per·di·tion /pər'disʜən/ ▶ n. **1** (in Christian belief) a state of eternal damnation into which a sinful person who has not repented passes after death. **2** complete and utter ruin: *the spending plan dooms the state to fiscal perdition.*

per·dur·a·ble /pər'd(y)ōōrəbəl/ ▶ adj. literary enduring continuously; permanent.

père /pe(ə)r/ ▶ n. used after a French surname to distinguish a father from a son of the same name.

per·e·gri·na·tion /,perigrə'nāsʜən/ ▶ n. literary a long or rambling journey: *a secret diary of their boozy peregrinations.* ■ **per·e·gri·nate** /'perigrə,nāt/ v. (old use).

per·e·grine /'perəgrin/ ▶ n. a powerful falcon with a bluish-gray back and wings and pale underparts.

per·emp·to·ry /pə'remptərē/ ▶ adj. **1** insisting on immediate attention or obedience, especially in an abrupt way: *she had come to dread his*

peremptory orders. **2** Law not open to appeal or challenge; final. ■ **per·emp·to·ri·ly** adv.

per·en·ni·al /pə'renēəl/ ▶ adj. **1** lasting or doing something for a long time or forever: *his perennial distrust of the media.* **2** (of a plant) living for several years. ▶ n. a plant that lives for several years. ■ **per·en·ni·al·ly** adv.

pe·re·stroi·ka /,perə'stroikə/ ▶ n. the economic and political reforms established in the former Soviet Union during the 1980s.

per·fect ▶ adj. /'pərfikt/ **1** having all the required elements or qualities: *she strove to be the perfect wife.* **2** free from any flaws or defects. **3** complete; absolute: *they were perfect strangers to him.* **4** Grammar (of a tense) describing a completed action or a state in the past, formed in English with *have* or *has* and the past participle, as in *they have eaten.* **5** Mathematics (of a number) equal to the sum of its positive divisors, e.g., the number 6, whose divisors (1, 2, 3) also add up to 6. ▶ v. /pər'fekt/ make something perfect or as good as possible: *she perfected her English by tuning in to American television.* ■ **per·fect·er** /pər'fektər/ n. **per·fect·i·ble** /pər'fektəbəl/ adj.

per·fec·tion /pər'feksʜən/ ▶ n. **1** the state of being excellent, complete, or flawless: *all the food was cooked to perfection.* **2** the action of making something perfect.

per·fec·tion·ist /pər'feksʜə,nist/ ▶ n. a person who refuses to be satisfied with something unless it is perfect. ■ **per·fec·tion·ism** n.

per·fect·ly /'pərfik(t)lē/ ▶ adv. **1** in a perfect way. **2** completely; absolutely (used for emphasis).

per·fect pitch ▶ n. the ability to recognize the pitch of a note or produce any given note.

per·fer·vid /pər'fərvid/ ▶ adj. literary intensely passionate or enthusiastic.

per·fid·i·ous /pər'fidēəs/ ▶ adj. literary deceitful and untrustworthy. ■ **per·fid·i·ous·ly** adv. **per·fid·i·ous·ness** n.

per·fi·dy /'pərfidē/ ▶ n. literary the state of being deceitful and untrustworthy.

per·fo·rate /'pərfə,rāt/ ▶ v. pierce and make a hole or holes in something. ■ **per·fo·ra·tion** /,pərfə'rāsʜən/ n. **per·fo·ra·tor** n.

per·force /pər'fôrs/ ▶ adv. formal necessarily; inevitably.

per·form /pər'fôrm/ ▶ v. **1** carry out or complete an action or function. **2** function or do something to a specified standard: *the car performs well at low speeds.* **3** present entertainment to an audience. ■ **per·form·a·ble** adj. **per·form·er** n.

per·for·mance /pər'fôrməns/ ▶ n. **1** the action of performing a task or function. **2** an act of performing a play, concert, song, etc. **3** the standard of functioning achieved by a machine or product. **4** informal an act that involves a great deal of time and effort, often when exaggerated or unnecessary: *she stayed behind, making a performance of wiping her shoes.*

per·for·mance art ▶ n. an art form that combines visual art with dramatic expression.

per·form·ing arts ▶ pl.n. forms of creative activity that are performed in front of an audience, such as drama, music, and dance.

per·fume /'pər,fyōōm, ,pər'fyōōm/ ▶ n. **1** a fragrant liquid used to give a pleasant smell to one's body. **2** a pleasant smell. ▶ v. **1** give a pleasant smell to something. **2** put perfume or a sweet-smelling ingredient on or into something.

■ **per·fumed** adj.

per·fum·er·y /pər'fyoomərē/ ▶ n. (pl.
perfumeries) 1 the process of producing and
selling perfumes. 2 a store that sells perfumes.
■ **per·fum·er** n.

per·func·to·ry /pər'fəNGktərē/ ▶ adj. carried out
with very little effort or interest: *they exchanged
a perfunctory handshake.* ■ **per·func·to·ri·ly**
/-'fəNGktərəlē/ adv.

per·fuse /pər'fyooz/ ▶ v. literary spread a liquid,
color, quality, etc., throughout something;
permeate. ■ **per·fu·sion** /-zHən/ n.

per·go·la /'pərgələ/ ▶ n. an arched structure
forming a framework for climbing plants.

per·haps /pər'(h)aps/ ▶ adv. 1 expressing
uncertainty or possibility. 2 used when making a
polite request or suggestion.

peri- ▶ prefix around; about: *perimeter.*

per·i·anth /'perē,aNTH/ ▶ n. the outer part of
a flower, consisting of the calyx (sepals) and
corolla (petals).

per·i·car·di·um /,peri'kärdēəm/ ▶ n. (pl.
pericardia /-'kärdēə/) the membrane enclosing
the heart. ■ **per·i·car·di·al** /-'kärdēəl/ adj.

per·i·carp /'peri,kärp/ ▶ n. the part of a fruit
formed from the wall of the ripened ovary.

per·i·dot /'peri,dät/ ▶ n. a green semiprecious
stone.

per·i·do·tite /'peridə,tīt, pə'ridə,tīt/ ▶ n. a dense
rock that is rich in magnesium and iron, thought
to be the main constituent of the earth's mantle.

per·i·gee /'perə,jē/ ▶ n. the point in the orbit of
the moon or a satellite at which it is nearest to
the earth. The opposite of **APOGEE.**

per·i·he·li·on /,perə'hēlyən, -'hēlēən/ ▶ n. (pl.
perihelia /-'hēlyə, -'hēlēə/) the point in the orbit
of a planet, asteroid, or comet at which it is
closest to the sun. The opposite of **APHELION.**

per·il /'perəl/ ▶ n. 1 a situation of serious and
immediate danger. 2 the risks or difficulties of a
situation or activity.
– PHRASES **at one's peril** at one's own risk. **in
peril of** very likely to suffer from; at risk of.

per·il·ous /'perələs/ ▶ adj. full of danger or risk.
■ **per·il·ous·ly** adv. **per·il·ous·ness** n.

pe·rim·e·ter /pə'rimitər/ ▶ n. 1 the outermost
parts or boundary of an area or object: *I drove
around the perimeter of the parking lot.* 2 the
continuous line forming the boundary of a
closed geometrical figure.

per·i·na·tal /,perə'nātl/ ▶ adj. relating to the
time immediately before and after a birth.
■ **per·i·na·tal·ly** adv.

per·i·ne·um /,perə'nēəm/ ▶ n. (pl. **perinea**
/,perə'nēə/) the area between the anus and the
scrotum or vulva. ■ **per·i·ne·al** /-'nēəl/ adj.

pe·ri·od /'pi(ə)rēəd/ ▶ n. 1 a length or portion
of time. 2 a portion of time with particular
characteristics: *the early medieval period.* 3 a
major division of geological time, forming part
of an era. 4 a punctuation mark (.) used at the
end of a sentence or an abbreviation. 5 a lesson
in a school. 6 (also **menstrual period**) a monthly
flow of blood and other material from the lining
of the uterus, occurring in women between
puberty and the menopause who are not
pregnant. 7 Physics the interval of time between
recurrences of a phenomenon. ▶ adj. belonging
to or typical of a past historical time: *period
furniture.*

pe·ri·od·ic /,pi(ə)rē'ädik/ ▶ adj. appearing

or occurring at intervals. ■ **pe·ri·o·dic·i·ty**
/,pi(ə)rēə'disitē/ n.

pe·ri·od·i·cal /,pi(ə)rē'ädikəl/ ▶ adj. occurring
or appearing at intervals. ▶ n. a magazine or
newspaper published at regular intervals.
■ **pe·ri·od·i·cal·ly** adv.

pe·ri·od·i·cal ci·ca·da ▶ n. an American cicada
whose nymphs emerge from the soil every
seventeen years in the north (**seventeen-year
locust**) or every thirteen years in the south.

pe·ri·od·ic ta·ble /,pi(ə)rē'ädik/ ▶ n. a table
of the chemical elements arranged in order of
atomic number, usually in rows, with elements
having similar atomic structure appearing in
vertical columns.

per·i·o·don·tics /,perēə'däntiks/ ▶ pl.n. (treated
as sing.) the branch of dentistry concerned with
the structures surrounding and supporting the
teeth. ■ **per·i·o·don·tal** /-'däntl/ adj.

pe·ri·od piece ▶ n. an object or work that is set
in or typical of an earlier historical period.

per·i·pa·tet·ic /,peripə'tetik/ ▶ adj. 1 traveling
from place to place. 2 Brit. (of a teacher)
working in more than one school or college.
■ **per·i·pa·tet·i·cal·ly** adv.

pe·riph·er·al /pə'rifərəl/ ▶ adj. 1 relating to or
situated on the outer limits of something. 2 of
secondary importance: *she saw their problems
as peripheral to her own.* 3 (of a device) able to
be attached to and used with a computer. ▶ n. a
device that is able to be attached to and used
with a computer. ■ **pe·riph·er·al·i·ty** /-,rifə'ralitē/
n. **pe·riph·er·al·ly** adv.

pe·riph·er·al nerv·ous sys·tem ▶ n. the
nervous system outside the brain and spinal
cord.

pe·riph·er·al vi·sion ▶ n. side vision; what
is seen on the side by the eye when looking
straight ahead.

pe·riph·er·y /pə'rifərē/ ▶ n. (pl. **peripheries**)
1 the outer limits or edge of an area or object.
2 a part of a subject, group, or area of activity
that is of secondary importance: *she's content to
stay on the periphery of music.*

pe·riph·ra·sis /pə'rifrəsis/ ▶ n. (pl. **periphrases**
/-,sēz/) the use of indirect and roundabout
language. ■ **per·i·phras·tic** /,perə'frastik/ adj.

per·i·scope /'perə,skōp/ ▶ n. a tube attached to
a set of mirrors or prisms, by which an observer
in a submerged submarine or behind an obstacle
can see things that are otherwise out of sight.

per·ish /'perish/ ▶ v. 1 literary die, especially in a
violent or sudden way. 2 literary be completely
ruined or destroyed. 3 chiefly Brit. (of rubber, food,
etc.) rot or decay.
– PHRASES **perish the thought** informal used to
say that a suggestion or idea is ridiculous or
unwelcome.

per·ish·a·ble /'perishəbəl/ ▶ adj. (of food) likely
to rot quickly. ▶ n. (**perishables**) perishable
foods.

per·i·stal·sis /,perə'stôlsis, -'stal-/ ▶ n. the
contraction and relaxation of the muscles
of the intestines, creating movements that
push the contents of the intestines forward.
■ **per·i·stal·tic** /-'stôltik/ adj.

per·i·style /'perə,stīl/ ▶ n. a row of columns
surrounding a courtyard or internal garden or
edging a veranda or porch.

per·i·to·ne·um /,peritn'ēəm/ ▶ n. (pl.
peritoneums or **peritonea** /-'nēə/) the
membrane lining the cavity of the abdomen and

covering the abdominal organs. ■ **per·i·to·ne·al** /-ˈēəl/ adj.

per·i·to·ni·tis /ˌperitnˈītis/ ► n. inflammation of the peritoneum.

per·i·wig /ˈperiˌwig/ ► n. a wig of a kind worn in the 17th and 18th centuries.

per·i·win·kle¹ /ˈperiˌwiNGkəl/ ► n. a plant with flat five-petaled flowers and glossy leaves.

per·i·win·kle² ► n. another term for WINKLE.

per·jure /ˈpərjər/ ► v. 1 (**perjure oneself**) deliberately tell a lie in a court of law after one has sworn to tell the truth. 2 (as adj. **perjured**) (of evidence) involving deliberate untruth. ■ **per·jur·er** n.

per·ju·ry /ˈpərjərē/ ► n. the offense of deliberately telling a lie in a court of law when having sworn to be truthful.

perk¹ /pərk/ ► v. (**perk up** or **perk something up**) become or make more cheerful or lively.

perk² ► n. informal a benefit, especially one that a person receives from their job.

perk³ ► v. informal (of coffee) percolate.

perk·y /ˈpərkē/ ► adj. (**perkier, perkiest**) cheerful and lively. ■ **perk·i·ly** adv. **perk·i·ness** n.

per·lite /ˈpərlīt/ ► n. a form of obsidian (volcanic rock) consisting of glassy globules, used as insulation or in a mixture with plant compost.

perm /pərm/ ► n. (also **permanent wave**) a method of setting the hair in curls and treating it with chemicals so that the style lasts for several months. ► v. set the hair in a perm.

per·ma·cul·ture /ˈpərməˌkəlCHər/ ► n. the development of agricultural ecosystems that are intended to be sustainable and self-sufficient.

per·ma·frost /ˈpərməˌfrôst, -ˌfräst/ ► n. a thick layer beneath the surface of the soil that remains frozen throughout the year.

per·ma·nent /ˈpərmənənt/ ► adj. lasting or intending to last for a long time or forever: *he had never settled down in a permanent job.* ■ **per·ma·nence** n. **per·ma·nen·cy** n. **per·ma·nent·ly** adv.

per·ma·nent wave ► n. see PERM.

per·ma·nent way ► n. Brit. the finished foundation of a railroad together with the track.

per·man·ga·nate /pərˈmaNGgəˌnāt/ ► n. a salt of manganese, oxygen, and another element such as potassium, used as an oxidizing agent in some tanning preparations and disinfectants.

per·me·a·ble /ˈpərmēəbəl/ ► adj. allowing liquids or gases to pass through. ■ **per·me·a·bil·i·ty** /ˌpərmēəˈbilitē/ n.

per·me·ate /ˈpərmēˌāt/ ► v. spread throughout something: *the aroma of soup permeated the air.* ■ **per·me·a·tion** /ˌpərmēˈāSHən/ n.

Per·mi·an /ˈpərmēən/ ► adj. Geology relating to the last period of the Palaeozoic era, about 290 to 245 million years ago, a time when reptiles increased rapidly in number.

per·mis·si·ble /pərˈmisəbəl/ ► adj. allowable; permitted. ■ **per·mis·si·bil·i·ty** /-ˌmisəˈbilitē/ n.

per·mis·sion /pərˈmiSHən/ ► n. the action of officially allowing something; authorization.

per·mis·sive /pərˈmisiv/ ► adj. allowing or characterized by freedom of behavior, especially in sexual matters: *the permissive society of the 60s.* ■ **per·mis·sive·ly** adv. **per·mis·sive·ness** n.

permit ► v. /pərˈmit/ (**permits, permitting, permitted**) 1 officially allow someone to do

something. 2 (also formal **permit of**) make possible: *the parking lot was too rutted to permit ball games.* ► n. /ˈpərmit/ an official document allowing someone to do something.

per·mu·ta·tion /ˌpərmyo͞oˈtāSHən/ ► n. 1 each of several possible ways in which things can be ordered or arranged. 2 Mathematics the action of changing the arrangement of a set of items. ■ **per·mu·ta·tion·al** adj. **per·mu·tate** v.

per·mute /pərˈmyo͞ot/ (also **permutate** /ˈpərmyo͞oˌtāt/) ► v. technical alter the sequence of a set or group of things.

per·ni·cious /pərˈniSHəs/ ► adj. having a harmful effect, especially in a gradual or subtle way: *the pernicious influences of the mass media.* ■ **per·ni·cious·ly** adv. **per·ni·cious·ness** n.

per·ni·cious a·ne·mi·a ► n. a deficiency in the production of red blood cells through a lack of vitamin B_{12}.

pe·ro·gi ► n. variant spelling of PIROGI.

per·o·ra·tion /ˌperəˈrāSHən/ ► n. the concluding part of a speech; the summing up.

per·ox·ide /pəˈräksīd/ ► n. 1 Chemistry a compound containing two oxygen atoms bonded together. 2 hydrogen peroxide, a chemical used as a bleach for the hair. ► v. bleach hair with peroxide.

per·pen·dic·u·lar /ˌpərpənˈdikyələr/ ► adj. 1 at an angle of 90° to a given line, plane, or surface, or to the ground. 2 (**Perpendicular**) referring to the latest stage of English Gothic architecture (late 14th to mid 16th centuries), characterized by large windows with vertical tracery. ► n. a straight line at an angle of 90° to a given line, plane, or surface. ■ **per·pen·dic·u·lar·i·ty** /-ˌdikyəˈlaritē/ n. **per·pen·dic·u·lar·ly** adv.

per·pe·trate /ˈpərpəˌtrāt/ ► v. carry out a bad or illegal act. ■ **per·pe·tra·tion** /ˌpərpəˈtrāSHən/ n. **per·pe·tra·tor** n.

> **USAGE**
> Do not confuse **perpetrate** and **perpetuate**. **Perpetrate** means 'carry out a bad or illegal act' (*a crime has been perpetrated against a sovereign state*), whereas **perpetuate** means 'make something continue for a considerable time' (*a monument to perpetuate the memory of those killed in the war*).

per·pet·u·al /pərˈpeCHo͞oəl/ ► adj. 1 never ending or changing. 2 so frequent as to seem continual: *their perpetual money worries.* ■ **per·pet·u·al·ly** adv.

per·pet·u·al mo·tion ► n. the motion of a hypothetical machine that, once activated, would run forever unless subject to an external force or to wear.

per·pet·u·ate /pərˈpeCHo͞oˌāt/ ► v. make something continue for a considerable time. ■ **per·pet·u·a·tion** /pərˌpeCHo͞oˈāSHən/ n. **per·pet·u·a·tor** n.

> **USAGE**
> On the difference between **perpetuate** and **perpetrate**, see the note at PERPETRATE.

per·pe·tu·i·ty /ˌpərpiˈt(y)o͞oitē/ ► n. (pl. **perpetuities**) 1 the state or quality of lasting forever. 2 a bond or other security with no fixed maturity date. – PHRASES **in** (or **for**) **perpetuity** forever.

per·plex /pərˈpleks/ ► v. make someone feel baffled or very puzzled.

per·plex·i·ty /pərˈpleksitē/ ► n. (pl. **perplexities**) 1 the state of being puzzled. 2 a puzzling thing.

per·qui·site /'pərkwəzit/ ▶ n. formal a benefit or right enjoyed as a result of one's job or position.

per se /pər 'sā/ ▶ adv. by or in itself or themselves.

per·se·cute /'pərsə,kyōot/ ▶ v. 1 treat someone in a cruel or unfair way, especially because of their race or beliefs. 2 persistently harass someone. ■ **per·se·cu·tion** /,pərsə'kyōoshən/ n. **per·se·cu·tor** n.

per·se·vere /,pərsə'vi(ə)r/ ▶ v. continue in a course of action in spite of difficulty or lack of success: *he persevered with subjects that he found disagreeable.* ■ **per·se·ver·ance** /,pərsə'vi(ə)rəns/ n.

Per·sian /'pərzhən/ ▶ n. 1 a person from Persia (now Iran). 2 the language of ancient Persia or modern Iran. 3 a long-haired breed of domestic cat. ▶ adj. relating to Persia or Iran.

Per·sian car·pet ▶ n. a carpet or rug with a traditional Persian design incorporating stylized symbolic designs.

Per·sian lamb ▶ n. the silky, tightly curled fleece of the karakul (an Asian sheep), used to make clothing.

per·si·flage /'pərsə,fläzh/ ▶ n. formal light mockery or banter.

per·sim·mon /pər'simən/ ▶ n. an edible fruit resembling a large tomato, with very sweet flesh.

per·sist /pər'sist/ ▶ v. 1 continue doing something in spite of difficulty or opposition: *the minority of drivers who persist in drinking.* 2 continue to exist.

per·sist·ent /pər'sistənt/ ▶ adj. 1 continuing to do something in spite of difficulty or opposition. 2 continuing or recurring for a long time. ■ **per·sist·ence** n. **per·sist·ent·ly** adv.

per·sist·ent veg·e·ta·tive state ▶ n. a condition in which a patient is kept alive by medical means but displays no sign of higher brain function.

per·snick·et·y /pər'snikitē/ ▶ adj. informal 1 placing excessive emphasis on minor details; fussy. 2 requiring a precise or careful approach.

per·son /'pərsən/ ▶ n. (pl. **people** /'pēpəl/ or **persons**) 1 a human being regarded as an individual. 2 a human being's body: *a bottle of wine concealed on his person.* 3 Grammar a category used to classify pronouns or verb forms according to whether they indicate the speaker (**first person**), the person spoken to (**second person**), or a third party (**third person**). – PHRASES **in person** with the presence or action of the person specified.

USAGE
The words **people** and **persons** are not used in exactly the same way. **People** is by far the most common and is used in ordinary writing (*a group of people*). However, **persons** is now found chiefly in official or formal writing: *this vehicle is authorized to carry twenty persons.*

-person ▶ comb.form used as a neutral alternative to *-man* in nouns referring to role or status: *salesperson.*

per·so·na /pər'sōnə/ ▶ n. (pl. **personas** or **personae** /-'sōnē/) 1 the aspect of a person's character that is presented to others: *her public persona.* 2 a role or character adopted by an author or actor.

per·son·a·ble /'pərsənəbəl/ ▶ adj. having a pleasant appearance and character. ■ **per·son·a·bly** /-blē/ adv.

per·son·age /'pərsənij/ ▶ n. an important or high-ranking person.

per·son·al /'pərsənəl/ ▶ adj. 1 relating or belonging to a particular person. 2 done by a particular person rather than someone else: *a personal appearance.* 3 concerning a person's private rather than professional life. 4 referring to a person's character or appearance in an offensive way: *he had the gall to make personal remarks.* 5 relating to a person's body. 6 Grammar relating to one of the three persons. ▶ n. (**personals**) advertisements or messages in the personal column of a newspaper.

per·son·al as·sis·tant ▶ n. a secretary or administrative assistant working for one particular person.

per·son·al col·umn ▶ n. a section of a newspaper containing private advertisements or messages.

per·son·al com·pu·ter ▶ n. a microcomputer designed for use by one person.

per·son·al i·den·ti·fi·ca·tion num·ber ▶ n. a number allocated to a person and used with a bank card to validate electronic transactions.

per·son·al·i·ty /,pərsə'nalitē/ ▶ n. (pl. **personalities**) 1 the characteristics or qualities that form a person's character. 2 lively or interesting personal qualities: *she's always had loads of personality.* 3 a celebrity.

per·son·al·i·ty dis·or·der ▶ n. Psychiatry a deeply ingrained pattern of behavior causing long-term difficulties in relationships or in functioning in society.

per·son·al·ize /'pərsənəl,īz/ ▶ v. 1 design or produce something to meet someone's individual requirements. 2 mark something to show that it belongs to a particular person. 3 cause an issue or argument to become concerned with personalities or feelings: *the media's tendency to personalize politics.* ■ **per·son·al·i·za·tion** /,pərsənəli'zāshən/ n.

per·son·al·ly /'pərsənəlē/ ▶ adv. 1 in person. 2 from one's own viewpoint. – PHRASES **take something personally** interpret a remark or action as directed against oneself and be upset by it.

per·son·al pro·noun ▶ n. each of the pronouns in English (*I, you, he, she, it, we, they, me, him, her, us,* and *them*) that show person, gender, number, and case.

USAGE
I, we, they, he, and **she** are **subjective** personal pronouns, which means they are used as the subject of a sentence, often coming before the verb (*she lives in Paris*). **Me, us, them, him,** and **her** are **objective** personal pronouns, which means that they are used as the object of a verb or preposition (*John hates me*). This explains why it is wrong to use *me* in *John and me went to the store*: the personal pronoun is in the subject position, so it must be **I.**
Where a personal pronoun is used alone, the situation is more difficult. Some people say that statements such as *she's younger than me* are wrong and that the correct form is *she's younger than I.* This is based on the fact that **than** is a conjunction and so the personal pronoun is still in the subject position even though there is no verb (in full it would be *she's younger than I am*). Yet for most people the supposed 'correct' form does not sound natural and it is mainly found in very formal writing; it is usually perfectly acceptable to say *she's younger than me.*

per·son·al pro·per·ty ▶ n. Law all of someone's property except land and buildings. Compare with REAL PROPERTY.

per·son·al·ty /'pərsənəltē/ ▶ n. Law a person's personal property. Compare with REALTY.

per·so·na non gra·ta /pər'sōnə nän 'grätə/ ▶ n. (pl. **personae non gratae** /pər'sōnē nän 'grätē/) a person who is not welcome somewhere because they have done something unacceptable.

per·son·ate /'pərsə,nāt/ ▶ v. formal pretend to be someone else, especially for fraudulent purposes. ■ **per·son·a·tion** /,pərsə'nāSHən/ n.

per·son·i·fy /pər'sänə,fī/ ▶ v. (**personifies, personifying, personified**) **1** represent a quality or concept by a figure in human form: *dramas in which vices and virtues were personified.* **2** give a personal nature or human characteristics to something nonhuman. ■ **per·son·i·fi·ca·tion** /pər,sänəfi'kāSHən/ n.

per·son·nel /,pərsə'nel/ ▶ pl.n. people who work for an organization or one of the armed forces.

per·son·nel car·ri·er ▶ n. an armored vehicle for transporting troops.

per·spec·tive /pər'spektiv/ ▶ n. **1** the art of representing three-dimensional objects on a two-dimensional surface so as to convey the impression of height, width, depth, and relative distance. **2** a particular point of view. **3** understanding of the relative importance of things: *we must keep a sense of perspective about what he's done.* ■ **per·spec·tiv·al** /-tivəl/ adj.

per·spi·ca·cious /,pərspi'kāSHəs/ ▶ adj. quickly gaining insight into and understanding of things. ■ **per·spi·ca·cious·ly** adv. **per·spi·cac·i·ty** /-'kasitē/ n.

per·spic·u·ous /pər'spikyōōwəs/ ▶ adj. **1** clearly expressed and easily understood; lucid. **2** expressing things clearly. ■ **per·spi·cu·i·ty** /,pərspi'kyōōitē/ n. **per·spic·u·ous·ly** adv.

per·spi·ra·tion /,pərspə'rāSHən/ ▶ n. **1** sweat. **2** the process of sweating.

per·spire /pər'spīr/ ▶ v. give out sweat through the pores of the skin.

per·suade /pər'swād/ ▶ v. use reasoning or argument to make someone do or believe something: *he persuaded her to go out with him.* ■ **per·suad·a·ble** adj. **per·suad·er** n.

per·sua·sion /pər'swāZHən/ ▶ n. **1** the process of persuading someone or of being persuaded. **2** a belief or set of beliefs: *writers of all political persuasions.* **3** a group or sect holding a particular religious belief.

per·sua·sive /pər'swāsiv, -ziv/ ▶ adj. **1** good at persuading someone to do or believe something. **2** providing sound reasons or arguments: *an informative and persuasive speech.* ■ **per·sua·sive·ly** adv. **per·sua·sive·ness** n.

pert /pərt/ ▶ adj. **1** attractively lively or cheeky. **2** (especially of a part of the body) attractively small and well shaped. **3** impudent or cheeky. ■ **pert·ly** adv. **pert·ness** n.

per·tain /pər'tān/ ▶ v. **1** (**pertain to**) be relevant or appropriate to: *matters pertaining to the organization of government.* **2** formal be in effect or existence at a particular place or time.

per·ti·na·cious /,pərtn'āSHəs/ ▶ adj. formal persistent and determined. ■ **per·ti·na·cious·ly** adv. **per·ti·nac·i·ty** /-'asitē/ n.

per·ti·nent /'pərtn-ənt/ ▶ adj. relevant or appropriate: *she asked a lot of pertinent questions.* ■ **per·ti·nence** n. **per·ti·nent·ly** adv.

per·turb /pər'tərb/ ▶ v. **1** make someone anxious or unsettled. **2** alter the normal or regular state or path of a system, moving object, etc.

per·tur·ba·tion /,pərtər'bāSHən/ ▶ n. **1** anxiety or uneasiness. **2** an alteration in the normal or regular state or path of a system, moving object, etc.

per·tus·sis /pər'təsis/ ▶ n. medical term for WHOOPING COUGH.

pe·ruke /pə'rōōk/ ▶ n. old use a wig or periwig.

pe·ruse /pə'rōōz/ ▶ v. formal read or examine something thoroughly or carefully. ■ **pe·rus·al** n. **pe·rus·er** n.

USAGE
The verb **peruse** means 'read something thoroughly and carefully.' It is sometimes taken to mean 'read through something quickly,' but this is a mistake.

Pe·ru·vi·an /pə'rōōvēən/ ▶ n. a person from Peru. ▶ adj. relating to Peru.

perv /pərv/ (also **perve**) ▶ n. informal a sexual pervert. ■ **perv·y** adj.

per·vade /pər'vād/ ▶ v. spread or be present throughout: *a smell of cabbage pervaded the air.*

per·va·sive /pər'vāsiv/ ▶ adj. spreading widely through an area or group of people; widespread: *ageism is pervasive in our society.* ■ **per·va·sive·ly** adv. **per·va·sive·ness** n.

per·verse /pər'vərs/ ▶ adj. **1** showing a deliberate desire to behave in a way that other people find difficult or unacceptable. **2** contrary to what is accepted or expected. **3** sexually perverted. ■ **per·verse·ly** adv. **per·verse·ness** n. **per·ver·si·ty** /-'vərsitē/ n. (pl. **perversities**).

per·ver·sion /pər'vərZHən/ ▶ n. **1** the action of perverting something. **2** abnormal or unacceptable sexual behavior.

per·vert /pə'vərt/ ▶ v. **1** change the original form or meaning of something so that it is no longer what it should be. **2** lead someone away from doing what is right, natural, or acceptable. ▶ n. /'pər,vərt/ a person whose sexual behavior is abnormal and unacceptable.

per·vert·ed /pər'vərtid/ ▶ adj. sexually abnormal or unacceptable.

per·vi·ous /'pərvēəs/ ▶ adj. allowing water to pass through; permeable.

Pe·sach /'pä,säk/ ▶ n. the Passover festival.

pe·se·ta /pə'sātə/ ▶ n. (until the introduction of the euro in 2002) the basic unit of money of Spain.

pes·ky /'peskē/ ▶ adj. (**peskier, peskiest**) informal annoying.

pe·so /'pāsō/ ▶ n. (pl. **pesos**) the basic unit of money of several Latin American countries and of the Philippines.

pes·sa·ry /'pesərē/ ▶ n. (pl. **pessaries**) **1** a small solid block of a medical preparation designed to dissolve after being inserted into the vagina, used to treat an infection or as a contraceptive. **2** a device inserted into the vagina to support the uterus.

pes·si·mism /'pesə,mizəm/ ▶ n. **1** lack of hope or confidence in the future. **2** Philosophy a belief that this world is as bad as it could be or that evil will ultimately triumph over good. ■ **pes·si·mist** n. **pes·si·mis·tic** /,pesə'mistik/ adj. **pes·si·mis·ti·cal·ly** /,pesə'mistik(ə)lē/ adv.

pest /pest/ ▶ n. **1** a destructive animal or insect that attacks crops, food, or livestock. **2** informal an annoying person or thing.

pes·ter /'pestər/ ▶ v. trouble or annoy someone with persistent requests or interruptions.

pes·ti·cide /'pestə,sīd/ ▶ n. a substance for destroying insects or other pests.

pes·tif·er·ous /pe'stifərəs/ ▶ adj. 1 literary carrying infection and disease. 2 humorous annoying.

pes·ti·lence /'pestələns/ ▶ n. old use a deadly epidemic disease, especially bubonic plague.

pes·ti·lent /'pestələnt/ ▶ adj. 1 deadly. 2 informal, dated annoying.

pes·ti·len·tial /,pestə'lencHəl/ ▶ adj. 1 relating to or tending to cause infectious diseases. 2 very widespread and troublesome: *pestilential weeds*. 3 informal annoying.

pes·tle /'pestl, 'pesəl/ ▶ n. a heavy implement with a rounded end, used for crushing and grinding substances in a mortar.

pes·to /'pestō/ ▶ n. a sauce of crushed basil leaves, pine nuts, garlic, Parmesan cheese, and olive oil, served with pasta.

PET /pet/ ▶ abbr. 1 polyethylene terephthalate. 2 positron emission tomography.

pet[1] /pet/ ▶ n. 1 an animal or bird kept for companionship or pleasure. 2 a person treated with special favor or affection: *the teacher's pet*. ▶ adj. 1 relating to or kept as a pet. 2 treated with special attention or arousing particularly strong feelings: *my pet hate*. ▶ v. (**pets, petting, petted**) 1 stroke or pat an animal. 2 caress someone sexually.

pet[2] ▶ n. a fit of sulking or bad temper.

PETA /pētə/ ▶ abbr. People for the Ethical Treatment of Animals.

peta- ▶ comb. form referring to a factor of one quadrillion (10^{15}).

pet·al /'petl/ ▶ n. each of the segments forming the outer part of a flower.

pe·tard /pi'tärd/ ▶ n. historical a small bomb made of a metal or wooden box filled with powder. – PHRASES **be hoist with** (or **by**) **one's own petard** find that one's schemes to cause trouble for other people backfire on one.

pe·ter /'pētər/ ▶ v. (usu. **peter out**) gradually come to an end: *the storm had petered out*.

Pe·ter Pan /,pētər 'pan/ ▶ n. a person who continues to have youthful characteristics, or one who is immature, especially one who is averse to growing up.

peth·i·dine /'peтHi,dēn, 'peтHə,dēn/ ▶ n. a painkiller used especially for women giving birth.

pé·til·lant /,pāti'yän/ ▶ adj. (of wine) slightly sparkling.

pet·i·ole /'petē,ōl/ ▶ n. the stalk that joins a leaf to a stem.

pet·it bour·geois /'petē bŏŏr'zHwä, pə'tē/ ▶ adj. characteristic of the lower middle class, especially in being conventional and conservative. ▶ n. (pl. **petits bourgeois** pronunc. same) a petit bourgeois person.

pe·tite /pə'tēt/ ▶ adj. (of a woman) attractively small and slim.

pe·tite bour·geoi·sie /pə'tēt ,bŏŏrzHwä'zē/ (also **petit bourgeoisie**) ▶ n. the lower middle class.

pe·tit four /'petē 'fôr/ ▶ n. (pl. **petits fours** /'petē 'fôrz/) a very small fancy cake, cookie, or candy.

pe·ti·tion /pə'tisHən/ ▶ n. 1 a formal written appeal or request concerning a particular cause, signed by many people and presented to an authority. 2 an appeal or prayer to a deity or someone in authority. 3 Law an application to a court for a writ, judicial action, etc.: *a divorce petition*. ▶ v. make or present a petition to: *they petitioned the government for a total ban on pesticide use*. ■ **pe·ti·tion·er** n.

pe·tit mal /'petē 'mäl/ ▶ n. a mild form of epilepsy with only very brief spells of unconsciousness. Compare with GRAND MAL.

pe·tit point /'petē ,point/ ▶ n. embroidery on canvas, using small diagonal stitches.

pet name ▶ n. a name used to express affection or familiarity.

pet·rel /'petrəl/ ▶ n. a black-and-white seabird that typically flies far from land.

pe·tri dish /'pētrē/ ▶ n. a shallow transparent dish with a flat lid, used in laboratories for the culture of microorganisms.

pet·ri·fy /'petrə,fī/ ▶ v. (**petrifies, petrifying, petrified**) 1 make someone so frightened that they are unable to move. 2 change organic matter into stone by encrusting or replacing its original substance with a mineral deposit. ■ **pet·ri·fac·tion** /,petrə'faksHən/ n. **pet·ri·fi·ca·tion** /,petrəfi'kāsHən/ n.

pet·ro·chem·i·cal /,petrō'kemikəl/ ▶ adj. relating to the chemical properties and processing of petroleum and natural gas. ▶ n. a chemical obtained from petroleum and natural gas.

pet·ro·dol·lar /'petrō,dälər/ ▶ n. a unit of currency used for calculating the money earned by a country from the export of petroleum.

pet·ro·glyph /'petrə,glif/ ▶ n. a rock carving.

pe·trog·ra·phy /pə'trägrəfē/ ▶ n. the study of the composition and properties of rocks. ■ **pe·trog·ra·pher** n. **pet·ro·graph·ic** /,petrə'grafik/ adj.

pet·rol /'petrəl/ ▶ n. chiefly Brit. gasoline.

pet·ro·la·tum /,petrə'lātəm/ ▶ n. another term for PETROLEUM JELLY.

pe·tro·le·um /pə'trōlēəm/ ▶ n. a hydrocarbon oil found in layers of rock and extracted and refined to produce fuels including gasoline, paraffin, and diesel oil.

pe·tro·le·um jel·ly ▶ n. a translucent solid substance obtained from petroleum, used as a lubricant or ointment.

pe·trol·o·gy /pə'träləjē/ ▶ n. the study of the origin, structure, and composition of rocks. ■ **pet·ro·log·i·cal** /,petrə'läjikəl/ adj. **pe·trol·o·gist** /-jist/ n.

pet·ti·coat /'petē,kōt/ ▶ n. a woman's light, loose undergarment in the form of a skirt or dress.

pet·ti·fog /'petē,fôg, 'petē,fäg/ ▶ v. (**pettifogs, pettifogging, pettifogged**) old use quibble about trivial points. ■ **pet·ti·fog·ger·y** /,petē'fôgərē, -'fäg-/ n.

pet·ti·fog·ging /'petē,fôgiNG, -,fäg-/ ▶ adj. petty or trivial.

pet·tish /'petisH/ ▶ adj. childishly sulky. ■ **pet·tish·ly** adv.

pet·ty /'petē/ ▶ adj. (**pettier, pettiest**) 1 of little importance; trivial. 2 (of a person's behavior) small-minded. 3 of secondary or lesser importance, rank, or scale: *petty theft*. ■ **pet·ti·ly** adv. **pet·ti·ness** n.

pet·ty bour·geois ▶ n. variant of PETIT BOURGEOIS.

pet·ty bour·geoi·sie ▶ n. variant of PETITE BOURGEOISIE.

pet·ty cash ▶ n. a small amount of money kept in an office for minor payments.

pet·ty of·fi·cer ▸ n. a rank of noncommissioned officer in the navy, above seaman and below chief petty officer.

pet·u·lant /ˈpeсн∂l∂nt/ ▸ adj. childishly sulky or bad-tempered. ■ **pet·u·lance** n. **pet·u·lant·ly** adv.

pe·tu·nia /p∂ˈt(y)o͞ony∂/ ▸ n. a South American plant with white, purple, or red funnel-shaped flowers.

pew /pyo͞o/ ▸ n. (in a church) a long bench with a back.

pew·ter /ˈpyo͞ot∂r/ ▸ n. a gray alloy of tin with copper and antimony (formerly, tin and lead).

pe·yo·te /pāˈyōtē/ ▸ n. **1** a small cactus native to Mexico and the southern US. **2** a hallucinogenic drug prepared from this, containing mescaline.

PFC (also **Pfc.**) ▸ abbr. Private First Class.

pfen·nig /ˈfenig/ ▸ n. (pl. same or **pfennigs**) a former unit of money of Germany, equal to one hundredth of a mark.

pfft /ft/ ▸ exclam. used to represent a dull abrupt sound like that of a small impact or explosion.
– PHRASES **go pfft** informal fail to work properly or at all.

PG ▸ abbr. parental guidance (a movie rating indicating that some parents may find certain material in the movie unsuitable for their children).

PG-13 ▸ symbol a movie rating indicating that some material may be inappropriate for children under 13.

pH ▸ n. Chemistry a figure expressing how acid or alkaline a substance is (7 is neutral, lower values are more acid, and higher values are more alkaline).

pha·e·ton /ˈfā-itn/ ▸ n. historical a light, open four-wheeled horse-drawn carriage.

phage /fāj/ ▸ n. a kind of virus that acts as a parasite of bacteria, infecting them and reproducing inside them.

phag·o·cyte /ˈfag∂ˌsīt/ ▸ n. a type of body cell that surrounds and absorbs bacteria and other small particles. ■ **phag·o·cyt·ic** /ˌfag∂ˈsitik/ adj.

pha·lan·ge·al /f∂ˈlanjē∂l/ ▸ adj. Anatomy relating to a phalanx or the phalanges.

pha·lanx /ˈfālaNGks, ˈfal-/ ▸ n. (pl. **phalanxes**) **1** a group of similar people or things: *the phalanx of waiting reporters.* **2** a body of troops or police officers in close formation. **3** (pl. **phalanges** /f∂ˈlanjēz, fāˈlanjēz/) Anatomy a bone of the finger or toe.

phal·lic /ˈfalik/ ▸ adj. relating to or resembling a penis, especially when erect.

phal·lo·cen·tric /ˌfalōˈsentrik/ ▸ adj. focused on the penis as a symbol of male dominance.

phal·lus /ˈfal∂s/ ▸ n. (pl. **phalli** /ˈfalī, -lē/ or **phalluses**) **1** a penis, especially when erect. **2** a representation of an erect penis as a symbol of fertility or potency.

Phan·er·o·zo·ic /ˌfan∂r∂ˈzōik/ ▸ adj. Geology relating to the eon covering the whole of time since the beginning of the Cambrian period, and comprising the Paleozoic, Mesozoic, and Cenozoic eras.

phan·tasm /ˈfantaz∂m/ ▸ n. literary a thing that exists only in the imagination. ■ **phan·tas·mal** /fanˈtazm∂l/ adj.

phan·tas·ma·go·ri·a /fanˌtazm∂ˈgôrē∂/ ▸ n. a sequence of real or imaginary images like that seen in a dream. ■ **phan·tas·ma·gor·ic** /-gôrik/ adj. **phan·tas·ma·gor·i·cal** /-gôrik∂l/ adj.

phan·tom /ˈfant∂m/ ▸ n. **1** a ghost. **2** a thing that exists only in the imagination. ▸ adj. apparently real but not actually so: *a phantom conspiracy.*

phan·tom limb ▸ n. a sensation experienced by a person who has had a limb amputated that the limb is still there.

phan·tom preg·nan·cy ▸ n. a condition in which signs of pregnancy are present in a woman who is not pregnant.

phar·aoh /ˈfar,ō, ˈfe(∂)r,ō, ˈfā,rō/ ▸ n. a ruler in ancient Egypt. ■ **phar·a·on·ic** /ˌfarāˈänik, ˌfe(∂)r-/ adj.

Phar·i·see /ˈfarəsē/ ▸ n. **1** a member of an ancient Jewish sect noted for following traditional and written Jewish law very strictly. **2** a self-righteous or hypocritical person. ■ **Phar·i·sa·ic** /ˌfarəˈsāik/ adj. **Phar·i·sa·i·cal** /ˌfarəˈsāik∂l/ adj.

phar·ma·ceu·ti·cal /ˌfärm∂ˈso͞otik∂l/ ▸ adj. relating to medicinal drugs. ▸ n. a manufactured medicinal drug. ■ **phar·ma·ceu·ti·cal·ly** adv.

phar·ma·cist /ˈfärm∂sist/ ▸ n. a person qualified to prepare and dispense medicinal drugs.

phar·ma·col·o·gy /ˌfärm∂ˈkäl∂jē/ ▸ n. the branch of science concerned with the uses, effects, and action of drugs. ■ **phar·ma·co·log·ic** /ˌfärm∂k∂ˈläjik/ adj. **phar·ma·co·log·i·cal** /-ˈläjik∂l/ adj. **phar·ma·col·o·gist** n.

phar·ma·co·pe·ia /ˌfärm∂k∂ˈpē∂/ ▸ n. **1** a book containing a list of medicinal drugs with directions for their use. **2** a stock of medicinal drugs.

phar·ma·cy /ˈfärm∂sē/ ▸ n. (pl. **pharmacies**) **1** a place where medicinal drugs are prepared or sold. **2** the science or practice of preparing and dispensing medicinal drugs.

pharm·ing /ˈfärmiNG/ ▸ n. **1** the genetic modification of plants and animals so that they produce substances that can be used as pharmaceuticals. **2** a criminal activity in which Internet users are redirected to a website that has been set up to steal identity information.

pha·ryn·ge·al /f∂ˈrinj(ē)∂l, ˌfarinˈjē∂l/ ▸ adj. relating to the pharynx.

phar·ynx /ˈfariNGks/ ▸ n. (pl. **pharynges** /f∂ˈrinjēz/) the cavity behind the nose and mouth, connecting them to the esophagus.

phase /fāz/ ▸ n. **1** a distinct period or stage in a process of change or development: *the final phases of the war.* **2** each of the forms in which the moon or a planet appears, according to the amount that is lit up. **3** Physics the stage that a regularly varying quantity (e.g., an alternating electric current) has reached in relation to zero or another chosen value. ▸ v. **1** carry something out in gradual stages. **2** (**phase something in/out**) gradually introduce or withdraw something: *the changes will be phased in over 10 years.*
– PHRASES **in** (or **out of**) **phase** working (or not working) together in the correct or a harmonious way.

phat·ic /ˈfatik/ ▸ adj. (of words) used for general social interaction rather than to convey information or ask questions.

PhD ▸ abbr. Doctor of Philosophy.

pheas·ant /ˈfez∂nt/ ▸ n. a large long-tailed game bird, the male of which has brightly colored plumage.

phen·cy·cli·dine /fenˈsīkliˌdēn, -ˈsik-/ ▸ n. a drug used in veterinary medicine as an anesthetic and in hallucinogenic drugs such as angel dust.

phe·no·bar·bi·tal /ˌfēnōˈbärbiˌtôl/ ▶ n. a sedative drug used to treat epilepsy.

phe·nol /ˈfēˌnôl, -ˌnäl/ ▶ n. a poisonous white crystalline solid obtained from coal tar. Also called CARBOLIC ACID. ■ **phe·no·lic** /fiˈnälik/ adj.

phe·nom·e·nal /fəˈnämənəl/ ▶ adj. 1 remarkable or outstanding: *the town expanded at a phenomenal rate.* 2 able to be perceived by the senses: *the phenomenal world.*
■ **phe·nom·e·nal·ly** adv.

phe·nom·e·nol·o·gy /fiˌnäməˈnäləjē/ ▶ n. Philosophy 1 the study of phenomena (things that can be observed) as distinct from that of the nature of being (ontology). 2 an approach that concentrates on the study of consciousness and the objects of direct experience.
■ **phe·nom·e·no·log·i·cal** /-ˌnämənəˈläjikəl/ adj. **phe·nom·e·nol·o·gist** /-ˈnäləjist/ n.

phe·nom·e·non /fəˈnäməˌnän, -nən/ ▶ n. (pl. **phenomena** /fəˈnämənə/) 1 a fact or situation that is observed to exist or happen: *natural phenomena such as clouds or the wind.* 2 a remarkable person or thing: *the band was a pop phenomenon for their sales figures alone.* 3 Philosophy the object of a person's perception.

USAGE
The singular form is **phenomenon** and the plural form is **phenomena**. Do not use **phenomena** as if it were a singular form; say *this is a strange phenomenon* not *this is a strange phenomena.*
---

phe·no·type /ˈfēnəˌtīp/ ▶ n. Biology the observable characteristics of an individual determined by its genetic makeup and the environment.

phen·yl /ˈfenəl, ˈfē-/ ▶ n. Chemistry the radical $-C_6H_5$, obtained from benzene.

pher·o·mone /ˈferəˌmōn/ ▶ n. a chemical substance produced by an animal and causing a response in others of its species.

phew /fyoō/ ▶ exclam. informal expressing relief.

phi·al /ˈfīəl/ ▶ n. another term for VIAL.

phil·a·del·phus /ˌfiləˈdelfəs/ ▶ n. a mock orange (shrub).

phi·lan·der /fəˈlandər/ ▶ v. (of a man) have many casual sexual relationships with women.
■ **phi·lan·der·er** n.

phi·lan·thro·pist /fəˈlanTHrəpist/ ▶ n. a person who helps other people, especially by giving money to good causes.

phi·lan·thro·py /fəˈlanTHrəpē/ ▶ n. the practice of helping other people, especially by giving money to good causes. ■ **phil·an·throp·ic** /ˌfilənˈTHräpik/ adj. **phil·an·throp·i·cal·ly** /-(ə)lē/ adv.

phi·lat·e·ly /fəˈlatl-ē/ ▶ n. the collection and study of postage stamps. ■ **phil·a·tel·ic** /ˌfiləˈtelik/ adj. **phi·lat·e·list** /-ist/ n.

-phile ▶ comb.form referring to a person or thing having a liking for a particular thing: *bibliophile.*

phil·har·mon·ic /ˌfilärˈmänik, ˌfilhär-/ ▶ adj. (in the names of orchestras) devoted to music.

-philia ▶ comb.form referring to a liking for something, especially an abnormal love for or inclination toward something: *pedophilia.*

phi·lip·pic /fəˈlipik/ ▶ n. a bitter verbal attack.

Phil·ip·pine /ˈfiləˌpēn/ ▶ adj. relating to the Philippines.

Phil·is·tine /ˈfiləˌstēn, -ˌstīn/ ▶ n. 1 a member of a people of ancient Palestine who came into conflict with the Israelites. 2 (**philistine**) a person who is hostile toward or uninterested

in culture and the arts. ■ **phil·is·tin·ism** /ˈfiləstēˌnizəm, fəˈlistə-/ n.

Phil·lips /ˈfiləps/ ▶ adj. trademark referring to a screw with a cross-shaped slot for turning, or a corresponding screwdriver.

phi·lo·den·dron /ˌfiləˈdendrən/ ▶ n. (pl. **philodendrons** or **philodendra** /-drə/) a tropical American climbing plant grown as a greenhouse or indoor plant.

phi·lol·o·gy /fəˈläləjē/ ▶ n. the study of the structure and historical development of languages. ■ **phi·lo·log·i·cal** /ˌfiləˈläjikəl/ adj. **phi·lol·o·gist** n.

phi·los·o·pher /fəˈläsəfər/ ▶ n. a person engaged or learned in philosophy.

phil·o·soph·i·cal /ˌfiləˈsäfikəl/ ▶ adj. 1 relating to the study of philosophy. 2 calm in difficult circumstances. ■ **phil·o·soph·ic** adj. **phil·o·soph·i·cal·ly** adv.

phi·los·o·phize /fəˈläsəˌfīz/ ▶ v. talk about serious issues, especially in a boring or pompous way.

phi·los·o·phy /fəˈläsəfē/ ▶ n. (pl. **philosophies**) 1 the study of the fundamental nature of knowledge, reality, and existence. 2 the theories of a particular philosopher. 3 a theory or attitude that guides a person's behavior. 4 the study of the theoretical basis of a branch of knowledge or experience: *the philosophy of science.*

phil·ter /ˈfiltər/ ▶ n. a love potion.

phish·ing /ˈfishiNG/ ▶ n. a type of Internet fraud in which a person impersonates a reputable company in order to persuade others to reveal personal information, such as passwords and credit card numbers, online.

phle·bi·tis /fləˈbītis/ ▶ n. inflammation of the walls of a vein.

phle·bot·o·my /fləˈbätəmē/ ▶ n. (pl. **phlebotomies**) the surgical opening or puncture of a vein to withdraw blood or introduce a fluid.
■ **phle·bot·o·mist** n.

phlegm /flem/ ▶ n. 1 a thick substance produced by the mucous membranes of the nose and throat, especially when one has a cold. 2 (in medieval science and medicine) one of the four bodily humors, believed to be associated with a calm or apathetic temperament. 3 calmness of temperament. ■ **phlegm·y** adj.

phleg·mat·ic /flegˈmatik/ ▶ adj. calm and unemotional. ■ **phleg·mat·i·cal·ly** adv.

phlo·em /ˈflōˌem/ ▶ n. the tissue in plants that conducts nutrients downward from the leaves.

phlo·gis·ton /flōˈjistän, -tən/ ▶ n. a substance supposed by 18th-century chemists to exist in all combustible bodies, and to be released in combustion.

phlox /fläks/ ▶ n. a plant with clusters of colorful scented flowers.

-phobe ▶ comb.form referring to a person having a fear or dislike of a specified thing: *technophobe.*

pho·bi·a /ˈfōbēə/ ▶ n. an extreme or irrational fear of something. ■ **pho·bic** /ˈfōbik/ adj. & n.

-phobia ▶ comb.form extreme or irrational fear or dislike of a specified thing: *arachnophobia.*
■ **-phobic** comb.form.

phoe·be /ˈfēbē/ ▶ n. a mainly gray-brown or blackish American tyrant flycatcher.

Phoe·ni·cian /fəˈnēsHən/ ▶ n. a member of an ancient people living in Phoenicia in the eastern Mediterranean. ▶ adj. relating to Phoenicia.

phoe·nix /'fēniks/ ▶ n. (in classical mythology) a bird that periodically burned itself on a funeral pyre and was born again from the ashes.

phone /fōn/ ▶ n. a telephone. ▶ v. make a telephone call to someone.

-phone ▶ comb.form 1 referring to an instrument using or connected with sound: *megaphone*. 2 referring to a person who uses a specified language: *francophone*.

phone book ▶ n. a telephone directory.

phone card ▶ n. another term for CALLING CARD (sense 2).

phone-in ▶ n. another term for CALL-IN.

phone jack ▶ n. a socket designed to receive the plug from a telephone, fax machine, etc.

pho·neme /'fōnēm/ ▶ n. any of the distinct units of sound that distinguish one word from another, e.g., *p*, *b*, *d*, and *t* in *pad*, *pat*, *bad*, and *bat*.

pho·net·ic /fə'netik/ ▶ adj. 1 relating to speech sounds. 2 (of a system of spelling) closely matching the sounds represented. ■ **pho·net·i·cal·ly** adv.

pho·net·ics /fə'netiks/ ▶ pl.n. (treated as sing.) the study and classification of speech sounds.

pho·ney /'fōnē/ ▶ adj. & n. variant spelling of PHONY.

phon·ic /'fänik/ ▶ adj. relating to speech sounds.

phon·ics /'fäniks/ ▶ pl.n. (treated as sing.) a method of teaching people to read by associating letters or groups of letters with particular sounds.

pho·no /'fōnō/ ▶ adj. referring to a type of plug used with audio and video equipment, in which one conductor is cylindrical and the other is a central prong that extends beyond it.

phono- ▶ comb.form relating to sound: *phonograph*.

pho·no·graph /'fōnə,graf/ ▶ n. 1 old use a record player. 2 historical an early form of gramophone. ■ **pho·no·graph·ic** /,fōnə'grafik/ adj.

pho·nol·o·gy /fə'näləjē, fō-/ ▶ n. the system of relationships between the basic speech sounds of a language. ■ **pho·no·log·i·cal** /,fōnə'läjikəl/ adj.

pho·ny /'fōnē/ (also **phoney**) informal ▶ adj. (**phonier**, **phoniest**) not genuine. ▶ n. (pl. **phonies**) a person or thing that is not genuine. ■ **pho·ni·ness** n.

phoo·ey /'foōē/ informal ▶ exclam. used to express scorn or disbelief. ▶ n. nonsense.

phos·gene /'fäsjēn/ ▶ n. a poisonous gas formerly used in warfare.

phos·phate /'fäsfāt/ ▶ n. Chemistry a salt or ester of phosphoric acid.

phos·phine /'fäsfēn/ ▶ n. a foul-smelling gas formed from phosphorus and hydrogen.

phos·phor /'fäsfər/ ▶ n. 1 a synthetic fluorescent or phosphorescent substance. 2 old-fashioned term for PHOSPHORUS.

phos·pho·res·cence /,fäsfə'resəns/ ▶ n. light given out by a substance without burning or heat, or with so little heat that it cannot be felt. ■ **phos·pho·resce** v. **phos·pho·res·cent** adj.

phos·phor·ic /fäs'fôrik/ ▶ adj. relating to or containing phosphorus.

phos·phor·ic ac·id ▶ n. a crystalline acid obtained by treating phosphates with sulfuric acid.

phos·pho·rus /'fäsfərəs/ ▶ n. a poisonous nonmetallic chemical element in the form of a yellowish waxy solid that ignites spontaneously in air and glows in the dark. ■ **phos·pho·rous** adj.

pho·to /'fōtō/ ▶ n. (pl. **photos**) a photograph.

photo- ▶ comb.form 1 relating to light. 2 relating to photography.

pho·to·cell /'fōtō,sel/ ▶ n. short for PHOTOELECTRIC CELL.

pho·to·chem·is·try /,fōtō'keməstrē/ ▶ n. the branch of chemistry concerned with the chemical effects of light. ■ **pho·to·chem·i·cal** /,fōtō'kemikəl/ adj.

pho·to·chro·mic /,fōtə'krōmik/ ▶ adj. (of glass, lenses, etc.) undergoing a reversible change in color when exposed to bright light.

pho·to·cop·i·er /'fōtə,käpēər/ ▶ n. a machine for making photocopies.

pho·to·cop·y /'fōtə,käpē/ ▶ n. (pl. **photocopies**) a photographic copy of something produced by a process involving the action of light on a specially prepared surface. ▶ v. (**photocopies**, **photocopying**, **photocopied**) make a photocopy of something. ■ **pho·to·cop·i·a·ble** adj.

pho·to·e·lec·tric /,fōtōi'lektrik/ ▶ adj. involving the emission of electrons from a surface by the action of light.

pho·to·e·lec·tric cell ▶ n. a device using a photoelectric effect to generate current.

pho·to fin·ish ▶ n. a close finish of a race in which the winner can be identified only from a photograph of competitors crossing the line.

pho·to·gen·ic /,fōtə'jenik/ ▶ adj. 1 looking attractive in photographs. 2 Biology producing or giving out light.

pho·to·graph /'fōtə,graf/ ▶ n. a picture made with a camera, in which an image is focused onto film and then made visible and permanent by chemical treatment. ▶ v. take a photograph of someone or something. ■ **pho·tog·ra·pher** /fə'tägrəfər/ n. **pho·to·graph·ic** /,fōtə'grafik/ adj.

pho·to·graph·ic mem·o·ry /,fōtə'grafik/ ▶ n. an ability to remember information or visual images in great detail.

pho·tog·ra·phy /fə'tägrəfē/ ▶ n. the taking and processing of photographs.

pho·to·gra·vure /,fōtəgrə'vyōōr/ ▶ n. a printing process in which the type or image is produced from a photographic negative transferred to a metal plate and etched in.

pho·to·jour·nal·ism /,fōtō'jərnə,lizəm/ ▶ n. the taking and publishing of photographs as a means of communicating news. ■ **pho·to·jour·nal·ist** n.

pho·to·mon·tage /,fōtōmän'täzн/ ▶ n. a picture consisting of a number of separate photographs placed together or overlapping.

pho·ton /'fōtän/ ▶ n. Physics a particle representing a quantum of light or other electromagnetic radiation. ■ **pho·ton·ic** adj.

pho·to op·por·tu·ni·ty (also **photo op**) ▶ n. an occasion on which famous people pose for photographers by arrangement.

pho·to·re·al·ism /'fōtō'rēə,lizəm/ ▶ n. a style of art and sculpture characterized by a very detailed and unidealized portrayal of ordinary life. ■ **pho·to·re·al·ist** n. & adj. **pho·to·re·al·is·tic** /,fōtō,rēə'listik/ adj.

pho·to·re·cep·tor /,fōtōri'septər/ ▶ n. a structure in an animal or plant that responds to light.

pho·to·sen·si·tive /,fōtə'sensitiv/ ▶ adj. responding to light. ■ **pho·to·sen·si·tiv·i·ty**

/-,sensə'tivitē/ n.

pho·to·stat /'fōtō,stat/ ▶ n. trademark **1** a type of machine for making photocopies on special paper. **2** a copy made by a photostat.
▶ v. (**photostats, photostatting, photostatted**) copy something with a photostat.

pho·to·syn·the·sis /,fōtō'sinthəsis/ ▶ n. the process by which green plants use sunlight to form nutrients from carbon dioxide and water. ■ **pho·to·syn·the·size** /,fōtō'sinthə,sīz/ v. **pho·to·syn·thet·ic** /-,sin'thetik/ adj.

pho·tot·ro·pism /,fōtə'trōpizəm, fō'tätrə,pizəm/ ▶ n. the turning of a plant or other organism either toward or away from a source of light. ■ **pho·to·trop·ic** /,fōtə'trōpik, -'träpik/ adj.

pho·to·vol·ta·ic /,fōtəvōl'tāik, ,fōtōvāl-/ ▶ adj. relating to the production of electric current at the junction of two substances exposed to light.

phras·al verb ▶ n. a verb combined with an adverb or preposition to give a new meaning that cannot be worked out from the individual parts, e.g., *break down* or *see to.*

phrase /frāz/ ▶ n. **1** a small group of words forming a unit within a clause. **2** Music a group of notes forming a distinct unit within a longer passage. **3** a group of words that have a particular meaning when used together.
▶ v. **1** put into a particular form of words: *it's important to phrase the question correctly.* **2** (often as n. **phrasing**) divide music into phrases in a particular way. ■ **phras·al** adj.
– PHRASES **turn of phrase** a particular or characteristic manner of expression.

phrase book ▶ n. a book listing useful expressions in a foreign language and their translations.

phra·se·ol·o·gy /,frāzē'äləjē/ ▶ n. (pl. **phraseologies**) a particular or characteristic way in which words are used: *legal phraseology.*

phre·nol·o·gy /fre'näləjē/ ▶ n. chiefly historical the study of the shape and size of a person's skull as a supposed indication of their character.
■ **phre·nol·o·gist** n.

Phryg·i·an /'frijēən/ ▶ n. a person from Phrygia, an ancient region of west central Asia Minor (the western peninsula of Asia). ▶ adj. relating to Phrygia.

phthi·sis /'thīsis, 'tī-/ ▶ n. old use tuberculosis or a similar disease.

phy·la /'fīlə/ ▶ plural of PHYLUM.

phy·lac·ter·y /fi'laktərē/ ▶ n. (pl. **phylacteries**) a small leather box containing biblical passages written in Hebrew, worn by Jewish men at morning prayer.

phyl·lo /'felō/ ▶ n. variant spelling of FILO.

phyl·lo·qui·none /,filō'kwinōn, -kwi'nōn/ ▶ n. vitamin K₁, a compound found in cabbage, spinach, and other leafy green vegetables, and essential for blood-clotting.

phyl·lox·e·ra /fi'läksərə, ,filək'si(ə)rə/ ▶ n. an insect that is a pest of vines.

phy·lum /'fīləm/ ▶ n. (pl. **phyla** /-lə/) a category in the classification of animals and plants that ranks above class and below kingdom.

phys·ic /'fizik/ ▶ n. old use medicinal drugs or medical treatment.

phys·i·cal /'fizikəl/ ▶ adj. **1** relating to the body as opposed to the mind. **2** relating to things that can be seen, heard, or touched. **3** involving bodily contact or activity: *a physical relationship.*

4 relating to physics or the operation of natural forces. ▶ n. a medical examination to establish how healthy or fit a person is. ■ **phys·i·cal·i·ty** /,fizi'kalitē/ n. **phys·i·cal·ly** adv.

phys·i·cal chem·is·try ▶ n. the branch of chemistry concerned with the application of the techniques and theories of physics to the study of chemical systems.

phys·i·cal ed·u·ca·tion ▶ n. instruction in physical exercise and games, especially in schools.

phys·i·cal ge·og·ra·phy ▶ n. the branch of geography concerned with natural features.

phys·i·cal sci·ences ▶ pl.n. the sciences concerned with the study of inanimate natural objects, including physics, chemistry, and astronomy.

phys·i·cal ther·a·py ▶ n. the treatment of disease or injury by physical methods such as massage and exercise. ■ **phys·i·cal ther·a·pist** n.

phy·si·cian /fi'zishən/ ▶ n. a person qualified to practice medicine.

phys·ics /'fiziks/ ▶ pl.n. (treated as sing.) **1** the branch of science concerned with the nature and properties of matter and energy. **2** the physical properties and nature of something.
■ **phys·i·cist** /'fizəsist/ n.

phys·i·og·no·my /,fizē'ä(g)nəmē/ ▶ n. (pl. **physiognomies**) a person's facial features or expression, especially when seen as an indication of character.

phys·i·ol·o·gy /,fizē'äləjē/ ▶ n. **1** the branch of biology concerned with the normal functions of living organisms and their parts. **2** the way in which a living organism or bodily part functions. ■ **phys·i·o·log·i·cal** /,fizēə'läjikəl/ adj. **phys·i·ol·o·gist** n.

phys·i·o·ther·a·py /,fizēō'therəpē/ ▶ n. British term for PHYSICAL THERAPY. ■ **phys·i·o·ther·a·pist** n.

phy·sique /fi'zēk/ ▶ n. the form, size, and development of a person's body.

phy·to·chem·i·cal /,fītō'kemikəl/ ▶ n. any of a group of compounds found in plants that are believed to have beneficial effects.

phy·to·es·tro·gen /,fītō'estrəjən/ ▶ n. a substance found in certain plants which can produce effects like that of the hormone estrogen when ingested.

phy·to·plank·ton /,fītō'plaNGktən/ ▶ n. plankton consisting of microscopic plants.

PI ▶ abbr. private investigator.

pi /pī/ ▶ n. **1** the sixteenth letter of the Greek alphabet (Π, π), represented as 'p.' **2** the numerical value of the ratio of the circumference of a circle to its diameter (approximately 3.14159).

pi·a /'pīə, 'pēə/ (in full **pia mater** /'pīə 'mātər, 'pēə 'mätər/) ▶ n. the delicate innermost membrane enveloping the brain and spinal cord.

pi·a·nism /'pēə,nizəm/ ▶ n. skill or artistry in playing the piano or composing music for the piano. ■ **pi·a·nis·tic** /,pēə'nistik/ adj.

pi·a·nis·si·mo /,pēə'nisi,mō/ ▶ adv. & adj. Music very soft or softly.

pi·an·o¹ /pē'anō/ ▶ n. (pl. **pianos**) a large keyboard musical instrument with metal strings that are struck by hammers when the keys are pressed.
■ **pi·an·ist** /'pēənist, pē'anist/ n.

pi·an·o² /pē'änō, pē'anō/ ▶ adv. & adj. Music soft or softly.

pi·an·o·forte /pē′ˌanōˈfôrtā, pēˈanōˌfôrt/ ▶ n. formal term for PIANO¹.

pi·a·no·la /ˌpēəˈnōlə/ ▶ n. trademark a piano equipped to be played automatically with a roll of perforated paper that controls the movement of the keys to produce a tune.

pi·as·ter /pēˈastər/ (also **piastre**) ▶ n. a unit of money of several Middle Eastern countries.

pi·az·za /pēˈätsə, pēˈazə/ ▶ n. a public square or marketplace, especially in Italy.

pic /pik/ ▶ n. informal a photograph or movie.

pi·ca /ˈpīkə/ ▶ n. Printing 1 a unit of type size and line length equal to 12 points (about 1/6 inch or 4.2 mm). 2 a size of letter in typewriting, with 10 characters to the inch (about 3.9 to the centimeter).

pi·ca·dor /ˈpikəˌdôr/ ▶ n. (in bullfighting) a person on horseback who goads the bull with a lance.

pic·a·resque /ˌpikəˈresk/ ▶ adj. relating to fiction dealing with the adventures of a dishonest but appealing hero.

pic·a·yune /ˌpikiˈyo͞on/ informal ▶ adj. of little value or importance. ▶ n. an unimportant person or thing.

pic·ca·lil·li /ˈpikəˌlilē/ ▶ n. (pl. **piccalillies** or **piccalillis**) an Indian relish made of chopped vegetables, mustard, and hot spices.

pic·co·lo /ˈpikəˌlō/ ▶ n. (pl. **piccolos**) a small flute an octave higher than the ordinary one.

pick¹ /pik/ ▶ v. 1 (also **pick something up**) take hold of something and move it: *he picked a match out of the ash tray.* 2 remove a flower or fruit from where it is growing. 3 choose someone or something from a number of alternatives: *he was picked for the debate team.* 4 remove unwanted matter from one's nose or teeth with a finger or a pointed instrument. ▶ n. 1 an act of selecting something: *take your pick from our extensive menu.* 2 (**the pick of**) informal the best person or thing in a particular group: *he was the pick of the bunch.* ∎ **pick·er** n.

– PHRASES **pick and choose** select only the best from among a number of alternatives. **pick at 1** repeatedly pull at something with one's fingers. 2 eat food in small amounts. **pick someone's brain** informal obtain information by questioning someone who is better informed about a subject. **pick a fight** provoke an argument or fight. **pick holes in** find fault with. **pick a lock** open a lock with an instrument other than the proper key. **pick someone/thing off** shoot one of a group from a distance. **pick on** single someone out for unfair treatment. **pick someone/thing out 1** distinguish someone or something from among a group. 2 play a tune slowly or with difficulty on a guitar or similar instrument. **pick over** (or **pick through**) sort through a number of items carefully. **pick someone's pockets** steal something from a person's pocket. **pick up** improve or increase. **pick someone/thing up 1** go to collect someone or something. 2 informal casually strike up a relationship with someone with a sexual purpose in mind. 3 return to an earlier point or topic. 4 obtain, acquire, or learn something: *he had picked up a little Russian from his father.* 5 become aware of or sensitive to something. 6 detect or receive a signal or sound. **pick one's way** walk slowly and carefully.

pick² (also **pickax** /ˈpikˌaks/) ▶ n. 1 a tool consisting of a curved iron bar with one or both ends pointed, fixed at right angles to its handle, used for breaking up hard ground or rock. 2 a plectrum.

pick·a·nin·ny /ˈpikəˌninē/ ▶ n. (pl. **pickaninnies**) offensive a small black child.

pick·ax /ˈpikˌaks/ (also **pickaxe**) ▶ n. another term for PICK² (sense 1).

pick·et /ˈpikit/ ▶ n. 1 a person or group of people standing outside a workplace with the aim of persuading other people not to work during a strike. 2 a soldier or small group of troops sent out to watch for the enemy. 3 a pointed wooden stake driven into the ground. ▶ v. (**pickets, picketing, picketed**) act as a picket outside a workplace.

pick·ings /ˈpikiNGz/ ▶ pl.n. profits or gains, especially those made easily or dishonestly.

pick·le /ˈpikəl/ ▶ n. 1 a small cucumber preserved in vinegar, brine, or a similar solution. 2 liquid used to preserve food or other perishable items. 3 (**a pickle**) informal a difficult situation. ▶ v. 1 preserve food in vinegar, brine, or a similar solution. 2 (as adj. **pickled**) informal, dated drunk.

pick-me-up ▶ n. informal a thing that makes one feel more energetic or cheerful.

pick·pock·et /ˈpikˌpäkət/ ▶ n. a person who steals from people's pockets.

pick·up /ˈpikˌəp/ ▶ n. 1 (also **pickup truck**) a small truck with an enclosed cab and open back. 2 an act of picking up or collecting a person or goods. 3 informal a casual encounter with someone, with a view to having a sexual relationship. 4 an improvement in an economic indicator. 5 the cartridge of a record player, carrying the stylus. 6 a device on an electric guitar that converts sound vibrations into electrical signals for amplification.

pick·y /ˈpikē/ ▶ adj. (**pickier, pickiest**) informal fussy: *a picky eater.*

pic·nic /ˈpikˌnik/ ▶ n. a packed meal eaten outdoors, or an occasion when such a meal is eaten. ▶ v. (**picnics, picnicking, picnicked**) have or take part in a picnic. ∎ **pic·nick·er** n.

– PHRASES **be no picnic** informal be difficult or unpleasant.

pico- ▶ comb.form referring to a factor of one million millionth (10^{-12}): *picosecond.*

pi·cot /ˈpēkō/ ▶ n. a small loop or series of loops in lace or embroidery, typically used to decorate a border.

Pict /pikt/ ▶ n. a member of an ancient people living in northern Scotland in Roman times.

pic·to·graph /ˈpiktəˌgraf/ (also **pictogram** /-ˌgram/) ▶ n. 1 a picture or symbol representing a word or phrase. 2 a pictorial representation of statistics on a chart, graph, or computer screen. ∎ **pic·to·graph·ic** /ˌpiktəˈgrafik/ adj.

pic·to·ri·al /pikˈtôrēəl/ ▶ adj. relating to or using pictures. ▶ n. a newspaper or magazine that has pictures as a main feature. ∎ **pic·to·ri·al·ly** adv.

pic·ture /ˈpikCHər/ ▶ n. 1 a painting, drawing, or photograph. 2 an image on a television screen. 3 a movie. 4 (**the pictures**) the movies. 5 an impression formed from an account or description of something: *a full picture of the disaster had not yet emerged.* ▶ v. 1 represent someone or something in a picture. 2 form a mental image of; visualize: *she pictured him waiting and smiled.*

– PHRASES (**as**) **pretty as a picture** very pretty. **in the picture** informal informed about something.

pic·ture-post·card ▸ adj. (of a view) prettily picturesque.

pic·tur·esque /ˌpikcHəˈresk/ ▸ adj. attractive in a quaint or charming way: *miles of picturesque beaches.* ◾ **pic·tur·esque·ly** adv. **pic·tur·esque·ness** n.

pic·ture win·dow ▸ n. a large window consisting of one pane of glass.

pid·dle /ˈpidl/ ▸ v. informal **1** urinate. **2** (**piddle around/about**) spend time in unimportant activities.

pid·dling /ˈpidliNG/ (also **piddly**) ▸ adj. informal ridiculously small or unimportant.

pidg·in /ˈpijən/ ▸ n. a simplified form of a language with elements taken from local languages, used for communication between people not sharing a common language.

pie /pī/ ▸ n. a baked dish of fruit, or meat and vegetables, encased in or topped with pastry.
− PHRASES **pie in the sky** informal a pleasant future event or idea that is very unlikely to happen.

pie·bald /ˈpīˌbôld/ ▸ adj. (of a horse) having irregular patches of two colors, typically black and white. ▸ n. a piebald horse.

piece /pēs/ ▸ n. **1** a portion separated from the whole. **2** an item used in constructing something or forming part of a set: *a piece of luggage.* **3** a musical or written work. **4** a figure or token used to make moves in a board game. **5** a coin of specified value. **6** informal a firearm. ▸ v. (**piece something together**) assemble something from individual parts.
− PHRASES **go to pieces** become so upset that one cannot function normally. **in one piece** not harmed or damaged. (**all**) **of a piece** (**with something**) entirely) consistent (with something). **say one's piece** give one's opinion.

pièce de ré·sis·tance /pēˈes də ˌrəziˈstäns, -räziˈstäns/ ▸ n. the most important or impressive feature of something: *the garden was her pièce de résistance.*

piece·meal /ˈpēsˌmēl/ ▸ adj. & adv. done in stages over a period of time.

piece·work /ˈpēsˌwərk/ ▸ n. work paid for according to the amount produced.

pie chart ▸ n. a diagram in which a circle is divided into sectors that each represent a proportion of the whole.

pied /pīd/ ▸ adj. having two or more different colors.

pied-à-terre /pēˌyäd ə ˈter/ ▸ n. (pl. **pieds-à-terre** pronunc. same) a small apartment or house kept for occasional use, one's permanent home being elsewhere.

pied·mont /ˈpēdmänt/ ▸ n. a gentle slope leading from the base of mountains to a region of flat land.

Pied Pip·er /pīd ˈpīpər/ ▸ n. a person who entices others to follow them in a course of action, especially one with disastrous results.

pie-eyed ▸ adj. informal very drunk.

pier /pi(ə)r/ ▸ n. **1** a structure leading out to sea and used as a landing stage for boats or as a place of entertainment. **2** a pillar supporting an arch or a bridge. **3** a wall between windows or other adjoining openings.

pierce /pi(ə)rs/ ▸ v. **1** make a hole in or through something with a sharp object. **2** force a way through: *a shrill voice pierced the air.* **3** (as adj. **piercing**) very sharp, cold, or high-pitched. ◾ **pierc·er** n.

Pi·er·rot /ˌpēəˈrō/ ▸ n. a male character in French pantomime, with a sad white-painted face, a loose white costume, and a pointed hat.

pi·e·ty /ˈpīitē/ ▸ n. (pl. **pieties**) **1** the quality of being deeply religious. **2** a conventional belief that is accepted without thinking.

pi·e·zo /pīˈēzō, pēˈäzō/ ▸ adj. piezoelectric.

pi·e·zo·e·lec·tric /pēˌäzōˌilekˈtrik, pīˌēz-/ ▸ adj. relating to electric polarization produced in certain crystals by the application of mechanical stress.

pif·fle /ˈpifəl/ ▸ n. informal nonsense.

pif·fling /ˈpifliNG/ ▸ adj. informal trivial; unimportant.

pig /pig/ ▸ n. **1** a domesticated mammal with sparse bristly hair and a flat snout, kept for its meat. **2** informal a greedy, dirty, or unpleasant person. **3** informal, derogatory a police officer. **4** an oblong mass of iron or lead from a smelting furnace. ▸ v. (**pigs, pigging, pigged**) informal (often **pig out**) gorge oneself with food. ◾ **pig·let** /ˈpiglit/ n.
− PHRASES **make a pig of oneself** informal overeat. **a pig in a poke** something that is bought without first being seen.

pi·geon /ˈpijən/ ▸ n. a fat bird with a small head and a cooing voice.

pi·geon·hole /ˈpijənˌhōl/ ▸ n. **1** each of a set of small compartments where letters or messages may be left for people. **2** a category into which someone or something is placed. ▸ v. place in a particular category, especially a restrictive one: *I was pigeonholed as a 'youth writer.'*

pi·geon-toed ▸ adj. having the toes or feet turned inward.

pig·ger·y /ˈpigərē/ ▸ n. (pl. **piggeries**) **1** a farm or enclosure where pigs are kept. **2** greed or unpleasantness, regarded as characteristic of pigs.

pig·gish /ˈpigisH/ ▸ adj. greedy, dirty, or unpleasant.

pig·gy /ˈpigē/ ▸ n. (pl. **piggies**) a child's word for a pig. ▸ adj. resembling a pig, especially in features or appetite.

pig·gy·back /ˈpigēˌbak/ ▸ n. a ride on someone's back and shoulders. ▸ adv. on the back and shoulders of another person. ▸ v. link to or take advantage of an existing system or body of work: *they have piggybacked their own networks onto the system.*

pig·gy bank ▸ n. a container for saving money, shaped like a pig.

pig·head·ed /ˈpigˌhedid/ ▸ adj. stupidly obstinate.

pig i·ron ▸ n. crude iron as first obtained from a smelting furnace.

pig·ment /ˈpigmənt/ ▸ n. **1** a natural substance that gives animal or plant tissue its color. **2** a substance used for coloring or painting. ◾ **pig·men·tar·y** /-ˌterē/ adj. **pig·men·ta·tion** /ˌpigmənˈtāsHən/ n.

pig·ment·ed /ˈpigˌmentid, ˌpigˈmentid/ ▸ adj. colored with or as if with pigment.

pig·my ▸ n. variant spelling of PYGMY.

pig·pen /ˈpigˌpen/ ▸ n. **1** a pen or enclosure for pigs. **2** a very dirty or untidy house or room.

pig·skin /ˈpigˌskin/ ▸ n. **1** leather made from the hide of a pig. **2** informal a football.

pig·sty /ˈpigˌstī/ ▸ n. (pl. **pigsties**) **1** an enclosure for a pig or pigs. **2** a very dirty or untidy house or room.

pig·tail /ˈpigˌtāl/ ▶ n. a braided length of hair worn singly at the back or on each side of the head. ■ **pig·tailed** adj.

pike[1] /pīk/ ▶ n. (pl. same) a predatory freshwater fish with a long body and sharp teeth.

pike[2] ▶ n. historical a weapon with a pointed metal head on a long wooden shaft.

pike[3] ▶ n. a jackknife position in diving or gymnastics.

pike[4] ▶ n. short for TURNPIKE.
– PHRASES **come down the pike** appear on the scene; come to someone's notice.

pik·er /ˈpīkər/ ▶ n. informal 1 a gambler who makes only small bets. 2 a miserly or cautious person.

pike·staff /ˈpīkˌstaf/ ▶ n. historical the wooden shaft of a pike.
– PHRASES **(as) plain as a pikestaff** very obvious.

pi·laf /pəˈläf, ˈpēläf/ (also **pilau** /-ˈlô, -lou/, **pulao** /-lô, -lou/) ▶ n. a Middle Eastern or Indian dish of spiced rice, often with vegetables or meat added.

pi·las·ter /pəˈlastər/ ▶ n. a rectangular column incorporated within and projecting slightly from a wall.

Pi·la·tes /piˈlätēz/ ▶ n. a system of exercises designed to improve physical strength, flexibility, and posture, and to enhance mental awareness.

pil·chard /ˈpilcHərd/ ▶ n. a small edible sea fish of the herring family.

pile[1] /pīl/ ▶ n. 1 a heap of things laid or lying one on top of another. 2 informal a large amount. 3 a large imposing building. ▶ v. 1 place things one on top of the other. 2 (**pile up**) form a pile or very large quantity. 3 (**pile something on**) informal exaggerate something for effect. 4 (**pile into/out of**) get into or out of a vehicle in a disorganized way.

pile[2] ▶ n. a heavy stake or post driven into the ground as a foundation or support for a structure.

pile[3] ▶ n. the soft projecting surface of a carpet or a fabric, consisting of the cut ends of many small threads.

pile driv·er ▶ n. a machine for driving piles into the ground.

piles /pīlz/ ▶ pl.n. hemorrhoids.

pile·up /ˈpīlˌəp/ ▶ n. 1 a crash involving several vehicles. 2 a large collection of something.

pil·fer /ˈpilfər/ ▶ v. steal things of little value. ■ **pil·fer·age** n.

pil·grim /ˈpilgrəm/ ▶ n. 1 a person who journeys to a holy place for religious reasons. 2 (**Pilgrim**) a member of a group of English Puritans who sailed in the *Mayflower* and founded Plymouth in 1620.

pil·grim·age /ˈpilgrəmij/ ▶ n. 1 a pilgrim's journey to a holy place. 2 a journey to a place of interest or importance.

pill /pil/ ▶ n. 1 a small round mass of solid medicine for swallowing whole. 2 (**the pill**) a contraceptive pill.
– PHRASES **a bitter pill** something that is unpleasant but must be accepted. **sweeten the pill** chiefly Brit. make an unpleasant necessity easier to accept.

pil·lage /ˈpilij/ ▶ v. rob a place or steal something with violence, especially in wartime. ▶ n. the action of pillaging a place or property. ■ **pil·lag·er** n.

pil·lar /ˈpilər/ ▶ n. 1 a tall vertical structure used as a support for a building or as an ornament. 2 a person or thing providing reliable support: *he was a pillar of his local community.*

■ **pil·lared** adj.
– PHRASES **from pillar to post** from one place to another in an unsatisfactory way.

pill·box /ˈpilˌbäks/ ▶ n. 1 a woman's hat with straight sides, a flat top, and no brim. 2 a small round box for holding pills. 3 a small, partly underground, concrete fort.

pil·lion /ˈpilyən/ ▶ n. a seat for a passenger behind a motorcyclist.

pil·lo·ry /ˈpilərē/ ▶ n. (pl. **pillories**) a wooden framework with holes for the head and hands, in which offenders were formerly imprisoned and exposed to public abuse. ▶ v. (**pillories**, **pillorying**, **pilloried**) 1 attack or ridicule someone publicly. 2 put someone in a pillory.

pil·low /ˈpilō/ ▶ n. a rectangular cloth bag stuffed with soft material, used to support the head when lying down or sleeping. ▶ v. support the head on something soft. ■ **pil·low·y** adj.

pil·low·case /ˈpilōˌkās/ ▶ n. a removable cloth cover for a pillow.

pil·low talk ▶ n. intimate conversation between lovers in bed.

pi·lot /ˈpīlət/ ▶ n. 1 a person who operates the flying controls of an aircraft. 2 a person with local knowledge who is qualified to take charge of a ship entering or leaving a harbor. 3 something done or produced as a test before introducing it more widely: *a pilot for a Channel 4 sitcom.* ▶ v. (**pilots**, **piloting**, **piloted**) 1 act as a pilot of an aircraft or ship. 2 test a scheme, program, etc., before introducing it more widely. ■ **pi·lot·age** n.

pi·lot light ▶ n. 1 a small gas burner kept alight permanently to light a larger burner when needed. 2 an electric indicator light or control light.

pi·lot whale ▶ n. a black toothed whale with a square bulbous head.

Pil·sner /ˈpilznər/ ▶ n. a lager beer with a strong hop flavor, originally brewed at Pilsen (Plzeň) in the Czech Republic.

PIM ▶ abbr. personal information manager.

pi·mien·to /pəˈm(y)entō/ (also **pimento** /pəˈmentō/) ▶ n. (pl. **pimientos**) a red sweet pepper.

pimp /pimp/ ▶ n. a man who controls prostitutes and arranges clients for them, taking a percentage of their earnings in return. ▶ v. 1 act as a pimp. 2 informal make something, especially a car, more showy or impressive.

pim·per·nel /ˈpimpərˌnel, -pərnəl/ ▶ n. a low-growing plant with bright five-petaled flowers.

pim·ple /ˈpimpəl/ ▶ n. a small hard inflamed spot on the skin. ■ **pim·pled** adj. **pim·ply** adj.

PIN /pin/ (also **PIN number**) ▶ abbr. personal identification number.

pin /pin/ ▶ n. 1 a thin piece of metal with a sharp point at one end and a round head at the other, used for fastening pieces of cloth, paper, etc. 2 a metal projection from an electric plug or an integrated circuit. 3 a small brooch or badge. 4 a steel rod used to join the ends of fractured bones while they heal. 5 Golf a stick with a flag placed in a hole to mark its position. 6 a metal peg in a hand grenade that prevents it from exploding. 7 (in bowling) one of a set of bottle-shaped wooden pieces arranged in an upright position at the end of a lane. 8 (**pins**) informal legs. ▶ v. (**pins**, **pinning**, **pinned**) 1 attach or fasten something with a pin or pins. 2 hold someone firmly so they are unable to move. 3 (**pin someone**

down) force someone to be specific about their intentions. **4** (**pin someone down**) restrict the actions of an enemy by firing at them. **5** (**pin something on**) place blame or responsibility on someone.
– PHRASES **pin one's hopes on** rely heavily on.

pi·ña co·la·da /ˈpēnyə kəˈlädə/ ▶ n. a cocktail made with rum, pineapple juice, and coconut.

pin·a·fore /ˈpinəˌfôr/ ▶ n. **1** a collarless, sleeveless dress worn over a blouse or sweater. **2** Brit. a loose sleeveless piece of clothing worn over other clothes to keep them clean.

pin·ball /ˈpinˌbôl/ ▶ n. a game in which small metal balls are shot across a sloping board to strike targets.

pince-nez /ˈpans,nā, ˈpins/ ▶ n. (treated as sing. or pl.) a pair of glasses with a nose clip instead of earpieces.

pin·cer /ˈpinsər/ ▶ n. **1** (**pincers**) a tool made of two pieces of metal with blunt inward-curving jaws, used for gripping and pulling things. **2** a front claw of a lobster or similar type of shellfish.

pin·cer move·ment ▶ n. an attack in which an army approaches the enemy from two sides at the same time.

pinch /pinCH/ ▶ v. **1** grip flesh tightly between the finger and thumb. **2** (of a shoe) hurt a foot by being too tight. **3** informal steal something. **4** informal arrest someone. ▶ n. **1** an act of pinching. **2** an amount of an ingredient that can be held between the fingers and thumb: *a pinch of salt.*
– PHRASES **in a pinch** if absolutely necessary. **feel the pinch** experience financial hardship.

pinch-hit ▶ v. **1** Baseball bat in place of another player, typically at a critical point in the game. **2** informal act as a substitute for someone, especially in an emergency: *last year I briefly pinch-hit for a movie critic on leave.*

pin·cush·ion /ˈpinˌko͝oSHən/ ▶ n. a small pad for holding pins.

pine[1] /pīn/ ▶ n. (also **pine tree**) an evergreen coniferous tree having clusters of long needle-shaped leaves.

pine[2] ▶ v. **1** (often **pine away**) feel very distressed or weak because one misses someone so much. **2** (**pine for**) miss or long for: *some members still pine for the old days.*

pin·e·al gland /ˈpinēəl, ˈpī-/ (also **pineal body**) ▶ n. a small gland at the base of the skull within the brain, producing a hormonelike substance in some mammals.

pine·ap·ple /ˈpīˌnapəl/ ▶ n. a large tropical fruit with juicy yellow flesh surrounded by a tough skin and topped with a tuft of leaves.

pine cone ▶ n. the conical or rounded woody fruit of a pine tree.

pine mar·ten ▶ n. a dark brown weasellike mammal that lives in trees.

pine nut ▶ n. the edible seed of various pine trees.

pine sis·kin /ˈsiskin/ ▶ n. a North American finch with dark-streaked plumage, a notched tail, and touches of yellow on its wings and tail.

pine·y /ˈpīnē/ (also **piny**) ▶ adj. relating to, resembling, or full of pines.

ping /pinG/ ▶ n. an abrupt high-pitched ringing sound. ▶ v. make an abrupt high-pitched ringing sound.

ping-pong /ˈpinG ˌpônG, -ˌpänG/ (also trademark **Ping-Pong**) ▶ n. informal table tennis.

pin·head /ˈpinˌhed/ ▶ n. **1** the flattened head of a pin. **2** informal a stupid person.

pin·hole /ˈpinˌhōl/ ▶ n. a very small hole.

pin·ion[1] /ˈpinyən/ ▶ n. the outer part of a bird's wing including the flight feathers. ▶ v. **1** tie or hold someone by the arms or legs. **2** cut off the pinion of a bird to prevent it from flying.

pin·ion[2] ▶ n. a small gear or spindle that engages with a large gear.

pink[1] /pinGk/ ▶ adj. **1** of a color between red and white. **2** informal, often derogatory left-wing. **3** relating to homosexuals: *the pink economy.* ▶ n. **1** pink color or material. **2** (**the pink**) informal the best condition: *he's in the pink of health.* ■ **pink·ish** adj. **pink·y** adj.

pink[2] ▶ n. a plant with sweet-smelling pink or white flowers and narrow gray-green leaves.

pink[3] ▶ v. cut a zigzag edge on something.

pink[4] ▶ v. Brit. (of a vehicle engine) make rattling sounds as a result of over-rapid combustion in the cylinders.

pink·ie /ˈpinGkē/ (also **pinky**) ▶ n. (pl. **pinkies**) informal the little finger.

pink·ing shears ▶ pl. n. scissors with a serrated blade, used to cut a zigzag edge in fabric.

pink·o /ˈpinGkō/ ▶ n. (pl. **pinkos** or **pinkoes**) informal, derogatory a left-wing or liberal person.

pink slip informal ▶ n. a notice of dismissal from employment. ▶ v. (**pink-slip**) dismiss someone from employment.

pin mon·ey ▶ n. a small sum of money for spending on items that are not essential.

pin·na /ˈpinə/ ▶ n. (pl. **pinnae** /ˈpinē/) the external part of the ear; the auricle.

pin·nace /ˈpinis/ ▶ n. chiefly historical a small boat forming part of the equipment of a larger ship.

pin·na·cle /ˈpinəkəl/ ▶ n. **1** the most successful point: *the pinnacle of his career.* **2** a high pointed piece of rock. **3** a small pointed turret on a roof.

pin·nate /ˈpināt, -it/ ▶ adj. Botany & Zoology having leaflets or other parts arranged on either side of a stem or axis.

PIN num·ber ▶ n. see PIN.

Pi·not /ˈpēnō, pēˈnō/ ▶ n. any of several varieties of wine grape, which are either red (**Pinot Noir** /nwär/) or white (**Pinot Blanc** /bläNGk/).

pin·point /ˈpinˌpoint/ ▶ v. find or identify exactly: *it is difficult to pinpoint a single cause for violence like this.* ▶ n. a tiny dot or point. ▶ adj. absolutely precise.

pin·prick /ˈpinˌprik/ ▶ n. **1** a prick caused by a pin. **2** a cause of minor irritation.

pins and nee·dles ▶ pl. n. (treated as sing.) a tingling sensation in a limb recovering from numbness.

pin·stripe /ˈpinˌstrīp/ ▶ n. a very narrow stripe in cloth, used especially for suits. ■ **pin-striped** adj.

pint /pīnt/ ▶ n. **1** a unit of liquid or dry capacity equal to one half of a quart. **2** chiefly Brit. informal a pint of beer.

pin·tail /ˈpinˌtāl/ ▶ n. a duck with a long pointed tail.

pin·to /ˈpintō/ ▶ n. (pl. **pintos**) a piebald horse.

pin·to bean ▶ n. a medium-sized speckled variety of kidney bean.

pint-sized (also **pint-size**) ▶ adj. informal very small.

pin-tuck ▶ n. a very narrow ornamental tuck in an item of clothing.

pin·up /ˈpinˌəp/ ▸ n. a poster featuring a sexually attractive person.

pin·wheel /ˈpinˌ(h)wēl/ ▸ n. **1** a child's toy consisting of a stick with colored vanes that twirl in the wind. **2** something shaped or rotating like a pinwheel.

Pin·yin /ˈpinˈyin/ ▸ n. the standard system for transliterating Chinese characters into the Roman alphabet.

pi·ña·ta /pēnˈyätə/ ▸ n. (especially in Spanish-speaking communities) a papier mâché figure of an animal, hung in the air at festivals so that children can smash it with sticks and share the contents.

pi·ñon /ˈpinyən, ˌpinˈyōn/ (also **pinyon**) ▸ n. **1** a small pine tree with edible seeds, native to Mexico and the southwestern US. **2** (also **piñon nut**) a pine nut from this tree.

pi·on /ˈpīˌän/ ▸ n. Physics a meson (subatomic particle) with a mass around 270 times that of the electron.

pi·o·neer /ˌpīəˈni(ə)r/ ▸ n. **1** a person who explores or settles in a new region. **2** a person who develops new ideas or techniques.
▸ v. develop or be the first to use: *the company pioneered the use of the computer in the courtroom.*

pi·ous /ˈpīəs/ ▸ adj. **1** deeply religious. **2** pretending to be good or religious so as to impress. **3** (of a hope) sincere but unlikely to be fulfilled. ∎ **pi·ous·ly** adv. **pi·ous·ness** n.

pip[1] /pip/ ▸ n. a small hard seed in a fruit.

pip[2] ▸ n. **1** Brit. a star indicating rank on the shoulder of an army officer's uniform. **2** any of the spots on a playing card, dice, or domino.

pip[3] ▸ n. a disease of poultry or other birds causing thick mucus in the throat.

pip[4] ▸ v. (of a young bird) crack (the shell of the egg) when hatching.

pipe /pīp/ ▸ n. **1** a tube used to carry water, gas, oil, etc. **2** a device for smoking tobacco, consisting of a narrow tube that opens into a small bowl in which the tobacco is burned. **3** a wind instrument consisting of a single tube with holes along its length that are covered by the fingers to produce different notes. **4** one of the tubes by which notes are produced in an organ. **5** (**pipes**) bagpipes. ▸ v. **1** convey something through a pipe. **2** transmit music, a program, or a signal by wire or cable. **3** play a tune on a pipe. **4** sing or say something in a high, shrill voice. **5** decorate food, clothing, or furnishings with piping.
– PHRASES **pipe down** informal be less noisy. **pipe up** say something suddenly. **put that in your pipe and smoke it** informal said to emphasize that someone will have to accept a particular situation, even if it is unwelcome.

pipe-clay ▸ n. a fine white clay, used for making tobacco pipes or for whitening leather.

pipe clean·er ▸ n. a piece of wire covered with fiber, used to clean a tobacco pipe.

piped-in mu·sic ▸ n. prerecorded background music played through loudspeakers.

pipe dream ▸ n. a hope or scheme that will never be realized.

pipe·line /ˈpīpˌlīn/ ▸ n. a long pipe for carrying oil, gas, or water over a long distance. ▸ v. carry oil, gas, or water by a pipeline.

– PHRASES **in the pipeline** in the process of being developed.

pipe or·gan ▸ n. an organ using pipes instead of or as well as reeds.

pip·er /ˈpīpər/ ▸ n. a person who plays a pipe or bagpipes.

– PHRASES **pay the piper** bear the consequences of an action or activity that one has enjoyed.

pi·pette /pīˈpet/ ▸ n. a narrow tube used in a laboratory for handling small quantities of liquid, the liquid being drawn into the tube by suction.

pip·ing /ˈpīpiNG/ ▸ n. **1** lengths of pipe. **2** lines of icing or whipped cream, used to decorate cakes and desserts. **3** thin cord covered in fabric and inserted along a seam or hem for decoration.
– PHRASES **piping hot** (of food or water) very hot.

pip·i·strelle /ˌpipəˈstrel, ˈpipəˌstrel/ ▸ n. a small insect-eating bat.

pip·it /ˈpipit/ ▸ n. a songbird of open country, typically having brown streaky plumage.

pip·pin /ˈpipin/ ▸ n. a red and yellow dessert apple.

pip·squeak /ˈpipˌskwēk/ ▸ n. informal an insignificant person.

pi·quant /ˈpēkənt, -känt/ ▸ adj. **1** having a pleasantly sharp or spicy taste. **2** stimulating or interesting: *legal arguments punctuated by piquant asides.* ∎ **pi·quan·cy** n. **pi·quant·ly** adv.

pique /pēk/ ▸ n. irritation or resentment arising from hurt pride. ▸ v. (**piques, piquing, piqued**) **1** arouse someone's interest. **2** (**be piqued**) feel irritated or resentful.

pi·qué /pēˈkā, pi-/ ▸ n. stiff cotton fabric woven in a ribbed or raised pattern.

pi·quet /piˈkā, ˈket/ ▸ n. a trick-taking card game for two players.

pi·ra·cy /ˈpīrəsē/ ▸ n. **1** the practice of attacking and robbing ships at sea. **2** the use or reproduction of a movie, recording, or other material without permission and in order to make a profit.

pi·ra·nha /pəˈränə/ ▸ n. a freshwater fish with very sharp teeth.

pi·rate /ˈpīrət/ ▸ n. **1** a person who attacks and robs ships at sea. **2** a person who reproduces the work of another for profit without permission. ▸ adj. **1** (of a movie, recording, or other material) that has been reproduced and used for profit without permission: *pirate videos.* **2** (of an organization) broadcasting without official permission: *a pirate radio station.* ▸ v. **1** reproduce (another's work) for profit without permission. **2** dated rob or plunder a ship. ∎ **pi·rat·ic** /pīˈratik, pi-/ adj.

pi·ro·gi /piˈrōgē/ (also **perogi**) ▸ n. (pl. same or **pirogies**) a dough dumpling stuffed with a filling such as potato or cheese.

pi·rogue /piˈrōg/ ▸ n. (in Central America and the Caribbean) a long narrow canoe made from a single tree trunk.

pir·ou·ette /ˌpiro͞oˈet/ ▸ n. (especially in ballet) an act of spinning on one foot. ▸ v. spin around on one foot.

pis·ca·to·ri·al /ˌpiskəˈtôrēəl/ (also **piscatory** /ˈpiskəˌtôrē/) ▸ adj. formal relating to fishing.

Pis·ces /ˈpīsēz, ˈpisēz/ ▸ n. **1** a constellation and the twelfth sign of the zodiac (the Fish or Fishes), which the sun enters about February 20. **2** (**a Pisces**) a person born when the sun is in this sign. ■ **Pis·ce·an** /-sēən/ n. & adj.

pis·ci·cul·ture /ˈpisiˌkəlCHər/ ▶ n. the controlled breeding and rearing of fish.

pis·cine /ˈpīsēn, ˈpisīn/ ▶ adj. relating to fish.

pis·civ·o·rous /piˈsivərəs/ ▶ adj. (of an animal) feeding on fish. ■ **pis·ci·vore** /ˈpisiˌvôr/ n.

piss /pis/ vulgar slang ▶ v. urinate. ▶ n. **1** urine. **2** an act of urinating. ■ **piss·er** n.
– PHRASES **piss off** chiefly Brit. go away. **piss someone off** annoy someone. **piss something away** waste something.

pissed /pist/ ▶ adj. vulgar slang **1** (also **pissed off**) very annoyed. **2** chiefly Brit. drunk.

pis·tach·i·o /pəˈstasHēˌō/ ▶ n. (pl. **pistachios**) the edible pale green seed of an Asian tree.

piste /pēst/ ▶ n. a ski trail of compacted snow.

pis·til /ˈpistl/ ▶ n. the female organs of a flower, comprising the stigma, style, and ovary.

pis·tol /ˈpistl/ ▶ n. a small gun designed to be held in one hand.

pis·tol-whip ▶ v. (**pistol-whips, pistol-whipping, pistol-whipped**) hit or beat someone with the butt of a pistol.

pis·ton /ˈpistn/ ▶ n. **1** a disk or short cylinder fitting closely inside a tube in which it moves up and down, used especially in an internal combustion engine to make other parts of the engine move. **2** a valve in a brass instrument that is pressed down to alter the pitch of a note.

pit¹ /pit/ ▶ n. **1** a large hole in the ground. **2** a mine or quarry for coal, gravel, etc. **3** a hollow or indentation in a surface. **4** a sunken area in a workshop floor allowing access to a car's underside. **5** an area at the side of a track where race cars are serviced and refueled. **6** a part of a theater where an orchestra plays. **7** a part of the floor of an exchange in which a particular stock or commodity is traded. **8** historical an enclosure in which animals were made to fight as a form of entertainment. **9** (**the pits**) informal a very bad place or situation. **10** (**the pit**) literary hell. ▶ v. (**pits, pitting, pitted**) **1** (**pit someone/thing against**) test someone or something in a contest or struggle against: *pit your wits against the world champions.* **2** make a hollow in the surface of something. ■ **pit·ted** adj.
– PHRASES **the pit of one's stomach** the lower part of the abdomen, regarded as the seat of strong feelings, especially anxiety.

pit² ▶ n. the stone of a fruit. ▶ v. (**pits, pitting, pitted**) remove the stone from fruit.

pi·ta /ˈpētə/ (also **pita bread**) ▶ n. a type of flat bread that can be split open to hold a filling.

pit-a-pat /ˈpit ə ˌpat/ (also **pitapat**) ▶ adv. with a sound like quick light taps.

pit bull (in full **pit bull terrier**) ▶ n. a fierce American type of bull terrier.

pitch¹ /piCH/ ▶ n. **1** the extent to which a sound or tone is high or low. **2** a particular level of intensity: *he's keyed up to the highest pitch of concentration.* **3** Baseball a legal delivery of the ball by the pitcher. **4** particular words used to sell or promote something: *a sales pitch.* **5** the steepness of a roof. **6** the movement up and down of the front of a ship or aircraft. ▶ v. **1** Baseball throw (the ball) for the batter to try to hit. **2** throw or fall heavily or roughly. **3** set one's voice or a piece of music at a particular pitch. **4** set or aim at a particular level, target, or audience: *he should pitch his talk at a suitable level.* **5** set up and fix something in position. **6** (**pitch in**) informal join in

enthusiastically with a task or activity. **7** (of the front of a moving ship or aircraft) move up and down. **8** (as adj. **pitched**) (of a roof) sloping.
– PHRASES **make a pitch** make an attempt at or bid for something.

pitch² ▶ n. a sticky black substance that hardens on cooling, made from tar or turpentine and used for waterproofing.

pitch-black (also **pitch-dark**) ▶ adj. completely dark.

pitch·blende /ˈpiCHˌblend/ ▶ n. a mineral found in dark pitchlike masses and containing radium.

pitched bat·tle /ˈpiCHt ˈbatl/ ▶ n. a fierce fight involving a large number of people.

pitch·er¹ /ˈpiCHər/ ▶ n. a large jug.

pitch·er² ▶ n. Baseball the player who throws the ball for the batter to hit.

pitch·er plant ▶ n. a plant with a deep pitcher-shaped pouch containing fluid in which insects are trapped and absorbed.

pitch·fork /ˈpiCHˌfôrk/ ▶ n. a farm tool with a long handle and sharp metal prongs, used for lifting hay. ▶ v. **1** lift something with a pitchfork. **2** thrust suddenly into an unexpected and difficult situation: *he was pitchforked into the job for six months.*

pitch-per·fect ▶ adj. exactly right in tone, mood, or pitch: *a pitch-perfect performance.*

pitch pine ▶ n. a pine tree with hard, heavy, resinous wood.

pitch·y /ˈpiCHē/ ▶ adj. (**pitchier, pitchiest**) resembling pitch, especially in being sticky or dark.

pit·e·ous /ˈpitēəs/ ▶ adj. deserving or arousing pity: *piteous cries.* ■ **pit·e·ous·ly** adv. **pit·e·ous·ness** n.

pit·fall /ˈpitˌfôl/ ▶ n. **1** a hidden or unsuspected danger or difficulty: *the pitfalls of setting up an office at home.* **2** a covered pit used to trap animals.

pith /piTH/ ▶ n. **1** spongy white tissue lining the rind of citrus fruits. **2** spongy tissue in the stems and branches of many plants. **3** the essential part of something: *puzzling over the pith of the problem.* **4** conciseness and clarity in expressing a point.

pith hel·met ▶ n. a head covering made from the dried pith of a tropical plant, used for protection from the sun.

pith·y /ˈpiTHē/ ▶ adj. (**pithier, pithiest**) **1** (of language or style) concise and expressing a point clearly. **2** (of a fruit or plant) containing much pith. ■ **pith·i·ly** adv. **pith·i·ness** n.

pit·i·a·ble /ˈpitēəbəl/ ▶ adj. **1** deserving or arousing pity. **2** ridiculously poor or small. ■ **pit·i·a·bly** /-əblē/ adv.

pit·i·ful /ˈpitifəl/ ▶ adj. **1** deserving or arousing pity. **2** very small or poor; inadequate. ■ **pit·i·ful·ly** adv. **pit·i·ful·ness** n.

pit·i·less /ˈpitilis/ ▶ adj. showing no pity; harsh or cruel. ■ **pit·i·less·ly** adv. **pit·i·less·ness** n.

pi·ton /ˈpētän/ ▶ n. a peg or spike driven into a crack to support a climber or a rope.

pit stop ▶ n. **1** (in auto racing) a stop in the pits for servicing and refueling. **2** a brief rest during a journey.

pit·tance /ˈpitns/ ▶ n. a very small or inadequate amount of money.

pit·ter-pat·ter /ˈpitər ˈpatər/ ▶ n. a sound of quick light steps or taps. ▶ adv. with a sound of quick light steps or taps.

pi·tu·i·tar·y gland /pə't(y)ōōə͵terē/ (also **pituitary body**) ▸ n. a pea-sized gland attached to the base of the brain, important in controlling growth and development.

pit·y /'pitē/ ▸ n. (pl. **pities**) 1 a feeling of sorrow and sympathy caused by the sufferings of others. 2 a cause for regret or disappointment: *what a pity we can't be friends.* ▸ v. (**pities, pitying, pitied**) feel pity for someone.

piv·ot /'pivət/ ▸ n. 1 the central point, pin, or shaft on which a mechanism turns or balances. 2 a person or thing playing a central part in an activity or organization. ▸ v. (**pivots, pivoting, pivoted**) 1 turn on a central point. 2 (**pivot on**) depend on: *success pivots on the performance of the sales force.* ■ **piv·ot·a·ble** adj.

piv·ot·al /'pivətl/ ▸ adj. 1 of central importance; vital: *Japan's pivotal role in the world economy.* 2 fixed or turning on a pivot.

pix·el /'piksəl/ ▸ n. any of the tiny areas of light on a display screen that make up an image.

pix·el·ate /'piksəlāt/ (also **pixellate** or **pixilate**) ▸ v. 1 divide an image into pixels, for display or for storage in a digital format. 2 display a person's image as a small number of large pixels in order to disguise their identity. ■ **pix·el·a·tion** /͵piksə'lāshən/ n.

pix·ie /'piksē/ (also **pixy**) ▸ n. (pl. **pixies**) a supernatural being in folklore. ■ **pix·ie·ish** adj.

pix·il·at·ed /'piksə͵lātid/ (Brit. **pixillated**) ▸ adj. informal crazy; confused.

piz·za /'pētsə/ ▸ n. a dish consisting of a flat, round base of dough baked with a topping of tomatoes, cheese, and other ingredients.

piz·zazz /pə'zaz/ (also **pizazz** or **pzazz**) ▸ n. informal a combination of liveliness and style.

piz·ze·ri·a /͵pētsə'rēə/ ▸ n. a pizza restaurant.

piz·zi·ca·to /͵pitsi'kätō/ ▸ adv. & adj. plucking the strings of a violin or other stringed instrument with the finger.

PJs ▸ abbr. pajamas.

pkg. ▸ abbr. (pl. **pkgs.**) package.

pl. ▸ abbr. 1 (also **Pl.**) place. 2 plural.

plac·ard /'plakärd, -ərd/ ▸ n. a sign for public display, either fixed on a wall or carried during a demonstration. ▸ v. cover something with placards.

pla·cate /'plākāt/ ▸ v. make someone less angry or hostile. ■ **pla·ca·to·ry** /-kə͵tôrē, 'plakə-/ adj.

place /plās/ ▸ n. 1 a particular position or area; a location. 2 a portion of space occupied by or set aside for someone or something: *Jack had saved her a place.* 3 a vacancy or available position. 4 a position in a sequence: *I finished in second place.* 5 the position of a figure in a decimal number. 6 (in place names) a square or short street. 7 informal a person's home. ▸ v. 1 put in a particular position or situation: *enemy officers were placed under arrest.* 2 find an appropriate place or role for someone or something. 3 allocate a specified position in a sequence to: *a survey placed the company 13th for achievement.* 4 remember where one has seen someone or something. 5 arrange for an order, bet, etc., to be carried out. ■ **plac·er** n.
– PHRASES **go places** informal be increasingly successful. **in place** established and working or ready. **in place of** instead of. **keep someone in**

his (or **her**) **place** keep someone from becoming too self-important. **out of place** 1 not in the proper position. 2 in a situation where one does not fit in. **put someone in his** (or **her**) **place** make someone feel less proud or arrogant. **take place** happen; occur. **take the place of** replace someone or something.

pla·ce·bo /plə'sēbō/ ▸ n. (pl. **placebos**) 1 a medicine given to a patient to make them feel better psychologically rather than for any physical effect. 2 a substance that has no medicinal effect, used as a control in testing new drugs.

place-kick /'plās͵kik/ Football ▸ n. a kick made after the ball is first placed on the ground. ▸ v. take a place kick. ■ **place-kick·er** n.

place·ment /'plāsmənt/ ▸ n. the action of placing someone or something.

pla·cen·ta /plə'sentə/ ▸ n. (pl. **placentae** /-tē/ or **placentas**) an organ that forms in the uterus of a pregnant mammal and that supplies blood and nourishment to the fetus through the umbilical cord. ■ **pla·cen·tal** /plə'sentl/ adj.

plac·id /'plasid/ ▸ adj. 1 not easily upset or excited. 2 with little movement or activity; calm: *the placid waters of the lake.* ■ **pla·cid·i·ty** /plə'siditē/ n. **plac·id·ly** adv.

plack·et /'plakit/ ▸ n. 1 an opening in an item of clothing, covering fastenings or for access to a pocket. 2 a flap of material used to strengthen such an opening.

pla·gia·rize /'plājə͵rīz/ ▸ v. take the work or idea of someone else and pass it off as one's own. ■ **pla·gia·rism** /'plājə͵rizəm/ n. **pla·gia·rist** n. **pla·gia·riz·er** /'plājə͵rizər/ n.

plague /plāg/ ▸ n. 1 a contagious disease spread by bacteria and causing fever and delirium. 2 an unusually large quantity of destructive insects or animals. ▸ v. (**plagues, plaguing, plagued**) 1 cause continual trouble to: *he grew up in a neighborhood plagued by crime.* 2 pester someone continually.

plaice /plās/ ▸ n. (pl. same) an edible brown marine flatfish with orange spots.

plaid /plad/ ▸ n. fabric woven in a checkered or tartan design.

plain /plān/ ▸ adj. 1 not decorated or elaborate; simple or ordinary: *good plain food.* 2 without a pattern or in only one color. 3 without identification; unmarked: *a plain envelope.* 4 easy to see or understand; clear. 5 (of language) clearly expressed, without the use of difficult terms. 6 (of a woman or girl) not beautiful or attractive. 7 sheer; simple: *the problem was plain exhaustion.* 8 (of a knitting stitch) made by putting the needle through the front of the stitch from left to right. Compare with PURL[1]. ▸ adv. informal used for emphasis: *that's plain stupid.* ▸ n. a large area of flat land with few trees. ■ **plain·ly** adv. **plain·ness** n.

plain-clothes /'plān͵klōᴛʜz/ ▸ pl.n. ordinary clothes rather than uniform, especially when worn by police officers.

plain·song /'plān͵sôNG, -säNG/ (also **plainchant**) ▸ n. unaccompanied medieval church music sung by a number of voices together.

plain-spo·ken ▸ adj. outspoken; blunt.

plaint /plānt/ ▸ n. 1 Law, Brit. an accusation or charge. 2 chiefly literary a complaint or lament.

plain·tiff /'plāntif/ ▸ n. a person who brings a

case against another in a court of law. Compare with **defendant**.

plain·tive /'plāntiv/ ▶ adj. sounding sad and mournful. ■ **plain·tive·ly** adv. **plain·tive·ness** n.

plait /plăt, plat/ ▶ n. a single length of hair, rope, or other material made up of three or more interlaced strands. ▶ v. form hair or other material into a plait or plaits.

plan /plan/ ▶ n. **1** a detailed proposal for doing or achieving something. **2** an intention or decision about what one is going to do. **3** a scheme for making regular payments toward a pension, insurance policy, etc. **4** a map or diagram. **5** a scale drawing of a horizontal section of a building. ▶ v. (**plans, planning, planned**) **1** decide on and arrange something in advance. **2** (**plan for**) make preparations for. **3** make a plan of something to be made or built.

pla·nar /'plānər/ ▶ adj. Mathematics relating to or in the form of a plane.

plan·chette /plan'sнet/ ▶ n. a small board on casters and fitted with a vertical pencil, used in seances to convey supposed messages from spirits.

plane¹ /plān/ ▶ n. **1** technical a flat surface on which a straight line joining any two points would wholly lie. **2** a level of existence or thought: *many believe there is a higher plane of existence.* ▶ adj. **1** completely level or flat. **2** relating to two-dimensional surfaces or magnitudes. ▶ v. **1** (especially of a bird) soar without moving the wings; glide. **2** (of a boat, surfboard, etc.) skim over the surface of water.

plane² ▶ n. an airplane.

plane³ (also **planer**) ▶ n. a tool consisting of a block with a projecting steel blade, used to smooth a wooden surface by paring shavings from it. ▶ v. smooth a surface with a plane.

plane⁴ (also **plane tree**) ▶ n. a tall spreading tree with maplelike leaves and a peeling bark.

plan·et /'planit/ ▶ n. **1** a large round object in space that orbits around a star. **2** (**the planet**) the earth. ■ **plan·e·tar·y** /'plani,terē/ adj. **plan·e·tol·o·gy** /,plani'täləjē/ n.

plan·e·tar·i·um /,plani'te(ə)rēəm/ ▶ n. (pl. **planetariums** or **planetaria** /-'te(ə)rēə/) a building in which images of stars, planets, and constellations are projected onto a domed ceiling.

plan·et·oid /'plani,toid/ ▶ n. another term for **asteroid**.

plan·gent /'planjənt/ ▶ adj. literary (of a sound) resonant and mournful. ■ **plan·gen·cy** n. **plan·gent·ly** adv.

plank /planGk/ ▶ n. **1** a long, flat piece of timber, used in flooring. **2** a fundamental part of a political or other program: *crime reduction is a central plank of the manifesto.* ■ **planked** adj.
– PHRASES **walk the plank** be forced by pirates to walk blindfolded along a plank over the side of a ship to one's death in the sea.

plank·ing /'planGkinG/ ▶ n. planks used for flooring or as part of a boat.

plank·ton /'planGktən/ ▶ n. small and microscopic organisms living in the sea or fresh water. ■ **plank·tic** adj. **plank·ton·ic** /-'tänik/ adj.

planned e·con·o·my ▶ n. another term for **command economy**.

plan·ner /'planər/ ▶ n. **1** a person who controls or plans urban development: *city planners.* **2** a person who plans their activities thoroughly.

3 a book or chart with information that is an aid to planning: *my day planner.*

plan·ning /'planinG/ ▶ n. **1** the process of making plans for something. **2** the control of development in cities and towns by local government.

plant /plant/ ▶ n. **1** a living organism that grows in the ground, having roots with which it absorbs substances and leaves in which it makes nutrients by photosynthesis. **2** a place where an industrial or manufacturing process takes place. **3** machinery used in an industrial or manufacturing process. **4** a person placed in a group as a spy. **5** a thing put among someone's belongings to make them appear guilty of wrongdoing. ▶ v. **1** place a seed, bulb, or plant in the ground so that it can grow. **2** place or fix someone or something in a specified position. **3** secretly place a bomb somewhere. **4** put or hide something among someone's belongings to make them appear guilty of wrongdoing. **5** send someone to join a group to act as a spy. **6** establish an idea in someone's mind. ■ **plant·let** /-lit/ n.

Plan·tag·e·net /plan'tajənit/ ▶ n. a member of the English royal dynasty that ruled from 1154 until 1485.

plan·tain¹ /'plantən/ ▶ n. a low-growing plant, with a rosette of leaves and green flowers.

plan·tain² ▶ n. a type of banana that is harvested green and cooked as a vegetable.

plan·tar /'plantər/ ▶ adj. Anatomy relating to the sole of the foot.

plan·ta·tion /plan'tāsнən/ ▶ n. **1** a large estate on which crops such as coffee, sugar, and tobacco are grown. **2** an area in which trees have been planted.

plant·er /'plantər/ ▶ n. **1** a manager or owner of a plantation. **2** a decorative container in which plants are grown.

plaque /plak/ ▶ n. **1** an ornamental tablet fixed to a wall in commemoration of a person or event. **2** a sticky deposit on teeth that encourages the growth of bacteria.

plash /plasн/ ▶ n. a splashing sound. ▶ v. make or hit with a splash. ■ **plash·y** adj.

plas·ma /'plazmə/ ▶ n. **1** the colorless fluid part of blood, lymph, or milk, in which corpuscles or fat globules are suspended. **2** Physics a gas of positive ions and free electrons with little or no overall electric charge. ■ **plas·mat·ic** /plaz'matik/ adj. **plas·mic** /-mik/ adj.

plas·ma screen ▶ n. a flat display screen that uses an array of cells containing a gas plasma to produce different colors in each cell.

plas·ter /'plastər/ ▶ n. **1** a soft mixture of lime with sand or cement and water for spreading on walls and ceilings to form a smooth hard surface when dried. **2** (also **plaster of Paris**) a hard white substance made by adding water to powdered gypsum, used for setting broken bones and making sculptures and casts. ▶ v. **1** cover a wall or ceiling with plaster. **2** coat thickly with a substance: *a face plastered in heavy makeup.* **3** make hair lie flat by dampening it. **4** display widely and prominently: *her story was plastered all over the December issue.* ■ **plas·ter·er** n.

plas·ter·board /'plastər,bôrd/ ▶ n. board made of plaster set between two sheets of heavy paper, used to line interior walls and ceilings.

plas·tered /'plastərd/ ▶ adj. informal very drunk.

plas·tic /'plastik/ ► n. **1** a material produced by chemical processes that can be molded into shape while soft and then set into a rigid or slightly elastic form. **2** informal credit cards or other plastic cards that can be used as money. ► adj. **1** made of plastic. **2** easily shaped or molded. **3** artificial or false: *a sales rep with a plastic smile.* **4** relating to molding or modeling in three dimensions: *the plastic arts.* ■ **plas·ti·cal·ly** /-(ə)lē/ adv. **plas·tic·i·ty** /pla'stisitē/ n.

plas·tic ex·plo·sive ► n. a puttylike explosive capable of being molded by hand.

plas·ti·cine /'plastə,sēn/ ► n. trademark a soft modeling material.

plas·ti·cize /'plastə,sīz/ ► v. **1** treat or coat something with plastic. **2** make something plastic or able to be molded. ■ **plas·ti·ci·za·tion** /,plastəsi'zāshən/ n. **plas·ti·ciz·er** n.

plas·tick·y /'plastikē/ ► adj. **1** resembling plastic. **2** artificial or of poor quality.

plas·tic sur·ger·y ► n. surgery performed to repair or reconstruct parts of the body damaged by injury or for cosmetic reasons.

plas·tique /pla'stēk/ ► n. plastic explosive.

plate /plāt/ ► n. **1** a flat dish from which food is eaten or served. **2** bowls, cups, and other utensils made of gold or silver. **3** a thin, flat piece of metal used to join or strengthen something or forming part of a machine. **4** a small, flat piece of metal with a name or other writing on it, fixed to a wall or door. **5** a sheet of metal or other material with an image of type or illustrations on it, from which multiple copies are printed. **6** a printed photograph or illustration in a book. **7** Baseball short for HOMEPLATE. **8** a thin, flat structure in a plant or animal. **9** each of the several rigid pieces of the earth's crust and upper mantle that together make up the earth's surface. ► v. **1** cover a metal object with a thin coating of a different metal. **2** put food on a plate before a meal. ■ **plat·er** n. **plat·ing** n.

– PHRASES **on a plate** informal with little or no effort. **on one's plate** occupying one's time or energy.

pla·teau /pla'tō/ ► n. (pl. **plateaux** /-'tōz/ or **plateaus**) **1** an area of fairly level high ground. **2** a period of little or no change following a period of activity or progress. ► v. (**plateaus, plateauing, plateaued**) reach a period of little or no change following activity or progress: *after making a huge jump in the rankings his game has really plateaued.*

plate glass ► n. thick fine-quality glass used for store windows and doors.

plate·let /'plāt-lit/ ► n. a small disk-shaped cell fragment without a nucleus, found in large numbers in blood and involved in clotting.

plat·en /'platn/ ► n. **1** a cylindrical roller in a typewriter against which the paper is held. **2** a plate in a small letterpress printing press that presses the paper against the type.

plate tec·ton·ics ► n. another term for TECTONICS.

plat·form /'platfòrm/ ► n. **1** a raised level surface on which people or things can stand. **2** a raised structure along the side of a railroad track where passengers get on and off trains. **3** a raised structure standing in the sea from which oil or gas wells can be drilled. **4** the declared policy of a political party or group: *seeking election on a platform of low taxes.* **5** an opportunity for the expression or exchange of views. **6** a very thick sole on a shoe. **7** a standard for the hardware of a computer system that determines the kinds of software it can run.

plat·i·num /'platn-əm/ ► n. a precious silvery-white metallic chemical element used in jewelry and in some electrical and laboratory equipment. ► adj. grayish-white or silvery.

plat·i·num blonde ► adj. (of hair) silvery-blond.

plat·i·tude /'plati,t(y)ōōd/ ► n. a remark or statement that has been used too often to be interesting or thoughtful. ■ **plat·i·tu·di·nous** /,plati't(y)ōōdn-əs/ adj.

Pla·ton·ic /plə'tänik/ ► adj. **1** relating to the ancient Greek philosopher Plato or his ideas. **2** (**platonic**) (of love or friendship) intimate and affectionate but not sexual. ■ **pla·ton·i·cal·ly** adv.

Pla·to·nism /'plātn,izəm/ ► n. the philosophy of Plato, especially his theories on the relationship between abstract ideas or entities and their corresponding objects or forms in the material world. ■ **Pla·to·nist** n. & adj.

pla·toon /plə'tōōn/ ► n. a subdivision of a company of soldiers, usually commanded by a lieutenant and divided into two or more sections.

plat·ter /'platər/ ► n. **1** a large flat serving dish. **2** a selection of food served on a platter: *a seafood platter.*

– PHRASES **on a** (**silver**) **platter** informal with little or no effort.

plat·y·pus /'platəpəs, -,pŏŏs/ (also **duck-billed platypus**) ► n. (pl. **platypuses**) an egg-laying Australian mammal with a ducklike bill and webbed feet, living partly on land and partly in water.

plau·dits /'plôdits/ ► pl.n. enthusiastic approval; praise.

plau·si·ble /'plôzəbəl/ ► adj. **1** seeming reasonable or probable. **2** skilled at producing persuasive arguments: *a plausible liar.* ■ **plau·si·bil·i·ty** /,plôzə'bilitē/ n. **plau·si·bly** adv.

play /plā/ ► v. **1** take part in games or other activities for enjoyment. **2** take part in a sport or contest. **3** compete against another player or team. **4** take a specified position on a sports team: *he played goalie.* **5** act the role of a character in a play or movie. **6** perform on a musical instrument or perform a piece of music. **7** move a piece or display a playing card in one's turn in a game. **8** make a CD, tape, or record produce sounds. **9** be cooperative: *he needs financial backing, but the banks won't play.* **10** move lightly and quickly; flicker: *a smile played about her lips.* ► n. **1** games and other activities that one takes part in for enjoyment. **2** the progress of an athletic match: *bad weather stopped play.* **3** a move or maneuver in a sport or game. **4** the state of being active or effective: *luck came into play.* **5** a dramatic work written for the stage or to be broadcast. **6** freedom of movement in a mechanism. **7** constantly changing movement: *the play of light across the surface.* ■ **play·a·ble** adj.

– PHRASES **make great play of** chiefly Brit. draw attention to something in an exaggerated way. **make a play for** informal attempt to attract someone or gain something. **play around** (or **about**) behave in a casual or irresponsible way. **play along** pretend to cooperate with someone. **play something by ear 1** perform music without having seen a score. **2** (**play it by ear**) informal proceed according to circumstances rather than following rules or a plan. **play something down** disguise the importance of something.

play fast and loose behave irresponsibly or immorally. **play for time** use excuses or unnecessary activities to gain time. **play into someone's hands** give someone an advantage without meaning to do so. **play someone against another** cause someone to compete with or oppose another for one's own advantage. **play on** exploit someone's weak point. **a play on words** a pun. **play** (or **play it**) **safe** avoid taking risks. **play up to** humor or flatter someone. **play something up** emphasize the extent or importance of something. **play with** treat someone inconsiderately for one's own amusement. **play with fire** take foolish risks.

play·act·ing ▶n. behavior that is exaggerated for pretense.

play·back /'plā,bak/ ▶n. the replaying of previously recorded sound or moving images.

play·bill /'plā,bil/ ▶n. 1 a poster announcing a theatrical performance. 2 a theater program.

play·boy /'plā,boi/ ▶n. a wealthy man who spends his time enjoying himself.

play-by-play ▶n. a detailed running commentary on an athletic contest.

play·er /'plāər/ ▶n. 1 a person taking part in a sport or game. 2 a person who plays a musical instrument. 3 a device for playing compact discs, tapes, or records. 4 a person who is influential in an area of activity: *a major player in political circles.* 5 an actor.

play·er pi·an·o ▶n. a piano fitted with an apparatus that enables it to be played automatically.

play·ful /'plāfəl/ ▶adj. 1 fond of playing; full of fun. 2 made or done in fun; not serious: *a playful punch on the arm.* ■ **play·ful·ly** adv. **play·ful·ness** n.

play·ground /'plā,ground/ ▶n. an outdoor area provided for children to play on.

play·group /'plā,grōōp/ ▶n. a regular play session for preschool children.

play·house /'plā,hous/ ▶n. 1 a theater. 2 a toy house for children to play in.

play·ing card ▶n. each of a set of rectangular pieces of card with numbers and symbols on one side, used to play various games.

play·ing field ▶n. a field used for outdoor team games.

play·list /'plā,list/ ▶n. a list of songs or pieces of music chosen to be broadcast on a radio station.

play·mak·er /'plā,mākər/ ▶n. a player in a team game who leads attacks or brings teammates into attacking positions.

play·mate /'plā,māt/ ▶n. a friend with whom a child plays.

play·off /'plā,ôf/ ▶n. 1 an additional match played to decide the outcome of a contest. 2 (**playoffs**) a series of contests played to determine the winner of a championship, as between the leading teams in different divisions or leagues.

play·pen /'plā,pen/ ▶n. a small portable enclosure in which a baby or small child can play safely.

play·thing /'plā,THiNG/ ▶n. 1 a person who is treated as amusing but unimportant. 2 a toy.

play·time /'plā,tīm/ ▶n. a period in the school day when children are allowed to go outside and play.

play·wright /'plā,rīt/ ▶n. a person who writes plays.

pla·za /'plazə, 'pläzə/ ▶n. 1 a public square or similar open space in a town or city. 2 a shopping center.

plc (also **PLC**) ▶abbr. Brit. public limited company.

plea /plē/ ▶n. 1 a request made in an urgent and emotional way. 2 a formal statement made by or on behalf of a person charged with an offense in a court of law. 3 a claim that one should not be blamed for or have to do something because of particular circumstances.

plea bar·gain·ing ▶n. Law an arrangement between a prosecutor and a person charged with an offense in which the latter pleads guilty to a lesser charge in the expectation of a less severe sentence.

plead /plēd/ ▶v. (past and past part. **pleaded** or **pled**) 1 make an urgent and emotional request. 2 argue in support of: *he visited the country to plead his cause.* 3 state formally in a court of law whether one is guilty or not guilty of the offense with which one is charged. 4 Law give a reason or a point of law as an accusation or defense. 5 present an excuse for doing or not doing something: *she pleaded family commitments as a reason for not attending.* ■ **plead·er** n.

USAGE

In a law court a person can **plead guilty** or **plead not guilty**. The phrase **plead innocent** is not a legal term, although it is found in general use.

plead·ing /'plēdiNG/ ▶adj. earnestly appealing. ▶n. (usu. **pleadings**) a formal statement of a case presented by each party in a lawsuit. ■ **plead·ing·ly** adv.

pleas·ant /'plezənt/ ▶adj. 1 enjoyable, pleasing, or attractive: *a pleasant town on a river.* 2 friendly and likable. ■ **pleas·ant·ly** adv. **pleas·ant·ness** n.

pleas·ant·ry /'plezntrē/ ▶n. (pl. **pleasantries**) 1 a conventional remark made as part of a polite conversation. 2 a mildly amusing joke.

please /plēz/ ▶v. 1 make someone feel happy and satisfied. 2 wish or desire: *do as you please.* 3 (**please oneself**) do as one wishes, without considering anyone else. ▶adv. used in polite requests or questions, or to accept an offer.

pleased /plēzd/ ▶adj. 1 feeling or showing pleasure and satisfaction. 2 (**pleased to do**) willing or glad to do something.

pleas·ing /'plēziNG/ ▶adj. pleasant, satisfying, or attractive. ■ **pleas·ing·ly** adv.

pleas·ur·a·ble /'plezHərəbəl/ ▶adj. pleasing; enjoyable. ■ **pleas·ur·a·bly** /-blē/ adv.

pleas·ure /'plezHər/ ▶n. 1 a feeling of happy satisfaction and enjoyment. 2 an enjoyable event or activity. 3 sexual satisfaction. ▶adj. intended for entertainment rather than business: *pleasure boats.* ▶v. arouse someone sexually. – PHRASES **at someone's pleasure** formal as and when someone wishes.

pleat /plēt/ ▶n. a fold in fabric or an item of clothing, held by stitching the top or side. ▶v. fold or form fabric into pleats.

pleb /pleb/ ▶n. informal, derogatory a lower-class person. ■ **pleb·by** adj.

plebe /plēb/ ▶n. informal a newly entered cadet or freshman, especially at a military academy.

ple·be·ian /pli'bēən/ ▶adj. lower-class or unsophisticated: *I've got very plebeian tastes.* ▶n. 1 a lower-class person. 2 (in ancient Rome) a commoner.

pleb·i·scite /'plebə,sīt/ ▶n. a vote made by all the

members of an electorate on an important public issue. ■ **ple·bis·ci·tar·y** /pləˈbisiˌterē/ adj.

plec·trum /ˈplektrəm/ ▶ n. (pl. **plectrums** or **plectra**) a thin flat piece of plastic or tortoiseshell used to pluck the strings of a guitar or similar musical instrument.

pled /pled/ ▶ past and past participle of PLEAD.

pledge /plej/ ▶ n. **1** a solemn promise to do something. **2** something valuable given as a guarantee that a debt will be paid or a promise kept. **3** (**the pledge**) a solemn vow not to drink alcohol. **4** a thing given as a token of love, favor, or loyalty. ▶ v. **1** solemnly promise to do or give something. **2** give something valuable as a guarantee on a loan.

Pleis·to·cene /ˈplīstəˌsēn/ ▶ adj. Geology relating to the first epoch of the Quaternary period (from 1.64 million to about 10,000 years ago), a time that included the ice ages and the appearance of humans.

ple·na·ry /ˈplenərē/ ▶ adj. **1** full; absolute: *plenary powers.* **2** (of a meeting at a conference or assembly) to be attended by all participants. ▶ n. a meeting attended by all participants at a conference or assembly.

plen·i·po·ten·ti·ar·y /ˌplenəpəˈtensHē,erē, -ˈtensHərē/ ▶ n. (pl. **plenipotentiaries**) a person given full power by a government to act on its behalf. ▶ adj. **1** having full power to take independent action. **2** (of power) absolute.

plen·i·tude /ˈpleniˌt(y) o͞od/ ▶ n. formal a large amount of something; an abundance.

plen·te·ous /ˈplentēəs/ ▶ adj. literary plentiful; abundant.

plen·ti·ful /ˈplentəfəl/ ▶ adj. existing in great quantities; abundant: *countries with plentiful supplies of oil.* ■ **plen·ti·ful·ly** adv.

plen·ty /ˈplentē/ ▶ pron. a large amount or quantity, or as much as is needed. ▶ n. a situation in which food and other necessities are available in large quantities. ▶ adv. informal used to emphasize the degree or extent of something: *she has plenty more ideas.*

ple·num /ˈplenəm, ˈplēnəm/ ▶ n. **1** an assembly of all the members of a group or committee. **2** Physics a space completely filled with matter, or the whole of space regarded in such a way.

ple·o·nasm /ˈplēəˌnazəm/ ▶ n. the use of more words than are necessary to express meaning (e.g., *I saw her with my own eyes*). ■ **ple·o·nas·tic** /ˌplēəˈnastik/ adj.

pleth·o·ra /ˈpleTHərə/ ▶ n. an excessive amount: *a plethora of complaints.*

pleu·ra /ˈplo͝orə/ ▶ n. (pl. **pleurae** /ˈplo͝orē/) each of a pair of membranes covering the lungs. ■ **pleu·ral** adj.

pleu·ri·sy /ˈplo͝orəsē/ ▶ n. inflammation of the membranes around the lungs, causing pain during breathing.

Plex·i·glas /ˈpleksiˌglas/ (also **plexiglas** or **plexiglass**) ▶ n. trademark a tough transparent plastic used as a substitute for glass.

plex·us /ˈpleksəs/ ▶ n. (pl. same or **plexuses**) **1** a network of nerves or vessels in the body. **2** an intricate network or weblike formation.

pli·a·ble /ˈplīəbəl/ ▶ adj. **1** easily bent; flexible. **2** easily influenced: *pliable teenage minds.* ■ **pli·a·bil·i·ty** /ˌplīəˈbilitē/ n.

pli·ant /ˈplīənt/ ▶ adj. easily bent or influenced; pliable. ■ **pli·an·cy** n. **pli·ant·ly** adv.

pli·é /plēˈā/ ▶ n. Ballet a movement in which a dancer bends the knees and straightens them again, having the feet turned out and heels firmly on the ground.

pli·ers /ˈplīərz/ ▶ pl.n. pincers with parallel flat jaws, used for gripping small objects or bending wire.

plight[1] /plīt/ ▶ n. a dangerous or difficult situation.

plight[2] ▶ v. old use **1** solemnly promise faith or loyalty. **2** (**be plighted to**) be engaged to be married to.

plim·soll /ˈplimsəl, -sōl/ (also **plimsole**) ▶ n. Brit. a light rubber-soled canvas sports shoe.

plink /plinGk/ ▶ v. make a short, sharp, metallic ringing sound. ▶ n. a short, sharp, metallic ringing sound. ■ **plink·y** adj.

plinth /plinTH/ ▶ n. **1** a heavy base supporting a statue or vase. **2** the lower square slab at the base of a column.

Pli·o·cene /ˈplīəˌsēn/ ▶ adj. Geology relating to the last epoch of the Tertiary period (5.2 to 1.64 million years ago), when the first hominids appeared.

PLO ▶ abbr. Palestine Liberation Organization.

plod /pläd/ ▶ v. (**plods, plodding, plodded**) **1** walk slowly with heavy steps. **2** work slowly but determinedly at a dull task. ▶ n. a slow, heavy walk. ■ **plod·der** n.

plonk /plänGk/ informal ▶ v. **1** set something down heavily or carelessly. **2** play unskillfully on a musical instrument. ▶ n. a sound like that of something being set down heavily.

plop /pläp/ ▶ n. a sound like that of a small solid object dropping into water. ▶ v. (**plops, plopping, plopped**) fall or drop with a plop.

plo·sive /ˈplōsiv/ ▶ adj. referring to a consonant (e.g., *d* or *p*) that is produced by stopping the flow of air from the mouth with the lips, teeth, or palate and then suddenly releasing it.

plot /plät/ ▶ n. **1** a secret plan to do something illegal or wrong. **2** the main sequence of events in a play, novel, or movie. **3** a small piece of ground marked out for building, gardening, etc. **4** a graph showing the relation between two variables. ▶ v. (**plots, plotting, plotted**) **1** secretly make plans to carry out something illegal or wrong. **2** invent the plot of a play, novel, or movie. **3** mark a route or position on a chart or graph. ■ **plot·less** adj. **plot·ter** n.

plough, etc. /plou/ ▶ n. & v. British spelling of PLOW, etc.

plov·er /ˈpləvər, ˈplō-/ ▶ n. a wading bird with a short bill.

plow /plou/ (Brit. **plough**) ▶ n. a large farming implement with one or more blades fixed in a frame, drawn over soil to turn it over and cut furrows. ▶ v. **1** turn up earth with a plow. **2** (**plow through/into**) (of a vehicle) move in a fast or uncontrolled way through or into someone or something. **3** move forward or progress with difficulty: *the students are plowing through grammar exercises.* **4** (**plow something in**) invest money in a business. ■ **plow·a·ble** adj. **plow·man** /ˈploumən/ n. (pl. **plowmen**).

plow·share /ˈplouˌsHe(ə)r/ ▶ n. the main cutting blade of a plow.

ploy /ploi/ ▶ n. a cunning plan or action intended to gain an advantage.

pluck /plək/ ▶ v. **1** take hold of something and quickly remove it from its place. **2** pull out a

hair, feather, etc. **3** pull the feathers from a bird's carcass to prepare it for cooking. **4** catch hold of: *she plucked at his sleeve.* **5** sound a stringed musical instrument with the finger or a plectrum. ▶ **n. 1** spirited and determined courage. **2** the heart, liver, and lungs of an animal as food.
– PHRASES **pluck up courage** summon up enough courage to do something frightening.

pluck·y /'pləkē/ ▶ **adj.** (**pluckier, pluckiest**) determined and brave in the face of difficulties. ▪ **pluck·i·ly adv. pluck·i·ness** n.

plug /pləg/ ▶ **n. 1** a piece of solid material fitting tightly into and blocking a hole. **2** a device consisting of an insulated casing with metal pins that fit into holes in a socket to make an electrical connection. **3** informal an electrical socket. **4** informal a piece of publicity promoting a product or event. **5** a piece of tobacco cut from a larger cake for chewing. ▶ **v.** (**plugs, plugging, plugged**) **1** block or fill in a hole or gap. **2** (**plug something in**) connect an electrical appliance by means of a socket. **3** (**plug into**) gain access to an information system or area of activity. **4** informal promote a product or event by mentioning it publicly: *during the show she plugged her new record.* **5** informal shoot or hit someone or something. **6** (**plug away**) informal proceed steadily with a task. ▪ **plug·ger** n.

plug-in ▶ **n.** a module or piece of software that can be added to an existing computer system to give extra features.

plum /pləm/ ▶ **n. 1** a soft oval fruit with purple, reddish, or yellow skin, containing a flattish pit. **2** a reddish-purple color. ▶ **adj.** informal highly desirable: *a plum job.*

plum·age /'plōōmij/ ▶ **n.** a bird's feathers.

plumb¹ /pləm/ ▶ **v. 1** explore or experience fully or to extremes: *using the Bible to plumb the spiritual depths of the human heart.* **2** measure the depth of water. **3** test an upright surface to determine the vertical. ▶ **n.** a lead ball or other heavy object attached to a line for finding the depth of water or determining the verticality of an upright surface. ▶ **adv.** informal **1** exactly: *plumb in the center.* **2** extremely or completely. ▶ **adj.** vertical.

plumb² ▶ **v.** install and connect water and drainage pipes.

plum·ba·go /pləm'bāgō/ ▶ **n.** (pl. **plumbagos**) an evergreen shrub or climber with gray or blue flowers.

plumb·er /'pləmər/ ▶ **n.** a person who installs and repairs the pipes and fittings of water supply, sanitation, or heating systems.

plumb·ing /'pləmiNG/ ▶ **n. 1** the system of pipes, tanks, and fittings required for the water supply, heating, and sanitation in a building. **2** the occupation of a plumber.

plumb line ▶ **n.** a line with a heavy weight attached to it, used to find the depth of water or to check that something is vertical.

plume /plōōm/ ▶ **n. 1** a long, soft feather or arrangement of feathers. **2** a long spreading cloud of smoke or vapor. ▶ **v. 1** (as adj. **plumed**) decorated with feathers. **2** (of smoke or vapor) spread out in a plume.

plum·met /'pləmit/ ▶ **v.** (**plummets, plummeting, plummeted**) **1** fall or drop straight down at high speed. **2** decrease

rapidly in value or amount: *foreign sales have plummeted.* ▶ **n. 1** a steep and rapid fall or drop. **2** a plumb line or weight.

plump¹ /pləmp/ ▶ **adj. 1** rather fat. **2** full and rounded in shape. ▶ **v.** (**plump something up**) make a cushion or pillow full and rounded. ▪ **plump·ish adj. plump·ness** n.

plump² ▶ **v. 1** set or sit down heavily and suddenly. **2** (**plump for**) make a definite choice: *offered drinks, he plumped for brandy.* ▶ **adv.** informal with a sudden or heavy fall: *she fell plump backwards.*

plum pud·ding ▶ **n.** a rich suet pudding containing raisins, currants, and spices.

plum to·ma·to ▶ **n.** an oval variety of tomato.

plun·der /'pləndər/ ▶ **v.** steal goods from a place by force, especially during war or rioting. ▶ **n. 1** goods obtained illegally and by force. **2** the forcible theft of goods. ▪ **plun·der·er** n.

plunge /plənj/ ▶ **v. 1** fall or move suddenly and uncontrollably. **2** jump or dive quickly and energetically. **3** (**plunge in**) begin a course of action without much thought. **4** (**be plunged into**) suddenly be brought into a specified condition or state: *the area was plunged into darkness.* **5** push or thrust something quickly. ▶ **n. 1** an act of plunging. **2** a sudden and marked fall in value or amount: *a 75% plunge in profits.*
– PHRASES **take the plunge** informal decide on a course of action that one feels nervous about.

plunge pool ▶ **n.** a deep basin at the foot of a waterfall formed by the action of the falling water.

plung·er /'plənjər/ ▶ **n. 1** a part of a device that can be pushed down. **2** a rubber cup on a long handle, used to clear blocked pipes by means of suction.

plunk /pləNGk/ informal ▶ **v. 1** play a keyboard or pluck a stringed instrument in a heavy-handed way. **2** put something down heavily. ▶ **n.** the sound of a stringed instrument being plucked.

plu·per·fect /,plōō'pərfikt/ ▶ **n.** Grammar another term for PAST PERFECT.

plu·ral /'plŏŏrəl/ ▶ **adj. 1** more than one in number. **2** Grammar (of a word or form) referring to more than one. **3** containing diverse elements: *a plural society.* ▶ **n.** Grammar a plural word or form. ▪ **plu·ral·ly adv.**

plu·ral·ism /'plŏŏrə,lizəm/ ▶ **n. 1** a political system of power-sharing among a number of political parties. **2** the existence or toleration in society of a number of different ethnic groups, cultures, and beliefs. **3** the holding of more than one ecclesiastical office or position at the same time by one person. ▪ **plu·ral·ist** n. & adj. **plu·ral·is·tic** /-'listik/ adj.

plu·ral·i·ty /plŏŏ'ralitē/ ▶ **n.** (pl. **pluralities**) **1** the state of being plural or more than one. **2** a large number of people or things. **3** the number of votes cast for a candidate who receives more than any other but does not receive an absolute majority.

plu·ral·ize /'plŏŏrə,līz/ ▶ **v. 1** make something more numerous. **2** give a plural form to a word. ▪ **plu·ral·i·za·tion** /,plŏŏrəli'zāshən/ n.

plus /pləs/ ▶ **prep. 1** with the addition of. **2** informal together with. ▶ **adj. 1** (after a number or amount) at least: *companies put losses at $500,000 plus.* **2** (after a grade) better than:

B-plus. **3** (before a number) above zero: *plus 60 degrees centigrade.* **4** having a positive electric charge. ▸ n. **1** (also **plus sign**) the symbol +, indicating addition or a positive value. **2** informal an advantage. ▸ conj. informal furthermore; also.

plus ça change /ˈploo säˈsHänzH/ ▸ exclam. used to acknowledge that certain things remain essentially unchanged.

plus fours /pləs fôrz/ ▸ pl.n. men's short baggy trousers that fit closely below the knee, formerly worn for hunting and golf.

plush /pləsH/ ▸ n. a rich fabric of silk, cotton, or wool, with a long, soft nap. ▸ adj. informal expensively luxurious. ■ **plush·y** adj.

plus-size ▸ adj. (of a woman or women's clothing) of a larger size than normal; outsize.

Plu·to /ˈplootō/ ▸ n. the most remote known planet of the solar system, ninth in order from the sun. ■ **Plu·to·ni·an** /plooˈtōnēən/ adj.

plu·toc·ra·cy /plooˈtäkrəsē/ ▸ n. (pl. **plutocracies**) **1** government by wealthy people. **2** a society governed by wealthy people. **3** a ruling class whose power is based on their wealth. ■ **plu·to·crat·ic** /ˌplootəˈkratik/ adj.

plu·to·crat /ˈplootə,krat/ ▸ n. often derogatory a person who is powerful because they are wealthy.

plu·ton·ic /plooˈtänik/ ▸ adj. (of igneous rock) formed by solidification at considerable depth beneath the earth's surface.

plu·to·ni·um /plooˈtōnēəm/ ▸ n. a radioactive metallic element used as a fuel in nuclear reactors and as an explosive in atomic weapons.

plu·vi·al /ˈploovēəl/ ▸ adj. technical relating to rainfall.

ply[1] /plī/ ▸ n. (pl. **plies**) **1** a thickness or layer of a folded or laminated material. **2** each of a number of multiple layers or strands of which something is made.

ply[2] ▸ v. (**plies, plying, plied**) **1** work steadily with a tool or at one's job. **2** (of a ship or vehicle) travel regularly over a route. **3** (**ply someone with**) provide someone with food or drink in an insistent way. **4** (**ply someone with**) repeatedly ask someone questions.

ply·wood /ˈplī,wood/ ▸ n. thin strong board consisting of two or more layers of wood glued together.

PM ▸ abbr. **1** post-mortem. **2** prime minister.

Pm ▸ symbol the chemical element promethium.

p.m. ▸ abbr. after noon.

PMS ▸ abbr. premenstrual syndrome.

pneu·mat·ic /n(y)ooˈmatik/ ▸ adj. containing or operated by air or gas under pressure: *a pneumatic drill.* ■ **pneu·mat·i·cal·ly** /n(y)ooˈmadʌk(ə)lē/ adv.

pneu·mat·ics /n(y)ooˈmatiks/ ▸ pl.n. (treated as sing.) the science of the mechanical properties of gases.

pneu·mo·coc·cus /ˌn(y)oomōˈkäkəs/ ▸ n. (pl. **pneumococci** /-ˈkäksī, -ˈkäksē/) a bacterium associated with pneumonia and some forms of meningitis. ■ **pneu·mo·coc·cal** adj.

pneu·mo·nia /n(y)ooˈmōnēə, -ˈmōnyə/ ▸ n. an infection causing inflammation of one or both lungs. ■ **pneu·mon·ic** /n(y)ooˈmänik/ adj.

PO ▸ abbr. **1** postal order. **2** Post Office.

Po ▸ symbol the chemical element polonium.

poach[1] /pōcH/ ▸ v. cook food by simmering it in a small amount of liquid.

poach[2] ▸ v. **1** take game or fish illegally from private or protected areas. **2** take or obtain in an unfair or underhanded way: *they tried to poach passengers by offering better seats.*

poach·er[1] /ˈpōcHər/ ▸ n. a pan for poaching eggs or other food.

poach·er[2] ▸ n. a person who poaches game or fish.

PO box ▸ n. a numbered box in a post office where mail for a person or organization is kept until collected.

po·chard /ˈpōcHərd/ ▸ n. a diving duck, the male of which has a reddish-brown head.

pock /päk/ ▸ n. a pockmark. ■ **pocked** adj.

pock·et /ˈpäkət/ ▸ n. **1** a small bag sewn into or on clothing, used for carrying small articles. **2** a small group or area that is set apart or different from its surroundings: *the advancing forces encountered only pockets of resistance.* **3** informal a person's financial resources: *gifts to suit every pocket.* **4** a pouchlike storage compartment in a suitcase, car door, etc. **5** an opening at the corner or on the side of a billiard table into which balls are driven. ▸ adj. of a suitable size for carrying in a pocket. ▸ v. (**pockets, pocketing, pocketed**) **1** put something into one's pocket. **2** take something belonging to someone else. **3** earn or win money: *he pocketed $1000 for a few hours' work.* **4** Billiards drive a ball into a pocket. ■ **pock·et·a·ble** adj.

– PHRASES **in someone's pocket** dependent on someone financially and therefore under their influence. **out of** (or **in**) **pocket** having lost (or gained) money.

pock·et·book /ˈpäkət,book/ ▸ n. a wallet, purse, or handbag.

pock·et·knife /ˈpäkət,nīf/ ▸ n. (pl. **pocketknives**) a penknife.

pock·et mon·ey ▸ n. a small amount of money for minor expenses.

pock·et ve·to ▸ n. an indirect veto of a legislative bill by retaining the bill unsigned until it is too late for it to be dealt with during the legislative session.

pock·et watch ▸ n. a watch on a chain, intended to be carried in a jacket or vest pocket.

pock·mark /ˈpäk,märk/ ▸ n. **1** a hollow scar or mark on the skin left by a pustule or pimple. **2** a hollow mark on a surface. ▸ v. cover something with hollow scars or marks.

pod[1] /päd/ ▸ n. **1** a long seed case of a pea, bean, or related plant. **2** a self-contained or detachable unit on an aircraft or spacecraft. ▸ v. (**pods, podding, podded**) **1** remove peas or beans from their pods before cooking. **2** (of a plant) form pods.

pod[2] ▸ n. a small group of whales or similar sea mammals.

po'd /ˌpēˈōd/ ▸ abbr. informal pissed off: *what was he po'd about?*

pod·cast /ˈpädkast/ ▸ n. a multimedia digital file made available on the Internet for downloading to a personal computer, portable media player, etc. ■ **pod·cast·er** n. **pod·cast·ing** n.

po·di·a·try /pəˈdīətrē/ ▸ n. another term for CHIROPODY. ■ **po·di·a·trist** /-trəst/ n.

po·di·um /ˈpōdēəm/ ▸ n. (pl. **podiums** or **podia** /-dēə/) a small platform on which a person stands when giving a speech or conducting an orchestra.

po·em /ˈpōəm, ˈpōim, pōm/ ▸ n. a piece of imaginative writing that combines elements of both speech and song, that is usually metaphorical, and that often exhibits meter and/or rhyme.

po·e·sy /ˈpōəzē, -sē/ ▶ n. old use or literary poetry.

po·et /ˈpōət, ˈpōit/ ▶ n. **1** a person who writes poems. **2** a person possessing special powers of imagination or expression. ■ **po·et·ess** n.

po·et·as·ter /ˈpōət͟,astər/ ▶ n. a person who writes very bad poetry.

po·et·ic /pōˈetik/ (also **poetical** /pōˈetikəl/) ▶ adj. relating to or resembling poetry. ■ **po·et·i·cal·ly** /-ik(ə)lē/ adv.

po·et·i·cize /pōˈetə,sīz/ ▶ v. **1** make something poetic. **2** write or speak poetically. ■ **po·et·i·cism** /-,sizəm/ n.

po·et·ic jus·tice ▶ n. suitable or deserved punishment or reward.

po·et·ic li·cense ▶ n. freedom to depart from the facts of a matter or from the accepted rules of language for artistic effect.

po·et·ics /pōˈetiks/ ▶ pl.n. (treated as sing.) the study of linguistic techniques in poetry and literature.

po·et lau·re·ate /ˈlôrēət/ ▶ n. (pl. **poets laureate**) a poet appointed to an honorary representative position in a state, country, or locality.

po·et·ry /ˈpōətrē, ˈpōitrē/ ▶ n. **1** poems as a whole or as a form of literature. **2** a quality of beauty or emotional intensity: *the sheer poetry of her tennis.*

po·go /ˈpōgō/ ▶ v. (**pogoes, pogoing, pogoed**) informal jump up and down as if on a pogo stick as a form of dancing to rock music.

po·go stick ▶ n. a toy for bouncing around on, consisting of a spring-loaded pole with a handle at the top and a bar to stand on near the bottom.

po·grom /ˈpōgrəm, pəˈgräm/ ▶ n. an organized massacre of an ethnic group, originally that of Jews in Russia or eastern Europe.

poign·ant /ˈpoinyənt/ ▶ adj. arousing a feeling of sadness or regret: *a poignant moment's silence for the dead football player.* ■ **poign·an·cy** n. **poign·ant·ly** adv.

poin·set·ti·a /poinˈset(ē)ə/ ▶ n. a small shrub with large showy scarlet modified leaves (bracts) surrounding the small yellow flowers.

point /point/ ▶ n. **1** the tapered, sharp end of a tool, weapon, or other object. **2** a particular place or moment: *at one point a shouting match broke out.* **3** an item, detail, or idea in a discussion, written work, etc. **4** (**the point**) the most important or relevant part of what is being discussed. **5** the advantage or purpose of something: *what's the point of it all?* **6** a particular feature or quality: *the building has its good points.* **7** a unit of scoring or of measuring value, achievement, or extent. **8** a decimal point. **9** a very small dot or mark on a surface. **10** (in geometry) something having position but not spatial extent, magnitude, dimension, or direction. **11** each of thirty-two directions marked at equal distances around a compass. **12** a narrow piece of land jutting out into the sea. **13** Printing a unit of measurement for type sizes and spacing (in the UK and US 0.351 mm, in Europe 0.376 mm). **14** (**points**) a set of electrical contacts in the distributor of a motor vehicle. ▶ v. **1** direct someone's attention in a particular direction by extending one's finger. **2** direct or aim something. **3** face in or indicate a particular direction: *a sign pointing left.* **4** (**point**

something out) make someone aware of something. **5** (**point to**) indicate that something is likely to happen: *everything pointed to an enemy attack.* **6** (**point something up**) reveal the true nature or importance of something. **7** give a sharp point to something. **8** fill in the joints of brickwork or tiling with mortar or cement.

– PHRASES **a case in point** an example that illustrates what is being discussed. **make a point of** make a special effort to do something. **on the point of** on the verge of. **take someone's point** accept that what someone is saying is valid. **up to a point** to some extent.

point-blank ▶ adj. & adv. **1** (of a shot or missile) fired from very close to its target. **2** in a blunt way, without explanation.

point·ed /ˈpointid/ ▶ adj. **1** having a sharpened or tapered tip or end. **2** (of a remark or look) directed toward a particular person and expressing a clear message. ■ **point·ed·ly** adv.

point·er /ˈpointər/ ▶ n. **1** a long, thin piece of metal on a scale or dial that moves to give a reading. **2** a rod used for pointing to features on a map or chart. **3** a hint or tip. **4** a breed of dog that on scenting game stands rigid looking toward it. **5** Computing a cursor or a link.

poin·til·lism /ˈpwantē,yizəm, ˈpointl,izəm/ ▶ n. a technique of neo-Impressionist painting using tiny dots of various pure colors, which become blended in the viewer's eye. ■ **poin·til·list** n. & adj.

point·ing /ˈpointiNG/ ▶ n. mortar or cement used to fill the joints of brickwork or tiling.

point·less /ˈpointlis/ ▶ adj. having little or no sense or purpose. ■ **point·less·ly** adv. **point·less·ness** n.

point man ▶ n. **1** the soldier at the head of a patrol. **2** (especially in a political context) a person at the forefront of an activity or endeavor.

point of de·par·ture ▶ n. the starting point of a line of thought or course of action.

point of or·der ▶ n. (pl. **points of order**) a query in a formal debate or meeting as to whether correct procedure is being followed.

point of view ▶ n. (pl. **points of view**) **1** a particular attitude or opinion. **2** the position from which something or someone is observed.

point spread ▶ n. a forecast of the number of points by which one sports team is expected to defeat another, used for betting purposes.

point-to-point ▶ n. (pl. **point-to-points**) Brit. an amateur cross-country steeplechase for horses used in hunting.

point·y /ˈpointē/ ▶ adj. (**pointier, pointiest**) informal having a pointed tip or end.

poise /poiz/ ▶ n. **1** a graceful and elegant way of holding the body. **2** calmness and confidence: *he had a moment to think, to recover his poise.* ▶ v. **1** be or cause to be balanced or suspended: *the world was poised between peace and war.* **2** (**be poised to do**) be ready and prepared to do something. **3** (as adj. **poised**) calm and elegant or confident.

poi·son /ˈpoizən/ ▶ n. **1** a substance that causes death or injury when swallowed or absorbed by a living organism. **2** a destructive influence: *the poison of fear.* ▶ v. **1** harm or kill a person or animal with poison. **2** contaminate something with poison. **3** have a destructive or harmful effect on: *the bad professors who poisoned the minds of a generation.* ■ **poi·son·er** n.

poi·son i·vy ▶ n. a North American climbing plant that produces an irritant oil in its leaves.

poi·son·ous /'poiz(ə)nəs/ ▶ adj. **1** (of an animal) producing poison. **2** (of a plant or substance) causing or capable of causing death or illness if taken into the body. **3** very unpleasant or spiteful. ■ **poi·son·ous·ly** adv.

poi·son pill ▶ n. a tactic used by a company threatened with an unwelcome takeover bid to make itself unattractive to the bidder.

poke¹ /pōk/ ▶ v. **1** prod someone or something with a finger or a sharp object. **2** make a hole by jabbing or prodding. **3** (**poke around**) look or search around. **4** push or stick out: *she poked her tongue out at him.* ▶ n. an act of poking.
– PHRASES **poke fun at** tease or make fun of. **poke one's nose into** informal take an unwelcome interest in.

poke² ▶ n. a bag or small sack.

pok·er¹ /'pōkər/ ▶ n. a metal rod with a handle, used for prodding and stirring an open fire.

pok·er² ▶ n. a card game in which the players bet on the value of the hands dealt to them, sometimes using bluffing.

pok·er face ▶ n. an emotionless expression that hides one's true feelings.

poke·weed /'pōk,wēd/ ▶ n. a North American plant with red stems, spikes of cream flowers, and purple berries.

pok·ey /'pōkē/ ▶ n. (usu. **the pokey**) informal prison.

pok·y /'pōkē/ (also **pokey**) ▶ adj. (**pokier, pokiest**) **1** annoyingly slow or dull. **2** (of a room or building) uncomfortably small and cramped.

po·lar /'pōlər/ ▶ adj. **1** relating to the North or South Poles of the earth or the areas around them. **2** having an electrical or magnetic field. **3** completely opposite in type.

po·lar bear ▶ n. a large white arctic bear that lives mainly on the pack ice.

po·lar·i·ty /pō'laritē, pə-/ ▶ n. (pl. **polarities**) **1** the state of having poles or opposites. **2** the direction of a magnetic or electric field.

po·lar·ize /'pōlə,rīz/ ▶ v. **1** divide into two groups with sharply contrasting opinions: *the nation's media are polarized in the controversy.* **2** Physics restrict the vibrations of a transverse wave, especially light, to one direction. **3** give magnetic or electric polarity to something.
■ **po·lar·i·za·tion** /,pōlərə'zāsHən/ n.

Po·lar·oid /'pōlə,roid/ ▶ n. trademark **1** a composite material that polarizes the light passing through it, produced in thin plastic sheets and used in sunglasses. **2** a type of camera that produces a finished print rapidly after each exposure. **3** a photograph taken with a Polaroid camera.

pol·der /'pōldər/ ▶ n. a piece of land reclaimed from the sea or a river, especially in the Netherlands.

Pole /pōl/ ▶ n. a person from Poland.

pole¹ /pōl/ ▶ n. **1** a long, thin, rounded piece of wood or metal, used as a support. **2** a fishing rod. ▶ v. move a boat along with a pole.

pole² ▶ n. **1** either of the two locations (**North Pole** or **South Pole**) at opposite ends of the earth's axis. **2** each of two opposing qualities or ideas: *these discs represent the opposite poles of rave culture.* **3** each of the two opposite points of

a magnet at which magnetic forces are strongest. **4** the positive or negative terminal of an electric cell or battery.
– PHRASES **be poles apart** have nothing in common.

pole·ax /'pōl,aks/ (also **poleaxe**) ▶ v. **1** knock down or stun someone with a heavy blow. **2** shock someone greatly: *she was poleaxed by the news.* ▶ n. **1** a battleaxe. **2** a butcher's ax used to slaughter animals.

pole build·ing ▶ n. a quickly constructed building in which vertical poles are secured in the ground to serve as both the foundation and framework.

pole·cat /'pōl,kat/ ▶ n. **1** a weasellike mammal with dark brown fur and an unpleasant smell. **2** a skunk.

pole danc·ing ▶ n. erotic dancing that involves swinging around a fixed pole. ■ **pole danc·er** n.

po·lem·ic /pə'lemik/ ▶ n. **1** a strong verbal or written attack: *a polemic against liberalism.* **2** (also **polemics**) the practice of engaging in fierce discussion. ▶ adj. (also **polemical** /pə'lemikəl/) relating to fierce discussion.
■ **po·lem·i·cist** /pə'leməsist/ n. **po·lem·i·cize** /pə'lemə,sīz/ v.

po·len·ta /pō'lentə/ ▶ n. (in Italian cooking) a paste or dough made from cornmeal, which is boiled and then fried or baked.

pole po·si·tion ▶ n. the most favorable position at the start of an automobile race.

pole·star /'pōl,stär/ ▶ n. the North Star.

pole vault ▶ n. an athletic event in which competitors attempt to vault over a high bar with the aid of a long flexible pole.

po·lice /pə'lēs/ ▶ n. (treated as pl.) **1** an official civic organization responsible for preventing and solving crime and maintaining public order. **2** the members of a police force. ▶ v. **1** maintain law and order in an area. **2** ensure that a law, rule, agreement, etc., is obeyed.

po·lice·man /pə'lēsmən/ (or **policewoman** /pə'lēs,wŏŏmən/) ▶ n. (pl. **policemen** or **policewomen**) a member of a police force.

po·lice of·fi·cer ▶ n. a policeman or policewoman.

po·lice state ▶ n. a state in which the police are required by the government to keep secret watch over and control citizens' activities.

po·lice sta·tion ▶ n. a building housing a local police force.

pol·i·cy¹ /'päləsē/ ▶ n. (pl. **policies**) **1** a course of action adopted or proposed by a political party, business, or other organization. **2** a principle that influences one's behavior: *his was a policy of live and let live.*

pol·i·cy² ▶ n. (pl. **policies**) a contract of insurance. ■ **pol·i·cy·hold·er** n.

pol·i·cy wonk ▶ n. full form of WONK.

po·li·o /'pōlē,ō/ ▶ n. short for POLIOMYELITIS.

po·li·o·my·e·li·tis /,pōlēō,mīə'lītis/ ▶ n. an infectious disease that affects the central nervous system and can cause temporary or permanent paralysis.

Pol·ish /'pōlisH/ ▶ n. the language of Poland. ▶ adj. relating to Poland.

pol·ish /'pälisH/ ▶ v. **1** make the surface of something smooth and shiny by rubbing. **2** improve or refine: *she's got to polish up her French for the job.* **3** (**polish something**

off) finish or consume something quickly.
▶ n. **1** a substance rubbed on something to make it smooth and shiny. **2** an act of polishing something. **3** smoothness or glossiness produced by polishing. **4** the quality of being skillful, elegant, or refined: *she has the confidence and polish of a veteran gymnast.* ■ **pol·ish·er** n.

po·lit·bu·ro /'pälət͵byŏŏrō, 'pō-/ ▶ n. (pl. **politburos**) the chief policy-making committee of a communist party, especially that of the former Soviet Union.

po·lite /pə'līt/ ▶ adj. (**politer**, **politest**) **1** respectful and considerate toward other people; courteous. **2** cultured or well bred: *polite society.* ■ **po·lite·ly** adv. **po·lite·ness** n.

pol·i·tesse /͵pälə'tes/ ▶ n. formal politeness.

pol·i·tic /'pälə͵tik/ ▶ adj. **1** (of an action) sensible and wise in the circumstances. **2** (also **politick**) old use (of a person) prudent and shrewd.
▶ v. (also **politick**) (**politics** or **politicks**, **politicking**, **politicked**) (usu. as n. **politicking**) often derogatory take part in political activity.

po·lit·i·cal /pə'litikəl/ ▶ adj. **1** relating to the government or public affairs of a country. **2** related to or interested in politics. **3** chiefly derogatory concerned with power or status within an organization rather than matters of principle: *they are paying the price for years of political infighting.* ■ **po·lit·i·cal·ly** /-ik(ə)lē/ adv.

po·lit·i·cal cor·rect·ness ▶ n. the avoidance of language or behavior considered to be discriminatory or offensive to certain groups of people.

po·lit·i·cal·ly cor·rect /pə'litik(ə)lē/ (or **incorrect**) ▶ adj. showing (or failing to show) political correctness.

po·lit·i·cal pris·on·er ▶ n. a person imprisoned for their political beliefs or actions.

po·lit·i·cal sci·ence ▶ n. the study of political activity and behavior.

pol·i·ti·cian /͵pälə'tisHən/ ▶ n. a person who is involved in politics as a job, as either a holder of or a candidate for an elected office.

po·lit·i·cize /pə'litə͵sīz/ ▶ v. **1** make someone politically aware; involve someone in politics. **2** make an issue or activity political in nature. ■ **po·lit·i·ci·za·tion** /pə͵litəsi'zäsHən/ n.

pol·i·tick ▶ v. variant spelling of **POLITIC**.

po·lit·i·co /pə'litikō/ ▶ n. (pl. **politicos**) informal, chiefly derogatory a politician.

pol·i·tics /'pälə͵tiks/ ▶ pl.n. (usu. treated as sing.) **1** the activities associated with governing a country or area, and with the political relations between countries. **2** the political beliefs of a person or organization. **3** activities aimed at gaining power within an organization: *office politics.* **4** the principles relating to or underlying a sphere or activity, especially when concerned with power and status.

pol·i·ty /'pälətē/ ▶ n. (pl. **polities**) **1** a particular form of government. **2** a state as having a distinct political existence.

pol·ka /'pō(l)kə/ ▶ n. a lively dance for couples in duple time.

pol·ka dot ▶ n. each of a number of round dots repeated to form a regular pattern.

poll /pōl/ ▶ n. **1** the process of voting in an election. **2** a record of the number of votes cast. **3** dialect a person's head. ▶ v. **1** record the opinion or vote of a number of people. **2** (of a candidate in an election) receive a specified number of votes. **3** Telecommunications & Computing check the status of a device, especially as part of a repeated cycle. **4** cut the horns off a young cow.

pol·lack /'päläk/ (also **pollock**) ▶ n. (pl. same or **pollacks**) an edible greenish-brown fish of the cod family.

pol·lard /'pälərd/ ▶ v. cut off the top and branches of a tree to encourage new growth. ▶ n. a pollarded tree.

pol·len /'pälən/ ▶ n. a powdery substance produced by the male part of a flower, containing the fertilizing agent.

pol·len count ▶ n. a measure of the amount of pollen in the air.

pol·li·nate /'pälə͵nāt/ ▶ v. carry pollen to a flower or plant and so fertilize it. ■ **pol·li·na·tion** /͵pälə'nāsHən/ n. **pol·li·na·tor** /-͵nātər/ n.

pol·lock ▶ n. variant spelling of **POLLACK**.

poll·ster /'pōlstər/ ▶ n. a person who carries out or analyzes opinion polls.

pol·lu·tant /pə'lŏŏtnt/ ▶ n. a substance that creates unpleasant or harmful effects in the air, soil, or water.

pol·lute /pə'lŏŏt/ ▶ v. **1** add harmful or unpleasant substances to soil, air, or water. **2** spoil or harm: *a society polluted by racism.* ■ **pol·lut·er** n.

pol·lu·tion /pə'lŏŏsHən/ ▶ n. the presence in the air, soil, or water of a substance with unpleasant or harmful effects.

Pol·ly·an·na /͵pälē'anə/ ▶ n. an excessively cheerful or optimistic person.

po·lo /'pōlō/ ▶ n. a game similar to hockey, played on horseback with a long-handled mallet.

po·lo·naise /͵pälə'nāz, ͵pō-/ ▶ n. a slow stately dance of Polish origin in triple time. ▶ adj. (of a dish) garnished with chopped hard-boiled egg yolk, breadcrumbs, and parsley.

po·lo·ni·um /pə'lōnēəm/ ▶ n. a rare radioactive metallic element.

po·lo shirt ▶ n. a casual short-sleeved shirt with a collar and two or three buttons at the neck.

pol·ter·geist /'pōltər͵gīst/ ▶ n. a supernatural being supposedly responsible for throwing objects around.

pol·troon /päl'trŏŏn/ ▶ n. old use a coward.

pol·y /'pälē/ ▶ n. (pl. **polys**) informal **1** polyethylene. **2** polytechnic.

poly- ▶ comb.form many; much: *polychrome.*

pol·y·am·ide /͵pälē'amīd/ ▶ n. a polymer of a type that includes many synthetic fibers such as nylon.

pol·y·an·dry /'pälē͵andrē/ ▶ n. the practice of having more than one husband at the same time. ■ **pol·y·an·drous** /͵pälē'andrəs/ adj.

pol·y·an·thus /͵pälē'anTHəs/ ▶ n. (pl. same) a flowering garden plant that is a hybrid of the wild primrose.

pol·y·car·bon·ate /͵päli'kärbə͵nāt, -nət/ ▶ n. a synthetic resin of a type that includes many molding materials and films.

pol·y·chro·mat·ic /͵pälikrō'matik/ ▶ adj. having several colors; multicolored.

pol·y·chrome /'päli͵krōm/ ▶ adj. painted, printed, or decorated in several colors. ▶ n. varied coloring. ■ **pol·y·chro·my** /'päli͵krōmē/ n.

pol·y·cot·ton /'pälē͵kätn/ ▶ n. fabric made from a mixture of cotton and polyester fiber.

pol·y·es·ter /'pälē,estər/ ▸ n. a synthetic resin of a type that is used chiefly to make textile fibers.

pol·y·eth·yl·ene /,pälē'eᴛʜəlēn/ ▸ n. a tough, light, synthetic resin used for plastic bags, food containers, and other packaging.

po·lyg·a·my /pə'ligəmē/ ▸ n. the practice of having more than one wife or husband at the same time. ■ **po·lyg·a·mist** n. **po·lyg·a·mous** adj.

pol·y·glot /'päli,glät/ ▸ adj. knowing, using, or written in several languages. ▸ n. a person who knows or uses several languages.

pol·y·gon /'päli,gän/ ▸ n. a plane figure with three or more straight sides and angles. ■ **po·lyg·o·nal** /pə'ligənl/ adj.

pol·y·graph /'päli,graf/ ▸ n. a machine that records changes in a person's physiological characteristics, such as pulse and breathing rates, used especially as a lie detector.

po·lyg·y·ny /pə'lijənē/ ▸ n. the practice of having more than one wife at the same time. ■ **po·lyg·y·nous** /pə'lijənəs/ adj.

pol·y·he·dron /,päli'hēdrən/ ▸ n. (pl. **polyhedra** /-'hēdrə/ or **polyhedrons**) a solid figure with many plane faces, typically more than six. ■ **pol·y·he·dral** /-'hēdrəl/ adj.

pol·y·math /'päli,maᴛʜ/ ▸ n. a person with a wide knowledge of many different subjects. ■ **pol·y·math·ic** /,päli'maᴛʜik/ adj.

pol·y·mer /'päləmər/ ▸ n. a substance with a molecular structure formed from many identical small molecules bonded together. ■ **pol·y·mer·ic** /,pälə'merik/ adj.

pol·y·mer·ase /pə'limə,rās, -,rāz/ ▸ n. an enzyme that brings about the formation of a particular polymer, especially DNA or RNA.

po·lym·er·ize /pə'limə,rīz, 'päləmə,rīz/ ▸ v. combine or cause to combine to form a polymer. ■ **po·lym·er·i·za·tion** /pə,limərə'zāsʜən, ,päləmərə-/ n.

pol·y·mor·phism /,päli'môr,fizəm/ ▸ n. the occurrence of something in several different forms. ■ **pol·y·mor·phic** /-'môrfik/ adj. **pol·y·mor·phous** /-'môrfəs/ adj.

Pol·y·ne·sian /,pälə'nēzʜən/ ▸ n. 1 a person from Polynesia, a large group of Pacific islands including New Zealand, Hawaii, and Samoa. 2 a group of languages spoken in Polynesia. ▸ adj. relating to Polynesia.

pol·y·no·mi·al /,pälə'nōmēəl/ ▸ n. Mathematics an expression consisting of several terms, especially terms containing different powers of the same variable.

pol·y·nos·ic /,päli'näsik/ ▸ n. a rayon-and-polyester yarn with a soft finish, used mainly in clothing.

pol·yp /'päləp/ ▸ n. 1 a simple sea creature that remains fixed in the same place, such as coral. 2 Medicine a small growth protruding from a mucous membrane.

pol·y·pep·tide /,päli'pep,tīd/ ▸ n. a peptide consisting of many amino acids bonded together in a chain, e.g., in a protein.

pol·y·phar·ma·cy /,pälē'färməsē/ ▸ n. (pl. **polypharmacies**) the simultaneous use of multiple drugs to treat a single illness or condition.

pol·y·phon·ic /,päli'fänik/ ▸ adj. 1 having many sounds or voices. 2 (especially of vocal music) in two or more parts, each having a melody of its own.

po·lyph·o·ny /pə'lifənē/ ▸ n. (pl. **polyphonies**) the combination in harmony of a number of musical parts, each forming an individual melody.

pol·y·ploid /'päli,ploid/ ▸ adj. (of a cell or nucleus) containing more than two matching sets of chromosomes.

pol·y·pro·pyl·ene /,päli'prōpə,lēn/ ▸ n. a synthetic resin that is a polymer of propylene.

pol·yp·tych /'pälip,tik/ ▸ n. a painting, especially an altarpiece, consisting of more than three panels joined by hinges or folds.

pol·y·rhythm /'päli,riᴛʜəm/ ▸ n. Music the use of two or more different rhythms simultaneously. ■ **pol·y·rhyth·mic** /,päli'riᴛʜmik/ adj.

pol·y·sac·cha·ride /,päli'sakə,rīd/ ▸ n. a carbohydrate (e.g., starch or cellulose) whose molecules consist of long chains of monosaccharide units.

pol·y·sty·rene /,päli'stīrēn/ ▸ n. a light synthetic material used especially as packaging.

pol·y·syl·lab·ic /,pälisə'labik/ ▸ adj. having more than one syllable.

pol·y·tech·nic /,päli'teknik/ ▸ n. a college offering courses in many subjects, especially vocational or technical subjects.

pol·y·the·ism /'päliᴛʜē,izəm/ ▸ n. the belief in or worship of more than one god. ■ **pol·y·the·ist** /-,ᴛʜēist/ n. **pol·y·the·is·tic** /,päliᴛʜē'istik/ adj.

pol·y·thene /'päləᴛʜēn/ ▸ n. Brit. another term for POLYETHYLENE.

pol·y·un·sat·u·rat·ed /,pälēən'sacʜə,rātid/ ▸ adj. referring to fats whose molecules contain several double or triple bonds, believed to be less healthy in the diet than monounsaturated fats. ■ **pol·y·un·sat·u·rates** /,pälēən'sacʜərits/ pl.n.

pol·y·u·re·thane /,päli'yo͝orə,ᴛʜān/ ▸ n. a synthetic resin used in paints and varnishes.

pol·y·va·lent /,päli'vālənt/ ▸ adj. having many different functions, forms, or aspects.

pol·y·vi·nyl chlo·ride /,päli'vīnl/ ▸ n. full form of PVC.

po·made /pō'mäd, -'mäd/ ▸ n. a scented oil or cream for making the hair smooth and glossy. ■ **po·mad·ed** adj.

po·man·der /pō'mandər, 'pō,mandər/ ▸ n. a ball or perforated container of mixed sweet-smelling substances used to perfume a room or cupboard.

pome·gran·ate /'päm(ə),granit, 'pəm-/ ▸ n. a round tropical fruit with a tough golden-orange skin and sweet red flesh containing many seeds.

pom·e·lo /'pämə,lō, 'päm-/ ▸ n. (pl. **pomelos**) a large citrus fruit similar to a grapefruit, with a thick yellow skin and bitter pulp.

Pom·er·a·ni·an /,pämə'rānēən/ ▸ n. a small breed of dog with long silky hair and a pointed muzzle.

pom·mel /'päməl, 'pəməl/ ▸ n. 1 the upward curving or projecting front part of a saddle. 2 a rounded knob on the end of the handle of a sword, dagger, or old-fashioned gun.

pommes frites /,päm 'frēt/ ▸ pl.n. very thin French fries.

pomp /pämp/ ▸ n. 1 the impressive clothes, music, and traditions that are part of a grand public ceremony. 2 (also **pomps**) old use a showy display of something, intended to impress other people.

pom·pa·dour /'pämpə,dôr, -,do͝or, pônpä'do͝or/ ▸ n. a hairstyle in which the hair is turned back off the forehead in a roll.

pom·pom /'päm,päm/ (also **pompon**) ▸ n. **1** a small woolen ball attached to a garment for decoration. **2** a cluster of brightly colored strands of yarn or plastic, waved in pairs by cheerleaders. **3** a dahlia, chrysanthemum, or aster with small tightly clustered petals.

pom-pom ▸ n. a large-caliber British machine gun, in service since 1930.

pomp·ous /'pämpəs/ ▸ adj. affectedly solemn or self-important. ■ **pom·pos·i·ty** /päm'päsətē/ n. **pomp·ous·ly** adv.

ponce /'pônsä/ Brit. informal ▸ n. **1** a man who lives off a prostitute's earnings. **2** derogatory an effeminate man. ▸ v. (**ponce about/around**) behave in a way that wastes time or looks affected or foolish. ■ **pon·cey** (also **poncy**) adj.

pon·cho /'pänCHō/ ▸ n. (pl. **ponchos**) a garment made of a large piece of woolen cloth with a slit in the middle for the head.

pond /pänd/ ▸ n. **1** a fairly small area of still water. **2** (**the pond**) humorous the Atlantic Ocean.

pon·der /'pändər/ ▸ v. consider something carefully.

pon·der·a·ble /'pändərəbəl/ ▸ adj. literary worthy of consideration; thought-provoking.

pon·der·o·sa /,pändə'rōsə/ (also **ponderosa pine**) ▸ n. a tall North American pine tree, grown for its wood and as an ornamental.

pon·der·ous /'pändərəs/ ▸ adj. **1** slow and clumsy because of great weight. **2** tediously solemn or long-winded: *the play's ponderous dialogue*. ■ **pon·der·ous·ly** adv.

pond·weed /'pänd,wēd/ ▸ n. a plant that grows in still or running water.

pons /pänz/ ▸ n. (pl. **pontes** /'pän,tēz/) the part of the brainstem that links the medulla oblongata and the thalamus.

pon·tiff /'päntəf/ ▸ n. the Pope.

pon·tif·i·cal /pän'tifikəl/ ▸ adj. **1** relating to the Pope; papal. **2** speaking as if one's own opinions are always correct; pompously dogmatic. ■ **pon·tif·i·cal·ly** adv.

pon·tif·i·cate ▸ v. /pän'tifi,kāt/ **1** express one's opinions in a pompous and overbearing or dogmatic way. **2** (in the Roman Catholic Church) officiate as bishop, especially at Mass. ▸ n. /-kət/ (also **Pontificate**) (in the Roman Catholic Church) the office or period of office of pope or bishop. ■ **pon·tif·i·ca·tor** /-,kātər/ n.

pon·toon /,pän'tōōn/ ▸ n. **1** a flat-bottomed boat or hollow metal cylinder used with others to support a temporary bridge or floating landing stage. **2** a bridge or landing stage supported by pontoons.

po·ny /'pōnē/ ▸ n. (pl. **ponies**) a horse of a small breed, especially one below 15 hands (58 inches).

po·ny·tail /'pōnē,tāl/ ▸ n. a hairstyle in which the hair is drawn back and tied at the back of the head.

poo ▸ exclam. & n. variant spelling of **POOH**.

pooch /pōōCH/ ▸ n. informal a dog.

poo·dle /'pōōdl/ ▸ n. **1** a breed of dog with a curly coat that is usually clipped. **2** Brit. a person who is too ready to do what someone else tells them to do.

pooh /pōō, pōō/ (also **poo**) informal ▸ exclam. expressing impatience or contempt. ▸ n. excrement.

pooh-bah /'pōō ,bä/ ▸ n. a pompous or self-important person who has a great deal of influence or holds many posts at the same time.

pooh-pooh /'pōō ,pōō, pōō 'pōō/ ▸ v. informal dismiss an idea or suggestion as being foolish or impractical.

pool[1] /pōōl/ ▸ n. **1** a small area of still water. **2** (also **swimming pool**) an artificial pool for swimming in. **3** a small, shallow patch of liquid lying on a surface: *a pool of blood*. **4** a deep place in a river.

pool[2] ▸ n. **1** a shared supply of vehicles, people, goods, or funds that is available when needed. **2** the total amount of players' stakes in gambling or sweepstakes. **3** a game played on a billiard table using 16 balls. **4** an arrangement between competing commercial organizations to fix prices and share business so as to eliminate competition. ▸ v. put money or other resources into a common fund to be used by a number of people: *they pooled their wages and bought food*.

pool·room /'pōōl,rōōm, -,rŏŏm/ ▸ n. (also **pool hall**) a commercial establishment where pool or billiard games are played.

pool·side /'pōōl,sīd/ ▸ n. the area immediately next to a swimming pool.

poop[1] /pōōp/ (also **poop deck**) ▸ n. a raised deck at the stern of a ship, especially a sailing ship.

poop[2] ▸ v. (often as adj. **pooped**) informal **1** exhaust someone. **2** (**poop out**) stop functioning.

poop[3] informal ▸ n. excrement. ▸ v. defecate.

poop[4] ▸ n. informal up-to-date or inside information.

pooped /pōōpd/ ▸ adj. informal exhausted.

poor /pŏŏr, pôr/ ▸ adj. **1** not having enough money to live at a comfortable or normal standard. **2** of a low standard or quality: *poor working conditions*. **3** (**poor in**) lacking in: *an acid soil that is poor in nutrients*. **4** deserving pity or sympathy: *he's driven the poor woman away*.
  – PHRASES **the poor man's ——** an inferior or cheaper substitute for the thing specified: *herring roe—the poor man's caviar*. **poor relation** a person or thing that is considered less good than others of the same type. **take a poor view of** regard someone or something with disapproval.

poor·house /'pŏŏr,hous, 'pôr-/ ▸ n. historical an institution where paupers were maintained with public funds.

poor·ly /'pŏŏrlē, 'pôr-/ ▸ adv. in a poor way: *schools that were performing poorly*. ▸ adj. chiefly Brit. unwell.

poor white ▸ n. derogatory a white person, especially in the southern US, who lacks money, education, or social status.

POP /päp/ ▸ abbr. **1** Computing point of presence, referring to the location at which equipment supporting access to the Internet is situated. **2** point of purchase, referring to products or promotions located adjacent to a retail checkout or cashier.

pop[1] /päp/ ▸ v. (**pops, popping, popped**) **1** make or cause to make a sudden short explosive sound. **2** go or come quickly or unexpectedly: *I might pop around later*. **3** quickly put something somewhere: *he popped a candy into his mouth*. **4** (of a person's eyes) open wide and appear to bulge. **5** informal take or inject a drug. ▸ n. **1** a sudden short explosive sound. **2** informal, dated a sweet carbonated soft drink. **3** Baseball a ball hit high but not deep, providing an easy catch.

– PHRASES **have** (or **take**) **a pop at** informal attack.
pop the question informal propose marriage.

pop² ▸n. (also **pop music**) popular modern commercial music, typically with a strong melody and beat. ▸adj. **1** relating to pop music. **2** often derogatory (especially of a scientific or academic subject) presented in a way that the general public will easily understand: *pop psychology*.

pop³ ▸n. informal term for FATHER.

po·pa·dom ▸n. variant spelling of POPPADOM.

pop art ▸n. art that uses styles and images from modern popular culture.

pop·corn /'päp,kôrn/ ▸n. corn kernels that swell up and burst open when heated and are then eaten as a snack.

pope /pōp/ ▸n. (**the Pope**) the Bishop of Rome as head of the Roman Catholic Church.

pop·er·y /'pōpərē/ ▸n. derogatory, chiefly old use Roman Catholicism.

pop-eyed ▸adj. informal having bulging or staring eyes.

pop·gun /'päp,gən/ ▸n. a child's toy gun that shoots a harmless pellet or cork.

pop·in·jay /'päpən,jā/ ▸n. dated a conceited person who is extremely concerned with their clothes and appearance.

pop·ish /'pōpiSH/ ▸adj. derogatory Roman Catholic.

pop·lar /'päplər/ ▸n. a tall, slender tree with soft wood.

pop·lin /'päplən/ ▸n. a cotton fabric with a finely ribbed surface.

pop·lit·e·al /päp'litēəl, ,päplə'tēəl/ ▸adj. relating to or situated in the hollow at the back of the knee.

pop·pa /'päpə/ ▸n. informal term for FATHER.

pop·pa·dom /'päpədəm/ (also **poppadum** or **popadom**) ▸n. (in Indian cooking) a large thin circular piece of unleavened spiced bread made from ground lentils and fried in oil until crisp.

pop·per /'päpər/ ▸n. informal **1** a pan or utensil for popping corn. **2** a small vial of amyl nitrite that is inhaled, making a popping sound when opened.

pop·py /'päpē/ ▸n. a plant with showy red, pink, or orange flowers and large seed capsules, including species that produce drugs such as opium and codeine.

pop·py·cock /'päpē,käk/ ▸n. informal nonsense.

Pop·si·cle /'päp,sikəl/ ▸n. trademark a piece of flavored ice or ice cream on a stick.

pop·u·lace /'päpyələs/ ▸n. (treated as sing. or pl.) the general public.

pop·u·lar /'päpyələr/ ▸adj. **1** liked or admired by many people or by a particular group: *one of the most popular girls in the school*. **2** intended for or suited to the taste or means of the general public: *the popular press*. **3** (of a belief or attitude) widely held among the general public. **4** (of political activity) carried on by the people as a whole: *a popular revolt*. ■ **pop·u·lar·i·ty** /,päpyə'laritē/ n. **pop·u·lar·ly** adv.

pop·u·lar front ▸n. a political party or coalition representing left-wing elements.

pop·u·lar·ize /'päpyələ,rīz/ ▸v. **1** make something popular: *his books have done much to popularize the sport*. **2** present something scientific or academic in a way that the general public will find interesting and understandable. ■ **pop·u·lar·i·za·tion** /,päpyələrə'zāSHən/ n.

pop·u·lar·iz·er n.

pop·u·late /'päpyə,lāt/ ▸v. **1** live in a place and form its population: *the island is populated by scarcely 40,000 people*. **2** cause people to settle in a place. **3** add data to a computer database.

pop·u·la·tion /,päpyə'lāSHən/ ▸n. **1** all the inhabitants of a place. **2** a particular group within this: *the country's immigrant population*. **3** Biology a community of animals or plants that interbreed.

pop·u·list /'päpyələst/ ▸adj. intended to appeal to or represent the interests and views of ordinary people. ▸n. a member of a political party that seeks to appeal to or represent the interests and views of ordinary people. ■ **pop·u·lism** /-,lizəm/ n.

pop·u·lous /'päpyələs/ ▸adj. having a large population.

pop-up ▸adj. **1** (of a book or greeting card) containing folded pictures that rise up to form a three-dimensional scene or figure when opened. **2** (of a computer menu or other feature) able to be superimposed on the screen being worked on and suppressed rapidly. ▸n. **1** a pop-up computer menu or other feature. **2** an Internet browser window that appears without having been requested, especially one containing an advertisement. **3** Baseball another term for POP¹ (sense 3 of the noun).

por·bea·gle /'pôr,bēgəl/ ▸n. a large shark found chiefly in the open seas of the North Atlantic and in the Mediterranean.

por·ce·lain /'pôrs(ə)lən/ ▸n. **1** a type of fine translucent china. **2** articles made of porcelain.

porch /pôrCH/ ▸n. a covered shelter projecting from the entrance of a building.

por·cine /'pôr,sīn/ ▸adj. relating to or resembling a pig or pigs.

por·ci·ni /pôr'CHēnē/ ▸pl.n. ceps (edible wild mushrooms).

por·cu·pine /'pôrkyə,pīn/ ▸n. a large rodent with protective spines or quills on the body and tail.

pore¹ /pôr/ ▸n. a tiny opening in the skin or other surface through which gases, liquids, or microscopic particles may pass.

pore² ▸v. (**pore over/through**) study or read something with close attention.

> **USAGE**
> Do not confuse **pore** and **pour**. **Pore** is used with **over** or **through** and means 'study or read something closely' (*I spend hours poring over cookbooks*), while **pour** means 'flow in a steady stream' (*water poured off the roof*).

pork /pôrk/ ▸n. the flesh of a pig used as food.

pork bar·rel ▸n. informal referring to the use of government funds for projects designed to win votes.

pork·er /'pôrkər/ ▸n. **1** a young pig raised and fattened for food. **2** informal, derogatory a fat person.

pork·pie hat ▸n. a hat with a flat crown and a brim turned up all around.

pork·y /'pôrkē/ informal ▸adj. (**porkier, porkiest**) fat.

porn /pôrn/ (also **porno**) informal ▸n. pornography. ▸adj. pornographic.

por·nog·ra·phy /pôr'nägrəfē/ ▸n. photographs, writing, movies, etc., intended to cause sexual excitement. ■ **por·nog·ra·pher** n. **por·no·graph·ic** /,pôrnə'grafik/ adj.

po·rous /'pôrəs/ ▸adj. (of a rock or other material) having tiny spaces through which liquid or air may pass. ■ **po·ros·i·ty** /pə'räsətē, pôr'äs-/ n.

por·phyr·i·a /pôr'fi(ə)rēə/ ▶n. a rare hereditary disease in which the body fails to break down hemoglobin properly, causing mental disturbance, extreme sensitivity to light, and excretion of dark pigments in the urine.

por·phy·ry /'pôrfərē/ ▶n. (pl. **porphyries**) a hard reddish igneous rock containing crystals of feldspar.

por·poise /'pôrpəs/ ▶n. a small toothed whale with a blunt rounded snout.

por·ridge /'pôrij/ ▶n. chiefly British term for **oatmeal** (sense 2).

por·rin·ger /'pôrənjər/ ▶n. historical a small bowl, often with a handle, used for soup or similar food.

port¹ /'pôrt/ ▶n. **1** a town or city with a harbor. **2** a harbor.
– PHRASES **port of call** a place where a ship or person stops on a journey.

port² (also **port wine**) ▶n. a sweet dark red fortified wine from Portugal.

port³ ▶n. the side of a ship or aircraft that is on the left when one is facing forward. The opposite of STARBOARD. ▶v. turn a ship or its helm to the port side.

port⁴ ▶n. **1** an opening in the side of a ship for boarding or loading. **2** a porthole. **3** an opening for the passage of steam, liquid, or gas. **4** an opening in the body of an aircraft or in a wall or armored vehicle through which a gun may be fired. **5** a socket in a computer network into which a device can be plugged.

port⁵ ▶v. **1** Computing transfer software from one system or machine to another. **2** Military carry a weapon diagonally across and close to the body with the barrel or blade near the left shoulder. ▶n. **1** Military the position required by an order to port a weapon. **2** Computing a transfer of software from one system or machine to another.

port·a·ble /'pôrtəbəl/ ▶adj. **1** able to be easily carried or moved. **2** (of a loan or pension) capable of being transferred. **3** Computing (of software) able to be ported. ■ **port·a·bil·i·ty** /,pôrtə'bilətē/ n.

por·tage /'pôrtij/ ▶n. **1** the carrying of a boat or its cargo overland between two navigable waterways. **2** a place at which this is necessary. ▶v. carry a boat or its cargo in this way.

por·tal /'pôrtl/ ▶n. **1** a large and imposing doorway, gate, or gateway. **2** an Internet site providing a directory of links to other sites.

por·tal vein ▶n. a vein carrying blood to the liver from the spleen, stomach, pancreas, and intestines.

por·ta·men·to /,pôrtə'men,tō/ ▶n. (pl. **portamentos** or **portamenti** /-tē/) Music a slide from one note to another, especially in singing or playing the violin.

port·cul·lis /pôrt'kələs/ ▶n. a strong, heavy grating that can be lowered to block a gateway to a castle.

por·tend /pôr'tend/ ▶v. be a sign or warning that something important or disastrous is likely to happen.

por·tent /'pôr,tent/ ▶n. a sign or warning that something important or disastrous is likely to happen: *many birds are regarded as portents of death.*

por·ten·tous /pôr'tentəs/ ▶adj. **1** important

as a sign or warning of what is likely to happen; of great significance: *this portentous year in their history.* **2** done in a pompous or excessively solemn way. ■ **por·ten·tous·ly** adv. **por·ten·tous·ness** n.

por·ter¹ /'pôrtər/ ▶n. **1** a person employed to carry luggage and other loads. **2** an attendant in a railroad sleeping car. **3** dark brown bitter beer brewed from charred or browned malt. ■ **por·ter·age** /'pôrtərij/ n.

por·ter² ▶n. chiefly Brit. an employee in charge of the entrance of a hotel, apartment complex, or other large building.

por·ter·house steak /'pôrtər,hous/ ▶n. a choice steak cut from the thick end of a sirloin.

port·fo·li·o /pôrt'fōlē,ō/ ▶n. (pl. **portfolios**) **1** a thin, flat case for carrying drawings, maps, etc. **2** a set of pieces of creative work intended to demonstrate a person's ability. **3** a range of investments held by a person or organization. **4** the position and duties of a government minister.

port·hole /'pôrt,hōl/ ▶n. **1** a small window on the outside of a ship or aircraft. **2** historical an opening for firing a cannon through.

por·ti·co /'pôrti,kō/ ▶n. (pl. **porticoes** or **porticos**) a roof supported by columns at regular intervals, built over the entrance to a building.

por·tion /'pôrshən/ ▶n. **1** a part or a share. **2** an amount of food suitable for or served to one person. **3** old use a person's destiny or fate. **4** old use a dowry. ▶v. divide something into portions and distribute it.

Port·land ce·ment /'pôrtlənd/ ▶n. cement made from limestone and clay that hardens under water.

port·ly /'pôrtlē/ ▶adj. (**portlier**, **portliest**) (especially of a man) rather fat. ■ **port·li·ness** n.

port·man·teau /pôrt'mantō/ ▶n. (pl. **portmanteaus** or **portmanteaux** /-tōz/) a large traveling bag made of stiff leather and opening into two equal parts. ▶adj. consisting of two or more aspects or qualities: *a portmanteau movie.*

port·man·teau word ▶n. a word blending the sounds and combining the meanings of two others, e.g., *brunch* from *breakfast* and *lunch.*

por·trait /'pôrtrət, -,trāt/ ▶n. **1** a painting, drawing, or photograph of a person, especially one depicting only the face or head and shoulders. **2** a written or filmed description. ▶adj. referring to a format for printed material that is higher than it is wide. Compare with LANDSCAPE. ■ **por·trait·ist** n. **por·trai·ture** /'pôrtricHər, -,cHŏŏr/ n.

por·tray /pôr'trā/ ▶v. **1** show or describe in a work of art or literature: *the suburban couples portrayed in this movie.* **2** describe in a particular way: *the book portrayed him as a relentless careerist.* **3** (of an actor) play the part of someone in a movie or play. ■ **por·tray·al** /-'trā(ə)l/ n. **por·tray·er** n.

Por·tu·guese /'pôrcHə,gēz/ ▶n. (pl. same) **1** a person from Portugal. **2** the language of Portugal and Brazil. ▶adj. relating to Portugal.

Por·tu·guese man-of-war ▶n. a floating sea creature like a jellyfish, with long stinging tentacles.

pose /pōz/ ▶v. **1** present or be a problem, danger, question, etc.: *the sheer number of visitors is posing a threat to the area.* **2** sit or stand in a particular position in order to be photographed, painted, or drawn. **3** (**pose as**) pretend to be:

two women posing as social workers forced their way into the house. **4** behave in a way intended to impress other people. ▶ n. **1** a position taken up in order to be painted, drawn, or photographed. **2** a way of behaving adopted in order to impress other people or give a false impression.

pos·er /ˈpōzər/ ▶ n. **1** a person who behaves or dresses in a way intended to impress other people. **2** a puzzling question or problem.

po·seur /pōˈzər/ ▶ n. another term for POSER (sense 1).

po·sey /ˈpōzē/ (also **posy**) ▶ adj. informal trying to impress other people; pretentious.

posh /päsH/ informal ▶ adj. **1** very elegant or luxurious. **2** chiefly Brit. upper-class. ■ **posh·ly** adv. **posh·ness** n.

pos·it /ˈpäzit/ ▶ v. (**posits, positing, posited**) put something forward as a fact or as a basis for argument.

po·si·tion /pəˈzisHən/ ▶ n. **1** a place where someone or something is located or has been put. **2** the correct place. **3** a way in which someone or something is placed or arranged: *he raised himself to a sitting position.* **4** a situation: *the company's financial position is grim.* **5** a person's place or level of importance in relation to other people: *she finished in second position.* **6** high rank or social standing. **7** a job. **8** a point of view or attitude: *the party's position on abortion.* **9** a place where part of a military force is posted. ▶ v. put or arrange in a particular position: *she positioned herself near the fireplace.* ■ **po·si·tion·al** /pəˈzisHənl/ adj. **po·si·tion·al·ly** adv.

pos·i·tive /ˈpäzitiv, ˈpäztiv/ ▶ adj. **1** characterized by the presence rather than the absence of distinguishing features: *a positive test result.* **2** expressing or implying confirmation, agreement, or permission. **3** constructive, optimistic, or confident: *a positive outlook on life.* **4** with no possibility of doubt; certain. **5** (of a quantity) greater than zero. **6** relating to, containing, or producing the kind of electric charge opposite to that carried by electrons. **7** (of a photographic image) showing light and shade or colors true to the original. **8** (of an adjective or adverb) expressing the basic degree of a quality. Contrasted with COMPARATIVE and SUPERLATIVE. ▶ n. a positive quality, attribute, or image. ■ **pos·i·tive·ly** adv. **pos·i·tive·ness** n. **pos·i·tiv·i·ty** /ˌpäzəˈtivətē/ n.

pos·i·tiv·ism /ˈpäzitivˌizəm, ˈpäztiv-/ ▶ n. a system of philosophy recognizing only that which can be scientifically verified or logically proved. ■ **pos·i·tiv·ist** n. & adj. **pos·i·tiv·is·tic** /ˌpäzətəˈvistik/ adj.

pos·i·tron /ˈpäzəˌträn/ ▶ n. Physics a subatomic particle with the same mass as an electron and a numerically equal but positive charge.

pos·se /ˈpäsē/ ▶ n. **1** historical a group of men summoned by a sheriff to enforce the law. **2** informal a group of people: *a posse of medical students.*

pos·sess /pəˈzes/ ▶ v. **1** have as property; own. **2** (also **be possessed of**) have as an ability, quality, or characteristic: *he did not possess a sense of humor.* **3** (of a demon or spirit) have complete power over someone. **4** (of an emotion, idea, etc.) dominate someone's mind. ■ **pos·ses·sor** n.

pos·ses·sion /pəˈzesHən/ ▶ n. **1** the state of having or owning something: *the book came into his possession.* **2** a thing owned: *my most precious*

possession. **3** the state of being possessed by a demon, emotion, etc. **4** (in sports) temporary control of the ball by a player or team.

pos·ses·sive /pəˈzesiv/ ▶ adj. **1** demanding someone's total attention and love. **2** unwilling to share one's possessions with other people. **3** Grammar expressing possession. ■ **pos·ses·sive·ly** adv. **pos·ses·sive·ness** n.

pos·ses·sive pro·noun ▶ n. Grammar a pronoun showing possession, e.g., *mine.*

pos·si·bil·i·ty /ˌpäsəˈbilətē/ ▶ n. (pl. **possibilities**) **1** a thing that is possible. **2** the state of being possible. **3** (**possibilities**) general qualities of a promising nature: *the house had possibilities.*

pos·si·ble /ˈpäsəbəl/ ▶ adj. **1** capable of existing, happening, or being done. **2** that may be so, but that is not certain: *the possible cause of the plane crash.* ▶ n. a possible candidate for a job or member of a team.

pos·si·bly /ˈpäsəblē/ ▶ adv. **1** perhaps. **2** in accordance with what is possible: *I try to do the job as well as I possibly can.*

pos·sum /ˈpäsəm/ ▶ n. **1** an Australasian marsupial that lives in trees. **2** informal an opossum.
– PHRASES **play possum** pretend to be unconscious, asleep, or unaware of something in order to trick someone.

post¹ /pōst/ ▶ n. **1** a long, strong, upright piece of timber or metal used as a support or a marker. **2** (**the post**) a starting post or winning post in a race. **3** a message sent to an Internet bulletin board or newsgroup. ▶ v. **1** display a notice in a public place. **2** announce or publish something: *the company posted a $460,000 loss.* **3** send a message to an Internet bulletin board or newsgroup. **4** achieve or record a particular score or result.

post² ▶ n. **1** an official service or system that delivers letters and parcels. **2** letters and parcels delivered. **3** a single collection or delivery of mail. ▶ v. **1** send a letter or parcel via the postal system. **2** (in bookkeeping) enter an item in a ledger.
– PHRASES **keep someone posted** keep someone informed of the latest developments or news.

post³ ▶ n. **1** a place where someone is on duty or where an activity is carried out. **2** a job. ▶ v. **1** station a soldier, police officer, etc., in a particular place. **2** send someone to a place to take up a job.

post- ▶ prefix after in time or order: *post-date.*

post·age /ˈpōstij/ ▶ n. **1** the sending of letters and parcels by mail. **2** the amount required to send something by mail.

post·age stamp ▶ n. an adhesive stamp stuck on a letter or parcel to show the amount of postage paid.

post·al /ˈpōstəl/ ▶ adj. relating to the post office or the mail.
– PHRASES **go postal** become crazed or violent, especially as a result of stress.

post·al code ▶ n. another term for POSTCODE.

post·bel·lum /pōstˈbeləm/ ▶ adj. occurring or existing after a war, in particular the American Civil War.

post·card /ˈpōstˌkärd/ ▶ n. a card for sending a message by mail without an envelope.

post·code /ˈpōstˌkōd/ ▶ n. Brit. a group of letters and numbers added to a mailing address to assist the sorting of mail.

post·co·i·tal /ˌpōstˈkōətl/ ▶ adj. occurring or done after sex. ■ **post·co·i·tal·ly** adv.

post·date /pōst'dāt/ ▶ v. **1** put a date later than the actual one on a document or check. **2** occur or come at a later date than: *Stonehenge was believed to postdate these structures.*

post·doc·tor·al /pōst'däktərəl/ ▶ adj. (of research) undertaken after the completion of a doctorate.

post·er /'pōstər/ ▶ n. a large printed picture or notice used for decoration or advertisement.

post·er child (or **poster boy** or **poster girl**) ▶ n. a person who epitomizes or represents a specified quality, cause, etc.: *he has become a poster boy for the antiglobalization movement.*

pos·te·ri·or /pä'sti(ə)rēər, pō-/ ▶ adj. **1** chiefly Anatomy further back in position; at or nearer the rear or hind end. The opposite of ANTERIOR. **2** formal coming after in time or order; later. ▶ n. humorous a person's buttocks.

pos·ter·i·ty /pä'steritē/ ▶ n. all future generations of people.

pos·tern /'pōstərn, 'päs-/ ▶ n. old use a back or side entrance.

pos·ter paint ▶ n. a thick opaque paint used for posters and children's paintings.

post·fem·i·nist /post'femənist/ ▶ adj. moving beyond or rejecting some of the earlier ideas of feminism as out of date.

post·grad·u·ate /pōst'grajōōit/ ▶ adj. relating to study undertaken after completing a first degree. ▶ n. a person engaged in postgraduate study.

post·haste /'pōst'hāst/ ▶ adv. with great speed.

post hoc /'pōst 'häk/ ▶ adj. & adv. occurring or done after the event: *a post hoc justification for the changes.*

post·hu·mous /'päschəməs, päst'(h)yōōməs/ ▶ adj. happening, awarded, or appearing after the person involved has died: *he was granted a posthumous pardon.* ■ **post·hu·mous·ly** adv.

pos·til·ion /pə'stilyən, pō-/ (also **postillion**) ▶ n. chiefly historical the rider of the leading nearside horse of a team or pair drawing a coach, when there is no coachman.

post·Im·pres·sion·ism ▶ n. a late 19th-century and early 20th-century style of art in which emphasis was placed on the emotions of the artist, as expressed by color, line, and shape. ■ **post·Im·pres·sion·ist** n. & adj.

post·in·dus·tri·al /ˌpōstin'dəstrēəl/ ▶ adj. (of an economy or society) no longer relying on heavy industry.

post·ing /'pōstiNG/ ▶ n. a message sent to an Internet bulletin board or newsgroup.

post·lude /'pōs(t)ˌlōōd/ ▶ n. a concluding piece of music.

post·man /'pōstmən/ (or **postwoman** /'pōstwŏŏmən/) ▶ n. (pl. **postmen** or **postwomen**) a mail carrier.

post·mark /'pōstˌmärk/ ▶ n. an official mark stamped on a letter or parcel, giving the date of mailing and canceling the postage stamp. ▶ v. stamp a letter or parcel with a postmark.

post·mas·ter /'pōstˌmastər/ (or **postmistress** /'pōstˌmistris/) ▶ n. a person in charge of a post office.

post·mod·ern·ism /pōst'mädərˌnizəm/ ▶ n. a style and movement in the arts characterized by distrust of theories and ideologies and by the deliberate mixing of different styles. ■ **post·mod·ern** adj. **post·mod·ern·ist** n. & adj. **post·mod·er·ni·ty** /ˌpōstmə'dərnətē/ n.

post·mor·tem /pōst'môrtəm/ ▶ n. **1** an examination of a dead body to establish the cause of death. **2** an analysis of an event made after it has happened: *an election postmortem.* ▶ adj. happening after death.

post·na·tal /pōst'nātl/ ▶ adj. happening in or relating to the period after childbirth.

post·nup·tial /pōst'nəpsнəl, -cнəl/ ▶ adj. after marriage.

post of·fice ▶ n. **1** the public department or corporation responsible for postal services and (in some countries) telecommunications. **2** a building where postal business is carried out.

post·op·er·a·tive /pōst'äp(ə)rətiv/ ▶ adj. relating to the period following a surgical operation.

post·paid /pōst'pād/ ▶ adj. & adv. (with reference to a letter or parcel) on which postage has already been paid.

post·par·tum /pōst'pärtəm/ ▶ adj. relating to the period following childbirth or the birth of young.

post·pone /pōst'pōn/ ▶ v. arrange for something to take place at a time later than that first planned. ■ **post·pone·ment** n.

post·pos·i·tive /ˌpōst'päzətiv/ ▶ adj. (of a word) placed after the word that it relates to.

post·pran·di·al /pōst'prandēəl/ ▶ adj. formal or humorous during or relating to the period after a meal.

post·punk ▶ n. a style of rock music inspired by punk but less aggressive in performance and musically more experimental.

post·script /'pōs(t)ˌskript/ ▶ n. an additional remark at the end of a letter, following the signature.

post·sea·son /'pōs(t)ˌsēzən/ ▶ adj. after the end of the regular season for a particular sport.

post·trau·mat·ic stress dis·or·der ▶ n. a condition of persistent stress occurring as a result of injury or severe psychological shock.

pos·tu·lant /'päscнələnt/ ▶ n. a person who wishes to enter a religious order.

pos·tu·late ▶ v. /'päscнəˌlāt/ suggest or assume that something exists or is true, as a basis for a theory or discussion. ▶ n. /'päscнələt/ a thing that is postulated. ■ **pos·tu·la·tion** /ˌpäscнə'lāsнən/ n.

pos·ture /'päscнər/ ▶ n. **1** a particular position of the body. **2** the usual way in which a person holds their body: *muscle tension can be the result of bad posture.* **3** an approach or attitude toward something: *labor unions adopted a more militant posture in wage negotiations.* ▶ v. behave in a way that is intended to impress or mislead other people. ■ **pos·tur·al** adj.

post·war /'pōst'wär/ ▶ adj. occurring or existing after a war.

po·sy[1] /'pōzē/ ▶ n. (pl. **posies**) a small bunch of flowers.

po·sy[2] ▶ adj. variant spelling of POSEY.

pot[1] /pät/ ▶ n. **1** a rounded or cylindrical container used for storage or cooking. **2** a container designed to hold a particular thing: *a lobster pot.* **3** (**the pot**) the total sum of the bets made on a round in poker and other card games. **4** Billiards a shot in which a player strikes a ball into a pocket. ▶ v. (**pots, potting, potted**) **1** plant something in a flowerpot. **2** preserve food in a sealed pot or jar. **3** Billiards strike a ball into a pocket. **4** informal hit or kill someone or

something by shooting.
– PHRASES **go to pot** informal deteriorate as a result of neglect.

pot² ▶ n. informal marijuana.

po·ta·ble /'pōtəbəl/ ▶ adj. formal (especially of water) safe to drink. ■ **po·ta·bil·i·ty** /ˌpōtə'bilətē/ n.

po·tage /pô'täzh/ ▶ n. thick soup.

po·tag·er /'pätijər/ ▶ n. a kitchen garden.

pot·ash /'pätˌash/ ▶ n. an alkaline potassium compound, used especially in making fertilizers.

po·tas·si·um /pə'tasēəm/ ▶ n. a soft silvery-white reactive metallic element.

po·tas·si·um hy·drox·ide ▶ n. a strongly alkaline white compound used in many industrial processes, e.g., soap manufacture.

po·tas·si·um ni·trate ▶ n. a white crystalline salt used in fertilizer, as a meat preservative, and as a constituent of gunpowder.

po·ta·tion /pō'tāshən/ ▶ n. old use or humorous **1** the action of drinking alcohol. **2** an alcoholic drink.

po·ta·to /pə'tātō/ ▶ n. (pl. **potatoes**) a starchy plant tuber that is cooked and eaten as a vegetable.

pot-au-feu /ˌpôt ō 'fœ/ ▶ n. (pl. same) a French soup of meat and vegetables cooked in a large pot.

pot·bel·ly /'pätˌbelē/ ▶ n. a large protruding stomach.

pot·boil·er /'pätˌboilər/ ▶ n. informal a book, movie, etc., produced purely to earn money quickly by appealing to popular taste.

pot-bound /pät bound/ ▶ adj. (of a plant) having roots that fill the flowerpot, leaving no room for them to expand.

po·teen /pə'tēn, -'chēn/ ▶ n. (in Ireland) whiskey that is made illicitly.

po·tent /'pōtnt/ ▶ adj. **1** having great power, influence, or effect: *a potent drug.* **2** (of a male) able to achieve an erection or to reach an orgasm. ■ **po·ten·cy** n. (pl. **potencies**) **po·tent·ly** adv.

po·ten·tate /'pōtnˌtāt/ ▶ n. a monarch or ruler.

po·ten·tial /pə'tenchəl/ ▶ adj. having the capacity to develop into something in the future: *a potential problem.* ▶ n. **1** qualities or abilities that may be developed and lead to future success or usefulness: *he showed great potential as an actor.* **2** (often **potential for/to do**) the possibility of something happening or of someone doing something in the future. **3** Physics the difference in voltage between two points in an electric field or circuit. ■ **po·ten·ti·al·i·ty** /pəˌtenchē'alətē/ n. **po·ten·tial·ly** adv.

po·ten·tial dif·fer·ence ▶ n. Physics the difference of electrical potential between two points.

po·ten·tial en·er·gy ▶ n. Physics energy possessed by a body as a result of its position or state. Compare with KINETIC ENERGY.

po·ten·ti·ate /pə'tenchēˌāt/ ▶ v. increase the power or effect of a drug, physiological reaction, etc.

po·ten·til·la /ˌpōtn'tilə/ ▶ n. a small shrub with yellow or red flowers.

po·ten·ti·om·e·ter /pəˌtenchē'ämətər/ ▶ n. an instrument for measuring or adjusting an electromotive force.

poth·er /'päTHər/ ▶ n. a commotion or fuss.

pot·hole /'pätˌhōl/ ▶ n. **1** a deep underground cave formed by water eroding the rock. **2** a hole

in a road surface. ■ **pot·holed** adj. **pot·hol·er** n.

po·tion /'pōshən/ ▶ n. a liquid with healing, magical, or poisonous properties.

pot·latch /'pätˌlach/ ▶ n. (among some North American Indian peoples) a ceremonial feast at which possessions are given away or destroyed as an indication of wealth.

pot·luck /'pätˌlək/ ▶ n. **1** the chance that whatever is available will prove to be good or acceptable. **2** a meal or party to which each of the guests contributes a dish.

pot pie ▶ n. **1** a meat and vegetable pie baked in a deep dish. **2** a stew with dumplings.

pot·pour·ri /ˌpōpə'rē, ˌpōpoo'rē/ ▶ n. (pl. **potpourris**) **1** a mixture of dried petals and spices placed in a bowl to perfume a room. **2** a mixture of things.

pot roast ▶ n. a piece of meat cooked slowly in a covered pot.

pot·sherd /'pätˌshərd/ ▶ n. a piece of broken pottery.

pot·shot /'pätˌshät/ ▶ n. a shot aimed unexpectedly or at random.

pot·tage /'pätij/ ▶ n. old use soup or stew.

pot·ted /'pätid/ ▶ adj. **1** grown or preserved in a pot. **2** informal intoxicated by drink or drugs.

pot·ter /'pätər/ ▶ n. a person who makes pottery.

pot·ter's wheel ▶ n. a flat revolving disk on which wet clay is shaped into pots, bowls, etc.

pot·ter·y /'pätərē/ ▶ n. (pl. **potteries**) **1** articles made of clay baked in a kiln. **2** the craft of making such articles. **3** a factory or workshop where such articles are made.

pot·ting shed ▶ n. a shed used for potting plants and storing garden tools and supplies.

pot·ty¹ /'pätē/ ▶ adj. (**pottier**, **pottiest**) informal, chiefly Brit. **1** foolish; crazy. **2** extremely enthusiastic about someone or something. ■ **pot·ti·ness** n.

pot·ty² ▶ n. (pl. **potties**) a container for a child to urinate or defecate into.

pouch /pouch/ ▶ n. **1** a small flexible bag, typically carried in a pocket or attached to a belt. **2** a pocket of skin in an animal's body, especially that in which marsupials carry their young. ■ **pouched** adj. **pouch·y** adj.

pouf¹ /poof/ ▶ n. variant spelling of POUFFE.

pouf² ▶ n. **1** a part of a dress in which a large mass of material has been gathered so that it stands away from the body. **2** a bouffant hairstyle.

pouffe /poof/ (also **pouf**) ▶ n. a large, firm cushion used as a seat or stool.

poult /pōlt/ ▶ n. a young domestic fowl being raised for food.

poul·tice /'pōltəs/ ▶ n. a soft moist mass, traditionally of flour, bran, and herbs, applied to the skin to reduce inflammation.

poul·try /'pōltrē/ ▶ n. chickens, turkeys, ducks, and geese.

pounce¹ /pouns/ ▶ v. **1** spring or swoop suddenly so as to seize or attack someone or something. **2** take swift advantage of a mistake or sign of weakness: *the press pounced on his words.* ▶ n. an act of pouncing.

pounce² ▶ n. a fine powder formerly used to prevent ink from spreading on paper or to prepare parchment for writing.

pound¹ /pound/ ▶ n. **1** a unit of weight equal to 16 oz avoirdupois (0.4536 kg), or 12 oz troy

(0.3732 kg). **2** (also **pound sterling**) (pl. **pounds sterling**) the basic unit of money of the UK, equal to 100 pence. **3** the basic monetary unit of several Middle Eastern countries, equal to 100 piasters. ■ **pound·er** n.

– PHRASES **one's pound of flesh** something that one is owed but, if given, would cause suffering or trouble to the person who owes it.

pound² ▶ v. **1** strike or hit heavily and repeatedly: *the men pounded him with their fists.* **2** beat or throb with a strong regular rhythm. **3** walk or run with heavy steps. **4** (**pound something out**) produce a document or piece of music with heavy strokes on a keyboard or instrument. **5** crush or grind something into a powder or paste.

pound³ ▶ n. a place where stray dogs or illegally parked vehicles may officially be taken and kept until claimed.

pound·age /'poundij/ ▶ n. **1** weight. **2** Brit. a charge made for every pound weight of something, or for every pound sterling in value.

pound cake ▶ n. a rich cake originally made with a pound of each chief ingredient.

pound sign ▶ n. **1** the sign (#), representing a pound as a unit of weight or mass. **2** the sign (£), representing a British pound sterling.

pour /pôr/ ▶ v. **1** flow or cause to flow in a steady stream. **2** (of rain) fall heavily. **3** prepare and serve a drink. **4** come or go in a steady stream: *people poured out of the train.* **5** (**pour something out**) express one's feelings freely. ■ **pour·er** n.

> **USAGE**
> On the confusion of **pour** and **pore**, see the note at PORE².

pous·sin /pōō'sen, -'saɴ/ ▶ n. a chicken killed young for eating.

pout /pout/ ▶ v. push one's lips forward as an expression of sulky annoyance or in order to make oneself look sexually attractive. ▶ n. a pouting expression. ■ **pout·y** adj.

pout·er /'poutər/ ▶ n. a kind of pigeon that is able to puff up its crop to a considerable extent.

pov·er·ty /'pävərtē/ ▶ n. **1** the state of being extremely poor. **2** the state of being inadequate in quality or amount: *the poverty of her imagination.*

pov·er·ty-strick·en ▶ adj. extremely poor.

POW ▶ abbr. prisoner of war.

pow·der /'poudər/ ▶ n. **1** fine dry particles produced by the grinding, crushing, or disintegration of a solid substance. **2** a cosmetic in this form for use on the face. **3** dated a medicine in this form. **4** gunpowder. ▶ v. **1** sprinkle or cover something with powder. **2** (often as adj. **powdered**) make something into a powder: *powdered milk.* ■ **pow·der·y** adj.

– PHRASES **keep one's powder dry** remain cautious and ready for a possible emergency.

pow·der blue ▶ n. a soft, pale blue.

pow·der keg ▶ n. **1** a situation that may suddenly become dangerous or violent. **2** a barrel of gunpowder.

pow·der puff ▶ n. a soft pad for applying powder to the face.

pow·der room ▶ n. euphemistic a women's lavatory in a public building.

pow·er /'pou(-ə)r/ ▶ n. **1** the ability to do something or act in a particular way: *the power*

of speech. **2** the ability to control or influence people or events. **3** the right or authority to do something: *police have the power to seize equipment.* **4** political authority or control. **5** physical strength or force. **6** a country viewed in terms of its international influence and military strength: *a world power.* **7** capacity or performance of an engine or other device. **8** energy that is produced by mechanical, electrical, or other means. **9** Physics the rate of doing work, measured in watts or horse power. **10** Mathematics the product obtained when a number is multiplied by itself a certain number of times. ▶ v. **1** supply a device with mechanical or electrical energy. **2** (**power something up/down**) switch a device on or off. **3** move with speed or force. ■ **pow·ered** adj.

– PHRASES **the powers that be** the authorities.

pow·er·boat /'pou(-ə)r,bōt/ ▶ n. a fast motorboat. ■ **pow·er·boat·ing** n.

pow·er brok·er ▶ n. a person who influences the balance of political or economic power.

pow·er·ful /'pou(-ə)rfəl/ ▶ adj. **1** having great power. **2** having a strong effect: *powerful anti-war images.* ■ **pow·er·ful·ly** adv.

pow·er·house /'pou(-ə)r,hous/ ▶ n. a person or thing having great energy or power.

pow·er·less /'pou(-ə)rləs/ ▶ adj. without ability, influence, or power. ■ **pow·er·less·ly** adv. **pow·er·less·ness** n.

pow·er line ▶ n. a cable carrying electrical power.

pow·er of at·tor·ney ▶ n. the authority to act for another person in particular legal or financial matters.

pow·er pack ▶ n. **1** a unit that stores and supplies electrical power. **2** a transformer for converting an alternating current to a direct current at a different voltage.

pow·er plant ▶ n. a power station.

pow·er play ▶ n. **1** tactics exhibiting or intended to increase a person's power or influence. **2** tactics in a team sport involving the concentration of players at a particular point. **3** Ice Hockey a situation in which a team has a numerical advantage over its opponents while one or more players is serving a penalty.

pow·er pop ▶ n. a style of pop music characterized by a strong melody line, heavy use of guitars, and simple rhythm.

pow·er rat·ing ▶ n. **1** the amount of electrical power required for a particular device. **2** a numerical representation of a sports team's strength for betting purposes.

pow·er sta·tion ▶ n. a building where electrical power is generated.

pow·er steer·ing ▶ n. steering aided by power from the vehicle's engine.

pow·wow /'pou,wou/ ▶ n. **1** informal a meeting for discussion. **2** a North American Indian ceremony involving feasting and dancing. ▶ v. informal meet to discuss something.

pox /päks/ ▶ n. **1** any disease caused by a virus and producing a rash of pus-filled pimples that leave pockmarks on healing. **2** (**the pox**) informal syphilis. **3** (**the pox**) historical smallpox.

pp ▶ abbr. **1** (**pp.**) pages. **2** (also **p.p.**) per procurationem (used when signing a letter on someone else's behalf). **3** Music pianissimo.

ppm ▶ abbr. **1** part(s) per million. **2** page(s) per minute, a measure of the speed of a computer printer.

PPS ▸ abbr. post (additional) postscript.

PPV ▸ abbr. pay-per-view.

PR ▸ abbr. 1 proportional representation. 2 public relations.

Pr ▸ symbol the chemical element praseodymium.

prac·ti·ca·ble /'praktikəbəl/ ▸ adj. able to be done or put into effect successfully: *it was not practicable to call her as a witness.* ■ **prac·ti·ca·bil·i·ty** /,praktikə'bilətē/ n. **prac·ti·ca·bly** adv.

prac·ti·cal /'praktikəl/ ▸ adj. 1 relating to the actual doing or use of something rather than theory: *the candidate should have practical management experience.* 2 likely to be effective or successful: *practical solutions to transport problems.* 3 suitable for a particular purpose. 4 realistic or sensible in one's approach to a situation. 5 skilled at making or doing things. 6 almost complete; virtual: *it was a practical certainty that he would raise more money.*

prac·ti·cal·i·ty /,prakti'kalətē/ ▸ n. (pl. **practicalities**) 1 the quality or state of being practical. 2 (**practicalities**) the aspects of a situation that involve action or experience rather than theories or ideas.

prac·ti·cal joke ▸ n. a trick played on someone to make them look foolish.

prac·ti·cal·ly /'praktik(ə)lē/ ▸ adv. 1 virtually; almost. 2 in a practical way.

prac·ti·cal nurse ▸ n. a nurse who has completed a training course of a lower standard than a registered nurse.

prac·tice /'praktəs/ ▸ n. 1 the use or application of an idea or method, as opposed to the theories relating to it: *putting policy into practice.* 2 the usual way of doing something. 3 the work, business, or place of work of a doctor, dentist, or lawyer. 4 the action of doing something repeatedly so as to become more skillful in it: *math improves with practice.* ▸ v. (Brit. **practise**) 1 do something repeatedly in order to become skillful in it: *I need to practice my French.* 2 carry out an activity or custom regularly. 3 work in a particular profession: *she began to practice law.* 4 observe the teaching and rules of a religion.

prac·ticed /'praktəst/ (Brit. **practised**) ▸ adj. expert in something as the result of much experience.

prac·tise ▸ v. British spelling of PRACTICE (verb).

prac·ti·tion·er /prak'tishənər/ ▸ n. a person who practices a particular profession or activity.

prae·tor /'prētər/ (also **pretor**) ▸ n. each of two ancient Roman magistrates ranking below consul. ■ **prae·to·ri·an** /prē'tôrēən/ adj. & n.

prae·to·ri·an guard ▸ n. (in ancient Rome) the bodyguard of the emperor.

prag·mat·ic /prag'matik/ ▸ adj. 1 dealing with things in a realistic and practical way. 2 relating to philosophical pragmatism. ■ **prag·mat·i·cal·ly** /-ik(ə)lē/ adv.

prag·ma·tism /'pragmə,tizəm/ ▸ n. 1 a realistic and practical attitude or approach. 2 a philosophical approach that evaluates theories in terms of the success of their practical application. ■ **prag·ma·tist** n.

prai·rie /'pre(ə)rē/ ▸ n. a large open area of grassland.

prai·rie dog ▸ n. a type of rodent that lives in burrows in the grasslands of North America.

praise /prāz/ ▸ v. 1 express warm approval of or admiration for: *he praised the work being* done by the security forces. 2 express respect and gratitude toward God or a god. ▸ n. 1 the expression of approval or admiration. 2 the expression of respect and gratitude as an act of worship.

– PHRASES **praise someone/thing to the skies** praise someone or something very highly or enthusiastically.

praise·wor·thy /'prāz,wərṮHē/ ▸ adj. deserving approval and admiration. ■ **praise·wor·thi·ly** adv. **praise·wor·thi·ness** n.

pra·line /'prä,lēn/ ▸ n. a smooth substance made from nuts boiled in sugar, used as a filling for chocolates.

pram /pram/ ▸ n. Brit. a four-wheeled vehicle for a baby, pushed by a person on foot.

prance /prans/ ▸ v. 1 move quickly with exaggerated steps. 2 (of a horse) move with high springy steps.

pran·di·al /'prandēəl/ ▸ adj. formal during or relating to a meal.

prang /praNG/ Brit. informal ▸ v. crash a motor vehicle or aircraft. ▸ n. a collision or crash.

prank /praNGk/ ▸ n. a practical joke or mischievous act. ■ **prank·ish** adj.

prank·ster /'praNGkstər/ ▸ n. a person who is fond of playing pranks.

pra·se·o·dym·i·um /,prāzēō'dimēəm/ ▸ n. a silvery-white metallic chemical element of the lanthanide series.

prate /prāt/ ▸ v. talk too much in a foolish or boring way.

prat·fall /'prat,fôl/ ▸ n. informal 1 a fall onto one's buttocks. 2 an embarrassing mistake.

prat·tle /'pratl/ ▸ v. talk too much in a foolish or trivial way. ▸ n. foolish or trivial talk.

prawn /prôn/ ▸ n. an edible shellfish that resembles a large shrimp.

prax·is /'praksəs/ ▸ n. 1 practice, as distinguished from theory. 2 accepted practice or custom, especially in religion.

pray /prā/ ▸ v. 1 say a prayer to God or a god. 2 wish or hope strongly for: *after days of rain, we were praying for sun.* ▸ adv. formal or old use please: *pray continue.*

prayer /pre(ə)r/ ▸ n. 1 a request for help or expression of thanks addressed to God or a god. 2 (**prayers**) a religious service at which people gather to pray together. 3 an earnest hope or wish.

prayer·ful /'pre(ə)rfəl/ ▸ adj. 1 relating to praying or prayers. 2 tending to pray; devout. ■ **prayer·ful·ly** adv.

prayer wheel ▸ n. a small revolving cylinder inscribed with or containing prayers, used by Tibetan Buddhists.

pray·ing man·tis ▸ n. see MANTIS.

PRC ▸ abbr. People's Republic of China.

pre- ▸ prefix before: *prearrange.*

preach /prēCH/ ▸ v. 1 give a religious talk to a gathering of people. 2 strongly recommend a course of action: *my parents always preached tolerance.* 3 (**preach at**) give moral advice to someone in a pompous way. ■ **preach·er** n.

preach·y /'prēCHē/ ▸ adj. giving moral advice in a pompous or overbearing way.

pre·am·ble /'prē,ambəl/ ▸ n. an opening statement; an introduction.

pre·am·pli·fi·er /prē'amplə,fīər/ (also **preamp**) ▸ n. an electronic device that amplifies a very weak signal and transmits it to a main amplifier.

pre·ar·range /ˌprēəˈrānj/ ▶v. arrange or agree upon something in advance.

Pre·cam·bri·an /prēˈkambrēən, -kām-/ ▶adj. Geology relating to the earliest period of the earth's history, ending about 570 million years ago, a time when living organisms first appeared.

pre·can·cer·ous /prēˈkansərəs/ ▶adj. (of a cell or medical condition) likely to develop into cancer if untreated.

pre·car·i·ous /priˈke(ə)rēəs/ ▶adj. **1** likely to fall or to cause someone to fall. **2** not safe or stable; uncertain: *the country's precarious financial position.* ■ **pre·car·i·ous·ly** adv. **pre·car·i·ous·ness** n.

pre·cast /ˈprēˈkast/ ▶adj. (especially of concrete) cast in its final shape before positioning.

pre·cau·tion /priˈkôSHən/ ▶n. **1** something done in advance to avoid problems or danger: *the best ways to foil hackers is to take a few simple precautions.* **2** (**precautions**) informal contraception. ■ **pre·cau·tion·ar·y** /-ˌnerē/ adj.

pre·cede /priˈsēd/ ▶v. **1** come before in time, order, or position: *read the chapters that precede the recipes.* **2** go in front or ahead of someone. ■ **pre·ced·ing** adj.

prec·e·dence /ˈpresədəns, priˈsēdns/ ▶n. the state of coming before other people or things in order or importance: *his desire for power took precedence over everything.*

prec·e·dent ▶n. /ˈpresid(ə)nt/ **1** an earlier event or action that acts as an example to be followed in a similar situation. **2** a previous legal case or decision that may or must be followed in subsequent similar cases. ▶adj. /priˈsēd(ə)nt/ coming before in time, order, or importance.

pre·cept /ˈprēˌsept/ ▶n. **1** a general rule regulating behavior or thought. **2** a writ or warrant.

pre·cep·tor /ˈprēˌseptər, priˈseptər/ ▶n. (fem. **preceptress** /ˈprēˌseptris/) a teacher or instructor.

pre·ces·sion /prəˈseSHən/ ▶n. **1** the slow movement of the axis of a spinning body around another axis. **2** the earlier occurrence of the equinoxes each year. ■ **pre·cess** /prēˈses, ˈprēˌses/ v. **pre·ces·sion·al** /priˈseSHənl/ adj.

pre·cinct /ˈprēˌsiNGkt/ ▶n. **1** one of the districts into which a city or town is divided for elections or policing purposes. **2** the area within the walls or boundaries of a place. **3** an enclosed area around a cathedral, church, or college.

pre·ci·os·i·ty /ˌpresHēˈäsətē/ ▶n. affectation or pretentiousness in language or art.

pre·cious /ˈpresHəs/ ▶adj. **1** very valuable. **2** greatly loved or treasured: *my daughter's very precious to me.* **3** ironic considerable: *a precious lot you know!* **4** sophisticated in an affected or exaggerated way. ■ **pre·cious·ly** adv. **pre·cious·ness** n.
– PHRASES **precious little** (or **few**) informal very little (or few).

pre·cious met·al ▶n. a valuable metal such as gold, silver, or platinum.

pre·cious stone ▶n. a very attractive and valuable piece of mineral, used in jewelry.

prec·i·pice /ˈpresəpəs/ ▶n. a tall and very steep rock face or cliff.

pre·cip·i·tant /priˈsipətənt/ ▶n. a cause of an action or event.

pre·cip·i·tate ▶v. /priˈsipəˌtāt/ **1** cause something undesirable to happen suddenly or prematurely. **2** cause to move suddenly and with force: *the ladder broke, precipitating them down into a heap.* **3** Chemistry cause a substance to be deposited in solid form from a solution. **4** cause moisture in the atmosphere to condense and fall as rain, snow, sleet, or hail. ▶adj. /priˈsipətət/ done or occurring suddenly or without careful consideration. ▶n. /priˈsipətət, -əˌtāt/ Chemistry a substance precipitated from a solution. ■ **pre·cip·i·tate·ly** /priˈsipətətlē/ adv. **pre·cip·i·ta·tor** /priˈsipəˌtātər/ n.

pre·cip·i·ta·tion /priˌsipəˈtāsHən/ ▶n. **1** rain, snow, sleet, or hail. **2** Chemistry the action of precipitating a substance from a solution. **3** old use sudden and unthinking action.

pre·cip·i·tous /priˈsipətəs/ ▶adj. **1** dangerously high or steep. **2** (of a change to a worse situation) sudden and dramatic. **3** done suddenly and without consideration; precipitate. ■ **pre·cip·i·tous·ly** adv.

pré·cis /prāˈsē, ˈprāsē/ (also **precis**) ▶n. (pl. same) a summary of a written work or speech. ▶v. (**précises**, **précising**, **précised**) make a summary of a piece of writing or a speech.

pre·cise /priˈsīs/ ▶adj. **1** expressed in a detailed and accurate way: *precise directions.* **2** very attentive to detail. **3** exact; particular: *at that precise moment the car stopped.* ■ **pre·cise·ly** adv. **pre·cise·ness** n.

> **USAGE**
>
> **Precise** does not mean exactly the same thing as **accurate**. **Accurate** means 'correct in all details,' while **precise** contains an idea of trying to specify details exactly: if you say 'It's 4:04 and 12 seconds' you are being *precise*, but not necessarily *accurate* (your watch might be slow).

pre·ci·sion /priˈsiZHən/ ▶n. the quality or fact of being precise. ▶adj. very accurate: *a precision instrument.*

pre·clude /priˈklo͞od/ ▶v. prevent something from happening or someone from doing something. ■ **pre·clu·sion** /-ˈklo͞oZHən/ n.

pre·co·cious /priˈkōSHəs/ ▶adj. (of a child) having developed certain abilities or ways of behaving at an earlier age than usual. ■ **pre·co·cious·ly** adv. **pre·co·cious·ness** n. **pre·coc·i·ty** /priˈkäsətē/ n.

pre·cog·ni·tion /ˌprēkägˈniSHən/ ▶n. knowledge of an event before it happens, especially through supposed paranormal means. ■ **pre·cog·ni·tive** /prēˈkägnətiv/ adj.

pre·con·ceived /ˌprēkənˈsēvd/ ▶adj. (of an idea or opinion) formed before full knowledge or evidence is available.

pre·con·cep·tion /ˌprēkənˈsepSHən/ ▶n. an idea or opinion that is formed before full knowledge or evidence is available.

pre·con·di·tion /ˌprēkənˈdiSHən/ ▶n. something that must exist or happen before other things can happen or be done.

pre·cook /ˈprēˈko͝ok/ ▶v. cook something in advance.

pre·cur·sor /ˈprēˌkərsər, priˈkər-/ ▶n. a person or thing that comes before another of the same kind: *the game was a precursor of baseball.* ■ **pre·cur·so·ry** adj.

pre·da·cious /priˈdāSHəs/ (also **predaceous**) ▶adj. (of an animal) predatory.

pre·date /prēˈdāt/ ▶ v. exist or occur at a date earlier than something.

pre·da·tion /priˈdāsHən/ ▶ n. the preying of one animal on others.

pred·a·tor /ˈpredətər/ ▶ n. 1 an animal that hunts and kills other animals for food. 2 a person who exploits others: *a sexual predator.*

pred·a·to·ry /ˈpredəˌtôrē/ ▶ adj. 1 (of an animal) hunting and killing other animals for food. 2 (of a person) exploiting other people.

pre·dawn /prēˈdôn/ ▶ adj. relating to or taking place before dawn.

pre·de·cease /ˌprēdiˈsēs/ ▶ v. formal die before another person.

pred·e·ces·sor /ˈpredəˌsesər, ˈprē-/ ▶ n. 1 a person who held a job or office before the current holder. 2 a thing that has been followed or replaced by another: *the chapel was built on the site of its predecessor.*

pre·des·ti·na·tion /prēˌdestəˈnāsHən/ ▶ n. the Christian belief that everything has been decided or planned in advance by God.

pre·des·tine /prēˈdestin/ ▶ v. (usu. as adj. **predestined**) (of God or fate) decide in advance that something will happen or that someone will have a particular fate.

pre·de·ter·mine /ˌprēdiˈtərmən/ ▶ v. establish or decide something in advance. ■ **pre·de·ter·mi·na·tion** /-ˌtərməˈnāsHən/ n.

pre·de·ter·min·er /ˌprēdiˈtərmənər/ ▶ n. Grammar a word or phrase that occurs before a determiner, for example *both* or *a lot of.*

pre·dic·a·ment /priˈdikəmənt/ ▶ n. a difficult or embarrassing situation.

pred·i·cate ▶ n. /ˈpredikət/ 1 Grammar the part of a sentence or clause containing a verb and stating something about the subject (e.g., *went home* in *John went home*). 2 Logic something that is declared or denied concerning an argument of a proposition. ▶ v. /ˈpredəˌkāt/ 1 (**predicate something on**) found or base something on: *the oil's low price is predicated on tax exemptions.* 2 declare or assert something as true or existing. ■ **pred·i·ca·tion** /ˌpredəˈkāsHən/ n.

pred·i·ca·tive /ˈpredəˌkātiv, -ikətiv/ ▶ adj. Grammar (of an adjective or noun) forming part or the whole of the predicate and coming after a verb, for example *old* in *the dog is old*. Contrasted with ATTRIBUTIVE. ■ **pred·i·ca·tive·ly** adv.

pre·dict /priˈdikt/ ▶ v. state that an event will happen in the future. ■ **pre·dic·tive** adj. **pre·dic·tor** n.

pre·dict·a·ble /priˈdiktəbəl/ ▶ adj. 1 able to be predicted. 2 always behaving or occurring in the way expected and therefore boring. ■ **pre·dict·a·bil·i·ty** /-ˌdiktəˈbilətē/ n. **pre·dict·a·bly** adv.

pre·dic·tion /priˈdiksHən/ ▶ n. 1 a thing predicted; a forecast. 2 the action of predicting something.

pre·di·gest /ˌprēdīˈjest, ˌprēdə-/ ▶ v. 1 (of an animal) treat food by a process similar to digestion to make it more easily digestible when subsequently eaten. 2 simplify information so that it is easier to absorb.

pre·di·lec·tion /ˌpredlˈeksHən, ˌprēdl-/ ▶ n. a preference or special liking for something.

pre·dis·pose /ˌprēdiˈspōz/ ▶ v. make someone likely to do, be, or think something: *certain people are predisposed to become drug abusers.* ■ **pre·dis·po·si·tion** /ˌprēˌdispəˈzisHən/ n.

pre·dom·i·nant /priˈdämənənt/ ▶ adj. 1 present as the main element: *the bird's predominant color was white.* 2 having the greatest control or power. ■ **pre·dom·i·nance** n. **pre·dom·i·nant·ly** adv.

pre·dom·i·nate /priˈdäməˌnāt/ ▶ v. 1 be the main element in something: *small-scale producers predominate in the south.* 2 have control or power.

pre·dom·i·nate·ly /priˈdämənətlē/ ▶ adv. mainly; for the most part.

pre·ec·lamp·sia /ˌprē-iˈklampsēə/ ▶ n. a condition in pregnancy characterized especially by high blood pressure. ■ **pre·ec·lamp·tic** /-ˈklamptik/ adj. & n.

pree·mie /ˈprēmē/ ▶ n. (pl. **preemies**) informal a baby born prematurely.

pre·em·i·nent /prēˈemənənt/ ▶ adj. better than all others; outstanding. ■ **pre·em·i·nence** n. **pre·em·i·nent·ly** adv.

pre·empt /prēˈempt/ ▶ v. 1 take action in order to prevent something from happening. 2 prevent someone from saying something by speaking first. ■ **pre·empt·ive** adj. **pre·empt·or** n.

pre·emp·tion /prēˈempsHən/ ▶ n. 1 the action of preventing something from happening. 2 the buying of goods or shares before the opportunity is offered to others.

preen /prēn/ ▶ v. 1 (of a bird) tidy and clean its feathers with its beak. 2 make oneself look attractive and then admire one's appearance. 3 (**preen oneself**) congratulate or pride oneself: *he's preening himself on having such a pretty girlfriend.*

pre·ex·ist /ˌprē-igˈzist/ ▶ v. (usu. as adj. **preexisting**) exist before or from an earlier time. ■ **pre·ex·ist·ence** n. **pre·ex·ist·ent** adj.

pre·fab /ˈprēˈfab, ˈprēˌfab/ ▶ n. informal a prefabricated building.

pre·fab·ri·cat·ed /prēˈfabriˌkātid/ ▶ adj. (of a building) made in sections that can be easily assembled on site. ■ **pre·fab·ri·ca·tion** /-ˌfabrəˈkāsHən/ n.

pref·ace /ˈprefəs/ ▶ n. 1 an introduction to a book, stating its subject, scope, or aims. 2 a preliminary explanation. ▶ v. 1 (**preface something with/by**) begin a speech or event with or by doing something. 2 provide a book with a preface. ■ **pref·a·to·ry** /ˈprefəˌtôrē/ adj.

pre·fect /ˈprēˌfekt/ ▶ n. a chief officer, magistrate, or regional governor in certain countries. ■ **pre·fec·to·ri·al** /ˌprēˌfekˈtôrēəl/ adj.

pre·fec·ture /ˈprēˌfekcHər/ ▶ n. 1 a district governed by a prefect. 2 the office or residence of a prefect. ■ **pre·fec·tur·al** /prēˈfekcHərəl/ adj.

pre·fer /priˈfər/ ▶ v. (**prefers, preferring, preferred**) 1 like someone or something better than another or others: *I prefer Greece to Spain.* 2 put forward a formal accusation for consideration by a court of law. 3 old use promote someone to an important position.

pref·er·a·ble /ˈpref(ə)rəbəl/ ▶ adj. more desirable or suitable. ■ **pref·er·a·bil·i·ty** /ˌpref(ə)rəˈbilətē/ n.

pref·er·a·bly /ˈpref(ə)rəblē/ ▶ adv. ideally; if possible.

pref·er·ence /ˈpref(ə)rəns/ ▶ n. 1 a greater liking for one alternative over another or others. 2 a thing preferred. 3 favor shown to one person over another or others: *preference is given to those who make a donation.*

pref·er·en·tial /ˌprefəˈrenCHəl/ ▸ adj. favoring a particular person or group: *he was giving his son-in-law preferential treatment.*
■ **pref·er·en·tial·ly** adv.

pre·fer·ment /priˈfərmənt/ ▸ n. promotion or appointment to a job or office.

pre·ferred stock ▸ n. stock that entitles the holder to a fixed dividend, whose payment takes priority over that of common-stock dividends.

pre·fig·ure /prēˈfigyər/ ▸ v. be an early indication or version of: *the fall of Jericho was thought to prefigure the Last Judgment.* ■ **pre·fig·u·ra·tion** /ˌprēˌfigyəˈrāSHən/ n.

pre·fix /ˈprēˌfiks/ ▸ n. **1** a word, letter, or number placed before another. **2** a letter or group of letters placed at the beginning of a word to alter its meaning (e.g., *non-*, *re-*). **3** a title placed before a name (e.g., *Mr.*). ▸ v. add letters or numbers to the beginning of a word or number.

pre·game /prēˈgām/ ▸ adj. in or relating to the period before a sporting event.

preg·nan·cy /ˈpregnənsē/ ▸ n. (pl. **pregnancies**) the condition or period of being pregnant.

preg·nant /ˈpregnənt/ ▸ adj. **1** (of a woman or female animal) having a child or young developing in the uterus. **2** full of meaning; significant: *a pregnant pause.*

pre·heat /prēˈhēt/ ▸ v. heat something beforehand.

pre·hen·sile /prēˈhensəl, -ˌsīl/ ▸ adj. (chiefly of an animal's limb or tail) capable of grasping things.

pre·his·tor·ic /ˌprē(h)iˈstôrik/ ▸ adj. relating to the period before written records.

pre·his·to·ry /prēˈhist(ə)rē/ ▸ n. **1** the period of time before written records. **2** the early stages of the development of something: *the prehistory of capitalism.* ■ **pre·his·to·ri·an** /-ˈstôrēən/ n.

pre·in·dus·tri·al /ˌprē-inˈdəstrēəl/ ▸ adj. before the development of industries on a large scale.

pre·judge /prēˈjəj/ ▸ v. make a judgment about someone or something without having all the necessary information.

prej·u·dice /ˈprejədəs/ ▸ n. **1** an opinion that is not based on reason or actual experience: *widespread prejudice against foreigners.* **2** dislike or unjust behavior based on this. **3** chiefly Law harm that may result from an action or judgment. ▸ v. **1** influence someone so that they have a biased or unfair opinion: *the statement might prejudice the jury.* **2** have a harmful effect on a situation. ■ **prej·u·diced** adj.
– PHRASES **without prejudice** Law without adversely affecting any existing right or claim.

prej·u·di·cial /ˌprejəˈdiSHəl/ ▸ adj. harmful to someone or something.

pre·kin·der·gar·ten /prēˈkindərˌgärtn, -ˌgärdn/ ▸ n. day care with some educational content for children younger than five.

pre·lap·sar·i·an /ˌprēlapˈse(ə)rēən/ ▸ adj. chiefly literary before the Fall of Man, when humans lapsed into a state of sin; innocent and unspoiled.

prel·ate /ˈprelət/ ▸ n. formal a bishop or other high-ranking Christian priest.

pre·lim·i·nar·y /priˈliməˌnerē/ ▸ adj. happening before or done in preparation for a main action or event: *preliminary talks.* ▸ n. (pl. **preliminaries**) **1** an action or event that comes before or is done in preparation for something. **2** a preliminary round in a sports competition.

pre·lit·er·ate /prēˈlitərət/ ▸ adj. relating to a society or culture that has not developed the use of writing.

prel·ude /ˈprel,(y) o͞od, ˈprā,l(y)o͞od/ ▸ n. **1** an action or event acting as an introduction to something more important: *the talks should be the prelude to a final agreement.* **2** a piece of music acting as an introduction to a longer work. ▸ v. act as an introduction to something.

pre·mar·i·tal /prēˈmaritl/ ▸ adj. happening before marriage.

pre·ma·ture /ˌprēməˈCHo͝or, -ˈt(y)o͝or/ ▸ adj. **1** happening or done before the proper time: *the sun can cause premature aging.* **2** (of a baby) born before the normal length of pregnancy is completed. ■ **pre·ma·ture·ly** adv. **pre·ma·tu·ri·ty** /-ˈCHo͝orətē, -ˈt(y)o͝or-/ n.

pre·med·i·ca·tion /ˌprēˌmedəˈkāSHən/ ▸ n. medication given in preparation for an operation or other treatment.

pre·med·i·tat·ed /priˈmedəˌtātid, prē-/ ▸ adj. (of an action, especially a crime) planned in advance. ■ **pre·med·i·ta·tion** /-ˌmedəˈtāSHən/ n.

pre·men·stru·al /prēˈmenstr(o͞o)əl/ ▸ adj. occurring or experienced before a menstrual period.

pre·men·stru·al syn·drome ▸ n. a complex of symptoms (including emotional tension and fluid retention) experienced by some women before a menstrual period.

pre·mier /prēˈm(y)i(ə)r, ˈprēmēər, ˈprēˌmi(ə)r/ ▸ adj. first in importance, order, or position. ▸ n. a prime minister or other head of government.

pre·miere /prēˈmyer, -ˈmi(ə)r/ ▸ n. the first performance of a play or musical work or the first showing of a movie. ▸ v. present the premiere of a play, musical work, or movie.

pre·mier·ship /prēˈm(y)irˌSHip, ˈprēmēər-, ˈprēˌmi(ə)r-/ ▸ n. the office or position of a prime minister or other head of government.

prem·ise /ˈpremis/ ▸ n. a statement or idea that forms the basis for a theory, argument, or line of reasoning. ▸ v. (**premise something on**) base an argument, theory, etc., on something.

prem·is·es /ˈpreməsəz/ ▸ pl.n. a building, together with its land and outbuildings, occupied by a business.

pre·mi·um /ˈprēmēəm/ ▸ n. (pl. **premiums**) **1** an amount paid for an insurance policy. **2** a sum added to a basic price or other payment. ▸ adj. (of a product) superior and more expensive: *premium beers.*
– PHRASES **at a premium 1** scarce and in demand. **2** above the usual price. **put** (or **place**) **a premium on** regard something as particularly important.

pre·mo·lar /prēˈmōlər/ ▸ n. a tooth between the canines and molar teeth.

pre·mo·ni·tion /ˌprēməˈniSHən, ˌprem-/ ▸ n. a strong feeling that something is about to happen. ■ **pre·mon·i·to·ry** /prēˈmänəˌtôrē/ adj.

pre·na·tal /prēˈnātl/ ▸ adj. before birth. ■ **pre·na·tal·ly** adv.

pre·nup /prēˈnəp/ ▸ n. informal a prenuptial agreement.

pre·nup·tial /prēˈnəpSHəl, -CHəl/ ▸ adj. before marriage.

pre·nup·tial a·gree·ment ▸ n. an agreement made by a couple before they marry concerning the ownership of their respective assets should the marriage fail.

pre·oc·cu·pa·tion /ˌprēˌäkyə'pāsHən/ ▶ n. **1** the state of thinking about something continuously and ignoring everything else. **2** a matter that fills someone's mind completely.

pre·oc·cu·py /prē'äkyəˌpī/ ▶ v. (**preoccupies, preoccupying, preoccupied**) fill someone's mind completely, so that they ignore everything else: *her mother was preoccupied with paying the bills.*

pre·or·dain /ˌprēôr'dān/ ▶ v. decide or determine something beforehand.

prep /prep/ informal ▶ v. prepare; make ready. ▶ n. preparation.

pre·pack·aged /prē'pakijd/ ▶ adj. (of goods) packed or wrapped before they are sold.

pre·paid /prē'pād/ ▶ past and past participle of **PREPAY.**

prep·a·ra·tion /ˌprepə'rāsHən/ ▶ n. **1** the action of preparing or the state of being prepared: *the preparation of a draft contract.* **2** something done to get ready for something else. **3** a substance that has been prepared for use as a medicine, cosmetic, or food.

pre·par·a·tive /prē'pe(ə)rətiv, -'par-/ ▶ adj. done in order to prepare for something; preparatory.

pre·par·a·to·ry /pri'pe(ə)rəˌtôrē, -'parə-, 'prep(ə)rə-/ ▶ adj. done in order to prepare for something.

pre·par·a·to·ry school ▶ n. a private school that prepares students for college or university.

pre·pare /pri'pe(ə)r/ ▶ v. **1** make something ready for use. **2** make something from other parts, ingredients, or substances: *I had to prepare the evening meal.* **3** make or get ready to do or deal with something: *she took time off to prepare for her exams.* **4** (**be prepared to do**) be willing to do. ■ **pre·par·er** n.

pre·par·ed·ness /prə'pe(ə)r(ə)dnis/ ▶ n. a state of readiness, especially for war.

pre·pay /prē'pā/ ▶ v. (past and past part. **prepaid**) pay for something in advance. ■ **pre·pay·ment** n.

pre·plan /'prē'plan/ ▶ v. plan something in advance.

pre·pon·der·ance /pri'pändərəns/ ▶ n. the state of being greater in number: *the preponderance of women among older people.*

pre·pon·der·ant /pri'pändərənt/ ▶ adj. greater in number or importance. ■ **pre·pon·der·ant·ly** adv.

pre·pon·der·ate /pri'pändəˌrāt/ ▶ v. be greater in number or importance: *the advantages preponderate over this apparent disadvantage.*

prep·o·si·tion /ˌprepə'zisHən/ ▶ n. Grammar a word used with a noun or pronoun to show place, position, time, or method. ■ **prep·o·si·tion·al** adj.

> **USAGE**
> A preposition (a word such as *from, to, on, after,* etc.) usually comes before a noun or pronoun and gives information about how, when, or where something has happened (*she arrived after dinner*). Some people believe that a preposition should never come at the end of a sentence, as in *where do you come from?*, and that you should say *from where do you come?* instead. However, this can result in English that sounds very awkward and unnatural, and is not a rule that has to be followed as long as the meaning of what you are saying is clear.

pre·pos·sess·ing /ˌprēpə'zesiNG/ ▶ adj. attractive or appealing in appearance: *he was not a prepossessing sight.*

pre·pos·ter·ous /pri'päst(ə)rəs/ ▶ adj. completely ridiculous or outrageous. ■ **pre·pos·ter·ous·ly** adv. **pre·pos·ter·ous·ness** n.

prep·py /'prepē/ (also **preppie**) informal ▶ adj. (**preppier, preppiest**) typical of a student at an expensive preparatory school, especially with reference to their neat style of dress. ▶ n. (pl. **preppies**) **1** a student attending an expensive preparatory school. **2** a person with a preppy style.

pre·pran·di·al /prē'prandēəl/ ▶ adj. formal or humorous done or taken before dinner.

pre·pro·duc·tion /ˌprēprə'dəksHən/ ▶ n. work done on a product, movie, or broadcast program before full-scale production begins.

pre·pro·gram /prē'prōˌgram, -grəm/ ▶ v. (**preprograms, preprogramming, preprogrammed**) program a computer in advance for ease of use.

prep school ▶ n. a preparatory school.

pre·pu·ber·tal /prē'pyōōbərtl/ ▶ adj. another term for **PREPUBESCENT.** ■ **pre·pu·ber·ty** n.

pre·pu·bes·cent /ˌprēpyōō'besənt/ ▶ adj. relating to or in the period before puberty.

pre·puce /'prēˌpyōōs/ ▶ n. **1** technical term for **FORESKIN. 2** the fold of skin surrounding the clitoris.

pre·quel /'prēkwəl, -kwil/ ▶ n. a story or movie containing events that happen before those of an existing work.

Pre-Raph·a·el·ite /'rafēəˌlīt, -räfē-, -'räfē-/ ▶ n. a member of a group of English 19th-century artists who painted in the style of Italian artists from before the time of Raphael. ▶ adj. **1** relating to the Pre-Raphaelites. **2** (of a woman) resembling one depicted in a Pre-Raphaelite painting, typically in having long auburn hair and pale skin. ■ **Pre-Raph·a·el·it·ism** /-ˌlīt,izəm/ n.

pre·re·cord /ˌprēri'kôrd/ ▶ v. (often as adj. **prerecorded**) record sound or film in advance.

pre·req·ui·site /prē'rekwəzət/ ▶ n. a thing that must exist or happen before something else can exist or happen: *an education is a prerequisite for getting a well-paid job.* ▶ adj. required before something else can exist or happen.

pre·rog·a·tive /pri'rägətiv, pə'räg-/ ▶ n. a right or privilege belonging to a particular person or group: *owning a car used to be the prerogative of the rich.*

Pres. ▶ abbr. President.

pres·age /'presij, pri'sāj/ ▶ v. be a sign or warning of an event that is about to happen. ▶ n. a sign or warning of an event that is about to happen; an omen.

pres·by·ter /'prezbitər, 'pres-/ ▶ n. **1** formal (in Presbyterian Churches) an elder. **2** historical an elder or minister of the Christian Church. ■ **pres·byt·er·al** /prez'bitərəl, pres-/ adj. **pres·by·te·ri·al** /ˌprezbi'ti(ə)rēəl, ˌpres-/ adj.

Pres·by·te·ri·an /ˌprezbə'tirēən, ˌpres-/ ▶ adj. relating to a Protestant Church or branch governed by elders, all of equal rank. ▶ n. a member of a Presbyterian Church. ■ **Pres·by·te·ri·an·ism** /ˌprezbə'tirēəˌnizəm, ˌpres-/ n.

pres·by·ter·y /'prezbəˌterē, 'pres-, -bətrē/ ▶ n. (pl. **presbyteries**) **1** (treated as sing. or pl.) a group of Church elders. **2** the house of a Roman Catholic parish priest. **3** the eastern part of a church near the altar.

pre·school /'prē'skool/ ▸ adj. relating to the time before a child is old enough to go to school. ▸ n. a school for children younger than those attending elementary school.

pre·scient /'preSH(ē)ənt, 'prē-/ ▸ adj. having knowledge of events before they take place. ■ **pre·science** n. **pre·scient·ly** adv.

pre·scribe /pri'skrīb/ ▸ v. **1** recommend and authorize the use of a medicine or treatment. **2** (often as adj. **prescribed**) state authoritatively that something should be done: *doing things in the prescribed way.*

> **USAGE**
> On the confusion between **prescribe** and **proscribe**, see the note at PROSCRIBE.

pre·scrip·tion /pri'skripSHən/ ▸ n. **1** a doctor's written instruction authorizing a patient to be issued with a medicine or treatment. **2** the action of prescribing a medicine or treatment. **3** an authoritative recommendation.

pre·scrip·tive /pri'skriptiv/ ▸ adj. **1** relating to the enforcement of a rule or method. **2** (of a right, title, etc.) legally established by long usage. ■ **pre·scrip·tiv·ism** /-'skriptə,vizəm/ n. **pre·scrip·tiv·ist** /-vist/ n. & adj.

pre·sea·son /'prē'sēzən/ ▸ adj. before the start of the season for a particular sport.

pres·ence /'prezəns/ ▸ n. **1** the state or fact of being present: *my presence in the apartment made her happy.* **2** a person's impressive manner or appearance. **3** a person or thing that is present but not seen. **4** a group of soldiers or police stationed in a particular place: *the US would maintain a presence in the region.*
– PHRASES **presence of mind** the ability to remain calm and take quick, sensible action in a difficult situation.

pres·ent¹ /'prezənt/ ▸ adj. **1** being or occurring in a particular place. **2** existing or occurring now. **3** Grammar (of a tense or participle) expressing an action now going on or a condition now existing. ▸ n. **1** (**the present**) the period of time now occurring. **2** Grammar a present tense or form of a verb.
– PHRASES **at present** now. **for the present** for now; temporarily. **these presents** Law, formal this document.

pres·ent² /pri'zent/ ▸ v. **1** give something to someone formally or at a ceremony. **2** offer for acceptance or consideration: *he stopped and presented his passport.* **3** formally introduce someone to someone else. **4** put a show or exhibition before the public. **5** introduce and appear in a television or radio show. **6** be the cause of a problem. **7** give a particular impression to others: *the EU presented a united front over the crisis.* **8** (**present oneself**) appear at or attend a formal occasion.
– PHRASES **present arms** hold a rifle vertically in front of the body as a salute.

pres·ent³ /'prezənt/ ▸ n. a thing given to someone as a gift.

pre·sent·a·ble /pri'zentəbəl/ ▸ adj. clean, well-dressed, or decent enough to be seen in public.

pres·en·ta·tion /,prē,zen'tāSHən, ,prezən-, ,prēzon-/ ▸ n. **1** the action of showing or giving something to someone. **2** the way in which something is presented: *the presentation of food is designed to stimulate your appetite.* **3** a talk or meeting at which a new product, idea, or piece of work is shown to an audience.
■ **pres·en·ta·tion·al** adj. **pres·en·ta·tion·al·ly** adv.

pre·sen·ti·ment /pri'zentəmənt/ ▸ n. a feeling that something undesirable is going to happen.

pres·ent·ly /'prezntlē/ ▸ adv. **1** after a short time; soon. **2** at the present time; now.

pres·ent par·ti·ci·ple ▸ n. Grammar the form of a verb, ending in -*ing*, that is used in forming tenses describing continuous action (e.g., *I'm thinking*), as a noun (e.g., *good thinking*), and as an adjective (e.g., *running water*).

pres·er·va·tion /,prezər'vāSHən/ ▸ n. **1** the action of preserving something. **2** the degree to which something has been preserved: *the chapel is in a poor state of preservation.*

pres·er·va·tion·ist /,prezər'vāSHənəst/ ▸ n. a person who supports the preservation of historic buildings or works of art.

pre·ser·va·tive /pri'zərvətiv/ ▸ n. a substance used to prevent food or other materials from decaying. ▸ adj. preventing something from decaying.

pre·serve /pri'zərv/ ▸ v. **1** keep something in its original or existing state. **2** keep a quality, situation, memory, etc., in existence: *a fight to preserve local democracy.* **3** keep something safe from harm. **4** treat food or other material to prevent it from decaying. ▸ n. **1** (usu. **preserves**) food made with fruit boiled in sugar, such as jam or marmalade. **2** something regarded as reserved for a particular person or group: *jobs that used to be the preserve of men.* **3** a place where game is protected and kept for private hunting.
■ **pre·serv·a·ble** adj. **pre·serv·er** n.

pre·set /'prē'set/ ▸ v. (**presets, presetting, preset**) set the controls of a device at a certain level before using it. ▸ n. a control or level that is set or adjusted before use.

pre·shrunk /'prē'SHrəNGk/ ▸ adj. (of a fabric or an item of clothing) shrunk during manufacture to prevent further shrinking when in use.

pre·side /pri'zīd/ ▸ v. **1** be in charge of a meeting, court, etc. **2** (**preside over**) be in charge of a situation.

pres·i·den·cy /'prez(ə)dənsē, 'prezə,densē/ ▸ n. (pl. **presidencies**) **1** the office or position of president. **2** the period of time that a president is in office.

pres·i·dent /'prez(ə)dənt, 'prezə,dent/ ▸ n. **1** the elected head of a republic. **2** the head of a society or similar organization. **3** the head of a bank or business. ■ **pres·i·den·tial** /,prezə'denCHəl/ adj.

pres·i·dent-e·lect ▸ n. (pl. **presidents-elect**) a person who has been elected president but has not yet taken office.

pre·sid·i·um /pri'sidēəm, -'zid-/ (also **praesidium**) ▸ n. a standing executive committee in a communist country.

press¹ /pres/ ▸ v. **1** move into contact with something by using steady physical force: *he pressed his face to the glass.* **2** push something to operate a device. **3** apply pressure to something to flatten or shape it. **4** move along by pushing. **5** (**press on/ahead**) continue to do something. **6** forcefully put forward an opinion or claim. **7** make strong efforts to persuade someone to do something: *the directors were pressed to justify their expenditure.* **8** extract juice or oil by crushing or squeezing fruit, vegetables, etc. **9** (of time) be short. ▸ n. **1** a device for crushing, flattening, or shaping something. **2** a printing press. **3** (**the press**) (treated as sing. or pl.) newspapers or journalists as a whole. **4** coverage in newspapers and magazines: *the government has had bad press for years.* **5** a closely packed mass of people or things. ■ **press·er** n.

– PHRASES **be pressed for** have very little of something, especially time. **go to press** go to be printed.

press² ▸v. historical force someone to serve in the army or navy.
– PHRASES **press someone/thing into service** put someone or something to a specified use as a temporary measure.

press con·fer·ence ▸n. a meeting held with journalists in order to make an announcement or answer questions.

press gang ▸n. historical a group of men employed to force other men to serve in the army or navy. ▸v. (**press-gang**) force someone to do something: *we press-ganged Simon into playing.*

press·ing /'presɪŋ/ ▸adj. **1** requiring urgent action. **2** expressing something strongly. ▸n. a record or other object made by molding material under pressure.

press·man /'pres,mən, ,man/ ▸n. (pl. **pressmen**) chiefly Brit. a journalist.

press re·lease ▸n. an official statement issued to journalists.

pres·sure /'preshər/ ▸n. **1** the steady force brought to bear on an object by something in contact with it. **2** the use of persuasion or intimidation to make someone do something. **3** a feeling of stress caused by having many demands on one's time or resources: *she resigned due to the pressure of work.* **4** the force per unit area applied by a fluid against a surface. ▸v. try to persuade or force someone to do something.

pres·sure cook·er ▸n. an airtight pot in which food can be cooked quickly under steam pressure.

pres·sure group ▸n. a group that tries to influence government policy and public opinion in the interest of a particular cause.

pres·sur·ize /'preshə,rīz/ ▸v. **1** keep the air pressure in an aircraft cabin the same as it is at ground level. **2** try to persuade or force someone to do something. ■ **pres·sur·i·za·tion** /,preshərə'zāshən/ n.

pres·ti·dig·i·ta·tion /,prestə,dijə'tāshən/ ▸n. formal magic tricks performed as entertainment. ■ **pres·ti·dig·i·ta·tor** /-'dijə,tātər/ n.

pres·tige /pres'tēzн, -'tēj/ ▸n. respect and admiration resulting from achievements or high quality: *her prestige in Europe was tremendous.*

pres·tig·ious /pre'stijəs, -'stē-/ ▸adj. having or bringing respect and admiration.

pres·to /'prestō/ ▸adv. & adj. Music in a quick tempo. ▸exclam. suggesting that something has been done so easily that it seems to be magic.

pre·stressed /prē'strest/ ▸adj. (of concrete) strengthened by means of rods or wires inserted under tension before setting.

pre·sum·a·bly /pri'zōōməblē/ ▸adv. as may be supposed; probably.

pre·sume /pri'zōōm/ ▸v. **1** suppose that something is probably the case. **2** be bold enough to do something that one does not have the right to do: *don't presume to give me orders in my own house.* **3** (**presume on/upon**) take advantage of someone's friendship or good nature. ■ **pre·sum·a·ble** adj.

pre·sump·tion /pri'zəmpshən/ ▸n. **1** an act of presuming something to be the case. **2** an idea that is presumed to be true. **3** disrespectful or excessively bold behavior.

pre·sump·tive /pri'zəmptiv/ ▸adj. **1** presumed in the absence of further information. **2** behaving with disrespectful boldness; presumptuous. ■ **pre·sump·tive·ly** adv.

pre·sump·tu·ous /pri'zəmpcн(ōō)əs/ ▸adj. behaving with disrespectful boldness. ■ **pre·sump·tu·ous·ly** adv. **pre·sump·tu·ous·ness** n.

pre·sup·pose /,prēsə'pōz/ ▸v. **1** depend on something in order to exist or be true. **2** assume something to be the case. ■ **pre·sup·po·si·tion** /,prē,səpə'zishən/ n.

pre·tend /pri'tend/ ▸v. **1** make it appear that something is the case when in fact it is not: *she turned the pages and pretended to read.* **2** (of a child) play an imaginative game. **3** give the appearance of feeling an emotion or having a quality. **4** (**pretend to**) claim to have a quality or title. ▸adj. informal imaginary; make-believe.

pre·tend·er /pri'tendər/ ▸n. a person who claims to have a right to a title or position.

pre·tense /'prē,tens, pri'tens/ ▸n. **1** an attempt to make something that is not the case appear true: *his anger was masked by a pretense that all was well.* **2** affected and pretentious behavior. **3** (**pretense to**) a claim to have or be something.

pre·ten·sion /pri'tenchən/ ▸n. **1** (often **pretensions**) a claim to a quality: *an aging rocker with literary pretensions.* **2** the action of trying to appear more important or better than one actually is.

pre·ten·tious /pri'tenchəs/ ▸adj. attempting to impress others by pretending to be more important or better than one actually is. ■ **pre·ten·tious·ly** adv. **pre·ten·tious·ness** n.

pret·er·it /'pretərit/ (also **preterite**) Grammar ▸adj. expressing a past action or state. ▸n. a simple past tense or form.

pre·term /prē'tərm/ ▸adj. & adv. after a pregnancy significantly shorter than normal: *babies born during preterm labor.*

pre·ter·nat·u·ral /,prētər'nacн(ə)rəl/ ▸adj. beyond what is normal or natural. ■ **pre·ter·nat·u·ral·ly** adv.

pre·text /'prē,tekst/ ▸n. a false reason used to justify an action.

pre·tor /'prētər/ ▸n. variant spelling of PRAETOR.

pre·treat /prē'trēt/ ▸v. treat something with a chemical before use. ■ **pre·treat·ment** n.

pret·ti·fy /'pritə,fī/ ▸v. (**prettifies, prettifying, prettified**) make something appear pretty. ■ **pret·ti·fi·ca·tion** /,pritəfə'kāshən/ n.

pret·ty /'pritē/ ▸adj. (**prettier, prettiest**) **1** (of a woman or girl) attractive in a delicate way. **2** pleasant in appearance: *a pretty dress.* **3** informal used to express displeasure: *a pretty state of affairs.* ▸adv. informal to a certain extent; fairly. ▸n. (pl. **pretties**) informal a pretty object. ■ **pret·ti·ly** adv. **pret·ti·ness** n.
– PHRASES **be sitting pretty** informal be in a favorable position. **a pretty penny** informal a large sum of money.

pret·zel /'pretsəl/ ▸n. a crisp or soft bread baked in the shape of a knot or stick and flavored with salt.

pre·vail /pri'vāl/ ▸v. **1** be widespread or current: *a friendly atmosphere prevailed among the crowds.* **2** be more powerful: *it is hard for logic to prevail over emotion.* **3** (**prevail on**) persuade someone to do something. ■ **pre·vail·ing** adj.

pre·vail·ing wind ▸n. a wind from the predominant or most usual direction.

prev·a·lent /'prevələnt/ ▶ adj. widespread in a particular area at a particular time. ■ **prev·a·lence** n.

pre·var·i·cate /pri'vari,kāt/ ▶ v. avoid giving a direct answer to a question. ■ **pre·var·i·ca·tion** /pri,vari'kāshən/ n. **pre·var·i·ca·tor** n.

pre·vent /pri'vent/ ▶ v. **1** stop something from happening or arising. **2** stop someone from doing something. ■ **pre·vent·a·ble** adj. **pre·vent·er** n. **pre·ven·tion** /pri'venchən/ n.

pre·ven·tive /pri'ventiv/ (also **preventative**) ▶ adj. designed to prevent something from happening. ▶ n. a medicine or other treatment intended to prevent disease or poor health.

pre·view /'prē,vyōō/ ▶ n. **1** a viewing or display of something before it becomes generally available. **2** a publicity article or trailer of a forthcoming movie, book, etc. ▶ v. provide or have a preview of a product, movie, etc. ■ **pre·view·er** n.

pre·vi·ous /'prēvēəs/ ▶ adj. **1** coming before in time or order. **2** informal too hasty in acting. ■ **pre·vi·ous·ly** adv.
– PHRASES **previous to** before.

pre·war /prē'wôr/ ▶ adj. occurring or existing before a war.

prey /prā/ ▶ n. **1** an animal hunted and killed by another for food. **2** a person who is easily exploited or harmed. **3** a person prone to experiencing distressing emotions. ▶ v. (**prey on**) **1** hunt and kill another animal for food. **2** take advantage of someone. **3** cause constant distress to: *the problem had begun to prey on my mind.*

pri·ap·ic /prī'apik, -'āpik/ ▶ adj. **1** relating to male sexuality. **2** relating to an erect penis. ■ **pri·a·pism** /'prīə,pizəm/ n.

price /prīs/ ▶ n. **1** the amount of money for which something is bought or sold. **2** something unwelcome that has to be done or given in order to achieve an aim: *some inequality would be a fair price to pay for a society where there is no poverty.* **3** the odds in betting. ▶ v. decide the price of something.
– PHRASES **at any price** no matter what is involved. **at a price** at a high cost. **what price something?** what has become of or what is the chance of something?

price·less /'prīsləs/ ▶ adj. **1** very valuable or precious. **2** informal very amusing.

price tag ▶ n. the cost of something.

pric·ey /'prīsē/ ▶ adj. (**pricier, priciest**) informal expensive.

prick /prik/ ▶ v. **1** make a small hole in something with a sharp point. **2** feel as though a sharp point or points were sticking into one. **3** cause mental or emotional discomfort to: *her conscience pricked her when she lied.* ▶ n. **1** an act of pricking someone or something. **2** a sharp pain, hole, or mark caused by pricking. **3** vulgar slang a man's penis. **4** vulgar slang a stupid or unpleasant man. ■ **prick·er** n.
– PHRASES **kick against the pricks** hurt oneself by continuing to resist something that cannot be changed. **prick up one's ears 1** (of a horse or dog) make the ears stand erect when alert. **2** (of a person) suddenly begin to pay attention.

prick·le /'prikəl/ ▶ n. **1** a small thorn on a plant or a short spine on an animal. **2** a tingling or mildly painful feeling on the skin. ▶ v. have a tingling feeling on the skin.

prick·ly /'prik(ə)lē/ ▶ adj. (**pricklier, prickliest**) **1** covered in prickles. **2** having or causing a prickling feeling. **3** easily offended.

prick·ly heat ▶ n. an itchy skin rash experienced in hot moist weather.

prick·ly pear ▶ n. a cactus that produces prickly, pear-shaped fruits.

pride /prīd/ ▶ n. **1** deep pleasure or satisfaction gained from achievements, qualities, or possessions. **2** a cause or source of deep pleasure or satisfaction: *the swimming pool was the pride of the village.* **3** a feeling of self-respect. **4** an excessively high opinion of oneself. **5** a group of lions forming a social unit. ▶ v. (**pride oneself on**) be especially proud of a quality or skill. ■ **pride·ful** /-fəl/ adj.
– PHRASES **pride of place** the most noticeable position.

prie-dieu /prē 'dyə(r), -'dyœ/ ▶ n. (pl. **prie-dieux** pronunc. same) a piece of furniture used for prayer, consisting of a kneeling surface and a narrow upright front with a rest for the elbows or for books.

priest /prēst/ ▶ n. **1** an ordained minister of the Catholic, Orthodox, or Anglican Church, authorized to perform certain ceremonies. **2** a person who performs ceremonies in a non-Christian religion. ■ **priest·hood** /'prēst,hŏŏd, 'prē,stŏŏd/ n. **priest·ly** adj.

priest·ess /'prēstis/ ▶ n. a female priest of a non-Christian religion.

prig /prig/ ▶ n. a person who behaves as if they are morally superior to others. ■ **prig·gish** adj.

prim /prim/ ▶ adj. (**primmer, primmest**) very formal and correct and disapproving of anything improper or rude. ■ **prim·ly** adv. **prim·ness** n.

pri·ma bal·le·ri·na /'prēmə/ ▶ n. the chief female dancer in a ballet or ballet company.

pri·ma·cy /'prīməsē/ ▶ n. the fact of being primary or most important.

pri·ma don·na /,primə 'dänə, ,prēmə/ ▶ n. **1** the chief female singer in an opera or opera company. **2** a very temperamental and self-important person.

pri·ma fa·ci·e /,prīmə 'fāshə, 'fāshē, 'fāshē,ē/ ▶ adj. & adv. Law accepted as correct until proved otherwise.

pri·mal /'prīməl/ ▶ adj. **1** at a very primitive or early stage of development; primeval. **2** Psychology relating to feelings or behavior believed to form the origins of emotional life: *primal fears.*

pri·ma·ri·ly /prī'me(ə)rəlē/ ▶ adv. for the most part; mainly.

pri·ma·ry /'prī,merē, 'prīm(ə)rē/ ▶ adj. **1** of chief importance; principal. **2** earliest in time or order. **3** relating to education for children between the ages of about five and eleven. ▶ n. (pl. **primaries**) a preliminary election to appoint delegates to a party conference or to select candidates for an election.

pri·ma·ry care ▶ n. health care received by people making an initial approach to a doctor or nurse for treatment.

pri·ma·ry col·or ▶ n. any of a group of colors from which all others can be obtained by mixing.

pri·ma·ry in·dus·try ▶ n. an industry concerned with obtaining or providing raw materials, such as mining or agriculture.

pri·mate /'prī,māt, 'prīmət/ ▶ n. **1** a mammal of an order including monkeys, apes, and humans. **2** (in the Christian Church) an archbishop.

pri·ma·tol·o·gy /ˌprīməˈtäləjē/ ▶ n. the branch of zoology concerned with monkeys and other primates. ■ **pri·ma·tol·o·gist** n.

prime¹ /prīm/ ▶ adj. 1 most important; main. 2 of the highest quality; excellent. 3 (of a number) that can be divided only by itself and one (e.g., 2, 3, 5, 7). ▶ n. 1 a time of greatest vigor or success in a person's life. 2 a prime number.

prime² ▶ v. 1 prepare someone for a situation by giving them relevant information. 2 make something, especially a firearm or bomb, ready for use or action. 3 cover a surface with primer. 4 pour or spray liquid into a pump to make it operate more easily.
– PHRASES **prime the pump** stimulate the growth or success of something with funding.

prime min·is·ter ▶ n. the head of the elected government in some countries, such as the UK and Canada.

prime mov·er ▶ n. a person who originates a plan or project.

prim·er¹ /ˈprīmər/ ▶ n. a substance painted on a surface as a base coat.

prim·er² ▶ n. a book providing a basic introduction to a subject or used for teaching reading.

prime rate ▶ n. the lowest rate of interest at which money may be borrowed commercially.

prime time ▶ n. the time at which a radio or television audience is expected to be greatest.

pri·me·val /prīˈmēvəl/ ▶ adj. 1 relating to the earliest time in history. 2 (of behavior or emotion) not based on reason; instinctive.

prim·i·tive /ˈprimitiv/ ▶ adj. 1 relating to the earliest times in history or stages in development of something: *primitive mammals.* 2 referring to a simple form of society that has not yet developed writing or industry. 3 offering a very basic level of comfort or convenience. 4 (of behavior or emotion) not based on reason; instinctive. ▶ n. 1 a person belonging to a primitive society. 2 a painter who deliberately uses a simple, naive style that rejects conventional techniques. ■ **prim·i·tive·ly** adv. **prim·i·tive·ness** n.

prim·i·tiv·ism /ˈprimitivˌizəm/ ▶ n. 1 a belief in the value of what is simple and unsophisticated, expressed especially through art or literature. 2 instinctive and unreasoning behavior. ■ **prim·i·tiv·ist** n. & adj.

pri·mo·gen·i·ture /ˌprīmōˈjeniˌCHər, -ˌCHŏŏr/ ▶ n. 1 the state of being the firstborn child. 2 the system by which the firstborn child, especially the eldest son, inherits all his parents' property.

pri·mor·di·al /prīˈmôrdēəl/ ▶ adj. existing at or from the beginning of time; primeval.

pri·mor·di·al soup ▶ n. a solution rich in organic compounds from which life on earth is supposed to have originated.

primp /primp/ ▶ v. make minor adjustments to one's hair, clothes, or makeup.

prim·rose /ˈprimˌrōz/ ▶ n. 1 a plant of European woodlands with pale yellow flowers. 2 a pale yellow color.
– PHRASES **primrose path** the pursuit of pleasure, especially when bringing undesirable consequences.

prim·u·la /ˈprimyələ/ ▶ n. a plant of a genus that includes primroses, cowslips, and polyanthus.

prince /prins/ ▶ n. 1 a son or other close male relative of a monarch. 2 a male monarch of a small country. 3 (in some European countries) a nobleman. ■ **prince·dom** /dəm/ n.

Prince Charm·ing ▶ n. a handsome and honorable young male lover.

prince con·sort ▶ n. the husband of a reigning queen who is himself a prince.

prince·ling /ˈprinsliNG/ ▶ n. 1 the ruler of a small or unimportant country. 2 a young prince.

prince·ly /ˈprinslē/ ▶ adj. 1 relating to or suitable for a prince. 2 (of a sum of money) generous.

Prince of Dark·ness ▶ n. the Devil.

Prince of Wales ▶ n. a title granted to the heir apparent to the British throne (usually the eldest son of the monarch).

prin·cess /ˈprinsəs, ˈprinˌses, prinˈses/ ▶ n. 1 a daughter or other close female relative of a monarch. 2 the wife or widow of a prince. 3 a female monarch of a small country.

prin·ci·pal /ˈprinsəpəl/ ▶ adj. most important; main. ▶ n. 1 the most important person in an organization or group. 2 the head of a school. 3 a sum of money lent or invested, on which interest is paid. 4 a person for whom another acts as a representative. 5 Law a person directly responsible for a crime. ■ **prin·ci·pal·ship** /-ˌSHip/ n.

> **USAGE**
> Do not confuse **principal** and **principle**. **Principal** is usually an adjective meaning 'main or most important' (*the country's principal cities*), whereas **principle** is a noun that usually means 'a truth or general law used as the basis for something' (*the basic principles of democracy*).

prin·ci·pal·i·ty /ˌprinsəˈpalətē/ ▶ n. (pl. **principalities**) a country ruled by a prince.

prin·ci·pal·ly /ˈprinsəp(ə)lē/ ▶ adv. for the most part; mainly.

prin·ci·ple /ˈprinsəpəl/ ▶ n. 1 a truth or general law that is used as a basis for a theory or system of belief: *the basic principles of democracy.* 2 (usu. **principles**) a rule or belief governing a person's behavior. 3 morally correct behavior: *a man of principle.* 4 a general scientific theorem or natural law. 5 a fundamental quality or basis of something. 6 Chemistry an active or characteristic constituent of a substance.
– PHRASES **in principle** in theory. **on principle** because of one's beliefs about what is right and wrong.

prin·ci·pled /ˈprinsəpəld/ ▶ adj. (of actions or behavior) based on one's beliefs about what is right and wrong.

print /print/ ▶ v. 1 produce books, newspapers, etc., by a process involving the transfer of words or images to paper. 2 produce words or an image by printing. 3 produce a paper copy of information stored on a computer. 4 produce a photographic print from a negative. 5 write words clearly without joining the letters. 6 transfer a colored design onto fabric or another surface. ▶ n. 1 the printed words appearing in a book, newspaper, etc. 2 a mark where something has pressed or touched a surface: *paw prints.* 3 a printed picture or design. 4 a photograph printed on paper from a negative or transparency. 5 a copy of a motion picture on film. 6 a piece of fabric with a colored design. ■ **print·a·ble** adj.
– PHRASES **in print 1** (of a book) available from the publisher. 2 in published form. **out of print** (of a book) no longer available from the publisher.

print·ed cir·cuit ▶ n. an electronic circuit based on thin strips of a conductor on an insulating board.

print·er /'printər/ ▶ n. 1 a person or business involved in printing. 2 a machine for printing, especially one linked to a computer.

print·ing /'printiNG/ ▶ n. 1 the production of books, newspapers, etc. 2 all the copies of a book printed at one time. 3 handwriting in which the letters are written separately.

print·ing press ▶ n. a machine for printing from type or plates.

print·mak·er /'print,mākər/ ▶ n. a person who creates and prints pictures or designs from plates or blocks. ■ **print·mak·ing** n.

print·out /'print,out/ ▶ n. a page of printed material from a computer's printer.

print run ▶ n. the number of copies of a book, magazine, etc., printed at one time.

pri·on /'prē,än/ ▶ n. a protein particle believed to be the cause of certain brain diseases, such as BSE.

pri·or¹ /'prīər/ ▶ adj. coming before in time, order, or importance: *the government denied having any prior knowledge of the attack.*
– PHRASES **prior to** before.

pri·or² ▶ n. (fem. **prioress** /'prīərəs/) 1 (in an abbey) the person next in rank below an abbot (or abbess). 2 the head of a house of friars (or nuns).

pri·or·i·tize /prī'ôrə,tīz, 'prīərə-/ ▶ v. 1 treat something as most important. 2 decide the order of importance of items or tasks. ■ **pri·or·i·ti·za·tion** /,prī,ôrətə'zāsHən/ n.

pri·or·i·ty /prī'ôrətē/ ▶ n. (pl. **priorities**) 1 the condition of being treated as more important: *safety should take priority over any other matter.* 2 a thing regarded as more important than others.

pri·or re·straint ▶ n. Law suppression of material before it is published or broadcast, on the grounds that it is libelous or harmful.

pri·o·ry /'prīərē/ ▶ n. (pl. **priories**) a monastery or nunnery governed by a prior or prioress.

prise ▶ v. variant spelling of PRIZE².

prism /'prizəm/ ▶ n. 1 a transparent object with triangular ends that breaks light up into the colors of the rainbow. 2 a solid geometric figure whose two ends are parallel and of the same size and shape, and whose sides are parallelograms.

pris·mat·ic /priz'matik/ ▶ adj. 1 relating to or in the shape of a prism. 2 (of colors) formed or distributed by a prism.

pris·on /'prizən/ ▶ n. a building in which criminals or people awaiting trial are confined.

pris·on camp ▶ n. a camp where prisoners of war or political prisoners are kept.

pris·on·er /'priz(ə)nər/ ▶ n. 1 a person found guilty of a crime and sent to prison. 2 a person captured and kept confined. 3 a person trapped by a situation: *he was a prisoner of his own fame.*
– PHRASES **take no prisoners** be ruthless in attempting to achieve one's objectives.

pris·on·er of con·science ▶ n. a person imprisoned for their political or religious views.

pris·on·er of war ▶ n. a person captured and imprisoned by the enemy in war.

pris·sy /'prisē/ ▶ adj. (**prissier**, **prissiest**) excessively concerned with behaving in a respectable way. ■ **pris·si·ly** adv. **pris·si·ness** n.

pris·tine /'pris,tēn, pri'stēn/ ▶ adj. 1 in its original condition; unspoiled: *two miles of pristine beaches.* 2 clean and fresh as if new. ■ **pris·tine·ly** adv.

pri·va·cy /'prīvəsē/ ▶ n. a state in which one is not watched or disturbed by others.

pri·vate /'prīvit/ ▶ adj. 1 for or belonging to one particular person or group only: *his private plane.* 2 (of thoughts or feelings) not to be revealed to others. 3 not revealing thoughts and feelings to others. 4 (of a service or industry) provided by a person or commercial business rather than the government. 5 working for oneself rather than for the government or an organization. 6 not connected with one's work or official position: *the president visited the country in a private capacity.* 7 (of a place) free from people who may overhear or interrupt.
▶ n. 1 (also **private soldier**) a soldier of the lowest rank in the army. 2 (**privates**) informal private parts; genitals. ■ **pri·vate·ly** adv.
– PHRASES **in private** with no one else present.

pri·vate en·ter·prise ▶ n. business or industry managed by independent companies rather than by the government.

pri·va·teer /,prīvə'tir/ ▶ n. historical a privately owned armed ship, authorized by a government for use in war.

pri·vate eye ▶ n. informal a private investigator.

pri·vate in·ves·ti·ga·tor (also **private detective**) ▶ n. a detective who is not a police officer and who carries out investigations for private clients.

pri·vate life ▶ n. a person's personal relationships, interests, etc., as distinct from their work or public life.

pri·vate parts ▶ pl.n. euphemistic a person's genitals.

pri·vate school ▶ n. 1 a school supported by a private organization or individuals. 2 Brit. an independent school that is wholly financed by fees paid by students.

pri·vate sec·re·tar·y ▶ n. 1 a secretary who deals with the personal matters of their employer. 2 a civil servant acting as an assistant to a senior government official.

pri·vate sec·tor ▶ n. the part of a country's economy not under direct government control.

pri·va·tion /prī'vāsHən/ ▶ n. a state in which essentials such as food are lacking.

pri·va·tize /'prīvə,tīz/ ▶ v. transfer a business or industry from public to private ownership. ■ **pri·va·ti·za·tion** /,prīvətə'zāsHən/ n.

priv·et /'privit/ ▶ n. a shrub with small dark green leaves.

priv·i·lege /'priv(ə)lij/ ▶ n. 1 a special right or advantage granted or available to a particular person or group. 2 an opportunity to do something regarded as a special honor: *she had the privilege of giving the opening lecture.* 3 the rights and advantages of rich and powerful people: *a young man of wealth and privilege.*

priv·i·leged /'priv(ə)lijd/ ▶ adj. 1 having a special right or advantage. 2 (of information) legally protected from being made public.

priv·y /'privē/ ▶ adj. (**privy to**) sharing in the knowledge of something secret. ▶ n. (pl. **privies**) a toilet in a small shed outside a house. ■ **priv·i·ly** adv.

prix fixe /'prē 'fēks, 'fiks/ ▶ n. a meal of several courses costing a fixed price.

prize¹ /'prīz/ ▶ n. 1 something given as a reward

to a winner or to recognize an outstanding achievement. **2** something of great value that is worth struggling to achieve: *the prize will be victory in the election.* ▸ **adj. 1** having been or likely to be awarded a prize. **2** outstanding of its kind. ▸ **v.** value highly: *the berries were prized for their healing properties.*

prize² /prīz/ (also **prise**) ▸ **v. 1** force something open or apart. **2** (**prize something out of/from**) obtain something from someone with difficulty.

prize·fight /'prīz‚fīt/ ▸ **n.** a boxing match for prize money. ■ **prize·fight·er** n.

pro¹ /prō/ ▸ **n.** (pl. **pros**) informal a professional. ▸ **adj.** professional.

pro² ▸ **n.** (pl. **pros**) (usu. in phrase **pros and cons**) an advantage or argument in favor of something. ▸ **prep. & adv.** in favor of.

pro-¹ ▸ **prefix 1** in favor of; supporting: *pro-choice.* **2** referring to movement forward, out, or away: *propel.* **3** acting as a substitute for: *proconsul.*

pro-² ▸ **prefix** before in time or order: *proactive.*

pro·ac·tive /prō'aktiv/ ▸ **adj.** creating or controlling a situation rather than just responding to it. ■ **pro·ac·tive·ly** adv.

pro-am /'prō 'am/ ▸ **adj.** (of a sports event) involving both professionals and amateurs.

prob·a·bi·lis·tic /‚präbəbə'listik/ ▸ **adj.** based on a theory of probability; involving chance.

prob·a·bil·i·ty /‚präbə'bilətē/ ▸ **n.** (pl. **probabilities**) **1** the extent to which something is likely to happen or be the case: *rain will make the probability of postponement even greater.* **2** a probable or the most probable event.
– PHRASES **in all probability** most probably.

prob·a·ble /'präbəbəl/ ▸ **adj.** likely to happen or be the case. ▸ **n.** a person likely to become or do something.

prob·a·bly /'präbəblē, 'präblē/ ▸ **adv.** almost certainly.

pro·bate /'prō‚bāt/ ▸ **n. 1** the official process of proving that a will is valid. **2** a verified copy of a will with a certificate as handed to the executors.

pro·ba·tion /prō'bāsHən/ ▸ **n. 1** the release of an offender from detention or prison on condition that they behave well and report regularly to a supervisor. **2** a period of training and testing a person in a new job or role. ■ **pro·ba·tion·ar·y** /-‚nerē/ adj.

pro·ba·tion·er /prō'bāsHənər/ ▸ **n. 1** a person serving a period of probation in a job or role. **2** an offender on probation from detention or prison.

pro·ba·tion of·fi·cer ▸ **n.** a person who supervises offenders on probation.

probe /prōb/ ▸ **n. 1** a thorough investigation: *a probe into political corruption.* **2** a blunt-ended surgical instrument for exploring a wound or part of the body. **3** a small measuring or testing device, especially an electrode. **4** an unmanned exploratory spacecraft. ▸ **v. 1** investigate something thoroughly. **2** explore or examine something with the hands or an instrument. ■ **prob·er** n. **prob·ing** adj.

pro·bi·ot·ic /‚prōbī'ätik/ ▸ **n.** a substance that stimulates the growth of beneficial microorganisms, especially the natural bacteria in the intestines.

pro·bi·ty /'prōbitē/ ▸ **n.** the quality of having strong moral principles; honesty and good character.

prob·lem /'präbləm/ ▸ **n. 1** a thing that is difficult to deal with or understand. **2** a question that can be resolved by using logical thought or mathematics.

prob·lem·at·ic /‚präblə'matik/ ▸ **adj.** difficult to deal with or understand; presenting a problem. ■ **prob·lem·at·i·cal** adj. **prob·lem·at·i·cal·ly** adv.

prob·lem·a·tize /'präbləmə‚tīz/ ▸ **v.** make something into or regard something as a problem.

pro bo·no /‚prō 'bônô, 'bōnō/ ▸ **adv. & adj.** referring to legal work undertaken without charge.

pro·bos·cis /prə'bäsəs, -'bäskəs/ ▸ **n.** (pl. **proboscises** /-'bäsēz/ or **proboscises**) **1** the long flexible nose of a mammal, such as an elephant's trunk. **2** an elongated sucking organ or mouthpart of an insect or worm.

pro·bos·cis mon·key ▸ **n.** a monkey native to the forests of Borneo, the male of which has a large dangling nose.

pro·caine /'prō‚kān/ ▸ **n.** a synthetic compound used as a local anesthetic.

pro·car·y·ote ▸ **n.** variant spelling of PROKARYOTE.

pro·ce·dure /prə'sējər/ ▸ **n. 1** an established or official way of doing something. **2** a series of actions carried out in a certain way. **3** a surgical operation. ■ **pro·ce·dur·al** adj. **pro·ce·dur·al·ly** adv.

pro·ceed /prə'sēd, prō-/ ▸ **v. 1** begin a course of action. **2** do something after something else: *she got up and proceeded to cook us breakfast.* **3** (of an action) continue. **4** move forward. **5** start a lawsuit against someone.

pro·ceed·ings /prə'sēdiNGz, prō-/ ▸ **pl.n. 1** an event or a series of activities with a set procedure. **2** action taken in a court of law to settle a dispute. **3** a report of a set of meetings or a conference.

pro·ceeds /'prō‚sēdz/ ▸ **pl.n.** money obtained from an event or activity.

proc·ess¹ /'prä‚ses, 'präsəs, 'prō-/ ▸ **n. 1** a series of actions or steps taken toward achieving a particular end. **2** a natural series of changes: *the aging process.* **3** a summons to appear in a court of law. **4** a natural projection or growth on the body or in an organism. ▸ **v. 1** treat raw material, food, etc., in order to change or preserve it. **2** deal with by means of an established procedure: *an administrator is needed to process applications.* **3** operate on data by means of a computer program.

proc·ess² /prə'ses/ ▸ **v.** (of people or vehicles) move forward in an orderly way.

pro·ces·sion /prə'sesHən/ ▸ **n. 1** a number of people or vehicles moving forward in an orderly way. **2** the action of moving forward in an orderly way. **3** a large number of people or things coming one after the other.

pro·ces·sion·al /prə'sesHənl/ ▸ **adj.** relating to a religious or ceremonial procession. ▸ **n.** a book of litanies and hymns used in Christian religious processions.

proc·es·sor /'präs‚esər, 'präsəsər, 'prō-/ ▸ **n. 1** a machine that processes something. **2** a central processing unit in a computer.

pro-choice /prō'CHois/ ▸ **adj.** supporting the right of a woman to choose to have an abortion.

pro·claim /prə'klām, prō-/ ▸ **v. 1** announce something officially or publicly. **2** declare someone officially or publicly to be: *he proclaimed James as King of England.* **3** show clearly; be a sign of: *his high forehead proclaimed his strength of mind.* ■ **proc·la·ma·tion** /ˌpräklə'māsнən/ n.

pro·cliv·i·ty /prō'klivətē, prə-/ ▶ n. (pl. **proclivities**) a tendency to do something regularly; an inclination.

pro·con·sul /prō'känsəl/ ▶ n. 1 a governor or deputy consul of a colony. 2 a governor of a province in ancient Rome.

pro·cras·ti·nate /prə'krastəˌnāt, prō-/ ▶ v. delay or postpone action. ■ **pro·cras·ti·na·tion** /prəˌkrastə'nāsнən, prō-/ n. **pro·cras·ti·na·tor** /-ˌnātər/ n.

pro·cre·ate /'prōkrēˌāt/ ▶ v. produce young; reproduce. ■ **pro·cre·a·tion** /ˌprōkrē'āsнən/ n. **pro·cre·a·tive** /-krēˌātiv/ adj.

Pro·crus·te·an /prə'krəstēən, prō-/ ▶ adj. literary enforcing uniformity regardless of natural variation or individuality.

proc·tol·o·gy /präk'täləjē/ ▶ n. the branch of medicine concerned with the anus and rectum. ■ **proc·to·log·i·cal** /ˌpräktə'läjikəl/ adj. **proc·tol·o·gist** n.

proc·tor /'präktər/ ▶ n. a person who monitors students during an examination.

proc·u·ra·tor /'präkyəˌrātər/ ▶ n. an agent representing others in a court of law.

pro·cure /prə'kyŏŏr, prō-/ ▶ v. 1 get or obtain something. 2 Law persuade or cause someone to do something. 3 provide a prostitute for someone. ■ **pro·cur·a·ble** adj. **pro·cure·ment** n. **pro·cur·er** n.

prod /präd/ ▶ v. (**prods, prodding, prodded**) 1 poke someone or something with a finger or pointed object. 2 persuade someone who is reluctant or slow to do something. ▶ n. 1 a poke. 2 a reminder to do something. 3 a pointed implement used to drive cattle.

prod·i·gal /'prädəgəl/ ▶ adj. 1 using money or resources in a wasteful way. 2 (**prodigal with**) having lavish amounts of something. ▶ n. 1 a wasteful and extravagant person. 2 (also **prodigal son**) a person who leaves home and lives a wasteful and extravagant life but returns repentant. ■ **prod·i·gal·i·ty** /ˌprädə'galətē/ n. **prod·i·gal·ly** adv.

pro·di·gious /prə'dijəs/ ▶ adj. impressively large. ■ **pro·di·gious·ly** adv.

prod·i·gy /'prädəjē/ ▶ n. (pl. **prodigies**) 1 a young person with exceptional abilities. 2 an outstanding example of a quality: *his book is a prodigy of information gathering.*

pro·duce ▶ v. /prə'd(y)ōōs, prō-/ 1 make, manufacture, or create something. 2 cause to happen or exist: *a report has concluded that richer colleges produce better results.* 3 show or provide something for inspection or use. 4 administer the financial and managerial aspects of a movie or broadcast or the staging of a play. 5 supervise the making of a musical recording. ▶ n. /'präd(y)ōōs, 'prō-/ things that have been produced or grown: *fresh produce from the garden.* ■ **pro·duc·er** n. **pro·duc·i·ble** adj.

prod·uct /'prädəkt/ ▶ n. 1 an article or substance manufactured for sale. 2 a result of an action or process: *the arrests were the product of a lengthy investigation.* 3 a substance produced during a natural, chemical, or manufacturing process. 4 Mathematics a quantity obtained by multiplying quantities together.

pro·duc·tion /prə'dəksнən, prō-/ ▶ n. 1 the action of producing something or the process of being produced. 2 the amount of something produced. 3 a movie, play, or music recording viewed in terms of the way it is made or staged: *a new production of* Hamlet.

pro·duc·tion line ▶ n. an assembly line in a factory.

pro·duc·tive /prə'dəktiv, prō-/ ▶ adj. 1 producing or able to produce large amounts of goods or crops. 2 achieving or producing a significant amount or result: *a long and productive career.* ■ **pro·duc·tive·ly** adv. **pro·duc·tive·ness** n.

pro·duc·tiv·i·ty /ˌprō,dək'tivətē, ˌprädək-, prə,dək-/ ▶ n. 1 the state of being productive. 2 the efficiency with which things are produced: *workers boosted productivity by 30 percent.*

prod·uct place·ment ▶ n. a practice in which companies pay for their products to be featured in movies and television programs.

pro·fane /prə'fān, prō-/ ▶ adj. 1 not holy or religious; secular. 2 not showing respect for God or holy things. 3 (of language) blasphemous or obscene. ▶ v. treat something holy with disrespect. ■ **prof·a·na·tion** /ˌpräfə'nāsнən, ˌprō-/ n.

pro·fan·i·ty /prə'fanətē, prō-/ ▶ n. (pl. **profanities**) 1 behavior that shows a lack of respect for God or holy things. 2 a swear word.

pro·fess /prə'fes, prō-/ ▶ v. 1 claim, often falsely, that something is true or the case: *she lied, cheated, and then professed her undying love.* 2 state openly that one has a particular feeling, opinion, etc. 3 belong to a particular religion.

pro·fessed /prə'fest, prō-/ ▶ adj. 1 (of a quality or feeling) claimed openly but often falsely. 2 openly declared to be: *a professed liberal.* ■ **pro·fess·ed·ly** /prə'fesədlē, -'festlē/ adv.

pro·fes·sion /prə'fesнən/ ▶ n. 1 an occupation that involves training and a formal qualification. 2 (treated as sing. or pl.) a group of people working in a profession: *the legal profession.* 3 a claim that is often false. 4 a declaration of belief in a religion.

pro·fes·sion·al /prə'fesнənl/ ▶ adj. 1 relating or belonging to a profession. 2 engaged in a sport or other activity as a paid occupation rather than as an amateur. 3 appropriate to a professional person; competent or skillful. ▶ n. 1 a person who is engaged or qualified in a profession. 2 a person who is very skilled in a particular activity. ■ **pro·fes·sion·al·ize** /prə'fesнənlˌīz/ v. **pro·fes·sion·al·ly** adv.

pro·fes·sion·al·ism /prə'fesнənlˌizəm/ ▶ n. the competence or skill expected of a professional.

pro·fes·sor /prə'fesər/ ▶ n. 1 a college or university teacher. 2 a university academic of the highest rank. 3 a person who openly declares their faith. ■ **pro·fes·so·ri·al** /ˌpräfə'sôrēəl/ adj. **pro·fes·sor·ship** /-ˌsнip/ n.

prof·fer /'präfər/ ▶ v. offer something to someone for acceptance.

pro·fi·cient /prə'fisнənt/ ▶ adj. competent or skilled in doing or using something: *she's proficient in Urdu.* ■ **pro·fi·cien·cy** n. **pro·fi·cient·ly** adv.

pro·file /'prōˌfīl/ ▶ n. 1 an outline of something, especially a face, as seen from one side. 2 a descriptive article about someone. 3 the extent to which a person or organization attracts

public notice: *her high profile as a pop star.*
▶ v. **1** describe someone in an article. **2** (**be profiled**) appear in outline. ■ **pro·fil·er** n.
– PHRASES **in profile** as seen from one side. **keep a low profile** try not to attract attention.

pro·fil·ing /ˈprōˌfīliNG/ ▶ n. the analysis of a person's psychological and behavioral characteristics.

prof·it /ˈpräfit/ ▶ n. **1** a financial gain, especially the difference between the amount earned and the costs involved in producing, buying, or operating something. **2** the advantage or benefit gained from something. ▶ v. (**profits, profiting, profited**) benefit, especially financially: *the only people to profit from the episode were the lawyers.* ■ **prof·it·less** adj.

prof·it·a·ble /ˈpräfitəbəl/ ▶ adj. **1** (of a business or activity) making a profit. **2** beneficial; useful: *he'd had a profitable day.* ■ **prof·it·a·bil·i·ty** /ˌpräfitəˈbilətē/ n. **prof·it·a·bly** adv.

prof·it and loss ac·count ▶ n. an account to which incomes and gains are added and expenses and losses taken away, so as to show the net profit or loss.

prof·it·eer·ing /ˌpräfəˈti(ə)riNG/ ▶ n. the making of an excessive profit in an unfair or dishonest way. ■ **prof·it·eer** /ˌpräfəˈti(ə)r/ n.

pro·fit·er·ole /prəˈfitəˌrōl/ ▶ n. a small hollow pastry filled with cream and covered with chocolate sauce.

prof·it mar·gin ▶ n. the difference between the cost of producing something and the price for which it is sold.

prof·it-shar·ing ▶ n. a system in which the people who work for a company receive a direct share of its profits.

prof·li·gate /ˈpräfligət, -ləˌgāt/ ▶ adj. **1** recklessly extravagant or wasteful. **2** indulging excessively in physical pleasures; licentious. ▶ n. a licentious or wasteful person. ■ **prof·li·ga·cy** /ˈpräfligəsē/ n.

pro for·ma /prō ˈfôrmə/ ▶ adv. & adj. as a matter of form or politeness. ▶ n. a standard document or form.

pro·found /prəˈfound, prō-/ ▶ adj. (**profounder, profoundest**) **1** very great or intense: *profound feelings of disquiet.* **2** showing great knowledge or insight. **3** demanding deep study or thought. **4** old use very deep. ■ **pro·found·ly** adv.

pro·fun·di·ty /prəˈfəndətē/ ▶ n. (pl. **profundities**) **1** great depth of insight or knowledge. **2** intensity of a state, quality, or emotion.

pro·fuse /prəˈfyōōs, prō-/ ▶ adj. done or appearing in large quantities; abundant: *I offered my profuse apologies.* ■ **pro·fuse·ly** adv.

pro·fu·sion /prəˈfyōōzHən, prō-/ ▶ n. a large quantity of something; an abundance.

pro·gen·i·tor /prōˈjenətər, prō-/ ▶ n. **1** an ancestor or parent. **2** a person who originates a cultural or intellectual movement. ■ **pro·gen·i·to·ri·al** /-jenəˈtôrēəl/ adj.

prog·e·ny /ˈpräjənē/ ▶ n. (treated as sing. or pl.) the offspring of a person or animal.

pro·ges·ter·one /prōˈjestəˌrōn, prə-/ ▶ n. a hormone that stimulates the uterus to prepare for pregnancy.

pro·ges·to·gen /prōˈjestəjən/ ▶ n. a hormone that maintains pregnancy and prevents further ovulation, used in oral contraceptives.

prog·na·thous /ˈprägnəTHəs, prägˈnā-/ ▶ adj. (of a jaw or chin) projecting.

prog·no·sis /prägˈnōsəs/ ▶ n. (pl. **prognoses**

/-ˌsēz/) a forecast, especially of the likely course of a medical condition.

prog·nos·tic /prägˈnästik/ ▶ adj. predicting the likely course of a medical condition. ■ **prog·nos·ti·cal·ly** /-ik(ə)lē/ adv.

prog·nos·ti·cate /prägˈnästəˌkāt/ ▶ v. make a forecast about a future event. ■ **prog·nos·ti·ca·tion** /prägˌnästəˈkāsHən/ n. **prog·nos·ti·ca·tor** /-ˌkātər/ n.

pro·gram /ˈprōˌgram, -grəm/ (Brit. **programme**) ▶ n. **1** a planned series of events. **2** a radio or television broadcast. **3** a set of related measures or activities with a long-term aim: *a program of reforms.* **4** a sheet or booklet giving details of a performance or event. **5** (Brit. **program**) a series of coded software instructions to control the operation of a computer or other machine. ▶ v. (**programs, programming, programmed**; or **programing, programed**) (Brit. **program**) provide a computer with a program. **2** cause a person or animal to behave in a predetermined way. **3** arrange something according to a plan or schedule. ■ **pro·gram·ma·ble** /ˈprōˌgraməbəl, prōˈgram-/ adj. **pro·gram·mer** n.

pro·gram·mat·ic /ˌprōgrəˈmatik/ ▶ adj. relating to a program, schedule, or method. ■ **pro·gram·mat·i·cal·ly** /-ik(ə)lē/ adv.

prog·ress ▶ n. /ˈprägrəs, ˈprägˌres, ˈprōˌgres/ **1** forward movement toward a destination. **2** development toward an improved or more advanced condition: *some states had made significant progress in nuclear technology.* ▶ v. /prəˈgres/ **1** move toward a destination. **2** develop toward a more advanced condition.

pro·gres·sion /prəˈgresHən/ ▶ n. **1** a gradual movement or development toward a destination or a more advanced state. **2** a number of things in a series. **3** a sequence of numbers following a mathematical rule. ■ **pro·gres·sion·al** adj.

pro·gres·sive /prəˈgresiv/ ▶ adj. **1** happening or developing gradually: *a progressive decline in popularity.* **2** favoring social reform or original thinking. **3** (of tax) at a rate increasing with the sum taxed. **4** (of a lens) allowing an infinite number of focusing distances for near, intermediate, and far vision. ▶ n. **1** a person who favors social reform. **2** (**progressives**) progressive lenses, or eyeglasses with such lenses. ■ **pro·gres·sive·ly** adv. **pro·gres·sive·ness** n.

pro·hib·it /prəˈhibit, prō-/ ▶ v. (**prohibits, prohibiting, prohibited**) **1** formally forbid someone from doing something by law or a rule. **2** make impossible; prevent: *the budget agreement had prohibited any tax cuts.* ■ **pro·hib·i·to·ry** /-ˌtôrē/ adj.

pro·hi·bi·tion /ˌprō(h)əˈbisHən/ ▶ n. **1** the action of formally forbidding something. **2** an order that forbids something. **3** (**Prohibition**) the prevention by law of the manufacture and sale of alcohol in the US from 1920 to 1933. ■ **Pro·hi·bi·tion·ist** n.

pro·hib·i·tive /prəˈhibitiv, prō-/ ▶ adj. **1** forbidding or preventing something. **2** (of a price) so high as to prevent something from being done or bought. ■ **pro·hib·i·tive·ly** adv.

proj·ect ▶ n. /ˈpräjˌekt, -ikt/ **1** an enterprise that is carefully planned to achieve a particular aim. **2** a piece of research work by a student. **3** a government-subsidized housing development. ▶ v. /prəˈjekt, prōˈjekt/ **1** estimate or forecast something on the basis of present trends.

2 plan a scheme. **3** stick out beyond something else. **4** throw or send something forward or outward. **5** cause light, shadow, or an image to fall on a surface. **6** present a particular image or impression: *he strives to project an image of youth.* **7** (**project something onto**) think that another person has the same feelings or emotions as oneself, especially unconsciously.

pro·jec·tile /prə'jektl, -ˌtīl/ ▶ n. a missile fired or thrown at a target. ▶ adj. **1** relating to a projectile. **2** propelled with great force.

pro·jec·tion /prə'jeksʜən/ ▶ n. **1** an estimate or forecast based on present trends. **2** a thing that sticks out from something. **3** the projecting of an image or sound. **4** the presentation of someone or something in a particular way: *the legal profession's projection of an image of altruism.* **5** a method for representing part of the surface of a solid object on a flat surface, used especially for making maps. ■ **pro·jec·tive** /prə'jektiv/ adj. **pro·jec·tion·ist** n.

pro·jec·tor /prə'jektər/ ▶ n. a device for projecting slides or film onto a screen.

pro·kar·y·ote /prō'karē,ōt/ (also **procaryote**) ▶ n. Biology a single-celled organism with neither a distinct nucleus with a membrane nor other specialized structures. Compare with EUKARYOTE.

pro·lapse /prō'laps, 'prō,laps/ ▶ n. **1** a condition in which a part or organ of the body has slipped forward or down. **2** a part or organ that has slipped forward or down. ■ **pro·lapsed** adj.

prole /prōl/ ▶ n. informal, derogatory a working-class person.

pro·le·gom·e·non /ˌprōlə'gämə,nän, -nən/ ▶ n. (pl. **prolegomena** /-nə/) a critical or discursive introduction to a book.

pro·le·tar·i·an /ˌprōli'te(ə)rēən/ ▶ adj. relating to workers or working-class people. ▶ n. a working-class person.

pro·le·tar·i·at /ˌprōli'te(ə)rēət/ ▶ n. (treated as sing. or pl.) workers or working-class people.

pro-life /prō'līf/ ▶ adj. opposing abortion and euthanasia. ■ **pro-lif·er** n.

pro·lif·er·ate /prə'lifə,rāt/ ▶ v. **1** increase rapidly in number: *the rave clubs that proliferated in the late Eighties.* **2** (of a cell or organism) reproduce rapidly. ■ **pro·lif·er·a·tion** /prə,lifə'rāsʜən/ n. **pro·lif·er·a·tive** /-,rātiv/ adj.

pro·lif·ic /prə'lifik/ ▶ adj. **1** producing much fruit or foliage or many offspring. **2** (of an artist, author, or composer) producing many works. **3** present in large quantities; plentiful. ■ **pro·lif·i·cal·ly** /-ik(ə)lē/ adv.

pro·lix /prō'liks/ ▶ adj. (of speech or writing) long and boring. ■ **pro·lix·i·ty** /-'liksətē/ n.

pro·logue /'prō,lôg, -,läg/ ▶ n. **1** an introductory section or scene in a book, play, or musical work. **2** an event or action leading to another.

pro·long /prə'lôNG, -'läNG/ ▶ v. cause to last longer: *the council prolonged the deadline to March 9th.* ■ **pro·lon·ga·tion** /prō,lôNG'gāsʜən, prə-/ n.

pro·longed /prə'lôNGd, -'läNGd/ ▶ adj. continuing for a long time; lengthy.

prom /präm/ ▶ n. a formal dance at a high school or college.

prom·e·nade /ˌprämə'nād, -'näd/ ▶ n. **1** a paved public walk along a seafront. **2** a leisurely walk taken for social reasons. ▶ v. take a leisurely walk for social reasons. ■ **prom·e·nad·er** n.

Pro·me·the·an /prə'mēтнēən/ ▶ adj. daring or skillful like Prometheus, a minor god in Greek mythology who stole fire from the gods and gave it to the human race.

pro·me·thi·um /prō'mēтнēəm/ ▶ n. an unstable radioactive metallic chemical element of the lanthanide series.

prom·i·nence /'prämənəns/ ▶ n. **1** the state of being important, famous, or noticeable. **2** a thing that projects or sticks out.

prom·i·nent /'prämənənt/ ▶ adj. **1** important; famous. **2** projecting or sticking out from something. **3** particularly noticeable: *the statue occupies a prominent position in the Sculpture Garden.* ■ **prom·i·nent·ly** adv.

pro·mis·cu·ous /prə'miskyo͞oəs/ ▶ adj. **1** having many sexual partners. **2** not selective in approach; indiscriminate: *a promiscuous mixing of styles.* ■ **prom·is·cu·i·ty** /ˌprämə'skyo͞oitē, prə,mis'kyo͞o-/ n. **prom·is·cu·ous·ly** adv.

prom·ise /'präməs/ ▶ n. **1** an assurance that one will do something or that something will happen. **2** indications of future excellence or success: *he showed some promise as an actor.* **3** a sign that something is likely to happen. ▶ v. **1** assure someone that one will do something or that something will happen. **2** make something seem likely: *it promised to be a night to remember.*

Prom·ised Land ▶ n. **1** the land of Canaan, promised to Abraham and his descendants in the Bible (Book of Genesis, chapter 12). **2** (**the promised land**) a place or situation where great happiness is expected.

prom·is·ee /ˌprämə'sē/ ▶ n. Law a person to whom a promise is made.

prom·is·ing /'präməsiNG/ ▶ adj. showing signs of future excellence or success. ■ **prom·is·ing·ly** adv.

prom·i·sor /'präməsər/ ▶ n. Law a person who makes a promise.

prom·is·so·ry note /'prämə,sôrē/ ▶ n. a signed document containing a written promise to pay a stated sum.

pro·mo /'prōmō/ ▶ n. (pl. **promos**) informal a promotional film, video, etc.

prom·on·to·ry /'prämən,tôrē/ ▶ n. (pl. **promontories**) a point of high land jutting out into the sea or a lake.

pro·mote /prə'mōt/ ▶ v. **1** support or actively encourage a cause, venture, or aim. **2** publicize a product or celebrity. **3** appoint someone to a higher position or rank. **4** transfer a sports team to a higher division.

pro·mot·er /prə'mōtər/ ▶ n. **1** the organizer of a sporting event or theatrical production. **2** a supporter of a cause or aim.

pro·mo·tion /prə'mōsʜən/ ▶ n. **1** activity that supports or encourages something: *the promotion of human rights.* **2** the publicizing of a product or celebrity. **3** (**promotions**) the activity or business of publicizing a product or celebrity. **4** the action of promoting someone or something to a higher position or rank. ■ **pro·mo·tion·al** adj.

prompt /prämpt/ ▶ v. **1** cause something to happen. **2** (**prompt someone to/to do**) cause someone to do something. **3** encourage a hesitating speaker to say something. **4** supply a forgotten word or line to an actor. ▶ n. **1** an act of prompting a speaker or actor. **2** a word or phrase used to prompt an actor. **3** a word or symbol that appears on a computer screen to show that input is required. ▸ **adj.** done or acting without delay. ■ **prompt·ly** adv. **prompt·ness** n.

prompt·er /'prämptər/ ▸ n. a person who prompts the actors during a play.

prom·ul·gate /'prämǝl‚gāt, prō'mǝl-/ ▸ v. **1** make something widely known. **2** put a law or decree into effect by an official announcement. ■ **prom·ul·ga·tion** /‚prämǝl'gāsнǝn, ‚prōmǝl-/ n. **prom·ul·ga·tor** n.

pro·nate /'prō‚nāt/ ▸ v. technical **1** put or hold (a hand, foot, or limb) with the palm or sole turned downward. Compare with SUPINATE. **2** walk or run with most of the weight on the outside of the feet. ■ **pro·na·tion** /'prō‚nāsнǝn/ n.

prone /prōn/ ▸ adj. **1** (**prone to/to do**) likely or liable to suffer from, do, or experience something unpleasant or undesirable. **2** lying flat, especially face downward. ■ **prone·ness** n.

prong /prôNG/ ▸ n. **1** each of two or more projecting pointed parts on a fork or other article. **2** each of the separate parts of an attack, argument, or scheme.

prong·horn /'prôNG‚hôrn/ (also **pronghorn antelope**) ▸ n. a fast-running North American mammal resembling but unrelated to an antelope.

pro·nom·i·nal /prō'nämǝnl/ ▸ adj. relating to or acting as a pronoun. ■ **pro·nom·i·nal·ly** adv.

pro·noun /'prō‚noun/ ▸ n. a word used instead of a noun to indicate someone or something already mentioned or known, e.g., *I, she, this.*

pro·nounce /prǝ'nouns/ ▸ v. **1** make the sound of a word or part of a word. **2** declare or announce something in a formal or solemn way. **3** (**pronounce on**) pass judgment or make a decision on. ■ **pro·nounce·a·ble** adj. **pro·nounc·er** n.

pro·nounced /prǝ'nounst/ ▸ adj. very noticeable. ■ **pro·nounc·ed·ly** /-'nounsǝdlē, -'nounstlē/ adv.

pro·nounce·ment /prǝ'nounsmǝnt/ ▸ n. a formal public statement.

pron·to /'präntō/ ▸ adv. informal promptly; quickly.

pro·nun·ci·a·tion /prǝ‚nǝnsē'āsнǝn/ ▸ n. the way in which a word is pronounced.

> **USAGE**
> **Pronunciation** should be pronounced with **-nun-** as the second syllable, and not as though it were spelled **-noun-**.

proof /proof/ ▸ n. **1** evidence that proves that a fact or statement is true. **2** the action of proving that something is true. **3** a series of stages in the solving of a mathematical or philosophical problem. **4** a copy of a printed page used for making corrections before final printing. **5** a trial photographic print. **6** a standard used to measure the strength of distilled alcoholic liquor. ▸ adj. (in combination) able to resist: *bulletproof.* ▸ v. **1** make a proof of a printed work. **2** proofread something. **3** make something waterproof.

proof pos·i·tive ▸ n. final or absolute proof of something.

proof·read /'proof‚rēd/ ▸ v. read printer's proofs and mark any errors. ■ **proof·read·er** n.

proof spir·it ▸ n. a mixture of alcohol and water used as a standard of strength of distilled alcoholic liquor.

prop[1] /präp/ ▸ n. **1** a pole or beam used as a temporary support. **2** a source of support or

assistance. ▸ v. (**props, propping, propped**) **1** support something with a prop. **2** lean something against something else. **3** (**prop someone/thing up**) support or help someone or something that would otherwise fail.

prop[2] ▸ n. a portable object used on the set of a play or movie.

prop[3] ▸ n. informal an aircraft propeller.

prop·a·gan·da /‚präpǝ'gandǝ/ ▸ n. information that is often biased or misleading, used to promote a political cause or point of view.

prop·a·gan·dist /‚präpǝ'gandist/ chiefly derogatory ▸ n. a person who spreads propaganda. ▸ adj. consisting of or spreading propaganda. ■ **prop·a·gan·dize** /‚präpǝ'gan‚dīz/ v.

prop·a·gate /'präpǝ‚gāt/ ▸ v. **1** produce a new plant naturally from the parent stock. **2** promote an idea or knowledge widely. **3** transmit motion, light, sound, etc., in a particular direction. ■ **prop·a·ga·tion** /‚präpǝ'gāsнǝn/ n.

prop·a·ga·tor /'präpǝ‚gātǝr/ ▸ n. **1** a covered, heated container of earth or compost, used for germinating seedlings. **2** a person who spreads an idea or knowledge.

pro·pane /'prō‚pān/ ▸ n. a flammable gas present in natural gas and used as bottled fuel.

pro·pel /prǝ'pel/ ▸ v. (**propels, propelling, propelled**) **1** drive or push someone or something forward. **2** send or force into a particular situation: *his doctorate propelled him into prominence.*

pro·pel·lant /prǝ'pelǝnt/ ▸ n. **1** a compressed gas that forces out the contents of an aerosol. **2** a substance used to provide thrust in a rocket engine. ▸ adj. capable of propelling something.

pro·pel·ler /prǝ'pelǝr/ (also **propellor**) ▸ n. a revolving shaft with two or more angled blades, for propelling a ship or aircraft.

pro·pen·si·ty /prǝ'pensǝtē/ ▸ n. (pl. **propensities**) a tendency to behave in a particular way.

prop·er /'präpǝr/ ▸ adj. **1** truly what something is said or regarded to be; genuine. **2** (after a noun) according to the precise meaning of the term: *the World Cup proper.* **3** suitable, right, or correct: *an artist needs the proper tools.* **4** respectable, especially excessively so. **5** (**proper to**) belonging particularly to: *the degree of certainty proper to mathematics.*

prop·er frac·tion ▸ n. a fraction that is less than one, with the numerator less than the denominator.

prop·er·ly /'präpǝrlē/ ▸ adv. **1** in a proper way. **2** in the precise sense. **3** informal, chiefly Brit. completely.

prop·er noun (also **proper name**) ▸ n. a name for a particular person, place, or organization, having an initial capital letter. Often contrasted with COMMON NOUN.

prop·er·tied /'präpǝrtēd/ ▸ adj. owning property and land.

prop·er·ty /'präpǝrtē/ ▸ n. (pl. **properties**) **1** a thing or things belonging to someone. **2** a building and the land belonging to it. **3** Law the right to possess, use, or dispose of something; ownership. **4** a characteristic or quality: *a perfumed oil with calming properties.*

proph·e·cy /'präfǝsē/ ▸ n. (pl. **prophecies**) **1** a prediction of a future event. **2** the power of prophesying the future.

proph·e·sy /'präfə,sī/ ▶ v. (**prophesies, prophesying, prophesied**) predict a future event.

USAGE
The words **prophesy** and **prophecy** are often confused. **Prophesy** is the spelling that should be used for the verb (*how can I prophesy the coming of a God in which I do not believe?*), whereas **prophecy** is the correct spelling for the noun (*a bleak prophecy of war*).

proph·et /'präfit/ ▶ n. (fem. **prophetess** /'präfətəs/) **1** (in some religions) a person believed to have been sent by God to teach people about his intentions. **2** a person who predicts the future. **3** a person who promotes or supports a new belief or theory.

pro·phet·ic /prə'fetik/ ▶ adj. **1** accurately predicting the future. **2** relating to a prophet or prophecy. ■ **pro·phet·i·cal** adj. **pro·phet·i·cal·ly** /-ik(ə)lē/ adv.

pro·phy·lac·tic /,prōfə'laktik/ ▶ adj. intended to prevent disease. ▶ n. **1** a medicine or course of action that is intended to prevent disease. **2** a condom.

pro·phy·lax·is /,prōfə'laksəs/ ▶ n. action taken to prevent disease.

pro·pin·qui·ty /prə'piNGkwətē/ ▶ n. nearness in time or space; proximity.

pro·pi·ti·ate /prə'pishē,āt/ ▶ v. win or regain the favor of a person, god, or spirit. ■ **pro·pi·ti·a·tion** /prə,pishē'āsHən/ n. **pro·pi·ti·a·to·ry** /-'pishēə,tôrē/ adj.

pro·pi·tious /prə'pishəs/ ▶ adj. giving or indicating a good chance of success; favorable: *it was a propitious moment for a global telephone network.* ■ **pro·pi·tious·ly** adv. **pro·pi·tious·ness** n.

prop·o·lis /'präpələs/ ▶ n. a substance collected by honeybees from tree buds for constructing and varnishing honeycombs.

pro·po·nent /prə'pōnənt/ ▶ n. a person who supports a theory, proposal, or project.

pro·por·tion /prə'pôrsHən/ ▶ n. **1** a part, share, or number considered in relation to a whole. **2** the relationship of one thing to another in terms of size or quantity; a ratio. **3** the correct or pleasing relationship of things or between the parts of a whole: *keep the size of the vase and the size of the flowers in your arrangement in proportion.* **4** (**proportions**) dimensions; size. ▶ v. formal adjust something so as to have a particular or suitable relationship to something else. ■ **pro·por·tioned** adj.
– PHRASES **in** (or **out of**) **proportion** regarded without (or with) exaggeration. **sense of proportion** the ability to judge the relative importance of things.

pro·por·tion·al /prə'pôrsHənl/ ▶ adj. corresponding in size or amount to something else. ■ **pro·por·tion·al·i·ty** /prə,pôrsHə'nalətē, pər,pôrsHə'nalədē/ n. **pro·por·tion·al·ly** adv.

pro·por·tion·al rep·re·sen·ta·tion ▶ n. an electoral system in which parties gain seats in proportion to the number of votes cast for them.

pro·por·tion·ate /prə'pôrsHənət/ ▶ adj. another term for PROPORTIONAL. ■ **pro·por·tion·ate·ly** adv.

pro·pos·al /prə'pōzəl/ ▶ n. **1** a plan or suggestion put forward for consideration. **2** the action of proposing something. **3** an offer of marriage.

pro·pose /prə'pōz/ ▶ v. **1** put forward an idea or plan for consideration. **2** nominate someone for an office or position. **3** put forward a motion to a lawmaking body or committee. **4** plan or intend to do something. **5** make an offer of marriage to someone. ■ **pro·pos·er** n.

prop·o·si·tion /,präpə'zisHən/ ▶ n. **1** a statement expressing a judgment or opinion. **2** a proposed scheme or plan. **3** a problem or task to be dealt with: *keeping weight off for life is a difficult proposition.* **4** Mathematics a formal statement of a theorem or problem. ▶ v. informal **1** make an offer or suggestion to someone. **2** ask someone to have sex. ■ **prop·o·si·tion·al** adj.

pro·pound /prə'pound/ ▶ v. put forward an idea or theory for consideration. ■ **pro·pound·er** n.

pro·pri·e·tar·y /p(r)ə'prī·i,terē/ ▶ adj. **1** relating to an owner or ownership. **2** behaving as if one owned something or someone: *he looked around with a proprietary air.* **3** (of a product) marketed under a registered trade name.

pro·pri·e·tar·y name ▶ n. a name of a product or service registered as a trademark.

pro·pri·e·tor /p(r)ə'prī·ətər/ ▶ n. (fem. **proprietress** /p(r)ə'prī·ətrəs/) **1** the owner of a business. **2** a holder of property.

pro·pri·e·to·ri·al /p(r)ə,prī·ə'tôrēəl/ ▶ adj. behaving as if one owned someone or something; possessive: *he draped his arm across her shoulders in a proprietorial way.* ■ **pro·pri·e·to·ri·al·ly** /p(r)ə,prī·ə'tôrēəlē/ adv.

pro·pri·e·ty /p(r)ə'prī·ətē/ ▶ n. (pl. **proprieties**) **1** correctness of behavior or morals. **2** (**proprieties**) the generally accepted details or rules of behavior. **3** the quality of being appropriate or right: *they questioned the propriety of investments made by the council.*

props /präps/ ▶ pl. n. informal respect or credit due to a person: *Erika gets props for the great work she did on the music.*

pro·pul·sion /prə'pəlsHən/ ▶ n. the action of propelling or driving something forward. ■ **pro·pul·sive** /-siv/ adj. **pro·pul·sive·ly** adv.

pro·pyl·ene /'prōpə,lēn/ ▶ n. a hydrocarbon gas obtained by cracking petroleum, used for making plastics and other chemicals.

pro ra·ta /prō 'rätə, 'rātə, 'ratə/ ▶ adj. proportional. ▶ adv. proportionally.

pro·rate /prō'rāt, 'prō,rāt/ ▶ v. allocate, distribute, or assess pro rata: *bonuses are prorated over the life of a player's contract.*

pro·rogue /p(r)ə'rōg/ ▶ v. (**prorogues, proroguing, prorogued**) discontinue a session of a parliament without dissolving it. ■ **pro·ro·ga·tion** /,prōrə'gāsHən/ n.

pro·sa·ic /prō'zāik/ ▶ adj. **1** (of language) not imaginative or original. **2** ordinary, dull, or mundane: *a prosaic travel experience.* ■ **pro·sa·i·cal·ly** /-ik(ə)lē/ adv.

pro·sce·ni·um /prə'sēnēəm, prō-/ ▶ n. (pl. **prosceniums** or **proscenia** /-nēə/) **1** the part of a stage in front of the curtain. **2** (also **proscenium arch**) an arch that frames the opening between the stage and the auditorium.

pro·sciut·to /prə'sHōōtō/ ▶ n. raw cured Italian ham.

pro·scribe /prō'skrīb/ ▶ v. **1** officially forbid something. **2** criticize or condemn someone or something. **3** historical outlaw someone. ■ **pro·scrip·tion** /-'skripsHən/ n. **pro·scrip·tive** /-'skriptiv/ adj.

prose /prōz/ ▸ n. ordinary written or spoken language. ▸ v. talk in a boring way.

pros·e·cute /'präsi,kyōōt/ ▸ v. 1 take legal action against someone or with respect to an offense. 2 continue a course of action with a view to completing it. ■ **pros·e·cut·a·ble** adj.

pros·e·cu·tion /,präsi'kyōōshən/ ▸ n. 1 the process of taking legal action against someone. 2 (**the prosecution**) (treated as sing. or pl.) the party prosecuting someone in a lawsuit. 3 the continuation of a course of action.

pros·e·cu·tor /'präsi,kyōōtər/ ▸ n. 1 a person, especially a public official, who takes legal action against someone. 2 a lawyer who conducts the case against a person accused of a crime. ■ **pros·e·cu·to·ri·al** /,präsikyə'tôrēəl/ adj.

pros·e·lyte /'präsə,līt/ ▸ n. a person who has converted from one opinion, religion, or party to another. ■ **pros·e·lyt·ism** /-lə,tizəm/ n.

pros·e·lyt·ize /'präsələ,tīz/ ▸ v. convert someone from one religion, belief, or opinion to another. ■ **pros·e·lyt·i·za·tion** /,präsələti'zāshən/ n. **pros·e·lyt·iz·er** n.

pros·o·dy /'präsədē, 'präzədē/ ▸ n. 1 the patterns of rhythm and sound used in poetry. 2 the theory or study of these patterns, or the rules governing them. 3 the patterns of stress and intonation in a language. ■ **pro·sod·ic** /prə'sädik, -zädik/ adj. **pros·o·dist** /'präsədist, 'präz-/ n.

pros·pect /'präs,pekt/ ▸ n. 1 the possibility or likelihood of a future event occurring: *there was no prospect of a reconciliation.* 2 a mental picture of a future or expected event. 3 (**prospects**) chances for success. 4 a person regarded as likely to be successful: *he was seen as a leading medal prospect for the Olympics.* 5 a wide view of landscape. ▸ v. (**prospect for**) search for mineral deposits, especially by means of drilling and excavation. ■ **pros·pec·tor** n.

pro·spec·tive /prə'spektiv/ ▸ adj. likely to happen or be something in the future: *a prospective buyer.* ■ **pro·spec·tive·ly** adv.

pro·spec·tus /prə'spektəs/ ▸ n. (pl. **prospectuses**) a printed booklet advertising a school or university or giving details of a stock offering.

pros·per /'präspər/ ▸ v. succeed or flourish, especially financially.

pros·per·ous /'präspərəs/ ▸ adj. rich and successful. ■ **pros·per·i·ty** /prä'speritē/ n. **pros·per·ous·ly** adv.

pros·ta·glan·din /,prästə'glandin/ ▸ n. any of a group of compounds with various biological effects, such as causing contractions of the uterus.

pros·tate /'präs,tāt/ ▸ n. a gland that surrounds the neck of the bladder in male mammals and produces a component of semen. ■ **pros·tat·ic** /prä'statik/ adj.

pros·the·sis /'präs'THēsis/ ▸ n. (pl. **prostheses** /-sēz/) an artificial body part.

pros·thet·ics /präs'THetiks/ ▸ pl.n. 1 artificial body parts. 2 pieces of flexible material applied to actors' faces to change their appearances. 3 (treated as sing.) the branch of medicine concerned with making and fitting artificial body parts. ■ **pros·thet·ic** /-'THetik/ adj. **pros·the·tist** /'präsTHətist/ n.

pros·ti·tute /'prästə,t(y)ōōt/ ▸ n. a person who has sex with people for money. ▸ v. (often **prostitute oneself**) 1 do something unworthy or corrupt for the sake of money or personal advantage: *he decided that he would no longer prostitute his talent to win popularity.* 2 offer someone or work as a prostitute. ■ **pros·ti·tu·tion** /,prästə't(y)ōōshən/ n.

pros·trate /'präs,trāt/ ▸ adj. 1 lying stretched out on the ground with the face downward. 2 completely overcome with distress or exhaustion. 3 (of a plant) growing along the ground. ▸ v. 1 (**prostrate oneself**) throw oneself flat on the ground, especially as an act of worship. 2 (**be prostrated**) be completely overcome with stress or exhaustion. ■ **pros·tra·tion** /prä'strāshən/ n.

pro·sum·er /prō'sōōmər/ ▸ n. 1 an amateur who purchases equipment suitable for professional use. 2 a well-informed and proactive consumer.

pros·y /'prōzē/ ▸ adj. (of speech or writing) dull and unimaginative.

prot·ac·tin·i·um /,prō,tak'tinēəm/ ▸ n. a rare radioactive metallic chemical element.

pro·tag·o·nist /prō'tagənist, prə-/ ▸ n. 1 the leading character in a play, movie, or novel. 2 an important person in a real situation. 3 an active supporter of a cause or idea.

pro·te·a /'prōtēə/ ▸ n. a chiefly South African shrub with large conelike flowerheads surrounded by brightly colored modified leaves (bracts).

pro·te·an /'prōtēən, prō'tēən/ ▸ adj. tending or able to change or adapt; variable or versatile.

pro·tect /prə'tekt/ ▸ v. 1 keep safe from harm or injury: *he tried to protect her from the attack.* 2 shield a country's own industry from foreign competition by taxing imported goods. 3 (as adj. **protected**) (of a threatened plant or animal species) safeguarded through laws against collecting or hunting.

pro·tect·ant /prə'tektənt/ ▸ n. a substance that provides protection, for example against ultraviolet radiation.

pro·tec·tion /prə'tekshən/ ▸ n. 1 the action of protecting or the state of being protected: *the vehicle provides protection against anti-personnel mines.* 2 a thing that protects someone or something. 3 the payment of money to criminals to prevent them from attacking oneself or one's property.

pro·tec·tion·ism /prə'tekshə,nizəm/ ▸ n. the theory or practice of shielding a country's own industries from foreign competition by taxing imports. ■ **pro·tec·tion·ist** n. & adj.

pro·tec·tive /prə'tektiv/ ▸ adj. 1 intended to protect someone or something from harm or injury. 2 having a strong wish to protect someone from harm or injury. ■ **pro·tec·tive·ly** adv. **pro·tec·tive·ness** n.

pro·tec·tive or·der ▸ n. a court order instructing a person to stop abusing or harassing a particular individual.

pro·tec·tor /prə'tektər/ ▸ n. 1 a person or thing that protects someone or something. 2 (**Protector**) historical a regent in charge of a kingdom when the monarch is away, ill, or too young to reign. ■ **pro·tect·ress** /prə'tektrəs/ n.

pro·tec·tor·ate /prə'tektərət/ ▶ n. **1** a country that is controlled and protected by another. **2** (**Protectorate**) historical the position or period of office of a Protector, in particular that of Oliver Cromwell and his son Richard as heads of state in England 1653–59.

pro·té·gé /'prōtə,zhā, ,prōtə'zhā/ ▶ n. (fem. **protégée** pronunc. same) a person who is guided and supported by an older and more experienced person.

pro·tein /'prō,tē(ə)n/ ▶ n. any of a group of organic compounds forming part of body tissues and forming an important part of the diet.

pro tem /prō 'tem/ ▶ adv. & adj. for the time being.

Prot·er·o·zo·ic /,prōtərə'zōik/ ▶ adj. Geology relating to the later part of the Precambrian eon (about 2,500 to 570 million years ago), in which the earliest forms of life evolved.

pro·test ▶ n. /'prō,test/ **1** a statement or action expressing disapproval or objection. **2** an organized public demonstration objecting to an official policy or course of action. ▶ v. /prə'test, prō'test, 'prō,test/ **1** express an objection to what someone has said or done. **2** take part in a public protest. **3** state strongly in response to an accusation or criticism: *she has always protested her innocence.* ■ **pro·test·er** /'prō,testər, prə'tes-/ (also **protestor**) n.

Prot·es·tant /'prätəstənt/ ▶ n. a member or follower of any of the Western Christian Churches that are separate from the Roman Catholic Church. ▶ adj. relating or belonging to any of the Protestant Churches. ■ **Prot·es·tant·ism** /'prätəstənt,izəm/ n.

Prot·es·tant eth·ic (also **Protestant work ethic**) ▶ n. another term for WORK ETHIC.

prot·es·ta·tion /,prätə'stāshən, ,prō,tes'tā-/ ▶ n. **1** a strong declaration that something is or is not the case. **2** an objection or protest.

pro·ti·um /'prōtēəm, 'prōsн(ē)əm/ ▶ n. Chemistry the common, stable isotope of hydrogen.

proto- ▶ comb. form **1** original; primitive: *prototype.* **2** first: *protozoan.*

pro·to·col /'prōtə,kôl, -,käl/ ▶ n. **1** the official system of rules governing affairs of state or diplomatic occasions. **2** the accepted code of behavior in a particular situation. **3** the original draft of a diplomatic document, especially of the terms of a treaty. **4** a formal record of scientific experimental observations. **5** Computing a set of rules governing the exchange or transmission of data between devices.

pro·ton /'prō,tän/ ▶ n. Physics a subatomic particle with a positive electric charge, occurring in all atomic nuclei.

pro·to·plasm /'prōtə,plazəm/ ▶ n. the material comprising the living part of a cell, including the cytoplasm and nucleus. ■ **pro·to·plas·mic** /,prōtə'plazmik/ adj.

pro·to·type /'prōtə,tīp/ ▶ n. **1** a first or preliminary version of a device or vehicle from which other versions are developed or copied. **2** the first or typical form of something. ■ **pro·to·typ·i·cal** /,prōtə'tipikəl/ adj. **pro·to·typ·i·cal·ly** /,prōtə'tipik(ə)lē/ adv.

pro·to·zo·an /,prōtə'zōən/ ▶ n. a single-celled microscopic animal such as an amoeba.

pro·tract /prə'trakt, prō-/ ▶ v. (often as adj. **protracted**) make something longer than

expected or normal: *a protracted dispute.*

pro·trac·tion /prə'trakshən, prō-/ ▶ n. the action of prolonging something or the state of being prolonged.

pro·trac·tor /'prō,traktər/ ▶ n. an instrument for measuring angles, typically in the form of a flat semicircle marked with degrees along the curved edge.

pro·trude /prə'trood, prō-/ ▶ v. extend or stick out beyond or above a surface.

pro·tru·sion /prə'troozhən, prō-/ ▶ n. **1** something that protrudes or sticks out. **2** the action of protruding.

pro·tu·ber·ance /prə't(y)oob(ə)rəns, prō-/ ▶ n. a thing that protrudes or sticks out.

pro·tu·ber·ant /prə't(y)oob(ə)rənt, prō-/ ▶ adj. sticking out or bulging.

proud /proud/ ▶ adj. **1** feeling pride or satisfaction in one's own achievements or those of someone close to one. **2** causing pride: *his proudest moment was when his son married Mandy.* **3** having or showing a high opinion of oneself. **4** having self-respect or dignity: *I was too proud to go home.* ■ **proud·ly** adv. – PHRASES **do someone proud** informal **1** make someone feel pleased or satisfied. **2** treat or entertain someone very well.

prove /proov/ ▶ v. (past part. **proved** or **proven** /'proovən/) **1** demonstrate by evidence or argument that something is true or exists. **2** show or be seen to be: *the scheme has proved a great success.* **3** (**prove oneself**) demonstrate one's abilities or courage. **4** Law establish the genuineness and validity of a will. **5** subject a gun to a testing process. **6** (of bread dough) rise through the action of yeast. ■ **prov·a·ble** adj. **prov·er** n.

> **USAGE**
> **Prove** has two past participles, **proved** and **proven**. You can correctly use either in sentences such as *this hasn't been proved yet* or *this hasn't been proven yet.* However, you should always use **proven** when the word is used as an adjective coming before the noun: *a proven talent* (not *a proved talent*).

prov·e·nance /'prävənəns/ ▶ n. **1** the origin or earliest known history of something. **2** a record of ownership of a work of art or an antique.

Pro·ven·çal /,prävən'säl, ,prō-/ ▶ adj. relating to Provence in southern France. ▶ n. **1** a person from Provence. **2** the language of Provence.

pro·ven·cale /,prävən'säl, ,prō-/ ▶ adj. (after a noun) cooked in a sauce made with tomatoes, garlic, and herbs.

prov·en·der /'prävəndər/ ▶ n. animal fodder.

prov·erb /'prä,vərb/ ▶ n. a short saying that states a general truth or piece of advice.

pro·ver·bi·al /prə'vərbēəl/ ▶ adj. **1** referred to in a proverb or saying. **2** well known, especially so as to be stereotypical: *he was the proverbial, consummate showman.* ■ **pro·ver·bi·al·ly** adv.

pro·vide /prə'vīd/ ▶ v. **1** make something available for use; supply something. **2** (**provide someone with**) equip or supply someone with something useful or necessary. **3** (**provide for**) make adequate preparation or arrangements for: *new qualifications must provide for changes in technology.* **4** state something in a will or other legal document. ■ **pro·vid·er** n.

pro·vid·ed /prə'vīdid/ ▶ conj. on the condition or understanding that.

prov·i·dence /'prävə,dens, -dəns/ ▸ n. the protective care of God or of nature as a spiritual power.

prov·i·dent /'prävədənt, -,dent/ ▸ adj. careful in preparing for the future. ■ **prov·i·dent·ly** adv.

prov·i·den·tial /,prävə'denchəl/ ▸ adj. **1** happening by chance at a favorable time; opportune: *it was providential that he was on call to provide free legal advice.* **2** involving divine foresight or intervention. ■ **prov·i·den·tial·ly** adv.

pro·vid·ing /prə'vīdiNG/ ▸ conj. on the condition or understanding that.

prov·ince /'prävins/ ▸ n. **1** a chief administrative division of a country or empire. **2 (the provinces)** the whole of a country outside the capital, especially when regarded as unsophisticated or narrow-minded. **3 (one's province)** one's particular area of knowledge, interest, or responsibility.

pro·vin·cial /prə'vinshəl/ ▸ adj. **1** relating to a province or the provinces. **2** unsophisticated or narrow-minded. ▸ n. **1** an inhabitant of a province. **2** an inhabitant of the regions outside the capital city of a country. ■ **pro·vin·cial·ism** /prə'vinchə,lizəm/ n. **pro·vin·ci·al·i·ty** /prə,vinshē'alətē/ n. **pro·vin·cial·ly** adv.

prov·ing ground ▸ n. an area or situation in which a person or thing is tested or proved.

pro·vi·sion /prə'vizHən/ ▸ n. **1** the action of providing or supplying something. **2** something supplied or provided. **3 (provision for/against)** arrangements for future events or requirements: *people must make provision for their retirement.* **4 (provisions)** supplies of food, drink, or equipment, especially for a journey. **5** a condition or requirement in a legal document. ▸ v. supply someone or something with provisions.

pro·vi·sion·al /prə'vizHənl/ ▸ adj. **1** arranged or existing for the present, possibly to be changed later. **2 (Provisional)** relating to the unofficial wings of the Irish Republican Army and Sinn Fein. ▸ n. **(Provisional)** a member of the unofficial wing of the Irish Republican Army or Sinn Fein. ■ **pro·vi·sion·al·i·ty** /prə,vizHə'nalətē/ n. **pro·vi·sion·al·ly** /-zHənl-ē/ adv.

pro·vi·so /prə'vīzō/ ▸ n. (pl. **provisos**) a condition attached to an agreement.

pro·vi·ta·min /prō'vītəmən/ ▸ n. a substance that is converted into a vitamin within an organism.

prov·o·ca·tion /,prävə'kāsHən/ ▸ n. **1** action or speech that makes someone angry or arouses a strong reaction. **2** the action of provoking someone.

pro·voc·a·tive /prə'väkətiv/ ▸ adj. **1** deliberately causing annoyance or anger. **2** intended to arouse sexual desire or interest. ■ **pro·voc·a·tive·ly** adv. **pro·voc·a·tive·ness** n.

pro·voke /prə'vōk/ ▸ v. **1** arouse a strong or unwelcome reaction or emotion in someone: *the decision provoked a storm of protest.* **2** deliberately make someone annoyed or angry. **3** make someone do or feel something, especially by arousing their anger.

pro·vo·lo·ne /,prōvə'lōnē, 'prōvə,lōn/ ▸ n. an Italian soft smoked cheese.

pro·vost /'prō,vōst/ ▸ n. **1** a senior administrative officer in certain colleges and universities. **2** Brit. the head of certain university colleges and private schools. **3** the head of a chapter in a cathedral.

pro·vost mar·shal ▸ n. the officer in charge of military police in camp or on active service.

prow /prou/ ▸ n. the pointed front part of a ship; the bow.

prow·ess /'prou-əs, 'prōəs/ ▸ n. **1** skill or expertise in a particular activity or field. **2** bravery in battle.

prowl /proul/ ▸ v. move about in a stealthy or restless way, especially in search of prey. ■ **prowl·er** n.
– PHRASES **on the prowl** moving around in a stealthy way.

prox·i·mal /'präksəməl/ ▸ adj. chiefly Anatomy situated nearer to the center of the body or the point of attachment. The opposite of DISTAL. ■ **prox·i·mal·ly** adv.

prox·i·mate /'präksəmit/ ▸ adj. closest in space, time, or relationship.

prox·im·i·ty /präk'simətē/ ▸ n. nearness in space, time, or relationship.

prox·y /'präksē/ ▸ n. (pl. **proxies**) **1** the authority to represent someone else, especially in voting. **2** a person authorized to act on behalf of someone else.

Pro·zac /'prō,zak/ ▸ n. trademark fluoxetine, a drug that is taken to treat depression.

prude /prōōd/ ▸ n. a person who is easily shocked by matters relating to sex or nudity. ■ **prud·ish** adj. **prud·er·y** /'prōōdərē/ n.

pru·dent /'prōōdnt/ ▸ adj. acting with or showing care and thought for the future. ■ **pru·dence** n. **pru·dent·ly** adv.

pru·den·tial /prōō'denchəl/ ▸ adj. involving or showing care and forethought, especially in business. ■ **pru·den·tial·ly** adv.

prune[1] /prōōn/ ▸ n. a dried plum with a black, wrinkled appearance.

prune[2] ▸ v. **1** trim a tree, shrub, or bush by cutting away dead or overgrown branches or stems. **2** make smaller by removing unwanted parts: *staff numbers have been pruned.* ▸ n. an instance of pruning something. ■ **prun·er** n.

pru·ri·ent /'prōōrēənt/ ▸ adj. having or encouraging too great an interest in sexual matters. ■ **pru·ri·ence** n. **pru·ri·ent·ly** adv.

pru·ri·tus /prōō'rītəs/ ▸ n. severe itching of the skin. ■ **pru·rit·ic** /-'ritik/ adj.

Prus·sian /'prəsHən/ ▸ n. a person from the former German kingdom of Prussia. ▸ adj. relating to Prussia.

Prus·sian blue ▸ n. a deep blue pigment.

prus·sic ac·id /'prəsik/ ▸ n. old-fashioned term for HYDROCYANIC ACID.

pry[1] /prī/ ▸ v. (**pries, prying, pried**) inquire too intrusively into a person's private affairs. ■ **pry·ing** adj. & n.

pry[2] ▸ v. (**pries, prying, pried**) use force to move or open something, or to separate something from something else.

PS ▸ abbr. **1** police sergeant. **2** postscript. **3** public school.

psalm /sä(l)m/ ▸ n. a religious song or hymn, in particular any of those contained in the Book of Psalms in the Bible. ■ **psalm·ist** n.

psal·ter /'sôltər/ ▸ n. a copy of the Book of Psalms in the Bible.

psal·ter·y /'sôltərē/ ▸ n. (pl. **psalteries**) an ancient and medieval musical instrument like a dulcimer but played by plucking the strings.

PSAT ▸ abbr. Preliminary Scholastic Aptitude Test.

pse·phol·o·gy /sē'fäləjē/ ▶ n. the statistical study of elections and trends in voting.
■ **pse·phol·o·gist** n.

pseud /sōōd/ ▶ n. Brit. informal a person who tries to impress others by pretending to have knowledge, especially about art or literature.

pseu·do /'sōōdō/ ▶ adj. informal not genuine; fake, pretentious, or insincere.

pseudo- (also **pseud-** before a vowel) ▶ comb.form false; not genuine: *pseudonym*.

pseu·do·e·phed·rine /,sōōdōə'fedrin/ ▶ n. a drug used as a nasal decongestant.

pseu·do·nym /'sōōdn-im/ ▶ n. a false name, especially one used by an author.

pseu·don·y·mous /sōō'dänəməs/ ▶ adj. writing or written under a false name. ■ **pseu·do·nym·i·ty** /,sōōdn'imətē/ n. **pseu·don·y·mous·ly** adv.

pseu·do·sci·ence /,sōōdō'sīəns/ ▶ n. beliefs or practices mistakenly regarded as being based on scientific methods. ■ **pseu·do·sci·en·tif·ic** /-,sīən'tifik/ adj.

p.s.i. ▶ abbr. pounds per square inch.

psil·o·cy·bin /,sīlə'sībin/ ▶ n. a substance that causes hallucinations, found in certain toadstools.

psit·ta·cine /'sitə,sīn/ Ornithology ▶ adj. relating to birds of the parrot family. ▶ n. a bird of the parrot family.

psit·ta·co·sis /,sitə'kōsəs/ ▶ n. a contagious disease of birds, which can be passed (especially from parrots) to human beings as a form of pneumonia.

pso·ri·a·sis /sə'rīəsəs/ ▶ n. a skin disease marked by red, itchy, scaly patches. ■ **pso·ri·at·ic** /,sôrē'atik/ adj.

PST ▶ abbr. Pacific Standard Time.

psych /sīk/ ▶ v. informal **1** (**psych someone up**) mentally prepare someone for a difficult task or occasion: *we had to psych ourselves up for the race.* **2** (**psych someone out**) intimidate an opponent or rival by appearing very confident or aggressive.

psy·che /'sīkē/ ▶ n. the human soul, mind, or spirit.

psych·e·de·lia /,sīkə'dēlyə/ ▶ n. music, culture, or art based on the experiences produced by psychedelic drugs.

psy·che·del·ic /,sīkə'delik/ ▶ adj. **1** (of drugs) producing hallucinations. **2** (of rock music) experimental and having drug-related lyrics. **3** having an intense, bright color or a swirling abstract pattern. ■ **psy·che·del·i·cal·ly** /-ik(ə)lē/ adv.

psy·chi·a·trist /sə'kīətrist, sī-/ ▶ n. a doctor specializing in the diagnosis and treatment of mental illness.

psy·chi·a·try /sə'kīətrē, sī-/ ▶ n. the branch of medicine concerned with the study and treatment of mental disorders. ■ **psy·chi·at·ric** /,sīkē'atrik/ adj. **psy·chi·at·ri·cal·ly** /-ik(ə)lē/ adv.

psy·chic /'sīkik/ ▶ adj. **1** relating to abilities or phenomena that cannot be explained by natural laws, especially involving telepathy or clairvoyance. **2** (of a person) appearing or considered to be telepathic or clairvoyant. **3** relating to the soul or mind. ▶ n. a person considered or claiming to have psychic powers; a medium. ■ **psy·chi·cal** /'sīkikəl/ adj. **psy·chi·cal·ly** /'sīkik(ə)lē/ adv.

psy·cho /'sīkō/ ▶ n. (pl. **psychos**) informal a psychopath.

psycho- ▶ comb.form relating to the mind or psychology: *psychometrics.*

psy·cho·ac·tive /,sīkō'aktiv/ ▶ adj. affecting the mind.

psy·cho·a·nal·y·sis /,sīkōə'naləsəs/ ▶ n. a method of treating mental disorders by investigating the conscious and unconscious elements in the mind and bringing repressed fears and conflicts into the conscious mind. ■ **psy·cho·an·a·lyst** /,sīkō'anl-əst/ n. **psy·cho·an·a·lyt·ic** /,sīkō,anl'itik/ adj.

psy·cho·an·a·lyze /,sīkō'anl,īz/ ▶ v. treat someone using psychoanalysis.

psy·cho·bab·ble /'sīkō,babəl/ ▶ n. informal, derogatory jargon used in popular psychology.

psy·cho·dra·ma /,sīkō'drämə, -'dramə/ ▶ n. **1** a form of psychotherapy in which patients act out events from their past. **2** a play, movie, or novel in which psychological elements are the main interest.

psy·cho·ki·ne·sis /,sīkōkə'nēsis/ ▶ n. the supposed ability to move objects by mental effort alone. ■ **psy·cho·ki·net·ic** /-'netik/ adj.

psy·cho·log·i·cal /,sīkə'läjəkəl/ ▶ adj. **1** relating to or affecting the mind. **2** relating to psychology. ■ **psy·cho·log·i·cal·ly** /-ik(ə)lē/ adv.

psy·cho·log·i·cal war·fare ▶ n. actions intended to reduce an opponent's confidence.

psy·chol·o·gy /sī'käləjē/ ▶ n. **1** the scientific study of the human mind and its functions. **2** the mental characteristics or attitude of a person. ■ **psy·chol·o·gist** n.

psy·cho·met·rics /,sīkə'metriks/ ▶ pl.n. (treated as sing.) the science of measuring mental abilities and processes. ■ **psy·cho·met·ric** adj.

psy·cho·path /'sīkə,paTH/ ▶ n. a person suffering from a serious mental disorder that causes them to commit violent or antisocial acts.
■ **psy·cho·path·ic** /,sīkə'paTHik/ adj.

psy·cho·pa·thol·o·gy /,sīkōpə'THäləjē, -paTH'äl-/ ▶ n. **1** the scientific study of mental disorders. **2** mental or behavioral disorder.
■ **psy·cho·path·o·log·i·cal** /-paTHō'läjikəl/ adj.

psy·chop·a·thy /sī'käpəTHē/ ▶ n. mental illness or disorder.

psy·cho·sex·u·al /,sīkō'seksHŌŌəl/ ▶ adj. relating to or involving the psychological aspects of a person's sexual feelings. ■ **psy·cho·sex·u·al·ly** adv.

psy·cho·sis /sī'kōsəs/ ▶ n. (pl. **psychoses** /-,sēz/) a mental disorder in which a person's perception of reality is severely distorted.

psy·cho·so·cial /,sīkō'sōsHəl/ ▶ adj. relating to the way in which social factors and individual thought and behavior are connected or linked.
■ **psy·cho·so·cial·ly** adv.

psy·cho·so·mat·ic /,sīkōsə'matik/ ▶ adj. **1** (of a physical illness) caused or made worse by a mental factor such as stress. **2** relating to the way in which the mind and body affect each other. ■ **psy·cho·so·mat·i·cal·ly** /-ik(ə)lē/ adv.

psy·cho·sur·ger·y /,sīkō'sərjərē/ ▶ n. brain surgery used to treat severe mental disorder.
■ **psy·cho·sur·gi·cal** /-'sərjikəl/ adj.

psy·cho·ther·a·py /,sīkō'THerəpē/ ▶ n. the treatment of mental disorder by psychological rather than medical means.
■ **psy·cho·ther·a·peu·tic** /-,THerə'pyōōtik/ adj. **psy·cho·ther·a·pist** n.

psy·chot·ic /sī'kätik/ ▸ adj. relating to or having a mental disorder in which a person's perception of reality is severely distorted. ▪ n. a person with such a disorder. ▪ **psy·chot·i·cal·ly** /-ik(ə)lē/ adv.

psy·cho·tro·pic /ˌsīkə'trōpik, -'träpik/ ▸ adj. (of drugs) affecting a person's mental state.

PT ▸ abbr. physical therapy.

Pt ▸ abbr. **1** Part. **2** (**pt**) pint. **3** (in scoring) point. **4** Printing point (as a unit of measurement). **5** (**Pt.**) Point (on maps). **6** (**pt**) port (a side of a ship or aircraft). ▸ symbol the chemical element platinum.

p.t. ▸ abbr. **1** past tense. **2** post town. **3** pro tempore. **4** part time.

PTA ▸ abbr. Parent–Teacher Association.

ptar·mi·gan /'tärməgən/ ▸ n. a grouse of northern mountains and the Arctic, whose gray and black plumage changes to white in winter.

pter·o·dac·tyl /ˌterə'daktəl/ ▸ n. a pterosaur (extinct flying reptile) of the late Jurassic period, with a long slender head and neck.

pter·o·saur /'terə,sôr/ ▸ n. an extinct flying reptile of the Jurassic and Cretaceous periods.

PTO ▸ abbr. **1** Parent–Teacher Organization. **2** chiefly Brit. please turn over.

Ptol·e·ma·ic /ˌtälə'mā-ik/ ▸ adj. **1** relating to the 2nd-century Greek astronomer Ptolemy. **2** relating to the Ptolemies, rulers of Egypt 304–30 BC.

Ptol·e·ma·ic sys·tem (also **Ptolemaic theory**) ▸ n. the former theory that the earth is the stationary center of the universe. Compare with COPERNICAN SYSTEM.

pto·maine /'tō,mān, tō'mān/ ▸ n. any of a group of organic compounds with an unpleasant taste and smell formed in decaying animal and vegetable matter.

PTSD ▸ abbr. post-traumatic stress disorder.

Pu ▸ symbol the chemical element plutonium.

pub /pəb/ ▸ n. **1** chiefly Brit. a tavern or bar. **2** Austral. a hotel.

pube /pyo͞ob/ ▸ n. vulgar slang a pubic hair.

pu·ber·ty /'pyo͞obərtē/ ▸ n. the period during which adolescents reach sexual maturity and become able to have children. ▪ **pu·ber·tal** /-bərtl/ adj.

pu·bes ▸ n. **1** /'pyo͞obēz, pyo͞obz/ (pl. same) the lower part of the abdomen at the front of the pelvis, covered with hair from puberty. **2** /'pyo͞obēz/ plural of PUBIS. **3** /pyo͞obz/ vulgar slang plural of PUBE.

pu·bes·cent /pyo͞o'besənt/ ▸ adj. **1** relating to a person at or approaching the age of puberty. **2** Botany & Zoology covered with short, soft hair; downy. ▪ **pu·bes·cence** n.

pu·bic /'pyo͞obik/ ▸ adj. relating to the pubes or pubis.

pu·bis /'pyo͞obəs/ ▸ n. (pl. **pubes** /-bēz/) either of a pair of bones forming the two sides of the pelvis.

pub·lic /'pəblik/ ▸ adj. **1** relating to or available to the people as a whole: *a campaign to raise public awareness of the problem.* **2** relating to or involved in the affairs of the community, especially in government or entertainment: *a public figure.* **3** intended to be seen or heard by people in general: *a public apology.* **4** provided by the government rather than an independent commercial company. ▸ n. **1** (**the public**) (treated as sing. or pl.) ordinary people in society in general. **2** a group of people with a shared

interest or activity: *the moviegoing public.* ▪ **pub·lic·ly** adv.

– PHRASES **go public 1** reveal details about something that was previously secret or private. **2** become a public company. **in public** when other people are present. **the public eye** the state of being well known to people in general, especially through the media.

pub·lic ad·dress sys·tem ▸ n. a system of microphones, amplifiers, and loudspeakers used to amplify speech or music.

pub·li·can /'pəblikən/ ▸ n. **1** chiefly Brit. a person who owns or manages a bar. **2** Austral. a person who owns or manages a hotel. **3** (in ancient Roman and biblical times) a tax collector.

pub·li·ca·tion /ˌpəbli'kāsHən/ ▸ n. **1** the action or process of publishing something. **2** a published book or journal.

pub·lic de·fend·er ▸ n. Law a lawyer employed by the government in a criminal trial to represent a defendant who is unable to afford legal assistance.

pub·lic en·e·my ▸ n. **1** a notorious wanted criminal. **2** a person or thing regarded as the greatest threat to a group or community.

pub·lic house ▸ n. Brit. formal term for PUB.

pub·li·cist /'pəbləsist/ ▸ n. a person responsible for publicizing a product or celebrity.

pub·lic·i·ty /pə'blisətē/ ▸ n. **1** attention given to someone or something by the media. **2** information that is given out about a product, person, company, etc., in order to advertise or promote them.

pub·li·cize /'pəblə,sīz/ ▸ v. **1** make widely known: *their attempts to publicize the dangers of pesticides.* **2** advertise or promote something.

pub·lic nui·sance ▸ n. **1** an act that is illegal because it interferes with the rights of the public generally. **2** informal an unpleasant or dangerous person or group.

pub·lic pros·e·cu·tor ▸ n. a district attorney.

pub·lic re·la·tions ▸ pl.n. (treated as sing.) the business of creating and maintaining a good public image for an organization or well-known person.

pub·lic school ▸ n. **1** (chiefly in North America) a school supported by public funds. **2** (in the UK) a private fee-paying secondary school.

pub·lic sec·tor ▸ n. the part of an economy that is controlled by the government.

pub·lic serv·ant ▸ n. a person who works for the government.

pub·lic-spir·it·ed ▸ adj. showing a willingness to do things that will help other people in society.

pub·lic trans·por·ta·tion ▸ n. buses, trains, and other forms of transport that are available to the public, charge set fares, and run on fixed routes.

pub·lic u·til·i·ty ▸ n. an organization supplying the community with electricity, gas, water, or sewerage.

pub·lish /'pəblisH/ ▸ v. **1** prepare and issue a book, newspaper, piece of music, etc., for public sale. **2** print something in a book, newspaper, or journal so as to make it generally known. **3** formally announce or read an edict or marriage banns. ▪ **pub·lish·a·ble** adj. **pub·lish·ing** n.

pub·lish·er /'pəblisHər/ ▸ n. **1** a company or person that prepares and issues books, newspapers, journals, or music for sale. **2** a newspaper proprietor.

puce /pyo͞os/ ▶ n. a dark red or purple-brown color.

puck[1] /pək/ ▶ n. a black disk made of hard rubber, used in ice hockey.

puck[2] ▶ n. a mischievous or evil spirit.

puck·er /'pəkər/ ▶ v. tightly gather or contract into wrinkles or small folds: *she puckered her lips.* ▶ n. a wrinkle or small fold.

puck·ish /'pəkiSH/ ▶ adj. playful and mischievous.

pud·ding /'po͝odiNG/ ▶ 1 a dessert with a creamy consistency. 2 chiefly Brit. a dessert, especially a cooked one. 3 chiefly Brit. the dessert course of a meal. 4 a sweet or savory steamed dish made with flour. 5 Brit. the intestines of a pig or sheep stuffed with oatmeal, spices, and meat and boiled. ■ **pud·ding·y** adj.

pud·dle /'pədl/ ▶ n. 1 a small pool of liquid, especially of rainwater on the ground. 2 clay and sand mixed with water and used as a watertight covering or lining for embankments or canals. ▶ v. 1 cover with or form puddles. 2 (usu. as n. **puddling**) historical stir molten iron with iron oxide in a furnace, to produce wrought iron.

pu·den·dum /pyo͞o'dendəm/ ▶ n. (pl. **pudenda** /-'dendə/) the external genitals, especially those of a woman.

pudg·y /'pəjē/ ▶ adj. (**pudgier, pudgiest**) informal fat or flabby.

pueb·lo /'pweblō/ ▶ n. (pl. **pueblos**) 1 a town or village in Spain, Latin America, or the southwestern US, especially an American Indian settlement. 2 (**Pueblo**) (pl. same or **Pueblos**) a member of any of various American Indian peoples living in pueblos, chiefly in New Mexico and Arizona.

pu·er·ile /'pyo͞o(ə)rəl, 'pyo͞or,īl/ ▶ adj. childishly silly and trivial. ■ **pu·er·il·i·ty** /pyo͞o(ə)'rilətē/ n. (pl. **puerilities**).

pu·er·per·al fe·ver /pyo͞o'ərpərəl/ ▶ n. fever caused by infection of the uterus after childbirth.

Puer·to Ri·can /,pôrtə 'rēkən, ,pwertə/ ▶ n. a person from Puerto Rico. ▶ adj. relating to Puerto Rico.

puff /pəf/ ▶ n. 1 a small amount of air or smoke blown from somewhere. 2 an act of drawing quickly on a pipe, cigarette, or cigar. 3 a light pastry case, typically filled with cream or jam. 4 informal (usu. **puff piece**) an overly complimentary review or advertisement. ▶ v. 1 breathe in repeated short gasps. 2 move with short, noisy puffs of air or steam: *a train puffed steadily across the bridge.* 3 smoke a pipe, cigarette, or cigar. 4 (**puff out/up** or **puff something out/up**) swell or cause to swell: *he puffed his chest out.* ■ **puff·er** n.

puff ad·der ▶ n. a large African viper that inflates the upper part of its body and hisses loudly when threatened.

puff·ball /'pəf,bôl/ ▶ n. a fungus that produces a large round fruiting body that bursts when ripe to release a cloud of spores.

puff·er·fish /'pəfər,fiSH/ ▶ n. (pl. same or **pufferfishes**) a fish with a spiny body that can inflate itself like a balloon when threatened.

puff·er·y /'pəfərē/ ▶ n. exaggerated or false praise.

puf·fin /'pəfən/ ▶ n. a seabird of the North Atlantic with a large head and a massive brightly colored triangular bill.

puff pas·try ▶ n. light flaky pastry.

puff·y /'pəfē/ ▶ adj. (**puffier, puffiest**) 1 softly rounded: *puffy clouds.* 2 (of a part of the body) swollen and soft. ■ **puff·i·ness** n.

pug /pəg/ ▶ n. a small dog with a broad flat nose and deeply wrinkled face.

pu·gi·list /'pyo͞ojəlist/ ▶ n. chiefly humorous a boxer. ■ **pu·gi·lism** /-,lizəm/ n. **pu·gi·lis·tic** /,pyo͞ojə'listik/ adj.

pug·na·cious /pəg'nāSHəs/ ▶ adj. eager or quick to argue, quarrel, or fight. ■ **pug·nac·i·ty** /,pəg'nasətē/ n.

pug nose ▶ n. a short nose with an upturned tip.

pu·is·sance /'pwisəns, 'pwē-, pyo͞o'isəns/ ▶ n. 1 a show jumping competition that tests a horse's ability to jump large, high obstacles. 2 old use or literary great power or skill. ■ **pu·is·sant** /'pwisənt, 'pwēsənt, 'pyo͞oəsənt/ adj. (old use or literary).

pu·ja /'po͞ojə/ ▶ n. a Hindu ceremonial offering.

puke /pyo͞ok/ ▶ v. & n. informal vomit. ■ **puk·ey** adj.

puk·ka /'pəkə/ (also **pukkah**) ▶ adj. informal 1 authentic or genuine. 2 socially acceptable. 3 informal excellent.

pu·lao /pə'lou, pə'lō, 'pərlo͞o/ ▶ n. variant spelling of PILAF.

pul·chri·tude /'pəlkrə,t(y)o͞od/ ▶ n. literary beauty. ■ **pul·chri·tu·di·nous** /,pəlkrə't(y)o͞odn-əs/ adj.

pule /pyo͞ol/ ▶ v. (often as adj. **puling**) literary cry feebly or in a complaining way.

pull /po͝ol/ ▶ v. 1 apply force to someone or something so as to move them toward oneself or the origin of the force. 2 remove by pulling: *she pulled a handkerchief from her pocket.* 3 move steadily: *the bus pulled away.* 4 move oneself with effort or against resistance: *she tried to pull away from him.* 5 strain a muscle or ligament. 6 (**pull at/on**) inhale deeply while drawing on a cigarette. 7 attract as a customer: *a DJ who is expected to pull in the crowds.* 8 informal cancel an event or withdraw an advertisement. 9 informal bring out a weapon for use. 10 deliberately slow the speed of a horse to make it lose a race. ▶ n. 1 an act of pulling. 2 a deep drink of something, or an act of taking a deep breath from a cigarette, pipe, etc. 3 a force, influence, or attraction: *the pull of her home town was a strong one.* ■ **pull·er** n.

– PHRASES **pull back** retreat or withdraw. **pull something down** demolish a building. **pull someone/thing in** 1 succeed in securing or obtaining something. 2 informal arrest someone. **pull someone's leg** deceive someone playfully. **pull something off** informal succeed in achieving or winning something difficult. **pull out** withdraw or retreat. **pull the plug on** informal prevent something from happening or continuing. **pull (one's) punches** be less forceful, severe, or critical than one could be. **pull strings** make use of one's influence to gain an advantage. **pull through** get through an illness or other difficult situation. **pull oneself together** regain one's self-control. **pull up** (of a vehicle) come to a halt. **pull someone up** make someone stop or pause. **pull one's weight** do one's fair share of work.

pul·let /'po͝olət/ ▶ n. a young hen, especially one less than one year old.

pul·ley /'po͝olē/ ▶ n. (pl. **pulleys**) a wheel with a grooved rim around which a rope, chain, or belt passes, used to raise heavy weights.

Pull·man /'po͝olmən/ ▶ n. (pl. **Pullmans**) a luxurious railroad car.

pull·out /'pŏŏl,out/ ▶ adj. (of a section of a magazine or newspaper) designed to be detached and kept. ▶ n. **1** a pullout section of a magazine or newspaper. **2** a withdrawal from military involvement or a commercial venture.

pull·o·ver /'pŏŏl,ōvər/ ▶ n. a knitted garment put on over the head and covering the top half of the body.

pul·lu·late /'pəlyə,lāt/ ▶ v. **1** reproduce or spread so as to become abundant. **2** be filled with life and activity.

pul·mo·nar·y /'pŏŏlmə,nerē, 'pəl-/ ▶ adj. relating to the lungs.

pulp /pəlp/ ▶ n. **1** a soft, wet mass of crushed or pounded material. **2** the soft fleshy part of a fruit. **3** a soft, wet mass of fibers obtained from rags or wood, used in making paper. ▶ v. **1** crush something into a pulp. **2** withdraw a publication from the market and recycle the paper. ▶ adj. referring to popular or sensational books or magazines, often regarded as being badly written: *pulp fiction*. ■ **pulp·y** adj.

pul·pit /'pŏŏl,pit, 'pəl-, -pət/ ▶ n. a raised enclosed platform in a church or chapel from which the preacher gives a sermon.

pul·sar /'pəl,sär/ ▶ n. an object in outer space, thought to be a rapidly rotating neutron star, that gives off regular rapid pulses of radio waves.

pul·sate /'pəl,sāt/ ▶ v. **1** expand and contract with strong regular movements. **2** produce a regular throbbing sensation or sound. **3** (as adj. **pulsating**) very exciting: *a pulsating semi-final*. ■ **pul·sa·tion** /,pəl'sāshən/ n.

pulse¹ /pəls/ ▶ n. **1** the regular throbbing of the arteries as blood is sent through them. **2** each successive throb of the arteries. **3** a single vibration or short burst of sound, electric current, or light. **4** a musical beat or other regular rhythm. **5** the center of activity in a particular area or field: *those close to the economic pulse*. ▶ v. **1** pulsate. **2** convert a wave or beam into a series of pulses.

pulse² ▶ n. the edible seeds of certain plants of the pea family, e.g., lentils.

pul·ver·ize /'pəlvə,rīz/ ▶ v. **1** crush something into fine particles. **2** informal defeat utterly: *he pulverized the opposition*. ■ **pul·ver·iz·er** n.

pu·ma /'p(y)ōōmə/ ▶ n. another term for COUGAR.

pum·ice /'pəməs/ ▶ n. a light and porous form of solidified lava, used to remove hard skin.

pum·mel /'pəməl/ ▶ v. (**pummels, pummeling, pummeled**) strike someone or something repeatedly with the fists.

pump¹ /pəmp/ ▶ n. a mechanical device using suction or pressure to raise or move liquids, compress gases, or force air into inflatable objects. ▶ v. **1** force liquid or gas to move by using a pump or by means of something that works like a pump: *the heart pumps blood around the body*. **2** (of liquid) flow as if being forced by a pump. **3** fill something with liquid or gas. **4** move or cause to move vigorously up and down: *we had to pump the handle like mad*. **5** (**pump something out**) produce something in large quantities or amounts: *carnival bands pumping out music*. **6** informal try to obtain information from someone by persistent questioning. **7** (as adj. **pumped up**) informal very enthusiastic or excited.
– PHRASES **pump iron** informal exercise with weights.

pump² ▶ n. a lightweight women's shoe, with a low-cut upper and a medium heel.

pump-ac·tion ▶ adj. referring to a firearm capable of firing several shots in succession without reloading, in which a new round is brought into the chamber by a slide action in line with the barrel.

pum·per·nick·el /'pəmpər,nikəl/ ▶ n. a dark, dense German bread made from whole-grain rye.

pump·kin /'pəm(p)kən, 'pəŋkən/ ▶ n. **1** a large rounded orange-yellow fruit with a thick rind and edible flesh. **2** Brit. another term for SQUASH².

pun /pən/ ▶ n. a joke playing on the different meanings of a word or exploiting the fact that there are words of the same sound and different meanings. ▶ v. (**puns, punning, punned**) make a pun. ■ **pun·ster** /'pənstər/ n.

punch¹ /pənCH/ ▶ v. **1** strike someone or something with the fist. **2** press a button or key on a machine. ▶ n. **1** a blow with the fist. **2** informal effectiveness or impact: *photos give their argument an extra visual punch*. ■ **punch·er** n.
– PHRASES **beat someone to the punch** informal anticipate or forestall someone's actions.

punch² ▶ n. **1** a device or machine for making holes in paper, leather, metal, etc. **2** a tool or machine for stamping a design on a material. ▶ v. pierce a hole in paper, leather, metal, etc.

punch³ ▶ n. a drink made from fruit juices, spices, etc., and usually wine or liquor.

punch·bowl /'pənCH,bōl/ ▶ n. **1** a deep bowl for mixing and serving punch. **2** chiefly Brit. a deep round hollow in a hilly area.

punch·card /'pənCH,kärd/ ▶ n. a perforated card used to control the operation of a machine or (formerly) to program computers.

punch-drunk ▶ adj. confused or dazed as a result of a series of heavy blows to the head.

pun·cheon /'pənCHən/ ▶ n. **1** a short post, especially one used for supporting the roof in a coal mine. **2** another term for PUNCH².

punching bag ▶ n. a stuffed suspended bag used for punching as exercise or training, especially by boxers.

punch·line /'pənCH,līn/ ▶ n. the final part of a joke or story, providing the humor or climax.

punch-up ▶ n. informal, chiefly Brit. a brawl.

punch·y /'pənCHē/ ▶ adj. (**punchier, punchiest**) **1** having an immediate impact; forceful. **2** another term for PUNCH-DRUNK.

punc·til·i·o /,pəNGK'tilē,ō/ ▶ n. (pl. **punctilios**) **1** a fine or trivial point of behavior or procedure. **2** punctilious behavior.

punc·til·i·ous /,pəNGK'tilēəs/ ▶ adj. showing great attention to detail or correct behavior. ■ **punc·til·i·ous·ly** adv. **punc·til·i·ous·ness** n.

punc·tu·al /'pəNGKCHŏŏəl/ ▶ adj. happening at or keeping to the arranged time. ■ **punc·tu·al·i·ty** /,pəNGKCHŏŏ'alitē/ n. **punc·tu·al·ly** adv.

punc·tu·ate /'pəNGKCHŏŏ,āt/ ▶ v. **1** occur or interrupt at intervals throughout: *the country's history has been punctuated by coups*. **2** put punctuation marks in a piece of writing.

punc·tu·a·tion /,pəNGKCHŏŏ'āshən/ ▶ n. the marks, such as period, comma, and parentheses, used in writing to separate sentences and their parts and to make meaning clear.

punc·ture /'pəNGKCHər/ ▶ n. a small hole caused by a sharp object, especially one in a tire. ▶ v. **1** make a puncture in something. **2** destroy a mood, feeling, etc.

pun·dit /'pəndit/ ▶ n. 1 an expert who frequently gives opinions about a subject in public. 2 variant spelling of PANDIT. ■ **pun·dit·ry** n.

pun·gent /'pənjənt/ ▶ adj. 1 having a sharply strong taste or smell. 2 (of remarks or humor) sharp and strongly worded. ■ **pun·gen·cy** n. **pun·gent·ly** adv.

Pu·nic /'pyŏŏnik/ ▶ adj. relating to ancient Carthage. ▶ n. the language of ancient Carthage.

pun·ish /'pənisH/ ▶ v. 1 cause someone to experience something unpleasant as a result of a criminal or wrongful act. 2 treat harshly or unfairly: *a rise in prescription charges would punish the poor.* ■ **pun·ish·a·ble** adj.

pun·ish·ment /'pənisHmənt/ ▶ n. 1 an unpleasant experience imposed on someone as a result of a criminal or wrongful act. 2 the action of punishing someone. 3 harsh or rough treatment.

pu·ni·tive /'pyŏŏnətiv/ ▶ adj. 1 imposing or intended as punishment. 2 (of a tax or other charge) extremely high. ■ **pu·ni·tive·ly** adv. **pu·ni·tive·ness** n.

Pun·ja·bi /ˌpənˈjäbē, pŏŏn-/ (also **Panjabi** /ˌpən-/) ▶ n. (pl. **Punjabis**) 1 a person from Punjab, a region of NW India and Pakistan. 2 the language of Punjab. ▶ adj. relating to Punjab.

punk /pəNGk/ ▶ n. 1 (also **punk rock**) a loud, fast form of rock music characterized by aggressive lyrics and behavior. 2 (also **punk rocker**) an admirer or player of punk music, typically having colored spiked hair and clothing decorated with safety pins and zippers. 3 informal a worthless person; a thug or criminal. ▶ adj. relating to punk rock and its admirers. ■ **punk·ish** adj. **punk·y** adj.

pun·kah /'pəNGkə/ ▶ n. chiefly historical (in India) a large cloth fan on a frame suspended from the ceiling, worked by a cord or electrically.

punt¹ /pənt/ ▶ n. a long, narrow, flat-bottomed boat, square at both ends and propelled with a long pole. ▶ v. travel in a punt. ■ **punt·er** n.

punt² ▶ v. 1 Football, etc. kick the ball after it has dropped from the hands and before it reaches the ground. 2 (of an offensive team) turn possession over to the defensive team by punting the ball after failing to make a first down. 3 delay in answering or taking action. ▶ n. a kick of this kind. ■ **punt·er** n.

punt³ ▶ v. 1 (in some gambling card games) lay a stake against the bank. 2 Brit. informal bet on or make a risky investment in something. ▶ n. Brit. informal a bet. ■ **punt·er** n.

pu·ny /'pyŏŏnē/ ▶ adj. (**punier, puniest**) 1 physically small and weak. 2 not impressive in quality, amount, or size: *their puny efforts.* ■ **pu·ni·ly** adv. **pu·ni·ness** n.

pup /pəp/ ▶ n. 1 a young dog. 2 a young wolf, seal, rat, or other mammal. 3 dated an impudent or arrogant boy or young man. ▶ v. (**pups, pupping, pupped**) give birth to a pup or pups.

pu·pa /'pyŏŏpə/ ▶ n. (pl. **pupae** /-ˌpē, -ˌpī/) an insect in its inactive stage of development between larva and adult, e.g., a chrysalis. ■ **pu·pal** adj.

pu·pate /'pyŏŏˌpāt/ ▶ v. (of an insect) become a pupa. ■ **pu·pa·tion** /pyŏŏ'pāsHən/ n.

pu·pil¹ /'pyŏŏpəl/ ▶ n. a person, especially a schoolchild, who is taught by someone; a student.

pu·pil² ▶ n. the dark circular opening in the

center of the iris of the eye, which controls the amount of light reaching the retina.

pup·pet /'pəpət/ ▶ n. 1 a model of a person or animal that can be moved either by strings or by a hand inside it. 2 a person under someone else's control. ■ **pup·pet·eer** /ˌpəpə'tir/ n. **pup·pet·ry** n.

pup·py /'pəpē/ ▶ n. (pl. **puppies**) 1 a young dog. 2 informal, dated a conceited or arrogant young man. ■ **pup·py·ish** adj.

pup·py love ▶ n. intense but short-lived feelings of love for someone, associated with adolescents.

pup tent ▶ n. a small triangular tent with room for one or two people.

pur·blind /'pər,blīnd/ ▶ adj. literary 1 lacking awareness or understanding. 2 partially sighted.

pur·chase /'pərchəs/ ▶ v. buy something. ▶ n. 1 the action of buying something. 2 a thing bought. 3 firm contact or grip. 4 a pulley or similar device for moving heavy objects. ■ **pur·chas·a·ble** adj. **pur·chas·er** n.

pur·dah /'pərdə/ ▶ n. the practice in certain Muslim and Hindu societies of screening women from men or strangers by means of a curtain or clothes that completely conceal their bodies.

pure /pyŏŏr/ ▶ adj. 1 not mixed with any other substance or material: *the jacket was pure wool.* 2 free of contamination. 3 innocent or morally good. 4 complete; nothing but: *a shout of pure anger.* 5 theoretical rather than practical: *pure mathematics.* 6 (of a sound) perfectly in tune and with a clear tone. ■ **pure·ly** adv.

pure·bred /'pyŏŏr,bred/ ▶ adj. (of an animal) bred from parents of the same breed or variety.

pu·rée /pyŏŏ'rā, -'rē/ ▶ n. a thick smooth substance made of crushed or liquidized fruit or vegetables. ▶ v. (**purées, puréeing, puréed**) make a purée of fruit or vegetables.

pure play ▶ n. 1 a company whose products are available only through the Internet. 2 a company that focuses exclusively on one particular market or commodity.

pur·ga·tion /ˌpər'gāsHən/ ▶ n. 1 purification. 2 emptying of the bowels brought about by laxatives.

pur·ga·tive /'pərgətiv/ ▶ adj. having a strong laxative effect. ▶ n. a laxative.

pur·ga·to·ry /'pərgəˌtôrē/ ▶ n. (pl. **purgatories**) 1 (in Catholic belief) a place or state of suffering inhabited by the souls of sinners who are atoning for their sins before going to heaven. 2 extreme distress or mental anguish. ■ **pur·ga·to·ri·al** /ˌpərgə'tôrēəl/ adj.

purge /pərj/ ▶ v. 1 rid of unwanted or undesirable things: *years of analysis had purged him of anger.* 2 remove a group of people considered to be undesirable from an organization. 3 empty one's bowels, especially as a result of taking a laxative. 4 Law atone for or wipe out contempt of court. ▶ n. 1 an act of removing a group of people from an organization. 2 dated a laxative.

pu·ri /'pŏŏrē/ ▶ n. (pl. **puris**) (in Indian cooking) a small, round piece of unleavened bread that puffs up when deep-fried.

pu·ri·fy /'pyŏŏrəˌfī/ ▶ v. (**purifies, purifying, purified**) make something pure by removing harmful, dirty, or unwanted substances. ■ **pu·ri·fi·ca·tion** /ˌpyŏŏrəfi'kāsHən/ n. **pu·ri·fi·er** n.

Pu·rim /'pŏŏrim, pŏŏ'rēm/ ▶ n. a Jewish festival held in spring to commemorate the defeat of Haman's plot to massacre the Jews.

pur·ist /'pyŏŏrist/ ▶ n. a person who insists on following traditional rules, especially in language or style. ■ **pur·ism** /'pyŏŏr,izəm/ n.

pu·ri·tan /'pyŏŏritn/ ▶ n. 1 (**Puritan**) a member of a group of English Protestants in the 16th and 17th centuries who sought to simplify and regulate forms of worship. 2 a person with strict moral beliefs who is critical of self-indulgent behavior. ▶ adj. 1 (**Puritan**) relating to the Puritans. 2 characteristic of a puritan. ■ **pu·ri·tan·ism** /'pyŏŏritə,nizəm/ (also **Puritanism**) n.

pu·ri·tan·i·cal /,pyŏŏri'tanikəl/ ▶ adj. having a very strict or critical attitude toward self-indulgent behavior.

pu·ri·ty /'pyŏŏritē/ ▶ n. the state of being pure.

purl[1] /'pərl/ ▶ adj. (of a knitting stitch) made by putting the needle through the front of the stitch from right to left. Compare with **PLAIN** (sense 8 of the adjective). ▶ v. knit with a purl stitch.

purl[2] ▶ v. literary (of a stream or river) flow with a swirling movement and a continuous murmuring sound.

pur·lieu /'pərl(y)ŏŏ/ ▶ n. (pl. **purlieus**) 1 (**purlieus**) the area near or surrounding a place. 2 a person's usual haunts.

pur·lin /'pərlən/ ▶ n. a horizontal beam along the length of a roof, supporting the rafters.

pur·loin /pər'loin/ ▶ v. formal or humorous steal something.

pur·ple /'pərpəl/ ▶ n. 1 a color between red and blue. 2 (**the purple**) the scarlet official dress of a cardinal. ▶ adj. of a color between red and blue. ■ **pur·plish** adj. **pur·ply** adj.

Pur·ple Heart ▶ n. a US military decoration for members of the armed forces wounded or killed in action.

pur·ple pas·sage ▶ n. an extremely ornate or elaborate passage in a literary work.

pur·ple prose ▶ n. prose that is too ornate.

pur·port ▶ v. /pər'pôrt/ appear or claim to be someone or do something: *she is not the person she purports to be.* ▶ n. /'pər,pôrt/ 1 the meaning of something. 2 the purpose of something. ■ **pur·port·ed** adj. **pur·port·ed·ly** adv.

pur·pose /'pərpəs/ ▶ n. 1 the reason for which something is done or for which something exists: *the purpose of the meeting is to appoint a trustee.* 2 determination: *there was a sense of purpose in her step as she set off.* ▶ v. formal have something as one's aim or intention.
– PHRASES **on purpose** intentionally.

pur·pose·ful /'pərpəsfəl/ ▶ adj. 1 having or showing determination. 2 having a useful purpose. ■ **pur·pose·ful·ly** adv. **pur·pose·ful·ness** n.

pur·pose·less /'pərpəslis/ ▶ adj. done with or having no purpose. ■ **pur·pose·less·ly** adv. **pur·pose·less·ness** n.

pur·pose·ly /'pərpəslē/ ▶ adv. deliberately; on purpose.

pur·pos·ive /'pərpəsiv, pər'pō-/ ▶ adj. having or done with a purpose. ■ **pur·pos·ive·ly** adv. **pur·pos·ive·ness** n.

purr /pər/ ▶ v. 1 (of a cat) make a low continuous sound in the throat, especially when happy or contented. 2 (of a vehicle or engine) move or run smoothly while making a similar sound. ▶ n. a purring sound.

purse /pərs/ ▶ n. 1 a handbag. 2 a small pouch for carrying money. 3 money available for spending; funds. 4 a sum of money given as a prize in a sporting contest. ▶ v. pucker one's lips into a tight, round shape.
– PHRASES **hold the purse strings** have control of expenditure.

purs·er /'pərsər/ ▶ n. a ship's officer who keeps the accounts, especially on a passenger vessel.

purse seine ▶ n. a large seine (fishing net) that may be drawn into the shape of a bag, used for catching fish swimming in shoals.

purs·lane /'pərslən, -,slān/ ▶ n. a small plant with fleshy leaves that grows in damp or marshy areas.

pur·su·ance /pər'sŏŏəns/ ▶ n. formal the carrying out of a plan or action.

pur·su·ant /pər'sŏŏənt/ ▶ adv. (**pursuant to**) formal in accordance with a law or legal resolution.

pur·sue /pər'sŏŏ/ ▶ v. (**pursues, pursuing, pursued**) 1 follow in order to catch or attack: *police officers pursued the car along I-95.* 2 try to achieve a goal. 3 engage in or continue with an activity or course of action: *he took a degree before pursuing his professional sports career.* 4 continue to investigate or discuss something. ■ **pur·su·er** n.

pur·suit /pər'sŏŏt/ ▶ n. 1 the action of pursuing someone or something. 2 a leisure or sporting activity.

pu·ru·lent /'pyŏŏr(y)ələnt/ ▶ adj. consisting of, containing, or discharging pus.

pur·vey /pər'vā/ ▶ v. formal provide or supply food or drink as one's business. ■ **pur·vey·or** n.

pur·view /'pər,vyŏŏ/ ▶ n. formal 1 the scope of the influence or concerns of something: *such crimes are not within the purview of the tribunal.* 2 a range of experience or thought.

pus /pəs/ ▶ n. a thick yellowish or greenish liquid produced in infected tissue.

push /pŏŏsh/ ▶ v. 1 apply force to someone or something so as to move them away from oneself or from the source of the force. 2 move one's body or a part of it forcefully into a particular position: *she pushed her hands into her pockets.* 3 move forward by using force: *he pushed his way through the crowd.* 4 drive oneself or urge someone to greater effort. 5 (**push for**) make persistent demands for something: *some legislators are pushing for tighter border controls.* 6 informal promote the use, sale, or acceptance of something. 7 informal sell a drug illegally. 8 (**be pushed**) informal have very little of something, especially time. 9 (**be pushing**) informal be nearly a particular age: *she's pushing forty.* ▶ n. 1 an act of pushing. 2 a great effort: *one last push for success.* ■ **push·er** n.
– PHRASES **push ahead** proceed with or continue a course of action. **push off** exert pressure so as to move a boat out from shore or away from another vessel. **when push comes to shove** informal when one has no choice but to act or make a decision.

push·cart /'pŏŏsh,kärt/ ▶ n. a small cart that is pushed or drawn by hand.

push·o·ver /'pŏŏsh,ōvər/ ▶ n. informal 1 a person who is easy to influence or defeat. 2 a thing that is easily done.

push-start ▶ v. start a motor vehicle by pushing it in order to make the engine turn.

push·up /'pŏŏsh,əp/ ▶ n. an exercise in which a

person lies facing the floor and raises their body by pressing down on their hands.

push·y /'pŏŏSHē/ ▸adj. (**pushier, pushiest**) too self-assertive or ambitious. ■ **push·i·ness** n.

pu·sil·lan·i·mous /ˌpyŏŏsəˈlanəməs/ ▸adj. timid or cowardly. ■ **pu·sil·la·nim·i·ty** /-ləˈnimətē/ n.

puss¹ /pŏŏs/ ▸n. informal **1** a cat. **2** a girl or young woman: *a glamour puss*.

puss² ▸n. informal a person's face or mouth.

pus·sy /'pŏŏsē/ ▸n. (pl. **pussies**) **1** informal a cat. **2** vulgar slang a woman's genitals. **3** vulgar slang women considered sexually. **4** vulgar slang sexual intercourse with a woman. **5** informal a weak, cowardly, or effeminate man.

pus·sy·cat /'pŏŏsē,kat/ ▸n. informal **1** a cat. **2** a mild-tempered or easy-going person.

pus·sy·foot /'pŏŏsē,fŏŏt/ ▸v. (**pussyfoots, pussyfooting, pussyfooted**) act very cautiously.

pus·sy wil·low ▸n. a willow with soft fluffy catkins that appear before the leaves.

pus·tule /'pəscHŏŏl, 'pəst(y)ŏŏl/ ▸n. a small blister or pimple containing pus. ■ **pus·tu·lar** adj.

put /pŏŏt/ ▸v. (**puts, putting, put**) **1** move to or place in a particular position: *he put down his cup.* **2** bring into a particular state or condition: *she tried to put me at ease.* **3** (**put something on**) make someone or something subject to something: *commentators put the blame on Congress.* **4** give a value, figure, or limit to something. **5** express something in a particular way: *to put it bluntly, we've been framed.* **6** (of a ship) proceed in a particular direction: *the boat put out to sea.* **7** throw a shot or weight as an athletic sport. ▸n. a throw of the shot or weight as a sport.
– PHRASES **be put upon** informal be taken advantage of as a result of one's good nature. **put about** (of a ship) turn on the opposite tack. **put someone down** informal criticize someone. **put something down 1** suppress a rebellion, coup, or riot by force. **2** kill a sick, old, or injured animal. **3** pay a sum as a deposit. **put something down to** attribute something to. **put one's hands together** applaud. **put someone off 1** cause someone to feel dislike or lose enthusiasm. **2** distract someone. **put something off** postpone something. **put something on 1** present or provide a play, service, etc. **2** become heavier by a particular amount. **3** adopt a particular expression, accent, etc. **put someone out** inconvenience, upset, or annoy someone. **put something out** dislocate a joint. **put one over on** informal deceive someone into accepting something that is not true. **put someone through 1** subject someone to an unpleasant experience. **2** connect someone by telephone to another person or place. **put something to** offer or submit something to someone for consideration: *he put the proposal to his daughter.* **put someone up 1** give someone temporary accommodations. **2** propose someone for election or adoption. **put something up** present, provide, or offer something: *the sponsors are putting up $5,000.* **put someone up to** informal encourage someone to do something wrong or unwise. **put up with** tolerate or endure: *I'm too tired to put up with any nonsense.*

pu·ta·tive /'pyŏŏtətiv/ ▸adj. generally considered or believed to be: *the putative father of her children.* ■ **pu·ta·tive·ly** adv.

put-down ▸n. informal a humiliating or critical remark.

pu·tre·fy /'pyŏŏtrə,fī/ ▸v. (**putrefies, putrefying, putrefied**) decay or rot and produce a very unpleasant smell. ■ **pu·tre·fac·tion** /ˌpyŏŏtrəˈfaksHən/ n.

pu·tres·cent /pyŏŏˈtresənt/ ▸adj. becoming putrid; rotting.

pu·trid /'pyŏŏtrid/ ▸adj. **1** decaying or rotting and giving off a very unpleasant smell. **2** informal very unpleasant.

putsch /pŏŏcH/ ▸n. a violent attempt to overthrow a government.

putt /pət/ ▸v. (**putts, putting, putted**) strike a golf ball gently so that it rolls into or near a hole. ▸n. a stroke of this kind.

put·ta·nes·ca /ˌpŏŏtəˈneskə, ˌpŏŏtnˈeskə/ ▸n. a pasta sauce made with tomatoes, garlic, olives, anchovies, etc.

put·tee /ˌpəˈtē/ ▸n. a long strip of cloth wound around the leg from ankle to knee for protection and support.

put·ter¹ /'pətər/ ▸n. a golf club designed for putting.

put·ter² ▸n. the rapid intermittent sound of a small gasoline engine. ▸v. move with or make such a sound.

put·ter³ ▸v. **1** occupy oneself by doing minor, pleasant tasks in a relaxed way. **2** move or go in a casual, unhurried way.

put·ting green /'pətiNG/ ▸n. a smooth area of short grass surrounding a hole on a golf course.

put·to /'pŏŏtō/ ▸n. (pl. **putti** /'pŏŏtē/) a representation of a naked child, especially a cherub or a cupid in Renaissance art.

put·ty /'pətē/ ▸n. a paste that is easily pressed into shape and gradually hardens as it sets, used for sealing glass in window frames, filling holes in wood, etc.
– PHRASES **be (like) putty in someone's hands** be easily manipulated by someone.

putz /'pəts, 'pŏŏts/ ▸n. informal a stupid person.

puz·zle /'pəzəl/ ▸v. **1** make someone feel confused as a result of being difficult to understand: *I was very puzzled by his reply.* **2** think hard about something that is difficult to understand: *he puzzled over this problem for years.* ▸n. **1** a game, toy, or problem designed to test mental skills or knowledge. **2** a person or thing that is difficult to understand. ■ **puz·zle·ment** n. **puz·zler** n.

PVA ▸abbr. polyvinyl acetate, a synthetic resin used in paints and glues.

PVC ▸abbr. polyvinyl chloride, a tough synthetic resin used for a wide variety of products including pipes and floor coverings.

PVS ▸abbr. Medicine persistent vegetative state.

Pvt. ▸abbr. (in the US Army and in company names) private.

PWR ▸abbr. pressurized-water reactor.

PX ▸abbr. post exchange.

pyg·my /'pigmē/ ▸n. (pl. **pygmies**) **1** (**Pygmy**) a member of certain peoples of very short stature in equatorial Africa. **2** chiefly derogatory a very small person or thing. **3** a person who is lacking in a particular respect: *intellectual pygmies.* ▸adj. very small; dwarf.

py·ja·mas /pəˈjäməz, -ˈjaməz/ ▸pl.n. British spelling of PAJAMAS.

py·lon /'pī,län, -lən/ ▸n. (also **electricity pylon**) a tall towerlike metal structure for carrying power lines.

py·lo·rus /pī'lôrəs, pə-/ ▸ n. (pl. **pylori** /-'lôr,ī, -'lôrē/) the opening from the stomach into the small intestine. ▪ **py·lor·ic** /pī'lôrik, pə-/ adj.

py·ra·can·tha /,pīrə'kanтнə/ ▸ n. a thorny evergreen shrub with white flowers and bright red or yellow berries.

pyr·a·mid /'pirə,mid/ ▸ n. **1** a huge stone structure with a square or triangular base and sloping sides that meet in a point at the top, especially one built as a royal tomb in ancient Egypt. **2** Geometry a polyhedron of which one face is a polygon and the other faces are triangles with a common vertex. **3** a pyramid-shaped thing or pile of things. ▪ **py·ram·i·dal** /pi'ramidl/ adj.

pyr·a·mid scheme ▸ n. a system of selling goods in which agency rights are sold to an increasing number of distributors at successively lower levels.

pyre /pīr/ ▸ n. a large pile of wood on which a dead body is placed and burned as part of a funeral ceremony.

py·re·thrum /pī'rēтнrəm, -'reтнrəm/ ▸ n. **1** a plant of the daisy family, typically with brightly colored flowers. **2** an insecticide made from the dried flowers of these plants.

py·ret·ic /pī'retik/ ▸ adj. feverish or causing fever.

Py·rex /'pī,reks/ ▸ n. trademark a hard heat-resistant type of glass.

py·rex·i·a /pī'reksēə/ ▸ n. raised body temperature; fever.

pyr·i·dox·ine /,piri'däk,sēn/ ▸ n. vitamin B₆, a compound present chiefly in cereals, liver oils, and yeast.

py·rite /'pī,rīt/ (also **iron pyrites** or **pyrites** /pə'rītēz, pī-/) ▸ n. a shiny yellow mineral that is a compound of iron and sulfur.

pyro- ▸ comb.form relating to fire: *pyromania*.

py·ro·clas·tic /,pīrō'klastik/ ▸ adj. Geology relating to rock fragments or ash erupted by a volcano, especially as a hot, dense, destructive flow.

py·rog·ra·phy /pī'rägrəfē/ ▸ n. the art or technique of decorating wood or leather by burning a design on the surface with a heated metallic point.

py·ro·ma·ni·a /,pīrō'mānēə/ ▸ n. an obsessive desire to set fire to things. ▪ **py·ro·ma·ni·ac** /-'mānē,ak/ n.

py·ro·tech·nic /,pīrə'teknik/ ▸ adj. **1** relating to fireworks. **2** brilliant or spectacular. ▪ **py·ro·tech·ni·cal** adj.

py·ro·tech·nics /,pīrə'tekniks/ ▸ pl.n. **1** a firework display. **2** (treated as sing.) the art of making fireworks or staging firework displays. **3** a spectacular performance or display: *vocal pyrotechnics*.

pyr·rhic /'pirik/ ▸ adj. (of a victory) won at too great a cost to have been worthwhile for the victor.

Py·thag·o·re·an the·o·rem /pə,тнagə'rēən, pī-/ ▸ n. the theorem that the square of the hypotenuse of a right triangle is equal in area to the sum of the squares of the other two sides.

Py·thag·o·re·an /pi,тнagə'rēən, pī-/ ▸ adj. relating to the Greek philosopher and mathematician Pythagoras (c. 580–500 BC) or his philosophy.

py·thon /'pī,тнän, 'pīтнən/ ▸ n. a large nonvenomous snake that kills its prey by squeezing and crushing it.

pyx /piks/ (also **pix**) ▸ n. Christian Church the container in which the consecrated bread used in the service of Holy Communion is kept.

p·zazz /pə'zaz/ ▸ n. variant spelling of PIZZAZZ.

Qq

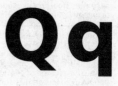

Q¹ (also **q**) ▸ n. (pl. **Qs** or **Q's**) the seventeenth letter of the alphabet.

Q² ▸ abbr. **1** queen (used especially in card games and chess). **2** question.

Qa·ba·lah /kə'bälə/ ▸ n. variant spelling of KABBALAH.

Qa·tar·i /'kätärē, kə'tärē/ ▸ n. (pl. **Qataris**) a person from Qatar, a country in the Persian Gulf. ▸ adj. relating to Qatar.

QC ▸ abbr. **1** quality control. **2** Quebec.

QED ▸ abbr. quod erat demonstrandum, used to state that something proves the truth of one's claim.

qi /CHē/ ▸ n. variant spelling of CHI.

qi·gong /,CHē'gäNG, -'gôNG/ ▸ n. a Chinese system of physical exercises and breathing control related to t'ai chi.

QT ▸ n. (in phrase **on the QT**) informal secretly.

qt. ▸ abbr. quart(s).

qty. ▸ abbr. quantity.

qua /kwä/ ▸ conj. formal in the capacity of; as being.

quack¹ /kwak/ ▸ n. the harsh sound made by a duck. ▸ v. make a quack.

quack² ▸ n. **1** an unqualified person who dishonestly claims to have medical knowledge. **2** informal a doctor perceived as one who prescribes wrong, useless, or harmful treatments. ■ **quack·er·y** n.

quad /kwäd/ ▸ n. **1** a quadrangle. **2** a quadruplet.

quad·ran·gle /'kwä,draNGgəl/ ▸ n. **1** a square or rectangular courtyard enclosed by buildings. **2** a four-sided geometrical figure, especially a square or rectangle. ■ **quad·ran·gu·lar** /kwä'draNGgyələr/ adj.

quad·rant /'kwädrənt/ ▸ n. **1** each of four parts of a circle, plane, object, etc., divided by two lines or planes at right angles. **2** historical an instrument for measuring altitude in astronomy and navigation.

quad·ra·phon·ic /,kwädrə'fänik/ (also **quadrophonic**) ▸ adj. (of sound reproduction) transmitted through four channels. ■ **qua·draph·o·ny** /kwä'dräfənē/ n.

quad·rate /'kwä,drāt, -rət/ ▸ adj. roughly square or rectangular.

quad·rat·ic /kwä'dratik/ ▸ adj. Mathematics involving the second and no higher power of an unknown quantity or variable.

quad·ren·ni·al /kwä'drenēəl/ ▸ adj. lasting for or recurring every four years.

quadri- ▸ comb.form four; having four: *quadriplegia.*

quad·ri·ceps /'kwädrə,seps/ ▸ n. (pl. same) a large muscle at the front of the thigh.

quad·ri·lat·er·al /,kwädrə'latərəl/ ▸ n. a four-sided figure. ▸ adj. having four straight sides.

quad·rille¹ /kwä'dril, k(w)ə-/ ▸ n. a square dance performed by four couples.

quad·rille² ▸ n. a trick-taking card game for four players, fashionable in the 18th century.

quad·ril·lion /kwä'drilyən/ ▸ cardinal number **1** a thousand raised to the power of five (10^{15}). **2** (also **quadrillions**) informal a very large number or amount. ■ **quad·ril·lionth** /kwä'drilyənTH/ ordinal number.

quad·ri·par·tite /,kwädrə'pärtīt/ ▸ adj. **1** consisting of four parts. **2** shared by or involving four parties.

quad·ri·ple·gi·a /,kwädrə'plēj(ē)ə/ ▸ n. paralysis of all four limbs. ■ **quad·ri·ple·gic** /-'plējik/ adj. & n.

quad·roon /kwä'drōon/ ▸ n. offensive a person who has one parent who is black and the other who has one black parent and one white one.

quad·ro·phon·ic /,kwädrə'fänik/ ▸ adj. variant spelling of QUADRAPHONIC.

quad·ru·ped /'kwädrə,ped/ ▸ n. an animal that has four feet, especially a mammal. ■ **quad·ru·pe·dal** /,kwädrə'pedl, kwä'drōopədl/ adj.

quad·ru·ple /kwä'drōopəl/ ▸ adj. **1** consisting of four parts or elements. **2** four times as much or as many. **3** (of time in music) having four beats in a bar. ▸ v. multiply or be multiplied by four. ▸ n. a quadruple number or amount.

quad·ru·plet /kwä'drōoplit/ ▸ n. each of four children born at one birth.

quad·ru·pli·cate /kwä'drōopləkit/ ▸ adj. consisting of four parts. – PHRASES **in quadruplicate** in four copies.

quaff /kwäf/ ▸ v. drink something heartily. ■ **quaff·a·ble** adj. **quaff·er** n.

quag·ga /'kwagə/ ▸ n. an extinct South African zebra with a yellowish-brown coat with darker stripes.

quag·mire /'kwag,mīr/ ▸ n. **1** a soft boggy area of land that gives way underfoot. **2** a complex or difficult situation: *a quagmire of unresolved issues.*

quail¹ /kwāl/ ▸ n. (pl. same or **quails**) a small short-tailed game bird, typically with brown plumage.

quail² ▸ v. feel or show fear or worry.

quaint /kwānt/ ▸ adj. attractively unusual or old-fashioned. ■ **quaint·ly** adv. **quaint·ness** n.

quake /kwāk/ ▸ n. informal an earthquake. ▸ v. **1** shudder with fear. **2** (especially of the earth) shake or tremble.

Quak·er /'kwākər/ ▸ n. a member of the Religious Society of Friends, a Christian movement that is strongly opposed to war and violence and that meets without any formal ceremony. ■ **Quak·er·ism** /-izəm/ n.

qual·i·fi·ca·tion /ˌkwäləfəˈkāsHən/ ▶ n. **1** a pass of an exam or an official completion of a course. **2** the action of qualifying or the fact of becoming qualified: *England needs to beat Poland to ensure qualification for the World Cup finals.* **3** a quality that makes someone suitable for a job or activity. **4** an official requirement. **5** a statement that restricts the meaning of another.

qual·i·fi·er /ˈkwäləˌfīər/ ▶ n. **1** a person or team that qualifies for a competition or its final rounds. **2** a match or contest to decide which people or teams qualify for a competition or its final rounds. **3** Grammar a word or phrase, especially an adjective, used to describe another word, especially a noun.

qual·i·fy /ˈkwäləˌfī/ ▶ v. (**qualifies, qualifying, qualified**) **1** meet the necessary standard or conditions to be entitled to do or receive something: *it's the best chance in years for the team to qualify for a major tournament.* **2** certify or license someone as able to practice a particular profession or activity. **3** make someone competent or knowledgeable enough to do something: *I'm not qualified to write on the subject.* **4** add restrictions to a statement to limit its meaning. **5** Grammar (of a word or phrase) describe another word in a particular way in order to restrict its meaning (e.g., in *the open door, open* is an adjective qualifying *door*).

qual·i·ta·tive /ˈkwäləˌtātiv/ ▶ adj. relating to or measured by quality. ■ **qual·i·ta·tive·ly** adv.

qual·i·ta·tive a·nal·y·sis ▶ n. Chemistry the identification of the constituents present in a substance.

qual·i·ty /ˈkwälətē/ ▶ n. (pl. **qualities**) **1** the standard of how good something is as measured against other similar things: *an improvement in product quality.* **2** general excellence. **3** a distinctive feature or characteristic: *strong leadership qualities.* **4** old use high social standing. ▶ adj. informal of good quality; excellent: *he's a quality player.*

qual·i·ty con·trol ▶ n. a system of maintaining quality in manufactured products by testing a sample to see if it meets the required standard.

qual·i·ty time ▶ n. time spent in giving one's full attention to one's child or partner, in order to strengthen the relationship.

qualm /kwä(l)m, kwô(l)m/ ▶ n. **1** a feeling of doubt or unease, especially about one's behavior: *he had no qualms about divorcing her.* **2** old use a brief faint or sick feeling.

quan·da·ry /ˈkwänd(ə)rē/ ▶ n. (pl. **quandaries**) a state of uncertainty over what to do in a difficult situation.

quan·ta /ˈkwäntə/ ▶ plural of QUANTUM.

quan·ti·fy /ˈkwäntəˌfī/ ▶ v. (**quantifies, quantifying, quantified**) express or measure the quantity of: *the method used to quantify how much acid rain it takes to damage ecosystems.* ■ **quan·ti·fi·a·ble** /ˈkwäntəˌfīəbəl/ adj. **quan·ti·fi·ca·tion** /ˌkwäntəfiˈkāsHən/ n. **quan·ti·fi·er** /ˈkwäntəˌfīər/ n.

quan·ti·ta·tive /ˈkwäntəˌtātiv/ ▶ adj. relating to or measured by quantity. ■ **quan·ti·ta·tive·ly** adv.

quan·ti·ta·tive a·nal·y·sis ▶ n. Chemistry the measurement of the quantities of particular constituents present in a substance.

quan·ti·ty /ˈkwäntətē/ ▶ n. (pl. **quantities**) **1** a certain amount or number of something. **2** the aspect of something that is measurable in

number, amount, size, or weight: *wages depended on quantity of output.* **3** a considerable number or amount.

quan·tize /ˈkwänˌtīz/ ▶ v. Physics apply quantum theory to; in particular restrict the number of possible values of a quantity or states of a system. ■ **quan·ti·za·tion** /ˌkwäntəˈzāsHən/ n. **quan·tiz·er** n.

quan·tum /ˈkwäntəm/ ▶ n. (pl. **quanta** /ˈkwäntə/) **1** Physics a distinct quantity of energy corresponding to that involved in the absorption or emission of energy by an atom. **2** a share or portion.

quan·tum com·put·er ▶ n. a hypothetical computer that makes use of the quantum states of subatomic particles to store information.

quan·tum dot ▶ n. Physics a nanoscale particle of semiconducting material that can be embedded in cells or organisms for various experimental purposes, such as labeling proteins.

quan·tum leap (also **quantum jump**) ▶ n. a sudden large increase or advance.

quan·tum me·chan·ics ▶ pl.n. (treated as sing.) the branch of physics concerned with describing the behavior of subatomic particles in terms of quanta.

quan·tum the·o·ry ▶ n. a theory of matter and energy based on the idea of quanta.

quar·an·tine /ˈkwôrənˌtēn/ ▶ n. a state or period of isolation for people or animals that have or may have a disease. ▶ v. put a person or animal in quarantine.

quark¹ /kwärk/ ▶ n. Physics any of a group of subatomic particles that carry a fractional electric charge and are believed to be building blocks of protons, neutrons, and other particles.

quark² ▶ n. a type of low-fat curd cheese.

quar·rel¹ /ˈkwôrəl, ˈkwä-/ ▶ n. **1** an angry argument or disagreement. **2** a reason for disagreement: *his quarrel is with those who exaggerate the benefits of the project.* ▶ v. (**quarrels, quarreling, quarreled**) **1** have a quarrel. **2** (**quarrel with**) disagree with.

quar·rel² ▶ n. historical a short heavy square-headed arrow or bolt for a crossbow.

quar·rel·some /ˈkwôrəlsəm, ˈkwä-/ ▶ adj. tending or likely to quarrel.

quar·ry¹ /ˈkwôrē, ˈkwä-/ ▶ n. (pl. **quarries**) an area of the earth's surface that has been dug open so that stone or other materials can be obtained. ▶ v. (**quarries, quarrying, quarried**) take stone or other materials from a quarry. ■ **quar·ri·er** n.

quar·ry² ▶ n. (pl. **quarries**) **1** an animal being hunted. **2** a person or thing being chased or looked for.

quar·ry³ ▶ n. (pl. **quarries**) **1** (also **quarry tile**) an unglazed floor tile. **2** a diamond-shaped pane in a lattice window.

quart /kwôrt/ ▶ n. a unit of liquid capacity equal to a quarter of a gallon or two pints, equivalent to approximately 0.94 liter (or 1.13 liters in the UK).

quar·ter /ˈkwôrtər/ ▶ n. **1** each of four equal parts into which something is divided. **2** a period of three months, used especially in reference to financial transactions. **3** a school term of 12 weeks. **4** a period of fifteen minutes; a quarter of an hour: *a quarter past nine.* **5** one fourth of a pound weight, equal to 4 ounces avoirdupois. **6** a part of a town or city with a specific character or use: *the business quarter.* **7** (**quarters**) rooms or lodgings. **8** a US or Canadian coin worth 25 cents. **9** one fourth of a hundredweight (US 25 lb or Brit. 28 lb). **10** a person, group, or area regarded as the source of something: *help came from an unexpected quarter.* **11** mercy shown to an opponent: *they gave the enemy no quarter.* **12** (**quarters**) the haunches or hindquarters of a horse. **13** the direction of one of the points of the compass. ▶v. **1** divide something into quarters. **2** (**be quartered**) be lodged somewhere. **3** historical cut the body of an executed person into four parts. **4** range over an area in all directions.

quar·ter·back /'kwôrtər,bak/ ▶n. Football a player stationed behind the center who directs a team's offensive play.

quar·ter·deck /'kwôrtər,dek/ ▶n. the part of a ship's upper deck near the stern, traditionally reserved for officers or for ceremonial use.

quar·ter·fi·nal /'kwôrtər,fīnl/ ▶n. a match or round of a tournament preceding the semifinal. ■ **quar·ter·fi·nal·ist** /'kwôrtər,fīnl-ist/ n.

quar·ter-hour ▶n. **1** (also **quarter of an hour**) a period of fifteen minutes. **2** a point of time fifteen minutes before or after a full hour of the clock.

quar·ter·ly /'kwôrtərlē/ ▶ adj. & adv. produced or occurring once every quarter of a year. ▶ n. (pl. **quarterlies**) a publication produced four times a year.

quar·ter·mas·ter /'kwôrtər,mastər/ ▶n. **1** a regimental officer in charge of providing accommodations and supplies. **2** a naval petty officer responsible for steering and signals.

quar·ter note ▶n. a musical note having the time value of half a half note, represented by a solid dot with a plain stem.

quar·tet /kwôr'tet/ (also **quartette**) ▶n. **1** a group of four people playing music or singing together. **2** a composition for a quartet. **3** a set of four people or things.

quar·tile /'kwôr,tīl, 'kwôrtl/ ▶ n. Statistics each of four equal groups into which a population can be divided according to the distribution of values of a particular variable.

quar·to /'kwôrtō/ ▶n. (pl. **quartos**) a page or paper size resulting from folding a sheet into four leaves, typically 10 inches × 8 inches (254 × 203 mm).

quartz /kwôrts/ ▶n. a hard mineral consisting of silica, typically occurring as colorless or white hexagonal prisms.

quartz clock (or **watch**) ▶n. a clock (or watch) regulated by vibrations of an electrically driven quartz crystal.

quartz·ite /'kwôrt,sīt/ ▶n. a compact, hard, granular rock consisting mainly of quartz.

qua·sar /'kwā,zär/ ▶n. a massive and extremely remote object in space that emits huge amounts of energy.

quash /kwôsh, kwäsh/ ▶v. **1** officially reject a legal decision as invalid. **2** put an end to; suppress: *rumors of job losses were quashed.*

quasi- /,kwä,zī, ,kwäzē-/ ▶comb.form **1** seemingly: *quasi-scientific.* **2** being partly or almost: *quasicrystalline.*

quas·sia /'kwäsн(ē)ə/ ▶n. a South American shrub or small tree whose wood, bark, or root yields a bitter medicinal tonic and insecticide.

quat·er·nar·y /'kwätər,nerē/ ▶adj. **1** fourth in

order or rank. **2** (**Quaternary**) Geology relating to the most recent period in the Cenozoic era, from about 1.64 million years ago to the present.

quat·rain /'kwä,trān/ ▶n. a stanza of four lines, typically with alternate rhymes.

quat·re·foil /'katər,foil, 'katrə-/ ▶n. an ornamental design of four lobes or leaves, resembling a clover leaf.

quat·tro·cen·to /,kwätrō'cнentō/ ▶n. the 15th century as a period of Italian art or architecture.

qua·ver /'kwāvər/ ▶v. (of a voice) tremble. ▶n. a tremble in a voice. ■ **qua·ver·y** adj.

quay /kē, k(w)ā/ ▶n. a platform lying alongside or projecting into water for loading and unloading ships.

quay·side /'kē,sīd, 'k(w)ā-/ ▶n. a quay and the area around it.

quea·sy /'kwēzē/ ▶adj. (**queasier, queasiest**) **1** feeling sick; nauseous. **2** slightly nervous or uneasy. ■ **quea·si·ly** adv. **quea·si·ness** n.

Quech·ua /'kecнwə/ ▶n. (pl. same or **Quechuas**) **1** a member of an American Indian people of Peru and neighboring countries. **2** the language of the Quechua. ■ **Quech·uan** adj. & n.

queen /kwēn/ ▶n. **1** the female ruler of an independent country, especially one who inherits the position by birth. **2** (also **queen consort**) a king's wife. **3** the best or most important woman or thing in a field of activity or group. **4** a playing card bearing a picture of a queen, ranking next below a king. **5** the most powerful chess piece, able to move in any direction. **6** a reproductive female in a colony of ants, bees, wasps, or termites. **7** informal, often derogatory a homosexual man, especially an effeminate or flamboyant one. ▶v. **1** (**queen it**) (of a woman) act in an unpleasantly superior way. **2** Chess convert a pawn into a queen when it reaches the opponent's end of the board. ■ **queen·dom** /-dəm/ n. **queen·ly** /'kwēnlē/ adj. **queen·ship** /-,sнip/ n.

Queen Anne ▶adj. referring to a style of English furniture or architecture characteristic of the early 18th century.

Queen Anne's lace ▶n. the uncultivated form of the carrot, with broad round heads of tiny white flowers that resemble lace.

queen bee ▶n. **1** the single reproductive female in a colony of honeybees. **2** informal a dominant woman in a group.

queen moth·er ▶n. the widow of a king and mother of the current sovereign.

queen post ▶n. either of two upright timbers between the tie beam and main rafters of a roof truss.

Queens·ber·ry Rules /'kwēnz,berē/ ▶pl.n. the standard rules of boxing.

Queen's Eng·lish ▶n. the English language as correctly written and spoken in Britain.

queen-sized (also **queen-size**) ▶adj. (of a bed) of a larger size than the standard but smaller than king-sized.

queer /kwi(ə)r/ ▶adj. **1** strange; odd. **2** informal, derogatory (of a man) homosexual. **3** informal, dated slightly ill. ▶n. informal, derogatory a homosexual man. ▶v. informal spoil or ruin something. ■ **queer·ish** adj. **queer·ly** adv. **queer·ness** n. – PHRASES **queer someone's pitch** Brit. informal spoil someone's plans or chances of doing something.

quell /kwel/ ▶ v. **1** put an end to a rebellion or other disorder. **2** stop or reduce a strong or unpleasant feeling: *I hurried to quell her fears.*

quench /kwench/ ▶ v. **1** satisfy thirst by drinking. **2** satisfy a desire. **3** extinguish a fire. **4** stop or reduce a strong feeling. **5** rapidly cool hot metal. ■ **quench·er** n.

que·nelle /kə'nel/ ▶ n. a small ball of ground meat or fish.

quer·u·lous /'kwer(y)ələs/ ▶ adj. complaining in a petulant or irritable way. ■ **quer·u·lous·ly** adv. **quer·u·lous·ness** n.

que·ry /'kwi(ə)rē/ ▶ n. (pl. **queries**) **1** a question expressing doubt or asking for information. **2** chiefly Printing a question mark. ▶ v. (**queries**, **querying**, **queried**) **1** ask a question to express doubt or obtain information. **2** put a query or queries to someone.

que·sa·dil·la /ˌkāsə'dēyə/ ▶ n. a hot tortilla with a spicy cheese filling.

quest /kwest/ ▶ n. **1** a long or difficult search: *the quest for a better life.* **2** (in medieval romance) an expedition by a knight to accomplish a specific task. ▶ v. search for something. ■ **quest·er** (also **questor**) n.

ques·tion /'kweschən/ ▶ n. **1** a sentence worded or expressed so as to obtain information. **2** a doubt as to whether something is true or valid. **3** the raising of a doubt or objection: *he obeyed without question.* **4** a problem that needs to be resolved. **5** a matter that depends on conditions: *it's only a question of time before something changes.* ▶ v. **1** ask someone questions. **2** express doubt about or object to something. ■ **ques·tion·er** n.
– PHRASES **come** (or **bring**) **into question** become (or raise) an issue for further consideration or discussion. **in question 1** being considered. **2** in doubt. **no question of** no possibility of. **out of the question** not possible.

ques·tion·a·ble /'kweschənəbəl/ ▶ adj. **1** open to doubt. **2** likely to be dishonest or morally wrong: *questionable financial deals.* ■ **ques·tion·a·bly** /-əblē/ adv.

ques·tion mark ▶ n. a punctuation mark (?) indicating a question.

ques·tion·naire /ˌkweschə'ne(ə)r/ ▶ n. a set of questions, usually with a choice of answers, written for a survey or statistical study.

quet·zal /ket'säl/ ▶ n. a long-tailed tropical American bird with iridescent green plumage.

queue /kyoo/ ▶ n. **1** chiefly Brit. a line of people or vehicles awaiting their turn for something or to continue. **2** Computing a list of data items, commands, etc., stored so as to be retrievable in a definite order. ▶ v. (**queues, queuing** or **queueing, queued**) chiefly Brit. wait in line.

quib·ble /'kwibəl/ ▶ n. **1** a minor objection or criticism. **2** old use a pun. ▶ v. argue about a trivial matter.

quiche /kēsh/ ▶ n. a dish made with eggs, milk, and various savory fillings, baked in a pie crust.

quick /kwik/ ▶ adj. **1** moving fast. **2** lasting or taking a short time: *a quick worker.* **3** with little or no delay; prompt. **4** able to think, learn, or notice things promptly; intelligent. **5** (of temper) easily roused. ▶ n. **1** (**the quick**) the tender flesh below the growing part of a fingernail or toenail. **2** (as pl. n. **the quick**) old use people who are living. ■ **quick·ly** adv. **quick·ness** n.
– PHRASES **a quick one** informal a rapidly consumed alcoholic drink. **cut someone to the quick** upset someone very much: *his laughter cut us to the quick.* **quick with child** old use at a stage of pregnancy when the fetus can be felt to move.

quick·en /'kwikən/ ▶ v. **1** make or become quicker. **2** stimulate or be stimulated: *my interest quickened.* **3** old use reach a stage in pregnancy when the fetus can be felt to move.

quick-fire ▶ adj. **1** unhesitating and rapid. **2** (of a gun) firing shots in rapid succession.

quick fix ▶ n. a solution that is implemented quickly but that is not good enough for the long term.

quick·ie /'kwikē/ informal ▶ n. **1** a rapidly consumed alcoholic drink. **2** a brief act of sex. ▶ adj. done or made quickly.

quick·lime /'kwik,līm/ ▶ n. a white caustic alkaline substance consisting of calcium oxide, obtained by heating limestone.

quick march ▶ n. a brisk military march.

quick·sand /'kwik,sand/ ▶ n. (also **quicksands**) loose wet sand that sucks in anything resting on it.

quick·set /'kwik,set/ ▶ n. Brit. hedging, especially of hawthorn, grown from cuttings.

quick·sil·ver /'kwik,silvər/ ▶ n. liquid mercury. ▶ adj. moving or changing rapidly and unexpectedly.

quick·step /'kwik,step/ ▶ n. a fast foxtrot (dance) in 4/4 time.

quick-tem·pered ▶ adj. easily angered.

quick-wit·ted ▶ adj. able to think or respond quickly.

quid¹ /kwid/ ▶ n. (pl. same) Brit. informal one pound sterling.
– PHRASES **quids in** Brit. informal profiting or likely to profit from something.

quid² ▶ n. a lump of chewing tobacco.

quid·di·ty /'kwidətē/ ▶ n. (pl. **quiddities**) the essential nature of a person or thing.

quid pro quo /'kwid ,prō 'kwō/ ▶ n. (pl. **quid pro quos**) a favor given in return for something.

qui·es·cent /kwē'esnt, kwī-/ ▶ adj. in a state or period of inactivity. ■ **qui·es·cence** n. **qui·es·cent·ly** adv.

qui·et /'kwīət/ ▶ adj. (**quieter, quietest**) **1** making little or no noise. **2** free from activity, disturbance, or excitement. **3** without being disturbed or interrupted: *a quiet drink.* **4** discreet, moderate, or restrained: *we wanted a quiet wedding.* **5** (of a person) calm and shy. ▶ n. absence of noise or disturbance. ▶ v. make or become quiet. ■ **qui·et·ly** adv. **qui·et·ness** n.
– PHRASES **keep quiet** say nothing or keep something secret. **on the quiet** informal secretly or without attracting attention.

qui·et·en /ˈkwīətn/ ▶ v. chiefly Brit. make or become quiet and calm.

qui·e·tude /ˈkwīəˌt(y)o͞od/ ▶ n. a state of calmness and quiet.

qui·e·tus /ˈkwīətəs/ ▶ n. (pl. **quietuses**) literary death or a cause of death, regarded as a release from life.

quill /kwil/ ▶ n. **1** a main wing or tail feather of a bird. **2** the hollow shaft of a feather. **3** a pen made from a main wing or tail feather of a bird. **4** a spine of a porcupine, hedgehog, etc.

quilt /kwilt/ ▶ n. **1** a warm bed covering made of padding enclosed between layers of fabric and kept in place by lines of decorative stitching. **2** a bedspread with decorative stitching. ▶ v. (usu. as adj. **quilted**) stitch padding between layers of fabric to form a quilt or item of clothing. ■ **quilt·er** n. **quilt·ing** n.

quince /kwins/ ▶ n. the hard, acid, pear-shaped fruit of a tree originally from Asia.

quin·cen·ten·ar·y /ˌkwinsenˈtenərē, kwinˈsentəˌnerē/ ▶ n. (pl. **quincentenaries**) a five-hundredth anniversary. ■ **quin·cen·ten·ni·al** /ˌkwinsenˈtenēəl/ n. & adj.

quin·cunx /ˈkwinˌkəNGks/ ▶ n. (pl. **quincunxes**) an arrangement of five objects with four at the corners of a square or rectangle and the fifth at its center. ■ **quin·cun·cial** /ˌkwinˈkənsHəl/ adj.

qui·nine /ˈkwīˌnīn/ ▶ n. a bitter compound present in cinchona bark, formerly used to treat malaria.

qui·none /ˈkwinōn/ ▶ n. any of a class of organic chemical compounds related to benzene but having two hydrogen atoms replaced by oxygen.

quin·quen·ni·al /kwiNGˈkwenēəl/ ▶ adj. lasting for or recurring every five years. ■ **quin·quen·ni·al·ly** adv.

quin·sy /ˈkwinzē/ ▶ n. inflammation of the throat, especially an abscess near the tonsils.

quint /kwint/ ▶ n. a quintuplet.

quin·ta /ˈkwintə/ ▶ n. **1** (in Spain, Portugal, and Latin America) a large country house. **2** a wine-growing estate, especially in Portugal.

quin·tal /ˈkwintl/ ▶ n. **1** a unit of weight equal to a hundredweight (112 lb) or, formerly, 100 lb. **2** a unit of weight equal to 100 kg.

quin·tes·sence /kwinˈtesəns/ ▶ n. **1** the most perfect or typical example of a quality or type: *he's emerged as the quintessence of cool.* **2** a refined essence or extract of a substance.

quin·tes·sen·tial /ˌkwintəˈsenCHəl/ ▶ adj. representing the most perfect or typical example of a quality or type. ■ **quin·tes·sen·tial·ly** adv.

quin·tet /kwinˈtet/ ▶ n. **1** a group of five people playing music or singing together. **2** a composition for a quintet. **3** a set of five people or things.

quin·til·lion /kwinˈtilyən/ ▶ cardinal number a thousand raised to the power of six (10^{18}). ■ **quin·til·lionth** /-yənTH/ ordinal number.

quin·tu·ple /kwinˈt(y)o͞opəl, -ˈtəpəl/ ▶ adj. **1** consisting of five parts or elements. **2** five times as much or as many. **3** (of time in music) having five beats in a bar. ▶ v. multiply or be multiplied by five. ▶ n. a quintuple number or amount.

quin·tu·plet /kwinˈtəplət, -ˈt(y)o͞oplət/ ▶ n. each of five children born at one birth.

quip /kwip/ ▶ n. a witty remark. ▶ v. (**quips, quipping, quipped**) make a witty remark. ■ **quip·ster** /-stər/ n.

quire /kwīr/ ▶ n. **1** 24 or 25 sheets of paper; one twentieth of a ream. **2** four sheets of paper folded to form eight leaves, as in medieval manuscripts.

quirk /kwərk/ ▶ n. **1** a peculiar aspect of a person's behavior. **2** a strange thing that happens by chance: *a quirk of fate.* **3** a sudden twist or curve.

quirk·y /ˈkwərkē/ ▶ adj. (**quirkier, quirkiest**) having peculiar or unexpected habits or qualities: *a quirky sense of humor.* ■ **quirk·i·ly** adv. **quirk·i·ness** n.

quirt /kwərt/ ▶ n. a short-handled riding whip with a braided leather lash.

quis·ling /ˈkwizliNG/ ▶ n. a traitor collaborating with an occupying enemy force.

quit /kwit/ ▶ v. (**quits, quitting, quitted** or **quit**) **1** leave a place, especially permanently. **2** resign from a job. **3** informal stop doing something. – PHRASES **be quit of** be rid of someone or something.

quite /kwīt/ ▶ adv. **1** to a certain extent; moderately. **2** to the greatest extent or degree; completely: *I quite agree.* ▶ exclam. (also **quite so**) expressing agreement. – PHRASES **quite a ——** a remarkable or impressive person or thing.

quits /kwits/ ▶ adj. on equal terms because a debt or score has been settled. – PHRASES **call it quits 1** decide to stop doing something. **2** agree that terms are now equal.

quit·ter /ˈkwitər/ ▶ n. informal a person who gives up easily.

quiv·er¹ /ˈkwivər/ ▶ v. shake or vibrate with a slight rapid movement. ▶ n. a quivering movement or sound. ■ **quiv·er·y** adj.

quiv·er² ▶ n. an archer's case for carrying arrows.

qui vive /ˌkē ˈvēv/ ▶ n. (in phrase **on the qui vive**) on the alert or lookout.

quix·ot·ic /kwikˈsätik/ ▶ adj. unselfish and idealistic to an impractical extent: *the quixotic desire to do good.* ■ **quix·ot·i·cal·ly** /-ik(ə)lē/ adv. **quix·o·tism** /ˈkwiksəˌtizəm/ n.

quiz /kwiz/ ▶ n. (pl. **quizzes**) **1** a game or competition involving a set of questions as a test of knowledge. **2** informal, chiefly Brit. a period of questioning. ▶ v. (**quizzes, quizzing, quizzed**) question someone.

quiz·mas·ter /ˈkwizˌmastər/ ▶ n. a person in charge of a quiz, especially someone who hosts a quiz show.

quiz show ▶ n. a television or radio program in which people compete in a quiz, usually for cash or other prizes.

quiz·zi·cal /ˈkwizəkəl/ ▶ adj. showing mild or amused puzzlement. ■ **quiz·zi·cal·i·ty** /ˌkwiziˈkalətē/ n. **quiz·zi·cal·ly** adv.

quoin /k(w)oin/ ▶ n. **1** an external angle of a wall or building. **2** a cornerstone. ■ **quoin·ing** n.

quoit /k(w)oit/ ▶ n. **1** a ring thrown in a game

with the aim of landing it over an upright peg. **2** (**quoits**) (treated as sing.) a game of throwing quoits.

quon·dam /'kwändəm, -ˌdam/ ▶ adj. formal that once was; former.

Quon·set /'kwänsət/ (usu. **Quonset hut**) ▶ n. trademark a prefabricated building with a semicylindrical corrugated roof.

quo·rum /'kwôrəm/ ▶ n. (pl. **quorums**) the minimum number of members that must be present at a meeting to make its business valid.

quo·ta /'kwōtə/ ▶ n. **1** a limited quantity of a product that may be produced, exported, or imported. **2** a share that a person or group is entitled to receive or has to contribute: *her weekly quota of articles is two for newspapers and one for a magazine.* **3** a fixed number of a group allowed to do something, e.g., immigrants entering a country.

quot·a·ble /'kwōtəbəl/ ▶ adj. suitable for or worth quoting. ■ **quot·a·bil·i·ty** /ˌkwōtə'bilətē/ n.

quo·ta·tion /ˌkwō'tāsHən/ ▶ n. **1** a passage or remark repeated by someone other than the person who originally said or wrote it. **2** a short musical passage or visual image taken from one piece of music or work of art and used in another. **3** the action of quoting from a speech, artistic work, etc. **4** a formal statement of the estimated cost of a job or service. **5** a registration granted to a company enabling their shares to be officially listed and traded on a stock exchange.

quo·ta·tion mark ▶ n. each of a set of punctuation marks, single (' ') or double (" "), used to mark the beginning and end of a title or quotation, or to set off a word or phrase regarded as slang or jargon.

quote /kwōt/ ▶ v. **1** repeat or copy out a passage or remark by another person. **2** (**quote something as**) mention something as an example to support a point: *the figures were quoted as more evidence for the failure of our schools.* **3** give someone an estimate for a job or service. **4** (**quote someone/thing at/as**) name someone or something at specified odds. **5** give a company a listing on a stock exchange. ▶ n. **1** a quotation. **2** (**quotes**) quotation marks.
– PHRASES **quote —— unquote** informal used in speech to indicate the start and end of a quotation: *the second sentence of the statement says, quote, There has never been a better time to invest, unquote.*

quoth /kwōTH/ ▶ v. old use or humorous said (used only in first and third person singular before the subject).

quo·tid·i·an /kwō'tidēən/ ▶ adj. **1** happening every day; daily. **2** ordinary or everyday.

quo·tient /'kwōsHənt/ ▶ n. **1** Mathematics a result obtained by dividing one quantity by another. **2** a degree or amount of a specified quality: *my coolness quotient evaporated on the spot.*

Qu·r'an /kə'rän, -'ran/ (also **Quran**) ▶ n. Arabic spelling of KORAN.

q.v. ▶ abbr. used to direct a reader to another part of a written work for further information.

qwer·ty /'kwərtē/ ▶ adj. referring to the standard layout on English-language typewriters and keyboards, having *q*, *w*, *e*, *r*, *t*, and *y* as the first keys on the top row of letters.

Rr

R[1] (also **r**) ▶ n. (pl. **Rs** or **R's**) the eighteenth letter of the alphabet.
– PHRASES **the three Rs** reading, writing, and arithmetic, regarded as the fundamentals of learning.

R[2] ▶ abbr. **1** rand. **2** (®) registered as a trademark. **3** (**R.**) River. **4** roentgen(s). **5** rook (in chess). **6** Baseball (on scorecards) run(s). **7** Brit. Regina or Rex.

r ▶ abbr. **1** radius. **2** right.

RA ▶ abbr. **1** (in the UK) Royal Academician or Royal Academy. **2** (in the UK) Royal Artillery.

Ra ▶ symbol the chemical element radium.

rab·bet /'rabit/ ▶ n. a step-shaped recess cut into wood, to which the edge or tongue of another piece may be joined. ▶ v. (**rabbets, rabbeting, rabbeted**) **1** make a rabbet in. **2** join or fix with a rabbet.

rab·bi /'rab‚ī/ ▶ n. (pl. **rabbis**) **1** a Jewish scholar or teacher, especially of Jewish law. **2** a Jewish religious leader. ■ **rab·bin·ate** /'rabənət, -‚nāt/ n.

rab·bin·ic /rə'binik, ra-/ ▶ adj. relating to rabbis or to Jewish law or teachings. ■ **rab·bin·i·cal** /rə'binikəl, ra-/ adj.

rab·bit /'rabit/ ▶ n. **1** a burrowing mammal with long ears and a short tail. **2** a hare. **3** the fur of the rabbit. ▶ v. (**rabbits, rabbiting, rabbited**) (usu. as n. **rabbiting**) hunt rabbits. ■ **rab·bit·y** adj.

rab·bit punch ▶ n. a sharp chop with the edge of the hand to the back of the neck.

rab·ble /'rabəl/ ▶ n. **1** a disorderly crowd. **2** (**the rabble**) ordinary people regarded as common or uncouth.

rab·ble-rous·er ▶ n. a person who stirs up popular opinion, especially for political reasons.

Rab·e·lai·sian /‚rabə'lāzʜən/ ▶ adj. relating to or like the French satirist François Rabelais or his writings, especially in being very imaginative and full of earthy humor.

rab·id /'rabəd, 'rā-/ ▶ adj. **1** extreme; fanatical: *rabid football fans.* **2** relating to or affected with rabies. ■ **rab·id·ly** adv.

ra·bies /'rābēz/ ▶ n. a dangerous disease of dogs and other mammals, caused by a virus that can be transmitted through an animal's saliva to humans, causing madness and convulsions.

rac·coon /ra'kōōn, rə-/ (also **racoon**) ▶ n. a grayish-brown American mammal with a black face and a ringed tail.

race[1] /rās/ ▶ n. **1** a competition between runners, horses, vehicles, etc., to see which is fastest over a set course. **2** a situation in which people compete to be first to achieve something: *the race for governor.* **3** a strong current flowing through a narrow channel. **4** a water channel, especially one in a mill or mine. **5** a smooth ring-shaped groove or guide for a ball bearing or roller bearing. ▶ v. **1** compete in a race. **2** have a race with someone. **3** prepare and enter an animal or car for races. **4** move or progress swiftly: *I raced into the house.* **5** (of machinery) operate at excessive speed. ■ **rac·er** n.

race[2] ▶ n. **1** each of the major divisions of humankind, having distinct physical characteristics. **2** racial origin or distinction. **3** a group of people sharing the same culture, language, etc.; an ethnic group. **4** a group of people or things with a shared feature: *a race of intelligent computers.* **5** Biology a subdivision of a species.

> **USAGE**
> Some people feel that the word **race** should be avoided, because of its associations with the now discredited theories of 19th-century anthropologists and physiologists about supposed racial superiority. Terms such as **people, community,** or **ethnic group** are less likely to cause offense.

race·car /'rās‚kär/ ▶ n. a car built for racing.

race·course /'rās‚kôrs/ ▶ n. a racetrack.

race·horse /'rās‚hôrs/ ▶ n. a horse bred and trained for racing.

ra·ceme /rā'sēm, rə-/ ▶ n. a flower cluster with the separate flowers attached by short stalks along a central stem, the lower flowers developing first. Compare with CYME.

race re·la·tions ▶ pl.n. relations between members of different races within a country.

race·track /'rās‚trak/ ▶ n. **1** a ground or track for horse or dog racing. **2** a track for motor racing.

race·way /'rās‚wā/ ▶ n. **1** a racetrack. **2** a water channel, especially an artificial one in which fish are reared. **3** a pipe or channel enclosing electric wires.

ra·cial /'rāshəl/ ▶ adj. **1** relating to race. **2** relating to differences or relations between races. ■ **ra·cial·ly** adv.

ra·cial·ism /'rāshə‚lizəm/ ▶ n. racism. ■ **ra·cial·ist** n. & adj.

ra·cial·ize /'rāshə‚līz/ ▶ v. make something racial or racist in nature or outlook.

rac·ing /'rāsiNG/ ▶ n. a sport that involves competing in races. ▶ adj. moving swiftly.

ra·ci·no /rə'sēnō/ ▶ n. a building complex or grounds having a racetrack and gambling facilities traditionally associated with a casino.

rac·ism /'rā‚sizəm/ ▶ n. **1** the belief that each race has certain qualities or abilities, giving rise to the view that some races are better than others. **2** discrimination against or hostility toward other races. ■ **rac·ist** n. & adj.

rack[1] /rak/ ▶ n. **1** a framework for holding or storing things. **2** a bar with cogs or teeth that fit

into a wheel or pinion. **3** a triangular frame for positioning pool balls. **4** a single game of pool. **5 (the rack)** historical an instrument of torture consisting of a frame on which the victim was tied by the wrists and ankles and stretched. ▸ v. **1** (also **wrack**) cause great pain or distress to someone. **2** place something in or on a rack. **3 (rack something up)** accumulate or achieve a score or amount.
− PHRASES **rack** (or **wrack**) **one's brains** think very hard.

> USAGE
> The words **rack** and **wrack** are often confused. The noun is always spelled **rack** (a magazine rack). The verb can be spelled **rack** or **wrack**, but only when it means 'cause great pain to someone' (he was racked/wracked with guilt) or in the phrase **rack** (or **wrack**) **one's brains**.

rack² ▸ n. a cut of meat, especially lamb, including the front ribs.

rack³ ▸ n. (in phrase **go to rack and ruin**) gradually fall into a bad condition.

rack⁴ ▸ v. draw off wine, beer, etc., from the sediment in the barrel.

rack-and-pin·ion ▸ adj. (of a mechanism) using a fixed bar with cogs or teeth that fit into a smaller cog.

rack·et¹ /ˈrakit/ (also **racquet**) ▸ n. a bat consisting of an oval or round frame with strings stretched across it, used in tennis, badminton, and squash.

rack·et² ▸ n. **1** a loud unpleasant noise. **2** informal a dishonest scheme for obtaining money: *a protection racket.* **3** informal a person's line of business. ▸ v. (**rackets, racketing, racketed**) make a loud unpleasant noise. ■ **rack·et·y** adj.

rack·et·eer /ˌrakiˈti(ə)r/ ▸ n. a person who makes money from dishonest activities. ■ **rack·et·eer·ing** n.

rac·on·teur /ˌrakänˈtər, -ənˈ/ ▸ n. a person who tells stories in an interesting way.

ra·coon ▸ n. variant spelling of RACCOON.

rac·quet /ˈrakit/ ▸ n. variant spelling of RACKET¹.

rac·quet·ball /ˈrakitˌbôl/ ▸ n. a game played with a rubber ball and a short-handled racket in a four-walled court.

rac·y /ˈrāsē/ ▸ adj. (**racier, raciest**) lively or exciting, especially in a sexual way. ■ **rac·i·ly** adv. **rac·i·ness** n.

rad¹ /rad/ ▸ abbr. radian(s).

rad² ▸ adj. informal excellent or impressive.

ra·dar /ˈrāˌdär/ ▸ n. a system for detecting the position and speed of aircraft, ships, etc., by sending out pulses of radio waves that are reflected off the object back to the source.

ra·dar gun ▸ n. a hand-held radar device used by traffic police to estimate a vehicle's speed.

ra·dar trap ▸ n. an area of road in which radar is used by the police to detect speeding vehicles.

ra·di·al /ˈrādēəl/ ▸ adj. **1** relating to or arranged in lines coming out from a central point to the edge of a circle: *radial markings resembling spokes.* **2** (of a tire) in which the layers of fabric have their cords running at right angles to the circumference of the tire. ▸ n. a radial tire. ■ **ra·di·al·ly** adv.

ra·di·al sym·me·try ▸ n. chiefly Biology symmetry about a central axis, as in a starfish.

ra·di·an /ˈrādēən/ ▸ n. an angle of 57.3 degrees, equal to that at the center of a circle formed by

an arc equal in length to the radius.

ra·di·ant /ˈrādēənt/ ▸ adj. **1** shining or glowing brightly. **2** showing great joy, love, or health: *a radiant smile.* **3** (of electromagnetic energy, especially heat) transmitted by radiation, rather than conduction or convection. **4** (of an appliance) emitting radiant energy for cooking or heating. ■ **ra·di·ance** n. **ra·di·ant·ly** adv.

ra·di·ate /ˈrādēˌāt/ ▸ v. **1** (with reference to light, heat, or other energy) send out or be sent out in rays or waves. **2** show a strong feeling or quality: *she radiated an aura of ambition.* **3** spread out from a central point: *rows of cells radiated from a central hall.* ■ **ra·di·a·tive** /-ˌātiv/ adj.

ra·di·a·tion /ˌrādēˈāsHən/ ▸ n. **1** the action or process of radiating. **2** energy sent out as electromagnetic waves or subatomic particles.

ra·di·a·tion sick·ness ▸ n. illness caused when a person is exposed to X-rays, gamma rays, or other radiation.

ra·di·a·tion ther·a·py ▸ n. the treatment of cancer or other disease using X-rays or similar radiation.

ra·di·a·tor /ˈrādēˌātər/ ▸ n. **1** a thing that radiates light, heat, or sound. **2** a heating device consisting of a metal case through which hot water circulates, or one heated by electricity or oil. **3** a cooling device in a vehicle or aircraft engine consisting of a bank of thin tubes in which circulating water is cooled by the surrounding air.

rad·i·cal /ˈradikəl/ ▸ adj. **1** relating to the basic nature of something; fundamental: *she made radical changes in her life.* **2** supporting complete political or social reform. **3** departing from tradition; innovative or progressive. **4** Mathematics relating to the root of a number or quantity. ▸ n. **1** a person who supports radical political or social reform. **2** Chemistry a group of atoms behaving as a unit in certain compounds. ■ **rad·i·cal·ism** /-ˌlizəm/ n. **rad·i·cal·ize** /ˈradikəˌlīz/ v. **rad·i·cal·ly** adv.

rad·i·cal chic ▸ n. superficial and purely fashionable support for radical left-wing views.

rad·i·cal sign ▸ n. Mathematics the sign $\sqrt{}$, which indicates the square root of the number following (or a higher root indicated by a raised numeral before the symbol).

ra·dic·chi·o /raˈdēkēˌō, rəˈ-/ ▸ n. (pl. **radicchios**) a variety of chicory with dark red leaves.

rad·i·cle /ˈradikəl/ ▸ n. the part of a plant embryo that develops into the primary root.

ra·di·i /ˈrādēˌī/ ▸ plural of RADIUS.

ra·di·o /ˈrādēˌō/ ▸ n. (pl. **radios**) **1** the sending and receiving of electromagnetic waves carrying sound messages. **2** broadcasting in sound: *she's written plays for radio.* **3** a broadcasting station or channel. **4** a device for receiving radio programs or for sending and receiving radio messages. ▸ v. (**radioes, radioing, radioed**) **1** send a message by radio. **2** communicate with a person or place by radio.

radio- ▸ comb.form **1** referring to radio waves or broadcasting: *radiogram.* **2** connected with rays, radiation, or radioactivity: *radiography.*

ra·di·o·ac·tive /ˌrādēōˈaktiv/ ▸ adj. emitting ionizing radiation or particles. ■ **ra·di·o·ac·tive·ly** adv.

ra·di·o·ac·tiv·i·ty /ˌrādēōakˈtivətē/ ▸ n. **1** the emission of ionizing radiation or particles, caused when atomic nuclei disintegrate spontaneously. **2** radioactive particles.

ra·di·o as·tron·o·my ▸ n. the branch of astronomy concerned with radio emissions from stars and other celestial objects.

ra·di·o·car·bon /ˌrādēōˈkärbən/ ▸ n. a radioactive isotope of carbon used in carbon dating.

ra·di·o·car·bon dat·ing ▸ n. another term for CARBON DATING.

ra·di·o·con·trolled ▸ adj. controllable from a distance by radio.

ra·di·o·gram /ˈrādēōˌgram/ ▸ n. Brit. dated a combined radio and record player.

ra·di·o·graph /ˈrādēōˌgraf/ ▸ n. an image produced on a sensitive plate or film by X-rays or other radiation. ■ **ra·di·o·graph·ic** adj.

ra·di·og·ra·phy /ˌrādēˈägrəfē/ ▸ n. the process of taking radiographs to assist in medical examinations. ■ **ra·di·og·ra·pher** /ˌrādēˈägrəfər/ n.

ra·di·o·i·so·tope /ˌrādēōˈīsəˌtōp/ ▸ n. a radioactive isotope.

ra·di·ol·o·gy /ˌrādēˈäləjē/ ▸ n. the science of X-rays and similar radiation, especially as used in medicine. ■ **ra·di·o·log·ic** /ˌrādēəˈläjik/ adj. **ra·di·o·log·i·cal** /ˌrādēəˈläjikəl/ adj. **ra·di·ol·o·gist** /-jist/ n.

ra·di·om·e·ter /ˌrādēˈämitər/ ▸ n. an instrument for detecting or measuring radiation. ■ **ra·di·om·e·try** /-trē/ n.

ra·di·o·met·ric /ˌrādēəˈmetrik/ ▸ adj. relating to the measurement of radioactivity.

ra·di·o·nu·clide /ˌrādēōˈn(y)ōōˌklīd/ ▸ n. a radioactive isotope.

ra·di·o·phon·ic /ˌrādēōˈfänik/ ▸ adj. relating to sound that is produced electronically.

ra·di·o·tel·e·phone /ˌrādēōˈteləfōn/ ▸ n. a telephone using radio transmission.

ra·di·o·tel·e·scope ▸ n. an instrument used to detect radio emissions from space.

ra·di·o·ther·a·py /ˌrādēōˈᴛʜerəpē/ ▸ n. radiation therapy. ■ **ra·di·o·ther·a·pist** n.

ra·di·o wave ▸ n. an electromagnetic wave having a frequency in the range 10^4 to 10^{11} or 10^{12} hertz.

rad·ish /ˈradisʜ/ ▸ n. the small, hot-tasting, red root of a plant that is eaten raw as a salad vegetable.

ra·di·um /ˈrādēəm/ ▸ n. a reactive, radioactive metallic chemical element.

ra·di·us /ˈrādēəs/ ▸ n. (pl. **radii** /ˈrādēˌī/ or **radiuses**) **1** a straight line from the center to the circumference of a circle or sphere. **2** a specified distance from a center in all directions: *hydrants within a two-mile radius.* **3** the thicker and shorter of the two bones in the human forearm.

ra·don /ˈrāˌdän/ ▸ n. a chemical element that is a rare radioactive gas.

RAF ▸ abbr. (in the UK) Royal Air Force.

raf·fi·a /ˈrafēə/ ▸ n. fiber from the leaves of a tropical palm tree, used for making hats, baskets, etc.

raff·ish /ˈrafisʜ/ ▸ adj. slightly disreputable, but in an attractive way.

raf·fle /ˈrafəl/ ▸ n. a lottery with goods rather than money as prizes. ▸ v. offer something as a prize in a raffle.

raft¹ /raft/ ▸ n. **1** a flat structure of pieces of timber fastened together, used as a boat or floating platform. **2** a small inflatable boat.

▸ v. travel or transport on a raft. ■ **raft·ing** n.

raft² ▸ n. a large amount: *she speaks a raft of languages.*

raft·er¹ /ˈraftər/ ▸ n. a beam forming part of the internal framework of a roof. ■ **raft·ered** adj.

raft·er² ▸ n. a person who travels by raft.

rag¹ /rag/ ▸ n. **1** a piece of old cloth. **2** (**rags**) old or tattered clothes. **3** informal a low-quality newspaper. ▸ v. (**rags, ragging, ragged**) give a decorative effect to a painted surface by applying paint with a rag.

rag² ▸ v. (**rags, ragging, ragged**) **1** (usu. **rag on someone**) tease or make fun of someone. **2** rebuke someone harshly.

rag³ ▸ n. a piece of ragtime music.

ra·ga /ˈrägə/ (also **rag** /räg/) ▸ n. (in Indian classical music) each of the six basic musical modes that express different moods in certain characteristic progressions.

rag·a·muf·fin /ˈragəˌməfən/ ▸ n. **1** a person in ragged, dirty clothes. **2** (also **raggamuffin**) a person who performs or likes ragga dance music.

rag doll ▸ n. a soft doll made from pieces of cloth.

rage /rāj/ ▸ n. **1** violent uncontrollable anger. **2** (in combination) anger or aggression associated with conflict arising from a particular situation: *air rage.* **3** a very popular person or thing: *remember when bell-bottoms were the rage?* **4** a strong desire: *a rage for order and purity.* ▸ v. **1** feel or express violent anger. **2** continue with great force or intensity: *the battle raged for six hours.* ■ **ra·ger** n.
– PHRASES **all the rage** temporarily very popular or fashionable.

rag·ga /ˈragə/ ▸ n. a style of dance music in which a DJ improvises lyrics over a backing track.

rag·ga·muf·fin /ˈragəˌməfən/ ▸ n. variant spelling of RAGAMUFFIN.

rag·ged /ˈragid/ ▸ adj. **1** (of cloth or clothes) old and torn. **2** wearing ragged clothes. **3** having a rough or irregular surface or edge. **4** not steady or uniform: *her breath came in ragged gasps.* **5** exhausted or stressed. ■ **rag·ged·ly** adv. **rag·ged·y** adj.
– PHRASES **run someone ragged** exhaust someone.

rag·gle-tag·gle /ˈragəl ˌtagəl/ ▸ adj. untidy and scruffy.

rag·gy /ˈragē/ ▸ adj. informal ragged or shabby.

rag·lan /ˈraglən/ ▸ adj. having or referring to sleeves that continue in one piece up to the neck of a garment.

ra·gout /raˈgōō/ ▸ n. a spicy stew of meat and vegetables.

rag·pick·er /ˈragˌpikər/ ▸ n. chiefly historical a person who collects and sells rags.

rag rug ▸ n. a rug made from small strips of fabric hooked into or pushed through a material such as hessian.

rag·tag /ˈragˌtag/ ▸ adj. untidy, disorganized, or very varied: *a ragtag group of idealists.*

rag·time /ˈragˌtīm/ ▸ n. an early form of jazz with a syncopated melody, played especially on the piano.

rag trade ▸ n. informal the clothing or fashion industry.

rag·weed /ˈragˌwēd/ ▸ n. a North American plant of the daisy family, whose pollen is a major cause of hay fever.

rag·wort /'rag,wərt, -,wôrt/ ▶ n. a yellow-flowered plant with ragged leaves.

rah /rä/ ▶ exclam. informal a cheer of encouragement or approval.

rai /rī/ ▶ n. a style of music blending Arabic and Algerian folk elements with Western rock.

raid /rād/ ▶ n. 1 a sudden attack on an enemy or on a building to commit a crime. 2 a surprise visit by police to arrest suspects or seize illegal goods. ▶ v. 1 make a raid on a place. 2 take something from a place in a secretive way: *she crept downstairs to raid the pantry.* ∎ **raid·er** n.

rail¹ /rāl/ ▶ n. 1 a bar or bars fixed on upright supports or attached to a wall or ceiling, forming part of a fence or used to hang things on. 2 each of the two metal bars laid on the ground to form a railroad track. 3 railroads as a means of transport. ▶ v. 1 provide or enclose something with a rail or rails. 2 convey goods by rail.
– PHRASES **go off the rails** informal begin behaving in an odd or unacceptable way. **on the rails** 1 informal functioning normally. 2 (of a racehorse or jockey) in a position on the racetrack nearest the inside fence.

rail² ▶ v. (**rail against/at**) complain or protest strongly about something.

rail³ ▶ n. a secretive gray and brown waterside bird.

rail car ▶ n. a railroad car.

rail·head /'rāl,hed/ ▶ n. a point at which a railroad ends.

rail·ing /'rāliNG/ ▶ n. a fence made of rails.

rail·ler·y /'rālərē/ ▶ n. good-humored teasing.

rail·road /'rāl,rōd/ ▶ n. 1 a track made of rails along which trains run. 2 a system of such tracks with the trains, organization, and staff required to run it. ▶ v. informal 1 rush or force someone into doing something. 2 cause a measure to be approved quickly by putting pressure on a group: *the bill was railroaded through the Senate.*

rail·road tie ▶ n. each of the wooden or concrete beams on which a railroad track rests.

rail·way /'rāl,wā/ ▶ n. chiefly Brit. a railroad.

rai·ment /'rāmənt/ ▶ n. old use or literary clothing.

rain /rān/ ▶ n. 1 the condensed moisture of the atmosphere falling in drops. 2 (**rains**) falls of rain. 3 a large quantity of things falling or descending: *a rain of blows.* ▶ v. 1 (**it rains, it is raining, it rained**) rain falls. 2 (**be rained out**) (of an event) be canceled or interrupted because of rain. 3 fall or cause to fall in large quantities.
– PHRASES **be as right as rain** be perfectly fit and well. **rain cats and dogs** rain heavily.

rain·bow /'rān,bō/ ▶ n. an arch of colors seen in the sky, caused by the refraction and dispersion of the sun's light by water droplets in the atmosphere.

rain·bow co·a·li·tion ▶ n. a political alliance of different groups, representing ethnic and other minorities.

rain·bow trout ▶ n. a large trout with reddish sides, native to western North America and introduced elsewhere.

rain check ▶ n. a ticket given for later use when an outdoor event is rained off.
– PHRASES **take a rain check** refuse an offer but imply that one may take it up later.

rain·coat /'rān,kōt/ ▶ n. a coat made from waterproofed or water-resistant fabric.

rain date ▶ n. an alternative date for an event in case of bad weather.

rain·drop /'rān,dräp/ ▶ n. a single drop of rain.

rain·fall /'rān,fôl/ ▶ n. the quantity of rain falling within an area in a given time.

rain·for·est /'rān,fôrəst/ ▶ n. a dense forest found in tropical areas with consistently heavy rainfall.

rain gauge ▶ n. a device for collecting and measuring the amount of rain that falls.

rain·mak·er /'rān,mākər/ ▶ n. informal a person who generates income for a business by brokering deals or attracting clients or funds.

rain·proof /'rān,prōōf/ ▶ adj. (especially of a building or garment) impervious to rain.

rain·storm /'rān,stôrm/ ▶ n. a storm with heavy rain.

rain·swept /'rān,swept/ ▶ adj. frequently or recently exposed to rain and wind.

rain·wa·ter /'rān,wôtər, -,wätər/ ▶ n. water that has fallen as rain.

rain·wear /'rān,we(ə)r/ ▶ n. waterproof or water-resistant clothes for wearing in the rain.

rain·y /'rānē/ ▶ adj. (**rainier, rainiest**) having a great deal of rain.
– PHRASES **a rainy day** a time in the future when money may be needed.

raise /rāz/ ▶ v. 1 lift or move someone or something upward or into an upright position. 2 increase the amount, level, or strength of: *she had to raise her voice to be heard.* 3 cause to be heard, felt, or considered: *doubts have been raised.* 4 collect or bring together money or resources. 5 bring up a child. 6 breed or grow animals or plants. 7 abandon a blockade, embargo, etc. 8 bring someone back from death. 9 (**raise something to**) Mathematics multiply a quantity to a specified power. ▶ n. an increase in salary. ∎ **rais·er** n.
– PHRASES **raise hell** informal make a noisy disturbance. **raise the roof** make a great deal of noise, especially by cheering.

raised ranch ▶ n. a style of house similar to a ranch, but with a split level.

rai·sin /'rāzən/ ▶ n. a partially dried grape. ∎ **rai·sin·y** adj.

rai·son d'ê·tre /rā'zôN 'detr(ə)/ ▶ n. (pl. **raisons d'être** /rā'zôN(z)/) the most important reason or purpose for someone's or something's existence.

rai·ta /'rītə/ ▶ n. an Indian side dish of spiced yogurt containing chopped cucumber or other vegetables.

Raj /räj/ ▶ n. (**the Raj**) historical the period of British rule in India.

ra·jah /'räjə, 'räzHə/ (also **raja**) ▶ n. historical an Indian king or prince.

Raj·put /'räj,pōōt, 'räzH-/ ▶ n. a member of a Hindu military caste.

rake¹ /rāk/ ▶ n. a tool consisting of a pole with metal prongs at the end, used for drawing together leaves, cut grass, etc., or smoothing soil or gravel. ▶ v. 1 draw together leaves or grass or smooth soil with a rake. 2 scratch something with a long sweeping movement. 3 pull or drag through something with a sweeping movement: *I raked a comb through my hair.* 4 sweep the air with gunfire or a beam of light. 5 (**rake through**) search through something. ∎ **rak·er** n.
– PHRASES **rake something in** informal make a lot of money.

rake² ▶ n. a fashionable or wealthy man who leads an immoral life.

rake³ ▶ v. set something at a sloping angle.
▶ n. the angle at which something slopes.

rake-off ▶ n. informal a share of the profits from a deal, especially one that is underhanded or illegal.

ra·ki /'rəˌkē, 'rakē, 'räkē/ ▶ n. a strong alcoholic drink made in eastern Europe or the Middle East.

rak·ish /'rākish/ ▶ adj. 1 dashing, jaunty, or slightly disreputable: *a cap set at a rakish angle.* 2 (of a boat or car) smart and streamlined.
■ **rak·ish·ly** adv.

ral·len·tan·do /ˌrälən'tändō, ˌralən'tandō/ ▶ adv. & adj. Music another term for RITARDANDO.

ral·ly /'ralē/ ▶ v. (**rallies, rallying, rallied**) 1 (with reference to troops) bring or come together again so as to continue fighting. 2 bring or come together as support or for united action: *my family rallied around.* 3 recover in health, spirits, or composure: *he floundered for a moment, then rallied again.* 4 (of share, currency, or commodity prices) increase after a fall. 5 drive in a motor rally. ▶ n. (pl. **rallies**) 1 a mass meeting held as a protest or in support of a cause. 2 a long-distance race for motor vehicles over roads or rough country. 3 an open-air event for people who own a particular kind of vehicle. 4 a quick or marked recovery: *the market staged a late rally.* 5 (in tennis and other racket sports) an exchange of several strokes between players.
■ **ral·ly·ist** n.

ral·ly·ing /'ralēing/ ▶ n. the action or sport of participating in a motor rally. ▶ adj. having the effect of calling people to action: *a rallying cry.*

RAM /ram/ ▶ abbr. Computing random-access memory.

ram /ram/ ▶ n. 1 an uncastrated adult male sheep. 2 a battering ram. 3 a striking or plunging device in some machines. ▶ v. (**rams, ramming, rammed**) 1 roughly force something into place. 2 strike or be struck with force. ■ **ram·mer** n.

Ram·a·dan /'rämə,dän, 'ramə,dan/ (also **Ramadhan**) ▶ n. the ninth month of the Muslim year, during which Muslims fast from dawn to sunset.

ram·ble /'rambəl/ ▶ v. 1 walk for pleasure in the countryside. 2 talk or write in an unfocused way for a long time: *he rambled on about Norman archways.* 3 (of a plant) grow over walls, fences, etc. ▶ n. a walk taken for pleasure in the countryside. ■ **ram·bler** n.

Ram·bo /'rambō/ ▶ n. an extremely tough and aggressive man.

ram·bunc·tious /ram'bəngkshəs/ ▶ adj. informal uncontrollably exuberant.

ram·bu·tan /ram'bo͞otn/ ▶ n. the red, plum-sized fruit of a tropical tree, with soft spines and a slightly sour taste.

ram·e·kin /'ramikən/ ▶ n. a small dish for baking and serving an individual portion of food.

ra·men /'rämən/ ▶ pl.n. (in oriental cuisine) quick-cooking noodles.

ram·ie /'ramē, 'rä-/ ▶ n. a vegetable fiber from a tropical Asian plant, used in making textiles.

ram·i·fi·ca·tion /ˌraməfə'kāshən/ ▶ n. 1 (**ramifications**) complex consequences of an action or event: *the ramifications of global environmental changes.* 2 a subdivision of a complex structure or process.

ram·i·fy /'ramə,fī/ ▶ v. (**ramifies, ramifying, ramified**) chiefly technical form parts that branch out.

ram·jet /'ram,jet/ ▶ n. a type of jet engine in which the air drawn in for combustion is compressed solely by the forward motion of the aircraft.

ramp /ramp/ ▶ n. 1 a sloping surface joining two different levels. 2 a movable set of steps for entering or leaving an aircraft. 3 an inclined road leading to or from a main highway.
▶ v. 1 (**ramp something up**) increase the level or amount of something: *the company plans to ramp up production of TVs.* 2 (as adj. **ramped**) provided with a ramp.

ram·page ▶ v. /ˌram'pāj/ rush around in a wild and violent way. ▶ n. /'ram,pāj/ a period of wild and violent behavior.

ramp·ant /'rampənt/ ▶ adj. 1 flourishing or spreading in an uncontrolled way: *rampant inflation.* 2 unrestrained or wild: *rampant sex.* 3 (after a noun) Heraldry (of an animal) shown standing on its left hind foot with its forefeet in the air. ■ **ramp·ant·ly** adv.

ram·part /'ram,pärt/ ▶ n. a defensive wall of a castle or city, having a broad top with a walkway.

ram·rod /'ram,räd/ ▶ n. 1 a rod for ramming down the charge of a muzzle-loading firearm. 2 used to describe a person's erect posture: *he stood ramrod straight.*

ram·shack·le /'ram,shakəl/ ▶ adj. in a very bad condition.

ran /ran/ ▶ past of RUN.

ranch /ranch/ ▶ n. 1 a large farm where cattle or other animals are bred. 2 (also **ranch house**) a single-story house. ▶ v. run a ranch.

ranch dress·ing ▶ n. a type of thick white salad dressing made with sour cream or buttermilk.

ranch·er /'ranchər/ ▶ n. 1 a person who owns or runs a ranch. 2 a ranch house.

ran·che·ro /ran'cherō/ ▶ n. (pl. **rancheros**) a person who farms or works on a ranch, especially in the southwestern US and Mexico.

ran·cid /'ransid/ ▶ adj. 1 (of fatty or oily foods) stale and smelling or tasting unpleasant. 2 highly unpleasant. ■ **ran·cid·i·ty** /ran'sidətē/ n.

ran·cor /'rangkər/ (Brit. **rancour**) ▶ n. bitter feeling or resentment. ■ **ran·cor·ous** adj.

rand /rand, ränd, ränt/ ▶ n. the basic unit of money of South Africa.

R & B ▶ abbr. 1 rhythm and blues. 2 a kind of pop music with a vocal style derived from soul.

R & D ▶ abbr. research and development.

ran·dom /'randəm/ ▶ adj. done or happening without a deliberate order, purpose, or decision: *the trees had been planted in a random pattern.*
■ **ran·dom·ly** adv. **ran·dom·ness** n.
– PHRASES **at random** without thinking or planning in advance.

ran·dom ac·cess ▶ n. the process of storing or finding information on a computer without having to access items in a fixed sequence.

ran·dom·ize /'randə,mīz/ ▶ v. (usu. as adj. **randomized**) technical make a random selection in an experiment, trial, etc.

R & R ▶ abbr. informal rest and recreation.

rand·y /'randē/ ▶ adj. (**randier, randiest**) informal, chiefly Brit. sexually aroused or excited.

rang /raNG/ ▶ past of RING².

range /rānj/ ▶ n. **1** the area of variation between limits on a particular scale: *the car's outside my price range.* **2** a set of different things of the same general type. **3** the scope or extent of a person's or thing's abilities or capacity: *he has shown his range in a number of roles.* **4** the distance within which something is able to operate or be effective. **5** a line of mountains or hills. **6** a large area of open land for grazing or hunting. **7** an area used as a testing ground for military equipment or for shooting practice. **8** a large cooking stove with several burners and an oven. ▶ v. **1** vary between specified limits. **2** arrange people or things in a row or rows or in a particular way. **3** (**range someone against** or **be ranged against**) set oneself or be set in opposition to: *Japan ranged herself against the European nations.* **4** travel over a wide area. **5** cover a wide number of different topics.

range·find·er /'rānj,fīndər/ ▶ n. an instrument for estimating the distance of an object.

rang·er /'rānjər/ ▶ n. **1** a keeper of a park, forest, or area of countryside. **2** a member of a body of armed men.

rang·y /'rānjē/ ▶ adj. (of a person) tall and slim with long limbs.

rank¹ /raNGk/ ▶ n. **1** a position within the armed forces or an organization. **2** high social standing. **3** a line or row of people or things positioned side by side. **4** (**ranks**) the members of a group: *the ranks of the unemployed.* **5** (**the ranks**) members of the armed forces who are not commissioned officers. **6** each of the eight rows of eight squares running from side to side across a chessboard. Compare with FILE¹. ▶ v. **1** give someone or something a rank within a grading system: *rank the samples in order of preference.* **2** hold a specified rank: *he now ranks third in the US.* **3** arrange things in a row or rows.
– PHRASES **break rank** (or **ranks**) fail to support a group to which you belong. **close ranks** unite so as to defend common interests. **pull rank** use your senior position to take advantage of someone. **rank and file** the ordinary members of an organization.

rank² ▶ adj. **1** smelling very unpleasant. **2** complete and utter: *a rank amateur.* **3** (of vegetation) growing too thickly.

rank·ing /'raNGkiNG/ ▶ n. a position on a scale of importance or achievement. ▶ adj. having a specified rank: *high-ranking officers.*

ran·kle /'raNGkəl/ ▶ v. (of a comment or fact) cause continuing annoyance or resentment.

ran·sack /'ran,sak, ran'sak/ ▶ v. **1** go hurriedly through a place stealing things and causing damage. **2** search something in a thorough and harmful way.

ran·som /'ransəm/ ▶ n. a sum of money demanded or paid for the release of a captive. ▶ v. **1** obtain the release of someone by paying a ransom. **2** hold a captive and demand payment for their release.
– PHRASES **hold someone to ransom** chiefly Brit. force someone to do something by threatening damaging action. **a king's ransom** a huge amount of money.

rant /rant/ ▶ v. speak or shout in an angry or uncontrolled way. ▶ n. a spell of ranting. ■ **rant·er** n.

rap /rap/ ▶ v. (**raps, rapping, rapped**) **1** hit a hard surface several times. **2** hit someone or something sharply. **3** informal criticize someone severely. **4** say sharply: *he rapped out an order.* **5** perform rap music. ▶ n. **1** a quick, sharp knock or blow. **2** a type of popular music of African-American origin in which words are spoken rapidly and rhythmically over an instrumental backing. **3** informal a criminal charge: *a murder rap.* ■ **rap·per** n.
– PHRASES **take the rap** informal be punished or blamed for something.

ra·pa·cious /rə'pāSHəs/ ▶ adj. very greedy or grasping. ■ **ra·pa·cious·ly** adv. **ra·pa·cious·ness** n. **ra·pac·i·ty** /rə'pasətē/ n.

rap·a·my·cin /,rapə'mīsin/ ▶ n. an antibiotic used as an immunosuppressant, especially to prevent organ rejection in transplants.

rape¹ /rāp/ ▶ v. (of a man) force someone to have sex with him against their will. ▶ n. **1** the crime of raping someone. **2** the spoiling or destruction of a place: *the rape of the countryside.*

rape² ▶ n. a plant with bright yellow flowers, especially a variety (**oilseed rape**) grown for its oil-rich seed.

rape·seed /'rāp,sēd/ ▶ n. seeds of the rape plant, used to make oil.

rap·id /'rapid/ ▶ adj. **1** happening in a short time: *several shots fired in rapid succession.* **2** (of an action) very fast. ▶ n. (usu. **rapids**) a part of a river where the water flows very fast, often over rocks. ■ **ra·pid·i·ty** /rə'pidətē/ n. **rap·id·ly** adv.

ra·pi·er /'rāpēər/ ▶ n. a thin, light sharp-pointed sword used for thrusting.

rap·ine /'rapən, -īn/ ▶ n. literary the violent seizure of property.

rap·ist /'rāpist/ ▶ n. a man who commits rape.

rap·pel /rə'pel/ ▶ v. (**rappels, rappelling, rappelled**) climb down a steep rock face using a rope coiled around the body and attached at a higher point.

rap·port /ra'pôr, rə-/ ▶ n. a close relationship in which people understand each other and communicate well.

rap·por·teur /,ra,pôr'tər/ ▶ n. a person appointed by an organization to report on its meetings.

rap·proche·ment /,rap,rōsh'män, -,rôsh-/ ▶ n. a renewal of friendly relations between countries or groups.

rap·scal·lion /rap'skalyən/ ▶ n. old use a mischievous person.

rapt /rapt/ ▶ adj. **1** completely fascinated and absorbed: *they listened with rapt attention.* **2** literary filled with an intense and pleasant emotion. ■ **rapt·ly** adv.

rap·tor /'raptər/ ▶ n. a bird of prey. ■ **rap·to·ri·al** /rap'tôrēəl/ adj.

rap·ture /'rapCHər/ ▶ n. **1** great pleasure or joy. **2** (**raptures**) expressions of great pleasure or enthusiasm.

rap·tur·ous /'rapCHərəs/ ▶ adj. feeling or expressing great pleasure or enthusiasm. ■ **rap·tur·ous·ly** adv.

ra·ra a·vis /,re(ə)rə 'āvis, ,rärə 'äwis/ ▶ n. another term for RARE BIRD.

rare¹ /re(ə)r/ ▶ adj. (**rarer, rarest**) **1** not occurring or found very often: *a rare genetic disorder.* **2** unusually good.

rare² ▶ adj. (**rarer, rarest**) (of red meat) lightly cooked, so that the inside is still red.

rare bird ▶ n. an exceptional or unusual person or thing.

rare·bit /ˈre(ə)rbit/ (also **Welsh rarebit** or **Welsh rabbit**) ▶ n. a dish of melted cheese on toast.

rare earth ▶ n. any of a group of chemically similar metallic elements including the lanthanide elements together with (usually) scandium and yttrium.

rar·e·fied /ˈrerəˌfīd/ ▶ adj. 1 (of air) of lower pressure than usual; thin. 2 distant from the lives and concerns of ordinary people; esoteric: *rarefied scholarly pursuits.*

rare·ly /ˈre(ə)rlē/ ▶ adv. not often; seldom.

rar·ing /ˈre(ə)riNG/ ▶ adj. informal very eager to do something: *she was raring to go.*

rar·i·ty /ˈre(ə)ritē/ ▶ n. (pl. **rarities**) 1 a rare or unusual thing. 2 the state or quality of being rare.

ras·cal /ˈraskəl/ ▶ n. 1 a mischievous or impudent person. 2 a dishonest man. ■ **ras·cal·i·ty** /rasˈkalətē/ n. **ras·cal·ly** adj.

rash[1] /rasн/ ▶ adj. acting or done without careful consideration: *a rash decision.* ■ **rash·ly** adv. **rash·ness** n.

rash[2] ▶ n. 1 an area of red spots or patches on a person's skin. 2 a series of unwelcome things happening within a short time: *a rash of strikes.*

rash·er /ˈrashər/ chiefly Brit. ▶ n. a thin slice of bacon.

rasp /rasp/ ▶ v. 1 make a harsh, grating sound: *cicadas rasped in the surrounding pines.* 2 say something in a harsh, grating tone. 3 (of a rough object) scrape something. 4 file something with a rasp. ▶ n. 1 a coarse file for use on metal or other hard material. 2 a harsh, grating noise. ■ **rasp·y** adj.

rasp·ber·ry /ˈrazˌberē, -b(ə)rē/ ▶ n. (pl. **raspberries**) 1 an edible reddish-pink soft fruit related to the blackberry. 2 informal a sound made with the tongue and lips, expressing scorn or contempt.

Ras·ta /ˈrastə/ ▶ n. & adj. informal short for RASTAFARIAN.

Ras·ta·far·i·an /ˌrastəˈfe(ə)rēən, -ˈfärēən/ ▶ adj. relating to a religious movement of Jamaican origin believing that Haile Selassie (the former emperor of Ethiopia) was the Messiah and that black people are the chosen people. ▶ n. a member of the Rastafarian movement. ■ **Ras·ta·far·i·an·ism** n.

Ras·ta·man /ˈrastəˌman/ ▶ n. (pl. **Rastamen**) informal a male Rastafarian.

ras·ter /ˈrastər/ ▶ n. a rectangular pattern of parallel scanning lines followed by the electron beam on a television screen or computer monitor.

rat /rat/ ▶ n. 1 a long-tailed rodent resembling a large mouse, often considered a serious pest. 2 informal an unpleasant person, especially one who is deceitful or disloyal. 3 informal an informant. 4 informal a person who is associated with or often visits a particular place: *a mall rat.* ▶ v. (**rats, ratting, ratted**) 1 (**rat on**) informal inform on someone. 2 (**rat on**) informal break an agreement or promise. 3 hunt or kill rats.

rat·a·ble /ˈrātəbəl/ ▶ adj. variant spelling of RATEABLE.

rat-a-tat /ˈrat ə ˌtat/ (also **rat-a-tat-tat** /ˌrat ə ˌtat ˈtat/) ▶ n. a rapping sound, as of knocking on a door, or the sound of gunfire.

ra·ta·touille /ˌratəˈto͞o-ē, ˌräˌtä-/ ▶ n. a dish consisting of onions, zucchini, tomatoes, eggplant, and peppers, stewed in oil.

rat·bag /ˈratˌbag/ ▶ n. informal an unpleasant or disliked person.

ratch·et /ˈrachit/ ▶ n. a device consisting of a bar or wheel with a set of angled teeth in which a cog, tooth, or pivoted bar fits, allowing motion in one direction only. ▶ v. (**ratchets, ratcheting, ratcheted**) 1 (**ratchet something up/down**) make something rise (or fall) as a step in an inevitable process: *the bank ratcheted up interest rates again.* 2 operate something by means of a ratchet.

rate /rāt/ ▶ n. 1 a measure, quantity, or frequency measured against another quantity or measure: *the island has the lowest crime rate in the world.* 2 the speed with which something moves or happens. 3 a fixed price paid or charged for something. 4 the amount of a charge or payment expressed as a percentage of another amount, or as a basis of calculation: *our current interest rates are very competitive.* ▶ v. 1 give a standard or value to something according to a particular scale. 2 consider to be of a certain quality or standard: *scouts rate him as the No. 1 player overall.* 3 be worthy of or merit something. 4 informal have a high opinion of someone or something.
– PHRASES **at any rate** whatever happens or may have happened. **at this rate** if things continue in this way.

rate·a·ble /ˈrātəbəl/ (also **ratable**) ▶ adj. able to be rated or estimated.

rate of ex·change ▶ n. another term for EXCHANGE RATE.

rath·er /ˈraᴛʜər/ ▶ adv. 1 (**would rather**) would prefer: *I'd rather you didn't tell him.* 2 to a certain extent; quite. 3 used to correct something you have said or to be more precise: *I walked, or rather, limped home.* 4 instead of. ▶ exclam. Brit. dated used to emphasize that you agree with or accept something.

rat·i·fy /ˈratəˌfī/ ▶ v. (**ratifies, ratifying, ratified**) give formal consent to an agreement, making it officially valid. ■ **rat·i·fi·ca·tion** /ˌratəfəˈkāSHən/ n.

rat·ing /ˈrātiNG/ ▶ n. 1 a classification or ranking based on quality, standard, or performance. 2 (**ratings**) the estimated audience size of a television or radio program.

ra·tio /ˈrāSHō, ˈrāSHēˌō/ ▶ n. (pl. **ratios**) the quantitative relationship between two amounts showing the number of times one value contains or is contained within the other.

ra·ti·oc·i·na·tion /ˌratēˌōsəˈnāSHən/ ▶ n. formal the formation of judgments by logic; reasoning. ■ **ra·ti·oc·i·nate** /ˌratēˈōsəˌnāt, ˌrasHē-/ v. **ra·ti·oc·i·na·tive** /-ˈōsəˌnātiv, ˈäs-/ adj.

ra·tion /ˈrasHən, ˈrā-/ ▶ n. 1 a fixed amount of food, fuel, or a similar commodity, officially allowed to each person during a shortage. 2 (**rations**) a regular allowance of food supplied to members of the armed forces. ▶ v. 1 limit the supply of a commodity to fixed rations. 2 (**ration someone to**) allow someone to have only a fixed amount of a commodity.

ra·tion·al /ˈrasHənl, ˈrasHnəl/ ▶ adj. 1 based on reason or logic: *a rational explanation.* 2 able to think sensibly or logically. 3 having the capacity to reason. 4 Mathematics (of a number or quantity) able to be expressed as a ratio of whole numbers. ■ **ra·tion·al·i·ty** /ˌrasHəˈnalətē/ n. **ra·tion·al·ly** adv.

ra·tion·ale /ˌrashəˈnal/ ▸ n. a set of reasons for a course of action or a belief.

ra·tion·al·ism /ˈrashənlˌizəm, ˈrashnəˌlizəm/ ▸ n. the belief that opinions and actions should be based on reason and knowledge rather than on religious belief or emotions. ■ **ra·tion·al·ist** n.

ra·tion·al·ize /ˈrashənlˌīz, ˈrashnəˌlīz/ ▸ v. **1** try to find a logical reason for an action or attitude: *rationalize your fear by thinking about it positively.* **2** make a company or industry more efficient by disposing of unwanted staff or equipment. ■ **ra·tion·al·i·za·tion** /ˌrashənlə'zāshən, ˌrashnələ-/ n. **ra·tion·al·iz·er** n.

rat race ▸ n. informal a way of life that is a fiercely competitive struggle for wealth or power.

rat·tan /raˈtan, rə-/ ▸ n. the thin, pliable stems of a tropical climbing palm, used to make furniture.

rat·tle /ˈratl/ ▸ v. **1** make or cause to make a rapid series of short, sharp knocking sounds. **2** move with a knocking sound. **3** informal make someone nervous or irritated. **4** (**rattle something off**) say or produce something quickly and easily: *he rattled off some safety tips.* **5** (**rattle on**/**away**) talk rapidly and at length. ▸ n. **1** a rattling sound. **2** a device or toy that makes a rattling sound. ■ **rat·tly** adj.

rat·tler /ˈratl-ər, ˈratlər/ ▸ n. informal a rattlesnake.

rat·tle·snake /ˈratlˌsnāk/ ▸ n. an American viper with a series of horny rings on the tail that produce a rattling sound.

rat·tle·trap /ˈratlˌtrap/ ▸ n. informal an old or rickety vehicle.

rat·tling /ˈratl-iNG, ˈratliNG/ ▸ adj. informal, dated very: *a rattling good story.*

rat·trap /ˈratˌtrap/ ▸ n. **1** a trap for catching rats. **2** informal a shabby or squalid building or establishment.

rat·ty /ˈratē/ ▸ adj. **1** resembling or like a rat. **2** informal in bad condition; shabby.

rau·cous /ˈrôkəs/ ▸ adj. **1** (of a sound) loud and harsh. **2** noisy or rowdy: *a raucous late-night dinner.* ■ **rau·cous·ly** adv. **rau·cous·ness** n.

raunch /rônCH, ränCH/ ▸ n. informal explicit earthiness or sexuality.

raun·chy /ˈrônCHē, ˈrän-/ ▸ adj. (**raunchier, raunchiest**) informal earthy and sexually explicit. ■ **raunch·i·ly** adv. **raunch·i·ness** n.

rav·age /ˈravij/ ▸ v. cause severe damage to someone or something. ▸ n. (**ravages**) the destructive effects of something.

rave /rāv/ ▸ v. **1** talk in a wild or angry way. **2** speak or write very enthusiastically about: *critics raved about his technique.* ▸ n. informal **1** a very enthusiastic review. **2** a very large party or similar event with dancing to loud, fast electronic music.

rav·el /ˈravel/ ▸ v. (**ravels, raveling, raveled**) **1** (**ravel something out**) untangle something. **2** confuse or complicate a situation.

ra·ven /ˈrāvən/ ▸ n. a large black crow. ▸ adj. (of hair) black and glossy.

rav·en·ing /ˈravəniNG/ ▸ adj. (especially of a wild animal) very hungry and searching for food.

rav·en·ous /ˈravənəs/ ▸ adj. very hungry. ■ **rav·en·ous·ly** adv.

rav·er /ˈrāvər/ ▸ n. informal **1** a person who regularly goes to raves. **2** a person who talks wildly or incoherently.

rave-up ▸ n. Brit. informal a lively, noisy party.

ra·vine /rəˈvēn/ ▸ n. a deep, narrow gorge with steep sides.

rav·ing /ˈrāviNG/ ▸ n. (**ravings**) wild talk that makes no sense. ▸ adj. & adv. informal used for emphasis: *she was no raving beauty.*

ra·vi·o·li /ˌravēˈōlē/ ▸ pl.n. small pasta cases filled with cheese, ground meat, etc.

rav·ish /ˈravish/ ▸ v. **1** (**be ravished**) literary be filled with great pleasure: *ravished by a sunny afternoon, she had agreed without thinking.* **2** dated rape someone. **3** old use seize and carry off someone by force.

rav·ish·ing /ˈravishiNG/ ▸ adj. very beautiful or delightful: *a ravishing film star.* ■ **rav·ish·ing·ly** adv.

raw /rô/ ▸ adj. **1** (of food) uncooked. **2** (of a material or substance) not processed or finished: *turn under the raw edges of the fabric.* **3** (of data) not organized or evaluated. **4** (of the skin) red and painful from being rubbed or scraped. **5** (of a person's nerves) very sensitive. **6** (of an emotion or quality) strong and undisguised: *raw masculinity.* **7** (of the weather) cold and damp. **8** new to an activity or job and therefore lacking experience. ■ **raw·ly** adv. **raw·ness** n. – PHRASES **in the raw 1** in its true state. **2** informal naked. **a raw deal** informal unfair or harsh treatment.

raw·hide /ˈrôˌhīd/ ▸ n. stiff leather that has not been tanned.

raw ma·te·ri·al ▸ n. a basic material from which a product is made.

ray¹ /rā/ ▸ n. **1** a line of light coming from the sun or any luminous object. **2** the straight line in which radiation travels to a given point. **3** (**rays**) a specified form of nonluminous radiation: *ultraviolet rays.* **4** a slight indication of a welcome quality: *a ray of hope.*

ray² ▸ n. a broad flat fish with winglike pectoral fins and a long thin tail.

ray·on /ˈrāˌän/ ▸ n. a synthetic fiber or fabric made from viscose.

raze /rāz/ ▸ v. completely destroy a building, town, etc.

ra·zor /ˈrāzər/ ▸ n. an implement with a sharp blade, used to shave hair from the face or body. ▸ v. cut hair with a razor.

ra·zor·back /ˈrāzərˌbak/ ▸ n. **1** a pig of a half-wild breed common in the southern US, with the back formed into a high, narrow ridge. **2** (also **razorback ridge**) a steep-sided, narrow ridge of land.

ra·zor·bill /ˈrāzərˌbil/ ▸ n. a black-and-white auk (seabird) with a deep bill.

ra·zor clam ▸ n. a burrowing mollusk with a long straight shell.

ra·zor wire ▸ n. metal wire with sharp edges or studded with small sharp blades, used as a barrier.

razz /raz/ ▸ v. informal tease someone playfully.

raz·zle /ˌrazəl/ ▸ n. (in phrase **on the razzle**) Brit. informal out celebrating or enjoying oneself.

raz·zle-daz·zle /ˌrazəl ˈdazəl/ ▸ n. informal exciting or noisy activity, intended to attract attention.

razz·ma·tazz /ˈrazməˌtaz/ (also **razzamatazz**) ▸ n. informal another term for RAZZLE-DAZZLE.

Rb ▸ symbol the chemical element rubidium.

RC ▸ abbr. **1** Red Cross. **2** Electronics resistance/capacitance (or resistor/capacitor). **3** Roman Catholic.

Rd. ▶ abbr. Road (used in street names).

RDA ▶ abbr. recommended daily (or dietary) allowance.

RDS ▶ abbr. respiratory distress syndrome.

Re ▶ symbol the chemical element rhenium.

re[1] /rā, rē/ ▶ prep. 1 in the matter of (used in headings or to introduce a reference). 2 about; concerning.

re[2] ▶ n. Music the second note of a major scale, coming after 'do' and before 'mi.'

re- ▶ prefix 1 once more; anew: *reactivate.* 2 with return to a previous state: *restore.*

> **USAGE**
>
> Words formed with the prefix (word beginning) **re-** are usually spelled without a hyphen (*react*). However, if the word to which **re-** is attached begins with **e**, then a hyphen is used to make it clear (*re-examine, re-enter*). You should also use a hyphen when the word formed with **re-** would be exactly the same as a word that already exists; use **re-cover** to mean 'cover again' and **recover** to mean 'get well again.'

're ▶ abbr. informal are (usually after *you, we,* and *they*).

reach /rēCH/ ▶ v. 1 stretch out an arm to touch or grasp something. 2 be able to touch something with an outstretched arm or leg. 3 arrive at a place. 4 achieve or extend to a specified point, level, or state: *unemployment reached a peak in 1933.* 5 succeed in achieving: *I hope we will be able to reach agreement.* 6 make contact with someone. ▶ n. 1 an act of reaching. 2 the distance to which someone can stretch out their arm. 3 the extent to which someone or something has power, influence, or the ability to do something: *college was out of her reach.* 4 (often **reaches**) a continuous extent of water, especially a stretch of river between two bends. ■ **reach·a·ble** adj.

re·ac·quaint /ˌrēəˈkwānt/ ▶ v. (**reacquaint someone/oneself with**) make someone familiar or acquainted with again: *she came here to reacquaint herself with existing customers.*

re·act /rēˈakt/ ▶ v. 1 respond to something in a particular way: *he reacted angrily to the news of his dismissal.* 2 suffer from harmful effects after eating, breathing, or touching a substance. 3 interact and undergo a chemical or physical change.

re·ac·tance /rēˈaktəns/ ▶ n. Physics the nonresistive component of impedance in an alternating-current circuit, arising from inductance and/or capacitance.

re·ac·tant /rēˈaktənt/ ▶ n. Chemistry a substance that takes part in and undergoes change during a chemical reaction.

re·ac·tion /rēˈakSHən/ ▶ n. 1 something done or experienced as a result of an event or situation: *her first reaction was one of relief.* 2 (**reactions**) a person's ability to respond to an event. 3 a response by the body to a drug or substance to which someone is allergic. 4 a way of thinking or behaving that is deliberately different from that of the past: *a reaction against austerity.* 5 opposition to political or social progress: *the forces of reaction.* 6 a process in which substances interact causing chemical or physical change. 7 Physics a force exerted in opposition to an applied force.

re·ac·tion·ar·y /rēˈakSHəˌnerē/ ▶ adj. opposing political or social progress or reform. ▶ n. (pl. **reactionaries**) a person holding reactionary views.

re·ac·ti·vate /rēˈaktivāt/ ▶ v. bring something back into action. ■ **re·ac·ti·va·tion** /rēˌaktiˈvāSHən/ n.

re·ac·tive /rēˈaktiv/ ▶ adj. 1 showing a response to a stimulus. 2 acting in response to a situation rather than creating or controlling it. 3 having a tendency to react chemically. ■ **re·ac·tiv·i·ty** /ˌrēˌakˈtivətē/ n.

re·ac·tor /rēˈaktər/ ▶ n. 1 (also **nuclear reactor**) a structure or piece of equipment in which suitable material can be made to undergo a controlled nuclear reaction, so releasing nuclear energy. 2 a container or device in which substances are made to react chemically.

read /rēd/ ▶ v. (past and past part. **read** /red/) 1 look at and understand the meaning of written or printed matter by interpreting its characters or symbols. 2 speak written or printed words aloud. 3 have a particular wording: *the placard read 'We want justice.'* 4 discover information by reading: *I read about the course in the paper.* 5 habitually read a particular newspaper or magazine. 6 understand or interpret the nature or significance of: *he didn't dare look away in case this was read as a sign of weakness.* 7 (**read something into**) think that something has a meaning or significance that it may not possess. 8 (**read up on**) gain information about a subject by reading. 9 chiefly Brit. study an academic subject at a university. 10 look at and record the figure indicated on a measuring instrument. 11 present a bill or other measure before a lawmaking body. 12 (of a computer) copy or transfer data. 13 hear and understand the words of someone speaking on a radio transmitter. ▶ n. 1 informal a book that is interesting or enjoyable to read. 2 a period or act of reading. ■ **read·a·ble** adj.

– PHRASES **read between the lines** look for or find a meaning that is not explicitly stated. **read someone's mind** know what someone else is thinking.

read·er /ˈrēdər/ ▶ n. 1 a person who reads. 2 a person who assesses the quality of manuscripts submitted for publication. 3 a book containing extracts of another book or books for teaching purposes. 4 a device that produces a readable image from microfiche or microfilm on a screen. ■ **read·er·ly** adj.

read·er·ship /ˈrēdərˌSHip/ ▶ n. (treated as sing. or pl.) the readers of a publication as a group.

read·i·ly /ˈredlē/ ▶ adv. 1 without hesitation; willingly. 2 without difficulty; easily.

read·ing /ˈrēdiNG/ ▶ n. 1 the action or skill of reading. 2 an instance of something being read to an audience. 3 a way of interpreting something: *his reading of the situation was justified.* 4 a figure recorded on a measuring instrument. 5 a stage of debate in a legislature through which a bill must pass before it can become law.

reading age ▶ n. a child's reading ability, measured by comparing it with the average ability of children of a particular age.

re·ad·just /ˌrēəˈjəst/ ▶ v. 1 set or adjust something again. 2 adjust or adapt to a changed situation or environment. ■ **re·ad·just·ment** n.

read-on·ly mem·o·ry /rēd/ ▶ n. Computing memory read at high speed but not capable of being changed by program instructions.

read·out /ˈrēdˌout/ ▶ n. a visual record or display of the output from a computer or scientific instrument.

read-write /'rēd 'rīt/ ▶ adj. Computing capable of reading existing data and accepting alterations or further input.

read·y /'redē/ ▶ adj. (**readier, readiest**) **1** prepared for an activity or situation. **2** made suitable and available for immediate use: *dinner's ready.* **3** easily available or obtained; within reach. **4** (**ready to/for**) willing to do or having a desire for. **5** immediate, quick, or prompt: *his ready wit.* ▶ v. (**readies, readying, readied**) prepare someone or something for an activity or purpose. ■ **read·i·ness** n.
– PHRASES **at the ready** prepared or available for immediate use. **make ready** prepare.

read·y-made ▶ adj. **1** made to a standard size or specification rather than to order. **2** easily available: *ready-made answers.*

read·y-mixed ▶ adj. (of concrete, paint, food, etc.) having some or all of the constituents already mixed together.

read·y mon·ey ▶ n. money in the form of cash that is immediately available.

read·y reck·on·er ▶ n. a book, table, etc., listing standard numerical calculations or other kinds of information.

read·y-to-wear ▶ adj. (of clothes) sold through stores rather than made to order for an individual customer.

re·af·firm /,rēə'fərm/ ▶ v. **1** state something again. **2** confirm the validity of something already established. ■ **re·af·fir·ma·tion** /,rē,afər'māsHən/ n.

re·a·gent /rē'ājənt/ ▶ n. a substance or mixture used to cause a chemical reaction, used especially to test for the presence of another substance.

re·al[1] /'rē(ə)l/ ▶ adj. **1** actually existing or occurring; not imagined or supposed. **2** not artificial; genuine: *real diamonds.* **3** worthy of the description; proper: *he's my idea of a real man.* **4** significant; serious: *a real danger of war.* **5** adjusted for changes in the value of money: *real incomes had fallen by 30 percent.* **6** Mathematics (of a number or quantity) having no imaginary part. ▶ adv. informal really; very. ■ **real·ness** n.

re·al[2] /rā'äl/ ▶ n. **1** the basic unit of money of Brazil since 1994, equal to 100 centavos. **2** a former coin and unit of money of various Spanish-speaking countries.

real es·tate ▶ n. property in the form of land or buildings.

re·a·lign /,rēə'līn/ ▶ v. **1** change or restore something to a different or former position or state. **2** (**realign oneself with**) change one's opinions so as to share those of another person, group, etc. ■ **re·a·lign·ment** n.

re·al·ism /'rēə,lizəm/ ▶ n. **1** the practice of accepting a situation as it is and dealing with it accordingly. **2** (in art or literature) the representation of things in a way that is accurate and true to life. **3** Philosophy the theory that abstract ideas have their own existence, independent of the mind. Often contrasted with NOMINALISM. ■ **re·al·ist** n. & adj.

re·al·is·tic /,rēə'listik/ ▶ adj. **1** having a sensible and practical idea of what can be achieved or expected. **2** representing things in a way that is accurate and true to life. ■ **re·al·is·ti·cal·ly** /-ik(ə)lē/ adv.

re·al·i·ty /rē'alətē/ ▶ n. (pl. **realities**) **1** the state of things as they actually exist, as opposed to how one might like them to be: *he refuses to face reality.* **2** a thing that is actually experienced or seen: *the harsh realities of life in a farming community.* **3** the state or quality of having existence or substance. ▶ adj. referring to television programs based on real people or situations, intended to be entertaining rather than informative: *reality TV.*

re·al·ize /'rē(ə),līz/ ▶ v. **1** become fully aware of as a fact; understand clearly: *he realized his mistake at once.* **2** achieve something desired or anticipated: *he finally realized his lifelong ambition.* **3** (**be realized**) (of something one is afraid will happen) happen: *their worst fears were realized.* **4** give actual or physical form to something. **5** be sold for a particular amount. **6** convert property, shares, etc., into money by selling them. ■ **re·al·i·za·ble** /,rēə'līzəbəl/ adj. **re·al·i·za·tion** /,rē(ə)lə'zāsHən/ n.

real life ▶ n. life as it is lived in reality, as distinct from a fictional or ideal world.

re·al·ly /'rē(ə)lē/ ▶ adv. **1** in reality; in actual fact. **2** very; thoroughly. ▶ exclam. expressing interest, surprise, or protest.

realm /relm/ ▶ n. **1** literary or Law a kingdom. **2** a field of activity or interest: *the realm of chemistry.*

re·al·po·li·tik /rā'äl,pōli,tēk/ ▶ n. politics based on practical considerations rather than moral or ideological principles.

real prop·er·ty ▶ n. Law property consisting of land or buildings. Compare with PERSONAL PROPERTY.

real time ▶ n. the actual time during which something occurs. ▶ adj. (**real-time**) (of a computer system) in which input data is processed extremely fast so that it is available virtually immediately as feedback to the process from which it is coming, e.g., in a missile guidance system.

re·al·tor /'rē(ə)ltər, -,tôr, 'rē(ə)lətər/ ▶ n. a person who acts as an agent for the sale and purchase of buildings and land; a real estate agent.

re·al·ty /'rē(ə)ltē/ ▶ n. Law a person's real property. Compare with PERSONALTY.

ream[1] /rēm/ ▶ n. **1** 500 (formerly 480) sheets of paper. **2** (**reams**) a large quantity of something, especially paper.

ream[2] ▶ v. widen a bore or hole with a special tool. ■ **ream·er** n.

re·an·a·lyze /rē'anl,īz/ ▶ v. carry out a further analysis of something. ■ **re·a·nal·y·sis** /,rēə'naləsəs/ n.

re·an·i·mate /rē'anə,māt/ ▶ v. bring someone back to life or consciousness. ■ **re·an·i·ma·tion** /,rē,anə'māsHən/ n.

reap /rēp/ ▶ v. **1** cut or gather a crop or harvest. **2** receive something as a result of one's own or others' actions: *the company is poised to reap the benefits of this investment.*

reap·er /'rēpər/ ▶ n. **1** a person or machine that harvests a crop. **2** (**the Reaper** or **the Grim Reaper**) a representation of death as a cloaked skeleton holding a large scythe.

re·ap·pear /,rēə'pi(ə)r/ ▶ v. appear again. ■ **re·ap·pear·ance** /,rēə'pi(ə)rəns/ n.

re·ap·point /,rēə'point/ ▶ v. appoint someone again to a position they previously held. ■ **re·ap·point·ment** n.

re·ap·praise /,rēə'prāz/ ▶ v. appraise something again or differently. ■ **re·ap·prais·al** n.

rear¹ /ri(ə)r/ ▶ n. **1** the back part of something. **2** (also **rear end**) informal a person's buttocks. ▶ adj. at the back.
– PHRASES **bring up the rear 1** be at the very end of a line. **2** come last in a race.

rear² ▶ v. **1** bring up and care for offspring. **2** breed or cultivate animals or plants. **3** (of an animal) raise itself upright on its hind legs. **4** (of a building, mountain, etc.) extend or appear to extend to a great height. **5** (**rear up**) show anger or irritation.

rear ad·mir·al ▶ n. a rank of naval officer, above captain and below vice admiral.

rear·guard /'ri(ə)r,gärd/ ▶ n. **1** the soldiers at the rear of a body of troops, especially those protecting a retreating army. **2** a reactionary or conservative group in an organization.

rear·guard ac·tion ▶ n. a defensive action carried out by a retreating army.

re·arm /rē'ärm/ ▶ v. provide with or obtain a new supply of weapons. ■ **re·ar·ma·ment** /rē'ärməmənt/ n.

rear·most /'ri(ə)r,mōst/ ▶ adj. furthest back.

re·ar·range /,rēə'rānj/ ▶ v. arrange something again in a different way. ■ **re·ar·range·ment** n.

re·ar·rest /,rēə'rest/ ▶ v. arrest someone again.

rear·view mir·ror /'ri(ə)r,vyōō/ ▶ n. a mirror fixed inside the windshield of a vehicle, enabling the driver to see the vehicle or road behind.

rear·ward /'ri(ə)rwərd/ ▶ adj. directed toward the back. ▶ adv. (also **rearwards**) toward the back.

rear-wheel drive ▶ n. a transmission system that provides power to the rear wheels of a motor vehicle.

rea·son /'rēzən/ ▶ n. **1** a cause, explanation, or justification. **2** good or obvious cause to do something: *we have reason to celebrate.* **3** the power to think, understand, and form judgments logically. **4** (**one's reason**) one's sanity. **5** what is right, practical, or possible: *I'll answer anything, within reason.* ▶ v. **1** think, understand, and form judgments logically. **2** (**reason something out**) find a solution to a problem by considering possible options. **3** (**reason with**) persuade someone by using logical argument. ■ **rea·soned** adj.
– PHRASES **by reason of** formal because of. **listen to reason** be persuaded to act sensibly. **it stands to reason** it is obvious or logical.

rea·son·a·ble /'rēz(ə)nəbəl/ ▶ adj. **1** fair and sensible. **2** as much as is appropriate or fair in a particular situation: *they have had a reasonable time to reply.* **3** fairly good; average. **4** not too expensive. ■ **rea·son·a·ble·ness** n. **rea·son·a·bly** adv.

re·as·sem·ble /,rēə'sembəl/ ▶ v. put something back together. ■ **re·as·sem·bly** /-blē/ n.

re·as·sert /,rēə'sərt/ ▶ v. state or declare something again. ■ **re·as·ser·tion** /,rēə'sərSHən/ n.

re·as·sess /,rēə'ses/ ▶ v. consider or assess someone or something again, in the light of new or different factors. ■ **re·as·sess·ment** n.

re·as·sign /,rēə'sīn/ ▶ v. assign someone or something again or differently. ■ **re·as·sign·ment** n.

re·as·sure /,rēə'SHŏŏr/ ▶ v. make someone feel less worried or afraid. ■ **re·as·sur·ance** n. **re·as·sur·ing** adj.

re·at·tach /,rēə'tacH/ ▶ v. attach something again. ■ **re·at·tach·ment** n.

re·a·wak·en /,rēə'wākən/ ▶ v. awaken again.

re·bal·ance /rē'baləns/ ▶ v. restore the correct balance to someone or something.

re·bar /'rē,bär/ ▶ n. reinforcing steel, especially as rods in concrete.

re·bar·ba·tive /rə'bärbətiv/ ▶ adj. formal unattractive and unpleasant or offensive.

re·bate ▶ n. /'rē,bāt/ **1** a partial refund to someone who has paid too much for tax, rent, etc. **2** a deduction or discount on a sum of money due. ▶ v. /'rē,bāt, ri'bāt/ pay money back as a rebate.

re·bec /'rē,bek, 'reb,ek/ ▶ n. a medieval three-stringed instrument played with a bow.

reb·el ▶ n. /'rebəl/ a person who rebels. ▶ v. /ri'bel/ (**rebels**, **rebelling**, **rebelled**) **1** fight against or refuse to obey an established government or ruler. **2** resist authority, control, or accepted behavior.

re·bel·lion /ri'belyən/ ▶ n. **1** an act of rebelling against an established government or ruler. **2** defiance of authority or control.

re·bel·lious /ri'belyəs/ ▶ adj. rebelling or showing a desire to rebel. ■ **re·bel·lious·ly** adv. **re·bel·lious·ness** n.

re·birth /rē'bərTH, 'rē,bərTH/ ▶ n. **1** the process of being reincarnated or born again. **2** a period of new life, growth, or activity: *the rebirth of a defeated nation.*

re·birth·ing /rē'bərTHiNG/ ▶ n. a form of therapy involving controlled breathing intended to imitate the traumatic experience of being born.

re·boot /rē'bōōt/ ▶ v. boot a computer system again.

re·born /rē'bôrn/ ▶ adj. **1** brought back to life or activity. **2** newly converted to a personal faith in Jesus; born-again.

re·bound ▶ v. /ri'bound, 'rē,bound/ **1** bounce back after hitting a hard surface. **2** recover in value, amount, or strength. **3** (**rebound on**) have an unexpected and unpleasant consequence for: *his tricks are rebounding on him.* ▶ n. /'rē,bound/ **1** a ball or shot that rebounds. **2** Basketball the act of gaining possession of a rebounding ball. **3** an instance of recovering in value, amount, or strength: *shares rose sharply in anticipation of an economic rebound.*
– PHRASES **on the rebound** while still distressed after the ending of a romantic relationship.

re·brand /rē'brand/ ▶ v. change the corporate image of a company or organization.

re·buff /ri'bəf/ ▶ v. reject someone or something in an abrupt or ungracious way: *they rebuffed his attempt to negotiate a new deal.* ▶ n. an abrupt or unkind rejection.

re·build /rē'bild/ ▶ v. (past and past part. **rebuilt**) build something again.

re·buke /ri'byōōk/ ▶ v. criticize or reprimand someone sharply. ▶ n. a sharp criticism.

re·bus /'rēbəs/ ▶ n. (pl. **rebuses**) a puzzle in which words are represented by combinations of pictures and letters.

re·but /ri'bət/ ▶ v. (**rebuts**, **rebutting**, **rebutted**) claim or prove that evidence or an accusation is false.

re·but·tal /ri'bətl/ ▶ n. an act of rebutting evidence or an accusation.

rec /rek/ ▶ n. informal recreation: (as adj.) *the rec center.*

rec. ▶ abbr. **1** record; recorder; recording. **2** recipe. **3** receipt. **4** (in prescriptions) fresh.

re·cal·ci·trant /ri'kalsətrənt/ ▶ adj. obstinately uncooperative or disobedient. ■ **re·cal·ci·trance** n. **re·cal·ci·trant·ly** adv.

re·cal·cu·late /rē'kalkyə‚lāt/ ▶ v. calculate something again or differently. ■ **re·cal·cu·la·tion** /‚rē‚kalkyə'lāsнən/ n.

re·call ▶ v. /ri'kôl/ **1** remember something. **2** cause one to remember or think of someone or something. **3** officially order to return: *the ambassador was recalled from Peru.* **4** (of a manufacturer) request all the purchasers of a product to return it, as a result of the discovery of a fault. **5** select an athlete as a member of a team from which they have previously been dropped, or bring an inactive player back to an active status. **6** call up stored computer data. ▶ n. /'rē‚kôl, ri'kôl, rē'kôl/ **1** the action of remembering or the ability to remember. **2** an act of officially recalling someone or something. – PHRASES **beyond recall** in such a way that restoration to the original state is impossible.

re·cant /ri'kant/ ▶ v. state that one no longer holds an opinion or belief. ■ **re·can·ta·tion** /‚rē‚kan'tāsнən/ n.

re·cap /rē'kap/ ▶ v. (**recaps, recapping, recapped**) recapitulate. ▶ n. a recapitulation.

re·ca·pit·u·late /‚rēkə'picнə‚lāt/ ▶ v. summarize and state again the main points of a speech, argument, etc.

re·ca·pit·u·la·tion /‚rēkə‚picнə'lāsнən/ ▶ n. **1** an act of recapitulating something. **2** Music a part of a movement in which themes from the exposition are repeated.

re·cap·ture /rē'kapcнər/ ▶ v. **1** capture a person or animal that has escaped. **2** recover something taken or lost. **3** experience a past time, event, or feeling again: *the programs give viewers a chance to recapture their own childhoods.* ▶ n. an act of recapturing someone or something.

re·cast /rē'kast/ ▶ v. (past and past part. **recast**) **1** present something in a different form or style: *his thesis has been recast for the general reader.* **2** give roles in a play, movie, or television show to different actors. **3** cast metal again or differently.

rec·ce /'rekē/ Brit. informal ▶ n. an act of reconnoitering a place or area. ▶ v. (**recces, recceing, recced**) reconnoiter a place or area.

re·cede /ri'sēd/ ▶ v. **1** move back or further away. **2** gradually diminish: *her panic receded.* **3** (of a man's hair) stop growing at the temples and above the forehead. **4** (as adj. **receding**) (of a facial feature) sloping backward: *a receding chin.*

re·ceipt /ri'sēt/ ▶ n. **1** the action of receiving something or the fact of its being received. **2** a written statement confirming that something has been paid for or received. **3** (**receipts**) an amount of money received over a period by an organization.

re·ceiv·a·ble /ri'sēvəbəl/ ▶ adj. able to be received. ▶ pl.n. (**receivables**) amounts owed to a business, regarded as assets.

re·ceive /ri'sēv/ ▶ v. **1** be given, presented with, or paid: *they received a $100,000 advance.* **2** accept or take delivery of something sent or offered. **3** form an idea or impression from an experience. **4** suffer, experience, or meet with: *the event received wide press coverage.* **5** (as adj. **received**) widely accepted as true or correct. **6** entertain someone as a guest. **7** admit someone as a member: *hundreds of converts were received into the Church.* **8** detect or pick up broadcast signals. **9** (in tennis and similar games) be the player to whom the server serves the ball. **10** buy or accept goods known to be stolen. **11** serve as a container for something. – PHRASES **be at** (or **on**) **the receiving end** informal be subjected to something unpleasant.

re·ceiv·er /ri'sēvər/ ▶ n. **1** a person or thing that receives something. **2** a piece of radio or television equipment converting broadcast signals into sound or images. **3** a telephone handset, in particular the part that converts electrical signals into sounds. **4** Football a player who catches a pass or kick. **5** a person appointed to manage the financial affairs of a bankrupt business.

re·ceiv·er·ship /ri'sēvər‚sнip/ ▶ n. the state of being managed financially by a receiver.

re·cent /'rēsənt/ ▶ adj. **1** having happened or been done lately; belonging to a period of time not long ago. **2** (**Recent**) Geology another term for HOLOCENE. ■ **re·cent·ly** adv.

re·cep·ta·cle /ri'septikəl/ ▶ n. **1** an object or space used to contain something. **2** Botany the base of a flower or flowerhead.

re·cep·tion /ri'sepsнən/ ▶ n. **1** the action or process of receiving someone or something. **2** the way in which someone or something is received: *an enthusiastic reception.* **3** a formal social occasion held to welcome someone or celebrate an event. **4** the area in a hotel, office, etc., where visitors are greeted. **5** the quality with which broadcast signals are received.

re·cep·tion·ist /ri'sepsнənist/ ▶ n. a person who greets and deals with clients and visitors to an office, hotel, doctor's office, etc.

re·cep·tive /ri'septiv/ ▶ adj. **1** able or willing to receive something. **2** willing to consider new suggestions and ideas. ■ **re·cep·tiv·i·ty** /‚rē‚sep'tivətē/ n.

re·cep·tor /ri'septər/ ▶ n. an organ or cell in the body that responds to external stimuli such as light or heat and transmits signals to a sensory nerve.

re·cess /'rē‚ses, ri'ses/ ▶ n. **1** a small space set back in a wall or into a surface. **2** a hollow space inside something. **3** (**recesses**) remote, secluded, or secret places. **4** a break between sessions of a congress, court of law, etc. **5** a break between school classes. ▶ v. (often as adj. **recessed**) set a fixture back into a wall or surface.

re·ces·sion /ri'sesнən/ ▶ n. a temporary economic decline during which trade and industrial activity are reduced. ■ **re·ces·sion·ar·y** /-‚nerē/ adj.

re·ces·sion·al /ri'sesнənl, ri'sesнnəl/ ▶ n. a hymn sung while the clergy and choir withdraw after a service.

re·ces·sive /ri'sesiv/ ▶ adj. (of a gene) appearing in offspring only if a contrary gene is not also inherited. Compare with DOMINANT.

re·charge /rē'cнärj/ ▶ v. charge a battery or a battery-operated device again. ■ **re·charge·a·ble** adj. **re·charg·er** n.

re·check /rē'cнek/ ▶ v. check something again.

re·cher·ché /rə‚sнer'sнā, rə'sнer‚sнā/ ▶ adj. too unusual or obscure to be easily understood.

re·chris·ten /rē'krisən/ ▶ v. give a new name to someone or something.

re·cid·i·vist /ri'sidəvist/ ▶ n. a person who repeatedly commits crimes and is not discouraged by being punished. ■ **re·cid·i·vism** /-ˌvizəm/ n.

rec·i·pe /ˈresəˌpē/ ▶ n. **1** a list of ingredients and instructions for preparing a dish. **2** something likely to lead to a particular outcome: *high interest rates are a recipe for disaster.*

re·cip·i·ent /riˈsipēənt/ ▶ n. a person who receives something.

re·cip·ro·cal /riˈsiprəkəl/ ▶ adj. **1** given, felt, or done in return: *he showed no reciprocal interest.* **2** (of an agreement or arrangement) affecting two parties equally. **3** Grammar (of a pronoun or verb) expressing mutual action or relationship (e.g., *each other, they kissed*). ▶ n. Mathematics the quantity obtained by dividing the number one by a given quantity. ■ **re·cip·ro·cal·ly** /-ək(ə)lē/ adv.

re·cip·ro·cate /riˈsiprəˌkāt/ ▶ v. respond to a gesture, action, or emotion with a corresponding one. ■ **re·cip·ro·ca·tion** /riˌsiprəˈkāSHən/ n.

rec·i·proc·i·ty /ˌresəˈpräsətē/ ▶ n. the practice of exchanging things with other parties to the benefit or advantage of both.

re·cir·cu·late /rēˈsərkyəˌlāt/ ▶ v. circulate something again. ■ **re·cir·cu·la·tion** /rēˌsərkyəˈlāsHən/ n.

re·cit·al /riˈsītl/ ▶ n. **1** the performance of a program of music by a soloist or small group. **2** a long account of a series of connected things: *a recital of Adam's failures.* ■ **re·cit·al·ist** n.

rec·i·ta·tive /ˌres(ə)təˈtēv/ ▶ n. the narrative and dialogue passages in an opera or oratorio, sung in a way that reflects the rhythms of ordinary speech.

re·cite /riˈsīt/ ▶ v. **1** repeat a poem or passage aloud from memory in front of an audience. **2** state a series of names, facts, etc., in order. ■ **rec·i·ta·tion** /ˌresiˈtāsHən/ n. **re·cit·er** n.

reck·less /ˈrekləs/ ▶ adj. without thought or care for the consequences of an action. ■ **reck·less·ly** adv. **reck·less·ness** n.

reck·on /ˈrekən/ ▶ v. **1** be of the opinion; think: *I reckon he'll win.* **2** (**be reckoned**) be considered to be: *their goalkeeper was reckoned to be the best in the world.* **3** calculate something. **4** (**reckon on**) rely on or expect: *no one had reckoned on a strike.* **5** (**reckon with** or **without**) take (or fail to take) something into account.
– PHRASES **to be reckoned with** not to be ignored or underestimated.

reck·on·ing /ˈrekəniNG/ ▶ n. **1** the action of calculating or estimating something. **2** an opinion or judgment. **3** punishment or retribution for one's actions.

re·claim /riˈklām/ ▶ v. **1** recover possession of something. **2** make wasteland or land formerly under water usable for growing crops. ▶ n. the action of reclaiming something. ■ **rec·la·ma·tion** /ˌrekləˈmāsHən/ n.

re·clas·si·fy /rēˈklasəˌfī/ ▶ v. (**reclassifies, reclassifying, reclassified**) classify someone or something differently. ■ **re·clas·si·fi·ca·tion** /rēˌklasəfəˈkāsHən/ n.

re·cline /riˈklīn/ ▶ v. **1** lean or lie back in a relaxed position. **2** (of a seat) have a back able to move into a sloping position. ■ **re·clin·a·ble** adj.

re·clin·er /riˈklīnər/ ▶ n. an upholstered armchair that can be tilted backward, especially one with a footrest.

rec·luse /ˈrekˌlōōs, riˈklōōs, ˈrekˌlōōz/ ▶ n. a person who avoids other people and lives a solitary life.

re·clu·sive /riˈklōōsiv, -ziv/ ▶ adj. tending to avoid the company of other people: *a reclusive former rock star.*

rec·og·ni·tion /ˌrekigˈnisHən/ ▶ n. **1** the action of recognizing or the process of being recognized. **2** appreciation or acknowledgment of something. **3** (also **diplomatic recognition**) formal acknowledgment by a country that another country has the status of an independent nation.

re·cog·ni·zance /riˈkägnəzəns, -ˈkänəzəns/ ▶ n. Law a bond by which a person undertakes before a court or magistrate to observe a particular condition, especially to appear when summoned.

rec·og·nize /ˈrekigˌnīz, ˈrekə(g)ˌnīz/ ▶ v. **1** identify or know someone or something from having come across them before. **2** accept or acknowledge the existence, validity, or legality of: *he was recognized as an international authority.* **3** show official appreciation of: *his work was recognized by an honorary degree from Albertus Magnus.* ■ **rec·og·niz·a·ble** adj.

re·coil /riˈkoil/ ▶ v. **1** suddenly spring back or flinch in fear, horror, or disgust. **2** spring back as a result of the force of impact or elasticity. **3** (of a gun) move abruptly backward as a reaction on firing a bullet or shell. **4** (**recoil on**) (of an action) have an unwelcome result or effect on the person responsible. ▶ n. the action of recoiling.

rec·ol·lect[1] /ˌrekəˈlekt/ ▶ v. remember something.

re·col·lect[2] /ˌrēkəˈlekt/ ▶ v. **1** collect something again. **2** (**recollect oneself**) manage to control one's feelings.

rec·ol·lec·tion /ˌrekəˈleksHən/ ▶ n. **1** the action of remembering, or the ability to remember. **2** a memory.

re·com·bi·nant /rēˈkämbənənt, ri-/ ▶ adj. relating to genetic material formed by recombination.

re·com·bi·na·tion /rēˌkämbəˈnāsHən/ ▶ n. **1** the process of recombining. **2** the rearrangement of genetic material, especially by exchange between chromosomes or by the artificial joining of DNA segments from different organisms.

re·com·bine /ˌrēkəmˈbīn/ ▶ v. combine again or differently.

re·com·mence /ˌrēkəˈmens/ ▶ v. begin again.

rec·om·mend /ˌrekəˈmend/ ▶ v. **1** state that someone or something is good or would be suitable for a purpose or role. **2** advise as a course of action: *he recommended that I leave the country.* **3** make appealing or desirable: *the house had much to recommend it.* ■ **rec·om·mend·a·ble** adj.

rec·om·men·da·tion /ˌrekəmənˈdāsHən, -ˌmen-/ ▶ n. **1** a suggestion or proposal as to the best course of action. **2** the action of recommending.

re·com·mis·sion /ˌrēkəˈmisHən/ ▶ v. commission something again.

rec·om·pense /ˈrekəmˌpens/ ▶ v. **1** compensate or make amends to someone for loss or harm suffered. **2** pay or reward someone for effort or work. ▶ n. compensation or reward.

re·con informal ▶ n. /ˈrēˌkän, riˈkän/ short for RECONNAISSANCE. ▶ v. /riˈkän/ (**recons, reconning, reconned**) short for RECONNOITER.

rec·on·cile /ˈrekənˌsīl/ ▶ v. **1** restore friendly relations between people. **2** make apparently incompatible things able to exist to together without problems or conflict: *an attempt to reconcile freedom with commitment.*

3 (**reconcile someone to**) make someone accept an unwelcome or unpleasant situation. ■ **rec·on·cil·a·ble** adj.

rec·on·cil·i·a·tion /ˌrekənˌsilēˈāsHən/ ▶ n. **1** the end of a disagreement and the return to friendly relations. **2** the action of reconciling.

rec·on·dite /ˈrekənˌdīt, riˈkän-/ ▶ adj. not known about or understood by many people.

re·con·di·tion /ˌrēkənˈdisHən/ ▶ v. **1** condition something again. **2** overhaul or repair an engine or other piece of equipment.

re·con·fig·ure /ˌrēkənˈfigyər/ ▶ v. configure something differently. ■ **re·con·fig·u·ra·tion** /ˌrēkənˌfigyəˈrāsHən/ n.

re·con·nais·sance /riˈkänəzəns, -səns/ ▶ n. military observation of an area carried out to locate an enemy or gain information.

re·con·nect /ˌrēkəˈnekt/ ▶ v. connect someone or something again. ■ **re·con·nec·tion** /ˌrēkəˈneksHən/ n.

re·con·noi·ter /ˌrēkəˈnoitər, ˌrek-/ (Brit. **reconnoitre**) ▶ v. make a military observation of an area. ▶ n. an act of reconnoitering an area.

re·con·sid·er /ˌrēkənˈsidər/ ▶ v. consider something again, with a view to changing a decision that has been made. ■ **re·con·sid·er·a·tion** /ˌrēkənˌsidəˈrāsHən/ n.

re·con·sti·tute /rēˈkänstəˌt(y) o͞ot/ ▶ v. **1** change the form and organization of an institution. **2** restore dried food to its original state by adding water. **3** reconstruct something. ■ **re·con·sti·tu·tion** /ˌrēˌkänstəˈt(y)o͞osHən/ n.

re·con·struct /ˌrēkənˈstrəkt/ ▶ v. **1** construct something again. **2** re-enact or form an impression of a past event from the evidence available. ■ **re·con·struc·tion** /ˌrēkənˈstrəksHən/ n. **re·con·struc·tive** /-tiv/ adj.

re·con·vene /ˌrēkənˈvēn/ ▶ v. come or bring together again for a meeting or activity.

re·con·vert /ˌrēkənˈvərt/ ▶ v. change something back to a former state. ■ **re·con·ver·sion** /-ˈvərzHən/ n.

re·cord ▶ n. /ˈrekərd/ **1** a piece of evidence or information forming a permanent account of something that has happened, been said, etc. **2** a thin plastic disk carrying recorded sound in grooves on each surface, for reproduction by a record player. **3** the previous behavior or performance of a person or thing: *the team preserved their unbeaten home record.* **4** the best performance or most remarkable event of its kind that has been officially recognized. **5** (also **criminal record**) a list of a person's previous criminal convictions. ▶ v. /riˈkôrd/ **1** put in writing or some other permanent form for later reference: *they were asked to keep a diary and record everything they ate or drank.* **2** convert sound, a broadcast, etc., into permanent form to be reproduced later. ■ **re·cord·a·ble** /rəˈkôrdəbəl, rē-/ adj. **re·cord·ist** /riˈkôrdist/ n.
– PHRASES **for the record** so that the true facts are recorded or known. **on record** officially measured and noted. **on** (or **off**) **the record** made (or not made) as an official statement. **put** (or **set**) **the record straight** correct a mistaken belief.

re·cord-break·ing ▶ adj. beating a record or best-ever achievement. ■ **re·cord-break·er** n.

re·cord·er /riˈkôrdər/ ▶ n. **1** a device for recording sound, pictures, or data. **2** a person who keeps records. **3** a simple woodwind

instrument without keys, played by blowing air through a shaped mouthpiece.

re·cord·ing /riˈkôrdiNG/ ▶ n. **1** a piece of music or film that has been recorded. **2** the process of recording something.

record play·er ▶ n. a device for playing records, with a turntable and a stylus that picks up sound from the groove.

re·count[1] /riˈkount/ ▶ v. tell someone about an event or experience.

re·count[2] ▶ v. /rēˈkount, ˈrē-/ count something again. ▶ n. /ˈrēˌkount/ an act of counting something again.

re·coup /riˈko͞op/ ▶ v. get back an amount of money that has been spent or lost. ■ **re·coup·a·ble** adj. **re·coup·ment** n.

re·course /ˈrēˌkôrs, riˈkôrs/ ▶ n. **1** a source of help in a difficult situation. **2** (**recourse to**) the use of someone or something as a source of help.

re·cov·er /riˈkəvər/ ▶ v. **1** return to a normal state of health, mind, or strength. **2** find or regain possession or control of: *he recovered his balance.* **3** regain or secure money by legal means or the making of profits. **4** remove or extract a substance from waste material for recycling or reuse. ■ **re·cov·er·a·ble** /riˈkəvərəbəl/ adj.

re·cov·er /rēˈkəvər, ˈrē-/ ▶ v. put a new cover or covering on something.

re·cov·er·y /riˈkəvərē/ ▶ n. (pl. **recoveries**) an act or the process of recovering.

re·cov·er·y po·si·tion ▶ n. a position used to prevent an unconscious person from choking, the body being placed face downward and slightly to the side, supported by the bent limbs.

rec·re·ant /ˈrekrēənt/ old use ▶ adj. **1** cowardly. **2** disloyal. ▶ n. a recreant person.

re·cre·ate /ˌrēkrēˈāt/ ▶ v. make or do something again.

rec·re·a·tion[1] /ˌrekrēˈāsHən/ ▶ n. enjoyable leisure activity. ■ **rec·re·a·tion·al** adj.

rec·re·a·tion[2] /ˈˌrēkrēˈāsHən/ ▶ n. the action of recreating something.

re·crim·i·na·tion /riˌkriməˈnāsHən/ ▶ n. (usu. **recriminations**) an accusation made in response to one from someone else.

re·cru·des·cence /ˌrēkro͞oˈdesns/ ▶ v. formal a renewed outbreak or occurrence of something. ■ **re·cru·des·cent** adj.

re·cruit /riˈkro͞ot/ ▶ v. **1** enlist someone in the armed forces. **2** enroll someone as a member or worker in an organization. **3** informal persuade someone to do or help with something. ▶ n. a newly recruited person. ■ **re·cruit·er** n. **re·cruit·ment** n.

rec·tal /ˈrektəl/ ▶ adj. relating to the rectum. ■ **rec·tal·ly** adv.

rec·tan·gle /ˈrekˌtaNGgəl/ ▶ n. a plane figure with four straight sides and four right angles. ■ **rec·tan·gu·lar** /rekˈtaNGgyələr/ adj.

rec·ti·fi·er /ˈrektəˌfīər/ ▶ n. an electrical device converting an alternating current into a direct one by allowing it to flow in one direction only.

rec·ti·fy /ˈrektəˌfī/ ▶ v. (**rectifies, rectifying, rectified**) **1** put something right. **2** convert alternating current to direct current. ■ **rec·ti·fi·a·ble** adj. **rec·ti·fi·ca·tion** /ˌrektəfiˈkāsHən/ n.

rec·ti·lin·e·ar /ˌrektəˈlinēər/ ▸ adj. contained by, consisting of, or moving in a straight line or lines.

rec·ti·tude /ˈrektəˌt(y)o͞od/ ▸ n. morally correct behavior.

rec·to /ˈrektō/ ▸ n. (pl. **rectos**) a right-hand page of an open book, or the front of a loose document. Contrasted with VERSO.

rec·tor /ˈrektər/ ▸ n. 1 (in an Anglican Church) a member of the clergy in charge of a parish. 2 (in the Roman Catholic Church) a priest in charge of a church or a religious institution. 3 the head of certain universities, colleges, and schools.
■ **rec·to·ri·al** /rekˈtôrēəl/ adj. **rec·tor·ship** /-ˌSHip/ n.

rec·to·ry /ˈrektərē/ ▸ n. (pl. **rectories**) a rector's house.

rec·tum /ˈrektəm/ ▸ n. (pl. **rectums** or **recta** /-tə/) the final section of the large intestine, ending at the anus.

re·cum·bent /riˈkəmbənt/ ▸ adj. 1 lying down. 2 (of a plant) growing close to the ground.
■ **re·cum·ben·cy** n.

re·cu·per·ate /riˈko͞opəˌrāt/ ▸ v. 1 recover from illness or physical exertion. 2 regain something lost. ■ **re·cu·per·a·tion** /riˌko͞opəˈrāSHən/ n. **re·cu·per·a·tive** /riˈko͞opəˌrātiv/ adj.

re·cur /riˈkər/ ▸ v. (**recurs, recurring, recurred**) 1 happen again or repeatedly. 2 (of a thought, image, etc.) come back to one's mind.
■ **re·cur·rence** /riˈkərəns, -ˈkə-rəns/ n.

re·cur·rent /riˈkərənt, -ˈkə-rənt/ ▸ adj. happening often or repeatedly. ■ **re·cur·rent·ly** adv.

re·cur·sion /riˈkərZHən/ ▸ n. chiefly Mathematics & Linguistics the repeated application of a procedure or rule to successive results of the process.
■ **re·cur·sive** /riˈkərsiv/ adj.

re·cuse /riˈkyo͞oz/ ▸ v. (**recuse oneself**) (of a judge) excuse oneself from a case because of a possible lack of impartiality.

re·cy·cle /rēˈsīkəl/ ▸ v. 1 convert waste into reusable material. 2 use something again.
■ **re·cy·cla·ble** /rēˈsīk(ə)ləbəl/ adj. & n. **re·cy·cler** /-k(ə)lər/ n.

red /red/ ▸ adj. (**redder, reddest**) 1 of the color of blood, fire, or rubies. 2 (of a person's face) red due to embarrassment, anger, or heat. 3 (of hair or fur) of a reddish-brown color. 4 (of wine) made from dark grapes and colored by their skins. 5 informal, chiefly derogatory communist or socialist. ▸ n. 1 red color or material. 2 informal, chiefly derogatory a communist or socialist. ■ **red·dish** adj. **red·dy** adj. **red·ly** adv. **red·ness** n.
– PHRASES **in the red** having spent more than is in one's bank account. **the red planet** Mars. **see red** informal suddenly become very angry.

re·dact /riˈdakt/ ▸ v. edit something for publication. ■ **re·dac·tion** /riˈdakSHən/ n. **re·dac·tor** n.

red blood cell ▸ n. less technical term for ERYTHROCYTE.

red-blood·ed ▸ adj. (of a man) full of strength and energy; virile.

red-brick ▸ adj. chiefly Brit. (of a British university) founded in the late 19th or early 20th century and often with buildings of red brick rather than stone, so being distinct from the older universities.

red·cap /ˈredˌkap/ ▸ n. 1 a railroad porter. 2 Brit. informal a member of the military police.

red card ▸ n. (especially in soccer) a red card shown by the referee to a player being sent off

the field.

red car·pet ▸ n. a long, narrow red carpet for an important visitor to walk along.

red cell ▸ n. less technical term for ERYTHROCYTE.

red-coat /ˈredˌkōt/ ▸ n. historical a British soldier.

Red Cres·cent ▸ n. a national branch in Muslim countries of the International Movement of the Red Cross and the Red Crescent.

Red Cross ▸ n. the International Movement of the Red Cross and the Red Crescent, an organization bringing relief to victims of war or natural disaster.

red deer ▸ n. a deer with a rich red-brown summer coat that turns brownish-gray in winter, the male having large antlers.

red·den /ˈredn/ ▸ v. 1 make or become red. 2 blush.

red dwarf ▸ n. Astronomy a small, old, relatively cool star.

re·dec·o·rate /rēˈdekəˌrāt/ ▸ v. decorate something again or differently.
■ **re·dec·o·ra·tion** /rēˌdekəˈrāSHən/ n.

re·deem /riˈdēm/ ▸ v. 1 make up for the faults or bad aspects of: *a poor debate redeemed by an outstanding speech.* 2 (**redeem oneself**) make up for one's poor performance or behavior in the past. 3 save someone from sin, error, or evil. 4 repay or clear a debt: *owners were unable to redeem their mortgages.* 5 exchange a coupon for goods or money. 6 gain or regain possession of something in exchange for payment. 7 fulfill a pledge or promise. ■ **re·deem·a·ble** adj.

re·deem·er /riˈdēmər/ ▸ n. 1 a person who redeems someone or something. 2 (**the Redeemer**) Jesus.

re·de·fine /ˌrēdiˈfīn/ ▸ v. define something again or differently. ■ **re·def·i·ni·tion** /ˌrēˌdefəˈniSHən/ n.

re·demp·tion /riˈdempSHən/ ▸ n. 1 the action of redeeming or the process of being redeemed. 2 a thing that saves someone from error or evil.
■ **re·demp·tive** /riˈdemptiv/ adj.

re·de·ploy /ˌrēdəˈploi/ ▸ v. move troops, employees, or resources to a new place or task.
■ **re·de·ploy·ment** n.

re·de·sign /ˌrēdiˈzīn/ ▸ v. design something again or differently. ▸ n. the action or process of redesigning.

re·de·vel·op /ˌrēdiˈveləp/ ▸ v. 1 develop something again or differently. 2 construct new buildings in an area, especially after demolishing the existing buildings. ■ **re·de·vel·op·er** n. **re·de·vel·op·ment** n.

red-faced ▸ adj. embarrassed or ashamed.

red flag ▸ n. 1 a warning of danger. 2 the symbol of socialist revolution.

red gi·ant ▸ n. a very large luminous star with a low surface temperature.

red-hand·ed ▸ adj. in or just after the act of doing something wrong.

red·head /ˈredˌhed/ ▸ n. a person, especially a woman, with red hair. ■ **red·head·ed** adj.

red heat ▸ n. the temperature or state of something so hot that it gives off red light.

red her·ring ▸ n. a clue or piece of information that is misleading or distracting.

red-hot ▸ adj. 1 so hot as to glow red. 2 extremely exciting or of great interest. 3 very passionate.

red-hot pok·er ▸ n. a plant with tall erect spikes of tubular flowers, the upper ones of which are red and the lower ones yellow.

re·di·al /rē′dīl/ ▶ v. (**redials, redialing, redialed**) dial a telephone number again.

re·did /rē′did/ ▶ past of REDO.

red ink ▶ n. used in reference to financial deficit or debt: *a project that has left the state awash in red ink.*

re·di·rect /ˌrēdə′rekt, -ˌdī-/ ▶ v. direct something to a new or different place or purpose. ■ **re·di·rec·tion** /-′reksʜən/ n.

re·dis·cov·er /ˌrēdis′kəvər/ ▶ v. discover something forgotten or ignored again. ■ **re·dis·cov·er·y** n.

re·dis·tri·bute /ˌrēdə′strib‚yōōt/ ▶ v. distribute something again or in a different way. ■ **re·dis·tri·bu·tion** /ˌrēˌdistrə′byōōsʜən/ n. **re·dis·trib·u·tive** /-′stribyətiv/ adj.

red-let·ter day ▶ n. an important or memorable day.

red light ▶ n. a red light instructing moving vehicles to stop.

red-light dis·trict ▶ n. an area with many brothels, strip clubs, etc.

red·line /′red‚līn/ ▶ v. informal **1** drive with a car's engine at its maximum rpm. **2** refuse a loan or insurance to someone because they live in an area considered to be a bad financial risk.

red meat ▶ n. meat that is red when raw, e.g., beef or lamb.

red mul·let ▶ n. a food fish with long, thin growths (barbels) on the chin, living in warmer seas.

red·neck /′red‚nek/ ▶ n. informal, derogatory a working-class white person from the southern US, especially one with politically conservative views.

re·do /rē′dōō/ ▶ v. (**redoes** /rē′dəz/, **redoing** /rē′dōōiNG/; past **redid** /rē′did/; past part. **redone** /rē′dən/) do something again or differently.

red·o·lent /′redl-ənt/ ▶ adj. **1** (**redolent of/with**) strongly suggesting or making one think of something: *names redolent of history and tradition.* **2** (**redolent of/with**) literary strongly smelling of something. **3** old use or literary fragrant. ■ **red·o·lence** n.

re·dou·ble /rē′dəbəl/ ▶ v. make or become greater, more intense, or more numerous: *we will redouble our efforts.*

re·doubt /ri′dout/ ▶ n. a temporary or additional fortification.

re·doubt·a·ble /ri′doutəbəl/ ▶ adj. often humorous (of a person) worthy of respect or fear, especially as an opponent. ■ **re·doubt·a·bly** /-′blē/ adv.

re·dound /ri′dound/ ▶ v. (**redound to**) formal contribute greatly to a person's credit or honor.

re·dox /′rē‚däks/ ▶ adj. Chemistry involving the process of both oxidation and reduction.

red pep·per ▶ n. a ripe sweet pepper, red in color and eaten as a vegetable.

re·draft /rē′draft/ ▶ v. draft a document again in a different way.

re·draw /rē′drô/ ▶ v. (past **redrew** /rē′drōō/; past part. **redrawn** /rē′drôn/) draw or draw up again or in a different way: *strategists will have to redraw their plans.*

re·dress /ri′dres, ′rē‚dres/ ▶ v. put an undesirable or unfair situation right. ▶ n. compensation for a grievance or an unjust act: *redress for victims of discrimination.*

– PHRASES **redress the balance** restore equality in a situation.

red salm·on ▶ n. the sockeye salmon.

red snap·per ▶ n. a reddish edible marine fish.

red squir·rel ▶ n. a small squirrel with a reddish coat.

red·start /′red‚stärt/ ▶ n. a small songbird of the warbler family.

red tape ▶ n. time-consuming or complicated official rules and procedures.

re·duce /ri′d(y)ōōs/ ▶ v. **1** make or become smaller or less in amount, degree, or size. **2** (**reduce someone/thing to**) bring someone or something to a particular state or action: *she had been reduced to near poverty.* **3** (**reduce something to**) change something to a simpler or more basic form. **4** boil a sauce or other liquid so that it becomes thicker and more concentrated. **5** Chemistry cause a substance to combine chemically with hydrogen. **6** Chemistry cause a substance to undergo a reaction in which electrons are gained from another substance or molecule. The opposite of OXIDIZE. ■ **re·duc·er** n. **re·duc·i·ble** adj.

– PHRASES **reduced circumstances** a state of poverty after one has been relatively wealthy. **reduce someone to the ranks** demote a non-commissioned officer to an ordinary soldier.

re·duc·ti·o ad ab·sur·dum /rə′dəktē‚ō ˌad əb′sərdəm, -′dáksʜē‚ō/ ▶ n. a method of proving that an argument or theory is false by showing that its logical consequence is absurd or contradictory.

re·duc·tion /ri′dəksʜən/ ▶ n. **1** the action of reducing something. **2** the amount by which something is reduced. **3** a smaller copy of a picture or photograph. **4** a thick and concentrated liquid or sauce.

re·duc·tion·ism /ri′dəksʜəˌnizəm/ ▶ n. often derogatory the analysis or explanation of something complex in terms of its simplest or most basic elements. ■ **re·duc·tion·ist** n. & adj.

re·duc·tive /ri′dəktiv/ ▶ adj. **1** often derogatory tending to present a subject or problem in an oversimplified form. **2** relating to chemical reduction. ■ **re·duc·tive·ly** adv. **re·duc·tive·ness** n.

re·dun·dant /ri′dəndənt/ ▶ adj. **1** not or no longer needed or useful: *many of the old skills had become redundant.* **2** Brit. (of a person) no longer employed because there is no more work available. ■ **re·dun·dan·cy** n. (pl. **redundancies**) **re·dun·dant·ly** adv.

re·du·pli·cate /ri′d(y)ōōpliˌkāt, ′rē-/ ▶ v. repeat or copy something so as to form another of the same kind. ■ **re·du·pli·ca·tion** /riˌd(y)ōōpli′kāsʜən, ˌrē-/ n.

re·dux /rē′dəks, ′rē‚dəks/ ▶ adj. (after a noun) revived or restored.

red·wing /′red‚wiNG/ ▶ n. a small thrush of northern Europe, having orange-red patches on its sides.

red·wood /′red‚wŏŏd/ ▶ n. a giant coniferous tree with reddish wood, native to California and Oregon.

re·ech·o ▶ v. echo again or repeatedly.

reed /rēd/ ▶ n. **1** a tall, slender-leaved plant with a hollow stem, growing in water or on marshy ground. **2** a piece of thin cane or metal that vibrates in a current of air to produce the sound of various musical instruments, as in the mouthpiece of a clarinet or at the base of some organ pipes. **3** a wind instrument played with a reed. ■ **reed·ed** adj.

re·e·dit ▶ v. edit something again.

reed or·gan ▶ n. a keyboard instrument similar to a harmonium, in which air is drawn upward past metal reeds.

re·ed·u·cat·e ▶ v. educate or train someone to behave or think differently. ■ **re·ed·u·ca·tion** n.

reed·y /'rēdē/ ▶ adj. (**reedier, reediest**) **1** (of a sound or voice) high and thin in tone. **2** full of or edged with reeds. **3** (of a person) tall and thin.

reef /rēf/ ▶ n. **1** a ridge of jagged rock or coral just above or below the surface of the sea. **2** a vein of gold or other ore. **3** each of several strips across a sail that can be taken in or rolled up to reduce the area exposed to the wind. ▶ v. take in one or more reefs of a sail.

reef·er /'rēfər/ ▶ n. informal a marijuana cigarette.

reek /rēk/ ▶ v. **1** have a very unpleasant smell. **2** (**reek of**) suggest something unpleasant or undesirable: *the whole thing reeks of hypocrisy.* ▶ n. a very unpleasant smell.

reel /rēl/ ▶ n. **1** a cylinder on which film, wire, etc., can be wound. **2** a part of a movie. **3** a lively Scottish folk dance. ▶ v. **1** (**reel something in**) bring something toward one by turning a reel. **2** (**reel something off**) say or recite something rapidly and with ease. **3** stagger or lurch violently. **4** feel shocked or bewildered: *workers are still reeling at the news that the factory is to close.*

re·e·lect ▶ v. elect someone to a further term of office. ■ **re·e·lec·tion** n.

reel-to-reel ▶ adj. (of a tape recorder) in which the tape passes between two reels mounted separately rather than within a cassette.

re·e·merge ▶ v. emerge again; begin to exist or become prominent once more. ■ **re·e·mer·gence** n. **re·e·mer·gent** adj.

re·em·pha·size ▶ v. emphasize something again. ■ **re·em·pha·sis** n.

re·en·act ▶ v. **1** act out a past event. **2** bring a law into effect again when the original statute has been repealed or has expired. ■ **re·en·act·ment** n.

re·en·gin·eer ▶ v. **1** redesign a machine. **2** restructure a company or its operations.

re·en·list /,rē-ən'list/ ▶ v. enlist again in the armed forces. ■ **re·en·list·er** n.

re·en·ter ▶ v. enter again: *women who wish to re-enter the labor market.* ■ **re·en·trance** n.

re·entrant ▶ adj. (of an angle) pointing inward. The opposite of **SALIENT**.

re·en·try /rē 'entrē/ ▶ n. (pl. **re·entries**) **1** the action or process of re-entering. **2** the return of a spacecraft or missile into the earth's atmosphere.

reeve¹ /rēv/ ▶ n. historical a local official, in particular the chief magistrate of a town or district in Anglo-Saxon England.

reeve² ▶ n. a female ruff (bird).

re·ex·am·ine ▶ v. **1** examine something again or further. **2** Law examine one's own witness again, after cross-examination by the opposing counsel. ■ **re·ex·am·i·na·tion** n.

re·export /rē'ek,spôrt, rē-ek'spôrt/ ▶ v. export imported goods, typically after further processing or manufacture. ▶ n. the action of re-exporting goods.

ref /ref/ ▶ n. informal (in sports) a referee.

ref. ▶ abbr. **1** reference. **2** refer to.

re·face /rē'fās/ ▶ v. put a new facing on a building.

re·fec·tion /ri'feksHən/ ▶ n. literary or old use **1** the process of refreshing oneself by eating or drinking. **2** a light meal.

re·fec·to·ry /ri'fekt(ə)rē/ ▶ n. (pl. **refectories**) a large room in an educational or religious institution in which people eat meals together.

re·fer /ri'fər/ ▶ v. (**refers, referring, referred**) **1** (**refer to**) write or speak about; mention: *her mother never referred to him again.* **2** (**refer someone to**) direct the attention of someone to something. **3** (**refer to**) (of a word or phrase) describe someone or something. **4** (**refer someone/thing to**) pass a person or matter to an authority or specialist for a decision. ■ **ref·er·a·ble** /'ref(ə)rəbəl, ri'fər-/ adj. **re·fer·rer** n.

ref·er·ee /,refə'rē/ ▶ n. **1** an official who supervises a game or match to ensure that players keep to the rules. **2** a person appointed to examine and assess an academic work submitted for publication. ▶ v. (**referees, refereeing, refereed**) act as referee of something.

ref·er·ence /'ref(ə)rəns/ ▶ n. **1** the action of referring to something. **2** a note in a book or article giving the source of a particular piece of information. **3** a letter from a previous employer giving information about someone's ability or reliability, used when applying for a new job. **4** a person providing such a letter. ▶ v. **1** provide a book or article with references. **2** mention or refer to someone or something.
– PHRASES **with** (or **in**) **reference to** in relation to.

ref·er·ence li·brar·y ▶ n. a library in which the books are to be consulted in the building rather than borrowed.

ref·er·ence point ▶ n. a basis or standard for assessment or comparison.

ref·er·en·dum /,refə'rendəm/ ▶ n. (pl. **referendums** or **referenda** /-də/) a general vote by a country's electorate on a single political question that has been referred to them for a direct decision.

ref·er·ent /'ref(ə)rənt/ ▶ n. Linguistics the thing that a word or phrase refers to or stands for.

ref·er·en·tial /,refə'rencHəl/ ▶ adj. containing or taking the form of a reference or references.

re·fer·ral /ri'fərəl/ ▶ n. the action of referring someone or something to a specialist or higher authority.

re·ferred pain ▶ n. pain felt in a part of the body other than its actual source.

re·fi /rē'fī/ ▶ v. (**refies, refied, refying**) refinance (a mortgage). ▶ adj. relating to refinancing and the refinancing market: *the refi boom is over.*

re·fill ▶ v. /rē'fil/ fill a container again. ▶ n. /'rē,fil/ an act of refilling a container, or a glass that is refilled. ■ **re·fill·a·ble** adj.

re·fi·nance /,rēfə'nans, rē'fī,nans/ ▶ v. finance something again, typically with new loans at a lower rate of interest.

re·fine /ri'fīn/ ▶ v. **1** remove impurities or unwanted elements from something. **2** make minor changes to something so as to improve it: *he gradually refined his technique.* ■ **re·fin·er** n.

re·fined /ri'fīnd/ ▶adj. **1** with impurities or unwanted elements having been removed by processing. **2** well educated, polite, and having good taste and manners.

re·fine·ment /ri'fīnmənt/ ▶n. **1** the process of refining. **2** an improvement brought about by the making of small changes. **3** the quality of being well educated, polite, and having good taste and manners.

re·fin·er·y /ri'fīnərē/ ▶n. (pl. **refineries**) an industrial establishment where a substance is refined.

re·fin·ish /rē'finish/ ▶v. apply a new finish to a surface or object.

re·fit /rē'fit/ ▶v. (**refits, refitting, refitted**) replace or repair machinery, equipment, and fittings in a ship, building, etc. ▶n. an act of refitting something.

re·flate /ri'flāt/ ▶v. (of a government) increase an economy's level of output. ■ **re·fla·tion** /ri'flāshən/ n. **re·fla·tion·ar·y** /ri'flāshə,nerē/ n.

re·flect /ri'flekt/ ▶v. **1** throw back heat, light, or sound without absorbing it. **2** (of a mirror or shiny surface) show an image of: *he could see himself reflected in Keith's glasses.* **3** represent in a realistic or appropriate way: *the letters reflect all aspects of his life.* **4** (**reflect well/badly on**) bring about a good or bad impression of someone or something. **5** (**reflect on**) think deeply or carefully about.

re·flect·ance /ri'flektəns/ ▶n. Physics a property of a surface equal to the proportion of the light shining on it that it reflects or scatters.

re·flect·ing tel·e·scope ▶n. a telescope in which a mirror is used to collect and focus light.

re·flec·tion /ri'flekshən/ ▶n. **1** the phenomenon of light, heat, sound, etc., being reflected. **2** an image formed by reflection. **3** a consequence or result of something: *healthy skin is a reflection of good health.* **4** a source of shame or blame: *his behavior was no reflection on his wife.* **5** serious thought or consideration.

re·flec·tive /ri'flektiv/ ▶adj. **1** providing or produced by reflection. **2** thoughtful. ■ **re·flec·tive·ly** adv. **re·flec·tiv·i·ty** /ri,flek'tivətē, ,rē,flek-/ n.

re·flec·tor /ri'flektər/ ▶n. **1** a piece of material that reflects light, e.g., a piece of red glass or plastic on the back of a motor vehicle or bicycle. **2** an object or device that reflects radio waves, sound, or other waves. **3** a reflecting telescope.

re·flex /'rē,fleks/ ▶n. **1** an action or movement performed without conscious thought as a response to something. **2** a thing that reproduces the essential features or qualities of something else: *politics was no more than a reflex of economics.* ▶adj. **1** performed as a reflex. **2** (of an angle) more than 180°.

re·flex cam·er·a ▶n. a camera with a focusing screen on which the image given by the lens is reflected by an angled mirror, so that the scene viewed is the same as that photographed.

re·flex·ion /ri'flekshən/ ▶n. old-fashioned spelling of REFLECTION.

re·flex·ive /ri'fleksiv/ ▶adj. **1** Grammar (of a pronoun) referring back to the subject of the clause in which it is used, e.g., *myself.* **2** Grammar (of a verb or clause) having a reflexive pronoun as its object (e.g., *wash oneself*). **3** performed without conscious thought; reflex. ■ **re·flex·ive·ly** adv. **re·flex·iv·i·ty** /ri,flek'sivətē,

,rē,flek/ n.

re·flex·ol·o·gy /,rē,flek'säləjē/ ▶n. a system of massage used to relieve tension and treat illness, based on the theory that there are points on the feet, hands, and head linked to every part of the body. ■ **re·flex·ol·o·gist** n.

re·flux /'rē,fləks/ ▶n. **1** technical the flowing back of a liquid, especially that of a fluid in the body. **2** Chemistry the process of boiling a liquid so that any vapor is liquefied and returned to the stock of liquid.

re·fo·cus /rē'fōkəs/ ▶v. (**refocuses, refocusing, refocused** or **refocusses, refocussing, refocussed**) **1** adjust the focus of a lens or one's eyes. **2** focus attention or resources on something new or different.

re·for·est·a·tion /rē,fôrə'stāshən, -'färə-/ ▶n. the process of planting new trees in an area of land that was formerly a forest. ■ **re·for·est** /rē'fôrəst, -'färəst/ v.

re·form /ri'fôrm/ ▶v. **1** make changes in something in order to improve it: *a copyright law that needs to be reformed.* **2** abandon an immoral or criminal lifestyle, or make someone do this. ▶n. the action or process of reforming something: *a major reform of the tax system.* ■ **re·form·er** n.

re·for·mat /rē'fôr,mat/ ▶v. (**reformats, reformatting, reformatted**) chiefly Computing give a new format to something.

ref·or·ma·tion /,refər'māshən/ ▶n. **1** the action or process of reforming. **2** (**the Reformation**) a 16th-century movement for the reform of the Roman Catholic Church, ending in the establishment of the Reformed and Protestant Churches.

re·form·a·to·ry /ri'fôrmə,tôrē/ ▶n. (pl. **reformatories**) (especially in names) a prison: *Illinois State Reformatory.*

Re·formed Church ▶n. a Church that has accepted the principles of the Reformation, especially a Calvinist Church (as distinct from a Lutheran one).

re·form·ist /ri'fôrmist/ ▶adj. supporting or recommending gradual political or social reform. ▶n. a person who supports or recommends such a policy. ■ **re·form·ism** /-,mizəm/ n.

re·form school ▶n. historical an institution to which young offenders were sent as an alternative to prison.

re·for·mu·late /rē'fôrmyə,lāt/ ▶v. formulate something again or differently. ■ **re·for·mu·la·tion** /rē,fôrmyə'lāshən/ n.

re·fract /ri'frakt/ ▶v. (of water, air, or glass) make a ray of light change direction when it enters at an angle.

re·fract·ing tel·e·scope ▶n. a telescope that uses a lens to collect and focus the light.

re·frac·tion /ri'frakshən/ ▶n. the fact or phenomenon of light changing direction when it enters water, air, or glass at an angle.

re·frac·tive /ri'fraktiv/ ▶adj. relating to or involving refraction. ■ **re·frac·tive·ly** adv.

re·frac·tive in·dex ▶n. the ratio of the velocity of light in a vacuum to its velocity in a specified medium.

re·frac·tor /ri'fraktər/ ▶n. **1** a lens or other object that causes refraction. **2** a refracting telescope.

re·frac·to·ry /ri'fraktərē/ ▸ adj. **1** formal stubborn or difficult to control. **2** (of a disease or medical condition) not responding to treatment. **3** technical heat-resistant; hard to melt or fuse. ■ **re·frac·to·ri·ness** n.

re·frain[1] /ri'frān/ ▸ v. (**refrain from**) stop oneself from doing something.

re·frain[2] ▸ n. a repeated line or section in a poem or song, typically at the end of each verse.

re·fresh /ri'fresh/ ▸ v. **1** give new strength or energy to someone. **2** revise or update skills, knowledge, or information. **3** prompt someone's memory by going over previous information.

re·fresh·er /ri'freshər/ ▸ n. a course or activity intended to update or improve one's skills or knowledge.

re·fresh·ing /ri'freshiNG/ ▸ adj. **1** giving new energy or strength. **2** welcome because new or different: *a refreshing change of pace.* ■ **re·fresh·ing·ly** adv.

re·fresh·ment /ri'freshmənt/ ▸ n. **1** a light snack or drink. **2** the giving of fresh strength or energy.

re·frig·er·ant /ri'frijərənt/ ▸ n. a substance used for cooling things. ▸ adj. causing cooling or refrigeration.

re·frig·er·ate /ri'frijə,rāt/ ▸ v. chill food or drink in order to preserve it. ■ **re·frig·er·a·tion** /ri,frijə'rāsHən/ n.

re·frig·er·a·tor /ri'frijə,rātər/ ▸ n. an appliance or compartment in which food and drink is stored at a low temperature.

re·f·uel /rē'fyoo(ə)l/ ▸ v. (**refuels, refueling, refueled**) supply or be supplied with more fuel.

ref·uge /'ref,yooj, -,yoozH/ ▸ n. **1** a place or state of safety from danger or trouble: *he took refuge in the French embassy.* **2** a place that provides a temporary home for those in need of protection or shelter.

ref·u·gee /,refyoo'jē, 'refyoo,jē/ ▸ n. a person who has been forced to leave their country in order to escape war, persecution, or natural disaster.

re·ful·gent /ri'fooljənt, -'fəl-/ ▸ adj. literary shining very brightly. ■ **re·ful·gence** n. **re·ful·gent·ly** adv.

re·fund ▸ v. /ri'fənd, 'rē,fənd/ pay a sum of money back to someone. ▸ n. /'rē,fənd/ a repayment of a sum of money. ■ **re·fund·a·ble** adj.

re·fur·bish /ri'fərbish/ ▸ v. renovate and redecorate a building or room. ■ **re·fur·bish·ment** n.

re·fus·al /ri'fyoozəl/ ▸ n. **1** an act of refusing to do something. **2** an expression of unwillingness to accept or grant an offer or request.

re·fuse[1] /ri'fyooz/ ▸ v. **1** state that one is unwilling to do something. **2** state that one is unwilling to grant or accept something offered or requested. **3** (of a horse) be unwilling to jump a fence or other obstacle. ■ **re·fus·er** n.

ref·use[2] /'ref,yoos, -,yooz/ ▸ n. matter thrown away as worthless.

re·fuse·nik /ri'fyooznik/ ▸ n. **1** a Jew in the former Soviet Union who was refused permission to emigrate to Israel. **2** a person who refuses to follow orders or obey the law as a protest.

re·fute /ri'fyoot/ ▸ v. **1** prove a statement, theory, or person to be wrong. **2** deny a statement or accusation. ■ **re·fut·a·ble** adj. **ref·u·ta·tion** /,refyoo'tāsHən/ n.

> **USAGE**
> Strictly speaking, **refute** means 'prove a statement or theory to be wrong' (*attempts to refute Einstein's theory*). However, it is often now used to mean simply 'deny a statement or accusation' (*I absolutely refute the charges made against me*): although some people object to this use, it is widely accepted in standard English.

re·gain /ri'gān/ ▸ v. **1** get something back after losing control or possession of it. **2** get back to a place or position.

re·gal /'rēgəl/ ▸ adj. relating to or fit for a monarch, especially in being magnificent or dignified. ■ **re·ga·li·ty** n. **re·gal·ly** adv.

re·gale /ri'gāl/ ▸ v. **1** entertain someone with conversation. **2** supply someone with generous amounts of food or drink.

re·ga·li·a /ri'gālyə/ ▸ pl.n. (treated as sing. or pl.) **1** objects such as a crown and scepter, symbolizing royalty and used at coronations or other occasions. **2** the distinctive clothing and objects of an office, activity, or group, worn at formal occasions: *full yachting regalia.*

re·gard /ri'gärd/ ▸ v. **1** think of in a particular way: *he regarded London as his base.* **2** look at someone or something in a particular way. **3** old use pay attention to someone or something. ▸ n. **1** care or concern: *she rescued him without regard for herself.* **2** high opinion; respect. **3** a steady look. **4** (**regards**) best wishes. – PHRASES **as regards** concerning. **in this** (or **that**) **regard** in connection with the point previously mentioned. **with** (or **in**) **regard to** as concerns.

re·gard·ing /ri'gärdiNG/ ▸ prep. about; concerning.

re·gard·less /ri'gärdləs/ ▸ adv. despite the current situation: *they were determined to carry on regardless.* – PHRASES **regardless of** without care or concern for.

re·gat·ta /ri'gätə, ri'gatə/ ▸ n. a sporting event consisting of a series of boat or yacht races.

re·gen·cy /'rējənsē/ ▸ n. (pl. **regencies**) **1** the office or period of government by a regent. **2** (**the Regency**) the period when George, Prince of Wales, acted as regent in Britain (1811–20). ▸ adj. (**Regency**) relating to the neoclassical style of British architecture and furniture popular during the late 18th and early 19th centuries.

re·gen·er·ate ▸ v. /ri'jenə,rāt/ **1** bring new and more vigorous life to an area, industry, or institution. **2** grow new tissue. ▸ adj. /ri'jenərət/ reborn, especially in a spiritual sense. ■ **re·gen·er·a·tion** /ri,jenə'rāsHən, ,rē-/ n. **re·gen·er·a·tive** /ri'jenərətiv, -,rātiv/ adj. **re·gen·er·a·tor** /-,rātər/ n.

re·gent /'rējənt/ ▸ n. a person appointed to rule a country because the monarch is too young or unfit to rule, or is absent. ▸ adj. (after a noun) acting as regent: *Prince Regent.*

reg·gae /'regā, 'rāgā/ ▸ n. a style of popular music with a strong beat, originating in Jamaica.

reg·i·cide /'rejə,sīd/ ▸ n. **1** the killing of a king. **2** a person who kills a king. ■ **reg·i·cid·al** /,rejə'sīdl/ adj.

re·gime /ri'zHēm, rā-/ ▸ n. **1** a government, especially one that strictly controls a country. **2** an ordered way of doing something; a system: *our approach is to simplify the licensing regime.*

3 a regimen.

reg·i·men /'rejəmən, 'rezн-/ ▶ n. a course of diet, exercise, or medical treatment that is followed to improve one's health.

reg·i·ment ▶ n. /'rejəmənt/ **1** a permanent unit of an army, typically divided into several smaller units. **2** a large number of people or things. ▶ v. /'rejə,ment/ organize according to a strict system: *every aspect of their life is strictly regimented.* ■ **reg·i·men·ta·tion** /,rejəmən'tāsнən, -,men-/ n.

reg·i·men·tal /,rejə'mentl/ ▶ adj. relating to an army regiment. ▶ n. (**regimentals**) military uniform, especially that of a particular regiment. ■ **reg·i·men·tal·ly** /-'mentl-ē/ adv.

Re·gi·na /rə'jēnə/ ▶ n. a reigning queen (used following a name).

re·gion /'rējən/ ▶ n. **1** an area of a country or the world having particular characteristics: *the equatorial regions.* **2** an administrative district of a city, state, or country. **3** a part of the body. – PHRASES **in the region of** approximately.

re·gion·al /'rējənl, 'rējnəl/ ▶ adj. relating to or typical of a region. ■ **re·gion·al·ize** /'rējənl,īz, 'rējnə,līz/ v. **re·gion·al·ly** /'rējənl-ē, 'rējnəlē/ adv.

re·gion·al·ism /'rējənl,izəm, 'rējnə-/ ▶ n. **1** loyalty to one's own region in cultural and political terms, rather than to central government. **2** a feature of language specific to a particular region. ■ **re·gion·al·ist** n. & adj.

reg·is·ter /'rejəstər/ ▶ n. **1** an official list or record. **2** a record of attendance, for example of students in a class. **3** the level and style of a piece of writing or speech, varying according to the situation in which it is used. **4** a particular part of the range of a voice or musical instrument. **5** a sliding device controlling a set of organ pipes, or a set of organ pipes controlled by such a device. **6** (in electronic devices) a location in a store of data. ▶ v. **1** enter someone or something in a register. **2** put one's name on an official list. **3** officially report one's arrival as a guest at a hotel or a departing passenger at an airport. **4** express an opinion or emotion. **5** (of an emotion) show in a person's face or gestures. **6** become aware of: *he had not even registered her presence.* **7** (of an instrument) detect and show a reading automatically. ■ **reg·is·tra·ble** /-st(ə)rəbəl/ adj.

reg·is·tered mail ▶ n. a postal service in which the sender can claim compensation if the item sent is damaged, late, or lost.

reg·is·tered nurse ▶ n. a nurse who has graduated from a college or a school of nursing. Compare with PRACTICAL NURSE.

reg·is·trant /'rejəstrənt/ ▶ n. a person who registers for something.

reg·is·trar /'rejə,strär/ ▶ n. **1** an official responsible for keeping official records. **2** the chief administrative officer in a college or university.

reg·is·tra·tion /,rejə'strāsнən/ ▶ n. **1** the action of registering or recording someone or something. **2** a certificate that attests to the registering of a person, a motor vehicle, etc. **3** (also **registration number**) the series of letters and figures identifying a motor vehicle, displayed on a license plate.

reg·is·try /'rejəstrē/ ▶ n. (pl. **registries**) **1** a place where official records are kept. **2** the registration

of someone or something.

reg·nant /'regnənt/ ▶ adj. **1** reigning; ruling. **2** formal currently having the greatest influence; dominant.

re·gress ▶ v. /ri'gres/ **1** return to a former or less advanced state. **2** return mentally to a former stage of life or a supposed previous life. ▶ n. /'rē,gres/ a return to a former or less advanced state.

re·gres·sion /ri'gresнən/ ▶ n. **1** a return to a former or less advanced state. **2** the action of returning mentally to an earlier stage of life or a supposed previous life.

re·gres·sive /ri'gresiv/ ▶ adj. **1** returning to a former or less advanced state. **2** (of a tax) taking a proportionally greater amount from people with lower incomes. ■ **re·gres·sive·ly** adv. **re·gres·sive·ness** n.

re·gret /ri'gret/ ▶ v. (**regrets**, **regretting**, **regretted**) feel or express sorrow or disappointment about something one has done or which one should have done. ▶ n. **1** a feeling of sorrow or disappointment: *she expressed her regret at Ann's death.* **2** (often **one's regrets**) used in polite expressions of apology or sadness.

re·gret·ful /ri'gretfəl/ ▶ adj. feeling or showing regret. ■ **re·gret·ful·ness** n.

re·gret·ful·ly /ri'gretfəlē/ ▶ adv. **1** in a regretful way. **2** it is regrettable or undesirable that.

> **USAGE**
> The main sense of **regretfully** is 'in a regretful way' (*he sighed regretfully*). However, it is now also used to mean 'it is regrettable or undesirable that' (*regretfully, mounting costs forced the branch to close*), although some people object to this use.

re·gret·ta·ble /ri'gretəbəl/ ▶ adj. giving rise to regret; undesirable. ■ **re·gret·ta·bly** /-blē/ adv.

re·group /rē'grōōp/ ▶ v. gather into organized groups again, typically after being attacked or defeated. ■ **re·group·ment** n.

re·grow /rē'grō/ ▶ v. (past **regrew** /rē'grōō/; past part. **regrown** /rē'grōn/) grow or cause to grow again. ■ **re·growth** /rē'grōтн/ n.

reg·u·lar /'regyələr, 'reg(ə)lər/ ▶ adj. **1** following or arranged in a pattern, especially with the same space between one thing and the next: *the association holds regular meetings.* **2** doing the same thing often: *regular worshipers.* **3** done or happening frequently. **4** following or controlled by an accepted standard: *the buying and selling of shares through regular channels.* **5** usual or customary. **6** Grammar (of a word) following the normal pattern of inflection. **7** (of food or clothing) of average size. **8** belonging to the permanent professional armed forces of a country. **9** of an ordinary kind. **10** (of a geometrical figure) having all sides and all angles equal. **11** (of a member of the Christian clergy) belonging to a religious or monastic order. **12** informal, dated rightly so called; absolute: *this place is a regular fisherman's paradise.* ▶ n. a regular customer, member of a team, etc. ■ **reg·u·lar·i·ty** /,regyə'laritē/ n. (pl. **regularities**) **reg·u·lar·ly** adv.

reg·u·lar can·on ▶ n. see CANON².

reg·u·lar·ize /'regyələ,rīz/ ▶ v. **1** make something regular. **2** place a temporary or provisional arrangement on an official or correct basis. ■ **reg·u·lar·i·za·tion** /,regyələrə'zāsнən/ n.

reg·u·late /'regyə,lāt/ ▶ v. **1** control or maintain the rate or speed of a machine or process.

2 control something, especially a business activity, by means of rules. ■ **reg·u·la·tive** /-ˌlātiv/ adj. **reg·u·la·tor** n. **reg·u·la·to·ry** /'regyələˌtôrē/ adj.

reg·u·la·tion /ˌreg(y)ə'lāsHən/ ▶ n. **1** a rule or order made and enforced by an authority. **2** the action of regulating something. ▶ adj. informal in accordance with expectations or conventions: *regulation blond hair.*

re·gur·gi·tate /ri'gərjəˌtāt/ ▶ v. **1** bring swallowed food up again to the mouth. **2** repeat information without analyzing or understanding it. ■ **re·gur·gi·ta·tion** /riˌgərjə'tāsHən/ n.

re·hab /'rēˌhab/ ▶ n. a course of rehabilitative treatment, especially for drug addiction or injury. ▶ v. (**rehabs, rehabbing, rehabbed**) rehabilitate or restore.

re·ha·bil·i·tate /ˌrē(h)ə'biləˌtāt/ ▶ v. **1** prepare someone who has been injured, ill, in prison, or addicted to drugs to resume normal life by training and therapy. **2** restore someone to their former status or reputation after being out of favor. **3** restore something to a former condition. ■ **re·ha·bil·i·ta·tion** /-ˌbilə'tāsHən/ n. **re·ha·bil·i·ta·tive** /-ˌtātiv/ adj.

re·hash /rē'hasH/ ▶ v. reuse old ideas or material without significant change or improvement. ▶ n. a reuse of old ideas or material.

re·hears·al /ri'hərsəl/ ▶ n. **1** a trial performance of a play or other work for later public performance. **2** the action of rehearsing.

re·hearse /ri'hərs/ ▶ v. **1** practice a play, piece of music, or other work for later public performance. **2** state a list of points that have been made many times before.

re·heat /rē'hēt/ ▶ v. heat something again.

re·house /rē'houz/ ▶ v. provide someone with new housing.

re·hy·drate /rē'hīˌdrāt/ ▶ v. absorb or cause to absorb moisture after dehydration. ■ **re·hy·dra·tion** /ˌrēhī'drāsHən/ n.

re·i·fy /'rēəˌfī/ ▶ v. (**reifies, reifying, reified**) formal make something abstract more real or physical. ■ **re·i·fi·ca·tion** /ˌrēəfə'kāsHən/ n.

reign /rān/ ▶ v. **1** rule as monarch. **2** be the dominant quality or aspect: *while the company remains silent, confusion reigns supreme.* **3** (as adj. **reigning**) (of an athlete or team) currently holding a particular title. ▶ n. **1** the period of rule of a monarch. **2** the period during which someone or something is best or most important.

USAGE
On the confusion of **reign** and **rein**, see the note at REIN.

rei·ki /'rākē/ ▶ n. a healing technique based on the belief that the therapist can channel energy into the patient by means of touch, to activate the natural healing processes of the patient's body.

re·im·burse /ˌrēim'bərs/ ▶ v. repay money to a person who has spent or lost it. ■ **re·im·burs·a·ble** adj. **re·im·burse·ment** n.

rein /rān/ ▶ n. **1** a long, narrow strap attached at one end to a horse's bit, used in pairs to control a horse. **2** (**reins**) the power to direct and control: *a new manager will soon take over the reins.* ▶ v. **1** control a horse by pulling on its reins. **2** keep under control; restrain: *he has failed to rein in his own security forces.*
− PHRASES (**a**) **free rein** freedom of action. **keep a tight rein on** exercise strict control over.

USAGE
The phrase **a free rein**, which comes from the meaning of allowing a horse to move freely without being controlled by reins, is often misinterpreted and wrongly spelled as *a free reign.*

re·in·car·nate /ˌrēin'kärˌnāt/ ▶ v. cause someone to be born again in another body.

re·in·car·na·tion /ˌrēinkär'nāsHən/ ▶ n. **1** the rebirth of a soul in a new body. **2** a person in whom a soul is believed to have been reborn.

rein·deer /'rānˌdi(ə)r/ ▶ n. (pl. same or **reindeers**) a deer with large branching antlers, native to the northern tundra and subarctic regions.

re·in·fect /ˌrēin'fekt/ ▶ v. infect someone or something again. ■ **re·in·fec·tion** /-'feksHən/ n.

re·in·force /ˌrēin'fôrs/ ▶ v. **1** strengthen or support an object. **2** strengthen or intensify a feeling, idea, etc. **3** strengthen a military force with additional personnel or equipment. ■ **re·in·forc·er** n.

re·in·forced con·crete ▶ n. concrete in which metal bars or wire are embedded to strengthen it.

re·in·force·ment /ˌrēin'fôrsmənt/ ▶ n. **1** the action of reinforcing something. **2** (**reinforcements**) extra personnel sent to strengthen an army or similar force.

re·in·stall /ˌrēin'stôl/ (Brit. **reinstal**) ▶ v. install again (used especially of software). ▶ n. a reinstallation of software. ■ **re·in·stal·la·tion** /ˌrēinstə'lāsHən/ n. **re·in·stall·er** n.

re·in·state /ˌrēin'stāt/ ▶ v. restore someone or something to a former position or state. ■ **re·in·state·ment** n.

re·in·sure /ˌrēin'sHŏŏr/ ▶ v. (of an insurer) transfer all or part of a risk to another insurer to provide protection against the risk of the first insurance. ■ **re·in·sur·ance** n. **re·in·sur·er** n.

re·in·te·grate /rē'intəˌgrāt/ ▶ v. **1** restore distinct elements into a whole. **2** integrate someone back into society. ■ **re·in·te·gra·tion** /ˌrēintə'grāsHən/ n.

re·in·ter·pret /ˌrēin'tərprət/ ▶ v. (**reinterprets, reinterpreting, reinterpreted**) interpret something in a new or different light. ■ **re·in·ter·pre·ta·tion** n.

re·in·tro·duce /ˌrē-intrə'd(y)ōōs/ ▶ v. **1** bring something into effect again. **2** put a species of animal or plant back into a place where it once lived. ■ **re·in·tro·duc·tion** /-'dəksHən/ n.

re·in·vent /ˌrēin'vent/ ▶ v. change something so much that it appears entirely new. ■ **re·in·ven·tion** /-'vensHən/ n.
− PHRASES **reinvent the wheel** waste a great deal of time or effort in creating something that already exists.

re·in·vest /ˌrēin'vest/ ▶ v. put the profit on a previous investment back into the same scheme. ■ **re·in·vest·ment** n.

re·in·vig·or·ate /ˌrēin'vigəˌrāt/ ▶ v. give new energy or strength to someone or something. ■ **re·in·vig·or·a·tion** /ˌrē-inˌvigə'rāsHən/ n.

re·is·sue /rē'isHōō/ ▶ v. (**reissues, reissuing, reissued**) make a new supply or different form of a book, record, or other product available for sale. ▶ n. a new issue of a product.

re·it·er·ate /rē'itəˌrāt/ ▶ v. say something again or repeatedly. ■ **re·it·er·a·tion** /rēˌitə'rāsHən/ n.

re·ject ▶ v. /ri'jekt/ **1** dismiss as unsatisfactory or faulty: *union negotiators rejected a 1.5 percent* *pay increase.* **2** refuse to consider or agree to something. **3** fail to show proper affection or concern for someone. **4** (of the body) show a damaging immune response to a transplanted organ or tissue. ▶ n. /'rē,jekt/ a rejected person or thing. ■ **re·jec·tion** /ri'jeksHən/ n.

re·jig /rē'jig/ ▶ v. (**rejigs, rejigging, rejigged**) rearrange something.

re·joice /ri'jois/ ▶ v. feel or show great joy.

re·join[1] /rē'join, 'rē-/ ▶ v. **1** join things together again. **2** return to a companion, organization, or route that one has left.

re·join[2] /ri'join/ ▶ v. say something in reply; retort.

re·join·der /ri'joindər/ ▶ n. a sharp or witty reply.

re·ju·ve·nate /ri'jōōvə,nāt/ ▶ v. make someone or something appear or feel younger, better, or more lively. ■ **re·ju·ve·na·tion** /ri,jōōvə'nāsHən/ n. **re·ju·ve·na·tor** n.

re·kin·dle /rē'kindəl/ ▶ v. **1** revive a past feeling, relationship, or interest. **2** relight a fire.

re·laid /rē'lād, 'rē-/ ▶ past and past participle of RELAY[2].

re·lapse ▶ v. /ri'laps, 'rē,laps/ **1** (of a sick or injured person) become ill again after a period of improvement. **2** (**relapse into**) return to a worse or less active state. ▶ n. /'rē,laps/ a return to poor health after a temporary improvement.

re·late /ri'lāt/ ▶ v. **1** make or show a connection between: *many drowning accidents are related to alcohol use.* **2** (**be related**) be connected by blood or marriage. **3** (**relate to**) have to do with; concern. **4** (**relate to**) feel sympathy for. **5** give an account of something. ■ **re·lat·er** (also **relator**) n.

re·lat·ed /ri'lātid/ ▶ adj. belonging to the same family, group, or type; connected. ■ **re·lat·ed·ness** n.

re·la·tion /ri'lāsHən/ ▶ n. **1** the way in which two or more people or things are connected or related. **2** (**relations**) the way in which two or more people or groups feel about and behave toward each other: *the meetings helped cement Anglo-American relations.* **3** a relative by blood or marriage. **4** (**relations**) formal sex or a sexual relationship. **5** the action of telling a story. ■ **re·la·tion·al** adj.
– PHRASES **in relation to** in connection with.

re·la·tion·ship /ri'lāsHən,sHip/ ▶ n. **1** the way in which two or more people or things are connected, or the state of being connected: *the relationship between art and architecture.* **2** the way in which two or more people or groups feel about and behave toward each other. **3** a loving and sexual association between two people.

rel·a·tive /'relətiv/ ▶ adj. **1** considered in relation or in proportion to something else. **2** existing only in comparison to something else: *months of relative calm ended in April.* **3** Grammar (of a pronoun, determiner, or adverb) referring to an earlier noun, sentence, or clause (e.g., *who* in *a contestant who qualified in the first round*). **4** Grammar (of a clause) connected to a main clause by a relative pronoun, determiner, or adverb. ▶ n. **1** a person connected by blood or marriage. **2** a species related to another.
– PHRASES **relative to 1** compared with or in relation to. **2** about; concerning.

rel·a·tive a·tom·ic mass ▶ n. the ratio of the average mass of one atom of an element to one twelfth of the mass of an atom of carbon-12.

rel·a·tive hu·mid·i·ty ▶ n. the amount of water vapor present in air expressed as a percentage of the amount needed for saturation at the same temperature.

rel·a·tive·ly /'relətivlē/ ▶ adv. in relation, comparison, or proportion to something else: *the room was relatively clean.*

rel·a·tive mo·lec·u·lar mass ▶ n. the ratio of the average mass of one molecule of an element or compound to one twelfth of the mass of an atom of carbon-12.

rel·a·tiv·ism /'relətə,vizəm/ ▶ n. the belief that knowledge, truth, and morality exist in relation to culture, society, or historical context, and are not always the same. ■ **rel·a·tiv·ist** n.

rel·a·tiv·i·ty /,relə'tivətē/ ▶ n. **1** the state of being relative in comparison to something else. **2** Physics a description of matter, energy, space, and time according to Einstein's theories based on the importance of relative motion and the principle that the speed of light is constant for all observers.

rel·a·tiv·ize /'relətə,vīz/ ▶ v. make or treat something as relative to or dependent on something else. ■ **rel·a·tiv·i·za·tion** /,relətəvə'zāsHən/ n.

re·launch /rē'lônCH, -'länCH/ ▶ v. launch a product again or in a different form. ▶ n. an instance of relaunching a product.

re·lax /ri'laks/ ▶ v. **1** make or become less tense, anxious, or rigid. **2** rest from work or engage in a leisure activity. **3** make a rule or restriction less strict.

re·lax·ant /ri'laksənt/ ▶ n. a drug that causes relaxation or reduces tension. ▶ adj. causing relaxation.

re·lax·a·tion /ri,lak'sāsHən, rē-/ ▶ n. **1** the state of being free from tension and worry. **2** the action of making something less strict.

re·lay[1] ▶ n. /'rē,lā/ **1** a group of people or animals performing a task for a period of time and then replaced by a similar group. **2** a race between teams of runners, each team member in turn covering part of the total distance. **3** an electrical device that opens or closes a circuit in response to a current in another circuit. **4** a device to receive, reinforce, and transmit a signal again. ▶ v. /ri'lā, 'rē,lā/ **1** receive and pass on information or a message. **2** broadcast something by means of a relay.

re·lay[2] /,rē'lā/ ▶ v. (past and past part. **relaid** /'rē,lād/) lay something again or differently.

re·lease /ri'lēs/ ▶ v. **1** set someone free from imprisonment or confinement. **2** free someone from a duty. **3** allow to move freely: *she released his arm and pushed him aside.* **4** allow information to be generally available. **5** make a movie or recording available to the public. **6** make property, money, or a right available to someone else. ▶ n. **1** the action of releasing or freeing someone or something. **2** a movie or recording released to the public. **3** a handle or catch that releases part of a mechanism. ■ **re·leas·a·ble** adj. **re·leas·er** n.

rel·e·gate /'relə,gāt/ ▶ v. place someone or something in a less important rank or position. ■ **rel·e·ga·tion** /,relə'gāsHən/ n.

re·lent /ri'lent/ ▶ v. **1** finally agree to something after first refusing it. **2** become less severe or intense.

re·lent·less /ri'lentləs/ ▶ adj. **1** never stopping or becoming weaker: *the relentless pursuit of* *wealth.* **2** refusing to give up; determined or strict. ■ **re·lent·less·ly** adv. **re·lent·less·ness** n.

rel·e·vant /'reləvənt/ ▶ adj. closely connected or appropriate to the current matter. ■ **rel·e·vance** n. **rel·e·van·cy** n. **rel·e·vant·ly** adv.

re·li·a·ble /ri'līəbəl/ ▶ adj. able to be depended on or trusted. ■ **re·li·a·bil·i·ty** /ri,līə'bilətē/ n. **re·li·a·bly** /-blē/ adv.

re·li·ance /ri'līəns/ ▶ n. dependence on or trust in someone or something. ■ **re·li·ant** adj.

rel·ic /'relik/ ▶ n. **1** an interesting object that has survived from the past. **2** a person or thing that has survived from the past but is now outdated. **3** a part of a holy person's body or belongings kept and treated as holy after their death.

rel·ict /'relikt/ ▶ n. **1** an organism or other thing that has survived from an earlier period. **2** old use a widow.

re·lief /ri'lēf/ ▶ n. **1** a feeling of reassurance and relaxation following release from anxiety or distress: *the rise of profits was greeted with relief.* **2** a cause of relief. **3** the action of removing or reducing pain, distress, or discomfort. **4** a temporary break in a tense or boring situation. **5** financial or practical assistance given to people in need or difficulty: *famine relief.* **6** a person or group replacing others who have been on duty. **7** the action of lifting a siege on a town. **8** the quality of being more noticeable than surrounding objects: *the sun threw the peaks into relief.* **9** a way of cutting a design into wood, stone, etc., so that parts of it stand out from the surface.

re·lief map ▶ n. a map that shows hills and valleys by shading rather than by contour lines alone.

re·lieve /ri'lēv/ ▶ v. **1** reduce or remove pain, distress, or difficulty. **2** cause someone to stop feeling distressed or anxious. **3** take over from someone who is on duty. **4** (**relieve someone of**) take a responsibility from someone. **5** make less boring or monotonous: *the bird's body is black, relieved only by white under the tail.* **6** bring military support for a besieged place. **7** (**relieve oneself**) formal or euphemistic urinate or defecate. ■ **re·liev·er** n.

re·light /rē'līt, 'rē-/ ▶ v. (past and past part. **relighted** or **relit** /-'lit/) light something again.

re·li·gion /ri'lijən/ ▶ n. **1** the belief in and worship of a God or gods. **2** a particular system of faith and worship. **3** a pursuit or interest that is very important to someone.

re·li·gi·os·i·ty /ri,lijē'äsətē/ ▶ n. the state of being excessively religious. ■ **re·li·gi·ose** /ri'lijē,ōs/ adj.

re·li·gious /ri'lijəs/ ▶ adj. **1** relating to or believing in a religion. **2** treated as very important or done with great care: *a boy with an almost religious devotion to fishing.* ▶ n. (pl. same) a monk or nun. ■ **re·li·gious·ly** adv. **re·li·gious·ness** n.

re·lin·quish /ri'liNGkwish/ ▶ v. willingly give something up. ■ **re·lin·quish·ment** n.

rel·i·quar·y /'relə,kwerē/ ▶ n. (pl. **reliquaries**) a container for holy relics.

rel·ish /'relish/ ▶ n. **1** great enjoyment. **2** a pleasant feeling of looking forward to something: *he was waiting with relish for her promised visit.* **3** a condiment eaten with plain food to add flavor. ▶ v. **1** enjoy something greatly. **2** look forward to something with pleasure.

re·live /rē'liv, 'rē-/ ▶ v. live through an experience or feeling again in one's imagination.

re·load /rē'lōd/ ▶ v. load something, especially a gun, again.

re·lo·cate /rē'lō,kāt, ,rēlō'kāt/ ▶ v. move to a new place and establish one's home or business there. ■ **re·lo·ca·tion** /,rēlō'kāSHən/ n.

re·luc·tance /ri'ləktəns/ ▶ n. unwillingness to do something.

re·luc·tant /ri'ləktənt/ ▶ adj. unwilling and hesitant. ■ **re·luc·tant·ly** adv.

re·ly /ri'lī/ ▶ v. (**relies, relying, relied**) (**rely on**) **1** have complete trust or confidence in someone or something. **2** be dependent on: *the charity has to rely on public donations.*

REM /rem/ ▶ abbr. rapid eye movement, referring to a kind of sleep that occurs at intervals during the night and is characterized by rapid eye movement and more dreaming.

re·made /rē'mād, 'rē-/ ▶ past and past participle of REMAKE.

re·main /ri'mān/ ▶ v. **1** stay in the same place or condition during further time. **2** continue to have a particular quality or fill a particular role. **3** be left over or outstanding after others or other parts have been dealt with or used: *a more difficult problem remains.*

re·main·der /ri'māndər/ ▶ n. **1** a part, number, or quantity that is left over. **2** a part that is still to come: *the remainder of the year.* **3** the number that is left over when one quantity does not exactly divide another. **4** a copy of a book left unsold when demand has fallen. ▶ v. put an unsold book on sale at a reduced price.

re·mains /ri'mānz/ ▶ pl.n. **1** things remaining. **2** historical or archaeological relics. **3** a person's body after death.

re·make ▶ v. /rē'māk, 'rē-/ (past and past part. **remade** /rē'mād, 'rē-/) make something again or differently. ▶ n. /'rē,māk/ a movie or piece of music that has been filmed or recorded anew and re-released.

re·mand /ri'mand/ Law ▶ v. place a person charged with a crime on bail or in custody to await their trial. ▶ n. the process of remanding someone to await trial.

re·mark /ri'märk/ ▶ v. **1** say something as a comment; mention something. **2** notice someone or something. ▶ n. **1** a comment. **2** the fact of being noticed or commented on: *the landscape was not worthy of remark.*

re·mark·a·ble /ri'märkəbəl/ ▶ adj. worthy of attention; extraordinary or striking. ■ **re·mark·a·bly** /-blē/ adv.

re·mar·ry /rē'marē/ ▶ v. (**remarries, remarrying, remarried**) marry again. ■ **re·mar·riage** /rē'marij/ n.

re·mas·ter /rē'mastər/ ▶ v. make a new or improved master of a sound recording.

re·match /'rē,maCH/ ▶ n. a second match or game between two sports teams or players.

re·me·di·al /ri'mēdēəl/ ▶ adj. **1** intended to set right or cure something: *an obligation to take remedial action in case animals are suffering.* **2** provided or intended for children with learning difficulties.

re·me·di·a·tion /ri,mēdē'āsHən/ ▶ n. **1** the action of setting something right, in particular environmental damage. **2** the giving of remedial teaching or therapy to children with learning difficulties. ■ **re·me·di·ate** /ri'mēdē,āt/ v.

rem·e·dy /'remədē/ ▶ n. (pl. **remedies**) **1** a medicine or treatment for a disease or injury. **2** a way of setting right or improving an undesirable situation. **3** a means of gaining legal amends for a wrong. ▶ v. (**remedies, remedying, remedied**) set right an undesirable situation. ■ **re·me·di·a·ble** /ri'mēdēəbəl/ adj.

re·mem·ber /ri'membər/ ▶ v. **1** have in or bring to one's mind someone or something from the past. **2** keep something necessary in mind: *remember to mail the letters.* **3** bear someone in mind by making them a gift or by mentioning them in prayer: *he remembered the boy in his will.* **4** (**remember someone to**) pass on greetings from one person to another.

re·mem·brance /ri'membrəns/ ▶ n. **1** the action of remembering. **2** a memory. **3** a thing kept or given as a reminder of someone.

re·mind /ri'mīnd/ ▶ v. **1** cause someone to remember something. **2** (**remind someone of**) cause someone to think of someone or something because they are similar in some way.

re·mind·er /ri'mīndər/ ▶ n. **1** a thing that causes someone to remember something. **2** chiefly Brit. a letter sent to remind someone to pay a bill.

rem·i·nisce /,remə'nis/ ▶ v. think or talk contentedly about the past.

rem·i·nis·cence /,remə'nisəns/ ▶ n. **1** a story told by a person about a past event that they remember. **2** the enjoyable recollection of past events.

rem·i·nis·cent /,remə'nisənt/ ▶ adj. **1** tending to remind one of someone or something; similar: *the leaves have a fresh taste reminiscent of cucumber.* **2** with one's mind full of memories. ■ **rem·i·nis·cent·ly** adv.

re·miss /ri'mis/ ▶ adj. lacking care or attention to duty.

re·mis·sion /ri'mishən/ ▶ n. **1** the cancellation of a debt, charge, or penalty. **2** a temporary period during which a serious illness becomes less severe. **3** formal forgiveness of sins.

re·mit ▶ v. /ri'mit/ (**remits, remitting, remitted**) **1** send money in payment. **2** cancel a debt or punishment. **3** refer a matter for decision to an authority. **4** forgive a sin.

re·mit·tance /ri'mitns/ ▶ n. **1** a sum of money sent in payment. **2** the action of sending payment.

re·mix ▶ v. /rē'miks, 'rē-/ **1** mix something again. **2** produce a different version of a musical recording by altering the balance of the separate tracks. ▶ n. /'rē,miks/ a remixed musical recording. ■ **re·mix·er** n.

rem·nant /'remnənt/ ▶ n. **1** a small remaining part or quantity. **2** a piece of cloth left when the greater part has been used or sold.

re·mod·el /rē'mädl/ ▶ v. (**remodels, remodeling, remodeled**) **1** change the structure or form of something. **2** shape an object again or differently.

re·mon·strance /ri'mänstrəns/ ▶ n. a strongly critical protest.

re·mon·strate /ri'män,strāt, 'remən-/ ▶ v. make a strongly critical protest. ■ **re·mon·stra·tion** /ri,män'strāsнən, ,remən-/ n.

re·mo·ra /'remərə, ri'môrə/ ▶ n. a slender sea fish that attaches itself to large fish by means of a sucker on top of the head.

re·morse /ri'môrs/ ▶ n. deep regret or guilt for a wrong that one has done.

re·morse·ful /ri'môrsfəl/ ▶ adj. filled with deep regret or guilt. ■ **re·morse·ful·ly** adv.

re·morse·less /ri'môrsləs/ ▶ adj. **1** (of something unpleasant) never ending or improving; relentless. **2** without regret or guilt. ■ **re·morse·less·ly** adv. **re·morse·less·ness** n.

re·mort·gage /rē'môrgij/ ▶ v. take out another or a different mortgage on a property. ▶ n. a different or additional mortgage.

re·mote /ri'mōt/ ▶ adj. (**remoter, remotest**) **1** far away in space or time. **2** situated far from the main cities or towns. **3** distantly related. **4** having very little connection: *the theory seems rather remote from everyday experience.* **5** (of a chance or possibility) unlikely to occur. **6** aloof and unfriendly. **7** (of an electronic device) operating or operated by means of radio or infrared signals. **8** Computing (of a device) that can only be accessed by means of a network. ▶ n. a remote control device. ■ **re·mote·ly** adv. **re·mote·ness** n.

re·mote con·trol ▶ n. **1** control of a device from a distance by means of signals transmitted from a radio or electronic device. **2** a device that controls another device in this way. ■ **re·mote-con·trolled** adj.

re·mou·lade /,rämə'läd, -mōō-/ ▶ n. a salad or seafood dressing made with hard-boiled egg yolks, oil, vinegar, and seasoning.

re·mount ▶ v. /rē'mount, 'rē-/ **1** get on a horse or vehicle again. **2** attach something to a new frame or setting. **3** organize or begin a course of action again. ▶ n. /'rē,mount/ a fresh horse for a rider.

re·move /ri'mōōv/ ▶ v. **1** take something off or away from the position occupied. **2** abolish or get rid of something. **3** dismiss someone from a job. **4** (**be removed from**) be very different from. **5** (as adj. **removed**) separated by a particular number of steps of descent: *his second cousin once removed.* ▶ n. the extent to which people or things are separated or remote from each other: *he kept himself at a certain remove from the confrontations.* ■ **re·mov·a·ble** adj. **re·mov·al** n. **re·mov·er** n.

re·mu·ner·ate /ri'myōōnə,rāt/ ▶ v. pay someone for services rendered or work done. ■ **re·mu·ner·a·tive** /-rətiv, -,rātiv/ adj.

re·mu·ner·a·tion /ri,myōōnə'rāsнən/ ▶ n. money paid for work or a service.

Ren·ais·sance /'renə,säns, -,zäns/ ▶ n. **1** the revival of European art and literature under the influence of classical styles in the 14th–16th centuries. **2** (**renaissance**) a revival of or renewed interest in something.

Ren·ais·sance man ▶ n. a person with a wide range of talents or interests.

re·nal /'rēnl/ ▶ adj. relating to the kidneys.

re·name /rē'nām, 'rē-/ ▶ v. give a new name to someone or something.

re·nas·cent /ri'nasənt, -'nāsənt/ ▶ adj. becoming active again. ■ **re·nas·cence** n.

rend /rend/ ▶ v. (past and past part. **rent**) literary **1** tear something to pieces. **2** cause great distress to someone.

rend·er /'rendər/ ▶ v. **1** provide a service, help, etc. **2** present something for inspection, consideration, or payment. **3** cause to be or become: *I was rendered speechless.* **4** perform or represent musically or artistically: *the children in the painting are very sensitively rendered.* **5** translate something into another language. **6** literary hand something over. **7** melt down fat so as to separate out its impurities. **8** cover stone or brick with a coat of plaster. ■ **ren·der·er** n.

rend·er·ing /'rendəriNG/ ▶n. **1** a performance of a piece of music or a role in a play. **2** a translation. **3** a first coat of plaster.

ren·dez·vous /'rändi,vōō, -dä-/ ▶n. (pl. same /-vōō/ or /-vōōz/) **1** a meeting at an agreed time and place. **2** a meeting place. ▶v. (**rendezvouses** /-,vōōz/, **rendezvousing** /-,vōōiNG/, **rendezvoused** /-,vōōd/) meet at an agreed time and place.

ren·di·tion /ren'dishən/ ▶n. **1** a way that something is rendered, performed, or represented, especially a performance of a dramatic role or a musical work: *a quick rendition of 'Happy Birthday.'* **2** a translation. **3** (also **extraordinary rendition**) the sending of a foreign criminal or terrorist suspect to be interrogated in a country with less rigorous controls on the treatment of prisoners.

ren·e·gade /'reni,gād/ ▶n. a person who deserts and betrays an organization, country, or set of principles. ▶adj. having treacherously changed allegiance.

re·nege /ri'neg, -'nig/ ▶v. go back on a promise or contract.

re·ne·go·ti·ate /,rēnə'gōshē,āt/ ▶v. negotiate something again in order to change the original agreed terms. ■ **re·ne·go·ti·a·ble** /-'gōsh(ē)əbəl/ adj. **re·ne·go·ti·a·tion** /-,gōshē'āshən, -,gōsē-/ n.

re·new /ri'n(y)ōō/ ▶v. **1** begin something again after an interruption. **2** (usu. as adj. **renewed**) give fresh life or intensity to: *a renewed interest in exercise.* **3** extend the period for which a license, subscription, or contract is valid. **4** replace something broken or worn out. ■ **re·new·al** n. **re·new·er** n.

re·new·a·ble /ri'n(y)ōōəbəl/ ▶adj. **1** capable of being renewed. **2** (of energy or its source) not exhausted when used. ■ **re·new·a·bil·i·ty** /ri,n(y)ōōə'bilətē/ n.

ren·min·bi /'ren'min'bē/ ▶n. (pl. same) **1** the system of currency of China. **2** a yuan.

ren·net /'renit/ ▶n. a substance made from curdled milk from the stomach of a calf, used in curdling milk for cheese.

re·nounce /ri'nouns/ ▶v. **1** formally state that one has given up a claim, right, or possession. **2** state publicly that one no longer has a particular belief or supports a particular cause. **3** abandon a bad habit or way of life. ■ **re·nounce·a·ble** adj. **re·nounce·ment** n. **re·nounc·er** n.

ren·o·vate /'renə,vāt/ ▶v. restore something old to a good state of repair. ■ **ren·o·va·tion** /,renə'vāshən/ n. **ren·o·va·tor** n.

re·nown /ri'noun/ ▶n. the state of being famous and respected. ■ **re·nowned** adj.

rent¹ /rent/ ▶n. **1** a tenant's regular payment to a landlord for the use of property or land. **2** a payment for the rental of equipment. ▶v. **1** pay someone for the use of something. **2** let someone use something in return for payment. ■ **rent·a·ble** adj. **rent·er** n.

rent² ▶n. a large tear in a piece of fabric.

rent³ ▶ past and past participle of REND.

ren·tal /'rentl/ ▶n. **1** the action of renting something. **2** a rented house or car. **3** an amount paid or received as rent. ▶adj. relating to or available for rent.

re·num·ber /rē'nəmbər/ ▶v. change the number or numbers given to something.

re·nun·ci·a·tion /ri,nənsē'āshən/ ▶n. the formal giving up of a claim, belief, or course of action.

re·oc·cu·py /rē'äkyə,pī/ ▶v. (**reoccupies, reoccupying, reoccupied**) occupy a place or position again. ■ **re·oc·cu·pa·tion** /,rē,äkyə'pāshən/ n.

re·oc·cur /,rēə'kər/ ▶v. (**reoccurs, reoccurring, reoccurred**) occur again or repeatedly. ■ **re·oc·cur·rence** /rēə'kərəns/ n.

re·of·fend /,rēə'fend/ ▶v. commit a further offense. ■ **re·of·fend·er** n.

re·o·pen /rē'ōpən/ ▶v. open again: *the house was reopened to the public.*

re·or·der /rē'ōrdər/ ▶v. **1** order goods again. **2** arrange something again or differently. ▶n. a repeated order for goods.

re·or·gan·ize /rē'ōrgə,nīz/ ▶v. change the way in which something is organized. ■ **re·or·gan·i·za·tion** /,rē,ōrgənə'zāshən/ n. **re·or·gan·iz·er** n.

re·or·i·ent /rē'ōrē,ent/ ▶v. **1** change the focus or direction of something. **2** (**reorient oneself**) find one's position again in relation to one's surroundings. ■ **re·o·ri·en·tate** /-ēən,tāt/ v. **re·o·ri·en·ta·tion** /,rē,ōrēən'tāshən/ n.

rep¹ /rep/ informal ▶n. a representative.

rep² ▶n. informal **1** repertory. **2** a repertory theater or company.

rep³ (also **repp**) ▶n. a fabric with a ribbed surface, used in curtains and upholstery.

rep⁴ ▶n. (in weight training) a repetition of a set of exercises.

rep⁵ ▶n. informal short for REPUTATION.

Rep. ▶abbr. **1** (in the federal or a state legislature) Representative. **2** Republic. **3** a Republican.

re·pack·age /rē'pakij/ ▶v. package or present something again or differently.

re·paid /rē'pād/ ▶ past and past participle of REPAY.

re·paint /rē'pānt/ ▶v. cover something with a new coat of paint.

re·pair¹ /ri'pe(ə)r/ ▶v. **1** restore something damaged, worn, or faulty to a good condition. **2** set right a breakdown in relations. ▶n. **1** the action of repairing something. **2** a part that has been repaired. **3** the relative condition of something: *the cottages were in good repair.* ■ **re·pair·a·ble** adj. **re·pair·er** n.

re·pair² ▶v. (**repair to**) formal or humorous go to a place.

re·pair·man /ri'pe(ə)r,man, -mən/ ▶n. (pl. **repairmen**) a person who repairs vehicles, machinery, or appliances.

rep·a·ra·ble /'rep(ə)rəbəl/ ▶adj. able to be repaired or rectified.

rep·a·ra·tion /,repə'rāshən/ ▶n. **1** the making of amends for a wrong: *sinners who make reparation for their sins.* **2** (**reparations**) compensation for war damage paid by a defeated country or faction. ■ **re·par·a·tive** /ri'parətiv/ adj.

rep·ar·tee /ˌrepərˈtē, ˌrepˌärˈtē, -ˈtā/ ▸ n. conversation characterized by quick, witty comments or replies.

re·past /riˈpast, ˈrēˌpast/ ▸ n. formal a meal.

re·pa·tri·ate /rēˈpātrēˌāt, rēˈpa-/ ▸ v. send someone back to their own country. ■ **re·pa·tri·a·tion** /ˌrēˌpātrēˈāsHən, ˌrēˌpa-/ n.

re·pay /rēˈpā/ ▸ v. (past and past part. **repaid**) **1** pay back a loan that is owed to someone. **2** do or give something as reward for a favor or kindness received. ■ **re·pay·a·ble** adj. **re·pay·ment** n.

re·peal /riˈpēl/ ▸ v. officially cancel a law or congressional act. ▸ n. the action of repealing a law or congressional act.

re·peat /riˈpēt/ ▸ v. **1** say something again. **2** do something again or more than once. **3** (**repeat itself**) occur again in the same way: *I don't intend to let history repeat itself.* **4** (of food) be tasted again after being swallowed, as a result of indigestion. ▸ n. **1** something that occurs or is done again. **2** a repeated broadcast of a television or radio program. **3** a musical passage that is to be repeated. ▸ adj. happening, done, or used more than once: *a repeat performance.* ■ **re·peat·a·ble** adj. **re·peat·ed·ly** adv. **re·peat·er** n.

re·peat·ing dec·i·mal ▸ n. a decimal fraction in which a figure or group of figures is repeated indefinitely, as in *0.333 ....*

re·pel /riˈpel/ ▸ v. (**repels, repelling, repelled**) **1** drive or force an attack or attacker back or away. **2** make someone feel disgust or horror. **3** (of a substance) be able to keep something out or be unable to mix with something: *boots with leather uppers to repel moisture.* **4** (of a magnetic pole or electric field) force away something similarly magnetized or charged. ■ **re·pel·ler** n.

re·pel·lent /riˈpelənt/ (also **repellant**) ▸ adj. **1** able to repel a particular thing: *water-repellent nylon.* **2** disgusting or distasteful. ▸ n. **1** a substance that deters insects or other pests. **2** a substance used to treat something to make it repel water. ■ **re·pel·lence** n. **re·pel·len·cy** n. **re·pel·lent·ly** adv.

re·pent /riˈpent/ ▸ v. feel or express sincere regret or remorse about something bad or wrong that one has done. ■ **re·pent·ance** n. **re·pent·ant** adj. **re·pent·er** n.

re·per·cus·sions /ˌrēpərˈkəsHənz, ˌrep-/ ▸ pl.n. the consequences of an event or action.

rep·er·toire /ˈrepə(r)ˌtwär/ ▸ n. the plays, operas, or other items known or regularly performed by a performer or company.

rep·er·to·ry /ˈrepə(r)ˌtôrē/ ▸ n. (pl. **repertories**) **1** the performance by a company of the plays, operas, or ballets in its repertoire at regular short intervals. **2** another term for REPERTOIRE.

rep·er·to·ry the·a·ter ▸ n. a theatrical company that performs plays from its repertoire for regular, short periods of time, moving on from one play to another.

rep·e·ti·tion /ˌrepəˈtisHən/ ▸ n. **1** the action of repeating something. **2** a thing that has been said or done before.

rep·e·ti·tious /ˌrepəˈtisHəs/ ▸ adj. having too much repetition; repetitive. ■ **rep·e·ti·tious·ly** adv. **rep·e·ti·tious·ness** n.

re·pet·i·tive /riˈpetətiv/ ▸ adj. repeated many times or too much. ■ **re·pet·i·tive·ly** adv. **re·pet·i·tive·ness** n.

re·pet·i·tive strain in·ju·ry ▸ n. a condition in which prolonged repetitive action causes pain or weakening in the tendons and muscles involved.

re·phrase /rēˈfrāz/ ▸ v. express something in an alternative way.

re·pine /riˈpīn/ ▸ v. literary be discontented; fret.

re·place /riˈplās/ ▸ v. **1** take the place of someone or something. **2** provide a substitute for something that is faulty, old, or damaged. **3** remove from a role and substitute with someone or something different: *he was replaced by a lightweight who knew nothing about the case.* **4** put something back in the place it occupied before. ■ **re·place·a·ble** adj. **re·plac·er** n.

re·place·ment /riˈplāsmənt/ ▸ n. **1** the action of replacing someone or something. **2** a person or thing that takes the place of another.

re·plant /rēˈplant, ˈrē-/ ▸ v. **1** plant a tree or other plant in a new pot or site. **2** provide an area with new plants.

re·play /rēˈplā, ˈrē-/ ▸ n. **1** an instance of playing a recording again. **2** a match or contest that is played again because the previous game was a draw. **3** an event that closely follows the pattern of a previous event. ▸ v. **1** play back a recording. **2** play a match or contest again.

re·plen·ish /riˈplenisH/ ▸ v. **1** fill something up again. **2** restore a stock or supply to a former level. ■ **re·plen·ish·er** n. **re·plen·ish·ment** n.

re·plete /riˈplēt/ ▸ adj. **1** (**replete with**) filled or well supplied with: *a courtyard replete with cacti.* **2** very full with food. ■ **re·ple·tion** /riˈplēsHən/ n.

rep·li·ca /ˈreplikə/ ▸ n. an exact copy or model of something, especially one on a smaller scale.

rep·li·cate ▸ v. /ˈrepliˌkāt/ **1** make an exact copy of something. **2** (**replicate itself**) (of genetic material or a living organism) reproduce or give rise to a copy of itself. **3** repeat an experiment to obtain a consistent result. ▸ n. /-kit/ a close or exact copy; a replica. ■ **rep·li·ca·ble** /ˈreplikəbəl/ adj. **rep·li·ca·tion** /ˌrepliˈkāsHən/ n. **rep·li·ca·tor** /ˈrepliˌkātər/ n.

re·ply /riˈplī/ ▸ v. (**replies, replying, replied**) **1** say or write something as an answer to something. **2** respond with a similar action: *they replied to the shelling with a mortar attack.* ▸ n. (pl. **replies**) **1** a spoken or written answer. **2** the action of answering or responding to someone or something. ■ **re·pli·er** n.

re·po /ˈrēˌpō/ informal ▸ n. (pl. **repos**) **1** another term for REPURCHASE AGREEMENT. **2** a car or other item that has been repossessed. ▸ v. (**repo's, repo'd, repoing**) repossess (a car or other item) when a buyer defaults on payments.

re·pop·u·late /rēˈpäpyəˌlāt/ ▸ v. **1** introduce a population into an area previously deserted. **2** populate or fill again: *probiotics repopulate your gut with healthy bacteria.* ■ **re·pop·u·la·tion** /ˌrēˌpäpyəˈlāsHən/ n.

re·port /riˈpôrt/ ▸ v. **1** give a spoken or written account of something. **2** cover an event or situation as a journalist. **3** (**be reported**) be said or rumored. **4** make a formal complaint about someone or something. **5** present oneself as having arrived somewhere or as ready to do something: *he had to report to the boss at 9 a.m.* **6** (**report to**) be responsible to a supervisor or manager. ▸ n. **1** an account given of a matter after investigation or consideration. **2** a description of an event or situation. **3** a teacher's written assessment of a student's work and progress. **4** a sudden loud noise, especially of gunfire. ■ **re·port·a·ble** adj.

re·port·age /rə'pôrtij, ,repôr'täzн/ ▶ n. **1** the reporting of news by the media. **2** factual, journalistic writing in a book.

re·port card ▶ n. **1** a teacher's written assessment of a student's work and progress. **2** an evaluation of performance: *legislators fared poorly in a recent report card.*

re·port·ed speech ▶ n. a speaker's words reported with the required changes of person and tense (e.g., *he said that he would go,* based on *I will go*). Contrasted with DIRECT SPEECH.

re·port·er /ri'pôrtər/ ▶ n. a person who reports news for a newspaper or broadcasting company.

rep·or·to·ri·al /,repə(r)'tôrēəl, ,rē-/ ▶ adj. of or characteristic of newspaper reporters: *reportorial ambition and curiosity.*

re·pose¹ /ri'pōz/ ▶ n. **1** a state of rest or tranquillity. **2** the state of being calm and composed. ▶ v. formal **1** lie down and rest. **2** be situated or kept in a particular place.

re·pose² ▶ v. (**repose something in**) place one's confidence or trust in.

re·po·si·tion /,rēpə'zisнən/ ▶ v. **1** alter the position of someone or something. **2** change the image of a company, product, etc., to target a different market.

re·pos·i·to·ry /ri'päzə,tôrē/ ▶ n. (pl. **repositories**) **1** a place or container for storage. **2** a person or thing that is full of information or a particular quality: *the lighthouse keeper is a repository of local history.*

re·pos·sess /,rēpə'zes/ ▶ v. retake possession of something when a buyer fails to make the required payments. ■ **re·pos·ses·sion** /-'zesнən/ n. **re·pos·ses·sor** n.

re·pot /rē'pät, 'rē-/ ▶ v. (**repots, repotting, repotted**) put a plant in another pot.

re·pous·sé /rə,pōō'sā/ ▶ adj. (of metalwork) hammered into relief from the reverse side.

repp /rep/ ▶ n. variant spelling of REP³.

rep·re·hend /,repri'hend/ ▶ v. reprimand someone. ■ **rep·re·hen·sion** /-'hencнən/ n.

rep·re·hen·si·ble /,repri'hensəbəl/ ▶ adj. wrong or bad and deserving condemnation. ■ **rep·re·hen·si·bil·i·ty** /-,hensə'bilətē/ n. **rep·re·hen·si·bly** /-blē/ adv.

rep·re·sent /,repri'zent/ ▶ v. **1** be entitled or appointed to act and speak on behalf of someone. **2** be an elected member of a lawmaking body for a constituency or party. **3** constitute; amount to: *this figure represents eleven percent of total sales.* **4** be a specimen or typical example of something. **5** (**be represented**) be present to a particular degree: *abstract art is well represented in this exhibition.* **6** portray in a particular way: *they were represented as being in need of protection.* **7** depict a subject in a work of art. **8** be a symbol of something.

rep·re·sen·ta·tion /,repri,zen'täsнən, -zən-/ ▶ n. **1** the action or an instance of representing someone or something. **2** an image, model, or other depiction of something. **3** (**representations**) statements made to an authority to express an opinion or register a protest.

rep·re·sen·ta·tion·al /,repri,zen'täsнənl/ ▶ adj. **1** relating to representation. **2** relating to art that shows the physical appearance of things.

■ **rep·re·sen·ta·tion·al·ly** /,repri,zen'täsнənl-ē/ adv.

rep·re·sen·ta·tive /,repri'zentətiv/ ▶ adj. **1** typical of a class or group. **2** containing typical examples of many or all types: *a representative sample.* **3** (of a lawmaking body) consisting of people chosen to act and speak on behalf of a wider group. **4** serving as a portrayal or symbol of something. ▶ n. **1** a person chosen to act and speak on behalf of another or others. **2** an agent of a firm who visits potential clients to sell its products. **3** an example of a class or group. ■ **rep·re·sent·a·tive·ly** adv. **rep·re·sent·a·tive·ness** n.

re·press /ri'pres/ ▶ v. **1** use force to control or stop: *the regime continues to repress political parties.* **2** prevent or restrict the expression or development of something. **3** try not to allow a thought or feeling to enter one's conscious mind. ■ **re·press·er** n. **re·press·i·ble** /-əbəl/ adj. **re·pres·sion** /ri'presнən/ n.

re·pressed /ri'prest/ ▶ adj. **1** (of a thought or feeling) not acknowledged; kept unconscious in one's mind. **2** tending to suppress one's feelings and desires.

re·pres·sive /ri'presiv/ ▶ adj. severely restricting personal freedom; oppressive. ■ **re·pres·sive·ly** adv. **re·pres·sive·ness** n.

re·prieve /ri'prēv/ ▶ v. **1** cancel the punishment of someone. **2** chiefly Brit. abandon or postpone plans to close something: *the threatened mines could be reprieved.* ▶ n. **1** the cancellation of a punishment. **2** a brief delay before something undesirable happens.

rep·ri·mand /'reprə,mand/ ▶ n. a formal expression of disapproval; a rebuke. ▶ v. formally tell someone that they have done something wrong.

re·print ▶ v. /rē'print, 'rē-/ print something again or in a revised form. ▶ n. /'rē,print/ **1** an act of reprinting. **2** a copy of a book or other material that has been reprinted.

re·pris·al /ri'prīzəl/ ▶ n. a violent or aggressive act done in return for a similar act.

re·prise /ri'prēz, -'prīz/ ▶ n. **1** a repeated passage in music. **2** a repeat of something: *Mets fans had hoped for a reprise of the last Series.* ▶ v. repeat a piece of music or a performance.

re·proach /ri'prōcн/ ▶ v. **1** express one's disapproval of or disappointment with someone. **2** (**reproach someone with**) accuse someone of. ▶ n. an expression of disapproval or disappointment. ■ **re·proach·a·ble** adj. – PHRASES **above** (or **beyond**) **reproach** so perfect as to be beyond criticism.

re·proach·ful /ri'prōcнfəl/ ▶ adj. expressing disapproval or disappointment. ■ **re·proach·ful·ly** adv.

rep·ro·bate /'reprə,bāt/ ▶ n. a person who behaves in an immoral way. ■ **rep·ro·ba·tion** /,reprə'bāsнən/ n.

re·proc·ess /rē'präs,es, -'präsəs, -'prō-/ ▶ v. process something again or differently in order to reuse it.

re·pro·duce /,rēprə'd(y)ōōs/ ▶ v. **1** produce a copy of something. **2** produce something similar to something else in a different situation. **3** (of an organism) produce offspring. ■ **re·pro·duc·er** n. **re·pro·duc·i·ble** adj.

re·pro·duc·tion /,rēprə'dəksнən/ ▶ n. **1** the action of reproducing. **2** a copy of a work of art, especially a print made of a painting. ▶ adj. made to imitate the style of an earlier period or particular craftsman: *reproduction furniture.* ■ **re·pro·duc·tive** /-'dəktiv/ adj.

re·proof /ri'pro͞of/ ▶ n. a criticism or rebuke.

re·prove /ri'pro͞ov/ ▶ v. rebuke or reprimand someone.

rep·tile /'reptəl, 'rep,tīl/ ▶ n. a cold-blooded vertebrate animal of a class that includes snakes, lizards, crocodiles, turtles, and tortoises, typically having a dry scaly skin and laying soft-shelled eggs. ■ **rep·til·i·an** /rep'tilēən, -'tilyən/ adj. & n.

re·pub·lic /ri'pəblik/ ▶ n. a state in which power is held by the people and their elected representatives, and that has a president rather than a monarch.

re·pub·li·can /ri'pəblikən/ ▶ adj. 1 belonging to or typical of a republic. 2 supporting the principles of a republic. 3 (**Republican**) supporting the Republican Party. ▶ n. 1 a person in favor of republican government. 2 (**Republican**) a member or supporter of the Republican Party. ■ **re·pub·li·can·ism** /-,nizəm/ n.

Re·pub·li·can Par·ty ▶ n. one of the two main US political parties (the other being the Democratic Party), favoring a conservative stance, limited central government, and a strong national defense.

re·pu·di·ate /ri'pyo͞odē,āt/ ▶ v. 1 refuse to accept something. 2 deny the truth or validity of: *he repudiated allegations that he was a shirker.* 3 chiefly Law refuse to fulfill an agreement, obligation, or debt. 4 old use disown or divorce one's wife. ■ **re·pu·di·a·tion** /ri,pyo͞odē'āsHən/ n. **re·pu·di·a·tor** n.

re·pug·nance /ri'pəgnəns/ ▶ n. intense disgust. ■ **re·pug·nan·cy** n.

re·pug·nant /ri'pəgnənt/ ▶ adj. unpleasant and completely unacceptable.

re·pulse /ri'pəls/ ▶ v. 1 drive back an attacking enemy by force. 2 reject or refuse to accept an offer or the person making it. 3 cause someone to feel intense distaste or disgust. ▶ n. 1 the action of driving back an attack. 2 a rejection or refusal of an offer or approach.

re·pul·sion /ri'pəlsHən/ ▶ n. 1 a feeling of intense distaste or disgust. 2 Physics a force under the influence of which objects tend to move away from each other, e.g., through having the same magnetic polarity.

re·pul·sive /ri'pəlsiv/ ▶ adj. 1 arousing intense distaste or disgust. 2 Physics relating to repulsion between objects. ■ **re·pul·sive·ly** adv. **re·pul·sive·ness** n.

re·pur·chase a·gree·ment ▶ n. Finance a contract in which the vendor of a security agrees to repurchase it from the buyer at an agreed price.

re·pur·pose /rē'pərpəs/ ▶ v. adapt something for use in a different purpose.

rep·u·ta·ble /'repyətəbəl/ ▶ adj. having a good reputation. ■ **rep·u·ta·bly** /-blē/ adv.

rep·u·ta·tion /,repyə'tāsHən/ ▶ n. 1 the beliefs or opinions that are generally held about someone or something. 2 a high public opinion of someone or something: *they have damaged the reputation of public service broadcasting.*

re·pute /ri'pyo͞ot/ ▶ n. 1 the opinion generally held of someone or something. 2 the state of being highly regarded. ▶ v. 1 (**be reputed**) be generally regarded as having done something

or as having particular characteristics. 2 (as adj. **reputed**) generally believed to exist: *the reputed flatness of the country.* ■ **re·put·ed·ly** adv.

re·quest /ri'kwest/ ▶ n. 1 an act of asking politely or formally for something. 2 a thing that is asked for politely or formally. ▶ v. politely or formally ask for something or ask someone to do something. ■ **re·quest·er** n.

req·ui·em /'rekwēəm, 'rā-/ ▶ n. 1 (especially in the Roman Catholic Church) a Mass for the souls of the dead. 2 a musical composition setting parts of such a Mass.

re·quire /ri'kwīr/ ▶ v. 1 need something for a purpose. 2 instruct or expect someone to do something. 3 specify as compulsory: *the minimum car insurance required by law.* 4 (**require something of**) regard an action or quality as due from someone because of the position they hold.

re·quire·ment /ri'kwīrmənt/ ▶ n. 1 something required; a need. 2 something that is compulsory.

req·ui·site /'rekwəzət/ ▶ adj. made necessary by particular circumstances or regulations: *some lack the requisite skills to succeed.* ▶ n. a thing that is necessary for a purpose.

req·ui·si·tion /,rekwə'zisHən/ ▶ n. 1 an official order enabling property or materials to be taken and used. 2 the taking of goods for military or public use. 3 a formal written demand that something should be done or put into operation. ▶ v. demand the use or supply of something by an official order.

re·quite /ri'kwīt/ ▶ v. formal give or do something suitable in return for a favor, love, kindness, etc. ■ **re·quit·al** n.

re·ran /rē'ran/ ▶ past of RERUN.

re·read /rē'rēd/ ▶ v. (past and past part. **reread** /rē'red/) read a written work or passage again.

rere·dos /'rerə,däs, 'ri(ə)rə-/ ▶ n. (pl. same) an ornamental screen at the back of an altar in a church.

re·re·lease /,rē-ri'lēs/ ▶ v. release a recording or movie again. ▶ n. a re-released recording or movie.

re·route /rē'ro͞ot, rē'rout/ ▶ v. send someone or something by or along a different route.

re·run /rē'rən/ ▶ v. (**reruns, rerunning, reran** /rē'ran/; past part. **rerun**) show, stage, or perform something again. ▶ n. an event or program that is run again.

re·sale /'rē,sāl/ ▶ n. the sale of a thing previously bought. ■ **re·sale·a·ble** (also **resalable**) adj.

re·sat /rē'sat/ ▶ past and past participle of RESIT.

re·sched·ule /rē'skejo͞o(ə)l/ ▶ v. 1 change the time of a planned event. 2 arrange a new scheme of repayments of a debt.

re·scind /ri'sind/ ▶ v. formally cancel a law, order, or agreement. ■ **re·scind·a·ble** adj.

re·scis·sion /ri'sizHən/ ▶ n. formal the official canceling of a law, order, or agreement.

res·cue /'reskyo͞o/ ▶ v. (**rescues, rescuing, rescued**) save someone or something from a dangerous or difficult situation. ▶ n. an act of rescuing someone or something. ■ **res·cu·a·ble** adj. **res·cu·er** n.

re·seal /rē'sēl/ ▶ v. seal something again. ■ **re·seal·a·ble** adj.

re·search ▶ n. /'rē,sərcH, ri'sərcH/ the systematic study of materials and sources in order to

establish facts and reach new conclusions.
▶v. **1** carry out research into a subject.
2 discover or check information for a book, program, etc. ■ **re·search·er** n.

re·search and de·vel·op·ment ▶n. (in industry) work directed toward new ideas and improvement of products and processes.

re·se·lect /ˌrēsəˈlekt/ ▶v. select someone or something again or differently. ■ **re·se·lec·tion** /ˌrēsəlˈeksʜən/ n.

re·sell /rēˈsel/ ▶v. (past and past part. **resold**) sell something one has bought to someone else. ■ **re·sell·er** n.

re·sem·blance /riˈzembləns/ ▶n. **1** the fact of looking like or being similar to someone or something: *he bears a strong resemblance to his mother*. **2** a way in which things are alike.

re·sem·ble /riˈzembəl/ ▶v. be similar to someone or something in appearance or qualities.

re·sent /riˈzent/ ▶v. feel bitter or angry toward someone or something.

re·sent·ful /riˈzentfəl/ ▶adj. feeling bitter or angry about something, especially unfair treatment. ■ **re·sent·ful·ly** adv. **re·sent·ful·ness** n.

re·sent·ment /riˈzentmənt/ ▶n. bitterness or anger at unfair treatment.

res·er·va·tion /ˌrezərˈvāsʜən/ ▶n. **1** the action of reserving something. **2** an arrangement in which something is reserved. **3** an area of land set aside for occupation by North American Indians or Australian Aboriginals. **4** an expression of doubt qualifying overall approval of a plan or statement: *some generals voiced reservations about making air strikes*.

re·serve /riˈzərv/ ▶v. **1** keep something for future use. **2** arrange for a seat, ticket, etc., to be kept for a particular person. **3** retain or hold a right or entitlement. **4** hold back from delivering a decision without proper consideration or evidence: *I'll reserve my views on his ability until he's played again.* ▶n. **1** a supply of something available for use if required. **2** funds kept available by a bank, company, or government. **3** a military force withheld from action to protect others, or additional to the regular forces and available in an emergency. **4** an extra player on a team, serving as a possible substitute. **5** (**the reserves**) the second-choice team. **6** an area of land set aside for occupation by a native people. **7** a protected area for wildlife. **8** a lack of warmth or openness: *he smiled and some of her natural reserve melted.* ■ **re·serv·a·ble** adj.

re·serve bank ▶n. a regional bank operating under and implementing the policies of the Federal Reserve.

re·serve cur·ren·cy ▶n. a strong currency widely used in international trade that a central bank is prepared to hold as part of its foreign exchange reserves.

re·served /riˈzərvd/ ▶adj. slow to reveal emotion or opinions. ■ **re·serv·ed·ly** adv. **re·serv·ed·ness** n.

re·serve price ▶n. the price set as the lowest acceptable by the seller for an item sold at auction.

re·serv·ist /riˈzərvist/ ▶n. a member of a military reserve force.

res·er·voir /ˈrezə(r),vwär, -,v(w)ôr/ ▶n. **1** a large lake used as a source of water supply. **2** a place where fluid collects, especially in rock strata or in the body. **3** a container or part of a machine designed to hold fluid. **4** a supply or source

of something: *the country's vast reservoir of computer scientists.*

re·set /rēˈset/ ▶v. (**resets, resetting, reset**) **1** set something again or differently. **2** set a counter, timer, etc., to zero. ■ **re·set·ta·ble** adj.

re·set·tle /rēˈsetl/ ▶v. settle or cause to settle in a different place. ■ **re·set·tle·ment** n.

re·shape /rēˈsʜāp/ ▶v. shape or form something differently or again.

re·shuf·fle /rēˈsʜəfəl/ ▶v. **1** change around the positions of members of a team, especially government officials. **2** rearrange something. ▶n. an act of reshuffling.

re·side /riˈzīd/ ▶v. **1** live in a particular place. **2** (of a right or legal power) belong to a person or body. **3** (**reside in**) (of a quality) be present in: *intelligence and judgment reside in old men.*

res·i·dence /ˈrez(ə)dəns, ˈrezə,dens/ ▶n. **1** the fact of living somewhere. **2** a person's home. **3** the official house of a government official.
– PHRASES **artist** (or **writer**) **in residence** an artist or writer who is based for a set period within a college or other institution and is available for teaching purposes.

res·i·den·cy /ˈrez(ə)dənsē, ˈrezə,densē/ ▶n. (pl. **residencies**) **1** the fact of living in a place. **2** a residential post held by an artist or writer. **3** a period of specialized medical training in a hospital.

res·i·dent /ˈrez(ə)dənt, ˈrezə,dent/ ▶n. **1** a person who lives somewhere on a long-term basis. **2** a medical graduate engaged in specialized practice under supervision in a hospital. **3** a bird, butterfly, or other animal of a species that does not migrate. ▶adj. **1** living somewhere on a long-term basis. **2** having living quarters at one's place of work. **3** attached to and working regularly for a particular institution.

res·i·den·tial /ˌrezəˈdenchəl/ ▶adj. **1** designed for people to live in. **2** (of a job, course, etc.) requiring someone to live in a particular place. **3** (of an area) occupied by private houses. ■ **res·i·den·tial·ly** adv.

re·sid·u·a /riˈzijōōə/ ▶ plural of RESIDUUM.

re·sid·u·al /riˈzijōōəl/ ▶adj. remaining after the greater part or quantity has gone or been removed. ▶n. a quantity remaining after the greater part has gone or been removed. ■ **re·sid·u·al·ly** adv.

res·i·due /ˈrezə,d(y)ōō/ ▶n. **1** a small amount of something that remains after the main part has gone or been taken or used. **2** Law the part of an estate that is left after the payment of charges, debts, and bequests. **3** a substance that remains after a process such as combustion or evaporation.

re·sid·u·um /riˈzijōōəm/ ▶n. (pl. **residua** /-ˈzijōōə/) technical a chemical residue.

re·sign /riˈzīn/ ▶v. **1** voluntarily leave a job or position of office. **2** (**be resigned**) accept that something undesirable cannot be avoided.

res·ig·na·tion /ˌrezigˈnāsʜən/ ▶n. **1** an act of resigning from a job. **2** a letter stating one's intention to resign. **3** acceptance of something undesirable that cannot be avoided: *he confronted old age with his usual resignation.*

re·sil·ient /riˈzilyənt/ ▶adj. **1** able to recoil or spring back into shape after bending, stretching, or being compressed. **2** (of a person) able to recover quickly from difficult conditions. ■ **re·sil·ience** n. **re·sil·ient·ly** adv.

res·in /ˈrezən/ ▸ n. **1** a sticky substance produced by some trees. **2** a synthetic polymer used as the basis of plastics, adhesives, varnishes, etc. ■ **res·in·ous** adj.

re·sist /riˈzist/ ▸ v. **1** withstand the action or effect of something. **2** try to prevent something by action or argument. **3** stop oneself from having or doing something tempting: *I couldn't resist taking a peek.* **4** struggle or fight back when attacked. ■ **re·sist·er** n. **re·sist·i·ble** adj.

re·sist·ance /riˈzistəns/ ▸ n. **1** the action of resisting. **2** the ability not to be affected by something undesirable. **3** the impeding or stopping effect that one material thing has on another: *air resistance was reduced by streamlining.* **4** the degree to which a material or device opposes the passage of an electric current. **5** (also **resistance movement**) a secret organization that fights against authority in an occupied country. ■ **re·sist·ant** adj.
– PHRASES **the path of least resistance** the easiest course of action.

re·sis·tive /riˈzistiv/ ▸ adj. **1** technical able to resist something. **2** relating to electrical resistance. ■ **re·sis·tiv·i·ty** /ˌriˌzisˈtivətē/ n.

re·sis·tor /riˈzistər/ ▸ n. a device that resists the passage of an electric current.

re·sit /rēˈsit/ Brit. ▸ v. (**resits, resitting, resat**) take an exam again after failing. ▸ n. an exam that is taken again for this reason.

re·size /rēˈsīz/ ▸ v. alter the size of something, especially a computer window or image.

re·skill /rēˈskil/ ▸ v. teach someone new skills.

re·sold /rēˈsōld/ ▸ past and past participle of RESELL.

res·o·lute /ˈrezəˌlo͞ot, -lət/ ▸ adj. admirably purposeful and determined. ■ **res·o·lute·ly** adv. **res·o·lute·ness** n.

res·o·lu·tion /ˌrezəˈlo͞oSHən/ ▸ n. **1** a firm decision. **2** a formal expression of opinion or intention agreed on by a lawmaking body. **3** the quality of being resolute or determined. **4** the resolving of a problem or dispute. **5** the process of separating something into its component parts. **6** the degree of detail visible in a photographic or television image. **7** the smallest interval between adjacent objects that is measurable by a telescope or other scientific instrument.

re·solve /riˈzälv, -ˈzólv/ ▸ v. **1** settle or find a solution to a problem. **2** decide firmly on a course of action. **3** (of a lawmaking body) take a decision by a formal vote. **4** (**resolve something into**) separate something into its component parts. **5** (of something seen at a distance) turn into a different form when seen more clearly. **6** (of optical or photographic equipment) separate or distinguish between objects that are close together. ▸ n. firm determination to do something. ■ **re·solv·a·ble** adj. **re·solv·er** n.

re·solv·ing pow·er ▸ n. the ability of an optical instrument or type of film to distinguish small or closely adjacent images.

res·o·nance /ˈrezənəns/ ▸ n. **1** the quality in a sound of being deep, clear, and reverberating. **2** the power to suggest images, emotions, or a quality. **3** Physics the reinforcement or prolongation of sound by reflection from a surface or by the vibration of an adjacent object at the same time.

res·o·nant /ˈrezənənt/ ▸ adj. **1** (of sound) deep, clear, and continuing to reverberate.

2 (of a room, musical instrument, or hollow body) tending to reinforce or prolong sounds. **3** (**resonant with**) filled or resounding with a sound. **4** suggesting images, emotions, or a quality: *a name resonant with Hollywood glamour.* ■ **res·o·nant·ly** adv.

res·o·nate /ˈrezənˌāt/ ▸ v. produce or be filled with a deep, clear reverberating sound. ■ **res·o·na·tor** n.

re·sort /riˈzórt/ ▸ n. **1** a place visited for vacations or recreation. **2** the adoption of a course of action in a difficult situation: *achieving desired outcomes without resort to war.* **3** a strategy or course of action. ▸ v. (**resort to**) adopt a course of action, especially an undesirable one, so as to resolve a difficult situation.
– PHRASES **as a first** (or **last** or **final**) **resort** before anything else is attempted (or when all else has failed).

re·sound /riˈzound/ ▸ v. **1** fill or be filled with a ringing, booming, or echoing sound. **2** (of fame, success, etc.) be much talked about. **3** (as adj. **resounding**) emphatic; definite: *a resounding success.*

re·source /ˈrēˌsórs, ˈrēˌzórs, riˈsórs, riˈzórs/ ▸ n. **1** (**resources**) a stock or supply of materials or assets that can be drawn on when required. **2** (**resources**) a country's means of supporting itself or becoming wealthier, as represented by its minerals, land, and other assets. **3** a source of help or information: *the database could be used as a teaching resource.* **4** a strategy adopted in a difficult situation. **5** (**resources**) personal qualities that help one to cope in a difficult situation. ▸ v. provide someone or something with resources.

re·source·ful /riˈsórsfəl, -ˈzórs-/ ▸ adj. able to find quick and clever ways to overcome difficulties. ■ **re·source·ful·ly** adv. **re·source·ful·ness** n.

re·spect /riˈspekt/ ▸ n. **1** a feeling of admiration for someone or something because of their qualities or achievements. **2** consideration for the feelings or rights of others. **3** (**respects**) polite greetings. **4** a particular aspect or point: *the government's record in this respect is a mixed one.* ▸ v. **1** feel or have respect for someone or something. **2** avoid harming or interfering with something. **3** agree to recognize and observe a law or rule. ■ **re·spect·er** n.
– PHRASES **with respect to** (or **in respect of**) as regards; with reference to.

re·spect·a·ble /riˈspektəbəl/ ▸ adj. **1** regarded by society to be proper, correct, and good. **2** adequate or acceptable; fairly good. ■ **re·spect·a·bil·i·ty** /riˌspektəˈbilətē/ n. **re·spect·a·bly** adv.

re·spect·ful /riˈspektfəl/ ▸ adj. feeling or showing respect or consideration. ■ **re·spect·ful·ly** adv. **re·spect·ful·ness** n.

re·spect·ing /riˈspektiNG/ ▸ prep. with reference to.

re·spec·tive /riˈspektiv/ ▸ adj. belonging or relating separately to each of two or more people or things: *they chatted about their respective lives.*

re·spec·tive·ly /riˈspektivlē/ ▸ adv. separately and in the order already mentioned.

re·spell /rēˈspel/ ▸ v. (past and past part. **respelled** or chiefly Brit. **respelt**) spell a word differently, especially to show how to pronounce it.

res·pi·ra·tion /ˌrespəˈrāSHən/ ▸ n. **1** the action of breathing. **2** a single breath. **3** the processes in living organisms involving the production of energy, typically with the intake of oxygen and the release of carbon dioxide.

res·pi·ra·tor /'respə,rātər/ ▶ n. **1** a device worn over the face to prevent the inhalation of smoke or other harmful substances. **2** a device that enables someone to breathe artificially.

res·pi·ra·to·ry /'respərə,tôrē, ri'spīrə-/ ▶ adj. relating to breathing.

res·pi·ra·to·ry tract ▶ n. the passage formed by the mouth, nose, throat, and lungs, through which air passes during breathing.

re·spire /ri'spī(ə)r/ ▶ v. **1** breathe. **2** (of a plant) carry out the process of respiration. ■ **res·pi·ra·ble** adj.

res·pite /'respət, ri'spīt/ ▶ n. a short period of rest or relief from something difficult or unpleasant.

re·splend·ent /ri'splendənt/ ▶ adj. attractive and colorful in an impressive way. ■ **re·splend·ence** n. **re·splend·ent·ly** adv.

re·spond /ri'spänd/ ▶ v. **1** say something in reply. **2** do something as a reaction to someone or something. ■ **re·spond·er** n.

re·spond·ent /ri'spändənt/ ▶ n. **1** Law a person against whom a petition is filed, especially one in an appeal or a divorce case. **2** a person who responds to a questionnaire or an advertisement.

re·sponse /ri'späns/ ▶ n. **1** a spoken or written answer. **2** a reaction to something. **3** technical a physical reaction to a stimulus or situation.

re·spon·si·bil·i·ty /ri,spänsə'bilətē/ ▶ n. (pl. **responsibilities**) **1** the state of being responsible for someone or something. **2** the opportunity or ability to act independently and make decisions without authorization. **3** a thing that one is required to do as part of a job or legal obligation.

re·spon·si·ble /ri'spänsəbəl/ ▶ adj. **1** having a duty to do something, or having control over or care for someone. **2** being the cause of something and so able to be blamed or credited for it: *the president is ultimately responsible for this situation.* **3** capable of being trusted. **4** (of a job or position) involving important duties or decisions or control over others. **5** (**responsible to**) having to report to a senior person. ■ **re·spon·si·ble·ness** n. **re·spon·si·bly** /-blē/ adv.

re·spon·sive /ri'spänsiv/ ▶ adj. **1** responding readily and with interest. **2** in response; answering. ■ **re·spon·sive·ly** adv. **re·spon·sive·ness** n.

rest¹ /rest/ ▶ v. **1** stop work or activity in order to relax or recover strength. **2** place or be placed so as to stay in a specified position. **3** (**rest on**) depend or be based on. **4** (**rest something in/on**) place trust, hope, or confidence in or on. **5** (**rest with**) be the responsibility of or belong to: *the final say rests with the city council.* **6** (of an issue) be left without further investigation or discussion. ▶ n. **1** the state or a period of resting. **2** an object that is used to hold or support something. **3** Music an interval of silence of a specified duration.

– PHRASES **rest one's case** conclude one's presentation of evidence and arguments in a lawsuit.

rest² ▶ n. **1** the remaining part of something. **2** (treated as pl.) the remaining people or things; the others. ▶ v. remain or be left in a specified condition: *rest assured we will do everything we can.*

re·start ▶ v. /rē'stärt/ start again. ▶ n. /'rē,stärt/ a new start or beginning.

re·state /rē'stāt/ ▶ v. state something again or differently.

res·tau·rant /'rest(ə)rənt, 'restə,ränt, 'res,tränt/ ▶ n. a place where people pay to sit and eat meals that are cooked on the premises.

res·tau·ra·teur /,restərə'tər/ ▶ n. a person who owns and manages a restaurant.

> USAGE
> Although **restaurateur** is related to *restaurant*, it is not spelled with an *n*.

rest·ful /'restfəl/ ▶ adj. having a quiet and soothing quality. ■ **rest·ful·ly** adv.

rest home ▶ n. an institution where old or frail people live and are cared for.

res·ti·tu·tion /,restə't(y)o͞osHən/ ▶ n. **1** the restoration of something lost or stolen to its proper owner. **2** payment to compensate for injury or loss. **3** the restoration of something to its original state. ■ **res·ti·tu·tive** /'restə,t(y)o͞otiv/ adj.

res·tive /'restiv/ ▶ adj. unable to keep still or unwilling to submit to control: *the republic's restive minorities.* ■ **res·tive·ly** adv. **res·tive·ness** n.

rest·less /'restləs/ ▶ adj. **1** unable to rest or relax as a result of anxiety or boredom. **2** offering no physical or emotional rest: *a restless night.* ■ **rest·less·ly** adv. **rest·less·ness** n.

re·stock /rē'stäk/ ▶ v. replenish a store with fresh stock or supplies.

res·to·ra·tion /,restə'rāsHən/ ▶ n. **1** the action of returning something to a former condition, place, or owner. **2** the process of repairing or renovating a building, work of art, etc. **3** the reinstatement of a previous practice, right, or situation. **4** the return of a monarch to a throne, a head of state to government, or a regime to power. **5** (**the Restoration**) the re-establishment of Charles II as King of England in 1660, or the period following this.

re·stor·a·tive /ri'stôrətiv/ ▶ adj. having the ability to restore health, strength, or well-being. ▶ n. a medicine or drink that restores health, strength, or well-being. ■ **re·stor·a·tive·ly** adv.

re·store /ri'stôr/ ▶ v. **1** bring back a previous practice, right, or situation. **2** return to a former condition, place, or owner: *he was restored to full favor.* **3** repair or renovate a building, work of art, etc. ■ **re·stor·a·ble** adj. **re·stor·er** n.

re·strain /ri'strān/ ▶ v. **1** keep someone or something under control or within limits. **2** prevent someone from moving or acting as they wish. **3** control a strong emotion. ■ **re·strain·a·ble** adj. **re·strain·er** n.

re·strained /ri'strānd/ ▶ adj. **1** reserved or unemotional. **2** not highly decorated or brightly colored.

re·straint /ri'strānt/ ▶ n. **1** a rule, measure, or fact that limits or controls: *the financial restraints of the budget.* **2** the action of restraining someone or something. **3** a device that limits or prevents freedom of movement. **4** unemotional or controlled behavior.

re·strict /ri'strikt/ ▶ v. **1** put a limit on something; keep something under control. **2** prevent someone from moving or acting as they wish.

re·strict·ed /ri'striktid/ ▶ adj. **1** limited in extent, number, or scope. **2** not revealed or made public for reasons of national security.

re·stric·tion /ri'strikshən/ ▶ n. **1** a limiting rule, measure, or condition. **2** the limitation or control of someone or something, or the state of being restricted.

re·stric·tive /ri'striktiv/ ▶ adj. limiting or controlling freedom of action or movement. ■ **re·stric·tive·ly** adv. **re·stric·tive·ness** n.

re·string /rē'striNG, 'rē-/ ▶ v. (past and past part. **restrung**) fit new strings to a musical instrument or sports racket.

rest·room /'rest,rōōm, -,rŏŏm/ ▶ n. a lavatory in a public building.

re·struc·ture /rē'strəkchər/ ▶ v. **1** organize something differently. **2** convert a debt into another debt that is repayable at a later time.

re·struc·tur·ing /rē'strəkchəriNG/ ▶ n. a reorganization of a company with a view to achieving greater efficiency and profit.

re·style ▶ v. /rē'stīl/ **1** give something a new shape or layout. **2** give a new description or name to someone or something. ▶ n. /'rēstīl/ an instance of restyling something.

re·sult /ri'zəlt/ ▶ n. **1** a thing that is caused or produced by something else; an outcome. **2** a quantity or another item of information obtained by experiment or calculation. **3** a final score, mark, or placing in a sporting event or exam. **4** a satisfactory or favorable outcome: *determination and persistence guarantee results.* **5** the outcome of a business's trading over a particular period, expressed as a statement of profit or loss. ▶ v. **1** happen because of something else. **2** (**result in**) have a specified outcome.

re·sult·ant /ri'zəltnt/ ▶ adj. happening or produced as a result.

re·sume /ri'zōōm/ ▶ v. **1** begin again or continue after a pause or interruption. **2** return to a seat or place.

ré·su·mé /'rezə,mā, ,rezə'mā/ ▶ n. **1** a summary of a person's education, qualifications, and previous jobs, sent with a job application; a curriculum vitae. **2** a summary of something.

re·sump·tion /ri'zəmpshən/ ▶ n. the action of beginning something again after an interruption.

re·sup·ply /,rēsə'plī/ ▶ v. (**resupplies, resupplying, resupplied**) provide with or obtain a fresh supply.

re·sur·face /rē'sərfəs/ ▶ v. **1** put a new coating on a surface. **2** come back up to the surface of deep water. **3** arise or become evident again: *the old animosities have resurfaced.*

re·sur·gent /ri'sərjənt/ ▶ adj. becoming stronger, or more active or popular again. ■ **re·sur·gence** n.

res·ur·rect /,rezə'rekt/ ▶ v. **1** restore a dead person to life. **2** revive something inactive, disused, or forgotten.

res·ur·rec·tion /,rezə'rekshən/ ▶ n. **1** the action of resurrecting or reviving someone or something. **2** (**the Resurrection**) (in Christian belief) the time when Jesus rose from the dead.

re·sus·ci·tate /ri'səsə,tāt/ ▶ v. **1** revive someone from unconsciousness. **2** make something active again. ■ **re·sus·ci·ta·tion** /ri,səsə'tāshən/ n. **re·sus·ci·ta·tive** /-,tātiv/ adj. **re·sus·ci·ta·tor** /-,tātər/ n.

re·tail /'rē,tāl/ ▶ n. the sale of goods to the general public (rather than to a wholesaler). ▶ v. **1** sell goods to the public. **2** (**retail at/for**) be sold by retail for a specified price. **3** describe the details of an incident to others. ■ **re·tail·er** n.

re·tain /ri'tān/ ▶ v. **1** continue to have or own something. **2** absorb and continue to hold a substance. **3** keep something in place. **4** keep someone as an employee. **5** obtain the services of an attorney with a preliminary payment. ■ **re·tain·a·ble** adj.

re·tain·er /ri'tānər/ ▶ n. **1** a thing that holds something in place. **2** a fee paid in advance to an attorney to obtain their services. **3** a servant who has worked for someone for a long time.

re·tain·ing wall ▶ n. a wall that holds back earth or water on one side of it.

re·take /rē'tāk, 'rē-/ ▶ v. (past **retook** /rē'tŏŏk/; past part. **retaken**) **1** take a test or exam again. **2** regain possession or control of something. ▶ n. **1** a test or exam that is retaken. **2** an instance of filming a scene or recording a piece of music again.

re·tal·i·ate /ri'talē,āt/ ▶ v. make an attack in return for a similar attack. ■ **re·tal·i·a·tion** /ri,talē'āshən/ n. **re·tal·i·a·tive** /ri'talē,ātiv, -ēativ/ adj. **re·tal·i·a·tor** /-,ātər/ n. **re·tal·i·a·to·ry** /ri'talēə,tôrē/ adj.

re·tard ▶ v. /ri'tärd/ hold back the development or progress of someone or something. ▶ n. /'rē,tärd/ offensive a person who has a mental disability. ■ **re·tar·da·tion** /,rē,tär'dāshən, ri-/ n. **re·tard·er** n.

re·tar·dant /ri'tärdnt/ ▶ adj. preventing or inhibiting: *fire-retardant polymers.* ▶ n. a fabric or substance that prevents or inhibits the outbreak of fire.

re·tard·ed /ri'tärdid/ ▶ adj. chiefly offensive less advanced in mental, physical, or social development than is usual for one's age.

retch /rech/ ▶ v. make the sound and movement of vomiting. ▶ n. an instance of retching.

re·tell /rē'tel/ ▶ v. (past and past part. **retold** /rē'tōld/) tell a story again or differently.

re·ten·tion /ri'tenchən/ ▶ n. **1** the action of keeping or holding something or the fact of being retained. **2** failure to remove a substance from the body.

re·ten·tive /ri'tentiv/ ▶ adj. **1** (of a person's memory) good at storing facts and impressions. **2** (of a substance) able to absorb and hold moisture. ■ **re·ten·tive·ly** adv. **re·ten·tive·ness** n. **re·ten·tiv·i·ty** /,rē,ten'tivətē, ri-/ n.

re·think /rē'THiNGk/ ▶ v. (past and past part. **rethought**) consider a policy or course of action again. ▶ n. an instance of rethinking.

ret·i·cent /'retəsənt/ ▶ adj. not revealing one's thoughts or feelings readily. ■ **ret·i·cence** n. **ret·i·cent·ly** adv.

re·tic·u·lat·ed /ri'tikyə,lātid/ ▶ adj. arranged or marked like a net or network.

re·tic·u·la·tion /ri,tikyə'lāshən/ ▶ n. a pattern or arrangement of interlacing lines resembling a net.

ret·i·cule /'reti,kyōōl/ ▶ n. chiefly historical a woman's small handbag, closed with a drawstring.

re·tie /rē'tī/ ▶ v. (**reties, retying, retied**) tie something again.

ret·i·na /'retn-ə/ ▶ n. (pl. **retinas** or **retinae** /'retn,ē, 'retn,ī/) a layer at the back of the eyeball containing cells that are sensitive to light and from which impulses are sent to the brain. ■ **ret·i·nal** /'retn-əl/ adj.

ret·i·nol /'retnôl, -,ōl/ ▶ n. vitamin A.

ret·i·nop·a·thy /ˌretnˈäpəTHē/ ▶ n. disease of the retina of the eye that results in impairment or loss of vision.

ret·i·nue /ˈretnˌ(y) o͞o/ ▶ n. a group of advisers or assistants accompanying an important person.

re·tire /riˈtīr/ ▶ v. **1** leave one's job and stop working, especially because one has reached a particular age. **2** Baseball put out a batter or side. **3** leave a place, especially so as to go somewhere more private: *it was Mr. Theil's habit to retire to his sitting room and stay there.* **4** go to bed. **5** (of a jury) leave the courtroom to decide the verdict of a trial. ▪ **re·tir·ee** /riˌtīˈrē/ n. **re·tired** adj.

re·tire·ment /riˈtīrmənt/ ▶ n. **1** the action or fact of retiring. **2** the period of one's life after retiring from work. **3** the state of being private; seclusion.

re·tire·ment plan ▶ n. another term for PENSION¹ (sense 1 of the noun).

re·tir·ing /riˈtīriNG/ ▶ adj. tending to avoid other people; shy.

re·ti·tle /rēˈtītl/ ▶ v. give a different title to a book, play, movie, etc.

re·told /rēˈtōld/ ▶ past and past participle of RETELL.

re·took /rēˈto͝ok/ ▶ past of RETAKE.

re·tool /rēˈto͞ol/ ▶ v. **1** equip (a factory) with new or adapted tools. **2** alter the form or character of: *he has a little time to retool his candidacy.*

re·tort¹ /riˈtôrt/ ▶ v. say something sharp or witty in answer to a remark or accusation. ▶ n. a sharp or witty reply.

re·tort² ▶ n. **1** a container or furnace for carrying out a chemical process on a large or industrial scale. **2** historical a glass container with a long neck, used in distilling liquids and other chemical operations.

re·touch /rēˈtəCH/ ▶ v. improve a painting, photograph, or other image by making slight additions or alterations. ▪ **re·touch·er** n.

re·trace /rēˈtrās/ ▶ v. **1** go back over the same route that one has just taken. **2** discover and follow a route taken by someone else. **3** trace something back to its source or beginning.

re·tract /riˈtrakt/ ▶ v. **1** withdraw a statement or accusation because it is not supported by evidence. **2** go back on an agreement or promise. **3** draw or be drawn back. ▪ **re·tract·a·ble** adj. **re·trac·tion** /riˈtraksHən/ n. **re·trac·tor** n.

re·trac·tile /riˈtraktəl, -ˌtīl/ ▶ adj. capable of being retracted or drawn back: *retractile claws.*

re·train /rēˈtrān/ ▶ v. teach or learn new skills.

re·trans·mit /ˌrētransˈmit, -tranz-/ ▶ v. (**retransmits, retransmitting, retransmitted**) transmit data, a radio signal, or a broadcast again or onto another receiver. ▪ **re·trans·mis·sion** /-ˈmisHən/ n.

re·tread /rēˈtred/ ▶ v. **1** (past **retrod** /rēˈträd/; past part. **retrodden** /rēˈträdn/) go back over a path or one's steps. **2** (past and past part. **retreaded**) put a new tread on a worn tire. ▶ n. a tire that has been given a new tread.

re·treat /riˈtrēt/ ▶ v. **1** (of an army) withdraw from an attack on enemy forces. **2** move away or back. **3** go to a quiet or secluded place. **4** change one's mind as a result of criticism or difficulty. ▶ n. **1** an act of retreating. **2** a quiet or secluded place. **3** a place where a person goes for a time in order to be quiet and pray or meditate. **4** a military musical ceremony carried out at sunset.

re·trench /riˈtrenCH/ ▶ v. reduce costs or spending in response to economic difficulty. ▪ **re·trench·ment** n.

re·tri·al /rēˈtrīəl, ˈrēˌtrīəl/ ▶ n. a second or further trial on the same issues and with the same parties.

ret·ri·bu·tion /ˌretrəˈbyo͞osHən/ ▶ n. severe punishment in revenge for a wrong or criminal act. ▪ **re·trib·u·tive** /riˈtribyətiv/ adj. **re·trib·u·to·ry** /riˈtribyəˌtôrē/ adj.

re·trieve /riˈtrēv/ ▶ v. **1** get or bring something back. **2** (of a dog) find and bring back game that has been shot. **3** find or extract information stored in a computer. **4** make a difficult situation better. ▪ **re·triev·a·ble** adj. **re·triev·al** n.

re·triev·er /riˈtrēvər/ ▶ n. a dog of a breed used for finding and bringing back game that has been shot.

ret·ro /ˈretrō/ ▶ adj. imitative of a style from the recent past. ▶ n. retro clothes, music, or style.

retro- ▶ comb.form **1** back or backward: *retrogression.* **2** behind: *retrorocket.*

ret·ro·ac·tive /ˌretrōˈaktiv/ ▶ adj. (especially of a law) taking effect from a date in the past. ▪ **ret·ro·ac·tive·ly** adv.

re·trod /rēˈträd/ ▶ past of RETREAD (sense 1 of the verb).

re·trod·den /rēˈträdn/ ▶ past participle of RETREAD (sense 1 of the verb).

ret·ro·fit /ˌretrōˈfit/ ▶ v. (**retrofits, retrofitting, retrofitted**) fit something with a component or accessory not fitted during manufacture. ▶ n. an act of fitting a component or accessory to something after manufacture.

ret·ro·fu·tur·ist·ic (also **retrofuturist**) ▶ adj. of or resembling a futuristic style or aesthetic from an earlier era; having both retro and futuristic elements.

ret·ro·grade /ˈretrəˌgrād/ ▶ adj. **1** directed or moving backward. **2** going back to an earlier and worse situation: *reconsidering these concepts would be a retrograde step.* **3** (of the order of something) reversed. **4** chiefly Astronomy (of the apparent motion of a planet) in a reverse direction from normal (from east to west). ▶ v. go back in position or time. ▪ **ret·ro·gra·da·tion** /ˌretrōgrāˈdāsHən/ n.

ret·ro·gres·sion /ˌretrəˈgresHən/ ▶ n. the process of returning to an earlier state, especially a worse one. ▪ **ret·ro·gres·sive** /-ˈgresiv/ adj.

ret·ro·rock·et /ˈretrōˌräkit/ ▶ n. a small auxiliary rocket on a spacecraft or missile, fired in the direction of travel to slow it down.

ret·ro·spect /ˈretrəˌspekt/ ▶ n. (in phrase **in retrospect**) when looking back on a past event; with hindsight. ▪ **ret·ro·spec·tion** /ˌretrəˈspeksHən/ n.

ret·ro·spec·tive /ˌretrəˈspektiv/ ▶ adj. **1** looking back on or dealing with past events. **2** (of an exhibition) showing the development of an artist's work over a period of time. **3** (of a statute or legal decision) taking effect from a date in the past. ▶ n. an exhibition showing the development of an artist's work over time. ▪ **ret·ro·spec·tive·ly** adv.

ret·rous·sé /rəˌtro͞oˈsā, ˌretro͞o-/ ▶ adj. (of a person's nose) turned up at the tip.

ret·ro·vi·rus /ˌretrōˈvīrəs, ˈretrōˌvīrəs/ ▶ n. any of a group of RNA viruses that insert a DNA copy of their genetic material into the host cell in order to replicate, e.g., HIV. ■ **ret·ro·vi·ral** adj.

ret·si·na /ret'sēnə/ ▶ n. a Greek white wine flavored with resin.

re·tune /rē't(y)ōon/ ▶ v. tune a radio, musical instrument, etc., again or differently.

re·turn /ri'tərn/ ▶ v. **1** come or go back to a place. **2** (**return to**) go back to a particular state or activity. **3** give, send, or put back: *she returned the spider to the garden.* **4** feel, say, or do the same feeling, action, etc., in response: *she didn't return my phone calls.* **5** (in tennis) hit or send the ball back to an opponent. **6** (of a judge or jury) state a verdict in response to a formal request. **7** yield or make a profit. **8** (of voters) elect a person or party to office. ▶ n. **1** an act or the action of returning. **2** a profit from an investment. **3** (also **return match** or **game**) a second sporting contest between the same opponents. **4** a piece of merchandise that has been returned because it is no longer wanted. **5** an official report submitted in response to a formal demand: *census returns.* ■ **re·turn·a·ble** adj. **re·turn·er** n.
– PHRASES **many happy returns** a greeting to someone on their birthday.

re·turn·ee /ri,tər'nē/ ▶ n. **1** a person who returns to their own country from abroad. **2** a person who returns to work after a long absence.

re·ty·ing /rē'tīiNG/ ▶ present participle of RETIE.

re·type /rē'tīp/ ▶ v. type words again, especially to correct a mistake.

re·u·ni·fy /rē'yōōnə,fī/ ▶ v. (**reunifies, reunifying, reunified**) restore political unity to a place or group. ■ **re·u·ni·fi·ca·tion** /,rē,yōōnəfi'kāsHən/ n.

re·un·ion /rē'yōōnyən/ ▶ n. **1** the action of coming or bringing together again after a period of separation. **2** a social gathering of people who have not seen each other for some time.

re·u·nite /,rēyōō'nīt/ ▶ v. bring or come together again after a period of separation.

re·use ▶ v. /rē'yōōz/ use something again or more than once. ▶ n. /rē'yōōs/ the action of using something again. ■ **re·us·a·ble** /rē'yōōzəbəl/ adj.

rev /rev/ informal ▶ n. (**revs**) the number of revolutions of an engine per minute. ▶ v. (**revs, revving, revved**) increase the running speed of an engine by pressing the accelerator.

Rev. ▶ abbr. Reverend.

re·val·ue /rē'valyōō/ ▶ v. (**revalues, revaluing, revalued**) **1** assess the value of something again. **2** adjust the official value of a currency in relation to other currencies. ■ **re·val·u·a·tion** /rē,valyōō'āsHən/ n.

re·vamp ▶ v. /rē'vamp/ alter something so as to improve its appearance. ▶ n. /'rē,vamp/ an act of improving the appearance of something.

re·vanch·ism /rə'väN,SHizəm/ ▶ n. a policy of retaliation, especially to recover lost territory. ■ **re·vanch·ist** adj. & n.

re·veal[1] /ri'vēl/ ▶ v. **1** make information that was previously unknown or secret known to others. **2** cause or allow to be seen: *the clouds were breaking up to reveal a clear blue sky.* ■ **re·veal·er** n.

re·veal[2] ▶ n. either side surface of an opening in a wall for a door or window.

re·veal·ing /ri'vēliNG/ ▶ adj. **1** making interesting information known to others. **2** (of an item of clothing) allowing much of the wearer's body to

be seen. ■ **re·veal·ing·ly** adv.

rev·eil·le /'revəlē/ ▶ n. a signal sounded on a bugle or drum to wake personnel in the armed forces.

rev·el /'revəl/ ▶ v. (**revels, reveling, reveled**) **1** enjoy oneself with others in a lively and noisy way. **2** (**revel in**) gain great pleasure from. ▶ n. (**revels**) lively and noisy celebrations. ■ **rev·el·er** n. **rev·el·ry** n. (pl. **revelries**).

rev·e·la·tion /,revə'lāsHən/ ▶ n. **1** the revealing of something previously secret or unknown. **2** a surprising and previously unknown fact: *revelations about his personal life.* **3** the revealing of knowledge to humans by God. **4** (**Revelation** or informal **Revelations**) the last book of the New Testament, describing God's revelation of the future to St. John. ■ **rev·e·la·tion·al** adj.

rev·e·la·to·ry /'revələ,tôrē, ri'vel-/ ▶ adj. revealing something previously unknown.

rev·e·nant /'revə,näN, -nənt/ ▶ n. a person who has returned, especially supposedly from the dead.

re·venge /ri'venj/ ▶ n. harmful action taken in return for an injury or wrong: *he would some day take his revenge on reporters.* ▶ v. **1** (**revenge oneself** or **be revenged**) take harmful action against someone for an injury or wrong done to oneself. **2** take revenge on behalf of someone else for a wrong or injury.

re·venge·ful /ri'venjfəl/ ▶ adj. eager for revenge.

rev·e·nue /'revə,n(y)ōō/ ▶ n. **1** the income received by an organization. **2** a country's or state's annual income, received especially from taxes, from which public expenses are met.

re·ver·ber·ate /ri'vərbə,rāt/ ▶ v. **1** (of a loud noise) be repeated as an echo. **2** have continuing serious effects: *the effects of his suicide reverberated around the globe.* ■ **re·ver·ber·ant** /-rənt/ adj. **re·ver·ber·a·tion** /ri,vərbə'rāsHən/ n.

re·vere /ri'vi(ə)r/ ▶ v. respect or admire someone or something deeply.

rev·er·ence /'rev(ə)rəns/ ▶ n. **1** deep respect or admiration for someone or something. **2** (**His/Your Reverence**) a title given to a member of the clergy, especially a priest in Ireland. ▶ v. respect or admire someone or something deeply.

rev·er·end /'rev(ə)rənd, 'revərnd/ ▶ adj. a title or form of address to members of the Christian clergy. ▶ n. informal a clergyman.

rev·er·ent /'rev(ə)rənt, 'revərnt/ ▶ adj. showing deep respect. ■ **rev·er·en·tial** /,revə'renchəl/ adj. **rev·er·ent·ly** adv.

rev·er·ie /'revərē/ ▶ n. a daydream.

re·vers /ri'vi(ə)r, -'ve(ə)r/ ▶ n. (pl. same) the turned-back edge of a garment revealing the underside, especially at the lapel.

re·ver·sal /ri'vərsəl/ ▶ n. **1** a change to an opposite direction, position, or course of action. **2** an adverse change of fortune.

re·verse /ri'vərs/ ▶ v. **1** move backward. **2** make something the opposite of what it was: *the damage done to the ozone layer may be reversed.* **3** turn something the other way around or up or inside out. **4** cancel or annul a judgment by a lower court or authority. **5** (of an engine) work in an opposite direction from normal. ▶ adj. **1** going in or turned toward the opposite direction. **2** operating or behaving in a way opposite to that which is usual or expected.

▶ n. **1** a complete change of direction or action. **2** (**the reverse**) the opposite to that previously stated. **3** a setback or defeat. **4** the opposite side or face to the observer. **5** the side of a coin or medal bearing the value or secondary design. **6** reverse gear.

– PHRASES **reverse the charges** make the person who receives a telephone call responsible for paying for it.

re·verse en·gi·neer·ing ▶ n. the reproduction of another manufacturer's product after detailed examination of how it is made.

re·verse gear ▶ n. a gear making a vehicle or piece of machinery move or work backward.

re·vers·i·ble /ri'vərsəbəl/ ▶ adj. **1** able to be returned to an original state or position: *the rise in crime is reversible.* **2** (of a garment or fabric) able to be turned inside out and worn or used with either side visible. ■ **re·vers·i·bil·i·ty** /ri,vərsə'bilətē/ n. **re·vers·i·bly** adv.

re·ver·sion /ri'vərZHən/ ▶ n. **1** a return to a previous state, practice, or belief. **2** Biology the action of an organism returning to a former or ancestral type. **3** the legal right, especially of the original owner, to possess or succeed to property when the present possessor dies or a lease ends. ■ **re·ver·sion·ar·y** /-,nerē/ adj.

re·vert /ri'vərt/ ▶ v. (**revert to**) **1** return to a previous state, condition, or subject. **2** Biology (of an organism) return to a former or ancestral type. **3** (of property) legally return to the original owner.

re·vet·ment /ri'vetmənt/ ▶ n. **1** a retaining wall of masonry that supports or protects a rampart, wall, etc. **2** a barricade of earth or sandbags providing protection from a blast or to prevent aircraft from overrunning when landing.

re·view /ri'vyoo/ ▶ n. **1** a formal assessment of something with the intention of making changes if necessary. **2** a critical assessment of a book, play, or other work. **3** a report on a past event. **4** Law a reconsideration of a judgment, sentence, etc. by a higher court or authority. **5** a ceremonial display and formal inspection of military or naval forces. ▶ v. **1** assess something formally with the intention of making changes if necessary. **2** write a review of a play, book, or other work. **3** Law submit a sentence, case, etc., for reconsideration by a higher court or authority. **4** view something again. ■ **re·view·a·ble** adj. **re·view·er** n.

re·vile /ri'vīl/ ▶ v. criticize someone in an abusive or scornful way.

re·vise /ri'vīz/ ▶ v. **1** reconsider and alter an opinion or judgment in the light of further evidence. **2** examine and amend a piece of writing. ▶ n. Printing a proof including corrections made in an earlier proof. ■ **re·vis·er** n.

re·vi·sion /ri'viZHən/ ▶ n. **1** the action of revising something. **2** a revised edition or form of something. ■ **re·vi·sion·ar·y** /-,nerē/ adj.

re·vi·sion·ism /ri'viZHə,nizəm/ ▶ n. often derogatory the reconsideration or modification of accepted theories or principles. ■ **re·vi·sion·ist** n. & adj.

re·vis·it /rē'vizit/ ▶ v. (**revisits, revisiting, revisited**) **1** come back to or visit a place again. **2** consider a situation again or from a different perspective.

re·vi·tal·ize /rē'vītl,īz/ ▶ v. give new life and vitality to someone or something. ■ **re·vi·tal·i·za·tion** /rē,vītl-ə'zāsHən/ n.

re·viv·al /ri'vīvəl/ ▶ n. **1** an improvement in the condition, strength, or popularity of something: *an economic revival.* **2** a new production of a play that has not been performed for some time. **3** a reawakening of religious faith brought about by evangelistic meetings.

re·viv·al·ism /ri'vīvə,lizəm/ ▶ n. **1** the promotion of a revival of religious faith. **2** a tendency or desire to revive a former custom or practice. ■ **re·viv·al·ist** n. & adj.

re·vive /ri'vīv/ ▶ v. **1** make someone conscious, healthy, or strong again. **2** restore interest in or the popularity of: *this style was revived in the 1970s.* **3** improve the condition of something. ■ **re·viv·a·ble** adj. **re·viv·er** n.

re·viv·i·fy /rē'vivə,fī/ ▶ v. (**revivifies, revivifying, revivified**) give new life or strength to someone or something. ■ **re·viv·i·fi·ca·tion** /,rē,vivəfə'kāsHən/ n.

re·voke /ri'vōk/ ▶ v. officially cancel a decree or decision. ■ **rev·o·ca·ble** /'revəkəbəl, ri'vōkəbəl/ adj. **rev·o·ca·tion** /,revə'kāsHən, ri,vō-/ n.

re·volt /ri'vōlt/ ▶ v. **1** take violent action against a government or ruler. **2** refuse to acknowledge someone or something as having authority: *the new chefs began to revolt against classic haute cuisine.* **3** make someone feel disgust. ▶ n. **1** an attempt to overthrow a government or ruler by violent action. **2** a refusal to continue to obey something: *a revolt over tax increases.* ■ **re·volt·ing** adj.

rev·o·lu·tion /,revə'looSHən/ ▶ n. **1** a forcible overthrow of a government or social order, in favor of a new system. **2** a great and far-reaching change: *marketing underwent a revolution.* **3** movement in orbit or in a circular course around a central point. **4** a complete circular movement around a central point. ■ **rev·o·lu·tion·ist** n.

rev·o·lu·tion·ar·y /,revə'looSHə,nerē/ ▶ adj. **1** involving or causing great change: *a revolutionary new drug.* **2** engaged in or relating to political revolution. ▶ n. (pl. **revolutionaries**) a person who starts or supports a political revolution.

rev·o·lu·tion·ize /,revə'looSHə,nīz/ ▶ v. change something greatly or completely.

re·volve /ri'välv, ri'vôlv/ ▶ v. **1** move in a circle around a central point. **2** (**revolve around/about**) move in a circular orbit around. **3** (**revolve around**) treat as the most important aspect: *her life revolved around her husband.*

re·volv·er /ri'välvər, -'vôl-/ ▶ n. a pistol with revolving chambers enabling several shots to be fired without reloading.

re·volv·ing door ▶ n. an entrance to a large building in which four partitions turn about a central point.

re·vue /ri'vyoo/ ▶ n. a theatrical show with short sketches, songs, and dances, typically dealing satirically with topical issues.

re·vul·sion /ri'vəlsHən/ ▶ n. a feeling of disgust and horror.

re·ward /ri'wôrd/ ▶ n. **1** a thing given in recognition of service, effort, or achievement. **2** a fair return for good or bad behavior: *a slap on the face was the reward for his crude remark.* **3** a sum of money offered for helping to find a criminal or handing in lost property. ▶ v. **1** give a reward to someone to show appreciation of their service, qualities, or achievements. **2** (**be**

rewarded) receive what one deserves.

re·ward·ing /ri'wôrdiNG/ ▶adj. providing satisfaction. ■ **re·ward·ing·ly** adv.

re·wind /rē'wīnd/ ▶v. (past and past part. **rewound** /rē'wound/) wind a film or tape back to the beginning. ▶n. a mechanism for rewinding a film or tape. ■ **re·wind·er** n.

re·wire /rē'wīr/ ▶v. provide a building, device, or vehicle with new electric wiring. ■ **re·wir·a·ble** adj.

re·word /rē'wərd/ ▶v. put something into different words.

re·work /rē'wərk/ ▶v. change something in order to improve or update it.

re·wound /rē'wound/ ▶ past and past participle of REWIND.

re·writ·a·ble /rē'rītəbəl/ ▶adj. Computing (of a storage device) enabling previously recorded data to be overwritten.

re·write /rē'rīt/ ▶v. (past **rewrote** /rē'rōt/; past part. **rewritten** /rē'ritn/) write something again so as to change or improve it. ▶n. an instance of rewriting something.

Reye's syn·drome /rīz, rāz/ ▶n. a life-threatening metabolic disorder in young children, involving encephalitis and liver failure.

Rf ▶symbol the chemical element rutherfordium.

RFD ▶abbr. rural free delivery.

RFID ▶abbr. radio frequency identification, denoting technologies that use radio waves to identify people or objects carrying encoded microchips.

RFP ▶abbr. request for proposal, a detailed specification of goods or services required by an organization, sent to potential contractors or suppliers.

Rg ▶symbol the chemical element roentgenium.

Rh ▶abbr. rhesus (factor).

r.h. ▶abbr. right hand.

rhap·so·dize /'rapsə,dīz/ ▶v. express great enthusiasm about someone or something.

rhap·so·dy /'rapsədē/ ▶n. (pl. **rhapsodies**) 1 an expression of great joy or enthusiasm: *rhapsodies of praise.* 2 a musical composition that is full of feeling and is not regular in form. 3 (in ancient Greece) an epic poem of a suitable length for recitation at one time. ■ **rhap·sod·ic** /rap'sädik/ adj.

rhe·a /rēə/ ▶n. a large flightless bird of South American grasslands, resembling a small ostrich with grayish-brown plumage.

rhe·ni·um /'rēnēəm/ ▶n. a rare silvery-white metallic element.

rhe·ol·o·gy /rē'äləjē/ ▶n. the branch of physics concerned with the deformation and flow of matter. ■ **rhe·o·log·i·cal** /,rēə'läjikəl/ adj. **rhe·ol·o·gist** n.

rhe·o·stat /'rēə,stat/ ▶n. an instrument used to control the current in an electrical circuit by varying the amount of resistance in it. ■ **rhe·o·stat·ic** /,rēə'statik/ adj.

rhe·sus fac·tor /'rēsəs/ ▶n. a substance in red blood cells that can cause disease in a newborn baby whose blood contains the factor (i.e., is **rhesus positive**) while the mother's blood does not (i.e., is **rhesus negative**).

rhe·sus mon·key ▶n. a small brown macaque with red skin on the face and rump, native to southern Asia.

rhet·o·ric /'retərik/ ▶n. 1 the art of effective or persuasive speaking or writing. 2 persuasive or impressive language that is insincere or meaningless: *I was sick of empty nationalist rhetoric.*

rhe·tor·i·cal /rə'tôrikəl/ ▶adj. 1 relating to rhetoric. 2 (of a statement) intended to persuade or impress. 3 (of a question) asked for effect or to make a statement rather than to obtain an answer. ■ **rhe·tor·i·cal·ly** adv.

rhet·o·ri·cian /,retə'risHən/ ▶n. 1 an expert in the art of effective or persuasive speaking or writing. 2 a speaker whose words are intended to impress or persuade.

rheum /rōōm/ ▶n. chiefly literary a watery fluid that collects in or drips from the nose or eyes. ■ **rheum·y** adj.

rheu·mat·ic /rōō'matik/ ▶adj. relating to or having rheumatism. ▶n. a person with rheumatism. ■ **rheu·ma·tick·y** adj. (informal).

rheu·mat·ic fe·ver ▶n. an acute fever marked by inflammation and pain in the joints, caused by a bacterial infection.

rheu·ma·tism /'rōōmə,tizəm/ ▶n. any disease marked by inflammation and pain in the joints, muscles, or fibrous tissue.

rheu·ma·toid /'rōōmə,toid/ ▶adj. relating to or resembling rheumatism.

rheu·ma·toid ar·thri·tis ▶n. a disease that gradually worsens, causing inflammation in the joints and painful swelling and immobility.

rheu·ma·tol·o·gy /,rōōmə'täləjē/ ▶n. the study of rheumatism, arthritis, and other disorders of the joints, muscles, and ligaments. ■ **rheu·ma·to·log·i·cal** /,rōōmətl'äjikəl/ adj. **rheu·ma·tol·o·gist** n.

rhine·stone /'rīn,stōn/ ▶n. an imitation diamond.

rhi·ni·tis /rī'nītis/ ▶n. inflammation of the mucous membrane of the nose, caused by infection with a virus or an allergic reaction.

rhi·no /'rīnō/ ▶n. (pl. same or **rhinos**) informal a rhinoceros.

rhi·noc·er·os /rī'näs(ə)rəs/ ▶n. (pl. same or **rhinoceroses**) a large plant-eating mammal with one or two horns on the nose and thick folded skin, native to Africa and South Asia.

rhi·no·plas·ty /'rīnō,plastē/ ▶n. (pl. **rhinoplasties**) plastic surgery performed on the nose.

rhi·zome /'rī,zōm/ ▶n. a horizontal underground plant stem bearing both roots and shoots.

Rho·de·sian /rō'dēzHən/ ▶n. a person from Rhodesia (now Zimbabwe). ▶adj. relating to Rhodesia.

Rhodes Schol·ar·ship /rōdz/ ▶n. any of several scholarships awarded annually for study at Oxford University by students from certain Commonwealth countries, the US, and Germany. ■ **Rhodes schol·ar** n.

rho·di·um /'rōdēəm/ ▶n. a hard, dense silvery-white metallic element.

rho·do·den·dron /,rōdə'dendrən/ ▶n. a shrub with large clusters of colorful trumpet-shaped flowers and large evergreen leaves.

rhom·bi /'räm,bī, -,bē/ ▶ plural of RHOMBUS.

rhom·bo·he·dron /,rämbō'hēdrən/ ▶n. (pl. **rhombohedra** /-drə/ or **rhombohedrons**) a solid figure whose faces are six equal rhombuses.

■ **rhom·bo·he·dral** /ˌrämbō'hēdrəl/ adj.

rhom·boid /'räm,boid/ ▶ adj. having or resembling the shape of a rhombus. ▶ n. a parallelogram in which adjacent sides are unequal. ■ **rhom·boi·dal** /räm'boidl/ adj.

rhom·bus /'rämbəs/ ▶ n. (pl. **rhombuses** or **rhombi** /-ˌbī, -ˌbē/) a quadrilateral whose sides all have the same length.

rhu·barb /'roō,bärb/ ▶ n. 1 the thick reddish or green leaf stalks of a plant, which are cooked and eaten as a fruit. 2 informal, dated a heated dispute.

rhum·ba ▶ n. variant spelling of RUMBA.

rhyme /rīm/ ▶ n. 1 a word that has the same sound or ends with the same sound as another. 2 similarity of sound between words or the endings of words. 3 a short poem with rhyming lines. ▶ v. 1 (of a word, syllable, or line) have or end with the same sound as another. 2 (**rhyme something with**) put a word together with another word that has a similar sound. 3 literary compose poetry. ■ **rhym·er** n.
– PHRASES **rhyme or reason** logical explanation: *there's no rhyme or reason to it.*

rhyme·ster /'rīmstər/ ▶ n. a person who composes simple or inferior rhymes.

rhym·ing slang ▶ n. a type of slang that replaces words with rhyming words or phrases, typically with the rhyming element omitted (e.g., *butcher's*, short for *butcher's hook*, meaning 'look').

rhy·thm /'riᴛʜəm/ ▶ n. 1 a strong, regular repeated pattern of music, sound, or movement. 2 a particular pattern formed by musical rhythm: *a slow waltz rhythm.* 3 the measured flow of words and phrases in verse or prose as determined by the length of and stress on syllables. 4 a regularly recurring sequence of events or processes: *the twice daily rhythms of the tides.* ■ **rhythm·less** adj.

rhy·thm and blues ▶ n. popular music of US black origin, arising from a combination of blues with jazz rhythms.

rhyth·mic /'riᴛʜmik/ ▶ adj. 1 having or relating to rhythm. 2 occurring regularly. ■ **rhyth·mi·cal** adj. **rhyth·mi·cal·ly** /-ik(ə)lē/ adv. **rhyth·mic·i·ty** /ˌriᴛʜ'misətē/ n.

rhy·thm meth·od ▶ n. a method of birth control in which sex is restricted to the times of a woman's menstrual cycle when ovulation is least likely to occur.

rhy·thm sec·tion ▶ n. the part of a pop or jazz group supplying the rhythm, in particular the bass, drums, and sometimes piano, other keyboards, or guitar.

RI ▶ abbr. Rhode Island.

ri·a /'rēə/ ▶ n. a long narrow inlet formed by the partial submerging of a river valley by the sea.

ri·al /rē'ôl, rē'äl/ (also **riyal**) ▶ n. 1 the basic unit of money of Iran and Oman. 2 (usu. **riyal**) the basic unit of money of Saudi Arabia, Qatar, and Yemen.

rib /rib/ ▶ n. 1 each of a series of thin bones attached in pairs to the spine and curving around to protect the chest and its organs. 2 a curved structure that supports a vault. 3 a curved strut forming part of the framework of a ship's hull. 4 a vein of a leaf or an insect's wing. 5 a combination of alternate plain and purl knitting stitches producing a ridged, slightly elastic fabric. ▶ v. (**ribs, ribbing, ribbed**) 1 mark with or form into ridges: *the road was ribbed with furrows of slush.* 2 informal tease someone good-

naturedly.

rib·ald /'ribəld, 'rib,ôld, 'rī,bôld/ ▶ adj. referring to sex in an amusingly coarse way.

rib·ald·ry /'ribəldrē, 'rī-/ ▶ n. coarse humorous talk or behavior.

ribbed /ribd/ ▶ adj. 1 having a pattern of raised bands. 2 (of a vault or other structure) strengthened with ribbing.

rib·bing /'ribiNG/ ▶ n. 1 a riblike structure or pattern. 2 informal good-natured teasing.

rib·bon /'ribən/ ▶ n. 1 a long, narrow strip of fabric, used for tying something or for decoration. 2 a ribbon of a special color or design awarded as a prize or worn to indicate the holding of an honor. 3 something that is long and narrow in shape. 4 a narrow band of inked material on a spool, used to produce the characters in some typewriters and computer printers. ■ **rib·boned** adj.
– PHRASES **cut** (or **tear**) **something to ribbons** severely damage something.

rib·by /'ribē/ ▶ adj. having prominent ribs.

rib·cage /'rib,kāj/ ▶ n. the bony frame formed by the ribs.

ri·bo·fla·vin /ˌrībə'flāvin, 'rībə,flā-/ ▶ n. vitamin B₂, a compound essential for energy production and present in milk, liver, and green vegetables.

ri·bo·nu·cle·ic ac·id /ˌrībōn(y)ōō'klē-ik, -'klā-ik/ ▶ n. see RNA.

rib·tick·ler ▶ n. informal a very amusing joke or story.

rice /rīs/ ▶ n. the grains of a cereal plant that is grown for food on wet land in warm countries. ▶ v. force cooked potatoes or other vegetables through a sieve or similar utensil. ■ **ric·er** n.

rice pa·per ▶ n. thin edible paper made from the flattened and dried pith of a shrub, used in oriental painting and in baking cookies and cakes.

rich /riCH/ ▶ adj. 1 having a great deal of money or assets. 2 (of a country or region) having valuable natural resources or a successful economy. 3 made of expensive materials: *rich mahogany furniture.* 4 existing in plentiful quantities; abundant. 5 having or producing something in large amounts: *fruits rich in vitamins.* 6 (of food) containing much fat, sugar, etc. 7 (of a color, sound, or smell) pleasantly deep and strong. 8 (of soil or land) fertile. 9 (of the mixture in an internal-combustion engine) containing a high proportion of fuel. 10 informal (of a remark) causing ironic amusement or indignation. ■ **rich·ness** n.

rich·es /'riCHiz/ ▶ pl.n. 1 material wealth. 2 valuable natural resources.

rich·ly /'riCHlē/ ▶ adv. 1 in a rich way. 2 fully: *a richly deserved vacation.*

Rich·ter scale /'riktər/ ▶ n. a scale for expressing the magnitude of an earthquake.

ri·cin /'rīsən, 'ris-/ ▶ n. a highly toxic protein obtained from the seeds of the castor oil plant.

rick /rik/ ▶ n. a stack of hay, cereal, or straw, especially one built into a regular shape.

rick·ets /'rikits/ ▶ n. (treated as sing. or pl.) a disease of children caused by a lack of vitamin D, in which the bones become softened and distorted.

rick·ett·si·a /ri'ketsēə/ ▶ n. (pl. **rickettsiae** /-sē,ē, -sē,ī/ or **rickettsias**) any of a group of very small bacteria of which some cause typhus and similar diseases in humans. ■ **rick·ett·si·al** adj.

rick·et·y /'rikitē/ ▸ adj. poorly made and likely to collapse. ■ **rick·et·i·ness** n.

rick·rack /'rik,rak/ ▸ n. braided trimming in a zigzag pattern, used on clothes.

rick·shaw /'rik,shô/ ▸ n. a light two-wheeled hooded vehicle drawn by one or more people, used in Asian countries.

ric·o·chet /'rikə,shā, -,shet/ ▸ v. (**ricochets** /'rikə,shāz, -,shets/, **ricocheting** /-,shā-iNG, -,sheting/, **ricocheted** /-,shād, -,shetid/) (of a bullet or other fast moving object) rebound off a surface. ▸ n. **1** a shot or hit that rebounds off a surface. **2** the action of rebounding off a surface.

ri·cot·ta /ri'kätə/ ▸ n. a soft white unsalted Italian cheese.

ric·tus /'riktəs/ ▸ n. a fixed grimace or grin. ■ **ric·tal** adj.

rid /rid/ ▸ v. (**rids, ridding, rid**) **1** (**rid someone/ thing of**) make someone or something free of an unwanted person or thing. **2** (**be** (or **get**) **rid of**) be or make oneself free of someone or something that is unwanted or annoying.

rid·dance /'ridns/ ▸ n. (in phrase **good riddance**) said to express relief at being rid of someone or something.

rid·den /'ridn/ past participle of **RIDE** ▸ adj. (in combination) full of a particular thing: *guilt-ridden.*

rid·dle[1] /'ridl/ ▸ n. **1** a question or statement that is worded in such a way that one needs to think hard to find its answer or meaning. **2** a puzzling person or thing. ■ **rid·dler** n.

rid·dle[2] ▸ v. **1** make many holes in someone or something. **2** fill with something undesirable: *my foot is now riddled with arthritis.* **3** pass a substance through a large coarse sieve. ▸ n. a large coarse sieve.

ride /rīd/ ▸ v. (past **rode**; past part. **ridden**) **1** sit on and control the movement of a horse, bicycle, or motorcycle. **2** (usu. **ride in/on**) travel in a vehicle or on a horse. **3** travel over an area on horseback or on a bicycle or motorcycle. **4** be carried or supported by: *surfers rode the waves.* **5** sail or float: *a ship rode at anchor in the dock.* **6** (**ride on**) depend on. **7** (**ride something out**) come safely through a difficult situation. **8** (**ride up**) (of an item of clothing) gradually move upward out of its proper position. **9** yield to a blow so as to reduce its impact. **10** (**be ridden**) be full of or dominated by: *people ridden by ill health.* ▸ n. **1** an act of riding. **2** a roller coaster, merry-go-round, etc., ridden at a fair or amusement park. **3** a path for horse riding. ■ **ride·a·ble** (also **ridable**) adj.

– PHRASES **be riding for a fall** informal be acting in a reckless way that invites failure. **let something ride** take no immediate action over something. **ride high** be successful. **a rough** (or **easy**) **ride** a difficult (or easy) time. **take someone for a ride** informal deceive someone.

rid·er /'rīdər/ ▸ n. **1** a person who rides a horse, bicycle, motorcycle, etc. **2** a condition added to something already agreed. ■ **rid·er·less** adj.

ridge /rij/ ▸ n. **1** a long narrow hilltop or mountain range. **2** a narrow raised strip on a surface. **3** Meteorology a long, narrow region of high pressure. **4** the edge formed where the two sloping sides of a roof meet at the top. ▸ v. (often as adj. **ridged**) form something into ridges. ■ **ridg·y** adj.

ridge tent ▸ n. a tent with a central ridge

supported by a pole or frame at each end.

rid·i·cule /'ridi,kyōōl/ ▸ n. the use of language to make fun of someone or something in an unkind way: *he became an object of ridicule among his own aides.* ▸ v. mock or make fun of someone or something.

ri·dic·u·lous /ri'dikyələs/ ▸ adj. very silly or unreasonable; absurd. ■ **ri·dic·u·lous·ly** adv. **ri·dic·u·lous·ness** n.

rid·ing /'rīdiNG/ ▸ n. the sport or activity of riding horses.

rid·ing crop ▸ n. a short flexible whip with a loop for the hand, used when riding horses.

rid·ing hab·it ▸ n. a woman's riding dress, consisting of a skirt and a double-breasted jacket.

Ries·ling /'rēzliNG, 'rēs-/ ▸ n. a dry white wine made from a variety of grape grown especially in Germany and Austria.

rife /rīf/ ▸ adj. **1** (especially of something undesirable) widespread: *drug addiction is rife.* **2** (**rife with**) full of something, especially something undesirable.

riff /rif/ ▸ n. a short repeated phrase in popular music or jazz. ▸ v. play riffs.

rif·fle /'rifəl/ ▸ v. **1** turn over the pages of a book or document quickly and casually. **2** (**riffle through**) search quickly through. ▸ n. an act of turning over pages or searching through something.

riff·raff /'rif,raf/ ▸ n. people who are considered disreputable or socially unacceptable.

ri·fle[1] /'rīfəl/ ▸ n. **1** a gun having a long spirally grooved barrel to make a bullet spin and thereby increase accuracy over a long distance. **2** (**rifles**) troops armed with rifles. ▸ v. **1** (usu. as adj. **rifled**) make spiral grooves in a gun or its barrel or bore. **2** hit or kick a ball hard and straight.

ri·fle[2] ▸ v. **1** search through something hurriedly to find or steal something. **2** steal something.

ri·fle·man /'rīfəlmən/ ▸ n. (pl. **riflemen**) a soldier armed with a rifle.

ri·fle range ▸ n. a place for practicing shooting with rifles.

ri·fling /'rīf(ə)liNG/ ▸ n. spiral grooves on the inside of a rifle barrel.

rift /rift/ ▸ n. **1** a crack, split, or break. **2** a serious break in friendly relations.

rift val·ley ▸ n. a steep-sided valley formed by subsidence of the earth's surface between nearly parallel faults.

rig[1] /rig/ ▸ v. (**rigs, rigging, rigged**) **1** provide a boat with sails and rigging. **2** assemble and adjust the equipment of a sailboat, aircraft, etc., in readiness for operation. **3** set up a device or structure, often in a makeshift way: *he'd rigged up a sort of tent.* **4** (**rig someone out**) dress someone in a particular outfit. ▸ n. **1** the arrangement of a boat's sails and rigging. **2** equipment or a device for a particular purpose: *a lighting rig.* **3** an oil rig or drilling rig. **4** a person's costume or outfit. **5** a truck. ■ **rigged** adj.

rig[2] ▸ v. (**rigs, rigging, rigged**) manage or arrange in a dishonest way so as to gain an advantage: *the results of the elections had been rigged.*

rig·a·to·ni /,rigə'tōnē/ ▸ pl.n. pasta in the form of short hollow fluted tubes.

rig·ger /'rigər/ ▸ n. **1** (in combination) a ship rigged in a particular way: *a square-rigger*. **2** a person who erects and maintains scaffolding or cranes. **3** a person who works on or helps to build an oil rig.

rig·ging /'rigiNG/ ▸ n. **1** the system of ropes or chains supporting a ship's masts and controlling or setting the yards and sails. **2** the ropes and wires supporting the structure of a hang-glider or parachute.

right /rīt/ ▸ adj. **1** on, toward, or relating to the side of a person or thing that is to the east when the person or thing is facing north. **2** morally good, justified, or acceptable: *I hope we're doing the right thing*. **3** factually correct. **4** most appropriate: *the right man for the job*. **5** in a satisfactory, sound, or normal condition. **6** relating to a right-wing person or group.
▸ adv. **1** on or to the right side. **2** to the furthest extent or degree; completely: *the car spun right off the track*. **3** exactly; directly. **4** in a correct or satisfactory way. **5** informal without delay; immediately. ▸ n. **1** that which is morally right. **2** a moral or legal entitlement to have or do something: *you have every right to be angry*. **3** (**rights**) the authority to perform, publish, or film a particular work or event. **4** (**the right**) the right-hand part, side, or direction. **5** a right turn. **6** a person's right fist, or a blow given with it. **7** (often **the Right**) (treated as sing. or pl.) a group or political party favoring conservative views. ▸ v. **1** return someone or something to a normal or upright position. **2** return to a normal or correct condition: *righting the economy demanded cuts in defense spending*. **3** make amends for a wrong. ■ **right·er** n. **right·ish** adj. **right·most** /'rīt,mōst/ adj. **right·ness** n. **right·ward** /'rītwərd/ adj. & adv. **right·wards** /'rītwərdz/ adv.
– PHRASES **by rights** if things were fair or correct. **in one's own right** as a result of one's own qualifications or efforts. **put** (or **set**) **someone right** tell someone the true facts of a situation. **put** (or **set**) **something to rights** return something to its correct or normal state. **right** (or **straight**) **away** immediately. **right on** informal **1** expressing support, approval, or encouragement. **2** (**right-on**) informal precisely correct: *I think the Japanese have it the most right-on*. **3** (**right-on**) Brit. informal, often derogatory in keeping with fashionable liberal or left-wing opinions and values.

right an·gle ▸ n. an angle of 90°, as in a corner of a square. ■ **right-an·gled** adj.
– PHRASES **at right angles to** forming an angle of 90° with.

right-click ▸ v. press the right-hand button on a computer mouse. ▸ n. an act of right-clicking.

right·eous /'rīCHəs/ ▸ adj. **1** morally right or justifiable: *righteous indignation about pay and conditions*. **2** (of a person) morally good; virtuous. ■ **right·eous·ly** adv. **right·eous·ness** n.

right field ▸ n. Baseball **1** the part of the outfield to the right of center field from the perspective of home plate. **2** the position of the defensive player stationed in right field.

right·ful /'rītfəl/ ▸ adj. **1** having a legal or moral right to something. **2** rightly claimed; appropriate: *helping the sport reach its rightful place in the Olympics*. ■ **right·ful·ly** adv. **right·ful·ness** n.

right hand ▸ n. **1** the region or direction on the right side of someone or something. **2** the most

important position next to someone. ▸ adj. **1** on or toward the right side. **2** done with or using the right hand.

right-hand·ed ▸ adj. **1** (of a person) using the right hand more naturally than the left. **2** done with the right hand. **3** turning to the right; toward the right. **4** (of a screw) that is to be turned clockwise.

right-hand·er /'handər/ ▸ n. **1** a right-handed person. **2** a blow struck with a person's right hand.

right-hand man ▸ n. a person's chief assistant.

right·ism /'rīt,izəm/ ▸ n. the political views or policies of the right. ■ **right·ist** /'rītist/ n. & adj.

right·ly /'rītlē/ ▸ adv. **1** in accordance with what is true, morally right, or just. **2** with good reason.

right-mind·ed (also **right-thinking**)
▸ adj. having views and principles that most people approve of.

right of way ▸ n. **1** the legal right to pass along a specific route through another's property. **2** a public path through another's property. **3** the right of a vehicle or ship to go before another.

Right Rev·er·end ▸ adj. a title given to a bishop, especially in the Anglican Church.

right side ▸ n. the side of something intended to be at the top or front.
– PHRASES **on the right side of 1** in favor with. **2** rather less than a specified age.

right-size /'rīt,sīz/ ▸ v. convert something to an appropriate size, especially by reducing staff levels in an organization.

rights of·fer·ing ▸ n. an issue of shares offered at a special price by a company to its existing shareholders.

right-to-die ▸ adj. relating to or advocating the right to refuse extraordinary measures intended to prolong someone's life when they are terminally ill or comatose.

right-to-life ▸ adj. another term for PRO-LIFE.

right whale ▸ n. a whale with a large head and a deeply curved jaw, of Arctic and temperate waters.

right wing ▸ n. **1** the conservative or reactionary section of a political party or system. **2** the right side of a sports team on the field or of an army. ■ **right-wing·er** n.

rig·id /'rijid/ ▸ adj. **1** unable to bend or be forced out of shape. **2** not able to be changed or adapted: *rigid rules governing the production of certain wines*. **3** stiff and unmoving, especially with fear. ■ **ri·gid·i·fy** /rə'jidə,fī/ v. (**rigidifies, rigidifying, rigidified**) **ri·gid·i·ty** /rə'jidətē/ n. **rig·id·ly** adv.

rig·ma·role /'rig(ə)mə,rōl/ ▸ n. **1** a lengthy and complicated procedure. **2** a long, rambling story.

rig·or /'rigər/ (Brit. **rigour**) ▸ n. **1** the quality of being thorough or severe: *his analysis is lacking in rigor*. **2** (**rigors**) demanding or extreme conditions.

rig·or mor·tis /,rigər 'môrtəs/ ▸ n. stiffening of the joints and muscles a few hours after death, lasting from one to four days.

rig·or·ous /'rigərəs/ ▸ adj. **1** very thorough or accurate. **2** (of a rule or system) strictly applied or followed. **3** strictly following a belief or system. **4** harsh and demanding: *rigorous military training*. ■ **rig·or·ous·ly** adv. **rig·or·ous·ness** n.

rijst·ta·fel /'rī,stäfəl/ ▸n. a meal of SE Asian food consisting of a selection of spiced rice dishes.

rile /rīl/ ▸v. informal annoy or irritate someone.

Ri·ley /'rīlē/ ▸n. (in phrase **the life of Riley**) informal a luxurious or carefree existence.

rill /ril/ ▸n. a small stream.

rim /rim/ ▸n. **1** the upper or outer edge of something circular. **2** (also **wheel rim**) the outer edge of a wheel, on which the tire is fitted. **3** a stain or deposit left on a surface by dirty water. ▸v. (**rims, rimming, rimmed**) provide or mark with a rim: *a lake rimmed by glaciers*. ■ **rim·less** adj.

rime /rīm/ ▸n. technical & literary hoar frost. ▸v. literary cover something with hoar frost. ■ **rim·y** adj.

rind /rīnd/ ▸n. the tough skin of some fruit, or the hard outer edge of cheese or bacon. ■ **rind·ed** adj. **rind·less** adj.

ring[1] /riNG/ ▸n. **1** a small circular metal band worn on a finger. **2** a circular band, object, or mark. **3** an enclosed space in which a sport, performance, or show takes place. **4** a group of people or things arranged in a circle. **5** a group of people involved in a shared activity, especially one that is illegal or secret: *a drug ring.* **6** a number of atoms bonded together to form a closed loop in a molecule. ▸v. **1** surround someone or something. **2** chiefly Brit. draw a circle around something. ■ **ringed** adj.
– PHRASES **run rings around** informal outclass or outwit easily.

ring[2] ▸v. (past **rang**; past part. **rung**) **1** make or cause to make a clear resounding sound. **2** (**ring with**) be filled or resound with a sound. **3** telephone someone. **4** call for attention by sounding a bell. **5** sound the hour or a peal on a bell or bells. **6** (of the ears) be filled with a buzzing or humming sound due to a blow or loud noise. **7** convey a specified impression or quality: *her honesty rings true.* **8** (**ring something up**) record an amount on a cash register. ▸n. **1** an act of ringing. **2** a resounding sound or tone. **3** informal a telephone call: *give me a ring.* **4** a quality conveyed by something heard: *the tale had a ring of truth.* **5** a set of bells, especially church bells.
– PHRASES **ring down** (or **up**) **the curtain 1** lower (or raise) a theater curtain. **2** mark the end (or beginning) of something.

ring bind·er ▸n. a loose-leaf binder with ring-shaped clasps that can be opened to pass through holes in the paper.

ring·er /'riNGər/ ▸n. **1** a person or device that rings. **2** informal another term for DEAD RINGER. **3** informal an athlete or horse fraudulently substituted for another in a competition.

ring fin·ger ▸n. the finger next to the little finger of the left hand, on which the wedding ring is worn.

ring·ing /'riNGiNG/ ▸adj. **1** having a clear resounding tone or sound. **2** (of a statement) forceful and completely clear. ■ **ring·ing·ly** adv.

ring·lead·er /'riNG,lēdər/ ▸n. a person who leads others in crime or causing trouble.

ring·let /'riNGlit/ ▸n. a corkscrew-shaped curl of hair. ■ **ring·let·ted** (also **ringleted**) adj.

ring·mas·ter /'riNG,mastər/ ▸n. the person who directs a circus performance.

ring mold ▸n. a ring-shaped open-topped container used for making molds and cakes.

ring road ▸n. Brit. a bypass encircling a town.

ring·side /'riNG,sīd/ ▸n. the area beside a boxing ring or circus ring. ■ **ring·sid·er** n.

ring·side seat ▸n. a very good position from which to observe something.

ring·tone /'riNG,tōn/ ▸n. a sound made by a cell phone when an incoming call is received.

ring·worm /'riNG,wərm/ ▸n. a skin disease occurring in small circular itchy patches, caused by various fungi and affecting chiefly the scalp or feet.

rink /riNGk/ ▸n. **1** (also **ice rink**) an enclosed area of ice for skating, ice hockey, or curling. **2** (also **roller rink**) a smooth enclosed floor for roller skating. **3** (also **bowling rink**) the strip of a lawn bowling green used for a match. **4** a team in curling or lawn bowling.

rinse /rins/ ▸v. **1** wash something with clean water to remove soap or dirt. **2** (often **rinse something off/out**) remove soap or dirt by rinsing. ▸n. **1** an act of rinsing. **2** a liquid for conditioning or coloring the hair. **3** an antiseptic liquid for cleaning the mouth. ■ **rins·er** n.

Ri·o·ja /rē'ōhä/ ▸n. a wine produced in La Rioja, Spain.

ri·ot /'rīət/ ▸n. **1** a violent public disturbance by a crowd of people. **2** a large or varied display or combination: *the garden was a riot of color.* **3** (**a riot**) informal a highly amusing or entertaining person or thing. ▸v. take part in a riot. ■ **ri·ot·er** n.
– PHRASES **read someone the Riot Act** give someone a severe warning or reprimand. **run riot 1** behave in a violent and uncontrolled way. **2** spread uncontrollably.

ri·ot·ous /'rīətəs/ ▸adj. **1** involving uncontrolled behavior, especially in celebration of something: *a riotous party.* **2** having a vivid, varied appearance. **3** involving public disorder. ■ **ri·ot·ous·ly** adv. **ri·ot·ous·ness** n.

RIP ▸abbr. rest in peace (used on graves).

rip[1] /rip/ ▸v. (**rips, ripping, ripped**) **1** tear or pull something forcibly away from something or someone. **2** make a tear or hole in something. **3** move forcefully and rapidly: *a fire ripped through the building.* **4** (**rip someone off**) informal cheat someone. **5** (**rip something off**) informal steal or copy something. ▸n. a long tear or cut. ■ **rip·per** n.
– PHRASES **let rip** informal **1** do something without restraint. **2** express oneself forcefully or angrily.

rip[2] (also **rip tide**) ▸n. a stretch of fast-flowing and rough water caused by the meeting of currents.

ri·par·i·an /ri'pe(ə)rēən, rī-/ ▸adj. relating to or situated on the banks of a river.

rip·cord /'rip,kôrd/ ▸n. a cord that is pulled to open a parachute.

ripe /rīp/ ▸adj. **1** (of fruit or grain) ready for harvesting and eating. **2** (of a cheese or wine) full-flavored and mature. **3** (**ripe for**) having reached a fitting time for: *land ripe for development.* **4** (**ripe with**) full of something. ■ **ripe·ly** adv. **ripe·ness** n.
– PHRASES **ripe old age** a person's age that is very old.

rip·en /'rīpən/ ▸v. become or make ripe or ready for eating.

rip-off ▸n. informal **1** an article that is greatly overpriced. **2** a poor-quality copy of something.

ri·poste /ri'pōst/ ▸n. **1** a quick clever reply to a critical or insulting remark. **2** a quick return thrust in fencing. ▶ v. make a quick clever reply to an insult or criticism.

rip·ple /ˈripəl/ ▶ n. **1** a small wave or series of waves. **2** a sound or feeling that spreads through a person, group, or place: *a ripple of laughter went around the hall.* **3** a type of ice cream with wavy lines of colored flavored syrup running through it. **4** a small periodic variation in voltage. ▶ v. **1** form or move with a series of small waves. **2** (of a sound or feeling) spread through a person, group, or place. ■ **rip·ply** adj.

rip-roar·ing ▶ adj. full of energy and excitement.

rip·saw /ˈripˌsô/ ▶ n. a coarse saw for cutting wood along the grain.

rip·stop /ˈripˌstäp/ ▶ n. nylon fabric that is woven so that a tear will not spread.

RISC /risk/ ▶ n. reduced instruction set computer; computing based on a form of microprocessor designed to perform a limited set of operations very quickly.

rise /rīz/ ▶ v. (past **rose** /rōz/; past part. **risen** /ˈrizən/) **1** come up or go up. **2** get up from lying, sitting, or kneeling. **3** increase in number, size, intensity, or quality: *house prices had risen.* **4** (of land) slope upward. **5** (of the sun, moon, or stars) appear above the horizon. **6** reach a higher social or professional position. **7** (**rise above**) succeed in not being restricted by: *try to rise above prejudice.* **8** (**rise to**) respond well to a challenging situation. **9** (often **rise up**) rebel against authority. **10** (of a river) have its source in a particular place. ▶ n. **1** an act of rising. **2** an increase in number, size, amount, or degree. **3** an upward slope or hill. **4** the vertical height of a step or slope.
– PHRASES **get a rise out of** informal provoke an angry or irritated response from. **on the rise 1** increasing. **2** becoming more successful. **rise and shine** informal wake up and get out of bed promptly. **rise from the dead** come to life again.

ris·er /ˈrīzər/ ▶ n. **1** a person who usually gets out of bed at a particular time of the morning: *an early riser.* **2** a vertical section between the treads of a staircase. **3** a vertical pipe for the upward flow of liquid or gas.

ris·i·ble /ˈrizəbəl/ ▶ adj. causing laughter; ridiculous. ■ **ris·i·bil·i·ty** /ˌrizəˈbilətē/ n. **ris·i·bly** /-blē/ adv.

ris·ing /ˈrīziNG/ ▶ n. a rebellion or revolt. ▶ adj. approaching a specified age.

risk /risk/ ▶ n. **1** a situation that could be dangerous or have an undesirable outcome: *outdoor activities carry an element of risk.* **2** the possibility that something unpleasant will happen. **3** a person or thing regarded as a likely source of danger or harm: *gloss paint can pose a fire risk.* ▶ v. **1** expose someone or something to danger, harm, or loss. **2** act in such a way as to make an undesirable outcome possible: *children risk serious injury as a result of strenuous gymnastics training.* **3** take a risk by engaging in a particular activity.
– PHRASES **at one's** (**own**) **risk** taking responsibility for one's own safety or possessions. **run** (or **take**) **a risk** (or **risks**) act in such a way as to make an undesirable outcome possible.

risk cap·i·tal ▶ n. another term for VENTURE CAPITAL.

risk·y /ˈriskē/ ▶ adj. (**riskier, riskiest**) involving the possibility of danger, failure, or loss.

■ **risk·i·ly** adv. **risk·i·ness** n.

ri·sot·to /riˈzôtō, -ˈsôtō/ ▶ n. (pl. **risottos**) an Italian dish of rice cooked in stock with ingredients such as meat or seafood.

ris·qué /riˈskā/ ▶ adj. referring to sex in an indecent or slightly shocking way.

ris·sole /riˈsōl, ˈrisˌōl/ ▶ n. chiefly Brit. a small cake or ball of meat and spices, coated in breadcrumbs and fried.

ri·tar·dan·do /ˌrētärˈdändō, ˌri-/ ▶ adv. & adj. Music with a gradual decrease of speed.

rite /rīt/ ▶ n. **1** a religious or other solemn ceremony or act. **2** a set of customary practices typical of a Church or a part of it: *the celebration of the full Roman rite.*
– PHRASES **rite of passage** a ceremony or event, e.g., marriage, marking an important stage in someone's life.

rit·u·al /ˈriCHŌōəl/ ▶ n. **1** a religious or solemn ceremony involving a series of actions performed according to a set order. **2** a set order of performing such a ceremony. **3** a series of actions done regularly and without variation: *it became a ritual to take her out every week to the hairdresser.* ▶ adj. relating to or done as a ritual. ■ **rit·u·al·ly** adv.

rit·u·al·is·tic /ˌriCHŌōəˈlistik/ ▶ adj. relating to or followed as part of a religious or other ritual: *a ritualistic act of worship.* ■ **rit·u·al·is·ti·cal·ly** adv. **rit·u·al·ism** /ˈriCHŌōəˌlizəm/ n.

rit·u·al·ize /ˈriCHŌōəˌlīz/ ▶ v. make something into a ritual by following a pattern of actions or behavior. ■ **rit·u·al·i·za·tion** /ˌriCHŌōələˈzāSHən/ n.

ritz·y /ˈritsē/ ▶ adj. (**ritzier, ritziest**) informal expensively stylish.

ri·val /ˈrīvəl/ ▶ n. **1** a person or thing competing with another for the same objective or to be better than the other. **2** a person or thing equal to another in quality: *she has no rivals as a female rock singer.* ▶ v. (**rivals, rivaling, rivaled**) be equal or comparable to: *a weekly TV ad budget that rivals that of any Broadway musical.* ■ **ri·val·rous** /ˈrīvəlrəs/ adj.

ri·val·ry /ˈrīvəlrē/ ▶ n. (pl **rivalries**) a situation in which two people or groups are competing for the same thing.

rive /rīv/ ▶ v. (past **rived** /rīvd/; past part. **riven** /ˈrivən/) (usu. **be riven**) literary tear apart or split.

riv·er /ˈrivər/ ▶ n. **1** a large natural flow of water traveling along a channel to the sea, a lake, or another river. **2** a large quantity of a flowing liquid.
– PHRASES **sell someone down the river** informal betray someone.

riv·er·bank /ˈrivərˌbaNGk/ ▶ n. the bank of a river.

riv·er·bed /ˈrivərˌbed/ ▶ n. the bed or channel in which a river flows.

riv·er·boat /ˈrivərˌbōt/ ▶ n. a boat designed for use on rivers.

riv·er·ine /ˈrivəˌrīn, -ˌrēn/ ▶ adj. technical or literary relating to or situated on a river or riverbank.

riv·er·side /ˈrivərˌsīd/ ▶ n. the ground along a riverbank.

riv·et /ˈrivit/ ▶ n. a short metal pin or bolt for holding together two metal plates, its headless end being beaten out or pressed down when in place. ▶ v. (**rivets, riveting, riveted**) **1** join metal plates with a rivet or rivets. **2** hold someone's interest or attention completely: *moviegoers*

have been riveted by great car chases for years.
■ **riv·et·er** n. **riv·et·ing** adj.

riv·i·er·a /ˌrivē'e(ə)rə, ri'vye(ə)rə/ ▶ n. a coastal region with a subtropical climate and vegetation, especially that of southern France and northern Italy.

riv·u·let /'riv(y)ələt/ ▶ n. a very small stream.

ri·yal /rē'(y)ôl, rē'(y)äl/ ▶ n. variant spelling of RIAL.

RN ▶ abbr. **1** registered nurse. **2** (in the UK) Royal Navy.

Rn ▶ symbol the chemical element radon.

RNA ▶ n. ribonucleic acid, a substance in living cells that carries instructions from DNA for controlling the synthesis of proteins.

roach[1] /rōch/ ▶ n. informal **1** a cockroach. **2** the butt of a marijuana cigarette.

■ **roach**[2] ▶ n. (pl. same) a common freshwater fish of the carp family.

road /rōd/ ▶ n. **1** a wide way between places, especially one with a hard surface for vehicles to travel on. **2** a way to achieving a particular outcome: *he's well on the road to recovery.* **3** (usu. **roads**) a partly sheltered stretch of water near the shore in which ships can ride at anchor.
■ **road·less** adj.
– PHRASES **one for the road** informal a final alcoholic drink before leaving. **on the road 1** on a long journey or series of journeys. **2** (of a car) able to be driven.

road·bed /'rōd,bed/ ▶ n. **1** material laid down to form a road, or on which railroad tracks are laid. **2** the part of a road on which vehicles travel.

road·block /'rōd,bläk/ ▶ n. a barrier put across a road by the police or army to stop and examine traffic.

road hog ▶ n. informal a motorist who makes it difficult for others to pass.

road·hold·ing /'rōd,hōldiNG/ ▶ n. chiefly Brit. the ability of a moving vehicle to remain stable, especially when cornering at high speeds.

road·house /'rōd,hous/ ▶ n. a tavern or restaurant on a country road.

road·ie /'rōdē/ ▶ n. informal a person employed by a touring pop or rock group to set up and maintain equipment.

road·kill /'rōd,kil/ ▶ n. animals killed on the road by a vehicle.

road·map /'rōd,map/ ▶ n. **1** a map showing the roads of an area. **2** a document setting out the procedure for achieving a goal: *a roadmap for peace.*

road pric·ing ▶ n. the practice of charging motorists to use busy roads at certain times, especially to relieve congestion.

road rage ▶ n. violent anger arising from conflict with the driver of another motor vehicle.

road·run·ner /'rōd,rənər/ ▶ n. a slender fast-running bird of the cuckoo family, found chiefly in arid country from the southern US to Central America.

road·show /'rōd,SHō/ ▶ n. **1** each of a series of radio or television programs broadcast on location from different places. **2** a touring political or promotional campaign.

road·side /'rōd,sīd/ ▶ n. the strip of land beside a road.

road·stead /'rōd,sted/ ▶ n. another term for ROAD (sense 3).

road·ster /'rōdstər/ ▶ n. an open-top car with two seats.

road test ▶ n. **1** a test of the performance of a vehicle or engine on the road. **2** a test of a driver's competence, required for obtaining a driver's license. **3** a test of equipment carried out in working conditions. ▶ v. (**road-test**) **1** test a vehicle or engine on the road. **2** try out something under working conditions, especially before it is made generally available: *we road-tested a new laptop computer.*

road·way /'rōd,wā/ ▶ n. **1** a road. **2** the part of a road intended for vehicles, in contrast to a sidewalk or median.

road·work /'rōd,wərk/ ▶ pl.n. repairs to roads or to pipes or cables under roads.

road·wor·thy /'rōd,wərTHē/ ▶ adj. (of a vehicle) fit to be used on the road. ■ **road·wor·thi·ness** n.

roam /rōm/ ▶ v. **1** travel aimlessly over a wide area. **2** (of the eyes or hands) pass lightly over something without stopping. ■ **roam·er** n.

roam·ing /'rōmiNG/ ▶ n. the use of or ability to use a cell phone outside of its network area.

roan /rōn/ ▶ adj. (of a horse or cow) having a coat that is mainly bay, chestnut, or black mixed with another color, typically white. ▶ n. a roan animal.

roar /rôr/ ▶ n. **1** a long, deep sound such as that made by a lion, natural force, or engine. **2** a loud, deep sound uttered by a person, especially as an expression of pain, anger, or amusement. ▶ v. **1** make a roar. **2** laugh loudly. **3** move, act, or happen fast or decisively: *Korean stocks roared back, closing with a gain of almost five percent.*

roar·ing /'rôriNG/ ▶ adj. informal complete: *a roaring success.* ■ **roar·ing·ly** adv.
– PHRASES **do a roaring trade** informal, chiefly Brit. do very good business. **the roaring forties** stormy ocean areas between latitudes 40° and 50° south. **the roaring twenties** the prosperous years of the 1920s.

roast /rōst/ ▶ v. **1** cook meat or vegetables in an oven or over a fire. **2** process coffee beans, nuts, etc., in intense heat. **3** make or become very warm. **4** informal criticize or reprimand someone severely. **5** informal offer a mocking tribute to someone. ▶ adj. (of food) having been roasted. ▶ n. **1** a cut of meat that has been roasted or that is intended for roasting. **2** the process of roasting something, especially coffee. **3** an outdoor party at which food is roasted: *a pig roast.* **4** a banquet to honor a person with good-natured ridicule. ■ **roast·er** n.

roast·ing /'rōstiNG/ informal ▶ adj. very hot and dry. ▶ n. a severe criticism or reprimand.

rob /räb/ ▶ v. (**robs**, **robbing**, **robbed**) **1** take property unlawfully from a person or place by force or threat of force. **2** (**rob someone of**) deprive someone of something needed, deserved, or important. **3** informal overcharge someone. ■ **rob·ber** n.
– PHRASES **rob Peter to pay Paul** deprive one person of something in order to pay another.

rob·ber·y /'räb(ə)rē/ ▶ n. (pl. **robberies**) **1** the action of robbing a person or place. **2** informal blatant overcharging.

robe /rōb/ ▶ n. **1** a loose outer garment reaching to the ankles, often worn on formal or ceremonial occasions as an indication of the wearer's rank, office, or profession. **2** a bathrobe. ▶ v. dress someone or oneself in a robe.

rob·in /'räbən/ ▶ n. **1** (also **American robin**) a

large North American thrush with an orange-red breast. **2** a small European songbird with a red breast and brown back and wings.

ro·bot /ˈrōˌbät, ˈrōbət/ ▶ n. a machine capable of carrying out a complex series of actions automatically, especially one programmable by a computer. ■ **ro·bot·ize** /ˈrōbəˌtīz/ v.

ro·bot·ic /rōˈbätik/ ▶ adj. **1** relating to robots. **2** mechanical, stiff, or unemotional. ■ **ro·bot·i·cal·ly** /-ik(ə)lē/ adv.

ro·bot·ics /rōˈbätiks/ ▶ pl.n. (treated as sing.) the branch of technology concerned with the design, construction, and use of robots.

ro·bust /rōˈbəst, ˈrōˌbəst/ ▶ adj. **1** able to withstand heavy use; sturdy. **2** strong and healthy. **3** determined and forceful: *a robust approach to reform.* **4** (of wine or food) strong and rich in flavor or smell. ■ **ro·bust·ly** adv. **ro·bust·ness** n.

ro·bus·ta /rōˈbəstə/ ▶ n. a type of coffee bean from a West African species of coffee plant, used especially in making instant coffee.

rock¹ /räk/ ▶ n. **1** the hard mineral material of the earth's crust. **2** a mass of rock projecting out of the ground or water. **3** a boulder. **4** Geology any natural material with a distinctive composition of minerals. **5** informal a diamond or other precious stone.
– PHRASES **on the rocks** informal **1** in difficulties and likely to fail. **2** (of a drink) served undiluted and with ice cubes.

rock² ▶ v. **1** move gently to and fro or from side to side. **2** shake violently, especially because of an earthquake or explosion. **3** shock or distress greatly: *the company was rocked by the resignation of its chairman.* **4** informal dance to or play rock music. **5** (often as adj. **rocking**) informal (of a place) be exciting or full of social activity. ▶ n. **1** rock music. **2** rock and roll music. **3** a rocking movement.

rock·a·bil·ly /ˈräkəˌbilē/ ▶ n. a type of popular music combining rock and roll and country music.

rock and roll (also **rock 'n' roll**) ▶ n. a type of popular dance music originating in the 1950s, having a heavy beat and simple melodies.

rock-bot·tom ▶ adj. at the lowest possible level.

rock climb·ing ▶ n. the sport or pastime of climbing rock faces, especially with ropes and special equipment.

rock crys·tal ▶ n. transparent quartz, typically in the form of colorless hexagonal crystals.

rock dove ▶ n. a mainly blue-gray pigeon found on cliffs, the ancestor of domestic and wild pigeons.

rock·er /ˈräkər/ ▶ n. **1** a person who performs or enjoys rock music. **2** a rocking chair. **3** a curved bar or similar support on which something such as a chair can rock. **4** a rocking device forming part of a mechanism.
– PHRASES **off one's rocker** informal mad.

rock·et¹ /ˈräkit/ ▶ n. **1** a cylindrical missile or spacecraft propelled to a great height or distance by a stream of burning gases. **2** a firework or signal propelled in this way. ▶ v. (**rockets**, **rocketing**, **rocketed**) **1** increase very rapidly and suddenly. **2** move or progress very rapidly: *he rocketed to national stardom.* **3** attack something with rocket-propelled missiles.

rock·et² ▶ n. another term for ARUGULA.

rock·et·ry /ˈräkətrē/ ▶ n. the branch of science and technology concerned with rockets.

rock·et sci·ence ▶ n. humorous something very difficult to understand. ■ **rock·et sci·en·tist** n.

rock face ▶ n. a vertical surface of bare rock.

rock gar·den ▶ n. a heaped arrangement of rocks with soil between them, planted with rock plants.

rock·ing chair ▶ n. a chair mounted on rockers or springs.

rock·ing horse ▶ n. a model of a horse mounted on rockers or springs for a child to ride on.

rock music ▶ n. a form of popular music with a strong beat, played on electric guitars, drums, etc.

rock pool ▶ n. a pool of water among rocks along a shoreline.

rock salt ▶ n. common salt occurring naturally as a mineral.

rock-sol·id ▶ adj. completely firm or stable.

rock wool ▶ n. inorganic material made into matted fiber, used especially for insulation or soundproofing.

rock·y¹ /ˈräkē/ ▶ adj. (**rockier, rockiest**) **1** consisting of rock. **2** full of rocks.

rock·y² ▶ adj. (**rockier, rockiest**) unsteady or unstable.

ro·co·co /rəˈkōkō, ˌrōkəˈkō/ ▶ adj. **1** relating to an elaborately ornate style of European furniture or architecture of the 18th century. **2** (of music or literature) highly or excessively ornate. ▶ n. the rococo style of architecture, furniture, etc.

rod /räd/ ▶ n. **1** a thin straight bar, especially of wood or metal. **2** a fishing rod. **3** (**the rod**) the use of a stick for caning or flogging someone. **4** one of two types of light-sensitive cell in the retina of the eye, responsible mainly for monochrome vision in poor light. Compare with CONE.

rode /rōd/ ▶ past of RIDE.

ro·dent /ˈrōdnt/ ▶ n. a mammal of a large group including rats, mice, and squirrels and distinguished by strong constantly growing incisors.

ro·den·ti·cide /rōˈdentəˌsīd/ ▶ n. a poison used to kill rodents.

ro·de·o /ˈrōdēˌō, rəˈdāō/ ▶ n. (pl. **rodeos**) **1** a contest or entertainment in which cowboys show their skill at riding broncos, roping calves, etc. **2** a competitive display of other skills, such as motorcycle riding.

roe¹ /rō/ ▶ n. **1** (also **hard roe**) the mass of eggs contained in the ovaries of a female fish or shellfish, especially when ripe and used as food. **2** (**soft roe**) the ripe testes of a male fish, especially when used as food.

roe² (also **roe deer**) ▶ n. (pl. same or **roes**) a small deer with a reddish summer coat that turns grayish in winter.

roe·buck /ˈrōˌbək/ ▶ n. a male roe deer.

roent·gen /ˈrentgən, ˈrənt-, -jən/ ▶ n. a unit of quantity of ionizing radiation.

roent·gen·i·um /rentˈgenēəm, rənt-, -ˈje-/ ▶ n. a radioactive element produced artificially.

ro·gan josh /ˈrōgən ˈjäsH/ ▶ n. an Indian dish of curried meat in a rich tomato-based sauce.

rog·er /ˈräjər/ ▶ exclam. your message has been received (used in radio communication).

rogue /rōg/ ▸ n. **1** a dishonest or immoral man. **2** a mischievous but likable person. ▸ adj. **1** (of an elephant or other large wild animal) destructive and living apart from the herd. **2** behaving in a faulty, unpredictable, or dangerous way: *a rogue state.*

rogue di·al·ing ▸ n. the illicit use of software to command a computer to call premium-rate telephone numbers over the Internet.

ro·guer·y /ˈrōgərē/ ▸ n. (pl. **rogueries**) dishonest, immoral, or mischievous behavior.

rogues' gal·ler·y ▸ n. informal a collection of photographs of known criminals, used by police to identify suspects.

ro·guish /ˈrōgiSH/ ▸ adj. playfully mischievous: *a roguish smile.* ■ **ro·guish·ly** adv. **ro·guish·ness** n.

roil /roil/ ▸ v. **1** make a liquid muddy by disturbing the sediment. **2** (of a liquid) move in a turbulent way.

roist·er /ˈroistər/ ▸ v. enjoy oneself or celebrate in a noisy or boisterous way. ■ **roist·er·er** n. **roist·er·ous** adj.

role /rōl/ ▸ n. **1** an actor's part in a play, movie, etc. **2** a person's or thing's function in a particular situation: *religion plays a vital role in society.*

> USAGE
> Do not confuse **role** with **roll**. **Role** means 'a part played by an actor,' whereas **roll** mainly means 'move by turning over and over' or 'a rolling movement' (*a roll of the dice*).

role mod·el ▸ n. a person whom others look to as an example to be imitated.

role-play·ing (also **role-play**) ▸ n. the acting out of a particular role, either consciously (as a technique in psychotherapy or training) or unconsciously (in accordance with the expectations of society).

Rolf·ing /ˈrôlfiNG/ ▸ n. a deep massage technique aimed at releasing muscular tension by manipulating connective tissue.

roll /rōl/ ▸ v. **1** move by turning over and over on an axis. **2** move forward on wheels or with a smooth, wavelike motion: *the fog rolled across the fields.* **3** (of a moving ship, aircraft, or vehicle) sway from side to side. **4** (of a machine or device) begin operating. **5** (often **roll something up**) turn something flexible over and over on itself to form a cylindrical or round shape. **6** (**roll up**) curl up tightly. **7** flatten something by passing a roller over it or by passing it between rollers. **8** (of a loud, deep sound) resound or reverberate. **9** pronounce a consonant, typically an *r*, with a trill. ▸ n. **1** a cylinder formed by rolling flexible material. **2** a rolling movement. **3** a gymnastic exercise in which the body is rolled into a tucked position and turned in a forward or backward circle. **4** a long, deep, reverberating sound. **5** (in drumming) a sustained, rapid alternation of single or double strokes of each stick. **6** a very small loaf of bread. **7** an official list or register of names.
– PHRASES **a roll in the hay** informal an act of sex. **be rolling in it** (or **money**) informal be very rich. **on a roll** informal experiencing a prolonged spell of success or good luck. **roll in** informal **1** be received in large amounts. **2** arrive in a casual way in spite of being late. **roll of honor** a list of people whose deeds are honored, especially a list of those who have died in battle. **roll something**

out officially launch a new product. **roll something over** extend a financial arrangement. **roll up** informal arrive. **roll up one's sleeves** prepare to work or fight.

roll·back /ˈrōlˌbak/ ▸ n. **1** a reduction or decrease. **2** a reversion to a previous state or situation: *they opposed a rollback to Stalinism.* **3** Computing the process of restoring a database or program to a previous state, typically to recover from an error. ▸ v. Computing restore a database to a previous state.

roll bar ▸ n. a metal bar running up the sides and across the top of a vehicle, protecting the occupants if the car overturns.

roll call ▸ n. the reading aloud of a list of names to establish who is present.

rolled gold ▸ n. gold in the form of a thin coating applied to a nonprecious metal by rolling.

rolled oats ▸ pl.n. oats that have had the husks removed and been crushed.

roll·er /ˈrōlər/ ▸ n. **1** a rotating cylinder used to move, flatten, or spread something. **2** a small cylinder on which hair is rolled to produce curls. **3** a long swelling wave that appears to roll steadily toward the shore.

roll·er·ball /ˈrōlərˌbôl/ ▸ n. **1** a ballpoint pen using thinner ink than other such pens. **2** Computing an input device containing a ball that is moved with the fingers to control the cursor.

roll·er bear·ing ▸ n. a bearing similar to a ball bearing but using small rollers instead of balls.

Roll·er·blade /ˈrōlərˌblād/ ▸ n. trademark a skate with wheels fixed in a single line. ▸ v. skate using Rollerblades. ■ **roll·er·blad·er** n. **roll·er·blad·ing** n.

roll·er coast·er ▸ n. a fairground attraction consisting of a light railroad track with many tight turns and steep slopes, on which people ride in small open cars.

roll·er rink ▸ n. see RINK (sense 2).

roll·er skate ▸ n. each of a pair of boots having four or more small wheels and used for gliding across a hard surface. ■ **roll·er skat·er** n. **roll·er skat·ing** n.

rol·lick·ing /ˈrälikiNG/ ▸ adj. lively and amusing in a high-spirited way.

roll·ing /ˈrōliNG/ ▸ adj. **1** (of land) extending in a series of gently rounded hills. **2** done in regular stages over a period of time: *a rolling program of reforms.*

roll·ing pin ▸ n. a cylinder for rolling out dough.

roll·ing stock ▸ n. locomotives, cars, or other vehicles used on a railroad.

roll·ing stone ▸ n. a person who is unwilling to settle for long in one place.
– PHRASES **a rolling stone gathers no moss** proverb a person who does not settle in one place will not accumulate wealth, status, responsibilities, or commitments.

roll neck ▸ n. a high loosely turned-over collar.

roll-on ▸ adj. (of a deodorant or cosmetic) applied by means of a rotating ball in the neck of the container.

roll·out /ˈrōlˌout/ ▸ n. **1** the unveiling of a new aircraft or spacecraft. **2** the official launch of a new product or service. **3** Football a play in which the quarterback runs toward the sideline before attempting to pass or advance.

roll·o·ver /ˈrōlˌōvər/ ▸ n. the extension or transfer of a debt or other financial arrangement: *the* *plan does not allow for rollover of outstanding loans.*

roll·top desk /'rōl,täp/ ▸ n. a writing desk with a semicircular flexible cover sliding in curved grooves.

roll-up ▸ n. an article of food rolled up and sometimes with a filling: *ham roll-ups.*

ro·ly-po·ly /'rōlē 'pōlē/ ▸ adj. informal round and plump.

ROM /räm/ ▸ abbr. Computing read-only memory.

ro·maine /rō'mān/ ▸ n. a variety of lettuce with crisp narrow leaves.

Ro·man /'rōmən/ ▸ adj. 1 relating to the ancient city of Rome or its empire or people. 2 relating to the modern city of Rome. 3 referring to the alphabet used for writing Latin, English, and most European languages. 4 (**roman**) (of type) of a plain upright kind used in ordinary print. ▸ n. 1 an inhabitant of Rome. 2 (**roman**) roman type.

ro·man-à-clef /rō,män ä 'klā/ ▸ n. (pl. **romans-à-clef** pronunc. same) a novel in which real people or events appear with invented names.

Ro·man can·dle ▸ n. a firework giving off flaming colored balls and sparks.

Ro·man Cath·o·lic ▸ adj. relating to the Roman Catholic Church. ▸ n. a member of the Roman Catholic Church. ■ **Ro·man Ca·thol·i·cism** n.

Ro·man Cath·o·lic Church ▸ n. the part of the Christian Church that has the Pope as its head.

Ro·mance /rō'mans, 'rō,mans/ ▸ n. the group of languages descended from Latin, such as French, Spanish, Portuguese, and Italian.

ro·mance /rō'mans, 'rō,mans/ ▸ n. 1 a pleasurable feeling of excitement and wonder associated with love. 2 a love affair. 3 a book or movie dealing with love in a sentimental or idealized way. 4 a quality or feeling of mystery, excitement, and remoteness from everyday life: *the romance of the past.* 5 a medieval story dealing with the adventures of knights. ▸ v. 1 try to win someone's love. 2 informal seek someone's custom or attention: *he's being romanced by the big boys in New York.* 3 deal with something in an idealized way. ■ **ro·manc·er** n.

Ro·man Em·pire ▸ n. the empire under Roman rule established in 27 BC and divided into two parts in AD 395.

Ro·man·esque /,rōmə'nesk/ ▸ adj. relating to a style of architecture prevalent in Europe *c.* 900–1200, with massive vaulting and round arches.

Ro·ma·ni·an /rō'mānēən, rōō-/ (also **Rumanian** /rōō'mānēən, -nyən/) ▸ n. 1 a person from Romania. 2 the language of Romania. ▸ adj. relating to Romania.

ro·man·ize /'rōmə,nīz/ ▸ v. put written words into the Roman alphabet or into roman type. ■ **ro·man·i·za·tion** /,rōmənə'zāSHən/ n.

Ro·man law ▸ n. the law code of the ancient Romans forming the basis of civil law in many countries today.

Ro·man nose ▸ n. a nose with a high bridge.

Ro·man num·er·al ▸ n. any of the letters representing numbers in the ancient Roman system: I = 1, V = 5, X = 10, L = 50, C = 100, D = 500, M = 1,000.

Ro·ma·no /rə'mänō/ ▸ n. a strong-tasting hard cheese, originally made in Italy.

ro·man·tic /rō'mantik, rə-/ ▸ adj. 1 relating to or likely to lead to love or romance: *a romantic dinner for two.* 2 showing or regarding life in an idealized and unrealistic way: *Buffalo Bill is largely responsible for our romantic view of the Old West.* 3 (**Romantic**) relating to the artistic and literary movement of romanticism. ▸ n. 1 a person who is emotional and has an unrealistic view of life or love. 2 (**Romantic**) a writer or artist of the Romantic movement. ■ **ro·man·ti·cal·ly** /-ik(ə)lē/ adv.

ro·man·ti·cism /rō'mantə,sizəm, rə-/ ▸ n. a literary and artistic movement that began in the late 18th century and emphasized creative inspiration and individual feeling. ■ **ro·man·ti·cist** n.

ro·man·ti·cize /rō'mantə,sīz, rə-/ ▸ v. deal with or describe in an idealized or unrealistic way: *folklore romanticizes pirates, who made their living by murder and robbery.* ■ **ro·man·ti·ci·za·tion** /rō,mantəsə'zāSHən, rə-/ n.

Rom·a·ny /'rämənē, 'rō-/ ▸ n. (pl. **Romanies**) 1 the language of the Gypsies. 2 a Gypsy.

rom·com /'räm,käm/ ▸ n. informal (in movies or television) a romantic comedy.

Ro·me·o /'rōmē,ō/ ▸ n. (pl. **Romeos**) an attractive, passionate male lover.

romp /rämp, rômp/ ▸ v. 1 play around roughly and energetically. 2 informal achieve or win something easily. 3 informal engage in sexual activity. ▸ n. 1 a spell of romping. 2 a lighthearted movie or other work. 3 informal an easy victory.

romp·er suit /'rämpər, 'rôm-/ (also **rompers** /'rämpər, 'rôm-/) ▸ n. a young child's one-piece outer garment.

ron·deau /'rändō, rän'dō/ ▸ n. (pl. **rondeaux** pronunc. same or /-dōz, 'dōz/) a poem of ten or thirteen lines with only two rhymes throughout and with the opening words used twice as a refrain.

ron·do /'rändō, rän'dō/ ▸ n. (pl. **rondos**) a musical form with a recurring leading theme, often found in the final movement of a sonata or concerto.

rönt·gen ▸ n. variant spelling of ROENTGEN.

roo /rōō/ ▸ n. Austral. informal a kangaroo.

rood /rōōd/ ▸ n. 1 a crucifix, especially one in a church. 2 chiefly Brit. a former measure of land area equal to a quarter of an acre.

rood screen ▸ n. a screen of wood or stone separating the nave from the chancel of a church.

roof /rōōf, rôôf/ ▸ n. (pl. **roofs**) 1 the structure forming the upper covering of a building or vehicle. 2 the top inner surface of a covered area or space. 3 the upper limit or level of prices or wages. ▸ v. cover a building with a roof. ■ **roof·er** n. **roof·less** adj.
– PHRASES **go through the roof** informal (of prices or figures) reach very high levels. **hit** (or **go through**) **the roof** informal suddenly become very angry. **the roof of the mouth** the palate.

roof·ing /'rōōfiNG, 'rôôf-/ ▸ n. material for constructing the roof of a building.

roof·line /'rōōf,līn, 'rôôf-/ ▸ n. the design or proportions of the roof of a building or vehicle.

roof rack ▸ n. a framework for carrying luggage or equipment on the roof of a vehicle.

roof·top /ˈro͞ofˌtäp, ˈro͞of-/ ▶ n. the outer surface of a building's roof.

rook[1] /ro͝ok/ ▶ n. a crow with black plumage and a bare face, nesting in colonies in treetops. ▶ v. informal swindle or overcharge someone.

rook[2] ▶ n. a chess piece, typically with its top in the shape of a battlement, that can move in any direction along a rank or file on which it stands.

rook·er·y /ˈro͝okərē/ ▶ n. (pl. **rookeries**) 1 a collection of rooks' nests high in a clump of trees. 2 a breeding colony of birds (especially seabirds), seals, or turtles.

rook·ie /ˈro͝okē/ ▶ n. informal a new recruit or member, especially in the army or police or a sports team.

room /ro͞om, ro͝om/ ▶ n. 1 a part of a building enclosed by walls, floor, and ceiling. 2 empty space that can be occupied or where something can be done: *there was no room to move.* 3 opportunity or scope: *there's room for improvement in kayak design.* ▶ v. share a room or apartment, especially at a college or similar institution.

room·ie /ˈro͞omē, ˈro͝omē/ ▶ n. informal a roommate.

room·ing house ▶ n. a private house providing rented accommodations.

room·mate /ˈro͞omˌmāt, ˈro͝om-/ ▶ n. 1 a person occupying the same room as another. 2 a person occupying the same apartment or house as another.

room serv·ice ▶ n. provision of food and drink to hotel guests in their rooms.

room tem·per·a·ture ▶ n. a comfortable indoor temperature, generally taken as about 70°F.

room·y /ˈro͞omē, ˈro͝omē/ ▶ adj. (**roomier**, **roomiest**) having plenty of room; spacious. ■ **room·i·ness** n.

roost /ro͞ost/ ▶ n. a place where birds or bats regularly settle to rest. ▶ v. (of a bird or bat) settle or gather for rest.

roost·er /ˈro͞ostər, ˈro͝ostər/ ▶ n. a male domestic fowl; a cock.

root[1] /ro͞ot, ro͝ot/ ▶ n. 1 a part of a plant normally below ground, which acts as a support and collects water and nutrients. 2 the part of a bodily organ or structure such as a hair that is embedded in tissue. 3 the basic cause, source, or origin: *money is the root of all evil.* 4 (**roots**) a person's family, ethnic, or cultural origins. 5 a form from which words have been made by adding prefixes or suffixes or by other modification. 6 Mathematics a number or quantity that when multiplied by itself one or more times gives a specified number or quantity. ▶ v. 1 (of a plant or cutting) establish roots. 2 establish deeply and firmly: *vegetarianism is rooted in Indian culture.* 3 (**be rooted**) stand completely still through fear or amazement. 4 (**root something out/up**) find and get rid of something. ■ **root·less** adj.
– PHRASES **at root** basically; fundamentally. **put down roots** begin to have a settled life in a place. **root and branch** Brit. (of a process or operation) thorough or radical. **take root** become established.

root[2] ▶ v. 1 (of an animal) turn up the ground with its snout in search of food. 2 search through something; rummage. 3 (**root for**) informal support a person or team enthusiastically.

root beer ▶ n. a carbonated drink made from an extract of the roots and bark of certain plants.

root ca·nal ▶ n. 1 the pulp-filled cavity in the root of a tooth. 2 a procedure to replace infected pulp in a root canal with an inert material.

root mean square ▶ n. Mathematics the square root of the arithmetic mean of the squares of a set of values.

root sign ▶ n. Mathematics the radical sign.

root·stock /ˈro͞otˌstäk, ˈro͝ot-/ ▶ n. 1 a rhizome. 2 a plant onto which another variety is grafted.

root·sy /ˈro͞otsē, ˈro͝ot-/ ▶ adj. informal (of music) not commercialized and emphasizing its traditional or ethnic origins.

root veg·e·ta·ble ▶ n. a carrot or other vegetable that grows as the root of a plant.

rope /rōp/ ▶ n. 1 a length of thick cord made by twisting together strands of hemp, nylon, etc. 2 a quantity of objects strung together: *a rope of pearls.* 3 (**the ropes**) the ropes enclosing a boxing or wrestling ring. 4 (**the ropes**) informal the established way of doing something: *I showed her the ropes.* ▶ v. 1 catch or tie someone or something with rope. 2 (**rope someone in/into**) persuade someone to take part in something.
– PHRASES **on the ropes 1** Boxing forced against the ropes by the opponent's attack. 2 in a state of near collapse.

rope lad·der ▶ n. two long ropes connected by short crosspieces, used as a ladder.

rop·y /ˈrōpē/ (also **ropey**) ▶ adj. (**ropier, ropiest**) 1 resembling a rope. 2 Brit. informal poor in quality or health. ■ **rop·i·ly** adv. **rop·i·ness** n.

Roque·fort /ˈrōkfərt/ ▶ n. trademark a soft blue cheese made from ewes' milk.

ror·qual /ˈrôrkwəl, -ˌkwôl/ ▶ n. a whale of a small group with pleated skin on the underside, e.g., the blue whale.

Ror·schach test /ˈrôrˌsHäk/ ▶ n. a test used in psychoanalysis, in which a standard set of symmetrical ink blots is presented to a person, who is asked to describe what they suggest or resemble.

ro·sa·ce·a /rōˈzāsH(ə)ə/ ▶ n. a condition in which some facial blood vessels enlarge, giving the cheeks and nose a flushed appearance.

ro·sa·ceous /rōˈzāsHəs/ ▶ adj. relating to plants of the rose family.

ro·sa·ry /ˈrōzərē/ ▶ n. (pl. **rosaries**) 1 (in the Roman Catholic Church) a form of devotion in which five (or fifteen) sets of ten Hail Marys are repeated. 2 a string of beads for keeping count of prayers said.

rose[1] /rōz/ ▶ n. 1 a sweet-smelling flower that grows on a prickly bush. 2 a perforated cap attached to a shower, the spout of a watering can, or the end of a hose to produce a spray. 3 a warm pink or light crimson color.
– PHRASES **come up roses** (of a situation) develop in a very favorable way. **come up** (or **out**) **smelling like roses** keep one's good reputation after involvement in a difficult situation.

rose[2] ▶ past of RISE.

ro·sé /rōˈzā/ ▶ n. deep pink wine colored by only brief contact with red grape skins.

ro·se·ate /ˈrōzēət, -ˌāt/ ▶ adj. literary rose-colored.

rose·bud /ˈrōzˌbəd/ ▶ n. the bud of a rose.

rose-col·ored (also **rose-tinted**) ▶ adj. (of a person's viewpoint) unrealistic and naive: *such thinking is the ultimate in rose-colored analysis.*

rose hip ▶ n. fuller form of HIP².

rose·mar·y /ˈrōzˌme(ə)rē/ ▶ n. an evergreen shrub of southern Europe, the leaves of which are used as an herb in cooking.

rose of Shar·on /ˈsharən, ˈsHe(ə)r-/ ▶ n. 1 a hardy hibiscus with pink or lavender flowers. 2 a low-growing St. John's wort with dense foliage and large golden-yellow flowers.

ro·sette /rōˈzet/ ▶ n. 1 a rose-shaped decoration made of ribbon, worn by supporters of a team or political party or awarded as a prize. 2 a design or object resembling a rose.

rose wa·ter ▶ n. scented water made with rose petals.

rose win·dow ▶ n. a circular window in a church with tracery radiating in a roselike pattern.

rose·wood /ˈrōzˌwo͝od/ ▶ n. a close-grained timber of a tropical tree, used for making furniture and musical instruments.

Rosh Ha·sha·nah /ˌrōsH (h)əˈsHōnə, ˌräsH, -ˈsHänə/ (also **Rosh Hashana**) ▶ n. the Jewish New Year festival.

Ro·si·cru·cian /ˌrōzəˈkro͞osHən, -ˌräzə-/ ▶ n. a member of a secretive 17th- and 18th-century society devoted to the study of alchemy and the occult. ▶ adj. relating to the Rosicrucians. ■ **Ro·si·cru·cian·ism** /-ˌnizəm/ n.

ros·in /ˈräzən/ ▶ n. a kind of resin produced by distilling oil of turpentine, used for treating the bows of stringed instruments. ▶ v. (**rosins, rosining, rosined**) rub or treat something with rosin.

ros·ter /ˈrästər, ˈrô-/ ▶ n. 1 a list of people's names together with the jobs they have to do at a particular time. 2 a list of athletes available for team selection. ▶ v. put a person's name on a roster.

ros·trum /ˈrästrəm, ˈrô-/ ▶ n. (pl. **rostra** /ˈrästrə, ˈrô-/ or **rostrums**) 1 a raised platform on which a person stands to make a public speech, play music, or conduct an orchestra. 2 a platform for supporting a movie or television camera.

ros·y /ˈrōzē/ ▶ adj. (**rosier, rosiest**) 1 (especially of a person's skin) pink. 2 promising or hopeful: *he painted a rosy picture of the future.* ■ **ros·i·ly** adv. **ros·i·ness** n.

rot /rät/ ▶ v. (**rots, rotting, rotted**) 1 (of organic matter) decompose by the action of bacteria and fungi; decay. 2 gradually get worse: *the education system has been allowed to rot.* ▶ n. 1 the process of decaying. 2 rotten or decayed matter. 3 a disease that causes tissue decay, especially in plants. 4 informal, chiefly Brit. nonsense; rubbish: *don't talk rot.*

Ro·ta·ry /ˈrōtərē/ ▶ n. a worldwide charitable society of business and professional people organized into local Rotary clubs. ■ **Ro·tar·i·an** /rōˈte(ə)rēən/ n. & adj.

ro·ta·ry /ˈrōtərē/ ▶ adj. 1 revolving around a center or axis. 2 having a rotating part or parts: *a rotary mower.*

ro·tate /ˈrōˌtāt/ ▶ v. 1 move in a circle around a central point or axis. 2 pass to each member of a group in a regularly recurring order: *the job of chairing the meeting rotates.* 3 grow different crops one after the other on the same area of land. ■ **ro·tat·a·ble** /ˈrōˌtātəbəl, rōˈtāt-/ adj.

ro·ta·tor /ˈrōˌtātər/ n. **ro·ta·to·ry** /ˈrōtəˌtôrē/ adj.

ro·ta·tion /rōˈtāsHən/ ▶ n. 1 the action of rotating around a central point. 2 the action or system of changing people or things in a repeated sequence: *crop rotation.* 3 a complete circular movement around a central point. ■ **ro·ta·tion·al** adj. **ro·ta·tion·al·ly** adv.

ROTC /ˈrätsē/ ▶ abbr. Reserve Officers' Training Corps.

rote /rōt/ ▶ n. regular repetition of something to be learned: *a poem learned by rote.*

rot·gut /ˈrätˌgət/ ▶ n. informal poor-quality alcoholic drink.

ro·ti /ˈrōtē/ ▶ n. (pl. **rotis**) (in Indian cooking) bread, especially a flat round bread cooked on a griddle.

ro·tis·ser·ie /rōˈtisərē/ ▶ n. 1 a rotating spit for roasting and barbecuing meat. 2 a restaurant specializing in roasted or barbecued meat.

ro·tor /ˈrōtər/ ▶ n. 1 the rotating part of a turbine, electric motor, or other device. 2 a hub with a number of blades spreading out from it that is rotated to provide the lift for a helicopter.

ro·to·till·er /ˈrōtəˌtilər/ ▶ n. trademark a machine with rotating blades for breaking up or tilling the soil. ■ **ro·to·till** v.

rot·ten /ˈrätn/ ▶ adj. 1 rotting or decaying. 2 morally or politically corrupt. 3 informal very bad or unpleasant. ▶ adv. informal very much: *your mother spoiled you rotten.* ■ **rot·ten·ness** n.

Rott·wei·ler /ˈrätˌwīlər, ˈrôtˌvīlər/ ▶ n. a large powerful black-and-tan breed of dog.

ro·tund /rōˈtənd, ˈrōˌtənd/ ▶ adj. having a large and rounded body or shape. ■ **ro·tun·di·ty** /-ˈtəndətē/ n. **ro·tund·ly** adv.

ro·tun·da /rōˈtəndə/ ▶ n. a round building or room, especially one with a dome.

rou·ble /ˈro͞obəl/ ▶ n. variant spelling of RUBLE.

rou·é /ro͞oˈā/ ▶ n. a man who leads an immoral life.

rouge /ro͞ozH/ ▶ n. a red powder or cream used as a cosmetic for coloring the cheeks. ▶ v. color the cheeks with rouge. ▶ adj. (of wine) red.

rough /rəf/ ▶ adj. 1 having an uneven or irregular surface; not smooth or level. 2 not gentle or careful; violent: *rough treatment.* 3 (of weather or the sea) wild and stormy. 4 not finished tidily; plain and basic: *rough wooden tables.* 5 not worked out or correct in every detail; approximate: *a rough guess.* 6 harsh in sound or taste. 7 not sophisticated or cultured. 8 informal difficult and unpleasant. ▶ n. 1 a basic, preliminary state: *we'll ask the designer for some roughs to start with.* 2 chiefly Brit. a violent person. 3 (on a golf course) the area of longer grass around the fairway and the green. ▶ v. 1 (**rough something out**) make a basic, preliminary version of something. 2 make something uneven. 3 (**rough it**) informal live in discomfort with only basic necessities. 4 (**rough someone up**) informal beat someone up. ■ **rough·ness** n.
 – PHRASES **in the rough** in a natural state. **rough and ready 1** basic but effective. 2 not sophisticated or refined. **rough edges** small flaws in something that is otherwise satisfactory. **rough justice** treatment that is not fair or in accordance with the law.

rough·age /ˈrəfij/ ▶ n. fiber in vegetables, cereals, and fruit that cannot be digested and which helps food and waste products to pass through the gut.

rough and tum·ble ▶ n. a situation without rules or organization.

rough·cast /'rəf,kast/ ▶ n. plaster of lime, cement, and gravel, used on outside walls. ▶ adj. coated with roughcast. ▶ v. coat a wall with roughcast.

rough·en /'rəfən/ ▶ v. make or become rough.

rough-hewn ▶ adj. (of a person) unsophisticated or uncouth.

rough·house informal ▶ n. /'rəf,hous/ a violent disturbance. ▶ v. /'rəf,hous, -,houz/ act or treat in a rough, violent way.

rough·ly /'rəflē/ ▶ adv. **1** in a rough or harsh way. **2** not exactly; approximately.

rough·neck /'rəf,nek/ ▶ n. informal **1** a rough, uncouth person. **2** an oil-rig worker.

rough·shod /'rəf,sнäd/ ▶ adj. (in phrase **ride roughshod over**) fail to consider a person's wishes or feelings.

rough trade ▶ n. informal male homosexual prostitution, especially when involving brutality or sadism.

rou·lade /rōō'läd/ ▶ n. a piece of meat, sponge cake, or other food, spread with a filling and rolled up.

rou·lette /rōō'let/ ▶ n. a gambling game in which a ball is dropped onto a revolving wheel with numbered compartments, the players betting on the number at which the ball will come to rest.

round /round/ ▶ adj. **1** shaped like a circle, cylinder, or sphere. **2** having a curved shape: *round red cheeks.* **3** (of a person's shoulders) bent forward. **4** (of a voice or musical tone) rich and mellow. **5** (of a number) expressed in convenient units rather than exactly, for example to the nearest whole number. **6** frank and truthful: *she berated him in round terms.* ▶ n. **1** a circular piece or shape. **2** a route by which a number of places or places are visited or inspected in turn: *hospital ward rounds.* **3** a regularly recurring sequence of activities: *their lives were a daily round of housework and laundry.* **4** each of a sequence of sessions in a process, especially in a sports contest. **5** a single division of a boxing or wrestling match. **6** a set of drinks bought for all the members of a group. **7** the amount of ammunition needed to fire one shot. **8** a song for three or more unaccompanied voices or parts, each singing the same theme but starting one after another. **9** a thick disk of beef cut from the haunch for a roast. ▶ adv. chiefly Brit. variant of AROUND (adverb). ▶ prep. chiefly Brit. variant of AROUND (preposition). ▶ v. **1** pass and go around something. **2** make a figure less exact but more convenient for calculations: *round the weight up to the nearest ounce.* **3** make or become round in shape. ■ **round·ish** adj. **round·ness** n.
– PHRASES **in the round 1** (of theater) with the audience placed on at least three sides of the stage. **2** (of sculpture) standing free, rather than carved in relief. **3** fully and thoroughly. **round something off 1** smooth the edges of something. **2** complete something in a satisfying or suitable way. **round someone/thing up** drive or collect people or animals together.

round·a·bout /'roundə,bout/ ▶ adj. **1** not following a direct route; circuitous. **2** not saying what is meant clearly and directly. ▶ n. Brit. **1** a merry-go-round. **2** a road junction at which traffic moves in one direction around a central island to reach one of the roads converging on it.

round·ed /'roundid/ ▶ adj. **1** round or curved. **2** well developed in all aspects; balanced: *a rounded human being.*

roun·del /'roundl/ ▶ n. **1** a small disk, especially a decorative medallion. **2** a circular identifying mark painted on military aircraft.

Round·head /'round,hed/ ▶ n. historical a member or supporter of the Parliamentary party in the English Civil War.

round·house /'round,hous/ ▶ n. **1** a railroad locomotive maintenance shed built around a turntable. **2** informal a blow given with a wide sweep of the arm.

round·ly /'roundlē/ ▶ adv. **1** in an emphatic or blunt way. **2** so as to form a circular shape.

round rob·in ▶ n. **1** a tournament in which each competitor plays in turn against every other. **2** a petition, especially one with signatures written in a circle to conceal the order of writing.

round ta·ble ▶ n. (usu. before another noun) a meeting at which parties meet on equal terms for discussion.

round-the-clock ▶ adj. lasting all day and all night: *round-the-clock surveillance.*

round trip ▶ n. a journey to a place and back again.

round·up /'round,əp/ ▶ n. **1** a gathering together of people or things. **2** a summary of facts or events.

round·worm /'round,wərm/ ▶ n. a parasitic worm found in the intestines of some mammals.

rouse /rouz/ ▶ v. **1** bring or come out of sleep. **2** cause someone to move or take interest after being inactive. **3** stir up or arouse: *his evasiveness roused my curiosity.*

rous·ing /'rouziNG/ ▶ adj. exciting; stirring: *a rousing speech.* ■ **rous·ing·ly** adv.

roust /roust/ ▶ v. informal make someone get up or start moving.

roust·a·bout /'roustə,bout/ ▶ n. an unskilled or casual worker, especially a laborer on an oil rig or in a circus.

rout¹ /rout/ ▶ n. **1** a disorderly retreat of defeated troops. **2** a decisive defeat. ▶ v. defeat someone decisively and force them to retreat.

rout² ▶ v. cut a groove in a hard surface.

route /rōōt, rout/ ▶ n. **1** a way taken in getting from a starting point to a destination. **2** a method or process that leads to a particular result: *a fast-track route to a coaching career.* ▶ v. (**routes, routing, routed**) send someone or something along a particular course.

rout·er¹ /'routər/ ▶ n. a power tool with a rotating shaped cutter, used in carpentry for making grooves, decorative moldings, etc.

rout·er² /'rōōtər, 'routər/ ▶ n. a device that forwards data packets to the appropriate parts of a computer network.

rou·tine /rōō'tēn/ ▶ n. **1** a sequence of actions regularly followed. **2** a set sequence in a dance or comedy act. ▶ adj. **1** performed as part of a regular procedure: *a routine inspection.* **2** without variety; dull. ■ **rou·tine·ly** adv.

rout·ing code ▶ n. **1** a numeric code that directs telephone calls or Internet traffic. **2** the magnetically encoded numbers on a check.

rou·tin·ize /rōō'tē,nīz, 'rōōtn,īz/ ▶ v. make something into a matter of routine; subject to a routine. ■ **rou·tin·i·za·tion** /-,tēnə'zāsнən, ,rōōtn-ə-/ n.

roux /rōō/ ▶ n. (pl. same) Cooking a mixture of fat (especially butter) and flour used in making sauces.

rove /rōv/ ▶ v. 1 travel constantly without a fixed destination; wander. 2 (of a person's eyes) look around in all directions. ■ **rov·er** n.

row¹ /rō/ ▶ n. a number of people or things in a line.
– PHRASES **in a row** informal one after the other; in succession.

row² /rō/ ▶ v. 1 propel a boat with oars. 2 row a boat as a sport. ▶ n. a spell of rowing. ■ **row·er** n.

row³ /rou/ chiefly Brit. ▶ n. 1 an angry quarrel. 2 a serious dispute. 3 a loud noise or uproar. ▶ v. have an angry quarrel.

row·an /'rōən/ ▶ n. a small tree with white flowers and red berries.

row·boat /'rō,bōt/ (Brit. **rowing boat**) ▶ n. a small boat propelled by oars.

row·dy /'roudē/ ▶ adj. (**rowdier, rowdiest**) noisy and disorderly. ▶ n. (pl. **rowdies**) a rowdy person. ■ **row·di·ly** /'roudl-ē/ adv. **row·di·ness** n. **row·dy·ism** /-,izəm/ n.

row·el /'rou(ə)l/ ▶ n. a spiked revolving disk at the end of a spur.

row house /rō / ▶ n. any of a row of houses joined by common side walls.

row·ing ma·chine ▶ n. an exercise machine with a handle to pull to simulate rowing a boat.

roy·al /'roiəl/ ▶ adj. 1 relating to or having the status of a king or queen or a member of their family. 2 of a quality or size suitable for a king or queen; splendid. 3 informal real; complete: *she's a royal pain in the butt*. ▶ n. informal a member of the royal family. ■ **roy·al·ly** adv.

roy·al blue ▶ n. a deep, vivid blue.

roy·al·ist /'roiəlist/ ▶ n. a person who supports the principle of rule by a king or queen. ■ **roy·al·ism** /-,izəm/ n.

roy·al jel·ly ▶ n. a substance produced by honeybee workers and fed by them to larvae that are being raised as potential queen bees.

roy·al·ty /'roiəltē/ ▶ n. (pl. **royalties**) 1 people of royal blood or status. 2 the status or power of a king or queen: *the insignia of royalty*. 3 a sum paid for the use of a patent or to an author or composer for each copy of a work sold or for each public performance.

RPI ▶ abbr. retail price index.

rpm ▶ abbr. revolutions per minute.

RR ▶ abbr. 1 railroad. 2 rural route.

RSI ▶ abbr. repetitive strain injury.

RSS ▶ n. Computing really simple syndication, a system for the distribution or syndication of Internet content from an online publisher to Web users.

RSVP ▶ abbr. répondez s'il vous plaît; please reply (used at the end of invitations).

rte. ▶ abbr. route.

RTF ▶ abbr. Computing rich text format.

Ru ▶ symbol the chemical element ruthenium.

RU-486 ▶ n. trademark for MIFEPRISTONE.

rub /rəb/ ▶ v. (**rubs, rubbing, rubbed**) 1 move back and forth over a surface while pressing against it. 2 apply with a rubbing action: *she rubbed some cream on her nose.* 3 (**rub something down**) dry, smooth, or clean something by rubbing. 4 (**rub something**

in/into) work an ingredient into a mixture by breaking and blending it with the fingertips. ▶ n. 1 an act of rubbing. 2 an ointment for rubbing into the skin. 3 (**the rub**) the central or most important difficulty.
– PHRASES **rub one's hands** show satisfaction. **rub it in** (or **rub someone's nose in something**) informal forcefully draw someone's attention to an embarrassing fact. **rub off** be transferred: *she hoped that some of his confidence would rub off on her*. **rub shoulders with** associate or come into contact with someone. **rub someone the wrong way** irritate someone.

ru·ba·to /rōō'bätō/ ▶ n. (pl. **rubatos** or **rubati** /-'bätē/) Music temporary disregard for strict tempo to allow an expressive quickening or slackening.

rub·ber¹ /'rəbər/ ▶ n. 1 a tough elastic substance made from the latex of a tropical tree or synthetically. 2 informal a condom. 3 Brit. a rubber eraser. ■ **rub·ber·ize** v. **rub·ber·y** adj.

rub·ber² ▶ n. 1 a contest consisting of a series of matches between the same sides in certain games. 2 (in Davis Cup tennis) a match forming part of a contest ('tie') between two nations. 3 Bridge a unit of play in which one side scores bonus points for winning the best of three games. 4 Baseball an oblong piece of rubber embedded in the pitcher's mound, on which the pitcher must keep one foot while delivering the ball.

rub·ber band ▶ n. a loop of rubber for holding things together.

rub·ber bul·let ▶ n. a bullet made of rubber, used in riot control.

rub·ber·neck /'rəbər,nek/ informal ▶ v. turn one's head to stare at something in a foolish way. ▶ n. a person who stares in a foolish way. ■ **rub·ber·neck·er** n.

rub·ber plant ▶ n. an evergreen tree with large dark green shiny leaves, native to SE Asia and formerly grown as a source of rubber.

rub·ber stamp ▶ n. 1 a hand-held device for stamping dates, addresses, etc., on a surface. 2 an instance of automatic approval given without proper consideration. ▶ v. (**rubber-stamp**) approve something automatically without proper consideration.

rub·ber tree ▶ n. a tree that produces the latex from which rubber is manufactured, native to the Amazonian rainforest.

rub·bing /'rəbiNG/ ▶ n. an impression of a design on brass or stone, made by placing a sheet of paper over it and rubbing it with chalk, wax, or a pencil.

rub·bing al·co·hol ▶ n. denatured alcohol, typically perfumed, used as an antiseptic or in massage.

rub·bish /'rəbish/ ▶ n. 1 waste material; refuse or litter. 2 unimportant or inferior material: *wasn't their last album rubbish?* 3 ridiculous or foolish talk or ideas; nonsense.

rub·ble /'rəbəl/ ▶ n. rough fragments of stone, brick, concrete, etc., especially as the debris from the demolition of buildings. ■ **rub·bly** adj.

rube /rōōb/ ▶ n. informal a country bumpkin.

Rube Gold·berg /'gōld,bərg/ ▶ adj. unnecessarily or comically complex in design.

ru·bel·la /rōō'belə/ ▶ n. a disease transmitted by a virus and with symptoms like mild measles; German measles.

Ru·bi·con /'rōōbə,kän/ ▶ n. a point of no return.

ru·bi·cund /'rōōbə,kənd/ ▸ adj. having a reddish complexion.

ru·bid·i·um /rōō'bidēəm/ ▸ n. a rare soft silvery reactive metallic element.

ru·ble /'rōōbəl/ (also chiefly Brit. **rouble**) ▸ n. the basic unit of money of Russia and some other former republics of the Soviet Union.

ru·bric /'rōōbrik/ ▸ n. 1 a heading on a document. 2 a set of instructions or rules. 3 a direction as to how a church service should be conducted.

ru·by /'rōōbē/ ▸ n. (pl. **rubies**) 1 a precious stone that is typically deep red in color. 2 a deep red color.

ruche /rōōsн/ ▸ n. a frill or pleat of fabric. ■ **ruched** adj. **ruch·ing** n.

ruck·sack /'rək,sak, 'rōōk-/ ▸ n. a bag with two shoulder straps that allow it to be carried on the back.

ruck·us /'rəkəs/ ▸ n. an argument or commotion.

ruc·tion /'rəksнən/ ▸ n. informal a disturbance or quarrel.

rud·beck·i·a /rōōd'bekēə, ,rəd-/ ▸ n. a North American plant of the daisy family, with yellow or orange flowers and a dark cone-shaped center.

rud·der /'rədər/ ▸ n. 1 a flat hinged upright piece at the back of a boat, used for steering. 2 an upright airfoil pivoted from the tailplane of an aircraft, used for steering.

rud·der·less /'rədərləs/ ▸ adj. lacking a clear sense of one's aims or direction.

rud·dy /'rədē/ ▸ adj. (**ruddier, ruddiest**) 1 (of a person's face) having a healthy red color. 2 reddish in color. ■ **rud·di·ness** n.

rude /rōōd/ ▸ adj. 1 offensively impolite or bad-mannered. 2 referring to sex or bodily functions in an offensive way. 3 very abrupt: *the war came as a rude awakening*. 4 dated roughly made or done. 5 old use ignorant and uneducated. ■ **rude·ly** adv. **rude·ness** n. **ru·der·y** /-ərē/ n.

ru·di·ment /'rōōdəmənt/ ▸ n. 1 (**rudiments**) the basic facts of a subject. 2 (**rudiments**) a basic or primitive form of something. 3 Biology an undeveloped or immature part or organ.

ru·di·men·ta·ry /,rōōdə'ment(ə)rē/ ▸ adj. 1 involving only the basic facts or elements: *a rudimentary education*. 2 not highly or fully developed: *a rudimentary stage of evolution*. ■ **ru·di·men·ta·ri·ly** /-men'te(ə)rəlē, -'ment(ə)rəlē/ adv.

rue¹ /rōō/ ▸ v. (**rues, rueing** or **ruing, rued**) bitterly regret a past event or action.

rue² ▸ n. an evergreen shrub with bitter strong-scented leaves that are used in herbal medicine.

rue·ful /'rōōfəl/ ▸ adj. expressing regret: *a rueful smile*. ■ **rue·ful·ly** adv. **rue·ful·ness** n.

ruff¹ /rəf/ ▸ n. 1 a projecting starched frill worn around the neck, especially in Elizabethan and Jacobean times. 2 a ring of feathers or hair around the neck of a bird or mammal. 3 (pl. same or **ruffs**) a wading bird, the male of which has a large ruff and ear tufts in the breeding season.

ruff² ▸ v. (in bridge and whist) play a trump in a trick that was led in a different suit. ▸ n. an act of playing such a trump.

ruf·fi·an /'rəfēən/ ▸ n. a violent or lawless person. ■ **ruf·fi·an·ism** /-,nizəm/ n. **ruf·fi·an·ly** adj.

ruf·fle /'rəfəl/ ▸ v. 1 disrupt the smooth surface of something. 2 irritate or upset someone. 3 (as adj. **ruffled**) gathered into a frill. ▸ n. a gathered frill on a garment.

ru·fi·yaa /'rōōfē,yä/ ▸ n. (pl. same) the basic unit of money of the Maldives.

ru·fous /'rōōfəs/ ▸ adj. (especially of an animal or bird) reddish brown in color.

rug /rəg/ ▸ n. 1 a small carpet. 2 informal, humorous a toupee.

– PHRASES **pull the rug out from under someone** abruptly withdraw support from someone.

rug·by /'rəgbē/ (also **rugby football**) ▸ n. a team game played with an oval ball that may be kicked, carried, and passed by hand, in which points are won by scoring a try or by kicking the ball over the crossbar of the opponents' goal.

rug·ged /'rəgid/ ▸ adj. 1 having a rocky and uneven surface. 2 (of clothing or equipment) strong and capable of withstanding rough handling. 3 having or requiring toughness and determination: *a stubborn, rugged individualist*. 4 (of a man) having attractively strong features. ■ **rug·ged·ly** adv. **rug·ged·ness** n.

ru·in /'rōōin/ ▸ n. 1 the physical destruction or collapse of something. 2 the remains of a building that has decayed or suffered much damage. 3 a severe downfall or decline: *such action can only result in the utter ruin of our nation*. 4 the complete loss of a person's money and other assets. ▸ v. 1 destroy or severely damage a building or other structure. 2 have a very damaging effect on: *the expressway has ruined village life*. 3 make someone very poor or bankrupt.

ru·in·a·tion /,rōōə'nāsнən/ ▸ n. the action of ruining someone or something or the state of being ruined.

ru·in·ous /'rōōənəs/ ▸ adj. 1 disastrous or destructive. 2 costing far more than a person can afford. 3 (of a building) in ruins. ■ **ru·in·ous·ly** adv.

rule /rōōl/ ▸ n. 1 a regulation or statement controlling behavior or procedure within a particular area of activity. 2 control of a country or people: *British rule*. 3 a code of practice and discipline for a religious community. 4 (**the rule**) the normal or usual state of things. 5 a ruler for measuring things. 6 a thin printed line or dash. ▸ v. 1 control or govern a people or country. 2 have a powerful and restricting influence on: *her whole life was ruled by fear*. 3 state with legal authority that something is the case. 4 informal be very good or the best. 5 make parallel lines on paper.

– PHRASES **as a rule** usually, but not always. **rule of thumb** a broadly accurate guide or principle, based on practice rather than theory. **rule something out/in** exclude (or include) something as a possibility. **rule the roost** be in complete control.

rul·er /'rōōlər/ ▸ n. 1 a person who rules a people or country. 2 a straight strip of rigid material, marked at regular intervals and used to draw straight lines or measure distances.

rul·ing /'rōōliNG/ ▸ n. a decision or statement made by someone in authority. ▸ adj. in control; governing.

rum /rəm/ ▸ n. an alcoholic liquor distilled from sugarcane residues or molasses.

Ru·ma·ni·an /rōō'mānēən, -nyən/ ▸ adj. & n. variant spelling of ROMANIAN.

rum·ba /'rəmbə, 'rōōm-, 'rōōm-/ (also **rhumba**) ▸ n. 1 a rhythmic dance with Spanish and African elements, originating in Cuba. **2** a ballroom dance based on the Cuban rumba.

rum·ble /ˈrəmbəl/ ▶ v. make or move with a continuous deep sound. ▶ n. **1** a continuous deep sound like distant thunder. **2** informal a street fight between rival gangs. ■ **rum·bler** n.

rum·ble strip ▶ n. one of a series of raised strips set in a road to warn drivers to slow down or to indicate that they have deviated from their lane.

ru·mi·nant /ˈroōmənənt/ ▶ n. a mammal of a type that chews the cud, such as cattle, sheep, or deer. ▶ adj. relating to mammals that chew the cud.

ru·mi·nate /ˈroōmənāt/ ▶ v. **1** think deeply about something. **2** (of a cow, sheep, etc.) chew the cud. ■ **ru·mi·na·tion** /ˌroōməˈnāsʜən/ n. **ru·mi·na·tive** /-ˌnātiv/ adj.

rum·mage /ˈrəmij/ ▶ v. search for something in an unmethodical way. ▶ n. an act of rummaging.

rum·mage sale ▶ n. a sale of various secondhand goods, especially for charity.

rum·my /ˈrəmē/ ▶ n. a card game in which the players try to form sets and sequences of cards.

ru·mor /ˈroōmər/ (Brit. **rumour**) ▶ n. a story spread among a number of people that is unconfirmed and may be false. ▶ v. (**be rumored**) be spread as a rumor.

rump /rəmp/ ▶ n. **1** the hind part of the body of a mammal or the lower back of a bird. **2** a small or unimportant part left over from something larger.

rum·ple /ˈrəmpəl/ ▶ v. make something untidy or disheveled. ■ **rum·pled** adj.

rum·pus /ˈrəmpəs/ ▶ n. (pl. **rumpuses**) a noisy disturbance.

run /rən/ ▶ v. (**runs, running, ran** /ran/; past part. **run**) **1** move fast using the legs. **2** move or pass something in a particular direction: *Helen ran her fingers through her hair.* **3** move forcefully or fast: *the tanker ran aground.* **4** be in charge of people or an organization. **5** continue, operate, or proceed: *everything's running according to plan.* **6** function or cause to function. **7** pass into or reach a specified state or level: *inflation is running at 11 percent.* **8** (of a liquid) flow. **9** send out a liquid. **10** (**run in**) (of a quality) be common in members of a family. **11** stand as a candidate in an election. **12** enter or be entered in a race. **13** (of dye or color) dissolve and spread when wet. **14** (of a bus, train, etc.) make a regular journey on a particular route. **15** transport someone in a car. **16** publish or be published in a newspaper or magazine. **17** smuggle goods. **18** (of a stocking or pair of tights) develop a vertical strip of unraveling. ▶ n. **1** an act or spell of running. **2** a running pace. **3** a journey or route. **4** a short trip in a car. **5** a course or track made or regularly used: *a ski run.* **6** a spell or stretch of something: *a run of bad luck.* **7** an enclosed area in which animals or birds may run freely in the open. **8** (**the run of**) free and unrestricted use of or access to somewhere. **9** (**the run**) the average or usual type: *she stood out from the general run of Harvard women.* **10** a rapid series of musical notes. **11** a sequence of cards of the same suit. **12** Baseball a point scored by the batter returning to the home plate after touching the bases. **13** a vertical strip of unraveled fabric in stockings or tights. **14** (**the runs**) informal diarrhea. ■ **run·na·ble** adj.

– PHRASES **be run off one's feet** be very busy.

give someone/thing a (good) run for their money provide someone or something with challenging competition. **have a (good) run for one's money** receive reward or enjoyment in return for one's efforts. **on the run 1** escaping from arrest. **2** while running or moving. **run across** meet or find by chance. **run after** informal pursue persistently. **run along** informal go away. **run away 1** escape from a person, place, or situation. **2** try to avoid facing up to danger or difficulty. **run away with 1** be out of the control of: *her imagination was running away with her.* **2** win a competition or prize easily. **run before one can walk** attempt something difficult before one has grasped the basic skills. **run something by** (or **past**) tell someone about something to find out their opinion. **run something down** (or **run down**) **1** gradually lose or cause to lose power. **2** reduce or be reduced in size or resources. **3** get worse or cause to get worse in quality. **run someone/thing down 1** knock someone or something down with a vehicle. **2** criticize someone or something. **run someone in** informal arrest someone. **run into 1** collide with. **2** meet someone by chance. **3** experience a problem. **run something off 1** produce a copy on a machine. **2** write or recite something quickly and with little effort. **run on** continue without stopping. **run out 1** use up or be used up. **2** become no longer valid. **run over** (of a container or its contents) overflow. **run someone/thing over** knock someone or something down with a vehicle. **run through** (or **over**) go over quickly or briefly as a rehearsal or reminder. **run to 1** extend to or reach an amount or size. **2** show a tendency toward. **run something up 1** allow a bill, score, etc., to build up. **2** make something quickly or hurriedly. **3** raise a flag. **run up against** experience or meet a problem.

run·a·bout /ˈrənəˌbout/ ▶ n. a small car or light aircraft, especially one used for short journeys.

run·a·round /ˈrənəˌround/ ▶ n. informal (in phrase **give someone the runaround**) treat someone badly by misleading them or failing to do or provide something.

run·a·way /ˈrənəˌwā/ ▶ n. a person who has run away from their home or an institution. ▶ adj. **1** (of an animal or vehicle) running out of control. **2** happening or done quickly or uncontrollably: *the runaway success of his first novel.*

run·down /ˈrənˌdoun/ ▶ n. a brief analysis or summary. ▶ adj. (**run-down**) **1** in a poor or neglected state. **2** tired and rather unwell, especially through overwork.

rune /roōn/ ▶ n. **1** a letter of an ancient Germanic alphabet used especially in Scandinavia. **2** a symbol with mysterious or magical significance. ■ **ru·nic** adj.

rung[1] /rəNG/ ▶ n. **1** a horizontal bar on a ladder to stand on. **2** a level or rank in society, a profession, etc.: *a youth on a low rung at the Foreign Office.* **3** a strengthening crosspiece in the structure of a chair.

rung[2] ▶ past participle of RING[2].

run-in ▶ n. informal a disagreement or fight.

run·nel /ˈrənl/ ▶ n. **1** a gutter. **2** a brook or stream.

run·ner /ˈrənər/ ▶ n. **1** a person or animal that runs. **2** a rod, groove, blade, or roller on which something slides. **3** a messenger or collector, especially for a bookmaker. **4** a shoot of a plant that grows along the ground and can take root at points along its length. **5** a long, narrow rug.

run·ner bean ▸ n. a climbing bean plant with scarlet flowers and long green edible pods.

run·ner-up ▸ n. (pl. **runners-up**) a competitor or team taking second place in a contest.

run·ning /'rəniNG/ ▸ adj. **1** (of water) flowing naturally or supplied through pipes and taps. **2** producing liquid or pus. **3** continuous or recurring: *a running joke.* **4** done while running. **5** (after a noun) in succession: *the third week running.*
– PHRASES **in** (or **out of**) **the running** in (or no longer in) with a chance of success.

run·ning bat·tle ▸ n. a battle that does not occur at a fixed location.

run·ning board ▸ n. a footboard extending along the side of a vehicle.

run·ning com·men·ta·ry ▸ n. a spoken description of events, given as they occur.

run·ning head ▸ n. a heading printed at the top of each page of a book or chapter.

run·ning mate ▸ n. an election candidate for the lesser of two linked political offices.

run·ning re·pairs ▸ pl.n. Brit. minor or temporary repairs carried out on machinery while it is in use.

run·ning stitch ▸ n. a simple needlework stitch consisting of a line of small even stitches that run back and forth through the cloth.

run·ning to·tal ▸ n. a total that is continually adjusted to take account of further items.

run·ny /'rənē/ ▸ adj. (**runnier, runniest**) **1** more liquid in consistency than is usual or expected. **2** (of a person's nose) producing thin mucus.

run·off /'rən,ôf/ ▸ n. **1** a further contest after a clear winner has not emerged in a previous one. **2** rainfall or other liquid that drains away from the surface of an area.

run-of-the-mill ▸ adj. lacking unusual or special aspects; ordinary.

runt /rənt/ ▸ n. a small pig or other animal, especially the smallest in a litter. ■ **runt·ish** adj. **runt·y** adj.

run-through ▸ n. **1** a rehearsal. **2** a brief summary.

run-up ▸ n. **1** a period of preparation before an important event. **2** an act of running briefly to gain momentum before bowling, performing a jump, etc.

run·way /'rən,wā/ ▸ n. **1** a strip of hard ground along which aircraft take off and land. **2** a catwalk in a fashion show.

ru·pee /rōō'pē, 'rōō,pē/ ▸ n. the basic unit of money of India, Pakistan, Sri Lanka, and some other countries.

rup·ture /'rəpchər/ ▸ v. **1** break or burst suddenly. **2** (**be ruptured** or **rupture oneself**) suffer a hernia in the abdomen. **3** disturb good relations. ▸ n. **1** a sudden breaking or bursting of something. **2** a hernia in the abdomen.

ru·ral /'rōōrəl/ ▸ adj. relating to or typical of the countryside rather than the town. ■ **ru·ral·i·ty** /rōō'ralitē/ n. **ru·ral·ize** v. **ru·ral·ly** adv.

Ru·ri·ta·ni·an /,rōōri'tānēən/ ▸ adj. relating to or typical of romantic adventure or its setting.

ruse /rōōz, rōōs/ ▸ n. an action intended to deceive someone; a trick.

rush[1] /rəsh/ ▸ v. **1** move or act with urgent haste. **2** deliver or produce something with urgent haste. **3** deal with hurriedly: *panic measures were rushed through the legislature.* **4** (of air or a liquid) flow strongly. **5** try to attack or capture a person or place suddenly. ▸ n. **1** a sudden quick movement or flow: *there was a rush for the door.* **2** a flurry of hasty activity. **3** a sudden strong demand for a product. **4** a sudden intense feeling. **5** informal a sudden thrill experienced after taking certain drugs. **6** (**rushes**) the first prints made of a movie after a period of shooting.

rush[2] ▸ n. a marsh or waterside plant with slender pith-filled leaves, some kinds of which are used for matting, baskets, etc. ■ **rush·y** adj.

rush hour ▸ n. a time at the start and end of the working day when traffic is at its heaviest.

rush·light /'rəsh,līt/ ▸ n. historical a candle made by dipping the pith of a rush in tallow.

rusk /rəsk/ ▸ n. a dry slice of rebaked bread, especially one eaten by babies.

rus·set /'rəsət/ ▸ adj. reddish brown. ▸ n. **1** a reddish-brown color. **2** a variety of dessert apple with a slightly rough greenish-brown skin. ■ **rus·set·y** adj.

Rus·sian /'rəshən/ ▸ n. **1** a person from Russia. **2** the language of Russia. ▸ adj. relating to Russia.

Rus·sian doll ▸ n. each of a set of brightly painted hollow wooden dolls that fit inside each other.

Rus·sian Or·tho·dox Church ▸ n. the national Church of Russia.

Rus·sian rou·lette ▸ n. a dangerous game of chance in which a person loads a bullet into one chamber of a revolver, spins the cylinder, and then pulls the trigger while pointing the gun at their own head.

Russ·ki /'rəskē, 'rōōskē/ (also **Russky**) ▸ n. (pl. **Russkis** or **Russkies**) informal, chiefly derogatory a Russian.

rust /rəst/ ▸ n. **1** a reddish-brown flaky coating of iron oxide that is formed on iron or steel by the action of water and oxygen. **2** a disease of plants caused by a fungus, which results in reddish or brownish patches. **3** a reddish-brown color. ▸ v. be affected with rust. ■ **rust·less** adj.

rust belt ▸ n. informal (especially in the American Midwest and NE states) a region where heavy industry is in decline and the population is falling.

rust buck·et ▸ n. informal a vehicle or ship that is old and badly rusted.

rus·tic /'rəstik/ ▸ adj. **1** relating to or typical of the country, especially in being attractively simple or unsophisticated: *hearty rustic dishes.* **2** (of furniture) made of rough branches or timber. ▸ n. often derogatory an unsophisticated country person. ■ **rus·ti·cal·ly** /-ik(ə)lē/ adv. **rus·tic·i·ty** /rə'stisətē/ n.

rus·ti·cate /'rəsti,kāt/ ▸ v. **1** go to, live in, or spend time in the country. **2** (usu. as adj. **rusticated**) shape masonry in large blocks with sunken joints and a roughened surface. ■ **rus·ti·ca·tion** /,rəsti'kāshən/ n.

rus·tle /'rəsəl/ ▸ v. **1** make or move with a soft crackling sound like that caused by the movement of dry leaves. **2** round up and steal cattle, horses, or sheep. **3** (**rustle something**

up) informal produce food or a drink quickly. ▶ n. a rustling sound. ■ **rus·tler** n.

rust·proof /ˈrəstˌpro͞of/ ▶ adj. not able to be corroded by rust. ▶ v. make something rustproof.

rust·y /ˈrəstē/ ▶ adj. (**rustier, rustiest**) **1** affected by rust. **2** (of knowledge or a skill) less good than it used to be because of lack of practice. **3** rust-colored; reddish-brown. ■ **rust·i·ly** adv. **rust·i·ness** n.

rut[1] /rət/ ▶ n. **1** a long deep track made by the repeated passage of the wheels of vehicles. **2** a pattern of behavior that has become dull but is hard to change: *here's me, stuck in a rut with Roger after all these years.* ■ **rut·ted** adj. **rut·ty** adj.

rut[2] ▶ n. an annual period of sexual activity in deer and some other mammals, during which the males fight each other for access to the females. ▶ v. (**ruts, rutting, rutted**) be in such a period of activity.

ru·ta·ba·ga /ˈro͞otəˌbāgə, ˈro͞ot-/ ▶ n. a round yellow root vegetable related to the turnip.

ru·the·ni·um /ro͞oˈTHēnēəm/ ▶ n. a hard silvery-white metallic chemical element.

ruth·er·for·di·um /ˌrəTHərˈfôrdēəm/ ▶ n. a very unstable chemical element made by high-energy atomic collisions.

ruth·less /ˈro͞oTHləs/ ▶ adj. having or showing no pity or sympathy; hard and selfish. ■ **ruth·less·ly** adv. **ruth·less·ness** n.

RV ▶ abbr. recreational vehicle.

R·V·er /ˈärˈvēər/ ▶ n. a user of a recreational vehicle.

Rwan·dan /ro͞oˈändən, rəˈwändən/ (also **Rwandese** /-dēz, -dēs/) ▶ n. a person from Rwanda, a country in central Africa. ▶ adj. relating to Rwanda.

rye /rī/ ▶ n. **1** a cereal plant resembling wheat, that grows in poor soils. **2** whiskey in which much of the grain used in distilling it is fermented rye.

rye bread ▶ n. a dense, chewy bread made with rye flour.

rye·grass /ˈrīˌgras/ ▶ n. a grass used for fodder and lawns.

Ss

S¹ (also **s**) ▶ n. (pl. **Ss** or **S's**) the nineteenth letter of the alphabet.

S² ▶ abbr. **1** (chiefly in Catholic use) Saint. **2** siemens. **3** small (as a clothes size). **4** South or Southern. ▶ symbol the chemical element sulfur.

s ▶ abbr. **1** second or seconds. **2** shilling or shillings.

's ▶ contr. informal **1** is: *she's an editor.* **2** has: *he's just gone.* **3** us: *let's be honest.* **4** does: *what's he want?*

-'s ▶ suffix **1** showing possession in singular nouns, also in plural nouns not ending in -s: *John's car | the children's school.* **2** forming the plural of a letter or symbol: *9's.*

SA ▶ abbr. **1** Salvation Army. **2** South Africa. **3** South America. **4** South Australia.

sab·ba·tar·i·an /ˌsabə'te(ə)rēən/ ▶ n. a person who strictly observes the sabbath. ■ **sab·ba·tar·i·an·ism** /-ˌnizəm/ n.

sab·bath /'sabəTH/ ▶ n. (often **the Sabbath**) a day intended for religious worship and rest from work, kept by Jews from Friday evening to Saturday evening, and by most Christians on Sunday.

sab·bat·i·cal /sə'batikəl/ ▶ n. a period of paid leave granted to a college or university teacher for study or travel. ▶ adj. relating to a sabbatical.

sa·ber /'sābər/ (Brit. **sabre**) ▶ n. **1** a heavy cavalry sword with a curved blade and a single cutting edge. **2** a light fencing sword with a tapering, typically curved blade.

sa·ber-rat·tling ▶ n. the display or threat of military force.

sa·ber-tooth /'sābər,tōōTH/ (also **saber-toothed tiger**) ▶ n. a large extinct member of the cat family with huge curved upper canine teeth.

sa·ble /'sābəl/ ▶ n. **1** a marten with a short tail and dark brown fur, native to Japan and Siberia. **2** the fur of the sable. ▶ adj. literary or Heraldry black.

sab·ot /sa'bō, 'sabō/ ▶ n. a kind of simple wooden shoe resembling a clog.

sab·o·tage /'sabə,täzh/ ▶ v. deliberately destroy, damage, or hinder: *they might try and sabotage the deal.* ▶ n. the action of sabotaging something.

sab·o·teur /ˌsabə'tər/ ▶ n. a person who sabotages something.

sa·bra /'säbrə/ ▶ n. a Jew born in Israel (or before 1948 in Palestine).

sa·bre, etc. /'sābər/ ▶ n. British spelling of SABER, etc.

SAC /sak/ ▶ abbr. Strategic Air Command.

sac /sak/ ▶ n. a hollow, flexible structure in the body or a plant, resembling a bag or pouch and containing air or liquid.

sac·cha·rin /'sak(ə)rən/ ▶ n. a synthetic substance used as a low-calorie sweetener.

sac·cha·rine /'sak(ə)rin, -rēn, -rīn/ ▶ adj. very sweet or sentimental: *horribly saccharine*

sitcoms. ▶ n. saccharin.

sac·er·do·tal /ˌsasər'dōtl, ˌsakər-/ ▶ adj. relating to priests or the priesthood.

sa·chem /'sāchəm/ ▶ n. **1** (among some American Indian peoples) a chief. **2** informal a boss or leader.

sa·chet /sa'shā/ ▶ n. a small perfumed bag used to scent clothes in a drawer or closet.

sack¹ /sak/ ▶ n. **1** a large bag made of strong fabric, paper, or plastic, used for storing and carrying goods. **2** (**the sack**) informal dismissal from employment: *he got the sack for swearing.* **3** (**the sack**) informal bed. ▶ v. informal dismiss someone from employment. ■ **sack·a·ble** adj. **sack·ful** /'sak,fōol/ n.

– PHRASES **hit the sack** informal go to bed.

sack² ▶ v. (in historical contexts) plunder and destroy a town or building. ▶ n. the plundering and destruction of a place.

sack³ ▶ n. historical a white wine formerly imported into Britain from Spain.

sack·but /'sak,bət/ ▶ n. an early form of trombone used in Renaissance music.

sack·cloth /'sak,klôTH, -,kläTH/ ▶ n. a coarse fabric woven from flax or hemp.

– PHRASES **sackcloth and ashes** an expression of extreme sorrow or remorse.

sack·ing /'sakiNG/ ▶ n. coarse material for making sacks; sackcloth.

sack lunch ▶ n. a lunch packed in a paper bag and carried to work, school, etc.

sa·cra /'sakrə, 'sā-/ ▶ plural of SACRUM.

sa·cral /'sakrəl, 'sā-/ ▶ adj. **1** Anatomy relating to the sacrum in the lower back. **2** relating to sacred rites or symbols.

sac·ra·ment /'sakrəmənt/ ▶ n. **1** (in the Christian Church) a religious ceremony in which the participants receive the grace of God, such as Holy Communion. **2** (also **the Blessed Sacrament** or **the Holy Sacrament**) (in Roman Catholic use) the consecrated bread and wine used in Holy Communion. ■ **sac·ra·men·tal** /ˌsakrə'mentl/ adj.

sa·cred /'sākrid/ ▶ adj. **1** connected with God or a god and treated as holy. **2** (of a text) containing the doctrines of a religion. **3** religious rather than secular: *sacred music.* **4** regarded as too valuable to be interfered with: *nothing is sacred, no name is beyond reach.* ■ **sa·cred·ly** adv. **sa·cred·ness** n.

sa·cred cow ▶ n. an idea, custom, or institution regarded as being above criticism (with reference to the Hindu belief that the cow is a sacred animal).

sac·ri·fice /'sakrə,fīs/ ▶ n. **1** an act of killing an animal or person or giving up a possession as an offering to a god or goddess. **2** an animal, person, or object offered to a god or goddess. **3** an act of giving up something you value for the sake of something more important: *parents make sacrifices to give their children an education.* ▶ v. offer or give up someone or something as a sacrifice. ■ **sac·ri·fi·cial** /ˌsakrəˈfishəl/ adj.

sac·ri·lege /ˈsakrəlij/ ▶ n. the treating of something sacred or highly valued with great disrespect. ■ **sac·ri·le·gious** /ˌsakrəˈlijəs/ adj.

sac·ris·tan /ˈsakristən/ ▶ n. a person in charge of a church sacristy.

sac·ris·ty /ˈsakristē/ ▶ n. (pl. **sacristies**) a room in a church where a priest prepares for a service, and where things used in worship are kept.

sac·ro·sanct /ˈsakrōˌsaNG(k)t/ ▶ adj. regarded as too important or valuable to be changed or questioned: *the protection of free speech by the constitution is sacrosanct.* ■ **sac·ro·sanc·ti·ty** /ˌsakrōˈsaNG(k)titē/ n.

sac·rum /ˈsakrəm, ˈsā-/ ▶ n. (pl. **sacra** /ˈsakrə, ˈsā-/ or **sacrums**) Anatomy a triangular bone in the lower back situated between the two hipbones of the pelvis.

SAD ▶ abbr. seasonal affective disorder, depression that is associated with late autumn and winter and thought to be caused by a lack of light.

sad /sad/ ▶ adj. (**sadder, saddest**) 1 feeling sorrow; unhappy. 2 causing or characterized by sorrow or regret: *the sad story of his life.* 3 informal very inadequate or unfashionable; pathetic. ■ **sad·ness** n.

SADD ▶ abbr. Students Against Drunk Driving.

sad·den /ˈsadn/ ▶ v. make someone unhappy.

sad·dle /ˈsadl/ ▶ n. 1 a seat with a raised ridge at the front and back, fastened on the back of a horse for riding. 2 a seat on a bicycle or motorcycle. 3 a low part of a hill or mountain ridge between two higher points. 4 a cut of meat consisting of the two loins. ▶ v. 1 put a saddle on a horse. 2 (**be saddled with**) be burdened with: *he's saddled with debts of $2 million.* – PHRASES **in the saddle** 1 on horseback. 2 in a position of control or responsibility.

sad·dle·back /ˈsadlˌbak/ ▶ n. 1 a hill with a ridge along the top that dips in the middle. 2 a pig of a black breed with a white stripe across the back.

sad·dle·bag /ˈsadlˌbag/ ▶ n. a bag attached to a saddle.

sad·dle horse ▶ n. a horse kept for riding only.

sad·dler /ˈsadlər/ ▶ n. a person who makes, repairs, or deals in equipment for horses.

sad·dler·y /ˈsadlərē, -əlrē/ ▶ n. (pl. **saddleries**) 1 saddles, bridles, and other equipment for horses. 2 the making or repairing of such equipment. 3 a saddler's premises.

sad·dle soap ▶ n. a kind of soft soap used for cleaning leather.

sad·dle·sore /ˈsadlˌsôr/ ▶ n. a sore on a horse's back, caused by an ill-fitting saddle. ▶ adj. chafed by riding on a saddle.

sad·dle stitch ▶ n. 1 a stitch of thread or a wire staple passed through the fold of a magazine or booklet. 2 (in needlework) a decorative stitch made with long stitches on the upper side of the cloth alternated with short stitches on the underside.

Sad·du·cee /ˈsajəˌsē, ˈsadyə-/ ▶ n. a member of an ancient Jewish sect that denied the resurrection of the dead and the existence of spirits, and that emphasized acceptance of the written Law rather than oral tradition.

sa·dhu /ˈsädōō/ ▶ n. Indian a holy man or wise man.

sa·dism /ˈsāˌdizəm/ ▶ n. the desire to gain sexual or other pleasure from hurting or humiliating other people. ■ **sa·dist** n. **sa·dis·tic** /səˈdistik/ adj. **sa·dis·ti·cal·ly** /səˈdistik(ə)lē/ adv.

sad·ly /ˈsadlē/ ▶ adv. 1 in a sad way. 2 it is sad or regrettable that: *sadly, I never spoke to Jenny again.*

sa·do·mas·o·chism /ˌsādōˈmasəˌkizəm, ˌsadō-/ ▶ n. sexual activity or psychological tendency that combines sadism and masochism. ■ **sa·do·mas·o·chist** n. **sa·do·mas·o·chis·tic** /ˌsādōˌmasəˈkistik, ˌsadō-/ adj.

sad sack ▶ n. informal an inept, blundering person.

sa·fa·ri /səˈfärē/ ▶ n. (pl. **safaris**) an expedition to observe or hunt animals in their natural habitat.

safe /sāf/ ▶ adj. 1 protected from danger or risk. 2 not leading to harm; not risky: *a safe investment providing regular income.* 3 providing security or protection: *keep your valuables in a safe place.* 4 (of a statement, verdict, etc.) based on good reasons or evidence and not likely to be wrong. ▶ n. a strong fireproof cabinet with a complex lock, used for storing valuables. ■ **safe·ly** adv. – PHRASES **safe and sound** with no harm done; uninjured. **to be on the safe side** so as to avoid the risk of something bad happening.

safe con·duct ▶ n. the official protection of someone from arrest or harm when passing through an area.

safe de·pos·it box (also **safety deposit box**) ▶ n. a metal box for valuables in a bank or hotel.

safe·guard /ˈsāfˌgärd/ ▶ n. a measure taken to protect or prevent something. ▶ v. protect against something undesirable: *a program to safeguard the future of endangered species.*

safe house ▶ n. a house in a secret location, used by spies or criminals in hiding.

safe·keep·ing /ˈsāfˈkēpiNG/ ▶ n. the keeping of something in a safe place.

safe pe·ri·od ▶ n. the time during and near a woman's menstrual period when conception is least likely.

safe room ▶ n. a room that is safe from attack, from which security operations can be directed.

safe sex (also **safer sex**) ▶ n. sexual activity in which people take precautions to protect themselves against sexually transmitted diseases.

safe·ty /ˈsāftē/ ▶ n. the condition of being safe: *the survivors were airlifted to safety.* ▶ adj. designed to prevent injury or damage: *a safety barrier.*

safe·ty belt ▶ n. another term for SEAT BELT.

safe·ty catch ▶ n. a device that prevents a gun being fired or a machine being operated accidentally.

safe·ty cur·tain ▶ n. a fireproof curtain that can be lowered between the stage and the main part of a theater to prevent the spread of fire.

safe·ty glass ▶ n. glass that has been toughened or laminated so that it is less likely to splinter when broken.

safe·ty match ▶ n. a match that can be lit only by striking it on a special surface, such as that on the side of a matchbox.

safe·ty net ▶ n. 1 a net placed to catch an acrobat in case of a fall. 2 a safeguard against hardship or risk: *a safety net of measures to protect vulnerable children.*

safe·ty pin ▸ n. a pin with a point that is bent back to the head and is held in a guard when closed.

safe·ty ra·zor ▸ n. a razor with a guard to reduce the risk of cutting the skin.

safe·ty valve ▸ n. **1** a valve that opens automatically to relieve excessive pressure. **2** a means of releasing feelings of tension or stress in a harmless way.

Saf·fir-Simp·son scale /ˌsafiər'simpsən/ ▸ n. a scale used for classifying hurricanes that form in the Atlantic and northern Pacific Oceans east of the International Date Line.

saf·flow·er /'saf,lou(-ə)r/ ▸ n. an orange-flowered plant resembling a thistle, with seeds that are used to produce an edible oil.

saf·fron /'safrən/ ▸ n. an orange-yellow spice and food coloring made from the dried stigmas of a crocus.

sag /sag/ ▸ v. (**sags, sagging, sagged**) **1** sink downward gradually under weight or pressure. **2** hang down loosely or unevenly. **3** (often as adj. **sagging**) weaken or decline: *the company is trying to boost sagging sales.* ▸ n. an instance of sagging. ■ **sag·gy** adj.

sa·ga /'sägə/ ▸ n. **1** a long story describing heroic adventures, especially a medieval Norse or Icelandic one. **2** a long, involved story or series of incidents.

sa·ga·cious /sə'gāSHəs/ ▸ adj. having or showing good judgment; wise. ■ **sa·ga·cious·ly** adv. **sa·gac·i·ty** /sə'gasitē/ n.

sage¹ /sāj/ ▸ n. a Mediterranean plant with grayish-green leaves that are used as an herb in cooking.

sage² ▸ n. a very wise man. ▸ adj. very wise. ■ **sage·ly** adv.

sage·brush /'sāj,brəSH/ ▸ n. **1** a shrubby aromatic North American plant of the daisy family. **2** semi-arid scrub dominated by sagebrush.

Sag·it·tar·i·us /ˌsajǐ'te(ə)rēəs/ ▸ n. **1** a constellation and the ninth sign of the zodiac (the Archer), which the sun enters about November 22. **2** (**a Sagittarius**) a person born when the sun is in this sign. ■ **Sag·it·ta·ri·an** /-'te(ə)rēən/ n. & adj.

sa·go /'sāgō/ ▸ n. flour or starchy granules obtained from a palm tree, often cooked with milk to make a pudding.

sa·gua·ro /sə'(g)wärō/ ▸ n. (pl. **saguaros**) a giant cactus whose branches are shaped like a candelabrum, native to Mexico and the southwestern US.

Sa·har·an /sə'harən, -'he(ə)rən, -'härən/ ▸ adj. relating to the Sahara Desert in North Africa.

Sa·hel·i·an /sə'hālēən, -'hēlēən, -'helēən/ ▸ adj. relating to the Sahel, a semiarid region bordering the southern Sahara Desert in North Africa.

sa·hib /'sä(h)ib/ ▸ n. Indian a polite way of addressing a man.

said /sed/ past and past participle of SAY. ▸ adj. referring to someone or something already mentioned: *the said agreement.*

sail /sāl/ ▸ n. **1** a piece of material spread on a mast to catch the wind and propel a boat or ship. **2** a trip in a sailboat or ship. **3** a wind-catching structure attached to the arm of a windmill. ▸ v. **1** travel in a sailboat as a sport or pastime.

2 travel in any ship or boat. **3** begin a voyage. **4** navigate or control a boat or ship. **5** move smoothly or confidently: *she sailed into the room.* **6** (**sail through**) informal achieve something easily.
– PHRASES **sail close to the wind 1** behave or operate in a risky way. **2** sail as nearly against the wind as possible. **under sail** with the sails hoisted.

sail·board /'sāl,bôrd/ ▸ n. a board with a mast and a sail, used in windsurfing. ■ **sail·board·er** n. **sail·board·ing** n.

sail·boat /'sāl,bōt/ (Brit. **sailing boat**) ▸ n. a boat propelled by sails.

sail·cloth /'sāl,klôTH, -ˌkläTH/ ▸ n. **1** canvas or other strong fabric used for making sails. **2** a similar strong fabric used for making clothes.

sail·fish /'sāl,fiSH/ ▸ n. (pl. same or **sailfishes**) an edible marine fish with a high sail-like fin on its back.

sail·or /'sālər/ ▸ n. **1** a person who works as a member of the crew of a ship or boat. **2** a person who sails as a sport or pastime. **3** (**a good/bad sailor**) a person who rarely (or often) becomes seasick.

sail·or suit ▸ n. a boy's blue and white suit resembling the traditional uniform of a sailor.

sail·plane /'sāl,plān/ ▸ n. a glider designed to fly for long distances.

saint /sānt/ ▸ n. **1** a very good or holy person who Christians believe will go to heaven after they die. **2** a very good or holy person who is officially declared to be a saint by the Christian Church after they die. **3** informal a very kind or patient person. ■ **saint·hood** /-ˌho͝od/ n.

St. Ber·nard ▸ n. a breed of very large dog originally kept to rescue travelers by the monks of the hospice on the Great St. Bernard, a pass across the Alps.

saint·ed /'sāntid/ ▸ adj. very good or kind, like a saint.

St. El·mo's fire /'elmōz/ ▸ n. a luminous electrical discharge sometimes seen on a ship or aircraft during a storm.

St. John's wort ▸ n. an herbaceous plant or shrub with yellow flowers.

saint·ly /'sāntlē/ ▸ adj. very holy or good. ■ **saint·li·ness** n.

St. Vi·tus's dance /'vītəsiz/ ▸ n. old-fashioned term for SYDENHAM'S CHOREA.

saith /seTH, 'sāiTH/ ▸ old-fashioned third person singular present of SAY.

sake¹ /sāk/ ▸ n. (**for the sake of**) **1** so as to achieve (something); in the interest of: *they moved to the coast for the sake of her health.* **2** out of consideration for or to help (someone).
– PHRASES **for old times' sake** in memory of former times. **for God's/goodness sake** expressing impatience or desperation.

sa·ke² /'säkē/ ▸ n. a Japanese alcoholic drink made from fermented rice.

sa·laam /sə'läm/ ▸ n. a gesture of greeting or respect in Arabic-speaking and Muslim countries, consisting of a low bow with the hand or fingers touching the forehead. ▸ v. make a gesture of salaam.

sal·a·ble /'sāləbəl/ ▸ adj. variant spelling of SALEABLE.

sa·la·cious /sə'lāSHəs/ ▸ adj. having or showing too much interest in sexual matters. ■ **sa·la·cious·ly** adv.

sal·ad /'saləd/ ▸ n. a cold dish of mixed raw vegetables.
– PHRASES **one's salad days** the period when one is young and inexperienced.

sal·ad dress·ing ▸ n. see DRESSING (sense 1).

sa·lade ni·çoise /sə'läd nē'swäz/ ▸ n. (pl. **salades niçoises** pronunc. same) a salad made typically from hard-boiled eggs, tuna, black olives, and tomatoes.

sal·a·man·der /'salə,mandər/ ▸ n. **1** a long-tailed amphibian resembling a newt, typically with bright markings. **2** a mythical lizardlike creature said to live in fire.

sa·la·mi /sə'lämē/ ▸ n. (pl. same or **salamis**) a type of spicy preserved sausage.

sal·a·ried /'salərēd/ ▸ adj. earning or offering a salary: *a salaried job.*

sal·a·ry /'salərē/ ▸ n. (pl. **salaries**) a fixed regular payment made by an employer to an employee, especially a professional or white-collar worker.

sale /sāl/ ▸ n. **1** the exchange of something for money: *cars for sale at reasonable prices.* **2** (**sales**) the activity or profession of selling. **3** a period in which goods are sold at reduced prices. **4** a public event at which goods are sold or auctioned.

sale·a·ble /'sāləbəl/ (also **salable**) ▸ adj. fit or able to be sold. ■ **sale·a·bil·i·ty** /,sālə'bilitē/ n.

sales·clerk ▸ n. a store assistant.

sales·girl /'sālz,gərl/ ▸ n. a female store assistant.

sales·man /'sālzmən/ (or **saleswoman** /'sālz,wŏŏmən/) ▸ n. (pl. **salesmen** or **saleswomen**) a person whose job involves selling or promoting goods. ■ **sales·man·ship** /-,ship/ n.

sales·per·son /'sālz,pərsən/ ▸ n. (pl. **salespeople** or **salespersons**) a salesman or saleswoman.

sales·room /'sālz,rŏŏm, -,rŏŏm/ ▸ n. a room in which auctions are held.

sales tax ▸ n. a tax on sales or on the receipts from sales.

sal·i·cyl·ic ac·id /,salə'silik/ ▸ n. a bitter substance present in certain plants, used in making aspirin and dyes.

sa·li·ent /'sālyənt, -lēənt/ ▸ adj. **1** most important: *the salient points of the case.* **2** (of an angle) pointing outward. The opposite of RE-ENTRANT. ▸ n. **1** a piece of land or section of fortification that juts out to form an angle. **2** an outward bulge in a military line. ■ **sa·li·ence** n. **sa·li·en·cy** n.

sa·line /'sā,lēn, -,līn/ ▸ adj. **1** containing salt. **2** chiefly Medicine (of a solution) containing sodium chloride and/or other salts, especially in the same concentration as in the body. ▸ n. a saline solution. ■ **sa·lin·i·ty** /sə'linitē/ n. **sal·i·ni·za·tion** /,salənə'zāshən/ n.

Sa·lish /'sālish/ ▸ n. (pl. same) a member of a group of American Indian peoples of the northwestern US and the west coast of Canada. ■ **Sa·lish·an** /-ən/ adj.

sa·li·va /sə'līvə/ ▸ n. a watery liquid produced by glands in the mouth, helping chewing, swallowing, and digestion. ■ **sal·i·var·y** /'salə,verē/ adj.

sal·i·vate /'salə,vāt/ ▸ v. **1** produce saliva. **2** show great delight at the sight or prospect of something: *companies are salivating over the promise of the new technology.* ■ **sal·i·va·tion** /,salə'vāshən/ n.

sal·low /'salō/ ▸ adj. (of a person's face or complexion) yellowish or pale brown in color.

sal·ly /'salē/ ▸ n. (pl. **sallies**) **1** a sudden charge out of a place surrounded by an enemy. **2** a witty or lively reply. ▸ v. (**sallies, sallying, sallied**) set out: *they sallied forth to battle with disease.*

salm·on /'samən/ ▸ n. (pl. same or **salmons**) a large fish with edible pink flesh, that matures in the sea and migrates to freshwater streams to spawn.

sal·mo·nel·la /,salmə'nelə/ ▸ n. **1** a bacterium that occurs mainly in the gut and can cause food poisoning. **2** food poisoning caused by this bacterium.

salm·on pink ▸ n. a pale orange-pink color.

sa·lon /sə'län, sa'lôn/ ▸ n. **1** a place where a hairdresser, beautician, or fashion designer carries out their work. **2** a reception room in a large house. **3** chiefly historical a regular gathering of writers, artists, etc., held in a fashionable household.

sa·loon /sə'lŏŏn/ ▸ n. **1** dated a bar, especially one associated with the American West of the 19th century. **2** a large public lounge on a ship.

sa·lo·pettes /,salə'pets/ ▸ pl.n. padded pants with a high waist and shoulder straps, worn for skiing.

sal·sa /'sälsə/ ▸ n. **1** a type of Latin American dance music incorporating elements of jazz and rock. **2** a dance performed to this music. **3** a spicy tomato condiment or dip.

sal·si·fy /'salsəfē, -,fī/ ▸ n. a plant with a long edible root like that of a parsnip.

SALT /sôlt/ ▸ abbr. Strategic Arms Limitation Talks.

salt /sôlt/ ▸ n. **1** (also **common salt** or **table salt**) sodium chloride, a white substance in the form of crystals used for seasoning or preserving food. **2** any chemical compound formed by the reaction of an acid with a base, with the hydrogen of the acid replaced by a metal or equivalent group. ▸ adj. containing or treated with salt: *salt water.* ▸ v. **1** season or preserve something with salt. **2** sprinkle a road or path with salt to melt snow or ice. **3** (**salt something away**) informal secretly put money away for future use. ■ **salt·less** adj. **salt·ness** n.
– PHRASES **rub salt into the wound** make a painful experience even more distressing. **the salt of the earth** a very kind, honest, or reliable person. **take something with a grain of salt** be aware that something may be exaggerated. **worth one's salt** good or competent at one's job.

salt-and-pep·per ▸ adj. speckled with a mixture of dark and light shades.

salt·box /'sôlt,bäks/ ▸ n. a style of house with two or three stories in the front and one fewer in the back, with a deeply pitched roof.

salt·bush /'sôlt,bŏŏsh/ ▸ n. a salt-tolerant plant, sometimes planted on saline soils to provide grazing.

salt·cel·lar /'sôlt,selər/ (also **salt cellar**) ▸ n. **1** a dish or other container for serving or storing salt. **2** a salt shaker.

salt flats ▸ pl.n. areas of flat land covered with a layer of salt.

sal·tire /'sal,tīr, 'sôl-/ ▸ n. Heraldry an X-shaped cross.

salt lick ▸ n. **1** a place where animals go to lick salt from the ground. **2** a block of salt provided for animals to lick.

salt marsh ▶ n. an area of coastal grassland that is regularly flooded by seawater.

salt pan ▶ n. a shallow container or hollow in the ground in which salt water evaporates to leave a deposit of salt.

salt·pe·ter /'sôlt'pētər/ (Brit. **saltpetre**) ▶ n. potassium nitrate or (**Chile saltpeter**) sodium nitrate.

salt shak·er ▶ n. a container with a perforated lid for sprinkling salt.

salt·wa·ter /'sôlt,wôtər, -,wätər/ ▶ adj. relating to or found in salt water; living in the sea.

salt·y /'sôltē/ ▶ adj. (**saltier, saltiest**) 1 tasting of or containing salt. 2 (of language or humor) racy or coarse: *recounting salty anecdotes.* ■ **salt·i·ly** adv. **salt·i·ness** n.

sa·lu·bri·ous /sə'lōōbrēəs/ ▶ adj. 1 good for the health; healthy. 2 (of a place) clean, well kept and pleasant. ■ **sa·lu·bri·ous·ly** adv. **sa·lu·bri·ty** /-britē/ n.

sa·lu·ki /sə'lōōkē/ ▶ n. (pl. **salukis**) a tall, slender breed of dog with a silky coat and large drooping ears.

sal·u·tar·y /'salyə,terē/ ▶ adj. 1 (of something unpleasant) beneficial because providing an opportunity to learn from experience: *the cut and thrust over pricing proved a salutary experience for the company.* 2 dated health-giving.

sal·u·ta·tion /,salyə'tāsHən/ ▶ n. formal a greeting.

sa·lute /sə'lōōt/ ▶ n. 1 a gesture of respect or acknowledgment. 2 a movement, typically a raising of a hand to the head, made as a formal gesture of respect by a member of a military or similar force. 3 the firing of a gun or guns as a formal or ceremonial sign of respect or celebration. ▶ v. 1 make a formal salute to a member of a military or similar force. 2 greet someone with a gesture. 3 express admiration and respect for: *we salute his genius.*

Sal·va·dor·ean /,salvə'dôrēən/ ▶ n. a person from El Salvador, a country in Central America. ▶ adj. relating to El Salvador.

sal·vage /'salvij/ ▶ v. 1 rescue a ship or its cargo from loss at sea. 2 save from possible loss, harm, or failure: *his latest stunt will do nothing to salvage his reputation.* ▶ n. 1 the rescue of a ship or its cargo from loss at sea. 2 cargo, property, or other items that have been saved from loss or harm. 3 Law payment made or due to a person who has salvaged a ship or its cargo. ■ **sal·vage·a·ble** adj. **sal·vag·er** n.

sal·va·tion /sal'vāsHən/ ▶ n. 1 the saving or protection of someone or something from harm or ruin. 2 (**one's salvation**) a means of being saved from harm or ruin: *his only salvation was to outwit the enemy.* 3 (in Christian belief) deliverance from sin and its consequences, believed to be brought about by faith in Jesus.

sal·va·tion·ist /sal'vāsHənist/ ▶ n. (**Salvationist**) a member of the Salvation Army, a Christian evangelical organization. ▶ adj. 1 relating to salvation in Christian belief. 2 (**Salvationist**) relating to the Salvation Army.

salve /sav, säv/ ▶ n. 1 an ointment used to help the skin to heal. 2 something that helps to reduce distress, guilt, etc.: *shopping is the perfect salve for my wounded ego.* ▶ v. do something to feel less guilty: *charity salves our conscience.*

sal·ver /'salvər/ ▶ n. a tray, typically one made of silver and used on formal occasions.

sal·vi·a /'salvēə/ ▶ n. a plant of a large group that includes sage, especially one grown for its bright scarlet flowers.

sal·vo /'sal,vō/ ▶ n. (pl. **salvos** or **salvoes**) 1 a simultaneous firing of artillery or other guns in a battle. 2 a sudden vigorous or aggressive series of acts: *a salvo of accusations.*

sal vo·la·ti·le /,sal və'latl-ē/ ▶ n. a scented solution of ammonium carbonate in alcohol, used as smelling salts.

SAM /sam/ ▶ abbr. surface-to-air missile.

Sa·mar·i·tan /sə'maritn, -'me(ə)r-/ ▶ n. 1 (**good Samaritan**) a charitable or helpful person. 2 a member of a people inhabiting Samaria, an ancient city and region of Palestine, in biblical times.

sa·mar·i·um /sə'me(ə)rēəm/ ▶ n. a hard silvery-white metallic chemical element of the lanthanide series.

sam·ba /'sambə, 'säm-/ ▶ n. a Brazilian dance of African origin. ▶ v. (**sambas, sambaing** /-bə,iNG/, **sambaed** /-bəd/) dance the samba.

sam·bal /'sämbäl/ ▶ n. (in oriental cooking) a spicy vegetable or fruit relish.

sam·bu·ca /sam'bōōkə/ ▶ n. an Italian anise-flavored liqueur.

same /sām/ ▶ adj. 1 (**the same**) exactly alike; not different or changed. 2 (**this/that same**) referring to a person or thing just mentioned: *that same year I went to Boston.* ▶ pron. (**the same**) 1 the same thing as previously mentioned. 2 identical people or things. ▶ adv. in the same way. ■ **same·ness** n.

– PHRASES **all** (or **just**) **the same** in spite of this; even so.

Sa·mi /'sämē/ ▶ pl.n. the people of Lapland in northern Scandinavia.

> **USAGE**
> **Sami** is the term by which the Lapps themselves prefer to be known.

sam·ite /'samīt, 'sā-/ ▶ n. historical a rich silk fabric interwoven with gold and silver threads.

sam·iz·dat /'sämiz,dät, səmyiz'dät/ ▶ n. (especially in the former Soviet Union) the secret copying and distribution of literature banned by the government.

Sa·mo·an /sə'mōən/ ▶ n. 1 a person from Samoa. 2 the Polynesian language of Samoa. ▶ adj. relating to Samoa.

sa·mo·sa /sə'mōsə/ ▶ n. a triangular fried Indian pastry containing spiced vegetables or meat.

sam·o·var /'samə,vär/ ▶ n. a decorated Russian urn used to heat water for tea.

Sam·o·yed /'samə,yed, sə'moiyid/ ▶ n. 1 a white Arctic breed of dog. 2 a member of a group of mainly nomadic peoples of northern Siberia.

sam·pan /'sam,pan/ ▶ n. a small boat propelled with an oar at the stern, used in the Far East.

sam·phire /'sam,fīr/ ▶ n. an edible fleshy-leaved plant that grows on rocks near the sea.

sam·ple /'sampəl/ ▶ n. 1 a small part or quantity intended to show what the whole is like. 2 a specimen of a substance taken for scientific testing or analysis. 3 a sound created by sampling. ▶ v. 1 take a sample or samples of something. 2 experience something briefly to see what it is like: *we finally got a chance to sample the New Orleans nightlife.* 3 (often as n. **sampling**) record or extract a small piece of music or sound digitally for use in a different piece of music.

sam·pler /'samplər/ ▶ n. **1** a piece of embroidery worked in various stitches to demonstrate a person's skill. **2** a representative collection or example of something. **3** an electronic device for sampling music and sound.

sam·u·rai /'samə,rī/ ▶ n. (pl. same) historical a member of a military class in Japan.

San /sän/ ▶ n. (pl. same) **1** a member of the Bushmen (a number of aboriginal peoples) of southern Africa. **2** the languages spoken by the San.

san·a·to·ri·um /,sanə'tôrēəm/ ▶ n. (pl. **sanatoriums** or **sanatoria** /-rēə/) another term for **SANITARIUM**.

San·cerre /sän'ser/ ▶ n. a light white wine produced in Sancerre, in the Loire region of France.

sanc·ti·fy /'saNG(k)tə,fī/ ▶ v. (**sanctifies**, **sanctifying**, **sanctified**) **1** make or declare something holy; consecrate. **2** make official or binding by a religious ceremony: *their love is sanctified by the sacrament of marriage.* **3** free someone or something from sin. ■ **sanc·ti·fi·ca·tion** /-fi'kāsHən/ n.

sanc·ti·mo·ni·ous /,saNG(k)tə'mōnēəs/ ▶ adj. derogatory making a show of being morally better than other people. ■ **sanc·ti·mo·ni·ous·ly** adv. **sanc·ti·mo·ni·ous·ness** n. **sanc·ti·mo·ny** /'saNG(k)tə,mōnē/ n.

sanc·tion /'saNG(k)sHən/ ▶ n. **1** a threatened penalty or punishment for disobeying a law or rule. **2** (**sanctions**) measures taken by a country to try to force another to do or obey something. **3** official permission or approval. ▶ v. **1** give official permission for: *the scheme was sanctioned by the court.* **2** impose a penalty on someone or something. ■ **sanc·tion·a·ble** adj.

sanc·ti·ty /'saNG(k)titē/ ▶ n. **1** the state or quality of being holy. **2** the state of being highly valued and worthy of great respect: *the sanctity of human life.*

sanc·tu·ar·y /'saNG(k)cHōō,erē/ ▶ n. (pl. **sanctuaries**) **1** a place or state of safety or protection: *they fled abroad, where they were offered sanctuary.* **2** a nature reserve. **3** a place where injured or unwanted animals are cared for. **4** a holy place. **5** the part of the chancel of a church containing the high altar.

sanc·tum /'saNG(k)təm/ ▶ n. (pl. **sanctums**) **1** a sacred or holy place. **2** a room to which a person can go for privacy and quiet: *the inner sanctum of the library.*

Sanc·tus /'saNG(k)təs/ ▶ n. (in the Christian Church) a hymn beginning *Sanctus, sanctus, sanctus* (Holy, holy, holy) forming a set part of the Mass.

sand /sand/ ▶ n. **1** a substance consisting of very fine particles resulting from the erosion of rocks, found on beaches, riverbeds, the seabed, and deserts. **2** (**sands**) a wide area of sand. ▶ v. **1** smooth something with sandpaper or a sander. **2** sprinkle something with sand.

san·dal /'sandl/ ▶ n. a shoe with a partly open upper or straps attaching the sole to the foot. ■ **san·daled** adj.

san·dal·wood /'sandl,wŏŏd/ ▶ n. the sweet-smelling wood of an Indian or SE Asian tree.

sand·bag /'san(d),bag/ ▶ n. a bag of sand, used for protection against floods or explosions.

▶ v. (**sandbags**, **sandbagging**, **sandbagged**) **1** protect or reinforce something with sandbags. **2** informal cause severe harm or damage to: *they saw their marriage sandbagged by problems.* ■ **sand·bag·ger** n.

sand·bank /'san(d),baNGk/ ▶ n. a buildup of sand forming a raised bank in the sea or a river.

sand·bar /'san(d),bär/ ▶ n. a long, narrow sandbank.

sand·blast /'san(d),blast/ ▶ v. roughen or clean something with a jet of sand driven by compressed air or steam. ■ **sand·blast·er** n.

sand·board /'san(d),bôrd/ ▶ n. a long, narrow board, often a modified snowboard, used for sliding down sand dunes. ■ **sand·board·er** n. **sand·board·ing** n.

sand·box /'san(d),bäks/ ▶ n. a shallow box or hollow containing sand for children to play in.

sand·cas·tle /'san(d),kasəl/ ▶ n. a model of a castle built out of sand.

sand·er /'sandər/ ▶ n. a power tool used for smoothing a surface.

sand·er·ling /'sandərliNG/ ▶ n. a small sandpiper, typically seen running after waves on the beach.

sand·fly /'san(d),flī/ ▶ n. (pl. **sandflies**) a small biting fly of tropical and subtropical regions that transmits a number of diseases.

S&H ▶ abbr. shipping and handling.

San·di·nis·ta /,sandə'nēstə/ ▶ n. a member of a left-wing Nicaraguan political organization, in power from 1979 until 1990.

sand·man /'san(d),man/ ▶ n. (**the sandman**) (in stories) a man supposed to make children sleep by sprinkling sand in their eyes.

sand mar·tin ▶ n. a small swallow with dark brown and white plumage, which digs nest holes in sandy banks near water.

sand·pa·per /'san(d),pāpər/ ▶ n. paper with sand or another rough substance stuck to it, used for smoothing surfaces. ▶ v. smooth something with sandpaper. ■ **sand·pa·per·y** adj.

sand·pi·per /'san(d),pīpər/ ▶ n. a wading bird with a long bill and long legs, found in coastal areas.

sand·pit /'san(d),pit/ ▶ n. a quarry from which sand is excavated.

sand·stone /'san(d),stōn/ ▶ n. red, yellow, or brown rock consisting of sand or quartz grains cemented together.

sand·storm /'san(d),stôrm/ ▶ n. a strong wind in a desert carrying clouds of sand.

sand·wich /'san(d)wicH/ ▶ n. two pieces of bread with a filling between them. ▶ v. **1** place in a restricted space between two other people or things: *the house was sandwiched between a store and a clinic.* **2** (**sandwich things together**) squeeze two things together.

sand·wich board ▶ n. a pair of advertisement boards connected by straps by which they are hung over a person's shoulders.

sand·y /'sandē/ ▶ adj. (**sandier**, **sandiest**) **1** covered in or consisting of sand. **2** light yellowish brown.

sane /sān/ ▶ adj. **1** having a normal mind; not mad. **2** reasonable or sensible: *a sane discussion of important issues.* ■ **sane·ly** adv.

sang /saNG/ ▶ past of **SING**.

sang·froid /säNG'frwä/ ▶ n. the ability to stay calm in difficult circumstances.

San·gio·vese /ˌsanjōˈvāzē/ ▶ n. an Italian red wine made from a variety of black wine grape.

san·gri·a /saNGˈgrēə/ ▶ n. a Spanish drink of red wine, lemonade, fruit, and spices.

san·gui·nar·y /ˈsaNGgwəˌnerē/ ▶ adj. chiefly literary involving or causing much bloodshed.

san·guine /ˈsaNGgwin/ ▶ adj. 1 cheerfully confident about the future. 2 (in medieval medicine) having a predominance of blood among the bodily humors, supposedly marked by a ruddy complexion and an optimistic disposition.

San·hed·rin /sanˈhedrən, -ˈhēdrin, sän- / ▶ n. the highest court of justice and the supreme council in ancient Jerusalem.

san·i·tar·i·um /ˌsaniˈte(ə)rēəm/ ▶ n. (pl. **sanitariums** or **sanitaria** /-ˈte(ə)rēə/) a place for the care of people who are recovering from an illness or who are chronically ill.

san·i·tar·y /ˈsaniˌterē/ ▶ adj. 1 relating to sanitation: *a sanitary engineer*. 2 hygienic and clean. 3 referring to sanitary napkins and tampons.

san·i·tary nap·kin (Brit. **sanitary towel**) ▶ n. a pad worn by women to absorb blood during a menstrual period.

san·i·ta·tion /ˌsaniˈtāsHən/ ▶ n. arrangements to protect public health, especially the provision of clean drinking water and the disposal of sewage.

san·i·tize /ˈsaniˌtīz/ ▶ v. 1 make something hygienic. 2 (often as adj. **sanitized**) derogatory make more acceptable by removing inappropriate or unpleasant material: *sanitized versions of raunchy CDs*. ■ **san·i·tiz·er** n.

san·i·ty /ˈsanitē/ ▶ n. 1 the condition of being mentally healthy. 2 reasonable and rational behavior.

sank /saNGk/ ▶ past of **SINK**[1].

sans /sanz/ ▶ prep. literary without: *she plays her role sans accent*.

sans-cu·lotte /ˌsanz k(y)ōōˈlät/ ▶ n. an extreme republican or revolutionary.

san·sei /ˈsänsā/ ▶ n. (pl. same) a person born in the US or Canada whose grandparents were immigrants from Japan. Compare with **NISEI** and **ISSEI**.

San·skrit /ˈsanˌskrit/ ▶ n. an ancient language of India, still used as a language of religion and scholarship.

sans ser·if /ˌsan(z) ˈserəf/ ▶ n. a style of type without serifs (small projections on the letters).

San·ta Claus /ˈsantə ˌklôz/ (also informal **Santa**) ▶ n. an imaginary figure said to bring presents for children at Christmas.

sap[1] /sap/ ▶ n. the fluid that circulates in plants, consisting chiefly of water with nutrients.
▶ v. (**saps**, **sapping**, **sapped**) 1 gradually weaken a person's strength or power. 2 (**sap someone of**) drain someone of strength or power: *they were sapped of stamina and their self-belief*.

sap[2] ▶ n. historical a tunnel or trench dug to conceal the approach of an attacker to a fortified place.

sap[3] ▶ n. informal a foolish person.

sap·id /ˈsapid/ ▶ adj. having a strong and pleasant taste.

sa·pi·ent /ˈsāpēənt/ ▶ adj. formal wise or intelligent.

sap·ling /ˈsapliNG/ ▶ n. a young, slender tree.

sap·o·dil·la /ˌsapəˈdilə/ ▶ n. 1 a large evergreen tropical American tree with hard wood and a milky latex that is used to make chewing gum. 2 the sweet brownish bristly fruit of the sapodilla.

sa·pon·i·fy /səˈpänəˌfī/ ▶ v. (**saponifies, saponifying, saponified**) turn fat or oil into soap by reaction with an alkali. ■ **sa·pon·i·fi·ca·tion** /səˌpänəfiˈkāsHən/ n.

sap·per /ˈsapər/ ▶ n. a military engineer who lays or detects and disarms mines.

sap·phic /ˈsafik/ ▶ adj. 1 (**Sapphic**) relating to the ancient Greek poet Sappho, or her poetry expressing love and affection for women. 2 formal or humorous relating to lesbians.

sap·phire /ˈsafˌī(ə)r/ ▶ n. 1 a transparent blue precious stone. 2 a bright blue color.

sap·py /ˈsapē/ ▶ adj. (**sappier, sappiest**) 1 informal excessively sentimental. 2 (of a plant) containing a lot of sap.

sap·ro·phyte /ˈsaprəˌfīt/ ▶ n. a plant, fungus, or microorganism that lives on decaying matter. ■ **sap·ro·phyt·ic** /ˌsaprəˈfitik/ adj.

sap·wood /ˈsapˌwŏŏd/ ▶ n. the soft outer layers of new wood between the heartwood and the bark of a tree.

sar·a·band /ˈsarəˌband/ (also **sarabande**) ▶ n. a slow, stately Spanish dance in triple time.

Sar·a·cen /ˈsarəsən/ ▶ n. an Arab or Muslim at the time of the Crusades.

sa·ra·pe ▶ n. variant of **SERAPE**.

sar·casm /ˈsärˌkazəm/ ▶ n. a way of using words that say the opposite of what one means, in order to mock someone.

sar·cas·tic /särˈkastik/ ▶ adj. using words that say the opposite of what one means, in order to mock someone. ■ **sar·cas·ti·cal·ly** /-ik(ə)lē/ adv.

sar·co·ma /särˈkōmə/ ▶ n. (pl. **sarcomas** or **sarcomata** /-mətə/) a cancerous tumor of a kind found chiefly in connective tissue.

sar·coph·a·gus /särˈkäfəgəs/ ▶ n. (pl. **sarcophagi** /-ˌjī/) a stone coffin.

sar·dine /särˈdēn/ ▶ n. a young pilchard or other young or small herringlike fish.

Sar·din·i·an /särˈdinēən/ ▶ n. 1 a person from Sardinia. 2 the language of Sardinia. ▶ adj. relating to Sardinia.

sar·don·ic /särˈdänik/ ▶ adj. showing a mocking or cynical attitude. ■ **sar·don·i·cal·ly** /-ik(ə)lē/ adv. **sar·don·i·cism** /-ˈdänəˌsizəm/ n.

sar·don·yx /särˈdäniks/ ▶ n. onyx (a semiprecious stone) in which white layers alternate with yellow or reddish ones.

sar·gas·so /särˈgasō/ (also **sargassum** /särˈgasəm/) ▶ n. a brown seaweed with fronds that contain sacs filled with air, typically floating in large masses.

sarge /särj/ ▶ n. informal sergeant.

sa·ri /ˈsärē/ (also **saree**) ▶ n. (pl. **saris** or **sarees**) an item of clothing consisting of a length of cotton or silk draped around the body, worn by women from the Indian subcontinent.

sa·rin /ˈsärēn/ ▶ n. a nerve gas developed during World War II.

sa·rong /səˈrông, -ˈräNG/ ▶ n. an item of clothing consisting of a long piece of cloth wrapped around the body and tucked at the waist or under the armpits.

SARS /särz/ (also **Sars**) ▶ abbr. severe acute respiratory syndrome.

sar·sa·pa·ril·la /ˌsärs(ə)pəˈrilə, ˌsaspə-/ ▶ n. 1 a preparation of the dried roots of a tropical plant, used as a flavoring. **2** a sweet drink flavored with sarsaparilla.

sar·sen /'särsən/ ▶ n. a sandstone boulder of a kind used to construct Stonehenge and other prehistoric monuments in southern England.

sar·to·ri·al /sär'tôrēəl/ ▶ adj. relating to clothes or a person's style of dress: *their sartorial splendor has been emulated around the world.* ■ **sar·to·ri·al·ly** adv.

SASE ▶ abbr. self-addressed stamped envelope.

sash¹ /sash/ ▶ n. a long strip of cloth worn over one shoulder or around the waist.

sash² ▶ n. a frame holding the glass in a window.

sa·shay /sa'shā/ ▶ v. informal walk in a confident way, swinging the hips from side to side.

sa·shi·mi /sä'shēmē/ ▶ n. a Japanese dish of small pieces of raw fish eaten with soy sauce and horseradish paste.

sash win·dow ▶ n. a window with one or two sashes (frames of glass) that can be slid up or down to open it.

Sas·quatch /'saskwäch, -kwach/ ▶ n. another name for BIGFOOT.

sass /sas/ informal ▶ n. disrespectful behavior; impertinence. ▶ v. be impertinent or rude to (someone).

sas·sa·fras /'sasə,fras/ ▶ n. an extract of the aromatic leaves or bark of a North American tree, used in medicines and perfumes.

Sas·se·nach /'sasə,nak/ Scottish & Irish derogatory ▶ n. an English person. ▶ adj. English.

sas·sy /'sasē/ ▶ adj. (**sassier, sassiest**) informal lively, confident, or impudent. ■ **sas·si·ness** n.

SAT ▶ abbr. trademark (formerly and variously 'Scholastic Assessment Test' and 'Scholastic Aptitude Test') a test of a student's academic skills, used for admission to US colleges.

sat /sat/ ▶ past and past participle of SIT.

Sa·tan /'sātn/ ▶ n. the Devil.

sa·tan·ic /sə'tanik, sā'-/ ▶ adj. **1** relating to or typical of Satan, especially in being evil. **2** connected with satanism.

sa·tan·ism /'sātn,izəm/ ▶ n. the worship of Satan. ■ **sa·tan·ist** n. & adj.

sa·tay /'sä,tā/ (also **saté**) ▶ n. a SE Asian dish consisting of small pieces of meat broiled on a skewer and served with spiced peanut sauce.

satch·el /'sachəl/ ▶ n. a shoulder bag with a long strap and typically closed by a flap.

sate /sāt/ ▶ v. **1** satisfy a desire fully. **2** supply with as much or more than is desired: *the child slept, sated with food.*

sa·teen /sa'tēn/ ▶ n. a cotton fabric with a glossy surface.

sat·el·lite /'satl,īt/ ▶ n. **1** an artificial object placed in orbit around the earth or another planet to collect information or for communication. **2** a natural object orbiting a planet. **3** (usu. before another noun) a country, community, or organization dependent on or controlled by a larger or more powerful one: *satellite offices in London and New York.*

sat·el·lite dish ▶ n. a bowl-shaped aerial with which signals are transmitted to or received from a communications satellite.

sat·el·lite tel·e·vi·sion ▶ n. television in which the signals are broadcast via satellite.

sa·ti /sə'tē, 'sə,tē/ (also **suttee** pronunc. same) ▶ n. the former Hindu practice of a widow

throwing herself onto her husband's funeral pyre.

sa·ti·ate /'sāshē,āt/ ▶ v. give someone as much as or more than they want. ■ **sa·ti·a·tion** /,sāshē'āshən/ n.

sa·ti·e·ty /sə'tīətē/ ▶ n. the feeling or state of being fully satisfied.

sat·in /'satn/ ▶ n. a smooth, glossy fabric, usually of silk. ▶ adj. having a smooth, glossy surface or finish. ■ **sat·in·y** adj.

sat·in·wood /'satn,wŏŏd/ ▶ n. the glossy yellowish wood of a tropical tree, used in making furniture.

sat·ire /'sa,tīr/ ▶ n. **1** the use of humor, irony, or exaggeration as a form of mockery or criticism. **2** a play, novel, etc., using satire. ■ **sat·i·rist** /'satərist/ n.

sa·tir·i·cal /sə'ti(ə)rikəl/ (also **satiric** /-'ti(ə)rik/) ▶ adj. using humor, irony, or exaggeration to mock or criticize. ■ **sa·tir·i·cal·ly** adv.

sat·i·rize /'satə,rīz/ ▶ v. mock or criticize by using humor, irony, or exaggeration: *the movie satirized the idea of national superiority.*

sat·is·fac·tion /,satis'fakshən/ ▶ n. **1** the state of being pleased because one's needs have been met or one has achieved something. **2** Law the payment of a debt or fulfillment of a duty or claim. **3** something due to one to make up for an injustice: *the work will stop if they don't get satisfaction.*

sat·is·fac·to·ry /,satis'fakt(ə)rē/ ▶ adj. acceptable, but not outstanding or perfect. ■ **sat·is·fac·to·ri·ly** adv.

sat·is·fied /'satis,fīd/ ▶ adj. contented; pleased: *satisfied customers.*

sat·is·fy /'satis,fī/ ▶ v. (**satisfies, satisfying, satisfied**) **1** please someone by meeting their expectations, needs, or desires: *I've never been satisfied with my job.* **2** fulfill a desire, demand, or need. **3** provide someone with adequate information or proof of something. **4** meet or comply with a condition or duty: *he had ceased to satisfy the conditions for residence.*

sat·phone /'sat,fōn/ ▶ n. a telephone that transmits its signal via a communications satellite.

sat·trap /'sā,trap, 'sa-/ ▶ n. **1** a subordinate or local ruler. **2** a provincial governor in the ancient Persian empire.

sat·su·ma /sat'sōōmə, 'satsə,mä/ ▶ n. a variety of tangerine with a loose skin.

sat·u·rate ▶ v. /'sachə,rāt/ **1** soak someone or something thoroughly with water or other liquid. **2** fill a market with so many products that demand is fully satisfied and no more products can be sold. **3** Chemistry cause a substance to combine with, dissolve, or hold the greatest possible quantity of another substance. ▶ n. /-rət/ a saturated fat.

sat·u·rat·ed /'sachə,rātid/ ▶ adj. **1** (of fats) having only single bonds between carbon atoms in their molecules and as a result being less easily processed by the body. **2** Chemistry (of a solution) containing the largest possible amount of the substance dissolved in it. **3** (of color) bright and rich.

sat·u·ra·tion /,sachə'rāshən/ ▶ n. the state of being so full that nothing else can be added: *a bid for market saturation.* ▶ adj. to the fullest extent: *saturation coverage by the press of police shootings.*

sat·u·ra·tion point ▶ n. the stage beyond which no more can be absorbed or accepted.

Sat·ur·day /'satər,dā, -dē/ ▶ n. the day of the week before Sunday and following Friday.

Sat·urn /'satərn/ ▶ n. a planet of the solar system, sixth in order from the sun and circled by broad flat rings. ■ **Sa·tur·ni·an** /sə'tərnēən/ adj.

Sat·ur·na·li·a /,satər'nālēə, -nālyə/ ▶ n. (treated as sing. or pl.) **1** the ancient Roman festival of the god Saturn in December, a period of wild celebration. **2** (**saturnalia**) literary a period or spell of wild celebration or self-indulgence. ■ **sat·ur·na·li·an** adj.

sat·ur·nine /'satər,nīn/ ▶ adj. **1** gloomy or serious. **2** (of looks) dark and moody.

sa·tyr /'satər, 'sātər/ ▶ n. **1** (in Greek Mythology) a lustful, drunken woodland god, represented as a man with a horse's ears and tail or (in Roman myth) with a goat's ears, tail, legs, and horns. **2** a man with strong sexual desires. ■ **sa·tyr·ic** /sə'tirik/ adj.

sauce /sôs/ ▶ n. **1** a liquid substance served with food to add moistness and flavor. **2** informal, chiefly Brit. impudent language or behavior; impudence. ▶ v. **1** provide with a sauce: *the noodles are sauced with a fish curry.* **2** informal, chiefly Brit. be impertinent or impudent to someone.

sauce·boat /'sôs,bōt/ ▶ n. a long, narrow vessel for serving sauce or gravy.

sauce·pan /'sôs,pan/ ▶ n. a deep cooking pan with a long handle and a lid.

sau·cer /'sôsər/ ▶ n. a shallow dish with a central circular hollow, on which a cup is placed.

sau·cy /'sôsē/ ▶ adj. (**saucier, sauciest**) informal **1** sexually suggestive in a lighthearted way: *saucy postcards.* **2** impudent. ■ **sau·ci·ly** adv. **sau·ci·ness** n.

Sau·di /'soudē, 'sô-/ ▶ n. (pl. **Saudis**) a person from Saudi Arabia, or a member of its ruling dynasty. ▶ adj. relating to Saudi Arabia or its ruling dynasty. ■ **Sau·di A·ra·bi·an** n. & adj.

sau·er·kraut /'sou(ə)r,krout/ ▶ n. a German dish of chopped pickled cabbage.

sau·na /'sônə, 'sou-/ ▶ n. **1** a small room used as a hot-air or steam bath for cleaning and refreshing the body. **2** a session in a sauna.

saun·ter /'sôntər/ ▶ v. walk in a slow, relaxed way. ▶ n. a leisurely stroll.

sau·ri·an /'sôrēən/ ▶ adj. relating to or like a lizard.

sau·ro·pod /'sôrə,päd/ ▶ n. a very large plant-eating dinosaur with a long neck and tail and a small head.

sau·sage /'sôsij/ ▶ n. **1** a short tube of raw minced meat encased in a skin, that is broiled or fried before eating. **2** a tube of spicy minced meat that is cooked or preserved and eaten cold in slices. **3** a cylindrical object.

sau·té /sō'tā, sô-/ (also **saute**) ▶ adj. fried quickly in a little hot fat. ▶ n. a dish of sautéed food. ▶ v. (**sautés, sautéing, sautéed** /-'tād/ or **sautéd**) fry food quickly in a little hot fat.

Sau·ternes /sō'tərn, sô-/ ▶ n. a sweet white wine from Sauternes in the Bordeaux region of France.

Sau·vi·gnon /,sōvin'yôn, -vē'nyôn/ (also **Sauvignon Blanc**) ▶ n. a white wine made from the Sauvignon variety of grape.

sav·age /'savij/ ▶ adj. **1** fierce and violent. **2** cruel or highly damaging: *a savage attack on*

the president. **3** primitive; uncivilized. ▶ n. **1** a member of a people regarded as primitive and uncivilized. **2** a brutal or vicious person. ▶ v. **1** (especially of a dog) attack someone or something ferociously. **2** criticize someone or something harshly. ■ **sav·age·ly** adv. **sav·age·ry** /-rē/ n.

sa·van·na /sə'vanə/ (also **savannah**) ▶ n. a grassy plain in tropical and subtropical regions, with few trees.

sa·vant /sa'vänt, sə-/ ▶ n. a very knowledgeable person.

save¹ /sāv/ ▶ v. **1** rescue someone or something from harm or danger. **2** prevent someone from dying. **3** store or keep something for future use. **4** keep data in a computer. **5** avoid the need to use up or spend: *computers save time.* **6** avoid something or prevent someone from doing or experiencing something: *this approach saves wear and tear on the books.* **7** (in Christian use) protect a person's soul from damnation. **8** Baseball (of a relief pitcher) finish a game while preserving a leading score. **9** chiefly Soccer & Hockey prevent an opponent from scoring a goal or point. ▶ n. **1** Baseball an instance of a relief pitcher saving a game. **2** chiefly Soccer & Hockey an act of preventing an opponent from scoring.
– PHRASES **save one's breath** not bother to say something pointless. **save someone's skin** (or **neck** or **bacon**) rescue someone from difficulty.

save² ▶ prep. & conj. formal or literary except; other than.

sav·er /'sāvər/ ▶ n. **1** a person who regularly saves money through a bank or recognized scheme. **2** something that prevents a resource from being used up: *a space-saver.*

sav·ing /'sāviNG/ ▶ n. **1** a reduction in use of a resource such as money or time. **2** (**savings**) money saved. ▶ adj. (in combination) preventing waste of a resource: *energy-saving.* ▶ prep. not including; except.

sav·ing grace ▶ n. a good quality that makes up for the faults of someone or something.

sav·ings ac·count ▶ n. a bank account that earns interest.

sav·ings and loan (also **savings and loan association**) ▶ n. an institution that pays interest on money deposited and lends money to savers.

sav·ings bank ▶ n. a bank that pays interest on deposits into savings accounts.

sav·ings bond ▶ n. a bond issued by the government and sold to the general public.

sav·ior /'sāvyər/ (Brit. **saviour**) ▶ n. **1** a person who saves someone or something from danger or harm. **2** (**the/our Savior**) (in Christianity) God or Jesus.

sav·oir faire /,savwär 'fe(ə)r/ ▶ n. the ability to act appropriately in social situations.

sa·vor /'sāvər/ (Brit. **savour**) ▶ v. **1** taste food or drink and enjoy it to the full. **2** enjoy or appreciate to the full: *I wanted to savor every moment.* **3** (**savor of**) have a suggestion or trace of an undesirable quality. ▶ n. **1** a characteristic taste or smell. **2** a trace, especially of something undesirable.

sa·vor·y¹ /'sāv(ə)rē/ ▶ n. a plant of the mint family, used as an herb in cooking.

sa·vor·y² (Brit. **savoury**) ▶ adj. **1** (of food) salty or spicy rather than sweet. **2** morally wholesome or acceptable: *the less savory aspects of the story.*

sa·voy /sə'voi/ ▸ n. a cabbage of a variety with wrinkled leaves.

sav·vy /'savē/ informal ▸ n. common sense or shrewdness. ▸ adj. (**savvier, savviest**) having common sense; shrewd. ▸ v. (**savvies, savvying, savvied**) know or understand something.

saw[1] /sô/ ▸ n. **1** a hand tool for cutting wood or other hard materials, having a long, thin toothed blade. **2** a mechanical power-driven cutting tool with a toothed rotating disk or moving band. ▸ v. (past part. **sawed** or **sawn**) **1** cut or make something with a saw. **2** cut something roughly. **3** make rapid movements like those of a saw.

saw[2] ▸ past of SEE[1].

saw[3] ▸ n. a proverb or wise saying.

saw·buck /'sô,bək/ ▸ n. **1** a sawhorse. **2** informal a $10 bill.

saw·dust /'sô,dəst/ ▸ n. powdery particles of wood produced by sawing.

sawed-off (also **sawn-off**) ▸ adj. **1** (of a gun) having had the barrel shortened for ease of handling and a wider field of fire. **2** informal (of an item of clothing) having been cut short.

saw·fish /'sô,fish/ ▸ n. (pl. same or **sawfishes**) a large tropical fish with a long flattened snout bearing large blunt teeth along each side.

saw·fly /'sô,flī/ ▸ n. (pl. **sawflies**) an insect related to the wasps, with a sawlike tube used in laying eggs in plant tissue.

saw·horse /'sô,hôrs/ ▸ n. a frame or trestle that supports wood for sawing.

saw·mill /'sô,mil/ ▸ n. a factory in which logs are sawn by machine.

sawn /sôn/ ▸ past participle of SAW[1].

saw·tooth /'sô,tōōTH/ (also **sawtoothed**) ▸ adj. shaped like the teeth of a saw.

saw·yer /'sôyər/ ▸ n. a person who saws timber.

sax /saks/ ▸ n. informal a saxophone. ■ **sax·ist** n.

sax·i·frage /'saksə,frij, -,frāj/ ▸ n. a low-growing plant of rocky or stony ground, bearing small white, yellow, or red flowers.

Sax·on /'saksən/ ▸ n. **1** a member of a Germanic people that conquered and settled in much of southern England in the 5th–6th centuries. **2** a person from modern Saxony in Germany. **3** (**Old Saxon**) the language of the ancient Saxons. ▸ adj. **1** relating to the Anglo-Saxons or their period of dominance in England (5th–11th centuries). **2** relating to modern Saxony.

sax·o·phone /'saksə,fōn/ ▸ n. a member of a family of metal wind instruments with a reed like a clarinet, used especially in jazz. ■ **sax·o·phon·ic** /,saksə'fänik/ adj. **sax·o·phon·ist** /-,fōnist/ n.

say /sā/ ▸ v. (**says** /sez/, **saying** /'sāiNG/, **said** /sed/) **1** speak words so as to convey information, an opinion, an instruction, etc. **2** (of a piece of writing or a symbol) convey information or instructions. **3** (of a clock or watch) indicate a time. **4** (**be said**) be claimed or reported. **5** (**say something for**) present a consideration in favor of or excusing: *he had nothing to say for himself.* **6** suggest as an example, possibility, or a basis for a theory: *let's say the fine is $79.* ▸ n. an opportunity to state one's opinion or to influence events. ■ **say·a·ble** adj. **say·er** n.
– PHRASES **go without saying** be obvious. **say the word** give permission or instructions. **there is no saying** it is impossible to know. **when all**

is said and done when everything is taken into account.

say·ing /'sāiNG/ ▸ n. a short, well-known expression containing advice or wisdom.

say-so ▸ n. informal the power to decide or allow something: *an owner can only close an area with the say-so of the council.*

Sb ▸ symbol the chemical element antimony.

SBA ▸ abbr. Small Business Administration.

SBS ▸ abbr. **1** sick building syndrome. **2** Special Boat Service.

SC ▸ abbr. South Carolina.

Sc ▸ symbol the chemical element scandium.

scab /skab/ ▸ n. **1** a dry protective crust that forms over a cut or wound during healing. **2** mange or a similar skin disease in animals. **3** a plant disease caused by a fungus, in which rough patches develop. **4** informal, derogatory a person who refuses to take part in a strike. ■ **scabbed** adj. **scab·by** adj.

scab·bard /'skabərd/ ▸ n. **1** a sheath for the blade of a sword or dagger. **2** a sheath for a gun or tool.

sca·bies /'skābēz/ ▸ n. a contagious skin disease marked by itching and small raised red spots, caused by a mite.

sca·bi·ous /'skābēəs/ ▸ n. a plant with blue, pink, or white pincushion-shaped flowers.

scab·rous /'skabrəs/ ▸ adj. **1** indecent or sordid: *scabrous Hollywood gossip.* **2** rough and covered with scabs.

scads /skadz/ ▸ pl.n. informal a large number or quantity.

scaf·fold /'skafəld, -,fōld/ ▸ n. **1** a raised wooden platform formerly used for public executions. **2** a structure made using scaffolding. ▸ v. attach scaffolding to a building. ■ **scaf·fold·er** n.

scaf·fold·ing /'skafəldiNG, -,fōl-/ ▸ n. **1** a temporary structure made of wooden planks and metal poles, used while building, repairing, or cleaning a building. **2** the materials used in scaffolding.

scal·a·ble /'skāləbəl/ (also **scaleable**) ▸ adj. **1** able to be climbed. **2** able to be changed in size or scale. **3** technical able to be graded according to a scale. ■ **scal·a·bil·i·ty** /,skālə'bilitē/ n.

sca·lar /'skālər/ Mathematics & Physics ▸ adj. having only magnitude, not direction. ▸ n. a quantity having only magnitude, not direction.

scal·a·wag /'skālə,wag/ (also **scallywag**) ▸ n. informal a mischievous person; a rascal.

scald /skôld/ ▸ v. **1** burn someone or something with very hot liquid or steam. **2** heat a liquid to near boiling point. **3** dip something briefly in boiling water. ▸ n. a burn caused by hot liquid or steam.

scale[1] /skāl/ ▸ n. **1** each of the small overlapping plates protecting the skin of fish and reptiles. **2** a thick dry flake of skin. **3** limescale in a kettle, boiler, etc. **4** tartar formed on teeth. ▸ v. **1** remove scale or scales from something. **2** (often as n. **scaling**) (especially of the skin) form or flake off in scales.

scale[2] ▸ n. **1** (usu. **scales**) an instrument or device for weighing. **2** either of the dishes on a simple scale balance.
– PHRASES **tip the scales** (or **balance**) be the deciding factor.

scale[3] ▸ n. **1** a range of values forming a standard system for measuring or grading something: *a pay scale.* **2** a measuring instrument with a

series of marks at regular intervals. **3** relative size or extent: *he operated on a grand scale.* **4** a ratio of size in a map, model, drawing, or plan. **5** an arrangement of the notes in a system of music in ascending or descending order of pitch. ▶v. **1** climb up or over something high and steep. **2** (**scale something back**/**down** or **up**) reduce (or increase) something in size, number, or extent. **3** (usu. as adj. **scaled**) represent in measurements that are in proportion to the size of the original: *a strictly scaled depiction of Scotland's regions.*
– PHRASES **to scale** reduced or enlarged in proportion to something.

scale in·sect ▶n. a small bug that produces a shieldlike scale and spends its life attached to a single plant.

sca·lene /ˈskāˌlēn/ ▶adj. (of a triangle) having sides unequal in length.

scal·lion /ˈskalyən/ ▶n. a long-necked onion with a small bulb, especially a green onion.

scal·lop /ˈskäləp, ˈskal-/ ▶n. **1** an edible shellfish with two hinged fan-shaped shells. **2** each of a series of small curves resembling the edge of a scallop shell, forming a decorative edging.
▶v. (**scallops, scalloping, scalloped**) (usu. as adj. **scalloped**) decorate something with a series of small curves.

scal·ly·wag /ˈskalēˌwag/ ▶n. variant spelling of SCALAWAG.

scalp /skalp/ ▶n. **1** the skin covering the top and back of the head. **2** historical the scalp with the hair cut away from an enemy's head as a battle trophy, a former practice among American Indians. ▶v. **1** historical take the scalp of an enemy. **2** informal resell a ticket for a popular event at a price higher than the official one. ■ **scalp·er** n.

scal·pel /ˈskalpəl/ ▶n. a knife with a small sharp blade, used by a surgeon.

scal·y /ˈskālē/ ▶adj. **1** covered in scales. **2** (of skin) dry and flaking.

scam /skam/ informal ▶n. a dishonest scheme; a fraud. ▶v. (**scams, scamming, scammed**) swindle someone. ■ **scam·mer** n.

scamp /skamp/ ▶n. informal a mischievous person, especially a child. ■ **scamp·ish** adj.

scamp·er /ˈskampər/ ▶v. run with quick light steps, especially through fear or excitement. ▶n. an act of scampering.

scam·pi /ˈskampē/ ▶n. (treated as sing. or pl.) a dish consisting of the tails of a kind of large shrimp, typically fried in butter and garlic and topped with breadcrumbs.

scan /skan/ ▶v. (**scans, scanning, scanned**) **1** look over something quickly in order to find relevant features or information. **2** move a detector or electromagnetic beam across someone or something, especially to obtain an image. **3** convert a document or picture into digital form for storage or processing on a computer. **4** analyze the meter of a line of verse. **5** (of verse) follow metrical principles. ▶n. **1** an act of scanning. **2** a medical examination using a scanner. **3** an image obtained by scanning. ■ **scan·na·ble** adj.

scan·dal /ˈskandl/ ▶n. **1** behavior or a situation regarded as wrong or unacceptable and causing general outrage. **2** outrage or gossip arising from such behavior: *the media's craving for scandal.*

scan·dal·ize /ˈskandlˌīz/ ▶v. shock or horrify someone by acting in an immoral or unacceptable way.

scan·dal·mon·ger /ˈskandlˌməNGgər, -ˌmäNGgər/ ▶n. a person who spreads rumors or spiteful gossip.

scan·dal·ous /ˈskandl-əs/ ▶adj. **1** causing general outrage by being wrong or unacceptable. **2** (of a situation) disgracefully bad. ■ **scan·dal·ous·ly** adv.

Scan·di·na·vi·an /ˌskandəˈnāvēən/ ▶adj. relating to Scandinavia. ▶n. **1** a person from Scandinavia. **2** the northern branch of the Germanic languages, comprising Danish, Norwegian, Swedish, Icelandic, and Faeroese.

scan·di·um /ˈskandēəm/ ▶n. a soft silvery-white metallic chemical element.

scan·ner /ˈskanər/ ▶n. **1** a machine that examines the body through the use of radiation, ultrasound, etc., used to aid diagnosis. **2** a device that scans documents and converts them into digital data.

scan·sion /ˈskansHən/ ▶n. **1** the action of scanning a line of verse to determine its rhythm. **2** the rhythm of a line of verse.

scant /skant/ ▶adj. **1** not enough; hardly any: *he paid scant attention to the needs of his wife.* **2** only just reaching the amount specified: *she weighed a scant two pounds.* ■ **scant·ly** adv.

scant·y /ˈskantē/ ▶adj. (**scantier, scantiest**) too little in quantity or amount. ▶pl.n. (**scanties**) informal women's skimpy panties. ■ **scant·i·ly** adv.

scape·goat /ˈskāpˌgōt/ ▶n. **1** a person who is blamed for the wrongdoings or mistakes of others. **2** (in the Bible) a goat sent into the wilderness after the Jewish chief priest had symbolically laid the sins of the people on it.
▶v. blame someone for the wrongdoings or mistakes of others.

scap·u·la /ˈskapyələ/ ▶n. (pl. **scapulae** /-ˌlē/ or **scapulas**) technical term for SHOULDER BLADE.

scap·u·lar /ˈskapyələr/ ▶adj. relating to the shoulder or shoulder blade. ▶n. a short cloak worn by monks, covering the shoulders.

scar /skär/ ▶n. **1** a mark left on the skin or within body tissue after a wound or burn has healed. **2** a lasting effect left following an unpleasant experience. **3** a mark left at the point where a leaf or other part has separated from a plant.
▶v. (**scars, scarring, scarred**) **1** mark someone or something with a scar or scars. **2** have a lasting and unpleasant effect on: *he was so traumatized by his childhood that he was scarred for life.*

scar·ab /ˈskarəb/ ▶n. **1** a large dung beetle, treated as sacred in ancient Egypt. **2** an ancient Egyptian gem in the form of a scarab.

scarce /ske(ə)rs/ ▶adj. **1** (of a resource) available in quantities that are too small to meet the demand for it. **2** occurring in small numbers or quantities; rare. ■ **scar·ci·ty** /ˈskersitē/ n.
– PHRASES **make oneself scarce** informal leave a place, especially so as to avoid a difficult situation.

scarce·ly /ˈske(ə)rslē/ ▶adv. **1** only just. **2** only a very short time before. **3** used to suggest that something is unlikely: *they could scarcely all be wrong.*

scare /ske(ə)r/ ▶v. **1** frighten or become frightened: *just seeing those needles scared me to death.* **2** (**scare someone away**/**off**) drive or keep someone away by fear. ▶n. **1** a sudden attack of fright. **2** a period of general anxiety or alarm: *a bomb scare.*

scare·crow /'ske(ə)r,krō/ ▶ n. an object made to resemble a person, set up to scare birds away from a field where crops are growing.

scared /ske(ə)rd/ ▶ adj. feeling or showing fear or nervousness.

scared·y-cat /'ske(ə)rdē ,kat/ ▶ n. informal a timid person.

scare·mon·ger /'ske(ə)r,məNGgər, -,mäNGgər/ ▶ n. a person who spreads frightening rumors. ■ **scare·mon·ger·ing** n.

scare quotes ▶ pl.n. quotation marks used around a word or phrase for emphasis or to express doubt.

scarf¹ /skärf/ ▶ n. (pl. **scarves** /skärvz/ or **scarfs**) a length or square of fabric worn around the neck or head. ■ **scarfed** /skärft/ (also **scarved** /skärvd/) adj.

scarf² ▶ v. join the ends of two pieces of wood or metal by beveling or notching them so that they fit together. ▶ n. a joint made by scarfing.

scarf³ ▶ v. informal eat or drink hungrily or enthusiastically: *he scarfed down the waffles.*

scar·i·fy /'skarə,fī/ ▶ v. (**scarifies, scarifying, scarified**) **1** make shallow cuts in the skin. **2** break up the surface of (soil or a road or sidewalk. **3** break up and remove matted vegetation from a lawn. **4** criticize someone harshly. ■ **scar·i·fi·ca·tion** /-fi'kāshən/ n. **scar·i·fi·er** n.

scar·la·ti·na /,skärlə'tēnə/ ▶ n. another term for SCARLET FEVER.

scar·let /'skärlit/ ▶ n. a bright red color.

scar·let fe·ver ▶ n. an infectious disease that particularly affects children, caused by bacteria and marked by fever and a scarlet rash.

scar·let wom·an ▶ n. chiefly humorous a woman known for having many sexual relationships.

scarp /skärp/ ▶ n. a very steep bank or slope; an escarpment.

scarp·er /'skärpər/ ▶ v. Brit. informal run away.

Scart /skärt/ (also **SCART**) ▶ n. a 21-pin socket used to connect video equipment.

scarves /skärvz/ ▶ plural of SCARF¹.

scar·y /'ske(ə)rē/ ▶ adj. (**scarier, scariest**) informal causing fear; frightening. ■ **scar·i·ly** adv.

scat¹ /skat/ ▶ v. (**scats, scatting, scatted**) informal go away; leave.

scat² ▶ n. improvised jazz singing in which the voice is used to imitate an instrument. ▶ v. (**scats, scatting, scatted**) sing using the voice to imitate an instrument.

scath·ing /'skāᴛʜiNG/ ▶ adj. harshly critical or scornful. ■ **scath·ing·ly** adv.

scat·o·log·i·cal /,skatl'äjikəl/ ▶ adj. concerned or obsessed with excrement and excretion. ■ **sca·tol·o·gy** /skə'täləjē/ n.

scat·ter /'skatər/ ▶ v. **1** throw a number of things in various random directions. **2** (of a group of people or animals) separate and move off in different directions. **3** (**be scattered**) occur or be found at various places rather than all together: *more than 73,000 cell phone masts are scattered across the landscape.*

scat·ter·brained /'skatər,brānd/ ▶ adj. disorganized and unable to concentrate on things.

scat·ter·gun /'skatər,gən/ ▶ n. a shotgun. ▶ adj. another term for SCATTERSHOT.

scat·ter·ing /'skatəriNG/ (also **scatter**) ▶ n. a small amount or number of things spread over an area: *a scattering of chairs and tables on the sidewalk.*

scat·ter·shot /'skatər,shät/ ▶ adj. (also **scattergun**) covering a broad range in an unsystematic way: *the scattershot approach to selecting material.*

scav·enge /'skavənj/ ▶ v. **1** search for and collect anything usable from rubbish. **2** (of an animal or bird) search for and eat dead animals.

scav·eng·er /'skavənjər/ ▶ n. **1** an animal that feeds on dead animals or waste material. **2** a person who searches for and collects usable items from rubbish.

sce·nar·i·o /sə'ne(ə)rē,ō, -'när-/ ▶ n. (pl. **scenarios**) **1** a suggested sequence of events: *in the worst-case scenario, he could be looking at assault charges.* **2** a written outline of a movie, novel, play, etc., giving details of the plot and individual scenes.

scene /sēn/ ▶ n. **1** the place where an incident occurs or occurred. **2** a view or landscape as seen by a spectator. **3** an incident or situation of a particular kind: *scenes of violence.* **4** a sequence of continuous action in a play, movie, opera, book, etc. **5** a public display of emotion or anger: *she was loath to make a scene in the office.* **6** a specified area of activity or interest: *the literary scene.* **7** the scenery used in a play or opera. – PHRASES **behind the scenes** out of public view. **come** (or **appear** or **arrive**) **on the scene** arrive; appear.

scen·er·y /'sēn(ə)rē/ ▶ n. **1** the natural features of a landscape considered in terms of their appearance. **2** the painted background used to represent a place on a stage or movie set. – PHRASES **chew the scenery** informal (of an actor) overact.

sce·nic /'sēnik/ ▶ adj. **1** relating to impressive or beautiful natural scenery: *the scenic route.* **2** relating to theatrical scenery. ■ **sce·ni·cal·ly** /-ik(ə)lē/ adv.

scent /sent/ ▶ n. **1** a distinctive smell, especially one that is pleasant. **2** pleasant-smelling liquid worn on the skin; perfume. **3** a trail indicated by the smell of an animal. ▶ v. **1** give a pleasant scent to something. **2** find or recognize something by the sense of smell. **3** sense that something exists or is about to happen: *the general scented victory last night.* ■ **scent·ed** adj.

scep·ter /'septər/ (Brit. **sceptre**) ▶ n. a staff carried by a king or queen on ceremonial occasions. ■ **scep·tered** adj.

scep·tic, etc. /'skeptik/ ▶ n. British spelling of SKEPTIC, etc.

scha·den·freu·de /'sнädən,froidə/ ▶ n. pleasure that someone gains from another person's misfortune.

sched·ule /'skejōol, -jəl/ ▶ n. **1** a plan that lists the intended tasks, events, and times needed to achieve something. **2** a timetable. **3** chiefly Law an appendix to a formal document or statute. ▶ v. arrange or plan for something to happen or for someone to do something. ■ **sched·ul·er** n. – PHRASES **on** (or **to** or **according to**) **schedule** on time; as planned.

sched·uled /'skejōold, -əld/ ▶ adj. **1** forming part of or included on a schedule. **2** (of an airline or flight) forming part of a regular service rather than specially chartered.

sched·uled caste ▶ n. the official name given in India to the caste considered 'untouchable' in orthodox Hindu scriptures and practice, officially regarded as socially disadvantaged.

sche·ma /'skēmə/ ▶ n. (pl. **schemata** /-mətə/ or **schemas**) technical an outline of a plan or theory.

sche·mat·ic /skə'matik, skē-/ ▶ adj. 1 (of a diagram) outlining the main features of something; simplified. 2 following a fixed pattern or plan: *the plot feels manipulative and schematic.* ■ **sche·mat·i·cal·ly** /-ik(ə)lē/ adv.

sche·ma·tize /'skēmə,tīz/ ▶ v. arrange or represent something in a schematic or simplified form.

scheme /skēm/ ▶ n. 1 a systematic plan for achieving a particular aim. 2 a secret or underhanded plan; a plot. 3 an ordered system or pattern: *a classical rhyme scheme.* ▶ v. make plans in an underhanded way; plot. ■ **schem·er** n.

scher·zo /'skertsō/ ▶ n. (pl. **scherzos** or **scherzi** /-tsē/) a lively, light, or playful musical composition, typically comprising a movement in a symphony or sonata.

schil·ling /'sHiliNG/ ▶ n. (until the introduction of the euro in 2002) the basic unit of money of Austria.

schism /'s(k)izəm/ ▶ n. 1 a split between strongly opposed groups within an organization, caused by differences of opinion or belief. 2 the formal separation of a Church into two Churches owing to differences in belief. ■ **schis·mat·ic** /s(k)iz'matik/ adj. & n.

schist /sHist/ ▶ n. a coarse-grained metamorphic rock that consists of layers of different minerals.

schis·to·so·mi·a·sis /sHistōsə'mīəsis/ ▶ n. another term for BILHARZIA.

schiz·oid /'skit,soid/ ▶ adj. 1 referring to a personality type characterized by emotional coldness, eccentric behavior, and withdrawal into a fantasy world. 2 informal mad or crazy. ▶ n. a person with a schizoid personality.

schiz·o·phre·ni·a /,skitsə'frēnēə, -'frenēə/ ▶ n. a long-term mental disorder whose symptoms include a disintegration in the process of thinking and withdrawal from reality into fantasy.

schiz·o·phren·ic /,skitsə'frenik/ ▶ adj. 1 having schizophrenia. 2 informal having inconsistent or contradictory elements. ▶ n. a person with schizophrenia.

schle·miel /sHlə'mēl/ (also **shlemiel**) ▶ n. informal a stupid, awkward, or unlucky person.

schlep /sHlep/ (also **schlepp**) informal ▶ v. (**schleps, schlepping, schlepped**) 1 haul or carry something heavy or awkward. 2 go or move reluctantly or with effort. ▶ n. a boring or difficult journey.

schlock /sHläk/ ▶ n. informal cheap or inferior goods or material; rubbish. ■ **schlock·y** adj.

schmaltz /sHmälts, sHmólts/ ▶ n. informal excessive sentimentality. ■ **schmaltz·y** adj.

schmooze /sHmōōz/ informal ▶ v. 1 chat, especially at a social event. 2 talk in a friendly way to someone in order to gain an advantage. ■ **schmooz·er** n. **schmooz·y** adj.

schmuck /sHmək/ ▶ n. informal a stupid or worthless person.

schnapps /sHnäps, sHnaps/ ▶ n. a strong alcoholic drink resembling gin.

schnau·zer /'sHnouzər/ ▶ n. a German breed of dog with a close wiry coat and heavy whiskers around the muzzle.

schnit·zel /'sHnitsəl/ ▶ n. a thin slice of veal or other pale meat, coated in breadcrumbs and fried.

schol·ar /'skälər/ ▶ n. 1 a person who studies a particular subject in detail; an academic. 2 a college student holding a scholarship.

schol·ar·ly /'skälərlē/ ▶ adj. 1 relating to serious academic study. 2 devoted to academic studies; learned.

schol·ar·ship /'skälər,sHip/ ▶ n. 1 serious academic study. 2 a grant made to support a student's education, awarded on the basis of achievement.

scho·las·tic /skə'lastik/ ▶ adj. 1 relating to schools and education. 2 relating to medieval scholasticism. ▶ n. a follower of medieval scholasticism.

scho·las·ti·cism /skə'lasti,sizəm/ ▶ n. the system of theology and philosophy taught in medieval European universities, based mainly on Aristotle's philosophy and logic and the works of early Christian religious writers.

school¹ /skōōl/ ▶ n. 1 an institution for educating children. 2 a day's work at school. 3 any institution at which instruction is given in a particular subject. 4 a department or faculty of a university. 5 informal a college or university. 6 a group of artists, writers, or philosophers who share similar ideas or methods. ▶ v. 1 formal send someone to school. 2 train in a particular skill or activity: *he schooled her in horsemanship.*
– PHRASES **school of thought** a particular way of thinking.

school² ▶ n. a large group of fish or sea mammals.

school board ▶ n. a local board or authority responsible for providing and maintaining schools.

school·boy /'skōōl,boi/ (or **schoolgirl**) ▶ n. a boy (or girl) attending school.

school·child /'skōōl,CHīld/ ▶ n. (pl. **schoolchildren** /'skōōl,CHildrən/) a child attending school.

school·days /'skōōl,dāz/ ▶ pl.n. the period in someone's life when they attended school.

school·house /'skōōl,hous/ ▶ n. a building used as a school, especially in a small community.

school·ing /'skōōliNG/ ▶ n. education received at school.

school·marm /'skōōl,mä(r)m/ ▶ n. old use a schoolmistress, especially one who is prim and strict.

school·mas·ter /'skōōl,mastər/ (or **schoolmistress** /'skōōl,mistris/) ▶ n. chiefly Brit. a teacher in a school.

school·mate /'skōōl,māt/ ▶ n. informal a fellow student.

school·room /'skōōl,rōōm, -,rŏŏm/ ▶ n. a room in which a class of students is taught.

school·teach·er /'skōōl,tēCHər/ ▶ n. a person who teaches in a school.

school vouch·er ▶ n. a government-funded voucher redeemable for tuition fees at a school other than the public school that a student could attend free.

school·work /'skōōl,wərk/ ▶ n. work assigned to students by their teachers in school.

schoon·er /'skōōnər/ ▶ n. 1 a sailing ship with two or more masts, typically with a mainmast that is larger than the the mast nearer the front. **2** a large glass for beer or ale.

schot·tische /'sHätisH/ ▶n. a dance resembling a slow polka.

schuss /sHŏŏs, sHŏŏs/ ▶n. a straight downhill run on skis. ▶v. make a straight downhill run on skis.

schwa /sHwä/ ▶n. Phonetics an unstressed vowel (as in *a* moment *ago*), represented by the symbol (ə) in the International Phonetic Alphabet.

sci·at·ic /sī'atik/ ▶adj. **1** relating to the hip. **2** affecting the sciatic nerve. **3** suffering from sciatica.

sci·at·i·ca /sī'atikə/ ▶n. pain affecting the back, hip, and outer side of the leg, caused by pressure on the sciatic nerve root in the lower back.

sci·at·ic nerve ▶n. a major nerve extending from the lower end of the spinal cord down the back of the thigh.

sci·ence /'sīəns/ ▶n. **1** the systematic study of the structure and behavior of the physical and natural world through observation and experiment. **2** an organized body of knowledge on any subject.

sci·ence fic·tion ▶n. fiction set typically in the future and dealing with imagined scientific, technological, or social developments.

sci·ence park ▶n. an area devoted to scientific research or the development of science-based industries.

sci·en·tif·ic /,sīən'tifik/ ▶adj. **1** relating to or based on science. **2** done in a methodical or organized way. ■ **sci·en·tif·i·cal·ly** /-ik(ə)lē/ adv.

sci·en·tist /'sīəntist/ ▶n. a person who has expert knowledge of one or more of the natural or physical sciences.

Sci·en·tol·o·gy /,sīən'täləjē/ ▶n. trademark a religious system based on the seeking of self-knowledge and spiritual fulfillment through courses of study and training. ■ **Sci·en·tol·o·gist** n.

sci-fi /'sī 'fī/ ▶n. informal short for SCIENCE FICTION.

scil·la /'silə/ ▶n. a plant with small blue star- or bell-shaped flowers and glossy leaves.

scim·i·tar /'simətər, -,tär/ ▶n. a short sword with a curved blade that broadens toward the point, first used in Eastern countries.

scin·til·la /sin'tilə/ ▶n. a tiny trace or amount: *not a scintilla of doubt.*

scin·til·late /'sin(t)l,āt/ ▶v. give off flashes of light; sparkle. ■ **scin·til·lant** /-ənt/ adj. & n. **scin·til·la·tion** /,sin(t)l'āsHən/ n.

scin·til·lat·ing /'sin(t)l,ātiNG/ ▶adj. **1** very clever, skillful, or exciting: *a scintillating performance.* **2** sparkling brightly.

sci·on /'sīən/ ▶n. **1** a young shoot or twig of a plant that is cut off to create a new plant. **2** a descendant of an important or famous family.

scis·sor /'sizər/ ▶v. **1** cut something with scissors. **2** move the legs back and forward in a way that resembles the action of scissors.

scis·sors /'sizərz/ ▶pl.n. (also **a pair of scissors**) a tool for cutting cloth and paper, consisting of two crossing blades pivoted in the middle. ▶adj. (also **scissor**) (of an action) in which two things cross each other or open and close like a pair of scissors: *a scissor kick.*

scle·ra /'skli(ə)rə/ ▶n. the white outer layer of the eyeball.

scle·ro·der·ma /,skli(ə)rə'dərmə, ,skler-/ ▶n. a medical condition in which the skin and

connective tissue hardens and contracts.

scle·ro·sis /sklə'rōsis/ ▶n. **1** abnormal hardening of body tissue. **2** (in full **multiple sclerosis**) a disease involving damage to the sheaths of nerve cells in the brain and spinal cord, leading to partial or complete paralysis.

scle·rot·ic /sklə'rätik/ ▶adj. **1** Medicine relating to or having sclerosis. **2** unable to adapt; rigid: *sclerotic management.*

scoff¹ /skôf, skäf/ ▶v. speak about someone or something in a scornful way. ■ **scoff·er** n.

scoff² ▶v. informal eat something quickly and greedily.

scold /skōld/ ▶v. angrily tell someone that they have done something wrong. ▶n. old use a woman who nags or grumbles constantly.

sco·li·o·sis /,skōlē'ōsis/ ▶n. Medicine abnormal lateral curvature of the spine.

sconce /skäns/ ▶n. a candle holder attached to a wall with an ornamental bracket.

scone /skōn, skän/ ▶n. a small plain cake made from flour, fat, and milk.

scoop /skōōp/ ▶n. **1** a utensil resembling a spoon, having a short handle and a deep bowl. **2** the bowl-shaped part of a digging machine or dredger. **3** informal a piece of news published by a newspaper or broadcast by a television or radio station before its rivals know about it. ▶v. **1** pick something up with a scoop. **2** create a hollow in something. **3** pick up in a swift, smooth movement: *he scooped her up in his arms.* **4** informal publish a news story before a rival. **5** informal win a prize.

scoop neck ▶n. a deeply curved wide neckline on a woman's garment.

scoot /skōōt/ ▶v. informal go or leave somewhere quickly.

scoot·er /'skōōtər/ ▶n. **1** (also **motor scooter**) a light two-wheeled motorcycle. **2** a child's toy consisting of a footboard mounted on two wheels and a long steering handle, moved by pushing one foot against the ground. ▶v. travel or ride on a scooter.

scope¹ /skōp/ ▶n. **1** the opportunity or possibility for doing something: *there is clearly scope for development in the future.* **2** the range of the area or subject matter that something deals with: *these matters are beyond the scope of this book.*

scope² ▶n. informal a telescope, microscope, or other device having a name ending in -*scope.*

-scope ▶comb.form referring to an instrument for observing or examining: *telescope.*

scor·bu·tic /skôr'byōōtik/ ▶adj. relating to or affected with scurvy.

scorch /skôrCH/ ▶v. **1** burn or become burned on the surface or edges. **2** (as adj. **scorched**) dried out and withered as a result of extreme heat. **3** informal move very fast: *a car scorching along the highway.* ▶n. the burning of the surface of something.

scorched earth pol·i·cy ▶n. a military strategy of burning or destroying all crops and other resources that might be of use to an invading enemy force.

scorch·er /'skôrCHər/ ▶n. informal a day or period of very hot weather.

score /skôr/ ▶n. **1** the number of points, goals, runs, etc., achieved by a person or side in a game. **2** (pl. same) a group or set of twenty. **3** (**scores of**) a large number of. **4** the written music

for a composition, showing all the vocal and instrumental parts. **5** (**the score**) informal the real situation or facts: *I'm not thick, I know the score.* **6** a notch or line cut into a surface. ▶v. **1** gain a point, goal, run, etc., in a game. **2** be worth a number of points. **3** record the score during a game. **4** cut or scratch a mark on a surface. **5** (**score something out/through**) delete part of a piece of writing by drawing a line through it. **6** orchestrate or arrange a piece of music. **7** informal succeed in obtaining illegal drugs. **8** informal succeed in attracting a sexual partner. ■ **score·less** adj. **scor·er** n.
– PHRASES **settle a score** take revenge on someone.

score·board /'skôr,bôrd/ ▶n. a large board on which the score in a game or match is displayed.

score·card /'skôr,kärd/ ▶n. **1** (also **scoresheet** /'skôr,SHēt/) a card or sheet or paper in which scores are recorded. **2** a card listing the names and positions of players in a team.

scorn /skôrn/ ▶n. a strong feeling that someone or something is worthless; contempt. ▶v. **1** express contempt for someone or something. **2** reject in a scornful way: *I have never scorned newspapers as many people do.*

scorn·ful /'skôrnfəl/ ▶adj. showing that one feels someone or something is worthless; contemptuous. ■ **scorn·ful·ly** adv.

Scor·pi·o /'skôrpē,ō/ ▶n. **1** the eighth sign of the zodiac (the Scorpion), which the sun enters about October 23. **2** (**a Scorpio**) a person born when the sun is in this sign. ■ **Scor·pi·an** /-pēən/ n. & adj.

scor·pi·on /'skôrpēən/ ▶n. a creature related to spiders, with pincers and a poisonous sting at the end of its tail.

scor·zo·ne·ra /,skôrzə'ni(ə)rə/ ▶n. the purple-brown root of a plant of the daisy family, eaten as a vegetable.

Scot /skät/ ▶n. **1** a person from Scotland. **2** a member of a Gaelic people that migrated from Ireland to Scotland around the late 5th century.

Scotch /skäcн/ ▶n. (also **Scotch whiskey**) whiskey made in Scotland. ▶adj. old-fashioned term for SCOTTISH.

scotch /skäcн/ ▶v. decisively put an end to: *they were quick to scotch talk of a disagreement.*

Scotch broth ▶n. a traditional Scottish soup made from meat stock with pearl barley and vegetables.

Scotch pine ▶n. a pine tree widely grown for timber and other products.

Scotch tape ▶n. trademark transparent adhesive tape. ▶v. fasten or stick something with transparent adhesive tape.

Scotch whis·key ▶n. another term for SCOTCH.

scot-free ▶adv. without suffering any punishment or injury: *the people who kidnapped her will get off scot-free.*

Scots /skäts/ ▶adj. another term for SCOTTISH. ▶n. the form of English used in Scotland.

Scots·man /'skätsmən/ (or **Scotswoman** /'skäts,woomən/) ▶n. (pl. **Scotsmen** or **Scotswomen**) a person from Scotland.

Scot·ti·cism /'skäti,sizəm/ ▶n. a characteristically Scottish word or phrase.

Scot·tie /'skätē/ ▶n. informal a Scottish terrier.

Scot·tish /'skätisн/ ▶adj. relating to Scotland or its people. ▶n. (as pl. n. **the Scottish**) the people

of Scotland. ■ **Scot·tish·ness** n.

Scot·tish ter·ri·er ▶n. a small rough-haired breed of terrier.

scoun·drel /'skoundrəl/ ▶n. a person who takes advantage of or deceives others; a rogue. ■ **scoun·drel·ly** adj.

scour¹ /skou(ə)r/ ▶v. **1** clean something by rubbing it with a detergent or something rough. **2** (of running water) wear away rock to form a channel or pool. ■ **scour·er** n.

scour² ▶v. search a place thoroughly.

scourge /skərj/ ▶n. **1** a cause of great trouble or suffering: *the plague was the scourge of the Middle Ages.* **2** historical a whip used to punish people. ▶v. **1** cause great suffering to someone or something. **2** historical whip someone as a punishment.

scout /skout/ ▶n. **1** a person sent ahead of a main force to gather information about the enemy. **2** (also **Scout**) a member of the Boy Scouts or Girl Scouts, organizations that aim to develop character through outdoor and other activities. **3** a talent scout. **4** an instance of searching somewhere to gather information. ▶v. **1** search a place in order to discover something. **2** explore or examine so as to gather information: *they are keen to scout out business opportunities.* **3** act as a talent scout. ■ **scout·ing** n.

scout·mas·ter /'skout,mastər/ ▶n. the adult in charge of a group of Boy Scouts.

scow /skou/ ▶n. a flat-bottomed boat for transporting cargo to and from ships in harbor.

scowl /skoul/ ▶n. an angry or bad-tempered expression. ▶v. frown in an angry or bad-tempered way.

scrab·ble /'skrabəl/ ▶v. **1** grope around with the fingers to find or hold onto something. **2** move quickly and awkwardly; scramble. ▶n. (**Scrabble**) trademark a board game in which players build up words from small lettered squares or tiles.

scrag·gly /'skrag(ə)lē/ (also **scraggy** /'skragē/) ▶adj. **1** thin and bony. **2** ragged or untidy in appearance.

scram /skram/ ▶v. (**scrams, scramming, scrammed**) informal go away or leave quickly.

scram·ble /'skrambəl/ ▶v. **1** move or make one's way quickly and awkwardly, using the hands as well as the feet. **2** make or become jumbled or confused. **3** put a broadcast transmission or telephone conversation into a form that can only be understood if received by a decoding device. **4** cook beaten eggs with a little liquid in a pan. **5** informal act in a hurried or undignified way: *firms scrambled to win contracts.* **6** (of fighter aircraft) take off immediately in an emergency or for action. ▶n. **1** an act of scrambling up or over something. **2** a hasty or undignified struggle to achieve or get something.

scram·bler /'skramb(ə)lər/ ▶n. a device for scrambling a broadcast transmission or telephone conversation. ■ **scram·bling** n.

scrap¹ /skrap/ ▶n. **1** a small piece or amount of something, especially one that is left over after the rest has been used. **2** (**scraps**) bits of uneaten food left after a meal. **3** waste metal and other material that can be reprocessed. ▶v. (**scraps, scrapping, scrapped**) **1** abolish or cancel a plan, policy, or law. **2** remove something from use so as to convert it to scrap metal.

scrap² informal ▸ n. a brief or minor fight or quarrel. ▸ v. (**scraps**, **scrapping**, **scrapped**) have a brief or minor fight or quarrel. ■ **scrap·per** n.

scrap·book /'skrap,bŏŏk/ ▸ n. a book of blank pages for sticking cuttings, drawings, or pictures in.

scrap·book·ing /'skrap,bŏŏkɪNG/ ▸ n. the activity or hobby of keeping a scrapbook.

scrape /skrāp/ ▸ v. **1** drag or pull a hard or sharp implement across a surface or object to remove dirt or waste matter. **2** damage something by rubbing against a rough or hard surface. **3** just manage to achieve, succeed, or pass: *he now scrapes a living from a roadside stand.* **4** (**scrape something together/up**) collect or accumulate something with difficulty. **5** (**scrape by/along**) manage to live with difficulty. ▸ n. **1** an act or sound of scraping. **2** an injury or mark caused by scraping. **3** informal an embarrassing or difficult situation that one has caused oneself. ■ **scrap·er** n.
– PHRASES **scrape the barrel** (or **the bottom of the barrel**) informal be forced to use the last and poorest resources because nothing else is available.

scrap·heap /'skrap,hēp/ ▸ n. a pile of things that have been thrown away as rubbish.
– PHRASES **on the scrapheap** rejected as no longer wanted or useful.

scrap·ie /'skrāpē/ ▸ n. a disease of sheep involving the central nervous system, in which the animals suffer from a lack of coordination.

scrap·py¹ /'skrapē/ ▸ adj. (**scrappier**, **scrappiest**) disorganized, untidy, or incomplete. ■ **scrap·pi·ly** adv. **scrap·pi·ness** n.

scrap·py² ▸ adj. (**scrappier**, **scrappiest**) inclined to fight; aggressive and quarrelsome. ■ **scrap·pi·ly** adv. **scrap·pi·ness** n.

scrap·yard /'skrap,yärd/ ▸ n. a place where waste metal and other material is collected before being discarded or recycled.

scratch /skracH/ ▸ v. **1** make a long mark or wound on a surface with something sharp. **2** rub a part of one's body with one's fingernails to relieve itching. **3** cross out writing. **4** cancel or abandon a plan or project. **5** withdraw from a competition. **6** make a living or achieve something with difficulty: *he was just scratching a living from the black market.* **7** (as n. **scratching**) the technique, used in rap music, of stopping a record by hand and moving it back and forth to give a rhythmic scratching effect. **8** (of a bird or mammal) rake the ground with the beak or claws in search of food. ▸ n. **1** a mark or wound made by scratching. **2** an act or spell of scratching. **3** informal a slight wound or injury. ▸ adj. put together from whatever is available: *we were a scratch team at best.* ■ **scratch·er** n.
– PHRASES **from scratch** from the very beginning. **scratch the surface** deal with a matter only in the most superficial way. **up to scratch** up to the required standard; satisfactory.

scratch card ▸ n. a card with a section or sections coated in a waxy substance that may be scraped away to reveal whether a prize has been won.

scratch·y /'skracHē/ ▸ adj. (**scratchier**, **scratchiest**) **1** rough in texture and causing scratching. **2** (of a voice or sound) rough; grating.

scrawl /skrôl/ ▸ v. write in a hurried, careless way. ▸ n. hurried, careless handwriting.

scrawn·y /'skrônē/ ▸ adj. (**scrawnier**, **scrawniest**) unattractively thin and bony.

scream /skrēm/ ▸ v. **1** make a long, loud, piercing cry or sound expressing strong emotion or pain. **2** move very rapidly, especially with a loud, high-pitched sound. **3** present in an urgent or obvious way: *the headlines screamed 'he offered me sex'.* ▸ n. **1** a long, loud, piercing cry or sound. **2** (**a scream**) informal a very funny person or thing. ■ **scream·er** n.

scream·ing·ly /'skrēmɪNGlē/ ▸ adv. to a very great extent; extremely: *screamingly funny television.*

scree /skrē/ ▸ n. a mass of small loose stones that form or cover a slope on a mountain.

screech /skrēcH/ ▸ v. **1** make a loud, harsh cry. **2** move fast with a loud, harsh sound. ▸ n. a loud, harsh cry or sound. ■ **screech·er** n. **screech·y** adj.

screech owl ▸ n. a small American owl with a screeching call and distinctive ear tufts.

screed /skrēd/ ▸ n. **1** a long speech or piece of writing. **2** a layer of material applied to level a floor or other surface.

screen /skrēn/ ▸ n. **1** an upright partition used to divide a room, give shelter, or conceal something. **2** a thing that shelters or conceals: *his jeep was parked behind a screen of trees.* **3** the flat front surface of a television or monitor, on which images and data are displayed. **4** a blank surface on which movies are projected. **5** (often **the screen**) movies or television: *a star of stage and screen.* ▸ v. **1** conceal, protect, or shelter with a screen: *her hair swung across to screen her face.* **2** show a movie or video or broadcast a television program. **3** protect someone from something dangerous or unpleasant. **4** test someone to find out whether or not they have a disease. **5** investigate someone to assess their suitability for a job. ■ **screen·er** n. **screen·ful** /-,fŏŏl/ n.

screen·play /'skrēn,plā/ ▸ n. the script of a movie, including acting instructions and scene directions.

screen-print ▸ v. force ink onto a surface through a prepared piece of fine material such as silk or nylon so as to create a picture or pattern. ▸ n. (**screen print**) a picture or design produced by screen-printing.

screen sav·er ▸ n. a computer program that replaces an unchanging screen display with a moving image to prevent damage to the phosphor.

screen test ▸ n. a filmed test to assess whether an actor is suitable for a movie or television role. ▸ v. (**screen-test**) give a screen test to an actor.

screen·writ·er /'skrēn,rītər/ ▸ n. a person who writes a screenplay for a movie. ■ **screen·writ·ing** n.

screw /skrŏŏ/ ▸ n. **1** a metal pin with a spiral thread running around it and a slotted head, used to join things together by being turned and pressed in. **2** a cylinder with a spiral ridge or thread running around the outside that can be turned to seal an opening, apply pressure, adjust position, etc. **3** (also **screw propeller**) a ship's or aircraft's propeller. **4** informal, derogatory a prison guard. **5** vulgar slang an act of having sex. ▸ v. **1** fasten or tighten something with a screw or screws. **2** turn something so as to attach or remove it by means of a spiral thread. **3** informal cheat or swindle someone. **4** vulgar slang have sex with someone.
– PHRASES **have one's head screwed on** (**the right way**) informal have common sense. **have a screw loose** informal be slightly eccentric or

mentally disturbed. **screw someone up** informal make someone emotionally disturbed. **screw something up 1** crush something into a tight mass. **2** informal make something go wrong.

screw·ball /'skro͞o,bôl/ informal ▸ n. a mad or eccentric person. ▸ adj. **1** crazy; absurd. **2** referring to a movie style of fast-moving comedy involving eccentric characters or ridiculous situations.

screw·driv·er /'skro͞o,drīvər/ ▸ n. **1** a tool with a shaped tip that fits into the head of a screw to turn it. **2** a cocktail made from vodka and orange juice.

screw·y /'skro͞oē/ ▸ adj. (**screwier, screwiest**) informal rather odd or eccentric.

scrib·ble /'skribəl/ ▸ v. **1** write or draw something carelessly or hurriedly. **2** informal write for a living or as a hobby. ▸ n. a piece of writing or a picture produced carelessly or hurriedly. ■ **scrib·bler** n.

scribe /skrīb/ ▸ n. **1** historical a person who copied out documents. **2** informal, often humorous a writer, especially a journalist. **3** historical a Jewish record-keeper or, later, a professional religious and legal expert. **4** (also **scriber**) a pointed instrument used for making marks to guide a saw or in signwriting. ▸ v. **1** literary write something. **2** mark something with a pointed instrument. ■ **scrib·al** adj.

scrim /skrim/ ▸ n. strong, coarse fabric used for heavy-duty lining or upholstery.

scrim·mage /'skrimij/ ▸ n. **1** a confused struggle or fight. **2** Football offensive play begun with the ball on the ground between the offensive and defensive lines with its longest axis at right angles to the goal line. **3** chiefly Football a practice session in which a simulated game is played.

scrimp /skrimp/ ▸ v. be very careful with money; economize.

scrim·shaw /'skrim,shô/ ▸ n. decorative work consisting of carved designs on the bones and teeth of marine mammals or on similar materials.

scrip /skrip/ ▸ n. **1** a certificate that demonstrates ownership of stocks, shares, and bonds, especially a certificate relating to an issue of additional shares to shareholders in proportion to the shares they already hold. **2** such certificates as a whole.

script /skript/ ▸ n. **1** the written part of a play, movie, or television or radio broadcast. **2** handwriting as distinct from print. **3** writing using a particular alphabet: *Russian script.* ▸ v. write a script for a play, movie, or television or radio broadcast.

scrip·tur·al /'skripchərəl/ ▸ adj. relating to the Bible.

scrip·ture /'skripchər/ (also **scriptures**) ▸ n. **1** the sacred writings of Christianity contained in the Bible. **2** the sacred writings of a religion other than Christianity.

script·writ·er /'skript,rītər/ ▸ n. a person who writes a script for a play, movie, or television or radio broadcast. ■ **script·writ·ing** n.

scriv·ener /'skriv(ə)nər/ ▸ n. historical a person who made a living by writing out documents; a clerk or scribe.

scrof·u·la /'skrôfyələ, 'skräf-/ ▸ n. historical a disease characterized by swollen glands, probably a form of tuberculosis. ■ **scrof·u·lous** adj.

scroll /skrōl/ ▸ n. **1** a roll of parchment or paper for writing or painting on. **2** an ornamental design or carving resembling a partly unrolled scroll of parchment. ▸ v. move displayed writing or graphics on a computer screen in order to view different parts of them. ■ **scroll·a·ble** adj. **scroll·er** n.

scroll bar ▸ n. a long, thin section at the edge of a computer display by which material can be scrolled using a mouse.

scrolled /skrōld/ ▸ adj. having an ornamental design or carving resembling a scroll.

scroll·work /'skrōl,wərk/ ▸ n. decoration consisting of spiral lines or patterns.

Scrooge /skro͞oj/ ▸ n. a person who is stingy with money.

scro·tum /'skrōtəm/ ▸ n. (pl. **scrota** or **scrotums**) the pouch of skin containing the testicles. ■ **scro·tal** /'skrōtl/ adj.

scrounge /skrounj/ ▸ v. informal try to get something from someone without having to pay or work for it. ■ **scroung·er** n.

scrub¹ /skrəb/ ▸ v. (**scrubs, scrubbing, scrubbed**) **1** rub someone or something hard so as to clean them. **2** (**scrub up**) thoroughly clean one's hands and arms before performing surgery. **3** informal cancel or abandon something. ▸ n. **1** an act of scrubbing. **2** a cosmetic lotion used to remove dead cells and cleanse the skin. **3** (**scrubs**) hygienic clothing worn by surgeons during operations.

scrub² ▸ n. **1** vegetation consisting mainly of brushwood or stunted trees. **2** land covered with brushwood or stunted trees. ▸ adj. referring to a shrubby or small form of a plant: *scrub oak.* ■ **scrub·by** adj.

scrub·ber /'skrəbər/ ▸ n. **1** a brush for scrubbing. **2** a device that uses water or a solution for purifying gases.

scrub·land /'skrəb,land/ ▸ n. (also **scrublands**) land consisting of brushwood or stunted trees.

scruff /skrəf/ ▸ n. the back of a person's or animal's neck.

scruff·y /'skrəfē/ ▸ adj. (**scruffier, scruffiest**) shabby and untidy or dirty. ■ **scruff·i·ly** /-əlē/ adv. **scruff·i·ness** n.

scrum /skrəm/ Rugby ▸ n. an ordered formation of players in which the forwards of each team push against each other with heads down and the ball is thrown in. ▸ v. (**scrums, scrumming, scrummed**) form or take part in a scrum.

scrump·tious /'skrəm(p)shəs/ ▸ adj. informal very delicious or attractive.

scrunch /skrənch/ ▸ v. **1** make a loud crunching noise. **2** crush or squeeze something into a tight mass. ▸ n. a loud crunching noise.

scrunch·ie /'skrənchē/ (also **scrunchy**) ▸ n. (pl. **scrunchies**) a circular band of fabric-covered elastic used for fastening the hair.

scru·ple /'skro͞opəl/ ▸ n. **1** a feeling of doubt as to whether an action is morally right: *I had no scruples about eavesdropping.* **2** historical a unit of weight equal to 20 grains. ▸ v. hesitate to do something that one thinks may be wrong: *she doesn't scruple to ask her parents for money.*

scru·pu·lous /'skro͞opyələs/ ▸ adj. **1** very careful and thorough. **2** very concerned to avoid doing wrong. ■ **scru·pu·los·i·ty** /,skro͞opyə'läsitē/ n. **scru·pu·lous·ly** adv. **scru·pu·lous·ness** n.

scru·ti·nize /'skro͞otn,īz/ ▸ v. examine someone or something closely and thoroughly.

scru·ti·ny /ˈskro͞otn-ē/ ▶ n. (pl. **scrutinies**) close and critical observation or examination.

scry /skrī/ ▶ v. (**scries, scrying, scried**) foretell the future with a crystal ball.

SCSI /ˈskəzē/ ▶ abbr. small computer system interface.

scu·ba /ˈsko͞obə/ ▶ n. self-contained underwater breathing apparatus; a portable breathing apparatus for divers, consisting of cylinders of compressed air attached to a mouthpiece or mask.

scu·ba div·ing ▶ n. the sport or pastime of swimming underwater using a scuba.

scud /skəd/ ▶ v. (**scuds, scudding, scudded**) move fast because driven by the wind: *clouds scudded across the sky.* ▶ n. literary clouds or spray driven by the wind.

scuff /skəf/ ▶ v. **1** scrape a shoe or other object against something. **2** mark a surface by scraping it. **3** drag one's feet when walking. ▶ n. a mark made by scraping a surface or object.

scuf·fle /ˈskəfəl/ ▶ n. a short, confused fight or struggle. ▶ v. **1** take part in a scuffle. **2** move in a hurried way, making a rustling or shuffling sound.

scull /skəl/ ▶ n. **1** each of a pair of small oars used by a single rower. **2** an oar placed over the back of a boat and moved from side to side to propel it. **3** a light, narrow boat propelled with a scull or a pair of sculls. ▶ v. propel a boat with sculls. ■ **scul·ler** n.

scul·ler·y /ˈskəl(ə)rē/ ▶ n. (pl. **sculleries**) a small kitchen or room at the back of a house used for washing dishes and other dirty household work.

scul·lion /ˈskəlyən/ ▶ n. old use a servant given the most menial tasks in a kitchen.

sculpt /skəlpt/ ▶ v. make a sculpture of someone or something.

sculp·tor /ˈskəlptər/ ▶ n. (fem. **sculptress**) an artist who makes sculptures.

sculp·ture /ˈskəlpCHər/ ▶ n. **1** the art of making three-dimensional figures and shapes by carving stone or wood or casting metal. **2** a work made by carving stone or wood or casting metal. ▶ v. **1** make something by carving stone or wood or casting metal. **2** (as adj. **sculptured**) having strong, smooth curves: *sculptured bodies doing pushups.* ■ **sculp·tur·al** /ˈskəlpCHərəl/ adj.

scum /skəm/ ▶ n. **1** a layer of dirt or froth on the surface of a liquid. **2** informal a worthless or hated person or group of people. ▶ v. (**scums, scumming, scummed**) cover the surface of a liquid with a layer of dirt or froth. ■ **scum·my** adj.

scum·bag /ˈskəmˌbag/ ▶ n. informal a hated or unpleasant person.

scum·ble /ˈskəmbəl/ Art ▶ v. give a softer or duller effect to a painting or color by applying a very thin coat of paint. ▶ n. a very thin coat of paint applied to a painting or color.

scup·per¹ /ˈskəpər/ ▶ n. a hole in a ship's side to allow water to run away from the deck.

scup·per² ▶ v. chiefly Brit. **1** informal prevent from working or succeeding; thwart: *the unions scuppered the plan.* **2** sink a ship deliberately.

scurf /skərf/ ▶ n. flakes on the surface of the skin, occurring especially as dandruff. ■ **scurf·y** adj.

scur·ril·ous /ˈskərələs/ ▶ adj. rude and insulting, and intended to damage someone's reputation: *a*

scurrilous attack. ■ **scur·ril·i·ty** /skəˈrilitē/ n. (pl. **scurrilities**).

scur·ry /ˈskərē/ ▶ v. (**scurries, scurrying, scurried**) move hurriedly with short, quick steps. ▶ n. a situation of hurried and confused movement.

scur·vy /ˈskərvē/ ▶ n. a disease caused by a lack of vitamin C, characterized by bleeding gums and the opening of previously healed wounds. ▶ adj. (**scurvier, scurviest**) old use worthless or contemptible.

scut·tle¹ /ˈskətl/ ▶ n. a metal container with a lid and a handle, used to store coal for a domestic fire.

scut·tle² ▶ v. run with short, quick steps. ▶ n. an act or sound of scuttling.

scut·tle³ ▶ v. **1** deliberately cause a scheme to fail. **2** sink one's own ship deliberately. ▶ n. an opening with a lid in a ship's deck or side.

scut·tle·butt /ˈskətlˌbət/ ▶ n. informal rumor; gossip.

scuz·zy /ˈskəzē/ ▶ adj. (**scuzzier, scuzziest**) informal disgustingly dirty or unpleasant. ■ **scuzz** /skəz/ n.

scythe /sīTH/ ▶ n. a tool used for cutting crops such as grass or wheat, with a long curved blade at the end of a long pole. ▶ v. **1** cut crops with a scythe. **2** move through something rapidly and forcefully.

Scyth·i·an /ˈsiTHēən/ ▶ n. a person from Scythia, an ancient region of SE Europe and Asia. ▶ adj. relating to Scythia.

SD ▶ abbr. South Dakota.

SDI ▶ abbr. Strategic Defense Initiative.

SE ▶ abbr. **1** southeast. **2** southeastern.

Se ▶ symbol the chemical element selenium.

sea /sē/ ▶ n. **1** the large continuous area of salt water that covers most of the earth's surface and surrounds its landmasses. **2** a particular area of sea: *the Black Sea.* **3** a vast expanse or quantity: *a sea of faces.* ■ **sea·ward** /ˈsēwərd/ adj. & adv. **sea·wards** /ˈsēwərdz/ adv.

– PHRASES **at sea 1** sailing on the sea. **2** confused; uncertain. **one's sea legs** one's ability to keep one's balance and not feel seasick on board a ship.

sea a·nem·o·ne ▶ n. a sea creature with a tube-shaped body that bears a ring of stinging tentacles around the mouth.

sea bass /bas/ ▶ n. a sea fish with a spiny fin on its back, resembling the freshwater perch.

sea·bed /ˈsēˌbed/ ▶ n. the ground under the sea; the ocean floor.

sea·bird /ˈsēˌbərd/ ▶ n. a bird that lives near the sea or coast.

sea·board /ˈsēˌbôrd/ ▶ n. a region bordering the sea; the coastline.

sea·bor·gi·um /sēˈbôrgēəm/ ▶ n. a very unstable chemical element made by high-energy atomic collisions.

sea·borne /ˈsēˌbôrn/ ▶ adj. transported or traveling by sea.

sea bream ▶ n. a sea fish that resembles the freshwater bream.

sea breeze ▶ n. **1** a breeze blowing toward the land from the sea. **2** a cocktail consisting of vodka, grapefruit juice, and cranberry juice.

sea change ▶ n. a great and very noticeable change in a situation.

sea cow ▶ n. a manatee or similar mammal that lives in the sea.

sea cu·cum·ber ▸ n. a sea creature having a thick wormlike body with tentacles around the mouth.

sea dog ▸ n. informal an old or experienced sailor.

sea·far·ing /'sē,fe(ə)riNG/ ▸ adj. (of a person) regularly traveling by sea. ▸ n. travel by sea.
■ **sea·far·er** n.

sea·food /'sē,fo͞od/ ▸ n. shellfish and sea fish as food.

sea·front /'sē,frənt/ ▸ n. the part of a coastal town next to and facing the sea.

sea·go·ing /'sē,gōiNG/ ▸ adj. **1** (of a ship) suitable for voyages on the sea. **2** relating to travel by sea.

sea green ▸ n. a pale bluish-green color.

sea·gull /'sē,gəl/ ▸ n. a gull.

sea·horse /'sē,hôrs/ ▸ n. a small sea fish that swims upright and has a head that resembles that of a horse.

sea·kale /'sē,kāl/ ▸ n. a coastal plant of the cabbage family, grown for its edible shoots.

SEAL /sēl/ (also **Seal**) ▸ n. a member of an elite force within the US Navy.

seal[1] /sēl/ ▸ n. **1** a device or substance used to join two things together or to prevent anything from passing between them. **2** a piece of wax or lead with a design stamped into it, attached to a document as a guarantee that it is genuine. **3** a confirmation or guarantee: *the scheme has the government's seal of approval.* ▸ v. **1** fasten or close something securely. **2** (**seal something off**) isolate an area by preventing people from entering or leaving it. **3** apply a coating to a surface to prevent something from passing through it. **4** make definite; finalize: *the consortium said they hoped to seal a deal within two weeks.* **5** fix a seal to a document to show that it is genuine. ■ **seal·a·ble** adj.
– PHRASES **my lips are sealed** I will not discuss or reveal something. **put** (or **set**) **the seal on** finally confirm or complete something.

seal[2] ▸ n. a fish-eating mammal that lives in the sea, with flippers and a streamlined body. ▸ v. (usu. as n. **sealing**) hunt for seals.

seal·ant /'sēlənt/ ▸ n. material used to make something airtight or watertight.

sea lav·en·der ▸ n. another term for **STATICE**.

seal·er[1] /'sēlər/ ▸ n. a device or substance used to make something airtight or watertight.

seal·er[2] ▸ n. a ship or person engaged in hunting seals.

sea lev·el ▸ n. the level of the sea's surface, used in calculating the height of geographical features such as hills.

seal·ing wax ▸ n. a mixture of shellac and rosin with turpentine, used to make seals.

sea li·on ▸ n. a large seal of the Pacific Ocean, the male of which has a mane on the neck and shoulders.

seal·skin /'sēl,skin/ ▸ n. the skin or prepared fur of a seal, used for making clothes.

seam /sēm/ ▸ n. **1** a line where two pieces of fabric are sewn together. **2** a line where the edges of two pieces of wood or other material touch each other. **3** an underground layer of a mineral such as coal or gold. **4** a supply of something valuable: *they've got a rich seam of experienced players.* ▸ v. join things with a seam.

sea·man /'sēmən/ ▸ n. (pl. **seamen**) a sailor, especially one below the rank of officer.
■ **sea·man·like** /-,līk/ adj. **sea·man·ship** /'sēmən,SHip/ n.

seam·less /'sēmlis/ ▸ adj. smooth and without seams or obvious joins. ■ **seam·less·ly** adv.

seam·stress /'sēmstris/ ▸ n. a woman who sews, especially as a job.

seam·y /'sēmē/ ▸ adj. (**seamier**, **seamiest**) immoral and unpleasant; sordid.

se·ance /'sā,äns/ ▸ n. a meeting at which people attempt to make contact with the spirits of people who are dead.

sea·plane /'sē,plān/ ▸ n. an aircraft with floats or skis instead of wheels, designed to land on and take off from water.

sea·port /'sē,pôrt/ ▸ n. a town or city with a harbor for seagoing ships.

sear /si(ə)r/ ▸ v. **1** burn or scorch something with a sudden intense heat. **2** (of pain) be experienced as a sudden burning sensation. **3** brown food quickly at a high temperature. ▸ adj. variant spelling of **SERE**.

search /sərCH/ ▸ v. **1** try to find someone or something by looking carefully and thoroughly. **2** examine thoroughly in order to find something or someone: *she searched the house from top to bottom.* **3** look for information in a computer network or database by using a search engine. **4** (as adj. **searching**) investigating very thoroughly: *searching questions.* ▸ n. an act of searching. ■ **search·a·ble** adj. **search·er** n.
– PHRASES **search me!** informal I do not know.

search en·gine ▸ n. a computer program that searches for and identifies specified items in a database, used especially for searching the Internet.

search·light /'sərCH,līt/ ▸ n. a powerful outdoor electric light with a beam that can be turned in the required direction.

search par·ty ▸ n. a group of people organized to look for someone or something.

search war·rant ▸ n. a legal document authorizing a police officer or other official to enter and search a place.

sea salt ▸ n. salt produced by the evaporation of seawater.

sea·scape /'sē,skāp/ ▸ n. a view or picture of an area of sea.

sea·shell /'sē,SHel/ ▸ n. the shell of a marine shellfish.

sea·shore /'sē,SHôr/ ▸ n. an area of sandy or rocky land next to the sea.

sea·sick /'sē,sik/ ▸ adj. suffering from nausea caused by the motion of a ship at sea.
■ **sea·sick·ness** n.

sea·side /'sē,sīd/ ▸ n. a beach area or vacation resort.

sea·son /'sēzən/ ▸ n. **1** each of the four divisions of the year (spring, summer, autumn, and winter) marked by particular weather patterns and daylight hours. **2** a period of the year with particular weather or when a particular activity is done: *the football season.* **3** (**the season**) the time of year traditionally marked by fashionable upper-class social events. ▸ v. **1** add salt, herbs, or spices to food. **2** make more lively or interesting: *his conversation is seasoned with punchlines.* **3** keep wood so as to dry it for use as firewood or lumber. **4** (as adj. **seasoned**) used to particular conditions; experienced: *a seasoned traveler.*
– PHRASES **in season 1** (of a fruit, vegetable, or other food) ready to eat and in good condition

at a particular time of year. **2** (of a female mammal) ready to mate.

sea·son·a·ble /'sēzənəbəl/ ▸ adj. usual for or appropriate to a particular season of the year.

sea·son·al /'sēzənəl/ ▸ adj. **1** relating to or typical of a particular season of the year. **2** changing according to the season. ▪ **sea·son·al·i·ty** /,sēzə'nalitē/ n. **sea·son·al·ly** adv.

sea·son·al af·fec·tive dis·or·der ▸ n. full form of SAD.

sea·son·ing /'sēzəniNG/ ▸ n. salt, herbs, or spices added to food to improve the flavor.

sea·son tick·et ▸ n. a ticket allowing travel within a particular period or admission to a series of events.

sea squirt ▸ n. a sea animal that has a baglike body with openings through which water flows in and out.

seat /sēt/ ▸ n. **1** a thing made or used for sitting on. **2** the part of a chair for sitting on. **3** a sitting place for a passenger in a vehicle or for a member of an audience. **4** a person's buttocks. **5** a place in an elected legislature or council. **6** a place where someone or something is based or something is carried out: *the town is the island's seat of government.* **7** the way in which a person sits on a horse. **8** a part of a machine that supports or guides another part. ▸ v. **1** arrange for someone to sit somewhere. **2** (**seat oneself** or **be seated**) sit down. **3** (of a place) have sufficient seats for a specified number of people. ▪ **seat·ing** n. **seat·less** adj.

seat belt ▸ n. a belt used to secure someone in the seat of a motor vehicle or aircraft.

sea ur·chin ▸ n. a sea animal that has a shell covered in spines.

sea wall ▸ n. a wall built to prevent the sea from flowing over an area of land.

sea·wa·ter /'sē,wôtər, -,wätər/ ▸ n. water in or taken from the sea.

sea·way /'sē,wā/ ▸ n. a waterway or channel used by seagoing ships.

sea·weed /'sē,wēd/ ▸ n. large algae growing in the sea or on rocks at the edge of the sea.

sea·wor·thy /'sē,wərTHē/ ▸ adj. (of a boat) in a good enough condition to sail on the sea. ▪ **sea·wor·thi·ness** n.

se·ba·ceous /sə'bāSHəs/ ▸ adj. technical **1** relating to a sebaceous gland. **2** relating to oil or fat.

se·ba·ceous gland ▸ n. a gland in the skin that produces an oily substance to lubricate the skin and hair.

seb·or·rhe·a /,sebə'rēə/ (Brit. **seborrhoea**) ▸ n. Medicine excessive discharge of sebum from the sebaceous glands.

se·bum /'sēbəm/ ▸ n. an oily substance produced by the sebaceous glands.

SEC ▸ abbr. Securities and Exchange Commission.

sec¹ /sek/ ▸ abbr. secant.

sec² ▸ n. informal a second or a very short space of time.

sec³ ▸ adj. (of wine) dry.

sec. ▸ abbr. second(s).

se·cant /'sē,kant, -kənt/ ▸ n. **1** Mathematics (in a right triangle) the ratio of the hypotenuse to the shorter side adjacent to an acute angle. **2** Geometry a straight line that cuts a curve in two or more parts.

se·cede /si'sēd/ ▸ v. withdraw formally from membership of a federation of states or other

alliance. ▪ **se·ced·er** n.

se·ces·sion /sə'seSHən/ ▸ n. the action of withdrawing from a federation or other alliance.

se·clude /si'klo͞od/ ▸ v. keep someone or oneself away from other people.

se·clud·ed /si'klo͞odid/ ▸ adj. **1** (of a place) not seen or visited by many people; sheltered and private. **2** (of a person's life) having little contact with other people.

se·clu·sion /si'klo͞oZHən/ ▸ n. the state of being private and away from other people.

sec·ond¹ /'sekənd/ ▸ ordinal number **1** that is number two in a sequence; 2nd. **2** lower in position, rank, or importance: *New York is second only to Los Angeles for air pollution.* **3** (**seconds**) goods of less than perfect quality. **4** (**seconds**) informal a second helping of food at a meal. **5** secondly (used to introduce a second point). **6** a person who assists a contestant in a boxing match or duel. ▸ v. **1** formally support a proposal, nomination, etc., before it is voted on or discussed further. **2** express agreement with someone or something. ▪ **sec·ond·er** n.

sec·ond² /'sekənd/ ▸ n. **1** the unit of time in the SI system, equal to one-sixtieth of a minute. **2** informal a very short time. **3** (also **arc second** or **second of arc**) a measurement of an angle equal to one sixtieth of a minute.

sec·ond³ /si'känd/ ▸ v. Brit. temporarily transfer an employee to another position or role. ▪ **se·cond·ment** n.

sec·ond·ar·y /'sekən,derē/ ▸ adj. **1** coming after, less important than, or resulting from someone or something that is first or most important: *a secondary road.* **2** relating to education for children from the age of eleven to sixteen or eighteen. ▪ **sec·ond·ar·i·ly** /-,derəlē/ adv.

sec·ond·ar·y col·or ▸ n. a color that is a result of mixing two primary colors.

sec·ond·ar·y sex·u·al char·ac·ter·is·tics ▸ pl.n. physical characteristics developed at puberty that distinguish between the sexes but are not involved in reproduction.

sec·ond best ▸ adj. next after the best. ▸ n. a less adequate or less desirable alternative.

sec·ond class ▸ n. **1** a set of people or things grouped together as the second best. **2** the second-best accommodations on an aircraft, train, or ship. ▸ adj. & adv. relating to the second class.

Sec·ond Com·ing ▸ n. (in Christian belief) the prophesied return of Jesus to Earth at the Last Judgment.

sec·ond cous·in ▸ n. see COUSIN.

sec·ond-de·gree ▸ adj. **1** (of burns) that cause blistering but not permanent scars. **2** Law (of a crime, especially a murder) less serious than a first-degree crime.

sec·ond-gen·er·a·tion ▸ adj. **1** referring to the children of parents who have emigrated from one country to another. **2** of a more advanced stage of technology than previous models or systems.

sec·ond-guess ▸ v. predict someone's actions or thoughts by guessing.

sec·ond·hand /'sekən(d)'hand/ ▸ adj. & adv. **1** (of goods) having had a previous owner; not new. **2** accepted on another person's authority and not from original investigation: *authors have had to make do with secondhand information.*

– PHRASES **at second hand** on the basis of what others have said rather than direct observation or experience.

sec·ond hand ▸ n. an extra hand in some watches and clocks that moves around to indicate the seconds.

sec·ond in com·mand ▸ n. the officer next in authority to the commanding or chief officer.

sec·ond lieu·ten·ant ▸ n. a rank of officer in the US Army, Air Force, and Marine Corps above chief warrant officer and below first lieutenant.

sec·ond·ly /'sekən(d)lē/ ▸ adv. in the second place; second.

sec·ond name ▸ n. Brit. a surname.

sec·ond na·ture ▸ n. something that one does very easily or naturally because one has done it so often or is particularly suited to it.

sec·ond per·son ▸ n. see PERSON (sense 3).

sec·ond-rate ▸ adj. poor in quality. ■ **sec·ond-rat·er** n.

sec·ond read·ing ▸ n. a second presentation of a bill to a lawmaking assembly.

sec·ond sight ▸ n. the supposed ability to predict future events or to know what is happening in a different place.

sec·ond string ▸ n. (often in phrase **a second string to one's bow**) an alternative resource or course of action in case another one fails.

sec·ond thoughts ▸ pl.n. a change of opinion or decision after considering something again.

sec·ond wind /wind/ ▸ n. fresh energy that enables one to continue with an activity after being tired.

se·cret /'sēkrit/ ▸ adj. **1** kept from or not known or seen by others. **2** fond of keeping secrets; secretive. ▸ n. **1** something that others do not know about. **2** a method of achieving something that is not generally known: *the secret of a happy marriage is compromise.* **3** something that is not fully understood; a mystery: *the secrets of the universe.* ■ **se·cre·cy** /'sēkrəsē/ n. **se·cret·ly** adv.

se·cret a·gent ▸ n. a spy acting for a country.

sec·re·taire /ˌsekri'te(ə)r/ ▸ n. a small writing desk.

sec·re·tar·i·at /ˌsekri'te(ə)rēət/ ▸ n. a governmental administrative office or department.

sec·re·tar·y /'sekriˌterē/ ▸ n. (pl. **secretaries**) **1** a person employed to deal with letters and telephone calls, make arrangements, and keep records. **2** an official of a society or other organization who deals with its correspondence and keeps its records. **3** an official in charge of a government department: *the defense secretary is in Cairo.* **4** a writing desk with shelves on top of it. ■ **sec·re·tar·i·al** /-'te(ə)rēəl/ adj.

sec·re·tar·y bird ▸ n. a slender long-legged African bird of prey, having a crest resembling a quill pen stuck behind the ear.

sec·re·tary gen·er·al ▸ n. (pl. **secretaries general**) the chief administrator of some organizations.

sec·re·tar·y of state ▸ n. the head of the State Department, responsible for foreign affairs.

se·crete¹ /si'krēt/ ▸ v. (of a cell, gland, or organ) produce and discharge a substance. ■ **se·cre·tor** /-tər/ n. **se·cre·to·ry** /-'tərē/ adj.

secrete² ▸ v. conceal or hide something.

se·cre·tion /si'krēsHən/ ▸ n. **1** a process by which substances are produced and discharged from a cell, gland, or organ for a particular function in the organism or for excretion. **2** a substance discharged by this process.

se·cre·tive /'sēkritiv/ ▸ adj. inclined to keep information secret or to hide one's feelings and intentions. ■ **se·cre·tive·ly** adv. **se·cre·tive·ness** n.

se·cret po·lice ▸ n. (treated as pl.) a police force working in secret against a government's political opponents.

se·cret sauce ▸ n. informal a special feature or technique kept secret by an organization and regarded as being the chief factor in its success.

se·cret serv·ice ▸ n. **1** a government department concerned with spying. **2** (**Secret Service**) a branch of the Treasury Department dealing with counterfeiting and providing protection for the president.

se·cret so·ci·e·ty ▸ n. an organization whose members are sworn to secrecy about its activities.

sect /sekt/ ▸ n. a group of people with different religious beliefs from those of a larger group to which they belong.

sec·tar·i·an /sek'te(ə)rēən/ ▸ adj. **1** relating to a religious sect or sects. **2** resulting from the differences that exist between members of different sects: *sectarian killings.* ▸ n. a member of a sect. ■ **sec·tar·i·an·ism** /-ˌnizəm/ n.

sec·tion /'seksHən/ ▸ n. **1** any of the parts into which something is divided or from which it is made up. **2** a distinct group within a larger body of people or things: *eco-warriors enjoyed widespread support from large sections of the population.* **3** the shape resulting from cutting a solid by or along a plane. **4** a representation of the internal structure of something as if it has been cut through. **5** a thin slice of plant or animal tissue prepared for examination with a microscope. **6** a separation by surgical cutting. ▸ v. **1** divide something into sections. **2** divide something by surgical cutting.

sec·tion·al /'seksHənl/ ▸ adj. of or relating to a section. ▸ n. a sofa made in sections that can be used separately as chairs. ■ **sec·tion·al·ize** /-ˌīz/ v. **sec·tion·al·ly** adv.

sec·tor /'sektər/ ▸ n. **1** an area or part that is distinct from others. **2** a distinct part of an economy, society, or field of activity: *the government aimed to reassure the commercial sector.* **3** a subdivision of an area for military operations. **4** a part of a circle between two lines drawn from its center to its circumference. ■ **sec·tor·al** /-rəl/ adj.

sec·u·lar /'sekyələr/ ▸ adj. **1** not religious or spiritual. **2** (of Christian clergy) not belonging to or living in a monastic or other community. ■ **sec·u·lar·ism** /-ˌrizəm/ n. **sec·u·lar·ist** /-rist/ n. **sec·u·lar·ize** /-ˌrīz/ v. **sec·u·lar·ly** adv.

se·cure /si'kyŏor/ ▸ adj. **1** likely to continue or to remain safe: *the days of secure staff jobs are over.* **2** fixed or fastened so as not to give way, become loose, or be lost. **3** feeling confident and free from fear or anxiety. **4** protected against attack or other criminal activity. **5** (of a prison or similar establishment) having measures in place to prevent the escape of inmates. ▸ v. **1** protect someone or something from danger or threat. **2** fix or fasten something securely. **3** succeed in obtaining: *he has secured a place on the ballot.*

4 guarantee a loan by having the right to take possession of property or goods if the borrower is unable to repay the money. ■ **se·cure·ly** adv.

se·cu·ri·ty /si'kyŏŏritē/ ▶ n. (pl. **securities**) **1** the state of being or feeling secure: *long-term job security*. **2** the safety of a state or organization against criminal activity such as terrorism. **3** something that is promised as a guarantee that a loan will be repaid. **4** a certificate proving ownership of stocks or bonds.

se·cu·ri·ty blan·ket ▶ n. a blanket or other familiar object that is a comfort to someone, typically a child.

se·dan /si'dan/ ▶ n. **1** an enclosed chair carried between two horizontal poles, used especially in the 17th and 18th centuries. **2** a car for four or more people.

se·date¹ /si'dāt/ ▶ adj. **1** slow, calm, and relaxed. **2** serious, quiet, and rather dull: *sedate small-town life*. ■ **se·date·ly** adv. **se·date·ness** n.

sedate² ▶ v. give someone a drug to make them calm or fall asleep.

se·da·tion /si'dāsHən/ ▶ n. the giving of a sedative drug to someone to calm them or make them sleep.

sed·a·tive /'sedətiv/ ▶ n. a drug that makes someone calm or sleepy. ▶ adj. making someone calm or sleepy.

sed·en·tar·y /'sedn,terē/ ▶ adj. **1** (of work or a way of life) involving much sitting and little exercise. **2** tending to sit down a lot; taking little exercise: *healthy but sedentary young men*. **3** (of an animal or people) tending to stay in the same place for much of the time.

sedge /sej/ ▶ n. a grasslike plant with triangular stems and small flowers, growing in wet ground.

sed·i·ment /'sedəmənt/ ▶ n. **1** matter that settles to the bottom of a liquid. **2** material carried in particles by water or wind and deposited on the land surface or seabed. ▶ v. settle or deposit as sediment. ■ **sed·i·men·ta·tion** /,sedəmən'tāsHən/ n.

sed·i·men·ta·ry /,sedə'mentərē/ ▶ adj. Geology (of rock) formed from sediment deposited by water or wind.

se·di·tion /si'disHən/ ▶ n. actions or speech that encourage rebellion against the authority of a government or ruler. ■ **se·di·tious** adj.

se·duce /si'd(y)ōōs/ ▶ v. **1** tempt someone into sexual activity. **2** persuade someone to do something unwise: *she was almost seduced into believing him*. ■ **se·duc·er** n. **se·duc·tion** /si'dəksHən/ n.

se·duc·tive /si'dəktiv/ ▶ adj. tempting and attractive. ■ **se·duc·tive·ly** adv. **se·duc·tive·ness** n.

se·duc·tress /si'dəktris/ ▶ n. a woman who seduces someone, especially into sexual activity.

sed·u·lous /'sejələs/ ▶ adj. showing dedication and great care or effort. ■ **sed·u·lous·ly** adv.

se·dum /'sēdəm/ ▶ n. a plant of a large group having fleshy leaves and small star-shaped flowers.

see¹ /sē/ ▶ v. (**sees** /sēz/, **seeing** /'sē-iNG/; past **saw** /sô/; past part. **seen** /sēn/) **1** become aware of someone or something with the eyes. **2** experience or witness an event or situation. **3** meet someone one knows socially or by chance. **4** form an opinion or conclusion after thinking or from information: *I saw that he was right*. **5** regard in a particular way: *he saw himself as a good teacher*. **6** view as a possibility: *I can't*

see him earning any more anywhere else. **7** meet someone regularly as a boyfriend or girlfriend. **8** consult a specialist or professional. **9** give someone an interview or consultation. **10** guide or take someone somewhere: *don't bother seeing me out*. **11** (**see to**) deal with something. **12** (**see that**) ensure that.
– PHRASES **see about** deal with something. **see someone off** accompany a person who is leaving to their point of departure. **see someone out** accompany a person to the door upon their leaving. **see something out** come to the end of a period of time or undertaking. **see through** realize someone's or something's true nature. **see someone through** support someone during a difficult period. **see something through** carry on with an undertaking until it is completed.

see² ▶ n. the district or position of a bishop or archbishop, centered on a cathedral church.

seed /sēd/ ▶ n. **1** a flowering plant's unit of reproduction, capable of developing into another such plant. **2** the beginning of a feeling, process, or condition: *the conversation sowed a seed of doubt in his mind*. **3** any of a number of stronger competitors in a sports tournament who have been given a position in an ordered list to ensure that they do not play each other in the early rounds. **4** old use a man's semen. **5** old use (chiefly in the Bible) a person's offspring or descendants. ▶ v. **1** sow land with seeds. **2** produce or drop seeds. **3** remove the seeds from vegetables or fruit. **4** make a competitor a seed in a sports tournament. ■ **seed·less** adj.
– PHRASES **go** (or **run**) **to seed 1** (of a plant) stop flowering as the seeds develop. **2** deteriorate, especially as a result of neglect: *he had gone to seed after his wife left him*.

seed·bed /'sēd,bed/ ▶ n. a bed of fine soil in which seedlings are germinated.

seed corn ▶ n. good-quality corn kept for seed.

seed head ▶ n. a flowerhead when it is producing seeds.

seed leaf ▶ n. a cotyledon.

seed·ling /'sēdliNG/ ▶ n. a young plant raised from seed.

seed mon·ey (also **seed capital**) ▶ n. money provided to start up a project.

seed pearl ▶ n. a very small pearl.

seed po·ta·to ▶ n. a potato intended for replanting to produce a new plant.

seed·y /'sēdē/ ▶ adj. (**seedier**, **seediest**) **1** sordid or immoral: *his seedy affair with a soft-porn starlet*. **2** shabby, dirty, and unpleasant: *a seedy bar*. **3** dated unwell. ■ **seed·i·ly** adv. **seed·i·ness** n.

see·ing /'sē-iNG/ ▶ conj. because; since.

seek /sēk/ ▶ v. (past and past part. **sought**) **1** try to find or obtain: *she may decide to seek alternative employment*. **2** (**seek someone/thing out**) search for and find someone or something. **3** ask for: *we are seeking legal advice*. **4** (**seek to do**) try or want to do: *they had never sought to interfere with her freedom*. ■ **seek·er** n.

seem /sēm/ ▶ v. **1** give the impression of being: *she seemed annoyed*. **2** (**cannot seem to do**) appear to be unable to do something, despite having tried.

seem·ing /'sēmiNG/ ▶ adj. appearing to be real or true; apparent. ■ **seem·ing·ly** adv.

seem·ly /'sēmlē/ ▶ adj. in keeping with good taste or correct behavior. ■ **seem·li·ness** n.

seen /sēn/ ▶ past participle of **SEE**¹.

seep /sēp/ ▶ v. (of a liquid) flow or leak slowly through or into something. ■ **seep·age** /'sēpij/ n.

seer /'sēər, si(ə)r/ ▶ n. a person who is supposedly able to see visions of the future.

seer·suck·er /'si(ə)r,səkər/ ▶ n. a fabric with a puckered surface.

see·saw /'sē,sô/ ▶ n. **1** a long plank balanced on a fixed support, on each end of which children sit and move up and down by pushing the ground with their feet. **2** a situation characterized by repeated changes from one state or condition to another: *the emotional seesaw of a first love affair.* ▶ v. repeatedly change from one state or condition to another and back again.

seethe /sēTH/ ▶ v. **1** be filled with strong but unexpressed anger. **2** be crowded with people or things. **3** (of a liquid) boil or churn as if boiling.

see-through ▶ adj. transparent or translucent.

seg·ment ▶ n. /'segmənt/ **1** each of the parts into which something is divided. **2** Geometry a part of a circle cut off by a chord, or a part of a sphere cut off by a plane not passing through the center. ▶ v. /'seg,ment, seg'ment/ divide something into segments. ■ **seg·men·tal** adj. **seg·men·ta·tion** /,segmən'tāsHən/ n.

seg·re·gate /'segri,gāt/ ▶ v. **1** set apart from the rest or from each other: *disabled people should not be segregated from the rest of society.* **2** separate people along racial, sexual, or religious lines.

seg·re·ga·tion /,segri'gāsHən/ ▶ n. **1** the action of segregating or the state of being segregated. **2** the enforced separation of different racial groups in a country, community, or place. ■ **seg·re·ga·tion·al** /-sHənl/ adj. **seg·re·ga·tion·ist** /-ist/ adj. & n.

se·gue /'segwā, 'sā-/ ▶ v. (**segues** /'segwāz, 'sā-/, **segueing** /'segwā-iNG, 'sā-/ or **seguing** /'segwiNG, 'sā-/, **segued** /'segwād, 'sā-/) (in music, movies, television, etc.) move without interruption from one song, melody, or scene to another. ▶ n. an instance of this.

sei·cen·to /sā'CHen,tō/ ▶ n. the style of Italian art and literature of the 17th century.

sei·gneur /sān'yər/ ▶ n. a feudal lord; a lord of a medieval manor. ■ **sei·gneu·ri·al** /-'yərēəl/ adj.

seine /sān, sen/ ▶ n. a fishing net that hangs vertically in the water with floats at the top and weights at the bottom edge, the ends being drawn together to encircle the fish. ▶ v. fish with a seine.

seis·mic /'sīzmik/ ▶ adj. **1** relating to earthquakes or other vibrations of the earth and its crust. **2** very great in size or effect: *seismic shifts in the global economy.* ■ **seis·mi·cal·ly** /-ik(ə)lē/ adv. **seis·mic·i·ty** /sīz'misitē/n.

seis·mo·graph /'sīzmə,graf/ ▶ n. an instrument that measures and records details of earthquakes, such as force and duration.

seis·mol·o·gy /sīz'mäləjē/ ▶ n. the branch of science concerned with earthquakes. ■ **seis·mo·log·i·cal** /,sīzmə'läjikəl/ adj. **seis·mol·o·gist** n.

seis·mom·e·ter /sīz'mämitər/ ▶ n. another term for SEISMOGRAPH.

seize /sēz/ ▶ v. **1** take hold of someone or something suddenly and forcibly. **2** take possession of something by force. **3** (of the police or another authority) officially take possession of: *customs officers seized drugs with*

a street value of over $300 million. **4** take an opportunity eagerly and decisively. **5** (**seize on**) take eager advantage of. **6** (often **seize up**) (of a machine or part in a machine) become jammed.

sei·zure /'sēzHər/ ▶ n. **1** the action of seizing. **2** a sudden attack of illness, especially a stroke or an epileptic fit.

sel·dom /'seldəm/ ▶ adv. not often; rarely.

se·lect /sə'lekt/ ▶ v. carefully choose someone or something as being the best or most suitable. ▶ adj. **1** carefully chosen as being among the best. **2** used by or consisting of wealthy or sophisticated people: *a select area of Boston.* ■ **se·lect·a·ble** adj.

se·lect com·mit·tee ▶ n. a small legislative committee appointed for a special purpose.

se·lec·tion /sə'leksHən/ ▶ n. **1** the action of selecting. **2** a thing or number of things that have been chosen from a wider group. **3** a range of things from which a choice may be made: *a wide selection of hot and cold dishes.*

se·lec·tive /sə'lektiv/ ▶ adj. **1** relating to or involving selection. **2** tending to choose carefully: *he's very selective in his reading.* **3** affecting some things and not others: *modern pesticides are selective in effect.* ■ **se·lec·tive·ly** adv. **se·lec·tiv·i·ty** /səlek'tivitē/ n.

se·lec·tive serv·ice ▶ n. service in the armed forces under conscription.

se·lec·tor /sə'lektər/ ▶ n. a device for selecting a particular gear or other setting of a machine or device.

se·le·ni·um /sə'lēnēəm/ ▶ n. a gray crystalline nonmetallic chemical element with semiconducting properties.

self /self/ ▶ n. (pl. **selves** /selvz/) **1** a person's essential being that distinguishes them from other people. **2** a person's particular nature or personality: *he was back to his old self.* ▶ pron. (pl. **selves**) oneself. ▶ adj. (of a trim, woven design, etc.) of the same material or color as the rest of the item.

self- ▶ comb.form **1** relating to or directed toward oneself or itself: *self-hatred.* **2** by one's own efforts; by its own action: *self-adjusting.* **3** on, in, for, or relating to oneself or itself: *self-adhesive.*

self-ab·sorbed ▶ adj. preoccupied with one's own emotions, interests, or situation. ■ **self-ab·sorp·tion** n.

self-a·buse /ə'byōos/ ▶ n. **1** behavior that causes damage or harm to oneself. **2** dated masturbation.

self-ad·dressed ▶ adj. (of an envelope) addressed to oneself.

self-ad·he·sive ▶ adj. sticking without needing to be moistened.

self-ad·just·ing ▶ adj. (chiefly of machinery) adjusting itself to meet changing requirements.

self-ag·gran·dize·ment ▶ n. the action of increasing one's own power or importance. ■ **self-ag·gran·diz·ing** adj.

self-ap·point·ed ▶ adj. having taken on a position or role without the agreement of other people.

self-as·sem·bly ▶ n. the construction of a piece of furniture from materials sold in kit form. ■ **self-as·sem·ble** v.

self-as·ser·tion ▶ n. the quality of being confident or forceful in the expression of one's opinions. ■ **self-as·ser·tive** adj. **self-as·ser·tive·ness** n.

self·as·sess·ment ▶ n. the process of judging oneself or one's actions or performance.

self·as·sur·ance ▶ n. confidence in one's own abilities or character. ■ **self-as·sured** adj.

self·a·ware·ness ▶ n. conscious knowledge and understanding of one's own character, feelings, and motives. ■ **self-a·ware** adj.

self·cen·sor·ship ▶ n. the exercising of control over what one says and does.

self·cen·tered ▶ adj. preoccupied with oneself and one's own feelings or needs. ■ **self-cen·tered·ness** n.

self·col·ored ▶ adj. **1** of a single uniform color. **2** (of a trim or accessory) of the same color as the rest of the item.

self·con·fessed ▶ adj. openly admitting to having certain characteristics: *a self-confessed alcoholic.*

self·con·fi·dence ▶ n. a feeling of trust in one's abilities, qualities, and judgment. ■ **self-con·fi·dent** adj. **self-con·fi·dent·ly** adv.

self·con·grat·u·la·tion ▶ n. too much pride in one's achievements or qualities. ■ **self-con·grat·u·la·to·ry** adj.

self·con·scious ▶ adj. **1** nervous, awkward, or embarrassed as a result of being worried about how one appears to other people. **2** done deliberately and with full awareness of the effect produced. ■ **self-con·scious·ly** adv. **self-con·scious·ness** n.

self·con·sis·tent ▶ adj. not having conflicting parts or aspects; consistent. ■ **self-con·sis·ten·cy** n.

self·con·tained ▶ adj. **1** complete, or having all that is needed, in itself. **2** not depending on or influenced by other people.

self·con·tra·dic·tion ▶ n. inconsistency between aspects or parts of a whole.

self·con·trol ▶ n. the ability to control one's emotions or behavior in difficult situations. ■ **self-con·trolled** adj.

self·de·cep·tion ▶ n. the tendency to deceive oneself into believing that a false or unfounded feeling, idea, or situation is true.

self·de·feat·ing ▶ adj. (of an action or policy) preventing rather than achieving a desired result.

self·de·fense ▶ n. the defending of oneself or one's interests, especially through the use of physical force, which is permitted in certain cases as an answer to a charge of violent crime. ■ **self-de·fen·sive** adj.

self·de·ni·al ▶ n. the action of going without or not doing something that one desires to have or do. ■ **self-de·ny·ing** adj.

self·dep·re·cat·ing ▶ adj. modest about or critical of oneself. ■ **self-dep·re·ca·tion** n. **self-dep·re·ca·to·ry** adj.

self·de·struct ▶ v. (of a device) destroy itself by exploding or disintegrating automatically, having been preset to do so.

self·de·struc·tive ▶ adj. causing harm to oneself. ■ **self-de·struc·tion** n. **self-de·struc·tive·ly** adv.

self·de·ter·mi·na·tion ▶ n. **1** the process by which a country gains independence and forms its own government and political system. **2** the right or ability of a person to control their own life.

self·di·rect·ed ▶ adj. **1** (of an emotion, statement, or activity) directed at oneself. **2** (of

an activity) under one's own control. ■ **self-di·rec·tion** n.

self·dis·ci·pline ▶ n. the ability to control one's feelings and overcome one's weaknesses. ■ **self-dis·ci·plined** adj.

self·doubt ▶ n. lack of confidence in oneself and one's abilities.

self·ed·u·cat·ed ▶ adj. educated largely through one's own efforts, rather than by formal instruction. ■ **self-ed·u·ca·tion** n.

self·ef·fac·ing ▶ adj. not seeking to attract attention to oneself or one's abilities or achievements. ■ **self-ef·face·ment** n.

self·em·ployed ▶ adj. working for oneself as a freelance or the owner of a business rather than for an employer. ■ **self-em·ploy·ment** n.

self·es·teem ▶ n. confidence in one's own worth or abilities.

self·e·val·u·a·tion ▶ n. another term for SELF-ASSESSMENT.

self·ev·i·dent ▶ adj. not needing to be demonstrated or explained; obvious.

self·ex·am·i·na·tion ▶ n. **1** the study of one's own behavior and motivations. **2** the examination of one's own body for any signs of illness.

self·ex·plan·a·to·ry ▶ adj. not needing explanation; clearly understood.

self·ex·pres·sion ▶ n. the expression of one's feelings or thoughts, especially in writing, art, music, or dance.

self·fer·tile ▶ adj. (of a plant) capable of self-fertilization.

self·fer·ti·li·za·tion ▶ n. the fertilization of plants and some invertebrate animals by their own pollen or sperm. ■ **self-fer·ti·lize** v.

self·fi·nanc·ing ▶ adj. (of an organization or enterprise) having or generating enough income to finance itself. ■ **self-fi·nanced** adj.

self·ful·fill·ing ▶ adj. (of a prediction) bound to become true because people expect it to and so act in a way that will make it happen.

self·gov·ern·ing ▶ adj. (of a former colony or dependency) administering its own affairs. ■ **self-gov·ern·ment** n.

self·harm ▶ n. deliberate injury to oneself, typically as a sign of psychological or psychiatric disorder. ▶ v. commit self-harm. ■ **self-harm·er** n.

self·help ▶ n. the use of one's own efforts and resources to achieve things without relying on other people.

self·hood /'self.hŏŏd/ ▶ n. the quality that forms a person's individual character.

self·im·age ▶ n. the idea one has of one's abilities, appearance, and personality.

self·im·por·tance ▶ n. an exaggerated sense of one's own value or importance. ■ **self-im·por·tant** adj.

self·im·prove·ment ▶ n. the improvement of one's knowledge, status, or character by one's own efforts.

self·in·duced ▶ adj. brought about by oneself.

self·in·dul·gent ▶ adj. allowing oneself to do or have what one wants, especially to an excessive extent. ■ **self-in·dul·gence** n.

self·in·flict·ed ▶ adj. (of a wound or other harm) caused by oneself.

self·in·ter·est ▶ n. one's personal interest or advantage, especially when pursued without concern for other people. ■ **self·in·ter·est·ed** adj.

self·in·volved ▶ adj. wrapped up in oneself or one's own thoughts.

self·ish /'selfɪSH/ ▶ adj. concerned mainly with one's own needs or wishes at the expense of consideration for other people. ■ **self·ish·ly** adv. **self·ish·ness** n.

self·less /'selfləs/ ▶ adj. concerned more with the needs and wishes of other people than with one's own. ■ **self·less·ly** adv. **self·less·ness** n.

self·lim·it·ing ▶ adj. (of a disease or condition) ultimately resolving itself without medical treatment.

self·love ▶ n. care or concern for one's own well-being and happiness.

self·made ▶ adj. having become successful or rich by one's own efforts.

self·med·i·cate ▶ v. treat oneself with medicine without seeking any medical supervision. ■ **self·med·i·ca·tion** n.

self·mo·ti·vat·ed ▶ adj. motivated to do something because of one's own enthusiasm or interest, without needing pressure from others. ■ **self·mo·ti·va·tion** n.

self·mu·ti·la·tion ▶ n. deliberate injury to one's own body.

self·o·pin·ion·at·ed ▶ adj. having too high a regard for one's own opinions and unwilling to listen to those of other people.

self·per·pet·u·at·ing ▶ adj. able to continue indefinitely without the assistance of anything or anyone else.

self·pit·y ▶ n. excessive concern with and unhappiness over one's own troubles. ■ **self·pit·y·ing** adj.

self·po·lic·ing ▶ n. the process of keeping order or maintaining control within a community without being accountable to an outside authority.

self·pol·li·na·tion ▶ n. the pollination of a flower by pollen from the same plant. ■ **self·pol·li·nate** v.

self·por·trait ▶ n. a portrait by an artist of himself or herself.

self·pos·sessed ▶ adj. calm, confident, and in control of one's feelings. ■ **self·pos·ses·sion** n.

self·pres·er·va·tion ▶ n. the protection of oneself from harm or death, regarded as a basic instinct in human beings and animals.

self·pro·claimed ▶ adj. describing oneself as something, without the agreement or approval of other people: *self-proclaimed experts.*

self·pro·pelled ▶ adj. moving or able to move without external propulsion. ■ **self·pro·pel·ling** adj.

self·re·al·i·za·tion ▶ n. fulfillment of one's own potential.

self·ref·er·en·tial ▶ adj. (especially of a literary or other creative work) making references to itself, its author or creator, or their other work.

self·re·gard ▶ n. **1** consideration for oneself. **2** too much pride in oneself; vanity. ■ **self·re·gard·ing** adj.

self·reg·u·lat·ing ▶ adj. regulating itself without intervention from external organizations, systems, etc. ■ **self·reg·u·la·tion** n. **self·reg·u·la·to·ry** adj.

self·re·li·ance ▶ n. reliance on one's own powers and resources rather than those of other people. ■ **self·re·li·ant** adj.

self·re·spect ▶ n. pride and confidence in oneself. ■ **self·re·spect·ing** adj.

self·re·straint ▶ n. self-control.

self·right·eous ▶ adj. certain that one is totally correct or morally superior to other people. ■ **self·right·eous·ly** adv. **self·right·eous·ness** n.

self·ris·ing flour ▶ n. flour that contains baking powder.

self·rule ▶ n. government of a country, state, or region by its own people.

self·sac·ri·fice ▶ n. the giving up of one's own interests or wishes in order to help other people. ■ **self·sac·ri·fic·ing** adj.

self·same /'self,sām/ ▶ adj. (**the selfsame**) the very same.

self·sat·is·fied ▶ adj. smugly pleased with oneself. ■ **self·sat·is·fac·tion** n.

self·seed ▶ v. (of a plant) propagate itself by the seed it produces, without human intervention. ■ **self·seed·er** n.

self·seek·ing ▶ adj. chiefly British term for SELF-SERVING. ■ **self·seek·er** n.

self·se·lect ▶ v. choose for oneself. ▶ adj. allowing users to select. ■ **self·se·lec·tion** n.

self·serv·ice ▶ adj. (of a store or restaurant) in which customers choose goods for themselves and pay at a checkout.

self·serv·ing ▶ adj. concerned with one's own welfare and interests rather than those of other people. ■ **self·serv·er** n.

self·start·er ▶ n. an ambitious person who acts on their own initiative.

self·styled ▶ adj. using a description or title that one has given oneself: *self-styled experts.*

self·suf·fi·cient ▶ adj. **1** able to support oneself or produce what one needs without outside help. **2** emotionally and intellectually independent. ■ **self·suf·fi·cien·cy** n.

self·sup·port·ing ▶ adj. **1** having the resources to be able to survive without outside help. **2** staying up or upright without being supported by something else.

self·sus·tain·ing ▶ adj. able to continue in a healthy state without outside help. ■ **self·sus·tained** adj.

self·tap·ping ▶ adj. (of a screw) able to cut a thread in the material into which it is inserted.

self·taught ▶ adj. having gained knowledge or skill by reading or experience rather than through formal teaching or training.

self·tim·er ▶ n. a mechanism in a camera that introduces a delay between the operation of the shutter release and the opening of the shutter, enabling the photographer to be included in the photograph.

self·willed ▶ adj. determined to have one's own way, without concern for the wishes of other people.

self·worth ▶ n. self-esteem.

sell /sel/ ▶ v. (past and past part. **sold**) **1** hand over something in exchange for money. **2** offer goods or property for sale. **3** (of goods) be bought in particular amounts or for a particular price: *the book didn't sell well.* **4** (**sell out**) sell all of one's stock of something. **5** (**sell up**) sell all of one's property or assets. **6** persuade someone that something has particular good qualities. **7** (**sell out**) abandon one's principles because it is expedient to do so. **8** (**sell someone out**) betray someone for one's own financial or material benefit. ■ **sell·a·ble** adj.

– PHRASES **sell someone/thing short** fail to recognize or describe the true value of someone or something.

sell-by date ▶ n. **1** a date marked on packaged food indicating the recommended time by which it should be sold. **2** informal a time after which something or someone is no longer considered desirable or effective.

sell·er /'selər/ ▶ n. **1** a person who sells something. **2** a product that sells in a particular way.

sell·ing point ▶ n. a feature of a product for sale that makes it attractive to customers.

sell-off ▶ n. a sale of business assets at a low price, carried out in order to dispose of them rather than as part of normal trading.

sell-out /'sel,out/ ▶ n. **1** the selling of the whole stock of something. **2** an event for which all tickets are sold. **3** a sale of a business or company. **4** a betrayal.

selt·zer /'seltsər/ (also **seltzer water**) ▶ n. soda water.

sel·vage /'selvij/ (chiefly Brit. also **selvedge**) ▶ n. an edge produced on woven fabric during manufacture that prevents it from unraveling.

selves /selvz/ ▶ plural of SELF.

se·man·tic /sə'mantik/ ▶ adj. relating to the meaning of words and sentences. ■ **se·man·ti·cal·ly** /-ik(ə)lē/ adv.

se·man·tics /sə'mantiks/ ▶ n. (usu. treated as sing.) **1** the branch of linguistics concerned with meaning. **2** the meaning of a word, phrase, sentence, or piece of writing.

sem·a·phore /'semə,fôr/ ▶ n. **1** a system of sending messages by holding one's arms or two flags or poles in certain positions that represent letters of the alphabet. **2** a device for sending messages in this way, consisting of an upright with movable parts. ▶ v. send a message by semaphore or by signals resembling semaphore.

sem·blance /'sembləns/ ▶ n. the outward appearance or apparent form of something.

se·men /'sēmən/ ▶ n. the fluid containing spermatozoa that is produced by men and male animals.

se·mes·ter /sə'mestər/ ▶ n. a half-year term in a school or college.

sem·i /'semī/ ▶ n. (pl. **semis**) informal **1** a tractor-trailer. **2** a semifinal.

semi- ▶ prefix **1** half: *semicircular.* **2** partly; in some degree: *semiconscious.*

sem·i·au·to·mat·ic /,semē,ôtə'matik, ,semī-/ ▶ adj. **1** partially automatic. **2** (of a firearm) able to load bullets automatically but not fire continuously.

sem·i·cir·cle /'semē,sərkəl, 'semī-/ ▶ n. a half of a circle or of its circumference. ■ **sem·i·cir·cu·lar** /,semē'sərkyələr, ,semī'sərkyələr/ adj.

sem·i·cir·cu·lar ca·nals ▶ pl.n. a system of three fluid-filled bony channels in the inner ear, involved in sensing and maintaining balance.

sem·i·co·lon /'semi,kōlən, 'semī-/ ▶ n. a punctuation mark (;) indicating a longer pause than that indicated by a comma.

sem·i·con·duc·tor /'semēkən,dəktər, 'semī-/ ▶ n. a solid, e.g., silicon, whose capacity to conduct electricity is limited but increases with temperature. ■ **sem·i·con·duct·ing** adj.

sem·i·con·scious /,semē'känsнəs, ,semī-/ ▶ adj. partially conscious.

sem·i·dou·ble /,semē'dəbəl, ,semī-/ ▶ adj. (of a flower) intermediate between single and double, with the additional petals not completely concealing the center of the flower.

sem·i·fi·nal /,semē'fīnl, ,semī-/ ▶ n. (in sports) a match or round immediately preceding the final. ■ **sem·i·fi·nal·ist** n.

sem·i·flu·id /,semē'floo-id, ,semī-/ ▶ adj. having a thick consistency between solid and liquid.

sem·i·liq·uid /,semē'likwid, ,semī-/ ▶ adj. another term for SEMIFLUID.

sem·i·nal /'semənl/ ▶ adj. **1** (of a work, event, or idea) strongly influencing later developments. **2** referring to semen. **3** relating to the seed of a plant. ■ **sem·i·nal·ly** adv.

sem·i·nar /'semə,när/ ▶ n. **1** a conference or other meeting for discussion or training. **2** a college class in which a small group of students meet to discuss topics with a teacher.

sem·i·nar·y /'semə,nerē/ ▶ n. (pl. **seminaries**) a college that prepares students to be priests, ministers, or rabbis. ■ **sem·i·nar·i·an** /,semə'ne(ə)rēən/ n.

se·mi·ol·o·gy /,sēmē'äləjē, ,semē-, ,sēmī-/ ▶ n. another term for SEMIOTICS. ■ **se·mi·o·log·i·cal** /-ə'läjikəl/ adj. **se·mi·ol·o·gist** n.

se·mi·ot·ics /,sēmē'ätiks, ,semē-, ,sēmī-/ ▶ pl.n. (treated as sing.) the study of signs and symbols and their use or interpretation. ■ **se·mi·ot·ic** adj. **se·mi·o·ti·cian** /,sēmēə'tisнən, ,sēmēə-/ n.

sem·i·per·me·a·ble /,semē'pərmēəbəl, ,semī-/ ▶ adj. (of a cell membrane) allowing small molecules to pass through but not large ones.

sem·i·pre·cious /,semē'presнəs, ,semī-/ ▶ adj. referring to minerals that can be used as gems but are considered to be less valuable than precious stones.

sem·i·pro·fes·sion·al /,semēprə'fesнənl, ,semī-/ ▶ adj. receiving payment for an activity but not relying entirely on it for a living. ▶ n. a person who is engaged in an activity on such a basis.

sem·i·re·tired /,semēri'tī(ə)rd, ,semī-/ ▶ adj. having retired from employment but continuing to work part-time or occasionally. ■ **sem·i·re·tire·ment** /-'tī(ə)rmənt/ n.

sem·i·skilled /,semē'skild, ,semī-/ ▶ adj. (of work or a worker) needing or having some, but not extensive, training.

sem·i·sol·id /,semē'sälid, ,semī-/ ▶ adj. having a very thick, sticky consistency; slightly thicker than semifluid.

Sem·ite /'semīt/ ▶ n. a member of a people speaking a Semitic language, in particular the Jews and Arabs.

Se·mit·ic /sə'mitik/ ▶ n. a family of languages that includes Hebrew, Arabic, and Aramaic. ▶ adj. relating to these languages or their speakers.

sem·i·tone /'semē,tōn, 'semī-/ ▶ n. chiefly British term for HALF STEP.

sem·i·trail·er /'semē,trālər, 'semī-/ ▶ n. **1** a trailer having wheels at the back but supported at the front by a towing vehicle. **2** a tractor trailer.

sem·o·li·na /ˌseməˈlēnə/ ▶ n. the hard grains left after the milling of flour, used in puddings and in pasta.

sem·pi·ter·nal /ˌsempəˈtərnl/ ▶ adj. literary eternal and unchanging; everlasting.

Sem·tex /ˈsemˌteks/ ▶ n. a type of plastic explosive.

Sen. ▶ abbr. 1 Senate. 2 Senator. 3 Senior.

sen·ate /ˈsenit/ ▶ n. 1 a lawmaking or governing body, especially the smaller upper assembly in the US, US states, France, and other countries. 2 the governing body of a college or university. 3 the state council of the ancient Roman republic and empire.

sen·a·tor /ˈsenitər/ ▶ n. a member of a senate. ■ **sen·a·to·ri·al** /ˌsenəˈtôrēəl/ adj. **sen·a·tor·ship** /-ˌSHip/ n.

send /send/ ▶ v. (past and past part. **sent**) 1 cause something to go or be taken to a destination. 2 order or instruct someone to go somewhere. 3 move something sharply or quickly. 4 cause to be in a particular state: *the traffic nearly sent me crazy.* ■ **send·er** n.
– PHRASES **send for 1** order someone to come. 2 order something by mail. **send word** send a message to someone.

send-off ▶ n. a gathering of people to wish good luck to someone who is leaving.

send-up /ˈsendˌəp/ ▶ n. informal an exaggerated imitation of someone or something, done in order to make fun of them.

Sen·e·ga·lese /ˌsenəɡəˈlēz, -ˈlēs/ ▶ n. (pl. **Senegalese**) a person from Senegal, a country on the coast of West Africa. ▶ adj. relating to Senegal.

se·nes·cence /səˈnesəns/ ▶ n. the process by which a living thing gradually deteriorates with age. ■ **se·nes·cent** adj.

sen·e·schal /ˈsenəSHəl/ ▶ n. 1 the steward of a noble's or monarch's house in medieval times. 2 chiefly historical a governor or other administrative or judicial officer.

se·nile /ˈsēˌnīl, ˈsen-/ ▶ adj. having the weaknesses or diseases of old age, especially a loss of mental abilities. ■ **se·nil·i·ty** /siˈnilitē/ n.

se·nile de·men·tia ▶ n. severe mental deterioration in old age, with loss of memory and lack of control of bodily functions.

sen·ior /ˈsēnyər/ ▶ adj. 1 relating to older people. 2 high or higher in rank or status. 3 relating to the final of four years of high school or college. 4 (after a name) referring to the elder of two with the same name in a family. ▶ n. 1 a person who is a specified number of years older than someone else: *she was two years his senior.* 2 a student in the fourth and final year of high school or college. 3 (in sports) a competitor of above a certain age or of the highest status. 4 a senior citizen. ■ **sen·ior·i·ty** /sēnˈyôritē, -ˈyär-/ n.

sen·ior cit·i·zen ▶ n. an elderly person, especially one who is retired.

sen·ior mo·ment ▶ n. humorous a temporary mental lapse.

sen·na /ˈsenə/ ▶ n. a laxative prepared from the dried pods of the cassia tree.

sen·sate /ˈsenˌsāt/ ▶ adj. becoming aware of things through the senses.

sen·sa·tion /senˈsāSHən/ ▶ n. 1 a physical feeling resulting from something that happens to or comes into contact with the body. 2 the ability to have such feelings. 3 a general awareness or impression not caused by anything that can be seen or defined: *the eerie sensation that she was being watched.* 4 a widespread reaction of interest and excitement, or a person or thing causing it.

sen·sa·tion·al /senˈsāSHənl/ ▶ adj. 1 causing or intending to cause great public interest and excitement. 2 informal very impressive or attractive. ■ **sen·sa·tion·al·ly** adv.

sen·sa·tion·al·ism /senˈsāSHənlˌizəm/ ▶ n. (in the media) the use of exciting or shocking stories or language at the expense of accuracy, in order to arouse public interest or excitement. ■ **sen·sa·tion·al·ist** n. & adj. **sen·sa·tion·al·is·tic** /senˌsāSHənlˈistik/ adj.

sen·sa·tion·al·ize /senˈsāSHənlˌīz/ ▶ v. present information in an exaggerated way in order to make it seem more interesting or exciting.

sense /sens/ ▶ n. 1 any of the faculties of sight, smell, hearing, taste, and touch, by which the body becomes aware of external things. 2 a feeling that something is the case. 3 (**sense of**) awareness of or sensitivity to: *a sense of direction.* 4 a sensible and practical attitude to situations or problems. 5 reason or purpose; good judgment: *there's no sense in standing in the rain.* 6 a meaning of a word or expression or the way in which a word or expression can be interpreted. ▶ v. 1 become aware of something by a sense or senses. 2 be vaguely aware of something. 3 (of a machine or similar device) detect something.
– PHRASES **come to one's senses 1** regain consciousness. 2 think and behave reasonably or sensibly again. **make sense** be understandable, justifiable, or sensible. **make sense of** manage to understand something.

sen·sei /ˈsenˌsā, senˈsā/ ▶ n. (pl. same) (in martial arts) a teacher.

sense·less /ˈsensləs/ ▶ adj. 1 lacking meaning, purpose, or common sense. 2 unconscious. ■ **sense·less·ly** adv. **sense·less·ness** n.

sense or·gan ▶ n. an organ of the body that responds to external stimuli by sending impulses to the brain.

sen·si·bil·i·ty /ˌsensəˈbilitē/ ▶ n. (pl. **sensibilities**) 1 the ability to appreciate and respond to complex emotions, especially as expressed in art and literature. 2 (**sensibilities**) a person's feelings that are liable to be easily shocked or offended.

sen·si·ble /ˈsensəbəl/ ▶ adj. 1 having or showing common sense. 2 practical and functional rather than decorative. 3 (**sensible of/to**) formal or dated aware of: *I am very sensible to your concerns.* ■ **sen·si·bly** /-blē/ adv.

sen·si·tive /ˈsensitiv/ ▶ adj. 1 quick to detect, respond to, or be affected by slight changes or influences. 2 appreciating the feelings of other people. 3 easily offended or upset. 4 (of a subject or issue) needing careful handling because likely to cause offense or controversy. 5 (of information) kept secret to avoid endangering national security. ■ **sen·si·tive·ly** adv. **sen·si·tive·ness** n.

sen·si·tive plant ▶ n. a tropical American plant of the pea family, whose leaves bend down when touched.

sen·si·tiv·i·ty /ˌsensiˈtivitē/ ▶ n. (pl. **sensitivities**) 1 the quality or condition of being sensitive. 2 (**sensitivities**) a person's feelings that might be easily offended or hurt.

sen·si·tize /'sensi,tīz/ ▶ v. make someone or something sensitive to or aware of something. ■ **sen·si·ti·za·tion** /,sensiti'zāsHən/ n. **sen·si·tiz·er** n.

sen·sor /'sensər/ ▶ n. a device that detects or measures a physical property.

sen·so·ry /'sensərē/ ▶ adj. relating to sensation or the senses. ■ **sen·so·ri·ly** /-rəlē/ adv.

sen·su·al /'sensHŌŌəl/ ▶ adj. relating to the physical senses as a source of pleasure, especially sexual pleasure. ■ **sen·su·al·ist** n. **sen·su·al·i·ty** /,sensHŌŌ'alitē/ n. **sen·su·al·ly** adv.

> **USAGE**
> Strictly speaking there is a difference between **sensual** and **sensuous**. **Sensual** is used in relation to pleasure experienced through the senses, especially sexual pleasure, while **sensuous** is a more neutral term, meaning 'relating to the senses rather than the intellect'.

sen·su·ous /'sensHŌŌəs/ ▶ adj. **1** relating to or affecting the senses rather than the intellect. **2** attractive or pleasing physically, especially sexually. ■ **sen·su·ous·ly** adv. **sen·su·ous·ness** n.

sent¹ /sent/ ▶ past and past participle of SEND.

sent² ▶ n. a unit of money of Estonia, equal to one hundredth of a kroon.

sen·tence /'sentns/ ▶ n. **1** a set of words that is complete in itself, conveying a statement, question, exclamation, or command. **2** the punishment given to someone found guilty by a court. ▶ v. declare in a court that a person found guilty is to receive a particular punishment.

sen·ten·tious /sen'tencHəs/ ▶ adj. given to making pompous comments on moral issues. ■ **sen·ten·tious·ly** adv. **sen·ten·tious·ness** n.

sen·tient /'sencH(ē)ənt/ ▶ adj. able to perceive or feel things. ■ **sen·tience** n.

sen·ti·ment /'sen(t)əmənt/ ▶ n. **1** a view, opinion, or feeling. **2** exaggerated and self-indulgent feelings of tenderness, sadness, or nostalgia.

sen·ti·men·tal /,sen(t)ə'men(t)l/ ▶ adj. **1** connected with or caused by feelings of tenderness, sadness, or nostalgia: he had a sentimental attachment to the place. **2** having or causing such feelings in a way that is exaggerated or self-indulgent: a sentimental love song. ■ **sen·ti·men·tal·ism** /,sen(t)ə'men(t)l,izəm/ n. **sen·ti·men·tal·ist** n. **sen·ti·men·tal·i·ty** /,sen(t)əmen'talitē, -mən-/ n. **sen·ti·men·tal·ly** adv.

sen·ti·men·tal·ize /,sen(t)ə'men(t)l,īz/ ▶ v. present or treat something in a sentimental way.

sen·ti·men·tal val·ue ▶ n. the value of an object that comes from its personal or emotional associations rather than its material worth.

sen·ti·nel /'sentn-əl/ ▶ n. a soldier or guard whose job is to stand and keep watch.

sen·try /'sentrē/ ▶ n. (pl. **sentries**) a soldier stationed to keep guard or to control access to a place.

sen·try box ▶ n. a structure with an open front, providing shelter for a standing sentry.

se·ñor /sān'yôr, sen-/ ▶ n. a title or form of address for a Spanish-speaking man, corresponding to Mr. or sir.

se·ño·ra /sān'yôrə, sen-/ ▶ n. a title or form of address for a Spanish-speaking woman, corresponding to Mrs. or madam.

se·ño·ri·ta /,sānyə'rētə, ,sen-/ ▶ n. a title or form of address for a Spanish-speaking unmarried woman, corresponding to Miss.

se·pal /'sēpəl/ ▶ n. each of the leaflike parts of a flower that surround the petals, enclosing them when the flower is in bud.

sep·a·ra·ble /'sep(ə)rəbəl/ ▶ adj. able to be separated or treated separately. ■ **sep·a·ra·bil·i·ty** /,sep(ə)rə'bilitē/ n.

sep·a·rate ▶ adj. /'sep(ə)rit/ **1** forming or seen as a unit apart or by itself; not joined or united with others. **2** different; distinct. ▶ v. /'sepə,rāt/ **1** move or come apart. **2** form a distinction or boundary between: a footpath separated their yard from the shore. **3** stop living together as a couple. **4** divide into component parts: the milk had separated into curds and whey. **5** extract or remove something for use or because it is unwanted. **6** distinguish between or from others; consider individually: it is impossible to separate belief from emotion. ▶ n. /'sep(ə)rit/ (**separates**) individual items of clothing designed to be worn in different combinations. ■ **sep·a·rate·ly** adv. **sep·a·rate·ness** n. **sep·a·ra·tor** /'sepə,rātər/ n.

sep·a·ra·tion /,sepə'rāsHən/ ▶ n. **1** the action of separating or the state of being separated. **2** the state in which a husband and wife remain married but live apart.

sep·a·ra·tist /'sep(ə)rətist/ ▶ n. a person who supports the separation of a particular group from a larger body on the basis of ethnic origin, religion, etc. ▶ adj. relating to such separation or people who support it. ■ **sep·a·ra·tism** /'sep(ə)rə,tizəm/ n.

Se·phar·di /sə'färdē/ ▶ n. (pl. **Sephardim** /-'färdim, -,fär'dēm/) a Jew of Spanish or Portuguese descent. Compare with ASHKENAZI. ■ **Se·phar·dic** /-dik/ adj.

se·pi·a /'sēpēə/ ▶ n. **1** a reddish-brown color, associated particularly with early photographs. **2** a brown pigment prepared from cuttlefish ink, used in drawing and in watercolors.

se·poy /'sē,poi/ ▶ n. historical an Indian soldier serving under British or other European orders.

sep·pu·ku /'sepŌŌ,kŌŌ, sə'pŌŌkŌŌ/ ▶ n. another term for HARA-KIRI.

sep·sis /'sepsis/ ▶ n. the presence in tissues of harmful bacteria, typically through infection of a wound.

Sept. ▶ abbr. September.

sep·ta /'septə/ ▶ plural of SEPTUM.

sep·tal /'septl/ ▶ adj. relating to a septum or septa.

Sep·tem·ber /sep'tembər/ ▶ n. the ninth month of the year.

sep·tet /sep'tet/ ▶ n. a group of seven people playing music or singing together.

sep·tic /'septik/ ▶ adj. (of a wound or a part of the body) infected with bacteria.

> **USAGE**
> Do not confuse **septic** with **skeptic**. **Septic** means 'infected with bacteria' (a septic finger), whereas **skeptic** means 'a person who tends to question or doubt accepted opinions' (numerous skeptics poured scorn on his claim).

sep·ti·ce·mi·a /,septi'sēmēə/ (Brit. **septicaemia**) ▶ n. blood poisoning caused by bacteria.

sep·tic tank ▶ n. an underground tank in which sewage is allowed to decompose through the action of bacteria before draining away into the ground.

sep·tu·a·ge·nar·i·an /ˌsepˌto͞oəjəˈne(ə)rēən/ ▶ n. a person who is between 70 and 79 years old.

Sep·tu·a·gint /ˈsepto͞oəjint/ ▶ n. a Greek version of the Hebrew Bible (or Old Testament), including the Apocrypha, produced in the 3rd and 2nd centuries BC.

sep·tum /ˈseptəm/ ▶ n. (pl. **septa** /-tə/) a partition separating two cavities in the body, such as that between the nostrils.

sep·tup·let /sepˈtəplit, sepˈt(y)o͞o-/ ▶ n. each of seven children born at one birth.

sep·ul·cher /ˈsepəlkər/ (Brit. **sepulchre**) ▶ n. a stone tomb or monument in which a dead person is laid or buried.

se·pul·chral /səˈpəlkrəl/ ▶ adj. **1** gloomy and solemn: *a speech delivered in sepulchral tones.* **2** relating to a tomb or burial. ■ **se·pul·chral·ly** adv.

se·quel /ˈsēkwəl/ ▶ n. **1** a book, movie, or television program that continues the story or develops the theme of an earlier one. **2** something that takes place after or as a result of an earlier event.

se·que·la /siˈkwelə/ ▶ n. (pl. **sequelae** /-ˈkwelē, -ˈkwelī/) a medical condition that is the consequence of a previous disease or injury.

se·quence /ˈsēkwəns/ ▶ n. **1** a particular order in which related things follow each other. **2** a set of related things that follow each other in a particular order. **3** a part of a movie or television program dealing with one particular event or topic. **4** Music a repetition of a phrase or melody at a higher or lower pitch. ▶ v. **1** arrange something in a sequence. **2** play or record music with a sequencer.

se·quenc·er /ˈsēkwənsər/ ▶ n. an electronic device for storing sequences of musical notes, chords, or rhythms and transmitting them to an electronic musical instrument.

se·quen·tial /siˈkwenCHəl/ ▶ adj. forming or following in a logical order or sequence. ■ **se·quen·tial·ly** adv.

se·ques·ter /səˈkwestər/ ▶ v. **1** isolate or hide away: *he sequestered himself in his studio.* **2** another term for SEQUESTRATE.

se·ques·trate /ˈsēkwiˌstrāt, ˈsek-, səˈkwesˌtrāt/ ▶ v. **1** take legal possession of assets until a debt has been paid or other claims have been met. **2** take forcible possession of something. ■ **se·ques·tra·tion** /ˌsēkwiˈstrāsHən, ˌsek-/ n. **se·ques·tra·tor** n.

se·quin /ˈsēkwin/ ▶ n. a small shiny disk sewn onto clothing for decoration. ■ **se·quined** (also **sequinned**) adj.

se·quoi·a /səˈk(w)oi-ə/ ▶ n. a redwood tree, especially the California redwood.

se·ra /ˈsi(ə)rə/ ▶ plural of SERUM.

se·ragl·io /səˈrälyō/ ▶ n. (pl. **seraglios**) **1** the women's rooms in a Muslim house or palace. **2** a harem.

se·ra·pe /səˈräpē/ (also **sarape**) ▶ n. a shawl or blanket worn as a cloak by people from Latin America.

ser·aph /ˈserəf/ ▶ n. (pl. **seraphim** /ˈserəˌfim/ or **seraphs**) a type of angel associated with light and purity. ■ **se·raph·ic** /səˈrafik/ adj. **se·raph·i·cal·ly** /səˈrafik(ə)lē/ adv.

Serb /sərb/ ▶ n. a person from Serbia.

Ser·bi·an /ˈsərbēən/ ▶ n. **1** the language of the Serbs. **2** a Serb. ▶ adj. relating to Serbia.

Ser·bo-Cro·at /ˈsərbō ˈkrōˌät, ˈkrōt/ (also **Serbo-Croatian** /krōˈāsHən/) ▶ n. the language spoken in Serbia, Croatia, and elsewhere in the former Yugoslavia.

sere /si(ə)r/ (also **sear**) ▶ adj. literary (of a plant) withered.

ser·e·nade /ˌserəˈnäd/ ▶ n. a piece of music sung or played in the open air at night, especially by a man under the window of the woman he loves. ▶ v. entertain someone with a serenade. ■ **ser·e·nad·er** n.

ser·en·dip·i·ty /ˌserənˈdipitē/ ▶ n. the occurrence of events by chance in a beneficial or lucky way: *many cancer drugs have been discovered through serendipity.* ■ **ser·en·dip·i·tous** /-ˈdipitəs/ adj. **ser·en·dip·i·tous·ly** adv.

se·rene /səˈrēn/ ▶ adj. calm, peaceful, and untroubled; tranquil. ■ **se·rene·ly** adv. **se·ren·i·ty** /səˈrenitē/ n.

serf /sərf/ ▶ n. (in the feudal system) an agricultural laborer who was tied to working on a particular estate. ■ **serf·dom** /-dəm/ n.

serge /sərj/ ▶ n. a hard-wearing woolen or worsted fabric.

ser·geant /ˈsärjənt/ ▶ n. **1** a rank of noncommissioned officer in the army or air force, above corporal. **2** a police officer ranking below a lieutenant.

ser·geant-at-arms (also Brit. **serjeant-at-arms**) ▶ n. (pl. **sergeants-at-arms**) an official of a lawmaking body whose duties include maintaining order and security.

ser·geant ma·jor ▶ n. a high-ranking noncommissioned officer in the US Army or Marine Corps, above master sergeant and below warrant officer.

se·ri·al /ˈsi(ə)rēəl/ ▶ adj. **1** consisting of or taking place in a series. **2** repeatedly committing the same offense or following a characteristic behavior pattern: *a serial killer.* **3** Computing (of a device) involving the transfer of data as a single sequence of bits. ▶ n. a story or play published or broadcast in regular instalments. ■ **se·ri·al·i·ty** /ˌsi(ə)rēˈalitē/ n. **se·ri·al·ly** adv.

se·ri·al·ism /ˈsi(ə)rēəˌlizəm/ ▶ n. a technique of musical composition using the twelve notes of the chromatic scale (one that rises or falls by half steps) in a fixed order that is subject to change only in specific ways. ■ **se·ri·al·ist** adj. & n.

se·ri·al·ize /ˈsi(ə)rēəˌlīz/ ▶ v. **1** publish or broadcast a story or play in regular instalments. **2** arrange something in a series. ■ **se·ri·al·i·za·tion** /ˌsi(ə)rēələˈzāsHən/ n.

se·ri·al num·ber ▶ n. an identification number showing the position of a manufactured item in a series.

se·ries /ˈsi(ə)rēz/ ▶ n. (pl. same) **1** a number of similar or related things coming one after another. **2** a sequence of related television or radio programs. **3** Geology a range of rock strata corresponding to an epoch in time: *the Pliocene series.* **4** Mathematics a set of quantities constituting a progression or having values determined by a common relation.
– PHRASES **in series** (of electrical components or circuits) arranged so that the current passes through each in turn.

ser·if /ˈserəf/ ▶ n. a slight projection finishing off a stroke of a letter, as in T contrasted with T.

se·ri·o·com·ic /ˌsi(ə)rē-ō-ʹkämik/ (also **serio-comic**) ▶ adj. combining serious and comic elements.

se·ri·ous /ʹsi(ə)rēəs/ ▶ adj. **1** dangerous or very bad: *serious injury.* **2** needing or showing careful consideration or action: *marriage is a serious matter.* **3** solemn or sensible. **4** sincere and in earnest. **5** informal substantial in size, number, or quality: *every minute is costing you serious money.* ■ **se·ri·ous·ness** n.

se·ri·ous·ly /ʹsi(ə)rēəslē/ ▶ adv. **1** in a serious way. **2** very; extremely: *he's seriously rich.*

ser·mon /ʹsərmən/ ▶ n. **1** a talk on a religious or moral subject, especially one given during a church service. **2** informal a long or boring reprimand. ■ **ser·mon·ic** /sərʹmänik/ adj.

ser·mon·ize /ʹsərməˌnīz/ ▶ v. give a long talk about morals to someone.

se·rol·o·gy /siʹräləjē/ ▶ n. the scientific study or examination of blood serum. ■ **se·ro·log·ic** /ˌsi(ə)rəʹläjik/ adj. **se·ro·log·i·cal** adj. **se·rol·o·gist** n.

se·ro·pos·i·tive /ˌsi(ə)rōʹpäzitiv/ (or **seronegative** /ˌsi(ə)rōʹnegətiv/) ▶ adj. giving a positive (or negative) result in a test of blood serum, especially for the presence of a virus.

ser·o·to·nin /ˌserəʹtōnən, ˌsi(ə)r-/ ▶ n. a compound in blood that constricts the blood vessels and brings about the transfer of impulses from one nerve to another.

se·rous /ʹsi(ə)rəs/ ▶ adj. relating to, resembling, or producing serum.

ser·pent /ʹsərpənt/ ▶ n. literary a large snake.

ser·pen·tine /ʹsərpənˌtēn, -ˌtīn/ ▶ adj. like a serpent or snake, especially in being winding or twisting. ▶ n. a dark green mineral that is often mottled or spotted like a snake's skin.

ser·ra·no /səʹränō/ ▶ n. a small, red or yellow, very hot chili that is used fresh or dried in Mexican cooking.

ser·rat·ed /ʹserˌātid, səʹrātid/ ▶ adj. having a jagged edge like the teeth of a saw.

ser·ra·tion /seʹrāsHən/ ▶ n. a tooth or point of a jagged edge.

ser·ried /ʹserēd/ ▶ adj. (of rows of people or things) standing close together.

se·rum /ʹsi(ə)rəm/ ▶ n. (pl. **sera** /ʹsi(ə)rə/ or **serums**) the thin amber-colored liquid that separates out when blood has clotted.

serv·ant /ʹsərvənt/ ▶ n. **1** a person employed to perform domestic duties in a household or for a person. **2** a person providing support or service for an organization or person: *he was a great servant of the community.*

serve /sərv/ ▶ v. **1** perform duties or provide a service for: *the hospital serves a large area of Central New York.* **2** be employed as a member of the armed forces. **3** spend a period in office, in an apprenticeship, or in prison. **4** present someone with food or drink. **5** attend to a customer in a store. **6** fulfill a purpose. **7** treat in a specified way: *homeowners wonder if they are being fairly served.* **8** (of food or drink) be enough for a specified number of people. **9** Law formally deliver a summons or writ to the person to whom it is addressed. **10** (in tennis and other racket sports) hit the ball or shuttlecock to begin play for each point of a game. **11** (of a male breeding animal) mate with a female. ▶ n. an act of serving in tennis, badminton, etc.
– PHRASES **if** (**my**) **memory serves** (**me**) if I

remember correctly. **serve someone right** be someone's deserved punishment or bad luck.

serv·er /ʹsərvər/ ▶ n. **1** a person or thing that serves. **2** a computer or program that controls or supplies information to a computer network.

serv·ice /ʹsərvis/ ▶ n. **1** the action of serving, helping, or providing: *he complained about the poor service in the hotel.* **2** a period of employment with an organization. **3** assistance or advice given to customers. **4** a ceremony of religious worship that follows a set form. **5** a system supplying a public need such as transportation, or utilities such as water. **6** a department or organization run by the government: *the parks service.* **7** (**the services**) the armed forces. **8** (often in phrase **in service**) employment as a servant. **9** a set of matching dishes used for serving a particular meal. **10** (in tennis, badminton, etc.) a serve. **11** a regular inspection and maintenance of a vehicle or other machine. ▶ v. **1** perform regular maintenance or repair work on a vehicle or machine. **2** provide a service or services for someone. **3** pay interest on a debt. **4** (of a male animal) mate with a female animal.
– PHRASES **in** (or **out of**) **service** available (or not available) for use.

serv·ice·a·ble /ʹsərvəsəbəl/ ▶ adj. **1** usable or in working order. **2** useful and hard-wearing rather than attractive. ■ **serv·ice·a·bil·i·ty** /ˌsərvəsəʹbilitē/ n.

serv·ice ar·e·a ▶ n. **1** a roadside area where services are available to motorists. **2** the area in which a subscriber can use their cell phone.

serv·ice charge ▶ n. **1** a charge added to a bill for service in a restaurant. **2** a charge made for other services, such as maintenance on a leased property.

serv·ice in·dus·try ▶ n. a business that provides a service for a customer rather than manufacturing goods.

serv·ice·man /ʹsərvəsˌman, -ˌman/ (or **servicewoman** /ʹsərvəsˌwŏŏmən/) ▶ n. (pl. **servicemen** or **servicewomen**) **1** a person serving in the armed forces. **2** a person providing maintenance for machinery.

serv·ice pack ▶ n. a periodically released update to software from a manufacturer, consisting of requested enhancements and fixes for known bugs.

serv·ice pro·vid·er ▶ n. a company that provides access to the Internet for its subscribers.

serv·ice road ▶ n. a minor road running parallel to a main road and giving access to houses, stores, or businesses.

serv·ice sta·tion ▶ n. a garage selling gasoline and oil and sometimes offering vehicle maintenance.

ser·vi·ette /ˌsərvēʹet/ ▶ n. chiefly Brit. a table napkin.

ser·vile /ʹsərvəl, -ˌvīl/ ▶ adj. **1** excessively willing to serve or please others. **2** relating to a slave or slaves. ■ **ser·vile·ly** adv. **ser·vil·i·ty** /sərʹvilitē/ n.

serv·ing /ʹsərviNG/ ▶ n. a quantity of food suitable for or served to one person.

ser·vi·tude /ʹsərviˌt(y)ŏŏd/ ▶ n. the state of being a slave or of being under the complete control of someone more powerful.

serv·let /ʹsərvlit/ ▶ n. Computing a small, server-resident program that typically runs automatically in response to user input.

ser·vo·mech·an·ism /ˈsərvōˌmekəˌnizəm/ ▶ n. a powered mechanism producing motion or forces at a higher level of energy than the input level, e.g., in the brakes and steering of large motor vehicles.

ser·vo·mo·tor /ˈsərvōˌmōtər/ ▶ n. the element in a servomechanism that provides mechanical motion.

ses·a·me /ˈsesəmē/ ▶ n. a tall plant of tropical and subtropical areas, grown for its oil-rich seeds.
– PHRASES **open ses·a·me** a free or unrestricted means of entering or accessing something.

ses·qui·pe·da·li·an /ˌseskwəpəˈdālyən/ ▶ adj. formal **1** (of a word) having many syllables; long. **2** full of long words; long-winded.

ses·sile /ˈsesəl, -īl/ ▶ adj. technical **1** (of an organism, e.g., a barnacle) fixed in one place; immobile. **2** (of a plant or animal structure) attached directly by its base without a stalk or similar structure.

ses·sion /ˈseSHən/ ▶ n. **1** a period devoted to a particular activity: *a training session.* **2** a meeting of a council, court, or lawmaking body to carry out its business. **3** a period during which council and other meetings are regularly held. **4** an academic year. ■ **ses·sion·al** adj.

ses·sion mu·si·cian ▶ n. a freelance musician hired to play on recording sessions.

ses·tet /sesˈtet/ ▶ n. the last six lines of a sonnet.

set¹ /set/ ▶ v. (**sets, setting, set**) **1** put, lay, or stand something in a specified place or position. **2** put or bring into a specified state: *the hostages were set free.* **3** cause to start doing something: *the incident set me thinking.* **4** give someone a task. **5** decide on or fix a time, value, or limit. **6** establish something as an example or record. **7** adjust a device as required: *don't set the volume too loud.* **8** prepare a table for a meal by placing utensils, dishes, etc., on it. **9** harden into a solid, semisolid, or fixed state. **10** arrange damp hair into the required style. **11** put a broken or dislocated bone or limb into the correct position for healing. **12** (of the sun or moon) appear to move toward and below the earth's horizon. **13** arrange type or written material for printing as required. **14** (of blossom or a tree) form into or produce fruit.
– PHRASES **set about** start doing something in an energetic or determined way. **set someone apart** make someone seem superior to others. **set something aside 1** keep something for a particular purpose. **2** formally cancel a legal decision or order. **set someone back** informal cost someone a particular amount of money. **set something down** record something in writing. **set forth** dated begin a journey. **set something forth** state something in writing or speech. **set in** (of something unwelcome) begin and seem likely to continue. **set off** begin a journey. **set something off 1** cause a bomb or alarm to go off. **2** make something more attractive by being placed near to something else. **set on** attack someone violently. **set out 1** begin a journey. **2** intend to do something. **set something out** arrange or display something. **set sail 1** begin a voyage. **2** hoist the sails of a boat. **set to** begin doing something in an energetic way. **set something to music** provide music for a written work. **set something up 1** place or erect something in position. **2** establish a business or other organization. **set someone up 1** establish someone in a particular enterprise or role.

2 informal make an innocent person appear guilty.

set² ▶ n. **1** a number of things or people grouped together as similar or forming a unit. **2** a group of people with shared interests or occupations: *the literary set.* **3** the way in which something is set or positioned: *that cold set of his jaw.* **4** a radio or television receiver. **5** (in tennis and other games) a group of games counting as a unit toward a match. **6** a collection of scenery, stage furniture, etc., used for a scene in a play, movie, etc. **7** (in jazz or popular music) a sequence of songs or pieces forming part or all of a live show or recording. **8** Mathematics a collection of distinct entities satisfying specified conditions and regarded as a unit. **9** a cutting, young plant, or bulb used to produce new plants: *an onion set.*

set³ ▶ adj. **1** fixed or arranged in advance. **2** firmly fixed and unchanging: *set ideas about race and culture.* **3** having a fixed wording. **4** ready or likely to do something: *we're all set for tonight!* **5** (**set on**) determined to do something.

set-a·side ▶ n. **1** the policy of taking land out of production to reduce crop surpluses. **2** a portion of funds or other resources reserved for a particular purpose.

set·back /ˈsetˌbak/ ▶ n. a problem that prevents or holds up progress.

set piece ▶ n. a part of a novel, movie, play, piece of music, etc., that is arranged in a recognized or elaborate way to create a particular effect.

set play ▶ n. Sport a prearranged maneuver carried out from a restart by the team who have the advantage.

set point ▶ n. (in tennis and other sports) a point that if won by one of the players will also win them a set.

set square ▶ n. a right-angled triangular plate for drawing lines, especially at 90°, 45°, 60°, or 30°.

set·tee /seˈtē/ ▶ n. a long upholstered seat for more than one person, typically with a back and arms.

set·ter /ˈsetər/ ▶ n. a breed of large dog with long hair, trained to stand rigid when scenting game.

set the·o·ry ▶ n. the branch of mathematics concerned with the properties and applications of sets.

set·ting /ˈsetiNG/ ▶ n. **1** the way or place in which something is set: *the islands offer a perfect setting for a family vacation.* **2** a piece of metal in which a precious stone or gem is fixed to form a piece of jewelry. **3** a piece of vocal or choral music composed for particular words. **4** (also **place setting**) a complete set of dishes and utensils for one person at a meal.

set·tle /ˈsetl/ ▶ v. **1** reach agreement on something disputed. **2** decide or arrange something finally: *they hadn't settled on a date for the wedding.* **3** make one's home in a new place. **4** (often **settle down**) adopt a more steady or secure life. **5** become or make calmer or quieter. **6** sit or place so as to be comfortable or secure: *she settled her bag on her shoulder.* **7** sink or fall slowly downward: *dust from the mill had settled on the roof.* **8** (often **settle in**) begin to feel comfortable in a new situation. **9** pay a debt or bill. **10** (**settle for**) accept something less than satisfactory. **11** (**settle down to**) begin to concentrate on an activity. **12** (**settle something on**) give money or property to someone through a legal document such as a will.

set·tle·ment /ˈsetlmənt/ ▶ n. **1** the action of settling. **2** an official agreement intended to settle a dispute or conflict. **3** a place where people establish a community. **4** a legal arrangement by which a person gives money or property to someone else: *a divorce settlement.*

set·tler /'setl-ər, 'setlər/ ▶ n. a person who establishes a community in a new area.

set·tlor /'setl-ər, 'setlər/ ▶ n. a person who makes a legal arrangement to transfer property to establish a trust.

set-to ▶ n. (pl. **set-tos**) informal a fight or argument.

set-top box ▶ n. a device that converts a digital television signal to an analog one, so that it can be viewed on a conventional set.

set·up /'set,əp/ ▶ n. informal **1** the way in which something is organized. **2** an organization. **3** a scheme intended to trick someone or make it appear that they have done something wrong.

sev·en /'sevən/ ▶ cardinal number one more than six; 7. (Roman numeral: **vii** or **VII.**) ■ **sev·en·fold** /'sevən,fōld/ adj. & adv.

– PHRASES **the seven deadly sins** (in Christian tradition) the sins of pride, covetousness, lust, anger, gluttony, envy, and sloth. **the seven seas** all the oceans of the world (the Arctic, Antarctic, North Pacific, South Pacific, North Atlantic, South Atlantic, and Indian Oceans). **the seven-year itch** a tendency to be unfaithful, supposed to arise after seven years of marriage.

Sev·en Sis·ters (the Seven Sisters) ▶ **1** Astronomy the star cluster of the Pleiades. **2** a group of seven women's (or formerly women's) colleges in the eastern US having high academic and social prestige.

sev·en·teen /,sevən'tēn, 'sevən,tēn/ ▶ cardinal number one more than sixteen; 17. (Roman numeral: **xvii** or **XVII.**) ■ **sev·en·teenth** /,sevən'tēnTH, 'sevən,tēnTH/ adj. & n.

sev·en·teen-year lo·cust ▶ n. the nymph of the northern species of the periodical cicada. See PERIODICAL CICADA.

sev·enth /'sevənTH/ ▶ ordinal number **1** that is number seven in a sequence; 7th. **2** (**a seventh/ one seventh**) each of seven equal parts into which something is divided. **3** a musical interval spanning seven consecutive notes in a scale.

Sev·enth-Day Ad·vent·ist ▶ n. a member of a strict Protestant sect that preaches that Jesus is about to return to earth and that observes Saturday as the sabbath.

sev·en·ty /'sevəntē/ ▶ cardinal number (pl. **seventies**) ten less than eighty; 70. (Roman numeral: **lxx** or **LXX.**) ■ **sev·en·ti·eth** /-tēəTH/ ordinal number.

sev·en·ty-eight ▶ n. an old phonograph record designed to be played at 78 rpm.

sev·er /'sevər/ ▶ v. **1** cut something off or into pieces. **2** put an end to a connection or relationship.

sev·er·al /'sev(ə)rəl/ ▶ determiner & pron. more than two but not many. ▶ adj. separate or respective: *the two levels of government sorted out their several responsibilities.* ■ **sev·er·al·ly** adv.

sev·er·ance /'sev(ə)rəns/ ▶ n. **1** the ending of a connection or relationship. **2** the state of being separated or cut off.

sev·er·ance pay ▶ n. money paid to an employee upon dismissal or discharge from employment.

se·vere /sə'vi(ə)r/ ▶ adj. **1** (of something bad or difficult) very great; intense. **2** strict or harsh: *severe penalties for hackers.* **3** very plain in style or appearance. ■ **se·vere·ly** adv. **se·ver·i·ty** /-'veritē/ n.

se·viche ▶ n. variant spelling of CEVICHE.

Se·ville or·ange /sə'vil/ ▶ n. a bitter orange used for marmalade.

Sè·vres /'sevrə/ ▶ n. a type of elaborately decorated fine porcelain.

sew /sō/ ▶ v. (past part. **sewn** or **sewed**) **1** join or repair something by making stitches with a needle and thread or a sewing machine. **2** (**sew something up**) informal bring something to a favorable conclusion.

sew·age /'sōōij/ ▶ n. waste water and excrement that is carried away in sewers.

sew·age treat·ment plant (also **sewage plant**) ▶ n. a place where sewage is treated.

sew·er¹ /'sōōər/ ▶ n. an underground pipe for carrying off drainage water and waste matter.

sew·er² /'sōər/ ▶ n. a person who sews.

sew·er·age /'sōōərij/ ▶ n. **1** the provision of drainage by sewers. **2** another term for SEWAGE.

sew·ing ma·chine ▶ n. a machine with a mechanically driven needle for sewing cloth.

sewn /sōn/ ▶ past participle of SEW.

sex /seks/ ▶ n. **1** either of the two main categories (male and female) into which humans and most other living things are divided on the basis of their reproductive functions. **2** sexual intercourse. **3** the fact of being male or female. **4** the group of all members of either sex: *her efforts to improve the condition of her sex.* ▶ v. **1** (**sex something up**) informal present something in a more interesting or lively way. **2** (**sex someone up**) informal have sex with someone. **3** determine the sex of an animal. ■ **sex·er** n.

USAGE
On the difference between the words **sex** and **gender**, see the note at GENDER.

sex·a·ge·nar·i·an /,seksəjə'ne(ə)rēən/ ▶ n. a person between 60 and 69 years old.

sex ap·peal ▶ n. the quality of being attractive in a sexual way.

sex change ▶ n. a change in a person's physical sexual characteristics by surgery and hormone treatment.

sex chro·mo·some ▶ n. a chromosome concerned in determining the sex of an organism (in mammals the X and Y chromosomes).

sexed /sekst/ ▶ adj. having specified sexual appetites: *highly sexed men.*

sex hor·mone ▶ n. a hormone affecting sexual development or reproduction, such as estrogen or testosterone.

sex·ism /'sek,sizəm/ ▶ n. prejudice or discrimination, typically against women, on the basis of a person's sex. ■ **sex·ist** adj. & n.

sex kit·ten ▶ n. informal a young woman who is very sexually attractive.

sex·less /'seksləs/ ▶ adj. **1** not sexually attractive or active. **2** neither male nor female.

sex life ▶ n. a person's sexual activity and relationships considered as a whole.

sex ob·ject ▶ n. a person regarded purely in terms of their sexual attractiveness or availability.

sex·ol·o·gy /sek'sälǝjē/ ▶ n. the study of people's sexual behavior. ■ **sex·o·log·i·cal** /,seksə'läjikəl/

adj. **sex·ol·o·gist** n.

sex·ploi·ta·tion /ˌseksploiˈtāsнən/ ▶ n. informal the commercial exploitation of sex, sexual attractiveness, or sexually explicit material.

sex·pot /ˈseksˌpät/ ▶ n. informal a sexy person.

sex sym·bol ▶ n. a person famous for their sexual attractiveness.

sex·tant /ˈsekstənt/ ▶ n. an instrument for measuring the angular distances between objects, used for navigation and surveying.

sex·tet /sekˈstet/ ▶ n. 1 a group of six people playing music or singing together. 2 a composition for a sextet. 3 a set of six.

sex·ton /ˈsekstən/ ▶ n. a person who looks after a church and churchyard, sometimes acting as bell-ringer and formerly as gravedigger.

sex tour·ism ▶ n. the organization of vacations abroad with the aim of taking advantage of the lack of restrictions on sexual activity and prostitution in some countries.

sex·tu·ple /sekˈst(y)ōōpəl, -ˈtəpəl/ ▶ adj. 1 consisting of six parts. 2 six times as much or as many.

sex·tu·plet /sekˈstəplit, -ˈst(y)ōōplət/ ▶ n. each of six children born at one birth.

sex·u·al /ˈseksнōōəl/ ▶ adj. 1 relating to sex or to physical attraction or intimate contact between people or animals. 2 relating to the two sexes or to gender. 3 (of reproduction) involving the fusion of male and female cells. ■ **sex·u·al·ize** /ˈseksнōōəˌlīz/ v. **sex·u·al·ly** adv.

sex·u·al ha·rass·ment ▶ n. the making of unwanted sexual advances or obscene remarks to a person, especially at work.

sex·u·al in·ter·course ▶ n. sexual contact in which a man puts his erect penis into a woman's vagina.

sex·u·al·i·ty /ˌseksнōōˈalitē/ ▶ n. (pl. **sexualities**) 1 a person's capacity for sexual feelings. 2 a person's sexual preference.

sex·u·al o·ri·en·ta·tion ▶ n. a person's sexual attraction toward members of the same, opposite, or both genders: *a draft ordinance that would prohibit discrimination on the basis of sexual orientation.*

sex work·er ▶ n. euphemistic a prostitute.

sex·y /ˈseksē/ ▶ adj. (**sexier, sexiest**) 1 sexually attractive or exciting. 2 sexually aroused. 3 informal exciting or appealing: *a sexy marketing buzzword.* ■ **sex·i·ly** adv. **sex·i·ness** n.

sez /sez/ ▶ v. nonstandard spelling of "says," used in representing uneducated speech: *"Oh Lordy!" sez de man.*

SF ▶ abbr. science fiction.

SFX ▶ abbr. special effects.

SG ▶ abbr. Physics specific gravity.

Sg ▶ symbol the chemical element seaborgium.

SGML ▶ abbr. Computing Standard Generalized Markup Language, a system for encoding electronic texts so that they can be displayed in any format.

shab·by /ˈsнabē/ ▶ adj. (**shabbier, shabbiest**) 1 in poor condition because of long use or neglect. 2 dressed in old or worn clothes. 3 mean and unfair: *a shabby trick.* ■ **shab·bi·ly** adv. **shab·bi·ness** n.

shack /sнak/ ▶ n. a roughly built hut or cabin. ▶ v. (**shack up with**) informal live with someone as a lover.

shack·le /ˈsнakəl/ ▶ n. 1 (**shackles**) a pair of metal rings connected by a chain, used to fasten a prisoner's wrists or ankles together. 2 (**shackles**) something that restricts freedom: *the human need to be free of the shackles of oppression.* 3 a metal link closed by a bolt, used to secure a chain or rope to something. ▶ v. 1 chain someone with shackles. 2 restrain or limit someone or something.

shad /sнad/ ▶ n. (pl. same or **shads**) an edible herringlike sea fish.

shad·dock /ˈsнadək/ ▶ n. another term for POMELO.

shade /sнād/ ▶ n. 1 an area that is dark and cool because it is sheltered from direct sunlight. 2 a form of a color with regard to how light or dark it is: *various shades of blue.* 3 a slightly different variety of something. 4 a lampshade. 5 (**shades**) informal sunglasses. 6 literary a ghost. ▶ v. 1 screen someone or something from direct light. 2 block all or some of the light coming from something. 3 represent a darker area in a picture with pencil or a block of color. 4 pass or change gradually: *outrage began to shade into dismay.* ■ **shade·less** adj. **shad·er** n.
– PHRASES **a shade** a slight amount: *I felt a shade anxious.* **shades of —** similar to or reminiscent of. **put someone/thing in the shade** be much better or more impressive than someone or something.

shad·ing /ˈsнādiNG/ ▶ n. 1 the representation of light and shade on a drawing or map. 2 a very slight variation in something.

shad·ow /ˈsнadō/ ▶ n. 1 a dark area or shape produced by an object coming between light rays and a surface. 2 partial or complete darkness. 3 a feeling of sadness or gloom. 4 the slightest trace: *without a shadow of a doubt.* 5 a weak or less good version: *she was a shadow of her former self.* 6 a position of less importance: *he lived in the shadow of his father.* 7 a person who constantly accompanies or secretly follows another. ▶ v. 1 cast a shadow over someone or something. 2 follow and observe someone secretly. 3 accompany an employee in their daily activities to gain experience of a job. ■ **shad·ow·er** n. **shad·ow·less** adj.

shad·ow·box /ˈsнadōˌbäks/ ▶ v. box against an imaginary opponent as a form of training. ▶ n. (also **shadow box**) a case with compartments for displaying small collectible or decorative objects.

shad·ow e·con·o·my ▶ n. illicit economic activity existing alongside a country's official economy.

shad·ow·land /ˈsнadōˌland/ (also **shadowlands**) ▶ n. literary a place or situation that is vague or that exists on the boundaries of other places or states.

shad·ow·y /ˈsнadōē/ ▶ adj. (**shadowier, shadowiest**) 1 full of shadows. 2 not well known; full of mystery: *the shadowy world of computer hacking.* ■ **shad·ow·i·ness** n.

shad·y /ˈsнādē/ ▶ adj. (**shadier, shadiest**) 1 situated in or full of shade. 2 giving shade from the sun. 3 informal seeming to be dishonest or illegal. ■ **shad·i·ness** n.

shaft /sнaft/ ▶ n. 1 a long, narrow part forming the handle of a tool or club, the body of a spear or arrow, or similar object. 2 a ray of light or bolt of lightning. 3 a long, narrow passage giving access to a mine, accommodating a lift, or providing ventilation. **4** each of the pair of poles between which a horse is harnessed to a vehicle. **5** a cylindrical rotating rod for the transmission of mechanical power in a machine. **6** the part of a column between the base and capital. **7** a sudden flash of a quality or feeling: *a shaft of inspiration.* **8** a witty or hurtful remark. ▶v. **1** (of light) shine in beams. **2** informal treat someone harshly or unfairly. ■ **shaft·ed** adj.

shag¹ /ʃag/ ▶n. **1** a thick, tangled hairstyle. **2** coarse cut tobacco. ▶adj. **1** (of a carpet or rug) having a long, rough pile. **2** (of pile on a carpet) long and rough.

shag² ▶n. a cormorant (seabird) with greenish-black plumage and a long curly crest.

shag³ Brit. vulgar slang ▶v. (**shags, shagging, shagged**) have sex with someone. ▶n. an act of sex. ■ **shag·ger** n.

shag·gy /ˈʃagē/ ▶adj. (**shaggier, shaggiest**) **1** (of hair or fur) long, thick, and untidy. **2** having shaggy hair or fur. ■ **shag·gi·ly** adv. **shag·gi·ness** n.
– PHRASES **shaggy-dog story** a long, rambling story or joke, amusing only because it is pointless.

sha·green /ʃəˈgrēn/ ▶n. **1** sharkskin used for decoration or for cleaning or polishing hard surfaces. **2** a kind of leather that has not been tanned, with a rough surface.

shah /ʃä/ ▶n. historical a title of the former king of Iran.

shake /ʃāk/ ▶v. (past **shook**; past part. **shaken**) **1** move quickly and jerkily up and down or to and fro. **2** tremble uncontrollably with strong emotion. **3** make a threatening gesture with: *he shook his fist.* **4** remove something by shaking. **5** shock or astonish someone. **6** get rid of or put an end to: *old habits he couldn't shake off.* ▶n. **1** an act of shaking. **2** an amount sprinkled from a container. **3** informal a milkshake. **4** (**the shakes**) informal a fit of trembling.
– PHRASES **in two shakes (of a lamb's tail)** informal very quickly. **no great shakes** informal not very good. **shake down** settle down. **shake hands (with someone)** hold someone's right hand in one's own when meeting or leaving them, to congratulate them, or to show agreement. **shake on it** informal confirm an agreement by shaking hands. **shake someone up** stir someone into action. **shake something up** make major changes to an organization or system.

shake·down /ˈʃākˌdoun/ ▶n. informal **1** a thorough search. **2** a major change or restructuring. **3** an act of swindling someone. **4** a makeshift bed.

shake·out /ˈʃākˌout/ ▶n. informal an upheaval or reorganization of a business, market, or organization due to competition and typically involving streamlining and layoffs.

shak·er /ˈʃākər/ ▶n. **1** a container for mixing ingredients by shaking them. **2** a container with a pierced top from which a powdered substance such as flour is poured by shaking. **3** (**Shaker**) a member of an American Christian sect living simply in celibate mixed communities. ▶adj. (**Shaker**) referring to a style of elegant but functional furniture traditionally produced by Shakers.

Shake·spear·e·an /ʃākˈspi(ə)rēən/ (also **Shakespearian**) ▶adj. relating to the English dramatist William Shakespeare. ▶n. an expert in

or student of Shakespeare's works.

shake-up ▶n. informal a major reorganization.

shak·o /ˈʃakō, ˈʃā-/ ▶n. (pl. **shakos**) a cylindrical military hat with a peak and a plume or pompom.

Shak·ti /ˈʃäktē/ ▶n. Hinduism female creative power or divine energy.

shak·y /ˈʃākē/ ▶adj. (**shakier, shakiest**) **1** shaking or trembling. **2** not steady or stable. **3** likely to fail or falter: *after a shaky start the team made superb efforts.* ■ **shak·i·ly** adv. **shak·i·ness** n.

shale /ʃāl/ ▶n. soft rock formed from compressed mud or clay, that can be split into thin layers. ■ **shal·y** (also **shaley**) adj.

shall /ʃal/ ▶modal v. (3rd sing. present **shall**) **1** used with *I* and *we* to express the future tense. **2** expressing a strong statement, intention, or order. **3** used in questions to make offers or suggestions.

> **USAGE**
> The traditional rule is that when forming the future tense, **shall** should be used with **I** and **we** (*I shall be late*), while **will** should be used with **you, he, she, it,** and **they** (*he will not be there*). However, when telling someone what to do or showing determination, this rule is reversed: **will** is used with **I** and **we** (*I will not tolerate this*), and **shall** is used with **you, he, she, it,** and **they** (*you shall go to school*). Nowadays, people do not follow these rules so strictly and are more likely to use the shortened forms **I'll, she'll,** etc., especially when speaking.

shal·lot /ʃəˈlät, ˈʃalət/ ▶n. a small vegetable of the onion family.

shal·low /ˈʃalō/ ▶adj. **1** having a short distance between the top and the bottom; not deep. **2** not thinking or thought out seriously or in detail: *a shallow analysis of society.* ▶n. (**shallows**) a shallow area of water. ■ **shal·low·ly** adv. **shal·low·ness** n.

sha·lom /ʃäˈlōm, ʃə-/ ▶exclam. said by Jews at meeting or parting.

shalt /ʃalt/ ▶ old-fashioned second person singular of SHALL.

sham /ʃam/ ▶n. **1** a thing that is not as good or as genuine as it seems to be: *our current free health service is a sham.* **2** a person who pretends to be something that they are not. ▶adj. not genuine; false. ▶v. (**shams, shamming, shammed**) pretend or pretend to be: *people who are shamming insanity.*

sha·man /ˈʃāmən, ˈshä-/ ▶n. (pl. **shamans**) (especially among some peoples of northern Asia and North America) a person who is believed to be able to contact good and evil spirits. ■ **sha·man·ic** /ʃəˈmanik/ adj. **sha·man·ism** /-ˌnizəm/ n. **sha·man·is·tic** /ˌʃäməˈnistik, ˌʃā-/ adj.

sham·ble /ˈʃambəl/ ▶v. walk in a slow, shuffling, awkward way. ▶n. a slow, shuffling walk.

sham·bles /ˈʃambəlz/ ▶pl.n. **1** informal a state of complete disorder. **2** old use a butcher's slaughterhouse.

shame /ʃām/ ▶n. **1** a feeling of humiliation or distress arising from one's awareness that one has done something wrong or foolish. **2** loss of respect; dishonor: *the incident had brought shame on his family.* **3** a cause of shame or dishonor. **4** a cause for regret or disappointment: *what a shame Ellie won't be here.* ▶v. make someone feel ashamed.

– PHRASES **put someone to shame** make someone feel ashamed by being much better than them.

shame·faced /'shām,fāst/ ▶ adj. showing shame. ■ **shame·fac·ed·ly** /-,fāsidlē, -,fāstlē/ adv. **shame·fac·ed·ness** /-,fāsidnis/ n.

shame·ful /'shāmfəl/ ▶ adj. causing or worthy of shame or disgrace: *a shameful secret.* ■ **shame·ful·ly** adv. **shame·ful·ness** n.

shame·less /'shāmlis/ ▶ adj. not feeling ashamed, even though one has done something wrong or foolish. ■ **shame·less·ly** adv. **shame·less·ness** n.

sham·my /'shamē/ ▶ n. (pl. **shammies**) informal a chamois leather.

sham·poo /sham'pōō/ ▶ n. **1** a liquid soap for washing the hair. **2** a similar liquid for cleaning a carpet, car, etc. **3** an act of washing with shampoo. ▶ v. (**shampoos, shampooing, shampooed**) wash or clean something with shampoo.

sham·rock /'sham,räk/ ▶ n. a cloverlike plant with three rounded leaves on each stem, the national emblem of Ireland.

shang·hai /'shang'hī/ ▶ v. (**shanghais, shanghaiing** /-,hī-iNG/, **shanghaied** /-,hīd/) **1** informal force or trick someone into doing something. **2** historical force someone to join a ship's crew.

Shan·gri-La /'shanggri 'lä/ ▶ n. a very pleasant or unspoiled place.

shank /shangk/ ▶ n. **1** the lower part of a person's leg. **2** the lower part of an animal's foreleg, especially as a cut of meat. **3** the shaft or stem of a tool, spoon, etc. **4** the band of a ring rather than the setting. ■ **shanked** adj.

shan't /shant/ ▶ contr. shall not.

shan·tung /shan'təng/ ▶ n. a type of soft silk with a coarse surface.

shant·y¹ /'shantē/ ▶ n. (pl. **shanties**) a small roughly built shack.

shant·y² ▶ n. (pl. **shanties**) variant spelling of CHANTEY.

shan·ty·town ▶ n. a settlement in or near a city where poor people live in makeshift houses or shacks.

shape /shāp/ ▶ n. **1** the outward form of someone or something as produced by their outline. **2** a geometric figure such as a rectangle. **3** a piece of material or paper made or cut in a particular form. **4** the correct or original form of something: *the wheels are out of shape and not perfectly circular.* **5** organized or well-defined structure or arrangement. **6** a particular condition or state: *the house was in poor shape.* **7** good physical condition. ▶ v. **1** give a shape to something. **2** determine the nature of. **3** develop in a particular way: *it was shaping up to be another bleak year.* **4** (**shape up**) improve one's fitness, performance, or behavior. ■ **shaped** adj. **shap·er** n.

– PHRASES **lick** (or **knock**) **someone/thing into shape** take forceful action to improve someone or something. **take shape** develop into something more definite or organized.

shape·less /'shāplis/ ▶ adj. lacking a definite or attractive shape. ■ **shape·less·ly** adv. **shape·less·ness** n.

shape·ly /'shāplē/ ▶ adj. (**shapelier, shapeliest**) having an attractive or well-proportioned shape: *shapely legs.* ■ **shape·li·ness** n.

shape-shift·er ▶ n. an imaginary being who is able to change their physical form when they want to. ■ **shape-shift·ing** n. & adj.

shard /shärd/ ▶ n. a sharp piece of broken pottery, metal, glass, etc.

share /she(ə)r/ ▶ n. **1** a part of a larger amount that is divided among or contributed by a number of people. **2** any of the equal parts into which a company's capital is divided, which can be bought by people in return for a proportion of the profits. **3** an amount regarded as normal or acceptable: *the new system had more than its fair share of problems.* **4** a person's contribution to an activity. ▶ v. **1** have or give a share of something. **2** possess or use jointly with others: *they shared an apartment.* **3** (**share in**) participate in an activity. **4** tell someone about something. ■ **share·a·ble** (also **sharable**) adj. **shar·er** n.

share·crop·per /'she(ə)r,kräpər/ ▶ n. a tenant farmer who gives a part of each crop as rent.

share·hold·er /'she(ə)r,hōldər/ ▶ n. a stockholder. ■ **share·hold·ing** n.

share·ware /'she(ə)r,we(ə)r/ ▶ n. computer software that is available free of charge and often distributed informally for users to evaluate.

sha·ri·a /shä'rēə/ ▶ n. Islamic law, based on the teachings of the Koran and the traditions of Muhammad.

shark¹ /shärk/ ▶ n. a large sea fish with a triangular fin on its back, many kinds of which prey on other animals.

shark² ▶ n. informal a person who exploits or swindles others.

shark·skin /'shärk,skin/ ▶ n. a stiff, slightly shiny synthetic fabric.

sharp /shärp/ ▶ adj. **1** having a cutting or piercing edge or point. **2** tapering to a point or edge. **3** sudden and rapid: *a sharp increase in interest rates.* **4** clear and definite: *the mood is in sharp contrast to last year's summit.* **5** (of a feeling or emotion) sudden and intense. **6** quick to understand, notice, or respond. **7** (of a food, taste, or smell) strong and slightly bitter. **8** (of a sound) sudden and penetrating. **9** (of a person or remark) critical or hurtful. **10** quick to take advantage, especially in a dishonest way. **11** making a sudden change of direction. **12** informal smart and stylish. **13** (after a noun) (of a note or key) higher by a half step than a specified note or key: *F sharp.* ▶ adv. **1** precisely: *the meeting starts at 7:30 sharp.* **2** suddenly or abruptly. ▶ n. **1** a musical note raised a half step above natural pitch, shown by the sign #. **2** an object with a sharp point. **3** a card sharp. ■ **sharp·ish** adj. **sharp·ly** adv. **sharp·ness** n.

sharp·en /'shärpən/ ▶ v. make or become sharp. ■ **sharp·en·er** n.

sharp·er /'shärpər/ ▶ n. informal a swindler, especially at cards; a card sharp.

sharp·shoot·er /'shärp,shōōtər/ ▶ n. a person skilled in shooting.

sharp-tongued ▶ adj. using harsh or critical language.

sharp-wit·ted ▶ adj. intelligent and quick to notice things.

shat /shat/ ▶ past and past participle of SHIT.

shat·ter /'shatər/ ▶ v. **1** break suddenly and violently into pieces. **2** damage or destroy: *he broke her heart and shattered her dreams.* **3** upset someone greatly. ■ **shat·ter·er** n.

shave /shāv/ ▶ v. **1** remove hair from the face or body by cutting it off close to the skin with a razor. **2** cut a thin slice or slices from something. **3** reduce by a small amount: *21 percent was shaved off the research budget.* **4** pass very close to something. ▶ n. an act of shaving.

shav·en /ˈshāvən/ ▶ adj. (of a part of the body) shaved.

shav·er /ˈshāvər/ ▶ n. **1** an electric razor. **2** *informal, dated* a young lad.

Sha·vi·an /ˈshāvēən/ ▶ adj. relating to or in the style of the Irish dramatist George Bernard Shaw. ▶ n. an admirer of Shaw or his work.

shav·ing /ˈshāving/ ▶ n. a thin strip cut off a surface.

Sha·vu·ot /shəˈvoŏˌōt, ˌshävoŏˈōt, shəˈvoŏəs/ ▶ n. a major Jewish festival held fifty days after the second day of Passover.

shawl /shôl/ ▶ n. a large piece of fabric worn by women over the shoulders or head or wrapped around a baby. ■ **shawled** adj.

Shaw·nee /shôˈnē/ ▶ n. (pl. same or **Shawnees**) a member of an American Indian people now living chiefly in Oklahoma.

she /shē/ ▶ pron. (third person sing.) **1** used to refer to a woman, girl, or female animal previously mentioned or easily identified. **2** used to refer to a ship, country, or other thing regarded as female. ▶ n. a female; a woman.

s/he /ˈshē ər ˈhē, ˈshēˈhē/ ▶ pron. a written representation of "he or she" used as a neutral alternative to indicate someone of either sex.

sheaf /shēf/ ▶ n. (pl. **sheaves** /shēvz/) **1** a bundle of papers. **2** a bundle of grain stalks tied together after reaping. ▶ v. tie grain stalks into bundles.

shear /shi(ə)r/ ▶ v. (past part. **shorn** or **sheared**) **1** cut the wool off a sheep or other animal. **2** cut off hair or wool with scissors or shears. **3** (**be shorn of**) have something taken away: *he was shorn of nearly $2 billion.* **4** break off because of a structural strain. ▶ n. a strain produced by pressure in the structure of a substance, so that each layer slides over the next. ■ **shear·er** n.

> **USAGE**
> Do not confuse **shear** and **sheer**. **Shear** means 'cut the wool off a sheep'. As a verb, **sheer** means 'change course quickly' (*the boat sheered off*); **sheer** is also an adjective meaning 'nothing but; absolute' (*sheer hard work*).

shears /shi(ə)rz/ (also **a pair of shears**) ▶ pl.n. a cutting instrument resembling a very large pair of scissors.

shear·wa·ter /ˈshi(ə)rˌwôtər, -ˌwätər/ ▶ n. a long-winged seabird related to the petrels.

sheath /shēth/ ▶ n. (pl. **sheaths** /shēthz, shēths/) **1** a cover for the blade of a knife or sword. **2** a condom. **3** a close-fitting covering or protective structure. **4** (also **sheath dress**) a close-fitting dress.

sheathe /shēth/ ▶ v. **1** put a knife or sword into a sheath. **2** cover in a close-fitting or protective covering: *her legs were sheathed in black stockings.*

sheath·ing /ˈshēthing/ ▶ n. a protective casing or covering.

sheaves /shēvz/ ▶ plural of **SHEAF**.

she·bang /shəˈbang/ ▶ n. (in phrase **the whole shebang**) *informal* the whole thing; everything.

she·been /shəˈbēn/ ▶ n. (especially in Ireland, Scotland, and South Africa) a place that sells alcoholic drink illegally.

shed[1] /shed/ ▶ n. **1** a simple building used for storage or to shelter animals. **2** a larger structure, typically with one or more sides open, for storing vehicles or machinery.

shed[2] ▶ v. (**sheds, shedding, shed**) **1** get rid of: *exercise helps you shed pounds.* **2** cast or give off light. **3** allow leaves, hair, skin, etc., to fall off naturally. **4** take off clothes. **5** be able to repel water. ■ **shed·der** n.
– PHRASES **shed tears** cry.

she'd /shēd/ ▶ contr. she had; she would.

she-dev·il ▶ n. a malicious or spiteful woman.

sheen /shēn/ ▶ n. a soft shine on a surface. ■ **sheen·y** adj.

sheep /shēp/ ▶ n. (pl. same) a grass-eating mammal with a thick woolly coat, kept in flocks for its wool or meat. ■ **sheep·like** /-ˌlīk/ adj.
– PHRASES **like sheep** (of people) easily led or influenced.

sheep dip ▶ n. **1** a liquid in which sheep are dipped to clean and disinfect their wool. **2** a place where sheep are dipped in this liquid.

sheep·dog /ˈshēpˌdôg, -ˌdäg/ ▶ n. **1** a dog trained to guard and herd sheep. **2** a breed of dog suitable for guarding and herding sheep.

sheep·ish /ˈshēpish/ ▶ adj. embarrassed as a result of having done something foolish. ■ **sheep·ish·ly** adv. **sheep·ish·ness** n.

sheep·shank /ˈshēpˌshangk/ ▶ n. a knot made in a rope to shorten it temporarily.

sheep·skin /ˈshēpˌskin/ ▶ n. **1** a sheep's skin with the wool on, made into a garment or rug. **2** *informal* a diploma.

sheer[1] /shi(ə)r/ ▶ adj. **1** nothing but; absolute: *sheer hard work.* **2** (of a cliff, wall, etc.) vertical or almost vertical. **3** (of a fabric) very thin and almost transparent. ▶ adv. vertically; perpendicularly. ■ **sheer·ly** adv. **sheer·ness** n.

> **USAGE**
> On the confusion of **sheer** and **shear**, see the note at SHEAR.

sheer[2] ▶ v. **1** (especially of a boat) swerve or change course quickly. **2** avoid or move away from an unpleasant topic.

sheet[1] /shēt/ ▶ n. **1** a large rectangular piece of cotton or other fabric, used on a bed to lie on or under. **2** a broad flat piece of metal or glass. **3** a rectangular piece of paper. **4** a wide expanse or moving mass of water, ice, flame, etc. ▶ v. **1** cover something with a sheet of cloth. **2** (of rain) fall heavily.

sheet[2] ▶ n. a rope attached to the lower corner of a sail, to hold and adjust it.
– PHRASES **two** (or **three**) **sheets to the wind** *informal* drunk.

sheet·ing /ˈshēting/ ▶ n. material formed into or used as a sheet.

sheet light·ning ▶ n. lightning seen as a broad area of light in the sky.

sheet met·al ▶ n. metal formed into thin sheets.

sheet mu·sic ▶ n. music published on loose sheets of paper and not bound into a book.

sheikh /shēk, shāk/ (also **shaykh** or **sheik**) ▶ n. **1** the leader of an Arab tribe, family, or village. **2** a leader in a Muslim community or organization. ■ **sheikh·dom** /-dəm/ n.

shei·la /SHēlə/ ▶ n. Austral./NZ informal a girl or woman.

shek·el /'SHekəl/ ▶ n. 1 the basic unit of money of modern Israel. 2 (**shekels**) informal money; wealth.

shel·duck /'SHel,dək/ ▶ n. (pl. same or **shelducks**) a large gooselike duck with brightly colored plumage.

shelf /SHelf/ ▶ n. (pl. **shelves**) 1 a flat length of wood or other rigid material fixed horizontally to a wall or forming part of a piece of furniture and used to display or store things. 2 a ledge of rock or protruding strip of land.
– PHRASES **off the shelf** taken from existing stock, not made to order.

shelf life ▶ n. the length of time for which an item is expected to remain able to be eaten, used, or sold.

shell /SHel/ ▶ n. 1 the hard protective outer case of an animal such as a snail, shellfish, or turtle. 2 the outer covering of an egg, nut kernel, or seed. 3 a metal case filled with explosives, to be fired from a large gun. 4 a hollow case, especially one used as a container for fireworks, cartridges, etc. 5 an outer structure or framework of a building or vehicle. 6 a light racing boat. 7 (also **shell program**) a program that provides an interface between the user and the operating system. ▶ v. 1 fire explosive shells at something. 2 remove the shell or pod from a nut or seed. 3 (**shell something out**) informal pay an amount of money. ■ **shell·less** adj. **shell·like** /-,līk/ adj.
shell·y /'SHelē/ adj.
– PHRASES **come out of one's shell** stop being shy.

she'll /SHēl/ ▶ contr. she will; she shall.

shel·lac /SHə'lak/ ▶ n. lac resin melted into thin flakes, used for making varnish. ▶ v. (**shellacs, shellacking, shellacked**) 1 varnish something with shellac. 2 informal defeat someone decisively.

shell·fire /'SHel,fīr/ ▶ n. bombardment by explosive shells.

shell·fish /'SHel,fiSH/ ▶ n. a creature such as a crab or oyster that has a shell and lives in water, especially an edible one.

shell shock ▶ n. dated a mental disorder that can affect soldiers who have been in battle for a long time. ■ **shell-shocked** adj.

Shel·ta /'SHeltə/ ▶ n. an ancient secret language used by Irish and Welsh tinkers and Gypsies, based on altered Irish or Gaelic words.

shel·ter /'SHeltər/ ▶ n. 1 a place giving protection from bad weather or danger. 2 a place providing food and accommodations for homeless people. 3 protection from something unpleasant or dangerous: *he waited in the shelter of a rock.* ▶ v. 1 provide someone or something with shelter. 2 take cover from bad weather or danger. 3 (as adj. **sheltered**) protected from the more unpleasant aspects of life.

shelve[1] /SHelv/ ▶ v. 1 place something on a shelf. 2 decide not to continue with; cancel or postpone: *the company shelved plans for a big pay raise for its CEO.* 3 fit something with shelves. ■ **shelv·er** n.

shelve[2] ▶ v. (of ground) slope downward.

shelves /SHelvz/ ▶ plural of SHELF.

shelv·ing /'SHelviNG/ ▶ n. shelves as a whole.

she·nan·i·gans /SHə'nanəgənz/ ▶ pl.n. informal 1 secret or dishonest activity. 2 high-spirited or mischievous behavior.

shep·herd /'SHepərd/ ▶ n. 1 a person who looks after sheep. 2 a member of the clergy regarded as providing spiritual care and guidance for a congregation. ▶ v. 1 guide or direct somewhere: *she shepherded them through the door.* 2 look after sheep. ■ **shep·herd·ess** /'SHepərdis/ n.

shep·herd's pie ▶ n. a dish of minced meat under a layer of mashed potato.

sher·bet /'SHərbit/ ▶ n. a frozen dessert made with fruit juice; sorbet.

sherd /SHərd/ ▶ n. another term for POTSHERD.

sher·iff /'SHerif/ ▶ n. an elected officer in a county or town, responsible for keeping the peace.

Sher·pa /'SHərpə/ ▶ n. (pl. same or **Sherpas**) a member of a Himalayan people living on the borders of Nepal and Tibet.

sher·ry /'SHerē/ ▶ n. (pl. **sherries**) a fortified wine originally from southern Spain.

she's /SHēz/ ▶ contr. she is; she has.

Shet·land po·ny /'SHetlənd/ ▶ n. a small breed of pony with a rough coat.

shew /SHō/ ▶ v. old-fashioned variant of SHOW.

Shi·a /'SHē,ä/ (also **Shi'a**) ▶ n. (pl. same or **Shias**) 1 one of the two main branches of Islam, the other being Sunni. 2 a Muslim who follows the Shia branch of Islam.

shi·at·su /SHē'ätsoo/ ▶ n. a Japanese therapy in which pressure is applied with the hands to points on the body.

shib·bo·leth /'SHibəlith, -,leTH/ ▶ n. a long-standing belief or principle that many people regard as outdated or no longer important: *the conflict challenged a series of military shibboleths.*

shied /SHīd/ ▶ past and past participle of SHY[2].

shield /SHēld/ ▶ n. 1 a broad piece of armor held for protection against blows or missiles. 2 a person or thing that provides protection. 3 a sporting trophy consisting of an engraved metal plate mounted on a piece of wood. 4 a drawing or model of a shield used for displaying a coat of arms. 5 a police officer's badge. ▶ v. 1 protect someone or something from something dangerous, unpleasant, or risky. 2 prevent from being seen: *the runners were shielded from view by the tunnel.* 3 enclose machinery or a source of sound, light, or radiation to protect the user.

shift /SHift/ ▶ v. 1 move or change from one position or direction to another: *the warming Gulf Stream could shift away from the UK.* 2 transfer responsibility, blame, or power to someone else. 3 change gear in a vehicle. 4 informal sell goods quickly or in large quantities. 5 Brit. informal move quickly. ▶ n. 1 a slight change in position, direction, or tendency: *a shift in public opinion.* 2 a period of time worked by a group of workers who start work as another group finishes. 3 a straight dress without a waist. 4 a key used to switch between two sets of characters or functions on a keyboard. 5 a gear lever or gear-changing mechanism. 6 old use a clever or crafty plan. ■ **shift·er** n.

shift·less /'SHiftlis/ ▶ adj. lazy and lacking ambition. ■ **shift·less·ness** n.

shift·y /'SHiftē/ ▶ adj. (**shiftier, shiftiest**) informal appearing untrustworthy or dishonest. ■ **shift·i·ly** adv. **shift·i·ness** n.

Shih Tzu /'SHē 'dzoo/ ▶ n. a dog of a breed with long, silky, erect hair and short legs.

shi·i·ta·ke /SHē'täkē, SHē-ē'täke/ ▶ n. an edible mushroom grown in Japan and China.

Shi·ite /'SHē,īt/ (also **Shi'ite**) ▶ n. a follower of the Shia branch of Islam. ▶ adj. relating to the Shia branch of Islam. ∎ **Shi·ism** /'SHē,izəm/ n.

shik·sa /'SHiksə/ ▸ n. derogatory (in Jewish use) a non-Jewish girl or woman.

shill /SHil/ informal ▸ n. an accomplice of a hawker, gambler, or swindler who acts as an enthusiastic customer to entice or encourage others. ▸ v. act or work as such a person.

shil·le·lagh /SHə'lālē/ ▸ n. (in Ireland) a wooden cudgel.

shil·ling /'SHiliNG/ ▸ n. **1** a former British coin and unit of money equal to one twentieth of a pound or twelve pence. **2** the basic unit of money of Kenya, Tanzania, and Uganda.

shil·ly-shal·ly /'SHilē ,SHalē/ ▸ v. (**shilly-shallies, shilly-shallying, shilly-shallied**) be unable to make up one's mind.

shim /SHim/ ▸ n. a washer or thin strip of material used in machinery to fill a space between parts or reduce wear. ▸ v. (**shims, shimming, shimmed**) fill up a space with a shim.

shim·mer /'SHimər/ ▸ v. shine with a soft wavering light. ▸ n. a soft wavering light or reflected light. ∎ **shim·mer·y** adj.

shim·my /'SHimē/ ▸ v. (**shimmies, shimmying, shimmied**) **1** walk or move with a smooth swaying motion. **2** shake or vibrate abnormally. **3** dance the shimmy. ▸ n. (pl. **shimmies**) a kind of ragtime dance in which the dancer shakes or sways the whole body.

shin /SHin/ ▸ n. **1** the front of the leg below the knee. **2** a cut of beef from the lower part of a cow's leg. ▸ v. (**shins, shinning, shinned**) (**shin up/down**) climb quickly up or down by gripping with the arms and legs.

shin·bone /'SHin,bōn/ ▸ n. the tibia.

shin·dig /'SHin,dig/ ▸ n. informal **1** a large, lively party. **2** a noisy disturbance or quarrel.

shine /SHīn/ ▸ v. (past and past part. **shone** or **shined**) **1** give out or reflect light. **2** point a torch or other light in a particular direction. **3** (of a person's eyes) be bright with an emotion. **4** be very good at something: *she shines at comedy.* **5** (**shine through**) (of a quality or skill) be clearly evident. **6** (past and past part. **shined**) polish something. ▸ n. **1** a quality of brightness produced by reflected light. **2** an act of polishing.
– PHRASES **take the shine off** make something seem less good or exciting. **take a shine to** informal develop a liking for someone.

shin·er /'SHīnər/ ▸ n. informal a black eye.

shin·gle¹ /'SHiNGgəl/ ▸ n. **1** a tile of asphalt composite, wood, metal, or slate used on walls or roofs. **2** dated a woman's short haircut, tapering from the back of the head to the nape of the neck. **3** a signboard, especially one outside a lawyer's or doctor's office: *Ol' Doc Green hung out his shingle in 1902.* ▸ v. **1** roof or clad something with shingles. **2** dated cut hair in a shingle.

shin·gle² ▸ n. a mass of small rounded pebbles, especially on a seashore. ∎ **shin·gly** /-g(ə)lē/ adj.

shin·gles /'SHiNGgəlz/ ▸ pl.n. (treated as sing.) a disease caused by a virus, in which painful blisters form along the path of a nerve or nerves.

shin·ny¹ /'SHinē/ ▸ v. (**shinnies, shinnied**) another term for SHIN: *he loved to shinny up that tree.*

shin·ny² (also **shinny hockey**) ▸ n. an informal form of ice hockey played especially by children, on the street or on ice, often with a ball or other object in place of a puck: *we used to play shinny on the canal with tin cans.*

shin splints ▸ pl.n. (treated as sing. or pl.) pain in the shin and lower leg caused by prolonged running on hard surfaces.

Shin·to /'SHin,tō/ ▸ n. a Japanese religion involving the worship of ancestors and nature spirits. ∎ **Shin·to·ism** /-izəm/ n. **Shin·to·ist** /-ist/ n.

shin·y /'SHinē/ ▸ adj. (**shinier, shiniest**) reflecting light because very smooth, clean, or polished. ∎ **shin·i·ly** adv. **shin·i·ness** n.

ship /SHip/ ▸ n. **1** a large boat for transporting people or goods by sea. **2** a sailboat with a bowsprit and three or more square-rigged masts. ▸ v. (**ships, shipping, shipped**) **1** transport people or goods on a ship or by other means. **2** make a product available for sale. **3** (of a boat) take in water over the side. **4** take oars from the oarlocks and lay them inside a boat. **5** (of a sailor) be employed on a ship. ∎ **ship·load** /'SHip,lōd/ n. **ship·per** n.
– PHRASES **when someone's ship comes in** when someone's fortune is made.

-ship ▸ suffix forming nouns referring to: **1** a quality or condition: *companionship.* **2** status or office: *citizenship.* **3** a skill: *workmanship.* **4** the members of a group: *membership.*

ship·board /'SHip,bôrd/ ▸ adj. used or occurring on board a ship.

ship·build·er /'SHip,bildər/ ▸ n. a person or company that designs and builds ships. ∎ **ship·build·ing** n.

ship·mate /'SHip,māt/ ▸ n. a fellow member of a ship's crew.

ship·ment /'SHipmənt/ ▸ n. **1** the action of transporting goods. **2** a quantity of goods shipped.

ship·ping /'SHipiNG/ ▸ n. **1** ships as a whole. **2** the transport of goods.

ship·shape /'SHip,SHāp/ ▸ adj. in good order; neat and clean.

ship·wreck /'SHip,rek/ ▸ n. **1** the sinking or breaking up of a ship at sea. **2** a ship that has sunk or been destroyed at sea. ▸ v. (**be shipwrecked**) **1** be left somewhere after one's ship has sunk or been destroyed. **2** (of a ship) suffer a shipwreck.

ship·wright /'SHip,rīt/ ▸ n. a shipbuilder.

ship·yard /'SHip,yärd/ ▸ n. a place where ships are built and repaired.

Shi·raz /SHi'räz/ ▸ n. a red wine made from a variety of black wine grape.

shire /SHī(ə)r/ ▸ n. **1** Brit. a county in England. **2** (**the Shires**) the rural areas of the English Midlands, regarded as strongholds of traditional country life. **3** Austral. a rural area with its own elected council.

shire horse ▸ n. a heavy powerful breed of horse, used for pulling loads.

shirk /SHərk/ ▸ v. avoid or neglect work or a duty. ∎ **shirk·er** n.

shirr /SHər/ ▸ v. (usu. as adj. **shirred**) **1** gather fabric by means of drawn or elastic threads in parallel rows. **2** bake an egg without its shell.

shirt /SHərt/ ▸ n. **1** an item of clothing for the upper body, with a collar and sleeves and buttons down the front. **2** a similar top of light material without full fastenings, worn for sports and leisure: *a polo shirt.* ∎ **shirt·ed** adj.
– PHRASES **keep your shirt on** informal stay calm. **lose one's shirt** informal lose all one's money.

shirt·dress ▶ n. a dress with a collar and button fastening in the style of a shirt, without a seam at the waist.

shirt·front /'sнәrt,frәnt/ ▶ n. the breast of a shirt, in particular the part that shows when a suit is worn.

shirt·sleeve /'sнәrt,slēv/ ▶ n. the sleeve of a shirt. ■ **shirt·sleeved** adj.
– PHRASES **in (one's) shirtsleeves** wearing a shirt without a jacket over it.

shirt·tail ▶ n. the curved part of a shirt that comes below the waist.

shirt·waist /'sнәrt,wāst/ ▶ n. **1** a woman's blouse that resembles a shirt. **2** (also **shirtwaister**) a shirt dress with a seam at the waist.

shish ke·bab /'sнɪsн kә,bäb/ ▶ n. a dish of pieces of meat and vegetables cooked and served on skewers.

shit /sнɪt/ vulgar slang ▶ v. (**shits, shitting, shitted** or **shit** or **shat** /sнat/) **1** pass feces from the body. **2** (**shit oneself**) be very frightened. ▶ n. **1** feces. **2** something worthless; rubbish. **3** an unpleasant or disliked person. ▶ exclam. expressing disgust or annoyance. ■ **shit·ty** adj.

shit·load /'sнɪt,lōd/ ▶ n. vulgar slang a large amount or number: *I have a shitload of work to do this week.*

Shi·va /'sнēvә/ (also **Siva**) ▶ (in Indian religion) a god regarded by some as the supreme being and by others as one of a supreme triad, and associated with the powers of reproduction and dissolution.

shiv·er¹ /'sнɪvәr/ ▶ v. shake slightly and uncontrollably from cold, fear, or excitement. ▶ n. **1** a brief trembling movement. **2** (**the shivers**) a spell of shivering from fear or cold. ■ **shiv·er·y** adj.

shiv·er² ▶ n. a splinter or fragment of a material such as glass. ▶ v. break into splinters or fragments.

Sho·ah /'sнōә, sнō'ä/ ▶ n. (in Jewish use) the Holocaust.

shoal¹ /sнōl/ ▶ n. a large number of fish swimming together. ▶ v. (of fish) swim together in a shoal.

shoal² ▶ n. **1** an area of shallow water. **2** a submerged sandbank that is visible at low tide. ▶ v. (of water) become shallower.

shock¹ /sнäk/ ▶ n. **1** a sudden upsetting or surprising event or experience: *her illness has come as a great shock to all of us.* **2** an unpleasant feeling of surprise and distress. **3** a serious medical condition associated with a fall in blood pressure, caused by loss of blood, severe injury, or sudden emotional stress. **4** a violent shaking movement caused by an impact, explosion, or earthquake. **5** an electric shock. ▶ v. **1** make someone feel very surprised and upset. **2** make someone feel outraged or disgusted. **3** cause someone to be in a state of medical shock. ■ **shock·a·ble** adj.

shock² ▶ n. an untidy or thick mass of hair.

shock³ ▶ n. a group of sheaves of grain placed upright and supporting each other to allow the grain to dry and ripen.

shock ab·sorb·er ▶ n. a device for absorbing jolts and vibrations, especially on a vehicle.

shock·er /'sнäkәr/ ▶ n. informal a thing that shocks, especially through being unacceptable or sensational.

shock·ing /'sнäkɪNG/ ▶ adj. **1** causing great surprise or disgust. **2** Brit. informal very bad. ■ **shock·ing·ly** adv.

shock·ing pink ▶ n. a very bright shade of pink.

shock·proof /'sнäk,proŏf/ ▶ adj. **1** designed to resist damage when dropped or knocked: *a shockproof watch.* **2** not easily shocked: *her shockproof attitude toward ignorance.*

shock tac·tics ▶ pl.n. the use of sudden violent or extreme action to shock someone into doing something.

shock ther·a·py (also **shock treatment**) ▶ n. treatment of certain mental illnesses by giving controlled electric shocks to the brain.

shock troops ▶ pl.n. troops trained to carry out sudden attacks.

shock wave ▶ n. a moving wave of very high pressure caused by an explosion or by something traveling faster than sound.

shod /sнäd/ ▶ past and past participle of SHOE.

shod·dy /'sнädē/ ▶ adj. (**shoddier, shoddiest**) **1** badly made or done. **2** dishonest or underhanded: *a shoddy political deal.* ■ **shod·di·ly** adv. **shod·di·ness** n.

shoe /sнoŏ/ ▶ n. **1** a covering for the foot with a stiff sole, ending just below the ankle. **2** a horseshoe. **3** a socket on a camera for fitting a flash unit. **4** a brake shoe. ▶ v. (**shoes, shoeing, shod**) **1** fit a horse with a shoe or shoes. **2** (**be shod**) be wearing shoes of a specified kind: *his large feet were shod in moccasins.*
– PHRASES **be** (or **put oneself**) **in someone else's shoes** imagine oneself in another person's situation.

shoe·box /'sнoŏ,bäks/ ▶ n. informal a very small room or space.

shoe·horn /'sнoŏ,hôrn/ ▶ n. a curved piece of metal or plastic, used for easing one's heel into a shoe. ▶ v. force into a space that is too small: *seven lecturers shoehorned into an office designed for one person.*

shoe·lace /'sнoŏ,lās/ ▶ n. a cord or leather strip passed through holes or hooks on opposite sides of a shoe and pulled tight to fasten it.

shoe·mak·er /'sнoŏ,mākәr/ ▶ n. a person who makes footwear as a profession.

shoe·shine /'sнoŏ,sнīn/ ▶ n. an act of polishing someone's shoes. ■ **shoe·shin·er** n.

shoe·string /'sнoŏ,strɪNG/ ▶ n. **1** a shoelace. **2** informal a small or inadequate amount of money: *living on a shoestring.*

shoe tree ▶ n. a shaped block put into a shoe when it is not being worn to keep it in shape.

sho·gun /'sнōgәn/ ▶ n. (formerly, in Japan) a hereditary commander-in-chief of the army. ■ **sho·gun·ate** /-gәnit, -gә,nāt/ n.

shone /sнän/ ▶ past and past participle of SHINE.

shoo /sнoŏ/ ▶ exclam. used to drive away an animal or person. ▶ v. (**shoos, shooing, shooed**) drive a person or animal away by saying 'shoo' or otherwise acting in a discouraging way.

shoo-in ▶ n. informal a person or thing that is certain to succeed or win.

shook /sнoŏk/ past of SHAKE

shoot /sнoŏt/ ▶ v. (past and past part. **shot** /sнat/) **1** kill or wound a person or animal with a bullet or arrow. **2** fire a missile from a weapon. **3** move suddenly and rapidly: *the car shot forward.* **4** glance at or say something to someone quickly or abruptly. **5** film or photograph a scene, movie,

etc. **6** (in sports) kick, hit, or throw the ball or puck in an attempt to score a goal. **7** (as adj.) **shooting**) (of a pain) sudden and piercing. **8** (of a boat) sweep swiftly down or under rapids, a waterfall, or a bridge. **9** (of a plant) send out buds or shoots. ▶ n. **1** a new part growing from the main trunk or stem of a tree or other plant. **2** an occasion of taking photographs professionally or making a movie or video: *a fashion shoot.* **3** an occasion when a group of people hunt and shoot game for sport. **4** Brit. land used for shooting game. **5** variant spelling of CHUTE¹.
– PHRASES **shoot the breeze** informal have a casual conversation. **shoot oneself in the foot** informal accidentally make a situation worse for oneself. **shoot one's mouth off** informal talk boastfully or too freely. **the whole shooting match** informal everything. **shoot up** informal inject oneself with a narcotic drug.

shoot·er /ˈSHo͞otər/ ▶ n. **1** a person who uses a gun. **2** informal a gun. **3** (in basketball) a player whose role is to attempt to score goals.

shoot·ing gal·ler·y ▶ n. **1** a room or fairground booth for shooting at targets. **2** informal a place used for taking drugs, especially by injection.

shoot·ing range ▶ n. an area provided with targets for the controlled practice of shooting.

shoot·ing star ▶ n. a small, rapidly moving meteor that burns up on entering the earth's atmosphere.

shoot-out ▶ n. **1** a gun battle that continues until one side is killed or defeated. **2** Soccer a tiebreaker decided by each side taking a specified number of penalty kicks.

shop /SHäp/ ▶ n. **1** a building or part of a building where goods or services are sold; a store. **2** a place where things are manufactured or repaired; a workshop. ▶ v. (**shops, shopping, shopped**) **1** go to a store or stores to buy goods. **2** (**shop around**) look for the best available price or rate for something.
– PHRASES **talk shop** discuss work matters with a colleague when one is not at work.

shop·a·hol·ic /ˌSHäpəˈhôlik, -ˈhälik/ ▶ n. informal a person with an uncontrollable urge to go shopping.

shop class ▶ n. a class in which practical skills such as carpentry or metalwork are taught.

shop floor ▶ n. the part of a factory where things are made or assembled.

shop·keep·er /ˈSHäpˌkēpər/ ▶ n. the owner and manager of a store.

shop·lift·ing /ˈSHäpˌlifting/ ▶ n. the theft of goods from a store by someone pretending to be a customer. ■ **shop·lift** v. **shop·lift·er** n.

shop·per /ˈSHäpər/ ▶ n. a person who is shopping.

shop·ping /ˈSHäping/ ▶ n. **1** the buying of goods from stores. **2** goods bought from stores.

shop·ping cen·ter ▶ n. a group of stores situated together, sometimes under one roof.

shop stew·ard ▶ n. a person elected by workers in a factory to represent them in dealings with management.

shop·worn /ˈSHäpˌwôrn/ ▶ adj. (of an article) dirty or damaged from being displayed or handled in a store.

shore¹ /SHôr/ ▶ n. **1** the land along the edge of a sea, lake, or large river. **2** (also **shores**) literary a foreign country: *distant shores.* ■ **shore·ward** adj. & adv. **shore·wards** adv.

– PHRASES **on shore** ashore; on land.

shore² ▶ v. (**shore something up**) **1** support or strengthen something weak or in difficulties: *the company will cut its investment program to shore up its shaky finances.* **2** support something with a prop or beam. ▶ n. a prop or beam set up against something to support it. ■ **shor·ing** n.

shore leave ▶ n. leisure time spent ashore by a sailor.

shore·line /ˈSHôrˌlīn/ ▶ n. the line along which the sea or other large body of water meets the land.

shorn /SHôrn/ ▶ past participle of SHEAR.

short /SHôrt/ ▶ adj. **1** of a small length in space or time. **2** (of a person) small in height. **3** smaller than is usual or expected: *a short speech.* **4** (**short of/on**) not having enough of something. **5** not available in sufficient quantities; scarce. **6** rude and abrupt. **7** (of a ball in sports) traveling a small distance, or not far enough. **8** (of odds in betting) reflecting a high level of probability. **9** (of a vowel) pronounced in a way that takes a shorter time than a long vowel in the same position (e.g., in standard English the vowel sound in *good*). **10** (of pastry) containing a high proportion of fat to flour and therefore crumbly. ▶ adv. not as far as the point aimed at: *you threw the ball short.* ▶ n. a short movie as opposed to a feature film. ▶ v. experience a short circuit. ■ **short·ish** adj. **short·ness** n.
– PHRASES **be caught short** be put at a disadvantage. **bring** (or **pull**) **someone up short** make someone stop or pause abruptly. **for short** as an abbreviation or nickname. **in short** to sum up; briefly. **in short order** immediately; rapidly: *the debt will be totally paid off in short order.* **in the short run** (or **term**) in the near future. **in short supply** (of a commodity) scarce. **make short work of** achieve, eat, or drink something quickly. **run short** not have enough of something. **short for** an abbreviation or nickname for. **short of 1** less than. **2** not reaching as far as. **3** without going so far as doing something extreme. **a short one** a drink of beer or liquor served in a measure smaller than usual. **stop short** stop suddenly.

short·age /ˈSHôrtij/ ▶ n. a situation in which there is not enough of something needed.

short·bread /ˈSHôrtˌbred/ ▶ n. a crisp, rich, crumbly type of cookie made with butter, flour, and sugar.

short·cake /ˈSHôrtˌkāk/ ▶ n. a small circular sponge cake or cake made of biscuit dough that is served with fruit and whipped cream as a dessert.

short·change ▶ v. **1** cheat someone by giving them less than the correct change. **2** treat unfairly by withholding something deserved: *women have been shortchanged by our education system.*

short cir·cuit ▶ n. a faulty connection in an electrical circuit in which the current flows along a shorter route than it should. ▶ v. (**short-circuit**) **1** cause or suffer a short circuit. **2** shorten a process by using a more direct but irregular method.

short·com·ing /ˈSHôrtˌkəming/ ▶ n. a failure to meet a certain standard; a fault or weakness: *the shortcomings of the legal system.*

short·cut ▶ n. **1** an alternative route that is shorter than the one usually taken. **2** a way of achieving something that is quicker than usual.

short·en /ˈsHôrtn/ ▶ v. make or become shorter.

short·en·ing /ˈsHôrtniNG, ˈsHôrtn-iNG/ ▶ n. fat used for making pastry.

short·fall /ˈsHôrtˌfôl/ ▶ n. a situation in which there is less of something than is required or expected.

short fuse ▶ n. informal a quick temper.

short·hand /ˈsHôrtˌhand/ ▶ n. 1 a method of rapid writing by means of abbreviations and symbols, used for recording what someone is saying. 2 a short and simple way of expressing or referring to something: *she learned that 'HS' is military shorthand for mustard gas.*

short-hand·ed ▶ adj. not having enough or the usual number of staff.

short haul ▶ n. a relatively short distance in terms of travel or the transport of goods.

short·horn /ˈsHôrtˌhôrn/ ▶ n. a breed of cattle with short horns.

short·list /ˈsHôrtˌlist/ ▶ n. a list of selected candidates from which a final choice is made. ▶ v. put someone or something on a shortlist.

short-lived /ˈlivd, ˈlīvd/ ▶ adj. lasting only a short time.

short·ly /ˈsHôrtlē/ ▶ adv. 1 in a short time; soon. 2 abruptly or sharply.

short or·der ▶ n. an order or dish of food that can be quickly prepared and served.
– PHRASES **in short order** see SHORT.

short-range ▶ adj. 1 able to be used or be effective only over short distances. 2 relating to a period of future time that is near to the present: *a short-range weather forecast.*

shorts /sHôrts/ ▶ pl. n. 1 short pants that reach to the knees or thighs. 2 men's underpants.

short shrift ▶ n. abrupt and unsympathetic treatment: *he gave short shrift to admirers who praised his courage.*

short·sight·ed /ˈsHôrtˈsītid/ ▶ adj. 1 not thinking carefully about the consequences of something. 2 Brit. nearsighted. ■ **short·sight·ed·ly** adv. **short·sight·ed·ness** n.

short-staffed ▶ adj. not having enough or the usual number of staff.

short·stop /ˈsHôrtˌstäp/ ▶ n. Baseball a fielder positioned between second and third base.

short-tem·pered ▶ adj. having a tendency to lose one's temper quickly.

short-term ▶ adj. occurring over or relating to a short period of time: *it might be a wise short-term investment.*

short-term·ism /ˈtərmizəm/ ▶ n. a policy of gaining profit or benefit in the near future without concern for more far-reaching effects.

short·wave ▶ n. 1 a radio wave of a wavelength between about 10 and 100 meters (and a frequency of about 3 to 30 megahertz). 2 broadcasting using a wavelength between about 10 and 100 meters.

short-wind·ed /ˈwindid/ ▶ adj. out of breath, or tending to run out of breath quickly.

short·y /ˈsHôrtē/ (also **shortie**) ▶ n. (pl. **shorties**) informal 1 a short person. 2 a short dress, nightdress, or raincoat.

Sho·sho·ne /sHōˈsHōnē/ ▶ n. (pl. same or **Shoshones**) a member of an American Indian people living chiefly in Wyoming, Idaho, and Nevada.

shot¹ /sHät/ ▶ n. 1 the firing of a gun or cannon. 2 a hit, stroke, or kick of the ball in sports, especially as an attempt to score. 3 informal an attempt to do something. 4 a photograph. 5 a film sequence photographed continuously by one camera. 6 a person with a specified level of ability in shooting: *he was an excellent shot.* 7 (also **lead shot**) tiny lead pellets used in a single charge or cartridge in a shotgun. 8 (pl. same) a ball of stone or metal fired from a large gun or cannon. 9 a heavy ball thrown by a shotputter. 10 the launch of a rocket: *a moon shot.* 11 informal a small drink of liquor. 12 informal an injection of a drug or vaccine.
– PHRASES **give it one's best shot** informal do the best that one can. **like a shot** informal without hesitation. **a shot in the arm** informal a source of encouragement.

shot² past and past participle of SHOOT ▶ adj. 1 (of cloth) woven with a warp and weft of different colors, giving a contrasting effect when looked at from different angles. 2 interspersed with a different color: *dark hair shot with silver.* 3 informal ruined or worn out.
– PHRASES **shot through with** filled with a quality or feature.

shot glass ▶ n. a small glass for serving liquor.

shot·gun /ˈsHätˌgən/ ▶ n. a gun for firing small shot at short range.

shot·gun wed·ding (also **shotgun marriage**) ▶ n. informal an enforced or hurried wedding, especially because the bride is pregnant.

shot put ▶ n. an athletic contest in which a very heavy round ball is thrown as far as possible. ■ **shot-put·ter** n. **shot-put·ting** n.

should /sHŏŏd/ ▶ modal v. (3rd sing. **should**) 1 used to indicate what is right or ought to be done. 2 used to indicate what is probable. 3 formal used to state what would happen if something else was the case: *if you should change your mind, I'll be at the hotel.*

shoul·der /ˈsHōldər/ ▶ n. 1 the joint between the upper arm or forelimb and the main part of the body. 2 a cut of meat from the upper foreleg and shoulder blade of an animal. 3 a steep sloping side of a mountain. ▶ v. 1 put something heavy over one's shoulder or shoulders to carry it. 2 take on a responsibility. 3 push someone or something out of one's way with one's shoulder. ■ **shoul·dered** adj.
– PHRASES **put one's shoulder to the wheel** set to work in a determined way. **shoulder arms** hold a rifle against the right side of the body, barrel upward. **shoulder to shoulder** side by side or acting together.

shoul·der bag ▶ n. a bag with a long strap that is hung over the shoulder.

shoul·der blade ▶ n. either of the large, flat triangular bones at the top of the back; the scapula.

shoul·der pad ▶ n. a pad sewn into the shoulder of a jacket, dress, etc., to provide shape or give protection.

shoul·der strap ▶ n. 1 a narrow strip of material going over the shoulder from front to back of a dress or top. 2 a long strap attached to a bag for carrying it over the shoulder.

should·n't /ˈsHŏŏdnt/ ▶ contr. should not.

shout /sHout/ ▶ v. 1 speak or call out very loudly. 2 (**shout at**) speak angrily and loudly to someone. 3 (**shout someone down**) prevent someone from speaking or being heard by shouting. ▶ n. a loud cry or call.

shout-out ▶ n. informal a message of congratulation, support, or appreciation.

shove /SHəv/ ▶ v. **1** push someone or something roughly. **2** put something somewhere carelessly or roughly. **3** (**shove off**) informal go away. **4** (**shove off**) push away from the shore in a boat. ▶ n. a strong push.

shov·el /'SHəvəl/ ▶ n. a tool resembling a spade with a broad blade and upturned sides, used for moving earth, snow, etc. ▶ v. (**shovels, shoveling, shoveled**) **1** move earth, snow, etc., with a shovel. **2** (**shovel something down/in**) informal eat food quickly and in large quantities.

shov·el·er /'SHəv(ə)lər/ (also **shoveller**) ▶ n. a duck with a long, broad bill.

show /SHō/ ▶ v. (past part. **shown** or **showed**) **1** be or make visible: *wrinkles were starting to show on her face*. **2** offer something to be inspected or viewed. **3** present an image of: *a postcard showing Mount Etna*. **4** display a quality, emotion, or characteristic. **5** be evidence of or prove something. **6** treat someone in a particular way. **7** make someone understand something by explaining it or doing it oneself. **8** lead or guide: *show them in, please*. **9** (also **show up**) informal arrive for an appointment. ▶ n. **1** a theatrical performance, especially a musical. **2** a light entertainment program on television or radio. **3** an event or competition involving the public display of animals, plants, or products. **4** an impressive or attractive sight or display. **5** a display of a quality or feeling. **6** an outward display intended to give a false impression. **7** a ridiculous display: *don't make a show of yourself*. **8** informal a project or organization: *I run the show*.
– PHRASES **for show** for the sake of appearance rather than use. **get the show on the road** informal begin a project or enterprise. **show one's hand** reveal one's plans. **show off** try to impress others by talking about one's abilities or possessions. **show something off** display something that one is proud of. **show of hands** a vote carried out by the raising of hands. **show oneself** (or **one's face**) appear in public. **show someone around** point out interesting features in a place or building to someone. **show someone/thing up 1** reveal someone or something as being bad or at fault. **2** informal embarrass or humiliate someone.

show biz /'SHō,biz/ ▶ n. informal show business. ■ **show-biz·zy** adj.

show·boat /'SHō,bōt/ ▶ n. **1** a river steamboat on which theatrical performances are given. **2** informal a show-off; an exhibitionist. ▶ v. informal show off: (as adj. **showboating**) *a lot of showboating politicians*. ■ **show·boat·er** n.

show busi·ness ▶ n. the world of movies, television, pop music, and the theater as a profession or industry.

show·case /'SHō,kās/ ▶ n. **1** an occasion for presenting someone or something favorably to the public. **2** a glass case for displaying articles in a store or museum. ▶ v. put on display: *he made a short film to showcase his directing talents*.

show·down /'SHō,doun/ ▶ n. a final test or confrontation intended to settle a dispute.

show·er /'SHou(-ə)r/ ▶ n. **1** a brief fall of rain or snow. **2** a mass of small things falling at once. **3** a large number of things arriving at the same

time: *a shower of awards*. **4** a piece of equipment that creates a spray of water under which a person stands to wash. **5** an act of washing in a shower. **6** a party at which presents are given to a woman who is about to get married or have a baby. ▶ v. **1** fall or cause to fall in a shower. **2** (**shower someone with** or **shower something on**) give a large number of things to someone. **3** wash oneself in a shower.

show·er·proof /'SHou(-ə)r,proof/ ▶ adj. (of a raincoat or jacket) able to keep out light rain.

show·er·y /'SHou(-ə)rē/ ▶ adj. with frequent showers of rain.

show·girl /'SHō,gərl/ ▶ n. an actress who sings and dances in a musical or variety show.

show·ground /'SHō,ground/ ▶ n. an area of land on which a show takes place.

show·ing /'SHō-iNG/ ▶ n. **1** a presentation of a movie or television program. **2** a performance of a particular quality: *poor opinion poll showings*.

show jump·ing ▶ n. the competitive sport of riding horses over a course of fences and other obstacles in an arena. ■ **show jump·er** n.

show·man /'SHōmən/ ▶ n. (pl. **showmen**) **1** the manager or presenter of a circus, fair, etc. **2** a person who is skilled at entertaining people or gaining their attention. ■ **show·man·ship** /-,SHip/ n.

shown /SHōn/ ▶ past participle of **show**.

show-off ▶ n. informal a person who tries to impress others by talking about their own abilities or possessions.

show·piece /'SHō,pēs/ ▶ n. **1** an outstanding example of something: *the harbor is one of the showpieces of the city*. **2** an item of work put on exhibition or display.

show·place /'SHō,plās/ ▶ n. a beautiful or interesting place that attracts many visitors.

show·room /'SHō,rōōm, -,rŏŏm/ ▶ n. a room used to display cars, furniture, or other goods for sale.

show·stop·per ▶ n. informal something that is very impressive, striking, or appealing. ■ **show-stop·ping** adj.

show tri·al ▶ n. a trial that is held in public to produce a preordained verdict and to influence or satisfy public opinion, rather than to ensure that justice is done.

show·y /'SHō-ē/ ▶ adj. (**showier, showiest**) very bright or colorful and attracting much attention. ■ **show·i·ly** adv. **show·i·ness** n.

shrank /SHraNGk/ ▶ past of **shrink**.

shrap·nel /'SHrapnəl/ ▶ n. small metal fragments thrown out by the explosion of a shell, bomb, etc.

shred /SHred/ ▶ n. **1** a strip of material that has been torn, cut, or scraped from something larger. **2** a very small amount: *not a shred of evidence*. ▶ v. (**shreds, shredding, shredded**) tear or cut something into shreds.

shred·der /'SHredər/ ▶ n. **1** a machine or other device for shredding something, especially documents. **2** informal a snowboarder.

shrew /SHrōō/ ▶ n. **1** a small mammal resembling a mouse, with a long pointed snout and tiny eyes. **2** a bad-tempered woman.

shrewd /SHrōōd/ ▶ adj. having or showing sharp powers of judgment; astute: *he's a shrewd businessman who knows how to make money*. ■ **shrewd·ly** adv. **shrewd·ness** n.

shrew·ish /ˈSHrōōiSH/ ▸ adj. (of a woman) bad-tempered or nagging. ■ **shrew·ish·ly** adv. **shrew·ish·ness** n.

shriek /SHrēk/ ▸ v. make a high-pitched piercing cry or sound. ▸ n. a high-pitched piercing cry or sound. ■ **shriek·er** n.

shrike /SHrīk/ ▸ n. a songbird with a hooked bill that often impales its prey on thorns.

shrill /SHril/ ▸ adj. 1 (of a voice or sound) high-pitched and piercing. 2 (of a complaint or demand) loud and forceful. ▸ v. make a high-pitched piercing noise. ■ **shrill·ness** n. **shril·ly** adv.

shrimp /SHrimp/ ▸ n. 1 (pl. same or **shrimps**) a small edible shellfish with ten legs. 2 informal, derogatory a small weak person. ▸ v. (often as n. **shrimping**) fish for shrimp. ■ **shrimp·er** n.

shrine /SHrīn/ ▸ n. 1 a place regarded as holy because it is connected to a holy person or event. 2 a place or receptacle containing a religious statue or holy object. 3 a place regarded as notable because it is associated with a particular person or thing: *the room was a shrine to middle-class taste.*

shrink /SHriNGk/ ▸ v. (past **shrank** /SHraNGk/; past part. **shrunk** /SHrəNGk/ or (especially as adj.) **shrunken** /ˈSHrəNGkən/) 1 become or make smaller in size or amount. 2 (of clothes or material) become smaller as a result of being washed in water that is too hot. 3 move back or away in fear or disgust. 4 (**shrink from**) be unwilling to do: *I don't shrink from my responsibilities.* ▸ n. informal a psychiatrist. ■ **shrink·a·ble** adj.

shrink·age /ˈSHriNGkij/ ▸ n. 1 the process of shrinking or the amount by which something has shrunk. 2 an allowance made for reduction in the takings of a business due to theft or wastage.

shrink·ing vi·o·let ▸ n. informal a very shy person.

shrink-wrap ▸ v. package an object in clinging plastic film. ▸ n. (**shrink wrap**) clinging plastic film used to package an object.

shrive /SHrīv/ ▸ v. (past **shrove** /SHrōv/; past part. **shriven** /ˈSHrivən/) old use (of a priest) hear a person's confession, give them a religious duty, and declare them free from sin.

shriv·el /ˈSHrivəl/ ▸ v. (**shrivels, shriveling, shriveled**) wrinkle and shrink through loss of moisture.

shroud /SHroud/ ▸ n. 1 a length of cloth in which a dead person is wrapped for burial. 2 a thing that surrounds or hides someone or something: *a shroud of mist often envelops the island.* 3 (**shrouds**) a set of ropes supporting the mast or topmast of a sailboat. ▸ v. surround so as to cover or hide: *his early life is shrouded in mystery.*

shrove /SHrōv/ ▸ past of **SHRIVE**.

Shrove Tues·day /SHrōv/ ▸ n. the day before Ash Wednesday.

shrub /SHrəb/ ▸ n. a woody plant that is smaller than a tree and divided into separate stems at or near the ground. ■ **shrub·by** adj.

shrub·ber·y /ˈSHrəb(ə)rē/ ▸ n. (pl. **shrubberies**) 1 shrubs collectively. 2 an area planted with shrubs.

shrug /SHrəg/ ▸ v. (**shrugs, shrugging, shrugged**) 1 raise one's shoulders slightly and briefly as a sign that one does not know or care about something. 2 (**shrug something off**) dismiss something as unimportant. ▸ n. 1 an act

of shrugging one's shoulders. 2 a woman's close-fitting cardigan or jacket, cut short at the front and back so that only the arms and shoulders are covered.

shrunk /SHrəNGk/ (also **shrunken**) ▸ past participle of **SHRINK**.

shtick /SHtik/ ▸ n. informal 1 a performer's routine or gimmick. 2 a person's talent or typical behavior: *he has developed a distinctive courtroom shtick.*

shuck /SHək/ ▸ v. 1 remove the husks or shells from corn or shellfish. 2 informal get rid of something. 3 informal take off an item of clothing. ▸ n. 1 the husk of an ear of corn. 2 the shell of an oyster, scallop, or clam.

shucks /SHəks/ ▸ exclam. informal used to express surprise, regret, etc.

shud·der /ˈSHədər/ ▸ v. tremble or shake violently, especially as a result of fear or disgust. ▸ n. an act of shuddering. ■ **shud·der·y** adj.

shuf·fle /ˈSHəfəl/ ▸ v. 1 walk without lifting the feet completely from the ground. 2 move restlessly while sitting or standing. 3 rearrange a deck of cards by sliding them over each other quickly. 4 rearrange people or things. 5 (**shuffle through**) look through a number of things hurriedly. ▸ n. 1 a shuffling walk or sound. 2 an act of shuffling a deck of cards. 3 a rearrangement of people or things; a reshuffle. 4 a dance performed with a quick dragging movement of the feet. ■ **shuf·fler** n.

shuf·fle·board /ˈSHəfəlˌbôrd/ ▸ n. a game played by pushing disks with a long-handled cue over a marked surface.

shun /SHən/ ▸ v. (**shuns, shunning, shunned**) avoid, ignore, or reject: *he shunned fashionable society.*

shunt /SHənt/ ▸ v. 1 slowly push or pull a railroad vehicle or vehicles from one set of tracks to another. 2 push or shove someone or something. 3 divert to a less important place or position: *amateurs were gradually being shunted to filing jobs.* ▸ n. 1 an act of shunting. 2 an electrical conductor joining two points of a circuit. 3 Surgery an alternative path for the flow of blood or other body fluid. ■ **shunt·er** n.

shush /SHŏŏSH, SHəSH/ ▸ exclam. be quiet. ▸ n. 1 an utterance of 'shush'. 2 a soft swishing or rustling sound. ▸ v. 1 tell or signal someone to be silent. 2 move with a soft swishing or rustling sound.

shut /SHət/ ▸ v. (**shuts, shutting, shut**) 1 move something into position to block an opening. 2 (**shut someone/thing in/out**) keep someone or something in or out by closing a door, gate, etc. 3 prevent access to a place or along a route. 4 stop operating for business: *we shut the store for lunch.* 5 close a book, curtains, etc.
– PHRASES **be** (or **get**) **shut of** informal be (or get) rid of. **shut down** stop operating or opening for business. **shut something off** stop something from flowing or working. **shut something out** prevent oneself from thinking about something. **shut up** informal stop talking.

shut·down /ˈSHətˌdoun/ ▸ n. an act of closing a factory or of turning off a machine.

shut-eye ▸ n. informal sleep.

shut-in ▸ n. 1 a person confined indoors, especially as a result of physical or mental disability. 2 a state or period in which an oil or gas well has available but unused capacity.

shut·out /ˈSHət,out/ ▸n. a competition or game in which the losing side fails to score.

shut·ter /ˈSHətər/ ▸n. **1** each of a pair of hinged panels fixed inside or outside a window that can be closed for security or to keep out the light. **2** a device that opens and closes to expose the film in a camera. ▸v. close the shutters of a window or building.

shut·tle /ˈSHətl/ ▸n. **1** a form of transportation that travels regularly between two places. **2** (in weaving) a bobbin used for carrying the weft thread across the cloth between the warp threads. **3** a bobbin carrying the lower thread in a sewing machine. ▸v. travel or transport someone or something regularly between places.

shut·tle·cock /ˈSHətl,käk/ ▸n. a light cone-shaped object consisting of a rounded piece of cork with feathers attached, or a similar object made of plastic, struck with rackets in badminton.

shut·tle di·plo·ma·cy ▸n. negotiations conducted by a person who travels between two or more countries that are reluctant to hold direct discussions.

shy¹ /SHī/ ▸adj. (**shyer, shyest**) **1** nervous or timid in the company of other people. **2** (**shy about/of**) slow or reluctant to do something. **3** (in combination) having a specified dislike: *camera-shy.* **4** (**shy of**) informal less than; short of: *the car weighs just shy of 3,000 pounds.* ▸v. (**shies, shying, shied**) **1** (of a horse) suddenly turn aside in fright. **2** (usu. **shy away from**) avoid something through nervousness or lack of confidence. ■ **shy·ly** adv. **shy·ness** n.

shy² ▸v. (**shies, shying, shied**) throw something at a target.

shy·ster /ˈSHīstər/ ▸n. informal a dishonest or deceitful person, especially a lawyer.

SI ▸abbr. Système International, the international system of units of measurement based on the meter, kilogram, second, ampere, kelvin, candela, and mole.

Si ▸symbol the chemical element silicon.

Si·a·mese /ˌsīəˈmēz/ ▸n. (pl. same) **1** (also **Siamese cat**) a breed of cat that has short pale fur with a darker face, ears, feet, and tail. **2** dated a person from Siam (now Thailand) in SE Asia. ▸adj. dated relating to Thailand.

Siam·ese twins ▸pl.n. twins whose bodies are joined at birth.

> **USAGE**
> The technical term is **conjoined twins**.

sib /sib/ ▸n. a brother or sister; a sibling.

Si·be·ri·an /sīˈbi(ə)rēən/ ▸n. a person from Siberia. ▸adj. relating to Siberia.

sib·i·lant /ˈsibələnt/ ▸adj. making a soft hissing sound. ▸n. a speech sound made with a hissing effect, for example *s, sh.* ■ **sib·i·lance** n.

sib·ling /ˈsibliNG/ ▸n. a brother or sister.

sib·yl /ˈsibəl/ ▸n. (in ancient Greece and Rome) a woman supposedly able to pass on the messages and prophecies of a god. ■ **sib·yl·line** /ˈsibə,līn, -,lēn/ adj.

sic¹ /sik/ ▸adv. (after a copied or quoted word that appears odd or wrong) written exactly as it stands in the original.

sic² (also **sick**) ▸v. (**sics, sicced, siccing**, or **sicks, sicked, sicking**) **1** set a dog or other animal on someone or something. **2** informal set someone to pursue, keep watch on, or accompany someone else.

Si·cil·ian /siˈsilyən/ ▸n. a person from Sicily. ▸adj. relating to Sicily.

sick¹ /sik/ ▸adj. **1** affected by physical or mental illness. **2** feeling nauseous and wanting to vomit. **3** (**sick of**) bored by or annoyed with someone or something because one has had too much of them. **4** informal behaving in an abnormal or cruel way. **5** informal (of humor) dealing with unpleasant subjects in a cruel or upsetting way. – PHRASES **be sick 1** be ill. **2** vomit.

sick² ▸v. variant spelling of **sic**².

sick·bay /ˈsik,bā/ ▸n. a room or building in a school or on a ship that is set aside for sick people.

sick·bed /ˈsik,bed/ ▸n. the bed of a person who is ill.

sick build·ing syn·drome ▸n. a condition affecting office workers, including headaches and breathing problems, which is said to be caused by factors such as poor ventilation.

sick·en /ˈsikən/ ▸v. **1** make someone feel disgusted or appalled. **2** become ill. **3** (**be sickening for**) Brit. be showing the first symptoms of an illness. **4** (as adj. **sickening**) informal very annoying. ■ **sick·en·ing·ly** adv.

sick·le /ˈsikəl/ ▸n. a farming tool with a short handle and a semicircular blade, used for cutting cereals or grass.

sick leave ▸n. permission to be absent from work because of illness.

sick·le-cell a·ne·mi·a (also **sickle-cell disease**) ▸n. a severe hereditary form of anemia in which the red blood cells are distorted into a crescent shape at low oxygen levels.

sick·ly /ˈsiklē/ ▸adj. (**sicklier, sickliest**) **1** often ill; in poor health. **2** showing or causing poor health. **3** (of flavor, color, etc.) so bright or sweet as to be unpleasant or make one feel sick. **4** excessively sentimental. ■ **sick·li·ness** n.

sick·ness /ˈsiknis/ ▸n. **1** the state of being ill. **2** a particular type of illness or disease. **3** nausea or vomiting.

sick·o /ˈsikō/ ▸n. (pl. **sickos**) informal a perverted person.

sick·room /ˈsik,rŏŏm/ ▸n. a room occupied by or set apart for people who are unwell.

side /sīd/ ▸n. **1** a position to the left or right of an object, place, or central point. **2** either of the two halves into which something can be divided: *she lay on her side of the bed.* **3** an upright or sloping surface of a structure or object that is not the top, bottom, front, or back. **4** each of the flat surfaces of a solid object. **5** either of the two surfaces of something flat and thin, e.g., paper. **6** a part or area near the edge of something. **7** a person or group opposing another or others in a dispute or contest. **8** a sports team. **9** a particular aspect: *he had a disagreeable side.* **10** either of the two faces of a record or of the corresponding parts of a cassette tape. **11** Geometry each of the lines forming the boundary of a plane rectilinear figure. **12** a person's line of descent as traced through either their father or mother. ▸adj. additional or less important: *a side dish.* ▸v. (**side with/against**) support or oppose one person or group in a conflict or dispute. ■ **sid·ed** adj. **side·ward** /ˈsīdwərd/ adj. & adv. **side·wards** /ˈsīdwərdz/ adv.

– PHRASES **on the side 1** informal in addition to one's regular job. **2** informal as a secret additional sexual relationship. **3** (of food) served separately from the main dish. **side by side** close together and facing the same way. **side on** on, from, or toward the side. **take sides** support one person or cause against another.

side·arm ▸ n. a weapon worn at a person's side, such as a pistol or other small firearm (or, formerly, a sword or bayonet).

side·band /ˈsīdˌband/ ▸ n. Telecommunications one of two frequency bands on either side of the carrier wave, containing the modulated signal.

side·bar /ˈsīdˌbär/ ▸ n. **1** a short piece of additional information placed alongside a main article in a newspaper or magazine. **2** a courtroom discussion between the lawyers and the judge held out of earshot of the jury.

side·board /ˈsīdˌbôrd/ ▸ n. **1** a flat-topped piece of furniture with cupboards and drawers, used for storing dishes, glasses, etc. **2** (**sideboards**) Brit. sideburns.

side·burns /ˈsīdˌbərnz/ ▸ pl.n. a strip of hair growing down each side of a man's face in front of his ears.

side·car /ˈsīdˌkär/ ▸ n. a small, low vehicle attached to the side of a motorcycle for carrying passengers.

side ef·fect ▸ n. a secondary, typically undesirable effect of a drug or medical treatment.

side·kick /ˈsīdˌkik/ ▸ n. informal a person's assistant.

side·light /ˈsīdˌlīt/ ▸ n. **1** (**sidelights**) a ship's navigation lights. **2** a narrow pane of glass alongside a door or larger window.

side·line /ˈsīdˌlīn/ ▸ n. **1** an activity done in addition to a person's main job. **2** either of the two lines forming the boundaries of the longer sides of a football field, basketball court, etc. **3** (**the sidelines**) a position of observing a situation rather than being directly involved in it. ▸ v. **1** prevent a player from playing in a team or game. **2** remove from an influential position: *our committee has been sidelined and excluded from decision-making.*

side·long /ˈsīdˌlông/ ▸ adj. & adv. (especially of a look) to or from one side; sideways.

side·man /ˈsīdˌman/ ▸ n. (pl. **sidemen**) a supporting musician in a jazz band or rock group.

si·de·re·al /sīˈdi(ə)rēəl/ ▸ adj. relating to the distant stars or their apparent positions in the sky.

si·de·re·al time ▸ n. Astronomy time reckoned from the motion of the earth (or a planet) relative to the distant stars (rather than with respect to the sun).

side road ▸ n. a minor road joining or branching from a main road.

side·sad·dle ▸ adv. (of a woman rider) sitting with both feet on the same side of the horse.

side·show /ˈsīdˌshō/ ▸ n. **1** a small show or stall at an exhibition, fair, or circus. **2** a minor incident or issue that diverts attention from the main subject.

side·split·ting ▸ adj. informal very amusing.

side·step /ˈsīdˌstep/ ▸ v. (**sidesteps, sidestepping, sidestepped**) **1** avoid someone or something by stepping sideways. **2** avoid dealing with or discussing: *he neatly sidestepped the questions about riots.* ▸ n. a step to one side to avoid someone or something.

side street ▸ n. a minor street.

side·swipe /ˈsīdˌswīp/ ▸ v. strike something, especially a motor vehicle, with a glancing blow. ▸ n. a critical remark made while discussing another matter.

side·track /ˈsīdˌtrak/ ▸ v. distract someone from an urgent or important issue.

side·view mir·ror ▸ n. a mirror projecting from the side of a vehicle, enabling the driver to see vehicles approaching alongside.

side·walk /ˈsīdˌwôk/ ▸ n. a paved path for pedestrians at the side of a road.

side·ways /ˈsīdˌwāz/ (also **sidewise** /ˈsīdˌwīz/) ▸ adv. & adj. **1** to, toward, or from the side. **2** not conventional; alternative: *a sideways look at life.*

side·wind·er /ˈsīdˌwīndər/ ▸ n. a burrowing rattlesnake of North American deserts that moves sideways by throwing its body into S-shaped curves.

sid·ing /ˈsīdiNG/ ▸ n. **1** cladding material for the outside of a building. **2** a short track beside and opening onto a main railroad line, where trains are shunted or left.

si·dle /ˈsīdl/ ▸ v. walk in a stealthy or uncertain way.

SIDS /sidz/ ▸ abbr. sudden infant death syndrome (technical term for CRIB DEATH).

siege /sēj/ ▸ n. **1** a military operation in which enemy forces try to capture a town or building by surrounding it and cutting off essential supplies. **2** a similar operation by a police team to force an armed person to surrender.
– PHRASES **lay siege to** begin a siege of a place. **under siege** under constant pressure or attack: *the farmed salmon industry is under siege.*

siege men·tal·i·ty ▸ n. a defensive or paranoid attitude based on the belief that others are hostile toward one.

sie·mens /ˈsēmənz/ ▸ n. Physics the SI unit of conductance.

si·en·na /sēˈenə/ ▸ n. a kind of earth used as a pigment in painting, normally yellowish-brown (**raw sienna**) or deep reddish-brown when roasted (**burnt sienna**).

si·er·ra /sēˈerə/ ▸ n. (in Spanish-speaking countries or the western US) a long jagged mountain chain.

Si·er·ra Le·o·ne·an /sēˌerə lēˈōnēən/ ▸ n. a person from Sierra Leone, a country in West Africa. ▸ adj. relating to Sierra Leone.

si·es·ta /sēˈestə/ ▸ n. an afternoon rest or nap, especially one taken regularly in hot countries.

sieve /siv/ ▸ n. a utensil consisting of a wire or plastic mesh held in a frame, used for straining solids from liquids or separating coarser particles from finer ones. ▸ v. put a substance through a sieve.

sie·vert /ˈsēvərt/ ▸ n. Physics the SI unit of dose equivalent, equal to an effective dose of a joule of energy per kilogram of recipient mass.

sift /sift/ ▸ v. **1** put a fine or loose substance through a sieve so as to remove lumps or large particles. **2** examine something thoroughly to sort out what is important or useful. ■ **sift·er** n.

sigh /sī/ ▸ v. **1** let out a long, deep breath expressing sadness, relief, tiredness, etc. **2** (**sigh**

for) literary long for someone or something. ▸ n. an act of sighing.

sight /sīt/ ▸ n. **1** the faculty of seeing. **2** the action of seeing: *I hate the sight of blood.* **3** the area or distance within which someone can see or something can be seen. **4** a thing that is seen. **5** (**sights**) places of interest to tourists and other visitors. **6** (**a sight**) informal a ridiculous or unattractive person or thing. **7** (also **sights**) a device that one looks through to aim a gun or to see with a telescope or similar instrument. ▸ v. **1** manage to see or glimpse: *two suspicious men had been sighted in the area.* **2** take aim by looking through the sights of a gun. ■ **sight·er** n. **sight·ing** n.
– PHRASES **at first sight** on the first impression. **catch sight of** manage to glimpse. **in sight** close to being achieved. **in** (or **within**) **sight of 1** so as to see or be seen from. **2** close to achieving. **in** (or **within**) **one's sights** within the scope of one's ambitions or expectations. **lose sight of** fail to consider, be aware of, or remember. **on** (or **at**) **sight** as soon as someone or something has been seen. **raise** (or **lower**) **one's sights** increase (or lower) one's expectations. **set one's sights on** hope strongly to achieve. **a sight** —— informal considerably: *she is a sight cleverer than Sarah.* **a sight for sore eyes** informal a person or thing that one is very pleased or relieved to see.

> **USAGE**
> For an explanation of the difference between **sight** and **site**, see the note at SITE.

sight·ed /'sītid/ ▸ adj. **1** having the ability to see; not blind. **2** having a specified kind of sight: *keen-sighted.*

sight·less /'sītlis/ ▸ adj. unable to see; blind.

sight line ▸ n. an imaginary line from someone's eye to what is seen.

sight-read /'sīt,rēd/ ▸ v. read a musical score and perform it without preparation.

sight·see·ing /'sīt,sēiNG/ ▸ n. the activity of visiting places of interest. ■ **sight·se·er** n.

sign /sīn/ ▸ n. **1** a thing whose presence or occurrence indicates that something exists, is happening, or may happen: *dark circles under the eyes are a sign of stress.* **2** a signal, gesture, or notice giving information or an instruction. **3** a symbol or word used to represent something in algebra, music, or other subjects. **4** each of the twelve equal sections into which the zodiac is divided. ▸ v. **1** write one's name on a letter, document, etc., in order to show that one has written it or that one authorizes its contents. **2** recruit an athlete, musician, etc., by signing a contract with them. **3** use gestures to give information or instructions. ■ **sign·er** n.
– PHRASES **sign off** conclude a letter, broadcast, or other message. **sign on** commit oneself to a job or other undertaking. **sign someone on** employ someone. **sign up** commit oneself to a job, course of study, etc.

sign·age /'sīnij/ ▸ n. commercial or public display signs.

sig·nal¹ /'signəl/ ▸ n. **1** a gesture, action, or sound giving information or an instruction. **2** a sign of a particular situation: *pain is a warning signal, telling you that something is wrong.* **3** an electrical impulse or radio wave transmitted or received. **4** a device that uses lights or a movable arm, used to tell drivers to stop or beware on a road or railroad. ▸ v. (**signals, signaling, signaled**) give information or an instruction to someone by means of a signal. ■ **sig·nal·er** n.

sig·nal² ▸ adj. striking in extent, seriousness, or importance. ■ **sig·nal·ly** adv.

sig·nal-to-noise ra·tio ▸ n. the ratio of the strength of an electrical or other signal carrying information to that of unwanted interference, generally given in decibels.

sig·na·to·ry /'signə,tôrē/ ▸ n. (pl. **signatories**) a person, organization, state, or country that has signed an agreement.

sig·na·ture /'signəCHər, -,CHŏŏr/ ▸ n. **1** a person's name written in a distinctive way, used in signing a document, letter, etc. **2** the action of signing something. **3** a distinctive product or quality by which someone or something can be recognized: *the chef produced the pâté that was his signature.* **4** Music a key signature or time signature.

sig·na·ture tune ▸ n. a piece of music used to introduce a particular television or radio program; theme tune.

sign·board /'sīn,bôrd/ ▸ n. a board displaying the name or logo of a business or product.

sig·net /'signit/ ▸ n. historical a small seal, especially one set in a ring, used to authorize an official document.

sig·net ring ▸ n. a ring with letters or a design set into it.

sig·nif·i·cance /sig'nifikəns/ ▸ n. **1** the quality of being significant; importance. **2** the meaning of something: *he took in the full significance of Peter's remarks.*

sig·nif·i·cant /sig'nifikənt/ ▸ adj. **1** important or large enough to be noticed. **2** having a particular meaning: *it's significant that he set the story in Italy.* **3** having a meaning that is not stated directly: *a significant look.* ■ **sig·nif·i·cant·ly** adv.

sig·nif·i·cant fig·ure ▸ n. Mathematics each of the digits of a number that are used to express it to the required degree of accuracy.

sig·nif·i·cant oth·er ▸ n. a person with whom someone has an established romantic or sexual relationship.

sig·ni·fy /'signə,fī/ ▸ v. (**signifies, signifying, signified**) **1** be an indication of something. **2** be a symbol of something. **3** make a feeling or intention known. **4** be of importance: *the locked door doesn't necessarily signify.* ■ **sig·ni·fi·ca·tion** /,signəfi'kāsHən/ n.

sign·ing /'sīniNG/ ▸ n. **1** an event at which an author signs copies of their book to gain publicity and sales. **2** sign language.

sign lan·guage ▸ n. a system of communication used among and with deaf people, consisting of gestures and signs made by the hands and face.

si·gnor /sēn'yôr/ ▸ n. a title or form of address for an Italian-speaking man, corresponding to *Mr.* or *sir.*

si·gno·ra /sēn'yôrə/ ▸ n. a title or form of address for an Italian-speaking married woman, corresponding to *Mrs.* or *madam.*

si·gno·ri·na /,sēnyə'rēnə/ ▸ n. a title or form of address for an Italian-speaking unmarried woman, corresponding to *Miss.*

sign·post /'sīn,pōst/ ▸ n. a sign on a post, giving information such as the direction and distance to a nearby town.

si·ka /'sēkə/ ▶ n. a deer with a grayish coat that turns yellowish-brown with white spots in summer, native to Japan and SE Asia.

Sikh /sēk/ ▶ n. a member of a religion (**Sikhism** /'sēkizəm/) that has one God and was founded in the Punjab in the 15th century by Guru Nanak. ▶ adj. relating to Sikhs or Sikhism.

si·lage /'sīlij/ ▶ n. grass or other green crops that are stored in airtight conditions without first being dried, used as animal feed in the winter.

si·lence /'sīləns/ ▶ n. 1 complete lack of sound. 2 a situation in which someone refuses or fails to speak: *he withdrew into sullen silence.* ▶ v. 1 prevent someone from speaking. 2 make something silent.

si·lenc·er /'sīlənsər/ ▶ n. a device for reducing the noise made by a mechanism, especially a gun.

si·lent /'sīlənt/ ▶ adj. 1 not making or accompanied by any sound. 2 not speaking or not spoken aloud: *a silent prayer.* 3 (of a movie) without an accompanying soundtrack. 4 (of a letter) written but not pronounced, e.g., *b* in *doubt.* ■ **si·lent·ly** adv.

si·lent part·ner ▶ n. a partner who invests money in a business but is not involved in running it.

sil·hou·ette /ˌsiloo'et/ ▶ n. 1 the dark shape and outline of someone or something visible against a lighter background. 2 a representation of someone or something that shows them as a black shape on a light background. ▶ v. show as a silhouette: *the castle was silhouetted against the sky.*

sil·i·ca /'silikə/ ▶ n. silicon dioxide, a hard colorless compound that occurs as quartz and in sandstone and many other rocks. ■ **si·li·ceous** /sə'lisHəs/ adj.

sil·i·ca gel ▶ n. hydrated silica in a hard granular form that absorbs moisture from the air.

sil·i·cate /'silə,kāt, -kit/ ▶ n. a compound of silica combined with a metal oxide.

sil·i·con /'silə,kän, -kən/ ▶ n. a gray nonmetallic chemical element with semiconducting properties, used in making electronic circuits.

> **USAGE**
> Do not confuse **silicon** with **silicone**. **Silicon** is a chemical element used in electronic circuits and microchips, while **silicone** is the material used in cosmetic implants.

sil·i·con chip ▶ n. a microchip.

sil·i·cone /'silə,kōn/ ▶ n. a synthetic resin made from silicon, used to make cosmetic implants, plastic, paints, etc.

sil·i·co·sis /ˌsilə'kōsis/ ▶ n. a lung disease caused by breathing dust containing silica.

silk /silk/ ▶ n. 1 a fine, soft fiber produced by silkworms. 2 thread or fabric made from silk. 3 (**silks**) clothes made from silk, worn by a jockey.

silk·en /'silkən/ ▶ adj. 1 smooth, soft, and shiny like silk: *her silken hair.* 2 made of silk.

silk·screen /'silk,skrēn/ ▶ n. a piece of fine material used in screen printing. ▶ v. print, decorate, or reproduce something using a silkscreen.

silk·worm /'silk,wərm/ ▶ n. a caterpillar that spins a silk cocoon from which silk fiber is obtained.

silk·y /'silkē/ ▶ adj. (**silkier**, **silkiest**) 1 smooth, soft, and shiny like silk. 2 (of a person's voice) smooth and gentle or persuasive. ■ **silk·i·ly** adv. **silk·i·ness** n.

sill /sil/ ▶ n. 1 a shelf or slab of stone, wood, or metal at the foot of a window or doorway. 2 a horizontal piece of metal that forms part of the frame of a vehicle. 3 Geology a sheet of igneous rock intruded between and parallel with existing strata. Compare with **DYKE**[1].

sil·ly /'silē/ ▶ adj. (**sillier**, **silliest**) showing a lack of common sense or judgment; foolish. ▶ n. (pl. **sillies**) informal a silly person. ■ **sil·li·ness** n.

si·lo /'sīlō/ ▶ n. (pl. **silos**) 1 a tall tower on a farm, used to store grain. 2 a pit or other airtight structure in which green crops are stored as silage. 3 an underground chamber in which a guided missile is kept ready for firing.

silt /silt/ ▶ n. fine sand, clay, or other material carried by running water and deposited as a sediment. ▶ v. (usu. **silt up** or **silt something up**) fill or block something with silt. ■ **sil·ta·tion** /sil'tāsHən/ n. **silt·y** adj.

Si·lu·ri·an /si'loorēən, sī-/ ▶ adj. Geology referring to the third period of the Palaeozoic era (about 439 to 409 million years ago), when the first fish and land plants appeared.

sil·ver /'silvər/ ▶ n. 1 a precious grayish-white metallic chemical element. 2 a shiny gray-white color like that of silver. 3 coins made from silver or from a metal that resembles silver. 4 silver dishes, containers, or cutlery. ▶ v. 1 coat or plate something with silver. 2 literary give a silvery appearance to: *the dome was silvered with frost.* 3 (of a person's hair) turn gray or white. ■ **sil·ver·i·ness** n. **sil·ver·y** adj.
– PHRASES **be born with a silver spoon in one's mouth** be born into a wealthy upper-class family. **the silver screen 1** a movie screen. 2 motion pictures.

sil·ver birch ▶ n. a birch tree with silver-gray bark.

sil·ver·fish /'silvər,fisH/ ▶ n. (pl. same or **silverfishes**) a small silvery wingless insect that lives in buildings.

sil·ver ju·bi·lee ▶ n. the twenty-fifth anniversary of an important event.

sil·ver med·al ▶ n. a medal made of or colored silver, awarded for second place in a race or competition.

sil·ver plate ▶ n. 1 a thin layer of silver applied as a coating to another metal. 2 plates, dishes, etc., made of or plated with silver.

sil·ver·smith /'silvər,smiTH/ ▶ n. a person who makes silver articles. ■ **sil·ver·smith·ing** n.

sil·ver tongue ▶ n. an ability to be eloquent and persuasive in speaking. ■ **sil·ver-tongued** adj.

sil·ver·ware /'silvər,wer/ ▶ n. 1 dishes, containers, or cutlery made of or coated with silver. 2 eating and serving utensils made of any material.

sil·vi·cul·ture /'silvi,kəlcHər/ ▶ n. the growing and cultivation of trees. ■ **sil·vi·cul·tur·al** /ˌsilvi'kəlcHərəl/ adj.

SIM /sim/ (also **SIM card**) ▶ n. subscriber identification module, a smart card inside a cell phone, carrying an identification number unique to the user, storing personal data, and preventing operation of the phone if removed.

sim·i·an /'simēən/ ▶ adj. relating to or resembling apes or monkeys. ▶ n. an ape or monkey.

sim·i·lar /'simələr/ ▶ adj. **1** like something else in appearance, character, etc., but not exactly the same: *a soft cheese similar to Brie.* **2** (of geometrical figures) having the same angles and proportions, though of different sizes. ■ **sim·i·lar·i·ty** n. (pl. **similarities**) **sim·i·lar·ly** adv.

> **USAGE**
> It is not good English to say **similar as** (*I've had similar problems as yourself*); use **similar to** instead (*I've had problems similar to yours*).

sim·i·le /'siməlē/ ▶ n. a figure of speech in which one thing is compared to another of a different kind (e.g., *our team was solid as a rock*).

si·mil·i·tude /si'milə,t(y)ood/ ▶ n. the quality or state of being similar.

SIMM /sim/ ▶ abbr. Computing single inline memory module.

sim·mer /'simər/ ▶ v. **1** stay or keep just below boiling point while bubbling gently. **2** be filled with anger or another strong emotion that is only just kept under control. **3** (**simmer down**) become calmer and quieter. ▶ n. a state or temperature just below boiling point.

si·mo·ny /'sīmənē, 'si-/ ▶ n. chiefly historical the buying or selling of pardons and other Church privileges.

sim·pa·ti·co /sim'päti,kō/ ▶ adj. (of a person) likable and easy to get along with; having or characterized by shared attributes or interests.

sim·per /'simpər/ ▶ v. smile in a coy or affected way. ▶ n. a coy or affected smile. ■ **sim·per·ing** adj.

sim·ple /'simpəl/ ▶ adj. (**simpler**, **simplest**) **1** easily understood or done. **2** plain and basic or uncomplicated in form, nature, or design: *a simple white blouse.* **3** of low or ordinary status: *she's a simple country girl.* **4** of very low intelligence. **5** consisting of a single element; not compound. **6** (of interest) payable on the sum loaned only. Compare with **COMPOUND**[1]. **7** (of a leaf or stem) not divided. ▶ n. chiefly historical an herb with healing properties, or a medicine made from one. ■ **sim·ple·ness** n.

sim·ple frac·ture ▶ n. an injury in which a broken bone does not pierce the skin.

sim·ple·mind·ed /'simpəl'mīndid/ ▶ adj. having or showing very little intelligence or judgment. ■ **sim·ple·mind·ed·ly** adv. **sim·ple·mind·ed·ness** n.

sim·ple·ton /'simpəltən/ ▶ n. a foolish or unintelligent person.

sim·plex /'simpleks/ ▶ adj. technical made up of a single part or structure.

sim·plic·i·ty /sim'plisitē/ ▶ n. the quality or condition of being simple.

sim·pli·fy /'simplə,fī/ ▶ v. (**simplifies**, **simplifying**, **simplified**) make something easier to use or understand. ■ **sim·pli·fi·ca·tion** /,simpləfi'kāsHən/ n.

sim·plis·tic /sim'plistik/ ▶ adj. treating complex issues and problems as simpler than they really are. ■ **sim·plis·ti·cal·ly** adv.

sim·ply /'simplē/ ▶ adv. **1** in a simple way. **2** merely; just. **3** absolutely; completely.

sim·u·la·crum /,simyə'läkrəm, -'lak-/ ▶ n. (pl. **simulacra** /-'läkrə, -'lakrə/ or **simulacrums**) **1** an image or representation of someone or something. **2** an unsatisfactory copy or substitute.

sim·u·late /'simyə,lāt/ ▶ v. **1** imitate the appearance or nature of: *red ocher intended to simulate blood.* **2** use a computer to create conditions resembling those in real life. **3** pretend to feel an emotion. ■ **sim·u·la·tion** /,simyə'lāsHən/ n.

sim·u·la·tor /'simyə,lātər/ ▶ n. a machine that imitates the controls and conditions of a real vehicle, process, etc., used for training or testing.

sim·ul·cast /'sīməl,kast/ ▶ n. a broadcast of the same program on radio and television at the same time, or on two or more channels at the same time. ▶ v. broadcast a program in this way.

si·mul·ta·ne·ous /,sīməl'tānēəs/ ▶ adj. happening, operating, or done at the same time. ■ **si·mul·ta·ne·i·ty** /,sīməltə'nēitē/ n. **si·mul·ta·ne·ous·ly** adv.

si·mul·ta·ne·ous e·qua·tions ▶ pl.n. equations involving two or more unknowns that are to have the same values in each equation.

sin[1] /sin/ ▶ n. **1** an act considered to break a religious or moral law. **2** an act regarded as a serious offense. ▶ v. (**sins**, **sinning**, **sinned**) commit a sin.
– PHRASES **live in sin** informal, dated (of an unmarried couple) live together.

sin[2] /sīn/ ▶ abbr. sine.

sin bin ▶ n. informal (in sports) a box or bench to which offending players can be sent as a penalty during a game.

since /sins/ ▶ prep. in the period between a time in the past and the present. ▶ conj. **1** during or in the time after. **2** for the reason that; because. ▶ adv. **1** from the time mentioned until the present. **2** ago.

sin·cere /sin'si(ə)r/ ▶ adj. (**sincerer**, **sincerest**) showing genuine feelings; free from deceit or pretense. ■ **sin·cere·ly** adv. **sin·cer·i·ty** /sin'seritē/ n.

sine /sīn/ ▶ n. (in a right triangle) the ratio of the side opposite a particular acute angle to the hypotenuse.

si·ne·cure /'sīnə,kyŏŏr, 'si-/ ▶ n. a position for which the holder is paid but which involves little or no work.

si·ne qua non /,sinē ,kwä 'nōn, ,sinī ,kwä 'nän/ ▶ n. a thing that is absolutely essential.

sin·ew /'sinyoo/ ▶ n. a piece of tough fibrous tissue that joins muscle to bone; a tendon or ligament. ■ **sin·ew·y** adj.

sin·fo·ni·a /,sinfə'nēə/ ▶ n. **1** a symphony. **2** (in baroque music) an orchestral piece used as an introduction to an opera, cantata, or suite. **3** a small symphony orchestra.

sin·fo·niet·ta /,sinfən'yetə/ ▶ n. Music **1** a short or simple symphony. **2** a small symphony orchestra.

sin·ful /'sinfəl/ ▶ adj. **1** wicked and immoral. **2** disgraceful: *a sinful waste.* ■ **sin·ful·ly** adv. **sin·ful·ness** n.

sing /sing/ ▶ v. (past **sang**; past part. **sung**) **1** make musical sounds with the voice in the form of a song or tune. **2** (of a bird) make characteristic tuneful whistling and twittering sounds. **3** make a high-pitched whistling sound. ■ **sing·a·ble** adj. **sing·er** n.
– PHRASES **sing the praises of** express enthusiastic approval or admiration of.

sing. ▶ abbr. singular.

sing·a·long /'sinGə,lông, 'sinGə,läng/ ▶ n. an informal occasion when people sing together in a group.

Sin·ga·po·re·an /ˌsiNGə'pôrēən/ ▶ n. a person from Singapore. ▶ adj. relating to Singapore.

singe /sinj/ ▶ v. (**singes, singeing, singed**) burn the surface of something lightly. ▶ n. a slight burn.

Sin·gha·lese /ˌsiNGGə'lēz, -'lēs/ ▶ n. & adj. variant spelling of SINHALESE.

sin·gle /'siNGGəl/ ▶ adj. **1** only one; not one of several. **2** designed or suitable for one person: *a single bed*. **3** consisting of one part. **4** not involved in an established romantic or sexual relationship. **5** regarded as distinct or separate from others in a group: *alcohol is the single most important cause of violence*. **6** even one: *they didn't receive a single reply*. ▶ n. **1** a single person or thing. **2** a short record or CD featuring one main song. **3** (**singles**) a game or competition for individual players. ▶ v. (**single someone/thing out**) choose someone or something from a group for special treatment. ■ **sin·gle·ness** n. **sin·gly** adv.

sin·gle bond ▶ n. a chemical bond in which one pair of electrons is shared between two atoms.

sin·gle-breast·ed ▶ adj. (of a jacket or coat) fastened by one row of buttons at the center of the front.

sin·gle com·bat ▶ n. fighting between two people.

sin·gle cur·ren·cy ▶ n. **1** a currency used by all the members of an economic federation. **2** (also **single European currency**) the currency (the euro) that replaced the national currencies of twelve member countries of the European Union in 2002.

sin·gle file ▶ n. a line of people or things arranged one behind another.

sin·gle-hand·ed ▶ adv. & adj. done without help from other people. ■ **sin·gle-hand·ed·ly** adv.

sin·gle-lens re·flex ▶ adj. referring to a reflex camera in which the lens that forms the image on the film also provides the image in the viewfinder.

sin·gle malt ▶ n. malt whiskey that has been produced by one distillery and is not blended with any other malt whiskey.

sin·gle mar·ket ▶ n. an association of countries that have few or no restrictions on the movement of goods, money, or people within the association.

sin·gle-mind·ed ▶ adj. concentrating with determination on one particular aim. ■ **sin·gle-mind·ed·ly** adv. **sin·gle-mind·ed·ness** n.

sin·gle par·ent ▶ n. a person bringing up a child or children without a partner.

sin·gle·ton /'siNGGəltən/ ▶ n. **1** a single person or thing of the kind under consideration. **2** informal a person who is not in a long-term relationship. **3** (in card games) a card that is the only one of its suit in a hand.

sin·gle trans·fer·a·ble vote ▶ n. an electoral system of proportional representation in which a person's vote can be transferred to a further choice of candidate.

sing·song /'siNG,sôNG/ ▶ adj. (of a person's voice) having a repeated rising and falling rhythm.

sin·gu·lar /'siNGgyələr/ ▶ adj. **1** Grammar (of a word or form) referring to just one person or thing. **2** very good or great; remarkable. **3** strange or eccentric. ▶ n. Grammar the singular form of a word. ■ **sin·gu·lar·ly** adv.

sin·gu·lar·i·ty /ˌsiNGgyə'laritē/ ▶ n. (pl. **singularities**) the state, fact, quality, or condition of being singular; a peculiarity or odd trait.

Sin·ha·lese /ˌsinhə'lēz, -'lēs/ (also **Singhalese** /ˌsiNGGə-/, **Sinhala** /'sinhələ/) ▶ n. (pl. same) **1** a member of an Indian people now forming the majority of the population of Sri Lanka. **2** the language spoken by the Sinhalese. ▶ adj. relating to the Sinhalese.

sin·is·ter /'sinistər/ ▶ adj. **1** giving the impression that something harmful or evil will happen or is happening: *a dark building with a sinister air*. **2** old use & Heraldry on or toward the bearer's left-hand side of a coat of arms. The opposite of DEXTER. ■ **sin·is·ter·ly** adv.

sink¹ /siNGk/ ▶ v. (past **sank** /saNGk/ or **sunk** /səNGk/; past part. **sunk**) **1** go down below the surface of liquid. **2** (with reference to a ship) go or cause to go to the bottom of the sea. **3** drop downward. **4** lower oneself or drop down gently: *she sank back onto her pillow*. **5** gradually decrease in amount or intensity. **6** (**sink in**) (of words or facts) become fully understood or realized. **7** (**sink something into**) force something sharp through a surface: *the dog sank its teeth into her arm*. **8** insert something beneath a surface. **9** pass into a particular state or condition: *she sank into sleep*. **10** (**sink something in/into**) put money or resources into.
– PHRASES **a sinking feeling** an unpleasant feeling caused by the realization that something unpleasant or undesirable has happened or will happen. **sink or swim** fail or succeed by one's own efforts.

sink² ▶ n. **1** a fixed basin with a water supply and outflow pipe. **2** a sinkhole.

sink·er /'siNGkər/ ▶ n. a weight used to keep a fishing line beneath the water.

sink·hole /'siNGk,hōl/ ▶ n. a cavity in the ground caused by water erosion and providing a route for surface water to disappear underground.

sink·ing fund ▶ n. a fund formed by regularly setting aside money in order to pay off a particular debt.

sin·ner /'sinər/ ▶ n. a person who sins.

Sino- /'sīnō/ ▶ comb. form Chinese; Chinese and ...: *Sino-American*.

si·nol·o·gy /sī'näləjē/ ▶ n. the study of Chinese language, history, and culture. ■ **si·nol·o·gist** n.

sin·ter /'sin(t)ər/ ▶ n. a hard substance that is deposited from mineral springs. ▶ v. make a powdered material form a solid mass by heating and compressing it.

sin·u·ous /'sinyōoəs/ ▶ adj. **1** having many curves and turns. **2** lithe and supple. ■ **sin·u·os·i·ty** /ˌsinyōo'äsitē/ n. **sin·u·ous·ly** adv.

si·nus /'sīnəs/ ▶ n. a hollow space within a bone or other tissue, especially one in the bones of the face or skull that connects with the inside of the nose.

si·nus·i·tis /ˌsīnə'sītis/ ▶ n. inflammation of a sinus that connects with the inside of the nose.

Sioux /sōō/ ▶ n. (pl. same) a member of a North American Indian people of the northern Mississippi valley area.

sip /sip/ ▶ v. (**sips, sipping, sipped**) drink something by taking small mouthfuls. ▶ n. a small mouthful of liquid. ■ **sip·per** n.

si·phon /'sīfən/ (also **syphon**) ▶ n. a tube used to convey liquid upward from a container and then down to a lower level, using the different fluid pressures at the tube openings to maintain the flow. ▶v. **1** draw off or convey liquid by means of a siphon. **2** take small amounts of money from a source over a period of time, especially illicitly. ∎ **si·phon·age** /-nij/ n. **si·phon·ic** /sī'fänik/ adj.

sir /sər/ (also **Sir**) ▶n. **1** a polite form of address to a man. **2** used to address a man at the beginning of a formal letter. **3** used as a title before the first name of a knight or baronet.

sire /sīr/ ▶n. **1** the male parent of an animal. **2** literary a father or other male ancestor. **3** old use a respectful form of address to someone of high social status, especially a king. ▶v. **1** be the male parent of an animal. **2** literary be the father of a child.

si·ren /'sīrən/ ▶n. **1** a device that makes a long, loud signal or warning sound. **2** Greek Mythology each of a group of female creatures whose singing lured unwary sailors onto rocks. **3** a woman whose sexual attractiveness is regarded as dangerous to men.

sir·loin /'sərloin/ ▶n. good-quality beef cut from the upper part of the loin.

si·roc·co /sə'räkō/ ▶n. (pl. **siroccos**) a hot wind blowing from North Africa to southern Europe.

sis /sis/ ▶n. informal sister.

si·sal /'sīsəl, 'sī-/ ▶n. fiber made from the leaves of a tropical Mexican plant, used especially for ropes or matting.

sis·sy /'sisē/ (also **cissy**) informal ▶n. (pl. **sissies**) a weak or effeminate person. ▶adj. (**sissier**, **sissiest**) weak or effeminate. ∎ **sis·si·fied** /'sisə,fīd/ adj.

sis·ter /'sistər/ ▶n. **1** a woman or girl in relation to other children of her parents. **2** a female friend or fellow member of a group or organization. **3** (often **Sister**) a member of a religious order of women. **4** (often **Sister**) Brit. a senior female nurse. ▶adj. belonging to the same group or type as something else: *a sister company.* ∎ **sis·ter·ly** adj.

sis·ter·hood /'sistər,hood/ ▶n. **1** the relationship between sisters. **2** a feeling of closeness and loyalty to a group of women or all women. **3** a group of women linked by a shared interest, belief, trade, etc.

sis·ter-in-law ▶n. (pl. **sisters-in-law**) **1** the sister of one's wife or husband. **2** the wife of one's brother or brother-in-law.

Sis·y·phe·an /,sisə'fēən/ ▶adj. (of a task) unending.

sit /sit/ ▶v. (**sits, sitting**; past and past part. **sat**) **1** be or put in a position in which one's weight is supported by one's buttocks and one's back is upright. **2** be or remain in a particular position or state: *the fridge was sitting in a pool of water.* **3** (of an animal) rest with the hind legs bent and the body close to the ground. **4** (of a legislature, committee, or court of law) be carrying on its business. **5** serve as a member of a council, jury, or other official body. **6** (of a table or room) have enough seats for: *the dining room sat 200 people.* **7** (**sit for**) pose for an artist or photographer. ▶n. a period of sitting.
– PHRASES **sit in for** temporarily carry out someone else's duties. **sit something out** not take part in something. **sit tight** informal **1** remain firmly in one's place. **2** hold back from taking action.

si·tar /si'tär/ ▶n. a large Indian lute with a long neck. ∎ **si·tar·ist** n.

sit·com /'sit,käm/ ▶n. a television or radio series in which the same set of characters are involved in amusing situations.

sit-down ▶adj. **1** (of a meal) eaten sitting at a table. **2** (of a protest) in which demonstrators occupy their workplace or sit down on the ground in a public place. ▶n. a period of sitting down.

site /sīt/ ▶n. **1** an area of ground on which something is or will be located. **2** a place where a particular event or activity is happening or has happened. **3** a website. ▶v. build or locate something in a particular place.

> **USAGE**
> Do not confuse **site** and **sight**. As a noun, **site** means 'a place where something is located or has happened' (*the site of the battle*), while **sight** chiefly means 'the ability to see' (*he lost his sight as a baby*).

sit-in ▶n. a form of protest in which demonstrators occupy a place until their demands are met.

Sit·ka /'sitkə/ ▶n. a fast-growing North American spruce tree, grown for its strong lightweight wood.

sit·ter /'sitər/ ▶n. **1** a person who poses for an artist or photographer. **2** a person who looks after children, pets, or a house while the parents or owners are away.

sit·ting /'sitiNG/ ▶n. **1** a period of being seated. **2** a period of time when a group of people are served a meal. **3** a period of time during which a committee, parliament, or court of law is carrying out its normal business. ▶adj. **1** in a seated position. **2** (of an elected representative) currently present or in office.

sit·ting duck ▶n. informal a person or thing with no protection against attack.

sit·ting room ▶n. a room for sitting and relaxing in.

sit·u·ate /'sicHoō,āt/ ▶v. **1** put in a particular place or context. **2** (**be situated**) be in a particular situation or set of circumstances: *she is now comfortably situated.*

sit·u·a·tion /,sicHoō'āsHən/ ▶n. **1** a set of circumstances that exist at a particular time and in a particular place: *the political situation in Russia.* **2** the location and surroundings of a place. **3** formal a job. ∎ **sit·u·a·tion·al** adj.

sit·u·a·tion com·e·dy ▶n. full form of **sitcom**.

sit·u·a·tion·ism /,sicHoō'āsHə,nizəm/ ▶n. a radical cultural and political movement of the mid 20th century that rejected conventional politics and aimed to transform attitudes to all aspects of everyday life. ∎ **sit·u·a·tion·ist** n. & adj.

sit-up ▶n. an exercise designed to strengthen the abdominal muscles, in which a person sits up from a horizontal position without using the arms.

sitz bath /sits/ ▶n. a bath in which only the buttocks and hips are immersed in water.

six /siks/ ▶cardinal number one more than five; 6. (Roman numeral: **vi** or **VI.**) ∎ **six·fold** /'siks,fōld/ adj. & adv.
– PHRASES **at sixes and sevens** in a state of confusion or disorganization. **six of one, (and) half a dozen of the other** a situation in which there is not much difference between two alternatives.

six-gun ▶n. another term for **six-shooter**.

six-pack ▶n. **1** a pack of six cans of beer. **2** informal a man's set of well-developed abdominal muscles.

six·pence /'siks,pens, -pəns/ ▶ n. Brit. a small coin worth six old pence (2½ p), withdrawn in 1980.

six-shoot·er ▶ n. a revolver with six chambers.

six·teen /sik'stēn, 'sik,stēn/ ▶ cardinal number one more than fifteen; 16. (Roman numeral: **xvi** or **XVI**.) ■ **six·teenth** /sik'stēnTH, 'sik,stēnTH/ ordinal number.

six·teenth note ▶ n. a musical note having the time value of a sixteenth of a whole note or half an eighth note, represented by a solid dot with a two-hooked stem.

sixth /siksTH/ ▶ ordinal number **1** that is number six in a sequence; 6th. **2** (**a sixth**/**one sixth**) each of six equal parts into which something is divided. **3** a musical interval spanning six consecutive notes in a scale.

sixth sense ▶ n. a supposed ability to know things by intuition or instinct rather than by sight, smell, hearing, etc.

six·ty /'sikstē/ ▶ cardinal number (pl. **sixties**) ten more than fifty; 60. (Roman numeral: **lx** or **LX**.) ■ **six·ti·eth** /-iTH/ ordinal number.

six·ty-four thou·sand dol·lar ques·tion (usually **$64,000 question**) ▶ n. informal something that is not known and on which a great deal depends.

siz·a·ble /'sīzəbəl/ (also **sizeable**) ▶ adj. fairly large.

size[1] /sīz/ ▶ n. **1** the overall measurements or extent of something. **2** each of a series of standard measurements in which articles are made or sold. ▶ v. **1** group or sort items according to their size. **2** (**size someone**/**thing up**) form a judgment of someone or something. ■ **sized** adj.

size[2] ▶ n. a sticky solution used to glaze paper, stiffen textiles, and prepare plastered walls for papering. ▶ v. treat something with size.

size·ism /'sīz,izəm/ ▶ n. prejudice or discrimination against people on the grounds of their size. ■ **size·ist** adj.

siz·zle /'sizəl/ ▶ v. **1** (of food) make a hissing sound when frying or roasting. **2** (as adj. **sizzling**) informal very hot or exciting. ▶ n. the sound of food sizzling. ■ **siz·zler** n.

SK ▶ abbr. Saskatchewan.

ska /skä/ ▶ n. a style of fast popular music originating in Jamaica in the 1960s.

skank /skaNGk/ ▶ n. a dance performed to reggae music, characterized by rhythmically bending forward, raising the knees, and extending the hands palms-downward. ▶ v. play reggae music or dance in this style.

skank·y /'skaNGkē/ ▶ adj. informal very unpleasant.

skate[1] /skāt/ ▶ n. an ice skate or roller skate. ▶ v. **1** glide on ice skates or roller skates. **2** ride on a skateboard. **3** (**skate over**/**around**) pass over or refer only briefly to a subject or problem. ■ **skat·er** n. **skat·ing** n.

skate[2] ▶ n. (pl. same or **skates**) an edible sea fish with a flattened diamond-shaped body.

skate·board /'skāt,bôrd/ ▶ n. a short, narrow board with two small wheels fixed to the bottom of either end, on which a person can ride. ▶ v. ride on a skateboard. ■ **skate·board·er** n. **skate·board·ing** n.

skate·park /'skāt,pärk/ ▶ n. an area set aside and equipped for skateboarding.

ske·dad·dle /ski'dadl/ ▶ v. informal leave hurriedly.

skeet /skēt/ (also **skeet shooting**) ▶ n. a shooting sport in which a clay target is thrown from a trap.

skein /skān/ ▶ n. **1** a length of thread or yarn, loosely coiled and knotted. **2** a flock of wild geese or swans in flight.

skel·e·tal /'skelətl/ ▶ adj. **1** relating to a skeleton. **2** extremely thin. **3** existing only in outline or as a framework: *a skeletal plot for a novel.* ■ **skel·e·tal·ly** adv.

skel·e·ton /'skelitn/ ▶ n. **1** a framework of bone, cartilage, or other rigid material supporting or containing the body of an animal. **2** a supporting framework or basic structure: *the concrete skeleton of an unfinished building.* ▶ adj. referring to an essential or minimum number of people or things: *a skeleton staff.* ■ **skel·e·ton·ize** /-,īz/ v. – PHRASES **skeleton in the closet** an embarrassing or shocking fact that someone wishes to keep secret.

skel·e·ton key ▶ n. a key designed to fit many locks.

skep·tic /'skeptik/ (Brit. **sceptic**) ▶ n. **1** a person who tends to question or doubt accepted opinions. **2** a person who doubts the truth of Christianity and other religions; an atheist. ■ **skep·ti·cism** /'skeptə,sizəm/ n.

> **USAGE**
> Do not confuse **skeptic** with **septic**. See the note at SEPTIC.

skep·ti·cal /'skeptikəl/ ▶ adj. not easily convinced; having doubts. ■ **skep·ti·cal·ly** /-ik(ə)lē/ adv.

sketch /skecH/ ▶ n. **1** a rough or unfinished drawing or painting. **2** a short, funny, self-contained scene in a comedy show. **3** a brief written or spoken account or description of something. ▶ v. **1** make a sketch of someone or something. **2** give a brief account or description of: *he sketched out his business plan.* ■ **sketch·er** n.

sketch·book /'skecH,bŏŏk/ (also **sketch pad**) ▶ n. a pad of drawing paper for sketching on.

sketch·y /'skecHē/ ▶ adj. (**sketchier, sketchiest**) not thorough or detailed. ■ **sketch·i·ly** adv. **sketch·i·ness** n.

skew /skyōō/ ▶ v. **1** suddenly change direction or move at an angle. **2** change or influence something so that it is not accurate, normal, or fair. ▶ n. **1** a slant. **2** a bias toward one particular group or subject: *the paper had a working-class skew.* ■ **skew·ness** n.

skew·bald /'skyōō,bôld/ ▶ adj. (of a horse) with irregular patches of white and another color, typically a shade of brown. ▶ n. a skewbald horse.

skew·er /'skyōōər/ ▶ n. a long piece of wood or metal used for holding pieces of food together during cooking. ▶ v. hold something in place or pierce something with a skewer or other pointed object.

ski /skē/ ▶ n. (pl. **skis**) **1** each of a pair of long, narrow pieces of wood, metal, or plastic attached to boots for traveling over snow. **2** a similar device attached beneath a vehicle or aircraft. ▶ v. (**skis, skiing, skied**) travel over snow on skis. ■ **ski·a·ble** adj. **ski·er** n. **ski·ing** n.

skid /skid/ ▶ v. (**skids, skidding, skidded**) **1** (of a vehicle) slide sideways on slippery ground or as a result of stopping or turning too quickly. **2** slip

or slide. ▶ n. **1** an act of skidding. **2** a runner attached to the underside of an aircraft for use when landing on snow or grass. **3** a braking device consisting of a wooden or metal shoe that prevents a wheel from revolving.
– PHRASES **hit the skids** informal begin a rapid decline. **on the skids** informal in a bad state; failing.

skid row /rō/ ▶ n. informal a run-down part of a town inhabited by homeless people, drug addicts, and alcoholics.

skiff /skif/ ▶ n. a light rowboat, usually for one person.

ski jump ▶ n. a steep slope leveling off before a sharp drop to allow a skier to leap through the air.

ski lift ▶ n. a system used to carry skiers up a slope to the top of a run, consisting of moving seats attached to an overhead cable.

skill /skil/ ▶ n. **1** the ability to do something well. **2** a particular ability: *practical skills such as cooking.*

skilled /skild/ ▶ adj. **1** having or showing skill. **2** (of work) requiring special skills.

skil·let /'skilit/ ▶ n. a frying pan.

skill·ful /'skilfəl/ (Brit. **skilful**) ▶ adj. having or showing skill. ■ **skill·ful·ly** adv. **skill·ful·ness** n.

skill set ▶ n. a person's range of skills or abilities.

skim /skim/ ▶ v. (**skims, skimming, skimmed**) **1** remove a substance from the surface of a liquid. **2** move quickly and lightly over or on a surface or through the air. **3** read through something quickly, noting only the important points. **4** (**skim over**) deal with a subject briefly or superficially. **5** throw a flat stone so that it bounces several times on the surface of water. **6** (usu. as n. **skimming**) fraudulently copy credit or debit card details with an electronic device.

ski mask ▶ n. a protective covering for the head and face, with holes for the eyes, nose, and mouth.

skim·mer /'skimər/ ▶ n. **1** a utensil, device, or craft for removing a substance from the surface of water or other liquid. **2** a vessel such as a hydroplane that has little or no displacement when traveling. **3** a long-winged seabird that feeds by flying low with the lower half of its beak skimming through the water. **4** a flat, broad-brimmed straw hat. **5** informal a fitted dress, often sleeveless and with a flared skirt. **6** a broad-bodied dragonfly found at ponds and swamps.

skim milk (also **skimmed milk**) ▶ n. milk from which the cream has been removed.

skimp /skimp/ ▶ v. spend less money or use less of something than is really necessary in an attempt to economize: *don't skimp on vacation insurance.*

skimp·y /'skimpē/ ▶ adj. (**skimpier, skimpiest**) **1** providing or consisting of less than is necessary; meager. **2** (of clothes) small and not covering much of the body.

skin /skin/ ▶ n. **1** the thin layer of tissue forming the natural outer covering of the body of a person or animal. **2** the skin of a dead animal used as material for clothing or other items. **3** the peel or outer layer of a fruit or vegetable. **4** an outer layer. ▶ adj. informal referring to pornography: *the skin trade.* ▶ v. (**skins, skinning, skinned**) **1** remove the skin from

something. **2** graze a part of one's body. ■ **skin·less** adj.
– PHRASES **by the skin of one's teeth** by a very narrow margin; only just. **get under someone's skin** informal annoy someone greatly. **have a thick** (or **thin**) **skin** be insensitive (or oversensitive) to criticism or insults. **have skin in the game** informal have a personal investment in an organization or undertaking and therefore a vested interest in its success. **it's no skin off my** (or **his**, etc.) **nose** someone is not annoyed or upset about something.

skin·care /'skin,ke(ə)r/ ▶ n. the use of cosmetics to care for the skin.

skin-deep ▶ adj. not deep or lasting; superficial.

skin-div·ing ▶ n. the activity of swimming under water without a diving suit, typically using scuba equipment and flippers. ■ **skin-div·er** n.

skin flick (also **skinflick**) ▶ n. informal a pornographic movie.

skin·flint /'skin,flint/ ▶ n. informal a very miserly person.

skin·head /'skin,hed/ ▶ n. a young man of a group with close-cropped hair, especially one who is aggressive and openly racist.

skin·ny /'skinē/ ▶ adj. (**skinnier, skinniest**) **1** very thin. **2** (of a piece of clothing) tight-fitting. ■ **skin·ni·ness** n.

skin·ny-dip ▶ v. informal swim naked.

skin test ▶ n. a test to discover whether an immune reaction occurs when a substance is applied to or injected into the skin.

skin·tight /'skin'tīt/ ▶ adj. (of a piece of clothing) very close-fitting.

skip /skip/ ▶ v. (**skips, skipping, skipped**) **1** move along lightly, stepping from one foot to the other with a little jump. **2** jump repeatedly over a rope that is held at both ends and turned over the head and under the feet. **3** leave out or move quickly over a section of something being read or watched. **4** not have or do something that one should have or do: *try not to skip breakfast.* ▶ n. a skipping movement.

ski pants ▶ pl.n. women's stretch pants with tapering legs and an elastic stirrup under each foot.

skip·jack /'skip,jak/ ▶ n. (also **skipjack tuna**) a small tuna with dark horizontal stripes.

ski pole ▶ n. either of two lightweight poles held by a skier to help them balance or move along.

skip·per /'skipər/ informal ▶ n. **1** the captain of a ship, boat, or aircraft. **2** the captain of a sports team. ▶ v. be the captain of a ship, boat, aircraft, or sports team.

skirl /skərl/ ▶ n. a shrill sound, especially that made by bagpipes. ▶ v. (of bagpipes) make a shrill sound.

skir·mish /'skərmish/ ▶ n. a brief period of unplanned fighting. ▶ v. take part in a skirmish. ■ **skir·mish·er** n.

skirt /skərt/ ▶ n. **1** a woman's outer garment that hangs from the waist and covers part or all of the legs. **2** the part of a coat or dress that hangs below the waist. **3** a surface that conceals or protects the wheels or underside of a vehicle or aircraft. **4** dated, informal women regarded as sexually desirable. ▶ v. (also **skirt around**) **1** go around or past the edge of something. **2** avoid dealing with: *they are both skirting the issue.*

skirt·ing /'skərting/ (also **skirting board**) ▶ n. chiefly Brit. a baseboard.

skit /skit/ ▶ n. a short comedy sketch or piece of humorous writing, especially one that makes fun of someone or something by imitating them.

skit·ter /'skitər/ ▶ v. move lightly and quickly.

skit·ter·y /'skitərē/ ▶ adj. restless; skittish.

skit·tish /'skitisH/ ▶ adj. 1 (of a horse) excitable or easily frightened and therefore difficult to control. 2 playful and unpredictable. ■ **skit·tish·ly** adv. **skit·tish·ness** n.

skit·tle /'skitl/ ▶ n. 1 (**skittles**) (treated as sing.) a game played with wooden pins set up at the end of an alley to be bowled down with a wooden ball. 2 a pin used in the game of skittles. 3 (also **table skittles**) a game played with similar pins set up on a board to be knocked down by swinging a suspended ball.

skiv·vies /'skivēz/ ▶ pl. n. trademark an undershirt and underpants as a set, or just the underpants.

sku·a /'skyo͞oə/ ▶ n. a large predatory seabird that pursues other birds to make them regurgitate fish.

skul·dug·ger·y /skəl'dəgərē/ (also **skullduggery**) ▶ n. underhanded or dishonest behavior.

skulk /skəlk/ ▶ v. hide or move around in a stealthy or furtive way. ■ **skulk·er** n.

skull /skəl/ ▶ n. 1 the bone framework that surrounds and protects the brain of a person or animal. 2 informal a person's head or brain.
– PHRASES **skull and crossbones** a representation of a skull with two thigh bones crossed below it, used formerly by pirates and now as a warning symbol.

skull·cap /'skəl,kap/ ▶ n. a small close-fitting cap without a peak.

skunk /skəNGk/ ▶ n. a black-and-white striped American mammal able to spray foul-smelling liquid at attackers.

sky /skī/ ▶ n. (pl. **skies**) 1 the region of the upper atmosphere seen from the earth. 2 literary heaven. ▶ v. (**skies**, **skying**, **skied**) informal hit a ball high into the air. ■ **sky·ward** /'skīwərd/ adj. & adv. **sky·wards** /'skīwərdz/ adv.
– PHRASES **the sky is the limit** there is practically no limit.

sky blue ▶ n. a bright, clear blue.

sky·box /'skī,bäks/ ▶ n. a luxurious enclosed seating area located high in a sports arena.

sky·cap /'skī,kap/ ▶ n. a porter at an airport.

sky·div·ing /'skī,dīviNG/ ▶ n. the sport of jumping from an aircraft and performing acrobatic maneuvers in the air before landing by parachute. ■ **sky·div·er** n.

sky-high ▶ adv. & adj. very high.

sky·lark /'skī,lärk/ ▶ n. a common Old World lark that sings while rising slowly high into the air. ▶ v. behave in a playful or mischievous way.

sky·light /'skī,līt/ ▶ n. a window set in a roof or ceiling.

sky·line /'skī,līn/ ▶ n. an outline of land and buildings seen against the sky.

sky·rock·et /'skī,räkit/ ▶ v. (**skyrockets**, **skyrocketing**, **skyrocketed**) informal (of a price or amount) increase very quickly.

sky·scrap·er /'skī,skrāpər/ ▶ n. a very tall building.

sky·walk /'skī,wôk/ ▶ n. an enclosed overhead walkway between buildings.

sky·way /'skī,wā/ ▶ n. 1 a route used by aircraft. 2 (also **skywalk** /'skī,wôk/) a covered overhead walkway between buildings.

slab /slab/ ▶ n. 1 a large, thick, flat piece of stone, concrete, or other hard material. 2 a thick slice or piece of food.

slack /slak/ ▶ adj. 1 not taut or held tightly in position; loose. 2 (of business or trade) not busy; quiet. 3 careless or lazy: *slack accounting procedures.* 4 (of a tide) neither ebbing nor flowing. ▶ n. 1 the part of a rope or line that is not held taut. 2 (**slacks**) casual trousers. ▶ v. 1 make slower or less intense: *the horse slacked his pace.* 2 (**slack off/up**) become slower or less intense. ■ **slack·en** v. **slack·ly** adv. **slack·ness** n.
– PHRASES **take** (or **pick**) **up the slack** 1 improve the use of resources in a business. 2 pull on the loose part of a rope to make it taut.

slack·er /'slakər/ ▶ n. informal a person who is lazy and avoids work.

slack wa·ter ▶ n. the state of the tide when it is turning.

slag /slag/ ▶ n. stony waste matter that is left when metal has been separated from ore by smelting or refining.

slag heap ▶ n. a large pile of waste material from a mine or industrial site.

slain /slān/ ▶ past participle of SLAY.

slake /slāk/ ▶ v. satisfy a desire, one's thirst, etc.

slaked lime ▶ n. calcium hydroxide, a soluble substance produced by combining quicklime with water.

sla·lom /'släləm/ ▶ n. a skiing, canoeing, or sailing race following a winding course marked out by poles. ▶ v. move or race in a winding path, avoiding obstacles.

slam¹ /slam/ ▶ v. (**slams, slamming, slammed**) 1 shut something forcefully and loudly. 2 push, put, or hit with great force: *she slammed down the phone.* 3 put into action suddenly or forcefully: *I slammed on the brakes.* 4 informal criticize someone or something severely. ▶ n. a loud bang caused by the forceful shutting of something. ▶ adv. (also **slam bang**) informal suddenly and forcefully.

slam² ▶ n. Bridge the bidding and winning of a grand slam (all thirteen tricks) or a small slam (twelve tricks).

slam-dance ▶ v. a form of dancing to rock music in which the dancers deliberately collide with one another.

slam dunk ▶ n. 1 Basketball a shot thrust down through the basket. 2 informal a foregone conclusion or certainty. ▶ v. (**slam-dunk**) Basketball thrust the ball down through the basket.

slam·mer /'slamər/ ▶ n. 1 informal prison. 2 (also **tequila slammer**) a cocktail made with tequila and champagne or another fizzy drink, which is covered, slammed on the table, and then drunk in one swallow.

slan·der /'slandər/ ▶ n. 1 the action or crime of making untrue statements that damage a person's reputation. Compare with LIBEL. 2 a statement of this kind. ▶ v. make untrue and damaging statements about someone. ■ **slan·der·er** n. **slan·der·ous** adj.

slang /slaNG/ ▶ n. very informal words and phrases that are more common in speech than in writing and are used by a particular group of people. ■ **slang·y** adj.

slant /slant/ ▶ v. 1 slope or lean in a particular direction. 2 present information from a

particular angle, especially in an unfair way.
▶ n. **1** a sloping position. **2** a point of view: *a new slant on science.* ▶ adj. at an angle; sloping.
■ **slant·wise** /'slant,wīz/ adj. & adv.

slant top desk ▶ n. a writing desk with drawers and a sloping top that opens downward to form a writing surface.

slap /slap/ ▶ v. (**slaps, slapping, slapped**) **1** hit someone or something with the palm of the hand or a flat object. **2** hit against something with a slapping sound. **3** (**slap something on**) put something on a surface quickly, carelessly, or forcefully. **4** (**slap something on**) informal impose a fine or other penalty on. ▶ n. a blow with the palm of the hand.
– PHRASES **slap in the face** an unexpected rejection. **slap on the back** an instance of congratulating or praising someone. **slap on the wrist** a mild reprimand.

slap·dash /'slap,dash/ ▶ adj. & adv. done too hurriedly and carelessly.

slap·hap·py /'slap,hapē/ (also **slap-happy**) ▶ adj. informal **1** casual or flippant in a cheerful and often irresponsible way. **2** (of an action or operation) unmethodical; poorly thought out. **3** dazed or stupefied from happiness or relief.

slap·stick /'slap,stik/ ▶ n. comedy based on deliberately clumsy actions and embarrassing events.

slash /slash/ ▶ v. **1** cut someone or something with a forceful sweeping movement. **2** informal reduce a price, quantity, or amount greatly.
▶ n. **1** a cut made with a sweeping stroke. **2** a bright patch or flash of color or light. **3** a slanting stroke (/) used chiefly between alternatives and in fractions and ratios. ■ **slash·er** n.

slash-and-burn ▶ adj. (of agriculture) in which vegetation is cut down and burned off before new seeds are sown.

slat /slat/ ▶ n. each of a series of thin, narrow pieces of wood or other material, arranged so as to overlap or fit into each other. ■ **slat·ted** adj.

slate /slāt/ ▶ n. **1** a gray, green, or bluish-purple rock easily split into smooth, flat plates, used as roofing material. **2** a plate of slate formerly used in schools for writing on. **3** a bluish-gray color. **4** a list of candidates for election to a post or office. ▶ v. **1** schedule or plan something. **2** cover a roof with slates. ■ **slat·er** n.

slath·er /'slaᴛʜər/ ▶ v. informal spread or smear a substance thickly or liberally.

slat·tern /'slatərn/ ▶ n. dated a dirty, untidy woman. ■ **slat·tern·ly** adj.

slaugh·ter /'slôtər/ ▶ n. **1** the killing of farm animals for food. **2** the killing of a large number of people in a cruel or violent way. ▶ v. **1** kill animals for food. **2** kill many people in a cruel or violent way. **3** informal defeat an opponent thoroughly. ■ **slaugh·ter·er** n.

slaugh·ter·house /'slôtər,hous/ ▶ n. a place where animals are killed for food.

Slav /släv/ ▶ n. a member of a group of peoples in central and eastern Europe who speak Slavic languages.

slave /slāv/ ▶ n. **1** a person who is the legal property of another and is forced to obey them. **2** a person who is strongly influenced by or controlled by something: *she was no slave to fashion.* ▶ v. work excessively hard.

slave driv·er ▶ n. informal a person who makes

others work very hard.

slave la·bor ▶ n. work that is demanding and very poorly paid.

slav·er[1] /'slāvər/ ▶ n. **1** a person dealing in or owning slaves. **2** a ship used for transporting slaves.

slav·er[2] /'slavər/ ▶ v. **1** let saliva run from the mouth. **2** show excessive desire or admiration: *the press corps is slavering over the idea of a real election battle.* ▶ n. saliva running from the mouth.

slav·er·y /'slāvərē/ ▶ n. **1** the state of being a slave. **2** the practice or system of owning slaves.

slave trade ▶ n. the buying, transporting, and selling of people, especially black Africans, as slaves.

Slav·ic /'slävik/ ▶ n. the group of languages that includes Russian, Polish, Czech, Bulgarian, and Serbo-Croat. ▶ adj. relating to Slavic or the Slavs.

slav·ish /'slāvish/ ▶ adj. **1** following or copying something without trying to be original: *he's a slavish follower of White House policy.* **2** obeying someone in a servile way. ■ **slav·ish·ly** adv.

Sla·von·ic /slə'vänik/ ▶ n. & adj. another term for **SLAVIC**.

slaw /slô/ ▶ n. coleslaw.

slay /slā/ ▶ v. (past **slew** /slo͞o/; past part. **slain** /slān/) **1** old use or literary kill a person or animal in a violent way. **2** murder someone. ■ **slay·er** n.

sleaze /slēz/ ▶ n. informal **1** immoral or dishonest behavior or activities, especially in politics or business. **2** a dishonest or immoral person.

slea·zy /'slēzē/ ▶ adj. (**sleazier, sleaziest**) **1** dishonest or immoral. **2** (of a place) dirty and seedy. ■ **slea·zi·ly** adv. **slea·zi·ness** n.

sled /sled/ ▶ n. a vehicle on runners for traveling over snow or ice, either pushed, pulled, or allowed to slide downhill. ▶ v. (**sleds, sledding, sledded**) ride on a sled.

sledge[1] /slej/ ▶ n. a sledgehammer.

sledge[2] chiefly Brit. ▶ n. & v. British term for **SLED**.

sledge·ham·mer /'slej,hamər/ ▶ n. a large, heavy hammer used for breaking rocks, driving in posts, etc. ▶ adj. very powerful, forceful, or unsubtle: *sledgehammer blows.*

sleek /slēk/ ▶ adj. **1** (of hair or fur) smooth and glossy. **2** wealthy and smart in appearance. **3** elegant and streamlined: *a sleek black car.* ▶ v. make hair smooth and glossy. ■ **sleek·ly** adv. **sleek·ness** n.

sleep /slēp/ ▶ n. **1** a state of rest in which the eyes are closed, the muscles are relaxed, the nervous system is inactive, and the mind is unconscious. **2** a gummy substance found in the corners of the eyes after sleep. ▶ v. (past and past part. **slept**) **1** be asleep. **2** (**sleep something off**) recover from something by going to sleep. **3** (**sleep in**) remain asleep or in bed later than usual in the morning. **4** provide a specified number of people with beds or bedrooms. **5** (**sleep with**) have sex or be in a sexual relationship with someone. **6** (**sleep around**) have many casual sexual partners. ■ **sleep·less** adj.
– PHRASES **put something to sleep** kill an animal painlessly.

sleep·er /'slēpər/ ▶ n. **1** a sleeping car or a train carrying sleeping cars. **2** a movie, book, or play that suddenly achieves success after first attracting little attention.

sleep·er cell ▶ n. a secretive group with

suspected links to a terrorist organization that is planning or believed capable of carrying out an attack.

sleep·ing bag ▶ n. a warm padded bag to sleep in, especially when camping.

sleep·ing car ▶ n. a railroad car provided with beds or berths.

sleep·ing pill ▶ n. a tablet of a drug that helps a person to sleep.

sleep·ing sick·ness ▶ n. a tropical disease transmitted by the bite of the tsetse fly, causing extreme tiredness.

sleep·o·ver /'slēp,ōvər/ ▶ n. a night spent by children or young people at a friend's house.

sleep·walk /'slēp,wôk/ ▶ v. walk around while asleep. ■ **sleep·walk·er** n.

sleep·y /'slēpē/ ▶ adj. (**sleepier, sleepiest**) 1 needing or ready for sleep. 2 (of a place) without much activity. ■ **sleep·i·ly** adv. **sleep·i·ness** n.

sleet /slēt/ ▶ n. rain containing some ice, or snow melting as it falls. ▶ v. (**it sleets, it is sleeting, it sleeted**) sleet falls. ■ **sleet·y** adj.

sleeve /slēv/ ▶ n. 1 the part of a piece of clothing that wholly or partly covers the arm. 2 a protective cover for a record. 3 a protective or connecting tube fitting over a rod, spindle, or smaller tube. ■ **sleeved** adj. **sleeve·less** adj.
– PHRASES **up one's sleeve** kept secret and ready for use when needed.

sleigh /slā/ ▶ n. a sled drawn by horses or reindeer. ■ **sleigh·ing** n.

sleigh bell ▶ n. a tinkling bell attached to the harness of a sleigh horse.

sleight /slīt/ ▶ n. (in phrase **sleight of hand**) 1 skillful use of the hands, typically in performing conjuring tricks. 2 the use of cunning to deceive people.

slen·der /'slendər/ ▶ adj. (**slenderer, slenderest**) 1 thin in a graceful and attractive way. 2 barely enough: *a slender majority.* ■ **slen·der·ly** adv. **slen·der·ness** n.

slept /slept/ ▶ past and past participle of SLEEP.

sleuth /slōōTH/ informal ▶ n. a detective. ▶ v. (usu. as n. **sleuthing**) carry out a search or investigation.

slew¹ /slōō/ ▶ v. turn or slide violently or uncontrollably. ▶ n. a violent or uncontrollable turn or slide.

slew² ▶ past of SLAY.

slew³ ▶ n. informal a large number or quantity: *he won a slew of awards for his film.*

slice /slīs/ ▶ n. 1 a thin, broad piece of food cut from a larger portion. 2 a portion or share. 3 (in sports) a stroke or shot that makes the ball spin to one side. ▶ v. 1 cut something into slices. 2 cut something with a sharp implement. 3 move easily and quickly: *a missile sliced through the air.* 4 (in sports) hit the ball at a slight angle so that it spins and curves as it travels. ■ **slic·er** n.

slice-and-dice ▶ adj. informal involving the quick rearrangement of elements; able to be analyzed in a number of different ways.

slick /slik/ ▶ adj. 1 done or operating in an impressively smooth and efficient way: *a slick piece of software.* 2 self-confident but shallow or insincere. 3 smooth, wet, and slippery or glossy: *his face was slick with sweat.* ▶ n. 1 an oil slick. 2 an application or amount of a glossy or oily substance. ▶ v. make hair smooth and glossy with water, oil, or cream. ■ **slick·ly** adv. **slick·ness** n.

slick·er /'slikər/ ▶ n. 1 a raincoat. 2 informal a cheat or swindler.

slide /slīd/ ▶ v. (past and past part. **slid**) 1 move along a smooth surface while remaining in contact with it. 2 move smoothly, quickly, or without being noticed. 3 change gradually to a worse condition or lower level: *shares in the company slid to a ten-year low.* ▶ n. 1 a structure with a smooth sloping surface for children to slide down. 2 a smooth stretch of ice or packed snow for sliding on. 3 an act of sliding. 4 a rectangular piece of glass on which an object is placed to be viewed under a microscope. 5 a small piece of photographic film set in a frame and viewed with a projector.

slid·er /'slīdər/ ▶ n. 1 a North American freshwater turtle with a red or yellow patch on the side of the head. 2 Baseball a pitch that breaks slightly as it nears home plate. 3 a knob or lever that is moved horizontally or vertically to control a variable, such as the volume of a radio; a computer icon that mimics such a knob or lever.

slide rule ▶ n. a ruler with a sliding central strip, marked with logarithmic scales and used for making calculations.

slid·ing scale ▶ n. a scale of fees, wages, etc., that varies according to particular conditions.

slight /slīt/ ▶ adj. 1 small in degree: *a slight increase in inflation.* 2 not sturdy and strongly built. 3 rather trivial or superficial. ▶ v. insult someone by treating them without proper respect. ▶ n. an insult. ■ **slight·ly** adv. **slight·ness** n.

slim /slim/ ▶ adj. (**slimmer, slimmest**) 1 thin in a graceful way; slender. 2 small in width and long and narrow in shape. 3 very small: *a slim chance of success.* ▶ v. (**slims, slimming, slimmed**) 1 make or become thinner, especially by dieting. 2 (usu. **slim down**) reduce a business to a smaller size to make it more efficient. ■ **slim·mer** n. **slim·ness** n.

slime /slīm/ ▶ n. an unpleasantly moist, soft, and slippery substance. ▶ v. cover something with slime.

slim·line /'slim,līn/ ▶ adj. slender in design.

slim·y /'slīmē/ ▶ adj. (**slimier, slimiest**) 1 covered by or resembling slime. 2 informal flattering in an unpleasantly insincere way.

sling¹ /sliNG/ ▶ v. (past and past part. **slung** /sləNG/) 1 hang or carry loosely: *he had a huge bag slung over his shoulder.* 2 informal throw something casually. 3 hurl something from a sling or similar weapon. ▶ n. 1 a flexible loop of fabric used to support or raise a hanging weight. 2 a weapon in the form of a strap or loop, used to hurl stones or other small missiles. ■ **sling·er** n.

sling² ▶ n. a sweetened drink of liquor, especially gin, and water.

sling·shot /'sliNG,SHät/ ▶ n. a forked stick with an elastic strap fastened to the two prongs, used for shooting small stones.

slink /sliNGk/ ▶ v. (past and past part. **slunk** /sləNGk/) move smoothly and quietly in a stealthy way. ▶ n. an act of slinking.

slink·y /'sliNGkē/ ▶ adj. (**slinkier, slinkiest**) informal 1 (of an item of clothing) fitting closely to the curves of the body. 2 moving in a graceful and sensuous way: *slinky models sashayed down the catwalk.*

slip¹ /slip/ ▶ v. (**slips, slipping, slipped**) 1 lose one's balance or footing and slide for a short

distance. **2** accidentally slide or move out of position or from someone's grasp: *the paper slipped from his fingers*. **3** fail to grip or make proper contact with a surface. **4** move or place quietly, quickly, or stealthily: *we slipped out by the back door*. **5** gradually become worse. **6** (usu. **slip up**) make a careless error. **7** escape or get free from something. **8** fail to be remembered by someone's mind. **9** release the clutch of a motor vehicle slightly or for a moment. **10** Knitting move a stitch to the other needle without knitting it. ▶ n. **1** an act of slipping. **2** a minor or careless mistake. **3** a loose-fitting undergarment worn under a dress or skirt. **4** a space in which to dock a boat or ship. ■ **slip·page** /'slipij/ n.
– PHRASES **give someone the slip** informal avoid or escape from someone. **let something slip** reveal something accidentally in conversation. **slip of the tongue** (or **the pen**) a minor mistake in speech (or writing).

slip² ▶ n. **1** a small piece of paper for writing on or that gives printed information. **2** a cutting taken from a plant for grafting or planting.
– PHRASES **a slip of a thing/boy/girl** a small, slim young person.

slip³ ▶ n. a creamy mixture of clay, water, and typically a pigment, used for decorating earthenware.

slip·case /'slip,kās/ ▶ n. a close-fitting case open at one side or end for an object such as a book.

slip·cov·er /'slip,kəvər/ ▶ n. **1** a detachable fitted cover for a chair or sofa. **2** a jacket for a book.

slip knot ▶ n. a knot that can be undone by a pull, or that can slide along the rope on which it is tied.

slip-on ▶ adj. (of shoes or clothes) having no fastenings and able to be put on and taken off quickly.

slipped disk (also **slipped disc**) ▶ n. an instance of the inner material of a disk between the bones of the spine protruding through the outer coat, pressing on nearby nerves and causing pain.

slip·per /'slipər/ ▶ n. a comfortable slip-on shoe that is worn indoors. ■ **slip·pered** adj.

slip·per·y /'slipərē/ ▶ adj. **1** difficult to hold firmly or stand on through being smooth, wet, or slimy. **2** (of a person) not able to be relied on or trusted. ■ **slip·per·i·ness** n.
– PHRASES **slippery slope** a course of action very likely to lead to something undesirable: *she was on the slippery slope to alcoholism*.

slip·per·y elm ▶ n. a North American elm tree with a slimy inner bark that is used in herbal medicine.

slip·shod /'slip,shäd/ ▶ adj. careless, thoughtless, or disorganized.

slip stitch ▶ n. (in sewing) a loose stitch used to join layers of fabric, invisible from the outside of the garment.

slip·stream /'slip,strēm/ ▶ n. **1** a current of air or water driven back by a revolving propeller or jet engine. **2** the partial vacuum created behind a moving vehicle. ▶ v. (especially in motor racing) follow in the slipstream of a vehicle to assist in overtaking it.

slip-up ▶ n. informal a mistake.

slip·way /'slip,wā/ ▶ n. a slope leading into water, used for launching and landing boats and ships or for building and repairing them.

slit /slit/ ▶ n. a long, narrow cut or opening.
▶ v. (**slits, slitting, slit**) **1** make a slit in

something. **2** (past and past part. **slitted**) narrow one's eyes into slits; squint.

slith·er /'sliTHər/ ▶ v. **1** move smoothly over a surface with a twisting motion. **2** slide unsteadily on a loose or slippery surface. ▶ n. **1** a sliding or twisting movement. **2** a small, narrow piece of something; a sliver. ■ **slith·er·y** adj.

sliv·er /'slivər/ ▶ n. a small, narrow piece cut or split off a larger piece. ▶ v. cut or break something into slivers.

sliv·o·vitz /'slivə,vits/ ▶ n. a type of plum brandy made chiefly in the former Yugoslavia and in Romania.

slob /släb/ informal ▶ n. a lazy and untidy person. ■ **slob·bish** adj. **slob·by** adj.

slob·ber /'släbər/ ▶ v. **1** have saliva dripping from the mouth. **2** (**slobber over**) show excessive enthusiasm for someone or something. ▶ n. excessive saliva dripping from the mouth. ■ **slob·ber·y** adj.

sloe /slō/ ▶ n. **1** the small bluish-black fruit of the blackthorn, with a sharp sour taste. **2** another term for BLACKTHORN.

sloe-eyed ▶ adj. having attractive dark almond-shaped eyes.

slog /släg/ informal ▶ v. (**slogs, slogging, slogged**) **1** work hard over a period of time. **2** walk or move with difficulty or effort. **3** hit something forcefully but wildly. ▶ n. a spell of difficult, tiring work or traveling. ■ **slog·ger** n.

slo·gan /'slōgən/ ▶ n. a short, memorable phrase used in advertising or associated with a political party or other group.

slo-mo /'slō 'mō/ ▶ n. short for SLOW MOTION.

sloop /sloōp/ ▶ n. a type of sailboat with one mast.

slop /släp/ ▶ v. (**slops, slopping, slopped**) **1** (of a liquid) spill over the edge of a container. **2** apply something casually or carelessly. **3** feed slops to an animal, especially a pig. ▶ n. (**slops**) **1** waste water that has to be emptied by hand. **2** unappetizing semiliquid food. **3** semiliquid kitchen refuse, often used as animal food.

slope /slōp/ ▶ n. **1** a surface with one end or side at a higher level than another. **2** a part of the side of a hill or mountain. ▶ v. (of a surface) be at an angle so that one end is higher than another.

slop·py /'släpē/ ▶ adj. (**sloppier, sloppiest**) **1** careless and disorganized: *the organization's sloppy management is hindering its work*. **2** slovenly. **3** (of a substance) containing too much liquid; watery. **4** (of a piece of clothing) casual and loose-fitting. **5** informal excessively sentimental. ■ **slop·pi·ly** adv. **slop·pi·ness** n.

slosh /släsh/ ▶ v. **1** (of liquid in a container) move around with a splashing sound. **2** move through liquid with a splashing sound. **3** pour liquid clumsily. ▶ n. an act or sound of splashing. ■ **slosh·y** adj.

sloshed /släsht/ ▶ adj. informal drunk.

slot /slät/ ▶ n. **1** a long, narrow opening into which something may be placed or fitted. **2** a place given to someone or something in an arrangement or scheme: *her show is taking its rightful place in the Saturday evening slot*. ▶ v. (**slots, slotting, slotted**) **1** place or be placed into a slot. **2** (**slot in/into**) fit easily into a new role or situation. ■ **slot·ted** adj.

sloth /slôth, släth, slōth/ ▶ n. **1** reluctance to work or make an effort; laziness. **2** a slow-moving tropical American mammal that hangs upside down from branches. ■ **sloth·ful** adj.

slot ma·chine ▶ n. a coin-operated gambling machine that generates combinations of symbols, with certain combinations winning money for the player.

slouch /slouCH/ ▶ v. stand, move, or sit in a lazy, drooping way. ▶ n. a lazy, drooping way of standing or sitting. ■ **slouch·y** adj.
– PHRASES **be no slouch** informal be good or fast at something.

slouch hat ▶ n. a hat with a wide, flexible brim.

slough[1] /slou, slōō/ ▶ n. **1** a swamp. **2** a situation in which there is no progress or activity.

slough[2] /sləf/ ▶ v. **1** (of an animal, especially a snake) shed an old skin. **2** (**slough something off**) get rid of something that is unwanted.

Slo·vak /'slōväk, -vak/ ▶ n. **1** a person from Slovakia. **2** the language of Slovakia.

Slo·va·ki·an /slō'väkēən/ ▶ n. a person from Slovakia. ▶ adj. relating to Slovakia.

Slo·vene /'slōvēn/ ▶ n. **1** a person from Slovenia. **2** the language of Slovenia. ■ **Slo·ve·ni·an** /slō'vēnēən/ n. & adj.

slov·en·ly /'sləvənlē, 'slä-/ ▶ adj. **1** untidy and dirty. **2** excessively casual; careless. ■ **slov·en·li·ness** n.

slow /slō/ ▶ adj. **1** moving or capable of moving only at a low speed. **2** taking a long time. **3** (of a clock or watch) showing a time earlier than the correct time. **4** not quick to understand, think, or learn. **5** showing little activity: *sales were slow.* **6** (of photographic film) needing long exposure. **7** (of an oven) giving off heat gently. ▶ v. (often **slow down/up**) reduce one's speed or the speed of a vehicle or process. **2** work or live less actively or intensely. ■ **slow·ly** n. **slow·ness** n.

> **USAGE**
>
> **Slow** is normally used as an adjective (*a slow learner*). It is also used as an adverb in certain situations, including compounds such as **slow-acting** and in the expression **go slow**. However, it is not the best style to use **slow** as an adverb in other ways (e.g. *he drives too slow*): in these cases, you should use **slowly** instead.

slow cook·er ▶ n. a large electric pot used for cooking food very slowly.

slow·down /'slō,doun/ ▶ n. a reduction in speed or activity, especially economic activity.

slow mo·tion ▶ n. the action of showing film or video more slowly than it was made or recorded, so that the action appears much slower than in real life.

slow·poke /'slō,pōk/ ▶ n. informal a person who acts or moves slowly, especially in an annoying or inconvenient way.

slow-worm ▶ n. a small snakelike lizard without legs.

SLR ▶ abbr. **1** self-loading rifle. **2** single-lens reflex.

sludge /sləj/ ▶ n. **1** thick, soft, wet mud. **2** semisolid industrial waste. ■ **sludg·y** adj.

slug[1] /sləg/ ▶ n. **1** a small mollusk that resembles a snail without a shell. **2** a small amount of an alcoholic drink. **3** a bullet. ▶ v. (**slugs, slugging, slugged**) gulp a drink, especially an alcoholic one.

slug[2] informal ▶ v. (**slugs, slugging, slugged**) **1** hit someone hard. **2** (**slug it out**) settle a dispute or contest by fighting or competing fiercely. ▶ n. a hard blow.

slug·gard /'sləgərd/ ▶ n. a lazy, inactive person. ■ **slug·gard·ly** adj.

slug·ger /'sləgər/ ▶ n. **1** a person who throws hard punches. **2** a baseball player who consistently hits for power, especially home runs and doubles.

slug·gish /'sləgiSH/ ▶ adj. **1** slow-moving or inactive. **2** lacking energy or alertness. ■ **slug·gish·ly** adv. **slug·gish·ness** n.

sluice /slōōs/ ▶ n. **1** (also **sluice gate**) a sliding gate or other device for controlling the flow of water. **2** (also **sluiceway**) an artificial channel for carrying off surplus water. **3** an act of rinsing with water. ▶ v. wash or rinse someone or something with water.

slum /sləm/ ▶ n. **1** a run-down and overcrowded area of a city or town inhabited by very poor people. **2** a house or building that is unfit to be lived in. ▶ v. (**slums, slumming, slummed**) (**slum it**) informal accept conditions that are worse than those one is used to. ■ **slum·mer** n. **slum·my** adj.

slum·ber /'sləmbər/ literary ▶ v. be asleep. ▶ n. a sleep. ■ **slum·ber·ous** /-bərəs/ (also **slumbrous** /-brəs/) adj.

slump /sləmp/ ▶ v. **1** sit, lean, or fall heavily and limply. **2** decline greatly or over a prolonged period: *prices slumped due to sluggish demand.* ▶ n. **1** a sudden or severe drop in the price or value of something. **2** a prolonged period of abnormally low economic activity. **3** a period of poor performance.

slung /sləNG/ ▶ past and past participle of **SLING**[1].

slunk /sləNGk/ ▶ past and past participle of **SLINK**.

slur /slər/ ▶ v. (**slurs, slurring, slurred**) **1** speak words in an unclear way, with the sounds running into one another. **2** perform a group of musical notes so that each runs smoothly into the next. **3** make damaging or false statements about someone. ▶ n. **1** an insult or accusation intended to damage someone's reputation. **2** an act of speaking indistinctly. **3** a curved line indicating that musical notes are to be performed so that each runs into the next.

slurp /slərp/ ▶ v. eat or drink something with a loud sucking sound. ▶ n. an act or sound of slurping.

slur·ry /'slərē/ ▶ n. (pl. **slurries**) a semiliquid mixture of manure, cement, or coal and water.

slush /sləSH/ ▶ n. **1** partially melted snow or ice. **2** informal excessive sentiment in novels, movies, etc. ▶ v. make a soft splashing sound. ■ **slush·y** adj.

slush fund ▶ n. a reserve of money used for underhanded or dishonest purposes, especially political bribery.

slut /slət/ ▶ n. a woman who has many sexual partners. ■ **slut·tish** adj. **slut·ty** adj.

sly /slī/ ▶ adj. (**slyer, slyest**) **1** having a cunning and deceitful nature. **2** (of a remark, glance, or expression) suggesting that one has secret knowledge that may be damaging or embarrassing: *slip the doorman a note with a sly grin.* **3** (of an action) done secretly. ■ **sly·ly** adv. **sly·ness** n.
– PHRASES **on the sly** in a secret way.

SM ▶ abbr. **1** sadomasochism. **2** Sergeant Major.

Sm ▶ symbol the chemical element samarium.

smack[1] /smak/ ▶ n. **1** a sharp blow given with the palm of the hand. **2** a loud, sharp sound. **3** a loud

smack kiss. ▶ v. **1** hit someone or something sharply with the palm of the hand. **2** hit or smash something into something else. **3** part the lips noisily. ▶ adv. informal **1** in a sudden and violent way. **2** exactly; precisely.

smack² ▶ v. (**smack of**) **1** seem to contain or involve something wrong or undesirable: *such writing smacks of racism.* **2** taste of something. ▶ n. (**a smack of**) a taste or suggestion of something.

smack³ ▶ n. informal heroin.

smack⁴ ▶ n. Brit. a sailboat with one mast, used for fishing.

smack·er /'smakər/ (also **smackeroo** /ˌsmakə'rōō/) ▶ n. informal **1** a loud kiss. **2** dated one dollar.

small /smôl/ ▶ adj. **1** not large in size, amount, or number. **2** not great in strength, importance, or power: *a small voice.* **3** not fully grown or developed; young. **4** (of a business or its owner) operating on a modest scale: *a small farmer.* ▶ adv. into small pieces. ■ **small·ness** n.
– PHRASES **feel** (or **look**) **small** feel (or look) foolish or unimportant. **the small of the back** the part of a person's back where the spine curves in at the level of the waist. **the small screen** television.

small arms ▶ pl.n. portable firearms.

small change ▶ n. **1** coins of low value. **2** something trivial.

small claims court ▶ n. a local court in which claims for small sums of money can be heard and decided quickly and cheaply, without using a lawyer.

small fry ▶ pl.n. **1** unimportant people or things. **2** young or small fish.

small in·tes·tine ▶ n. the part of the intestine that runs between the stomach and the large intestine.

small-mind·ed ▶ adj. having a narrow outlook; petty.

small·pox /'smôlˌpäks/ ▶ n. a serious disease spread by a virus, with fever and blisters that leave permanent scars.

small print ▶ n. important details or conditions in an agreement or contract that are printed in small type so that they are not easily noticed.

small-scale ▶ adj. of limited size or extent.

small talk ▶ n. polite conversation about unimportant matters.

small-time ▶ adj. informal unimportant; minor.

smarm·y /'smärmē/ ▶ adj. (**smarmier, smarmiest**) informal friendly or flattering in an insincere or excessive way. ■ **smarm·i·ly** adv. **smarm·i·ness** n.

smart /smärt/ ▶ adj. **1** informal intelligent. **2** informal quick-witted and clever. **3** clever in an impudent or sarcastic way. **4** clean, tidy, and stylish. **5** (of a place) fashionable and upmarket. **6** attractive and new in appearance: *smart bathroom furniture.* **7** quick; brisk: *I set off at a smart pace.* ▶ v. **1** feel a sharp, stinging pain. **2** feel upset and annoyed. ▶ n. **1** a sharp, stinging pain. **2** (**smarts**) informal intelligence or shrewdness. ■ **smart·ly** adv. **smart·ness** n.
– PHRASES **look smart** chiefly Brit. be quick.

smart al·eck /'alik/ (also **smart alec**) ▶ n. informal a person who is irritating because they behave as if they know everything.

smart-ass ▶ n. informal another term for SMART ALECK.

smart bomb ▶ n. a radio-controlled or laser-guided bomb, often with a built-in computer.

smart card ▶ n. a plastic card on which information is stored in electronic form, used for financial transactions.

smart dust ▶ n. a collection of very small computerized sensors capable of wireless communication, designed to act as a dispersed network.

smart·en /'smärtn/ ▶ v. (**smarten up**) make or become smarter.

smart growth ▶ n. planned economic and community development that attempts to curb urban sprawl and worsening environmental conditions.

smart·phone /'smärtˌfōn/ ▶ n. a cell phone that incorporates a palmtop computer.

smart·y /'smärtē/ ▶ n. (pl. **smarties**) informal a person who behaves as if they know everything.

smart·y-pants ▶ n. another term for SMARTY.

smash /smaSH/ ▶ v. **1** break violently into pieces. **2** hit or collide forcefully. **3** crash and severely damage a vehicle. **4** (in sports) hit the ball very hard. **5** completely defeat, destroy, or put an end to: *police smashed a major crime network.* ▶ n. **1** an act or sound of smashing. **2** (also **smash hit**) informal a very successful song, movie, or show.

smashed /smaSHt/ ▶ adj. informal very drunk.

smash·ing /'smaSHiNG/ ▶ adj. Brit. informal excellent; wonderful.

smat·ter·ing /'smatəriNG/ ▶ n. **1** a small amount. **2** a slight knowledge of a language or subject.

smear /smi(ə)r/ ▶ v. **1** coat or mark someone or something with a greasy or sticky substance. **2** blur or smudge something. **3** damage a person's reputation by false accusations. ▶ n. **1** a greasy or sticky mark. **2** a false accusation. **3** a sample thinly spread on a slide for examination under a microscope. ■ **smear·y** adj.

smell /smel/ ▶ n. **1** the faculty of sensing things by means of the organs in the nose. **2** something sensed by the nose; a scent or odor. **3** an act of smelling. ▶ v. (past and past part. **smelt** or **smelled**) **1** sense the scent or odor of someone or something. **2** sniff at something in order to find out its smell. **3** have a particular scent or odor: *the room smelled of dampness.* **4** have a strong or unpleasant odor. **5** sense or suspect that something exists or is about to happen: *I can smell trouble.* ■ **smell·er** n.
– PHRASES **smell a rat** informal suspect a trick.

smell·ing salts ▶ pl.n. chiefly historical a chemical mixed with perfume, sniffed by someone who feels faint.

smell·y /'smelē/ ▶ adj. (**smellier, smelliest**) having a strong or unpleasant smell. ■ **smell·i·ness** n.

smelt¹ /smelt/ ▶ v. extract metal from its ore by a process involving heating and melting. ■ **smelt·er** n.

smelt² ▶ past and past participle of SMELL.

smelt³ ▶ n. (pl. same or **smelts**) a small silvery fish that lives both in fresh water and the sea.

smid·gen /'smijin/ (also **smidgeon** or **smidgin**) ▶ n. informal a tiny amount of something.

smi·lax /'smīlaks/ ▶ n. **1** a climbing shrub with hooks and tendrils, grown as ornamentals or for their sarsaparilla-yielding roots. **2** a climbing asparagus with decorative foliage.

smile /smīl/ ▶v. **1** form the features of the face into a pleased, friendly, or amused expression, with the corners of the mouth turned up. **2** (**smile at/on**) be favorable to: *luck was smiling on them as they carried out their plan.* ▶n. an act of smiling.

smil·ey /'smīlē/ ▶adj. informal smiling; cheerful. ▶n. (pl. **smileys**) a symbol that represents a smiling face, formed by the characters :-) and used in emails and similar electronic communications.

smirch /smərcH/ ▶v. **1** make someone or something dirty. **2** damage a person's reputation.

smirk /smərk/ ▶v. smile in a smug or silly way. ▶n. a smug or silly smile. ■ **smirk·er** n. **smirk·y** adj.

smite /smīt/ ▶v. (past **smote** /smōt/; past part. **smitten** /'smitn/) **1** (**be smitten**) be affected severely by a disease or feeling. **2** (**be smitten**) be strongly attracted to someone or something: *Vince had been smitten with Tess for years.* **3** literary hit someone or something with a hard blow. **4** old use defeat or conquer an opponent.

smith /smiTH/ ▶n. **1** a person who works in metal. **2** a blacksmith. ▶v. treat metal by heating, hammering, and forging it.

smith·er·eens /ˌsmiTHə'rēnz/ ▶pl.n. informal small pieces.

smith·y /'smiTHē/ ▶n. (pl. **smithies**) a blacksmith's workshop.

smit·ten /'smitn/ ▶ past participle of SMITE.

smock /smäk/ ▶n. **1** a loose dress or blouse with the upper part closely gathered in smocking. **2** a loose garment worn to protect one's clothes. ▶v. decorate a dress or blouse with smocking.

smock·ing /'smäkiNG/ ▶n. decoration on a garment created by gathering a section of the material into tight pleats and holding them together with a pattern of parallel stitches.

smog /smäg/ ▶n. fog or haze intensified by smoke or other pollution in the atmosphere. ■ **smog·gy** adj.

smoke /smōk/ ▶n. **1** a visible vapor in the air, produced by a burning substance. **2** an act of smoking a cigarette or cigar. **3** informal a cigarette or cigar. ▶v. **1** give out smoke. **2** breathe the smoke of a cigarette, pipe, etc., in and out. **3** cure or preserve meat or fish by hanging it in smoke. **4** (**smoke someone/thing out**) drive someone or something out of a place by using smoke. **5** (as adj. **smoked**) (of glass) treated so as to darken it. ■ **smok·a·ble** adj. **smoke·less** /'smōkləs/ adj. **smok·er** n.

– PHRASES **go up in smoke** informal **1** be destroyed by fire. **2** (of a plan) come to nothing. **where there's smoke, there's fire** there is always a reason for a rumor.

smoke alarm ▶n. a device that detects and gives a warning of the presence of smoke.

smoke-free ▶adj. **1** without smoke: *a smoke-free environment.* **2** where smoking is not permitted: *a smoke-free train.*

smoke·screen /'smōkˌskrēn/ ▶n. **1** something intended to disguise someone's real intentions or activities. **2** a cloud of smoke created to conceal military operations.

smoke·stack /'smōkˌstak/ ▶n. a chimney or funnel for discharging smoke from a locomotive, ship, or factory.

smok·ing gun ▶n. a piece of evidence that

proves without doubt that someone is guilty of wrongdoing.

smok·ing jack·et ▶n. a man's comfortable jacket, formerly worn while smoking after dinner.

smok·y /'smōkē/ (also **smokey**) ▶adj. (**smokier, smokiest**) **1** producing or filled with smoke. **2** having the taste or smell of smoked food. **3** resembling smoke in color or appearance: *smoky gray eyeshadows.* ■ **smok·i·ly** adv. **smok·i·ness** n.

smol·der /'smōldər/ (Brit. **smoulder**) ▶v. **1** burn slowly with smoke but no flame. **2** feel intense and barely concealed anger, hatred, lust, etc.

smolt /smōlt/ ▶n. a young salmon or trout after the parr stage (two years old), when it migrates to the sea for the first time.

smooch /smōōcH/ informal ▶v. kiss and cuddle amorously. ▶n. a spell of kissing and cuddling. ■ **smooch·er** n. **smooch·y** adj.

smooth /smōōTH/ ▶adj. **1** having an even and regular surface. **2** (of a liquid) without lumps. **3** (of movement) without jerks. **4** happening without problems: *the organizers deserve thanks for the smooth running of the festival.* **5** charming in very confident or flattering way. **6** (of a flavor) not harsh or bitter. ▶v. **1** make something smooth. **2** deal successfully with a problem: *these disputes were smoothed over.* ■ **smooth·ly** adv. **smooth·ness** n.

smooth·bore /'smōōTHˌbôr/ ▶n. a gun with a barrel that is not rifled.

smooth·ie /'smōōTHē/ ▶n. **1** a thick, smooth drink of fresh fruit puréed with milk, yogurt, or ice cream. **2** informal a charming and confident man who is often not sincere.

smooth-talk·ing ▶adj. informal using very persuasive or flattering language. ■ **smooth-talk·er** n.

smor·gas·bord /'smôrgəsˌbôrd/ ▶n. a buffet offering a variety of meats, salads, hors d'oeuvres, etc.

smote /smōt/ ▶ past of SMITE.

smoth·er /'smaTHər/ ▶v. **1** suffocate someone by covering the nose and mouth. **2** (**smother someone/thing in/with**) cover someone or something entirely with something. **3** prevent from developing or being expressed: *she smothered a sigh.* **4** make someone feel overwhelmed by treating them too protectively. **5** put out a fire by covering it.

smoul·der /'smōldər/ ▶v. British spelling of SMOLDER.

SMS ▶abbr. Short Message (or Messaging) Service, a system that enables cell-phone users to send and receive text messages. ▶n. a message sent or received using SMS.

SMTP ▶abbr. Simple Mail Transfer (or Transport) Protocol, a standard for the transmission of email on a computer network.

smudge /sməj/ ▶v. make or become blurred or smeared. ▶n. a blurred or smeared mark. ■ **smudg·y** adj.

smug /sməg/ ▶adj. (**smugger, smuggest**) pleased with oneself in an irritating way; self-satisfied. ■ **smug·ly** adv. **smug·ness** n.

smug·gle /'sməgəl/ ▶v. **1** move goods illegally into or out of a country. **2** take someone or something secretly to or from a place. ■ **smug·gler** n. **smug·gling** n.

smut /smət/ ▸ n. **1** a small flake of soot or dirt. **2** indecent or obscene talk, writing, or pictures. **3** a disease of cereal crops caused by a fungus, in which affected parts change to black powder.

smut·ty /'smətē/ ▸ adj. (**smuttier, smuttiest**) **1** indecent or obscene. **2** dirty or sooty.

Sn ▸ symbol the chemical element tin.

snack /snak/ ▸ n. a small quantity of food eaten between meals or instead of a meal. ▸ v. eat a snack.

snack bar ▸ n. a place where snacks or quickly prepared light meals are sold.

snaf·fle /'snafəl/ ▸ n. a simple bit on a horse's bridle, used with a single set of reins.

sna·fu /sna'fōō/ ▸ n. informal a situation that is confused, disorganized, or that has gone wrong.

snag /snag/ ▸ n. **1** an unexpected difficulty or drawback. **2** a sharp or jagged projection. **3** a small tear in fabric. ▸ v. (**snags, snagging, snagged**) **1** catch or tear something on a sharp projection. **2** informal manage to get or obtain something. ■ **snag·gy** adj.

snag·gle-toothed /'snagəl,tōōтнt/ ▸ adj. having irregular or projecting teeth.

snail /snāl/ ▸ n. a slow-moving mollusk with a spiral shell into which it can withdraw its whole body.
– PHRASES **snail's pace** a very slow speed or rate of progress.

snail mail ▸ n. informal the ordinary postal service as opposed to email.

snake /snāk/ ▸ n. a reptile with a long, slender limbless body, many kinds of which have a venomous bite. ▸ v. move or extend with the twisting motion of a snake: *the road snakes inland.*
– PHRASES **snake in the grass** a person who pretends to be friendly but is secretly working against someone.

snake·bite /'snāk,bīt/ ▸ n. Brit. a drink consisting of draft cider and lager in equal proportions.

snake charm·er ▸ n. an entertainer who appears to make snakes move by playing music.

snake·head /'snāk,hed/ ▸ n. a member of a Chinese criminal network chiefly involved in smuggling illegal immigrants.

snake·skin /'snāk,skin/ ▸ n. the skin of a snake.

snak·y /'snākē/ (also **snakey**) ▸ adj. (**snakier, snakiest**) **1** long and winding. **2** cold and cunning.

snap /snap/ ▸ v. (**snaps, snapping, snapped**) **1** break with a sharp cracking sound. **2** open or close with a brisk movement or sharp sound. **3** (of an animal) make a sudden bite. **4** (**snap someone/thing up**) quickly obtain someone or something that is desirable or in short supply. **5** suddenly lose one's self-control. **6** say something quickly and irritably. **7** (**snap out of**) informal get out of a bad mood by a sudden effort. **8** take a snapshot of someone or something. ▸ n. **1** an act or sound of snapping. **2** a snapshot. **3** a crisp, brittle cookie. **4** a children's card game in which players compete to call 'snap' as soon as two cards of the same type are exposed. ▸ adj. done or taken on the spur of the moment: *a snap decision.*

snap·drag·on /'snap,dragən/ ▸ n. a plant with brightly colored flowers that have a mouthlike opening.

snap fas·ten·er ▸ n. a small fastener with two parts that fit together when pressed.

snap-lock ▸ adj. (of a device or part) that fastens automatically when pushed into position.

snap·per /'snapər/ ▸ n. an edible sea fish noted for snapping its toothed jaws.

snap·ping tur·tle ▸ n. a large American freshwater turtle with a long neck and strong hooked jaws.

snap·pish /'snapisн/ ▸ adj. informal irritable; snappy. ■ **snap·pish·ly** adv. **snap·pish·ness** n.

snap·py /'snapē/ ▸ adj. (**snappier, snappiest**) informal **1** irritable and sharp. **2** cleverly brief and to the point: *a comedy loaded with snappy dialogue.* **3** neat and stylish: *a snappy dresser.* ■ **snap·pi·ly** adv.
– PHRASES **make it snappy** do it quickly.

snap·shot /'snap,sнät/ ▸ n. an informal photograph, taken quickly.

snare /sne(ə)r/ ▸ n. **1** a trap for catching small animals, consisting of a loop of wire or cord that pulls tight. **2** something likely to lure someone into harm or trouble. **3** (also **snare drum**) a drum with a length of wire, gut, or hide stretched across the head to make a rattling sound. ▸ v. catch someone or something in a snare or trap.

snarl[1] /snärl/ ▸ v. **1** growl with bared teeth. **2** say something aggressively. ▸ n. an act or sound of snarling. ■ **snarl·y** adj.

snarl[2] ▸ v. (**snarl something up**) **1** tangle something up. **2** hinder something. ▸ n. a knot or tangle.

snarl-up ▸ n. Brit. informal **1** a traffic jam. **2** a muddle.

snatch /snacн/ ▸ v. **1** grab something in a rude or eager way. **2** informal steal something or kidnap someone suddenly. **3** quickly take when the chance presents itself: *I snatched a few hours' sleep.* ▸ n. **1** an act of snatching. **2** a fragment of music or talk. ■ **snatch·er** n.

snaz·zy /'snazē/ ▸ adj. (**snazzier, snazziest**) informal smart and stylish.

sneak /snēk/ ▸ v. (past and past part. **sneaked** or informal **snuck** /snək/) **1** move or take in a stealthy or secretive way. **2** do or achieve in a stealthy way: *she sneaked a glance at her watch.* ▸ n. informal a person who behaves in a secretive and underhanded way. ▸ adj. acting or done secretly or unofficially: *a sneak preview.*

sneak·er /'snēkər/ ▸ n. a soft shoe worn for sports or casual occasions.

sneak·ing /'snēkiNG/ ▸ adj. (of a feeling) remaining in one's mind.

sneak·y /'snēkē/ ▸ adj. (**sneakier, sneakiest**) secretive in a sly or guilty way. ■ **sneak·i·ly** adv. **sneak·i·ness** n.

sneer /sni(ə)r/ ▸ n. a scornful or mocking smile, remark, or tone. ▸ v. smile or speak in a scornful or mocking way.

sneeze /snēz/ ▸ v. suddenly expel air from the nose and mouth due to irritation of the nostrils. ▸ n. an act or the sound of sneezing. ■ **sneez·er** n. **sneez·y** adj.
– PHRASES **not to be sneezed at** informal not to be rejected without careful consideration.

snick·er /'snikər/ ▸ v. **1** give a smothered scornful laugh. **2** (of a horse) make a gentle high-pitched neigh. ▸ n. an act of snickering; a gentle high-pitched neigh.

snide /snīd/ ▸ adj. disrespectful or mocking in an indirect way. ■ **snide·ly** adv. **snide·y** adj.

sniff /snif/ ▸ v. **1** draw in air audibly through the

nose. **2** (**sniff around/round**) informal investigate something secretly. **3** (**sniff something out**) informal discover something by investigation. ▶ n. **1** an act or sound of sniffing. **2** informal a hint or sign: *they're off at the first sniff of trouble.* **3** informal a slight chance. ■ **sniff·er** n.

– PHRASES **not to be sniffed at** informal worth having or considering.

sniff·er dog ▶ n. a dog trained to find drugs or explosives by smell.

snif·fle /'snifəl/ ▶ v. sniff slightly or repeatedly, typically because of a cold or fit of crying. ▶ n. **1** an act of sniffling. **2** (also **the snuffles**) a slight head cold. ■ **snif·fly** adj.

snif·fy /'snifē/ ▶ adj. (**sniffier, sniffiest**) informal scornful; contemptuous. ■ **sniff·i·ly** adv.

snif·ter /'sniftər/ ▶ n. a footed glass that is wide at the bottom and tapers to the top, used especially for brandy.

snip /snip/ ▶ v. (**snips, snipping, snipped**) cut something with scissors using small, quick strokes. ▶ n. **1** an act of snipping. **2** a small piece that has been cut off. **3** (**snips**) hand shears for cutting metal.

snipe /snīp/ ▶ v. (usu. **snipe at**) **1** shoot at someone from a hiding place at long range. **2** criticize someone or something in a sly or petty way. ▶ n. (pl. same or **snipes**) a wading bird with brown plumage and a long straight bill. ■ **snip·er** n.

snip·pet /'snipit/ ▶ n. a small piece or brief extract.

snip·py /'snipē/ ▶ adj. informal curt or sharp.

snitch /sniCH/ informal ▶ v. **1** steal something. **2** inform on someone. ▶ n. an informer.

sniv·el /'snivəl/ ▶ v. (**snivels, sniveling, sniveled**) **1** cry and sniffle. **2** complain in a whining or tearful way. ▶ n. a spell of sniveling. ■ **sniv·el·er** n.

snob /snäb/ ▶ n. **1** a person who greatly respects upper-class or rich people and who looks down on people of a lower class. **2** a person who believes that their tastes in a particular area are superior to others: *a wine snob.* ■ **snob·ber·y** /-bərē/ n. (pl. **snobberies**) **snob·bism** /-,bizəm/ n. **snob·by** adj. (**snobbier, snobbiest**).

snob·bish /'snäbiSH/ ▶ adj. relating to or typical of a snob: *his snobbish contempt for the lower classes.* ■ **snob·bish·ly** adv.

snood /snood/ ▶ n. **1** an ornamental hairnet or pouch worn over the hair at the back of a woman's head. **2** a wide ring of knitted material worn as a hood or scarf.

snook /snook/ ▶ n. (in phrase **cock a snook at**) informal, chiefly Brit. **1** openly show contempt or a lack of respect for someone or something. **2** place one's hand so that the thumb touches one's nose and the fingers are spread out, as a gesture of contempt.

snook·er /'snookər/ ▶ n. **1** a game played with cue sticks on a billiard table, in which the players use a white cue ball to pocket the other balls in a set order. **2** a position in a game of snooker or pool in which a player cannot make a direct shot at any permitted ball. ▶ v. **1** (in snooker and pool) put an opponent in a position in which they cannot make a direct shot at any permitted ball. **2** (**be snookered**) informal be tricked or deceived: *they get snookered into signing away their paychecks.*

snoop /snoop/ informal ▶ v. look around or investigate secretly to try to find out private information. ▶ n. an act of snooping. ■ **snoop·er** n.

snoot·y /'snootē/ ▶ adj. (**snootier, snootiest**) informal treating people as if they are socially inferior; snobbish. ■ **snoot·i·ly** adv. **snoot·i·ness** n.

snooze /snooz/ informal ▶ n. a short, light sleep. ▶ v. sleep lightly and briefly. ■ **snooz·er** n. **snooz·y** adj.

snooze but·ton ▶ n. a control on a clock that sets an alarm to repeat after a short interval.

snore /snôr/ ▶ n. a snorting sound in a person's breathing while they are asleep. ▶ v. make a snorting sound while asleep. ■ **snor·er** n.

snor·kel /'snôrkəl/ ▶ n. a tube for a swimmer to breathe through while under water. ▶ v. (**snorkels, snorkeling, snorkeled**) (often as n. **snorkeling**) swim using a snorkel. ■ **snor·kel·er** n.

snort /snôrt/ ▶ n. **1** an explosive sound made by the sudden forcing of breath through the nose. **2** informal an amount of cocaine that is breathed in through the nose. **3** informal a measure of an alcoholic drink. ▶ v. **1** make a snort, especially to express anger or mockery. **2** informal inhale cocaine. ■ **snort·er** n.

snot /snät/ ▶ n. informal **1** mucus in the nose. **2** an unpleasant person.

snot·ty /'snätē/ ▶ adj. (**snottier, snottiest**) informal **1** full of or covered with mucus from the nose. **2** having a superior or arrogant attitude. ■ **snot·ti·ly** adv. **snot·ti·ness** n.

snout /snout/ ▶ n. **1** the projecting nose and mouth of an animal. **2** the projecting front or end of something such as a pistol. ■ **snout·ed** adj.

snow /snō/ ▶ n. **1** frozen water vapor in the atmosphere that falls in light white flakes. **2** (**snows**) falls of snow. **3** a mass of flickering white spots on a television or radar screen, caused by interference or a poor signal. ▶ v. **1** (**it snows, it is snowing, it snowed**) snow falls. **2** (**be snowed in/up**) be unable to leave somewhere due to heavy snow. **3** (**be snowed under**) be overwhelmed with a large quantity of something, especially work. ■ **snow·less** adj.

snow·ball /'snō,bôl/ ▶ n. **1** a ball of packed snow. **2** a cocktail containing advocaat and lemonade. ▶ v. **1** increase rapidly in size, intensity, or importance: *my enthusiasm quickly snowballed.* **2** throw snowballs at someone.

snow·bird /'snō,bərd/ ▶ n. **1** informal a person who moves from Canada or a northern US state to a warmer southern US state in the winter. **2** a kind of junco with gray or brown upper parts and a white belly.

snow blind·ness ▶ n. temporary blindness caused by the glare of light reflected by a large expanse of snow.

snow·board /'snō,bôrd/ ▶ n. a board resembling a short, broad ski, used for sliding downhill on snow. ■ **snow·board·er** n. **snow·board·ing** n.

snow·bound /'snō,bound/ ▶ adj. **1** prevented from traveling or going out by snow. **2** (of a place) cut off because of snow.

snow·capped ▶ adj. (of the top of a mountain) covered with snow.

snow·drift /'snō,drift/ ▶ n. a bank of deep snow heaped up by the wind.

snow·drop /'snō,dräp/ ▶ n. a plant that bears drooping white flowers during late winter.

snow·fall /'snō,fôl/ ▶ n. **1** a fall of snow. **2** the quantity of snow falling within a particular area in a given time.

snow·field /ˈsnōˌfēld/ ▶ n. a permanent wide expanse of snow in mountainous or polar regions.

snow·flake /ˈsnōˌflāk/ ▶ n. each of the many feathery ice crystals that fall as snow.

snow goose ▶ n. a goose that breeds in Arctic Canada and Greenland, having white plumage with black wing tips.

snow job ▶ n. informal an attempt to deceive or persuade someone, especially by using flattery.

snow leop·ard ▶ n. a rare large cat that has pale gray fur patterned with dark blotches and rings, living in mountainous parts of central Asia.

snow·line /ˈsnōˌlīn/ ▶ n. the altitude above which some snow remains on the ground throughout the year.

snow·man /ˈsnōˌman/ ▶ n. (pl. **snowmen**) a model of a human figure created with compressed snow.

snow·mo·bile /ˈsnōmōˌbēl/ ▶ n. a motor vehicle with runners or caterpillar tracks for traveling over snow.

snow pea ▶ n. a variety of pea with an edible pod.

snow·plow /ˈsnōˌplou/ (Brit. **snowplough**) ▶ n. 1 a device or vehicle for clearing roads of snow. 2 an act of turning the points of one's skis inward in order to slow down or turn.

snow·shoe /ˈsnōˌSHoō/ ▶ n. a flat device resembling a tennis racket, which is attached to the sole of a boot and used for walking on snow.

snow·storm /ˈsnōˌstôrm/ ▶ n. a heavy fall of snow accompanied by a high wind.

snow·y /ˈsnōē/ ▶ adj. (**snowier**, **snowiest**) 1 covered with snow. 2 (of weather or a period of time) characterized by snowfall. 3 like snow, especially in being pure white.

snow·y owl ▶ n. a large northern owl, the male being entirely white.

snub /snəb/ ▶ v. (**snubs**, **snubbing**, **snubbed**) ignore or reject someone or something scornfully. ▶ n. an act of snubbing someone or something. ▶ adj. (of a person's nose) short and turned up at the end.

snuck /snək/ informal ▶ past and past participle of **SNEAK**.

snuff[1] /snəf/ ▶ v. 1 put out a candle. 2 (**snuff something out**) abruptly put an end to something. ▶ n. the charred part of a candle wick.

snuff[2] ▶ n. powdered tobacco that is sniffed up the nostril. ▶ v. inhale or sniff at something.
– PHRASES **up to snuff** informal 1 up to the required standard. 2 in good health.

snuff·er /ˈsnəfər/ ▶ n. a small hollow metal cone on the end of a handle, used to put out a candle by smothering the flame.

snuf·fle /ˈsnəfəl/ ▶ v. 1 breathe noisily through a partially blocked nose. 2 (of an animal) make repeated sniffing sounds. ▶ n. 1 a snuffling sound. 2 (also **the snuffles**) informal a cold. ■ **snuf·fly** adj.

snuff mov·ie ▶ n. informal a pornographic movie or video recording of an actual murder.

snug /snəg/ ▶ adj. (**snugger**, **snuggest**) 1 warm and cozy. 2 close-fitting. ■ **snug·ly** adv. **snug·ness** n.

snug·gle /ˈsnəgəl/ ▶ v. settle into a warm, comfortable position.

so[1] /sō/ ▶ adv. 1 to such a great extent. 2 extremely; very much. 3 to the same extent: *he isn't so bad as you'd think.* 4 referring back to something previously mentioned.
5 similarly: *times have changed and so have I.* 6 in the way described or demonstrated; thus. ▶ conj. 1 therefore. 2 (**so that**) with the result or aim that. 3 and then. 4 introducing a question or concluding statement. 5 in the same way.
– PHRASES **and so on** (or **forth**) and similar things; et cetera. **or so** approximately. **so long!** informal goodbye. **so much as** even: *without so much as a word.*

so[2] ▶ n. variant of **SOL**[1].

So. ▶ abbr. South.

soak /sōk/ ▶ v. 1 make or become thoroughly wet by leaving or remaining in liquid. 2 (of a liquid) penetrate or spread through completely: *the rain soaked their hair.* 3 (**soak something up**) absorb a liquid. 4 (**soak something up**) expose oneself to something beneficial or enjoyable: *soak up the Mediterranean sun.* 5 (**soak oneself in**) involve oneself deeply in a particular experience. ▶ n. 1 an act or period of soaking. 2 informal a heavy drinker.

soak·ing /ˈsōkiNG/ (also **soaking wet**) ▶ adj. very wet.

so-and-so ▶ n. (pl. **so-and-sos**) informal 1 a person or thing whose name the speaker does not know or need to specify. 2 an unpleasant or disliked person (used instead of an offensive word): *a nosy so-and-so.*

soap /sōp/ ▶ n. 1 a substance used with water for washing and cleaning, made of natural oils or fats combined with an alkali, and typically perfumed. 2 informal a soap opera. ▶ v. wash someone or something with soap.

soap·box /ˈsōpˌbäks/ ▶ n. 1 a box or crate used as a stand when making a speech in public. 2 an opportunity for someone to express their views publicly: *I tend to get up on my soapbox about this issue.*

soap op·er·a ▶ n. a television or radio drama serial dealing with daily events in the lives of the same group of characters.

soap pow·der ▶ n. powdered detergent for washing clothes.

soap·stone /ˈsōpˌstōn/ ▶ n. a soft rock consisting largely of the mineral talc.

soap·suds /ˈsōpˌsədz/ ▶ pl.n. another term for **SUDS**.

soap·y /ˈsōpē/ ▶ adj. (**soapier**, **soapiest**) 1 containing or covered with soap. 2 like soap.

soar /sôr/ ▶ v. 1 fly or rise high into the air. 2 maintain height in the air by gliding. 3 increase rapidly above the usual level.

So·a·ve /ˈswävā/ ▶ n. a dry white Italian wine.

SOB ▶ abbr. son of a bitch.

sob /säb/ ▶ v. (**sobs**, **sobbing**, **sobbed**) 1 cry making loud gasping noises. 2 say something while sobbing. ▶ n. an act or sound of sobbing.

so·ber /ˈsōbər/ ▶ adj. (**soberer**, **soberest**) 1 not affected by alcohol; not drunk. 2 serious and sensible or thoughtful. 3 (of a color) not bright or conspicuous. ▶ v. 1 (usu. **sober up** or **sober someone up**) become or make sober after being drunk. 2 (often as adj. **sobering**) make or become serious: *a sobering thought.* ■ **so·ber·ly** adv.

so·bri·e·ty /səˈbrīətē, sō-/ ▶ n. the state of being sober.

so·bri·quet /ˈsōbriˌkā, -ˌket/ (also **soubriquet**) ▶ n. a person's nickname.

sob sto·ry ▶ n. informal a story intended to arouse sympathy.

Soc. ▸abbr. **1** Socialist. **2** Society.

so·ca /'sōkə/ ▸n. calypso music with elements of soul, originally from Trinidad.

so-called ▸adj. called by the name or term specified (often in the speaker's view, inappropriately): *her so-called friends.*

soc·cer /'säkər/ ▸n. a game played by two teams of eleven players with a round ball that may not be handled during play except by the goalkeepers, the object being to score goals by kicking or heading the ball into the opponents' goal.

so·cia·ble /'sōsHəbəl/ ▸adj. **1** liking to talk to and join in activities with other people. **2** friendly and welcoming: *a very sociable little village.*
■ **so·cia·bil·i·ty** /ˌsōsHə'bilitē/ n. **so·cia·bly** adv.

so·cial /'sōsHəl/ ▸adj. **1** relating to society and its organization. **2** needing the company of other people; suited to living in communities. **3** relating to or designed for activities in which people meet each other for pleasure. **4** (of birds, insects, or mammals) breeding or living in colonies or organized communities. ▸n. an informal social gathering organized by the members of a club or group. ■ **so·ci·al·i·ty** /ˌsōsHē'alitē/ n. **so·cial·ly** /'sōsHələ/ adv.

so·cial climb·er ▸n. derogatory a person who is anxious to gain a higher social status.

so·cial con·tract (also **social compact**) ▸n. an unspoken agreement among the members of a society to cooperate for the benefit of everyone, for example by sacrificing some individual freedom in return for government protection.

so·cial de·moc·ra·cy ▸n. a socialist system of government achieved by democratic means.

so·cial·ism /'sōsHəˌlizəm/ ▸n. a political and economic theory of social organization that holds that a country's land, transportation, natural resources, and chief industries should be owned or controlled by the community as a whole. ■ **so·cial·ist** n. & adj. **so·cial·is·tic** /ˌsōsHə'listik/ adj.

so·cial·ite /'sōsHəˌlīt/ ▸n. a person who mixes in fashionable society.

so·cial·ize /'sōsHəˌlīz/ ▸v. **1** mix socially with other people. **2** make someone behave in a way that is acceptable to society. ■ **so·cial·i·za·tion** /ˌsōsHəli'zāsHən/ n.

so·cial mar·ket e·con·o·my (also **social market**) ▸n. an economic system based on a free market operating together with a welfare state to protect people who are unable to sell their labor, such as the elderly or unemployed.

so·cial net·work·ing ▸n. the use of a dedicated website to communicate informally with other members of the site, by posting messages, photographs, etc.

so·cial re·al·ism ▸n. the realistic portrayal in art of contemporary life, as a means of commenting on the social or political situation.

so·cial sci·ence ▸n. **1** the scientific study of human society and social relationships. **2** a subject within this field, such as economics.

So·cial Se·cu·ri·ty ▸n. a federal insurance program that provides benefits to retired persons, the unemployed, and the disabled.

so·cial ser·vi·ces ▸pl.n. services provided by the government for the community, such as education and medical care.

so·cial stud·ies ▸pl.n. (treated as sing.) the study of human society.

so·cial work ▸n. work carried out by people trained to help improve the conditions of people who are poor, old, or socially deprived. ■ **so·cial work·er** n.

so·ci·e·ty /sə'sīətē/ ▸n. (pl. **societies**) **1** all the people living together in a more or less ordered community. **2** a particular community of people living in a country or region, and having shared customs, laws, and organizations. **3** (also **high society**) people who are fashionable, wealthy, and influential, viewed as a distinct social group. **4** an organization or club formed for a particular purpose or activity. **5** the situation of being in the company of other people: *she shunned the society of others.* ■ **so·ci·e·tal** /sə'sīitl/ adj.

so·ci·o·bi·ol·o·gy /ˌsōsēōˌbī'äləjē/ ▸n. the scientific study of the biological aspects of social behavior in animals and humans. ■ **so·ci·o·bi·o·log·i·cal** /-ˌbīə'läjikəl/ adj. **so·ci·o·bi·ol·o·gist** n.

so·ci·o·cul·tur·al /ˌsōsēō'kəlcHərəl/ ▸adj. combining social and cultural factors.

so·ci·o·ec·o·nom·ic /ˌsōsēōˌēkə'nämik, -ekə-/ ▸adj. relating to the interaction of social and economic factors.

so·ci·ol·o·gy /ˌsōsē'äləjē/ ▸n. the study of the structure and functioning of human society. ■ **so·ci·o·log·i·cal** /ˌsōsēō'läjikəl/ adj. **so·ci·ol·o·gist** n.

so·ci·o·path /'sōsēōˌpaTH/ ▸n. a person with a personality disorder showing itself in extreme antisocial attitudes and behavior. ■ **so·ci·o·path·ic** /ˌsōsēō'paTHik/ adj.

so·ci·o·po·lit·i·cal /ˌsōsēōpə'litikəl/ ▸adj. combining social and political factors.

sock /säk/ ▸n. **1** a knitted garment for the foot and lower part of the leg. **2** informal a hard blow. ▸v. informal hit someone or something hard.
– PHRASES **put a sock in it** informal stop talking. **sock it to** informal make a forceful impression on someone.

sock·et /'säkit/ ▸n. **1** a hollow in which something fits or revolves. **2** an electrical device into which a plug or light bulb is fitted.

sock·eye /'säkˌī/ ▸n. a North Pacific salmon that is an important food fish.

So·crat·ic /sə'kratik/ ▸adj. relating to the ancient Greek philosopher Socrates or his ideas.

sod /säd/ ▸n. **1** grass-covered ground; turf. **2** a piece of turf.

so·da /'sōdə/ ▸n. **1** a carbonated soft drink. **2** (also **soda water**) carbonated water (originally made with sodium bicarbonate). **3** sodium carbonate.

so·da bread ▸n. bread in which baking soda is used as the raising agent.

so·da foun·tain ▸n. **1** a device dispensing soda water or soft drinks. **2** a cafe or counter selling soft drinks, ice creams, etc.

sod·den /'sädn/ ▸adj. **1** soaked through. **2** (in combination) having drunk too much of an alcoholic drink: *whiskey-sodden.*

so·di·um /'sōdēəm/ ▸n. a soft silver-white metallic chemical element of which common salt and soda are compounds.

so·di·um bi·car·bon·ate ▸n. a soluble white powder used chiefly in fire extinguishers and effervescent drinks and as a raising agent in baking.

so·di·um chlo·ride ▸n. the chemical name for common salt.

so·di·um hy·drox·ide ▶n. a strongly alkaline white compound used in many industrial processes; caustic soda.

so·di·um-va·por lamp (also **sodium lamp**) ▶n. a lamp in which an electrical discharge in sodium vapor gives a yellow light.

sod·om·ite /'sädə,mīt/ ▶n. a person who engages in sodomy.

sod·om·y /'sädəmē/ ▶n. anal or oral sex. ■ **sod·om·ize** /'sädə,mīz/ v.

so·fa /'sōfə/ ▶n. a long upholstered seat with a back and arms, for two or more people.

so·fa bed ▶n. a sofa that can be converted into a bed.

sof·fit /'säfit/ ▶n. the underside of an arch, a balcony, overhanging eaves, etc.

soft /sôft/ ▶adj. 1 easy to mold, cut, compress, or fold. 2 not rough or coarse in texture. 3 quiet and gentle. 4 (of light or color) not harsh. 5 sympathetic or lenient; not strict or strict enough. 6 informal (of a job or way of life) needing little effort. 7 informal foolish. 8 (**soft on**) informal having romantic feelings for someone. 9 (of a drink) not alcoholic. 10 (of a drug) not likely to cause addiction. 11 (of water) free from mineral salts. 12 (of a group within a political party) willing to compromise. 13 (also **soft-core**) (of pornography) suggestive but not explicit. ■ **soft·ish** adj. **soft·ly** adv. **soft·ness** n. – PHRASES **have a soft spot for** be fond of. **a soft** (or **easy**) **touch** informal a person who is easily persuaded or imposed on.

soft·back /'sôf(t),bak/ ▶adj. & n. another term for PAPERBACK.

soft·ball /'sôf(t),bôl/ ▶n. a form of baseball played on a smaller field with a larger, softer ball.

soft-boiled ▶adj. (of an egg) lightly boiled, leaving the yolk soft or liquid.

soft·cov·er /'sôf(t),kəvər/ ▶adj. & n. another term for PAPERBACK.

soft·en /'sôfən/ ▶v. 1 make or become soft or softer. 2 (often **soften someone up**) make someone more likely to do something. ■ **soft·en·er** n.

soft fo·cus ▶n. deliberate slight blurring or lack of definition in a photograph or movie.

soft·heart·ed /'sôft'härtid/ ▶adj. kind, caring and sympathetic.

soft·ie /'sôftē/ (also **softy**) ▶n. (pl. **softies**) informal a weak or softhearted person.

soft pal·ate /'palit/ ▶n. the fleshy, flexible part toward the back of the roof of the mouth.

soft-ped·al ▶v. play down the unpleasant aspects of something. ▶n. (**soft pedal**) a pedal on a piano that can be pressed to soften the tone.

soft rock ▶n. a style of rock music with a less persistent beat and more emphasis on lyrics and melody than hard rock.

soft sell ▶n. the selling of something in a gentle and persuasive way.

soft-soap ▶v. informal use flattery to persuade someone to do something.

soft-spo·ken ▶adj. speaking or said with a gentle, quiet voice.

soft tar·get ▶n. a person or thing that is relatively unprotected or vulnerable.

soft·ware /'sôft,we(ə)r/ ▶n. programs and other operating information used by a computer.

soft·wood /'sôft,wŏŏd/ ▶n. the wood from conifers as opposed to that of broadleaved trees.

soft·y ▶n. variant spelling of SOFTIE.

sog·gy /'sägē/ ▶adj. (**soggier, soggiest**) very wet and soft. ■ **sog·gi·ly** adv. **sog·gi·ness** n.

soh /sō/ ▶n. variant of SOL¹.

soi-di·sant /,swä dē'zän(t)/ ▶adj. using a description or title that one has given oneself; self-styled: *a soi-disant novelist.*

soi·gné /swän'yā/ ▶adj. (fem. **soignée** pronunc. same) elegant and well groomed.

soil¹ /soil/ ▶n. 1 the upper layer of earth in which plants grow. 2 the territory of a particular nation.

soil² ▶v. 1 make something dirty. 2 damage someone's reputation. ▶n. waste matter, especially sewage.

soi·rée /swä'rā/ ▶n. an evening social gathering, typically in a private house, for conversation or music.

so·journ /'sōjərn/ literary ▶n. a temporary stay. ▶v. stay somewhere temporarily. ■ **so·journ·er** n.

sol¹ /sōl/ ▶n. Music the fifth note of a major scale, coming after 'fa' and before 'la'.

sol² /säl, sōl/ ▶n. Chemistry a liquid containing a colloid in suspension.

sol³ /sōl, sôl/ ▶n. (pl. **soles** /'sōlāz, 'sôles/) the basic unit of money of Peru.

sol·ace /'sälis/ ▶n. comfort or consolation given in a time of difficulty or sadness. ▶v. give solace to someone.

so·lar /'sōlər/ ▶adj. relating to the sun or its rays, or using the sun's energy.

so·lar bat·ter·y (also **solar cell**) ▶n. a device that converts the sun's radiation into electricity.

so·lar e·clipse ▶n. an eclipse in which the sun is hidden by the moon.

so·lar en·er·gy ▶n. energy in the form of radiation given off by the sun.

so·lar flare ▶n. a brief eruption of intense high-energy radiation from the sun's surface.

so·lar·i·um /sə'le(ə)rēəm, sō-/ ▶n. (pl. **solariums** or **solaria** /-'le(ə)rēə/) 1 a room equipped with sunlamps or sunbeds. 2 a room with large areas of glass to let in sunlight.

so·lar·ize /'sōlə,rīz/ ▶v. Photography change the relative darkness of a part of an image by overexposure to light.

so·lar pan·el ▶n. a panel designed to absorb the sun's rays as a source of energy for generating electricity or heating.

so·lar plex·us /'pleksəs/ ▶n. a network of nerves at the pit of the stomach.

so·lar pow·er ▶n. power obtained by controlling and using the energy of the sun's rays.

so·lar sys·tem ▶n. the sun together with the planets, asteroids, comets, etc., in orbit around it.

so·lar wind ▶n. a continuous flow of charged particles from the sun, spreading throughout the solar system.

so·lar year ▶n. the time between one spring or autumn equinox and the next, or between one winter or summer solstice and the next (365 days, 5 hours, 48 minutes, and 46 seconds).

sold /sōld/ ▶ past and past participle of SELL.

sol·der /'sädər/ ▶n. an alloy, especially one based on lead and tin, that is heated and melted and used to join pieces of metal together. ▶v. join pieces of metal with solder.

sol·der·ing i·ron ▶n. an electrical tool for melting and applying solder.

sol·dier /'sōljər/ ▶ n. 1 a person who serves in an army. 2 (also **common soldier** or **private soldier**) a private in an army. ▶ v. 1 serve as a soldier. 2 (**soldier on**) informal continue doing something in spite of difficulty. ■ **sol·dier·ly** adj.
– PHRASES **soldier of fortune** a professional soldier hired to serve in a foreign army.

sole¹ /sōl/ ▶ n. 1 the underside of a person's foot. 2 the section forming the underside of a piece of footwear. 3 the underside of a tool or implement such as a plane. ▶ v. replace the sole on a shoe.

sole² ▶ n. (pl. same) an edible flatfish.

sole³ ▶ adj. 1 one and only. 2 belonging or restricted to one person or group.

sol·e·cism /'sälə,sizəm, 'sō-/ ▶ n. 1 a grammatical mistake. 2 an instance of bad manners or incorrect behavior.

sole·ly /'sōl(l)ē/ ▶ adv. not involving anyone or anything else; only.

sol·emn /'säləm/ ▶ adj. 1 formal and dignified. 2 not cheerful; serious. 3 deeply sincere: *a solemn oath.* ■ **sol·emn·ly** adv.

so·lem·ni·ty /sə'lemnitē/ ▶ n. (pl. **solemnities**) 1 the state or quality of being solemn. 2 (**solemnities**) formal, dignified rites or ceremonies.

sol·em·nize /'säləm,nīz/ ▶ v. 1 perform a ceremony, especially that of marriage. 2 mark an occasion with a formal ceremony. ■ **sol·em·ni·za·tion** /,säləmni'zāsʜən/ n.

so·le·noid /'sōlə,noid/ ▶ n. a cylindrical coil of wire that becomes magnetic when an electric current is passed through it.

sole·plate /'sōl,plāt/ ▶ n. 1 a metal plate forming the base of an electric iron, jigsaw, or other machine. 2 a horizontal timber at the base of a wall frame.

sol·fa /,sōl 'fä/ ▶ n. short for TONIC SOL-FA.

so·lic·it /sə'lisit/ ▶ v. (**solicits, soliciting, solicited**) 1 ask for or try to obtain something from someone: *he called a meeting to solicit their views.* 2 (of a prostitute) approach someone and offer sex for money. ■ **so·lic·i·ta·tion** /sə,lisə'tāsʜən/ n.

so·lic·i·tor /sə'lisitər/ ▶ n. 1 a person who contacts businesses to sell them supplies, services, or advertising. 2 the chief law officer of a city, town, or government department. 3 Brit. a lawyer qualified to deal with conveyancing, draw up wills, advise clients and instruct barristers, and represent clients in lower courts. Compare with BARRISTER.

so·lic·i·tor gen·er·al ▶ n. (pl. **solicitors general**) the law officer directly below the attorney general in the US Department of Justice.

so·lic·i·tous /sə'lisitəs/ ▶ adj. showing interest or concern about a person's well-being. ■ **so·lic·i·tous·ly** adv. **so·lic·i·tous·ness** n.

so·lic·i·tude /sə'lisi,t(y)ōōd/ ▶ n. care or concern for someone or something.

sol·id /'sälid/ ▶ adj. (**solider, solidest**) 1 firm and stable in shape; not liquid or fluid. 2 strongly built or made. 3 not hollow or having spaces or gaps. 4 consisting of the same substance throughout. 5 (of time) continuous: *two solid hours of entertainment.* 6 able to be relied on: *solid evidence.* 7 Geometry three-dimensional.
▶ n. 1 a solid substance or object. 2 (**solids**) food that is not liquid. 3 a three-dimensional body or geometric figure. ■ **so·lid·i·ty** /sə'liditē/ n. **sol·id·ly** adv. **sol·id·ness** n.

sol·i·dar·i·ty /,sälə'de(ə)ritē/ ▶ n. unity and mutual support resulting from shared interests, feelings, or opinions.

sol·i·di /'säli,dī/ ▶ plural of SOLIDUS.

so·lid·i·fy /sə'lidə,fī/ ▶ v. (**solidifies, solidifying, solidified**) make or become hard or solid. ■ **so·lid·i·fi·ca·tion** /sə,lidəfi'kāsʜən/ n.

sol·id state ▶ adj. (of an electronic device) using solid semiconductors, e.g., transistors, as opposed to valves.

sol·i·dus /'sälidəs/ ▶ n. (pl. **solidi** /-,dī/) another term for SLASH (sense 3 of the noun).

so·lil·o·quy /sə'liləkwē/ ▶ n. (pl. **soliloquies**) a speech in a play in which a character speaks their thoughts aloud when alone on stage. ■ **so·lil·o·quize** /-,kwīz/ v.

sol·ip·sism /'sälip,sizəm/ ▶ n. 1 the view that the self is all that can be known to exist. 2 the quality of being selfish. ■ **sol·ip·sist** n. **sol·ip·sis·tic** /,sälip'sistik/ adj.

sol·i·taire /'sälə,te(ə)r/ ▶ n. 1 any of various card games for one person, played by trying to use up all one's cards by forming certain sequences. 2 a single diamond or other gem in a piece of jewelry.

sol·i·tar·y /'sälə,terē/ ▶ adj. 1 done or existing alone. 2 (of a place) secluded or isolated. 3 single: *not a solitary shred of evidence.* ▶ n. (pl. **solitaries**) 1 a person who lives alone for personal or religious reasons. 2 informal solitary confinement. ■ **sol·i·tar·i·ness** n.

sol·i·tar·y con·fine·ment ▶ n. the isolating of a prisoner in a separate cell as a punishment.

sol·i·tude /'sälə,t(y)ōōd/ ▶ n. 1 the state of being alone. 2 a lonely or uninhabited place.

sol·mi·za·tion /,sälmi'zāsʜən, sōl-/ ▶ n. a system of associating each note of a musical scale with a particular syllable (typically the sequence do, re, mi, fa, sol, la, ti), especially to teach singing.

so·lo /'sōlō/ ▶ n. (pl. **solos**) 1 a song, dance, or piece of music for one performer. 2 a flight undertaken by a single pilot. 3 (also **solo whist**) a card game resembling whist in which the players make bids and the highest bidder plays against the others. ▶ adj. & adv. for or done by one person. ▶ v. (**soloes, soloing, soloed**) perform a solo.

so·lo·ist /'sōlōist/ ▶ n. a musician or singer who performs a solo.

Sol·o·mon's seal ▶ n. a plant with arching stems bearing a double row of broad leaves and drooping green and white flowers.

sol·stice /'sōlstis/ ▶ n. each of the two times in the year, respectively at midsummer and midwinter, when the sun reaches its highest or lowest point in the sky at noon, marked by the longest and shortest days.

sol·u·ble /'sälyəbəl/ ▶ adj. 1 (of a substance) able to be dissolved, especially in water. 2 (of a problem) able to be solved. ■ **sol·u·bil·i·ty** /,sälyə'bilitē/ n.

sol·ute /'säl,yōōt/ ▶ n. the minor component in a solution, dissolved in the solvent.

so·lu·tion /sə'lōōsʜən/ ▶ n. 1 a means of solving a problem. 2 the correct answer to a puzzle. 3 a mixture formed when a substance (the solute) is dissolved in a liquid (the solvent). 4 the process of dissolving or the state of being dissolved.

solve /sälv, sôlv/ ▶ v. find an answer to, explanation for, or way of dealing with a problem or mystery. ■ **solv·a·ble** adj. **solv·er** n.

sol·vent /'sälvənt/ ▶ adj. **1** having more money than one owes. **2** able to dissolve other substances. ▶ n. **1** a liquid that can dissolve other substances. **2** the liquid in which another substance is dissolved to form a solution. ■ **sol·ven·cy** n.

sol·vent a·buse ▶ n. the deliberate inhalation of the intoxicating fumes of certain solvents such as glue.

so·ma /'sōmə/ ▶ n. **1** Biology the parts of an organism other than the reproductive cells. **2** the body as distinct from the soul or mind.

So·ma·li /sə'mälē, sō-/ ▶ n. (pl. **Somalis**) **1** a person from Somalia. **2** a member of a mainly Muslim people of Somalia. **3** the language of the Somali. ■ adj. relating to Somalia. ■ **So·ma·li·an** adj. & n.

so·mat·ic /sə'matik, sō-/ ▶ adj. relating to the body, especially as distinct from the mind.

som·ber /'sämbər/ (Brit. **sombre**) ▶ adj. **1** dark or dull. **2** serious and sad. ■ **som·ber·ly** adv. **som·ber·ness** n.

som·bre·ro /säm'bre(ə)rō/ ▶ n. (pl. **sombreros**) a broad-brimmed hat, typically worn in Mexico and the southwestern US.

some /səm/ ▶ determiner **1** an unspecified amount or number of. **2** referring to an unknown or unspecified person or thing. **3** (used with a number) approximately. **4** a considerable amount or number of. **5** a certain small amount or number of. **6** expressing admiration: *that was some goal.* ▶ pron. **1** an unspecified number or amount of people or things. **2** a certain small number or amount of people or things.

some·bod·y /'səmbədē, 'səm,bädē/ ▶ pron. someone.

some·day /'səm,dā/ ▶ adv. at some time in the future.

some·how /'səm,hou/ ▶ adv. **1** by one means or another. **2** for an unknown or unspecified reason.

some·one /'səm,wən/ ▶ pron. **1** an unknown or unspecified person. **2** an important or famous person.

some·place /'səm,plās/ ▶ adv. & pron. informal somewhere.

som·er·sault /'səmər,sôlt/ ▶ n. an acrobatic movement in which a person turns head over heels in the air or on the ground and finishes on their feet. ▶ v. perform a somersault.

some·thing /'səm,THiNG/ ▶ pron. **1** an unspecified or unknown thing. **2** an unspecified or unknown amount or degree. ▶ adv. informal used for emphasis: *my back hurts something terrible.*

some·time /'səm,tīm/ ▶ adv. at some unspecified or unknown time. ▶ adj. former: *the sometime editor of the paper.*

some·times /'səm,tīmz/ ▶ adv. occasionally.

some·what /'səm,(h)wät/ ▶ adv. to some extent; rather.

some·where /'səm,(h)we(ə)r/ ▶ adv. **1** in or to an unspecified or unknown place. **2** used to indicate an approximate amount. ▶ pron. some unspecified place.

– PHRASES **get somewhere** informal make progress.

som·me·lier /,səməl'yā/ ▶ n. a waiter who serves wine.

som·nam·bu·lism /säm'nambyə,lizəm/ ▶ n. sleepwalking. ■ **som·nam·bu·lant** adj. **som·nam·bu·list** n. **som·nam·bu·lis·tic**

/-,nambyə'listik/ adj.

som·no·lent /'sämnələnt/ ▶ adj. **1** sleepy. **2** causing sleepiness. ■ **som·no·lence** n. **som·no·lent·ly** adv.

son /sən/ ▶ n. **1** a boy or man in relation to his parents. **2** a male descendant. **3** (**the Son** or **the Son of Man**) Jesus. **4** (also **my son**) a form of address for a boy or younger man.

so·nar /'sō,när/ ▶ n. **1** a system for detecting objects under water based on the emission and reflection of sound pulses. **2** a device used in this system.

so·na·ta /sə'nätə/ ▶ n. a piece of classical music for a solo instrument, often with a piano accompaniment.

song /sôNG/ ▶ n. **1** a poem or other set of words set to music. **2** singing: *they broke into song.* **3** the musical sounds made by some birds, whales, and insects. **4** literary a poem.

– PHRASES **for a song** informal very cheaply. **a song and dance** informal a fuss.

song·bird /'sôNG,bərd/ ▶ n. a bird with a musical song.

song cy·cle ▶ n. a set of related songs forming a single musical work.

song·smith /'sôNG,smiTH/ ▶ n. informal a writer of popular songs.

song·ster /'sôNGstər/ ▶ n. (fem. **songstress**) a person who sings.

song·writ·er /'sôNG,rītər/ ▶ n. a writer of songs or the music for them.

son·ic /'sänik/ ▶ adj. relating to or using sound waves. ■ **son·i·cal·ly** /-ik(ə)lē/ adv.

son·ic boom ▶ n. an explosive noise caused by the shock wave from an aircraft or other object traveling faster than the speed of sound.

son·ics /'säniks/ ▶ pl.n. musical sounds artificially produced or reproduced.

son-in-law ▶ n. (pl. **sons-in-law**) the husband of one's daughter.

son·net /'sänit/ ▶ n. a poem of fourteen lines using any of a number of fixed rhyme schemes.

son·ny /'sənē/ ▶ n. informal a familiar form of address to a boy or young man.

son·o·gram /'sänə,gram/ ▶ n. **1** a graph showing the distribution of energy at different frequencies in a sound. **2** a visual image produced from an ultrasound examination. ■ **son·o·graph·ic** /,sänə'grafik/ adj. **so·nog·ra·phy** /sə'nägrəfē/ n.

so·no·rous /sə'nôrəs, 'sänərəs/ ▶ adj. **1** (of a sound) deep and full. **2** (of speech) using grand or impressive language. ■ **so·nor·i·ty** /sə'nôritē/ n. **so·no·rous·ly** adv.

soon /sōōn/ ▶ adv. **1** in or after a short time. **2** early. **3** used to indicate a preference: *I'd just as soon Tim did it.* ■ **soon·ish** adv.

– PHRASES **no sooner than** at the very moment that. **sooner or later** eventually.

> **USAGE**
> The phrase **no sooner** should be followed by **than** rather than **when** in standard English: *we had no sooner arrived than we had to leave*, not *we had no sooner arrived when we had to leave*. This is because **sooner** is a comparative form, and comparative forms should be followed by **than**.

soot /sŏŏt/ ▶ n. a black powdery or flaky substance produced when an organic substance such as coal is burned.

sooth /sōōth/ ▶ n. old use truth.
– PHRASES **in sooth** truly.

soothe /sōōth/ ▶ v. **1** gently calm a person or their fears. **2** relieve pain or discomfort.
■ **sooth·er** n. **sooth·ing** adj.

sooth·say·er /'sōōth,sāər/ ▶ n. a person supposed to be able to foresee the future. ■ **sooth·say·ing** n.

soot·y /'sōōtē/ ▶ adj. (**sootier, sootiest**) covered with or colored like soot.

SOP ▶ abbr. standard operating procedure.

sop /säp/ ▶ n. a thing of no great value given or done in an attempt to appease someone who is angry or disappointed. ▶ v. (**sops, sopping, sopped**) (**sop something up**) soak up liquid.

soph. ▶ abbr. sophomore.

soph·ism /'säfizəm/ ▶ n. a clever but false argument, especially one used to deceive other people.

soph·ist /'säfist/ ▶ n. a person who uses clever but false arguments. ■ **so·phis·tic** /sə'fistik/ adj. **so·phis·ti·cal** /sə'fistikəl/ adj.

so·phis·ti·cate ▶ n. /sə'fistə,kit, -kāt/ a person having experience and taste in matters of fashion and culture. ▶ v. /sə'fistə,kāt/ make someone or something more sophisticated.
■ **so·phis·ti·ca·tion** /sə,fisti'kāsнən/ n.

so·phis·ti·cat·ed /sə'fisti,kātid/ ▶ adj. **1** having or showing experience and taste in matters of culture or fashion. **2** appealing to sophisticated people. **3** (of a machine, system, or technique) highly developed and complex.

soph·ist·ry /'säfəstrē/ ▶ n. (pl. **sophistries**) **1** the use of clever false arguments, especially to deceive other people. **2** a clever but false argument.

soph·o·more /'säf(ə),môr/ ▶ n. a second-year high-school or college student.

soph·o·mor·ic /,säf(ə)'môrik/ ▶ adj. **1** relating to or characteristic of a sophomore. **2** pretentious or juvenile: *sophomoric humor.*

sop·o·rif·ic /,säpə'rifik/ ▶ adj. causing drowsiness or sleep. ▶ n. a drug or other substance that causes drowsiness or sleep.

sop·ping /'säpiNG/ (also **sopping wet**) ▶ adj. wet through.

sop·py /'säpē/ ▶ adj. (**soppier, soppiest**) informal **1** sentimental in a silly or self-indulgent way. **2** rather weak and feeble. ■ **sop·pi·ly** adv. **sop·pi·ness** n.

so·pran·o /sə'pranō/ ▶ n. (pl. **sopranos**) the highest singing voice. ▶ adj. (of an instrument) of a high or the highest pitch in its family: *a soprano saxophone.*

sor·bet /sôr'bā, 'sôrbit/ ▶ n. a frozen dessert consisting of fruit juice or purée in a sugar syrup.

sor·cer·er /'sôrsərər/ ▶ n. (fem. **sorceress** /'sôrsəris/) a person believed to practice magic; a wizard. ■ **sor·cer·y** /'sôrsərē/ n.

sor·did /'sôrdid/ ▶ adj. **1** dishonest or immoral; morally distasteful: *the truth about his sordid past.* **2** dirty or squalid. ■ **sor·did·ly** adv. **sor·did·ness** n.

sore /sôr/ ▶ adj. **1** painful or aching. **2** great; urgent: *we're in sore need of him.* **3** informal upset and angry. ▶ n. a raw or painful place on the body. ▶ adv. old use extremely: *sore afraid.*
■ **sore·ness** n.
– PHRASES **sore point** an issue about which someone feels distressed or annoyed. **stand (or

stick) out like a sore thumb be quite obviously different.

sore·ly /'sôrlē/ ▶ adv. extremely; greatly.

sor·ghum /'sôrgəm/ ▶ n. a cereal native to warm regions, grown for grain and animal feed.

so·ror·i·ty /sə'rôritē, -'rä-/ ▶ n. (pl. **sororities**) a society for female students in a college or university.

sor·rel[1] /'sôrəl/ ▶ n. an edible plant of the dock family with arrow-shaped leaves and a bitter flavor.

sor·rel[2] ▶ n. **1** a light reddish-brown color. **2** a horse with a sorrel coat.

sor·row /'särō, 'sôrō/ ▶ n. **1** deep distress caused by loss or disappointment. **2** a cause of sorrow. ▶ v. feel sorrow.

sor·row·ful /'särəfəl, ,sôrō-/ ▶ adj. **1** feeling or showing sorrow. **2** causing sorrow.
■ **sor·row·ful·ly** adv.

sor·ry /'särē, 'sô-/ ▶ adj. (**sorrier, sorriest**) **1** feeling distress or pity through sympathy with someone else's misfortune. **2** feeling or expressing regret. **3** in a poor or pitiful state. **4** unpleasant and regrettable: *a sorry business.*
■ **sor·ri·ness** n.

sort /sôrt/ ▶ n. **1** a category of people or things with a common feature or features. **2** informal a person with a particular nature: *he was a friendly sort.* ▶ v. **1** arrange systematically in groups: *he sorted the contents of the desk into two piles.* **2** (often **sort something out**) separate something from a mixed group. **3** (**sort something out**) resolve a problem or difficulty. **4** (**sort someone out**) informal deal with a troublesome person. ■ **sort·er** n.
– PHRASES **of a sort** (or **of sorts**) of a somewhat unusual or inferior kind. **out of sorts** slightly unwell or unhappy. **sort of** informal to some extent.

> **USAGE**
> The expression **these sort of**, as in *I don't want to answer these sort of questions*, does not follow traditional grammar and should be avoided in formal writing. This is because **these** is plural and normally agrees with a plural noun; the preferred usage is *these sorts of questions*. See also the note at KIND[1].

sort·ie /,sôr'tē, 'sôrtē/ ▶ n. **1** an attack made by troops coming out from a position of defense. **2** a flight by a single aircraft on a military operation. **3** a short trip.

SOS ▶ n. **1** an international signal of extreme distress, used especially by ships at sea. **2** an urgent appeal for help.

so-so ▶ adj. neither very good nor very bad.

sot /sät/ ▶ n. a person who is regularly drunk.
■ **sot·tish** adj.

sot·to vo·ce /'sätō 'vōchē/ ▶ adv. & adj. in a quiet voice.

sou /sōō/ ▶ n. dated, informal a very small amount of money.

sou·brette /sōō'bret/ ▶ n. a pert maidservant or similar minor female role in a comedy.

sou·bri·quet ▶ n. variant spelling of SOBRIQUET.

souf·flé /sōō'flā/ ▶ n. a light, spongy baked dish made by mixing egg yolks and another ingredient such as cheese or fruit with stiffly beaten egg whites.

sought /sôt/ ▶ past and past participle of SEEK.
– PHRASES **sought af·ter** in great demand.

souk /sōōk/ ▶ n. an Arab market.

soul /sōl/ ▶ n. **1** the spiritual element of a

person, believed to be immortal. **2** a person's moral or emotional nature. **3** emotional or intellectual energy or power: *their performance lacked soul.* **4** a person regarded as a perfect example of a particular quality: *she's the soul of discretion.* **5** an individual person: *I'll never tell a soul.* **6** (also **soul music**) a kind of music that incorporates elements of gospel music and rhythm and blues, popularized by black Americans.

soul-des·troy·ing ▶ adj. unbearably dull and repetitive.

soul food ▶ n. food traditionally associated with black people of the southern US.

soul·ful /'sōlfəl/ ▶ adj. expressing deep and usually sorrowful feeling. ■ **soul·ful·ly** adv. **soul·ful·ness** n.

soul·less /'sōl,lis/ ▶ adj. **1** lacking character and individuality: *soulless postwar apartment blocks.* **2** (of an activity) dull and uninspiring. **3** lacking human feelings.

soul·mate /'sōl,māt/ ▶ n. a person ideally suited to another.

soul-search·ing ▶ n. close examination of one's emotions and motives.

sound¹ /sound/ ▶ n. **1** vibrations that travel through air or water and are sensed by the ear. **2** a thing that can be heard. **3** music, speech, and sound effects accompanying a movie or broadcast. **4** an idea or impression given by words: *you've had a hard day, by the sound of it.* ▶ v. **1** make a sound. **2** make a sound to show or warn of something. **3** give a particular impression: *the job sounds great.* **4** (**sound off**) express one's opinions loudly or forcefully. ■ **sound·less** adj.

sound² ▶ adj. **1** in good condition. **2** based on reason or good judgment. **3** financially secure. **4** competent or reliable. **5** (of sleep) deep and unbroken. **6** severe or thorough: *a sound thrashing.* ▶ adv. in a sound way. ■ **sound·ly** adv. **sound·ness** n.

sound³ ▶ v. **1** find out the depth of water in the sea, a lake, etc., by means of a line or pole or using sound echoes. **2** (**sound someone out**) question someone discreetly or cautiously about their opinions or feelings. **3** examine the bladder or another part of the body with a long surgical probe. ■ **sound·er** n.

sound⁴ ▶ n. a narrow stretch of water forming an inlet or connecting two larger areas of water.

sound-and-light ▶ adj. referring to an nighttime entertainment held at a historic monument or building, telling its history by the use of lighting effects and recorded sound.

sound bar·ri·er ▶ n. the point at which an aircraft reaches the speed of sound, causing reduced control, an explosive noise, and various other effects.

sound bite ▶ n. a short, memorable extract from a speech or interview.

sound·board /'soun(d),bôrd/ (also **sounding board**) ▶ n. a thin board over which the strings of a piano or similar instrument are positioned to increase the sound produced.

sound·box /'sound,bäks/ ▶ n. the hollow chamber that forms the body of a stringed instrument and makes the sound resonate.

sound·check /'soun(d),CHek/ ▶ n. a test of sound equipment before a musical performance or recording.

sound ef·fect ▶ n. a sound other than speech or music made artificially for use in a play, movie, etc.

sound·ing /'soundiNG/ ▶ n. **1** the action of sounding the depth of water. **2** a measurement taken by sounding. **3** (**soundings**) information or evidence found out before taking action.

sound·ing board ▶ n. **1** a person or group with whom new ideas or opinions are discussed to test their validity or likelihood of success. **2** a board over or behind a pulpit or stage to reflect a speaker's voice forward. **3** a soundboard.

sound·ing line ▶ n. a weighted line used to measure the depth of water under a boat.

sound-proof /'soun(d),prōōf/ ▶ adj. preventing sound getting in or out. ▶ v. make something soundproof.

sound-scape /'soun(d),skāp/ ▶ n. a piece of music considered in terms of the different sounds of which it is composed.

sound sys·tem ▶ n. a set of equipment for reproducing and amplifying sound.

sound·track /'soun(d),trak/ ▶ n. the sound accompaniment to a movie.

sound wave ▶ n. a wave of alternate compression and reduction in density by which sound travels through air or water.

soup /sōōp/ ▶ n. a savory liquid dish made by boiling meat, fish, or vegetables in stock or water. ▶ v. (**soup something up**) informal **1** increase the power and efficiency of an engine or other machine. **2** make something more elaborate or impressive.
– PHRASES **in the soup** informal in trouble.

soup·çon /sōōp'sôN/ ▶ n. a very small amount of something.

soup kitch·en ▶ n. a place where free food is served to homeless or destitute people.

soup·y /'sōōpē/ ▶ adj. (**soupier, soupiest**) **1** having the appearance or consistency of soup. **2** informal foolishly sentimental.

sour /'sou(ə)r/ ▶ adj. **1** having a sharp taste like lemon or vinegar. **2** tasting or smelling unpleasant as a result of fermentation or staleness. **3** resentful, bitter, or angry. ▶ v. make or become sour. ▶ n. a cocktail made by mixing liquor with lemon or lime juice. ■ **sour·ly** adv. **sour·ness** n.
– PHRASES **go** (or **turn**) **sour** become less pleasant; turn out badly. **sour grapes** an attitude in which someone pretends to despise or dislike something because they cannot have it themselves.

source /sôrs/ ▶ n. **1** a place, person, or thing from which something originates. **2** a person, book, or document that provides information or evidence. **3** the spring or other place from which a river or stream begins. ▶ v. get something from a particular place: *the milk is sourced from local farms.*

source·book /'sôrs,bŏŏk/ ▶ n. a collection of writings and articles on a particular subject, especially one used as a basic introduction to that subject.

sour cream ▶ n. cream deliberately made sour by the addition of certain bacteria.

sour·dough /'sou(ə)r,dō/ ▶ n. bread made from fermenting dough, originally that left over from a previous baking.

sour·puss /'sou(ə)r,pŏŏs/ ▶ n. informal a bad-tempered or grumpy person.

sour·sop /'sou(ə)r,säp/ ▶ n. a large acidic custard apple with white fibrous flesh.

sou·sa·phone /'sōōzə,fōn/ ▶ n. a form of tuba with a wide end that points forward above the player's head.

souse /sous/ ▶ v. 1 soak or drench something with liquid. 2 (as adj. **soused**) (of gherkins, fish, etc.) pickled or marinated: *soused herring.* 3 (as adj. **soused**) informal drunk. ▶ n. liquid used for pickling.

sou·tane /sōō'tän/ ▶ n. a type of cassock worn by Roman Catholic priests.

south /souTH/ ▶ n. 1 the direction toward the point of the horizon 90° clockwise from east. 2 the southern part of a place. ▶ adj. 1 lying toward, near, or facing the south. 2 (of a wind) blowing from the south. ▶ adv. to or toward the south. ■ **south·bound** /'souTH,bound/ adj. & adv.

South Af·ri·can ▶ n. a person from South Africa. ▶ adj. relating to South Africa.

South A·mer·i·can ▶ n. a person from South America. ▶ adj. relating to South America.

south·east /,souTH'ēst/ ▶ n. the direction or region halfway between south and east. ▶ adj. 1 lying toward, near, or facing the southeast. 2 (of a wind) from the southeast. ▶ adv. to or toward the southeast. ■ **south·east·ern** adj.

south·east·er·ly /,souTH'ēstərlē/ ▶ adj. & adv. in a southeastward position or direction. ▶ n. a wind blowing from the southeast.

south·east·ward /,souTH'ēstwərd/ ▶ adv. (also **southeastwards**) toward the southeast. ▶ adj. in, toward, or facing the southeast.

south·er·ly /'səTHərlē/ ▶ adj. & adv. 1 facing or moving toward the south. 2 (of a wind) blowing from the south. ▶ n. (pl. **southerlies**) a south wind.

south·ern /'səTHərn/ ▶ adj. 1 situated in, directed toward, or facing the south. 2 (usu. **Southern**) relating to or typical of the south. ■ **south·ern·most** /-,mōst/ adj.

south·ern·er /'səTHərnər/ ▶ n. a person from the south of a region or country.

South·ern Lights ▶ pl.n. the aurora australis.

south·paw /'souTH,pô/ ▶ n. 1 informal a left-handed person. 2 a left-handed boxer who leads with the right hand.

south-south·east ▶ n. the direction halfway between south and southeast.

south-south·west ▶ n. the direction halfway between south and southwest.

south·ward /'souTHwərd/ ▶ adj. in a southerly direction. ▶ adv. (also **southwards**) toward the south.

south·west /,souTH'west/ ▶ n. the direction or region halfway between south and west. ▶ adj. 1 lying toward or facing the southwest. 2 (of a wind) from the southwest. ▶ adv. to or toward the southwest. ■ **south·west·ern** adj.

south·west·er·ly /,souTH'westərlē/ ▶ adj. & adv. in a southwestward position or direction. ▶ n. (pl. **southwesterlies**) a wind blowing from the southwest.

south·west·ward /,souTH'westwərd/ ▶ adv. (also **southwestwards**) toward the southwest. ▶ adj. in, toward, or facing the southwest.

sou·ve·nir /,sōōvə'ni(ə)r/ ▶ n. a thing that is kept as a reminder of a person, place, or event.

sou'·west·er /,sou'westər/ ▶ n. a waterproof hat with a broad brim or flap covering the back of the neck.

sov·er·eign /'säv(ə)rən/ ▶ n. 1 a king or queen who is the supreme ruler of a country. 2 a former British gold coin worth one pound sterling. ▶ adj. 1 possessing supreme power. 2 (of a nation or its affairs) acting or done independently.

sov·er·eign·ty /'säv(ə)rəntē/ ▶ n. (pl. **sovereignties**) 1 supreme power or authority. 2 a self-governing country.

so·vi·et /'sōvēit, -,et/ ▶ n. 1 (**Soviet**) a citizen of the former Soviet Union. 2 an elected council in the former Soviet Union. ▶ adj. (**Soviet**) relating to the former Soviet Union. ■ **So·vi·et·ism** /-,tizəm/ n. **So·vi·et·ize** /-,tīz/ v.

So·vi·et·ol·o·gist /,sōvēi'täləjist/ ▶ n. an expert on the former Soviet Union.

sow[1] /sō/ ▶ v. (past **sowed**; past part. **sown** or **sowed**) 1 plant seed by scattering it on or in the earth. 2 spread or introduce something unwelcome: *the new policy has sown confusion and doubt.* ■ **sow·er** n.

sow[2] /sou/ ▶ n. an adult female pig.

soy /soi/ ▶ n. another term for **SOYBEAN.** ▶ adj. made from soybeans: *soy burgers.*

soy·bean /'soi,bēn/ (also **soya bean** /'soiə/) ▶ n. an edible bean that is high in protein.

soy·meal /'soi,mēl/ ▶ n. a high-protein foodstuff made from soybeans, used in livestock feeds and as a raw ingredient in some processed foods.

soy milk /soi/ (also **soya milk** /soiə/) ▶ n. a liquid made from soybean flour in water, used as a substitute for milk.

soy sauce /soi/ ▶ n. a sauce made with fermented soybeans, used in Chinese and Japanese cooking.

SP ▶ abbr. 1 starting price. 2 service pack.

spa /spä/ ▶ n. 1 a place or resort with a mineral spring that is considered to have health-giving properties. 2 a place offering a range of health and beauty treatments. 3 (also **spa bath** or **pool**) a bath containing hot aerated water.

space /spās/ ▶ n. 1 a continuous area or expanse that is free or unoccupied. 2 the dimensions of height, depth, and width within which all things exist and move. 3 (also **outer space**) the physical universe beyond the earth's atmosphere. 4 an interval of time (indicating that it is short): *forty men died in the space of two days.* 5 a blank between typed or written words or characters. 6 the freedom to live and develop as one wishes. ▶ v. 1 position things at a distance from one another. 2 (**be spaced out**) informal be in a state of great happiness or confusion, especially from taking drugs. ■ **spac·er** n. **spac·ing** n.

space age ▶ n. (**the space age**) the era that started when the exploration of space became possible. ▶ adj. (**space-age**) very modern; technologically advanced.

space bar ▶ n. a long key on a typewriter or computer keyboard for making a space.

space ca·det ▶ n. informal a person regarded as being out of touch with reality.

space cap·sule ▶ n. a small spacecraft or the part of a larger one that contains the instruments or crew, designed to be returned to earth.

space·craft /'spās,kraft/ ▶ n. (pl. same or **spacecrafts**) a vehicle used for traveling in space.

space heat·er ▶ n. a self-contained appliance, usually electric, for heating an enclosed room. ■ **space heat·ing** n.

space·man /'spās,man, -mən/ ▸ n. (pl. **spacemen**) a male astronaut.

space probe ▸ n. an unmanned spacecraft used for exploration.

space·ship /'spā(s),ship/ ▸ n. a manned spacecraft.

space shut·tle ▸ n. a rocket-launched spacecraft able to land like an unpowered aircraft, used to make repeated journeys between earth and craft orbiting the earth.

space sta·tion ▸ n. a large artificial satellite used as a long-term base for manned operations in space.

space·suit /'spās,soot/ ▸ n. a sealed and pressurized suit designed to allow an astronaut to survive in space.

space–time ▸ n. Physics the concepts of time and three-dimensional space regarded as forming a four-dimensional continuum.

space·walk /'spās,wôk/ ▸ n. a period of activity by an astronaut outside a spacecraft. ■ **space·walk·er** n.

spac·ey /'spāsē/ (also **spacy**) ▸ adj. (**spacier**, **spaciest**) informal **1** out of touch with reality. **2** (of popular music) drifting and unworldly.

spa·cial ▸ adj. variant spelling of SPATIAL.

spa·cious /'spāshəs/ ▸ adj. (of a room or building) having plenty of space. ■ **spa·cious·ly** adv. **spa·cious·ness** n.

spade /spād/ ▸ n. a tool with a rectangular metal blade and a long handle, used for digging. ▸ v. dig or move earth with a spade. – PHRASES **call a spade a spade** speak plainly and frankly.

spades /spādz/ ▸ n. one of the four suits in a deck of playing cards, represented by an upside-down black heart shape with a small stalk. – PHRASES **in spades** informal in large amounts or to a high degree.

spade·work /'spād,wərk/ ▸ n. hard or routine work done to prepare for something.

spa·dix /'spādiks/ ▸ n. (pl. **spadices** /-dəsēz/) Botany a spike of tiny flowers closely arranged around a fleshy stem and typically enclosed in a spathe (large modified leaf).

spa·ghet·ti /spə'getē/ ▸ pl.n. pasta made in long strands.

spa·ghet·ti bo·lo·gnese /,bōlən'yēz, -'yāz/ ▸ n. a dish of spaghetti with a sauce of ground beef, tomato, onion, and herbs.

spa·ghet·ti west·ern ▸ n. informal a western (movie) filmed in Europe by an Italian director.

spake /spāk/ old use ▸ past of SPEAK.

spam /spam/ ▸ n. **1** email that has not been requested, sent to large numbers of Internet users. **2** (**Spam**) trademark a canned meat product made mainly from ham. ▸ v. (**spams, spamming, spammed**) send email that has not been requested to large numbers of Internet users. ■ **spam·mer** n.

span /span/ ▸ n. **1** the length of time for which something lasts: *he scored twice within a span of four minutes.* **2** the full extent of something from end to end. **3** a part of a bridge between the uprights supporting it. **4** a wingspan of a bird or aircraft. **5** (also **handspan**) the maximum distance between the tips of the thumb and little finger. ▸ v. (**spans, spanning, spanned**) **1** extend from side to side of something. **2** extend across a period of time or a range of subjects:

their interests span almost all the conventional disciplines.

span·dex /'spandeks/ ▸ n. a type of stretchy synthetic fabric.

span·drel /'spandrəl/ ▸ n. Architecture the roughly triangular space between the curve of an arch and the ceiling or framework above.

span·gle /'spanggəl/ ▸ n. **1** a small thin piece of glittering material, used to decorate an item of clothing; a sequin. **2** a spot of bright color or light. ▸ v. (usu. as adj. **spangled**) cover an item of clothing with spangles. ■ **span·gly** adj.

Span·iard /'spanyərd/ ▸ n. a person from Spain.

span·iel /'spanyəl/ ▸ n. a breed of dog with a long, silky coat and drooping ears.

Span·ish /'spanish/ ▸ n. the main language of Spain and of much of Central and South America. ▸ adj. relating to Spain or Spanish. ■ **Span·ish·ness** n.

Span·ish fly ▸ n. a toxic preparation of the dried bodies of a kind of beetle, sometimes used as an aphrodisiac.

Span·ish gui·tar ▸ n. the standard six-stringed acoustic guitar, used especially for classical and folk music.

Span·ish om·e·let ▸ n. an omelet containing chopped vegetables, served open rather than folded.

Span·ish on·ion ▸ n. a large onion with a mild flavor.

spank /spangk/ ▸ v. slap someone on the buttocks with the open hand or a flat object, especially as a punishment. ▸ n. a slap or series of slaps on the buttocks.

spank·ing /'spangking/ ▸ adj. **1** lively; brisk: *a spanking pace.* **2** informal impressive or pleasing. ▸ n. a series of spanks on the buttocks.

span·ner /'spanər/ ▸ n. chiefly Brit. a wrench (tool).

spar[1] /spär/ ▸ n. a thick, strong pole used as a mast or yard on a ship.

spar[2] ▸ v. (**spars, sparring, sparred**) **1** make the motions of boxing without landing heavy blows, as a form of training. **2** argue with someone without hostility. ▸ n. a period of sparring.

spar[3] ▸ n. a crystalline transparent or semitransparent mineral that is easily split.

spare /spe(ə)r/ ▸ adj. **1** not currently being used or needed: *the spare bedroom was filled with boxes.* **2** (of time) not taken up by one's usual work or activities. **3** with no excess fat; thin. **4** elegantly simple: *her clothes are smart and spare in style.* ▸ n. an item kept in case another of the same type is lost, broken, or worn out. ▸ v. **1** give something that one has enough of to someone. **2** make free or available: *can you spare me a moment?* **3** hold back from killing or harming someone. **4** protect someone from something unpleasant. ■ **spare·ly** adv. **spare·ness** n. – PHRASES **spare no expense** be prepared to pay any amount. **to spare** left over.

spare·ribs ▸ pl.n. trimmed ribs of pork.

spare tire ▸ n. **1** an extra tire carried in a motor vehicle in case of a puncture. **2** informal a roll of fat around a person's waist.

spar·ing /'spe(ə)ring/ ▸ adj. using or giving only a little of something: *sparing use of hair sprays.* ■ **spar·ing·ly** adv.

spark /spärk/ ▸ n. **1** a small fiery particle

produced by burning or caused by friction.
2 a flash of light produced by an electrical discharge. **3** an electrical discharge that ignites the explosive mixture in an internal-combustion engine. **4** a small amount of an intense feeling: *a tiny spark of anger.* **5** a sense of liveliness and excitement. ▶ v. **1** produce sparks. **2** ignite a fire. **3** (also **spark off**) cause to happen: *the announcement sparked off protests.* ■ **spark·y** adj.

spar·kle /'spärkəl/ ▶ v. **1** shine brightly with flashes of light. **2** be lively and witty. **3** (as adj. **sparkling**) (of drink) fizzy. ▶ n. **1** a glittering flash of light. **2** liveliness and wit. ■ **spar·kly** adj.

spar·kler /'spärk(ə)lər/ ▶ n. a hand-held firework that gives out sparks.

spark plug ▶ n. a device for firing the explosive mixture in an internal combustion engine.

spar·row /'sparō/ ▶ n. a small bird with brown and gray plumage.

spar·row hawk /'sparō,hôk/ ▶ n. a small hawk that preys on small birds.

sparse /spärs/ ▶ adj. present in small amounts or numbers and often thinly scattered: *Australia's relatively sparse animal population.* ■ **sparse·ly** adv. **sparse·ness** n. **spar·si·ty** /'spärsitē/ n.

Spar·tan /'spärtn/ ▶ adj. **1** relating to Sparta, a city-state in ancient Greece. **2** (**spartan**) not comfortable or luxurious; basic: *spartan barracklike hotels.* ▶ n. a citizen of Sparta.

spasm /'spazəm/ ▶ n. **1** a sudden and uncontrollable tightening of a muscle. **2** a sudden brief spell of an activity or feeling.

spas·mod·ic /spaz'mädik/ ▶ adj. occurring or done in brief, irregular bursts: *spasmodic fighting.* ■ **spas·mod·i·cal·ly** /-ik(ə)lē/ adv.

spas·tic /'spastik/ ▶ adj. **1** relating to or affected by muscle spasm. **2** relating to cerebral palsy, which makes it difficult for a person to control their muscles and movements. ▶ n. offensive **1** a person with cerebral palsy. **2** informal an incompetent person. ■ **spas·ti·cal·ly** adv. **spas·tic·i·ty** /spa'stisitē/ n.

> **USAGE**
> You should not use the word **spastic** as a noun, because many people feel it is offensive; say *person with cerebral palsy* instead.

spat[1] /spat/ ▶ past and past participle of SPIT[1].

spat[2] ▶ n. a cloth covering formerly worn by men over the ankles and shoes.

spat[3] ▶ n. informal a petty quarrel.

spate /spāt/ ▶ n. **1** a large number of similar things coming quickly one after the other. **2** chiefly Brit. a sudden flood in a river.

spathe /spāт͟H/ ▶ n. Botany a large bract (modified leaf) enclosing the flower cluster of certain plants.

spa·tial /'spāSHəl/ (also **spacial**) ▶ adj. relating to space: *a map showing spatial distribution of species of birds.* ■ **spa·ti·al·i·ty** /,spāSHē'alitē/ n. **spa·tial·ly** adv.

spat·ter /'spatər/ ▶ v. cover someone or something with drops or spots of a liquid or substance. ▶ n. a spray or splash of a liquid or substance.

spat·u·la /'spaCHələ/ ▶ n. **1** an implement with a broad flat blunt blade, used for mixing or spreading food, plaster, paint, etc. **2** a kitchen utensil with a long handle and a broad flat square or rectangular blade, sometimes slotted, used for flipping and lifting pancakes, etc.

spat·u·late /'spaCHələt/ ▶ adj. having a broad rounded end.

spawn /spôn/ ▶ v. **1** (of a fish, frog, etc.) release or deposit eggs. **2** give rise to: *overeating has spawned a weight-loss industry that reaps $40 billion per year.* ▶ n. the eggs of fish, frogs, etc. ■ **spawn·er** n.

spay /spā/ ▶ v. sterilize a female animal by removing the ovaries.

speak /spēk/ ▶ v. (**speaks**, **speaking**, **spoke**; past part. **spoken**) **1** say something. **2** (**speak to**) talk to someone in order to pass on information, advise them, etc. **3** communicate in or be able to communicate in a specified language: *my mother spoke Russian.* **4** (**speak up**) speak more loudly. **5** (**speak out/up**) express one's opinions frankly and publicly. **6** (**speak for**) express the views or position of another person. **7** be evidence of: *the islands speak of history.* **8** (**speak to**) appeal or relate to someone. **9** make a speech.
– PHRASES **speak in tongues** speak in an unknown language during religious worship. **speak one's mind** express one's opinions frankly. **speak volumes** express a great deal without using words.

speak·eas·y /'spēk,ēzē/ ▶ n. (pl. **speakeasies**) informal (during Prohibition) a secret illegal drinking club.

speak·er /'spēkər/ ▶ n. **1** a person who speaks. **2** a person who speaks a particular language. **3** a person who makes a speech. **4** (**Speaker**) the officer in charge of proceedings in a legislative assembly. **5** a loudspeaker.

speak·er·phone /'spēkər,fōn/ ▶ n. a telephone with a loudspeaker and microphone, which does not need to be held in the hand.

speak·ing /'spēkiNG/ ▶ adj. **1** used for or engaged in speech. **2** able to speak a particular language.
– PHRASES **on speaking terms** polite or friendly toward someone, especially after an argument.

spear /spi(ə)r/ ▶ n. **1** a weapon with a pointed metal tip set on a long shaft. **2** a stem of asparagus or broccoli. ▶ v. pierce or hit someone or something with a spear or other pointed object.

spear·head /'spi(ə)r,hed/ ▶ v. lead a campaign, activity, or attack. ▶ n. a person or group that leads a campaign, activity, or attack.

spear·mint /'spi(ə)r,mint/ ▶ n. the common garden mint, used in cooking as an herb and as a flavoring.

spec[1] /spek/ ▶ n. (in phrase **on spec**) informal in the hope of success but without any specific preparation or plan.

spec[2] informal ▶ n. a detailed working description; a specification. ▶ v. (**specs**, **speccing**, **specced**) construct something to a specified standard.

spe·cial /'speSHəl/ ▶ adj. **1** better, greater, or otherwise different from what is usual: *they make a special effort at Christmas.* **2** organized or intended for a particular purpose. **3** belonging or particular to a specific person or thing: *we want to preserve the town's special character.* **4** (of education) for children with particular needs, especially those with learning difficulties. ▶ n. **1** something designed or organized for a particular occasion or purpose. **2** a dish not on a restaurant's regular menu but served on a particular day. ■ **spe·cial·ness** n.

spe·cial ef·fects ▶ pl.n. illusions created for movies and television by camerawork, computer graphics, etc.

Spe·cial For·ces ▶ pl.n. an elite force within the US Army specializing in guerrilla warfare and counterinsurgency.

spe·cial·ist /'speSHəlist/ ▶ n. a person who is highly skilled or knowledgeable in a particular field. ▶ adj. relating to or involving detailed knowledge within a field. ■ **spe·cial·ism** /-ˌlizəm/ n.

spe·ci·al·i·ty /ˌspeSHē'alitē/ ▶ n. (pl. **specialities**) chiefly British term for SPECIALTY.

spe·cial·ize /'speSHəˌlīz/ ▶ v. 1 concentrate on and become expert in a particular skill or area: *he could specialize in neurosurgery.* 2 focus on providing a particular product or service. 3 (**be specialized**) (of an organ or part) be adapted or set apart to serve a special function. ■ **spe·cial·i·za·tion** /ˌspeSHəli'zāSHən/ n.

spe·cial·ly /'speSHəlē/ ▶ adv. 1 for a special purpose. 2 informal in particular; chiefly.

USAGE

For an explanation of the difference between **specially** and **especially**, see the note at ESPECIALLY.

spe·cial needs ▶ pl.n. particular educational requirements of children with learning difficulties, a physical disability, or emotional and behavioral difficulties.

spe·cial·ty /'speSHəltē/ ▶ n. (pl. **specialties**) 1 a pursuit, area of study, or skill to which someone has devoted themselves and in which they are expert. 2 a product for which a person or region is famous. 3 a branch of medicine or surgery.

spe·ci·a·tion /ˌspēSHē'āSHən, ˌspēsē-/ ▶ n. Biology the formation of new and distinct species in the course of evolution.

spe·cie /'spēSHē, -sē/ ▶ n. money in the form of coins rather than notes.

spe·cies /'spēsēz, -sHēz/ ▶ n. (pl. same) 1 a group of living organisms consisting of similar individuals capable of breeding with each other. 2 a kind or sort: *they reject this species of feminism.*

spe·cies bar·ri·er ▶ n. the natural mechanisms that prevent a virus, disease, etc., from spreading from one species to another.

spe·cif·ic /spə'sifik/ ▶ adj. 1 clearly defined or identified. 2 precise and clear. 3 (**specific to**) belonging or relating only to: *the term is specific to Canada.* 4 relating to species or a species. ▶ n. (**specifics**) precise details. ■ **spe·cif·i·cal·ly** adv. **spec·i·fic·i·ty** /ˌspesə'fisitē/ n.

spec·i·fi·ca·tion /ˌspesəfi'kāSHən/ ▶ n. 1 the action of identifying something precisely or of stating a precise requirement. 2 (usu. **specifications**) a detailed description of the design and materials used to make something. 3 a standard of workmanship and materials required to be met in a piece of work.

spe·cif·ic grav·i·ty ▶ n. technical the ratio of the density of a substance to a standard density, usually that of water or air.

spec·i·fy /'spesəˌfī/ ▶ v. (**specifies, specifying, specified**) state or identify clearly and definitely: *the company can't specify a delivery date.* ■ **spec·i·fi·a·ble** adj. **spec·i·fi·er** n.

spec·i·men /'spesəmən/ ▶ n. 1 an animal, plant,

object, etc., used as an example of its species or type for scientific study or display. 2 a sample for medical testing, especially of urine. 3 a typical example of something. 4 informal a person or animal of a specific type: *this odd female specimen.*

spe·cious /'spēSHəs/ ▶ adj. 1 seeming reasonable or plausible, but actually wrong: *a specious argument.* 2 misleading in appearance. ■ **spe·cious·ly** adv. **spe·cious·ness** n.

speck /spek/ ▶ n. a tiny spot or particle. ▶ v. mark something with small spots.

speck·le /'spekəl/ ▶ n. a small spot or patch of color. ▶ v. (often as adj. **speckled**) mark with speckles: *a speckled brown egg.*

specs /'speks/ ▶ pl.n. informal a pair of spectacles.

spec·ta·cle /'spektəkəl/ ▶ n. a visually impressive performance or display.
– PHRASES **make a spectacle of oneself** draw attention to oneself by behaving in a ridiculous way in public.

spec·ta·cles /'spektəkəlz/ ▶ pl.n. a pair of eyeglasses. ■ **spec·ta·cled** adj.

spec·tac·u·lar /spek'takyələr/ ▶ adj. very impressive, striking, or dramatic. ▶ n. a large-scale and impressive performance or event. ■ **spec·tac·u·lar·ly** adv.

spec·tate /'spektāt/ ▶ v. watch an event; be a spectator.

spec·ta·tor /'spekˌtātər/ ▶ n. a person who watches at a show, game, or other event.

spec·ter /'spektər/ (Brit. **spectre**) ▶ n. 1 a ghost. 2 a possible unpleasant or dangerous situation.

spec·tra /'spektrə/ ▶ plural of SPECTRUM.

spec·tral[1] /'spektrəl/ ▶ adj. relating to or like a specter or ghost. ■ **spec·tral·ly** adv.

spec·tral[2] ▶ adj. relating to spectra or the spectrum. ■ **spec·tral·ly** adv.

spec·tre ▶ n. British spelling of SPECTER.

spec·tro·graph /'spektrəˌgraf/ ▶ n. a device for photographing or otherwise recording spectra. ■ **spec·tro·graph·ic** /ˌspektrə'grafik/ adj.

spec·trom·e·ter /spek'trämitər/ ▶ n. a device used for recording and measuring spectra, especially as a method of analysis. ■ **spec·tro·met·ric** /ˌspektrə'metrik/ adj. **spec·trom·e·try** /spek'trämətrē/ n.

spec·tro·scope /'spektrəˌskōp/ ▶ n. a device for producing and recording spectra for examination.

spec·tros·co·py /spek'träskəpē/ ▶ n. the branch of science concerned with the investigation and measurement of spectra produced when matter interacts with or emits electromagnetic radiation. ■ **spec·tro·scop·ic** /ˌspektrə'skäpik/ adj. **spec·tros·co·pist** /-pist/ n.

spec·trum /'spektrəm/ ▶ n. (pl. **spectra** /-trə/) 1 a band of colors produced by separating light into elements with different wavelengths, e.g., in a rainbow. 2 the entire range of wavelengths of electromagnetic radiation (such as light and radio waves). 3 the components of a sound or other phenomenon arranged according to frequency, energy, etc. 4 a range of beliefs, ideas, qualities, etc.: *the idea could gain support across the political spectrum.*

spec·u·la /'spekyələ/ ▶ plural of SPECULUM.

spec·u·late /'spekyəˌlāt/ ▶ v. 1 form a theory or opinion without firm evidence. 2 invest in stocks, property, or other ventures in the hope

of making a profit but with the risk of loss.
■ **spec·u·la·tion** /ˌspekyə'lāSHən/ n. **spec·u·la·tor** /-ˌlātər/ n.

spec·u·la·tive /'spekyəˌlātiv, -lətiv/ ▶ adj. **1** based on theory or guesswork rather than knowledge. **2** (of an investment) involving a high risk of loss. ■ **spec·u·la·tive·ly** adv. **spec·u·la·tive·ness** n.

spec·u·lum /'spekyələm/ ▶ n. (pl. **specula** /-lə/) Medicine a metal instrument that is used to widen an opening or passage in the body to allow inspection.

sped /sped/ ▶ past and past participle of **SPEED**.

speech /spēCH/ ▶ n. **1** the expression of thoughts and feelings using spoken language. **2** a formal talk delivered to an audience. **3** a sequence of lines written for one character in a play.

speech·i·fy /'spēCHəˌfī/ ▶ v. (**speechifies**, **speechifying, speechified**) deliver a speech in a boring or pompous way. ■ **speech·i·fi·er** n.

speech·less /'spēCHlis/ ▶ adj. unable to speak, especially as a result of shock or strong emotion. ■ **speech·less·ly** adv. **speech·less·ness** n.

speech rec·og·ni·tion ▶ n. the process of enabling a computer to identify and respond to the sounds produced in human speech.

speech ther·a·py ▶ n. treatment to help people with speech and language problems. ■ **speech ther·a·pist** n.

speed /spēd/ ▶ n. **1** the rate at which someone or something moves or operates: *the car has a top speed of 147 mph.* **2** a fast rate of movement or action. **3** each of the possible gear ratios of a bicycle. **4** the light-gathering power of a camera lens. **5** the sensitivity of photographic film to light. **6** informal an amphetamine drug.
▶ v. (past and past part. **sped** /sped/ or **speeded**) **1** move quickly. **2** (**speed up**) move or work more quickly. **3** (usu. **speed something up**) cause something to happen more quickly. **4** (of a motorist) travel at a speed greater than the legal limit. **5** old use make prosperous or successful: *may God speed you.* ■ **speed·er** n.
– PHRASES **up to speed** informal fully informed or up to date.

speed·boat /'spēdˌbōt/ ▶ n. a motorboat designed for high speed.

speed bump (Brit. also **speed hump**) ▶ n. a ridge set in a road to control the speed of vehicles.

speed cam·era ▶ n. a roadside camera designed to catch speeding vehicles.

speed dat·ing (trademark **SpeedDating**) ▶ n. an organized activity in which a person has short conversations with a series of people to see if they like each other enough to begin a relationship.

speed di·al ▶ n. a function on some telephones that allows numbers to be entered into a memory and dialed with the push of a single button. ▶ v. (**speed-dial**) dial a telephone number by using a speed dial function.

speed lim·it ▶ n. the maximum speed at which a vehicle may legally travel on a particular stretch of road.

speed·om·e·ter /spə'dämitər/ ▶ n. an instrument on a vehicle's dashboard that indicates its speed.

speed·ster /'spēdstər/ ▶ n. informal a person or thing that operates well at high speed.

speed·way /'spēdˌwā/ ▶ n. **1** a stadium or track used for automobile or motorcycle racing. **2** Brit. a form of motorcycle racing in which the riders race laps around an oval dirt track.

speed·well /'spēdˌwel/ ▶ n. a small creeping plant with blue or pink flowers.

speed·y /'spēdē/ ▶ adj. (**speedier, speediest**) **1** done or occurring quickly. **2** moving or able to move quickly. ■ **speed·i·ly** adv. **speed·i·ness** n.

spe·le·ol·o·gy /ˌspēlē'äləjē/ ▶ n. the study or exploration of caves. ■ **spe·le·o·log·i·cal** /ˌspēlēə'läjikəl/ adj. **spe·le·ol·o·gist** n.

spell¹ /spel/ ▶ v. (past and past part. **spelled** or chiefly Brit. **spelt**) **1** write or name the letters that form a word in the correct order. **2** (of letters) form a word. **3** be a sign of; lead to: *the plans would spell disaster.* **4** (**spell something out**) explain something clearly.

spell² ▶ n. **1** a form of words thought to have magical power. **2** a very attractive or fascinating quality: *those who fell under the spell of his undeniable charm.*

spell³ ▶ n. a short period of time. ▶ v. allow someone to rest briefly by taking over from them in an activity.

spell·bind /'spelˌbīnd/ ▶ v. (past and past part. **spellbound** /'spelˌbound/) hold someone's complete attention: *the singer held the audience spellbound.* ■ **spell·bind·er** n.

spell·check·er /'spelˌCHekər/ ▶ n. a computer program that checks the spelling of words in a computer document. ■ **spell·check** v. & n.

spell·er /'spelər/ ▶ n. **1** a person who spells with a specified ability: *a good speller.* **2** a book for teaching spelling. **3** another term for SPELL-CHECKER.

spell·ing /'speliNG/ ▶ n. **1** the way in which a word is spelled. **2** a person's ability to spell.

spell·ing bee ▶ n. a spelling competition.

spelt /spelt/ ▶ n. an old kind of wheat with bearded ears and spikelets that each contain two narrow grains, used especially in health foods.

spe·lunk·ing /spi'ləNGkiNG/ ▶ n. the exploration of caves, especially as a hobby. ■ **spe·lunk·er** /-kər/ n.

spend /spend/ ▶ v. (past and past part. **spent**) **1** pay out money to buy or hire goods or services. **2** use or use up energy or resources. **3** pass time in a specified way: *she spent a lot of time traveling.* ■ **spend·a·ble** adj. **spend·er** n.

spend·thrift /'spen(d)ˌTHrift/ ▶ n. a person who spends money in an extravagant and irresponsible way.

spent /spent/ past and past participle of SPEND ▶ adj. used up; exhausted.

sperm /spərm/ ▶ n. (pl. same or **sperms**) **1** semen. **2** a spermatozoon (male sex cell).

sper·ma·cet·i /ˌspərmə'setē/ ▶ n. a white waxy substance obtained from an organ in the head of the sperm whale, formerly used in candles and ointments.

sper·ma·to·zo·on /ˌspərmətə'zōən, spər'ma-/ ▶ n. (pl. **spermatozoa** /-'zōə/) the male sex cell of an animal, which fertilizes the ovum (female reproductive cell).

sperm count ▶ n. the number of spermatozoa in a measured amount of semen, used as an indication of a man's fertility.

sper·mi·cide /'spərməˌsīd/ ▶ n. a substance that kills sperm, used as a contraceptive.
■ **sper·mi·cid·al** /ˌspərmə'sīdl/ adj.

sperm whale ▸ n. a toothed whale with a massive head, feeding largely on squid.

spew /spyo͞o/ ▸ v. **1** pour out or discharge rapidly and in large quantities: *a fax machine spewed out information.* **2** informal vomit. ▸ n. informal vomit. ■ **spew·er** n.

SPF ▸ abbr. sun protection factor.

sphag·num /'sfagnəm, 'spag-/ ▸ n. a type of moss that grows on bogs.

sphere /sfi(ə)r/ ▸ n. **1** a round solid figure in which every point on the surface is at an equal distance from the center. **2** an area of activity, interest, or expertise: *political reforms to match those in the economic sphere.* **3** a particular section of society.

spher·i·cal /'sfi(ə)rikəl, 'sfer-/ ▸ adj. shaped like a sphere. ■ **spher·i·cal·ly** adv.

sphe·roid /'sfi(ə)r,oid/ ▸ n. an object that is roughly the same shape as a sphere. ■ **sphe·roi·dal** /sfi'roidl/ adj.

spher·ule /'sfi(ə)r(y)o͞ol, 'sfer-/ ▸ n. a small sphere. ■ **spher·u·lar** /-yo͞olər/ adj.

sphinc·ter /'sfiNGktər/ ▸ n. a ring of muscle that surrounds an opening such as the anus, and can be tightened to close it.

sphinx /sfiNGks/ ▸ n. an ancient Egyptian stone figure with a lion's body and a human or animal head.

sphyg·mo·ma·nom·e·ter /,sfigmōmə'nämitər/ ▸ n. an instrument for measuring blood pressure, consisting of an inflatable rubber cuff that is fitted around the arm and connected to a column of mercury next to a graduated scale.

spic /spik/ ▸ n. informal, offensive a Spanish-speaking person from Central or South America or the Caribbean.

spice /spīs/ ▸ n. **1** a strong-tasting vegetable substance used to flavor food. **2** something that adds interest and excitement: *shared highs and lows can add spice to your relationship.* ▸ v. **1** flavor something with spice. **2** (**spice something up**) make something more exciting or interesting.

spick-and-span ▸ adj. neat, clean, and well looked after.

spic·ule /'spik,yo͞ol/ ▸ n. chiefly Zoology a small needlelike object or structure.

spic·y /'spīsē/ ▸ adj. (**spicier, spiciest**) **1** strongly flavored with spice. **2** mildly indecent: *spicy jokes.* ■ **spic·i·ly** adv. **spic·i·ness** n.

spi·der /'spīdər/ ▸ n. **1** an eight-legged arachnid (insectlike creature), most kinds of which spin webs in which to capture insects. **2** a long-legged rest for a billiard cue that can be placed over a ball without touching it.

spi·der crab ▸ n. a crab with long, thin legs and a compact pear-shaped body.

spi·der mite ▸ n. a plant-feeding mite resembling a tiny spider.

spi·der mon·key ▸ n. a South American monkey with very long limbs and a long tail that it can use for grasping.

spi·der plant ▸ n. a plant having long, narrow leaves with a central yellow stripe, popular as a house plant.

spi·der·y /'spīdərē/ ▸ adj. long and thin, like a spider's legs: *spidery writing.*

spiel /spēl, sHpēl/ ▸ n. informal an elaborate and insincere speech made to persuade someone to buy or believe something.

spiff·y /'spifē/ ▸ adj. (**spiffier, spiffiest**) informal smart or stylish. ■ **spif·fi·ly** adv.

spig·ot /'spigət/ ▸ n. **1** a faucet. **2** a small peg or plug, especially for putting into the vent of a cask. **3** the plain end of a section of a pipe fitting into the socket of the next one.

spike¹ /spīk/ ▸ n. **1** a thin pointed piece of metal or wood. **2** each of several metal points set into the sole of a sports shoe to prevent slipping. **3** a sharp increase: *a spike in demand.* ▸ v. **1** impale on or pierce with something sharp: *she spiked another oyster.* **2** form something into or cover something with sharp points. **3** informal secretly add alcohol or a drug to drink or food. **4** put an end to a plan or undertaking. **5** increase and then decrease sharply: *oil prices would spike and then fall again.*

spike² ▸ n. Botany a flower cluster formed of many flowerheads attached directly to a long stem.

spike·nard /'spīk,närd/ ▸ n. historical an expensive perfumed ointment made from the rhizome (underground stem) of a Himalayan plant.

spik·y /'spīkē/ ▸ adj. (**spikier, spikiest**) **1** like a spike or spikes or having many spikes: *short spiky hair.* **2** informal easily annoyed; irritable. ■ **spik·i·ly** adv. **spik·i·ness** n.

spill¹ /spil/ ▸ v. (past and past part. **spilled** or **spilt**) **1** flow or cause to flow over the edge of a container. **2** move or empty out from a place: *students began to spill out of the building.* **3** informal reveal private or personal information. ▸ n. **1** an instance of a liquid spilling or the quantity spilled. **2** a fall from a horse or bicycle. ■ **spill·age** /'spilij/ n. **spill·er** n.

– PHRASES **spill the beans** informal reveal secret information. **spill blood** kill or wound people.

spill² ▸ n. a thin strip of wood or paper used for lighting a fire.

spill·o·ver /'spil,ōvər/ ▸ n. **1** a thing that overflows or has spread into another area. **2** (usu. before another noun) an unexpected result or effect of something.

spill·way /'spil,wā/ ▸ n. a passage for surplus water from a dam.

spin /spin/ ▸ v. (**spins, spinning, spun** /spən/) **1** turn around quickly. **2** (of a person's head) have a feeling of dizziness. **3** (of a ball) move through the air with a revolving motion. **4** draw out and twist the fibers of wool, cotton, etc., to convert them into yarn. **5** (of a spider or a silkworm or other insect) produce a web, silk, or cocoon by forcing out a fine thread from a special gland. **6** (**spin something out**) make something last as long as possible. ▸ n. **1** a spinning motion. **2** informal a brief trip in a vehicle for pleasure. **3** a favorable slant given to a news story. ■ **spin·ner** n.

– PHRASES **spin a yarn** tell a far-fetched story.

spi·na bif·i·da /'spīnə 'bifidə/ ▸ n. a condition present from birth in which part of the spinal cord is exposed through a gap in the backbone, and which can cause paralysis and other problems.

spin·ach /'spinicH/ ▸ n. a vegetable with large dark green leaves.

spi·nal /'spīnl/ ▸ adj. relating to the spine. ■ **spi·nal·ly** adv.

spi·nal col·umn ▸ n. the spine.

spi·nal cord ▸ n. the cylindrical bundle of nerve fibers in the spine that connects all parts of the body to the brain.

spin·dle /'spindl/ ▶ n. **1** a slender rounded rod with tapered ends, used in spinning wool, flax, etc., by hand. **2** a rod serving as an axis that revolves or on which something revolves.

spin·dly /'spin(d)lē/ ▶ adj. long or tall and thin.

spin doc·tor ▶ n. informal a spokesperson for a political party or politician employed to present events in a favorable way to the media.

spin·drift /'spin,drift/ ▶ n. **1** spray blown from the crests of waves by the wind. **2** driving snow.

spine /spīn/ ▶ n. **1** a series of vertebrae (bones) extending from the skull to the small of the back, enclosing the spinal cord; the backbone. **2** the part of a book that encloses the inner edges of the pages. **3** a central or strengthening feature: *Norway's mountainous spine.* **4** a hard pointed projection found on certain plants (e.g., cacti) and animals (e.g., hedgehogs).

spine-chill·er ▶ n. a story or movie that causes terror and excitement. ■ **spine-chill·ing** adj.

spine·less /'spīnlis/ ▶ adj. **1** lacking courage and determination. **2** (of an animal) having no backbone; invertebrate. **3** (of an animal or plant) lacking spines. ■ **spine·less·ly** adv. **spine·less·ness** n.

spin·et /'spinit/ ▶ n. a type of small harpsichord popular in the 18th century.

spine-tin·gling ▶ adj. informal thrilling or pleasurably frightening.

spin·i·fex /'spinə,feks/ ▶ n. a grass with spiny flowerheads that break off and are blown about, occurring from east Asia to Australia.

spin·na·ker /'spinəkər/ ▶ n. a large three-cornered sail set in front of the mainsail of a racing yacht when the wind is coming from behind.

spin·ner·et /,spinə'ret/ ▶ n. an organ through which the silk, gossamer, or thread of spiders, silkworms, and certain other insects is produced.

spin·ning jen·ny ▶ n. historical a machine for spinning with more than one spindle at a time.

spin·ning wheel ▶ n. a machine for spinning yarn or thread with a spindle driven by a wheel attached to a crank or treadle.

spin-off ▶ n. **1** a product or benefit produced during or after the main activity. **2** a book, movie, television program, etc., based on another book, movie, program, etc.

spin·ster /'spinstər/ ▶ n. chiefly derogatory a single woman beyond the usual age for marriage. ■ **spin·ster·hood** /-,hŏod/ n. **spin·ster·ish** adj.

spin·y /'spīnē/ ▶ adj. (**spinier**, **spiniest**) full of or covered with prickles. ■ **spin·i·ness** n.

spin·y ant·eat·er ▶ n. another term for ECHIDNA.

spi·ra·cle /'spirəkəl, 'spī-/ ▶ n. an external opening used for breathing in certain insects, fish, and other animals. ■ **spi·rac·u·lar** /spī'rakyələr, spī-/ adj.

spi·rae·a /spī'rēə/ ▶ n. chiefly Brit. variant spelling of SPIREA.

spi·ral /'spīrəl/ ▶ adj. winding in a continuous curve around a central point or axis. ▶ n. **1** a spiral curve, shape, or pattern. **2** a continuous increase or decrease in prices, wages, etc., that gradually gets faster: *a downward spiral of crippling debt.* ▶ v. (**spirals**, **spiraling**, **spiraled**) **1** move in a spiral course. **2** show a continuous and rapid increase or decrease. ■ **spi·ral·ly** adv.

spi·ral-bound ▶ adj. (of a book or notepad)

bound with a spiral wire threaded through a row of holes along one edge.

spire /spī(ə)r/ ▶ n. a tall pointed structure on the top of a church tower or other building.

spi·re·a /spī'rēə/ (also **spiraea**) ▶ n. a shrub with clusters of small white or pink flowers.

spir·it /'spirit/ ▶ n. **1** the part of a person that consists of their character and feelings rather than their body, often believed to survive after their body is dead. **2** a ghost or other supernatural being. **3** the typical or dominant character, quality, or mood: *they shared her spirit of adventure.* **4** (**spirits**) a person's mood. **5** courage, energy, and determination. **6** the real meaning of something as opposed to its strict interpretation: *the rule had been broken in spirit if not in letter.* **7** chiefly Brit. strong distilled alcoholic drink, such as rum. **8** purified distilled alcohol, such as methylated spirit. ▶ v. (**spirits**, **spiriting**, **spirited**) (**spirit someone/thing away**) take someone or something away rapidly and secretly.
– PHRASES **when the spirit moves someone** when someone feels inclined to do something.

spir·it·ed /'spiritid/ ▶ adj. **1** full of energy, enthusiasm, and determination. **2** having a specified character: *a generous-spirited man.* ■ **spir·it·ed·ly** adv. **spir·it·ed·ness** n.

spir·it gum ▶ n. a quick-drying solution of gum, used by actors to attach false hair to their faces.

spir·it·less /'spiritlis/ ▶ adj. lacking courage, energy, or determination. ■ **spir·it·less·ly** adv. **spir·it·less·ness** n.

spir·it lev·el ▶ n. see LEVEL (sense 6 of the noun).

spir·it·u·al /'spirichŏoəl/ ▶ adj. **1** relating to the human spirit as opposed to material or physical things: *I'm responsible for his spiritual welfare.* **2** relating to religion or religious belief. ▶ n. (also **Negro spiritual**) a religious song of a kind associated with black Christians of the southern US. ■ **spir·it·u·al·i·ty** /,spirichŏo'alitē/ n. **spir·it·u·al·ize** /'spirichŏoə,līz/ v. **spir·it·u·al·ly** adv.

spir·it·u·al·ism /'spirichŏoə,lizəm/ ▶ n. the belief that it is possible to communicate with the spirits of the dead, especially through mediums. ■ **spir·it·u·al·ist** n. **spir·it·u·al·is·tic** /,spirichŏoə'listik/ adj.

spi·ro·gy·ra /,spīrə'jīrə/ ▶ n. a type of algae consisting of long green threads.

spit¹ /spit/ ▶ v. (**spits**, **spitting**, **spat** /spat/ or **spit**) **1** force saliva, food, or liquid from the mouth. **2** say something in a hostile way. **3** (of a fire or food being cooked) give out small bursts of sparks or hot fat. ▶ n. **1** saliva. **2** an act of spitting. ■ **spit·ter** n.
– PHRASES **be the spitting image of** informal look exactly like. **spit and polish** thorough cleaning and polishing. **spit blood** feel or express strong anger. **spit it out** informal say it quickly; stop hesitating.

spit² ▶ n. **1** a thin metal rod pushed through meat in order to hold and turn it while it is roasted. **2** a narrow point of land projecting into the sea.

spit·ball /'spit,bôl/ ▶ n. **1** a ball of chewed paper used as a missile. **2** Baseball an illegal pitch made with a ball moistened with saliva or other substance to make it move erratically. ▶ v. informal throw out a suggestion for discussion: *I'm just spitballing a few ideas.* ■ **spit·ball·er** n.

spite /spīt/ ▶ n. a desire to hurt, annoy, or offend

someone. ▶ v. deliberately hurt, annoy, or offend someone.
– PHRASES **in spite of 1** without being affected by. **2** without regard for. **in spite of oneself** although one did not want or expect to do so.

spite·ful /'spītfəl/ ▶ adj. deliberately hurtful; malicious. ■ **spite·ful·ly** adv. **spite·ful·ness** n.

spit·fire /'spit,fīr/ ▶ n. a person with a fierce temper.

spit·tle /'spitl/ ▶ n. saliva; spit.

spit·toon /spi'tŏon/ ▶ n. a container for spitting into.

splash /splasH/ ▶ v. **1** (with reference to a liquid) fall or cause to fall in scattered drops: *wine splashed onto the bed.* **2** make someone or something wet with scattered drops. **3** move around in water, causing it to fly about. **4** (**splash down**) (of a spacecraft) land on the sea. **5** display a story or photograph very noticeably in a newspaper or magazine. ▶ n. **1** an instance or sound of splashing. **2** a small quantity of liquid that has splashed onto a surface. **3** a small quantity of liquid added to a drink. **4** a bright patch of color. **5** informal a noticeable or sensational news story. ■ **splash·y** adj. (**splashier, splashiest**).
– PHRASES **make a splash** informal attract a great deal of attention.

splash·down /'splasH,doun/ ▶ n. the moment at which a spacecraft lands on the sea.

splat /splat/ informal ▶ n. a sound of something soft and wet or heavy striking a surface. ▶ v. (**splats, splatting, splatted**) hit or land with a splat.

splat·ter /'splatər/ ▶ v. splash someone or something with a sticky or thick liquid. ▶ n. a splash of a sticky or thick liquid.

splay /splā/ ▶ v. spread or be spread out or further apart: *he stood with his legs splayed out.* ▶ adj. turned outward or widened: *she sat splay-legged.*

splay-foot·ed ▶ adj. having a broad flat foot turned outward.

spleen /splēn/ ▶ n. **1** an organ in the abdomen that is involved in the production and removal of blood cells and forms part of the immune system. **2** bad temper; spite.

splen·did /'splendid/ ▶ adj. **1** magnificent; very impressive. **2** informal excellent; very good. ■ **splen·did·ly** adv.

splen·dif·er·ous /splen'difərəs/ ▶ adj. informal, humorous very good; splendid.

splen·dor /'splendər/ (Brit. **splendour**) ▶ n. magnificent and impressive quality or appearance: *the splendor of Mount Everest.*

sple·net·ic /splə'netik/ ▶ adj. bad-tempered or spiteful.

splen·ic /'splēnik, 'sple-/ ▶ adj. relating to the spleen.

splice /splīs/ ▶ v. **1** join a rope or ropes by weaving the strands together at the ends. **2** join pieces of wood, film, or tape at the ends. ▶ n. a place where film, rope, etc., has been spliced together. ■ **splic·er** n.

spliff /splif/ ▶ n. informal a marijuana cigarette.

spline /splīn/ ▶ n. a rectangular key fitting into grooves in the hub and shaft of a wheel. ▶ v. secure a part with a spline.

splint /splint/ ▶ n. a strip of rigid material for supporting a broken bone when it has been set. ▶ v. secure a broken limb with a splint or splints.

splin·ter /'splin(t)ər/ ▶ n. a small, thin sharp piece of wood, glass, etc., broken off from a larger piece. ▶ v. **1** break into splinters. **2** (of a group) divide into smaller separate groups: *the company splintered into seven regional operating companies.* ■ **splin·ter·y** adj.

splin·ter group ▶ n. a small organization that has broken away from a larger one.

split /split/ ▶ v. (**splits, splitting, split**) **1** break into parts by force. **2** divide into parts or groups: *once again the family was split up.* **3** (often **split up**) end a marriage or other relationship. **4** informal leave a place, especially suddenly. **5** (**be splitting**) informal (of a person's head) be suffering from a bad headache. ▶ n. **1** a tear or crack. **2** an instance of splitting or dividing: *a 75–25 split of the proceeds.* **3** a division between members of a group or an end of a relationship: *a split in the ruling party.* **4** (**the splits**) (in gymnastics and dance) an act of leaping in the air or sitting down with the legs straight and at right angles to the body. ■ **split·ter** n.
– PHRASES **split the difference** take the average of two proposed amounts. **split one's sides** informal laugh heartily or uncontrollably.

split end ▶ n. a tip of a person's hair that has split from dryness or ill-treatment.

split in·fin·i·tive ▶ n. a sentence consisting of the infinitive of a verb with an adverb or other word placed between *to* and the verb, e.g., *she seems to really like it.*

> **USAGE**
> Many people still think that splitting infinitives (putting a word between *to* and the verb) is wrong. They think that it is better to say *she used secretly to admire him* rather than *she used to secretly admire him*, although this sometimes sounds awkward or gives a different emphasis to what is being said. For this reason, the rule about not splitting infinitives is not followed so strictly today, although it is best not to split them in formal writing.

split-lev·el ▶ adj. **1** (of a room or building) having the floor divided into different levels. **2** (of a range) having the oven and stovetop in separate units.

split pea ▶ n. a pea dried and split in half for cooking.

split screen ▶ n. a movie, television, or computer screen on which two or more separate images are displayed.

split sec·ond ▶ n. a very brief moment of time. ▶ adj. (**split-second**) very rapid or accurate: *split-second timing.*

splits·ville /'splits,vil/ (also **Splitsville**) ▶ n. informal the termination of a relationship, especially a romantic one: *her parents are headed for Splitsville.*

splosh /splasH/ informal ▶ v. move with a soft splashing sound. ▶ n. a splash.

splotch /splacH/ informal ▶ n. a spot, splash, or smear of something. ▶ v. mark something with a spot, splash or smear. ■ **splotch·y** adj.

splurge /splərj/ informal ▶ v. spend extravagantly: *this is a good place to splurge on extravagant materials.* ▶ n. a sudden spell of spending money extravagantly.

splut·ter /'splatər/ ▶ v. **1** make a series of short explosive spitting or choking sounds. **2** say something in a rapid and unclear way. ▶ n. a spluttering sound. ∎ **splut·ter·er** n.

spoil /spoil/ ▸ v. (past and past part. **spoiled** or (chiefly Brit.) **spoilt**) **1** make less good or enjoyable: *I am not going to let her spoil my day.* **2** harm a child's character by not treating them strictly enough. **3** treat someone with great or excessive kindness. **4** (of food) become unfit for eating. **5** (**be spoiling for**) be very eager for: *Cooper was spoiling for a fight.* ▸ n. (**spoils**) stolen goods.

spoil·age /'spoilij/ ▸ n. the decay of food and other perishable goods.

spoil·er /'spoilər/ ▸ n. **1** a part fitted to a car in order to improve roadholding at high speeds. **2** a flap on an aircraft wing that can be raised to create drag and so reduce speed. **3** a news story published with the intention of reducing the impact of a similar item published in a rival paper. **4** a part of the storyline of a book, movie, etc., the knowledge of which would reveal too much to someone who has not yet read the book or viewed the movie.

spoil·sport /'spoil,spôrt/ ▸ n. a person who spoils the pleasure of others.

spoils sys·tem ▸ n. the practice of a successful political party giving public office to its supporters.

spoke[1] /spōk/ ▸ n. **1** each of the bars or wire rods connecting the center of a wheel to its rim. **2** each of the metal rods in an umbrella to which the material is attached.

spoke[2] ▸ past of SPEAK.

spo·ken /'spōkən/ past participle of SPEAK ▸ adj. (in combination) speaking in a specified way: *a soft-spoken man.*
– PHRASES **be spoken for 1** be already claimed or reserved. **2** already have a romantic relationship.

spoke·shave /'spōk,SHāv/ ▸ n. a small plane with a handle on each side of its blade, used for shaping curved surfaces.

spokes·man /'spōksmən/ (or **spokeswoman** /'spōks,wŏŏmən/) ▸ n. (pl. **spokesmen** or **spokeswomen**) a person who makes statements on behalf of a group.

spokes·per·son /'spōks,pərsən/ ▸ n. (pl. **spokespersons** or **spokespeople** /-,pēpəl/) a spokesman or spokeswoman.

spo·li·a·tion /,spōlē'āsHən/ ▸ n. **1** the action of destroying or ruining something. **2** the action of plundering a place.

spon·dee /'spändē/ ▸ n. a foot (unit of poetic meter) consisting of two long (or stressed) syllables.

spon·dy·li·tis /,spändə'lītis/ ▸ n. arthritis in the backbone, especially (**ankylosing spondylitis**) a form in which the vertebrae (bones) become fused.

sponge /spənj/ ▸ n. **1** an invertebrate sea creature with a soft porous body. **2** a piece of a light absorbent substance used for washing, as padding, etc. ▸ v. (**sponges, sponging** or **spongeing, sponged**) **1** wipe or clean someone or something with a wet sponge or cloth. **2** (usu. **sponge off**) informal obtain money or food from others without giving anything in return. ∎ **sponge·like** /'spənj,līk/ adj.

sponge cake ▸ n. a very light cake made with eggs, sugar, and flour but little or no fat.

spong·er /'spənjər/ ▸ n. informal a person who lives by obtaining money or food from others.

spon·gi·form /'spänji,fôrm/ ▸ adj. technical having

a porous structure or consistency like that of a sponge.

spon·gy /'spənjē/ ▸ adj. (**spongier, spongiest**) like a sponge in being porous, absorbent, or compressible. ∎ **spon·gi·ness** n.

spon·sor /'spänsər/ ▸ n. **1** a person or organization that pays for or contributes to the costs of an event or a radio or television program in return for advertising. **2** a person who promises to give money to a charity after another person has participated in a fund-raising activity. **3** a person who introduces and supports a proposal for a new law. **4** a person taking official responsibility for the actions of another. **5** a godparent at a child's baptism. ▸ v. be a sponsor for a person, event, or fund-raising activity. ∎ **spon·sor·ship** /-,SHip/ n.

spon·ta·ne·ous /spän'tānēəs/ ▸ adj. **1** done or occurring as a result of an unplanned impulse: *the crowd broke into spontaneous applause.* **2** open, natural, and uninhibited. **3** (of a process or event) happening naturally, without being made to do so. ∎ **spon·ta·ne·i·ty** /,späntə'nēitē, -'nā-/ n. **spon·ta·ne·ous·ly** adv.

spon·ta·ne·ous com·bus·tion ▸ n. the burning of organic matter caused by chemical changes within the substance itself.

spoof /spŏŏf/ informal ▸ n. **1** a humorous imitation of something in which its typical features are exaggerated: *a spoof of Bond films.* **2** a trick played on someone as a joke. ▸ v. **1** imitate something while exaggerating its typical features. **2** trick someone. ∎ **spoof·er** n. **spoof·er·y** /'spŏŏfərē/ n.

spook /spŏŏk/ informal ▸ n. **1** a ghost. **2** a spy. ▸ v. frighten someone or something.

spook·y /'spŏŏkē/ ▸ adj. (**spookier, spookiest**) informal sinister or ghostly. ∎ **spook·i·ly** adv. **spook·i·ness** n.

spool /spŏŏl/ ▸ n. a cylindrical device on which thread, film, etc., can be wound. ▸ v. **1** wind or be wound onto a spool. **2** Computing send data for printing or processing on a peripheral device to an intermediate store.

spoon /spŏŏn/ ▸ n. an implement consisting of a small shallow bowl on a long handle, used for eating, stirring, and serving food. ▸ v. **1** transfer food with a spoon. **2** informal, dated (of a couple) kiss and cuddle amorously. ∎ **spoon·ful** /-,fŏŏl/ n.

spoon·bill /'spŏŏn,bil/ ▸ n. a tall wading bird having a long bill with a very broad flat tip.

spoon·er·ism /'spŏŏnə,rizəm/ ▸ n. an error in speech in which the initial sounds or letters of two or more words are accidentally swapped around, as in *you have hissed the mystery lectures.*

spoon-feed ▸ v. **1** provide someone with so much help or information that they do not need to think for themselves. **2** feed a baby with a spoon.

spoor /spŏŏr, spô(ə)r/ ▸ n. the track or scent of an animal.

spo·rad·ic /spə'radik/ ▸ adj. occurring at irregular intervals or only in a few places: *sporadic fighting broke out.* ∎ **spo·rad·i·cal·ly** /-ik(ə)lē/ adv.

spore /spôr/ ▸ n. a tiny reproductive cell produced by plants without vascular systems (such as mosses and algae), fungi, etc.

spor·ran /'spärən, 'spôr-/ ▸ n. a small pouch worn around the waist so as to hang in front of the kilt as part of men's Scottish Highland dress.

sport /spôrt/ ▶ n. **1** an activity involving physical effort and skill in which a person or team competes against another or others. **2** informal a person who behaves in a good or specified way when teased or defeated: *go on, be a sport!* **3** success or pleasure derived from an activity such as hunting. **4** dated entertainment; fun. **5** Biology an animal or plant that is markedly different from the parent type as a result of mutation. ▶ v. **1** wear or display a distinctive item. **2** literary play in a lively way. ■ **sport·er** n.
– PHRASES **the sport of kings** horse racing.

sport coat ▶ n. another term for **SPORTS JACKET**.

sport·ing /spôrtiNG/ ▶ adj. **1** connected with or interested in sports. **2** fair and generous toward others. ■ **sport·ing·ly** adv.

sport·ing chance ▶ n. a reasonable chance of winning or succeeding.

spor·tive /spôrtiv/ ▶ adj. playful; light-hearted.

sports car /spôrts/ ▶ n. a low-built fast car.

sports·cast /spôrts,kast/ ▶ n. a broadcast of sports news or a sports event. ■ **sports·cast·er** n. **sports·cast·ing** n.

sports jack·et /spôrts/ ▶ n. a man's informal jacket resembling a suit jacket.

sports·man /spôrtsmən/ (or **sportswoman** /spôrts,wŏŏmən/) ▶ n. (pl. **sportsmen** or **sportswomen**) **1** a person who takes part in a sport, especially as a professional. **2** a person who behaves in a fair and generous way toward others. ■ **sports·man·like** /-,līk/ adj. **sports·man·ship** /-,SHip/ n.

sports·per·son /spôrts,pərsən/ ▶ n. (pl. **sportspersons** or **sportspeople** /-,pēpəl/) a sportsman or sportswoman.

sport·ster /spôrtstər/ ▶ n. a sports car.

sports·wear /spôrts,we(ə)r/ ▶ n. clothes worn for sport or for casual use.

sport u·til·i·ty ve·hi·cle ▶ n. a high-performance four-wheel-drive vehicle.

sport·y /spôrtē/ ▶ adj. (**sportier, sportiest**) informal **1** fond of or good at sports. **2** (of clothing) suitable for sport or casual wear. **3** (of a car) compact and with fast acceleration. ■ **sport·i·ness** n.

spot /spät/ ▶ n. **1** a small round mark on a surface. **2** a pimple. **3** a particular place, point, or position: *an ideal picnic spot.* **4** a place for an individual item in a show. **5** informal, chiefly Brit. a small amount: *have a spot of tea.* ▶ v. (**spots, spotting, spotted**) **1** notice or recognize someone or something that is difficult to find or that one is searching for. **2** mark something with spots. **3** (**it spots, it is spotting, it spotted**) light rain falls. ■ **spot·ted** adj.
– PHRASES **on the spot 1** immediately. **2** at the scene of an event. **put someone on the spot** informal force someone into a situation in which they must respond or act. **spot on** informal completely accurate or accurately.

spot check ▶ n. a test made without warning on a person or thing selected at random. ▶ v. (**spot-check**) make a random check on someone or something without warning.

spot·less /spätlis/ ▶ adj. **1** absolutely clean. **2** without any mistakes or moral faults; perfect: *the defendant has a spotless record.* ■ **spot·less·ly** adv. **spot·less·ness** n.

spot·light /spät,līt/ ▶ n. **1** a lamp projecting a narrow, intense beam of light directly onto a place or person. **2** (**the spotlight**) intense public attention. ▶ v. (past and past part. **spotlighted** or **spotlit** /-lit/) **1** light up someone or something with a spotlight. **2** direct attention to a problem or situation.

spot·ted dick ▶ n. Brit. a suet pudding containing currants.

spot·ter /spätər/ ▶ n. **1** (usu. in combination) a person who observes or looks for a particular thing as a hobby or job: *a talent spotter.* **2** a pilot or aircraft employed in spotting enemy positions.

spot·ty /spätē/ ▶ adj. (**spottier, spottiest**) **1** marked with or having spots. **2** of uneven quality.

spous·al /spouzəl/ ▶ adj. Law relating to marriage or to a husband or wife.

spouse /spous/ ▶ n. a husband or wife.

spout /spout/ ▶ n. **1** a projecting tube or lip through or over which liquid can be poured from a container. **2** a stream of liquid flowing out with great force. ▶ v. **1** send out or flow forcibly in a stream: *water spouted from a pipe.* **2** express one's views in a lengthy or emphatic way. ■ **spout·ed** adj. **spout·er** n.

sprain /sprān/ ▶ v. wrench the ligaments of a joint so as to cause pain and swelling. ▶ n. the result of wrenching a joint.

sprang /spraNG/ ▶ past of **SPRING**.

sprat /sprat/ ▶ n. a small edible sea fish of the herring family.

sprawl /sprôl/ ▶ v. **1** sit, lie, or fall with the limbs spread out in an awkward way. **2** (often as adj. **sprawling**) spread out irregularly over a large area: *a sprawling city.* ▶ n. **1** the disorganized expansion of an urban or industrial area into the nearby countryside. **2** a relaxed or awkward position with the limbs spread out.

spray[1] /sprā/ ▶ n. **1** liquid sent through the air in tiny drops. **2** a liquid that can be forced out of an aerosol or other container in a spray. ▶ v. **1** apply liquid in a spray. **2** cover or treat someone or something with a spray. **3** (of liquid) be sent through the air in a spray. **4** scatter over an area or object with force: *the gunmen sprayed bullets at all three cars.* ■ **spray·er** n.

spray[2] ▶ n. **1** a stem or small branch of a tree or plant, bearing flowers and leaves. **2** a bunch of cut flowers arranged in an attractive way.

spray gun ▶ n. a device resembling a gun that is used to spray a liquid such as paint under pressure.

spray-paint ▶ v. paint an image or message on to a surface with a spray, or paint a surface with a spray.

spread /spred/ ▶ v. (past and past part. **spread**) **1** open something out so as to increase its surface area, width, or length. **2** stretch out limbs, hands, fingers, or wings so that they are far apart. **3** extend or distribute over a large or increasing area: *rain will spread southeast during the day.* **4** reach or cause to reach more and more people: *panic spread among the crowd.* **5** apply a substance in an even layer. ▶ n. **1** the action of spreading over an area. **2** the extent, width, or area covered by something. **3** the range of something: *a wide spread of ages.* **4** a soft paste that can be spread on bread. **5** an article or advertisement covering several columns or pages of a newspaper or magazine. **6** informal a large and impressive meal. **7** a large farm or ranch.

■ **spread·a·ble** adj. **spread·er** n.

spread bet·ting ▶ n. a form of betting in which money is won or lost according to the degree by which the score or result of a sporting event varies from the spread of expected values quoted by the bookmaker.

spread-ea·gle ▶ v. (**be spread-eagled**) be stretched out with the arms and legs spread wide.

spread·sheet /'spred,sHet/ ▶ n. a computer program in which figures arranged in a grid can be manipulated and used in calculations.

spree /sprē/ ▶ n. a spell of unrestrained activity: *a shopping spree.*

sprig /sprig/ ▶ n. **1** a small stem bearing leaves or flowers, taken from a bush or plant. **2** a descendant or younger member of a family or social class. **3** a small molded decoration applied to a piece of pottery before firing. ■ **sprigged** adj.

spright·ly /'sprītlē/ ▶ adj. (**sprightlier, sprightliest**) (especially of an old person) lively; energetic. ■ **spright·li·ness** n.

spring /sprinG/ ▶ v. (past **sprang** /spranG/ or **sprung** /spronG/; past part. **sprung**) **1** move suddenly or rapidly upward or forward. **2** move or do suddenly: *the door sprang open.* **3** (**spring from**) originate or arise from: *his short film sprang from a midlife crisis.* **4** (**spring up**) suddenly develop or appear. **5** (as adj. **sprung**) (of a vehicle or item of furniture) having springs. **6** (**spring something on**) present something suddenly or unexpectedly to someone. **7** informal bring about the escape or release of a prisoner. ▶ n. **1** the season after winter and before summer. **2** a spiral metal coil that can be pressed or pulled but returns to its former shape when released. **3** a sudden jump upward or forward. **4** a place where water wells up from an underground source. **5** the ability to spring back strongly; elastic quality. ■ **spring·less** adj. **spring·like** /-ˌlīk/ adj.
– PHRASES **spring a leak** (of a boat or container) develop a leak.

spring·board /'sprinG,bôrd/ ▶ n. **1** a flexible board from which a diver or gymnast may jump in order to push off more strongly. **2** a thing that starts off an activity or enterprise: *a book can be a springboard for discussions with children about their own lives.*

spring·bok /'sprinG,bäk/ ▶ n. **1** a southern African gazelle that leaps when disturbed. **2** (**the Springboks**) the South African international rugby union team.

spring chick·en ▶ n. **1** informal a young person: *I'm no spring chicken.* **2** a young chicken for eating (originally available only in spring).

spring clean·ing ▶ n. a thorough cleaning of a house or room. ▶ v. (**spring-clean**) clean a house or room thoroughly.

spring·er span·iel /'sprinGər/ ▶ n. a small spaniel of a breed originally used to drive game birds out of cover.

spring-load·ed ▶ adj. containing a compressed or stretched spring pressing one part against another.

spring on·ion ▶ n. chiefly Brit. a green onion; a scallion.

spring roll ▶ n. an Asian snack or appetizer consisting of rice paper filled with vegetables and sometimes meat, rolled into a cylinder and deep-fried.

spring·tail /'sprinG,tāl/ ▶ n. a minute wingless insect that uses a springlike organ under the abdomen to leap when disturbed.

spring tide /'sprinG ˌtīd/ ▶ n. a tide just after a new or full moon, when there is the greatest difference between high and low water.

spring·time /'sprinG,tīm/ ▶ n. the season of spring.

spring·y /'sprinGē/ ▶ adj. (**springier, springiest**) **1** springing back quickly when squeezed or stretched. **2** (of movements) light and confident. ■ **spring·i·ly** adv. **spring·i·ness** n.

sprin·kle /'sprinGkəl/ ▶ v. **1** scatter or pour small drops or particles over an object or surface. **2** distribute something randomly throughout: *the city is sprinkled with factories producing computers.* ▶ n. a small amount that is sprinkled over something.

sprin·kler /'sprinGk(ə)lər/ ▶ n. **1** a device for watering lawns. **2** an automatic fire extinguisher installed in a ceiling.

sprin·kling /'sprinGk(ə)linG/ ▶ n. a small, thinly distributed amount of something.

sprint /sprint/ ▶ v. run at full speed over a short distance. ▶ n. **1** an act of sprinting. **2** a short, fast race. ■ **sprint·er** n.

sprit /sprit/ ▶ n. a small pole reaching diagonally from a mast to the upper outer corner of a sail.

sprite /sprīt/ ▶ n. **1** an elf or fairy. **2** a computer graphic that can be moved on-screen and otherwise manipulated as a single entity.

sprit·sail /'sprit,sāl, -səl/ ▶ n. a sail that is extended diagonally from the mast by a small pole reaching to the upper outer corner.

spritz /sprits/ ▶ v. spray liquid in quick short bursts at or onto something. ▶ n. an act of spraying a short burst of liquid.

spritz·er /'spritsər/ ▶ n. a mixture of wine and soda water.

sprock·et /'spräkit/ ▶ n. **1** each of several projections on the rim of a wheel that fit into the links of a chain or holes in film, tape, or paper. **2** (also **sprocket wheel**) a wheel with sprockets.

sprout /sprout/ ▶ v. **1** (of a plant) produce shoots. **2** start to grow something, especially hair. **3** appear or develop in large numbers: *multiplexes are sprouting up around the country.* ▶ n. **1** a shoot of a plant. **2** a Brussels sprout.

spruce¹ /sproōs/ ▶ adj. neat and smart. ▶ v. (**spruce someone/thing up**) make someone or something neater.

spruce² ▶ n. a conical coniferous tree that has hanging cones.

sprue /sproō/ ▶ n. **1** a channel through which metal or plastic is poured into a mold. **2** a piece of metal or plastic that has solidified in a sprue.

sprung /sprənG/ ▶ past participle and past of SPRING.

spry /sprī/ ▶ adj. (**spryer, spryest**, or **srier, sriest**) (especially of an old person) lively.

spud /spəd/ ▶ n. informal a potato.

spu·man·te /spə'mäntē, spyə-/ ▶ n. an Italian sparkling white wine.

spume /spyoōm/ literary ▶ n. froth or foam that is found on waves. ▶ v. form froth or foam.

spun /spən/ ▶ past and past participle of SPIN.

spunk /spənGk/ ▶ n. informal courage and determination. ■ **spunk·y** adj. (**spunkier, spunkiest**).

spur /spər/ ▶ n. **1** a device with a small spike or a

spiked wheel, worn on a rider's heel for urging a horse forward. **2** a thing that encourages an act or activity: *wars act as a spur to invention.* **3** a projection from a mountain. **4** a short branch road or railroad line. **5** Botany a slender tubular projection from the base of a flower. ▶v. (**spurs, spurring, spurred**) **1** encourage someone to do something or cause something to speed up: *governments should be providing incentives to spur economic growth.* **2** urge a horse forward with spurs.
– PHRASES **on the spur of the moment** on an impulse; without thinking.

spurge /spərj/ ▶n. a plant or shrub with milky latex and small greenish flowers.

spur gear ▶n. a gearwheel with teeth projecting parallel to the wheel's axis.

spu·ri·ous /'spyŏŏrēəs/ ▶adj. **1** not being what it seems to be; false. **2** (of reasoning) apparently but not actually correct. ■ **spu·ri·ous·ly** adv. **spu·ri·ous·ness** n.

spurn /spərn/ ▶v. reject someone or something with contempt.

spurt /spərt/ ▶v. **1** gush out in a sudden stream. **2** move with a sudden burst of speed. ▶n. **1** a sudden gushing stream. **2** a sudden burst of activity or speed.

sput·nik /'spətnik, 'spŏŏt-/ ▶n. each of a series of Soviet artificial satellites, the first of which was the first to be placed in orbit.

sput·ter /'spətər/ ▶v. **1** make a series of soft explosive sounds. **2** say something in a rapid and unclear way; splutter. ▶n. a sputtering sound.

spu·tum /'spyŏŏtəm/ ▶n. a mixture of saliva and mucus coughed up from the throat or lungs.

spy /spī/ ▶n. (pl. **spies**) **1** a person employed to collect and report secret information on an enemy or competitor. **2** a person or device that observes people secretly. ▶v. (**spies, spying, spied**) **1** work as a spy. **2** (**spy on**) watch someone secretly. **3** be able to see; notice: *he could spy a figure in the distance.* **4** (**spy something out**) collect information about something before deciding how to act.

spy·glass /'spī,glas/ ▶n. a small telescope.

spy·ware /'spī,we(ə)r/ ▶n. software that enables someone to gather information about another's computer activities by transmitting data secretly from their hard drive.

sq. ▶abbr. square.

SQL ▶abbr. Structured Query Language, a computer language used for database manipulation.

squab /skwäb/ ▶n. a young pigeon that is yet to leave the nest.

squab·ble /'skwäbəl/ ▶n. a quarrel about an unimportant matter. ▶v. quarrel about an unimportant matter.

squad /skwäd/ ▶n. (treated as sing. or pl.) **1** a division of a police force dealing with a particular type of crime: *the vice squad.* **2** a group of athletes from which a team is chosen. **3** a small number of soldiers assembled for drill or given a particular task.

squad car ▶n. a police patrol car.

squad·ron /'skwädrən/ ▶n. **1** an operational unit in an air force. **2** a main division of an armored or cavalry regiment. **3** a group of warships on a particular duty.

squal·id /'skwälid/ ▶adj. **1** very dirty and

unpleasant. **2** highly immoral or dishonest: *a squalid attempt to buy votes.*

squall /skwôl/ ▶n. **1** a sudden violent gust of wind or localized storm. **2** a loud cry. ▶v. (of a baby or small child) cry noisily and continuously. ■ **squal·ly** adj.

squal·or /'skwälər/ ▶n. the state of being dirty and unpleasant.

squan·der /'skwändər/ ▶v. waste money, time, or an opportunity in a reckless or foolish way.

square /skwe(ə)r/ ▶n. **1** a plane figure with four equal straight sides and four right angles. **2** an open four-sided area surrounded by buildings. **3** an area within a military barracks or camp that is used for drill. **4** the product of a number multiplied by itself. **5** an L-shaped or T-shaped instrument used for obtaining or testing right angles. **6** informal, dated an old-fashioned or boringly conventional person. ▶adj. **1** having the shape of a square. **2** having or forming a right angle. **3** (of a unit of measurement) equal to the area of a square whose side is of the unit specified: *1,500 square meters of land.* **4** (after a noun) referring to the length of each side of a square shape or object: *the room was ten meters square.* **5** at right angles. **6** (of two or more things) level or parallel. **7** broad and solid in shape. **8** fair and honest: *she'd been as square with him as anybody could be.* **9** informal, dated old-fashioned or boringly conventional. ▶adv. directly; straight. ▶v. **1** make something square or rectangular. **2** (as adj. **squared**) marked out in squares. **3** multiply a number by itself. **4** (**square with**) agree or be consistent with: *do those claims square with the facts?* **5** settle a bill or debt. **6** make the score of a match or game even. **7** informal pay someone money in order to obtain their cooperation. **8** bring the shoulders into a position in which they appear square and broad. ■ **square·ness** n. **squar·er** n. **squar·ish** adj.
– PHRASES **back to square one** informal back to where one started. **a square deal** see DEAL¹. **a square peg in a round hole** see PEG. **square up 1** take up the position of a person about to fight. **2** (**square up to**) tackle a difficulty with determination.

square dance ▶n. a country dance that starts with four couples facing one another in a square.

square knot ▶n. a type of double knot that holds very securely but can be easily undone.

square·ly /'skwe(ə)rlē/ ▶adv. **1** not at an angle; directly. **2** without any doubt; firmly: *he put the blame squarely on your shoulders.*

square meal ▶n. a large and satisfying meal.

square meas·ure ▶n. a unit of measurement relating to area.

square-rigged ▶adj. (of a sailing ship) having the main sails at right angles to the length of the ship.

square root ▶n. a number that produces a specified quantity when multiplied by itself.

squash¹ /skwäsh, skwôsh/ ▶v. **1** crush or squeeze something so that it becomes flat, soft, or out of shape. **2** force someone or something into a restricted space. **3** put an end to: *he squashed reports that the firm had changed its mind.* ▶n. **1** a state of being squashed. **2** (also **squash rackets**) a game in which two players use rackets to hit a small rubber ball against the walls of a closed court. ■ **squash·y** adj.

squash² ▶n. (pl. same or **squashes**) a gourd

with flesh that can be cooked and eaten as a vegetable.

squat /skwät/ ▶ v. (**squats, squatting, squatted**) **1** crouch or sit with the knees bent and the heels close to the buttocks or thighs. **2** unlawfully occupy an uninhabited building or area of land. ▶ adj. (**squatter, squattest**) short and wide or broad. ▶ n. **1** a squatting position. **2** a building occupied unlawfully. ■ **squat·ter** n.

squat thrust ▶ n. an exercise in which the legs are thrust backward to their full extent from a squatting position with the hands on the floor.

squaw /skwô/ ▶ n. offensive an American Indian woman or wife.

squawk /skwôk/ ▶ v. **1** (of a bird) make a loud, harsh noise. **2** say something in a loud, shrill tone. ▶ n. an act of squawking. ■ **squawk·er** n.

squeak /skwēk/ ▶ n. **1** a short, high-pitched sound or cry. **2** a single communication or sound: *I didn't hear a squeak from him.* ▶ v. **1** make a squeak. **2** say something in a high-pitched tone. **3** informal only just manage to succeed or to achieve something: *the bill squeaked through with just six votes to spare.* ■ **squeak·er** n. **squeak·y** adj. (**squeakier, squeakiest**).

squeak·y clean ▶ adj. informal **1** completely clean. **2** morally correct; very virtuous.

squeal /skwēl/ ▶ v. **1** make a long, high-pitched cry or noise. **2** say something in a high-pitched tone. **3** (often **squeal on**) informal inform on someone. **4** informal complain about something. ▶ n. a long, high-pitched cry or noise. ■ **squeal·er** n.

squeam·ish /'skwēmish/ ▶ adj. **1** easily disgusted or made to feel sick. **2** having very firm moral views. ■ **squeam·ish·ly** adv. **squeam·ish·ness** n.

squee·gee /'skwē jē/ ▶ n. a scraping tool with a rubber-edged blade, used for cleaning windows. ▶ v. (**squeegees, squeegeeing, squeegeed**) clean something with a squeegee.

squeeze /skwēz/ ▶ v. **1** firmly press something from opposite or all sides. **2** extract liquid or a soft substance from something by squeezing. **3** (**squeeze in/into/through**) manage to get into or through a restricted space. **4** (**squeeze someone/thing in**) manage to find time for someone or something. **5** obtain by pressure, force, etc.: *a series of con games designed to squeeze money out of the government.* ▶ n. **1** an act of squeezing or the state of being squeezed. **2** a hug. **3** a small amount of liquid that is squeezed out. **4** a strong financial demand or pressure: *a squeeze on profits.* **5** (usu. **main squeeze**) informal a person's girlfriend or boyfriend. ■ **squeez·a·ble** adj. **squeez·er** n. – PHRASES **put the squeeze on** informal pressure someone into doing something.

squeeze·box ▶ n. informal an accordion or concertina.

squelch /skwelch/ ▶ v. **1** make a soft sucking sound such as that made by treading in thick mud. **2** informal forcefully silence someone or put an end to something. ▶ n. a squelching sound. ■ **squelch·y** adj.

squib /skwib/ ▶ n. **1** a small firework that hisses before exploding. **2** a short piece of satirical writing.

squid /skwid/ ▶ n. (pl. same or **squids**) a mollusk that lives in the sea, with a long body, eight arms, and two long tentacles.

squig·gle /'skwigəl/ ▶ n. a short line that curls and loops irregularly. ■ **squig·gly** adj.

squill /skwil/ ▶ n. **1** (also **sea squill**) a Mediterranean plant with broad leaves and white flowers. **2** a small plant resembling a hyacinth, with clusters of violet-blue or blue-striped flowers.

squint /skwint/ ▶ v. **1** look at someone or something with partly closed eyes. **2** partly close the eyes. **3** have an eye that looks in a different direction to the other eye. ▶ n. **1** a permanent condition in which one eye does not look in the same direction as the other. **2** informal a quick look. ■ **squint·y** adj.

squire /'skwīr/ ▶ n. **1** a country gentleman, especially the chief landowner in an area. **2** historical a young nobleman acting as an attendant to a knight before becoming a knight himself. ▶ v. (of a man) accompany or escort a woman.

squire·ar·chy /'skwīrärkē/ ▶ n. (pl. **squirearchies**) country landowners as a group.

squirm /skwərm/ ▶ v. **1** wriggle or twist the body from side to side, especially from nervousness or discomfort. **2** be embarrassed or ashamed. ▶ n. a wriggling movement. ■ **squirm·y** adj.

squir·rel /'skwər(ə)l/ ▶ n. an agile rodent with a bushy tail that lives in trees. ▶ v. (**squirrels, squirreling, squirreled**) (**squirrel something away**) hide or keep money or valuables in a safe place.

squir·rel·ly /'skwər(ə)lē/ ▶ adj. **1** relating to or resembling a squirrel. **2** informal restless or nervous.

squirt /skwərt/ ▶ v. **1** force out liquid in a thin jet from a small opening. **2** wet someone or something with a jet of liquid. ▶ n. **1** a thin jet of liquid. **2** informal a weak or insignificant person.

squish /skwish/ ▶ v. **1** make a soft squelching sound. **2** informal squash something. ▶ n. a soft squelching sound. ■ **squish·y** adj.

Sr ▶ symbol the chemical element strontium.

Sr. ▶ abbr. senior (in names): *E. T. Krebs, Sr.*

SRAM /'es,ram/ ▶ abbr. Electronics static random-access memory.

Sri Lan·kan /,srē 'läNGkən, ,SHrē, 'laNGkən/ ▶ n. a person from Sri Lanka. ▶ adj. relating to Sri Lanka.

SRO ▶ abbr. **1** standing room only. **2** single room occupancy.

SS¹ ▶ abbr. **1** Saints. **2** steamship. **3** social security. **4** Baseball shortstop.

SS² ▶ n. the Nazi special police force.

SSA ▶ abbr. **1** Social Security Act. **2** Social Security Administration.

SSE ▶ abbr. south-southeast.

SSRI ▶ abbr. selective serotonin reuptake inhibitor, any of a group of antidepressant drugs that prevent the uptake of serotonin in the brain.

SST ▶ abbr. supersonic transport.

SSW ▶ abbr. south-southwest.

St. ▶ abbr. **1** Saint. **2** Street.

stab /stab/ ▶ v. (**stabs, stabbing, stabbed**) **1** thrust a knife or other pointed weapon into someone. **2** make a short, forceful movement with a pointed object: *I stabbed at my salad in irritation.* **3** (of a pain) cause a sudden sharp feeling. ▶ n. **1** an act of stabbing. **2** a sudden sharp feeling or pain. **3** (**a stab at**) informal an attempt to do something. ■ **stab·ber** n. – PHRASES **stab someone in the back** betray someone.

sta·bil·i·ty /stə'bilitē/ ▶ n. the state of being stable, steady, or unchanging.

sta·bi·lize /'stābə,līz/ ▶ v. make or become stable, steady, or unchanging. ■ **sta·bi·li·za·tion** /,stābəli'zāsнən/ n.

sta·bi·liz·er /'stābə,līzər/ ▶ n. **1** a device used to stabilize a ship or aircraft. **2** a substance preventing the breakdown of emulsions in food or paint. **3** a mood stabilizer.

sta·ble[1] /'stābəl/ ▶ adj. (**stabler, stablest**) **1** not likely to give way or overturn; firmly fixed. **2** not likely to change or fail: *a stable relationship*. **3** not worsening in health after an injury or operation. **4** not easily upset or disturbed; sane and sensible. **5** not liable to undergo chemical decomposition or radioactive decay. ■ **sta·bly** /-b(ə)lē/ adv.

stable[2] ▶ n. **1** a building for housing horses. **2** a place where racehorses are kept and trained. **3** an organization or place that produces particular types of people or things: *the magazine is from the same stable as* Vogue. ▶ v. put or keep a horse in a stable.

sta·ble·mate /'stābəl,māt/ ▶ n. **1** a horse from the same stable as another. **2** a person or product from the same organization or background as another.

sta·bling /'stāb(ə)liNG/ ▶ n. accommodations for horses.

stac·ca·to /stə'kätō/ ▶ adv. & adj. Music with each sound or note sharply separated from the others. ▶ n. (pl. **staccatos**) **1** Music a staccato passage or performance. **2** a series of short detached sounds or words.

stack /stak/ ▶ n. **1** a neat pile of objects. **2** a rectangular or cylindrical pile of hay, straw, etc. **3** informal a large quantity of something. **4** a chimney. ▶ v. **1** arrange things in a stack. **2** fill or cover a place with stacks of things. **3** cause aircraft to fly at different altitudes while waiting to land. **4** shuffle or arrange a deck of cards dishonestly. **5** (**be stacked against/in favor of**) (of a situation) be very likely to produce an unfavorable or favorable outcome for: *the odds were stacked against Fiji in the World Cup.* ■ **stack·a·ble** adj. **stack·er** n.

sta·di·um /'stādēəm/ ▶ n. (pl. **stadiums** or **stadia** /-dēə/) a sports arena with tiers of seats for spectators.

staff /staf/ ▶ n. **1** (treated as sing. or pl.) the employees of an organization. **2** (treated as sing. or pl.) a group of officers assisting a commanding officer. **3** a long stick used as a support or weapon. **4** a rod or scepter held as a sign of office or authority. **5** Music a stave. ▶ v. provide an organization with staff.
– PHRASES **the staff of life** a basic food, especially bread.

staff·er /'stafər/ ▶ n. a member of a staff, especially of a newspaper.

staff of·fi·cer ▶ n. a military officer serving on the staff of a headquarters or government department.

staff ser·geant ▶ n. a rank of noncommissioned officer in the US armed forces, just above sergeant.

stag /stag/ ▶ n. **1** a fully adult male deer. **2** a social gathering attended by men only. **3** a person who attends a social gathering without a partner. ▶ adv. without a partner at a social gathering: *we decided to go stag.*

stag bee·tle ▶ n. a large dark beetle, the male of which has large branched jaws resembling antlers.

stage /stāj/ ▶ n. **1** a part, period, or point in a process: *she was in the early stages of pregnancy.* **2** a raised floor or platform on which actors, entertainers, or speakers perform. **3** (**the stage**) the theater as a profession or form of entertainment. **4** a part of a journey. **5** an area of public activity: *his aim is to put Latin American art back on the world stage.* **6** a floor or level of a structure. **7** each of two or more sections of a rocket or spacecraft that are jettisoned in turn when their fuel is exhausted. **8** Electronics a part of a circuit containing a single amplifying transistor or valve. ▶ v. **1** present a performance of a play or other show. **2** organize and participate in a public event. **3** cause something dramatic or unexpected to happen. ■ **stage·a·ble** adj.
– PHRASES **set the stage for** prepare the conditions for something to happen.

stage·coach /'stāj,kōch/ ▶ n. a closed horse-drawn vehicle formerly used to carry passengers and often mail along a regular route.

stage·craft /'stāj,kraft/ ▶ n. skill in writing or staging plays.

stage di·rec·tion ▶ n. an instruction in a play script indicating the position or tone of an actor, or specifying sound effects, lighting, etc.

stage door ▶ n. an actors' and workmen's entrance from the street to the backstage area of a theater.

stage fright ▶ n. nervousness before or during a performance.

stage·hand /'stāj,hand/ ▶ n. a person dealing with scenery or props during a play.

stage-man·age ▶ v. **1** arrange and control carefully to create a particular effect: *he stage-managed his image with astounding success.* **2** be the stage manager of a play or other production. ■ **stage man·age·ment** n.

stage man·ag·er ▶ n. the person responsible for lighting and other technical arrangements for a stage play.

stage name ▶ n. a name used by an actor for professional purposes.

stage-struck ▶ adj. having a passionate wish to become an actor.

stage whis·per ▶ n. a loud whisper by an actor on stage, intended to be heard by the audience.

stag·e·y ▶ adj. variant spelling of STAGY.

stag·fla·tion /,stag'flāsнən/ ▶ n. high inflation combined with high unemployment and stagnant demand in a country's economy.

stag·ger /'stagər/ ▶ v. **1** walk or move unsteadily, as if about to fall. **2** astonish someone greatly. **3** spread payments, events, etc., over a period of time. **4** arrange objects or parts so that they are not in line. ▶ n. an act of staggering.

stag·ing /'stājiNG/ ▶ n. **1** a way of staging a play or similar production. **2** a temporary platform for working or standing on.

stag·ing ar·e·a (also **staging point** or **staging post**) ▶ n. a stopping place or assembly point en route to a destination.

stag·nant /'stagnənt/ ▶ adj. **1** (of water or air) completely still and often having an unpleasant smell. **2** showing little activity: *a stagnant economy.*

stag·nate /'stag,nāt/ ▶ v. **1** stop developing;

become inactive: *while the economy has stagnated, individual savings have increased.* **2** (of water or air) become still or stagnant. ■ **stag·na·tion** /stag'nāsнən/ n.

stag party ▶ n. an all-male celebration, especially one held for a man about to be married.

stag·y /'stājē/ (also **stagey**) ▶ adj. excessively theatrical or exaggerated. ■ **stag·i·ly** adv. **stag·i·ness** n.

staid /stād/ ▶ adj. respectable, serious, and unadventurous.

stain /stān/ ▶ v. **1** mark or discolor something with something that is difficult to remove. **2** damage the reputation of someone or something. **3** color something with a dye or chemical. ▶ n. **1** a discolored patch or dirty mark that is difficult to remove. **2** a thing that damages a person's reputation: *I left the court without a stain on my character.* **3** a dye or chemical used to color materials. ■ **stain·a·ble** adj. **stain·er** n.

stained glass ▶ n. colored glass used to form pictures or designs, typically used for church windows.

stain·less /'stānlis/ ▶ adj. unmarked by or resistant to stains.

stain·less steel ▶ n. a form of steel containing chromium, resistant to tarnishing and rust.

stair /ste(ə)r/ ▶ n. **1** each of a set of fixed steps. **2** (**stairs**) a set of fixed steps leading from one floor of a building to another.

stair·case /'ste(ə)r,kās/ (also **stairway**) ▶ n. a set of stairs and its surrounding structure.

stair·climb·er /'ste(ə)r,klīmər/ ▶ n. an exercise machine on which the user simulates the action of climbing a staircase.

stair·lift /'ste(ə)r,lift/ ▶ n. a lift in the form of a chair that can be raised or lowered at the edge of a staircase.

stair·way /'ste(ə)r,wā/ ▶ n. a set of steps or stairs and its surrounding walls or structure.

stair·well /'ste(ə)r,wel/ ▶ n. a shaft in which a staircase is built.

stake¹ /stāk/ ▶ n. **1** a strong post with a point at one end, driven into the ground to support a tree, form part of a fence, etc. **2** (**the stake**) historical a wooden post to which a person was tied before being burned alive. ▶ v. **1** support a plant with a stake. **2** (**stake something out**) state one's position or assert one's rights forcefully. **3** (**stake someone/thing out**) informal keep a place or person under secret observation. – PHRASES **stake a claim** assert one's right to something.

stake² ▶ n. **1** a sum of money gambled. **2** a share or interest in a business or situation. **3** (**stakes**) prize money. **4** (**stakes**) a competitive situation: *one step ahead in the fashion stakes.* ▶ v. gamble money or something of value. – PHRASES **at stake 1** at risk. **2** in question.

stake·hold·er /'stāk,hōldər/ ▶ n. a person with an interest or concern in a business or similar venture. ▶ adj. (of an organization or system) in which all those people involved are seen as having an interest in its success: *a stakeholder economy.* ■ **stake·hold·ing** n. & adj.

stake-out ▶ n. informal a period of secret observation.

sta·lac·tite /'stə'lak,tīt/ ▶ n. a tapering structure hanging from the roof of a cave, formed of

calcium salts deposited by dripping water.

sta·lag·mite /'stə'lag,mīt/ ▶ n. a tapering column rising from the floor of a cave, formed of calcium salts deposited by dripping water.

stale /stāl/ ▶ adj. (**staler, stalest**) **1** (of food) no longer fresh or pleasant to eat. **2** no longer new and interesting: *their marriage had gone stale.* **3** (of a person) no longer performing well because of having done something for too long. ▶ v. make or become stale. ■ **stale·ly** /'stā(l)lē/ adv. **stale·ness** n.

stale·mate /'stāl,māt/ ▶ n. **1** a situation in which further progress by opposing sides seems impossible. **2** Chess a position counting as a draw, in which a player is not in check but can only move into check. ▶ v. cause a situation to reach stalemate. ■ **stalk·er** n.

Sta·lin·ism /'stälə,nizəm/ ▶ n. the ideology and policies adopted by the Soviet Communist Party leader and head of state Joseph Stalin, based on dictatorial state control and the pursuit of communism. ■ **Sta·lin·ist** n. & adj.

stalk¹ /stôk/ ▶ n. **1** the main stem of a plant. **2** the attachment or support of a leaf, flower, or fruit. **3** a slender support or stem of an object. ■ **stalk·like** /-,līk/ adj. **stalk·y** adj.

stalk² ▶ v. **1** follow someone or something stealthily. **2** harass someone with unwanted and obsessive attention. **3** stride in a proud, stiff, or angry way. **4** chiefly literary move silently or threateningly through a place: *fear stalks the streets.* ■ **stalk·er** n.

stalk·ing horse ▶ n. a person or thing that is used to disguise a person's real intentions.

stall /stôl/ ▶ n. **1** a stand, booth, or compartment for the sale of goods in a market. **2** an individual compartment for an animal in a stable or cowshed. **3** a stable or cowshed. **4** a compartment for one person in a set of toilets or shower cubicles. **5** (also **starting stall**) a compartment in which a horse is held before the start of a race. **6** a seat in the choir or chancel of a church, enclosed at the back and sides. ▶ v. **1** (of a motor vehicle or its engine) stop running. **2** stop making progress. **3** be vague or indecisive in order to gain time to deal with something: *she was stalling for time.* **4** (of an aircraft) be moving too slowly to allow it to be controlled effectively.

stal·lion /'stalyən/ ▶ n. an adult male horse that has not been castrated.

stal·wart /'stôlwərt/ ▶ adj. **1** loyal, reliable, and hard-working. **2** dated sturdy and strongly built. ▶ n. a loyal and reliable supporter or member of an organization.

sta·men /'stāmin/ ▶ n. the male fertilizing organ of a flower, typically consisting of a pollen-containing anther on a very thin stalk.

stam·i·na /'stamənə/ ▶ n. the ability to keep up physical or mental effort over a long period.

stam·mer /'stamər/ ▶ v. speak or say something with difficulty, repeating the first letters of words and often pausing. ▶ n. a tendency to stammer. ■ **stam·mer·er** n.

stamp /stamp/ ▶ v. **1** bring the foot down heavily on the ground or an object. **2** walk with heavy, forceful steps. **3** (**stamp something out**) put an end to something by taking decisive action. **4** press a device against something in order to leave a mark or pattern. **5** (**stamp something on**) fix something in the mind: *the date was* *stamped on his memory.* **6** stick a postage stamp on a letter or parcel. ▶ n. **1** a small piece of paper that is stuck to a letter or parcel to show that postage has been paid. **2** an instrument for stamping a pattern or mark. **3** a mark or pattern made by a stamp. **4** a distinctive impression or quality: *the whole project has the stamp of authority.* **5** a particular class or type: *he went around with men of his own stamp.* **6** an act of stamping the foot. ■ **stamp·er** n.

stamp duty ▶ n. a duty that must be paid in order for certain documents to be legally recognized.

stam·pede /stam'pēd/ ▶ n. **1** a sudden panicked or excited rush of a group of people or animals. **2** a situation in which a large number of people are trying to respond to something at once: *he tried in vain to stem the stampede toward modernism.* ▶ v. **1** (of animals or people) rush in a sudden mass panic. **2** rush someone into doing something: *she claimed to have been stampeded into making wrong decisions.* ■ **stam·ped·er** n.

stamp·ing ground ▶ n. chiefly British term for STOMPING GROUND.

stance /stans/ ▶ n. **1** the way in which someone stands. **2** an attitude toward something; a standpoint.

stanch /stônch, stänch/ (Brit. also **staunch**) ▶ v. stop or restrict the flow of something, especially blood from a wound.

stan·chion /'stanchən/ ▶ n. an upright bar, post, or frame forming a support or barrier.

stand /stand/ ▶ v. (past and past part. **stood** /stŏŏd/) **1** be in or rise to an upright position, supported by the feet. **2** place or be situated in a particular position. **3** move in a standing position to a specified place: *I stood aside to let him enter.* **4** be in a particular state or condition: *since grandad's death the house has stood empty.* **5** remain motionless or unchanged. **6** remain valid: *my decision stands.* **7** withstand an experience without being damaged. **8** tolerate or like: *I can't stand brandy.* **9** be likely to do something: *investors stood to lose heavily.* **10** adopt a particular attitude toward an issue. **11** take a particular role: *he stood security for the government's borrowings.* ▶ n. **1** an attitude toward a particular issue: *the party's tough stand in immigration.* **2** a determined effort to hold one's ground or resist something. **3** a rack, base, or item of furniture for holding or displaying something. **4** a large structure for spectators to sit or stand in at different levels. **5** a small stall from which goods are sold or displayed. **6** a raised platform for a band, orchestra, or speaker. **7** (**the stand**) a witness box in a court of law. **8** a stopping of movement or progress. **9** a place where vehicles wait for passengers. **10** a group of trees of the same kind.
– PHRASES **stand by 1** watch something bad without becoming involved. **2** support someone or keep a promise. **3** be ready to take action if required. **stand down 1** (also **stand aside**) resign from or leave a job or office. **2** relax after a state of readiness. **stand for 1** be an abbreviation of or symbol for. **2** put up with; tolerate. **stand in** take someone's place; deputize. **stand on** be very concerned to follow correct behavior: *one doesn't stand on rights when driving in Japan.* **stand on one's own (two) feet** be or become independent. **stand out 1** project or be easily noticeable. **2** be clearly better. **stand to** Military stand ready for an attack.

stand trial be tried in a court of law. **stand someone up** informal fail to keep a date with someone. **stand up for** speak or act in support of. **stand up to 1** resist someone in a spirited way. **2** resist the harmful effects of.

stand·a·lone /'standə,lōn/ ▶ adj. (of computer hardware or software) able to operate independently of other hardware or software.

stand·ard /'standərd/ ▶ n. **1** a level of quality or achievement: *the restaurant offers a high standard of service.* **2** a required or accepted level of quality or achievement. **3** something used as a measure in order to make comparisons. **4** (**standards**) principles of morally acceptable behavior. **5** a military or ceremonial flag. **6** a popular tune or song that has become well established. **7** (usu. before another noun) a shrub grafted on an upright stem and trained to grow in the shape of a tree: *a standard rose.* ▶ adj. **1** used or accepted as normal or average. **2** (of a size, measure, etc.) regularly used or produced. **3** (of a work, writer, etc.) viewed as authoritative and so widely read. ■ **stand·ard·ly** adv.

stand·ard-bear·er ▶ n. **1** a leading figure in a cause or movement. **2** a soldier carrying the flag of a unit, regiment, or army.

stand·ard·ize /'standər,dīz/ ▶ v. make things of the same type have the same features or qualities. ■ **stand·ard·i·za·tion** /,standərdi'zāshən/ n.

stand·ard of liv·ing ▶ n. the amount of money and level of comfort available to a person or community.

stand·ard time ▶ n. a uniform time for places in approximately the same longitude.

stand·by /'stan(d),bī/ ▶ n. (pl. **standbys**) **1** readiness for duty or immediate action. **2** a person or thing ready to be used in an emergency. ▶ adj. (of tickets for a journey or performance) sold only at the last minute if still available.

stand·ee /stan'dē/ ▶ n. a person who is standing rather than seated.

stand-in ▶ n. a person who stands in or deputizes for another.

stand·ing /'standing/ ▶ n. **1** the position, status, or reputation of someone or something. **2** the length of time that something has existed: *a problem of long standing.* ▶ adj. **1** remaining in force or use: *a standing invitation.* **2** (of a jump or start of a race) performed from rest or an upright position. **3** (of water) stagnant or still.
– PHRASES **leave someone/thing standing** informal be much better or faster than someone or something.

stand·ing joke ▶ n. something that regularly causes amusement.

stand·ing or·der ▶ n. **1** an order placed on a regular basis with a retailer. **2** an order or ruling that governs the procedures of a society, council, etc. **3** a military order or ruling that is retained even under changing circumstances.

stand·ing o·va·tion ▶ n. a period of prolonged applause during which the audience rise to their feet.

stand·ing stone ▶ n. another term for MENHIR.

stand·off /'stand,ôf, -,äf/ ▶ n. a situation in a dispute in which no agreement can be reached.

stand·off·ish /,stand'ôfish, -'äfish/ ▶ adj. informal cold and unfriendly.

stand·out /'stand,out/ ► n. informal an outstanding person or thing.

stand·pipe /'stan(d),pīp/ ► n. a vertical pipe extending from a water supply, connecting a temporary tap to the mains.

stand·point /'stan(d),point/ ► n. 1 an attitude toward a particular issue. 2 the position from which a person can view a scene or an object.

stand·still /'stan(d),stil/ ► n. a situation without movement or activity.

stand-up ► adj. 1 (of comedy or a comedian) performed or performing by telling jokes to an audience. 2 informal brave and fiercely loyal: a *stand-up guy*. 3 designed to stay upright or erect: *a stand-up collar*. 4 involving or used by people standing up.

stank /staNGk/ ► past of STINK.

stan·za /'stanzə/ ► n. a group of lines forming the basic recurring unit in a poem; a verse.

staph·y·lo·coc·cus /,staf(ə)lō'käkəs/ ► n. (pl. **staphylococci** /-'käk,sī, -,sē/) a bacterium of a group including many kinds that cause pus to be formed.

sta·ple¹ /'stāpəl/ ► n. 1 a small U-shaped piece of wire used to fasten papers together. 2 a small U-shaped metal bar with pointed ends, driven into wood to hold things such as wires in place. ► v. secure something with a staple or staples.

staple² ► n. 1 a main item of trade or production. 2 a main or important element of something. 3 the fiber of cotton or wool considered in terms of its length and fineness. ► adj. main or important: *a staple food*.

sta·pler /'stāp(ə)lər/ ► n. a device for fastening papers together with staples.

star /stär/ ► n. 1 a huge mass of burning gas that is visible as a glowing point in the night sky. 2 a shape with five or six points representing a star, often used to indicate a category of excellence. 3 a famous or talented entertainer or athlete. 4 an outstanding person or thing in a group. 5 Astrology a planet, constellation, etc., considered to influence one's fortunes or personality: *his destiny was written in the stars*. ► v. (**stars**, **starring**, **starred**) 1 (of a movie, play, etc.) have someone as a leading performer. 2 (of a performer) have a leading role in a movie, play, etc. 3 mark, decorate, or cover something with star-shaped marks or objects.
– PHRASES **see stars** seem to see flashes of light as a result of a blow on the head.

star an·ise ► n. a small star-shaped fruit with an anise flavor, used in Asian cooking.

star·board /'stär,bôrd/ ► n. the side of a ship or aircraft on the right when one is facing forward. The opposite of PORT³.

star·burst /'stär,bərst/ ► n. 1 a pattern of lines or rays radiating from a central point. 2 a period of intense activity in a galaxy involving the formation of stars.

starch /stärCH/ ► n. 1 a carbohydrate that is obtained chiefly from cereals and potatoes and is an important constituent of the human diet. 2 powder or spray made from starch, used to stiffen fabric. ► v. stiffen fabric with starch.

starch·y /'stärCHē/ ► adj. (**starchier**, **starchiest**) 1 (of food) containing a lot of starch. 2 informal (of a person) stiff and formal in manner or behavior. ■ **starch·i·ly** adv. **starch·i·ness** n.

star-crossed ► adj. literary fated to be unlucky.

star·dom /'stärdəm/ ► n. the state or status of being a famous or talented entertainer or athlete.

stare /ste(ə)r/ ► v. 1 look fixedly at someone or something with the eyes wide open. 2 (**stare someone out**) look fixedly at someone until they feel forced to look away. ► n. an act of staring. ■ **star·er** n.
– PHRASES **be staring someone in the face** be obvious.

star·fish /'stär,fiSH/ ► n. (pl. same or **starfishes**) a sea creature having a flattened body with five or more arms.

star·fruit /'stär,frōōt/ ► n. another term for CARAMBOLA.

star·gaz·er /'stär,gāzər/ ► n. informal an astronomer or astrologer.

stark /stärk/ ► adj. 1 severe or bare in appearance. 2 unpleasantly or sharply clear. 3 complete; sheer: *stark terror*. ■ **stark·ly** adv. **stark·ness** n.
– PHRASES **stark naked** completely naked. **stark raving mad** informal completely mad.

stark·ers /'stärkərz/ ► adj. Brit. informal completely naked.

star·let /'stärlit/ ► n. informal a promising young actress or performer.

star·light /'stär,līt/ ► n. light coming from the stars. ■ **star·lit** /'stär,lit/ adj.

star·ling /'stärliNG/ ► n. a songbird with dark shiny plumage.

Star of Da·vid /'dāvid/ ► n. a six-pointed figure consisting of two interlaced equilateral triangles, used as a Jewish and Israeli symbol.

star route ► n. a postal delivery route served by a private contractor.

star·ry /'stärē/ ► adj. (**starrier**, **starriest**) 1 full of or lit by stars. 2 informal relating to stars in entertainment.

star·ry-eyed ► adj. full of unrealistic hopes and dreams about someone or something.

Stars and Bars ► pl.n. (treated as sing.) historical the flag of the Confederate States of America.

Stars and Stripes ► pl.n. (treated as sing.) the national flag of the US.

star·ship /'stär,SHip/ ► n. (in science fiction) a large manned spaceship for travel between the stars.

star sign ► n. a sign of the zodiac.

star-span·gled ► adj. informal impressively successful.

star·struck ► adj. fascinated and very impressed by famous people.

star-stud·ded ► adj. featuring a number of famous people.

START /stärt/ ► abbr. Strategic Arms Reduction Talks.

start /stärt/ ► v. 1 begin to do, be, happen, or engage in: *she started talking to him*. 2 begin to operate or work. 3 make something happen or operate. 4 begin to move or travel. 5 jump or jerk from surprise. ► n. 1 the point at which something begins. 2 an act of beginning. 3 an advantage consisting in having set out in a race or on a journey before one's rivals or opponents. 4 a sudden movement of surprise.
– PHRASES **for a start** in the first place. **start at** cost at least a specified amount. **start out** (or **up**) begin a venture or undertaking. **to start with** as the first thing to be taken into account.

start·er /'stärtər/ ▶n. **1** a person or thing that starts. **2** chiefly Brit. the first course of a meal. **3** an automatic device for starting a machine. **4** a competitor taking part in a race or game at the start. **5** a topic or question with which to start a discussion or course of study.
– PHRASES **for starters** informal first of all. **under starter's orders** waiting for the signal to start a race.

start·er home ▶n. a small house or apartment designed for people buying their first home.

start·ing block ▶n. a block against which runners brace their feet at the start of a race.

start·ing gate ▶n. a barrier raised at the start of a horse race to ensure that all the competitors start at the same time.

start·ing price ▶n. the final odds at the start of a horse race.

star·tle /'stärtl/ ▶v. make someone feel sudden shock or alarm. ■ **star·tled** adj.

star·tling /'stärtl-iNG/ ▶adj. very surprising or remarkable. ■ **star·tling·ly** adv.

start·up ▶n. **1** the action of starting something. **2** a newly established business.

starve /stärv/ ▶v. **1** suffer or die from hunger. **2** make someone starve by preventing them from eating. **3** (**be starving** or **starved**) informal feel very hungry. **4** (**be starved of**) be deprived of: *the arts are being starved of funds.* ■ **star·va·tion** /-'vāsHən/ n.

stash /stasH/ informal ▶v. store something safely in a secret place. ▶n. a secret store of something.

sta·sis /'stāsis, 'sta-/ ▶n. **1** formal or technical a period or state when there is no change or development. **2** Medicine a stopping of the normal flow of a body fluid.

state /stāt/ ▶n. **1** the condition of someone or something at a particular time. **2** a nation or territory considered as an organized political community under one government. **3** a community or area forming part of a federal republic. **4** (**the States**) the United States of America. **5** the government of a country. **6** the grand ceremonial procedures associated with monarchy or government: *he was buried in state.* **7** (**a state**) informal an agitated, untidy, or dirty condition. ▶v. express something definitely or clearly in speech or writing. ■ **state·hood** /'stāt,hŏŏd/ n.
– PHRASES **state of affairs** a situation. **state-of-the-art** using the newest ideas and most up-to-date features. **state of emergency** a situation of national danger or disaster in which a government suspends normal constitutional procedures. **state of grace** a state of being free from sin.

state·craft /'stāt,kraft/ ▶n. the skillful management of state affairs.

State De·part·ment ▶n. the department of foreign affairs.

state house (also **statehouse**) ▶n. the building where a state legislature meets.

state·less /'stātlis/ ▶adj. not recognized as a citizen of any country.

state·ly /'stātlē/ ▶adj. (**statelier**, **stateliest**) dignified, grand, or impressive. ■ **state·li·ness** n.

state·ment /'stātmənt/ ▶n. **1** a definite or clear expression of something in speech or writing.

2 a formal account of facts or events, especially one given to the police or in court. **3** a document setting out items of debit and credit between a bank or other organization and a customer.

state·room /'stāt,rŏŏm, -,rŏŏm/ ▶n. **1** a large room in a palace or public building, for use on formal occasions. **2** a private room on a ship.

state school ▶n. another term for STATE UNIVERSITY.

state's ev·i·dence ▶n. Law evidence for the prosecution given by a participant in or accomplice to the crime being tried.

state·side /'stāt,sīd/ ▶adj. & adv. informal relating to, in, or toward the US.

states·man /'stātsmən/ (or **stateswoman** /'stāts,wŏŏmən/) ▶n. (pl. **statesmen** or **stateswomen**) an experienced and respected political leader. ■ **states·man·like** /-,līk/ adj. **states·man·ship** /-,sHip/ n.

states' rights ▶pl.n. the rights and powers held by individual US states rather than by the federal government.

state u·ni·ver·si·ty ▶n. a university managed by the authorities of a particular US state.

state·wide /'stāt'wīd/ ▶adj. & adv. extending throughout a particular US state.

stat·ic /'statik/ ▶adj. **1** not moving, changing, or active: *they believed in a static social order.* **2** Physics concerned with bodies at rest or forces in equilibrium. Often contrasted with DYNAMIC. **3** (of an electric charge) acquired by objects that cannot conduct a current. ▶n. **1** static electricity. **2** crackling or hissing on a telephone, radio, etc. ■ **stat·i·cal·ly** /-ik(ə)lē/ adv.

stat·ice /'statisē, 'statis/ ▶n. a plant with small pink or lilac funnel-shaped flowers, growing mainly in coastal areas.

stat·ic e·lec·tric·i·ty ▶n. stationary electric charge produced by friction, causing sparks or crackling or the attraction of dust or hair.

stat·ics /'statiks/ ▶pl.n. (usu. treated as sing.) the branch of mechanics concerned with bodies at rest and forces in equilibrium.

stat·in /'statn/ ▶n. any of a group of drugs that act to reduce levels of cholesterol in the blood.

sta·tion /'stāsHən/ ▶n. **1** a place where passenger trains stop on a railroad line, typically with platforms and buildings. **2** a place where a particular activity or service is based: *a radar station.* **3** a broadcasting company. **4** the place where someone or something stands or is placed for a particular purpose or duty. **5** a person's social rank or position. **6** Austral./NZ a large sheep or cattle farm. ▶v. put in or send to a particular place: *troops were stationed in the town.*

sta·tion·ar·y /'stāsHə,nerē/ ▶adj. **1** not moving. **2** not changing in quantity or condition.

USAGE
Do not confuse **stationary** and **stationery**: **stationary** is an adjective meaning 'not moving or changing' (*the truck crashed into a stationary car*), while **stationery** is a noun meaning 'paper and other writing materials'.

sta·tion break ▶n. a pause between broadcast programs for an announcement of the identity of the station transmitting them.

sta·tion·er /'stāsH(ə)nər/ ▶n. a person who sells stationery.

sta·tion·er·y /'stāsHə,nerē/ ▶n. paper and other materials needed for writing.

sta·tion·mas·ter /ˈstāsнən‚mastər/ ▶ n. a person in charge of a railroad station.

Sta·tion of the Cross ▶ n. each of a series of fourteen pictures representing incidents during Jesus's progress from Pilate's house to his entombment.

sta·tion wag·on ▶ n. a car that has a large carrying area behind the seats and an extra door at the rear.

stat·ism /ˈstāt‚izəm/ ▶ n. a political system in which the government has a great deal of central control over social and economic affairs. ■ **stat·ist** n. & adj.

sta·tis·tic /stəˈtistik/ ▶ n. a fact or piece of data obtained from a study of a large quantity of numerical information.

sta·tis·ti·cal /stəˈtistikəl/ ▶ adj. relating to statistics. ■ **sta·tis·ti·cal·ly** adv.

sta·tis·tics /stəˈtistiks/ ▶ pl.n. (treated as sing.) the collection and analysis of large quantities of numerical information. ■ **stat·is·ti·cian** /‚stati'stisнən/ n.

stats /stats/ ▶ pl.n. informal statistics.

stat·u·ar·y /ˈstacнōō‚erē/ ▶ n. statues considered as a group.

stat·ue /ˈstacнōō/ ▶ n. a carved or cast figure of a person or animal, especially one that is life-size or larger.

stat·u·esque /‚stacнōō'esk/ ▶ adj. (of a woman) attractively tall, graceful, and dignified.

stat·u·ette /‚stacнōō'et/ ▶ n. a small statue.

stat·ure /ˈstacнər/ ▶ n. 1 a person's natural height when standing. 2 the importance or reputation gained by a person as a result of their ability or achievements: *an architect of international stature.*

sta·tus /ˈstātəs, ˈstatəs/ ▶ n. 1 a person's social or professional standing in relation to other people. 2 high rank or social standing. 3 the situation at a particular time during a process. 4 the official classification given to someone or something.

sta·tus quo /ˈstātəs ˈkwō, ˈstatəs/ ▶ n. the existing situation.

sta·tus sym·bol ▶ n. a possession seen as an indication of a person's wealth or high social or professional status.

stat·ute /ˈstacнōōt/ ▶ n. 1 a written law passed by a parliament or other legislative assembly. 2 a rule of an organization or institution.

stat·ute book ▶ n. (**the statute book**) the whole of a nation's laws.

stat·ute law ▶ n. all the written laws of a legislature, country, etc., considered as a group.

stat·ute of lim·i·ta·tions ▶ n. a law that limits the period in which certain kinds of actions can be brought.

stat·u·to·ry /ˈstacнə‚tôrē/ ▶ adj. 1 required, permitted, or enacted by law. 2 having come to be required or expected as a result of being done regularly: *the statutory Christmas phone call to his mother.* ■ **stat·u·to·ri·ly** /-‚tôrəlē/ adv.

stat·u·to·ry rape ▶ n. Law sexual intercourse with a minor.

staunch[1] /stôncн, stäncн/ ▶ adj. very loyal and committed. ■ **staunch·ly** adv.

staunch[2] ▶ v. British variant spelling of STANCH.

stave /stāv/ ▶ n. 1 any of the lengths of wood fixed side by side to make a barrel, bucket, etc. 2 a strong stick, post, or pole. 3 (also **staff**)

Music a set of five parallel lines on or between any of which a note is written to indicate its pitch. 4 a verse or stanza of a poem. ▶ v. 1 (past and past part. **staved** or **stove** /stōv/) (**stave something in**) break something by forcing it inward or piercing it roughly. 2 (past and past part. **staved**) (**stave something off**) prevent or delay something undesirable: *emergency measures were introduced to stave off a crisis.*

stay[1] /stā/ ▶ v. 1 remain in the same place. 2 remain in a particular state or position: *inflation will stay down.* 3 live somewhere temporarily as a visitor or guest. 4 stop, delay, or prevent something. ▶ n. 1 a period of staying somewhere. 2 a suspension or postponement of judicial or legal proceedings: *a stay of execution.* 3 (**stays**) historical a corset made of two pieces laced together and stiffened by strips of whalebone. ▶ v. 1 ...
– PHRASES **stay the course** (or **distance**) 1 keep going to the end of a race or contest. 2 continue with a difficult task or activity to the end. **stay on** continue to study, work, or be somewhere after others have left. **stay over** stay for the night as a visitor or guest. **stay put** remain somewhere without moving.

stay[2] ▶ n. 1 a large rope, wire, or rod used to support a ship's mast or other upright pole. 2 a supporting wire or cable on an aircraft.

stay·ing pow·er ▶ n. endurance or stamina.

stay·sail /ˈstāsəl, -‚sāl/ ▶ n. a triangular sail fastened on a stay.

stead /sted/ ▶ n. (in phrase **in someone's/something's stead**) instead of someone or something: *she was appointed in his stead.*
– PHRASES **stand someone in good stead** be useful to someone over time or in the future.

stead·fast /ˈsted‚fast/ ▶ adj. completely unwavering in one's attitudes or aims. ■ **stead·fast·ly** adv. **stead·fast·ness** n.

stead·y /ˈstedē/ ▶ adj. (**steadier**, **steadiest**) 1 firmly fixed, supported, or balanced. 2 not faltering or wavering: *a steady gaze.* 3 sensible and reliable. 4 regular, even, and continuous in development, frequency, or strength: *a steady decline in the national birth rate.* ▶ v. (**steadies**, **steadying**, **steadied**) make or become steady. ▶ exclam. (also **steady on!**) a warning to keep calm or take care. ■ **stead·i·ly** adv. **stead·i·ness** n.
– PHRASES **go steady** informal have a regular romantic or sexual relationship with someone.

steak /stāk/ ▶ n. 1 high-quality beef from the hindquarters of the animal, cut into thick slices for broiling or frying. 2 a thick slice of other meat or fish. 3 poorer-quality beef for braising or stewing.

steak·house /ˈstāk‚hous/ ▶ n. a restaurant that specializes in serving steaks.

steak tar·tare /tä(r)ˈtär/ ▶ n. a dish consisting of raw ground steak mixed with raw egg.

steal /stēl/ ▶ v. (past **stole** /stōl/; past part. **stolen** /ˈstōlən/) 1 take something without permission or legal right and without intending to return it. 2 move somewhere quietly or surreptitiously. ▶ n. informal a bargain. ■ **steal·er** n.
– PHRASES **steal a look** (or **glance**) take a quick and surreptitious look at someone or something. **steal a march** on gain an advantage over someone by acting before they do. **steal the show** attract the most attention and praise. **steal someone's thunder** win the praise or attention expected by someone else by acting or speaking

before them.

stealth /stelTH/ ▶ n. cautious and surreptitious action or movement. ▶ adj. (of aircraft) designed to be difficult to detect by radar or sonar: *a stealth bomber.*

stealth tax ▶ n. a tax charged in such a way that it is not noticed as a tax.

stealth·y /'stelTHē/ ▶ adj. (**stealthier, stealthiest**) cautious and surreptitious. ■ **stealth·i·ly** adv. **stealth·i·ness** n.

steam /stēm/ ▶ n. **1** the hot vapor into which water is converted when heated, which condenses in the air into a mist of minute water droplets. **2** power for machines produced by steam under pressure. **3** energy or force of movement; momentum: *the dispute gathered steam.* ▶ v. **1** give off or produce steam. **2** (**steam up**) mist over with steam. **3** cook food by heating it in steam from boiling water. **4** clean or treat something with steam. **5** (of a ship or train) travel somewhere under steam power. **6** informal move somewhere rapidly or forcefully. **7** (**be/get steamed up**) informal be or become very agitated or angry.
– PHRASES **get up** (or **pick up**) **steam 1** generate enough pressure to drive a steam engine. **2** (of an activity, project, etc.) gradually gain momentum. **let off steam** informal get rid of pent-up energy or strong emotion. **run out of steam** informal lose momentum or enthusiasm. **under one's own steam** without help from other people.

steam bath ▶ n. a room filled with hot steam for cleaning and refreshing the body.

steam·boat /'stēm,bōt/ ▶ n. a boat propelled by a steam engine, especially a paddle-wheel craft of a type used on rivers in the 19th century.

steam en·gine ▶ n. **1** an engine that uses the expansion or rapid condensation of steam to generate power. **2** a steam locomotive.

steam·er /'stēmər/ ▶ n. **1** a ship or boat powered by steam. **2** a type of saucepan in which food can be steamed.

steam i·ron ▶ n. an electric iron that gives off steam from holes in its flat surface.

steam·roll·er /'stēm,rōlər/ ▶ n. a heavy, slow-moving vehicle with a roller, used to flatten the surfaces of roads during construction. ▶ v. (also **steamroll** /'stēm,rōl/) **1** force someone into doing or accepting something. **2** (of a government or other authority) forcibly pass a law by limiting debate or overriding opposition.

steam·ship /'stēm,SHip/ ▶ n. a ship that is powered by a steam engine.

steam·y /'stēmē/ ▶ adj. (**steamier, steamiest**) **1** producing, filled with, or clouded with steam. **2** hot and humid. **3** informal involving passionate sexual activity. ■ **steam·i·ly** adv. **steam·i·ness** n.

ste·ar·ic ac·id /stē'arik, 'stī(ə)r-/ ▶ n. a solid saturated fatty acid obtained from animal or vegetable fats.

ste·a·tite /'stēə,tīt/ ▶ n. the mineral talc occurring especially as soapstone.

steed /stēd/ ▶ n. old use or literary a horse.

steel /stēl/ ▶ n. **1** a hard, strong gray or bluish-gray alloy of iron with carbon and usually other elements, used as a structural material and in manufacturing. **2** strength and determination: *nerves of steel.* ▶ v. mentally prepare oneself to do or face something difficult.

steel band ▶ n. a band that plays music on steel drums.

steel drum (also **steel pan**) ▶ n. a percussion instrument made out of an oil drum with one end beaten down and divided into sections to give different notes.

steel·head /'stēl,hed/ (also **steelhead trout**) ▶ n. a rainbow trout of a large migratory variety.

steel wool ▶ n. fine strands of steel matted together into a mass, used for polishing or cleaning hard surfaces.

steel·work /'stēl,wərk/ ▶ n. articles made of steel.

steel·works /'stēl,wərks/ ▶ pl.n. (usu. treated as sing.) a factory where steel is manufactured.

steel·y /'stēlē/ ▶ adj. (**steelier, steeliest**) **1** resembling steel in color, brightness, or strength. **2** coldly determined. ■ **steel·i·ness** n.

steel·yard /'stēl,yärd/ ▶ n. a weighing device that has a short arm taking the item to be weighed and a long graduated arm along which a weight is moved until it balances.

steep¹ /stēp/ ▶ adj. **1** rising or falling sharply; almost perpendicular. **2** (of a rise or fall in an amount) very large or rapid. **3** informal (of a price or demand) not reasonable; excessive. ▶ n. chiefly literary a steep mountain slope. ■ **steep·ly** adv. **steep·ness** n.

steep² ▶ v. **1** soak something in water or other liquid. **2** (**be steeped in**) be filled with a particular quality: *a castle steeped in history.*

steep·en /'stēpən/ ▶ v. become or make steeper.

stee·ple /'stēpəl/ ▶ n. **1** a church tower and spire. **2** a spire on the top of a church tower or roof. ▶ v. place the fingers or hands together so that they form an upward-pointing V-shape.

stee·ple·chase /'stēpəl,CHās/ ▶ n. **1** a horse race run on a racetrack that has ditches and hedges as jumps. **2** a running race in which runners must clear hurdles and water jumps. ■ **stee·ple·chas·er** n. **stee·ple·chas·ing** n.

stee·ple·jack /'stēpəl,jak/ ▶ n. a person who climbs tall structures such as chimneys and steeples in order to carry out repairs.

steer¹ /sti(ə)r/ ▶ v. **1** guide or control the movement of a vehicle, ship, or aircraft. **2** direct or guide: *he steered her to a chair.* ▶ n. informal a piece of advice or information. ■ **steer·a·ble** adj. **steer·er** n.
– PHRASES **steer clear of** take care to avoid.

steer² ▶ n. a bullock.

steer·age /'sti(ə)rij/ ▶ n. **1** historical the cheapest accommodations in a ship. **2** old use or literary the action of steering a boat.

steer·ing /'sti(ə)riNG/ ▶ n. the mechanism in a vehicle, ship, or aircraft that allows it to be steered.

steer·ing col·umn ▶ n. a shaft that connects the steering wheel of a vehicle to the rest of the steering mechanism.

steer·ing com·mit·tee (also **steering group**) ▶ n. a committee that decides on the priorities or order of business of an organization.

steer·ing wheel ▶ n. a wheel that a driver turns in order to steer a vehicle.

steers·man /'sti(ə)rzmən/ ▶ n. (pl. **steersmen**) a person who steers a boat or ship.

steg·o·saur /'stegə,sôr/ (also **stegosaurus** /,stegə'sôrəs/) ▶ n. a plant-eating dinosaur with a double row of large bony plates along the back.

stein /stīn/ ▶ n. a large earthenware beer mug.

ste·la /'stēlə/ (also **stele** /stēl/) ▶ n. (pl. **stelae** /-ˌlē/) Archaeology an upright stone slab or column with an inscription or design.

stel·lar /'stelər/ ▶ adj. **1** relating to a star or stars. **2** informal featuring or having the quality of a star performer. **3** informal excellent; outstanding.

stem[1] /stem/ ▶ n. **1** the main body or stalk of a plant or shrub. **2** the stalk supporting a fruit, flower, or leaf. **3** a long, thin supporting or main section of something, such as that of a wine glass or tobacco pipe. **4** a vertical stroke in a letter or musical note. **5** Grammar the root or main part of a word, to which other elements are added. **6** the main upright timber or metal piece at the bow of a ship. ▶ v. (**stems**, **stemming**, **stemmed**) (**stem from**) come from or be caused by: *depression stemming from domestic difficulties.*
– PHRASES **from stem to stern** from one end to the other, especially of a ship.

stem[2] ▶ v. (**stems**, **stemming**, **stemmed**) stop or restrict the flow or progress of something.

stem cell ▶ n. an undifferentiated cell within an organism that can divide to produce more cells of the same kind or develop into a specialized cell.

stem·ware /'stemˌwe(ə)r/ ▶ n. goblets and stemmed drinking glasses regarded collectively.

stench /stenCH/ ▶ n. a strong and very unpleasant smell.

sten·cil /'stensəl/ ▶ n. a thin sheet of card, plastic, or metal with a pattern or letters cut out of it, used to produce a design on the surface below by applying ink or paint through the holes.
▶ v. (**stencils**, **stenciling**, **stenciled**) decorate something with a stencil.

ste·nog·ra·pher /stə'nägrəfər/ ▶ n. a shorthand typist.

stent /stent/ ▶ n. Medicine **1** a tubular support placed temporarily inside a blood vessel, canal, or duct to aid healing or relieve an obstruction. **2** an impression or cast of a part or body cavity, used to maintain pressure so as to promote healing, especially of a skin graft.

sten·to·ri·an /sten'tôrēən/ ▶ adj. (of a person's voice) loud and powerful.

step /step/ ▶ n. **1** an act of lifting and putting down the foot or alternate feet, as in walking. **2** the distance covered by a step. **3** a flat surface on which to place one's foot when moving from one level to another. **4** a measure or action taken to deal with or achieve something: *the local authority must take steps to protect the children.* **5** a position or grade in a scale or series. **6** a block fixed to a boat's keel to take the base of a mast or other fitting. ▶ v. (**steps**, **stepping**, **stepped**) lift and put down one's foot or alternate feet.
– PHRASES **in** (or **out of**) **step 1** walking, marching, or dancing in the same (or a different) rhythm and pace as other people. **2** conforming (or not conforming) to what other people are doing or thinking. **mind** (or **watch**) **one's step** walk or act carefully. **step down** (or **aside**) withdraw or resign from a position or job. **step forward** offer one's help or services. **step in 1** become involved in a difficult situation, especially in order to help. **2** act as a substitute for someone. **step on it** informal go faster. **step out of line** behave inappropriately or disobediently. **step something up** increase the amount, speed, or strength of something.

step- ▶ comb.form referring to a relationship resulting from a remarriage: *stepmother.*

step aer·o·bics ▶ pl.n. a type of aerobics that involves stepping up onto and down from a portable block.

step·broth·er /'step,brəTHər/ ▶ n. a son of one's stepparent by a marriage other than that with one's own father or mother.

step·child /'step,CHīld/ ▶ n. (pl. **stepchildren**) a child of one's husband or wife by a previous marriage.

step·daugh·ter /'step,dôtər, 'step,dätər/ ▶ n. a daughter of one's husband or wife by a previous marriage.

step·fa·ther /'step,fäTHər/ ▶ n. a man who is married to one's mother after the divorce of one's parents or the death of one's father.

steph·a·no·tis /,stefə'nōtis/ ▶ n. a climbing plant with fragrant waxy white flowers.

step·lad·der /'step,ladər/ ▶ n. a short folding ladder with flat steps and a small platform.

step·moth·er /'step,məTHər/ ▶ n. a woman who is married to one's father after the divorce of one's parents or the death of one's mother.

step·par·ent /'ste(p),parənt, -,pe(ə)r-/ ▶ n. a stepfather or stepmother.

steppe /step/ ▶ n. a large area of flat grassland without trees in SE Europe or Siberia.

step·ping-stone /'steping,stōn/ ▶ n. **1** a raised stone on which to step when crossing a stream or muddy area. **2** an action that helps someone make progress toward a goal.

step·sis·ter /'step,sistər/ ▶ n. a daughter of one's stepparent by a marriage other than that with one's own father or mother.

step·son /'step,sən/ ▶ n. a son of one's husband or wife by a previous marriage.

step·wise /'step,wīz/ ▶ adv. & adj. **1** in a series of distinct stages; not continuously: *the concentrations tend to decrease stepwise.* **2** Music (of melodic motion) moving by adjacent scale steps rather than leaps.

ster·e·o /'sterē-ō, 'sti(ə)r-/ ▶ n. (pl. **stereos**) **1** sound that is directed through two or more speakers so that it seems to surround the listener and come from more than one source. **2** a CD player, record player, etc., that has two or more speakers and produces this type of sound. ▶ adj. relating to or producing this type of sound.

ster·e·o·phon·ic /,sterēə'fänik, ,sti(ə)r-/ ▶ adj. full form of STEREO.

ster·e·o·scope /'sterēə,skōp, 'sti(ə)r-/ ▶ n. a device by which two photographs of the same object taken at slightly different angles are viewed together, creating a three-dimensional impression.

ster·e·o·scop·ic /,sterēə'skäpik, ,sti(ə)r-/ ▶ n. **1** able to see objects as three-dimensional forms. **2** relating to a stereoscope.

ster·e·o·type /'sterēə,tīp, 'sti(ə)r-/ ▶ n. a widely held but oversimplified idea of the typical characteristics of a person or thing. ▶ v. view or represent someone or something as a stereotype.

ster·e·o·typ·i·cal /,sterēə'tipikəl/ ▶ adj. relating to or resembling a stereotype: *stereotypical images of femininity.* ■ **ster·e·o·typ·i·cal·ly** adv.

ster·ile /'sterəl/ ▶ adj. **1** not able to produce children, young, crops, or fruit. **2** free from bacteria or other living microorganisms. **3** lacking imagination, creativity, or excitement. ■ **ste·ril·i·ty** /stə'rilitē/ n.

ster·i·lize /'sterə,līz/ ▶ v. **1** make something

free from bacteria. **2** make a person or animal unable to produce offspring by removing or blocking the sex organs. ■ **ster·i·li·za·tion** /ˌsterəl(ə)'zāsHən/ n.

ster·ling /'stərliNG/ ▶ n. **1** an item or set of items, especially flatware, made of sterling silver: *get out the sterling for dinner*. **2** British money. ▶ adj. **1** made of sterling silver. **2** excellent; of great value: *they do sterling work for charity*.

ster·ling sil·ver ▶ n. silver of at least 92¼ percent purity.

stern[1] /stərn/ ▶ adj. **1** serious and strict. **2** severe; demanding: *the team are facing a stern test*. ■ **stern·ly** adv. **stern·ness** n.

stern[2] ▶ n. the rearmost part of a ship or boat.

ster·num /'stərnəm/ ▶ n. (pl. **sternums** or **sterna** /-nə/) the breastbone.

ste·roid /'ster,oid, 'sti(ə)r-/ ▶ n. **1** any of a large class of organic compounds that includes certain hormones and vitamins. **2** an anabolic steroid. ■ **ste·roi·dal** /ste'roidl, sti-/ adj.

ste·rol /'sterôl, -äl, 'sti(ə)r-/ ▶ n. Biochemistry any of a group of naturally occurring unsaturated steroid alcohols, such as cholesterol.

ster·to·rous /'stərtərəs/ ▶ adj. (of breathing) noisy and labored. ■ **ster·to·rous·ly** adv.

stet /stet/ ▶ v. let it stand (used as an instruction on a printed proof to ignore a correction).

steth·o·scope /'steTHə,skōp/ ▶ n. a medical instrument for listening to the action of someone's heart or breathing, having a small disk that is placed against the chest and two tubes connected to earpieces.

Stet·son /'stetsən/ ▶ n. trademark a hat with a high crown and a very wide brim, traditionally worn by cowboys in the US.

ste·ve·dore /'stēvə,dôr/ ▶ n. a person employed at a dock to load and unload ships.

ste·vi·a /'stēvēə, 'stev-/ ▶ n. a composite herb native to South America whose leaves are the source of a noncaloric sweetener.

stew /st(y)oo/ ▶ n. **1** a dish of meat and vegetables cooked slowly in liquid in a closed dish. **2** informal a state of anxiety or agitation. ▶ v. **1** cook food slowly in liquid in a closed dish. **2** informal be in a heated or stuffy atmosphere. **3** informal be anxious or agitated.
– PHRASES **stew in one's own juices** informal be left to suffer the consequences of one's own actions.

stew·ard /'st(y)ooərd/ ▶ n. **1** a person who looks after the passengers on a ship or aircraft. **2** an official who supervises arrangements at a large public event. **3** a person employed to manage a large house or estate. **4** a person responsible for supplies of food to a college, club, etc. ▶ v. act as a steward of something. ■ **stew·ard·ship** /-,SHip/ n.

stew·ard·ess /'st(y)ooərdis/ ▶ n. a woman who looks after the passengers on a ship or aircraft.

stick[1] /stik/ ▶ n. **1** a thin piece of wood that has fallen or been cut off a tree. **2** a piece of trimmed wood used for support in walking or as a weapon. **3** (in hockey, polo, etc.) a long, thin implement used to hit or direct the puck or ball. **4** a long, thin object or piece: *a stick of dynamite*. **5** (**the sticks**) informal, derogatory country areas far from towns or cities.

stick[2] ▶ v. (past and past part. **stuck** /stək/) **1** (**stick something in/into/through**) insert or push a pointed object into or through something.

2 (**stick in/into/through**) (of a pointed object) be or remain fixed with its point embedded in something. **3** protrude or extend in a particular direction: *his front teeth stick out*. **4** fasten or become fastened to something: *she stuck the stamp on the envelope*. **5** informal put something somewhere in a quick or careless way. **6** (**be stuck**) be fixed in a particular position or unable to move or be moved. **7** (**be stuck**) be unable to continue with a task or find the answer or solution.
– PHRASES **be stuck on** informal be infatuated with. **be stuck with** informal be unable to get rid of or escape from. **stick around** informal remain in or near a place. **stick at** informal persevere with something. **stick by** continue to support or be loyal to someone. **stick in one's throat** (or **craw**) be difficult or impossible to accept. **stick it out** informal put up with or persevere with something difficult or unpleasant. **stick one's neck out** informal risk criticism or anger by acting or speaking boldly. **stick out** be extremely noticeable. **stick to** continue doing or using something rather than changing to something else: *I'll stick to tap water*. **stick together** informal (of two or more people) support and remain loyal to each other. **stick up for** support or defend a person or cause.

stick·ball /'stik,bôl/ ▶ n. an informal game resembling baseball, played with a stick and a (usually rubber) ball.

stick·er /'stikər/ ▶ n. a sticky label or notice.

stick·er price ▶ n. the advertised retail price of an item, especially the price listed on a sticker attached to the window of a new automobile.

stick·er shock ▶ n. informal shock or dismay experienced by the potential buyers of a particular product on discovering its high or increased price.

stick·ing point ▶ n. an obstacle that prevents progress toward an agreement or goal.

stick in·sect ▶ n. another term for WALKING STICK (sense 2).

stick-in-the-mud ▶ n. informal a person who is unwilling to try anything new or exciting.

stick·le·back /'stikəl,bak/ ▶ n. a small freshwater or coastal fish with sharp spines along its back.

stick·ler /'stik(ə)lər/ ▶ n. a person who insists on a certain quality or type of behavior: *Susan was a stickler for punctuality*.

stick shift ▶ n. a gear lever or manual gearbox.

stick·up /'stik,əp/ ▶ n. informal an armed robbery in which a gun is used to threaten people.

stick·y /'stikē/ ▶ adj. (**stickier, stickiest**) **1** tending or designed to stick to things on contact; adhesive. **2** (of a substance) like glue in texture. **3** (of the weather) hot and humid; muggy. **4** informal difficult or awkward: *the relationship is going through a sticky patch*. ▶ n. (pl. **stickies**) a piece of paper with an adhesive strip on one side, used for leaving notes. ■ **stick·i·ly** adv. **stick·i·ness** n.

stiff /stif/ ▶ adj. **1** not easily bent; rigid. **2** not moving freely; difficult to turn or operate. **3** unable to move easily and without pain. **4** (of a person or their manner) not relaxed or friendly. **5** severe or difficult: *the company faces stiff competition for the contracts*. **6** (of an alcoholic drink) strong. **7** (—— **stiff**) informal having a particular unpleasant feeling to an extreme extent: *scared stiff*. ▶ n. informal a dead body.

■ **stiff·ly** adv. **stiff·ness** n.

– PHRASES **stiff upper lip** the tendency to endure difficulty without complaining or showing one's feelings.

stiff·en /ˈstifən/ ▶ v. **1** make or become stiff. **2** make or become stronger. ■ **stiff·en·er** n.

stiff-necked ▶ adj. proud and stubborn.

sti·fle¹ /ˈstīfəl/ ▶ v. **1** prevent someone from breathing freely. **2** smother or suppress: *she stifled a giggle.*

stifle² ▶ n. a joint in the legs of horses and other animals, equivalent to the knee in humans.

sti·fling /ˈstīf(ə)liNG/ ▶ adj. unpleasantly hot and stuffy. ■ **sti·fling·ly** adv.

stig·ma /ˈstigmə/ ▶ n. (pl. **stigmas** or in sense 2 **stigmata** /stigˈmätə, ˈstigmətə/) **1** a mark or sign of disgrace. **2** (**stigmata**) (in Christian tradition) marks on a person's body corresponding to those left on Jesus's body by the Crucifixion. **3** the part of a plant's pistil that receives the pollen during pollination.

stig·mat·ic /stigˈmatik/ ▶ adj. relating to a stigma or stigmas. ▶ n. a person with stigmata.

stig·ma·tize /ˈstigmə,tīz/ ▶ v. regard or treat someone or something as worthy of disgrace or great disapproval. ■ **stig·ma·ti·za·tion** /ˌstigməti'zāsHən/ n.

stile /stīl/ ▶ n. an arrangement of steps set into a fence or wall that allows people to climb over.

sti·let·to /stəˈletō/ ▶ n. (pl. **stilettos**) **1** (also **stiletto heel**) a thin, high tapering heel on a woman's shoe. **2** a short dagger with a tapering blade.

still¹ /stil/ ▶ adj. **1** not moving. **2** (of air or water) not disturbed by wind, sound, or currents. ▶ n. **1** a state of deep and quiet calm. **2** a photograph or a single shot from a movie. ▶ adv. **1** even now or at a particular time. **2** nevertheless. **3** even: *better still.* ▶ v. make or become still. ■ **still·ness** n.

still² ▶ n. a piece of equipment for distilling alcoholic drinks such as whiskey.

still·birth /ˈstil,bərTH/ ▶ n. the birth of a baby that has died in the uterus.

still·born /ˈstil,bôrn/ ▶ adj. **1** (of a baby) born dead. **2** (of a proposal or plan) having failed to develop or succeed.

still life ▶ n. (pl. **still lifes**) a painting or drawing of an arrangement of objects such as flowers or fruit.

stilt /stilt/ ▶ n. **1** either of a pair of upright poles with supports for the feet enabling the user to walk raised above the ground. **2** each of a set of posts supporting a building. **3** a wading bird with very long, slender legs.

stilt·ed /ˈstiltid/ ▶ adj. (of speech or writing) not natural, relaxed, or flowing easily. ■ **stilt·ed·ly** adv. **stilt·ed·ness** n.

Stil·ton /ˈstiltn/ ▶ n. trademark a kind of strong, rich blue cheese.

stim·u·lant /ˈstimyələnt/ ▶ n. **1** a substance that acts to increase levels of physiological or nervous activity in the body. **2** something that increases activity, interest, or enthusiasm. ▶ adj. acting as a stimulant.

stim·u·late /ˈstimyə,lāt/ ▶ v. **1** help something to develop or become more active: *policies designed to stimulate economic growth.* **2** encourage or arouse interest or enthusiasm in someone. **3** raise levels of physiological or nervous activity in the body. ■ **stim·u·la·tion** /ˌstimyə'lāsHən/ n. **stim·u·la·tor** /-,lātər/ n. **stim·u·la·to·ry** /-lə,tôrē/ adj.

stim·u·lus /ˈstimyələs/ ▶ n. (pl. **stimuli** /-,lī/) **1** something that causes a specific reaction in an organ or tissue of the body. **2** something that encourages activity, interest, or enthusiasm.

sting /stiNG/ ▶ n. **1** a small sharp-pointed organ of an insect, capable of inflicting a painful wound by injecting poison. **2** any of a number of minute hairs on certain plants, causing inflammation if touched. **3** a wound from a sting. **4** a sharp tingling sensation or hurtful effect. **5** informal a carefully planned undercover operation. ▶ v. (past and past part. **stung**) **1** wound someone or something with a sting. **2** produce a stinging sensation. **3** make someone feel angry or upset. **4** (**sting someone into**) provoke someone to do something by causing annoyance or offense. **5** informal swindle or overcharge someone.

sting·er /ˈstiNGər/ ▶ n. **1** the part of an insect or animal that holds a sting. **2** an insect or animal that stings, such as a bee or jellyfish. **3** informal a painful blow: *he suffered a stinger on his right shoulder.* **4** a cocktail including crème de menthe and brandy.

sting·ing net·tle ▶ n. a nettle covered in stinging hairs.

sting·ray /ˈstiNG,rā/ ▶ n. a ray (fish) with a long poisonous serrated spine at the base of the tail.

stin·gy /ˈstinjē/ ▶ adj. (**stingier, stingiest**) informal not generous. ■ **stin·gi·ly** adv. **stin·gi·ness** n.

stink /stiNGk/ ▶ v. (past **stank** /staNGk/ or **stunk** /stəNGk/; past part. **stunk**) **1** have a strong, unpleasant smell. **2** informal seem very bad, unpleasant, or dishonest. ▶ n. **1** a strong, unpleasant smell. **2** informal a commotion or fuss.

stink bomb ▶ n. a small container that when broken releases a substance with a very unpleasant smell.

stink·er /ˈstiNGkər/ ▶ n. informal a very unpleasant person or thing.

stink·horn /ˈstiNGk,hôrn/ ▶ n. a fungus with a rounded head that turns into a foul-smelling slimy substance containing the spores.

stink·ing /ˈstiNGkiNG/ ▶ adj. **1** smelling very unpleasant. **2** informal very bad or unpleasant. ▶ adv. informal extremely: *stinking rich.*

stink·y /ˈstiNGkē/ ▶ adj. (**stinkier, stinkiest**) informal having a strong, unpleasant smell.

stint /stint/ ▶ v. (also **stint on**) be very economical or stingy about spending or providing something: *he doesn't stint on wining and dining.* ▶ n. **1** a period of work: *his career included a stint as a musician.* **2** limited supply or effort.

sti·pend /ˈstī,pend, -pənd/ ▶ n. a fixed regular sum paid as a salary or allowance to a clergyman, teacher, or public official.

sti·pen·di·ar·y /stīˈpendē,erē/ ▶ adj. **1** receiving a stipend; working for pay rather than voluntarily. **2** relating to a stipend.

stip·ple /ˈstipəl/ ▶ v. **1** mark a surface with numerous small dots or specks. **2** produce a decorative effect on paint or other material by roughening its surface when wet.

stip·u·late /ˈstipyə,lāt/ ▶ v. demand or specify something as part of a bargain or agreement. ■ **stip·u·la·tion** /ˌstipyə'lāsHən/ n.

stir¹ /stər/ ▶ v. (**stirs, stirring, stirred**) **1** move an implement around and around in a liquid or soft substance to mix it thoroughly. **2** move slightly or begin to be active. **3** wake up or get out of bed. **4** (often **stir someone up**) arouse a strong feeling in someone. ▶n. **1** an act of stirring. **2** a disturbance or commotion: *the event caused quite a stir.* ■ **stir·rer** n.

stir² ▶n. informal prison.

stir·cra·zy ▶adj. informal psychologically disturbed as a result of being imprisoned.

stir-fry ▶v. fry food rapidly over a high heat while stirring it briskly.

stir·ring /'stəriNG/ ▶adj. causing great excitement or strong emotion. ▶n. a first sign of activity, movement, or emotion.

stir·rup /'stərəp, 'stə-rəp, 'stir-/ ▶n. **1** each of a pair of metal loops attached at either side of a horse's saddle to support the rider's foot. **2** a pair of metal supports for the ankles used during gynecological examinations.

stitch /stiCH/ ▶n. **1** a loop of thread or yarn made by a single pass of the needle in sewing, knitting, or crocheting. **2** a method of sewing, knitting, or crocheting producing a particular pattern. **3** informal the smallest item of clothing: *a voluptuous woman without a stitch on.* **4** a sudden sharp pain in the side of the body, caused by vigorous exercise. ▶v. make or mend something with stitches. ■ **stitch·er** n. **stitch·ing** n.
– PHRASES **in stitches** informal laughing uncontrollably.

stoat /stōt/ ▶n. a small mammal of the weasel family, with chestnut fur (white in northern animals in winter), white underparts, and a black-tipped tail.

sto·chas·tic /stə'kastik/ ▶adj. technical not precisely predictable; random or affected by chance.

stock /stäk/ ▶n. **1** a supply of goods or materials available for sale or use. **2** farm animals bred and kept for their meat or milk; livestock. **3** the capital of a company raised through the selling of shares. **4** (**stocks**) a portion of a company's stock held by an individual or group as an investment. **5** water in which bones, meat, fish, or vegetables have been slowly simmered. **6** a person's ancestry. **7** a breed, variety, or population of an animal or plant. **8** the trunk or woody stem of a tree or shrub. **9** a plant with sweet-smelling white, pink, or lilac flowers. **10** (**the stocks**) (treated as sing. or pl.) historical a wooden structure with holes for securing a person's feet and hands, in which criminals were locked as a public punishment. **11** the part of a rifle or other gun to which the barrel and firing mechanism are attached, held against the shoulder when firing. **12** a band of material worn around the neck. ▶adj. **1** (of a product) usually kept in stock and so regularly available for sale. **2** (of a phrase or expression) used too regularly: *a stock response.* **3** referring to a conventional character type that recurs in a particular genre of literature, theater, or movies. ▶v. **1** have or keep a supply of a product. **2** (also **stock something up**) fill something with a supply of goods. **3** (**stock up**) obtain supplies of something for future use.
– PHRASES **in** (or **out of**) **stock** available (or unavailable) for immediate sale or use. **take stock** make an overall assessment of a particular situation.

stock·ade /stä'kād/ ▶n. **1** a barrier or enclosure formed from upright wooden posts. **2** a military prison.

stock·breed·er /'stäk,brēdər/ ▶n. a farmer who breeds livestock.

stock·brok·er /'stäk,brōkər/ ▶n. a person who buys and sells stocks and shares on behalf of clients. ■ **stock·brok·ing** n.

stock car ▶n. an ordinary car that has been strengthened for use in a race in which the competing cars collide with each other.

stock com·pa·ny ▶n. a repertory company that is largely based in one theater.

stock cube ▶n. a cube of dried meat, vegetable, or fish stock for use in cooking.

stock ex·change ▶n. a market in which stocks and shares are bought and sold.

stock·hold·er /'stäk,hōldər/ ▶n. an owner of shares in a company.

stock·i·nette /,stäkə'net/ ▶n. a soft, loosely knitted stretchy fabric.

stock·ing /'stäkiNG/ ▶n. **1** either of a pair of separate close-fitting nylon garments covering the foot and leg, worn by women. **2** a long sock worn by men. **3** a long sock or sock-shaped receptacle hung up by children on Christmas Eve to be filled with presents. **4** a white marking of the lower part of a horse's leg. ■ **stock·inged** adj.
– PHRASES **in one's stocking feet** without shoes.

stock·ing cap ▶n. a knitted hat with a long tapered end that hangs down.

stock·ing stitch ▶n. a knitting stitch consisting of alternate rows of plain and purl stitch.

stock·ing stuff·er ▶n. a small present suitable for putting in a Christmas stocking.

stock-in-trade ▶n. the typical subject or item a person, company, or profession uses or deals in.

stock·man /'stäkmən, -,man/ ▶n. (pl. **stockmen**) **1** a person who looks after livestock. **2** an owner of livestock.

stock mar·ket ▶n. a stock exchange.

stock op·tion ▶n. an option for an employee to buy stock in their company at a discount or at a stated fixed price.

stock·pile /'stäk,pīl/ ▶n. a large supply of goods or materials that has been gathered together. ▶v. gather together and keep a large supply of goods or materials.

stock·pot /'stäk,pät/ ▶n. a pot in which stock is prepared by long, slow cooking.

stock·room /'stäk,rōōm, -,rŏŏm/ ▶n. a room in which stocks of goods or materials are stored.

stock split ▶n. an issue of new shares in a company to existing shareholders in proportion to their current holdings.

stock-still ▶adv. without any movement; completely still.

stock swap ▶n. **1** acquisition of a company in which payment consists of stock in the buying company. **2** a means of exercising stock options in which shares already owned are traded for a greater number of shares at the exercise price.

stock·tak·ing /'stäk,tākiNG/ ▶n. the action or process of recording the amount of stock held by a business. ■ **stock·take** n. & v.

stock·y /'stäkē/ ▶adj. (**stockier, stockiest**) (especially of a person) short and sturdy. ■ **stock·i·ly** adv. **stock·i·ness** n.

stock·yard /'stäk,yärd/ ▶n. a large yard containing pens and sheds in which livestock is kept.

stodg·y /'stäjē/ ▶adj. **1** (of food) heavy and filling. **2** rather serious and dull. ■ **stodg·i·ness** n.

sto·gie /ˈstōgē/ (also **stogy**) ▶ n. (pl. **stogies**) a long, thin, inexpensive cigar.

sto·ic /ˈstō-ik/ ▶ n. **1** a stoical person. **2** (**Stoic**) a member of the ancient philosophical school of Stoicism. ▶ adj. **1** stoical. **2** (**Stoic**) relating to the Stoics or Stoicism.

sto·i·cal /ˈstō-ikəl/ ▶ adj. enduring pain and hardship without showing one's feelings or complaining. ■ **sto·i·cal·ly** /-ik(ə)lē/ adv.

sto·i·cism /ˈstō-iˌsizəm/ ▶ n. **1** stoical behavior. **2** (**Stoicism**) an ancient Greek school of philosophy that taught that it is wise to remain indifferent to changes of fortune and to pleasure and pain.

stoke /stōk/ ▶ v. **1** add coal to a fire, furnace, etc. **2** encourage or stir up a strong emotion. **3** (**stoke up**) informal eat a large quantity of food to give oneself energy.

stok·er /ˈstōkər/ ▶ n. a person who tends the furnace on a steamship or steam train.

stole¹ /stōl/ ▶ n. **1** a woman's long scarf or shawl, worn loosely over the shoulders. **2** a priest's garment worn over the shoulders.

stole² ▶ past of STEAL.

sto·len /ˈstōlən/ ▶ past participle of STEAL.

stol·id /ˈstälid/ ▶ adj. calm, dependable, and showing little emotion or reaction. ■ **sto·lid·i·ty** /stəˈliditē/ n. **stol·id·ly** adv.

stol·len /ˈstōlən, ˈsHtō-/ ▶ n. a rich German fruit and nut cake.

sto·ma /ˈstōmə/ ▶ n. (pl. **stomas** or **stomata** /-mətə, ˌstōˈmätə/) technical **1** a minute pore in the leaf or stem of a plant, allowing gases to move in and out. **2** a small mouthlike opening in some invertebrate animals. **3** an artificial opening made into a hollow organ, especially the gut.

stom·ach /ˈstəmək/ ▶ n. **1** the organ of the body in which the first part of digestion occurs. **2** the abdominal area of the body; the belly. **3** an appetite or desire for something: *they had no stomach for a fight.* ▶ v. **1** consume food or drink without feeling or being sick: *he cannot stomach milk.* **2** endure or accept: *what I won't stomach is thieving.*
– PHRASES **a strong stomach** an ability to see or do unpleasant things without feeling sick or squeamish.

stom·ach·ache /ˈstəmək.āk/ ▶ n. a pain in a person's belly.

sto·mach pump ▶ n. a syringe attached to a long tube, used for extracting the contents of a person's stomach (for example, if they have swallowed poison).

sto·ma·ta /ˈstōmətə, stōˈmätə/ ▶ plural of STOMA.

stomp /stämp, stômp/ ▶ v. tread or stamp heavily and noisily.

stomp·ing ground (chiefly Brit. also **stamping ground**) ▶ n. a place that a person regularly visits or spends time at.

stone /stōn/ ▶ n. **1** the hard, solid nonmetallic mineral matter that rock is made of. **2** a small piece of stone found on the ground. **3** a piece of stone shaped as a memorial or to mark out a boundary. **4** a gem or jewel. **5** a hard seed in certain fruits. **6** (pl. same) Brit. a unit of weight equal to 14 lb (6.35 kg). **7** a whitish or brownish-gray color. ▶ v. **1** throw stones at someone. **2** remove the stone from a fruit. ▶ adv. extremely or totally: *stone cold.*
– PHRASES **leave no stone unturned** try

everything possible in order to achieve something. **a stone's throw** a short distance.

Stone Age ▶ n. a prehistoric period that came before the Bronze Age, when weapons and tools were made of stone.

stone-broke ▶ adj. informal having no money at all.

stone cir·cle ▶ n. a prehistoric monument consisting of stones arranged in a circle.

stone·crop /ˈstōn.kräp/ ▶ n. a plant with star-shaped yellow or white flowers that grows among rocks or on walls.

stoned /stōnd/ ▶ adj. informal strongly affected by drugs or alcohol.

stone-faced ▶ adj. informal revealing no emotions through the expressions of the face.

stone-ground /ˈstōnˈground/ ▶ adj. (of flour) ground with millstones.

stone·ma·son /ˈstōnˌmāsən/ ▶ n. a person who cuts, prepares, and builds with stone.

stone·wall /ˈstōnˌwôl/ ▶ v. delay or block a person or process by refusing to answer questions or by giving evasive replies.

stone·ware /ˈstōnˌwe(ə)r/ ▶ n. a type of hard and impermeable pottery.

stone·washed /ˈstōnˌwôsHt, -ˌwäsHt/ (also **stonewash**) ▶ adj. (of a garment or fabric) washed with small stones to produce a worn or faded appearance.

stone·work /ˈstōnˌwərk/ ▶ n. the parts of a building that are made of stone.

ston·y /ˈstōnē/ ▶ adj. (**stonier**, **stoniest**) **1** full of stones. **2** made of or resembling stone. **3** cold and unfeeling: *a stony glare.* ■ **ston·i·ly** adv.
– PHRASES **fall on stony ground** (of words or a suggestion) be ignored or badly received.

stood /stood/ ▶ past and past participle of STAND.

stooge /stōōj/ ▶ n. informal **1** derogatory a less important person used by another to do routine or unpleasant work. **2** a performer whose act involves being the butt of a comedian's jokes.

stool /stōōl/ ▶ n. **1** a seat without a back or arms. **2** chiefly Medicine a piece of feces.

stool·ie /ˈstōōlē/ ▶ n. informal short for STOOL PIGEON.

stool pi·geon ▶ n. informal a police informer.

stoop¹ /stōōp/ ▶ v. **1** bend the head or body forward and downward. **2** have the head and shoulders permanently bent forward. **3** lower one's moral standards to do something wrong: *Craig wouldn't stoop to thieving.* ▶ n. a stooping posture.

stoop² ▶ n. a porch with steps in front of a building.

stop /stäp/ ▶ v. (**stops, stopping, stopped**) **1** come or bring to an end. **2** prevent something from happening, moving, or operating. **3** prevent someone from doing something. **4** no longer move or operate: *my watch has stopped.* **5** (of a bus or train) call at a particular place to pick up or set down passengers. **6** block or close up a hole or leak. **7** withhold or deduct: *they stopped the strikers' wages.* **8** ask a bank to withhold payment on a check. **9** obtain the required pitch from the string of a musical instrument by pressing at the appropriate point with the finger. ▶ n. **1** an act of stopping. **2** a place where a bus or train regularly stops. **3** an object or part of a mechanism that prevents movement. **4** a set of organ pipes of a particular tone and range of pitch. **5** a knob that controls such a set of organ pipes.

– PHRASES **pull out all the stops** make a very great effort to achieve something. **stop off** (or **over**) pay a short visit to a place on the way to somewhere else.

stop-and-go ▶ adj. having progress marked by alternate stopping and restarting: *stop-and-go driving.*

stop·cock /'stäp‚käk/ ▶ n. an externally operated valve regulating the flow of a liquid or gas through a pipe.

stop·gap /'stäp‚gap/ ▶ n. a temporary solution or substitute.

stop·light /'stäp‚līt/ ▶ n. **1** another term for TRAFFIC LIGHT. **2** a red traffic light.

stop-mo·tion ▶ n. a technique of film animation in which the camera is repeatedly stopped and started to give the impression of movement.

stop-off ▶ n. another term for STOPOVER.

stop·o·ver /'stäp‚ōvər/ ▶ n. a break in a journey.

stop·page /'stäpij/ ▶ n. **1** an instance of stopping. **2** an instance of industrial action. **3** a blockage.

stop·per /'stäpər/ ▶ n. **1** a plug for sealing a container. **2** a person or thing that stops something: *a conversation stopper.* ▶ v. seal a container with a stopper.

stop·watch /'stäp‚wäch/ ▶ n. a special watch with buttons that start and stop the display, used to time races.

stor·age /'stôrij/ ▶ n. **1** the action of storing something. **2** space available for storing: *we put most of the furniture into storage.*

stor·age heat·er ▶ n. Brit. an electric heater that stores up heat during the night and releases it during the day.

store /stôr/ ▶ n. **1** a retail establishment selling different types of goods. **2** a quantity or supply of something kept for use as needed. **3** a place where things are kept for future use or sale: *a grain store.* **4** (**stores**) supplies of equipment and food kept for use by members of an army, navy, or other institution. **5** a computer memory. ▶ v. **1** keep for future use: *a small room used for storing furniture.* **2** enter or keep information in the memory of a computer. **3** (**store something up**) fail to deal with something, especially when this results in future problems.

– PHRASES **in store** about to happen. **set store by** consider to be of a particular level of importance: *he set great store by teamwork.*

store brand ▶ n. a product manufactured specially for a retailer and bearing the retailer's name.

store·front /'stôr‚frənt/ ▶ n. **1** the part of a store that faces the street. **2** a commercial establishment, such as a store or restaurant, occupying space facing the street on the ground floor of a building.

store·house /'stôr‚hous/ ▶ n. **1** a building used for storing goods. **2** a thing that contains a large store of something: *the CD is an interactive storehouse of garden information.*

store·keep·er /'stôr‚kēpər/ ▶ n. **1** a person who owns or runs a store. **2** a person responsible for stored goods.

store·room /'stôr‚rōōm, -‚rŏŏm/ ▶ n. a room in which items are stored.

sto·rey /'stôrē/ ▶ n. Brit. variant spelling of STORY².

sto·ried /'stôrēd/ ▶ adj. literary celebrated in or associated with stories or legends.

stork /stôrk/ ▶ n. a tall long-legged bird with a long heavy bill and white and black plumage.

storm /stôrm/ ▶ n. **1** a violent disturbance of the atmosphere with strong winds and rain, and often thunder, lightning, or snow. **2** an uproar or controversy. **3** an intense outburst of a specified feeling or reaction: *the comedy attracted a storm of criticism.* ▶ v. **1** move angrily or forcefully: *he stormed out of the house.* **2** (of troops) suddenly attack and capture a place. **3** shout angrily.

– PHRASES **take something by storm 1** capture a place by a sudden attack. **2** have great and rapid success in a place.

storm cloud ▶ n. **1** a large dark rain cloud. **2** (**storm clouds**) a sign of problems or trouble to come: *storm clouds are looming over the PC market.*

storm door (or **storm window**) ▶ n. an additional outer door (or window) for protection in bad weather.

storm pet·rel ▶ n. a small petrel (bird) with blackish plumage, formerly believed to be a sign of bad weather to come.

storm sew·er (also **storm drain**) ▶ n. a sewer built to carry away excess water in times of heavy rain.

storm troops ▶ pl.n. another term for SHOCK TROOPS. ■ **storm troop·er** n.

storm win·dow ▶ n. a window fixed outside a normal window for protection and insulation in bad weather or winter.

storm·y /'stôrmē/ ▶ adj. (**stormier, stormiest**) **1** affected by a storm. **2** full of angry or violent outbursts of feeling. ■ **storm·i·ly** adv. **storm·i·ness** n.

sto·ry¹ /'stôrē/ ▶ n. (pl. **stories**) **1** an account of imaginary or real people and events told for entertainment. **2** a description of past events, experiences, etc.: *he issued a dossier giving his side of the story.* **3** an item of news. **4** a plot or storyline. **5** informal a lie.

sto·ry² (Brit. **storey**) ▶ n. (pl. **stories** or **storeys**) a floor or level of a building.

sto·ry·board /'stôrē‚bôrd/ ▶ n. a sequence of drawings representing the shots planned for a movie or television production.

sto·ry·book /'stôrē‚bŏŏk/ ▶ n. a book containing a story or stories for children. ▶ adj. perfect, as things typically are in children's stories: *a storybook romance.*

sto·ry·line /'stôrē‚līn/ ▶ n. the plot of a novel, play, movie, etc.

sto·ry·tell·er /'stôrē‚telər/ ▶ n. a person who tells stories. ■ **sto·ry·tell·ing** n.

stoup /stōōp/ ▶ n. a basin for holy water in a church.

stout /stout/ ▶ adj. **1** rather fat or heavily built. **2** (of an object) sturdy and thick. **3** brave and determined: *he put up a stout defense.* ▶ n. a kind of strong, dark beer brewed with roasted malt or barley. ■ **stout·ly** adv. **stout·ness** n.

stout·heart·ed /'stout'härtid/ ▶ adj. courageous or determined.

stove¹ /stōv/ ▶ n. a piece of equipment for cooking or heating that operates by burning fuel or using electricity.

stove² ▶ past and past participle of STAVE.

stove·pipe /'stōv‚pīp/ ▶ n. a pipe taking the smoke and gases from a stove up through a roof or to a chimney.

stove·pipe hat ▶ n. a type of tall top hat.

stow /stō/ ▶ v. **1** pack or store an object tidily in a particular place. **2** (**stow away**) hide oneself on a ship, aircraft, etc., so as to travel secretly or without paying. ■ **stow·age** /'stōij/ n.

stow·a·way /'stōə,wā/ ▶ n. a person who stows away on a ship, aircraft, etc.

stra·bis·mus /strə'bizməs/ ▶ n. Medicine the condition of having a squint.

strad·dle /'stradl/ ▶ v. **1** sit or stand with one leg on either side of something or someone. **2** extend across both sides of: *the plain straddles the border between Alaska and the Yukon.*

Strad·i·var·i·us /ˌstradə've(ə)rēəs/ ▶ n. a violin or other stringed instrument made by the Italian violin-maker Antonio Stradivari or his followers.

strafe /strāf/ ▶ v. attack something with machine-gun fire or bombs from low-flying aircraft.

strag·gle /'stragəl/ ▶ v. **1** trail slowly behind the person or people in front. **2** grow or spread out in an irregular, untidy way. ▶ n. an irregular and untidy group. ■ **strag·gler** /'strag(ə)lər/ n. **strag·gly** /'strag(ə)lē/ adj.

straight /strāt/ ▶ adj. **1** extending uniformly in one direction only; without a curve or bend. **2** properly positioned so as to be level, upright, or symmetrical. **3** in proper order or condition: *it'll take a long time to get the place straight.* **4** honest and direct. **5** in continuous succession: *his fourth straight win.* **6** (of an alcoholic drink) undiluted. **7** informal conventional or respectable. **8** informal heterosexual. **9** (of drama) serious as opposed to comic or musical. ▶ adv. **1** in a straight line or in a straight way. **2** without delay or diversion. **3** clearly and logically: *I'm so tired I can't think straight.* ▶ n. **1** the straight part of something. **2** informal a conventional person. **3** informal a heterosexual person. ■ **straight·ly** adv. **straight·ness** n.
– PHRASES **go straight** live an honest life after being a criminal. **the straight and narrow** the honest and morally acceptable way of living. **straight off** (or **out**) informal without hesitating.

> **USAGE**
> Do not confuse **straight** with **strait**. **Straight** means 'without a curve or bend' (*a long, straight road*), whereas **strait** means 'a narrow passage of water' (*the Straits of Gibraltar*) or 'trouble or difficulty' (*the economy is in dire straits*).

straight·a·way /'strātə,wā/ ▶ adv. immediately. ▶ adj. extending or moving in a straight line. ▶ n. a straight section of a road or racetrack.

straight·edge /'strāt,ej/ ▶ n. a bar with one edge accurately straight, used for testing straightness.

straight·en /'strātn/ ▶ v. **1** make or become straight. **2** stand or sit up straight after bending.

straight-faced ▶ adj. having a blank or serious facial expression. ■ **straight face** n.

straight·for·ward /ˌstrāt'fôrwərd/ ▶ adj. **1** easy to do or understand. **2** honest and open. ■ **straight·for·ward·ly** adv. **straight·for·ward·ness** n.

straight·jack·et ▶ n. variant spelling of STRAITJACKET.

straight-laced ▶ adj. variant spelling of STRAIT-LACED.

straight man ▶ n. a person in a show whose role is to provide a comedian with opportunities to make jokes.

straight-up ▶ adj. informal honest; trustworthy.

strain¹ /strān/ ▶ v. **1** force a part of one's body or oneself to make an unusually great effort. **2** injure a limb, muscle, or organ by making it work too hard. **3** make severe or excessive demands on: *he strained her tolerance to the limit.* **4** pull or push forcibly at something. **5** pour a mainly liquid substance through a sieve or similar device to separate out any solid matter. ▶ n. **1** a force tending to pull or stretch something to an extreme degree. **2** an injury caused by straining a muscle, limb, etc. **3** a severe demand on strength or resources: *the large order is already putting a strain on the airline.* **4** a state of tension or exhaustion caused by severe demands on a person's strength or resources. **5** the sound of a piece of music as it is played.

strain² ▶ n. **1** a distinct breed or variety of an animal, plant, or other organism. **2** a tendency in a person's character. **3** a type or kind of something: *the Tibetan strain of Buddhism.*

strained /strānd/ ▶ adj. **1** tense, tired, or uneasy. **2** produced by deliberate effort; artificial or forced: *a strained conversation.*

strain·er /'strānər/ ▶ n. a device for straining liquids, having holes punched in it or made of wire mesh.

strait /strāt/ ▶ n. **1** (also **straits**) a narrow passage of water connecting two seas or other large areas of water. **2** (**straits**) a situation of trouble or difficulty: *the economy is in dire straits.*

> **USAGE**
> On the confusion of **strait** and **straight**, see the note at STRAIGHT.

strait·ened /'strātnd/ ▶ adj. restricted because of poverty: *they lived in straitened circumstances.*

strait·jack·et /'strāt,jakət/ (also **straightjacket**) ▶ n. **1** a strong garment with long sleeves that can be tied together to confine the arms of a violent prisoner or mental patient. **2** something that severely restricts freedom of action or development.

strait-laced (also **straight-laced**) ▶ adj. having very strict moral attitudes.

strand¹ /strand/ ▶ v. **1** drive or leave a boat, person, or sea creature aground on a shore. **2** leave something without the means to move from a place: *the trucks are stranded in France.* ▶ n. literary or Irish the shore of a sea, lake, or large river.

strand² ▶ n. **1** a single thin length of thread, wire, etc. **2** a single hair or thin lock of hair. **3** a part of a complex whole: *the two main strands of feminism.*

strange /strānj/ ▶ adj. **1** unusual or surprising and often difficult to understand. **2** not previously visited, seen, or encountered; unfamiliar: *finding ATMs in a strange city can be a problem.* ■ **strange·ly** adv. **strange·ness** n.

stran·ger /'strānjər/ ▶ n. **1** a person one does not know. **2** a person who does not know, or is not known in, a particular place.
– PHRASES **be no** (or **a**) **stranger to** be familiar (or not familiar) with a feeling or situation.

stran·gle /'stranggəl/ ▶ v. **1** kill or injure someone by squeezing their neck. **2** prevent from happening or developing: *industry is being strangled by high diesel taxes.* ■ **stran·gler** /'strangg(ə)lər/ n.

stran·gle·hold /'stranggəl,hōld/ ▶ n. **1** a grip around a person's neck that deprives them of oxygen and so can kill them. **2** complete control over something.

stran·gu·late /'straNGgyə,lāt/ ▶ v. (usu. as adj. **strangulated**) Medicine squeeze a part of the body so tightly that blood cannot circulate through it.

stran·gu·la·tion /,straNGgyə'lāshən/ ▶ n. 1 the action of strangling someone or the state of being strangled. 2 a medical condition in which a part of the body is squeezed so tightly that blood cannot circulate through it.

strap /strap/ ▶ n. 1 a strip of flexible material used for fastening, securing, carrying, or holding onto someone or something. 2 (**the strap**) punishment by beating with a leather strap. ▶ v. (**straps, strapping, strapped**) 1 fasten or secure someone or something with a strap. 2 beat someone with a leather strap. 3 (as adj. **strapped**) informal short of money: *I'm constantly strapped for cash.* ■ **strap·less** adj. **strap·py** adj.

strap·hang·er /'strap,haNGər/ ▶ n. informal 1 a standing passenger in a bus or train. 2 a person who commutes to work by public transportation.

strap·ping¹ /'strapiNG/ ▶ adj. (of a person) big and strong.

strap·ping² ▶ n. 1 adhesive plaster for strapping injuries. 2 strips of flexible material or metal used to fasten or strengthen something.

stra·ta /'strätə, 'stratə/ ▶ plural of STRATUM.

strat·a·gem /'stratəjəm/ ▶ n. a plan or scheme intended to outwit an opponent.

stra·te·gic /strə'tējik/ ▶ adj. 1 forming part of a long-term plan to achieve a specific purpose. 2 relating to the gaining of long-term military advantage. 3 (of weapons) intended to be fired at enemy industrial areas and communication centers rather than used in a battle. Often contrasted with TACTICAL. ■ **stra·te·gi·cal·ly** /-ik(ə)lē/ adv.

strat·e·gy /'stratəjē/ ▶ n. (pl. **strategies**) 1 a plan designed to achieve a particular long-term aim. 2 the art of planning and directing military activity in a war or battle. Often contrasted with TACTICS (see TACTIC). ■ **strat·e·gist** n.

strat·i·fy /'stratə,fī/ ▶ v. (**stratifies, stratifying, stratified**) (usu. as adj. **stratified**) 1 form or arrange something into strata, layers, or levels. 2 arrange or classify someone or something. ■ **strat·i·fi·ca·tion** /,stratəfi'kāshən/ n.

stra·tig·ra·phy /strə'tigrəfē/ ▶ n. the branch of geology concerned with the order and relative dating of rock strata. ■ **strat·i·graph·ic** /,stratə'grafik/ adj. **strat·i·graph·i·cal** /,stratə'grafikəl/ adj.

stra·to·cu·mu·lus /,stratō'kyoomyələs, ,strä-/ ▶ n. cloud forming a low layer of clumped or broken gray masses.

strat·o·sphere /'stratə,sfi(ə)r/ ▶ n. 1 the layer of the earth's atmosphere above the troposphere and below the mesosphere. 2 informal the very highest levels of something. ■ **strat·o·spher·ic** /,stratə'sfi(ə)rik, -'sferik/ adj.

stra·tum /'strātəm, 'stra-/ ▶ n. (pl. **strata** /'strātə, 'strä-/) 1 a layer or a series of layers of rock. 2 a thin layer within any structure. 3 a level or class of society. ■ **stra·tal** adj.

> **USAGE**
> Remember that, as in Latin, the singular form in English is **stratum** and the plural is **strata**: it is incorrect to create the form **stratas** as the plural.

stra·tus /'strātəs, 'stra-/ ▶ n. cloud forming a continuous horizontal gray sheet, often with rain or snow.

straw /strô/ ▶ n. 1 dried stalks of grain, used as fodder or bedding for animals and for thatching, packing, or weaving. 2 a single dried stalk of grain. 3 a thin hollow tube of paper or plastic for sucking drink from a container. 4 a pale yellow color.
– PHRASES **grasp** (or **clutch**) **at straws** turn in desperation to something that is unlikely to be helpful. **draw the short straw** be chosen to perform an unpleasant task. **the last** (or **final**) **straw** a further minor difficulty that comes after a series of difficulties and makes a situation unbearable.

straw·ber·ry /'strô,berē, -b(ə)rē/ ▶ n. (pl. **strawberries**) a sweet soft red fruit with many seeds on the surface.

straw·ber·ry blond (also **strawberry blonde**) ▶ adj. (of hair) light reddish-blond in color. ▶ n. a person with strawberry blond hair.

straw poll (also **straw vote**) ▶ n. an unofficial test of opinion.

straw pur·chase ▶ n. a crime in which a person who is not allowed to buy a gun for themselves induces another person to buy it.

stray /strā/ ▶ v. 1 move away aimlessly from a group or from the right course or place: *the child had strayed from home and was lost in the desert.* 2 (of the eyes or a hand) move idly in a particular direction. 3 dated be unfaithful to a husband, wife, or lover. ▶ adj. 1 not in the right place; separated from a group. 2 (of a domestic animal) having no home or having wandered away from home. ▶ n. a stray person or thing, especially a domestic animal.

streak /strēk/ ▶ n. 1 a long, thin mark. 2 an element of a particular kind in someone's character: *Lucy had a ruthless streak.* 3 a spell of successes or failures: *he hit a winning streak.* ▶ v. 1 mark something with streaks. 2 move very fast. 3 informal run naked in a public place so as to cause shock or amusement. ■ **streak·er** n. **streak·ing** n.

streak·y /'strēkē/ ▶ adj. (**streakier, streakiest**) having streaks. ■ **streak·i·ly** adv. **streak·i·ness** n.

stream /strēm/ ▶ n. 1 a small, narrow river. 2 a continuous flow of liquid, air, gas, people, etc. ▶ v. 1 run or move in a continuous flow. 2 run with tears, sweat, or other liquid: *I woke up in the night, streaming with sweat.* 3 float at full extent in the wind.
– PHRASES **on stream** in or into production or operation.

stream·er /'strēmər/ ▶ n. a long, narrow strip of material used as a decoration or flag.

stream·ing /'strēmiNG/ ▶ adj. (of a cold) accompanied by running of the nose and eyes. ▶ n. a method of relaying data (especially video and audio material) over a computer network as a steady continuous stream.

stream·line /'strēm,līn/ ▶ v. 1 (usu. as adj. **streamlined**) design or form in a way that presents very little resistance to a flow of air or water: *a streamlined train.* 2 make an organization or system more efficient by employing faster or simpler working methods.

stream of con·scious·ness ▶ n. a literary style that records the continuous flow of thoughts and reactions in the mind of a character.

street /strēt/ ▶ n. a public road in a city, town, or village. ▶ adj. 1 relating to fashionable young people living in cities and towns: *street style.*

2 homeless: *street children.*

– PHRASES **on the streets 1** homeless. **2** working as a prostitute.

street·car /ˈstrētˌkär/ ▸ n. a trolley car.

street·light /ˈstrētˌlīt/ (also **streetlamp**) ▸ n. a light illuminating a road, typically mounted on a tall pole.

street-smart ▸ adj. another term for STREETWISE.
▸ n. (**street smarts**) the skills and knowledge necessary for dealing with the difficulties of modern city life.

street val·ue ▸ n. the price for which something that is illegal or has been illegally obtained, especially drugs, can be sold.

street·walk·er /ˈstrētˌwôkər/ ▸ n. a prostitute who seeks clients in the street.

street·wise /ˈstrētˌwīz/ ▸ adj. informal having the skills and knowledge necessary for dealing with the difficulties of modern city life.

strength /streNG(k)TH, strenTH/ ▸ n. **1** the quality or state of being strong or powerful. **2** a good or valuable quality. **3** the number of people making up a group. **4** the number of people that makes a group complete: *we are now 30 staff below strength.*

– PHRASES **in strength** in large numbers. **on the strength of** on the basis of. **tower** (or **pillar**) **of strength** a person who can be relied on to support and comfort others.

strength·en /ˈstreNG(k)THən, ˈstren-/ ▸ v. make or become stronger. ■ **strength·en·er** n.

stren·u·ous /ˈstrenyōōəs/ ▸ adj. requiring or using great effort or exertion. ■ **stren·u·ous·ly** adv. **stren·u·ous·ness** n.

strep /strep/ ▸ n. informal short for STREPTOCOCCUS.

strep·to·coc·cus /ˌstreptəˈkäkəs/ ▸ n. (pl. **streptococci** /-ˈkäksī, -sē/) a bacterium of a large genus including those causing scarlet fever, pneumonia, and tooth decay. ■ **strep·to·coc·cal** /-ˈkäkəl/ adj.

strep·to·my·cin /ˌstreptəˈmīsin/ ▸ n. an antibiotic used against tuberculosis.

stress /stres/ ▸ n. **1** pressure or tension exerted on an object. **2** a state of mental or emotional strain. **3** particular emphasis or importance. **4** emphasis given to a syllable or word in speech.
▸ v. **1** emphasize a point, statement, etc., when speaking or writing. **2** give emphasis to a syllable or word when pronouncing it. **3** subject to strain, tension, or pressure: *this type of workout does stress the knee joints.*

stress·ful /ˈstresfəl/ ▸ adj. causing mental or emotional stress.

stretch /strecH/ ▸ v. **1** (of something soft or elastic) be made or be able to be made longer or wider without tearing or breaking. **2** pull something tightly from one point to another. **3** extend the body or a part of the body to its full length. **4** extend over an area or period of time: *the beach stretches for over four miles.* **5** last longer than expected. **6** (of finances or resources) be enough for a particular purpose. **7** make demands on: *directors churned out pictures that failed to stretch the imagination.*
▸ n. **1** a continuous area or period of time: *a treacherous stretch of road.* **2** an act of stretching. **3** the capacity to stretch or be stretched; elasticity. **4** the fact or state of being stretched. **5** informal a period of time spent in prison. ▸ adj. informal (of a car) much longer than usual and seating more people: *a stretch limo.*

■ **stretch·y** adj. (**stretchier, stretchiest**).

– PHRASES **at full stretch** using the maximum amount of one's resources or energy. **at a stretch 1** in one continuous period. **2** just possible but with difficulty. **stretch one's legs** go for a short walk. **stretch a point** allow or do something not usually acceptable.

stretch·er /ˈstrecHər/ ▸ n. **1** a framework of two poles with a long piece of canvas slung between them, used for carrying sick, injured, or dead people. **2** a brick or stone laid with its long side along the face of a wall. ▸ v. carry someone on a stretcher.

stretch marks ▸ pl.n. marks on the skin, especially on the abdomen, caused by stretching of the skin from obesity or during pregnancy.

strew /strōō/ ▸ v. (past part. **strewn** or **strewed**) **1** scatter things untidily over a surface or area. **2** (**be strewn with**) be covered with untidily scattered things.

stri·a /ˈstrīə/ ▸ n. (pl. **striae** /ˈstrī-ē/) technical a line, ridge, or groove, especially one of a number of similar parallel features.

striated /ˈstrīˌātid/ ▸ adj. technical **1** marked with a series of ridges or grooves. **2** striped or streaked. ■ **stri·a·tion** /strīˈāsHən/ n.

strick·en /ˈstrikən/ past participle of STRIKE
▸ adj. **1** seriously affected by something unpleasant. **2** (of a face or look) showing great distress.

strict /strikt/ ▸ adj. **1** demanding that rules about behavior are obeyed. **2** (of a rule) that must be obeyed exactly. **3** (of a person) following rules or beliefs exactly. **4** very exact and clearly defined: *the characters are not soldiers in the strict sense of the word.* ■ **strict·ly** adv. **strict·ness** n.

stric·ture /ˈstrikcHər/ ▸ n. **1** a rule restricting behavior or action. **2** a sternly critical remark. **3** Medicine abnormal narrowing of a passage or duct in the body: *a colonic stricture.*

stride /strīd/ ▸ v. (past **strode** /strōd/; past part. **stridden** /ˈstridn/) walk with long, decisive steps. ▸ n. **1** a long, decisive step. **2** the length of a step in running or walking. **3** a step made toward an aim: *the company has made huge strides in product quality.* **4** (**one's stride**) a good or regular rate of progress, especially after a slow start.

– PHRASES **take something in one's stride** deal calmly with something difficult.

stri·dent /ˈstrīdnt/ ▸ adj. **1** loud and harsh. **2** presenting a point of view in an excessively forceful way. ■ **stri·den·cy** n. **stri·dent·ly** adv.

strid·u·late /ˈstrijəˌlāt/ ▸ v. (of a grasshopper or similar insect) make a shrill sound by rubbing the legs, wings, or other parts of the body together. ■ **strid·u·la·tion** /ˌstrijəˈlāsHən/ n.

strife /strīf/ ▸ n. angry or bitter disagreement; conflict.

strike /strīk/ ▸ v. (past and past part. **struck** /strək/) **1** deliver a hard blow to someone or something. **2** come forcefully into contact with someone or something. **3** (in sports) hit or kick a ball. **4** (of a disaster, disease, etc.) occur suddenly and have harmful effects on: *a major earthquake struck the island.* **5** attack someone or something suddenly. **6** (**strike something into**) cause a strong emotion in someone. **7** cause to become suddenly: *he was struck dumb.* **8** suddenly come into the mind of someone. **9** (**be struck by/ with**) find particularly interesting or impressive:

she was struck by the beauty of the scene. **10** light a match by rubbing it against a rough surface. **11** (of employees) refuse to work as a form of organized protest. **12** go somewhere vigorously or purposefully: those who could swim struck out for the bank. **13** (**strike out**) start out on a new or independent course. **14** reach an agreement or compromise. **15** cross something out with a pen. **16** (**strike someone off**) officially remove someone from membership of a professional group. **17** (of a clock) indicate the time by sounding a chime or stroke. **18** make a coin or medal by stamping metal. **19** discover gold, minerals, or oil by drilling or mining. **20** take down a tent or camp. ▶ n. **1** an act of striking by employees. **2** a refusal to do something, as a form of organized protest: a rent strike. **3** a sudden attack. **4** (in sports) an act of striking a ball. **5** an act of striking gold, minerals, or oil.
– PHRASES **strike an attitude** (or **pose**) hold one's body in a particular position to create an impression. **strike up** begin to play a piece of music. **strike something up** begin a friendship or conversation with someone. **strike while the iron is hot** make use of an opportunity immediately.

strike·break·er /ˈstrīkˌbrākər/ ▶ n. a person who works or is employed in place of others who are on strike.

strike·out /ˈstrīkˌout/ ▶ n. Baseball an out called when a batter accumulates three strikes. ▶ adj. Computing (of text) having a horizontal line through the middle; crossed out.

strik·er /ˈstrīkər/ ▶ n. **1** an employee on strike. **2** (chiefly in soccer) a forward or attacker.

strike zone ▶ n. Baseball an area over home plate through which the ball must be pitched in order for a strike to be called.

strik·ing /ˈstrīkiNG/ ▶ adj. **1** attracting attention; noticeable. **2** very attractive. ■ **strik·ing·ly** adv.

string /striNG/ ▶ n. **1** material consisting of threads twisted together to form a thin length. **2** a piece of string. **3** a length of catgut or wire on a musical instrument, producing a note by vibration. **4** (**strings**) the stringed instruments in an orchestra. **5** a piece of nylon or similar material interwoven with others to form the head of a sports racket. **6** a set of things tied or threaded together on a thin cord. **7** a sequence of similar items or events: a string of burglaries. **8** Computing a sequence of characters or other data. **9** a G-string or thong. ▶ v. (past and past part. **strung** /strəNG/) **1** hang or thread things on a string. **2** (**be strung** or **be strung out**) be arranged in a long line. **3** fit a string or strings to a musical instrument, a racket, or a bow. ■ **stringed** adj.
– PHRASES **be strung out** informal **1** be tense or nervous. **2** be under the influence of alcohol or drugs. **no strings attached** informal there are no special conditions. **string someone along** informal mislead someone deliberately over a period of time. **string someone up** kill someone by hanging.

string bass /bās/ ▶ n. (especially among jazz musicians) a double bass.

string bean ▶ n. any of various beans eaten in their fibrous pods; a runner bean.

strin·gent /ˈstrinjənt/ ▶ adj. (of regulations or requirements) very strict; that must be obeyed. ■ **strin·gen·cy** n. **strin·gent·ly** adv.

string·er /ˈstriNGər/ ▶ n. **1** informal a journalist who is not on the regular staff of a newspaper, but who reports part-time on a particular place.

2 a structural piece running lengthwise in a framework, especially that of a ship or aircraft.

string quar·tet ▶ n. **1** a chamber music group consisting of a first and second violin, viola, and cello. **2** a composition for a string quartet.

string·y /ˈstriNGē/ ▶ adj. (**stringier**, **stringiest**) **1** long and thin. **2** (of food) containing chewy fibers.

strip¹ /strip/ ▶ v. (**strips**, **stripping**, **stripped**) **1** remove all coverings or clothes from someone or something. **2** take off one's clothes. **3** remove all the contents from a room, vehicle, etc. **4** (**strip someone of**) deprive someone of rank, power, or property. **5** remove paint or varnish from a surface. **6** sell off a company's assets for profit. ▶ n. an act of undressing.

strip² ▶ n. **1** a long, narrow piece of cloth, paper, or other material. **2** a long, narrow area of land. **3** a main road lined with stores and other facilities.

stripe /strīp/ ▶ n. **1** a long narrow band of a different color or texture from its surroundings. **2** a chevron on a uniform, showing military rank. **3** a type or category. ▶ v. mark someone or something with stripes. ■ **striped** adj. **strip·y** (also **stripey**) adj.

striped bass /bas/ ▶ n. a large migrating bass of North American coastal waters, with dark horizontal stripes along the upper sides.

strip·ling /ˈstripliNG/ ▶ n. old use or humorous a young man.

strip mine ▶ n. an open-pit mine. ▶ v. (**strip-mine**) obtain ore or coal by open-pit mining.

stripped-down ▶ adj. **1** reduced to essentials: a stripped-down funding bill. **2** (of a machine, motor vehicle, etc.) having had all internal parts removed; dismantled.

strip·per /ˈstripər/ ▶ n. **1** a striptease performer. **2** a device or substance for stripping paint, varnish, etc.

strip-search ▶ v. search someone for concealed drugs, weapons, or other items, by stripping off their clothes.

strip·tease /ˈstripˌtēz/ ▶ n. a form of entertainment in which a performer gradually undresses to music in a sexually exciting way.

strive /strīv/ ▶ v. (past **strove** /strōv/ or **strived**; past part. **striven** /ˈstrivən/ or **strived**) make great efforts, especially to achieve or prevent something: the charity strives to keep costs low. ■ **striv·er** n.

strobe /strōb/ ▶ n. a stroboscope. ▶ v. flash at rapid intervals.

stro·bo·scope /ˈstrōbəˌskōp/ ▶ n. an instrument that shines a bright light at rapid intervals so that a moving person or object appears stationary. ■ **stro·bo·scop·ic** /ˌstrōbəˈskäpik/ adj.

strode /strōd/ ▶ past of STRIDE.

stro·ga·noff /ˈstrōgəˌnôf, ˈstrō-/ ▶ n. a dish in which the main ingredient, typically beef, is cooked in a sour cream sauce.

stroke /strōk/ ▶ n. **1** an act of hitting. **2** a mark made by drawing a pen, pencil, or paintbrush once across paper or canvas. **3** a line forming part of a written or printed character. **4** a short diagonal line separating characters or figures. **5** a sudden disabling attack or loss of consciousness caused by an interruption in the flow of blood to the brain. **6** a sound made by a striking clock. **7** an act of stroking with the hand. **8** one of a series of repeated movements, especially in

swimming or rowing. **9** a style of moving the arms and legs in swimming. **10** the way in which the oar is moved in rowing. **11** Golf an act of hitting the ball with a club, as a unit of scoring. ▶ v. gently move one's hand over someone or something. ■ **strok·er** n.
– PHRASES **stroke of genius** an outstandingly original idea. **stroke of luck** a lucky and unexpected event.

stroke play ▶ n. golf in which the score is reckoned by counting the number of strokes taken overall. Compare with MATCH PLAY.

stroll /strōl/ ▶ v. **1** walk in a leisurely way. **2** informal in sports, achieve a victory easily. ▶ n. **1** a short leisurely walk. **2** informal a victory that is easily achieved.

stroll·er /'strōlər/ ▶ n. a folding chair on wheels, in which a young child can be pushed along.

strong /strông, sträng/ ▶ adj. (**stronger, strongest**) **1** physically powerful. **2** done with or exerting great force: *a strong current.* **3** able to withstand great force or pressure. **4** secure, stable, or firmly established. **5** great in power, influence, or ability: *a strong leader.* **6** (of something smelled, tasted, etc.) very intense. **7** (of language) forceful and using swear words. **8** (of a solution or drink) containing a large proportion of a substance. **9** used after a number to indicate the size of a group: *a crowd several thousands strong.* **10** (of verbs) forming the past tense and past participle by a change of vowel within the stem rather than by adding an ending or suffix (e.g., *swim, swam, swum*). ■ **strong·ly** adv.
– PHRASES **going strong** informal continuing to be healthy, vigorous, or successful. **strong on 1** good at. **2** possessing large quantities of. **one's strong point** (or **suit**) something one is very good at.

strong-arm ▶ adj. using force or violence. ▶ v. use force or violence against someone.

strong·box /'strông,bäks/ ▶ n. a small lockable metal box in which valuables may be kept.

strong·hold /'strông,hōld/ ▶ n. **1** a place of strong support for a cause or political party. **2** a place that has been fortified against attack.

strong·man /'strông,man/ ▶ n. (pl. **strongmen**) **1** a very strong man, especially one who performs feats of strength for entertainment. **2** a leader who rules by force or violence.

strong·room /'strông,rōōm, -,rŏŏm/ ▶ n. a room, typically one in a bank, designed to protect valuable items against fire and theft.

strong suit ▶ n. **1** (in bridge) a holding of a number of high cards of one suit in a hand. **2** a desirable quality that is particularly prominent in someone's character or an activity at which they excel.

stron·ti·um /'stränCHēəm, -tēəm/ ▶ n. a soft silver-white metallic chemical element.

strop /sträp/ ▶ n. a strip of leather for sharpening razors. ▶ v. (**strops, stropping, stropped**) sharpen a razor on or with a strop.

strove /strōv/ ▶ past of STRIVE.

struck /strək/ ▶ past and past participle of STRIKE.

struc·tur·al /'strəkCHərəl/ ▶ adj. relating to or forming part of a structure. ■ **struc·tur·al·ly** adv.

struc·tur·al·ism /'strəkCHərə,lizəm/ ▶ n. a theory that pieces of writing, languages, and social systems should be seen as a structure whose various parts have meaning only when considered in relation to each other.

■ **struc·tur·al·ist** n. & adj.

struc·ture /'strəkCHər/ ▶ n. **1** the arrangement of and relations between the parts of something complex: *changes to the company's organizational structure.* **2** a building or other object constructed from several parts. **3** the quality of being well organized. ▶ v. organize or arrange something according to a plan or system.

stru·del /'strōōdl/ ▶ n. a dessert of thin pastry rolled up around a fruit filling and baked.

strug·gle /'strəgəl/ ▶ v. **1** make forceful efforts to get free. **2** try hard to do something under difficult circumstances. **3** make one's way with difficulty. ▶ n. **1** an act of struggling. **2** a conflict or contest: *a power struggle for the leadership.* **3** a very difficult task. ■ **strug·gler** /'strəg(ə)lər/ n.

strum /strəm/ ▶ v. (**strums, strumming, strummed**) play a guitar or similar instrument by sweeping the thumb or a plectrum up or down the strings.

strum·pet /'strəmpət/ ▶ n. old use or humorous a woman who has many sexual partners.

strung /strəNG/ ▶ past and past participle of STRING.

strut /strət/ ▶ n. **1** a bar used to support or strengthen a structure. **2** an arrogant or very confident walk. ▶ v. (**struts, strutting, strutted**) **1** walk in an arrogant or very confident way, with one's back straight and head up. **2** brace something with a strut or struts.

strych·nine /'strik,nīn, -,nēn/ ▶ n. a bitter and highly poisonous substance obtained from the seeds of nux vomica (an Asian tree).

Stu·art /'st(y)ōōərt/ (also **Stewart** pronunc. same) ▶ adj. belonging or relating to the royal family ruling Scotland 1371–1714 and Britain 1603–1714 (interrupted by the Commonwealth 1649–60). ▶ n. a member of the Stuart family.

stub /stəb/ ▶ n. **1** the remnant of a pencil, cigarette, or similar-shaped object after use. **2** a shortened or unusually short thing. **3** the counterfoil of a check, ticket, or other document. ▶ v. (**stubs, stubbing, stubbed**) **1** accidentally hit one's toe against something. **2** (often **stub something out**) put a cigarette out by pressing the lighted end against something.

stub·ble /'stəbəl/ ▶ n. **1** short, stiff hairs growing on a man's face when he has not shaved for a while. **2** the cut stalks of cereal plants left in the ground after harvesting. ■ **stub·bly** adj.

stub·born /'stəbərn/ ▶ adj. **1** determined not to change one's attitude or position. **2** difficult to move, remove, or cure: *a stubborn stain.* ■ **stub·born·ly** adv. **stub·born·ness** n.

stub·by /'stəbē/ ▶ adj. (**stubbier, stubbiest**) short and thick.

stuc·co /'stəkō/ ▶ n. fine plaster used for coating wall surfaces or molding into architectural decorations. ■ **stuc·coed** adj.

stuck /stək/ ▶ past participle of STICK².

stuck-up ▶ adj. informal unfriendly toward others because one believes that one is superior to them.

stud¹ /stəd/ ▶ n. **1** a large-headed piece of metal that pierces and projects from a surface, especially for decoration. **2** a small piece of jewelry that is pushed through a pierced ear or nostril. **3** a device consisting of two buttons joined with a bar, used to fasten a collar to a shirt. ▶ v. (**studs, studding, studded**) **1** decorate something with studs or similar small objects.

2 cover or scatter with many small things: *the sky was studded with stars.* ■ **stud·ding** n.

stud² ▶ n. **1** an establishment where horses or other domesticated animals are kept for breeding. **2** (also **stud horse**) a stallion. **3** informal a man who has many sexual partners or is considered sexually desirable.

stu·dent /ˈst(y)oōdnt/ ▶ n. **1** a person studying at a school or college. **2** a person who takes a particular interest in a subject. ▶ adj. referring to a person who is studying to enter a particular profession: *a student nurse.*

stu·di·o /ˈst(y)oōdē,ō/ ▶ n. (pl. **studios**) **1** a room from which television or radio programs are broadcast, or in which they are recorded. **2** a place where film or sound recordings are made. **3** a room where an artist works or where dancers practice.

stu·di·o a·part·ment ▶ n. an apartment containing one main room.

stu·di·ous /ˈst(y)oōdēəs/ ▶ adj. **1** spending a lot of time studying or reading. **2** done deliberately or with great care. ■ **stu·di·ous·ly** adv. **stu·di·ous·ness** n.

studly /ˈstədlē/ ▶ adj. (**studlier, studliest**) informal (of a man) sexually attractive in a strongly masculine way.

stud·y /ˈstədē/ ▶ n. (pl. **studies**) **1** the activity of learning or gaining knowledge, typically by reading or research. **2** a detailed investigation and analysis of a subject or situation: *a recent study of army recruits.* **3** a room for reading, writing, or academic work. **4** a drawing or painting done for practice or before creating a larger picture. **5** a piece of music designed to develop a player's technical skill. ▶ v. (**studies, studying, studied**) **1** gain knowledge of a subject. **2** investigate and analyze a subject or situation in detail. **3** concentrate on gaining knowledge. **4** look at closely: *she bent her head to study the plans.* **5** (as adj. **studied**) done deliberately and carefully: *she takes a studied approach to her work.*
– PHRASES **a study in** a good example of a quality or emotion.

stuff /stəf/ ▶ n. **1** substance, things, or activities that one does not know the name of or that one does not need to specify. **2** basic characteristics: *Helen was made of sterner stuff.* **3** (**one's stuff**) informal the things that one has knowledge of or experience in. ▶ v. **1** fill a container or space tightly or hastily with something. **2** fill out the skin of a dead animal or bird with material to restore its original shape and appearance. **3** fill the inside of an item of food with a savory or sweet mixture. **4** (**be stuffed up**) informal have one's nose blocked up with mucus as the result of a cold. **5** (**stuff oneself**) informal eat greedily.

stuffed shirt ▶ n. informal a pompous or conventional person.

stuff·ing /ˈstəfiNG/ ▶ n. **1** a mixture used to stuff poultry or meat before cooking. **2** padding used to stuff cushions, furniture, or soft toys.
– PHRASES **knock the stuffing out of** informal severely damage someone's confidence or strength.

stuff·y /ˈstəfē/ ▶ adj. (**stuffier, stuffiest**) **1** lacking fresh air or ventilation. **2** conventional and narrow-minded. **3** (of a person's nose) blocked up. ■ **stuff·i·ly** adv. **stuff·i·ness** n.

stul·ti·fy /ˈstəltə,fī/ ▶ v. (**stultifies, stultifying,**

stultified) (usu. as adj. **stultifying**) make someone feel bored or drained of energy. ■ **stul·ti·fi·ca·tion** /ˌstəltəfiˈkāsHən/ n. **stul·ti·fy·ing·ly** adv.

stum·ble /ˈstəmbəl/ ▶ v. **1** trip and briefly lose one's balance. **2** walk unsteadily. **3** make a mistake or mistakes in speaking. **4** (**stumble across/on/upon**) find someone or something by chance. ▶ n. an act of stumbling.

stum·bling block ▶ n. an obstacle.

stump /stəmp/ ▶ n. **1** the part of a tree trunk left projecting from the ground after the rest has fallen or been cut down. **2** a part of something that remains after the rest has been cut off or worn away. ▶ v. **1** informal baffle someone. **2** walk stiffly and noisily.

stump·er /ˈstəmpər/ ▶ n. informal a puzzling question.

stump·y /ˈstəmpē/ ▶ adj. short and thick; squat.

stun /stən/ ▶ v. (**stuns, stunning, stunned**) **1** make a person or animal unconscious or dazed by hitting them on the head. **2** astonish or shock someone so that they are temporarily unable to react.

stung /stəNG/ ▶ past and past participle of STING.

stun gun ▶ n. a device that makes an attacker unable to move, typically by giving them a nonfatal electric shock.

stunk /stəNGk/ ▶ past and past participle of STINK.

stun·ner /ˈstənər/ ▶ n. informal a strikingly beautiful or impressive person or thing.

stun·ning /ˈstəniNG/ ▶ adj. very impressive or attractive. ■ **stun·ning·ly** adv.

stunt¹ /stənt/ ▶ v. slow down the growth or development of someone or something.

stunt² ▶ n. **1** an action displaying spectacular skill and daring. **2** something unusual done to attract attention: *a publicity stunt.*

stunt·man /ˈstənt,man/ (or **stuntwoman** /ˈstənt,woōmən/) ▶ n. (pl. **stuntmen** or **stuntwomen**) a person who takes an actor's place in performing dangerous stunts.

stu·pa /ˈstoōpə/ ▶ n. a Buddhist shrine in the form of a dome-shaped building.

stu·pe·fy /ˈst(y)oōpə,fī/ ▶ v. (**stupefies, stupefying, stupefied**) **1** make someone unable to think or feel properly. **2** astonish and shock someone. ■ **stu·pe·fac·tion** /ˌst(y)oōpəˈfaksHən/ n.

stu·pen·dous /st(y)oōˈpendəs/ ▶ adj. very impressive. ■ **stu·pen·dous·ly** adv.

stu·pid /ˈst(y)oōpid/ ▶ adj. (**stupider, stupidest**) **1** lacking intelligence or common sense. **2** informal used to express annoyance or boredom: *your stupid paintings!* **3** dazed and unable to think clearly. ■ **stu·pid·i·ty** /st(y)oōˈpiditē/ n. **stu·pid·ly** adv.

stu·por /ˈst(y)oōpər/ ▶ n. a state of being dazed or nearly unconscious. ■ **stu·por·ous** /-rəs/ adj.

stur·dy /ˈstərdē/ ▶ adj. (**sturdier, sturdiest**) **1** strongly and solidly built or made. **2** confident and determined: *the townspeople have a sturdy independence.* ■ **stur·di·ly** adv. **stur·di·ness** n.

stur·geon /ˈstərjən/ ▶ n. a very large river or sea fish with bony plates on the body, from whose roe caviar is made.

Sturm und Drang /ˌsHtoŏrm oŏn(t) ˈdräNG/ ▶ n. **1** an 18th-century German literary and artistic movement characterized by the expression of emotional unrest. **2** a state or situation of emotional upheaval or stress: *the Sturm und Drang of adolescence.*

stut·ter /'stətər/ ▶ v. **1** have difficulty speaking as a result of the involuntary repetition of the first sounds of a word. **2** (of a machine or gun) produce a series of short, sharp sounds. ▶ n. a tendency to stutter while speaking. ■ **stut·ter·er** n.

sty¹ /stī/ ▶ n. (pl. **sties**) a pigsty.

sty² (also **stye**) ▶ n. (pl. **sties** or **styes**) an inflamed swelling on the edge of an eyelid.

Styg·i·an /'stijēən/ ▶ adj. literary very dark.

style /stīl/ ▶ n. **1** a way of doing something. **2** a distinctive appearance, design, or arrangement: *new styles in jewelry.* **3** a way of painting, writing, etc., characteristic of a particular period, person, or movement. **4** elegance and sophistication. **5** an official or legal title. **6** a narrow extension of a plant's ovary, bearing the stigma. ▶ v. **1** design, make, or arrange in a particular form: *he styled my hair differently this time.* **2** give a particular name, description, or title to someone or something. ■ **style·less** /'stīl(l)is/ adj. **styl·er** n.

sty·li /'stīlī/ ▶ plural of STYLUS.

styl·ish /'stīlish/ ▶ adj. **1** having or showing a good sense of style. **2** fashionably elegant. ■ **styl·ish·ly** adv. **styl·ish·ness** n.

styl·ist /'stīlist/ ▶ n. **1** a person who cuts hair or designs fashionable clothes. **2** a person whose job is to arrange and coordinate food, clothes, etc., in an attractive way in photographs, movies, etc.

styl·is·tic /stī'listik/ ▶ adj. relating to style, especially literary style. ■ **styl·is·ti·cal·ly** /-ik(ə)lē/ adv.

styl·is·tics /stī'listiks/ ▶ pl.n. (treated as sing.) the study of the literary styles of particular writers or types of literature.

styl·ized /'stī,līzd/ ▶ adj. represented or treated in a nonrealistic style. ■ **styl·i·za·tion** /,stīli'zāsHən/ n.

sty·lus /'stīləs/ ▶ n. (pl. **styli** /-,lī/) **1** a pointed implement used for scratching or tracing letters or engraving. **2** a penlike device used to input handwriting directly into a computer. **3** a hard point following a groove in a phonograph record and transmitting the recorded sound for reproduction.

sty·mie /'stīmē/ ▶ v. (**stymies, stymying** or **stymieing, stymied**) informal prevent or hinder the progress of someone or something.

styp·tic /'stiptik/ ▶ adj. able to stop bleeding. ▶ n. a substance that stops bleeding.

sty·rene /'stī,rēn/ ▶ n. Chemistry an unsaturated liquid hydrocarbon obtained as a petroleum byproduct and used to make plastics.

sty·ro·foam /'stīrə,fōm/ ▶ n. trademark a kind of expanded polystyrene, used for making food containers.

sua·sion /'swāzHən/ ▶ n. formal persuasion as opposed to force.

suave /swäv/ ▶ adj. (**suaver, suavest**) (of a man) charming, confident, and elegant. ■ **suave·ly** adv. **suave·ness** n. **suav·i·ty** /-itē/ n. (pl. **suavities**).

sub /səb/ informal ▶ n. **1** a submarine. **2** a substitute, especially for a teacher in a school or for a player on a sports team. **3** a submarine sandwich. ▶ v. (**subs, subbing, subbed**) act as a substitute.

sub- ▶ prefix **1** under: *submarine.* **2** lower in rank or importance: *subaltern.* **3** below; less than: *subzero.* **4** subsequent or secondary: *subdivision.*

sub·al·tern /səb'ôltərn/ ▶ n. an officer in the British army below the rank of captain.

sub·a·quat·ic /,səbə'kwätik, -'kwa-/ ▶ adj. underwater: *subaquatic life forms.*

sub·a·que·ous /səb'äkwēəs, -'ak-/ ▶ adj. existing, formed, or taking place under water.

sub·arc·tic /,səb'ärktik, -'ärtik/ ▶ adj. relating to the region immediately south of the Arctic Circle.

sub·as·sem·bly /,səbə'semblē/ ▶ n. (pl. **subassemblies**) a unit assembled separately but designed to be incorporated with other units into a larger manufactured product.

sub·a·tom·ic /,səbə'tämik/ ▶ adj. smaller than or occurring within an atom.

sub·a·tom·ic par·ti·cle ▶ n. a particle smaller than an atom (for example, a neutron) or a cluster of such particles. Compare with ELEMENTARY PARTICLE.

sub·cat·e·go·ry /'səb,katə,gôrē/ ▶ n. (pl. **subcategories**) a secondary or less important category.

sub·com·mit·tee /'səbkə,mitē/ ▶ n. a committee consisting of some members of a larger committee, formed in order to study a subject in more detail.

sub·com·pact /səb'kämpakt/ ▶ n. a motor vehicle that is smaller than a compact.

sub·con·scious /səb'känsHəs/ ▶ adj. relating to the part of the mind of which one is not fully aware but which influences one's actions and feelings. ▶ n. (**one's/the subconscious**) this part of the mind. ■ **sub·con·scious·ly** adv. **sub·con·scious·ness** n.

sub·con·ti·nent /,səb'käntənənt/ ▶ n. a large part of a continent considered as a particular area, such as North America. ■ **sub·con·ti·nen·tal** /-,käntə'nen(t)l/ adj.

sub·con·tract ▶ v. /səb'käntrakt, ,səbkən'trakt/ employ a firm or person outside one's company to do work as part of a larger project. ▶ n. /səb'käntrakt/ a contract to do work for another company as part of a larger project. ■ **sub·con·trac·tor** n.

sub·cul·ture /'səb,kəlcHər/ ▶ n. a distinct group within a society or class, having beliefs or interests that are different from those of the larger group. ■ **sub·cul·tur·al** adj.

sub·cu·ta·ne·ous /,səbkyōō'tānēəs/ ▶ adj. situated or applied under the skin. ■ **sub·cu·ta·ne·ous·ly** adv.

sub·di·vide /'səbdə,vīd/ ▶ v. divide into smaller parts something that has already been divided.

sub·di·vi·sion /'səbdə,vizHən/ ▶ n. **1** the action of subdividing something. **2** a secondary or less important division.

sub·duc·tion /səb'dəksHən/ ▶ n. Geology the sideways and downward movement of the edge of a plate of the earth's crust into the mantle beneath another plate.

sub·due /səb'd(y)ōō/ ▶ v. (**subdues, subduing, subdued**) **1** overcome, quiet, or bring under control: *she managed to subdue an instinct to applaud.* **2** bring a country under control by force.

sub·dued /,səb'd(y)ōōd/ ▶ adj. **1** quiet and rather thoughtful or depressed. **2** (of color or lighting) soft; muted.

sub·fam·i·ly /'səb,fam(ə)lē/ ▶ n. (pl. **subfamilies**) a subdivision of a group, especially the taxonomic category that ranks below family and above tribe or genus.

sub·group /'səb,grōōp/ ▶ n. a small group that is part of a larger one.

sub·head·ing /'səb,hediNG/ (also **subhead**)
▶ n. a heading given to a section within a larger piece of writing.

sub·hu·man /səb'(h)yōōmən/ ▶ adj. not having the normal qualities of a human being, especially so as to be lacking in intelligence.
▶ n. a subhuman creature or person.

subj. ▶ abbr. **1** subject. **2** subjective. **3** subjectively. **4** subjunctive.

sub·ject ▶ n. /'səbjəkt/ **1** a person or thing that is being discussed, studied, or dealt with. **2** a branch of knowledge studied or taught in a school, college, etc. **3** Grammar the word or words in a sentence that name who or what performs the action of the verb. **4** a member of a country or state other than its ruler. ▶ adj. /'səbjəkt/ (**subject to**) **1** likely or having a tendency to be affected by something unpleasant or unwelcome: *he was subject to bouts of depression.* **2** dependent or conditional on: *the merger is subject to shareholders' approval.* **3** under someone's or something's control or authority. ▶ adv. /'səbjəkt/ (**subject to**) if certain conditions are fulfilled. ▶ v. /səb'jekt/ (usu. **subject someone/thing to**) **1** make someone or something undergo an unpleasant experience. **2** bring a person or country under one's control or authority. ■ **sub·jec·tion** /səb'jeksHən/ n.

sub·jec·tive /səb'jektiv/ ▶ adj. **1** based on or influenced by personal feelings, tastes, or opinions. **2** Grammar relating to a case of nouns and pronouns used for the subject of a sentence. ■ **sub·jec·tive·ly** adv. **sub·jec·tiv·i·ty** /,səbjek'tivitē/ n.

sub·ject mat·ter ▶ n. the thing dealt with or represented in a book, speech, work of art, etc.

sub ju·di·ce /,sōōb 'yōōdi,kā, ,səb 'jōōdi,sē/
▶ adj. being considered by a court of law.

sub·ju·gate /'səbjə,gāt/ ▶ v. conquer or gain control of someone or something.
■ **sub·ju·ga·tion** /,səbjə'gāsHən/ n.

sub·junc·tive /səb'jəNG(k)tiv/ Grammar ▶ adj. (of a form of a verb) expressing what is imagined or wished or possible. ▶ n. a subjunctive form of a verb.

> **USAGE**
> The **subjunctive** form of a verb is used to express what is imagined, wished, or possible. It is usually the same as the ordinary (**indicative**) form of the verb except in the third person singular (*he, she,* or *it*), where the normal **-s** ending is omitted. For example, you should say *face* rather than *faces* in the sentence *the report recommends that he face the tribunal.* The subjunctive is also different from the indicative when using the verb 'to be'; for example, you should say *I were* rather than *I was* in the sentence *I wouldn't try it if I were you.* See also LEST.

sub·lease ▶ n. /'səb,lēs/ a lease of a property by a tenant to a subtenant. ▶ v. /'səb'lēs/ another term for SUBLET.

sub·let /'səb'let/ ▶ v. (**sublets, subletting, sublet**) let a property or part of a property that one is already renting to someone else.

sub·li·mate /'səblə,māt/ ▶ v. **1** direct an instinctive impulse, especially sexual energy, into a more socially acceptable activity.
2 transform something into a purer or idealized

form. **3** Chemistry another term for SUBLIME.
■ **sub·li·ma·tion** /,səblə'māsHən/ n.

sub·lime /sə'blīm/ ▶ adj. (**sublimer, sublimest**)
1 of such excellence or beauty as to inspire great admiration or awe. **2** extreme: *the sublime confidence of youth.* ▶ v. Chemistry (with reference to a solid substance) change directly into vapor when heated, typically forming a solid deposit again on cooling. ■ **sub·lime·ly** adv. **sub·lim·i·ty** /sə'blimitē/ n.

sub·lim·i·nal /sə'blimənl/ ▶ adj. (of a stimulus or mental process) affecting someone's mind without their being aware of it.
■ **sub·lim·i·nal·ly** adv.

sub·ma·chine gun /,səbmə'sHēn/ ▶ n. a hand-held lightweight machine gun.

sub·ma·rine /,səbmə'rēn, 'səbmə,rēn/ ▶ n. a streamlined warship designed to operate under the surface of the sea for long periods.
▶ adj. existing, happening, done, or used under the surface of the sea. ■ **sub·ma·rin·er** /səb'marənər, -mə'rēnər/ n.

sub·ma·rine sand·wich ▶ n. a sandwich made of a long roll typically filled with meat, cheese, and vegetables such as lettuce, tomato, and onions.

sub·merge /səb'mərj/ ▶ v. **1** push or hold someone or something under water. **2** go down below the surface of water. **3** completely cover or hide something. ■ **sub·mer·gence** n.

sub·merse /səb'mərs/ ▶ v. technical submerge something.

sub·mers·i·ble /səb'mərsəbəl/ ▶ adj. designed to operate under water. ▶ n. a small boat or craft that is submersible.

sub·mer·sion /səb'mərzHən, -sHən/ ▶ n. the action of submerging or the state of being submerged.

sub·mi·cro·scop·ic /,səbmīkrə'skäpik/ ▶ adj. too small to be seen by an ordinary microscope.

sub·mis·sion /səb'misHən/ ▶ n. **1** the action of submitting something. **2** a proposal or application submitted for consideration.

sub·mis·sive /səb'misiv/ ▶ adj. meekly obedient or passive. ■ **sub·mis·sive·ly** adv. **sub·mis·sive·ness** n.

sub·mit /səb'mit/ ▶ v. (**submits, submitting, submitted**) **1** accept or give in to someone's or something's authority, control, or greater strength. **2** present a proposal or application to a person or group of people for consideration or assessment. **3** subject someone or something to a particular process or treatment. **4** (especially in the context of a court of law) suggest or argue.

sub·nor·mal /səb'nôrməl/ ▶ adj. not meeting standards or reaching a level regarded as normal or usual. ■ **sub·nor·mal·i·ty** /,səbnôr'malitē/ n.

sub·op·ti·mal /səb'äptəməl/ ▶ adj. technical of less than the highest standard or quality.

sub·or·der /'səb,ôrdər/ ▶ n. Biology a taxonomic category that ranks below order and above family.

sub·or·di·nate ▶ adj. /sə'bôrdnit/ **1** lower in rank or position. **2** less important. ▶ n. /sə'bôrdnit/ a person under the authority or control of someone else. ▶ v. /-,āt/ treat or regard as less important: *economic reforms should be subordinated to financial constraints.*
■ **sub·or·di·na·tion** /-,bôrdn'āsHən/ n.

sub·or·di·nate clause ▶ n. a clause that forms part of and is dependent on a main clause (e.g., *when it rang* in *she answered the phone when it rang*).

sub·orn /sə'bôrn/ ▶ v. persuade or bribe someone to commit an unlawful act such as perjury.

sub·plot /'səb,plät/ ▶ n. a plot in a play, novel, etc., that is secondary to the main plot.

sub·poe·na /sə'pēnə/ ▶ n. a written order instructing a person to attend a court of law. ▶ v. (**subpoenas, subpoenaing, subpoenaed** or **subpoena'd**) summon someone with a subpoena.

sub·prime /'səb,prīm/ ▶ adj. referring to credit or loan arrangements for borrowers with a poor credit history, incurring higher than usual risk and so involving high rates of interest.

sub·ro·ga·tion /,səbrə'gāshən/ ▶ n. Law the substitution of one person or group by another in respect of a debt or insurance claim, accompanied by the transfer of any associated rights and duties.

sub ro·sa /,səb 'rōzə/ ▶ adj. & adv. formal happening or done in secret.

sub·rou·tine /'səbrōō,tēn/ ▶ n. Computing a set of instructions designed to perform a frequently used operation within a program.

sub-Sa·har·an ▶ adj. from or forming part of the African regions south of the Sahara Desert.

sub·scribe /səb'skrīb/ ▶ v. 1 (often **subscribe to**) arrange to receive something, especially a magazine, on a regular basis by paying in advance. 2 (**subscribe to**) contribute a sum of money to a project or cause on a regular basis. 3 apply to take part in: *the course is fully subscribed.* 4 apply to buy shares in a company. 5 (**subscribe to**) express agreement with an idea or proposal. ■ **sub·scrib·er** n.

sub·script /'səb,skript/ ▶ adj. (of a letter, figure, or symbol) written or printed below the line.

sub·scrip·tion /səb'skripshən/ ▶ n. 1 an advance payment made in order to receive or take part in something, or as a donation. 2 the action or fact of subscribing.

sub·sec·tion /'səb,seksHən/ ▶ n. a division of a section.

sub·sense /'səb,sens/ ▶ n. a related but less important sense of a word defined in a dictionary.

sub·se·quent /'səbsəkwənt/ ▶ adj. coming after something in time. ■ **sub·se·quent·ly** adv.

sub·ser·vi·ent /səb'sərvēənt/ ▶ adj. 1 too willing to obey other people. 2 less important. ■ **sub·ser·vi·ence** n.

sub·set /'səb,set/ ▶ n. 1 a part of a larger group of related things. 2 Mathematics a set of which all the elements are contained in another set.

sub·side /səb'sīd/ ▶ v. 1 become less intense, violent, or severe. 2 (of water) go down to a lower or the normal level. 3 (of a building) sink lower into the ground. 4 (of the ground) cave in; sink. 5 (**subside into**) give way to a strong feeling.

sub·sid·ence /səb'sīdns, 'səbsidns/ ▶ n. the gradual caving in or sinking of an area of land.

sub·sid·i·a·ri·ty /,səb,sidē'aritē/ ▶ n. (in politics) the principle that a central authority should carry out only those tasks that cannot be carried out at a more local level.

sub·sid·i·ar·y /səb'sidē,erē/ ▶ adj. 1 related but

less important. 2 (of a company) controlled by a holding or parent company. ▶ n. (pl. **subsidiaries**) a subsidiary company.

sub·si·dize /'səbsə,dīz/ ▶ v. 1 support an organization or activity financially. 2 pay part of the cost of producing something to help keep the price low. ■ **sub·si·di·za·tion** /,səbsədi'zāsHən/ n.

sub·si·dy /'səbsidē/ ▶ n. (pl. **subsidies**) 1 a sum of money given to an industry or business from public funds to help keep the price of a product or service low. 2 a sum of money granted to support an activity or undertaking that is held to be in the public interest. 3 a grant or contribution of money.

sub·sist /səb'sist/ ▶ v. 1 manage to stay alive, especially with limited resources. 2 chiefly Law remain in force or effect.

sub·sist·ence /səb'sistəns/ ▶ n. the action or fact of subsisting. ▶ adj. referring to production at a level that is only enough for one's own use, without any surplus for trade: *subsistence agriculture.*

sub·sist·ence lev·el (also **subsistence wage**) ▶ n. a standard of living (or wage) that provides only the basic necessities of life.

sub·soil /'səb,soil/ ▶ n. the soil lying immediately under the surface soil.

sub·son·ic /,səb'sänik/ ▶ adj. relating to or flying at a speed or speeds less than that of sound.

sub·spe·cies /'səb,spēsHēz, -sēz/ ▶ n. (pl. same) Biology a subdivision of a species.

subst. ▶ abbr. 1 substantive. 2 substantively. 3 substitute.

sub·stance /'səbstəns/ ▶ n. 1 a type of solid, liquid, or gas that has particular properties. 2 the real physical matter of which a person or thing consists. 3 solid basis in reality or fact: *the claim has no substance.* 4 the most important or essential part or meaning. 5 the quality of being important or significant: *nothing of substance was achieved.* 6 the subject matter of a piece of writing or work of art. 7 an intoxicating or narcotic drug, especially an illegal one.
– PHRASES **in substance** with regard to the fundamental points; essentially.

sub·stand·ard /'səb'standərd/ ▶ adj. below the usual or required standard.

sub·stan·tial /səb'stanCHəl/ ▶ adj. 1 of great importance, size, or value. 2 strongly built or made. 3 concerning the essential points of something: *there was substantial agreement on changing policies.* 4 real and tangible rather than imaginary. ■ **sub·stan·ti·al·i·ty** /-,stanCHē'alitē/ n.

sub·stan·tial·ly /səb'stanCHəlē/ ▶ adv. 1 to a great extent. 2 for the most part; mainly: *things will remain substantially the same.*

sub·stan·ti·ate /səb'stanCHē,āt/ ▶ v. provide evidence to prove that something is true. ■ **sub·stan·ti·a·tion** /-,stanCHē'āsHən/ n.

sub·stan·tive /'səbstəntiv/ ▶ adj. important or meaningful. ▶ n. Grammar, dated a noun. ■ **sub·stan·tive·ly** adv.

sub·sta·tion /'səb,stāsHən/ ▶ n. 1 a set of equipment reducing the high voltage of electrical power transmission to that suitable for supply to consumers. 2 a small police station or fire station.

sub·sti·tute /'səbsti,t(y)ōōt/ ▶ n. 1 a person or thing acting or used in place of another. 2 an athlete who may replace another after a match has begun. ▶v. **1** use one person or thing instead of another. **2** replace one person or thing with another. **3** replace an athlete with a substitute during a match. ■ **sub·sti·tut·a·ble** adj. **sub·sti·tu·tion** /ˌsəbstiˈt(y)ōōsHən/ n.

USAGE
Traditionally, **substitute** is followed by **for** and means 'use one person or thing instead of another', as in *she substituted the fake vase for the real one*. It may also be used with **with** or **by** to mean 'replace something with something else', as in *she substituted the real vase with the fake one*. This can be confusing, since the two sentences shown above mean the same thing, yet the object of the verb and the object of the preposition have swapped positions. Despite the potential confusion, the second, newer use is acceptable, although still disapproved of by some people.

sub·strate /ˈsəbˌstrāt/ ▶n. **1** the surface or material on which an organism lives, grows, or feeds. **2** the substance on which an enzyme acts.

sub·stra·tum /ˈsəbˌstrātəm, -ˌstra-/ ▶n. (pl. **substrata** /ˈsəbˌstrātə, -ˌstra-/) **1** an underlying layer or substance, in particular a layer of rock or soil beneath the surface of the ground. **2** a foundation or basis.

sub·struc·ture /ˈsəbˌstrəkcHər/ ▶n. an underlying or supporting structure.

sub·sume /səbˈsōōm/ ▶v. include something in a larger category or group.

sub·ten·ant /ˈsəbˈtenənt/ ▶n. a person who rents property from a tenant.

sub·tend /səbˈtend/ ▶v. Geometry (of a line, arc, etc.) form an angle at a particular point when straight lines from its extremities meet.

sub·ter·fuge /ˈsəbtərˌfyōōj/ ▶n. secret or dishonest actions used in order to achieve an aim.

sub·ter·ra·ne·an /ˌsəbtəˈrānēən/ ▶adj. existing or happening under the earth's surface. ■ **sub·ter·ra·ne·ous** adj.

sub·text /ˈsəbˌtekst/ ▶n. an underlying theme in a speech or piece of writing.

sub·ti·tle /ˈsəbˌtītl/ ▶n. **1** (**subtitles**) captions displayed at the bottom of a movie or television screen that translate the dialogue. **2** a secondary title of a published work. ▶v. provide something with a subtitle or subtitles.

sub·tle /ˈsətl/ ▶adj. (**subtler**, **subtlest**) **1** so delicate or precise that it is difficult to analyze or describe: *a subtle distinction.* **2** cleverly achieving an effect in a way that is not immediately obvious: *subtle lighting.* **3** making use of clever and indirect methods to achieve something. **4** able to make fine distinctions: *a subtle mind.* ■ **sub·tle·ty** /ˈsətltē/ n. (pl. **subtleties**) **sub·tly** adv.

sub·to·tal /ˈsəbˌtōtl/ ▶n. the total of one set within a larger group of figures to be added.

sub·tract /səbˈtrakt/ ▶v. take one number or amount away from another to calculate the difference between them. ■ **sub·trac·tion** /səbˈtraksHən/ n. **sub·trac·tive** /-tiv/ adj.

sub·trop·i·cal /ˌsəbˈträpikəl/ ▶adj. relating to the regions of the earth that are near or next to the tropics. ■ **sub·trop·ics** /ˈsəbˈträpiks/ pl.n.

sub·u·nit /ˈsəbˌyōōnit/ ▶n. a distinct component of something.

sub·urb /ˈsəbərb/ ▶n. a residential district on the outskirts of a city.

sub·ur·ban /səˈbərbən/ ▶adj. **1** relating to or like a suburb. **2** boringly conventional. ■ **sub·ur·ban·ize** /səˈbərbəˌnīz/ v.

sub·ur·ban·ite /səˈbərbəˌnīt/ ▶n. a person who lives in a suburb.

sub·ur·bi·a /səˈbərbēə/ ▶n. suburbs and the way of life of the people who live in them.

sub·ven·tion /səbˈvencHən/ ▶n. a grant of money, especially from a government.

sub·ver·sive /səbˈvərsiv/ ▶adj. trying or intended to damage or weaken the power of an established system or institution. ▶n. a subversive person. ■ **sub·ver·sive·ly** adv. **sub·ver·sive·ness** n.

sub·vert /səbˈvərt/ ▶v. damage or weaken the power of an established system or institution. ■ **sub·ver·sion** /-ˈvərzHən, -sHən/ n. **sub·vert·er** n.

sub·way /ˈsəbˌwā/ ▶n. **1** an underground electric railroad. **2** Brit. a tunnel under a road for pedestrians to use.

sub·woof·er /ˈsəbˌwōōfər/ ▶n. a part of a loudspeaker designed to reproduce very low bass frequencies.

sub·ze·ro /ˌsəbˈzi(ə)rō/ ▶adj. (of temperature) lower than zero; (on the Celsius scale) below freezing.

suc·ceed /səkˈsēd/ ▶v. **1** achieve an aim or purpose. **2** gain fame, wealth, or social status. **3** take over a position or title from someone else. **4** become the new rightful holder of a position or title: *James I succeeded to the throne in 1603.* **5** come after and take the place of: *her embarrassment was succeeded by fear.*

suc·cess /səkˈses/ ▶n. **1** the achievement of an aim or purpose. **2** the gaining of fame, wealth, or social status. **3** a person or thing that achieves success.

suc·cess·ful /səkˈsesfəl/ ▶adj. **1** having achieved an aim or purpose. **2** having achieved fame, wealth, or social status. ■ **suc·cess·ful·ly** adv.

suc·ces·sion /səkˈsesHən/ ▶n. **1** a number of people or things following one after the other. **2** the action or right of inheriting a position or title.
– PHRASES **in quick succession** following one another at short intervals. **in succession** following one after the other without interruption.

suc·ces·sive /səkˈsesiv/ ▶adj. following one another or following others. ■ **suc·ces·sive·ly** adv.

suc·ces·sor /səkˈsesər/ ▶n. a person or thing that succeeds another.

success sto·ry ▶n. informal a successful person or thing.

suc·cinct /sə(k)ˈsiNG(k)t/ ▶adj. expressed clearly and in few words. ■ **suc·cinct·ly** adv. **suc·cinct·ness** n.

suc·cor /ˈsəkər/ (Brit. **succour**) ▶n. help given to someone who is suffering or in difficulty. ▶v. help someone who is suffering or in difficulty.

suc·co·tash /ˈsəkəˌtasH/ ▶n. a dish of corn and lima beans cooked together.

suc·cu·bus /ˈsəkyəbəs/ ▶n. (pl. **succubi** /-ˌbī/) a female demon believed to have sex with sleeping men.

suc·cu·lent /ˈsəkyələnt/ ▶adj. **1** (of food) tender, juicy, and tasty. **2** (of a plant) having thick fleshy leaves or stems adapted to storing water. ▶n. a succulent plant. ■ **suc·cu·lence** n. **suc·cu·lent·ly** adv.

suc·cumb /sə'kəm/ ▸ v. **1** give in to pressure, temptation, etc. **2** die from the effect of a disease or injury.

such /sɒCH/ ▸ determiner, predeterminer, & pron. **1** of the type previously mentioned. **2** (**such —— as/that**) of the type about to be mentioned: *there's no such thing as a free lunch.* **3** to so high a degree; so great. – PHRASES **as such** in the exact sense of the word. **such-and-such** an unspecified person or thing. **such as 1** for example. **2** of a kind that; like.

such·like /'sɒCH,līk/ ▸ pron. things of the type mentioned. ▸ determiner of the type mentioned.

suck /sək/ ▸ v. **1** draw liquid or air into the mouth by tightening the lip muscles and breathing in. **2** hold something in the mouth and draw at it by tightening the lip and cheek muscles. **3** pull forcefully: *he was sucked under the surface of the river.* **4** (**suck someone in/into**) involve someone in a situation or activity, especially against their will. **5** (**suck up to**) informal try to please someone in authority in order to gain advantage for oneself. **6** informal be very bad or unpleasant. ▸ n. an act or sound of sucking.

suck·er /'səkər/ ▸ n. **1** a rubber cup that sticks to a surface by suction. **2** a flat or concave organ that enables an animal to cling to a surface by suction. **3** informal a gullible person. **4** (**a sucker for**) informal a person who is especially influenced by or fond of a particular thing: *I was a sucker for flattery.* **5** a shoot springing from the base of a tree or other plant, especially one coming from the root at some distance from the trunk.

suck·er punch informal ▸ n. an unexpected punch or blow. ▸ v. (**sucker-punch**) punch or hit someone unexpectedly.

suck·le /'səkəl/ ▸ v. (with reference to a baby or young animal) feed from the breast or udder.

suck·ling /'səkliNG/ ▸ n. a baby or young animal that is still feeding on its mother's milk.

su·crose /'soo,krōs/ ▸ n. a compound that is the chief component of cane or beet sugar.

suc·tion /'səkSHən/ ▸ n. the process of removing air or liquid from a space or container, creating a partial vacuum that causes something else to be sucked in or that causes surfaces to stick together. ▸ v. remove something using suction.

Su·da·nese /,soodn'ēz, -'ēs/ ▸ n. a person from Sudan. ▸ adj. relating to Sudan.

sud·den /'sədn/ ▸ adj. happening or done quickly and unexpectedly. ■ **sud·den·ly** adv. **sud·den·ness** n. – PHRASES (**all**) **of a sudden** suddenly.

sud·den death ▸ n. a means of deciding the winner in a tied match, in which play continues and the winner is the first side or player to score.

sud·den in·fant death syn·drome ▸ n. technical term for CRIB DEATH.

su·do·ku /soo'dōkoo/ ▸ n. a puzzle in which one must fill a grid of nine squares by nine squares (subdivided into nine regions of three by three squares) with the numbers one to nine, in such a way that no number is repeated in any horizontal line, vertical line, or three-by-three subdivision.

Su·dra /'soo,drə/ ▸ n. a member of the worker caste, lowest of the four Hindu castes.

suds /sədz/ ▸ pl. n. froth made from soap and water. ■ **suds·y** adj.

sue /soo/ ▸ v. (**sues, suing, sued**) **1** take legal action against a person, institution, etc., typically in order to get compensation for something. **2** (**sue for**) formal appeal formally to a person for: *the rebels were forced to sue for peace.*

suede /swād/ ▸ n. leather with the flesh side rubbed to make a velvety nap.

su·et /'sooit/ ▸ n. the hard white fat on the kidneys of cattle, sheep, and other animals, used as a shortening in pastry, etc., and as a food for wild birds. ■ **su·et·y** adj.

suf·fer /'səfər/ ▸ v. **1** experience or be subjected to something bad or unpleasant. **2** (**suffer from**) be affected by or subject to an illness or condition. **3** become or appear worse in quality: *his relationship with her did suffer.* **4** old use tolerate someone or something. **5** old use allow someone to do something. ■ **suf·fer·er** n.

suf·fer·ance /'səf(ə)rəns/ ▸ n. lack of objection rather than genuine approval; toleration.

suf·fice /sə'fīs/ ▸ v. be enough or adequate: *a quick look should suffice.* – PHRASES **suffice** (**it**) **to say** used to indicate that one is withholding details in order to be brief or discreet.

suf·fi·cien·cy /sə'fiSHənsē/ ▸ n. (pl. **sufficiencies**) **1** the condition or quality of being sufficient. **2** an adequate amount, especially of something essential.

suf·fi·cient /sə'fiSHənt/ ▸ adj. & determiner enough; adequate. ■ **suf·fi·cient·ly** adv.

suf·fix /'səfiks/ ▸ n. a letter or group of letters added at the end of a word to form another word (e.g., *-ation*).

suf·fo·cate /'səfə,kāt/ ▸ v. **1** die or cause to die from lack of air or inability to breathe. **2** have or cause to have difficulty in breathing. ■ **suf·fo·ca·tion** /,səfə'kāSHən/ n.

suf·fra·gan /'səfrəgən/ (also **suffragan bishop**) ▸ n. a bishop appointed to help the bishop in charge of a diocese.

suf·frage /'səfrij/ ▸ n. the right to vote in political elections.

suf·fra·gette /,səfrə'jet/ ▸ n. historical a woman who campaigned for women to be given the right to vote in political elections.

suf·fra·gist /'səfrəjist/ ▸ n. historical a person in favor of women being given the right to vote in political elections.

suf·fuse /sə'fyooz/ ▸ v. gradually spread through or over: *her cheeks were suffused with color.* ■ **suf·fu·sion** /sə'fyooZHən/ n.

Su·fi /'soofē/ ▸ n. (pl. **Sufis**) a member of a mystic Muslim group. ■ **Su·fism** /'soo,fizəm/ n.

sug·ar /'SHoogər/ ▸ n. **1** a sweet crystalline substance obtained especially from sugarcane and sugar beet. **2** any of the class of soluble crystalline sweet-tasting carbohydrates found in plant and animal tissue, including sucrose and glucose. ▸ v. sweeten, sprinkle, or coat something with sugar. ■ **sug·ar·less** adj. – PHRASES **sugar the pill** see PILL.

sug·ar beet ▸ n. a type of beet (plant) from which sugar is extracted.

sug·ar·cane /'SHoogər,kān/ ▸ n. a tropical grass with tall thick stems from which sugar is extracted.

sug·ar·coat·ed /'SHoogər,kōtid/ ▸ adj. superficially attractive or acceptable.

sug·ar dad·dy ▸ n. informal a rich older man who lavishes gifts on a much younger woman.

sug·ar ma·ple ▶ n. a North American maple, which yields the sap from which maple sugar and maple syrup are made.

sug·ar·plum /'sHŏŏgər,pləm/ ▶ n. a small round candy of flavored boiled sugar.

sug·ar snap (also **sugar snap pea**) ▶ n. a type of snow pea with thick, rounded pods.

sug·ar·y /'sHŏŏgərē/ ▶ adj. **1** containing much sugar. **2** coated in sugar. **3** too sentimental.

sug·gest /sə(g)'jest/ ▶ v. **1** put an idea or plan forward for consideration. **2** make someone think that something exists or is the case: *evidence suggests that he died soon after 1190.* **3** say or express indirectly: *are you suggesting that I should ignore her?* **4** (**suggest itself**) (of an idea) come into one's mind.

sug·gest·i·ble /sə(g)'jestəbəl/ ▶ adj. quick to accept other people's ideas or suggestions; easily influenced. ■ **sug·gest·i·bil·i·ty** /sə(g),jestə'bilitē/ n.

sug·ges·tion /sə(g)'jescHən/ ▶ n. **1** an idea or plan put forward for consideration. **2** something that implies or indicates a certain fact or situation: *there is no suggestion that she was involved in wrongdoing.* **3** a slight trace or indication: *a suggestion of a smile.* **4** Psychology the process by which a person is led to accept an idea or belief uncritically, especially as a technique in hypnosis.

sug·ges·tive /sə(g)'jestiv/ ▶ adj. **1** bringing ideas, images, etc., to mind: *flavors suggestive of coffee and blackberry.* **2** (of a remark, joke, etc.) hinting at sexual matters; mildly indecent. ■ **sug·ges·tive·ly** adv. **sug·ges·tive·ness** n.

su·i·cid·al /,sŏŏi'sīdl/ ▶ adj. **1** deeply unhappy or depressed and likely to commit suicide. **2** likely to have a disastrously damaging effect on oneself or one's interests: *a suicidal career move.* ■ **su·i·cid·al·ly** adv.

su·i·cide /'sŏŏi,sīd/ ▶ n. **1** the action of killing oneself deliberately. **2** a person who commits suicide. **3** a course of action that is likely to be very damaging to one's career, position in society, etc. ▶ adj. referring to a military operation carried out by people who do not expect to survive it: *a suicide bomber.*

su·i·cide pact ▶ n. an agreement between two or more people to commit suicide together.

su·i ge·ne·ris /,sŏŏ,ī 'jenərəs, ,sŏŏē/ ▶ adj. unique.

suit /sŏŏt/ ▶ n. **1** a set of outer clothes made of the same fabric and designed to be worn together, consisting of a jacket and pants or a jacket and a skirt. **2** a set of clothes for a particular activity. **3** any of the sets into which a deck of playing cards is divided (spades, hearts, diamonds, and clubs). **4** a lawsuit. **5** informal a high-ranking business executive. **6** the process of trying to win a woman's affection with a view to marriage. ▶ v. **1** be convenient for or acceptable to: *what time would suit you?* **2** (of clothes, colors, etc.) go well with or be right for someone's features or figure. **3** (**suit oneself**) do exactly as one wants. **4** (as adj. **suited**) right or appropriate for a particular person, purpose, or situation: *washable wallpaper ideally suited to bathrooms and kitchens.*

suit·a·ble /'sŏŏtəbəl/ ▶ adj. right or appropriate for a particular person, purpose, or situation. ■ **suit·a·bil·i·ty** /,sŏŏtə'bilitē/ n. **suit·a·bly** /-blē/ adv.

suit·case /'sŏŏt,kās/ ▶ n. a case with a handle and

a hinged lid, used for carrying clothes and other personal possessions.

suite /swēt/ ▶ n. **1** a set of rooms for one person's or family's use or for a particular purpose. **2** a set of furniture of the same design. **3** a set of pieces of instrumental music to be played in succession. **4** a set of pieces from an opera or musical arranged as one instrumental work.

suit·or /'sŏŏtər/ ▶ n. a man who wishes to marry a particular woman.

sul·fa drugs /'səlfə/ (chiefly Brit. also **sulpha drugs**) ▶ pl.n. the sulfonamide family of drugs.

sul·fate /'səl,fāt/ (Brit. **sulphate**) ▶ n. Chemistry a salt or ester of sulfuric acid.

sul·fide /'səl,fīd/ (Brit. **sulphide**) ▶ n. Chemistry a compound of sulfur with another element or group.

sul·fon·a·mide /səl'fänə,mīd/ (Brit. **sulphonamide**) ▶ n. any of a class of sulfur-containing drugs that are able to prevent the multiplication of certain bacteria.

sul·fur /'səlfər/ (Brit. **sulphur**) ▶ n. a nonmetallic chemical element that easily catches fire, typically occurring as yellow crystals.

sul·fur di·ox·ide ▶ n. a colorless strong-smelling poisonous gas formed by burning sulfur.

sul·fu·ric /səl'fyŏŏrik/ ▶ adj. containing sulfur or sulfuric acid.

sul·fu·ric a·cid ▶ n. a strong corrosive acid made by oxidizing solutions of sulfur dioxide.

sul·fur·ous /'səlfərəs/ ▶ adj. containing or obtained from sulfur.

sulk /səlk/ ▶ v. be silent, bad-tempered, and resentful as a result of annoyance or disappointment. ▶ n. a period of sulking.

sulk·y /'səlkē/ ▶ adj. (**sulkier, sulkiest**) silent, bad-tempered, and resentful. ■ **sulk·i·ly** adv. **sulk·i·ness** n.

sul·len /'sələn/ ▶ adj. bad-tempered and sulky. ■ **sul·len·ly** adv. **sul·len·ness** n.

sul·ly /'səlē/ ▶ v. (**sullies, sullying, sullied**) literary **1** damage someone's or something's purity or reputation. **2** make something dirty.

sul·pha drugs ▶ pl.n. British spelling of SULFA DRUGS.

sul·phate ▶ pl.n. British spelling of SULFATE.

sul·phide ▶ pl.n. British spelling of SULFIDE.

sul·phon·a·mide ▶ pl.n. British spelling of SULFONAMIDE.

sul·phur, etc. ▶ n. British spelling of SULFUR, etc.

sul·tan /'səltn/ ▶ n. the title given to a ruler in some Muslim countries.

sul·tan·a /səl'tanə/ ▶ n. **1** a small light brown seedless raisin; a golden raisin. **2** a wife of a sultan.

sul·tan·ate /'səltn,āt/ ▶ n. **1** the rank or position of a sultan. **2** the territory ruled by a sultan.

sul·try /'səltrē/ ▶ adj. (**sultrier, sultriest**) **1** (of the weather) hot and humid. **2** displaying or suggesting sexual passion.

sum /səm/ ▶ n. **1** a particular amount of money. **2** (also **sum total**) the total amount resulting from the addition of two or more numbers or amounts. **3** an arithmetical calculation. ▶ v. (**sums, summing, summed**) (**sum someone/thing up**) **1** concisely describe someone's or something's nature or character. **2** (**sum something up** or **sum up**) summarize something briefly. **3** Law (of a judge) review the evidence at the end of a case, and direct the jury about points of law.

– PHRASES **in sum** to sum up.

su·mac /'sōōmak, 'shōō-/ (also **sumach**) ▶ n. a shrub or small tree with clusters of fruits that are ground and used as a spice in Middle Eastern cooking.

Su·ma·tran /sə'mätrən/ ▶ n. a person from the Indonesian island of Sumatra. ▶ adj. relating to Sumatra.

Su·me·ri·an /sə'merēən, -'miər-/ ▶ adj. relating to Sumer, an ancient region of what is now Iraq. ▶ n. a person from Sumer.

sum·ma·rize /'səmə,rīz/ ▶ v. give a brief statement of the main points of something.

sum·ma·ry /'səmərē/ ▶ n. (pl. **summaries**) a brief statement of the main points of something. ▶ adj. 1 not including unnecessary details or formalities. 2 (of a legal process or judgment) done or made without the normal legal formalities. ■ **sum·mar·i·ly** /sə'me(ə)rəlē, 'səmərəlē/ adv.

> USAGE
> Do not confuse **summary** and **summery**. A **summary** is a brief statement of the main points of something (*a summary of today's news*), whereas **summery** is an adjective meaning 'typical of or suitable for summer' (*summery weather*).

sum·ma·tion /sə'māshən/ ▶ n. 1 the process of adding things together. 2 the action of summing something up. 3 a summary.

sum·mer /'səmər/ ▶ n. the season after spring and before autumn, when the weather is warmest. ▶ v. spend the summer in a particular place. ■ **sum·mer·y** adj.

sum·mer·house /'səmər,hous/ ▶ n. 1 a house or cottage used as a second residence during the summer months. 2 a small building in a garden or park, used for sitting in during the summer months.

sum·mer school ▶ n. courses held during school summer vacations.

sum·mer squash ▶ n. a squash that is eaten before the seeds and rind have hardened.

sum·mer·time /'səmər,tīm/ ▶ n. the season or period of summer.

sum·ming-up ▶ n. 1 a summary. 2 a judge's review of evidence at the end of a case, with a direction to the jury about points of law.

sum·mit /'səmit/ ▶ n. 1 the highest point of a hill or mountain. 2 the highest possible level of achievement. 3 a meeting between heads of government.

sum·mon /'səmən/ ▶ v. 1 instruct someone to be present. 2 order someone to appear in a court of law. 3 urgently ask for help. 4 call people to attend a meeting. 5 produce a quality or reaction from within oneself by making an effort: *she managed to summon up a smile.*

sum·mons /'səmənz/ ▶ n. (pl. **summonses**) 1 an order to appear in a court of law. 2 an act of instructing someone to be present. ▶ v. chiefly Law serve someone with a summons.

su·mo /'sōōmō/ ▶ n. Japanese wrestling in which a wrestler must not go outside a circle or touch the ground with any part of his body except the soles of his feet.

sump /səmp/ ▶ n. 1 the base of an internal-combustion engine, which serves as a reservoir of oil for the lubrication system. 2 a hollow in the floor of a mine or cave in which water collects. 3 a cesspool.

sump·tu·ous /'səm(p)chōōəs/ ▶ adj. splendid and expensive-looking. ■ **sump·tu·ous·ly** adv. **sump·tu·ous·ness** n.

sum to·tal ▶ n. another term for **sum** (sense 2 of the noun).

sun /sən/ ▶ n. 1 (also **Sun**) the star around which the earth orbits. 2 any similar star, with or without planets. 3 the light or warmth received from the sun. ▶ v. (**suns, sunning, sunned**) (**sun oneself**) sit or lie in the sun. ■ **sun·less** adj.

– PHRASES **under the sun** in existence.

sun-baked ▶ adj. exposed to the heat of the sun.

sun·bathe /'sən,bāTH/ ▶ v. sit or lie in the sun to get a suntan. ■ **sun·bath·er** n.

sun·beam /'sən,bēm/ ▶ n. a ray of sunlight.

sun·belt /'sən,belt/ ▶ n. a strip of territory receiving a high amount of sunshine, especially the southern US from California to Florida.

sun·block /'sən,bläk/ ▶ n. a cream or lotion for protecting the skin from sunburn.

sun·burn /'sən,bərn/ ▶ n. inflammation of the skin caused by too much exposure to the ultraviolet rays of the sun. ■ **sun·burned** (or **sunburnt**) adj.

sun·burst /'sən,bərst/ ▶ n. 1 a design or ornament representing the sun and its rays. 2 a sudden brief appearance of the full sun from behind clouds.

sun·cream /'sən,krēm/ ▶ n. a cream rubbed onto the skin to protect it from sunburn.

sun·dae /'sən,dā/ ▶ n. a dish of ice cream with added ingredients such as fruit, nuts, and syrup.

Sun·day /'səndā, -dē/ ▶ n. the day of the week before Monday and following Saturday, observed by most Christians as a day of religious worship.

Sun·day best ▶ n. a person's best clothes.

Sun·day school ▶ n. a class held on Sundays to teach children about Christianity or Judaism.

sun deck ▶ n. 1 the deck of a yacht or cruise ship that is open to the sky. 2 a terrace or balcony positioned to catch the sun.

sun·der /'səndər/ ▶ v. literary 1 split something apart. 2 break the connection or relationship between two or more people or things.

sun·dew /'sən,d(y)ōō/ ▶ n. a small carnivorous plant found in boggy places, with leaves bearing sticky hairs for trapping insects.

sun·di·al /'sən,dīl/ ▶ n. a device used for telling the time, consisting of a pointer that casts a shadow on a surface marked with hours like a clock.

sun·down /'sən,doun/ ▶ n. sunset.

sun·dress /'sən,dres/ ▶ n. a light, loose sleeveless dress.

sun-dried ▶ adj. dried in the sun, as opposed to by artificial heat.

sun·dry /'səndrē/ ▶ adj. of various kinds. ▶ pl. n. (**sundries**) various items not important enough to be mentioned individually.

sun·fish /'sən,fish/ ▶ n. (pl. same or **sunfishes**) a large sea fish with tall fins near the rear of the body.

sun·flow·er /'sən,flou(-ə)r/ ▶ n. a tall plant bearing very large yellow flowers with edible seeds from which an oil used in cooking, margarine, etc., is extracted.

sung /səNG/ ▶ past participle of SING.

sun·glass·es /'sən,glasiz/ ▶ pl.n. glasses tinted to protect the eyes from sunlight or glare.

sunk /səNGk/ ▶ past participle of SINK¹.

sunk·en /'səNGkən/ ▶ adj. **1** having sunk. **2** at a lower level than the surrounding area. **3** (of a person's cheeks or eyes) hollow or appearing set back into the face as a result of age, disease, etc.

sun-kissed ▶ adj. made warm or brown by the sun.

sun·lamp /'sən,lamp/ ▶ n. a lamp giving off ultraviolet rays, used chiefly to produce an artificial suntan.

sun·light /'sən,līt/ ▶ n. light from the sun. ■ **sun·lit** /'sən,lit/ adj.

Sun·na /'soōnə, 'sənə/ ▶ n. the traditional part of Muslim law based on Muhammad's words or acts, accepted as authoritative by Muslims.

Sun·ni /'soōnē/ ▶ n. (pl. same or **Sunnis**) **1** one of the two main branches of Islam, the other being Shia. **2** a Muslim who follows the Sunni branch of Islam.

sun·ny /'sənē/ ▶ adj. (**sunnier, sunniest**) **1** bright with or receiving much sunlight. **2** cheerful.

sun·ny side ▶ n. **1** the side of something that receives the sun for longest. **2** the more cheerful or pleasant aspect of something.
– PHRASES **sunny side up** (of an egg) fried on one side only.

sun·rise /'sən,rīz/ ▶ n. **1** the time in the morning when the sun rises. **2** the colors and light visible in the sky at sunrise.

sun·roof /'sən,roōf, -,roŏf/ ▶ n. a panel in the roof of a car that can be opened for extra ventilation.

sun·screen /'sən,skrēn/ ▶ n. a cream or lotion rubbed onto the skin to protect it from the sun.

sun·set /'sən,set/ ▶ n. **1** the time in the evening when the sun sets. **2** the colors and light visible in the sky at sunset.

sun·shade /'sən,SHād/ ▶ n. a parasol, awning, or other device giving protection from the sun.

sun·shine /'sən,SHīn/ ▶ n. sunlight unbroken by cloud. ■ **sun·shin·y** adj.

sun·spot /'sən,spät/ ▶ n. a temporary darker and cooler patch on the sun's surface.

sun·stroke /'sən,strōk/ ▶ n. heatstroke caused by spending too much time exposed to hot sunlight.

sun·tan /'sən,tan/ ▶ n. a golden-brown coloring of the skin caused by spending time in the sun. ■ **sun·tanned** adj.

sun·up /'sən,əp/ ▶ n. sunrise.

sup /səp/ ▶ v. (**sups, supping, supped**) dated eat supper.

su·per /'soōpər/ ▶ adj. informal excellent.

super- ▶ comb.form **1** above; over; beyond: *superstructure*. **2** to a great or extreme degree: *superabundant*. **3** extra large of its kind: *superpower*.

su·per·a·bun·dant /,soōpərə'bəndənt/ ▶ adj. formal occurring in very large quantities. ■ **su·per·a·bun·dance** n.

su·per·an·nu·a·ted /,soōpər'anyoō,ātid/ ▶ adj. **1** (of an employee) discharged from a job with a pension. **2** too old to be effective or useful.

su·per·an·nu·a·tion /,soōpər,anyoō'āsHən/ ▶ n. regular payment made into a fund by an employee toward a future pension.

su·perb /soŏ'pərb, sə-/ ▶ adj. extremely good or impressive. ■ **su·perb·ly** adv.

su·per·bike /'soōpər,bīk/ ▶ n. a high-performance motorcycle.

su·per·bug /'soōpər,bəg/ ▶ n. informal a bacterium, insect, etc., that has become resistant to antibiotics or pesticides.

su·per·car /'soōpər,kär/ ▶ n. a high-performance sports car.

su·per·cen·ter /'soōpər,sentər/ ▶ n. a superstore.

su·per·charge /'soōpər,CHärj/ ▶ v. (usu. as adj. **supercharged**) **1** provide an engine with a supercharger. **2** give extra power, energy, or intensity to: *a supercharged collection of dance tracks*.

su·per·charg·er /'soōpər,CHärjər/ ▶ n. a device that increases the efficiency of an internal-combustion engine by raising the pressure of the fuel-air mixture supplied to it.

su·per·cil·i·ous /,soōpər'sileəs/ ▶ adj. behaving as though one thinks one is superior to other people. ■ **su·per·cil·i·ous·ly** adv. **su·per·cil·i·ous·ness** n.

su·per·com·put·er /'soōpərkəm,pyoōtər/ ▶ n. a particularly powerful mainframe computer.

su·per·con·duc·tiv·i·ty /,soōpər,kän,dək'tiv itē/ ▶ n. Physics the property of zero electrical resistance in some substances at very low temperatures. ■ **su·per·con·duct·ing** /-kən'dəktiNG/ adj. **su·per·con·duc·tor** /'soōpərkən,dəktər/ n.

su·per·con·ti·nent /'soōpər,käntn-ənt/ ▶ n. a huge landmass believed to have divided in the geological past to form some of the present continents.

su·per·cool /,soōpər'koōl/ ▶ v. Chemistry cool a liquid below its freezing point without solidification or crystallization.

su·per·crit·i·cal /,soōpər'kritikəl/ ▶ adj. Physics greater than or above a critical threshold such as critical mass or temperature.

su·per·du·per /'soōpər 'doōpər/ ▶ adj. humorous **1** very good; marvelous. **2** tremendous or colossal in size or degree.

su·per·e·go /,soōpər'ēgō/ ▶ n. (pl. **superegos**) the part of the mind that acts as a conscience, reflecting social standards that have been learned. Compare with EGO and ID.

su·per·e·rog·a·to·ry /,soōpərə'rägə,tōrē/ ▶ adj. more than what is needed or required; superfluous.

su·per·fam·i·ly /'soōpər,fam(ə)lē/ ▶ n. (pl. **superfamilies**) Biology a taxonomic category that ranks above family and below order.

su·per·fi·cial /,soōpər'fisHəl/ ▶ adj. **1** existing or happening at or on the surface. **2** appearing to exist or be true until examined more closely: *the resemblance is superficial*. **3** not thorough: *a superficial knowledge of the system*. **4** lacking depth of character or understanding; not concerned with serious matters. ■ **su·per·fi·ci·al·i·ty** /-,fisHē'alitē/ n. (pl. **superficialities**) **su·per·fi·cial·ly** adv.

su·per·flu·ous /soŏ'pərfləwəs/ ▶ adj. more than is needed; unnecessary. ■ **su·per·flu·i·ty** n. (pl. **superfluities**) **su·per·flu·ous·ly** adv.

su·per·food /'soōpər,foōd/ ▶ n. a food considered especially nutritious or otherwise beneficial to health and well-being.

su·per·glue /'soōpər,gloō/ ▶ n. a very strong quick-setting glue.

su·per·heat /,soōpər'hēt/ ▶ v. Physics **1** heat a liquid under pressure above its boiling point without vaporization. **2** heat steam or other vapor above the temperature of the liquid from which it was formed.

su·per·he·ro /'sōōpər,hirō/ ▶ n. (pl. **superheroes**) a fictional hero with superhuman powers.

su·per·high·way /'sōōpər,hīwā, ,sōōpər'hī,wā/ ▶ n. an expressway.

su·per·hu·man /,sōōpər'(h)yōōmən/ ▶ adj. having or showing exceptional ability or powers. ■ **su·per·hu·man·ly** adv.

su·per·im·pose /,sōōpərim'pōz/ ▶ v. place or lay one thing over another. ■ **su·per·im·po·si·tion** /-,impə'zishən/ n.

su·per·in·tend /,sōōpərin'tend/ ▶ v. manage or oversee an activity, organization, etc. ■ **su·per·in·tend·ence** n.

su·per·in·tend·ent /,sōōpərin'tendənt/ ▶ n. **1** a person who supervises or is in charge of an activity, organization, etc. **2** the head custodian of a building. **3** (in the UK) a police officer ranking above chief inspector. **4** (in the US) the chief of a police department.

su·pe·ri·or /sə'pi(ə)rēər/ ▶ adj. **1** higher in status, quality, or power. **2** of a high standard or quality. **3** having or showing a belief that one is better than other people: *he had a rather superior manner*. **4** (of a letter, figure, or symbol) written or printed above the line. **5** chiefly Anatomy higher in position. ▶ n. **1** a person of higher rank. **2** the head of a monastery or other religious institution.

su·pe·ri·or·i·ty /sə,pi(ə)rē'ôritē, -'äritē/ ▶ n. the state of being superior.

su·per·la·tive /sə'pərlətiv/ ▶ adj. **1** of the highest quality or degree. **2** Grammar (of an adjective or adverb) expressing the highest degree of a quality (e.g., *bravest*, *most fiercely*). Contrasted with POSITIVE and COMPARATIVE. ▶ n. an exaggerated expression of praise. ■ **su·per·la·tive·ly** adv.

su·per·man /'sōōpər,man/ (or **superwoman** /'sōōpər,wŏŏmən/) ▶ n. (pl. **supermen** or **superwomen**) informal a person with exceptional physical or mental abilities.

su·per·mar·ket /'sōōpər,märkit/ ▶ n. a large self-service store selling foods and household goods.

su·per·max /'sōōpər,maks/ ▶ n. an extremely high-security prison or part of a prison, intended for particularly dangerous prisoners. ▶ adj. (of a prison) having extremely high-security features or facilities: *12 percent of prisoners live in supermax units*.

su·per·mod·el /'sōōpər,mädl/ ▶ n. a very successful and famous fashion model.

su·per·nat·u·ral /,sōōpər'nacH(ə)rəl/ ▶ adj. referring or relating to events, forces, or powers that cannot be explained by science or the laws of nature. ▶ n. (**the supernatural**) supernatural events, forces, or powers. ■ **su·per·nat·u·ral·ly** adv.

su·per·no·va /,sōōpər,nōvə/ ▶ n. (pl. **supernovae** /-,nōvē/ or **supernovas**) a star that undergoes an explosion, becoming suddenly very much brighter.

su·per·nu·mer·ar·y /,sōōpər'n(y)ōōmə,rerē/ ▶ adj. **1** more than is normally needed; extra. **2** not belonging to a regular staff but employed for extra work. ▶ n. (pl. **supernumeraries**) an extra person or thing.

su·per·or·di·nate /,sōōpər'ôrdn-ət/ ▶ n. a thing that represents a higher order or category within a system of classification.

su·per·pose /,sōōpər'pōz/ ▶ v. place something on or above something else. ■ **su·per·po·si·tion** /-pə'zishən/ n.

su·per·pow·er /'sōōpər,pouər/ ▶ n. a very powerful and influential nation.

su·per·script /'sōōpər,skript/ ▶ adj. (of a letter, figure, or symbol) written or printed above the line.

su·per·sede /,sōōpər'sēd/ ▶ v. take the place of someone or something previously in authority or use.

> **USAGE**
> The ending of **supersede** is spelled **-sede**, not *-cede*; it is the only verb that has this ending.

su·per·size /'sōōpər,sīz/ ▶ v. produce or serve (something) in a larger size: *click here to supersize the picture.* ▶ adj. larger than normal.

su·per·son·ic /,sōōpər'sänik/ ▶ adj. involving or referring to a speed greater than that of sound. ■ **su·per·son·i·cal·ly** /-ik(ə)lē/ adv.

su·per·star /'sōōpər,stär/ ▶ n. an extremely famous and successful performer or athlete. ■ **su·per·star·dom** /-dəm/ n.

su·per·state /'sōōpər,stāt/ ▶ n. a large and powerful state formed from a federation or union of several nations.

su·per·sti·tion /,sōōpər'stishən/ ▶ n. **1** irrational belief in supernatural events. **2** a widely held but irrational belief that certain objects, actions, or events bring good or bad luck.

su·per·sti·tious /,sōōpər'stishəs/ ▶ adj. believing in the supernatural and its influence in bringing good or bad luck. ■ **su·per·sti·tious·ly** adv.

su·per·store /'sōōpər,stôr/ ▶ n. a retail store with more than the average amount of space and variety of stock.

su·per·struc·ture /'sōōpər,strəkcHər/ ▶ n. **1** a structure built on top of something else. **2** the part of a building above its foundations. **3** the parts of a ship, other than masts and rigging, above its hull and main deck.

su·per·tank·er /'sōōpər,taNGkər/ ▶ n. a very large oil tanker.

su·per·vene /,sōōpər'vēn/ ▶ v. happen so as to interrupt or change an existing situation. ■ **su·per·ven·ient** /-'vēnyənt/ adj. **su·per·ven·tion** /-'vencHən/ n.

su·per·vil·lain /'sōōpər,vilən/ ▶ n. a very wicked fictional character, especially one with superhuman powers.

su·per·vise /'sōōpər,vīz/ ▶ v. observe and direct the performance of a task or the work of a person. ■ **su·per·vi·sion** /,sōōpər'vizHən/ n. **su·per·vi·sor** /-,vīzər/ n. **su·per·vi·so·ry** /,sōōpər'vīzərē/ adj.

su·pi·nate /'sōōpə,nāt/ ▶ v. technical **1** put or hold (a hand, foot, or limb) with the palm or sole turned upward. Compare with PRONATE. **2** walk or run with most of the weight on the inside of the feet. ■ **su·pi·na·tion** /,sōōpə'nāshən/ n.

su·pi·na·tor /'sōōpə,nātər/ ▶ n. **1** a muscle whose contraction produces or assists in the supination of a limb or part of a limb. **2** any of several specific muscles in the forearm. **3** one who supinates when walking or running.

su·pine /'sōō,pīn/ ▶ adj. **1** lying face upward. **2** failing to act as a result of laziness or weakness. ■ **su·pine·ly** adv. **su·pine·ness** n.

sup·per /'səpər/ ▶ n. a light or informal evening meal.
– PHRASES **sing for one's supper** provide a service in return for a benefit.

sup·plant /sə'plant/ ▶ v. take the place of: *another technology might supplant the CD.* ■ **sup·plant·er** n.

sup·ple /'səpəl/ ▶ adj. (**suppler**, **supplest**) able to bend or move easily; flexible. ■ **sup·ple·ness** n.

sup·ple·ment /'səpləmənt/ ▶ n. **1** a thing added to something else to improve or complete it. **2** a separate section added to a newspaper or magazine. **3** an additional charge payable for an extra service or facility. ▶ v. add an extra element or amount to something. ■ **sup·ple·men·tal** /ˌsəplə'mentl/ adj. **sup·ple·men·ta·tion** /ˌsəplə,men'tāshən/ n.

sup·ple·men·ta·ry /ˌsəplə'mentərē/ ▶ adj. provided in addition to something so as to complete or improve it: *supplementary information.*

sup·pli·ant /'səplēənt/ ▶ n. a person who makes a humble request.

sup·pli·cate /'səpli,kāt/ ▶ v. humbly ask or beg for something. ■ **sup·pli·cant** /-kənt/ n. **sup·pli·ca·tion** /ˌsəpli'kāshən/ n. **sup·pli·ca·to·ry** /-kə,tôrē/ adj.

sup·ply /sə'plī/ ▶ v. (**supplies**, **supplying**, **supplied**) make something needed available to someone; provide someone with something. ▶ n. (pl. **supplies**) **1** a stock or amount of something supplied or available. **2** the action of supplying something. **3** (**supplies**) provisions and equipment necessary for an army or expedition. ■ **sup·pli·er** n.
– PHRASES **supply and demand** the amount of goods or services available and the desire of buyers for them, considered as factors deciding their price.

sup·ply-side ▶ adj. Economics (of a policy) designed to increase output and employment by reducing taxation.

sup·port /sə'pôrt/ ▶ v. **1** bear all or part of the weight of someone or something. **2** give help, encouragement, or approval to: *many famous women have supported her cause.* **3** provide someone with a home and the necessities of life. **4** provide enough food and water for life to exist. **5** confirm the truth of; back up: *the studies support our findings.* **6** (of a pop or rock group or performer) appear before the main act at a concert. **7** (as adj. **supporting**) of secondary importance to the leading roles in a play, movie, etc. ▶ n. **1** a person or thing that supports someone or something. **2** the action of supporting or the state of being supported. **3** help, encouragement, or approval: *her loyal support of her husband.* ■ **sup·port·a·ble** adj.

sup·port·er /sə'pôrtər/ ▶ n. a person who supports a political party, etc.

sup·port·ive /sə'pôrtiv/ ▶ adj. providing encouragement or emotional help. ■ **sup·port·ive·ly** adv. **sup·port·ive·ness** n.

sup·pose /sə'pōz/ ▶ v. **1** think that something is true or probable, but without proof. **2** (of a theory or argument) assume or require that something is the case as a necessary condition: *the procedure supposes that a will has already been proved.* **3** (**be supposed to do**) be required

or expected to do something.

sup·pos·ed·ly /sə'pōzidlē/ ▶ adv. according to what is generally believed.

sup·po·si·tion /ˌsəpə'zishən/ ▶ n. a belief held without proof or certain knowledge; an assumption or hypothesis.

sup·pos·i·to·ry /sə'päzə,tôrē/ ▶ n. (pl. **suppositories**) a small piece of a medicinal substance that dissolves after being placed in the rectum or vagina.

sup·press /sə'pres/ ▶ v. **1** forcibly put an end to an activity that threatens an established authority. **2** prevent from acting or developing: *the immune system is suppressed with powerful drugs.* **3** prevent something from being published. **4** consciously avoid thinking of an unpleasant idea or memory. ■ **sup·pres·sion** /sə'preshən/ n. **sup·pres·sive** adj. **sup·pres·sor** n.

sup·pres·sant /sə'presənt/ ▶ n. a drug or other substance that prevents a bodily function from working.

sup·pu·rate /'səpyə,rāt/ ▶ v. (of a wound, ulcer, etc.) form or discharge pus. ■ **sup·pu·ra·tion** /ˌsəpyə'rāshən/ n. **sup·pu·ra·tive** /-,rātiv/ adj.

su·pra /'sōōprə/ ▶ adv. formal used in academic or legal texts to refer to someone or something mentioned above or earlier.

su·pra·na·tion·al /ˌsōōprə'nashənl/ ▶ adj. having power or influence that goes beyond national boundaries or governments.

su·prem·a·cist /sə'preməsist, sōō-/ ▶ n. a person who believes that a particular group, especially a racial group, is superior to all others. ▶ adj. relating to the belief that a particular group is superior to all others. ■ **su·prem·a·cism** /sə'premə,sizəm, sōō-/ n.

su·prem·a·cy /sə'preməsē, sōō-/ ▶ n. the state of being superior to all others in authority, power, or status.

su·preme /sə'prēm, sōō-/ ▶ adj. **1** highest in authority, rank, or importance. **2** very great or greatest: *the chapel is a supreme example of medieval architecture.* ▶ n. (also **suprême**) a rich cream sauce or a dish served in a cream sauce. ■ **su·preme·ly** adv.

supreme court ▶ n. the highest court of law in a country or state.

su·pre·mo /sə'prē,mō, sōō-/ ▶ n. (pl. **supremos**) Brit. informal **1** a person in charge of an organization. **2** a person with great skill in a particular area: *a marketing supremo.*

Supt. ▶ abbr. Superintendent.

sur- ▶ prefix equivalent to SUPER-.

su·ra /'sōōrə/ (also **surah**) ▶ n. a chapter or section of the Koran.

sur·cease /sər'sēs/ ▶ n. **1** the ending or stopping of something. **2** relief from something unpleasant.

sur·charge /'sər,CHärj/ ▶ n. an additional charge or payment. ▶ v. make someone pay an additional charge.

surd /sərd/ ▶ n. Mathematics a number that cannot be expressed as a ratio of two whole numbers.

sure /SHŏŏr/ ▶ adj. **1** completely confident that one is right. **2** (**sure of/to do**) certain to receive, get, or do: *the menu is sure to please everyone.* **3** undoubtedly true; completely reliable. **4** steady and confident. ▶ adv. informal certainly. ■ **sure·ness** n.
– PHRASES **be sure to do** do not fail to do. **for**

sure informal without doubt. **make sure** confirm or ensure that something is the case or is done. **to be sure** certainly; it must be admitted.

sure-fire ▶ adj. informal certain to succeed.

sure-foot·ed ▶ adj. **1** unlikely to stumble or slip. **2** confident and competent.

sure·ly /'sHŏŏrlē/ ▶ adv. **1** it must be true that. **2** without doubt; certainly. **3** in a confident way. **4** informal of course.

sure·ty /'sHŏŏritē/ ▶ n. (pl. **sureties**) **1** a person who accepts responsibility if another person fails to pay a debt, appear in court, etc. **2** money given as a guarantee that someone will do something. **3** the state of being sure or certain of something.

surf /sərf/ ▶ n. waves that break and form foam on a seashore or reef. ▶ v. **1** stand or lie on a surfboard and ride on the crest of a wave toward the shore. **2** move from site to site on the Internet. **3** channel-surf. ■ **surf·er** n. **surf·ing** n.

sur·face /'sərfis/ ▶ n. **1** the outside part or uppermost layer of something. **2** the upper limit of a body of liquid. **3** the outward appearance of someone or something as distinct from less obvious aspects: *Tom was a womanizer, but on the surface he remained respectable.* ▶ adj. **1** relating to or occurring on the surface. **2** (of transportation) by sea or overland rather than by air. **3** outward or superficial: *surface politeness.* ▶ v. **1** rise or come up to the surface. **2** become apparent: *the row first surfaced two years ago.* **3** provide something, especially a road, with a particular surface. **4** informal appear after having been asleep.

sur·face ten·sion ▶ n. the tension of the surface film of a liquid, which tends to minimize surface area.

sur·fac·tant /sər'faktənt/ ▶ n. a substance, such as a detergent, that is added to a liquid to increase its spreading or wetting properties by reducing its surface tension.

surf·board /'sərf,bôrd/ ▶ n. a long, narrow board used in surfing.

sur·feit /'sərfit/ ▶ n. **1** an excessive amount of something. **2** old use an illness caused by excessive eating or drinking. ▶ v. (**surfeits, surfeiting, surfeited**) make someone want no more of something as a result of having consumed or done it to excess: *I am surfeited with shopping.*

surge /sərj/ ▶ n. **1** a sudden powerful forward or upward movement. **2** a sudden large temporary increase. **3** a powerful rush of an emotion. ▶ v. **1** move suddenly and powerfully forward or upward. **2** increase suddenly and powerfully: *shares surged to a record high.*

sur·geon /'sərjən/ ▶ n. a medical practitioner qualified to practice surgery.

sur·geon gen·er·al ▶ n. (pl. **surgeons general**) the head of a public health service or of an armed forces medical service.

sur·ger·y /'sərjərē/ ▶ n. (pl. **surgeries**) **1** the medical treatment of injuries or disorders by cutting open the body and removing or repairing parts. **2** Brit. a place where a doctor or nurse treats or advises patients.

sur·gi·cal /'sərjikəl/ ▶ adj. **1** relating to or used in surgery. **2** worn to correct or relieve an injury, illness, or deformity. **3** done with great precision: *surgical bombing.* ■ **sur·gi·cal·ly** /-ik(ə)lē/ adv.

Su·ri·na·mese /,sŏŏrənə'mēz, -'mēs/ ▶ adj. relating

to Suriname, a country on the NE coast of South America.

sur·ly /'sərlē/ ▶ adj. (**surlier, surliest**) bad-tempered and unfriendly. ■ **sur·li·ly** /-ləlē/ adv. **sur·li·ness** n.

sur·mise /sər'mīz/ ▶ v. believe something to be true without having evidence. ▶ n. a belief that something is true without having evidence to confirm it.

sur·mount /sər'mount/ ▶ v. **1** overcome a difficulty or obstacle. **2** stand or be placed on top of something. ■ **sur·mount·a·ble** adj.

sur·name /'sər,nām/ ▶ n. an inherited name shared by members of a family, as distinct from a personal name.

sur·pass /sər'pas/ ▶ v. **1** be greater or better than: *demand for the college's Latin courses has surpassed expectations.* **2** (as adj. **surpassing**) old use or literary outstanding; very great. ■ **sur·pass·a·ble** adj.

sur·plice /'sərplis/ ▶ n. a loose white garment worn over a cassock by Christian clergy and members of church choirs.

sur·plus /'sərpləs/ ▶ n. **1** an amount left over when requirements have been met. **2** the amount by which the amount of money received is greater than the amount of money spent over a specific period. ▶ adj. more than what is needed or used; extra.

sur·prise /sə(r)'prīz/ ▶ n. **1** a feeling of mild astonishment or shock caused by something unexpected. **2** an unexpected or astonishing thing. ▶ v. **1** make someone feel mild astonishment or shock. **2** capture, attack, or discover suddenly and unexpectedly: *he surprised a gang stealing scrap metal.* ■ **sur·prised** adj. **sur·pris·ing** adj. **sur·pris·ing·ly** adv. – PHRASES **take someone by surprise** happen when someone is not prepared. **take someone/ thing by surprise** attack or capture someone or something unexpectedly.

sur·re·al /sə'rēəl/ ▶ adj. having ideas or images mixed together in a strange way; like a dream: *a surreal road movie.* ■ **sur·re·al·ly** adv.

sur·re·al·ism /sə'rēə,lizəm/ ▶ n. a 20th-century movement in art and literature in which images or events are combined in a strange or irrational way. ■ **sur·re·al·ist** n. & adj. **sur·re·al·is·tic** /sə,rēə'listik/ adj.

sur·ren·der /sə'rendər/ ▶ v. **1** stop resisting an opponent and put oneself under their control. **2** give up a person, right, or possession when demanded to do so. **3** (**surrender to**) give in completely to a powerful emotion or influence. **4** cancel a life insurance policy and receive back a proportion of the premiums paid. ▶ n. the action or an act of surrendering: *the final surrender of Germany on May 8, 1945.*

sur·rep·ti·tious /,sərəp'tisHəs/ ▶ adj. done secretly. ■ **sur·rep·ti·tious·ly** adv.

sur·ro·gate /'sərəgit, -,gāt/ ▶ n. a substitute, especially a person who stands in for another in a role or office. ■ **sur·ro·ga·cy** /'sərəgəsē/ n.

sur·ro·gate moth·er ▶ n. a woman who bears a child on behalf of another woman, either from her own egg or from having a fertilized egg from the other woman implanted in her uterus.

sur·round /sə'round/ ▶ v. **1** be all around or encircle someone or something. **2** be associated

with: *the killings were surrounded by controversy.*
▶ n. **1** a border or edging. **2** (**surrounds**) the area around something; surroundings.

sur·round·ings /sə'roundɪŋz/ ▶ pl.n. the area or conditions around a person or thing: *a school in rural surroundings.*

sur·tax /'sər,taks/ ▶ n. an additional tax on something already taxed, especially at a higher rate of tax on incomes above a certain level.

surtitle /'sər,tītl/ ▶ n. a caption projected on a screen above the stage in an opera, translating the words being sung. ▶ v. provide with surtitles.

sur·veil·lance /sər'vāləns/ ▶ n. close observation, especially of a suspected spy or criminal.

sur·vey ▶ v. /sər'vā, 'sər,vā/ **1** look carefully and thoroughly at someone or something. **2** examine and record the features of an area of land to produce a map or description. **3** question a group of people to investigate their opinions.
▶ n. /'sər,vā/ **1** a general view, examination, or description. **2** an investigation of the opinions or experience of a group of people, based on a series of questions. **3** an act of surveying an area of land. **4** a map or report obtained by surveying.

sur·vey·or /sər'vāər/ ▶ n. a person who surveys land as a profession.

sur·viv·al /sər'vīvəl/ ▶ n. **1** the state or fact of surviving: *the animal's chances of survival were low.* **2** an object or practice that has survived from an earlier time.
– PHRASES **survival of the fittest** the principle that only the people or things that are best adapted to their situation or environment will continue to exist.

sur·viv·al·ist /sər'vīvəlist/ ▶ n. a person who practices outdoor survival skills as a sport or hobby. ■ **sur·viv·al·ism** /sər'vīvə,lizəm/ n.

sur·viv·al kit ▶ n. **1** a pack of emergency equipment, including food, medical supplies, and tools. **2** a collection of items to help someone in a particular situation: *a substitute teacher survival kit.*

sur·vive /sər'vīv/ ▶ v. **1** continue to live or exist. **2** continue to live in spite of an accident or ordeal. **3** remain alive after the death of someone. ■ **sur·viv·a·bil·i·ty** /sər,vīvə'bilətē/ n. **sur·viv·a·ble** /sər'vīvəbəl/ adj.

sur·vi·vor /sər'vīvər/ ▶ n. a person who survives, especially one who remains alive after an accident or ordeal.

sus·cep·ti·bil·i·ty /sə,septə'bilitē/ ▶ n. (pl. **susceptibilities**) **1** the state of being easily harmed or influenced. **2** (**susceptibilities**) a person's sensitive feelings.

sus·cep·ti·ble /sə'septəbəl/ ▶ adj. **1** likely to be influenced or harmed by a particular thing: *patients with liver disease may be susceptible to infection.* **2** easily influenced by feelings or emotions. **3** (**susceptible of**) capable of something. ■ **sus·cep·ti·bly** /-blē/ adv.

su·shi /'sōōshē/ ▶ n. a Japanese dish consisting of small balls or rolls of cold rice with vegetables, egg, or raw seafood.

sus·pect ▶ v. /sə'spekt/ **1** believe to be probable or possible: *if you suspect a problem with the thermostat, call a repair technician.* **2** believe that someone is guilty of a crime or offense, without definite proof. **3** doubt that something is genuine or true. ▶ n. /'səs,pekt/ a person suspected of a crime or offense. ▶ adj. /'səs,pekt/ possibly dangerous or false.

sus·pend /sə'spend/ ▶ v. **1** stop something temporarily. **2** temporarily bar someone from a job or from attending school, as a punishment or during investigation. **3** postpone or delay an action, event, or judgment. **4** (as adj. **suspended**) Law (of a sentence) not enforced as long as no further offense is committed within a specified period. **5** hang from somewhere. **6** (**be suspended**) technical (of particles) be dispersed throughout a fluid.

sus·pend·ed an·i·ma·tion ▶ n. a state in which most of the functions of an animal or plant stop for a time, without death.

sus·pend·ed ceil·ing ▶ n. a ceiling with a space between it and the floor above from which it hangs.

sus·pend·ers /sə'spendərz/ ▶ pl.n. a pair of straps passing over the shoulders and fastening to the top of a pair of pants to hold them up.

sus·pense /sə'spens/ ▶ n. a state or feeling of excited or anxious uncertainty about what may happen. ■ **sus·pense·ful** /-fəl/ adj.

sus·pen·sion /sə'spenshən/ ▶ n. **1** the action of suspending or the state of being suspended. **2** the temporary barring of someone from a job or from school, especially as a punishment. **3** the system of springs and shock absorbers that supports a vehicle on its wheels. **4** technical a mixture in which particles are dispersed throughout a fluid.

sus·pen·sion bridge ▶ n. a bridge in which the deck is suspended from cables running between towers.

sus·pi·cion /sə'spishən/ ▶ n. **1** a feeling or thought that something is true or probable: *she had a suspicion that he was laughing at her.* **2** a feeling or belief that someone has done something wrong. **3** distrust of someone or something. **4** a very slight trace: *a suspicion of a smile.*
– PHRASES **above suspicion** too good or honest to be thought capable of wrongdoing. **under suspicion** suspected of wrongdoing.

sus·pi·cious /sə'spishəs/ ▶ adj. **1** having a feeling that someone has done something wrong. **2** (also **suspicious of**) not able to trust someone or something. **3** seeming to be dishonest or dangerous: *a suspicious package.* ■ **sus·pi·cious·ly** adv. **sus·pi·cious·ness** n.

suss /səs/ ▶ v. (**susses, sussing, sussed**) chiefly Brit. informal (often **suss someone/thing out**) realize or understand the true nature of someone or something.

sus·tain /sə'stān/ ▶ v. **1** support someone physically or mentally. **2** cause to continue for some time: *he cannot sustain a normal conversation.* **3** suffer something unpleasant. **4** decide that a claim is valid. **5** bear the weight of an object. ■ **sus·tain·er** n. **sus·tain·ment** n.

sus·tain·a·ble /sə'stānəbəl/ ▶ adj. **1** able to be sustained or continued. **2** (of industry, development, or agriculture) not making excessive use of natural resources.
■ **sus·tain·a·bil·i·ty** /sə,stānə'bilitē/ n. **sus·tain·a·bly** /-blē/ adv.

sus·te·nance /'səstənəns/ ▶ n. **1** food and drink as needed to keep someone alive. **2** the process of making something continue.

su·tra /'sōōtrə/ ▶ n. **1** a rule or saying in Sanskrit literature, or a set of these on grammar or Hindu law or philosophy. **2** a Buddhist or Jainist scripture.

sut·tee /sə'tē, 'sə,tē/ ▶ n. variant spelling of SATI.

su·ture /'sōōCHər/ ▶ n. **1** a stitch or stitches holding together the edges of a wound or surgical cut. **2** a thread or wire used for stitching a wound or cut. ▶ v. stitch up a wound or cut with a suture.

SUV ▶ abbr. sport utility vehicle.

su·ze·rain·ty /'sōōzərəntē, 'sōōzə,rāntē/ ▶ n. the right of one country to rule over another country that has its own ruler but is not fully independent. ■ **su·ze·rain** /'sōōzərən, 'sōōzə,rān/ n.

s.v. ▶ abbr. (in references in written works) under the word or heading given.

svelte /svelt, sfelt/ ▶ adj. slender and elegant.

Sven·ga·li /sven'gälē, sfen-/ ▶ n. a person who exercises a controlling influence on another, especially for a sinister purpose.

SW ▶ abbr. **1** southwest. **2** southwestern.

swab /swäb/ ▶ n. **1** an absorbent pad used for cleaning wounds or taking a sample from the body for testing. **2** a sample taken with a swab. ▶ v. (**swabs, swabbing, swabbed**) **1** clean a wound with an absorbent pad. **2** wash a floor or ship's deck with a mop or cloth.

swad·dle /'swädl/ ▶ v. wrap someone in clothes or cloth.

swad·dling clothes /'swädliNG/ ▶ pl.n. strips of cloth formerly wrapped around a newborn baby to calm it.

swag /swag/ ▶ n. **1** a decorative garland of flowers, fruit, and greenery. **2** a curtain or piece of fabric fastened to hang in a drooping curve. **3** informal money or goods taken by a thief or burglar. ▶ v. (**swags, swagging, swagged**) arrange fabric so as to hang in a drooping curve.

swag·ger /'swagər/ ▶ v. walk or behave in a very confident or arrogant way. ▶ n. a very confident or arrogant way of walking. ▶ adj. (of a coat or jacket) cut with a loose flare from the shoulders.

swag·ger stick ▶ n. a short cane carried by a military officer.

Swa·hi·li /swä'hēlē/ ▶ n. (pl. same) **1** a Bantu language widely spoken in East Africa. **2** a member of a people of Zanzibar and nearby coastal regions.

swain /swān/ ▶ n. **1** literary a young male lover. **2** old use a country youth.

swal·low¹ /'swälō/ ▶ v. **1** pass food, drink, or saliva down the throat. **2** take in or cover completely: *the dark mist swallowed her up.* **3** use the throat muscles as if swallowing, especially because of nervousness. **4** completely use up money or resources. **5** put up with unfair treatment. **6** believe something untrue without question. **7** hide a feeling: *he swallowed his pride.* ▶ n. an act of swallowing. ■ **swal·low·er** n.

swallow² ▶ n. a swift-flying migratory songbird with a forked tail.

swal·low·tail /'swälō,tāl/ ▶ n. a large brightly colored butterfly with tail-like projections on the hind wings.

swam /swam/ ▶ past of SWIM.

swa·mi /'swämē/ ▶ n. (pl. **swamis**) a male Hindu religious teacher.

swamp /swämp/ ▶ n. a bog or marsh. ▶ v. **1** overwhelm or flood something with water. **2** overwhelm with too much of something; inundate: *the country was swamped with goods from abroad.* ■ **swamp·y** adj.

swamp·land /'swämp,land/ ▶ n. (also **swamplands**) land consisting of swamps.

swan /swän/ ▶ n. a large white waterbird with a long flexible neck and webbed feet.

swan dive ▶ n. a dive performed with the arms outspread until close to the water.

swank /swaNGk/ informal ▶ v. try to impress others with one's wealth, knowledge, or achievements. ▶ n. behavior or talk intended to impress others.

swank·y /'swaNGkē/ ▶ adj. (**swankier, swankiest**) informal **1** stylishly luxurious and expensive. **2** inclined to show off.

swans·down /'swänz,doun/ ▶ n. the fine soft feathers of a swan, used for trimmings and powder puffs.

swan·song /'swän,sôNG/ ▶ n. the final performance or activity of a person's career.

swap /swäp/ (also Brit. **swop** pronunc. same) ▶ v. (**swaps, swapping, swapped**) exchange or substitute one thing or person for another. ▶ n. an act of exchanging one thing or person for another.

swap meet ▶ n. **1** a gathering at which people trade or exchange items of common interest: *a computer swap meet.* **2** a flea market.

sward /swôrd/ ▶ n. literary an expanse of short grass.

swarm /swôrm/ ▶ n. **1** a large group of insects flying closely together. **2** a large number of honeybees that leave a hive with a queen in order to establish a new colony. **3** a large group of people or things. ▶ v. **1** move in or form a swarm. **2** (**swarm with**) be crowded or overrun with: *the place was swarming with police.* **3** (**swarm up**) climb rapidly by gripping something with one's hands and feet.

swarth·y /'swôrTHē/ ▶ adj. (**swarthier, swarthiest**) having a dark complexion. ■ **swarth·i·ness** n.

swash·buck·ling /'swôsH,bəkliNG, 'swäsH-/ ▶ adj. engaging in or showing daring and romantic adventures: *he made eight swashbuckling films.* ■ **swash·buck·ler** /'swôsH,bəklər, 'swäsH-/ n.

swas·ti·ka /'swästikə/ ▶ n. an ancient symbol in the form of an equal-armed cross with each arm continued at a right angle, used (in clockwise form) as the emblem of the German Nazi party.

swat /swät/ ▶ v. (**swats, swatting, swatted**) hit someone or something with a sharp blow from a flat object.

swatch /swäCH/ ▶ n. **1** a piece of fabric used as a sample. **2** a number of fabric samples bound together.

swath /swäTH, swôTH/ (also **swathe** /swāTH, swäTH/) ▶ n. (pl. **swaths** /swäTHs, swôTHs/ or **swathes** /swäTHz, swäTHz/) **1** a broad strip or area: *vast swathes of countryside.* **2** a row or line of grass, wheat, etc., as it falls when mown or reaped.

swathe /swäTH, swāTH/ ▶ v. wrap someone or something in several layers of fabric. ▶ n. a strip of material in which something is wrapped.

SWAT team /swät/ ▶ n. a group of police marksmen who specialize in high-risk tasks such as hostage rescue.

sway /swā/ ▶ v. **1** move slowly and rhythmically backward and forward or from side to side. **2** make someone change their opinion. ▶ n. **1** a swaying movement. **2** power, influence, or control: *he fell under the sway of a* *revolutionary scientist.*

– PHRASES **hold sway** have great power or influence.

swear /swe(ə)r/ ▸ v. (past **swore**; past part. **sworn**) 1 state or promise something solemnly or on oath. 2 make someone promise to do something: *I am sworn to secrecy.* 3 use offensive or obscene language. ■ **swear·er** n.

– PHRASES **swear by** informal be certain that something is very good or useful. **swear someone in** admit someone to a new post or job by making them take a formal oath. **swear off** informal promise to stop doing or to give up something. **swear to** say that something is definitely the case.

swear word ▸ n. an offensive or obscene word.

sweat /swet/ ▸ n. 1 moisture given out through the pores of the skin, especially in reaction to heat, physical effort, or anxiety. 2 informal hard work. 3 informal a state of anxiety or distress. ▸ v. (past and past part. **sweated** or **sweat**) 1 produce sweat. 2 make a great deal of effort: *I've sweated over this for six months.* 3 be very anxious. 4 (of a substance) give off moisture. 5 cook chopped vegetables slowly in a pan with a small amount of fat.

– PHRASES **break a sweat** informal make a great physical effort. **no sweat** informal all right; no problem. **sweat blood** informal make a very great effort. **sweat bullets** informal be extremely anxious or nervous.

sweat·band /'swet,band/ ▸ n. a band of absorbent material worn to soak up sweat.

sweat·er /'swetər/ ▸ n. a knitted garment worn over the upper body, typically with long sleeves.

sweat gland ▸ n. a small gland that secretes sweat, situated in the dermis of the skin.

sweat·pants /'swet,pants/ ▸ pl.n. loose, warm trousers with an elastic or drawstring waist, worn for exercise or leisure.

sweat·shirt /'swet,sнərt/ ▸ n. a loose, heavy, collarless shirt, typically made of cotton and worn for exercise or leisure.

sweat·shop /'swet,sнäp/ ▸ n. a factory or workshop employing workers for long hours in poor conditions.

sweat·suit /'swet,sσ̄ot/ ▸ n. an outfit consisting of a sweatshirt and sweatpants, worn when exercising or as leisurewear.

sweat·y /'swetē/ ▸ adj. (**sweatier**, **sweatiest**) soaked in or causing sweat. ■ **sweat·i·ly** adv. **sweat·i·ness** n.

Swede /swēd/ ▸ n. a person from Sweden.

Swed·ish /'swēdisн/ ▸ n. the Scandinavian language of Sweden. ▸ adj. relating to Sweden.

sweep /swēp/ ▸ v. (past and past part. **swept** /swept/) 1 clean an area by brushing away dirt or litter. 2 move forcefully: *I was swept along by the crowd.* 3 move swiftly and smoothly. 4 affect swiftly and widely: *violence swept the country.* 5 (**sweep something away/aside**) remove or abolish something quickly and suddenly. 6 search an area. 7 extend continuously in an arc or curve: *forests swept down the hillsides.* ▸ n. 1 an act of sweeping. 2 a long, swift curving movement. 3 a long curved stretch of road, river, etc. 4 the range or scope of something: *the whole sweep of the history of the USA.* 5 a chimney sweep. 6 informal a sweepstake.

– PHRASES **sweep the board** win every event or prize in a contest.

sweep·er /'swēpər/ ▸ n. 1 a person or device that cleans by sweeping. 2 Soccer a player stationed behind the other defenders, free to defend at any point across the field.

sweep·ing /'swēpiNG/ ▸ adj. 1 extending or performed in a long, continuous curve. 2 wide in range or effect. 3 (of a statement) too general. ▸ n. (**sweepings**) dirt or refuse collected by sweeping. ■ **sweep·ing·ly** adv.

sweep·stakes /'swēp,stāks/ (also **sweepstake**) ▸ n. a form of gambling in which the winner receives all the money bet by the other participants.

sweet /swēt/ ▸ adj. 1 having the pleasant taste of sugar or honey. 2 having a pleasant smell; fragrant. 3 pleasant or satisfying: *the sweet life.* 4 kind or thoughtful. 5 charming and endearing. 6 working or done smoothly or easily: *the sweet handling of this motorcycle.* 7 (of air, water, etc.) fresh and pure. 8 (**sweet on**) informal, dated in love with someone. ▸ n. 1 (**sweets**) sweet foods, collectively. 2 Brit. a small piece of candy. 3 Brit. a dessert. ■ **sweet·ish** adj. **sweet·ly** adv.

sweet-and-sour ▸ adj. cooked with sugar and either vinegar or lemon.

sweet·bread /'swēt,bred/ ▸ n. the thymus gland or pancreas of an animal, used for food.

sweet corn ▸ n. a variety of corn with sweet kernels that are eaten as a vegetable.

sweet·en /'swētn/ ▸ v. 1 make or become sweet or sweeter. 2 make something more acceptable. 3 (**sweeten someone up**) informal be pleasant to someone in order to make them agree to something, help, etc.

sweet·en·er /'swētn-ər, 'swētnər/ ▸ n. 1 a substance used to sweeten food or drink. 2 informal a bribe.

sweet·heart /'swēt,härt/ ▸ n. a person who is loved by someone. ▸ adj. informal agreed privately by two sides in their own interests at others' expense: *a sweetheart deal.*

sweet·ie /'swētē/ ▸ n. informal used as a term of affection.

sweet·meat /'swēt,mēt/ ▸ n. old use a candy or item of sweet food.

sweet·ness /'swētnis/ ▸ n. the quality of being sweet.

– PHRASES **sweetness and light** pleasantness or harmony.

sweet pea ▸ n. a climbing plant of the pea family with colorful fragrant flowers.

sweet pep·per ▸ n. a variety of pepper with a mild or sweet flavor.

sweet po·ta·to ▸ n. the edible tuber of a tropical climbing plant, with pinkish-orange flesh.

sweet-talk ▸ v. informal use charm or flattery to persuade someone to do something.

sweet tooth ▸ n. (pl. **sweet tooths**) a great liking for sweet foods.

sweet wil·liam ▸ n. a fragrant plant with clusters of vivid red, pink, or white flowers.

swell /swel/ ▸ v. (past part. **swollen** /'swōlən/ or **swelled**) 1 become larger or rounder in size. 2 increase in intensity, amount, or volume: *the low murmur swelled to a roar.* ▸ n. 1 a full or gently rounded form. 2 a gradual increase in sound, amount, or intensity. 3 a slow, regular movement of the sea in rolling waves that do not break. 4 informal, dated a fashionable upper-class person. ▸ adj. informal, dated excellent; very good.

swell·ing /'sweliNG/ ▶ n. a place on the body that has swollen as a result of illness or an injury.

swel·ter /'sweltər/ ▶ v. be uncomfortably hot.

swept /swept/ past and past participle of **sweep** ▶ adj. (also **swept back**) (of an aircraft's wings) directed backward from the fuselage.

swerve /swərv/ ▶ v. abruptly depart from a straight course. ▶ n. an abrupt change of course.

swift /swift/ ▶ adj. **1** happening quickly or promptly. **2** moving or capable of moving at high speed. ▶ n. a fast-flying bird with long, slender wings, spending most of its life flying. ■ **swift·ly** adv. **swift·ness** n.

swig /swig/ informal ▶ v. (**swigs, swigging, swigged**) drink something in large gulps. ▶ n. a large gulp of a drink.

swill /swil/ ▶ v. informal drink something in large quantities. ▶ n. waste food mixed with water for feeding to pigs.

swim /swim/ ▶ v. (**swims, swimming, swam** /swam/; past part. **swum** /swəm/) **1** propel oneself through water by moving the arms and legs. **2** be immersed in or covered with liquid. **3** experience a dizzily confusing feeling. ▶ n. an act or period of swimming. ■ **swim·mer** n.
– PHRASES **in the swim** involved in or aware of current events.

swim·ming·ly /'swimiNGlē/ ▶ adv. informal smoothly and satisfactorily.

swim·ming pool ▶ n. an artificial pool for swimming in.

swim·suit /'swim,sŏŏt/ ▶ n. a garment worn for swimming.

swim trunks (also **swimming trunks**) ▶ pl.n. shorts worn by men for swimming.

swim·wear /'swim,we(ə)r/ ▶ n. clothing worn for swimming.

swin·dle /'swindl/ ▶ v. use deception to obtain money or possessions from someone. ▶ n. a scheme or act designed to obtain money dishonestly. ■ **swin·dler** n.

swine /swīn/ ▶ n. **1** (pl. same) a pig. **2** (pl. same or **swines**) informal an unpleasant person. ■ **swin·ish** adj.

swine fe·ver ▶ n. an intestinal disease of pigs, caused by a virus.

swine·herd /'swīn,hərd/ ▶ n. chiefly historical a person who tends pigs.

swing /swiNG/ ▶ v. (past and past part. **swung** /swəNG/) **1** move back and forth or from side to side while hanging from a fixed point. **2** move by grasping a support and leaping. **3** move in a smooth, curving line: *the cab swung into the car park.* **4** (**swing at**) attempt to punch someone. **5** shift from one opinion, mood, or situation to another: *opinion swung in the senator's favor.* **6** have a decisive influence on a vote or decision. **7** informal succeed in bringing something about. **8** informal swap sexual partners or engage in group sex. **9** informal be lively, exciting, or fashionable. ▶ n. **1** a seat hanging from ropes or chains, on which someone can sit and swing. **2** an act of swinging. **3** a clear change in public opinion, especially in an election. **4** a style of jazz or dance music with an easy flowing rhythm. ■ **swing·er** n. **swing·y** adj.
– PHRASES **get into the swing of things** informal become used to an activity. **in full swing** at the height of activity.

swing bridge ▶ n. a bridge that can be swung to one side to allow ships to pass.

swing·ing /'swiNGiNG/ ▶ adj. informal **1** lively, exciting, and fashionable. **2** sexually liberated.

swing·ing door ▶ n. a door that can be opened in either direction and is closed by a spring device when released.

swipe /swīp/ informal ▶ v. **1** hit or try to hit someone or something with a swinging blow. **2** steal something. **3** pass a swipe card through an electronic reader. ▶ n. **1** a sweeping blow. **2** an act of criticizing someone or something.

swipe card ▶ n. a plastic card carrying coded information that is read when the card is slid through an electronic device.

swirl /swərl/ ▶ v. move in a twisting or spiraling pattern. ▶ n. a swirling movement or pattern. ■ **swirl·y** adj.

swish /swiSH/ ▶ v. move with a soft rushing sound. ▶ n. a soft rushing sound or movement. ■ **swish·y** adj.

Swiss /swis/ ▶ adj. relating to Switzerland or its people. ▶ n. (pl. same) a person from Switzerland.

Swiss chard ▶ n. see **CHARD**.

Swiss cheese ▶ n. **1** cheese of a style originating in Switzerland, typically containing large holes. **2** used figuratively to refer to something that is full of holes, gaps, or defects.

switch /swiCH/ ▶ n. **1** a device for making and breaking an electrical connection. **2** a change from one thing to another. **3** a slender, flexible shoot cut from a tree. **4** a set of points on a railroad track. ▶ v. **1** change from one thing to another: *she worked as a librarian and then switched to teaching.* **2** exchange one thing for another. **3** (**switch something off/on**) turn an electrical device off or on. **4** (**switch off**) informal cease to pay attention. ■ **switch·a·ble** adj. **switch·er** n.

switch·back /'swiCH,bak/ ▶ n. **1** a 180° bend in a road or path, especially one leading up the side of a mountain; a hairpin turn. **2** Brit. a road with alternate sharp ascents and descents.

switch·blade /'swiCH,blād/ ▶ n. a knife with a blade that springs out from the handle when a button is pressed.

switch·board /'swiCH,bôrd/ ▶ n. a device for routing telephone calls within an organization.

switch-hit·ter ▶ n. **1** Baseball a batter who can hit from either side of home plate. **2** informal a bisexual.

switch·yard /'swiCH,yärd/ ▶ n. a large railroad yard in which freight cars are organized into trains.

swiv·el /'swivəl/ ▶ v. (**swivels, swiveling, swiveled**) turn around, or around a central point. ▶ n. a connecting device between two parts enabling one to revolve without turning the other.

swiz·zle stick /'swizəl/ ▶ n. a stick used for frothing up or taking the fizz out of drinks.

swol·len /'swōlən/ ▶ past participle of **SWELL**.

swoon /swŏŏn/ literary ▶ v. faint, especially from extreme emotion. ▶ n. an instance of fainting.

swoop /swŏŏp/ ▶ v. **1** move rapidly downward through the air. **2** carry out a sudden raid. ▶ n. a swooping or snatching movement or action.
– PHRASES **at (or in) one fell swoop** see **FELL**[3].

swoosh /swŏŏSH, swŏŏSH/ ▶ n. **1** the sound produced by a sudden rush of air or liquid. **2** an emblem or design representing a flash or stripe of color. ▶ v. move with a rushing sound.

swop /swäp/ ▶ v. & n. British variant spelling of SWAP.

sword /sôrd/ ▶ n. **1** a weapon with a long metal blade and a handle, used for thrusting or striking. **2** (**the sword**) literary military power; violence.
– PHRASES **put someone to the sword** kill someone, especially in war.

sword·fish /'sôrd,fisн/ ▶ n. (pl. same or **swordfishes**) a large sea fish with a long swordlike snout.

sword of Dam·o·cles /'damə,klēz/ ▶ n. something bad that threatens to happen at any time.

sword·play /'sôrd,plā/ ▶ n. fencing with swords or foils.

swords·man /'sôrdzmən/ ▶ n. (pl. **swordsmen**) a man who fights with a sword. ■ **swords·man·ship** /-,ship/ n.

swore /swôr/ ▶ past of SWEAR.

sworn /swôrn/ past participle of SWEAR ▶ adj. **1** given under oath. **2** determined to remain the specified thing: *sworn enemies.*

swum /swəm/ ▶ past participle of SWIM.

swung /swəNG/ ▶ past and past participle of SWING.

syb·a·rite /'sibə,rīt/ ▶ n. a person who is very fond of luxury and pleasure. ■ **syb·a·rit·ic** /,sibə'ritik/ adj.

syc·a·more /'sikə,môr/ ▶ n. **1** an American plane tree. **2** a large maple tree native to central and southern Europe.

syc·o·phant /'sikəfənt, -,fant/ ▶ n. a person who flatters someone important in order to try to gain favor with them. ■ **syc·o·phan·cy** /-fənsē, -,fansē/ n. **syc·o·phan·tic** /,sikə'fantik/ adj.

Sy·den·ham's cho·rea /'sidnəmz kô'rēə/ ▶ n. a form of chorea (disorder of the nervous system) chiefly affecting children and associated with rheumatic fever.

syl·la·bar·y /'silə,berē/ ▶ n. (pl. **syllabaries**) a set of written characters representing syllables and (in some languages or stages of writing) serving the purpose of an alphabet.

syl·lab·ic /sə'labik/ ▶ adj. **1** relating to or based on syllables. **2** (of a consonant) that forms a whole syllable, such as the *l* in *bottle*. ■ **syl·lab·i·cal·ly** /-ik(ə)lē/ adv.

syl·lab·i·fy /sə'labə,fī/ ▶ v. (**syllabifies**, **syllabifying**, **syllabified**) divide words into syllables. ■ **syl·lab·i·fi·ca·tion** /sə,labəfi'kāshən/ n.

syl·la·ble /'siləbəl/ ▶ n. a unit of pronunciation having one vowel sound and forming all or part of a word (e.g., *butter* has two syllables).

syl·la·bub /'silə,bəb/ ▶ n. a whipped cream dessert, typically flavored with white wine or sherry.

syl·la·bus /'siləbəs/ ▶ n. (pl. **syllabuses** or **syllabi** /-,bī/) the subjects covered in a course of study or teaching.

syl·lo·gism /'silə,jizəm/ ▶ n. a form of reasoning in which a conclusion is drawn from two propositions (premises) (e.g., *all dogs are animals; all animals have four legs; therefore all dogs have four legs*). ■ **syl·lo·gis·tic** /,silə'jistik/ adj.

sylph /silf/ ▶ n. **1** an imaginary spirit of the air. **2** a slender woman or girl. ■ **sylph·like** /'silf,līk/ adj.

syl·van /'silvən/ ▶ adj. chiefly literary consisting of or relating to woods; wooded.

sym. ▶ abbr. **1** symbol. **2** Chemistry symmetrical. **3** symphony. **4** symptom.

sym·bi·ont /'simbē,änt, -bī-/ ▶ n. Biology either of two organisms that live in symbiosis with one another.

sym·bi·o·sis /,simbē'ōsis, -bī-/ ▶ n. (pl. **symbioses** /-,sēz/) **1** Biology a situation in which two different organisms live with and are dependent on each other, to the advantage of both. **2** a relationship between different people or groups that is beneficial to both: *his dances celebrate the symbiosis of music and dance.* ■ **sym·bi·ot·ic** /-'ätik/ adj.

sym·bol /'simbəl/ ▶ n. **1** a thing or person that represents or stands for something else: *the limousine was a symbol of his wealth.* **2** a sign, letter, or mark that has a fixed meaning, especially in music, science, or mathematics.

sym·bol·ic /sim'bälik/ ▶ adj. **1** acting as a symbol: *a repeating design symbolic of eternity.* **2** involving the use of symbols or symbolism. ■ **sym·bol·i·cal·ly** /-ik(ə)lē/ adv.

sym·bol·ism /'simbə,lizəm/ ▶ n. **1** the use of symbols to represent ideas or qualities. **2** (**Symbolism**) an artistic and poetic movement or style using symbolic images and indirect suggestion to express mystical ideas, emotions, and states of mind. ■ **sym·bol·ist** n. & adj.

sym·bol·ize /'simbə,līz/ ▶ v. **1** be a symbol of: *the ceremonial dagger symbolizes justice.* **2** represent something by means of symbols. ■ **sym·bol·i·za·tion** /,simbəli'zāshən/ n.

sym·bol·o·gy /sim'bäləjē/ ▶ n. **1** the study or use of symbols. **2** symbols as a whole.

sym·met·ri·cal /sə'metrikəl/ ▶ adj. made up of exactly similar parts facing each other or around an axis; showing symmetry. ■ **sym·met·ric** adj. **sym·met·ri·cal·ly** /-ik(ə)lē/ adv.

sym·me·try /'simitrē/ ▶ n. (pl. **symmetries**) **1** the quality of being made up of exactly similar parts facing each other or around an axis. **2** the quality of being the same or very similar: *the political symmetry between the two debates.* **3** correct or pleasing proportion of the parts of something.

sym·pa·thet·ic /,simpə'тнetik/ ▶ adj. **1** feeling or expressing kindness or understanding toward someone. **2** showing that one approves of an idea or action: *many people are sympathetic to the idea of globalization.* **3** pleasing or likable. **4** referring to the part of the nervous system supplying the internal organs, blood vessels, and glands. ■ **sym·pa·thet·i·cal·ly** /-ik(ə)lē/ adv.

sym·pa·thize /'simpə,тнīz/ ▶ v. **1** feel or express sympathy. **2** support an opinion or political movement. ■ **sym·pa·thiz·er** n.

sym·pa·thy /'simpəтнē/ ▶ n. (pl. **sympathies**) **1** the feeling of being sorry for someone who is unhappy or in difficulty: *they had great sympathy for the flood victims.* **2** support for or approval of an idea, cause, etc. **3** understanding between people who have similar views or interests.
– PHRASES **in sympathy 1** relating harmoniously to something else; in keeping. **2** happening in a way that corresponds to something else.

> **USAGE**
> On the difference between **sympathy** and **empathy**, see the note at EMPATHY.

sym·phon·ic /sim'fänik/ ▶ adj. relating to or having the form of a symphony.

sym·pho·ny /'simfənē/ ▶ n. (pl. **symphonies**) an

elaborate musical composition for full orchestra, typically in four movements.

sym·pho·ny or·ches·tra ▶ n. a large classical orchestra, including string, woodwind, brass, and percussion instruments.

sym·po·si·um /sim'pōzēəm/ ▶ n. (pl. **symposia** /-zēə/ or **symposiums**) **1** a conference to discuss a particular academic or specialist subject. **2** a collection of related papers by a number of contributors.

symp·tom /'sim(p)təm/ ▶ n. **1** a change in the body or mind that is the sign of a disease. **2** an indication of an undesirable situation.

symp·to·mat·ic /,sim(p)tə'matik/ ▶ adj. acting as a symptom or sign of something: *these difficulties are symptomatic of fundamental problems.* ■ **symp·to·mat·i·cal·ly** /-ik(ə)lē/ adv.

syn·a·gogue /'sinə,gäg/ ▶ n. a building where Jewish people meet for religious worship and instruction.

syn·apse /'sin,aps/ ▶ n. a gap between two nerve cells, across which impulses are conducted. ■ **syn·ap·tic** /sə'naptik/ adj.

sync /sinGk/ (also **synch** pronunc. same) informal ▶ n. synchronization. ▶ v. synchronize something with something else.
– PHRASES **in** (or **out of**) **sync** working well (or badly) together.

syn·chro·mesh /'sinGkrō,mesh/ ▶ n. a system of gear changing in which the gearwheels are made to revolve at the same speed during engagement.

syn·chron·ic /sinG'kränik/ ▶ adj. concerned with something, especially a language, as it exists at one point in time: *synchronic narratives.* Often contrasted with DIACHRONIC.

syn·chro·nic·i·ty /,sinGkrə'nisitē/ ▶ n. the occurrence of events at the same time, which appear to be related but have no obvious connection.

syn·chro·nize /'sinGkrə,nīz/ ▶ v. cause to occur or operate at the same time or rate: *synchronize your hand gestures with your main points.* ■ **syn·chro·ni·za·tion** /,sinGkrənə'zāsHən/ n. **syn·chro·niz·er** n.

syn·chro·nized swim·ming ▶ n. a sport in which teams of swimmers perform coordinated movements in time to music.

syn·chro·nous /'sinGkrənəs/ ▶ adj. existing or occurring at the same time. ■ **syn·chro·nous·ly** adv.

syn·chro·ny /'sinGkrənē/ ▶ n. the state of operating or developing at the same time or rate as something else.

syn·cline /'sin,klīn/ ▶ n. a ridge or fold of rock in which the strata slope upward from the axis. Compare with ANTICLINE.

syn·co·pat·ed /'sinGkə,pātid/ ▶ adj. (of music or a rhythm) having the beats or accents altered so that strong beats become weak and vice versa. ■ **syn·co·pa·tion** /,sinGkə'pāsHən/ n.

syn·co·pe /'sinGkəpē/ ▶ n. **1** Medicine fainting caused by low blood pressure. **2** Grammar the omission of sounds or letters from within a word, for example when *library* is pronounced /'lī,brē/.

syn·cre·tism /'sinGkrə,tizəm/ ▶ n. the combining of different religions, cultures, or schools of thought. ■ **syn·cret·ic** /sinG'kretik/ adj. **syn·cre·tist** n. & adj. **syn·cre·tis·tic** /,sinGkrə'tistik/ adj.

syn·cre·tize /'sinGkri,tīz/ ▶ v. attempt to combine

differing religious beliefs, cultures, or schools of thought. ■ **syn·cre·ti·za·tion** /,sinGkritə'zāsHən/ n.

syn·di·cal·ism /'sindəkə,lizəm/ ▶ n. a movement that believes in transferring the ownership and control of industry and business to workers' unions. ■ **syn·di·cal·ist** n. & adj.

syn·di·cate ▶ n. /'sindikit/ **1** a group of people or organizations that combine to promote a common interest. **2** an agency that supplies items to a number of news media at the same time. **3** (**the syndicate**) organized crime.
▶ v. /'sindi,kāt/ **1** publish or broadcast material in a number of media at the same time.
2 control or manage something by a syndicate. ■ **syn·di·ca·tion** /,sindi'kāsHən/ n.

syn·drome /'sin,drōm/ ▶ n. **1** a group of medical symptoms that consistently occur together. **2** a set of opinions or behavior that is typical of a particular group of people.

syn·ec·do·che /si'nekdəkē/ ▶ n. a figure of speech in which a part is made to represent the whole or vice versa, as in *England lost by six wickets* (meaning 'the English cricket team').

syn·er·gy /'sinərjē/ (also **synergism** /-,jizəm/) ▶ n. cooperation of two or more people or things to produce a combined effect that is greater than the sum of their separate effects: *the synergy between artist and record company.* ■ **syn·er·get·ic** /,sinər'jetik/ adj.

syn·od /'sinəd/ ▶ n. an official meeting of the ministers and other members of a Christian Church. ■ **syn·od·al** /'sinədl/ adj. **syn·od·i·cal** /sə'nädikəl/ adj.

syn·o·nym /'sinə,nim/ ▶ n. a word or phrase that means the same as another word or phrase in the same language. ■ **syn·on·y·my** /sə'nänəmē/ n.

syn·on·y·mous /sə'nänəməs/ ▶ adj. **1** (of a word or phrase) having the same meaning as another word or phrase in the same language. **2** closely associated with something: *his name was synonymous with victory.* ■ **syn·on·y·mous·ly** adv.

syn·op·sis /sə'näpsis/ ▶ n. (pl. **synopses** /-,sēz/) a brief summary or outline.

syn·op·tic /sə'näptik/ ▶ adj. **1** relating to a synopsis. **2** (**Synoptic**) referring to the Gospels of Matthew, Mark, and Luke, which describe events from a similar point of view, as contrasted with that of John.

syn·o·vi·al /sə'nōvēəl/ ▶ adj. relating to a type of joint in the body that is enclosed in a flexible membrane containing a lubricating fluid.

syn·tax /'sin,taks/ ▶ n. **1** the arrangement of words and phrases to create well-formed sentences. **2** a set of rules for the formation of sentences. ■ **syn·tac·tic** /sin'taktik/ adj. **syn·tac·ti·cal** /sin'taktikəl/ adj. **syn·tac·ti·cal·ly** /-ik(ə)lē/ adv.

synth /sinTH/ ▶ n. informal a synthesizer. ■ **synth·y** adj.

syn·the·sis /'sinTHəsis/ ▶ n. (pl. **syntheses** /-,sēz/) **1** the combination of parts to form a connected whole. **2** the production of chemical compounds by reaction from simpler materials. ■ **syn·the·sist** n.

syn·the·size /'sinTHi,sīz/ ▶ v. **1** combine things into a connected whole. **2** make something by chemical synthesis. **3** produce sound electronically.

syn·the·siz·er /'sinTHə,sīzər/ ▶ n. an electronic musical instrument that produces sounds by generating and combining signals of different frequencies.

syn·thet·ic /sin'THetik/ ▶ **adj. 1** made by chemical synthesis, especially to imitate a natural product: *synthetic rubber.* **2** not genuine; insincere. ▶ **n.** a synthetic substance. ■ **syn·thet·i·cal·ly** /-ik(ə)lē/ **adv.**

syph·i·lis /'sifəlis/ ▶ **n.** a serious sexually transmitted disease spread by bacteria. ■ **syph·i·lit·ic** /ˌsifə'litik/ **adj. & n.**

syphon▶ n. & v. variant spelling of SIPHON.

Syr·i·an /'si(ə)rēən/ ▶ **n.** a person from Syria. ▶ **adj.** relating to Syria.

sy·ringe /sə'rinj, 'sirinj/ ▶ **n.** a tube with a nozzle and piston for sucking in and forcing out liquid in a thin stream, often one fitted with a hollow needle for injecting drugs or withdrawing bodily fluids. ▶ **v.** (**syringes**, **syringing**, **syringed**) spray liquid into or over something with a syringe.

syr·up /'sirəp, 'sər-/ ▶ **n. 1** a thick sweet liquid made by dissolving sugar in boiling water. **2** a thick sweet liquid containing medicine or used as a drink.

syr·up·y /'sirəpē, 'sər-/ ▶ **adj. 1** thick or sweet, like syrup. **2** excessively sentimental.

sys·tem /'sistəm/ ▶ **n. 1** a set of things working together as a mechanism or network: *the railroad system.* **2** an organized scheme or method by which something is done. **3** a person's body.

4 the state of being well organized. **5** (**the system**) the rules or people that control a country or society, especially when regarded as restrictive or unfair. **6** Computing a group of related hardware units or programs or both. **7** Geology a major range of rock strata that corresponds to a period in time: *the Devonian system.*

sys·tem·at·ic /ˌsistə'matik/ ▶ **adj.** done or acting according to a system; methodical. ■ **sys·tem·at·i·cal·ly** /-ik(ə)lē/ **adv. sys·tem·a·tist** /'sistəməˌtist/ **n.**

sys·tem·at·ics /ˌsistə'matiks/ ▶ **pl.n.** (treated as sing.) the branch of biology that deals with classification and nomenclature; taxonomy.

sys·tem·a·tize /'sistəməˌtīz/ ▶ **v.** arrange things according to an organized system. ■ **sys·tem·a·ti·za·tion** /ˌsistəməti'zāsHən/ **n.**

sys·tem·ic /sə'stemik/ ▶ **adj. 1** relating to a system as a whole. **2** (of an insecticide or fungicide) entering the plant via the roots or shoots and passing through the tissues. ■ **sys·tem·i·cal·ly** /-ik(ə)lē/ **adv.**

sys·tems an·a·lyst /'sistəmz/ ▶ **n.** a person who analyzes a complex process or operation in order to improve its efficiency. ■ **sys·tems a·nal·y·sis n.**

sys·to·le /'sistəlē/ ▶ **n.** the phase of the heartbeat when the heart muscle contracts and pumps blood into the arteries. Often contrasted with DIASTOLE. ■ **sys·tol·ic** /si'stälik/ **adj.**

Tt

T¹ (also **t**) ▶ n. (pl. **Ts** or **T's**) the twentieth letter of the alphabet.
– PHRASES **to a T** informal to perfection; exactly.

T² ▶ abbr. **1** tera- (10¹²). **2** tesla. **3** tablespoon(s); tablespoonful(s).

t ▶ abbr. **1** ton(s). **2** teaspoon(s); teaspoonful(s).

TA ▶ abbr. teaching assistant; a graduate student who assists a college professor.

Ta /tä/ ▶ symbol the chemical element tantalum.

ta /tä/ ▶ exclam. Brit. informal thank you.

tab¹ /tab/ ▶ n. **1** a small flap or strip of material attached to something, used to give information or to hold it, fasten it, etc. **2** informal a tally of items ordered in a bar or restaurant. **3** informal a restaurant or bar bill. **4** a ring on a can that is pulled to open it. ▶ v. (**tabs, tabbing, tabbed**) mark something with a tab.
– PHRASES **keep tabs on someone** informal monitor someone's activities. **pick up the tab** informal pay for something.

tab² ▶ n. short for TABULATOR. ▶ v. (**tabs, tabbing, tabbed**) short for TABULATE.

tab³ ▶ n. informal a tablet, especially one containing an illegal drug.

Ta·bas·co /tə'baskō/ ▶ n. trademark a very hot sauce made from a type of pepper.

tab·bou·leh /tə'bōōlē/ ▶ n. a Middle Eastern salad of cracked wheat mixed with finely chopped tomatoes, onions, parsley, etc.

tab·by /'tabē/ ▶ n. (pl. **tabbies**) a gray or brownish cat with dark stripes.

tab·er·nac·le /'tabər,nakəl/ ▶ n. **1** a place of worship used by some Protestants or Mormons. **2** (in a Roman Catholic church) a box or cabinet in which the bread consecrated for Holy Communion may be placed. **3** (in the Bible) a tent used by the Israelites to house the Ark of the Covenant during the Exodus.

ta·bla /'täblə/ ▶ n. a pair of small hand drums fixed together, used in Indian music.

tab·la·ture /'tabləCHər, -,CHŏŏr/ ▶ n. a form of musical notation indicating fingering rather than the pitch of notes.

ta·ble /'tābəl/ ▶ n. **1** a piece of furniture with a flat top supported by legs, for eating, writing, or working at. **2** a set of facts or figures displayed in rows or columns. **3** (**tables**) multiplication tables. **4** food provided in a restaurant or household: *food includes a lunchtime buffet table.* ▶ v. **1** postpone consideration of: *we'll table this discussion until next week.* **2** Brit. formally present something for discussion at a meeting.
– PHRASES **on the table** available for discussion. **turn the tables** turn a situation of disadvantage to oneself into one of advantage.

tab·leau /,ta'blō/ ▶ n. (pl. **tableaux** or **tableaus** /,ta'blōz/) a group of models or motionless

figures representing a scene from a story or from history.

tab·leau vi·vant /tä'blō vē'vän, -'vänt/ ▶ n. (pl. **tableaux vivants** pronunc. same) a silent and motionless group of people arranged to represent a scene.

ta·ble·cloth /'tābəl,klôTH, -,kläTH/ ▶ n. a cloth spread over a table, especially during meals.

ta·ble d'hôte /,täbəl 'dōt, ,täblə, ,tabəl/ ▶ n. a restaurant menu or meal offered at a fixed price and with limited choices.

ta·ble·land /'tābəl,(l)and/ ▶ n. a broad, high, level region; a plateau.

ta·ble man·ners ▶ pl.n. behavior that is considered polite while eating at a table.

ta·ble salt ▶ n. see SALT.

ta·ble·spoon /'tābəl,spōōn/ ▶ n. **1** a large spoon for serving food. **2** the amount held by a tablespoon, equivalent to 3 teaspoons, 1/2 fluid ounce, or 15 milliliters. ■ **ta·ble·spoon·ful** n.

tab·let /'tablit/ ▶ n. **1** a slab of stone, clay, or wood on which an inscription is written. **2** a writing pad. **3** a pill.

ta·ble ten·nis ▶ n. an indoor game played with small bats and a small hollow ball hit across a table divided by a net.

ta·ble·top /'tābəl,täp/ ▶ n. the horizontal top part of a table.

ta·ble·ware /'tābəl,wer/ ▶ n. dishes, utensils, and glassware used for serving and eating meals.

ta·ble wine ▶ n. wine of moderate quality considered suitable for drinking with a meal.

tab·loid /'tab,loid/ ▶ n. a newspaper having pages half the size of those of a broadsheet, written in a popular style and typically dominated by sensational stories. ■ **tab·loid·i·za·tion** /,tabloidə'zāsHən/ n.

ta·boo /tə'bōō, ta-/ ▶ n. (pl. **taboos**) a social or religious custom placing a ban or restriction on a particular thing or person. ▶ adj. banned or restricted by social custom: *sex was a taboo subject.* ▶ v. (**taboos, tabooing, tabooed**) put a ban or taboo on someone or something.

ta·bor /'tābər/ ▶ n. historical a small drum, especially one played at the same time as a simple pipe.

tab·u·lar /'tabyələr/ ▶ adj. **1** (of data) consisting of or presented in columns or tables. **2** broad and flat, like the top of a table.

ta·bu·la ra·sa /'täbyŏŏlə 'räsə, 'räzə/ ▶ n. **1** an absence of preconceived ideas. **2** a person's mind, especially at birth, regarded as being empty of ideas.

tab·u·late /'tabyə,lāt/ ▶ v. arrange data in columns or tables. ■ **tab·u·la·tion** /,tabyə'lāsHən/ n.

tab·u·la·tor /'tabyəlātər/ ▶ n. a facility in a word-processing program, or a device on a typewriter, for advancing to set positions when producing tables of data.

tach /tak/ ▸ n. informal short for TACHOMETER.

ta·chom·e·ter /ta'kämitər, tə-/ ▸ n. an instrument that measures the working speed of an engine, typically in revolutions per minute.

tach·y·car·di·a /,taki'kärdēə/ ▸ n. an abnormally rapid heart rate.

tac·it /'tasit/ ▸ adj. understood or suggested without being stated: *your silence may be taken to mean tacit agreement.* ■ **tac·it·ly** adv.

tac·i·turn /'tasi,tərn/ ▸ adj. saying little; uncommunicative. ■ **tac·i·tur·ni·ty** /,tasi'tərnitē/ n. **tac·i·turn·ly** adv.

tack¹ /tak/ ▸ n. 1 a course of action: *the board changed tack and recommended that shareholders accept a takeover.* 2 a small broad-headed nail. 3 a thumbtack. 4 a long stitch used to fasten fabrics together temporarily. 5 a sailboat's course relative to the direction of the wind: *the ketch swung to the opposite tack.* ▸ v. 1 fasten or fix something with tacks. 2 (**tack something on**) add something to something that already exists. 3 change the direction of a sailboat so that the wind blows into the sails from the opposite side.

tack² ▸ n. equipment used in horse riding, including the saddle and bridle.

tack·le /'takəl/ ▸ v. 1 make a determined effort to deal with a problem or difficult task: *police launched an initiative to tackle rising crime.* 2 begin to discuss a difficult issue with someone. 3 (in football) seize and stop or throw down an opposing player. 4 (in soccer, rugby, etc.) try to take the ball from or prevent the movement of an opponent. ▸ n. 1 the equipment required for a task or sport. 2 a mechanism consisting of ropes, pulley blocks, and hooks for lifting heavy objects. 3 (in sports) an act of tackling an opponent. 4 the rigging and pulleys used to work a boat's sails. ■ **tack·ler** /'tak(ə)lər/ n.

tack·y¹ /'takē/ ▸ adj. (**tackier, tackiest**) (of glue, paint, etc.) slightly sticky because not fully dry. ■ **tack·i·ness** n.

tack·y² ▸ adj. (**tackier, tackiest**) informal showing poor taste and quality. ■ **tack·i·ness** n.

ta·co /'täkō/ ▸ n. (pl. **tacos**) a Mexican dish consisting of a folded tortilla filled with seasoned meat or beans.

tact /takt/ ▸ n. sensitivity and skill in dealing with others or with difficult issues.

tact·ful /'tak(t)fəl/ ▸ adj. having or showing skill and sensitivity in dealing with others or with difficult issues. ■ **tact·ful·ly** adv. **tact·ful·ness** n.

tac·tic /'taktik/ ▸ n. 1 an action or plan that is intended to achieve a specific result. 2 (**tactics**) the art of directing and organizing the movement of armed forces and equipment during a war. Often contrasted with STRATEGY. ■ **tac·ti·cian** /tak'tisHən/ n.

tac·ti·cal /'taktikəl/ ▸ adj. 1 done or planned to achieve a particular result. 2 (of weapons) for use in direct support of military or naval operations. Often contrasted with STRATEGIC. 3 relating to military tactics. ■ **tac·ti·cal·ly** adv.

tac·tile /'taktl, 'tak,tīl/ ▸ adj. 1 relating to the sense of touch. 2 liking to touch others in a friendly or sympathetic way. ■ **tac·til·i·ty** /tak'tilitē/ n.

tact·less /'taktləs/ ▸ adj. thoughtless and insensitive. ■ **tact·less·ly** adv. **tact·less·ness** n.

tad /tad/ informal ▸ adv. (**a tad**) to a minor extent; rather. ▸ n. a small amount of something.

tad·pole /'tad,pōl/ ▸ n. the larva of an amphibian such as a frog or toad, at the stage when it lives

in water and has gills and a tail.

tae-bo /'tī 'bō/ ▸ n. trademark an exercise system combining elements of aerobics and kick-boxing.

tae kwon do /'tī 'kwän 'dō/ ▸ n. a modern Korean martial art similar to karate.

taf·fe·ta /'tafitə/ ▸ n. a fine shiny silk or similar synthetic fabric.

taf·fy /'tafē/ ▸ n. (pl. **taffies**) 1 a candy similar to toffee, made from sugar or molasses, boiled with butter and pulled until glossy. 2 dated, informal insincere flattery.

tag¹ /tag/ ▸ n. 1 a label used to identify something or to give other information about it. 2 an electronic device attached to someone to monitor their movements. 3 a nickname or description by which someone or something is widely known. 4 a nickname or other identifying mark written as the signature of a graffiti artist. 5 a frequently repeated quotation or phrase. 6 Computing a character or set of characters attached to an item of data in order to identify it. ▸ v. (**tags, tagging, tagged**) 1 attach a tag or label to someone or something. 2 (**tag something on**) add something to the end of something else as an afterthought. 3 (**tag along**) accompany someone without being invited. 4 (of a graffiti artist) write a tag or nickname on a surface.

tag² ▸ n. a children's game in which one player chases the rest, and anyone who is caught then becomes the person doing the chasing.

Ta·ga·log /tə'gäləg, -lôg/ ▸ n. 1 a member of a people from the Philippine Islands. 2 the language of the Tagalogs, the basis of Filipino.

ta·gli·a·tel·le /,tälyə'telē/ ▸ pl.n. pasta in narrow ribbons.

tag line ▸ n. informal a catchphrase, slogan, or punchline.

ta·hi·ni /tə'hēnē/ ▸ n. a Middle Eastern paste or spread made from ground sesame seeds.

Ta·hi·tian /tə'hēsHən/ ▸ n. 1 a person from Tahiti. 2 the language of Tahiti. ▸ adj. relating to Tahiti.

t'ai chi /'tī 'CHē, 'jē/ (also **t'ai chi ch'uan** /'tī ,CHē 'CHwän, jē/) ▸ n. a Chinese martial art and system of exercises, consisting of sequences of very slow controlled movements.

tai·ga /'tīgə/ ▸ n. swampy coniferous forest of high northern latitudes, especially that between the tundra and steppes of Siberia.

tail¹ /tāl/ ▸ n. 1 the part at the rear of an animal that sticks out from the rest of the body. 2 something that resembles an animal's tail in shape or position. 3 the rear part of an aircraft, with the horizontal stabilizer and rudder. 4 the final, more distant, or weaker part: *the tail of a hurricane.* 5 (**tails**) the side of a coin without the image of a head on it. 6 (**tails**) informal a tailcoat, or a man's formal evening suit with such a coat. 7 informal a person secretly following another to observe their movements. ▸ v. 1 informal secretly follow and observe someone. 2 (**tail off/away**) gradually become smaller or weaker. ■ **tail·less** adj.

– PHRASES **on someone's tail** informal following someone closely. **with one's tail between one's legs** informal feeling dejected or humiliated.

USAGE
Do not confuse **tail** with **tale**. Tail means 'the rear or end part of an animal or thing' (*the dog wagged its tail*), whereas **tale** means 'a story' (*a fairy tale*).

tail² ▸ n. Law, chiefly historical limitation of ownership of an estate or title to a person and their direct descendants.

tail·coat /'tāl,kŏt/ ▶ n. a man's formal coat, with a long skirt divided at the back into tails and cut away in front.

tail end ▶ n. the last or rear part of something.

tail fin ▶ n. **1** a fin at the rear of a fish's body. **2** a projecting vertical surface on the tail of an aircraft, providing stability. **3** an upswept projection on each rear corner of a car, popular in the 1950s.

tail·gate /'tāl,gāt/ ▶ n. **1** a hinged flap at the back of a truck. **2** the door at the back of a station wagon or hatchback. ▶ v. informal **1** drive too closely behind another vehicle. **2** eat a meal served from the back of a parked vehicle. ■ **tail·gat·er** n.

tail·light ▶ n. a red light at the rear of a vehicle.

tai·lor /'tālər/ ▶ n. a person whose occupation is making men's clothing for individual customers. ▶ v. **1** make clothes to fit individual customers. **2** make or adapt for a particular purpose or person: *the database has been tailored to meet the needs of the restaurant industry.*

tai·lored /'tālərd/ ▶ adj. (of clothes) smart, fitted, and well cut.

tai·lor·ing /'tāləriNG/ ▶ n. **1** the activity or occupation of a tailor. **2** the style or cut of an item of clothing.

tai·lor-made ▶ adj. **1** made or adapted for a particular purpose or person. **2** (of clothes) made by a tailor for a particular customer.

tail·piece /'tāl,pēs/ ▶ n. **1** the final or end part of something. **2** a part added to the end of a piece of writing. **3** a small decorative design at the foot of a page or the end of a chapter or book.

tail·pipe /'tāl,pīp/ ▶ n. the rear section of the exhaust pipe of a motor vehicle.

tail·spin /'tāl,spin/ ▶ n. a fast revolving motion made by a rapidly descending aircraft.

tail·wind /'tāl,wind/ ▶ n. a wind blowing in the direction that a vehicle or aircraft is traveling in.

taint /tānt/ ▶ v. **1** affect with an undesirable quality: *his reputation was tainted by scandal.* **2** contaminate or pollute something. ▶ n. a trace of an undesirable quality or substance.

Tai·wan·ese /,tīwə'nēz, -wä-, -'nēs/ ▶ n. (pl. same) a person from Taiwan. ▶ adj. relating to Taiwan.

Ta·jik /tä'jik/ (also **Tadzhik**) ▶ n. **1** a member of a mainly Muslim people inhabiting Tajikistan and parts of neighboring countries. **2** a person from the republic of Tajikistan.

take /tāk/ ▶ v. (past **took** /tŏŏk/; past part. **taken** /'tākən/) **1** reach for and hold something. **2** occupy a place or position. **3** carry or bring someone or something with one. **4** remove someone or something from a place. **5** bring into a particular state: *the invasion took Europe to the brink of war.* **6** perform an action or undertake a task. **7** accept or receive someone or something. **8** require or use up: *the journey took four hours in all.* **9** experience or be affected by something. **10** consume something as food, drink, medicine, or drugs. **11** acquire or assume a position, state, or form. **12** act on an opportunity. **13** use something as a route or a means of transport. **14** hold or accommodate: *the hotel takes just twenty guests.* **15** view or deal with in a specified way: *he took it as an insult.* **16** subtract

something from something else. **17** tolerate or endure: *I can't take it any more.* **18** gain possession of something by force. **19** study a subject. **20** submit answers to an exam or test. **21** make a photograph with a camera. ▶ n. **1** a sequence of sound or part of a movie filmed or recorded continuously. **2** a particular version of or approach to something: *his whimsical take on life.* **3** an amount gained or acquired from one source or in one session. ■ **tak·er** n.
– PHRASES **be on the take** informal take bribes. **take after** resemble a parent or ancestor. **take something back** withdraw a statement. **take five** informal have a short break. **take someone in** cheat or deceive someone. **take something in 1** make an item of clothing tighter by altering its seams. **2** include or understand something. **take someone in hand** undertake to control or reform someone. **take something in hand** start dealing with a task. **take it out of** exhaust someone. **take off 1** become airborne. **2** leave hastily. **take someone off** imitate someone. **take something off** remove clothing. **take someone on** engage an employee. **take something on 1** undertake a task. **2** begin to have a particular meaning or quality. **take something out on** relieve one's frustration or anger by mistreating someone. **take over** assume control of or responsibility for something. **take one's time** not hurry. **take to 1** get into the habit of. **2** form a liking or develop an ability for. **3** go to a place to escape danger. **take something up 1** become interested in a pursuit. **2** occupy time, space, or attention. **3** pursue a matter further. **take someone up on** accept an offer or challenge from someone. **take up with** begin to associate with someone.

take·a·way /'tākə,wā/ ▶ n. Brit. takeout.

take·down /'tāk,doun/ ▶ n. **1** a wrestling maneuver in which an opponent is swiftly brought to the mat from a standing position. **2** informal a police raid or arrest. **3** (as adj.) denoting a firearm with the capacity to have the barrel and magazine detached from the stock.

take-home pay ▶ n. the pay received by an employee after tax and insurance have been deducted.

take·off /'tāk,ôf, -,äf/ ▶ n. **1** an act of becoming airborne. **2** informal an act of imitating someone or something.

take·out /'tāk,out/ ▶ n. a meal of prepared food purchased from a restaurant, deli, etc., and eaten elsewhere.

take·o·ver /'tāk,ōvər/ ▶ n. an act of taking control of something such as a company from someone else.

take-up ▶ n. **1** a device for taking up slack or excess: (as adj.) *a take-up reel.* **2** chiefly Brit. the acceptance of something offered: *practices that discourage take-up of legal advice.*

tak·ing /'tākiNG/ ▶ n. (**takings**) the amount of money earned by a business from the sale of goods or services. ▶ adj. dated pleasant and charming.
– PHRASES **for the taking** available to take advantage of.

talc /talk/ ▶ n. **1** talcum powder. **2** a soft mineral that is a form of magnesium silicate.

tal·cum pow·der /'talkəm/ ▶ n. the mineral talc in powdered form used on the skin to make it feel smooth and dry.

tale /tāl/ ▶ n. **1** a fictional or true story. **2** a lie.

ta·leg·gio /tə'lejē-ō/ ▶ n. a soft Italian cheese made from cow's milk.

tal·ent /'talənt/ ▶ n. **1** natural ability or skill. **2** people possessing natural ability or skill. **3** an ancient weight and unit of currency. **4** chiefly Brit. informal people regarded in terms of their sexual attractiveness or availability. ■ **tal·ent·ed** adj. **tal·ent·less** adj.

tal·ent scout ▶ n. a person whose job is searching for talented performers, especially in sports and entertainment.

tal·is·man /'talismən, -iz-/ ▶ n. (pl. **talismans**) an object thought to have magic powers and to bring good luck. ■ **tal·is·man·ic** /,taliz'manik/ adj.

talk /tôk/ ▶ v. **1** speak in order to give information or express ideas or feelings. **2** be able to speak. **3** (**talk something over/through**) discuss something thoroughly. **4** (**talk back**) reply in a defiant or insolent way. **5** (**talk down to**) speak to someone in a way that suggests one feels superior to them. **6** (**talk someone around/round**) persuade someone to accept or agree to something. **7** (**talk someone into/out of**) convince someone to do or not to do something. **8** reveal secret or private information. ▶ n. **1** conversation or discussion. **2** a speech or lecture. **3** (**talks**) formal discussions or negotiations. **4** rumor, gossip, or speculation: *there's talk of a conspiracy.* ■ **talk·er** n. – PHRASES **you should talk** informal used to tell someone that the criticism they are making applies equally well to them. **now you're talking** informal expressing enthusiastic agreement or approval. **talk the talk** informal speak in a way intended to convince or impress someone.

talk·a·tive /'tôkətiv/ ▶ adj. fond of talking. ■ **talk·a·tive·ly** adv. **talk·a·tive·ness** n.

talk·ie /'tôkē/ ▶ n. informal a movie with a soundtrack, as distinct from a silent movie.

talk·ing book ▶ n. a recorded reading of a book.

talk·ing head ▶ n. informal a commentator or reporter on television who speaks to the camera and is viewed in closeup.

talk·ing point ▶ n. a topic that causes discussion or argument.

talk·ing-to ▶ n. informal a sharp reprimand.

talk ra·di·o ▶ n. a type of radio program in which topical issues are discussed by the host and by listeners who phone in.

talk show ▶ n. a television or radio program in which celebrities or other guests talk informally to a host.

talk·time /'tôk,tīm/ ▶ n. the time during which a cell phone is in use to handle calls, especially as a measure of the duration of the battery.

tall /tôl/ ▶ adj. **1** of great or more than average height. **2** measuring a specified distance from top to bottom. ■ **tall·ish** adj. **tall·ness** n. – PHRASES **a tall order** an unreasonable or difficult demand. **a tall story** (or **tale**) an account that is difficult to believe and seems unlikely to be true.

tall·boy /'tôl,boi/ ▶ n. a tall chest of drawers in two sections, one standing on the other.

tal·low /'talō/ ▶ n. a hard substance made from animal fat, used (especially in the past) in making candles and soap. ■ **tal·low·y** adj.

tall ship ▶ n. a sailing ship with a high mast or masts.

tal·ly /'talē/ ▶ n. (pl. **tallies**) **1** a current score or amount. **2** a record of a score or amount. **3** (also **tally stick**) historical a piece of wood marked with notches as a record of the items in an account. ▶ v. (**tallies, tallying, tallied**) **1** agree or correspond: *this account does not tally with accounts from local people.* **2** calculate the total number of something.

tal·ly·ho ▶ exclam. a huntsman's cry to the hounds on sighting a fox.

Tal·mud /'täl,mŏŏd, 'talməd/ ▶ n. a collection of ancient writings on Jewish civil and ceremonial law and legend. ■ **Tal·mud·ic** /tal'm(y)ŏŏdik, -'mŏŏdik/ adj. **Tal·mud·ist** /'tälmŏŏdist, 'talməd-/ n.

tal·on /'talən/ ▶ n. a claw of a bird of prey. ■ **tal·oned** adj.

ta·lus¹ /'täləs/ ▶ n. (pl. **tali** /'tālī/) the bone in the ankle that forms a movable joint with the shinbone.

talus² ▶ n. (pl. **taluses**) a sloping mass of rock fragments at the foot of a cliff.

tam /tam/ ▶ n. a tam-o'-shanter.

ta·ma·le /tə'mälē/ ▶ n. a Mexican dish of seasoned meat wrapped in cornmeal dough and steamed or baked in corn husks.

tam·a·rack /'tamə,rak/ ▶ n. a slender North American larch.

ta·ma·ril·lo /,tamə'rilō, -'rē-ō/ ▶ n. (pl. **tamarillos**) the red egg-shaped fruit of a tropical South American plant.

tam·a·rin /'tamərin, -,ran/ ▶ n. a small monkey native to forests in South America.

tam·a·rind /'tamə,rind/ ▶ n. sticky brown acidic pulp from the pod of a tropical African tree, used in Asian cooking.

tam·a·risk /'tamə,risk/ ▶ n. a shrub or small tree with tiny scalelike leaves on slender branches.

tam·bour /'tam,bŏŏr/ ▶ n. **1** historical a small drum. **2** a circular frame for holding fabric taut while it is being embroidered.

tam·bou·rine /,tambə'rēn/ ▶ n. a percussion instrument resembling a shallow drum with metal disks around the edge, played by being shaken or hit with the hand.

tame /tām/ ▶ adj. **1** (of an animal) not dangerous or frightened of people. **2** not exciting or adventurous: *Saturday night TV is a pretty tame affair.* **3** informal (of a person) willing to cooperate. ▶ v. **1** make an animal tame. **2** control or make less powerful: *the battle to tame inflation.* ■ **tame·ly** adv. **tame·ness** n. **tam·er** n.

Tam·il /'taməl/ ▶ n. **1** a member of a people living in parts of South India and Sri Lanka. **2** the language of the Tamils.

tam-o'-shan·ter /'tam ə ,sнantər/ ▶ n. a round Scottish cap with a pompom in the center.

ta·mox·i·fen /tə'mäksəfən/ ▶ n. a synthetic drug used to treat breast cancer and infertility in women.

tamp /tamp/ ▶ v. firmly ram or pack a substance down or into something.

tam·per /'tampər/ ▶ v. (**tamper with**) interfere with something without permission or so as to cause damage. ■ **tam·per·er** n.

tam·pon /'tam,pän/ ▶ n. a plug of soft material put into the vagina to absorb blood during a woman's period.

tan¹ /tan/ ▶ n. **1** a golden-brown shade of skin

developed by pale-skinned people after being in the sun. **2** a yellowish-brown color. ▶ v. (**tans, tanning, tanned**) **1** become golden brown after being in the sun. **2** convert animal skin into leather. **3** informal, dated beat someone as a punishment. ■ **tan·ner** n.

tan² ▶ abbr. tangent.

tan·a·ger /'tanəjər/ ▶ n. a brightly colored American songbird.

tan·dem /'tandəm/ ▶ n. a bicycle with seats and pedals for two riders, one behind the other.
– PHRASES **in tandem** together or at the same time.

tan·door /tan'do͝or, tän-/ ▶ n. a clay oven of a type used originally in northern India and Pakistan.

tan·door·i /tan'do͝orē, tän-/ ▶ adj. (of Indian food) cooked in a tandoor.

tang /taNG/ ▶ n. **1** a strong taste, flavor, or smell. **2** the projection on the blade of a knife or other tool by which the blade is held firmly in the handle.

tan·gent /'tanjənt/ ▶ n. **1** a straight line or plane that touches a curve or curved surface at a point, but if extended does not cross it at that point. **2** Mathematics the ratio of the sides (other than the hypotenuse) opposite and adjacent to an angle in a right triangle. **3** a completely different line of thought or action: *her mind went off on a tangent.* ■ **tan·gen·cy** n.

tan·gen·tial /tan'jenCHəl/ ▶ adj. **1** only slightly connected or relevant: *such concoctions have only a tangential relationship with food as eaten in India.* **2** relating to or along a tangent. ■ **tan·gen·tial·ly** adv.

tan·ge·rine /ˌtanjə'rēn/ ▶ n. **1** a small citrus fruit with a loose orange-red skin. **2** a deep orange-red color.

tan·gi·ble /'tanjəbəl/ ▶ adj. **1** able to be perceived by touch. **2** clear and definite; real: *I was seeing tangible benefits from working out.* ■ **tan·gi·bil·i·ty** /ˌtanjə'bilitē/ n. **tan·gi·bly** /-blē/ adv.

tan·gle /'taNGgəl/ ▶ v. **1** twist strands together into a confused mass. **2** (**tangle with**) informal become involved in a conflict with. ▶ n. **1** a confused mass of something twisted together. **2** a confused or complicated state. ■ **tan·gly** adj.

tan·go /'taNGgō/ ▶ n. (pl. **tangos**) **1** a Latin American ballroom dance characterized by marked rhythms and postures and abrupt pauses. **2** a piece of music in the style of a tango. ▶ v. (**tangoes, tangoing, tangoed**) dance the tango.

tang·y /'taNGē/ ▶ adj. (**tangier, tangiest**) having a strong, sharp flavor or smell. ■ **tang·i·ness** n.

tank /taNGk/ ▶ n. **1** a large container or storage chamber for holding liquid or gas. **2** the container holding the fuel supply in a motor vehicle. **3** a container with transparent sides in which to keep fish. **4** a heavy armored fighting vehicle carrying guns and moving on a continuous metal track. ▶ v. (**be/get tanked up**) informal drink heavily or become drunk. ■ **tank·ful** /-ˌfo͝ol/ n.

tan·kard /'taNGkərd/ ▶ n. a tall beer mug with a handle and sometimes a hinged lid.

tank·er /'taNGkər/ ▶ n. a ship, road vehicle, or aircraft for carrying liquids in bulk.

tank top ▶ n. a close-fitting sleeveless top.

tan·ner·y /'tanərē/ ▶ n. (pl. **tanneries**) a place where animal hides are tanned.

tan·nic ac·id /'tanik/ ▶ n. another term for TANNIN.

tan·nin /'tanin/ ▶ n. a bitter yellowish or brownish substance present in tea, grapes, and the bark of some trees. ■ **tan·nic** adj.

tan·ning bed ▶ n. a piece of equipment for acquiring an artificial tan, consisting of two banks of sunlamps between which a person lies or stands.

tan·sy /'tanzē/ ▶ n. a plant with yellow flat-topped buttonlike flowerheads.

tan·ta·lize /'tantlˌīz/ ▶ v. torment or tease someone by showing or promising them something that they cannot have. ■ **tan·ta·li·za·tion** /ˌtantli'zāsHən/ n. **tan·ta·liz·ing** adj.

tan·ta·lum /'tantl-əm/ ▶ n. a hard silver-gray metallic chemical element.

tan·ta·mount /'tantəˌmount/ ▶ adj. (**tantamount to**) equivalent in seriousness to: *the resignations were tantamount to an admission of guilt.*

tan·tra /'tantrə, 'tan-/ ▶ n. **1** a Hindu or Buddhist written work dealing with mystical or magical practices. **2** the fact of following the principles of these works, involving mantras, meditation, yoga, and ritual. ■ **tan·tric** /-trik/ adj. **tan·trism** /-ˌtrizəm/ n.

tan·trum /'tantrəm/ ▶ n. an uncontrolled outburst of anger and frustration.

Tan·za·ni·an /ˌtanzə'nēən/ ▶ n. a person from Tanzania, a country in East Africa. ▶ adj. relating to Tanzania.

Taoi·seach /'tēsHək, -sHəkH, 'THē-/ ▶ n. the prime minister of the Republic of Ireland.

Tao·ism /'douˌizəm, 'tou-/ ▶ n. a Chinese philosophy based on the belief that everything in the universe is connected and that a person should try to balance the opposing principles of yin and yang to reach a calm acceptance of life. ■ **Tao·ist** n. & adj.

tap¹ /tap/ ▶ n. **1** a device for controlling a flow of liquid or gas from a pipe or container. **2** a device connected to a telephone for listening secretly to conversations. ▶ v. (**taps, tapping, tapped**) **1** make use of a resource or supply: *clients seeking to tap the agency's resources of expertise.* **2** connect a device to a telephone in order to listen to conversations secretly. **3** draw liquid through the tap or spout of a cask, barrel, etc. **4** draw sap from a tree by cutting into it. **5** informal obtain money or information from someone. ■ **tap·pa·ble** adj.
– PHRASES **on tap** informal freely available whenever needed.

tap² ▶ v. (**taps, tapping, tapped**) **1** hit someone or something with a quick, light blow or blows. **2** strike something lightly and repeatedly against something else. ▶ n. **1** a quick, light blow. **2** a piece of metal attached to the toe and heel of a tap dancer's shoe. **3** tap dancing. ■ **tap·per** n.

ta·pas /'täpəs/ ▶ pl.n. small Spanish savory dishes, typically served with drinks at a bar.

tap dance ▶ n. a dance performed wearing shoes fitted with metal taps, characterized by rhythmical tapping of the toes and heels. ■ **tap danc·er** n. **tap-dancing** n.

tape /tāp/ ▶ n. **1** light, flexible material in a narrow strip, used to hold, fasten, or mark off something. **2** (also **adhesive tape**) a strip of paper or plastic coated with adhesive, used to stick things together. **3** a kind of tape with magnetic properties, used for recording sound, pictures, or computer data. **4** a cassette or reel containing magnetic tape. ▶v. **1** record sound or pictures on magnetic tape. **2** fasten, attach, or mark off something with tape.

tape deck ▶n. a piece of equipment for playing audiotapes, especially as part of a stereo system.

tape meas·ure ▶n. a strip of tape marked at regular intervals for measuring something.

ta·pe·nade /ˌtäpəˈnäd/ ▶n. a Provençal savory paste or dip, made from black olives, capers, and anchovies.

ta·per /ˈtāpər/ ▶v. **1** reduce in thickness toward one end. **2** (**taper off**) gradually lessen. ▶n. **1** a long, thin candle. **2** a wick coated with wax, or a long piece of paper or wood, used for lighting a lamp, candle, etc.

tape re·cord·er ▶n. a device for recording sounds on magnetic tape and then reproducing them. ■ **tape-re·cord** v. **tape re·cord·ing** n.

tap·es·try /ˈtapistrē/ ▶n. (pl. **tapestries**) a piece of thick fabric with pictures or designs woven or embroidered on it. ■ **tap·es·tried** adj.

tape·worm /ˈtāpˌwərm/ ▶n. a flatworm with a long ribbonlike body, the adult of which lives as a parasite in the intestines.

tap·i·o·ca /ˌtapēˈōkə/ ▶n. a starchy substance in the form of hard white grains, obtained from cassava and used for puddings and other dishes.

ta·pir /ˈtāpər/ ▶n. a piglike mammal with a long flexible snout, native to tropical America and Malaysia.

tap·pet /ˈtapit/ ▶n. a moving part in a machine that transmits motion in a straight line between a cam and another part.

tap·room /ˈtapˌro͞om, -ˌro͝om/ ▶n. a room in which beer is available on tap; a bar in a hotel or inn.

tap·root /ˈtapˌro͞ot, -ˌro͝ot/ ▶n. a tapering root growing straight downward and forming the center from which smaller roots spring.

tap wa·ter ▶n. water from a piped supply; water from a faucet.

tar[1] /tär/ ▶n. **1** a dark, thick flammable liquid distilled from wood or coal, used in road-making and for preserving timber. **2** a similar substance formed by burning tobacco or other material. ▶v. (**tars, tarring, tarred**) cover something with tar.
– PHRASES **tar and feather someone** smear someone with tar and then cover them with feathers as a punishment. **tar people with the same brush** consider certain people to have the same faults.

tar[2] ▶n. informal, dated a sailor.

ta·ra·ma·sa·la·ta (also **taramosalata**) /ˌtärəməsəˈlätə/ ▶n. a dip made from the roe of cod or other fish, olive oil, and seasoning.

tar·an·tel·la /ˌtarənˈtelə/ ▶n. a rapid whirling dance originating in southern Italy.

ta·ran·tu·la /təˈranCHələ/ ▶n. **1** a very large hairy spider found chiefly in tropical and subtropical America. **2** a large black spider of southern Europe.

tar·boosh /tärˈbo͞osh/ ▶n. a hat similar to a fez worn by Muslim men in some countries.

tar·dy /ˈtärdē/ ▶adj. (**tardier, tardiest**) **1** late in happening. **2** slow to act or respond: *the law may be tardy in reacting to changing attitudes.* ■ **tar·di·ly** adv. **tar·di·ness** n.

tare[1] /te(ə)r/ ▶n. **1** a vetch (plant). **2** (in the Bible) a type of weed.

tare[2] ▶n. **1** the weight of a vehicle without its fuel or load. **2** an allowance made for the weight of the packaging in determining the net weight of goods.

tar·get /ˈtärgit/ ▶n. **1** a person, object, or place selected as the aim of an attack. **2** a board marked with a series of circles sharing the same center, aimed at in archery or shooting. **3** a goal or result that one aims to achieve: *a sales target.* ▶v. (**targets, targeting, targeted**) **1** select someone or something as an object of attention or attack. **2** aim or direct something. ■ **tar·get·a·ble** adj.
– PHRASES **on** (or **off**) **target** succeeding (or not succeeding) in hitting or achieving the thing aimed at.

tar·iff /ˈtarif/ ▶n. **1** a tax or duty to be paid on a particular class of imports or exports. **2** a list of the fixed prices charged by a business such as a hotel or restaurant. **3** Law a scale of sentences and damages for crimes and injuries of varying degrees of seriousness. ▶v. fix the price of something according to a tariff.

tar·mac /ˈtärˌmak/ ▶n. **1** trademark material used for surfacing roads or other outdoor areas, consisting of broken stone mixed with tar. **2** (**the tarmac**) a runway or other area surfaced with tarmac. ▶v. (**tarmacs, tarmacking, tarmacked**) surface an area with tarmac.

tarn /tärn/ ▶n. a small mountain lake.

tar·na·tion /tärˈnāsHən/ ▶n. & exclam. dated used as a euphemism for "damnation."

tar·nish /ˈtärnisH/ ▶v. **1** (of metal) become dull as a result of exposure to air or moisture. **2** cause harm or a loss of respect to: *they will make up negative stories to tarnish my image.* ▶n. a film or stain formed on an exposed surface of a mineral or metal. ■ **tar·nish·a·ble** adj.

ta·ro /ˈtärō, ˈte(ə)rō/ ▶n. the starchy corm of a tropical Asian plant, eaten as a vegetable.

ta·rot /ˈtärō, ˈte(ə)rō, təˈrō/ ▶n. a set of special playing cards used for fortune-telling.

tarp /tärp/ ▶n. informal a tarpaulin sheet or cover.

tar·pau·lin /tärˈpôlən, ˈtärpə-/ ▶n. **1** heavy-duty waterproof cloth. **2** a sheet of tarpaulin used as a covering.

tar·pon /ˈtärpən/ ▶n. a large tropical sea fish resembling a herring in appearance.

tar·ra·gon /ˈtarəˌgän, -gən/ ▶n. a plant with narrow strong-tasting leaves, used as an herb in cooking.

tar·ry[1] /ˈtärē/ ▶adj. relating to or covered with tar. ■ **tar·ri·ness** n.

tar·ry[2] /ˈtarē/ ▶v. (**tarries, tarrying, tarried**) literary stay longer than intended.

tar·sal /ˈtärsəl/ ▶adj. relating to the tarsus. ▶n. a bone of the tarsus.

tar·si·er /ˈtärsēər/ ▶n. a small tree-dwelling primate (mammal) with very large eyes, native to the islands of SE Asia.

tar·sus /ˈtärsəs/ ▶n. (pl. **tarsi** /ˈtärsī, -sē/) the group of small bones in the ankle and upper foot.

tart[1] /tärt/ ▶n. an open pastry case containing a sweet or savory filling. ■ **tart·let** /-lit/ n.

tart[2] informal ▶n. **1** derogatory a woman who has many sexual partners. **2** a prostitute. ▶v. informal, chiefly Brit. **1** (**tart oneself up**) make oneself look attractive with clothes or makeup. **2** (**tart something up**) improve the appearance of something. ■ **tart·y** adj. (**tartier, tartiest**).

tart[3] ► adj. **1** sharp or acid in taste. **2** (of a remark or tone of voice) sharp or sarcastic. ■ **tart·ly** adv. **tart·ness** n.

tar·tan /'tärtn/ ► n. **1** a pattern of colored checks and intersecting lines, especially one associated with a particular Scottish clan. **2** a woolen cloth with a tartan pattern.

Tar·tar /'tärtər/ ► n. **1** historical a member of a group of central Asian peoples who conquered much of Asia and eastern Europe in the early 13th century. **2** (**tartar**) a person who is fierce or difficult to deal with.

tar·tar /'tärtər/ ► n. **1** a hard deposit that forms on the teeth and contributes to their decay. **2** a deposit of impure cream of tartar formed during the fermentation of wine.

tar·tare /tär'tär, 'tärtər/ ► adj. (of fish or meat) served raw, seasoned and shaped into small cakes: *steak tartare.*

tar·tar·ic ac·id /tär'tarik/ ► n. an organic acid found especially in unripe grapes and used in baking powders and as a food additive.

tar·tar sauce (also **tartare sauce**) ► n. mayonnaise mixed with chopped onions, pickles, and capers, typically eaten with fish.

tar·tra·zine /'tärtrə,zēn, -zin/ ► n. a bright yellow synthetic dye made from tartaric acid and used to color food, drugs, and cosmetics.

Tar·zan /'tärzan, -zən/ ► n. a very strong and agile man.

task /task/ ► n. a piece of work to be done.
– PHRASES **take someone to task** reprimand or criticize someone.

task force ► n. **1** an armed force organized for a special operation. **2** a group of people specially organized for a task.

task·mas·ter /'task,mastər/ ► n. (fem. **taskmistress**) a person who makes someone work very hard.

Tas·ma·ni·an dev·il /taz'mānēən, -'mānyən/ ► n. a heavily built aggressive marsupial with a large head, powerful jaws, and mainly black fur, found only on the Australian island of Tasmania.

tas·sel /'tasəl/ ► n. **1** a tuft of hanging threads, knotted together at one end and used for decoration in soft furnishing and clothing. **2** the tufted head of some plants. ■ **tas·seled** adj.

taste /tāst/ ► n. **1** the sensation of flavor perceived in the mouth on contact with a substance. **2** the sense by which taste is perceived. **3** a small amount of food or drink taken as a sample. **4** a brief experience of something: *it was his first taste of artistic success.* **5** a person's liking for something. **6** the ability to judge what is of good quality or of a high artistic standard. **7** (**taste for**) a liking for or interest in something. **8** (often **in good** (or **bad**) **taste**) the quality of being (or not being) acceptable: *a joke in bad taste.* ► v. **1** perceive the flavor of something. **2** have a specified flavor. **3** test the flavor of something by eating or drinking a small amount of it. **4** have a brief experience of: *the team has not yet tasted victory.*
– PHRASES **a bad** (or **bitter**) **taste in someone's mouth** a feeling of distress or disgust following an experience. **to taste** according to one's personal liking.

taste bud ► n. any of the clusters of nerve endings on the tongue and in the lining of the mouth that provide the sense of taste.

taste·ful /'tāstfəl/ ► adj. showing good judgment as to quality, appearance, or appropriate behavior. ■ **taste·ful·ly** adv. **taste·ful·ness** n.

taste·less /'tāstlis/ ► adj. **1** lacking flavor. **2** lacking in judgment as to quality, appearance, or appropriate behavior. ■ **taste·less·ly** adv. **taste·less·ness** n.

tast·er /'tāstər/ ► n. a person who tests food or drink by tasting it.

-tastic ► comb.form informal forming adjectives referring to someone or something that is excellent in a particular respect: *poptastic.*

tast·y /'tāstē/ ► adj. (**tastier, tastiest**) **1** (of food) having a pleasant, distinct flavor. **2** informal, chiefly Brit. attractive or appealing. ■ **tast·i·ly** adv. **tast·i·ness** n.

ta·ta·mi /tə'tämē/ ► n. (pl. same or **tatamis**) a rush-covered straw mat forming a traditional Japanese floor covering.

Ta·tar /'tätər/ ► n. **1** a member of a Turkic people living in Tatarstan and other parts of Russia and Ukraine. **2** the Turkic language of this people.

ta·ter /'tātər/ ► n. informal a potato.

tat·tered /'tatərd/ ► adj. **1** old and torn. **2** ruined; in tatters.

tat·ters /'tatərz/ ► pl.n. irregularly torn pieces of cloth, paper, etc.
– PHRASES **in tatters** destroyed; ruined.

tat·ting /'tatiNG/ ► n. **1** a kind of knotted lace made by hand with a small shuttle. **2** the process of making such lace.

tat·tle /'tatl/ ► n. gossip; casual talk. ► v. gossip about someone or something. ■ **tat·tler** n.

tat·tle·tale /'tatl,tāl/ ► n. a person who reports other people's wrongdoings or reveals their secrets.

tat·too[1] /ta'too/ ► n. (pl. **tattoos**) a permanent design made on the skin by making small holes in it with a needle and filling them with colored ink. ► v. (**tattoos, tattooing, tattooed**) mark a person's skin in this way. ■ **tat·too·er** n. **tat·too·ist** n.

tat·too[2] ► n. (pl. **tattoos**) **1** an evening drum or bugle signal recalling soldiers to their quarters. **2** a rhythmic tapping or drumming.

tat·ty /'tatē/ ► adj. (**tattier, tattiest**) informal worn and shabby. ■ **tat·ti·ly** adv. **tat·ti·ness** n.

taught /tôt/ ► past and past participle of TEACH.

taunt /tônt/ ► n. a remark made in order to anger, upset, or provoke someone. ► v. provoke or upset someone with taunts. ■ **taunt·er** n. **taunt·ing** adj. **taunt·ing·ly** adv.

taupe /tōp/ ► n. a gray color tinged with brown.

Tau·rus /'tôrəs/ ► n. **1** a constellation and the second sign of the zodiac (the Bull), which the sun enters about April 21. **2** (**a Taurus**) a person born when the sun is in this sign. ■ **Tau·re·an** /'tôrēən, tô'rēən/ n. & adj.

taut /tôt/ ► adj. **1** stretched or pulled tight. **2** (of muscles or nerves) tense. **3** (of writing, music, etc.) concise and controlled. ■ **taut·en** v. **taut·ly** adv. **taut·ness** n.

tau·tog /tô'tôg, tô'täg/ ► n. a grayish-olive edible wrasse found off the Atlantic coast of North America.

tau·tol·o·gy /tô'täləjē/ ► n. (pl. **tautologies**) the saying of the same thing over again in different words, considered as a fault of style (e.g., *they arrived one after the other in succession*). ■ **tau·to·log·i·cal** /,tôtl'äjikəl/

adj. **tau·to·log·i·cal·ly** /ˌtôtl'äjik(ə)lē/ adv.
tau·tol·o·gist /-jist/ n. **tau·tol·o·gize** /-ˌjīz/ v.
tau·tol·o·gous /-gəs/ adj.

tav·ern /'tavərn/ ▸ n. a bar, especially one that sells food.

ta·ver·na /tə'vərnə/ ▸ n. a small Greek restaurant.

taw·dry /'tôdrē/ ▸ adj. (**tawdrier, tawdriest**)
1 showy but cheap and of poor quality. **2** sleazy or unpleasant: *the tawdry business of politics.*
■ **taw·dri·ly** adv. **taw·dri·ness** n.

taw·ny /'tônē/ ▸ adj. (**tawnier, tawniest**)
orange-brown or yellowish-brown in color.
■ **taw·ni·ness** n.

tax /taks/ ▸ n. money that must be paid to the government. ▸ v. **1** put a tax on something, or make someone pay a tax. **2** pay tax on a vehicle. **3** make heavy demands on: *the ordeal would tax her strength.* **4** accuse someone of wrongdoing.
■ **tax·a·ble** adj.

tax·a /'taksə/ ▸ plural form of TAXON.

tax·a·tion /tak'sāsHən/ ▸ n. **1** the imposing of tax on someone or something. **2** money paid as tax.

tax a·void·ance ▸ n. the arrangement of one's financial affairs so as to pay only the minimum of tax that is legally required.

tax break ▸ n. informal a tax reduction or advantage allowed by the government.

tax-de·duct·i·ble ▸ adj. permitted to be deducted from income before the amount of tax to be paid is calculated.

tax e·va·sion ▸ n. the illegal nonpayment or underpayment of tax.

tax-ex·empt ▸ adj. not liable to tax. ■ **tax ex·emp·tion** n.

tax ha·ven ▸ n. a country or independent area where taxes are low.

tax·i /'taksē/ ▸ n. (pl. **taxis**) a motor vehicle licensed to carry passengers to the place of their choice in return for payment of a fare.
▸ v. (**taxies, taxiing** or **taxying, taxied**) (of an aircraft) move slowly along the ground before takeoff or after landing.

tax·i·cab /'taksēˌkab/ ▸ n. a taxi.

tax·i·der·my /'taksəˌdərmē/ ▸ n. the art of preparing, stuffing, and mounting the skins of animals so that they appear lifelike.
■ **tax·i·der·mic** /ˌtaksə'dərmik/ adj. **tax·i·der·mist** /'taksəˌdərmist/ n.

tax·i·me·ter /'taksēˌmētər/ ▸ n. a device used in taxis that automatically records the distance traveled and the fare to be paid.

tax·ing /'taksiNG/ ▸ adj. physically or mentally demanding.

tax·i stand (Brit. **taxi rank**) ▸ n. a place where taxis park while waiting to be hired.

tax·i·way /'taksēˌwā/ ▸ n. a route along which an aircraft taxies when moving to or from a runway.

tax·man /'taksˌman/ ▸ n. (pl. **taxmen**) informal, chiefly Brit. an inspector or collector of taxes.

tax·on /'taksän/ ▸ n. (pl. **taxa** /'taksə/) Biology a taxonomic group of any rank, such as a species, family, or class.

tax·on·o·my /tak'sänəmē/ ▸ n. **1** the branch of science concerned with the classification of things, especially plants and animals.
2 a particular scheme of classification.
■ **tax·o·nom·ic** /ˌtaksə'nämik/ adj. **tax·on·o·mist**

/-mist/ n.

tax·pay·er /'taksˌpāər/ ▸ n. a person who pays taxes.

tax re·turn ▸ n. a form on which a taxpayer makes a statement of their income and personal circumstances, used to assess how much tax they should pay.

tax shel·ter ▸ n. a financial arrangement made to avoid or minimize taxes.

tax year ▸ n. a period of twelve months used for calculating taxes.

TB ▸ abbr. tubercle bacillus; tuberculosis.

Tb ▸ symbol the chemical element terbium.

TBA ▸ abbr. to be announced (or arranged).

T-bar ▸ n. **1** a beam or bar shaped like the letter T. **2** (also **T-bar lift**) a type of ski lift in the form of a series of inverted T-shaped bars for towing two skiers at a time uphill.

T-bone ▸ n. a large choice piece of loin steak containing a T-shaped bone.

tbsp. (also **Tbsp**) (pl. same or **tbsps**)
▸ abbr. tablespoonful.

Tc ▸ symbol the chemical element technetium.

T-cell ▸ n. Physiology a lymphocyte of a type produced or processed by the thymus gland and actively participating in the immune response.

TCP/IP ▸ abbr. trademark transmission control protocol/Internet protocol, used to govern the connection of computer systems to the Internet.

TD ▸ abbr. **1** Football touchdown. **2** technical drawing. **3** Treasury Department.

Te ▸ symbol the chemical element tellurium.

tea /tē/ ▸ n. **1** a hot drink made by infusing the dried, crushed leaves of an evergreen Asian shrub (the tea plant) in boiling water. **2** the dried leaves used to make tea. **3** a drink made from the leaves, fruits, or flowers of other plants. **4** chiefly Brit. a light afternoon meal consisting of sandwiches, cakes, etc., with tea to drink.

tea bag ▸ n. a small porous bag containing tea leaves, onto which boiling water is poured to make tea.

teach /tēcH/ ▸ v. (past and past part. **taught**)
1 give information about a particular subject to a class or student. **2** show someone how to do something. **3** make someone realize or understand something: *the experience taught me the real value of money.* ■ **teach·a·ble** adj. **teach·ing** n.

teach·er /'tēcHər/ ▸ n. a person who teaches in a school. ■ **teach·er·ly** adj.

tea co·zy ▸ n. a thick or padded cover placed over a teapot to keep the tea hot.

tea·cup /'tēˌkəp/ ▸ n. a cup from which tea is drunk.

teak /tēk/ ▸ n. hard wood used in shipbuilding and for making furniture, obtained from a tree native to India and SE Asia.

teal /tēl/ ▸ n. (pl. same or **teals**) **1** a small freshwater duck, typically with a bright blue-green patch on the wing plumage. **2** (also **teal blue**) a dark greenish-blue color.

team /tēm/ ▸ n. **1** a group of players forming one side in a competitive game or sport. **2** two or more people working together. **3** two or more horses harnessed together to pull a vehicle.
▸ v. **1** (**team up**) join with another person or group to do or achieve something. **2** (**team something with**) wear an item of clothing with

another: *a pinstripe suit teamed with a white shirt.*

> **USAGE**
> Do not confuse **team** with **teem**. Team means 'a group of people playing or working together' or 'join with another person or group to achieve something' (*she teamed up with other singers to form the group*), while **teem** means 'be full of something' (*every garden is teeming with wildlife*) or 'pour down' (*rain teemed down all morning*).

team·mate /'tē(m),māt/ ▶ n. a fellow member of a team.

team play·er ▶ n. a person who plays or works well as a member of a team.

team spir·it ▶ n. feelings of trust and cooperation among the members of a team.

team·ster /'tēmstər/ ▶ n. **1** a truck driver. **2** a member of the International Brother of Teamsters (a major US labor union). **3** a driver of a team of animals.

team·work /'tēm,wərk/ ▶ n. the effective action of a team of people working together.

tea·pot /'tē,pät/ ▶ n. a pot with a handle, spout, and lid, in which tea is prepared.

tear[1] /te(ə)r/ ▶ v. (past **tore** /tôr/; past part. **torn** /tôrn/) **1** (often **tear something up**) pull something apart or into pieces: *I tore up the letter.* **2** rip a hole or split in something. **3** remove something by pulling it roughly or forcefully: *he tore a page from his notebook.* **4** damage a muscle or ligament by overstretching it. **5** (**tear something down**) demolish or destroy something. **6** (**tear something apart**) destroy good relations between people. **7** (**tear oneself away**) leave despite a strong desire to stay. **8** (**be torn**) be unable to choose between two options. **9** informal move very quickly and in a reckless or excited way. **10** (**tear into**) attack someone verbally. ▶ n. a hole or split caused by tearing. ■ **tear·a·ble** adj.

tear[2] /ti(ə)r/ ▶ n. a drop of clear salty liquid produced by glands in a person's eye when they are crying or when the eye is irritated. ■ **tear·y** adj.
– PHRASES **in tears** crying.

tear·drop /'ti(ə)r,dräp/ ▶ n. a single tear. ▶ adj. shaped like a tear.

tear duct /ti(ə)r/ ▶ n. a passage through which tears pass from the glands that produce them to the eye, or from the eye to the nose.

tear·ful /'ti(ə)rfəl/ ▶ adj. **1** crying or about to cry. **2** causing tears; sad: *a tearful farewell.* ■ **tear·ful·ly** adv. **tear·ful·ness** n.

tear gas /ti(ə)r/ ▶ n. gas that causes severe irritation to the eyes, used in warfare and riot control.

tear·jerk·er /'ti(ə)r,jərkər/ ▶ n. informal a story or movie intended to arouse feelings of sadness in an audience.

tea·room ▶ n. a small restaurant or cafe where tea and other light refreshments are served.

tea rose ▶ n. a garden rose having a delicate scent resembling that of tea.

tease /tēz/ ▶ v. **1** make fun of someone in a playful way or in order to annoy or embarrass them. **2** tempt someone sexually, without intending to have sex with them. **3** (**tease something out**) find out something by searching through a mass of information. **4** gently pull or comb tangled wool, hair, etc., into separate strands. **5** comb hair in the reverse direction of its growth to make it look fuller. ▶ n. informal **1** a person who teases. **2** an act of teasing someone.

tea·sel /'tēzəl/ (also **teazle** or **teazel**) ▶ n. a tall prickly plant with spiny purple flowerheads.

teas·er /'tēzər/ ▶ n. informal a tricky question or task.

tea set ▶ n. a set of dishes for serving tea.

tea·spoon /'tē,spo͞on/ ▶ n. **1** a small spoon used for adding sugar to and stirring hot drinks. **2** the amount held by a teaspoon, equivalent to 1/6 fluid ounce or 5 milliliters. ■ **tea·spoon·ful** n.

teat /tēt/ ▶ n. a nipple of the mammary gland of a female animal's body from which milk is sucked by the young.

tea·time /'tē,tīm/ ▶ n. chiefly Brit. the time in the afternoon when tea is served.

tea tow·el ▶ n. chiefly Brit. a dish towel.

tea-tree oil ▶ n. an oil obtained from a species of tea tree, used in soaps and other products for its refreshing fragrance and antiseptic properties.

tech /tek/ ▶ n. informal **1** technology. **2** a technician. **3** Basketball a technical foul.

tech·ie /'tekē/ ▶ n. (pl. **techies**) informal a person who is an expert in technology, especially computing.

tech·ne·ti·um /tek'nēsH(ē)əm/ ▶ n. an unstable radioactive metallic element made by high-energy collisions.

tech·nic /'teknik/ ▶ n. **1** technique. **2** (**technics**) (treated as sing. or pl.) technical terms, details, and methods. ■ **tech·ni·cist** /-nisist/ n.

tech·ni·cal /'teknikəl/ ▶ adj. **1** relating to a particular subject, art, or craft, or its practical skills and techniques. **2** relating to the practical use of machinery and methods in science and industry. **3** requiring specialized knowledge in order to be understood. **4** according to a strict application or interpretation of the law or rules: *a technical violation of the treaty.* **5** Basketball a technical foul. ■ **tech·ni·cal·ly** adv.

tech·ni·cal foul ▶ n. Basketball a violation of certain rules of the game, not usually involving physical contact.

tech·ni·cal·i·ty /,tekni'kalitē/ ▶ n. (pl. **technicalities**) **1** a small formal detail within a set of rules, as contrasted with the intent or purpose of the rules. **2** (**technicalities**) the details of how something works or is done: *the technicalities of police procedure.* **3** the use of technical terms or methods.

tech·ni·cal knock·out ▶ n. Boxing the ending of a fight by the referee because a contestant is judged to be unable to continue, the opponent being declared the winner.

tech·ni·cian /tek'nishən/ ▶ n. **1** a person employed to look after technical equipment or do practical work in a laboratory. **2** a person skilled in the technique of an art, science, craft, or sport.

Tech·ni·col·or /'tekni,kələr/ ▶ n. **1** trademark a process of producing motion pictures in color by using synchronized monochrome films, each of a different color, to produce a color print. **2** (**technicolor**) informal vivid color.

tech·nique /tek'nēk/ ▶ n. **1** a method or skill used for carrying out a particular task. **2** a person's level of skill in a particular field. **3** a skillful or efficient way of doing or achieving something.

tech·no /'teknō/ ▶ n. a style of fast electronic

dance music, with a strong beat and few or no vocals.

tech·no·bab·ble /'teknō‚babəl/ ▶ n. informal incomprehensible technical jargon.

tech·noc·ra·cy /tek'näkrəsē/ ▶ n. (pl. **technocracies**) a social or political system in which scientific or technical experts hold a great deal of power. ■ **tech·no·crat** /'teknə‚krat/ n. **tech·no·crat·ic** /‚teknə'kratik/ adj.

tech·nol·o·gy /tek'näləjē/ ▶ n. (pl. **technologies**) 1 the application of scientific knowledge for practical purposes. 2 machinery and equipment developed from such scientific knowledge. 3 the branch of knowledge concerned with applied sciences. ■ **tech·no·log·i·cal** /‚teknə'läjikəl/ adj. **tech·no·log·i·cal·ly** /-ik(ə)lē/ adv. **tech·nol·o·gist** n.

tech·nol·o·gy trans·fer ▶ n. the transfer of new technology from the originator to a secondary user, especially from developed to underdeveloped countries.

tech·no·phile /'teknə‚fīl/ ▶ n. a person who is enthusiastic about new technology. ■ **tech·no·phil·i·a** /‚teknə'filēə/ n. **tech·no·phil·ic** /‚teknə'filik/ adj.

tech·no·phobe /'teknə‚fōb/ ▶ n. a person who dislikes or fears new technology. ■ **tech·no·pho·bi·a** /‚teknə'fōbēə/ n. **tech·no·pho·bic** /‚teknə'fōbik/ adj.

tech·no·speak /'teknə‚spēk/ ▶ n. another term for **TECHNOBABBLE**.

tec·ton·ic /tek'tänik/ ▶ adj. 1 Geology relating to the structure of the earth's crust and the large-scale processes that take place within it. 2 relating to building or construction. 3 (of an event, especially a change) very significant or considerable. ■ **tec·ton·i·cal·ly** /-ik(ə)lē/ adv.

tec·ton·ics /tek'täniks/ ▶ pl.n. (treated as sing. or pl.) Geology large-scale processes affecting the structure of the earth's crust.

ted·dy /'tedē/ ▶ n. (pl. **teddies**) 1 (also **teddy bear**) a soft toy bear. 2 a woman's all-in-one undergarment.

Te De·um /tā 'dāəm, tē 'dēəm/ ▶ n. a Christian hymn beginning *Te Deum laudamus*, 'We praise Thee, O God', sung at matins or on special occasions such as a thanksgiving.

te·di·ous /'tēdēəs/ ▶ adj. too long or slow; dull. ■ **te·di·ous·ly** adv. **te·di·ous·ness** n.

te·di·um /'tēdēəm/ ▶ n. the state of being tedious.

tee¹ /tē/ ▶ n. 1 a cleared space on a golf course, from which the ball is struck at the beginning of play for each hole. 2 a small peg placed in the ground to support a golf ball before it is struck from a tee. 3 a mark aimed at in lawn bowling, quoits, curling, etc. ▶ v. (**tees, teeing, teed**) Golf 1 (**tee up**) place the ball on a tee ready to make the first stroke of the round or hole. 2 (**tee off**) begin a round or hole by playing the ball from a tee. 3 (**tee someone off**) informal make someone angry or annoyed.

tee² ▶ n. informal a T-shirt.

tee-hee /‚tē 'hē/ ▶ n. a giggle or laugh.

teem¹ /tēm/ ▶ v. (**teem with**) be full of or swarming with.

> **USAGE**
> On the confusion of **teem** and **team**, see the note at **TEAM**.

teem² ▶ v. (of rain) pour down; fall heavily.

teen /tēn/ informal ▶ adj. relating to teenagers.

▶ n. a teenager.

-teen ▶ suffix forming the names of numerals from 13 to 19.

teen·age /'tēn‚āj/ ▶ adj. relating to a teenager or teenagers. ■ **teen·aged** adj.

teen·ag·er /'tēn‚ājər/ ▶ n. a person aged between 13 and 19 years.

teens /tēnz/ ▶ pl.n. the years of a person's age from 13 to 19.

teen·sy /'tēnsē/ ▶ adj. (**teensier, teensiest**) informal very tiny.

tee·ny /'tēnē/ ▶ adj. (**teenier, teeniest**) informal tiny.

tee·ny·bop·per ▶ n. informal a young teenager who follows the latest fashions in clothes and pop music.

tee·ny-wee·ny /'tēnē 'wēnē/ (also **teensy-weensy**) ▶ adj. informal very tiny.

tee·pee ▶ n. variant spelling of **TEPEE**.

tee shirt ▶ n. variant spelling of **T-SHIRT**.

tee·ter /'tētər/ ▶ v. 1 move or balance unsteadily. 2 be unable to decide between different options.

teeth /tēth/ ▶ plural of **TOOTH**.

teethe /tēTH/ ▶ v. (of a baby) develop its first teeth.

teeth·ing ring /'tēTHiNG/ ▶ n. a small ring for a baby to bite on while teething.

tee·to·tal /'tē‚tōtl/ ▶ adj. choosing never to drink alcohol. ■ **tee·to·tal·ism** /-‚izəm/ n. **tee·to·tal·er** n.

Tef·lon /'tef‚län/ ▶ n. trademark a tough synthetic resin used to make seals and bearings and to coat nonstick cooking utensils.

tel·co /'telkō/ ▶ n. (pl. **telcos**) a telecommunications company.

tele- ▶ comb.form 1 to or at a distance: *telecommunication*. 2 relating to television: *telegenic*. 3 done by means of the telephone: *telemarketing*.

tel·e·cast /'telə‚kast/ ▶ n. a television broadcast. ▶ v. broadcast a program by television. ■ **tel·e·cast·er** n.

tel·e·com /'telə‚käm/ (Brit. also **telecoms**) ▶ pl.n. (treated as sing.) telecommunications.

tel·e·com·mu·ni·ca·tion /‚teləkə‚myōōni'kāshən/ ▶ n. 1 long-distance communication by means of cable, telephone, broadcasting, satellite, etc. 2 (**telecommunications**) (treated as sing.) the technology concerned with this.

tel·e·com·mut·ing /‚teləkə'myōōtiNG/ ▶ n. the practice of working from home, communicating with a central workplace by telephone, email, and fax. ■ **tel·e·com·mute** v. **tel·e·com·mut·er** n.

tel·e·coms /'telə‚kämz/ (also **telecomms**) ▶ pl.n. (treated as sing.) telecommunications.

tel·e·con·fer·ence /'telə‚känf(ə)rəns/ ▶ n. a conference in which participants in different locations are linked by telecommunication devices. ■ **tel·e·con·fer·enc·ing** n.

tel·e·e·van·ge·list ▶ n. variant of **TELEVANGELIST**.

tel·e·gen·ic /‚telə'jenik/ ▶ adj. having an appearance or manner that is attractive on television.

tel·e·gram /'telə‚gram/ ▶ n. a message sent by telegraph and delivered in written or printed form.

tel·e·graph /'telə‚graf/ ▶ n. a system or device for transmitting messages from a distance along a wire, especially one creating signals by making and breaking an electrical connection. ▶ v. **1** send a message to someone by telegraph. **2** convey a message by one's facial expression or body language. ■ **te·leg·ra·pher** /təˈlegrəfər/ n. **tel·e·graph·ic** /ˌteləˈgrafik/ adj. **te·leg·ra·phist** /təˈlegrəfist/ n. **te·leg·ra·phy** /təˈlegrəfē/ n.

tel·e·ki·ne·sis /ˌteləkiˈnēsis/ ▶ n. the supposed ability to move objects at a distance by mental power or other nonphysical means. ■ **tel·e·ki·net·ic** /-ˈnetik/ adj.

tel·e·mark /ˈteləˌmärk/ Skiing ▶ n. a turn in downhill skiing or a landing style in ski jumping with one ski advanced and the knees bent. ▶ v. perform such a turn while skiing.

tel·e·mar·ket·ing /ˌteləˈmärkitiNG/ ▶ n. the marketing of goods or services by telephoning potential customers. ■ **tel·e·mar·ket·er** n.

tel·e·mat·ics /ˌteləˈmatiks/ ▶ pl.n. (treated as sing.) the branch of information technology that deals with the long-distance transmission of computerized information. ■ **tel·e·mat·ic** adj.

tel·e·med·i·cine /ˌteləˈmedisin/ ▶ n. the diagnosis and treatment of patients at a distance by means of telecommunications technology.

te·lem·e·ter /təˈlemitər, ˈteləˌmētər/ ▶ n. a piece of equipment for recording the readings of an instrument and transmitting them by radio. ■ **tel·e·met·ric** /ˌteləˈmetrik/ adj. **te·lem·e·try** /təˈlemitrē/ n.

tel·e·ol·o·gy /ˌtelēˈäləjē, ˌtēlē-/ ▶ n. (pl. **teleologies**) **1** the philosophical theory that all natural phenomena can be explained with reference to their purpose. **2** the theological doctrine that there is evidence of design and purpose in the natural world. ■ **tel·e·o·log·i·cal** /-əˈläjikəl/ adj.

te·lep·a·thy /təˈlepəTHē/ ▶ n. the supposed communication of thoughts or ideas without using speech, writing, or any other normal method. ■ **tel·e·path** /ˈteləpaTH/ n. **tel·e·path·ic** /ˌteləˈpaTHik/ adj.

tel·e·phone /ˈteləˌfōn/ ▶ n. **1** a system for transmitting voices over a distance using wire or radio, by converting sound vibrations to electrical signals. **2** a piece of equipment used as part of such a system, typically having a handset with a transmitting microphone and a set of numbered buttons by which a connection can be made to another such piece of equipment. ▶ v. contact someone by telephone. ■ **tel·e·phon·ic** adj. **tel·e·phon·i·cal·ly** adv.

tel·e·phone booth ▶ n. a public booth or enclosure in which a pay phone is situated.

tel·e·phone di·rec·to·ry ▶ n. a book listing the names, addresses, and telephone numbers of the people and businesses in a particular area.

tel·e·phone ex·change ▶ n. a set of equipment that connects telephone lines during a call.

tel·e·phone num·ber ▶ n. a number given to a particular telephone and used in making connections to it.

tel·e·phone pole ▶ n. a tall pole used to carry telephone wires and other utility lines above the ground.

te·leph·o·nist /təˈlefōnist, təˈlefə-/ ▶ n. Brit. a switchboard operator.

te·leph·o·ny /təˈlefənē, ˈteləˌfōnē/ ▶ n. the working or use of telephones.

tel·e·pho·to lens /ˈteləˌfōtō/ ▶ n. a lens with a longer focal length than standard, producing a

magnified image of a distant object.

tel·e·port /ˈteləˌpôrt/ ▶ n. a center providing connections between different forms of telecommunications, especially one that links satellites to ground-based communications. ▶ v. (especially in science fiction) transport or be transported across space and time instantly. ■ **tel·e·por·ta·tion** /ˌteləpôrˈtāsHən/ n.

tel·e·pres·ence /ˈteləˌprezəns/ ▶ n. the use of virtual reality technology, especially for the remote control of machinery or to produce the impression of being in another location.

tel·e·print·er /ˈteləˌprin(t)ər/ ▶ n. Brit. a device for transmitting telegraph messages as they are keyed, and for printing messages received.

tel·e·promp·ter /ˈteləˌpräm(p)tər/ (also **TelePrompTer**) ▶ n. trademark a device used in television to project a speaker's script out of sight of the audience.

tel·e·sales /ˈteləˌsālz/ ▶ pl.n. chiefly Brit. the selling of goods or services over the telephone.

tel·e·scope /ˈteləˌskōp/ ▶ n. an optical instrument designed to make distant objects appear nearer, containing an arrangement of lenses, or of curved mirrors and lenses, by which rays of light are collected and focused and the resulting image magnified. ▶ v. **1** (of an object made of several tubular parts fitting into each other) slide into itself so as to become smaller. **2** condense or combine so as to occupy less space or time: *at sea the years are telescoped into hours.* ■ **tel·e·scop·ic** /ˌteləˈskäpik/ adj. **tel·e·scop·i·cal·ly** /-ik(ə)lē/ adv.

tel·e·sur·ger·y /ˈteləˌsərjərē/ ▶ n. surgery performed by a doctor considerably distant from the patient, using medical robotics and multimedia image communication. ■ **tel·e·sur·geon** /ˈteləˌsərjən/ n.

tel·e·text /ˈteləˌtekst/ ▶ n. a news and information service transmitted to televisions with appropriate receivers.

tel·e·thon /ˈteləˌTHän/ ▶ n. a long television program broadcast to raise money for a charity.

tel·e·type /ˈteləˌtīp/ ▶ n. trademark a kind of teleprinter.

tel·e·van·ge·list /ˌteləˈvanjəlist/ (also **tele-evangelist**) ▶ n. an evangelical preacher who appears regularly on television.

tel·e·vise /ˈteləˌvīz/ ▶ v. broadcast something on television.

tel·e·vi·sion /ˈteləˌvizHən/ ▶ n. **1** a system for converting visual images (with sound) into electrical signals, transmitting them by radio or other means, and displaying them electronically on a screen. **2** (also **television set**) a device with a screen for receiving television signals. **3** the process or business of broadcasting programs on television.

tel·e·vis·u·al /ˌteləˈvizHŌŌəl/ ▶ adj. relating to or suitable for television. ■ **tel·e·vi·su·al·ly** adv.

tel·e·work·ing /ˈteləˌwərkiNG/ ▶ n. another term for TELECOMMUTING. ■ **tel·e·work·er** n.

tel·ex /ˈteleks/ ▶ n. **1** an international system of telegraphy in which printed messages are transmitted and received by teleprinters. **2** a machine used for this. **3** a message sent by telex. ▶ v. send a message to someone by telex.

tell /tel/ ▶ v. (past and past part. **told** /tōld/) **1** communicate information to someone. **2** order or advise someone to do something. **3** express something in words: *tell me the story* *again.* **4** (**tell someone off**) informal reprimand someone. **5** establish that something is the case: *you can tell they're in love.* **6** be able to recognize a difference. **7** (of an experience or period of time) have a noticeable effect on someone. **8** (**tell on**) informal inform someone about a person's wrongdoings.

– PHRASES **tell tales** gossip about another person's secrets or wrongdoings. **tell time** (or **tell the time**) be able to read the time from the face of a clock or watch.

tell·er /'telǝr/ ▶ n. **1** a person who deals with customers' transactions in a bank. **2** a person who tells something. **3** a person appointed to count votes.

tell·ing /'teliNG/ ▶ adj. having a striking or revealing effect; significant. ■ **tell·ing·ly** adv.

tell·ing-off ▶ n. (pl. **tellings-off**) Brit. informal a reprimand.

tell·tale /'tel,tāl/ ▶ adj. revealing something: *the telltale signs of a woman in love.* ▶ n. Brit. a tattletale.

tel·lu·ric /tǝ'lŏŏrik/ ▶ adj. **1** relating to the earth as a planet. **2** relating to the soil.

tel·lu·ri·um /tǝ'lŏŏrēǝm/ ▶ n. a silvery-white crystalline nonmetallic element with semiconducting properties.

tel·ly /'telē/ ▶ n. (pl. **tellies**) Brit. informal term for TELEVISION.

tel·net /'tel,net/ ▶ n. Computing a network protocol or program that allows a user on one computer to log in to another computer that is part of the same network.

tel·o·mere /'tēlǝ,mi(ǝ)r, 'telǝ-/ ▶ n. Genetics a compound structure at the end of a chromosome. ■ **tel·o·mer·ic** /,tēlǝ'merik, ,telǝ-/ adj.

te·maz·e·pam /tǝ'mazǝ,pam/ ▶ n. a sedative drug.

te·mer·i·ty /tǝ'meritē/ ▶ n. excessively confident or bold behavior.

temp /temp/ informal ▶ n. a person working in an office who is employed on a temporary basis. ▶ v. work as a temp.

temp. ▶ abbr. temperature.

tem·peh /'tempā/ ▶ n. an Indonesian dish consisting of deep-fried fermented soybeans.

tem·per /'tempǝr/ ▶ n. **1** a person's state of mind in terms of their being angry or calm: *she regained her temper.* **2** a tendency to become angry easily. **3** an angry state of mind. **4** the degree of hardness and elasticity in steel or another metal. ▶ v. **1** balance or modify something so as to make it less extreme: *their idealism is tempered with realism.* **2** improve the hardness and elasticity of a metal by reheating and then cooling it.

– PHRASES **keep** (or **lose**) **one's temper** manage (or fail to manage) to control one's anger.

tem·per·a /'tempǝrǝ/ ▶ n. a method of painting that uses powdered colors mixed with egg yolk.

tem·per·a·ment /'temp(ǝ)rǝmǝnt/ ▶ n. a person's nature in terms of the effect it has on their behavior.

tem·per·a·men·tal /,temp(ǝ)rǝ'mentl/ ▶ adj. **1** liable to unreasonable changes of mood. **2** relating to or caused by a person's temperament. ■ **tem·per·a·men·tal·ly** adv.

tem·per·ance /'temp(ǝ)rǝns/ ▶ n. the practice of never drinking alcohol.

tem·per·ate /'temp(ǝ)rǝt/ ▶ adj. **1** (of a region or climate) having mild temperatures. **2** showing moderation or self-restraint.

tem·per·ate zone ▶ n. each of the two regions of the earth between the Arctic Circle and the Tropic of Cancer and the Antarctic Circle and the Tropic of Capricorn.

tem·per·a·ture /'temp(ǝ)rǝchǝr, -,chŏŏr/ ▶ n. **1** the degree or intensity of heat present in a place, substance, or object. **2** a body temperature above normal. **3** the degree of excitement or tension in a situation or discussion: *the temperature of the debate lowered.*

tem·pest /'tempist/ ▶ n. a violent windy storm.

– PHRASES **a tempest in a teapot** great anger or excitement about a trivial matter.

tem·pes·tu·ous /tem'peschŏŏǝs/ ▶ adj. **1** very stormy. **2** full of strong and changeable emotions: *a tempestuous relationship.*
■ **tem·pes·tu·ous·ly** adv. **tem·pes·tu·ous·ness** n.

tem·pi /'tempē/ ▶ plural of TEMPO.

Tem·plar /'templǝr/ ▶ n. historical a member of the Knights Templar, a powerful religious and military order.

tem·plate /'templǝt/ ▶ n. **1** a shaped piece of rigid material used as a pattern for processes such as cutting out, shaping, or drilling. **2** something that acts as a model or example for others to copy.

tem·ple[1] /'tempǝl/ ▶ n. **1** a building used for the worship of a god or gods. **2** (**the Temple**) either of two ancient religious buildings of the Jews in Jerusalem.

tem·ple[2] ▶ n. the flat part of either side of the head between the forehead and the ear.

tem·po /'tempō/ ▶ n. (pl. **tempos** or **tempi** /-pē/) **1** the speed at which a passage of music is played. **2** the pace of an activity or process.

tem·po·ral[1] /'temp(ǝ)rǝl/ ▶ adj. **1** relating to time. **2** relating to the physical world rather than to spiritual matters. ■ **tem·po·ral·ly** adv.

tem·po·ral[2] ▶ adj. relating to or situated in the temples of the head.

tem·po·ral bone ▶ n. either of a pair of bones that form part of the side of the skull on each side and enclose the middle and inner ear.

tem·po·ral lobe ▶ n. each of the paired lobes of the brain lying beneath the temples, including areas concerned with the understanding of speech.

tem·po·rar·y /'tempǝ,rerē/ ▶ adj. lasting for only a short or limited time. ■ **tem·po·rar·i·ly** adv. **tem·po·rar·i·ness** n.

tem·po·rize /'tempǝ,rīz/ ▶ v. be evasive or delay making a decision in order to gain time.

tempt /tem(p)t/ ▶ v. **1** try to persuade someone to do something appealing but wrong or unwise. **2** (**be tempted to do**) have an urge or inclination to do something: *I was tempted to look at my watch.* **3** entice or attract: *programs designed to tempt young people into engineering.*
■ **tempt·er** n. **tempt·ing** adj.

– PHRASES **tempt fate** (or **providence**) do something risky or dangerous.

temp·ta·tion /tem(p)'tāshǝn/ ▶ n. **1** the action of tempting or the state of being tempted. **2** a tempting thing.

tempt·ress /'tem(p)tris/ ▶ n. a sexually attractive woman who sets out to make a man desire her.

tem·pu·ra /'tempǝrǝ, tem'pŏŏrǝ/ ▶ n. a Japanese dish of fish, shellfish, or vegetables, fried in batter.

ten /ten/ ▶ **cardinal number** one more than nine; 10. (Roman numeral: **x** or **X**.) ■ **ten·fold** /'ten,fōld/ **adj. & adv.**
- PHRASES **ten out of ten** referring to an excellent performance. **ten to one** very probably.

ten·a·ble /'tenəbəl/ ▶ **adj. 1** able to be defended against attack or objection. **2** (of a post, grant, etc.) able to be held or used for a particular period: *a scholarship tenable for three years.*

te·na·cious /tə'nāsHəs/ ▶ **adj. 1** holding firmly to something. **2** continuing to exist or do something for longer than might be expected: *a tenacious belief.* ■ **te·na·cious·ly** adv. **te·nac·i·ty** /-'nasitē/ n.

ten·an·cy /'tenənsē/ ▶ n. (pl. **tenancies**) the possession or occupation of land or property as a tenant.

ten·ant /'tenənt/ ▶ n. **1** a person who rents land or property from a landlord. **2** Law a person privately owning land or property. ▶ v. occupy property as a tenant.

ten·ant farm·er ▶ n. a person who farms rented land.

tench /tencH/ ▶ n. (pl. same) a freshwater fish of the carp family.

Ten Com·mand·ments ▶ pl.n. (in the Bible) the rules of conduct given by God to Moses on Mount Sinai.

tend¹ /tend/ ▶ v. **1** frequently behave in a particular way or have a certain characteristic: *men tend to marry younger women.* **2** go or move in a particular direction.

tend² ▶ v. care for or look after: *ambulance crews were tending to the injured.*

ten·den·cy /'tendənsē/ ▶ n. (pl. **tendencies**) **1** an inclination toward a particular characteristic or type of behavior. **2** a group within a larger political party or movement.

ten·den·tious /ten'densHəs/ ▶ adj. expressing a strong opinion, especially a controversial one. ■ **ten·den·tious·ly** adv. **ten·den·tious·ness** n.

ten·der¹ /'tendər/ ▶ adj. (**tenderer, tenderest**) **1** gentle and kind. **2** (of food) easy to cut or chew. **3** (of a part of the body) painful to the touch. **4** young and vulnerable: *he started sailing at the tender age of ten.* **5** (of a plant) easily damaged by severe weather. ■ **ten·der·ly** adv. **ten·der·ness** n.

ten·der² ▶ v. **1** offer or present something formally: *he tendered his resignation.* **2** make a formal written offer to carry out work, supply goods, etc., for a stated fixed price. **3** give money as payment for something. ▶ n. a formal offer to carry out work, supply goods, etc. for a stated fixed price. ■ **ten·der·er** n.
- PHRASES **put something out to tender** ask for offers to carry out work, supply goods, etc. to be submitted.

ten·der³ ▶ n. **1** a boat used to ferry people and supplies to and from a ship. **2** a railroad car attached to a steam locomotive, carrying fuel and water.

ten·der·foot /'tendər,fŏŏt/ ▶ n. (pl. **tenderfoots** or **tenderfeet**) a person who is new to and lacks experience in an activity or situation.

ten·der·heart·ed /'tendər'härtid/ ▶ adj. having a kind, gentle, or sentimental nature.

ten·der·ize /'tendə,rīz/ ▶ v. make meat more tender by beating it or cooking it slowly. ■ **ten·der·iz·er** n.

ten·der·loin /'tendər,loin/ ▶ n. the tenderest part of a loin of beef, pork, etc., taken from under the short ribs in the hindquarters.

ten·di·ni·tis /,tendə'nītis/ (also **tendonitis**) ▶ n. inflammation of a tendon.

ten·don /'tendən/ ▶ n. **1** a band of strong fibrous tissue that attaches a muscle to a bone. **2** the hamstring of a four-legged mammal.

ten·dril /'tendrəl/ ▶ n. **1** a slender threadlike part of a climbing plant, which stretches out and twines around any suitable support. **2** a slender ringlet of hair.

ten·e·brous /'tenəbrəs/ ▶ adj. literary dark; shadowy.

ten·e·ment /'tenəmənt/ ▶ n. **1** (also **tenement house**) a large house divided into several separate apartments. **2** a room or set of rooms forming a separate home within a house or apartment block.

ten·et /'tenit/ ▶ n. one of the principles or beliefs of a religion, philosophy, etc.

ten-gal·lon hat ▶ n. a large, broad-brimmed hat, traditionally worn by cowboys.

ten·ner /'tenər/ ▶ n. Brit. informal a ten-pound note.

ten·nis /'tenis/ ▶ n. a game for two or four players, who use rackets to strike a ball over a net stretched across a grass or clay court.

ten·nis el·bow ▶ n. inflammation of the tendons of the elbow caused by overuse of the forearm muscles.

ten·nis shoe ▶ n. a light canvas or leather soft-soled shoe suitable for tennis or casual wear.

ten·on /'tenən/ ▶ n. a projecting piece of wood made to fit into a mortise in another piece of wood.

ten·or¹ /'tenər/ ▶ n. a singing voice between baritone and alto or countertenor, the highest of the ordinary adult male range. ▶ adj. referring to an instrument of the second or third lowest pitch in its family: *a tenor sax.*

ten·or² ▶ n. the general meaning or nature of something: *the even tenor of life in the village.*

ten·o·syn·o·vi·tis /,tenō,sinə'vītis/ ▶ n. inflammation and swelling of a tendon, especially in the wrist, often caused by repetitive movements such as those made when typing.

ten·pin bowl·ing ▶ n. a game in which ten wooden pins are set up at the end of a track and knocked down by rolling a hard, heavy ball at them.

TENS /tenz/ ▶ abbr. transcutaneous electrical nerve stimulation, a technique for relieving pain by applying electrodes to the skin.

tense¹ /tens/ ▶ adj. **1** feeling, causing, or showing anxiety and nervousness. **2** (especially of a muscle) stretched tight or rigid. ▶ v. make or become tense. ■ **tense·ly** adv. **tense·ness** n.

tense² ▶ n. Grammar a set of forms taken by a verb to indicate the time or completeness of the action.

ten·sile /'tensəl, -,sīl/ ▶ adj. **1** relating to tension or being stretched. **2** capable of being drawn out or stretched.

ten·sile strength ▶ n. the resistance of a material to breaking when being stretched.

ten·sion /'tensHən/ ▶ n. **1** a situation in which there is conflict or distrust because of differing views, aims, or needs: *months of tension between the military and the government.* **2** a feeling of anxiety and mental pressure. **3** the state of being stretched tight. **4** the degree of stitch tightness in knitting and machine sewing. **5** voltage of a particular magnitude: *high tension*. ■ **ten·sion·al** adj.

tent /tent/ ▶ n. a portable shelter made of cloth, supported by one or more poles and stretched tight by cords attached to pegs driven into the ground.

ten·ta·cle /ˈtentəkəl/ ▶ n. a long, thin flexible part extending from the body of an animal, used for feeling or holding things, or for moving about. ■ **ten·ta·cled** adj. **ten·tac·u·lar** /tenˈtakyələr/ adj.

ten·ta·tive /ˈtentətiv/ ▶ adj. **1** done without confidence; hesitant: *a few tentative steps*. **2** not certain or fixed; provisional: *a tentative arrangement*. ■ **ten·ta·tive·ly** adv. **ten·ta·tive·ness** n.

tent cat·er·pil·lar ▶ n. a moth caterpillar that lives in groups inside communal silken webs in a tree, which it often defoliates.

ten·ter·hook /ˈtentərˌho͝ok/ ▶ n. (in phrase **on tenterhooks**) in a state of nervous suspense.

tenth /tenTH/ ▶ ordinal number **1** that is number ten in a sequence; 10th. **2** (**a tenth/one tenth**) each of ten equal parts into which something is divided. **3** a musical interval spanning an octave and a third in a scale. ■ **tenth·ly** adv.

tent stitch ▶ n. a series of parallel diagonal stitches.

ten·u·ous /ˈtenyo͞oəs/ ▶ adj. **1** very slight or weak: *a sick woman with only a tenuous grasp of reality*. **2** very slender or fine. ■ **ten·u·ous·ly** adv. **ten·u·ous·ness** n.

ten·ure /ˈtenyər, -ˌyo͝or/ ▶ n. **1** the conditions under which land or buildings are held or occupied. **2** the holding of a job or position. **3** guaranteed permanent employment, especially in a teaching post at a college or university. –PHRASES **security of tenure** the right of a tenant of property to occupy it after the lease expires (unless a court should order otherwise).

ten·ured /ˈtenyərd, -ˌyo͝ord/ ▶ adj. (especially of a professor) having a permanent post.

te·pee /ˈtēˌpē/ (also **teepee** or **tipi**) ▶ n. a cone-shaped tent made of skins or cloth on a frame of poles, as used by American Indians.

tep·id /ˈtepid/ ▶ adj. **1** (especially of a liquid) lukewarm. **2** unenthusiastic: *a tepid response*. ■ **te·pid·i·ty** /təˈpiditē/ n. **tep·id·ly** adv.

te·qui·la /təˈkēlə/ ▶ n. a Mexican alcoholic spirit made from the agave plant.

te·qui·la sun·rise ▶ n. a cocktail of tequila, orange juice, and grenadine.

ter- ▶ comb. form three; having three: *tercentenary*.

tera- ▶ comb. form **1** referring to a factor of one million million (10¹²): *terawatt*. **2** Computing referring to a factor of 2⁴⁰: *terabyte*.

ter·a·byte /ˈterəˌbīt/ ▶ n. a unit of information stored in a computer equal to one million million (10¹²) or (strictly) 2⁴⁰ bytes.

ter·a·flop /ˈterəˌfläp/ ▶ n. a unit of computing speed equal to one million million floating-point operations per second.

te·rat·o·gen /teˈratəjən, -ˌjen, ˈterətəjən/ ▶ n. a substance or factor that causes abnormalities to develop in an embryo. ■ **te·rat·o·gen·ic** /təˌratəˈjenik, ˌterətə-/ adj.

ter·bi·um /ˈtərbēəm/ ▶ n. a silvery-white metallic chemical element.

ter·cen·ten·ni·al /ˌtərsenˈtenēəl/ ▶ n. (pl. **tercentennials**) a three-hundredth anniversary.

ter·gi·ver·sa·tion /ˌtərjivərˈsāsHən/ ▶ n. the use of language that is evasive or ambiguous. ■ **ter·gi·ver·sate** /ˈtərjivərˌsāt, ˈtərjivər-/ v.

ter·i·ya·ki /ˌterēˈyäkē/ ▶ n. a Japanese dish of fish or meat marinated in soy sauce and broiled.

term /tərm/ ▶ n. **1** a word or phrase used to describe a thing or to express an idea. **2** (**terms**) language used on a particular occasion: *a protest in the strongest possible terms*. **3** (**terms**) requirements or conditions laid down or agreed. **4** (**terms**) relations between people: *we're on good terms*. **5** each of the periods in the year during which teaching is given in a school or college or during which a court of law holds sessions. **6** a period for which something lasts or is intended to last. **7** (also **full term**) the completion of a normal length of pregnancy. **8** Mathematics each of the quantities in a ratio, series, or mathematical expression. **9** Logic a word or words that may be the subject or predicate of a proposition. ▶ v. call by a particular word or phrase: *these are termed "reactive" treatments*. –PHRASES **come to terms with** become able to accept or deal with something. **in terms of** (or **in —— terms**) with regard to a particular aspect of something: *there are benefits to be gained in terms of cost*. **the —— term** a period that is a specified way into the future: *in the long term*. **on —— terms** in a specified relation or on a specified footing: *we are once again on speaking terms*.

ter·ma·gant /ˈtərməgənt/ ▶ n. a bad-tempered or overbearing woman.

ter·mi·na·ble /ˈtərmənəbəl/ ▶ adj. **1** able to be terminated. **2** coming to an end after a certain time.

ter·mi·nal /ˈtərmənəl/ ▶ adj. **1** relating to, forming, or situated at the end. **2** (of a disease) predicted to lead to a person's death. **3** informal extreme and usually beyond cure or alteration: *an industry in terminal decline*. ▶ n. **1** the station at the end of a railroad or other transport route. **2** a departure and arrival building for passengers at an airport. **3** a point of connection for closing an electric circuit. **4** a piece of equipment, usually consisting of a keyboard and a screen, that is connected to a central computer system. **5** a place where oil or gas is stored at the end of a pipeline or at a port. ■ **ter·mi·nal·ly** adv.

ter·mi·nal ve·loc·i·ty ▶ n. Physics the constant speed that a freely falling object reaches when the resistance of the medium through which it is falling prevents it from moving any faster.

ter·mi·nate /ˈtərməˌnāt/ ▶ v. **1** bring something to an end. **2** end a pregnancy at an early stage by a medical procedure. **3** (of a train or bus service) end its journey. **4** (**terminate in**) (of a thing) have its end at a particular place or in a particular form: *the cord terminates in a five-pin plug*. ■ **ter·mi·na·tion** /ˌtərməˈnāsHən/ n. **ter·mi·na·tor** /ˈtərməˌnātər/ n.

ter·mi·nol·o·gy /ˌtərməˈnäləjē/ ▶ n. (pl. **terminologies**) the set of terms used in a particular subject, profession, etc. ■ **ter·mi·no·log·i·cal** /-nəˈläjikəl/ adj.

ter·mi·nus /ˈtərmənəs/ ▶ n. (pl. **termini** /-nī/ or **terminuses**) chiefly Brit. a railroad or bus terminal.

ter·mite /ˈtərˌmīt/ ▶ n. a small, soft-bodied insect that feeds on wood and lives in colonies in large nests of earth.

term life in·sur·ance ▶n. life insurance that pays a benefit in the event of the death of the insured during a specified term. Compare with WHOLE LIFE INSURANCE.

term pa·per ▶n. a student's lengthy essay on a subject drawn from the work done during a school or college term.

tern /tərn/ ▶n. a seabird resembling a gull, with long pointed wings and a forked tail.

ter·na·ry /'tərnərē/ ▶adj. 1 composed of three parts. 2 Mathematics using three as a base.

ter·pene /'tər,pēn/ ▶n. Chemistry any of a large group of unsaturated hydrocarbons found in the essential oils of conifers and other plants.

terp·si·cho·re·an /,tərpsikə'rēən, -'kôrēən/ ▶adj. formal or humorous relating to dancing.

terr. ▶abbr. 1 territory. 2 territorial. 3 terrace.

ter·race /'teris/ ▶n. 1 a level paved area next to a building; a patio. 2 each of a series of flat areas on a slope, used for growing crops. 3 Brit. a block of row houses. ▶v. make sloping land into terraces. ■ **ter·rac·ing** n.

ter·raced /'terist/ ▶adj. (of land) having been formed into terraces.

ter·ra cot·ta /'terə 'kätə/ ▶n. 1 brownish-red earthenware that has not been glazed, used as a decorative building material and in modeling. 2 a strong brownish-red color.

ter·ra fir·ma /'terə 'fərmə/ ▶n. dry land; the ground.

ter·rain /tə'rān/ ▶n. a stretch of land, especially seen in terms of its physical features: *mountainous terrain.*

ter·ra in·cog·ni·ta /'terə ,inkäg'nētə, in'kägnitə/ ▶n. unknown territory.

ter·ra·pin /'terə,pin/ ▶n. 1 a small edible turtle with lozenge-shaped markings on its shell, found in coastal marshes of the eastern US. 2 a small freshwater turtle.

ter·rar·i·um /tə're(ə)rēəm/ ▶n. (pl. **terrariums** or **terraria** /-'re(ə)rēə/) 1 a glass-fronted case in which to keep small reptiles or amphibians. 2 a sealed transparent globe or similar container in which plants are grown.

ter·raz·zo /tə'räzō, tə'rätsō/ ▶n. flooring material consisting of chips of marble or granite set in concrete and polished smooth.

ter·res·tri·al /tə'restrēal, -'resCHəl/ ▶adj. 1 relating to the earth or dry land. 2 (of an animal or plant) living on or in the ground. 3 (of television broadcasting) using ground-based equipment rather than a satellite. ■ **ter·res·tri·al·ly** adv.

ter·ri·ble /'terəbəl/ ▶adj. 1 extremely bad, serious, or unpleasant. 2 troubled, guilty, or unwell: *I felt terrible about forgetting her name.* 3 causing terror.

ter·ri·bly /'terəblē/ ▶adv. 1 extremely. 2 very badly.

ter·ri·er /'terēər/ ▶n. a small breed of dog originally used for hunting animals that live underground.

ter·rif·ic /tə'rifik/ ▶adj. 1 of great size, amount, or strength. 2 informal excellent. ■ **ter·rif·i·cal·ly** /-ik(ə)lē/ adv.

ter·ri·fy /'terə,fī/ ▶v. (**terrifies, terrifying, terrified**) make someone feel terror. ■ **ter·ri·fy·ing** adj.

ter·rine /tə'rēn/ ▶n. 1 a mixture of chopped meat, fish, or vegetables pressed into a container and served cold. 2 an earthenware container for such a dish.

ter·ri·to·ri·al /,teri'tôrēəl/ ▶adj. 1 relating to the ownership of an area of land or sea: *a territorial dispute.* 2 (of an animal) having and defending a territory. ■ **ter·ri·to·ri·al·i·ty** /-,tôrē'alitē/ n. **ter·ri·to·ri·al·ly** adv.

ter·ri·to·ri·al wa·ters ▶pl.n. the part of the sea legally under the control of a state or country, especially those within a stated distance from its coast.

ter·ri·to·ry /'terə,tôrē/ ▶n. (pl. **territories**) 1 an area under the control of a ruler or country. 2 an organized division of a country not having the full rights of a state. 3 an area defended by an animal against others of the same sex or species. 4 an area of land of a particular type: *a campaign in mountainous territory.* 5 an area in which a person has particular rights, responsibilities, experience, or knowledge: *the Oscars are familiar territory for this actor.*

ter·roir /ter'wär/ ▶n. the complete natural environment in which a particular wine is produced, including factors such as the soil and climate.

ter·ror /'terər/ ▶n. 1 extreme fear. 2 a cause of terror. 3 the use or threat of violence to cause extreme fear: *a campaign of terror.* 4 informal a person who is annoying or difficult to control.

ter·ror·ism /'terə,rizəm/ ▶n. the unofficial or unauthorized use of violence and intimidation in the attempt to achieve political aims. ■ **ter·ror·ist** n. & adj.

ter·ror·ize /'terə,rīz/ ▶v. threaten and frighten someone over a period of time.

ter·ry /'terē/ ▶n. (pl. **terries**) fabric with raised loops of thread on both sides, used for towels.

terse /tərs/ ▶adj. (**terser, tersest**) using few words; abrupt. ■ **terse·ly** adv. **terse·ness** n.

ter·ti·ar·y /'tərsHē,erē, -sHərē/ ▶adj. 1 third in order or level. 2 (of medical treatment) provided at a specialist institution. 3 (**Tertiary**) Geology relating to the first period of the Cenozoic era, about 65 to 1.64 million years ago.

TESL /'tesəl/ ▶abbr. teaching of English as a second language.

tes·la /'teslə/ ▶n. Physics the SI unit of magnetic flux density.

TESOL /'te,säl, -,sôl, 'tesəl/ ▶abbr. teaching of English to speakers of other languages.

tes·sel·lat·ed /'tesə,lātid/ ▶adj. (of a floor) decorated with mosaics. ■ **tes·sel·la·tion** /,tesə'lāsHən/ n.

tes·ser·a /'tesərə/ ▶n. (pl. **tesserae** /'tesərē/) a small tile or block of stone used in a mosaic.

tes·si·tu·ra /,tesi'to͞orə/ ▶n. the range within which most musical notes of a vocal part fall.

test¹ /test/ ▶n. 1 a procedure intended to establish the quality, performance, or reliability of something. 2 a short examination of a person's skill or knowledge. 3 a means of testing something. 4 a difficult situation that reveals the strength or quality of someone or something: *this is the first serious test of the peace agreement.* 5 an examination of part of the body or a body fluid for medical purposes. 6 Chemistry a procedure for identifying a substance or revealing whether it is present. ▶v. 1 make someone or something undergo a test. 2 touch or taste something

before taking further action. **3** severely try a person's endurance or patience. ■ **test·a·ble** adj.
– PHRASES **test the water** find out people's feelings or opinions before taking further action.

test² ▶ n. Zoology the shell or tough outer covering of some invertebrates and protozoans.

tes·ta /'testə/ ▶ n. (pl. **testae** /-tē/) Botany the protective outer covering of a seed.

tes·ta·ment /'testəmənt/ ▶ n. **1** a person's will. **2** evidence of a fact, event, or quality: *the show's success is a testament to her talent.* **3** (**Testament**) a division of the Bible (see OLD TESTAMENT, NEW TESTAMENT).

tes·ta·men·ta·ry /ˌtestə'men(t)ərē/ ▶ adj. relating to a will.

tes·tate /'tes,tāt/ ▶ adj. having made a valid will before dying.

tes·ta·tor /'testātər/ ▶ n. (fem. **testatrix** /te'stātriks/) a person who has made a will or given a legacy.

test bed ▶ n. a piece of equipment for testing new devices.

test case ▶ n. a legal case whose result is used as an example when decisions are being made on similar cases in the future.

test-drive ▶ v. drive a motor vehicle to judge its performance and other qualities.

test·er¹ /'testər/ ▶ n. **1** a person or device that tests something. **2** a sample of a product allowing customers to try it before buying.

tes·ter² ▶ n. a canopy over a four-poster bed.

tes·tes /'testēz/ ▶ plural form of TESTIS.

test flight ▶ n. a flight during which the performance of an aircraft or its equipment is tested. ■ **test-fly** v.

tes·ti·cle /'testikəl/ ▶ n. either of the two oval organs that produce sperm in male mammals, enclosed in the scrotum behind the penis. ■ **tes·tic·u·lar** /te'stikyələr/ adj.

tes·ti·fy /'testə,fī/ ▶ v. (**testifies, testifying, testified**) **1** give evidence as a witness in a court of law. **2** (**testify to**) be evidence or proof of: *luxurious villas testify to the wealth here.*

tes·ti·mo·ni·al /ˌtestə'mōnēəl/ ▶ n. **1** a formal statement of a person's character and qualifications. **2** a public tribute to someone. **3** (in sports) a game or event held in honor of a player, who receives part of the income generated.

tes·ti·mo·ny /'testə,mōnē/ ▶ n. (pl. **testimonies**) **1** a formal statement, especially one given in a court of law. **2** (**testimony to**) evidence or proof of something.

tes·tis /'testis/ ▶ n. (pl. **testes** /-,tēz/) an organ that produces sperm.

tes·tos·ter·one /te'stästə,rōn/ ▶ n. a steroid hormone that stimulates the development of male secondary sexual characteristics.

test pi·lot ▶ n. a pilot who flies new or modified aircraft to test their performance.

test tube ▶ n. a thin glass tube closed at one end, used to hold material for laboratory testing or experiments.

test-tube ba·by ▶ n. informal a baby conceived by in vitro fertilization.

tes·ty /'testē/ ▶ adj. (**testier, testiest**) easily irritated; irritable. ■ **tes·ti·ly** adv. **tes·ti·ness** n.

tet·a·nus /'tetn-əs/ ▶ n. a disease causing the muscles to stiffen and go into spasms, spread by bacteria. ■ **te·tan·ic** /te'tanik/ adj.

tetch·y /'tecHē/ ▶ adj. (**tetchier, tetchiest**) bad-tempered and irritable. ■ **tetch·i·ly** adv. **tetch·i·ness** n.

tête-à-tête /'tāt ə 'tāt, 'tet ə 'tet/ ▶ n. (pl. same or **tête-à-têtes** pronunc. same) a private conversation between two people.

teth·er /'teTHər/ ▶ v. tie an animal with a rope or chain so as to restrict its movement. ▶ n. a rope or chain used to tether an animal.

tetra- (also **tetr-** before a vowel) ▶ comb.form four; having four: *tetrahedron.*

tet·ra·cy·cline /ˌtetrə'sī,klēn, -klin/ ▶ n. Medicine any of a large group of antibiotics with a molecular structure containing four rings.

tet·rad /'te,trad/ ▶ n. technical a group or set of four.

tet·ra·he·dron /ˌtetrə'hēdrən/ ▶ n. (pl. **tetrahedra** /-drə/ or **tetrahedrons**) a solid having four plane triangular faces. ■ **tet·ra·he·dral** /-drəl/ adj.

te·tral·o·gy /te'träləjē/ ▶ n. (pl. **tetralogies**) a group of four related books, operas, plays, etc.

te·tram·e·ter /te'tramitər/ ▶ n. a line of verse made up of four metrical feet.

tet·ra·pod /'tetrə,päd/ ▶ n. an animal of a group that includes all vertebrates apart from fish.

Teu·ton /'t(y)ōōtn/ ▶ n. **1** a member of an ancient Germanic people who lived in Jutland. **2** often derogatory a German.

Teu·ton·ic /t(y)ōō'tänik/ ▶ adj. **1** informal, often derogatory displaying qualities regarded as typical of Germans. **2** relating to the Teutons.

Tex·as hold 'em /'hōldəm/ ▶ n. a form of poker in which each player is dealt two cards face down and combines these with any of five community cards to make the best available five-card hand.

Tex-Mex /'teks 'meks/ ▶ adj. (especially of food or music) having a blend of Mexican and southern American features. ▶ n. Tex-Mex music or food.

text /tekst/ ▶ n. **1** a book or other written or printed work. **2** the main body of a written work as distinct from appendices, illustrations, etc. **3** written or printed words or computer data. **4** a written work chosen as a subject of study. **5** a passage from the Bible, especially as the subject of a sermon. **6** a text message. ▶ v. send a text message to someone. ■ **text·er** n. **text·ing** n.

text·book /'teks(t),bŏŏk/ ▶ n. a book used as a standard work for the study of a subject. ▶ adj. done in exactly the recommended way: *a textbook example of damage control.*

text ed·i·tor ▶ n. Computing a system or program that allows a user to edit text.

tex·tile /'tek,stīl/ ▶ n. a type of cloth or woven fabric. ▶ adj. relating to fabric or weaving.

text mes·sage ▶ n. an electronic message sent and received by cell phone. ■ **text mes·sag·ing** n.

tex·tu·al /'teksCHŌŌəl/ ▶ adj. relating to a text or texts. ■ **tex·tu·al·ly** adv.

tex·tu·al·i·ty /ˌteksCHŌŌ'alitē/ ▶ n. the quality or use of language that is typical of written works as distinct from spoken usage.

tex·ture /'teksCHər/ ▶ n. **1** the feel, appearance, or consistency of a surface, substance, or fabric. **2** the quality created by the combination of elements in a work of music or literature: *a closely knit symphonic texture.* ▶ v. give a rough or raised texture to a surface. ■ **tex·tur·al** adj.

tex·tur·ize /'teksCHə,rīz/ ▶ v. give a particular texture to something.

TFT ▶ abbr. thin-film transistor, used to make flat color display screens.

TGV ▶ n. a French high-speed passenger train.

Th ▶ symbol the chemical element thorium.

Thai /tī/ ▶ n. (pl. same or **Thais**) **1** a person from Thailand. **2** the official language of Thailand.

thal·a·mus /ˈtʜaləməs/ ▶ n. (pl. **thalami** /-ˌmī/) each of two masses of gray matter in the front part of the brain, relaying sensory information to other parts of the brain.

tha·las·so·ther·a·py /tʜəˌlasōˈtʜerəpē, ˌtʜalasō-/ ▶ n. the use of seawater in cosmetic and health treatment.

tha·lid·o·mide /tʜəˈlidəˌmīd/ ▶ n. a drug formerly used as a sedative, but found to cause malformation of the fetus when taken in early pregnancy.

thal·li·um /ˈtʜalēəm/ ▶ n. a soft silvery-white metallic chemical element whose compounds are very poisonous.

thal·lus /ˈtʜaləs/ ▶ n. (pl. **thalli** /ˈtʜalī/) a plant body that lacks true roots and a vascular system, typical of algae, fungi, and lichens.

than /tʜan, tʜən/▶ conj. & prep. **1** used to introduce the second part of a comparison: *he was smaller than his son.* **2** used to introduce an exception or contrast: *insects other than bees.* **3** used in expressions indicating one thing happening immediately after another: *no sooner were we seated than we had to move.*

> **USAGE**
> For an explanation of whether to use **I** and **we** or **me** and **us** after **than**, see the note at **PERSONAL PRONOUN**.

than·a·tol·o·gy /ˌtʜanəˈtäləjē/ ▶ n. the scientific study of death and practices associated with it.

thank /tʜangk/ ▶ v. **1** express gratitude to someone. **2** ironic blame or hold responsible: *you have only yourself to thank.*
– PHRASES **thank goodness** (or **God** or **heavens**) an expression of relief. **thank you** a polite expression of gratitude.

thank·ful /ˈtʜangkfəl/ ▶ adj. **1** pleased and relieved. **2** expressing gratitude.
■ **thank·ful·ness** n.

thank·ful·ly /ˈtʜangkfəlē/ ▶ adv. **1** in a thankful way. **2** luckily; fortunately.

> **USAGE**
> The traditional sense of **thankfully** is 'in a thankful way' (*she accepted the offer thankfully*). The newer use, meaning 'luckily; fortunately' (*thankfully, we didn't have to wait*) is now by far the most common, although some people think that it is incorrect.

thank·less /ˈtʜangklis/ ▶ adj. **1** (of a job or task) unpleasant and unlikely to be appreciated by others. **2** not showing or feeling gratitude.

thanks /tʜangks/ ▶ pl. n. **1** an expression of gratitude. **2** thank you.
– PHRASES **no thanks to** despite the unhelpfulness of. **thanks to** due to.

thanks·giv·ing /ˌtʜangksˈgiving/
▶ n. **1** the expression of gratitude to God. **2** (**Thanksgiving**) an annual national holiday in the US held on the fourth Thursday in November, commemorating the Pilgrims' harvest festival in 1621; a similar holiday in Canada held on the second Monday in October.

that /tʜat, tʜət/ ▶ pron. & determiner **1** (pl. **those**) used to refer to a person or thing seen or heard by the speaker or already mentioned or known. **2** (pl. **those**) referring to the more distant of two things near to the speaker. **3** (pl. **those**) used in singling out someone or something with a particular feature. **4** (as pronoun) (pl. **that**) used instead of which, who, when, etc., to introduce a clause that defines or identifies something: *the woman that owns the place.* ▶ adv. **1** to such a degree. **2** informal very: *he wasn't that far away.*
▶ conj. **1** introducing a subordinate clause (one that depends on a main clause): *she said that she'd be late.* **2** literary expressing a wish or regret.
– PHRASES **that is** (or **that is to say**) a set expression introducing or following an explanation. **that said** even so. **that's that** there is nothing more to do or say about the matter.

> **USAGE**
> When is it right to use **that** and when should you use **which**? The general rule is that when introducing clauses that define or identify something, **that** is the preferred relative pronoun: *a book that aims to simplify scientific language.* You should use **which**, but never **that**, to introduce a clause preceded by a comma and giving additional information: *the book, which costs $15, has sold over a million copies* (not the book, that costs $15, has sold over a million copies).

thatch /tʜacʜ/ ▶ n. **1** a roof covering of straw, reeds, or similar material. **2** informal a person's hair. ▶ v. cover a roof or building with thatch.
■ **thatch·er** n.

thaw /tʜô/ ▶ v. **1** become or make liquid or soft after being frozen. **2** (**it thaws, it is thawing, it thawed**) the weather becomes warmer and causes snow and ice to melt. **3** (of a part of the body) become warm enough to stop feeling numb. **4** make or become friendlier. ▶ n. **1** a period of warmer weather that thaws ice and snow. **2** an improvement in relations or an increase in friendliness.

the /tʜē, tʜə/ ▶ determiner **1** used to refer to one or more people or things already mentioned or easily understood; the definite article. **2** used to refer to someone or something that is unique: *the sun.* **3** used to refer to something in a general rather than a specific way: *he plays the violin.* **4** used to explain which person or thing is being referred to: *the house at the end of our street.* **5** enough of: *I don't have the money to buy a house.*

the·a·ter /ˈtʜēətər/ (also **theatre**) ▶ n. **1** a building in which plays and other dramatic performances are given. **2** the writing and production of plays. **3** a play considered in terms of its dramatic quality: *this is intense, moving theater.* **4** (also **lecture theater**) a room for lectures with seats in tiers. **5** Brit. an operating room. **6** the area in which something happens: *a new theater of war has opened up.*

the·at·ri·cal /tʜēˈatrikəl/ ▶ adj. **1** relating to acting, actors, or the theater. **2** exaggerated and excessively dramatic: *he looked over his shoulder with theatrical caution.* ▶ n. **1** (**theatricals**) theatrical performances or behavior. **2** a professional actor or actress. ■ **the·at·ri·cal·i·ty** /-ˌatriˈkalitē/ n. **the·at·ri·cal·ly** /-ik(ə)lē/ adv.

the·at·rics /tʜēˈatriks/ ▶ pl. n. theatrical performances or behavior; theatricals.

thee /tʜē/ ▶ pron. old use or dialect you (as the singular object of a verb or preposition).

theft /tʜeft/ ▶ n. the action or crime of stealing.

their /tʜe(ə)r/ ▶ possessive determiner **1** belonging to or associated with the people or things

previously mentioned or easily identified.
2 belonging to or associated with a person whose sex is not specified (used in place of either 'his' or 'his or her'). **3** (**Their**) used in titles.

> **USAGE**
>
> Do not confuse **their**, **there**, and **they're**. **Their** means 'belonging to them' (*I went around to their house*), while **there** means 'in, at, or to that place' (*it will take an hour to get there*), and **they're** is short for 'they are' (*they're going to be late*).
>
> On the use of **their** in the singular to mean 'his or her', see the note at **THEY**.

theirs /THE(ə)rz/ ▶ possessive pron. used to refer to something belonging to or associated with two or more people or things previously mentioned.

> **USAGE**
>
> There is no apostrophe: the spelling should be **theirs** not *their's*.

the·ism /'THē,izəm/ ▶ n. belief in the existence of a god or gods, specifically of a creator who intervenes in the universe. Compare with **DEISM**. ■ **the·ist** n. **the·is·tic** /THē'istik/ adj.

them /THem, THəm/ ▶ pron. (third person pl.) **1** used as the object of a verb or preposition to refer to two or more people or things previously mentioned or easily identified. **2** referring to a person whose sex is not specified (used in place of either 'him' or 'him or her').

> **USAGE**
>
> For an explanation of the use of **them** in the singular to mean 'his or her', see the note at **THEY**.

the·mat·ic /THi'matik/ ▶ adj. arranged according to subject or relating to a subject. ■ **the·mat·i·cal·ly** /-ik(ə)lē/ adv.

theme /THēm/ ▶ n. **1** the subject of a talk, piece of writing, etc. **2** a prominent or frequently recurring melody or group of notes in a musical composition. **3** an idea that often recurs in a work of art or literature: *the theme of journeys is apparent throughout the book.* **4** (also **theme song** or **music**) a piece of music played at the beginning and end of a movie, television show, etc. ▶ adj. (of a restaurant, bar, or leisure venue) designed in the style of a particular country, historical period, etc. ▶ v. (often as adj. **themed**) give a particular setting or style to: *an American-themed restaurant.*

theme park ▶ n. a large amusement park based around a particular idea.

them·self /THəm'self, THem-/ ▶ pron. (third person sing.) informal used instead of 'himself' or 'herself' to refer to a person whose sex is not specified.

> **USAGE**
>
> The standard reflexive pronoun (a word such as *myself* or *herself*) corresponding to **they** and **them** is **themselves**, as in *they can do it themselves.* The singular form **themself** has been used recently to correspond to the singular use of **they** when referring to a person whose sex is not specified (*helping someone to help themself*). However, **themself** is not good English, and you should use **themselves** instead.

them·selves /THəm'selvz, THem-/ ▶ pron. (third person pl.) **1** used as the object of a verb or preposition to refer to a group of people or things previously mentioned as the subject of the clause. **2** they or them personally. **3** used instead of 'himself' or 'herself' to refer to a person whose sex is not specified.

then /THen/ ▶ adv. **1** at that time. **2** after that; next. **3** also; in addition. **4** in that case; therefore. – PHRASES **but then** (**again**) on the other hand. **then and there** immediately.

thence /THens/ (also **from thence**) ▶ adv. formal **1** from a place or source previously mentioned. **2** as a consequence.

thence·forth /THens'fôrTH/ (also **thenceforward**) ▶ adv. old use or literary from that time, place, or point onward.

the·oc·ra·cy /THē'äkrəsē/ ▶ n. (pl. **theocracies**) a system of government in which priests rule in the name of God or a god. ■ **the·o·crat·ic** /THēə'kratik/ adj.

the·od·o·lite /THē'ädə,līt/ ▶ n. a surveying instrument with a rotating telescope for measuring horizontal and vertical angles.

the·o·lo·gian /THēə'lōjən/ ▶ n. a person expert in or studying theology.

the·ol·o·gy /THē'äləjē/ ▶ n. (pl. **theologies**) **1** the study of God and religious belief. **2** a system of religious beliefs and theory. ■ **the·o·log·i·cal** /THēə'läjikəl/ adj. **the·o·log·i·cal·ly** /-ik(ə)lē/ adv. **the·ol·o·gist** n.

the·o·rem /'THēərəm, 'THi(ə)r-/ ▶ n. **1** Physics & Mathematics a general proposition or rules that can be proved by reasoning. **2** Mathematics a rule expressed by symbols or formulae.

the·o·ret·i·cal /THēə'retikəl/ (also **theoretic** /THēə'retik/) ▶ adj. **1** concerned with the theory of a subject rather than its practical application. **2** based on theory rather than experience or practice: *the theoretical possibility of a chain reaction.* ■ **the·o·ret·i·cal·ly** /-ik(ə)lē/ adv.

the·o·re·ti·cian /,THēərə'tiSHən, ,THi(ə)rə-/ ▶ n. a person who develops or studies the theory of a subject.

the·o·rize /'THēə,rīz, 'THi(ə)r,īz/ ▶ v. form a theory or theories about something. ■ **the·o·rist** /'THēərist, 'THi(ə)r-/ n. **the·o·ri·za·tion** /,THēərə'zāSHən, ,THi(ə)r-/ n.

the·o·ry /'THēərē, 'THi(ə)rē/ ▶ n. (pl. **theories**) **1** a reasoned set of ideas that is intended to explain why something happens or exists. **2** an idea that explains or justifies something: *I have this theory that these guys were mean because they had silly names.* **3** a set of principles on which an activity is based: *a theory of education.* – PHRASES **in theory** in a possible situation, but probably not in reality.

the·os·o·phy /THē'äsəfē/ ▶ n. a philosophy that believes that a person may achieve knowledge of God through such things as intuition, meditation, and prayer, especially the movement called the Theosophical Society. ■ **the·o·soph·i·cal** /,THēə'säfikəl/ adj. **the·os·o·phist** n.

ther·a·peu·tic /,THerə'pyōōtik/ ▶ adj. **1** relating to the healing of disease. **2** having a good effect on the body or mind. ■ **ther·a·peu·ti·cal·ly** /-ik(ə)lē/ adv. **ther·a·peu·tics** pl.n.

ther·a·py /'THerəpē/ ▶ n. (pl. **therapies**) **1** treatment intended to relieve or heal a physical disorder. **2** the treatment of mental or emotional problems by psychological means. ■ **ther·a·pist** n.

Ther·a·va·da /,THerə'vädə/ ▶ n. the more conservative of the two major traditions of Buddhism (the other being Mahayana), practiced mainly in Sri Lanka, Burma (Myanmar), Thailand, Cambodia, and Laos.

there /THe(ə)r/ ▶ adv. **1** in, at, or to that place or position. **2** on that issue. **3** used in attracting

attention to someone or something. **4** (usu. **there is/are**) used to indicate the fact or existence of something. ▶ **exclam. 1** used to focus attention. **2** used to comfort someone.
– PHRASES **so there** informal used to express defiance. **there and then** immediately.

> USAGE
> For an explanation of the difference between **there**, **their**, and **they're**, see the note at THEIR.

there·a·bouts /'THE(ə)rə,bouts/ (also **thereabout**) ▶ **adv.** near that place, time, or figure.

there·af·ter /THE(ə)r'aftər/ ▶ **adv.** formal after that time.

there·at /THE(ə)r'at/ ▶ **adv.** old use or formal **1** at that place. **2** on account of or after that.

there·by /THE(ə)r'bī/ ▶ **adv.** by that means; as a result of that.

there·fore /'THE(ə)r,fôr/ ▶ **adv.** for that reason; consequently.

there·from /THE(ə)r'frəm/ ▶ **adv.** old use or formal from that or that place.

there·in /THE(ə)r'in/ ▶ **adv.** formal in that place, document, or respect.

ther·e·min /'THErə,min/ ▶ **n.** an electronic musical instrument in which the tone is generated by two high-frequency oscillators and the pitch controlled by the movement of the performer's hand toward and away from the circuit.

there·of /THE(ə)r'əv/ ▶ **adv.** formal of the thing just mentioned; of that.

there·on /THE(ə)r'än, -'ôn/ ▶ **adv.** formal on or following from the thing just mentioned.

there's /THE(ə)rz/ ▶ **contr. 1** there is. **2** there has.

there·to /THE(ə)r'tōō/ ▶ **adv.** formal to that or that place.

there·un·der /THE(ə)r'əndər/ ▶ **adv.** chiefly formal in accordance with the thing mentioned.

there·un·to /,THE(ə)r,ən'tōō/ ▶ **adv.** old use or formal to that.

there·up·on /'THE(ə)rə,pän/ ▶ **adv.** formal immediately or shortly after that.

there·with /THE(ə)r'wiTH, -'wiTH/ ▶ **adv.** old use or formal **1** with or in the thing mentioned. **2** soon or immediately after that.

therm /THərm/ ▶ **n.** a unit of heat, equivalent to 100,000 Btu or 1.055×10^8 joules.

ther·mal /'THərməl/ ▶ **adj. 1** relating to heat. **2** (of an item of clothing) made of a fabric that provides good insulation to keep the body warm. ▶ **n. 1** an upward current of warm air, used by birds, gliders, and balloonists to gain height. **2** (**thermals**) thermal clothing, especially underwear. ■ **ther·mal·ly adv.**

ther·mal im·ag·ing ▶ **n.** the technique of using the heat given off by an object to produce an image of it or locate it.

ther·mal spring ▶ **n.** a spring of naturally hot water.

ther·mic /'THərmik/ ▶ **adj.** relating to heat.

therm·i·on·ic /,THərmī'änik/ ▶ **adj.** relating to the emission of electrons from substances heated to very high temperatures.

ther·mi·on·ic valve ▶ **n.** Electronics a vacuum tube giving a flow of thermionic electrons in one direction, used in rectifying a current and in radio reception.

therm·is·tor /'THər,mistər/ ▶ **n.** an electrical resistor whose resistance is greatly reduced by heating, used for measurement and control.

ther·mo·cou·ple /'THərmō,kəpəl/ ▶ **n.** a device for measuring or sensing a temperature difference, consisting of two wires of different metals connected at two points, between which a voltage is developed in proportion to any temperature difference.

ther·mo·dy·nam·ics /,THərmōdī'namiks/ ▶ **pl.n.** (treated as sing.) the branch of science concerned with the relations between heat and other forms of energy involved in physical and chemical processes. ■ **ther·mo·dy·nam·ic adj. ther·mo·dy·nam·i·cal·ly** /-ik(ə)lē/ **adv.**

ther·mo·e·lec·tric /,THərmō-i'lektrik/ ▶ **adj.** producing electricity by a difference of temperatures.

ther·mo·gen·e·sis /,THərmō'jenəsis/ ▶ **n.** technical the production of bodily heat. ■ **ther·mo·gen·ic** /-mə'jenik/ **adj.**

ther·mog·ra·phy /THər'mägrəfē/ ▶ **n.** a printing technique in which a resinous powder is dusted onto wet ink and fused by heating to produce a raised impression. ■ **ther·mo·graph·ic** /,THərmə'grafik/ **adj.**

ther·mom·e·ter /THər'mämitər/ ▶ **n.** an instrument for measuring temperature, typically consisting of a glass tube marked with a temperature scale and containing mercury or alcohol, which expands when heated.

ther·mo·nu·cle·ar /,THərmō'n(y)ōōklēər, -kli(ə)r/ ▶ **adj.** relating to or using nuclear fusion reactions that occur at very high temperatures.

ther·mo·pile /'THərmə,pīl/ ▶ **n.** a set of thermocouples arranged for measuring small quantities of radiant heat.

ther·mo·plas·tic /,THərmə'plastik/ ▶ **adj.** (of a substance) becoming plastic when heated.

ther·mo·reg·u·la·tion /,THərmō,regyə'lāshən/ ▶ **n.** technical the regulation of bodily temperature.

ther·mos /'THərməs/ (also **Thermos**) ▶ **n.** trademark a container that keeps a substance hot or cold by means of a double wall enclosing a vacuum.

ther·mo·set·ting /'THərmō,setiNG/ ▶ **adj.** (of a substance) setting permanently when heated.

ther·mo·sphere /'THərmō,sfir/ ▶ **n.** the upper region of the atmosphere above the mesosphere.

ther·mo·stat /'THərmə,stat/ ▶ **n.** a device that automatically regulates temperature or activates a device at a set temperature. ■ **ther·mo·stat·ic** /,THərmə'statik/ **adj. ther·mo·stat·i·cal·ly** /,THərmə'statik(ə)lē/ **adv.**

the·sau·rus /THə'sôrəs/ ▶ **n.** (pl. **thesauri** /-'sôrī/ or **thesauruses**) a book containing lists of words that have the same, similar, or a related meaning.

these /THēz/ ▶ plural of THIS.

the·sis /'THēsis/ ▶ **n.** (pl. **theses** /-sēz/) **1** a statement or theory put forward to be supported or proved. **2** a long essay involving personal research, written as part of a university degree.

thes·pi·an /'THespēən/ ▶ **adj.** relating to drama and the theater. ▶ **n.** an actor or actress.

they /THā/ ▶ **pron.** (third person pl.) **1** used to refer to two or more people or things previously mentioned or easily identified. **2** people in general. **3** informal people in authority regarded as a whole. **4** used to refer to a person whose sex is not specified (in place of either 'he' or 'he or she').

they'd /ᴛʜād/ ► contr. **1** they had. **2** they would.
they'll /ᴛʜāl/ ► contr. **1** they will. **2** they shall.
they're /ᴛʜe(ə)r/ ► contr. they are.

they've /ᴛʜāv/ ► contr. they have.
thi·a·mine /'ᴛʜīəmin, -mēn/ (also **thiamin** /-min/) ► n. vitamin B₁, found in unrefined cereals, beans, and liver, a deficiency of which causes beriberi.
thick /ᴛʜik/ ► adj. **1** with opposite sides or surfaces relatively far apart. **2** (of a garment or fabric) made of heavy material. **3** made up of a large number of things or people close together: *thick forest.* **4** (**thick with**) densely filled or covered with something. **5** (of the air or atmosphere) heavy, or difficult to see through. **6** (of a liquid or a semiliquid substance) relatively firm in consistency; not flowing freely. **7** informal of low intelligence; stupid. **8** (of a voice) hoarse or husky. **9** (of an accent) very marked and difficult to understand. **10** informal having a very close, friendly relationship. ► n. (**the thick**) the middle or the busiest part: *in the thick of battle.* ■ **thick·ly** adv.
– PHRASES **thick and fast** rapidly and in great numbers. (**as**) **thick as thieves** informal very close or friendly. **through thick and thin** under all circumstances, no matter how difficult.
thick·en /'ᴛʜikən/ ► v. make or become thick or thicker. ■ **thick·en·er** n.
– PHRASES **the plot thickens** the situation is becoming more complicated and puzzling.
thick·en·ing /'ᴛʜikəniNG/ ► n. **1** a thicker area or part. **2** a substance added to a liquid to make it thicker.
thick·et /'ᴛʜikit/ ► n. a dense group of bushes or trees.
thick·head·ed /'ᴛʜik,hedid/ ► n. informal dull and stupid.
thick·ness /'ᴛʜiknis/ ► n. **1** the distance through an object, as distinct from width or height. **2** the state or quality of being thick. **3** a layer of material. **4** a thicker part of something: *beams set into the thickness of the wall.*
thick·set /'ᴛʜik,set/ ► adj. heavily or solidly built; stocky.
thief /ᴛʜēf/ ► n. (pl. **thieves** /ᴛʜēvz/) a person who steals another person's property.
thieve /ᴛʜēv/ ► v. be a thief; steal things. ■ **thiev·er·y** /'ᴛʜēv(ə)rē/ n. **thiev·ish** adj.
thigh /ᴛʜī/ ► n. the part of the leg between the hip and the knee.
thigh bone ► n. the femur.
thim·ble /'ᴛʜimbəl/ ► n. a small metal or plastic cap, worn to protect the finger and push the needle in sewing.
thim·ble·ful /'ᴛʜimbəl,fŏŏl/ ► n. a small quantity of something.
thin /ᴛʜin/ ► adj. (**thinner**, **thinnest**) **1** having opposite surfaces or sides close together. **2** (of a garment or fabric) made of light material. **3** having little flesh or fat on the body. **4** having few parts or members in relation to the area covered or filled: *a thin crowd.* **5** (especially of the air) not dense or heavy. **6** containing much liquid and not much solid substance. **7** (of a sound) faint and high-pitched. **8** lacking substance; weak and inadequate: *the evidence is rather thin.* ► v. (**thins**, **thinning**, **thinned**) **1** make or become less thick. **2** (often **thin something out**) remove some plants from a row or area to allow the others more room to grow. ■ **thin·ly** adv. **thin·ness** n.
– PHRASES **into thin air** so as to become invisible or nonexistent.
thine /ᴛʜīn/ old use ► possessive pron. yours. ► possessive determiner (before a vowel) your.
thing /ᴛʜiNG/ ► n. **1** an unspecified object, action, creature, etc. **2** an object as distinct from a living creature. **3** (**one's things**) a person's belongings or clothing. **4** (**things**) unspecified circumstances or matters: *how are things?* **5** (**the thing**) informal what is needed, acceptable, or fashionable. **6** (**one's thing**) informal one's special interest.
thing·a·ma·jig /'ᴛʜiNGəmə,jig/ (also **thingamabob** /-,bäb/) ► n. a person or thing whose name one has forgotten, does not know, or does not wish to mention.
thing·y /'ᴛʜiNGē/ ► n. (pl. **thingies**) another term for **THINGAMAJIG**.
think /ᴛʜiNGk/ ► v. (past and past part. **thought** /ᴛʜôt/) **1** have a particular opinion, belief, or idea about someone or something. **2** use the mind to form connected ideas about someone or something. **3** (**think of/about**) take someone or something into account or consideration. **4** (**think of/about**) consider the possibility or advantages of: *I was thinking of going home.* **5** (**think of**) have a particular opinion of: *she thought of him as a friend.* **6** (**think of**) call something to mind. ► n. an act of thinking. ■ **think·a·ble** adj. **think·er** n.
– PHRASES **think better of** decide not to do something after reconsideration. **think nothing of** consider an activity others regard as odd, wrong, or difficult as easy or normal. **think something over** consider something carefully. **think something through** consider every aspect of something before acting. **think twice** consider a course of action carefully before going ahead with it. **think something up** informal invent something.
think·ing /'ᴛʜiNGkiNG/ ► n. a person's ideas or opinions. ► adj. using thought or rational judgment; intelligent.
– PHRASES **put on one's thinking cap** informal think carefully about a problem.
think tank ► n. a group of experts providing advice and ideas on specific political or economic problems.
thin·ner /'ᴛʜinər/ (also **thinners**) ► n. a solvent used to thin paint or other solutions.
thin·nings /'ᴛʜiniNGz/ ► pl.n. seedlings, trees, or fruit that have been thinned out to improve the growth of those remaining.
third /ᴛʜərd/ ► ordinal number **1** that is number three in a sequence; 3rd. **2** (**a third/one third**) each of three equal parts into which something is divided. **3** a musical interval spanning three consecutive notes in a scale. ■ **third·ly** adv.

third class ▸ n. **1** a set of people or things grouped together as the third best. **2** a cheap class of mail for advertising and other unsealed printed material. **3** chiefly historical the cheapest and least comfortable accommodations in a train or ship. ▸ adj. & adv. relating to the third class.

third cous·in ▸ n. see COUSIN.

third-de·gree ▸ adj. **1** (of burns) being of the most severe kind, affecting tissue below the skin. **2** Law (of a crime, especially murder) in the least serious category. ▪ n. (**the third degree**) long and harsh questioning to obtain information or a confession.

third-gen·er·a·tion ▸ adj. (of a broadband digital telephone technology) that supports Internet connection and multimedia services.

third par·ty ▸ n. a person or group besides the two main ones involved in a situation or dispute.

third per·son ▸ n. **1** a third party. **2** see PERSON (sense 3).

third-rate ▸ adj. of very poor quality; inferior.

third read·ing ▸ n. a third presentation of a bill to a lawmaking assembly, in the US to consider it for the last time and in the UK to debate committee reports.

Third Reich /rīk, rīкн/ ▸ n. the Nazi regime in Germany, 1933–45.

Third World ▸ n. the developing countries of Asia, Africa, and Latin America.

thirst /тнərst/ ▸ n. **1** a feeling of needing or wanting to drink. **2** the state of not having enough water to stay alive. **3** (**thirst for**) a strong desire for something. ▸ v. **1** (**thirst for/after**) have a strong desire for: *an opponent thirsting for revenge.* **2** old use feel a need to drink.

thirst·y /ˈтнərstē/ ▸ adj. (**thirstier, thirstiest**) **1** feeling or causing a need to drink: *modeling is thirsty work.* **2** (**thirsty for**) having or showing a strong desire for something. **3** (of an engine or plant) consuming a lot of fuel or water. ▪ **thirst·i·ly** adv. **thirst·i·ness** n.

thir·teen /ˌтнərˈtēn, ˈтнərˌtēn/ ▸ cardinal number one more than twelve; 13. (Roman numeral: **xiii** or **XIII**.) ▪ **thir·teenth** /ˌтнərˈtēnтн, ˈтнərˌtēnтн/ ordinal number.

Thir·teen Col·o·nies ▸ the British colonies that ratified the Declaration of Independence in 1776 and became founding states of the US.

thir·ty /ˈтнərtē/ ▸ cardinal number (pl. **thirties**) ten less than forty; 30. (Roman numeral: **xxx** or **XXX**.) ▪ **thir·ti·eth** /-ітн/ ordinal number.

thir·ty-eight ▸ n. a revolver of .38 caliber.

thir·ty-sec·ond note ▸ n. a musical note having the time value of half a sixteenth note, represented by a solid dot with a three-hooked stem.

this /тнis/ ▸ pron. & determiner (pl. **these** /тнēz/) **1** used to identify a specific person or thing close at hand, just mentioned, or being indicated or experienced. **2** referring to the nearer of two things close to the speaker. **3** (as determiner) used with periods of time related to the present. ▸ adv. to the degree or extent indicated: *they can't handle a job this big.*

this·tle /ˈтнisəl/ ▸ n. a plant with a prickly stem and leaves and rounded heads of purple flowers.

this·tle·down /ˈтнisəlˌdoun/ ▸ n. the light fluffy down of thistle seeds, which enables them to be blown about in the wind.

thith·er /ˈтнiтнər, ˈтнi-/ ▸ adv. old use or literary to or toward that place.

tho /тнō/ ▸ conj. & adv. informal spelling of THOUGH.

thong /тнôNG, тнäNG/ ▸ n. **1** a narrow strip of leather or other material, used as a fastening or as the lash of a whip. **2** a pair of panties or skimpy bathing suit like a G-string. **3** a light sandal or flip-flop.

tho·rac·ic /тнəˈrasik/ ▸ adj. relating to the thorax.

tho·rax /ˈтнôraks/ ▸ n. (pl. **thoraces** /ˈтнôrəˌsēz/ or **thoraxes**) **1** the part of the body between the neck and the abdomen. **2** the middle section of the body of an insect, bearing the legs and wings.

tho·ri·um /ˈтнôrēəm/ ▸ n. a white radioactive metallic chemical element.

thorn /тнôrn/ ▸ n. **1** a stiff, sharp-pointed woody projection on the stem or other part of a plant. **2** a thorny bush, shrub, or tree. – PHRASES **a thorn in someone's side** (or **flesh**) a source of continual annoyance or trouble.

thorn·y /ˈтнôrnē/ ▸ adj. (**thornier, thorniest**) **1** having many thorns or thorn bushes. **2** causing difficulty or trouble: *the thorny issue of censorship.*

thor·ough /ˈтнərō/ ▸ adj. **1** complete with regard to every detail. **2** done with or showing great care and completeness. **3** absolute; utter: *he is a thorough nuisance.* ▪ **thor·ough·ly** adv. **thor·ough·ness** n.

thor·ough·bred /ˈтнərəˌbred/ ▸ adj. **1** (especially of a horse) of pure breed. **2** informal of outstanding quality. ▸ n. a thoroughbred animal.

thor·ough·fare /ˈтнərəˌfe(ə)r/ ▸ n. a road or path forming a route between two places.

thor·ough·go·ing /ˈтнərəˌgōiNG/ ▸ adj. **1** involving or dealing with every detail or aspect. **2** complete; absolute.

those /тнōz/ ▸ plural of THAT.

thou[1] /тнou/ ▸ pron. old use or dialect you (as the singular subject of a verb).

thou[2] /тнou/ ▸ n. (pl. same or **thous**) **1** informal a thousand. **2** one thousandth of an inch.

though /тнō/ ▸ conj. **1** despite the fact that; although. **2** however; but. ▸ adv. however: *he was able to write, though.*

thought[1] /тнôt/ ▸ n. **1** an idea or opinion produced by thinking, or that suddenly comes into the mind. **2** the process of thinking. **3** (**one's thoughts**) one's mind or attention. **4** careful consideration: *I haven't given much thought to sexism.* **5** (**thought of**) an intention, hope, or idea of: *they had no thought of surrender.* **6** the formation of opinions, especially as a system of ideas, or the opinions so formed: *traditions of Western thought.*

thought[2] ▸ past and past participle of THINK.

thought·ful /ˈтнôtfəl/ ▸ adj. **1** thinking deeply. **2** showing careful consideration. **3** considerate toward other people. ▪ **thought·ful·ly** adv. **thought·ful·ness** n.

thought·less /ˈтнôtləs/ ▸ adj. **1** not considerate toward other people. **2** without considering the consequences: *to think a few minutes of thoughtless pleasure could end in this.* ▪ **thought·less·ly** adv. **thought·less·ness** n.

thought po·lice ▸ n. (treated as pl.) a group of people who aim to suppress ideas that depart from the way of thinking that they believe to be correct.

thought·pro·vok·ing ▶ adj. stimulating careful consideration or attention: *thought-provoking questions.*

thou·sand /ˈтʜouzənd/ ▶ cardinal number **1** (**a/one thousand**) the number equivalent to the product of a hundred and ten; 1,000. (Roman numeral: **m** or **M.**) **2** (**thousands**) informal an unspecified large number.
– PHRASES **bat a thousand** see BAT¹.
■ **thou·sand·fold** /-ˌfōld/ adj. & adv. **thou·sandth** /ˈтʜouzən(t)тʜ/ ordinal number.

Thou·sand Is·land dress·ing ▶ n. a dressing for salad or seafood consisting of mayonnaise with ketchup and chopped pickles.

thrall /тʜrôl/ ▶ n. the state of being in another's power: *she was in thrall to her husband.*
■ **thral·dom** /-dəm/ (also **thralldom**) n.

thrash /тʜrash/ ▶ v. **1** beat someone or something repeatedly and violently with a stick or whip. **2** move in a violent or uncontrolled way: *he lay thrashing around in pain.* **3** informal defeat someone heavily. **4** (**thrash something out**) discuss an issue frankly and thoroughly so as to reach a decision. ▶ n. **1** a violent or noisy movement. **2** (also **thrash metal**) a style of fast, loud, harsh-sounding rock music.

thrash·er¹ /ˈтʜrashər/ ▶ n. a person or thing that thrashes.

thrash·er² ▶ n. a thrushlike American songbird with mainly brown or gray plumage, a long tail, and a down-curved bill.

thread /тʜred/ ▶ n. **1** a long, thin strand of cotton, nylon, or other fibers used in sewing or weaving. **2** a long, thin line or piece of something. **3** (also **screw thread**) a spiral ridge on the outside of a screw, bolt, etc., or on the inside of a cylindrical hole, to allow two parts to be screwed together. **4** a theme running through a situation or piece of writing. **5** (**threads**) informal clothes. ▶ v. **1** pass a thread through the eye of a needle. **2** move or weave in and out of obstacles: *I threaded my way through the tables.* **3** (as adj. **threaded**) (of a hole, screw, etc.) having a screw thread. ■ **thread·er** n. **thread·y** adj.

thread·bare /ˈтʜredˌber/ ▶ adj. **1** (of cloth, clothing, etc.) old, thin, and shabby. **2** lacking originality or freshness: *threadbare clichés.*

thread·worm /ˈтʜredˌwərm/ ▶ n. a very thin worm that lives as a parasite in the intestines of humans and animals.

threat /тʜret/ ▶ n. **1** a stated intention to harm someone, especially if they do not do what one wants. **2** a likely cause of damage or danger. **3** the possibility of trouble or danger: *their culture is under threat from logging and dams.*

threat·en /ˈтʜretn/ ▶ v. **1** state that one intends to harm someone or cause trouble if one does not get what one wants. **2** put at risk: *a broken finger threatened his career.* **3** (of a situation or the weather) seem likely to produce an unwelcome result. ■ **threat·en·ing** adj.

three /тʜrē/ ▶ cardinal number one more than two; 3. (Roman numeral: **iii** or **III**.) ■ **three·fold** /ˈтʜrēˌfōld/ adj. & adv.

three-di·men·sion·al ▶ adj. **1** having or appearing to have length, breadth, and depth. **2** lifelike or real.

3G ▶ adj. (of telephone technology) third-generation.

three-leg·ged race /ˈlegəd/ ▶ n. a race run by pairs of people, one member of each pair having their left leg tied to the right leg of the other.

three-piece ▶ adj. **1** (of a set of furniture) consisting of a sofa and two armchairs. **2** (of a set of clothes) consisting of pants or a skirt with a vest and jacket.

three-quar·ter ▶ n. Rugby each of four players in a team positioned across the field behind the halfbacks.

three-ring cir·cus ▶ n. informal a confused or disorganized situation.

three·score /ˈтʜrēˈskôr/ ▶ cardinal number literary sixty.

three·some /ˈтʜrēsəm/ ▶ n. a group of three people.

three-way ▶ adj. involving three directions, processes, or participants: *a three-way race for the presidency.*

three-wheel·er ▶ n. a vehicle with three wheels, especially a child's tricycle.

thren·o·dy /ˈтʜrenədē/ ▶ n. (pl. **threnodies**) a song, piece of music, or poem expressing grief or regret.

thresh /тʜresh/ ▶ v. **1** separate grains of cereals from the rest of the plant. **2** move violently; thrash. ■ **thresh·er** n.

thresh·old /ˈтʜreshˌ(h)ōld/ ▶ n. **1** a strip of wood or stone forming the bottom of a doorway. **2** a level or point at which something would begin or come into effect: *he was on the threshold of a dazzling career.*

threw /тʜrōō/ ▶ past of THROW.

thrice /тʜrīs/ ▶ adv. old use or literary **1** three times. **2** extremely; very: *I was thrice blessed.*

thrift /тʜrift/ ▶ n. **1** carefulness and economy in the use of money and other resources. **2** a plant that forms low-growing tufts of slender leaves with rounded pink flowerheads, found on sea cliffs and mountains.

thrift·less /ˈтʜriftlis/ ▶ adj. spending money in an extravagant and wasteful way.

thrift shop (also **thrift store**) ▶ n. a store selling secondhand clothes and other household goods.

thrift·y /ˈтʜriftē/ ▶ adj. (**thriftier, thriftiest**) careful with money; economical. ■ **thrift·i·ly** adv.

thrill /тʜril/ ▶ n. **1** a sudden feeling of excitement and pleasure. **2** an exciting or pleasurable experience. **3** a wave of emotion or sensation: *a thrill of excitement ran through her.* ▶ v. **1** give someone a sudden feeling of excitement and pleasure. **2** (**thrill to**) experience something exciting. ■ **thrill·ing** adj.

thrill·er /ˈтʜrilər/ ▶ n. a novel, play, or movie with an exciting plot that involves crime or spying.

thrips /тʜrips/ (also **thrip**) ▶ n. (pl. same) a minute black insect that sucks plant sap, noted for swarming on warm, still summer days.

thrive /тʜrīv/ ▶ v. (past **thrived** or **throve** /тʜrōv/; past part. **thrived** or **thriven** /ˈтʜrivən/) **1** grow or develop well or vigorously. **2** be successful; flourish: *she has managed to thrive in a fickle sport.*

thro' /тʜrōō/ ▶ prep., adv., & adj. literary or informal spelling of THROUGH.

throat /тʜrōt/ ▶ n. **1** the passage that leads from the back of the mouth, through which food passes to the esophagus and air passes to the lungs. **2** the front part of the neck.
– PHRASES **be at each other's throats** quarrel or fight persistently. **force something down someone's throat** force something on a person's

attention. **stick in one's throat** be unwelcome or difficult to accept.

throat·y /ˈTHrōtē/ ▸ adj. (**throatier, throatiest**) (of a voice or other sound) deep and husky. ■ **throat·i·ly** adv. **throat·i·ness** n.

throb /THräb/ ▸ v. (**throbs, throbbing, throbbed**) 1 beat or sound with a strong, regular rhythm. 2 feel pain in a series of regular beats. ▸ n. a strong, regular beat or sound.

throes /THrōz/ ▸ pl.n. intense or violent pain and struggle.
– PHRASES **in the throes of** in the middle of experiencing or doing something difficult.

throm·bo·sis /THräm'bōsis/ ▸ n. (pl. **thromboses** /-ˌsēz/) the formation of a blood clot in a blood vessel or the heart. ■ **throm·bot·ic** /-'bätik/ adj.

throne /THrōn/ ▸ n. 1 a ceremonial chair for a sovereign or bishop. 2 (**the throne**) the power or rank of a sovereign.

throng /THrÔNG, THräNG/ ▸ n. a large, densely packed crowd. ▸ v. gather somewhere in large numbers.

throt·tle /ˈTHrätl/ ▸ n. a device controlling the flow of fuel or power to an engine. ▸ v. 1 attack or kill someone by choking or strangling them. 2 control an engine or vehicle with a throttle.

through /THro͞o/ ▸ prep. & adv. 1 moving in one side and out of the other side of an opening or location. 2 so as to make a hole or passage in. 3 (prep.) expressing the location of something beyond an opening or an obstacle. 4 continuing in time toward: *she struggled through until payday.* 5 from beginning to end of an experience or activity. 6 so as to inspect all or part of: *he read the letter through carefully.* 7 by means of. 8 (adv.) so as to be connected by telephone. 9 expressing the extent of turning from one direction to another. ▸ adj. 1 (of public transportation or a ticket) continuing or valid to the final destination. 2 (of traffic, roads, etc.) passing straight through a place. 3 having successfully passed to the next stage of a competition. 4 informal having finished an activity, relationship, etc.
– PHRASES **through and through** thoroughly or completely.

through·out /THro͞o'out/ ▸ prep. & adv. all the way through.

through·put /ˈTHro͞oˌpo͝ot/ ▸ n. the amount of material or items passing through a system or process.

through·way ▸ n. another spelling of THRUWAY.

throve /THrōv/ ▸ past of THRIVE.

throw /THrō/ ▸ v. (past **threw** /THro͞o/; past part. **thrown** /THrōn/) 1 send something from one's hand through the air by a rapid movement of the arm and hand. 2 move or place quickly, hurriedly, or forcefully: *the door was thrown open.* 3 direct, or cast light, an expression, etc., in a particular direction. 4 send suddenly into a particular state: *the country was thrown into chaos.* 5 disconcert or confuse someone. 6 have a fit or tantrum. 7 hold a party. 8 make a clay pot, dish, etc., on a potter's wheel. 9 (of a horse) cause its rider to fall off. 10 project one's voice so that it appears to come from somewhere else. 11 informal lose a race or contest on purpose. ▸ n. 1 an act of throwing. 2 a light cover for furniture. 3 a light blanket, used especially when sitting. 4 (**a throw**) informal a single turn, round, or item: *on-the-spot portraits at $25 a throw.* ■ **throw·er** n.

– PHRASES **throw something away 1** get rid of something useless or unwanted. **2** fail to make use of an opportunity or advantage. **throw one's hand in** withdraw; give up. **throw something in 1** include something extra with something that is being sold or offered. **2** interrupt a conversation with a casual remark. **throw in the towel 1** (in boxing) throw a towel into the ring as a sign of defeat. **2** admit defeat. **throw oneself into** start to do something in an enthusiastic way. **throw something open** make something generally accessible. **throw someone out** force someone to leave. **throw something out 1** get rid of something useless or unwanted. **2** (of a court, lawmaking body, etc.) dismiss or reject something. **throw someone over** abandon or reject a lover. **throw up** informal vomit.

throw·a·way /ˈTHrōəˌwā/ ▸ adj. 1 intended to be thrown away after being used once or a few times. 2 (of a remark) said in a casual way.

throw·back /ˈTHrōˌbak/ ▸ n. a person or thing that resembles someone or something that existed in the past.

throw-in ▸ n. Soccer & Rugby the act of throwing the ball from the sideline to restart the game after the ball has gone out of play.

throw rug ▸ n. a small decorative rug designed to be placed with a casual effect and moved as required.

thru /THro͞o/ ▸ prep., adv., & adj. informal spelling of THROUGH.

thrum /THrəm/ ▸ v. (**thrums, thrumming, thrummed**) 1 make a continuous rhythmic humming sound. 2 strum the strings of a musical instrument in a rhythmic way. ▸ n. a continuous rhythmic humming sound.

thrush[1] /THrəsH/ ▸ n. a small or medium-sized songbird with a brown back and spotted breast.

thrush[2] ▸ n. infection of the mouth and throat or the genitals by a yeastlike fungus.

thrust /THrəst/ ▸ v. (past and past part. **thrust**) 1 push suddenly or forcibly: *she thrust her hands into her pockets.* 2 make one's way forcibly. 3 (**thrust something on**) force someone to accept or deal with something. 4 extend or project: *the jetty thrust out into the water.* ▸ n. 1 a sudden or violent lunge or attack. 2 the main theme of a course of action or argument: *the thrust of the book is to guard young men from folly.* 3 the force produced by an engine to propel a jet or rocket. ■ **thrust·er** n.

thru·way /ˈTHro͞oˌwā/ (also **throughway**) ▸ n. a major road or highway.

thud /THəd/ ▸ n. a dull, heavy sound. ▸ v. (**thuds, thudding, thudded**) move, fall, or hit something with a thud.

thug /THəg/ ▸ n. 1 a violent and aggressive man. 2 (**Thug**) historical a member of an organization of robbers and assassins in India. ■ **thug·ger·y** /ˈTHəgərē/ n. **thug·gish** adj.

thu·li·um /ˈTH(y)o͞olēəm/ ▸ n. a soft silvery-white metallic chemical element.

thumb /THəm/ ▸ n. the short, thick first digit of the hand, set lower and apart from the other four. ▸ v. 1 press, touch, or indicate something with the thumb. 2 turn over pages with the thumb. 3 (as adj. **thumbed**) (of a book's pages) worn or dirty by repeated handling. 4 request a free ride in a passing vehicle by signaling with the thumb; hitchhike.
– PHRASES **thumb one's nose at** informal show

contempt for. **thumbs up** (or **down**) informal an indication of satisfaction or approval (or of rejection or failure). **under someone's thumb** completely under someone's influence.

thumb drive ▶ n. another term for USB FLASH DRIVE.

thumb in·dex ▶ n. a set of lettered notches cut down the side of a book to make it easier to find the required section.

thumb·nail /'THəm,nāl/ ▶ n. the nail of the thumb. ▶ adj. brief or concise: *a thumbnail sketch.*

thumb·print /'THəm,print/ ▶ n. 1 a mark made by the inner part of the top joint of the thumb. 2 an identifying characteristic.

thumb·screw /'THəm,skrōō/ ▶ n. an instrument of torture that crushes the thumbs.

thumb·tack /'THəm,tak/ ▶ n. a short flat-headed pin for fastening paper to a surface.

thump /THəmp/ ▶ v. 1 hit someone or something heavily with the fist or a blunt object. 2 put down or move forcefully or noisily: *he thumped the gun down on the counter.* 3 (of a person's heart or pulse) beat strongly. 4 informal defeat someone heavily. ▶ n. a heavy, dull blow or noise. ■ **thump·er** n.

thump·ing /'THəmpiNG/ ▶ adj. informal impressively large: *a thumping 64 percent majority.*

thun·der /'THəndər/ ▶ n. 1 a loud rumbling or crashing noise heard after a lightning flash due to the expansion of rapidly heated air. 2 a loud deep resounding noise. ▶ v. 1 (**it thunders, it is thundering, it thundered**) produce thunder. 2 make or move with a loud deep noise. 3 speak loudly and angrily. ■ **thun·der·y** adj.

thun·der·bolt /'THəndər,bōlt/ ▶ n. a flash of lightning with a crash of thunder at the same time.

thun·der·clap /'THəndər,klap/ ▶ n. a crash of thunder.

thun·der·cloud /'THəndər,kloud/ ▶ n. a cumulus cloud with a towering or spreading top, charged with electricity and producing thunder and lightning.

thun·der·head /'THəndər,hed/ ▶ n. a rounded, projecting head of a cumulus cloud, which is a sign of a thunderstorm.

thun·der·ing /'THəndəriNG/ ▶ adj. informal very great or impressive: *he's a thundering bore.*

thun·der·ous /'THənd(ə)rəs/ ▶ adj. 1 relating to or resembling thunder. 2 (of a person's expression or mood) very angry or menacing. ■ **thun·der·ous·ly** adv.

thun·der·show·er /'THəndər,sHou(-ə)r/ ▶ n. a brief rain shower accompanied by thunder and lightning.

thun·der·storm /'THəndər,stôrm/ ▶ n. a storm with thunder and lightning.

thun·der·struck /'THəndər,strək/ ▶ adj. very surprised or shocked.

thunk¹ /THəNGk/ ▶ n. & v. informal term for THUD.

thunk² ▶ v. informal or humorous past and past participle of THINK: *who would've thunk it?*

thu·ri·ble /'THŏŏrəbəl/ ▶ n. a container in which incense is burned; a censer.

Thurs·day /'THərzdā, -dē/ ▶ n. the day of the week before Friday and following Wednesday.

thus /THəs/ ▶ adv. literary or formal 1 as a result of this; therefore. 2 in this way. 3 to this point; so.

thwack /THwak/ ▶ v. hit someone or something with a sharp blow. ▶ n. a sharp blow.

thwart /THwôrt/ ▶ v. 1 prevent someone from accomplishing something. 2 prevent something from succeeding. ▶ n. a crosspiece forming a seat for a rower in a boat.

thy /THĪ/ (also **thine** /THĪn/ before a vowel) ▶ possessive determiner old use or dialect belonging to you; your.

thyme /tīm/ ▶ n. a low-growing plant of the mint family, used as an herb in cooking.

thy·mine /'THĪ,mēn, -min/ ▶ n. Biochemistry a compound that is one of the four constituent bases of nucleic acids.

thy·mol /'THĪ,mól, -,mōl/ ▶ n. a white crystalline compound present in oil of thyme and used as a flavoring and preservative.

thy·mus /'THĪməs/ ▶ n. (pl. **thymi** /-mī/) a gland in the neck that produces white blood cells for the immune system. ■ **thy·mic** /'THĪmik/ adj.

thy·roid /'THĪ,roid/ (also **thyroid gland**) ▶ n. a large gland in the neck that produces hormones regulating growth and development through the rate of metabolism.

thy·self /THĪ'self/ ▶ pron. (second person sing.) old use or dialect yourself.

Ti ▶ symbol the chemical element titanium.

ti /tē/ ▶ n. Music the seventh note of a major scale, coming after 'la'.

ti·ar·a /tē'ärə, -'ärə, -'e(ə)rə/ ▶ n. 1 a semicircular jeweled ornamental band worn on the front of a woman's hair. 2 a crown with three tiers worn by a pope.

Ti·bet·an /tə'betn/ ▶ n. 1 a person from Tibet. 2 the language of Tibet. ▶ adj. relating to Tibet.

tib·i·a /'tibēə/ ▶ n. (pl. **tibiae** /'tibē,ē/ or **tibias**) the inner and typically larger of the two bones between the knee and the ankle, parallel with the fibula. ■ **tib·i·al** adj.

tic /tik/ ▶ n. a recurring spasm of the muscles, most often in the face.

tick¹ /tik/ ▶ n. 1 a regular short, sharp sound, such as made by a clock. 2 Brit. informal a moment. 3 Brit. a check mark. ▶ v. 1 make regular short, sharp sounds. 2 (**tick away/by/past**) (of time) pass. 3 chiefly Brit. mark something with a check mark. 4 (**tick over**) (of an engine) run slowly while the vehicle is not moving. 5 (**tick over**) work or operate slowly or at a minimum level. 6 (**tick someone off**) informal make someone annoyed or angry. – PHRASES **what makes someone tick** informal what motivates someone.

tick² ▶ n. a tiny creature related to the spiders, which attaches itself to the skin and sucks blood.

tick·er /'tikər/ ▶ n. informal 1 a person's heart. 2 informal a watch.

tick·er tape ▶ n. a paper strip on which messages are recorded in an electronic or telegraphic machine.

tick·et /'tikit/ ▶ n. 1 a piece of paper or card giving the holder a right to be admitted to a place or event or to travel on public transportation. 2 an official notice of a parking or driving offense. 3 a label attached to an item in a store, giving its price, size, etc. 4 a set of policies supported by a party in an election: *he ran on a right-wing ticket.* 5 (**the ticket**) informal the desirable thing. ▶ v. (**tickets, ticketing, ticketed**) issue someone with a ticket.

■ **tick·et·less** adj.

tick·ing /'tikiNG/ ► n. a hard-wearing material used to cover pillows and mattresses.

tick·le /'tikəl/ ► v. 1 lightly touch someone in a way that causes them to itch, twitch, or laugh. 2 be appealing or amusing to: *I was tickled by the idea.* ► n. an act of tickling or the feeling of being tickled. ■ **tick·ler** /'tik(ə)lər/ n. **tick·ly** /'tik(ə)lē/ adj.

– PHRASES **be tickled pink** informal be very amused or pleased.

tick·lish /'tik(ə)lisH/ ► adj. 1 sensitive to being tickled. 2 (of a situation or problem) needing careful handling; tricky.

tic-tac-toe /'tik ,tak 'tō/ (also **tick-tack-toe**) ► n. a game in which each of two players tries to be the first to complete a row, column, or diagonal with either three O's or three X's on a nine-square grid.

tid·al /'tīdl/ ► adj. relating to or affected by tides. ■ **tid·al·ly** adv.

tid·al bore ► n. another term for BORE³.

tid·al wave ► n. 1 an exceptionally large ocean wave, especially one caused by an underwater earthquake or volcanic eruption. 2 an overwhelming or widespread occurrence of an activity, emotion, or reaction: *a tidal wave of patriotism swept the nation.*

tid·bit /'tid,bit/ (Brit. **titbit** /'tit,bit/) ► n. 1 a small piece of tasty food. 2 a small item of very interesting information.

tid·dly /'tidlē/ ► adj. (**tiddlier, tiddliest**) Brit. informal slightly drunk.

tid·dl·ywinks /'tidlē,wiNGks/ ► pl.n. (treated as sing.) a game in which small plastic counters are flicked into a central container, using a larger counter.

tide /tīd/ ► n. 1 the alternate rising and falling of the sea due to the attraction of the moon and sun. 2 a powerful surge of feeling or trend of events: *the rising tide of urban violence.* ► v. (**tide someone over**) help someone through a difficult period.

tide·line /'tīd,līn/ (also **tidemark** /'tīd,märk/) ► n. a line left or reached by the sea on a shore at the highest point of a tide.

tide·wa·ter /'tīd,wôtər, -,wätər/ ► n. water brought to or affected by tides.

ti·dings /'tīdiNGz/ ► pl.n. literary news; information.

ti·dy /'tīdē/ ► adj. (**tidier, tidiest**) 1 arranged neatly and in order. 2 liking to keep oneself and one's possessions neat and in order. 3 informal (of a sum of money) considerable. ► v. (**tidies, tidying, tidied**) 1 (often **tidy someone/thing up**) make someone or something tidy. 2 (**tidy something away**) put away for the sake of tidiness. ► n. (pl. **tidies**) a container for holding small objects. ■ **ti·di·ly** adv. **ti·di·ness** n.

tie /tī/ ► v. (**ties, tying, tied**) 1 attach or fasten someone or something with string, cord, etc. 2 form a string, lace, etc., into a knot or bow. 3 restrict or limit to a particular situation or place: *he didn't want to be tied down by a full-time job.* 4 connect or link: *Canada's economy is closely tied to that of the US.* 5 achieve the same score or ranking as another competitor. 6 hold things together by a crosspiece or tie. ► n. (pl. **ties**) 1 a thing that ties. 2 a necktie. 3 a result in a game or match in which two or more competitors are equal. 4 a rod or beam holding parts of a structure together. 5 Music a curved line above

or below two notes of the same pitch indicating that they are to be played as one note.

– PHRASES **tie in** fit or be in harmony: *her ideas don't tie in with mine.* **tie someone up** 1 restrict someone's movement by binding their limbs or tying them to something. 2 informal occupy someone so that they have no time for any other activity. **tie something up** 1 settle something in a satisfactory way. 2 invest capital so that it is not immediately available for use.

tie-back ► n. a decorative strip of fabric or cord used for holding an open curtain back from the window.

tie-break·er /'tī,brākər/ (also **tiebreak** /'tī,brāk/) ► n. a means of deciding a winner from competitors who are equal at the end of a game or match.

tie-dye ► v. produce patterns on fabric by tying knots in it before it is dyed.

tie-in ► n. 1 a connection or association. 2 a product produced to take commercial advantage of a related movie, book, etc.

tie·pin /'tī,pin/ ► n. a tie tack.

tier /ti(ə)r/ ► n. 1 one of a series of rows or levels placed one above and behind the other. 2 a level or grade within an organization or system. ■ **tiered** adj.

tie tack ► n. an ornamental pin for holding a tie in place.

tie-up ► n. a link or connection.

TIFF /tif/ ► abbr. Computing tagged image file format.

tiff /tif/ ► n. informal a trivial quarrel.

ti·ger /'tīgər/ ► n. 1 a large member of the cat family with a yellow-brown coat striped with black, native to the forests of Asia. 2 (also **tiger economy**) a dynamic economy of an East Asian country such as Taiwan or South Korea.

ti·ger cat ► n. 1 a small forest cat that has a light brown coat with dark stripes and blotches, native to Central and South America. 2 a domestic cat with markings like a tiger's.

ti·ger·ish /'tīgərisH/ ► adj. resembling a tiger, especially in being fierce.

ti·ger lil·y ► n. a tall Asian lily with orange flowers spotted with black or purple.

ti·ger moth ► n. a moth with boldly spotted and streaked wings.

ti·ger's eye (also **tiger eye**) ► n. a yellowish-brown semiprecious variety of quartz.

ti·ger shrimp ► n. a large edible shrimp marked with dark bands.

tight /tīt/ ► adj. 1 fixed, closed, or fastened firmly. 2 (of clothes) close-fitting. 3 well sealed against something such as water or air. 4 (of a rope, fabric, or surface) stretched so as to leave no slack. 5 (of an area or space) allowing little room for maneuver: *a tight parking spot.* 6 (of people or things) closely packed together. 7 (of a community or other group) having a close relationship between its members. 8 (of a form of control) strictly imposed: *security was tight.* 9 (of money or time) limited. 10 (of a bend, turn, or angle) changing direction sharply. 11 informal not generous, especially with money; stingy. 12 informal drunk. ► adv. very firmly, closely, or tensely. ■ **tight·ly** adv. **tight·ness** n.

– PHRASES **a tight ship** a strictly controlled organization or operation. **a tight corner** (or **spot**) a difficult situation.

tight·en /'tītn/ ► v. make or become tight or

tighter.

tight·fist·ed ▶ adj. informal not willing to spend or give much money; stingy.

tight-knit (also **tightly knit**) ▶ adj. (of a group of people) closely linked by strong relationships and shared interests.

tight-lipped ▶ adj. unwilling to reveal information or express emotion.

tight·rope /'tīt,rōp/ ▶ n. a rope or wire stretched high above the ground, on which acrobats balance.

tights /tīts/ ▶ pl.n. a close-fitting garment made of stretchy material, covering the hips, legs, and feet.

tight·wad /'tīt,wäd/ ▶ n. informal a mean or miserly person.

ti·gress /'tīgris/ ▶ n. a female tiger.

tike ▶ n. variant spelling of TYKE.

tik·ka /'tika, 'tē-/ ▶ n. an Indian dish of pieces of meat or vegetables marinated in a spice mixture.

ti·la·pi·a /tə'läpēə/ ▶ n. an African freshwater fish, introduced in other parts of the world for food.

til·de /'tildə/ ▶ n. an accent (~) placed over Spanish *n* or Portuguese *a* or *o* to show that they should be pronounced in a particular way.

tile /tīl/ ▶ n. **1** a thin square or rectangular piece of baked clay, concrete, cork, etc., used for covering roofs, floors, or walls. **2** a thin, flat piece used in Scrabble, mah-jongg, and other games. ▶ v. cover a surface with tiles. ■ **til·er** n.

til·ing /'tīliNG/ ▶ n. **1** a surface covered by tiles. **2** the tiles used to cover a surface.

till[1] /til/ ▶ prep. & conj. less formal way of saying UNTIL.

> **USAGE**
> Although **till** and **until** have the same meaning, **till** is more informal and is used more often in speech than in writing. It is also more usual to use **until** at the beginning of a sentence.

till[2] ▶ n. a cash register or drawer for money in a store, bank, or restaurant.

till[3] ▶ v. prepare and cultivate land for crops. ■ **till·a·ble** adj. **till·age** /'tilij/ n.

till·er[1] /'tilər/ ▶ n. a horizontal bar fitted to the head of a boat's rudder post and used for steering.

till·er[2] ▶ n. an implement or machine for breaking up soil, such as a plow.

tilt /tilt/ ▶ v. **1** move into a sloping position. **2** change in attitude or tendency: *the balance of power tilted toward the workers.* **3** (**tilt at**) historical (in jousting) thrust at someone with a lance or other weapon. ▶ n. **1** a sloping position or movement. **2** (**tilt at**) an attempt to win something. **3** a bias or tendency. **4** historical a joust. ■ **tilt·er** n.

– PHRASES (**at**) **full tilt** with maximum speed or force. **tilt at windmills** attack imaginary enemies.

tilth /tilTH/ ▶ n. the condition of soil that has been prepared for growing crops.

tim·bale /'timbəl, tim'bäl/ ▶ n. a dish of finely ground meat or fish cooked with other ingredients in a mold or a pastry shell.

tim·ber /'timbər/ ▶ n. **1** wood prepared for use in building and carpentry. **2** a wooden beam used in building. ■ **tim·bered** adj. **tim·ber·ing** n.

tim·ber·land /'timbər,land/ ▶ n. (also

timberlands) land covered with forest suitable or managed for timber.

tim·ber·line /'timbər,līn/ ▶ n. another term for TREELINE.

tim·ber wolf ▶ n. a wolf of a large variety found mainly in northern North America, with tawny-gray fur.

tim·bre /'tambər, 'tăNbrə/ ▶ n. **1** the quality of a musical sound or voice as distinct from its pitch and intensity. **2** distinctive quality or character: *the phrase had the right bureaucratic timbre.*

tim·brel /'timbrəl/ ▶ n. old use a tambourine or similar instrument.

time /tīm/ ▶ n. **1** the unlimited continued progress of existence and events in the past, present, and future, regarded as a whole. **2** (also **times**) a particular point or period of time: *Victorian times.* **3** a point of time as measured in hours and minutes past midnight or noon. **4** the right or appropriate moment to do something: *it was time to go.* **5** (**a time**) an indefinite period. **6** the length of time taken to complete an activity. **7** time as available or used: *a waste of time.* **8** (**one's time**) a period regarded as characteristic of a stage of one's life. **9** an instance of something happening or being done: *the nurse came in four times a day.* **10** (**times**) (following a number) expressing multiplication. **11** the rhythmic pattern or tempo of a piece of music. **12** the normal rate of pay for time spent working. **13** informal a prison sentence. ▶ v. **1** arrange a time for: *the first race is timed for 11:15.* **2** perform an action at a particular time. **3** measure the time taken by someone or something. **4** (**time something out**) (of a computer or a program) cancel an operation automatically because a set interval of time has passed.

– PHRASES **about time** used to say that something should have happened earlier. **at the same time** nevertheless. **at a time** separately in the specified groups or numbers: *he took the stairs two at a time.* **behind the times** not aware of or using the latest ideas or techniques. **for the time being** until some other arrangement is made. **have no time for** dislike or disapprove of someone or something. **in time 1** not late. **2** eventually. **3** in accordance with the appropriate musical rhythm or tempo. **keep good time 1** (of a clock or watch) record time accurately. **2** be punctual. **keep time** play or accompany music in time. **on time** punctual; punctually. **pass the time of day** exchange greetings or casual remarks. **time immemorial** a time in the past that is so long ago that people cannot remember it. **the time of one's life** a very enjoyable period or occasion. **time will tell** the truth about something will be established in the future.

time-and-mo·tion stud·y ▶ n. a study of the efficiency of a company's working methods.

time bomb ▶ n. **1** a bomb designed to explode at a set time. **2** a situation that is likely to cause serious problems if action is not taken: *the treatment of refugees had become a political time bomb.*

time cap·sule ▶ n. a container holding a selection of objects chosen as being typical of the present time, buried for discovery in the future.

time·card /'tīm'kärd/ ▶ n. a card used to record an employee's starting and quitting times, usually stamped by a time clock.

time clock ▸ n. a clock with a device for recording employees' times of arrival and departure.

time-con·sum·ing ▸ adj. taking a lot of or too much time.

time frame ▸ n. a specified period of time.

time-hon·ored ▸ adj. (of a custom or tradition) respected or valued because it has existed for a long time.

time-keep·er /'tīm,kēpər/ ▸ n. **1** a person who records the amount of time taken by a process or activity. **2** a person regarded in terms of how punctual they are. **3** a watch or clock regarded in terms of how accurate it is. ■ **time-keep·ing** n.

time lag ▸ n. see LAG¹.

time-lapse ▸ adj. (of a photographic technique) taking a sequence of frames at set intervals to record changes that take place slowly over time.

time·less /'tīmlis/ ▸ adj. not affected by the passage of time or changes in fashion. ■ **time·less·ly** adv. **time·less·ness** n.

time·line /'tīm,līn/ (also **time line**) ▸ n. a graphic representation of the passage of time as a line.

time·ly /'tīmlē/ ▸ adj. done or occurring at a favorable or appropriate time. ■ **time·li·ness** n.

time ma·chine ▸ n. (in science fiction) a machine capable of taking a person to the past or future.

time off ▸ n. time that is not occupied with one's usual work or studies.

time out ▸ n. **1** time for rest or leisure. **2** (**timeout**) a brief break from play in a game or sport. **3** a temporary suspension of activities, especially as a punishment for a child who has misbehaved while playing with others.

time·piece /'tīm,pēs/ ▸ n. an instrument for measuring time; a clock or watch.

tim·er /'tīmər/ ▸ n. **1** an automatic device for stopping or starting a machine at a preset time. **2** a person or device that records the amount of time taken by something. **3** indicating how many times someone has done something: *a first-timer*.

time·scale /'tīm,skāl/ ▸ n. the time allowed for or taken by a process or sequence of events.

time·share /'tīm,sHe(ə)r/ ▸ n. an arrangement in which joint owners use a property as a vacation home at different specified times.

time sheet ▸ n. a piece of paper for recording the number of hours worked.

time sig·na·ture ▸ n. a sign in the form of two numbers at the start of a piece of music showing the number of beats in a bar.

time switch ▸ n. a switch that is automatically activated at a set time.

time·ta·ble /'tīm,tābəl/ ▸ n. a list or plan of times at which events are scheduled to take place. ▸ v. schedule something to happen at a particular time.

time tri·al ▸ n. (in various sports) a test of a competitor's individual speed over a set distance.

time warp ▸ n. (especially in science fiction) a situation in which it is possible for people or things belonging to one period to move to another.

time·worn ▸ adj. damaged or made less interesting as a result of age or a great deal of use.

time zone ▸ n. see ZONE (sense 2 of the noun).

tim·id /'timid/ ▸ adj. (**timider, timidest**) not brave or confident. ■ **ti·mid·i·ty** /tə'miditē/ n. **tim·id·ly** adv. **tim·id·ness** n.

tim·ing /'tīmiNG/ ▸ n. **1** the quality of being able to judge the right time to do something: *a politician with an unerring sense of timing.* **2** a particular time when something happens.

tim·or·ous /'timərəs/ ▸ adj. lacking in courage or confidence; nervous. ■ **tim·or·ous·ly** adv. **tim·or·ous·ness** n.

tim·pa·ni /'timpənē/ (also **tympani**) ▸ pl.n. kettledrums. ■ **tim·pa·nist** n.

tin /tin/ ▸ n. **1** a silvery-white metallic chemical element. **2** an airtight container with a lid, made of tinplate or aluminum. **3** Brit. a tinplate or aluminum container for preserving food; a can. ▸ v. (**tins, tinning, tinned**) cover something with a thin layer of tin.

tin can ▸ n. a tinplate or aluminum container for preserving food, especially an empty one.

tinc·ture /'tiNGkcHər/ ▸ n. **1** a medicine made by dissolving a drug in alcohol. **2** a slight trace of something. ▸ v. (**be tinctured**) be tinged with a slight trace of: *his affability was tinctured with faint sarcasm.*

tin·der /'tindər/ ▸ n. dry, flammable material used for lighting a fire.

tin·der·box /'tindər,bäks/ ▸ n. **1** a situation that is likely to become dangerous: *some prisons are tinderboxes of violence.* **2** historical a box containing tinder, flint, a steel, and other items for lighting a fire.

tine /'tīn/ ▸ n. a prong or sharp point, especially of a fork.

tin·e·a /'tinēə/ ▸ n. technical term for RINGWORM.

tin·foil /'tin,foil/ ▸ n. metal foil used for covering or wrapping food.

ting /tiNG/ ▸ n. a sharp, clear ringing sound. ▸ v. make a sharp, clear ringing sound.

tinge /tinj/ ▸ v. (**tinges, tinging** or **tingeing, tinged**) **1** color something slightly. **2** affect with a small amount of a quality: *a visit tinged with sadness.* ▸ n. a slight trace of a color, feeling, or quality.

tin·gle /'tiNGgəl/ ▸ v. experience a slight prickling or stinging sensation. ▸ n. a slight prickling or stinging sensation. ■ **tin·gly** /'tiNGg(ə)lē/ adj.

tin·horn /'tin,hôrn/ informal ▸ n. a contemptible person, especially one pretending to have money, influence, or ability. ▸ adj. pretending to be more significant or influential than one really is; small-time: *tinhorn dictators who turn out to be military incompetents.*

tin·ker /'tiNGkər/ ▸ n. **1** a traveling mender of pots, kettles, etc. **2** an act of tinkering with something. ▸ v. (**tinker with**) try to repair or improve something by making many small changes. ■ **tin·ker·er** n.

tin·kle /'tiNGkəl/ ▸ v. make a light, clear ringing sound. ▸ n. a light, clear ringing sound. ■ **tin·kly** /-k(ə)lē/ adj.

tin·ni·tus /'tinitəs, ti'nī-/ ▸ n. Medicine ringing or buzzing in the ears.

tin·ny /'tinē/ ▸ adj. **1** having a thin, metallic sound. **2** made of thin or poor-quality metal. **3** having an unpleasantly metallic taste. ■ **tin·ni·ly** adv. **tin·ni·ness** n.

Tin Pan Al·ley ▸ n. **1** a district in New York City where many songwriters, arrangers, and music publishers were formerly based. **2** the world of composers and publishers of popular music.

tin·plate /'tin,plāt/ ▸ n. sheet steel or iron coated with tin. ■ **tin·plat·ed adj.**

tin·pot /'tin,pät/ ▸ adj. informal not significant or effective: *a tinpot dictator.*

tin·sel /'tinsəl/ ▸ n. **1** a form of decoration consisting of thin strips of shiny metal foil attached to a length of thread. **2** superficial attractiveness or glamour: *the phony tinsel of Hollywood.* ■ **tin·seled adj. tin·sel·ly adj.**

Tin·sel·town /'tinsəl,toun/ ▸ n. the glamorous but artificial world of Hollywood and its film industry.

tin·smith /'tin,smiTH/ ▸ n. a person who makes or repairs articles made of tin or tinplate.

tin·snips /'tin,snips/ ▸ pl.n. a pair of clippers for cutting sheet metal.

tint /tint/ ▸ n. **1** a shade of a color. **2** a dye for coloring the hair. ▸ v. **1** color slightly: *the clouds were tinted with crimson.* **2** dye the hair.

tin·tin·nab·u·la·tion /,tintə,nabyə'lāSHən/ ▸ n. a ringing or tinkling sound.

ti·ny /'tīnē/ ▸ adj. (**tinier, tiniest**) very small. ▸ n. (pl. **tinies**) informal a very young child. ■ **ti·ni·ly adv. ti·ni·ness n.**

tip¹ /tip/ ▸ n. **1** the pointed or rounded end of something thin or tapering. **2** a small part fitted to the end of an object. ▸ v. (**tips, tipping, tipped**) (usu. as adj. **tipped**) attach to or cover the tip of: *a tipped cigarette.*
– PHRASES **on the tip of one's tongue** almost but not quite spoken or coming to mind.

tip² ▸ v. (**tips, tipping, tipped**) **1** overbalance so as to fall or turn over. **2** be or put in a sloping position. **3** empty out the contents of a container by holding it at an angle. **4** hit or touch lightly: *his shot was tipped over the bar by Nixon.*
– PHRASES **tip one's hat** raise or touch one's hat as a greeting or mark of respect.

tip³ ▸ n. **1** a small extra sum of money given to someone to reward good service. **2** a piece of practical advice. **3** a piece of expert information about the likely winner of a race or contest. ▸ v. (**tips, tipping, tipped**) **1** give a tip to someone as a reward for good service. **2** (**tip someone off**) informal give someone secret information.

tipi ▸ n. variant spelling of TEPEE.

tip-off ▸ n. informal a piece of secret information.

tip·per /'tipər/ ▸ n. a person who leaves a tip of a specified amount: *a good tipper.*

tip·ple /'tipəl/ ▸ v. drink alcohol regularly. ▸ n. informal an alcoholic drink. ■ **tip·pler** /'tip(ə)lər/ n.

tip·py·toe /'tipē/ ▸ v. informal tiptoe.

tip·ster /'tipstər/ ▸ n. a person who gives tips as to the likely winner of a race or contest.

tip·sy /'tipsē/ ▸ adj. (**tipsier, tipsiest**) slightly drunk. ■ **tip·si·ly adv. tip·si·ness n.**

tip·toe /'tip,tō/ ▸ v. (**tiptoes, tiptoeing, tiptoed**) walk quietly and carefully with the heels raised and the weight on the balls of the feet.
– PHRASES **on tiptoe** (or **tiptoes**) with the heels raised and the weight on the balls of the feet.

tip-top ▸ adj. of the very best quality; excellent.

ti·rade /'tī,rād, ,tī'rād/ ▸ n. a long angry speech criticizing someone or something.

tir·a·mi·su /,tirəmē'soō, -'mēsoō/ ▸ n. an Italian dessert consisting of layers of sponge cake soaked in coffee and brandy, with powdered

chocolate and mascarpone cheese.

tire¹ /tīr/ ▸ v. **1** make or become in need of rest or sleep. **2** make someone feel impatient or bored. **3** (**tire of**) become impatient or bored with: *she will stay with him until she tires of her.*

tire² /tī(ə)r/ (Brit. **tyre**) ▸ n. a rubber covering that is inflated or that surrounds an inflated inner tube, fitted around a wheel to form a soft contact with the road.

tired /tīrd/ ▸ adj. **1** in need of sleep or rest; weary. **2** (**tired of**) bored with someone or something. **3** (of a statement or idea) boring or uninteresting because used too often. ■ **tired·ly adv. tired·ness n.**

tire iron ▸ n. a steel lever for removing tires from wheel rims.

tire·less /'tīrlis/ ▸ adj. having or showing great effort or energy. ■ **tire·less·ly adv. tire·less·ness n.**

tire·some /'tīrsəm/ ▸ adj. annoying or boring. ■ **tire·some·ly adv. tire·some·ness n.**

'tis ▸ contr. chiefly literary it is.

ti·sane /ti'zan, -'zän/ ▸ n. an herbal tea.

tis·sue /'tishoō/ ▸ n. **1** any of the distinct types of material of which animals or plants are made, consisting of specialized cells. **2** tissue paper. **3** a paper handkerchief. **4** delicate gauzy fabric. ■ **tis·su·ey adj.**
– PHRASES **a tissue of lies** a story that is full of lies.

tis·sue cul·ture ▸ n. Biology & Medicine the growing of cells from a living organism in an artificial medium outside the organism.

tis·sue pa·per ▸ n. very thin, soft paper.

tit¹ /tit/ ▸ n. a small insect-eating songbird; a titmouse.

tit² ▸ n. vulgar slang a woman's breast.

tit³ ▸ n. (in phrase **tit for tat**) a situation in which a person insults or hurts someone to retaliate for something they have done.

Ti·tan /'tītn/ ▸ n. **1** any of a family of giant gods in Greek mythology. **2** (**titan**) a very strong, intelligent, or important person.

ti·tan·ic /tī'tanik/ ▸ adj. very strong, large, or powerful: *a titanic struggle for survival.* ■ **ti·tan·i·cal·ly** /-ik(ə)lē/ adv.

ti·ta·ni·um /tī'tānēəm/ ▸ n. a hard silver-gray metal used in strong corrosion-resistant alloys.

tithe /tīTH/ ▸ n. **1** one tenth of the amount people produced or earned in a year, formerly taken as a tax to support the Church. **2** (in certain religious denominations) a tenth of a person's income pledged to the Church. ▸ v. pay a tenth of one's income as a tithe.

Ti·tian /'tishən/ ▸ adj. (of hair) bright golden auburn.

tit·il·late /'titl,āt/ ▸ v. interest or excite someone, especially in a sexual way. ■ **tit·il·la·tion** /,titl'āSHən/ n.

tit·i·vate /'titə,vāt/ ▸ v. informal make someone or something neater or more attractive. ■ **tit·i·va·tion** /,titə'vāSHən/ n.

ti·tle /'tītl/ ▸ n. **1** the name of a book, musical composition, or other work. **2** a name that describes someone's position or job. **3** a word, such as *Dr., Mrs.,* or *Prince,* used before or instead of someone's name to indicate their rank, profession, or status. **4** the position of being the winner of a competition, especially of being the champion of a sports competition: *he won the world title.* **5** a caption or credit in a movie or television broadcast. **6** the legal right to own something, especially land or property. ▶ v. give a title to someone or something.

ti·tled /'tītld/ ▶ adj. having a title indicating nobility or rank.

ti·tle deed ▶ n. a legal document providing evidence of a person's right to own a property.

ti·tle role ▶ n. the role in a play, movie, or television show from which the work's title is taken.

tit·mouse /'tit‚mous/ ▶ n. (pl. **titmice** /'tit‚mīs/) another term for TIT¹.

ti·trate /'tī‚trāt/ ▶ v. Chemistry calculate the amount of a substance in a solution by measuring the volume of a standard reagent required to react with it. ■ **ti·tra·tion** /‚tī'trāsHən/ n.

tit·ter /'titər/ ▶ v. give a short, quiet laugh. ▶ n. a short, quiet laugh.

tit·tle /'titl/ ▶ n. a tiny amount or part of something.

tit·tle-tat·tle ▶ n. trivial talk; gossip. ▶ v. engage in gossip.

tit·u·lar /'ticHələr/ ▶ adj. **1** holding a formal position or title without any real authority: *the queen is titular head of the Church of England.* **2** relating to a title. ■ **tit·u·lar·ly** adv.

tiz·zy /'tizē/ ▶ n. (pl. **tizzies**) informal a state of nervous excitement or agitation.

TKO ▶ abbr. Boxing technical knockout.

Tl ▶ symbol the chemical element thallium.

TLC ▶ abbr. informal tender loving care.

TM ▶ abbr. **1** trademark. **2** trademark Transcendental Meditation.

Tm ▶ symbol the chemical element thulium.

TN ▶ abbr. Tennessee.

TNC ▶ abbr. transnational corporation.

TNT ▶ abbr. trinitrotoluene, a high explosive.

to /tōō/ ▶ prep. **1** in the direction of. **2** situated in the direction mentioned: *there are mountains to the north.* **3** so as to reach a particular state. **4** identifying the person or thing affected by an action: *you were unkind to her.* **5** indicating that people or things are related, linked, or attached. **6** (in telling the time) before the hour specified: *it's four minutes to six.* **7** indicating a rate of return: *the car only does ten miles to the gallon.* **8** introducing the second part of a comparison: *the club's nothing to what it once was.* ▶ infinitive marker used with the base form of a verb to indicate that the verb is in the infinitive. ▶ adv. so as to be closed or nearly closed: *he pulled the door to.*
– PHRASES **to and fro** in a constant movement backward and forward or from side to side.

> **USAGE**
> Do not confuse **to** with **too** or **two. To** mainly means 'in the direction of' (*the next train to London*), while **too** means 'excessively' (*she was driving too fast*) or 'in addition' (*is he coming too?*). **Two** is a number meaning 'one less than three' (*we met two years ago*).

toad /tōd/ ▶ n. **1** a tailless amphibian with a short stout body and short legs. **2** a very unpleasant or disliked person.

toad·flax /'tōd‚flaks/ ▶ n. a plant with yellow or purplish flowers that resemble those of the snapdragon.

toad·stool /'tōd‚stōōl/ ▶ n. a fungus, typically in the form of a rounded cap on a stalk.

toad·y /'tōdē/ ▶ n. (pl. **toadies**) a person who behaves in an excessively respectful way toward another in order to gain their favor. ▶ v. (**toadies, toadying, toadied**) act in an excessively respectful way to gain someone's favor.

toast /tōst/ ▶ n. **1** sliced bread that has been browned by putting it close to a source of heat, such as a broiler or fire. **2** an act of raising glasses at a gathering and drinking together in honor of a person or thing. **3** a person who is respected or admired: *he was the toast of the baseball world.* ▶ v. **1** make bread or other food brown by putting it under a broiler or close to another source of heat. **2** drink a toast to someone. **3** (of a DJ) accompany reggae music with improvised rhythmic speech.
– PHRASES **be toast** informal be finished, defunct, or dead.

toast·er /'tōstər/ ▶ n. an electrical device for making toast.

toast·mas·ter /'tōs(t)‚mastər/ (or **toastmistress** /'tōs(t)‚mistris/) ▶ n. an official responsible for proposing toasts and making other formal announcements at a large social event.

toast·y /'tōstē/ ▶ adj. **1** of or resembling toast. **2** comfortably warm.

to·bac·co /tə'bakō/ ▶ n. (pl. **tobaccos**) the dried nicotine-rich leaves of an American plant, used for smoking or chewing.

to·bac·co·nist /tə'bakənist/ ▶ n. a merchant who sells cigarettes and tobacco.

to·bog·gan /tə'bägən/ ▶ n. a light, long, narrow sled used for sliding downhill over snow or ice. ▶ v. ride on a toboggan.

toc·ca·ta /tə'kätə/ ▶ n. a musical composition for a keyboard instrument designed to display the performer's touch and technique.

to·coph·er·ol /tə'käfə‚rôl, -‚räl/ ▶ n. vitamin E.

toc·sin /'täksən/ ▶ n. old use an alarm bell or signal.

to·day /tə'dā/ ▶ adv. **1** on or during this present day. **2** at the present period of time; nowadays. ▶ n. **1** this present day. **2** the present period of time.

tod·dle /'tädl/ ▶ v. **1** (of a young child) move with short unsteady steps while learning to walk. **2** informal go somewhere in a casual or leisurely way. ▶ n. an act of toddling.

tod·dler /'tädlər/ ▶ n. a young child who is just beginning to walk.

tod·dy /'tädē/ ▶ n. (pl. **toddies**) a drink made of liquor with hot water and sugar.

to-do /tə 'dōō/ ▶ n. informal a commotion or fuss.

toe /tō/ ▶ n. **1** any of the five digits at the end of the foot. **2** the lower end or tip of something. ▶ v. (**toes, toeing, toed**) push or touch someone or something with the toes. ■ **toe·less** adj.
– PHRASES **make someone's toes curl** informal make someone feel very embarrassed. **on one's toes** ready and alert. **toe the line** obey authority.

> **USAGE**
> The phrase **toe the line**, which comes from the meaning 'stand with the tips of the toes exactly touching a line', is often misinterpreted and wrongly spelled as tow the line.

toe·cap /'tō‚kap/ ▶ n. a piece of steel or leather on the front part of a boot or shoe.

toe·hold /'tō‚hōld/ ▶ n. **1** a relatively minor position from which further progress may be made: *the initiative is helping companies to gain a toehold in the Gulf.* **2** (in climbing) a small foothold.

toe·nail /'tō͟,nāl/ ▶ n. a nail on the upper surface of the tip of each toe.

toe-tap·ping ▶ adj. informal (of music) lively.

toff /täf/ ▶ n. Brit. informal, derogatory a rich upper-class person.

tof·fee /'tôfē, 'täfē/ ▶ n. a kind of firm candy that softens when sucked or chewed, made by boiling together sugar and butter.

to·fu /'tōfōō/ ▶ n. a soft white substance made from mashed soybeans, used in Asian and vegetarian cooking.

tog /täg/ informal ▶ n. (**togs**) clothes. ▶ v. (**be togged up/out**) be fully dressed for a particular occasion or activity.

to·ga /'tōgə/ ▶ n. a loose outer garment made of a single piece of cloth, worn by the citizens of ancient Rome.

to·geth·er /tə'geṯHər/ ▶ adv. **1** with or near to another person or people. **2** so as to touch, combine, or be united. **3** regarded as a whole. **4** (of two people) married or in a sexual relationship. **5** at the same time. **6** without interruption. ▶ adj. informal sensible, calm, or well organized. ■ **to·geth·er·ness** n.
– PHRASES **together with** as well as.

tog·gle /'tägəl/ ▶ n. **1** a narrow piece of wood or plastic attached to a coat or jacket, pushed through a loop to act as a fastener. **2** Computing a key or command that is used to alternate between one effect, feature, or state and another. ▶ v. Computing switch from one effect, feature, or state to another by using a toggle.

tog·gle switch ▶ n. an electric switch operated by means of a projecting lever that is moved up and down.

To·go·lese /,tōgō'lēz, ,tōgə-, -'lēs/ ▶ n. (pl. same) a person from Togo, a country in West Africa. ▶ adj. relating to Togo.

toil /toil/ ▶ v. **1** work very hard. **2** move along slowly and with difficulty. ▶ n. exhausting work. ■ **toil·er** n.

toile /twäl/ ▶ n. **1** an early version of a finished garment made up in cheap material so that the design can be tested. **2** a semitransparent fabric.

toi·let /'toilit/ ▶ n. **1** a large bowl for urinating or defecating into. **2** a bathroom.

toi·let pa·per ▶ n. paper in sheets or on a roll for wiping oneself clean after using a toilet.

toi·let·ries /'toilitrēz/ ▶ pl.n. articles used in washing and taking care of the body, such as soap and shampoo.

toi·lette /twä'let/ ▶ n. old-fashioned term for TOILET (sense 2).

toi·let-train ▶ v. teach a young child to use the toilet.

toi·let wa·ter ▶ n. a diluted form of perfume.

toil·some /'toilsəm/ ▶ adj. old use or literary involving hard work or effort.

To·kay /tō'kā/ ▶ n. a sweet aromatic wine, originally made near Tokaj in Hungary.

toke /tōk/ informal ▶ n. a draw on a cigarette or pipe, especially one containing marijuana. ▶ v. smoke cannabis or tobacco.

to·ken /'tōkən/ ▶ n. **1** a thing that represents a fact, quality, or feeling: *the gift of a plant*

is a token of love. **2** a voucher that can be exchanged for goods or services. **3** a disk used to operate a machine or in exchange for certain goods or services. ▶ adj. **1** done for the sake of appearances: *cases like this often bring token fines.* **2** chosen by way of tokenism to represent a particular group.
– PHRASES **by the same token** in the same way or for the same reason.

to·ken·ism /'tōkə,nizəm/ ▶ n. the practice of doing something in a superficial way, so as to be seen to be obeying the law or satisfying a particular group of people. ■ **to·ken·is·tic** /,tōkə'nistik/ adj.

told /tōld/ ▶ past and past participle of TELL.

tol·er·a·ble /'tälərəbəl/ ▶ adj. **1** able to be tolerated or endured. **2** fairly good.
■ **tol·er·a·bil·i·ty** /,täl(ə)rə'bilitē/ n. **tol·er·a·bly** /-blē/ adv.

tol·er·ance /'täl(ə)rəns/ ▶ n. **1** the ability to accept things that one dislikes or disagrees with. **2** the ability to endure specified conditions or treatment: *the plant's tolerance to pests and herbicides.* **3** an allowable amount of variation of a measurement, especially in the dimensions of a machine or part.

tol·er·ant /'tälərənt/ ▶ adj. **1** able to accept things that one dislikes or disagrees with. **2** able to endure specified conditions or treatment. ■ **tol·er·ant·ly** adv.

tol·er·ate /'tälə,rāt/ ▶ v. **1** allow something that one dislikes or disagrees with to exist or continue: *the organization will not tolerate racism.* **2** patiently endure someone or something that is unpleasant or annoying. **3** be able to be exposed to a drug, toxin, etc., without a bad reaction. ■ **tol·er·a·tion** /,tälə'rāsHən/ n.

toll[1] /tōl/ ▶ n. **1** a charge payable to use a bridge or road or for a long-distance telephone call. **2** the number of deaths or casualties arising from an accident, disaster, etc. **3** the cost or damage resulting from something: *the policy's environmental toll has been high.*
– PHRASES **take its toll** (or **take a heavy toll**) have a very harmful effect.

toll[2] ▶ v. **1** (of a bell) sound with slow, even strokes. **2** (of a bell) ring to announce the time, a service, or a person's death. ▶ n. a single ring of a bell.

toll·booth /'tōl,bōōTH/ ▶ n. a booth at which drivers must stop to pay a toll.

toll·gate /'tōl,gāt/ ▶ n. a barrier across a road where a toll must be paid to pass through.

Tol·tec /'tōl,tek, 'täl-/ ▶ n. a member of an American Indian people that flourished in Mexico before the Aztecs. ■ **Tol·tec·an** /tōl'tekən, täl-/ adj.

tol·u·ene /'tälyōō,ēn/ ▶ n. a liquid hydrocarbon resembling benzene, present in coal tar and petroleum.

tom /täm/ ▶ n. the male of various animals, especially a domestic cat.

tom·a·hawk /'tämə,hôk/ ▶ n. a light ax formerly used as a tool or weapon by American Indians.

to·ma·to /tə'mātō, -'mätō/ ▶ n. (pl. **tomatoes**) a glossy red or yellow edible fruit, eaten as a vegetable or in salads.

tomb /tōōm/ ▶ n. **1** a burial place consisting of a stone structure above ground or a large underground vault. **2** a monument to a dead person, erected over their burial place. **3** (**the tomb**) literary death.

tom·boy /'täm,boi/ ▶ n. a girl who enjoys rough, noisy activities traditionally associated with boys. ■ **tom·boy·ish** adj.

tomb·stone /'tōōm,stōn/ ▶ n. a large, flat inscribed stone standing or laid over a grave.

tom·cat /'täm,kat/ ▶ n. a male domestic cat.

Tom Col·lins /täm 'kälənz/ ▶ n. a cocktail made from gin mixed with soda water, sugar, and lemon or lime juice.

Tom, Dick, and Har·ry /'täm 'dik and 'harē/ ▶ n. ordinary people in general.

tome /tōm/ ▶ n. chiefly humorous a book, especially a large, serious one.

tom·fool·er·y /täm'fōōl(ə)rē/ ▶ n. silly behavior.

Tom·my /'tämē/ ▶ n. (pl. **Tommies**) informal a British private soldier.

tom·my gun /'tämē/ ▶ n. informal a type of submachine gun.

to·mog·ra·phy /tə'mägrəfē/ ▶ n. a technique for displaying a cross section through a human body or other solid object using X-rays or ultrasound. ■ **to·mo·gram** /'tōmə,gram/ n. **to·mo·graph·ic** /,tōmə'grafik/ adj.

to·mor·row /tə'môrō, -'märō/ ▶ adv. **1** on the day after today. **2** in the near future. ▶ n. **1** the day after today. **2** the near future.

tom-tom ▶ n. a drum beaten with the hands, associated with North American Indian, African, or Eastern cultures.

ton /tən/ ▶ n. **1** (also **short ton**) a unit of weight equal to 2,000 lb avoirdupois (907.19 kg). **2** (also **long ton**) a unit of weight equal to 2,240 lb avoirdupois (1,016.05 kg). **3** a metric ton. **4** (also **displacement ton**) a unit of measurement of a ship's weight equal to 2,240 lb or 35 cubic feet (0.99 cubic meters). **5** (also **tons**) informal a large number or amount of something.

ton·al /'tōnl/ ▶ adj. **1** relating to tone. **2** (of music) written using conventional keys and harmony. ■ **ton·al·ly** adv.

to·nal·i·ty /tō'nalitē/ ▶ n. (pl. **tonalities**) **1** the character of a piece of music as determined by the key in which it is played or the relationships between the notes of a scale or key. **2** the use of conventional keys and harmony as the basis of musical composition.

ton·do /'tändō/ ▶ n. (pl. **tondi** /-dē/) a circular painting.

tone /tōn/ ▶ n. **1** a musical or vocal sound with reference to its pitch, quality, and strength: *they spoke in hushed tones.* **2** the sound of a person's voice, expressing a feeling or mood. **3** the general character of something: *trust her to lower the tone of the conversation.* **4** (also **whole tone**) a basic interval in classical Western music, equal to two semitones. **5** the particular quality of brightness or deepness of a shade of a color. **6** the normal level of firmness in a resting muscle. ▶ v. **1** (often **tone something up**) make the body or a muscle stronger or firmer. **2** (**tone something down**) make something less harsh, extreme, or intense: *he toned down his criticisms.* **3** (**tone with**) match the color of something. ■ **tone·less** adj.

tone arm ▶ n. the movable arm supporting the pickup of a record player.

tone-deaf ▶ adj. unable to recognize differences of musical pitch accurately.

tone po·em ▶ n. a piece of orchestral music, typically in one movement, describing a subject taken from mythology, literature, history, etc.

ton·er /'tōnər/ ▶ n. **1** a liquid applied to the skin to reduce oiliness and improve its condition. **2** a powder used in photocopiers. **3** a chemical solution used to change the tone of a photographic print.

tong /tôNG, täNG/ ▶ n. a Chinese association or secret society associated with organized crime.

Ton·gan /'täNGgən/ ▶ n. **1** a person from Tonga, a group of islands in the South Pacific. **2** the Polynesian language spoken in Tonga. ▶ adj. relating to Tonga.

tongs /tôNGz, täNGz/ ▶ pl.n. a tool with two movable arms that are joined at one end, used for picking up and holding things.

tongue /təNG/ ▶ n. **1** the fleshy muscular organ in the mouth, used for tasting, licking, swallowing, and (in humans) producing speech. **2** the tongue of an animal as food. **3** a person's style or way of speaking: *his sharp tongue.* **4** a particular language. **5** a strip of leather or fabric under the laces in a shoe. **6** the clapper of a bell. **7** a long, low promontory of land. **8** a projecting strip on a wooden board that fits into a groove on another. **9** the vibrating reed of a musical instrument or organ pipe. ▶ v. (**tongues**, **tonguing**, **tongued**) **1** sound a note distinctly on a wind instrument by interrupting the air flow with the tongue. **2** lick something with the tongue.

– PHRASES **the gift of tongues** the power of speaking in unknown languages, believed by some Christians to be one of the gifts of the Holy Spirit. **have lost one's tongue** be silent, especially as a result of shock, shyness, etc. **hold one's tongue** dated remain silent. (**with**) **tongue in cheek** not seriously meaning what one is saying.

tongue and groove ▶ n. wooden planking in which adjacent boards are joined by means of interlocking ridges and grooves down their sides.

tongue de·pres·sor ▶ n. an instrument used by health practitioners to press down the tongue in order to allow inspection of the mouth or throat.

tongue-in-cheek ▶ adj. & adv. with ironic or flippant intent.

tongue-lash·ing ▶ n. a severe scolding.

tongue-tied ▶ adj. too shy or embarrassed to speak.

tongue-twist·er ▶ n. a sequence of words that are difficult to pronounce quickly and correctly.

ton·ic /'tänik/ ▶ n. **1** a medicinal drink taken to make a person feel healthier or more energetic. **2** anything that makes a person feel better: *a vacation is just the tonic you need to shake off those midwinter blues.* **3** short for TONIC WATER. **4** the first note in a musical scale that, in conventional harmony, provides the keynote of a piece of music.

ton·ic sol-fa /,sōl 'fä/ ▶ n. a system of naming the notes of the scale used to teach singing, with do as the keynote of all major keys and la as the keynote of all minor keys.

ton·ic wa·ter ▶ n. a bitter carbonated soft drink made with quinine, used especially as a mixer with gin or other liquors.

to·night /tə'nīt/ ▶ adv. on the evening or night of

the present day. ▶ n. the evening or night of the present day.

ton·nage /'tənij/ ▶ n. **1** weight in tons. **2** the size or carrying capacity of a ship measured in tons.

tonne /tən/ ▶ n. another term for METRIC TON.

ton·sil /'tänsəl/ ▶ n. either of two small masses of tissue in the throat, one on each side of the root of the tongue.

ton·sil·lec·to·my /ˌtänsə'lektəmē/ ▶ n. (pl. **tonsillectomies**) a surgical operation to remove the tonsils.

ton·sil·li·tis /ˌtänsə'lītis/ ▶ n. inflammation of the tonsils.

ton·so·ri·al /tän'sôrēəl/ ▶ adj. chiefly humorous relating to hairdressing.

ton·sure /'tänshər/ ▶ n. a circular area on a monk's or priest's head where the hair is shaved off. ■ **ton·sured** adj.

Ton·y /'tōnē/ ▶ n. (pl. **Tonys**) any of a number of awards given annually for outstanding achievement in the theater.

ton·y /'tōnē/ ▶ adj. (**tonier, toniest**) informal fashionable, stylish, or high-class.

too /tōō/ ▶ adv. **1** to a higher degree than is desirable, allowed, or possible. **2** in addition; also: *is he coming too?* **3** informal very: *you're too kind.*
– PHRASES **none too** —— not very: *she was none too pleased.*

> **USAGE**
> On the confusion of **too** with **to** or **two**, see the note at TO.

took /tŏŏk/ ▶ past of TAKE.

tool /tōōl/ ▶ n. **1** a piece of equipment, especially a hand-held one, used to carry out a particular function. **2** a thing used to help achieve something or perform a job: *a dictionary is an invaluable tool while you are learning a language.* **3** a person used or controlled by another.
▶ v. **1** make a decorative design on a leather book cover by using a heated tool. **2** provide a factory with the equipment needed to do or make something. **3** informal drive around in a casual or leisurely way.

tool·bar /'tōōl,bär/ ▶ n. Computing a strip of icons used to perform certain functions.

tool·box /'tōōl,bäks/ ▶ n. **1** a box or container for tools. **2** Computing the set of programs or functions accessible from a single menu.

tool kit ▶ n. **1** a set of tools. **2** Computing a set of software tools.

tool·mak·er /'tōōl,mākər/ ▶ n. a person who makes and repairs tools for use in a manufacturing process.

toot /tōōt/ ▶ n. **1** a short, sharp sound made by a horn, trumpet, or similar instrument. **2** informal a spell of carousing; a spree. **3** informal cocaine, or a snort of cocaine. ▶ v. **1** make a short, sharp sound with a horn, trumpet, or similar instrument. **2** informal snort cocaine.

tooth /tōōTH/ ▶ n. (pl. **teeth** /tēTH/) **1** each of a set of hard enamel-coated structures in the jaws, used for biting and chewing. **2** a projecting part, especially a cog on a gearwheel or a point on a saw or comb. **3** (**teeth**) genuine power or effectiveness: *the Charter would be fine if it had teeth.* ■ **toothed** adj.
– PHRASES **armed to the teeth** having many weapons. **fight tooth and nail** fight very fiercely. **get one's teeth into** work energetically

and enthusiastically on a particular task. **in the teeth of 1** directly against the wind. **2** in spite of opposition or difficulty.

tooth·ache /'tōōTH,āk/ ▶ n. pain in a tooth or teeth.

tooth·brush /'tōōTH,brəSH/ ▶ n. a small brush with a long handle, used for cleaning the teeth.

toothed whale ▶ n. any of the large group of predatory whales with teeth, including sperm whales, killer whales, and dolphins.

tooth fair·y ▶ n. a fairy said to take children's milk teeth after they fall out and leave a coin under their pillow.

tooth·less /'tōōTHlis/ ▶ adj. **1** having no teeth. **2** lacking genuine power or effectiveness: *laws that are well intentioned but toothless.*

tooth·paste /'tōōTH,pāst/ ▶ n. a paste used on a brush for cleaning the teeth.

tooth·pick /'tōōTH,pik/ ▶ n. a short pointed piece of wood or plastic used for removing bits of food stuck between the teeth.

tooth·some /'tōōTHsəm/ ▶ adj. **1** (of food) appetizing or tasty. **2** informal attractive; appealing.

tooth·y /'tōōTHē/ ▶ adj. (**toothier, toothiest**) having or showing numerous, large, or prominent teeth. ■ **tooth·i·ly** adv.

too·tle /'tōōtl/ ▶ v. **1** casually make a series of sounds on a horn, trumpet, etc. **2** informal go or travel in a leisurely way. ▶ n. **1** an act or sound of tootling. **2** informal a leisurely journey.

toot·sie /'tōōtsē/ (also **tootsy**) ▶ n. (pl. **tootsies**) informal **1** a person's foot. **2** a young woman.

top¹ /täp/ ▶ n. **1** the highest or uppermost point, part, or surface. **2** a thing placed on, fitted to, or covering the upper part of something. **3** (**the top**) the highest or most important rank, level, or position. **4** the utmost degree: *she shouted at the top of her voice.* **5** an item of clothing covering the upper part of the body. **6** (**tops**) informal a particularly good person or thing.
▶ adj. highest in position, rank, or degree: *the top floor.* ▶ v. (**tops, topping, topped**) **1** be more, better, or taller than: *sales topped $500,000 last year.* **2** be at the highest place or rank in: *the album topped the charts for five weeks.* **3** provide something with a top or topping. **4** reach the top of a hill, slope, etc. ▶ adv. (**tops**) informal at the most. ■ **top·most** /'täp,mōst/ adj.
– PHRASES **on top** in addition. **on top of 1** so as to cover. **2** very near to. **3** in command or control of. **4** in addition to. **on top of the world** informal very happy. **over the top 1** informal to an excessive or exaggerated degree. **2** chiefly historical over the parapet of a trench and into battle. **top something off** finish something in a memorable way. **top something out** put the highest structural feature on a building. **top something up** fill up a partly full container.

top² ▶ n. a toy with a rounded top and pointed base, that can be made to spin when turned around very quickly.

to·paz /'tōpaz/ ▶ n. **1** a colorless, yellow, or pale blue precious stone. **2** a dark yellow color.

top brass ▶ n. see BRASS.

top·coat /'täp,kōt/ ▶ n. **1** an overcoat. **2** an outer coat of paint.

top dog ▶ n. informal a person who is successful or dominant in their field.

top-down ▶ adj. **1** referring to a system in which actions and policies are initiated at the highest level; hierarchical. **2** proceeding from the general to the particular: *a top-down approach to research.*

top draw·er ▶ adj. informal of the highest quality or social class.

tope[1] /tōp/ ▶ v. old use or literary regularly drink too much alcohol. ■ **top·er** n.

tope[2] ▶ n. a small shark found chiefly in coastal waters.

top flight ▶ n. the highest rank or level.

top·gal·lant /täp'galənt, tə'gal-/ ▶ n. **1** the section of a square-rigged sailing ship's mast immediately above the topmast. **2** a sail set on a topgallant mast.

top hat ▶ n. a man's formal black hat with a high cylindrical crown.

top-heav·y ▶ adj. **1** too heavy at the top and therefore likely to fall over or be unstable. **2** (of an organization) having too many senior executives compared to the number of ordinary workers.

to·pi·ar·y /'tōpē,erē/ ▶ n. (pl. **topiaries**) **1** the art of clipping bushes or trees into decorative shapes. **2** bushes or trees clipped into decorative shapes.

top·ic /'täpik/ ▶ n. a subject of a piece of writing, speech, conversation, etc.

top·i·cal /'täpikəl/ ▶ adj. **1** relating to or dealing with current affairs. **2** relating to a particular subject. **3** (of a medicine) applied to part of the body. ■ **top·i·cal·i·ty** /,täpə'kalitē/ n. **top·i·cal·ly** /-ik(ə)lē/ adv.

top·knot /'täp,nät/ ▶ n. **1** a section of hair tied up on the top of the head. **2** a tuft or crest of hair or feathers on the head of an animal or bird.

top·less /'täpləs/ ▶ adj. having the breasts uncovered.

top·lev·el ▶ adj. of the highest level of importance.

top·mast /'täp,mast, -məst/ ▶ n. the second section of a square-rigged sailing ship's mast, immediately above the lower mast.

top-notch ▶ adj. informal of the highest quality.

to·pog·ra·phy /tə'pägrəfē/ ▶ n. (pl. **topographies**) **1** the arrangement of the physical features of an area. **2** a detailed representation of the physical features of an area on a map. ■ **to·pog·ra·pher** n. **top·o·graph·ic** /,täpə'grafik/ adj. **top·o·graph·i·cal** /,täpə'grafikəl/ adj.

to·poi /'tōpoi/ ▶ plural of TOPOS.

to·pol·o·gy /tə'päləjē/ ▶ n. (pl. **topologies**) **1** Mathematics the study of geometrical properties and spatial relations that remain unaffected by smooth changes in shape or size of figures. **2** the way in which the parts of something are interrelated or arranged. ■ **top·o·log·i·cal** /,täpə'läjikəl/ adj.

top·o·nym /'täpə,nim/ ▶ n. a place name, especially one derived from a physical feature of the area.

top·os /'tōpōs/ ▶ n. (pl. **topoi** /-poi/) a traditional theme in literature.

top·ping /'täpiNG/ ▶ n. a layer of food poured or spread over another food.

top·ple /'täpəl/ ▶ v. **1** overbalance and fall over. **2** remove a government or leader from power.

top round ▶ n. a cut of meat from an inner section of a round of beef.

top·sail /'täpsəl, -,sāl/ ▶ n. **1** a sail set on a ship's topmast. **2** a sail set lengthwise, above the gaff.

top se·cret ▶ adj. of the highest secrecy.

top-shelf ▶ adj. of a high quality; excellent: *top-shelf vocal talent.*

top·side /'täp,sīd/ ▶ n. the upper part of a ship's side, above the waterline.

top·soil /'täp,soil/ ▶ n. the top layer of soil.

top·spin /'täp,spin/ ▶ n. a fast forward spin given to a moving ball, often resulting in a curved path or a strong forward motion on rebounding.

top·sy-tur·vy /'täpsē 'tərvē/ ▶ adj. & adv. **1** upside down. **2** in a state of confusion.

top-tier ▶ adj. of the highest level or quality: *Canada's top-tier athletes.*

top-up ▶ n. Brit. an additional or extra amount or portion that restores something to a former level.

toque /tōk/ ▶ n. **1** a woman's small hat, typically having a narrow, closely turned-up brim. **2** a tall white hat with a full crown, worn by chefs.

tor /tôr/ ▶ n. a steep hill or rocky peak.

To·rah /'tôrə, 'tô-, tô'rä/ ▶ n. (in Judaism) the law of God as revealed to Moses and recorded in the Pentateuch.

torch /tôrCH/ ▶ n. **1** chiefly historical a piece of wood or cloth soaked in tallow and ignited. **2** British term for a FLASHLIGHT (sense 1). **3** a valuable quality, principle, or cause that needs to be protected and maintained: *the torch of freedom.* ▶ v. informal set fire to something.
– PHRASES **carry a torch for** be in love with someone who does not return one's love.

torch·light /'tôrCH,līt/ ▶ n. the light of a torch or torches. ■ **torch·lit** /-lit/ adj.

torch song ▶ n. a sad or sentimental romantic song.

tore /tôr/ ▶ past of TEAR[1].

tor·e·a·dor /'tôrēə,dôr/ ▶ n. a bullfighter, especially one on horseback.

to·ri /'tôrī/ ▶ plural of TORUS.

tor·ment ▶ n. /'tôrment/ **1** great physical or mental suffering. **2** a cause of great suffering. ▶ v. /tôr'ment/ **1** make someone suffer greatly. **2** annoy or tease a person or animal in a cruel or unkind way. ■ **tor·men·tor** /tôr'mentər/ n.

torn /tôrn/ ▶ past participle of TEAR[1].

tor·na·do /tôr'nādō/ ▶ n. (pl. **tornadoes** or **tornados**) a storm with violently rotating winds having the appearance of a funnel-shaped cloud.

to·roi·dal /tô'roidl/ ▶ adj. Geometry of or resembling a torus.

tor·pe·do /tôr'pēdō/ ▶ n. (pl. **torpedoes**) a long, narrow self-propelled underwater missile designed to be fired from a ship, submarine, or an aircraft. ▶ v. (**torpedoes, torpedoing, torpedoed**) **1** attack a ship with a torpedo or torpedoes. **2** ruin a plan or project.

tor·pe·do boat ▶ n. a small, fast, light warship armed with torpedoes.

tor·pid /'tôrpid/ ▶ adj. **1** mentally or physically inactive; lacking energy. **2** (of an animal) dormant, especially during hibernation. ■ **tor·pid·i·ty** /tôr'piditē/ n. **tor·pid·ly** adv.

tor·por /'tôrpər/ ▶ n. the state of being inactive and lacking in energy.

torque /tôrk/ ▶ n. a force that tends to cause rotation.

tor·rent /'tôrənt, 'tär-/ ▶ n. **1** a strong and fast-moving stream of water or other liquid. **2** an overwhelming outpouring of something: *a* *torrent of abuse.*

tor·ren·tial /tò'renCHəl, tə-/ ▶ adj. (of rain) falling rapidly and heavily. ■ **tor·ren·tial·ly** adv.

tor·rid /'tôrəd, 'tär-/ ▶ adj. 1 very hot and dry. 2 full of sexual passion. ■ **tor·rid·ly** adv.

tor·rid zone ▶ n. the hot central region of the earth bounded by the tropics of Cancer and Capricorn.

tor·sion /'tôrsHən/ ▶ n. the action of twisting or the state of being twisted, especially of one end of an object in relation to the other. ■ **tor·sion·al** adj.

tor·sion bar ▶ n. a bar forming part of a vehicle suspension, twisting in response to the motion of the wheels and absorbing their vertical movement.

tor·so /'tôrsō/ ▶ n. (pl. **torsos**) 1 the trunk of the human body. 2 a statue of a torso.

tort /tôrt/ ▶ n. Law a wrongful act or a violation of a right (other than under contract) leading to legal liability.

torte /tôrt, 'tôrtə/ ▶ n. a rich, sweet cake or tart.

tor·tel·li·ni /,tôrtl'ēnē/ ▶ pl.n. small pieces of pasta stuffed with meat, cheese, vegetables, etc., and then rolled and formed into the shape of rings.

tor·til·la /tôr'tē(y)ə/ ▶ n. 1 (in Mexican cooking) a thin, flat corn pancake. 2 (in Spanish cooking) an omelet.

tor·toise /'tôrtəs/ ▶ n. a slow-moving land reptile with a scaly or leathery domed shell into which it can draw its head and legs.

tor·toise·shell /'tôrtə(s),sHel/ ▶ n. 1 the semitransparent mottled yellow and brown shell of certain turtles, used to make jewelry or ornaments. 2 a domestic cat with markings resembling tortoiseshell. 3 a butterfly with mottled orange, yellow, and black markings.

tor·tu·ous /'tôrCHōōəs/ ▶ adj. 1 full of twists and turns. 2 extremely long and complicated: *a tortuous legal battle.* ■ **tor·tu·os·i·ty** /,tôrCHōō'äsitē/ n. **tor·tu·ous·ly** adv. **tor·tu·ous·ness** n.

tor·ture /'tôrCHər/ ▶ n. 1 the action of causing someone severe pain as a punishment or a means of persuasion. 2 great suffering or anxiety. ▶ v. subject someone to torture. ■ **tor·tur·er** n.

tor·tur·ous /'tôrCHərəs/ ▶ adj. involving or causing pain or suffering.

to·rus /'tôrəs/ ▶ n. (pl. **tori** /'tôrī/ or **toruses**) 1 Geometry a surface or solid resembling a ring-shaped doughnut, formed by rotating a closed curve about a line that lies in the same plane but does not intersect it. 2 a ring-shaped object or chamber. 3 Architecture a large convex molding with a semicircular cross section.

To·ry /'tôrē/ ▶ n. (pl. **Tories**) 1 a member or supporter of the British Conservative Party. 2 a member of the English political party that opposed the exclusion of James II from the succession and later gave rise to the Conservative Party. ■ **To·ry·ism** /-,izəm/ n.

toss /tòs, täs/ ▶ v. 1 throw something lightly or casually. 2 move from side to side or back and forth. 3 jerk one's head or hair sharply backward. 4 throw a coin into the air so as to make a decision, based on which side of the coin faces uppermost when it lands. 5 shake or turn food in a liquid to coat it lightly. ▶ n. an act of tossing something.
– PHRASES **toss something off** 1 drink something rapidly or all at once. 2 produce something rapidly or without thought or effort.

toss-up ▶ n. informal 1 a situation in which any of two or more outcomes is equally possible. 2 the tossing of a coin to make a decision.

tos·ta·da /tō'städə/ (also **tostado** /-dō/) ▶ n. (pl. **tostadas** also **tostados**) a Mexican deep-fried tortilla topped with a mixture of beans, ground meat, and vegetables.

tot[1] /tät/ ▶ n. 1 a very young child. 2 chiefly Brit. a small drink of liquor.

tot[2] ▶ v. (**tots, totting, totted**) (**tot something up**) chiefly Brit. 1 add up numbers or amounts. 2 accumulate something over time: *he totted up 180 League appearances.*

to·tal /'tōtl/ ▶ adj. 1 being the whole number or amount. 2 complete; absolute: *a total stranger.* ▶ n. the whole number or amount of something. ▶ v. (**totals, totaling, totaled**) 1 amount to a total number: *debts totaling $6,000.* 2 find the total of: *the scores were totaled.* 3 informal damage something beyond repair. ■ **to·tal·ly** adv.

to·tal e·clipse ▶ n. an eclipse in which the whole of the disk of the sun or moon is obscured.

to·tal·i·tar·i·an /tō,tali'te(ə)rēən/ ▶ adj. (of a system of government) consisting of only one leader or party that has complete power and control and permits no opposition. ▶ n. a person in favor of a totalitarian system of government. ■ **to·tal·i·tar·i·an·ism** /-,nizəm/ n.

to·tal·i·ty /tō'talitē/ ▶ n. 1 the whole of something. 2 the time during which the sun or moon is totally obscured during an eclipse.

to·tal·i·za·tor /'tōtl-i,zātər/ (or **totalizer** /'tōtl,īzər/) ▶ n. 1 a device showing the number and amount of bets staked on a race. 2 another term for TOTE[2].

to·tal re·call ▶ n. the ability to remember with clarity every detail of the events of one's life or of a particular event, object, or experience.

to·tal war ▶ n. a war that is unrestricted in terms of the weapons used, the territory or combatants involved, or the objectives pursued.

tote[1] /tōt/ ▶ v. informal carry something. ▶ n. informal a tote bag.

tote[2] ▶ n. (**the tote**) informal a system of betting based on the use of a totalizator, in which winnings are calculated according to the amount staked rather than odds offered.

tote bag ▶ n. a large bag for carrying a number of items.

to·tem /'tōtəm/ ▶ n. a natural object or animal believed by a particular society to have spiritual significance and adopted by it as an emblem. ■ **to·tem·ic** /tō'temik/ adj.

to·tem pole ▶ n. a pole on which totems are hung or on which the images of totems are carved.

tot·ter /'tätər/ ▶ v. 1 move in an unsteady way. 2 shake or rock as if about to collapse. 3 be insecure or on the point of failure. ▶ n. an unsteady walk. ■ **tot·ter·y** adj.

tou·can /'tōō,kan, -,kän/ ▶ n. a tropical American fruit-eating bird with a massive bill and brightly colored plumage.

tou·ch /təCH/ ▶ v. 1 come into or be in contact with someone or something. 2 bring one's hand or another part of one's body into contact with someone or something. 3 handle in order to harm or interfere with: *I didn't touch any of her* *stuff.* **4** use or consume: *he barely touched the food on his plate.* **5** have an effect on someone or something. **6** produce feelings of affection, gratitude, or sympathy in: *she was touched by his loyalty.* **7** have any dealings with. **8** informal be comparable to in quality, skill, etc.: *no one can touch him at judo.* **9** (as adj. **touched**) informal slightly mad. ▶ n. **1** an act or way of touching. **2** the ability to be aware of something through physical contact, especially with the fingers. **3** a small amount. **4** a distinctive detail or feature. **5** a distinctive or skillful way of dealing with something: *a sure political touch.* **6** Soccer & Rugby the area beyond the sidelines, out of play. ■ **touch·a·ble** adj.

– PHRASES **in touch 1** in or into communication. **2** having up-to-date knowledge about a particular subject, situation, etc. **lose touch 1** no longer be in communication. **2** stop being aware of or informed about a particular subject, situation, etc. **out of touch** lacking awareness of or up-to-date knowledge about a particular subject, situation, etc. **touch down** (of an aircraft or spacecraft) land. **touch someone for** informal ask someone for money as a loan or gift. **touch something off 1** cause something to ignite or explode by touching it with a match. **2** make something happen suddenly: *the incident touched off a global banking crisis.* **touch on** deal briefly with a subject. **touch something up** make small improvements to something.

touch-and-go ▶ adj. (of an outcome) possible but very uncertain.

touch·back /ˈtəCHˌbak/ ▶ n. Football a ball downed deliberately behind one's own goal line or kicked through one's end zone.

touch·down /ˈtəCHˌdoun/ ▶ n. **1** the moment at which an aircraft lands. **2** Football & Rugby an act of scoring by touching the ball down behind the opponents' goal line.

tou·ché /tōōˈSHā/ ▶ exclam. **1** used to acknowledge a good or clever point made at one's expense. **2** (in fencing) used to acknowledge a hit by one's opponent.

touch foot·ball ▶ n. a form of football in which a ball carrier is downed by touching instead of tackling.

touch·ing /ˈtəCHiNG/ ▶ adj. arousing gratitude or sympathy; moving. ▶ prep. concerning. ■ **touch·ing·ly** adv.

touch·line /ˈtəCHˌlīn/ ▶ n. Soccer & Rugby the boundary line on each side of the field.

touch·point /ˈtəCHˌpoint/ ▶ n. **1** Commerce any point of contact between a buyer and a seller. **2** a condition or circumstance likely to precipitate a highly unfavorable outcome.

touch screen ▶ n. a display device that allows the user to interact with a computer by touching areas on the screen.

touch·stone /ˈtəCHˌstōn/ ▶ n. **1** a standard or criterion by which something may be judged. **2** a piece of stone formerly used for testing alloys of gold by observing the color of the mark that they made on it.

touch-tone ▶ adj. (of a telephone) having buttons that produce different sounds when pushed, rather than a dial.

touch-type ▶ v. type without looking at the keys.

touch·y /ˈtəCHē/ ▶ adj. (**touchier**, **touchiest**) **1** quick to take offense; oversensitive. **2** (of a situation or issue) requiring careful handling.

■ **touch·i·ly** adv. **touch·i·ness** n.

touch·y-feel·y /ˈfēlē/ ▶ adj. informal, often derogatory openly expressing affection or other emotions, especially through physical contact.

tough /təf/ ▶ adj. **1** strong enough to withstand wear and tear. **2** able to endure hardship, difficulty, or pain. **3** involving difficulty or hardship: *the training has been quite tough.* **4** strict and uncompromising: *tough anti-smoking laws.* **5** (of a person) rough or violent. **6** used to express a lack of sympathy. ▶ n. informal a rough and violent man. ■ **tough·ness** n.

– PHRASES **tough it out** informal endure a period of hardship or difficulty.

tough·en /ˈtəfən/ ▶ v. make or become tough.

tough love ▶ n. the practice of helping a person by adopting a strict attitude toward them or requiring them to take responsibility for their actions.

tough-mind·ed ▶ adj. realistic and unsentimental.

tou·pee /tōōˈpā/ ▶ n. a small wig or artificial hairpiece worn to cover a bald spot.

tour /tōōr/ ▶ n. **1** a journey for pleasure in which several different places are visited. **2** a short trip made to view or inspect something. **3** a journey made by performers or a sports team, in which they perform or play in several different places. **4** (also **tour of duty**) a period of duty on military or diplomatic service. ▶ v. make a tour of an area.

tour de force /ˌtōōr də ˈfôrs/ ▶ n. (pl. **tours de force** pronunc. same) a performance or achievement that has been accomplished with great skill.

Tou·rette's syn·drome /tōōˈrets/ ▶ n. a disorder of the nervous system characterized by involuntary muscle spasms and in some cases the compulsive utterance of obscene words.

tour·ism /ˈtōōrˌizəm/ ▶ n. the business of organizing and running vacations and visits to places of interest.

tour·ist /ˈtōōrist/ ▶ n. a person who travels for pleasure. ■ **tour·is·tic** /tōōˈristik/ adj.

tour·ist class ▶ n. the cheapest accommodations or seating in a ship, aircraft, or hotel.

tour·ist·y /ˈtōōristē/ ▶ adj. informal, often derogatory appealing to or visited by many tourists.

tour·ma·line /ˈtōōrmələn, -ˌlēn/ ▶ n. a brittle gray or black mineral used as a gemstone and in electrical devices.

tour·na·ment /ˈtərnəmənt, ˈtōōr-/ ▶ n. **1** a series of contests between a number of competitors, competing for an overall prize. **2** a medieval sporting event in which knights jousted with blunted weapons for a prize.

tour·ne·dos /ˈtōōrnəˌdō/ ▶ n. (pl. same) a small, round, thick piece of meat cut from a fillet of beef.

tour·ney /ˈtərnē, ˈtōōr-/ ▶ n. (pl. **tourneys**) a medieval joust.

tour·ni·quet /ˈtərnikit, ˈtōōr-/ ▶ n. a cord or tight bandage that is tied around a limb to stop a wound from bleeding.

tour op·er·a·tor ▶ n. a travel agent specializing in package tours.

tou·sle /ˈtouzəl/ ▶ v. make a person's hair untidy.

tout /tout/ ▶ v. **1** attempt to sell something, typically by using a direct or persistent approach. **2** attempt to persuade people of the

tow value or merit of someone or something: *she was touted as a potential prime minister.* **3** offer horse-racing tips for a share of the winnings. **4** British term for SCALP (sense 2 of the verb). ▸ n. a person who touts.

tow¹ /tō/ ▸ v. use a vehicle or boat to pull another vehicle or boat along. ▸ n. an act of towing a vehicle or boat. ■ **tow·a·ble** adj.
– PHRASES **in tow 1** (also **on tow**) being towed. **2** accompanying or following someone.

USAGE
On the confusion of **tow** and **toe**, see the note at TOE.

tow² ▸ n. short, coarse fibers of flax or hemp, used for making yarn.

to·ward /tôrd, t(ə)'wôrd/ (also **towards** /tôrdz, t(ə)'wôrdz/) ▸ prep. **1** in the direction of. **2** getting nearer to a time or aim. **3** in relation to. **4** contributing to the cost of.

tow bar ▸ n. a bar fitted to the back of a vehicle, used in towing a trailer or camper.

tow·el /'toul/ ▸ n. a piece of thick absorbent cloth or paper used for drying. ▸ v. (**towels, toweling, toweled**) dry someone or something with a towel.

tow·er /'tou(ə)r/ ▸ n. **1** a tall, narrow building, either freestanding or forming part of a building such as a church or castle. **2** a tall structure that houses machinery, operators, etc. **3** a tall structure used as a container or for storage. ▸ v. rise to or reach a great height.

tow·er·ing /'tou(-ə)riNG/ ▸ adj. **1** very tall. **2** of very high quality: *a towering performance.* **3** very strong or intense: *a towering rage.*

tow·head /'tō,hed/ ▸ n. a person with very light blond hair. ■ **tow·head·ed** adj.

town /toun/ ▸ n. **1** a settlement larger than a village and generally smaller than a city, with defined boundaries and local government. **2** the central part of a town or city, with its business or shopping area. **3** densely populated areas, especially as contrasted with the country or suburbs. **4** the permanent residents of a college town, as distinct from the students.
– PHRASES **go to town** informal do something thoroughly or enthusiastically. **on the town** informal enjoying the nightlife of a city or town.

town car ▸ n. a large, luxurious car; a limousine.

town clerk ▸ n. a public official in charge of the records of a town.

town coun·cil ▸ n. the elected governing body in a town or district. ■ **town coun·ci·lor** n.

town cri·er ▸ n. historical a person employed to make public announcements in the streets.

town hall ▸ n. a building housing local government offices.

town·house /'toun,hous/ ▸ n. **1** a tall, narrow traditional row house, generally having three or more floors. **2** a house in a town or city owned by a person who owns another property in the country.

town·ie /'tounē/ ▸ n. informal **1** a person who lives in a town, especially as distinct from one who lives in the country. **2** a resident in a college town, rather than a college student.

town plan·ning ▸ n. the planning and control of the construction, growth, and development of a town or other urban area. ■ **town plan·ner** n.

town·scape /'toun,skāp/ ▸ n. a view or picture of a town or city.

towns·folk /'tounz,fōk/ ▸ pl.n. another term for TOWNSPEOPLE.

town·ship /'toun,SHip/ ▸ n. **1** a division of a county that has certain powers of local administration. **2** (in South Africa) a suburb or city occupied chiefly by black people, formerly officially designated for black occupation by apartheid laws.

towns·man /'tounzmən/ (or **townswoman** /'tounz,wŏomən/) ▸ n. (pl. **townsmen** or **townswomen**) a person living in a particular town or city.

towns·peo·ple /'tounz,pēpəl/ (also **townsfolk** /'tounz,fōk/) ▸ pl.n. the people living in a particular town or city.

tow·path /'tō,paTH/ ▸ n. a path beside a river or canal, originally used as a pathway for horses towing barges.

tow rope ▸ n. a rope, cable, etc., used in towing.

tow truck ▸ n. a truck used to tow or pick up disabled vehicles.

tox·e·mi·a /täk'sēmēə/ (Brit. **toxaemia**) ▸ n. **1** blood poisoning by toxins from a local bacterial infection. **2** a condition in pregnancy characterized especially by high blood pressure; preeclampsia.

tox·ic /'täksik/ ▸ adj. **1** poisonous. **2** relating to or caused by poison. ■ **tox·ic·i·ty** /täk'sisitē/ n.

tox·i·cant /'täksikənt/ ▸ n. a toxic substance introduced into the environment, e.g., a pesticide.

tox·i·col·o·gy /,täksi'käləjē/ ▸ n. the branch of science concerned with the nature, effects, and detection of poisons. ■ **tox·i·co·log·i·cal** /,täksikə'läjikəl/ adj. **tox·i·col·o·gist** n.

tox·ic shock syn·drome ▸ n. acute blood poisoning in women, typically caused by bacterial infection from a tampon that has been kept in the body for too long.

tox·in /'täksin/ ▸ n. a poison produced by a microorganism or other organism, to which the body reacts by producing antibodies.

tox·o·car·i·a·sis /,täksəkə'rīəsis/ ▸ n. infection of a human with the larvae of a worm that is a parasite of dogs, cats, and other animals, causing illness and a risk of blindness.

tox·o·plas·mo·sis /,täksōplaz'mōsis/ ▸ n. a disease caused by a parasite, transmitted chiefly through undercooked meat, soil, or cat feces.

toy /toi/ ▸ n. **1** an object for a child to play with. **2** a gadget or machine that provides amusement for an adult. ▸ adj. (of a breed or variety of pet dog) very small in full-grown size. ▸ v. (**toy with**) **1** consider an idea casually or indecisively. **2** handle absentmindedly or nervously: *she was toying with a loose strand of hair.* **3** eat or drink something in an unenthusiastic way. ■ **toy·like** /-,līk/ adj.

toy boy ▸ n. Brit. informal a male lover who is much younger than his partner.

trace¹ /trās/ ▸ v. **1** find someone or something by careful investigation. **2** find or describe the origin or development: *the book traces his flying career with the RAF.* **3** follow the course or position of something with one's eye, mind, or finger. **4** copy a drawing, map, or design by drawing over its lines on a piece of transparent paper placed on top of it. **5** draw a pattern or outline. ▸ n. **1** a mark or other indication of the existence or passing of something: *the aircraft disappeared without a trace.* **2** a very small quantity. **3** a barely noticeable indication: *a trace of a smile touched his lips.* **4** a line or pattern on a paper or screen corresponding to something that is being recorded or measured. **5** a procedure to trace something, such as the place from which a telephone call was made. ■ **trace·a·ble** adj.

trace² ► n. each of the two side straps, chains, or ropes by which a horse is attached to a vehicle that it is pulling.

trace el·e·ment ► n. a chemical element present or required only in minute amounts.

trace min·er·al ► n. a trace element required for nutrition.

trac·er /'trāsər/ ► n. **1** a bullet or shell whose course is made visible by a trail of flames or smoke, used to assist in aiming. **2** a substance that is introduced into the body and whose subsequent progress can be followed from its color, radioactivity, or other distinctive property.

trac·er·y /'trāsərē/ ► n. (pl. **traceries**) **1** a decorative design of holes and outlines in stone, especially in the upper part of a window. **2** a delicate branching pattern. ■ **trac·er·ied** adj.

tra·che·a /'trākēə/ ► n. (pl. **tracheae** /-kē,ē/ or **tracheas**) the tube conveying air between the larynx and the lungs; the windpipe. ■ **tra·che·al** adj.

tra·che·ot·o·my /,trākē'ätəmē/ (also **tracheostomy** /-'ästəmē/) ► n. (pl. **tracheotomies**) a surgical cut in the windpipe, made to enable someone to breathe when the windpipe is blocked.

tra·cho·ma /trə'kōmə/ ► n. a contagious infection transmitted by a bacterium and causing inflammation of the inner surface of the eyelids.

trac·ing /'trāsiNG/ ► n. **1** a copy of a drawing, map, etc., made by tracing. **2** a faint or delicate mark or pattern.

track /trak/ ► n. **1** a rough path or minor road. **2** a prepared course or circuit for racing. **3** a mark or line of marks left by a person, animal, or vehicle in passing. **4** a continuous line of rails on a railroad. **5** a section of a record, compact disc, or cassette tape containing one song or piece of music. **6** a strip or rail along which something such as a curtain may be moved. **7** a jointed metal band around the wheels of a heavy vehicle. **8** the transverse distance between a vehicle's wheels. ► v. **1** follow the course or movements of: *he tracked the flight of two military aircraft.* **2** (**track someone/thing down**) find someone or something after a thorough or difficult search. **3** follow a particular course. **4** (of a movie or television camera) move in relation to the subject being filmed. ■ **track·er** n. **track·less** adj.
– PHRASES **keep** (or **lose**) **track of** keep (or fail to keep) fully aware of or informed about. **make tracks** informal leave. **on the right** (or **wrong**) **track** following a course likely to result in success (or failure). **stop** (or **be stopped**) **in one's tracks** informal come (or be brought) to a sudden and complete halt. **the wrong side of the tracks** informal a poor or less prestigious part of town.

track and field ► n. athletic events that take place on a running track and a nearby field; track events and field events.

track·ball /'trak,bôl/ ► n. a small ball set in a holder that can be rotated by hand to move a cursor on a computer screen.

track·ing /'trakiNG/ ► n. **1** Electronics the maintenance of a constant difference in

frequency between connected circuits or components. **2** the alignment of the wheels of a vehicle.

track rec·ord ► n. the past achievements or performance of a person, organization, or product.

track·suit /'trak,soot/ ► n. a warm, loose-fitting outfit consisting of a sweatshirt or light jacket and pants with an elastic or drawstring waist.

track·way /'trak,wā/ ► n. a path formed by the repeated treading of people or animals.

tract¹ /trakt/ ► n. **1** a large area of land. **2** a system of organs or tubes in the body that are connected and that have a particular purpose: *the digestive tract.*

tract² ► n. a pamphlet containing a short piece of writing on a political or religious topic.

trac·ta·ble /'traktəbəl/ ► adj. **1** easy to control or influence. **2** (of a situation or problem) easy to deal with. ■ **trac·ta·bil·i·ty** /,traktə'bilitē/ n.

trac·tion /'traksHən/ ► n. **1** the action of pulling a thing along a surface. **2** the power used for pulling. **3** the applying of a sustained pull on a limb or muscle, especially to maintain the position of a fractured bone or to correct a deformity. **4** the grip of a tire on a road or a wheel on a rail.

trac·tor /'traktər/ ► n. a powerful motor vehicle with large rear wheels, used chiefly on farms for pulling equipment and trailers.

trac·tor-trai·ler ► n. a vehicle consisting of a tractor or cab with an engine and a separate, attached trailer in which goods can be transported.

trade /trād/ ► n. **1** the buying and selling of goods or services. **2** a commercial activity of a particular kind: *the tourist trade.* **3** a job requiring manual skills and special training. **4** (**the trade**) (treated as sing. or pl.) the people engaged in a particular area of business. **5** a trade wind. ► v. **1** buy and sell goods or services; operate as a business or company. **2** buy or sell a particular item or product. **3** exchange something for something else, typically as a commercial transaction. **4** (**trade something in**) exchange a used article in part payment for another. **5** (**trade on**) take advantage of: *the government is trading on fears of inflation.* ■ **trad·a·ble** (or **tradeable**) adj.

trade def·i·cit ► n. the amount by which the cost of a country's imports exceeds the value of its exports.

trad·ed op·tion ► n. an option on a stock exchange or futures exchange that can itself be bought and sold.

trade-in ► n. (usu. as adj.) a used article accepted by a retailer in partial payment for another: *the trade-in value of the car.*

trade jour·nal (also **trade magazine**) ► n. a periodical containing news and items of interest concerning a particular trade.

trade·mark /'trād,märk/ ► n. **1** a symbol, word, or words chosen to represent a company or product, legally registered or established by use. **2** a distinctive characteristic or object: *the murder had all the trademarks of a Mafia hit.*

trade name ► n. **1** a name that has the status of a trademark. **2** a name by which something is known in a particular trade or profession.

trade-off ► n. a balance achieved between two desirable but conflicting features; a compromise.

trad·er /'trādər/ ▶ n. **1** a person who trades goods, currency, or shares. **2** a merchant ship.

trad·es·can·tia /ˌtradə'skanċH(ē)ə, -tēə/ ▶ n. an American plant with triangular flowers.

trade se·cret ▶ n. a secret device or technique used by a company in manufacturing its products.

trades·man /'trādzmən/ ▶ n. (pl. **tradesmen**) a person engaged in trading or in a skilled profession.

trade sur·plus ▶ n. the amount by which the value of a country's exports exceeds the cost of its imports.

trade un·ion (Brit. also **trades union**) ▶ n. a labor union.

trade wind /wind/ ▶ n. a wind blowing steadily toward the equator from the northeast in the northern hemisphere or from the southeast in the southern hemisphere, especially at sea.

trad·ing card ▶ n. each of a set of picture cards that are collected and traded.

trad·ing post ▶ n. a store or small settlement established for trading in a remote place.

tra·di·tion /trə'disHən/ ▶ n. **1** the passing on of customs or beliefs from generation to generation. **2** a long-established custom or belief passed on in this way. **3** an artistic or literary method or style established by an artist, writer, or movement, and subsequently followed by other people.

tra·di·tion·al /trə'disHənl/ ▶ adj. relating to or following customs or beliefs that have been passed from generation to generation: *traditional Irish music*. ■ **tra·di·tion·al·ly** adv.

tra·di·tion·al·ism /trə'disHənl,izəm/ ▶ n. the support of tradition, especially so as to resist change. ■ **tra·di·tion·al·ist** n. & adj.

tra·duce /trə'd(y)o͞os/ ▶ v. say unpleasant or untrue things about someone.

traf·fic /'trafik/ ▶ n. **1** vehicles moving on public roads. **2** the movement of ships or aircraft. **3** the commercial transportation of goods or passengers. **4** the messages or signals sent through a communications system. **5** the action of trading in something illegal. ▶ v. (**traffics, trafficking, trafficked**) deal or trade in something illegal. ■ **traf·fick·er** n.

traf·fic cir·cle ▶ n. a road junction at which traffic moves in one direction around a central island.

traf·fic is·land ▶ n. a small raised area in the middle of a road that provides a safe place for pedestrians to stand.

traf·fic jam ▶ n. a line or lines of traffic at or virtually at a standstill.

traf·fic light (also **traffic lights**) ▶ n. a set of automatically operated colored lights for controlling traffic.

tra·ge·di·an /trə'jēdēən/ ▶ n. **1** (fem. **tragedienne** /trəˌjēdē'en/) an actor who plays tragic roles. **2** a writer of tragedies.

trag·e·dy /'trajidē/ ▶ n. (pl. **tragedies**) **1** an event causing great suffering and distress. **2** a serious play with an unhappy ending, especially one concerning the downfall of the main character.

trag·ic /'trajik/ ▶ adj. **1** extremely distressing or sad. **2** relating to tragedy in a literary work. ■ **trag·i·cal·ly** /-ik(ə)lē/ adv.

trag·i·com·e·dy /ˌtrajə'kämidē/ ▶ n. (pl. **tragicomedies**) a play or novel containing elements of both comedy and tragedy. ■ **trag·i·com·ic** /-'kämik/ adj.

trail /trāl/ ▶ n. **1** a mark or a series of signs left behind by the passage of someone or something. **2** a track or scent used in following someone or hunting an animal. **3** a beaten path through rough country. **4** a route planned or followed for a particular purpose: *the tourist trail*. **5** a long, thin part stretching behind or hanging down from something. ▶ v. **1** draw or be drawn along behind someone or something: *her robe trailed along the ground*. **2** follow someone's or something's trail. **3** walk or move slowly or wearily. **4** (**trail away/off**) (of a person's voice) fade gradually before stopping. **5** be losing to an opponent in a contest. **6** (of a plant) grow along the ground or so as to hang down. **7** give advance publicity to a movie, television show, etc., with a trailer.

trail·blaz·er /'trāl,blāzər/ ▶ n. **1** a person who is the first to do something. **2** a person who makes a new track through wild country. ■ **trail·blaz·ing** n. & adj.

trail·er /'trālər/ ▶ n. **1** an unpowered vehicle towed by another. **2** the rear section of a tractor-trailer. **3** an extract from a movie or television show used for advance advertising. **4** (also **travel trailer**) a vehicle equipped for living in, designed to be towed by a car.

trail·er park (also **trailer court**) ▶ n. **1** an area where trailers are parked and used for recreation or as permanent homes. **2** (as adj.) lacking refinement, taste, or quality: *her trailer-park bleached perm*.

trail·er trash ▶ n. offensive poor, lower-class white people, typically regarded as living in mobile homes.

trail·er truck ▶ n. a tractor-trailer.

trail·ing edge ▶ n. the rear edge of a moving object, especially an airfoil.

trail mix ▶ n. a mixture of dried fruit and nuts eaten as a snack.

train /trān/ ▶ v. **1** teach a person or animal a particular skill or type of behavior through regular practice and instruction. **2** be taught in such a way: *he trained as a plumber*. **3** make or become physically fit through a course of exercise and diet. **4** (**train something on**) point something at: *he trained his gun on the side door*. **5** make a plant grow in a particular direction or shape. ▶ n. **1** a series of railroad cars moved as a unit by a locomotive or by integral motors. **2** a number of vehicles or load-carrying animals moving in a line. **3** a series of connected events or thoughts. **4** a long piece of trailing material attached to the back of a formal dress or robe. **5** a group of attendants accompanying an important person. ■ **train·a·ble** adj. **train·ing** n. **train·load** /'trān,lōd/ n.
− PHRASES **in train** in progress.

train·ee /trā'nē/ ▶ n. a person undergoing training for a particular job or profession. ■ **train·ee·ship** /-,sHip/ n.

train·er /'trānər/ ▶ n. **1** a person who trains people or animals. **2** (also **training shoe**) Brit. a soft shoe, suitable for sports or casual wear.

train·ing wheels ▶ n. a pair of small supporting wheels fitted on a child's bicycle.

train·spot·ter /'trān,spätər/ ▶ n. Brit. a person who collects locomotive numbers as a hobby. ■ **train·spot·ting** n.

traipse /trāps/ ▸ v. walk or move wearily or reluctantly. ▸ n. a boring or tiring walk.

trait /trāt/ ▸ n. **1** a distinguishing quality or characteristic. **2** a genetically determined characteristic.

trai·tor /'trātər/ ▸ n. a person who betrays their country, a cause, etc. ■ **trai·tor·ous** adj.

tra·jec·to·ry /trə'jektərē/ ▸ n. (pl. **trajectories**) the path followed by a moving object under the action of given forces.

tram /tram/ (also **tramcar** /'tram,kär/) ▸ n. Brit. a trolley car; a cable car.

tram·mel /'traməl/ ▸ v. (**trammels, trammeling, trammeled**) restrict someone's freedom of action. ▸ pl.n. (**trammels**) literary things that restrict someone's freedom of action.

tramp /tramp/ ▸ v. **1** walk heavily or noisily. **2** walk wearily or reluctantly over a long distance. ▸ n. **1** a homeless person who travels around and lives by begging or doing casual work. **2** the sound of heavy steps. **3** a long walk. **4** a cargo ship running between many different ports rather than sailing a fixed route. **5** informal a promiscuous woman. ■ **tramp·er** n. **tramp·y** adj. (informal).

tram·ple /'trampəl/ ▸ v. **1** tread on something and crush it. **2** (**trample on/over**) treat someone or something with disrespect or contempt: *a statesman ought not to trample on the opinions of his advisers.*

tram·po·line /'trampə,lēn/ ▸ n. a strong fabric sheet connected by springs to a frame, used as a springboard and landing area in doing acrobatic or gymnastic exercises. ■ **tram·po·lin·ing** n.

tram·way /'tram,wā/ ▸ n. Brit. **1** a set of rails for a trolley car. **2** a trolley car system.

trance /trans/ ▸ n. **1** a half-conscious state in which someone does not respond to external stimuli, typically as brought about by hypnosis. **2** a state in which someone is not paying attention to what is happening around them. **3** (also **trance music**) a type of electronic dance music characterized by hypnotic rhythms.

tranche /träNSH/ ▸ n. any of the parts into which something, especially an amount of money or an issue of shares in a company, is divided.

tran·nie /'tranē/ (also **tranny**) ▸ n. (pl. **trannies**) informal **1** a transvestite. **2** a transmission in a motor vehicle.

tran·quil /'traNGkwəl/ ▸ adj. free from disturbance; calm. ■ **tran·quil·i·ty** /,traNG'kwilitē/ n. **tran·quil·ly** adv.

tran·quil·ize /'traNGkwə,līz/ ▸ v. make a person or animal calm or unconscious, especially by giving them a sedative drug.

tran·quil·iz·er /'traNGkwə,līzər/ ▸ n. a drug taken to reduce tension or anxiety.

trans- ▸ prefix **1** across; beyond: *transcontinental.* **2** on or to the other side of: *transatlantic.* **3** into another state or place: *translate.*

trans·act /tran'sakt, -'zakt/ ▸ v. do business with a person or organization.

trans·ac·tion /tran'saksHən, -'zak-/ ▸ n. **1** an act of buying or selling something. **2** the action of carrying out business. ■ **trans·ac·tion·al** adj.

trans·at·lan·tic /,transət'lantik, ,tranz-/ ▸ adj. **1** crossing the Atlantic. **2** concerning countries on both sides of the Atlantic, typically Britain and the US. **3** relating to or situated on the other side of the Atlantic.

trans·ax·le /'trans,aksəl, tranz-/ ▸ n. an integral driving axle and differential gear in a motor vehicle.

trans·ceiv·er /tran'sēvər/ ▸ n. a combined radio transmitter and receiver.

tran·scend /tran'send/ ▸ v. **1** be or go beyond the range or limits of: *an issue transcending party politics.* **2** be better than a person or achievement.

tran·scend·ent /tran'sendənt/ ▸ adj. **1** going beyond normal or physical human experience. **2** (of God) existing apart from and not limited by the physical universe. ■ **tran·scend·ence** n. **tran·scend·ent·ly** adv.

tran·scen·den·tal /,transen'dentl/ ▸ adj. relating to a spiritual area that is beyond human experience or knowledge. ■ **tran·scen·den·tal·ly** adv.

Tran·scen·den·tal Med·i·ta·tion ▸ n. trademark a technique for relaxation and promoting harmony by meditation and repetition of a mantra.

trans·con·ti·nen·tal /,transkäntə'nentl, ,tranz-/ ▸ adj. crossing or extending across a continent or continents.

tran·scribe /tran'skrīb/ ▸ v. **1** put thoughts, speech, or data into written or printed form. **2** make a copy of something, especially in another alphabet or language. **3** arrange a piece of music for a different instrument or voice. ■ **tran·scrib·er** n.

tran·script /'tran,skript/ ▸ n. a written or printed version of material that was originally spoken or presented in another form.

tran·scrip·tion /tran'skripsHən/ ▸ n. **1** a written or printed version of something; a transcript. **2** the action of transcribing something. **3** a piece of music transcribed for a different instrument or voice.

trans·der·mal /trans'dərməl, tranz-/ ▸ adj. relating to the application of a medicine or drug through the skin, especially by means of an adhesive patch.

trans·duc·er /trans'd(y)o͞osər, tranz-/ ▸ n. a device that converts variations in a physical quantity (such as pressure or brightness) into an electrical signal, or vice versa. ■ **trans·duc·tion** /-'dəksHən/ n.

tran·sect /tran'sekt/ technical ▸ v. cut across or make a transverse section in something. ▸ n. a straight line or narrow cross section through an object or across the earth's surface, along which observations or measurements are made. ■ **tran·sec·tion** /-'seksHən/ n.

tran·sept /'tran,sept/ ▸ n. (in a cross-shaped church) either of the two parts extending at right angles from the nave.

tran·sex·u·al /tran'seksHo͞oəl/ ▸ n. & adj. variant spelling of TRANSSEXUAL.

trans-fat /'trans'fat/ ▸ n. an unsaturated fatty acid found especially in margarines and cooking oils.

trans·fer ▸ v. /trans'fər, 'transfər/ (**transfers, transferring, transferred**) **1** move from one place to another: *transfer the rice to a saucepan.* **2** move to another department, job, team, etc. **3** change to another place, route, or means of transportation during a journey. **4** officially pass property, or a right or responsibility, to another person. **5** (as adj. **transferred**) (of the sense of a word or phrase) changed by extension or metaphor. ▸ n. /'transfər/ **1** an act of transferring someone or something. **2** a small colored picture or design on paper, which can be transferred to another surface by being pressed or heated.

■ **trans·fer·a·ble** /trans'fərəbəl, 'transfərə-/ adj. **trans·fer·ee** /ˌtransfə'rē/ n. **trans·fer·or** /'transfərər, 'transfərər/ (chiefly Law) n. **trans·fer·ral** /trans'fərəl/ n.

trans·fer·ence /trans'fərəns, 'transfərəns/ ▶ n. **1** the action of transferring something. **2** Psychoanalysis the redirection to a substitute, usually a therapist, of emotions originally felt in childhood.

trans·fig·u·ra·tion /trans,figyə'rāsHən/ ▶ n. **1** a complete transformation into a more beautiful or spiritual state. **2** (**the Transfiguration**) Jesus's appearance in glory to three of his disciples (in the gospels of Matthew and Mark).

trans·fig·ure /trans'figyər/ ▶ v. (**be transfigured**) be transformed into something more beautiful or spiritual.

trans·fix /trans'fiks/ ▶ v. **1** make someone motionless with horror, wonder, or astonishment. **2** pierce someone or something with a sharp implement.

trans·form /trans'fôrm/ ▶ v. **1** change or be changed in appearance, form, or nature: *expressways have transformed our lives.* **2** change the voltage of an electric current.
■ **trans·form·a·tive** /-mətiv/ adj.

trans·for·ma·tion /ˌtransfər'māsHən/ ▶ n. a marked change in nature, form, or appearance.
■ **trans·for·ma·tion·al** adj.

trans·form·er /trans'fôrmər/ ▶ n. a device for changing the voltage of an alternating current.

trans·fu·sion /trans'fyo͞ozHən/ ▶ n. **1** the medical process of transferring blood or its components from one person or animal to another. **2** a transfer of something vital, especially money: *the country's economy will receive a transfusion of at least $1 billion.* ■ **trans·fuse** /trans'fyo͞oz/ v.

trans·gen·der /tranz'jendər, trans-/ (also **transgendered**) ▶ adj. transsexual.

trans·gen·ic /tranz'jenik, tranz-/ ▶ adj. containing genetic material into which DNA from a different organism has been artificially added.
■ **trans·gene** /trans'jēn, tranz-/ n. **trans·gen·ics** pl.n.

trans·gress /trans'gres, tranz-/ ▶ v. go beyond the limits of what is morally, socially, or legally acceptable. ■ **trans·gres·sion** /-'gresHən/ n. **trans·gres·sive** adj. **trans·gres·sor** n.

tran·ship ▶ v. variant spelling of TRANSSHIP.

trans·hu·mance /trans'(h)yo͞oməns, tranz-/ ▶ n. the action or practice of moving livestock seasonally from one grazing ground to another.
■ **trans·hu·mant** adj.

tran·sient /'transHənt, -zHənt, -zēənt/ ▶ adj. **1** lasting only for a short time. **2** staying or working in a place for a short time only. ▶ n. a person who stays or works in a place for a short time. ■ **tran·sience** n. **tran·sien·cy** n. **tran·sient·ly** adv.

tran·sis·tor /tran'zistər/ ▶ n. **1** a semiconductor device with three connections, able to amplify or rectify an electric current. **2** (also **transistor radio**) a portable radio using circuits containing transistors. ■ **tran·sis·tor·ize** /tran'zistə,rīz/ v.

tran·sit /'tranzit/ ▶ n. **1** the carrying of people or things from one place to another. **2** an act of passing through or across a place. ▶ v. (**transits, transiting, transited**) pass across or through

an area.

tran·si·tion /tran'zisHən, -'sisHən/ ▶ n. the process or a period of changing from one state or condition to another: *the rituals marked the transition from boyhood to manhood.*
■ **tran·si·tion·al** adj.

tran·si·tion met·al ▶ n. any of the set of metallic chemical elements occupying the central block in the periodic table, e.g., iron, manganese, chromium, and copper.

tran·si·tion se·ries ▶ n. Chemistry the set of transition metals in the periodic table.

tran·si·tive /'transitiv, 'tranz-/ ▶ adj. (of a verb) able to take a direct object, e.g., *saw* in *he saw the donkey.* The opposite of INTRANSITIVE. ■ **tran·si·tive·ly** adv. **tran·si·tiv·i·ty** /ˌtransə'tivitē, -zə-/ n.

tran·si·to·ry /'transi,tôrē, 'tranzi-/ ▶ adj. lasting for a short time; not permanent. ■ **tran·si·to·ri·ly** adv. **tran·si·to·ri·ness** n.

trans·late /trans'lāt, tranz-/ ▶ v. **1** express the sense of words or writing in another language. **2** be expressed or be able to be expressed in another language. **3** (**translate into**) convert or be converted into another form: *they were unable to translate their concert success into record sales.* ■ **trans·lat·a·ble** adj. **trans·la·tor** n.

trans·la·tion /trans'lāsHən, tranz-/ ▶ n. **1** the action of translating something. **2** a word or written work that is translated into another language.

trans·lit·er·ate /trans'litə,rāt, tranz-/ ▶ v. write a letter or word using the closest corresponding letters of a different alphabet or language.
■ **trans·lit·er·a·tion** /trans,litə'rāsHən, tranz-/ n.

trans·lo·cate /trans'lō,kāt, tranz-/ ▶ v. chiefly technical move from one place to another.
■ **trans·lo·ca·tion** /trans,lō'kāsHən, tranz-/ n.

trans·lu·cent /trans'lo͞osnt, tranz-/ ▶ adj. allowing light to pass through partially; semitransparent.
■ **trans·lu·cence** n. **trans·lu·cen·cy** n.

trans·mi·gra·tion /ˌtrans,mī'grāsHən, ˌtranz-/ ▶ n. (in some beliefs) the passing of a person's soul after their death into another body.

trans·mis·si·ble /tranz'misəbəl/ ▶ adj. (especially of a disease, virus, etc.) able to be transmitted.
■ **trans·mis·si·bil·i·ty** /-ˌmisə'bilitē/ n.

trans·mis·sion /trans'misHən, tranz-/ ▶ n. **1** the action of passing something from one person or place to another. **2** a program or signal that is transmitted. **3** the mechanism by which power is transmitted from an engine to the axle in a motor vehicle.

trans·mit /tranz'mit, trans-/ ▶ v. (**transmits, transmitting, transmitted**) **1** pass from one place or person to another: *the disease is transmitted by mosquitoes.* **2** broadcast or send out an electrical signal or a radio or television program. **3** allow heat, light, or other energy to pass through a medium. ■ **trans·mit·tal** n.

trans·mit·ter /trans'mitər, tranz-/ ▶ n. a device used to produce and transmit electromagnetic waves carrying messages or signals, especially those of radio or television.

trans·mog·ri·fy /trans'mägrə,fī, tranz-/ ▶ v. (**transmogrifies, transmogrifying, transmogrified**) chiefly humorous change into someone or something completely different: *alchemists strove to transmogrify base metals into gold.*
■ **trans·mog·ri·fi·ca·tion** /-ˌmägrəfi'kāsHən/ n.

trans·mute /trans'myōōt, tranz-/ ▶v. change in form, nature, or substance. ■ **trans·mu·ta·tion** /ˌtransmyōō'tāsHən, ˌtranz-/ n.

trans·na·tion·al /trans'nasHənl, tranz-/ ▶adj. extending or operating across national boundaries. ▶n. a multinational company.

trans·o·ce·an·ic /ˌtransōsHē'anik, ˌtranz-/ ▶adj. crossing an ocean.

tran·som /'transəm/ ▶n. 1 the flat surface forming the stern of a boat. 2 a strengthening crossbar above a window or door.
– PHRASES **over the transom** informal offered or sent without prior agreement; unsolicited.

tran·som win·dow ▶n. a window set above the transom of a door or larger window; a fanlight.

tran·son·ic /tran'sänik/ ▶adj. referring to speeds close to that of sound.

trans·par·en·cy /tran'sparənsē/ ▶n. (pl. **transparencies**) 1 the condition of being transparent. 2 a positive transparent photograph printed on plastic or glass, and viewed using a slide projector.

trans·par·ent /tran'spe(ə)rənt, -'spar-/ ▶adj. 1 allowing light to pass through so that objects behind can be distinctly seen. 2 obvious or evident: *the company's transparent attempt to woo back women customers.* ■ **trans·par·ent·ly** adv.

trans·per·son·al /trans'pərsənl, tranz-/ ▶adj. relating to states of consciousness beyond the limits of personal identity.

tran·spire /tran'spī(ə)r/ ▶v. 1 come to be known or prove to be the case. 2 happen; occur. 3 Botany (of a plant or leaf) give off water vapor through the stomata (tiny pores). ■ **tran·spi·ra·tion** /-spə'rāsHən/ n.

> USAGE
> The standard sense of **transpire** is 'come to be known' (*it transpired that he had bought a house*). From this, a newer sense developed, meaning 'happen' (*I'm going to find out what transpired*). This sense, although very common, is sometimes criticized for being an unnecessarily long word used where **occur** or **happen** would do just as well.

trans·plant ▶v. /ˌtrans'plant/ 1 transfer someone or something to another place or situation. 2 take living tissue or an organ and implant in another part of the body or in another body. ▶n. /'transˌplant/ 1 an operation in which an organ or tissue is transplanted. 2 a person or thing that has been transferred to another place or situation. ■ **trans·plant·a·ble** /trans'plantəbəl/ adj. **trans·plan·ta·tion** /-ˌplan'tāsHən/ n.

tran·spon·der /tran'spändər/ ▶n. a device for receiving a radio signal and automatically transmitting a different signal.

trans·port ▶v. /ˌtrans'pôrt/ 1 carry people or goods from one place to another by means of a vehicle, aircraft, or ship. 2 (**be transported**) be overwhelmed with a strong emotion: *she was transported with pleasure.* 3 historical send a convict to a distant country as a punishment. ▶n. /'transˌpôrt/ 1 a system or means of transporting people or goods. 2 the action of transporting people or goods. 3 a large vehicle, ship, or aircraft for carrying troops or stores. 4 (**transports**) overwhelmingly strong emotions. ■ **trans·port·a·bil·i·ty** /ˌtransˌpôrtə'bilitē/ n. **trans·port·a·ble** /trans'pôrtəbəl/ adj.

trans·por·ta·tion /ˌtranspər'tāsHən/ ▶n. 1 a system or means of transporting people or goods. 2 the action of transporting people or goods. 3 historical the action or practice of transporting convicts to a penal colony.

trans·port·er /trans'pôrtər/ ▶n. a large vehicle used to carry heavy objects.

trans·pose /trans'pōz/ ▶v. 1 cause two or more things to exchange places. 2 transfer to a different place or situation: *the play is transposed to America.* 3 write or play music in a different key from the original. ■ **trans·pos·a·ble** adj. **trans·po·si·tion** /ˌtranspə'zisHən/ n.

trans·sex·u·al /tran(s)'seksHōōəl/ (also **transexual** /tran'seksHōōəl/) ▶n. a person born with the physical characteristics of one sex who emotionally and psychologically feels that they belong to the opposite sex. ▶adj. relating to a transsexual person. ■ **trans·sex·u·al·ism** /-ˌlizəm/ n. **trans·sex·u·al·i·ty** /-ˌseksHōō'alitē/ n.

trans·ship /tran(s)'sHip/ (also **tranship**) ▶v. transfer cargo from one ship or other form of transport to another. ■ **trans·ship·ment** n.

tran·sub·stan·ti·a·tion /ˌtransəbˌstansHē'āsHən/ ▶n. (in Christian belief) the doctrine that when the bread and wine of Holy Communion have been consecrated they are converted into the body and blood of Jesus.

trans·u·ran·ic /ˌtransyə'ranik, tranz-/ ▶adj. (of a chemical element) having a higher atomic number than uranium (92).

trans·verse /trans'vərs, tranz-/ ▶adj. situated or extending across something. ■ **trans·verse·ly** adv.

trans·ves·tite /trans'ves,tīt, tranz-/ ▶n. a person, typically a man, who gains pleasure from dressing in clothes usually worn by the opposite sex. ■ **trans·ves·tism** /-ˌtizəm/ n.

trap /trap/ ▶n. 1 a device, pit, or enclosure designed to catch and hold animals. 2 an unpleasant situation from which it is difficult to escape. 3 a trick that causes someone to do something that they do not intend or that will harm them: *the police set a trap for two local gangs.* 4 a container or device used to collect a specified thing. 5 a curve in the waste pipe from a bath, basin, or toilet that is always full of liquid to prevent the upward passage of gases. 6 a light, two-wheeled carriage pulled by a horse or pony. 7 the compartment from which a greyhound is released at the start of a race. 8 a device for hurling an object such as a clay pigeon into the air. 9 informal a person's mouth. ▶v. (**traps, trapping, trapped**) 1 catch or hold in a trap: *twenty workers were trapped by the flames.* 2 trick someone into doing something.

trap·door /'trap,dôr/ ▶n. a hinged or removable panel in a floor, ceiling, or roof.

tra·peze /trə'pēz, tra-/ ▶n. (also **flying trapeze**) a horizontal bar hanging by two ropes high above the ground, used by acrobats in a circus.

tra·pe·zi·um /trə'pēzēəm/ ▶n. (pl. **trapezia** /-zēə/ or **trapeziums**) Geometry 1 a quadrilateral with no sides parallel. 2 British term for TRAPEZOID (sense 1).

tra·pe·zi·us /trə'pēzēəs/ ▶n. (pl. **trapezii** /-zē,ī/) either of a pair of large triangular muscles extending over the back of the neck and shoulders and moving the head and shoulder blade.

trap·e·zoid /'trapi,zoid/ ▶n. Geometry 1 a quadrilateral with one pair of sides parallel.

2 British term for **trapezium** (sense 1).
■ **trap·e·zoi·dal** /ˌtrapiˈzoidl/ adj.

trap·per /ˈtrapər/ ▶ n. a person who traps wild animals, especially for their fur.

trap·pings /ˈtrapiNGz/ ▶ pl.n. **1** the signs or objects associated with a particular situation or role: *I had the trappings of success.* **2** a horse's ornamental harness.

Trap·pist /ˈtrapist/ ▶ n. a monk belonging to a branch of the Cistercian order of monks who speak only in certain situations.

trash /trasH/ ▶ n. **1** waste material; refuse. **2** poor-quality writing, art, etc. **3** a person or people regarded as being of very low social standing.
▶ v. informal wreck or destroy something.

trash can ▶ n. a receptacle for trash; a garbage can.

trash talk informal ▶ n. insulting or boastful speech intended to intimidate or humiliate someone.
▶ v. (**trash-talk**) use insulting or boastful speech for such a purpose. ■ **trash talk·er** n.

trash·y /ˈtrasHē/ ▶ adj. (**trashier**, **trashiest**) of poor quality: *trashy movies.* ■ **trash·i·ness** n.

trat·to·ri·a /ˌträtəˈrēə/ ▶ n. an Italian restaurant.

trau·ma /ˈtroumə, ˈtrô-/ ▶ n. (pl. **traumas**) **1** a deeply distressing experience. **2** emotional shock following a stressful event. **3** Medicine physical injury. ■ **trau·mat·ic** /trəˈmatik, trou-, trô-/ adj. **trau·mat·i·cal·ly** /-ik(ə)lē/ adv.

trau·ma·tize /ˈtroumə,tīz, ˈtrô-/ ▶ v. cause someone to experience lasting shock as a result of a disturbing experience or injury.

tra·vail /trəˈvāl, ˈtrav,āl/ (also **travails**) ▶ n. literary a situation or experience that involves much hard work or difficulty: *the museum records the town's wartime travails.*

trav·el /ˈtravəl/ ▶ v. (**travels, traveling, traveled**) **1** go from one place to another, especially over a long distance. **2** go along a road or through a region. **3** move at a particular speed, in a particular direction, or over a particular distance: *light travels faster than sound.* **4** remain in good condition after a journey: *certain wines do not travel well.* ▶ n. **1** the action of traveling. **2** (**travels**) journeys, especially abroad. **3** the range or motion of a part of a machine. ▶ adj. (of a device) small enough to be packed for use when traveling: *a travel iron.*

trav·el a·gen·cy ▶ n. an agency that makes the necessary arrangements for travelers. ■ **trav·el a·gent** n.

trav·eled /ˈtravəld/ ▶ adj. **1** having traveled to many places. **2** used by people traveling: *a well-traveled route.*

trav·el·er /ˈtrav(ə)lər/ (Brit. **traveller**) ▶ n. a person who is traveling or who often travels.

trav·el·er's check ▶ n. a check for a fixed amount that may be exchanged for cash or used to pay for things abroad.

trav·el·ing sales·man ▶ n. a representative of a firm who visits businesses to show samples and gain orders.

tra·vel kit ▶ n. a waterproof bag for holding toothpaste, soap, etc., when traveling.

trav·e·logue /ˈtravə,lôg, -,läg/ ▶ n. a movie, book, or illustrated talk about a person's travels.

trav·el trail·er ▶ n. see **trailer** (sense 4).

trav·erse /trəˈvərs/ ▶ v. **1** travel or extend across or through: *he traversed the forest.* **2** move something back and forth or sideways.

▶ n. **1** an act of traversing something. **2** a part of a structure that extends or is fixed across something. ■ **tra·vers·a·ble** adj. **tra·vers·al** n.

trav·er·tine /ˈtravər,tēn, -tin/ ▶ n. white or light-colored rock deposited from mineral springs, used in building.

trav·es·ty /ˈtravistē/ ▶ n. (pl. **travesties**) an absurd or distorted representation: *the trial was a travesty of justice.* ▶ v. (**travesties, travestying, travestied**) represent someone or something in an absurd or distorted way.

tra·vois /trəˈvoi, ˈtrav,oi/ ▶ n. (pl. same) a V-shaped frame of poles pulled by a horse, formerly used by North American Indians to carry goods.

trawl /trôl/ ▶ v. **1** search widely and thoroughly: *he trawled the bars of Athens for a drink.* **2** catch fish with a trawl net or seine. ▶ n. **1** a thorough search. **2** (also **trawl net**) a large wide-mouthed fishing net dragged by a boat along the bottom of the sea or a lake.

trawl·er /ˈtrôlər/ ▶ n. a fishing boat used for trawling. ■ **trawl·er·man** /ˈtrôlər,mən/ n. (pl. **trawlermen**)

tray /trā/ ▶ n. a flat, shallow container with a raised rim, used for carrying things.

treach·er·ous /ˈtrecHərəs/ ▶ adj. **1** not loyal or able to be trusted. **2** having hidden or unpredictable dangers: *treacherous currents.* ■ **treach·er·ous·ly** adv.

treach·er·y /ˈtrecHərē/ ▶ n. (pl. **treacheries**) behavior that involves betraying someone's trust.

trea·cle /ˈtrēkəl/ ▶ n. **1** excessively sweet sentimentality or flattery. **2** Brit. molasses. ■ **trea·cly** /ˈtrēk(ə)lē/ adj.

tread /tred/ ▶ v. (past **trod** /träd/ /träd/; past part. **trodden** /ˈträdn/ or **trod**) **1** walk in a specified way. **2** press down or crush something with the feet. **3** walk on or along something. ▶ n. **1** a person's way of walking or the sound made by this: *I heard the heavy tread of Dad's boots.* **2** the top surface of a step or stair. **3** the part of a vehicle tire that grips the road. **4** the part of the sole of a shoe that rests on the ground.
– PHRASES **tread carefully** (or **lightly** or **warily**) take action in a cautious or restrained way. **tread on someone's toes** offend someone by getting involved in something that is their responsibility. **tread water 1** stay in an upright position in deep water by moving the feet with a walking movement. **2** fail to make progress.

trea·dle /ˈtredl/ ▶ n. a lever worked by the foot to operate a machine.

tread·mill /ˈtred,mil/ ▶ n. **1** a device used for exercise, consisting of a continuous moving belt on which to walk or run. **2** a job or situation that is tiring, boring, and difficult to escape from: *they were on a never-ending treadmill of duty.* **3** a large wheel turned by the weight of people or animals treading on steps fitted into it, formerly used to drive machinery.

trea·son /ˈtrēzən/ (also **high treason**) ▶ n. the crime of betraying one's country, especially by attempting to kill or overthrow the sovereign or government. ■ **trea·son·a·ble** adj. **trea·son·ous** adj.

treas·ure /ˈtrezhər/ ▶ n. **1** a quantity of precious metals, gems, or other valuable objects. **2** a very valuable object. **3** informal a much loved or highly valued person. ▶ v. **1** look after a valuable or valued item carefully. **2** value someone or something highly.

treas·ure hunt ▶ n. a game in which players search for hidden objects by following a trail of clues.

treas·ur·er /'trezhərər/ ▶ n. a person appointed to manage the finances of a society, company, or other organization.

treas·ure trove ▶ n. a collection or store of valuable or pleasant things.

treas·ur·y /'trezhərē/ ▶ n. (pl. **treasuries**) **1** the funds or income of a country, state, institution, or society. **2** (**Treasury**) (in some countries) the government department responsible for the overall management of the economy. **3** a place where treasure is stored. **4** a collection of valuable or pleasant things.

Treas·ur·y bill ▶ n. a government security that does not pay interest, but is issued at a price that is less than the value it can be redeemed at.

treat /trēt/ ▶ v. **1** behave toward or deal with in a particular way: *he treated her with courtesy.* **2** give medical care or attention to a person, illness, etc. **3** apply a process or a substance to something. **4** present or discuss a subject. **5** (**treat someone to**) pay for someone's food, drink, or entertainment. **6** (**treat oneself**) do or have something very enjoyable. ▶ n. **1** a surprise gift, event, etc., that gives great pleasure. **2** (**one's treat**) an act of paying for someone's food, drink, or entertainment. ■ **treat·a·ble** adj. **treat·er** n.

trea·tise /'trētis/ ▶ n. a written work dealing formally and systematically with a subject.

treat·ment /'trētmənt/ ▶ n. **1** a way of behaving toward someone or dealing with something. **2** medical care for an illness or injury. **3** the use of a substance or process to preserve or give particular properties to something: *the treatment of hazardous waste.* **4** the presentation or discussion of a subject.

trea·ty /'trētē/ ▶ n. (pl. **treaties**) a formal agreement between nations.

tre·ble¹ /'trebəl/ ▶ adj. **1** consisting of three parts. **2** multiplied or occurring three times. ▶ n. a threefold quantity or thing. ▶ pron. an amount that is three times as large as usual. ▶ v. make or become three times as large or as many.

treble² ▶ n. **1** a high-pitched voice, especially a boy's singing voice. **2** the high-frequency output of a radio or audio system.

tre·ble clef ▶ n. Music a clef placing G above middle C on the second-lowest line of the stave.

tree /trē/ ▶ n. **1** a woody perennial plant consisting of a trunk and branches, that can typically grow to a considerable height. **2** a branching structure. ■ **tree·less** adj.

tree·creep·er /'trē,krēpər/ ▶ n. a small brown songbird that creeps about on the trunks of trees to search for insects.

tree di·a·gram ▶ n. a diagram with a structure of branching connecting lines.

tree fern ▶ n. a large palmlike fern with a stem that resembles a tree trunk.

tree frog ▶ n. a tree-living frog that has long toes with adhesive disks and is typically small and brightly colored.

tree house ▶ n. a structure built in the branches of a tree for children to play in.

tree-hug·ger ▶ n. informal, derogatory an

environmental campaigner. ■ **tree-hug·ging** n.

tree·line /'trē,līn/ ▶ n. the height on a mountain above which trees are unable to grow.

tree ring ▶ n. each of a number of rings in the cross section of a tree trunk, representing a single year's growth.

tree sur·geon ▶ n. a person who prunes and treats old or damaged trees in order to preserve them. ■ **tree sur·ger·y** n.

tree·top /'trē,täp/ ▶ n. the uppermost part of a tree.

tre·foil /'trē,foil, 'tref,oil/ ▶ n. **1** a small plant with yellow flowers and cloverlike leaves. **2** an ornamental design in the form of three rounded arcs like a clover leaf, used typically in stone tracery.

trek /trek/ ▶ n. a long, difficult journey, especially one made on foot. ▶ v. (**treks, trekking, trekked**) go on a trek. ■ **trek·ker** n.

trel·lis /'trelis/ ▶ n. a framework of bars used as a support for climbing plants. ■ **trel·lised** adj.

trem·ble /'trembəl/ ▶ v. **1** shake uncontrollably as a result of fear, excitement, or weakness. **2** be very worried or frightened. **3** (of a thing) shake slightly. ▶ n. a trembling feeling, movement, or sound. ■ **trem·bly** /'tremb(ə)lē/ adj. (informal).

tre·men·dous /trə'mendəs/ ▶ adj. **1** very great in amount, scale, or intensity. **2** informal very good or impressive. ■ **tre·men·dous·ly** adv.

trem·o·lo /'tremə,lō/ ▶ n. (pl. **tremolos**) a wavering effect in singing or created when playing some musical instruments.

trem·or /'tremər/ ▶ n. **1** an uncontrollable quivering movement. **2** (also **earth tremor**) a slight earthquake. **3** a sudden feeling of fear or excitement.

trem·u·lous /'tremyələs/ ▶ adj. **1** shaking or quivering slightly. **2** timid; nervous. ■ **trem·u·lous·ly** adv. **trem·u·lous·ness** n.

trench /trenCH/ ▶ n. **1** a long, narrow ditch. **2** a long ditch dug by troops to provide shelter from enemy fire. **3** (also **ocean trench**) a long, narrow, deep depression in the ocean bed. ▶ v. dig a trench or trenches in the ground.

trench·ant /'trenCHənt/ ▶ adj. (of speech or writing) expressed forcefully and clearly. ■ **trench·an·cy** n. **trench·ant·ly** adv.

trench coat ▶ n. a double-breasted raincoat with a belt.

trench·er¹ /'trenCHər/ ▶ n. historical a wooden plate or platter.

trench·er² ▶ n. a machine used to dig trenches.

trench·er·man /'trenCHərmən/ ▶ n. (pl. **trenchermen**) humorous a person who eats heartily.

trench war·fare ▶ n. warfare in which opposing troops fight from trenches facing each other.

trend /trend/ ▶ n. **1** a general direction in which something is developing or changing: *an upward trend in sales.* **2** a fashion. ▶ v. develop in a particular direction.

trend·set·ter /'tren(d),setər/ ▶ n. a person who leads the way in fashion or ideas. ■ **trend·set·ting** adj.

trend·y /'trendē/ informal ▶ adj. (**trendier, trendiest**) very fashionable or up to date. ▶ n. (pl. **trendies**) a fashionable person. ■ **trend·i·ly** adv. **trend·i·ness** n.

tre·pan /trə'pan/ chiefly historical ▶ n. a saw used by surgeons for perforating the skull.

▶ v. (**trepans, trepanning, trepanned**) perforate a person's skull with a trepan. ■ **trep·a·na·tion** /ˌtrepəˈnāsнən/ n.

trep·i·da·tion /ˌtrepiˈdāsнən/ ▶ n. a feeling of fear or nervousness about something that may happen.

trep·i·da·tious /ˌtrepiˈdāsнəs/ ▶ adj. informal apprehensive or nervous.

tres·pass /ˈtrespəs, -ˌpas/ ▶ v. **1** enter someone's land or property without their permission. **2** (**trespass on**) take advantage of someone's good nature, help, etc. **3** (**trespass against**) old use commit an offense against a person or law. ▶ n. **1** Law entry to a person's land or property without their permission. **2** old use a sin or other morally wrong act. ■ **tres·pass·er** n.

tress /tres/ ▶ n. a long lock of a woman's hair.

tres·tle /ˈtresəl/ ▶ n. a framework consisting of a horizontal beam supported by two pairs of sloping legs, used in pairs to support a flat surface such as a table top.

tres·tle ta·ble ▶ n. a table consisting of a board or boards laid on trestles.

tri- ▶ comb.form three; having three: *triathlon*.

tri·a·ble /ˈtrīəbəl/ ▶ adj. (of an offense or case) liable to trial in a court of law.

tri·ac·e·tate /trīˈasiˌtāt/ ▶ n. a form of cellulose acetate used as a basis for synthetic fibers.

tri·ad /ˈtrīˌad/ ▶ n. **1** a group of three related people or things. **2** (also **Triad**) a Chinese secret society involved in organized crime. ■ **tri·ad·ic** /trīˈadik/ adj.

tri·age /trēˈäzн, ˈtrēˌäzн/ ▶ n. (in a hospital or in war) the assessment of the seriousness of wounds or illnesses to decide the order in which a large number of patients should be treated. ▶ v. (**triages, triaging, triaged**) decide the order of treatment of patients.

tri·al /ˈtrī(ə)l/ ▶ n. **1** a formal examination of evidence in a court of law to decide if someone accused of a crime is guilty or not. **2** a test of performance, qualities, or suitability. **3** a sports match to test the ability of players eligible for selection to a team. **4** (**trials**) an event in which horses or dogs compete or perform. **5** a test of a person's endurance or patience. ▶ v. (**trials, trialing, trialed**) test something to assess its suitability or performance.
– PHRASES **on trial 1** being tried in a court of law. **2** being tested for suitability or performance. **trial and error** the process of experimenting with various methods until one finds the most successful.

tri·al·ist /ˈtrīəlist/ (Brit. **triallist**) ▶ n. a person who participates in a sports trial.

tri·al run ▶ n. a preliminary test of a new system or product.

tri·an·gle /ˈtrīˌaNGgəl/ ▶ n. **1** a plane figure with three straight sides and three angles. **2** a thing shaped like a triangle. **3** a musical instrument consisting of a steel rod bent into a triangle, played by hitting it with a rod. **4** an emotional relationship involving a couple and a third person with whom one of them is involved.

tri·an·gu·lar /trīˈaNGgyələr/ ▶ adj. **1** shaped like a triangle. **2** involving three people or groups. ■ **tri·an·gu·lar·i·ty** /trīˌaNGgyəˈlaritē/ n. **tri·an·gu·lar·ly** adv.

tri·an·gu·late /trīˈaNGgyəˌlāt/ ▶ v. (in surveying) divide an area into triangles in order to determine the distances and relative positions of

points. ■ **tri·an·gu·la·tion** /trīˌaNGgyəˈlāsнən/ n.

Tri·as·sic /trīˈasik/ ▶ adj. Geology relating to the earliest period of the Mesozoic era (about 245 to 208 million years ago), when the first dinosaurs, ammonites, and primitive mammals appeared.

tri·ath·lon /trīˈaтнlən, -ˌlän/ ▶ n. an athletic contest consisting of three different events, typically swimming, cycling, and long-distance running. ■ **tri·ath·lete** /trīˈaтнˌlēt/ n.

trib·al /ˈtrībəl/ ▶ adj. relating to or typical of a tribe or tribes. ■ **trib·al·ly** adv.

trib·al·ism /ˈtrībəˌlizəm/ ▶ n. behavior and attitudes that are based on a person's loyalty to a tribe or other social group. ■ **trib·al·ist** adj.

tri·band ▶ adj. (of a cell phone) having three frequencies, enabling it to be used in different regions.

tribe /trīb/ ▶ n. **1** a social group in a traditional society consisting of linked families or communities with a common culture and dialect. **2** derogatory a group with a shared interest, profession, etc.: *a tribe of speechwriters*. **3** (**tribes**) informal large numbers of people. **4** a category in scientific classification that ranks above genus and below family.

> **USAGE**
> The word **tribe** can cause offense when used to refer to a community living within a traditional society today, and it is better in such cases to use alternative terms such as **community** or **people**. However, when talking about such communities in the past, it is perfectly acceptable to say **tribe**: *the area was inhabited by Slavic tribes.*

tribes·man /ˈtrībzmən/ (or **tribeswoman** /ˈtrībzˌwठomən/) ▶ n. (pl. **tribesmen** or **tribeswomen**) a member of a tribe in a traditional society.

trib·u·la·tion /ˌtribyəˈlāsнən/ ▶ n. a cause or state of great trouble or distress: *the tribulations of work and family*.

tri·bu·nal /trīˈbyठonl, trə-/ ▶ n. a court of justice.

trib·une /ˈtribyठon, triˈbyठon/ ▶ n. **1** (in ancient Rome) an official chosen by the ordinary people to protect their interests. **2** literary a champion of people's rights.

trib·u·tar·y /ˈtribyəˌterē/ ▶ n. (pl. **tributaries**) **1** a river or stream flowing into a larger river or lake. **2** historical a person or nation that pays money to another more powerful ruler or nation.

trib·ute /ˈtribyठot/ ▶ n. **1** an act, statement, or gift that is intended to show gratitude, respect, or admiration. **2** something that indicates the worth of something else: *his victory was a tribute to his persistence*. **3** historical payment made regularly by one nation or ruler to a more powerful one.

trice /trīs/ ▶ n. (in phrase **in a trice**) in a moment; very quickly.

tri·cen·ten·ni·al /ˌtrīsenˈtenēəl/ ▶ n. the three-hundredth anniversary of a significant event. ▶ adj. relating to a three-hundredth anniversary: *the tricentennial year*.

tri·ceps /ˈtrīˌseps/ ▶ n. (pl. same) the large muscle at the back of the upper arm.

tri·cer·a·tops /trīˈserəˌtäps/ ▶ n. a large plant-eating dinosaur having a huge head with two large horns, a smaller horn on the snout, and a bony frill above the neck.

trich·i·no·sis /ˌtrikəˈnōsis/ ▶ n. a disease caught from infected meat, especially pork, characterized by digestive disturbance, fever, and muscular rigidity.

tri·chol·o·gy /triˈkäləjē/ ▶ n. the branch of medicine concerned with the hair and scalp. ■ **trich·o·log·i·cal** /ˌtrikəˈläjikəl/ adj. **tri·chol·o·gist** n.

tri·chro·mat·ic /ˌtrīkrōˈmatik/ ▶ adj. **1** having or using three colors. **2** having normal color vision, which is sensitive to all three primary colors. ■ **tri·chro·ma·tism** /-ˈkrōməˌtizəm/ n.

trick /trik/ ▶ n. **1** an act or scheme intended to deceive or outwit someone. **2** a skillful act performed for entertainment. **3** an illusion: *there was nothing there—it had only been a trick of the light.* **4** a habit or mannerism: *he had an odd trick of blowing through his lips when he was listening.* **5** (in bridge, whist, etc.) a sequence of cards forming a single round of play. ▶ v. **1** cunningly deceive or outwit someone. **2** (**trick someone into/out of**) deceive someone into doing or parting with something. ▶ adj. intended to trick or to create an illusion: *a trick question.* ■ **trick·er** n. **trick·er·y** n. – PHRASES **do the trick** informal achieve the required result. **trick or treat** a children's custom of calling at houses in costume at Halloween with the threat of pranks if they are not given candy. **tricks of the trade** special clever techniques used in a profession or craft.

trick·le /ˈtrikəl/ ▶ v. **1** (of a liquid) flow in a small stream. **2** come or go slowly or gradually: *details began to trickle out.* **3** (**trickle down**) (of wealth) gradually spread from the richest to the poorest people in society. ▶ n. **1** a small flow of liquid. **2** a small group or number of people or things moving slowly.

trick·le-down ▶ n. the theory that the poorest people in society gradually benefit as a result of the increasing wealth of the richest.

trick·ster /ˈtrikstər/ ▶ n. a person who cheats or deceives people.

trick·y /ˈtrikē/ ▶ adj. (**trickier, trickiest**) **1** difficult or awkward to do or deal with: *he knew how to handle tricky media questions.* **2** deceitful or crafty. ■ **trick·i·ly** adv. **trick·i·ness** n.

tri·col·or /ˈtrīˌkələr/ ▶ n. a flag with three bands of different colors, especially the French national flag with equal bands of blue, white, and red. ▶ adj. (also **tricolored**) having three colors.

tri·corn /ˈtrīˌkôrn/ (also **tricorne**) ▶ n. a hat with a brim turned up on three sides.

tri·cot /ˈtrēkō/ ▶ n. a fine knitted fabric.

tri·cus·pid /trīˈkəspid/ ▶ n. a tooth with three cusps or points.

tri·cy·cle /ˈtrīsikəl, -ˌsikəl/ ▶ n. a vehicle similar to a bicycle, but having three wheels, two at the back and one at the front.

tri·cy·clic /trīˈsīklik, -ˈsik-/ ▶ n. any of a class of drugs used to treat depression.

tri·dent /ˈtrīdnt/ ▶ n. a three-pronged spear.

tried /trīd/ ▶ past and past participle of **TRY**.

tri·en·ni·al /trīˈenēəl/ ▶ adj. lasting for or recurring every three years. ■ **tri·en·ni·al·ly** adv.

tri·er /ˈtrī(ə)r/ ▶ n. a person who always makes an effort, however unsuccessful they may be.

tri·fid /ˈtrīfid/ ▶ adj. technical (of part of a plant or animal) divided into three parts by a deep cleft.

tri·fle /ˈtrīfəl/ ▶ n. **1** a thing of little value or importance. **2** a cold dessert of sponge cake and fruit covered with layers of custard, gelatin, and cream. ▶ v. (**trifle with**) treat without seriousness or respect: *he was not a man to be trifled with.* ■ **tri·fler** n. – PHRASES **a trifle** slightly; rather.

tri·fling /ˈtrīf(ə)liNG/ ▶ adj. unimportant or trivial. ■ **tri·fling·ly** adv.

tri·fo·li·ate /trīˈfōlē-it, -ˌāt/ ▶ adj. (of a compound leaf) having three small leaves.

trig /trig/ ▶ n. informal trigonometry.

trig·ger /ˈtrigər/ ▶ n. **1** a device that releases a spring or catch and so fires a gun or sets off a mechanism. **2** an event that causes something to happen. ▶ v. **1** (also **trigger something off**) cause to happen: *house dust may trigger an asthma attack.* **2** cause a device to function.

trig·ger-hap·py ▶ adj. apt to shoot someone or take other violent action on the slightest provocation.

tri·glyc·er·ide /trīˈglisəˌrīd/ ▶ n. a compound formed from glycerol and three fatty acid groups, e.g., the main constituents of natural fats and oils.

trig·o·nom·e·try /ˌtrigəˈnämitrē/ ▶ n. the branch of mathematics concerned with the relations of the sides and angles of triangles and with the functions of angles. ■ **trig·o·no·met·ric** /-nəˈmetrik/ adj. **trig·o·no·met·ri·cal** /-nəˈmetrikəl/ adj.

trike /trīk/ ▶ n. informal a tricycle.

tri·lat·er·al /trīˈlatərəl/ ▶ adj. **1** shared by or involving three parties: *trilateral talks.* **2** Geometry on or with three sides.

tril·by /ˈtrilbē/ ▶ n. (pl. **trilbies**) chiefly Brit. a soft felt hat with a narrow brim and indented crown.

tri·lin·gual /trīˈliNGgwəl/ ▶ adj. **1** speaking three languages fluently. **2** written or carried out in three languages. ■ **tri·lin·gual·ism** /-ˌlizəm/ n.

trill /tril/ ▶ n. a quavering or warbling sound, especially a rapid alternation of notes. ▶ v. make a quavering or warbling sound.

tril·lion /ˈtrilyən/ ▶ cardinal number (pl. **trillions** or (with numeral or quantifying word) same) **1** a million million (1,000,000,000,000 or 10^{12}). **2** Brit. dated a million million million (1,000,000,000,000,000,000 or 10^{18}). **3** (**trillions**) informal a very large number or amount. ■ **tril·lionth** /ˈtrilyənTH/ ordinal number.

tri·lo·bite /ˈtrīləˌbīt/ ▶ n. a fossil marine arthropod (invertebrate creature) with a rear part divided into three segments.

tril·o·gy /ˈtriləjē/ ▶ n. (pl. **trilogies**) a group of three related novels, plays, or movies.

trim /trim/ ▶ v. (**trims, trimming, trimmed**) **1** cut away unwanted or irregular parts from something. **2** reduce the size, amount, or number of: *the company aims to trim production costs.* **3** decorate something, especially along its edges. **4** adjust a boat's sail to take advantage of the wind. ▶ n. **1** decoration, especially along the edges of something. **2** the upholstery or interior lining of a car. **3** an act of cutting something. **4** the state of being in good order. ▶ adj. (**trimmer, trimmest**) **1** neat and smart. **2** slim and fit. ■ **trim·ly** adv. **trim·mer** n. **trim·ness** n. – PHRASES **in trim** slim and fit. **trim one's sails (to the wind)** make changes to suit one's new situation.

tri·ma·ran /ˈtrīməˌran/ ▶ n. a sailboat or other boat with three hulls side by side.

tri·mes·ter /trī'mestər, 'trī,mes-/ ▶ n. **1** a period of three months as a division of the duration of pregnancy. **2** each of the three terms in an academic year.

trim·ming /'trimiNG/ ▶ n. **1** (**trimmings**) small pieces trimmed off. **2** decoration, especially for clothing. **3** (**the trimmings**) the traditional accompaniments to something: *roast turkey with all the trimmings.*

Trin·i·da·di·an /,trinə'dadēən, -'dādē-/ ▶ n. a person from Trinidad. ▶ adj. relating to Trinidad.

Trin·i·tar·i·an /,trinə'te(ə)rēən/ ▶ adj. relating to the Christian doctrine of the Trinity. ▶ n. a Christian who believes in the doctrine of the Trinity. ■ **Trin·i·tar·i·an·ism** /-,nizəm/ n.

trin·i·ty /'trinitē/ ▶ n. (pl. **trinities**) **1** (**the Trinity** or **the Holy Trinity**) (in Christian belief) the three persons (Father, Son, and Holy Spirit) that together make up God. **2** a group of three people or things.

trin·ket /'triNGkit/ ▶ n. a small ornament or item of jewelry that is of little value.

tri·o /'trē-ō/ ▶ n. (pl. **trios**) **1** a set or group of three. **2** a group of three musicians.

tri·ode /'trī,ōd/ ▶ n. a semiconductor device with three connections, typically allowing the flow of current in one direction only.

tri·ox·ide /trī'äk,sīd/ ▶ n. Chemistry an oxide containing three atoms of oxygen.

trip /trip/ ▶ v. (**trips, tripping, tripped**) **1** catch one's foot on something and stumble or fall. **2** (**trip up** or **trip someone up**) make or cause to make a mistake. **3** walk, run, or dance with quick light steps. **4** (of words) flow lightly and easily: *a name that trips off the tongue.* **5** activate a mechanism, especially by contact with a switch. **6** (of part of an electric circuit) disconnect automatically as a safety measure. **7** informal experience hallucinations as a result of taking a drug such as LSD. ▶ n. **1** a journey or excursion. **2** an instance of tripping or falling. **3** informal a period of hallucinations caused by taking a drug. **4** informal a self-indulgent attitude or activity: *a power trip.* **5** a device that trips a mechanism or circuit.
– PHRASES **trip the light fantastic** humorous dance.

tri·par·tite /trī'pär,tīt/ ▶ adj. **1** consisting of three parts. **2** shared by or involving three parties.

tripe /trīp/ ▶ n. **1** the first or second stomach of a cow or sheep used as food. **2** informal nonsense; rubbish.

trip ham·mer ▶ n. a large, heavy hammer used in forging, which is raised and then allowed to drop on the metal being worked.

Tri·pit·a·ka /tri'pitəkə/ ▶ n. the sacred writings of Theravada Buddhism.

tri·plane /'trī,plān/ ▶ n. an early type of aircraft with three pairs of wings, one above the other.

tri·ple /'tripəl/ ▶ adj. **1** consisting of or involving three things or people. **2** having three times the usual size, quality, or strength. ▶ predeterminer three times as much or as many. ▶ n. a thing that is three times as large as usual or is made up of three parts. ▶ v. make or become three times as much or as many. ■ **trip·ly** /'triplē/ adv.

tri·ple bond ▶ n. a chemical bond in which three pairs of electrons are shared between two atoms.

Trip·le Crown ▶ n. an award or honor for winning a group of three important events in a sport.

tri·ple jump ▶ n. **1** an athletic event in which

competitors attempt to jump as far as possible by performing a hop, a step, and a jump from a running start. **2** a jump in which a skater makes three full turns while in the air.

tri·ple play ▶ n. Baseball a defensive play in which three runners are put out.

tri·ple point ▶ n. Chemistry the temperature and pressure at which the solid, liquid, and vapor phases of a pure substance can coexist in equilibrium.

tri·plet /'triplit/ ▶ n. **1** each of three children or animals born at the same time. **2** a group of three equal musical notes to be performed in the time of two or four. **3** a set of three rhyming lines of verse.

tri·ple time ▶ n. musical time with three beats to the bar.

tri·plex /'tripleks, 'trī-/ ▶ n. a residential building divided into three apartments. ▶ adj. having three parts.

trip·li·cate ▶ adj. /'triplikit/ existing in three copies or examples. ▶ v. /-,kāt/ **1** make three copies of something. **2** multiply something by three. ■ **trip·li·ca·tion** /,triplə'kāsHən/ n. **tri·plic·i·ty** /tri'plisitē/ n.

tri·pod /'trīpäd/ ▶ n. **1** a three-legged stand for supporting a camera or other piece of equipment. **2** old use a stool, table, or cauldron set on three legs.

trip·py /'tripē/ ▶ adj. (**trippier, trippiest**) informal resembling or causing the hallucinations experienced after taking a drug such as LSD: *trippy dance music.*

trip·tych /'triptik/ ▶ n. **1** a picture or carving on three panels, typically hinged together vertically and used as an altarpiece. **2** a set of three related artistic, literary, or musical works.

trip·wire /'trip,wīr/ ▶ n. a wire that is stretched close to the ground and activates a trap, explosion, or alarm when disturbed.

tri·reme /'trī,rēm/ ▶ n. an ancient Greek or Roman warship with three banks of oars.

tri·sect /trī'sekt/ ▶ v. divide something into three parts. ■ **tri·sec·tion** /-'seksHən/ n.

tris·mus /'trizməs/ ▶ n. technical term for LOCKJAW.

tris·tesse /trē'stes/ ▶ n. literary a state of melancholy sadness.

trite /trīt/ ▶ adj. (of a remark or idea) unoriginal and dull because of overuse. ■ **trite·ly** adv. **trite·ness** n.

trit·i·um /'tritēəm, 'trisH-/ ▶ n. Chemistry a radioactive isotope of hydrogen with a mass approximately three times that of the usual isotope.

trit·u·rate /'tricHə,rāt/ ▶ v. technical grind a substance to a fine powder. ■ **trit·u·ra·tion** /,tricHə'rāsHən/ n.

tri·umph /'trīəmf/ ▶ n. **1** a great victory or achievement. **2** the state of being victorious or successful. **3** joy or satisfaction resulting from a success or victory. **4** a highly successful example: *their marriage was a triumph of togetherness.* **5** a ceremonial procession of a victorious general into ancient Rome. ▶ v. **1** achieve victory or success. **2** rejoice in a victory or success: *she stopped triumphing over Mary's failure.* ■ **tri·um·phal** /trī'əmfəl/ adj.

tri·um·phal·ism /trī'əmfə,lizəm/ ▶ n. excessive rejoicing over one's own success or achievements. ■ **tri·um·phal·ist** adj. & n.

tri·um·phant /trī'əmfənt/ ▶ adj. **1** having won a battle or contest; victorious. **2** joyful after a victory or achievement. ■ **tri·um·phant·ly** adv.

tri·um·vir /trī'əmvər/ ▶ n. (in ancient Rome) each of three public officials jointly responsible for overseeing any of the administrative departments.

tri·um·vi·rate /trī'əmvərit, -ˌrāt/ ▶ n. **1** a group of three powerful or important people or things. **2** (in ancient Rome) a group of three men holding power.

tri·une /'trī,(y)ōōn/ ▶ adj. (especially with reference to the Christian Trinity) consisting of three in one.

triv·et /'trivit/ ▶ n. **1** a metal stand on which hot dishes are placed. **2** an iron tripod placed over a fire for a cooking pot or kettle to stand on.

triv·i·a /'trivēə/ ▶ pl.n. unimportant details or pieces of information.

triv·i·al /'trivēəl/ ▶ adj. not very important or serious: *doctors can find it frustrating to be called out on trivial matters.* ■ **triv·i·al·i·ty** /ˌtrivē'alitē/ n. (pl. **trivialities**) **triv·i·al·ly** adv.

triv·i·al·ize /'trivēəˌlīz/ ▶ v. make something seem less important or complex than it really is. ■ **triv·i·al·i·za·tion** /ˌtrivēəli'zāsHən/ n.

tro·chee /'trōkē/ ▶ n. a foot (unit of poetic meter) consisting of one long or stressed syllable followed by one short or unstressed syllable. ■ **tro·cha·ic** /trō'kā-ik/ adj.

trod /träd/ ▶ past and past participle of TREAD.

trod·den /'trädn/ ▶ past participle of TREAD.

trog·lo·dyte /'träglə,dīt/ ▶ n. **1** a person who lives in a cave. **2** a person who is ignorant or old-fashioned. ■ **trog·lo·dyt·ic** /ˌträglə'ditik/ adj.

troi·ka /'troikə/ ▶ n. **1** a Russian vehicle pulled by a team of three horses side by side. **2** a group of three political leaders or managers working together.

troil·ism /'troiˌlizəm/ ▶ n. sexual activity involving three participants.

Tro·jan /'trōjən/ ▶ n. an inhabitant of ancient Troy in the western peninsula of Asia. ▶ adj. relating to Troy.
– PHRASES **work like a Trojan** work very hard.

Tro·jan Horse ▶ n. something intended to weaken or defeat an enemy secretly.

troll¹ /trōl/ ▶ n. (in folklore) an ugly giant or dwarf that lives in a cave.

troll² ▶ v. fish by trailing a baited line along behind a boat. ■ **troll·er** n.

trol·ley /'trälē/ ▶ n. (pl. **trolleys**) **1** a trolley car or trolleybus. **2** (also **trolley wheel**) a wheel attached to a pole, used for collecting current from an overhead electric wire to drive a trolley car. **3** a large metal basket or frame on wheels, used for transporting heavy or bulky items such as luggage. **4** Brit. a shopping cart. **5** a small table on wheels, used to convey food and drink.
– PHRASES **off one's trolley** informal mad; insane.

trol·ley bus /'trälē,bəs/ ▶ n. a bus powered by electricity obtained from overhead wires by means of a trolley wheel.

trol·ley car ▶ n. a passenger vehicle powered by electricity obtained from an overhead cable by means of a trolley wheel.

trol·lop /'träləp/ ▶ n. dated or humorous a woman who has many sexual partners.

trom·bone /träm'bōn, trəm-/ ▶ n. a large

brass wind instrument with a sliding tube that is moved to produce different notes. ■ **trom·bon·ist** n.

trompe l'œil /ˌtrômp 'loi/ ▶ n. (pl. **trompe l'œils** pronunc. same) a painting or method of painting that creates the illusion of a three-dimensional object or space.

troop /trōōp/ ▶ n. **1** (**troops**) soldiers or armed forces. **2** a group of people or animals of a particular kind. **3** a unit of an armored or cavalry division. **4** a unit of Girl or Boy Scouts organized under a troop leader. ▶ v. come or go as a group: *the girls trooped in for dinner.*

troop car·ri·er ▶ n. a large aircraft or armored vehicle designed for transporting troops.

troop·er /'trōōpər/ ▶ n. **1** a state police officer. **2** a mounted police officer. **3** a private soldier in a cavalry or armored unit. **4** chiefly Brit. a ship for transporting troops.

troop·ship /'trōōp,sHip/ ▶ n. a ship for transporting troops.

trope /trōp/ ▶ n. a figurative or metaphorical use of a word or expression.

tro·phy /'trōfē/ ▶ n. (pl. **trophies**) **1** a cup or other decorative object awarded as a prize. **2** a souvenir of an achievement, such as a head of an animal killed when hunting.

tro·phy wife ▶ n. informal, derogatory a young, attractive wife regarded as a status symbol for an older man.

trop·ic /'träpik/ ▶ n. **1** the line of latitude 23°26′ north (**tropic of Cancer**) or south (**tropic of Capricorn**) of the equator. **2** (**the tropics**) the region between the tropics of Cancer and Capricorn. ▶ adj. relating to the tropics; tropical.

trop·i·cal /'träpəkəl/ ▶ adj. **1** relating to the tropics. **2** very hot and humid. ■ **trop·i·cal·ly** adv.

trop·i·cal storm ▶ n. a localized, very intense low-pressure wind system with winds just below that of hurricane force, forming over tropical oceans.

tro·pism /'trō,pizəm/ ▶ n. Biology the turning of all or part of an organism toward or away from an external stimulus such as light.

trop·o·sphere /'träpə,sfi(ə)r, 'trō-/ ▶ n. the lowest region of the atmosphere, extending from the earth's surface to a height of about 6–10 km (the lower boundary of the stratosphere). ■ **trop·o·spher·ic** /ˌträpə'sfi(ə)rik, -'sferik, ˌtrō-/ adj.

trop·po /'träpō/ ▶ adv. Music too much; excessively.

trot /trät/ ▶ v. (**trots, trotting, trotted**) **1** (of a horse) move at a pace faster than a walk, lifting each diagonal pair of legs alternately. **2** (of a person) run at a moderate pace with short steps. **3** (**trot something out**) informal produce an account that has been produced many times before. ▶ n. **1** a trotting pace. **2** an act of trotting. **3** (**the trots**) informal diarrhea.

troth /trôtH, trōtH/ ▶ n. old use or formal faith or loyalty when pledged in a solemn agreement.
– PHRASES **pledge** (or **plight**) **one's troth** make a solemn promise, especially to marry someone.

Trot·sky·ism /'trätskē,izəm/ ▶ n. the political or economic principles of the Russian revolutionary Leon Trotsky, especially the theory that socialism should be established throughout the world by continuing revolution. ■ **Trot·sky·ist** n. & adj. **Trot·sky·ite** /'trätskē,īt/ n. & adj. (derogatory).

trot·ter /'trätər/ ▶ n. **1** a horse bred or trained for the sport of trotting. **2** a pig's foot.

trot·ting /'träting/ ▸ n. racing for horses pulling a two-wheeled vehicle and driver.

trou·ba·dour /'trōōbəˌdôr, -ˌdŏŏr/ ▸ n. (in medieval France) a performing poet who composed and sang in Provençal, especially on the theme of courtly love.

trou·ble /'trəbəl/ ▸ n. **1** difficulty or problems. **2** effort made to do something: *I've gone to a lot of trouble to help you.* **3** a cause of worry or inconvenience. **4** a situation in which a person is likely to be punished or blamed: *he's been in trouble with the police.* **5** public unrest or disorder. ▸ v. **1** cause distress or inconvenience to someone. **2** (as adj. **troubled**) showing or experiencing problems or anxiety. **3** (**trouble about/over/with**) be anxious about someone or something. **4** (**trouble to do**) make the effort to do: *oh, don't trouble to answer.*
– PHRASES **look for trouble** informal deliberately try to start an argument or fight.

trou·ble·mak·er /'trəbəlˌmākər/ ▸ n. a person who often causes trouble, especially by encouraging others to defy people in authority.

trou·ble·shoot /'trəbəlˌSHŌŌt/ ▸ v. **1** analyze and solve problems for an organization. **2** trace and correct faults in a mechanical or electronic system. ■ **trou·ble·shoot·er** n.

trou·ble·some /'trəbəlsəm/ ▸ adj. causing difficulty or annoyance. ■ **trou·ble·some·ness** n.

trou·ble spot ▸ n. a place where difficulties or conflict regularly occur.

trough /trôf/ ▸ n. **1** a long, narrow open container for animals to eat or drink out of. **2** a channel used to convey a liquid. **3** Meteorology a long, narrow region of low pressure. **4** a point of low activity or achievement: *peaks and troughs in demand.* **5** a hollow between two wave crests in the sea.

trounce /trouns/ ▸ v. defeat someone heavily in a contest.

troupe /trōōp/ ▸ n. a group of dancers, actors, or other entertainers who tour to different venues.

troup·er /'trōōpər/ ▸ n. **1** an entertainer with long experience. **2** a reliable and uncomplaining person.

trou·sers /'trouzərz/ ▸ pl.n. an outer garment covering the body from the waist to the ankles, with a separate part for each leg; pants. ▸ adj. (**trouser**) relating to trousers: *his trouser pocket.* ■ **trou·sered** adj.

trous·seau /'trōōˌsō, ˌtrōō'sō/ ▸ n. (pl. **trousseaux** pronunc. same, or **trousseaus** /-ˌsōz/) the clothes, linen, and other belongings collected by a bride for her marriage.

trout /trout/ ▸ n. (pl. same or **trouts**) an edible fish of the salmon family, found chiefly in fresh water.

trove /trōv/ ▸ n. a store of valuable or pleasant things.

trow /trō/ ▸ v. old use think or believe something.

trow·el /'trouəl/ ▸ n. **1** a small garden tool with a curved scoop for lifting plants or earth. **2** a small tool with a flat, pointed blade, used to apply and spread mortar or plaster. ▸ v. (**trowels, troweling, troweled**) apply or spread something with a trowel.

troy /troi/ (also **troy weight**) ▸ n. a system of weights used mainly for precious metals and

gems, with a pound of 12 ounces or 5,760 grains. Compare with AVOIRDUPOIS.

tru·ant /'trōōənt/ ▸ n. a student who stays away from school without permission or explanation. ▸ adj. wandering; straying. ■ **tru·an·cy** n.

truce /trōōs/ ▸ n. an agreement between enemies to stop fighting for a certain time.

truck¹ /trək/ ▸ n. **1** a large road vehicle for carrying goods or troops. **2** Brit. an open railroad car. ▸ v. convey goods by truck.

truck² ▸ n. (in phrase **have no truck with**) refuse to deal or be associated with.

truck·er /'trəkər/ ▸ n. a long-distance truck driver.

truck farm ▸ n. a place where vegetables and fruit are grown for sale. ■ **truck farm·er** n.

truck·le /'trəkəl/ ▸ v. submit or behave obsequiously.

truck stop ▸ n. a large roadside service station and restaurant for truck drivers on interstate highways.

truc·u·lent /'trəkyələnt/ ▸ adj. quick to argue or fight. ■ **truc·u·lence** n. **truc·u·lent·ly** adv.

trudge /trəj/ ▸ v. walk slowly and with heavy steps. ▸ n. a long and tiring walk.

true /trōō/ ▸ adj. (**truer, truest**) **1** in accordance with fact or reality. **2** rightly so called; genuine: *true love.* **3** real or actual: *she guessed my true intentions.* **4** accurate and exact. **5** (**true to**) in keeping with a standard or expectation: *true to his threats, he retaliated.* **6** loyal or faithful. **7** correctly positioned or aligned; upright or level. ▸ v. (**trues, truing** or **trueing, trued**) bring something into the exact shape or position required. ■ **true·ness** n.
– PHRASES **come true** actually happen or become the case. **out of true** not in the correct or exact shape or alignment. **true to form** (or **type**) being or behaving as expected.

true-blue ▸ adj. very loyal or traditional.

true north ▸ n. north according to the earth's axis, not magnetic north.

truf·fle /'trəfəl/ ▸ n. **1** an underground fungus that resembles a rough-skinned potato, eaten as a delicacy. **2** a soft chocolate candy.

tru·ism /'trōōˌizəm/ ▸ n. a statement that is obviously true and says nothing new or interesting.

tru·ly /'trōōlē/ ▸ adv. **1** in a truthful way. **2** genuinely or properly. **3** in actual fact; really. **4** absolutely or completely (used for emphasis): *a truly dreadful song.*
– PHRASES **yours truly 1** used as a formula for ending a letter. **2** humorous used to refer to oneself.

trump¹ /trəmp/ ▸ n. **1** (in bridge, etc.) a playing card of the suit chosen to rank above the others, which can win a trick where a card of a different suit has been led. **2** (also **trump card**) a valuable resource that may be used, especially as a surprise, to gain an advantage. **3** informal, dated a helpful or admirable person. ▸ v. **1** play a trump on a card of another suit. **2** beat by saying or doing something better: *this sequel trumps the original movie.* **3** (**trump something up**) invent a false accusation or excuse.

trump² ▸ n. old use a trumpet or a sound made by one.

trump·er·y /'trəmpərē/ old use ▸ n. (pl. **trumperies**) things that are superficially attractive or appealing but have little real worth. ▶ adj. showy but worthless.

trum·pet /'trəmpit/ ▶ n. **1** a brass musical instrument with a flared end. **2** something shaped like a trumpet, especially the central part of a daffodil flower. **3** the loud cry of an elephant. ▶ v. (**trumpets, trumpeting, trumpeted**) **1** announce widely or enthusiastically: *researchers trumpeted a major medical breakthrough.* **2** (of an elephant) make its loud cry. **3** play a trumpet. ■ **trum·pet·er** n.

trun·cate /'trəŋˌkāt/ ▶ v. shorten something by cutting off the top or the end. ■ **trun·ca·tion** /ˌtrəŋˈkāsHən/ n.

trun·cheon /'trənCHən/ ▶ n. chiefly Brit. a short, thick stick carried as a weapon by a police officer.

trun·dle /'trəndl/ ▶ v. move or roll along slowly and heavily.

trun·dle bed ▶ n. a low bed on wheels that can be stored under a larger bed.

trunk /trəŋk/ ▶ n. **1** (also **tree trunk**) the main woody stem of a tree. **2** a person's or animal's body apart from the limbs and head. **3** the long nose of an elephant. **4** a large box with a hinged lid for storing or transporting clothes and other articles. **5** the space at the back of a car for carrying luggage and other goods. ▶ adj. relating to the main routes of a transport or communication network: *a trunk road.*

trunks /trəŋks/ ▶ pl. n. men's shorts worn for swimming or boxing.

truss /trəs/ ▶ n. **1** a padded belt worn to support a hernia. **2** a framework of rafters, posts, and struts that supports a roof, bridge, or other structure. **3** a compact cluster of flowers or fruit growing on one stalk. **4** a large projection of stone or timber, typically one supporting a cornice. ▶ v. **1** tie someone up tightly. **2** tie up the wings and legs of a chicken or other bird before cooking. **3** support something with a truss or trusses.

trust /trəst/ ▶ n. **1** firm belief that someone or something is reliable, true, or able to do something: *the need to restore trust in the police.* **2** acceptance of the truth of a statement without evidence or investigation. **3** the state of being responsible for someone or something. **4** a legal arrangement whereby a person (a trustee) holds property as its nominal owner for the good of one or more other people. **5** an organization managed by trustees. ▶ v. **1** firmly believe to be reliable, true, or able to do something: *they trusted their neighbors to protect them.* **2** (**trust someone with**) have the confidence to allow someone to have, use, or look after someone or something. **3** (**trust someone/thing to**) give someone or something to another person for safekeeping. **4** (**trust to**) rely on luck, fate, etc. **5** hope: *I trust that you are well.* ■ **trust·a·ble** adj. **trust·ed** adj.

trust com·pa·ny ▶ n. a company formed to act as a trustee or to deal with trusts.

trust·ee /trəˈstē/ ▶ n. a person given legal powers to hold and manage property in trust for the benefit of another person or people. ■ **trust·ee·ship** n.

trust·ful /'trəs(t)fəl/ ▶ adj. having or showing total trust in someone. ■ **trust·ful·ly** adv. **trust·ful·ness** n.

trust fund ▶ n. a fund consisting of money or property that is held and managed for another person or people by a trust.

trust·ing /'trəstiNG/ ▶ adj. tending to trust others; not suspicious. ■ **trust·ing·ly** adv. **trust·ing·ness** n.

trust·wor·thy /'trəstˌwərTHē/ ▶ adj. able to be relied on as honest and truthful. ■ **trust·wor·thi·ness** n.

trust·y /'trəstē/ ▶ adj. (**trustier, trustiest**) old use or humorous having been used or known for a long time and regarded as reliable: *my trusty old typewriter.*

truth /trōōTH/ ▶ n. (pl. **truths** /trōōTHz, trōōTHs/) **1** the state of being true: *no one could doubt the truth of his claims.* **2** (also **the truth**) that which is true; actual facts. **3** a fact or belief that is accepted as true.
– PHRASES **in truth** really; in fact.

truth·ful /'trōōTHfəl/ ▶ adj. **1** telling or expressing the truth; honest. **2** realistic; lifelike. ■ **truth·ful·ly** adv. **truth·ful·ness** n.

try /trī/ ▶ v. (**tries, trying, tried**) **1** make an attempt or effort to do something. **2** (also **try something out**) test something new or different to see if it is suitable, effective, or pleasant. **3** attempt to open a door or window. **4** (**try something on**) put on an item of clothing to see if it fits or suits one. **5** make severe demands on: *Mary tried everyone's patience to the limit.* **6** put someone on trial. **7** investigate and decide a case or issue in a formal trial. ▶ n. (pl. **tries**) **1** an attempt to do something. **2** a test of something new or different.
– PHRASES **tried and true** (or **tested**) having proved effective or reliable before. **try one's hand at** attempt to do something for the first time.

> **USAGE**
> The expressions **try to** and **try and** both mean the same thing, but it is better to use **try to** in writing (*we should try to help them* rather than *we should try and help them*).

try·ing /'trī-iNG/ ▶ adj. difficult or annoying.

try·out /'trī,out/ ▶ n. a test of the potential of someone or something, especially in sports.

tryp·to·phan /'triptəˌfan/ ▶ n. an amino acid that is a constituent of most proteins and is an essential nutrient in the diet of vertebrates.

try square ▶ n. an implement used to check and mark right angles in construction work.

tryst /trist/ literary ▶ n. a private, romantic meeting between lovers. ▶ v. meet privately with a lover.

tsar /zär/ (also **czar** or **tzar**) ▶ n. **1** an emperor of Russia before 1917. **2** a person with great authority or power in a particular area: *America's new drug tsar.* ■ **tsar·ist** n. & adj.

tsa·ri·na /zäˈrēnə, (t)sä-/ (also **czarina** or **tzarina**) ▶ n. an empress of Russia before 1917.

tset·se /'(t)setsē, '(t)set-/ (also **tsetse fly**) ▶ n. an African bloodsucking fly that transmits sleeping sickness and other diseases.

T-shirt (also **tee shirt**) ▶ n. a short-sleeved casual top, having the shape of a T when spread out flat.

tsp. ▶ abbr. (pl. same or **tsps.**) teaspoonful.

T-square ▶ n. a T-shaped instrument for drawing or testing right angles.

TSS ▶ abbr. toxic shock syndrome.

tsu·na·mi /(t)sŏōˈnämē/ ▶ n. (pl. same or **tsunamis**) a tidal wave caused by an earthquake or other disturbance.

TT ▶ abbr. Trust Territories.

TTL ▶ abbr. **1** transistor transistor logic, a widely used technology for making integrated electronic circuits. **2** (of a camera focusing system) through-the-lens.

Tua·reg /'twä,reg/ ▶ n. (pl. same or **Tuaregs**) a member of a Berber people of the western and central Sahara.

tub /təb/ ▶ n. **1** a low, wide, open container with a flat bottom. **2** a small plastic or cardboard container for food. **3** informal a bath. **4** informal a short, broad boat that is awkward to handle.

tu·ba /'t(y)oobə/ ▶ n. a large low-pitched brass wind instrument.

tub·al /'t(y)oobəl/ ▶ adj. relating to or occurring in a tube, especially the Fallopian tubes.

tub·by /'təbē/ ▶ adj. (**tubbier**, **tubbiest**) informal (of a person) short and rather fat. ■ **tub·bi·ness** n.

tube /t(y)oob/ ▶ n. **1** a long, hollow cylinder for conveying or holding something. **2** a flexible metal or plastic container sealed at one end and having a cap at the other: *a tube of toothpaste.* **3** a hollow cylindrical organ or structure in an animal or plant. **4** Brit. trademark (**the Tube**) the underground railroad system in London. **5** a sealed container containing two electrodes between which an electric current can be made to flow. **6** a cathode ray tube, especially in a television set. **7** (**the tube**) informal television. ▶ v. (usu. as adj. **tubed**) provide something with a tube or tubes.

– PHRASES **go down the tube** (or **tubes**) informal be completely lost or wasted.

tu·ber /'t(y)oobər/ ▶ n. **1** a thickened underground part of a stem or rhizome, e.g., that of the potato, bearing buds from which new plants grow. **2** a thickened fleshy root, e.g., of the dahlia.

tu·ber·cle /'t(y)oobərkəl/ ▶ n. **1** a small lump on a bone or on the surface of an animal or plant. **2** a small rounded swelling in the lungs or other tissues, characteristic of tuberculosis.

tu·ber·cu·lar /t(y)oo'bərkyələr/ ▶ adj. **1** relating to or affected with tuberculosis. **2** having or covered with tubercles.

tu·ber·cu·lin /t(y)oo'bərkyəlin/ ▶ n. a sterile protein extract produced from cultures of tubercle bacillus, used to test for tuberculosis.

tu·ber·cu·lo·sis /tə,bərkyə'lōsis, t(y)oo-/ ▶ n. an infectious disease transmitted by a bacterium, in which tubercles (small swellings) appear in the tissues, especially the lungs.

tu·ber·ose /'t(y)oobə,rōs, -,rōz/ ▶ n. a Mexican plant with heavily scented white waxy flowers and a bulblike base.

tu·ber·ous /'t(y)oobərəs/ ▶ adj. **1** (of a plant) resembling, forming, or having a tuber or tubers. **2** Medicine having rounded swellings.

tub·ing /'t(y)oobiNG/ ▶ n. a length or lengths of material in the form of tubes.

tu·bu·lar /'t(y)oobyələr/ ▶ adj. **1** long, round, and hollow like a tube. **2** made from a tube or tubes.

tu·bu·lar bells ▶ pl.n. an orchestral instrument consisting of a row of hanging metal tubes struck with a mallet.

tu·bule /'t(y)oo,byool/ ▶ n. a very small tube, especially in an animal or plant.

tuck /tək/ ▶ v. **1** push, fold, or turn under or between two surfaces: *he tucked his shirt into his trousers.* **2** (**tuck someone in/up**) settle someone in bed by pulling the edges of the bedclothes firmly under the mattress. **3** store

or locate in a safe or hidden place: *a French restaurant tucked away in an arcade.* **4** (**tuck in/into**) informal eat food heartily. **5** make a flattened, stitched fold in a garment or material. ▶ n. a flattened, stitched fold in a garment or material.

tuck·er /'təkər/ ▶ n. **1** historical a piece of lace or linen worn on a bodice or as an insert at the front of a low-cut dress: *wear your best bib and tucker.* **2** Austral./NZ informal food. ▶ v. (**be tuckered out**) informal be exhausted or worn out.

Tu·dor /'t(y)oodər/ ▶ adj. **1** relating to the English royal family that held the throne from 1485 to 1603. **2** referring to the main architectural style of the Tudor period, characterized by half-timbering. ▶ n. a member of the Tudor family.

Tues·day /'t(y)oozdā, -dē/ ▶ n. the day of the week before Wednesday and following Monday.

tu·fa /'t(y)oofə/ ▶ n. **1** a porous rock composed of calcium carbonate and formed as a deposit from mineral springs. **2** another term for TUFF.

tuff /təf/ ▶ n. a light, porous rock formed from volcanic ash.

tuf·fet /'təfit/ ▶ n. **1** a tuft or clump. **2** a footstool or low seat.

tuft /təft/ ▶ n. a bunch of threads, grass, or hair, held or growing together at the base. ■ **tuft·ed** adj. **tuft·y** adj.

tug /təg/ ▶ v. (**tugs**, **tugging**, **tugged**) pull something hard or suddenly. ▶ n. **1** a hard or sudden pull. **2** (also **tugboat** /'təg,bōt/) a small, powerful boat for towing larger boats and ships.

tug of war ▶ n. a contest in which two teams pull at opposite ends of a rope until one drags the other over a central line.

tu·i·tion /t(y)oo'isHən/ ▶ n. **1** a sum of money charged for teaching or instruction by a school, college, or university. **2** teaching or instruction, especially of individuals or small groups.

tu·la·re·mi·a /,t(y)oolə'rēmēə/ (Brit. **tularaemia**) ▶ n. a severe bacterial disease of animals transmissible to humans, characterized by ulcers, fever, and loss of weight.

tu·lip /'t(y)ooləp/ ▶ n. a spring-flowering plant with boldly colored cup-shaped flowers.

tu·lip tree ▶ n. **1** a North American tree with large leaves and small tuliplike flowers. **2** informal a magnolia tree or shrub.

tulle /tool/ ▶ n. a soft, fine net material, used for making veils and dresses.

tum·ble /'təmbəl/ ▶ v. **1** fall suddenly, clumsily, or headlong. **2** move in an uncontrolled way. **3** decrease rapidly in amount or value: *property prices tumbled.* **4** rumple; disarrange. **5** (**tumble to**) informal suddenly realize something. ▶ n. **1** a sudden or clumsy fall. **2** an untidy or confused arrangement or state: *a tumble of untamed curls.* **3** an acrobatic feat such as a cartwheel.

tum·ble·down /'təmbəl,doun/ ▶ adj. (of a building) falling or fallen into ruin.

tum·bler /'təmblər/ ▶ n. **1** a drinking glass with straight sides and no handle or stem. **2** an acrobat. **3** a part of a lock that holds the bolt until lifted by a key. **4** an electrical switch worked by pushing a small sprung lever.

tum·ble·weed /'təmbəl,wēd/ ▶ n. a plant of dry regions that breaks off near the ground in late summer, forming light masses blown about by the wind.

tum·bril /'təmbrəl/ (also **tumbrel**) ► n. historical an open cart that tilted backward to empty out its load, especially one used to take prisoners to the guillotine during the French Revolution.

tu·mes·cent /t(y) o͞o'mesənt/ ► adj. swollen or becoming swollen. ■ **tu·mes·cence** n.

tu·mid /'t(y)o͞omid/ ► adj. **1** (of a part of the body) swollen. **2** (of language) pompous.

tum·my /'təmē/ ► n. (pl. **tummies**) informal a person's stomach or abdomen.

tum·my but·ton ► n. informal a person's navel.

tu·mor /'t(y)o͞omər/ (Brit. **tumour**) ► n. a swelling of a part of the body caused by an abnormal growth of tissue. ■ **tu·mor·ous** adj.

tu·mult /'t(y)o͞o,məlt/ ► n. **1** a loud, confused noise, as caused by a large mass of people. **2** confusion or disorder.

tu·mul·tu·ous /t(y)o͞o'məlcHo͞oəs, tə-/ ► adj. **1** very loud or uproarious: *tumultuous applause.* **2** excited, confused, or disorderly. ■ **tu·mul·tu·ous·ly** adv.

tu·mu·lus /'t(y)o͞omyə,ləs/ ► n. (pl. **tumuli** /-,lī/) an ancient burial mound.

tun /tən/ ► n. a large beer or wine cask.

tu·na /'t(y)o͞onə/ ► n. (pl. same or **tunas**) a large edible fish of warm seas.

tun·dra /'təndrə/ ► n. a vast, flat, treeless Arctic region of Europe, Asia, and North America in which the subsoil is permanently frozen.

tune /t(y)o͞on/ ► n. a sequence of notes that forms a piece of music; a melody. ► v. **1** (also **tune up**) adjust a musical instrument to the correct pitch. **2** adjust a radio or television to a particular frequency. **3** (**tune in**) watch or listen to a television or radio broadcast. **4** adjust an engine or balance mechanical parts so that they run smoothly and efficiently. **5** adjust or adapt to a purpose or situation: *the animals are finely tuned to life in the desert.* ■ **tun·a·ble** (also **tuneable**) adj.
– PHRASES **in** (or **out of**) **tune** in (or not in) the correct musical pitch. **to the tune of** informal amounting to or involving a particular sum of money.

tune·ful /'t(y)o͞onfəl/ ► adj. having a pleasing tune; melodious. ■ **tune·ful·ly** adv. **tune·ful·ness** n.

tune·less /'t(y)o͞onləs/ ► adj. not pleasing to listen to. ■ **tune·less·ly** adv. **tune·less·ness** n.

tun·er /'t(y)o͞onər/ ► n. **1** a person who tunes musical instruments, especially pianos. **2** an electronic device used for tuning. **3** an electronic device in a stereo system that receives radio signals and supplies them to an audio amplifier.

tune·smith /'t(y)o͞on,smiTH/ ► n. informal a composer of popular music or songs.

tung·sten /'təNGstən/ ► n. a hard gray metallic element with a very high melting point, used to make electric light filaments.

tung·sten car·bide ► n. a very hard gray compound used in making engineering dies, cutting and drilling tools, etc.

tu·nic /'t(y)o͞onik/ ► n. **1** a loose sleeveless garment reaching to the thighs or knees. **2** a close-fitting short coat worn as part of a uniform.

tu·ni·cate /'t(y)o͞oni,kāt/ ► n. Zoology a marine invertebrate with a rubbery or hard outer coat. ► adj. (usu. **tunicated**) Botany (of a plant bulb, such as an onion) having concentric layers.

tun·ing fork ► n. a two-pronged steel device

used for tuning instruments, which vibrates when hit against a surface to give a note of specific pitch.

Tu·ni·sian /t(y)o͞o'nēzHən/ ► n. a person from Tunisia. ► adj. relating to Tunisia.

tun·nel /'tənl/ ► n. an underground passage, built through a hill or under a building or dug by a burrowing animal. ► v. (**tunnels, tunneling, tunneled**) dig or force a passage underground or through something. ■ **tun·nel·er** n.

tun·nel vi·sion ► n. **1** a condition in which a person cannot see things properly if they are not straight ahead. **2** informal the tendency to focus only on a single or limited aspect of a subject or situation.

tu·pe·lo /'t(y)o͞opə,lō/ ► n. (pl. **tupelos**) a North American or Asian tree of damp and swampy habitats that yields useful timber.

Tu·pi /'to͞opē, to͞o'pē/ ► n. (pl. same or **Tupis**) **1** a member of a group of American Indian peoples of the Amazon valley. **2** any of the languages of the Tupi. ■ **Tu·pi·an** adj.

Tu·pi-Gua·ra·ni /'to͞o'pē ,gwärə'nē/ ► n. a South American Indian language family whose main members are Guarani and the Tupian languages.

tup·pence /'təpəns/ ► n. Brit. variant spelling of TWOPENCE.

Tup·per·ware /'təpər,wer/ ► n. trademark a range of plastic containers used chiefly for storing food.

tur·ban /'tərbən/ ► n. a long length of material wound around a cap or the top of the head, worn especially by Muslim and Sikh men. ■ **tur·baned** (also **turbanned**) adj.

tur·bid /'tərbid/ ► adj. **1** (of a liquid) cloudy or muddy; not clear. **2** confused or unclear in meaning. ■ **tur·bid·i·ty** /tər'biditē/ n.

tur·bine /'tər,bīn, -bin/ ► n. a machine for producing power in which a wheel or rotor is made to revolve by a fast-moving flow of water, steam, gas, or air.

tur·bo /'tərbō/ ► n. (pl. **turbos**) short for TURBOCHARGER.

tur·bo·charge /'tərbō,CHärj/ ► v. (often as adj. **turbocharged**) **1** equip an engine or vehicle with a turbocharger. **2** make more powerful, fast, or exciting: *turbocharged business growth.*

tur·bo·charg·er /'tərbō,CHärjər/ ► n. a supercharger driven by a turbine powered by the engine's exhaust gases.

tur·bo·fan /'tərbō,fan/ ► n. a jet engine in which a turbine-driven fan provides additional thrust.

tur·bo·jet /'tərbō,jet/ ► n. a jet engine in which the jet gases also operate a turbine-driven compressor for compressing the air drawn into the engine.

tur·bo·prop /'tərbō,präp/ ► n. a jet engine in which a turbine is used to drive a propeller.

tur·bot /'tərbət/ ► n. (pl. same or **turbots**) an edible flatfish of inshore waters, which has large bony swellings on the body.

tur·bu·lence /'tərbyələns/ ► n. **1** violent or unsteady movement of air or water, or of another fluid. **2** upheaval, conflict, or confusion: *Europe emerged from a long period of political turbulence.*

tur·bu·lent /'tərbyələnt/ ► adj. **1** involving much conflict, upheaval, or confusion. **2** (of air or water) moving violently or unsteadily. ■ **tur·bu·lent·ly** adv.

turd /tərd/ ► n. vulgar slang **1** a lump of excrement.

2 an unpleasant or disliked person.

tu·reen /t(y)o͞oˈrēn/ ▶n. a deep covered dish from which soup is served.

turf /tərf/ ▶n. (pl. **turfs** or **turves** /tərvz/) **1** grass and the surface layer of earth held together by its roots. **2** a piece of turf cut from the ground. **3** (**the turf**) horse racing or racetracks generally. **4** (**someone's turf**) informal a place or area of activity regarded as someone's personal territory or responsibility: *he did not like poachers on his turf.* ▶v. cover ground with turf.

tur·gid /ˈtərjid/ ▶adj. **1** (of language or style) pompous and boring. **2** swollen or full: *a turgid river.* ■ **tur·gid·i·ty** /tərˈjiditē/ n. **tur·gid·ly** adv.

Turk /tərk/ ▶n. **1** a person from Turkey. **2** a member of any of the ancient peoples who spoke Turkic languages.

tur·key /ˈtərkē/ ▶n. (pl. **turkeys**) **1** a large game bird native to North America, that is bred for food. **2** informal something that is very unsuccessful or of very poor quality. – PHRASES **talk turkey** informal talk frankly and openly.

tur·key·cock /ˈtərkēˌkäk/ ▶n. a male turkey.

tur·key vul·ture ▶n. a common American vulture with black plumage and a bare red head.

Tur·kic /ˈtərkik/ ▶adj. referring to a large group of languages of western and central Asia, including Turkish, Kazakh, and Uzbek.

Turk·ish /ˈtərkish/ ▶n. the language of Turkey. ▶adj. relating to Turkey or its language.

Turk·ish bath ▶n. **1** a cleansing treatment that involves sitting in a room filled with very hot air or steam, followed by washing and massage. **2** a building or room where a Turkish bath is available.

Turk·ish cof·fee ▶n. very strong black coffee served with the fine grounds in it.

Turk·ish de·light ▶n. a candy made of gelatin coated in powdered sugar.

tur·mer·ic /ˈtərmərik/ ▶n. a bright yellow powder obtained from a plant of the ginger family, used as a spice in Asian cooking.

tur·moil /ˈtərˌmoil/ ▶n. a state of great disturbance, confusion, or uncertainty.

turn /tərn/ ▶v. **1** move in a circular direction around a central point. **2** move so as to face or go in a different direction. **3** change in nature, state, form, or color: *the drizzle turned into a downpour.* **4** pass or reach a particular age or time. **5** (of the tide) change from flood to ebb or vice versa. **6** twist or sprain an ankle. **7** make a profit. **8** shape something on a lathe. **9** (usu. as adj. **turned**) give a pleasing form to: *finely turned phrases.* **10** (of milk) become sour. ▶n. **1** an act of turning. **2** a bend in a road, river, etc. **3** a place where a road meets or branches off another; a turning. **4** a time when a member of a group must or is allowed to do something: *it was her turn to speak.* **5** a time when one period of time ends and another begins: *the turn of the century.* **6** a change in a situation. **7** a brief feeling of illness: *a funny turn.* **8** a short performance, especially one of a number given by different performers. **9** a short walk or ride. **10** one round in a coil of rope or other material. ■ **turn·er** n. – PHRASES **at every turn** on every occasion; continually. **be turned out** be dressed in the specified way. **by turns** alternately. **do someone a good turn** do something that is helpful for someone. **in turn** one after the other. **out**

of turn at a time when it is inappropriate or not one's turn. **take turns** (or Brit. **take it in turns**) (of two or more people) do something alternately or one after the other. **to a turn** to exactly the right degree. **turn something around** make an organization successful after a period of poor performance. **turn someone away** refuse to allow someone to enter a place. **turn someone/thing down 1** reject something offered or proposed by someone. **2** reduce the volume or strength of sound, heat, etc., produced by a device by adjusting its controls. **turn in** informal go to bed in the evening. **turn someone/thing in** hand someone or something over to the authorities. **turn off** leave one road in order to join another. **turn someone off** informal make someone feel bored or disgusted. **turn something off** (or **on**) stop (or start) the operation of something by means of a tap, switch, or button. **turn of mind** a particular way of thinking. **turn on** suddenly attack someone or something. **turn someone on** informal excite someone, especially sexually. **turn out 1** prove to be the case. **2** attend a meeting, go to vote, etc. **turn something out 1** switch off an electric light. **2** produce something. **3** empty something, especially one's pockets. **turn over** (of an engine) start or continue to run properly. **turn someone over** hand someone over to the custody or care of someone in authority. **turn something over 1** transfer control or management of something to someone else. **2** (of a business) have a turnover of a particular amount. **turn tail** informal turn around and run away. **turn to 1** start doing or becoming involved with something. **2** go to someone for help or information. **turn up 1** be found, especially by chance. **2** put in an appearance; arrive. **turn something up 1** increase the volume or strength of sound, heat, etc., produced by a device by adjusting its controls. **2** reveal or discover something.

turn·a·bout /ˈtərnəˌbout/ ▶n. a sudden and complete change or reversal of opinion or of a situation.

turn·a·round /ˈtərnəˌround/ ▶n. **1** an abrupt or unexpected change. **2** the process of completing a task, or the time needed to do this.

turn·coat /ˈtərnˌkōt/ ▶n. a person who deserts one party or cause in order to join an opposing one.

turn·down /ˈtərnˌdoun/ ▶n. **1** a rejection or refusal. **2** a decline; a downturn.

turn·ing /ˈtərning/ ▶n. **1** a place where a road branches off another. **2** the action or skill of using a lathe. **3** (**turnings**) shavings of wood resulting from turning wood on a lathe.

turn·ing cir·cle ▶n. the smallest circle in which a vehicle or boat can turn without reversing.

turn·ing point ▶n. a time when a decisive change happens, especially one with good results.

tur·nip /ˈtərnəp/ ▶n. a round root vegetable with white or cream flesh.

turn·key /ˈtərnˌkē/ ▶n. (pl. **turnkeys**) old use a jailer.

turn·off ▶n. (also **turn-off**) **1** a junction at which a road branches off another. **2** informal a person or thing that makes one feel bored or disgusted.

turn·on ▶n. informal a person or thing that makes one feel excited or sexually aroused.

turn·out /ˈtərnˌout/ ▶n. the number of people

attending or taking part in an event.

turn·o·ver /ˈtərnˌōvər/ ▶ n. **1** the amount of money taken by a business in a particular period. **2** the rate at which employees leave a workforce and are replaced. **3** the rate at which goods are sold and replaced in a store. **4** a small pie made by folding a piece of pastry over on itself to enclose a filling.

turn·pike /ˈtərnˌpīk/ ▶ n. **1** an expressway, especially one on which a toll is charged. **2** historical a tollgate. **3** historical a road on which a toll was collected.

turn sig·nal ▶ n. a flashing light on a vehicle to show that it is about to change lanes or turn.

turn·stile /ˈtərnˌstīl/ ▶ n. a mechanical gate with revolving horizontal arms that allow only one person at a time to pass through.

turn·stone /ˈtərnˌstōn/ ▶ n. a small short-billed sandpiper noted for turning over stones to find small animals.

turn·ta·ble /ˈtərnˌtābəl/ ▶ n. **1** a circular revolving plate supporting a record as it is played. **2** a circular revolving platform for turning a railroad locomotive.

tur·pen·tine /ˈtərpənˌtīn/ ▶ n. **1** a substance produced by certain trees, distilled to make oil of turpentine. **2** (also **oil of turpentine**) a strong-smelling oil distilled from this substance, used in mixing and thinning paints and varnishes and for cleaning paintbrushes.

tur·pi·tude /ˈtərpiˌt(y)o͞od/ ▶ n. formal wicked behavior or character: *acts of moral turpitude.*

turps /tərps/ ▶ n. informal turpentine.

tur·quoise /ˈtərˌk(w)oiz/ ▶ n. **1** a greenish-blue or sky-blue semiprecious stone. **2** a greenish-blue color.

tur·ret /ˈtərit/ ▶ n. **1** a small tower at the corner of a building or wall, especially of a castle. **2** an armored tower, usually one that revolves, for a gun and gunners in a ship, aircraft, or tank. ■ **tur·ret·ed** adj.

tur·tle /ˈtərtl/ ▶ n. a sea or freshwater reptile with a bony or leathery shell and flippers or webbed toes. – PHRASES **turn turtle** (chiefly of a boat) turn upside down.

tur·tle·dove ▶ n. a small dove with a soft purring call.

tur·tle·neck /ˈtərtlˌnek/ ▶ n. a high, close-fitting, turned-over collar on a knit shirt, sweater, or similar garment.

turves /tərvz/ ▶ plural of TURF.

Tus·can /ˈtəskən/ ▶ adj. **1** relating to Tuscany in central Italy. **2** relating to a classical order of architecture resembling the Doric but lacking all decoration. ▶ n. a person from Tuscany.

tush¹ /təsh/ ▶ exclam. old use or humorous expressing disapproval, impatience, or dismissal.

tush² /to͞osh/ ▶ n. informal a person's buttocks.

tusk /təsk/ ▶ n. a long pointed tooth that protrudes from a closed mouth, as one of a pair in the elephant, walrus, or wild boar. ■ **tusked** adj.

tusk·er /ˈtəskər/ ▶ n. an elephant or wild boar with well-developed tusks.

tus·sle /ˈtəsəl/ ▶ n. a vigorous struggle or scuffle. ▶ v. take part in a tussle.

tus·sock /ˈtəsək/ ▶ n. a dense clump or tuft of grass. ■ **tus·sock·y** adj.

tus·sore /ˈtəsôr/ ▶ n. a strong but coarse kind of silk.

tu·tee /t(y)o͞oˈtē/ ▶ n. a student of a tutor.

tu·te·lage /ˈt(y)o͞otl-ij/ ▶ n. **1** protection of or authority over someone or something: *the organizations remained under firm government tutelage.* **2** instruction; tuition.

tu·te·lar·y /ˈt(y)o͞otlˌerē/ ▶ adj. **1** acting as a protector, guardian, or patron. **2** relating to protection or a guardian.

tu·tor /ˈt(y)o͞otər/ ▶ n. **1** a private teacher who teaches a single student or a very small group. **2** chiefly Brit. a college or university teacher responsible for the teaching and supervision of students assigned to them. ▶ v. act as a tutor to one student or a very small group.

tu·to·ri·al /t(y)o͞oˈtôrēəl/ ▶ n. **1** a period of instruction given by a tutor. **2** a book or computer program giving information about a subject or explaining how to do something. ▶ adj. relating to a tutor or tuition.

Tut·si /ˈto͞otsē/ ▶ n. (pl. same or **Tutsis**) a member of a people forming a minority of the population of Rwanda and Burundi.

tut·ti /ˈto͞otē/ ▶ adv. & adj. Music with all voices or instruments together.

tut·ti-frut·ti /ˈto͞otē ˈfro͞otē/ ▶ n. (pl. **tutti-fruttis**) a type of ice cream containing mixed fruits.

tu·tu /ˈto͞oˌto͞o/ ▶ n. a female ballet dancer's costume consisting of a bodice attached to a very short, stiff skirt made of many layers of fabric and projecting horizontally from the waist.

Tu·va·lu·an /to͞oˈvälo͞oən/ ▶ n. a person from Tuvalu, a country made up of a number of islands in the SW Pacific. ▶ adj. relating to Tuvalu.

tux /təks/ ▶ n. informal a tuxedo.

tux·e·do /təkˈsēdō/ ▶ n. (pl. **tuxedos** or **tuxedoes**) **1** a man's dinner jacket. **2** a formal evening suit including a dinner jacket. ■ **tux·e·doed** adj.

TV ▶ abbr. television.

TVP ▶ abbr. trademark textured vegetable protein, a protein obtained from soybeans and made to resemble ground meat.

twad·dle /ˈtwädl/ ▶ n. dated, informal trivial or foolish speech or writing; nonsense.

twain /twān/ ▶ cardinal number old-fashioned term for TWO.

twang /twaNG/ ▶ n. **1** a strong ringing sound such as that made by the plucked string of a musical instrument. **2** a distinctive nasal way of speaking. ▶ v. make a twang. ■ **twang·y** adj.

'twas ▶ contr. old use or literary it was.

twat /twät/ ▶ n. vulgar slang **1** a woman's genitals. **2** a stupid or unpleasant person.

tweak /twēk/ ▶ v. **1** twist or pull something with a small sharp movement. **2** informal improve a mechanism or system by making fine adjustments. ▶ n. **1** an act of tweaking. **2** informal a fine adjustment. ■ **tweak·er** n.

tweed /twēd/ ▶ n. **1** a rough woolen cloth flecked with mixed colors. **2** (**tweeds**) clothes made of tweed.

tweed·y /ˈtwēdē/ ▶ adj. (**tweedier, tweediest**) **1** made of tweed cloth. **2** informal of a refined, traditional, upscale character. ■ **tweed·i·ness** n.

tween /twēn/ (also **tweenager** /ˈtwēnˌājər/) ▶ n. informal a child between the ages of about 10 and 14.

'tween ▶ contr. old use or literary between.

tweet /twēt/ ▶ n. the chirp of a small bird. ▶ v. make a chirping noise.

tweet·er /'twētər/ ▶ n. a loudspeaker designed to reproduce high frequencies.

tweeze /twēz/ ▶ v. pluck or pull something with tweezers.

tweez·ers /'twēzərz/ ▶ pl.n. (also **pair of tweezers**) a small instrument like a pair of pincers for plucking out hairs or embedded slivers and picking up small objects.

twelfth /twelfTH/ ▶ ordinal number **1** that is number twelve in a sequence; 12th. **2** (**a twelfth/one twelfth**) each of twelve equal parts into which something is divided. **3** a musical interval spanning an octave and a fifth in a scale. ■ **twelfth·ly** adv.

Twelfth Night ▶ n. **1** January 6, the Christian feast of the Epiphany. **2** the evening of January 5, formerly the twelfth and last day of Christmas festivities.

twelve /twelv/ ▶ cardinal number two more than ten; 12. (Roman numeral: **xii** or **XII**.)

twelve·month /'twelv,mənTH/ ▶ n. old use a year.

twelve-step ▶ adj. denoting or referring to a process of recovery from addiction by following a twelve-stage program, especially one modeled on that of Alcoholics Anonymous. ▶ v. (often as n. **twelve-stepping**) (of an addict) undergo such a program.

twen·ty /'twentē/ ▶ cardinal number (pl. **twenties**) ten less than thirty; 20. (Roman numeral: **xx** or **XX**.) ■ **twen·ti·eth** /'twentēiTH/ ordinal number.

24-7 (also **24/7**) ▶ adv. informal twenty-four hours a day, seven days a week; all the time.

twen·ty-one ▶ n. the card game blackjack.

twen·ty-twen·ty vi·sion (also **20/20 vision**) ▶ n. normal sharpness of vision.

'twere ▶ contr. old use or literary it were.

twerp /twərp/ ▶ n. informal a silly or annoying person.

twice /twīs/ ▶ adv. **1** two times. **2** double in degree or quantity.

twid·dle /'twidl/ ▶ v. play or fiddle with something in an aimless or nervous way. ▶ n. an act of twiddling. ■ **twid·dler** n. **twid·dly** adj. – PHRASES **twiddle one's thumbs** have nothing to do.

twig /twig/ ▶ n. a slender woody shoot growing from a branch or stem of a tree or shrub. ■ **twigged** adj. **twig·gy** adj.

twi·light /'twī,līt/ ▶ n. **1** the soft glowing light from the sky when the sun is below the horizon. **2** a period or state of gradual decline: *he was in the twilight of his career.* ▶ adj. mysterious, secret, or unreal: *the twilight world of drugs.*

twi·light zone ▶ n. **1** a conceptual area that is undefined, uncertain, or intermediate. **2** the lowest level of the ocean to which light can penetrate.

twi·lit /'twī,lit/ ▶ adj. dimly lit.

twill /twil/ ▶ n. a fabric so woven as to have a surface of diagonal parallel ridges. ■ **twilled** adj.

'twill ▶ contr. old use or literary it will.

twin /twin/ ▶ n. **1** one of two children or animals born at the same birth. **2** a thing that is exactly like another. ▶ adj. **1** forming or being one of a pair of twins or matching things: *the twin problems of economic failure and social decline.* **2** (of a bedroom) containing two single beds. ▶ v. (**twins, twinning, twinned**) link or combine

things as a pair.

twin bed ▶ n. a bed designed or suitable for one person; a single bed.

twine /twīn/ ▶ n. strong thread or string consisting of strands of hemp or cotton twisted together. ▶ v. wind something around something else.

twinge /twinj/ ▶ n. **1** a sudden, sharp pain. **2** a brief, sharp pang of emotion. ▶ v. (**twinges, twingeing** or **twinging, twinged**) suffer a sudden, sharp pain.

twin·kle /'twiNGkəl/ ▶ v. **1** (of a star or light) shine with a gleam that changes constantly from bright to faint. **2** (of a person's eyes) sparkle with amusement or liveliness. **3** (of a person's feet) move lightly and rapidly. ▶ n. a twinkling sparkle or gleam. ■ **twin·kly** /-k(ə)lē/ adj. – PHRASES **in the twinkling of an eye** in an instant.

twirl /twərl/ ▶ v. spin quickly and lightly around. ▶ n. **1** an act of twirling. **2** a spiral shape. ■ **twirl·er** n. **twirl·y** adj.

twist /twist/ ▶ v. **1** form something into a bent, curled, or distorted shape. **2** turn or bend around or into a different direction: *she twisted in her seat to look at the buildings.* **3** force out of the natural position by a twisting action: *he twisted his ankle.* **4** take or have a winding course. **5** deliberately distort the meaning of words. **6** (as adj. **twisted**) strange or abnormal in an unpleasant way; perverted. **7** dance the twist. ▶ n. **1** an act of twisting. **2** a thing with a spiral or curved shape. **3** a new or unexpected development or way of treating something: *the plot includes a clever twist.* **4** (**the twist**) a dance with a twisting movement of the body, popular in the 1960s. **5** a fine strong thread consisting of twisted fibers. **6** a carpet with a tightly curled pile. ■ **twist·y** adj. – PHRASES **twist someone's arm** informal forcefully persuade someone to do something that they are reluctant to do.

twist·er /'twistər/ ▶ n. a tornado.

twit¹ /twit/ ▶ n. informal, chiefly Brit. a foolish person. ■ **twit·tish** adj.

twit² ▶ v. (**twits, twitting, twitted**) informal tease someone good-humoredly.

twitch /twicH/ ▶ v. make a short jerking movement. ▶ n. **1** a twitching movement. **2** a pang: *he felt a twitch of annoyance.*

twitch·y /'twicHē/ ▶ adj. (**twitchier, twitchiest**) informal nervous; anxious.

twit·ter /'twitər/ ▶ v. **1** (of a bird) make a series of short high sounds. **2** talk rapidly in a nervous or trivial way. ▶ n. **1** a twittering sound. **2** informal an agitated or excited state. ■ **twit·ter·y** adj.

'twixt ▶ contr. betwixt; between.

two /tōō/ ▶ cardinal number one less than three; 2. (Roman numeral: **ii** or **II**.) ■ **two·fold** /'tōō,fōld/ adj. & adv. – PHRASES **put two and two together** draw an obvious conclusion from the available evidence. **two by two** side by side in pairs. **two-horse race** a contest in which only two of the competitors are likely winners.

> **USAGE**
> For an explanation of the difference between **two**, **to**, and **too**, see the note at **TO**.

two-bit ▶ adj. informal unimportant, cheap, or worthless.

two-by-four ▸ n. a length of wood with a rectangular cross section approximately two inches by four inches.

two-di·men·sion·al ▸ adj. 1 having or appearing to have length and breadth but no depth. 2 lacking depth; superficial: *two-dimensional bad guys.*

two-faced ▸ adj. insincere and deceitful.

two-fist·ed ▸ adj. strong, virile, and straightforward.

two-hand·ed ▸ adj. & adv. having, using, or requiring the use of two hands.

two-pence /'təpəns/ (also **tuppence**) ▸ n. Brit. 1 the sum of two pence, especially before decimalization (1971). 2 informal anything at all: *he didn't care twopence for her.*

two-piece ▸ adj. consisting of two matching items.

two·some /'tōōsəm/ ▸ n. a set of two people or things.

two-step ▸ n. a dance with sliding steps in march or polka time.

two-stroke ▸ adj. (of an internal-combustion engine) having its power cycle completed in one up-and-down movement of the piston.

two-time ▸ v. informal be unfaithful to a lover or spouse. ■ **two-tim·er** n.

two-tone (also **two-toned**) ▸ adj. having two different shades or colors: *a two-tone jacket.*

'twould ▸ contr. old use it would.

two-way ▸ adj. 1 involving movement or communication in opposite directions. 2 (of a switch) permitting a current to be switched on or off from either of two points.
– PHRASES **two-way street** a situation involving shared action or responsibility: *trust is a two-way street.*

two-way mir·ror ▸ n. a panel of glass that can be seen through from one side and is a mirror on the other.

twp. ▸ abbr. township.

TX ▸ abbr. Texas.

ty·coon /tī'kōōn/ ▸ n. a wealthy, powerful person in business or industry.

ty·ing /'tī-iNG/ ▸ present participle of TIE.

tyke /tīk/ (also **tike**) ▸ n. informal a mischievous child.

ty·lo·sin /'tīlə,sin/ ▸ n. an antibiotic that is fed to livestock as a growth promoter.

tym·pa·ni ▸ pl.n. variant spelling of TIMPANI.

tym·pa·num /'timpənəm/ ▸ n. (pl. **tympanums** or **tympana** /-nə/) 1 the eardrum. 2 Architecture a space enclosed between the lintel of a doorway and an arch over it, or the triangle enclosed by a classical pediment. ■ **tym·pan·ic** /tim'panik/ adj.

type /tīp/ ▸ n. 1 a category of people or things that share particular qualities or features. 2 informal a person of a specified character or nature: *sporty types in tracksuits.* 3 a person or thing that is a typical example of something: *she described his sayings as the type of modern wisdom.* 4 printed characters or letters. 5 pieces of metal with raised letters or characters on their upper surface, for use in letterpress printing.
▸ v. 1 write using a typewriter or computer. 2 Medicine determine the type to which a person or their blood or tissue belongs. ■ **typ·ing** n.

type·cast /'tīp,kast/ ▸ v. (past and past part. **typecast**) 1 repeatedly cast an actor in the same type of role because their appearance is appropriate or they are known for such roles. 2 regard as fitting a stereotype: *she didn't want to be typecast as an angst-ridden female rock musician.*

type·face /'tīp,fās/ ▸ n. a particular design of printed letters or characters.

type·script /'tīp,skript/ ▸ n. a typed copy of a written work.

type·set /'tīp,set/ ▸ v. (**typesets, typesetting, typeset**) arrange or generate the data or type for written material to be printed. ■ **type·set·ter** n. **type·set·ting** n.

type·writ·er /'tīp,rītər/ ▸ n. an electric, electronic, or manual machine with keys for producing characters similar to printed ones. ■ **type·writ·ing** /-,rītiNG/ n. **type·writ·ten** /-,ritn/ adj.

ty·phoid /'tī,foid/ (also **typhoid fever**) ▸ n. an infectious fever caused by a bacterium, resulting in red spots on the chest and abdomen and severe irritation of the intestines.

ty·phoon /tī'fōōn/ ▸ n. a tropical storm with very high winds, occurring in the region of the Indian Ocean and the western Pacific Ocean.

ty·phus /'tīfəs/ ▸ n. an infectious disease caused by a bacterium, resulting in a purple rash, headaches, fever, and usually delirium.

typ·i·cal /'tipikəl/ ▸ adj. 1 having the distinctive qualities of a particular type of person or thing: *a typical example of a small American town.* 2 behaving or happening in the expected or usual way: *a typical day began with breakfast at 7:30 a.m.* ■ **typ·i·cal·i·ty** /,tipi'kalitē/ n. **typ·i·cal·ly** adv.

typ·i·fy /'tipə,fī/ ▸ v. (**typifies, typifying, typified**) be a typical example or feature of: *their furniture is typified by its functional design.* ■ **typ·i·fi·ca·tion** /,tipəfi'kāsHən/ n.

typ·ist /'tīpist/ ▸ n. a person skilled in typing and employed for this purpose.

ty·po /'tīpō/ ▸ n. (pl. **typos**) informal a small mistake in typed or printed writing.

ty·pog·ra·phy /tī'pägrəfē/ ▸ n. 1 the art or process of preparing material for printing, especially of designing how printed text will appear. 2 the style and appearance of printed matter. ■ **ty·pog·ra·pher** n. **ty·po·graph·ic** /,tīpə'grafik/ adj. **ty·po·graph·i·cal** /,tīpə'grafikəl/ adj.

ty·pol·o·gy /tī'päləjē/ ▸ n. (pl. **typologies**) a classification of things according to general type. ■ **ty·po·log·i·cal** /,tīpə'läjikəl/ adj. **ty·pol·o·gist** n.

ty·ran·ni·cal /tə'ranikəl/ ▸ adj. exercising power in a cruel and unfair way. ■ **ty·ran·ni·cal·ly** adv.

ty·ran·ni·cide /tə'rani,sīd/ ▸ n. 1 the killing of a tyrant. 2 the killer of a tyrant. ■ **ty·ran·ni·cid·al** /tə,rani'sīdl/ n.

tyr·an·nize /'tirə,nīz/ ▸ v. rule or dominate someone in a cruel or oppressive way.

ty·ran·no·sau·rus /tə,ranə'sôrəs/ (also **tyrannosaurus rex** /reks/) ▸ n. a very large meat-eating dinosaur with powerful jaws and small clawlike front legs.

tyr·an·ny /'tirənē/ ▸ n. (pl. **tyrannies**) 1 cruel and oppressive government or rule. 2 a nation under cruel and oppressive government. 3 cruel and unfair use of power or control: *a young man liberated from the tyranny of his father.* ■ **tyr·an·nous** adj.

ty·rant /ˈtīrənt/ ▶ n. **1** a cruel and oppressive ruler. **2** a person who uses their power in a cruel and unfair way.

tyre, etc. ▶ n. British spelling of TIRE², etc.

ty·ro /ˈtīrō/ ▶ n. (pl. **tyros**) a beginner or novice.

ty·ro·sine /ˈtīrəˌsēn/ ▶ n. an amino acid that is a constituent of most proteins and is important in the synthesis of some hormones.

tzar ▶ n. variant spelling of TSAR.

tza·ri·na ▶ n. variant spelling of TSARINA.

tza·tzi·ki /tsäˈtsēkē/ ▶ n. a Greek side dish of yogurt with cucumber, garlic, and often mint.

Uu

U¹ (also **u**) ▶ n. (pl. **Us** or **U's**) the twenty-first letter of the alphabet.

U² ▶ symbol the chemical element uranium.

UAE ▶ abbr. United Arab Emirates.

UAV ▶ abbr. unmanned aerial vehicle.

uber- /'ōōbər/ (also **über-** /'ȳbər/) ▶ prefix referring to an outstanding or supreme example of a person or thing: *an uberbabe.*

Über·mensch /'ōōbər,menCH, 'ȳbər-/ ▶ n. the ideal superior man of the future who could rise above conventional Christian morality to create and impose his own values.

u·biq·ui·tous /yōō'bikwətəs/ ▶ adj. present, appearing, or found everywhere: *ubiquitous coffee shops.* ■ **u·biq·ui·tous·ly** adv. **u·biq·ui·tous·ness** n. **u·biq·ui·ty** n.

U-boat ▶ n. a German submarine of World War I or II.

u.c. ▶ abbr. upper case.

ud·der /'ədər/ ▶ n. the milk-producing gland of female cattle, sheep, goats, horses, etc., hanging near the hind legs as a baglike organ with two or more teats.

u·don /'ōō,dän/ ▶ n. (in Japanese cooking) large noodles made from wheat flour.

UFO ▶ n. (pl. **UFOs**) a mysterious object seen in the sky for which it is claimed no scientific explanation can be found, believed by some to be a vehicle carrying beings from outer space. ■ **u·fol·o·gist** /yōō'fäləjist/ n. **u·fol·o·gy** /yōō'fäləjē/ n.

U·gan·dan /yōō'gandən/ ▶ n. a person from Uganda. ▶ adj. relating to Uganda.

ugh /əg, əкн, ōōкн/ ▶ exclam. informal used to express disgust or horror.

Ug·li fruit /'əglē/ ▶ n. (pl. same) trademark a mottled green and yellow citrus fruit that is a cross between a grapefruit and a tangerine.

ug·li·fy /'əglə,fī/ ▶ v. (**uglifies, uglifying, uglified**) make something ugly.

ug·ly /'əglē/ ▶ adj. (**uglier, ugliest**) **1** unpleasant or unattractive in appearance. **2** involving violence or other unpleasantness: *an ugly scene was averted.* **3** disturbing or disagreeable: *the whole ugly truth of slavery.* ■ **ug·li·ness** n.

ug·ly duck·ling ▶ n. a person who unexpectedly turns out to be beautiful or talented.

UHF ▶ abbr. ultrahigh frequency.

uh-huh /ə 'hə, ən 'hən/ ▶ exclam. used to express agreement or as a noncommittal response to a question or remark.

UHT ▶ abbr. ultrahigh temperature (a process used to extend the shelf life of certain foods, particularly milk).

uil·lean pipes /'ilən, 'ilyən/ ▶ pl.n. Irish bagpipes played using bellows worked by the elbow.

UK ▶ abbr. United Kingdom.

u·kase /yōō'kās, -'kāz/ ▶ n. **1** historical a decree with the force of law, issued by the tsarist Russian government. **2** a dictatorial command.

uke /yōōk/ ▶ n. informal short for **UKULELE**.

U·krain·i·an /yōō'krānēən/ ▶ n. **1** a person from Ukraine. **2** the language of Ukraine. ▶ adj. relating to Ukraine.

u·ku·le·le /,yōōkə'lālē/ (also **ukelele**) ▶ n. a small four-stringed guitar of Hawaiian origin.

u·la·ma ▶ n. variant spelling of **ULEMA**.

ul·cer /'əlsər/ ▶ n. an open sore on an external or internal surface of the body, caused by a break in the skin or mucous membrane that fails to heal. ■ **ul·cered** adj. **ul·cer·ous** adj.

ul·cer·ate /'əlsə,rāt/ ▶ v. develop into or become affected by an ulcer. ■ **ul·cer·a·tion** /,əlsə'rāshən/ n. **ul·cer·a·tive** /-rətiv, -,rātiv/ adj.

u·le·ma /'ōōlə,mä/ (also **ulama**) ▶ n. **1** (treated as sing. or pl.) a group of Muslim scholars recognized as having specialist knowledge of Islamic sacred law and theology. **2** a member of an ulema.

ul·lage /'əlij/ ▶ n. **1** the amount by which a container falls short of being full. **2** loss of liquid by evaporation or leakage.

ul·na /'əlnə/ ▶ n. (pl. **ulnae** /-,nē, -,nī/ or **ulnas**) the thinner and longer of the two bones in the human forearm. ■ **ul·nar** adj.

ul·ster /'əlstər/ ▶ n. a long, loose overcoat made of rough cloth, worn by men.

Ul·ster·man /'əlstərmən/ (or **Ulsterwoman** /'əlstər,wōōmən/) ▶ n. (pl. **Ulstermen** or **Ulsterwomen**) a person from Northern Ireland or Ulster.

ul·te·ri·or /,əl'ti(ə)rēər/ ▶ adj. other than what is obvious or has been admitted: *she had some ulterior motive in coming.*

ul·ti·mate /'əltəmit/ ▶ adj. **1** being or happening at the end of a process; final. **2** being the best or most extreme example of its kind: *climbing Mount Everest is the ultimate challenge.* **3** basic or fundamental: *atoms are the ultimate constituents of anything that exists.* ▶ n. (**the ultimate**) the best of its kind: *the scooter was the ultimate in continental chic.* ■ **ul·ti·ma·cy** /-məsē/ n. **ul·ti·mate·ly** adv.

ul·ti·ma·tum /,əltə'mātəm, -'mät-/ ▶ n. (pl. **ultimatums** or **ultimata** /-'mātə, -'mätə/) a final warning that action will be taken against someone unless they agree to another party's demands.

ul·tra /'əltrə/ ▶ n. informal a person with extreme political or religious views.

ultra- ▶ prefix **1** to an extreme degree; very: *ultralight.* **2** beyond; on the other side of: *ultramarine.*

ultra·high fre·quen·cy ▶ n. (in radio) a

frequency of 300–3,000 megahertz.

ul·tra·light /ˈəltrəˌlīt, ˈəltrəˌlīt/ ▶ adj. very lightweight.

ul·tra·ma·rine /ˌəltrəməˈrēn/ ▶ n. a brilliant deep blue pigment and color.

ul·tra·mon·tane /ˌəltrəˈmänˌtān, -ˈmänˌtān/ ▶ adj. **1** (in the Roman Catholic Church) believing that the pope should have supreme authority in matters of faith and discipline. **2** situated on the other side of the Alps from the speaker. ▶ n. a person who believes that the pope should have supreme authority. ■ **ul·tra·mon·ta·nism** /-ˈmäntəˌnizəm/ n.

ul·tra·son·ic /ˌəltrəˈsänik/ ▶ adj. involving sound waves with a frequency above the upper limit of human hearing. ■ **ul·tra·son·i·cal·ly** /-ik(ə)lē/ adv.

ul·tra·son·ics /ˌəltrəˈsäniks/ ▶ pl. n. **1** (treated as sing.) the science and application of sound waves with a frequency above the upper limit of human hearing. **2** (treated as sing. or pl.) ultrasonic waves; ultrasound.

ul·tra·so·nog·ra·phy /ˌəltrəsəˈnägrəfē/ ▶ n. a medical technique that uses echoes of ultrasound pulses to show objects or areas of different density in the body. ■ **ul·tra·son·o·graph·ic** /əltrəˌsänəˈgrafik, -ˌsōnə-/ adj.

ul·tra·sound /ˈəltrəˌsound/ ▶ n. **1** sound or other vibrations having a frequency above the upper limit of human hearing, particularly as used in medical scans. **2** an ultrasound scan, especially one of a pregnant woman's fetus.

ul·tra·struc·ture /ˈəltrəˌstrəkCHər/ ▶ n. Biology a fine structure, especially within a cell, that is so small that it can be seen only with an electron microscope. ■ **ul·tra·struc·tur·al** /-CHərəl/ adj.

ul·tra·vi·o·let /ˌəltrəˈvī(ə)lət/ ▶ n. electromagnetic radiation having a wavelength just shorter than that of violet light but longer than that of X-rays. ▶ adj. referring to such radiation.

ul·tra vi·res /ˌəltrə ˈvīrēz/ ▶ adj. & adv. Law beyond the legal power or authority of a person or organization.

ul·u·late /ˈəlyəˌlāt, ˈyōōl-/ ▶ v. howl or wail, especially to express grief. ■ **ul·u·la·tion** /ˌəlyəˈlāsHən, ˌyōōl-/ n.

um·bel /ˈəmbəl/ ▶ n. Botany a flower cluster in which stalks spring from a common center and form a flat or curved surface.

um·bel·lif·er /ˌəmˈbeləfər/ ▶ n. Botany a plant of the parsley family, having its flowers arranged in umbels. ■ **um·bel·lif·er·ous** /-bəˈlif(ə)rəs/ adj.

um·ber /ˈəmbər/ ▶ n. a natural pigment, normally dark yellowish-brown (**raw umber**) or dark brown when roasted (**burnt umber**).

um·bil·i·cal /ˌəmˈbilikəl/ ▶ adj. **1** relating to the navel or the umbilical cord. **2** (of a relationship) very close; inseparable: *the umbilical connection between land and people.* ■ **um·bil·i·cal·ly** adv.

um·bil·i·cal cord ▶ n. a flexible cordlike structure containing blood vessels, attaching a fetus to the placenta while it is in the uterus.

um·bil·i·cus /ˌəmˈbilikəs/ ▶ n. (pl. **umbilici** /-ˌkī, -ˌsī, -ˌkē/ or **umbilicuses**) the navel.

um·bra /ˈəmbrə/ ▶ n. (pl. **umbras** or **umbrae** /-ˌbrē, -ˌbrī/) the darkest inner part of a shadow, especially the dark central part of the shadow cast by the earth or the moon in an eclipse. ■ **um·bral** adj.

um·brage /ˈəmbrij/ ▶ n. (in phrase **take umbrage**) take offense or become annoyed.

um·brel·la /ˌəmˈbrelə/ ▶ n. **1** a device consisting of a circular fabric canopy on a folding metal frame supported by a central rod, used as protection against rain. **2** a thing that includes or contains a range of different parts or aspects: *the concepts embodied under the broad umbrella of personality disorder.* **3** a protecting force or influence. ▶ adj. including or involving different parts or aspects: *an umbrella organization.*

um·laut /ˈo͝omˌlout/ ▶ n. a mark (¨) used over a vowel in German and some other languages to indicate how it should be pronounced.

um·ma /ˈo͝omə/ (also **ummah**) ▶ n. the whole community of Muslims bound together by ties of religion.

ump /əmp/ ▶ n. & v. informal short for UMPIRE.

umph ▶ n. variant spelling of OOMPH.

um·pire /ˈəmˌpī(ə)r/ ▶ n. **1** (in certain sports) an official who supervises a game to ensure that players keep to the rules and who settles disputes arising from the play. **2** a person chosen to settle a dispute. ▶ v. act as an umpire of a game.

ump·teen /ˈəm(p)ˌtēn/ ▶ cardinal number informal very many. ■ **ump·teenth** /-ˌtēnTH/ ordinal number.

UN ▶ abbr. United Nations.

un-¹ ▶ prefix **1** (added to adjectives, participles, and their derivatives) not; the reverse of: *unacceptable* | *unselfish.* **2** (added to nouns) a lack of: *untruth.*

> **USAGE**
> For an explanation of the difference between the prefixes (word beginnings) **un-** and **non-**, see the note at NON-.

un-² ▶ prefix added to verbs. **1** referring to the reversal or cancellation of an action or state: *unsettle.* **2** referring to deprivation, separation, or change to a lesser state: *unmask.* **3** referring to release: *unhand.*

'un ▶ contr. informal one.

un·a·bashed /ˌənəˈbasHt/ ▶ adj. not embarrassed or ashamed. ■ **un·a·bash·ed·ly** adv.

un·a·bat·ed /ˌənəˈbātid/ ▶ adj. without any reduction in intensity or strength.

un·a·ble /ˌənˈābəl/ ▶ adj. lacking the skill, means, strength, or opportunity to do something.

un·a·bridged /ˌənəˈbrijd/ ▶ adj. (of a novel, play, or other written work) not cut or shortened; complete.

un·ac·cent·ed /ˌənˈakˌsentid, ˌanakˈsen-/ ▶ adj. having no accent, stress, or emphasis.

un·ac·cept·a·ble /ˌənəkˈseptəbəl/ ▶ adj. not satisfactory or allowable. ■ **un·ac·cept·a·bil·i·ty** /-ˌseptəˈbilətē/ n. **un·ac·cept·a·bly** adv.

un·ac·com·pa·nied /ˌənəˈkəmp(ə)nēd/ ▶ adj. **1** having no companion or escort. **2** without instrumental accompaniment. **3** happening without something else occurring at the same time: *no happiness comes unaccompanied by sorrow.*

un·ac·count·a·ble /ˌənəˈkountəbəl/ ▶ adj. **1** unable to be explained. **2** not responsible for the outcome of something or required to justify actions or decisions. ■ **un·ac·count·a·bil·i·ty** /-ˌkountəˈbilətē/ n. **un·ac·count·a·bly** /-blē/ adv.

un·ac·count·ed /ˌənəˈkountid/ ▶ adj. (**unaccounted for**) not taken into consideration or explained.

un·ac·cus·tomed /ˌənə'kəstəmd/ ▸ adj. **1** not usual or customary. **2** (**unaccustomed to**) not familiar with or used to something. ■ **un·ac·cus·tomed·ly** adv.

un·ac·knowl·edged /ˌənak'nälijd/ ▸ adj. **1** existing or having taken place but not accepted or admitted to. **2** (of a person or their work) deserving recognition but not receiving it.

un·ac·quaint·ed /ˌənə'kwāntid/ ▸ adj. **1** (**unacquainted with**) having no experience of or familiarity with something. **2** not having met before.

un·a·dorned /ˌənə'dôrnd/ ▸ adj. not decorated; plain.

un·a·dul·ter·at·ed /ˌənə'dəltəˌrātid/ ▸ adj. **1** not mixed with any different or inferior substances. **2** complete; total: *pure, unadulterated happiness.*

un·ad·ven·tur·ous /ˌənad'venCHərəs, ˌənəd-/ ▸ adj. not offering, involving, or eager for new or exciting things. ■ **un·ad·ven·tur·ous·ly** adv.

un·ad·vis·ed·ly /ˌənəd'vīzidlē/ ▸ adv. in an unwise or rash way.

un·aes·thet·ic /ˌənes'THetik/ (also **unesthetic**) ▸ adj. not visually pleasing; unattractive.

un·af·fect·ed /ˌənə'fektid/ ▸ adj. **1** feeling or showing no effects. **2** (of a person) sincere and genuine. ■ **un·af·fect·ed·ly** adv.

un·af·fil·i·at·ed /ˌənə'filēˌātid/ ▸ adj. not officially attached to or connected with an organization.

un·af·ford·a·ble /ˌənə'fôrdəbəl/ ▸ adj. too expensive to be afforded by the average person.

un·a·fraid /ˌənə'frād/ ▸ adj. feeling no fear.

un·aid·ed /ˌən'ādid/ ▸ adj. needing or having no help.

un·a·ligned /ˌənə'līnd/ ▸ adj. **1** not placed or arranged in a straight line or in correct relative positions. **2** not allied with or supporting an organization or cause.

un·a·like /ˌənə'līk/ ▸ adj. differing from each other; not similar.

un·al·loyed /ˌənə'loid/ ▸ adj. **1** complete; total: *unalloyed delight.* **2** (of metal) not alloyed; pure.

un·al·ter·a·ble /ˌən'ôlt(ə)rəbəl/ ▸ adj. not able to be changed. ■ **un·al·ter·a·bly** /-blē/ adv.

un·al·tered /ˌən'ôltərd/ ▸ adj. remaining the same.

un·am·big·u·ous /ˌənam'bigyōōəs/ ▸ adj. not open to more than one interpretation; clear in meaning. ■ **un·am·big·u·ous·ly** adv.

un·am·bi·tious /ˌənam'bisHəs/ ▸ adj. **1** not motivated by a strong desire to succeed. **2** (of a plan or piece of work) not involving anything new, exciting, or demanding.

un·A·mer·i·can /ˌənə'merikən/ ▸ adj. **1** not American in nature. **2** US against the interests of the US and therefore treasonable.

u·nan·i·mous /yōō'nanəməs/ ▸ adj. **1** (of people) fully in agreement. **2** (of an opinion, decision, or vote) held or carried by everyone involved. ■ **u·na·nim·i·ty** /ˌyōōnə'nimətē/ n. **u·nan·i·mous·ly** adv.

un·an·nounced /ˌənə'nounst/ ▸ adj. without warning or notice: *he often dropped in unannounced.*

un·an·swer·a·ble /ˌən'ans(ə)rəbəl/ ▸ adj. **1** unable to be answered. **2** unable to be questioned or disagreed with: *an unanswerable case for investment.*

un·an·swered /ˌən'ansərd/ ▸ adj. not answered or responded to.

un·a·pol·o·get·ic /ˌənəˌpälə'jetik/ ▸ adj. not sorry for one's actions. ■ **un·a·pol·o·get·i·cal·ly** /-ik(ə)lē/ adv.

un·ap·peal·ing /ˌənə'pēliNG/ ▸ adj. not inviting or attractive. ■ **un·ap·peal·ing·ly** adv.

un·ap·pe·tiz·ing /ˌən'apəˌtīziNG/ ▸ adj. not inviting or attractive. ■ **un·ap·pe·tiz·ing·ly** adv.

un·ap·pre·ci·at·ed /ˌənə'prēsHēˌātid/ ▸ adj. not fully understood, recognized, or valued.

un·ap·pre·ci·a·tive /ˌənə'prēsH(ē)ətiv/ ▸ adj. not fully understanding or recognizing something.

un·ap·proach·a·ble /ˌənə'prōCHəbəl/ ▸ adj. not welcoming or friendly.

un·ap·proved /ˌənə'prōōvd/ ▸ adj. not officially accepted or permitted.

un·ar·gu·a·ble /ˌən'ärgyōōəbəl/ ▸ adj. not open to disagreement; certain. ■ **un·ar·gu·a·bly** /-blē/ adv.

un·armed /ˌən'ärmd/ ▸ adj. not equipped with or carrying weapons.

un·a·shamed /ˌənə'sHāmd/ ▸ adj. feeling or showing no guilt or embarrassment. ■ **un·a·sham·ed·ly** /-'sHāmidlē/ adv.

un·asked /ˌən'as(k)t/ ▸ adj. **1** (of a question) not asked. **2** without being invited or asked: *we'd never have entered the house unasked.*

un·as·sail·a·ble /ˌənə'sāləbəl/ ▸ adj. unable to be attacked, questioned, or defeated. ■ **un·as·sail·a·bil·i·ty** /-ˌsālə'bilətē/ n. **un·as·sail·a·bly** /-blē/ adv.

un·as·ser·tive /ˌənə'sərtiv/ ▸ adj. not having or showing a confident and forceful personality.

un·as·sist·ed /ˌənə'sistid/ ▸ adj. not helped by anyone or anything.

un·as·so·ci·at·ed /ˌənə'sōsHēˌātid, -'sōsē-/ ▸ adj. not connected or associated: *they perform music previously unassociated with the saxophone.*

un·as·sum·ing /ˌənə'sōōmiNG/ ▸ adj. not wanting to draw attention to oneself or one's abilities. ■ **un·as·sum·ing·ly** adv.

un·at·tached /ˌənə'taCHt/ ▸ adj. **1** not married or having an established lover. **2** not working for or belonging to a particular organization.

un·at·tain·a·ble /ˌənə'tānəbəl/ ▸ adj. not able to be reached or achieved. ■ **un·at·tain·a·bly** /-blē/ adv.

un·at·tend·ed /ˌənə'tendid/ ▸ adj. without the owner or a responsible person present; not being supervised or looked after.

un·at·trac·tive /ˌənə'traktiv/ ▸ adj. not pleasing, appealing, or inviting. ■ **un·at·trac·tive·ly** adv. **un·at·trac·tive·ness** n.

un·at·trib·ut·ed /ˌənə'tribyətid/ ▸ adj. (of a quotation, story, or work of art) of unknown or unpublished origin. ■ **un·at·trib·ut·a·ble** /-'yətəbəl/ adj.

un·au·thor·ized /ˌən'ôTHəˌrīzd/ ▸ adj. not having official permission or approval.

un·a·vail·a·ble /ˌənə'vāləbəl/ ▸ adj. **1** not able to be used or obtained. **2** not free to do something: *he was unavailable for comment.* ■ **un·a·vail·a·bil·i·ty** /ˌənəˌvālə'bilitē/ n.

un·a·vail·ing /ˌənə'vāliNG/ ▸ adj. achieving little or nothing. ■ **un·a·vail·ing·ly** adv.

un·a·void·a·ble /ˌənə'voidəbəl/ ▸ adj. not able to be avoided or prevented; inevitable. ■ **un·a·void·a·bil·i·ty** /-ˌvoidə'bilətē/ n. **un·a·void·a·bly** /-blē/ adv.

un·a·ware /ˌənə'we(ə)r/ ▸ adj. having no knowledge of a situation or fact.

■ **un·a·ware·ness** n.

un·a·wares /ˌənəˈwe(ə)rz/ (also **unaware**) ▶ adv. so as to surprise someone; unexpectedly: *modern life has caught that woman completely unawares.*

un·bal·ance /ˌənˈbaləns/ ▶ v. **1** upset the balance or stability of: *judo unbalances an opponent before throwing him.* **2** (as adj. **unbalanced**) mentally or emotionally disturbed. **3** (as adj. **unbalanced**) not giving equal coverage or treatment to all aspects of something.

un·bear·a·ble /ˌənˈbe(ə)rəbəl/ ▶ adj. not able to be endured or tolerated. ■ **un·bear·a·bly** /-blē/ adv.

un·beat·a·ble /ˌənˈbētəbəl/ ▶ adj. **1** not able to be bettered or beaten: *CDs at unbeatable prices.* **2** very good. ■ **un·beat·a·bly** /-blē/ adv.

un·beat·en /ˌənˈbētn/ ▶ adj. not defeated or bettered.

un·be·com·ing /ˌənbiˈkəmiNG/ ▶ adj. **1** (especially of clothing) not flattering. **2** (of behavior) not appropriate or acceptable. ■ **un·be·com·ing·ly** adv.

un·be·known /ˌənbiˈnōn/ (also **unbeknownst** /-ˈnōnst/) ▶ adj. (**unbeknown to**) without the knowledge of someone.

un·be·lief /ˌənbəˈlēf/ ▶ n. lack of religious belief.

un·be·liev·a·ble /ˌənbəˈlēvəbəl/ ▶ adj. **1** so extreme as to be difficult to believe; extraordinary: *the rent is unbelievable!* **2** not likely to be true. ■ **un·be·liev·a·bly** /-ˈlēvəblē/ adv.

un·be·liev·er /ˌənbəˈlēvər/ ▶ n. a person who does not believe in God or a particular religion.

un·be·liev·ing /ˌənbəˈlēviNG/ ▶ adj. feeling or showing that one does not believe someone or something.

un·bend /ˌənˈbend/ ▶ v. (past and past part. **unbent**) **1** make or become straight. **2** become less formal or strict.

un·bend·ing /ˌənˈbendiNG/ ▶ adj. strict and unwilling to change one's views; inflexible.

un·bi·ased /ˌənˈbīəst/ ▶ adj. showing no prejudice; impartial.

un·bid·den /ˌənˈbidn/ ▶ adj. **1** without having been invited. **2** (of a thought or feeling) arising without conscious effort.

un·bleached /ˌənˈblēCHt/ ▶ adj. (especially of paper, cloth, or flour) not bleached.

un·blem·ished /ˌənˈblemiSHt/ ▶ adj. not damaged or marked in any way.

un·blink·ing /ˌənˈbliNGkiNG/ ▶ adj. (of a description or look) direct, thorough, and honest: *an unblinking portrait of the man and the writer.* ■ **un·blink·ing·ly** adv.

un·block /ˌənˈbläk/ ▶ v. remove an obstruction from something.

un·blush·ing /ˌənˈbləSHiNG/ ▶ adj. not feeling or showing embarrassment or shame. ■ **un·blush·ing·ly** adv.

un·bolt /ˌənˈbōlt/ ▶ v. open a door or window by drawing back a bolt.

un·born /ˌənˈbôrn/ ▶ adj. (of a baby) not yet born.

un·bos·om /ˌənˈbo͞ozəm/ ▶ v. old use (**unbosom oneself**) reveal one's thoughts or secrets.

un·bound /ˌənˈbound/ ▶ adj. **1** not restricted or tied up: *they were unbound by convention.* **2** (of printed pages) not bound together.

un·bound·ed /ˌənˈboundid/ ▶ adj. having no limits.

un·bowed /ˌənˈboud/ ▶ adj. not having given in to pressure or defeat.

un·break·a·ble /ˌənˈbrākəbəl/ ▶ adj. not liable to break or able to be broken.

un·breath·a·ble /ˌənˈbreT͟Həbəl/ ▶ adj. (of air) not fit or pleasant to breathe.

un·bridge·a·ble /ˌənˈbrijəbəl/ ▶ adj. (of a gap or difference between people or opinions) not able to be closed or made less significant.

un·bri·dled /ˌənˈbrīdld/ ▶ adj. not controlled; unrestrained: *a night of unbridled passion.*

un·bro·ken /ˌənˈbrōkən/ ▶ adj. **1** not broken; intact. **2** not interrupted or disturbed. **3** (of a record) not beaten. **4** (of a horse) not broken in.

un·buck·le /ˌənˈbəkəl/ ▶ v. unfasten the buckle of a belt, shoe, etc.

un·built /ˌənˈbilt/ ▶ adj. (of buildings or land) not yet built or built on.

un·bun·dle /ˌənˈbəndl/ ▶ v. **1** market or charge for items or services separately rather than as part of a package. **2** split a company or conglomerate into its constituent businesses, especially before selling them off.

un·bur·den /ˌənˈbərdn/ ▶ v. **1** (**unburden oneself**) talk to someone about a worry or problem, so that one feels less anxious. **2** (**be unburdened**) not burdened or worried.

un·burned /ˌənˈbərnd/ (also chiefly Brit. **unburnt** /ˌənˈbərnt/) ▶ adj. not damaged or destroyed by fire.

un·but·ton /ˌənˈbətn/ ▶ v. **1** unfasten the buttons of an item of clothing. **2** informal relax and become less inhibited.

un·called /ˌənˈkôld/ ▶ adj. (**uncalled for**) not desirable, justified, or necessary: *we got a reprimand that was totally uncalled for.*

un·can·ny /ˌənˈkanē/ ▶ adj. (**uncannier**, **uncanniest**) **1** strange or mysterious. **2** so accurate or intense as to be unsettling: *he bore an uncanny resemblance to the current prime minister.* ■ **un·can·ni·ly** adv.

un·cared /ˌənˈke(ə)rd/ ▶ adj. (**uncared for**) not looked after properly.

un·car·ing /ˌənˈke(ə)riNG/ ▶ adj. not sympathetic to or concerned about others. ■ **un·car·ing·ly** adv.

un·cas·trat·ed /ˌənˈkastrātid/ ▶ adj. (of a male animal) not castrated.

un·ceas·ing /ˌənˈsēsiNG/ ▶ adj. not stopping; continuous. ■ **un·ceas·ing·ly** adv.

un·cer·e·mo·ni·ous /ˌənserəˈmōnēəs/ ▶ adj. lacking courtesy; rude or abrupt. ■ **un·cer·e·mo·ni·ous·ly** adv.

un·cer·tain /ˌənˈsərtn/ ▶ adj. **1** not known, reliable, or definite: *an uncertain future.* **2** not completely confident or sure. ■ **un·cer·tain·ly** adv.

– PHRASES **in no uncertain terms** clearly and forcefully.

un·cer·tain·ty /ˌənˈsərtntē/ ▶ n. (pl. **uncertainties**) **1** the state of being uncertain. **2** something that is uncertain or makes one feel uncertain.

un·chal·lenge·a·ble /ˌənˈCHalənjəbəl/ ▶ adj. not able to be questioned or opposed.

un·chal·lenged /ˌənˈCHalənjd/ ▶ adj. **1** not questioned or opposed: *the report's findings did not go unchallenged.* **2** not called on to prove one's identity.

un·chal·leng·ing /ˌənˈCHalənjiNG/ ▶ adj. not demanding or testing one's abilities.

un·change·a·ble /ˌənˈcHānjəbəl/ ▸ adj. not liable to change or able to be altered.

un·changed /ˌənˈcHānjd/ ▸ adj. not changed; unaltered.

un·chang·ing /ˌənˈcHānjiNG/ ▸ adj. remaining the same. ■ **un·chang·ing·ly** adv.

un·char·ac·ter·is·tic /ˌənkariktəˈristik/ ▸ adj. not typical of a particular person or thing. ■ **un·char·ac·ter·is·ti·cal·ly** /-ik(ə)lē/ adv.

un·char·is·mat·ic /ˌənkarizˈmatik/ ▸ adj. lacking the charm that can inspire admiration in others.

un·char·i·ta·ble /ˌənˈcHaritəbəl/ ▸ adj. unkind or unsympathetic to others. ■ **un·char·i·ta·bly** /-blē/ adv.

un·chart·ed /ˌənˈcHärtid/ ▸ adj. (of an area of land or sea) not mapped or surveyed.

un·checked /ˌənˈcHekt/ ▸ adj. (of something undesirable) not controlled or restrained.

un·chiv·al·rous /ˌənˈsHivəlrəs/ ▸ adj. (of a man) discourteous, especially toward women.

un·chris·tian /ˌənˈkrischən/ ▸ adj. 1 not in accordance with the teachings of Christianity. 2 unkind or unfair: *she felt an unchristian hope that he stepped on a sea urchin.*

un·ci·al /ˈənsHəl, -sēəl/ ▸ adj. written in rounded separated letters similar to modern capital letters, as found in manuscripts of the 4th–8th centuries. ▸ n. an uncial letter or manuscript.

un·cir·cum·cised /ˌənˈsərkəmˌsīzd/ ▸ adj. (of a boy or man) not circumcised.

un·civ·il /ˌənˈsivəl/ ▸ adj. not polite; discourteous.

un·civ·i·lized /ˌənˈsivəˌlīzd/ ▸ adj. 1 not having developed a modern culture or way of life. 2 not behaving in accordance with accepted moral or social standards.

un·clad /ˌənˈklad/ ▸ adj. not wearing any clothes; naked.

un·claimed /ˌənˈklāmd/ ▸ adj. not having been claimed.

un·clasp /ˌənˈklasp/ ▸ v. 1 unfasten a clasp or similar device. 2 release the grip of: *I unclasped her fingers from my hair.*

un·clas·si·fi·a·ble /ˌənˈklasəˌfīəbəl/ ▸ adj. not able to be put into a particular category.

un·clas·si·fied /ˌənˈklasəˌfīd/ ▸ adj. 1 not put into categories. 2 not officially classed as secret.

un·cle /ˈəNGkəl/ ▸ n. the brother of one's father or mother or the husband of one's aunt.

un·clean /ˌənˈklēn/ ▸ adj. 1 not clean; dirty. 2 morally wrong. 3 (of food) regarded in a particular religion as impure and unfit to be eaten.

un·clean·li·ness /ˌənˈklenlēnis/ ▸ n. the state of being dirty.

un·clear /ˌənˈkli(ə)r/ ▸ adj. 1 difficult to see, hear, or understand. 2 confused or not certain about something: *we are unclear about how to classify this activity.*

un·cleared /ˌənˈkli(ə)rd/ ▸ adj. 1 (of land) not cleared of vegetation. 2 (of a check) not having passed through a clearinghouse and been paid into a person's account.

un·clench /ˌənˈklencH/ ▸ v. release a clenched part of the body.

Un·cle Sam /sam/ ▸ n. the US or its federal government, often shown as a man with a tall hat and a white beard.

Un·cle Tom /täm/ ▸ n. derogatory a black man considered to be excessively obedient or servile to white people.

un·climbed /ˌənˈklīmd/ ▸ adj. (of a mountain or rock face) not previously climbed. ■ **un·climb·a·ble** /-ˈklīməbəl/ adj.

un·clip /ˌənˈklip/ ▸ v. (**unclips, unclipping, unclipped**) release something from being fastened or held with a clip.

un·clog /ˌənˈkläg, -ˈkläg/ ▸ v. (**unclogs, unclogging, unclogged**) remove a blockage from something.

un·clothed /ˌənˈklōᴛʜd/ ▸ adj. wearing no clothes; naked.

un·cloud·ed /ˌənˈkloudid/ ▸ adj. 1 (of the sky) not dark or overcast. 2 not troubled or spoiled by anything.

un·clut·tered /ˌənˈklətərd/ ▸ adj. not cluttered by too many objects or unnecessary items.

un·coil /ˌənˈkoil/ ▸ v. straighten from a coiled position.

un·col·ored /ˌənˈkələrd/ ▸ adj. 1 having no color. 2 not influenced: *her views were uncolored by her husband's.*

un·combed /ˌənˈkōmd/ ▸ adj. (of a person's hair) not combed.

un·com·fort·a·ble /ˌənˈkəmfərtəbəl, -ˈkəmftərbəl/ ▸ adj. 1 causing slight physical discomfort. 2 uneasy or awkward: *an uncomfortable silence.* ■ **un·com·fort·a·bly** /-blē/ adv.

un·com·mer·cial /ˌənkəˈmərsHəl/ ▸ adj. not making or intended to make a profit.

un·com·mon /ˌənˈkämən/ ▸ adj. 1 out of the ordinary; unusual. 2 remarkably great. ■ **un·com·mon·ly** adv.

un·com·mu·ni·ca·tive /ˌənkəˈmyōōnəkətiv, -ˌkātiv/ ▸ adj. unwilling to talk or give out information.

un·com·pet·i·tive /ˌənkəmˈpetətiv/ ▸ adj. not cheaper or better than others and therefore not able to compete commercially.

un·com·plain·ing /ˌənkəmˈplāniNG/ ▸ adj. not complaining about an unpleasant situation. ■ **un·com·plain·ing·ly** adv.

un·com·pli·cat·ed /ˌənˈkämpləˌkātid/ ▸ adj. simple or straightforward.

un·com·pli·men·ta·ry /ˌənkämpləˈmentərē, -ˈmentrē/ ▸ adj. not expressing praise; rude or insulting.

un·com·pre·hend·ing /ˌənˌkämpriˈhendiNG/ ▸ adj. not able to understand something. ■ **un·com·pre·hend·ing·ly** adv.

un·com·pro·mis·ing /ˌənˈkämprəˌmīziNG/ ▸ adj. 1 unwilling to change one's mind or behavior; resolute. 2 harsh or relentless: *uncompromising club music.* ■ **un·com·pro·mis·ing·ly** adv.

un·con·cealed /ˌənkənˈsēld/ ▸ adj. (especially of an emotion) not concealed; obvious.

un·con·cern /ˌənkənˈsərn/ ▸ n. a lack of worry or interest.

un·con·cerned /ˌənkənˈsərnd/ ▸ adj. not concerned or interested. ■ **un·con·cern·ed·ly** /-ˈsərnədlē/ adv.

un·con·di·tion·al /ˌənkənˈdisHənl, -ˈdisHnəl/ ▸ adj. not subject to any conditions or requirements. ■ **un·con·di·tion·al·ly** adv.

un·con·di·tioned /ˌənkənˈdisHənd/ ▸ adj. (of behavior) not formed or influenced by conditioning or learning; instinctive.

un·con·fi·dent /ˌənˈkänfədənt, -fəˌdent/ ▸ adj. not confident; shy or hesitant.

un·con·fined /ˌənkənˈfīnd/ ▸adj. **1** not confined to a limited space. **2** (of joy or excitement) very great.

un·con·firmed /ˌənkənˈfərmd/ ▸adj. not yet confirmed as true or valid.

un·con·gen·ial /ˌənkənˈjēnyəl/ ▸adj. **1** not friendly or pleasant to be with. **2** not suitable for or encouraging something: *the atmosphere was uncongenial to good conversation.*

un·con·nect·ed /ˌənkəˈnektid/ ▸adj. **1** not joined together or to something else. **2** not associated or linked in a sequence.

un·con·quer·a·ble /ˌənˈkäNGk(ə)rəbəl/ ▸adj. not able to be conquered or overcome.

un·con·scion·a·ble /ˌənˈkänsH(ə)nəbəl/ ▸adj. **1** not morally right. **2** excessive: *he takes an unconscionable time to get there.* ■ **un·con·scion·a·bly** /-blē/ adv.

un·con·scious /ˌənˈkänsHəs/ ▸adj. **1** not awake and aware of and responding to one's surroundings. **2** done or existing without realizing. **3** (**unconscious of**) unaware of. ▸n. (**the unconscious**) the part of the mind that cannot be accessed by the conscious mind but that affects behavior and emotions. ■ **un·con·scious·ly** adv. **un·con·scious·ness** n.

un·con·se·crat·ed /ˌənˈkänsiˌkrātid/ ▸adj. not made or declared to be holy or sacred.

un·con·sid·ered /ˌənkənˈsidərd/ ▸adj. **1** not thought about carefully. **2** not fully appreciated.

un·con·sti·tu·tion·al /ˌənˌkänstəˈt(y)o͞osHənl/ ▸adj. not in accordance with the constitution of a country or the rules of an organization. ■ **un·con·sti·tu·tion·al·ly** adv.

un·con·strained /ˌənkənˈstrānd/ ▸adj. not restricted or limited.

un·con·sum·mat·ed /ˌənˈkänsəˌmātid/ ▸adj. (of a marriage or relationship) not having been consummated by having sex.

un·con·tain·a·ble /ˌənkənˈtānəbəl/ ▸adj. (especially of an emotion) very strong.

un·con·tam·i·nat·ed /ˌənkənˈtaməˌnātid/ ▸adj. not contaminated by something impure or harmful.

un·con·ten·tious /ˌənkənˈtenCHəs/ ▸adj. not causing or likely to cause disagreement or controversy.

un·con·test·ed /ˌənkənˈtestid/ ▸adj. not contested or challenged.

un·con·trived /ˌənkənˈtrīvd/ ▸adj. not appearing artificial.

un·con·trol·la·ble /ˌənkənˈtrōləbəl/ ▸adj. not able to be controlled. ■ **un·con·trol·la·bly** adv.

un·con·trolled /ˌənkənˈtrōld/ ▸adj. not controlled or restricted.

un·con·tro·ver·sial /ˌənˌkäntrəˈvərsHəl/ ▸adj. not causing debate or conflicting opinions. ■ **un·con·tro·ver·sial·ly** adv.

un·con·ven·tion·al /ˌənkənˈvensHənl/ ▸adj. not in accordance with what is generally done or believed: *his unconventional approach to life.* ■ **un·con·ven·tion·al·i·ty** /-ˌvensHəˈnalətē/ n. **un·con·ven·tion·al·ly** adv.

un·con·vinced /ˌənkənˈvinst/ ▸adj. not certain that something is true or can be relied on.

un·con·vinc·ing /ˌənkənˈvinsiNG/ ▸adj. failing to convince or impress. ■ **un·con·vinc·ing·ly** adv.

un·cooked /ˌənko͝okt/ ▸adj. not cooked; raw.

un·cool /ˌənˈko͞ol/ ▸adj. informal not fashionable or impressive.

un·co·op·er·a·tive /ˌənkōˈäp(ə)rətiv/ ▸adj. unwilling to help others or do what they ask.

un·co·or·di·nat·ed /ˌənkōˈôrdnˌātid/ ▸adj. **1** badly organized. **2** (of a person or their movements) clumsy.

un·cork /ˌənˈkôrk/ ▸v. pull the cork out of a bottle.

un·cor·rob·o·rat·ed /kəˈräbəˌrātid/ ▸adj. not supported or confirmed by evidence.

un·count·a·ble /ˌənˈkountəbəl/ ▸adj. too many to be counted.

un·count·ed /ˌənˈkountid/ ▸adj. **1** not counted. **2** very numerous.

un·cou·ple /ˌənˈkəpəl/ ▸v. disconnect something from something else.

un·couth /ˌənˈko͞oTH/ ▸adj. lacking good manners or sophistication.

un·cov·er /ˌənˈkəvər/ ▸v. **1** remove a cover or covering from someone or something. **2** discover something previously secret or unknown.

un·cov·ered /ˌənˈkəvərd/ ▸adj. not covered by something.

un·crit·i·cal /ˌənˈkritikəl/ ▸adj. not willing to criticize or judge someone or something. ■ **un·crit·i·cal·ly** /-ik(ə)lē/ adv.

un·cross /ˌənˈkrôs, -ˈkräs/ ▸v. move something back from a crossed position.

un·crowd·ed /ˌənˈkroudid/ ▸adj. (of a place) not crowded.

un·crowned /ˌənˈkround/ ▸adj. not formally crowned as a monarch.

unc·tion /ˈəNG(k)sHən/ ▸n. **1** formal the smearing of someone with oil or ointment as a religious ceremony. **2** excessive politeness or flattery.

unc·tu·ous /ˈəNG(k)CHo͞oəs/ ▸adj. excessively flattering or friendly. ■ **unc·tu·ous·ly** adv. **unc·tu·ous·ness** n.

un·cul·ti·vat·ed /ˌənˈkəltəˌvātid/ ▸adj. **1** (of land) not used for growing crops. **2** not highly educated.

un·cul·tured /ˌənˈkəlCHərd/ ▸adj. not having good taste, manners, or education.

un·cured /ˌənˈkyo͝ord/ ▸adj. (of food) not preserved by salting, drying, or smoking.

un·curl /ˌənˈkərl/ ▸v. straighten from a curled position.

un·cut /ˌənˈkət/ ▸adj. **1** not cut or shaped by cutting. **2** (of a written work, movie, or performance) left in its complete form; not censored or abridged.

un·dam·aged /ˌənˈdamijd/ ▸adj. not harmed or damaged.

un·dat·ed /ˌənˈdātid/ ▸adj. not provided or marked with a date.

un·daunt·ed /ˌənˈdôntid, -ˈdänt-/ ▸adj. not discouraged by difficulty, danger, or disappointment.

un·de·ceive /ˌəndiˈsēv/ ▸v. tell someone that an idea or belief is mistaken.

un·de·cid·ed /ˌəndiˈsīdid/ ▸adj. **1** not having made a decision; uncertain. **2** not settled or resolved: *the ship's fate is still undecided.* ■ **un·de·cid·ed·ly** adv.

un·de·ci·pher·a·ble /ˌəndiˈsīf(ə)rəbəl/ ▸adj. (of speech or writing) not able to be read or understood.

un·de·feat·ed /ˌəndiˈfētid/ ▸adj. not defeated.

un·de·fend·ed /ˌəndiˈfendid/ ▸adj. not defended.

un·de·fined /ˌəndiˈfīnd/ ▸adj. not clear or

defined. ■ **un·de·fin·a·ble** adj.

un·de·mand·ing /ˌəndəˈmandiNG, ˌəndēˈmandiNG/ ▶ adj. (especially of a task) not demanding.

un·dem·o·crat·ic /ˌəndeməˈkratik/ ▶ adj. not according to democratic principles. ■ **un·dem·o·crat·i·cal·ly** /-ik(ə)lē/ adv.

un·de·mon·stra·tive /ˌəndiˈmänstrətiv/ ▶ adj. not tending to express feelings openly.

un·de·ni·a·ble /ˌəndiˈnīəbəl/ ▶ adj. unable to be denied or questioned. ■ **un·de·ni·a·bly** /-blē/ adv.

un·der /ˈəndər/ ▶ prep. 1 extending or directly below. 2 below or behind something covering or protecting. 3 at a lower level, layer, or grade than. 4 lower than a specified amount, rate, or norm. 5 expressing submission or control: *I was under his spell.* 6 as provided for by the rules of; in accordance with. 7 used to express grouping or classification. 8 undergoing a process. ▶ adv. 1 extending or directly below something. 2 affected by an anesthetic; unconscious. – PHRASES **under way 1** having started and making progress. 2 (of a boat) moving through the water.

under- ▶ prefix 1 below; beneath: *undercover.* 2 lower in status: *undersecretary.* 3 insufficiently; incompletely: *undernourished.*

un·der·a·chieve /ˌəndərəˈCHēv/ ▶ v. do less well than is expected. ■ **un·der·a·chieve·ment** n. **un·der·a·chiev·er** n.

un·der·age /ˌəndərˈāj/ ▶ adj. too young to take part legally in a particular activity.

un·der·arm /ˈəndərˌärm/ ▶ adj. & adv. (of a throw or stroke in sports) made with the arm or hand below shoulder level. ▶ n. a person's armpit.

un·der·bel·ly /ˈəndərˌbelē/ ▶ n. (pl. **underbellies**) 1 the soft underside or abdomen of an animal. 2 a hidden and unpleasant or criminal part of society.

un·der·bid /ˌəndərˈbid/ ▶ v. (**underbidding**; past and past part. **underbid**) (especially when trying to secure a contract) make a lower bid than someone else.

un·der·bite /ˈəndərˌbīt/ ▶ n. the projection of the lower teeth beyond the upper.

un·der·brush /ˈəndərˌbrəSH/ ▶ n. undergrowth in a forest.

un·der·car·riage /ˈəndərˌkarij/ ▶ n. 1 a wheeled structure beneath an aircraft that supports the aircraft on the ground. 2 the supporting frame under the body of a vehicle.

un·der·charge /ˌəndərˈCHärj/ ▶ v. charge someone a price or amount that is too low.

un·der·class /ˈəndərˌklas/ ▶ n. the lowest social class in a country or community, consisting of the poor and unemployed.

un·der·clothes /ˈəndərˌklō(TH)z/ ▶ pl.n. clothes worn under others next to the skin. ■ **un·der·cloth·ing** n.

un·der·coat /ˈəndərˌkōt/ ▶ n. a layer of paint applied after the primer and before the topcoat.

un·der·cook /ˌəndərˈko͝ok, ˈəndərˌko͝ok/ ▶ v. cook food for too short a time.

un·der·cov·er /ˌəndərˈkəvər/ ▶ adj. & adv. involving secret work for the purposes of investigation or spying.

un·der·croft /ˈəndərˌkrôft, -ˌkräft/ ▶ n. the crypt of a church.

un·der·cur·rent /ˈəndərˌkərənt/ ▶ n. 1 a hidden or underlying feeling or influence: *I sensed an undercurrent of resentment among the other girls.* 2 a current of water below the surface, moving in a different direction from any surface current.

un·der·cut /ˌəndərˈkət/ ▶ v. (**undercutting**; past and past part. **undercut**) 1 offer goods or services at a lower price than a competitor. 2 weaken or undermine: *his authority was being undercut.* 3 cut or wear away the part below or under something.

un·der·de·vel·oped /ˌəndərdiˈveləpt/ ▶ adj. 1 not fully developed. 2 (of a country or region) not economically advanced. ■ **un·der·de·vel·op·ment** n.

un·der·dog /ˈəndərˌdôg, -ˌdäg/ ▶ n. a competitor thought to have little chance of winning a fight or contest.

un·der·done /ˌəndərˈdən/ ▶ adj. (of food) not cooked for long enough.

un·der·dress /ˌəndərˈdres/ ▶ v. (**be underdressed**) be dressed too plainly or too informally for a particular occasion.

un·der·em·ployed /ˌəndərimˈploid/ ▶ adj. not having enough work, or not having work that makes full use of one's abilities. ■ **un·der·em·ploy·ment** n.

un·der·es·ti·mate /ˌəndərˈestəˌmāt/ ▶ v. 1 estimate something to be smaller or less important than it really is. 2 regard someone as less capable than they really are. ▶ n. /-mit/ an estimate that is too low. ■ **un·der·es·ti·ma·tion** /-ˌestəˈmāSHən/ n.

un·der·ex·pose /ˌəndərikˈspōz/ ▶ v. expose photographic film for too short a time. ■ **un·der·ex·po·sure** /-ˈspōzHər/ n.

un·der·fed /ˌəndərˈfed/ ▶ adj. having had too little to eat.

un·der·foot /ˌəndərˈfo͝ot/ ▶ adv. 1 under one's feet; on the ground. 2 constantly present and in one's way.

un·der·fund /ˌəndərˈfənd/ ▶ v. fail to provide an organization, project, etc., with enough funding. ■ **un·der·fund·ing** n.

un·der·gar·ment /ˈəndərˌgärmənt/ ▶ n. an item of underclothing.

un·der·glaze /ˈəndərˌglāz/ ▶ n. color or decoration applied to pottery before the glaze is applied.

un·der·go /ˌəndərˈgō/ ▶ v. (**undergoes**; past **underwent** /ˌəndərˈwent/; past part. **undergone** /ˌəndərˈgôn/) experience or be subjected to something unpleasant or difficult.

un·der·grad /ˈəndərˌgrad/ ▶ n. informal an undergraduate.

un·der·grad·u·ate /ˌəndərˈgrajəwit/ ▶ n. /-mit/ a student at a college or university who has not yet earned a bachelor's degree.

un·der·ground /ˌəndərˈground/ ▶ adj. & adv. 1 beneath the surface of the ground. 2 in secrecy or hiding. 3 favoring alternative or experimental forms of lifestyle or artistic expression. ▶ n. 1 a group or movement organized secretly to work against an existing government. 2 Brit. a subway.

un·der·growth /ˈəndərˌgrōTH/ ▶ n. a dense growth of shrubs and other plants.

un·der·hand /ˈəndərˌhand/ ▶ adj. 1 underarm. 2 (usu. **underhanded**) acting or done in a secret or dishonest way.

un·der·lay¹ ▶ n. /ˈəndərˌlā/ material laid under a carpet for protection or support. ▶ v. /ˌəndərˈlā/ (past and past part. **underlaid**) place something under something else, especially to support or raise it.

un·der·lay² /ˌəndərˈlā/ ▶ past tense of **UNDERLIE**.

un·der·lie /ˌəndərˈlī/ ▶ v. (**underlying**; past **underlay**; past part. **underlain**) lie or be situated under something. ■ **un·der·ly·ing** adj.

un·der·line /ˈəndərˌlīn/ ▶ v. **1** draw a line under a word or phrase to give emphasis. **2** emphasize: *he underlined the importance of spending on health and education.* ▶ n. a line drawn under a word or phrase.

un·der·ling /ˈəndərliNG/ ▶ n. chiefly derogatory a person of lower rank or status.

un·der·lit /ˌəndərˈlit/ ▶ adj. not having enough light or lighting; dim.

un·der·man /ˌəndərˈman/ ▶ v. (**undermans, undermanning, undermanned**) fail to provide an organization with enough workers.

un·der·mine /ˌəndərˈmīn, ˈəndərˌmīn/ ▶ v. **1** damage or weaken: *an attempt to undermine the president's authority.* **2** wear away the base or foundation of a rock formation. **3** dig or excavate beneath a building or fortification so as to make it collapse.

un·der·neath /ˌəndərˈnēth/ ▶ prep. & adv. **1** situated directly below. **2** so as to be partly or wholly concealed by. ▶ n. the part or side facing toward the ground.

un·der·nour·ished /ˌəndərˈnərisht, -ˈnə-risht/ ▶ adj. not having enough food or the right type of food for good health. ■ **un·der·nour·ish·ment** n.

un·der·paid /ˌəndərˈpād/ ▶ past and past participle of **UNDERPAY**.

un·der·pants /ˈəndərˌpan(t)s/ ▶ pl.n. an undergarment covering the lower part of the torso and having two holes for the legs.

un·der·part /ˈəndərˌpärt/ ▶ n. a lower part or portion.

un·der·pass /ˈəndərˌpas/ ▶ n. a road or pedestrian tunnel passing under another road or a railroad.

un·der·pay /ˌəndərˈpā/ ▶ v. (past and past part. **underpaid**) pay someone too little, or pay less than is due for something.

un·der·per·form /ˌəndərpərˈfôrm/ ▶ v. perform less well than expected. ■ **un·der·per·for·mance** n.

un·der·pin /ˌəndərˈpin/ ▶ v. (**underpins, underpinning, underpinned**) **1** support, justify, or form the basis for an argument, claim, etc. **2** support a structure from below by laying a solid foundation or replacing weak materials with stronger ones.

un·der·play /ˌəndərˈplā, ˈəndərˌplā/ ▶ v. represent something as being less important than it really is.

un·der·priv·i·leged /ˌəndərˈpriv(ə)lijd/ ▶ adj. not enjoying the same rights or standard of living as the majority of the population.

un·der·rate /ˌəndə(r)ˈrāt/ ▶ v. (often as adj. **underrated**) fail to recognize the quality, value, or importance of someone or something.

un·der·re·port /ˌəndə(r)riˈpôrt/ ▶ v. fail to report news or data fully.

un·der·rep·re·sent /ˌəndə(r)ˌrepriˈzent/ ▶ v. (**be underrepresented**) form a disproportionately small percentage: *women are underrepresented in the Senate.*

un·der·re·sourced /ˌəndə(r)ˈrēˌsôrst, -ˈriˌsôrst/ ▶ adj. provided with insufficient resources.

un·der·score /ˈəndərˌskôr, ˌəndərˈskôr/ ▶ v. & n. another term for **UNDERLINE**.

un·der·sea /ˌəndərˈsē/ ▶ adj. relating to or situated below the sea or the surface of the sea.

un·der·sec·re·tar·y /ˌəndərˈsekriˌterē/ ▶ n. (pl. **undersecretaries**) **1** (in the US) the chief assistant to a member of the cabinet. **2** (in the UK) a junior minister or senior civil servant.

un·der·sell /ˌəndərˈsel/ ▶ v. (past and past part. **undersold**) **1** sell something at a lower price than a competitor. **2** fail to represent someone's or something's true quality or worth.

un·der·sexed /ˌəndərˈsekst/ ▶ adj. having unusually weak sexual desires.

un·der·shirt /ˈəndərˌSHərt/ ▶ n. an undergarment worn under a shirt.

un·der·shoot /ˌəndərˈSHo͞ot/ ▶ v. (past and past part. **undershot**) **1** (of an aircraft) land short of the runway. **2** fall short of a point or target.

un·der·shorts /ˈəndərˌSHôrts/ ▶ pl.n. men's underpants.

un·der·side /ˈəndərˌsīd/ ▶ n. the bottom or lower side or surface of something.

un·der·signed /ˈəndərˌsīnd/ ▶ n. (**the undersigned**) formal the person or people who have signed the document in question.

un·der·sized /ˌəndərˈsīzd/ (also **undersize**) ▶ adj. smaller than the usual size.

un·der·skirt /ˈəndərˌskərt/ ▶ n. a petticoat.

un·der·sold /ˌəndərˈsōld/ ▶ past and past participle of **UNDERSELL**.

un·der·spend /ˌəndərˈspend/ ▶ v. (past and past part. **underspent**) spend too little or less than planned.

un·der·staffed /ˌəndərˈstaft/ ▶ adj. (of an organization) having too few members of staff to operate effectively.

un·der·stand /ˌəndərˈstand/ ▶ v. (past and past part. **understood**) **1** know or realize the intended meaning of words, a language, or a speaker. **2** be aware of the significance, explanation, or cause of something: *he didn't understand why we were laughing.* **3** be sympathetically aware of: *I understand how you feel.* **4** interpret or view something in a particular way. **5** believe to be the case from information received: *I understand you're at art school.* **6** assume that something is present or is the case: *he liked to play the field, that was understood.*

un·der·stand·a·ble /ˌəndərˈstandəbəl/ ▶ adj. **1** able to be understood. **2** to be expected; natural, reasonable, or forgivable. ■ **un·der·stand·a·bly** /-blē/ adv.

un·der·stand·ing /ˌəndərˈstandiNG/ ▶ n. **1** the ability to understand something. **2** the power of abstract thought; intellect. **3** a person's interpretation or judgment of a situation. **4** sympathetic awareness or tolerance. **5** an informal or unspoken agreement or arrangement. ▶ adj. sympathetically aware of other people's feelings. ■ **un·der·stand·ing·ly** adv.

un·der·state /ˌəndərˈstāt/ ▶ v. describe or represent something as being smaller or less important than it really is. ■ **un·der·state·ment** n.

un·der·stat·ed /ˌəndərˈstātid/ ▶ adj. presented or expressed in a subtle and effective way. ■ **un·der·stat·ed·ly** adv.

un·der·steer /ˌəndərˈsti(ə)r/ ▶ v. (of a motor vehicle) have a tendency to turn less sharply than is intended.

un·der·stood /ˌəndər'sto͝od/ ▸ past and past participle of UNDERSTAND.

un·der·sto·ry /'əndərˌstôrē/ ▸ n. (pl. **understories**) Ecology a layer of vegetation beneath the top branches of the trees in a forest.

un·der·stud·y /'əndərˌstədē/ ▸ n. (pl. **understudies**) an actor who learns another's role in order to be able to act in their absence. ▸ v. (**understudies, understudying, understudied**) be an understudy for another actor.

un·der·take /ˌəndər'tāk/ ▸ v. (past **undertook** /ˌəndər'to͝ok/; past part. **undertaken** /ˌəndər'tākn/) **1** make oneself responsible for carrying out a project, activity, etc.; take something on: *a firm of builders undertook the construction work.* **2** formally guarantee or promise to do something.

un·der·tak·er /'əndərˌtākər/ ▸ n. a funeral director.

un·der·tak·ing /'əndərˌtākiNG, ˌəndər'tā-/ ▸ n. **1** a formal promise to do something. **2** a task or project that is taken on by someone. **3** the management of funerals as a profession.

un·der·tone /'əndərˌtōn/ ▸ n. **1** a subdued or muted tone of sound or color. **2** an underlying quality or feeling.

un·der·tow /'əndərˌtō/ ▸ n. another term for UNDERCURRENT.

un·der·use ▸ v. /ˌəndər'yo͞oz/ fail to make enough use of something. ▸ n. /ˌəndər'yo͞os/ insufficient use of something. ∎ **un·der·used** adj.

un·der·u·ti·lize /ˌəndər'yo͞otlˌīz/ ▸ v. underuse something.

un·der·val·ue /ˌəndər'valyo͞o/ ▸ v. (**undervalues, undervalued, undervaluing**) **1** fail to recognize someone's or something's importance or worth. **2** underestimate something's financial value.

un·der·wa·ter /ˌəndər'wôtər, -'wätər/ ▸ adj. & adv. situated or happening beneath the surface of the water.

un·der·way /ˌəndər'wā/ ▸ adj. variant of UNDER WAY (SEE UNDER).

> USAGE
> The spelling **underway** is best avoided in formal writing: use **under way** instead.

un·der·wear /'əndərˌwer/ ▸ n. clothing worn under other clothes next to the skin.

un·der·weight /'əndərˌwāt, ˌəndər'wāt/ ▸ adj. below a weight considered normal or desirable.

un·der·went /ˌəndər'went/ ▸ past of UNDERGO.

un·der·whelm /ˌəndər'(h)welm/ ▸ v. humorous fail to impress or make a positive impact on someone.

un·der·wire /'əndərˌwīr/ ▸ n. a semicircular wire support stitched under each cup of a bra. ▸ adj. (of a bra) having such a wire.

un·der·world /'əndərˌwərld/ ▸ n. **1** the world of criminals or of organized crime. **2** (in myths and legends) the home of the dead, imagined as being under the earth.

un·der·write /'əndə(r)ˌrīt, ˌəndə(r)'rīt/ ▸ v. (past **underwrote** /'əndə(r)ˌrōt, ˌəndə(r)'rōt/; past part. **underwritten** /'əndə(r)ˌritn, ˌəndə(r)'ritn/) **1** sign and accept liability under an insurance policy. **2** undertake to finance or otherwise support or guarantee something. ∎ **un·der·writ·er** n.

un·de·scend·ed /ˌəndi'sendid/ ▸ adj. (of a testicle) remaining in the abdomen instead of descending normally into the scrotum.

un·de·served /ˌəndi'zərvd/ ▸ adj. not deserved or earned. ∎ **un·de·serv·ed·ly** /-'zərvədlē/ adv.

un·de·serv·ing /ˌəndi'zərviNG/ ▸ adj. not deserving or worthy of something.

un·de·sir·a·ble /ˌəndi'zīrəbəl/ ▸ adj. not wanted or desirable because harmful, offensive, or unpleasant. ▸ n. an unpleasant or offensive person. ∎ **un·de·sir·a·bil·i·ty** n. **un·de·sir·a·bly** /-blē/ adv.

un·de·sired /ˌəndi'zīrd/ ▸ adj. not wanted or desired.

un·de·tect·a·ble /ˌəndi'tektəbəl/ ▸ adj. not able to be detected.

un·de·tect·ed /ˌəndi'tektid/ ▸ adj. not detected or discovered.

un·de·ter·mined /ˌəndi'tərmənd/ ▸ adj. not firmly decided or settled.

un·de·terred /ˌəndi'tərd/ ▸ adj. persevering despite setbacks.

un·de·vel·oped /ˌəndi'veləpt/ ▸ adj. not having developed or been developed.

un·de·vi·at·ing /ˌən'dēvēˌātiNG/ ▸ adj. showing no deviation; constant and steady.

un·di·ag·nosed /ˌən'dīəgˌnōst/ ▸ adj. not diagnosed.

un·did /ˌən'did/ ▸ past of UNDO.

un·dies /'əndēz/ ▸ pl.n. informal articles of underwear.

un·dif·fer·en·ti·at·ed /ˌənˌdifə'renchēˌātid/ ▸ adj. not different or differentiated.

un·di·gest·ed /ˌəndə'jestəd, -ˌdī-/ ▸ adj. **1** (of food) not digested. **2** (of information) not having been properly understood or absorbed.

un·dig·ni·fied /ˌən'digniˌfīd/ ▸ adj. appearing foolish; lacking in dignity.

un·di·lut·ed /ˌəndi'lo͞otid, -dī-/ ▸ adj. **1** (of a liquid) not diluted. **2** (of a feeling or quality) not mixed or combined with any other: *pure, undiluted happiness.*

un·di·min·ished /ˌəndi'miniSHt/ ▸ adj. not reduced or lessened.

un·dimmed /ˌən'dimd/ ▸ adj. not dimmed; still bright or intense.

un·dip·lo·mat·ic /ˌənˌdiplə'matik/ ▸ adj. insensitive and tactless. ∎ **un·dip·lo·mat·i·cal·ly** /-ik(ə)lē/ adv.

un·di·rect·ed /ˌəndə'rektəd, -ˌdī-/ ▸ adj. lacking a proper plan or purpose.

un·dis·cern·ing /ˌəndi'sərniNG/ ▸ adj. lacking judgment or taste.

un·dis·ci·plined /ˌən'disəplind/ ▸ adj. uncontrolled in behavior or manner.

un·dis·closed /ˌəndis'klōzd/ ▸ adj. not revealed or made known.

un·dis·cov·ered /ˌəndis'kəvərd/ ▸ adj. not discovered.

un·dis·crim·i·nat·ing /ˌəndis'krimənˌātiNG/ ▸ adj. lacking good judgment or taste.

un·dis·guised /ˌəndis'gīzd/ ▸ adj. (of a feeling) not disguised or concealed; open.

un·dis·mayed /ˌəndis'mād/ ▸ adj. not dismayed or discouraged by a setback.

un·dis·put·ed /ˌəndi'spyo͞otid/ ▸ adj. not disputed or called into question.

un·dis·tin·guished /ˌəndi'stiNGgwiSHt/ ▸ adj. lacking distinction; not very good or impressive.

un·dis·turbed /ˌəndis'tərbd/ ▸ adj. not disturbed.

un·di·vid·ed /ˌəndə'vīdid/ ▸ adj. **1** not divided, separated, or broken into parts. **2** devoted completely to one person or thing: *you have my undivided attention.*

un·do /ən'dōō/ ▶ v. (**undoes** /ən'dəs/; past **undid** /ən'did/; past part. **undone** /ən'dən/) **1** unfasten or loosen. **2** cancel or reverse the effects of (a previous action or measure). **3** formal cause the downfall or ruin of.

un·do·cu·ment·ed /ən'däkyə‚mentid/ ▶ adj. not recorded in or proved by documents.

un·do·ing /ən'dōō-iNG/ ▶ n. a person's ruin or downfall.

un·done /ən'dən/ ▶ adj. **1** not tied or fastened. **2** not done or finished. **3** formal or humorous ruined by a disastrous setback.

un·doubt·ed /ən'doutid/ ▶ adj. not questioned or doubted by anyone. ■ **un·doubt·ed·ly** adv.

un·dreamed /ən'drēmd/ (also **undreamt** /-'dremt/) ▶ adj. (**undreamed of**) not previously thought to be possible.

un·dress /ən'dres/ ▶ v. **1** (also **get undressed**) take off one's clothes. **2** take the clothes off someone else. ▶ n. **1** the state of being naked or only partially clothed. **2** Military ordinary clothing or uniform, as opposed to full dress.

un·dressed /ən'drest/ ▶ adj. **1** wearing no clothes; naked. **2** not treated, processed, or prepared for use. **3** (of food) not having a dressing.

un·drink·a·ble /ən'driNGkəbəl/ ▶ adj. not fit to be drunk because of impurity or poor quality.

un·due /ən'd(y)ōō/ ▶ adj. more than is reasonable or necessary; excessive. ■ **un·du·ly** adv.

un·du·lant /'ənjələnt, 'əndyə-/ ▶ adj. undulating.

un·du·late /'ənjə‚lāt, 'əndyə-/ ▶ v. **1** move with a smooth wavelike motion. **2** have a wavy form or outline. ■ **un·du·la·tion** /‚ənjə'lāSHən, ‚əndyə-/ n. **un·du·la·to·ry** /'ənjələ‚tôrē, 'əndyə-/ adj.

un·dyed /ən'dīd/ ▶ adj. (of fabric) not dyed; of its natural color.

un·dy·ing /ən'dī-iNG/ ▶ adj. lasting forever.

un·earned /ən'ərnd/ ▶ adj. not earned or deserved.

un·earned in·come ▶ n. income from private means (such as investments) rather than from work.

un·earth /ən'ərTH/ ▶ v. **1** find something in the ground by digging. **2** discover something by investigation or searching.

un·earth·ly /ən'ərTHlē/ ▶ adj. **1** unnatural or mysterious. **2** informal unreasonably early or inconvenient: *an unearthly hour.*

un·ease /ən'ēz/ ▶ n. anxiety or discontent.

un·eas·y /ən'ēzē/ ▶ adj. (**uneasier, uneasiest**) **1** anxious or uncomfortable. **2** liable to change; not settled: *an uneasy truce.* ■ **un·eas·i·ly** adv. **un·eas·i·ness** n.

un·eat·a·ble /ən'ētəbəl/ ▶ adj. not fit to be eaten.

un·eat·en /ən'ētn/ ▶ adj. not eaten.

un·ec·o·nom·ic /‚ən‚ekə'nämik, -‚ēkə-/ ▶ adj. not profitable or making efficient use of resources.

un·ec·o·nom·i·cal /‚ən‚ekə'nämikəl, -‚ēkə-/ ▶ adj. wasteful of money or other resources; not economical.

un·ed·i·fy·ing /ən'edə‚fī-iNG/ ▶ adj. arousing disapproval; distasteful or unpleasant.

un·ed·it·ed /ən'editid/ ▶ adj. (of material for publication or broadcasting) not edited.

un·ed·u·cat·ed /ən'ejə‚kātid/ ▶ adj. poorly educated.

un·e·lect·ed /‚əni'lektid/ ▶ adj. (of an official) not elected.

un·em·bar·rassed /‚ənem'barəst/ ▶ adj. not feeling or showing embarrassment.

un·e·mo·tion·al /‚əni'mōSHənl/ ▶ adj. not having or showing strong feelings. ■ **un·e·mo·tion·al·ly** adv.

un·em·ploy·a·ble /‚ənim'ploi-əbəl/ ▶ adj. not able or likely to get paid employment because of a lack of skills or qualifications.

un·em·ployed /‚ənim'ploid/ ▶ adj. **1** without a paid job but available to work. **2** (of a thing) not in use.

un·em·ploy·ment /‚ənim'ploimənt/ ▶ n. **1** the state of being unemployed. **2** the number or proportion of unemployed people.

un·em·ploy·ment ben·e·fit ▶ n. payment made by a government or labor union to an unemployed person.

un·en·closed /‚ənen'klōzd/ ▶ adj. (especially of land) not enclosed.

un·en·cum·bered /‚ənen'kəmbərd/ ▶ adj. not burdened or prevented from moving or acting freely.

un·end·ing /ən'endiNG/ ▶ adj. seeming to last or continue for ever.

un·en·dur·a·ble /‚ənin'd(y)ōōrəbəl/ ▶ adj. not able to be tolerated or endured.

un·en·force·a·ble /‚ənen'fôrsəbəl/ ▶ adj. (especially of a law) impossible to enforce.

un·en·light·ened /‚ənen'lītnd/ ▶ adj. not enlightened in outlook.

un·en·ter·pris·ing /ən'entər‚prīziNG/ ▶ adj. lacking initiative or resourcefulness.

un·en·thu·si·as·tic /‚ənen‚THōōzē'astik/ ▶ adj. not having or showing enthusiasm. ■ **un·en·thu·si·as·ti·cal·ly** /-ik(ə)lē/ adv.

un·en·vi·a·ble /ən'envēəbəl/ ▶ adj. difficult, undesirable, or unpleasant.

un·e·qual /ən'ēkwəl/ ▶ adj. **1** not equal in quantity, size, or value. **2** not fair, evenly balanced, or having equal advantage. **3** (**unequal to**) not having the ability or resources to meet a challenge. ■ **un·e·qual·ly** adv.

un·e·qualed /ən'ēkwəld/ (Brit. **unequalled**) ▶ adj. better or greater than all others of the same kind.

un·e·quiv·o·cal /‚əni'kwivəkəl/ ▶ adj. leaving no doubt; completely clear in meaning. ■ **un·e·quiv·o·cal·ly** /-ək(ə)lē/ adv.

un·err·ing /ən'əriNG, -'er-/ ▶ adj. always right or accurate. ■ **un·err·ing·ly** adv.

UNESCO /yōō'neskō/ ▶ abbr. United Nations Educational, Scientific, and Cultural Organization.

un·es·sen·tial /‚ənə'senCHəl/ ▶ adj. not essential or absolutely necessary.

un·eth·i·cal /ən'eTHikəl/ ▶ adj. not morally correct or acceptable. ■ **un·eth·i·cal·ly** /-ik(ə)lē/ adv.

un·e·ven /ən'ēvən/ ▶ adj. **1** not level or smooth. **2** not regular, consistent, or equal. ■ **un·e·ven·ly** adv. **un·e·ven·ness** n.

un·e·vent·ful /‚əni'ventfəl/ ▶ adj. not marked by interesting or exciting events. ■ **un·e·vent·ful·ly** adv. **un·e·vent·ful·ness** n.

un·ex·am·ined /‚ənig'zamind/ ▶ adj. not investigated or examined.

un·ex·cep·tion·a·ble /‚ənik'sepSH(ə)nəbəl/

▶ adj. not open to objection, but not particularly new or exciting.

un·ex·cep·tion·al /ˌənik'sepsHənl/ ▶ adj. not out of the ordinary; usual. ■ **un·ex·cep·tion·al·ly** adv.

un·ex·cit·ing /ˌənik'sītiNG/ ▶ adj. not exciting; dull.

un·ex·pect·ed /ˌənik'spektid/ ▶ adj. not expected or regarded as likely to happen. ■ **un·ex·pect·ed·ly** adv. **un·ex·pect·ed·ness** n.

un·ex·plained /ˌənik'splānd/ ▶ adj. not made clear or accounted for. ■ **un·ex·plain·a·ble** adj.

un·ex·plod·ed /ˌənik'splōdid/ ▶ adj. (of an explosive device) not having exploded.

un·ex·plored /ˌənik'splôrd/ ▶ adj. not explored, investigated, or evaluated.

un·ex·pressed /ˌənik'sprest/ ▶ adj. (of a thought or feeling) not communicated or made known.

un·ex·pur·gat·ed /ˌən'ekspər,gātid/ ▶ adj. (of a text) complete and containing all the original material; not censored.

un·fail·ing /ˌən'fāliNG/ ▶ adj. 1 without error. 2 reliable or constant. ■ **un·fail·ing·ly** adv.

un·fair /ˌən'fe(ə)r/ ▶ adj. not based on or showing fairness. ■ **un·fair·ly** adv. **un·fair·ness** n.

un·faith·ful /ˌən'fāTHfəl/ ▶ adj. 1 not faithful; disloyal. 2 having sex with a person other than one's husband, wife, or established partner. ■ **un·faith·ful·ly** adv. **un·faith·ful·ness** n.

un·fal·ter·ing /ˌən'fôltəriNG/ ▶ adj. not faltering; steady or resolute. ■ **un·fal·ter·ing·ly** adv.

un·fa·mil·iar /ˌənfə'milyər/ ▶ adj. 1 not known or recognized; uncharacteristic. 2 (**unfamiliar with**) not having knowledge or experience of something. ■ **un·fa·mil·i·ar·i·ty** /-ˌmilē'e(ə)ritē, -fəmil'yer-/ n.

un·fash·ion·a·ble /ˌən'fasHənəbəl/ ▶ adj. not fashionable or popular. ■ **un·fash·ion·a·bly** /-blē/ adv.

un·fas·ten /ˌən'fasən/ ▶ v. open the fastening of something.

un·fath·om·a·ble /ˌən'faTHəməbəl/ ▶ adj. 1 too strange or difficult to be understood. 2 impossible to measure the depth or extent of. ■ **un·fath·om·a·bly** /-blē/ adv.

un·fa·vor·a·ble /ˌən'fāv(ə)rəbəl/ (Brit. **unfavourable**) ▶ adj. 1 expressing lack of approval. 2 unlikely to lead to a successful outcome: *unfavorable economic conditions.* ■ **un·fa·vor·a·bly** /-blē/ adv.

un·fazed /ˌən'fāzd/ ▶ adj. informal not disconcerted or worried by something unexpected.

un·fea·si·ble /ˌən'fēzəbəl/ ▶ adj. inconvenient or impractical. ■ **un·fea·si·bly** adv.

un·feel·ing /ˌən'fēliNG/ ▶ adj. unsympathetic, harsh, or callous.

un·feigned /ˌən'fānd/ ▶ adj. genuine; sincere.

un·fer·ment·ed /ˌənfər'mentid/ ▶ adj. not fermented.

un·fer·ti·lized /ˌən'fərtl,īzd/ ▶ adj. not fertilized.

un·fet·tered /ˌən'fetərd/ ▶ adj. unrestrained or uninhibited.

un·filled /ˌən'fild/ ▶ adj. not filled; vacant or empty.

un·fin·ished /ˌən'finisHt/ ▶ adj. 1 not finished; incomplete. 2 not having been given an attractive surface appearance in manufacture.

un·fit /ˌən'fit/ ▶ adj. 1 unsuitable or inadequate for something. 2 not in good physical condition.

un·fit·ted /ˌən'fitid/ ▶ adj. unfit for something.

un·fit·ting /ˌən'fitiNG/ ▶ adj. unsuitable or unbecoming.

un·fixed /ˌən'fikst/ ▶ adj. 1 unfastened; loose. 2 uncertain or variable.

un·flag·ging /ˌən'flagiNG/ ▶ adj. not becoming tired or weak; remaining strong. ■ **un·flag·ging·ly** adv.

un·flap·pa·ble /ˌən'flapəbəl/ ▶ adj. informal calm in a crisis.

un·flat·ter·ing /ˌən'flatəriNG/ ▶ adj. not flattering. ■ **un·flat·ter·ing·ly** adv.

un·flinch·ing /ˌən'flincHiNG/ ▶ adj. not afraid or hesitant. ■ **un·flinch·ing·ly** adv.

un·fo·cused /ˌən'fōkəst/ (also **unfocussed**) ▶ adj. 1 not focused; out of focus. 2 without a specific aim or direction.

un·fold /ˌən'fōld/ ▶ v. 1 open or spread out from a folded position. 2 reveal or be revealed.

un·forced /ˌən'fôrst/ ▶ adj. 1 produced naturally and without effort. 2 (of an action) not done as a result of pressure from another person.

un·fore·seen /ˌənfôr'sēn, -fər-/ ▶ adj. not anticipated or predicted. ■ **un·fore·see·a·ble** adj.

un·for·get·ta·ble /ˌənfər'getəbəl/ ▶ adj. so enjoyable, impressive, etc., that it is impossible to forget. ■ **un·for·get·ta·bly** /-blē/ adv.

un·for·giv·a·ble /ˌənfər'givəbəl/ ▶ adj. so bad as to be unable to be forgiven or excused. ■ **un·for·giv·a·bly** /-blē/ adv.

un·for·giv·ing /ˌənfər'giviNG/ ▶ adj. 1 not willing to forgive or excuse faults. 2 (of conditions) harsh or hostile.

un·formed /ˌən'fôrmd/ ▶ adj. 1 without a definite form. 2 not fully developed.

un·forth·com·ing /ˌənfôrTH'kəmiNG/ ▶ adj. 1 not willing to reveal information. 2 not available when needed.

un·for·tu·nate /ˌən'fôrcHənət/ ▶ adj. 1 having or marked by bad luck; unlucky. 2 regrettable or inappropriate: *an unfortunate remark.* ▶ n. a person who suffers bad fortune. ■ **un·for·tu·nate·ly** adv.

un·found·ed /ˌən'foundid/ ▶ adj. having no basis in fact: *an unfounded rumor.*

un·freeze /ˌən'frēz/ ▶ v. (past **unfroze** /ˌən'frōz/; past part. **unfrozen** /ˌən'frōzən/) 1 thaw something frozen. 2 remove restrictions on the use of an asset.

un·friend·ly /ˌən'fren(d)lē/ ▶ adj. (**unfriendlier, unfriendliest**) not friendly. ■ **un·friend·li·ness** n.

un·frock /ˌən'fräk/ ▶ v. another term for DEFROCK.

un·ful·filled /ˌənfoŏ(l)'fild/ ▶ adj. not fulfilled. ■ **un·ful·fill·a·ble** adj. **un·ful·fill·ing** adj.

un·fund·ed /ˌən'fəndid/ ▶ adj. not receiving funds; not having a fund.

un·fun·ny /ˌən'fənē/ ▶ adj. (**unfunnier, unfunniest**) (of something meant to be funny) not amusing.

un·furl /ˌən'fərl/ ▶ v. spread out from a rolled or folded state.

un·fur·nished /ˌən'fərnisHt/ ▶ adj. without furniture.

un·gain·ly /ˌən'gānlē/ ▶ adj. clumsy or awkward. ■ **un·gain·li·ness** n.

un·gen·er·ous /ˌən'jenərəs/ ▶ adj. not generous; stingy.

un·gen·tle·man·ly /ˌən'jentlmənlē/ ▶ adj. (of a man's behavior) not well-mannered or pleasant.

un·glazed /ˌənˈglāzd/ ▸ **adj.** not glazed.

un·glued /ˌənˈglo͞od/ ▸ **adj.** not or no longer stuck.
– PHRASES **come unglued** informal **1** end in failure. **2** become confused or upset.

un·god·ly /ˌənˈgädlē/ ▸ **adj.** **1** immoral or sinful. **2** informal unreasonably early or inconvenient: *telephone calls at ungodly hours.* ■ **un·god·li·ness n.**

un·gov·ern·a·ble /ˌənˈgəvərnəbəl/ ▸ **adj.** impossible to control or govern.

un·grace·ful /ˌənˈgrāsfəl/ ▸ **adj.** lacking in grace; clumsy. ■ **un·grace·ful·ly adv.**

un·gra·cious /ˌənˈgrāSHəs/ ▸ **adj.** not polite, kind, or pleasant. ■ **un·gra·cious·ly adv.**

un·gram·mat·i·cal /ˌəngrəˈmatikəl/ ▸ **adj.** not following grammatical rules. ■ **un·gram·mat·i·cal·ly** /-ik(ə)lē/ **adv.**

un·grate·ful /ˌənˈgrātfəl/ ▸ **adj.** not feeling or showing gratitude. ■ **un·grate·ful·ly adv.** **un·grate·ful·ness n.**

un·guard·ed /ˌənˈgärdid/ ▸ **adj.** **1** without protection or a guard. **2** not well considered; careless: *an unguarded remark.*

un·guent /ˈəNGgwənt/ ▸ **n.** a soft substance, especially a perfumed oil, used as ointment or for lubrication.

un·gu·late /ˈəNGgyələt, -ˌlāt/ ▸ **n.** Zoology a mammal that has hoofs.

un·hand /ˌənˈhand/ ▸ **v.** old use or humorous release someone from one's grasp.

un·hap·py /ˌənˈhapē/ ▸ **adj.** (**unhappier, unhappiest**) **1** not happy. **2** not lucky; unfortunate. ■ **un·hap·pi·ly adv. un·hap·pi·ness n.**

un·harmed /ˌənˈhärmd/ ▸ **adj.** not harmed; uninjured.

UNHCR ▸ **abbr.** United Nations High Commission for Refugees.

un·health·y /ˌənˈhelTHē/ ▸ **adj.** (**unhealthier, unhealthiest**) **1** not in good health. **2** likely to lead to illness or bad health: *an unhealthy diet.* ■ **un·health·i·ly adv. un·health·i·ness n.**

un·heard /ˌənˈhərd/ ▸ **adj.** **1** not heard or listened to. **2** (**unheard of**) previously unknown.

un·heed·ed /ˌənˈhēdid/ ▸ **adj.** heard or noticed but ignored.

un·heed·ing /ˌənˈhēdiNG/ ▸ **adj.** not paying attention.

un·help·ful /ˌənˈhelpfəl/ ▸ **adj.** not helpful. ■ **un·help·ful·ly adv. un·help·ful·ness n.**

un·her·ald·ed /ˌənˈherəldid/ ▸ **adj.** not previously announced; without warning.

un·hes·i·tat·ing /ˌənˈheziˌtātiNG/ ▸ **adj.** without doubt or hesitation. ■ **un·hes·i·tat·ing·ly adv.**

un·hinge /ˌənˈhinj/ ▸ **v.** make someone mentally unbalanced.

un·his·tor·i·cal /ˌənhiˈstôrikəl, -ˈstär-/ ▸ **adj.** not in accordance with history or historical analysis.

un·ho·ly /ˌənˈhōlē/ ▸ **adj.** (**unholier, unholiest**) **1** sinful; wicked. **2** (of an alliance) unnatural and likely to be dangerous or harmful. **3** informal very bad: *an unholy row.*

un·hook /ˌənˈho͝ok/ ▸ **v.** unfasten or detach something held by a hook.

un·hoped /ˌənˈhōpt/ ▸ **adj.** (**unhoped for**) beyond one's hopes or expectations.

un·horse /ˌənˈhôrs/ ▸ **v.** make someone fall from a horse.

un·hur·ried /ˌənˈhərēd, -ˈhə-rēd/ ▸ **adj.** moving, acting, or taking place without haste or urgency. ■ **un·hur·ried·ly adv.**

un·hurt /ˌənˈhərt/ ▸ **adj.** not hurt or harmed.

un·hy·gi·en·ic /ˌənhīˈjēnik, ˌənhīˈjēnik/ ▸ **adj.** not hygienic.

uni- ▸ **comb.form** one; having or consisting of one: *unicycle.*

U·ni·ate /ˈyo͞onēˌat, -it, -ˌāt/ or **Uniat** /ˈyo͞onēˌat, -it/ ▸ **adj.** referring to any Christian community in eastern Europe or the Near East that acknowledges the supremacy of the pope but has its own liturgy.

u·ni·cam·er·al /ˌyo͞onəˈkam(ə)rəl/ ▸ **adj.** (of a lawmaking assembly) having a single chamber.

u·ni·cast /ˈyo͞oniˌkast/ ▸ **n.** transmission of a data package or an audiovisual signal to a single recipient.

UNICEF /ˈyo͞onəˌsef/ ▸ **abbr.** United Nations Children's Fund (originally United Nations International Children's Emergency Fund).

u·ni·cel·lu·lar /ˌyo͞onəˈselyələr/ ▸ **adj.** Biology consisting of a single cell.

u·ni·corn /ˈyo͞onəˌkôrn/ ▸ **n.** a mythical animal represented as a horse with a single straight horn projecting from its forehead.

u·ni·cy·cle /ˈyo͞onəˌsīkəl/ ▸ **n.** a cycle with a single wheel, chiefly used by acrobats. ■ **u·ni·cy·clist** /-ˌsīklist/ **n.**

un·i·den·ti·fi·a·ble /ˌənīˈdentəˌfīəbəl/ ▸ **adj.** unable to be identified.

un·i·den·ti·fied /ˌənīˈdentəˌfīəd/ ▸ **adj.** not recognized or identified.

un·id·i·o·mat·ic /ˌənˌidēəˈmatik/ ▸ **adj.** not using or containing expressions natural to a native speaker of a language.

u·ni·di·rec·tion·al /ˌyo͞onidiˈreksHənl/ ▸ **adj.** moving or operating in a single direction.

u·ni·fi·ca·tion /ˌyo͞onəfiˈkāsHən/ ▸ **n.** the process of being unified.

u·ni·form /ˈyo͞onəˌfôrm/ ▸ **adj.** not varying in form or character; the same in all cases and at all times. ▸ **n.** the distinctive clothing worn by members of the same organization or by children attending certain schools. ■ **u·ni·formed adj. u·ni·form·i·ty** /ˌyo͞onəˈfôrmətē/ **n. u·ni·form·ly adv.**

u·ni·fy /ˈyo͞onəˌfī/ ▸ **v.** (**unifies, unifying, unified**) make or become united or uniform. ■ **u·ni·fi·er n.**

u·ni·lat·er·al /ˌyo͞onəˈlatərəl, -ˈlatrəl/ ▸ **adj.** **1** performed by or affecting only one person, group, etc. **2** relating to or affecting only one side of an organ, the body, etc. ■ **u·ni·lat·er·al·ism** /ˌyo͞onəˈlatərəˌlizəm, -ˈlatrə-/ **n. u·ni·lat·er·al·ist n. & adj. u·ni·lat·er·al·ly adv.**

un·im·ag·i·na·ble /ˌənəˈmaj(ə)nəbəl/ ▸ **adj.** impossible to imagine or understand. ■ **un·im·ag·i·na·bly** /-blē/ **adv.**

un·im·ag·i·na·tive /ˌənəˈmaj(ə)nətiv/ ▸ **adj.** not using or displaying imagination; dull. ■ **un·im·ag·i·na·tive·ly adv.**

un·im·paired /ˌənimˈpe(ə)rd/ ▸ **adj.** not weakened or damaged.

un·im·peach·a·ble /ˌənimˈpēCHəbəl/ ▸ **adj.** not able to be doubted, questioned, or criticized. ■ **un·im·peach·a·bly** /-blē/ **adv.**

un·im·ped·ed /ˌənimˈpēdid/ ▸ **adj.** not obstructed or hindered.

un·im·por·tant /ˌənimˈpôrtnt/ ▸ **adj.** lacking in importance. ■ **un·im·por·tance n.**

un·im·pressed /ˌənimˈprest/ ▸ **adj.** not impressed.

un·im·pres·sive /ˌənim'presiv/ ▸ adj. not impressive.

un·im·proved /ˌənim'prōōvd/ ▸ adj. (of land) not cleared or cultivated.

un·in·cor·po·rat·ed /ˌənin'kôrpəˌrātid, ˌəniNG-/ ▸ adj. 1 not formed into a legal corporation. 2 not included as part of a whole.

un·in·form·a·tive /ˌənin'fôrmətiv/ ▸ adj. not providing useful or interesting information.

un·in·formed /ˌənin'fôrmd/ ▸ adj. lacking awareness or understanding of the facts.

un·in·hab·it·a·ble /ˌənin'habətəbəl/ ▸ adj. not suitable for living in.

un·in·hab·it·ed /ˌənin'habitid/ ▸ adj. without inhabitants.

un·in·hib·it·ed /ˌənin'hibitid/ ▸ adj. expressing oneself or acting freely and naturally. ■ **un·in·hib·it·ed·ly** adv.

un·in·i·ti·at·ed /ˌənə'nisHēˌātid/ ▸ adj. without special knowledge or experience.

un·in·jured /ˌən'injərd/ ▸ adj. not harmed or damaged.

un·in·spired /ˌənin'spīrd/ ▸ adj. 1 not original or imaginative; dull. 2 not excited.

un·in·spir·ing /ˌənin'spīriNG/ ▸ adj. not exciting or interesting.

un·in·stall /ˌənin'stôl/ ▸ v. remove an application or file from a computer. ■ **un·in·stall·er** n.

un·in·sur·a·ble /ˌənin'sHŏŏrəbəl/ ▸ adj. not eligible for insurance cover.

un·in·sured /ˌənin'sHŏŏrd/ ▸ adj. not covered by insurance.

un·in·tel·li·gent /ˌən'inteləjənt/ ▸ adj. lacking intelligence.

un·in·tel·li·gi·ble /ˌənin'teləjəbəl/ ▸ adj. impossible to understand. ■ **un·in·tel·li·gi·bil·i·ty** /-ˌteləjə'bilətē/ n. **un·in·tel·li·gi·bly** /-blē/ adv.

un·in·tend·ed /ˌənin'tendid/ ▸ adj. not planned or meant.

un·in·ten·tion·al /ˌənin'tencHənl/ ▸ adj. not done on purpose. ■ **un·in·ten·tion·al·ly** adv.

un·in·ter·est·ed /ˌən'intristid, -'intəˌrestid/ ▸ adj. not interested or concerned.

> **USAGE**
> For an explanation of the meaning and use of **uninterested** and **disinterested**, see the note at **DISINTERESTED**.

un·in·ter·est·ing /ˌən'intristiNG, -'intəˌrestiNG/ ▸ adj. not interesting; dull.

un·in·ter·rupt·ed /ˌənˌintə'rəptid/ ▸ adj. 1 continuous. 2 not obstructed: *an uninterrupted view*. ■ **un·in·ter·rupt·ed·ly** adv.

un·in·vit·ed /ˌənin'vītid/ ▸ adj. arriving or acting without invitation.

un·in·vit·ing /ˌənin'vītiNG/ ▸ adj. not attractive; unpleasant.

un·in·volved /ˌənin'välvd/ ▸ adj. not involved.

un·ion /'yōōnyən/ ▸ n. 1 the action of uniting or the fact of being united: *he supported closer economic union with Europe*. 2 a labor union. 3 a society or association formed by people with a common interest or purpose. 4 (also **Union**) a political unit consisting of a number of states or provinces with the same central government. 5 (**the Union**) the northern states of the US in the American Civil War. 6 a state of harmony or agreement. 7 a marriage.

un·ion·ist /'yōōnyənist/ ▸ n. 1 a member of a

labor union. 2 (**Unionist**) a person in favor of the union of Northern Ireland with Great Britain. ■ **un·ion·ism** /-ˌnizəm/ n.

un·ion·ize /'yōōnyəˌnīz/ ▸ v. join or cause to join a labor union. ■ **un·ion·i·za·tion** /ˌyōōnyəni'zāsHən, -ˌnī'zā-/ n.

Un·ion Jack (also **Union flag**) ▸ n. the national flag of the UK.

un·ion shop ▸ n. a place of work where employers may hire nonunion workers who must join a labor union within an agreed time.

un·ion suit ▸ n. dated a single undergarment combining shirt and pants.

u·ni·po·lar /ˌyōōnə'pōlər/ ▸ adj. having or relating to a single pole or extremity.

u·nique /yōō'nēk/ ▸ adj. 1 being the only one of its kind; unlike anything else. 2 (**unique to**) belonging or connected to one particular person, group, or place. 3 very special or unusual. ■ **u·nique·ly** adv. **u·nique·ness** n.

> **USAGE**
> Strictly speaking, since the main meaning of **unique** is 'being the only one of its kind', it is impossible to use adverbs with it that modify its meaning, such as **really** or **quite**. However, **unique** has a less precise sense in addition to its main meaning: 'very special or unusual' (*a really unique opportunity*). Here, **unique** does not relate to an absolute state that cannot be modified, and so the use of **really** and similar adverbs is acceptable.

u·ni·sex /'yōōnəˌseks/ ▸ adj. designed for both sexes.

u·ni·son /'yōōnəsən, -zən/ ▸ n. 1 the fact of two or more things being said or happening at the same time. 2 a coincidence in pitch of musical sounds or notes.

u·nit /'yōōnit/ ▸ n. 1 an individual thing or person that is complete in itself but that can also form part of a larger whole. 2 a device, part, or item of furniture with a particular function: *a sink unit*. 3 a self-contained or distinct section of a building or group of buildings. 4 a subdivision of a larger military grouping. 5 a standard quantity in terms of which other quantities may be expressed. 6 one as a number or quantity. ■ **u·nit·ize** v.

u·ni·tard /'yōōnəˌtärd/ ▸ n. a tight-fitting one-piece garment covering the whole body.

U·ni·tar·i·an /ˌyōōni'te(ə)rēən/ ▸ n. a member of a Christian Church that believes in the unity of God and rejects the idea of the Trinity. ■ **U·ni·tar·i·an·ism** /-ˌnizəm/ n.

u·ni·tar·y /'yōōniˌterē/ ▸ adj. 1 forming a single entity or unit. 2 relating to a unit or units.

u·nite /yōō'nīt/ ▸ v. come or bring together for a common purpose or to form a whole: *councilors were united in their opposition to the plans*. ■ **u·nit·ed** adj. **u·ni·tive** /'yōōnətiv, yōō'nī-/ adj.

u·ni·ty /'yōōnətē/ ▸ n. (pl. **unities**) 1 the state of being united or forming a whole. 2 a thing forming a complex whole. 3 Mathematics the number one.

u·ni·ver·sal /ˌyōōnə'vərsəl/ ▸ adj. affecting or done by all people or things in the world or in a particular group; applicable to all cases: *the incidents caused universal concern*. ■ **u·ni·ver·sal·i·ty** /-vər'salətē/ n. **u·ni·ver·sal·ly** adv.

u·ni·ver·sal·ist /ˌyōōnə'vərsəlist/ ▸ n. (in

Christian belief) a person who believes that all humankind will eventually be saved. ■ **u·ni·ver·sal·ism** /-ˌlizəm/ n. **u·ni·ver·sal·is·tic** /-ˌvərsə'listik/ adj.

u·ni·ver·sal·ize /ˌyōōnə'vərsəˌlīz/ ▶ v. make something universal, or make something available for all. ■ **u·ni·ver·sal·i·za·tion** /-ˌvərsəli'zāsʜən/ n.

u·ni·ver·sal joint ▶ n. a joint that can transmit rotary power by a shaft at any selected angle.

U·ni·ver·sal Time (also **Universal Time Coordinated**) ▶ another term for GREENWICH MEAN TIME.

u·ni·verse /'yōōnəˌvərs/ ▶ n. **1** all existing matter and space considered as a whole; the cosmos. **2** a particular sphere of activity or experience.

u·ni·ver·si·ty /ˌyōōnə'vərsətē/ ▶ n. (pl. **universities**) a high-level educational institution in which students study for degrees and academic research is carried out.

U·NIX /'yōōniks/ (also **Unix**) ▶ n. trademark a widely used multiuser computer operating system.

un·just /ˌən'jəst/ ▶ adj. not just; unfair. ■ **un·just·ly** adv.

un·jus·ti·fi·a·ble /ˌən'jəstəˌfīəbəl, -ˌjəstə'fī-/ ▶ adj. impossible to justify. ■ **un·jus·ti·fi·a·bly** /-blē/ adv.

un·jus·ti·fied /ˌən'jəstəˌfīd/ ▶ adj. not justified.

un·kempt /ˌən'kem(p)t/ ▶ adj. having an untidy or disheveled appearance.

un·kind /ˌən'kīnd/ ▶ adj. not sympathetic, caring, or kind. ■ **un·kind·ly** adv. **un·kind·ness** n.

un·know·a·ble /ˌən'nōəbəl/ ▶ adj. not able to be known. ■ **un·know·a·bil·i·ty** /-ˌnōə'bilətē/ n.

un·know·ing /ˌən'nō-iNG/ ▶ adj. not knowing or aware. ▶ n. literary ignorance. ■ **un·know·ing·ly** adv.

un·known /ˌən'nōn/ ▶ adj. not known or familiar. ▶ n. an unknown person or thing.
– PHRASES **unknown to** without someone's knowledge.

un·known quan·ti·ty ▶ n. a person or thing whose nature, value, or significance is not known.

Un·known Sol·dier ▶ n. an unidentified representative member of a country's armed forces killed in war, buried with special honors in a national memorial.

un·la·beled /ˌən'lābəld/ (Brit. **unlabelled**) ▶ adj. without a label.

un·lace /ˌən'lās/ ▶ v. undo the laces of a shoe or garment.

un·lad·en /ˌən'lādn/ ▶ adj. not carrying a load.

un·la·dy·like /ˌən'lādēˌlīk/ ▶ adj. not appropriate for or behaving like a well-bred woman.

un·la·ment·ed /ˌənlə'mentid/ ▶ adj. not mourned or regretted.

un·latch /ˌən'lacʜ/ ▶ v. unfasten the latch of a door or gate.

un·law·ful /ˌən'lôfəl/ ▶ adj. not conforming to or permitted by law or rules. ■ **un·law·ful·ly** adv. **un·law·ful·ness** n.

USAGE
For an explanation of the difference between **unlawful** and **illegal**, see the note at ILLEGAL.

un·lead·ed /ˌən'ledid/ ▶ adj. (of gasoline) without added lead.

un·learn /ˌən'lərn/ ▶ v. (past and past part. **unlearned** or **unlearnt**) attempt to forget something that

has been learned.

un·learn·ed[1] /ˌən'lərnid/ ▶ adj. not well educated.

un·learn·ed[2] /ˌən'lərnd/ (also **unlearnt** /ˌən'lərnt/) ▶ adj. not having been learned.

un·leash /ˌən'lēsʜ/ ▶ v. **1** release an animal from a leash. **2** allow something strong or destructive to happen: *the US unleashed a full-scale military attack.*

un·leav·ened /ˌən'levənd/ ▶ adj. (of bread) made without yeast or other raising agent.

un·less /ən'les, ən-/ ▶ conj. except when; if not.

un·let·tered /ˌən'letərd/ ▶ adj. poorly educated or illiterate.

un·li·censed /ˌən'līsənst/ ▶ adj. not having an official license, especially for the sale of alcoholic drinks.

un·like /ˌən'līk/ ▶ prep. **1** different from; not like. **2** in contrast to. **3** uncharacteristic of. ▶ adj. different from each other. ■ **un·like·ness** n.

USAGE
It is not good English to use **unlike** as a conjunction (a word connecting words or clauses of a sentence together), as in *she was behaving unlike she'd ever behaved before.* Use **as** with a negative instead: *she was behaving as she'd never behaved before.*

un·like·ly /ˌən'līklē/ ▶ adj. (**unlikelier, unlikeliest**) not likely to happen or be the case; improbable. ■ **un·like·li·hood** n.

un·lim·it·ed /ˌən'limitid/ ▶ adj. not limited or restricted; infinite.

un·lined[1] /ˌən'līnd/ ▶ adj. not marked with lines or wrinkles.

un·lined[2] ▶ adj. without a lining.

un·list·ed /ˌən'listid/ ▶ adj. not included on a list, especially of telephone numbers or stock exchange prices.

un·lit /ˌən'lit/ ▶ adj. **1** not provided with lighting. **2** not having been lit.

un·liv·a·ble /ˌən'livəbəl/ ▶ adj. not able to be lived in; uninhabitable.

un·lived /ˌən'livd/ ▶ adj. (**unlived in**) not appearing to be inhabited.

un·load /ˌən'lōd/ ▶ v. **1** remove goods from a vehicle, ship, etc. **2** remove ammunition from a gun or film from a camera. **3** informal get rid of something.

un·lock /ˌən'läk/ ▶ v. **1** unfasten the lock of a door, container, etc., using a key. **2** make something previously inaccessible or unexploited available.

un·looked /ˌən'lŏŏkt/ ▶ adj. (**unlooked for**) unexpected; unforeseen.

un·loose /ˌən'lōōs/ ▶ v. undo or release something.

un·loos·en /ˌən'lōōsən/ ▶ v. another term for UNLOOSE.

un·loved /ˌən'ləvd/ ▶ adj. loved by no one.

un·love·ly /ˌən'ləvlē/ ▶ adj. not attractive; ugly.

un·luck·y /ˌən'ləkē/ ▶ adj. (**unluckier, unluckiest**) having, bringing, or resulting from bad luck. ■ **un·luck·i·ly** adv.

un·made /ˌən'mād/ ▶ adj. (of a bed) not arranged tidily.

un·man /ˌən'man/ ▶ v. (**unmans, unmanning, unmanned**) literary deprive a man of qualities traditionally associated with men, such as self-control or courage.

un·man·age·a·ble /ˌən'manijəbəl/

▸ **adj.** difficult or impossible to manage or control. ■ **un·man·age·a·bly** /-blē/ **adv.**

un·man·ly /,ən'manlē/ ▸ **adj.** not manly.

un·manned /,ən'mand/ ▸ **adj.** not having or needing a crew or staff.

un·man·ner·ly /,ən'manərlē/ ▸ **adj.** not well mannered.

un·marked /,ən'märkt/ ▸ **adj. 1** not marked. **2** not noticed.

un·mar·ried /,ən'marēd/ ▸ **adj.** not married; single.

un·mask /,ən'mask/ ▸ **v.** reveal someone's or something's true character or nature.

un·matched /,ən'macHt/ ▸ **adj.** not matched or equaled.

un·men·tion·a·ble /,ən'menCHənəbəl/ ▸ **adj.** too embarrassing or offensive to be spoken about.

un·mer·ci·ful /,ən'mərsəfəl/ ▸ **adj.** showing no mercy. ■ **un·mer·ci·ful·ly adv.**

un·mer·it·ed /,ən'meritid/ ▸ **adj.** not deserved.

un·met /,ən'met/ ▸ **adj.** (of a requirement) not achieved or fulfilled.

un·mind·ful /,ən'mīn(d)fəl/ ▸ **adj.** (**unmindful of**) not conscious or aware of something.

un·miss·a·ble /,ən'misəbəl/ ▸ **adj.** that should not or cannot be missed.

un·mis·tak·a·ble /,ənmə'stākəbəl/ (also **unmistakeable**) ▸ **adj.** not able to be mistaken for anything else. ■ **un·mis·tak·a·bly** /-blē/ **adv.**

un·mit·i·gat·ed /,ən'mitə,gātid/ ▸ **adj.** absolute; complete: *an unmitigated disaster.* ■ **un·mit·i·gat·ed·ly adv.**

un·mixed /,ən'mikst/ ▸ **adj.** not mixed.

un·mod·er·at·ed /,ən'mädə,rātid/ ▸ **adj.** (of an Internet bulletin board or chat room) not monitored for inappropriate or offensive content.

un·moor /,ən'mŏŏr/ ▸ **v.** release the moorings of a boat or ship.

un·mo·ti·vat·ed /,ən'mōtə,vātid/ ▸ **adj. 1** not motivated or enthusiastic. **2** without apparent motive: *an unmotivated attack.*

un·moved /,ən'mŏŏvd/ ▸ **adj. 1** not affected by emotion or excitement. **2** not changed in purpose or position.

un·mov·ing /,ən'mŏŏviNG/ ▸ **adj. 1** not moving; staying still. **2** not evoking emotion or excitement.

un·mu·si·cal /,ən'myŏŏzikəl/ ▸ **adj. 1** not pleasing to the ear. **2** not enjoying or skilled at playing music.

un·name·a·ble /,ən'nāməbəl/ (also **unnamable**) ▸ **adj.** unmentionable.

un·named /,ən'nāmd/ ▸ **adj.** not named.

un·nat·u·ral /,ən'nacH(ə)rəl/ ▸ **adj. 1** contrary to what is found in nature; abnormal or artificial. **2** different from what is normal or expected. ■ **un·nat·u·ral·ly adv. un·nat·u·ral·ness n.**

un·nav·i·ga·ble /,ən'navəgəbəl/ ▸ **adj.** not able to be sailed on by ships or boats.

un·nec·es·sar·y /,ən'nesə,serē/ ▸ **adj.** not necessary, or more than is necessary. ■ **un·nec·es·sar·i·ly** /-,nesə'se(ə)rəlē/ **adv.**

un·nerve /,ən'nərv/ ▸ **v.** make someone feel nervous or frightened. ■ **un·nerv·ing adj.**

un·no·tice·a·ble /,ən'nōtisəbəl/ ▸ **adj.** not easily observed or noticed.

un·no·ticed /,ən'nōtist/ ▸ **adj.** not noticed.

un·num·bered /,ən'nəmbərd/ ▸ **adj. 1** not given a number. **2** not counted, or not able to be counted.

un·ob·served /,ənəb'zərvd/ ▸ **adj.** not observed; unseen.

un·ob·struct·ed /,ənəb'strəktid, -äb-/ ▸ **adj.** not obstructed.

un·ob·tain·a·ble /,ənəb'tānəbəl/ ▸ **adj.** not able to be obtained.

un·ob·tru·sive /,ənəb'trŏŏsiv/ ▸ **adj.** not conspicuous or attracting attention. ■ **un·ob·tru·sive·ly adv. un·ob·tru·sive·ness n.**

un·oc·cu·pied /,ən'äkyə,pīd/ ▸ **adj.** not occupied.

un·of·fi·cial /,ənə'fisHəl/ ▸ **adj.** not officially authorized or confirmed. ■ **un·of·fi·cial·ly adv.**

un·o·pened /,ən'ōpənd/ ▸ **adj.** not opened.

un·op·posed /,ənə'pōzd/ ▸ **adj.** not opposed; unchallenged.

un·or·gan·ized /,ən'ôrgə,nīzd/ ▸ **adj.** not organized.

un·o·rig·i·nal /,ənə'rijənl/ ▸ **adj.** lacking originality. ■ **un·o·rig·i·nal·i·ty** /-,rijə'nalətē/ **n. un·o·rig·i·nal·ly adv.**

un·or·tho·dox /,ən'ôrTHə,däks/ ▸ **adj.** different from what is usual, traditional, or accepted. ■ **un·or·tho·dox·y n.**

un·os·ten·ta·tious /,ənästən'tāsHəs/ ▸ **adj.** not ostentatious or showy. ■ **un·os·ten·ta·tious·ly adv.**

un·pack /,ən'pak/ ▸ **v. 1** remove the contents of a suitcase, bag, container, etc. **2** separate something into its different elements in order to make it easier to understand.

un·paid /,ən'pād/ ▸ **adj. 1** (of a debt) not yet paid. **2** (of work or leave) done or taken without payment. **3** not receiving payment for work done.

un·paired /,ən'pe(ə)rd/ ▸ **adj. 1** not arranged in pairs. **2** not forming one of a pair.

un·pal·at·a·ble /,ən'palətəbəl/ ▸ **adj. 1** not pleasant to taste. **2** difficult to put up with or accept.

un·par·al·leled /,ən'parə,leld/ ▸ **adj.** having no parallel or equal; exceptional.

un·par·don·a·ble /,ən'pärdn-əbəl, -'pärdnə-/ ▸ **adj.** (of a fault or offense) unforgivable. ■ **un·par·don·a·bly** /-blē/ **adv.**

un·par·lia·men·ta·ry /,ən,pärlə'mentərē/ ▸ **adj.** (especially of language or procedures) against the rules of behavior of a parliament.

un·pas·teur·ized /,ən'pascHə,rīzd/ ▸ **adj.** not pasteurized.

un·pa·tri·ot·ic /,ən,pātrē'ätik/ ▸ **adj.** not patriotic. ■ **un·pa·tri·ot·i·cal·ly** /-(ə)lē/ **adv.**

un·paved /,ən'pāvd/ ▸ **adj.** not having a paved surface.

un·peo·pled /,ən'pēpəld/ ▸ **adj.** empty of people.

un·per·son /,ən'pərsən, -,pər-/ ▸ **n.** (pl. **unpersons**) a person whose name or existence is officially denied or ignored.

un·per·turbed /,ənpər'tərbd/ ▸ **adj.** not perturbed or worried.

un·pick /,ən'pik/ ▸ **v. 1** undo the stitches from a piece of sewing. **2** carefully analyze the different elements of something.

un·pin /,ən'pin/ ▸ **v.** (**unpins, unpinning, unpinned**) unfasten or detach something by removing a pin or pins.

un·pit·y·ing /,ən'pitē-iNG/ ▸ **adj.** not feeling or showing pity.

un·placed /ˌənˈplāst/ ▶ adj. chiefly Horse Racing not one of the first three (sometimes four) to finish in a race.

un·planned /ˌənˈpland/ ▶ adj. not planned.

un·play·a·ble /ˌənˈplāəbəl/ ▶ adj. 1 not able to be played or played on: *the field was unplayable.* 2 (of music) too difficult to perform.

un·pleas·ant /ˌənˈplezənt/ ▶ adj. 1 not pleasant. 2 not friendly or kind. ■ **un·pleas·ant·ly** adv.

un·pleas·ant·ness /ˌənˈplezəntnəs/ ▶ n. 1 the state or quality of being unpleasant. 2 bad feeling or quarreling between people.

un·plowed /ˌənˈploud/ ▶ adj. (of land) not having been plowed.

un·plug /ˌənˈpləg/ ▶ v. (**unplugs, unplugging, unplugged**) 1 disconnect an electrical device by removing its plug from a socket. 2 remove an obstacle or blockage from something.

un·plugged /ˌənˈpləgd/ ▶ adj. trademark (of pop or rock music) performed or recorded with acoustic rather than electrically amplified instruments.

un·plumbed /ˌənˈpləmd/ ▶ adj. 1 not provided with plumbing. 2 not fully explored or understood. ■ **un·plumb·a·ble** adj.

un·pol·ished /ˌənˈpälisht/ ▶ adj. 1 not having a polished surface. 2 (of a performance or piece of work) not having been refined or perfected.

un·pop·u·lar /ˌənˈpäpyələr/ ▶ adj. not liked or popular. ■ **un·pop·u·lar·i·ty** /-ˌpäpyəˈlaritē/ n.

un·pop·u·lat·ed /ˌənˈpäpyəˌlātid/ ▶ adj. without inhabitants.

un·pow·ered /ˌənˈpou(-ə)rd/ ▶ adj. (of a vehicle, boat, etc.) not propelled by burning a fuel such as gasoline.

un·prac·ticed /ˌənˈpraktist/ (Brit. **unpractised**) ▶ adj. not trained or experienced.

un·prec·e·dent·ed /ˌənˈpresəˌdentid/ ▶ adj. never done or known before. ■ **un·prec·e·dent·ed·ly** adv.

un·pre·dict·a·ble /ˌənpriˈdiktəbəl/ ▶ adj. 1 not able to be predicted. 2 changeable or unreliable. ■ **un·pre·dict·a·bil·i·ty** /-ˌdiktəˈbilətē/ n. **un·pre·dict·a·bly** /-blē/ adv.

un·prej·u·diced /ˌənˈprejədist/ ▶ adj. without prejudice; unbiased.

un·pre·med·i·tat·ed /ˌənpriˈmedəˌtātid, -prē-/ ▶ adj. not thought out or planned beforehand.

un·pre·pared /ˌənpriˈpe(ə)rd/ ▶ adj. 1 not ready or able to deal with something. 2 not made ready for use.

un·pre·pos·ses·sing /ˌənˌprēpəˈzesiNG/ ▶ adj. not attractive or appealing in appearance.

un·pres·sur·ized /ˌənˈpreshəˌrīzd/ ▶ adj. 1 (of a gas or its container) not having raised pressure that is produced or maintained artificially. 2 (of an aircraft cabin) not having normal atmospheric pressure maintained at a high altitude.

un·pre·ten·tious /ˌənpriˈtenchəs/ ▶ adj. not pretentious; modest or unassuming. ■ **un·pre·ten·tious·ly** adv. **un·pre·ten·tious·ness** n.

un·prin·ci·pled /ˌənˈprinsəpəld/ ▶ adj. not acting in accordance with moral principles.

un·print·a·ble /ˌənˈprintəbəl/ ▶ adj. (of words, comments, or thoughts) too offensive or shocking to be published.

un·prob·lem·at·ic /ˌənˌpräbləˈmatik/ ▶ adj. not presenting a problem or difficulty. ■ **un·prob·lem·at·i·cal·ly** /-ik(ə)lē/ adv.

un·proc·essed /ˌənˈpräˌsest, -səst-, -ˈprō-/ ▶ adj. not processed.

un·pro·duc·tive /ˌənprəˈdəktiv/ ▶ adj. 1 not producing or able to produce large amounts of goods, crops, etc. 2 not achieving much; not very useful.

un·pro·fes·sion·al /ˌənprəˈfeshənl/ ▶ adj. not in accordance with the standards expected in a particular profession. ■ **un·pro·fes·sion·al·ly** adv.

un·prof·it·a·ble /ˌənˈpräfitəbəl/ ▶ adj. 1 not making a profit. 2 not beneficial or useful.

un·prom·is·ing /ˌənˈpräməsiNG/ ▶ adj. not giving hope of future success or good results.

un·prompt·ed /ˌənˈpräm(p)tid/ ▶ adj. said or done without being prompted by someone else.

un·pro·nounce·a·ble /ˌənprəˈnounsəbəl/ ▶ adj. too difficult to pronounce.

un·pro·tect·ed /ˌənprəˈtektid/ ▶ adj. 1 not protected or kept safe from harm. 2 (of sex) performed without a condom.

un·prov·en /ˌənˈprōōvən/ (also **unproved**) ▶ adj. 1 not shown by evidence or argument to be true or to exist. 2 not tried and tested.

un·pro·voked /ˌənprəˈvōkt/ ▶ adj. (of an attack, crime, etc.) not directly provoked.

un·pub·lished /ˌənˈpəblisht/ ▶ adj. 1 (of a work) not published. 2 (of an author) having no writings published. ■ **un·pub·lish·a·ble** adj.

un·pun·ished /ˌənˈpənisht/ ▶ adj. (of an offense or offender) not receiving any punishment or penalty.

un·put·down·a·ble /ˌənˌpŏŏtˈdounəbəl/ ▶ adj. informal (of a book) so absorbing that one cannot stop reading it.

un·qual·i·fied /ˌənˈkwälәˌfīd/ ▶ adj. 1 not having the necessary qualifications or requirements. 2 without limitation; total: *an unqualified success.*

un·quan·ti·fi·a·ble /ˌənˈkwäntәˌfīәbәl, -ˌkwäntәˈfī-/ ▶ adj. impossible to express or measure.

un·quench·a·ble /ˌənˈkwenchəbəl/ ▶ adj. not able to be quenched or satisfied.

un·ques·tion·a·ble /ˌənˈkweschәnәbәl/ ▶ adj. not able to be disputed or doubted. ■ **un·ques·tion·a·bly** /-blē, -ˈkwesH-/ adv.

un·ques·tioned /ˌənˈkweschәnd/ ▶ adj. 1 not disputed or doubted; certain. 2 accepted without question. ■ **un·ques·tion·ing** adj.

un·qui·et /ˌənˈkwīət/ ▶ adj. 1 unable to be still; restless. 2 uneasy or anxious.

un·quote /ˌənˈkwōt, ˈənˌkwōt/ ▶ v. see QUOTE. —— **UNQUOTE** at QUOTE.

un·quot·ed /ˌənˈkwōtid/ ▶ adj. not quoted or listed on a stock exchange.

un·ranked /ˌənˈraNGkt/ ▶ adj. not having achieved or been given a rank or ranking.

un·rav·el /ˌənˈravəl/ ▶ v. (**unravels, unraveling, unraveled**) 1 undo twisted, knitted, or woven threads. 2 become undone. 3 investigate and solve a mystery or puzzle. 4 begin to fail or collapse: *the peace process began to unravel.*

un·reach·a·ble /ˌənˈrēcHəbəl/ ▶ adj. unable to be reached or contacted.

un·re·ac·tive /ˌənrēˈaktiv/ ▶ adj. having little tendency to react chemically.

un·read /ˌənˈred/ ▶ adj. not having been read.

un·read·a·ble /ˌənˈrēdəbəl/ ▶ adj. 1 not clear enough to read; illegible. 2 too dull or difficult to be worth reading. ■ **un·read·a·bil·i·ty**

/-ˌrēdəˈbilətē/ **n. un·read·a·bly** /-blē/ **adv.**

un·read·y /ˌənˈredē/ ▶ **adj.** not ready or prepared.

un·re·al /ˌənˈrē(ə)l/ ▶ **adj. 1** imaginary or not seeming real. **2** unrealistic. ■ **un·re·al·i·ty** /-rēˈalətē/ **n.**

un·re·al·is·tic /ˌənrēəˈlistik/ ▶ **adj. 1** not having a sensible idea of what can be achieved or expected. **2** not representing things in a realistic way. ■ **un·re·al·is·ti·cal·ly** /-ik(ə)lē/ **adv.**

un·re·al·ized /ˌənˈrēəˌlīzd/ ▶ **adj. 1** not achieved or created. **2** not converted into money: *unrealized property assets.*

un·rea·son /ˌənˈrēzən/ ▶ **n.** lack of reasonable thought; irrationality.

un·rea·son·a·ble /ˌənˈrēz(ə)nəbəl/ ▶ **adj. 1** not guided by or based on good sense. **2** beyond the limits of what is acceptable or achievable. ■ **un·rea·son·a·ble·ness n. un·rea·son·a·bly** /-blē/ **adv.**

un·rea·son·ing /ˌənˈrēz(ə)niNG/ ▶ **adj.** not guided by or based on reason; illogical.

un·re·cep·tive /ˌənriˈseptiv/ ▶ **adj.** not receptive.

un·rec·og·niz·a·ble /ˌənˈrekəgˌnīzəbəl/ ▶ **adj.** not able to be recognized. ■ **un·rec·og·niz·a·bly** /-blē/ **adv.**

un·rec·og·nized /ˌənˈrekəgˌnīzd/ ▶ **adj. 1** not identified from previous encounters or knowledge. **2** not acknowledged as valid.

un·re·con·struct·ed /ˌənˌrēkənˈstrəktid/ ▶ **adj.** not reconciled or converted to the current political theory or movement.

un·re·cord·ed /ˌənriˈkôrdid/ ▶ **adj.** not recorded.

un·reel /ˌənˈrēl/ ▶ **v. 1** unwind something. **2** (of movie film) wind from one reel to another during projection.

un·re·fined /ˌənriˈfīnd/ ▶ **adj. 1** not processed to remove impurities. **2** not elegant or cultured.

un·re·gen·er·ate /ˌənriˈjenərət/ ▶ **adj.** not reforming or showing repentance; obstinately wrong or bad.

un·reg·is·tered /ˌənˈrejəstərd/ ▶ **adj.** not officially recognized and recorded.

un·reg·u·lat·ed /ˌənˈregyəˌlātid/ ▶ **adj.** not controlled or supervised by regulations or laws.

un·re·hearsed /ˌənriˈhərst/ ▶ **adj.** not rehearsed.

un·re·lat·ed /ˌənriˈlātid/ ▶ **adj.** not related.

un·re·leased /ˌənriˈlēst/ ▶ **adj.** (especially of a movie or recording) not released.

un·re·lent·ing /ˌənriˈlenting/ ▶ **adj. 1** not stopping or becoming weaker. **2** refusing to relent or give in. ■ **un·re·lent·ing·ly adv.**

un·re·li·a·ble /ˌənriˈlīəbəl/ ▶ **adj.** not able to be relied on. ■ **un·re·li·a·bil·i·ty** /ˌənriˌlīəˈbilətē/ **n. un·re·li·a·bly** /-blē/ **adv.**

un·re·lieved /ˌənriˈlēvd/ ▶ **adj.** lacking variation or change; monotonous. ■ **un·re·liev·ed·ly** /-ˈlēvidlē/ **adv.**

un·re·mark·a·ble /ˌənriˈmärkəbəl/ ▶ **adj.** not particularly interesting or surprising.

un·re·marked /ˌənriˈmärkt/ ▶ **adj.** not noticed or remarked on.

un·re·mit·ting /ˌənriˈmiting/ ▶ **adj.** never relaxing or slackening. ■ **un·re·mit·ting·ly adv.**

un·re·mu·ner·a·tive /ˌənriˈmyōōnərətiv, -ˌrātiv/ ▶ **adj.** bringing little or no profit or income.

un·re·peat·a·ble /ˌənriˈpētəbəl/ ▶ **adj. 1** not able to be repeated. **2** too offensive or shocking to be said again.

un·re·pent·ant /ˌənriˈpentənt/ ▶ **adj.** showing no regret for one's wrongdoings. ■ **un·re·pent·ant·ly adv.**

un·re·port·ed /ˌənriˈpôrtəd/ ▶ **adj.** not reported.

un·rep·re·sent·a·tive /ˌənˌrepriˈzentətiv/ ▶ **adj.** not typical of a class or group.

un·re·quit·ed /ˌənriˈkwītid/ ▶ **adj.** (of love) not returned.

un·re·served /ˌənriˈzərvd/ ▶ **adj. 1** without reservations; complete. **2** frank and open. **3** not set apart for a particular purpose or booked in advance. ■ **un·re·serv·ed·ly adv.**

un·re·solved /ˌənriˈzälvd, -ˈzôlvd/ ▶ **adj.** (of a problem, dispute, etc.) not resolved.

un·re·spon·sive /ˌənriˈspänsiv/ ▶ **adj.** not responsive. ■ **un·re·spon·sive·ness n.**

un·rest /ˌənˈrest/ ▶ **n.** a state of rebellious dissatisfaction in a group of people: *years of industrial unrest.*

un·re·strained /ˌənriˈstrānd/ ▶ **adj.** not restrained or restricted. ■ **un·re·strain·ed·ly** /-ˈstrānidlē/ **adv.**

un·re·strict·ed /ˌənriˈstriktid/ ▶ **adj.** not limited or restricted.

un·re·ward·ing /ˌənrəˈwôrding/ ▶ **adj.** not rewarding or satisfying.

un·ripe /ˌənˈrīp/ ▶ **adj.** not ripe.

un·ri·valed /ˌənˈrīvəld/ (Brit. **unrivalled**) ▶ **adj.** greater or better than all others.

un·roll /ˌənˈrōl/ ▶ **v.** open or cause to open out from a rolled-up state.

un·ro·man·tic /ˌənrōˈmantik, ˌənrə-/ ▶ **adj.** not romantic.

un·ruf·fled /ˌənˈrəfəld/ ▶ **adj. 1** (of a person) calm and unperturbed. **2** not disordered or disturbed.

un·ru·ly /ˌənˈrōōlē/ ▶ **adj.** (**unrulier, unruliest**) disorderly and disruptive; difficult to control. ■ **un·ru·li·ness n.**

un·sad·dle /ˌənˈsadl/ ▶ **v.** remove the saddle from a horse.

un·safe /ˌənˈsāf/ ▶ **adj. 1** not safe; dangerous. **2** Law (of a verdict or conviction) not based on reliable evidence and likely to constitute a miscarriage of justice. **3** (of sexual activity) in which people do not take precautions to protect themselves against sexually transmitted diseases such as AIDS.

un·said /ˌənˈsed/ past and past participle of UNSAY ▶ **adj.** not said or expressed.

un·sal·a·ble /ˌənˈsāləbəl/ (also **unsaleable**) ▶ **adj.** not able to be sold.

un·salt·ed /ˌənˈsôltid/ ▶ **adj.** without added salt.

un·san·i·tar·y /ˌənˈsaniˌterē/ ▶ **adj.** not hygienic.

un·sat·is·fac·to·ry /ˌənˌsatəsˈfakt(ə)rē/ ▶ **adj. 1** not good enough. **2** Law another term for UNSAFE. ■ **un·sat·is·fac·to·ri·ly** /-ˈfakt(ə)rəlē/ **adv.**

un·sat·is·fied /ˌənˈsatisˌfīd/ ▶ **adj.** not satisfied.

un·sat·is·fy·ing /ˌənˈsatisˌfīiNG/ ▶ **adj.** not satisfying.

un·sat·u·rat·ed /ˌənˈsaCHəˌrātid/ ▶ **adj.** Chemistry (of fats) having double and triple bonds between carbon atoms in their molecules and as a consequence being more easily processed by the body.

un·sa·vor·y /ˌənˈsāv(ə)rē/ (Brit. **unsavoury**) ▶ **adj. 1** unpleasant to taste, smell, or look at. **2** not morally respectable; disreputable.

un·say /ˌənˈsā/ ▶ **v.** (past and past part. **unsaid**) withdraw or retract a statement.

un·say·a·ble /ˌənˈsāəbəl/ ▶ **adj.** not able to

un·scarred /ˌənˈskärd/ ▶ adj. not scarred or damaged.

un·scathed /ˌənˈskāT͟Hd/ ▶ adj. without suffering any injury, damage, or harm.

un·scent·ed /ˌənˈsentid/ ▶ adj. not scented.

un·sched·uled /ˌənˈskejo͞old, -əld/ ▶ adj. not scheduled.

un·schooled /ˌənˈsko͞old/ ▶ adj. **1** lacking schooling or training. **2** not affected; natural and spontaneous.

un·sci·en·tif·ic /ˌənˌsīənˈtifik/ ▶ adj. not in accordance with scientific principles or methods. ■ **un·sci·en·tif·i·cal·ly** /-ik(ə)lē/ adv.

un·scram·ble /ˌənˈskrambəl/ ▶ v. restore a scrambled broadcast, message, etc., to an intelligible or readable state.

un·screened /ˌənˈskrēnd/ ▶ adj. **1** not subjected to testing or investigation by screening. **2** not shown or broadcast.

un·screw /ˌənˈskro͞o/ ▶ v. unfasten something by twisting it.

un·script·ed /ˌənˈskriptid/ ▶ adj. said or delivered without a prepared script; impromptu.

un·scru·pu·lous /ˌənˈskro͞opyələs/ ▶ adj. without moral principles; dishonest or unfair. ■ **un·scru·pu·lous·ly** adv. **un·scru·pu·lous·ness** n.

un·seal /ˌənˈsēl/ ▶ v. remove or break the seal of something.

un·sealed /ˌənˈsēld/ ▶ adj. not sealed.

un·sea·son·a·ble /ˌənˈsēzənəbəl/ ▶ adj. (of weather) unusual for the time of year. ■ **un·sea·son·a·bly** /-blē/ adv.

un·sea·son·al /ˌənˈsēzənəl/ ▶ adj. (especially of weather) unusual or inappropriate for the time of year.

un·sea·soned /ˌənˈsēzənd/ ▶ adj. **1** (of food) not flavored with salt, pepper, or other spices. **2** (of lumber) not treated for building purposes. **3** (of firewood) not aged or dry; green.

un·seat /ˌənˈsēt/ ▶ v. **1** make someone fall from a saddle or seat. **2** remove a government or person in authority from power.

un·se·cured /ˌənsiˈkyo͞ord/ ▶ adj. **1** (of a loan) made without an asset given as security. **2** not made secure or safe.

un·seed·ed /ˌənˈsēdid/ ▶ adj. (of a competitor in a sports tournament) not seeded.

un·see·ing /ˌənˈsēiNG/ ▶ adj. with one's eyes open but without noticing or seeing anything. ■ **un·see·ing·ly** adv.

un·seem·ly /ˌənˈsēmlē/ ▶ adj. (of behavior or actions) not proper or appropriate. ■ **un·seem·li·ness** n.

un·seen /ˌənˈsēn/ ▶ adj. not seen or noticed.

un·self·con·scious /ˌənˌselfˈkänsHəs/ ▶ adj. not shy or embarrassed. ■ **un·self·con·scious·ly** adv. **un·self·con·scious·ness** n.

un·sel·fish /ˌənˈselfisH/ ▶ adj. not selfish. ■ **un·self·ish·ly** adv. **un·self·ish·ness** n.

un·sen·ti·men·tal /ˌənˌsentəˈmen(t)l/ ▶ adj. not displaying or influenced by sentimental feelings. ■ **un·sen·ti·men·tal·ly** adv.

un·se·ri·ous /ˌənˈsi(ə)rēəs/ ▶ adj. not serious; lighthearted.

un·ser·vice·a·ble /ˌənˈsərvəsəbəl/ ▶ adj. not in working order; unfit for use.

un·set·tle /ˌənˈsetl/ ▶ v. make anxious or uneasy;

disturb: *the crisis has unsettled financial markets.* ■ **un·set·tling** adj.

un·set·tled /ˌənˈsetld/ ▶ adj. **1** changeable or likely to change: *unsettled weather.* **2** agitated; uneasy. **3** not yet resolved.

un·sex /ˌənˈseks/ ▶ v. deprive someone of their gender, sexuality, or the characteristic features of one or the other sex.

un·shack·le /ˌənˈsHakəl/ ▶ v. release someone from shackles or other restraints.

un·shak·a·ble /ˌənˈsHākəbəl/ (also **unshakeable**) ▶ adj. (of a belief, feeling, etc.) firm and unable to be changed or disputed.

un·shak·en /ˌənˈsHākən/ ▶ adj. not having changed or weakened: *their trust in him remains unshaken.*

un·shav·en /ˌənˈsHāvən/ ▶ adj. not having shaved or been shaved.

un·sheathe /ˌənˈsHēT͟H/ ▶ v. pull a knife or similar weapon out of a sheath.

un·shed /ˌənˈsHed/ ▶ adj. (of tears) welling in a person's eyes but not falling.

un·shelled /ˌənˈsHeld/ ▶ adj. not extracted from its shell.

un·ship /ˌənˈsHip/ ▶ v. (**unships, unshipping, unshipped**) **1** remove an oar, mast, or other object from a fixed or regular position. **2** unload cargo from a ship or boat.

un·shock·a·ble /ˌənˈsHakəbəl/ ▶ adj. impossible to shock.

un·shorn /ˌənˈsHôrn/ ▶ adj. (of hair or wool) not cut or shorn.

un·sight·ed /ˌənˈsītid/ ▶ adj. **1** lacking the power of sight. **2** (especially in sports) prevented from having a clear view.

un·sight·ly /ˌənˈsītlē/ ▶ adj. unpleasant to look at; ugly. ■ **un·sight·li·ness** n.

un·signed /ˌənˈsīnd/ ▶ adj. **1** not identified or authorized by a person's signature. **2** (of a musician or athlete) not having signed a contract of employment.

un·sink·a·ble /ˌənˈsiNGkəbəl/ ▶ adj. unable to be sunk.

un·skilled /ˌənˈskild/ ▶ adj. not having or requiring special skill or training.

un·skill·ful /ˌənˈskilfəl/ (Brit. also **unskilful**) ▶ adj. not having or showing skill. ■ **un·skill·ful·ly** adv.

un·sling /ˌənˈsliNG/ ▶ v. (past and past part. **unslung**) remove something from the place where it has been slung or suspended.

un·smil·ing /ˌənˈsmīliNG/ ▶ adj. not smiling; serious or unfriendly. ■ **un·smil·ing·ly** adv.

un·so·cia·ble /ˌənˈsōsHəbəl/ ▶ adj. **1** not enjoying the company of other people. **2** not contributing to friendly relationships between people.

un·so·cial /ˌənˈsōsHəl/ ▶ adj. antisocial.

un·sold /ˌənˈsōld/ ▶ adj. (of an item) not sold.

un·so·lic·it·ed /ˌənsəˈlisitid/ ▶ adj. not asked for.

un·solved /ˌənˈsälvd, -ˈsôlvd/ ▶ adj. not solved.

un·so·phis·ti·cat·ed /ˌənsəˈfistəˌkātid/ ▶ adj. **1** lacking experience or taste in matters of culture or fashion. **2** not complicated or highly developed; basic.

un·sort·ed /ˌənˈsôrtid/ ▶ adj. not sorted or arranged.

un·sound /ˌənˈsound/ ▶ adj. **1** not safe or strong; in poor condition. **2** not based on reliable evidence or reasoning; unreliable or unacceptable.

un·spar·ing /ˌənˈspe(ə)riNG/ ▶ adj. merciless; severe. ■ **un·spar·ing·ly** adv.

un·speak·a·ble /ˌənˈspēkəbəl/ ▶ adj. **1** not able to be expressed in words. **2** too bad or horrific to express in words. ■ **un·speak·a·bly** /-blē/ adv.

un·spe·cif·ic /ˌənspəˈsifik/ ▶ adj. not specific; vague.

un·spec·i·fied /ˌənˈspesəˌfīd/ ▶ adj. not stated clearly or exactly.

un·spec·tac·u·lar /ˌənspekˈtakyələr, -spək-/ ▶ adj. not spectacular; unremarkable.

un·spoiled /ˌənˈspoild/ (Brit. also **unspoilt** /ˌənˈspoilt/) ▶ adj. not spoiled, in particular (of a place) largely unaffected by building or development.

un·spo·ken /ˌənˈspōkən/ ▶ adj. understood without being expressed in speech: *an unspoken agreement.*

un·spool /ˌənˈspo͞ol/ ▶ v. unwind or be unwound from a spool.

un·sport·ing /ˌənˈspôrtiNG/ ▶ adj. not fair or sportsmanlike. ■ **un·sport·ing·ly** adv.

un·sports·man·like /ˌənˈspôrtsmənˌlīk/ ▶ adj. not behaving according to the spirit of fair play in a particular sport.

un·sprung /ˌənˈsprəNG/ ▶ adj. not provided with springs.

un·sta·ble /ˌənˈstābəl/ ▶ adj. (**unstabler**, **unstablest**) **1** likely to change or collapse; not stable. **2** prone to sudden changes of mood or mental health problems.

un·stained /ˌənˈstānd/ ▶ adj. not stained.

un·stat·ed /ˌənˈstātid/ ▶ adj. not stated or declared.

un·stead·y /ˌənˈstedē/ ▶ adj. (**unsteadier**, **unsteadiest**) **1** liable to fall or shake. **2** not regular or controlled. ■ **un·stead·i·ly** adv. **un·stead·i·ness** n.

un·stick /ˌənˈstik/ ▶ v. (past and past part. **unstuck** /ˌənˈstək/) separate a thing that is stuck to another.

un·stint·ing /ˌənˈstintiNG/ ▶ adj. given or giving without restraint. ■ **un·stint·ed** adj. **un·stint·ing·ly** adv.

un·stop·pa·ble /ˌənˈstäpəbəl/ ▶ adj. impossible to stop or prevent. ■ **un·stop·pa·bly** /-blē/ adv.

un·stop·per /ˌənˈstäpər/ ▶ v. remove the stopper from a container.

un·stressed /ˌənˈstrest/ ▶ adj. (of a syllable) not pronounced with stress.

un·string /ˌənˈstriNG/ ▶ v. (past and past part. **unstrung** /ˌənˈstrəNG/) **1** (usu. as adj. **unstrung**) unnerve or upset: *a mind unstrung by loneliness.* **2** remove or relax the string or strings of a bow or musical instrument.

un·struc·tured /ˌənˈstrəkchərd/ ▶ adj. without formal organization or structure.

un·stuck /ˌənˈstək/ ▶ past and past participle of UNSTICK.
– PHRASES **come unstuck** informal fail.

un·stud·ied /ˌənˈstədēd/ ▶ adj. not forced or artificial; natural.

un·stuff·y /ˌənˈstəfē/ ▶ adj. friendly, informal, and approachable.

un·sub·scribe /ˌənsəbˈskrīb/ ▶ v. cancel a subscription, especially to an electronic mailing list.

un·sub·stan·tial /ˌənsəbˈstanCHəl/ ▶ adj. having little or no solidity, reality, or factual basis.

un·sub·stan·ti·at·ed /ˌənsəbˈstanCHēˌātid/ ▶ adj. not supported or proven by evidence.

un·sub·tle /ˌənˈsətl/ ▶ adj. not subtle; obvious. ■ **un·sub·tly** adv.

un·suc·cess·ful /ˌənsəkˈsesfəl/ ▶ adj. not successful. ■ **un·suc·cess·ful·ly** adv.

un·suit·a·ble /ˌənˈso͞otəbəl/ ▶ adj. not right or appropriate for a particular purpose or occasion. ■ **un·suit·a·bil·i·ty** /-ˌso͞otəˈbilətē/ n. **un·suit·a·bly** /-blē/ adv.

un·suit·ed /ˌənˈso͞otid/ ▶ adj. lacking the right or necessary qualities for something: *he was totally unsuited for the job.*

un·sul·lied /ˌənˈsəlēd/ ▶ adj. not spoiled or made impure.

un·sung /ˌənˈsəNG/ ▶ adj. not celebrated or praised: *unsung heroes.*

un·su·per·vised /ˌənˈso͞opərˌvīzd/ ▶ adj. not done or acting under supervision.

un·sup·port·a·ble /ˌənsəˈpôrtəbəl/ ▶ adj. insupportable.

un·sup·port·ed /ˌənsəˈpôrtid/ ▶ adj. **1** not supported. **2** not proven to be true by evidence or facts.

un·sure /ˌənˈSHo͝or/ ▶ adj. **1** lacking confidence. **2** not fixed or certain. ■ **un·sure·ly** adv. **un·sure·ness** n.

un·sur·faced /ˌənˈsərfist/ ▶ adj. (of a road or path) not provided with a hard-wearing upper layer.

un·sur·pass·a·ble /ˌənsərˈpasəbəl/ ▶ adj. not able to be bettered or exceeded.

un·sur·passed /ˌənsərˈpast/ ▶ adj. better or greater than any other.

un·sur·pris·ing /ˌənsə(r)ˈprīziNG/ ▶ adj. expected and so not causing surprise. ■ **un·sur·pris·ing·ly** adv.

un·sus·pect·ed /ˌənsəˈspektid/ ▶ adj. **1** not known or thought to exist; not imagined as possible. **2** not regarded with suspicion.

un·sus·pect·ing /ˌənsəˈspektiNG/ ▶ adj. not aware of the presence of danger; feeling no suspicion. ■ **un·sus·pect·ing·ly** adv.

un·sus·tain·a·ble /ˌənsəˈstānəbəl/ ▶ adj. **1** not able to be maintained at the current rate or level. **2** not able to be upheld or defended. **3** upsetting the ecological balance by depleting natural resources. ■ **un·sus·tain·a·bly** /-blē/ adv.

un·swayed /ˌənˈswād/ ▶ adj. not influenced or affected.

un·sweet·ened /ˌənˈswētnd/ ▶ adj. (of food or drink) without added sugar or other sweetener.

un·swerv·ing /ˌənˈswərviNG/ ▶ adj. not changing or becoming weaker. ■ **un·swerv·ing·ly** adv.

un·sym·met·ri·cal /ˌənsəˈmetrikəl/ ▶ adj. not symmetrical.

un·sym·pa·thet·ic /ˌənˌsimpəˈTHetik/ ▶ adj. **1** not sympathetic. **2** not showing approval of an idea or action. **3** not likable. ■ **un·sym·pa·thet·i·cal·ly** /-ik(ə)lē/ adv.

un·sys·tem·at·ic /ˌənˌsistəˈmatik/ ▶ adj. not done or acting according to a fixed plan or system. ■ **un·sys·tem·at·i·cal·ly** /-ik(ə)lē/ adv.

un·taint·ed /ˌənˈtān(t)id/ ▶ adj. not contaminated or tainted.

un·tamed /ˌənˈtāmd/ ▶ adj. not tamed or controlled. ■ **un·tame·a·ble** (also **untamable**) adj.

un·tan·gle /ˌənˈtaNGgəl/ ▶ v. **1** undo something

that has become twisted or tangled. **2** make something complicated or confusing easier to understand or deal with.

un·tapped /ˌən'tapt/ ▸ adj. (of a resource) not yet exploited or used.

un·tar·nished /ˌən'tärnisHt/ ▸ adj. **1** (of metal) not tarnished. **2** not spoiled or ruined.

un·tast·ed /ˌən'tāstid/ ▸ adj. (of food or drink) not sampled.

un·taught /ˌən'tôt/ ▸ adj. **1** not having been taught or educated. **2** not gained by teaching; natural or spontaneous.

un·ten·a·ble /ˌən'tenəbəl/ ▸ adj. not able to be maintained or defended against attack or objection.

un·tend·ed /ˌən'tendid/ ▸ adj. not cared for or looked after; neglected.

un·ten·ured /ˌən'tenyərd/ ▸ adj. (of a college teacher or post) without tenure; not permanent.

Un·ter·mensch /'o͞ontər,menCH/ ▸ n. (pl. **Untermenschen** /-,menCHən/) a person considered racially or socially inferior.

un·test·ed /ˌən'testid/ ▸ adj. not subjected to testing; unproven. ■ **un·test·a·ble** adj.

un·think·a·ble /ˌən'THiNGkəbəl/ ▸ adj. too unlikely or undesirable to be considered a possibility. ■ **un·think·a·bly** /-blē/ adv.

un·think·ing /ˌən'THiNGkiNG/ ▸ adj. without proper consideration. ■ **un·think·ing·ly** adv.

un·thought /ˌən'THôt/ ▸ adj. (**unthought of**) not imagined or dreamed of.

un·threat·en·ing /ˌən'THretniNG/ ▸ adj. not threatening.

un·ti·dy /ˌən'tīdē/ ▸ adj. (**untidier, untidiest**) **1** not arranged tidily. **2** (of a person) not keeping things tidy or well organized. ■ **un·ti·di·ly** adv. **un·ti·di·ness** n.

un·tie /ˌən'tī/ ▸ v. (**unties, untying, untied**) undo or unfasten something tied.

un·til /ˌən'til, ən-/ ▸ prep. & conj. up to the point in time or the event mentioned.

> **USAGE**
> For an explanation of the difference between **until** and **till**, see the note at **TILL¹**.

un·time·ly /ˌən'tīmlē/ ▸ adj. **1** happening or done at an unsuitable time; inappropriate. **2** (of a death or end) happening too soon or sooner than normal. ■ **un·time·li·ness** n.

un·tir·ing /ˌən'tīriNG/ ▸ adj. continuing at the same rate without loss of energy. ■ **un·tir·ing·ly** adv.

un·ti·tled /ˌən'tītld/ ▸ adj. **1** (of a book or other work) having no title. **2** not having a title indicating high social or official rank.

un·to /'ənto͞o/ ▸ prep. **1** old-fashioned term for **TO**. **2** old-fashioned term for **UNTIL**.

un·told /ˌən'tōld/ ▸ adj. **1** too much or too many to be counted: *thieves caused untold damage.* **2** not told or recounted.

un·touch·a·ble /ˌən'təCHəbəl/ ▸ adj. **1** not able to be touched or affected. **2** unable to be matched or rivaled. ▸ n. a member of the lowest caste in Hindu society. ■ **un·touch·a·bil·i·ty** /-,təCHə'bilitē/ n.

> **USAGE**
> The use of the term **untouchable** to refer to a member of the lowest caste in Hindu society was declared illegal in the constitution of India in 1949 and of Pakistan in 1953. The official term today is **scheduled caste**.

un·touched /ˌən'təCHt/ ▸ adj. **1** not handled, used, or tasted. **2** not affected, changed, or damaged in any way.

un·to·ward /ˌən'tôrd, -t(ə)'wôrd/ ▸ adj. unexpected and inappropriate or unwelcome.

un·trace·a·ble /ˌən'trāsəbəl/ ▸ adj. unable to be found or traced.

un·tracked /ˌən'trakt/ ▸ adj. (of land) without a path or tracks.

un·trained /ˌən'trānd/ ▸ adj. not having been trained in a particular skill.

un·tram·meled /ˌən'traməld/ (Brit. also **untrammelled**) ▸ adj. not restricted or hampered.

un·trans·lat·a·ble /ˌən,trans'lātəbəl, -,tranz-/ ▸ adj. not able to be translated.

un·treat·a·ble /ˌən'trētəbəl/ ▸ adj. for whom or which no medical care is available or possible.

un·treat·ed /ˌən'trētid/ ▸ adj. **1** not given medical care. **2** not treated by the use of a chemical, physical, or biological process, substance, etc.

un·tried /ˌən'trīd/ ▸ adj. not yet tested; inexperienced.

un·trod·den /ˌən'trädn/ ▸ adj. not having been walked on.

un·trou·bled /ˌən'trəbəld/ ▸ adj. not troubled.

un·true /ˌən'tro͞o/ ▸ adj. **1** false or incorrect. **2** not faithful or loyal.

un·trust·wor·thy /ˌən'trəst,wərTHē/ ▸ adj. unable to be trusted. ■ **un·trust·wor·thi·ness** n.

un·truth /ˌən'tro͞oTH/ ▸ n. (pl. **untruths**) **1** a lie. **2** the quality of being false.

un·truth·ful /ˌən'tro͞oTHfəl/ ▸ adj. not truthful. ■ **un·truth·ful·ly** adv. **un·truth·ful·ness** n.

un·tucked /ˌən'təkt/ ▸ adj. with the edges or ends hanging loose; not tucked in.

un·tu·tored /ˌən't(y)o͞otərd/ ▸ adj. not formally taught or trained.

un·twist /ˌən'twist/ ▸ v. open something from a twisted position.

un·ty·ing /ˌən'tī-iNG/ ▸ present participle of **UNTIE**.

un·typ·i·cal /ˌən'tipikəl/ ▸ adj. unusual or uncharacteristic. ■ **un·typ·i·cal·ly** /-ik(ə)lē/ adv.

un·us·a·ble /ˌən'yo͞ozəbəl/ ▸ adj. not fit to be used.

un·used ▸ adj. **1** /ˌən'yo͞ozd/ not used. **2** /ˌən'yo͞ost/ (**unused to**) not accustomed to something.

un·u·su·al /ˌən'yo͞oZHo͞oəl/ ▸ adj. **1** not habitually or commonly done or occurring. **2** remarkable; exceptional. ■ **un·u·su·al·ly** adv. **un·u·su·al·ness** n.

un·ut·ter·a·ble /ˌən'ətərəbəl/ ▸ adj. too great or awful to describe. ■ **un·ut·ter·a·bly** /-blē/ adv.

un·ut·tered /ˌən'ətərd/ ▸ adj. not spoken or expressed.

un·var·ied /ˌən've(ə)rēd/ ▸ adj. not varied.

un·var·nished /ˌən'värnisHt/ ▸ adj. **1** not varnished. **2** plain and straightforward: *the unvarnished truth.*

un·var·y·ing /ˌən've(ə)rē-iNG/ ▸ adj. not varying. ■ **un·var·y·ing·ly** adv.

un·veil /ˌən'vāl/ ▸ v. **1** show or announce publicly for the first time: *he unveiled plans to crack down on crime.* **2** remove a veil or covering from a new monument or work of art as part of a public ceremony. **3** remove a veil from someone's face.

un·ven·ti·lat·ed /ˌən'ventl,ātid/ ▸ adj. not ventilated.

un·ver·i·fi·a·ble /ˌən'verə,fīəbəl, ˌən,verə'fī-/

▸ **adj.** unable to be verified.

un·ver·i·fied /ˌənˈverəˌfīd/ ▸ **adj.** not verified.

un·versed /ˌənˈvərst/ ▸ **adj.** (**unversed in**) not experienced or skilled in.

un·vi·a·ble /ˌənˈvīəbəl/ ▸ **adj.** not capable of working successfully.

un·voiced /ˌənˈvoist/ ▸ **adj.** 1 not expressed in words. 2 (of a speech sound) produced without vibration of the vocal cords.

un·want·ed /ˌənˈwäntid, -ˈwônt-/ ▸ **adj.** not wanted.

un·war·rant·a·ble /ˌənˈwôrəntəbəl, -ˈwär-/ ▸ **adj.** unjustifiable. ■ **un·war·rant·a·bly** /-blē/ **adv.**

un·war·rant·ed /ˌənˈwôrəntid, -ˈwär-/ ▸ **adj.** not warranted.

un·war·y /ˌənˈwe(ə)rē/ ▸ **adj.** not cautious. ■ **un·war·i·ly** **adv.**

un·washed /ˌənˈwôsht, -ˈwäsht/ ▸ **adj.** not washed.
– PHRASES **the (great) unwashed** derogatory ordinary people; the masses.

un·watch·a·ble /ˌənˈwäCHəbəl/ ▸ **adj.** too disturbing or boring to watch.

un·watched /ˌənˈwäCHt/ ▸ **adj.** not watched.

un·wa·ver·ing /ˌənˈwāvəriNG/ ▸ **adj.** not wavering; steady or resolute. ■ **un·wa·ver·ing·ly** **adv.**

un·weaned /ˌənˈwēnd/ ▸ **adj.** not weaned.

un·wea·ried /ˌənˈwi(ə)rēd/ ▸ **adj.** not wearied.

un·wea·ry·ing /ˌənˈwi(ə)rē-iNG/ ▸ **adj.** never tiring or slackening.

un·wed /ˌənˈwed/ ▸ **adj.** not married.

un·wel·come /ˌənˈwelkəm/ ▸ **adj.** not welcome.

un·wel·com·ing /ˌənˈwelkəmiNG/ ▸ **adj.** unfriendly or inhospitable.

un·well /ˌənˈwel/ ▸ **adj.** physically or mentally ill.

un·whole·some /ˌənˈhōlsəm/ ▸ **adj.** not wholesome.

un·wield·y /ˌənˈwēldē/ ▸ **adj.** (**unwieldier, unwieldiest**) hard to move or manage because of its size, shape, or weight. ■ **un·wield·i·ness** **n.**

un·will·ing /ˌənˈwiliNG/ ▸ **adj.** not willing. ■ **un·will·ing·ly** **adv.** **un·will·ing·ness** **n.**

un·wind /ˌənˈwīnd/ ▸ **v.** (past and past part. **unwound**) 1 undo something that has been wound. 2 relax after a period of work or tension.

un·win·na·ble /ˌənˈwinəbəl/ ▸ **adj.** not winnable.

un·wis·dom /ˌənˈwizdəm/ ▸ **n.** foolishness.

un·wise /ˌənˈwīz/ ▸ **adj.** foolish. ■ **un·wise·ly** **adv.**

un·wit·ting /ˌənˈwitiNG/ ▸ **adj.** 1 not aware of the full facts. 2 unintentional. ■ **un·wit·ting·ly** **adv.**

un·wom·an·ly /ˌənˈwoomənlē/ ▸ **adj.** not womanly.

un·wont·ed /ˌənˈwôntid, ˌənˈwōntid/ ▸ **adj.** not usual or expected. ■ **un·wont·ed·ly** **adv.**

un·work·a·ble /ˌənˈwərkəbəl/ ▸ **adj.** not able to be done successfully; impractical.

un·worked /ˌənˈwərkt/ ▸ **adj.** not cultivated, mined, or carved.

un·world·ly /ˌənˈwərldlē/ ▸ **adj.** 1 not interested in money or other material things. 2 lacking experience of life. 3 not seeming to belong to this world. ■ **un·world·li·ness** **n.**

un·worn /ˌənˈwôrn/ ▸ **adj.** 1 not worn or damaged from much use. 2 (of an item of clothing) never worn.

un·wor·ried /ˌənˈwərēd/ ▸ **adj.** not worried or anxious.

un·wor·thy /ˌənˈwərT͟Hē/ ▸ **adj.** (**unworthier, unworthiest**) 1 not deserving respect or attention. 2 not appropriate to someone's good reputation or social position: *such a suggestion is unworthy of the gentleman.* ■ **un·wor·thi·ly** **adv.** **un·wor·thi·ness** **n.**

un·wound /ˌənˈwound/ ▸ past and past participle of UNWIND.

un·wound·ed /ˌənˈwoondid/ ▸ **adj.** not wounded.

un·wrap /ˌənˈrap/ ▸ **v.** (**unwraps, unwrapping, unwrapped**) remove the wrapping from something.

un·wrin·kled /ˌənˈriNGkəld/ ▸ **adj.** not wrinkled.

un·writ·a·ble /ˌənˈrītəbəl/ ▸ **adj.** not able to be written.

un·writ·ten /ˌənˈritn/ ▸ **adj.** 1 not recorded in writing. 2 (of a law, rule, agreement, etc.) generally accepted although not formally established.

un·yield·ing /ˌənˈyēldiNG/ ▸ **adj.** not yielding or giving way.

un·zip /ˌənˈzip/ ▸ **v.** (**unzips, unzipping, unzipped**) 1 unfasten the zipper of an item of clothing. 2 Computing expand a compressed file.

up /əp/ ▸ **adv.** 1 toward a higher place or position. 2 to the place where someone is: *I crept up behind him.* 3 at or to a higher level or value. 4 so as to be formed, finished, or brought together: *the government set up an inquiry.* 5 out of bed. 6 in a publicly visible place. 7 (of the sun) visible in the sky. 8 toward the north. 9 into a happy mood. 10 winning by a specified margin: *the Mets were up by 5 in the fourth inning.* 11 Brit. toward or in the capital or a major city. ▸ **prep.** 1 from a lower to a higher point of something. 2 from one end of a street or other area to another. ▸ **adj.** 1 directed or moving toward a higher place or position. 2 at an end. 3 (of the road) being repaired. 4 feeling cheerful. 5 (of a computer system) working properly. ▸ **v.** (**ups, upping, upped**) increase a level or amount. ▸ **n.** informal a period of success or happiness.
– PHRASES **be up on** be well informed about. **on the up and up** informal legitimate; honest and sincere. **something is up** informal something significant is happening. **up against 1** close to or touching. 2 informal confronted with. **up and down** in various places throughout. **up before** appearing for a hearing in the presence of a judge, magistrate, etc. **up for 1** available for. 2 being considered for. 3 due for. 4 (often **up for it**) informal ready to take part in something. **ups and downs** a mixture of both good and bad experiences. **up to 1** as far as a particular number, level, point, etc. 2 (also **up until**) until. 3 good enough for or capable of. 4 the duty or choice of. 5 informal occupied with. **what's up?** informal 1 what is going on? 2 what is the matter?

up- ▸ **prefix 1** (added to verbs and their derivatives) upward: *upturned.* 2 (added to verbs and their derivatives) to a more recent time: *update.* 3 (added to nouns) referring to motion up: *uphill.* 4 (added to nouns) higher: *upland.*

up-and-com·ing ▸ **adj.** likely to become successful. ■ **up-and-com·er** **n.**

U·pan·i·shad /(y)ŏŏˈpänəˌsHad, ŏŏˈpəniˌsHad/ ▸ **n.** each of a series of Hindu sacred books explaining the philosophy introduced in the Vedas (the oldest Hindu scriptures).

up·beat /ˈəpˌbēt/ ▸ **adj.** positive and cheerful or enthusiastic. ▸ **n.** (in music) an unstressed beat coming before a stressed beat.

up·braid /ˌəpˈbrād/ ▶v. criticize or scold someone.

up·bring·ing /ˈəpˌbriNGiNG/ ▶n. the way in which a child is cared for and taught how to behave while it is growing up.

UPC ▶abbr. Universal Product Code; a more formal term for BAR CODE.

up·chuck /ˈəpˌCHək/ informal ▶v. vomit. ▶n. matter vomited from the stomach.

up·com·ing /ˈəpˌkəmiNG/ ▶adj. about to happen; forthcoming.

up·coun·try /ˈəpˌkəntrē, ˌəpˈkəntrē/ ▶adv. & adj. in or toward the inland areas of a country.

up·date ▶v. /ˌəpˈdāt, ˈəpˌdāt/ 1 make something more modern. 2 give someone the latest information. ▶n. /ˈəpˌdāt/ an act of updating or an updated version. ■ **up·dat·a·ble** adj.

up·draft /ˈəpˌdraft/ (Brit. **updraught**) ▶n. an upward current or draft of air.

up·end /ˌəpˈend/ ▶v. set or turn something on its end or upside down.

up·field /ˌəpˈfēld/ ▶adv. Football another term for DOWNFIELD.

up·front /ˌəpˈfrənt/ informal ▶adv. (usu. **up front**) 1 at the front; in front. 2 (of a payment) in advance. ▶adj. 1 expressing one's thoughts and intentions openly; frank. 2 (of a payment) made in advance.

up·grade /ˈəpˌgrād, ˌəpˈgrād/ ▶v. 1 raise to a higher standard, level, etc.: *the company will be upgrading its services.* 2 promote an employee. ▶n. an act of upgrading or an upgraded version. ■ **up·grad·a·ble** (also **upgradeable**) adj. **up·grad·er** n.

up·heav·al /ˌəpˈhēvəl/ ▶n. a violent or sudden change or disruption.

up·hill /ˌəpˈhil/ ▶adv. toward the top of a slope. ▶adj. 1 sloping upward. 2 difficult: *an uphill struggle.*

up·hold /ˌəpˈhōld/ ▶v. (past and past part. **upheld** /ˌəpˈheld/) 1 support something and ensure that it continues to exist: *it is the sheriff's duty to uphold the law.* 2 (of a court of law or official body) agree that a previous decision was correct or that a request is reasonable. ■ **up·hold·er** n.

up·hol·ster /əpˈhōlstər, əˈpōl-/ ▶v. provide a sofa, chair, etc., with a soft, padded covering. ■ **up·hol·ster·er** n.

up·hol·ster·y /əpˈhōlst(ə)rē, əˈpōl-/ ▶n. 1 the soft, padded covering on a sofa, chair, etc. 2 the art or practice of upholstering furniture.

up·keep /ˈəpˌkēp/ ▶n. 1 the process of keeping something in good condition. 2 the cost of supporting a person or keeping something in good condition.

up·land /ˈəplənd/ ▶n. (also **uplands**) an area of high or hilly land.

up·lift ▶v. /ˌəpˈlift/ 1 lift something up. 2 (often as adj. **uplifting**) make more happy, spiritual, or moral: *tender and uplifting songs.* 3 (**be uplifted**) (of an island, mountain, etc.) be created by an upward movement of the earth's surface. ▶n. 1 an act of lifting or raising something. 2 support from a bra or similar garment for a woman's bust. 3 a feeling of new happiness, hope, or spirituality. ■ **up·lift·er** n.

up·light·er /ˈəpˌlītər/ ▶n. a lamp designed to throw light upward. ■ **up·light·ing** n.

up·link /ˈəpˌliNGk/ ▶n. a communications link to a satellite. ▶v. send something by a communications link to a satellite.

up·load /ˈəpˌlōd, ˌəpˈlōd/ ▶v. transfer data to a larger computer system. ▶n. the action or process of transferring data to a larger computer system.

up·mar·ket /ˈəpˌmärkit, ˈəpˌmär-/ ▶adj. & adv. expensive and of high quality; upscale.

up·on /əˈpän, əˈpôn/ ▶prep. more formal term for ON.

up·per /ˈəpər/ ▶adj. 1 situated above another part. 2 higher in position or status. 3 situated on higher ground. 4 (in place names) situated to the north. ▶n. 1 the part of a boot or shoe above the sole. 2 informal a stimulating drug, especially an amphetamine.
– PHRASES **have the upper hand** have an advantage or control.

up·per·case /ˈəpərˌkās/ ▶n. capital letters.

up·per class ▶n. (treated as sing. or pl.) the social group with the highest status, especially the aristocracy. ▶adj. relating to the upper class.

up·per·class·man /ˌəpərˈklasmən/ ▶n. (pl. **upperclassmen**) a junior or senior in high school or college.

up·per crust ▶n. (**the upper crust**) informal the upper classes.

up·per·cut /ˈəpərˌkət/ ▶n. a punch delivered with an upward motion and the arm bent.

up·per house (also **upper chamber**) ▶n. 1 one of two houses (often the smaller) in a bicameral legislature or parliament. 2 the Senate (of the US or of a US state). 3 (**the Upper House**) (in the UK) the House of Lords.

up·per·most /ˈəpərˌmōst/ ▶adj. highest in place, rank, or importance. ▶adv. at or to the uppermost position.

up·pi·ty /ˈəpətē/ ▶adj. informal self-important; arrogant.

up·raise /ˌəpˈrāz/ ▶v. raise something to a higher level.

up·rate /ˌəpˈrāt, ˈəpˌrāt/ ▶v. 1 increase the value of a payment. 2 improve the performance of something.

up·right /ˈəpˌrīt/ ▶adj. 1 vertical; erect. 2 greater in height than breadth. 3 strictly respectable or honest: *an upright member of the community.* 4 (of a piano) having vertical strings. ▶adv. in or into an upright position. ▶n. 1 a vertical post, structure, or line. 2 an upright piano. ■ **up·right·ly** adv. **up·right·ness** n.

up·ris·ing /ˈəpˌrīziNG/ ▶n. a rebellion or revolt against an established ruler or government.

up·riv·er /ˈəpˈrivər/ ▶adv. & adj. toward or situated at a point nearer the source of a river.

up·roar /ˈəpˌrôr/ ▶n. 1 a loud and emotional noise or disturbance. 2 a public expression of outrage.

up·roar·i·ous /ˌəpˈrôrēəs/ ▶adj. 1 very noisy or lively. 2 very funny. ■ **up·roar·i·ous·ly** adv. **up·roar·i·ous·ness** n.

up·root /ˌəpˈrōōt, -ˈrŏŏt/ ▶v. 1 pull a plant, tree, etc., out of the ground. 2 move someone from their home or usual surroundings.

up·rush /ˈəpˌrəSH/ ▶n. a sudden surge or flow, especially of a feeling.

UPS ▶abbr. Computing uninterruptible power supply.

up·scale /ˈəpˌskāl, ˌəpˈskāl/ ▶adj. & adv. expensive and of high quality or status.

up·set ▶v. /ˌəpˈset/ (**upsets**, **upsetting**, **upset**)

1 make someone unhappy, disappointed, or worried. **2** knock something over. **3** disrupt or disturb: *antibiotics can upset the balance of bacteria in the bowel.* ▶ n. /'əpset/ **1** an unexpected result or situation. **2** the state of being unhappy, disappointed, or worried. ▶ adj. **1** /,əp'set/ unhappy, disappointed, or worried. **2** /'əpset/ (of a person's stomach) having disturbed digestion. ■ **up·set·ting** adj.

up·shot /'əp,SHät/ ▶ n. the eventual outcome or conclusion of something.

up·side /'əp,sīd/ ▶ n. the positive aspect of a situation.

up·side down▶ adv. & adj. **1** with the upper part where the lower part should be. **2** in or into total disorder.

up·side-down cake ▶ n. a cake that is baked over a layer of fruit in syrup and turned out upside down for serving.

up·size /'əp,sīz/ ▶ v. increase in size or complexity.

up·stage /,əp'stāj/ ▶ v. **1** divert attention from someone else and toward oneself. **2** (of an actor) move toward the back of a stage to make another actor face away from the audience. ▶ adv. & adj. at or toward the back of a stage.

up·stairs /,əp'ste(ə)rz/ ▶ adv. on or to an upper floor. ▶ adj. situated on an upper floor. ▶ n. an upper floor.

up·stand·ing /,əp'standiNG, 'əp,stan-/ ▶ adj. respectable and honest.

up·start /'əp,stärt/ ▶ n. derogatory a person who has suddenly become important and behaves arrogantly.

up·state /'əp'stāt/ ▶ adj. & adv. in or to a part of a state remote from its large cities. ▶ n. an upstate area.

up·stream /,əp'strēm/▶ adv. & adj. situated or moving in the direction opposite to that in which a stream or river flows.

up·stroke /'əp,strōk/ ▶ n. an upward stroke.

up·surge /'əp,sərj/ ▶ n. a sudden large increase: *an upsurge in cases of domestic violence.*

up·swept /'əp,swept/ ▶ adj. (of the hair) brushed upward and off the face.

up·swing /'əp,swiNG/ ▶ n. an increase or improvement; an upward trend.

up·sy-dai·sy /'əpsē ,dāzē/ ▶ exclam. expressing encouragement to a child who has fallen or is being lifted.

up·take /'əp,tāk/ ▶ n. the action of taking up or making use of something.

– PHRASES **be quick (or slow) on the uptake** informal be quick (or slow) to understand things.

up·tem·po /'əp,tempō/▶ adj. & adv. Music played with a fast or increased tempo.

up·thrust /'əp,THrəst/ ▶ n. **1** something that has been thrust upward. **2** the upward movement of part of the earth's surface. ▶ v. thrust something upward.

up·tight /,əp'tīt/ ▶ adj. informal **1** nervously tense or angry. **2** unable to express one's feelings; repressed.

up·time /'əp,tīm/ ▶ n. time during which a machine, especially a computer, is in operation.

up to date ▶ adj. incorporating or aware of the latest developments and trends.

up·town ▶ adj. & adv. /,əp'toun/ in or typical of the residential area of a town or city, especially an area of affluence. ▶ n. /'əp,toun/ an uptown area.

up·trend /'əp,trend/ ▶ n. an upward tendency,

especially in economic matters.

up·turn /'əp,tərn/ ▶ n. an improvement or upward trend.

up·turned /'əp,tərnd, ,əp'tərnd/ ▶ adj. turned upward or upside down.

uPVC ▶ abbr. unplasticized polyvinyl chloride, a rigid form of PVC used for pipework and window frames.

up·ward /'əpwərd/ ▶ adv. (also **upwards**) toward a higher point or level. ▶ adj. moving or leading toward a higher point or level. ■ **up·ward·ly** adv.

– PHRASES **upwards of** more than.

up·ward·ly mo·bile ▶ adj. moving to a higher social class; acquiring wealth and status.

up·well·ing /,əp'weliNG/ ▶ n. an instance or amount of something rising or building up: *a strong upwelling of nationalism.*

up·wind /,əp'wind/▶ adv. & adj. into the wind.

u·ra·ni·um /yŏŏ'rānēəm/ ▶ n. a dense radioactive metallic chemical element used as a fuel in nuclear reactors.

U·ran·us /'yŏŏrənəs, yŏŏ'rā-/ ▶ n. a planet of the solar system, seventh in order from the sun. ■ **U·ra·ni·an** /yŏŏ'rānēən/ adj.

ur·ban /'ərbən/ ▶ adj. **1** relating to a town or city. **2** (of popular culture, especially dance music) of black origin. ■ **ur·ban·ism** /'ərbə,nizəm/ n. **ur·ban·ist** /'ərbənist/ n.

ur·bane /ər'bān/ ▶ adj. (of a man) confident, courteous, and sophisticated. ■ **ur·bane·ly** adv.

ur·ban·ite /'ərbə,nīt/ ▶ n. informal a person who lives in a town or city.

ur·ban·i·ty /,ər'banitē/ ▶ n. the quality of being confident, courteous, and sophisticated.

ur·ban·ize /'ərbə,nīz/ ▶ v. **1** build towns and cities in a country area. **2** make someone used to living in a city rather than a country area. ■ **ur·ban·i·za·tion** /,ərbənə'zāsHən/ n.

ur·ban leg·end (also **urban myth**) ▶ n. an entertaining story or piece of information of uncertain origin that is circulated as if it is true.

ur·chin /'ərcHin/▶ n. **1** a poor child dressed in ragged clothes. **2** short for SEA URCHIN.

Ur·du /'ŏŏrdōŏ, 'ər-/ ▶ n. a language closely related to Hindi, the official language of Pakistan and widely used in India.

u·re·a /yŏŏ'rēə/ ▶ n. a colorless crystalline compound that is excreted from the body in urine.

u·re·ter /'yŏŏritər, yŏŏ'rētər/ ▶ n. the duct by which urine passes from the kidney to the bladder.

u·re·thane /'yŏŏrə,THān/ ▶ n. a synthetic crystalline compound used to make pesticides and fungicides.

u·re·thra /yŏŏ'rēTHrə/ ▶ n. the duct by which urine passes out of the body, and which in males also carries semen. ■ **u·re·thral** adj.

u·re·thri·tis /,yŏŏrə'THrītis/ ▶ n. inflammation of the urethra.

urge /ərj/ ▶ v. **1** try earnestly or persistently to persuade someone to do something. **2** strongly recommend something. **3** encourage to move more quickly or in a particular direction: *he urged his pony on.* ▶ n. a strong desire or impulse.

ur·gent /'ərjənt/ ▶ adj. **1** requiring immediate action or attention. **2** earnest and insistent: *an urgent whisper.* ■ **ur·gen·cy** n. **ur·gent·ly** adv.

u·ric ac·id /'yŏŏrik/ ▶ n. an insoluble compound that is the main substance excreted by birds, reptiles, and insects.

u·ri·nal /'yŏŏrənl/ ▸ n. a bowl attached to the wall in a public toilet, into which men urinate.

u·ri·nar·y /'yŏŏrə,nerē/ ▸ adj. **1** relating to urine. **2** referring to the organs, structures, and ducts in which urine is produced and passed from the body.

u·ri·nate /'yŏŏrə,nāt/ ▸ v. pass urine from the body. ■ **u·ri·na·tion** /,yŏŏrə'nāsHən/ n.

u·rine /'yŏŏrən/ ▸ n. a yellowish fluid stored in the bladder and discharged through the urethra, consisting of excess water and waste substances removed from the blood by the kidneys.

URL ▸ abbr. uniform (or universal) resource locator, the address of a World Wide Web page.

urn /ərn/ ▸ n. **1** a tall, rounded vase with a stem and base, especially one for storing a cremated person's ashes. **2** a large metal container with a tap, in which tea or coffee is made and kept hot.

u·ro·gen·i·tal /,yŏŏrō'jenətl, ,yŏŏrə-/ ▸ adj. referring to both the urinary and genital organs.

u·rol·o·gy /yŏŏ'räləjē/ ▸ n. the branch of medicine concerned with the urinary system. ■ **u·ro·log·i·cal** /,yŏŏrə'läjikəl/ adj. **u·rol·o·gist** n.

ur·sine /'ər,sīn/ ▸ adj. relating to or resembling bears.

Ur·su·line /'ərs(y)əlin, -,lĭn, -,lēn/ ▸ n. a nun of an order founded in Italy for nursing the sick and teaching girls. ▸ adj. relating to the Ursulines.

ur·ti·car·i·a /,ərti'ke(ə)rēə/ ▸ n. technical term for HIVES.

U·ru·guay·an /,(y)ŏŏrə'gwīən, -'gwä-/ ▸ n. a person from Uruguay. ▸ adj. relating to Uruguay.

US ▸ abbr. United States.

us /əs/ ▸ pron. (first person pl.) **1** used by a speaker to refer to himself or herself and one or more others as the object of a verb or preposition. **2** used after the verb 'to be' and after 'than' or 'as'. **3** informal me.

> **USAGE**
> For an explanation of whether to use **us** or **we** after **than**, see the note at PERSONAL PRONOUN.

USA ▸ abbr. United States of America.

us·a·ble /'yŏŏzəbəl/ (also **useable**) ▸ adj. able to be used. ■ **us·a·bil·i·ty** /,yŏŏzə'bilətē/ n.

USAF ▸ abbr. United States Air Force.

us·age /'yŏŏsij, -zij/ ▸ n. **1** the action of using something or the fact of being used: *a survey of water usage*. **2** the way in which words are normally and correctly used in a language.

USB ▸ abbr. universal serial bus, a connector that enables any of a variety of peripheral devices to be plugged into a computer.

USB flash drive ▸ n. a small external flash drive that can be used with any computer with a USB port.

USDA ▸ abbr. United States Department of Agriculture.

use ▸ v. /yŏŏz/ **1** take, hold, or employ something as a means of achieving a purpose. **2** take or consume an amount from an available supply. **3** (**use something up**) consume the whole of something. **4** treat someone in a particular way. **5** take advantage of or exploit someone. **6** /yŏŏst/ (**used to**) did repeatedly or existed in the past: *this road used to be a track.* **7** /yŏŏst/ (**be/get used to**) be or become familiar with someone or something through experience. ▸ n. /yŏŏs/ **1** the action of using something or the state of being

used. **2** the ability or power to move or control something: *he lost the use of his legs*. **3** a purpose for or way in which something can be used. **4** the value or point of something: *what's the use of crying?*

– PHRASES **make use of** use or benefit from.

> **USAGE**
> Confusion can arise over whether to write **used to** or **use to**. It is correct to write **used to** except in negatives and questions: *we used to go to the cinema all the time.* However, in negatives and questions using the verb **do**, you should write **use to**: *I didn't use to like mushrooms.*

use·a·ble /'yŏŏzəbəl/ ▸ adj. variant spelling of USABLE.

use-by date ▸ n. a date marked on packaged food indicating the recommended date by which it should be eaten.

used /yŏŏzd/ ▸ adj. **1** having already been used. **2** secondhand.

use·ful /'yŏŏsfəl/ ▸ adj. able to be used for a practical purpose or in several ways. ■ **use·ful·ly** adv. **use·ful·ness** n.

use·less /'yŏŏsləs/ ▸ adj. **1** serving no purpose. **2** informal having little ability or skill. ■ **use·less·ly** adv. **use·less·ness** n.

Use·net /'yŏŏz,net/ ▸ n. an Internet service consisting of thousands of newsgroups.

us·er /'yŏŏzər/ ▸ n. a person who uses or operates something.

us·er-friend·ly ▸ adj. easy to use or understand. ■ **us·er-friend·li·ness** n.

us·er in·ter·face ▸ n. the method or software by which users communicate with computers, typically involving a graphic display with clickable items or dialog boxes.

ush·er /'əsHər/ ▸ n. **1** a person who shows people to their seats in a theater or church. **2** an official in a court of law who swears in jurors and witnesses and keeps order. ▸ v. **1** show or guide someone somewhere. **2** (**usher something in**) cause or mark the start of something new: *when the first jet crossed the Atlantic it ushered in a new era.*

ush·er·ette /,əsHə'ret/ ▸ n. a woman who shows people to their seats in a theater.

USMC ▸ abbr. United States Marine Corps.

USN ▸ abbr. United States Navy.

USO ▸ abbr. United Service Organizations.

USP ▸ abbr. unique selling point.

USPS ▸ abbr. United States Postal Service.

USS ▸ abbr. United States Ship.

USSR ▸ abbr. historical Union of Soviet Socialist Republics.

u·su·al /'yŏŏzHŏŏəl/ ▸ adj. happening or done most of the time or in most cases. ▸ n. informal **1** the thing that happens or is done most of the time. **2** (**the/one's usual**) the drink someone regularly prefers.

u·su·al·ly /'yŏŏzH(ŏŏ)əlē/ ▸ adv. **1** in a way that is usual or normal. **2** generally speaking; as a rule.

u·su·ri·ous /yŏŏ'zHŏŏrēəs/ ▸ adj. relating to the lending of money at unreasonably high rates of interest.

u·surp /yŏŏ'sərp, yŏŏ'zərp/ ▸ v. take over a person's position or power illegally or by force. ■ **u·sur·pa·tion** /,yŏŏsər'pāsHən/ n. **u·surp·er** n.

u·su·ry /'yŏŏzH(ə)rē/ ▸ n. the practice of lending money at unreasonably high rates of interest.

■ **u·su·rer** n.

UT ▶ abbr. Utah.

u·ten·sil /yōō'tensəl/ ▶ n. a tool or container, especially for household use.

u·ter·ine /'yōōtərin, -ˌrīn/ ▶ adj. relating to the uterus.

u·ter·us /'yōōtərəs/ ▶ n. (pl. **uteri** /'yōōtəˌrī, -ˌrē/) the organ in the body of a woman or female mammal in which offspring develop before birth; the womb.

u·til·i·tar·i·an /yōōˌtili'te(ə)rēən/ ▶ adj. **1** useful or practical rather than attractive. **2** relating to utilitarianism. ▶ n. a person who supports utilitarianism.

u·til·i·tar·i·an·ism /yōōˌtilə'te(ə)rēəˌnizəm/ ▶ n. the belief that the right course of action is the one that will lead to the greatest happiness of the greatest number of people.

u·til·i·ty /yōō'tilətē/ ▶ n. (pl. **utilities**) **1** the state of being useful, profitable, or beneficial: *the garden was treated as a combination of utility and beauty.* **2** an organization supplying electricity, gas, water, or sewerage to the public. ▶ adj. having several uses or functions.

u·til·i·ty knife ▶ n. a knife with a short, strong replaceable blade.

u·til·i·ty room ▶ n. a room in which a washing machine and other domestic equipment are kept.

u·til·i·ty ve·hi·cle (also **utility truck**) ▶ n. a truck with low sides, used for small loads.

u·ti·lize /'yōōtlˌīz/ ▶ v. make practical and effective use of something. ■ **u·ti·liz·a·ble** /ˌyōōtl'īzəbəl, 'yōōtlˌī-/ adj. **u·ti·li·za·tion** /ˌyōōtl-ə'zāsнən/ n.

ut·most /'ətˌmōst/ ▶ adj. most extreme; greatest. ▶ n. (**the utmost**) the greatest or most extreme extent or amount.

U·to·pi·a /yōō'tōpēə/ ▶ n, an imaginary place, society, or situation where everything is perfect.

u·to·pi·an /yōō'tōpēən/ ▶ adj. relating to or aiming for a situation in which everything is perfect. ▶ n. a person with idealistic views on reform. ■ **u·to·pi·an·ism** /-ˌnizəm/ n.

ut·ter[1] /'ətər/ ▶ adj. complete; absolute: *I stared at him in utter amazement.* ■ **ut·ter·ly** adv.

utter[2] ▶ v. **1** make a sound or say something. **2** Law put forged money into circulation. ■ **ut·ter·a·ble** adj. **ut·ter·er** n.

ut·ter·ance /'ətərəns/ ▶ n. **1** a word, statement, or sound uttered. **2** the action of uttering something.

ut·ter·most /'ətərˌmōst/ ▶ adj. & n. another term for UTMOST.

U-turn ▶ n. **1** the turning of a vehicle in a U-shaped course so as to face the opposite way. **2** a complete change of policy or behavior: *the government is doing a U-turn on road building.*

UV ▶ abbr. ultraviolet.

UVA ▶ abbr. ultraviolet radiation of relatively long wavelengths.

UVB ▶ abbr. ultraviolet radiation of relatively short wavelengths.

UVC ▶ abbr. ultraviolet radiation of very short wavelengths, which does not penetrate the earth's ozone layer.

u·vu·la /'yōōvyələ/ ▶ n. (pl. **uvulae** /-ˌlē, -ˌlī/) a fleshy part of the soft palate that hangs above the throat.

UWB ▶ abbr. ultra wideband, a radio communications technology for the transmission of signals over a very broad range of frequencies.

ux·o·ri·al /ˌək'sôrēəl, əg'zôr-/ ▶ adj. relating to a wife.

ux·o·ri·ous /ˌək'sôrēəs, əg'zôr-/ ▶ adj. (of a man) very or excessively fond of his wife. ■ **ux·o·ri·ous·ness** n.

Uz·bek /'ŏŏzˌbek, 'əz-, ŏŏz'bek/ ▶ n. **1** a person from Uzbekistan. **2** a member of a people living mainly in Uzbekistan. **3** the language of Uzbekistan.

U·zi /'ŏŏzē/ ▶ n. a type of submachine gun.

Vv

V¹ (also **v**) ▶ n. (pl. **Vs** or **V's**) **1** the twenty-second letter of the alphabet. **2** the Roman numeral for five.

V² ▶ abbr. volt(s). ▶ symbol **1** the chemical element vanadium. **2** voltage or potential difference. **3** (in mathematical formulae) volume.

v. ▶ abbr. **1** Grammar verb. **2** versus. **3** very. ▶ symbol (**v**) velocity.

VA ▶ abbr. Virginia.

vac /vak/ ▶ n. informal a vacuum cleaner.

va·can·cy /'vākənsē/ ▶ n. (pl. **vacancies**) **1** a job or position that is available for someone to do. **2** an available room in a hotel, guest house, etc. **3** empty space. **4** lack of intelligence or interest: *her wide-eyed vacancy.*

va·cant /'vākənt/ ▶ adj. **1** not occupied; empty. **2** (of a job or position) not filled. **3** showing no intelligence or interest. ■ **va·cant·ly** adv.

va·cate /'vā,kāt/ ▶ v. **1** go out of a place, leaving it empty. **2** give up a job or position.

va·ca·tion /vā'kāsнən, və-/ ▶ n. **1** an extended period of leisure, especially away from home. **2** a fixed period of time off between terms in schools and courts. **3** the action of leaving a place or job. ▶ v. take a vacation, especially away from home. ■ **va·ca·tion·er** n. **va·ca·tion·ist** n.

vac·ci·nate /'vaksə,nāt/ ▶ v. treat a person or animal with a vaccine to produce immunity against a disease. ■ **vac·ci·na·tion** /,vaksə'nāsнən/ n.

vac·cine /vak'sēn/ ▶ n. a substance made from the microorganisms that cause a disease, injected into the body to make it produce antibodies and so provide immunity against that disease.

vac·il·late /'vasə,lāt/ ▶ v. keep changing one's mind about something. ■ **vac·il·la·tion** /,vasə'lāsнən/ n.

vac·u·ole /'vakyōō,ōl/ ▶ n. Biology a space inside a cell, enclosed by a membrane and typically containing fluid.

vac·u·ous /'vakyəwəs/ ▶ adj. showing a lack of thought or intelligence. ■ **va·cu·i·ty** /va'kyōōətē, və-/ n. **vac·u·ous·ly** adv. **vac·u·ous·ness** n.

vac·u·um /'vak,yōō(ə)m, -yəm/ ▶ n. (pl. **vacuums** or **vacua** /-yōōə/) **1** a space that is completely empty of matter. **2** a space from which the air has been completely or partly removed. **3** a gap left by the loss or departure of someone or something important. **4** (pl. **vacuums**) a vacuum cleaner. ▶ v. clean something with a vacuum cleaner.
– PHRASES **in a vacuum** without relation to someone or something else; in isolation.

vac·u·um clean·er ▶ n. an electrical device that collects dust and other particles by means of suction.

vac·u·um-pack ▶ v. seal a product in a pack or wrapping with the air removed.

vac·u·um tube ▶ n. a sealed glass tube containing a near vacuum that allows the free passage of electric current.

va·de me·cum /,vädē 'mäkəm, ,vādē 'mē-/ ▶ n. a handbook or guide that a person carries with them to refer to.

vag·a·bond /'vagə,bänd/ ▶ n. a person who has no settled home or job; a vagrant.

va·gar·y /'vāgərē/ ▶ n. (pl. **vagaries**) a change that cannot be predicted or explained: *the vagaries of the weather.*

va·gi·na /və'jīnə/ ▶ n. the muscular tube leading from the external genitals to the cervix (neck of the uterus) in women and most female mammals. ■ **vag·i·nal** adj. **va·gi·nal·ly** adv.

va·grant /'vāgrənt/ ▶ n. a person who has no settled home or job. ▶ adj. relating to or living as a vagrant; wandering. ■ **va·gran·cy** n.

vague /vāg/ ▶ adj. **1** not clear, certain, or detailed: *vague promises of a better future.* **2** thinking or expressing oneself in an imprecise or unclear way. ■ **vague·ly** adv. **vague·ness** n.

vain /vān/ ▶ adj. **1** having an excessively high opinion of oneself. **2** not producing the required result; unsuccessful. ■ **vain·ly** adv.
– PHRASES **in vain** without success. **take someone's name in vain** use someone's name in a way that shows a lack of respect.

> **USAGE**
> Do not confuse **vain** with **vane** or **vein**. **Vain** means 'having an excessively high opinion of oneself' (*a vain woman with a touch of snobbery*) or 'unsuccessful' (*a vain attempt to tidy up*); **vane** means 'a broad blade forming part of a windmill, propeller, or turbine'; **vein** means 'a tube that carries blood around the body' or 'a particular way, style, or quality' (*he continued in a more serious vein*).

vain·glo·ry /'vān,glôrē, ,vān'glôrē/ ▶ n. literary excessive pride in oneself. ■ **vain·glo·ri·ous** /,vān'glôrēəs/ adj. **vain·glo·ri·ous·ly** /,vān'glôrēəslē/ adv.

Vais·ya /'vīsнyə, 'vīs-/ ▶ n. (also **Vaishya** pronunc. same) ▶ n. a member of the third of the four Hindu castes, comprising merchants and farmers.

val·ance /'valəns, 'vāləns/ ▶ n. **1** a length of fabric screening the curtain fittings above a window. **2** Brit. a bedskirt. ■ **val·anced** adj.

vale /vāl/ ▶ n. literary (except in place names) a valley.
– PHRASES **vale of tears** the world as a place of trouble or sorrow.

val·e·dic·tion /,valə'diksнən/ ▶ n. **1** the action of saying goodbye. **2** a farewell speech or statement.

val·e·dic·to·ri·an /,valə,dik'tôrēən/ ▶ n. a

student, typically having the highest academic achievements of their class, who delivers the valedictory at a graduation ceremony.

val·e·dic·to·ry /ˌvalə'dikt(ə)rē/ ▶ adj. related to saying goodbye. ▶ n. (pl. **valedictories**) a farewell speech.

va·lence /'vāləns/ (also **valency** /'vālənsē/) ▶ n. the combining power of a chemical element, as measured by the number of hydrogen atoms it can displace or combine with.

val·en·tine /'valən,tīn/ ▶ n. **1** a card sent on St. Valentine's Day (February 14) to a person one loves or is attracted to. **2** a person to whom one sends such a card.

va·le·ri·an /və'li(ə)rēən/ ▶ n. **1** a plant with clusters of small pink, red, or white flowers. **2** a sedative drug obtained from a valerian root.

val·et /va'lā, 'valā, 'valit/ ▶ n. **1** a man's male attendant, responsible for looking after his clothes and other personal needs. **2** a person employed to clean or park cars. ▶ v. (**valets, valeting, valeted**) **1** clean a car as a professional service. **2** act as a valet to a man.

val·e·tu·di·nar·i·an /ˌvalə,t(y)ōōdn'e(ə)rēən/ ▶ n. a person in poor health or who worries too much about their health.

Val·hal·la /val'halə, väl'hälə/ ▶ n. Scandinavian Mythology a palace in which heroes killed in battle feasted for eternity.

val·iant /'valyənt/ ▶ adj. showing courage or determination. ■ **val·iant·ly** adv.

val·id /'valid/ ▶ adj. **1** (of a reason, argument, etc.) based on what is true or logical. **2** officially acceptable or legally binding: a valid passport. ■ **va·lid·i·ty** /və'lidətē/ n. **val·id·ly** adv.

val·i·date /'valə,dāt/ ▶ v. **1** check or prove that something is true or valid. **2** make or declare something to be officially acceptable or legally binding. ■ **val·i·da·tion** /ˌvalə'dāsʜən/ n.

va·lise /və'lēs/ ▶ n. a small travel bag or suitcase.

Val·i·um /'valēəm/ ▶ n. trademark for DIAZEPAM.

Val·kyr·ie /val'ki(ə)rē, 'valkərē/ ▶ n. Scandinavian Mythology each of Odin's twelve handmaids who chose heroes killed in battle to take to Valhalla.

val·ley /'valē/ ▶ n. (pl. **valleys**) a low area between hills or mountains, typically with a river or stream flowing through it.

val·or /'valər/ (Brit. **valour**) ▶ n. great courage in the face of danger. ■ **val·or·ous** adj.

val·or·ize /'valə,rīz/ ▶ v. give value or validity to: the English valorize stupidity. ■ **val·or·i·za·tion** /ˌvalərə'zāsʜən/ n.

Val·po·li·cel·la /ˌval,pōlə'cʜelə, ˌväl-/ ▶ n. a red wine made in the Val Policella district of Italy.

val·u·a·ble /'valy(ōō)əbəl/ ▶ adj. **1** worth a great deal of money. **2** very useful or important. ▶ n. (**valuables**) valuable items. ■ **val·u·a·bly** /-blē/ adv.

val·u·a·tion /ˌvalyōō'āsʜən/ ▶ n. an estimate of how much something is worth, especially one carried out by a professional valuer.

val·ue /'valyōō/ ▶ n. **1** the amount of money that something is worth. **2** the importance or worth of something: he realized the value of education. **3** (**values**) beliefs about what is right and wrong and what is important. **4** Mathematics the amount represented by a letter, symbol, or number. **5** the relative duration of the sound represented by a musical note. ▶ v. (**values, valuing, valued**) **1** estimate the value of something. **2** consider to be important or worthwhile: she had come to

value her privacy. ■ **val·ue·less** adj.

val·ue-add·ed tax ▶ n. a tax on the amount by which a product rises in value at each stage of its production or distribution.

val·ue judg·ment ▶ n. an assessment of something as good or bad based on personal opinions rather than facts.

valve /valv/ ▶ n. **1** a device for controlling the flow of a liquid or gas through a pipe or duct. **2** a cylindrical mechanism used to vary the length of the tube in a brass musical instrument. **3** a structure in the heart or in a blood vessel that allows blood to flow in one direction only. **4** each of the two parts of the hinged shell of a bivalve mollusk such as an oyster or mussel.

val·vu·lar /'valvyələr/ ▶ adj. relating to or having a valve or valves.

va·moose /va'mōōs, və-/ ▶ v. informal leave somewhere hurriedly.

vamp¹ /vamp/ ▶ v. (**vamp something up**) informal improve something by adding something more interesting. ▶ n. the upper front part of a boot or shoe.

vamp² informal ▶ n. a woman who uses her sexual attractiveness to seduce and control men. ▶ v. blatantly set out to attract a man. ■ **vamp·ish** adj. **vamp·y** adj.

vam·pire /'vam,pī(ə)r/ ▶ n. **1** (in folklore) a dead person supposed to leave their grave at night to drink the blood of living people. **2** (also **vampire bat**) a small bat that feeds on blood by piercing the skin with its teeth, found mainly in tropical America. ■ **vam·pir·ic** /vam'pirik/ adj. **vam·pir·ism** /'vampī,rizəm/ n.

van¹ /van/ ▶ n. **1** a motor vehicle used for transporting goods or people. **2** Brit. a baggage or freight car on a train.

van² ▶ n. (**the van**) **1** the leading part of an advancing group of people. **2** the forefront: we have always been in the van of progress.

va·na·di·um /və'nādēəm/ ▶ n. a hard gray metallic chemical element, used to make alloy steels.

Van Al·len belt /'alən/ ▶ n. each of two regions of intense radiation partly surrounding the earth at heights of several thousand kilometers.

van·dal /'vandl/ ▶ n. a person who deliberately destroys or damages property. ■ **van·dal·ism** /'vandl,izəm/ n.

van·dal·ize /'vandl,īz/ ▶ v. deliberately destroy or damage property.

Van·dyke /van'dīk/ (also **Vandyke beard**) ▶ n. a neat pointed beard.

vane /vān/ ▶ n. **1** a broad blade attached to a rotating axis or wheel that pushes or is pushed by wind or water, forming part of a windmill, propeller, or turbine. **2** a weathervane.

> **USAGE**
> For an explanation of the difference between **vane, vain**, and **vein**, see the note at VAIN.

van·guard /'van,gärd/ ▶ n. **1** a group of people leading the way in new developments or ideas. **2** the leading part of an advancing army or naval force.

va·nil·la /və'nilə/ ▶ n. a substance obtained from the pods of a tropical orchid or produced artificially, used as a flavoring.

van·ish /'vanisʜ/ ▶ v. **1** disappear from view suddenly and completely. **2** stop existing: woodlands are vanishing. ■ **van·ish·ing** adj. & n.

van·ish·ing·ly adv.

van·ish·ing point ▸ n. the point in the distance at which receding parallel lines appear to meet.

van·i·ty /'vanətē/ ▸ n. (pl. **vanities**) **1** excessive pride in one's appearance or achievements. **2** the quality of being pointless or futile: *the vanity of human wishes*. **3** a vanity table.

van·i·ty case ▸ n. a small case fitted with a mirror and compartments for makeup.

van·i·ty ta·ble ▸ n. a dressing table.

van·i·ty u·nit ▸ n. a unit consisting of a washbasin set into a flat top with cupboards beneath.

van·quish /'vaNGkwiSH/ ▸ v. literary defeat someone or something completely. ■ **van·quish·er** n.

van·tage /'vantij/ (also **vantage point**) ▸ n. a place or position giving a good view.

vap·id /'vapid/ ▸ adj. not interesting or original: *vapid musical comedies*. ■ **va·pid·i·ty** /va'pidətē/ n. **vap·id·ly** adv.

va·por /'vāpər/ (Brit. **vapour**) ▸ n. **1** a liquid or substance that is suspended in the air in a mass of tiny drops or particles. **2** Physics a gaseous substance that can be made into liquid by pressure alone. **3** (**the vapors**) dated a fit of faintness, nervousness, or depression. ■ **va·por·ous** adj.

va·po·ret·to /,väpə'retō, ,vapə-/ ▸ n. (pl. **vaporetti** /-'retē/ or **vaporettos**) (in Venice) a canal boat used for public transportation.

va·por·ize /'vāpə,rīz/ ▸ v. convert a substance into vapor. ■ **va·por·i·za·tion** /,vāpərə'zāsHən, -,rī'zā-/ n.

va·por·iz·er /'vāpə,rīzər/ ▸ n. a device that is used to breathe in medicine in the form of a vapor.

va·por trail ▸ n. a trail of condensed water from an aircraft or rocket at high altitude, seen as a white streak against the sky.

va·pour, etc. /'vāpər/ ▸ n. British spelling of VAPOR, etc.

va·que·ro /vä'kerō/ ▸ n. (pl. **vaqueros**) (in Spanish-speaking parts of the US) a cowboy; a cattle driver.

VAR ▸ abbr. value-added reseller, a company that adds extra features to products it has bought before selling them to consumers.

var·i·a·ble /'ve(ə)rēəbəl/ ▸ adj. **1** often changing or likely to change; not consistent: *the photos are of variable quality*. **2** able to be changed or adapted. **3** Mathematics (of a quantity) able to take on different numerical values. ▸ n. a variable element, feature, or quantity. ■ **var·i·a·bil·i·ty** /,ve(ə)rēə'bilitē/ n. **var·i·a·bly** /-blē/ adv.

var·i·ance /'ve(ə)rēəns/ ▸ n. the amount by which something changes or is different from something else.
– PHRASES **at variance** (**with**) inconsistent with or opposing.

var·i·ant /'ve(ə)rēənt/ ▸ n. a form or version that varies from other forms of the same thing or from a standard type.

var·i·a·tion /,ve(ə)rē'āsHən/ ▸ n. **1** a change or slight difference in condition, amount, or level: *regional variations in house prices*. **2** a different or distinct form or version. **3** a new but still recognizable version of a musical theme. ■ **var·i·a·tion·al** adj.

var·i·col·ored /'ve(ə)ri,kələrd/ ▸ adj. consisting of several different colors.

var·i·cose /'varə,kōs/ ▸ adj. (of a vein, especially

in the leg) swollen, twisted, and lengthened, as a result of poor circulation.

var·ied /'ve(ə)rēd/ ▸ adj. involving a number of different types or elements: *a long and varied career*.

var·i·e·gat·ed /'ver(ē)ə,gātid/ ▸ adj. having irregular patches or streaks of different colors. ■ **var·i·e·ga·tion** /,ver(ē)i'gāsHən/ n.

va·ri·e·tal /və'rīətl/ ▸ adj. **1** (of a wine or grape) made from or belonging to a single specified variety of grape. **2** relating to or forming a variety of plant or animal.

va·ri·e·ty /və'rīətē/ ▸ n. (pl. **varieties**) **1** the quality or state of being different or varied. **2** (**a variety of**) a range of things of the same general type that are different in character: *the center offers a variety of activities*. **3** a type: *fifty varieties of pasta*. **4** a form of entertainment consisting of a series of different acts, such as singing, dancing, and comedy. **5** Biology a subspecies or cultivar.

var·i·ous /'ve(ə)rēəs/ ▸ adj. different from one another; of different kinds or sorts. ▸ determiner & pron. more than one; individual and separate. ■ **var·i·ous·ly** adv. **var·i·ous·ness** n.

var·let /'värlət/ ▸ n. **1** old use a rogue or rascal. **2** historical a male servant.

var·mint /'värmənt/ ▸ n. dated, informal or dialect a troublesome or mischievous person or wild animal.

var·nish /'värnisH/ ▸ n. resin dissolved in a liquid, applied to wood or metal to give a hard, clear, shiny surface when dry. ▸ v. **1** apply varnish to something. **2** disguise or gloss over a fact.

var·si·ty /'värsətē/ ▸ n. (pl. **varsities**) a sports team representing a school or college. ▸ adj. referring to a school's sports team, especially one made up of the school's more advanced players: *she made varsity basketball in her sophomore year*.

var·y /'ve(ə)rē/ ▸ v. (**varies, varying, varied**) **1** differ in size, degree, or nature from something else of the same general class: *the houses vary in price*. **2** change from one form or state to another. **3** modify something to make it less uniform: *he tried to vary his diet*.

vas /vas/ ▸ n. (pl. **vasa** /'vāsə, -zə/) a vessel or duct in the body.

vas·cu·lar /'vaskyələr/ ▸ adj. referring to the system of vessels for carrying blood or (in plants) sap, water, and nutrients.

vas de·fe·rens /,vas 'defərənz, -,renz/ ▸ n. (pl. **vasa deferentia** /,vāsə ,defə'rensн(ē)ə, ,vāzə/) either of the ducts that convey sperm from the testicles to the urethra.

vase /vās, vāz, väz/ ▸ n. a decorative container used as an ornament or for displaying cut flowers.

vas·ec·to·my /və'sektəmē, va-/ ▸ n. (pl. **vasectomies**) the surgical cutting and sealing of part of each vas deferens as a means of sterilization.

Vas·e·line /,vasə'lēn, 'vasə,lēn/ ▸ n. trademark a type of petroleum jelly used as an ointment and lubricant.

vas·sal /'vasəl/ ▸ n. **1** historical (in the feudal system) a man who promised to fight for a monarch or lord in return for holding a piece of land. **2** a country that is controlled by or dependent on another. ■ **vas·sal·age** /-əlij/ n.

vast /vast/ ▸ adj. of very great extent or quantity;

huge. ■ **vast·ly** adv. **vast·ness** n.

VAT /vat/ ▶ abbr. value added tax.

vat /vat/ ▶ n. a large container used to hold liquid.

vat·ic /'vatik/ ▶ adj. literary predicting what will happen in the future.

Vat·i·can /'vatikən/ ▶ n. the palace and official residence of the Pope in Rome. ■ & n.

vaude·ville /'vôd(ə),vil, -vəl/ ▶ n. a type of entertainment featuring a mixture of musical and comedy acts. ■ **vaude·vil·lian** /,vôd(ə)'vilyən/ adj. & n.

vault¹ /vôlt/ ▶ n. 1 a large room used for storing things securely, especially in a bank. 2 a room under a church or in a graveyard, used for burials. 3 a roof or ceiling in the form of an arch or a series of arches. ■ **vault·ed** adj.

vault² ▶ v. jump over something in a single movement, supporting or pushing oneself with the hands or a pole. ▶ n. an act of vaulting. ■ **vault·er** n.

vault·ing /'vôltiNG/ ▶ n. the arrangement of vaults in a roof or ceiling.

vault·ing horse ▶ n. a padded wooden block used for vaulting over in gymnastics.

vaunt /vônt, vänt/ ▶ v. (usu. as adj. **vaunted**) boast about or praise: *his vaunted gift for spotting talent.* ■ **vaunt·ing** adj.

va·va·voom /,vä vä 'vōōm/ informal ▶ n. the quality of being exciting, vigorous, or sexually attractive. ▶ adj. sexually attractive: *her va-va-voom figure.*

VC ▶ abbr. Victoria Cross.

V-chip ▶ n. a computer chip installed in a television receiver that can be programmed to block violent or sexually explicit material.

VCR ▶ abbr. videocassette recorder.

VD ▶ abbr. venereal disease.

VDT ▶ abbr. video display terminal.

've ▶ abbr. informal have.

veal /vēl/ ▶ n. meat from a young calf.

vec·tor /'vektər/ ▶ n. 1 Mathematics & Physics a quantity having direction as well as magnitude, especially as determining the position of one point in space relative to another. 2 an organism that transmits a disease or parasite from one animal or plant to another. ■ **vec·to·ri·al** /vek'tôrēəl/ adj.

Ve·da /'vādə, 'vēdə/ ▶ n. (treated as sing. or pl.) the earliest Hindu sacred writings. ■ **Ve·dic** adj.

Ve·dan·ta /vā'däntə, və-/ ▶ n. a Hindu philosophy based on the doctrine of the Upanishads. ■ **Ve·dan·tic** adj. **Ve·dan·tist** n.

V-E Day ▶ n. the day (May 8) marking the Allied victory in Europe in 1945.

vee /vē/ ▶ n. 1 the letter V. 2 a thing shaped like a V.

vee·jay /'vē jā/ ▶ n. informal a VJ.

veer /vi(ə)r/ ▶ v. 1 change direction suddenly. 2 suddenly change in opinion, subject, etc.: *the conversation veered away from theatrical things.* 3 (of the wind) change direction clockwise around the points of the compass. ▶ n. a sudden change of direction.

veg /vej/ ▶ n. (pl. same) Brit. informal vegetables, or a vegetable.

veg·an /'vēgən, 'vejən/ ▶ n. a person who does not eat or use any animal products. ■ **veg·an·ism** /'-ə,nizəm/ n.

veg·e·ta·ble /'vejtəbəl, 'vəjətə-/ ▶ n. 1 a plant or part of a plant used as food. 2 informal, derogatory a

person who is incapable of normal mental or physical activity as a result of brain damage.

veg·e·ta·ble oil ▶ n. an oil obtained from plants, e.g., olive oil or sunflower oil.

veg·e·tal /'vejətl/ ▶ adj. formal relating to plants.

veg·e·tar·i·an /,veji'te(ə)rēən/ ▶ n. a person who does not eat meat, and who may also choose to eat no other animal products. ▶ adj. eating or including no meat or other animal products. ■ **veg·e·tar·i·an·ism** /-,nizəm/ n.

veg·e·tate /'vejə,tāt/ ▶ v. spend time in a dull and inactive way that involves little mental stimulation.

veg·e·ta·tion /,vejə'tāsHən/ ▶ n. plants in general. ■ **veg·e·ta·tion·al** adj.

veg·e·ta·tive /'vejə,tātiv/ ▶ adj. 1 relating to vegetation or the growth of plants. 2 relating to reproduction or propagation by asexual means. 3 (of a person) alive but in a coma and showing no sign of brain activity or responsiveness.

veg·gie /'vejē/ ▶ n. & adj. 1 another term for VEGETABLE. 2 informal, chiefly Brit. another term for VEGETARIAN.

veg·gie burg·er (also trademark **Vegeburger**) ▶ n. a patty resembling a hamburger but made with vegetables or soybeans instead of meat.

ve·he·ment /'vēəmənt/ ▶ adj. showing strong feeling; forceful or passionate. ■ **ve·he·mence** n. **ve·he·ment·ly** adv.

ve·hi·cle /'vēəkəl, 'vē,hikəl/ ▶ n. 1 a thing used for transporting people or goods on land, such as a car or truck. 2 a means of expressing or achieving something: *she used paint as a vehicle for her ideas.* 3 a movie, television show, song, etc., intended to display the leading performer to the best advantage. ■ **ve·hic·u·lar** /vē'hikyələr/ adj.

veil /vāl/ ▶ n. 1 a piece of fine material worn to protect or hide the face. 2 a piece of fabric forming part of a nun's headdress, resting on the head and shoulders. 3 a thing that hides or disguises something: *an eerie veil of mist.* ▶ v. 1 cover someone or something with a veil. 2 cover or hide: *the country is still veiled in mystery.* 3 (as adj. **veiled**) not expressed directly or clearly: *a thinly veiled threat.* – PHRASES **draw a veil over** avoid discussing or drawing attention to something embarrassing or unpleasant. **take the veil** become a nun.

vein /vān/ ▶ n. 1 any of the tubes forming part of the circulation system by which blood is carried from all parts of the body toward the heart. 2 (in general use) a blood vessel. 3 a very thin rib running through a leaf. 4 (in insects) a hollow rib forming part of the supporting framework of a wing. 5 a streak of a different color in wood, marble, cheese, etc. 6 a fracture in rock containing a deposit of minerals or ore. 7 a particular way, style, or quality: *he did a number of engravings in a similar vein.* 8 a source of a quality: *a rich vein of satire.* ■ **veined** adj. **vein·ing** n. **vein·y** adj.

USAGE

For an explanation of the difference between **vein, vane,** and **vain,** see the note at VAIN.

ve·lar /'vēlər/ ▶ adj. (of a speech sound such as *k* or *g* in English) pronounced with the back of the tongue near the soft palate.

Vel·cro /'velkrō/ ▶ n. trademark a fastener consisting of two strips of fabric that stick to each other when pressed together. ▶ v. fasten or join something with Velcro.

veld /velt/ (also **veldt**) ▶ n. open, uncultivated country or grassland in southern Africa.

vel·lum /'veləm/ ▶ n. **1** fine parchment made from the skin of a sheep, goat, or calf. **2** smooth cream-colored writing paper.

ve·loc·i·pede /və'läsə‚pēd/ ▶ n. historical an early form of bicycle propelled by working pedals on cranks fitted to the front axle.

ve·loc·i·rap·tor /və'läsə‚raptər/ ▶ n. a small meat-eating dinosaur with a large slashing claw on each foot.

ve·loc·i·ty /və'läsətē/ ▶ n. (pl. **velocities**) **1** technical the speed of something in a given direction. **2** (in general use) speed.

ve·lo·drome /'velə‚drōm, 'vēlə-/ ▶ n. a cycle-racing track with steeply banked curves.

ve·lour /və'lŏŏr/ (also **velours**) ▶ n. a plush woven fabric resembling velvet.

ve·lou·té /‚valŏŏ'tā/ ▶ n. a white sauce made from a roux of butter and flour with chicken, veal, or pork stock.

vel·vet /'velvət/ ▶ n. **1** a fabric of silk, cotton, or nylon with a thick short pile on one side. **2** soft downy skin that covers a deer's antler while it is growing. ■ **vel·vet·y** adj.

vel·vet·een /‚velvə‚tēn, ‚velvə'tēn/ ▶ n. a cotton fabric with a pile resembling velvet.

ve·na ca·va /‚vēnə 'kävə, 'kāvə/ ▶ n. (pl. **venae cavae** /'vēnē 'kävē, 'kāvē, 'vēnī 'kāvī, 'kāvī/) each of two large veins carrying deoxygenated blood into the heart.

ve·nal /'vēnl/ ▶ adj. prepared to do dishonest or immoral things in return for money. ■ **ve·nal·i·ty** /vē'nalətē, və-/ n.

vend /vend/ ▶ v. **1** offer small items for sale. **2** Law or formal sell something.

ven·det·ta /ven'detə/ ▶ n. **1** a prolonged bitter quarrel with or campaign against someone. **2** a prolonged feud between families in which people are murdered in revenge for previous murders.

vend·ing ma·chine ▶ n. a machine that dispenses food, drinks, cigarettes, or other small articles when a coin or token is inserted.

ven·dor /'vendər, -‚dôr/ (also **vender**) ▶ n. **1** a person or company offering something for sale. **2** Law the person who is selling a property.

ve·neer /və'ni(ə)r/ ▶ n. **1** a thin decorative covering of fine wood applied to a coarser wood or other material. **2** an outer quality or attractive appearance that hides the true nature of someone or something: *the area's veneer of respectability has gone.* ▶ v. (usu. as adj. **veneered**) cover something with a veneer. ■ **ve·neer·ing** n.

ven·er·a·ble /'venərəbəl, 'venrə-/ ▶ adj. **1** greatly respected because of age, wisdom, or character. **2** (in the Anglican Church) a title given to an archdeacon. **3** (in the Roman Catholic Church) a title given to a dead person who has gained a certain degree of sanctity but has not been fully beatified or canonized.

ven·er·ate /'venə‚rāt/ ▶ v. regard someone or something with great respect. ■ **ven·er·a·tion** /‚venə'rāSHən/ n. **ven·er·a·tor** n.

ve·ne·re·al /və'ni(ə)rēəl/ ▶ adj. **1** relating to

sexually transmitted disease. **2** formal relating to sex or sexual desire.

ve·ne·re·al dis·ease ▶ n. a disease that is caught by having sex with a person who is already infected.

ven·er·y¹ /'venərē/ ▶ n. old use indulgence in sexual activity.

ven·er·y² ▶ n. old use hunting.

Ve·ne·tian /və'nēsHən/ ▶ adj. relating to Venice. ▶ n. a person from Venice.

ve·ne·tian blind ▶ n. a window blind consisting of horizontal slats that can be adjusted to control the amount of light that passes through.

Ven·e·zue·lan /‚venəz(ə)'wälən/ ▶ n. a person from Venezuela. ▶ adj. relating to Venezuela.

venge·ance /'venjəns/ ▶ n. punishment or harm caused to someone in return for an injury or wrong: *he'd had a terrible life and was now taking vengeance on humanity.*
– PHRASES **with a vengeance** with great intensity.

venge·ful /'venjfəl/ ▶ adj. wanting to punish or harm someone in return for a wrong or injury. ■ **venge·ful·ly** adv. **venge·ful·ness** n.

ve·ni·al /'vēnēəl, 'vēnyəl/ ▶ adj. **1** (of a fault or offense) minor and able to be forgiven. **2** Christian Theology (of a sin) that does not deprive the soul of God's grace. Often contrasted with **MORTAL**.

ven·i·son /'venəsən, -zən/ ▶ n. meat from a deer.

Venn di·a·gram /ven/ ▶ n. a diagram representing mathematical or logical sets as circles, common elements of the sets being represented by overlapping sections of the circles.

ven·om /'venəm/ ▶ n. **1** poisonous fluid produced by animals such as snakes and scorpions and typically injected by biting or stinging. **2** extreme hatred or bitterness: *her voice was full of venom.*

ven·om·ous /'venəməs/ ▶ adj. **1** (of an animal) producing or capable of injecting venom. **2** full of hate or bitterness. ■ **ven·om·ous·ly** adv.

ve·nous /'vēnəs/ ▶ adj. relating to a vein or the veins.

vent¹ /vent/ ▶ n. an opening that allows air, gas, or liquid to pass out of or into a confined space. ▶ v. **1** express a strong emotion freely. **2** discharge air, gas, or liquid through an outlet.
– PHRASES **give vent to** express a strong emotion.

vent² ▶ n. a slit in a garment, especially in the lower part of the seam at the back of a coat.

ven·ti·late /'ventə‚lāt/ ▶ v. **1** cause air to enter and circulate freely in a room or building. **2** discuss an opinion or issue in public. ■ **ven·ti·la·tion** /‚ventə'lāsHən/ n.

ven·ti·la·tor /'ventə‚lātər/ ▶ n. **1** a device or opening for ventilating a room or building. **2** a machine that pumps air in and out of a person's lungs to help them to breathe. ■ **ven·ti·la·to·ry** /'ventələ‚tôrē/ adj.

ven·tral /'ventrəl/ ▶ adj. technical on or relating to the underside or abdomen. Compare with **DORSAL**. ■ **ven·tral·ly** adv.

ven·tri·cle /'ventrəkəl/ ▶ n. **1** each of the two larger and lower cavities of the heart. **2** each of four connected fluid-filled cavities in the brain. ■ **ven·tric·u·lar** /ven'trikyələr/ adj.

ven·tril·o·quist /ven'trilə,kwist/ ▶ n. an entertainer who can make their voice seem to come from a dummy of a person or animal. ■ **ven·tri·lo·qui·al** /,ventrə'lōkwēəl/ adj. **ven·tril·o·quism** /-,kwizəm/ n. **ven·tril·o·quy** /-kwē/ n.

ven·ture /'venchər/ ▶ n. **1** a business enterprise involving considerable risk. **2** a risky or daring activity or undertaking. ▶ v. **1** dare to do something dangerous or risky. **2** dare to say something that may be considered bold. ■ **ven·tur·er** n.

ven·ture cap·i·tal ▶ n. capital invested in a business project in which there is a large element of risk.

ven·ture·some /'venchərsəm/ ▶ adj. willing to do something risky or difficult.

ven·ue /'ven,yōō/ ▶ n. the place where an event or meeting is held.

Ve·nus /'vēnəs/ ▶ n. a planet of the solar system, second in order from the sun and the brightest object in the sky after the sun and moon. ■ **Ve·nu·si·an** /və'n(y)ōōsH(ē)ən, -zHən, -sēən/ adj. & n.

Ve·nus fly·trap /'flī,trap/ ▶ n. a plant with hinged leaves that spring shut on and digest insects that land on them.

ve·ra·cious /və'rāsHəs/ ▶ adj. formal speaking or representing the truth.

ve·rac·i·ty /və'rasətē/ ▶ n. **1** the quality of being true or accurate. **2** the quality of telling the truth: *he devised a test of the agent's veracity.*

ve·ran·da /və'randə/ (also **verandah**) ▶ n. a roofed structure with an open front along the outside of a house, level with the ground floor.

verb /vərb/ ▶ n. a word used to describe an action, state, or occurrence, such as *hear, become,* or *happen.*

ver·bal /'vərbəl/ ▶ adj. **1** relating to or in the form of words. **2** spoken rather than written; oral. **3** relating to a verb. ▶ n. a word or words functioning as a verb. ■ **ver·bal·ly** adv.

ver·bal·ism /'vərbə,lizəm/ ▶ n. concentration on words rather than their meaning or content.

ver·bal·ize /'vərbə,līz/ ▶ v. express ideas or feelings in words. ■ **ver·bal·i·za·tion** /,vərbələ'zāsHən, -,lī'zā-/ n.

ver·bal noun ▶ n. a noun formed from a verb, such as *smoking* in *smoking is forbidden.*

ver·ba·tim /vər'bātəm/ ▶ adv. & adj. in exactly the same words as were used originally.

ver·be·na /vər'bēnə/ ▶ n. a garden plant with bright showy flowers.

ver·bi·age /'vərbē-ij/ ▶ n. excessively lengthy or technical speech or writing.

ver·bose /vər'bōs/ ▶ adj. using more words than are needed. ■ **ver·bose·ly** adv. **ver·bos·i·ty** /-'bäsətē/ n.

ver·bo·ten /fər'bōtn, vər-/ ▶ adj. forbidden by an authority.

ver·dant /'vərdnt/ ▶ adj. green with grass or other lush vegetation. ■ **ver·dan·cy** n. **ver·dant·ly** adv.

ver·dict /'vərdikt/ ▶ n. **1** a formal decision made by a jury in a court of law as to whether a person is innocent or guilty of an offense. **2** an opinion or judgment made after testing or considering

something.

ver·di·gris /'vərdə,grēs, -,gris, -,grē/ ▶ n. a bright bluish-green substance formed on copper or brass by oxidation.

ver·dure /'vərjər/ ▶ n. literary lush green vegetation.

verge /vərj/ ▶ n. **1** an edge or border. **2** a limit beyond which something will happen: *she was on the verge of tears.* ▶ v. (**verge on**) be very close to: *the speed at which they drove verged on lunacy.*

verg·er /'vərjər/ ▶ n. **1** an official in a church who acts as a caretaker and attendant. **2** an officer who carries a rod in front of a bishop or dean as a symbol of office.

ver·i·fy /'verə,fī/ ▶ v. (**verifies, verifying, verified**) **1** check that something is true or accurate. **2** confirm or show to be true or accurate: *our instrument readings verified his statement.* ■ **ver·i·fi·a·ble** /'verə,fīəbəl, ,verə'fī-/ adj. **ver·i·fi·ca·tion** /,verəfi'kāsHən/ n. **ver·i·fi·er** n.

ver·i·ly /'verəlē/ ▶ adv. old use truly; certainly.

ver·i·si·mil·i·tude /,verəsə'mili,t(y)ōōd/ ▶ n. the appearance of being true or real.

ve·ris·mo /və'rizmō, ve-/ ▶ n. realism or authenticity, especially in opera, art, or movies.

ver·i·ta·ble /'veritəbəl/ ▶ adj. rightly so called (used for emphasis): *a veritable army of backpackers.* ■ **ver·i·ta·bly** /-blē/ adv.

vé·ri·té /,veri'tā/ ▶ n. a genre of movies and television that emphasizes realism and naturalism.

ver·i·ty /'veritē/ ▶ n. (pl. **verities**) **1** a true principle or belief: *the eternal verities of history.* **2** literary the quality of being true; truth.

ver·mi·cel·li /,vərmə'cHelē, -'selē/ ▶ pl.n. pasta made in long thin threads.

ver·mic·u·lite /vər'mikyə,līt/ ▶ n. a yellow or brown mineral used for insulation or for growing plants in.

ver·mi·form /'vərmə,fôrm/ ▶ adj. technical resembling or having the shape of a worm.

ver·mi·fuge /'vərmə,fyōōj/ ▶ n. a medicine used to destroy worms that live in or on the bodies of people or animals.

ver·mil·ion /vər'milyən/ ▶ n. a brilliant red pigment or color.

ver·min /'vərmən/ ▶ n. (treated as pl.) **1** wild mammals and birds that are harmful to crops, farm animals, or game, or that carry disease. **2** worms or insects that live in or on the bodies of animals or people. **3** people who are very unpleasant or dangerous to society. ■ **ver·min·ous** adj.

ver·mouth /vər'mōōtH/ ▶ n. a red or white wine flavored with herbs.

ver·nac·u·lar /vər'nakyələr/ ▶ n. **1** the language or dialect spoken by the ordinary people of a country or region. **2** informal the vocabulary used by people in a particular group or activity: *baseball vernacular.* ▶ adj. **1** spoken as or using the language or dialect of the ordinary people. **2** (of architecture) concerned with simple, traditional structures such as houses and barns rather than large public buildings.

ver·nal /'vərnl/ ▶ adj. relating to the season of spring.

ver·nier /'vərnēər/ ▶ n. a small movable graduated scale for indicating fractions of the main scale on a measuring device.

ve·ron·i·ca /və'ränəkə/ ▶ n. a plant with narrow

pointed leaves and blue or purple flowers.

ver·ru·ca /vəˈrōōkə/ ▶ n. (pl. **verrucae** /-kē, -kī/ or **verrucas**) a contagious wart on the sole of the foot.

ver·sa·tile /ˈvərsətl/ ▶ adj. **1** having many different uses. **2** having a range of different skills: *one of our most versatile composers.* ■ **ver·sa·til·i·ty** /ˌvərsəˈtilətē/ n.

verse /vərs/ ▶ n. **1** writing arranged with a regular rhythm, and often having a rhyme. **2** a group of lines that form a unit in a poem or song. **3** each of the short numbered divisions of a chapter in the Bible or other scripture.

versed /vərst/ ▶ adj. (**versed in**) experienced or skilled in; knowledgeable about.

ver·si·fy /ˈvərsəˌfī/ ▶ v. (**versifies, versifying, versified**) turn writing or ideas into verse. ■ **ver·si·fi·ca·tion** /ˌvərsəfiˈkāSHən/ n. **ver·si·fi·er** n.

ver·sion /ˈvərzHən/ ▶ n. **1** a form of something that differs in some way from other forms of the same type of thing: *the car comes in two-door and four-door versions.* **2** an account of something told from a particular person's point of view. ▶ v. create a new version of something.

ver·so /ˈvərsō/ ▶ n. (pl. **versos**) a left-hand page of an open book, or the back of a loose document. Contrasted with **RECTO**.

ver·sus /ˈvərsəs, -səz/ ▶ prep. **1** against: *England versus France.* **2** as opposed to; in contrast to.

vert /vərt/ ▶ n. green, as a conventional heraldic color.

ver·te·bra /ˈvərtəbrə/ ▶ n. (pl. **vertebrae** /-ˌbrē, -ˌbrā/) each of the series of small bones forming the backbone. ■ **ver·te·bral** /-brəl, vərˈtē-/ adj.

ver·te·brate /ˈvərtəbrət, -ˌbrāt/ ▶ n. an animal having a backbone, including mammals, birds, reptiles, amphibians, and fish. ▶ adj. relating to vertebrates.

ver·tex /ˈvərˌteks/ ▶ n. (pl. **vertices** /-təˌsēz/ or **vertexes**) **1** the highest point; the top. **2** each angular point of a polygon, triangle, or other geometrical figure. **3** a meeting point of two lines that form an angle.

ver·ti·cal /ˈvərtikəl/ ▶ adj. at right angles to a horizontal line or surface; having the top directly above the bottom. ▶ n. **1** (**the vertical**) a vertical line or surface. **2** an upright structure. ■ **ver·ti·cal·i·ty** /ˌvərtiˈkalətē/ n. **ver·ti·cal·ly** adv.

ver·tig·i·nous /vərˈtijənəs/ ▶ adj. **1** very high or steep. **2** relating to or affected by vertigo. ■ **ver·tig·i·nous·ly** adv.

ver·ti·go /ˈvərtəgō/ ▶ n. a feeling of dizziness caused by looking down from a great height or by disease affecting the inner ear.

ver·vain /ˈvərˌvān/ ▶ n. a plant with small blue, white, or purple flowers, used in herbal medicine.

verve /vərv/ ▶ n. vigor, spirit, and style: *he writes with his usual verve.*

ver·vet mon·key /ˈvərvət/ ▶ n. a common African monkey with greenish-brown upper parts and a black face.

ver·y /ˈverē/ ▶ adv. **1** in a high degree. **2** used to emphasize a description: *the very best quality.* ▶ adj. **1** actual; precise. **2** used to emphasize an extreme point in time or space. **3** mere: *the very thought of drink made him feel sick.* **4** old use real; genuine.

very high fre·quen·cy ▶ n. (in radio) a frequency of 30-300 megahertz.

Ver·y light /ˈverē, ˈvi(ə)rē/ ▶ n. a flare fired into the air from a pistol for signaling.

Ver·y Rev·er·end ▶ adj. a title given to a dean in the Anglican Church.

ve·si·cle /ˈvesikəl/ ▶ n. **1** a small fluid-filled sac or cyst in an animal or plant. **2** a blister full of clear fluid. ■ **ve·sic·u·lar** /vəˈsikyələr/ adj.

ves·pers /ˈvespərz/ ▶ n. a service of evening prayer, especially in the Western Christian Church.

ves·sel /ˈvesəl/ ▶ n. **1** a ship or large boat. **2** a bowl, cup, or other container for liquids. **3** a tube or duct that carries a fluid within the body, or within a plant. **4** a person or thing that conveys or embodies a quality or feeling: *the written word is a safer vessel for love than the spoken word.*

vest /vest/ ▶ n. **1** a close-fitting, sleeveless waist-length garment typically having no collar and with buttons down the front. **2** a sleeveless garment worn for a particular purpose: *a bulletproof vest.* **3** Brit. a sleeveless undergarment worn on the upper part of the body. ▶ v. **1** (**vest something in**) give power, property, etc., to someone. **2** give someone the legal right to power, property, etc.: *the court was vested with extensive powers.*

ves·tal /ˈvestl/ ▶ adj. literary chaste; pure. ▶ n. a Vestal Virgin.

Ves·tal Vir·gin ▶ n. (in ancient Rome) a virgin dedicated to the goddess Vesta and vowed to chastity.

vest·ed in·ter·est ▶ n. **1** a personal reason for wanting something to happen, especially because one expects to gain advantage from it. **2** a person or group having such a reason. **3** Law an interest (usually in land or money held in trust) recognized as belonging to a particular person.

ves·ti·bule /ˈvestəˌbyōōl/ ▶ n. **1** a room or hall just inside the outer door of a building. **2** Anatomy a chamber or channel opening into another. ■ **ves·tib·u·lar** /veˈstibyələr, və-/ adj. (Anatomy).

ves·tige /ˈvestij/ ▶ n. **1** a remaining trace of something that once existed: *the last vestiges of true wilderness.* **2** the smallest amount.

ves·tig·i·al /veˈstij(ē)əl/ ▶ adj. remaining as the last small part of something: *he felt a vestigial flicker of anger from last night.* ■ **ves·tig·i·al·ly** adv.

vest·ment /ˈves(t)mənt/ ▶ n. **1** a robe worn by the clergy or members of the choir during church services. **2** old use a robe worn on ceremonial occasions.

ves·try /ˈvestrē/ ▶ n. (pl. **vestries**) a room in or attached to a church, used as an office and for changing into ceremonial robes.

vet[1] /vet/ ▶ n. informal a veterinarian. ▶ v. (**vets, vetting, vetted**) **1** check or examine something very carefully. **2** investigate a person's background in order to ensure that they are suitable for a job requiring secrecy, loyalty, or trustworthiness.

vet[2] ▶ n. informal a veteran.

vetch /vecH/ ▶ n. a plant with purple, pink, or yellow flowers, grown for silage or fodder.

vet·er·an /ˈvetərən, ˈvetrən/ ▶ n. **1** a person who has had long experience in a particular field. **2** a person who used to serve in the armed forces.

Vet·er·ans Day ▶ n. a US holiday held on November 11 to commemorate military veterans.

vet·er·i·nar·i·an /ˌvet(ə)rəˈne(ə)rēən/ ▶ n. a

person qualified to treat diseased or injured animals.

vet·er·i·nar·y /'vet(ə)rə,nerē/ ▶ adj. relating to the treatment of diseases and injuries in animals.

vet·er·i·nar·y sur·geon ▶ n. British term for VETERINARIAN.

vet·i·ver /'vetəvər/ ▶ n. a fragrant extract or essential oil obtained from the root of an Indian grass, used in perfumery and aromatherapy.

ve·to /'vētō/ ▶ n. (pl. **vetoes**) 1 a right to reject a decision or proposal made by a lawmaking body. 2 any refusal to allow something. ▶ v. (**vetoes**, **vetoing**, **vetoed**) 1 use a veto against a decision or proposal of a lawmaking body. 2 refuse to allow: *I vetoed the idea of a vacation.*

vex /veks/ ▶ v. make someone annoyed or worried. ■ **vex·a·tion** /vek'sāsHən/ n.

vex·a·tious /vek'sāsHəs/ ▶ adj. 1 causing annoyance or worry. 2 Law referring to an action or the bringer of an action that is brought without sufficient grounds for winning, purely to cause annoyance to the defendant.

vexed /vekst/ ▶ adj. 1 (of an issue) difficult to resolve and causing much debate: *the vexed question of Europe.* 2 annoyed or worried.

VGA ▶ abbr. videographics array, a standard for defining color display screens for computers.

vgc ▶ abbr. very good condition.

VHF ▶ abbr. very high frequency.

VHS ▶ abbr. trademark video home system (as used by home video recorders).

VI ▶ abbr. Virgin Islands.

via /'vīə, 'vēə/ ▶ prep. 1 traveling through a place en route to a destination. 2 by way of; through. 3 by means of.

vi·a·ble /'vīəbəl/ ▶ adj. 1 capable of working successfully: *the belief that there are no viable alternatives to formal schooling.* 2 (of a plant, animal, or cell) capable of surviving or living successfully. ■ **vi·a·bil·i·ty** /,vīə'bilətē/ n. **vi·a·bly** /-blē/ adv.

vi·a·duct /'vīə,dəkt/ ▶ n. a long bridgelike structure carrying a road or railroad across a valley or other low ground.

Vi·ag·ra /vī'agrə/ ▶ n. trademark a drug used to treat impotence in men.

vi·al /'vī(ə)l/ ▶ n. a small container used especially for holding liquid medicines.

vi·ands /'vīəndz/ ▶ pl.n. old use food.

vi·at·i·cum /vī'atikəm, vē-/ ▶ n. (pl. **viatica** /-kə/) (in the Christian Church) the Eucharist as given to a person who is dying or in danger of death.

vibe /vīb/ ▶ n. informal 1 (usu. **vibes**) the atmosphere of a place or a mood felt among a group of people: *a bar with good vibes.* 2 (**vibes**) short for VIBRAPHONE.

vi·brant /'vībrənt/ ▶ adj. 1 full of energy and enthusiasm. 2 (of sound) strong or resonant. 3 (of color) bright or bold. ■ **vi·bran·cy** n. **vi·brant·ly** adv.

vi·bra·phone /'vībrə,fōn/ ▶ n. a musical percussion instrument with a double row of metal bars that are hit by the player, each above a resonator with lids that open and close electrically, giving a vibrato effect. ■ **vi·bra·phon·ist** /-,fōnist/ n.

vi·brate /'vī,brāt/ ▶ v. 1 move with small movements rapidly to and fro. 2 (of a sound) resonate. ■ **vi·bra·to·ry** /'vībrə,tôrē/ adj.

vi·bra·tion /vī'brāsHən/ ▶ n. 1 an instance or the state of vibrating. 2 (**vibrations**) informal the atmosphere of a place or a mood felt among a group of people. ■ **vi·bra·tion·al** adj.

vi·bra·to /və'brätō, vī-/ ▶ n. a rapid, slight variation in pitch in singing or playing some musical instruments, producing a stronger or richer tone.

vi·bra·tor /'vī,brātər/ ▶ n. a device that vibrates, used for massage or sexual stimulation.

vi·bur·num /vī'bərnəm/ ▶ n. a shrub or small tree with clusters of small white flowers.

vic·ar /'vikər/ ▶ n. 1 (in the Church of England) a priest in charge of a parish. 2 (in other Anglican Churches) a member of the clergy deputizing for another. 3 (in the Roman Catholic Church) a representative or deputy of a bishop.

vic·ar·age /'vikərij/ ▶ n. the house of a vicar.

vic·ar gen·er·al ▶ n. (pl. **vicars general**) an official serving as a deputy or representative of a bishop or archbishop.

vi·car·i·ous /vī'kerēəs, vi-/ ▶ adj. 1 experienced in the imagination after watching or reading about another person's actions or feelings: *vicarious excitement.* 2 done by one person as a substitute for another. ■ **vi·car·i·ous·ly** adv.

vice¹ /vīs/ ▶ n. 1 immoral or wicked behavior. 2 criminal activities involving prostitution, pornography, or drugs. 3 an immoral or bad quality in a person's character. 4 a bad habit.

vice² ▶ n. British spelling of VISE.

vice- ▶ comb.form (often without hyphen) next in rank to and able to deputize for: *vice president.*

vice ad·mi·ral ▶ n. a high rank of naval officer, above rear admiral and below admiral.

vice chan·cel·lor ▶ n. a deputy chancellor, such as one in a British university who is in charge of its administration.

vice pres·i·dent ▶ n. an official or executive who serves as a deputy to a president.

vice·re·gal /,vīs'rēgəl/ ▶ adj. relating to a viceroy.

vice·roy /'vīs,roi/ ▶ n. a person who governs a colony on behalf of a sovereign.

vice squad ▶ n. a department of a police force that enforces laws against prostitution, drug abuse, illegal gambling, etc.

vice ver·sa /'vīs 'vərsə, 'vīsə/ ▶ adv. reversing the order of the items just mentioned.

vi·chys·soise /,vēsHē'swäz, ,vishē-, 'vēsHē,swäz, 'vishē-/ ▶ n. a soup made with potatoes, leeks, and cream and typically served chilled.

vi·cin·i·ty /və'sinətē/ ▶ n. (pl. **vicinities**) the area near or surrounding a place.
– PHRASES **in the vicinity of** in the region of a price or amount.

vi·cious /'visHəs/ ▶ adj. 1 cruel or violent. 2 full of hatred or anger: *a vicious campaign to discredit him.* 3 very severe or serious: *a vicious stomach bug.* 4 (of an animal) wild and dangerous. ■ **vi·cious·ly** adv. **vi·cious·ness** n.

vi·cious cir·cle ▶ n. a situation in which one problem leads to another, which then makes the first one worse.

vi·cis·si·tudes /və'sisə,t(y)ōōdz/ ▶ pl.n. changes of circumstances or fortune.

vi·comte /vē'kônt/ ▶ n. (pl. **vicomtes** pronunc. same) a French nobleman corresponding in rank to a viscount.

vic·tim /'viktəm/ ▶ n. 1 a person harmed or killed as a result of a crime or accident. 2 a person who has been tricked. **3** an animal or person killed as a religious sacrifice. ■ **vic·tim·hood** /-ˌho͝od/ n.

– PHRASES **fall victim to** be hurt, killed, or destroyed by someone or something.

vic·tim·ize /'viktəˌmīz/ ▶ v. single someone out for cruel or unfair treatment. ■ **vic·tim·i·za·tion** /ˌviktəmə'zāSHən/ n. **vic·tim·iz·er** n.

vic·tim·less /'viktəmləs/ ▶ adj. (of a crime) in which there is no injured party.

vic·tim·ol·o·gy /ˌviktə'mäləjē/ ▶ n. (pl. **victimologies**) the study of the victims of crime and the psychological effects on them.

vic·tor /'viktər/ ▶ n. a person who defeats an opponent in a battle, game, or competition.

Vic·to·ri·an /vik'tôrēən/ ▶ adj. **1** relating to the reign of Queen Victoria (1837–1901). **2** relating to the attitudes associated with the Victorian period, especially those of prudishness and strict morality. ▶ n. a person who lived during the Victorian period. ■ **Vic·to·ri·an·ism** /-ˌnizəm/ n.

Vic·to·ri·an·a /vik,tôrē'anə, -'änə/ ▶ pl.n. articles, especially collectors' items, from the Victorian period.

vic·to·ri·ous /vik'tôrēəs/ ▶ adj. **1** having won a victory. **2** relating to a victory; triumphant: *a victorious glance*. ■ **vic·to·ri·ous·ly** adv.

vic·to·ry /'vikt(ə)rē/ ▶ n. (pl. **victories**) an act of defeating an opponent in a battle, game, or other competition.

vict·ual /'vitl/ dated ▶ n. (**victuals**) food or provisions. ▶ v. (**victuals, victualing, victualed**) provide someone or something with food or other stores.

vi·cu·ña /vī'k(y)o͞onə və-, və-, 'ko͞onyə/ ▶ n. **1** a wild relative of the llama, having fine silky wool. **2** cloth made from the wool of the vicuña.

vid /vid/ ▶ n. informal short for VIDEO.

vi·de /'vēdē, 'vēˌdā, 'vīdē/ ▶ v. see (used as an instruction in a written work to refer the reader elsewhere).

vid·e·o /'vidēˌō/ ▶ n. (pl. **videos**) **1** a system of recording, reproducing, or broadcasting moving images using magnetic tape. **2** a movie or other recording on magnetic tape. **3** a cassette of videotape. ▶ v. (**videoes, videoing, videoed**) film an event or make a video recording of a television program.

vid·e·o ar·cade ▶ n. an indoor area containing coin-operated video games.

vid·e·o·con·fer·ence /'vidēōˌkänf(ə)rəns, -ˌkänf(ə)rns/ ▶ n. an arrangement in which television sets linked to telephone lines are used to enable a group of people to talk to and see each other. ■ **vid·e·o·con·fer·enc·ing** n.

vid·e·o·disc /'vidēōˌdisk/ (also **videodisk**) ▶ n. a CD-ROM or other disk used to store images.

vid·e·o dis·play ter·min·al ▶ n. a device for displaying information from a computer on a screen, typically a monitor.

vid·e·o game ▶ n. a computer game played on a television or other display screen.

vid·e·og·ra·phy /ˌvidē'ägrəfē/ ▶ n. the process or art of making video films. ■ **vid·e·og·ra·pher** n.

video jockey ▶ n. full form of VJ.

vid·e·o-on-de·mand ▶ n. a system in which viewers choose their own filmed entertainment, by means of a PC or interactive TV system.

vid·e·o·phile /'vidēəˌfīl/ ▶ n. a person who is very enthusiastic about video recordings or technology.

vid·e·o·phone /'vidēōˌfōn/ ▶ n. a telephone device that transmits and receives images as well as sound.

vid·e·o re·cord·er ▶ n. a machine linked to a television set, used for recording programs and playing videotapes.

vid·e·o·tape /'vidēōˌtāp/ ▶ n. **1** magnetic tape for recording and reproducing images and sound. **2** a cassette on which this magnetic tape is held. ▶ v. record or film something on videotape.

vie /vī/ ▶ v. (**vies, vying, vied**) compete eagerly with others in order to do or achieve something: *companies vying for a slice of the market*.

Vi·en·nese /ˌvēə'nēz, -'nēs/ ▶ n. (pl. same) a person from Vienna. ▶ adj. relating to Vienna.

Vi·et·nam·ese /ˌvē,etnə'mēz, ˌvyet-, ˌvēət-, -'mēs/ ▶ n. (pl. same) **1** a person from Vietnam. **2** the language of Vietnam. ▶ adj. relating to Vietnam.

view /vyo͞o/ ▶ n. **1** the ability to see something or to be seen from a particular position: *the mountains came into view*. **2** something seen from a particular position, especially beautiful scenery. **3** an attitude or opinion: *strong political views*. **4** an inspection of things for sale by prospective buyers. ▶ v. **1** look at or inspect someone or something. **2** regard in a particular way: *he viewed beggars as potential thieves*. **3** inspect a house or other property with the prospect of buying or renting it. **4** watch something on television. ■ **view·a·ble** adj.

– PHRASES **in full view** clearly visible. **in view** able to be seen; visible. **in view of** because or as a result of. **with a view to** with the aim or intention of.

view·er /'vyo͞oər/ ▶ n. **1** a person who views something. **2** a device for looking at film transparencies or similar photographic images.

view·er·ship /'vyo͞oərˌSHip/ ▶ n. (treated as sing. or pl.) the audience for a particular television program or channel.

view·find·er /'vyo͞oˌfīndər/ ▶ n. a device on a camera that the user looks through in order to see what will appear in the photograph.

view·point /'vyo͞oˌpoint/ ▶ n. **1** a point of view; an opinion. **2** a position giving a good view.

view·screen /'vyo͞oˌskrēn/ ▶ n. the screen on a television, computer, or similar device on which images and information are displayed.

vig·il /'vijəl/ ▶ n. **1** a period of staying awake during to keep watch or pray. **2** a stationary, peaceful demonstration in support of a cause.

vig·i·lant /'vijələnt/ ▶ adj. keeping careful watch for possible danger or difficulties. ■ **vig·i·lance** n. **vig·i·lant·ly** adv.

vig·i·lan·te /ˌvijə'lantē/ ▶ n. a member of a group of people who take it on themselves to prevent crime or punish offenders without legal authority. ■ **vig·i·lan·tism** /-ˌtizəm/ n.

vig·ne·ron /ˌvēnyə'rôn, -'rōn/ ▶ n. a person who grows grapes for winemaking.

vi·gnette /vin'yet/ ▶ n. **1** a brief, vivid description or episode. **2** a small illustration or portrait photograph that fades into its background without a definite border.

vig·or /'vigər/ (Brit. **vigour**) ▶ n. **1** physical strength and good health. **2** effort, energy, and enthusiasm.

vig·or·ous /'vig(ə)rəs/ ▶ adj. **1** strong, healthy, and full of energy. **2** involving effort, energy, or determination: *a vigorous election campaign*. **3** (of language) forceful. ■ **vig·or·ous·ly** adv.

vig·or·ous·ness n.

Vi·king /ˈvīkiNG/ ▶ n. a member of the Scandinavian seafaring people who raided and settled in parts of Britain and elsewhere in NW Europe between the 8th and 11th centuries.

vile /vīl/ ▶ adj. **1** very unpleasant. **2** morally bad; wicked. ■ **vile·ly** adv. **vile·ness** n.

vil·i·fy /ˈviləˌfī/ ▶ v. (**vilifies, vilifying, vilified**) speak or write about someone in a very abusive way. ■ **vil·i·fi·ca·tion** /ˌviləfiˈkāsHən/ n.

vil·la /ˈvilə/ ▶ n. **1** a rented vacation home, especially abroad. **2** (especially in continental Europe) a large country house in its own grounds. **3** (in Roman times) a large country house consisting of buildings arranged around a courtyard.

vil·lage /ˈvilij/ ▶ n. **1** a community in a country area that is smaller than a town. **2** a self-contained district or community within a town or city. ■ **vil·lag·er** n.

vil·lain /ˈvilən/ ▶ n. **1** a wicked person or a person guilty of a crime. **2** a bad character in a novel, play, movie, etc., whose evil actions are important to the plot. ■ **vil·lain·ous** adj. **vil·lain·y** n. (pl. **villainies**).

vil·la·nelle /ˌviləˈnel/ ▶ n. a poem of nineteen lines, with only two rhymes throughout, and some lines repeated.

vil·lein /ˈvilən, -ˌān/ ▶ n. (in medieval England) a poor man who had to work for a lord in return for a small piece of land on which to grow food.

vil·lus /ˈviləs/ ▶ n. (pl. **villi** /ˈvilī, ˈvilē/) any of many tiny fingerlike growths of tissue on some membranes of the body, especially the small intestine. ■ **vil·lous** /ˈviləs/ adj.

vim /vim/ ▶ n. informal energy; enthusiasm.

VIN /vin/ ▶ abbr. vehicle identification number.

vin·ai·grette /ˌvinəˈgret/ ▶ n. a salad dressing of oil, wine vinegar, and seasoning.

vin·di·cate /ˈvindəˌkāt/ ▶ v. **1** clear someone of blame or suspicion. **2** show to be right or justified: *more sober views were vindicated by events.* ■ **vin·di·ca·tion** /ˌvindəˈkāsHən/ n.

vin·dic·tive /vinˈdiktiv/ ▶ adj. having or showing a strong or spiteful desire for revenge. ■ **vin·dic·tive·ly** adv. **vin·dic·tive·ness** n.

vine /vīn/ ▶ n. **1** a climbing plant with a woody stem, especially one that produces grapes. **2** the slender stem of a climbing plant.

vin·e·gar /ˈvinəgər/ ▶ n. **1** a sour liquid made from wine, beer, or cider, used as a seasoning or for pickling. **2** bitterness or spitefulness: *she was bossy and full of vinegar.* ■ **vin·e·gar·y** adj.

vine·yard /ˈvinyərd/ ▶ n. a plantation of grapevines, producing grapes used in winemaking.

vingt-et-un /ˌvant ā ˈən, ˌvan tä ˈœn/ ▶ n. the card game blackjack or twenty-one.

vi·nho ver·de /ˈvinyō ˈverdē, ˈvēnyōō ˈverdə/ ▶ n. a young Portuguese wine, not allowed to mature.

vin·i·cul·ture /ˈvinəˌkəlCHər/ ▶ n. the growing of grapevines for winemaking.

vin·i·fi·ca·tion /ˌvinəfiˈkāsHən/ ▶ n. the conversion of grape juice or other vegetable extract into wine by fermentation.

vi·no /ˈvēnō/ ▶ n. (pl. **vinos**) informal wine.

vi·nous /ˈvīnəs/ ▶ adj. of, resembling, or associated with wine.

vin·tage /ˈvintij/ ▶ n. **1** the year or place in which wine was produced. **2** a wine of high quality made from the crop of a single specified district in a good year. **3** the harvesting of grapes for winemaking. **4** the grapes or wine of a particular season. **5** the time that something was produced: *rifles of various vintages.* ▶ adj. **1** referring to high-quality vintage wine. **2** (of something from the past) of high quality.

vint·ner /ˈvintnər/ ▶ n. a wine merchant.

vi·nyl /ˈvīnl/ ▶ n. **1** a type of strong plastic, used in making floor coverings, paint, and phonograph records. **2** Chemistry the unsaturated hydrocarbon radical $-CH=CH_2$, derived from ethylene.

vi·ol /ˈvīəl/ ▶ n. a musical instrument of the Renaissance and baroque periods, resembling a violin but with six strings and held vertically.

vi·o·la¹ /vēˈōlə/ ▶ n. an instrument of the violin family, larger than the violin and tuned a fifth lower.

vi·o·la² /ˈvīōlə, vē-, ˈvīələ/ ▶ n. a plant of a genus that includes pansies and violets.

vi·o·la da gam·ba /vēˈōlə də ˈgämbə, ˈgam-/ ▶ n. a viol, specifically a bass viol (corresponding to the modern cello).

vi·o·late /ˈvīəˌlāt/ ▶ v. **1** fail to obey a rule, law, or formal agreement. **2** fail to respect a person's privacy or rights. **3** treat something sacred with disrespect. **4** chiefly literary rape someone. ■ **vi·o·la·tion** /ˌvīəˈlāsHən/ n. **vi·o·la·tor** n.

vi·o·lence /ˈvī(ə)ləns/ ▶ n. **1** behavior involving physical force intended to hurt, damage, or kill. **2** the power of a destructive natural force. **3** strength of emotion: *the violence of her feelings.*

vi·o·lent /ˈvī(ə)lənt/ ▶ adj. **1** using or involving violence. **2** very intense or powerful: *violent dislike.* ■ **vi·o·lent·ly** adv.

vi·o·let /ˈvī(ə)lət/ ▶ n. **1** a small plant with purple, blue, or white five-petaled flowers. **2** a bluish-purple color.

vi·o·lin /ˌvīəˈlin/ ▶ n. a musical instrument having four strings and a body narrowed at the middle, played with a bow. ■ **vi·o·lin·ist** n.

vi·o·list /vēˈōlist/ ▶ n. a viola player.

vi·o·lon·cel·lo /ˌvīələnˈCHelō, ˌvē-/ ▶ n. formal term for CELLO.

VIP ▶ n. a very important person.

vi·per /ˈvīpər/ ▶ n. **1** a poisonous snake with large fangs and a body with dark patterns on a lighter background. **2** a spiteful or treacherous person. ■ **vi·per·ish** adj. **vi·per·ous** adj.

vi·ra·go /vəˈrägō, -ˈrä-/ ▶ n. (pl. **viragos** or **viragoes**) a domineering, violent, or bad-tempered woman.

vi·ral /ˈvīrəl/ ▶ adj. relating to or caused by a virus or viruses. ■ **vi·ral·ly** adv.

vi·ral mar·ket·ing ▶ n. a marketing technique whereby information about a product is passed electronically from one Internet user to another.

vi·re·mi·a /vīˈrēmēə/ (Brit. also **viraemia**) ▶ n. Medicine the presence of viruses in the blood.

vir·e·o /ˈvirēˌō/ ▶ n. (pl. **vireos**) a small American songbird, typically green or gray with yellow or white underparts.

vir·gin /ˈvərjən/ ▶ n. **1** a person who has never had sexual intercourse. **2** (**the Virgin**) the Virgin Mary, the mother of Jesus. **3** a person who is inexperienced in a particular activity: *a political virgin.* ▶ adj. **1** having had no sexual experience.

2 not yet used or exploited: *virgin forest.* **3** (of olive oil) made from the first pressing of olives.

vir·gin·al /'vərjənl/ ▶ adj. relating to or appropriate for a virgin: *virginal white.*

vir·gin·als /'vərjənlz/ ▶ pl.n. a type of small harpsichord popular in the 16th and 17th centuries.

Vir·gin Birth ▶ n. the Christian doctrine of Jesus's birth from a mother, Mary, who was a virgin.

Vir·gin·ia creep·er /vər'jinyə/ ▶ n. a North American climbing plant, grown for its red autumn foliage.

vir·gin·i·ty /vər'jinətē/ ▶ n. **1** the state of never having had sexual intercourse. **2** the state of being inexperienced in a particular activity.

Vir·go /'vərgō/ ▶ n. **1** a constellation and the sixth sign of the zodiac (the Virgin), which the sun enters about August 23. **2** (**a Virgo**) a person born when the sun is in this sign. ■ **Vir·go·an** /-gōən/ n. & adj.

vir·i·des·cent /ˌvirə'desənt/ ▶ adj. literary greenish or becoming green. ■ **vir·i·des·cence** n.

vi·rid·i·an /və'ridēən/ ▶ n. a bluish-green pigment or color.

vir·ile /'virəl/ ▶ adj. **1** (of a man) strong, energetic, and having a strong sex drive. **2** vigorous or powerful: *virile guitar bursts.* ■ **vi·ril·i·ty** /və'rilitē/ n.

vi·rol·o·gy /vī'räləjē/ ▶ n. the branch of science concerned with the study of viruses. ■ **vi·ro·log·i·cal** /ˌvīrə'läjikəl/ adj. **vi·rol·o·gist** n.

vir·tu·al /'vərchōōəl/ ▶ adj. **1** almost or nearly the thing described, but not completely: *the virtual absence of border controls.* **2** not existing in reality but made by computer software to appear to do so. ■ **vir·tu·al·i·ty** /ˌvərchōō'alitē/ n.

vir·tu·al·ize /'vərchōōəˌlīz/ ▶ v. convert something to a computer-generated version of reality. ■ **vir·tu·al·i·za·tion** /ˌvərchōōələ'zāsHən/ n.

vir·tu·al·ly /'vərchə(wə)lē/ ▶ adv. **1** nearly; almost. **2** Computing by means of virtual reality techniques.

vir·tu·al mem·o·ry (also **virtual storage**) ▶ n. Computing memory that appears to exist as main storage although most of it is supported by data held in secondary storage.

vir·tu·al re·al·i·ty ▶ n. a system in which images that look like real, three-dimensional objects are created by computer.

vir·tue /'vərchōō/ ▶ n. **1** behavior showing high moral standards. **2** a good or desirable personal quality. **3** a good or useful quality of a thing: *the virtues of village life.* **4** old use virginity or chastity. – PHRASES **by virtue of** as a result of.

vir·tu·o·so /ˌvərchōō'ōsō/ ▶ n. (pl. **virtuosi** /-sē/ or **virtuosos**) a person highly skilled in music or another artistic activity. ■ **vir·tu·os·ic** /-'äsik, -'ōsik/ adj. **vir·tu·os·i·ty** /-'äsitē/ n.

vir·tu·ous /'vərchəwəs/ ▶ adj. **1** having or showing high moral standards. **2** old use (especially of a woman) chaste. ■ **vir·tu·ous·ly** adv. **vir·tu·ous·ness** n.

vir·tu·ous cir·cle ▶ n. a situation in which one event leads to another, each one increasing the beneficial effect of the next.

vir·u·lent /'vir(y)ələnt/ ▶ adj. **1** (of a disease or poison) having a very severe or harmful effect. **2** (of a virus) highly infective. **3** bitterly hostile: *a virulent attack on liberalism.* ■ **vir·u·lence** n.

vir·u·lent·ly adv.

vi·rus /'vīrəs/ ▶ n. **1** a submicroscopic particle, typically consisting of nucleic acid coated in protein, that can cause infection or disease and can only multiply within the cells of a host organism. **2** an infection or disease caused by a virus. **3** (also **computer virus**) a piece of code introduced secretly into a computer system in order to damage or destroy data.

vi·sa /'vēzə/ ▶ n. a stamp or note on a passport indicating that the holder is allowed to enter, leave, or stay for a specified time in a country.

vis·age /'vizij/ ▶ n. literary a person's facial features or expression. ■ **vis·aged** adj.

vis-à-vis /'vēz ə 'vē/ ▶ prep. in relation to.

vis·cer·a /'visərə/ ▶ pl.n. the internal organs of the body, especially those in the abdomen.

vis·cer·al /'vis(ə)rəl/ ▶ adj. **1** relating to the body's internal organs. **2** (of a feeling) deep and instinctive rather than rational: *the voters' visceral fear of change.* ■ **vis·cer·al·ly** adv.

vis·cid /'visid/ ▶ adj. sticky in consistency.

vis·cose /'vis,kōs, -,kōz/ ▶ n. rayon fabric or fiber made from treating cellulose with certain chemicals.

vis·cos·i·ty /vi'skäsitē/ ▶ n. (pl. **viscosities**) the state of being thick, sticky, and semifluid in consistency.

vis·count /'vī,kount/ ▶ n. a British nobleman ranking above a baron and below an earl.

vis·count·ess /'vī,kountəs/ ▶ n. the wife or widow of a viscount, or a woman holding the rank of viscount in her own right.

vis·cous /'viskəs/ ▶ adj. having a thick, sticky consistency between solid and liquid.

vise /vīs/ (Brit. **vice**) ▶ n. a metal tool with movable jaws that are used to hold an object firmly in place while work is done on it.

vis·i·bil·i·ty /ˌvizə'bilitē/ ▶ n. **1** the state of being able to see or be seen. **2** the distance that a person can see, depending on light and weather conditions.

vis·i·ble /'vizəbəl/ ▶ adj. **1** able to be seen. **2** able to be noticed; prominent: *a more visible police presence could be the norm.* **3** (of light) within the range of wavelengths to which the eye is sensitive. ■ **vis·i·bly** /-blē/ adv.

Vis·i·goth /'vizə,gäTH/ ▶ n. a member of the branch of the Goths who invaded the Roman Empire between the 3rd and 5th centuries AD.

vi·sion /'vizHən/ ▶ n. **1** the ability to see. **2** the ability to think about the future with imagination or wisdom: *the organization has lost its vision and direction.* **3** an experience of imagining something, or of seeing someone or something in a dream or trance. **4** the images seen on a television screen. **5** a very beautiful person or sight.

vi·sion·ar·y /'vizHə,nerē/ ▶ adj. **1** thinking about the future with imagination or wisdom. **2** relating to supernatural or dreamlike visions. ▶ n. (pl. **visionaries**) a person with imaginative and original ideas about the future.

vis·it /'vizit/ ▶ v. (**visits, visiting, visited**) **1** go to see a person or place for a period of time. **2** go to see someone for a particular purpose, such as to receive advice: *I visited my doctor for a checkup.* **3** access and view a website or web page. **4** (as adj. **visiting**) (of an academic) working for a fixed period of time at another college or university. **5** literary cause something harmful or unpleasant to affect someone: *they were visited with an epidemic.* **6** (usu. **visit with**) informal chat with someone. ▶ n. **1** an act of going to see a person or place. **2** a temporary stay at a place.

vis·it·a·tion /ˌvizə'tāshən/ ▶ n. **1** an official or formal visit. **2** the appearance of a god or goddess or a supernatural being. **3** a disaster or difficulty regarded as a punishment from God: *a visitation of the plague.* **4** (**the Visitation**) the visit of the Virgin Mary to Elizabeth described in the Gospel of Luke, chapter 1.

vis·i·tor /'vizitər/ ▶ n. **1** a person visiting a person or place. **2** a bird that migrates to a particular area for only part of the year.

vi·sor /'vīzər/ (also **vizor**) ▶ n. **1** a movable part of a helmet that can be pulled down to cover the face. **2** a screen for protecting the eyes from unwanted light. **3** a stiff peak at the front of a cap. ▪ **vi·sored** adj.

VISTA /'vistə/ ▶ abbr. Volunteers in Service to America.

vis·ta /'vistə/ ▶ n. **1** a pleasing view. **2** an imagined future event or situation: *vistas of freedom seemed to open ahead of him.*

vis·u·al /'vizHŌŌəl/ ▶ adj. relating to seeing or sight. ▶ n. a picture, piece of film, or display used to illustrate or accompany something. ▪ **vis·u·al·ly** adv.

vis·u·al·ize /'vizH(ə)wəˌlīz/ ▶ v. form an image of someone or something in the mind. ▪ **vis·u·al·i·za·tion** /ˌvizH(ə)wələ'zāshən/ n. **vis·u·al·iz·er** n.

vi·tal /'vītl/ ▶ adj. **1** absolutely necessary; essential. **2** essential for life: *the vital organs.* **3** full of energy; lively. ▶ n. (**vitals**) the body's important internal organs. ▪ **vi·tal·ly** adv.

vi·tal force ▶ n. the energy or spirit that gives life to living creatures.

vi·tal·ism /'vītlˌizəm/ ▶ n. the theory that life is dependent on a force or principle distinct from purely chemical or physical forces. ▪ **vi·tal·ist** n. & adj. **vi·tal·is·tic** /ˌvītl'istik/ adj.

vi·tal·i·ty /vī'talitē/ ▶ n. the state of being full of energy; liveliness.

vi·tal·ize /'vītlˌīz/ ▶ v. give strength and energy to: *the drink is claimed to vitalize the body and mind.*

vi·tal signs ▶ pl. n. clinical measurements, specifically pulse rate, temperature, blood pressure, and rate of breathing, that indicate the state of a patient's essential body functions.

vi·tal sta·tis·tics ▶ pl. n. **1** statistics relating to the population, such as the number of births, marriages, and deaths. **2** informal the measurements of a woman's bust, waist, and hips.

vi·ta·min /'vītəmən/ ▶ n. any of a group of organic compounds that are present in many foods and are essential for normal nutrition.

vi·ta·min A ▶ n. retinol, a compound that is essential for growth and vision in dim light and is found in vegetables, egg yolk, and fish-liver oil.

vi·ta·min B ▶ n. any of a group of substances essential for the working of certain enzymes in the body, including thiamine (**vitamin B₁**), riboflavin (**vitamin B₂**), pyridoxine (**vitamin B₆**), and cyanocobalamin (**vitamin B₁₂**).

vi·ta·min C ▶ n. ascorbic acid, a compound found in citrus fruits and green vegetables, essential in maintaining healthy connective tissue.

vi·ta·min D ▶ n. any of a group of compounds found in liver and fish oils, essential for the absorption of calcium and including calciferol (**vitamin D₂**) and cholecalciferol (**vitamin D₃**).

vi·ta·min E ▶ n. tocopherol, a compound found in wheat-germ oil, egg yolk, and leafy vegetables and important in stabilizing cell membranes.

vi·ta·min K ▶ n. any of a group of compounds found mainly in green leaves and essential for the blood-clotting process, including phylloquinone (**vitamin K₁**) and menaquinone (**vitamin K₂**).

vi·ti·ate /'vishē,āt/ ▶ v. formal **1** make something less good or effective. **2** destroy or reduce the legal validity of something.

vit·i·cul·ture /'viti,kəlcHər/ ▶ n. **1** the cultivation of grapevines. **2** the study of grape cultivation. ▪ **vit·i·cul·tur·al** /ˌviti'kəlcHərəl/ adj. **vit·i·cul·tur·ist** /-'rist/ n.

vit·i·li·go /ˌvītl'īgō, -'ēgō/ ▶ n. a medical condition in which the pigment is lost from areas of the skin, causing whitish patches.

vit·re·ous /'vitrēəs/ ▶ adj. **1** resembling glass in appearance. **2** (of a substance) containing glass.

vit·re·ous hu·mor ▶ n. the transparent jellylike tissue filling the eyeball behind the lens.

vit·ri·fy /'vitrə,fī/ ▶ v. (**vitrifies, vitrifying, vitrified**) convert something into glass or a glasslike substance by exposure to heat. ▪ **vit·ri·fi·ca·tion** /ˌvitrəfi'kāshən/ n.

vit·ri·ol /'vitrēəl, -,ōl/ ▶ n. **1** extreme bitterness or malice: *a website where waiters vent their vitriol.* **2** old use sulfuric acid.

vit·ri·ol·ic /ˌvitrē'älik/ ▶ adj. filled with bitterness or malice: *a vitriolic attack on working mothers.* ▪ **vit·ri·ol·ic·al·ly** /-ik(ə)lē/ adv.

vi·tu·per·a·tion /və,t(y)ŌŌpə'rāsHən, vī-/ ▶ n. bitter and abusive language. ▪ **vi·tu·per·a·tive** /və't(y)ŌŌpə,rātiv, vī-, -p(ə)rətiv/ adj.

vi·va /'vēvə/ ▶ exclam. long live! (used to express praise or support).

vi·va·ce /vē'vä,CHā, -CHē/ ▶ adv. & adj. Music in a lively and brisk way.

vi·va·cious /və'vāsHəs, vī-/ ▶ adj. (especially of a woman) attractive and lively. ▪ **vi·va·cious·ly** adv. **vi·vac·i·ty** /və'vasitē, vī-/ n.

vi·var·i·um /vī've(ə)rēəm/ ▶ n. (pl. **vivaria** /-'ve(ə)rēə/) an enclosure or structure used for keeping animals in conditions similar to their natural environment for study or as pets.

vi·va vo·ce /ˌvēvə 'vōcHā, ,vīvə 'vōsē/ ▶ adj. (especially of an examination) oral rather than written. ▶ adv. orally rather than in writing.

viv·id /'vivid/ ▶ adj. **1** producing powerful feelings or strong, clear images in the mind: *a vivid description.* **2** (of a color) very deep or bright. ▪ **viv·id·ly** adv. **viv·id·ness** n.

viv·i·fy /'vivə,fī/ ▶ v. (**vivifies, vivifying, vivified**) make someone or something more lively or interesting. ▪ **viv·i·fi·ca·tion** /ˌvivəfi'kāshən/ n.

vi·vip·a·rous /vī'vip(ə)rəs, vi-/ ▶ adj. (of an animal) giving birth to live young that have developed inside the body of the parent. Compare with OVIPAROUS. ▪ **viv·i·par·i·ty** /ˌvivə'paritē, ,vīvə-/ n.

viv·i·sec·tion /ˌvivə'seksHən/ ▶ n. the practice of operating on live animals for scientific research (used by people opposed to such work). ▪ **viv·i·sec·tion·ist** n. & adj. **viv·i·sec·tor**

/'vivə‚sektər, ‚vivə'sektər/ n.

vix·en /'viksən/ ▸ n. **1** a female fox. **2** a spirited or quarrelsome woman. ■ **vix·en·ish** adj.

viz. /viz/ ▸ adv. namely; in other words.

vi·zier /və'zi(ə)r/ ▸ n. historical a high-ranking official in some Muslim countries.

vi·zor ▸ n. variant spelling of VISOR.

vizs·la /'vizHlə, 'vēzlə/ ▸ n. a breed of golden-brown pointer (dog) with large drooping ears.

VJ /'vē‚jā/ ▸ n. a person who introduces and plays popular music videos; a video jockey. ▸ v. (**VJ's**, **VJ'ing**, **VJ'd**) perform as a VJ.

V-J Day ▸ n. the day (August 15) in 1945 on which Japan ceased fighting in World War II, or the day (September 2) when Japan formally surrendered.

VLF ▸ abbr. very low frequency (referring to radio waves of frequency 3–30 kilohertz and wavelength 10–100 kilometers).

VLSI ▸ abbr. Electronics very large-scale integration, the process of integrating hundreds of thousands of components on a single silicon chip.

V-neck ▸ n. a neckline having straight sides meeting at a point to form a V-shape. ■ **V-necked** adj.

vo·cab·u·lar·y /vō'kabyə‚lerē, və-/ ▸ n. (pl. **vocabularies**) **1** all the words used in a particular language or area of activity: *business vocabulary.* **2** all the words known to an individual person. **3** a list of words and their meanings, accompanying a piece of foreign or specialist writing. **4** a range of artistic or stylistic forms or techniques: *his command of the vocabulary of classical ballet.*

vo·cal /'vōkəl/ ▸ adj. **1** relating to the human voice. **2** expressing opinions or feelings freely or loudly. **3** (of music) consisting of or including singing. ▸ n. (also **vocals**) a part of a piece of music that is sung. ■ **vo·cal·ly** adv.

vo·cal cords (also **vocal folds**) ▸ pl.n. the folds of the lining of the larynx whose edges vibrate in the airstream to produce the voice.

vo·cal·ic /vō'kalik, və-/ ▸ adj. Phonetics relating to or consisting of a vowel or vowels.

vo·cal·ist /'vōkəlist/ ▸ n. a singer, especially in jazz or popular music.

vo·cal·ize /'vōkə‚līz/ ▸ v. **1** make a sound or say a word. **2** express something with words. **3** sing with several notes to one vowel. ■ **vo·cal·i·za·tion** /‚vōkələ'zāsHən/ n.

vo·ca·tion /vō'kāsHən/ ▸ n. **1** a person's career or main occupation. **2** a profession. **3** a strong belief that one ought to pursue a particular career or occupation.

vo·ca·tion·al /vō'kāsHənl/ ▸ adj. relating to a particular occupation and its skills or knowledge. ■ **vo·ca·tion·al·ly** adv.

voc·a·tive /'väkətiv/ ▸ n. the grammatical case used in addressing a person or thing.

vo·cif·er·ous /və'sifərəs, vō-/ ▸ adj. expressing opinions in a loud and forceful way: *he was a vociferous opponent of the takeover.* ■ **vo·cif·er·ous·ly** adv. **vo·cif·er·ous·ness** n.

vo·cod·er /'vō‚kōdər/ ▸ n. an electronic synthesizer that produces sounds from an analysis of speech input.

VOD ▸ abbr. video-on-demand.

vod·ka /'vädkə/ ▸ n. a clear, originally Russian alcoholic spirit made from rye, wheat, or potatoes.

vogue /vōg/ ▸ n. the fashion or style current at a particular time. ■ **vogu·ish** adj.

voice /vois/ ▸ n. **1** the sound produced in a person's larynx and uttered through the mouth, as speech or song. **2** the ability to speak or sing: *I've lost my voice.* **3** the range of pitch or type of tone with which a person sings, e.g., soprano. **4** a vocal part in a musical composition. **5** an opinion or the right to express an opinion: *giving the people a voice in decision-making.* **6** Grammar a form of a verb showing the relation of the subject to the action: *the passive voice.* ▸ v. **1** express something in words. **2** (as adj. **voiced**) Phonetics (of a speech sound) produced with vibration of the vocal cords (e.g., b, d, v).

voice box ▸ n. the larynx.

voice·less /'voislis/ ▸ adj. **1** lacking a voice; speechless. **2** Phonetics (of a speech sound) produced without vibration of the vocal cords (e.g., f, k, p).

voice·mail /'vois‚māl/ ▸ n. a centralized electronic system that can store messages from telephone callers.

voice-o·ver ▸ n. a piece of narration in a movie or television broadcast that is spoken by a person who is not seen on the screen.

voice·print /'vois‚print/ ▸ n. a visual record of a person's speech, analyzed with respect to frequency, duration, and amplitude, used for identification.

void /void/ ▸ adj. **1** (especially of a contract or agreement) not valid or legally binding. **2** (**void of**) free from; lacking: *the tundra is seemingly void of life.* **3** completely empty. ▸ n. a completely empty space. ▸ v. **1** declare that something is not valid or legally binding. **2** discharge or drain away water, gases, waste matter, etc. ■ **void·a·ble** adj.

voi·la /vwä'lä/ ▸ exclam. there it is; there you are.

voile /voil/ ▸ n. a thin, semitransparent fabric of cotton, wool, or silk.

VOIP ▸ abbr. voice over Internet protocol, a technology for making telephone calls over the Internet in which speech sounds are converted into binary data.

vol·a·tile /'välətl/ ▸ adj. **1** liable to change rapidly and unpredictably, especially for the worse: *volatile currency markets.* **2** (of a substance) easily evaporated at normal temperatures. ▸ n. a substance that is easily evaporated at normal temperatures. ■ **vol·a·til·i·ty** /‚välə'tilitē/ n. **vol·a·til·ize** /'välətl‚īz/ v.

vol·a·tile oil ▸ n. another term for ESSENTIAL OIL.

vol-au-vent /‚vôl ō 'vän/ ▸ n. a small round case of puff pastry filled with a savory mixture.

vol·can·ic /väl'kanik, vôl-/ ▸ adj. **1** relating to or produced by a volcano or volcanoes. **2** (of a feeling or emotion) very intense and liable to burst out suddenly. ■ **vol·can·i·cal·ly** /-ik(ə)lē/ adv.

vol·can·ic glass ▸ n. obsidian (a volcanic rock).

vol·can·ism /'välkə‚nizəm, 'vôl-/ (also **vulcanism** /'vəlkə‚nizəm/) ▸ n. volcanic activity or phenomena.

vol·ca·no /väl'kānō, vôl-/ ▸ n. (pl. **volcanoes** or **volcanos**) a mountain having a crater or opening through which lava, rocks, hot vapor, and gas are or have been forced from the earth's crust.

vol·can·ol·o·gy /‚välkə'näləjē, ‚vôl-/ (also **vulcanology**) ▸ n. the scientific study of volcanoes. ■ **vol·can·ol·o·gist** /-jist/ n.

vole /vōl/ ▶ n. a small mouselike rodent with a rounded muzzle.

vo·li·tion /vəˈlishən, vō-/ ▶ n. a person's power to choose freely and make their own decisions: *he left Oxford of his own volition.* ■ **vo·li·tion·al** adj.

vol·ley /ˈvälē/ ▶ n. (pl. **volleys**) **1** a number of bullets or other missiles fired at one time. **2** a series of questions, insults, etc., directed at someone rapidly one after the other. **3** (in sports) a strike or kick of the ball made before it touches the ground. ▶ v. (**volleys, volleying, volleyed**) (in sports) hit or kick the ball before it touches the ground. ■ **vol·ley·er** n.

vol·ley·ball /ˈvälēˌbôl/ ▶ n. a team game in which a ball is hit by hand over a net and points are scored if the ball touches the ground on the opponent's side of the court.

volt /vōlt/ ▶ n. the SI unit of electromotive force, the difference of potential that would carry one ampere of current against a resistance of one ohm.

volt·age /ˈvōltij/ ▶ n. an electromotive force or potential difference expressed in volts.

vol·ta·ic /välˈtā-ik, vōl-, vôl-/ ▶ adj. referring to electricity produced by chemical action in a battery.

volte-face /ˌvält(ə) ˈfäs, ˌvōlt(ə), ˌvôlt(ə)/ ▶ n. **1** an abrupt and complete reversal of attitude or policy. **2** an act of turning around so as to face in the opposite direction.

volt·me·ter /ˈvōltˌmētər/ ▶ n. an instrument for measuring electric potential in volts.

vol·u·ble /ˈvälyəbəl/ ▶ adj. **1** speaking easily and at length. **2** expressed in many words: *voluble descriptions of horses.* ■ **vol·u·bil·i·ty** /ˌvälyəˈbilətē/ n. **vol·u·bly** adv.

vol·ume /ˈvälyəm, -ˌyōōm/ ▶ n. **1** the amount of space occupied by a substance or object or enclosed within a container. **2** the amount or quantity of something: *the growing volume of traffic.* **3** degree of loudness. **4** a book, especially one forming part of a larger work or series. **5** a consecutive sequence of issues of a periodical. **6** fullness or thickness of the hair.

vol·u·met·ric /ˌvälyəˈmetrik/ ▶ adj. relating to the measurement of volume. ■ **vol·u·met·ri·cal·ly** /-trik(ə)lē/ adv.

vo·lu·mi·nous /vəˈlōōmənəs/ ▶ adj. **1** (of clothing) loose and full. **2** (of writing) very lengthy and detailed. ■ **vo·lu·mi·nous·ly** adv.

vol·u·mize /ˈvälyəˌmīz, -yōō-/ ▶ v. give volume or body to hair.

vol·un·ta·rism /ˈväləntəˌrizəm/ ▶ n. the principle of relying on voluntary action or participation. ■ **vol·un·ta·rist** n. & adj.

vol·un·tar·y /ˈvälənˌterē/ ▶ adj. **1** done or acting of one's own free will: *a voluntary code of practice.* **2** willingly working or done without payment. **3** (of an action or part of the body) under the conscious control of the brain. ▶ n. (pl. **voluntaries**) an organ solo played before, during, or after a church service. ■ **vol·un·tar·i·ly** /ˌvälənˈte(ə)rəlē, ˈvälənˌter-/ adv.

vol·un·teer /ˌvälənˈtir/ ▶ n. **1** a person who freely offers to do something. **2** a person who willingly works for an organization without being paid. **3** a person who freely joins the armed forces. ▶ v. **1** freely offer to do something. **2** say or suggest something without being asked. **3** suggest someone for a task or activity without consulting them first.

vo·lup·tu·ar·y /vəˈləpCHōōˌerē/ ▶ n. (pl. **voluptuaries**) a person who enjoys sensual or sexual pleasure very much.

vo·lup·tu·ous /vəˈləpCHəwəs/ ▶ adj. **1** (of a woman) having a full, sexually attractive body. **2** giving sensual pleasure: *voluptuous fabrics.* ■ **vo·lup·tu·ous·ly** adv. **vo·lup·tu·ous·ness** n.

vo·lute /vəˈlōōt/ ▶ n. a decorative scroll shape typically found at the tops of columns in Ionic architecture.

vom·it /ˈvämət/ ▶ v. (**vomits, vomiting, vomited**) **1** bring up food and other matter from the stomach through the mouth. **2** send out in an uncontrolled flow: *the machine vomited sheet after sheet of paper.* ▶ n. food and other matter vomited from the stomach.

voo·doo /ˈvōōˌdōō/ ▶ n. a religious cult of African origin practiced chiefly in the Caribbean, involving sorcery, possession by spirits, and elements of Roman Catholic ritual.

vo·ra·cious /vəˈrāshəs/ ▶ adj. **1** wanting or eating great quantities of food. **2** doing something eagerly and enthusiastically: *his voracious reading of literature.* ■ **vo·ra·cious·ly** adv. **vo·rac·i·ty** /-ˈrasitē/ n.

-vorous ▶ comb.form feeding on a specified food: *carnivorous.* ■ **-vore** comb.form.

vor·tex /ˈvôrˌteks/ ▶ n. (pl. **vortexes** or **vortices** /-təˌsēz/) **1** a whirling mass of water or air. **2** a powerful feeling, force, or situation that is difficult to avoid or escape from: *the country could be drawn into the vortex of world politics.* ■ **vor·ti·cal** /ˈvôrtikəl/ adj. **vor·tic·i·ty** /vôrˈtisitē/ n.

vo·ta·ry /ˈvōtərē/ ▶ n. (pl. **votaries**) **1** a person who has taken vows to dedicate their life to God or religious service. **2** a devoted follower or supporter: *a votary of the arts.*

vote /vōt/ ▶ n. **1** a formal indication of a choice between two or more candidates or courses of action. **2** (**the vote**) the right to participate in an election. **3** (**the vote**) a particular group of voters or the votes cast by them: *the green vote.* ▶ v. **1** give or register a vote. **2** grant or permit something by vote. **3** *informal* suggest something: *I vote we have one more game.* ■ **vot·er** n.

– PHRASES **vote of (no) confidence** a vote showing that a majority continues to support (or no longer supports) the policy of a leader or governing body. **vote with one's feet** *informal* express an opinion by leaving voluntarily: *overtaxed Africans could vote with their feet, leaving to find farmland elsewhere.*

vo·tive /ˈvōtiv/ ▶ adj. offered to God or a god as a sign of gratitude. ▶ n. (also **votive candle**) any candle used as such an offering, or a short, thick candle used especially for decorative purposes.

vouch /vouCH/ ▶ v. (**vouch for**) **1** confirm that something is true or accurate. **2** say that someone is who they claim to be or that they are reliable or honest.

vouch·er /ˈvouCHər/ ▶ n. a piece of paper that entitles the holder to a discount, or that may be exchanged for goods or services.

vouch·safe /ˈvouCHˈsāf, ˈvouCHˌsāf/ ▶ v. give or reveal in a gracious or superior way: *you'd never vouchsafed that interesting fact before.*

vow /vou/ ▶ n. a solemn promise. ▶ v. solemnly promise to do something.

vow·el /ˈvou(ə)l/ ▶ n. **1** a speech sound in

which the mouth is open and the tongue is not touching the top of the mouth, the teeth, or the lips. **2** a letter representing such a sound, such as *a, e, i, o, u.*

vox pop·u·li /ˈväks ˈpäpyəˌlī, -ˌlē/ ▸ n. popular opinion as represented by informal comments from members of the public.

voy·age /ˈvoi-ij/ ▸ n. a long journey by sea or in space. ▸ v. go on a voyage. ■ **voy·ag·er** n.

vo·yeur /voiˈyər, vwä-/ ▸ n. **1** a person who gains sexual pleasure from watching others when they are naked or taking part in sexual activity. **2** a person who enjoys seeing the pain or distress of others. ■ **vo·yeur·ism** /ˈvoiyəˌrizəm, voiˈyərˌizəm, vwäˈyər-/ n. **voy·eur·is·tic** /ˌvoiyəˈristik, ˌvwäyə-/ adj. **voy·eur·is·ti·cal·ly** adv.

VP ▸ abbr. vice president.

VPN ▸ abbr. virtual private network.

VR ▸ abbr. virtual reality.

VRML ▸ abbr. Computing virtual reality modeling language.

vs. ▸ abbr. versus.

V-sign ▸ n. **1** a gesture symbolizing victory, made by holding up the hand with the palm facing outward and making a V-shape with the first two fingers. **2** Brit. a similar V-shape gesture, but meant to be rude, made by having the palm face inward.

VSOP ▸ abbr. Very Special Old Pale, a kind of brandy.

VT ▸ abbr. Vermont.

VTOL /ˈvēˌtäl, -ˌtȯl/ ▸ abbr. vertical takeoff and landing.

vul·can·ism /ˈvəlkəˌnizəm/ ▸ n. variant spelling of VOLCANISM.

vul·can·ite /ˈvəlkəˌnīt/ ▸ n. hard black vulcanized rubber.

vul·can·ize /ˈvəlkəˌnīz/ ▸ v. harden rubber by treating it with sulfur at a high temperature.

■ **vul·can·i·za·tion** /ˌvəlkənəˈzāsHən/ n.

vul·can·ol·o·gy /ˌvəlkəˈnäləjē/ ▸ n. variant spelling of VOLCANOLOGY.

vul·gar /ˈvəlgər/ ▸ adj. **1** lacking sophistication or good taste: *a vulgar striped suit.* **2** referring to sex or bodily functions in a rude way. **3** dated relating to or typical of ordinary people. ■ **vul·gar·i·ty** /ˌvəlˈgaritē/ n. (pl. **vulgarities**) **vul·gar·ly** adv.

vul·gar frac·tion ▸ n. British term for COMMON FRACTION.

vul·gar·i·an /ˌvəlˈge(ə)rēən/ ▸ n. a person who lacks good taste and sophistication, especially one who is wealthy.

vul·gar·ism /ˈvəlgəˌrizəm/ ▸ n. a word or expression that refers to sex or bodily functions in a rude way.

vul·gar·ize /ˈvəlgəˌrīz/ ▸ v. spoil something by making it ordinary or less refined. ■ **vul·gar·i·za·tion** /ˌvəlgərəˈzāsHən/ n.

vul·gar Lat·in ▸ n. informal Latin of classical times.

Vul·gate /ˈvəlˌgāt, -gət/ ▸ n. the main Latin version of the Bible, prepared in the 4th century and later revised and adopted as the official version for the Roman Catholic Church.

vul·ner·a·ble /ˈvəln(ə)rəbəl/ ▸ adj. exposed to the possibility of being attacked or harmed: *maneuver your opponent into a vulnerable position.* ■ **vul·ner·a·bil·i·ty** /ˌvəln(ə)rəˈbilitē/ n. (pl. **vulnerabilities**) **vul·ner·a·bly** /-blē/ adv.

vul·pine /ˈvəlˌpīn/ ▸ adj. relating to or resembling a fox or foxes.

vul·ture /ˈvəlcHər/ ▸ n. **1** a large bird of prey without feathers on the head and neck, that feeds on dead animals. **2** a person who tries to benefit from the difficulties of others.

vul·va /ˈvəlvə/ ▸ n. the female external genitals. ■ **vul·val** adj.

vy·ing /ˈvī-iNG/ ▸ present participle of VIE.

W w

W¹ (also **w**) ▶ n. (pl. **Ws** or **W's**) the twenty-third letter of the alphabet.

W² ▶ abbr. **1** watt(s). **2** West or Western. **3** (in tables of sports results) won. ▶ symbol the chemical element tungsten.

w (also **w/**) ▶ abbr. with.

WA ▶ abbr. Washington (State).

WAC /wak/ ▶ abbr. Women's Army Corps.

wack·o /'wakō/ (also **whacko**) informal ▶ adj. mad; insane. ▶ n. (pl. **wackos** or **wackoes**) a crazy person.

wack·y /'wakē/ (also **whacky**) ▶ adj. (**wackier, wackiest**) informal funny or amusing in a slightly odd way. ■ **wack·i·ly** adv. **wack·i·ness** n.

wad /wäd/ ▶ n. **1** a lump or bundle of a soft material, used for padding, stuffing, or wiping. **2** a bundle or roll of paper or banknotes.
▶ v. (**wads, wadding, wadded**) **1** compress a soft material into a wad. **2** line or fill something with soft material. ■ **wad·ding** n.

wad·dle /'wädl/ ▶ v. walk with short steps and a clumsy swaying motion. ▶ n. a waddling way of walking.

wade /wād/ ▶ v. **1** walk through water or mud. **2** (**wade through**) read or deal with something that is boring and takes a long time. **3** (**wade in/into**) informal attack or intervene in a forceful way: *he waded into the debate, calling for the policy to be scrapped.* ▶ n. an act of wading.

wad·er /'wādər/ ▶ n. **1** a long-legged bird that feeds in shallow water, such as a sandpiper. **2** (**waders**) high waterproof boots, used by anglers.

wa·di /'wädē/ ▶ n. (pl. **wadis**) (in Arabic-speaking countries) a valley, ravine, or channel that is dry except in the rainy season.

wad·ing pool ▶ n. a shallow artificial pool for children to paddle in.

wa·fer /'wāfər/ ▶ n. **1** a very thin, light, crisp cookie or cracker. **2** a thin disk of unleavened bread used in the Christian service of Holy Communion. **3** a very thin slice of a semiconductor crystal used in solid-state electric circuits.

wa·fer-thin ▶ adj. & adv. very thin or thinly.

waf·fle¹ /'wäfəl, 'wô-/ informal ▶ v. speak or write at length in a vague or trivial way. ▶ n. lengthy but vague or trivial talk or writing. ■ **waf·fler** n. **waf·fly** adj.

waf·fle² ▶ n. a small crisp batter cake with a squared pattern on both sides, eaten hot with butter or syrup.

waf·fle i·ron ▶ n. a utensil used for baking waffles.

waft /wäft, waft/ ▶ v. **1** move easily or gently through the air. **2** move along with a gliding motion: *models wafted down the catwalk in filmy skirts.* ▶ n. **1** a scent carried in the air. **2** a gentle movement of air.

wag¹ /wag/ ▶ v. (**wags, wagging, wagged**) move rapidly to and fro. ▶ n. a wagging movement.

wag² ▶ n. dated informal a person who likes making jokes.

wage /wāj/ ▶ n. (also **wages**) **1** a fixed regular payment for work, typically paid daily or weekly. **2** the result or effect of doing something wrong or unwise: *disasters are the wages of sin.* ▶ v. carry on a war or campaign. ■ **waged** adj.

wa·ger /'wājər/ ▶ n. & v. more formal term for BET.

wag·gish /'wagisH/ ▶ adj. informal humorous in a playful way. ■ **wag·gish·ly** adv.

wag·gle /'wagəl/ ▶ v. move with short quick movements from side to side or up and down.
▶ n. an act of waggling. ■ **wag·gler** n. **wag·gly** adj.

Wag·ne·ri·an /väg'ne(ə)rēən/ ▶ adj. relating to or typical of the German composer Richard Wagner or his work.

wag·on /'wagən/ (Brit. also **waggon**) ▶ n. **1** a vehicle, especially a horse-drawn one, for transporting goods. **2** a wheeled cart or stall used by a food vendor. **3** Brit. a car on a freight train. ■ **wag·on·er** n. **wag·on·load** n.
– PHRASES **on** (or **off**) **the wagon** informal not drinking (or drinking) alcohol.

wag·on-lit /'vägôn 'lē/ ▶ n. (pl. **wagons-lits** pronunc. same) a sleeping car on a train in continental Europe.

wag·tail /'wag,tāl/ ▶ n. a slender songbird with a long tail that wags up and down.

wah-wah /'wä 'wä/ ▶ n. a musical effect achieved on an electric guitar by use of a pedal and on brass instruments by alternately applying and removing a mute.

waif /wāf/ ▶ n. **1** a homeless and helpless person, especially a child. **2** a person who appears thin or pale. ■ **waif·ish** adj. **waif-like** adj.

wail /wāl/ ▶ n. **1** a long high-pitched cry of pain, grief, or anger. **2** a long high-pitched sound.
▶ v. make a long high-pitched cry or sound.
■ **wail·er** n.

wain /wān/ ▶ n. old use a wagon or cart.

wain·scot /'wänskət, -,skät, -skōt/ (also **wainscoting** or **wainscotting**) ▶ n. an area of wooden paneling on the lower part of the walls of a room. ■ **wain·scot·ed** (also **wainscotted**) adj.

waist /wāst/ ▶ n. **1** the part of the body below the ribs and above the hips. **2** a narrow part in the middle of something such as a violin. ■ **waist·ed** adj.

waist·band /'wās(t),band/ ▶ n. a strip of cloth forming the waist of a skirt or a pair of pants.

waist·coat /'wās(t),kōt, 'weskət/ ▶ n. Brit. a vest, especially one worn by men over a shirt and under a jacket.

waist·line /'wās(t),līn/ ▶ n. **1** the measurement around a person's body at the waist. **2** the shaping and position of the waist of an item of clothing.

wait /wāt/ ▶ v. **1** stay in a particular place or delay action until a particular time or event. **2** be delayed or postponed: *he needs a shirt but that can wait.* **3** (**wait on**) act as an attendant to. **4** serve food and drink to people at a meal or in a restaurant. ▶ n. a period of waiting.
– PHRASES **in wait** watching for someone and preparing to attack them.

wait·er /'wātər/ (or **waitress** /'wātris/) ▶ n. a person whose job is to serve customers at their tables in a restaurant.

wait·ing game ▶ n. a tactic in which one refrains from action in order to act more effectively later on: *policemen were playing a waiting game outside a country cottage.*

wait·ing list ▶ n. a list of people waiting for something that is not immediately available.

wait·ing room ▶ n. a room for people who are waiting, for example to see a doctor or to catch a train.

wait·per·son /'wāt,pərsən/ ▶ n. a waiter or waitress.

waive /wāv/ ▶ v. choose not to insist on or demand a right or claim.

> **USAGE**
> **Waive** is sometimes confused with **wave**. **Waive** means 'choose not to insist on or demand a right or claim' (*he waived all rights to the money*), whereas the much more common word **wave** means 'move to and fro' (*the flag waved in the wind*).

waiv·er /'wāvər/ ▶ n. **1** an act of not insisting on a right or claim. **2** a document recording this.

wake¹ /wāk/ ▶ v. (past **woke** /wōk/ or **waked**; past part. **woken** /'wōkən/ or **waked**) **1** (often **wake up**) stop or cause someone to stop sleeping. **2** bring to life; stir: *his voice wakes desire in others.* **3** (**wake up to**) realize or become alert to something. ▶ n. **1** (especially in Irish tradition) a party held after a funeral. **2** a watch held beside the body of someone who has died.

wake² ▶ n. a trail of disturbed water or air left by the passage of a ship or aircraft.
– PHRASES **in the wake of** following as a result of.

wake·board·ing /'wāk,bôrdiNG/ ▶ n. the sport of riding on a short, wide board resembling a surfboard while being towed behind a motorboat. ■ **wake·board** n. **wake·board·er** n.

wake·ful /'wākfəl/ ▶ adj. **1** unable or not needing to sleep. **2** alert and aware of possible danger. ■ **wake·ful·ness** n.

wak·en /'wākən/ ▶ v. wake someone from sleep.

wake-up call ▶ n. something that alerts people to an unsatisfactory situation.

Wal·dorf sal·ad /'wôl,dôrf/ ▶ n. a salad made from apples, walnuts, celery, and mayonnaise.

wale /wāl/ ▶ n. **1** a ridge on a textured fabric such as corduroy. **2** a horizontal wooden strip fitted to strengthen a boat's side.

walk /wôk/ ▶ v. **1** move on foot at a regular and fairly slow pace. **2** travel over a route or area on foot. **3** accompany or guide someone on foot. **4** take a dog out for exercise. **5** Baseball be awarded first base after not swinging at four balls pitched outside the strike zone. **6** Baseball allow or enable

a batter to walk. **7** informal be released from suspicion or from a charge. ▶ n. **1** a journey on foot. **2** an unhurried rate of movement on foot. **3** a route or path for walking. **4** a person's way of walking. **5** Baseball an instance of being awarded (or allowing a batter to reach) first base after not swinging at four balls pitched outside the strike zone. ■ **walk·a·ble** adj.
– PHRASES **walk it** informal achieve a victory easily. **walk off** (or **away**) **with** informal **1** steal something. **2** win something. **walk of life** the position within society that someone holds. **walk out** leave suddenly or angrily. **walk over** informal **1** treat someone thoughtlessly or unfairly. **2** defeat someone easily.

walk·a·bout /'wôkə,bout/ ▶ n. **1** chiefly Brit. an informal stroll among a crowd conducted by an important visitor. **2** a journey (originally on foot) undertaken by an Australian Aboriginal in order to live in the traditional way.

walk·er /'wôkər/ ▶ n. **1** a person who walks, especially for exercise or enjoyment. **2** a frame used for disabled or infirm people for support while walking.

walk·ie-talk·ie /'wôkē 'tôkē/ ▶ n. a portable two-way radio.

walk-in ▶ adj. (of a storage area) large enough to walk into.

walk·ing pa·pers ▶ pl.n. informal notice of dismissal from a job: *the reporter has been given his walking papers.*

walk·ing stick ▶ n. **1** a stick with a curved handle used for support when walking. **2** (also **walkingstick**) a long, slender, slow-moving insect that resembles a twig.

Walk·man /'wôkmən, -,man/ ▶ n. (pl. **Walkmans** or **Walkmen**) trademark a type of personal stereo.

walk-on ▶ adj. (of a part in a play or movie) small and not involving any speaking.

walk·out /'wôk,out/ ▶ n. a sudden angry departure, especially as a protest or strike.

walk·o·ver /'wôk,ōvər/ ▶ n. an easy victory.

walk-up ▶ adj. **1** (of a building) allowing access to the upper floors by stairs only; having no elevator. **2** easily accessible to pedestrians: *a walk-up food stand.* ▶ n. a building allowing access to the upper floors by stairs only.

walk·way /'wôk,wā/ ▶ n. a raised passageway in a building, or a wide path outdoors.

wall /wôl/ ▶ n. **1** a continuous upright structure forming the side of a building or room or enclosing or dividing an area of land. **2** a barrier or obstacle to progress: *police met a wall of silence from witnesses.* **3** Soccer a line of defenders forming a barrier against a free kick taken near the penalty area. **4** the outer layer or lining of a bodily organ or cavity. ▶ v. **1** enclose an area within walls. **2** (**wall something up**) block or seal a place with a wall. **3** (**wall someone/thing in/up**) surround or imprison someone or something with a wall or barrier. ■ **wall·ing** n.
– PHRASES **drive someone** (or **go**) **up the wall** informal make someone (or become) very irritated. **go to the wall** informal (of a business) fail. **off the wall** informal eccentric or unconventional. **wall-to-wall** **1** (of a carpet) fitted to cover an entire floor. **2** informal very numerous or plentiful.

wal·la·by /'wäləbē/ ▶ n. (pl. **wallabies**) an Australasian marsupial resembling a small kangaroo.

wal·lah /'wälə/ ▶ n. Indian or informal a person of a

specified kind or having a specified role: *an office wallah*.

wall·board /'wôl,bôrd/ ▶ n. a type of board used for covering walls and ceilings.

wall·cov·er·ing /'wôl,kəv(ə)riNG/ ▶ n. material such as wallpaper used as a decorative covering for interior walls.

wal·let /'wälit, 'wô-/ ▶ n. 1 a pocket-sized, flat, folding holder for money and plastic cards. 2 old use a bag for holding provisions when traveling.

wall·eye /'wôl,ī/ ▶ n. 1 an eye with a streaked or opaque white iris. 2 an eye directed abnormally outward. 3 a predatory freshwater fish with large, opaque silvery eyes. ■ **wall·eyed** adj.

wall·flow·er /'wôl,flou(-ə)r/ ▶ n. 1 a plant with fragrant flowers that bloom in early spring. 2 informal a girl who does not have a man to dance with at a dance or party.

Wal·loon /wä'lo͞on/ ▶ n. 1 a member of a people who speak a French dialect and live in southern and eastern Belgium and neighboring parts of France. 2 the French dialect spoken by the Walloons.

wal·lop /'wäləp/ informal ▶ v. (**wallops, walloping, walloped**) 1 hit someone or something very hard. 2 heavily defeat an opponent. 3 (as adj. **walloping**) very large or great: *walloping energy bills*. ▶ n. a heavy blow or punch.

wal·low /'wälō/ ▶ v. 1 roll around or lie in mud or shallow water. 2 (of a boat or aircraft) roll from side to side. 3 (**wallow in**) enjoy something without restraint: *he wallowed in self-pity*. ▶ n. 1 an act of wallowing. 2 an area of mud or shallow water where mammals go to wallow.

wall·pa·per /'wôl,pāpər/ ▶ n. 1 paper pasted in strips over the walls of a room to provide a decorative or textured surface. 2 an optional background pattern or picture on a computer or cell phone screen. ▶ v. apply wallpaper to a wall or room.

wal·nut /'wôl,nət/ ▶ n. 1 an edible wrinkled nut with a hard round shell. 2 the tree that produces walnuts, a source of valuable ornamental wood.

wal·rus /'wôlrəs, 'wä-/ ▶ n. a large sea mammal with two large downward-pointing tusks, found in the Arctic Ocean.

wal·rus mus·tache ▶ n. a long, thick, drooping moustache.

waltz /wôlts/ ▶ n. a dance in triple time performed by a couple, who turn around and around as they progress around the dance floor. ▶ v. 1 dance a waltz. 2 move or behave in a casual or inconsiderate way: *she waltzed in and took all the credit*. ■ **waltz·er** n.

wam·pum /'wämpəm/ ▶ n. historical a string of small cylindrical beads made by North American Indians from shells, worn as a decorative belt or used as money.

WAN /wan/ ▶ abbr. Computing wide area network.

wan /wän/ ▶ adj. 1 (of a person) pale and appearing ill or exhausted. 2 (of light) pale; weak. 3 (of a smile) lacking enthusiasm; strained. ■ **wan·ly** adv.

wand /wänd/ ▶ n. 1 a rod used in casting magic spells or performing conjuring tricks. 2 a staff or rod held as a symbol of office. 3 a hand-held electronic device passed over a bar code to read the data.

wan·der /'wändər/ ▶ v. 1 walk or move in a leisurely, casual, or aimless way. 2 move slowly away from a fixed point or place: *my attention had wandered*. ▶ n. an act or spell of wandering. ■ **wan·der·er** n. **wan·der·ings** pl.n.

wan·der·lust /'wändər,ləst/ ▶ n. a strong desire to travel.

wane /wān/ ▶ v. 1 (of the moon) appear to become smaller each day as a result of having a decreasing area of its surface illuminated by the sun. 2 decrease in strength or extent: *confidence in the dollar waned*. – PHRASES **on the wane** becoming smaller, or less important or common.

wan·gle /'waNGgəl/ informal ▶ v. obtain something desired by persuasion or cunning. ■ **wan·gler** n.

wank /waNGk/ Brit. vulgar slang ▶ v. (also **wank off**) masturbate. ▶ n. an act of masturbating.

wank·er /'waNGkər/ ▶ n. Brit. vulgar slang a stupid or disliked person.

wan·na /'wônə, 'wä-/ ▶ contr. informal want to; want a.

wan·na·be /'wänəbē, 'wô-/ ▶ n. informal, derogatory a person who wants to be like someone famous.

want /wänt, wônt/ ▶ v. 1 feel a need or desire to have or do something. 2 (**be wanted**) (of a suspected criminal) be sought by the police. 3 informal should or need to do something: *you don't want to believe all you hear*. 4 (often **want for**) literary lack something desirable or essential. 5 desire someone sexually. 6 informal, chiefly Brit. (of a thing) need something to be done: *the wheel wants greasing*. ▶ n. 1 a lack or shortage of something. 2 lack of essentials; poverty. 3 a desire.

want ad ▶ n. informal a classified advertisement, typically placed by someone wanting to hire a worker or to buy or sell an item.

want·ing /'wänting, wônt-/ ▶ adj. 1 lacking in something required or desired. 2 not good enough; unsatisfactory: *workers who are found wanting face dismissal*.

wan·ton /'wäntn/ ▶ adj. 1 (of a cruel or violent action) deliberate and unprovoked. 2 (especially of a woman) having many sexual partners. ▶ n. old use a woman who has many sexual partners. ■ **wan·ton·ly** adv. **wan·ton·ness** n.

WAP /wap/ ▶ abbr. Wireless Application Protocol, a means of enabling a cell phone to browse the Internet and display data.

wap·i·ti /'wäpitē/ ▶ n. (pl. **wapitis**) another term for ELK.

war /wôr/ ▶ n. 1 a state of armed conflict between different nations, states, or groups. 2 a state of hostility or intense competition between groups. 3 a campaign against something undesirable: *a war on drugs*. ▶ v. (**wars, warring, warred**) take part in a war.

War. ▶ abbr. Warwickshire.

war·ble /'wôrbəl/ ▶ v. 1 (of a bird) sing with a succession of constantly changing notes. 2 (of a person) sing in a trilling or quavering voice. ▶ n. a warbling sound.

war·ble fly ▶ n. a large fly that lays its eggs on cattle, horses, and other mammals, the larvae of which form a swelling or abscess beneath the skin.

war·bler /'wôrb(ə)lər/ ▶ n. a small songbird with a warbling song, typically living in trees and bushes.

war chest ▶ n. a reserve of funds used for fighting a war.

war crime ▶ n. an act carried out during a war

that violates accepted international rules of war.

ward /wôrd/ ▶ n. **1** a room or division in a hospital for one or more patients. **2** an administrative division of a city or borough that is represented by a councilor or councilors. **3** a child or young person under the care and control of a guardian appointed by their parents or a court. **4** any of the ridges or bars inside a lock that prevent the turning of any key without corresponding grooves. ▶ v. (**ward someone/thing off**) prevent someone or something from harming or affecting one. ■ **ward·ship** n.

-ward (also **-wards**) ▶ suffix **1** (usu. **-wards**) (forming adverbs) toward the specified place or direction: *homewards.* **2** (usu. **-ward**) (forming adjectives) turned or tending toward: *upward.*

war·den /'wôrdn/ ▶ n. **1** a person responsible for supervising a particular place or procedure. **2** the head official in charge of a prison. **3** Brit. the head of certain schools, colleges, or other institutions. ■ **war·den·ship** n.

ward·er /'wôrdər/ ▶ n. (fem. **wardress**) chiefly Brit. a prison guard.

ward·robe /'wôr,drōb/ ▶ n. **1** a large, tall cabinet for hanging clothes in. **2** a person's entire collection of clothes. **3** the costume department or costumes of a theater or movie company.

ward·room /'wôrd,rōōm, -,rŏŏm/ ▶ n. a room on board a warship in which commissioned officers eat and relax.

-wards ▶ suffix variant spelling of **-WARD**.

ware /we(ə)r/ ▶ n. **1** pottery of a specified type: *porcelain ware.* **2** manufactured articles of a specified type. **3** (**wares**) articles offered for sale.

ware·house /'we(ə)r,hous/ ▶ n. **1** a large building where raw materials or manufactured goods are stored. **2** a large wholesale or retail store. ▶ v. /-,hous, -,houz/ store goods in a warehouse.

war·fare /'wôr,fe(ə)r/ ▶ n. the activities involved in fighting a war.

war·fa·rin /'wôrfərin/ ▶ n. a compound used as a rat poison and as a drug to prevent blood clotting.

war game ▶ n. **1** a military exercise to test or improve tactical skill. **2** a mock military conflict carried out as a game or sport.

war·head /'wôr,hed/ ▶ n. the explosive head of a missile, torpedo, or similar weapon.

war·horse /'wôr,hôrs/ ▶ n. informal a veteran soldier, politician, etc., who has participated in many campaigns or contests.

war·like /'wôr,līk/ ▶ adj. **1** tending to wage war; hostile. **2** relating to or prepared for war.

war·lock /'wôr,läk/ ▶ n. a man who practices witchcraft.

war·lord /'wôr,lôrd/ ▶ n. a military commander, especially one who has complete control of a region. ■ **war·lord·ism** n.

warm /wôrm/ ▶ adj. **1** of or at a fairly high temperature. **2** (of clothes or coverings) made of a material that helps the body to retain heat. **3** enthusiastic, affectionate, or kind: *a warm welcome.* **4** (of a color) containing red, yellow, or orange tones. **5** (of a scent or trail) fresh and easy to follow. **6** close to finding or guessing something. ▶ v. **1** make or become warm. **2** (**warm to/toward**) become more interested in or enthusiastic about someone or something. ▶ n. **1** (**the warm**) a warm place or area. **2** an act of warming. ■ **warm·er** n. **warm·ly** adv.

warm·ness n.

– PHRASES **warm up 1** prepare for exercise by doing gentle stretches and exercises. **2** (of an engine or electrical device) reach a temperature high enough to operate efficiently. **warm something up** entertain an audience to make them more enthusiastic before the arrival of the main act.

warm-blood·ed ▶ adj. **1** (of animals, chiefly mammals and birds) maintaining a constant body temperature by their metabolism. **2** passionate or spirited.

warmheart·ed /'wôrm'härtəd/ ▶ adj. sympathetic and kind.

war·mon·ger /'wôr,məNGgər, -,mäNG-/ ▶ n. a person who tries to bring about war.

warmth /wôrmTH/ ▶ n. **1** the quality, state, or feeling of being warm. **2** enthusiasm, affection, or kindness. **3** intensity of emotion.

warm-up ▶ n. **1** a period or act of preparation for exercise. **2** a period before a stage performance in which the audience is entertained.

warn /wôrn/ ▶ v. **1** inform someone about a possible danger or problem. **2** advise someone not to do something wrong or foolish. **3** (**warn someone off**) order someone to keep away or to refrain from doing something.

warn·ing /'wôrniNG/ ▶ n. **1** a statement or event that indicates a possible danger or problem. **2** advice against doing something wrong or foolish. **3** advance notice: *he arrived without warning.* ■ **warn·ing·ly** adv.

warp /wôrp/ ▶ v. **1** make or become bent or twisted as a result of heat or dampness. **2** make abnormal or strange; distort: *his hatred has warped his judgment.* ▶ n. **1** a distortion or twist in shape. **2** (in weaving) the lengthwise threads on a loom over and under which the weft threads are passed to make cloth.

war·paint /'wôr,pānt/ ▶ n. **1** paint traditionally used to decorate the face and body before battle, especially by North American Indians. **2** informal or humorous elaborate or excessive makeup.

war·path /'wôr,paTH/ ▶ n. (in phrase **on the warpath**) in an angry or aggressive state.

war·plane /'wôr,plān/ ▶ n. an aircraft designed and equipped to take part in air combat or to drop bombs.

war·rant /'wôrənt, 'wä-/ ▶ n. **1** an official authorization giving the police or another body the power to make an arrest, search somewhere, etc. **2** a document entitling the holder to receive goods, money, or services. **3** justification or authority: *there is no warrant for this assumption.* **4** an official certificate of appointment issued to an officer of lower rank than a commissioned officer. ▶ v. **1** make necessary or justify a course of action. **2** officially state or guarantee something. ■ **war·rant·a·ble** adj.

– PHRASES **I** (or **I'll**) **warrant** dated no doubt.

war·rant of·fi·cer ▶ n. a rank of officer in the US armed forces below the commissioned officers and above the noncommissioned officers.

war·ran·ty /'wôrəntē, 'wä-/ ▶ n. (pl. **warranties**) **1** a written guarantee promising to repair or replace an article if necessary within a specified period. **2** a guarantee by a person who is insured that certain statements are true or that certain conditions shall be fulfilled, the breach of which will make the policy invalid.

war·ran·ty deed ▶n. Law a deed that guarantees a clear title to the buyer of a property.

war·ren /'wôrən, 'wä-/ ▶n. **1** a network of interconnecting rabbit burrows. **2** a complex network of paths or passages.

war·ri·or /'wôrēər/ ▶n. (especially in the past) a brave or experienced soldier or fighter.

war·ship /'wôr,SHip/ ▶n. a ship equipped with weapons and designed to take part in warfare at sea.

wart /wôrt/ ▶n. **1** a small, hard, growth on the skin, caused by a virus. **2** any rounded lump or growth on the skin of an animal or the surface of a plant. ■ **wart·y** adj.
– PHRASES **warts and all** informal including faults or unattractive qualities.

wart·hog /'wôrt,häg/ ▶n. an African wild pig with a large head, warty lumps on the face, and curved tusks.

war·time /'wôr,tīm/ ▶n. a period during which a war is taking place.

war-torn ▶adj. (of a place) racked or devastated by war.

war·y /'we(ə)rē/ ▶adj. (**warier, wariest**) (often **wary of**) cautious about possible dangers or problems. ■ **war·i·ly** adv. **war·i·ness** n.

was /wəz/ ▶ first and third person singular past of BE.

wa·sa·bi /wə'säbē/ ▶n. an edible Japanese plant with a thick green root that tastes like strong horseradish.

wash /wäSH, wôSH/ ▶v. **1** clean someone or something with water and, typically, soap or detergent. **2** (of flowing water) carry or move: *floods washed away the bridges.* **3** be carried by flowing water. **4** informal seem convincing or genuine: *excuses just don't wash with us.* **5** brush something with a thin coat of dilute paint or ink. ▶n. **1** an act of washing or an instance of being washed. **2** a quantity of clothes needing to be or just having been washed. **3** the water or air disturbed by a moving boat or aircraft. **4** a medicinal or cleansing liquid: *antiseptic skin wash.* **5** a thin coating of paint or metal. **6** silt or gravel carried by water and deposited as sediment. ■ **wash·a·ble** adj.
– PHRASES **be washed out** be postponed or canceled because of rain. **come out in the wash** informal be resolved eventually. **wash one's dirty linen in public** informal discuss one's personal affairs in public. **wash one's hands of** take no further responsibility for. **wash over** occur all around without greatly affecting: *she allowed the conversation to wash over her.* **wash up** clean oneself, especially one's hands: *nobody eats until everyone washes up.*

wash·ba·sin /'wäSH,bāsən, 'wôSH-/ ▶n. a basin used for washing the hands and face.

wash·board /'wäSH,bôrd, 'wôSH-/ ▶n. **1** a ridged or corrugated board against which clothes are scrubbed during washing. **2** a similar board played as a percussion instrument by scraping. ▶adj. (of a person's stomach) lean and with well-defined muscles.

wash·cloth /'wäSH,klôTH, 'wôSH-/ ▶n. a small cloth of toweling for washing oneself with.

washed-out ▶adj. **1** faded by repeated washing. **2** pale and tired.

washed-up ▶adj. informal no longer effective or successful.

wash·er /'wäSHər, 'wôSH-/ ▶n. **1** a person or device that washes. **2** a small flat ring fixed between a nut and bolt to spread the pressure or between two joining surfaces to prevent leakage.

wash·er·wom·an /'wäSHər,wŏŏmən, 'wôSH-/ ▶n. (pl. **washerwomen**) a woman whose occupation is washing clothes.

wash·ing /'wäSHiNG, 'wôSH-/ ▶n. a quantity of clothes, bed linen, etc., that is to be washed or has just been washed.

wash·ing ma·chine ▶n. a machine for washing clothes, bed linen, etc.

wash·ing so·da ▶n. sodium carbonate, used dissolved in water for washing and cleaning.

wash·out /'wäSH,out, 'wôSH-/ ▶n. informal a disappointing failure.

wash·room /'wäSH,rŏŏm, 'wôSH-, -,rŏŏm/ ▶n. a room with washing and toilet facilities.

wash·stand /'wäSH,stand, 'wôSH-/ ▶n. chiefly historical a piece of furniture designed to hold a jug, bowl, or basin for washing the hands and face.

wash·tub /'wäSH,təb, 'wôSH-/ ▶n. a large metal tub for washing laundry.

wash·y /'wäSHē, 'wôSHē/ ▶adj. (**washier, washiest**) **1** (of color) pale: *it's a washy sort of brown.* **2** thinly or unevenly colored, as if by watery paint: *a washy band of pale blue floats above.*

was·n't /'wəzənt/ ▶contr. was not.

Wasp /wäsp/ (also **WASP**) ▶n. an upper-class or middle-class American white Protestant, regarded as a member of the most powerful social group.

wasp /wäsp/ ▶n. a stinging winged insect that typically nests in complex colonies and has a black and yellow-striped body.

wasp·ie /'wäspē/ ▶n. (pl. **waspies**) a woman's corset or belt designed to emphasize a slender waist.

wasp·ish /'wäspiSH/ ▶adj. sharply irritable. ■ **wasp·ish·ly** adv. **wasp·ish·ness** n.

wasp-waist·ed ▶adj. having a very narrow waist.

was·sail /'wäsəl, -,säl/ old use ▶n. **1** spiced ale or mulled wine drunk during celebrations for Twelfth Night and Christmas Eve. **2** lively festivities involving the drinking of much alcohol. ▶v. **1** celebrate with much alcohol. **2** go from house to house at Christmas, singing carols.

wast /wəst, wäst/ old use or dialect ▶ second person singular past of BE.

wast·age /'wāstij/ ▶n. **1** the action of wasting something. **2** an amount wasted.

waste /wāst/ ▶v. **1** use more of something than is necessary or useful. **2** fail to make good use of: *we're wasted in this job.* **3** (**be wasted on**) not be appreciated by someone. **4** gradually become weaker and thinner: *she was wasting away from tuberculosis.* **5** informal kill someone. **6** (as adj. **wasted**) informal under the influence of alcohol or illegal drugs. ▶adj. **1** removed or discarded as no longer useful or required. **2** (of an area of land) not used, cultivated, or built on. ▶n. **1** an act or instance of wasting something: *it's a waste of time trying to feed him.* **2** unusable or unwanted material or byproducts. **3** a large area of barren, uninhabited land.
– PHRASES **go to waste** be wasted. **lay waste (to)** completely destroy a place.

waste·bas·ket /'wāst,baskit/ (also **wastepaper**

basket) ▶ n. a receptacle for small quantities of rubbish.

waste·ful /ˈwāstfəl/ ▶ adj. using or using up something carelessly or extravagantly. ■ **waste·ful·ly** adv. **waste·ful·ness** n.

waste·land /ˈwāstˌland/ ▶ n. 1 a barren or empty area of land. 2 a situation, time, or place lacking in culture, spirituality, or intellectual activity: *the mid 1970s are now seen as a cultural wasteland.*

wast·er /ˈwāstər/ ▶ n. 1 a wasteful person or thing. 2 informal a person who does little or nothing of value.

wast·rel /ˈwāstrəl/ ▶ n. literary a lazy person who spends their time and money in a careless way.

wat /wät/ ▶ n. (in SE Asia) a Buddhist monastery or temple.

watch /wäcн/ ▶ v. 1 look at someone or something with attention or interest. 2 keep someone or something under careful observation. 3 treat with caution or control: *watch what you say!* 4 (**watch for**) look out for. 5 (**watch out**) be careful. ▶ n. 1 a small timepiece usually worn on a strap on the wrist. 2 an act or instance of watching. 3 a period of keeping alert for danger or trouble during the night. 4 a fixed period of duty on a ship, usually lasting four hours. 5 a shift worked by firefighters or police officers. 6 (also **night watch**) historical a watchman or watchmen who patrolled the streets of a town at night. ■ **watch·er** n.
– PHRASES **keep watch** stay on the lookout for danger or trouble. **watch one's back** protect oneself against unexpected danger.

watch·a·ble /ˈwäcнəbəl/ ▶ adj. (of a movie or television program) fairly enjoyable to watch.

watch·dog /ˈwäcнˌdôg/ ▶ n. 1 a dog kept to guard private property. 2 a person or group that monitors the practices of companies providing a particular service.

watch·ful /ˈwäcнfəl/ ▶ adj. alert to possible difficulty or danger. ■ **watch·ful·ly** adv. **watch·ful·ness** n.

watch·mak·er /ˈwäcнˌmākər/ ▶ n. a person who makes and repairs watches and clocks. ■ **watch·mak·ing** n.

watch·man /ˈwäcнmən/ ▶ n. (pl. **watchmen**) a man employed to look after an empty building, especially at night.

watch·tow·er /ˈwäcнˌtou(-ə)r/ ▶ n. a tower built to create a high observation point.

watch·word /ˈwäcнˌwərd/ ▶ n. a word or phrase expressing the central aim or belief of a person or group.

wa·ter /ˈwôtər, ˈwä-/ ▶ n. 1 the liquid that forms the seas, lakes, rivers, and rain and is the basis of the fluids of living organisms. 2 (**waters**) an area of sea under the legal authority of a particular country. 3 (**the waters**) the water of a mineral spring used for medicinal purposes. 4 (**waters**) the fluid surrounding a fetus in the uterus, especially as passed from a woman's body shortly before she gives birth. 5 the quality of transparency and brilliance shown by a diamond or other gem. ▶ v. 1 pour water over a plant or an area of ground. 2 give a drink of water to an animal. 3 (of the eyes or mouth) produce tears or saliva: *the smell of bacon made my mouth water.* 4 dilute a drink with water. 5 (**water something down**) make something less forceful or controversial by changing or leaving out certain details. 6 (of a river) flow through an area. ■ **wa·ter·less** adj.
– PHRASES **hold water** (of a theory) seem valid or reasonable. **pass water** euphemistic urinate. **of the first water** of the highest degree: *she was a bore of the first water.* **under water** submerged; flooded. **water on the brain** informal hydrocephalus. **water under the bridge** past events that are over and done with.

wa·ter·based ▶ adj. (of a substance or solution) using or having water as a medium or main ingredient.

wa·ter·bed /ˈwôtərˌbed, ˈwä-/ ▶ n. a bed with a water-filled rubber or plastic mattress.

wa·ter·bird /ˈwôtərˌbərd, ˈwä-/ ▶ n. a bird that lives on or near water.

wa·ter birth ▶ n. a birth in which the mother spends the final stages of labor in a birthing pool.

wa·ter boat·man ▶ n. a bug that lives in water and swims on its back using its back legs as oars.

wa·ter·borne ▶ n. 1 (of a vehicle or goods) conveyed by, traveling on, or involving travel or transportation on water. 2 (of a disease) communicated or propagated by contaminated water.

wa·ter buf·fa·lo ▶ n. a large black Asian buffalo with heavy swept-back horns, used for carrying heavy loads.

wa·ter can·non ▶ n. a device that sends out a powerful jet of water, used to disperse a crowd.

wa·ter chest·nut ▶ n. the crisp, white-fleshed tuber of a tropical plant, used in oriental cooking.

wa·ter clos·et ▶ n. dated a flush toilet.

wa·ter·col·or /ˈwôtərˌkələr, ˈwä-/ (Brit. **watercolour**) ▶ n. 1 artists' paint that is thinned with water rather than oil. 2 a picture painted with watercolors. 3 the art of painting with watercolors. ■ **wa·ter·col·or·ist** n.

wa·ter cool·er ▶ n. 1 a dispenser of cooled drinking water. 2 (as adj.) informal denoting the type of informal conversation among office workers that takes place around a water cooler: *a water-cooler chat about the president.*

wa·ter·course /ˈwôtərˌkôrs, ˈwä-/ ▶ n. a brook, stream, or artificially constructed water channel.

wa·ter crack·er ▶ n. a thin, crisp unsweetened cracker made from flour and water.

wa·ter·craft /ˈwôtərˌkraft, ˈwä-/ ▶ n. (pl. same) 1 a boat or other vessel. 2 skill in sailing and other activities that take place on water.

wa·ter·cress /ˈwôtərˌkres, ˈwä-/ ▶ n. a cress that grows in running water and whose strong-tasting leaves are used in salad.

wa·ter·fall /ˈwôtərˌfôl, ˈwä-/ ▶ n. a stream of water falling from a height, formed when a river or stream flows over a precipice or steep slope.

wa·ter fea·ture ▶ n. a pond or fountain in a garden.

wa·ter·fowl /ˈwôtərˌfoul, ˈwä-/ ▶ pl.n. ducks, geese, or other large waterbirds.

wa·ter·front /ˈwôtərˌfrənt, ˈwä-/ ▶ n. a part of a town or city alongside a body of water.

wa·ter·hole /ˈwôtərˌhōl, ˈwä-/ ▶ n. a hollow in which water collects, typically one at which animals drink.

wa·ter·ing can ▶ n. a portable water container with a long spout and a detachable perforated cap, used for watering plants.

wa·ter·ing hole ▶ n. 1 a waterhole from which

animals regularly drink. **2** informal a tavern or bar.

wa·ter·ing place ▶ n. **1** a watering hole. **2** a spa or seaside resort.

wa·ter lev·el ▶ n. the height reached by the water in a river, tank, etc.

wa·ter li·ly ▶ n. a plant that grows in water, with large round floating leaves and large cup-shaped flowers.

wa·ter·line /'wôtər,līn, 'wä-/ ▶ n. **1** the level normally reached by the water on the side of a ship. **2** a line on a shore, riverbank, etc., marking the level reached by the sea or a river.

wa·ter·logged /'wôtər,lôgd, 'wä-/ ▶ adj. saturated with or full of water.

Wa·ter·loo /'wôtər,lōō, 'wä-, ,wôtər'lōō, ,wä-/ ▶ n. (usu. in phrase **meet one's Waterloo**) a decisive defeat or failure.

wa·ter main ▶ n. the main pipe in a water supply system.

wa·ter·man /'wôtərmən, 'wä-/ ▶ n. (pl. **watermen**) a person who provides transport by boat.

wa·ter·mark /'wôtər,märk, 'wä-/ ▶ n. a faint design made in some paper that is visible when held against the light, identifying the maker. ▶ v. mark paper with a watermark.

wa·ter mead·ow ▶ n. a meadow that is periodically flooded by a stream or river.

wa·ter·mel·on /'wôtər,melən, 'wä-/ ▶ n. a large melonlike fruit with smooth green skin, red pulp, and watery juice.

wa·ter·mill /'wôtər,mil, 'wä-/ ▶ n. a mill worked by a waterwheel.

wa·ter pis·tol ▶ n. a toy pistol that shoots a jet of water.

wa·ter po·lo ▶ n. a seven-a-side game played by swimmers in a pool, with a ball like a volleyball that the players try to throw into their opponents' net.

wa·ter·proof /'wôtər,prōōf, 'wä-/ ▶ adj. preventing water from passing through. ▶ v. make something waterproof.

wa·ter rat ▶ n. a large ratlike rodent that lives both on land and in water.

wa·ter-re·sis·tant ▶ adj. partially able to prevent water from passing through.

wa·ter·shed /'wôtər,sHed, 'wä-/ ▶ n. **1** an area or ridge of land that separates waters flowing to different rivers, basins, or seas. **2** a turning point in a situation: *the band's success produced a watershed in popular music.*

wa·ter·side /'wôtər,sīd, 'wä-/ ▶ n. the area next to a sea, lake, or river.

wa·ter·ski /'wôtər,skē, 'wä-/ ▶ n. (pl. **waterskis**) each of a pair of skis enabling the wearer to skim the surface of the water when towed by a motorboat. ▶ v. (**waterskis, waterskiing, waterskied**) travel on waterskis. ■ **wa·ter·ski·er** n.

wa·ter snake ▶ n. a harmless snake that spends part of its time in fresh water.

wa·ter·spout /'wôtər,spout, 'wä-/ ▶ n. a funnel-shaped column of water and spray formed by a whirlwind occurring over the sea.

wa·ter ta·ble ▶ n. the level below which the ground is saturated with water.

wa·ter·tight /'wôtər,tīt, 'wä-/ ▶ adj. **1** closely sealed, fastened, or fitted so as to prevent the passage of water. **2** (of an argument or account) unable to be disputed or questioned.

wa·ter tow·er ▶ n. a tower supporting a water tank at a height to create enough pressure to distribute the water through a system of pipes.

wa·ter·way /'wôtər,wā, 'wä-/ ▶ n. a river, canal, or other route for travel by water.

wa·ter·weed /'wôtər,wēd, 'wä-/ ▶ n. vegetation growing in water.

wa·ter·wheel /'wôtər,(h)wēl, 'wä-/ ▶ n. a large wheel driven by flowing water, used to work machinery or to raise water to a higher level.

wa·ter wings ▶ pl.n. inflated floats fixed to the arms of someone learning to swim.

wa·ter witch ▶ n. a person who searches for underground water with a divining rod; a dowser.

wa·ter·works /'wôtər,wərks, 'wä-/ ▶ pl.n. (treated as sing.) an establishment for managing a water supply.

– PHRASES **turn on the waterworks** informal start crying.

wa·ter·y /'wôtərē, 'wä-/ ▶ adj. **1** consisting of, containing, or resembling water. **2** (of food or drink) thin or tasteless as a result of containing too much water. **3** weak or pale: *watery sunlight.*

watt /wät/ ▶ n. the SI unit of power, equivalent to one joule per second and corresponding to the rate of energy in an electric circuit where the potential difference is one volt and the current is one ampere.

watt·age /'wätij/ ▶ n. an amount of electrical power expressed in watts.

wat·tle[1] /'wätl/ ▶ n. **1** a material for making fences, walls, etc., consisting of rods interlaced with twigs or branches. **2** an Australian acacia tree with long flexible branches.

wat·tle[2] ▶ n. a fleshy lobe hanging from the head or neck of the turkey and some other birds.

wat·tle and daub ▶ n. a material formerly used in building walls, consisting of wattle covered with mud or clay.

Wa·tu·si /wä'tōōsē/ ▶ v. **1** an energetic dance popular in the 1960s. **2** (treated as pl.) the Tutsi people as a group (now dated in English use).

wave /wāv/ ▶ v. **1** move one's hand to and fro in greeting or as a signal. **2** move something held in one's hand to and fro. **3** move or sway to and fro while remaining fixed to one point: *the flag waved in the wind.* **4** style hair so that it curls slightly. ▶ n. **1** a ridge of water moving along the surface of the sea or arching and breaking on the shore. **2** a sudden occurrence of or increase in a phenomenon or emotion: *a wave of panic swept over her.* **3** a gesture or signal made by waving one's hand. **4** a slightly curling lock of hair. **5** Physics a periodic disturbance of the particles of a substance without overall movement of the particles, as in the transmission of sound, light, heat, etc.

– PHRASES **make waves** informal **1** create a significant impression. **2** cause trouble.

> **USAGE**
> For an explanation of the confusion between **wave** and **waive**, see the note at **WAIVE**.

wave·band /'wāv,band/ ▶ n. a range of wavelengths between two given limits, used in radio transmission.

wave·form /'wāv,fôrm/ ▶ n. Physics a curve showing the shape of a wave at a given time.

wave·length /'wāv,leNG(k)TH/ ▶ n. **1** Physics the distance between successive crests of a wave of sound, light, radio waves, etc. **2** a person's way of thinking when communicated to another: *we weren't on the same wavelength.*

wave·let /'wāvlit/ ▶ n. a small wave.

wa·ver /'wāvər/ ▶ v. **1** move quiveringly; flicker. **2** begin to weaken; falter: *his love for her had never wavered.* **3** be undecided between two opinions or courses of action. ■ **wa·ver·er** n. **wa·ver·y** adj.

WAV file /wāv/ ▶ n. Computing a format for storing audio files that produces CD-quality audio.

wav·y /'wāvē/ ▶ adj. (**wavier, waviest**) having or consisting of a series of wavelike curves. ■ **wav·i·ness** n.

wax¹ /waks/ ▶ n. **1** a soft solid oily substance that melts easily, used for making candles or polishes. **2** a substance produced by bees to make honeycombs; beeswax. ▶ v. **1** polish or treat something with wax. **2** remove hair from a part of the body by applying melted wax and then peeling it off with the hairs. ■ **wax·er** n.

wax² ▶ v. **1** (of the moon) gradually have a larger part of its visible surface lit up, so that it appears to increase in size. **2** literary become larger or stronger. **3** speak or write in a particular way: *they waxed lyrical about the old days.*

waxed pa·per (also **wax paper**) ▶ n. paper treated with wax to make it waterproof or greaseproof.

wax·en /'waksən/ ▶ adj. **1** having a smooth, pale, semitransparent surface like that of wax. **2** old use or literary made of wax.

wax·wing /'waks,wiNG/ ▶ n. a crested songbird, mainly pinkish-brown and with bright red tips to some wing feathers.

wax·work /'waks,wərk/ ▶ n. **1** a lifelike dummy modeled in wax. **2** (**waxworks**) (treated as sing.) an exhibition of waxworks.

wax·y /'waksē/ ▶ adj. (**waxier, waxiest**) resembling wax in consistency or appearance. ■ **wax·i·ness** n.

way /wā/ ▶ n. **1** a method, style, or manner of doing something. **2** the typical manner in which someone behaves or in which something happens: *it was not his way to wait for things to happen.* **3** a road, track, path, or street. **4** a route or means taken in order to reach, enter, or leave a place. **5** the route along which someone or something is traveling or would travel if unobstructed: *he blocked her way.* **6** a specified direction: *we just missed a car coming the other way.* **7** the distance in space or time between two points. **8** a particular aspect. **9** a specified condition or state: *the family was in a poor way.* **10** informal a particular area: *they live somewhere around your way.* **11** (**ways**) parts into which something divides or is divided. **12** forward motion or momentum of a ship or boat through water. ▶ adv. informal at or to a considerable distance or extent.
– PHRASES **by the way** incidentally. **by way of 1** so as to pass through or across; via. **2** as a form of. **3** by means of. **come one's way** happen or become available to one. **get** (or **have**) **one's** (**own**) **way** get or do what one wants in spite of opposition. **give way 1** yield to someone or something. **2** collapse or break under pressure. **3** (**give way to**) be replaced or superseded by. **go one's way 1** (of events, circumstances, etc.) be favorable to one. **2** leave. **have a way with** have a particular talent for dealing with or ability in. **have one's way with** old use or humorous

have sex with. **in a way** (or **in some ways** or **in one way**) to a certain extent. **lead the way 1** go first along a route. **2** be the first to do something. **one way and another** (or **one way or the other**) **1** taking most considerations into account. **2** by some means. **on the** (or **one's** or **its**) **way** about to arrive or happen. **on the** (or **one's** or **its**) **way out** informal going out of fashion or favor. **the other way around** (or **round**) **1** in the opposite position or direction. **2** the opposite of what is expected or supposed. **out of the way 1** (of a place) remote. **2** dealt with or finished. **3** no longer an obstacle to someone's plans. **4** unusual or exceptional. **ways and means** the methods and resources for achieving something, especially raising revenue.

way·bill /'wā,bil/ ▶ n. a list of passengers or goods being carried on a vehicle.

way·far·er /'wā,fe(ə)rər/ ▶ n. literary a person who travels on foot. ■ **way·far·ing** n. & adj.

way·lay /'wā,lā/ ▶ v. (past and past part. **waylaid**) **1** intercept someone in order to attack them. **2** stop someone and keep them in conversation.

way·mark /'wā,märk/ ▶ n. (also **waymarker**) a sign forming one of a series used to mark out a footpath or similar route.

way-out ▶ adj. informal very unconventional or experimental.

-ways ▶ suffix forming adjectives and adverbs of direction or manner: *lengthways.*

way·side /'wā,sīd/ ▶ n. the edge of a road.
– PHRASES **fall by the wayside** fail to continue with an undertaking.

way sta·tion ▶ n. a stopping place on a journey.

way·ward /'wāwərd/ ▶ adj. difficult to control because of unpredictable or willful behavior. ■ **way·ward·ly** adv. **way·ward·ness** n.

Wb ▶ abbr. weber(s).

WBA ▶ abbr. World Boxing Association.

WBC ▶ abbr. World Boxing Council.

WC ▶ abbr. Brit. water closet.

we /wē/ ▶ pron. (first person pl.) **1** used by a speaker to refer to himself or herself and one or more other people considered together. **2** people in general. **3** used in formal situations for or by a royal person, or by a writer, to refer to himself or herself. **4** you (used in a superior way).

USAGE
On whether to use **we** or **us** following **than**, see the note at PERSONAL PRONOUN.

weak /wēk/ ▶ adj. **1** lacking physical strength and energy. **2** liable to break or give way under pressure. **3** not secure, stable, or firmly established: *a weak economy.* **4** lacking power, influence, or ability. **5** lacking intensity: *a weak light from a single streetlamp.* **6** (of a liquid or solution) heavily diluted. **7** not convincing or forceful: *a weak plot.* **8** (of verbs) forming the past tense and past participle by adding a suffix (in English, typically *-ed*).
– PHRASES **the weaker sex** (treated as sing. or pl.) dated women regarded as a group.

weak·en /'wēkən/ ▶ v. make or become weak.

weak-kneed ▶ adj. lacking determination or courage.

weak·ling /'wēkliNG/ ▶ n. a weak person or animal.

weak·ly /'wēklē/ ▶ adv. in a weak way.
▶ adj. (**weaklier, weakliest**) weak or sickly.

weak·ness /'wēknis/ ▶ n. **1** the state of being

weak. **2** a disadvantage or fault. **3** a person or thing that one cannot resist or likes too much. **4** (**weakness for**) a liking for something that is hard to resist: *his weakness for shrimp cocktails.*

weal¹ /wēl/ (also chiefly Medicine **wheal**) ▶ n. a red, swollen mark left on flesh by a blow or pressure.

weal² ▶ n. formal that which is best for someone or something: *guardians of the public weal.*

wealth /welTH/ ▶ n. **1** a large amount of money, property, or valuable possessions. **2** the state of being rich. **3** a large amount of a resource or desirable thing: *a wealth of information.*

wealth·y /'welTHē/ ▶ adj. (**wealthier, wealthiest**) having a great deal of money, resources, or assets; rich.

wean /wēn/ ▶ v. **1** make a young mammal used to food other than its mother's milk. **2** (often **wean someone off**) make someone give up a habit or addiction. **3** (**be weaned on**) be strongly influenced by something from an early age: *a generation weaned on television.*

wean·ling /'wēnliNG/ ▶ n. a newly weaned animal.

weap·on /'wepən/ ▶ n. **1** a thing designed or used to cause physical harm or damage. **2** a means of gaining an advantage or attacking someone or something: *the drug is a powerful new weapon to treat cancer.* ■ **weap·on·ry** n.

weap·on·ize ▶ v. convert to use as a weapon.

weap·on of mass de·struc·tion ▶ n. a nuclear, biological, or chemical weapon able to cause widespread destruction and loss of life.

wear /we(ə)r/ ▶ v. (past **wore** /wôr/; past part. **worn** /wôrn/) **1** have something on one's body as clothing, decoration, or protection. **2** display a particular facial expression. **3** damage or destroy something by friction or continued use. **4** withstand continued use to a specified degree: *the fabric wears well wash after wash.* **5** (**wear off**) become less effective or intense: *the drug's effects were wearing off.* **6** (**wear someone down**) overcome someone by persistence. **7** (**wear someone out**) exhaust someone. **8** (as adj. **wearing**) mentally or physically tiring. **9** (**wear on**) (of time) pass in a slow or boring way. ▶ n. **1** clothing suitable for a particular purpose or of a particular type: *evening wear.* **2** damage caused by continuous use. **3** the capacity for resisting continuous use without damage. **4** the wearing of something on the body: *tops for wear in the evening.* ■ **wear·a·ble** adj. **wear·er** n.

– PHRASES **wear thin** be gradually used up or become less acceptable.

wear·i·some /'wi(ə)rēsəm/ ▶ adj. making one feel tired or bored.

wear·y /'wi(ə)rē/ ▶ adj. (**wearier, weariest**) **1** feeling or showing tiredness. **2** causing tiredness. **3** reluctant to experience any more of: *he was weary of constant arguments.* ▶ v. (**wearies, wearying, wearied**) **1** make someone weary. **2** (**weary of**) grow tired of someone or something. ■ **wea·ri·ly** adv. **wea·ri·ness** n.

wea·sel /'wēzəl/ ▶ n. **1** a small slender meat-eating mammal related to the stoat. **2** informal a deceitful or treacherous person. ▶ v. (**weasels, weaseling, weaseled**) achieve something by cunning or deceit: *somehow he weaseled her into going.* ■ **wea·sel·ly** adj.

– PHRASES **weasel words** words or statements that are deliberately confusing or misleading.

weath·er /'weTHər/ ▶ n. the state of the atmosphere at a place and time as regards temperature, wind, rain, etc. ▶ adj. referring to the side from which the wind is blowing; windward. Contrasted with LEE. ▶ v. **1** wear away or change in form or appearance by long exposure to the weather: *his face was weathered and pockmarked.* **2** come safely through a difficult or dangerous situation.

– PHRASES **keep a weather eye on** be watchful for developments. **make heavy weather of** informal have unnecessary difficulty in dealing with a task or problem. **under the weather** informal slightly unwell or depressed.

weath·er bal·loon ▶ n. a balloon equipped with meteorological apparatus that is sent up into the atmosphere to provide information about the weather.

weath·er-beat·en ▶ adj. damaged, worn, or tanned by exposure to the weather.

weath·er·cock /'weTHər,käk/ ▶ n. a weathervane in the form of a rooster.

weath·er·man /'weTHər,man/ (or **weatherwoman**) ▶ n. (pl. **weathermen** or **weatherwomen**) a person who broadcasts a description and forecast of weather conditions.

weath·er·proof /'weTHər,pro͞of/ ▶ adj. resistant to the effects of bad weather. ▶ v. make something weatherproof.

weath·er sta·tion ▶ n. an observation post where weather conditions are observed and recorded.

weath·er·strip /'weTHər,strip/ ▶ n. a strip of rubber, metal, etc., used to seal the edges of a door or window against rain and wind. ▶ v. (**weatherstrips, weatherstripped, weatherstripping**) apply such a strip to (a door or window).

weath·er·vane /'weTHər,vān/ ▶ n. a revolving pointer that shows the direction of the wind.

weave¹ /wēv/ ▶ v. (past **wove** /wōv/; past part. **woven** /'wōvən/ or **wove**) **1** make fabric by interlacing long threads passing in one direction with others at a right angle to them. **2** make basketwork or a wreath by interlacing rods or flowers. **3** (**weave something into**) make facts, events, and other elements into a story. ▶ n. a particular way in which fabric is woven: *cloth of a very fine weave.*

weave² ▶ v. move from side to side to get around obstructions.

weav·er /'wēvər/ ▶ n. **1** a person who weaves fabric. **2** (also **weaver bird**) a songbird of tropical Africa and Asia that builds elaborately woven nests.

web /web/ ▶ n. **1** a network of fine threads made by a spider to catch its prey. **2** a complex system of interconnected elements: *the story's web of lies.* **3** (**the Web**) the World Wide Web. **4** a membrane between the toes of a swimming bird or other animal that lives in water.

webbed /webd/ ▶ adj. (of an animal's feet) having the toes connected by a web.

web·bing /'webiNG/ ▶ n. strong, closely woven fabric used for making straps and belts and for supporting the seats of upholstered chairs.

web·cam /'web,kam/ ▶ n. trademark a video camera connected to a computer, so that its images may be viewed by Internet users.

web·cast /ˈwebˌkast/ ▶ n. a live video broadcast of an event transmitted across the Internet.

we·ber /ˈwebər/ ▶ n. the SI unit of magnetic flux, sufficient to cause an electromotive force of one volt in a circuit of one turn when generated or removed in one second.

web·foot·ed ▶ adj. having webbed feet.

web host·ing ▶ n. the activity or business of providing storage space and access for websites.

web·link /ˈwebliNGk/ ▶ n. 1 another term for **HYPERLINK**. 2 a printed address of a website in a book, newspaper, etc.

web·log /ˈwebˌlôg, -ˌläg/ ▶ n. full form of **BLOG** (noun).

web·mas·ter /ˈwebˌmastər/ ▶ n. a person who is responsible for a particular server on the Internet.

web page ▶ n. a hypertext document that can be accessed via the Internet.

web·site /ˈwebˌsīt/ ▶ n. a location connected to the Internet that maintains one or more web pages.

web·zine /ˈwebˌzēn/ ▶ n. a magazine published on the Internet.

wed /wed/ ▶ v. (**weds, wedding;** past and past part. **wedded** or **wed**) 1 formal or literary marry or get married. 2 formal or literary give or join someone in marriage. 3 (as adj. **wedded**) relating to marriage: *wedded bliss.* 4 combine two desirable factors or qualities. 5 (**be wedded to**) be entirely devoted to an activity, belief, etc.

we'd /wēd/ ▶ contr. 1 we had. 2 we should or we would.

wed·ding /ˈwediNG/ ▶ n. a marriage ceremony.

wed·ding band ▶ n. a wedding ring.

wed·ding cake ▶ n. a rich iced cake, typically in multiple tiers, served at a wedding reception.

wed·ding march ▶ n. a piece of march music played at the entrance of the bride or the exit of the couple at a wedding.

wed·ding ring ▶ n. a ring worn by a married person, given to them by their spouse at their wedding.

wedge /wej/ ▶ n. 1 a piece of wood, metal, etc., with a thick end that tapers to a thin edge, that is driven between two objects or parts of an object to secure or separate them. 2 a wedge-shaped thing or piece. 3 a golf club with a low, angled face for hitting the ball as high as possible into the air. 4 a shoe with a fairly high heel forming a solid block with the sole. ▶ v. 1 fix something in position with a wedge. 2 force into a narrow space: *she wedged her carryall between two bags.* – PHRASES **drive a wedge between** cause a disagreement or hostility between. **the thin end of the wedge** informal an action unimportant in itself but which is likely to lead to more serious developments.

wedge is·sue ▶ n. a divisive political issue, especially one raised by a candidate for office in hopes of attracting or alienating an opponent's supporters.

wedg·ie /ˈwejē/ ▶ n. informal 1 a shoe with a wedged heel. 2 an act of pulling up the material of someone's underpants tightly between their buttocks as a practical joke.

Wedg·wood /ˈwejˌwo͝od/ ▶ n. trademark a type of pottery made by the English potter Josiah Wedgwood and his successors, especially a kind of powder-blue stoneware with white embossed cameos.

wed·lock /ˈwedˌläk/ ▶ n. formal the state of being married.
– PHRASES **born in** (or **out of**) **wedlock** born of married (or unmarried) parents.

Wednes·day /ˈwenzdā, -dē/ ▶ n. the day of the week before Thursday and following Tuesday.

wee /wē/ ▶ adj. (**weer, weest**) chiefly Scottish little.

weed /wēd/ ▶ n. 1 a wild plant growing where it is not wanted, especially among crops or garden plants. 2 informal marijuana. 3 (**the weed**) informal tobacco. 4 informal a thin and leggy person. ▶ v. 1 remove weeds from an area of ground. 2 (**weed someone/thing out**) remove inferior or unwanted items or members from a group or collection.

weed·kill·er /ˈwēdˌkilər/ ▶ n. a substance used to destroy weeds.

weed whack·er ▶ n. an electrically powered grass trimmer with a nylon cutting cord which rotates rapidly on a spindle.

weed·y /ˈwēdē/ ▶ adj. (**weedier, weediest**) 1 containing or covered with many weeds. 2 informal (of a person) thin and leggy.

wee hours ▶ pl.n. (**the wee hours**) the early hours of the morning after midnight.

week /wēk/ ▶ n. 1 a period of seven days. 2 the period of seven days generally reckoned from and to midnight on Saturday night. 3 the five days from Monday to Friday, or the time spent working during this period.

week·day /ˈwēkˌdā/ ▶ n. a day of the week other than Saturday or Sunday.

week·end /ˈwēkˌend/ ▶ n. Saturday and Sunday. ▶ v. informal spend a weekend somewhere.

week·end·er /ˈwēkˌendər/ ▶ n. a person who spends weekends away from their main home.

week·ly /ˈwēklē/ ▶ adj. 1 done, produced, or happening once a week. 2 calculated in terms of a week: *weekly income.* ▶ adv. once a week. ▶ n. (pl. **weeklies**) a newspaper or periodical issued every week.

wee·nie /ˈwēnē/ ▶ n. 1 another term for **WIENER** (sense 1). 2 vulgar slang a man's penis. 3 informal a weak, socially inept, or boringly studious person.

weep /wēp/ ▶ v. (past and past part. **wept**) 1 shed tears. 2 discharge liquid. 3 (as adj. **weeping**) used in names of trees and shrubs with drooping branches, e.g., **weeping willow.** ▶ n. a fit or spell of shedding tears. ■ **weep·er** n.

weep·ie /ˈwēpē/ (also **weepy**) ▶ n. (pl. **weepies**) informal a sentimental or emotional movie, novel, or song.

weep·y /ˈwēpē/ ▶ adj. (**weepier, weepiest**) informal 1 inclined to weep; tearful. 2 sentimental: *a weepy TV movie.* ■ **weep·i·ly** adv. **weep·i·ness** n.

wee·vil /ˈwēvəl/ ▶ n. a small beetle with a long snout, several kinds of which are pests of crops or stored foodstuffs.

weft /weft/ ▶ n. (in weaving) the crosswise threads that are passed over and under the warp threads on a loom to make cloth.

Wehr·macht /ˈverˌmäkt, -ˌmäKHt/ ▶ n. the German armed forces from 1921 to 1945.

weigh /wā/ ▶ v. 1 find out how heavy someone or something is. 2 have a specified weight. 3 (**weigh something out**) measure and take out a portion of a particular weight. 4 (**weigh someone down**) make someone feel stressed or anxious. 5 (**weigh on**) be depressing or worrying to someone. 6 (**weigh in**) (of a boxer

or jockey) be officially weighed before or after a contest. **7** (often **weigh something up**) assess the nature or importance of something. **8** (often **weigh against**) influence a decision or action: *the evidence weighed heavily against him.* **9** (**weigh in**) informal make a forceful contribution to a competition or argument. **10** (**weigh into**) join in or attack forcefully or enthusiastically: *he weighed into the companies for their high costs.*
– PHRASES **weigh anchor** (of a boat) take up the anchor when ready to sail.

weigh·bridge /ˈwāˌbrij/ ▶ n. a machine for weighing vehicles, set into the ground to be driven onto.

weigh-in ▶ n. an official weighing, e.g., of boxers before a fight.

weigh sta·tion ▶ n. a roadside station where commercial vehicles can be required to stop and be inspected.

weight /wāt/ ▶ n. **1** the amount that someone or something weighs. **2** the quality of being heavy. **3** a heavy object. **4** a unit or system of units used for expressing how much something weighs. **5** a piece of metal known to weigh a definite amount and used on scales to find out how heavy something is. **6** (**weights**) heavy blocks or disks used in weightlifting or weight training. **7** the ability to influence decisions or actions: *their recommendation will carry great weight.* **8** the importance attached to something. **9** a feeling of pressure or worry: *that'll be a weight off my mind.* **10** the surface density of cloth, used as a measure of its quality. **11** Physics the force exerted on the mass of a body by a gravitational field. ▶ v. **1** make something heavier or keep something in place with a weight. **2** attach importance or value to: *reading and writing should be weighted equally in the assessment.* **3** (**be weighted**) be planned or arranged so as to give one party an advantage.
– PHRASES **be worth one's weight in gold** be very useful or helpful. **throw one's weight around** informal assert oneself in an unpleasant way.

weight·ing /ˈwātiNG/ ▶ n. allowance or adjustment made to take account of special circumstances.

weight·less /ˈwātlis/ ▶ adj. (of a body) not apparently acted on by gravity. ■ **weight·less·ly** adv. **weight·less·ness** n.

weight·lift·ing /ˈwātˌliftiNG/ ▶ n. the sport or activity of lifting barbells or other heavy weights. ■ **weight·lift·er** n.

weight train·ing ▶ n. physical training that involves lifting weights.

weight-watch·er ▶ n. a person who is on a diet in order to lose weight.

weight·y /ˈwātē/ ▶ adj. (**weightier**, **weightiest**) **1** weighing a great deal; heavy. **2** very serious and important. ■ **weight·i·ly** adv. **weight·i·ness** n.

Weil's dis·ease /vīlz/ ▶ n. an infectious disease caused by a bacterium and transmitted by rats via contaminated water.

Wei·mar·an·er /ˈwīməˌränər, ˈvī-/ ▶ n. a thin-coated gray breed of pointer used as a gun dog.

weir /wi(ə)r/ ▶ n. **1** a low dam built across a river to raise the level of water upstream or control its flow. **2** an enclosure of stakes set in a stream as a trap for fish.

weird /wi(ə)rd/ ▶ adj. **1** informal very strange or unusual: *he's a weird little guy.* **2** mysterious

or strange in a frightening way. ■ **weird·ly** adv. **weird·ness** n.

weird·o /ˈwi(ə)rdō/ ▶ n. (pl. **weirdos**) informal a strange or eccentric person.

welch ▶ v. variant spelling of WELSH.

wel·come /ˈwelkəm/ ▶ n. **1** an instance or way of greeting someone. **2** a pleased or approving reaction. ▶ exclam. used to greet someone in a glad or friendly way. ▶ v. **1** greet someone who is arriving in a polite or friendly way. **2** be glad to receive or hear of: *the decision was widely welcomed.* ▶ adj. **1** (of a guest or new arrival) gladly received. **2** very pleasing because much needed or desired. **3** allowed or invited to do a particular thing: *you are welcome to join in.* **4** (**welcome to**) used to indicate relief at giving up something to another: *the job is all yours and you're welcome to it!* ■ **wel·com·er** n.

weld /weld/ ▶ v. **1** join metal parts together by heating the surfaces to the point of melting and pressing or hammering them together. **2** make an article by welding. **3** unite into a strong and effective whole: *they welded diverse ethnic groups into a single political system.* ▶ n. a welded joint. ■ **weld·er** n.

wel·fare /ˈwelˌfe(ə)r/ ▶ n. **1** the health, happiness, and fortunes of a person or group. **2** organized practical or financial help provided, typically by the government, to help people in need.

wel·fare state ▶ n. a system under which the government protects the health and well-being of its citizens by providing grants, pensions, and other benefits.

wel·far·ism /ˈwelfe(ə)ˌrizəm/ ▶ n. the principles or policies associated with a welfare state. ■ **wel·far·ist** n. & adj.

wel·kin /ˈwelkin/ ▶ n. literary the sky or heaven.

well¹ /wel/ ▶ adv. (**better** /ˈbetər/, **best** /best/) **1** in a good or satisfactory way. **2** in a thorough way: *add the mustard and mix well.* **3** to a great extent or degree; very much. **4** in a favorable or approving way. **5** in prosperity or comfort. **6** Brit. informal very; extremely: *he was well out of order.* **7** very probably. **8** without difficulty. **9** with good reason: *what, you may well ask, are they doing here?* **10** old use at a good time; luckily: *hail fellow, well met.* ▶ adj. (**better**, **best**) **1** in good health. **2** in a satisfactory state or position. **3** sensible; advisable. ▶ exclam. used to express surprise, anger, resignation, etc., or when pausing in speech.
– PHRASES **as well** in addition; too. **as well** (or **just as well**) **1** with equal reason or an equally good result. **2** sensible, appropriate, or desirable. **be well up on** know a great deal about something. **leave** (or **let**) **well enough alone** refrain from interfering with or trying to improve something. **well and truly** completely.

> **USAGE**
> As an adverb, **well** is often used with a past participle (such as *known* or *dressed*) to form compound adjectives: **well known**, **well dressed**, and so on. Such adjectives should be written without a hyphen when they are used immediately after a verb (*she is well known as a writer*) but with a hyphen when they come before a noun (*a well-known writer*).

well² ▶ n. **1** a shaft sunk into the ground to obtain water, oil, or gas. **2** a hollow made to hold liquid. **3** a plentiful source or supply: *a deep well of sympathy.* **4** an enclosed space in the middle of a building, giving room for stairs or an elevator or allowing in light or air. ▶ v. (often **well up**) **1** (of a liquid) rise up to the surface and spill or be about to spill. **2** (of an emotion) arise and become more intense.

we'll /wēl/ ▶ contr. we will; we shall.

well-ad·vised ▶ adj. sensible; wise.

well-ap·point·ed ▶ adj. (of a building or room) having a high standard of equipment or furnishing.

well-bal·anced ▶ adj. mentally and emotionally stable.

well-be·ing ▶ n. the state of being comfortable, healthy, or happy.

well-bred ▶ adj. polite and well brought up.

well-built ▶ adj. (of a person) strong and sturdy.

well-dis·posed ▶ adj. having a positive, sympathetic, or friendly attitude.

well-done ▶ adj. **1** carried out successfully or satisfactorily. **2** (of food) thoroughly cooked. ▶ exclam. (**well done**) used to express congratulation or approval.

well-en·dowed ▶ adj. **1** having plentiful supplies of a resource. **2** (of a woman) having large breasts.

well-found·ed ▶ adj. based on good evidence or reasons.

well·head /ˈwelˌhed/ ▶ n. **1** the place where a spring comes out of the ground. **2** the structure over an oil or gas well.

well-heeled ▶ adj. informal rich; wealthy.

wel·ling·ton /ˈweliNGtən/ (also **wellington boot**) ▶ n. Brit. a knee-length waterproof rubber or plastic boot.

well-known ▶ adj. known widely or thoroughly.

well-mean·ing (also **well-meant**) ▶ adj. having good intentions but not necessarily the desired effect.

well-nigh ▶ adv. almost.

well-off ▶ adj. **1** rich; wealthy. **2** in a favorable situation.

well-oiled ▶ adj. **1** operating smoothly. **2** informal drunk.

well-pre·served ▶ adj. (of an old person) showing little sign of aging.

well-read ▶ adj. very knowledgeable as a result of reading widely.

well-round·ed ▶ adj. **1** (of a person) having a pleasingly curved or plump shape. **2** having a mature personality and varied interests: *a well-rounded student.*

well-spo·ken ▶ adj. speaking in an educated and refined way.

well·spring /ˈwelˌspriNG/ ▶ n. literary **1** a plentiful source of something: *a wellspring of creativity.* **2** the place where a spring comes out of the ground.

well-to-do ▶ adj. wealthy; prosperous.

well-trav·eled ▶ adj. **1** (of a person) having traveled widely. **2** (of a route) much used by travelers.

well-tried ▶ adj. having been used often and therefore known to be reliable.

well-trod·den ▶ adj. (of a route) much used by travelers.

well-turned ▶ adj. **1** (of a phrase or compliment) elegantly expressed. **2** (of a woman's ankle or leg) attractively shaped.

well-wish·er ▶ n. a person who feels or expresses a desire that someone else finds happiness or

success.

well-worn ▶ adj. **1** showing signs of extensive use or wear. **2** (of a phrase or idea) used or repeated so often that it is no longer interesting or original.

Welsh /welsh/ ▶ n. the language of Wales. ▶ adj. relating to Wales. ■ **Welsh·man** n. (pl. **Welshmen**) **Welsh·ness** n. **Welsh·wom·an** n. (pl. **Welshwomen**).

welsh /welsh/ (also **welch**) ▶ v. (**welsh on**) fail to pay a debt or fulfill an obligation.

Welsh rare·bit (also **Welsh rabbit**) ▶ n. another term for RAREBIT.

welt /welt/ ▶ n. **1** a ribbed, reinforced, or decorative border on an item of clothing. **2** a weal. **3** a leather rim around the edge of the upper of a shoe, to which the sole is attached.

Welt·an·schau·ung /ˈveltˌänˌsHouˈəNG/ ▶ n. (pl. **Weltanschauungen** /-sHouˈəNGən/) a particular philosophy or view of life.

wel·ter /ˈweltər/ ▶ n. a large confused or disorganized mass or quantity: *a welter of new regulations.*

wel·ter·weight /ˈweltərˌwāt/ ▶ n. a weight in boxing and other sports between lightweight and middleweight.

wen /wen/ ▶ n. a boil or other swelling or growth on the skin.

wench /wenCH/ ▶ n. old use or humorous a girl or young woman.

wend /wend/ ▶ v. (**wend one's way**) go slowly or by an indirect route.

Wens·ley·dale /ˈwenzlēˌdāl/ ▶ n. a type of white cheese with a crumbly texture.

went /went/ ▶ past of GO[1].

wept /wept/ ▶ past and past participle of WEEP.

were /wər/ ▶ second person singular past, plural past, and past subjunctive of BE.

we're /wi(ə)r/ ▶ contr. we are.

weren't /wər(ə)nt/ ▶ contr. were not.

were·wolf /ˈwe(ə)rˌwŏŏlf/ ▶ n. (pl. **werewolves**) (in folklore) a person who periodically changes into a wolf, typically when there is a full moon.

wert /wərt/ ▶ old-fashioned second person singular past of BE.

Wes·ley·an /ˈwezlēən, ˈwes-/ ▶ adj. relating to the teachings of the English preacher John Wesley or the main branch of the Methodist Church, which he founded. ▶ n. a follower of Wesley or of the main Methodist tradition.

west /west/ ▶ n. **1** the direction in which the sun sets at the equinoxes, on the left-hand side of a person facing north. **2** the western part of a place. **3** (**the West**) Europe and North America seen in contrast to other civilizations. **4** (**the West**) historical the non-Communist countries of Europe and North America. **5** (**the West**) historical America's western frontier, especially during the 19th century. ▶ adj. **1** lying toward, near, or facing the west. **2** (of a wind) blowing from the west. ▶ adv. to or toward the west. ■ **west·bound** /ˈwestˌbound/ adj. & adv.

west·er·ly /ˈwestərlē/ ▶ adj. & adv. **1** facing or moving toward the west. **2** (of a wind) blowing from the west. ▶ n. (pl. **westerlies**) a wind blowing from the west.

west·ern /ˈwestərn/ ▶ adj. **1** situated in, directed toward, or facing the west. **2** (usu. **Western**) coming from or typical of the West, in particular Europe and North America. ▶ n. a movie or novel about cowboys in western North America. ■ **west·ern·most** /-ˌmōst/ adj.

West·ern Church ▶ n. the part of the Christian Church originating in the Western Roman Empire, including the Roman Catholic, Anglican, Lutheran, and Reformed Churches.

West·ern·er /'westərnər/ ▶ n. a person from the west, especially from western Europe or North America.

west·ern·ize /'westərˌnīz/ ▶ v. bring a country, system, etc., under the influence of the cultural, economic, or political systems of Europe and North America. ■ **west·ern·i·za·tion** /ˌwestərniˈzāshən/ n. **west·ern·iz·er** n.

West In·di·an ▶ n. a person from the West Indies, or a person of West Indian descent. ▶ adj. relating to the West Indies.

west-north·west ▶ n. the direction midway between west and northwest.

west-south·west ▶ n. the direction midway between west and southwest.

west·ward /'westwərd/ ▶ adj. toward the west. ▶ adv. (also **westwards**) in a westerly direction.

wet /wet/ ▶ adj. (**wetter**, **wettest**) 1 covered or saturated with liquid. 2 (of the weather) rainy. 3 (of paint, ink, etc.) not yet having dried or hardened. 4 (of a process) involving the use of water or liquid. 5 informal (of an area) allowing the free sale of alcoholic drink. ▶ v. (**wets**, **wetting**; past and past part. **wet** or **wetted**) 1 cover or touch someone or something with liquid. 2 urinate in or on something. 3 (**wet oneself**) urinate without intending to. ▶ n. 1 (**the wet**) rainy weather. 2 liquid that makes something damp. ■ **wet·ly** adv. **wet·ness** n.

– PHRASES **all wet** informal completely wrong. **wet behind the ears** informal lacking experience; immature. **wet one's whistle** informal have a drink.

wet·back /'wetˌbak/ ▶ n. informal, derogatory a Mexican living in the US, especially one who is an illegal immigrant.

wet blan·ket ▶ n. informal a person who spoils other people's enjoyment by being disapproving or unenthusiastic.

wet dream ▶ n. an erotic dream that causes a man to involuntarily ejaculate semen.

wet fly ▶ n. an artificial fishing fly designed to sink below the surface of the water.

weth·er /'weᴛʜər/ ▶ n. a castrated ram.

wet·land /'wetˌland, -lənd/ ▶ n. (also **wetlands**) swampy or marshy land.

wet nurse ▶ n. chiefly historical a woman employed to breastfeed another woman's child. ▶ v. (**wet-nurse**) 1 act as a wet nurse to. 2 informal look after someone as if they were a helpless infant: *I have no intention of wet-nursing you prima donnas.*

wet·suit /'wetˌso͞ot/ ▶ n. a close-fitting rubber garment covering the entire body, worn for warmth in water sports or diving.

we've /wēv/ ▶ contr. we have.

whack /(h)wak/ informal ▶ v. 1 strike someone or something forcefully with a sharp blow. 2 put something somewhere roughly or carelessly. 3 defeat an opponent heavily. ▶ n. 1 a sharp or resounding blow. 2 a try or attempt.

– PHRASES **out of whack** not working correctly. **top** (or **full**) **whack** chiefly Brit. the maximum price or rate.

whack·o ▶ adj. & n. (pl. **whackos**) variant spelling of **wacko**.

whack·y ▶ adj. variant spelling of **wacky**.

whale[1] /(h)wāl/ ▶ n. (pl. same or **whales**) a very large sea mammal with a horizontal tail fin and a blowhole on top of the head for breathing.

– PHRASES **a whale of a** —— informal an extremely good example of something. **have a whale of a time** informal enjoy oneself very much.

whale[2] ▶ v. informal beat; hit.

whale·bone /'(h)wālˌbōn/ ▶ n. 1 a horny substance that grows in a series of thin parallel plates in the upper jaw of some whales and is used by them to strain plankton from the seawater. 2 strips of this substance, formerly used to stiffen corsets.

whal·er /'(h)wālər/ ▶ n. 1 a ship used for hunting whales. 2 a sailor whose job is to hunt whales.

whal·ing /'(h)wāliNG/ ▶ n. the practice or industry of hunting and killing whales for their oil, meat, or whalebone.

wham /(h)wam/ informal ▶ exclam. used to express the sound of a forceful impact or the idea of a sudden and dramatic event. ▶ v. (**whams**, **whamming**, **whammed**) strike something forcefully.

wham·my /'(h)wamē/ ▶ n. (pl. **whammies**) informal 1 an event with a powerful and unpleasant effect; a blow. 2 an evil or unlucky influence; a curse: *I think that guy put the whammy on me.*

whap /(h)wap/ v. (**whaps**, **whapping**, **whapped**) v. & n. ▶ variant spelling of **whop**.

wharf /(h)wôrf/ ▶ n. (pl. **wharves** /(h)wôrvz/ or **wharfs**) a level quayside area to which a ship may be moored to load and unload.

what /(h)wət, (h)wät/ ▶ pron. & determiner 1 asking for information specifying something. 2 (as pronoun) asking for repetition of something not heard or confirmation of something not understood. 3 (as pronoun) the thing or things that. 4 no matter what; whatever. 5 used to emphasize something surprising or remarkable. ▶ adv. to what extent?

– PHRASES **give someone what for** informal punish or scold someone severely. **what for?** informal for what reason? **what's what** informal what is useful or important. **what with** because of.

what·cha·ma·call·it /'(h)wəchəməˌkôlit, '(h)wä-/ ▶ n. informal a person or thing whose name one has forgotten, does not know, or does not wish to mention.

what·ev·er /(h)wətˈevər, ˌ(h)wät-/ ▶ pron. & determiner used to emphasize a lack of restriction in referring to any thing; no matter what. ▶ pron. used for emphasis instead of 'what' in questions. ▶ adv. 1 at all; of any kind. 2 informal no matter what happens.

what·not /'(h)wətˌnät, '(h)wät-/ ▶ n. informal used to refer to an unidentified item or items having something in common with items already named.

whats·it /'(h)wətsit, '(h)wät-/ ▶ n. informal a person or thing whose name one cannot remember, does not know, or does not wish to specify.

what·so·ev·er /ˌ(h)wətsōˈevər, ˌ(h)wät-/ ▶ adv. at all. ▶ determiner & pron. old use whatever.

wheal /(h)wēl/ ▶ n. variant spelling of **weal**[1].

wheat /(h)wēt/ ▶ n. a cereal widely grown in temperate countries, the grain of which is ground to make flour.

wheat·ear /'(h)wētˌir/ ▶ n. a songbird with black

and gray, buff, or white plumage and a white rump.

wheat·en /'(h)wētn/ ▸ **adj.** made of wheat.

wheat germ ▸ **n.** a nutritious foodstuff consisting of the center parts of grains of wheat.

wheat·grass /'(h)wēt‚gras/ ▸ **n.** a relative of couch grass that is cultivated for its nutritional benefits.

whee·dle /'(h)wēdl/ ▸ **v.** use endearments or flattery to persuade someone to do something.

wheel /(h)wēl/ ▸ **n.** 1 a circular object that revolves on an axle, fixed below a vehicle to enable it to move along or forming part of a machine. 2 something resembling a wheel or having a wheel as its essential part. 3 (**the wheel**) a steering wheel. 4 (**wheels**) informal a car. 5 a turn or rotation. 6 a recurring cycle of events: *he attempted to stop the wheel of history.* ▸ **v.** 1 push or pull something with wheels. 2 carry or convey on something with wheels: *she was wheeled into the operating room.* 3 fly or turn in a wide circle or curve. 4 turn around quickly to face another way. 5 (**wheel something out**) informal resort to something that has been frequently seen or heard before.
– PHRASES **wheel and deal** take part in commercial or political scheming. **the wheel of Fortune** the wheel that the goddess Fortune is represented as turning as a symbol of random luck or change. **wheels within wheels** secret or indirect influences affecting a complex situation.

wheel·bar·row /'(h)wēl‚barō/ ▸ **n.** a small cart with a single wheel at the front and two supporting legs and two handles at the rear, used for carrying loads in building or gardening.

wheel·base /'(h)wēl‚bās/ ▸ **n.** the distance between the front and rear axles of a vehicle.

wheel·chair /'(h)wēl‚CHe(ə)r/ ▸ **n.** a chair on wheels for use by a person who cannot walk as the result of an illness, accident, etc.

wheel·er /'(h)wēlər/ ▸ **n.** (in combination) a vehicle having a specified number of wheels: *a three-wheeler.*

wheel·er-deal·er (also **wheeler and dealer**) ▸ **n.** a person who takes part in commercial or political scheming. ■ **wheel·er-deal·ing** n.

wheel·house /'(h)wēl‚hous/ ▸ **n.** a shelter for the person at the wheel of a boat or ship.

wheel·ie /'(h)wēlē/ ▸ **n.** informal a maneuver in which a bicycle or motorcycle is ridden for a short distance with the front wheel raised off the ground.

wheel·spin /'(h)wēl‚spin/ ▸ **n.** the rotation of a vehicle's wheels without movement of the vehicle forward or backward.

wheel·wright /'(h)wēl‚rīt/ ▸ **n.** chiefly historical a person who makes or repairs wooden wheels.

wheeze /(h)wēz/ ▸ **v.** 1 breathe with a whistling or rattling sound in the chest, as a result of a blockage in the air passages. 2 (of a device) make an irregular rattling or spluttering sound. ▸ **n.** a sound of a person wheezing. ■ **wheez·i·ly** adv. **wheez·i·ness** n. **wheez·y** adj.

whelk /(h)welk/ ▸ **n.** a large edible marine snail with a spiral shell that tapers into a long tubelike extension.

whelp /(h)welp/ ▸ **n.** chiefly old use 1 a puppy. 2 derogatory a boy or young man. ▸ **v.** give birth to a puppy.

when /(h)wen/ ▸ **adv.** 1 at what time? 2 how soon? 3 in what circumstances? 4 at which time or in which situation. ▸ **conj.** 1 at or during the time that. 2 at any time that; whenever. 3 after which; and just then. 4 in view of the fact that. 5 although; whereas.

whence /(h)wens/ (also **from whence**) ▸ **adv.** formal or old use 1 from what place or source? 2 from which; from where. 3 to the place from which. 4 as a consequence of which.

when·ev·er /(h)wən'evər/ ▸ **conj.** 1 at whatever time; on whatever occasion. 2 every time that. ▸ **adv.** used for emphasis instead of 'when' in questions.

when·so·ev·er /‚(h)wensō'evər/ ▸ **conj. & adv.** formal word for WHENEVER.

where /(h)we(ə)r/ ▸ **adv.** 1 in or to what place or position? 2 in what direction or respect? 3 at, in, or to which. 4 the place or situation in which. 5 in or to a place or situation in which.

where·a·bouts /'(h)we(ə)rə‚bouts/ ▸ **adv.** where or approximately where? ▸ **n.** (treated as sing. or pl.) the place where someone or something is.

where·af·ter /(h)we(ə)r'aftər/ ▸ **adv.** formal after which.

where·as /(h)we(ə)r'az/ ▸ **conj.** 1 in contrast or comparison with the fact that. 2 taking into consideration the fact that.

where·at /(h)we(ə)r'at/ ▸ **adv. & conj.** old use or formal at which.

where·by /(h)we(ə)r'bī/ ▸ **adv.** by which.

where·fore /'(h)we(ə)r‚fôr/ old use ▸ **adv.** for what reason? ▸ **adv. & conj.** as a result of which.

where·from /‚(h)we(ə)r'frəm/ ▸ **adv.** old use from which or from where.

where·in /(h)we(ə)r'in/ ▸ **adv.** formal 1 in which. 2 in what place or respect?

where·of /(h)we'räv, -'əv/ ▸ **adv.** formal of what or which.

where·on /(h)we(ə)r'än, -'ôn/ ▸ **adv.** old use on which.

where·so·ev·er /‚(h)we(ə)rsō'evər/ ▸ **adv. & conj.** formal word for WHEREVER.

where·to /(h)we(ə)r'tōō/ ▸ **adv.** old use or formal to which.

where·up·on /‚(h)we(ə)rə'pän, -'pôn/ ▸ **conj.** immediately after which.

wher·ev·er /(h)we(ə)r'evər/ ▸ **adv.** 1 in or to whatever place. 2 used for emphasis instead of 'where' in questions. ▸ **conj.** in every case when.

where·with /(h)we(ə)r'wiTH, -'wiTH/ ▸ **adv.** formal or old use with or by which.

where·with·al /'(h)we(ə)rwiTH‚ôl, -wiTH-/ ▸ **n.** the money or other resources needed for a particular purpose.

wher·ry /'(h)werē/ ▸ **n.** (pl. **wherries**) 1 a light rowboat used chiefly for carrying passengers. 2 Brit. a large, light barge.

whet /(h)wet/ ▸ **v.** (**whets, whetting, whetted**) 1 sharpen the blade of a tool or weapon. 2 arouse or stimulate someone's desire, interest, or appetite.

wheth·er /'(h)weTHər/ ▸ **conj.** 1 expressing a doubt or choice between alternatives. 2 expressing an inquiry or investigation. 3 indicating that a statement applies whichever of the alternatives mentioned is the case.

USAGE
For an explanation of the use of **whether** and **if**, see the note at IF.

whet·stone /'(h)wet‚stōn/ ▸ **n.** a fine-grained

stone used to sharpen cutting tools.

whey /(h)wā/ ▶ n. the watery part of milk that remains after curds have formed.

whey-faced ▶ adj. (of a person) pale.

which /(h)wicH/ ▶ pron. & determiner **1** asking for information specifying one or more people or things from a definite set. **2** used to refer to something previously mentioned when introducing a clause giving further information.

> **USAGE**
> For an explanation of the difference in use between **which** and **that**, see the note at **THAT**.

which·ev·er /,(h)wicH'evər/
▶ determiner & pron. **1** used to emphasize a lack of restriction in selecting one of a definite set of alternatives. **2** regardless of which.

whick·er /'(h)wikər/ ▶ v. (of a horse) give a soft breathy whinny. ▶ n. a sound of this type.

whiff /(h)wif/ ▶ n. **1** a smell that is smelled only briefly or faintly. **2** a trace or hint of something bad or exciting: *a whiff of danger.* **3** a puff or breath of air or smoke. ▶ v. get a brief or faint smell of something.

whif·fle /'(h)wifəl/ ▶ v. **1** blow or move lightly. **2** make a soft sound. ▶ n. a slight movement of air.

Whig /(h)wig/ ▶ n. **1** a member of a British political party that was succeeded in the 19th century by the Liberal Party. **2** an American colonist who supported the American Revolution. **3** a member of an American political party in the 19th century that was succeeded by the Republican Party. ■ **Whig·gish** adj. **Whig·gism** n.

while /(h)wīl/ ▶ n. **1** (**a while**) a period of time. **2** (**a while**) for some time. **3** (**the while**) at the same time; meanwhile. **4** (**the while**) literary during the time that. ▶ conj. **1** at the same time as. **2** whereas (indicating a contrast). **3** although. ▶ adv. during which. ▶ v. (**while something away**) pass time in a leisurely way.
– PHRASES **worth while** (or **worth one's while**) worth the time or effort spent.

whilst /(h)wīlst/ ▶ conj. & adv. chiefly Brit. while.

whim /(h)wim/ ▶ n. a sudden desire or change of mind.

whim·brel /'(h)wimbrəl/ ▶ n. a small curlew with a striped crown and a trilling call.

whim·per /'(h)wimpər/ ▶ v. make a series of low, feeble sounds expressing fear, pain, or discontent. ▶ n. a whimpering sound.

whim·si·cal /'(h)wimzikal/ ▶ adj. **1** playfully unusual or fanciful: *a whimsical sense of humor.* **2** showing sudden changes of behavior. ■ **whim·si·cal·i·ty** n. **whim·si·cal·ly** adv.

whim·sy /'(h)wimzē/ (also **whimsey**) ▶ n. (pl. **whimsies** or **whimseys**) **1** playfully unusual or fanciful behavior or humor. **2** a fanciful or odd thing. **3** a whim.

whine /(h)wīn/ ▶ v. **1** give or make a long, high-pitched complaining cry. **2** (especially of a machine) make a long, high-pitched unpleasant sound. **3** complain in a petulant way. ▶ n. **1** a whining cry or sound. **2** a petulant complaint. ■ **whin·er** n. **whin·y** (also **whiney**) adj.

whinge /(h)winj/ Brit. informal ▶ v. (**whinges, whingeing, whinged**) complain persistently and peevishly. ▶ n. an act of whingeing. ■ **whing·er** n.

whin·ny /'(h)winē/ ▶ n. (pl. **whinnies**) a gentle, high-pitched neigh. ▶ v. (**whinnies, whinnying, whinnied**) (of a horse) make such a sound.

whip /(h)wip/ ▶ n. **1** a strip of leather or length of cord fastened to a handle, used for beating a person or urging on an animal. **2** an official of a political party appointed to maintain discipline among its members in Congress or Parliament, especially to ensure attendance and voting. **3** a dessert made from cream or eggs beaten into a light fluffy mass. ▶ v. (**whips, whipping, whipped**) **1** beat a person or animal with a whip. **2** (of a flexible object or rain or wind) strike or beat violently: *the wind whipped their faces.* **3** move or take something out fast or suddenly. **4** beat cream, eggs, etc., into a froth. ■ **whip·per** n. **whip·ping** n.
– PHRASES **the whip hand** a position of power or control. **whip someone/thing up 1** make or prepare something very quickly. **2** deliberately excite or provoke someone. **3** stimulate a particular feeling in someone.

whip·cord /'(h)wip,kôrd/ ▶ n. **1** thin, tough, tightly twisted cord used for making the flexible end part of whips. **2** a closely woven ribbed fabric.

whip·lash /'(h)wip,lasH/ ▶ n. **1** the lashing action of a whip. **2** injury caused by a severe jerk to the head.

whip·per·snap·per /'(h)wipər,snapər/
▶ n. dated informal a young and inexperienced person who is disrespectful or overconfident.

whip·pet /'(h)wipit/ ▶ n. a small slender breed of dog used in racing.

whip·ping boy ▶ n. a person who is blamed or punished for other people's faults or mistakes.

whip·poor·will /'(h)wipər,wil/ ▶ n. a North and Central American nightjar with a distinctive call.

whip·py /'(h)wipē/ ▶ adj. flexible; springy.

whip·saw /'(h)wip,sô/ ▶ n. a saw with a narrow blade and a handle at both ends. ▶ v. (past part. **whipsawn** or **whipsawed**) **1** cut something with a whipsaw. **2** informal subject someone or something to two difficult situations or opposing pressures at the same time.

whir /(h)wər/ (also **whirr**) ▶ v. (**whirrs, whirring, whirred**) (of something rapidly rotating or moving to and fro) make a low, continuous, regular sound. ▶ n. a whirring sound.

whirl /(h)wərl/ ▶ v. **1** move rapidly around and around. **2** (of the head or mind) seem to spin around. ▶ n. **1** a rapid movement around and around. **2** frantic activity: *the mad social whirl.*
– PHRASES **give something a whirl** informal give something a try. **in a whirl** in a state of confusion.

whirl·i·gig /'(h)wərlē,gig/ ▶ n. **1** an object, especially a toy, that spins around, e.g., a top or pinwheel. **2** a process or activity characterized by constant change or hectic activity. **3** chiefly Brit. another term for **MERRY-GO-ROUND**. **4** (also **whirligig beetle**) a small black water beetle that typically swims rapidly in circles on the surface.

whirl·pool /'(h)wərl,pool/ ▶ n. **1** a quickly rotating mass of water in a river that may draw floating objects toward its center. **2** (also **whirlpool bath**) a heated pool in which hot bubbling water is continuously circulated.

whirl·wind /'(h)wərl,wind/ ▶ n. **1** a column of air moving rapidly around and around in a cylindrical or funnel shape. **2** a situation in which many things happen very quickly: *a whirlwind of activity.* ▶ adj. happening very quickly or suddenly: *a whirlwind romance.*

whisk /(h)wisk/ ▶v. **1** move or take suddenly and quickly: *he whisked her off to Paris.* **2** beat a substance with a light, rapid movement.
▶n. **1** a utensil for whisking eggs or cream. **2** (also **whisk broom**) a small, stiff, short-handled broom used especially to brush clothing or upholstery. **3** a bunch of grass, twigs, or bristles for flicking away dust or flies. **4** a brief, rapid action or movement.

whisk broom ▶n. a small, stiff broom used especially to brush clothing.

whis·ker /'(h)wiskər/ ▶n. **1** a long hair or bristle growing from the face or snout of an animal. **2** (**whiskers**) the hair growing on a man's face. **3** (**a whisker**) informal a very small amount. ■ **whis·kered** adj. **whis·ker·y** adj.

whis·key /'(h)wiskē/ (also chiefly Brit. **whisky**) ▶n. (pl. **whiskeys, whiskies**) a liquor distilled from malted grain, especially barley or rye.

whis·per /'(h)wispər/ ▶v. **1** speak very softly. **2** literary rustle or murmur softly. ▶n. **1** a whispered word or phrase, or a whispering tone of voice. **2** literary a soft rustling or murmuring sound. **3** a rumor or piece of gossip. **4** a slight trace. ■ **whis·per·er** n. **whis·per·y** adj.

whis·per·ing cam·paign ▶n. an attempt to to damage someone's reputation by systematically circulating a rumor about them.

whist /(h)wist/ ▶n. a card game in which points are scored according to the number of tricks won.

whis·tle /'(h)wisəl/ ▶n. **1** a clear, high-pitched sound made by forcing breath through pursed lips, or between one's teeth. **2** any similar high-pitched sound. **3** an instrument used to produce a whistling sound. ▶v. **1** produce a whistle: *the crowd cheered and whistled.* **2** produce a tune by whistling. **3** blow a whistle. **4** move rapidly through the air or a narrow opening with a whistling sound. **5** (**whistle for**) wish for or expect something in vain. ■ **whis·tler** n.
– PHRASES **blow the whistle on** informal bring an illicit activity to an end by informing on the person responsible. (**as**) **clean as a whistle** extremely clean or clear. **whistle in the dark** pretend to be unafraid.

whis·tle-blow·er ▶n. informal a person who informs on someone engaged in an illicit activity.

whis·tle-stop ▶adj. very fast and with only brief pauses.

whit /(h)wit/ ▶n. a very small part or amount.
– PHRASES **not a whit** not at all.

white /(h)wīt/ ▶adj. **1** of the color of milk or fresh snow. **2** very pale. **3** relating to the human group having light-colored skin. **4** (of food such as bread or rice) light in color through having been refined. **5** (of wine) made from white grapes, or dark grapes with the skins removed, and having a yellowish color. **6** morally or spiritually pure. **7** Brit. (of coffee or tea) served with milk or cream. ▶n. **1** white color. **2** (also **whites**) white clothes or material. **3** the visible pale part of the eyeball around the iris. **4** the outer part that surrounds the yolk of an egg; the albumen. **5** a member of a light-skinned people. **6** a white or cream butterfly. ▶v. (**white something out**) cover a mistake with white correction fluid. ■ **white·ly** adv. **white·ness** n. **whit·ish** adj.
– PHRASES **bleed someone/thing white** drain someone or something of wealth or resources.

whited sepulcher literary a hypocrite.

white ant ▶n. another term for TERMITE.

white-bait /'(h)wīt,bāt/ ▶n. the small silvery-white young of herrings, sprats, and similar sea fish as food.

white-beam /'(h)wīt,bēm/ ▶n. a tree related to the rowan, with red berries and hairy oval leaves that are white underneath.

white belt ▶n. a white belt worn by a beginner in judo or karate.

white blood cell ▶n. less technical term for LEUKOCYTE.

white-board /'(h)wīt,bôrd/ ▶n. a wipeable board with a white surface used for teaching or presentations.

white-bread ▶adj. informal bland and unchallenging in a way thought characteristic of the white middle classes.

white-cap /'(h)wīt,kap/ ▶n. a small wave with a foamy white crest.

white cell ▶n. less technical term for LEUKOCYTE.

white Christ·mas ▶n. a Christmas during which there is snow on the ground.

white-col·lar ▶adj. relating to the work done or people who work in an office or other professional environment.

white dwarf ▶n. Astronomy a small, very dense star.

white el·e·phant ▶n. a possession that is useless or unwanted, especially one that is expensive to maintain.

white·fish /'(h)wīt,fish/ ▶n. (pl. same or **whitefishes**) a mainly freshwater fish of the salmon family, widely used as food.

white flag ▶n. a white flag or cloth used as a symbol of surrender, truce, or a wish to negotiate.

white·fly /'(h)wīt,flī/ ▶n. (pl. **whiteflies**) a minute winged bug covered with powdery white wax, damaging plants by feeding on sap and coating them with honeydew.

white gold ▶n. a silver-colored alloy of gold with another metal.

white goods ▶pl.n. large domestic electrical goods such as refrigerators and washing machines. Compare with BROWN GOODS.

white·head /'(h)wīt,(h)ed/ ▶n. informal a pale or white-topped pustule on the skin.

white heat ▶n. the temperature or state of something that is so hot that it gives out white light.

white hope (also **great white hope**) ▶n. a person expected to bring much success to a team or organization.

white hors·es ▶pl.n. white-crested waves at sea.

white-hot ▶adj. so hot as to glow white.

white knight ▶n. a person or thing that comes to someone's aid.

white-knuck·le ▶adj. causing fear or nervous excitement.

white lie ▶n. a harmless lie told to avoid hurting someone's feelings.

white light ▶n. apparently colorless light containing all the wavelengths of the visible spectrum at equal intensity (such as ordinary daylight).

white mag·ic ▶n. magic used only for good purposes.

white meat ▶n. pale meat such as the breast

meat of chicken or turkey.

whit·en /'(h)wītn/ ▸ v. make or become white. ■ **whit·en·er** n.

white noise ▸ n. noise containing many frequencies with equal intensities.

white·out /'(h)wīt,out/ ▸ n. **1** a dense blizzard. **2** a weather condition in which the features and horizon of snow-covered country are indistinguishable.

white pa·per ▸ n. an official report giving information or proposals on a particular issue.

White Rus·sian ▸ n. **1** dated a person from Belarus (formerly Belorussia) in eastern Europe. **2** an opponent of the Bolsheviks during the Russian Civil War. **3** a cocktail made from vodka, coffee liqueur, and cream or milk. ▸ adj. relating to White Russians.

white sale ▸ n. a store's sale of household linens.

white sauce ▸ n. a sauce consisting of flour blended and cooked with butter and milk or stock.

white slave ▸ n. dated a white girl or woman tricked or forced into prostitution in a foreign country.

white spir·it ▸ n. Brit. a colorless liquid distilled from petroleum, used as a paint thinner and solvent.

white su·prem·a·cy ▸ n. the belief that white people are superior to those of all other races. ■ **white su·prem·a·cist** n. & adj.

white tie ▸ n. **1** a white bow tie worn by men as part of full evening dress. **2** a man's full evening dress. ▸ adj. (of an event) requiring full evening dress to be worn.

white trash ▸ n. derogatory poor white people.

white·wash /'(h)wīt,wäsh, -,wôsh/ ▸ n. **1** a solution of lime or chalk and water, used for painting walls white. **2** a deliberate concealment of someone's mistakes or faults. **3** informal a victory by the same side in every game of a series. ▸ v. **1** paint something with whitewash. **2** conceal unpleasant or incriminating facts about: *the editor and his newspaper have whitewashed the past.* **3** informal defeat an opposing side with a whitewash.

whitewa·ter /'(h)wīt'wôtər, -'wä-/ ▸ n. a fast shallow stretch of water in a river.

white wed·ding ▸ n. Brit. a traditional wedding at which the bride wears a formal white dress.

white witch ▸ n. a person who uses witchcraft to help other people.

whit·ey /'(h)wītē/ ▸ n. (pl. **whiteys**) informal, derogatory a white person.

whith·er /'(h)wiᴛʜər/ old use or literary ▸ adv. **1** to what place or state? **2** what is the likely future of? **3** to which (with reference to a place). **4** to whatever place.

whit·ing¹ /'(h)wītiNG/ ▸ n. (pl. same) a slender-bodied sea fish with edible white flesh.

whit·ing² ▸ n. ground chalk used for purposes such as whitewashing and cleaning metal plate.

whit·low /'(h)wit,lō/ ▸ n. an abscess in the soft tissue near a fingernail or toenail.

Whit·sun·day /'(h)wit,sən·dā/ ▸ n. another term for PENTECOST (sense 1).

whit·tle /'(h)witl/ ▸ v. **1** form a piece of wood into an object by repeatedly cutting small slices from it. **2** (**whittle something away**/**down**) reduce something by degrees.

whiz /(h)wiz/ (also **whizz**) ▸ v. (**whizzes, whizzing, whizzed**) **1** move quickly through the air with a whistling sound. **2** move or go fast.

3 (**whiz through**) do or deal with something quickly. ▸ n. **1** a whizzing sound. **2** informal a fast movement or brief journey. **3** (also **wiz**) informal a person who is extremely clever at something. ■ **whiz·zy** adj.

whiz kid ▸ n. informal a young person who is very successful or highly skilled.

WHO ▸ abbr. World Health Organization.

who /hoo/ ▸ pron. **1** what or which person or people? **2** introducing a clause giving further information about a person or people previously mentioned.

USAGE
According to formal grammar, **who** is used as the subject of a verb (*who decided this?*) and **whom** is used as the object of a verb or preposition (*to whom do you wish to speak?*). However, in modern English **who** is often used instead of **whom**, as in *who should we support?* and most people consider this to be acceptable.

whoa /wō/ ▸ exclam. used as a command to a horse to stop or slow down.

who'd /hood/ ▸ contr. **1** who had. **2** who would.

who·dun·it /hoo'dənit/ (Brit. **whodunnit**) ▸ n. informal a story or play about a murder in which the identity of the murderer is not revealed until the end.

who·ev·er /hoo'evər/ ▸ contr. **1** the person or people who; any person who. **2** regardless of who. **3** used for emphasis instead of 'who' in questions.

whole /hōl/ ▸ adj. **1** complete; entire. **2** emphasizing a large extent or number: *a whole range of issues.* **3** in an unbroken or undamaged state. ▸ n. **1** a thing that is complete in itself. **2** (**the whole**) all of something. ▸ adv. informal entirely; wholly: *a whole new meaning.* ■ **whole·ness** n.
– PHRASES **as a whole** as a single unit; in general. **on the whole** taking everything into account; in general. **the whole nine yards** informal everything possible or available.

whole·heart·ed /'hōl'härtid/ ▸ adj. completely sincere and committed. ■ **whole·heart·ed·ly** adv.

whole life in·sur·ance ▸ n. life insurance that pays a benefit on the death of the insured and also accumulates a cash value. Compare with TERM LIFE INSURANCE.

whole note ▸ n. a musical note having the time value of two half notes or four quarter notes, represented by a ring with no stem.

whole num·ber ▸ n. a number without fractions; an integer.

whole·sale /'hōl,sāl/ ▸ n. the selling of goods in large quantities to be sold to the public by others. ▸ adv. **1** being sold in such a way. **2** as a whole and in an indiscriminate way. ▸ adj. done on a large scale; extensive. ▸ v. sell goods wholesale. ■ **whole·sal·er** n.

whole·some /'hōlsəm/ ▸ adj. **1** good for health and physical well-being. **2** morally good or beneficial. ■ **whole·some·ly** adv. **whole·some·ness** n.

whole step ▸ n. Music an interval of a (whole) tone.

whole wheat ▸ n. whole grains of wheat including the husk.

whol·ly /'hōl(l)ē/ ▸ adv. entirely; fully.

whom /hoom/ ▸ pron. used instead of 'who' as the object of a verb or preposition.

for WHOEVER.

USAGE
For an explanation of the use of **who** and **whom**, see the note at **WHO**.

---

whom·ev·er /hŏŏm'evər/ ▸ **pron.** formal used instead of 'whoever' as the object of a verb or preposition.

whomp /(h)wämp, (h)wômp/ informal ▸ **v.** strike someone or something heavily. ▸ **n.** a thump.

whom·so·ev·er /ˌhŏŏmsō'evər/ ▸ **relative pron.** formal used instead of 'whosoever' as the object of a verb or preposition.

whoop /(h)wŏŏp, hŏŏp/ ▸ **n.** a loud cry of joy or excitement. ▸ **v.** give or make a whoop.
– PHRASES **whoop it up** informal enjoy oneself or celebrate enthusiastically.

whoop·ee /'(h)wŏŏpē, '(h)wŏŏ'pē/ ▸ **exclam.** informal expressing wild excitement or joy.
– PHRASES **make whoopee 1** celebrate wildly. **2** have sex.

whoop·ee cush·ion /'wŏŏpē/ ▸ **n.** a rubber cushion that makes a sound like the breaking of wind when someone sits on it.

whoop·er swan /'(h)wŏŏpər, 'hŏŏpər/ ▸ **n.** a large swan with a black and yellow bill and a loud trumpeting call, breeding in northern Eurasia and Greenland.

whoop·ing cough ▸ **n.** a contagious bacterial disease chiefly affecting children, characterized by convulsive coughs followed by a rasping indrawn breath.

whoop·ing crane ▸ **n.** a large mainly white crane with a trumpeting call.

whoops /wŏŏps, wŏŏps/ (also **whoops-a-daisy** /wŏŏps ə ˌdāzē, wŏŏps ə ˌdāzē/) ▸ **exclam.** informal another term for oops.

whoosh /(h)wŏŏsH, (h)wŏŏsH/ (also **woosh**) ▸ **v.** move quickly or suddenly and with a rushing sound. ▸ **n.** a whooshing movement.

whop /(h)wäp/ (also **whap**) informal ▸ **v.** (**whops, whopping, whopped**) hit someone or something hard. ▸ **n.** a heavy blow or its sound.

whop·per /'(h)wäpər/ ▸ **n.** informal **1** a very large thing. **2** a complete or blatant lie.

whop·ping /'(h)wäpiNG/ ▸ **adj.** informal extremely large.

whore /hôr/ derogatory ▸ **n. 1** a prostitute. **2** a woman who has many sexual partners. ■ **whor·ish** adj.

whore·house /'hôr,hous/ ▸ **n.** informal a brothel.

whorl /(h)wôrl/ ▸ **n. 1** each of the turns in the spiral shell of a mollusk. **2** a set of leaves, flowers, or branches springing from a stem at the same level and encircling it. **3** a complete circle in a fingerprint. ■ **whorled** adj.

who's /hŏŏz/ ▸ **contr. 1** who is. **2** who has.

USAGE
Do not confuse **who's** with **whose**. **Who's** is short for **who is** or **who has**, as in *he has a son who's a doctor,* or *who's locked the door?,* while **whose** means 'belonging to or associated with which person' or 'of whom or which', as in *whose coat is this?* or *a man whose opinion I respect.*

---

whose /hŏŏz/ ▸ **possessive determiner & pron. 1** belonging to or associated with which person. **2** (as possessive determiner) of whom or which.

whos·ev·er /ˌhŏŏz'evər/ ▸ **relative pron. & determiner** belonging to or associated with whichever person; whoever's.

who·so·ev·er /ˌhŏŏsō'evər/ ▸ **pron.** formal term

---

whup /(h)wŏŏp, (h)wəp/ ▸ **v.** (**whups, whupping, whupped**) informal thrash someone or something.

why /(h)wī/ ▸ **adv. 1** for what reason or purpose? **2** on account of which; the reason for which. ▸ **exclam.** expressing surprise or indignation, or used for emphasis. ▸ **n.** (pl. **whys**) a reason or explanation.

WI ▸ **abbr. 1** West Indies. **2** Wisconsin.

Wic·ca /'wikə/ ▸ **n.** the religious cult of modern witchcraft. ■ **Wic·can** adj. & n.

wick /wik/ ▸ **n.** a strip of porous material up which liquid fuel is drawn to the flame in a candle, lamp, or lighter. ▸ **v.** (usu. as adj. **wicking**) absorb or draw off liquid.
– PHRASES **get on someone's wick** Brit. informal annoy someone.

wick·ed /'wikid/ ▸ **adj.** (**wickeder, wickedest**) **1** evil or morally wrong. **2** playfully mischievous. **3** informal excellent; very good. ■ **wick·ed·ly** adv. **wick·ed·ness** n.

wick·er /'wikər/ ▸ **n.** flexible twigs, typically of willow, plaited or woven to make items such as furniture and baskets. ■ **wick·er·work** /'wikər,wərk/ n.

wick·et /'wikit/ ▸ **n. 1** a small door or gate, especially one beside or in a larger one. **2** one of the wire hoops on a croquet course. **3** Cricket each of the sets of three stumps with two bails across the top at either end of the pitch, defended by a batsman.

wide /wīd/ ▸ **adj.** (**wider, widest**) **1** of great or more than average width. **2** extending a specified distance from side to side. **3** open to the full extent. **4** including a great variety of people or things. **5** spread among a large number or over a large area. **6** (in combination) extending over the whole of: *industry-wide.* **7** at a great or specified distance from a point or target. ▸ **adv. 1** to the full extent. **2** far from a particular point or target. **3** (in field sports) at or near the side of the field. ■ **wide·ly** adv. **wide·ness** n.
– PHRASES **wide awake** fully awake. **wide of the mark** inaccurate.

wide-an·gle ▸ **adj.** (of a lens) having a short focal length and so covering a wider view than a standard lens.

wide ar·e·a net·work ▸ **n.** a computer network in which the computers connected may be far apart, generally having a radius of more than half a mile.

wide-eyed ▸ **adj. 1** having one's eyes wide open in amazement. **2** inexperienced; innocent.

wid·en /'wīdn/ ▸ **v.** make or become wider.

wide-rang·ing ▸ **adj.** covering an extensive range of subjects or issues.

wide·screen /'wīd,skrēn/ ▸ **n.** (often as adj.) a movie or television screen presenting a wide field of vision in relation to height: *widescreen TV.*

wide·spread /'wīd'spred/ ▸ **adj.** spread among a large number or over a large area.

widg·eon ▸ **n.** variant spelling of WIGEON.

widg·et /'wijit/ ▸ **n.** informal a small gadget or mechanical device.

wid·ow /'widō/ ▸ **n. 1** a woman whose husband has died and who has not married again. **2** humorous a woman whose husband is often away taking part in a particular sport or activity: *a golf widow.* ▸ **v.** (**be widowed**) become a widow or widower.

wid·ow·er /'widō-ər/ ▸ n. a man whose wife has died and who has not married again.

wid·ow·hood /'widō,hŏŏd/ ▸ n. the state or period of being a widow or widower.

wid·ow's mite ▸ n. a small monetary contribution from someone who is poor.

wid·ow's peak ▸ n. a V-shaped growth of hair toward the center of the forehead.

wid·ow's weeds ▸ pl.n. black clothes worn by a widow in mourning.

width /widтн, witтн/ ▸ n. 1 the measurement or extent of something from side to side. 2 a piece of something at its full extent from side to side. 3 wide range or extent.

width·wise /'widтн,wīz, 'witтн-/ (also **widthways** /'widтн,wāz, 'witтн-/) ▸ adv. in a direction parallel with a thing's width.

wield /wēld/ ▸ v. 1 hold and use a weapon or tool. 2 have and be able to use power or influence. ■ **wield·er** n.

wie·ner /'wēnər/ ▸ n. 1 a frankfurter or similar sausage. 2 another term for WEENIE (sense 3).

Wie·ner schnit·zel /'vēnər ,sнnitsəl/ ▸ n. a thin slice of veal that is breaded and fried.

wife /wīf/ ▸ n. (pl. **wives** /wīvz/) 1 a married woman in relation to her husband. 2 old use a woman. ■ **wife·ly** adj.

Wi-Fi /'wī 'fī/ ▸ abbr. Wireless Fidelity, a set of technical standards for transmitting data over wireless networks.

wig /wig/ ▸ n. a covering for the head made of real or artificial hair.

wig·eon /'wijən/ (also **widgeon**) ▸ n. a duck with reddish-brown and gray plumage, the male having a whistling call.

wig·gle /'wigəl/ ▸ v. move with short movements up and down or from side to side. ▸ n. a wiggling movement. ■ **wig·gler** n. **wig·gly** adj.

wig·wam /'wig,wäm/ ▸ n. a dome-shaped or conical dwelling made by fastening mats, skins, or bark over a framework of poles (as used formerly by some North American Indian peoples).

wi·ki /'wikē/ ▸ n. a website that allows its users to edit its content and structure.

wild /wīld/ ▸ adj. 1 (of animals or plants) living or growing in the natural environment; not domesticated or cultivated. 2 (of scenery or a region) not inhabited in or changed by people. 3 lacking discipline or control. 4 not civilized; primitive. 5 not based on reason or evidence: *a wild guess.* 6 (of looks, appearance, etc.) showing strong emotion. 7 informal very enthusiastic or excited. 8 informal very angry. ▸ n. 1 (**the wild**) a natural state. 2 (also **the wilds**) a remote area with few or no inhabitants. ■ **wild·ly** adv. **wild·ness** n.

– PHRASES **run wild** grow or behave in an uncontrolled way.

wild card ▸ n. 1 a playing card that can have any value, suit, color, or other property in a game according to the choice of the player holding it. 2 a person or thing whose qualities are uncertain. 3 Computing a character that will match any character or sequence of characters in a search. 4 an opportunity to enter a sports competition without taking part in qualifying matches or being ranked at a particular level.

wild·cat /'wīld,kat/ ▸ n. 1 a small Eurasian and African cat, typically gray with black markings and a bushy tail, believed to be the ancestor

of the domestic cat. 2 any of various North American cats, especially the bobcat. 3 an exploratory oil well. ▸ adj. (of a strike) sudden and unofficial.

wil·de·beest /'wildə,bēst/ ▸ n. (pl. same or **wildebeests**) another term for GNU.

wil·der·ness /'wildərnis/ ▸ n. 1 a wild, uninhabited, and inhospitable region. 2 a state of being out of political favor or office.

wild·fire /'wīld,fīr/ ▸ n. (in phrase **spread like wildfire**) spread with great speed.

wild·flow·er /'wīld,flou(-ə)r/ ▸ n. a flower of an uncultivated variety that grows freely without human intervention.

wild·fowl /'wīld,foul/ ▸ pl.n. birds that are hunted as game, especially waterbirds.

wild goose chase ▸ n. a hopeless search for or pursuit of something that is impossible to find or does not exist.

wild·life /'wīld,līf/ ▸ n. the native animals of a region.

wild rice ▸ n. a tall American grass with edible grains, related to rice and growing on wet land.

Wild West ▸ the western US during its lawless early history.

wiles /wīlz/ ▸ pl.n. cunning stratagems used by someone in order to get what they want.

will[1] /wil/ ▸ modal v. (3rd sing. present **will**; past **would**) 1 expressing the future tense. 2 expressing a strong intention or assertion about the future. 3 expressing inevitable events. 4 expressing a request. 5 expressing desire, consent, or willingness. 6 expressing facts about ability or capacity. 7 expressing habitual behavior. 8 expressing probability or expectation about something in the present.

USAGE

For an explanation of the difference between **will** and **shall**, see the note at SHALL.

---

will[2] ▸ n. 1 a person's power to decide on something and take action. 2 (also **willpower**) control or restraint deliberately exerted by a person: *a stupendous effort of will.* 3 a person's desire or intention in a particular situation: *the will to live.* 4 a legal document containing instructions about what should be done with a person's money and property after their death. ▸ v. 1 intend or desire to happen. 2 bring about by the exercise of mental powers. 3 bequeath in one's will.

– PHRASES **at will** at whatever time or in whatever way one pleases. **where there's a will there's a way** proverb determination will overcome any obstacle. **with a will** energetically and resolutely.

will·ful /'wilfəl/ (Brit. **wilful**) ▸ adj. 1 (of a bad or harmful act) deliberate. 2 stubborn and determined. ■ **will·ful·ly** adv. **will·ful·ness** n.

wil·lie ▸ n. variant spelling of WILLY.

wil·lies /'wilēz/ ▸ pl.n. (**the willies**) informal a strong feeling of nervousness or uneasiness.

will·ing /'wiliNG/ ▸ adj. 1 ready, eager, or prepared to do something. 2 given or done readily. ■ **will·ing·ly** adv. **will·ing·ness** n.

will-o'-the-wisp /'wil ə тнə 'wisp/ ▸ n. 1 a person or thing that is difficult or impossible to reach or catch. 2 a dim, flickering light seen hovering or floating at night on marshy ground, thought to result from the combustion of natural gases.

wil·low /ˈwilō/ ▸ n. a tree or shrub that typically grows near water, has narrow leaves and flexible branches, and bears catkins.

wil·low herb ▸ n. a plant with long narrow leaves and pink or pale purple flowers.

wil·low·ware /ˈwilō,we(ə)r/ ▸ n. blue and white pottery with a design featuring a Chinese scene typically including a willow tree and figures on a bridge.

wil·low·y /ˈwilōē/ ▸ adj. **1** (of a person) tall, slim, and graceful. **2** bordered, shaded, or covered by willows.

will·pow·er /ˈwil,pou(ə)r/ ▸ n. see WILL² (sense 2 of the noun).

wil·ly /ˈwilē/ (also **willie**) ▸ n. (pl. **willies**) Brit. informal a penis.

wil·ly-nil·ly /ˈwilē ˈnilē/ ▸ adv. **1** whether one likes it or not. **2** without direction or planning; haphazardly.

wilt¹ /wilt/ ▸ v. **1** (of a plant) become limp through heat, loss of water, or disease; droop. **2** (of a person) become tired and weak. ▸ n. any of a number of plant diseases that cause foliage to wilt.

wilt² ▸ old-fashioned second person singular of WILL¹.

wil·y /ˈwīlē/ ▸ adj. (**wilier**, **wiliest**) using cunning or crafty methods to gain an advantage. ■ **wil·i·ness** n.

wimp /wimp/ informal ▸ n. a weak and cowardly person. ▸ v. (**wimp out**) fail to do something as a result of fear or lack of confidence. ■ **wimp·ish** adj. **wimp·y** adj.

wim·ple /ˈwimpəl/ ▸ n. a cloth headdress covering the head, neck, and sides of the face, formerly worn by women and still by some nuns.

win /win/ ▸ v. (**winning**; past and past part. **won**) **1** be successful or victorious in a contest or conflict. **2** gain as a result of success in a contest, conflict, etc.: *you could win a trip to Australia.* **3** gain someone's attention, support, or love. **4** (**win someone over**) gain someone's support or favor. **5** (**win out/through**) manage to succeed or achieve something by effort. ▸ n. a victory in a game or contest. ■ **win·less** adj. **win·na·ble** adj.
– PHRASES **win the day** be victorious.

wince /wins/ ▸ v. give a slight involuntary grimace or flinch due to pain or distress. ▸ n. an instance of wincing.

winch /winCH/ ▸ n. **1** a hauling or lifting device consisting of a rope or chain winding around a horizontal rotating drum, turned by a crank or by motor. **2** the crank of a wheel or axle. ▸ v. hoist or haul something with a winch.

wind¹ /wind/ ▸ n. **1** the natural movement of the air, especially in the form of a current blowing from a particular direction. **2** breath as needed in physical exertion, speech, playing an instrument, etc. **3** air swallowed while eating or gas generated in the stomach and intestines by digestion. **4** meaningless talk. **5** (also **winds**) (treated as sing. or pl.) wind or woodwind instruments forming a band or section of an orchestra. ▸ v. make someone unable to breathe easily for a short time. ■ **wind·less** adj.
– PHRASES **get wind of** informal hear about something secret or private. **put the wind up** Brit. informal alarm or frighten someone. **sail close to** (or **near**) **the wind** informal come close to being indecent, dishonest, or disastrous. **take the**

wind out of someone's sails frustrate someone by doing or saying something they were not expecting.

wind² /wīnd/ ▸ v. (past and past part. **wound** /wound/) **1** move in or take a twisting or spiral course. **2** pass something around a thing or person so as to encircle or enfold them. **3** (of something long) twist or be twisted around itself or a core. **4** make a clockwork device operate by turning a key or handle. **5** turn a key or handle repeatedly. **6** move audiotape, videotape, or film back or forward to a desired point. **7** hoist or pull something with a winch, windlass, etc. ▸ n. a single turn made when winding. ■ **wind·er** n.
– PHRASES **wind down 1** (of a clockwork mechanism) gradually lose power. **2** (also **wind something down**) draw or bring something gradually to a close. **3** informal relax after stress or excitement. **wind up** informal end up in a particular state, situation, or place. **wind someone up 1** make someone agitated or excited: *the kids are too wound up to sleep.* **2** Brit. informal tease or irritate someone. **wind something up** gradually bring something to an end.

wind·bag /ˈwind,bag/ ▸ n. informal a person who talks a lot but says little of any value.

wind·break /ˈwind,brāk/ ▸ n. a row of trees, wall, or screen that provides shelter from the wind.

wind·break·er /ˈwind,brākər/ ▸ n. trademark a wind-resistant jacket with a close-fitting neck, waistband, and cuffs.

wind·chill /ˈwin(d),CHil/ ▸ n. the cooling effect of wind on a surface.

wind chimes /wind/ ▸ pl.n. pieces of glass, metal rods, or similar items, hung near a door or window so as to strike each other and make a ringing sound in the breeze.

wind·fall /ˈwind,fôl/ ▸ n. **1** a large amount of money that is received unexpectedly. **2** an apple or other fruit blown from a tree by the wind.

wind farm /wind/ ▸ n. an area containing a group of energy-producing windmills or wind turbines.

wind·ing /ˈwīndiNG/ ▸ adj. having a twisting or spiral course. ▸ n. **1** a twisting movement or course. **2** a thing that winds or is wound around something.

wind·ing sheet /ˈwīndiNG/ ▸ n. a sheet in which a dead body is wrapped for burial; a shroud.

wind in·stru·ment /wind/ ▸ n. **1** a musical instrument in which sound is produced by the vibration of air, typically by the player blowing into the instrument. **2** a woodwind instrument as distinct from a brass instrument.

wind·jam·mer /ˈwind,jamər/ ▸ n. historical a merchant sailing ship.

wind·lass /ˈwindləs/ ▸ n. a winch, especially one on a ship or in a harbor.

wind·mill /ˈwind,mil/ ▸ n. a building with sails or vanes that turn in the wind and produce power to grind grain, generate electricity, or draw water. ▸ v. move one's arms in a way that suggests the movement of a windmill's sails.

win·dow /ˈwindō/ ▸ n. **1** an opening in a wall or roof of a building, or in a vehicle, fitted with glass in a frame to let in light or air and allow people to see out. **2** an opening through which customers are served in a bank, ticket office, etc. **3** a framed area on a computer screen for viewing information. **4** a transparent panel in an envelope to show an address. **5** an interval or opportunity for action. ■ **win·dow·less** adj.

win·dow box ▶ n. a long narrow box in which flowers and other plants are grown on an outside windowsill.

win·dow dress·ing ▶ n. **1** the arrangement of a display in a store window. **2** the presentation of something in a superficially attractive way to give a good impression.

win·dow frame ▶ n. a frame holding the glass of a window.

win·dow ledge ▶ n. a windowsill.

win·dow·pane /'windō,pān/ ▶ n. a pane of glass in a window.

win·dow seat ▶ n. **1** a seat below a window, especially one in a bay or alcove. **2** a seat next to a window in an aircraft or train.

win·dow-shop ▶ v. look at the goods displayed in store windows, especially without intending to buy. ■ **win·dow-shop·per** n.

win·dow·sill /'windō,sil/ ▶ n. a ledge or sill forming the bottom part of a window.

wind·pipe /'wind,pīp/ ▶ n. the air passage from the throat to the lungs; the trachea.

wind·proof /'wind,proof/ ▶ adj. (of an item of clothing or fabric) giving protection from the wind.

wind·screen /'wind,skrēn/ ▶ n. Brit. a windshield.

wind·shield /'win(d),SHēld/ ▶ n. a window at the front of a motor vehicle.

wind·shield wip·er ▶ n. a device consisting of a rubber blade on an arm that moves in an arc, for keeping a windshield clear of rain and snow.

wind·sock /'wind,säk/ ▶ n. a light, flexible cylinder or cone mounted on a mast to show the direction and strength of the wind, especially at an airfield.

wind·storm /'wind,stôrm/ ▶ n. a storm with very strong wind but little or no rain or snow; a gale.

wind·surf·ing /'wind,sərfiNG/ ▶ n. the sport of riding on a sailboard on water. ■ **wind·surf** v. **wind·surf·er** n.

wind·swept /'wind,swept/ ▶ adj. **1** (of a place) exposed to strong winds. **2** (of a person's hair or appearance) untidy after being in the wind.

wind tun·nel /wind/ ▶ n. a tunnel-like device for producing an airstream, in order to investigate flow or the effect of wind on an aircraft or other object.

wind·up /'wīnd,əp/ ▶ n. **1** an act of bringing something to an end. **2** Baseball a pitching position in which one step is taken back or to either side, followed by one step forward during delivery of the ball.

wind·ward /'windwərd/ ▶ adj. & adv. facing the wind or on the side facing the wind. Contrasted with **LEEWARD**. ▶ n. the side from which the wind is blowing.

wind·y¹ /'windē/ ▶ adj. (**windier**, **windiest**) **1** marked by or exposed to strong winds: *a windy day*. **2** informal (of speaking or writing) using many words that sound impressive but mean little. ■ **wind·i·ly** adv. **wind·i·ness** n.

wind·y² /'windē/ ▶ adj. following a winding course.

wine /wīn/ ▶ n. **1** an alcoholic drink made from fermented grape juice. **2** a fermented alcoholic drink made from other fruits or plants. ■ **wine·y** (also **winy**) adj.
– PHRASES **wine and dine someone** entertain

someone with drinks and a meal.

wine cel·lar ▶ n. **1** a cellar for storing wine. **2** a stock of wine.

wine·glass ▶ n. a glass with a stem and foot, used for drinking wine.

wine·grow·er /'wīn,grōər/ ▶ n. a grower of grapes for wine.

wine list ▶ n. a list of the wines available in a restaurant.

wine·mak·er /'wīn,mākər/ ▶ n. a producer of wine. ■ **wine·mak·ing** n.

win·er·y /'wīnərē/ ▶ n. (pl. **wineries**) a place where wine is made.

wine·skin /'wīn,skin/ ▶ n. an animal skin sewn up and used to hold wine.

wine tast·ing ▶ n. an occasion when wine is tasted in order to assess its quality.

wine vin·e·gar ▶ n. vinegar made from wine rather than malt.

wing /wiNG/ ▶ n. **1** a modified forelimb or other part enabling a bird, bat, or insect to fly. **2** a rigid horizontal structure projecting from both sides of an aircraft and supporting it in the air. **3** a part of a large building, especially one that projects from the main part. **4** a group within an organization having particular views or a particular function: *the militant wing of a religious group.* **5** (**the wings**) the sides of a theater stage out of view of the audience. **6** the part of a soccer, rugby, or hockey field close to the sidelines. **7** (also **wing forward**) an attacking player positioned near the sidelines. ▶ v. **1** fly, or move quickly as if flying: *the prize will be winging its way to you soon.* **2** shoot a person or bird so as to wound in the arm or wing. **3** (**wing it**) informal speak or act without preparation. ■ **winged** adj. **wing·less** adj.
– PHRASES **in the wings** ready for use or action at the appropriate time. **on the wing** (of a bird or insect) in flight. **on a wing and a prayer** with only a small chance of success. **spread one's wings** extend one's activities and interests. **take wing** fly away. **under one's wing** in or into one's protective care.

wing·beat /'wiNG,bēt/ (also **wingstroke** /'wiNG,strōk/) ▶ n. one complete set of movements of a wing in flying.

wing chair ▶ n. an armchair with side pieces projecting forward from a high back.

wing col·lar ▶ n. a high stiff shirt collar with turned-down corners.

wing·er /'wiNGər/ ▶ n. **1** an attacking player on the wing in soccer, hockey, etc. **2** (in combination) a member of a specified political wing: *a religious right-winger.*

wing mir·ror ▶ n. a mirror projecting from the side of a vehicle; a side-view mirror.

wing nut ▶ n. a nut with a pair of projections for the fingers to turn it on a screw.

wing·span /'wiNG,span/ (also **wingspread** /-,spred/) ▶ n. the maximum extent from tip to tip of the wings of an aircraft, bird, etc.

wing tip ▶ n. a shoe with a toe cap having a backward extending point and curving sides.

wink /wiNGk/ ▶ v. **1** close and open one eye quickly as a signal of affection or greeting or to convey a message. **2** shine or flash on and off. ▶ n. an act of winking. ■ **wink·er** n.
– PHRASES **as easy as winking** informal very easy or easily. **in the wink of an eye** (or **in a wink**) very quickly. **not sleep a wink** (or **not get a**

wink of sleep) not sleep at all.

win·kle /'wiNGkəl/ ▶ n. a small edible sea snail with a spiral shell. ▶ v. (**winkle something out**) chiefly Brit. extract or obtain something with difficulty.

win·ner /'winər/ ▶ n. 1 a person or thing that wins something. 2 informal a thing that is a success or is likely to be successful.

win·ning /'winiNG/ ▶ adj. 1 gaining, resulting in, or relating to victory. 2 attractive; endearing. ▶ n. (**winnings**) money won, especially by gambling. ■ **win·ning·ly** adv.

win·ning post ▶ n. a post marking the end of a race.

win·now /'winō/ ▶ v. 1 reduce people or things from a group until only the best ones are left: *we had to winnow out the losers.* 2 blow air through grain in order to remove the chaff.

win·o /'wīnō/ ▶ n. (pl. **winos**) informal a person who drinks excessive amounts of cheap wine or other alcohol, especially one who is homeless.

win·some /'winsəm/ ▶ adj. attractive or appealing in a fresh or innocent way. ■ **win·some·ly** adv. **win·some·ness** n.

win·ter /'wintər/ ▶ n. the coldest season of the year, after autumn and before spring. ▶ v. spend the winter in a particular place. ▶ adj. (of crops) sown in autumn for harvesting the following year.

win·ter·green /'wintər,grēn/ ▶ n. 1 a North American shrub whose leaves produce oil. 2 (also **oil of wintergreen**) a pungent oil obtained from wintergreen or from birch bark, used as a medicine or flavoring.

win·ter·ize /'wintə,rīz/ ▶ v. adapt or prepare something for use in cold weather.

Win·ter O·lym·pics ▶ pl.n. an international contest of winter sports held every four years at a two-year interval from the Summer Olympic Games.

win·ter sports ▶ pl.n. sports performed on snow or ice.

win·ter·time /'wintər,tīm/ ▶ n. the season or period of winter.

win·try /'wintrē/ (also **wintery** /'wint(ə)rē/) ▶ adj. (**wintrier**, **wintriest**) typical of winter, especially in being very cold or bleak.

win–win ▶ adj. (of a situation) in which each party benefits.

wipe /wīp/ ▶ v. 1 clean or dry something by rubbing with a cloth or the hand. 2 remove dirt or moisture with a cloth or the hand. 3 erase data from a tape, computer, etc. ▶ n. 1 an act of wiping. 2 an absorbent disposable cleaning cloth. ■ **wipe·a·ble** adj. **wip·er** n.

– PHRASES **wipe the floor with** informal defeat someone completely. **wipe something off** subtract an amount from a value or debt. **wipe someone out 1** kill a large number of people. 2 (**be wiped out**) informal be exhausted or intoxicated. **wipe something out** remove or eliminate something. **wipe the slate clean** make a fresh start.

wipe·out /'wīp,out/ ▶ n. informal 1 an instance of complete destruction or failure. 2 a fall while surfing or skiing.

wire /wīr/ ▶ n. 1 metal drawn out into a thin flexible strand or rod. 2 a length or quantity of wire used for fencing, to carry an electric current, etc. 3 a concealed electronic listening device. 4 informal a telegram. ▶ v. 1 install electric circuits or wires in something. 2 provide, fasten, or reinforce something with wire. 3 informal send a telegram to someone.

– PHRASES **down to the wire** informal until the very last minute.

wire brush ▶ n. a brush with tough wire bristles for cleaning hard surfaces.

wired /wīrd/ ▶ adj. informal 1 making use of computers and information technology to transfer or receive information. 2 nervous, tense, or edgy. 3 under the influence of drugs or alcohol.

wire–haired ▶ adj. (especially of a dog breed) having wiry hair.

wire·less /'wīrlis/ ▶ adj. using radio, microwaves, etc. (as opposed to wires) to transmit signals. ▶ n. dated, chiefly Brit. 1 a radio. 2 broadcasting or telegraphy using radio signals. ■ **wire·less·ly** adv.

wire·less hot spot ▶ n. see HOT SPOT (sense 3).

wire serv·ice ▶ n. a news agency that supplies news stories to its subscribers, e.g., newspapers and radio and television stations.

wire·tap·ping /'wīr,tapiNG/ ▶ n. the practice of tapping a telephone line to monitor conversations secretly.

wire·worm /'wīr,wərm/ ▶ n. the wormlike larva of a kind of beetle, which feeds on roots and can cause damage to crops.

wir·ing /'wīriNG/ ▶ n. a system of wires providing electric circuits for a device or building.

wir·y /'wī(ə)rē/ ▶ adj. (**wirier**, **wiriest**) 1 resembling wire in form and texture. 2 lean, tough, and sinewy: *a small, wiry woman.*

wis·dom /'wizdəm/ ▶ n. 1 the quality of having experience, knowledge, and good judgment. 2 the body of knowledge and experience that develops within a particular society or period: *old Yankee wisdom.*

wis·dom tooth ▶ n. each of the four molars at the back of the mouth that usually appear at about the age of eighteen.

wise¹ /wīz/ ▶ adj. 1 having or showing experience, knowledge, and good judgment. 2 (**wise to**) informal aware of. ▶ v. (**wise up**) informal become aware of or informed about something. ■ **wise·ly** adv.

– PHRASES **be none** (or **not any**) **the wiser** not understand something, even though it has been explained.

wise² ▶ n. old use the way or extent of something.

-wise ▶ suffix 1 forming adjectives and adverbs of manner or respect: *clockwise.* 2 informal concerning: *security-wise.*

wise·a·cre /'wīz,ākər/ ▶ n. a person who pretends to be wise or knowledgeable.

wise·crack /'wīz,krak/ informal ▶ n. a witty remark or joke. ▶ v. make a wisecrack. ■ **wise·crack·er** n.

wise guy ▶ n. informal a person who makes sarcastic or sassy remarks to demonstrate their cleverness.

wish /wish/ ▶ v. 1 desire something that cannot or probably will not happen. 2 want to do something. 3 want someone to do something or something to be done. 4 express a hope that someone has happiness or success. 5 (**wish someone/thing on**) hope that someone has to deal with someone or something unpleasant. ▶ n. 1 a desire or hope: *a wish for a more leisurely life.* 2 (**wishes**) an expression of a hope for someone's happiness, success, or welfare. 3 a thing wished for.

wish·bone /'wɪsн,bōn/ ▸ n. a forked bone between the neck and breast of a cooked chicken or similar bird that, when broken by two people, entitles the holder of the longer portion to make a wish.

wish·ful /'wɪsнfəl/ ▸ adj. 1 having or expressing a wish for something to happen. 2 based on impractical wishes rather than facts: *without resources the proposals were merely wishful thinking.* ■ **wish·ful·ly** adv.

wish·ful·fill·ment ▸ n. the satisfying of wishes in dreams or fantasies.

wish·ing well ▸ n. a well into which one drops a coin and makes a wish.

wish·y-wash·y /'wɪsнē 'wäsнē, -'wôsнē/ ▸ adj. not firm or forceful; feeble: *wishy-washy liberalism.*

wisp /wɪsp/ ▸ n. a small thin bunch, strand, or amount of something. ■ **wisp·y** adj.

wist /wɪst/ ▸ past and past participle of **wɪт²**.

wis·te·ri·a /wi'sti(ə)rēə/ (also **wistaria** /-'ste(ə)r-/) ▸ n. a climbing shrub with hanging clusters of pale bluish-lilac flowers.

wist·ful /'wɪstfəl/ ▸ adj. having or showing a feeling of vague or regretful longing. ■ **wist·ful·ly** adv. **wist·ful·ness** n.

wit¹ /wɪt/ ▸ n. 1 (also **wits**) the capacity to think inventively and understand quickly; keen intelligence: *he needed all his wits to find the way back.* 2 a natural talent for using words and ideas in a quick, clever, and amusing way. 3 a witty person. ■ **wit·ted** adj.
− PHRASES **be at one's wits' end** be so worried that one does not know what to do. **have** (or **keep**) **one's wits about one** be constantly alert. **live by one's wits** earn money by clever and sometimes dishonest means.

wit² ▸ v. (**wot, witting, wist**) old use know someone or something.
− PHRASES **to wit** that is to say.

witch /wɪcн/ ▸ n. 1 a woman thought to have evil magic powers. 2 a person who follows or practices modern witchcraft. 3 informal an ugly or disliked old woman. ■ **witch·y** adj.

witch·craft /'wɪcн,kraft/ ▸ n. the practice of magic, especially the use of spells and the calling up of evil spirits. See also **wɪcca**.

witch doc·tor ▸ n. (among tribal peoples) a person believed to have magic powers of healing, seeing the future, etc.

witch·er·y /'wɪcнərē/ ▸ n. 1 the practice of magic. 2 bewitching quality or power.

witch ha·zel ▸ n. a cleansing and medicinal astringent made from the bark and leaves of a shrub.

witch-hunt ▸ n. a campaign directed against a person or group whose views are considered to be unacceptable or a threat to society.

witch·ing hour ▸ n. midnight, regarded as the time when witches are supposedly active.

with /wɪтн, wɪтн/ ▸ prep. 1 accompanied by. 2 possessing; having. 3 indicating the instrument used to perform an action or the material used for a purpose: *cut the fish with a knife.* 4 in relation to. 5 in opposition to or competition with. 6 indicating the way or attitude in which a person does something. 7 indicating responsibility: *leave it with me.* 8 in the same direction as. 9 affected by a particular fact or condition. 10 employed by. 11 using the services of. 12 indicating separation or removal from something: *their jobs were dispensed with.*

− PHRASES **be with someone** informal follow someone's meaning. **with it** informal 1 up to date or fashionable. 2 alert and able to understand.

with·al /wɪтн'ôl, wɪтн-/ ▸ adv. old use in addition.

with·draw /wɪтн'drô, wɪтн-/ ▸ v. (past **withdrew**; past part. **withdrawn**) 1 remove or take away something. 2 leave or cause to leave a place. 3 stop taking part in an activity or being a member of a team or organization. 4 discontinue something previously given or provided: *the party withdrew its support for the government.* 5 take back a statement. 6 take money out of an account. 7 go away to another place in order to be private or quiet. 8 stop taking an addictive drug.

with·draw·al /wɪтн'drôl, wɪтн-/ ▸ n. 1 the action of withdrawing. 2 the process of giving up an addictive drug.

with·drawn /wɪтн'drôn, wɪтн-/ past participle of **wɪтнdraw** ▸ adj. very shy or reserved.

with·er /'wɪтнər/ ▸ v. 1 (of a plant) become dry and shriveled. 2 become shrunken or wrinkled from age or disease. 3 gradually die out: *support for the UN strategy withered away.* 4 (as adj. **withering**) showing scorn or contempt. ■ **with·er·ing·ly** adv.

with·ers /'wɪтнərz/ ▸ pl.n. the highest part of a horse's back, lying at the base of the neck above the shoulders.

with·hold /wɪтн'hōld, wɪтн-/ ▸ v. (past and past part. **withheld** /wɪтн'held, wɪтн-/) 1 refuse to give someone something that they want or is due to them. 2 suppress or restrain an emotion or reaction. ■ **with·hold·er** n.

with·in /wɪтн'in, wɪ'тн-/ ▸ prep. 1 inside. 2 inside the range or bounds of: *we were within sight of the finish.* 3 occurring inside a particular period of time. 4 not further off than (used with distances). ▸ adv. 1 inside; indoors. 2 internally or inwardly.

with·out /wɪтн'out, wɪтн-/ ▸ prep. 1 not accompanied by or having the use of. 2 in circumstances in which the action mentioned does not happen. ▸ adv. old use outside.

with·stand /wɪтн'stand, wɪтн-/ ▸ v. (past and past part. **withstood** /wɪтн'stŏŏd, wɪтн-/) 1 remain undamaged or unaffected by something. 2 offer strong resistance to: *the city withstood the eastern invaders.*

with·y /'wɪтнē, 'wɪтнē/ ▸ n. (pl. **withies**) a tough flexible willow branch, used for tying things or making baskets.

wit·less /'wɪtlis/ ▸ adj. foolish; stupid. ■ **wit·less·ly** adv. **wit·less·ness** n.

wit·ness /'witnis/ ▸ n. 1 a person who sees an event take place. 2 a person giving sworn evidence to a court of law or the police. 3 a person who is present at the signing of a document and signs it themselves to confirm this. 4 (**witness to**) evidence or proof of: *the memorial service was witness to his wide circle of interests.* 5 open expression of a person's religious faith through words or actions.
▸ v. 1 be a witness to an event. 2 be the place or period in which an event takes place: *the 1960s witnessed a drop in churchgoing.*

wit·ness stand (Brit. **witness box**) ▸ n. the place in a court of law from where a witness gives evidence.

wit·ti·cism /'witi,sizəm/ ▸ n. a witty remark.

wit·ting /'witɪNG/ ▸ adj. 1 deliberate; on purpose.

2 aware of the full facts. ■ **wit·ting·ly** adv.

wit·ty /'witē/ ▶ adj. (**wittier, wittiest**) showing or having the ability to say clever and amusing things. ■ **wit·ti·ly** adv. **wit·ti·ness** n.

wives /wīvz/ ▶ plural of **WIFE**.

wiz /wiz/ ▶ n. variant spelling of **WHIZ** (sense 3 of the noun).

wiz·ard /'wizərd/ ▶ n. **1** a man who has magical powers, especially in legends and fairy tales. **2** a person who is very skilled in a particular area or activity: *a financial wizard.* **3** a computer software tool that automatically guides a user through a process. ■ **wiz·ard·ly** adj.

wiz·ard·ry /'wizərdrē/ ▶ n. **1** the art or practice of magic. **2** great skill in a particular area or activity.

wiz·ened /'wizənd, 'wē-/ ▶ adj. shriveled or wrinkled with age.

WLAN /'dəbəlyōō ˌlan/ ▶ abbr. Computing wireless local area network.

WMD ▶ abbr. weapon (or weapons) of mass destruction.

WNW ▶ abbr. west-northwest.

WO ▶ abbr. Warrant Officer.

woad /wōd/ ▶ n. a plant whose leaves were formerly used to make blue dye.

wob·ble /'wäbəl/ ▶ v. **1** move unsteadily from side to side. **2** (of the voice) tremble. **3** waver between different courses of action: *the president wobbled on Bosnia.* ▶ n. a wobbling movement or sound. ■ **wob·bler** n.

wob·bly /'wäb(ə)lē/ ▶ adj. (**wobblier, wobbliest**) **1** tending to wobble. **2** weak and unsteady from illness, tiredness, or anxiety. **3** uncertain or insecure: *the evening got off to a wobbly start.* ■ **wob·bli·ness** n.

woe /wō/ ▶ n. literary **1** great sorrow or distress. **2** (**woes**) troubles or problems.
– PHRASES **woe betide someone** a person will be in trouble if they do a specified thing.

woe·be·gone /'wōbiˌgôn, -ˌgän/ ▶ adj. looking sad or miserable.

woe·ful /'wōfəl/ ▶ adj. **1** very sad or miserable. **2** shockingly bad: *the woeful state of public education.* ■ **woe·ful·ly** adv.

wok /wäk/ ▶ n. a bowl-shaped frying pan used in Chinese cooking.

woke /wōk/ ▶ past of **WAKE**[1].

wok·en /'wōkən/ ▶ past participle of **WAKE**[1].

wold /wōld/ ▶ n. (especially in British place names) a piece of high, open, uncultivated land.

wolf /wŏŏlf/ ▶ n. (pl. **wolves** /wŏŏlvz/) **1** a wild animal of the dog family, that lives and hunts in packs. **2** informal a man who seduces many women. ▶ v. (usu. **wolf something down**) eat food quickly and greedily. ■ **wolf·ish** adj.
– PHRASES **cry wolf** raise repeated false alarms, so that a real cry for help is ignored. **keep the wolf from the door** have enough money to be able to buy food. **throw someone to the wolves** sacrifice someone in order to avoid trouble for oneself. **a wolf in sheep's clothing** a person who appears friendly but is really hostile.

wolf·hound /'wŏŏlfˌhound/ ▶ n. a dog of a large breed originally used to hunt wolves.

wolf·ram /'wŏŏlfrəm/ ▶ n. tungsten or its ore.

wolf whis·tle ▶ n. a whistle with a rising and falling pitch, used to express sexual attraction or admiration. ▶ v. (**wolf-whistle**) whistle at someone in this way.

wol·ver·ine /ˌwŏŏlvə'rēn, 'wŏŏlvəˌrēn/ ▶ n. a heavily built short-legged mammal with a long brown coat and a bushy tail, native to northern tundra and forests.

wolves /wŏŏlvz/ ▶ plural of **WOLF**.

wom·an /'wŏŏmən/ ▶ n. (pl. **women**) **1** an adult human female. **2** a female worker or employee. **3** a wife or lover. ■ **wom·an·li·ness** n. **wom·an·ly** adj.
– PHRASES **the little woman** a condescending way of referring to one's wife.

wom·an·hood /'wŏŏmənˌhŏŏd/ ▶ n. **1** the state or period of being a woman. **2** women as a group. **3** the qualities associated with women, such as femininity.

wom·an·ish /'wŏŏmənish/ ▶ adj. derogatory **1** suitable for or typical of a woman: *womanish indecision.* **2** (of a man) effeminate.

wom·an·ize /'wŏŏməˌnīz/ ▶ v. (usu. as n. **womanizing**) (of a man) have many casual sexual relationships with women. ■ **wom·an·iz·er** n.

wom·an·kind /'wŏŏmənˌkīnd/ ▶ n. women as a group.

womb /wŏŏm/ ▶ n. the uterus.

wom·bat /'wämˌbat/ ▶ n. a burrowing Australian marsupial that resembles a small bear with short legs.

wom·en /'wimin/ ▶ plural of **WOMAN**.

wom·en·folk /'wiminˌfōk/ ▶ pl.n. the women of a family or community considered as a group.

wom·en's lib·er·a·tion (also informal **women's lib**) ▶ n. a movement supporting the freedom of women to have the same rights, status, and treatment as men (now usually replaced by the term *feminism*).

wom·ens·wear /'wiminzˌwe(ə)r/ ▶ n. clothing for women.

won[1] /wən/ ▶ past and past participle of **WIN**.

won[2] /wän/ ▶ n. (pl. same) the basic unit of money of North and South Korea.

won·der /'wəndər/ ▶ v. **1** desire to know something. **2** feel doubt: *I wondered about the validity of his comments.* **3** feel amazement and admiration. ▶ n. **1** a feeling of surprise and admiration caused by something beautiful, unexpected, or unfamiliar. **2** a cause of wonder: *the wonders of the coral reef.* ▶ adj. having remarkable qualities or abilities: *a wonder drug.* ■ **won·der·er** n.
– PHRASES **no** (or **little** or **small**) **wonder** it is not surprising. **wonders will never cease** often ironic an exclamation of surprise and pleasure. **work** (or **do**) **wonders** have a very beneficial effect.

won·der·ful /'wəndərfəl/ ▶ adj. very good, pleasant, or remarkable. ■ **won·der·ful·ly** adv. **won·der·ful·ness** n.

won·der·land /'wəndərˌland/ ▶ n. a place full of wonderful things.

won·der·ment /'wəndərmənt/ ▶ n. a state of awed admiration or respect.

won·drous /'wəndrəs/ ▶ adj. literary causing amazement and admiration. ▶ adv. old use wonderfully; remarkably. ■ **won·drous·ly** adv.

wonk /wäNGk/ (also **policy wonk**) ▶ n. informal, derogatory a person who takes an excessive interest in minor details of political policy.

won·ky /'wäNGkē/ ▶ adj. (**wonkier, wonkiest**) informal **1** unsteady or faulty. **2** not straight; crooked. ■ **won·ki·ly** adv. **won·ki·ness** n.

wont /wônt, wōnt/ ▶ n. (**one's wont**) formal one's usual behavior. ▶ adj. (**wont to**) literary in the habit of doing something; accustomed.

won't /wōnt/ ▶ contr. will not.

wont·ed /'wôntid, 'wōn-/ ▶ adj. literary usual; normal.

won·ton /'wän,tän/ ▶ n. (in Chinese cooking) a small round dumpling with a savory filling, typically served in soup.

woo /wōō/ ▶ v. (**woos, wooing, wooed**) **1** try to gain a woman's love. **2** try to gain the support or custom of: *the store decided to woo customers with parking.* ■ **woo·er** n.

wood /wōōd/ ▶ n. **1** the hard fibrous material forming the trunk or branches of a tree or shrub, used for fuel or lumber. **2** (also **woods**) a small forest. **3** (**the wood**) wooden barrels used for storing alcoholic drinks. **4** a golf club with a wooden or other head that is relatively broad from face to back.
– PHRASES **be unable to see the wood for the trees** fail to grasp the main issue because of overattention to details. **out of the woods** out of difficulty. **knock on wood** said to prevent a confident statement from bringing bad luck, often accompanied by the old custom of knocking on or touching something wooden to prevent such bad luck.

wood·bine /'wōōd,bīn/ ▶ n. **1** another term for VIRGINIA CREEPER. **2** Brit. the common honeysuckle.

wood·block /'wōōd,bläk/ ▶ n. a block of wood from which woodcut prints are made.

wood·carv·ing /'wōōd,kärving/ ▶ n. **1** the action or skill of carving wood. **2** a carved wooden object. ■ **wood·carv·er** n.

wood·chip /'wōōd,CHip/ ▶ n. chiefly Brit. wallpaper with small chips of wood embedded in it to give a grainy surface texture.

wood·chuck /'wōōd,CHək/ ▶ n. a North American marmot (burrowing rodent) with a heavy body and short legs.

wood·cock /'wōōd,käk/ ▶ n. (pl. same) a long-billed woodland bird of the sandpiper family, with brown plumage.

wood·cut /'wōōd,kət/ ▶ n. a print of a type made from a design cut in relief in a block of wood.

wood·cut·ter /'wōōd,kətər/ ▶ n. a person who cuts down trees for wood.

wood·ed /'wōōdid/ ▶ adj. (of land) covered with woods.

wood·en /'wōōdn/ ▶ adj. **1** made of or resembling wood. **2** stiff and awkward in speech or behavior. ■ **wood·en·ly** adv. **wood·en·ness** n.

wood·grain /'wōōd,grān/ ▶ adj. (of a surface or finish) imitating the grain pattern of wood.

wood·land /'wōōdlənd/ ▶ n. (also **woodlands**) land covered with trees.

wood·louse /'wōōd,lous/ ▶ n. (pl. **woodlice**) a small insectlike creature with a gray segmented body that it is able to roll into a ball.

wood·peck·er /'wōōd,pekər/ ▶ n. a bird with a strong bill and a stiff tail, typically pecking at tree trunks to find insects.

wood pulp ▶ n. wood fiber reduced chemically or mechanically to pulp and used in the manufacture of paper.

wood·ruff /'wōōd,rəf/ (also **sweet woodruff**) ▶ n. a white-flowered plant with sweet-scented leaves used to flavor drinks and in perfumery.

wood·shed /'wōōd,SHed/ ▶ n. a shed where wood

for fuel is stored. ▶ v. informal practice a musical instrument.

woods·man /'wōōdzmən/ ▶ n. (pl. **woodsmen**) a forester, hunter, or woodcutter.

woods·y /'wōōdzē/ ▶ adj. (**woodsier, woodsiest**) relating to or characteristic of wood or woodlands.

wood·turn·ing /'wōōd,tərning/ ▶ n. the activity of shaping wood with a lathe. ■ **wood·turn·er** n.

wood·wind /'wōōd,wind/ ▶ n. (treated as sing. or pl.) wind instruments other than brass instruments forming a section of an orchestra, including flutes, oboes, and clarinets.

wood·work /'wōōd,wərk/ ▶ n. **1** the wooden parts of a room, building, or other structure. **2** Brit. woodworking. ■ **wood·work·er** n.
– PHRASES **come out of the woodwork** (of a disliked person or thing) suddenly appear, especially to take advantage of a situation.

wood·work·ing /'wōōd,wərking/ ▶ n. the activity or skill of making things from wood.

wood·worm /'wōōd,wərm/ ▶ n. **1** the wood-boring larva of a kind of small brown beetle. **2** the damaged condition of wood resulting from infestation with woodworm.

wood·y /'wōōdē/ ▶ adj. (**woodier, woodiest**) **1** covered with trees. **2** made of or resembling wood. ■ **wood·i·ness** n.

woof¹ /wōōf/ ▶ n. the barking sound made by a dog. ▶ v. (of a dog) bark.

woof² ▶ n. another term for WEFT.

woof·er /'wōōfər/ ▶ n. a loudspeaker designed to reproduce low frequencies.

wool /wōōl/ ▶ n. **1** the fine soft hair forming the coat of a sheep, goat, or similar animal, especially when shorn and made into cloth or yarn. **2** a metal or mineral made into a mass of fine fibers.
– PHRASES **pull the wool over someone's eyes** deceive someone.

wool·en /'wōōlən/ (Brit. **woollen**) ▶ adj. **1** made of wool. **2** relating to the production of wool. ▶ n. (**woolens**) woolen clothes.

wool·gath·er·ing ▶ n. aimless thought or daydreaming.

wool·ly /'wōōlē/ ▶ adj. (**woollier, woolliest**) **1** made of wool. **2** (of an animal or plant) covered with wool or hair resembling wool. **3** resembling wool in texture or appearance. **4** confused or unclear: *woolly thinking.* ▶ n. (pl. **woollies**) informal chiefly Brit. a woolen sweater or cardigan. ■ **wool·li·ness** n.

woosh ▶ v. & n. variant spelling of WHOOSH.

wooz·y /'wōōzē/ ▶ adj. (**woozier, wooziest**) informal unsteady, dizzy, or dazed. ■ **wooz·i·ly** adv. **wooz·i·ness** n.

wop /wäp/ ▶ n. informal, offensive an Italian or other southern European.

Worces·ter·shire sauce /'wōōstər,SHi(ə)r, -SHər/ ▶ n. a tangy sauce containing soy sauce and vinegar, first made in Worcester in England.

word /wərd/ ▶ n. **1** a single unit of language that has meaning and is used with others to form sentences. **2** a remark or statement. **3** (**a word**) even the smallest amount of something spoken or written: *don't believe a word.* **4** (**words**) angry talk. **5** (**the word**) a command or signal: *someone gave me the word to start playing.* **6** (**one's word**) a person's version of the truth. **7** (**one's word**) a promise. **8** news or information. ▶ v. express something in particular words. ■ **word·less** adj.

– PHRASES **have a word** speak briefly to someone. **in so many words** precisely in the way mentioned. **in a word** briefly. **a man** (or **woman**) **of his** (or **her**) **word** a person who keeps their promises. **on** (or **upon**) **my word** an exclamation of surprise or emphasis. **take someone at their word** assume that a person is speaking honestly or sincerely. **take the words out of someone's mouth** say what someone else was about to say. **take someone's word** (**for it**) believe what someone says or writes without checking for oneself. **word for word** in exactly the same or, when translated, exactly equivalent words. **word of honor** a solemn promise. **word of mouth** speech as a means of conveying information.

word class ▶ n. a part of speech.

word·ing /'wərdiNG/ ▶ n. the way in which something is expressed in words.

word-per·fect /'pərfəkt/ ▶ adj. (of an actor or speaker) knowing one's part or speech by heart.

word·play /'wərd,plā/ ▶ n. the witty use of words and their meanings, especially in puns.

word proc·es·sor ▶ n. a computer or program for creating, editing, storing, and printing a document. ■ **word proc·ess·ing** n.

word·smith /'wərd,smiTH/ ▶ n. a skilled user of words.

word·y /'wərdē/ ▶ adj. (**wordier**, **wordiest**) using or expressed in too many words. ■ **word·i·ly** adv. **word·i·ness** n.

wore /wôr/ ▶ past of WEAR.

work /wərk/ ▶ n. 1 activity involving mental or physical effort done in order to achieve a result. 2 the activity or job that a person does to earn money. 3 a task or tasks to be done. 4 a thing or things done or made; the result of an action: *her work hangs in the Wadsworth Atheneum.* 5 (**works**) (treated as sing., often in combination) a place where industrial or manufacturing processes are carried out: *they're hiring at the steel works.* 6 (**works**) the mechanism of a machine. 7 a defensive military structure. 8 Physics the exertion of force overcoming resistance or producing molecular change. 9 (**the works**) informal everything needed, wanted, or expected. ▶ v. (past and past part. **worked** or old use **wrought** /rôt/) 1 do work, especially as a job. 2 make someone do work. 3 (of a machine or system) function properly or effectively. 4 operate a machine. 5 have the desired result: *her plan worked admirably.* 6 bring a material or mixture to a desired shape or consistency. 7 move gradually or with difficulty: *they worked their way up the steep hill.* 8 produce an article or design using a specified material or sewing stitch. 9 cultivate land or extract materials from a mine or quarry. 10 bring into a specified emotional state: *he'd worked himself into a rage.* ■ **work·less** adj.

– PHRASES **get worked up** become excited, angry, or stressed. **have one's work cut out** (**for one**) be faced with a hard or lengthy task. **in the works** being planned or produced. **work something in** try to include something. **work something off** get rid of something through physical effort. **work out 1** develop in a good or specified way. 2 engage in vigorous physical exercise. **work something out 1** solve a sum or calculate an amount. 2 plan something in detail. **work to rule** chiefly Brit. follow official working rules and hours exactly in order to reduce output and efficiency, as a form of industrial action.

work up to proceed gradually toward something more advanced. **work something up** develop something gradually.

work·a·ble /'wərkəbəl/ ▶ adj. 1 able to be shaped, manipulated, or dug. 2 capable of producing the desired result: *a workable peace settlement.* ■ **work·a·bil·i·ty** /,wərkə'bilitē/ n. **work·a·bly** adv.

work·a·day /'wərkə,dā/ ▶ adj. not special or interesting; ordinary.

work·a·hol·ic /,wərkə'hôlik, -'hälik/ ▶ n. informal a person who works very hard and finds it difficult to stop working. ■ **work·a·hol·ism** /'wərkə,hôlizəm, -,häl-/ n.

work·a·round /'wərkə,round/ ▶ n. a method for overcoming a problem in a computer program or system.

work·bench /'wərk,benCH/ ▶ n. a bench at which carpentry or other mechanical or practical work is done.

work·book /'wərk,bŏŏk/ ▶ n. a student's book containing instruction and exercises.

work·day /'wərk,dā/ ▶ n. a day on which a person works.

work·er /'wərkər/ ▶ n. 1 a person who works. 2 a person who achieves a specified thing: *a miracle-worker.* 3 a neuter or undeveloped female bee, wasp, ant, etc., large numbers of which perform the basic work of a colony.

work eth·ic ▶ n. the belief that it is a person's moral duty to work hard.

work·flow /'wərk,flō/ ▶ n. the sequence of processes through which a piece of work passes from start to finish.

work·force /'wərk,fôrs/ ▶ n. (treated as sing. or pl.) the people engaged in or available for work in a particular area, organization, or industry.

work·horse /'wərk,hôrs/ ▶ n. a person or machine that works hard and reliably over a long period.

work·house /'wərk,hous/ ▶ n. historical (in the UK) a public institution in which poor people received food and lodging in return for work.

work·ing /'wərkiNG/ ▶ adj. 1 having paid employment. 2 doing manual work. 3 functioning or able to function. 4 used as the basis for work or discussion and likely to be changed later: *a working title.* ▶ n. 1 a mine or a part of a mine from which minerals are being extracted. 2 (**workings**) the way in which a machine, organization, or system operates. 3 (**workings**) a record of the calculations made in solving a mathematical problem.

work·ing cap·i·tal ▶ n. the capital of a business that is used in its day-to-day trading operations.

work·ing class ▶ n. the social group consisting largely of people who do manual or industrial work. ▶ adj. relating to the working class.

work·load /'wərk,lōd/ ▶ n. the amount of work to be done by someone or something.

work·man /'wərkmən/ ▶ n. (pl. **workmen**) 1 a person employed to do manual work. 2 a person who works in a specified way: *he's a good workman.*

work·man·like /'wərkmən,līk/ ▶ adj. showing efficient skill.

work·man·ship /'wərkmən,SHip/ ▶ n. the degree of skill with which a product is made or a job done.

work·mate /'wərk,māt/ ▶ n. chiefly Brit. a person

with whom one works; a colleague.

work of art ▶ n. a creative product with strong imaginative or artistic appeal.

work·out /'wərk,out/ ▶ n. a session of vigorous physical exercise.

work per·mit ▶ n. an official document giving a foreigner permission to take a job in a country.

work·piece /'wərk,pēs/ ▶ n. an object being worked on with a tool or machine.

work·place /'wərk,plās/ ▶ n. a place where people work.

work·room /'wərk,rōōm, -,rŏŏm/ ▶ n. a room for working in.

work·sheet /'wərk,SHēt/ ▶ n. **1** a paper listing questions or tasks for students. **2** a paper recording work done or in progress.

work·shop /'wərk,SHäp/ ▶ n. **1** a room or building in which goods are made or repaired. **2** a meeting for discussion and activity on a particular subject or project.

work·shy ▶ adj. unwilling to work.

work·space /'wərk,spās/ ▶ n. **1** space in which a person or people can work. **2** Computing a memory storage facility for temporary use.

work·sta·tion /'wərk,stāSHən/ ▶ n. a desktop computer terminal, typically one that is part of a network.

work sur·face ▶ n. another term for COUNTERTOP.

work·week /'wərk,wēk/ ▶ n. the total number of hours or days worked in a week.

world /wərld/ ▶ n. **1** (**the world**) the earth with all its countries and peoples. **2** a region or group of countries: *the English-speaking world*. **3** all that belongs to a particular period or area of activity: *the theater world*. **4** (**one's world**) a person's life and activities. **5** (**the world**) secular or material matters as opposed to spiritual or religious ones. **6** a planet. **7** (**a/the world of**) a very large amount of: *that makes a world of difference*.
– PHRASES **the best of both** (or **all possible**) **worlds** the benefits of widely differing situations, enjoyed at the same time. **man** (or **woman**) **of the world** a person with a great deal of experience of life and who is not easily shocked. **out of this world** informal very enjoyable or impressive.

world-beat·er ▶ n. a person or thing that is better than all others in its field. ■ **world-beat·ing** adj.

world-class ▶ adj. relating to or among the best in the world.

World Cup ▶ n. a competition between teams from many countries in a sport, in particular a soccer tournament held every four years.

world Eng·lish ▶ n. the English language including all of its regional varieties, such as North American, Australian, and South African English.

world-fa·mous ▶ adj. known throughout the world.

world·ly /'wərldlē/ ▶ adj. (**worldlier, worldliest**) **1** relating to material things rather than spiritual ones: *he gave up his worldly goods and left in search of enlightenment*. **2** having experience of life; sophisticated. ■ **world·li·ness** n.

world·ly-wise ▶ adj. having enough experience of life not to be easily shocked or cheated.

world mu·sic ▶ n. traditional music from the developing world, sometimes incorporating elements of Western popular music.

world or·der ▶ n. a system established internationally for preserving global political stability.

world pow·er ▶ n. a country that has significant influence in international affairs.

world-rank·ing ▶ adj. among the best in the world.

World Se·ries ▶ the championship for North American major league baseball, played between the champions of the American League and the National League.

world-shak·ing ▶ adj. very important.

world·view /'wərld,vyōō/ ▶ n. a particular philosophy of life or conception of the world.

world war ▶ n. a war involving many large nations in different parts of the world, especially the wars of 1914–18 and 1939–45.

world-wea·ry ▶ adj. bored with or cynical about life.

world-wide /'wərld'wīd/ ▶ adj. extending or applicable throughout the world. ▶ adv. throughout the world.

World Wide Web ▶ n. an extensive information system on the Internet providing facilities for documents to be connected to other documents by hypertext links.

WORM /wərm/ ▶ abbr. Computing write-once read-many.

worm /wərm/ ▶ n. **1** an earthworm or other creeping or burrowing invertebrate animal with a long, thin, soft body and no limbs. **2** (**worms**) parasites that live in the intestines. **3** a maggot regarded as eating dead bodies buried in the ground: *food for worms*. **4** informal a weak or disliked person. ▶ v. **1** (**worm one's way**) move by crawling or wriggling. **2** (**worm one's way into**) gradually move into a situation in order to gain an advantage. **3** (**worm something out of**) obtain information from someone by continual questions or cunning.

worm cast ▶ n. a coiled mass of soil, mud, or sand thrown up at the surface by a burrowing worm.

worm-eat·en ▶ adj. (of wood) full of holes made by woodworm.

worm gear ▶ n. a mechanical arrangement consisting of a toothed wheel worked by a short revolving cylinder (worm) bearing a screw thread.

worm·hole /'wərm,hōl/ ▶ n. **1** a hole made by a burrowing insect larva or worm in wood, fruit, etc. **2** Physics a hypothetical shortcut through space and time.

worm·wheel /'wərm,(h)wēl/ ▶ n. the wheel of a worm gear.

worm·wood /'wərm,wŏŏd/ ▶ n. a woody shrub with a bitter taste, used as an ingredient of vermouth and absinthe and in medicine.

worm·y /'wərmē/ ▶ adj. (**wormier, wormiest**) worm-eaten or full of worms.

worn /wôrn/ past participle of WEAR ▶ adj. **1** damaged by wear. **2** very tired.

worn out ▶ adj. **1** exhausted. **2** so damaged by wear as to be no longer usable.

wor·ried /'wərēd/ ▶ adj. feeling, showing, or expressing anxiety. ■ **wor·ried·ly** adv.

wor·ri·some /'wərē,səm/ ▶ adj. causing anxiety or concern.

wor·ry /'wərē/ ▶ v. (**worries, worrying, worried**)

1 feel or cause to feel troubled over actual or possible difficulties: *you worry about your children when they stay out late.* **2** annoy or disturb someone. **3** (of a dog) tear at or pull something with the teeth. **4** (of a dog) chase and attack sheep or other livestock. **5** (**worry at**) pull at or fiddle with repeatedly: *he began to worry at the knot in the cord.* ▶ n. (pl. **worries**) **1** the state of being troubled about actual or possible difficulties. **2** a source of anxiety. ■ **wor·ri·er** n. **wor·ry·ing** adj.

– PHRASES **no worries** informal, chiefly Austral. all right; fine.

wor·ry beads ▶ pl.n. a string of beads that a person fingers so as to stay calm and relaxed.

wor·ry·wart /'wərē,wôrt/ ▶ n. informal a person who tends to dwell unduly on difficulty or troubles.

worse /wərs/ ▶ adj. **1** less good, satisfactory, or pleasing. **2** more serious or severe. **3** more ill or unhappy. ▶ adv. **1** less well. **2** more seriously or severely. ▶ n. a worse event or situation.

– PHRASES **none the worse for** not affected badly or harmed by. **the worse for wear** informal **1** in a poor condition; worn. **2** feeling rather drunk. **worse off** less fortunate or wealthy.

wors·en /'wərsən/ ▶ v. make or become worse.

wor·ship /'wərsHəp/ ▶ n. **1** the practice of showing deep respect for and praying to a god or goddess. **2** religious rites and ceremonies. **3** great admiration or respect for someone. ▶ v. (**worships, worshiping, worshiped**) **1** offer praise and prayers to a god or goddess. **2** feel great admiration or respect for someone. ■ **wor·ship·er** n.

wor·ship·ful /'wərsHəpfəl/ ▶ adj. feeling or showing great respect and admiration.

worst /wərst/ ▶ adj. most bad, severe, or serious. ▶ adv. **1** most severely or seriously. **2** least well. ▶ n. the worst part, event, or situation. ▶ v. defeat or get the better of someone.

– PHRASES **at worst** in the worst possible case. **do one's worst** do as much damage as one can. **if worst comes to worst** if the most serious or difficult situation arises.

wor·sted /'wo͝ostid, 'wərstid/ ▶ n. smooth and close-textured woolen fabric made from a fine yarn.

wort /wərt, wôrt/ ▶ n. a sweet solution made from soaking ground malt or other grain before fermentation, used to produce beer.

worth /wərTH/ ▶ adj. **1** equivalent in value to the sum or item specified. **2** deserving to be treated or regarded in the way specified: *the museum is worth a visit.* **3** having income or property amounting to a specified sum. ▶ n. **1** the value or merit of someone or something. **2** an amount of a commodity equivalent to a specified sum of money: *a million dollars' worth of damage.*

– PHRASES **for all one is worth** informal as energetically or enthusiastically as one can.

worth·less /'wərTHlis/ ▶ adj. **1** having no real value or use. **2** having no good qualities. ■ **worth·less·ly** adv. **worth·less·ness** n.

worth·while /'wərTH'(h)wīl/ ▶ adj. worth the time, money, or effort spent.

wor·thy /'wərTHē/ ▶ adj. (**worthier, worthiest**) **1** deserving or good enough: *issues worthy of further consideration.* **2** deserving effort, attention, or respect. **3** well meaning but rather dull or unimaginative. ▶ n. (pl. **worthies**) often humorous a person important in a particular sphere:

local worthies. ■ **wor·thi·ly** adv. **wor·thi·ness** n.

-worthy ▶ comb.form **1** deserving of a specified thing: *newsworthy.* **2** suitable for a specified thing: *roadworthy.*

wot /wät/ ▶ singular present of WIT².

would /wo͝od/ ▶ modal v. (3rd sing. present **would**) **1** past of WILL¹, in various senses. **2** (expressing the conditional mood) indicating the result of an imagined event. **3** expressing a desire or inclination. **4** expressing a polite request. **5** expressing an opinion or assumption: *I would have to agree.* **6** literary expressing a wish or regret: *would that he had lived to finish it.*

> **USAGE**
> For an explanation of the difference between **would** and **should**, see the note at SHOULD.

would-be ▶ adj. often derogatory desiring or hoping to be a specified type of person: *a would-be actress.*

would·n't /'wo͝odnt/ ▶ contr. would not.

wouldst /wo͝odst/ ▶ old-fashioned second person singular of WOULD.

wound¹ /wo͞ond/ ▶ n. **1** an injury to the body caused by a cut, blow, or other impact. **2** mental pain caused to someone: *what I'm saying might open up old wounds.* ▶ v. **1** injure a person or part of the body. **2** hurt someone's feelings.

wound² /wound/ ▶ past and past participle of WIND².

wove /wōv/ ▶ past of WEAVE¹.

wo·ven /'wōvən/ ▶ past participle of WEAVE¹.

wow¹ /wou/ informal ▶ exclam. (also **wowee** /'wouē, 'wou'(w)ē/) expressing astonishment or admiration. ▶ v. impress and excite someone greatly. ▶ n. a sensational success.

wow² ▶ n. Electronics slow pitch variation in sound reproduction, perceptible in long notes. Compare with FLUTTER (sense 3 of the noun).

WP ▶ abbr. word processing or word processor.

wpm ▶ abbr. words per minute (used after a number to indicate typing speed).

wrack¹ /rak/ ▶ v. variant spelling of RACK¹.

> **USAGE**
> For an explanation of the difference between **wrack** and **rack**, see the note at RACK¹.

wrack² ▶ n. a coarse brown seaweed that grows on the shoreline.

wraith /rāTH/ ▶ n. a ghost or ghostly image of someone, especially one seen shortly before or after a person's death. ■ **wraith·like** adj.

wran·gle /'raNGgəl/ ▶ n. a long and complicated dispute or argument. ▶ v. **1** have a long and complicated dispute or argument. **2** round up or take charge of livestock. ■ **wran·gler** n.

wrap /rap/ ▶ v. (**wraps, wrapping, wrapped**) **1** cover or enclose someone or something in paper or soft material. **2** encircle or wind around: *he wrapped an arm around her waist.* **3** (in word processing, etc.) cause a word or words to be carried over to a new line automatically. **4** informal finish filming or recording. ▶ n. **1** a loose outer garment or piece of material. **2** paper or material used for wrapping. **3** a tortilla wrapped around a filling, eaten as a sandwich. **4** informal the end of a session of filming or recording. ■ **wrap·ping** n.

– PHRASES **be wrapped up in** be so absorbed in something that one does not notice other people or things. **under wraps** kept secret. **wrap up** (also **wrap someone up**) put on or dress someone in warm clothes. **wrap something up** end a discussion or complete a deal.

wrap·a·round ▸adj. **1** curving or extending around at the sides. **2** (of a skirt, dress, etc.) having one part overlapping another and fastened loosely.

wrap·per /'rapər/ ▸n. a piece of paper or other material used for wrapping something.

wrasse /ras/ ▸n. (pl. same or **wrasses**) a brightly colored sea fish with thick lips and strong teeth.

wrath /raᴛʜ/ ▸n. extreme anger.

wrath·ful /'raᴛʜfəl/ ▸adj. literary full of or showing great anger. ■ **wrath·ful·ly** adv.

wreak /rēk/ ▸v. **1** cause a great amount of damage or harm. **2** take revenge on someone.

> USAGE
> The past tense of **wreak** is **wreaked**, as in *rainstorms wreaked havoc yesterday*, not **wrought**. **Wrought** is in fact an old-fashioned past tense of **work**.

wreath /rēᴛʜ/ ▸n. (pl. **wreaths** /rēᴛʜz, rēᴛʜs/) **1** an arrangement of flowers, leaves, or stems fastened in a ring and used for decoration or for placing on a grave. **2** a curl or ring of smoke or cloud.

wreathe /rēᴛʜ/ ▸v. **1** envelop, surround, or encircle: *the mountain was wreathed in mist.* **2** (of smoke) move with a curling motion.

wreck /rek/ ▸n. **1** the destruction of a ship at sea; a shipwreck. **2** a ship destroyed at sea. **3** a building, vehicle, etc., that has been destroyed or badly damaged. **4** a person in a very bad physical or mental state. **5** a road or rail crash. ▸v. **1** cause a ship to sink or break up. **2** destroy or severely damage a structure or vehicle. **3** spoil completely: *the injury wrecked his chances.*

wreck·age /'rekij/ ▸n. the remains of something that has been badly damaged or destroyed.

wrecked /rekt/ ▸adj. informal **1** exhausted. **2** under the influence of drugs or alcohol: *she got wrecked on the champagne.*

wreck·er /'rekər/ ▸n. **1** a person or thing that wrecks something. **2** a person who breaks up damaged vehicles to obtain usable spares or scrap. **3** a tow truck.

wren /ren/ ▸n. a very small short-winged songbird with a cocked tail.

wrench /rench/ ▸v. **1** pull or twist suddenly and violently: *he wrenched the gun from my hand.* **2** injure a part of the body as a result of a sudden twisting movement. ▸n. **1** a sudden violent twist or pull. **2** a feeling of acute sadness and distress caused by leaving a person or place. **3** an adjustable tool used for gripping and turning nuts or bolts.

wrest /rest/ ▸v. **1** take power or control from someone after a struggle. **2** forcibly pull something from a person's grasp.

wres·tle /'resəl/ ▸v. **1** take part in a fight or contest that involves close grappling with one's opponent. **2** struggle with a difficulty or problem. **3** move or manipulate with difficulty: *she wrestled the keys out of the ignition.* ▸n. **1** a wrestling bout or contest. **2** a hard struggle. ■ **wres·tler** n. **wres·tling** n.

wretch /rech/ ▸n. **1** an unfortunate person. **2** informal a disliked or unpleasant person.

wretch·ed /'rechid/ ▸adj. (**wretcheder**, **wretchedest**) **1** in a very unhappy or unfortunate state; miserable. **2** very bad or unpleasant: *the wretched conditions of the*

slums. **3** used to express anger or annoyance: *she disliked the wretched man intensely.* ■ **wretch·ed·ly** adv. **wretch·ed·ness** n.

wrig·gle /'rigəl/ ▸v. **1** twist and turn with quick short movements. **2** (**wriggle out of**) manage to avoid doing something that one ought to do. ▸n. a wriggling movement. ■ **wrig·gler** n. **wrig·gly** adj.

wright /rīt/ ▸n. old use a maker or builder.

wring /riNG/ ▸v. (past and past part. **wrung** /rəNG/) **1** squeeze and twist something to force liquid from it. **2** twist and break an animal's neck. **3** squeeze someone's hand tightly. **4** (**wring something from/out of**) obtain something with difficulty or effort. – PHRASES **wring one's hands** clasp and twist one's hands together as a gesture of distress or despair.

wring·er /'riNGər/ ▸n. a device for wringing water from wet clothes or other objects. – PHRASES **put someone through the wringer** informal subject someone to a very stressful experience, especially a severe interrogation.

wring·ing /'riNGiNG/ ▸adj. extremely wet; soaked.

wrin·kle /'riNGkəl/ ▸n. **1** a slight line or fold, especially in fabric or the skin of the face. **2** informal a minor difficulty. ▸v. make or become wrinkled. ■ **wrin·kled** adj.

wrin·kly /'riNGk(ə)lē/ ▸adj. (**wrinklier**, **wrinkliest**) having many wrinkles.

wrist /rist/ ▸n. the joint connecting the hand with the forearm.

wrist·band /'rist,band/ ▸n. a band worn around the wrist, especially for identity purposes or to soak up sweat when playing sports.

wrist·watch /'rist,wäch/ ▸n. a watch worn on a strap around the wrist.

writ[1] /rit/ ▸n. an official document issued in the name of a court or other legal authority, ordering a person to do or not to do something.

writ[2] ▸v. old-fashioned past participle of WRITE. – PHRASES **writ large** in an obvious or exaggerated form.

write /rīt/ ▸v. (past **wrote**; past part. **written**) **1** mark letters, words, or other symbols on a surface, with a pen, pencil, or similar implement. **2** compose and send a letter to someone. **3** compose a book or other written work. **4** compose a musical work. **5** fill out or complete a check or similar document. **6** Computing enter data into a specified storage medium or location. ■ **writ·a·ble** adj. (chiefly Computing). – PHRASES **be written all over one's face** informal be obvious from one's expression. **write someone/thing off 1** dismiss someone or something as insignificant. **2** cancel a bad debt or acknowledge that an asset will not be recovered.

write-off ▸n. **1** a worthless or ineffectual person or thing. **2** Finance a bad debt that is taken as a loss or an asset that will not be recovered.

writ·er /'rītər/ ▸n. **1** a person who has written a particular work, or who writes books or articles as an occupation. **2** Computing a device that writes data to a storage medium.

writ·er·ly /'rītərlē/ ▸adj. **1** relating to or characteristic of a professional author. **2** deliberately literary in style.

writ·er's block ▸n. the condition of being

unable to think of what to write or how to proceed with writing.

writ·er's cramp ▸ n. pain or stiffness in the hand caused by writing for a long time.

write-up ▸ n. a newspaper review of a recent book, performance, product, etc.

writhe /rīŦH/ ▸ v. twist or squirm in pain or distress.

writ·ing /'rītiNG/ ▸ n. **1** the activity or skill of writing. **2** written work. **3** (**writings**) books or other written works by a particular author or on a particular subject. **4** a sequence of letters or symbols forming words.
– PHRASES **the writing** (or **handwriting**) **is on the wall** see HANDWRITING.

writ·ten /'ritn/ ▸ past participle of WRITE.

wrong /rôNG/ ▸ adj. **1** not correct or true; mistaken or in error. **2** unjust, dishonest, or immoral. **3** in a bad or abnormal condition: *something's wrong with the car.* ▸ adv. **1** in a mistaken or undesirable way or direction. **2** with an incorrect result. ▸ n. an unjust, dishonest, or immoral action. ▸ v. **1** act unjustly or dishonestly toward someone. **2** mistakenly attribute bad motives to someone. ■ **wrong·ly** adv. **wrong·ness** n.
– PHRASES **get hold of the wrong end of the stick** Brit. misunderstand something. **in the wrong** responsible for a mistake or offense. **on the wrong side of 1** out of favor with. **2** somewhat more than a particular age.

wrong·do·ing /'rôNG,dooiNG/ ▸ n. illegal or dishonest behavior. ■ **wrong·do·er** n.

wrong·ful /'rôNGfəl/ ▸ adj. not fair, just, or legal. ■ **wrong·ful·ly** adv.

wrong·head·ed /'rôNG,hedid/ ▸ adj. having or showing bad judgment; misguided.

wrote /rōt/ ▸ past tense of WRITE.

wroth /rôŦH/ ▸ adj. old use angry.

wrought /rôt/ ▸ adj. **1** (of metals) beaten out or shaped by hammering. **2** (in combination) made or fashioned in the specified way: *well-wrought.* **3** (**wrought up**) upset and anxious.

wrought i·ron ▸ n. a tough malleable form of iron suitable for forging or rolling rather than casting.

wrung /rəNG/ ▸ past and past participle of WRING.

wry /rī/ ▸ adj. (**wryer, wryest** or **wrier, wriest**) **1** using or expressing dry, especially mocking, humor: *a wry smile.* **2** (of a person's face) twisted into an expression of disgust, disappointment, or annoyance. **3** bending or twisted to one side. ■ **wry·ly** adv. **wry·ness** n.

WSW ▸ abbr. west-southwest.

wt ▸ abbr. weight.

WTO ▸ abbr. World Trade Organization.

wun·der·kind /'woondər,kind/ ▸ n. (pl. **wunderkinds** or **wunderkinder**) a person who achieves great success at a relatively young age.

Wur·litz·er /'wərlitsər/ ▸ n. trademark a large pipe organ or electric organ.

wuss /woos/ ▸ n. informal a weak or ineffectual person.

WV ▸ abbr. West Virginia.

WWI ▸ abbr. World War I.

WWII ▸ abbr. World War II.

WWF ▸ abbr. **1** World Wildlife Fund. **2** World Wrestling Federation.

WWW ▸ abbr. World Wide Web.

WY ▸ abbr. Wyoming.

WYSIWYG /'wizē,wig/ ▸ adj. Computing referring to the display of text on-screen in a form exactly corresponding to its appearance on a printout.

wy·vern /'wīvərn/ ▸ n. Heraldry a winged two-legged dragon with a barbed tail.

X¹ (also **x**) ▶ n. (pl. **Xs** or **X's**) **1** the twenty-fourth letter of the alphabet. **2** referring to an unknown or unspecified person or thing. **3** (usu. *x*) the first unknown quantity in an algebraic expression. **4** (usu. *x*) referring to the main or horizontal axis in a system of coordinates. **5** a cross-shaped written symbol, used to indicate a wrong answer or to symbolize a kiss. **6** the Roman numeral for ten.

X² ▶ symbol movies classified as suitable for adults only (replaced in 1990 by *NC–17*).

X chro·mo·some ▶ n. (in humans and other mammals) a sex chromosome, two of which are normally present in female cells (known as XX) and only one in male cells (known as XY). Compare with **Y CHROMOSOME**.

Xe ▶ symbol the chemical element xenon.

xe·bec /'zē,bek/ ▶ n. historical a small three-masted Mediterranean sailing ship.

xe·non /'zē,nän, 'zen,än/ ▶ n. an inert gaseous chemical element, present in trace amounts in the air and used in some kinds of electric light.

xen·o·pho·bi·a /,zēnə'fōbēə, ,zenə-/ ▶ n. intense or irrational dislike or fear of people from other countries. ■ **xen·o·phobe** /'zēnə,fōb, 'zenə-/ n. **xen·o·pho·bic** adj.

xen·o·trans·plan·ta·tion /,zenə,transplan'tāshən, ,zēnə-/ ▶ n. the process of grafting or transplanting organs or tissues between members of different species. ■ **xen·o·trans·plant** /-'trans,plant/ n.

X·er /'eksər/ ▶ n. a Generation Xer.

xe·ri·scape /'zi(ə)rə,skāp, 'zerə-/ ▶ n. **1** a style of landscape design needing little or no water or maintenance, used in arid regions. **2** a garden or landscape created in such a style. ▶ v. landscape an area in such a style.

xe·rog·ra·phy /zi'rägrəfē/ ▶ n. a dry copying process in which powder sticks to parts of a surface remaining electrically charged after being exposed to light from an image of the document to be copied. ■ **xe·ro·graph·ic** /,zi(ə)rə'grafik/ adj.

Xer·ox /'zi(ə)r,äks/ ▶ n. trademark **1** a xerographic copying process. **2** a copy made using such a process. ▶ v. (**xerox**) copy a document using xerography.

Xho·sa /'kōsə, 'kô-, 'кнō-, 'кнô-/ ▶ n. (pl. same or **Xhosas**) **1** a member of a South African people traditionally living in the Eastern Cape Province. **2** the Bantu language of the Xhosa.

XHTML ▶ abbr. Computing Extensible Hypertext Markup Language.

XL ▶ abbr. extra large (as a clothes size).

Xmas /'krisməs, 'eksməs/ ▶ n. informal Christmas.

XML ▶ abbr. Extensible Markup Language.

X-rat·ed /'eks ,rātid/ ▶ adj. **1** pornographic or indecent. **2** (formerly) referring to a movie given an X classification.

X-ray /'eks ,rā/ ▶ n. **1** an electromagnetic wave of very short wavelength, able to pass through many materials opaque to light and so make it possible to see into or through them. **2** an image of the internal structure of an object produced by passing X-rays through it. ▶ v. photograph or examine something or someone with X-rays.

xy·lem /'zīləm/ ▶ n. the tissue in plants that carries water and dissolved nutrients upward from the root and also helps to form the woody element in the stem.

xy·lene /'zī,lēn/ ▶ n. a liquid hydrocarbon obtained by distilling wood, coal tar, or petroleum, used in fuels and solvents.

xy·lo·phone /'zīlə,fōn/ ▶ n. a musical instrument played by striking a row of wooden bars of graduated length with small hammers.

Yy

Y¹ (also **y**) ▶ n. (pl. **Ys** or **Y's**) **1** the twenty-fifth letter of the alphabet. **2** referring to an unknown or unspecified person or thing (coming second after 'x'). **3** (usu. *y*) the second unknown quantity in an algebraic expression. **4** (usu. *y*) referring to the secondary or vertical axis in a system of coordinates.

Y² ▶ abbr. yen. ▶ symbol the chemical element yttrium.

y ▶ abbr. year(s).

Y2K ▶ abbr. year 2000 (with reference to the millennium bug).

yacht /yät/ ▶ n. **1** a medium-sized sailboat equipped for cruising or racing. **2** a powered boat or small ship equipped for cruising. ■ **yacht·ing** n.

yachts·man /'yätsmən/ (or **yachtswoman**) ▶ n. (pl. **yachtsmen** or **yachtswomen**) a person who sails yachts.

yack /yak/ ▶ n. & v. variant spelling of YAK².

ya·hoo¹ /'yä,hoo, yä'hoo/ ▶ n. informal a rude, coarse, or violent person.

ya·hoo² /yä'hoo/ ▶ exclam. expressing great joy or excitement.

Yah·weh /'yä,wä, -,we, -,vä/ ▶ n. a form of the Hebrew name of God used in the Bible.

yak¹ /yak/ ▶ n. a large ox with shaggy hair and large horns, used in Tibet to carry loads and for its milk, meat, and hide.

yak² (also **yack**) informal ▶ v. (**yaks, yakking, yakked**) talk at length about unimportant or boring subjects. ▶ n. a trivial or lengthy conversation.

ya·ku·za /yä'koozə, 'yäkoo,zä/ ▶ n. (pl. same) (**the Yakuza**) a powerful Japanese criminal organization.

Yale lock /yäl/ ▶ n. trademark a cylinder lock.

y'all /yôl/ ▶ contr. you-all.

yam /yam/ ▶ n. **1** the edible starchy tuber of a tropical and subtropical climbing plant, eaten as a vegetable. **2** a sweet potato.

yam·mer /'yamər/ informal ▶ v. **1** talk loudly and continuously. **2** make a loud, continuous noise. ▶ n. loud and continuous noise.

yang /yaNG, yäNG/ ▶ n. (in Chinese philosophy) the active male principle of the universe. Contrasted with YIN.

Yank /yaNGk/ ▶ n. informal short for YANKEE.

yank /yaNGk/ informal ▶ v. pull quickly and hard: *he yanked her to her feet.* ▶ n. a sudden hard pull.

Yan·kee /'yaNGkē/ ▶ n. informal **1** often derogatory an American. **2** a person from New England or one of the US northern states. **3** historical a Union soldier in the Civil War. **4** a bet on four or more horses to win (or be placed) in different races.

yap /yap/ ▶ v. (**yaps, yapping, yapped**) **1** give a sharp, shrill bark. **2** informal talk at length in an irritating way. ▶ n. a sharp, shrill bark. ■ **yap·py** adj. (informal).

yard¹ /yärd/ ▶ n. **1** a unit of length equal to 3 feet (0.9144 meter). **2** a square or cubic yard, especially of sand or other building materials. **3** a long pole slung across a ship's mast for a sail to hang from.
– PHRASES **by the yard** in large numbers or quantities.

yard² ▶ n. **1** a piece of ground adjoining a building or house. **2** an area of land used for a particular purpose or business: *they're out in the yard loading lumber.*

yard·age /'yärdij/ ▶ n. a distance or length measured in yards.

yard·arm /'yärd,ärm/ ▶ n. either end of the yard (long pole) slung across a ship's mast for a sail to hang from.

yard·bird /'yärd,bərd/ ▶ n. informal **1** a new military recruit, especially one given menial jobs to do. **2** a convict.

yard·man /'yärd,man/ ▶ n. (pl. **yardmen**) **1** a person working in a railroad or lumberyard. **2** a person who does various outdoor jobs.

yard sale ▶ n. a sale of miscellaneous secondhand items held on the grounds of the seller's home.

yard·stick /'yärd,stik/ ▶ n. **1** a standard used for judging the value or success of something: *test scores are not the only yardstick of a school's performance.* **2** a measuring rod a yard long.

yar·mul·ke /'yämə(l)kə, yärmə(l)kə/ (also **yarmulka**) ▶ n. a skullcap worn in public by Orthodox Jewish men or during prayer by other Jewish men.

yarn /yärn/ ▶ n. **1** spun thread used for knitting, weaving, or sewing. **2** informal a long or rambling story.

yar·row /'yarō/ ▶ n. a plant with feathery leaves and heads of small white or pale pink flowers, used in herbal medicine.

yash·mak /'yäsh,mäk, 'yasH,mak/ ▶ n. a veil concealing all of the face except the eyes, worn by some Muslim women in public.

yat·ter /'yatər/ informal ▶ v. talk continuously; chatter. ▶ n. continuous talk.

yaw /yô/ ▶ v. (of a moving ship or aircraft) turn to one side or from side to side. ▶ n. yawing movement of a ship or aircraft.

yawl /yôl/ ▶ n. a kind of two-masted sailboat.

yawn /yôn/ ▶ v. **1** involuntarily open one's mouth wide and inhale deeply due to tiredness or boredom. **2** (often as adj. **yawning**) wide open: *a yawning chasm.* ▶ n. **1** an act of yawning. **2** informal a boring or tedious thing or event.

yawp /yôp/ ▶ n. a harsh or hoarse cry or yelp. ▶ v. shout or exclaim hoarsely.

yaws /yôz/ ▶ pl.n. (treated as sing.) a contagious tropical disease caused by a bacterium that enters cuts on the skin and causes small lesions that may develop into deep ulcers.

Yb ▶ symbol the chemical element ytterbium.

Y chro·mo·some ▶ n. (in humans and other mammals) a sex chromosome that is normally present only in male cells, which are known as XY. Compare with x CHROMOSOME.

yd. ▶ abbr. yard (measure).

ye[1] /yē/ ▶ pron. (second person pl.) old use or dialect plural of THOU[1].

ye[2] ▶ determiner mock old-fashioned term for THE.

yea /yā/ old use or formal ▶ adv. yes. ▶ n. an answer indicating agreement.

yeah /'ye(ə), 'ya(ə)/ (also **yeh** /ye/) ▶ exclam. & n. informal variant of YES.

year /yi(ə)r/ ▶ n. **1** the time taken by the earth to make one complete orbit around the sun. **2** (also **calendar year**) the period of 365 days (or 366 days in leap years) starting from the first of January. **3** a period of the same length as this starting at a different point. **4** a similar period used for reckoning time according to other calendars. **5** (**one's years**) one's age or time of life. **6** (**years**) informal a very long time. **7** a set of students of similar ages who enter and leave a school or college at the same time: *we were in the same year at Choate.*
– PHRASES **year in, year out** continuously or repeatedly over a period of years.

year·book /'yi(ə)r,bŏŏk/ ▶ n. **1** an annual publication of the graduating class in a school or college, giving photographs of students and details of school activities in the previous year. **2** an annual publication giving details of events of the previous year, especially those connected with a particular area of activity.

year·ling /'yi(ə)rlING/ ▶ n. **1** an animal of a year old, or in its second year. **2** a racehorse in the calendar year after the year in which it was born. ▶ adj. having lived for a year.

year·long ▶ adj. lasting for or throughout a year.

year·ly /'yi(ə)rlē/ ▶ adj. & adv. happening or produced once a year or every year.

yearn /yərn/ ▶ v. have a strong feeling of loss and longing for something. ■ **yearn·ing** n. & adj.

year-on-year ▶ adj. (of figures, prices, etc.) as compared with the corresponding ones from a year earlier.

year-round ▶ adj. happening or continuing throughout the year.

yeast /yēst/ ▶ n. **1** a microscopic single-celled fungus capable of converting sugar into alcohol and carbon dioxide. **2** a grayish-yellow preparation of the yeast fungus, used to make bread dough rise and to ferment beer, wine, etc. **3** Biology any single-celled fungus that reproduces by budding or dividing in two. ■ **yeast·y** adj.

yell /yel/ ▶ n. a loud, sharp cry. ▶ v. shout loudly.

yel·low /'yelō/ ▶ adj. **1** of the color of egg yolks or ripe lemons. **2** offensive having a yellowish or olive skin (as used to describe Chinese or Japanese people). **3** informal cowardly. ▶ n. yellow color. ▶ v. (of paper, fabric, paint, etc.) become slightly yellow, especially with age. ■ **yel·low·ish** adj. **yel·low·ness** n. **yel·low·y** adj.

yel·low-bel·ly ▶ n. informal a coward. ■ **yel·low-bel·lied** adj.

yel·low card ▶ n. (especially in soccer) a yellow card shown by the referee to a player being cautioned.

yel·low fe·ver ▶ n. a tropical disease caused by a virus transmitted by mosquitoes, causing fever and jaundice and often fatal.

yel·low·fin /'yelō,fin/ (also **yellowfin tuna**) ▶ n. a tuna with yellow anal and dorsal fins that is an important food fish.

yel·low jack·et ▶ n. informal a wasp or hornet with bright yellow markings.

yel·low jer·sey ▶ n. (in a cycling race involving stages) a yellow jersey worn each day by the rider who is ahead on time over the whole race, and presented to the rider with the shortest overall time at the finish of the race.

yel·low jour·nal·ism ▶ n. journalism using sensationalism and crude exaggeration. ■ **yel·low jour·nal·ist** n.

Yel·low Pag·es (also **yellow pages**) ▶ pl.n. trademark (in the UK) a telephone directory printed on yellow paper and listing businesses and other organizations according to the goods or services they offer.

yelp /yelp/ ▶ n. a short, sharp cry. ▶ v. make a yelp or yelps.

Yem·e·ni /'yemənē/ ▶ n. a person from Yemen. ▶ adj. relating to Yemen.

Yem·en·ite /'yemə,nīt/ ▶ n. & adj. another term for YEMENI.

yen[1] /yen/ ▶ n. (pl. same) the basic unit of money of Japan.

yen[2] ▶ n. a strong desire to do or have something.

yeo·man /'yōmən/ ▶ n. (pl. **yeomen**) historical **1** a man owning a house and a small area of farming land. **2** a servant in a royal or noble household.

Yeo·man of the Guard ▶ n. a member of the British monarch's bodyguard (now having only ceremonial duties).

yep /yep/ (also **yup**) ▶ exclam. & n. nonstandard variant of YES, representing informal pronunciation.

yer·ba ma·té /'yerbə 'mä,tā, 'yər-/ ▶ n. another term for MATÉ.

yes /yes/ ▶ exclam. **1** used to confirm, agree to, or accept something. **2** used to reply to someone who is trying to attract one's attention. **3** used to express delight. ▶ n. (pl. **yeses** or **yesses**) an answer or vote in favor of something.

ye·shi·va /yə'sHēvə/ ▶ n. an orthodox Jewish college or seminary.

yes-man ▶ n. informal a person who always agrees with people in authority.

yes·ter·day /'yestər,dā, -dē/ ▶ adv. on the day before today. ▶ n. **1** the day before today. **2** the recent past.

yes·ter·year /'yestər,yir/ ▶ n. literary last year or the recent past.

yet /yet/ ▶ adv. **1** up until now or then. **2** as soon as the present or a specified time: *wait, don't go yet.* **3** from now into the future for a specified length of time. **4** referring to something that will or may happen in the future. **5** still; even (used for emphasis): *yet another diet book.* **6** in spite of that. ▶ conj. but at the same time.

yet·i /'yetē, 'yātē/ ▶ n. a large hairy manlike creature said to live in the highest part of the Himalayas.

yew /yōō/ ▶ n. a coniferous tree with poisonous red fruit and springy wood.

Yid·dish /'yidisH/ ▶ n. a language used by Jews in or from central and eastern Europe, originally a German dialect with words from Hebrew and several modern languages. ▸adj. relating to Yiddish. ■ **Yid·dish·er** n.

yield /yēld/ ▸v. **1** produce or provide a natural or industrial product. **2** produce a result, gain, or financial return. **3** give way to demands or pressure. **4** give up possession of: *residents vowed they will yield no more ground to increasing traffic.* **5** (of a mass or structure) give way under force or pressure. ▸n. an amount or result produced: *the milk yield was poor.* ■ **yield·er** n.

yin /yin/ ▸n. (in Chinese philosophy) the passive female principle of the universe. Contrasted with YANG.

yip·pee /'yipē, ,yip'ē/ ▸exclam. expressing excitement or delight.

y·lang-y·lang /'ē,läNG 'ē,läNG/ ▸n. a sweet-scented essential oil obtained from the flowers of a tropical tree, used in perfume and in aromatherapy.

YMCA ▸abbr. Young Men's Christian Association.

yo /yō/ ▸exclam. informal used to greet someone, attract their attention, or express excitement.

yo·del /'yōdl/ ▸v. (**yodels, yodeling, yodeled**) call or sing in a style that alternates rapidly between a normal voice and a very high one. ▸n. a song or call of this type. ■ **yo·del·er** n.

yo·ga /'yōgə/ ▸n. a Hindu spiritual discipline, a part of which, including breath control, simple meditation, and the holding of specific body positions, is widely practiced for health and relaxation. ■ **yo·gic** adj.

yo·gi /'yōgē/ ▸n. (pl. **yogis**) a person who is skilled in yoga.

yo·gurt /'yōgərt/ (also **yoghurt** or **yoghourt**) ▸n. a thick liquid food prepared from milk that has been fermented by adding bacteria to it.

yoke /yōk/ ▸n. **1** a piece of wood fastened over the necks of two animals and attached to a plow or cart in order for them to pull it. **2** something that restricts freedom or is difficult to bear: *the yoke of imperialism.* **3** a part of an item of clothing that fits over the shoulders and to which the main part of the garment is attached. **4** (pl. same or **yokes**) a pair of animals joined together with a yoke. **5** a frame fitting over a person's neck and shoulders, used for carrying buckets or baskets. ▸v. **1** join together or attach with a yoke. **2** bring people or things into a close relationship: *we are yoked to the fates of others.*

yo·kel /'yōkəl/ ▸n. an unsophisticated country person.

yolk /yōk/ ▸n. the yellow inner part of a bird's egg, which is rich in protein and fat and nourishes the developing embryo. ■ **yolked** adj. **yolk·y** adj.

Yom Kip·pur /'yôm ki'pŏŏr, 'yōm, 'yäm, 'kipər/ ▸n. the most solemn religious fast of the Jewish year, the last of the ten days of penitence that begin with Rosh Hashana (the Jewish New Year).

yon /yän/ literary or dialect ▸determiner & adv. yonder; that. ▸pron. that person or thing over there.

yon·der /'yändər/ old use or dialect ▸adv. over there. ▸determiner that or those (referring to something situated at a distance).

yo·ni /'yōnē/ ▸n. (pl. **yonis**) Hinduism the vulva, regarded as a symbol of divine reproductive energy and represented by a circular stone.

yoo-hoo /'yōō ,hōō/ ▸exclam. a call used to attract attention: *Yoo-hoo!—Is anyone there?* ▸v. make such a call.

yore /yôr/ ▸n. (in phrase **of yore**) literary of former times or long ago.

York·shire pud·ding ▸n. a baked batter pudding typically eaten with roast beef.

York·shire ter·ri·er ▸n. a small long-haired blue-gray and tan breed of terrier.

Yo·ru·ba /'yôrəbə/ ▸n. (pl. same or **Yorubas**) **1** a member of an African people of SW Nigeria and Benin. **2** the language of the Yoruba.

you /yōō/ ▸pron. (second person sing. or pl.) **1** used to refer to the person or people that the speaker is addressing. **2** used to refer to the person being addressed together with other people of the same type: *you Canadians.* **3** used to refer to any person in general.

you-all /'yōō ,ôl, yôl/ (also **y'all**) ▸pron. Southern US you (used to refer to more than one person).

you'd /yōōd/ ▸contr. **1** you had. **2** you would.

you'll /yōōl/ ▸contr. you will; you shall.

young /yəNG/ ▸adj. (**younger, youngest**) **1** having lived or existed for only a short time. **2** relating to or typical of young people. ▸n. (treated as pl.) young children or animals; offspring. ■ **young·ish** adj.

young gun ▸n. informal an energetic and confident young man.

young·ster /'yəNGstər/ ▸n. a child or young person.

Young Turk ▸n. a young person eager for complete social or political change.

your /yôr, yŏŏr/ ▸possessive determiner **1** belonging to or associated with the person or people that the speaker is addressing. **2** belonging to or associated with any person in general. **3** (**Your**) used when addressing the holder of certain titles.

> **USAGE**
> Do not confuse the possessive **your** meaning 'belonging to you' (*let me talk to your daughter*) with the form **you're**, which is short for **you are** (*you're a good cook*).

you're /yŏŏr, yôr/ ▸contr. you are.

yours /yôrz, yŏŏrz/ ▸possessive pron. used to refer to something belonging to or associated with the person or people that the speaker is addressing.

> **USAGE**
> There is no apostrophe: the spelling should be **yours** not *your's*.

your·self /yər'self, yôr-, yŏŏr-/ ▸pron. (second person sing.) (pl. **yourselves**) **1** used as the object of a verb or preposition when this is the same as the subject of the clause and the subject is the person or people being addressed. **2** (emphatic) you personally.

youth /yōōTH/ ▸n. (pl. **youths**) **1** the period between childhood and adult age. **2** the state or quality of being young, energetic, or immature: *men are attracted to youth and beauty.* **3** a young man. **4** (treated as sing. or pl.) young people.

youth cen·ter ▸n. a place or organization providing leisure activities for young people.

youth·ful /'yōōTHfəl/ ▸adj. **1** young or seeming young. **2** typical of young people; energetic, fresh, or immature. ■ **youth·ful·ly** adv. **youth·ful·ness** n.

youth hos·tel ▸n. a place providing inexpensive accommodations, aimed mainly at young people on vacation. ■ **youth-hos·tel·ing** n.

you've /yōōv/ ▸contr. you have.

yowl /youl/ ▶ n. a loud wailing cry of pain or distress. ▶ v. make a loud wailing cry.

yo-yo /ˈyō ˌyō/ ▶ n. (pl. **yo-yos**) trademark (in the UK) a toy consisting of a pair of joined disks with a deep groove between them in which string is attached and wound, which can be spun down and up by its weight as the string unwinds and rewinds. ▶ v. (**yo-yoes**, **yo-yoing**, **yo-yoed**) move up and down repeatedly; fluctuate: *the stock market has yo-yoed.*

YT ▶ abbr. Yukon Territory.

yt·ter·bi·um /iˈtərbēəm/ ▶ n. a silvery-white metallic chemical element.

yt·tri·um /ˈitrēəm/ ▶ n. a grayish-white metallic chemical element.

yu·an /yo͞oˈän/ ▶ n. (pl. same) the basic unit of money of China.

yuc·ca /ˈyəkə/ ▶ n. a plant with swordlike leaves and white bell-shaped flowers, native to warm regions of the US and Mexico.

yuck /yək/ (also **yuk**) informal ▶ exclam. used to express disgust. ▶ n. something messy or disgusting. ■ **yuck·y** (also **yukky**) adj.

Yu·go·slav /ˈyo͞ogōˌsläv, ˌyo͞ogōˈsläv, -gə-/ ▶ n. a person from any of the states of the former country of Yugoslavia. ■ **Yu·go·sla·vi·an** n. & adj.

Yule /yo͞ol/ (also **Yuletide**) ▶ n. old use Christmas.

yule log ▶ n. **1** a large log traditionally burned in the hearth on Christmas Eve. **2** a log-shaped cake eaten at Christmas.

yum /yəm/ (also **yum-yum**) informal ▶ exclam. used to express pleasure at eating, or at the prospect of eating, a particular food. ▶ adj. (of food) delicious.

yum·my /ˈyəmē/ ▶ adj. (**yummier, yummiest**) informal very good to eat; delicious.

yup /yəp/ ▶ exclam. & n. variant form of **YEP**.

Yu·pik /ˈyo͞opik/ ▶ n. (pl. same or **Yupiks**) **1** a member of an Eskimo people of Siberia, the Aleutian Islands, and Alaska. **2** any of the languages of the Yupik.

yup·pie /ˈyəpē/ (also **yuppy**) ▶ n. (pl. **yuppies**) informal, derogatory a well-paid young middle-class professional working in a city. ■ **yup·pie·dom** n.

yup·pie flu ▶ n. informal derogatory term for CHRONIC FATIGUE SYNDROME.

yup·pi·fy /ˈyəpəˌfī/ ▶ v. (**yuppifies, yuppifying, yuppified**) informal, derogatory make a place more upmarket or expensive, in keeping with the taste and lifestyle of yuppies. ■ **yup·pi·fi·ca·tion** /ˌyəpəfiˈkāsʜən/ n.

yurt /yo͞ort, yərt/ ▶ n. a circular tent of felt or skins used by nomads in Mongolia, Siberia, and Turkey.

YWCA ▶ abbr. Young Women's Christian Association.

Zz

Z /zed/ US /zē/ (also **z**) ▶ n. (pl. **Zs** or **Z's**) **1** the twenty-sixth letter of the alphabet. **2** (usu. z) the third unknown quantity in an algebraic expression. **3** used in repeated form to represent buzzing or snoring.

za·ba·glio·ne /ˌzäbəl'yōnē/ ▶ n. an Italian dessert made of whipped egg yolks, sugar, and wine.

zag /zag/ ▶ n. a sharp change of direction in a zigzag course: *we traveled in a series of zigs and zags.* ▶ v. (**zagged, zagging**) make a sharp change of direction: *a long path zigged and zagged through the woods.*

Za·ir·e·an /zä'i(ə)rēən/ (also **Zairian**) ▶ n. a person from the Democratic Republic of Congo (known as Zaire from 1971 to 1997). ▶ adj. relating to Zaire.

Zam·bi·an /'zambēən/ ▶ n. a person from Zambia. ▶ adj. relating to Zambia.

za·ny /'zānē/ ▶ adj. (**zanier, zaniest**) amusingly unconventional and individual. ■ **za·ni·ly** adv. **za·ni·ness** n.

zap /zap/ informal ▶ v. (**zaps, zapping, zapped**) **1** destroy or get rid of: *it's vital to zap stress fast.* **2** move or do suddenly and rapidly. **3** use a remote control to change television channels, operate a DVD player, etc. **4** cook or warm food or a beverage in a microwave oven. ▶ n. a sudden burst of energy or sound.

zap·per /'zapər/ ▶ n. informal **1** a remote control for a television, DVD player, etc. **2** an electronic device used for killing insects.

zap·py /'zapē/ ▶ adj. (**zappier, zappiest**) informal lively; energetic.

za·zen /ˌzä'zen/ ▶ n. Zen meditation.

zeal /zēl/ ▶ n. great energy or enthusiasm for a cause or aim.

zeal·ot /'zelət/ ▶ n. a person who follows a religion, cause, or policy very strictly or enthusiastically. ■ **zeal·ot·ry** n.

zeal·ous /'zeləs/ ▶ adj. having or showing great enthusiasm or energy for a cause or aim. ■ **zeal·ous·ly** adv. **zeal·ous·ness** n.

ze·bra /'zēbrə/ ▶ n. an African wild horse with black-and-white stripes and an erect mane.

ze·bu /'zē,b(y)ōō/ ▶ n. a breed of domesticated ox with a humped back.

zed /zed/ ▶ n. Brit. the letter Z.

zee /zē/ ▶ n. the letter Z.

zeit·geist /'tsīt,gīst, 'zīt-/ ▶ n. the characteristic spirit or mood of a particular period of history.

Zen /zen/ ▶ n. a Japanese school of Buddhism emphasizing the value of meditation and intuition.

ze·na·na /zə'nänə/ ▶ n. (in India and Iran) separate living quarters for women in a house.

ze·nith /'zēniTH/ ▶ n. **1** the time at which someone or something is most powerful or successful: *the designer reached his zenith in the sixties.* **2** the point in the sky directly overhead. **3** the highest point in the sky reached by the sun or moon. ■ **ze·nith·al** adj.

zeph·yr /'zefər/ ▶ n. literary a soft, gentle breeze.

Zep·pe·lin /'zep(ə)lən/ ▶ n. a large German airship of the early 20th century.

ze·ro /'zi(ə)rō, 'zē,rō/ ▶ cardinal number (pl. **zeros**) **1** the figure 0; naught. **2** a point on a scale or instrument from which a positive or negative quantity is calculated. **3** a temperature of 0°C (32°F), marking the freezing point of water. **4** the lowest possible amount or level: *I rated my chances as zero.* ▶ v. (**zeroes, zeroing, zeroed**) **1** (**zero in on**) target or focus attention on: *drugs that zero in on diseased cells.* **2** adjust an instrument to zero. **3** set the sights of a gun for firing.

ze·ro hour ▶ n. the time at which a military or other operation is set to begin.

ze·ro-sum ▶ adj. (of a game or situation) in which whatever is gained by one side is lost by the other.

ze·ro tol·er·ance ▶ n. strict enforcement of the law regarding any form of antisocial behavior.

zest /zest/ ▶ n. **1** great enthusiasm and energy: *her remarkable zest for life.* **2** the quality of being exciting or interesting. **3** the outer colored part of the peel of citrus fruit, used as flavoring. ■ **zest·ful** adj. **zest·y** adj.

zest·er /'zestər/ ▶ n. a kitchen utensil for scraping or peeling zest from citrus fruit.

zeug·ma /'zōōgmə/ ▶ n. a figure of speech in which a word applies to two others in different senses (e.g., *John and his driving license expired last week*).

zi·do·vu·dine /zī'dävyə,dēn, zə-, -'dō-/ ▶ n. an antiviral drug used to slow the growth of HIV infection in the body.

zig /zig/ ▶ n. a sharp change of direction in a zigzag course: *we traveled in a series of zigs and zags.* ▶ v. (**zigged, zigging**) make a sharp change of direction: *we zigged to the right.*

zig·gu·rat /'zigə,rat/ ▶ n. (in ancient Mesopotamia, part of present-day Iraq) a tower in the shape of a tiered pyramid, often with a temple on top.

zig·zag /'zig,zag/ ▶ n. a line or course having sharp alternate right and left turns. ▶ adj. & adv. veering to right and left alternately. ▶ v. (**zigzags, zigzagging, zigzagged**) take a zigzag course.

zilch /zilCH/ ▶ pron. informal nothing.

zil·lion /'zilyən/ ▶ cardinal number informal a very large number of people or things. ■ **zil·lion·aire** n. **zil·lionth** ordinal number.

Zim·bab·we·an /zim'bäbwēən, -wēən/

▶ n. a person from Zimbabwe. ▶ adj. relating to Zimbabwe.

zinc /ziNGk/ ▶ n. a silvery-white metallic chemical element that is used in making brass and for coating iron and steel as a protection against corrosion.

zine /zēn/ (also **'zine**) ▶ n. informal 1 a magazine, especially a fanzine. 2 a webzine.

Zin·fan·del /'zinfən‚del/ ▶ n. a variety of black wine grape grown in California, from which a red wine is made.

zing /ziNG/ informal ▶ n. energy, enthusiasm, or liveliness. ▶ v. move swiftly. ■ **zing·y** adj.

zing·er /'ziNGər/ ▶ n. informal 1 a striking or amusing remark. 2 an outstanding person or thing: *a zinger of a shot.*

zin·ni·a /'zinēə/ ▶ n. a plant of the daisy family with bright showy flowers.

Zi·on /'zīən/ (also **Sion** /'sīən/) ▶ n. 1 the Jewish people or religion. 2 (in Christian thought) the heavenly city or kingdom of heaven.

Zi·on·ism /'zīə‚nizəm/ ▶ n. a movement for the development and protection of a Jewish nation in Israel. ■ **Zi·on·ist** n. & adj.

zip /zip/ ▶ n. 1 informal energy or liveliness. 2 British term for ZIPPER. ▶ v. (**zips, zipping, zipped**) 1 fasten something with a zipper. 2 informal move at high speed. 3 Computing compress a file so that it takes up less space. ▶ pron. informal nothing at all.

zip code (also **ZIP code**) ▶ n. a five- or nine-digit postal code.

zip file ▶ n. a computer file whose contents are compressed for storage or transmission.

zip·per /'zipər/ ▶ n. a fastener consisting of two flexible strips of metal or plastic with interlocking projections that are closed or opened by pulling a slide along them. ▶ v. fasten something with a zipper.

zip·py /'zipē/ ▶ adj. (**zippier, zippiest**) informal 1 bright, fresh, or lively. 2 fast or speedy.

zir·con /'zər‚kän/ ▶ n. a brown or semitransparent mineral, used as a gem and in industry.

zir·co·ni·um /‚zər'kōnēəm/ ▶ n. a hard silver-gray metallic chemical element.

zit /zit/ ▶ n. informal a pimple on the skin. ■ **zit·ty** adj.

zith·er /'ziTHər, 'ziTH-/ ▶ n. a musical instrument with numerous strings stretched across a flat soundbox, placed horizontally and played with the fingers and a plectrum.

zlo·ty /'zlôtē, 'zlä-/ ▶ n. (pl. same, **zlotys**, or **zloties**) the basic unit of money of Poland.

Zn ▶ symbol the chemical element zinc.

zo·di·ac /'zōdē‚ak/ ▶ n. an area of the sky in which the sun, moon, and planets appear to lie, divided by astrologers into twelve equal divisions or signs. ■ **zo·di·a·cal** /zō'dīəkəl/ adj.

zom·bie /'zämbē/ ▶ n. 1 informal a person who seems to be barely aware of or interested in what is happening. 2 a corpse supposedly brought back to life by witchcraft. ■ **zom·bi·fy** v. (**zombifies, zombifying, zombified**).

zone /zōn/ ▶ n. 1 an area that has a particular characteristic or use, or is subject to certain restrictions. 2 (also **time zone**) a range of longitudes where a common standard time is used. ▶ v. divide an area into zones. ■ **zon·al** adj.

zonk /zäNGk, zôNGk/ ▶ v. informal 1 (**zonk out**) fall suddenly and heavily asleep. 2 hit someone or something heavily. 3 (as adj. **zonked**) under the influence of drugs or alcohol.

zoo /zoō/ ▶ n. 1 a place that keeps wild animals for study, conservation, or display to the public. 2 informal a confused or chaotic situation.

zoo·ge·og·ra·phy /‚zōəjē'ägrəfē/ ▶ n. the branch of zoology concerned with the geographical distribution of animals. ■ **zo·o·ge·og·ra·pher** n. **zo·o·ge·o·graph·ic** /‚zōə‚jēə'grafik/ adj. **zo·o·ge·o·graph·i·cal** /‚zōə‚jēə'grafikəl/ adj.

zo·oid /'zō‚oid/ ▶ n. Zoology an individual member of a colony of invertebrate animals.

zoo·keep·er /'zoō‚kēpər/ ▶ n. a person employed to look after the animals in a zoo.

zo·ol·o·gy /zō'äləjē, zoō-/ ▶ n. 1 the scientific study of animals. 2 the animal life of a particular region or period. ■ **zo·o·log·i·cal** /‚zōə'läjikəl, ‚zoōə-/ adj. **zo·o·log·i·cal·ly** /‚zōə'läjik(ə)lē, ‚zoōə-/ adv. **zo·ol·o·gist** n.

zoom /zoōm/ ▶ v. 1 move or travel very quickly. 2 (of a camera) change smoothly from a long shot to a closeup or vice versa.

zoom lens ▶ n. a lens allowing a camera to zoom by varying the distance between the center of the lens and its focus.

zo·o·mor·phic /‚zōə'môrfik/ ▶ adj. having or representing animal forms or gods of animal form: *zoomorphic art.*

zo·o·plank·ton /'zōə‚plaNGktən/ ▶ n. Biology plankton consisting of small animals and the immature stages of larger animals.

zoot suit /zoōt/ ▶ n. a man's suit typically having a long loose jacket with padded shoulders and high-waisted tapering trousers, popular in the 1940s.

Zo·ro·as·tri·an·ism /‚zôrō'astrēə‚nizəm/ ▶ n. a religion of ancient Persia based on the worship of a single god, founded by the prophet Zoroaster (also called Zarathustra) in Persia in the 6th century BC. ■ **Zo·ro·as·tri·an** adj. & n.

zouk /zoōk/ ▶ n. a style of popular music combining Caribbean and Western elements and having a fast heavy beat.

zounds /zoundz/ ▶ exclam. old use or humorous expressing surprise or indignation.

Zr ▶ symbol the chemical element zirconium.

zuc·chi·ni /zoō'kēnē/ ▶ n. (pl. same or **zucchinis**) a green variety of smooth-skinned summer squash.

Zu·lu /'zoōloō/ ▶ n. 1 a member of a South African people. 2 the Bantu language of the Zulus.

zy·de·co /'zīdə‚kō/ ▶ n. a kind of black American dance music originally from Louisiana, typically featuring accordion and guitar.

zy·gote /'zī‚gōt/ ▶ n. Biology a cell resulting from the fusion of two gametes. ■ **zy·got·ic** /zī'gätik/ adj.